TRITTON ON INTELLECTUAL PROPERTY IN EUROPE

TRITTON ON INTELLECTUAL PROPERTY IN EUROPE

FIFTH EDITION

RICHARD DAVIS
Hogarth Chambers

THOMAS ST QUINTIN
Hogarth Chambers

GUY TRITTON
Hogarth Chambers

SWEET & MAXWELL

THOMSON REUTERS

First edition published in 1996
Second edition published in 2002
Third edition published in 2008
Fourth edition published in 2014

Published in 2018 by Thomson Reuters, trading as Sweet & Maxwell.
(Registered in England & Wales, Company No 1679046.
Registered Office and address for service:
5 Canada Square, Canary Wharf, London E14 5AQ)

For further information on our products and services, visit
www.sweetandmaxwell.co.uk

Printed and bound in Great Britain by CPI Group (UK) Ltd,
Croydon, CR0 4YY

No natural forests were destroyed to make this product;
only farmed timber was used and re-planted.

A CIP catalogue record for this book is available from the British Library.

ISBN 9780414062696

CONTRIBUTORS

Ben Longstaff
(Patents, 4th edition)

Simon Malynicz QC
(Copyright, 2nd edition)

James Graham
(trade mark, 2nd edition)

Ashley Roughton
(Border Controls, 3rd edn; Jurisdiction 2nd edition)

Michael Edenborough QC
(Plant Variety Rights, 2nd editon)

.

FOREWORD

With the arrival of *Intellectual Property Law in Europe* in 1996, Guy Tritton set the bar for all comprehensive titles on intellectual property in the common market. Now in its fifth edition, it still towers above other titles in this field. What the authors have consistently managed to do is provide a comprehensive in-depth overview of a complex field of law that has so many facets—economic, international, European, domestic private, public, administrative and criminal. Today's IP specialist needs to be a centipede and will find much depth and detail in this book, yet for the purpose of legal education this book has remained surprisingly accessible, despite its growing volume. However, the publishers have performed a small miracle in maintaining the overall size of the book. One only needs to compare the first edition with the fifth in terms of the thickness of the paper and the smaller, yet legible font to appreciate the art of publishing.

The book's perspective has always been that of harmonisation of EU IP laws and the effect on domestic systems. It is ironic that the decision of the UK to leave the EU will place the authors of this book in a third country that is outside of the EU's legal order. Even in the realm of patents, and despite the UK's ratification of the Unified Patent Court Agreement, a common position on the scope of patent protection may not have taken firm root. It remains to be seen whether traditionally held common law beliefs on exhaustion will resurface in a new "Global Britain" trade policy.

Since 1996, much has been achieved in terms of perfecting the Common Market (now the EU) and defining the EU's international relations with third countries through free trade agreements. The 1995 WTO TRIPS Agreement also had a profound impact on enforcement and dispute settlement. Rule-based trade resulted in an unprecedented economic growth and with it came alignment of IP protection. With the role of the WTO as an enforcer of rules-based trade now under threat, the question is whether we will see a shift of forum to investor-state dispute settlement arbitration. The first ISDS arbitration cases involving IP as investment have been brought by large tobacco and pharmaceutical corporations that were unhappy with regulatory changes in respect of trade mark use or patentability standards. So far, these ISDS claims have not been very successful. However, the availability of ISDS through inclusion in trade arrangements has raised questions on the legitimacy of international investors being offered a "second bite of the cherry" when national avenues to challenge national governments before domestic courts have been exhausted.

For now, though, this fifth edition reflects the state of the art in EU and European intellectual property law. In a time where intellectual property is the new gold for developed economies, a comprehensive knowledge of the field is key. With the fourth industrial revolution resulting in a convergence of technologies and the development of new business models, intellectual property will be at the heart of this data-driven economy. This will also present new challenges in calibrating the IP system for this new environment. It is good to see that the authors are aware of what is to come whilst also remaining critical of the excesses of the system. A balance between the interests of right holders, users and societal interests is after all part of the fabric of the IP system. Public perception, however, is that the interests of right holders have been served by European harmonisation where "best practices" of enforcement prevail, but where the interests of citizens have been overlooked. Robotization, biotechnology and the use of artificial intelligence challenge the ethical framework of our societies resulting in a situation where the public acceptance of IP ownership and enforcement is no longer self-evident.

The public backlash against the Anti-Counterfeiting Trade Agreement and the balancing act the Commission had to undertake in order to appraise the functioning of the Biotechnology Directive only serve to highlight that large initiatives to develop IP policy, let alone enhanced protection, will be difficult to complete unless societal concerns are addressed. Director General of the World Intellectual Property Organization Francis Gurry has repeatedly observed that a fragmented and piecemeal approach to future IP development may be the only way forward for now. That may not even be a bad thing. Incremental improvements may yield unexpected and positive results. For incremental innovation, however, a deep understanding of the IP ecosystem is key. This is why this book remains essential.

Anselm Kamperman Sanders PhD
(Lond.)

Professor of Intellectual Property Law

Director Advanced Masters in Intellectual Property Law and Knowledge Management (LLM/MSc)

Maastricht University

The Netherlands

PREFACE

I write this preface in a bittersweet mood. On the one hand, I am delighted that the 5th edition is being published. The 1st edition of *Intellectual Property in Europe* was published in 1996. It is thus 22 years old and after years of nurturing and caring for it, I believe that it has now grown up and is an established title in the field of EU IP law. On the other hand, in June 2016, my country, the UK voted by the slenderest of margins to leave the EU. I do not intend to be diplomatic here. I believe that this was a protest vote which has gone very badly wrong and the UK, and to a lesser extent, the EU, will both be much the worse because of this outcome. Gone are the days when countries can act by themselves. The UK will learn this lesson the hard way.

I am delighted that Professor Anselm Kamperman Sanders of Maastricht University has written the Foreword for the 5th edition. He has singlehandedly created a superb and outstanding post-graduate LLM/MSc course in Intellectual Property Law and Knowledge Management at Maastricht. Students from around the world attend this course which is well structured and thought out. I have been involved with this course from its early beginnings and I am proud that since then, this book has been the main textbook for the students.

In the field of EU IP law, there have been no major earthquakes since the 4th edition was published in 2014. However, if the Unitary Patent and the Agreement on the Unified Patent Court comes into force, this will revolutionise the landscape of patents and patent litigation in the EU. I am very hopeful that this will happen and thus I have written extensively on them in Ch.2, "Patents in Europe". At present, it faces two main challenges: a constitutional challenge before the Bundesverfassungsgericht (German Constitutional Court) and Brexit. However, the UK has ratified the UPC Agreement, leaving only Germany to follow in order for it to come into force. At a lower level, the Court of Justice still is handing down judgments on the meaning of the Supplementary Protection Certificate Regulation. There is a desperate need for a Grand Unified Theory judgment from the Court of Justice on this difficult EU regulation. In the field of trade marks, changes to the EU Trade Mark Regulation are now all in force (and the changes in the new EU Trade Mark Directive must be implemented in Member States by January 2019). These include the removal of the need for a graphical representation of a trade mark, the introduction of a "goods in transit" exclusive right, the removal of the "company" own name defence, and the introduction of a EU certification mark (which is long overdue). In the field of copyright, there has been little change other than further judgments from the Court of Justice, mainly on the vexed meaning of the "communication to the public" right. Having made a rod for its own back with the introduction of the "new public" criterion, the Court of Justice struggles to apply it in its recent decisions. Perhaps it is time to go back to fundamentals. In the field of designs, the Court of Justice in Doceram has now handed down the long-awaited decision on the meaning of the "technical function" exclusion in the Design Regulation and Directive. As forecast, the multiplicity-of-forms theory has been rejected but it is somewhat unclear what is the proper approach to this most important of exclusions.

In the field of IP and competition law, national courts and the Court of Justice are getting to grips with patents which protect technological standards (what are called Standard Essential Patents ("SEPs")). Whilst it is recognised by all that it would be an abuse of a dominant position if SEPs are not licensed on FRAND

(Fair, Reasonable and Non-Discriminatory) terms, there has been much uncertainty as how a SEP holder and a potential licensee should negotiate FRAND licences. In *Huawei v ZTE*, the Court of Justice has clarified the approach. Also, although not well known, the US has updated its guidance on IP and Antitrust law in 2017. In IP and competition law, generally, where the US leads, the EU follows. In the field of jurisdiction, the Court of Justice continues to refine the thorny and tricky issue of jurisdiction for online IP infringements.

Finally, I would also like to thank Lesley Davis for her patience and hard work in editing this book (which I am told is a tough one as it is so long and detailed). I would also like to thank Stephen Wallace of Thomson Reuters for making sure that I kept to my deadlines (well, to be precise, his last deadline!). I would also like to thank my wife, Jane, and my three children, Lara, Luke and Jocelyn for their forbearance as I went to my "bunker" at the end of the garden many evenings and weekends to produce this edition.

I have endeavoured to state the law as of 1 May 2018.

Guy Tritton

Hogarth Chambers

TABLE OF CONTENTS

5. DESIGN PROTECTION IN EUROPE

6. PLANT VARIETY RIGHTS IN EUROPE

8. INTELLECTUAL PROPERTY AND ARTICLE 101

9. INTELLECTUAL PROPERTY AND TECHNOLOGY TRANSFER LICENCES

10. INTELLECTUAL PROPERTY AND HORIZONTAL AGREEMENTS

11.   Intellectual Property, Vertical Agreements

12. ABUSE OF A DOMINANT POSITION

13. ENFORCEMENT OF COMPETITION LAW IN THE EU

14. EU DEFENCES TO EXERCISE OF IPRS

15. PROCEDURES AND REMEDIES FOR ENFORCEMENT OF IPRS

CONTENTS

TABLE OF CASES

TABLE OF STATUTES

TABLE OF INTERNATIONAL AND EUROPEAN LEGISLATION, TREATIES AND CONVENTIONS

DIRECTIVES

DECISIONS

INTRODUCTION

TABLE OF CONTENTS

INTELLECTUAL PROPERTY RIGHTS IN THE 21ST CENTURY

In 2000, the direction of mankind seemed fairly certain. First, the political system **1-001** of western liberal democracy was seen as the inevitable outcome for countries throughout the world. Indeed, it was seen as the final form of human government—an inevitable Darwinian political destination.[1] Free trade and globalisation, the handmaiden of liberal democracy, was seen also as a strong force for good for the welfare of mankind. It too was seen as a kind of economic Darwinian destination.

In 2000, the same optimism and certainty applied to intellectual property rights **1-002** ("IPRs"). A primary goal of Western liberal democracies is to promote technological innovation and the creative arts and thereby enhance the welfare of its people. IPRs, which protect new ideas and works for the benefit of their creators, were seen as an essential tool to attain that goal. At the dawn of the 21st century, the prevailing view was that without the existence of IPRs, undertakings would not make the necessary investment in risky research and development projects whose fruits could easily be taken by third parties who have not incurred these costs. Similarly in the creative industries, although the argument was weaker, the view was that artists, composers, musicians and authors should have exclusive rights in their works to encourage them to create. More nobly, IPRs were seen as rewarding the creators for their new ideas and works. All of this encouraged the need to provide for strong IPRs.

Moreover, the belief at the start of the 21st century was that IPRs had never been **1-003** so important because of the ease in which new ideas or works could be misappropriated by persons other than their creators. There were a number of reasons for this belief. First, through the Internet, the public has access to information in an unprecedented way.[2] The effect of this combined with an increasingly educated world, particularly in India and China, means that creators of new ideas, concepts and works can no longer rely upon a built-in delay in the transmission of such ideas,

---

[1] See "The End of History and the Last Man" *Fukuyama*, 1992 (Free Press).
[2] The open-source *Wikipedia* is an excellent example of the current availability of information. Indeed, it has a very helpful discussion of what is meant by "intellectual property rights"!

concepts and works and the subsequent use of them so as to exploit their creations. IPRs protect ideas, concepts and works. Secondly, the world has become fiercely competitive. No longer can an undertaking rely upon the fact that it can make profits from inefficiencies in manufacturing, the supply chain or in capital investment, e.g. the cost of transport of goods or the lack of access to capital finance for building expensive infrastructure such as factories. This means that undertakings must increasingly look to safeguard their market share and profit by other means, in particular by being innovative and protecting their innovations. Here, IPRs are vital. Thirdly, and linked to the fiercely competitive nature of the world, the increasing wealth and knowledge of the consumer means that undertakings who supply consumer products can no longer simply supply a commodity but each must add value to that commodity in terms of technology, design and brand image to win and maintain market share. For instance, no longer are mobile telephones simply for telephoning people when away from the home or office. They are now promoted as being indicative of a lifestyle which the consumer can "buy into" if the consumer chooses to purchase them. IPRs, particular registered trade marks and designs, are vital to undertakings who wish to protect this added value. Thus, in 2000, it was said that:

> "In the new global economy of ideas, ownership, control, and access to creative works and scientific knowledge have considerable economic import, giving rise to fierce competition over intellectual and creative works, or what one analyst describes as the "knowledge wars."[3]

1-004   In Europe, a trading bloc which was shifting from a basic manufacturing and industrial stage to a sophisticated manufacturing and post-industrial stage, IPRs were seen as vital to maintaining the EU's "edge" over other less developed economies IPRs protected information, ideas and innovation—the lifeblood of a 21st century EU.

1-005   The sunny optimism that everyone had about IPRs at the dawn of the 21st century is also seen when in the year 2000, the Charter of Fundamental Rights was formally adopted by the European Parliament, Council of Ministers and the European Commission.[4] This sets out a series of rights and freedoms such as the right to a fair trial, the right of privacy and freedom of expression and information. Rights such as these are a cornerstone of a liberal democracy. Significantly, for the readers of this book, art.17(2) of the Charter says baldly and shortly

> "Intellectual property shall be protected".

1-006   IPRs had now become a fundamental right of undertakings and persons[5]. Indeed,

---

3   See the discussion paper submitted by Dr A.R. Chapman, "Approaching Intellectual Property as a Human Right: Obligations Related to Article 15(1)(c)" American Association for the Advancement of Science (AAAS), Washington, USA to the United Nations Economic and Social Committee, October 3, 2000 citing in part, S. Shulman, *Owning the Future* (Boston: Houghton Mifflin Company, 1999), p.4.

4   By the Treaty of Lisbon in 2007, the Charter became an integral part of EU law and has the same legal value as the Treaty of the Functioning of the European Union ("TFEU")—see art.6 EU Treaty.

5   There is some circularity here as the phrase "intellectual property" is understood as meaning a property right. Thus, it is a tautology to say that (intellectual) property is protected as protection (ownership) is intrinsic to the concept of property. Thus, one must conclude that what is meant here is that it is a fundamental right that new works and ideas that would be commonly understood as

art.17 Charter is entitled "Right to Property" which allows everyone the right to own and not be deprived of their possessions. The right to protection of the innovative or creative workings of the hand and mind was now the same as the right of a person to own their own home (and be able to exclude strangers from their property).

However, a series of events in the last 10 years has darkened the earlier sunny outlook. The banking crisis of 2008, large-scale immigration into the EU, the rise of the far-right politics in certain EU Member States, the vote of the UK to leave the EU, an increasingly aggressive Russia, the rise of a China as an economic superpower despite its refusal to become a liberal democracy, the advent of religious extremism and the election of the populist President Trump in the USA have created widespread *angst* about the direction of the Western world including the EU. Many started to doubt the prevailing orthodoxies. A largescale populist backlash began against the whole concept of Western liberal democracy, globalisation and free trade. Globalisation was viewed as creating a superclass at the expense of the squeezed middle classes and loss of jobs amongst the working classes. The high priests of free trade and globalisation began to recant and confess that maybe they were not the force for good that they had said they were.[6] Freedom of movement of persons had begun to alarm the electorate in the EU. This was seen as being the root cause of large scale immigration into Member States of the EU and from poorer Member States to richer Member States like the UK, Germany and Scandinavia. Undoubtedly, this was a prime reason for Brexit.

1-007

Perhaps unsurprisingly, in parallel, a backlash started against intellectual property rights. The oft-said mantra that intellectual property rights were necessary to promote technological innovation and foster a lively artistic and cultural scene increasingly came to be viewed by many as a hollow and empty saying. Instead, intellectual property rights were understood to inhibit technological growth and the free flow of information and ideas and also stifle creativity. In a book published in 1999, it was said that the "tentacles of intellectual property" spread over every aspect of human life.[7] From 2008, those tentacles seemed to be strangling every aspect of human life. Instead of being viewed as the engine for technological growth and development, and the necessary foundation for a vibrant creative industry, it appeared a force for bad. Economists began to doubt that a patent system encouraged innovation and invention.[8] In the field of information technology, weak patents and an epidemic of over-patenting has made follow-on innovation difficult and eroded many of the gains from knowledge creation.[9] Copyright began to be perceived as a method of monopolising knowledge and threatening traditional intellectual and artistic freedoms and hindering legitimate new forms of business. Thus,

1-008

---

being the subject matter of protection under widespread norms of patent, design, copyright, plant variety rights, etc. laws should be protected.

[6] See N. Saval, "Globalisation: the rise and fall of an idea that swept the world", *The Guardian*, 14 July 2017 (see *https://www.theguardian.com/world/2017/jul/14/globalisation-the-rise-and-fall-of-an-idea-that-swept-the-world* [Accessed 18 March 2018]).

[7] *Principles of Intellectual Property Law* Catherine Colston, Cavendish Publishing Limited, 1999, p.1.

[8] e.g. see M. Boldrin and D.K. Levine, "The Case Against Patents" *Boldrin/Levine* Working Paper 2012-035A (*https://files.stlouisfed.org/files/htdocs/wp/2012/2012-035.pdf* [Accessed 18 March 2018]). See also "A question of utility" *The Economist*, 8 August 2015. See also D. Baker, A. Jayadev and J. Stiglitz, "*Innovation, Intellectual Property and Development*", July 2017, Shuttleworth Foundation.

[9] D. Baker, A. Jayadev and J. Stiglitz, "*Innovation, Intellectual Property and Development*", July 2017, Shuttleworth Foundation, p.6

in a landmark copyright case of the Court of Justice, it had to consider whether a media monitoring and analysis business that scanned Danish newspaper articles, captured extracts from them and then sent summaries of them to customers by email, infringed copyright in the articles. The Court of Justice held, interpreting the Information Society Directive, a EU harmonising Directive on copyright, that even the reproduction of 11 words could infringe copyright in those articles.[10] The significance here is that the media monitoring business was in a different business to that of the newspapers. Indeed, it could be said that the sending of summaries of newspaper articles of interests to their customers was of benefit to the newspapers as it would encourage their customers to read the articles. In the field of software, it has been argued that the protection of software through copyright, threatens and impede the rapid evolution of software into a highly efficient and reliable product.[11] Arguments that copyright is needed to encourage innovation and development of software started to look thin. The widespread availability and robustness of open-source operating system software such as Linux was seen as having arisen precisely because many thousands of programmers were able to develop and evolve it without worrying about infringement of IPRs.[12] Both Linux and Wikipedia were seen as living proof that IPRs were not needed to encourage technical innovation or create ground-breaking literary works. Others considered that the need for copyright lasting 70 years after the death of author to encourage artistic creativity was over-stated. As said by a US judge in 2006, Van Gogh sold no paintings in his lifetime and was driven to create non-marketable works by an inner pressure.[13]

1-009   Judges in some countries started to pushback at the strangling tentacles of IP. Therefore, in an USA case, *Authors Guild v Hathitrust*,[14] the HathiTrust Digital Library (a spin-off of the Google Books Library Project) scanned and digitally copied books, some of which were not in the public domain. The primary purpose was to allow people to carry out full-text search on books using a search engine. The US courts held that such use did not infringe as it was "transformative" and thus allowed under the "fair use" doctrine in the US. However, there is no equivalent doctrine in the EU and such use would most likely infringe copyright.[15] In 2006, an influential US judge argued that the US had too many IPRs.[16]

1-010   In the EU, academics began to doubt whether IPRs should be a fundamental right—a belief that would have been considered heretical in 2000. Thus, in 2009, a well-known EU IP professor said that art.17(2) Charter "could contribute to amplifying the crisis of legitimacy that IP is currently facing in public opinion".[17] In essence, his argument was that there was no real justification in uplifting IP to that of a fundamental right.

---

[10] *Infopaq A/S v Danske Dagblades Forening* (C-5/08) ECLI:EU:C:2009:465.

[11] J. Ernstmeyer, "Does Strict Territoriality Toll the End of Software Patents" *Boston University Law Review* Vol. 89:1267 at 1274.

[12] R.J. Mann, "Commercialising Open Source Software: Do Property Rights Still Matter?" (2006) *Harvard Journal Law & Technology* (20)1, 21–22. Linux, the open source operating system is considered by many to be much quicker and more efficient than Windows.

[13] R.A. Posner (Judge of the US Court of Appeals, 7th Circuit), "Do We Have Too Many Intellectual Property Rights" *University of Chicago Law School* (2006), Vol: 9:2, 173–185, at 180.

[14] 755 F.3d 87 (2nd Cir., 2014).

[15] See Ch.4, "Copyright in Europe", paras 4-264, 4-338.

[16] R.A. Posner (Judge of the US Court of Appeals, 7th Circuit), "Do We Have Too Many Intellectual Property Rights" *University of Chicago Law School* (2006), Vol: 9:2, 173–185.

[17] C. Geiger, "Intellectual Property Shall be Protected!?—Article 17(2) of the Charter of Fundamental Rights of the European Union: a Mysterious Provision with an Unclear Scope" [2009] E.I.P.R. 114.

What is the insight and view of the authors of this book? Is the backlash justi-   **1-011**
fied or is it an over-reaction? Every area of law seeks to strike a balance between
competing interests. It is inevitable that over a period of time, the legal pendulum
will swing back and forth between those interests. Intellectual property is no
different. There are many competing interests in the field of intellectual property.
In recent times, the Court of Justice has recognised such in the field of IPR law. For
instance, in one case, the court took account not only of art.17(2) but also the right
of privacy, the protection of personal data, the right to conduct a business and
protect one's commercial interests, and the need to attain a single market.[18] To these
rights and freedoms, the reader should also be aware of art.11 Charter (freedom of
expression and information) and art.13 Charter (freedom of the arts and sciences)
as freedoms to be considered in appropriate IPR cases.

In the authors' view, the backlash is a healthy correction of the inexorable   **1-012**
increase in the breadth, strength and duration of IPRs that has marked the EU's lawmaking in the field of IPR. Since it is easier to create rights rather than take them
away, the tendency has been to force Member States to harmonise upwards to the
Member State with the greatest level of protection rather than downwards. A good
example of this is the Term Directive which harmonised copyright upwards to the
highest level of protection afforded in Germany—70 years after the death of the
author.[19] Since the first EU IP legislation (being the Trade Mark Directive),[20] the EU
lawmakers have increased the protection of IP in three dimensions across the EU.
First, they have required Member States to protect a wide variety of IPRs—
patents, industrial designs, trade marks, plant variety rights, copyright in literary,
dramatic and musical works, performers' rights, database rights, supplementary
protection certificates (for pharmaceutical patents), rights in sound recordings
(phonograms), films and broadcasts (terrestrial and satellite). Secondly, for the
above intellectual property, they have provided for a wide and ever-increasing range
of restricted acts—e.g. for copyright works, the following is reserved to the
copyright owner: the right of reproduction (including temporary electronic
reproduction), marketing, distribution, public performance, renting, lending, communication to the public (including making available on the Internet), and
broadcasting. Thirdly, as well as the extension of copyright to 70 years after death
discussed above, in 2011, the EU extended the term of protection for performers
and sound recordings to 70 years in the EU.[21] To the authors' knowledge, there has
not been one EU IP law which has over time overall weakened the level of IP
protection in the EU rather than strengthened it.

The authors of this book consider that there is much to be said for returning to   **1-013**
an earlier treaty than the Charter of Fundamental Rights. The latter was agreed at
the high noon of liberal democracy, free trade and the belief that IPRs were a force
for good. In the authors' view, art.27 of the Universal Declaration of Human Rights
1948 achieves a good balance. It says:

---

[18] e.g. see *Scarlet v SABAM* (C-70/10) [2011] E.C.R. I-11959 at [53] where the CJEU held in the
context of requiring an Internet Service Provider to install a filtering system that the national court
must strike a fair balance between the right to intellectual property, the freedom to conduct a business, the right to protection of personal data, and the freedom to receive or impart information.
[19] Dir.2006/116/EC. The Term Directive is discussed at para.4-097.
[20] Dir.89/104.
[21] Dir.2011/77/EU.

"27.1 Everyone has the right freely to participate in the cultural life of the community, to enjoy the arts and to share in scientific advancement and its benefits.

27.2 Everyone has the right to the protection of the moral and material interests resulting from any scientific, literary or artistic production of which he is the author."

1-014   The equal emphasis of the right of everyone to share in the cultural life of the community, enjoy the arts and share in the scientific advancement of a society in art.27.1 with that of protecting scientific, literary or artistic works in art.27.2 within the same article is welcome. It emphasises that IPRs are not "an end in themselves but only a means towards greater economic welfare for all".[22] This is unlike art.17(2) Charter which makes the protection of intellectual property an end in itself.[23] IPRs must and should be constantly evaluated to ensure that they act as the fuel and oil of an economy and not its brakes. Whilst arts 27.1 and 27.2 could be viewed, superficially, to be in stark conflict, they are not. For instance, a patent confers exclusive rights on someone in a defined area of technology. Does that not conflict with everyone sharing in scientific advancement and its benefits? The answer to that question will usually be no. First, the technology may not have existed but for the availability of patent protection, Secondly, the owner of a patent in valuable technology will have the self-interest to ensure that the technology is commercialised (whether by itself or through licensing third parties) for the benefit of business and the public. Therefore, the public will share in its benefits. Thirdly, the owner is also required to publish the patented technology in the patent application so that all are free to read it and learn of the scientific advancement.

1-015   There are signs that the EU is also recognising some of the legitimacy of the backlash against IPR. Consequently, in line with the increasing acknowledgment that copyright can inhibit rather than promote the growth of an economy, with the EU's Digital Single Market agenda, there has been some attempt to stem the tide of increasing IPR protection to allow for teaching, research, text and data mining and the preservation of cultural heritage by introducing mandatory exceptions.[24]

1-016   It may be that those in the field of intellectual property should remember the saying of Isaac Newton, who discovered the laws of gravity:

"If I have seen further it is by standing on the shoulders of giants."

Mankind needs to be able to stand on the shoulders of the giants of the past to carry it to the stars.

PLAN OF THIS BOOK

1-017   For the 1st edn of this book, a conscious decision was taken to examine and analyse the nature and extent of intellectual property protection in Europe in a "top-down" way. Then, such was a brave decision because so many of the laws of Member States were unharmonised and there were substantial differences. Yet now, it is safe to say that apart from one or two small but defined areas (e.g. unregistered rights in industrial designs and unfair competition), intellectual property law is now fully harmonised at a EU level. There is little point in examining the laws of Member States. They should be very similar although the existence of optional

---

[22] D. Baker, A. Jayadev and J. Stiglitz, "*Innovation, Intellectual Property and Development*", July 2017, Shuttleworth Foundation, p.70.

[23] As said at fn.5, art.17(2) is in truth, a tautology.

[24] See the proposal for a directive on copyright in the Digital Single Market COM (2016) 593.

provisions in EU harmonising Directives gives some freedom to Member States. However, even where optional provisions exist in such Directives, Member States have simply the option to adopt them or not. They cannot amend them or modify them. Thus, this book considers EU law in the field of intellectual property. In particular, it considers IPRs created by EU law. It then considers the impact of EU law on those rights. However, it would be a mistake to consider EU law in isolation. Whilst EU law is of superior status to the laws of Member States, it sits in the framework of international conventions. Of these, the most important is TRIPS. Prior to the Treaty of Lisbon, the European Convention of Human Rights was also of considerable importance. But now, in substance, the principles of the ECHR have been integrated into the EU via the Charter of Fundamental Rights which elevates human rights to EU law at the highest level.[25] That Charter expressly protects intellectual property. As discussed in the previous section, any consideration of EU laws of intellectual property cannot be done in isolation of other areas of EU law.

This book is split into a number of specific sections.   **1-018**

- The first section is concerned with the existence, nature and extent of IPRs in Europe. Patents, trade marks, copyright, design and plant variety rights are all examined in a European context, including a full analysis of international, European and EU conventions, laws and initiatives in each area.
- The second section concerns the effect of the free movement of goods and services provisions and the competition provisions of the Treaty of Functioning of European Union ("TFEU") on the enforcement and licensing of intellectual property.
- The third section considers enforcement of IPRs. Here the practice and procedure of enforcement of IPRs, whether through the courts or via customs seizure is discussed. A chapter on "Euro-defences" is also included which considers the availability of defences to IPR infringement actions where the defence does not arise from the IPR legislation itself.
- The fourth section examines the issue of jurisdiction and enforcement of judgments in the context of intellectual property litigation in Europe.

In the rest of this chapter, the reader is introduced to the EU, the European   **1-019** Economic Area ("EEA") and intellectual property conventions that affect Europe.

THE EU

History of the EU

On 25 March 1957, France, Germany, Belgium, the Netherlands, Luxembourg   **1-020** and Italy signed the Treaty of Rome, which gave birth to the European Economic Community (the "EEC"). The Treaty of Rome was intended to provide for closer economic ties between Member States and the establishment of a single customs union in the EEC. Although only concerned with economic co-operation, its parents were the two World Wars, and from the outset it was envisaged that the Treaty of Rome would lead to closer union between the Member States, eliminate nationalism and thus promote peace and prosperity.

---

[25] art.6(1) of the Treaty of European Union. The EU is still a signatory to the ECHR but as said at art.6(2), such does not affect the EU's competencies as defined in the Treaties.

1-021   Since 1957, the Treaty of Rome has evolved over the years. Originally, it established the European Commission, Council, European Parliament and Court of Justice. In these early years, the Commission represented the executive arm of the EEC, the Council represented the legislative arm of the EEC and the Court of Justice represented the judicial arm. The European Parliament (or Assembly, as it was then known) had little power.

1-022   However, since the 1980s, there has been substantial development. In 1986, the then 12 Member States signed the Single European Act (the "SEA"). The principal purpose of the SEA was to eliminate the remaining barriers to the single internal market within the self-imposed deadline of 31 December 1992, which was to be achieved by an immense programme of harmonisation. In addition, the SEA extended the sphere of Community competence and introduced a number of procedural changes designed to accelerate the Community decision-making process.

1-023   In 1992, the Treaty on European Union ("EU Treaty") was signed at Maastricht. It came into force on 1 November 1993. It is often called the "Maastricht Treaty". The extent of the EU Treaty was far wider than the original Treaty of Rome. The EU Treaty established the European Union ("EU") and the EC Treaty. The EU is not the same as the EC Treaty. The Maastricht Treaty made substantial amendments to the EEC Treaty which widened its scope and effect beyond its original economic field. In doing so, it re-named the EEC Treaty as the EC Treaty. The most important provision was to set a goal for full economic and monetary union, and the creation of a single currency by 1 January 1999.[26] As readers will now be aware, a single currency exists in most of the Member States of the EU. It also introduced the concept of citizenship of the Union.[27]

1-024   On 1 May 1999, the Treaty of Amsterdam came into force. It can be considered as an amending treaty to the Maastricht Treaty. It made substantial amendments to the EU Treaty and the EC Treaty. The main areas which it affected were: fundamental rights—it incorporated fundamental principles of liberty, democracy, respect for human rights and other fundamental freedoms and the rule of law; free movement of persons; non-discrimination, social policy, employment, civil justice, the environment and common foreign policy. Furthermore, there was an extension of the role of qualified majority voting. The Amsterdam Treaty restructured the EU Treaty. In addition, it permitted Member States to opt out of closer integration whilst allowing the rest to proceed.

1-025   The Treaty of Nice was signed on 26 February 2001. This made certain changes to the EU Treaty and paved the way for the increase of the EU to 27 countries, which again made various amendments to the EU Treaties. In 2007, the Treaty of Lisbon was signed. This came into force in 2009 and made significant changes to the EU and EC Treaty. They are now known as the Treaty on European Union (the "TEU") and the Treaty on the Functioning of the European Union (the "TFEU"). The Treaty of Lisbon introduced two significant changes. First, the Charter of Fundamental Rights was made an integral part of the EU Treaties.[28] Secondly, it increased the number of policy areas where the European Parliament plays a significant role in the enactment of legislation.[29] Qualified majority voting on a number of issues was introduced. However, an attempt to introduce a Constitution for Europe, although signed by Member States was never ratified by key European countries and can be considered dead.

---

[26]   Britain and Denmark were permitted to opt out of this provision.

[27]   art.8 EC Treaty.

[28]   art.6(1) TEU.

[29]   Known as the "ordinary legislative procedure".

As of March 2018, Austria, Belgium, Bulgaria, Croatia, Cyprus, Czech Republic, **1-026** Denmark, Estonia, Finland, France, Germany, Greece, Hungary, Ireland, Italy, Latvia, Lithuania, Luxembourg, Malta, the Netherlands, Poland, Portugal, Romania, Slovakia, Slovenia, Spain, Sweden and the UK are Member States.

For the purpose of this book, the reader need hardly go beyond the TFEU. The **1-027** TFEU is very detailed whereas the TEU is more political and general in nature. However, as said above, the Charter of Fundamental Rights is incorporated into the EU Treaties by the TEU and not the TFEU.

Brexit

On 23 June 2016, a referendum was held in the UK as to whether to remain in **1-028** or leave the EU. Thirty million people voted (71.8 per cent turnout) and 52 per cent voted to leave. In March 2017, the UK invoked art.50 TFEU to leave the EU.[30] This gives both sides two years to agree the terms of the split. Currently, it is very difficult to forecast what the terms of the split will be (although as of March 2018, substantial progress has been made in the negotiations). In the author's view, it is likely that the UK will maintain EU IP legislation unless there is good and compelling reason not to. Furthermore, it is likely that the UK will pay due deference to the judgments of the ECJ in interpreting such EU legislation.

Structure and framework of the TFEU

The EU's institutions broadly reflect the division in modern democratic countries **1-029** of power between the legislature, the executive and the judiciary. The TFEU provides for a European Parliament, a Council and a Commission. These are the three main institutions responsible for EU legislation. There is also the Court of Justice (Court of Justice of European Union) which consists of the Court of Justice[31] itself and a first instance court, the General Court (formerly known as the Court of First Instance). Lastly, there is also a Court of Auditors.

Council[32]

The Council consists of representatives of the Member States. Its main role is to **1-030** co-ordinate the broad economic policies of EU member countries, sign agreements between the EU and third countries, approve the annual EU budget, and develop the EU's foreign and defence policies. Only the Council has the power to pass EU legislation. By being the ultimate legislative body, the representatives of Member States have considerable control over the passing of EU legislation. However, it can only act on the basis of a proposal from the European Commission or European Parliament. Thus, the TFEU ensures considerable checks and balances in the passing of legislation. The legislative process of the EU is considered below. The Presidency of the Council is changed every six months and is cycled through the Member States.

As will be seen, in the case of some legislative proposals, qualified majority vot- **1-031** ing is permitted. The legislative decision-making process is considered below.

The Council only meets a few times a month but much of its work is done by **1-032**

---

[30] The European Union (Notification of Withdrawal) Act 2017.
[31] Sometimes known as the ECJ (to distinguish it from the General Court and the CJEU itself which is the name for the courts).
[32] arts 237–243 TFEU.

the Committee of Permanent Representatives ("COREPER"), which consists of representatives who scrutinise and sift proposals coming from the Commission prior to a final decision being made by the Council.

European Commission[33]

1-033   The European Commission represents the interests of the EU as a whole. It has a number of roles. First, it proposes new legislation to the European Parliament and the Council. Secondly, it acts as watchdog and policeman to ensure that EU laws are correctly applied in Member States and in certain areas, e.g. competition law, it enforces the law. It loosely approximates to the executive body of a democratic government. It has powers to formulate non-binding recommendations and opinions. Invariably, major legislation enacted by the Council will often originate from proposals from the Commission. It initiates and drafts legislation intended to put the EC Treaty's objectives into effect. The work of the Commission is carried out by Directorates-General. For the purposes of this book, the two relevant Directorates-General are DG COMP (Competition) and DG GROW (Internal Market, Industry, Entrepreneurship and SMEs (GROW)).

European Parliament

1-034   Originally, the European Parliament was known as the Assembly and consisted of representatives of members of parliaments of the Member States. Its functions were advisory and supervisory. In 1979, direct elections were introduced. Since then, the role of the European Parliament has been increased and it now plays a substantial role in the legislative process. Indeed, it was an intellectual property Directive, the Biotechnology Directive, which was the first legislative proposal that the European Parliament rejected using its veto powers following the introduction of the co-decision procedure.[34] Under the TFEU, its role in the legislative process has been increased and it now plays a robust and central role in the IPR legislative process, particularly where legislation must be passed according to the "ordinary legislative procedure" which is discussed later in this chapter.

The Court of Justice of the European Union[35]

1-035   The Court of Justice of the European Union plays a very important role in the interpretation of EU law and also the determination of validity of EU law. It is the supreme authority on all matters relating to EU law. It settles legal disputes between Member States and EU institutions. Also, individuals, companies and organisations can bring cases before the Court of Justice if they feel that their rights have been infringed by an EU institution. It also provides guidance on the interpretation or validity of EU law via the preliminary reference procedure from the courts of Member States.[36] The emphasis is very much on written rather than oral procedure.

1-036   Each country appoints one judge per EU country. There are also nine Advocate-

---

[33]   arts 244–250 TFEU.
[34]   G. Porter, *The Drafting History of the European Biotechnology Directive* (Oxford: OUP, 2009), pp.3–28.
[35]   arts 251–281.
[36]   art.267.

Generals whose job is to present opinions on the case brought before the court in an impartial manner. There is also a first instance court called the General Court (formerly called the Court of First Instance). The General Court does not have permanent Advocate-Generals. This importantly deals with appeals from European Intellectual Property Office ("EUIPO") (formerly known as OHIM) which is the body responsible for the grant of Community Registered Designs and EU Trade Marks. It also deals with appeals from the European Commission, particularly in the field of competition law. Appeals lie from the General Court to the Court of Justice.

The Court of Justice and General Court has played a very important role in the interpretation of the TFEU, its predecessors and secondary legislation in the field of intellectual property.   **1-037**

EU law

As discussed above, primary EU law consists of the TFEU and the TEU. For the   **1-038**
purpose of this book, the reader is only concerned with the TFEU but the Charter of Fundamental Rights is incorporated into the primary Treaty provisions via the TEU[37] and is accorded equal status to the TFEU and the TEU. The EU can conclude agreements with third countries or international organisations where the Treaty so provides or where the conclusion of an agreement is necessary in order to achieve, within the framework of the Union's policies, one of the objectives referred to in the Treaties. Such agreements are binding upon the institutions of the EU and its Member States.[38]

Article 288 TFEU allows the Council and Commission to put the objectives of   **1-039**
the TFEU into practice by enacting secondary legislation using the legislative procedures set out in art.288 TFEU. This provides as follows:

Regulations:	A Regulation has general application and is binding in its entirety and is directly applicable in all Member States.
Directives:	A Directive can be enacted. This is binding as to the result to be achieved, upon each Member State to which it is addressed, but leaves to the Member States the choice of form and method of implementation. In the field of IPR, directives are used to harmonise the laws of Member States.
Decisions:	A Decision is binding in its entirety but only upon those to whom they are addressed.[39]
Recommendations and Opinions:	These are only of persuasive effect and have no binding force.

---

[37] art.6 TEU.

[38] art.216.

[39] Decisions are not always declared as being as a "decision". The test as to whether a ruling is a Decision within the meaning of art.288 is whether it is a "measure emanating from the competent authority intended to produce legal effects and constituting the culmination of procedure within that authority, whereby the latter gives its final ruling in a form from which its nature can be identified"— *Compagnie de Forges de Châtillon, Commentry et Neuves-Maison v High Authority* (54/65) [1966] E.C.R. 185, [195]; [1966] C.M.L.R. 525.

The process of creating EU legislation

1-040   Under the Treaty of Rome, the power to create legislation rested firmly in the hands of the Commission and the Council. The Commission would make a legislative proposal and the Council would vote on it. The European Parliament played no effective role and was little more than a talking shop. Following the Maastricht Treaty, a co-decision procedure was introduced which gave a role to the European Parliament. Following the Treaty of Lisbon, the European Parliament now plays an integral and important role in the legislative process. For most legislation, a procedure called "the ordinary legislative procedure"[40] is adopted. This involves proposals going from the Commission to the European Parliament to the Council which then shuttle back and forth from the Parliament to the Council until a text is agreed. The other type of procedure is called the "special legislative procedure". This procedure is not defined in the TFEU and is a procedure which is referred to in certain articles of the TFEU and where the mechanism is set out in those articles.

1-041   In most areas, the Council must act by a qualified majority vote ("QMV"). However, in some areas it must act unanimously. A QMV proposal that comes from the European Commission must be supported by 55 per cent of Member States and Member States representing 65 per cent of the total EU population. Where the proposal does not come from the Commission, 72 per cent of Council members representing at least 65 per cent of the EU population must vote in favour.

1-042   Importantly, in the field of intellectual property, a number of different legislative mechanisms can be used and the route used will determine whether qualified majority voting is required rather than unanimous voting. The specific legislative mechanisms for passing legislation relating to IPR are discussed below.[41]

Direct applicability

1-043   Once a Member State has ratified the TFEU, the primary legislation of the TFEU becomes legally effective in the Member State without the need for further enactment. Thus, in the UK, s.2(1) of the European Communities Act 1972 provides that:

> "All such rights, powers, obligations and restrictions from time to time created or arising by or under the Treaties, and all such remedies and procedures from time to time provided for by or under the Treaties, as in accordance with the Treaties are without further enactment to be given legal effect or used in the United Kingdom shall be recognised and available in law, and be enforced, allowed and followed accordingly."

1-044   Other Member States which are dualist have enacted similar legislation. Monist States (i.e. a state whose domestic laws recognises the force of international conventions ratified by that state) will not have required such implementing legislation. EU law which automatically becomes become part of a Member State's legal order is said to be "directly applicable".

Direct effect

1-045   Much of EU legislation is addressed to Member States and does not prima facie impose any obligations or grant any rights to individuals of those states. Direc-

---

[40]   art.294 TFEU.
[41]   See para.1-100.

tives are often intended to give rights to individuals but require implementation by Member States for such rights to become domestic law. In such cases, individuals will not normally be able to rely upon them in legal proceedings. Provisions of EU law which are found to be capable of application by national courts at the suit of individuals are termed "directly effective".[42]

Traditionally, the expression "direct effect" has been used to describe the legal **1-046** issue as to whether, in national proceedings before the court of a Member State, a private party can rely upon a Directive which has not been implemented (at all or correctly). In reality, the principle of "direct effect" is about constriction of EU legislation of any kind. Thus, the courts of a Member State are concerned to determine whether a EU legislative act can be construed (i.e. interpreted) as being intended to be able to be relied upon by individuals. Thus, in *Consorzio del Prosciutto di Parma v Asda Stores Ltd*,[43] the House of Lords said that it had to consider whether, as a matter of construction, a EU act was intended to be directly enforceable in the courts of Member States at the suit of individuals. Generally, as is intimated by art.288 TFEU, Regulations are more likely to have direct effect than Directives, because, unlike Directives, they are not reliant upon implementation by Member States and there is no discretion as to the form and methods of implementation. However, even a Regulation must be directly effective to be enforceable by a private individual. The principal difference between on the one hand, Directives and on the other hand, Regulations and primary Treaty provisions having direct effect is that even if a Directive has direct effect, it can only be relied upon by an individual against a Member State (or its organs). It cannot be relied upon in a private action against another individual.[44] As is nowadays said, a Directive may have "vertical direct effect" but can never have "horizontal direct effect".

The Court of Justice has been asked many times to adjudicate whether a EU **1-047** legislative act has direct effect and what the consequences are of a provision being directly effective. Its case law, principally on the issue as to whether Directives could be relied on by individuals in national courts, establishes that for a EU provision to have direct effect, it must fulfil the following three conditions:

(i)   The provision must impose a clear and precise obligation on Member States.

(ii)   The provision must be unconditional, i.e. not accompanied by any reservation; if, however, it is subject to certain exceptions, they must be strictly defined and limited.

(iii)   The Member State must not have an effective power of discretionary judgment as to the application of the rule in question.[45]

In the context of Directives, it has been said that for these to be directly effec- **1-048**

---

[42]   The distinction between these two doctrines, direct effect and direct applicability, was first pointed out by J.A. Winter in "Direct Applicability and Direct Effect: two distinct and different concepts in Community law" (1972) 9(4) C.M.L.R. 425, 425–438.

[43]   [2001] C.M.L.R. 43; [2001] E.T.M.R. 53 HL.

[44]   See para.1-054.

[45]   These rules were first set out by Gand AG in *Alfons Lütticke GmbH v Hauptzollamt Saarlouis* (57/65) [1966] E.C.R. 205; [1971] C.M.L.R. 674. See also *Franz Grad v Finanzamt Traünstein* (9/70) [1970] E.C.R. 825, [1971] C.M.L.R. 1; *Van Duyn v Home Office* (41/75) [1974] E.C.R. 1337, [1975] 1 C.M.L.R. 1; *Verbond van Nederlandse Ondernemingen v Inspecteur der Invoerrechten en Accijnzen* (51/76) [1977] E.C.R. 113, [1977] 1 C.M.L.R. 413; *Pubblico Ministero v Ratti* (148/78) [1979] E.C.R. 1629, [1980] 1 C.M.L.R. 96; and *Mölkerel-Zentrale Westfalen Lippe v Hauptzollamt Paderborn* (28/67) [1968] E.C.R. 143. See also *Cooperative Agricola Zootecnica S Antonio v*

tive, the Court of Justice has said that it is settled case law that such must be unconditional and sufficiently precise.[46] It has been said that for a EU provision to be directly effective, it must be "capable of being applied by a court to a specific case."[47]

Articles of the TFEU

1-049   The Court of Justice has stated that the Treaty of Rome, the predecessor to the TFEU, is more than an agreement creating mutual obligations between Member States but also imposes obligations on individuals and also confers on them legal rights.[48] Although an article of the TFEU is directly applicable (i.e. it does not require the intervention of Member States to be law in Member States), whether an Article has direct effect depends on whether it fulfils the three conditions outlined above.[49] For the purposes of this book, all the Treaty provisions on the free movement of goods and services, competition and discrimination on the grounds of sex and nationality have direct effect.

Regulations

1-050   As described expressly in art.288, Regulations are directly applicable. By this, it means that they become part of the law of the Member State without the need for further intervention by the Member State. As such, a Regulation will usually also have direct effect. However, it is a matter of construction of a Regulation as to whether it is intended to confer an enforceable right on an individual.[50] Occasionally, a Regulation will need national implementation to create a legislative measure which is certain and clear enough to be directly effective.[51] In *Parma Ham*,[52] the House of Lords was concerned with whether two EU Regulations on the protection of geographical indications of origin ("GIO")[53] created a EU right which was enforceable in courts. In particular, under the Regulations, Parma Ham had been designated a GIO. Under the GIO specification for Parma Ham, it required that slicing and packaging of Parma Ham was done in accordance with Italian regulations. These requirements were challenged in UK courts as not being directly enforce-

---

Amministrazione delle Finanze dello State (C-246/94) [1996] E.C.R. I-4373, where the court said that "a Community provision is unconditional where it sets forth an obligation which is not qualified by any condition, or subject, in its implementation or effects, to the taking of any measure either by the Community institutions or by the Member States".

[46]   *Portgás—Sociedade de Produção e Distribuição de Gás SA v Ministério da Agricultura, do Mar, do Ambiente e do Ordenamento do Território* (C-425/12) ECLI:EU:C2013:329 at [18].

[47]   per Van Gerven AG in *H J Banks & Co Ltd v British Coal Corp* (C-128/92) [1994] E.C.R. I-1209 at [27]. Referred to by the House of Lords in *Parma Ham* [2001] 1 C.M.L.R. 43; [2001] E.T.M.R. 53 by Lord Hoffmann at [35].

[48]   *Van Gend en Loos v Nederlandse Administratie der Belastingen* (26/72) [1963] E.C.R. 1; [1963] C.M.L.R. 185.

[49]   e.g. see *Alfons Lütticke GmbH v Hauptzollamt Saarlouis* (57/65) [1966] E.C.R. 205; [1971] C.M.L.R. 674.

[50]   *Parma Ham* [2001] 1 C.M.L.R. 43; [2001] E.T.M.R. 53 per Lord Hoffmann (House of Lords, England).

[51]   e.g. See *Steinike und Weinlig v Germany* (C-78/76) [1977] E.C.R. 595; [1977] 2 C.M.L.R. 688. Here it was held that the inclusion of rules relating to state aids (which the CJEU have held do not have direct effect) into an agricultural regulation did not make those rules "directly effective" by their mere inclusion in a Community Regulation.

[52]   *Parma Ham* [2001] 1 C.M.L.R. 43; [2001] E.T.M.R. 53.

[53]   GIOs are discussed at para.3-855.

able by a private individual (in this case, the consortium of Parma Ham producers). It was argued that the GIO specification was uncertain and not transparent (i.e. not readily accessible) and, therefore, not of direct effect. The House of Lords split as to whether it was of direct effect and referred the matter to the Court of Justice. The Court of Justice held that in relation to the requirement of slicing and packaging, the GIO regulation was not directly effective as there was no adequate publicity in EU legislation of these requirements.[54]

Directives

A Directive is "binding as to the result to be achieved, upon each Member State to which it is addressed, but shall leave to the national authorities the choice of form and methods".[55] Accordingly, the TFEU never intended that Directives should be relied on by individuals in actions before national courts. Rather, it was intended that individuals rely upon the national legislation which implemented a Directive. However, in many cases, a Member State has failed to implement correctly, or in time, a Directive in breach of its obligations under the Directive. **1-051**

In such circumstances, the Court of Justice has held that Directives will be directly effective, provided that they fulfil the conditions described above.[56] Thus, a Directive will not be directly effective where the time limit for its implementation has not expired.[57] A Directive can be directly effective even if the relevant Member State has implemented it. Thus, where a Member State has not properly implemented a Directive, an individual can rely on the direct effect of a Directive.[58] **1-052**

Article 288 imposes an obligation on Member States to implement Directives. In *Marshall v South West Hampshire Area HA*,[59] the Court of Justice ruled that an individual may rely upon the direct effect of Directives against a Member State, regardless of the capacity in which the state was acting. However, it held that art.288 meant that a Directive did not itself impose obligations on an individual and that a provision of a Directive could not be relied upon *against* an individual in national courts.[60] The Court of Justice has subsequently said that a Directive may be relied upon against organisations or bodies which are subject to the authority or control of the state, or which have special powers beyond those which result from normal relations between individuals.[61] The failure by the Court of Justice to recognise that a Directive cannot impose obligations on individuals and thus cannot be relied upon **1-053**

---

[54] *Consorzio del Prosciutto di Parma v Asda Stores Ltd* (C-108/01) [2003] E.C.R. I-5121.

[55] art.288.

[56] See para.1-045, e.g. see *Cooperativa Agricola Zootecnica S. Antonio v Amministrazione delle Finanze dello Stato* (C-246/94) [1996] E.C.R. I-4373 for an example of a decision of the CJEU that an agricultural Directive was directly effective and thus a Member State was liable for its failure to implement it.

[57] *Pubblico Ministero v Ratti* (148/78) [1979] E.C.R. 1629; [1980] 1 C.M.L.R. 96.

[58] e.g. see *VNO v Inspecteur der Invoeerechten en Accijnzen* (51/76) [1977] E.C.R. 113; [1977] 1 C.M.L.R. 413.

[59] *Marshall v South West Hampshire Area HA* (152/84) [1986] 1 Q.B. 401; [1986] E.C.R. 723; [1986] 1 C.M.L.R. 688.

[60] This principle has been affirmed several times, e.g. see *El Corte Inglés SA v Cristina Blázquez Rivero* (C-192/94) [1996] E.C.R. I-1281 at [5]. *Portgás—Sociedade de Produção e Distribuição de Gás SA v Ministério da Agricultura, do Mar, do Ambiente e do Ordenamento do Território* (C-425/12) [2013] ECLI:EU:C:2013:829 at [18].

[61] *Foster v British Gas Plc* (C-188/89) [1990] E.C.R. 3313; [1990] 2 C.M.L.R. 833. However, see the English Court of Appeal's ruling in *Doughty v Rolls Royce Plc* [1992] I.R.L.R. 126, where it ruled that Rolls Royce, then a nationalised undertaking, did not fall within the concept of a public body

against individuals who breach the provisions of a Directive has been criticised. In *Paola Faccini Dori v Recreb Srl*,[62] the Court of Justice was asked to reconsider this principle. It declined to do so and said:

> "It need merely be noted here that, as is clear from the judgment in *Marshall*, cited above (paragraphs 48 and 49), the case law on the possibility of relying on directives against State entities is based on the fact that under Article [288] a directive is binding only in relation to 'each Member State to which it is addressed'. That case law seeks to prevent 'the State from taking advantage of its own failure to comply with EU law'.
>
> It would be unacceptable if a State, when required by the EU legislature to adopt certain rules intended to govern the State's relations-or those of State entities-with individuals and to confer certain rights on individuals, were able to rely on its own failure to discharge its obligations so as to deprive individuals of the benefits of those rights. Thus the Court has recognized that certain provisions of directives on conclusion of public works contracts and of directives on harmonization of turnover taxes may be relied on against the State (or State entities) (see the judgment in Case 103/88 *Fratelli Costanzo v Comune di Milano* [1989] E.C.R. 1839 and the judgment in Case 8/81 *Becker v Finanzamt Muenster-Innenstadt* [1982] E.C.R. 53).
>
> The effect of extending that case law to the sphere of relations between individuals would be to recognize a power in the EU to enact obligations for individuals with immediate effect, whereas it has competence to do so only where it is empowered to adopt regulations."[63]

1-054   This principle that a Directive only imposes obligations on a Member State and its organs but does not impose obligations on individuals has been applied many times and can be now considered settled law.[64]

Interpretation of national law in accordance with Directives

1-055   In *Von Colson and Kamann v Land NordRhein-Westfalen*[65] the Court of Justice ruled that national courts must interpret national law in such a way as to ensure that the objectives of a Directive are achieved. In *Marleasing SA v La Comercial Internacional de Alimentacion SA*,[66] the claimant sought a declaration that certain contracts were void under Spanish law on the grounds of lack of cause. The defendants contended that Dir.68/151, which should have been in force in Spain from the date of its accession and which provided an exhaustive list of situations in which nullity could be invoked, did not permit lack of cause as a ground. On reference to the Court of Justice, it said the national courts must, as far as possible, interpret national law in the light of the wording and purpose of the Directive in order to achieve the result pursued by the Directive. It added that this was regardless of whether the national provisions in question were adopted before or after the

---

such that an individual could rely on the direct effect of a Directive against it.

62   (C-91/92) [1994] E.C.R. I-3325.

63   See [22]–[24]. See also, *Unilever Italia SpA v Central Food SpA* (C-443/98) [2000] E.C.R. I-7535; *Marshall* (152/84) [1986] E.C.R. 723 at [48]; *Faccini Dori* (C-91/92) [1994] E.C.R. I-3325 at [20]; *El Corte Inglés* (C-192/94) [1996] E.C.R. I-1281 at [16] and [17]; *Wells* (C-201/02) [2004] E.C.R. I-723 at [56]; and *Pfeiffer* (C-397/01 to C-403/01) [2004] E.C.R. I-8835 at [108] and [109]) where the court has reiterated this approach.

64   e.g. see *Portgás—Sociedade de Produção e Distribuição de Gás SA v Ministério da Agricultura, do Mar, do Ambiente e do Ordenamento do Território* (C-425/12) [2013] ECLI:EU:C:2013:829 at [22]–[24] and cases cited there.

65   *Von Colson v Land Nordrhein-Westfahlen* (C-14/83) [1984] E.C.R. 1891; [1986] 2 C.M.L.R. 430.

66   (C-106/89) [1990] E.C.R. I-4315; [1992] 1 C.M.L.R. 305.

Directive. Accordingly, it would seem that the rule as expressed in *Von Colson* applies regardless as to whether the legislation in question was specifically introduced to implement the Directive or not. This obligation applies as much to national legislatives measures enacted to implement intellectual property directive as in other field. Thus, in *Björnekulla*, it was held that Swedish trade mark must be interpreted in the light of the wording and purpose of the Trade Mark Directive, even if such was contrary to the purpose as divined by the *travaux préparatoires* for the 1960 Swedish trade mark law.[67] Indeed, this obligation has led national courts to ignore home-grown legislative measures which have no counterpart in the founding Directive.[68] The need to interpret domestic legislation in the light of EU Directives that have legislated in the field of domestic legislation is, without doubt, a very strong one. Thus, as the Court of Justice said:

> "110. It is true that the obligation on a national court to refer to the content of a directive when interpreting and applying the relevant rules of domestic law is limited by general principles of law, particularly those of legal certainty and non-retroactivity, and that obligation cannot serve as the basis for an interpretation of national law contra legem (see, by analogy, Criminal proceedings against *Pupino* (C-105/03) [2006] Q.B. 83; [2005] 3 W.L.R. 1102; [2005] E.C.R. I-5285, paragraphs 44 and 47).
>
> 111. Nevertheless, the principle that national law must be interpreted in conformity with EU law requires national courts to do whatever lies within their jurisdiction, taking the whole body of domestic law into consideration and applying the interpretative methods recognised by domestic law, with a view to ensuring that the directive in question is fully effective and achieving an outcome consistent with the objective pursued by it (see *Pfeiffer*, paragraphs 115, 116, 118 and 119)."[69]

As said in the excerpt, the obligation on national courts to interpret domestic law **1-056** in the light of Directives is in part restrained by the general principles of law which form part of EU law and in particular the principles of legal certainty and non-retroactivity.[70] These principles apply where the application of the *Von Colson* principle would conflict with an individual's right to assume that domestic law is valid and subsisting. Moreover, national courts have resisted any tendency to construe national legislation in accordance with a Directive where such would clearly conflict with the plain wording and evident intention of the national legislature.[71] Thus, in a UK case where the issue was the interpretation of a section whose wording was very clear, the Court of Appeal considered a provision in domestic copyright legislation which stated that the showing or playing in public

---

[67] *Björnekulla v Procordia* (C-371/02) [2004] E.C.R. I-5791; [2005] 3 C.M.L.R. 16; [2004] E.T.M.R. 69; [2004] R.P.C. 45 at [13].

[68] Thus, in the UK, the Court of Appeal suggests that the home-grown defence of s.10(6) of the Trade Marks Act 1994 (reference to a registered trade mark for purpose of identifying goods or services of proprietor of mark) should be ignored because it has no counterpart in the Trade Mark Directive, e.g. see *O2 v Hutchison* [2006] EWCA Civ 1656 CA.

[69] *Adeneler v Ellinikos Organismos Galaktos (ELOG)* (C-212/04) [2006] E.C.R. I-6057; [2006] 3 C.M.L.R. 30.

[70] *Kolpinghuis Nijmegen* (80/86) [1987] E.C.R. 3969; [1989] 2 C.M.L.R. 18.

[71] In England, see *Duke v GEC Reliance Ltd* [1988] A.C. 618; *Webb v EMO (Air Cargo) Ltd* [1992] 4 All E.R. 929, HL; *R. v British Coal Corp* [1993] 1 C.M.L.R. 721. In Germany, see *Re a Rehabilitation Centre* [1992] 2 C.M.L.R. 21. Cf. *Litster v Forth Dry Dock & Engineering Co Ltd* [1990] 1 A.C. 546, where the House of Lords stated that where Regulations had been introduced specifically to implement an EC Directive, then UK courts must interpret domestic law to comply with the Directive, supplying the necessary words by implication in order to achieve a result compatible with EC law.

of a broadcast or cable programme to an audience that has not paid for admission to the place where the broadcast or cable programme is shown did not infringe copyright in the broadcast, any sound recording or film.[72] This provision had been amended by secondary legislation designed to implement Dir.2001/29 (the "Copyright Directive"). The problem was that no such defence existed in the Copyright Directive. Yet the words in the defence were clear even though there was good argument that the government had made a mistake in its understanding of the wide-ranging nature of the "communication to the public" right introduced by the Copyright Directive and that such would cover the showing or playing in public of broadcasts. The issue thus was whether the *Marleasing* principle could be extended, in effect, to delete a defence which was clearly intended to have some effect. The Court of Appeal said as follows:

"[52] The starting point is that the wording of s.72(1) is clear and unambiguous in embracing within its ambit any 'showing or playing in public of a broadcast' to an audience who have not paid for admission to the place where the broadcast is to be seen or heard. *The mere fact that statutory language is clear and unambiguous, if the words are given a literal meaning, is not necessarily an insuperable obstacle to a conforming interpretation in accordance with the Marleasing principle. In the present case, however, the language of s.72(1) must be seen in the context of the clear intention of the government, apparent from contemporaneous documentation, including its published conclusions on the 2002 consultation, to maintain to the fullest extent possible the United Kingdom's existing exceptions to copyright infringement. The retention of the same clear and unambiguous introductory language in s.72(1) after the Copyright Directive is a strong indication of the government's intention to make no alteration to its ambit (save in relation to excepted sound recordings). In short, the clear and unambiguous introductory wording to s.72(1) supports the proposition in the present case that the corollary of the government's mistake as to the ambit of s.72(1) is that the government did not intend to introduce a specific new limitation to its ambit other than the express provision relating to sound recording. That is supported by the following further considerations.*

...

[57] These consequences relate to an important part of the legislation. They cannot be described as minor or unimportant matters in the overall statutory scheme merely because they concern a limited number of sections. In considering the legitimate limits of a Marleasing conforming interpretation in the present case, the practical consequences of that interpretation, the plain absence of any intent on the part of the government to bring them about and its equally plain mistake as to the relationship between the amended s.20 and the amended s.72(1) and (1B), the impact on the coherence of the statutory scheme, and the lack of any certainty as to how the government or Parliament would have addressed those issues if they had appreciated them (including initiating a debate within the European Union), cannot simply be swept aside by pointing to an overall intention on the part of the government to comply with the Copyright Directive. *All those matters are a clear indication that to limit the clear and unambiguous introductory words in s.72(1) as FAPL suggests would go beyond legitimate interpretation by the Court and would encroach on Parliament's legislative role.*" [Emphasis supplied.]

---

[72] *FAPL v QC Leisure* [2013] F.S.R. 20.

Generally, in construing the meaning of a Directive, it is wrong to use the minutes of Council meetings as an aid to interpretation.[73]

1-057

Liability of a Member State in damages for failure to properly implement a Directive

The Court of Justice has held that a Member State must compensate an individual for its failure to implement a Directive. In *Francovich v Italy*,[74] Italy failed to implement a Directive which was designed to guarantee the payment of arrears of wages to employees in the event of their employer's insolvency. The time limit for the Directive's implementation had expired and the Court of Justice had already held, in art.258 TFEU proceedings, that Italy was in breach of its EU obligations in failing to implement the Directive. The Court of Justice held that the Directive was not directly effective as it was not sufficiently clear and precise. However, it held that a Member State who failed to implement a Directive was liable to compensate individuals if certain conditions were satisfied. These are:

1-058

(a) the Directive involved rights conferred on individuals;
(b) the contents of those rights could be identified on the basis of the provisions of the Directive; and
(c) there was a causal link between the state's failure and the damage suffered by the persons affected.[75]

It should be noted that the three conditions are not contingent on the Directive being directly effective. The above test is less stringent than the test for the direct effectiveness of Directives. In France, the Conseil d'État has awarded damages against the state for losses suffered as a result of a ministerial order in breach of an EU Directive.[76]

1-059

In *Brasserie du Pecheur v Germany; R v Secretary of State for Transport Ex p. Factortame Ltd*,[77] the Court of Justice expanded on the *Francovich* criteria. It held that Member States of the EU are liable to compensate individuals for damage caused by serious infringements of directly effective provisions of EU law. A German and an English case were referred to the Court of Justice under art.267. In both cases, national legislation had previously been held by the Court of Justice to infringe EU law.[78]

1-060

The court held that the principle of a Member State's liability for damage caused to individuals by infringements of EU law had been established in *Francovich v Italy*. It held that a right of reparation arose where the rule of EU law infringed was intended to confer rights on individuals, the breach was sufficiently serious and the breach directly caused damage to individuals. In determining whether the breach

1-061

---

[73] *Conseil National de L'Ordre Des Architectes v Egle* (310/90) [1992] E.C.R. I-177, [1992] 2 C.M.L.R. 113; *Re Business Transfer Directive: EC Commission v Belgium* (237/84) [1986] E.C.R. 1247, [1988] 2 C.M.L.R. 865; *R. v Immigration Appeal Tribunal Ex p. Antonissen* (C-292/89) [1991] E.C.R. I-745, [1991] 2 C.M.L.R. 373; and *Re Transport Workers: EC Commission v Greece* (C-306/89) [1991] E.C.R. I-5880, [1994] 1 C.M.L.R. 803.

[74] *Francovich v Italy* (C-6 and 9/90) [1991] E.C.R. I-5357; [1993] 2 C.M.L.R. 66.

[75] See also *Dillenkofer v Germany* (C-178/94) [1996] E.C.R. I-4845; [1996] 3 C.M.L.R. 469 and *Sweden v Stockholm Lindpark AB* (C-150/99) [2001] E.C.R. I-0493.

[76] *Rothmans & Philip Morris and Arizona* [1993] 1 C.M.L.R. 93, Conseil d'État.

[77] (C-46 and 48/93) [1996] E.C.R. I-1029; [1996] 1 C.M.L.R. 889.

[78] See *EC Commission v Germany* (178/84) [1987] E.C.R. 1227; [1988] 1 C.M.L.R. 780 and *Factortame (No.3)* (C-221/89) [1991] E.C.R. I-3905; 3 C.M.L.R. 589.

was sufficiently serious, the decisive test was whether the Member State manifestly and gravely disregarded the limits on its discretion. The court gave guidance on the factors which the national courts should consider with respect to this condition. These factors included the clarity and precision of the rule breached, the measure of discretion left to the national authorities, whether the infringement and damage caused were intentional or involuntary, whether any error of law was excusable, and whether the position taken by EU institutions may have contributed towards the Member State's breach of EU law. It held that a breach of EU law will clearly be sufficiently serious if it has persisted despite a judgment finding the infringement to be established or in the light of settled case law. It is a matter for the national court to decide whether a breach is sufficiently serious to justify the imposition of liability in damages. As regards the last condition, the national court must assess whether there was a direct causal link between the breach of the obligation borne by the state and the damage sustained by the applicant. In considering the extent of reparation, the court stated that it must be commensurate with the loss sustained, so as to ensure the effective protection of EU law rights. Provisions governing claims for compensation should not be less favourable than those applying to similar domestic claims, and they should include the right to exemplary damages for unconstitutional or oppressive conduct where this is provided for in national law for like claims.

Decisions

1-062   A decision is binding in its entirety upon those to whom it is addressed.[79] By their very nature, decisions only impose obligations on those to whom they are addressed. It is not thought that other persons can seek to rely upon such decisions in private actions for the same reasons as apply to Directives. Decisions intended for Member States are analogous to Directives and will be directly effective, provided the three conditions described above are met.[80]

Recommendations and opinions

1-063   Neither recommendations nor opinions have legal effect under the TFEU and are merely persuasive.[81] However, the Court of Justice has said that national courts are:

> "bound to take Community recommendations into consideration in deciding disputes submitted to them, in particular where they clarify the interpretation of national provisions adopted in order to implement them or where they are designed to supplement binding EEC measures".[82]

Supremacy of EU law

1-064   The TFEU and its predecessor Treaties are silent on the issue of whether EU law is superior to the domestic law of a Member State. In the early days, in several cases, this issue came before national courts and the Court of Justice. On a national

---

[79]   art.288.
[80]   See *Franz Grad v Finanzamt Traünstein* (9/70) [1970] E.C.R. 825; [1971] C.M.L.R. 1. See also fn.37.
[81]   art.288.
[82]   *Grimaldi v Fonds des Maladies Professionelles* (C-322/88) [1989] E.C.R. 4407; [1991] 2 C.M.L.R. 265.

level, initially, courts viewed the original Treaty of Rome as an international Convention which was recognised at a domestic level. If the Member State was monist, the Treaty became part of domestic law from the moment of ratification. If the Member State was dualist, it required incorporation by a domestic statute before becoming law in that state. However, whether a state was monist or dualist, the real issue was whether the various Treaties were merely another part of domestic law or whether, in fact, it had a higher authority.

The Court of Justice has consistently ruled that EU law takes precedence over national law. Thus, in *Costa v ENEL*,[83] there was a conflict between a number of treaty provisions and a later Italian statute. It was argued, on the basis of *lex posterior derogat priori*,[84] that the Italian law took priority. In *Internationale Handelgesellschaft mbH v Einfuhr-und Vorratsstelle für Getreide und Futtermittel*,[85] a claimant claimed in German proceedings that an EC Regulation was invalid because it conflicted with provisions of the German constitution. The Court of Justice was unequivocal when these cases concerning conflict between EEC laws and domestic laws were referred to it. It consistently ruled that laws derived from the EC Treaty must take precedence over domestic laws, whether constitutional in nature or otherwise. In *Simmenthal SpA v EC Commission*, a later case, the Italian constitutional court ruled that it would be prepared to declare any national law conflicting with EC law as invalid. However, in the case itself, where there was a conflict between EU and domestic law, the Italian judge was unsure as to whether he should wait for the domestic law to be declared invalid by the constitutional court or merely refuse to apply it. On reference to the Court of Justice,[86] the latter held that a national court was obliged to apply EU law and should refuse to apply any conflicting provisions of national legislation, even if adopted subsequently, and that it was not necessary to wait for the domestic law to be annulled. In the British case of *R v Secretary of State for Transport Ex p. Factortame Ltd (No.2)*,[87] the Court of Justice said, in the context of interlocutory proceedings, that a national court must refuse to apply a rule of national law if such would prevent it from giving interim relief based upon EU law.

1-065

For their part, the courts of Member States were initially slow to recognise the supremacy of EU law. In *Costa v ENEL* and *Internationale Handelgesellschaft*, as is clear from those authorities, the Italian and German constitutional courts did not consider that it was acte clair that EU law was supreme. However, there is no doubt that national courts now recognise the supremacy of EU law. In the UK, national courts have recognised the supremacy of EU law where it conflicts with domestic law.[88] In other Member States, courts have moved from their early stance so that EU law now takes precedence over national law although the matter is somewhat more nuanced in relation to the constitutions of Member States. Even the most

1-066

---

[83] (6/64) [1964] E.C.R. 585; [1964] C.M.L.R. 425.
[84] "The later law repeals the former law."
[85] (11/70) [1970] E.C.R. 1125; [1972] C.M.L.R. 255.
[86] (92/78) [1979] E.C.R. 777; [1980] 1 C.M.L.R. 25.
[87] [1990] 3 C.M.L.R. 867.
[88] See *Macarthys Ltd v Smith* [1979] I.C.R. 785 CA; *Garland v British Rail Engineering* [1983] 2 A.C. 751 HL; *Factortame Ltd v Secretary of State for Transport* [1989] 2 All E.R. 692 HL; *Pickstone v Freemans* [1989] A.C. 66 HL; *R. v Secretary of State for Transport Ex p. Factortame (No.2)* [1991] 1 All E.R. 106; *McKechnie v UBM Building Supplies (Southern) Ltd* [1991] I.C.R. 710, EAT. In contrast, see the early case of *Felixstowe Dock & Railway Co v British Transport Docks Board* [1976] 2 C.M.L.R. 655 CA. See also, *Thorburn v Sunderland CC* [2003] Q.B. 151.

chauvinist of Member States, France, now recognises the supremacy of EU law.[89] In Germany, the German constitutional court reversed its position taken in *Internationale Handelgesellschaft*,[90] and accept the supremacy of EU law where it is directly effective, provided that the latter respects fundamental rights.[91] In Italy, the constitutional court reversed its earlier position in *Costa v ENEL* and now recognises the supremacy of EU law but reserved its right to ensure that the fundamental principles of the Italian constitution were not infringed by Union law.[92] However, in Poland, the Constitutional Tribunal held that whilst EU law may override national statutes, it did not override the constitution of Poland and that in the case of conflict, Poland could make a sovereign decision as to how this conflict should be resolved.[93] In other countries, this issue has been resolved by amendments to their constitution.[94]

1-067   On a final note, the surrender of sovereignty to the EU by Member States is voluntary. Article 50 TFEU allows a Member State to leave the EU and in March 2017, the UK invoked the same.

Application and interpretation of EU law

1-068   As discussed earlier, the TFEU is not merely an international convention which is only addressed to Member States. It affects individuals conferring rights and obligations on them. It forms part of a Member State's domestic law and, provided the relevant provision is directly effective, can be relied upon in a national court. In the case of Articles of the TFEU and Regulations, if directly effective, they can be relied upon against other individuals. In the case of a Directive, if directly effective they can only be relied upon by individuals against the Member State who has failed to implement the Directive.

1-069   As well as private actions against individuals or Member States, the TFEU provides for the enforcement of EU laws in various other ways. First, under the TFEU and its secondary legislation, the European Commission is often empowered, especially in competition law, to enforce EU law against Member States and individuals. Secondly, the TFEU provides for various mechanisms to ensure that EU institutions and Member States comply with their obligations under the TFEU.

---

[89]   *Nicolo Semoules* [1990] C.M.L.R. 173; *Boisdet* [1991] 1 C.M.L.R. 3. In *Nicolo Semoules*, the French administrative courts which are separate to ordinary courts followed the decision in the Cour de Cassation (the highest ordinary court) in *Administration des Douanes v Societe 'Cafés Jacques Vabre et SARL Wiegel et Cie'* [1975] 2 C.M.L.R. 336. See also *Rothmans and Arizona Tobacco* [1993] 1 C.M.L.R. 253 where the Conseil d'État held that a Directive would prevail over a subsequently adopted statute.

[90]   *Internationale Handelgesellschaft (Solange I)* [1974] 2 C.M.L.R. 430.

[91]   *Application of Wunsche Handelgesellschaft (Solange II)* [1987] 3 C.M.L.R. 225; *Re Kloppenberg* [1988] 3 C.M.L.R. 1. However, the matter is nuanced. Thus, in *Brunner v The European Union Treaty* [1994] 1 C.M.L.R. 57, the FCC affirmed German constitutional sovereignty and its right to review the scope of Community competence. Where a Directive is not directly effective, the Bundesgerichtshof refused to interpret domestic law against its clear meaning to comply with an EU Directive—see *Re a Rehabilitation Centre* [1992] 2 C.M.L.R. 21.

[92]   *Frontini v Ministero delle Finanze*(232/89) [1974] 2 C.M.L.R. 372; *Spa Fragd v Amministrazione dell Finanze dello Stato*.

[93]   Verdict of the Constitutional Tribunal of Poland of 11 May 2005; K 18/04. See K. Kowalik-Bañczyk, "Should We Polish it Up? The Polish Constitutional Tribunal and the Idea of Supremacy of EU Law" (2005) *German Law Journal* 6(10), 1355–1366.

[94]   e.g. see art.10 of the Constitution of the Czech Republic which states that every international Treaty ratified by Parliament takes precedence over all other laws and in Ireland, the Third Amendment to the Constitution of Ireland which also provides explicitly for the supremacy of EU law.

Thus, art.258 enables the Commission to bring proceedings against Member States for failure to fulfil an obligation under the Treaty. Article 259 permits a Member State to bring an action against another Member State for the latter's failure to fulfil its Community obligations.

Furthermore, the TFEU provides for a number of mechanisms whereby the Court of Justice may consider issues of EU law and the acts of EU institutions. Under art.267 TFEU, a court may refer a question of EU law to the Court of Justice or the validity of acts of institutions of the EU. Article 263 permits an individual to request the Court of Justice to review the legality of acts done by EU institutions on the grounds of lack of competence, infringement of an essential procedural requirement, infringement of the TFEU or of any rule of law relating to its application, or misuse of powers. Similarly, under art.265, an individual can bring proceedings before the Court of Justice if a EU institution fails to act in infringement of the TFEU. Finally, under arts 268 and 340, the Court of Justice has jurisdiction to award damages in a case of non-contractual liability against an EU institution, where it or its servants act in breach of the general principles common to the laws of the Member States.

1-070

These mechanisms are now considered in more detail.

1-071

Preliminary references to the Court of Justice

Article 267 TFEU provides that:

1-072

"The Court of Justice of the European Union shall have jurisdiction to give preliminary rulings concerning:

(a) the interpretation of the Treaties;
(b) the validity and interpretation of acts of the institutions, bodies, offices or agencies of the Union;

Where such a question is raised before any court or tribunal of a Member State, that court or tribunal may, if it considers that a decision on the question is necessary to enable it to give judgment, request the Court to give a ruling thereon.

Where any such question is raised in a case pending before a court or tribunal of a Member State against whose decisions there is no judicial remedy under national law, that court or tribunal shall bring the matter before the Court.

If such a question is raised in a case pending before a court or tribunal of a Member State with regard to a person in custody, the Court of Justice of the European Union shall act with the minimum of delay."

It should be noted that the ability to make a reference under art.267 is limited. Only national courts have jurisdiction when it comes to the application of EU law to disputes between individuals. Accordingly, the Court of Justice will not rule on the application of EU law to a set of facts, even if that is the overriding issue in a case. Instead, it will put forward an abstract interpretation of the law.[95] The Court of Justice has emphasised that it can only answer the national court's question on the basis of the facts as they appear from the order for reference. Thus, in the context of proceedings raising an important point on the extent of a trade-mark owner's rights, the court said it would not depart from the stated facts because the owner of the mark, not being a party to the main proceedings, could not put its argument

1-073

---

[95] This often includes "helpful guidance" as the application of its interpretation to a particular set of facts!

to the court.[96] The Court of Justice will only rule in real disputes—it will not give a ruling on hypothetical questions.[97] Also, the Court of Justice is not an appellate court from the court of last instance of a Member State. If a party to proceedings considers that the court of last instance has wrongly applied EU law or refused to make a reference because it considers the interpretation of EU legislation to be clear and unambiguous, the party cannot appeal to the Court of Justice.

1-074   Any court or tribunal may refer an issue to the Court of Justice provided that the court or tribunal has a public element. Thus, an arbitrator appointed to settle privately a dispute between parties cannot make use of art.267.[98] The Greek Competition Commission was not a court or tribunal as it was not sufficiently independent of the Minister for Development.[99]

1-075   Under art.267, a distinction should be made between courts which fall within the second and third paragraph of art.267 (which are, for convenience's sake called arts 267(2) and 267(3)). Courts other than those of last resort have a discretion to refer to the Court of Justice when an issue as to interpretation arises, whereas the court of last resort is obliged in such circumstances to refer. A decision by an inferior court which is not capable of appeal is, for the purposes of art.267, a court that falls within art.267(3) and, thus, must refer to the Court of Justice if an issue as to the interpretation of EU law is raised.[100] However, where as a matter of procedural law of a Member State, a declaration of admissibility is required before a case can be appealed to the highest court from the court below and such will only be given if it is important for guidance in the application of the law or if there are special grounds for examination of the appeal, the Court of Justice has held that this did not mean that the court below was the court of last resort.[101] Inferior courts of a Member State are free to request a ruling from the Court of Justice, even if a clear domestic precedent or ruling given by a superior domestic court exists.[102]

1-076   The Court of Justice in *CILFIT Srl v Ministro della Sanità* has said that national courts (whether courts of last resort or not) need not refer automatically an issue to the Court of Justice when a question of the interpretation or validity of a EU law is raised. There is no need to refer when: (a) the question of EU law is irrelevant, (b) the EU provisions have already been interpreted by the Court of Justice, even though the questions at issue are not strictly identical, or (c) the correct application is so obvious as to leave no scope for reasonable doubt. In such circumstances, the matter is acte clair and there is need to refer.[103] The application of these three

---

[96] *Phytheron International SA v Jean Bourdon SA* (C-352/95) [1997] E.C.R. I-1729; [1997] F.S.R. 937.

[97] *Traunfellner* (C-421/01) [2003] E.C.R. I-11941 at [37].

[98] *Nordsee Deutsche Hochseefischerei GmbH v Reederei Mond Hochseefischerei Nordstern AG & Co KG* (102/81) [1982] E.C.R. 1095.

[99] *Synetairismos Farmakopoion Aitolias & Akarnanias (SYFAIT) v Glaxosmithkline* (C-53/03) [2005] E.C.R. I-4609 at [29]–[34]. In this case, the CJEU give detailed guidance as to what is a court or tribunal within the meaning of art.267.

[100] See *Costa v ENEL* (6/64) [1964] E.C.R. 585; [1964] C.M.L.R. 425, where the CJEU said that "national courts against whose decisions as in the present case there is no judicial remedy must refer the matter to the Court of Justice". In this case, the national court was an Italian magistrate's court.

[101] *Lyckeskog* (C-99/00) [2002] E.C.R. I-4839 (reference from Sweden). That has been followed in *Cartesio* (C-210/06) [2008] E.C.R. I-9641. In the UK, see *Magnavision NV v General Optical Council* [1987] 2 C.M.L.R. 262 and *Chiron v Murex Diagnostics (No.8)* [1995] F.S.R. 309 CA (leave to appeal from the Court of Appeal to Supreme Court was refused).

[102] *Rheinmühlen-Dusseldorf* (146/73) [1974] E.C.R. 139; [1974] 1 C.M.L.R. 523. Cf. Wood J's remarks to the contrary in *Enderby v Frenchay HA* [1991] I.C.R. 382, EAT.

[103] *CILFIT Srl v Ministra dello Sanita* (C-283/81) [1982] E.C.R. 3415; [1983] 1 C.M.L.R. 472. The

conditions must be assessed in the light of the specific characteristics of EU law, the particular difficulties to which its interpretation gives rise, and the risk of divergences in judicial decisions within the EU.[104]

A court other than that of last resort has discretion to refer. Factors like time, cost, workload of the Court of Justice, and the wishes of the parties should be taken into account.[105] Where the issue is raised at a court of last resort, then the issue as to whether the matter falls within the *CILFIT* criteria becomes of crucial importance. If such a court takes the view that there is no need to refer, then that is the end of the matter.[106]   **1-077**

Where the decision involves a ruling on the invalidity of a EU measure, the Court of Justice has stated that inferior national courts do not have jurisdiction to declare EU measures invalid and that, if they have any doubts, a reference must be made.[107] Furthermore, if a party seeks a reference under art.267 that a EU act is invalid, the Court of Justice may refuse jurisdiction if the party concerned could have brought proceedings under art.263 for annulment of the act but failed to do so within the two-month period.[108]   **1-078**

A procedural rule in a Member State that prevents a national court from considering of its own motion whether or not a measure of domestic law is compatible with a provision of EU law will normally be contrary to EU law.[109]   **1-079**

The Court of Justice has given useful guidance to national courts in relation to references under art.267, based on its case law.[110]   **1-080**

Judicial review of acts of EU institutions

Article 263 TFEU provides: **1-081**

"The Court of Justice of the European Union shall review the legality of legislative acts, of acts of the Council, of the Commission and of the European Central Bank, other than recommendations and opinions, and of acts of the European Parliament and of the European Council intended to produce legal effects vis-à-vis third parties. It shall also review the legality of acts of bodies, offices or agencies of the Union intended to produce legal effects vis-à-vis third parties.

It shall for this purpose have jurisdiction in actions brought by a Member State, the European Parliament, the Council or the Commission on grounds of lack of competence, infringement of an essential procedural requirement, infringement of the Treaties or of any rule of law relating to their application, or misuse of powers.

---

expression "acte clair" comes from French administrative law.

[104] For cases on "need to refer" in England, see *Bulmer v Bollinger* [1974] Ch. 401 CA; *R. v Henn* [1978] 1 W.L.R. 1031; *R. v Inner London Education Authority Ex p. Hinde* [1985] 1 C.M.L.R. 716 HC.

[105] See Lord Denning MR in *Bulmer v Bollinger* [1974] Ch. 401 CA.

[106] However, in Germany, the German Federal Constitutional Court will review decisions by courts of last instance where it is clear that the court's decision does not comply with the CILFIT criterion—see *Re VAT Directive* [1982] 1 C.M.L.R. 527, [1989] 1 C.M.L.R. 873; *Re Patented Feedingstuffs* [1989] 2 C.M.L.R. 902.

[107] *Foto-Frost v Hauptzollamt Lübeck-Ost* (314/85) [1987] E.C.R. 4199 at 4232; [1988] 3 C.M.L.R. 57.

[108] *TWD v Germany* (C-188/92) [1994] E.C.R. I-833.

[109] *Peterbroeck v Van Campenhout & Cie* (C-312/93) [1996] 1 C.M.L.R. 793. See, also, a similar case in *Van Schijndel v Stichting Pensioenfonds voor Fysiotherapeuten* (C-430–431/93) [1996] 1 C.M.L.R. 801.

[110] Information Notice on references from national courts for a preliminary ruling [2009] OJ C/297/01.

The Court shall have jurisdiction under the same conditions in actions brought by the Court of Auditors, by the European Central Bank and by the Committee of the Regions for the purpose of protecting their prerogatives.

Any natural or legal person may, under the conditions laid down in the first and second paragraphs, institute proceedings against an act addressed to that person or which is of direct and individual concern to them, and against a regulatory act which is of direct concern to them and does not entail implementing measures.

Acts setting up bodies, offices and agencies of the Union may lay down specific conditions and arrangements concerning actions brought by natural or legal persons against acts of these bodies, offices or agencies intended to produce legal effects in relation to them.

The proceedings provided for in this Article shall be instituted within two months of the publication of the measure, or of its notification to the plaintiff, or, in the absence thereof, of the day on which it came to the knowledge of the latter, as the case may be."

1-082   Article 263 permits individuals to challenge the legality of EU acts. Any act which produces legal effects for the parties concerned and brings about a change in their legal position is an act capable of annulment under art.263.[111]

1-083   For an individual to challenge an act of an EU institution, as set out in art.263, they must show that it is of direct and individual concern to them if it is not a decision addressed to them. The Court of Justice has given many decisions as to whether an individual has satisfied these criteria. In *Plaumann v EC Commission*,[112] a German importer of clementines sought to challenge a decision by the Commission addressed to the German government, whereby it refused the latter permission to reduce its customs duties on clementines. The Court of Justice held that, in order for the applicant to avail himself of art.263, he must show that the decision affects him because of certain characteristics which are peculiarly relevant to him, or by reason of circumstances in which he is differentiated from all other persons, and not by the mere fact that he belongs to a class of persons who are affected.[113] It is clear that the number of persons affected by an EU measure is not relevant.[114] However, if the applicant forms part of a "closed" class of persons to whom the measure is directed such that no one else is capable of entering that class or being affected by the same measure, then the case law of the Court of Justice suggests that the measure is one of "direct and individual" concern to that applicant.[115] Where the EU measure was issued as a result of proceedings initiated by the applicant, the latter

---

[111] *Re Noordwijks Cement Accoord* (8–11/66) [1967] E.C.R. 75; [1967] C.M.L.R. 77, CJEU (a registered letter was sent to companies by the Commission notifying them that their immunity from fines under EC competition law was at an end, was an act capable of review under art.267). Cf. *Nashua Corporation v EC Commission & Council* (C-133 and 150/87) [1990] 1 E.C.R. 719; [1990] 2 C.M.L.R. 6 (preliminary measures paving way for final decision not a reviewable act).

[112] (25/62) [1963] E.C.R. 95; [1964] C.M.L.R. 29, CJEU.

[113] See also, *Cassa Nazionale di Previdenza ed Assistenza a favore degli Avvocati e Procuratori v EU Council* (T-116/94R) [1995] E.C.R. II-0001. See also, *Campo Ebro Industrial SA v EU Council* (T-472/93) [1995] E.C.R. II-0421; [1996] 1 C.M.L.R. (action brought by Spanish isoglucose manufacturers to annul Community Reg.3814/92 was inadmissible).

[114] *Glucoseries Reunies v EC Commission* (1/64) [1964] E.C.R. 413; [1964] C.M.L.R. 596.

[115] e.g. see *Toepfer v EC Commission* (106/63) [1965] E.C.R. 405, [1966] C.M.L.R. 111; *International Fruit Co v EC Commission* (41/70) [1972] E.C.R. 1219, [1975] 2 C.M.L.R. 515; *Japanese Ballbearings* (113 & 118–121/77) [1979] E.C.R. 1185, [1979] 2 C.M.L.R. 257; *Sofrimport SARL v EC Commission* [1990] E.C.R. I-2477, [1990] 3 C.M.L.R. 80. See also, R. Greaves, "Locus Standi under Article [230] when seeking annulment of a Regulation" [1986] 11 E.L.Rev. 119.

will normally have little difficulty in showing that the measure is of direct and individual concern to them.[116]

In several cases, the Court of Justice, in ruling that the applicant does not have **1-084** locus standi, has said that the validity of EU acts is open to attack under art.277 in national proceedings.[117] The Court of Justice refused jurisdiction under art.263 where a party sought a reference that a EU decision addressed to the German government was invalid because the party had been informed of the decision and of their right to challenge it and had failed to do so within the two-month period provided for in art.263.[118]

Provided the action is brought within the two-month period, the court will review **1-085** the decision on the four grounds of lack of competence, infringement of an essential procedural requirement, infringement of the Treaty or any rule of law relating to its application, or misuse of powers. The Court of Justice does not interpret these provisions restrictively and will often show little reluctance in reviewing the reasoning behind the act or decision almost de novo. If the proceedings under art.263 are successful, the Court of Justice will declare the measure void under art.264.

Failure to act by institutions of the EU

Article 265 TFEU provides: **1-086**

"Should the European Parliament, the European Council, the Council, the Commission or the European Central Bank, in infringement of the Treaties, fail to act, the Member States and the other institutions of the Union may bring an action before the Court of Justice of the European Union to have the infringement established. This Article shall apply, under the same conditions, to bodies, offices and agencies of the Union which fail to act.

The action shall be admissible only if the institution, body, office or agency concerned has first been called upon to act. If, within two months of being so called upon, the institution, body, office or agency concerned has not defined its position, the action may be brought within a further period of two months.

Any natural or legal person may, under the conditions laid down in the preceding paragraphs, complain to the Court that an institution, body, office or agency of the Union has failed to address to that person any act other than a recommendation or an opinion."

Articles 263 and 265 are complementary in nature. Thus, where there is **1-087** uncertainty as to which Article should be invoked, it is not necessary to characterise the proceedings as being under one or the other Article, since both Articles merely prescribe one and the same method of recourse.[119] The institutions called upon to act must be under a clear and definable obligation for art.265 to be invoked.[120]

Although art.265 is silent on the issue of who has locus standi, the Court of **1-088**

---

[116] See *Metro-SB-Grössmarkte v EC Commission* (26/76) [1977] E.C.R. 1875; [1978] 2 C.M.L.R. 1.
[117] e.g. see *Koninklijke Scholten-Honig v EC Council and Commission* (101/76) [1977] E.C.R. 797; [1980] 2 C.M.L.R. 669 and *Royal Scholten-Honig (Holdings) Ltd v Intervention Board for Agriculture Produce* (C-103/77) [1978] E.C.R. 2037; [1979] 1 C.M.L.R. 675, where, in the first case, the CJEU held that the applicant had failed to establish locus standi but annulled the Regulation in the later case on reference under art.267.
[118] *TWD v Germany* (C-188/92) [1994] E.C.R. I-833.
[119] e.g. see *Chevalley v EC Commission* (15/70) [1970] E.C.R. 975.
[120] *European Parliament v EC Council* (13/83) [1985] E.C.R. 1513; [1986] 1 C.M.L.R. 138.

Justice has implied the condition under art.265 that the failure to act is of individual and direct concern to the applicant. In effect, the applicant must fulfil two conditions. First, that the act, if carried out, would be of direct and individual concern to the applicant, and secondly, that the applicant is legally entitled to demand action.[121]

1-089   Once the relevant institution is called upon to act, it may execute the act requested, define its position or do nothing. Usually, the relevant institution (normally the Commission) will define its position in a letter to the applicant. Often, this merely amounts to a refusal to act in writing. In such circumstances, art.265 is no longer relevant and the applicant is obliged to issue proceedings under art.263 for annulment of the communication which defines the institution's position.

1-090   If the applicant can satisfy the above requirements, the court will review whether the institution's failure to act constitutes an infringement of the Treaty. Often, it will rule that the institution has discretion in the pursuit of the objectives under the Treaty and, accordingly, the institution is under no obligation to act. However, often the applicant's procedural rights will have been infringed (i.e. the right of a complainant to a full hearing) and the court may order that such rights are respected.

1-091   If an action under art.265 is successful, then the court will order that the institution shall take all necessary measures to comply with the judgment of the Court of Justice.[122]

Incidental review of regulations before the Court of Justice

1-092   Article 277 TFEU provides that:

> "Notwithstanding the expiry of the period laid down in Article 263, sixth paragraph, any party may, in proceedings in which an act of general application adopted by an institution, body, office or agency of the Union is at issue, plead the grounds specified in Article 263, second paragraph, in order to invoke before the Court of Justice of the European Union the inapplicability of that act."

This provision permits parties to plead that any act of general application (normally a regulation) is inapplicable where such is incidental to the main proceedings in proceedings before the Court of Justice. In proceedings before national courts, parties are free to raise an issue as the validity of such a legislative act by reference to the Court of Justice under art.267. Article 277 cannot be used directly to attack an act of general application.[123] The Court of Justice will not permit art.277 to be used to evade time limits under other provisions.[124] However, where the validity of an act is based on the validity of a legislative act, then art.277 permits a party to claim that the act is inapplicable and, thus, the act invalid. Accordingly, art.277 is often used when allied to a claim under art.263, where the challenged act derives its valid-

---

[121] *Firma MackPrang v EC Commission* (15/71) [1971] E.C.R. 797, [1972] C.M.L.R. 52; *Bethell v EC Commission* (246/81) [1982] E.C.R. 2277, [1982] 3 C.M.L.R. 300; *Star Fruit Company SA v EC Commission* (247/87) [1989] E.C.R. 291, [1990] 1 C.M.L.R. 733; *Nordgetreide v EC Commission* (42/71) [1972] E.C.R. 105; [1973] C.M.L.R. 177.

[122] art.266 TFEU.

[123] *Milchwerke Heinz Wohrmann & Sohn v EC Commission* (31/62) [1962] E.C.R. 501; [1966] C.M.L.R. 152.

[124] See (31/62) [1962] E.C.R. 501; [1966] C.M.L.R. 152 and *EC Commission v Belgium* [1978] E.C.R. 1881.

ity from a Regulation which the applicant claims is invalid.[125] However, it can be used with art.265 where a failure to act is justified by resort to an invalid act of general application.[126]

The grounds for review are the same as in art.267. It should be noted that art.277 **1-093** only entitles the Court of Justice to rule that the legislative act is inapplicable inter partes. It does not result in the annulment of the relevant EU legislation.

THE EU AND INTELLECTUAL PROPERTY

Introduction

In 1958, following the entry into force of the Treaty of Rome (also then called **1-094** the European Economic Treaty), the view was that there was no EU competence to legislate in the field of intellectual property.[127] The view was therefore that any harmonisation of IPRs had to take place at an international and not at a EU level. This indeed occurred in relation to the European Patent Convention which was signed in 1973 and came into force in 1976. This is a regional European treaty and not an EU legislative measure. Attempts were made to develop regional treaties which were specific to EEC countries such as the Community Patent Convention (CPC). However, this was not intended to be a EU legislative measure. This never came into force despite being adopted at a conference in 1989. However, the aim and purpose of the CPC is now to be achieved via the Unified Patent which introduces a unitary EU patent similar to the EU Trade Mark, Community Design and Community Plant Variety Right. It is anticipated that will come into force in 2018 or 2019.[128]

The view that the EEC had no relevance to intellectual property was challenged **1-095** by lawyers and academics, who maintained that, in certain circumstances, industrial property and the exercise of their rights would result in anti-competitive practices and that the competition provisions of the Treaty of Rome applied as much to such practices as others.[129] Such academics drew inspiration from the founding Member States' laws which provided several solutions as to how to reconcile intellectual property with the freedom of goods and services and the competition provision of the EEC. Thus, German antitrust law prohibited restrictions in licences which extended beyond the "scope of the patent". Other commentators suggested that the traditional exclusionary effects of industrial protection rights should be restricted under the Treaty of Rome where parallel protection rights were held by the same person on the basis that an inventor should only have one opportunity to obtain remuneration for their invention.[130]

---

[125] e.g. see *Simmenthal SpA v EC Commission* (92/78) [1979] E.C.R. 777; [1980] 1 C.M.L.R. 25, CJEU.

[126] *SNUPAT v High Authority* (32/58) [1959] E.C.R. 127.

[127] G. Sen, *GRUR Int. 1958*, referred to at H. Johannes, *Industrial Property and Copyright in European Community Law* (Leyden: Sijthoff, 1976), p.7; V. Scordamaglia, "Constructing European Intellectual Property—Achievements and Perspectives" in C. Geiger (ed), *The legal framework of the legislative activity concerning intellectual property rights at European regional level* (Cheltenham: Edward Elgar, 2013), p.62. This view was taken by reason of arts 36 and 222 Treaty of Rome (now arts 36 and 345 TFEU). Article 222 states that the Treaty shall in no way prejudice the rules in Member States governing the system of property ownership.

[128] This is discussed at para.2-506.

[129] e.g. see V. van Themaat, *GRUR Int. 1964*, p.21.

[130] N. Koch and F. Froschmaier, "The Doctrine of Territoriality in Patent Law and the European Com-

1-096   Against this background, the Court of Justice began considering the relationship between IPRs and the Treaty of Rome in the 1960s when right holders brought
proceedings to prevent parallel imports between Member States. Initially, in the
1960s, the exercise of IPRs was considered under the competition provisions of the
Treaty of Rome but in the 1970s, a number of landmark judgments of the Court of
Justice made it clear that when considering the exercise of IPRs to prevent trade
between Member States, the most relevant provisions were the free movement of
goods provisions of the Treaty of Rome—arts 30–36 (now arts 34–36 TFEU). This
led to the development by the Court of Justice of the exhaustion of rights principle
whereby, as discussed in the previous paragraph, the owner of parallel rights should
only have one opportunity to obtain remuneration for their rights and thus could not
prevent parallel imports. The landmark cases of the Court of Justice are discussed
in Ch.7, "Intellectual Property and Free Movement of Goods".[131] In its decisions,
it was clear that two factors were important. First, that a fundamental objective of
the Treaty of Rome was a single (common) market with no customs barriers inside
it. Secondly, its clear view that EU law was of a superior status to the laws of
Member States. Such permitted the Court of Justice to take a robust view of the ability of the Treaty of Rome to prevent the exercise of IPRs granted under the domestic
laws of Member States. Thus, gradually, from its first decision in the mid-1960s in
Consten & Grundig,[132] the Court of Justice developed principles which delineated
the relationship between EU law and national IPRs. The most important principle
was that an IPR owner cannot exercise their rights to prevent the subsequent circulation of a product that has been placed on the market in the Community by them or
with their consent. This can be seen as the extension of a national doctrine of
exhaustion of rights to an EU-wide exhaustion of rights. These principles are looked
at in Ch.7, "Intellectual Property and Free Movement of Goods".

1-097   In parallel, in the 1970s, the European Commission formed the view, contrary
to the academic view discussed above, that harmonisation of the intellectual
property laws of Member States by the issuing of Directives was not prohibited by
the Treaty of Rome. It considered that it had power to issue harmonising Directives in the field of IPR where such was necessary for the purpose of attaining a
single market in the EEC.[133] The reasoning was that until the intellectual property
laws were harmonised, then trade in goods protected by IPRs within the common
market would be substantially hindered. Furthermore, the Commission took the
view that there was also power under the Treaty of Rome to issue regulations
providing for unitary Community-wide IPRs. Thus, in the early 1970s, it started
considering proposals for a trade mark directive which harmonised trade mark law
in the Member States of the EEC and also a regulation providing for a single
Community-wide trade mark (the Community Trade Mark). After very protracted
discussion and negotiation, a trade mark Directive was introduced in 1989 and a
Community Trademark regulation in 1993. There then followed a large number of

---

mon Market" (1965) *IDEA, the Patent, Trade mark and Copyright Journal of Research and Education*, Vol.9, 343.

[131] See para.7-009, et seq.

[132] *Etablissements Consten & Grundig v EC Commission* (56/64) [1966] E.C.R. 299; [1966] C.M.L.R.
418.

[133] art.100 EEC Treaty allows the issuing of Directives for the approximation of laws which have a direct
incidence on the establishment or functioning of the Common Market. It is the predecessor provision to art.114 TFEU.

harmonising Directives in the field of designs, copyright, databases, biotechnology patents and plant variety rights. Alongside these, the European Community introduced a Community Registered Design and a Community Plant Variety Right. After many fruitless years, the EU introduced via the "enhanced cooperation procedure" in the TFEU patent legislation which provides for a Unitary Patent that has yet to come into force, but when it comes into effect, provides for a patent with unitary effect in all Member States other than Spain and Croatia. This will sit alongside the Agreement on a Unified Patent Court which sets up a specialist pan-European court to hear infringement and validity proceedings on the Unitary Patent as well as "classic" European patents.

The consequence of the enactment of EU IPR Directives and regulations in the   **1-098**
field of IPRs is that the Court of Justice has much less reason to consider the legality under primary Treaty provisions law of the exercise of the IPRs. As the IPRs now owe their existence to EU Directives and Regulations, the conflict between the exercise of IPRs and the TFEU has been "internalised" within the Directives and Regulations. For instance, all IPR Directives have "internalised" the Court of Justice's doctrine of exhaustion of rights into IP Directives and EU unitary right regulations so that those Directives and Regulations provide a specific defence to an action for infringement of a particular right where the defendant is dealing in a product which has been placed on the market in the European Economic Area by the IPR owner or with their consent.[134] Indeed, the Court of Justice has taken the view that once a Directive is introduced which is intended to harmonise IPR law in a particular area via a Directive or Regulation, then it is not allowed to rely directly upon the free movement of goods provisions of TFEU as the Directive or Regulation is intended to *internalise* the tension at a treaty level between the exercise of IPR and the free movement of goods provisions *within* the Directive.[135]

It is thus now convenient in more detail to consider the legislative basis for the   **1-099**
enactment of these IPR legislative measures.

Legislative basis for EU intellectual property legislation

Harmonising Directives

The prime justification of the Commission for putting forward harmonising   **1-100**
provisions in the field of intellectual property has been to remove national differences and attain a single market. To this end, art.114 TFEU provides as follows:

> "1.   Save where otherwise provided in the Treaties, the following provisions shall apply for the achievement of the objectives set out in Article 26. The European Parliament and the Council shall, acting in accordance with the ordinary legislative procedure and after consulting the Economic and Social Committee, adopt the measures for the approximation of the provisions laid down by law, regulation or administrative action in Member States which have as their object the establishment and functioning of the internal market."

The predecessor to this provision was art.100 EEC Treaty and after that art.95   **1-101**

---

[134] The EEA Agreement extended the EU-wide doctrine to an EEA-wide doctrine. See para.7-335, et seq.
[135] This is discussed in more detail Ch.7 at para.7-093.

EC Treaty.[136] Recourse to art.114 as a legal basis is possible if the aim is to prevent the emergence of future obstacles to trade resulting from multifarious development of national laws of Member States, provided that the emergence of such obstacles is likely and the measure in question is designed to prevent them.[137] Thus, the legal basis on which a EU legislative act is adopted must be determined according to its main object.[138]

1-102 Article 114 (and its predecessors) has been used by EU institutions as the legal basis for issuing a substantial number of harmonising Directives in the field of intellectual property. This legal basis has been considered a number of times by the Court of Justice following challenges by Member States to the validity of such legislation. In *Spain v EU Council*,[139] the Kingdom of Spain challenged the validity of the EC Regulation which permitted patentees of pharmaceutical drugs to apply for a Supplemental Protection Certificate ("SPC") where there had been a delay in the grant of marketing authorisation for the pharmaceutical.[140] If a SPC is granted, it extends the protection of a pharmaceutical patent via sui generis protection. Spain argued that in the allocation of powers between the EU and Member States, the predecessor Articles to arts 36 and 345 TFEU[141] meant that Member States had exclusive sovereignty over industrial property matters and that the EU had no power to regulate substantive patent law. They submitted that the EU could only harmonise those aspects relating to the exercise of industrial property rights which are capable of having an effect upon the achievement of the general objectives laid down in the EC Treaty. They submitted that such action could not take the form of a new industrial property right, particularly one which, in effect, changed the duration of a patent. The Court of Justice rejected the argument that the predecessors to arts 36 and 345 reserved exclusively to Member States the ability to enact new IPRs. Moreover, the court said that the effect of these articles was to confer competence on the EU to harmonise national laws in the field of intellectual property.[142] Such provisions entitled the EU, in order to achieve the objectives of the Treaty, to legislate in the field of intellectual property, in particular, the attainment of an internal market without frontiers. The court held that the adoption of a Regulation conferring a SPC was aimed at harmonising differing national laws on the grant of a SPC. Thus, when it was adopted, two Member States had enacted for such a right and another state was preparing to do so. By providing for a EU-wide right, the Regulation was aimed at preventing the fragmentation of the internal market whereby the medicine would be protected in some states but not others.

1-103 Later in the 1990s, the Netherlands challenged the validity of the Biotechnology Directive, which sought to harmonise national laws of Member States relat-

---

136 In 1986, the Single European Act modified art.100 to permit qualified voting but was otherwise, in essence, the same (it then became art.100a). Article 100a became art.95 EC Treaty following the Amsterdam Treaty. In essence, all these provisions are the same insofar as they permit harmonising Directives in the field of IPR but the legislative mechanism (e.g. unanimous vs. qualified majority voting) differed.

137 *Spain v Council* (C-350/92) [1995] E.C.R. I-1985 at [35]; *Germany v Parliament and Council* (C-376/98) [2000] E.C.R. I-8419 at [86]; and *Netherlands, Italy and Norway v Parliament, Council & Commission* (C-377/98) [2001] E.C.R. I-7079 at [15].

138 *Commission v Council* (C-155/91) [1993] E.C.R. I-939 at [19]–[21]; (C-377/98) [2001] E.C.R. I-7079 at [27]–[28].

139 (C-350/92) [1995] E.C.R. I-1985; [1996] 1 C.M.L.R. 415.

140 This Regulation is discussed in Ch.2, para.2-603.

141 art.345 states that "This Treaty shall in no way prejudice the rules in Member States governing the system of property ownership".

142 Referring to *Opinion 1/94* [1994] E.C.R. I-5267 at [55]–[71].

ing to the controversial and difficult area of patent protection of biotechnological inventions.[143] As with the SPC Regulation, the Directive was enacted pursuant to the predecessor to art.114. The Netherlands States submitted that as Member States' patent laws were derived from the European Patent Convention ("EPC"), including the availability of patent protection for biotechnological inventions, then the European Union should have re-negotiated the EPC rather than, in effect, amend the EPC via the route of a harmonising Directive. The Court of Justice rejected this argument. It said that there was nothing to prevent the EU legislature from having recourse to harmonisation by means of a Directive in preference to the more indirect and unpredictable approach of seeking to amend the wording of the EPC.[144] The Italian government, intervening on behalf of the Netherlands, submitted that, as the chief aim of the Directive was concerned with supporting the industrial development of the EU and scientific research in the genetic engineering sector, then it should have been adopted on the basis of predecessor Articles to arts 173 and 179 TFEU.[145] The Court of Justice again rejected this argument, stating that the legal basis on which an act is adopted must be determined according to its main object.[146] It said that it was common ground that whilst the aim of the Biotechnological Directive was to promote research and development in the field of genetic engineering in the EC, the purpose of the Directive was to remove obstacles to such research and development which exist as a result of differences in national legislation and case law.[147]

However, art.114 has its limits. It cannot be relied upon solely on the basis that **1-104** there exist disparities between the laws of Member States in a particular field. If such were the only criterion for invoking art.114, it would allow the EU to issue harmonising Directives in every area of law. It must be shown that the harmonising legislative act does actually contribute to eliminating obstacles to the free movement of goods and to the freedom to provide services, and to removing distortions of competition.[148] In joined cases *Poland v Parliament and Council*,[149] *Pillbox 3(UK) Ltd v Secretary of State for Health* and *Philip Morris Brands Sàrl v Secretary of State for Health*,[150] Dir.2014/40/EU which required standardisation of labelling and packaging of tobacco products and also harmonised rules relating to e-cigarettes, the applicants sought to invalidate the Directive on the grounds that, inter alia, art.114 did not give the EU the right to enact such a Directive. The ECJ rejected this argument. It acknowledged that a mere finding of disparity between national rules is not sufficient to have recourse to art.114 but it must be shown that such differences obstruct the fundamental freedoms and have a direct effect on the

---

[143] *Netherlands v European Parliament and Council of the European Union* (C-377/98) [2001] E.C.R. I-7079. The biotechnological directive is discussed at para.2-578.

[144] See [25].

[145] art.173 is concerned with industrial development of the EU and art.179 is concerned with the objective of promoting research and development in the scientific sector.

[146] Citing *Commission v Council* (C-155/91) [1993] E.C.R. I-939.

[147] See [27].

[148] *Federal Republic of Germany v European Parliament and Council of the European Union* (C-376/98) [2000] E.C.R. I-8419. In this action, which was concerned with the validity of Dir.94/43 concerning the advertisement of tobacco products, the CJEU annulled the Directive on the basis that, in reality, it was not concerned with the removal of obstacles to trade between Member States.

[149] *Republic of Poland v European Parliament and Council of the European Union* (C-358/14) ECLI:EU:C:2016:323.

[150] *Philip Morris Brands SARL v Secretary of State for Health* (C-547/14) ECLI:EU:C:2016:325.

functioning of the internal market.[151] In these decisions, the Court of Justice said that recourse to art.114 was also allowed if the aim was to prevent the emergence of future obstacles to trade as a result of divergences in national laws. This would also be the case if it is likely that obstacles will emerge in future because Member States have taken, or are about to take, divergent measures with respect to protection of product.[152]

Unitary EU-wide IPRs

1-105   The EU has enacted three European regulations which provide for a EU-wide unitary intellectual property. These are the European Union Trade Mark Regulation, the Community Design Regulation and the Community Plant Variety Right Regulation.[153] Article 114 does not provide the legislative basis for such rights, as they are not concerned with the harmonisation of national laws of Member States but rather for creating new rights superimposed on national rights.[154]

1-106   Accordingly, another provision had to be found. This was art.352 TFEU (previously art.308 EC Treaty and prior to that, art.235 EEC Treaty). This provision states as follows:

> "1.   If action by the Union should prove necessary, within the framework of the policies defined in the Treaties, to attain one of the objectives set out in the Treaties, and the Treaties have not provided the necessary powers, the Council, acting unanimously on a proposal from the Commission and after obtaining the consent of the European Parliament, shall adopt the appropriate measures. Where the measures in question are adopted by the Council in accordance with a special legislative procedure, it shall also act unanimously on a proposal from the Commission and after obtaining the consent of the European Parliament."

1-107   This provision was used to pass the unitary-wide IPRs. It differed in one key respect to the enabling provision for IP Directives—namely that it required a unanimous vote of the Council. However, the Treaty of Lisbon introduced a specific provision into the TFEU which allowed the introduction of a unitary EU-wide IPR. Article 118 TFEU states as follows:

> "In the context of the establishment and functioning of the internal market, the European Parliament and the Council, acting in accordance with the ordinary legislative procedure, shall establish measures for the creation of European intellectual property rights to provide uniform protection of intellectual property rights throughout the Union and for the setting up of centralised Union-wide authorisation, coordination and supervision arrangements.
>
> The Council, acting in accordance with a special legislative procedure, shall by means of regulations establish language arrangements for the European intellectual property rights. The Council shall act unanimously after consulting the European Parliament."

1-108   As can be seen from art.118, there are two different legislative procedures. In

---

[151] (C-358/14), at [32]; (C-547/14), at [58].

[152] e.g. (C–547/14), at [62].

[153] The European Union Trade Mark Regulation ("EUTMR") was called the Community Trade Mark Regulation ("CTMR") but since the Lisbon Treaty, where the European Community was renamed the European Union, a new Regulation was issued. In the case of the Community Design Regulation and the Community Plant Variety Right Regulation, these have not been updated since the Lisbon Treaty and thus are still called by these names. All give rise to a single EU-wide right.

[154] *Opinion 1/94* [1994] E.C.R. I-5267 at [59]; (C-377/98) [2001] E.C.R. I-7079 at [24].

relation to the establishment of an EU-wide right, it only requires the use of the "ordinary legislative procedure". This has been discussed already and does not require unanimity of voting in the Council. However, because of the political difficulties over the language regime for these EU-wide rights, the language regime must be enacted via the special legislative procedure which requires unanimity and consultation with the European Parliament.[155] In *Kingdom of Spain v European Parliament and Council of the European Union*[156] the Court of Justice rejected an action from Spain against the EU Council and Parliament that art.118 TFEU was not an adequate legal basis for the adoption of Reg.1257/2012. This is the EU Regulation which allows the conversion of a European patent into a Unitary Patent. It held that the unitary patent protection established by Reg.1257/2012 was apt to prevent divergences in terms of patent protection in the participating Member States and thus fell within the first paragraph art.118.[157] It also rejected a parallel action from Spain concerning Reg.1260/2012 which sets out the language regime for the Unitary Patent. Spain alleged that the language regime discriminated against Spain (as it did not include the Spanish language). The Court of Justice held that whilst this regime did differentiate between the official languages of the EU, it pursued a legitimate objective which was the creation of a uniform and simple translation regime for the Unitary Patent.[158]

Enhanced co-operation

A legislative mechanism in the Treaty of the European Union called "enhanced co-operation"[159] permits Member States who wish to establish enhanced co-operation between themselves to make use of the EU institutions to pass EU laws confined to those Member States who wish to make use of the procedure. This was first introduced by the Treaty of Amsterdam as a means of permitting Member States interested in co-operating more closely on matters to embark upon a "fast track" procedure whilst those Member States who were not interested would not be involved. It was introduced as a mechanism to break deadlocks in negotiations between Member States. The Treaty of Nice and Lisbon extended this procedure and made it easier to use (e.g. the ability of a Member State to veto its use by other Member States was removed). It thus permits a multi-track Europe with some pro-integrationist countries being in the fast lane and others which are more Eurosceptic remaining in the slow lane.   **1-109**

The procedure for enhanced co-operation is set out in the TFEU.[160] In essence, those countries who wish to make use of the enhanced co-operation procedure must submit a proposal to the European Commission who may decide to support it. Ultimate authority for using this procedure lies with the European Council.   **1-110**

The enhanced procedure was used to enact the two EU regulations which gave birth to the Unitary Patent—Regs 1257/2012 and 1260/2012. It was seen as a way of avoiding the objections that certain Member States (then Spain and Italy) had with the proposed linguistic regime of English, French and German for the Unitary Patent. Twenty-five Member States indicated to the European Commission that they   **1-111**

---

[155] For discussion of the ordinary and special legislative procedure, see para.1-040.
[156] (C–146/13) EU:C:2015:298.
[157] See [51].
[158] *Kingdom of Spain v Council of the European Union* (C-147/13) ECLI:EU:C:2014:2381.
[159] art.20 TEU.
[160] arts 326–334.

wished to invoke the "enhanced co-operation" procedure for passing legislation on the Unitary Patent. By Council Decision 2011/167,[161] the European Council authorised these Member States to establish enhanced co-operation in this field. This then led to the passing of the two regulations.[162] Since then Italy has acceded to the Unitary Patent Regulations.

Competency of EU and Member States for IPRs

1-112   The TFEU sets out for a particular field of activity, whether (a) the EU has exclusive competence to legislate in that area, (b) the EU has shared competency with Member States, or (c) Member States have exclusive competency. As a starting point, the EU and Member States share competency to legislate in the field of intellectual property. This is because intellectual property laws of the EU are concerned with the internal market and art.4.2(a) TFEU says that such is a shared competency field.[163]

1-113   However, in the field of IPRs, the competency of Member States may be ousted so as to confer exclusive competency on the EU. This is now discussed.

Harmonising Directive

1-114   Where a harmonising IPR Directive has been enacted, Member States no longer have competency to enact legislation which is inconsistent with the Directive or, where the Directive is exhaustive in a particular field of intellectual property law, to legislate in that field.[164] This is discussed in more depth in the chapter on Intellectual Property and Free Movement.[165]

Common commercial policy

1-115   The EU has exclusive competence in the area of "common commercial policy".[166] This is concerned with the EU's action "on the international scene", i.e. trade with non-Member States and not trade in the internal market.[167] In particular, the common commercial policy includes "commercial aspects of intellectual property".[168] In *Daiichi Sankyo*, the Court of Justice held that the TRIPS agreement was concerned with "commercial aspects of intellectual property" and thus the EU had exclusive competency. The Court of Justice held that although TRIPS did not relate to the details, as regards customs or otherwise, of operations of international trade as such, the provisions of TRIPS have a specific link with international trade. The Court of Justice distinguished previous decisions on the

---

[161] [2011] OJ L76/53.

[162] Italy eventually withdrew its objection so that the two Regulations now apply to Italy.

[163] e.g. see Recital 12, Council Decision 2011/167 authorising enhanced co-operation in the area of the creation of unitary patent protection. See also *Daiichi Sankyo Co Ltd v DEMO* (C-414/11) ECLI:EU:C:2013:520 at [59].

[164] See *DR/TV2 Danmark* (C-510/10) EU:C:2012:244 at [31] and case law cited thereto; see [150], *Opinion 3/15 Treaty of Marrakesh/Competency* ECLI:EU:C:2016:657.

[165] See para.7-093.

[166] art.3.1(e) TFEU. As to what this means, see *Commission and Parliament v Council* (C-389/15) ECLI:EU:C:2017:798 at [65] where the court said that it is settled EU law that for an act to fall within "common commercial policy", it must be intended to promote, facilitate or govern trade and have "direct and immediate effects" on that trade.

[167] art.205 TFEU. See *Daiichi Sankyo*, at [50].

[168] art.207.1.

interpretation of predecessor Treaties where it had not found that the EU had exclusive competence in the field of TRIPS.[169] It held that the primary objective of the TRIPS agreement is to strengthen and harmonise the protection of IPRs on a worldwide scale. It said that TRIPS is an integral part of the WTO system and therefore has a specific link with international trade.[170] It therefore rejected the argument of most of the governments that the patentability provisions in TRIPS fell within the field of the internal market and not that of common commercial policy. The Court of Justice accepted that Member States were free to legislate on the subject of IPRs by virtue of such relating to the field of the internal market (for which, as said, there is shared competency between the EU and Member States), but said that they would have to comply with TRIPS.[171]

After *Daiichi Sankyo*, the European Commission requested the Court of Justice to give an opinion as to whether the EU had exclusive competence to agree the Marrakesh Treaty to Facilitate Access to Published Works for Persons Who are Blind, Visually Impaired or Otherwise Print Disabled, which was negotiated within the framework and under the aegis of the World Intellectual Property Organisation (WIPO). A central aspect of the Marrakesh Treaty is the imposition of a set of limitations and exceptions to the copyright laws of signatories to the treaty to allow blind and visually impaired persons access to literary works. In *Treaty of Marrakesh/Competency*, the Court of Justice held, not following the opinion of Wahl AG, that the Marrakesh Treaty was not concerned with "common commercial policy" of the EU. It held that the treaty was not specifically intended to promote, facilitate or govern international trade in accessible format copies but rather to improve the access of the blind and visually impaired to accessible format copies in other Contracting Parties.[172] It also rejected the Commission's bold argument that "commercial aspects of intellectual property" governed all intellectual property rights other than moral rights.[173] It held that the rules of the Marrakesh Treaty which provide for the introduction of an exception or limitation to the rights of reproduction, distribution and making available to the public did not have a specific link with international trade so as to concern the commercial aspects of intellectual property in art.207.[174] Recently, the Court of Justice held that the EU has exclusive competency to negotiate a revised Lisbon Agreement on geographical indications of origin.[175]

1-116

Article 3(2) TFEU and common rules

Article 3(2) TFEU provides that the EU has exclusive competency for the:

1-117

---

[169] The CJEU distinguished earlier law which governed the situation prior to the Lisbon Treaty, e.g. *Merck Genéricos–Produtos Farmacêuticos* (C-431/05) [2007] E.C.R. I-7001 and *Opinion 1/94* [1994] E.C.R. I-5267.

[170] See [53].

[171] See [59].

[172] See [89].

[173] See [85].

[174] See [86].

[175] (C-389/15) ECLI:EU:C:2017:798. See Ch.3, para.3-858.

"conclusion of an international agreement when its conclusion is provided for in a legislative act of the Union or is necessary to enable the Union to exercise its internal competence, or in so far as its conclusion may affect common rules or alter their scope".[176]

1-118   The logic of this aspect of art.3.2 is that once the EU has adopted common rules (through EU legislation), then Member States cannot negotiate an international agreement with third countries insofar as such negotiations could or would give rise to a need to change those common rules.[177] As said by Wahl AG, agreements between Member States and third countries "may easily create obstacles, both at the political and at the legal level, to the correct functioning and, possibly, the future development of EU law."[178] For the application of art.3(2), it is sufficient that a relevant area is already covered to a large extent by EU rules—there is no need for complete harmonisation of the area.[179] The "common rules" aspect of art.3(2) may be seen as the "international" legal bedfellow of the principle discussed above, that once the EU has issued a harmonising Directive in a legal field, Member States no longer have competence to pass laws in that field. If Member States could conclude an international agreement with third countries in the field which they are not able themselves to legislate, it would make no sense.

1-119   The EU has asserted its exclusive competency under art.3(2) in relation to international conventions on intellectual property where there has been some harmonisation. In *Commission and Parliament v Council*,[180] the ECJ had to consider a jurisdictional dispute between the Commission and the EU Council. In the context of international negotiations for the protection of the neighbouring rights of broadcasting organisations, the EU Council issued a decision mandating co-operation between the European Commission and the Council of Europe (which represents the Member States but which is not an institution of the EU).

1-120   The European Commission considered that the EU had exclusive competence and thus the decision was contrary to art.3(2) as the decision implied that there was shared competency with Member States. The Court of Justice agreed and annulled the decision. It held that the EU had already established via various Directives a regime with high and homogeneous protection for broadcasting organisations in connection with their broadcasts. Accordingly, there existed "common rules". The Court of Justice held that international negotiations would:

"fall within an area covered to a large extent by common EU rules and that those negotiations may affect common EU rules or alter their scope"[181]

and therefore, the decision of the EU Council was in breach of art.3(2) TFEU. In *Treaty of Marrakesh/Competency*, discussed at para.1-115, the Court of Justice was

---

[176] art.3(2) codifies the principle derived from *Commission v Council (ERTA)* (C-22/70) EU:C:1971:32—see [127], Advocate-General Opinion, *3/15 Treaty of Marrakesh/Competency* ECLI:EU:C:2016:657. A history of the "ebb and flow" of what is called the ERTA principle can be read at European Law Blog, 1 March 2017 *"Opinion 3/15 on the Marrakesh Treaty: ECJ Reaffirms Narrow "Minimum Harmonisation" Exception to ERTA Principle"* (*https://europeanlawblog.eu/ 2017/03/01/opinion-315-on-the-marrakesh-treaty-ecj-reaffirms-narrow-minimum-harmonisation-exception-to-erta-principle/* [Accessed 25 March 2018].

[177] e.g. see Sharpston AG's Opinion in (C-114/12), at [87]–[90]; judgment of the Court of Justice, at [102].

[178] See [125], *Opinion 3/15 Treaty of Marrakesh/Competency* ECLI:EU:C:2016:657.

[179] See [128], *Opinion 3/15* and authorities cited at fn.81.

[180] *European Commission and European Parliament v Council of the European Union* (C-114/12) ECLI:EU:C:2014:2151.

[181] See [102].

asked to give its opinion as to whether the Marrakesh Treaty to Facilitate Access to Published Works for Persons Who are Blind, Visually Impaired or Otherwise Print Disabled, which was negotiated within the framework of the World Intellectual Property Organisation ("WIPO") and which introduced a standard set of exceptions to copyright to allow the reproduction, distribution and making available of published works in formats accessible to such persons fell within art.3(2) and thus the EU had exclusive competency. The Information Society Directive (2001/29) had already substantially harmonised the legal framework for the protection of copyright and also had provided an exhaustive set of optional exceptions and limitations.[182] Yet, under Dir.2001/29, Member States were free to adopt all, some or none of the exceptions and limitations. By reason of this, it was argued by some Member States that art.3(2) did not apply as in substance, the EU had not sought to harmonise these exceptions and limitations.[183] The Court of Justice dismissed this argument by saying that although such option existed, it was granted by the EU legislature and was highly circumscribed.[184] Accordingly, it held that the Marrakesh Treaty fell within art.3(2).

EUROPEAN ECONOMIC AREA

History of the EEA

In 1960, the European Free Trade Association ("EFTA") was established for those states which did not wish to join the EEC but wished to participate in a free trade zone which was limited in scope. The founding members were Austria, Denmark, Norway, Portugal, Sweden, Switzerland, and the UK. Thereafter, Iceland, Finland and Liechtenstein joined. In 1973, Denmark and the UK joined the EC and the rest concluded bilateral Free Trade Agreements with the Community ("the 1972 FTAs"). In 1984, the Community, its Member States and EFTA countries started to consider co-operation in areas beyond the framework of the FTAs. In particular, the parties examined areas such as standardisation, simplification of trade documentation, research and development, mobility of workers, social and consumer matters and intellectual property. As EC integration grew apace, EFTA countries began to look at further integration. In 1989, the President of the Commission proposed that a new form of association between the EC and EFTA states was formed. This was to lead to the European Economic Area Agreement ("EEA Agreement"). The aim of this agreement was to provide for a much more systematic and thorough integration of EC and EFTA states, without actually having to extend EC membership to the EFTA countries.

1-121

In August 1991, the EC Commission asked the Court of Justice to rule on the compatibility with the EC Treaty of the judicial mechanism planned in the EEA Agreement. The Court of Justice gave an adverse opinion, stating that the EEA

1-122

---

[182] Dir.92/100 is discussed in Ch.4, para.4-264.
[183] This argument is based on what is called the "minimum harmonisation" exception to the *ERTA* rule—the latter which is codified in art.3(2). It was first raised in *Opinion 2/91 ILO Convention No. 170* EU:C:1993:106.
[184] See [126].

judicial system conflicted with the EC Treaty.[185] The negotiations reconvened and concluded fresh texts to which the Court of Justice gave its approval.[186]

1-123   On 2 May 1992, the EEA Agreement was signed by the European Community, the then 12 Member States and seven states of EFTA. The ratification process progressed smoothly until Switzerland, in a referendum, rejected the EEA Agreement. This resulted in a Protocol to the EEA Agreement to take this rejection into account. Eventually, the EEA Agreement and this Protocol were ratified by all remaining states and came into force on 1 January 1994.[187] Also on 2 May 1992, the EFTA states signed two agreements which established three new institutions—the EFTA Standing Committee (analogous to the EC Council and composed of representatives of the EFTA countries); an EFTA Surveillance Authority ("ESA"), an independent body equivalent to the EC Commission for ensuring that EFTA states fulfilled their EEA obligations; and the EFTA Court, which was to have a parallel jurisdiction to the Court of Justice.[188] These separate agreements were necessary because although the EC had its own institutions for overseeing the proper implementation of the EEA Treaty in its Member States, there were no equivalent institutions in the EFTA states.

1-124   It might be thought that the relevance of the EEA is marginal. Three of the EFTA states, Finland, Sweden and Austria, have left EFTA and become members of the EU. Thus, only Norway, Iceland and Liechtenstein are members of the EEA and not of the European Union. Switzerland is in a special position because it is still a member of EFTA but not of the EEA. However, with the departure of the UK from the EU, if it were to join the EEA, the significance of the EEA would become much more relevant.

Fundamental aspects of the EEA

1-125   The general objective of the EEA is to promote a continuous and balanced strengthening of trade and economic relations between the Contracting Parties, with equal conditions of competition and the respect of the same rules with a view to creating a homogeneous EEA.[189] The economic objective is to be attained through the extension of the EU rules to the EFTA states. The homogeneity objective is to be attained through the application of common rules and the permanent updating of these rules following the evolution of the EU rules. The fundamental provisions of the EEA Agreement replicate the provision of the EU Treaty in relation to the four freedoms of the EU, i.e. free movement of goods, person, services and capital, thus extending these freedoms to the EFTA countries. Also, other policies of the EU, such as environment and social policy, are included in the EEA Agreement. However, there is no enlargement of the EU policies in the field of agriculture, fiscal harmonisation and EU common policies towards third countries. As well as replication of the above provisions of the TFEU, the EEA Agreement includes much of the EU secondary legislation, whether Regulations, Directives or Decisions of the Court of Justice by annexing it to the EEA Agreement. This "bundle of law" is referred to as the *acquis communautaire* of the EEA Agreement.

---

[185] *Opinion 1/91* [1991] E.C.R. I-6079; [1992] 1 C.M.L.R. 245.
[186] *Opinion 1/92* [1992] E.C.R. I-282; [1992] 2 C.M.L.R. 217.
[187] [1994] OJ L1.
[188] Agreement on a Standing Committee of the EFTA States and Agreement between the EFTA states on the Establishment of a Surveillance Authority and a Court of Justice.
[189] art.1(1) EEA.

Special provisions are included as to the interpretation of this *acquis communautaire* in line with rulings of the Court of Justice. Also, the EEA Agreement envisages the addition of future EU legislation to its body of legislation.

In particular, for the purposes of this book, the EEA Agreement and its *acquis* **1-126** *communautaire* cover inter alia the fields of technical barriers to trade, intellectual property and competition.

Although many of the fundamental provisions of the EEA and TFEU are identi- **1-127** cal in nature, it would be a mistake to assume that their application will be identical under the two Treaties. The distinction between the EEA and the TFEU was expressed by the Court of Justice when giving its opinion on the compatibility of the intended judicial mechanism of an EEA Court with the then EC Treaty. The Court of Justice stated that the provision of the EC Treaty on free movement of goods and competition, far from being an end in themselves, must be interpreted as a means of achieving the objectives of the Treaty, namely the achievement of economic integration leading to an internal market and economic and monetary union. In contrast, there was no such objective in the EEA Treaty. Furthermore, the Court of Justice said that in relation to the objective of homogeneity in the EEA, the fact that provisions in the EEA were identical to those of the EU Treaty did not mean that they should be interpreted identically.[190]

The fact that identical provisions in the EEA and EU Treaties may not be **1-128** interpreted identically was graphically illustrated when the EFTA Court decided, in *Mag Instruments v Californian Trading Co*[191] that art.7(1) of Council Directive 89/104 (Trade Mark Directive), which had been incorporated into the EEA Treaty as *acquis communautaire*, should be interpreted as leaving it up to the EFTA states to decide whether to introduce or maintain the principle of international exhaustion of rights conferred by a trade mark with regard to goods originating from outside the EEA. Later, the Court of Justice decided in, *Silhouette v Hartlauer*, that art.7(1) prevented EC states from introducing or maintaining a principle of international exhaustion of rights.[192] It declined to follow *Mag Instruments*. As the Advocate-General said, EFTA did not have as one of its goals the attainment of a single market, whereas the EC Treaty did. A decade later, the EFTA Court revisited the issue in *L'Oréal Norge AS v Per Aarskog AS*.[193] The EFTA court concluded that whilst the court in *Mag Instruments* had attached importance to free trade and competition, in *Silhouette*, the Court of Justice had emphasised the need for facilitating free movement of goods and for ensuring the same level of protection throughout the EU. The EFTA court held that such were valid considerations in both an EU and an EEA context. It accordingly concluded that the differences between the EEA Agreement and the EC Treaty (as it then was) were not sufficient to constitute compelling grounds for divergent interpretation of art.7 of the Trade Mark Directive. It accordingly overruled *Mag Instruments* and held that EEA states (who were not members of the EU) were not free to adopt an international exhaustion of rights principle.

---

[190] See *Opinion 1/91* [1991] E.C.R. I-6079; [1992] C.M.L.R. 245.
[191] (E-2/97) [1998] E.T.M.R. 85; [1998] 1 C.M.L.R. 331.
[192] (C-355/96) [1998] E.C.R. I-4799.
[193] *L'Oréal Norge AS v Per Aarskog AS and L'Oréal SA v Smart Club AS* (E-9/07 and E-10/07) (judgment of EFTA Court date 8 July 2008) [2008] E.T.M.R. 60.

Structure and framework of the EEA Agreement

1-129   The EEA Agreement sets out the objectives of the EEA, non-discrimination provisions, the substantive provisions relating to the four freedoms, various other provisions relating to social policy, consumer protection, environment, statistics and company law, the institutional provisions including the decision-making procedure, measures safeguarding homogeneity, surveillance mechanism, settlement of disputes, and safeguard measures whilst the final part deals with the "cohesion fund". Appended to the agreement are 49 Protocols and 22 Annexes, which constitute the *acquis communautaire*. The two freedoms relating to the free movement of goods and competition law are discussed in the relevant chapters. The *acquis communautaire* relating to intellectual property is briefly discussed below, but the reader is referred to the relevant chapter for detailed information.

1-130   The Contracting Parties to the EEA are the EU, its Member States and the EFTA states.[194] Whilst the EEA Agreement is an agreement reached by the EU with the EFTA states under art.218 TFEU Treaty, there were certain areas, in particular, IPRs, in which Member States retained competences. Accordingly, Member States and EFTA states needed to be parties to the EEA. The EEA Agreement applies to the territories of the EU and EFTA states.

1-131   Under the EEA Agreement, adopted Regulations and Directives do not automatically become part of the internal order of the Contracting Parties. Under art.7, the EEA Agreement states that such provisions shall be binding upon the Contracting Parties and "be, or be made, part of their internal order" as follows:

(a)   an act corresponding to an EU Regulation shall as such be made part of the internal legal order of the Contracting Parties; and

(b)   an act corresponding to an EU Directive shall leave to the authorities of the Contracting Parties the choice of form and method of implementation.

1-132   This provision is similar to art.288 TFEU but does not refer to the direct applicability of Regulations. This omission, which was the result of intense argument from dualist states, suggests that Regulations may need to be enacted in EFTA states before they form part of domestic law. With regard to the "direct effect" of Directives in EFTA states, it is unclear whether art.6 of the EEA Agreement, which deems that in the case of identical provisions in the EEA and TFEU, the EEA provision should be interpreted according to Court of Justice case law, means that under the EEA Agreement, Directives shall have direct effect.[195]

Acquis communautaire

1-133   The EEA Agreement incorporates many EU secondary legislative acts and these are added to as new EU Directives and Regulations are adopted. This has been achieved by 22 Annexes. The incorporation of such legislation has been done by a reference technique with appropriate modifications rather than by actual incorporation. Those Regulations, Directives and Decisions which have been incorporated are binding on the Contracting Parties. Recommendations, notices, communications, guidelines, etc. are non-binding acts which the Contracting Parties must take note of.

---

[194] art.2(c).

[195] See T. Blanchet, R. Piipponen, M. Westman-Clément, *The Agreement on the EEA* (Oxford: OUP, 1994), p.21. For the meaning of "direct effect", see para.1-045, et seq.

In relation to intellectual property, art.65(2) of the EEA Treaty provides that **1-134** Protocol 28 and Annex 17, which contain specific provisions and arrangements concerning intellectual, industrial and commercial property, shall, unless otherwise specified, apply to all products and services. The reference to "intellectual" property which is not mentioned in the TFEU is in line with the Court of Justice's interpretation of "industrial and commercial property" in art.36 TFEU.

Protocol 28 sets out general provisions on intellectual property and is discussed **1-135** later.[196] Annex 17 refers to EU legislation on intellectual property which is included as *acquis communautaire*. At the cut-off date of 31 July 1991, only three EU legislative acts in the field of intellectual property were in force. These were the Semiconductor Directive, the Trade Mark Directive and the Software Directive. These were thus incorporated into the EEA Agreement as *acquis communautaire*. Since the cut-off date and the entry into force of the EEA, the EU has legislated further in the field of intellectual property. Whether such EU legislation in the field of intellectual property is included in EFTA depends on its adoption by the EEA Joint Committee. In broad terms, as a matter of policy, the EEA Joint Committee adopts all EU IPR Directives without any substantive amendments and all EU IPR Directives have been adopted although there is usually some time lag between the enactment of the Directive by the EU and its adoption into the EEA. If adopted, Annex 17 is then amended. A full list of the Directives incorporated into Annex 17 as *acquis communautaire* whether by the original EEA Agreement or by adoption by the EEA Joint Committee can be seen at the EFTA website.[197]

Institutions of the EEA

The EEA is intended to act as a two-pillar system, with the EU and the EFTA side **1-136** taking care of its own internal matters. Accordingly, the implementation, enforcement and interpretation of the EEA by the EU in its Member States is achieved by the institutions of the EU. On the EFTA side, new institutions have been established which parallel the institutions of the ECU so as to ensure the effective implementation of the EEA Act in EFTA states. Also, various joint bodies are established, in particular for joint decision making and dispute settlement.

Common EEA institutions

The common EU-EFTA bodies are the EEA Council, the EEA Joint Committee, **1-137** the EEA Parliamentary Committee, and the EEA Consultative Committee. The EEA Council, which consists of members of the EU Council, EU Commission and one member of the government of each EFTA state, is responsible for the implementation of the EEA Agreement and laying down general guidelines for the work of the EEA Joint Committee. The EEA Joint Committee has the task of ensuring the effective implementation and operation of the Agreement. Its most important role is that it is responsible for the introduction of new legislation into the EEA Agreement. In practice, this will mean being consulted by the EU Commission as to proposed EU legislation and the scrutiny of new EU legal acts to see whether they should be incorporated into the EEA Agreement. Finally, there is the EEA Joint Parliamentary

---

[196] See para.1-144.
[197] *www.efta.int* [Accessed 3 April 2018].

Committee, which does not have any powers concerning EEA legislation but is merely consultative in nature.

EFTA institutions

1-138 Under two Agreements signed at the same time as the EEA Agreement, the EFTA states undertook to set up an EFTA Surveillance Authority ("ESA"), analogous to the EU Commission, whose primary task is to ensure the fulfilment by the EFTA states of their obligations under the EEA Agreement—a EFTA court analogous to the Court of Justice and a Standing Committee of the EFTA states, whose role is to facilitate the elaboration of decisions taken on an EEA level.

1-139 Of importance is the division of jurisdiction between the Court of Justice and EFTA court. It was originally proposed to have an EEA court consisting of judges from the Court of Justice and EFTA states. However, this was not acceptable to the Court of Justice, which considered it incompatible with the EC Treaty—the predecessor to the TFEU. In its Opinion, the Court of Justice stated that, although many provisions of the EU and EEA Treaty were identical, that did not mean that they could be interpreted in the same way, because the EC Treaty's objectives were more integrative and profound than those of the EEA.[198] Accordingly, the Court of Justice was of the opinion that there would be a polluting effect. The judicial mechanism was then re-negotiated, which resulted in a two-pillar system, with the Court of Justice having competence on the EU side and the EFTA Court having responsibility on the EFTA side. The Court of Justice approved this arrangement in its second Opinion.[199]

1-140 The EFTA Court has competence[200] to rule on: whether, in ESA/EFTA state, an EFTA state has failed to fulfil its obligations under the EEA Agreement[201]; disputes between two EFTA states[202]; advisory opinions on the interpretation of the EEA Agreement[203]; proceedings brought by an EFTA state against a decision of the ESA on grounds of lack of competence, infringement of an essential requirement, infringement of the EEA Agreement or any rule of law relating to its application or misuse of powers[204]; similar proceedings brought by an individual member against a decision of ESA which is addressed to them or of direct and individual concern[205]; and proceedings brought by an EFTA state where the ESA fails to act in infringement of the EEA Agreement.[206] The above provisions have similar parallel provisions to the TFEU. However, they are not as extensive. For instance, whilst an individual can bring proceedings for the annulment of an ESA decision, they cannot bring proceedings for the annulment of other legislative acts, i.e. Regulations and Directives of EU law incorporated into the EEA by the EEA or the EEA Joint Committee.

---

[198] *Opinion 1/91* [1991] E.C.R. I-6079; [1992] 1 C.M.L.R. 245.
[199] *Opinion 1/92* [1992] E.C.R. I-282; [1992] 2 C.M.L.R. 217.
[200] In general, see art.108(2) of the EEA Agreement for general competence of the EFTA Court.
[201] ESA/Court Agreement art.31.
[202] ESA/Court Agreement art.32.
[203] ESA/Court Agreement art.34.
[204] ESA/Court Agreement art.36.
[205] ESA/Court Agreement art.36.
[206] ESA/Court Agreement art.37.

Uniform interpretation and surveillance of EEA and EU provisions

The EEA legal system is closely based on that of the EU system. Indeed, the **1-141** intention was that the former should, in key respects, be identical to the latter. In almost 60 years of the existence of the EU Treaty and its predecessor treaties, the Court of Justice has played a vital part in interpreting the provisions of the EU Treaty, particularly in the field of intellectual property. The drafters of the EEA Treaty were keen to ensure that there was uniform interpretation of identical provisions in both Treaties. In relation to rulings of the Court of Justice given prior to the signing of the agreement, art.6 of the EEA Agreement provides that:

> "Without prejudice to the future developments of case law, the provisions of this Agreement in so far as they are identical in substance to corresponding rules of the Treaty establishing the European Economic Community and the Treaty establishing the European Coal and Steel Community and the acts adopted in application of these two Treaties, shall, in the implementation and application be interpreted in conformity with the relevant rulings of the Court of Justice of the European Communities given prior to the date of signature of the Agreement."

In relation to identical provisions adopted after the signing of the Agreement, a **1-142** more complex procedure had to be adopted because of the Court of Justice's wariness of a joint "EEA Court" approach to the EU and EEA Agreement. Accordingly, the EEA Treaty sets up a system of exchange of information between the Court of Justice, EFTA Court, General Court and courts of last instance of EFTA states.[207] Most importantly, art.3(2) of the ESA/Court Agreement obliges the EFTA Court to "pay due account" to the principles laid down by the Court of Justice after the date of signature of the EEA Agreement which concern either the EEA or provisions identical in substance which appear in the EU Treaty. This means that the EFTA Court will rarely depart from an interpretation of the Court of Justice on an identical provision.[208]

Also, the EEA Treaty provides for co-operation between the EU Commission and **1-143** ESA.[209]

Intellectual property and the EEA

In the process of drafting the EEA Agreement, both EU and EFTA experts were **1-144** keen to have intellectual property provisions in the EEA Agreement. It was eventually agreed that the basic intellectual property provisions would go into a protocol (Protocol 28) and the secondary law into an annex (Annex 17). Article 65(2) of the main part of the Agreement provides a reference point to the Protocol and Annex by stating that they both contain specific provisions and arrangements concerning intellectual, industrial and commercial property, which, unless otherwise specified, apply to all products and services. The other explicit reference in the main part of the EEA Agreement is to "industrial and commercial property" in art.13 of the EEA, which replicates exactly art.36 TFEU.[210]

Protocol 28 contains nine articles which address three types of issue: level of **1-145**

---

[207] EEA art.106.

[208] See T. Blanchet, R. Piipponen, M. Westman-Clément, *The Agreement on the EEA* (Oxford: OUP, 1994), p.37.

[209] art.109 EEA.

[210] Including the omission of a reference to "intellectual" property.

protection, commitment to participate in or adhere to different EU measures or international conventions, and matters relating to third countries or to international activities.

1-146   On the question of level of protection, art.1(2) of Protocol 28 obliges Contracting Parties to adjust their legislation on intellectual property so as to make it compatible with the principles of free circulation of goods and services and with the level of protection of intellectual property attained in EU law, including the level of enforcement of those rights. Article 1(3) provides for a more specialised adjustment procedure whereby EFTA states are obliged, following a request and consultation with Contracting Parties, to adjust their legislation on intellectual property in order to reach "at least the level of protection of intellectual property prevailing in the Community upon signature of the Agreement".

1-147   Article 2 of the Protocol obliges Contracting Parties to respect the principle of exhaustion of rights developed in EU law by the Court of Justice.[211]

1-148   Article 3 of the Protocol obliges Contracting Parties to undertake to use their best endeavours to conclude, within a period of three years after the entry into force of the Agreement on the Community Patent,[212] negotiations with a view to the participation of the EFTA states. Furthermore, art.3 requires EFTA states to ensure that their patent laws comply with the substantive provisions of the EPC.[213] Article 4 makes certain provisions as to the extension of semi-conductor protection to persons from third countries.

1-149   Article 5 obliges Contracting Parties to obtain their adherence before 1 January 1995 to the Paris Convention (Stockholm 1967 revision), the Berne Convention (Paris 1971 revisions), the Rome Convention for the Protection of Performers, Producers of Phonograms and Broadcasting Organisation, the Madrid Protocol concerning trade marks, the Nice Agreement concerning the International Classification of Goods and Services (Geneva 1977, amended 1979), the Budapest Treaty on the International Recognition of the Deposit of Microorganisms for the purposes of Patent Procedure, and the Patent Cooperation Treaty. Additionally, Contracting Parties were required to ensure that their domestic legislation complied with their duties under the Paris, Berne and Rome Conventions upon entry into force of the EEA Agreement. Iceland, Norway and Liechtenstein have complied with these requirements.

1-150   Articles 6, 7 and 8 of Protocol 28 provide for a framework of co-operation between Contracting Parties in relation to future developments in intellectual property. Article 6 provides that Contracting Parties agree, without prejudice to the competence of the EU and its Member States in relation to intellectual property, to improve the regime established by the EEA Agreement as regards intellectual property in the GATT regime. Article 7 provides for consultation between Contracting Parties in the field of intellectual property. Article 8 provides that Contracting Parties agree to enter into negotiations in order to enable full participation of interested EFTA states in future measures concerning intellectual property which might be adopted in EU law.

1-151   Finally, art.9 safeguards the competence of the EU and its Member States in matters of intellectual property.

---

[211] In relation to patents, this provision takes effect, at the latest, one year after the entry into force of the EEA Agreement. The application of the exhaustion of rights principle in the EEA Agreement is discussed at para.7-335.

[212] "Agreement relating to Community Patent" [1989] OJ L401/1. In 1989, it was anticipated that the Community Patent Convention would become law and provide a unitary Community-wide patent.

[213] The EPC is discussed in detail in Ch.2.

Secondary EU intellectual property legislation is adopted via its inclusion in An- **1-152**
nex 17 (the *acquis communautaire* route) which has been discussed above.[214]

INTERNATIONAL CONVENTIONS AND EU LAW

International conventions, Member States and the EU

The importance of proper intellectual property protection to the economies of **1-153**
Member States of the EU has meant that almost all are members of the fundamental
intellectual property Conventions, namely the Paris Convention for the Protection
of Industrial Property, the Berne Convention for the Protection of Artistic and Literary Works, the Rome Convention for the Protection of Performers, Producers of
Phonograms and Broadcasting Organisations, the Madrid System concerning the
International Registration of Marks, the Patent Cooperation Treaty concerning the
obtaining of international patents, the European Patent Convention, the International
Convention for the Protection of New Varieties of Plants and the Hague Convention for the International Registration of Designs. These Conventions are discussed
in detail in the chapters on Patents, Trade Marks, Copyright, Designs and Plant
Variety Rights.

Furthermore, the TRIPS part of the WTO Agreement plays a very important role **1-154**
in providing for a minimum level of protection for all IPRs. It is discussed below
and in relation to individual rights, also in the relevant chapters.

Generally, whether or not an international convention confers rights on individu- **1-155**
als is a matter for the laws of Member States. In countries which have a dualist
tradition, international conventions only form part of the law of a Member State
when incorporated via an act of the national legislature.[215] Monist states recognise
international conventions as forming part of their domestic legal order without
further need for legislation.

The above Conventions have meant that, in many respects, intellectual property **1-156**
laws in European countries have been harmonised without the need for EU
legislation. Thus, the European Patent Convention has resulted in the harmonisation of the patent laws of European countries.

Most of the above Conventions are intended to harmonise national laws on intel- **1-157**
lectual property, ensure reciprocity of treatment to nationals of contracting states
or, in the case of certain Conventions, such as the Patent Cooperation Treaty and
the Madrid System, to provide for an easier and simpler system of obtaining
internationally protected IPRs. The interpretation and enforcement of rights is left
to the individual states. Even the European Patent Convention (the "EPC"), which
both harmonises contracting states' patent laws and provides for a centralised patent application system, does not provide for a patent appellate court responsible for
the interpretation of the Convention nor provide for a central enforcement procedure
of a European patent against potential infringers. In this respect, they must be
considered less profound and integrative than EU measures such as the EU Trade
Mark, the Community Registered Design, the Community Plant Variety Right and
the Unitary Patent.

---

[214] See para.1-133.
[215] Thus, in the UK, no Convention has force of law unless enacted by an act of Parliament.

Status of international conventions in EU law

1-158   Pursuant to art.216 TFEU, the EU may conclude an agreement with one or more third countries or international organisations where the EU Treaties provide or where the conclusion of an agreement is necessary in order to achieve, within the framework of the EU's policies, one of the objectives referred to in the EU Treaty or is provided for in a legally binding act of the EU. In particular, pursuant to art.217 TFEU, the EU may conclude international agreements which establish an association involving reciprocal rights and obligations. If the EU concludes such international agreements, then these agreements are binding upon the institutions of the EU and also on its Member States.[216]

1-159   Such agreements form an integral part of EU law and are applicable in the EU.[217] In general, the procedural mechanism for the EU acceding to an international convention is via a Council Decision.[218] There is some suggestion that if all Member States have signed up to an international convention, that the EU may be regarded as "having taken the place of [those] Member States".[219]

1-160   Even though an international agreement may form part of the legal order of the EU, such is not by itself sufficient to confer rights on individuals. It is necessary that for those provisions to have "direct effect",[220] they are, as regards their content, unconditional and sufficiently precise and their nature and broad logic must not preclude their being so relied on directly.[221] Thus, the Court of Justice held that decisions of the Council of Association established by an EC-Turkey Agreement were capable of being directly effective provided that regard was given to its wording and the purpose and nature of the agreement itself and the provision contained a clear and precise obligation which was not subject in its implementation or effects to the adoption of any subsequent measure.[222]

1-161   In the field of intellectual property, the EU has signed up to the following conventions:

- TRIPS (and the Protocol amending the TRIPS Agreement—the Doha Declaration).[223]
- The Protocol relating to the Madrid Agreement.[224]
- WIPO Copyright Treaty.[225]
- The WIPO Performances and Phonograms Treaty.[226]
- The European Convention relating to questions on Copyright Law and

---

[216] art.216(2).

[217] *Società Consortile Fonografici (SCF) v Del Corso R&V Haegeman Sprl v Belgium* (C-135/10) ECLI:EU:C:2012:140 at [39]. *Haegeman* (181/73) [1974] E.C.R. 449 at [5]; *Demirel* (12/86) [1987] E.C.R. 3719 at [7]; and *Bogiatzi* (C–301/08) [2009] E.C.R. I-10185 at [23].

[218] art.218 TFEU sets out the procedure for the EU acceding to an international convention.

[219] e.g. see *Società Consortile Fonografici*, at [41] applying *Commune de Mesquer* (C-188/07) [2008] E.C.R. I-4501 at [85]. It is beyond the scope of this book to discuss this further.

[220] For a discussion of "direct effect", see para.1-045.

[221] *Società Consortile*, at [43]–[44] and cases cited thereto.

[222] See *Sevince v Staatssecretaris van Justitie* (C-192/89) [1990] E.C.R. I-3461; [1992] 2 C.M.L.R. 57.

[223] TRIPS is discussed below at para.1-167.

[224] The Protocol to the Madrid Agreement is a trade mark international treaty and is discussed in the Trade Marks chapter at para.3-052.

[225] This Treaty is a special agreement under the Berne Convention that deals with the protection of works and the rights of their authorisation in the digital environment. See para.4-061.

[226] This Treaty is concerned with the protection of performances (actors, singers, musicians) and producers of phonograms. In particular, the focus is on the digital environment. See para.4-066.

Neighbouring Rights in the Framework of Transfrontier Broadcasting by Satellite.[227]

- Hague Agreement concerning the International Registration of Industrial Designs.[228]

Legality of EU measure in light of international convention

In certain cases, it has been argued in proceedings by private individuals or Member States that a EU legislative act does not comply with the provisions of an international convention and is thus invalid. Where the EU is not a party to the convention, such as the European Patent Convention, the Court of Justice has held that the lawfulness of a EU instrument does not depend on its conformity with an international agreement.[229]   **1-162**

On the other hand, where the EU is a party to the international convention, then a EU legislative act may be determined as being ultra vires but not simply because it does not comply with the provisions of such a convention. The Court of Justice set out the approach to determining whether an act of the EU, e.g. a Directive is to be considered invalid by reason of an international agreement which the EU has acceded to in *Air Transport Association of America v Secretary of State for Energy and Climate Change*.[230] First, the EU is free when acceding to an international convention to determine what effect the convention has in the internal legal order of Member States. It is only if such has not been done that the Court of Justice must consider the validity of the EU act in the same manner as any question of interpretation relating to the effect of the international agreement in EU law. Secondly, only the Court of Justice has jurisdiction to determine whether an act of the EU, e.g. a Directive is invalid by reason of an international convention. Thirdly, where international agreements are concluded by the EU pursuant to art. 216(2) TFEU, such prevail over the acts of the EU.[231] Fourthly, the provisions of the international convention which are relied upon for the purpose of attacking the validity of a EU act must be as regards their content, be unconditional and sufficiently precise. Such is satisfied where the provision relied upon contains a clear and precise obligation which is not subject, in its implementation or effects, to the adoption of any subsequent measure.[232]   **1-163**

A good example of the application of this jurisdiction in the field of intellectual property was the action brought by the Netherlands, Italy and Norway that the Biotechnology Directive did not comply with TRIPS. It was argued inter alia that the Biotechnology Directive required Member States to breach their own obligations under TRIPS—an international agreement which the Directive purported not to affect.[233] The EU and all Member States were parties to TRIPS. The Court of Justice held that TRIPS was not in principle, having regard to its nature and structure, among the rules in the light of which the court must review the lawful-   **1-164**

---

[227] This has yet to come into force.
[228] See para.5-016.
[229] *Netherlands v European Parliament and Council of the European Union* (C-377/98) [2001] E.C.R. I-7079 at [52].
[230] (C-366/10) [2011] E.C.R. I-13755.
[231] art.216 is discussed at para.1-158.
[232] See [48]–[56].
[233] *Netherlands v European Parliament and Council of the European Union* (C-377/98) [2001] E.C.R. I-7079 at [55].

ness of measures adopted by EU institutions.[234] However, the Court of Justice held that where a Directive imposes an obligation on a Member State to breach their own obligations under international law which the Directive claims not to affect, then the Court of Justice has jurisdiction under EU law to consider whether the relevant provisions of the Directive were valid.[235] The complainant Member States alleged that art.27(3)(b) TRIPS allowed Member States not to grant a patent for plants and animals other than micro-organisms whereas the Directive did not give the Member States that possibility. However, the Court of Justice held that TRIPS permitted a group of states to adopt a common position with a view to its application and that the Directive amounted, in effect, to the adoption of such a common position.[236]

Obligation to interpret EU and national legislation in light of international convention

1-165   In general, EU law must be interpreted in the light of international conventions.[237] More particularly, where the EU is a party to the international convention, EU secondary legislation must, so far as is possible, be interpreted in a manner that is consistent with the international agreements.[238] This obligation applies even though the international agreement does not have direct effect.[239]

1-166   As regards the interpretation of the legislation of Member States in the light of an international convention, a distinction is drawn between where the EU has already legislated in the field of the international convention and where it has not. In the former, the Court of Justice has said that courts of Member States are required to apply national laws as far as possible in the light of the wording and purpose of the international convention. In the latter, the Court of Justice has said, in the context of IPRs where there was no relevant EU legislation, that such does not fall within the scope of EU law. Thus, it said that EU law neither "requires nor forbids" a Member State from applying the international convention directly.[240]

TRIPS Agreement

1-167   Apart from the 1968 Stockholm Conference that adopted the revised Berne and Paris Conventions and created the World Intellectual Property Organization, the TRIPS Agreement is the most significant international Convention in the field of intellectual property in the 20th century. Like the Paris Convention, it affects a wide variety of IPRs. It deals with many difficult political issues and, in particular,

---

[234] See [52] applying *Portugal v Council* (C-149/96) [1999] E.C.R. I-8395 at [47].

[235] See [55]–[56].

[236] See [58].

[237] *Poulsen* (C-286/90) [1992] E.C.R. I-06019. This statement was not expressly limited to circumstances where the EU is a party to the international convention. However, in *Poulsen*, the EC Regulation was intended to implement international obligations of the Community.

[238] *Germany v EC Commission* (C-61/94) [1996] E.C.R. I-3989 at [52].

[239] See *Parfums Christian Dior SA v TUK Consultancy BV* (C-300 and 392/98) [2000] E.C.R. I-11307; [2001] E.T.M.R. 26; [2001] E.C.D.R 12 at [45]–[47].

[240] *Parfums Christina Dior*, at [49]. It should be noted that this case concerns TRIPS which the EU is a party to. This position is less clear where the EU has legislated in a field covered by the international convention but is not a party to the international convention. Finally, it should be noted that the reasoning was in part based on the competence of the Member State to legislate in the relevant field. In the case of TRIPS, it has now been held that since the TFEU came into force, the EU has exclusive competence. This is discussed at para.1-115.

enforcement.[241] With the failure of states to establish new intellectual property standards in the GATT (General Agreement on Tariffs and Trade) framework, a new impetus to harmonisation of intellectual property laws of countries was given by the Uruguay Round of Multilateral Trade Negotiations at Punta del Este. The Uruguay Round was a series of conferences and meetings which occurred between 1986 and 1994. On 15 April 1994, at Marrakesh, "The Final Act Embodying the Results of the Uruguay Round of Multilateral Trade Negotiations" was signed. It covers a number of areas that had been negotiated on. In particular, it gave birth to the World Trade Organization via the Marrakesh Agreement Establishing the World Trade Organization. Annex 1C of this agreement is the "Agreement on Trade-Related Aspects of Intellectual Property Rights". This is conveniently shorthanded to TRIPS. Accordingly, those countries who are members of the WTO are contracting states to TRIPS.

TRIPS covers copyright and neighbouring rights (i.e. performers' rights, produc- **1-168**
ers of sound recordings and broadcasting organisations); trade marks, including service marks; geographical indications of origin; industrial designs; patents; protection of new varieties of plants; the layout designs of integrated circuits; and confidential information.

The four main features of TRIPS are: **1-169**

(1)   minimum standards;
(2)   enforcement;
(3)   dispute settlement; and
(4)   criminal sanctions.

Minimum standards

In respect of each of the main areas of intellectual property covered by the TRIPS **1-170**
Agreement, TRIPS specifies the minimum standards of protection to be provided by each contracting state. Each of the main elements of protection is defined, namely the subject-matter to be protected, the rights to be conferred and permissible exceptions to those rights, and the minimum duration of protection. TRIPS outlines these standards by requiring, first, that the substantive obligations of the main Conventions of the WIPO, the Paris Convention for the Protection of Industrial Property (Paris Convention) and the Berne Convention for the Protection of Literary and Artistic Works (Berne Convention), in their most recent versions, must be complied with. With the exception of the provisions of the Berne Convention on moral rights, all of the main substantive provisions of these Conventions are incorporated by reference and, thus, become obligations under the TRIPS Agreement between contracting states.[242] Secondly, the TRIPS Agreement adds a substantial number of obligations on matters where the pre-existing Conventions are silent or are seen as being inadequate. The TRIPS Agreement is, thus, sometimes referred to as a Berne and Paris-plus agreement.

The provisions of TRIPS in each field of IP is discussed in more detail in the **1-171**
relevant chapter.

---

[241] A comprehensive account of the TRIPS Agreement, including the history of it, can be found in D. Gervais, *The TRIPS Agreement: Drafting History and Analysis*, 4th edn (London: Sweet & Maxwell, 2012).

[242] See arts 2.1 and 9.1 of TRIPS.

Enforcement

1-172   The second main set of provisions deals with domestic procedures and remedies for the enforcement of IPRs. The Agreement lays down certain general principles applicable to all IPR-enforcement procedures. In addition, it contains provisions on civil and administrative procedures and remedies, provisional measures, special requirements related to border measures and criminal procedures, which specify, in a certain amount of detail, the procedures and remedies that must be available so that right-holders can effectively enforce their rights.

1-173   The main provisions provided for by arts 41–50 are as follows:

- Enforcement procedures must be such as to permit effective action against any act of infringement of IPRs.
- Remedies available must be expeditious in order to prevent infringements and they must constitute a deterrent to further infringements.
- Procedures must be applied in such a manner as to avoid the creation of barriers to legitimate trade and to provide for safeguards against their abuse.
- The enforcement of IPRs must be fair and equitable, not too costly and not involve unreasonable time limits or unwarranted delays.
- Courts must be able to order disclosure of incriminating and relevant documents by an opposing party.
- Courts must have the right to grant injunctions to prevent infringements.
- Courts must have the right to award damages to compensate the IPR owner.[243]
- Courts must be able to order the disposal of infringing goods.
- Courts must be able to order the disclosure by the infringer of the identity of third parties who are involved in the production and supply of infringing goods.
- Courts must be able to order compensation to defendants who have been wrongly injuncted.
- Courts must have the right to grant immediate and effective provisional relief, including injunctive relief and preservation of evidence. This includes the right to grant ex parte relief (i.e. where the other party is not given notice of the proceedings) in circumstances where any delay is likely to cause irreparable harm or where there is a demonstrable risk of evidence being destroyed. Such provisional measures must cease if proceedings leading to a decision on the merits of the case are not initiated within a reasonable period. This period can either be determined by the court which ordered the measures or, if the court fails to make such a determination, it must not exceed 30 working days or 31 calendar days.[244]

Dispute settlement

1-174   The Agreement makes disputes between WTO Members about the respect of the TRIPS obligations subject to the WTO's dispute settlement procedures.

---

[243] art.45.1 gives the right to an award of damages to compensate the IPR owner where the infringer knew, or had reason to believe, that he was engaged in an infringing activity. Article 45.2 confers discretion on contracting states to permit courts to order recovery of profits and/or payment of pre-established damages even where the infringer did not know or had reason to believe that they were infringing. Of course in many countries such as the UK, compensatory damages are available, even

Criminal measures

TRIPS also handles criminal procedures. According to art.61, provision must be **1-175** made for these to be applied at least in cases of wilful trade-mark counterfeiting or copyright piracy on a commercial scale. TRIPS allows members to decide whether to provide for criminal procedures and penalties to be applied in other cases of infringement of IPRs, in particular where they are committed wilfully and on a commercial scale.

Sanctions must include imprisonment and/or monetary fines sufficient to provide **1-176** a deterrent, consistent with the level of penalties applied for crimes of a corresponding gravity. Criminal remedies in appropriate cases must also include seizure, forfeiture and destruction of the infringing goods and of materials and instruments used to produce them.

DOHA Declaration on TRIPS

In 2001, WTO members met in Doha, Qatar to address concerns from develop- **1-177** ing countries about the obstacles they faced when seeking to provide affordable medicine in poor countries. In particular, concerns were expressed about the effect of IPRs on prices of medicines in poor countries. A declaration was adopted by WTO members (the Doha Declaration) which sought to emphasise the flexibility of TRIPS to address public health concerns.[245] Article 6 also included the right to grant compulsory licences. However, as recognised in the Declaration, many poor countries had little or no manufacturing ability to make use of the compulsory licensing provisions. Thus, without more, such provisions provided little by way of comfort to poor countries. Accordingly, the WTO Members instructed the Council for TRIPS to find expeditiously solutions to this issue.

In 2003, the Council took the decision to implement art.6 by providing for a **1-178** temporary waiver of art.31(f) TRIPS whereby compulsory licensing had to be primarily for the domestic market. In 2005, WTO members reached agreement to make permanent this waiver. Thus, WTO members could issue compulsory licences to export generic versions of patented medicines to countries with insufficient or no manufacturing capacity in the pharmaceutical sector. In 2017, two thirds of WTO Members finally incorporated it and the Doha Declaration into TRIPS.[246]

TRIPS and EU law

The TRIPS Agreement was approved by Council Decision 94/800 of 22 **1-179** December 1994.[247] Accordingly, the European Community (now the EU) became a party to TRIPS as of 1 January 1995. Prior to the entry into force of the TFEU, as said by Jacobs AG in *Schieving-Nijstad*, as a matter of EU law, competence for concluding it was shared between the European Community and its Member

---

against innocent infringers.

[244] art.50. This provision has given rise to a couple of references to the CJEU concerning whether it has direct effect in Member States of the EU and whether national courts of Member States should take the provisions of art.50 into account, e.g. see *Parfums Christian Dior SA v TUK Consultancy BV* (C-300 and 392/98) [2000] E.C.R. 1–11307; [2001] E.T.M.R. 26; [2001] E.C.D.R. 12 at [45]–[47].

[245] See *http://www.wto.org* [Accessed 9 February 2018].

[246] See Ch.2, para.2-026 and fn.39 in that chapter.

[247] [1994] OJ L336/1.

States.[248] However, since the entry into force of the TFEU, it has now been held by the Court of Justice that the EU now has exclusive competence to legislate in the field of TRIPS as such forms part of the common commercial policy of the EU which under the TFEU, the EU has exclusive competence.[249] The Court of Justice has jurisdiction to give rulings on the interpretation of TRIPS.[250]

TRIPS: its place in EU law

1-180   As a matter of EU law, TRIPS does not create rights upon which individuals may rely directly before the courts.[251] However, as with other international conventions to which the EU has acceded to and despite the fact that it does not have direct effect, the accession of the EU to TRIPS on 1 January 1995 means that in a IP field in which the EU has legislated, national courts of Member States are required to interpret national provisions as far as possible in the light of the wording and purpose of the relevant provisions of TRIPS.[252] As, a fortiori, this rule only applies in a field in which the EU has already legislated, it means that national courts will need to interpret national measures in the light of both EU legislation and TRIPS. Thus, in *Anheuser-Busch Inc v Budějovický Budvar, národní podnik*, which concerned the right of an owner of a registered trade mark to enforce its trade mark rights against a defendant who used a similar sign as part of its trading name, the Court of Justice held that the national measure must be interpreted in the light of both the Trade Mark Directive and art.16(1) TRIPS.[253] The obligation to interpret EU legislation in the light of TRIPS applies even where the conduct of which complaint is made arose prior to 1 January 1996 (i.e. when the EU became a party to TRIPS), provided that the conduct continued after that date.[254]

1-181   In an area of IPR law where the EU had not legislated, prior to the TFEU coming into effect, the Court of Justice had said that in such a case, then EU law neither "requires nor forbids" Member States from pursuant to their domestic law, permitting individuals to rely directly upon a provision in TRIPS.[255] Thus, in *Merck Genéricos v Merck & Co*, pursuant to transitional provisions of Portuguese law concerning pharmaceutical patents, the period for protection was 15 years from date of issue of the grant of the patent. However, under art.33 TRIPS, the minimum

---

[248] *Schieving-Nijstad vof v Robert Groeneveld* (C-89/99) [2001] E.C.R. I-5851 at [9] citing *Opinion 1/94* [1994] E.C.R. I-5267 at [105].

[249] This is discussed at para.1-115.

[250] *Hermès* (C-53/89) [1998] E.C.R. I-3603 at [22]–[33].

[251] *Società Consortile Fonografici v Del Corso* (C-135/10) [2012] E.C.R. 0000 at [46]; *Monsanto Techology LLC v Cefetra BV* (C-428/08), at [71]; *Parfums Christian Dior* (C-300/98 & 392/08) [2000] E.C.R. I-11307 at [44]–[47]; *Merck Genéricos—Produtos Farmacêuticos v Merck* (C-431/05) [2007] E.C.R. I-7001 at [35]. See also last recital to Decision 94/800 which states that the WTO Agreement and its annexes (i.e. TRIPS) "is not susceptible to being directly invoked in Community or Member State courts". This recital must be seen as an application of the principle discussed earlier in this chapter at para.1-163 that the EU is free to decide when acceding to an international convention how it shall fit into the EU legal order.

[252] *Schieving-Nijstad* (C-89/99) [2001] E.C.R. I-5851 at [54]; *Hermès* (C-53/96) [1998] E.C.R. I-3603 at [28]; *Parfums Christian Dior* (C-300 & 392/98) [2000] E.C.R. I-11307, [2001] E.T.M.R. 26 at [45]–[47], [2001] E.C.D.R 12; *Heidelberger Bauchemie* (C-49/02) [2004] E.C.R. I-6129 at [20]; (C-245/02) [2004] E.C.R. I-10989 at [55]; *Monsanto Technology LLC v Cefetra* (C-428/08), at [72]; *Merck Genéricos* (C-431/05), at [35].

[253] (C-245/02) [2004] E.C.R. I-10989 at [57].

[254] (C-245/02) [2004] E.C.R. I-10989 at [53].

[255] *Merck Genéricos—Produtos Farmacêuticos Lda v Merck & Co Inc* (C-431/05), at [34]; *Parfums Christian Dior*, at [48].

period of protection is stipulated to be 20 years from the filing date. The Portuguese courts referred to the Court of Justice whether the patentee could rely directly upon art.33 TRIPS in domestic proceedings. The Court of Justice held that there had been no EU legislation which was relevant to the period of protection of patents.[256] Accordingly, it held that it was a matter of Portuguese law whether it should give direct effect to art.33 or not.

Exclusive competence of EU under the TFEU to legislate in the field of TRIPS

As discussed above, the Court of Justice has held that TRIPS concerns commercial aspects of intellectual property rights and thus, under the TFEU, the EU has exclusive competency.[257]   **1-182**

---

[256] Of course, there is under the EPC but such is not an EU measure.
[257] See para.1-115.

CHAPTER 2

PATENTS IN EUROPE

TABLE OF CONTENTS

INTRODUCTION

Patents are often considered the jewel in the crown of intellectual property rights. **2-001**
Unlike most other rights, patents protect ideas, albeit they must be technical rather
than abstract ideas. No other IPR affords such extensive protection. A trade mark
protects a brand but not a product; registered designs protect the appearance of a
product but not a product, and copyright is not an absolute right but merely a right
against copying. In contrast, if a patent protects a vital technological improvement, it can be a goldmine to its owner whether by permitting its owner to exploit
exclusively the improvement or by licensing. For instance, the patent rights for the
blue LED[1] invented by Shuji Nakamura of Nichia was adjudicated by a Japanese
court to be worth US$580 million to Nichia.

In Europe, patents play an important role in the economy. In a systematic analysis **2-002**
of the private economic value of patents in Europe, it was discovered that the mean
average of the value of a European patent was €3 million, the median average was
about €400,000 and the mode was around a few thousand Euros.[2] The huge difference between the mean, median and mode demonstrates that a few patents are billion dollar blockbusters but that most are worth very little or nothing. Unsurprisingly, Europe has a very developed patent system. Not only can an inventor apply
for national patents but the existence of the European Patent Convention allows the
inventor to apply for a single European patent which is prosecuted to grant before
the European Patent Office. Upon grant, it results in a basket of national patents.
Furthermore, the inventor can make use of the Patent Cooperation Treaty which is
an international patent treaty and designate contracting states to the EPC (all
European countries) as a single designated entity (called a Euro-PCT application).

---

[1]   Light emitting diode.
[2]   A. Gambardella, D. Harhoff and B. Verspagen, "The Value of European Patents" *European Manage-
       ment Review* [2008] 5, 69–84.

2-003   However, (and excitingly) and after many failed attempts, efforts to introduce an EU Unitary Patent which will apply to 26 Members States (all bar Spain and Croatia) similar to that which exists for EU Trade Marks and Community Designs are about to bear fruit. The EU Unitary Patent will be prosecuted as a European patent before the EPO. Following grant, it can be converted into a EU Unitary Patent.[3] In particular, the EU Unitary Patent regime greatly reduces the current cost of translation of a granted European patent into the official languages of the contracting states to the EPC.

2-004   Moreover, hand in hand with the introduction of a EU Unitary Patent, is the establishment of a Unified Patent Court ("UPC") which will have exclusive competence for both EU Unitary Patents and also European patents (for the latter, there is a transitional period of shared jurisdiction between the UPC and courts of Member States and the ability to opt-out). The UPC's rulings will have unitary effect in the territory of those countries which have ratified the UPC Agreement at the given time. The UPC will not have competence with regards to national patents.[4]

2-005   The underlying rationale behind the Agreement setting up the UPC is that it will confer on owners of European and EU Unitary Patents the ability to obtain "one-stop shop" injunctive and damages and other relief for all countries which have ratified the UPC Agreement without the need for parallel litigation in countries. Conversely, it will allow an undertaking to revoke a European patent or EU Unitary Patent in its entirety as opposed to country-by-country. This will greatly reduce the cost of enforcement and revocation of European patents. It will also allow the development of a truly European patent case law thereby enhancing legal certainty for all users.

2-006   As of 1st May 2018, the only ratification needed for the UPC Agreement to come into force is that of Germany. There is a constitutional challenge before the German Constitutional Court which has caused Germany to delay ratifying it. The other two cornerstone Member States—UK and France—have ratified it. A Protocol on the Provisional Application of the UPC Agreement has been agreed which will allow the provisional application of the institutional, financial and administrative provisions of the Unified Patent Court to come into effect. This means that the UPC should be fully operational and ready to hear cases on the day that the UPC Agreement formally comes into force.

2-007   Current predictions as to when the UPC Agreement will come into force are difficult to predict because of the constitutional challenge.

2-008   In keeping with the "top-down" approach of this book, this chapter does not set out the national patent laws of each European country. This should not deter the reader because the accession of all European countries to the Paris Convention, EPC and PCT and, in the case of EU countries, the accession of them all to EPC and the TFEU mean that there has been a high degree of harmonisation of substantive national patent law throughout Europe. Nowadays, national differences are most noticeable in two areas: the degree of ex officio search and examination of patent applications in national patent offices and the approach by courts of European countries to construction of claims in infringement and revocation proceedings.

2-009   This chapter therefore focuses on the international conventions which apply to patents in Europe. It examines in detail both the procedural and substantive law of

---

3   This is discussed in more detail at para.2-506.
4   This is discussed in more detail at para.2-534.

the PCT and EPC. It then looks at EU law in the field of patents. These are the EU Unitary Patent, the Biotechnology Directive and Supplementary Protection Certificates (which extend protection by up to five years for pharmaceuticals whose launch on the market was delayed by the need to obtain market authorisation). It also looks at the Agreement on the UPC, which although not EU legislation, is best considered together with the EU legislation establishing a EU Unitary Patent.

Paris Convention

The Paris Convention[5] represents the first efforts of several countries to adopt a common approach to intellectual property. It is the founding Convention in the field of patents. It was first entered into in 1883 and has since been amended several times.[6] The most recent revision is called the "Stockholm Act" revision. Most countries of the world and all European countries have now acceded to the Convention, which has had the effect of harmonising patent law to a considerable degree in Europe. Its main principles are as follows: **2-010**

(a) Nationals of a country belonging to the Convention ("contracting states") must enjoy the same rights with regard to intellectual property in other countries of the Convention as nationals of those other countries.[7]

(b) In relation to patents, the filing of a patent application in a contracting state gives the applicant a right of priority of 12 months in respect of other applications for the same invention in any other contracting state.[8] Thus, subsequent filings of patent applications in other contracting states will not be rendered invalid by any public disclosure of the invention in the 12-month "priority" period.[9]

(c) Contracting states have the right to enact measures providing for "compulsory licences" for abuses of the patent, in particular for failure to work. Such licences are not to be applied before the expiry of four years from the date of filing of the patent application or three years from the date of the grant of the patent, whichever is the later.[10]

(d) The Convention provides for minimum periods of grace for the payment of fees and for domestic legislation to provide for restoration of patents which have lapsed due to non-payment of fees.[11]

The Paris Convention also provides for an Assembly of the Union and an Executive Committee.[12] These two bodies are designed to ensure that the Convention is implemented in the contracting states and to develop the Convention in the future. Administrative tasks are performed by the World Intellectual Property Organization ("WIPO") which is a Specialised Agency of the United Nations whose task is to administer some 21 treaties in the field of intellectual property.[13] **2-011**

---

[5] The official name is: The Paris Convention for the Protection of Industrial Property.
[6] Brussels (1900), Washington (1911), The Hague (1925), London (1934), Lisbon (1958), and Stockholm (1967) as amended in 1979.
[7] Paris Convention art.2(1).
[8] art.4.
[9] art.4(B).
[10] art.5.
[11] art.5*bis*.
[12] arts 13, 14.
[13] For further information on WIPO, visit: *http://www.wipo.int* [Accessed 18 August 2017].

2-012   The Paris Convention has provided the framework for the Patent Cooperation Treaty ("PCT") and the European Patent Convention ("EPC"). Under art.19 of the Paris Convention, contracting states are allowed to enter into separate treaties provided that these agreements do not contravene the provisions of the Paris Convention. Therefore, the Patent Cooperation Treaty specifically states that none of its provision is to be interpreted as diminishing the rights of nationals or residents of contracting states under the Paris Convention.[14] Similarly, the preamble to the European Patent Convention states that it is a special agreement within art.19 of the Paris Convention.

TRIPS AGREEMENT

2-013   The TRIPS (Trade Related Aspects of Intellectual Property Rights) Agreement makes certain important provisions in respect of patents. The reader who is not familiar with TRIPS should see the overview contained in Ch.1.[15] Suffice to say that TRIPS is an agreement entered into between members of the World Trade Organisation ("WTO"), which includes all European countries. The patent section of TRIPS was one of the most difficult to negotiate as it involved a key number of North-South issues.[16] However, the result of such negotiations was impressive and TRIPS now provides a very important multilateral instrument in this field. The key points are discussed below.

Availability of patents for all inventions

2-014   Article 27 provides that patents shall be available for any inventions, whether products or processes in all fields of technology, provided that they are new, involve an inventive step and are capable of industrial application. This overriding provision corresponds in substance to national patent law throughout the world. As such, it merely consolidates the prior position. More important is that art.27 provides that patents shall be available and patent rights enjoyable "without discrimination as to the place of invention, the field of technology and whether products are imported or locally produced".[17]

2-015   Article 27 TRIPS was considered by the CJEU in *Monsanto v Cefetra*.[18] The facts of this case are discussed elsewhere in this chapter.[19] It was argued that art.9 of the Biotechnology Directive[20] was incompatible with art.27 TRIPS. The CJEU reiterated that TRIPS does not create rights upon which individuals may rely directly before the courts by reason of EU law.[21] However, it emphasised that EU law must be interpreted as far as possible in keeping with TRIPS (whilst not giving direct ef-

---

14   PCT art.1(2).
15   See para.1-167, et seq.
16   Generally, see D. Gervais, *The TRIPS Agreement: Drafting History and Analysis*, 4th edn (London: Sweet & Maxwell, 2012).
17   In relation to the "field of technology" provision, this requirement of non-discrimination is subject to art.27(3) which permits countries to exclude inventions in the medical, veterinarian and plant and animal fields from patentability. See para.2-017.
18   (C-428/08) [2010] E.C.R. I-6765.
19   See para.2-593.
20   This is discussed at para.2-593.
21   See [71]. Generally, see para.1-180.

fect to it).[22] The CJEU took the view however that art.9 of the Biotechnology Directive did not run counter to art.27 TRIPS.

The ban on discrimination by reference to the field of technology is considered **2-016** by some to mean that the exclusion under the EPC on the patenting of computer programs per se is illegal.[23] Furthermore, the ban on discrimination between local and imported products is important but should be read in the context of compulsory licences, and with reference to art.31(f) discussed at para.2-026.

Exceptions to patentability

There are important exceptions to the general requirement of patentability set out **2-017** in art.27. Thus, signatories to TRIPS *may* exclude from patentability the following:

(i)   inventions whose exploitation would be contrary to *ordre public* or morality, to protect human, animal or plant life or health, or to avoid serious prejudice to the environment provided that such exclusion is not made merely because the exploitation is prohibited by law[24];

(ii)   diagnostic, therapeutic and surgical methods for the treatment of humans or animals[25]; and

(iii) plants and animals other than micro-organisms, and essentially biological processes for the production of plants or animals other than non-biological and microbiological processes. However, members shall provide for the protection of plant varieties either by patents or by an effective sui generis system or by any combination thereof. Because it was considered that this provision could conflict with the Convention on Biological Diversity which inter alia seeks to ensure a fair and equitable sharing of benefits arising from the use of genetic resources, this provision was required to be reviewed four years after the date of entry into force of the WTO Agreement.[26]

These provisions correspond substantially to art.53(a)–(c) EPC. The main dif- **2-018** ference is that art.53(b) EPC excludes specifically from patent protection plant or animal *varieties* or essentially biological processes for the production of plants or animals (but not microbiological processes). It does not exclude per se patent protection for plants or animals (although such may be objectionable under other provisions such as *ordre public*).

Moreover, as the EPC excludes protection for plant varieties, the requirement **2-019** under art.27 TRIPS that protection be given to plant varieties means that signatories to the EPC must give protection via sui generis plant variety right protection rather

---

[22] See [72]. Again, see para.1-180.

[23] The removal of such a bar in the EPC was proposed at the Diplomatic Conference in 2000 on the revision of the EPC but it was not adopted. The patenting of computer programs under the EPC is considered at para.2-265.

[24] art.27(2). The wording of this exception is mirrored in art.53(a) EPC—see para.2-272.

[25] art.27(3)(a). The wording of this exception is mirrored in art.53(c) EPC and considerable case law has developed under the EPC as to its meaning—see para.2-275.

[26] art.27(3)(b). This also is mirrored in art.53(b) EPC—see para.2-294. For more information on the Convention of Biological Diversity, see *www.cbd.int* [Accessed 18 August 2017]. The WTO conducted a review on the relationship between TRIPS and the CBD in 2006 (IP/C/W/368 Rev.1 *https://www.wto.org/english/tratop_e/trips_e/ipcw368_e.pdf* [Accessed 18 August 2017]. In 2014, the Nagoya Protocol to the CBD came into force. This has now implemented in the EU by Reg.511/2014. See para.2-669.

than patent protection. Most European countries already have plant variety protection whether as a result of their obligations under the 1991 UPOV (International Union for the Protection of New Varieties of Plants) Convention or, in the case of the EU (which is a signatory to TRIPS), by reason of the Community Plant Variety Right.[27]

Rights conferred by a patent

2-020   Article 28(1) of TRIPS provides that a patent confers on its owner, the exclusive right:

"(a)   where the subject-matter of a patent is a product, to prevent third parties not having the owner's consent from the acts of: making, using, offering for sale, selling or importing for these purposes that product;

(b)   where the subject-matter of a patent is a process, to prevent third parties not having the owner's consent from the act of using the process, and from the acts of: using, offering for sale, selling or importing for these purposes at least the product obtained directly by that process."

2-021   Article 28(1) was inspired by art.19 of the draft Patent Law Treaty. It is an uncontroversial measure, as it accords with the law and practice of many countries. It should be noted that the mere possession of an infringing product is not in itself an infringing act. Many national laws do however provide for such a right if it is in the course of business, which is useful in practice to seize such products. However, many jurisdictions which do not have such a right will also permit the seizure of such products on the basis that there is a sufficient and reasonable fear that the products will be sold.[28]

Requirement of disclosure

2-022   Article 29(1) provides that an applicant for a patent must disclose the invention in a manner sufficiently clear and complete for the invention to be carried out by a person skilled in the art. This is often described as the obligation of sufficiency. Article 29(1) also provides that WTO members *may* require the applicant to indicate the best mode for carrying out the invention known to the inventor at the filing date or, where priority is claimed, at the priority date of the application.

2-023   The compulsory part of art.29 is common in patent laws of national countries and is a requirement in the EPC.[29] However, it is not an obligation in the Paris Convention and thus fills a lacuna in the latter convention. Its rationale is that the inventor provides full disclosure in exchange for a monopoly whose duration is limited in time so that others may exploit the invention without undue difficulty after the expiry of the patent. The optional provision of "best mode" in art.29 is not mirrored in the EPC and therefore the imposition of such an obligation by a state which is a member of the EPC would not be permissible under the EPC.[30]

---

[27] See Ch.6, "Plant Variety Rights in Europe".
[28] Thus, in England, one can obtain a quia timet injunction to restrain a future tortious act.
[29] See para.2-236 for detailed discussion as to this requirement in the EPC.
[30] The EPC requires all Members States to harmonise their law in accordance with the EPC. See para.2-100.

Exceptions to rights conferred

Article 30 states that: **2-024**

"Members may provide limited exceptions to the exclusive rights conferred by a patent, provided that such exceptions do not unreasonably conflict with a normal exploitation of the patent and do not unreasonably prejudice the legitimate interests of the patent owner, taking account of the legitimate interests of third parties."

Such a provision is, of course, very vague. The 1990 draft of art.30 gave   **2-025**
examples of what was in the legislator's mind. These were rights based on prior use; acts done privately and for non-commercial purposes; acts done for experimental purposes (such as preparation in a pharmacy in individual cases of a medicine in accordance with a prescription); and acts done by government for purposes merely of its own use. Such examples did not survive into the final Article but may give some indication as to the intention of the legislator in drafting art.30.[31] Certainly, it would appear that such acts (save the pharmacy exception) do not unreasonably conflict with the normal exploitation of the patent, do not unreasonably prejudice the legitimate interests of the patent owner, and represent legitimate interests of third parties.

Compulsory licences

Where the law of a WTO Member State provides for a compulsory licence of a   **2-026**
patent,[32] then art.31 provides that certain provisions must be respected in relation to the grant of that licence. These are numerous but include the following:

(a) the right to adequate remuneration in the circumstances of each case, taking into account the economic value of the authorisation[33];
(b) the consideration of each case on its merits[34];
(c) the applicant must have already sought a licence from the patentee on reasonable terms and conditions, with such efforts not proving successful within a reasonable period of time[35];
(d) the licence shall be limited in scope and duration of use in accordance with the purpose for which it was authorised[36];
(e) the licence must be non-exclusive and non-assignable (save where the underlying business is also assigned)[37];
(f) the compulsory licence should be used predominantly for the supply of the domestic market authorising such use[38]; and
(g) where the application for a compulsory licence is a patentee who requires

---

[31] Generally, see D. Gervais, *The TRIPS Agreement—Drafting History and Analysis*, 4th edn (London: Sweet & Maxwell, 2012).
[32] This provision is not concerned with limitations of the right of a patentee under art.30. See fn.7 to art.31. The two provisions are thus independent and standalone.
[33] art.31(h).
[34] art.31(a).
[35] art.31(b).
[36] art.31(c).
[37] art.31(d) and (e).
[38] art.31(f). A Protocol introducing art.31*bis* which amends art.31(f) has now come into force. Article 31*bis* deals with the problem caused by developing countries who do not have domestic manufacturing ability to produce pharmaceuticals (as recognised in the Doha Declaration of TRIPS Agreement and Public Health). The effect of art.31*bis* is to disapply art.31(f) where a compulsory licence

a licence from another patent so that the applicant can exploit their patent, then it must be shown that the invention claimed in the second patent involves an important technical advance of considerable economic significance in relation to the invention claimed in the first patent.[39] The owner of the first patent is entitled to a cross-licence in respect of the second patent and use authorised in respect of the first patent is non-assignable except with the assignment of the second patent.

Revocation/forfeiture of a patent

2-027 Article 32 provides that an opportunity for judicial review of any decision to revoke or forfeit a patent shall be made available.[40] The term "judicial" means that where the authority in question is not a court of law, it must follow the formal legal procedure of a court.[41] If read literally, the provision could lead to the absurd result that no decision could ever be final. The intent here is clearly to ensure that any tribunal decision to revoke or forfeit (which can occur automatically, i.e. by reason of non-payment of renewal fees) may be reviewed by judicial process. However, once such has occurred, normal rules would apply.[42]

Term of a patent

2-028 Article 33 stipulates a minimum period for protection under a patent, which is 20 years counted from the filing date. This provision harmonises member countries' patent laws, some of which previously counted from the date of grant. It is notable that art.33 does not lay down a maximum period. Under many countries' laws and under EU legislation, protection is extended for certain products where the marketing of those products has been delayed by the need for regulatory approval—in particular in the field of pharmaceuticals.

Burden of proof in actions for infringement of a process patent

2-029 In an action for infringement of a patent which is for a process for manufacturing a product, it is often difficult to prove that the patented process has been used. In such circumstances, art.34 provides that judicial authorities may order the defendant to prove that the process which produced an identical product was obtained by a different process.

2-030 Furthermore, where the product is identical to a product produced by the patented process, art.34 requires national patent laws of WTO members to provide "in at least one of the following circumstances" that there is an evidential presumption that the

---

is needed for the purpose of allowing an eligible importing Member State to import pharmaceuticals to address public health problems in that state. This amendment took effect on 23 January 2017 following acceptance by two thirds of WTO Members and replaces the 2003 "waiver"—see *https://www.wto.org/english/tratop_e/trips_e/amendment_e.htm* [Accessed 18 August 2017]. Those WTO Members had until 31 December 2017 to accept the amendment. See also para.7-079 (no discrimination allowed between Member States of the EU which would appear to contravene art.31(f)).

[39] art.31(l).
[40] See also art.41(4).
[41] See D. Gervais, *The TRIPS Agreement: Drafting History and Analysis*, 4th edn (London: Sweet & Maxwell, 2012), para.2-424.
[42] See D. Gervais, *The TRIPS Agreement: Drafting History and Analysis*, 4th edn (London: Sweet & Maxwell, 2012), para.2-424.

product was obtained via the patented process:

(a) if the product obtained by the patented process is new; or
(b) if there is a substantial likelihood that the identical product was made by the process and the owner of the patent has been unable through reasonable efforts to determine the process actually used.

Article 34(2) also permits any WTO member to provide that the presumption of infringement shall apply *only if* the condition in (a) or *only if* the condition in (b), is fulfilled.[43] **2-031**

Condition (b) may be difficult to fulfil in many cases. It is often customary for courts to order the defendant to describe the process that was used by it. Such a description is of course not proof in the formal sense. Clearly, where there is suspicion that the described process is not the actual process, art.34 will be of assistance to a patentee. Article 34(3) states that the "legitimate interests of defendants in protecting their manufacturing and business secrets shall be taken into account" where a defendant wishes to discharge the evidential burden by showing proof to the contrary. Such could be done by imposing a measure of controlled disclosure to the patentee of the evidence concerning the defendant's process.[44] **2-032**

It should be noted that in the Agreement for the Unified Patent Court, that the above provision has been implemented. Thus, art.55 stipulates that if the subject matter of a patent is a process for obtaining a new product, the burden of proof is reversed where either (a) or (b) is satisfied. **2-033**

PATENT COOPERATION TREATY

Fundamentals of the PCT

The Patent Cooperation Treaty ("PCT") was set up in order to provide a centralised procedure for the grant of patent applications for contracting states. Its aim is to centralise, simplify and render more economical patent applications for countries who are signatories to the PCT. In essence, it is a procedural treaty and does not concern itself with the actual grant of patents, which is left to national patent offices. It is a worldwide treaty to which as of April 2018, 152 countries have acceded, including almost all of the important industrial countries. The Treaty was signed on 19 June 1970 and came into force on 1 June 1978 and countries have been becoming members up to the present day.[45] All European countries have ratified the convention. Countries that have acceded to it are deemed to belong to the International Patent Cooperation Union.[46] **2-034**

Chapter I of the PCT permits an applicant to file an "International Application" **2-035**

---

[43] In other words, Contracting States cannot provide for presumptions of infringement other than when either of these two conditions are fulfilled.

[44] In England, the High Court is used to making such orders—see *Warner Lambert v Glaxo Laboratories* [1975] R.P.C. 354 where in a patent infringement action, an order was made that only certain nominated persons could have access to confidential documentation of the defendant which described the defendant's process and which was claimed to be highly confidential and upon appropriate contractual undertakings or undertakings to the court not to disclose the information or make use of it.

[45] The PCT Treaty was amended in 1979, 1984 and 2001. An up-to-date version can be found at: *http://www.wipo.int/treaties/en/registration/pct* [Accessed 18 August 2017].

[46] PCT art.1(1).

at their local national patent office, called the "Receiving Office".[47] All countries who are contracting states are automatically Designated States. Upon receipt of the application, the Receiving Office will check that the application complies with certain formalities. It will then remit copies to the International Bureau of WIPO in Geneva, which acts as the administrative office for the PCT.[48] It also sends copies of the application to a patent office which is designated as an International Searching Authority ("ISA").[49] This office will make a search of the prior art and then send the International Search Report ("ISR") to the International Bureau at WIPO and also to the applicant.[50] The ISA will also send a preliminary non-binding report as to the patentability of the invention in the light of the ISR—the International Preliminary Report on Patentability—or IPRP.

2-036   The applicant is given an opportunity, if necessary, to amend the patent application.[51]

2-037   An applicant who is a resident or national of a contracting state which has acceded to Chapter II of the PCT may make a demand that the application be subject to an international preliminary examination by the appropriate International Preliminary Examining Authority ("IPEA").[52] This is sometimes called a PCT-II application. The ISR will be sent to the IPEA. The IPEA will draw up an opinion to which the applicant can respond with argument or amendment prior to the IPEA drawing up an International Preliminary Examination Report ("IPER") which is sent to WIPO and the applicant.[53] Then those countries which the applicant has elected to receive the IPER (these must be countries which have acceded to Chapter II and are called "Elected States") will receive the IPER from WIPO and the international PCT phase ends.[54] The IPER constitutes a preliminary opinion on the patentability of the invention and is not binding on the patent offices of the Elected States ("the Elected Offices"). The applicant will generally wait until the end of the 30th month (or the 31st month in some cases) from the filing of the international application (or the priority date as the case may be) before filing translations with Elected Offices.

2-038   Since 2004, the attraction of seeking an IPER has lessened because, as said above, the ISA is also now required to prepare a written opinion on the patentability of the application—the International Preliminary Report on Patentability ("IPRP"). This is sent to the applicant at the same time as the ISR. This is not made available for public inspection until the end of 30 months from the priority date. Hence, it can provide a valuable and confidential early view as to the patentability of the application.

2-039   The international patent application and the ISR are then sent to the patent offices of the Designated States ("the Designated Offices") or if a PCT-II application, the "Elected Offices" and the international application enters the national phase.[55] This ends the international phase under the PCT.

2-040   At this point, the applicant will have a fair idea of the patentability of the inven-

---

[47] PCT arts 3, 10.
[48] PCT art.12(1).
[49] PCT arts 12(1), 16.
[50] PCT art.18(2). Note that since 1 January 2009 all applicants may also request a language-based "Supplementary International Search" under the new PCT Rule 45*bis*.
[51] PCT art.19(1).
[52] PCT art.31.
[53] PCT arts 34, 35.
[54] PCT art.36.
[55] PCT art.20.

tion and the countries for which they wish to obtain patent protection. Prior to the 30th or 31st month of the priority date of the international application,[56] it will enter the national phase.[57] This is done by paying a national fee and providing a copy of the international application and filing a translation (where necessary) of the application into the official language of the patent offices of the countries for which the applicant seeks protection.

The PCT procedure thus gives great advantages to the applicant compared with parallel applications in many national patent offices. Not only is it more cost-effective, but it gives the applicant a considerable period of time in which to consider the desirability of obtaining protection in foreign countries, having seen a reputable search report and a preliminary examination report as to the patentability of the claimed invention.
2-041

The procedural structure of the PCT complements the Paris Convention, which is concerned with rationalising the substantive patent laws of countries. However, the Treaty specifically states that none of its provision is to be interpreted as diminishing the rights of any national or resident of a country which is party to the Paris Convention.[58]
2-042

The PCT also complements the EPC. It permits applicants to designate states which have ratified the EPC (a "Euro-PCT" application). This in turn enables them to obtain a basket of corresponding national patents via the EPC route. The end result is the same to the applicant as designating the Member States individually. However, the application for those countries is prosecuted before the EPO and not in the national patent offices of the individual countries.
2-043

The PCT procedure is now explained in more detail. The legislation for the PCT is contained in the Treaty itself and the Implementing Regulations.[59] For practitioners, WIPO has published a looseleaf "*PCT Applicant's Guide*" which is continually updated.[60]
2-044

International application

Filing of international applications

Only those who are nationals or residents of contracting states of the PCT can apply for patent protection via the PCT.[61] International applications must be filed with the national office of the contracting state of which the applicant is a national or resident or at the International Bureau of WIPO at Geneva.[62] This office is called
2-045

---

[56] For whether or not not it is the 30th or 31st month, see *http://www.wipo.int/pct/en/texts/time_limits.html* [Accessed 18 August 2017] for relevant period. There is one exception to the 30th or 31st-month rule and that is Luxembourg which provides for a 20th-month rule where a request for an IPER under Chapter II of the PCT is not made.

[57] PCT art.22.

[58] PCT art.1(2).

[59] The abbreviation "PCT r" is used to denote a rule in the Implementing Regulations. These are available via the WIPO website at *http://www.wipo.int/pct/en/texts/rules/rtoc1.htm* [Accessed 18 August 2017].

[60] This is available at most national patent offices and copies can be obtained direct from WIPO, 34 Chemin des Colombettes, CH-1211 Geneva 20, Switzerland. It is also available from the WIPO website at: *http://www.wipo.int/pct/en/appguide* [Accessed 18 August 2017].

[61] PCT art.9.

[62] PCT r.19(1). Contracting states can make arrangements that nationals or those who reside in a contracting state can file at another contracting state's patent office. Thus, Switzerland acts as Receiv-

the Receiving Office.[63] The application must be on a printed form provided by the Receiving Office or WIPO, or presented as a computer printout.[64] The prescribed form provides a comprehensive checklist and should be completed carefully with the assistance of the guide-notes.[65]

2-046 If the applicant wishes to make a PCT-II application, i.e. to obtain an IPER in prosecuting their application in the elected states, then the applicant must be a resident or national of a contracting state which is bound by Chapter II of the PCT and make an application to the Receiving Office of that state or to the International Bureau.[66]

2-047 Following changes to the rules in 2004, an application results in automatic designation of all contracting states bound by the PCT.[67]

Language regime for international applications

2-048 The rules concerning languages under the PCT are somewhat complicated. The international application must be in a language permitted by the Receiving Office. WIPO's website for the PCT contains a table of languages that are allowed for each European Receiving Office.[68] A Receiving Office can designate one or more languages that they will indicate that they will accept. However, each Receiving Office must permit the filing in at least one language which is a "language of publication" (hence its name).[69] The current "languages of publication" are Arabic, Chinese, English, French, German, Japanese, Korean, Portuguese, Russian or Spanish.[70] If the international application is not filed in a language which is accepted by the designated ISA, then the applicant must file within one month from the date of receipt of the international application by the Receiving Office, a translation into a language accepted by the ISA.[71] The applicant must also file a translation in a language of publication.[72] If the application was not filed in a language of publication and has not been translated into a language of publication for the purpose of the ISR, then the applicant must file a translation of the application into any language of publication within 14 months from the priority date.[73]

2-049 The effect of the above rules means that the application will, by the time of international publication, have been translated into a "language of publication" (hence its name). That will then become the language in which the international application is published.[74] If the language of publication is not English, then the

---

ing Office for Liechtenstein.

[63] PCT art.10.

[64] PCT r.3. Certain Receiving Offices have telegraphic, facsimile and teleprinter facilities for filing. The reader should consult the *PCT Applicant's Guide*.

[65] An example of the prescribed form can be seen in the *PCT Applicant's Guide*.

[66] art.31(2)(a); PCT r.54.

[67] PCT rr.4.1, 4.9.

[68] See *http://www.wipo.int/pct/en/appguide/index.jsp* [Accessed 18 August 2017] for tables showing the receiving offices for each country. Clicking on the link under "Receiving Offices" to provide a page containing information including permissible languages for publication.

[69] PCT r.12.1(b).

[70] PCT r.48.3(a).

[71] PCT r.12.3(a).

[72] PCT r.12.3(a)(ii).

[73] PCT r.12.4(a).

[74] PCT r.48.

International Bureau will arrange for the title, abstract and the ISR to be translated into English.[75]

Procedure upon receipt of application

The Receiving Office, after satisfying itself that the formalities have been complied with, will notify the applicant and WIPO. Provided that the formalities have been complied with,[76] the Receiving Office will give an "international filing date" to the application. This is deemed to be a regular national filing date as defined by the Paris Convention and thus acts as the priority date.[77]   **2-050**

Contents of the international application

The description must disclose the invention in a manner sufficiently clear and complete for the invention to be carried out by a person skilled in the art.[78] It must specify the technical field to which the invention relates and the background art. Further it must disclose the invention as claimed and state the advantageous effects, if any, of the invention with reference to the background art. Where a designated state requires a "best mode" for carrying out the invention, then this must be set out as well. If it is not already clear, it must be shown how the invention is capable of being exploited industrially.   **2-051**

The claim or claims must define the matter for which protection is sought, they must be clear and concise and must be fully supported by the description.[79] Drawings must be provided where they are necessary for an understanding of the invention.[80] General claims by reference to the description or drawings are not permitted.[81] Claims must identify those features which form part of the prior art and must contain a characterising portion stating precisely the technical features which, in combination with the "prior art" features, the patent application is designed to protect.[82] Dependent claims are permissible, as are dependent claims which refer to more than one other claim, provided they refer to such claims in the alternative. However, multiple dependent claims cannot serve as a basis for any other multiple claim.[83]   **2-052**

The application must relate to only one invention.[84]   **2-053**

---

[75] PCT r.48.3(c).

[76] PCT r.11.

[77] PCT art.11(4).

[78] PCT art.5.

[79] PCT art.6.

[80] art.7.

[81] PCT r.6.2.

[82] PCT r.6.3. Generally this rule is not enforced in the international phase. However, it is a strong feature of the EPC.

[83] PCT r.6.4. For example, it is permissible to have a Claim 7 which is based on an inventive feature plus Claims 1–6. However, it is not theoretically permissible to have a Claim 8 which is based on Claims 1–7 plus another inventive feature, as Claim 7 is itself a multiple dependent claim. However, since such claims are permitted by the EPO (at least) in practice such claims are commonplace.

[84] PCT r.13.

Claiming priority

2-054 The PCT permits the claiming of priority from one or more earlier applications.[85] The substantive requirements are governed by art.4 of the Stockholm Act of the Paris Convention.[86] Thus, there is a grace period of 12 months during which the applicant may claim the priority of an earlier application.[87] The applicant may designate the same contracting state from which it is claiming priority by reason of an earlier application in that state. Where, in an international application, the priority of one or more national applications filed in or for a Designated State is claimed, or where the priority of an international application having designated only one state is claimed, the conditions for and the effect of the priority claim in that state is governed by the national law of that state.[88] A copy of the priority document must be provided within 16 months of the priority date to WIPO or the Receiving Office (or, if later, before the date of international publication).[89] If the application fails to claim priority, the situation would seem to be insoluble unless a new application with a valid priority claim can still be filed. Errors in the priority claim which relate to the date or country designation can only be corrected in the case where the correction is obvious. The application number of the priority claim may be furnished at any time up to 16 months from priority, which mechanism permits the correction of an incorrect number within such a period.[90]

Defects in the application

2-055 If the application is found by the Receiving Office not to have complied with the above formalities, then it must invite the applicant to file the required correction.[91] In most circumstances, the international filing date is then deemed to be the date of receipt of the required corrections.[92] The late payment of fees does not affect the deemed filing date, although it may result in the application being deemed to have been withdrawn.[93]

Designation of contracting states

2-056 Since 1 January 2004, all contracting states are automatically designated.[94]

International search

2-057 Each application is subject to an international search by an ISA. The relevant ISA is that prescribed by the Receiving Office.[95] The object of the search is to discover relevant prior art.[96] The ISA is usually a national patent office or an institution like the EPO. The ISA will not carry out a search if the international application relates

---

[85] art.8.
[86] See para.2-010.
[87] art.8.
[88] art.8(2)(b).
[89] PCT r.17.
[90] art.8(1), PCT r.4.10, and r.26*bis*.1.
[91] art.11(2)(a).
[92] arts 11(2)(a), 14 and PCT r.20.3(b)(i).
[93] arts 11(2), 14 and PCT r.27.
[94] PCT r.4.1, r.4.9(a)(i).
[95] PCT r.35, art.16.
[96] arts 15, 16.

to a subject-matter which it is not required to search. These categories correspond to inventions generally considered unpatentable by national laws. These include: scientific and mathematical theories; plant or animal varieties; methods for treatment of the human or animal body; and computer programs.[97] Furthermore, if more than one invention has been claimed for, the ISA may ask for additional fees to be paid in respect of each additional invention.

If the international application is not in a language accepted by the ISA, the applicant must furnish, to the Receiving Office, a translation of the international application into a language which is both a language accepted by the ISA and a language of publication.[98] As each Receiving Office and ISA is obliged to accept at least one language which is a language of publication, an applicant will always have the choice to file an application in a language which can be used by both the ISA and for the purpose of publication. **2-058**

An ISR will then be drawn up by the ISA within three months of receipt of the search copy by the ISA or nine months from the priority date, whichever is the later.[99] A copy is sent to the applicant and WIPO.[100] The ISR must be in the language in which the international application is to be published.[101] If the report is not in English, WIPO will, free of charge, prepare an English translation.[102] **2-059**

The ISA is under a duty to try to discover not just "as much of the relevant prior art as … facilities permit", but also to consult certain "documentation specified by the Regulations".[103] This consists of certain PCT applications and certain national patent documents.[104] The ISR must contain the citations of documents considered to be relevant and list the fields searched.[105] Copies of the cited documents may be sent to the applicant or the Receiving Office by request upon payment of the costs of the ISA in preparing and mailing the documents.[106] **2-060**

Since 1 July 2008, applicants can ask the ISA to take account not just of the results of an earlier search carried out by that ISA, but also of the results of an earlier search carried out by another ISA or national or regional Office.[107] **2-061**

The ISA will usually flag cited prior art documents with "X" if they are considered to be very close prior art. **2-062**

Supplementary International Search

Following amendments adopted in September 2007 by the PCT Assembly, all applicants are entitled to send a request for an ISA other than the one conducting the main international search to conduct a Supplementary International Search **2-063**

---

[97] PCT r.39. The ISA will search for prior art in computer programs if it is equipped to do so (see PCT r.39.1(vi)).

[98] See para.2-048.

[99] art.18, PCT r.42.

[100] art.18, PCT r.44.

[101] PCT r.43.4. For language of publication, see above, para.2-048.

[102] PCT r.45.

[103] art.15(4), PCT r.34.

[104] PCT r.34. These are stipulated to include international patents, published patent applications, national patents, and published applications of France in or after 1920, Germany, the Soviet Union, Switzerland, the UK and the USA; inventors' certificates of the Soviet Union; and utility certificates of France and patents and published applications in English, German, French and Spanish which have been made available to the ISA—see PCT r.34.1(c).

[105] PCT r.43.5.

[106] art.20(3), PCT r.44.3.

[107] PCT r.12bis.1, r.4.12, r.41.1.

("SIS").[108] Such a request must be made to the International Bureau, and must be made within 22 months of the priority date.[109] The purpose of this provision is to allow applicants to gain a better overview of the prior art by searching for documents in languages other than those likely to be searched as part of the main international search. The scope of the search is governed by the same rules as the main international search.[110] Individual ISAs have been allowed to choose whether or not to offer this service as a Supplementary International Search Authority ("SISA").[111] The applicant must furnish the International Bureau with a translation of the application into a language accepted by the SISA if the language of the application and any translations already furnished to the Receiving Office do not fall within that category.[112] SISs are subject to additional handling and search fees.[113] The SISA will, within 28 months from the priority date, either produce (or "establish") its supplementary international search report ("SISR") or else declare that no such report is to be produced, and on the same day transmit to both the applicant and the International Bureau either a copy of the SISR or the declaration as the case may be.[114]

Non-binding written opinion as to patentability (IPRP)

2-064   The ISA will issue a written opinion at the same time as it issues the ISR saying whether the invention is novel, inventive and industrially applicable and whether it complies with the requirements of the PCT.[115] This forms the basis of the International Preliminary Report on Patentability ("IPRP").[116] The IPRP is non-binding on Designated States. Applicants may submit comments on the IPRP to the International Bureau.[117] If the applicant demands that its application be internationally examined by an IPEA, then the IPRP is treated as a report by the IPEA and the applicant is invited to submit a response to the IPEA.[118] Thus, there is no reason to seek an IPER unless the applicant wishes to obtain an amended IPRP. Usually though, if there is an adverse IPRP, applicants tackle this during prosecution of the application during the national or regional phase.

Amendment of the claims

2-065   The applicant has only one opportunity to amend the claims upon receipt of the ISR and IPRP.[119] The amendments may not go beyond the disclosure in the international application as filed.[120] The applicant has an opportunity to file a brief

---

[108] PCT r.45 *bis*.

[109] PCT r.45*bis*.1(a).

[110] PCT r.33.2.

[111] As of January 2014, the ISAs that have given notice of their SISA status are: Austria, the EPO, Finland, the Russian Federation, Sweden, and the Nordic Patent Institute.

[112] PCT r.45 *bis* .1(c).

[113] PCT rr.45*bis*.2, 45*bis*.3.

[114] PCT rr.45*bis*.7, 45*bis*.8.

[115] PCT r.43*bis*.

[116] PCT r.44*bis*.1.

[117] *PCT Applicant's Guide*, paras 7.030–7.031.

[118] PCT r.43*bis*.1(c).

[119] art.19.

[120] art.19(2). If the national law of a designated state permits amendments to go beyond such disclosure, then failure to comply with such a requirement has no consequence in that state—art.19(3).

statement in the language of publication, explaining the amendments.[121] Such amendments must be made within two months of receipt of the ISR, or 16 months from the priority date or the date on which technical preparations for the publication of the application are deemed to have been completed, whichever time limit expires last.[122] Where the applicant wishes to submit a demand for preliminary examination, they should file the amendments with the demand if they wish, to the IPEA to consider the amendments for the purposes of examination or, where the time limit for examination has not expired, the applicant may apply to postpone the examination for such amendments to be made.[123] It should be noted that where an applicant chooses to have the application examined by an IPEA, they will have a second chance to amend the claims during the examination stage.[124] There is usually no need to file amendments at the search stage unless there is a particular desire to have the amendments included in the international publication.

Publication of the application

WIPO must publish the application, in the form of a pamphlet, promptly after the expiry of 18 months from the priority date of the application along with the search report and amendments.[125] If the search report or amendments of claims are not ready, this does not prevent the application being published. However, these will be published later.[126] The position regarding the language of publication and the need for translation has already been discussed.[127]   **2-066**

The bibliographic data, title and abstract are published in the *PCT Gazette* in electronic form in both English and French.[128]   **2-067**

The application will not be published if it is deemed withdrawn or notice of its withdrawal is received by the International Bureau before technical preparations for publication have been completed.[129] Generally, technical preparations are completed by the 15th day before the date of publication.[130] The notice of withdrawal may state that withdrawal is to be effective only on condition that international publication can be avoided.[131]   **2-068**

The effect of publication is that provisional protection for the applicant in a Designated State may arise as with the national publication of unexamined national applications.[132] However, contracting states can (and usually will) make such provisional protection run from the time that a translation of the international application into the language in which national applications of that contracting state   **2-069**

---

[121] art.19, PCT r.46.4.
[122] PCT r.46.
[123] PCT r.53.9, r.62. If the demand has already been sent off, then the applicant should file the amendments with the IPEA at the same time as filing the amendments with the International Bureau.
[124] art.34.
[125] art.21, PCT r.48.
[126] PCT r.48.2(g).
[127] See para.2-048.
[128] PCT r.86.2.
[129] art.21(5). An application will be deemed to have been withdrawn if it does not comply with the requirements of the PCT and its Implementing Regulations and the applicant has failed to notify the relevant body of the corrections—see PCT r.20.7.
[130] See *PCT Applicant's Guide*, "International Phase", para.9.014
[131] See *PCT Applicant's Guide*, "International Phase", para.9.023A.
[132] art.29(1).

is published and made available to the public or transmitted to the potential infringer.[133]

Communication to Designated Offices

2-070   The international application, along with the ISR, must be communicated by the International Bureau to each Designated Office (unless the latter waives such requirements).[134] This must be done promptly after publication of the international application or, in any event, within 19 months of the priority date.[135] The applicant is notified of the states that the international application has been sent to. The application is sent in the language in which it was published or, if different to that in which it was filed, at the request of the designated office, the language in which it was filed.[136]

Copy, translation and fee to Designated Offices—national phase

2-071   The general rule is that the applicant must furnish a copy of the international application (unless already provided by WIPO), a translation into an official language of the Designated Office and pay the required national fee for each of the Designated Offices in which they wish to obtain protection by the expiry of 30 months from the priority date.[137] However, certain countries declared art.22 (which makes this provision) as incompatible with their domestic law. As of January 2014, only one European country, Luxembourg, has stipulated 20 months as being the period for entry into the national phase. Other countries have provided, pursuant to art.22(3) for a longer period, namely 31 months.[138] No reminders are sent to applicants and failure to comply with these time limits is usually fatal. It is at this stage that the applicant decides, in effect, in which countries they wish to obtain protection. As said before, all contracting states are automatically designated upon application.

2-072   In general, Designated States will confer the same level of protection on an international application which has been subject to international publication as that conferred on a domestic application which is published.[139] This will usually mean that some degree of protection (usually the right to compensation) is afforded from the date of publication of the international application (assuming the application becomes a registered patent). However, if the language of the international publication is not a language permitted by the Designated Office, then protection will usually only arise once a translation of the application has been made into a permitted language of the Designated Office.[140]

2-073   The international application now enters the national phase and further prosecu-

---

[133] art.29(2). See *http://www.wipo.int/pct/guide/en* [Accessed 18 August 2017] which sets out the languages of publication of Designated Offices.

[134] art.20, PCT r.47.1.

[135] PCT r.47.1.

[136] PCT r.47.3.

[137] art.22, PCT r.49.

[138] For a full list of countries which have a time limit different to 30 months, see *http://www.wipo.int/pct/en/texts/time_limits.html* [Accessed 18 August 2017].

[139] art.29(1).

[140] art.29(3). Invariably, Designated States do not provide for protection earlier than the publication of a translation into a language permitted by that country. The prescribed languages for each designated state and the commencement of protection is set out at *http://www.wipo.int/pct/en/texts/time_*

tion is between the applicant and the national patent office of each designated state. The PCT leaves the Designated State to determine whether the application satisfies the criteria of patentability.[141] Thus, in this sense, the PCT is a procedural treaty.

The applicant will usually be permitted to further amend the claims during the examination phase of the application before the national patent office. In any event, the national office must permit the applicant to amend their claims up to one month from furnishing a copy of the international application and, where necessary, a translation to the Designated Office.[142] Generally, most Designated Offices permit an applicant to amend a PCT application which has entered the national phase at any period during the examination procedure.

2-074

International preliminary examination—Chapter II PCT

Introduction

For qualifying applications,[143] and where elected, an examining authority called the International Preliminary Examination Authority ("IPEA") will compile a report on the patentability of the international application. This is known as the International Preliminary Examination Report ("IPER"). It is important to note that the IPER is not binding on the Elected States and is essentially preliminary in nature.[144] To start with, this will be the non-binding written opinion ("IPRP") prepared by the ISA.[145]

2-075

In Europe, the designated IPEA of the vast majority of elected states is the EPO and its examination will normally mean that any subsequent examination during the national phase is a mere formality. Moreover, all European countries are signatories to Chapter II of the PCT and this has increased its usefulness in Europe. However, in many cases, there is no reduction in the national examination phase fee where an IPER has been prepared, so it will not be cheaper than a Chapter I international application. Moreover, now that the ISA (International Search Authority) also prepares a non-binding written opinion on patentability (the IPRP), the attractions of seeking an IPER have lessened. Thus, the reason for seeking an IPER would be only where the applicant wishes to challenge the IPRP or have the application re-examined, having filed amendments following receipt of the IPRP. If such is the case, as the time for entering the national phase is now (save Luxembourg) the same regardless of whether the applicant makes a demand for an IPER or not, there is no delay in seeking an IPER and may suit an applicant who wishes to obtain a favourable international opinion on patentability prior to entering the national phase. Since 1 July 2014, the IPEA will now conduct a top-up search to uncover prior art not available at the time that the ISR was carried out.[146]

2-076

The IPEA will examine the international application according to internationally accepted criteria for patentability which thus gives the applicant an early opportunity to evaluate the chances of obtaining patent protection in elected states. The

2-077

---

limits.html [Accessed 18 August 2017].

[141] art.27(5).

[142] art.28, PCT r.52.

[143] See para.2-078.

[144] art.33(1).

[145] See para.2-064.

[146] PCT r.66.1*ter*. It will not do where such would not serve any useful purpose, i.e. the ISR is sufficient to demonstrate lack of novelty.

objective of the examination is to formulate a preliminary and non-binding opinion on the question of whether the claimed invention appears to be novel, involves an inventive step and is industrially applicable.[147] It is not to determine whether the invention is patentable according to national law.[148] The IPER is confidential and is not made available to third parties,[149] so applicants need not fear the publication of an adverse report.

Eligible applicants

2-078   Only an applicant who is a national or resident of a contracting state bound by Chapter II of the PCT who has filed an international application at the Receiving Office of a contracting state bound by Chapter II (called an "elected" office) may "demand" that an International Preliminary Examination ("IPE") be undertaken by an International Preliminary Examining Authority ("IPEA").[150]

Time limits

2-079   The demand may be submitted at any time prior to the expiry of the later of the following two time limits: (i) three months from the date of transmittal to the Applicant of the ISR and written opinion of the ISA; or (ii) 22 months from the priority date.[151] This will normally permit the applicant to take into account the ISR and IPRP prepared by the ISA. However, in respect of certain states which require applications to enter the national phase by the expiry of 20 months from the priority date, then the demand for IPE must be made before the expiry of 19 months from the priority date regardless of whether an ISR or written opinion has been prepared.[152] This has the effect of postponing the deadline for entering the national phase to the expiry of 30 months from the priority date. In general, the earlier the demand for IPE, the better the quality of the report because the international preliminary report on patentability must in most cases be established before the expiry of 28 months from the priority date.[153]

2-080   However, this problem can be overcome for all European countries by making an "EP" designation for a patent under the EPC (a Euro-PCT application).[154] The time limit set by the EPO is 31 months from the priority date. These countries can then be designated as countries within the EP application.

The demand

2-081   The applicant must make a demand to WIPO for their international application to be examined.[155] This demand is separate from the international application and

---

[147] art.33(1).

[148] art.35(2).

[149] art.38, PCT r.94.

[150] art.31(2)(a). A list of contracting states which have ratified Chapter II of the PCT can be seen at *http://www.wipo.int/pct/en/appguide/index.jsp* [Accessed 18 August 2017]. PCT r.18.1 defines the concept of "residence" and "nationality".

[151] PCT r.54*bis*.1(a), PCT r.69.1(a)(iii), PCT r.69.2.

[152] art.39(1). This applies to countries which opted out of the new art.22—see para.2-071.

[153] See *PCT Applicant's Guide*, "International Phase", para.10.010.

[154] This is discussed at para.2-496.

[155] art.31(3).

must be submitted directly to the IPEA competent to carry out the IPE.[156] The competent IPEA will depend on which Receiving Office the international application was filed in and which language the application was filed in.[157]

The international application must be translated into a language accepted by the IPEA if it was not initially published or filed in such a language.[158] **2-082**

The demand must be in the language of the international application or if different, the language of publication. The demand must be signed by the applicant. The applicant must pay a handling fee to the IPEA.[159] Furthermore, the IPEA may require a preliminary examination fee.[160] Full details as to the requirements of the demand are set out in the *PCT Applicant's Guide*.[161] **2-083**

Substantive examination by the IPEA

The IPEA will start the IPE when it is in possession of both the demand and the ISR.[162] Substantive examination will not begin, however, until any defects in the demand have been corrected and unpaid fees have been settled. If an indication has been made in the demand that amendments under art.19 are to be taken into account, the IPEA will not start until it receives a copy of the amendments.[163] If the IPEA has been asked to delay the IPE until receipt of the amendments, it will not start examination until the earliest of: receipt of those amendments; receipt of a notice from the applicant that they do not wish to make amendments; or the expiry of 20 months from the priority date.[164] The IPEA shall take into consideration all of the documents cited in the ISR.[165] Everything made available by the public anywhere in the world by means of written disclosure, including drawings and other illustrations, is considered prior art, provided that it was made available before the priority date (whether that be the international filing date of the application or an earlier date by which it claims priority).[166] Non-written disclosure is not taken into account by the IPEA for the purposes of what is prior art but the report must call attention to such non-written disclosure.[167] Similarly, patent and patent applications which were published after the priority date of an international application but filed before such a date are not deemed part of the prior art either for the purposes of novelty or inventive step.[168] This is important, as most national laws and the EPC do take into account such publications when considering novelty but not inventive step. However, the IPER must draw attention to such applications.[169] The IPEA may **2-084**

---

[156] art.31, PCT r.59.

[157] PCT r.59. A list of which IPEA is competent depending on the Receiving Office or language is contained in Annex C and E of the *PCT Applicant's Guide* and at *http://www.wipo.int/pct/guide/en* [Accessed 18 August 2017].

[158] PCT r.55.2.

[159] PCT r.57.

[160] PCT r.58.

[161] See *PCT Applicant's Guide*, "International Phase", para.10.004, et seq.

[162] PCT r.69.1(a).

[163] PCT r.69.1(c).

[164] PCT r.69.1(d).

[165] art.33(6).

[166] PCT r.64.

[167] PCT r.64.2.

[168] PCT r.64.3, PCT r.65.2.

[169] PCT r.64.3, PCT r.70.10.

consider a "mosaic" of prior art, provided such a combination is obvious to a person skilled in the art.[170] The IPEA will use the IPRP as the starting point.

2-085   The IPEA will not carry out an IPE where the subject-matter of the invention comprises the following:

(i)   scientific and mathematical theories;

(ii)   plant or animal varieties or essentially biological processes for the production of plants and animals other than microbiological processes and the products of such processes;

(iii)   schemes, rules or methods of doing business, performing purely mental acts or playing games;

(iv)   methods for treatment of the human or animal body by surgery or therapy as well as diagnostic methods;

(v)   mere presentations of information; and

(vi)   computer programs to the extent that the IPEA is not equipped to carry out an IPE concerning such programs.[171]

2-086   The IPEA will prepare an opinion as to whether each claim is novel, inventive and has industrial applicability.[172] The IPRP prepared by the ISA will stand as the initial written opinion.[173] The applicant is given an opportunity to make written submissions and/or to amend the application if the IPEA forms the opinion that the application is not novel, inventive nor capable of industrial application or is otherwise defective.[174] The IPEA will also rule on the allowability of amendments filed during the examination of the patent.[175] The procedure at this stage is fluid and similar to examinations before national patent offices. Thus, amendments and arguments will be taken into account if they are submitted in sufficient time.[176]

2-087   An IPER must be prepared within 28 months from the priority date.[177] Thus, in normal circumstances, the applicant will receive the report two months before national processing at the Elected Offices starts. The report will state whether the criteria of novelty, inventive step and industrial applicability have been fulfilled.[178] Furthermore, it will cite relevant documents. Copies of the report are sent to the International Bureau and the applicant.[179] The IPER is prepared in the language of publication of the international application.[180] The International Bureau will then send the IPER to each Elected Office and, where necessary, if the IPER is not in an official language of the Elected Office, the latter may request that it be translated into English.[181]

---

[170] PCT r.65.1.

[171] art.34(4)(a)(i), PCT r.67.

[172] art.35(1)(2), PCT r.70.

[173] PCT r.66.1*bis*.

[174] art.34(2)(b), PCT r.66.3.

[175] PCT r.66.2(a)(iv).

[176] *PCT Applicant's Guide*, "International Phase", para.10.025.

[177] PCT r.69.2. However, it may be six months from the time provided under PCT r.69.1 (IPEA must be in possession of demand, fees and ISR or written opinion) or PCT r.55.2 (transmission of translation) if later than the expiry of 28 months.

[178] art.35(2), PCT r.70.6.

[179] PCT r.71.1.

[180] PCT r.70.17 and see para.2-048.

[181] art.36, PCT r.72.

Translation and national fee to Elected Offices—National Phase, Chapter II

Where an applicant has made a demand for IPER, the applicant must furnish to **2-088** the Elected Offices a copy of a translation of the international application not later than the expiry of 30 months from the priority date[182] or a longer period if stipulated by national laws.[183] Generally, amendments of the international application will be permissible during examination of the application before the national patent office.[184] A national fee will usually be payable. The IPER does not bind the national office but will be very persuasive, especially if drawn up by the EPO.

EUROPEAN PATENT CONVENTION

Structure of this chapter on EPC

The section in this chapter on the EPC is structured as follows: **2-089**

- Introduction to the EPC.
- The substantive requirements of the EPC, e.g. novelty, inventive step, industrial application, etc. These requirements are concerned with whether the patent application should lead to the grant of a patent or if granted, whether it is valid.
- The inventions that are not patentable under the EPC.
- Infringement of European patents.
- The practice and procedure of applying for a European patent before the EPO.

For those readers who wish to read about a European patent with unitary effect **2-090** (a EU Unitary Patent) and the effect of the Agreement on the Unified Patent Court on litigation of European patents and EU unitary patents, this is discussed later in this chapter.[185]

Introduction

The European Patent Convention ("EPC") was born from a political initiative for **2-091** a centralised system of granting patents in Europe, with all the attendant economies of scale and avoiding the duplication of work by several national patent offices. Certain countries, especially France, felt the need for a system which was more complete and rigorous than the PCT and thus in 1973 in Munich the EPC was born and entered into force in October 1977.

The EPC is a regional European patent treaty and is a special agreement within **2-092** the meaning of art.19 of the Paris Convention. It permits an applicant to make a filing at the European Patent Office (EPO) so as to obtain a basket of national patents in contracting states to the EPC. The EPO acts as the examination authority. If a European patent is granted, it results in the grant of national patents in all designated states (assuming certain formalities such as translation have been complied with). It differs from the PCT route in that the EPO's decision on patentability of an ap-

---

[182] art.39.
[183] art.39(1)(b). See *http://www.wipo.int/pct/en/appguide/index.jsp* [Accessed 18 August 2017]. Many countries have extended the period to 31 months.
[184] See *PCT Applicant's Guide*, "National Phase", para.58.
[185] See para.2-506.

plication cannot be reviewed by national patent offices although the granted patent can be subject to invalidity proceedings before the courts of Member States or via the EPO's post-grant opposition procedure.

2-093   It is now a very popular route to obtaining patents. In 2016, a total of 296,000 patent filings were made to the EPO and 96,000 patents were granted by the EPO. More than 50 per cent of European patent applications are now by non-European countries (predominantly USA, China, Japan, and South Korea). The "Tower of Babel" problem of a continent having over 20 languages is being solved by the development of high-quality machine translations (developed in co-operation with Google). It is anticipated that in about five to 10 years, this will permit high-quality translations into all of the languages of contracting states to the EPC. However, the success of the EPC has meant a substantial delay in the grant of patents. Thus, research shows that in 2014, the mean time from application to grant of a European patent is 52 months (with the median being 44 months). This falls short of the Paris Convention goal of 36 months.[186] However, some applications can take virtually the whole lifetime of a patent to be granted.[187]

2-094   Thirty-eight European countries are members of the EPC. The member countries are: Albania, Austria, Belgium, Bulgaria, Cyprus, Croatia, Czech Republic, Denmark, Estonia, Finland, Former Yugoslav Republic of Macedonia, France, Germany, Greece, Hungary, Iceland, Ireland, Italy, Latvia, Liechtenstein, Lithuania, Luxembourg, Malta, Monaco, Netherlands, Norway, Poland, Portugal, Romania, San Marino, Serbia, Slovakia, Slovenia, Spain, Sweden, Switzerland, Turkey and the UK. From this list, it can be seen that 10 contracting states are not EU members.

2-095   European patents may also be "extended" to Morocco, Bosnia-Herzegovina and Montenegro and also "validated" to the Republic of Moldova. These countries have entered into bilateral agreements with the EPO whereby an applicant can seek protection in both countries via the European patent system even though they are not members of the EPC. National law modelled on the EPC rather than the EPC itself is applied to the consideration of the patent application.[188]

EPC 2000

2-096   In November 2000, a diplomatic conference was held to revise the EPC in several areas. It was substantially successful and, as a result, a number of amendments were made to the EPC. The changes came into force on 13 December 2007 following ratification by the 15th contracting state.[189] Readers should be aware that in many old cases, the pre-EPC 2000 article is referred to. A full version of the EPC can be found at the EPO website.[190]

---

[186] *http://ipkitten.blogspot.co.uk/2016/03/epo-performance-1-application-pendency.html* [Accessed 18 August 2017].

[187] Thus, in *Managing patient care/CAREFUSION* (T 0823/11), the TBA held that examination proceedings which lasted 12 years were excessively long (citing *Tyvik AS v Norway* ECHR, (no.25498/08) judgment 2 May 2013, which held that protracted patent prosecutions was a breach of art.6(1) of the ECHR (right of access to court)).

[188] For further details on this system, see [1994] OJ EPO 72.

[189] EPO Notice, concerning deposit of the 15th instrument of ratification of the EPC Revision Act [2006] OJ EPO 138.

[190] See *http://www.epo.org/law-practice/legal-texts/html/epc/2016/e/index.html* l [Accessed 18 August 2017].

Scheme of the EPC

The EPC provides for a centralised prosecution up to grant at the European Pat- **2-097**
ent Office ("EPO") of patent applications in respect of Member States. This results
in the grant of national patents in those Member States which were designated by
the applicant. It also provides for the establishment of the EPO, whose headquarters
are in Munich.[191] Applicants who wish to obtain national patents in contracting
states (called "Designated States") can make an application under the EPC to the
EPO. The EPO will process the application, conduct a search on the application,
publish it, examine it and, if it is found patentable under the EPC, grant national
patents for the designated states. The EPC also provides for third parties to bring
opposition proceedings at the EPO to revoke the European patent within nine
months from the grant.[192] Such proceedings can carry on for years.[193]

Thus, the applicant obtains what is often called a "bundle" of national patents in **2-098**
the designated states. Once granted, the issues of validity and infringement post-
grant are matters for the national courts who theoretically will uniformly apply the
substantive law of the EPC (as enacted into domestic patent laws). However, as said
above, there is a post-grant EPO opposition procedure whereby third parties may
oppose the grant of the European patent. Furthermore, at the request of the proprietor, the EPO may amend the claims of a granted European patent.[194]

Readers should be aware that once the EU Unitary Patent is in force, the entity **2-099**
which is granted a European patent may convert such, within one month of grant,
into a single patent with effect for all EU countries (bar Spain and Croatia). The EU
Unitary Patent is discussed later in this chapter.[195]

Harmonisation of the patent laws of contracting states

The EPC governs the law relating to the patentability of an application for a **2-100**
European patent.[196] However, the EPC also has the effect of harmonising the
substantive patent law of the contracting states to the EPC. This is brought about
by the following five provisions:

- European patents have the same effect and are subject to the same conditions as national patents in Member States.[197]
- European patents confer on their proprietors the same rights as would be
  conferred by a national patent.[198]
- European patents are given the same or more protection upon publication
  of the application as that of a published national patent application.[199]
- European patents can only be revoked on grounds specified in the Treaty.[200]
  These are that the subject-matter of the European patent is not patentable;
  the European patent does not disclose the invention in a manner suf-

---

[191] The EPO also has offices at The Hague (which acts as a Receiving Office and Search Division),
Berlin, Vienna and Brussels.
[192] art.99.
[193] In fact it has been known for opposition appeal proceedings to last until after the expiry of the patent.
[194] art.105a.
[195] See para.2-506.
[196] art.2.
[197] art.2.
[198] art.64.
[199] art.67.
[200] art.138.

ficiently clear and complete for it to be carried out by a person skilled in the art; the subject-matter of the European patent extends beyond the content of the application as filed or, if the patent was granted on a divisional application, beyond the content of the earlier application as filed; the protection of the European patent has been extended; or if the proprietor of the European patent is not entitled to the patent.[201]

- European patents must have the same prior right effect as a national patent application and a national patent.[202]

2-101   The effect of the above requirements has meant that Member States have been compelled to harmonise their substantive patent laws in accordance with the EPC. Thus, in the UK, the Patents Act 1977 was enacted so that the UK could fulfil its obligations under the EPC.

Non-harmonisation by EPC

2-102   However, there are certain aspects which are not harmonised by the EPC. Generally, these are procedural aspects relating to enforcement of patents in national courts. Moreover, the EPC does not harmonise the acts which amount to infringing acts and acts that amount to indirect infringement.[203] The EPC does not harmonise the range of measures that a court can grant following a finding of infringement. The EPC does not determine which courts an alleged infringer can be sued in. The significance of these differences will lessen as the enforcement provisions of the Agreement on the UPC come into force for European patents.

Harmonisation within the EU

2-103   Within the EU, (28 members of the EPC are also EU Member States), there has been considerable harmonisation of the law on enforcement of patents as well as to a lesser extent, the substantive law of patents. Thus, within the EU:

(a)   The Enforcement Directive has substantially harmonised the range of measures that a court of an EU Member State can grant.[204]

(b)   The Recast Jurisdiction Regulation harmonises the jurisdictional aspects of patent litigation of European patents insofar as litigation is brought in the EU.[205] Furthermore, the Agreement on the Unified Patent Court has jurisdictional provisions in relation to the litigation of European patents and EU Unitary Patents).[206]

(c)   The Agreement on the Unified Patent Court harmonises the acts which amount to an infringement of a European patent and EU Unitary Patent.[207]

(d)   The Biotechnology Directive for biotechnology inventions and the Sup-

---

[201]   art.138.
[202]   art.139(1).
[203]   This should be distinguished from the scope of protection provided by the patent.
[204]   See Ch.15.
[205]   See Ch.16. The Jurisdiction Regulation has been amended to take account of the EU Unitary Patent and the Agreement on the UPC—Reg.542/2014 [2014] OJ L 163/1.
[206]   See para.2-541.
[207]   See para.2-541.

plementary Protection Certificate Regulation for the extension of patent protection for pharmaceuticals are EU legislative measures.[208]

(e) The EU has enacted two regulations to establish a European patent with unitary effect (the EU Unitary Patent).[209] These will come into effect when the Agreement on the UPC comes into effect but will not apply to Spain or Croatia.[210]

Essential features of a European patent

The essential features of European patents are that they provide for protection **2-104** for a period of 20 years from the date of filing of the application and are granted for inventions which are new, involve an inventive step and are susceptible of industrial application.[211] Certain types of inventions are precluded from patentability, e.g. business methods, presentation of information and computer programs, but only "as such".[212] The applicant can decide in which of the contracting states to the EPC it requires protection. An application for a European patent under the EPC will result in a grant of a basket of national patents. There is no need for "further processing" as with the PCT.

The EPC was amended in the 1990s to allow contracting states to extend the term **2-105** of a European patent, or to grant corresponding protection following immediately after the expiry of the term of the patent, in order to take account of delay in marketing of the invention caused by the invention requiring an authorisation order before it could be put on the market in a state.[213] This amendment to the EPC coincided with the European Commission's Regulation on Supplementary Protection Certificates which permitted the extension of protection for up to a maximum of five years where marketing authorisation was delayed. This regulation is discussed below.[214]

Legal documentation of the EPC

Besides the Treaty itself, the Articles of the EPC provide for secondary legisla- **2-106** tion called Implementing Regulations.[215] These form an integral part of the EPC but, in case of conflict, the EPC prevails.[216] Such considerations also apply to the Protocols appended to the EPC. The EPO publishes an Official Journal ("OJ EPO") which contains selected decisions of the Board of Appeal and Enlarged Board of Appeal and decisions and notices of the Administrative Council and President of the EPO. The EPO publishes *Guidelines for Examination in the European Patent Office*, which are of considerable assistance for applicants and professional representatives.[217] These are extensive but not binding, although they will generally be followed at first instance, at least. The EPO publishes considerable

---

[208] See paras 2-577 and 2-603.
[209] See para.2-506.
[210] Although Poland is bound by the EU Unitary Patent regulations, it has not signed up to the Agreement of the UPC which governs exclusively litigation of the EU Unitary Patent.
[211] arts 63, 53.
[212] See para.2-249, et seq.
[213] Act Revising art.63 of the Convention of the Grant of European Patents (EPC) [1992] OJ EPO 1.
[214] See para.2-603.
[215] Denoted as EPC r.
[216] art.164.
[217] Denoted as "Guid". The EPO publishes online all relevant legislation and the guidelines at *http://*

informational material, of which *How to Get a European Patent—Guide for Applicants* is a helpful and digestible source of information.[218] Furthermore, the EPO keeps a register known as the Register of European Patents which contains the required particulars of published European patent applications and European patents during opposition.[219] Entries made in the Register are published weekly in the *European Patent Bulletin*.[220] The EPO also publishes a Case Law publication that sets out the salient decisions of the Enlarged Board of Appeal and the Technical Boards of Appeal.[221]

2-107   The EPO allows for public inspection of published European patent applications upon payment of an administrative fee.[222] Access to the register is possible via telecommunications.

2-108   The EPO website at *http://www.epo.org* contains a wealth of information that the reader should make use of.

Administration of the EPC

2-109   The application of the EPC is run and managed by the EPO and the Administrative Council.[223] The task of the EPO is to grant European patents as supervised by the Administrative Council. Its seat is at Munich but it has offices at The Hague, Berlin, Vienna and Brussels. It has five divisions:

(1)   the Receiving Section, which is based at The Hague;

(2)   the Search Division, which is responsible for drawing up European search reports, which is also based at The Hague;

(3)   the Examining Division, which is responsible for the substantive examination of the application;

(4)   the Opposition Division, which is responsible for the examination of oppositions against any European patent; and

(5)   the Legal Division, which is concerned with legal questions on interpretation of the EPC, the Register of European Patents and the upkeep and maintenance of the list of European Patent Attorneys.[224]

2-110   Furthermore, there is a two-tiered appellate structure consisting of the Technical and Legal Boards of Appeal and the Enlarged Board of Appeal. The latter hears appeals on important points of law and ensures uniform application of the law, and also has a limited jurisdiction to overturn decisions of the Technical Board of Appeal ("TBA") where there has been a substantial procedural irregularity. Only the Board of Appeal or the President of the EPO may remit a question to the EBA and the latter only in specific circumstances.[225] The appellant has no right personally to demand a reference to the EBA but may request that a reference is made.[226]

2-111   The Administrative Council, which consists of representatives of Member States, is empowered under the EPC to carry out certain administrative duties including

---

www.epo.org/law-practice.html [Accessed 18 August 2017].

[218] See *http://www.epo.org/applying/european/Guide-for-applicants.html* [Accessed 18 August 2017].

[219] art.127, EPC r.92.

[220] art.129(a).

[221] *http://www.epo.org/law-practice/case-law-appeals/case-law.html* [Accessed 18 August 2017].

[222] art.128(4), EPC r.94.

[223] art.4(2)(b).

[224] arts 15–20.

[225] See G3/95 [1996] OJ EPO 169.

[226] arts 21–22, 112.

inter alia the establishment of sub-offices of the EPO, the election of the President of the EPO, the fixing of financial provisions, the criteria for professional representatives who are entitled to appear before the EPO, the recruitment of employees, and the accession of European states to the EPC. Furthermore, it is competent to amend the time limits laid down in the Convention and the Implementing Regulations.[227] The EPO essentially finances itself from fees for applications (including renewal fees for pending applications) and payments made by contracting states in respect of renewal fees for European Patents levied in those states.[228]

Relationship of the EPC to international conventions

The EPC is a regional convention for the grant of patents in Europe.[229] It constitutes a special agreement within the Paris Convention and a regional treaty within the Patent Cooperation Treaty.[230] European patents can be granted on the basis of an international application filed in accordance with the PCT (called a Euro-PCT filing).[231] In the Euro-PCT route, the initial part of the procedure is governed in accordance with the provisions of the PCT with the applicant designating the EPO as either as a Designated Office or Elected Office for countries which are members of the EPC. Besides being a Designated or Elected Office, the EPO will act as a Receiving Office as well as an International Searching Authority and International Preliminary Examining Authority under the PCT.

2-112

EPC and TRIPS

In *IBM/Computer Programs*,[232] the Technical Board of Appeal considered the application of various treaties in deciding how to approach the issue of patentability of inventions comprising computer programs and, in particular, the Agreement on Trade Related Aspects of Intellectual Property Rights ("TRIPS"). The TBA held that it was "not convinced" that TRIPS may be applied to the EPC. It held that there was no justification, in particular under the Vienna Convention on the Law of Treaties, for the direct application of TRIPS to the EPC. In particular, TRIPS was binding only on its Member States; the EPO was not a member of the WTO (World Trade Organization) and did not sign the TRIPS agreement. Moreover, there was not even full correspondence between the contracting states to the EPC and the Member States of TRIPS. However, the TBA did hold that it was appropriate to take it into consideration, since it was aimed at setting common standards and principles concerning the availability, scope and use of trade-related intellectual property rights and gave a clear indication of current trends.[233] However, in the final analysis, the TBA held that:

2-113

---

[227] arts 33, 35.

[228] art.37.

[229] Only European countries can be invited to join the EPC—art.166.1(b). Turkey is a contracting state to the EPC. It is normally considered to be part of Europe and Asia.

[230] See Preamble to the EPC and arts 150–158 EPC. See J15/80 (Priority/earlier deposit of industrial design) for an analysis of the relevance of the EPC being a special agreement within the meaning of art.19 of the Paris Convention in relation to priority rights.

[231] See arts 150–158, EPC r.157, Guid. E-VIII.

[232] *IBM/Computer Programs* (T-935/97) [1999] E.P.O.R. 301.

[233] Under TRIPS, there is no exclusion of patentability for computer-related inventions. See para.2-014 for further discussion.

"... the only source of substantive patent law for examining European patent applications at this moment is the European Patent Convention."[234]

2-114   This approach was followed by the Enlarged Board of Appeal in *Astrazeneca/ Priority from India*.[235] Thus, an applicant for a European patent was not entitled to claim priority from an application made in India, which at the relevant date was not a member of the Paris Convention but was a member of the WTO/TRIPS Agreement. It was common ground that the EPO itself was not a party to TRIPS. However, the issue was whether the EPO was bound by TRIPS because the EPC contracting states were. The EBA considered carefully this issue and reviewed the case law. It concluded:

> "In summary, therefore, TRIPs provisions, like decisions of the European and International Courts of Justice and national decisions, are elements to be taken into consideration by the boards of appeal but are not binding on them. Whereas it is legitimate for the boards of appeal to use the TRIPs Agreement as a means to interpret provisions of the EPC which admit of different interpretations, specific provisions of TRIPs cannot justify ignoring express and unambiguous provisions of the EPC. To do so would usurp the role of the legislator. This is confirmed by the fact that the legislator of EPC 2000 found it necessary to revise Article 87 EPC in order to implement the TRIPs Agreement."[236]

The EPC and EU

2-115   The European Patent Convention is a sui generis regional European treaty which has no legal connection with the EU or the TFEU. Thus, in *Philips/Publication of patent specification*[237] the applicant effectively complained about the obligation to translate a patent application into a wide variety of national languages under art.65 EPC for the patent to take effect in those countries. The applicant complained that the cost of such was that it offended arts 34–36 TFEU and that therefore a provision of German law which required translation of a European patent into German for the patent to take effect in Germany offended the EC Treaty, the predecessor treaty to the TFEU.[238] The EPO held that it was not a court or tribunal of the EU and had no right to refer a preliminary reference to the CJEU. It said that such an argument was to be raised in a national court. Indeed, precisely this occurred and the objection was held as unfounded by the CJEU.[239]

2-116   In *WARF/Stem Cells* (G2/06), the EBA was asked to refer various questions on the meaning of the implementing regulations concerning the patentability of stem cells to the CJEU on the basis that such repeated the wording of art.6(2)(c) of the Biotechnological Directive.[240] The EBA dismissed this application on the grounds that it had no power to do so. It said that the fact that the rules were implemented to correspond with that of the Directive could not be taken as imposing some new power to refer. Importantly, of course, EPC members do not have to be EU members (and 10 are not). In that sense, the CJEU would be giving a ruling on a matter which could purportedly affect non-EU members.

---

234 (T-935/97) [1999] E.P.O.R. 301 at [3].

235 *Astrazeneca/Priority from India* (G2 and 3/02) [2004] E.P.O.R. 39.

236 para.8.6 of EPC 2000 amended art.87 so that an applicant could claim priority from any country which was a Member of the WTO (which includes TRIPS).

237 *Philips/Publication of patent specification* (T-276/99) [2004] E.P.O.R. 3.

238 These are the free movement of goods provisions of the TFEU and are discussed in Ch.7.

239 *BASF v Präsident des Deutsche Patentamt* (C-44/98) [1999] E.C.R. I-6269; [2001] 2 C.M.L.R. 21.

240 *WARF/Stem Cells* (G2/06) [2009] E.P.O.R. 15. The Biotechnology Directive is an EU legislative measure and is discussed at para.2-577.

However, the distinction between the EPC and EU law has been eroded by EU legislation relating to the EU Unitary Patent and the Biotechnology Directive. Thus, where an applicant elects to convert the European patent into a EU Unitary Patent (once it comes into force), then the enforcement of a EU Unitary Patent will be governed by EU regulations. The EU Unitary Patent is discussed later in this chapter.[241] Moreover, whilst the UPC Agreement[242] is not itself an EU legislative act but an intergovernmental treaty between the participating states outside the framework of the EU (even though it is only open to accession by members of the EU), it envisages that the Unified Patent Court can make preliminary references to the CJEU on matters relating to the UPC Agreement and EU Unitary Patent. The relationship between the CJEU and the EU Unitary Patent and the UPC Agreement is discussed later in the chapter.[243]   **2-117**

Equally, in relation to the Biotechnology Directive, which seeks to harmonise the laws of EU Member States on the patentability of biotechnological inventions, the EPO has had to harmonise its law to conform with the Directive and indeed, the EPC Implementing Regulations state that the Directive should be used as a supplementary means of interpretation for its rules on biotechnological inventions.[244] Indeed, when in 2016, the EU Commission issued a non-binding Notice clarifying that, under the Biotechnology Directive, its view was that the products of essentially biological processes are not patentable. As a result, in July 2017, the EPO felt compelled to amend its rules to overturn its previous practice that such were indeed patentable.[245]   **2-118**

Substantive requirements for a European patent

The Guidelines say that there are four basic requirements for a European patent: **2-119**

(a)   there must be an invention belonging to any field of technology;
(b)   the invention is susceptible of industrial application;[246]
(c)   the invention must be new; and
(d)   the invention must involve an "inventive step".[247]

It also says that there are two further requirements. First, the disclosure in the patent must be such that it can be carried out by a person skilled in the art. This is often called the "sufficiency" requirement. Secondly, the invention must of a "technical character" to the extent that it must relate to a technical field, be concerned with a technical problem, and must have technical features in terms of which the matter for which protection is sought can be defined in the claim.[248] This second requirement can be considered as part of the requirement that the invention must belong in a field of technology. Thus, inventions relating to discoveries, mathematical methods, etc. are excluded "as such". Furthermore, there are two other exclusions which are not based on the requirement that the invention be technical. These are inventions for plant or animal varieties or essentially biological processes and also   **2-120**

---

[241] See para.2-506.
[242] Agreement on a Unified Patent Court [2013] OJ L175/1. See para.2-534.
[243] See para.2-537.
[244] See EPC r.26(1).
[245] See the Decision of Administrative Council CA/D 6/17 (29 June 2017) OJ EPO 2017, A56 amending EPC r.28(2). See generally, paras 2-302 to 2-304.
[246] art.52(1).
[247] See Guid. G-I-1.
[248] Guid. G-I-2.

methods for treatment of the human or animal body by surgery or therapy and diagnostic methods for such.

2-121 Finally, it is necessary to consider the sui generis principles that relate to biotechnology inventions which arise because the EU Biotechnology Directive has been implemented into the EPC.

2-122 Thus in the next sections, the following are considered:

- novelty,
- inventive step,
- industrial application,
- sufficiency,
- exclusions from patentability, and
- biotechnology inventions.

2-123 These provisions are now considered in detail. Readers should know that the EPO website provides two very useful texts for applying the above provisions: First, the Guidelines of Examination, and secondly the Case Law of the EPO Boards of Appeal. When considering a particular provision, the reader will find that these publications provide invaluable guidance.[249]

Novelty

Introduction

2-124 An invention is considered new if it does not form part of the state of the art.[250] The state of the art is held to comprise everything made "available to the public" by means of a written or oral description by use or in any other way before the date of filing or priority date (whichever is the earliest).[251] This is stipulated to include European patent applications filed before but published after the date of filing or priority date.[252] For the purposes of examination before the EPO, the state of the art will mainly consist of the documents listed in the search report. Examination for novelty will then amount to consideration of the prior art in the light of common general knowledge and also as against common general knowledge. Examiners are not entitled to use their own general knowledge unless it can be proven.[253] A matter forms part of the prior art if it is possible for members of the public to gain knowledge of the matter and there is no obligation of confidentiality.[254]

Absolute novelty

2-125 The requirement of novelty is an absolute one. Thus, it is not necessary to show that the public has actually seen the prior art provided that it is available to the

---

[249] For the EPO case law, see *http://www.epo.org/law-practice/case-law-appeals/case-law.html* [Accessed 18 August 2017] and for the Guidelines, see *http://www.epo.org/law-practice/legal-texts/html/guidelines/e/index.htm* [Accessed 18 August 2017].

[250] art.54(1).

[251] art.54(2), art.89.

[252] art.54(3)..

[253] *Kubat* (T-157/87) [1989] E.P.O.R. 221.

[254] See Guid. G-IV 7.2. For an example of where there was held to be no obligation of confidentiality, see *PRYSMIAN/Hydrogen-absorbing composition* (T-1464/05) [2010] E.P.O.R. 1.

public.[255] In certain circumstances, it may be unclear whether there has been an "enabling" disclosure to the public. Thus, it is necessary to consider whether the public understands the disclosure. In this respect, the TBA has held that "public" in this context means "skilled person".[256] An oral disclosure before a circle of persons who were unable to understand the technical teaching at a lecture did not constitute an enabling disclosure, as they would have been unable to reproduce such information to other skilled members of the public.[257] In contrast, it was held that an oral disclosure at an International Conference by a lecturer, which included an advance abstract, a subsequent paper, a poster presentation and workshop discussions, constituted prior art for the purpose of novelty.[258] A single non-confidential sale and delivery of a piece of equipment will disclose the structure of the equipment to the public provided that a person skilled in the art can determine the structure using their normal investigative capabilities.[259]

The concept of "enabling disclosure" is also applicable where a product is disclosed but not how to make it or what it is made of. This is particularly relevant in relation to pharmaceuticals. Thus, a chemical product may exist in the prior art but its composition not may not be known or how to make it. This is discussed below.[260]   **2-126**

Burden and standard of proof of prior art

Where a party alleges lack of novelty, the burden of proof is on that party to show that the relevant information was made available to the public.[261] The EPO operates a policy of proof which is described as the "free evaluation of evidence" which means that each piece of evidence is given an appropriate weight according to its probative value which is evaluated in view of the particular circumstances of each case.[262] The Guidelines say that the standard for assessing such circumstances is on the balance of probability and not beyond reasonable doubt.[263]   **2-127**

However, such is in conflict with earlier cases concerning prior art relying upon Internet website entries, where the TBA has said that proof must be beyond reasonable doubt.[264] Thus, in *Joint Ventures/Sekisui*,[265] the TBA said that whilst acknowledging that the standard of proof for prior public use was the balance of probability, where practically all of the evidence in support of an alleged prior public use lies within the power and knowledge of the opponent, the latter has to prove his case "up to the hilt".[266] Later, in *Gills' Cables*[267] an opponent relied upon witness statements relating to an instance of prior use. The patentee argued that   **2-128**

---

[255] *Japan Styrene Paper* (T-444/88) [1991] E.P.O.R. 94.
[256] *HOOPER/T-Cell Growth factor* (T-877/90) [1993] E.P.O.R. 6.
[257] (T-877/90) [1993] E.P.O.R. 6, 20 November 1996.
[258] *GENENTECH/Expression in yeast* (T-455/91) [1996] E.P.O.R. 87.
[259] *THOMSON/Electron Tube* (T-953/90) [1998] E.P.O.R. 415.
[260] See para.2-131.
[261] *APPLERA/Instrument for monitoring nucleic acid amplification reactions* (T-313/05).
[262] The principle of free evaluation of evidence was confirmed in *Identity of appellant* (G1/12) [31], applying *Opposition on behalf of a third party/INDUPACK* (G3/97).
[263] Guid. G-IV 7.5.2.
[264] *SAPPORO BREWERIES/Barley* (T-1875/06) [2008] E.O.P.R. 29, approving (T-1134/06). It is of note that in (T-1134/06), the TBA referred to proof of Internet use meeting the same criteria as for prior use or prior oral use, i.e. when was it made available, what was made available, and under what circumstances was it made available.
[265] *Joint Ventures/Sekisui* (T-472/92).
[266] See [3.1].

there was doubt about the credibility of the witnesses' statements and averred that there was no absolute proof. The TBA held the following (at 110):

> "It is to be noted in this context that the EPC does not contain any provisions restricting acceptable means of proof. Neither are there particular provisions about the evaluation of evidence or about how the outcome of taking of evidence should be assessed. In accordance with the case law of the Boards of Appeal, the principle of free evaluation of evidence applies. This means that the Board must reach its decision on the basis of the whole of the evidence provided and in the light of the conclusion it reaches after careful evaluation of that evidence.
>
> The decision need not be based on absolute proof, which, particularly where it is alleged that a prior use took place a long time ago, would amount to an unreasonable burden, *but should be based on a degree of probability, which, in human experience, verges on certainty*."[268] [Author's emphasis.]

2-129 These conflicting decisions were later recognised by the TBA who sought to reconcile them by saying that the right approach was that the prior art must be established with sufficient degree of certainty to convince the tribunal that the facts are correct.[269]

2-130 The Guidelines state that proof beyond reasonable doubt ("up to the hilt") of an alleged fact is not required.[270] In the author's view, the correct approach is indeed a flexible one based on the doctrine of "free evaluation". This approach allows a tribunal to determine the degree of cogency of evidence required depending on the facts of the case, e.g. where certain "prior uses" are inherently improbable, convincing evidence is required to overcome the inherent improbability of such prior uses.[271] Factors to be taken into account when determining the cogency required would include: (i) whether the facts and matters were solely within the knowledge of one party; (ii) the ability via investigation of the other party to disprove such facts; (iii) the inherent unlikelihood of the prior use (e.g. oral disclosure giving full details of an invention without contemporaneous written evidence); (iv) the credibility of the attesting evidence; and (v) the failure of the proving party to adduce corroborative evidence that one would have expected to have seen (e.g. witnesses to an oral disclosure).

---

[267] *GILLS' CABLES/Control cable assembly* (T-575/94) [1997] E.P.O.R. 100.

[268] See also *MAELZER/Adaptor* (T-441) [1997] E.P.O.R. 177 where the evidence of prior user was disregarded because of its flimsiness. In *SEKISUI/Shrinkable Sheet* (T-472/92) [1997] E.P.O.R. 432, it was held that the burden of proof in relation to evidence of prior use should be beyond reasonable doubt because there was unlikely to be any evidence available to the patentee to contradict it. See also *AT&T/Proof of prior publication* (T-750/94) [1997] E.P.O.R. 509.

[269] *Change capture for data warehousing/Oracle* (T-545/08) citing *AT&T/Proof of prior publication* (T-750/94) [1997] E.P.O.R. 509.

[270] Guid. 7.5.2.

[271] In *Re B Children* [2008] UKHL 35, the House of Lords of England and Wales had to deal with the tension between the balance of probability test ("more likely than not") in civil proceedings when certain allegations were inherently unlikely. The House of Lords reaffirmed the balance of probability test but at the same time approved the statement by Lord Nicholls in *In Re H (Minors) (Sexual Abuse: Standard of Proof)* [1996] A.C. 563 that:

> "the court will have in mind as a factor, to whatever extent is appropriate in the particular case, that the more serious the allegation the less likely it is that the event occurred and, hence, the stronger should be the evidence before the court concludes that the allegation is established on the balance of probability."

Enabling disclosure

In many cases, the prior art document may disclose a product but not how to **2-131** make the product. Thus, a document may disclose a chemical compound but not how to manufacture that compound. If the skilled person in the art cannot make it using their common general knowledge (or in the case of a product of nature, separate it), then such is not considered to be an enabling disclosure and therefore does not prejudice the patentability for the chemical compound.[272] Thus as said by the TBA:

"It is the view of the Board that a document does not effectively disclose a chemical compound, even though it states the structure and the steps by which it is produced, if the skilled person is unable to find out from the document or from common general knowledge how to obtain the required starting material or intermediates. Information, which can only be obtained after a comprehensive search, is not to be regarded as part of common general knowledge."[273]

Vice versa, a similar issue arises where the product itself (as opposed to a prior **2-132** art document referring to the product) is made available to the public but not its chemical composition. In *Availability to the Public: Reference by the President of the EPO*,[274] the EBA was asked whether the chemical composition of a product was made available to the public by virtue of the availability to the public of that product, irrespective of whether particular reasons can be identified to cause the skilled person to analyse the composition. In response to this question, the EBA said that there is no requirement that the public should have particular reasons for analysing the product put on the market. It said:

"Where it is possible for the skilled person to discover the composition or the internal structure of the product and to reproduce it without undue burden, then both the product and its composition or internal structure become state of the art...

It is the fact that direct and unambiguous access to some particular information is possible, which makes the latter available, whether or not there is any reason for looking for it."[275]

Therefore, motive to analyse the product for its chemical composition is ir- **2-133** relevant to the issue of novelty.[276] The EBA also held that a commercially available product per se does not implicitly disclose anything beyond its composition or internal structure. Thus extrinsic characteristics which are only revealed when the product is exposed to interaction with specifically chosen outside conditions,

---

[272] Guid. G-VI, 2.

[273] *Herbicides/ICI* (T-206/83) [1987] OJ EPO 5; [1986] E.P.O.R. 232. See also Guid. G-VI.4. and *Thickness of magnetic layers* (T-26/85) ECLI:EP:BA:1988:T002685.19880920 and *Caisse octogonale/OTOR* (T-491/99) ECLI:EP:BA:2000:T049199.20001024.

[274] G01/92 [1993] E.P.O.R. 241.

[275] See para.1.4. The EBA disapproved of the decision of *HOECHST/Polyvinylester dispension* (T-93/89) [1992] E.P.O.R. 155.

[276] This principle is applied many times. For a good example of its application, see *Packard/Liquid Scintillation* (T-952/92) [1997] E.P.O.R. 457 and *Fluid flow simulation/SIMCON* (T-2440/12) ECLI:EP:BA:2015:T244012:20150915. However, see *PU catalysts/AIR PRODUCTS* (T-2048/12) ECLI:EP:BA:2016:T204812.20160119, where the TBA distinguished G/01/92 by saying that the decision did not imply that all impurities and their relative amounts in a chemical product were disclosed merely because it was possible to identify and quantity them by analytical means(see 2.4–2.5).

e.g. reactants are not disclosed because "they point beyond the product per se as they are dependent on deliberate choices being made".[277] Thus, use of a known compound for a particular purpose is not merely disclosed by the product being available to the public.

2-134   It has been said that the test for determining whether a prior art document is an enabling disclosure cited for the purpose of novelty and inventive step is the same as the requirement under art.83 EPC that patent applications must disclose the invention in a manner sufficiently clear and complete for it to be carried out by a person skilled in the art.[278] Therefore, a prior art document which does not meet the sufficiency criteria is not enabling and must be disregarded as prior art.[279]

2-135   In many non-chemical cases, the prior art will be an enabling disclosure without more. Thus, in the case of mechanical apparatus, the placing of that apparatus on the market will invariably mean that via analysis and reverse engineering, its structure both physical and mechanical can be derived. Thus the act of disclosure of mechanical apparatus will invariably be an enabling one.

Selection inventions: novelty

2-136   In certain cases, an inventor may find that a particular product in a known range of products has a surprising and beneficial effect. This is usually called a selection invention. In this field, the issues of novelty and inventive step are often inextricably intertwined. If a product selected from a known range of products does not contain a surprising effect, it will often be adjudicated that the particular product is anticipated by disclosure of the class of products from which it comes, even though the issue of surprise or unexpectedness goes more to the question of obviousness. Selection inventions are most common in the chemical field.

2-137   In considering the area of selection inventions, the Guidelines make it clear that a generic disclosure does not take away the novelty of any specific example but that a specific disclosure does take away the novelty of a generic claim.[280]

> "In determining the novelty of a selection, it has to be decided, whether the selected elements are disclosed in an individualised (concrete) form in the prior art (see T-12/81). A selection from a single list of specifically disclosed elements does not confer novelty."[281]

2-138   However, matters become more complicated where the prior art discloses a range of products. For instance, a prior art patent specification may claim any organic compound with a trichloro- (CF_3) group on the basis that the trichloro- group has a beneficial effect.[282] Such could embody an infinite range of organic compounds. In these circumstances, what is the approach where a person discovers that out of this infinite range, a particular organic compound with the trichloro- grouping discloses the same beneficial effect but that the effect is much more marked than with other trichloro- compounds. A realistic approach would be to say that it would be unfair on the person to find that theoretically such a compound was disclosed

---

[277] See para.3.
[278] *Herbicides* (T-206/83) at [2]. This latter requirement is described as the "sufficiency" requirement and is discussed at para.2-236. This case has been cited many times, e.g. see *Porous inorganic oxide/ W.R. Grace & Co* (T-2026/10).
[279] e.g. see *Anti-Stokes-Leuchtstoffe/BUNDRESDRUCKEREI* (T-1026/10).
[280] Guid. G-VI 6.
[281] Guid. G-VI 8(i).
[282] These are sometimes called "Markush" claims.

in the prior art patent specification. However, at the other end, if there were only 10 organic compounds capable of having a trichloro- group, then it could be said that sooner or later, it would have been discovered that one of them had a marked and exaggerated beneficial effect. The EPO has dealt with this issue by taking a pragmatic ex ante approach. The TBA has said:

> "It is established jurisprudence of the Boards of Appeal that a sub-range selected from a broad range of numbers may be novel in respect to the latter. It is decisive to establish whether or not a skilled person would have "seriously contemplated" on the basis of the information derivable from [the prior art] in combination with his common general knowledge, applying the technical teaching of the prior art to the rather narrow selected sub-range.[283]"

The concept of "seriously contemplated" will involve a multi-factorial decision based on a number of facts. However, the focus is very much a technical one. Are there sufficient "technical pointers" in the prior art when combined with common general knowledge to mean that the skilled person, without the benefit of hindsight, would consider that it was technically worthwhile to investigate the sub-range? It is not thought that commercial matters such as the cost of investigating the matter or considering whether the value of the possible beneficial effect in the sub-range meant that it was worthwhile investigating the sub-range. In the author's view, the real issue is whether the "technical pointers" shine a beam towards the sub-range and not whether the skilled person would be motivated to follow that beam which could involve a very wide range of commercial factors.   **2-139**

Where a substance was known to have catalytic properties in a wide range of proportions, a patent application claiming a sub-range of that range will be novel if the sub-range is not merely an arbitrary selection of the wide range, but has some added technical feature, even if this feature can be produced by different proportions of the catalyst outside of the sub-range.[284] Where a specification in a prior art patent discloses two classes of starting substances which are combined to give a product and that specification contains examples of individual entities in each class, then nevertheless, a substance resulting from the reaction of a specific pair from the two lists can be regarded as novel.[285] In other words, the EPO will not deem the prior document to have disclosed every combination of the two starting classes.[286]   **2-140**

The fact that a sub-range of chemical compounds has a technical effect which differentiates it from the wider class does not per se mean that such is novel. Thus, the TBA held that a claim for a bleaching agent wherein the claim was for a C_6-C_{12} alkyl group as against the prior art, which disclosed a C_6-C_{15} alkyl group was not novel because a skilled person would have considered those compounds containing lower alkyl groups as being the most preferred compounds because of their easier accessibility and their better solubility in water. Here one sees the "blending" of the concepts of novelty and inventive stage.   **2-141**

---

[283] *UNILEVER/Interesterification process* (T-366/90) [1993] E.P.O.R. 383 applying *UNILEVER/ Washing Composition* [1992] E.P.O.R. 501 and *TOSHIBA/Thickness of magnetic layers* [1990] E.P.O.R. 267.

[284] *HOECHST* (T-198/84) [1985] OJ EPO 209, [1979–85] E.P.O.R. C987; *AGREVO/Triazole sulphonamides* [1996] E.P.O.R. 171; cf. *STAMICARBON/Cyclohexane oxidation* (T-247/91) [1996] E.P.O.R. 120

[285] *BAYER/Diastereoisomers* (T-12/81) [1979–85] E.P.O.R. B308; [1982] OJ EPO 296.

[286] *DRACO/Xanthenes* (T-7/86) [1989] E.P.O.R. 65; I.P.D. 11043, September 1988. This is known as the "two lists" principle—see Guid. G-VI-8(i).

2-142   It is necessary to show that all the chemical substances claimed in the sub-class have the unexpected and beneficial quality. In *AGREVO/Triazole sulphonamides*,[287] the TBA considered a patent for a group of triazole sulphonamides possessing herbicidal activity and claimed as chemical compounds per se. The claims were wide, including claims to a multitude of "substituted" triazole sulphonamides. The Examining Division rejected the claim inter alia on the basis that having regard to the fact that the technical effect claimed was herbicidal, "substituted" could not be given its ordinary technical meaning of substituted by absolutely anything. On appeal, the TBA considered a number of issues relating to claims for a broad category of chemical compounds. The TBA said that in order for a selection of compounds to be patentable it must not be arbitrary but justified by a hitherto unknown technical effect which is caused by those structural features which distinguish the claimed compounds from the numerous other compounds.

2-143   Finally, it should be said that in the case of selection inventions, there is a fine line between novelty and inventive step. If a particular product or sub-range is not considered disclosed by publication of the prior art range on the grounds that the skilled person would not have seriously contemplated applying the technical teaching of the prior art to that sub-range or product, then such will usually be determinative of the issue of inventive step. It is difficult to conclude that it is obvious to find a sub-range from the prior art range if the skilled person would not have seriously contemplated applying the prior art teaching to find that sub-range. Notwithstanding this, the Guidelines say that the concept of "seriously contemplated" is fundamentally different from the "reasonable expectation of success" test applied to determining inventive step.[288]

Confidential disclosure

2-144   If the disclosure is made to persons subject to a duty of confidentiality, the disclosure does not constitute prior art. Care must be taken to ensure that all parties are so bound. A factory-scale experiment conducted by the patentee around six months prior to the priority date in the opponent's works on account of the patentee's lack of available facilities for large-scale experiments, was held to be an enabling disclosure which invalidated the patent, as the parties were not subject to a tacit or express duty to maintain secrecy.[289]

Non-prejudicial disclosures

2-145   Certain disclosures of the invention itself prior to the date of filing are treated under the EPC as not being prejudicial provided they occurred no earlier than six months before the filing of the European patent application. These are oral disclosures due to evident abuse in relation to the applicant or their legal predecessor. There must be a relationship between the patentee and the discloser. This can produce a harsh result. Hence, the TBA held that a premature disclosure of an application of the closest prior art document by the Brazilian Patent Office was not an evident abuse which would prevent it being treated as prior art, despite

---

[287] *AGREVO/Triazole* [1996] E.P.O.R. 171.
[288] See para.2-228.
[289] *BAYER/Plasterboard* (T-602/91) [1996] E.P.O.R. 388. See also the decisions in *PRYSMIAN/ Hydrogen-absorbing composition* (T-1464/05) [2010] E.P.O.R. 1, and *UNOVA/Valve seat bushing* (T-163/03) [2008] E.P.O.R. 31.

the detriment suffered by the patentee as a result, because there existed no relationship between the patentee and the Brazilian Patent Office and the disclosure was a mere error.[290]If within the six-month period prior to filing the application, the invention is displayed at an official or officially recognised exhibition in terms of the convention on international exhibitions signed at Paris on 22 November 1928, this is not a relevant prior disclosure.[291]

Earlier non-published European patent applications

For the purposes of novelty but not obviousness, European patent applications **2-146** filed before the priority date but published afterwards are treated as constituting prior art for the purpose of novelty but not obviousness.[292] This is to prevent double patenting of the same invention.

Publication during priority period

Where a document is published during the priority interval, this will be treated **2-147** as prior art to the extent that priority is not validly claimed.[293] With regard to prior national rights where there has been no disclosure prior to the priority date, these are dealt with after grant of the patent according to the national patent law of the relevant contracting state.[294]

Second and further uses of a known product

Where the application claims a new use for a known substance, such a claim is **2-148** considered novel .[295] Equally, if a further novel use is found for the substance that may also be claimed if it is inventive.[296] Where the use is medical or therapeutic, the draughtsman must avoid claims which offend art.53(c) (methods for treatment of the human or animal body). Thus, as made clear by the last part of art.53(c), the claim must be to the substance for use in a medical/therapeutic method rather than use of a substance in, e.g. treating a medical condition. First and second medical and non-medical use inventions are discussed in detail elsewhere in this chapter.[297]

"Mosaicing" prior art: novelty

The Guidelines make it clear that in considering novelty, it is not permissible to **2-149** combine items of prior art together.[298] Indeed, the Guidelines say that it is not permissible to combine separate items belonging to different embodiments described in one and the same document unless such combination has been specifi-

---

[290] *UNILEVER/Deodorant Detergent* (T-385/92) [1996] E.P.O.R. 579.
[291] art.55. The EPO publishes annually in the OJ EPO a list of exhibitions falling within the terms of the Convention which have been registered by the International Exhibition Bureau.
[292] arts 54(3), 56.
[293] *Priority interval* (G-3/93) [1995] OJ EPO 18; [1994] E.P.O.R. 521 Vol.10/XV. See also G.W. Schlich, "Publish and be Damned? The EPO's enlarged board of appeal decision in G03/93" [1995] 17 E.I.P.R. 327 for a criticism of this decision.
[294] art.139(2); Guid. G-IV 6. See *BAYER/Polyether Polyols* (T-4/80) [1979–85] E.P.O.R. B260, [1982] OJ EPO 149; *Mobil Oil* (T-550/88) I.P.D. April 1992, 15045.
[295] art.54(4) (in relation to medical substances).
[296] art.54(5).
[297] See para.2-152.
[298] Guid. G-VI.1.

cally suggested.[299] However, material referred to explicitly in a document is treated as being incorporated into that document.[300] Claimed subject-matter which is derived directly and unambiguously from a prior art document will not be novel, but care must be taken not to treat the teaching of a document as including well-known equivalents in considering the novelty as opposed to the obviousness of a claimed invention.[301] In contrast, as the Guidelines make clear, mosaicing of prior art is permissible when considering inventive step.[302]

Invention anticipated by reason of inevitable outcome of prior instructions

2-150 In *ALLIED SIGNAL/Polyolefin fiber*[303] the TBA was concerned with whether certain prior art documents anticipated the claimed invention. The opponent claimed that the inevitable outcome of following the teaching of an express literal disclosure of certain documents was the anticipation of the claimed invention. The TBA said that the term "available to the public" clearly goes beyond literal or diagrammatic description and implies a communication, express or implicit, of technical information by other means as well. In the case where a prior art document fails explicitly to disclose something falling within a claim, availability in the sense of art.54 may still be established if the inevitable outcome of following the teaching of prior art falls within the ambit of that claim. The opponent accepted that there was a measure of uncertainty as to the outcome of the prior art documents but submitted that, on the balance of probability, it was more likely than not that the disclosure of the documents would inevitably lead to something falling within the claims in suit. The TBA rejected this approach and held that in deciding what is or is not the inevitable outcome of an express literal disclosure in a particular prior art document, a standard of proof "beyond all reasonable doubt" needs to be applied. If any such doubt existed as to what might or might not be the result of carrying out the literal disclosure and instructions of a prior art, then the case on anticipation failed.[304]

Common general knowledge

2-151 The prior art also includes Common General Knowledge ("CGK"). CGK is that body of knowledge which the person skilled in the art is deemed to know as part of the background to a particular field of technology. It has been said to be the unwritten "mental furniture" of the skilled person in the art.[305] The EPO's approach to CGK is as follows:

(i) Basic general knowledge as well as the ability to look up such knowledge in encyclopaedias and handbooks, as well as, in exceptional cases, in a series of relevant studies or in a scientific publication.

(ii) It is not expected that the skilled man will carry out a comprehensive search of the literature covering the whole state of the art. No undue ef-

---

[299] Guid. G-VI.1; *Grehal/Shear* (T-305/87) [1991] E.P.O.R. 389 at [5.3].

[300] Guid. G-VI 1. See *Amoco 1990* (T-153/85) [1988] OJ EPO 1; [1988] E.P.O.R. 116.

[301] Guid. G-VI 2.

[302] See para.2-207.

[303] *ALLIED SIGNAL/Polyolefin fiber* (T-793/93) [1996] E.P.O.R. 104.

[304] See application of this in *Precipitated silica/PPG INDUSTRIES OHIO, INC* (T-0685/09) where the TBA confirmed that the standard of proof was conviction and not balance of probability. See also para.2-127 on standard of proof in proving prior art.

[305] *Triazoles* (T-939/92).

fort in the way of such a search can be required from the person skilled in the art.

(iii)   The information found must be unambiguous and usable in a direct and straightforward manner without doubts or further research work.[306]

It will be rare that common general knowledge will come from the content of patent specifications. However, such will be the case where the specifications provide a consistent picture that a particular technical procedure was generally known and belonged to the common general knowledge in the art at the relevant date.[307] The concept of common general knowledge is relevant in two ways under the EPC. First, it may itself form the basis of an attack on the novelty or inventiveness of a patent. Thus, an opponent may claim that the inventions in the patent are obvious over common general knowledge as opposed to an identified item of prior art. This is sometimes called an "inherent obviousness" attack. However, where the common general knowledge relied upon has existed for many years prior to the inventions, such may be indicative of inventive step. That is because, unlike a prior art patent specification which may have been unknown to the skilled person as of the priority date, ex hypothesi, common general knowledge is always known to the skilled person. Secondly, when considering the issue of inventive step, such is considered from the viewpoint of the skilled person who possesses common general knowledge. Thus, if an invention consists of the application of common general knowledge to a prior art patent specification, then such would suggest that it was not inventive.

First and second medical use inventions

What is the position regarding novelty where the claim is to a *known* product for   **2-152**
a medical use which was hitherto *unknown*? Is the fact that a product is known (i.e. prior art) fatal to a claim to a medical use of the known product when that medical use was not known ("first medical use invention")? Furthermore, what is the position where the prior art consists of a *known* medical use of a *known* product but the patent claims a different hitherto *unknown* medical use unrelated to the *known* medical use? Does that preclude patenting for a second medical use of the same substance not known in the prior art ("second medical use invention")? Articles 54(5) and 54(5) deal with this issue.

Article 54(4) and 54(5) says that: **2-153**

"(4)   Paragraphs 2 and 3 [*the requirements of novelty*] shall not exclude the patentability of any substance or composition, comprised in the state of the art, for use in a method referred to in Article 53(c), provided that *its use* for *any* such method is not comprised in the state of the art.

(5)   Paragraphs 2 and 3 [*the requirements of novelty*] shall also not exclude the patentability of any substance or composition referred to in paragraph 4 *for any specific use in a method referred to in Article 53(c), provided that such use* is not comprised in the state of the art." [Author's emphasis.]

Before considering the effect of these provisions, it is instructive to consider the history of art.54(4) and (5).[308]

---

[306]   *Bayer/Chimeric Gene* (T-890/02) [2006] E.P.O.R. 10. See also Guid. G–VII-2, para.3.1.

[307]   *Glazing Inspection/Pilkington* (T-412/09) at [2.1.3].

[308]   art.54(1)–(5) is concerned with the definition of novelty.

History of the EPC's approach to first and second medical use inventions

2-154   Prior to EPC 2000, the only relevant provision was art.54(5) which read:

"The provisions of paragraphs 1 to 4 shall not exclude the patentability of any substance or composition, comprised in the state of the art, for use in a method referred to in Article 52, paragraph 4, provided that its use for *any* method referred to in that paragraph is not comprised in the state of the art." [Author's emphasis.]

2-155   In the Munich Diplomatic Conference on the European Patent Convention,[309] a conference preceded the actual signing of the EPC and therefore its notes must be considered *travaux préparatoires*. The chairman of the conference noted, in response to a statement from the Yugoslav delegation, the following:

"...in his opinion, the aim in paragraph 54(5) was to make clear that a known substance (or a known composition) which, since it formed part of the state of the art, was no longer patentable, nevertheless could be patented for the first use in a method for treatment of the human or animal body by surgery or therapy; however, a further patent could not be granted if a second possible use were found for the same substance, irrespective of whether the human or animal body was to be treated with it."

2-156   The chairman noted that his views were shared by the government delegations and that the Main Committee did not wish to endorse an opposite viewpoint put forward by the UNICE delegation. Thus, art.54(5) suggested that a first medical use invention was permissible but not a second medical use invention.

2-157   However, in *Second medical use/EISAI*,[310] the Enlarged Board of Appeal held that art.54(5) (as it then was) did not prevent the patenting of second medical indication inventions. The EBA said:

"Article 54(5) EPC alone provides only a partial compensation for the restriction of patent rights in the industrial and commercial field resulting from Article 52(4) EPC, first sentence. It should be added that the Enlarged Board does not deduce from the special provision of Article 54(5) EPC that there was any intention to exclude second (and further) medical indications from patent protection other than by a purpose-limited product claim. The rule of interpretation that if one thing is expressed the alternative is excluded (expressio unius est exclusio alterius), is a rule to be applied with very great caution as it can lead to injustice. No intention to exclude second (and further) medical indications generally from patent protection can be deduced from the terms of the European Patent Convention; nor can it be deduced from the legislative history of the articles in question.

For these reasons, the Enlarged Board considers that it is legitimate in principle to allow claims *directed to the use of a substance or composition for the manufacture of a medicament for a specified new and inventive therapeutic application*, even in a case in which the process of manufacture as such does not differ from known processes using the same active ingredient." [Emphasis supplied.]

2-158   The form of claim emphasised in the excerpt above is known as a "Swiss-style claim". It was a claim designed to overcome any objections that could be made under the old art.54(5). The EBA's decision in *Second medical use/EISAI* was relied upon in many subsequent cases.

---

[309] 10 February 1975.

[310] (G-05/83) [1985] OJ EPO 64; [1979–85] E.P.O.R. B241. There were seven parallel decisions of the EBA on the same point all delivered on 5 December 1984. Three of these were published in the [1985] OJ EPO 60, 64, 67 in German, English and French ((G-1/83), (G-5/83) and (G-6/83)).

The amendment in EPC2000 was to split old art.54(5) and the case law on it into 2-159 sections—art.54(4) dealing with first medical use inventions and art.54(5) dealing with second medical use inventions. New art.54(4) makes it clear that first use medical inventions can be broad claims to therapeutic use whilst the new art.54(5) by the addition of "specific" makes it clear that second and subsequent medical uses are permissible and that there is no need to couch such claims in a Swiss-style claim. The reason for the new art.54(5) was to eliminate any legal uncertainty on the patentability of further medical uses. The TBA has said that in relation to the new art.54(5) that "specific" is only used in contrast to the unspecific use allowable in a claim to a first medical use and not as requiring that any detailed criteria be met before a use for a therapy can be considered specific.[311]

First medical use

Article 54(4) makes it clear that patent protection for first medical use inventions is permissible even where the substance is known. The required novelty for the medicament which forms the subject-matter of the claim is derived from the new pharmaceutical use.[312] In a first medical use invention, an application may contain claims in terms of a broad statement of therapeutic purpose and does not need to be limited to a specifically disclosed individual therapeutic purpose, even if the description only discloses a specific therapeutic purpose.[313] Thus claims such as "Substance X for use as an active therapeutic substance" have been allowed.[314] Whilst the Guidelines say that a claim for a first medical indication invention should be in a form such as "substance of composition X" followed by the indication of the use, i.e. "for use as a medicament as an antibacterial agent or for curing disease Y",[315] the fact that a specific use is disclosed in the specification does not in itself call for a restriction of the purpose-limited product claim to that use.[316]

It is important that such a claim is distinguished from a claim "Use of substance 2-161 or composition X for the treatment of disease Y", which as such would be regarded as relating to a method for treatment explicitly excluded from patentability by art.53(c).[317]

Second and further medical use: "Swiss Claims" and (G-2/08)

As discussed above, pre-EPC 2000, old art.54(5) appeared to suggest that second 2-162 medical use inventions were not permissible but that the EPO had permitted Swiss-style claims to avoid such an exclusion. The TBA had noted that a Swiss-style claim would only give the patent proprietor a remedy against the maker or dealer. It continued by saying that if there is a well-established other therapeutic use (whether patented or not) for the composition, then the proprietor may find it difficult to find any target to sue for patent infringement. The TBA said that such would be a

---

[311] *Method of administration/GENENTECH* (T-1020/03) [2006] E.P.O.R. 9 at [51].

[312] *Second medical use EISAI* (G-05/83) [1985] OJ EPO 64; [1979–85] E.P.O.R. B241.

[313] *HOFFMANN-LA ROCHE/Pyrrolidine Derivatives* (T-128/82) [1979–85] E.P.O.R. C987; [1984] OJ EPO 164; I.P.D. 7050, July–August 1984. See also (T-36/83) [1987] E.P.O.R. 1; I.P.D. 9097, December 1986.

[314] *HOFFMANN-LA ROCHE/Pyrrolidine Derivatives* (T-128/82) [1979–85] E.P.O.R. C987; [1984] OJ EPO 164; I.P.D. 7050, July–August 1984.

[315] Guid. G-II 4.2.

[316] (T-128/82) [1979–85] E.P.O.R. C987.

[317] Guid. G-VI 7.1. See (G-05/83) [1985] OJ EPO 64; [1979–85] E.P.O.R. B241.

problem for the proprietor of the patent for the second medical indication and not for any physician, nurse or patient.[318]

2-163   Clearly, there was a high degree of artificiality in a Swiss-style claim and permitting Swiss-style claims rendered the old art.54(5) impotent. Furthermore, it appeared to be contrary to the intentions of the founding members of the EPC. It is unfortunate that the EBA did not refer specifically to the Minutes of the Munich Convention as, in the author's opinion, there can be deduced a general intention to ban second medical use inventions regardless of whether patents for such were couched as product or use claims.[319]

2-164   However, new art.54(5) appeared to suggest that there was no need for Swiss-style claims for second medical use invention. This was confirmed in *Abbott Respiratory/Dosage regime* (G-2/08)[320] where the EBA considered whether a known medicament could be patented under the provisions of arts 53(c) and 54(5) EPC for use in a different, new and inventive treatment by therapy of the same illness.[321] It held that such an invention was indeed patentable, even where the dosage regime is the only claimed feature which does not form part of the state of the art. Also, the EBA said that because of the change to art.54(5) which explicitly permits claims to a substance for a second use, the rationale for a Swiss-style claim no longer exists. Indeed, such claims are no longer permitted to have the format of a Swiss-type claim, since art.54(5) now permits purpose-related product protection. Accordingly, a "Swiss-type" claim is allowable only by way of transitional provisions if the application is new and inventive and has a filing or earliest priority date before 29 January 2011.[322] In *Treatment of Pompe's Disease/GENZYME*,[323] the Board of Appeal held that an EPC 2000 claim was wider in scope than a Swiss-style claim (and thus amendment to the former was not permissible after grant[324]). It held that in Swiss-style claims, the relevant purpose is limited to use in treating the indication specified on the packaging leaflet created during manufacture, whereas a EPC 2000 new art.54(5) claim, not being limited by the process of manufacture, would also encompass products used to treat the protected indication even if the product label only referred to non-protected indications.[325] In other words, any use of a pharmaceutical product regardless of what therapeutic use is described on the packaging or label would infringe the new art.54(5) whereas such is not true of Swiss-style claims.

2-165   Unlike the practice for first medical use inventions, where the claimed use may be simply therapeutic use, a claim to a second or further medical use must specify

---

[318] *Genentech* (T-1020/03) [2006] E.P.O.R. 9, [17]. In *Genentech*, the TBA casts doubt on a number of TBA decisions as not having been decided properly in the light of (G-05/83) or not having properly stated the principle in (G-05/83). These are *Procter & Gamble/Gastrointestinal Compositions* (T-317/95) [1999] E.P.O.R. 528, (T-56/97) (unpublished), (T-548/97) (unpublished); and *Sequus/Liposome Composition* (T-4/98) [2002] E.P.OR. 34; and (T-458/99) (unpublished). See also para.2-331 (infringement of second medical use claims).

[319] *The EISAI* case and the validity of Swiss-style claims were attacked strongly in *Bristol-Myers Squibb v Baker Norton Pharmaceutical Inc* [2001] R.P.C. 1 CA. The Court of Appeal of England noted the attack but did not have to decide the matter.

[320] [2010] E.P.O.R. 26.

[321] *ABBOTT RESPIRATORY/Dosage regime* (G-2/08) [2010] E.O.P.R. 26.

[322] See Guid. G-VI 7.1, and Notice from the EPO in OJ EPO [2010] at 514.

[323] *Treatment of Pomple's Disease/GENZYME* (T-1673/11) ECLI:EP:BA:2015:T167311.20151020.

[324] art.123(3) does not permit the broadening of protection of a claim after grant. See para. 2-440.

[325] See para.9.2.

the new and therapeutic application.[326] A claim for a second or further medical use must be specifically set out in the claim and the extent of protection will be so limited, as such an invention will be considered in accordance with the principles of selection inventions.[327] Claims for different uses are allowable, provided that they form a single general inventive concept.[328] When considering the inventiveness of second and further use medical inventions, the invention is not anticipated merely because the technical feature that is claimed may have inherently taken place in the course of carrying out what had previously been made available to the public if such is not known to be happening.[329]

Care must be taken to distinguish between a new therapeutic use and the discovery of a fact relating to a known therapeutic use.[330] Thus, in one case, a patent was applied for the use of a retinoid compound in conjunction with a corticosteroid for use in preventing skin atrophy.[331] As of the priority date, it was known that corticosteroids were used for the treatment of skin conditions such as psoriasis. It was known that skin atrophy was a well-recognised and fully documented clinical condition occurring after prolonged use of corticosteroids. It was, thus, an unfortunate side effect of the use of corticosteroids. It was also known that corticosteroid-retinoid compositions had also been used for the treatment of psoriasis and other dermatoses and that a medical practitioner would have treated patients using a corticosteroid-retinoid composition in the expectation that no skin atrophy would occur. The mere discovery by the applicant that such was due to the use of a retinoid did not and could not confer novelty on a known process, as the skilled person was already aware of the occurrence of the desired effect when applying the known process. Thus, the critical criterion for determining novelty is whether the skilled person was aware of the second medical use of a known product—it is not necessary to know the biochemical mechanism that was responsible for the second medical use.

2-166

Use of a known substance for a known use but administered via a new therapeutic administrative regime

In an English case, the Court of Appeal considered a Swiss-style claim for the use of a medicament (taxol) for the treatment of cancer which, when administered over a short period of time, had the effect of reducing neutropenia (hair loss).[332] The prior art disclosed the use of taxol for the treatment of cancer but did not specifically disclose that, if administered over a short period, it reduced neutropenia. The Court of Appeal held that when considering the novelty of second medical use inventions and applying EISAI, novelty must reside in the therapeutic purpose rather than in the method of use.[333] The court said that if novelty can lie in the nature of use, rather than in the end-result at which that use aims, then it was a method of treatment contrary to art.53(c) (previously art.52(4)).

2-167

---

[326] *Second medical use/EISAI* (G-5/83) at [2] Order; (T-1020/03) [2006] E.P.O.R. 9 at [7].
[327] See G. Paterson, "The Patentability of Further Uses of Known Product under the EPC" [1991] 1 E.I.P.R. 16.
[328] art.82 and Guid. G-VI 7.1.
[329] *Friction reducing additive/MOBIL OIL* (G-02/88) [1990] OJ EPO 93; [1990] E.P.O.R. 73.
[330] *Genentech* (T-1020/03) [2006] E.P.O.R. 9 at [8] which refers to (T-254/93), (T-189/95) and (T-486/01). Approved in (G-02/08), at [5.10.9].
[331] *ORTHO PHARMACEUTICAL/Prevention of skin atrophy* (T-254/93) [1999] E.P.O.R. 1.
[332] *Bristol Myers Squibb Co v Baker Norton Pharmaceuticals Inc* [2001] R.P.C. 1.
[333] per Buxton LJ.

2-168   However, in *Genentech Inc*,[334] in choosing not to follow the Court of Appeal in *Bristol-Myers*, the TBA held that Swiss-style claims directed to the use of a composition for manufacture of a medicament for a specified new and inventive therapeutic application where the novelty of the application lay only in the dose to be used or the manner of application were permissible.[335] In *Merck & Co Inc's Patents*,[336] Jacob J reluctantly followed *Bristol Myers* but said that if new and non-obvious methods of administration of known drugs for known diseases are not patentable in principle, then there would be less of a research incentive to find such methods even using a Swiss form claim. However, in *Actavis UK v Merck & Co Inc*[337] the Court of Appeal declined to follow Bristol Myers and instead followed the TBA in *Genentech Inc*.

2-169   In *Abbott Respiratory/Dosage Regime* (G2/08), discussed above,[338] the matter was put beyond doubt when the EBA held that where it is already known to use a medicament to treat an illness, art.54(5) EPC 2000 does not exclude the patenting of a medicament for use in a novel dosage regime for treatment of the same illness.[339]

New non-medical uses of a known product

2-170   Articles 54(4) and 54(5) make it clear that use of a substance or compositions for treatment of humans or animals is deemed novel provided that the use (as opposed to the substance or composition) is not in the prior art. However, many inventions concern a new and inventive use of a known product for a *non-medical* use. In relation to a claim for a *new* use of an *old* product for a particular non-medical purpose, there has been little dispute that such is patentable.[340] Greater dispute occurred over a claim for the known use of a known substance for a new purpose. The EBA had to consider this point in the case of *Friction reducing additive/MOBIL OIL*.[341] The respondent argued that a distinction should be drawn between a claim for a *new* use of an *old* substance for a *new* purpose and a claim for an *old* use of an *old* substance for a *new* purpose. It accepted that the former was capable of being novel but that the latter kind of claim could never be novel because the only novel feature of the claim was a "mental novelty" devoid of technical effect.[342]

2-171   However, the EBA held that what was important was whether the functional technical feature of the invention had been made available to the public. If the claim included a "new means of realisation" by which the new purpose could be achieved, then such was a novel technical feature.[343] In the declaratory part of its judgment, it held that a claim to the use of a known compound for a particular purpose, which is based on a technical effect that is described in the patent, should be interpreted as including that technical effect as a functional technical feature and accordingly was not open to objections of novelty, provided that the technical feature had not

---

[334] *Genentech* (T-1020/03) [2006] E.P.O.R. 9.

[335] See [72].

[336] *Merck & Co Inc's Patents* [2003] F.S.R. 298.

[337] [2008] R.P.C. 26 CA.

[338] See para.2-164.

[339] Order to Question 1.

[340] (G-05/83) [1985] OJ EPO 64; [1979–85] E.P.O.R. B241, EBA; (G-02/88) [1990] OJ EPO 93; [1990] E.P.O.R. 73, EBA. See also Guid. G-VI 7.2.

[341] (G-02/88) [1990] OJ EPO 93 as corrected by 969; I.P.D. 13029, March 1990, EBA.

[342] (G-02/88) [1990] OJ EPO 93 at [7.1].

[343] (G-02/88) [1990] OJ EPO 93.

been previously made available to the public. This test is rather more easily stated than applied. However, a distinction can be drawn between merely discovering a hitherto undiscovered effect arising out of the known use of a known substance (which is unpatentable) as opposed to applying that undiscovered effect to give rise to a technical effect (which may be patentable if the technical effect is novel and inventive). Thus, as the TBA said, if the patent in suit merely conveys additional information about a known process rather than teaching the person skilled in the art to do something which would not have been done absent the patent in suit, then it does not give rise to a new industrial application.[344]

This must be right. It is difficult (indeed meaningless) to draw a cogent distinc- **2-172** tion between a *new* use and a *new* purpose. Thus, in *BAYER/Plant Growth*,[345] the facts were that a compound X, which was previously known and used to affect plant growth, was found to be useful as a plant fungicide. The only possible novelty in the claimed invention lay in the use of the compound as a fungicide rather than as a growth regulator. The EBA held that the technical features of the claim and the underlying invention had not been made available to the public by the prior art and thus were novel. Here the new use is as a fungicide and the purpose of the invention is to kill fungi. The distinction between use and purpose is rather illusory.

The disclosure in the patent application of a new technical effect which was not **2-173** described before does not mean there is an inventive step. The issue of inventive step where a new use or new field-of-use has been established requires a careful factual analysis.[346]

Inventive step

An invention will be considered as involving an inventive step if having regard **2-174** to the state of the art, it is not obvious to a person skilled in the art.[347] The prior art is not to be taken for the purposes of inventiveness as including earlier European patent applications which are published after the filing date of the application in question.[348]

The Guidelines state: **2-175**

"Thus the question to consider, in relation to any claim defining the invention, is whether before the filing or priority date valid for that claim, having regard to the art known at the time, it would have been obvious to the person skilled in the art to arrive at something falling within the terms of the claim. If so, the claim is not allowable for lack of inventive step. The term 'obvious' means that which does not go beyond the normal progress of technology but merely follows plainly or logically from the prior art, i.e. something which does not involve the exercise of any skill or ability beyond that to be expected of the person skilled in the art. In considering inventive step, as distinct from novelty (see G-VI, 3), it is fair to construe any published document in the light of knowledge up to and including the day before the filing or priority date valid for the claimed invention and to have regard to all the knowledge generally available to the person skilled in the art up to and including that day."[349]

The issue of obviousness is much more fact-dependent than the issue of novelty. **2-176**

---

[344] *AMERICAN CYANAMID/Melamine derivatives* (T-279/93) [1999] E.P.O.R. 88.
[345] *BAYER/Plant Growth* (G-06/88) [1990] OJ EPO 114; [1990] E.P.O.R. 257.
[346] *FUJITSU/Silicon oxynitride semiconductor* (T-329/99) [1996] E.P.O.R. 224.
[347] art.56.
[348] arts 54(3), 56.
[349] Guid. G-VII.4.

Unlike novelty which concerns the determination of a concrete issue—namely, does the claimed invention exist in the prior art—the determination as to whether a claimed invention which does not exist in the prior art is inventive is more difficult. The tribunal determining the issue of inventiveness will need to consider a large number of factors (often called a multifactorial decision). Furthermore, it requires a degree of mental gymnastics. The tribunal must consider whether it is obvious to arrive at the claimed invention from the prior art which requires it to put itself in the shoes of the skilled person as of the priority date considering the prior art but who does not have knowledge of the claimed invention.

2-177   Notwithstanding the fact-dependent nature of the issue, the EPO has developed a number of principles. These are now discussed.

Objective approach

2-178   As in the case of novelty, inventive step is an objective concept, so when assessing inventive step, the case history of the invention is irrelevant. As the TBA said:

> "As in the case of novelty, inventive step is an objective concept. Objectivity in the assessment of inventive step is achieved by starting out from the objectively prevailing state of the art in the light of which the problem is determined which the invention addresses from an objective point of view and consideration is given to the question or obviousness of the disclosed solution to this problem as seen by the man skilled in the art and having those capabilities which can be objectively expected of him. This also avoids the retrospective approach which inadmissibly makes use of knowledge of the invention, as feared by the applicant."[350]

Problem and solution approach

2-179   In general, the EPO favours a problem-and-solution approach to obviousness. It has said that this should be applied save in exceptional cases. It is described in the Guidelines as follows[351]:

> "In order to assess inventive step in an objective and predictable manner, the so-called 'problem-and-solution approach' should be applied. Thus deviation from this approach should be exceptional.
>   In the problem-and-solution approach, there are three main stages:
>
> (i)   determining the 'closest prior art'
> (ii)   establishing the 'objective technical problem' to be solved
> (iii) considering whether or not the claimed invention, starting from the closest prior art and the objective technical problem, would have been obvious to the skilled person."

2-180   This approach has been applied in countless cases. It is intended to eliminate the problem of hindsight, i.e. considering the issue of inventive step by reference to the invention rather than from the prior art. The Guidelines give a helpful example of how it works:

Example
The problem of permanently marking farm animals such as cows without causing pain to the animals or damage to the hide has existed since farming began. The solution

---

[350] *BASF A.G.* (T-24/81) [1983] OJ EPO 133; I.P.D. 6020, April 1982.
[351] Guid. G-VII, section 5.

("freeze-branding") consists in applying the discovery that the hide can be permanently depigmented by freezing.[352]

Care must be taken when applying the problem to be solved. The Guidelines give an example of an invention lying into the arrival of an insight into the cause of an observed phenomenon (the practical use of this phenomenon then being obvious). **2-181**

Example
The agreeable flavour of butter is found to be caused by minute quantities of a particular compound. As soon as this insight has been arrived at, the technical application comprising adding this compound to margarine is immediately obvious.

However, it would be wrong to say that the problem and solution approach does not apply here. Rather, it is sometimes necessary to take care in formulating the problem. For instance, in the butter example, the problem was not how to use the particular compound to make margarine taste agreeable (which was obvious) but how does one make margarine taste like butter? Once formulated as such, the inventor's solution was to discover that the agreeable flavour of butter was due to minute quantities of a particular compound *and then to* add these minute quantities to margarine. Viewed overall as a solution to the stated problem, such is very likely to be found to be inventive. **2-182**

Despite this, not all inventions easily fit into the problem/solution approach. In particular, it may be artificial to say that the skilled person was aware of a problem in the prior art at all. The limits of the problem/solution approach are discussed below.[353] In *Method for manufacturing semiconductor substrate*,[354] the TBA held that a claim for manufacture of a semiconductor substrate comprising a silicon-germanium (SiGe) film was obvious over prior art which concerned the manufacture of a semiconductor substrate comprising a germanium (Ge) film. The TBA held that such difference could not be relevant because the problem-solution approach presupposed that the skilled person had a purpose in mind from the outset of the invention process, namely making a semiconductor comprising a silicon-germanium film. It thus held that it would be immediately apparent to the skilled person that what is disclosed in the prior art could be adapted *to the purpose of the claimed invention* in a straightforward manner (as SiGe films were known). **2-183**

In the author's view, the flaw is that the problem is identified by reference to the solution identified in the patent. The TBA referred by way of example to the fact that the appellant's argument was not persuasive because it was equivalent to saying that if the purpose was to make a salami sandwich, it was inventive to choose salami as the filling. This necessarily involves hindsight. For instance, if the claim was to an invention to make a sandwich using unexpected ingredients, e.g. flour in the bread made from the pollen of flowers, it hardly advances the analysis of inventive step to say that the problem was to make a sandwich from flour made of flower pollen. In particular, if sandwiches had been made from wheat flour for many years and no one had ever considered using a flour made from pollen (let us assume it has some non-allergenic qualities) for the sandwich, a holistic approach to **2-184**

---

[352] Guid. G-VII-9.
[353] See para.2-196.
[354] *Method for manufacturing semiconductor substrate/Shin-Etsu Chemical Co Ltd* (T-1841/11) ECLI:EP:BA:2015:T184111.20151203.

inventiveness would suggest that a sandwich made using flour from pollen is inventive.

2-185   In the author's view, the flaw in the TBA's reasoning is to define the problem too narrowly and with too close an eye to the solution claimed. A better approach would be to define the problem by reference to the disadvantage in the prior art. Thus, in *Method for manufacturing semiconductor substrate*, the advantage of SiGe over Ge was that it prevented lattice defects. Thus, in the author's view, a correct statement of the problem was how to improve a substrate comprising of a Ge layer so as to avoid lattice defects. It would appear from the decision that choosing a SiGe layer would have been an obvious step as SiGe films were known and also prior art methods for manufacturing them. Thus, the answer would have been the same if the stated problem with the prior art had been defined more broadly and with less hindsight.

Technical solution to a technical problem

2-186   For the purpose of applying the problem-and-solution approach, the problem must be a technical problem solved by a technical solution.[355] All the features in the claim should contribute to the solution, and the problem must be one that the skilled person in the particular technical field might be asked to solve at the priority date.[356] This requirement that the contribution of the invention be a technical contribution is important when considering whether an invention relating to excluded subject-matter under art.52 is patentable, e.g. computer-related inventions. This is discussed below.

2-187   It is rare that the EPO will be faced with claims which have no technical feature in them. Usually, the EPO will be considering claims which contain technical and non-technical features. In such circumstances, when applying the problem-and-solution approach, due care must be taken to define:

- the technical field to which the invention belongs;
- the scope of the technical expertise and skills expected to be applied by the technical person in the particular technical field; and
- the correct formulation of the technical problem actually solved.[357]

2-188   When it considers inventive step, the EPO will isolate the technical features of the invention even if they are intermingled in a mixed technical/non-technical claim.[358] The effect of this approach is to concentrate on the technical contribution disclosed by the patent rather than the ingeniousness of the draughtsman of the claims.

Inventive Step and Excluded Patent Subject Matter

2-189   Consistent with the approach of the EPO described in the previous section, the EPO has developed an approach whereby it must be shown that when considering inventive step, the contribution of the invention is not in a field excluded from

---

[355] e.g. *CONJUCHEM/Fusion peptide inhibitors* (T-433/05) [2007] E.P.O.R. 52.
[356] *Two identities/COMVIK* (T-641/00) [2004] E.P.O.R. 10 at [20]. See also *DUNS LICENSING ASSOCIATES/Estimating sales activity* (T-154/04) [2007] E.P.O.R. 38.
[357] e.g. see *SYSTRAN/Translating natural languages* (T-1177/97) [2005] E.P.O.R. 13.
[358] *Controlling pension benefits system/PBS partnership* (T-931/95) [2002] E.P.O.R. 52; *COMVIK/ Two identities* (T-641/00) [2004] E.P.O.R. 10 at [28].

patentability.[359] Here, the approach is to focus on the technical contribution to the prior art and determine whether this is inventive to the identified technical problem. Non-technical features, to the extent that they do not interact with the technical subject matter of the claim for solving a technical problem are ignored.

Thus, in *Duns Licensing Associates/Estimating sales activity*[360] the TBA said that a patentable invention "must provide a novel and inventive" *technical contribution* to the prior art. The TBA in *Duns Licensing* said that the "constant jurisprudence" of the Boards of Appeal when considering patentability and inventive step was as follows:

    2-190

"(a)   Article 52(1) EPC sets out four requirements to be fulfilled by a patentable invention: there must be an invention, and if there is an invention, it must satisfy the requirements of novelty, inventive step, and industrial applicability.

(b)   Having technical character is an implicit requisite of an 'invention' within the meaning of Art.52(1) EPC (requirement of 'technicality').

(c)   Article 52(2) EPC does not exclude from patentability any subject matter or activity having technical character, even if it is related to the items listed in this provision since these items are only excluded 'as such' (Art.52(3) EPC).

(d)   The four requirements invention, novelty, inventive step, and susceptibility of industrial application are essentially separate and independent criteria of patentability, which may give rise to concurrent objections. Novelty, in particular, is not a requisite of an invention within the meaning of Art.52(1) EPC, but a separate requirement of patentability.

(e)   For examining patentability of an invention in respect of a claim, the claim must be construed to determine the technical features of the invention, i.e. the features which contribute to the technical character of the invention.

(f)   It is legitimate to have a mix of technical and 'non-technical' features appearing in a claim, in which the non-technical features may even form a dominating part of the claimed subject matter. Novelty and inventive step, however, can be based only on technical features, which thus have to be clearly defined in the claim. Non-technical features, to the extent that they do not interact with the technical subject matter of the claim for solving a technical problem, i.e. non-technical features 'as such', do not provide a technical contribution to the prior art and are thus ignored in assessing novelty and inventive step.

(g)   For the purpose of the problem-and-solution approach, the problem must be a technical problem which the skilled person in the particular technical field might be asked to solve at the relevant priority date. The technical problem may be formulated using an aim to be achieved in a non-technical field, and which is thus not part of the technical contribution provided by the invention to the prior art. This may be done in particular to define a constraint that has to be met (even if the aim stems from an a posteriori knowledge of the invention)."

This approach was apparently approved in *Programs for computer/Admissibility* (G3/08).[361] The EBA said that whilst it was aware that rejection for lack of an inventive step based on the ground that the invention lay in a non-technical feature was "in some way distasteful to many people", it was an approach "which has been

    2-191

---

[359] *Hitachi/Auction Method* (T-258/03) [2004] E.P.O.R. 55 at [21] and cases cited there.
[360] (T-154/04) [2007] E.P.O.R. 38.
[361] [2010] E.P.O.R. 36 at [10.13.1]. The EBA said that whilst it was not the task of the EBA to determine whether such an approach was correct, it did say that it was evident from its frequent use that the list of "non-inventions" can play a very important role in determining whether claimed subject matter is inventive (see [10.13.1]).

consistently developed since T1173/97" and that it "has created a practicable system for delimiting the innovations for which a patent may be granted".[362]

2-192   The Guidelines set out the following approach to the determination of inventive step for an invention which has mix of technical and non-technical features as is often the case with computer-implemented inventions[363]:

(i)   The features which contribute to the technical character of the invention are determined on the basis of the technical effects achieved in the context of the invention (see G-II, 3.1 to 3.7).

(ii)   A suitable starting point in the prior art is selected as the closest prior art based on the features contributing to the technical character of the invention identified in step (i) (see G-VII, 5.1).

(iii)   The differences from the closest prior art are identified. The technical effect(s) of these differences, in the context of the claim as a whole, is/are determined in order to identify the features which make a technical contribution and those which do not.

(a)   If there are no differences (not even a non-technical difference), an objection under art.54 is raised.

(b)   If the differences do not make any technical contribution, an objection under art.56 is raised. The reasoning for the objection should be that the subject-matter of a claim cannot be inventive if there is no technical contribution to the prior art.

(c)   If the differences include features making a technical contribution, the following applies:

–   The objective technical problem is formulated on the basis of the technical effect(s) achieved by these features. In addition, if the differences include features making no technical contribution, these features, or any non-technical effect achieved by the invention, may be used in the formulation of the objective technical problem as part of what is "given" to the skilled person, in particular as a constraint that has to be met (see G-VII, 5.4.1).

–   If the claimed technical solution to the objective technical problem is obvious to the person skilled in the art, an objection under art.56 is raised.

2-193   Thus, in *Hitachi/Auction Method*[364] the application concerned a claim for an "automatic auction method executed in a server computer" comprising various steps which essentially described a Dutch auction.[365] Other claims included an apparatus claim "a computerised auction apparatus for performing an automatic auction via a network" and a claim to a "computer program, which when run on a computer network comprising client computers and a server" carried out the Dutch auction method. There were auxiliary requests as well.

2-194   The claimed contribution to the prior art was that it introduced a variant on the known Dutch auction and permitted the carrying out of a Dutch auction on computers. The heart of the invention appeared to be based on modifications to the

---

[362] See [10.13] and [10.13.2].

[363] Guid. G-VII, section 5.4.

[364] (T-258/03) [2004] E.P.O.R. 55.

[365] A Dutch auction consists of an auction whereby the price for a product is dropped iteratively until someone bids. If more than one person bids for the product at a particular price, then the auction enters a conventional auction and the price goes up until there is only one bidder.

known Dutch auction method including, in particular, dealing with a situation where two or more bidders bid at a particular price. However, as the TBA said, such a feature was fundamentally independent of the computer arrangement for performing the auction. They said that it could just as well be used for conducting a Dutch auction method without computer support, e.g. by collecting bids in writing. The TBA said that the invention could be regarded therefore as a mere automation of a non-technical activity. Any ingeniousness required to develop the rules for such an auction could not be considered for inventive step.[366] In contrast, a claim to a method in a computer system having a clipboard for performing data transfer in a clipboard format was patentable and consisted of inventive step.[367]

The approach in *Hitachi/Auction Method* appears to be the current favoured approach to the determination of inventive step for computer-related inventions.[368] It certainly has its attractions as it prevents applicants from avoiding the effect of art.52(1) by the wording of claims. Therefore, in relation to the issue of inventive step, it has found favour in the UK.[369]   **2-195**

Problem and solution approach questioned

The EPO Guidelines say that deviation from the problem-solution approach should only occur in exceptional circumstances.[370] What might those exceptional circumstances be? In *ALCAN/Aluminium alloys*[371] the TBA revisited the "problem-and-solution" approach. It pointed out that its weakness is that it relies on the results of a search of the relevant prior art, which is made with actual knowledge of the invention and is thus inherently based on hindsight. Therefore, it requires care in its application. Furthermore, the TBA pointed out that it can result in complicated multi-step reasoning where the facts are clear, either for or against inventiveness. Accordingly, the TBA said: **2-196**

"if an invention breaks entirely new ground, it may suffice to say that there is no close prior art, rather than constructing a problem based on what is tenuously regarded as the closest prior art."

The TBA went on to say that it saw a welcome trend in recent unreported decisions which have emphasised that the investigation of inventiveness should avoid formulating artificial and unrealistic technical problems and should normally start from the technical problems identified in the patent in suit.[372] The *Alcan/Aluminium Alloys* case was decided in the 20th century and it is fair to say that the EPO is still firmly wedded to the problem/solution approach. In the author's view, this is to be applauded because there is no question that in the majority of cases it   **2-197**

---

366 Citing *Two identities/COMVIK* (T-641/00) [2004] E.P.O.R. 10. See also *Matsushita/Remote-control* (T-244/00) [2005] E.P.O.R. 12.

367 *Microsoft/Clipboard formats I* (T-424/03) [2006] E.P.O.R. 39.

368 See *Programs for computers* (G3/08) at [10.13.2] where the EBA said that it has been cited in over 40 decisions by eight Technical Boards of Appeal and "that the Boards are in general quite comfortable with it".

369 See *CFPH LLC's Patent Applications* [2006] R.P.C. 5, High Ct. The divergence between the UK and the EPO relates to the proper interpretation of art.52 (excluded patentable subject matter) rather than art.56 (inventive step) when considering computer-related inventions. See para.2-267.

370 Guid. G-VII, section 5.

371 *ALCAN/Aluminium alloys* (T-465/92) [1995] E.P.O.R. 501.

372 See also *PENGULAN/Surface finish* (T-495/91) [1995] E.P.O.R. 516; *UENO/BON-3-acid* (T-741/91) [1995] E.P.O.R. 533.

works well. Equally though it is important that the examiner of inventive step should know when *not to use it*. This ensures a logical and structural approach to the issue of inventive step which does not jettison a useful intellectual tool simply because in some circumstances, it does not work.

2-198   A good example of where it does not work is where the invention lies in the realisation that *there is a problem.* This point was made by the English court in *Actavis v Novartis*[373] which considered in-depth the problem-and-solution approach. Lord Justice Jacob considered that the determination of the "problem" can be quite artificial and often guided by hindsight of the invention.[374] He then continued by saying:

> "[35]   Moreover the [person skilled in the art] does not really cope well with cases where the invention involves perceiving that there is a problem, or in appreciating that a known problem, perhaps 'put up with' for years, can be solved. Take for instance the 'Anywayup Cup' case, *Haberman v Jackel International* [1999] F.S.R. 683. The invention was a baby's drinker cup fitted with a known kind of valve to prevent it leaking. Babies drinker cups had been known for years. Parents all over the world had put up with the fact that if they were dropped they leaked. No-one had thought to solve the problem. So when the patentee had the technically trivial idea of putting in a valve, there was an immediate success. The invention was held non-obvious, a conclusion with which most parents would agree. Yet fitting reasoning to uphold the patent into a PSA approach would not really work. For by identifying the problem as leakage and suggesting it can be solved, one is halfway to the answer—put in a valve."

2-199   In an early case, the TBA said in *RIDER/Simethicone*[375]:

> "6.   The discovery of a yet unrecognised problem may, in certain circumstances, give rise to patentable subject- matter in spite of the fact that the claimed solution is retrospectively trivial and in itself obvious ('problem inventions'). For instance the so-called analogy processes in chemistry are only claimable as long as the problem, i.e. the need to provide certain patentable products as their effect, is not yet within the state of the art.
>
> 7.   The question regarding the inventive step, in relation to the modification of the layered tablet of the state of the art as suggested by the present applicants, is not whether the skilled man could have inserted a barrier between the layers but whether he would have done so in expectation of some improvement or advantage. Since the Yen tablet was, on the face of it and from what was assumed in view of its commercialisation, a satisfactory answer to the problem of undesirable migration, the addition of a barrier would have appeared superfluous, wasteful and devoid of any technical effect. In view of the recognition that a barrier has, after all, a substantial effect, the outcome was not predictable and the claimed modification involves an inventive step on this basis."

Furthermore, as said above,[376] even where it is apt and fitting to use the problem/solution approach, care should be taken not to define the problem with the prior art too closely by reference to the claimed solution but rather by reference to the disadvantage of the prior art.

---

[373]   [2010] EWCA Civ 82 CA.
[374]   See [33].
[375]   *RIDER/Simethicone Tablet* (T-2/83) [1984] OJ EPO 165; [1979–1985] E.P.O.R. Vol.C, 715.
[376]   See paras 2-181 to 2-182.

Could/would test

In certain cases, however, the EPO has formulated a "could/would" test for inventive step. This is used in tandem with the problem/solution approach. Thus, when considering the problem posed by the prior art and whether it was obvious to solve it via the invention, the EPO Guidelines (G-VII-5) considers whether:

2-200

> "[5.3] In the third stage the question to be answered is whether there is any teaching in the prior art as a whole that would (not simply could, but would) have prompted the skilled person, faced with the objective technical problem, to modify or adapt the closest prior art while taking account of that teaching, thereby arriving at something falling within the terms of the claims, and thus achieving what the invention achieves (see G-VII, 4).
>
> In other words, the point is not whether the skilled person *could* have arrived at the invention by adapting or modifying the closest prior art, but whether he *would* have done so because the prior art incited him to do so in the hope of solving the objective technical problem or in expectation of some improvement or advantage (see T-2/83 *RIDER/Simethicone tablet*)." [Emphasis supplied.]

As the Guidelines suggest, this approach was ventilated in *RIDER/Simethicone tablet*[377] which has already been considered above in relation to the limitations of the problem/solution approach.[378]

2-201

Care must be taken in applying the "would" test when the contribution claimed is simply arbitrary, i.e. from a technical viewpoint, it makes no positive technical contribution to the prior art. As said by the Board of Appeal:

2-202

> "... The could/would approach only applies if the 'would' part involves technical considerations. If it does not, the fact that the invention could be arrived at is sufficient to render it obvious.[379]"

The "could/would" approach recognises that in many cases, the inventive step lies in recognising that there is a problem with the prior art. This reflects discussion in the previous section that a defect in the problem/solution approach is that it assumes that the inventive step lies in the *solution* and not the recognition that there is a *problem*. It is concerned with *motivation* of the person skilled in the art to improve the prior art. If the prior art appears to provide a satisfactory answer, then there may be no motivation to improve it. Is there anything in the prior art that hints or teaches that there is in fact a problem in the prior art? If there is, then the person skilled in the art may be motivated to modify or adapt it. Such an approach avoids the pitfalls in constructing an artificial problem/solution approach where a skilled person perceives nothing wrong with the prior art.

2-203

Person skilled in the art

The person skilled in the art will be presumed to be an ordinary practitioner, aware of what was common general knowledge in the art at the relevant date. The Guidelines describe them as follows:

2-204

> "The 'person skilled in the art' should be presumed to be a skilled practitioner in the

---

[377] *RIDER/Simethicone Tablet* (T-2/83) [1984] OJ EPO 165; [1979-1985] E.P.O.R. Vol.C, 715.
[378] See para.2-199.
[379] *Toshiba/I C Card* (T-273/02) [2005] E.P.O.R. 52.

relevant field of technology, who is possessed of average knowledge and ability and is aware of what was common general knowledge in the art at the relevant date (see T-4/98, T-143/94 and T-426/88). He should also be presumed to have had access to everything in the 'state of the art', in particular the documents cited in the search report, and to have had at his disposal the means and capacity for routine work and experimentation which are normal for the field of technology in question. If the problem prompts the person skilled in the art to seek its solution in another technical field, the specialist in that field is the person qualified to solve the problem. The skilled person is involved in constant development in his technical field (see T-774/89 and T-817/95). He may be expected to look for suggestions in neighbouring and general technical fields (see T-176/84 and T-195/84) or even in remote technical fields, if prompted to do so (see T-560/89). Assessment of whether the solution involves an inventive step must therefore be based on that specialist's knowledge and ability (see T-32/81). There may be instances where it is more appropriate to think in terms of a group of persons, e.g. a research or production team, rather than a single person (see T-164/92 and T-986/96). It should be borne in mind that the skilled person has the same level of skill for assessing inventive step and sufficient disclosure (see T-60/89, T-694/92 and T-373/94)."[380]

2-205 The legal fiction that the person skilled in the art is presumed to have had access to everything which is prior art applies even though they would not, in the ordinary course of seeking to solve a problem, have considered a potential piece of prior art. Thus, where it was contended that a prior art document, disclosing a particular type of perfumed pack for volatile flavourants, was not addressed to a skilled person considering the problem of perfuming highly reactive washing powder, the EPO held that the state of the art to be considered is absolute and not to be confined to the alleged addressee of the document.[381]

2-206 A person skilled in a particular art will be deemed to be conversant with neighbouring fields of technology but not more remote fields.[382] Fields are neighbouring where they have contact points determined by function such that the skilled person of one is able to imagine solutions of a specific problem in the other field.[383] The skilled person does not have to be the same person for all aspects of obviousness. Thus, if it is obvious to a person skilled in a particular field to consult a specialist in another neighbouring field to solve a problem, then that specialist will become the person skilled in the art. Thus, in considering whether it was obvious to use glass fibre to replace components in a conveyor belt cleaning apparatus, the skilled person was the materials specialist and not the conveyor belt specialist.[384] Similarly, the TBA held that a patent was not inventive because it could be solved by a team consisting of a housing specialist and a plugged connections specialist and there was no synergistic effect arising from the interaction of the three claimed features in Claim 1.[385]

---

[380] Guid. G-VII, para.3.
[381] *Unilever's Application* (T-107/82) [1979-85] E.P.O.R. B534; I.P.D. 6114.
[382] See *MOBIUS* (T-176/84) [1986] OJ EPO 50, [1986] E.P.O.R. 117; and *KERBER* (T-28/87) [1989] OJ EPO 383, [1989] E.P.O.R. 377.
[383] *HOECHST/Pharmaceutical preparation* (T-01/85) [1999] E.P.O.R. 57. See also *AEG Kabel/Cable outer sheath* (T-118/84) [1999] E.P.O.R. 186.
[384] *Fives-Cail Babcock SA* (T-32/81) [1982] OJ EPO 225; [1979-85] E.P.O.R. B377; I.P.D. 5086, October 1982.
[385] *BOSCH/Diagnostic test system for motor vehicles* (T-141/87) [1996] E.P.O.R. 570.

Combining prior art

In certain jurisdictions like the UK, it is a heresy when considering inventive step **2-207** to combine two items of prior art unless one points to the other (although it is acceptable to combine *a* given piece of prior art with common general knowledge). However, in the EPO, the Guidelines say (G-VII-6): **2-208**

> "[5.2] In the context of the problem-solution approach, it is permissible to combine the disclosure of one or more documents, parts of documents or other pieces of prior art (e.g. a public prior use or unwritten general technical knowledge) with the closest prior art. However, the fact that more than one disclosure must be combined with the closest prior art in order to arrive at a combination of features may be an indication of the presence of an inventive step, e.g. if the claimed invention is not a mere aggregation of features (see G-VII, 7, para.6)."

Practitioners at the EPO will be very familiar with this approach. The Guidelines **2-209** give more guidance on this issue (G-VII-6):

> "[6] In determining whether it would be obvious to combine two or more distinct disclosures, the examiner should also have regard in particular to the following:
> (i) whether the content of the disclosures (e.g. documents) is such as to make it likely or unlikely that the person skilled in the art, when faced with the problem solved by the invention, would combine them-for example, if two disclosures considered as a whole could not in practice be readily combined because of inherent incompatibility in disclosed features essential to the invention, the combining of these disclosures should not normally be regarded as obvious;
> (ii) whether the disclosures, e.g. documents, come from similar, neighbouring or remote technical fields (see G-VII, 3);
> (iii) the combining of two or more parts of the same disclosure would be obvious if there is a reasonable basis for the skilled person to associate these parts with one another. It would normally be obvious to combine with a prior-art document a well-known textbook or standard dictionary; this is only a special case of the general proposition that it is obvious to combine the teaching of one or more documents with the common general knowledge in the art. It would, generally speaking, also be obvious to combine two documents one of which contains a clear and unmistakable reference to the other (for references which are considered an integral part of the disclosure, see G-IV, 5.1 and G-VI, 1). In determining whether it is permissible to combine a document with an item of prior art made public in some other way, e.g. by use, similar considerations apply."

A skilled person is unlikely to combine two documents if the methods that they **2-210** teach point in different directions, especially where one document refers to a technique that is more than 50 years old.[386]

Ex post facto analysis

The EPO Guidelines warn against examiners holding that an invention is obvi- **2-211** ous with the benefit of hindsight. Thus, they say:

> "[8] It should be remembered that an invention which at first sight appears obvious

---

[386] *CORNING GLASS/Moulding* (T-366/89) [1993] E.P.O.R. 266. In contrast, see *MITSUBISHI/ Endless power transmission* (T-169/84) [1987] E.P.O.R. 120 where the Examining Board combined a contemporary document with one from 90 years earlier.

might in fact involve an inventive step. Once a new idea has been formulated, it can often be shown theoretically how it might be arrived at, starting from something known, by a series of apparently easy steps. The examiner should be wary of ex post facto analysis of this kind. When combining documents cited in the search report, he should always bear in mind that the documents produced in the search have, of necessity, been obtained with foreknowledge of what matter constitutes the alleged invention. In all cases he should attempt to visualise the overall state of the art confronting the skilled person before the applicant's contribution, and he should seek to make a 'real-life' assessment of this and other relevant factors. He should take into account all that is known concerning the background of the invention and give fair weight to relevant arguments or evidence submitted by the applicant. If, for example, an invention is shown to be of considerable technical value, and particularly if it provides a technical advantage which is new and surprising and which is not merely achieved as a bonus effect in a 'one-way street' situation (see G-VII, 10.2), and this technical advantage can convincingly be related to one or more of the features included in the claim defining the invention, the examiner should be hesitant in pursuing an objection that such a claim lacks inventive step."[387]

2-212   The TBA criticised an opponent who appealed a finding of inventive step by saying that:

"in seeking to analyze retrospectively how a skilled person might have been able to arrive at the concept of the invention in two mental stages, the appellants are adopting a typical ex post facto approach which fails to do justice to the objective standards by which inventive step is to be assessed. The consistent case law of the Board requires that the question of obviousness be considered from the viewpoint of the existing technical problem."[388]

Mere allegation of claimed effect/plausibility

2-213   A mere allegation of a claimed effect is not sufficient to support an inventive step as required by art.56.[389] It must be shown that prima facie, such an effect is indeed achieved. Thus, where a patent claimed that a particular chemical would have a positive effect on the immune system but provided no data, the TBA said that whilst it was not necessary to explain the mechanism, "concrete evidence" that there was such an effect is required.[390]

2-214   In the UK, this consideration has led to a number of decisions whereby the UK courts have said that it must be "plausible" that the effect will be achieved across the scope of the claim.[391] The UK courts have pointed out that the test for plausibility is different to the requirement that there be a fair expectation of success for obviousness. As the Patents Court said in *Actavis v Eli Lilly*[392]:

"[177] In my judgment, the policy considerations underlying plausibility for sufficiency are different from those underlying fair expectation of success for obviousness, which indicates that the standard for assessment of plausibility is not the same as assessment of obviousness. For obviousness, a fair expectation of suc-

---

[387] Guid. G-VII-8.
[388] *Hydrocarbon mixtures/LINDE*(T-2/85). See also, *TORAY/Flame retarding polyester composition* (T-227/89) [1993] E.P.O.R. 107.
[389] *Deprenyl Animal Health/Use of deprenyl in dogs* (T-210/02) [2005] E.P.O.R. 18.
[390] (T-210/02) [2005] E.P.O.R. 18 at [43].
[391] e.g. see *Hospira v Genentech* [2014] EWCA Civ 1094.
[392] [2015] EWHC 3294.

cess is required because, in an empirical art, many routes may be obvious to try, without any real idea of whether they will work. The denial of patent protection based upon the 'obvious to try' criterion alone would provide insufficient incentive for research and development in, for example, pharmaceuticals and biotechnology, and would lead to the conclusion that a research program of uncertain outcome would deprive a patent of inventive step. The reason why the court requires that the invention of a patent should be plausible is different. It is to exclude speculative patents, based on mere assertion, where there is no real reason to suppose that the assertion is true."

However, the threshold for showing plausibility is low. It merely requires that it is "credible" that the claimed effects will be achieved. Thus, there is no requirement in the EPC that a patent should contain data or experimental proof to support its claim. It may therefore turn out that a "plausible" invention is in fact insufficient because tests show that the "credible" claimed effects are in fact not actually achieved (or not achieved across the scope of the claim).[393]   **2-215**

It should be said that plausibility in itself is not an express ground of invalidity. Rather, it falls to be taken into account when considering whether a patent is inventive or insufficient.[394]   **2-216**

Generalisation

Often, the inventive step lies in the inventor transforming the problem into a more general problem and drawing upon general prior art and applying it to the specific problem. In such cases, the TBA has warned its Examining Division against the danger of over-generalising the problem. It has said: **2-217**

"it will be possible in most cases by heightening the level of generalisation to define a problem which is the same for a certain state of the art and for the invention. But to transform the actual problem as stated in the description of the application into a more general problem may be said to be one of the hallmarks of inventive step. The ordinary skilled person is not endowed with such a power of generalisation. Therefore the teaching of a document may have narrower implications for persons skilled in the art and broader implications for a potential inventor who first perceives the problem which his future invention is intended to solve. The assessment of inventive step must look at the situation solely from the practical viewpoint of the skilled person."[395]

Long-felt want

The features of a claim may appear to be trivial and obvious in hindsight but may well be inventive if the combination of such features led to a process which fulfilled a long-felt need.[396] An invention satisfying a long-felt need is often considered to be a hallmark of invention. However, an applicant must prove, if they rely on commercial success to overcome an obviousness objection, that such success arose from   **2-218**

---

[393] A point made by Carr J in *Actavis v Eli Lilly*, at [178].
[394] *Actavis v Eli Lilly*, at [173].
[395] *UNION CARBIDE CORP* (T-124/82) [1979-85] E.P.O.R. B586.
[396] See *MICHAELSEN/Packing Machine* (T-106/84) [1979-85] E.P.O.R. C959, [1985] OJ EPO 132; *FRISCO FINDUS/Frozen fish* (T-90/89) [1991] E.P.O.R. 42.

the invention and not other causes like skilful advertising or lack of economic motivation to invent.[397] The Guidelines state[398]:

> "Where the invention solves a technical problem which workers in the art have been attempting to solve for a long time, or otherwise fulfils a long-felt need, this may be regarded as an indication of inventive step.
>
> Commercial success alone is not to be regarded as indicative of inventive step, but evidence of immediate commercial success when coupled with evidence of a long-felt want is of relevance provided the examiner is satisfied that the success derives from the technical features of the invention and not from other influences (e.g. selling techniques or advertising)."

2-219   Where an opponent argues that the invention merely represents the combination of techniques contained in two prior art documents, then the invention may well be non-obvious if the opponent was personally aware of all the prior art for some years before the priority date and yet did not think of combining the two together.[399]

Unexpected side effect/bonus effect

2-220   In *GKN SANKEY/Tractor Wheels*,[400] the TBA held that where the solution of the problem set out in the patent application was obvious, the patent was not saved by an unexpected side effect. In *Buckman Laboratories International/Synergistic combination*,[401] in revoking a patent, the Board of Appeal held that the problem was of improving the efficiency of a biocide mixture and as it was obvious to try out a particular and more effective biocide chemical, the fact that there was an unexpected synergistic effect was not sufficient to confer inventiveness.

2-221   The EPO has said that:

> "Whilst the existence of a surprising effect appears to be an essential condition for the inventive step, this may not necessarily override the conclusion of obviousness in another respect, particularly if the skilled man had had compelling reasons to consider the same entity as an inevitable or even unique solution of that or another known problem."[402]

2-222   The Guidelines put it as follows:

> "An unexpected technical effect may be regarded as an indication of inventive step. It must, however, derive from the subject-matter as claimed, not merely from some additional features which are mentioned only in the description. However, if, having regard to the state of the art, it would already have been obvious for a skilled person to arrive at something falling within the terms of a claim, for example due to a lack of alternatives thereby creating a 'one-way street' situation, the unexpected effect is merely a bonus ef-

---

[397] See *BASF* (T-24/86) [1983] OJ EPO 133, I.P.D. 6020; *MASCHINEFABRIEK G.J. NIJHUIS BV* (T-80/86) I.P.D. 11094, January/February 1989.

[398] Guid. G-VII-10.3.

[399] *AIR PRODUCTS & CHEMICALS INC* (T-271/84) [1987] E.P.O.R. 23; I.P.D. 10093, November 1987.

[400] *GKN SANKEY/Tractor Wheels* (T-386/89) [1996] E.P.O.R. 37 applying *ALLEN-BRADLEY/Electromagnetically operated switch* (T-21/81) [1979-85] E.P.O.R. B342.

[401] *Buckman Laboratories International/Synergistic combination* (T-393/01) [2005] E.P.O.R. 8.

[402] *MÖLYNYCKE AB* (T-102/82) [1979-85] E.P.O.R. B530, I.P.D. 6100, October 1983; cf. *TEKTRONIX* (T-699/91) [1995] E.P.O.R. 389.

fect which does not confer inventiveness on the claimed subject-matter (see T 231/97 and T 192/82)."[403]

Care must be applied in considering whether the effect is a mere side effect or the actual solution to an important aspect of a complex problem.[404] For example, a patent application for a sterile compress containing dry salt was held to be inventive and novel as against compresses using moist sodium chloride, as there were unexpected healing qualities and there had been no suggestion that such compresses could be improved merely by simply presenting them in a dry state rather than a wet state.[405] In other words, there was no obvious reason why the person skilled in the art would have used dry salt compresses in the first place.

2-223

Old prior art

The mere fact that there is a long period between the prior art and the invention does not per se demonstrate inventiveness but may assist if the patentee is able to prove that during that time there had existed an unsatisfied requirement that the invention solved.[406] Thus, if the old prior art came close to the invention but the development trend thereafter turned away from the invention and went in an entirely different direction, this may demonstrate an inventive step.[407]

2-224

Disadvantage of invention

What is the position where the claimed invention does not advance the prior art because it is less advantageous than the prior art? At a fundamental level, as the Guidelines make it clear, the validity of a patent does not depend per se on it entailing technical progress or indeed having any useful effect.[408] However, when it comes to considering inventive step, a claimed invention that does not confer a technical advantage or make a contribution to the art will normally be considered lacking in inventive step. As the Guidelines say:

2-225

"It should be noted that if the invention is the result of a foreseeable disadvantageous modification of the closest prior art, which the skilled person could clearly predict and correctly assess, and if this predictable disadvantage is not accompanied by an unexpected technical advantage, then the claimed invention does not involve an inventive step (see T 119/82 and T 155/85). In other words, a mere foreseeable worsening of the prior art does not involve an inventive step. However, if this worsening is accompanied by an unexpected technical advantage, an inventive step might be present. Similar considerations apply to the case where an invention is merely the result of an arbitrary non-functional modification of a prior-art device or of a mere arbitrary choice from a host of possible solutions (see T 72/95 and T 939/92)."[409]

---

[403] Guid. G-VII, para.10.2.
[404] *NGK/Insulators* (T-155/88) [1998] E.P.O.R. 161.
[405] (T-102/82) [1979-85] E.P.O.R. B530; I.P.D. 6100, October 1983.
[406] *VDO ADOLF SCHINDLING/Illuminating Device* (T-324/94) [1997] E.P.O.R. 146. See also *EISAI/ Benzodioxane derivatives* (T-964/92) [1997] E.P.O.R. 201 where it was held that the age of a cited document is a pointer to the presence of inventive step, but is only a subsidiary pointer where obviousness does not already follow from other reasons.
[407] *Tillott/Carminative preparation* (T-261/87) [2003] E.P.O.R. 18.
[408] Guid. G-I-3.
[409] Guid. G-VII-10.1.

2-226   However, in an interesting case, *L'AIR LIQUIDE/Gas separation*,[410] the claim was for the separation of gas mixtures by means of a semi-permeable membrane whereby the inventive part was balancing the partial pressure of one of the gas components on both sides of the membrane so that there was no partial pressure differential over the membrane. The Opposition Division rejected the patent because it noted that there was a much better way of achieving the same effect, namely adding sufficient concentrations of another gas to the feed side. However, upholding the appeal, the TBA held that the mere fact that there might be a much more effective way of carrying out the same task did not render the claim unpatentable. Indeed, it said that:

> "the apparent futility of achieving this by carrying out the claimed process cannot be said to be obvious. In fact in view of this futility, it could be said to be completely non-obvious."

2-227   It might be thought that this decision is in conflict with the Guidelines cited above. However, in the author's view it is not. It was not being suggested that the invention did not advance the prior art but rather that there was a more obvious way of advancing the prior art.

No real expectation of success

2-228   In many cases, particularly biotechnological inventions involving the isolation of a particular genetic sequence, prior art may indicate a particular research path but such a path would have been seen as giving rise to real difficulties and requiring long and complex technique. In such circumstances, even though a "signpost" exists to the invention, the person skilled in the art is unlikely to try it as they have no real expectation of success. As said in *Genentech/HIF-Gamma*[411]:

> "The Board is convinced that there is no sufficient certainty that the skilled person in this situation would have tried this method with any reasonable expectation of success. In other words, while someone might have chosen the route of the recombinant-DNA technique, he would only have attempted it despite success being very uncertain, for example because he trusted in his own luck, skill and inventive ingenuity to overcome the known and the as yet unknown problems involved, even though these problems were such that the average skilled person would expect to fail."[412]

2-229   In another case, *GENENTECH/t-PA*,[413] the invention was for a process which comprised the preparation of a protein which had a particular amino acid sequence. The patentee had found a method for cloning and expressing human t-PA in a recombinant host. The appellants argued that there was considerable interest in arriving at a solution to this problem and that the skilled person would have arrived at a solution by following the prior art. On the other hand, the patentees argued that all the uncertainties and problems that the skilled person had to face (low abundance of mRNA, size of mRNA, unknown amino acid sequence of human t-PA, and so on) showed that the solution to the problem was far from straightforward. The

---

[410] *L'AIR LIQUIDE/Gas separation* (T-1027/93) [1996] E.P.O.R. 188.

[411] *Genentech/HIF-Gamma* (T-223/92) [2003] E.P.O.R. 12.

[412] (T-223/92) [2003] E.P.O.R. 12 at [64].

[413] *GENENTECH/t-PA* (T-923/92) [1996] E.P.O.R. 275. (NB. national patents based on the same invention (although the claims were cast differently) were held invalid in England-see *GENENTECH/t-PA* [1987] R.P.C. 553 upheld on appeal [1989] R.P.C. 147.)

Technical Board of Appeal found that, although there was much incentive for solving the problem as the patentees had, the task was regarded as tough, the prospects of success were considered thin, and the announcement of the isolation by the patentees of a full-length clone encoding human t-PA was received in the interested milieus as a pleasant surprise. Accordingly, the Board concluded that there was an inventive step.[414]

Generally speaking, the more unexplored a technical field of research is, the lower the expectation of success. Conversely, where it was mere routine work for a skilled person to try with a reasonable expectation of success to create the invention, there was no inventive step.[415] Where facts are relied upon for the purpose of showing that the skilled person in the art would have been dissuaded from trying a particular line of research, it must be shown that such factors created a prejudice or constituted a real obstacle to trying out that line.[416]   **2-230**

Unreliable prior art

In certain cases, although there may be no argument about disclosure of a piece   **2-231** of prior art, the patentee has sought to argue that such a publication was inherently unreliable, i.e. because it is an unrefereed publication or because the authors had no experience in the relevant field and therefore the person skilled in the art would not have considered it. The EPO has rejected this argument because when considering inventive step, the skilled person is expected to be aware of everything made available to the public by any means and there is no rule that publications of less known authors are not taken seriously by other scientists. In every case, it was the technical content of a piece of prior art which was relevant.[417]

Selection inventions

As discussed earlier at para.2-136 when considering whether the selection of a   **2-232** particular product or sub-range from prior art which discloses a range of products is inventive, the issue of novelty and inventive step are very much intertwined. When considering the novelty of the selection invention, the issue is whether the skilled person would have seriously contemplated that the prior art identifies the product or sub-range. However, the Guidelines seek to differentiate the issue of novelty and inventive step. They say:

"The subject-matter of selection inventions differs from the closest prior art in that it represents selected sub-sets or sub-ranges. If this selection is connected to a particular technical effect, and if no hints exist leading the skilled person to the selection, then an inventive step is accepted (this technical effect occurring within the selected range may also be the same effect as attained with the broader known range, but to an unexpected degree). The criterion of 'seriously contemplating' mentioned in connection with the test for novelty of overlapping ranges should not be confused with the assessment of inventive step. For inventive step, it has to be considered whether the skilled person would have made the selection or would have chosen the overlapping range in the hope of solving the

---

[414] For cases where the TBA held that a one way street argument did succeed, see *BIOGEN/Hepatitis B virus* (T-886/91) [1999] E.P.O.R. 361; and *BIOGEN/Human beta-interferon* (T-207/94) [1999] E.P.O.R. 451.

[415] *Biogen/Hepatitis B virus e antigens* (T-717/89) [2003] E.P.O.R. 39.

[416] *Monsanto/Somatic changes* (T-333/97) [2003] E.P.O.R. 36.

[417] *British Technology Group/Newcastle disease virus* (T-145/95) [2003] E.P.O.R. 42.

underlying technical problem or in expectation of some improvement or advantage. If the answer is negative, then the claimed matter involves an inventive step."

2-233   The test of whether the skilled person "would have made the selection…in the hope of solving the underlying problem" is difficult to distinguish from the test as to whether the skilled person would have "seriously contemplated" applying the technical teaching of the prior art to the particular product or sub-range. If he would not have seriously contemplated applying that technical teaching on the basis that it did not "shine a beam" on the particular product or sub-range, it is difficult to see why it would be obvious to select the product or sub-range.

Industrial application

2-234   An invention must be capable of industrial application for it to be patentable under the EPC. This condition is satisfied if it can be made or used in any kind of industry, including agriculture.[418] This provision is interpreted widely. Industry is to be construed as meaning activities carried out continuously, independently and for financial gain.[419] Thus, use of a product in a beauty parlour has been held to constitute industrial application.[420] Article 57 requires the disclosure of a practical application. The disclosure of a means of production of a biological substance without disclosure of some profitable use for which that substance could be employed was contrary to art.57. The application did not disclose any practical way of exploiting the substance in any field of industrial activity.[421]

2-235   Indeed, it is difficult to imagine "inventions" which are not capable of industrial application which are not also excluded from patentability under art.52.[422] The Guidelines state that "industry" should be understood as meaning an activity which belongs to the useful or practical arts as distinct from the aesthetic arts. In the author's view, this is a rather rigid and somewhat meaningless distinction for the 21st century which has moved on from a rigid split between art and science. In the author's view, a useful starting point is not the distinction between art and science but rather an invention that has *in concreto* effects on the outside world (the environment) rather than being an abstract mental concept. This view might be said to owe rather too much to the philosophy of Descartes and his espousal of mind/body dualism.[423] However, it avoids the patenting of mere knowledge. Nonetheless, an invention that *does something* is not per se capable of industrial application within the meaning of the EPC. It must be shown that it does something *useful*, i.e. of benefit to mankind. The TBA declared in *Max-Planck/BDPI Phosphatase*,[424] which concerned a patent concerning the manufacture of a BDP1 polypeptide:

> "19.   No doubt exists that a BDP1 polypeptide could be 'made and used' as a further tool, in addition to the many already available in the art (cf. document D12), for exploring the complex cellular signal transduction pathways and their implications in the

---

[418]   art.57.

[419]   *Du Pont* (T-144/83) [1987] E.P.O.R. 6; I.P.D. 9098, December 1986.

[420]   *ROUSSEL-UCLAF* (T-36/83) [1986] OJ EPO 295; [1987] E.P.O.R. 1. See also *BTG/Contraceptive method* (T-74/93) [1995] E.P.O.R. 279, where there is a rather amusing discussion as to whether contraception as practised by a prostitute is capable of industrial application.

[421]   *Max-Planck/BDP1 Phosphatase* (T-870/04) [2006] E.P.O.R. 14 at [18]–[23].

[422]   A point made in the EPO Guidelines at G-III.1. Inventions excluded from patentability are discussed at para.2-249.

[423]   René Descartes was a 16th century French philosopher.

[424]   See fn.422.

regulation of cellular processes and, possibly, disease states. But the whole burden is left to the reader to guess or find a way to exploit it in industry by carrying out work in search for some practical application geared to financial gain, without any confidence that any practical application exists.

20. No suggestion or indication is given in the application of BDP1 acting as a tumour-suppressor ... the board considers that no such suggestion can be derived from the application itself or from the prior art.

21. In the board's judgment ... it identifies no practical way of exploiting it in at least one field of industrial activity. In this respect, it is considered that a vague and speculative indication of possible objectives that might or might not be achievable by carrying out further research with the tool as described is not sufficient for fulfilment of the requirement of industrial applicability. The purpose of granting a patent is not to reserve an unexplored field of research for an applicant.

22. ... This contrasts with the present case where the only practicable use suggested is to use what is claimed to find out more about the natural functions of what is claimed itself. This is not in itself an industrial application, but rather research undertaken either for its own sake or with the mere hope that some useful application will be identified."

Sufficiency

A detailed description of at least one way of carrying out the invention must be given.[425] It has always been accepted that as a matter of policy, the price for a 20-year monopoly for an invention is that the inventor must disclose a method of working that invention. Thus, as said by the TBA in *Serine protease/BAYER*,[426] "a basic principle of the patent system is that exclusive rights can only be granted in exchange for a full disclosure of the invention, which includes the need to indicate how to exploit the invention."[427] Unlike the US, it is not necessary to disclose the "best mode" of carrying out the invention under the EPC. This increases the attractiveness of the patent system because many inventors fear that the disadvantage of disclosure of their invention is not compensated for by the prospect that they may obtain patent protection. Thus, non-disclosure of the "best mode" gives them some security if the published patent application does not proceed to grant or is subsequently invalidated.   **2-236**

Under the EPC, art.83 requires that an invention is disclosed in a manner sufficiently clear and complete for it to be carried out by a person skilled in the art. The invention is defined by the claims of the patent. Thus, what is the position where the claims are sufficiently broad to encompass a wide variety of different types of apparatus or methods? The Guidelines say as follows: **2-237**

"... A single example may suffice, but where the claims cover a broad field, the application should not usually be regarded as satisfying the requirements of Art. 83 unless the description gives a number of examples or describes alternative embodiments or variations extending over the area protected by the claims. However, regard must be had to the facts and evidence of the particular case. There are some instances where even a very broad field is sufficiently exemplified by a limited number of examples or even one example (see also F-IV, 6.3). In these latter cases the application must contain, in addition to the examples, sufficient information to allow the person skilled in the art, using his common general knowledge, to perform the invention over the whole area claimed

---

[425] art.83, EPC r.42(1)(e).
[426] (T-1452/06).
[427] See [23].

without undue burden and without needing inventive skill (see T 727/95). In this context, the whole area claimed" is to be understood as substantially any embodiment falling within the ambit of a claim, even though a limited amount of trial and error may be permissible, e.g. in an unexplored field or when there are many technical difficulties (see T 226/85 and T 409/91)."[428]

2-238   Chemical compound cases can often cause difficulties because often the invention concerns a pharmacokinetic or therapeutic effect created by a particular structure. In such circumstances, the EPO takes the view that it is possible to support broad claims from a narrow base. Thus, it gives the example of an application as filed describing the preparation of a novel chemical compound having particular properties. A claim which defines that compound along with certain higher homologues may well be supported by such a description if the skilled person would have no reason to doubt the soundness of such a generalisation.[429]

2-239   The reference in the Guidelines to "undue burden and without needing inventive skill" and the need to perform the invention "over the whole area claimed" are the two key requirements under art.83. It is useful to use a mountaineering analogy. If the claims are very narrow, one can imagine a mountain with a small peak. In such circumstances, the patent must show a way up the mountain to the peak which is not too difficult. Provided at least one route is shown, it does not matter that there are other routes or indeed better routes to the peak. However, where the claims are wide, such may be because the claims seek to claim a generalised concept capable of being realised in a number of ways. This can be likened to a plateau at the top of the mountain (like Table Mountain in South Africa). Provided the disclosure in the patent has shown one way to the top, it is then easy to get to other parts of the plateau. On the other hands, the claims may be so wide as, in effect, to cover a mountain range of different peaks, i.e. they contain a discrete set of different (albeit related) inventions. In such circumstances, then it is necessary for the patent description to disclose how to get to each peak (i.e. each different discrete invention).

2-240   On these two subjects, the TBA has said the following:

"claims may not be considered allowable if they encompass subject-matter which in the light of disclosure provided by the description can be performed only with undue burden or with application of inventive skill. As for the amount of technical detail needed for a sufficient disclosure, this is a matter which depends on the correlation of the facts of each particular case with certain general parameters, such as the character of the technical field, the date on which the disclosure was presented and corresponding common general knowledge, and the amount of reliable technical detail disclosed in a document.

In certain cases, a description of one way of performing the claimed invention may be sufficient to support broad claims with functionally defined features, for example where the disclosure of a new technique constitutes the essence of the invention and the description of one way of carrying it out enables the skilled person to obtain without undue burden the same effect of the invention in a broad area by use of suitable variants of the component features. On other cases, more technical details and more than one example may be necessary in order to support claims of a broad scope, for example, where the achievement of a given technical effect by known techniques in different areas of application constitutes the essence of the invention and serious doubts exist as to whether the said effect can readily be obtained for the whole range of applications claimed. However, in all these cases, the guiding principle is always that the skilled person should, after read-

---

[428] Guid. F-III-1.
[429] *XEROX CORP* (T-133/85) [1989] E.P.O.R. 116.

ing of the description, be able to readily perform the invention over the whole area claimed without undue burden and without needing inventive skill. On the other hand, the objection of lack of sufficient disclosure presupposes that there are serious doubts, substantiated by verifiable facts, in this respect."[430]

If the person skilled in the art is unable to replicate the invention across the whole range of applications claimed without undue burden, then the application will generally be objectionable under both arts 83 and 84. Where reference is made in the description to a trade-marked product for the purpose of teaching how to perform the invention, such is dangerous because the technical nature of such a product might vary over time. However, where such a trade mark unambiguously refers to a very specific product and was available as of the priority date to the person skilled in the art, such is permissible.[431] In England. the Court of Appeal has held that where the technical contribution is one of general application, it would be wrong in principle to limit protections to the worked examples as such would make patent protection ineffectual.[432]

2-241

Plausibility of invention across the width of the claims Because of its increasing importance in patent litigation and disputes before the EPO, this section deals with arguments that the invention (as defined by the claims) is not "*plausible*" or "*credible*". This can be seen as part of the golden rule that a monopoly should correspond to, and be justified by the technical contribution to the art. In *AP-1complex/ Salk Institute for Biological Studies*,[433] the TBA rejected a claim for use of a steroid hormone for the preparation of a pharmaceutical for the treatment of tumour formation. The Board held that no hormone had been identified with such a quality and that the claim amounted to no more than invitation to set up further research programmes to see what hormones worked. In *Factor-9/John Hopkins University School of Medicine*,[434] the TBA concluded, in considering a claim to a polynucleotide encoding a polypeptide having GDF-9 activity, that the alleged invention proceeded on the basis that "GDF-9" activity belonged to a super-family with known beneficial effects.

2-242

The TBA held that there was not enough evidence in the application to show this and thus "*to make at least plausible that a solution was found to the problem which was purportedly solved*".[435]

2-243

However, the EPC requires no experimental proof for patentability or the disclosure of experimental data or results in the application when filed. Thus, where an objection is taken on the grounds that it is implausible that the claimed effect is achieved, the TBA said (in *Pancreatic cells/IPSEN*) that it is only relevant where there are doubts about the suitability of the claimed invention to solve the technical problem addressed. Where a patent application states that the invention achieves the claimed effect without providing any data to show that such is the case, such is not in itself a reason to find the invention implausible.[436] Thus, it is necessary to have substantiated doubts *for some reason other* than the lack of relevant experimental data or results in the patent application.

2-244

---

[430] *MYCOGEN/Plant Cells* (T-694/92) [1998] E.P.O.R. 114 at [5]. See also *Massachusetts Institute of Technology/Biopolymers* (T-639/95) [2003] E.P.O.R. 16 (incomplete references rendered claims insufficient in gene encoding invention).

[431] *Unilever/Antiperspirant composition* (T-67/94) [2003] E.P.O.R. 64.

[432] *Regeneron v Kymab* [2018] EWCA Civ 671.

[433] (T-609/02) ECLI:EP:BA:2004:T060902.20041027.

[434] (T-1329/04) ECLI:EP:BA:2005:T132904.20050628.

[435] See [11].

[436] *Pancreatic cells/IPSEN* (T-578/06) ECLI:EP:BA:2011:T057806.20110629 at [12]–[23].

2-245   Can the applicant rely upon evidence that a claim is plausible if such comes into existence after the date of filing or is published after the filing date? In *Factor 9/John Hopkins*, the applicant relied upon evidence published after the filing date which established that the polynucleotide did have the claimed beneficial effect. The TBA held that such evidence may not serve as the *sole* proof of plausibility.[437] The TBA said that the definition of an invention requires that that it is plausible by "*the disclosure in the application that its teaching solves the problem it purports to solve*". In contrast, in *Pancreatic cells/IPSEN* the TBA did take account of post-published literature to amount to some degree of proof that the claimed effects were plausible. However, this was in the case where the TBA had no reason to doubt the claimed effect and it was on that basis, it said that it could take account of post-published evidence.[438]

2-246   In *Warner-Lambert Co LLC v Generics (UK) Ltd*,[439] the Court of Appeal of England and Wales followed this approach and, by analogy to the Supreme Court of England and Wales' judgment in *Human Genome Science Inc v Eli Lilly & Co*,[440] held that the test was a low, threshold test.[441] It was not to be treated as the same as the "obvious to try" test for obviousness which is a higher, tougher test. The rationale as explained by the Court of Appeal is that:

> "[46] ... It is designed to prohibit speculative claiming, which would otherwise allow the armchair inventor a monopoly over a field of endeavour to which he has made no contribution. It is not designed to prohibit patents for good faith predictions which have some, albeit manifestly incomplete, basis. Such claims may turn out to be insufficient nonetheless if the prediction turns out to be untrue. A patent which accurately predicts that an invention will work is, however, not likely to be revoked on the ground that the prediction was based on the slimmest of evidence. Thus, the claims will easily be seen not to be speculative where the inventor provides a reasonably credible theory as to why the invention will or might work."

In *Warner-Lambert* the patent was found to be invalid because it was a claim to prevent pain and it was not plausible that the invention disclosed in the patent would be effective for all types of pain (it was only plausible that it would prevent inflammatory (central neuropathic) pain).

2-247   In an interesting case, *Epshtein v Comptroller-General of Patents, Designs and Trade Marks*,[442] concerning an application for a homeopathic invention, the UK Intellectual Property Office held that although the data showed that a therapeutic effect was plausible, it was rejected as the applicant for the patent did not provide a plausible explanation of the scientific theory as to how the therapeutic effect was achieved. On appeal, a deputy judge of the High Court upheld the appeal holding that it was not necessary to provide a coherent plausible theory as to why the therapeutic effect was achieved. According to the judge: "*If the therapeutic effect is plausible, then the claim is plausible even though the reason for the therapeutic*

---

[437] See [12].
[438] See [17]. The logic of this is not wholly clear as if the TBA had no reason to doubt the claimed effect in the patent application, then such suggests that there was no need for the Examining Division to consider implausibility at all.
[439] [2016] EWCA Civ 1006.
[440] [2011] UKSC 51.
[441] See [46].
[442] [2016] EWHC 1511.

effect cannot be explained."[443] Although this judgment might be seen as clashing with the excerpt in *Warner-Lambert* (cited above) that the inventor must provide a "*reasonable credible theory as to why the invention will work*", it does not. If an invention does work, then there has been a contribution to the art even if, on the current state of science, one is unable to explain why. Patents are concerned with matters practical and not matters theoretical.

The reader should not confuse classic insufficiency with plausibility. Insufficiency is concerned with the disclosure of a way to carry out the invention. Plausibility is concerned with whether it is plausible to believe that a product or process disclosed in an application achieves the claimed effect or advantage. A patent application may disclose a way of making a product but it may not be plausible that such a product has any beneficial effect or achieves the claimed effect. Thus, where a claim is to a pharmaceutical compound per se but the claim does not include the claimed effect, the patent may be classically sufficient but implausible and thus merely be a claim to a compound that does not advance the state of the art or have any practical utility. That is why plausibility is often taken in the EPO as an objection of lack of inventive step rather than one of insufficiency.[444] It could equally be said that an implausible invention is one that lacks industrial applicability.[445]

2-248

Unpatentable inventions

Introduction

As said in the start of the section on the substantive requirements under the EPC, an invention must be technical. Like other patent systems, the EPC is not concerned with inventive *concepts* per se but technical applications. As a consequence of this, art.52(2) states that the following are defined as not being inventions within the EPC:

2-249

(a) discoveries, scientific theories and mathematical methods;
(b) aesthetic creations;
(c) schemes, rules and methods for performing mental acts, playing games or doing business and programs for computers; and
(d) presentations of information.[446]

As said by the Guidelines, the items on this list are all either abstract and/or non-technical whereas an invention must be of both a concrete and technical character.[447] The most problematic of these exclusions is computer programs. Many would instinctively say that these are technical in nature. Unsurprisingly, it is this category which has caused the most difficulties and computer-related inventions are considered in a separate section. The EPC only excludes such categories from fulfilling the requirement of patentability if the alleged invention relates to the above

2-250

---

[443] See [55].
[444] As was done in (T-1329/04). See also *Pancreatic cells/IPSEN* (T-578/06) ECLI:EP:BA:2011:T057806.20110629. See para.2-213.
[445] See para.2-234 and in particular the excerpt cited there of the decision by the TBA in *Max-Planck/BDPI Phosphatase*.
[446] art.52(2).
[447] Guid. G-II-1.

categories "as such".[448] Thus, an invention which makes use of computer programs, mathematical modelling, etc. is not excluded from patentability merely because it incorporates such.

2-251   As well as the above exclusions, there are three other categories of inventions which are excluded:

- Inventions contrary to ordre public or morality.
- Surgery, therapy and diagnostic methods.
- Plants and animal varieties or essentially biological process for the production of plants or animals.[449]

2-252   In the following paragraphs we consider these exclusions. The exclusion of plants and animal varieties and essentially biological processes is considered in the section on biotechnological inventions.

Requirement of technical effect—art.52

2-253   The exclusions in art.52(2) can be considered as being aimed at preventing the patenting of inventions which are not technical. The TBA has said that the effect of art.52(3) (the "as such" provision) is that it would mean typically that "purely abstract concepts devoid of any technical implications" are excluded from protection.[450] However, the fact that a business method invention has practical utility does not mean that it avoids the art.52(2) exclusion.[451]

2-254   A mix of technical and non-technical features will suffice to avoid the exclusion under art.52.[452] Hence, the use of technical means for carrying out a method which is itself excluded, i.e. being a method for performing mental acts will usually render such a method a technical process or method and therefore an invention within the meaning of art.52(1).[453] Where claims contain non-technical elements and known technical elements, the claim will only be allowed if the interaction of the two types produces a technical effect.[454]

2-255   The technical character of an invention is assessed without regard to the prior art by the EPO.[455] This is in contrast to the "contribution" approach taken by some Member States, e.g. the UK's approach in relation to computer-related inventions.[456]

---

[448] art.52(3), Guid. G-II 2.

[449] The reader should be aware as well that if the invention is of a biotechnological nature, there are sui generis provisions which need to be considered. See para.2-281.

[450] *Hitachi/Auction Method* (T-258/03) [2004] E.P.O.R. 55 at [34].

[451] *Pitney Bowes/Undeliverable mail* (T-388/04) [2007] OJ EPO 16; [2007] E.P.O.R. 31.

[452] (T-258/03) [2004] E.P.O.R. 55.

[453] *IBM/Text clarity processing* (T-38/86) [1990] E.P.O.R. 606 cited in *Hitachi/Auction method*. See also *PBS Partnership/Controlling pension benefits systems* (T-931/95) [2002] E.P.O.R. 52 where it was held that an apparatus being a physical entity or concrete product suitable for performing or supporting an economic activity was an invention within the meaning of art.52(1).

[454] See *KOCH & STERZEL* (T-26/86) [1988] OJ EPO 19, [1988] E.P.O.R. 72; *BEATTIE/Marker* (T-158/88) [1992] E.P.O.R. 221.

[455] Guid.   G-II-2,   G-II-3.6;   *Computer   program   product/IBM*   (T-1173/97) ECLI:EP:BA:1998:T117397.19980701 confirmed in *Programs for computers* (G3/08) ECLI:EP:BA:2010:G000308.20100512.

[456] Discussed at para.2-267.

Mere Discovery

A discovery "as such" is not patentable. The EPO Guidelines say the following: **2-256**

"If a new property of a known material or article is found out, that is mere discovery and unpatentable because discovery as such has no technical effect and is therefore not an invention within the meaning of Art.52(1). If, however, that property is put to practical use, then this constitutes an invention which may be patentable. For example, the discovery that a particular known material is able to withstand mechanical shock would not be patentable, but a railway sleeper made from that material could well be patentable. To find a previously unrecognised substance occurring in nature is also mere discovery and therefore unpatentable. However, if a substance found in nature can be shown to produce a technical effect, it may be patentable. An example of such a case is that of a substance occurring in nature which is found to have an antibiotic effect. In addition, if a micro-organism is discovered to exist in nature and to produce an antibiotic, the micro-organism itself may also be patentable as one aspect of the invention. Similarly, a gene which is discovered to exist in nature may be patentable if a technical effect is revealed, e.g. its use in making a certain polypeptide or in gene therapy."[457]

It can be seen from the Guidelines that patentability lies in the wording of the claims. It is necessary to ensure that the claims maintain some particular use of the discovery whether in a particular method or its incorporation in apparatus. **2-257**

In relation to biotechnological inventions, the matter is complicated by the introduction of specific rules in the EPC which are themselves influenced by the EU Biotechnological Directive. Thus EPC r.23(c)(a) states that a biological material which is isolated from its natural environment or produced by means of a technical process even if it previously occurred in nature is patentable. Thus, a claim to a biological material which exists in nature is permissible because the claim is to the isolated material itself (and the isolation itself may be difficult) and not anything in nature which includes it. Biotechnological inventions are considered later in this chapter.[458] **2-258**

Aesthetic character

A painting may be highly innovative compared to what existed in the prior art. Thus, the Impressionist movement represented a radical change from classical art which ultimately aimed for photorealism. However, as made clear in the Guidelines, the aesthetic effect is not patentable.[459] A distinction should be drawn between the technical means used to achieve an aesthetic effect (which is patentable) and the aesthetic effect itself (which is not). According to the Guidelines: **2-259**

"For example, features relating solely to the aesthetic or artistic effect of the information content of a book, or to its layout or letterfont, would not be considered as technical features. Neither would features such as the aesthetic effect of the subject of a painting or the arrangement of its colours or its artistic (e.g. Impressionist) style be technical. Nevertheless, if an aesthetic effect is obtained by a technical structure or other technical means, although the aesthetic effect itself is not of a technical character, the means of obtaining it may be. For example, a fabric may be provided with an attractive appear-

---

[457] Guid. G-II-3.1.
[458] See para.2-281.
[459] Guid. G-II-3.4.

ance by means of a layered structure not previously used for this purpose, in which case a fabric incorporating such structure might be patentable."[460]

2-260   In a recent UK case, a claim in a patent was to a child's toy consisting of a water fusible polyhedral bead (i.e. gem-like) whereas the prior art was a water fusible round bead. The patent claimed that such was more aesthetic and less tiresome to a child.[461] The defendant sought to revoke the patent on the grounds that such was a claim to an invention of aesthetic character. The court rejected the argument, considering that the claim was not to a particular design or group of designs. It considered that a distinction needs to be drawn between an invention which contributes a new aesthetic effect (patentable) and one which claims an aesthetic creation as such (not patentable).[462] It held that the claim was of the former nature.

Presentation of information

2-261   In a number of decisions in Germany, the Bundesgerichtshof (BGH) has considered the patentability of user interface designs (see *X ZR* 47/07; *X ZR* 37/13 and *X ZR* 110/13). In particular, in *X ZR* 110/13, the BGH considered whether Apple's "slide to unlock" feature in its mobile phones was patentable. It held that the specific "swipe" gesture could be considered a technical contribution but not the feedback of that swipe gesture via an unlock image. Such distinctions are fine. In *X ZR* 37/13, which concerned an application whereby a capsule with a micro-camera could be swallowed and then would take a series of "stills" whilst travelling through the gastro-intestinal tract, the BGH considered that such took into account the physiological characteristics of human perception and reception of information and held that this was a technical solution to a technical problem.

Computer-related inventions

2-262   Article 52 of the EPC states that computer programs, along with mathematical methods, schemes, rules and methods for performing mental acts and presentations of information are not to be regarded as patentable. This is qualified by art.52(3), which states that this exclusion of patentability only applies to the extent that the European patent relates to such excluded subject-matter or activities "as such".

2-263   The interpretation of art.52 in the context of computer-related inventions has been very problematic with ultimately, a series of questions being referred to the EBA by the President of the EPO concerning what were said to be divergent decisions of the TBA in the determination of whether a computer-related invention was excluded from patentability. It was clear from the decisions of the TBA that there was a "soft" approach to art.52 whereby provided the claimed invention had some type of technical effect, it was permissible, whereas the "hard" approach (sometimes called the "contribution approach") considered whether the contribution of the claimed invention to the prior art was technical.

---

[460] Guid. G-II-3.4.
[461] *Epoch Co Ltd v Character Options Ltd* [2017] EWHC 556 (IPEC). The beads were used by a child to create aesthetically pleasing patterns that were fused together through the addition of water.
[462] See [48] citing inter alia *Hettling-Denker/Translucent building materials* (T-686/90) [2004] E.P.O.R. 5. In *Epoch v Character Options*, the defendant's argument was based on the "contribution" approach that the UK has adopted for computer-related inventions which differs to the EPO approach.

In *Opinion/Admissibility* (G3/08)[463] the EBA declined to answer the reference by   **2-264**
the President on the grounds that it was inadmissible as the case law was not in
conflict. However, in reaching that decision, it considered the case law and whether
such was divergent. In doing so, it held that in fact, the "hard approach" had been
rejected by various TBAs and that the "soft" approach was correct. In particular, it
reviewed the history of TBA decisions in this area as follows:

(a)   In *IBM/Computer Programs* (T-1173/97)[464] the TBA had said that a techni-
      cal effect was required which went beyond the normal physical interac-
      tions between the software and the hardware on which it is run and that what
      was required was a "further technical effect". However, in contrast, the TBA
      had specifically excluded consideration of whether the contribution over the
      prior art was of a technical nature. In (G3/08), the EBA sought to illustrate
      this point by saying that if a claim was to a "cup carrying a certain picture",
      according to the "contribution approach", cups are known so that the
      contribution to the art was only in a field excluded from patentibility by
      art.52 and thus should be refused. The EBA said that in (T-1173/97), the
      TBA had rejected the "contribution" approach and that issue of patent-
      ability and technical effect had to be considered without regard to the prior
      art.[465]

(b)   In *Hitachi/Auction Method* (T-258/03) and *Microsoft* (T-424/03) and other
      decisions since then, the decisions of the TBA had in fact *followed IBM/
      Computer Programs* (T-1173/97) insofar as it rejected the "contribution ef-
      fect" argument but they had *not followed* it on its requirement of "further
      technical effect". No decision of the TBA had followed *IBM/Computer
      Programs* (T-1173/97) on the requirement of "further technical effect" and
      the approach in *Microsoft* (T-424/03) and *Hitachi/Auction Methods* (T-258/
      03) which rejected the "further technical effect" had not been challenged in
      any later decisions.[466]

(c)   Accordingly, there was a consistent approach in the case law of the TBA that
      a claim to a particular kind of computer-readable medium memory with
      certain special properties, e.g. a Blu-Ray disk was "evidentially not
      excluded from patentability" by arts 52(2) and 52(3) regardless of whether
      such was new at the relevant date.[467] Thus, to take the example of the cup
      above, a claim to "a cup decorated with picture X" was not liable to be
      excluded from patentability under art.52.

(d)   Thus, the EBA said that the present position of the case law is that a claim
      in the area of computer programs can avoid exclusion under art.52 merely
      by explicitly mentioning the use of a computer or a computer-readable stor-
      age medium and that the approach in *IBM/Computer programs* (T-1173/
      97) of a requirement of a "further technical effect" was not the law and had
      not been followed since that decision.[468]

---

[463]   [2010] E.P.O.R. 36.
[464]   *IBM/Computer Programs* (T-1173/97).
[465]   See (G3/08) at [10.4]–[10.6].
[466]   Notwithstanding this, it is of note that the Guidelines still refer to the requirement of a further techni-
        cal effect (e.g. see Guid. G-II-3.6). It is unfortunate that the EBA considered that there was no need
        to clarify this issue.
[467]   See [10.8.5].
[468]   See [10.13].

(e) However, whilst it might be the case that one could overcome the exclusion of programs for computers by merely requiring formulation of the claim as a computer implemented method or computer program product, such was to ignore the fact that the question of "technical contribution" was legitimate to contemplate when considering whether the claim lacked inventive step. Whilst some may consider that distasteful, it is an approach which has been consistently applied[469] and it was legitimate to ask whether, when considering inventive step, there was a technical solution to a technical problem.

2-265   Since the decision in (G3/08), the approach by the TBA to computer-related inventions has been somewhat inconsistent. Thus, in *INTEL/Reduced flicker*[470] the TBA held that the EBA in (G3/08) had held that the definition of the "further technical effect" given in (T-1173/97) stood as the established case law citing (G3/98) at [10.3] and [10.4]. However, in fact, these paragraphs in (G3/98) were referring to the rejection of the "contribution approach" in (T-1173/97) and not the adoption of the "further technical effect". It is quite clear that in *Opinion/Admissibility* (G3/08), the EBA was of the view that the decision of the TBA in (T-1173/97) concerning the requirement of "further technical effect" had in fact not been followed in subsequent cases when considering the issue of exclusions of patentability.[471] As said by the EBA, the present position of the case law is that a claim in the area of computer programs can avoid exclusion under arts 52(2)(c) and (3) "merely by explicitly mentioning the use of a computer or a computer-readable storage medium" but that a claim which specifies no more than "Program X on a computer-readable storage medium" or "a method of operating a computer according to program X" will still fail to be patentable for lack of an inventive step under arts 52(1) and 56.[472] In contrast to *INTEL/Reduced flicker*, in *Microsoft/Digital rights management*[473] the TBA held that it was the established case law of the Boards of Appeal that method claims to a method being carried out by computer devices and a claim to a "computer-readable medium" were not excluded from patentability.[474]

2-266   Thus, in summary, in EPO proceedings, avoiding a ground of lack of patentability under art.52(2) and art.52(3) for computer-related inventions will be an easy task of ensuring that there is no claim to a computer program simpliciter but rather the operation of that computer program on hardware. However, the real ground of objection will come when considering whether there is an inventive step. At that point, it must be shown that the invention in the claim represents a technical solution to a technical problem and it will be no answer to that to merely say that the program is run on a computer.

---

[469]   At [10.13]. See also *DUNS* (T-154/04). The approach of the EPO to inventive step for computer-related inventions is considered at paras 2-189 to 2-195.

[470]   (T-979/06) [2011] E.P.O.R. 14.

[471]   e.g. see [10.7.1]–[10.8.2] and [10.13]. It should be said that in *INTEL/Reduced flicker*, the requirement of "Further technical effect" was held to be satisfied so that it made no difference to the outcome of the decision.

[472]   See [10.13].

[473]   (T-1658/06) [2011] E.P.O.R. 22.

[474]   Citing *Hitachi* (T-258/03) and *Microsoft* (T-424/03).

It should be noted that Member States have not all followed the above approach. **2-267**
Hence, in the UK, the "contribution" approach is applied. Thus, the Court of Appeal in *Aerotel v Telco; Macrossan*[475] has endorsed the following four-step test:

(1) properly construe the claim;
(2) identify the actual contribution;
(3) ask whether it falls solely within the excluded subject-matter; and
(4) check whether the actual or alleged contribution is actually "technical in nature".

It can be appreciated that the English approach is in reality to apply the approach in *Hitachi* but to art.52 rather than art.56 (inventive step). It probably matters little whether the assessment as to whether the contribution over the prior art is technical occurs under art.52 (patentability) or under art.56 (inventiveness). So, although the court rejected the EPO approach in *Hitachi*,[476] the difference is probably more academic than real. In both jurisdictions, a patent will not be granted unless the claims embody a technical contribution which is inventive over the prior art. **2-268**

Inventions contrary to ordre public or public morality

Article 53(a) excludes from patentability inventions, the publication or exploitation of which would be contrary to *ordre public* or morality, provided that the exploitation shall not be deemed to be so contrary merely because it is prohibited by law or regulation in some or all of the contracting states.[477] Any invention, the publication or exploitation of which would be contrary to *ordre public* or morality is specifically excluded from patentability. The purpose of this is to exclude from protection inventions likely to induce riot or public disorder, or to lead to criminal or other generally offensive behaviour; one "obvious" example of subject-matter given by the EPO Guidelines is an anti-personnel mine.[478] This provision is likely to be invoked only in rare and extreme cases.[479] A fair test to apply is to consider whether it is probable that the public in general would regard the invention as so abhorrent that the grant of patent rights would be inconceivable.[480] **2-269**

In some cases, where there is offensive material in the application, refusal of a patent may not be necessary. For instance, where the invention has both an offensive and a non-offensive use, e.g. a process for breaking open locked safes, its use by a burglar being offensive, but its use by a locksmith in the case of emergency, **2-270**

---

[475] *Aerotel v Telco; Macrossan* [2007] R.P.C. 7. See also *Symbian v The Comptroller General* [2008] EWCA Civ 1066.

[476] The court considered itself bound by its own earlier decisions under the doctrine of stare decisis. An appeal to the House of Lords was turned down.

[477] In the Biotechnological Directive, art.6(1) states that inventions shall be considered unpatentable where their commercial exploitation would be contrary to ordre public or morality. This provision is also largely mirrored in TRIPS art.27(2).

[478] This example is somewhat problematic. It would appear to suggest that military weapons designed to kill cannot be patented. Whilst the author has considerable sympathy to this, it seems unlikely that ordre public objections are intended to exclude military inventions as a class whose aim must be considered largely to destroy and kill the enemy. The EPO has allowed the patenting of weapons such as inventive firearms and missile launchers. Anti-personnel mines might be considered a particularly appalling type of weapon but they are no worse than any weapon whose purpose is to kill.

[479] Guid. G-II-4.1.

[480] Guid. G-II 4.1.

inoffensive. In such a case, no objection arises under art.53(a), but if the application contains an explicit reference to a use which is contrary to *ordre public* or morality, deletion of this reference will be required under the terms of EPC r.34(1)(a).

2-271 Specific public policy considerations apply to the patenting of biotechnological inventions relating to human cells because of sui generis rules in the implementing regulations. These are discussed later in this chapter.[481]

Surgery, therapy and diagnostic methods

2-272 Article 53(c) of the EPC provides as follows:

> "methods for treatment of the human or animal body by surgery or therapy and diagnostic methods practised on the human or animal body; this provision shall not apply to products, in particular substances or compositions, for use in any of these methods."

2-273 Prior to EPC 2000, art.53(c) was art.52(4) which deemed that such methods were not capable of industrial application. The wording of art.53(c) is an editorial adjustment which is not intended to create any substantive change. It was done to reflect the fact that art.52(4) was better considered as an exception to patentability for reasons of public health and not lack of industrial applicability.[482]

2-274 The policy behind the exclusion of such methods is that the medical treatment of humans or the veterinary treatment of animals should not be hampered by patents.[483] It has also been said by the Enlarged Board of Appeal that its intention is only to free from restraint non-commercial and non-industrial medical and veterinary medical activities.[484] The EPO have held that the exception to patentability in art.53(c) must be construed narrowly and does not apply to non-therapeutic treatments.[485] A method does not fall within art.53(c) if:

> "there is no functional link and hence no physical causality between its constituent steps carried out in relation to a therapy device and the therapeutic effect product on the body by the device."[486]

2-275 Thus, a method for controlling stimulation energy in a pacemaker did not fall within art.53(c) as such was a refinement which did not have the effect of preventing or treating a pathological condition.[487] "Therapy" means the curing of a disease or malfunction of the body and covers prophylactic treatment, e.g. immunisation against a certain disease.[488] It includes treatment with chemical substances or treat-

---

[481] See para.2-313.
[482] *Diagnostic methods* (G-1/04) [2006] E.P.O.R. 161 at [11]; *Genentech* (T-1020/03) [2006] E.P.O.R. 9 at [49].
[483] *BRUKER/Non-invasive measurement* (T-285/86) [1988] E.P.O.R. 3357; *NYCOMED/ Contrast Agent* (T-655/92) [1998] E.P.O.R. 206; *Diagnostic methods* (G-01/04) [2006] E.P.O.R. 15 at [4].
[484] *Eisai/Second Medical Indication* (G-05/83) [1979–85] E.P.O.R. Vol.B, 241.
[485] (T-144/83) [1987] E.P.O.R. 6; I.P.D. 9098, December 1986.
[486] *Siemens/Flow Measurement* (T-245/87) [1989] E.P.O.R. 241.
[487] *ELA Medical/Therapeutic Method* (T-789/96) [2003] E.P.O.R. 3 at [2.2].
[488] e.g. (T-36/83) [1987] E.P.O.R. 1; I.P.D. 9097, December 1986 (claim to use of chemical product for skin-cleansing did not relate to medical therapy); *WILLIAM RORER* (T-81/84) [1988] E.P.O.R. 297; I.P.D. 10054, July–August 1987 (treatment of menstrual discomfort held to be a therapeutic treatment).

ment with compositions in general.[489] In relation to inventions relating to cosmetic surgery, the Board of Appeal has said that the intention of the legislator was that only those treatments by therapy or surgery are excluded from patentability which:

"are suitable for or potentially suitable for maintaining or restoring the health, the physical integrity and the physical well being of a human being or an animal and to prevent diseases."[490]

Diagnostic methods

When considering whether the claim is to a diagnostic method, the EBA has said that it is necessary to bear in mind the various steps involved in diagnosis. These are: **2-276**

(i)   the examination phase involving the collection of data;
(ii) the comparison of these data with standard values;
(iii) the finding of any significant deviation, i.e. a symptom, during the comparison; and
(iv) the attribution of the deviation to a particular clinical picture, i.e. the deductive medical or veterinary decision phase.[491]

Claims will generally be allowed unless they consist of: **2-277**

(a) the actual intellectual diagnostic phase;
(b) the steps necessary to making such a diagnosis; and
(c) a step involving interaction with the human or animal body.[492]

In *Medi-Physics/Treatment by surgery*[493] the EBA had to consider the application of the above principles. In particular, it had to contemplate whether an imaging method for a diagnostic purpose which comprised or encompassed a step consisting of physical intervention practised on the human or animal body (namely the injection of a contrast agent into the heart) was excluded from patent protection under art.53(c). The EBA held that a claimed imaging method which comprised or encompassed an invasive step representing a substantial physical intervention on the body (which required professional medical expertise and which entailed a substantial health risk) was excluded from patentability under art.53(c). Moreover, where there were a number of steps and one of the steps included a step excluded from protection under art.53(c), then the whole claim was excluded. However, if such a step was disclaimed, the exclusion would not apply. **2-278**

Diagnostic methods do not cover all methods related to diagnosis. Methods for obtaining information (data, physical quantities) from the living human or animal body are not excluded by art.53(c) if the information obtained merely provides intermediate results which, on their own, do not enable a decision to be made on the treatment necessary. However, an invention is of a diagnostic character where the method includes an essential step or steps which are to be implemented by a **2-279**

[489] *EISAI* (G-05/83) [1985] OJ EPO 64; [1979–85] E.P.O.R. Vol.B, 241 at [10].
[490] *General Hospital Corp/Hair removal method* (T-383/90) [2005] E.P.O.R. 33.
[491] *Diagnostic methods* (G-1/04) [2006] E.P.O.R. 15 at [5].
[492] (G-1/04) [2006] E.P.O.R. 15 at [8].
[493] (G1/07) [2010] E.P.O.R. 25.

doctor or under their responsibility.[494] Generally such methods include X-ray and NMR investigations and blood pressure measurements.

Products for use in therapeutic or diagnostic methods

2-280   The last part of art.53(c) means that patents may be obtained for products, substances or compositions which are used in therapeutic or diagnostic methods. Thus, surgical, therapeutic and diagnostic instruments and claims to particular substances or composition for use in any surgical, therapeutic or diagnostic method are patentable.[495] However, a claim for the *use* of a substance or composition for the treatment of the human or animal body by therapy will fall within this prohibition.[496] The effect of this is that a doctor need not be concerned with whether or not there is a patent for product X when using X in a particular therapeutic, surgical or diagnostic procedure but only the patentee may manufacture X if it is to be used for such a procedure.

Biotechnological inventions

2-281   Many people consider that biotechnology inventions will make a large impact on all of our lives in the 21st century. Now that the Human Genome Project (the mapping of the human gene) has been completed, all that remains is to discover what function each part of the human genome performs (if any, as it is now recognised that much of the human genome has no obvious purpose at all). This is a huge undertaking, as the human gene sequence is incredibly long. Similarly, with animals and plants, biotechnology companies are keen to discover what effect each part of a gene has on the organism or its immediate environment (if any). Once the function of part of a gene is discovered, biotechnology companies can try and isolate such a sequence, if such has a beneficial effect, and insert it into other organisms to produce what is known as a transgenic organism. It is this aspect of biotechnology which is seen as very exciting. Biotechnology companies invest considerable resources into discovering the function of different parts of a gene. As a result, they will often seek patents to protect their efforts. Such patents will often seek to claim the discovered technical effect of part of a gene sequence of a product found in nature. Thus, a particular plant may have an anti-fungal effect. Biotechnological companies will usually put considerable effort into isolating that relevant sequence in the DNA of that plant which has such an effect. They would then seek to claim use of that particular sequence in producing an anti-fungal effect.

2-282   However, from the perspective of the patent lawyer, biotechnology inventions give rise to two concerns. The first concern is a moral concern, namely that biotechnology inventions can be concerned with, broadly put, the patenting of "life" and that such is objectionable—particularly, insofar as it relates to human life. In particular, this concern relates to new "Frankenstein" forms of life. The second

---

[494] (T-655/92) [1998] E.P.O.R. 206.

[495] Guid. G–II–4.2. See also, (G 05/83) *Second medical indication/EISAI* [1985] OJ EPO 64; [1979–85] E.P.O.R. Vol.B, 241 at [14]. See also *BAXTER/Blood Extraction Method* (T-329/44) [1998] E.P.O.R. 363 where the TBA said if the claimed subject-matter is actually confined to operating an apparatus for performing a method with the technical aim of facilitating blood flow towards a blood extraction point, the operation of the apparatus itself has no therapeutic purpose or effect and is therefore not excluded from patentability under art.53(c).

[496] *Second medical invention/EISAI* (G-05/83) [1985] OJ EPO 64; [1979–85] E.P.O.R. Vol.B, 241 at [12].

concern is that there has existed for many years the ability to obtain protection for plant varieties via plant breeders' rights and that it was inappropriate for there to be "double protection".

These concerns have meant that objections to biotechnology inventions have **2-283** arisen under art.53(a) (*ordre public*). This is discussed further below.[497] The second concern is that art.53(b) EPC says that European patents shall not be granted in respect of:

> "plant or animal varieties or essentially biological processes for the production of plants or animals; this provision does not apply to microbiological processes or the products thereof."

EU Biotech Directive

The issue of the patentability of biotechnological inventions has also been much **2-284** discussed within the EU. These discussions have resulted in the adoption of Dir.98/ 44/EC of 6 July 1998 on the legal protection of biotechnological inventions ("the Biotechnology Directive").[498] This Directive required Member States to harmonise their national patent laws in the area of patentability of biotechnological inventions by 2000. Although the EPO is not bound by EU law, it took the view that the Directive was essentially based on the case law of the Boards of Appeal and its interpretation of the EPC.[499] Accordingly, the EPO took the view that implementation of the Directive merely entailed framing an interpretation of the applicable provisions of the EPC specifically to comply with the Directive. Therefore, it was of the view that amendment of its Implementing Regulations was the appropriate instrument for implementing the Directive. Accordingly, a new chapter entitled "Chapter V Biotechnological Inventions" was added to the rules.[500] In essence, these rules repeat definitions set out in the Directive and expressly state that the Directive shall be used as a supplementary means of interpretation.[501] This means that the CJEU's judgments on the interpretation of the Biotechnology Directive are relevant but not binding to the interpretation of art.53(b) and the Implementing Regulations insofar as they relate to biotechnological inventions.

However, in 2016, a tension developed between the EPC's approach to patent- **2-285** ability of biotechnology inventions and that of the EU in relation to inventions for products derived from essentially biological processes. The EU Commission took the approach that such should not be patentable under the Biotechnology Directive and in November 2016, issued a non-binding notice to that effect. However, in earlier decisions, the EBA had taken the view that that such were patentable. Technically, at a legal level, there was no formal conflict as EU Commission Notices are not binding. Furthermore, the EPC makes it clear that that in the event of a conflict between the Implementing Regulations and the EPC, the latter prevails.[502] However, in June 2017, the EPO did an "about turn" and issued a notice that overturned earlier EBA decisions and by a decision of the Administrative Council, amended the Implementing Regulations to align them with the EU's ap-

---

[497] See para.2-313.
[498] See para.2-577.
[499] *EPO Notice dated 1 July 1999 concerning the amendment of the Implementing Regulations to the EPC* [1999] OJ EPO 572 at Recital 8.
[500] EPC rr.26–29.
[501] EPC r.26(1).
[502] art.164(2).

proach and thus overturn the EBA decisions. This illustrates the uneasy relationship between the EPC and EU law in the field of patents where there is an overlap. It is perhaps surprising that the EPO felt the need to overturn the decisions of the EBA based upon a non-binding notice from the EU Commission. It also undermines the EPO's initial view that the Directive is aligned with the case law of the EPO.

Definition of "biotechnological invention"

2-286   For the purpose of the EPC, a "biotechnological invention" is an invention which concerns a product consisting of or containing biological material or a process by means of which biological material is produced, processed or used. "Biological material" itself is defined as any material containing genetic information and is capable of reproducing itself or being reproduced in a biological system.[503]

Mere discovery

2-287   The EPC has always excluded discoveries from being patentable subject matter. In the field of biotechnology, a particular concern has been attempts to patent human DNA genetic sequences. In this regard, the EPO distinguishes between such claims simpliciter and claims to biological material which is isolated from its natural environment. Prior to the introduction of EPC rr.26–29, the EPO considered in *HOWARD FLOREY/Relaxin*,[504] in opposition proceedings, an objection by the Green Party of the European Parliament to the grant of a patent for H2-relaxin, which had had no previously recognised existence. The patentee had developed a process for obtaining H2-relaxin and the DNA encoding it, had characterised these products by their chemical structure and had found a use for the protein. A typical claim was for a DNA fragment which coded for a certain amino acid sequence. The Green Party claimed that the subject-matter of the opposed patent lacked novelty and were mere discoveries, since the gene that encodes relaxin has always been present in the female human body. The Opposition Division rejected this ground, stating that the claims to cDNAs (i.e. DNA copies of human mRNA encoding relaxin) did not occur in the human body. It went on to consider the claims to natural DNA fragments encoding H2-relaxin; the latter had not been known before and had no previously recognised existence. It said that it was established patent practice to recognise novelty for a natural substance which had been isolated for the first time and had no previously recognised existence.

2-288   Following the amendment of the implementing regulations to align the EPC with the Biotechnology Directive, the Implementing Regulations introduced various rules to permit the patenting of isolated biotechnology material. Thus, EPC r.27 stipulates that biotechnology inventions are patentable if they concern "biological material which is isolated from its natural environment or produced by means of a technical process even if it previously occurred in nature".[505]

2-289   In relation to the human body, EPC r.29 also says:

> "(1)   The human body, at the various stages of its formation and development, and the simple discovery of one of its elements, including the sequence or partial sequence of a gene, cannot constitute patentable inventions.
>
> (2)   An element isolated from the human body or otherwise produced by means of a

---

[503] EPC r.26(2), (3).
[504] [1995] E.P.O.R. 541.
[505] EPC r.27(a).

technical process, including the sequence or partial sequence of a gene, may constitute a patentable invention, even if the structure of that element is identical to that of a natural element."

It is significant at EPC r.29(2) that the EPC permits the patenting of DNA frag- **2-290** ments provided such is "isolated" from the human body. Thus, in relation to the human body, this approach mirrors what the EPO said in *Howard Florey/Relaxin* was established patent practice. However, the invention must still be capable of industrial application.[506]

Plant varieties and biotechnological inventions

As discussed in Ch.6, "Plant Variety Rights", plant varieties are protectable under **2-291** sui generis rights.[507] In particular, there exists an EU Regulation which confers a unitary EU Plant Variety Right. The legislative history behind the exclusion of plant variety rights in art.53(b) of the EPC was fully examined in *NOVARTIS II/ Transgenic Plant*,[508] a decision of the EBA. The EBA noted that art.53(b) was derived from art.2(b) of the Strasbourg Patent Convention. The EBA further noted that art.2(b) of the Strasbourg Patent Convention stipulated that contracting states were not bound to provide for the grant of patents in respect of plant varieties. In other words, it was left to the national legislator to decide whether or not to grant patents for plant varieties. The reason for this was that art.2(1) of the International Convention for the Protection of New Varieties 1961 (UPOV) (now superseded by the 1991 Convention) did not permit the simultaneous protection of both plant breeders' rights and a patent for a plant variety.[509] Accordingly, the legislator of the EPC decided to ban the grant of patents in respect of plant varieties. As noted by the EBA, the purpose of art.53(b) was to ban the grant of a European patent for which there existed plant variety protection under the 1961 UPOV Convention.[510] Thus, the EBA noted that there was nothing in the *travaux préparatoires* to suggest that art.53(b) could or should exclude subject-matter for which no protection under a plant breeders' rights system was available. The EPC and the 1961 UPOV Convention were intended to be entirely complementary. Indeed, in the amendments to the Implementing Regulations, "plant variety" has the same definition as that in the 1991 UPOV Convention and the EU Plant Variety Right.

In *NOVARTIS II/Transgenic plant*, the EBA had to consider certain questions **2-292** which had been referred by the TBA concerning the patentability of a transgenic plant. The application related to the control of plant pathogens in agricultural crops. It included claims to transgenic plants containing in their genomes specific foreign genes, the expression of which resulted in the production of antipathogenically active substances and to methods of preparing such plants. Thus the transgenic plants killed or inhibited the growth of pathogens. The nature of the invention was that one could produce a large number of different agricultural plants, each containing the antipathogenically-active gene. In effect, the product claims of the patent application covered *any* plant variety which contained the inserted foreign genes. Accordingly, the TBA considered that it was not patentable. The TBA did not accept

---

[506] See on this, para.2-234.
[507] See Ch.6 for a full discussion of plant variety rights.
[508] (G-1/98) [2000] OJ EPO 111; [2000] E.P.O.R. 303.
[509] The ban on double protection was abandoned in the 1991 UPOV Convention (see Ch.6, "Plant Variety Rights in Europe").
[510] *NOVARTIS II/Transgenic plant* (G-1/98) [2000] OJ EPO 111; [2000] E.P.O.R. 303 at [3.6].

the argument that if the claim comprised more than a single plant variety, it was therefore patentable, saying that such was contrary to the normal rules of logic. It said that the concept that specific embodiments of an invention, namely actual plant varieties, were not patentable but that a broad claim to plants which included all such varieties was patentable, was "a notion quite alien to patent law in general".

2-293   The matter was referred to the EBA. The crucial question which the TBA referred to the EBA was whether a claim which related to a transgenic plant avoided the prohibition on patenting in art.53(b), even though it embraced an infinite number of plant varieties. The EBA said that it is not the wording but the substance of a claim which is decisive in assessing the subject-matter to which the claim is directed. To do that, one must identify the underlying invention. Thus, it said that it is relevant how generic or specific the claimed invention is. It said that the inventor who has invented a fastening means, characterised in that they consist of a specific material, has invented neither a nail, nor a screw nor a bolt. Rather, their invention is directed to fastening means generally. Such is a generic claim and not merely a claim to a large number of different fastening means. The EBA then recited the definition of "plant variety" in art.1(vi) of the UPOV 1991 Convention and stated that such should be contrasted from a plant defined by single recombinant DNA sequence, which is not a concrete living being but an abstract and open definition embracing an *indefinite* number of individual entities defined by a part of its genotype or by a property bestowed on it by that part. Thus, the invention did not set out the characteristics necessary to assess the homogeneity or stability of varieties claimed. The EBA said that the claimed invention neither expressly nor implicitly defined a single variety or a multiplicity of varieties which necessarily consisted of several individual varieties. Hence the subject-matter of the invention was neither limited nor directed to a variety or varieties.[511] The EBA said that such an invention could not be protected by plant variety rights. The inventor in the genetic engineering field could not obtain appropriate protection because they would always be limited to a few varieties, even though they had provided the means for inserting the gene into all appropriate plant varieties. Accordingly, as the EBA had held that as the purpose of art.53(b) was to exclude from protection inventions which were protectable as plant varieties pursuant to the 1961 UPOV Convention, such an invention was not excluded from patentability under art.53(b). This decision is now reflected in EPC r.27(b) which states that biotechnological inventions are patentable if they concern:

"Without prejudice to Rule 28, paragraph 2, plants or animals if the technical feasibility of the invention is not confined to a particular plant or animal variety."

2-294   The reference to "Without prejudice to 28, paragraph 2" was inserted by a decision of the Administrative Council dated 29 June 2017 whereby the rules were changed to ban the patenting of animal or plant inventions which consisted of products derived from essentially biological processes. This is discussed below.[512]

2-295   The EPC rules define a "plant variety". The definition is:

"any plant grouping within a single botanical taxon of the lowest known rank, which grouping, irrespective of whether the conditions for the grant of a plant variety right are fully met, can be:

---

[511] See para.3.1 of the Decision.
[512] See para.2-302.

(a)   defined by the expression of the characteristics that results from a given genotype or combination of genotypes,
(b)   distinguished from any other plant grouping by the expression of at least one of the said characteristics, and
(c)   considered as a unit with regard to its suitability for being propagated unchanged.[513]"

As discussed above, this definition should be read in light of the purpose of   **2-296**
art.53(b) which is to exclude protection for plant varieties that qualify or could qualify for protection under plant breeders' rights.

In a subsidiary question in *NOVARTIS II/Transgenic Plant*, the EBA ruled that   **2-297**
the exception to patentability in art.53(b) applied to plant varieties irrespective of the way in which they were produced. Therefore, plant varieties containing genes introduced into an ancestral plant by recombinant gene technology are excluded from patentability. Protection under the UPOV Convention applied irrespective of how the variety was obtained.

Essentially biological processes

As well as plant and animal varieties, art.53(b) excludes the patentability of es-   **2-298**
sentially biological processes for the production of animals or plants but not for microbiological processes or their products. Such an exception is narrowly construed.[514] The Implementing Regulation defines a process for the production of plants or animals as being essentially biological if it consists "entirely of natural phenomena such as crossing or selection".[515] This of course points towards the traditional process of creating plant or animal varieties by selecting appropriate parent plants or animals with desirable traits or phenotypes for the purpose of creating a new hybrid offspring which combines such traits in a desirable manner. Crossing or selection are, of course, typical plant breeding techniques which do not require any human intervention at a genetic level. Plant breeders merely facilitate and encourage natural processes by planting pollen of one variety onto the stigma (the female receptor) of other flowers and modifying natural conditions such as temperature, humidity, etc. Prior to the new rules, the Board of Appeal, in the context of plants, stated that:

> "Whether or not a (non-micro-biological) process is to be considered as essentially biological within the meaning of Article 53(b) has to be judged on the basis of the essence of the invention taking into account the totality of human intervention and its impact on the result achieved. It is the opinion of the Board that the necessity for human intervention alone is not yet a sufficient criterion for its not being 'essentially biological'. Human interference may only mean that the process is not a 'purely biological' process, without contributing anything beyond a trivial level. It is further not a matter simply of whether such intervention is of a quantitative or qualitative character."[516]

The definition in the rules to "crossing or selection" finds echoes in *NOVARTIS*   **2-299**
II/Transgenic Plant, where the EBA said that:

---

[513] EPC r.26(4).
[514] (T-320/87) [1990] OJ EPO 3; [1990] E.P.O.R. 173 at [6].
[515] EPC r.26(5).
[516] (T-320/87) [1990] OJ EPO 3; [1990] E.P.O.R. 173. See also H-R Jaenichen and A. Schrell, "The European Patent Office's Recent Decisions on Patenting Plants" [1993] 12 E.I.P.R. 466, 469.

"varieties have been generally considered to be the result of the breeding process (Cf. *Boringer Industrial Property Rights and Biotechnology, Plant Variety Protection No. 55*, June 1988, page 45, point 1.1). In essence, this means that they are the result of the processes of selection and crossing, including modern techniques such as cell fusion which do not occur under natural conditions."[517]

2-300   Thus, the new definition appears aimed at excluding from patentability those processes which are normally deployed to create plant varieties. If so, then the ban on patenting essentially biological processes for the production of plants would appear to ban only those processes which are typically used for producing a plant variety. In other words, the EPC bans the patentability not only of plant varieties but also the method of creating a plant variety.[518] Hence, one should construe "essentially biological process" in the context of avoiding the grant of patents for which there exists protection under plant variety rights. There is therefore a symmetry of approach to the meanings of "plant variety" and "essentially biological".

2-301   The correctness of the approach whereby it was intended not to grant double protection under the sui generis plant variety laws and patents was confirmed in the joined cases of *Essentially biological processes* (G2/07) and (G1/08).[519] In those decisions, the EBA had to consider whether a non-microbiological process for the production of plants consisting of sexually crossing the whole genomes of plants and thereafter selecting plants fell under the exclusion of art.53(b). It held that such was excluded from patentability and that this kind of process did not escape such a conclusion merely because the method used contained a further step of a technical nature which served to enable or assist the performance of the steps of sexually crossing the whole genomes of plants. However, it held that if a trait was introduced into the genome or modified a trait in the genome of the patent produced in a manner which was not the result of mixing the genes of the plants chosen for sexual crossing, then the process was not excluded from patentability under art.53(b). In relation to this last step, it said that such a process leaves the realm of plant breeding which the legislator wanted to exclude from patentability.[520] However, it clarified that this could only apply where the step of introducing a trait into the genome was performed within the steps of sexually crossing and selection processes. If the trait was introduced upstream or downstream of such crossing and selection processes, this should be ignored when considering whether the invention is excluded by art.53(b).[521]

Products obtained from essentially biological processes

2-302   In the joined cases of *Broccoli II and Tomatoes II*,[522] the Enlarged Board of Appeal considered whether the exclusion in art.53(b) against the patenting of "essentially biological" processes applied to a patent claim for a product that is directly obtained and/or defined by an essentially biological process. Despite arguments that

---

[517] Point 3.1.
[518] art.64(2) EPC confers protection on products directly obtained by a patented process. Thus, a ban on the method of obtaining plant varieties prevents applicants from obtaining patent protection for plant varieties via the back door.
[519] [2011] E.P.O.R. 27.
[520] See [154] (E.P.O.R.).
[521] See [155] (E.P.O.R.).
[522] (G2/12) and (G2/13) ECLI:EP:BA:2015:G000213.20150325.

allowing claims for protection of a product-by-excluded process would permit evasion of art.53(b) by mere careful drafting of claims, it concluded that:

"the mere fact that an applicant or patent proprietor chooses a product claim or product-by-process claim instead of a method claim directed to an essentially biological process is not a matter of some sort of 'skilful claim drafting' or circumvention of legal hurdles but a legitimate choice to obtain patent protection for the claim subject-matter on conditions that the requirements for allowability of such a claim are met."

It thus held that such claims were permissible. This finding was made **2-303** notwithstanding that the only method available at the filing date for generating the claimed subject matter was an essentially biological process and thus the generation of the claimed product necessitated the use of an essentially biological process that had been excluded under art.53(b).[523]

However, on request from the European Parliament, the EU Commission is- **2-304** sued a non-binding notice in November 2016 that the intention of the EU legislators when adopting the Biotechnology Directive was to exclude such products from patentability.[524] The notice stated that whilst the decisions in (G2/13) and (G2/12) were in line with the intentions of the draughtsmen of the EPC, it was "questionable" whether the same result would have been reached in the EU context. It then proceeded to consider the Directive and concluded that the intention of the EU was to exclude from patentability plants and animals that are obtained by essentially biological processes.[525]

This led to the EPO staying all proceedings relating to such claims pending **2-305** review. On 29 June 2017, the Administrative Council took a decision to amend the Implementing Regulations to fall into line with the EU Commission notice.[526] These provisions took effect from 1 July 2017. Accordingly, as of that date, plants or animals exclusively obtained by means of an essentially biological process are not patentable.

Microbiological processes

Under art.53(b), the ban on patenting of "essentially biological" processes does **2-306** not apply to microbiological processes. The Implementing Regulations define a "microbiological process" as any process involving or performed upon or resulting in microbiological material.[527] Furthermore, the Regulations say that a

---

[523] However, see *Recombination cassettes/BASF Plant Science GmbH* (T-2323/11) which held that art.53(b) did prevent the patenting of a plant which resulted from natural breeding (meiosis) even though the parent plants were transgenic and the second parent contained a transgene that excised the defective target gene in the first parent.

[524] *EU Notice* [2016] OJ C411/03.

[525] Thereby reaching a different conclusion to that of the Dutch courts in *Cresco v Taste of Nature* (CA, The Hague, 28 May 2013) as to the interpretation of art.4(1)(b) of the Biotechnology Directive (see "Are changes to rules 27 and 28 EPC illegal?" *CIPA Journal* July–August 2017, Vol.46 11–14 for further discussion). This article raises important issues of the real difficulties caused by the EPO changing its rules to accord with the EU Commission's view and thereby overturning its own jurisprudence and the lack of ability of the EPO to refer issues of interpretation of EU law to the CJEU.

[526] Decision of Administrative Council CA/D 6/17 OJ EPO 2017 A56. EPC r.27(b) and 28(2) were the rules that were changed to give effect to this decision.

[527] EPC r.26(6).

microbiological or other technical process or a product obtained by means of such a process other than a plant or animal variety is a patentable invention.[528]

2-307   In *NOVARTIS II/Transgenic Plant*, the EBA held that genetic engineering is not identical with microbiological processes. The term "microbiological processes" was synonymous with processes using microorganisms which are different from the parts of living beings used for the genetic modification of plants.[529]

2-308   Thus, a real distinction is to be drawn between biological processes and microbiological processes. The former are not patentable but the latter are, even if they only involve natural phenomena (and not genetic engineering). Generally, microbiological processes using microorganisms do not lead to plant varieties. As explained above, the ban on the patenting of biological processes is to avoid the patenting of processes which lead to products that are protectable under plant variety rights legislation. Thus, it makes sense not to exclude microbiological processes from being patentable.

Biotechnological inventions and animal varieties

2-309   The question of what is meant by "animal varieties" in art.53(b) was highlighted in the *HARVARD/Onco-Mouse* European patent application.[530] In this case, oncogenic sequences had been incorporated into mice, thus producing transgenic mice. The oncogenic sequences made the mouse more susceptible to cancer and thus useful as a research subject. Therefore, the relevant claims were:

> "17.   A transgenic non-human mammalian animal whose germ cells and somatic cells contain an activated oncogeny sequence introduced into said animal, or an ancestor of said animal, at a stage no later than the 8-cell stage, said oncogeny optionally being further defined according to any one of Claims 3 to 10.
>
> 18.   An animal as claimed in Claim 17 which is a rodent."

2-310   The Examining Division had some difficulty with this claim owing to the fact that the phrase "animal varieties" in art.53(b), which in the German and French text was "*tierarten*" and "*races animales*" (all of which versions are equally authentic), had differing meanings. "*Tierarten*" means "species" in English, whilst "animal varieties" and "*races animales*" denote sub-categories below the species level.[531] Thus, the Examining Division held that art.53(b) precluded patent protection for animals in general. The TBA disagreed and invoked the well-established principles that exceptions to patentability must be construed narrowly and held that the exclusion of animal varieties did not exclude animals in general. The case was remitted back to the Examining Board, who held that as the claims were for non-human mammals and rodents, these were higher taxonomic units than either "*tierarten*" or "*races animales*" and thus the invention was patentable.

2-311   This approach was taken in later opposition proceedings regarding the same

---

[528] EPC r.27(c).

[529] *NOVARTIS II/Transgenic plant* (G-1/98) [2000] OJ EPO 111; [2000] E.P.O.R. 303 at [5.2] of Decision. The EBA took into account the fact that cells and parts thereof are treated like microorganisms under the current practice of the EPO (*PLANT GENETIC SYSTEMS/Plant Cells* (T-356/93) [1995] OJ EPO 545, points 32–34) but held that such did not mean that genetically modified plants should be treated as products of microbiological processes.

[530] *HARVARD/Onco-Mouse* (T-19/90) [1990] OJ EPO 476.

[531] For a more detailed analysis on the differences between these, see V. Vossius, "Patent Protection for Animals; Onco-Mouse/Harvard" [1990] 12(7) E.I.P.R. 250.

patent. In *HARVARD/transgenic animal*,[532] which was the consolidated appeal from the dismissal of the opposition of 17 groups opposed to the grant of the *Onco-Mouse* patent, the TBA recognised the problems caused by the different languages but said that it did not have to decide the matter because the highest taxonomic category ("*tierarten*") meant animal species and the claims were not to a species but wider than that. It also rejected a submission that the transgenic mice were a new species.[533]

It should be noted that in interpreting the ban on patenting "animal varieties", there is no protection via sui generis laws protecting such (unlike plant varieties). **2-312**

Biotechnological inventions and ordre public

As discussed earlier, inventions cannot be granted where their commercial exploitation is contrary to *ordre public* or public morals. In the case of biotechnological inventions, the Implementing Regulations set out certain rules to be applied when considering art.53(a) as it applies to biotechnological inventions. Like other provisions, these mirror the Biotechnological Directive concerning the interpretation of art.53(a). Thus, r.28.1(a)–(d) state that European patents will not be granted in respect of biotechnological inventions which, in particular, concern the following: **2-313**

    (a)   processes for cloning human beings;
    (b)   processes for modifying the germ line genetic identity of human beings;
    (c)   uses of human embryos for industrial or commercial purposes; and
    (d)   processes for modifying the genetic identity of animals which are likely to cause them suffering without any substantial medical benefit to man or animal, and also animals resulting from such processes.[534]

In *WARF/Stem Cells*[535] the EBA had to consider the application of the EPC r.28.1(c). The patent concerned a method of creating human stem cells which necessitated as part of the process, the use and destruction of human embryos. The claims were to stem cell cultures. However, the method for preparing those stem cell cultures was not part of the claims but as set out in the description, the production of the stem cell cultures necessitated the destruction of human embryos. The EBA held that the third condition applied and that the claims were not patentable. It pointed out that art.53(a) was concerned not with the mere fact of the patenting itself but the *performing* of the invention. It thus said that if such included a step of destroying human embryos, it had to be considered as contravening r.28.1(c). In *Brüstle v Greenpeace*[536] the CJEU had to consider the equivalent provision to EPC r.28.1(c) in the Biotechnology Directive.[537] The patentee was the holder of a German patent which concerned isolated and purified neural precursor cells which were produced from embryonic stem cells. The precursor cells were used for the treatment of neural defects. The German courts referred a number of questions to the CJEU. First, it was concerned as to the precise meaning of "embryo" and whether **2-314**

---

[532] (T-315/03) [2005] E.P.O.R. 31.
[533] See [13.3.1].
[534] This last provision appears to be derived from (T-19/90) [1990] OJ EPO 476, where the TBA put forward such a rule as an appropriate test under art.53(a).
[535] (G2/06) [2009] OJ EPO 306; [2006] E.P.O.R. 31.
[536] (C-34/10) ECLI:EU:C:2011:669, [2012] 1 C.M.L.R. 41.
[537] art.6(1)(c), "use of human embryos for industrial or commercial purposes".

such covered stems cells obtained from a human embryo at the blastocyst stage. The CJEU said that "embryo" means any fertilised human ovum, a non-fertilised human ovum into which the cell nucleus from a mature human cell has been transplanted, and a non-fertilised human ovum whose division and further development has been stimulated by parthogenesis.[538] The CJEU also followed the EBA in *WARF/Stem Cells* and held that where the technical teaching of a patent application requires the prior destruction of human embryos as base material, such meant that the invention was not patentable regardless of the stage at which that takes place and even if the description does not refer to human embryos.[539]

2-315   Rule 28.1(d) was extensively interpreted in *HARVARD/Transgenic Animals* (T 315/03). It said that a likelihood of suffering to animals was necessary to trigger r.28.1(d) and once triggered, it required a balancing exercise between the suffering to animals and the medical benefit to man or animal. This exercise consisted of considering whether animal suffering was likely, whether substantial medical benefit had been established, and whether the suffering and the medical benefit both exist in relation to the use of the same animals. Proof was required to show animal suffering and also for the likely medical benefit. In *HARVARD/Transgenic Animals*, the main request was rejected because it applied to all rodents and there was no evidence that there was any benefit in applying the claimed process to all rodents as opposed to merely mice. However, in granting auxiliary requests which related only to mice, the TBA held that there was evidence of medical benefit and held that the balancing exercise under r.28.1(d) favoured grant of the claim. In *HARVARD/Transgenic Animals*, the TBA made it clear that even if r.28.1(d) did not apply, art.53(a) could still apply. This necessitated an assessment of whether or not the invention was contrary to morality or *ordre public*. This was sufficiently flexible to allow consideration of views such as social order, environmental risk and accepted standards of behaviour in European culture. The essential test was that laid out in *HARVARD/Onco Mouse*[540] namely:

> "The decision as to whether or not Art.53(a) EPC is a bar to patenting the present invention would seem to depend mainly on a careful weighing up of the suffering of animals and possible risks to the environment on the one hand, and the invention's usefulness to mankind on the other."[541]

2-316   In rejecting the opponents' arguments that the invention was contrary to morality, the Board said that there was insufficient evidence of a risk to evolution. The existence of a limited patent monopoly would limit and not increase the number of transgenic mice and trade in them and there was insufficient evidence that the public found the use of genetically manipulated mice in medical research at the priority date as being morally unacceptable.[542]

---

[538] See [36].

[539] See [52].

[540] (T-19/90) [1990] E.P.O.R. 501.

[541] (T-19/90) [1990] E.P.O.R. 501 at [5] cited at (T-315/03) [2005] E.P.O.R. 31 at [10.5].

[542] For an interesting article on the interaction of patents and morality see P. Drahos, "Biotechnology Patents, Markets and Morality" [1999] 21(9) E.I.P.R. 441 where he forcefully argues that the patent community has retained a strong pro-patent attitude in constructing the relationship between morality and patenting in the field of biotechnology which undermines much of the argument. See also A. Warren, "A Mouse in Sheep's Clothing: The Challenge to the Patent Morality Criterion Posed by 'Dolly'" [1998] 20 E.I.P.R. 445.

In *International Stem Cell Corporation v Comptroller-General of Patents*,[543] the **2-317** Court of Justice considered the patentability under the Biotech Directive of a claim to unfertilised ova whose division and development had been stimulated by parthenogenesis and contained only pluripotent cells. The applicant had submitted two applications to the UK Intellectual Property Office for a method of producing pluripotent human stem cell lines from immature unfertilised ova (oocytes) which had been subject to parthenogenesis to produce parthenotes. The UK IPO rejected the application, applying *Brüstle* (C–34/10), on the basis that such ova were capable of commencing the process of development of a human being just as an embryo created by the fertilisation of an ovum could do. Accordingly, it held that it was contrary to art.6.2(c) of the Biotech Directive (use of human embryos for industrial or commercial purposes). The matter went on appeal to the High Court which referred the issue to the Court of Justice concerning the proper interpretation of *Brüstle*.

The CJEU held that a patent application for a human parthenote, such as was the **2-318** subject matter of the application, could only be rejected if such had, in the light of knowledge which was sufficiently tried and tested by international medical science, the "inherent capacity of developing into a human being".[544] Some confusion had arisen because in *Brüstle*, written observations had been made that an unfertilised human ovum which had been stimulated by parthenogenesis *did* have the capacity to develop into a human being. However, in *International Stem Cell Corporation*, all parties were agreed that in fact, it was not capable of commencing the process of development into a human being. This was because although a parthenote was capable of dividing and further developing, it could never develop to term in contrast with a fertilised ovum because it did not contain any paternal DNA which was required for the development of extra-embryonic tissue. Thus, human parthenotes could develop only to the blastocyst stage.

Finally, it should be noted that in June 2017, Rule 28 was amended to exclude **2-319** plants or animals exclusively obtained by means of an essentially biological process. This is discussed above.[545]

Protection afforded by European patent

Scope of protection

Article 69 of the EPC harmonises the scope of protection of European patents. **2-320** It states that the extent of protection of a European patent is determined by the claims.[546] As to how this is to be interpreted by the national courts when applying it in infringement proceedings, the Protocol on the Interpretation of art.69 of the Convention states that:

---

[543] (C–364/13) EU:C:2014:2451.

[544] See [36].

[545] See para.2-302.

[546] art.69 was amended by EPC 2000 to remove the words "the terms of the claims" and substitute merely "the claims". The explanation given for the change is that the expressions "*inhalt*", "terms" and "*teneur*" were unclear in scope and did not have the same meaning in all three official languages. Furthermore, the corresponding provision in the WIPO Basic Proposal for a Patent Law did not include such a construction and merely defined the extent of protection as that determined by the claims.

"**Article 1**

Article 69 should not be interpreted in the sense that the extent of the protection conferred by a European patent is to be understood as that defined by the strict, literal meaning of the wording used for the claims, the description and drawings being employed only for the purpose of resolving an ambiguity found in the claims. Neither should it be interpreted in the sense that the claims serve only as a guideline and that the actual protection conferred may extend only to what, from a consideration of the description and drawings by a person skilled in the art, the patentee has contemplated. On the contrary, it is to be interpreted as defining a position between these extremes which combines a fair protection for the patentee with a reasonable degree of certainty for third parties."

"**Article 2**

For the purposes of determining the extent of protection conferred by a European patent, due account shall be taken of any element which is equivalent to an element specified in the claims."

2-321   Instead, as said in *Actavis*, the Protocol bears "all the hallmarks of the product of a composite agreement". Article 1 is generally accepted as being a compromise between the literalist tradition of the UK and the "taking of the invention" tradition of Germany. The UK approach saw the wording of the claim as "ringfencing" the scope of the monopoly of the patent. The German approach was to see the wording of the claim as a guide to what was the invention to be protected. It should be noted that art.2 was introduced by EPC2000. Following the Diplomatic Conference on 20–29 November 2000 to amend the EPC, there was intense discussion about amending art.69 and the Protocol to art.69. The impetus to amend the Protocol arose out of concerns that national courts were not applying art.69 in as uniform an application as had been hoped.

2-322   The effect of the introduction of art.2 was considered by the UK Supreme Court in *Actavis UK Ltd v Eli Lilly and Co*.[547] This important judgment held (rather belatedly) that the UK's previous approach to infringement did not give sufficient weight to art.2 when considering whether a variant infringed. After a *tour d'horizon* of the practice of other EPC contracting states on the issue of whether a variant infringed, it held that the right approach to considering whether a variant infringed was a three-step test as follows[548]:

(i)   Notwithstanding that it is not within the literal meaning of the relevant claim(s) of the patent, does the variant achieve substantially the same result in substantially the same way as the invention, i.e. the inventive concept revealed by the patent?

(ii)   Would it be obvious to the person skilled in the art, reading the patent at the priority date, but knowing that the variant achieves substantially the same result as the invention, that it does so in substantially the same way as the invention?

(iii) Would such a reader of the patent have concluded that the patentee nonetheless intended that strict compliance with the literal meaning of the relevant claim(s) of the patent was an essential requirement of the invention?

2-323   In order to establish infringement in a case where there is no literal infringe-

---

[547] [2017] UKSC 48.
[548] See [65]. This three-step test was a reformulation of an earlier test set out in *Improver Corp v Remington Consumer Products* [199] F.S.R. 181 which was itself based upon *Catnic* [1982] R.P.C. 183.

ment, a patentee would have to establish that the answer to the first two questions was "yes" and that the answer to the third question was "no".

The UK Supreme Court decision is useful as it considers the approach taken by **2-324** other EPC states to the issue of infringement by a variant. Thus, in Germany, the Bundesgerichtshof has stated that a variant will infringe if (i) it solves the problem underlying the invention with modified but objectively equivalent means, (ii) this would be recognised by the person skilled in the art, and (iii) the person focusing on the essential meaning of the technical teaching protected in the patent would regard the variant as being equivalent to the solution offered by the invention.[549] In France, the doctrine of equivalents applied where the variant was "different in form but perform[s] the same function" as the invention but only where "the function [claimed in the patent] is a new one".[550] In Italy, the view was that a variant would be held to infringe if: (i) it reproduced the "inventive core" of the patent, (ii) it was an obvious variation, although (iii) the fact that the variant included some modifications which were not obvious and/or the fact that the variant did not include some of the elements of the patent claim did not necessarily prevent the variant infringing.[551] In the Netherlands, the doctrine of equivalents applied if: (i) the variant was foreseeable at the priority date, although such was not a necessary condition where the variant was, due to later developments, an obvious variant at a later date, (ii) the inventive concept was sufficiently broad to cover the variant, (iii) the variant made uses of and benefited from the inventive concept, and (iv) reasonable legal certainty is not unduly compromised.[552] Interestingly, many of the approaches taken by other EPC states owed their style to the pre-Actavis three-step test taken by the UK in the decision of *Improver Corp v Remington* which, in *Actavis*, the UK Supreme Court reformulated to take account of art.2 of the Protocol.[553] A good example of legal Darwinism.

It should be noted that, as said by the UK Supreme Court, the effect of art.2 to **2-325** the Protocol is that it extends protection beyond the normal meaning of the words of a claim. As said by Lord Neuberger, two issues arise when considering the issue of infringement by a variant: (i) does the variant infringe any of the claims as a matter of *normal* interpretation, and *if not* (ii) does the variant nonetheless infringe because it varies from the invention in a way/ways which is/are immaterial?[554] Thus, as Lord Neuberger said, the second issue involves not merely identifying what the words of a claim would mean in their context to the notional addresses but also considering the extent if any to which the scope of protected afforded by the claim should extend beyond the normal meaning of the words. He cited a former judge of the Patents Courts who said that the Protocol "is not concerned with the rules of construction of claims" but with "determining the scope of protection".[555]

Once the Agreement on the UPC comes into force, it is likely that one of the first **2-326**

---

[549] Case No *X ZR* 168/00, 2002 GRUR 519 (*Schniedmeser I*) at [30] (see *Actavis UK* at [44]).
[550] See *Actavis UK* at [45]. J. Azema and J-C Galloux, *Droit de la Propriété Industrielle*, 7th edn (Paris: Dalloz, 2012), p.442.
[551] This came from decisions of the Corte di Cassazione in Case No 257, *Forel SpA v Lisec* (13 January 2004), Case No 30234, *Barilla GER Fratelli SpA v Pastificio Fazion SpA* (30 December 2012) and Case No 622, *Entsorga Italia Srl v Ecodeco Srl* (11 January 2013) (see *Actavis UK* at [48]).
[552] Lecture from Judge Kalden, head of IP Division, Court of Appeal in the Hague, "Article 69—the Scylla and Charybdis of the European Patent Convention—Which Route did the Dutch Courts Take?" (2016 Symposium, German Bundespatentgericht). See *Actavis UK* at [51].
[553] See fn.548 and *Actavis UK*, at [43]–[44].
[554] See [54].
[555] See [56].

jobs of the UPC Appeal Court will be to give guidance on the proper interpretation of the Protocol to art.69. However, it would appear that currently, the approach now taken by EPC Contracting States to the important issue of variants is broadly aligned.

File wrapper estoppel

2-327   It should be noted in the negotiations for EPC 2000 that it had been proposed that the Protocol to art.69 should also include a section that statements made during the course of prosecution of the patent before the EPO which sought to limit the extent of protection conferred by a patent in proceedings during the grant or validity of the patent (in particular where it was made in order to overcome a citation of prior art) should be taken into account when construing the extent of protection (known in the United States as "file wrapper estoppel"). This was rejected in the Diplomatic Conference. The provision was sought because of a divergence among contracting states as to the extent to which a court or tribunal can have regard to statements made during the course of prosecution of a patent application. Thus, the doctrine generally does not apply in England save in exceptional cases.[556] In the Netherlands, the Hoge Raad in *Ciba Geigy A.G. v Ote Optics*, held that one may rely upon that part of the patent grant file which is accessible to the public to decide the extent of protection conferred by a European patent if the average skilled person still had reasonable doubts as to the interpretation to be given to claims.[557] In Germany, the courts have held that the prosecution history is of relevance in deciding the scope of claims. Thus, in *WEICHVORRICHTUNG II/Sleeping* device,[558] the Bundesgerichtshof held that where a patentee in opposition proceedings declares that they do not wish to seek protection for a particular embodiment and then in infringement proceedings seeks to make claims in respect of that particular embodiment, it is contrary to the principle of *venire contra factum proprium* for the patentee to so assert. In France, it would appear that it is only relevant in order to assess the understanding of a skilled person at the priority date.[559]

Relevant date

2-328   Although there had been some divergent authority in the past, it is now clear that the relevant date for determining the scope of protection of a patent and whether it

---

[556] The application of the file wrapper estoppel doctrine was considered by the UK Supreme Court in *Actavis UK Ltd v Eli Lilly & Co*. The court considered the approach to file wrapper estoppel in France, Germany, the Netherlands, Italy and Spain and commented that the French courts appeared more ready to refer to the prosecution history on interpretation or scope than the German or Dutch court (see [86]). It held that it was appropriate for the UK courts to adopt a "sceptical but not absolutist, attitude" to bear in mind the prosecution file when considering a question of infringement along substantially the same lines as the German and Dutch courts. The Supreme Court held that reference to the file would only be appropriate where the point at issue is "truly unclear if one confines oneself to the specification and claims of the patent and the contents of the file unambiguously resolve the point" or it would be contrary to the public interest for the contents of the file to be ignored. An example of the latter would be where the patentee had made it clear to the EPO that they were not seeking to contend that that their patent, if granted, would extend its scope to the sort of variant which they now claimed infringed (see [88]).

[557] *CIBA Geigy A.G. v Ote Optics BV* reported in summary at [1998] OJ EPO 142, and in Dutch [1995] Rechtspraak van de Week 176; in German [1995] G.R.U.R. Int. 727.

[558] *X ZR 73/95* reported at [1998] OJ EPO 141.

[559] See W. Tilmann, "Harmonisation of Invalidity and Scope-of-Protection Practice of National Courts of EPC Member States" [2006] E.I.P.R. 2006, 169–173.

would have been obvious to the person skilled in the art that the variant would achieve substantially the same result is the priority date of the patent.[560]

What infringes? Who infringes?

The EPC does not harmonise the question of *what acts* amount to infringement nor *who is liable* for acts of infringement. Thus, art.64(3) EPC states that the rights conferred by a European patent shall be those rights as conferred by a national patent. Ultimately, there is little difference in the laws of contracting states as to what acts amount to an infringement—generally, any exploitation whether by manufacturing, marketing, dealing in, offering for sale, or selling infringing goods amounts to an act of infringement. However, the issue becomes more complicated when considering the liability of accessories. Most countries do have laws that permit a patentee to target persons who provide essential means to enable a product to be made which infringes an apparatus patent or a process to be carried out which infringes a method patent. Thus, in the UK, the person who supplies or offers to supply any means relating to an: **2-329**

> "essential element of the invention for putting the invention into effect when he knows or it is obvious to a reasonable person in the circumstances that those means are suitable for putting and are intended to put the invention into effect in the United Kingdom"

is an infringer where the invention is patented.[561] A broadly similar approach to contributory infringement is taken in Germany, France, Italy and Spain.[562] Indeed, the Court of Appeal in the UK has referred to cases in Germany and elsewhere as an aid to interpretation of these provisions, saying that where such cases deal with points of obvious importance in patent law, their reasoning should be considered strongly persuasive and should be followed where it is not obviously wrong.[563]

However, it should be noted that harmonisation of what acts are capable of being infringing acts and accessory liability for supplying products which can implement an invention is covered by the Agreement on the Unified Patent Court. Once this is in force, then in all EU countries other than Spain and Poland, there will be harmonisation.[564] **2-330**

---

[560] *Actavis UK*, at [44]–[52], [63] and [65]. This does not mean that protection is limited to foreseeable variants as of priority date. *Actavis*, at [63]. It should be noted that the law of Member States was earlier on the issue of relevant date and much more fragmented. See W. Tilmann, "Harmonisation of Invalidity and Scope-of-Protection Practice of National Courts of EPC Member States" [2006] E.I.P.R. 2006, 169–173.

[561] Patents Act 1977 s.60(2). This approach has been adopted in the UPC Agreement—see para.2-561. For a recent consideration of the scope of s.60(2), see the Court of Appeal of England and Wales' decision in *Actavis v Eli Lilly* [2015] EWCA Civ 555 (upheld on appeal by the Supreme Court [2017] UKSC 48 at [103]–[112].

[562] N. Holder and J. Schmidt, "Indirect Patent Infringement—Latest Developments in Germany" [2006] 28(9) E.I.P.R. 2006, 480–484. *Actavis v Eli Lilly* [2015] EWCA Civ 555, where the Court of Appeal held that there was "no detectable difference in the laws of France, Italy and Spain" on the approach to contributory infringement—[93] (although this was said to be "common ground.").

[563] *Grimme Landmaschinenfabrik GmbH v Scott (t/a Scotts Potato Machinery)* [2010] EWCA Civ 1110; [2011] F.S.R. 7.

[564] The Agreement on the UPC is discussed at para.2-506.

Infringement of Swiss-style second medical use claims

2-331   Courts of Member States have had to consider infringement by manufacturers of pharmaceuticals of Swiss-style medical use claims. A Swiss-style medical use claim is discussed earlier in this chapter.[565] It is a claim phrased as follows: "*Use of Substance A for the preparation of a pharmaceutical composition for treating Condition X.*" Historically, prior to EPC 2000, Swiss-style medical use claims were necessary until EPC 2000 changed art.54(5) EPC to permit claims to "*Substance A for medical use X*".[566] Indeed, Swiss-style claims are no longer allowed.[567]

2-332   Regarding many Member States, the courts have had to consider the circumstances as to when a manufacturer of a pharmaceutical will be liable for infringement of a Swiss-style second medical use claim when it labels the pharmaceuticals with a "skinny label" that excludes reference to the patented indications or dosages from the product (as allowed under European medicines legislation). Unsurprisingly, doctors and pharmacists familiar with "skinny labels" may prescribe such medicines to be used for the protected indication regardless of what is said on the label. Equally unsurprisingly, manufacturers of "skinny label" pharmaceuticals know of this practice.

2-333   Against this background, the question then becomes "in what circumstances is the manufacturer liable?" A number of approaches need to be considered.

- The manufacturer is not liable unless, by an assessment of the acts of the manufacturer, it intended that the skinny label pharmaceutical should be prescribed to patients by doctors and pharmacists for the protected use (the *intention* approach).
- The manufacturer has a positive obligation to prevent doctors and pharmacists from prescribing the skinny label pharmaceutical for the protected use and has taken all reasonable steps to so prevent (the *all reasonable steps* approach).
- The manufacturer is liable if it is reasonably foreseeable that a significant number of doctors and pharmacists will prescribe the skinny label pharmaceutical for the protected use (the *reasonably foreseeable* approach).

2-334   The courts of Member States have found this issue difficult. In Germany, the German courts have favoured the intention approach but in a narrow form. In *Carvedilol II* (Bundesgerichtshof), *Chronic Hepatitis C Treatment* (Landgericht Düsseldorf) and *Warner-Lambert Co LLC v Aliud Pharma GmbH* (Landgericht Hamburg), the courts have sought to see whether packaging or the skinny label would induce the prescriber to prescribe the pharmaceutical for the protected use. This narrow approach was criticised by the English Court of Appeal in *Warner-Lambert Co LLC v Generics (UK) Ltd*[568] on the grounds that it is difficult to see why advertising should not be taken into account which induces the prescriber to prescribe for the patented use.[569] However, in proceedings in Hamburg, the Hamburg Regional Court granted an interim injunction on the same pregabalin patent as that considered in the UK on the grounds that generic companies had participated in tenders for rebate contracts without clarifying that the skinny-

---

[565] See para.2-162.
[566] See para.2-162.
[567] See para.2-164.
[568] [2016] EWCA Civ 1006 (on appeal to the Supreme Court).
[569] See [190].

labelled generic version could not be prescribed to patents for the protected indication.[570] This approach aligns itself with the "all reasonable steps" approach adopted in France.

In Spain, in *Wyeth v Arafarma and Qualtec*,[571] the Madrid Court of Appeal said that it was necessary to show that the manufacturer had carried out some act aimed at strengthening the use of the same for that indication. This is a variant of the "intention" approach. **2-335**

In France, in *Warner-Lambert v Sandoz* (C-15/58725), the Tribunal de Grande Instance held that the manufacturer had positive obligations to prevent the marketing of its pharmaceutical for the protected use. In that case, it was found that Sandoz had fulfilled that obligation by sending emails to doctors and pharmacists as how to prescribe the generic medicine. This is an application of the "all reasonable steps" approach. **2-336**

In *Warner-Lambert Co v Generics*, the English Court of Appeal, modifying its view in the interim proceedings in the same case on which principle the first instance judge had applied and found there to be no infringement, favoured the French approach. Strictly, this was obiter dicta, as the Court had found the patent to be invalid for insufficiency. The Court of Appeal said that the correct approach was: **2-337**

> "[208] ... The intention will be negatived where the manufacturer has taken all reasonable steps within his power to prevent the consequences occurring. In such circumstances his true objective is a lawful one, and one would be entitled to say that the foreseen consequences were not intended, but were an unintended incident of his otherwise lawful activity. I think this approach is in line with that adopted in the decision of the Tribunal de Grande Instance, in that it recognises an obligation on the manufacturer to take steps if he is to enter the market where he stands to benefit from the patentee's contribution to the art."

No court has favoured the *reasonably foreseeable* approach. This is unsurprising as it could render the manufacturer liable regardless of what steps were taken by the manufacturer to prevent use for the protected indication. **2-338**

On the issue of indirect infringement of Swiss-style medical use claim, the Court of Appeal of England and Wales in *Warner-Lambert v Generics* considered that it was possible that, given the nature of the claim which was the "*use of Substance A for the preparation of a pharmaceutical composition for treating Condition X*" that where a pharmacist labels a pharmaceutical supplied by the generic manufacturer for such a condition, such could be considered part of the claim as the process of preparing the composition can continue through any packaging step performed by the manufacturer and includes the labelling step performed by the pharmacist.[572] **2-339**

Interestingly, in Spain, the Barcelona Court of Appeal held in *Warner-Lambert v Laboratorios Cinfa SA* that where there was a real likelihood that the generic medicine would be used for the patented use, there would be indirect infringement. Commenting on this case, the Court of Appeal of England and Wales said in *Warner Lambert* that such appears to have proceeded on the basis that downstream direct infringement was not necessary for a finding of indirect infringement.[573] In the English court's view, there could not be indirect infringement if the act of labelling by the doctor or pharmacist did not form an element of the claim. **2-340**

---

[570] 2 April 2015. Docket No. 327/15 O67/15, Hamburg Landgericht.

[571] (647/2013) ES:TS:2014:4845.

[572] See [224].

[573] See [231].

2-341   A real issue is whether the approach to infringement of new art.54(5) second medical use claims will be the same or different to pre-EPC 2000 Swiss-form second medical use claims. As discussed earlier, in *Treament of Pompe's disease/ GENZYME*,[574] the EPO took the view that the former is wider in scope than the latter,[575] holding that new art.54(5) covered products used to treat the protected indication even if the product label only referred to non-protected indications. This must be right. A doctor or pharmacist would be liable for *direct infringement* for supplying a pharmaceutical to a person for use for the protected indication even if the label indicated use only for a non-protected indication. This would not be the case for Swiss-style claims which apply to the *manufacture* of a pharmaceutical.

Practice and procedure under the EPC

2-342   In this section, we consider the practice and procedure for applying for a European patent. As said in the introduction to the EPC, the grant of a European patent is done by the EPO with the result that if the application is successful, it results in a basket of national patents in contracting states to the EPC. Considerable assistance is given by the EPO at its website to the procedural requirements of obtaining a European patent.[576]

The Applicant

2-343   Unlike the Patent Cooperation Treaty or the Paris Convention, a European patent application can be filed by any natural or legal person regardless of their nationality or place of residence.[577] A European patent application may be filed by joint applicants or by two or more applicants designating different contracting states.[578] Applicants can, therefore, allocate different contracting states between themselves.

Entitlement to patent

2-344   The right to a European patent belongs to the inventor or their successor in title.[579] If the inventor is an employee, then the entitlement to a European patent shall be determined in accordance with the law of the state in which the employee is mainly employed or, if this is indeterminable, the state where the employer has their place of business to which the employee is attached.[580] In accordance with most contracting states' law, this will mean that the employer will be entitled to the patent provided that the employee was acting in the course of their employment when the employee made the invention.

---

[574] *Treatment of Pompe's disease/GENZYME* (T-1673/11) ECLI:EP:BA:2015:T167311.20151020.
[575] See para.2-164 for discussion of this.
[576] In particular, there is the very useful guide for applicants (see *http://www.epo.org/applying/european/ Guide-for-applicants.html* [Accessed 18 August 2017] which is a user-friendly compressed version of the Guidelines for Examinations themselves which also be accessed at the EPO website (*http:// www.epo.org/law-practice.html* [Accessed 18 August 2017]).
[577] art.58.
[578] art.59.
[579] art.60.
[580] art.60(1).

Protocol

The Protocol on Jurisdiction and the Recognition of Decisions in respect of the **2-345**
Right to the Grant of a European Patent (which is annexed to the EPC) provides
for a jurisdictional framework, through which a person may raise the question of
who has the right to the grant of a European patent. It forms an integral part of the
EPC.[581] It is only concerned with claims to the right to the grant of a European
patent.[582] Essentially, the Member State which is to have jurisdiction is determined
according to the following list (in descending order of priority):

(1) that jurisdiction to which the parties agreed in writing[583];
(2) if an employer/employee dispute, the state in which the employee is mainly
     employed, or if that cannot be determined, where the employer's place of
     business is[584];
(3) if the applicant has their place of business or residence in one of the Member
     States, then in that state[585];
(4) if the applicant has their place of business or residence outside the Member
     States, then the Member State where the party claiming the right to the grant
     of a European patent has their residence or principal place of business[586];
     and
(5) the Federal Republic of Germany.[587]

The court[588] which is seized of the matter must decide, of its own motion, whether
or not it has jurisdiction.[589] If an earlier application has been made to the court of
another Member State, then the court other than the first seized must decline
jurisdiction or, if the jurisdiction is challenged, stay the proceedings until determination of the issue.[590] It is not clear whether issues of residence, place of business and
the phrase "mainly employed" are to be determined according to national law or
private international law, or whether there should be an independent autonomous
approach.

Challenges based on the entitlement to the grant of a European patent can be **2-346**
made after grant of the European patent. Courts of other Member States must
recognise the decision of the appropriate court as to the entitlement to grant of a
European patent.[591] Even if it appears to another court that the court which gave out
the decision did not have jurisdiction, has applied the wrong law, or was otherwise
wrong, it cannot review the decision or refuse to recognise its validity.[592] The two
exceptions to this rule are that an applicant for a European patent can dispute the
recognition of an adverse decision if they were not notified early and sufficiently
enough to defend themselves, or if the decision is incompatible with another deci-

---

[581] EPC art.164.
[582] Protocol art.1.
[583] art.5. If it is an employee/employer dispute, then this Article only applies if the national law govern-
       ing the contract of employment permits such an agreement—art.5(2) Protocol.
[584] art.4; art.60.
[585] art.2.
[586] art.3.
[587] art.6.
[588] This is deemed to include authorities that have jurisdiction to decide such claims under national law
       (i.e. national patent offices)—art.1(2).
[589] Protocol art.7.
[590] arts 7 and 8.
[591] art.9 Protocol.
[592] art.9(2).

sion given in a Member State in proceedings between the same parties which were started before those in which the decision to be recognised was given.[593]

2-347   In England, the Court of Appeal, in construing the Patents Act 1977 s.82, which gives effect to the Protocol under English law, held that the phrase "right to be granted a European patent" should not be interpreted narrowly, and included the right to the patent or the fruits of the patent. Thus, where it was alleged that a party held a European patent application on constructive trust for another, the Court of Appeal held that it was a matter which went to the right to the grant of a European patent and, on the facts, declined jurisdiction.[594]

Relationship between the Recast Brussels Regulation and Protocol

2-348   There has been some debate as to whether the Protocol can be considered as a special jurisdictional agreement which overrides the jurisdiction rules of the Recast Brussels Regulation ("RBR") by virtue of art.71 of the latter.[595] The English courts take the view that art.71 applies.[596] However, a French court has taken the opposite view.[597] In the author's view, it is clear that the Protocol is a jurisdiction agreement that falls within art.71 RBR. First, it satisfies the test set out by the Court of Justice in *TNT Express Nederland BV v AXA Versicherung*[598] that the jurisdictional rules be "highly predictable, facilitate the sound administration of justice and enable the risk of concurrent proceedings to be minimised". Secondly, it applies to parties regardless whether they are domiciled in the EU whereas the RBR only applies if the defendant is domiciled in the EU. Therefore, it is clear that the RBR would not apply to *some* entitlement disputes over a European patent whereas the Protocol will apply to all.[599] Thirdly, the RBR has no provisions on entitlement to a patent (let alone a European patent). Fourthly, art.11 of the Protocol, which forms an integral part of the EPC which is ratified by all EU Member States, makes it clear that it is intended to override other jurisdictional agreements. Fifthly, the rules in the Protocol can be considered analogous to the sui generis jurisdictional rules in the EU Unitary Right regulations which have been held by the Court of Justice to have the character of lex specialis under the predecessor to the RBR.[600]

2-349   Upon issuing entitlement proceedings, the claimant should notify and provide proof to the EPO that they have begun proceedings against the applicant. The EPO will then stay proceedings, provided that publication has taken place.[601] If the court of the relevant state determines that someone other than the applicant has the right to the European patent application, then that person may, within three months of the decision being given, prosecute the application itself, file a new application, or

---

[593] art.10 Protocol.

[594] *Kakkar v Szelke* [1989] F.S.R. 225 CA.

[595] See Ch.17, para.17-214.

[596] *Innovia Films v Frito-Lay North America, Inc* [2012] R.P.C. 24; *Conductive Inkjet Technology Ltd v Uni-Pixel Displays Inc* [2013] EWHC 2968 (Ch.) (although it should be said that this was common ground between the parties).

[597] *NCAM Technologies Ltd v Solidanim*, Tribunal de Grande Instance, 24 November 2016, RG No. 15/15648 applying *TNT Express Nederland BV v AXA Versicherung AG* (C-533/08) ECLI:EU:C:2010:243.

[598] (C-533/08) ECLI:EU:C:2010:24 at [53].

[599] It should be noted that art.22(4) (exclusive jurisdiction) RBR (which applies regardless of the domicile of the defendant) does not apply to entitlement disputes—see para.17-129.

[600] *Nintendo Co Ltd v BigBen Interactive GmbH* (C-24/16, C-25/16) ECLI:EU:C:2017:724 at [42].

[601] EPC r.14(1).

request that the application be refused.[602] If the successful claimant chooses to file a new application, then the original application is deemed to be withdrawn on the date of filing of the new application.[603]

If there are two or more persons who have independently made the invention, then the right to the European patent belongs to the patent application which has either the earliest date of filing or priority date,[604] provided the earlier patent application is subsequently published. This provision only has effect in relation to the designated states specified in the patent application.   **2-350**

Languages under the EPC

English, French and German are the official languages of the EPO and European patent applications must be filed in one of these languages.[605] All proceedings must then be conducted up to grant in the language chosen for the application, which is called the language of the proceedings.[606]   **2-351**

The exceptions to the above rule are as follows: **2-352**

(a) If the applicant has a residence or principal place of business in a contracting state which has an official language other than English, French or German. In such a case, the applicant may file an application in an official language of that state.[607] However, a translation of the application must be filed within two months into one of the official languages, which then becomes the language of the proceedings.[608] During prosecution of the application, other documents which are required to be filed may be filed in the official language of the contracting state concerned but translations into an official language of the EPO must be filed within one month of the filing of the document.[609] If this is not done, the document is deemed not to have been received.[610]

(b) In written proceedings before the EPO, any of the official languages may be used.[611]

---

[602] art.61. If a new application is filed under art.61, it will be entitled to the priority date of the usurping application provided that the subject-matter of the new application does not extend beyond that of the usurping application. It is not necessary for the usurping application to be pending for art.61 to be applicable—see *LATCHWAYS/Unlawful Applicant* (G-3/92) [1995] E.P.O.R. 141.

[603] EPC r.17(1).

[604] arts 60(2), 87, 89.

[605] art.14(1). Note: If an international patent application has been filed and published under the PCT in one official language of the EPO, it is not possible, on entry into the European phase, to file a translation of the application into one of the other two EPO official languages; see *Language of the proceedings/MERIAL* (G-4/08).

[606] art.14(3). See also *Language of the proceedings/MERIAL* (G-4/08).

[607] art.14(4).

[608] art.14(4), EPC r.6.1. If not filed in time, the application is deemed to have been withdrawn—art.14(2).

[609] art.14(4), EPC rr.3(1), 6(2).

[610] art.14(4).

[611] EPC r.3(1). In written proceedings on a European patent application or an international application in the regional phase, EPO departments cannot use an EPO official language other than the language of proceedings used for the application pursuant to art.14(3) EPC; see *Language of the proceedings/ MERIAL* (G-4/08).

(c)   Documents for evidence may be filed in any language but the EPO may require them to be translated.[612]

(d)   Oral proceedings may be conducted in any one of the official languages provided one month's notice prior to the hearing is given to the EPO.[613] Furthermore, oral proceedings may be conducted in an official language of a contracting state provided that provision for interpretation into the language of the proceedings is made.[614]

2-353   Publication of the application takes place in the language of the proceedings.[615]

2-354   Generally, the EPC confers provisional protection to a patent application from the date of publication of the application.[616] However, the EPC gives a contracting state the power to stipulate that provisional protection in its state for published European applications, where that state has been designated, is conditional on the filing of translation of the claims into the official language of the state.[617] At grant, the patent is published in the language of the proceedings together with a translation of the claims into the other two official languages of the EPO.[618]

2-355   Importantly, a designated state may provide that at grant, translations of the entire text of the patent into the official language of the designated state must be provided within a certain time limit. Generally, this is three months from the date of publication of the patent although, in certain countries, such is extendible. Nineteen countries of the 38 countries to the EPC require a translation of the complete patent specification into their language. These countries are: Austria, Belgium, Bulgaria, Cyprus, the Czech Republic, Estonia, Greece, Ireland, Italy, Lithuania, Malta, Norway, Poland, Portugal, Romania, Serbia, Slovakia, Spain, and Turkey. The other 19 contracting states have ratified the London Agreement and thus have dispensed entirely or partly with the translation requirements of art.65 EPC. The London Agreement is now discussed.

London Agreement

2-356   The cost of translation of patent specifications into the languages of all contracting states (if protection is sought throughout the EPC countries) is extremely expensive. It is a very substantial deterrent to applicants. In an effort to reduce costs, Albania, Croatia, Denmark, Finland, France, Germany, Hungary, Iceland, Latvia, Liechtenstein, Lithuania, Luxembourg, Macedonia, Monaco, Netherlands, Slovenia, Sweden, Switzerland, and the UK have signed and ratified the London Agreement on art.65. The London Agreement allows Member States to dispense with translation requirements in certain situations, e.g. where the patent is granted in an official language of the EPO stipulated to be acceptable. Under art.1(1) of the London Agreement, some signatories to the Agreement have dispensed with the translational requirements under art.65 in their entirety—these being contracting states that have

---

[612]   EPC r.3(3).

[613]   EPC r.4.

[614]   EPC r.4(1).

[615]   art.14(5).

[616]   art.67(1).

[617]   art.67(3). The EPO publishes a list of the requirements of the contracting states as regards translation at: *http://www.epo.org/law-practice/legal-texts/html/natlaw/en/iv/index.htm* [Accessed 3 June 2018]. In general, at the very least, a contracting state requires translation of the claims (if not the whole description) into one of its official languages for provisional protection to be provided.

[618]   art.14(6).

an official language in common with one of the official languages of the EPO.[619] Other countries which do not have an official language in common with one of the official languages of the EPO have required that only the claims be translated into one of their official languages.[620] Some of these countries have dispensed with the requirement for further translation if the European patent is granted in English.[621] The EPO maintains a webpage which sets out the precise language requirements of the signatories to the London Agreement which the reader should consult as this is updated from time to time.[622]

EU Unitary Patent and languages

If the European patent is converted into a EU Unitary Patent following grant, then it is necessary to consider its language requirements of EU legislation. These are discussed later in this chapter when considering the EU Unitary Patent.[623]   **2-357**

Designation of contracting states

In an application, all contracting states are deemed to have been designated in the request for a grant of a European patent.[624] This now accords with PCT applications, which also automatically designates all PCT countries.[625] If no state at all is designated, then no date of filing will be recognised.[626] Owing to the importance of such a rule, the EPO has established a working practice in this area.[627] For applications filed on or after 1 April 2009, there is a flat designation fee covering all EPC contracting states, and the former system of charging designation fees for individual designated states no longer applies.[628] For European patent applications, the designation fees must be paid within six months of the date on which the European Patent Bulletin mentions the publication of the European search report.[629]   **2-358**

Priority

An applicant can claim priority for a European patent application for an earlier patent application filed in any state party to the Paris Convention within the previous 12 months.[630] If priority is validly claimed, the priority date will count as the date of filing of the European patent application in order to establish what is prior   **2-359**

---

[619] France, Germany, Ireland, Liechtenstein, Luxembourg, Monaco, Switzerland and the UK.
[620] Albania, Croatia, Denmark, Finland, Macedonia, Hungary, Iceland, Latvia, Lithuania, Netherlands, Sweden and Slovenia.
[621] Albania, Croatia, Denmark, Finland, Hungary, Iceland, Netherlands, Norway and Sweden. Macedonia, Latvia, Lithuania and Slovenia have not prescribed any language under art.1(2) of the London Agreement.
[622] See *http://www.epo.org/law-practice/legal-texts/london-agreement/key-points.html* [Accessed 18 August 2017]. See also the section on "National Law relating to the EPC" in the section on "Translation requirements after grant" (see *http://www.epo.org/law-practice/legal-texts/html/natlaw/en/iv/ index.htm* [Accessed on 3 June 2018]).
[623] See para.2-528.
[624] art.79.
[625] See para.2-047.
[626] art.80, EPC r.40.
[627] *Legal Advice 7* [1980] OJ EPO 395.
[628] Guid. A-III 11.2.1.
[629] EPC r.39(1). See Guid. A-III 11.2.1.
[630] EPC art.87(1).

art which could be used to challenge the application.[631] The rationale for claiming priority was recently considered by the EBA in *Infineum USA/Partial Priority* (G1/15). It held that the purpose of the priority right is to protect the applicant against third parties filing a patent application in respect of the same invention during the 12-month period after the first filing.[632] Furthermore, if the application claims the same invention as that disclosed in the priority document, then the subject matter of the priority document cannot be considered prior art as against the application. This is achieved by deeming the subsequent application to have been filed on the date of the first filing to the extent that it relates to the same subject matter as the first filing.[633] This provides a *"sort of barrier"* designed to prevent third parties from interfering with the applicant's right to obtain protection for the claimed subject matter which it disclosed first in the previous application. This is also true for the applicant (i.e. the priority rule prevents the priority document from being treated as prior art as against the applicant itself). Thus, as said by the EBA, the only circumstance in which a novelty objection can succeed is where priority cannot be recognised.[634]

2-360   The Legal Board of Appeal has held that the Paris Convention could not be interpreted as giving a right of priority for a patent application based on anything other than an earlier patent application.[635] Furthermore, the requirement that the state be a party to the Paris Convention is strict. Thus, where the priority application was made in India, which was not a member of the Paris Convention but was a member of TRIPS, this was fatal.[636]

Same invention

2-361   In order for priority to be conferred on an application, it is necessary that the later application must relate to the same invention and contain the same subject-matter as the application from which priority is being drawn.[637] The requirement of the "same invention" necessitates that a skilled person should be able to derive the subject-matter of the claim, directly and unambiguously, from the previous applicants as a whole (taking into account the common general knowledge).[638] This does not require identical wording but the essence of the disclosures must be the same. The Guidelines state that the requirement of "same invention" is the same as the test for determining whether an amendment is permissible.[639] The EPO will not concentrate on the claims but on the earlier application as a whole.[640]

---

631   arts 89, 54(2).
632   See [4.3.2].
633   See [4.3.3].
634   See [4.3.4].
635   *ARENHOLD* (J-15/80) [1981] OJ EPO 7 corrected at [1981] OJ EPO 546.
636   *Astrazeneca/Priorities from India* (G-2/03) [2004] E.P.O.R. 39. This case is discussed elsewhere on the issue of whether TRIPS applies to the interpretation of the EPC—see para.2-114.
637   art.87(1), (4).
638   *X/Same invention* (G-2/98) [2001] OJ EPO 413. For applications of this principle, see *CANON/Priority* (T-297/01) [2004] E.P.O.R. 380 and *Arch/copper pyrithione* (T-178/03) [2006] E.P.O.R. 41. See also (G1/15) at [6.2].
639   Guid F-VI 2.2. See also *Genetic Systems/Disclaimer* (G-01/03) [2004] E.P.O.R. 33 at [64].
640   *NGK INSULATORS* (T-184/84) [1986] E.P.O.R. 169; I.P.D. 9113, February 1987. See also art.88(4).

Partial and multiple priorities

Multiple priorities may be claimed for a European patent application.[641] If one **2-362**
or more priorities are claimed in respect of a European patent application, the right
of priority covers only those "elements" of the application which are disclosed in
the priority document (partial priority).[642] Here, "elements" do not mean a single
feature but subject matter as defined in a claim or disclosed in the form of an
embodiment or example.[643] Where a claim in the later application is broader than
an "element" disclosed in the priority document, then priority may be claimed for
such an element but not the other embodiments encompassed by the claim. It is irrelevant whether the partial priority is claimed from one element in one priority
document or a plurality of element in a plurality of priority documents.[644] There is
no requirement that in a claim which encompasses a priority element disclosed in
a priority document but goes wider than such to cover elements not disclosed in a
priority document, a priority claim is only permissible where it gives rise to the
claiming of "a limited number of clearly defined alternative subject matters".[645]
Thus, as made clear by the Enlarged Board of Appeal in (G1/15), under the EPC,
a claim to partial priority may only be refused for a claim that encompasses alternative subject matter (what is called a generic "OR" claim) if such matter is not
disclosed for the first time *directly, or at least implicitly, unambiguously and in an
enabling manner in the priority document*. No other substantive conditions or
limitations apply. This makes it clear that the concept of "poisonous priority" which
arose from the EBA's decision in (G2/98) is now dead.

By way of example, in a claim in an application which claims "metal" and the **2-363**
priority document claims "iron", then the claim in the application includes a claim
to iron. That aspect of the claim will be entitled to priority from the priority
document. As regard non-iron metal, the issue will be whether such is disclosed
directly or implicitly, unambiguously and in an enabling manner (applying the test
above) in the priority document. If it is not, then the claim to non-iron metal is not
entitled to priority but equally will be novel in the light of same priority document
and thus the priority document is not "poisonous" (i.e. rendering the claim for non-
iron metal as being anticipated for lack of novelty by the priority document under
art.54(3) EPC[646]). This is because, in essence, the test for claim for priority set out
above is now the same as for novelty. In short, if the priority document could be
cited as novelty—destroying prior art against all or part of a claim, then the priority claim is a legitimate one. If it cannot be cited in this fashion, then the priority
claim for all or part of a claim is an illegitimate one but that claim (or part of it)
will be novel as against the priority document. This is a welcome return to common sense and has a pleasing symmetry about it.

In a somewhat surprising decision, the TBA held that it was not possible to make **2-364**
several filings in respect of the same invention in one and the same country during

---

[641] art.88(2).
[642] art.88(3); (G1/15) at [5.1.2].
[643] (G1/15) at [5.1.2] citing (G2/98) at [4] and [6.2].
[644] (G1/15) at [5.1.3].
[645] This wording was suggested in (G2/98) and applied in a number of TBA decisions but in (G1/15),
   the EBA held that was not a requirement. Accordingly, these decisions are no longer good law.
[646] See para.2-146 for discussion of art.54(3).

the priority period and to claim separate priority for each of these applications.[647] However, this decision was not followed in *SDLO/Mystery Swine Disease*,[648] in which the TBA rejected an argument that there is a doctrine of "exhaustion of priority rights", namely that a right to priority is "exhausted" and cannot be claimed again in a later patent application in or for the same territory. In the light of (G1/15) it would appear that there is no scope for an "exhaustion of priority rights" doctrine as such makes it clear that there are no limitation or conditions on the right to be able to claim priority other than the "same invention" test.

Procedural conditions for claiming priority

2-365   The applicant claiming priority must file a declaration of priority, the state, the date of filing, the file number of the previous application, and a copy of the previous application certified by the national authority, along with a certificate stating the date of the filing of the previous application.[649] Failure to state the date of filing and in which state will result in automatic loss of priority.[650] The EPO will call on the applicant to correct other deficiencies.[651] The priority document (certified as correct by the authority with which it was filed) must be filed within 16 months after the earliest priority date.[652] In general, unless requested by the EPO, there is no need to translate the priority document into one of the official languages of the EPO. This will only be necessary where the EPO needs to determine the validity of the priority claim.[653]

Contents of the patent application

2-366   The accompanying notes with the printed form for a European patent application set out the main formalities that are required. These can be divided between the request for a European patent and the actual application itself. The request must include an indication that a European patent is sought and information identifying the applicant.[654]

2-367   The actual application must contain a description of the invention, one or more claims, any drawings referred to in the description of the claims and an abstract.[655] Furthermore, the application must designate the inventor[656] and, if the applicant is not the inventor, it must designate the origin of the applicant's right to the European patent.[657] These requirements are discussed below in more detail.

---

[647]   *L'Oréal/Skin equivalent* (T-998/99) [2005] E.P.O.R. 39.

[648]   *SDLO/Mystery Swine Disease* (T-15/01) [2005] E.P.O.R. 45. In doing so, it rejected the argument set out in (T-998/99) [2005] E.P.O.R. 39.

[649]   art.88, EPC r.52.

[650]   EPC rr.52(1), 57, 58.

[651]   art.91, EPC r.58.

[652]   EPC r.53(1).

[653]   Guid. F-VI-3.4, EPC r.53(3).

[654]   art.78, EPC r.41.

[655]   art.78.

[656]   art.81 and EPC r.21. Under r.21, an incorrect designation of an inventor can only be rectified with the consent of the wrongly designated person. Where the application failed to designate all the inventors, the consent of the already designated inventors was not required as they were not "wrongly designated" inventors—see *FUJITSU* (J-8/82) [1979–85] E.P.O.R. A111; I.P.D. 7038, June 1984.

[657]   EPC r.19.

The date of filing is deemed to be the date on which these requirements have been fulfilled.[658]   **2-368**

Description

The description must: **2-369**

(a) specify the technical field to which the invention relates;
(b) indicate the background art which, as far as known to the applicant, can be regarded as useful for understanding the invention, for drawing up the European search report and for the examination, and, preferably, cite the documents reflecting such art;
(c) disclose the invention, as claimed, in such terms that the technical problem (even if not expressly stated as such) and its solution can be understood, and state any advantageous effects of the invention with reference to the background art[659];
(d) briefly describe the figures in the drawings, if any;
(e) describe in detail at least one way of carrying out the invention claimed using examples where appropriate and referring to the drawings, if any; and
(f) indicate explicitly, when it is not obvious from the description or nature of the invention, the way in which the invention is capable of exploitation in industry.[660]

In relation to condition (e), the specification need not describe all ways of achieving the invention but it must disclose more than isolated examples and also a technical concept fit for generalisation which would enable the skilled person to achieve the invention without undue difficulty.[661] Whilst it is important that the description adequately allows a party to carry out the invention, errors can be corrected if the skilled person would have recognised the defect and remedied it without difficulty.[662]   **2-370**

The description forms the basis for the claims and along with the drawings is used to interpret the claims.[663] It is important that this requirement is complied with when filing the application. This is because the description cannot be amended so as to extend beyond the content of the application as filed.[664]   **2-371**

Claims

The claims of a patent are very important. They define the protection that is sought. There are three requirements for claims. They must: **2-372**

(i) define the matter for which protection is sought;
(ii) be clear and concise; and
(iii) be supported by the description.[665]

---

[658] art.80. Where the wrong documents are filed in error, such cannot be corrected under EPC r.88 and hence the filing date accorded will be the date when the correct documents are filed—*ATOTECH/ Correction* (G-02/95) [1997] E.P.O.R. 77.

[659] However such comparisons should not be disparaging.

[660] EPC r.42(1)(a)–(f).

[661] *UNILEVER* (T-435/91) [1994] OJ EPO 188.

[662] *AIR PRODUCTS* (T-171/84) [1986] OJ EPO 95; [1986] E.P.O.R. 210; I.P.D. 9087, November 1986.

[663] art.69(1).

[664] art.123(2). See para.2-419 for further discussion of the validity of amendments and the objection of "added matter".

[665] art.84.

2-373   The claims must be clear without need to refer to the description. The TBA has held that art.84 requires that the claims are clear in themselves when being read with the normal skills, including the knowledge about the prior art, but not including any knowledge derived from the description of the patent application or amended patent.[666] Claims can be to physical entities or physical activities, or can include features relating to both physical activities or physical entities but there need be no rigid demarcation between these type of claims.[667] A claim to an "electronic message" comprising a number of elements was held to be a valid claim as it was to a physical construct and not merely to the information content.[668]

2-374   The EPC states that wherever appropriate, the claims must comprise two parts—a pre-characterising ("prior art") portion and a characterising portion. The pre-characterising portion must contain the designation of the subject-matter of the invention and the technical features necessary to define the invention but which, in combination, form part of the prior art. The "characterising" portion designates the technical features that, when combined with the "prior art" features, it is desired to protect.[669] The mere inclusion of features in the "prior art" part of a claim will not be regarded by the EPO as a binding statement as to the lack of novelty in such features. The determination of novelty must be decided purely in the light of the objective facts of the case.[670] Thus, where an applicant finds that they have wrongly attributed a claimed feature to the pre-characterising section rather than the characterising section, the applicant may transpose the feature accordingly.[671] Where an applicant adds a section of "preferred features" in the specification, these are not to be treated as claims requiring claims fees.[672]

2-375   Claims to use stated for a particular purpose are proper alternatives to method claims for carrying out an activity.[673] If the subject-matter of a European patent is a process, the protection conferred by the patent extends to the products directly obtained by such process.[674] However, an actual claim for a products-by-process is not admissible unless the product itself fulfils the requirement for patentability.[675] Furthermore, a product-by-process is only allowable where the product cannot be defined by its structural features.[676]

2-376   Claims stating the essential features of an invention may be followed by one or more claims concerning particular embodiments of that invention.[677] Such dependent claims must contain, if possible, at the beginning a reference to the independ-

---

[666] *ICI/Optical sensing apparatus* (T-454/89) [1995] E.P.O.R. 600 at 609. It should be noted that art.84 will not be considered after grant of the patent in opposition proceedings unless an amendment is put forward and the objection of lack of clarity only arises out of the amendment—*Examination of clarity objection/Prosthetic Liner Process* (EBA) (G3/14). See para.2-419.

[667] (G-02/88) [1990] E.P.O.R. 73.

[668] *Lucent/Structured voicemail message* (T-858/02) [2006] E.P.O.R. 6.

[669] EPC r.43(1)(b).

[670] *SIEMENS* (T-6/81) [1979–85] E.P.O.R. B294; I.P.D. 5029, May 1982. See also *HUTCHINSON/Tyre locking device* (T-850/90) [1996] E.P.O.R. 439.

[671] (T-6/81) [1979–85] E.P.O.R. B294; I.P.D. 5029, May 1982.

[672] (G-05/83) [1985] OJ EPO 64; [1979–85] E.P.O.R. B241; *Neorx/Claims Fees* (J-15/88) [1991] E.P.O.R. 76. 13198.

[673] *PHARMUKA* (G-06/83) [1985] OJ EPO 67; (T-36/83) [1987] E.P.O.R. 1.

[674] art.64(2).

[675] *INTERNATIONAL FLAVOURS* (T-150/82) [1979–85] E.P.O.R. C629.

[676] *Sandvik/Cemented Carbide Body* (T-81/14).

[677] EPC r.43(3).

ent claim, and then state the additional features it is desired to protect.[678] Dependent claims can refer to other dependent claims but, if so, they should be grouped together in an appropriate way.[679] References to the description or drawing should not be used unless absolutely essential.[680] Provided that there is unity of invention, a European patent application may contain independent claims in different categories, i.e. product and process. Where the applicant wishes to file different claims for different states because of prior national rights in certain designated states, they should not file two or more sets of claims in their application, but should file broad claims and amend at the appropriate time. The EPC discourages applications with a large number of claims. In particular, it charges a claims fee for each claim over and above 15 claims, with the additional fees increasing sharply above 50 claims.[681]

Disclaimer

Disclaimers of prior art[682] may be contained in claims. Such disclaimers will be permitted if the subject-matter remaining in the claim cannot be defined more clearly and concisely by positive technical means.[683] This is so, even if the disclaimer relates to an earlier application which had not been published at the time of examination.[684] Disclaimers of prior art are often added by way of amendments during examination to avoid invalidation of the claim by prior art unknown to the applicant. The lawfulness of such amendments is discussed later.[685]   **2-377**

Drawings

Drawings often assist the reader in understanding the specification. Where the intelligibility of technical features in claims can be increased by use of reference numerals from the drawings, then they should be included in the claims. Such reference signs will not be construed as limiting the claim.[686] However, references to drawings in claims should not be used unless absolutely essential.[687]   **2-378**

Detailed provisions as to the layout and structure of drawings are laid down in the Rules and these should be consulted.[688]   **2-379**

Abstract

The abstract merely serves as technical information and cannot be taken into account for any other purpose. It must contain a precise summary of the disclosure as contained in the description, the claims and the drawings and the technical field   **2-380**

---

[678] EPC r.43(4).
[679] EPC r.43(4).
[680] EPC r.43(6), (7).
[681] EPC rr.43(5), 45(1), art.2 RFees
[682] See Guid. F-IV 4.20.
[683] *Genetic Systems/Disclaimer; PPG/Disclaimer* (G1-G2/03) [2004] E.P.O.R. 33 at [62].
[684] *BAYER/Polyether polyols* (T-04/80) [1979–85] E.P.O.R. B260.
[685] See para.2-437.
[686] EPC r.43(7).
[687] EPC r.43(6).
[688] EPC r.46.

to which the invention pertains. It should be drafted so as to constitute an efficient instrument for the purpose of searching in the particular technical field.[689]

Micro-organisms

2-381   Where an invention concerns a microbiological process or its product, then, unless the use of the micro-organism is available to the public or can be described in the application so that it can be carried out by a person skilled in the art, the micro-organism must be deposited with a recognised depositary institution not later than the date of filing of the application in order to comply with the requirement that the application should disclose the invention in a manner sufficiently clear and complete for it to be carried out by a person skilled in the art.[690] If the invention concerns the derivation of a product from strains within a class of micro-organisms, it is not necessary to deposit a preferred strain of that class according to the following rules if the description of the application contains a method to discover a preferred strain which would produce the desired product.[691]

2-382   The application as filed with the EPO must contain relevant information available to the applicant on the characteristics of the micro-organism and the depositary institution as well as the file number of the culture deposit.[692] The information relating to the depositary institution and file number must be filed within the earliest of the following periods: a period of 16 months from the filing date or priority date; by the date of submission of a request for early publication of the application; or within one month after the EPO has communicated to the applicant that a right to inspection of the files has arisen as the applicant has invoked rights against a third party.[693]

2-383   A person may request on a recognised form to the EPO, that the deposited culture be released to them after the date of publication of the European patent application.[694] The requester must use the culture or any culture derived therefrom for experimental purposes only and must not make the deposited culture available to third parties until the patent is no longer in force or the application has been withdrawn.[695] The applicant can indicate to the EPO that samples only be issued to an expert nominated by the requester prior to the date on which technical preparations for publication of the application are deemed to have been completed.[696] Such an expert can either be one approved by the applicant or one recognised as an expert by the President of the EPO.[697] The expert will be under the same obligations as the requester would have been.[698]

---

[689] art.85, EPC r.47(5).
[690] art.83, EPC r.31. A list of the recognised depositary institutions is available from the EPO.
[691] *NABISCO BRANDS INC* (T-239/87) [1988] E.P.O.R. 311; I.P.D. 11031, July–August 1988.
[692] EPC r.31(1)(b) and (c).
[693] EPC r.31(2).
[694] EPC r.33(1), (4). The requester is entitled to have the deposited culture made available prior to such a date if the applicant has invoked rights against it—art.128(2).
[695] EPC r.33(2). For the definition of derived culture, see EPC r.33(2).
[696] See EPC r.32(1).
[697] EPC r.32(2).
[698] EPC r.32(2).

Fees

The EPO provides for a series of fees to be paid within certain time limits. These **2-384** are laid down in the Rules relating to Fees (which are updated from time to time and should be checked carefully).[699] In summary, fees are paid during the stages of the European application—filing, designation of countries, search, divisional, examination and grant. Furthermore, renewal fees are payable for the application from the third and successive years from the date of filing.

The fee system is aimed at discouraging certain practices. Thus, a fee is charged **2-385** for each claim over 15 claims and this fee rises steeply for the 51st and subsequent claims. Additional fees are also payable for applications which exceed 35 pages. Where a deadline is extendible, then there will often be additional processing fees. The consequences of failing to pay fees in time are set out herebelow in relation to each stage.

Unity of invention

The European patent application must relate to one invention only or to a group **2-386** of inventions so linked as to form a single inventive concept.[700] EPC r.44 clarifies this by saying:

"(1) Where a group of inventions is claimed in one and the same European patent application, the requirement of unity of invention referred to in Article 82 shall be fulfilled only when there is a technical relationship among those inventions involving one or more of the same or corresponding special technical features. The expression "special technical features" shall mean those features which define a contribution which each of the claimed inventions considered as a whole makes over the prior art.

(2) The determination whether a group of inventions is so linked as to form a single general inventive concept shall be made without regard to whether the inventions are claimed in separate claims or as alternatives within a single claim."

In considering whether there is unity of invention, i.e. a technical relationship **2-387** among those inventions, the Boards of Appeal have said that as a pre-condition, it requires an analysis of the technical problem or problems underlying the respective group of inventions.[701]

This objection can only be raised by the EPO either by the Search Division or **2-388** the Examining Division. It cannot be raised as a ground for opposition or before the national courts as a ground for revocation.[702] The applicant must file a divisional application if they are not content to limit their application to the first invention.[703]

In chemical inventions involving claims for intermediates and end-products **2-389** where the intermediates were required for the preparation of the end-products, the EPO will permit the claiming of both intermediates and end-products claims as well as the preparation of the end-products, as such relates to a group of inventions so

---

[699] Referred to as RFees. For fees as of August 2017, see *http://www.epo.org/law-practice/legal-texts/official-journal/2016/etc/se2/p1.html* [Accessed 18 August 2017].
[700] art.82.
[701] See summary of decisions on this in *KENNEDY INSTITUTE/Autoimmune disorders* (T-188/04) [2005] E.P.O.R. 51.
[702] See arts 100, 138. For where the Search Division raises the question of unity, see para.2-400.
[703] See para.2-443.

linked as to form a single inventive concept.[704] Where the application claims two or more claims relating to differing uses for an inventive product, then the claims fall within a single inventive concept.[705]

Communication and filing with the EPO

2-390   The EPO allows communications by post, fax, hand or electronically. As regards the latter, this can be done either by the use of CD-R/DVD-R or using various EPO online portals such as the EPO Online Filing, its web-form filing service or EPO case management system.[706] Filing by email is not allowed.[707] With some contracting states, a European patent application may be filed at their central industrial property office.[708]

General provisions regarding the EPO's decision-making process

Decisions of the EPO

2-391   In any proceedings before it, the EPO must examine the facts of its own motion and is not restricted in its examination of an application to considering the facts, evidence and arguments provided by the parties.[709] It may disregard facts and evidence which are not submitted in due time by the parties.[710] However, the EPO may only make its decision based upon grounds or evidence on which the parties concerned have had an opportunity to present their comments.[711] It will only consider the European application or text in the text submitted to or agreed by the applicant or the proprietor of the patent.[712]

Taking of evidence

2-392   The means of taking and giving evidence may include the hearing of parties, requests for information, the production of documents, hearing of witnesses, opinions by experts, inspection, and sworn statements in writing.[713] Where the EPO considers it necessary to hear evidence orally, it will issue a summons to the person concerned to appear before it or request that the competent court in the country of residence of the person concerned take such evidence.[714] Such a summons must give at least two months' notice to the witness.[715] In general, in relation to critical declarations, the EPO should summon the maker of the declaration, in particular

---

[704] *BAYER AG* (T-57/82) [1979–85] E.P.O.R. B474; I.P.D. 5088, October 1982.
[705] *X/Fibre Fleece* (W-11/89) (decision of the TBA on the meaning of the equivalent provision in the Patent Cooperation Treaty).
[706] Guid. A-II-1.3 sets out in detail the various electronic methods for communication.
[707] Guid. A-II-1.4.
[708] Guid. A-II-1.1.
[709] art.114.
[710] art.114(2).
[711] art.113(1). See *MONSANTO COMPANY/Right to be heard* (T-922/02) [2004] E.P.O.R. 44 where the TBA emphasises this fundamental right.
[712] art.113(2).
[713] art.117(1).
[714] EPC r.118(1), (2).
[715] EPC r.118(2).

where it is on the evidence of prior user.[716] A witness summoned to the EPO may request that they give their evidence at a competent court in their country of residence.[717] The taking of oral evidence may be given on oath.[718] More detailed provisions for oral hearings generally are contained in the Implementing Regulations.[719]

Evaluation of evidence

The EPC is silent on the standard of proof of facts and what cogency of evidence is required to prove facts. However, considerable case law has developed concerning the evaluation of evidence. In *Identity of applicant* (G1/12),[720] the EBA confirmed that proceedings before the EPO are conducted in accordance with the principle of free evaluation of evidence.[721] As the evaluation of evidence concerning prior use where novelty is put in issue is often a thorny issue, this has already been discussed in the section on novelty.[722]

2-393

The Guidelines give good guidance as to the application of the "free evaluation" approach.

2-394

"When evidence is examined, since the EPC says nothing about how the outcome of taking of evidence should be assessed, the principle of unfettered consideration applies. This means that its content and its significance for the proceedings are assessed in the light of the particular circumstances of each individual case (e.g. time, place, type of evidence, position of witness in firm, etc.). The principle of unfettered consideration also means that EPO departments are empowered to evaluate evidence submitted by the parties in any appropriate manner, or indeed to disregard it as unimportant or irrelevant. In particular it has to be decided on a case-by-case basis when a particular piece of evidence is sufficient.

When deciding whether an alleged fact is accepted, the Division may use the criterion of the "balance of probabilities", which means that it is satisfied that one set of facts is more likely to be true than the other. Furthermore, the more serious the issue, the more convincing must be the evidence to support it (see T 750/94). For example, if a decision might result in revocation of the patent in a case concerning alleged prior use, the available evidence has to be very critically and strictly examined. In particular, in case of alleged prior use for which little if any evidence would be available to the patentee to establish that no prior use had taken place, the Division should cede to the stricter criterion close to absolute conviction, i.e. beyond any reasonable doubt (see T 97/94)."[723]

Observations from third parties

The EPO may also, following the publication of the application, take account of observations from third parties concerning the patentability of the invention. Such observations must be in writing and include a statement of grounds on which they are based. In such a case, the observations must be communicated to the applicant

2-395

---

[716] *ALTHIN MEDICAL/Declaration in lieu of oath* (T-474/04) [2005] E.P.O.R. 47. In that case, the declaration had given evidence via a German unsworn declaration ("*eidesstatliche Versicherungen*").
[717] EPC r.120.
[718] EPC r.120(3).
[719] EPC rr.115–124.
[720] [2014] OJ EPO A114.
[721] See [31] applying (G3/97).
[722] See para.2-127.
[723] Guid. E-III-4.3.

or proprietor of the patent for comment.[724] Such a third party cannot request an oral hearing as they are not deemed to be a party to the proceedings.[725]

Oral hearings

2-396   The EPO may have an oral hearing if it considers it to be expedient or if one of the parties to the proceedings requests one.[726] Generally speaking, the applicant will not be allowed more than one oral hearing on the same subject. However, the TBA has stressed that the right to an oral hearing is an extremely important procedural right which the EPO should take all steps to safeguard.[727] Thus, the EPO cannot issue a decision where there has been a request for an oral hearing.[728] Oral proceedings before the Receiving Section, the Examining Section and the Legal Division are not public.[729] However, oral proceedings before the Boards of Appeal and the Opposition Division are public, including the delivery of the decision, unless there would be serious and unjustified disadvantages in doing so.[730]

Loss of rights

2-397   Where a person loses rights as a result of a failure to comply with time limits, the EPO must communicate the loss of rights to the person concerned.[731] The person concerned may, within two months after the notification, apply for a decision on the matter by the EPO if they consider that the finding of the EPO is inaccurate.[732]

Prosecution of application before EPO

The filing of the patent application

2-398   The request for grant of a European patent application must be filed on the prescribed EPO form.[733] This is provided with an explanatory note and sets out the mandatory requirements for the request form. The application must be filed either at the EPO in Munich or its branch at The Hague or Berlin, or, if the national law permits, in the patent office of a contracting state.[734] However, divisional applications must be filed at the EPO.[735] The EPC's requirements regarding communication with it, its language regime and fees have already been discussed.[736]

---

[724] art.115, EPC r.114.
[725] arts 115, 116.
[726] art.116(1).
[727] *ASHLAND* (T-668/89), I.P.D. 13159, September 1990.
[728] *Thomassen/Tin Preservation* (T-560/88) [2003] E.P.O.R. 10. See also *Fujitsu/Oral Proceedings* (T-19/87) [1988] E.P.O.R. 393.
[729] art.116(3).
[730] art.116(4).
[731] art.119, EPC r.112(1).
[732] EPC r.112(2).
[733] EPC r.41(1).
[734] art.75.
[735] art.76.
[736] See paras 2-351, 2-384 and 2-390.

Preliminary examination of application

Once an application examination is filed, the Receiving Section examines whether the application satisfies the formal requirements and accords a date of filing.[737] Furthermore, it checks to see if the filing and search fees have been paid and, if necessary, whether a translation of the application in the language of the proceedings has been filed in time

2-399

Search under the EPC

Following the formal examination, the EPO then conducts a search on the basis of the claims with due regard to the description and any drawings.[738] The objective of the search is to discover the state of art which is relevant for the Examining Division to determine whether the claimed invention is new and involves an inventive step. The search is normally carried out only on European, PCT and certain national published patent applications. If the application arises from entry into the European phase of a PCT application, then the EPO will dispense with drawing up a supplementary search report if it was the ISA. Where the application claims more than one group of inventions and thus lacks unity,[739] the EPO will only search against the inventions first mentioned in the claim.[740] Once the search has been carried out, the EPO will prepare an opinion as to whether the application meets the requirements of the EPC. This is similar to the IPRP prepared by the ISA in a PCT application.[741] The search report and the opinion (called the Extended European Search Report "EESR") is then sent to the applicant. The applicant is then required to respond to the EESR or otherwise the application is deemed withdrawn within the time period for requesting examination of the application.[742] This could involve filing amendments and/or filing observations on the search opinion.

2-400

Publication of the application

The EPO is obliged to publish a European patent application as soon as possible after the expiry of a period of 18 months from the date of filing or, where relevant, the priority date, or at the request of the applicant before the expiry of that period.[743] This will include the search report if it is available. Otherwise the search report is published separately.[744] The publication will include any amended claims which are amended before the termination of the technical preparations for publication.[745]

2-401

Publication is important because it provides for provisional protection of the patent which cannot be less than that provided for national unexamined published applications and must give rise to at least the right to reasonable compensation in the

2-402

---

[737] arts 80, 90.
[738] Generally, see Guid. B for the search phase of an application.
[739] For lack of unity, see para.2-383.
[740] Guid. B-VII-1.1.
[741] See para.2-064.
[742] EPC r.70, r.70a(1).
[743] art.93.
[744] Guid. A-VI.
[745] EPC r.68(4).

event of infringement.[746] However, contracting states can provide that such provisional protection is not available until such time as a translation of the claims into one of its official languages has been made available to the public or has been communicated to the person using the invention in that state.[747] Once publication has occurred, the public may, on request, inspect the files relating to the application.[748] Finally, publication of an application can have serious consequences because the specification then becomes part of the prior art and could thus be fatal to a subsequent application based on the same invention. Publication of an application will not occur if the application is refused, withdrawn or deemed to have been withdrawn before the termination of the technical preparations for publication.[749] Such preparations are deemed to have been completed at the end of the day five weeks before the end of the 18-month period from the filing date or the priority date (if claimed).[750]

Examination of the application

2-403   The applicant must file a request for examination before the expiry of a period of six months after the date on which the European Patent Bulletin mentions the publication of the search report.[751] During this period, as discussed above, the applicant must have responded to the EESR.[752]

2-404   The Examining Division will then consider whether the application meets the substantive requirements of the EPC. The focus here will be here on comments and/or amendments filed by the application in response to the EESR. If it considers that the application is not patentable, it must invite the applicant "as often as necessary" to file observations or amendments.[753] The Examining Division's task is to consider, in the light of the search report and where available, the EESR, whether the application complies with the requirements of the EPC and, in particular, whether the invention is patentable.[754]

2-405   Where the applicant has indicated a desire for speedy examination, the examiner will try and issue its first communication within three months of receipt of the request for examination.[755]

2-406   The examining process involves a constructive dialogue between an examiner allocated to the application and the applicant as to the patentability of the invention. Thus the EPO has stated that the guiding principle of the examining procedure is that a decision on whether to grant a patent or refuse the application should be reached in as few actions as possible.[756]

2-407   If the Examining Division considers that a European patent cannot be granted, it will refuse the application. The decision is issued by the Examining Division as a whole and must contain the reasons for refusal. These reasons may only be based

---

[746] art.67(2).
[747] See para.2-354.
[748] art.128.
[749] EPC r.67(2).
[750] [2007] OJ EPO D1, Decision of President of EPO; Guid. A-VI-1.1.
[751] art.94(2); EPC r.70.
[752] See para.2-400.
[753] art.94(3).
[754] art.94(1).
[755] See *Guide for Applicants*, para.161: *http://www.epo.org/applying/european/Guide-for-applicants/html/e/index.html* [Accessed 18 August 2017]; Notice from EPO dated 30 September 2015.
[756] *Guide for Applicants*, para.162.

on grounds in respect of which the applicant has had an opportunity to put forward comments.

The decision-making process of the EPO is discussed in more detail elsewhere.[757]   **2-408**

Grant of the patent

If the Examining Division concludes that the application fulfils the require-   **2-409**
ments of the EPC, then it will grant a European patent provided that the applicant
has:

(a) approved the text in which it is intended to grant the patent;
(b) paid the fee for grant and printing and ensured, where applicable, renewal
     fees and claim fees have been paid in time; and
(c) filed translation of the claims in the two other official languages of the EPO
     in time.[758]

The actual procedure is that the EPO informs the applicant of the text in which   **2-410**
it intends to grant the patent and asks the applicant to indicate within four months
whether they approve the text notified (this is called the "Rule 71(3) communication"—previously r.51(4)) and invite them to pay the fees for grant, printing and
to provide translations of the claims into the two other official language. If the applicant pays the fees and files the translations, they are deemed to have approved
the text intended for grant.[759]

If the applicant is still unhappy with the application, it can file further amend-   **2-411**
ments or correction of errors within this two- to four-month period but must also
file translations of the amended claims into the two other official languages.[760]

The Examining Division will then either grant the patent in the approved form   **2-412**
(including any amendments if such are permissible) or refuse it. The actual grant
of a European patent takes effect on the date on which the European Patent Bulletin mentions the grant. The EPO will, at the same time, publish a specification of
the European patent containing the description, claims (in all three official
languages) and any drawings.[761]

Transfer into national patents

The grant of European patent results in the obtaining of a "bundle" of national   **2-413**
patents for the states designated in the application. Contracting states can stipulate
that owners of European patents must provide translations into an official language
of that state and that if they fail to do so, the patent is void ab initio in the relevant
state.[762]

Whether or not a translation of the description or claims is required into an of-   **2-414**
ficial language of a designated state depends on whether it is a party to the London
Agreement and/or what provision has been made by the contracting state. This has
been discussed earlier.[763]

---

[757] See para.2-391.
[758] Guid. C-V-I 1.1–1.5; 2.
[759] EPC r.71(3).
[760] EPC r.71(3).
[761] arts 97, 98, EPC r.71(a).
[762] art.65.
[763] See paras 2-351 to 2-357.

2-415   Once the Agreement on the UPC comes into effect, following grant, the applicant may request that the European patent be converted into a EU Unitary Patent for EU states that are participating Member States (all bar Spain and Croatia). This is discussed below.[764]

Amendments

Between receipt of search report and r.71(3) communication

2-416   Prior to receipt of the search report, the applicant is not entitled to amend the description, claims or drawings.[765] After receipt of the search report, the applicant may, of their own volition, amend the description, claims or drawings in response to the EESR.[766] Otherwise, save in response to communications from the EPO, consent of the Examining Division is required to file amendments.[767] In considering whether or not to give its consent, the Examining Division will balance the need for speedy grant against the commercial damage that would be inflicted upon the public by the existence of invalid patents.[768] Generally, the Examining Division will give its consent if the amendment complies with the substantive law of the EPC.

r.71(3) communication

2-417   Once the EPO has issued a r.71(3) intention to grant, the applicant may request amendments to the communicated text but such must be reasoned.[769] This should deal with why the amended application does not contravene the prohibition on added matter under art.123(2).[770] In the r.71(3) communication, the Examining Division may include amendments and corrections made on its own initiative which it may reasonably expect the application to accept.[771] The Examining Division will then issue a new communication under r.71(3) if it considers that the amendments are admissible and allowable. In general, the later that the application to amend is made, the harder it is to obtain the consent of the Examining Division.[772]

---

[764] See para.2-506.

[765] EPC r.137(1).

[766] EPC r.137(2), r.70(a), r.161.As to how amendments should be made, see Guid. C-III- 2. For EESR, see para.2-400.

[767] EPC r.137(3).

[768] *EURO-CELTIQUE* (T-675/90) [1994] 1 E.P.O.R. 66.

[769] Guid. C-V-4.3.

[770] Guid. C-V-4.3. The prohibition on "added matter" is considered at para.2-425, et seq.

[771] Generally see Guid. C-V-1.1 as to the types of amendments that the Examining Division will put forward of its own initiative.

[772] For an example of the exercise of the discretion under EPC r.71(3) (or its predecessor, r.51(4)), see *SITE MICROSURGICAL SYSTEMS/Ophthalmic microsurgical system* (T-375/90) [1993] E.P.O.R. 588 (amendment permissible after [r.71(3)] communication because the applicant was prompt and amendment sought to avoid narrow interpretation by competitor); *UNIVERSITY OF CALIFORNIA* (T-182/88) [1989] E.P.O.R. 147, I.P.D. 13085, June 1990 (addition of method claims specifically adapted for Austria after [r.71(3)] communication permissible as EPO's interest in speedy completion outweighed by A's interest in obtaining proper patent protection in Austria). See also *WHITBY II/late amendment* (G-7/93) [1995] E.P.O.R. 49, which states that discretion must be exercised restrictively balancing the interests of the applicant with that of the EPO's interest in bringing proceedings to a close. Cf. *EURO-CELTIQUE* (T-675/90) [1994] 1 E.P.O.R. 66 (these two cases concerned an application to amend following the old "Rule 51(6)" communication).

Auxiliary requests

At the examining stage or on appeal, the applicant will often put forward a **2-418** proposed set of alternative claims if the main claims ("the higher request") are held to be impermissible. Such claims are known as "auxiliary requests" and are often used. They act as fall-back positions. An applicant may put forward a number of auxiliary requests. Generally, such requests must be put forward in good time. Admission of the requests is a matter of discretion for the Examining Division or Appeal Board. At the appellate stage, there must be a good reason for permitting the request.[773] A Board of Appeal may refuse to consider amended claims constituting new requests which are filed at a late stage, for example, during oral proceedings, if such amended claims are not at first sight clearly allowable.[774] Amendments put forward during appeal or opposition proceedings are examined fully as to their compatibility with the EPC.[775] Care must be taken when putting forward a number of auxiliary requests during ex officio proceedings. This is because the Examining Division must know which text the applicant is putting forward.[776] Thus, where the Examining Division indicated to an applicant that it was not prepared to permit first and second-choice auxiliary requests but was prepared to permit a third-choice auxiliary request and invited the applicant to withdraw the first and second-choice requests, its refusal to do so meant that the Examining Division refused the application.[777] However, where the Examining Division indicates at a r.71(3) stage that it only intends to grant the patent in a low preference auxiliary request, the applicant is entitled to an explanation of the reasons why the higher ranking requests are not allowable.[778] Auxiliary requests must be properly formulated and the precise wording determined.[779]

Amendments in opposition proceedings

A different practice exists during opposition proceedings. In such proceedings, **2-419** the Opposition Division will rule on each request.[780] During opposition proceedings, which occur after grant of a patent, the patentee is more restricted in its ability to amend their patent. Thus, there is no general right to amend a patent. However, the patentee may amend the description, claims or drawings to overcome a ground of opposition specified in art.100 even if that ground is not invoked by the opponent.[781] If such is the case, then in general the principles applying to the grant of leave to amend a patent during examination apply to proceedings in opposition proceedings.[782] In *Novel Enhanced Coating for Prosthetic Lines/Freedom Innova-*

---

[773] *PROCTER/Oral Composition* (T-840/93) [1997] E.P.O.R. 60.

[774] *MITSUBISHI/Gas laser device* (T-926/93) [1998] E.P.O.R. 94 at [98].

[775] *Rohm & Haas/Power to examine (G-09/91)* [1993] E.P.O.R. 485.

[776] See *Bone care/Vitamin D derivatives* (T-549/96) [2003] E.P.O.R. 58 and *No.15/98 Legal Advice from EPO* [1998] OJ EPO 3/133.

[777] (T-549/96) [2003] E.P.O.R. 58.

[778] *APPLERA/Dibenzorrhodamine dye* (T-1255/04) [2005] E.P.O.R. 38 at [3.3]. This thus enables him to appeal the decision refusing the higher preference request. See also Guid. C-V-4.6.2 which sets out the procedure that the applicant should follow if it wishes the grant to be based on a higher request which has been refused pursuant to the first r.71(3) communication.

[779] *Ameron/Polysiloxane* (T-455/03) [2006] E.P.O.R. 20.

[780] (T-549/96) [2003] E.P.O.R. 58 at [4.2].

[781] EPC r.80.

[782] For the principles applying to the grant of leave to amend a patent during oral proceedings during

tions LLC (G3/14)[783] the EBA dealt with how the Opposition Division should manage lack of clarity objections to amendments put forward in opposition proceedings. It said that the Opposition Division should examine whether such claims are objectionable under art.84 for lack of clarity but only when, and then only, to the extent that the amendment itself introduces the possibility of non-compliance with art.84.

Amendments in divisional applications

2-420   Where amendments are put forward in divisional applications, then the permissibility of the amendment under art.123(2) needs to be considered not only with respect to the application as filed but also with respect to the parent application (and where appropriate, the grandparent application). The issue of amendments to divisional applications is considered in the section on divisional applications.[784]

Amendment on appeal

2-421   Once a patent is granted, the EPC does not allow any amendment to broaden the scope of protection of the claims.[785] In opposition proceedings, in response to an objection by the opponent or Opposition Division, a patentee may put forward claims that narrow the breadth of the claims (perhaps in response to new prior art unearthed by the opponent). These amendments may be accepted by the Opposition Division. The opponent may then appeal and argue that the amendments were unallowable because, e.g. they introduced added subject matter. In such circumstances, the patentee may wish to revert to the broader claims as granted and during the appeal, file such amendments. However, if the TBA allowed the patentee to do so, it would put the opponent/appellant in a worse position than if it had not appealed. This triggers the doctrine of *reformatio in peius* whereby an appellant cannot be put in a worse position than if it had not appealed. However, clearly, a rigid application of the doctrine could work very substantial injustice to the patentee. If the TBA forms the view that the amendment allowed by the Opposition Division did introduce added subject matter but equally, the patentee could not withdraw it, then it would be bound to revoke the patent.

2-422   The EBA had to deal with these issues in *Reformatio in peius* (G1/99).[786] It held that in principle, the doctrine of reformatio in peius applied to appellate proceedings from the Opposition Division. However, it held that an exception may be made to this principle where its strict application would mean that the patent as maintained in amended form would otherwise have to be revoked as a direct consequence of an inadmissible amendment held allowable by the Opposition Division. It said that in such circumstances, the patent proprietor should be allowed to file requests (i) for an amendment introducing the originally disclosed features which limited the scope of the patent as maintained, (ii) if such a limitation is not possible, for an amendment introducing one or more originally disclosed features which extend the scope of the patent as maintained (but within the limits

---

opposition proceedings, see *TERUMO/Production of peptides (amendments permitted)* (T-626/90) [1996] E.P.O.R. 194; *PROCTER/Oral compositions (amendments denied)* (T-28/92) [1996] E.P.O.R. 305.
[783] ECLI:EP:BA:2015:G000314.20150324.
[784] Discussed at paras 2-443, 2-446.
[785] See para.2-440.
[786] *Reformatio in peius* (G1/99) ECLI:EP:BA:2001:G000199.20010402.

of art.123(3)), or (iii) if such is not possible, the deletion of the inadmissible amendment (but again within the limit of art.123(3)).[787]

Centralised post-grant amendment

Following the introduction of the EPC 2000, the registered proprietor of a patent may surrender a granted European patent revoked or have it limited by way of amendment for all designated states.[788] It cannot do so if there are pending opposition proceedings.[789] Previously, proprietors who wished to amend European patents following grant had to do so in the national jurisdictions. This was obviously expensive and involved multiple proceedings. Accordingly, this was a very welcome change to the EPC.

2-423

The procedure is ex parte. The draft amendments are examined to ensure that the amended claims comply with art.84,[790] do not add subject-matter and do not extend the protection of the patent.[791] If the draft amendments do not satisfy this, the Examining Division gives the requester one opportunity to correct any deficiencies and amend the claims and where appropriate the description and drawings within a specified period.[792] Importantly, there is no other examination, e.g. of novelty or inventive step or of "discretionary" matters, e.g. the conduct of the patentee, delay, etc. If the proposed amendments satisfy the Examining Division, the amended patent specification is then published.[793]

2-424

Substantive law

Amendments prior to grant of the patent are only permissible if they do not contain subject-matter which extends beyond the content of the application as filed.[794] The basic principle has been stated in *Disclaimer/SCRIPPS* (G2/10)[795]:

2-425

"[4.3] The importance and the applicability, without exception, of Article 123(2) EPC was underlined in the jurisprudence of the Enlarged Board of Appeal as early as in its opinion G 3/89 and decision G 11/91 (OJ EPO 1993, 117 and 125, relating to amendments by way of correction). From these rulings it follows that any amendment to the parts of a European patent application or of a European patent relating to the disclosure (the description, claims and drawings) is subject to the mandatory prohibition on extension laid down in Article 123(2) EPC and can therefore, irrespective of the context of the amendment made, only be made within the limits of '*what a skilled person would derive directly and unambiguously, using common general knowledge, and seen objectively and relative to the date of filing, from the whole of these documents as filed ... .*'"

The underlined part of the above excerpt is said to be the"gold standard" for al-

2-426

---

[787] For a good example of the application of these exceptions, see *KCI Licensing Inc/Vacuum assisted tissue treatment system* (T-2129/14) ECLI:EP:BA:2016:T212914.20160601.

[788] art.105a EPC.

[789] art.105a(2).

[790] e.g. the claims are clear and concise, define the matter for which protection is sought and are supported by the description. See para.2-371.

[791] EPC r.95(2).

[792] EPC r.95(2).

[793] art.105c.

[794] art.123(2). Guid. H-IV, para.2.1.

[795] *Disclaimer/SCRIPPS (G2/10)* ECLI:EP:BA:2011:G000210.20110830; *Disclaimer III* (G1/16) ECLI:EP:BA:2017:G000116.20171218.

lowability of amendments under art.123(2) and apply to all amendments whatever their nature.[796] The idea underlying art.123(2) is that an applicant should not be allowed to improve his person by adding subject-matter not discussed in the application as filed, as this would give him an unwarranted advantage and could be damaging to the legal security of third parties relying upon the original content of the application.[797] It is a notorious fact that practitioners consider that the EPO is extremely strict on the allowability of amendments under art.123(3) with undue focus on the claims as filed and the proposed amended claim, rather than considering the disclosure as a whole of the patent application as filed. In new EPO Guidelines, which came into force on 1 November 2014, the EPO has sought to distance itself from this approach and issued new guidelines which state:

> "When assessing the conformity of the amended claims to the requirements of Art. 123(2), the focus should be placed on what is really disclosed to the skilled person by the documents as filed as directed to a technical audience. In particular, the examiner should avoid disproportionally focusing on the structure of the claims as filed to the detriment of the subject-matter that the skilled person would directly and unambiguously derive from the application as a whole."[798]

2-427   Despite these new guidelines, in *Samsung*,[799] the TBA held that the Guidelines do not change the law. It said that the above wording was taken from (T-2619/11) whose comments were made in the circumstances of the case and in (T-2619/11) the TBA did not intend to gloss over the existing "gold" standard. Nevertheless, in *Samsung*, the TBA did consider whether a passage in the description gave support for the amended claim but held that it did not.[800]

2-428   No distinction should be drawn between subject-matter in the specification or claims.[801] The above statement is one of general principle. However, the EPO has developed a number of sub-principles in relation to the deletion or addition of integers into claims. These are now discussed.

Deletion or replacement of feature in claim

2-429   Where the amendment seeks to replace or remove a feature from a claim, the Guidelines say that this is allowable under art.123(2) provided that:

> "The replacement or removal of a feature from a claim does not violate *Art. 123(2)* if the skilled person would directly and unambiguously recognise that:
>
> (i)   the feature was not explained as essential in the disclosure[802];
> (ii)   the feature is not, as such, indispensable for the function of the invention in the light of the technical problem the invention serves to solve; and

---

[796] See (G1/16), at [18]–[19].
[797] See (G1/16), at [36] citing (G1/03), at [9].
[798] Guid. H-IV-2.2.
[799] *Reinforcement for the top plate of a drum washing machine/SAMSUNG* (T-1363/12) ECLI:EP:BA:2014:T136312.20141212.
[800] See [1.4].
[801] *SWINTONS* (T-14/83) [1984] OJ EPO 105; *USS ENGINEERS* (T-139/83) [1979–85] E.P.O.R. C855; I.P.D. 6111, November 1983.
[802] For an illustration of whether a feature is essential, see *VAN DER LELY/Soil cultivating implement* (T-136/88) [1996] E.P.O.R. 67 where it was held that the deletion of a feature of Claim 1 during opposition proceedings was impermissible because the feature was clearly put forward as being necessary to solve the originally indicated problem and an invention without the feature was neither disclosed nor appeared intended by the description.

(iii) the replacement or removal requires no real modification of other features to compensate for the change.

In case of a replacement by another feature, the replacing feature must of course find support in the original application documents, so as not to contravene *Art. 123(2)* (see *T 331/87*)."[803]

In the case of replacement of one feature for another, the EPO held that for an **2-430** invention for winding apparatus, the substitution of the phrase "rotatable carrier" for "rotatable disc" was allowable. This was despite the fact that the original application made no mention of a "rotatable disc", because a skilled person would have understood immediately that the configuration of the carrier was of no consequence.[804] In contrast, in an application where an applicant wished to amend their claims to include a re-circulating copier in which odd-numbered sheets were copied and stored, whereas in the application as originally filed, it was the even numbered sheets that were copied and stored, the TBA held that the proposed claims contained information that went beyond the content of the application as filed and was therefore not allowable.[805]

Addition of a feature in claim

An applicant will sometimes put forward an amendment to limit the scope of a **2-431** claim by the addition of a limiting feature because of prior art that has been uncovered. In *KABUSHIKI KAISHA/Divisional application*,[806] the TBA held that prior to the grant of the application, the addition to a claim of an undisclosed limiting feature may or may not constitute subject-matter which extends beyond the content of the application as filed, depending on circumstances. Generally, if the added feature provides a technical contribution to the subject-matter (i.e. contributes to the inventiveness) and is not disclosed in the application, it will be impermissible. If, on the other hand, the feature in question merely excludes protection for part of the subject-matter, it will be permissible. In considering whether the added feature goes beyond providing a mere limitation but involves a technical contribution to the claimed invention, one must consider how it interacts with the other features of the claim so as to solve or assist the solution of the technical problem as it is understood by the skilled person.[807]

Intermediate generalisation/restriction

Even where the additional feature added to the claim is disclosed in the original **2-432** application, such may not be enough to avoid art.123(2). This is particularly the case where some but not all features of a particular embodiment are introduced by way

---

[803] Guid. H-V-3.1.

[804] *Rieter/Winding apparatus* (T-52/82) [1979–85] E.P.O.R. B459.

[805] See (T-133/85) [1989] E.P.O.R. 116. This case is interesting in that it discusses the relationship between art.84 (claims must be supported by description) and art.123(2) (amendment must not contain subject-matter which extends beyond the context of the application as filed).

[806] *KABUSHIKI KAISHA/Divisional Application* (T-873/94) [1998] E.P.O.R. 71; (G-01/93) [1995] E.P.O.R. 97.

[807] *ADVANCED SEMICONDUCTOR PRODUCTS/Optical membrane* (T-384/91) [1996] E.P.O.R. 125 applying (G-01/93) [1995] E.P.O.R. 97. See also *ALLEXON/Lubricating oil additive* [1995] E.P.O.R. 306.

of amendment into a claim. This is often called an "intermediate generalisation". This term is used because the applicant is not seeking to claim the embodiment per se but is seeking to "cherry-pick"[808] some features of the embodiment (usually to avoid a prior art citation) but omitting in the amended claim, all features of the embodiment. Thus, the applicant is putting forward a claim that falls between the original (wide) claim and a particular embodiment of that wide claim disclosed in the patent specification. In that sense, it is an "intermediate" claim which seeks to "generalise" the disclosed embodiment so that the claim would cover other embodiments other than the particular disclosed embodiment. It would probably be better to understand it as an "intermediate restriction" (as it restricts to some extent the original claim but not as far as restricting it to all the features of a disclosed embodiment).

2-433   With an amendment that is an intermediate generalisation, the applicant may often argue that the amendment is allowed because there is express disclosure of the added features in the patent description, e.g. an embodiment. However, it will be appreciated that if the applicant has cherry-picked features from an embodiment but discarded other features in the same embodiment and these features have some structural relationship with each other, then the amended claim may truly be said to claim an invention not disclosed in the application as filed. Thus, the Guidelines make it clear that the contents of the application as filed should not be considered a "reservoir" from which individual features pertaining to separate embodiments can be combined in order to artificially create a particular combination.[809]

2-434   The Guidelines set out a two-part test for the admissibility of such features.

(1)   The feature is not related or inextricably linked to the other features of that embodiment.

(3)   The overall disclosure justifies the generalising isolation of the feature and its introduction into the claim.[810]

2-435   The Guidelines give helpful examples drawn from TBA case law. One will suffice.

Example 3
Original claim 1 relates to a coating composition comprising at least one rosin compound, at least one polymer and an antifoulant.

After amendment a new claim was introduced relating to a method for preparing a coating composition comprising the mixing of at least one rosin compound, at least one polymer and an antifoulant. The only basis for the method is the examples. The Board observed that for some solutions the amount of added rosin was extremely low whereas for others it was extremely high. The subject-matter of the amended claim was considered to be an unallowable generalisation of the examples, since nothing in the description indicated to the person skilled in the art that the observed variations were not essential to make a coating composition.

2-436   The above example comes from a TBA case.[811] The amended claim drew from 20 examples given in the patent application whereby the polymer was mixed with

---

[808] A mildly prejudicial English expression which means to select those features/arguments/facts which favour one but ignore those which do not.
[809] Guid. H-V-3.2.1.
[810] Guid. H-V-3.2.1.
[811] This comes from the decision in *Anti-fouling/BASF* (T-200/04) ECLI:EP:BA:2006:T020004.20061024. See [10.1] to [10.4].

rosin in different ratios. The Board held that there were two possible readings—taking the examples as a whole, the variations across the 20 examples showed that *any* mixture was possible (and thus the generalisation was admissible) or alternatively, for *each* polymer solution, the ratio was critical. It held that it was not clear which was the right interpretation and therefore that the amendment was an impermissible generalisation as there was ambiguity and *"nothing in the description indicates to the person skilled in the art that the observed variations are not essential to make a coating composition"*.[812]

Disclaimers of prior art

Applicants may also seek to exclude prior art by eliminating from a general feature specific embodiments or areas. These are generally called disclaimers. These will usually take two forms—"undisclosed" and "disclosed" disclaimers. An "undisclosed" disclaimer occurs when a claim includes a disclaimer to take account of prior art not known to the applicant or subject matter that is unpatentable but where the disclaimed subject matter is not expressly mentioned in the patent application as filed. A "disclosed" disclaimer is one which disclaims subject matter expressly mentioned in the patent application as filed, e.g. as an example or embodiment. The EBA considered the lawfulness of "undisclosed" disclaimers in in *PPG/Disclaimer; GENETIC SYSTEMS/Disclaimer*[813] It held that an "undisclosed" disclaimer could not be refused under art.123(2) solely because the disclaimed subject matter had no basis in the application as filed. In short, the mere fact that the disclaimed prior art is not disclosed expressly in the application as filed is not fatal. This is important because often the claim will be to a class of products without disclosing every product that falls within the class. Thus, a claim may be to "fruit" and there is a need to disclaim tangerines which are not mentioned in the patent application as filed. However, the EBA made it clear that "undisclosed" disclaimers were only allowable in certain cases—to restore novelty against art.54(3) prior art,[814] accidental anticipation under art.54(2) or to disclaim subject matter which is excluded from patentability. The EBA said that if the disclaimer becomes relevant for the assessment of inventive step or sufficiency of disclosure, it adds subject matter contrary to art.123(2).

2-437

The permissibility of "disclosed" disclaimers was considered in the EBA's decision in *The Scripps Research Institute/Disclaimer*.[815] Here, the EBA held that an amendment which introduced a disclaimer whereby subject matter referred to in the application as filed was disclaimed would infringe art.123(2) if the remaining subject matter after introduction of the disclaimer was not explicitly or implicitly, directly and unambiguously disclosed to the skilled person in the application as filed, using common general knowledge. Determining whether that was the case required a technical assessment of the overall technical circumstances of the individual case under consideration, taking into account the nature and extent of the disclosure in the application as filed, the nature and extent of the disclaimed subject matter, and its relationship with the subject matter remaining in the claim after

2-438

---

[812] See [10.2.2].
[813] (G-1/03) and (G-2/03) [2004] E.P.O.R. 33.
[814] art.54(3) renders for the purpose of novelty but not inventive step European patent applications filed prior to the date of filing of a European patent application but published after that date.
[815] (G2/10) [2011] E.P.O.R. 45.

amendments.[816] Despite the above, the EBA said that normally a disclaimer does not change the teaching of the subject matter of the claim and does not tend to add information.[817]

2-439   It will be appreciated from the above that in the case of "undisclosed" disclaimers, the EBA in *PPG/Disclaimer* does not make it a requirement that the disclaimed prior art be disclosed expressly (whether by way of an example, embodiment, etc.) in the application as filed. Whereas, in *The Scripps Research Institute*, the EBA propounds a broad test that, in essence, requires the person skilled in the art to have understood that the amended claim with the disclaimer was a possible alternative to the original claim. This test is rarely likely to be satisfied for "undisclosed" disclaimers. Whilst it might be said that the EBA in *Scripps* was dealing with "disclosed" disclaimers in *PPG/Disclaimer* rather than "undisclosed" disclaimers, it hardly advances an argument to say that the test in *The Scripps Research* does not apply when it cannot be satisfied! Such has little logic. This tension led to a further referral to the EBA in *Disclaimer III* (G1/16) concerning whether the test in *The Scripps Research Institute* should be applied to both undisclosed as well as to disclosed disclaimers and thus whether *PPG/Disclaimer* is no longer good law for undisclosed disclaimers. Whilst holding that the gold standard to amendments applies, the EBA held *Disclaimer III* (G1/16) that for undisclosed disclaimers, the test is that set out in *PPG Disclaimer* (G1/03) whereas for disclosed disclaimers, it is *The Scripps Research Institute/Disclaimer* (G2/10).

Post-grant amendments

2-440   Amendments are possible after grant (i.e. during opposition proceedings or central amendment proceedings) but art.123(3) confers the additional requirements that any amendment must not extend the protection it confers. This condition is in addition to the requirement in art.100(c) that in opposition proceedings, the subject-matter of the patent must not extend beyond the content of the application as filed.[818] In *ADVANCED SEMICONDUCTOR PRODUCTS/Limiting feature*,[819] the EBA held there is no mutual relationship between art.123(2) and art.123(3). Thus, during opposition proceedings, if a limiting feature added during the prosecution of the patent was determined to be contrary to art.100(c) because it added subject-matter to the application, it could not be maintained in the patent, nor could it be removed without widening the scope of the claims contrary to art.123(3). The EBA noted that this could operate harshly against an applicant who amends their application to add a feature (thus limiting the protection conferred by the patent) during examination in response to an ex parte objection and then has that amendment challenged during opposition proceedings. The patentee will not be entitled to withdraw the limiting feature amendment, as this would widen the breadth of the claim, but as said by the EBA, such is prohibited by art.123(3). Hence, great care must be exercised by patent attorneys during the prosecution of a patent application not to put forward limiting features because of the discovery of a piece of prior art without considering very carefully whether it adds subject-

---

[816] See [91] (E.P.O.R.).

[817] See [54] (E.P.O.R.).

[818] art.100(c) corresponds to the pre-grant art.123(2) provision. Where the proceedings are central amendment proceedings, EPC r.95(2) requires that the Examining Division examine whether the amended claims are permissible under art.123(2) and (3). See para.2-423.

[819] (G-1/93).

matter. If in doubt, it is better to argue that the limitation feature is not required and keep the claims as wide as possible, as one can always narrow the claims in opposition proceedings.

It may be that one can avoid the "trap" by proposing to replace the offending **2-441** feature with another feature which does not extend the protection of the patent. However, whether this is permissible depends on whether the other feature offends art.123(2).[820] Alternatively, the applicant can file a divisional application.

In *Treatment of Pompe's Disease/GENZYME*,[821] the TBA held that a Swiss- **2-442** style second medical use claim could not be amended after grant to a purpose limited EPC 2000 claim[822] as the latter was wider in protection than the former. Thus, such an amendment would extend the protection of the claims as granted contrary to art.123(3).

Divisional applications

Where an application is considered by the EPO not to have unity of inven- **2-443** tion,[823] the objection can be overcome by filing a divisional application (or a number of them) based on the original application. Alternatively, a divisional application may be filed instead of amending claims which are objected to. The divisional application is treated as a separate application which claims priority from the original application.[824] A divisional application may be give rise to one or more divisional applications from it. Thus, it is possible to have second, third, etc. "generations" of divisional applications.

Compliance with art.76

Article 76 states that the divisional application can be filed only in respect of **2-444** subject-matter which does not extend beyond the content of the earlier application as filed.[825] In the case of a second-generation divisional application, such applications must not be filed in respect of subject-matter which extends beyond the content of the first divisional application.[826] In *SEIKO/Divisional application*, the TBA queried whether in the case of second or subsequent generation divisional applications, it had to be shown that *all the parents* of the second or subsequent generational application were validly filed and did not contravene art.76. In a number of cases, it had been held that if *any of* the parents did not comply with art.76, the child application was invalid. This is called the *impeccable pedigree* theory.[827] For example, in considering whether a third generation divisional application complied with art.76, the impeccable pedigree theory required the Examining Division to consider whether the first generation divisional application did not include subject matter which extended beyond the original application, whether the

---

[820] A helpful approach to dealing with the art.123(2)–(3) trap by replacing the offending feature with another feature is provided in the commentary on art.123(3) at para.3 of D. Visser, *The Annotated European Patent Convention*, 21st edn (Haarlem: H. Tel, 2013).

[821] (T-1673/11).

[822] See para.2-164.

[823] For "unity of invention", see para.2-386.

[824] art.76(1).

[825] art.76(1). Guid. A-IV 1; C-IX 1.

[826] *Seiko/divisional application* (T-720/02) [2006] E.P.O.R. 2.

[827] (T-904/97) (unpublished); *Brother/divisional application* (T-555/00) [2006] E.P.O.R. 33; *Tridonic/Divisional application* (T-1158/01) [2005] E.P.O.R. 32.

second generation divisional application did not include subject matter which extended beyond the first generation application and the original application, as well as whether the third generation divisional application did not include subject matter that extended beyond the original application, the first generation and the second generation divisional application.[828] The TBA referred this matter to the EBA. The EBA ruled that where there are a number of divisional applications, it is a *necessary and sufficient* condition that anything disclosed in the divisional application be directly, unambiguously and separately derivable from what is disclosed in *each* of the preceding applications as filed.[829] However, if this condition is satisfied for each divisional application, the EBA said that there is no need to show that the parent divisional applications themselves complied with art.76. This ties in with the decision in (G-1/05) (discussed in the next section) which permits amendments of invalid divisional applications.

2-445   Only contracting states designated in the earlier application may be so designated in the divisional application.[830]

Amendment of invalidly filed divisional application

2-446   For many years, the EPO permitted applicants to amend divisional applications even if the divisional application *as filed* offended art.76. However, this practice was questioned by a Board of Appeal which believed that such a practice might, in fact, be impermissible.[831] Accordingly, it referred the legitimacy of this practice to the EBA. In particular, the Board considered such a practice to be inconsistent with the "impeccable pedigree" approach discussed in the previous paragraph.[832] The TBA was particularly concerned that an ability to correct a divisional application which was filed contrary to art.76 meant that:

> "The mere filing of a divisional application relating to a pending earlier application but being invalid by virtue of Art.76(1) EPC at present in effect grants an applicant the opportunity to postpone the moment when he—in the course of amendments made to overcome an objection under Art.76(1)—freely selects which aspect of the earlier application is to be divided out. According to the present practice, provided the description of the invalid divisional application is the same as that of the earlier application as filed, the applicant at the time of the correction benefits from the very same freedom for formulating the amended divisional application as if he had not yet filed the divisional and as if the earlier application was still pending."[833]

2-447   However, on referral to the EBA, it held that it did not matter if, upon filing, the divisional application contained subject-matter extending the content of the earlier application. Thus, if the divisional application offended art.76 by including added matter, it was legitimate for the applicant to delete such added matter by way of amendment to the divisional application. The fact that the divisional application when filed offended against art.76 was not fatal to a subsequent application to

---

[828] As will be appreciated by those mathematically inclined, such would mean conducting n! (n factorial) evaluations where n equals the generation, e.g. where n=3 (a third generation application), n!=6.

[829] *Seiko/Division Application* (G-1/06) [2007] E.P.O.R. 47.

[830] art.76(2). In *YAKAZI/Divisional* (J-40/03) [2005] E.P.O.R. 5, the Board said that an applicant cannot designate a state in a divisional application if it has not been so designated in a parent application (or it has lapsed because the designation fee has not been paid).

[831] *Astropower/Divisional Application* (T-39/03) [2006] E.P.O.R. 1.

[832] This is discussed at para.2-443.

[833] (T-39/03) [2006] E.P.O.R. 1 at [23].

amend to cure the art.76 objection.[834] Furthermore, this could be done even if the earlier application was no longer pending.

Practice and procedure

A divisional application can only be filed by the original applicant.[835] There must **2-448** be exact correlation between the applicants for the parent and the applicants for the divisional. Thus, if the parent was filed by two or more applicants, the same applicants (or their successors) must file the divisional application.[836]

A divisional application can only be filed if there is a pending earlier European **2-449** patent application.[837] As a divisional application is itself a pending application, then a divisional application can be filed on a pending parent divisional application.[838] A failure to file a divisional application whilst the parent is pending is fatal and re-establishment of rights is not permissible.[839] An application is pending up to (but not including) the date that the European Patent Bulletin mentions the grant of the European patent, or until the date that it is refused, withdrawn or deemed withdrawn. In *SONY/Pending Application*[840] the EBA said that where an application for a European patent was refused and no appeal filed, the application remained pending until the expiry of the period for filing an appeal. Thus, a divisional application filed prior to the expiry of that period was a lawful application.

Divisional applications must be filed in the language of the proceedings for the **2-450** earlier application; if the latter is not an official language of the Office then a translation must be filed within two months of filing the divisional application.[841] Both filing and search fees must be paid in respect of each European divisional application within one month of the filing of the division application.[842] The designation fee must be paid within six months of the date on which the Bulletin mentions the publication of the search report being drawn up in respect of the divisional application.[843] Where designation fees are not paid, the application is deemed withdrawn.[844]

As the divisional application is treated as having the same date of filing as the **2-451** earlier application, renewal fees may be due upon the actual filing of the divisional application. If so, these and any other renewal fees which would fall due within a

---

[834] *Divisional/ASTROPOWER* (G1/05) [2008] OJ 271.
[835] As to the requirement that only the applicant can file a divisional, see *SULZERMEDICA/Identity of application of divisional application* (J-17–18/97) [2004] E.P.O.R. 8.
[836] *Trustees of Dartmouth College* (J-2/01) [2004] E.P.O.R. 54.
[837] EPC r.36.
[838] (T-720/02) [2006] E.P.O.R. 2. See also Guid. A-IV-1.1.1.1.
[839] *MICROSOFT/Concept of time limit* (J-18/04) [2006] E.P.O.R. 11. This held that substantive rights which were lost in the parent application cannot be re-established in the divisional application by applying art.122 EPC (which permits re-establishment of rights where a "time limit" has not been observed).
[840] (G1/09) [2011] E.P.O.R. 7. However, note *Ericsson Inc/Divisional Application* (J-28/03) [2005] E.P.O.R. 36. In that case, the patentee filed a Notice of Appeal against the grant of its own patent in order to create an artificial situation so as to be able to file a divisional application. This was considered an abusive appeal done to create an artificial pending parent application—see [11].
[841] EPC r.36(2).
[842] EPC r.36(3).
[843] EPC r.36(4).
[844] EPC rr.36(4).

period of four months from filing must be paid within that period to the EPO or within six months of the due date upon payment of an additional fee.[845]

Opposition proceedings

2-452   The EPC allows third parties to apply to revoke a European patent within nine months of the mention of its grant. Although, the European patent is now a "bundle" of national patents, the EPC specifically allows third parties to bring revocation proceedings before the EPO which, if successful, will result in the revocation of the European patent in toto in all of the designated states. Such proceedings are called opposition proceedings and are dealt with by the Opposition Division. Opposition proceedings may only be brought on the following grounds:[846]

(a) the subject-matter of the patent is not patentable under the EPC;

(b) the patent does not disclose the invention in a manner sufficiently clear and complete for it to be carried out by a person skilled in the art; and

(c) the subject-matter of the European patent extends beyond the content of the application as filed.

2-453   Thus, an opponent cannot object on the basis of lack of unity of invention, that the claims are not clear and concise or supported by description or that the patentee is not entitled to the patent. A European patent owner cannot bring opposition proceedings against their own patent.[847] Such used to be done because of the inability of patentees to centrally amend their patents. However, now that EPC 2000 permits the proprietor to request the EPO to revoke or limit a European patent, provided that opposition proceedings are not pending, the effect of this ruling will be much diminished.[848]

Practice and procedure

2-454   The party bringing opposition proceedings ("the opponent") must file a Notice of Opposition within the nine-month period from grant of the patent and pay an opposition fee.[849] The EPO recommends that parties use the pre-printed form available free of charge from the EPO. The Notice of Opposition must include a written reasoned statement of the grounds on which the opposition is based, as well as an indication of the facts, evidence and arguments presented in support of these grounds.[850] The Notice of Opposition must be in an official language of the EPO.[851] A third party may intervene after the expiry of the nine-month period where proceedings for infringement of the same patent have been issued against them, if they give notice of intervention within three months of the date on which the

---

[845] EPC r.51(3).

[846] art.100. An opponent cannot allege that a patent is invalid because of national prior rights *MOBIL/ Admissibility* (T-550/88) [1990] E.P.O.R. 391.

[847] *PEUGEOT & CITROEN* (G-9/93) [1995] OJ EPO 260; [1995] E.P.O.R. 10/XV 260, reversing *MOBIL OIL/Opposition by proprietor* (G-1/84) [1986] E.P.O.R. 39.

[848] See para.2-423.

[849] art.99(1), EPC rr.76, 77. Where an opposition is filed by a group, only one opposition fee is payable—*HOWARD FLOREY/Admissibility of Joint Opposition* (G-3/99) [2003] E.P.O.R. 1.

[850] ECP r.76, art.99(1).

[851] EPC r.3.

infringement proceedings were instituted.[852] An opponent cannot introduce during the procedure a new ground of opposition without the consent of the patent holder.[853]

The EPO will check that the formalities have been complied with.[854] If the formalities have been complied with, it will notify the patent owner of the opposition proceedings, provide the owner with the written statement, and invite them to file their observations and any amendments they consider necessary, within a certain period (usually four months).[855]

2-455

The opposition proceedings then enter a period of substantive examination.[856] Documentary evidence referred to by a party in opposition proceedings should be filed with the Notice of Opposition or written submissions. If not, they should be filed in "due time" upon invitation by the EPO, failing which the EPO may decide not to take into account any argument based on them.[857] In general, late submission of evidence will be accepted if it represents evidence more critically relevant against the validity of the patent than anything else previously raised.[858] Thus, even if an opponent submits documents outside the nine-month period, these will only be disregarded if it is clearly established that they could have been submitted earlier. Reasons for disregarding such documents must be given.[859] However, where an opponent failed to put forward evidence of its own prior use until after the expiry of the opposition period and in the absence of good reasons for the delay, the Board took the view that such amounted to an abuse of the proceedings and a breach of the principle of good faith and refused to take it into account.[860] The parties will be consulted and if requested, an oral hearing can be arranged.[861] The owner of the patent may, at this stage, also be invited to file an amended specification and/or claims.[862] A failure by an opponent to comment on auxiliary requests will amount to consent to the requests.[863]

2-456

In general, an opponent cannot freely transfer the opposition to a third party unless the transferee can be considered a successor to the opponent.[864] Thus, a company which, as of the date of filing the opposition, was a subsidiary of the opponent but subsequently carried on the business to which the opposed patent relates, cannot acquire the status of opponent if all its shares are assigned to another

2-457

---

[852] art.105; EPC r.89.

[853] *ROHM & HAAS/Power to examine* (G-10/91) [1993] E.P.O.R. 485.

[854] EPC r.77.

[855] EPC r.79(1). The patent proprietor cannot file amendments if the opposition is found to be inadmissible—see (T-550/88) [1990] E.P.O.R. 391.

[856] For a helpful guide to the principles to be applied in the opposition procedure, see *Opposition Procedure in the EPO* [2001] OJ EPO 131–181.

[857] art.114(2), EPC r.83.

[858] *AIR PRODUCTS/Pressure swing adsorption* (T-156/84) [1989] E.P.O.R. 47.

[859] (T-156/84) [1989] E.P.O.R. 47; I.P.D. 10103, February 1988. See also *DUPONT/Late submission* (T-951/91) [1995] E.P.O.R. 398 at 410, where the TBA refused to admit late evidence as there was no good reason for the delay. In that case, however, the TBA emphasised that the main criteria for deciding on the admissibility of a late filed document is its relevance (see 409).

[860] *GILLETTE/Public prior use* (T-17/91) [1998] E.P.O.R. 310.

[861] *Guide to applying for a European patent*, para.183.

[862] EPC r.81(3).

[863] *HOOGOVENS/Admissibility* (T-118/95) [1999] E.P.O.R. 467.

[864] *HOFFMAN-LA ROCHE/Transfer of opposition* (G-2/04) [2005] E.P.O.R. 35; *MAN/Transfer of opposition* (G-4/88) [1990] E.P.O.R. 1.

company (i.e. it ceases to be a subsidiary of the opponent).[865] Where the opponent dies, the heirs to the opponent can continue the opposition or its appeal but heirs must establish their right as heir by good evidence.[866] In general, the EPO will treat the issue of existence and successorship of legal entities such as companies as a matter of the law of the country of incorporation. Thus, where a UK company was dissolved under UK company law during the course of an opposition but then restored (and under UK law, a restored company is deemed to have continued its existence as if it had not ceased to exist) the EPO held that that it must recognise the retroactive nature of that provision of national law.[867]

2-458   The patent may either be maintained, revoked or maintained in an amended form.[868] If the patentee puts forward amendments to the claims to avoid the effect of facts or matters raised in the opposition, then the Opposition Division must satisfy itself that the amendments meet the requirement of the EPC.[869] However, the claims cannot be broadened.[870] Parties are given the right, if the EPO intends to maintain an amended patent, to submit observations within two months if they disapprove of the text in which it is intended to maintain the patent.[871] The owner of a patent amended during opposition proceedings must pay printing fees and file a translation of any amended claims in the other two official languages within three months from the expiry of the above period.[872] The EPO publishes the result of the opposition proceeding and any new specifications of amended European patents.[873] However, such amendments must not extend the protection conferred.[874]

2-459   The Opposition Division has the right to apportion costs in opposition proceedings. Such an apportionment, which will take into account the remuneration of the representatives, must only take into consideration the expenses necessary to assure proper protection of the rights involved.[875] There is no right of appeal on the sole issue of costs in opposition proceedings, unless the amount fixed is in excess of the Rules relating to Fees.

Appeals

Boards of Appeal

2-460   There are three appellate bodies. The Technical Board of Appeal ("TBA") is responsible for appeals from decisions concerning the refusal or grant of a European

---

[865] (G-2/04) [2005] E.P.O.R. 35.

[866] *Optiscan/Scanning confocal endoscope* (T-74/00) [2005] E.P.O.R. 43.

[867] *Party Status/Fischer-Tropsch Catalysts* (G1/13).

[868] art.101.

[869] art.101(3). Despite the apparent wording of art.101(3) which suggests that amended claims will be considered de novo as to lack of clarity under art.84, the EBA has made it clear (there were divergent TBA decisions on the matter) that where an amendment is put forward, the claims of the patent may be examined only for compliance with the requirements of art.84 "only when, and then only to the extent" that the amendment introduces non-compliance with art.84—*Examination of clarity objection/Prosthetic Liner Process* (G3/14). See para.2-419.

[870] art.123(3). See para.2-440.

[871] EPC r.82.

[872] EPC r.82(2). There is a further grace period of two months—see EPC r.82(3) but a surcharge is payable.

[873] art.103.

[874] art.123(3).

[875] EPC r.88. In practice, the amount awarded by the EPO is small.

patent or from decisions of an Opposition Division.[876] The Legal Board of Appeal ("LBA") is responsible for the few appeals which are purely on a matter of law and contain no technical element.[877] The Enlarged Board of Appeal ("EBA") is the highest appellate body in the EPO and is concerned with the uniform application of the law and where an important point of law arises.[878] Only the Board of Appeal or the President of the EPO can refer any question or point of law to the EBA.[879]

Following the much criticised decision in *Request with a view to revision*[880] in which the EBA held that it had no power to review the decision of a Board of Appeal, even where there was a substantial procedural irregularity, it was agreed at the Diplomatic Conference in November 2000 to permit a party to appeal to the EBA where there has been a "fundamental procedural defect" in the appeal proceedings. There are five separate grounds on which such a petition may be founded, including a "fundamental violation of Art.113 [right to be heard and basis of decisions]" and "any other fundamental procedural defect defined in the Implementing Regulations".[881]
    2-461

Finally, as discussed elsewhere in this chapter, the principle of *reformatio in peius* means that an appellant cannot be in a worse position on appeal than if it had never appealed. However, because of the hardship that this could cause to patent proprietors in opposition proceedings where limiting amendments are allowed by the Opposition Division, the EBA has established some exceptions to this rule.[882]
    2-462

Procedure

Appeals lie from the decisions of the Receiving Section, Examining Division, Opposition Division and the Legal Division and the filing of an appeal suspends the effect of such decisions.[883] Any party to proceedings adversely affected by a decision may appeal and other parties in the proceedings automatically become parties to the appeal.[884] The appeal lies from the decision and not from the grounds of the decision. Therefore, a party may raise fresh reasons even though they are unconnected with the reasons in the decision under appeal.[885]
    2-463

However, in relation to raising new grounds of appeal (as opposed to new reasons for supporting an existing ground), a distinction must be drawn between the ex parte pre-grant stage and the inter partes post-grant stage. In relation to the former, the Enlarged Board of Appeal has held that the Board of Appeal has the power to examine whether the application or the invention to which it relates meets the requirements of the EPC, even if the Examining Division did not take into account such matters in the examination proceedings or consider that such were
    2-464

---

[876] art.21.

[877] art.21(2).

[878] Decision numbers beginning with "T" are those of the TBA. Correspondingly, "J" indicates the Legal Board of Appeal and "G" indicates the EBA.

[879] art.112.

[880] *Request with a view to revision* (G-1/97) [2000] OJ EPO 322.

[881] art.112a.

[882] See para.2-421.

[883] art.106.

[884] art.107. A party who is successful at first instance is not adversely affected by obiter dicta remarks made in relation to grounds which are unsuccessfully raised: *Trutac/Entitlement to appeal* (T-981/01) [2005] E.P.O.R. 24.

[885] *MITSUI/Ethylen copolymer* (T-611/90) [1991] E.P.O.R. 481; I.P.D. 14144, August 1991.

met.[886] However, in relation to post-grant opposition procedure, the Enlarged Board of Appeal has held that a fresh ground of opposition which was not raised and substantiated in the notice of opposition and was not introduced into the opposition proceedings by a party or the Opposition Division could not be raised in appellate proceedings.[887] Thus, in appeal proceedings where only novelty and inventive steps were in issue, it was not open to the TBA to consider whether the invention was a patentable discovery because it represented unpatentable subject-matter based on art.52.[888] Only parties to the first instance decision or their successors may appeal a decision.[889]

2-465   A party may only appeal against an adverse interlocutory decision if it appeals the final decision, unless the interlocutory decision allows for a separate appeal.[890] This may force a party to accept an adverse interlocutory decision which may prejudice the presentation of its case, rather than wait to have the patent application refused and then appeal the decision with all the attendant risks and delay that such a course entails.

2-466   An appellant can challenge the inclusion of a member on the Board of Appeal where a reasonable onlooker would conclude, considering the circumstances of the cases, that the party might have good reasons to doubt the impartiality of the member objected to.[891]

2-467   A notice of appeal must be filed in writing with the EPO within two months of notification of the adverse decision. It must contain the name and address of the appellant and a statement identifying the decision and the extent to which amendment or cancellation of the decision is requested. An appeal fee must also be paid.[892] Within four months from the date of notification of the decision, a written statement setting out the grounds of the appeal must be filed.[893] These time limits cannot be extended.[894]

2-468   In practice, the appellate stage is primarily a written procedure and thus arguments should be fully developed in writing, although an oral hearing can be requested.[895] There is fundamentally little difference between the examination procedure and the appeal procedure and, accordingly, new evidence will generally be admissible in appeal proceedings.[896]

2-469   If the decision is ex parte (i.e. the appellant is not opposed by another party to the proceedings) against a department, then the department concerned shall be given

---

[886] *SIEMENS/Scope of examination* in *Ex p. appeal* (G-10/93) [1997] E.P.O.R. 227.

[887] *THOMAS DE LA RUE/Grounds for Opposition* (G-01/95) [1996] E.P.O.R. 601; *ETHICON/Coated surgical staple* (G-07/95) [1997] E.P.O.R. 89 applying (G-09/91); *ROHM & HAAS/Power to examine* (G-10/91) [1993] E.P.O.R. 485.

[888] (G-10/91) [1993] E.P.O.R. 485.

[889] *GENENCOR/Non-party appellant* (T-656/98) [2004] E.P.O.R. 11.

[890] art.106(2).

[891] *Discovision/Appealable Decision* (G-5/91) [1993] E.P.O.R. 120; *Exclusion and objection* (G-1/05) [2007] E.P.O.R. 17.

[892] art.108, EPC r.99.

[893] The grounds of appeal must give full reasons for their appeal otherwise they will be inadmissible—see *MEDICAL BIOLOGICAL SCIENCES/Oral Prosthesis* (J-22/86) [1987] OJ EPO 280, [1987] E.P.O.R. 87; *HULS* (T-220/83) [1986] OJ EPO 249, [1987] E.P.O.R. 87; and *NICOLON/Statement of Grounds* (T-145/88) [1991] E.P.O.R. 357, I.P.D. 14105, June 1991.

[894] art.108.

[895] art.116. See also RApp art.11, et seq.

[896] *BAYER/Carbonless copying paper* (T-1/80) [1981] OJ EPO 206; [1979–85] E.P.O.R. B250. However, the Appeal Board may disregard facts or evidence which were not submitted in due time—art.114(2).

an opportunity to rectify its decision if it is clear that there are fundamental deficiencies in the first instance proceedings, unless special reasons present themselves for doing otherwise.[897] The Boards of Appeal may reject or allow the appeal. If the latter, it can either exercise any power within the competence of the department which was responsible for the appealed decision or remit the case to the department for further prosecution.[898] It may also remit the matter back to the division below for renewed or further examination. The appeal fees may be reimbursed if the department concerned accepts its mistake or if there has been a substantial procedural violation.[899]

Where the case is remitted, the first instance department is bound by the ratio decidendi of the decision of the Board of Appeal.[900] **2-470**

Judicial review of EPO in a contracting state

In an interesting English case, the High Court held that a decision of the EPO **2-471** Boards of Appeal was not judicially reviewable in the UK.[901] This was then considered in a later case of the Court of Appeal in *Virgin Atlantic Airways Ltd v Jet Airways (India) Ltd & Comptroller General of Patents*,[902] where the EPO had accidentally designated the UK for a European patent even though a request had been made not to do so. The proprietor of the European patent then sued for patent infringement on the accidentally granted EP(UK) patent. Before the Court of Appeal in England, the defendants who had been found to have infringed the EP(UK) patent sought to argue that the UK register of patents should be rectified to remove the EP(UK) patent. The difficulty was that the grounds of revocation did not include such a ground.[903] The defendants argued that the mistaken grant was contrary to the defendants' human rights, particularly its right under art.6 ECHR (right to a fair trial). However, the Court of Appeal considered that the EPO had exclusive jurisdiction to decide matters (including the exclusive jurisdiction to make mistakes) and that Member States did not have the right in the course of infringement proceedings, to, in effect, correct a mistake of the EPO by providing a positive defence.

However, what is the position if the EPO granted a European patent following a **2-472** fraud on the EPO? In the Court of Appeal, it appeared to accept that if the UK Intellectual Property Office had granted a patent by reason of fraud, one could chal-

---

[897] art.109(1), art.10 RApp.

[898] art.111(1).

[899] EPC r.67. For an example of substantial procedural violation, see *PATRICK POSSO* (T-185/82) [1979–85] E.P.O.R. C696; I.P.D. 7049, July–August 1984 (the applicant confused dates of prior art in its submissions on obviousness and the EPO failed to notify the applicant of the error and refused application). For example of when appeal fees will not be refunded, see *SCIAKY BROS* (T-12/82) [1979–85] E.P.O.R. B395; I.P.D. 7042, June 1984—auxiliary claim submitted on appeal after the main claim had been rejected by Examining Board—case remitted to Examining Division for consideration of the auxiliary claim but the appellant was not entitled to have appeal fees reimbursed; *Compagnie Française de l'Azote* (T-27/83) (COFAZ) I.P.D. 6113, November 1983—rejection based on clear misunderstanding of the state of the art but no substantial procedural violation.

[900] *Genentech/Hepatitis B Antigen* (T-796/02) [2004] E.P.O.R. 56.

[901] In *R. v Comptroller General of Patents Ex p. Lenzing* [1997] R.P.C. 245. See also W. Cook, "Judicial Review of the EPO and the Direct Effect of TRIPS in the European Community" [1997] 19(7) E.I.P.R. 367.

[902] [2013] EWCA Civ 1713.

[903] s.72 of the Patents Act 1977 set out the grounds for revocation of a patent which were said to be the only grounds for revocation. This is based on the EPC.

lenge the grant of the patent by way of judicial review.[904] One might consider that such grounds would also apply to a fraud on the EPO. It is not clear from the judgment of the Court of Appeal whether they would have entertained such but the judgment suggests not.[905] The difficulty about judicial review based on fraud (however attractive it may sound) is that if the fraud is *material* to the grant of the patent, i.e. the applicant dishonestly said that some prior use was confidential when it was not, then there is no need for judicial review as the defendant could seek revocation on the grounds that in fact the prior use was not confidential. If however, there was some fraud which was immaterial to the grant of the patent, i.e. the applicant dishonestly lied in a statement about a product description of its own prior use relied upon by an opponent, but which, if he had told the truth, would not have affected the decision to grant patent, then in effect, the court would be imposing a ground of revocation based on the applicant not dealing with the EPO in good faith. Whilst this has its attractions, it is not difficult to see how such a ground could ultimately become very onerous on the applicant and encourage defendant infringers to conduct minute examination of the bona fides of the applicant in the prosecution of the patent before the EPO. This would be a dangerous road to embark upon and could encourage expensive US-style litigation where fraud on the USPTO is a ground of invalidation and has spun satellite litigation. It is better that such is properly thought out (if it be a problem) by the members of the EPC and appropriate remedies found to deal with what is no doubt a very rare occurrence.

Time limits

2-473   As with the prosecution of any patent application in any patent office, compliance with time limits is extremely important and the consequences of failure to do so can be fatal. Thus, although the above sections each contain information on time limits relevant to that stage of proceedings, general information concerning time limits is set out here.

Three types of time limits

2-474   There are three kinds of time limits which are provided for in the EPC:

(a)   Time limits laid down in the EPC or its Implementing Regulations which are computed from the date of filing or priority date.
(b)   Time limits whose duration is laid down in the EPC or its Implementing Regulations, but which are computed from an event other than the date of filing or the priority date.
(c)   Time limits set by the EPO during the proceedings.

2-475   With the exception of the time limits for the re-establishment of rights and further processing, the EPO will draw the attention of the applicant to each of the time limits in the second and third categories.[906]

---

[904]   See [171].
[905]   See [172].
[906]   *Guide for Applicants: How to get a European patent*, Annex VI. See: *http://www.epo.org/applying/european/Guide-for-applicants/html/e/index.html* [Accessed 18 August 2017].

Calculation of time

For the purposes of calculating time limits, the general principle is that time starts **2-476** on the day following the day on which the relevant event occurred. For time limits which start from the date of notification, the relevant date is generally the date of deemed receipt of the document notified (10 days after dispatch) unless a later date of receipt can be shown.[907] For the expiry of a time period where a particular date is not stated, the Implementing Regulations should be consulted.[908] In relation to documentation sent by post to the EPO, the relevant date is the actual date of receipt by the EPO. The EPO does not provide for a deemed day of receipt being a certain number of days after posting.[909] A general interruption or dislocation of the mail delivery service will postpone the relevant date.[910] However, where an applicant cannot prove such an interruption or dislocation but merely that there has been an unusual postal delay, this will not be sufficient to postpone the relevant date.[911] Notifications sent by the EPO to the applicant will usually be done by registered letter and are deemed to be delivered to the applicant on the 10th day after sending, unless the letter fails to reach the addressee or has reached them at a later date. If there is any dispute, the EPO must establish that the letter has reached its destination or establish the date on which it was received.[912]

Failure to observe time limits

Where the EPO has correctly assessed that the applicant has failed to observe a **2-477** time limit, the applicant may request further processing of the application within two months of the communication, pay the further processing fee and rectify the omission within the same period.[913] The EPO will grant that request unless by reason of EPC r.135(2), the failure relates to specific acts, e.g. failure to claim priority, failure to appeal in time, failure to seek petition for review, failure to make a deposit of biological material, etc.[914] In such circumstances, no further processing can be provided.

Loss of rights

Where a loss of rights occurs, no decision need be taken for this to happen but **2-478** the EPO must notify applicants of any loss of rights.[915] If the applicant considers that the EPO has wrongfully removed their rights, they may apply for a decision

---

[907] EPC r.126.
[908] See EPC rr.131 and 134.
[909] *ALLIED SIGNAL* (T-702/89) [1993] E.P.O.R. 580.
[910] EPC r.134(2).
[911] (T-702/89) [1993] E.P.O.R. 580 (postal delay of six days).
[912] EPC r.126(2).
[913] EPC r.136; art.121.
[914] The reader should consult EPC r.135(2).
[915] EPC r.112. See *AKZO* (T-26/88) [1990] E.P.O.R. 21 which held (in the context of a failure by a patentee within the time limit set by art.102(4) (now deleted) to pay printing fee and file translations of amended claims during opposition proceedings pursuant to EPC r.58(5) (now part of r.82)) that the patent was automatically revoked and thus the communication under EPC r.112 (then r.69) notifying of loss of rights was not a "decision" that could be appealed. Thus, the patentee's remedy lay in the re-establishment of rights and not by way of appeal against the communication notifying them of loss of rights or using the procedure set out in EPC r.112(2) (see below).

from the EPO within two months after notification of the communication of loss of rights.[916]

Restoration of rights

2-479   Where rights are lost as a result of a failure to comply with a time period, the applicant may seek to have their rights restored. Such will only occur if the applicant can show that "in spite of all due care required by the circumstances having been taken" the applicant was unable to observe a time limit.[917] Examples would include organisational upheavals or sudden serious illness.[918] Such an application must be filed within two months from the removal of the cause of non-compliance but, in any event, within a year following the expiry of the unobserved time limit.[919] However, where the failure to comply with time limits was brought about by the conduct of the EPO, the Legal Board of Appeal held that it was contrary to the principle of good faith governing relations between the EPO and the applicant and the principle of *venire contra factum proprium* to deem the application withdrawn. In such exceptional circumstances the late renewal fee was deemed to have been paid on time even though the "long stop" period for re-establishment of rights in relation to late payment of renewal fees (one year) had expired.[920] The application must state the grounds on which it is based and must set out the facts on which it relies.[921] Furthermore, the request for re-establishment of rights is not deemed to be filed until the fee is paid.[922]

2-480   However, there are certain situations where re-establishment of rights is not permissible.

- Where the time limit for re-establishment of rights has lapsed.[923]
- Where further processing is still available.[924]

Correction of errors

2-481   The Implementing Regulations permit, upon request, the correction of linguistic errors, errors of transcription and mistakes in any document filed with the EPO.[925] If the request for correction concerns a description, claims or drawings then the correction must be obvious in the sense that it is immediately evident that nothing else would have been intended than what is offered as the correction.

2-482   The Legal Board of Appeal has said that the following principles apply to an application to correct a mistake or error:

(a)   A mistake exists where a document filed with the EPO does not express the true intention of the parties.

---

[916] EPC r.112(2).

[917] art.122. "All due care" means all reasonable care, i.e. the standard of care that the notional reasonably competent patentee, applicant or representative would employ in all the relevant circumstances (*Re-establishment of rights/GRAIN PROCESSING CORP* (T-30/90) ECLI:EP:BA:2006:T020004.20061024).

[918] Generally, see guidance at Guid. E-VII-3.2.

[919] art.122(2). See *LION BREWERIES* (J-17/89) I.P.D. 13133, August 1990 on the interpretation of the date of removal on non-compliance.

[920] *EXPANDED METAL CO/Principle of good faith* (J-14/94) [1996] E.P.O.R. 327.

[921] EPC r.136(2).

[922] EPC r.136(1); art.2(1), (13) RFees.

[923] art.122(4).

[924] EPC r.136(3).

[925] EPC r.139.

(b) A mistake may be an incorrect statement or may result from an omission.

(c) The burden on the applicant of proving that a mistake has been made, what the mistake was and what the correction should be is a heavy one; r.139 (formerly r.88) may not be used to enable a person to give effect to a change of mind.

(d) The request for correction must be made promptly and, except in exceptional circumstances, sufficiently early for a warning to be included in the publication of the application.[926]

The EPO has been more generous in applying the test where there is no damage to public interest (i.e. third parties are unlikely to be adversely affected by the correction) than where there is. Thus, where an applicant's professional representatives had initially failed to claim priority from two priority dates rather than one, the LBA held, allowing the correction, that the mistake had been clearly explained, the applicants and their professional representatives had acted promptly to rectify the mistake, and there was no danger to the public interest because the published specification included on its front page a warning that a request had been made under r.88 to claim priority from a second application.[927] However, in relation to applications to amend descriptions and claims, the EPO is very strict indeed because of the possible effect on third parties. In particular, the EBA has held that the rule permitting corrections (EPC r.88) is subject to art.123(2) (amendments to a European patent application may only be allowed provided that the subject-matter does not extend beyond the content of the application as filed). Hence, a correction to the documents which make up the filed application (description, claims and where appropriate the drawings) may not be made if such is to breach art.123(2). Accordingly, where an agent had mistakenly filed the description and claims of another application in a request for grant, such documents cannot be replaced by way of a correction under EPC r.88 with the documents which the agents had intended to file with their request (and as a result, the application was not able to be accorded the original filing date).[928]   **2-483**

Once the patent has been granted but is later discovered to contain an error of wording, then it is not possible to amend the patent.[929]   **2-484**

---

[926] *Correction/Priority declaration* (J-09/91) [1998] E.P.O.R. 352. See also other decisions on priority errors: *UNI-CHARM/priority declaration (error)* (J-03/91) [1994] E.P.O.R. 566; *DU PONT/ Correction of priority date* (J-06/91) [1993] E.P.O.R. 318; and *UNITED STATES/Priority declaration* (J-02/92) [1994] E.P.O.R. 547.

[927] *YOSHIDA KOGYO KK* (J-4/82) [1982] OJ EPO 385; [1979–85] E.P.O.R. A102; I.P.D. 5103, December 1982–January 1983, LBA. See also *RIB LOC* (J-8/80) [1980] OJ EPO 293. Cf. *GENERAL DATACOMM INDUSTRIES* (J-13/80) [1979–85] E.P.O.R. A129; I.P.D. 5106, December 1982– January 1983, LBA where the LBA refused to allow an amendment under r.88 to include a reference to a computer program appended to a priority document that the applicant had failed to file.

[928] *ATOTECH/Correction* (G-02/95) [1997] E.P.O.R. 77.

[929] *Fisher-Rosemont/Request to correct patent* (G1/10) [2012] E.P.O.R. 43 (where the patentee sought to correct a granted patent after initiation of opposition proceedings to change "position" to "portion"). The EBA said that no recourse could be had to either EPC r.139 or EPC r.140 to correct the error.

Accelerated prosecution of European patents: PACE

2-485   The grant of a European patent is at present a lengthy process and the mean time from filing to grant is four years.[930] In many circumstances, the applicant needs a patent to be granted earlier.[931] In such circumstances, they may prefer to use a PCT or Euro-PCT route, as the EPO has said that it will give preference to PCT applications because of the strict time limits. If, however, the applicant uses the EPC route, there are several ways of accelerating the prosecution of a European patent application. To assist applicants requiring rapid search or examination, the EPO has improved and simplified its programme for accelerated prosecution of European patent applications, which is called PACE.[932] The programme also applies to international applications entering the European phase before the EPO ("Euro-PCT applications") unless otherwise indicated. The applicant must make a written request for acceleration. Where the applicant complies with the options available under PACE, they may considerably shorten the proceedings in comparison with the average processing time from filing-up to grant of a European patent. Full guidance as to how to accelerate the grant of a European patent is set out in the Guide for Applicants, Part 1.[933]

Revocation: national courts and Opposition Division

2-486   As discussed earlier, the EPO has no jurisdiction to determine infringement actions. However, in contrast both the Opposition Division of the EPO and national courts and tribunals have jurisdiction to revoke granted European patents granted for the country where the court or tribunal is situated. The former can revoke the European patent in toto whereas the national court or country can only revoke the European patent insofar as it designates the country of the court or tribunal. Because of the ability of the Opposition Division to revoke a European patent after grant and the length of time it takes for the Opposition Division to deal with cases, in many situations, there will often be parallel proceedings in national courts and the Opposition Division. Thus, a national patent court could be trying an infringement action whilst an application to revoke the same patent is pending before the Opposition Division. This can give and has given rise to particular problems which are now discussed.

2-487   The reader should note that the issue as to which countries have jurisdiction to revoke patents is discussed in Ch.17, Jurisdiction.[934]

Parallel jurisdiction

2-488   There is little doubt that the national courts and the EPO have parallel and independent jurisdictions to revoke a European patent. Thus, in *Beloit Technologies v Valmet Paper Machinery Inc*[935] where proceedings for infringement of a European patent and a counterclaim of invalidity of that patent were being tried at

---

[930] See para.2-093.
[931] Although art.67 gives provisional protection to published European applications, the deterrent effect of a granted patent is usually much more than a published application.
[932] See Notice from the EPO dated 30 November 2015 [2015] OJ EPO A93.
[933] Annex II. See *http://www.epo.org/applying/european/Guide-for-applicants/html/e/ga_aii.html* [Accessed 18 August 2017].
[934] See para.17-117.
[935] [1997] R.P.C. 489 CA.

the same time as appeals from the Opposition Division were being held in the EPO (and the possibility of the patent being amended in the appeal), it was argued that the UK court had no jurisdiction pending the outcome of the appeal of the Opposition Division. The Court of Appeal held that the Patents Act 1977 s.77(2) (which states that the provisions of the Patents Act 1977 do not affect the operation of any provisions of the EPC) did not remove the right of the UK courts to revoke an invalid European patent (UK) at any time after grant, even if there were current opposition proceedings in which the patentee was reserving their position about amending the patent. The patentee had the right to amend the patent in the UK proceedings. Thus, the court (upheld on appeal) revoked the EP(UK) patent.

Legal effect in Member State where Opposition Division revokes European patent

Notwithstanding the undoubted right of the courts of a Member State to revoke **2-489** a European patent designated for that Member State even where there are pending opposition proceedings, greater difficulties arise if the court of a Member State finds a patent valid and infringed and then subsequently, the Opposition Division revokes a European patent. Such has retrospective effect (i.e. ab initio). Should the decision of the court of the Member State stand despite the European patent being revoked or should the defendant be able to apply to discharge the finding of infringement and validity? This issue arose in the UK in *Virgin Atlantic v Zodiac*.[936] In that case, the defendant was found to have infringed a valid claim of the patentee. However, in parallel EPO opposition proceedings, the patent was subsequently amended to a form in which none of the claims would have been infringed by the defendant. Virgin, the patentee, then initiated, following their success, an inquiry as to damages. However, upon the Opposition Division amending the patent, the defendant sought to overturn the original judgment. The Court of Appeal found that cause of action estoppel (res judicata) prevented the defendant from challenging the earlier finding of infringement and validity. In short, the public policy interest in finality of litigation (*interest rei publicae ut sit finis litium*) outweighed the undoubted injustice of being found to have infringed a patent that in effect never existed. The Supreme Court overturned a line of authorities and reversed the judgment of the Court of Appeal. It held that that the matter was not res judicata as the revocation of the European patent by the opposition division was a decision in rem and determined the status of the patent *erga omnes*. It is less clear whether the Supreme Court would have adopted such a route if judgment had been given on the inquiry as to damages.

The above matter shows the danger of a court not staying proceedings pending **2-490** determination by the Opposition Division of the validity of a patent. However, whilst such is attractive, it ignores the fact that it is notorious that opposition proceedings can drag on for years in the EPO. If stays were automatically granted, it would potentially deny the right of a patentee to enforce their patent within a reasonable time against infringers.

Legal effect in Member State where Opposition Division refuses to revoke European patent

If national courts do decide to stay invalidity proceedings pending the decision **2-491** of the Opposition Division, will such courts be bound by the decision of the Op-

---

936 [2013] UKSC 46.

position Division if the European patent is not revoked? This issue has been decided negatively in both England and Germany, where unsuccessful opponents sought to raise the same grounds in the national proceedings as had been raised in the Opposition Division. Both courts (with the English Court of Appeal adopting the reasoning of the Bundesgerichtshof) held that opposition proceedings are not exactly equivalent to infringement proceedings in national courts. The former acts as an ex post facto examination of the protectability of a patent already granted and is not a truly inter partes proceedings concerning the validity of a granted patent. Furthermore, both held that the effect of the EPC, in particular art.138, is that final determination of the validity of a European patent rests with national courts.[937] Thus, in revocation proceedings in Germany, the Bundesgerichtshof took an opposite view to the Opposition Division on the issue of obviousness of a European patent.[938] The court said that the opinion of the Opposition Division should be taken into account as an expert opinion but is not binding. In particular and importantly, the court said that it is not the task of the Opposition Division to determine the scope of protection of a patent by interpreting the content of granted claims.[939]

Stay of national proceedings pending the outcome of opposition proceedings

2-492   As can be seen from the above discussions, where there are pending proceedings before the Opposition Division (or on appeal), the prudent and safe course for a national court seized of infringement proceedings is to stay pending the outcome of the Opposition Division. If there is any urgency, such can be dealt with by the grant of interim injunctions pending determination of the outcome. However, whilst such is no doubt prudent, it ignores the fact that the national court's jurisdiction is independent and parallel to the EPO; its jurisdiction extends to both infringement and validity; the right to a fair trial within a reasonable period under art.6 ECHR and that in certain countries, the ventilation of validity issues may be more extensive than before the Opposition Division (e.g. via cross examination, disclosure of documents, etc.). Perhaps more importantly, the length of time it takes for Opposition Division proceedings (and their appeals) to be heard are so considerable[940] that from a commercial viewpoint, it means that there is no resolution of the dispute within an acceptable time frame. Many would say that some justice is better than no justice or put another way, that some resolution is better than no resolution.

2-493   The Court of Appeal of England and Wales has given authoritative guidance on the question of whether to stay national proceedings in favour of EPO oppositions.[941] The court has a very wide discretion on whether or not to stay, but such discretion should always be exercised in the context of the EPC, recognising that proceedings may end up being duplicated. The length of stay that will be necessary (if granted) will likely be the weightiest factor in exercising the discretion, and if the national court is likely to produce a decisive result sooner than the EPO, a stay will usually be inappropriate. Following the Supreme Court's decision in *Virgin*

---

[937] *Buehler AG v Chronos Richardson Ltd* [1998] R.P.C. 609 CA; *Zahkranzfraser* (X ZR 29/93).

[938] *REGENBECKEN/Rainwater reservoir* (X ZR 57/96) [1999] OJ EPO at 245.

[939] (X ZR 57/96) [1999] OJ EPO, 325. Whilst this is true vis-à-vis infringement proceedings, the breadth of claims is clearly relevant to the validity of a patent and as such, will be relevant to the issue of validity.

[940] It may be that such proceedings are not concluded until after the expiry of the patent in issue.

[941] *Glaxo Group v Genentech* [2008] EWCA Civ 23, [2008] F.S.R. 18 at [79]–[88]; *IPCom v HTC* [2013] EWCA Civ 1496.

v Zodiac, which demonstrated the clear concerns that the Supreme Court had about national courts continuing with an action for infringement in the light of pending proceedings before the Opposition Division, the Court of Appeal gave the following guidance in *IPCom v HTC* in relation to the discretion to stay or not to stay:

"1.   The discretion, which is very wide indeed, should be exercised to achieve the balance of justice between the parties having regard to all the relevant circumstances of the particular case.

2.   The discretion is of the Patents Court, not of the Court of Appeal. The Court of Appeal would not be justified in interfering with a first instance decision that accords with legal principle and has been reached by taking into account all the relevant, and only the relevant, circumstances.

3.   Although neither the EPC nor the 1977 Act contains express provisions relating to automatic or discretionary stay of proceedings in national courts, they provide the context and condition the exercise of the discretion.

4.   It should thus be remembered that the possibility of concurrent proceedings contesting the validity of a patent granted by the EPO is inherent in the system established by the EPC. It should also be remembered that national courts exercise exclusive jurisdiction on infringement issues.

5.   *If there are no other factors, a stay of the national proceedings is the default option.* There is no purpose in pursuing two sets of proceedings simply because the Convention allows for it.

6.   It is for the party resisting the grant of the stay to show why it should not be granted. Ultimately it is a question of where the balance of justice lies.

7.   One important factor affecting the exercise of the discretion is the extent to which refusal of a stay will irrevocably deprive a party of any part of the benefit which the concurrent jurisdiction of the EPO and the national court is intended to confer. *Thus, if allowing the national court to proceed might allow the patentee to obtain monetary compensation which is not repayable if the patent is subsequently revoked, this would be a weighty factor in favour of the grant of a stay. It may, however, be possible to mitigate the effect of this factor by the offer of suitable undertakings to repay.*

8.   The Patents Court judge is entitled to refuse a stay of the national proceedings where the evidence is that some commercial certainty would be achieved at a considerably earlier date in the case of the UK proceedings than in the EPO. It is true that it will not be possible to attain certainty everywhere until the EPO proceedings are finally resolved, but some certainty, sooner rather than later, and somewhere, such as in the UK, rather than nowhere, is, in general, preferable to continuing uncertainty everywhere.

9.   It is permissible to take account of the fact that resolution of the national proceedings, whilst not finally resolving everything, may, by deciding some important issues, promote settlement.

10.   *An important factor affecting the discretion will be the length of time that it will take for the respective proceedings in the national court and in the EPO to reach a conclusion.* This is not an independent factor, but needs to be considered in conjunction with the prejudice which any party will suffer from the delay, and lack of certainty, and what the national proceedings can achieve in terms of certainty.

11.   The public interest in dispelling the uncertainty surrounding the validity of monopoly rights conferred by the grant of a patent is also a factor to be considered.

12.   In weighing the balance it is material to take into account the risk of wasted costs, but this factor will normally be outweighed by commercial factors concerned with early resolution.

13.   The hearing of an application for a stay is not to become a mini-trial of the vari-

ous factors affecting its grant or refusal. The parties' assertions need to be examined critically, but at a relatively high level of generality."[942] [Emphasis supplied.]

2-494   An example of the factors in play here can be seen in *Eli Lilly v Janssen Sciences*[943] where the High Court of England and Wales refused an application to stay Lilly's revocation and declaration of non-infringement action against Janssen's divisional patent pending the outcome of EPO proceedings. The European patent had been found invalid in the UK and also by the Opposition Division but it was under appeal to the TBA. The decision turned on its facts, including the interesting detail that Lilly wanted to apply for a marketing authorisation for its product (solanezumab) but did not want to do so if Janssen could use that marketing authorisation to apply for a SPC (unusually, it had no marketing authorisation of its own for the product) and thus extend the lifetime of protection for products covered by the basic patent. In short, Lilly had no interest in applying for a marketing authorisation if its product infringed the basic patent which could then be used by Janssen to extend the lifetime of the patent via the SPC route. Thus, Lilly appeared to be in a position of considerably commercial uncertainty which it wished to resolve as quickly as possible. These factors outweighed the fact that the Opposition Division's decision (on the divisional patent) and the Technical Board of Appeal's decision (on the parent patent) were due to be heard within five months of the hearing of the application to stay.

2-495   The above principles are clearly applicable to any Member State where the issue is one of discretion. To the above principles one might add that a court should take into account the possibility of interim injunctive relief being granted alongside a stay. However, interim injunctive relief that is of many years duration may be indistinguishable at a commercial plane to the grant of a permanent injunction. This is particularly true where the invention has a certain lifespan after which it is no longer of economic, technical or commercial interest to either party. It should be noted that other countries take different approaches to the overlapping jurisdiction problem: Austrian legislation states that proceedings for revocation must be stayed pending a decision in the Opposition Division.[944]

THE EPC, PCT AND EPO

Introduction

2-496   The EPC is a regional treaty for the purposes of the PCT.[945] The PCT provides that where a state which is designated or elected under the PCT is also a party to a regional treaty, then that application may be treated as an application for a regional patent.[946] Accordingly, the EPC permits the EPO to be a Designated Office and an Elected Office under the PCT.[947] This means that if a PCT applicant is considering obtaining European patents in those countries which are signatories to the EPC, they can obtain European patents in those countries by merely requesting a European patent in their PCT application. Once publication of the international application

---

[942] *IPCom v HTC*, at [68].
[943] [2016] EWHC 313.
[944] As recognised in *INDUPAK/Strawman* (T-301/95) [1998] E.P.O.R. 142.
[945] Preamble to EPC. PCT art.45(1).
[946] PCT art.45(1).
[947] See EPC arts 150–153 and EPC rr.159–163.

has been completed and the application sent in English, French or German to the EPO, the EPO will process the application and, if found patentable, grant European patents for the relevant Member States. This route is called the Euro-PCT route (although it should perhaps more accurately be known as the PCT-Euro route). A PCT application will enter the European regional phase within 31 months from the earliest claimed priority date of the PCT application or the filing date if no priority is claimed. Where the EPO is an Elected Office, it will make use of the IPER in the prosecution of the European application. Where it is simply a Designated Office, it will make use of the IPRP.

As a procedural way of obtaining national patents in many countries, the PCT **2-497** and EPC are fully compatible with each other and provide an extremely useful route for applicants who wish to obtain patent protection in a number of industrialised countries besides Europe. Indeed, the majority of applications to the EPO are via the Euro-PCT route.

The EPO can also act as a Receiving Office, International Search Authority **2-498** ("ISA") and International Preliminary Examining Authority ("IPEA") within the PCT, even when it is not a Designated Office or Elected Office (i.e. where the application is not a Euro-PCT application).[948]

The EPO publishes a very useful guide called the "Euro-PCT Guide".[949] There **2-499** is a reasonably complex interplay between the PCT and the EPC (and their respective implementing regulations) and this publication provides a very clear and easy-to-read guide to Euro-PCT applications.

Roles of the EPO

EPO as a Receiving Office

If the applicant is a resident or national of a state which is a signatory to both the **2-500** EPC and PCT, then the EPO may act as a Receiving Office.[950] The international application must be filed in English, French or German.[951] If the application is filed with an authority of a contracting state for onward transmittal to the EPO as the Receiving Office, then the contracting state must ensure that the application reaches the EPO not later than two weeks before the end of the 13th month after filing, or if priority is claimed, from the date of priority.[952] The EPO will then process the matter according to the PCT and PCT guidelines.

EPO as an ISA

The EPO will act as an ISA for applicants who are residents or nationals of a **2-501** contracting state to the EPC.[953] It will prepare an ISR and a written preliminary opinion of the patentability of the application (the IPRP). If the applicant requests, it will also carry out a supplementary international search (SIS). This is a more thorough search than the ISR.

---

[948] For meaning of these, see paras 2-034 to 2-044.
[949] This is accessible at: *http://www.epo.org/applying/international/guide-for-applicants.html* [Accessed 18 August 2017].
[950] EPC art.151. For meaning of "resident or national of a contracting state", see PCT r.18.
[951] EPC r.157(2).
[952] EPC r.157(3).
[953] EPC art.152.

EPO as an IPEA

2-502   The EPO will act as an IPEA for applicants who are residents or nationals of a contracting state to the EPC.[954] Applications must be made in English, French or German. There is a handling fee and a much larger preliminary examination fee.[955] As is made clear in the Euro-PCT Guide, international preliminary examination will, in general, have no added value unless amendments and/or arguments have been filed with the EPO following receipt of the ISR and the non-binding preliminary opinion issued by the EPO as ISA.[956]

EPO as a Designated or Elected Office: the Euro-PCT route[957]

2-503   The EPO will act as a Designated Office for any state which is a signatory to both the PCT and the EPC, and for which state the applicant wishes to obtain a European patent. It will also act as an Elected Office where the applicant has elected that state if the PCT application is a PCT-II application.[958] This is commonly called the Euro-PCT route for the applicant who files an international application under the PCT that requires protection in a large number of countries including European countries. In respect of those European countries, such is treated as an application before the EPO for a European patent for those countries.

2-504   If the applicant, after considering the ISR (and where requested, the supplemental search report) and the IPRP and where relevant the IPER, decides to pursue the international application before the EPO in order to obtain patent protection in countries which are signatories to the EPC, they must comply with certain requirements within 31 months from the filing date or, if priority has been claimed, from the earliest priority date.[959] Those requirements are set out in the Euro-PCT Guide and are contained within the EPC rules[960] but include the supply of a translation of the application (if not in an official language of the EPO) and payment of various fees (filing fee, designation fee, search fee and where relevant, examination fee and renewal fee).[961] If the applicant is not resident nor has its principal place of business within one of the EPC contracting states, a professional representative must be appointed. Amendments may be filed within set time limits prior to the application being examined.[962] Thereafter, the Euro-PCT application is processed in much the same way as an application for a European patent.

EPO acting in a combination of roles

2-505   The EPO can act as Receiving Office, International Searching Authority, International Preliminary Examining Authority, Designated Office, and Elected Office or combine any of these roles. In a Euro-PCT II application, the EPO could act

---

954 art.152.

955 However, the preliminary examination fee is much less than a regular examination fee under the EPC.

956 *How to get a European patent, Guide for Applicants, Part 2 (Euro-PCT Guide)*, para.302: *http:// www.epo.org/applying/international/guide-for-applicants.html* [Accessed 18 August 2017].

957 Generally, see Euro-PCT Guide, Section E.

958 EPC art.153(1).

959 EPC r.159(1); arts 22(1), (3), 39(1)(a) PCT.

960 EPC rr.159–162.

961 Generally, see Euro-PCT Guide, Section E.

962 See Euro-PCT Guide, Section E, IV.

as all bodies. If the applicant wishes to be restricted to obtaining patents in states which are Member States of both the PCT and EPC, then the apparent outcome, that is of patents being granted in these countries, is the same under both routes. The merits of the various routes are discussed below.[963]

EU Unitary Patent

Introduction

Unlike in the field of trade marks, designs and copyright, until recently the EU has played a relatively small role in the enactment of legislation which harmonises patent laws. Until 2012, the only harmonising EU legislative measures in the field of patents were the Biotechnology Directive and the Supplementary Protection Certificate regulation. However, this was not because of a lack of interest by the EU in patents. Indeed, it was recognised that the cost of patenting in Europe was very expensive because of the large number of countries and the translational requirements. Thus, for many decades, the European Commission had sought to introduce a unitary Community Patent similar to the EU Trade Mark and Community Registered Design.   **2-506**

As long ago as 1965, a complete draft of an EEC patent law not only provided for a centralised grant procedure for unitary European patents but also a system of law governing them. In 1969, following a break of four years due to political reasons caused by the UK's request to join the EEC, it was proposed that this draft be split into two conventions. The first was intended to create a centralised European procedure for any European country, regardless of whether or not it was a member of the EEC, which granted European patents that would have the legal value of a bundle of national patents. By the second convention, it was intended to create a European patent for the Common Market which was of a unitary and autonomous character and was governed by a common system of law.   **2-507**

The first convention led to the Munich Convention establishing the EPC. The second convention led to the Luxembourg Convention establishing the Community Patent Convention ("CPC") in 1975. This provided that the Community patent was of a unitary nature which could only be granted, transferred, revoked or allowed to lapse in respect of the whole Community. In 1977, the European Patent Convention entered into force. The CPC required the ratification of the nine EEC states that had signed it. However, Denmark and Ireland were not able to ratify the CPC for constitutional reasons. This deadlock and further difficulties over the ratification of the Convention by Spain in the 1980s led to two conferences in Luxembourg in 1985 and 1989. At the first conference, agreement was reached on the Protocol on Litigation and the Establishment of the Community Patent Appeal Court. These provisions essentially provided for national designated patents courts to adjudicate on the infringement and validity of Community patents and revoke them if necessary. However, the conferences provided for the establishment of the Community Patent Appeal Court ("COPAC"), which was to have exclusive jurisdiction to determine issues raised on appeals concerning certain provisions of the CPC   **2-508**

---

[963] See para.2-674.

and the validity of the Community Patent.[964] At the second conference in 1989, it was agreed that the CPC would only enter into force upon ratification by the 12 signatory EC states. However, because of the continuing difficulties caused by Denmark, Ireland and Spain, a Protocol for the Possible Modification of the Conditions of Entry into Force of the CPC was agreed. This provided that if the CPC had not entered force by 31 December 1991, another conference would be reconvened in order for the Member States to unanimously amend the number of states which had to ratify the CPC in order for it to come into force. Unfortunately, no agreement was reached at an Intergovernmental Conference in Lisbon in July 1992 in relation to this Protocol.[965]

2-509   It soon became fairly clear that the CPC was never going to become law. Interest waned. In part, the impetus behind the CPC was the fear that national intellectual property rights would be used to partition the EU. However, the jurisprudence of the CJEU in relation to the interaction of arts 34–36 and intellectual property rights had removed that fear.[966] There was thus little incentive to ratify the CPC and it was said that ratification of the 1989 Luxembourg Convention would have been equivalent to "putting a dead man on the throne".[967]

2-510   However, the need and yearning for a cheap, unitary, EU-wide patent still remained. Following a period of intensive consultation which led to the *Green Paper on the Community Patent and the Patent System in Europe*,[968] in 1999, the Commission set forward numerous proposals for patent reform in Europe,[969] which included the preparation of a draft Regulation providing for a unitary EU-wide patent. The legislative mechanism proposed required unanimous consent.[970] The Council Regulation would have direct applicability in all Member States.

2-511   The main aspects of the new Community Patent Regulation were as follows:

- The Community Patent would have a unitary nature and be effective throughout the Community.
- The EPO would manage the filing, prosecution and grant of a Community Patent.
- The patent would be granted and published in one of the working languages of the EPO (French, German and English) and the claims would be translated into the other two. This would reduce significantly the costs of obtaining a patent for Europe. However, unlike the EPC, there would be no option for Member States to ask for additional translations in their own

---

[964] For a detailed analysis of the jurisdictional rules on litigation under the CPC, see D. Young QC and C. Birss, "Forum Shopping under the Community Patent Convention" [1992] E.I.P.R. 361 and R. Foglia, "Procedural Aspects of Litigation under the Community Patent" [1990] 22 I.I.C. 970.

[965] The conference was very secret and non-governmental observers were excluded. It is thus not exactly clear what happened at the conference. See M. Burnside, "The Community Patent Convention; Is it Obsolete in its Present Form" [1993] 14 E.I.P.R. 285 at 288.

[966] See J.B. van Benthem, "The European Patent System and European Integration" [1993] I.I.C. 435 at 443 and M. Burnside, "The Community Patent Convention; Is it Obsolete in its Present Form" [1993] 14 E.I.P.R. 285 at 288.

[967] M. Burnside, "The Community Patent Convention; Is it Obsolete in its Present Form" [1993] 14 E.I.P.R. 285 at 287–288.

[968] *Green Paper on the Community Patent and the Patent System in Europe* COM (97) 314.

[969] COM (99) 197. *Communication from the Commission dated 5 February 1999 to the Council, European Parliament and the ECSC following A Resolution of the European Parliament dated 19 November 1998 on the Commission Green Paper.* These are reported respectively in [1999] OJ EPO 193 at 197.

[970] The provision relied upon is now art.352 TFEU (ex-art.308 and previously art.235).

language. As has been seen above, this requirement adds considerably to the costs of obtaining a patent and rarely is resort made to the national translations.

- Disputes on infringement and validity would be dealt with by a centralised Community tribunal within the framework of the CJEU. This would ensure that differing interpretations of the same patent in the Member States would not occur. This proposal would require an amendment to the European Community Treaty. It was not clear whether the central tribunal would be an appellate tribunal (as suggested by the European Parliament) or a first instance tribunal.

On 8 March 2004, a revised Community Patent Regulation was put forward. However, the real difficulty concerned the issue of compulsory translations of the Community Patent into the various languages of the EU and the effect of incorrect translations. In 2004, the Council failed to agree on the details of the Regulation and at the time of the 3rd edn of this book (2007), considerable pessimism reigned over the likelihood of implementation of the Community Patent Regulation because of the difficulties in getting unanimous consent to a simplified translation regime. In particular, it was clear that Spain and Italy were adamantly opposed to the proposed language regime. **2-512**

However, such pessimism has proved unfounded. In 2010, a group of Member States "discovered" the "enhanced co-operation" procedure in the TFEU[971] which permits a group of Member States to choose to co-operate on a specific topic. Twenty-six Member States have now chosen to use this procedure to set up a EU Unitary Patent. In March 2011, the Council authorised the adoption of this procedure for enacting EU legislation for a EU Unitary Patent. Spain and Italy brought actions before the CJEU for annulment of the Council's decision authorising the use of the enhanced co-operation procedure but these were unsuccessful.[972] Italy then opted into the UP Regulations leaving Spain on its own (Croatia has yet to opt in as it has only recently joined the EU but is expected to do so). On 11 December 2012, the European Council adopted two regulations using the enhanced co-operation procedure—one for the EU Unitary Patent[973] and the other for the translation arrangements for such protection[974]. These are called the Unitary Patent Regulations. **2-513**

However, the EU regulations did not provide for a system of litigating the EU Unitary Patent. There was a strong wish for a Europe-wide system for litigating both the proposed EU Unitary Patent and also classic European patents which would allow for a one-stop shop in one country but whose decision would have effect throughout EPC contracting states or EU participating Member States (for the EU Unitary Patent). There was considerable resistance to the non-technical Court of Justice having the right to rule on every aspect of substantive patent law. Furthermore, numerous contracting states to the EPC were not EU Member States. The European Commission put forward a proposal which was an international **2-514**

---

[971] arts 326–334 TFEU. See para.1-109.

[972] *Spain v Council* (C-274/11) and *Italy v Council* (C-295/11) (judgment of 16 April 2013). On 22 March 2013, Spain issued two further complaints (C-146/13 and C-147/13) which sought annulment of the EU Unitary Patent legislation. On 5 May 2015, the Court of Justice rejected the challenge by Spain in *Kingdom of Spain v European Parliament and Council of the European Union* (C–146/13 and C–147/13). See para.1-108.

[973] EU Regulation 1257/2012 [2012] OJ L361/1.

[974] EU Regulation 1260/2012 [2012] OJ L361/89.

agreement to be concluded between Member States, the EU and non-EU contracting states to the EPC. However, it was rejected by the CJEU as being incompatible with EU law.[975] This rejection led a new regional agreement open only to participating EU Member States (the three states which are not signatories are Spain, Poland and Croatia). This is called the Agreement on the Unified Patent Court ("the UPC Agreement").[976] It creates a specialised patent court (the Unified Patent Court) with exclusive jurisdiction for litigation relating to the EU Unitary Patent and also shared jurisdiction with national courts for litigation of "classic European patents" which have effect in participating Member States. The illegality of the earlier agreement under EU law has been cured by limiting the UPC Agreement to EU Member States and giving the CJEU jurisdiction to adjudicate on matters under the UPC Agreement that raise issues of EU law.[977]

2-515   The "EU Unitary Patent package" (i.e. the UP Regulations and the Agreement on a Unified Patent Court) will only apply from the date of entry into force of the Agreement on a United Patent Court. For the latter to come into force, the Agreement on a Unified Patent Court will need to be ratified by at least 13 states including Germany, the UK and France. As of 1 May 2018 , 13 Member States have ratified the UPC Agreement.[978] The UK and France have ratified it but not Germany. As regards Germany, a challenge has been made to the German Constitutional Court (*Bundesverfassungsgericht*) regarding the ratification by Germany of the UPC Agreement. This has led to the court making an informal request to the Office of the President of the German Republic to refrain from ratifying the UPC Agreement. It is unclear when the court will render its decision.

Brexit

2-516   Following the "Brexit" referendum in June 2016, there were doubts as to whether the UK would ratify the Agreement on the UPC. However, the UK has now ratified it.

2-517   Once the UK has left the EU there are concerns as to whether it can participate in the UPC Agreement. Accordingly, an opinion was therefore sought as to whether the UK could participate in the UPC Agreement. Concern was expressed about the fact that the Agreement includes a mechanism for referral to the CJEU. The view from UK constitutional lawyers[979] is rather tentative that it *"would be constitutionally possible for the UK to continue to participate in the UPCA after Brexit so long as it signs up to all of the provisions of the Agreement which protect EU constitutional principles"*. However, the opinion identifies that the CJEU could interpret the UPCA as precluding the participation of non-Member States. There is a risk that the CJEU would reach the opposite conclusion. The constitutional lawyers' view is that provided that the UK agrees to respect the supremacy of EU law (in patent disputes before the UPC), the possibility of claiming damages and/or instituting infringement proceedings for breach of EU law and the ability to make

---

[975] Opinion 1/09 [2011] E.C.R. I-1137.

[976] Agreement on a Unified Patent Court 2013/C/175/01. NB. This is not a EU legislative Act.

[977] Including a preliminary reference procedure, see art.21 UPC Agreement.

[978] A current list of Member States who have ratified the Agreement on the UPC can be found at: *http://www.consilium.europa.eu/en/documents-publications/agreements-conventions/agreement/?aid=2013001* [Accessed 25 April 2018]. This is updated regularly.

[979] *http://www.eip.com/assets/downloads/gordon-and-pascoe-advice-upca-34448129-1-.pdf* [Accessed on 18 August 2017].

references to the CJEU (the upshot of Opinion 1/09), then the UK could sign up to the UPC.

Finally, it should be said that one is here concerned with the Agreement on the **2-518** UPC. The EU Unitary Patent would not be available to the UK once it has exited the EU. This raises the issue as to what would happen to EU Unitary Patents as regards protection in the UK. This will be the same issue as already exists for the EU Trade Mark and EU Design which are both unitary rights. In that respect, it is known that the intention of the UK and EU is that Brexit will not lead to loss of rights in the UK. Rather, it is expected that a "Montenegro" option will occur whereby the EU unitary right will result, upon formal exit from the EU, in a "clone" UK right. As said by the EPO in its "Unitary Patent Guide",[980] it can be expected that appropriate solutions will be found that avoid any loss of rights as the protection of acquired rights and the preservation of legal certainty are general principles of law respected throughout Europe.[981]

The EU Unitary Patent and UPC Agreement: Fundamentals

To the uninformed reader, discussion about the EU Unitary Patent (officially **2-519** titled a "European patent with unitary effect") and the Agreement on the Unified Patent Court can be confusing. It is vital to distinguish between the two although they are intimately linked to each other, they are different in nature. It is also necessary to understand their relationship with the EPC and EPO.

On the one hand, the EU Unitary Patent is the creature of two EU legislative **2-520** measures that only apply to the 26 EU Member States who participated in the enhanced co-operation procedure under which the measures were taken ("participating Member States"). As of 1 May 2018, it does not apply to Spain or Croatia. Essentially, these measures create a unitary EU-wide patent similar in nature to the EU Trade Mark and EU Design (and indeed the EU Plant Variety Right). The nature of a unitary EU right is that there is only one registered right for the whole of the EU. It cannot be split or divided up into national EU registered rights. However, there are differences. First, unlike the EU Trade Mark and EU Design, where the substantive law of both of these is set out in EU Regulations, the substantive law of the EU Unitary Patent is the law of the EPC. Secondly, a EU Unitary Patent will only be granted on request after grant of the European patent. Thus, up to grant, there is no difference between a EU Unitary Patent and that of a "classic" European patent. The EPO has exclusive jurisdiction to decide on its grant and yet unlike EUIPO, the EPO is not an EU body. After grant of a European patent, a request to convert a European patent into a EU Unitary Patent must be made within one month of the date of grant of the European patent. Thirdly, unlike an EU Trade Mark or EU Design, a EU Unitary Patent will not apply to all EU countries as Spain and Croatia are not "participating Member States" (although they may join it in the future).

A EU Unitary Patent can sit alongside a classic European patent. Thus, an owner **2-521** could have a EU Unitary Patent in those countries which are Participating Member States with parallel national patents arising from the grant of the European patent in other EPC countries. Thus, the EU Unitary Patent is an additional option for pat-

---

[980] 1 August 2017. It can be accessed at *http://documents.epo.org/projects/babylon/eponet.nsf/0/ C3ED1E790D5E75E0C125818000325A9B/$File/Unitary_Patent_guide_en.pdf* [Accessed 18 August 2017].

[981] See para.15.

ent protection in Europe alongside the national route and the classic European patent.

2-522　On the other hand, the Agreement on the Unified Patent Court ("UPC Agreement") is not a EU measure but rather a regional agreement. It is intended to provide a framework for the enforcement of and litigation of both the EU Unitary Patent and classic European patents. The UPC is intended to provide for a one-stop shop for litigation of both the EU Unitary Patent and classic European patents. However, whilst there is no ability to opt out of use of the UPC to litigate a EU Unitary Patent, there are transitional and opt-out provisions for classic European patents. Furthermore, Spain, Poland and Croatia have not signed the UPC Agreement. In such circumstances, the UPC Agreement will not apply to Spain, Poland and Croatia and those states who have not ratified the UPC Agreement despite it coming into force.

2-523　The UPC's rulings will be truly pan-European. Its findings will have effect in the territories of all the contracting states that have ratified the UPCA. It can thus enforce a EU Unitary Patent or classic European patent on a pan-European basis and also revoke such patents on a pan-European basis.

2-524　Despite the UPC Agreement and the EU Unitary Patent being different legislative measures, the latter being a EU measure and the former being a European regional treaty, they are, as seen above, closely linked. The EU Unitary Patent relies upon the Agreement of the UPC as the legislative measure that governs litigation of it and accordingly, does not come into effect until the UPC Agreement comes into force.[982] Furthermore, under the UPC Agreement, the UPC has an ability to refer questions to the CJEU much as a national court has the ability to make a preliminary reference to the CJEU under art.267 for interpretation of a EU legislative measure.

2-525　In the next section, the law relating to the grant of the EU Unitary Patent are discussed. The section following that discusses the UPC Agreement as it applies to both the EU Unitary Patent and classic European patents.

EU Unitary Patent

Fundamentals

2-526　In essence, a EU Unitary Patent is a European patent which, following grant, is converted into a European patent with unitary effect in Member States of the EU that have participated in the "enhanced co-operation" procedure and are thus bound by the two EU Unitary Patent EU regulations: Regs 1257/2012 and 1260/2012 ("Participating Member States"). These are all EU countries other than Spain and Croatia. The first one deals with the establishment of the EU Unitary Patent whilst the latter deals with the language regime applicable to the EU Unitary Patent. The EU Unitary Patent system builds on the EPC. The pre-grant phase is exactly the same as for European patents. An applicant will file a European patent application seeking protection in EPC contracting states. Once a European patent is granted, the owner must initiate before the EPO a post-grant procedure with a view to obtaining a EU Unitary Patent. This is a simple procedure and there are few requirements. Assuming that the requirements are met, the EPO will grant a EU Unitary Patent and register it. The EU Unitary Patent has unitary character, meaning it provides

---

[982] Reg.1257/2012 art.18(2).

uniform protection and equal effect in all Participating Member States. Like the EU Trade Mark, it may only be limited, transferred or revoked or lapse in respect of all Participating Member States. However, it may be licensed in respect of the whole or part of the territories of all these states.

The procedure for grant of a EU Unitary Patent is now discussed in more detail. **2-527**

Languages

One of the real drivers for the EU Unitary Patent was the need to reduce the cost **2-528**
of translation. Whilst the London Agreement[983] had gone some way to achieving that, there was a genuine desire on behalf of EU countries to go further. The need to make the patent regime in the EU affordable to businesses was paramount. Inevitably, with English becoming the *lingua franca* of Europe, it was to play centre stage. Equally inevitably, countries such as Spain and Italy, whose languages are not official languages of the EPO, were concerned that any removal of the obligation to translate into Spanish and Italian would be adverse to national interests. This led to intense negotiation to come up with an acceptable language regime for any proposed EU Unitary Patent (which negotiations ultimately led to Spain choosing not to participate) between EU Member States.

The result is Reg.1260/2012 which governs the language requirements of the EU **2-529**
Unitary Patent. It must be remembered that this "sits" on top of the language regime of the EPO as the language rules of the EPC and its implementing regulations will govern the pre-grant phase of a EU Unitary Patent. Thus, upon grant of a European patent, under the EPC the claims will have been translated into the two official languages of the EPO other than the language of the proceedings. This means that the claims will already exist in English, French and German. A central theme of Reg.1260/2012 is to delay translation of the specification of a European patent until when such is necessary—in other words, when there is a dispute. This avoids the high cost of translating European patents which are never litigated upon and sit on a shelf gathering dust.

A request for a EU Unitary Patent must contain a translation of the European pat- **2-530**
ent as follows. If the language of the EPO proceedings was French or German, then a full translation of the specification of the European patent must be translated into English. Where the language of the proceedings was English, a full translation into any other official language of the EU is required.[984] The effect of the above is that there will always exist an English version of the EU Unitary Patent as well as one other EU official language (i.e. German or French). Compensation for translation costs is available for SMEs, natural persons, non-profit organisations, universities and public research organisations who have their residence or principal place of business in the EU.[985] It should be said that it is not intended that this regime continue forever. Rather, it is expected at some time in the future that a request for a EU Unitary Patent will require no further translation than that for the underlying

---

[983] See para.2-356.
[984] Reg.1260/2012 art.6(1).
[985] Reg.1260/2012 art.5. This is only available where the European patent application was filed in an official EU language other than English, German or French (Reg.1260/12 art.5).

European patent.[986] When this happens will depend on how good machine translations of patent applications become.[987] At present, this is some years away.

2-531   However, when a dispute arises concerning the infringement of a EU Unitary Patent, the intended defendant may request a full translation of the EU Unitary Patent into an official language of the EU country where the alleged infringement took place or the EU country in which it is domiciled.[988] The owner of the EU Unitary Patent may also be requested to translate it into the language used by a court adjudicating on the dispute.[989] The cost of these translations is borne by the owner of the patent.[990]

Request for EU Unitary Patent

2-532   Following mention of the grant of a European patent in the European Patent Bulletin, a request for the grant of a EU Unitary Patent must be made within one month. This is non-extendable.[991] Furthermore, a request can only be made if the European patent has been granted with the same set of claims in all 26 participating Member States.[992] The request must contain a translation of the patent as discussed in the previous section. Provided that the above requirements are satisfied, the EPO will grant a EU Unitary Patent. A detailed guidance as to the procedure is set out in the EPO's Unitary Patent Guide.[993]

Post-grant of the EU Unitary Patent

2-533   Once the EU Unitary Patent is granted, the EPO acts as a one-stop shop for its administration. Litigation of it is discussed in the following section on the UPC Agreement. Only one renewal fee per annum needs to be paid for the EU Unitary Patent which avoids the need to pay renewal fees for each Designated State. The renewal fee is set at the level equivalent to the combined renewal fee of the top four countries (Germany, France, the UK and the Netherlands).[994] The EPO will be responsible for the management of the EU Unified Patent including registering transfers, licences and other dealings in it. The UPC has an appellate function regarding decisions of the EPO in it carrying out its administrative tasks.[995]

Agreement on a Unified Patent Court

Introduction

2-534   All EU members other than Poland and Spain have signed the Agreement on a Unified Patent Court ("the UPC Agreement").[996] Croatia who joined the EU on 1 July 2013 has also yet to sign. For it to come into force, it requires ratification by

---

986   Reg.1260/2012 art.3.
987   Reg.1260/2012 art.6(3)–(5).
988   Reg.1260/2012 art.4.
989   Reg.1260/2012 art.4(2).
990   Reg.1260/2012 art.4(3).
991   Reg.1257/2012 art.9.
992   Reg. 1257/2012 art.3(1) Recital 7.
993   See fn.961.
994   See *EPO, Unitary Patent Guide*, paras 25–26.
995   Reg.1257/2012 art.9.
996   A copy of this is published in the Official Journal of the EPO—[2013] OJ C175/1.

at least 13 signatory countries, as well as France, Germany and UK. Save that Germany has yet to ratify it, these conditions are otherwise satisfied. This Agreement (which is not an EU measure) radically changes the landscape of patent litigation in Europe. The UPC Agreement creates a specialised patent court ("UPC") with exclusive jurisdiction for determining infringement and validity of EU Unitary Patents. It also has the same jurisdiction for classic European patents and European patent applications and Supplementary Protection Certificates which are alive or pending as of the date of entry into force of the UPC Agreement.[997] However, for these, the UPC Agreement shares jurisdiction between the UPC and national courts for seven years following it coming into force and also allows owners of the same to opt-out of the UPC Agreement. The exact nature of these transitional and opt-out provisions is discussed later.[998] Owners of the EU Unitary Patent cannot opt out of the UPC Agreement.

The UPC comprises a Court of First Instance, a Court of Appeal and a Registry. **2-535** The Court of First Instance will be composed of a central division with a seat in Paris and two sections in London and Munich, with several local and regional divisions in the contracting Member States to the Agreement. The Court of Appeal will be located in Luxembourg. The UPC may request preliminary rulings on the EU Unitary Patent Regulation and the Translational Requirements Regulation from the CJEU in accordance with art.267 TFEU.[999] However, it is important to emphasise that this is a sui generis mechanism. The Agreement on the UPC is not EU legislation.

The UPC Agreement does not only create the UPC which has exclusive jurisdic- **2-536** tion for European patents and EU Unitary Patents. It also sets out detailed provisions as regards: (i) litigation before the UPC, (ii) the allocation of jurisdiction amongst the contracting Member States, (iii) what acts are deemed infringing (including contributory infringement), and (iv) the remedies that a proprietor of a European or EU Unitary Patent can obtain. Its adoption is a tribute to the persistence and ambition of those who for many decades have considered that it was of paramount importance to Europe to provide a method of litigating patents in Europe which was attractive, effective, overcame the very real problems caused by the EU being a Tower of Babel, and which provided a convenient pan-European "one-stop shop" for patent litigation in the EU.

The UPC

The UPC consists of a Court of First Instance which is divided into central, **2-537** regional and local divisions.[1000] A local division is a court of a contracting state but two or more contracting states can choose to establish a regional division (e.g. covering the territories of Belgium, Luxembourg and The Netherlands). In general, infringement proceedings are brought before the local or regional division whereas actions for revocation of a European patent or EU Unitary Patent which are not by way of counterclaim to an infringement action are brought in the Central Division. The Central Division is based in Munich, London and Paris with these courts having allocated specialities (life sciences, pharmaceuticals, chemistry and metallurgy in London; mechanical engineering, lighting, heating, weapons and blasting

---

[997] art.3.
[998] See para.2-570.
[999] UPC Agreement arts 21, 23.
[1000] art.7.

in Munich; and performing operations, transporting, textiles, paper, fixed constructions, physics and electricity in Paris[1001]).

2-538   The UPC also has a Court of Appeal which is based in Luxembourg.[1002] It should also be noted that the UPC can refer preliminary references to the CJEU on points of EU law. As substantive patent law is not derived from EU law, questions of interpretation of the EPC cannot be referred to the Court of Justice.[1003] Despite this, the CJEU will continue to be involved in interpreting EU Directives and Regulations such as the Biotechnology Directive, the enforcement of IPRs and Supplementary Protection Certificates.

Applicable law

2-539   The UPC will apply a mixture of EU, EPC and national law to disputes before it.[1004] In essence, procedural rules governing the enforcement of EU Unitary Patents and classic European patents and SPCs is governed by the UPC Agreement, whereas the scope of protection and the validity of such is governed by the EPC.

2-540   As well as primary law, Rules of Procedure have been adopted which will apply as secondary legislation.[1005]

Jurisdiction of UPC to infringement and validity proceedings

2-541   The UPC has exclusive competence in respect of actual or threatened infringement actions of EU Unitary Patents together with declarations for non-infringement (including provisional and protective measures and injunctions), actions and counterclaims for revocation of these patents and declarations of invalidity of SPCs.[1006] It has shared jurisdiction with national courts for classic European patents for the first seven years from when it comes into force. Also, owners of classic European patents may opt out of its jurisdiction on a patent-by-patent basis.

2-542   In general, the determination of which division of the UPC court can hear actions for infringement and validity is determined by the Recast Brussels Regulation or (for non-EU Member States) by the Lugano Convention.[1007] However, the UPC Agreement also has its own *lex specialis* jurisdiction provisions (much like the EU Trade Mark and Community Registered Design regulations have their own special jurisdiction provisions) and these are fairly comprehensive. Thus, the jurisdictional provisions of the UPC Agreement "sit" within the Recast Brussels Regulation with the former taking precedence over the latter.

[1001] art.7; Annex II of Agreement.

[1002] arts 6, 9.

[1003] There were substantial fears expressed about incorporating substantive patent law into EU law by reason of the Court of Justice's inability to decide on complicated patent matters and the delays involved in preliminary references to the Court of Justice. Thus, measures which were intended to allow this were removed from the EU UP Regulations. For discussion of this, see M.J. Crowley, "Restoring Order in European Patent Law: A Proposal for the Reintroduction of the Substantive Patent Provisions of the Unitary Patent Package into EU Law" *NYU Journal of Intellectual Property and Entertainment Law* [2015] Vol.4(2), 197–225. This can be accessed at: *http://jipel.law.nyu.edu/vol-4-no-2-1-crowley/#_ftnref3* [Accessed 18 August 2017].

[1004] arts 20, 24.

[1005] These can be found at: *https://www.unified-patent-court.org/sites/default/files/upc_rules_of_procedure_18th_draft_15_march_2017_final_clear.pdf* [Accessed 18 August 2017].

[1006] art.32.

[1007] art.31. The jurisdictional rules are discussed in Ch.17 at para.17-223, et seq.

Infringement

In relation to actual or threatened infringement actions (and provisional and **2-543** protective measures thereto), actions for damages or compensation derived from the provisional protection conferred by a published European patent application and actions relating to the use of the invention prior to the grant of the patent (or rights based on prior use of the invention), hereinafter referred to as "the Infringement Actions", must be brought in one or more of the following courts:

Local/Regional Division	• The actual or threatened infringement has occurred or may occur in that Member State.[1008] A counterclaim for revocation can be brought in the same proceedings before the court of the local division seized with the actual or threatened infringement action.[1009] • The defendant (or, in the case of multiple defendants, one of the defendants) has its residence or principal place of business in that Member State. An action may be brought only against multiple defendants where the defendants have a commercial relationship and the action relates to the same alleged infringement.[1010] • The parties have agreed to bring such actions before the local division.[1011]
Central Division	Where there are no local or regional division courts in the Member State which would have jurisdiction under the above conditions.[1012]

Revocation or declaration of non-infringement

Where an undertaking wishes to revoke a EU Unitary Patent or a classical **2-544** European patent or wishes to obtain a declaration of non-infringement of such, an action must be brought before the Central Division and not the local or regional division.[1013] If however, an action for infringement relating to the same patent has already been brought before a local or regional division, then the action for revocation or declaration of non-infringement is treated as if it were a counterclaim and must be brought before the same division.[1014] As said above, if a local or regional UP court has jurisdiction over an infringement action, it has jurisdiction over a counterclaim to revoke the patent which is the subject matter of the infringement proceedings.

[1008] art.33(1)(a).
[1009] art.33(3).
[1010] art.33(1)(b).
[1011] art.33(7).
[1012] art.33(1), last paragraph.
[1013] art.33(4).
[1014] art.33(4).

Pending and associated actions

2-545   The UPC Agreement contains various provisions concerning the allocation of jurisdiction where there are pending actions for revocation or infringement or declarations for non-infringement before the Court of First Instance. These mirror somewhat parallel provisions in the EU Trade Mark and Community Registered Design regulations. The provisions split into mandatory obligations (i.e. the seized court must decline jurisdiction or stay the proceedings) and discretionary obligations (i.e. the seized court may in the exercise of its discretion decline jurisdiction or stay the proceedings).

Mandatory obligations	The seized court *must* decline jurisdiction and/or stay the proceedings in the following circumstances:
parallel infringement proceedings	(a) Where there is a pending action for infringement of a patent before a division of the Court of First Instance, then any action between the same parties on the same patent cannot be brought in any other division.[1015] (b) However, if the infringement action is pending before a regional division and the acts of infringement have occurred in three or more regional divisions, then, at the request of the defendant, the regional division concerned must refer the case to the central division.[1016] (c) Where an action has been brought between the same parties on the same patent in different divisions, then any division other than the first seized must declare the action inadmissible.[1017] (d) Where an action for declaration of non-infringement is pending before the central division, it shall be stayed if an infringement action on the same patent and between the same parties is brought within three months in a local or regional division of the date of commencement of the action for declaration of non-infringement in the central division.[1018]

[1015] art.33(2), first paragraph.
[1016] art.33(2), first paragraph.
[1017] art.33(2), first paragraph.
[1018] art.33(6).

Discretionary provisions *infringement/ revocation*	In circumstances where infringement proceedings are brought before a local or regional division and the defendant then issues a counterclaim for revocation of the same patent, the local or regional division *may do* one of three things: (a) it may choose to proceed with the action for infringement and counterclaim for revocation and request the assignment from the President of the CFI of a technically qualified judge with qualifications from the pool of judges; (b) refer the counterclaim to the central division (i.e. bifurcate the proceedings) and suspend or proceed with the action for infringement; or (c) with the agreement of the parties, refer the whole case to the central division.[1019]

Conversely where an action for revocation is pending before the central division, an action for infringement of the same patent and between the same parties may be brought in any local, regional or central division. However, if brought before a local or regional division, that division may choose to hear the infringement action, suspend the action for infringement, or with the agreement of the parties, refer the infringement proceedings to the central division.[1020]   **2-546**

EPO oppositions and UPC court

Oppositions are still possible for EU Unitary Patents and European Patents. The UPC may stay its proceedings when a "rapid decision" is expected from the EPO.[1021]   **2-547**

Territorial effect of decisions of the UPC

In the case of classical European patents, a decision of the UPC applies to all the territories of participating Member States which are also designated states of the European Patent.[1022] This is clearly a very revolutionary change from the current regime whereby a national court of a Member State may only order revocation of a European patent for that state.[1023] In the case of a EU Unitary Patent, it can only be revoked *in toto*. Infringement decisions will also have effect for all contracting Member States regardless whether the defendant is domiciled in the Member State where the proceedings are heard. Again, this is a radical change from the existing position which is governed by the Recast Brussels Regulation.[1024]   **2-548**

[1019] art.33(3).
[1020] art.33(5).
[1021] art.33.10.
[1022] art.34.
[1023] Generally, see Ch.17.
[1024] art.3 Reg.1257/2012.

Proceedings before the UPC court

2-549 The UPC Agreement has general provisions as to the issuing and conduct of proceedings before it. These are to be supplemented by rules of procedure which have been finalised.[1025]

2-550 The general provisions of the UPC Agreement provide that litigation shall be dealt in ways which are "proportionate to the importance and complexity thereof."[1026] The UPC court must actively manage the cases without impairing the freedom of the parties to determine the subject matter of, and the supporting evidence for, their case.[1027]

Parties entitled to bring proceedings

2-551 A patent proprietor, an exclusive licensee and a non-exclusive licensee which has express consent from the proprietor to do so may bring proceedings for infringement.[1028] Any natural or legal person may bring an action for revocation of a European or EU Unitary Patent.[1029] However, in infringement proceedings, the defendant cannot bring a counterclaim for revocation of the patent if the patent proprietor is not party to those proceedings. In such circumstances, a separate action for revocation must be brought against the patent proprietor.[1030]

Representation

2-552 Parties must be represented by lawyers authorised to practise before a court of a contracting Member State or European Patent Attorneys.[1031]

Language of proceedings

2-553 The language of proceedings before a local or regional division must be in an official EU language which is the official language of the contracting state of the local or regional division seized of the action.[1032] However, contracting states may designate one or more of the official languages of the EPO as the language of proceedings for their local or regional division.[1033] With agreement of the parties and the approval of the competent panel, the language in which the patent was granted may be used as the language of proceedings. If the panel objects, the parties may request referral of the case to the central division.[1034] At the request of one of the parties, the President of the CFI may on grounds of fairness and taking into account all relevant circumstances, designate the use of the language in which the patent was granted as the language of proceedings.[1035]

[1025] See *https://www.unified-patent-court.org/sites/default/files/upc_rules_of_procedure_18th_draft_15_march_2017_final_clear.pdf* [Accessed 18 August 2017] for the latest draft.
[1026] art.42.
[1027] art.43.
[1028] art.47(1)–(3).
[1029] art.46.
[1030] art.47(5).
[1031] art.48.
[1032] art.49(1).
[1033] art.49(2).
[1034] art.49(3).
[1035] art.49(5).

In relation to proceedings before the central division, the language of proceedings must be the language in which the patent concerned was granted.[1036] **2-554**

In relation to appeals, the language of proceedings is the language of proceedings of the Court of First Instance. This is the case unless either of the parties agree the use of the language in which the patent was granted or in exceptional cases, the Court of Appeal may decide on another official language of a contracting Member State.[1037] **2-555**

Provisions are applicable for translation of documents or oral proceedings.[1038] **2-556**

Written, interim and oral procedure

The UPC Agreement states that the proceedings before the UPC court shall consist of written, interim and an oral procedure.[1039] The purpose of the oral procedure is to give the parties the opportunity to explain properly their arguments but such may be dispensed with provided the parties agree.[1040] In broad terms, the current draft rules of procedure provide that there be full pleadings including a Statement of Claim and a Statement of Defence. These should set out all facts and matters relied upon, the evidence relied upon, arguments of law, and a list of documents relied upon.[1041] Similar provision is made for the Statement of Defence[1042] and also for Counterclaims for revocation[1043] and rebuttal pleadings. Once the written procedure has ended, there is an interim procedure whereby the judge-rapporteur shall explore possibilities of settlement, conferences with parties and further clarification of specific points. The third stage is the oral hearing. This is intended to be more similar to the continental system whereby judges can question witnesses or experts with the parties, also under the control of the presiding judge, being able to ask questions of witnesses or experts. It is then envisaged that judgment will be handed down within six weeks of the oral hearing.[1044] **2-557**

Means of evidence

The UPC Agreement provides for the giving or obtaining of evidence in a flexible manner. This may include the hearing of parties; requests for information; production of documents; hearing of witnesses; opinions by experts; inspection, comparative tests or experiments; and sworn statements.[1045] The court may appoint court experts to assist.[1046] There are also provisions for orders to produce evidence and/or to preserve evidence or to inspect premises.[1047] **2-558**

[1036] art.49(6).

[1037] art.50.

[1038] art.51.

[1039] art.52(1).

[1040] art.52(3).

[1041] Draft Rule 13. For UK practitioners, this means that they will be similar to pleadings in the Intellectual Property Enterprise Court and not like Patent Court pleadings.

[1042] Draft Rule 24.

[1043] Draft Rule 25.

[1044] Rule 118.6(a).

[1045] art.53.

[1046] art.57.

[1047] art.60.

Freezing Orders

2-559   The UPC Agreement also permits the grant of freezing orders whereby parties may be ordered not to remove from the jurisdiction any assets located therein or not to deal in any assets whether located within the jurisdiction or not.[1048]

Provisional or protective measures

2-560   The court may grant interim injunctions against an alleged infringer or an intermediary whose services are used by the alleged infringer which are intended to prevent any imminent infringement on a provisional basis. In such circumstances, the court may make the grant of such orders subject to the lodging of guarantees intended to ensure the compensation of the right holder. The UPC may also grant "search and seize" orders by way of protective measures.[1049]

Infringing acts

2-561   The Agreement on the UPC also harmonises the patent laws of the contracting Member States as regards what acts will infringe a EU Unitary Patent and a classical European patent. As stated earlier in this chapter,[1050] the EPC sets out the scope of protection of a European patent by reference to the Protocol to art.69 EPC but not what acts amount to an infringement. Thus, to date this has always been a matter of national law. The UPC Agreement harmonises the law in this regard. Thus art.25 provides that the following acts are acts of infringement:

- making, offering, placing on the market or using a product which is the subject-matter of the patent, or importing or storing the product for those purposes[1051];
- using a process which is the subject-matter of the patent or, where the third party knows, or should have known, that the use of the process is prohibited without the consent of the patent proprietor, offering the process for use within the territory of the contracting Member States in which that patent has effect[1052];
- offering, placing on the market, using, importing, or storing for those purposes a product obtained directly by a process which is the subject-matter of the patent[1053] are all deemed to be infringing acts; and[1054]
- in relation to contributory infringement, the UPC Agreement adopts the current UK approach in the Patents Act 1977.[1055] Thus, art.26 stipulates as follows:

  "1.   A patent shall confer on its proprietor the right to prevent any third party not having the proprietor's consent from supplying or offering to supply, within the territory of the Contracting Member States in which that patent has effect, any person other than a party entitled to exploit the patented

---

[1048] art.61, art.62(3).
[1049] See art.62.
[1050] See para.2-320.
[1051] art.25(a).
[1052] art.25(b).
[1053] art.25(c).
[1054] art.25.
[1055] see s.60(2) and (3) of the Patents Act 1977.

invention, with means, relating to an essential element of that invention, for putting it into effect therein, when the third party knows, or should have known, that those means are suitable and intended for putting that invention into effect.

2.   Paragraph 1 shall not apply when the means are staple commercial products, except where the third party induces the person supplied to perform any of the acts prohibited by Article 25."

The UPC Agreement also sets out a number of defences where the acts done by the defendant would otherwise infringe the patent. These include: acts done privately and for non-commercial purposes; acts done for experimental purposes relating to the subject matter of the patented invention; and the use of biological material for the purpose of breeding or discovering and developing other plant varieties and various other very specific defences (e.g. the "farmer's privilege to use patented material to propagate on his own holding").[1056] Those persons who qualify under these provisions are not considered as persons "entitled to exploit the patented invention" within the meaning of art.26(1).[1057]   **2-562**

Defences

The UPC Agreement provides for a number of defences. Thus, if a person had a "prior use" or "right of personal possession" defence under the laws of a contracting state, they continue to benefit from such a defence in that state.[1058] Furthermore, as with other EU unitary rights, the UPC Agreement provides for an exhaustion defence if a product covered by the European patent has been placed on the market in the EU by, or with the consent, of the patent proprietor unless there are legitimate grounds for the patent proprietor to oppose further commercialisation of the product.[1059] The UPC Agreement does not provide for exhaustion in relation to a EU Unitary Patent as such is provided in identical terms in Reg.1257/2012.[1060]   **2-563**

Remedies

The UPC Agreement sets out a range of remedies that can be granted upon a finding of infringement. These include injunctive relief (including against an intermediary), damages, delivery up of infringing products, destruction of tools used for making the infringement items, and declarations of infringement.[1061]   **2-564**

With respect of damages, the UPC Agreement states that it may order the infringer who knowingly or with reasonable grounds to know engaged in infringing a patent to pay damages appropriate to the harm actually suffered by the party as a result of the infringement.[1062] The purpose of damages is, as far as possible, to place the injured party in the position it would have been had no infringement had   **2-565**

[1056] art.27.

[1057] art.26(3).

[1058] See art.28.

[1059] art.29. The Court of Justice has developed an exhaustion of rights principle for national patents by reference to arts 34–36 TFEU (see Ch.7, para.7-025, et seq.). Undoubtedly, therefore, the proper interpretation of this provision engages EU law and in particular, the width of "legitimate grounds". Unlike trade mark law, where EU law provides for legitimate reasons to oppose further commercialisation where such would damage the reputation of the mark, it is difficult to see what such grounds would be for a European patent.

[1060] Reg.1257/2012 art.6.

[1061] art.63–68.

[1062] art.68.

taken place.[1063] Damages may not be punitive.[1064] An award of damages must take into account all appropriate aspects including negative economic consequences, lost profits, unfair profits made by the infringer, and elements other than economic factors, such as the moral prejudice caused to the injured party by the infringement. Alternatively damages may be awarded as a lump sum on the basis of a notional licence.[1065] These provisions echo in large part the Enforcement Directive.[1066] If the defendant did not knowingly, or with reasonable grounds know or engage in infringing activities, the court may order the recovery of profits or the payment of compensation.[1067]

2-566   The court may also order publication of the judgment at the defendant's expense.[1068]

Revocation of Unitary or European Patent

2-567   As discussed already,[1069] where a EU Unitary Patent or European Patent is revoked by the UPC, it is revoked in its entirety for all participating Member States. The UPC may revoke the patent entirely or partly. However, only the grounds referred to in arts 138(1) and 138(2) of the EPC may be relied upon.[1070] If the patent is revoked in part, then the patent is limited by a corresponding amendment of the claims. The effect of revocation is that the patent is invalid ab initio.[1071]

Costs

2-568   Reasonable and proportionate costs and other expenses incurred by the successful party will, as a general rule, be borne by the unsuccessful party up to a ceiling set by the Rules of Procedure.[1072] The court may order the applicant, at the request of the defendant, adequate security for its legal costs and expenses.[1073] A party who is a natural person may apply for legal aid.[1074]

Limitation periods

2-569   In general, actions relating to all forms of financial compensation may not be brought more than five years after the date on which the applicant became aware or had reasonable grounds to become aware of the *last fact* justifying the action.[1075] It is not clear how this is intended to apply where infringement has occurred continuously over a period of time in excess of five years when it comes to the ques-

---

[1063] art.68(2).
[1064] art.68(2).
[1065] art.68(3).
[1066] See Ch.15.
[1067] art.68(4).
[1068] art.80.
[1069] See para.2-519.
[1070] These are that the patent is excluded from patentability, lacks novelty or inventive step, lacks industrial application, the patent is insufficient, the patent consists of added matter, the protection has been unlawfully extended, or the proprietor of the patent is not entitled. It is of note that lack of clarity or support for the claims is not a ground of invalidity.
[1071] art.65(4).
[1072] art.69.
[1073] art.69(4).
[1074] art.71.
[1075] art.72.

tion of recovery of damages. If the infringing acts are continuing but the patentee has known about them for more than five years, is it prevented from bringing an action for financial compensation at all or merely in relation to the acts that occurred more than five years ago?[1076] If the former, such would be a harsh interpretation and may indeed find patentees issuing proceedings simply to preserve the right to recover financial compensation. Equally, it would be harsh to the defendant if the applicant is permitted to recover damages for all acts even if they occurred more than five years prior to the issue of proceedings on the somewhat arbitrary basis that when proceedings were issued, the last act occurred less than five years prior to the issue of proceedings. The fair and just result is that (where awareness of the applicant is proven) the patentee is limited to recover for damages for each infringing act that occurred five years or less prior to the issue of proceedings. It should be noted that the limitation provision is said to be without prejudice to art.24(2) and (3) which is concerned with the ability of the UPC to apply national law. Such suggests that the UPC may consider the national law of a contracting state applicable to limitation periods by applying private international law rules in preference to this provision for acts that occured in that state.

Transitional provisions and opt-out for classic European patents

At present, as discussed elsewhere,[1077] once a European patent is granted, it **2-570** becomes a basket of national patents and proceedings for infringement and revocation actions of such are the same as for national patents. However, as mentioned above, the UPC Agreement is intended to cover European patents and also Supplemental Protection Certificates. Such is truly revolutionary. However, there are clearly risks involved in the litigation before the UPC. A one-stop pan-European shop is great if one wins, but obviously not good if one loses. Many patent owners may not wish to risk revocation of their European patents on a European-wide basis but prefer to have them tested on a country by country basis.

The UPC Agreement thus has transitional provisions and also allows for own- **2-571** ers of classic European patents (but not the EU Unitary Patent) to opt out of the UPC Agreement.[1078] These provisions are not wholly clear so it is necessary to consider them in some detail.[1079]

Seven-year parallel jurisdiction

For a transitional period of seven years from the date of entry into force of the **2-572** UPC Agreement, infringement and revocation proceedings of classical European patents and also SPCs may be brought before national courts as well as the UPC.[1080] This means that both a patentee and an applicant for revocation have a choice of jurisdiction. Although not absolutely clear, it would appear that the intention is that where proceedings are brought before national courts, the UPC Agreement shall not apply at all but only national law. Thus, a national court would only have jurisdiction to revoke the European patent registered in its own country. Although it has

---

[1076] In the UK, the Limitation Act 1980 would simply bar the patentee from recovering damages for acts that occurred more than six years ago.

[1077] See para.2-047.

[1078] art.83.

[1079] For a detailed critique of the transitional provisions, see R. Pinckney, "Understanding the transitional provisions of the Agreement on the Unified Patent Court" (2015) E.I.P.R. 37(5), 268–277.

[1080] art.83(1).

been suggested that this provision only applies if the owner of a European patent has elected to opt out (see below), this seems an unlikely interpretation. There is no such condition attached to art.83(1). Secondly, it would be surprising if those wishing to litigate European patents were suddenly required to litigate them under the radically different UPC Agreement the moment that the UPC Agreement came into effect unless they had lodged and had registered their opt-out under art.83(3) before bringing national proceedings. In particular, there are no transitional provisions for the lodging of opt-outs prior to the UPC Agreement coming into force. Finally, if the provisions in art.83(1) are dependent on a patentee applying to opt-out under art.83(3), then art.83(1) is otiose and unnecessary as the opt-out provisions apply for the lifetime of the patent (or until the opt-out is withdrawn).

Opt-out

2-573   As well as the parallel jurisdiction provided for by art.83(1) above, art.83(3) allows the owner or applicant for a European patent to opt out of the "*exclusive competence of the [UPC]*" prior to the end of the transitional period set out in art.83(1). Indeed, the UPC rules allow for a patentee to opt out during a three-month "sunrise" period prior to the UPC Agreement coming into force.

2-574   Two interpretational difficulties arise here. First, does the opt-out last only for the duration of the transitional period or the lifetime of the patent? Secondly, does the opt-out relate only to the *exclusivity* of the UPC or does it exclude the whole UPC Agreement?

2-575   On the first point, it seems tolerably clear that the opt-out is intended to last for the lifetime of the patent or until withdrawn. The Preparatory Committee's view accords with this. As said by them, the contrary interpretation would make no sense as an opt-out can be notified right up to the end of the transitional period.[1081] Against this, it has been asked that if the "lifetime" view is right, why is the length of the transitional period important (in art.83(3))?[1082] In the author's view, the answer to this is that art.83(1) and art.83(3) serve two different purposes. Article 83(1) provides for shared jurisdiction for a finite period of time as patentees and their representatives get used to the advantages and disadvantages of the UPC and also avoid the many tripwires and mines that would exist if the UPC had automatic exclusive jurisdiction the moment that it came into effect. On the other hand, art.83(3) allows a patentee to opt out of the UPC once they have taken a considered decision as to the benefits of the UPC and decided whether or not they wish to take the efficient, cheaper but plainly riskier route of the UPC. Moreover, it must be remembered that an opt-out allows a European patent owner to prevent a third party from seeking pan-European revocation of its patent. Article 83(1) does not provide for such protection as it allows the third party to choose the UPC route. An opt-out under art.83(3) allows the patent owner to "lock out" that option to a third party. The reason for linking the end date for opting out in art.83(3) with the transitional period set out in art.83(1) is because after seven years of litigation of patents in both national courts and UPC, the patentee should have the ability to weigh up carefully the pros and cons of both jurisdictions. In short, art.83(3) confers on European patent owners a finite time (being seven years) to decide whether to opt out a European patent for its lifetime with the benefit of having seen litigation under the UPC play out in the UPC and national courts of the EU for that period.

[1081] See *https://www.unified-patent-court.org/faq/opt-out* [Accessed 18 August 2017].
[1082] See R. Pinckney, "Understanding the transitional provisions of the Agreement on the Unified Patent Court" (2015) E.I.P.R. 37(5), 268–277.

On the second point, it again seems tolerably clear that the intent of art.83(3) was **2-576** not to give national courts shared jurisdiction with the UPC if the owner of a European patent opted-out but rather to oust the UPC from having *any* jurisdiction. Again, this is the Preparatory Committee's view.[1083] As they say, at least for the transitional period, the contrary interpretation would mean that art.83(1) and 83(3) would have the same effect and thus be surprising. Another strong argument for the above view is that a patent owner cannot opt-out under art.83(3) if proceedings have already been bought before the UPC. There would be no need for this carve-out if an opt-out under art.83(3) did not deprive the UPC of jurisdiction but merely gave national courts *shared* jurisdiction with the UPC.

BIOTECHNOLOGICAL PATENT DIRECTIVE

Introduction

Since the 1980s, the European Commission had been seeking to enact a Direc-   **2-577** tive concerning the patentability of biotechnological inventions. The Commission was of the opinion that the protection for such inventions in Member States varied considerably and was generally less favourable than in the USA and Japan. The aim of the Directive was to increase the protection for such inventions and also to clarify what was patentable. In March 1995, the European Parliament rejected the proposed Directive, despite a Common Position being adopted on it. The main reason for its rejection was that it was considered by many to remove many restrictions on the patenting of life forms.

At the time, it was thought that the Commission would not seek to re-introduce   **2-578** a new Directive in the foreseeable future. However, the need for a Directive in this field was paramount and in December 1995 the Commission came up with an amended proposal which sought to take into account the ethical dimension of biotechnological inventions. The proposal then went through a very intensive legislative process. Thus, in July 1997, the European Parliament tabled 66 amendments to the December 1995 text. The substance of all 66 amendments was accepted by the European Commission, which then put forward an amended proposed Directive in August 1997. This proposal was accepted by the European Parliament and put before the Council in November 1997, which approved the proposal by a qualified majority (the Netherlands voted against it). Shortly thereafter, a Common Position was adopted on the Directive by the Commission and Parliament and on 16 June 1998, the Council of Ministers passed the Directive.[1084] It came into force on 30 July 1998 and Member States were given until 30 July 2000 to amend the laws to comply with the Directive.[1085] Many of the Articles of the Directive have been implemented into the Implementing Regulations of the EPC in order to ensure that the approach of the EPC to biotechnological inventions is the same under as the Directive.[1086]

The Biotechnology Directive is the only area of substantive patent law where the   **2-579** EPC and EU law overlap. Undoubtedly, this causes and has caused tension. The EPC is a regional patent convention that does not sit in a wider body of non-patent law (other than international patent conventions such as TRIPS). Put bluntly, the

---

[1083] See *https://www.unified-patent-court.org/faq/opt-out* [Accessed 18 August 2017].
[1084] Directive 98/44/EC [1998] OJ L213/13.
[1085] [1998] OJ L213/13 art.15.
[1086] See para.2-281, et seq.

EPO's business is the grant of patents for inventions. Insofar as there are exceptions to the patentability of inventions, they are construed narrowly. On the other hand, the Biotechnology Directive sits in a body of EU law which extends far beyond patent law and must take account of many fundamental principles of EU law which have nothing to do with patents. When the CJEU interprets a EU legislative measure, it does so against a host of fundamental principles enshrined in the EU Treaties (including the Charter of Fundamental Rights).

2-580   The Directive was borne out of a compromise between the EU Commission and the European Parliament, with the latter very concerned about the ethical issues raised by the patenting of life and nature. This is self-evident from the *travaux préparatoires*. In contrast, the main driver for art.53(b) EPC which bans patenting for plant or animal varieties or essentially biological processes for the production of plants or animals was to avoid double protection under plant variety rights laws and patent laws.[1087] Given such, it is perhaps unsurprising that a divergence of approach to the interpretation of identical provisions in the EPC and the Directive and the EU institutions has happened with the EU being more against the patenting of life forms than the EPO. This divergence happened on the issue as to whether or not the EPC and the Directive bans the patenting of products derived from essentially biological processes. Article 4.1(b) of the Directive and art.53(b) EPC both ban the patenting of "essentially biological processes for the production of plants or animals". As discussed earlier in this chapter, the Enlarged Board of Appeal ("EBA") held that such did not ban products derived from essentially biological processes as this exception should be construed narrowly.[1088] However, in its Notice,[1089] the EU Commission took a different view. It considered that the intention of the Directive was to ban the patenting of plants or animals that had been created by natural processes rather than technical means (i.e. genetic insertion). In coming to this conclusion, it considered the *travaux préparatoires* of the Directive which, of course, do not apply to the EPC. Thus, despite the wording of the two articles being the same, any teleological interpretation of the same wording was bound to be different. As discussed earlier in this chapter, the end result is that the EPO has amended its rules to align itself with the EU Commission's view (and thereby overturned the EBA decisions).

2-581   The EPO's approach to biotechnology inventions has already been considered.[1090] Accordingly, the reader should refer to that section as well.

Biotechnological inventions must be protected

2-582   The Directive required that Member States protect biotechnological inventions under national patent law.[1091] A biotechnological invention is not defined in the Articles of the Directive. It is generally recognised as involving the creation of a new life-form by altering the genetic code of an existing life-form. However, it is also used to apply to inventions relating to the discovery of part of a genetic sequence of a life-form which causes a particular effect, i.e. a rare medical disease. Apart from the Netherlands, no Member State had expressly banned the patenting of biotechnological inventions.

[1087] See para.2-291 for discussion of this.
[1088] See paras 2-302 to 2-305.
[1089] Commission Notice [2016] OJ C411/3.
[1090] See para.2-281.
[1091] art.1.

However, much uncertainty was caused by the fact that national patent laws of Member States (which conformed to the substantive law of the European Patent Convention) did not permit: (a) the patenting of animal or plant varieties or essentially biological processes for the product of plants and animals; (b) mere discoveries; and (c) inventions whose exploitation would be contrary to *ordre public*. One of the Directive's principal aims[1092] was to clarify the application of these EPC exceptions to biotechnological inventions.

2-583

The Directive expressly states that new inventions which involve an inventive step and are susceptible of industrial application shall be patentable even if they concern a product consisting of or containing biological material or a process by means of which biological material is produced, processed or used.[1093] "Biological material" is defined as meaning any material containing genetic information and being capable of reproducing itself or being reproduced in a biological system.[1094] The Directive makes it clear that biological material which is isolated from its natural environment or produced by means of a technical process may be the subject of an invention, even if it previously occurred in nature.[1095] This last provision is intended to clarify the distinction between a mere discovery of biological material (which is not patentable) and its industrial application. Thus the Recitals state that a mere DNA sequence without indication of a function does not contain any technical information and is therefore not a patentable invention.[1096] However, where the invention (in order to comply with the criterion that it must be capable of industrial application) states what the industrial application is, such may be patentable. In particular, where the sequence is used to produce a protein or part of a protein, it is necessary to specify what that protein or part of a protein is or what function it performs.[1097] The EPC has amended its Implementing Regulations to take into account these parts of the Directive. The EPC considers that the changes merely codify the Boards of Appeals' approach to the issues of patentability of biotechnological inventions.[1098]

2-584

The Directive makes specific reference to biotechnological inventions relating to genetic material derived from the human body. It states that the human body at the various stages of its formation and development, and the simple discovery of one of its elements, including the sequence or partial sequence of a gene, cannot constitute patentable inventions.[1099] It continues that an element isolated from the human body or otherwise produced by means of a technical process, including the sequence or partial sequence of a gene, *may* constitute a patentable invention, even if the structure of that element is identical to that of a natural element.[1100] The Recitals explain that isolated elements are only capable of being put into practice by human beings and nature is incapable of accomplishing this by itself.[1101] It is not clear whether these provisions relating to human beings are intended to add anything to (as opposed to clarifying) the general principle that one cannot patent the mere

2-585

[1092] See para.2-580.
[1093] art.3(1).
[1094] art.2(1)(a).
[1095] art.3(2).
[1096] Recital 23.
[1097] Recitals 22, 24.
[1098] For the discussion on the interactivity of the ban on discovery and biotechnological inventions in the context of the EPC, see para.2-287.
[1099] art.5(1).
[1100] art.5(2).
[1101] Recital 21.

discovery of a genetic sequence, only its industrial application. In other words, it is not clear whether any special treatment should be given to patents for a human DNA fragment rather than animal DNA. It is likely that these provisions were put into the Directive in order to make it expressly clear to all parties that the Directive would not permit the patenting of human DNA fragments per se.[1102] The more relevant provisions regarding the patentability of genetic material relating to humans are those dealt with below under the *ordre public*/morality provisions.[1103]

Biotechnological inventions, plant and animal varieties and essentially biological processes

2-586   The Directive confirms that plant and animal varieties and essentially biological processes for the production of plants and animals are not patentable.[1104] This mirrors art.53 of the EPC, which also so provides. The reason for this exclusion has already been discussed in this chapter.[1105] The Directive, however, seeks to clarify the interrelationship between such an exclusion and biotechnological inventions. Therefore, art.4(2) of the Directive states that inventions which concern plants or animals are patentable if the "technical feasibility of the invention is not confined to a particular plant or animal variety".[1106] This phrase is somewhat clarified in the Recitals, which state that the concept of "plant variety" is defined by the legislation protecting new varieties as being a variety which is defined by its whole genome and therefore possesses individuality and is clearly distinguishable from other varieties, whereas a plant grouping which is characterised by a particular gene and not its whole genome is not covered by the protection of new varieties and is therefore not excluded from patentability, even if it comprises new varieties of plants.[1107] The distinction between a plant variety and an invention which seeks to affect the genetic code of plants has been fully explored in a number of decisions of the Enlarged Board of Appeal ("EBA").[1108] Much of the judicial comment made in these cases closely mirrors the distinction made in the Directive between an invention which is for a plant variety per se and an invention which is for a plant grouping characterised by a particular gene. However, care should be taken in using the reasoning of the EBA in interpreting the Directive in relation to *animal varieties*, as the reasoning of the EBA was, in part, determined by the fact that the intention in excluding plant varieties from being patentable was because they were protected under the 1961 UPOV Convention and that convention did not permit the simultaneous protection of both plant variety rights and patent protection for a plant variety. Such reasoning, of course, does not apply to animal varieties, as there is no corresponding convention which provides sui generis protection for animal varieties. The wording of art.4(2) has been incorporated into the Implementing Regulations of the EPC.[1109]

[1102] It would seem from the Recitals that such was an expressed concern of the Group of Advisers on the Ethical Implications of Biotechnology to the European Commission (see Recital 19).
[1103] See para.2-588.
[1104] art.4(1).
[1105] See para.2-291, et seq.
[1106] art.4(2).
[1107] Recitals 30, 31.
[1108] *NOVARTIS II/Transgenic plant* (G-1/98). This case is discussed in detail at para.2-292.
[1109] EPC r.27(b).

Essentially biological processes

Article 4.1 bans alongside the ban on patenting of plant and animal varieties, essentially biological processes for the production of plants and animals. The meaning of "essentially biological" has been discussed within the context of art.53(b) EPC earlier in this chapter.[1110] However, in the Directive, it is expressly defined as "A process for the production of plants or animals" which consists "entirely of natural phenomena such as crossing or selection".[1111] In 2016, the Commission issued a Notice saying that on a proper interpretation of the Directive and its *travaux préparatoires*, it intended to exclude patent protection for plants and animals obtained by means of an essentially biological process as well as method patents for such processes.[1112] Resulting from this, the Administrative Council of the EPO changed the Implementing Regulations to align EPC law with this notice.[1113]

2-587

Biotechnological inventions, ordre public and morality

Article 6 of the Directive states that inventions shall be considered unpatentable where their commercial exploitation would be contrary to ordre public or morality. However, art.6 continues by saying that the mere fact that exploitation is contrary to law or a regulation is not sufficient reason for excluding an invention from being patentable. Article 6 clarifies that the following inventions shall be considered unpatentable:

2-588

(a) processes for cloning human beings;
(b) processes for modifying the germ line genetic identity of human beings;
(c) uses of human embryos for industrial or commercial purposes; and
(d) processes for modifying the genetic identity of animals which are likely to cause them suffering without any substantial medical benefit to man or animal, and also animals resulting from such processes.

These provisions are clearly important in an era where much progress is being made into discovering genetic sequences responsible for a number of genetic-related diseases such as cystic fibrosis and Hodgkinson's disease and the current debate on the use of human foetal material for the purpose of repairing worn-out organs of people. The above provisions have been legislated into the EPC rules in order to ensure harmony between the EPC and EU law. The CJEU has adjudicated on the meaning of "use of human embryos for industrial or commercial purposes" in both *Brüstle v Greenpeace*[1114] and *International Stem Cell Corporation v Comptroller-General of Patents*.[1115] This is discussed in the corresponding section on the EPC.[1116]

2-589

Ordre public, art.6 of the Biotech Directive and art.27(2) of TRIPS

Article 6 is largely in accordance with art.27(2) of the TRIPS Agreement which states that:

2-590

[1110] See para.2-298.
[1111] art.2.2.
[1112] This is discussed above at para.2-580.
[1113] See para.2-308.
[1114] *Oliver Brüstle v Greenpeace* (C-34/10) [2012] 1 C.M.L.R 41.
[1115] (C–364/13) EU:C:2014:2451.
[1116] See para.2-314.

"Members may exclude from patentability inventions, the prevention within their territory of the commercial exploitation of which is necessary to protect ordre public or morality, including to protect human, animal or plant life or health or to avoid serious prejudice to the environment, provided that such exclusion is not made merely because the exploitation is prohibited by their law."

2-591   A careful reading of art.27(2) of TRIPS reveals that two requirements must be proven before it is applicable. First, it must be shown that the commercial exploitation of the invention is contrary to *ordre public* and not merely the invention itself (or indeed the patent for the invention). Secondly, it must be shown that the prevention of commercial exploitation is necessary to protect *ordre public* before the exception can be invoked, whereas the Directive does not impose such a test. The word "necessary" has been interpreted by a WTO panel as meaning that a measure is justified only if no alternative measure could reasonably be expected to be employed.[1117] It is necessary to interpret the Directive in the light of the objectives and purpose of TRIPS.[1118]

Scope of protection of biotechnological patents

2-592   Where biological material possessing specific characteristics is patentable under the Directive, the protection conferred by that patent extends to any biological material derived from such biological material through propagation or multiplication in an identical or divergent form and possessing those same characteristics.[1119] In the case of a process patent, such protection extends to biological material directly obtained from that process ("first generation biological material") and any subsequent generation biological material derived from such material which possesses the same characteristics as the first generation biological material.[1120]

2-593   In the case of a patent for a product which contains or consists of genetic information, art.9 provides that protection extends to all material in which the product is incorporated and "in which the genetic information is contained and performs its function". This provision was considered by the CJEU in *Monsanto Technology v Cefetra*.[1121] The claimant, Monsanto, owned a patent for a class of herbicide-resistant enzymes. The genes encoding these enzymes were isolated from three different bacteria and then inserted into the DNA of a soy plant called Roundup Ready. This meant that the soy plant was resistant to the herbicide "Roundup". Roundup Ready soy beans were cultivated on a large scale in Argentina where there was no patent protection. The defendants imported three cargoes of soy bean meal into Europe. The tests showed that they produced the herbicide-resistant enzyme. The Dutch courts referred the question to the CJEU of whether the soy bean meal was covered by art.9. The CJEU held that it did not apply to soy bean meal as the enzymes in the soy bean meal could not perform the function for which they had been patented. In essence, the soy bean meal was dead material which could not be used to create more soy plants which were herbicide-resistant. Thus, art.9 does not protect any foodstuff derived from genetically-modified plants

---

[1117] "Thailand-Restrictions on Importation of an Internal Tax on Cigarettes", WTO Panel Report BISD 37S/200. The Panel's finding related inter alia to the word "necessary" in GATT art.XX(b). This Article uses the same expression as TRIPS art.27(2).

[1118] See para.1-179.

[1119] art.8.

[1120] art.8(2).

[1121] (C-428/08) [2010] E.C.R. I-6765.

but rather only those products which can be used to create the benefit that the genetical modification bestows. However, if art.9 would result in providing protection for the human body at its various stages of formation and developments, such is excluded from protection.[1122]

Exceptions

There are two basic exceptions to the above principle. The minor exception is that where the patentee places on the market in the EU biological material or consents to such placing on the market, the patentee cannot claim protection in biological material which:　　　　　　　　　　　　　　　　　　　　　　　　　　**2-594**

> "necessarily results from the application for which the biological material was marketed, provided that the material obtained is not used for other propagation or multiplication."[1123]

Thus, where genetically modified pest-resistant wheat seed is sold by the patentee or with their consent, the harvest from such seed is clearly second generation seed and, as such, is biological material derived from the pest-resistant seed and therefore would be protected by the patent. The sale of such harvested wheat grains to a miller would not constitute an infringement of the patent. However, the sale of such harvested seed to another farmer as seed would constitute infringement, as such would be for the purposes of subsequent propagation.　　　　　　　　　　　**2-595**

The major exception is the "farmer's exception" recognised under plant variety laws. The sale of plant propagating material subject to a patent to a farmer implies authorisation for the farmer to use the product of their harvest for propagation or multiplication by them on their own farm, the extent and conditions of this derogation corresponding to those under art.14 of Reg.2100/94.[1124] Similarly, where a patentee sells "breeding livestock" protected by a patent, the farmer is free to "use the protected livestock for an agricultural purpose".[1125]　　　　　　　**2-596**

Accordingly, a farmer can breed in perpetuity the protected "breeding livestock" and sell the livestock for, e.g. meat, but cannot sell the livestock to another farmer so that they can breed in perpetuity the livestock. The exact interpretation of this provision is determined by national laws, regulations and practices.[1126]　　　**2-597**

Compulsory cross licensing

It is clear from the Directive that biological material could be subject to both plant variety rights and patent protection. Thus, a popular potato variety may have　　　　　　　　　　　　　　　　　　　　　　　　　　　　　　**2-598**

[1122] art.9 excludes from protection products falling within the "human body" exceptions in art.5(1). See para.2-585. See also para.2-588 (*ordre public*).

[1123] art.10.

[1124] art.11(1). Regulation 2100/94 is the Council Regulation on Community Plant Variety Rights and is discussed in Ch.6. The farmer's right is discussed at para.6-103.

[1125] art.11(2).

[1126] art.11(3). The reason given for this rather loosely worded provision is that there is no Community legislation on animal variety rights—Recital 51. However, if there are considerable differences between the national practices laws and practices of Member States, such could give rise to arbitrary discrimination or disguised restrictions in trade between Member States and would thus be subject to review by the Court of Justice. It is therefore likely that this provision will not give carte blanche to Member States to widely interpret the phrase "agricultural purposes".

been genetically modified by the insertion of a gene to confer insect resistance.[1127] In such cases, there may exist plant variety rights and patent rights which are held by different people. The owner of one right would normally require the consent of the other right's owner to commercialise the product. Article 12 provides for a system of compulsory cross licences where the licence is "necessary" for the exploitation of the patent or plant variety. The licence will be granted on "reasonable terms".

2-599   Applicants for a compulsory licence must show that they have unsuccessfully applied to the holder of the other right and that the plant variety or invention constitutes significant technical progress of considerable economic interest compared with the corresponding invention claimed in the patent or the protected plant variety.[1128] As commented on, the word "unsuccessfully" is not defined. Does it mean, for example, that the applicant has been refused a licence at any price or that the two parties could not agree on the contractual terms?[1129] It is likely that it means that the holder of the patent or right would not agree to a licence on reasonable terms otherwise the provision would be devoid of any real effect. It is supposed that the requirement of "significant technical progress of considerable economic interest" is intended to prevent a licence of a valuable patent or plant variety right being compulsorily granted to the owner of a variety right or patent which is of little worth.[1130] This would be to penalise the owner of the former right. Therefore, the owner of a patent for a genetic modification that can slightly lighten the colour of a potato may not be able to justify the grant of a compulsory licence for a popular potato variety in which it is intended to genetically modify. Such would clearly give the patent owner a windfall by permitting the patent owner to make and sell a popular plant variety to modify it with a commercially minor important genetic modification. The contrary view would say that such asymmetries can be dealt with by differing cross-royalties. As commented on, it would appear to be the public's interest which is important here and not the individual person's.[1131]

Deposit of biological material

2-600   As is normal with biological material, the requirement in patent law that the patent must disclose to a skilled person the ability to reproduce the invention is deemed to be satisfied only if the biological material, the subject of the patent, is deposited at a recognised depositary institution.[1132] The Directive makes detailed provision as to the ability to access such deposits.[1133]

[1127] This is an example given by J. Ardley in "Compulsory Cross-Licensing: An Examination of Article 12 of the Biotechnology Directive" [1998/1999] *BioScience Law Review* 135.

[1128] art.11(3).

[1129] See J. Ardley, "Compulsory Cross-Licensing" [1998/1999] *BioScience Law Review* 135 at 136.

[1130] The requirements are similar to those set out in art.31 TRIPS for the owner of an improvement patent to obtain a licence for a basic patent. See para.2-026 (and the Directive must be interpreted in the light of TRIPS).

[1131] See J. Ardley, "Compulsory Cross-Licensing" [1998/1999] *BioScience Law Review* 135 at 137.

[1132] art.13.

[1133] art.13(2)–(4).

Proposals for a Directive approximating the laws of the Member States in relation to utility models

In 1999, the European Commission proposed a Directive approximating the legal arrangements for the protection of inventions by utility model.[1134] A utility model is generally regarded as a lesser form of patent where the duration of protection is shorter than a normal patent, there is no ex parte examination, and the requirement of inventiveness is considerably diluted. At present, utility model protection exists in a number of Member States but with differing requirements and conditions.[1135] The Commission considers that the utility model form of protection is more flexible and less burdensome than the patent and is more suitable for inventions which have a limited degree of inventiveness and a relatively short life span. They are particularly suited to SMEs (Small and Medium Enterprises) which are active in certain fields of innovation. The amended draft Directive proposes the harmonisation of utility model laws and that utility model protection shall be available for new inventions involving products or processes that involve an inventive step and are susceptible of industrial application. The following sets out the key proposals where such differs from the law pertaining to patents:

2-601

(a) the exceptions to utility model protection are substantially the same as for patents under the EPC save that there is a general ban on protection for inventions "relating to biological material" and "relating to chemical or pharmaceutical substances or processes";

(b) an invention shall be considered to have an inventive step if:

> "it exhibits an advantage and having regard to the state of the art, is not very obvious to a person skilled in the art"

The advantage must be:

> "practical or technical advantage for the use or manufacture of the product or process in question, or another benefit to the user, for example in the field of education or entertainment;"

(c) the examining authority need only examine that the formal requirements are met. The authority shall not examine for novelty, inventive step and industrial application;

(d) the duration of the utility model shall be six years from the date of filing of the application. This may be renewed on application for further two-year periods up to a maximum of 10 years from the date of filing of the application;

(e) a utility model rights-owner is deemed to have exhausted their rights in a product placed on the market in the EU by themselves or with their consent but such a principle is expressly held not to apply if that product was put on the market outside the EU by themselves or with their consent; and

(f) one can apply for both a utility model and patent but utility model protec-

---

[1134] COM (99) 309, adopted by the Commission on 30 June 1999.

[1135] Thus protection for utility models exists in the following countries under the following names: France, *Certificat d'Utilite*; Denmark, *Brugsmodel*; Belgium, *Brevet de Courte Duree/Octrooi van korte duur*; Germany, *Gebrauchsmuster*; Spain, *Modelo de Utilidad*; Ireland, *Short Term Patent*; Italy, *Brevetto per Modelli di Utilita*; Netherlands, *Zesjarig octrooi*; Austria, *Gebrauchsmuster*; Portugal, *Modelo de Utilidada* and, finally, Finland, *Nyttighetsmodellagen*.

tion is deemed to be ineffective where a patent relating to the same invention has been granted and published.

2-602   However, no progress has been made on this proposal and for the time being, must be considered a dead proposal.

Supplementary protection for patented pharmaceutical and plant protection products

Introduction

2-603   Most countries provide for a regulatory framework for the testing of pharmaceuticals prior to them being placed on the market. The European Commission has introduced two Directives in this field, one for medicinal products for human use[1136] and one for veterinary products.[1137] Often, there will be substantial delays prior to the product coming on the market.[1138] Clearly, where a pharmaceutical is the subject of a patent, this reduces the effective term of protection and often would make its exploitation uneconomic. A survey in 1988 of more than 300 pharmaceutical products showed that the effective patent life of pharmaceutical products in Europe was eight years.[1139] In the 1980s, several countries, including the US, Japan, Italy and France, introduced legislation which provided for the restoration of the patent term for pharmaceuticals. Such legislative measures were seen to have put many European pharmaceutical companies at a competitive disadvantage.

2-604   Thus, the Commission proposed that a regulation conferring supplementary protection for pharmaceuticals should be enacted. Eventually, Reg.1768/92 which created a supplementary protection certificate for medicinal products was passed and which came into force on 2 July 1993 in all Member States.[1140] This was subsequently replaced by Reg.469/2009 which codified Reg.1768/92 but made no substantive changes.

2-605   As well as a supplemental protection regime for pharmaceuticals for humans and animals, EU law also provides for a supplementary protection certificate for plant protection products.[1141] Plant protection products (e.g. herbicides, insecticides and pesticides) are also subject to an approval scheme under Reg.1107/2009.[1142] This too can delay the introduction of patented inventions in this field and thus it was considered appropriate to introduce SPCs for such products.

2-606   Both regulations in substance extend the lifetime of the protection afforded by

---

[1136] Dir.2001/83 [2001] OJ L311/67. This replaces earlier Directives.

[1137] Dir.2001/82 [2001] OJ L311/1. This replaces earlier Directives.

[1138] A "new" pharmaceutical (i.e. one which is not bioequivalent to an existing marketed product) will typically take some 12 years to reach the market—see R. Whaite and N. Jones, "Pharmaceutical Patent Term Restoration: the European Commission's Proposed Regulation" [1992] E.I.P.R. 324–326.

[1139] See R. Lelkes, A. von Uexküll and P. Tauchner, "Patent Term Restoration in Europe: Taking Advantage of the Supplementary Protection Certificate" *Patent World*, December 1992–January 1993, 14–23.

[1140] Council Reg.1768/92, [1992] OJ L182/1. For detailed commentary on this SPC Regulation, see R. Lelkes, A. von Uexküll and P. Tauchner, "Patent Term Restoration in Europe: Taking Advantage of the Supplementary Protection Certificate" *Patent World*, December 1992–January 1993, 14–23; R. Whaite and N. Jones, "Pharmaceutical Patent Term Restoration: the European Commission's Proposed Regulation" [1992] E.I.P.R. 324–326; T. Cook, "The Supplementary Protection Certificate—How is it Working in Practice" *Patent World*, February 1994, 29.

[1141] Reg.1610/96 [1996] OJ L198/30.

[1142] [2009] OJ L309/1 replacing Dirs 91/414 and 79/117.

the underlying patent to a maximum of 15 years of exclusivity from the date that the medicinal product in question first obtains authorisation to be placed on the market in the EU.[1143] There are a number of conditions which must be satisfied for such to occur which are discussed below. The proper interpretation of these conditions has been problematic and has resulted in a number of preliminary references from national courts and the issuing of a large number of judgments and Reasoned Orders.

Neither regulation extends the life of a basic patent as such. Instead, they provide for the grant of a sui generis supplementary protection certificate which is intended to have the same effect as an extension of the period of protection of the underlying patent.[1144] It is only available for patents relating to the active ingredients of medicinal or veterinary products used in human or animal healthcare or plant protection products.
2-607

A challenge by Spain to the vires of the SPC Regulation was dismissed by the CJEU.[1145]
2-608

Policy behind SPCs

In interpreting the various provisions of the SPC Regulations, the CJEU has emphasised two key objectives of these regulations. Thus, in *Eli Lilly v Human Genome Sciences*[1146] the CJEU said that:
2-609

> "[41] Moreover, it should be recalled that the SPC is designed simply to re-establish a sufficient period of effective protection of the basic patent by permitting the holder to enjoy an additional period of exclusivity on the expiry of that patent, which is intended to compensate, at least in part, for the delay to the commercial exploitation of his invention by reason of the time which has elapsed between the date on which the application for the patent was filed and the date on which the first MA in the European Union was granted (Case C-229/09 *Hogan Lovells International* [2010] E.C.R. I-11335, paragraph 50; Case C-443/12 *Actavis Group PTC and Actavis UK* [2013] E.C.R. I-0000, paragraph 31; and Case C-484/12 *Georgetown University* [2013] E.C.R. I-0000, paragraph 36)."

In other cases, the CJEU has emphasised the need to incentivise pharmaceutical companies to invest into pharmaceutical research. Thus, in *Medeva BV v Comptroller General of Patents, Designs and Trade Marks*[1147]:
2-610

> "[30] First, it must be noted that the fundamental objective of Regulation No 469/2009 is to ensure sufficient protection to encourage pharmaceutical research, which plays a decisive role in the continuing improvement in public health (see *Farmitalia*, paragraph 19, and *AHP Manufacturing*, paragraph 30).[1148]
>
> [31] The reason given for the adoption of that regulation is the fact that the period of effective protection under the patent is insufficient to cover the investment put into pharmaceutical research and the regulation thus seeks to make up for that insuf-

---

[1143] Recital 9, Reg.469/2009; Recital 11, Reg.1610/96.

[1144] See J.N. Adams, "Supplementary Protection Certificates: The Challenge to EC Regulation 1768/92" [1994] 8 E.I.P.R. 323 at 324.

[1145] *Kingdom of Spain v Council of the EU* (C-350/92) [1995] E.C.R. I-1985; [1996] C.M.L.R. 415; [1996] F.S.R. 73. The jurisdictional basis for the attack is discussed at length at para.1-102.

[1146] (C-493/12) [2013] ECLI:EU:C:2013:835.

[1147] (C-322/10) [2011] E.C.R. I-12051. See also Recital 4 to Reg.469/2009.

[1148] See also *Hogan Lovells* (C-229/09) [2010] E.C.R. I-11355 at [51]; *Bayer CropScience AG* (C-11/13) ECLI:EU:C:204:2010 at [39] where the same was said in relation to plant protection products.

ficiency by creating a SPC for medicinal products (see Case C-181/95 *Biogen* [1997] E.C.R. I-357, paragraphs 26, and *AHP Manufacturing*, paragraph 30)."

2-611 However, it would be a mistake to consider that the purpose of a SPC is to grant exactly the same period of protection as would have existed if the right holder had not needed to obtain marketing authorisation and thus could have exploited the patented invention from filing the application for a patent. As said in the recitals to Reg.469/2009, all interests at stake including those of public health need to be taken into account in a sector as complex and sensitive of the pharmaceutical sector. Thus, the period of protection granted by the SPC cannot exceed five years.[1149] This may be substantially less than the period of patent protection "lost" as a result of delays caused by the need to obtain marketing authorisation. Moreover, the period of protection is calculated from the date of first marketing authorisation in the EEA. It may be that for some Member States where the MA is granted several years after the first MA in the EEA, that there is little or no extension of protection.

2-612 Bringing these points together, it can be said that the purpose of SPCs is to confer an additional period of exclusivity for pharmaceutical manufacturers so as to incentivise them to carry out research by compensating them to some extent for the reduction in the period of exclusivity that they will have to exploit patented pharmaceutical inventions by reason of the need to obtain marketing authorisations for a pharmaceutical product.[1150] It will be appreciated from this that a SPC should not be granted for a pharmaceutical where there is no material delay in it being marketed by reason of the need to conduct clinical trials in order to obtain marketing authorisation.

2-613 However, because the SPC Regulation seeks to achieve a balanced solution taking due account of the various competing interests in the pharmaceutical sector (these being pharmaceutical research companies, generic manufacturers, patients and the state health sector), as said by one Advocate-General, some care must be taken in making a teleological interpretation of the individual provisions of the SPC Regulation.[1151]

2-614 The SPC Regulations are now considered in detail. As both SPC Regulations are very similar in structure, the SPC Regulation for medicinal products is considered.[1152] Where there are material differences, then both are discussed.

Conditions for grant of a SPC

2-615 For a SPC certificate to be granted, six substantive conditions must be satisfied:

(a) The basic patent is for an "active ingredient or combination of active ingredients of a medicinal product" or (in the case of the SPC regulation for plant protection products), substances or a combination of substances that

---

[1149] Recital 10.

[1150] Of course, it is not sufficient for pharmaceutical companies merely to recover the investment for the product for which a SPC is sought because many R&D projects will fail and not lead to commercially exploitable inventions. Thus, it is necessary to take into account "failed" projects as well.

[1151] *Neurim Pharmaceuticals v Comptroller-General of Patents* (C-130/11), EU:C:2012:268 Trstenjak AG at [41]–[42] cited in *Abraxis Bioscience LLC v The Comptroller-General of Patents* [2017] EWHC 14 (Pat) at [16].

[1152] Indeed, as said in *Massachusetts Institute of Technology* (C-431/04) [2006] E.C.R. I-4089, Recital 17 of the Plant Protection SPC Regulation can be used to interpret the SPC Regulation for medicinal products (which was then Reg.1768/92). See also *AHP Manufacturing BV v Bureau voor de Industriële Eigendom* (C-482/07) [2009] E.C.R. I-7295 at [23].

have a general or specific action against harmful organisms or plants, parts of plants or plant products.

(b) As of the date of application for the SPC, the product is protected by a basic patent in force.[1153]

(c) As of the date of application for the SPC, a valid authorisation to place the product on the market as a medicinal product has been granted in accordance with Dir.2001/83 or veterinary product in accordance with Dir.2001/82.[1154]

(d) As of the date of the application, the product has not already been the subject of a supplementary protection certificate.[1155]

(e) As of the date of the application, the authorisation relied upon is the first authorisation to place the product in the EEA as a medicinal product in accordance with Dir.2001/83 or veterinary product in accordance with Dir.2001/82.[1156]

(f) The application for a SPC is lodged within six months of the date of authorisation or six months from the date of grant of the patent (whichever is the latest).[1157]

The last condition is straightforward. The first five have proven not to be. These are now discussed.

Condition 1: Active ingredient in medicinal product

In the case of medicinal products for human or animals, it is necessary that the patent (the "basic" patent) protects "the active ingredients or a combination of active ingredients of a medicinal product".[1158] "Medicinal product" is defined as: **2-616**

> "any substance or combination of substances presented for treating or preventing disease in human beings or animals and any substance or combination of substances which may be administered to human beings or animals with a view to making a medical diagnosis or to restoring, correcting or modifying physiological functions in human beings or in animals."[1159]

In contrast, "active ingredient" is not defined in the SPC Regulation. Some guidance as what is meant by this comes from the Commission's Explanatory Memorandum for the predecessor regulation to Reg.469/2009 which said: **2-617**

> "11. The proposal for a Regulation therefore concerns only new medicinal products. It does not involve granting a certificate for all medicinal products that are authorized to be placed on the market. Only one certificate may be granted for any one product, a product being understood to mean an active substance in the strict sense. Minor changes to the medicinal product such as a new dose, the use of a different salt or ester or a different pharmaceutical form will not lead to the issue of a new certificate.

[1153] art.3(a).

[1154] art.3(b). See para.2-631 for explanation of these Directives.

[1155] art.3(c), art.1(d).

[1156] arts 3(d) and 13. Although art.13 mentions "the Community", by reason of Protocol 1 to the EEA Agreement, this extends to marketing in the EEA—see *Novartis v UK Patent Office; Millennium Pharmaceuticals Inc v Ministre de l'Économie* (C-207/03 & C-252/03) [2005] E.C.R. I-3209 at [26].

[1157] art.7.

[1158] art.3(a), art.1(b).

[1159] art.1(a) Reg.469/2009.

12. However, the proposal is not confined to new products only. A new process for obtaining the product or a new application of the product may also be protected by a certificate. All research, whatever the strategy or final result, must be given sufficient protection."

2-618   In *Massachusetts Institute of Technology*, the CJEU held that a substance which does not have any therapeutic effect of its own is not covered by the concept of "active ingredient".[1160] In that case, MIT had a patent which covered the alliance of two elements, an excipient (polifeprosan) and an ingredient (carmustine) which was used with inert excipients for the treatment of brain tumours. The excipient permitted the release of carmustine into the cranium in a slow and gradual manner. The excipient acted as a bioerodible matrix. The German patent office refused an application for SPC for carmustine+polifeprosan on the grounds that polifeprosan was not an active ingredient and accordingly, the SPC application was not for a combination of active ingredients. MIT had already obtained a marketing authorisation for carmustine on its own and thus time had expired for the grant of a SPC for carmustine on its own. Although the excipient, polifeprosan, rendered possible the administration of carmustine in a therapeutic efficacious way and influenced its therapeutic activity, the CJEU considered that as it did not have any therapeutic effect on its own, this meant that the application was not for a combination of active ingredients.[1161]

2-619   The decision of the Court of Justice in *Massachusetts Institute of Technology* was applied in *Arne Forsgren v Österreischisches Patentamt*.[1162] This case concerned an application for a SPC for a protein (Protein D) which was found in a pneumococcal vaccine for paediatric use called Synflorix. Protein D was the subject of a patent (the basic patent) but Synflorix and not Protein D had received marketing authorisation. Synflorix consisted of 10 serotypes conjugated to carrier proteins. In eight of the serotypes, Protein D was the carrier protein. The Austrian patent office refused the application on the grounds that Protein D was just an excipient. This was appealed and the Austrian appellate tribunal referred a number of questions to the Court of Justice including whether a SPC could be granted for a product where the active ingredient (Protein D) was covalently bonded to other active ingredients. The Court of Justice held that the fact that the active ingredient was covalently bonded was not in itself a reason to preclude the grant of a SPC. The real issue was whether Protein D had a pharmacological, immunological or metabolic action of its own regardless of whether or not it was covalently bonded to other active ingredients.

2-620   The above cases have led an English court to say that the interpretation of art.1(b) is *acte éclairé*.[1163] It held that a composition (nab-paclitaxel) consisting of paclitaxel

---

[1160] (C-431/04) ECLI:EU:2006:291 at [25].

[1161] See [27]–[31]. See also *Yissum* (C-202/05) ECLI:EU:C:2007:214 at [18] (Reasoned Order); *Glaxosmithkline Biologicals* (C-210/13) ECLI:EU:C:2013:762 (Reasoned Order) (where it was held that an adjuvant which had no therapeutic effect but enhanced the therapeutic effect of an antigen was not itself an active ingredient).

[1162] (C–631/13) EU:C:2015:13.

[1163] This means that the Court of Justice has already provided a clear explanation of the provision and thus does not require a further reference to it—see *Abraxis Bioscience LLC v The Comptroller-General of Patents* [2017] EWHC 14 (Pat). However, the court has referred to the Court of Justice on the meaning of art.3(d) and this referral is pending case *Abraxis Bioscience* (C-443/17). For art.3(d), see para.2-653.

formulated as albumin-coated nanoparticles was not an "active ingredient" but paclitaxel was. The albumin was merely a carrier.[1164]

In relation to the SPC regulation for plant protection products, the CJEU had to consider in *Bayer CropScience AG v Deutsche Patent-under Markenamt*[1165] whether a European patent for the use of a chemical compound as a "safener" was a product which was covered by the regulation. This depended on whether it was for an active substance or combination of substances that had a general or specific action against harmful organisms or plants, parts of plants or plant products.[1166] The CJEU held that a proper interpretation of "active substance" meant that it must have a "toxic, phytotoxic or plant protection action of [its] own". It held that when considering whether a safener had such properties, such were defined in Reg.1107/2009[1167] as substances or preparations which are added to a plant protection product to eliminate or reduce phytotoxic effects of the plant protection products. It then said that safeners increase the effectiveness of a plant protection product by limiting its toxic or ecotoxic effects. Although the CJEU said the matter was for the national court, their observations appear intended to suggest that safeners would amount to "products" within the SPC Regulation on plant protection products.[1168]

2-621

If a SPC is granted for a product that falls outside the definition of "product", then the SPC is invalid.[1169]

2-622

Condition 2: The product is protected by a basic patent in force as of the date of application

Article 3(a) of Reg.469/2009 states that a SPC cannot be applied for a product unless the product is "protected by a basic patent in force". The relevant date for this is the date of application for the SPC. Therefore, one cannot apply for a SPC if the basic patent has expired.[1170] This has led to considerable divergence on the proper interpretation and has resulted in several references to the Court of Justice. The reason for the large number of references has been because pharmaceutical companies like to file successive SPC applications based on pharmaceutical compounds which incorporate variants of the inventive active ingredient (or combination of active ingredient) referred to in the basic patent. Such has been justified on the grounds that the variants are all protected by the basic patent. The suspicion is that such companies are seeking to extend protection of the core active ingredient via a policy of filing successive SPCs applications. Thus, the real question is what is meant by "protected by the basic patent". The widest interpretation would mean that the product which is the subject of the SPC must infringe the claims of the patent ("the infringement test"). As will be seen, this approach has been rejected by the Court of Justice in favour of a test that requires a court to ask

2-623

[1164] See [55]–[59]. This was relevant as paclitaxel was already the subject of a marketing authorisation and thus the marketing authorisation for nab-paclitaxel which was relied upon for the SPC application was not the first marketing authorisation as required under art.3(d) (See *Abraxis*, at [2]–[4]).

[1165] (C-11/13) ECLI:EU:C:2014:2010

[1166] arts 1.8, 1.3.

[1167] The regulation which governs the marketing of plant protection products in the EU. See [2009] OJ L309/1 replacing Dirs 91/414 and 79/117.

[1168] See [32]–[37].

[1169] *Synthon BV v Merz Pharma GmBh v & Co* (C-195/09) [2011] E.C.R. I-07011 at [57].

[1170] This may happen where there is a very substantial delay in the grant of a marketing authorisation such that the patent has expired. This happened in *Merck Sharp & Dohme Corp v Comptroller-General of Patents, Designs and Trade Marks* (C-567/16) ECLI:EU:C:2017:948.

whether the claim relate "implicitly but necessarily and specifically to the active ingredient in question". This is a very Delphic test whose application is unclear.

2-624   It is useful to review the authorities. In an early case, *Farmitalia Carlo Erba*[1171] the CJEU held, in interpreting art.3(a) that in the absence of EU harmonisation, the extent of patent protection must be a matter of national law.[1172] This suggested that the "infringement" approach was correct. However, 10 years later, in *Medeva v Comptroller-General of Patents, Designs and Trade Marks*,[1173] the CJEU effectively rejected this approach. It said that Reg.469/2009 seeks to establish a uniform solution at EU level and thus aims to prevent the heterogeneous development of national laws leading to disparities. Without saying it explicitly, it is clear that implicitly it was rejecting the "infringement" approach in *Farmitalia*.[1174] It then said that art.3(a) prevents the grant of a SPC relating to active ingredients which are not "specified in the wording of the claims of the basic patent".[1175] However, the CJEU then made it clear that it was not sufficient merely for the active ingredient to be specified in the wording of the claim. Thus, it said that a SPC cannot be granted for a *single* active ingredient if the basic patent did not make any claim for an active ingredient individually but only in combination with another.[1176] The CJEU justified its reasoning on the basis that the explanatory memorandum to the first SPC regulation for medicinal products and the recitals to the SPC for plant protection products referred to the need for the products to be the subject of patent protection specifically covering them.[1177]

2-625   The reasoning in *Medeva* was followed in a number of Reasoned Orders. In *Yeda Research v Comptroller General of Patents, Designs and Trade Marks*,[1178] the patent was for a combination of two active ingredients (cetuximab and irinotecan) for the treatment of cancer. Yeda applied for a SPC for cetuximab alone. This was refused by the UK Patent Office on the grounds that cetuximab alone was not protected by the patent. Yeda argued that the patent permitted them to oppose any use by third parties from supplying cetuximab as such would amount to an indirect infringement (i.e. contributory infringement) of the patent as it would amount to the supply of an essential means. However, the CJEU considered that the matter was clear applying *Medeva*. It said that the infringement test could not apply because the provisions concerning infringement of patents were not the subject of harmonisation at EU level.[1179] It thus said that the SPC Regulation could not be interpreted in the light of unharmonised laws. It said that art.5 of the SPC Regulation was intended to confer the same rights as conferred by a basic patent and was subject to the same limitations and obligations. It thus held that art.3(a) precluded the grant of a SPC relating to active ingredients which are not specified in the word-

---

[1171] (C-392/97) [1999] E.C.R. I-5553; [2000] R.P.C. 580.

[1172] See [26]–[27].

[1173] (C-322/10) [2011] E.C.R. I-12051.

[1174] *Medeva* and the UK government both proposed that such was the test—see [20]. See also, M. Snodin, "Supplementary Protection Certificates: The CJEU issues its decision in two seminal cases" [2012] *BioScience Law Review* 12(2) at 58. See also *Eli Lilly v HGS* [2014] EWHC 2404 at [62].

[1175] See [25]. In support of this interpretation, it relied upon the Explanatory Memorandum to the proposal for a SPC Regulation where it said that what is "protected by a basic patent" refers "expressly and solely to the wording of the claims of the basic patent".

[1176] See [26].

[1177] See [27]. Here clearly, the active ingredient is specified in the claim but because such is in combination with another active ingredient, a single active ingredient would not infringe.

[1178] (C-518/10) [2011] E.C.R. I-12209.

[1179] See [34].

ings of the claims of the basic patent.[1180] It also said that if a patent claims that a product is composed of two active ingredients but does not make any claim in relation to one of those active ingredients individually, a SPC cannot be granted for one active ingredient considered in isolation.[1181]

In *University of Queensland v Comptroller General of Patents, Designs and Trade Marks*,[1182] the CJEU was concerned with the opposite of *Yeda*. In this case, a SPC was applied for which included active ingredients not identified in the wording of the claims of the basic patent. The CJEU also issued a Reasoned Order saying that art.3(a) precluded the grant of a SPC relating to active ingredients not identified in the wording of the claims of the basic patent relied on in support of the SPC application.[1183] In the same case, the CJEU considered whether a SPC could be obtained for a product obtained by the process protected in the basic patent. In general, patent law will prevent the marketing of products obtained directly from a patented process.[1184] The CJEU said that a patent protecting the process by why a product is obtained may enable a SPC to be granted for that process. However, this appears to forget that SPCs cannot be granted for processes.[1185] However, the CJEU said that art.3(a) prevented the grant of a SPC for a product not identified in the wording of the claim, even if the product is derived directly or indirectly from the process.[1186] This Reasoned Order is thus a much more emphatic rejection of the infringement test because unlike *Yeda*, it is difficult to say that a product for two active ingredients or derived directly from a process product does not infringe a patent for one of those ingredients or a process which leads directly to the product. The reasoning that a SPC cannot be applied for a combination of active ingredients where one or more of those ingredients are not identified in the wording of the claims of the basic patent was applied by way of reasoned order in *Daiichi Sankyo v Comptroller General of Patents, Designs & Patents*.[1187]

2-626

However, in 2013, the CJEU reviewed the approach to art.3(a) yet again in *Eli Lilly v HGS*.[1188] In that case, HGS was the holder of a European patent which related to the discovery of a new protein, neutrokine alpha, of which too much or too little was responsible for diseases of the immune system. One of the claims of the patent was for an antibody that bound to neutrokine-alpha, thereby neutralising it. Of significance was that the claim was defined in functional terms (i.e. any antibody that bound to neutrokine-alpha) rather than setting out the structural formal of the antibodies which did bind to neutrokine-alpha. HGS then applied for a SPC for a *specific* antibody which bound to neutrokine-alpha. Eli Lilly challenged the grant of such a SPC on the ground, relying upon Medeva, that the claims of the patent did not disclose the specific antibody in question and that for it to qualify for SPC protection, the patent would have to contain a structural definition of the antibody and the claims would have to be much more specific. However, the CJEU rejected this approach. It said it was not necessary for the active ingredient to be expressly identified in the claims by a structural formula. It said that the mere fact that the active ingredient is covered by a functional formula did not preclude an applica-

2-627

[1180] See [37]–[39].
[1181] See [38] applying *Medeva*, at [26].
[1182] (C-630/10) [2011] E.C.R. I-12231.
[1183] See [31].
[1184] e.g. see art.28(1)(b) TRIPS.
[1185] See art.3(a)–(d).
[1186] See [41].
[1187] (C-6/11) [2011] E.C.R. I-12255.
[1188] *Eli Lilly and Co Ltd v Human Genome Sciences Inc* (C-493/12) ECLI:EU:C:2013:835.

tion for a SPC. It was for the national court to determine whether "*the claims relate, implicitly but necessarily and specifically, to the active ingredient in question*".[1189] A key to the proper understanding of this somewhat Delphic phrase is contained in the CJEU's decision. It said as follows:

> "[43] In the light of the objective of Regulation No 469/2009, the refusal of an SPC application for an active ingredient which is not specifically referred to by a patent issued by the EPO relied on in support of such an application may be justified— *in circumstances such as those in the main proceedings and as observed by Eli Lilly—where the holder of the patent in question has failed to take any steps to carry out more in-depth research and identify his invention specifically*, making it possible to ascertain clearly the active ingredient which may be commercially exploited in a medicinal product corresponding to the needs of certain patients. In such a situation, if an SPC were granted to the patent holder, even though—since he was not the holder of the MA granted for the medicinal product developed from the specifications of the source patent—that patent holder had not made any investment in research relating to that aspect of his original invention, that would undermine the objective of Regulation No 469/2009, as referred to in recital 4 in the preamble thereto." [Emphasis supplied.]

2-628   On the return of *Eli Lilly* to the UK, the Patents Court held that the requirements of art.3(a) were satisfied.[1190] The Patents Court clearly found it difficult to interpret the CJEU's judgment but ultimately concluded that the CJEU was saying that a product that fell within a functional claim was sufficient to satisfy the requirement that "the claims relate, implicitly but necessarily, and specifically, to the active ingredient in question". It said that the CJEU was not saying that an "individualised description" of the SPC product was required. It said that the focus must be on the claims. In fact, a clue to the decision is that the patent had been held to be sufficient across the whole claim in issue and that there was an enabling disclosure of all the antibodies claimed.[1191] Furthermore, HGS, the patent holder, had carried out in-depth research to identify a commercial product resulting in a market authorisation order and that the research which led to the patent was important in achieving that MA.[1192] In other words, the CJEU appeared to be proceeding on a false factual basis.[1193] Thus, it would appear that HGS's application for a SPC did satisfy the policy rationale identified in [43] of the CJEU decision.

2-629   It is unlikely that *Eli Lilly v HGS* is the last word on this difficult issue.[1194] This is because the test in *Eli Lilly* is opaque and the policy behind art.3(a) is not well articulated by the Court of Justice as opposed to the policy behind SPCs in general. Indeed, as discussed above, it is not clear that one can talk about a policy behind the individual articles of art.3 of the SPC Regulation. Rather, all of the articles are

---

[1189] Order of CJEU.

[1190] *Eli Lilly v HGS* [2014] EWHC 2404.

[1191] See [31].

[1192] See [51]. It should be noted that the matter was complicated by the fact that the MA was not obtained by the patent holder. This was what was called the Third Party Issue (see in particular, the earlier decision *Eli Lilly v HGS* [2012] EWHC 2290).

[1193] See [50] where the High Court makes this point.

[1194] The Patents Court of England and Wales has referred to the Court of Justice in *Teva v Gilead Sciences Inc* [2017] EWHC 13 a question concerning the proper interpretation of *Eli Lilly* where the SPC was for a combination of AB+C but the basic patent did not mention expressly C although a dependent claim referred to A+B + a pharmaceutically acceptable carrier (which described C). This is pending case *Teva UK* (C-121/17).

intended *as a whole* to implement a policy of compensation for holders of pharmaceutical patents whose exploitation has been delayed by the need to obtain marketing authorisation. Perhaps, it would be better for the Court of Justice to make that clear and say that the SPC Regulation must as a whole be interpreted so that SPCs are not granted in a manner inconsistent with the above policy. This would avoid consideration of art.3(a)–(d) in isolation of each other but in aggregate. Thus, in *Eli Lilly*, there was no suggestion that Eli Lilly were seeking to obtain successive SPC protection for the same core inventive concept disclosed in the basic patent.

Finally, under art.3(a), in *Biogen Inc v SmithKline Beecham Biological SA*,[1195] it **2-630** was held that where a product is protected by a number of basic patents in force which belong to a number of patent holders, each of those patents could be designated for the purpose of the procedure for the grant of a SPC. This does not mean that more than one SPC can be obtained for a product as art.3(c) and (d) means that only one SPC can be granted for each product. This is discussed below.

Condition 3: A valid authorisation to place the product on the market as a medicinal product has been granted as of the date of application for the SPC

SPCs are only granted where there has been a delay in marketing a human or **2-631** animal pharmaceutical because of the need to get marketing authorisation. Directive 2001/83[1196] is the Directive concerning the grant of market authorisation for human medicines and Dir.2001/82[1197] is the equivalent for animal medicines. To obtain a SPC, there must be a earlier granted marketing authorisation ("MA") under either of these two Directives as of the date of application for the SPC.

As a preliminary matter, in *Yamanouchi Pharmaceuticals*,[1198] the CJEU made it **2-632** clear that the right to apply for a SPC depended on an authorisation to market the product being granted in the country in which the SPC is sought. In *Yamanouchi*, the French authorities had granted an authorisation to market the pharmaceutical for France but the UK authorities had refused it for the UK. The patentee applied for a SPC in the UK arguing that it was so entitled because an authorisation order had been granted for France. The CJEU said that art.3(b) must be interpreted as meaning that a patentee cannot apply for a SPC for a substance in a Member State unless authorisation has been given to market that substance *in that Member State*.

Article 3(b) requires that the product which is the subject of a SPC application **2-633** has been the subject of a marketing authorisation order under EU law. The wording suggests that one cannot apply for a SPC for a product unless *that* product has been granted a MA. However, in a number of cases, the CJEU have taken a teleological (purposive) approach to this requirement such that it is not necessary that there is identity between the product approved by the MA and the product for which a SPC is sought. Rather, the focus has been on whether the product which is the subject of a SPC application is protected by the basic patent. This is perhaps unfortunate because clearly art.3(b) is intended to be a distinct ground from art.3(a).

[1195] (C-181/95) [1997] E.C.R. 357; [1997] R.P.C. 833. See also *University of Queensland*, at [35]; *Medeva*, at [41] and *Georgetown University*, at [34].

[1196] Dir.2001/83/EC on the Community code relating to medicinal products for human use [2001] OJ L311/67. This has been amended by Dir.2010/84/EU.

[1197] Dir.2001/82/EC on the Community code relating to veterinary medicinal products [2001] OJ L311/1.

[1198] (C-110/95) [1997] E.C.R. I-3251.

2-634   The interpretation of art.3(b) was first considered in *Farmitalia Carlo Erba*.[1199] Farmitalia owned a German patent for a particular active ingredient in a pharmaceutical called idarubicin. In Germany, it obtained market authorisation for a pharmaceutical for the treatment of acute myelitic leukaemias in humans in which the active ingredient was idarubicin hydrochloride, a salt of idarubicin. Later, it sought a SPC for idarubicin both as a hydrochloride salt and more generally for idarubicin simpliciter. It obtained a SPC for the salt but the German Patent Office declined to issue a certificate for idarubicin simpliciter. This was because it considered that by applying art.3(b), no authorisation had been given for idarubicin simpliciter but only for a specific salt of it, namely the hydrochloride salt. On appeal, the Bundesgerichtshof referred to the CJEU the question of whether such an approach was correct. The CJEU said that to interpret the SPC Regulation as covering only the specific embodiment in the MA would frustrate the purpose of the SPC Regulation as it would permit a competitor to apply for and obtain a MA for a different salt of the same active ingredient. Moreover, the CJEU said the aim of a SPC was to confer the same rights as those conferred by the basic patent and thus if the basic patent covered the active ingredient and its salts and esters, then so should the SPC. Accordingly, it held that the SPC certificate is capable of covering the active ingredient simpliciter and is not confined to the product actually authorised by the MA.[1200]

2-635   A similar approach was taken in *Georgetown University et al v Comptroller General of Patents, Designs and Trade Marks*.[1201] In that case, Georgetown University was the owner of a patent for a vaccine for the prevention of the papillomavirus infection which comprised a number of different proteins which could induce neutralising antibodies against papillomavirus virions. A MA was granted comprising a product which contained a combination of several of these proteins. Georgetown University then filed SPC applications claiming each of the proteins individually. These applications were rejected on the grounds that they did not comply with art.3(b) as the MA contained more active ingredients than those for which SPC protection was sought. Thus, again, there was a lack of identity between the product for which medical authorisation was obtained and the products for which SPC applications were filed. The difference between *Georgetown* and *Farmitalia* was that in the latter, there was only one active ingredient in the MA. Notwithstanding that difference, the CJEU held that where the active ingredient was specified in the wording of the claims of the basic patent, the fact that the MA was for the active ingredient in combination with other active ingredients did not prevent a SPC application for the specific active ingredient. In other words, the fact that the patent expressly mentioned the active ingredient was sufficient to permit an application to be made for that ingredient *solus* even though the MA was for a combination of the active ingredient with other products.

2-636   In *Medeva v Comptroller General of Patents, Designs and Trade Marks*,[1202] Medeva had a patent for a vaccine that consisted of a combination of two antigens as active ingredients. Medeva then submitted MAs for medicinal products that consisted of the two antigens used in combination with other active ingredients.[1203] The Patent Office of the UK refused one application for a SPC on the basis that

---

[1199] (C-392/97) [1999] E.C.R. I-5553; [2000] R.P.C. 580.
[1200] See [18]–[22].
[1201] (C-422/10) [2011] E.C.R. I-12157.
[1202] (C-322/10) [2011] E.C.R. I-12051.
[1203] See [13]–[14].

there was not identity between the combination of active ingredients for which the SPC were sought and the MA. In short, the MA was for a medicinal product containing nine active ingredients which included the two antigens, whereas the SPC was for the two antigens on their own. Again, the CJEU adopted a teleological approach to whether the SPCs could be granted and held that identity of the active ingredients in the MA and SPC was not required. It said that such would undermine the fundamental objective of the SPC Regulation which was to ensure sufficient protection to encourage pharmaceutical research and play a decisive role in the continuing improvement in public health.[1204] It thus held that a distinction need to be drawn between the medicinal product for which a MA was granted and the product for which a SPC was sought.[1205] It thus held that a SPC could be granted for a combination of two active ingredients even where the MA was for a combination of the two active ingredients used in combination with other active ingredients.[1206]

However, in *Arne Forsgren v Österreischisches Patentamt*,[1207] the Court of **2-637** Justice returned to the policy behind SPC Regulations when considering the effect of art.3(b). This concerned the validity under art.3(b) of a SPC for the alleged active ingredient, Protein D, which was a carrier protein found in a pneumococcal vaccine or paediatric use called Synflorix. Synflorix had a marketing authorisation but the marketing authorisation did not relate to the use of Protein D. The Court of Justice said as follows:

"[38] ... since no trial or data concerning the therapeutic effects of Protein D against Haemophilus influenzae was integrated into the marketing authorisation procedure, that procedure was not able to delay the commercial use of the basic patent. In such circumstances, the grant of an SPC is contrary to the aim pursued by Regulation No 469/2009, which is to offset, at least in part, the delay to the commercial use of a patented invention on account of the time needed for the first marketing authorisation in the European Union to be granted.

[39] Accordingly, the answer to Question 2(a) is that Article 3(b) of Regulation No 469/ 2009 must be interpreted as precluding the grant of an SPC for an active ingredient whose effect does not fall within the therapeutic indications covered by the wording of the marketing authorisation."

This decision is welcome. The whole policy behind the grant of SPCs is to **2-638** compensate patentees for a delay in exploiting inventions which are the subject matter of a patent by the need to obtain a marketing authorisation. This requires a close nexus between the subject matter of the SPC and that of the marketing authorisation. Merely requiring a close nexus between the subject matter of the basic patent and the SPC (as would appear to be the approach of the Court of Justice in *Farmitalia* and *Georgetown*) is to ignore the fundamental policy of the SPC Regulation.

What type of medical authorisation?

In a number of cases the Court of Justice has had to consider precisely what type **2-639** of medical authorisation is necessary to be granted before a SPC can be applied for.

[1204] See [34].
[1205] See [37]–[38].
[1206] See also *University of Queensland*, at [35]–[36]. Reasoned Order, where this principle was applied.
[1207] (C-631/13) ECLI:EU:C:2015:13.

In *Hogan Lovells v Bayer CropScience*,[1208] the Court of Justice held that a provisional MA which could be granted for substances whose active ingredients were not listed in Dir.91/414 was a relevant marketing authorisation for the purpose of art.3(b).[1209] In contrast, in *Sumitomo Chemical v Deutsche Patent-under Markenamt*,[1210] an emergency medical authorisation order was granted for the active ingredient for a plant protection product. The CJEU held that an emergency MA could not found an application for a SPC because such is restricted to products which did not comply with the Directive permitting plant protection products to be placed on the market. Also, such did not require a prior scientific evaluation of the risks.[1211] In *Merck Sharpe & Dohme v Comptroller-General of Patents, Designs and Trade Marks*,[1212] the Court of Justice held that an "end of procedure" notice issued by a Member State under Dir. 2001/83 prior to the grant of a full marketing authorisation was not a marketing authorisation for the purpose of art.3(b).

2-640   In *Sumitomo*, the CJEU also held that a SPC could not be applied for before the date on which the plant protection product has obtained the medical authorisation order.[1213]

2-641   Finally, it should be said that if the product has been placed on the market in the EU as a medicinal product for human use prior to obtaining a market authorisation, then the SPC Regulation does not apply.[1214]

SPC wider than the MA

2-642   In *Pharmaq AS v Intervet International BV*,[1215] the EFTA court considered, on reference from the Norwegian courts, the position where a SPC had been granted too widely so that it covered improved vaccines that did not fall within the products subject to the medical authorisation order. It held that a SPC is invalid to the extent that it is granted a wider scope than that set out in the relevant MA. Applying this decision, the Norwegian Court of Appeal held that as such was the case, it had no option but to declare the entire SPC invalid.[1216] This was surprising to many who had assumed that EFTA court was merely saying that a SPC with a broad product definition was unenforceable to the extent that its scope was wider than the products authorised in the MA. As said in one article, many SPCs are granted with definitions that are not identical to the product definition in the marketing authorisation so this decision is worrying to SPC owners.[1217]

[1208] (C-229/09) [2010] E.C.R. I-11335.
[1209] See [44].
[1210] (C-210/12) ECLI:EU:C:2013:665.
[1211] See [36]–[38].
[1212] (C-567/16) ECLI:EU:C:2017:948. The patent expired a month before the full marketing authorisation was granted—see [27]–[29].
[1213] See [40]–[45].
[1214] art.2; *Generics (UK) Ltd v Synaptic* (C-427/09) [2011] E.C.R. I-7099; *Synthon* (C-195/09) [2011] E.C.R. I-7011. In this regard, it did not matter that authorisation had not been granted pursuant to the relevant EU Directive. As the court said in *Generics*, where the product had been on the market as a medicinal product for human use before obtaining marketing authorisation pursuant to the relevant EU Directive on authorisation of medical products for human use (then Dir.65/65 (now replaced by Dir.2001/83)), the product could not be the subject of a SPC.
[1215] (E-16/14).
[1216] *Pharmaq AS v Intervet International BV* 15-1705539ASD-BORG/01.
[1217] See D. Wise and N. Wegner-Cribbs, "SPC Summer Review: Part 2" *CIPA Journal* Vol.46, No.9, pp.24–25.

Condition 4: The product has not already been the subject of a certificate as of the date of application for the SPC

Article 3(c) requires that the product for which a SPC is sought is not already the subject of a SPC. The obvious purpose of this provision is to prevent successive extensions of protection for a product. For each product, there is the opportunity to extend protection via the SPC regime once up to a maximum period of five years. However, how broadly or narrowly should one define a "product" under art.3(c)? Can the patentee, having obtained a MA for one salt of the active ingredient, obtain a SPC for that salt and then having obtained a second MA for another salt of the active ingredient, apply for a second SPC even though the basic patent does not differentiate between these salts and sees them as all part of the same family of products incorporating the active ingredient? If such were allowed, it is clear that the SPC regime could be abused.

2-643

The jurisprudence of the CJEU concerning the interpretation of art.3(c) has been somewhat inconsistent. In *Biogen Inc v SmithKline Beecham Biologicals SA*,[1218] the CJEU was seized with the issue of interpretation of art.3(c) for the first time. The facts of the case were unusual. One of the questions referred by the Belgian courts was whether, where one and the same product is covered by several basic patents belonging to different holders, could a SPC be granted to each holder of a basic patent or not. The CJEU held that it would be wrong to confer preferential treatment on any of the holders of the patents and thus, it held answering the question referred to it by the Belgian court that each of those patents could be designated for the purpose of the procedure for the grant of a SPC.[1219] However, in a somewhat throwaway remark, which was unnecessary to the decision, it said that under art.3(c), only one certificate could be granted for each basic patent.[1220] In *AHP Manufacturing v BIE*,[1221] the CJEU applied its finding in *Biogen* and held that it was permissible to grant a SPC to each holder of a basic patent for the product even if SPCs had already been granted to other holders of other basic patents for the product. At the same time, without any need to do so for the purpose of its decision, it confirmed the throwaway remark in *Biogen* that only one SPC could be granted for each basic patent.[1222]

2-644

In *Takeda Chemical Application (SPC No.2)*,[1223] the English Patent Office was concerned about the meaning of the CJEU's statement in *Biogen* that only one SPC could be granted for each patent. The Patent Office said that if the court's remark was taken at face value, then it would mean that if more than one product was protected by a single basic patent, the applicant for a SPC would have to decide which of the products should benefit from SPC protection (i.e. which should be the "golden egg": see [21]). The Patent Office considered that such could not have been what the court intended and instead what it meant was that if a product was protected by more than one basic patent, it could not obtain more than one SPC for a particular product. The logic of this argument is plain and as will be seen, the CJEU has aligned itself with this position. Yet, the powerfulness of the argument is somewhat undermined by the fact that when deciding the scope of protection of

2-645

[1218] (C-181/95) [1997] E.C.R. I-357; [1997] R.P.C. 833 (ECJ) at [28].
[1219] See [28].
[1220] See [28].
[1221] *AHP Manufacturing* (C-482/07) [2009] E.C.R. I-7295 at [22] and [23].
[1222] See [22].
[1223] [2004] R.P.C. 2. This was decided prior to *AHP Manufacturing*.

a SPC (discussed below), the CJEU has interpreted such as extending beyond the mere product for which a SPC has been obtained to the protection offered by the claims of the basic patent. Thus, the problem of deciding which shall be the "golden egg" disappears if the SPC protects a wide variety of eggs, whichever "golden egg" is chosen.

2-646 In two cases handed down on the same day in December 2013, the CJEU had to deal with the question of attempts to obtain protection by successive SPC applications based on the same basic patent. In *Actavis Group v Sanofi*[1224], Sanofi was the owner of a European patent for a family of compounds whose active ingredient was irbesartan. The patent also contained a claim to a composition comprising irbesartan in association with a "diuretic". A MA was obtained for a medicine (Aprovel) which contained irbesartan as its single active ingredient for the purpose of treating hypertension. However, a year later, Sanofi obtained another MA for a compound medicine (CoAprovel) which combined irbesartan with a diuretic (HCTZ). This MA was also for treating hypertension. Sanofi then obtained SPCs for both irbesartan simpliciter and irbesartan with HCTZ. Actavis sought revocation of the CoAprovel SPC. It argued that the SPC for CoAprovel was invalid in the light of art.3(c) as Sanofi had already obtained a SPC for the basic patent (relying upon *Biogen* and *AHP Manufacturing*). The CJEU held that one could obtain SPCs for different products protected within the same basic patent.[1225] However, it considered that this did not apply where the holder of a basic patent could obtain successive SPCs each time they placed a combination of active ingredients on the market where one active ingredient was protected by the basic patent but not the other active ingredient. Technically, of course, irbesartan with HCTZ had not been the subject of a previous certificate. However, there was no dispute between the parties that Sanofi, relying upon the first SPC certificate for irbesartan solus, could have prevented the marketing of irbesartan combined with another ingredient. Thus, the effect of granting the second SPC would have been to extend protection for irbesartan + HCTZ beyond the term of the first SPC. Importantly, the basic patent did not protect HCTZ *alone* in the basic patent. Accordingly, the CJEU held that where a SPC has already been obtained for an active ingredient based on a MA for that ingredient, the patentee could not obtain a second SPC for a second MA where such was for the active ingredient combined with another active ingredient where the latter was *not* protected by the patent. As said by the CJEU:

> "[41] It should be recalled that the basic objective of Regulation No 469/2009 is to compensate for the delay to the marketing of what constitutes the core inventive advance that is the subject of the basic patent, namely, in the main proceedings, irbesartan. In the light of the need, referred to in recital 10 in the preamble to that regulation, to take into account all the interests at stake, including those of public health, if it were accepted that all subsequent marketing of that active ingredient in conjunction with an unlimited number of other active ingredients, not protected as such by the basic patent but simply referred to in the wording of the claims of the patent in general terms, such as, in the case of the patent in the main proceedings, 'beta-blocking compound', 'calcium antagonist', 'diuretic', 'non-steroidal anti-inflammatory' or 'tranquilizer', conferred entitlement to multiple SPCs, that would be contrary to the requirement to balance the interests of the pharmaceutical industry and those of public health as regards the encouragement of research within the European Union by the use of SPCs."

[1224] *Actavis Group pTC EHF, Actavis UK Ltd v Sanofi* (C-443/12) ECLI:EU:C:2013:833.
[1225] Citing *Georgetown University* which was handed down the same day and discussed in the next paragraph—see [29].

In contrast, in the second *Georgetown* case, *Georgetown v Octrooicentrum*   **2-647**
Nederland,[1226] the facts were that Georgetown had obtained a SPC in relation to a
combination of active ingredients on the basis that the basic patent and the MA
protected this combination. It then applied to obtain a SPC in respect of one of the
active ingredients which was also protected as such by the basic patent. Thus, the
distinction between the facts of this case and *Actavis* was that the basic patent
protected both the combination of the active ingredients and the individual
ingredients. OCN (the Dutch intellectual property office) argued that to grant a SPC
for the ingredient itself would in effect amount to a grant of a second SPC for the
same basic patent which it said the CJEU had said in earlier authorities was not
permissible.[1227] However, the CJEU considered that such a line of authorities was
distinguishable where the same basic patent could be considered as protecting a
number of products within the meaning of art.3(a) of the SPC Regulation. Where
such was the case, then there was nothing in principle which prevented the obtaining of several SPCs based on different products protected by the basic patent. It
made the powerful point that if such were not the case, then it would simply force
applicants to apply for a multitude of patents for each of their "products" thus causing unnecessary costs. Therefore, it held that the patentee could obtain a SPC for
an active ingredient which was protected by the basic patent even though it had
already obtained a SPC for a combination of ingredients which included the same
active ingredient where such was also protected by the basic patent.[1228]

However, what about the requirement cited in *Actavis v Sanofi* about not grant-   **2-648**
ing successive SPCs for the same product? This argument did not feature in
Georgetown. There may be two reasons for this. First, a SPC for a combination of
active ingredients does not prevent use of a single ingredient.[1229] Thus, obtaining a
second SPC for the single ingredient did not amount to successive extensions of
protection for the single ingredient. In contrast, *Actavis* was the other way round
with the first MA being for the active ingredient *solus* and then the second MA being for it in combination with another ingredient. As the SPC based on the first MA
would have given protection against the combination, the observation that such
amounted to repeated grants of SPCs for the active ingredient was clearly correct.
The second reason may be that the SPC application for the individual active ingredient in *Georgetown* was based upon the same MA for the combination.[1230] Thus, as
the extension of period of protection is a formula based on the difference between
the date of first medical authorisation and the date of application for the basic patent, there would have been no further extension of the period of protection. The only
effect of the second SPC application was to ensure that the individual active ingredient was protected via a SPC certificate as well as the combination. This factor appears to have been considered important by the CJEU.[1231] In contrast, in *Sanofi v
Actavis*, the effect was to extend the duration of protection for an active ingredient
and not merely the scope of protection.

[1226] (C-484/12) ECLI:EU:C:2013:745.
[1227] See [28] of the decision which cites *Biogen* (C-181/95) and *AHP Manufacturing* (C-482/07).
[1228] See [30].
[1229] Although it may be arguable that the supply of such could amount to contributory infringement under
national laws.
[1230] See [35].
[1231] e.g. see [35], [40]. See also M. Snodin, "Three CJEU decisions that answer some questions but pose
some more" [2014] JIPLP 9(7) 599 at 602.

2-649   In a later case, *Actavis v Boehringer*,[1232] Boehringer had obtained a patent for the active ingredient telmisartan (for treatment of high blood pressure). Originally, claims were to telmisartan and a salt of telmisartan. It obtained a marketing authorisation for telmisartan and a SPC for telmisartan. That SPC expired in 2013. In 2002, Boehringer obtained a marketing authorisation for telmisartan hydrochlorothiazide. Hydrochlorothiazide is a well-known active ingredient, being a diuretic and had been known to exist since 1958, as well as being in the public domain. It was mentioned *en passant* in the patent as one of a large number of active ingredients which could be combined with telmisartan without claiming any special inventive effect from the combination. In late 2002, following the grant of marketing authorisation for telmisartan hydrochlorothiazide, Boehringer applied for a SPC for the combination. The UK Intellectual Property Office suggested to Boehringer that they applied to amend the patent as it did not have a claim to the combination of telmisartan and hydrochlorothiazide (such having been disclosed in the basic patent). Boehringer followed this suggestion and accordingly, UKIPO granted a SPC for telmisartan hydrochlorothiazide. Actavis claimed that the combination SPC was invalid.

2-650   On reference to the Court of Justice, it held applying *Sanofi* that the application for the combination SPC was impermissible.

2-651   In summary, it is fairly clear in the CJEU's judgments in *Sanofi*, *Georgetown* and *Boehringer* that the CJEU is concerned about granting successive SPC protection for, in essence, the same inventive concept. Thus, in *Sanofi*, it was keen to emphasise that there was no bar absolute to protecting a combination of active ingredients[1233] provided that such covered a "totally separate innovation".[1234] Whether such is the case is not and should not be dependent on whether the two separate inventions are protected by one or more basic patents.[1235] Equally, it should not depend on whether the same inventive concept happens to be the subject of two or more marketing authorisations (for instance where the inventive active ingredient is combined with two different salts). The Court of Justice's approach is highly teleological and in line with the policy behind the SPC Regulation (discussed above). In brief, a delay in obtaining a MA for an inventive concept justifies the grant of a SPC but no more than one SPC.

2-652   This teleological approach was taken by the UK in a case in 2017. In *Teva UK Ltd v Merck Sharp & Dohme*,[1236] the Patents Court considered the case law of *Sanofi*, *Georgetown* and *Boehringer* and concluded that it was clear that art.3(c) precluded the grant of a SPC for a combination of active ingredients where one of those ingredients embodied the core invention in the basic patent and had already been the subject of a SPC unless that combination represented a "distinct invention protected by the patent".[1237] The court concluded that for this to be shown, it had to be highlighted in the patent that the combination was inventive over the single active ingredient which was the subject of the earlier authorisation. The judge considered that such was not the case as there was nothing in the basic patent to sug-

---

[1232] *Actavis Group PTC ehf v Boerhinger Ingelheim Pharma GmbH & Co KG* (C–577/13) EU:C:2015:165.

[1233] Indeed, art.1(b) permits such.

[1234] See [42].

[1235] The CJEU in [42] did mention that this needed to be the subject of new basic patent but clearly such remarks must be viewed in the light of *Georgetown* which permitted two SPCs based on the same patent where they were for two different products.

[1236] [2017] EWHC 539 (Pat).

[1237] See [34].

gest that the combination (which was the subject of a claim) represented a distinct invention over the single active ingredient. The court considered that it was necessary, for the purpose of a simple and transparent system for the grant of SPCs, that the patent disclosed that the combination was a distinct invention.[1238] This approach is in line with the policy identified in the previous paragraph—one invention, one SPC.

Condition Five: First authorisation to place the product on the market in the EEA

Article 3(d) requires that the application for the SPC is based on the first **2-653** authorisation to place the product (as defined in art.1(b)) on the market in the EEA. In *Neurim Pharmaceuticals v Comptroller-General of Patents, Designs and Trade Marks*,[1239] Neurim was the owner of a European patent for "melatonin". It applied for a SPC based on a MA for a medicinal product for human use. However, earlier, a MA had been granted for melatonin for use for a veterinary product (for sheep). The Comptroller rejected the application on the grounds that there was an earlier authorisation (namely the veterinary one) to the one relied upon for the purpose of the SPC. However, on a preliminary reference, the CJEU held that as the scope of the SPC could only cover the new use of the product (i.e. human use), that, in such circumstances, only the marketing authorisation for human use was relevant.[1240]

In an English case, *Abraxis Bioscience*, the Patents Court of England and Wales **2-654** had to consider an application for a SPC for a new therapeutic formulation (nab-paclitaxel) of an old active ingredient (paclitaxel). Abraxis had a patent and marketing authorisation for this new formulation. Difficulty arose because the active ingredient paclitaxel had already been the subject of a prior authorisation. Abraxis argued that *Neurim* should be extended to cover not only *new* uses of an active ingredient but also new *formulations* of an (old) active ingredient. The Comptroller-General argued that there was no new "product" (within the meaning of art.1(b)) as paclitaxel alone was the active ingredient. As that had already been granted a marketing authorisation within the EEA, art.3(d) prevented Abraxis from obtaining a SPC based on its MA for nab-paclitaxel. The Patents Court considered the matter unclear but its provisional view was that the Explanatory Memorandum of the EU Commission for the first SPC Regulation indicated that SPCs should be available for new applications (i.e. new therapeutic uses) but not for new formulations of old active ingredients.[1241] It will be interesting to see how the Court of Justice decides this. There is much merit in Abraxis' favour. Nab-paclitaxel was a new inventive formulation whose launch on the market had been delayed by the need for a marketing authorisation. As said by the Patents Court, it "fully acknowledge[d] the force" of Abraxis' argument that the primary purpose of the SPC Regulation is to reward innovative research and compensate patentees for delay.[1242] Such certainly favoured Abraxis' application for a SPC.

The date of first authorisation to place the product on the market in the EEA is **2-655**

[1238] See [168]–[171].

[1239] (C-103/11) [2013] R.P.C. 23.

[1240] See [22]–[27].

[1241] *Abraxis Bioscience LLC v The Comptroller-General of Patents* [2017] EWHC 14 (Pat). This referral is now pending case *Abraxis Bioscience* (C-443/17). The Explanatory Memorandum of the Commission is discussed at para.2-617.

[1242] *Abraxis*, at [63].

relevant to the calculation of the period of the SPC. This is discussed below. In *Seattle Genetics Inc v Österreiches Patentamt*[1243] the Court of Justice held that the date of first authorisation to place the product on the market in the EU in art.13(1) of Reg.469/2009 was to be determined by EU law and not the law of the Member State in which the marketing authorisation in question took effect. It then went on to say that under EU law, this is the date on which notification of the decision granting marketing authorisation was given to the addressee of the decision.

Subject-matter and scope of protection

2-656   Articles 4 and 5 of the SPC Regulation state as follows:

"**Article 4**
   Subject matter of protection
   Within the limits of the protection conferred by the basic patent, the protection conferred by a certificate shall extend only to the product covered by the authorisation to place the corresponding medicinal product on the market and for any use of the product as a medicinal product that has been authorised before the expiry of the certificate.

Article 5
   Effects of the certificate
   Subject to the provisions of Article 4, the certificate is to confer the same rights as conferred by the basic patent and to be subject to the same limitations and the same obligations."

2-657   The effect of art.5 is that the SPC confers the same rights and defences as would apply if the action were for infringement of the basic patent.[1244] Thus, if the basic patent extended protection to products obtained from process, then the SPC will also cover such products.[1245] However, art.5 specifically refers to art.4 which refers to the protection only extending to the product covered by the authorisation. This qualification should also be read in the light of Recital 10 which states that "*the protection granted should furthermore be strictly confined to the product which obtained authorisation to be placed on the market as a medicinal product*". Such would suggest that an alleged infringing product only infringes a SPC where two conditions are satisfied: (i) the alleged infringing product infringes the basic patent (if it had not expired); and (ii) the alleged infringing product is a product "covered" by the authorisation. One interpretation of this second condition might be that it is satisfied if the alleged infringing product *could* be placed on the market under the MA. However, as seen below, such an interpretation may be inadequate to properly protect the owner of a SPC.

2-658   However, the CJEU has avoided such over-literal interpretation and effectively ignored art.4. In *Novartis AG v Actavis UK Ltd*[1246] the facts were that Novartis had a basic patent for Valsartan which was used for treating hypertension. Claim 1 of the patent protected thousands of compounds including Valsartan. A MA was

---

[1243] (C–471/14) EU:C:2015:659.

[1244] e.g. see *Georgetown University v Octrooicentrum Nederland* (C-484/12), at [39].

[1245] See *University of Queensland v Comptroller General of Patents, Designs & Trade Marks*, at [39]. However, as discussed at para.2-623, a SPC cannot be applied for products which are not specifically mentioned in the claims of a process patent as such do not satisfy the conditions of art.3(a)—see [40].

[1246] (C-442/11) Order of Court dated 9 February 2012.

obtained for Valsartan as its sole active ingredient and a SPC was granted on that basis. Novartis also marketed and sold another medicinal product which combined Valsartan with hydrochlorothiazide, a diuretic which had blood pressure reducing properties. Actavis indicated its intention to market this combination product and argued that the SPC held by Novartis was for Valsartan as a sole active ingredient and did not cover the combination of Valsartan with another active ingredient. There was no issue that it would have infringed the basic patent. The CJEU considered the matter clear-cut and issued a Reasoned Order. It held that Novartis was entitled to prevent the marketing by Actavis of the combination product. As it said, such would ensure that, pursuant to art.5, the SPC conferred the same rights as that conferred by the basic patent.[1247]

A similar disregard of the requirement that the protection under a SPC be strictly confined to the product authorised under the MA was displayed in the EFTA Court decision in *Pharmaq v Intervet*.[1248] It held that a SPC can extend to cover a specific strain of virus included in the basic patent but not mentioned in the MA where the specific strain constitutes the same active ingredient as the approved medicinal product and had therapeutic effects which fell within the same therapeutic indications for which the MA had been granted. **2-659**

The decisions in *Novartis v Actavis* and to some extent, *Pharmaq v Intervnet* are understandable when one considers the broad justice. After all, there will invariably be a salt of the relevant active ingredient for which the SPC holder does not have a medical authorisation. Yet, equating the protection of the SPC to that of the basic patent risks conferring protection on the SPC holder that goes beyond merely permitting the SPC holder to recoup the investment lost due to the delay in marketing a medicinal product incorporating the active ingredient covered by the basic patent. One thing that is clear is that a SPC is not merely an extension of the term of protection of the basic patent for a further fixed period. Such an interpretation would represent a windfall to the owner of a basic patent. One is tempted to say that the fair approach (which gives force to art.4 and Recital 10) is that the scope of protection of a SPC extends to prohibiting the marketing of any third party medicinal product where: (i) it infringes the basic patent, *and* (ii) it contains the same active ingredient or combination of active ingredients as which was or were the subject of the medical authorisation order. **2-660**

Duration of protection

The certificate takes effect at the end of the lawful term of the basic patent. The period of protection is calculated as the period which elapsed between the date on which the application for a basic patent was lodged and the date of the *first* authorisation to place the product on the market in *the EEA* reduced by a period of five years.[1249] However, the duration of the certificate may not exceed five years from the date on which it takes effect.[1250] Thus, by way of example: **2-661**

[1247] Citing at [20]—*Medeva* (C-322/10) [2011] E.C.R. I-12051 at [39]; *Georgetown University* (C-422/10) [2011] E.C.R. I-12157 at [32]; and orders of 25 November 2011 in *University of Queensland and CSL* (C-630/10) [2011] E.C.R. I-12231, [34] and *Daiichi Sankyo* (C-6/11) [2011] E.C.R. I-12255 at [29].

[1248] (E-16/14).

[1249] art.13(1) as amended by Point 8 of Protocol 1 to the EEA Agreement (see *Novartis v UK Patent Office; Millennium Pharmaceuticals Inc v Ministre de l'Économie* (C-207/03 & C-252/03) [2005]

- Patent filed on 1 January 2000 and first MA granted for EEA on 1 January 2005, the period elapsed is five years and this must then be reduced by five years. Duration of SPC = 0 years.
- Patent filed on 1 January 2000 and first MA granted on 1 January 2010, the period elapsed is 10 years and then must be reduced by five years. Duration of SPC = five years.
- Patent filed on 1 January 2000 and first MA granted on 1 January 2015, the period elapsed is 15 years and then this must be reduced by five years to give 10 years. However, such exceeds the maximum extension and so the period of protection. Duration of SPC = five years.

2-662   Thus, if there is a considerable delay between the grant of the first authorisation order in a contracting state of the EEA and the grant of the authorisation order in the contracting state in which the application for a SPC is made, the duration of protection under the SPC may be seriously affected or indeed negated in certain countries where the obtaining of authorisation takes time.[1251] Despite attempts to challenge the unfairness of such, it has been made clear that the decisive factor is that the period of exclusive use is the same throughout the EEA.[1252]

2-663   Conversely, in *Merck Canada Inc v Accord*[1253] Merck Canada lodged an application for a patent for an active ingredient on 11 October 1991. The patent expired on 2 October 2013 which was under Portuguese law, 15 years after the date of grant of the patent (being 2 October 1998). The first MA for that product was obtained in Finland on 25 August 1997. Merck then applied for a SPC on 3 February 1999 for the active ingredient. Applying the approach under art.13, the extension of protection was the difference between 25 August 1997 and 11 October 1991 minus five years. Thus this equated to five years, 10 months and 15 days, minus five years, i.e. 10 months and 15 days. When this was added to the expiry of the basic patent,

---

E.C.R. I-3209). For those suffering from arithmetical fatigue, examples of calculations of the relevant period are given in R. Whaite and N. Jones, "Pharmaceutical Patent Term Restoration: the European Commission's Proposed Regulation" [1992] E.I.P.R. 324–326. Where the SPC was granted in a country prior to its accession to the EU but after the date of first authorisation of a SPC for the same product in the EU, such does not affect the rule that the duration is determined by first authorisation in the EU—see *F.Hoffmann-La Roche AG v Accord Healthcare OÜ* (C-572/15) ECLI:EU:C:2016:739.

[1250] art.13(2).

[1251] See *Novartis v UK Patent Office; Millennium Pharmaceuticals Inc v Ministre de l'Économie* (C-207/03 & C-252/03) [2005] E.C.R. I-3209, the Court of Justice held that authorisations by Swiss regulatory authorities which counted as authorisations for Liechtenstein under bilateral agreements amounted to an authorisation to market in the EEA. Liechtenstein is a member of EEA whereas Switzerland is not. Following this decision, Switzerland has changed the effect of its authorisation in Liechtenstein—see S. Moore, "EU Patents: ECJ clarifies effect of Swiss marketing authorizations on duration of SPCs" [2005] E.I.P.R. 27(8), N157–158. See application of this judgment in the Reasoned Order in *AstraZeneca AB v Comptroller General of Patents* (C-617/12) ECLI:EU:2013:761 where the CJEU held that it was irrelevant whether the MA holder had actually been able to market the medicinal product in question in Liechtenstein or that Switzerland had amended the bilateral agreement to exclude automatic recognition of Swiss authorisations in Liechtenstein (at [58]). However, the CJEU appeared to consider this irrelevant because Astrazeneca had already made sales of the active ingredient in an EEA state (at [56]) and because the amendment of the bilateral agreement post-dated the grant of the Swiss authorisation (at [58]). Paragraph 60 and the declaratory order referred to the fact that the Swiss authority's decision to issue an administrative authorisation was automatically recognised in Liechtenstein and it would appear that, if such had not been the case, then the reasoning of the CJEU would not have applied.

[1252] See Colomer's AG Opinion in *Novartis* [2005] E.C.R. I-3209.

[1253] (C-555/13) ECLI:EU:C:2014:92.

it resulted in a SPC expiring on 17 August 2014. However, this period exceeded 15 years from the date of grant of first authorisation in the EU (being 25 August 1997). Recital 9 of Reg.469/2009 stipulates that the holder of a patent and certificate should be able to enjoy a maximum period of 15 years of exclusivity from the time that the medicinal product in question first obtain authorisation to be obtained on the market in the EU. Thus, there was a stark conflict between Recital 9 and art.13. The CJEU considered that there was no doubt (and thus issued a Reasoned Order) that Recital 9 "trumped" art.13 and that regardless of the "theoretical validity period" of the certificate resulting from the application of art.13, the period of protection conferred overall could never exceed 15 years from the date of first authorisation within the EU.[1254]

Paediatric extension of six months

A SPC can be extended by six months as compensation for obtaining and submit-**2-664** ting data from paediatric clinical trials where the result of all studies have been conducted in compliance with an agreed paediatric investigation plan.[1255] In *Merck Sharp & Dohme v Deutsche Patent- und Markenamt*[1256] Merck applied for a SPC for a pharmaceutical substance covered by a basic patent. In fact, the MA had been granted four years eight months and 16 days from the application for the basic patent. Thus, no SPC could be granted as such was less than five years. However, Merck wished to extend the SPC by six months by reason of the authorisation of a paediatric investigation plan. The Bundespatentgericht were not sure whether: (i) the fact that the period between the filing of the patent and the grant of first MA was less than five years meant that no SPC could be granted; and (ii) if so, what was the relevant period? Could one have a negative SPC? The CJEU said that one could grant a SPC in such circumstances and that the period of the paediatric extension had to take into account a SPC of negative duration. Thus, in *Merck Sharp*, as the period between the application for the patent and the grant of MA was less than five years but more than four and a half years, the extension of time for the paediatric extension was two months and 16 days from the date of expiry of the patent.[1257]

Entitlement to a SPC

The holder of the basic patent or their successor in title is entitled to the grant of **2-665** a supplementary protection certificate.[1258] Although the Regulation does not address it, the prevailing opinion is that the applicant does not need to be the proprietor of the marketing authorisation.[1259] Thus, where a licensee holds the authorisation, application for the SPC could be made in the name of the patentee. Difficulties

---

[1254] See [33]–[34].

[1255] art.13(3) Reg.469/2009; art.36 Reg.1901/2006 on medicinal products for paediatric use.

[1256] (C-125/10) [2011] E.C.R. I-12987.

[1257] See [44].

[1258] art.7.

[1259] R. Lelkes, A. von Uexküll and P. Tauchner, "Patent Term Restoration in Europe: Taking Advantage of the Supplementary Protection Certificate" *Patent World*, December 1992–January 1993, 14 at 17. Thus, in *Biogen Inc v SmithKline*, the patent proprietor was Biogen and Smithkline were licensees who had obtained a marketing authorisation order. It appears to have been accepted *sub silentio* that such was not fatal to Biogen applying for an SPC. See also *Georgetown University v Octrooicentrum Nederland* where the MAs for the papillomavirus vaccine had been granted to Sanofi Pasteur and

may arise when independent parties each possess novel and inventive process patents for the same active ingredient. Under the Regulation, a supplementary protection certificate cannot be granted for a product if it is already the subject of a certificate. Once one party with a process patent has obtained a certificate following authorisation of the product, the other patent owner will not be able to obtain a certificate, even if it is the older patent.[1260]

Procedural conditions

2-666   These are set out in arts 8–11. In summary, application must be made to the patent office which granted the basic patent or on whose behalf it was granted (i.e. not the EPO if a European patent) and must include a copy of the authorisation order.[1261] A fee may be payable. Publication of the grant of a certificate will take place. National patent offices of Member States may require the payment of annual fees.[1262] As a certificate can only be granted if the basic patent is in force, applicants may be advised to make parallel applications in relation to several basic patents if the validity of some of those patents are in doubt.[1263]

Licences and SPC

2-667   The SPC Regulation does not expressly deal with the status during the SPC period of existing licences under the basic patent. It has been suggested that art.5, which states that the certificate shall be subject to the same limitations and obligations as that of the basic patent, means that the licence continues into the period covered by the SPC.[1264] Germany has specifically legislated that this is the case.[1265]

EPC and SPC Regulation

2-668   As mentioned earlier, art.63 EPC permits contracting Member States to extend the term of a European patent to take account of inter alia an administrative authorisation procedure required by law before the product can be put on the market in that state.[1266] This amendment is much broader in scope than the SPC Regulation, as it covers non-medical products. The SPC Regulation is not a harmonising Directive. However, there is little doubt that the intention of the SPC Regulation

---

also to GlaxoSmithKline, yet Georgetown had applied for the SPCs. In the UK, see *Eli Lilly v HGS*.

[1260] See arts 3(c), 4 and analysis in R. Lelkes, A. von Uexküll and P. Tauchner, "Patent Term Restoration in Europe: Taking Advantage of the Supplementary Protection Certificate" *Patent World*, December 1992–January 1993, 17–18.

[1261] In *Biogen Inc v SmithKline Beecham Biological SA* (C-181/95) [1997] E.C.R. 357; [1997] R.P.C. 833, it was held that where the owner of the marketing authorisation was different from the owner of the basic patent, the former was not required to provide the patent holder with a copy of that authorisation (see [38]). Equally, where the holder of the basic patent and the marketing authorisation are held by different persons and the patent holder is unable to provide a copy of the authorisation, an application for a certificate cannot be refused on that ground alone (see [47]).

[1262] art.12.

[1263] See T. Cook, "The Supplementary Protection Certificate—How is it Working in Practice" *Patent World*, February 1994, 29 at 30.

[1264] T. Cook, "The Supplementary Protection Certificate—How is it Working in Practice" *Patent World*, February 1994, 29 at 32.

[1265] R. Lelkes, A. von Uexküll and P. Tauchner, "Patent Term Restoration in Europe: Taking Advantage of the Supplementary Protection Certificate" *Patent World*, December 1992–January 1993, 14.

[1266] See para.2-105.

was to provide a harmonised EU law regarding the grant of SPC certificates.[1267] Thus, insofar as a contracting member is a member of both the EPC and the EU, it is doubtful that such a state can extend protection beyond that provided by the SPC Regulation for medicinal and veterinary products.

EU law and the Nagoya Protocol

On 12 October 2014, the Nagoya Protocol on Access to Genetic Resources and Fair and Equitable Sharing of Benefits Arising from Their Utilisation to the Convention on Biological Diversity entered into force. The purpose of this is to ensure that there is a sharing of benefit derived from genetic material discovered in countries and traditional knowledge associated with such where it is exploited commercially. The EU is a party to the Nagoya Protocol. Accordingly, the EU has enacted Reg.511/2014 and an implementing regulation, Reg.2015/1866 to implement the Nagoya Protocol in the EU.   **2-669**

It is beyond the scope of this book to discuss in detail these regulations. In brief, they envisage that users of genetic resource or traditional knowledge (e.g. researchers) have accessed such with the prior informed consent of states who can be considered to have rights to such and have agreed benefit sharing arrangements. A rather cumbersome "certificate of compliance" method is envisaged which confirms that a genetic resource or traditional knowledge has been accessed with the consent of the relevant states and that mutually agreed terms have been entered into concerning its use.   **2-670**

The relationship between these regulations and the grant and licensing of national patents in EU countries, European or EU Unitary Patents which claim inventions that make use of protected genetic material or traditional knowledge is unclear. For instance, where prior informed consent has not been obtained for the grant of a patent which makes use of such genetic material or traditional knowledge, it might be argued that those states with rights in such are entitled to be recorded as a co-owner of the patent or that profits made from the exploitation of the patent should be shared with those with rights in such.   **2-671**

There are currently no plans to amend the EPC or its rules to accommodate the Nagoya Protocol or indeed the EU regulations.   **2-672**

EEA PATENT LEGISLATION

In the field of patent law, the EU had not issued any legislation prior to the cut-off date of 31 July 1991 (when the annexes to the EEA Agreement listing the EEA relevant *acquis communautaire* were closed). Accordingly, no secondary legislation in the field of patent law was included as *acquis* into the EEA Agreement. Since the cut-off date, the EEA has sought to adopt all EU intellectual property legislation. An up-to-date list of the EU IP legislation that the EEA has adopted can be found   **2-673**

[1267] See Recital 7 which refers to the "a uniform solution at Community level should be provided". Moreover, the SPC Regulation was enacted pursuant to art.95 ECT (now art.114 TFEU) which permits the adoption of measures which have as their object the establishment and functioning of the internal market. See also art.21 Reg.446/2009 which states that the Regulation does not apply to certificates granted in accordance with the national legislation of a Member State before 2 January 1993. This plainly suggests that it is intended to apply to SPC certificates granted thereafter.

at the EFTA website at Annex 17.[1268] It should be noted that whilst EU IP legislation is adopted, unitary EU-wide rights do not extend to EEA countries which are not members of EU, so the EU Unitary Patent does not extend to Norway, Iceland and Liechtenstein. However, in the field of patents, it should be noted that EFTA states are also obliged to harmonise their patent laws with the substantive provisions of the EPC.[1269] Thus, although a EU Unitary Patent is not obtainable in these countries, a national patent via the EPC is obtainable.

COMPARISON OF NATIONAL, PCT, EPC AND EU UNITARY PATENT

2-674   It will be appreciated that there are a number of routes to obtaining patent protection in Europe. At its simplest, the applicant can file for a patent in one or more national patent offices of Member States. If protection is only sought in one or two countries, this may be the cheapest route to protection. Also, national patent offices tend to be less rigorous in their examination of applications than the EPO. Alternatively, where protection is sought in most contracting states, then the EPC route becomes cheapest. Generally, this route is cheapest once one wishes to obtain patent protection in three or more EPC countries. A further and attractive route is a Euro-PCT application whereby an applicant makes a home filing and 12 months later files an international application under the Patent Cooperation Treaty claiming priority from the home filing. That international application is then converted into a European application for Contracting States to the EPC.

2-675   Once the EU Unitary Patent comes into effect, the cost of obtaining and enforcing EU-wide patent protection will become considerably less because of the reduction in translational requirements and costs. This is a very attractive feature of the EU Unitary Patent. Where worldwide protection is sought, then the Euro-PCT route with conversion of the European patent into a EU Unitary Patent upon grant of the European patent becomes a very attractive route. However, the attractions of a one-stop shop conferred by the EU Unitary Patent are double-edged and high risk. Many would prefer to "test" the enforcement and validity of a classic European patent in a key European jurisdiction. If the patent is revoked, such order for revocation will only take effect in that country. With the EU Unitary Patent, an order for revocation would take effect throughout all 26 Participating Member States. It is precisely that risk which explains is why there is a seven-year transitional period and owners of a European patent can opt-out from the Agreement of the Unified Patent Court for the lifetime of a European patent and thus prevent revocation of a European patent throughout the Participating Member States by a single judgment of the UPC.

[1268] See *http://www.efta.int/media/documents/legal-texts/eea/the-eea-agreement/Annexes%20to%20the %20Agreement/annex17.pdf* [Accessed 18 August 2017].
[1269] art.3(4), Protocol 28.

CHAPTER 3

TRADE MARKS IN EUROPE

INTRODUCTION TO TRADE MARKS

Trade marks play an essential role in a market economy. By conferring exclusive **3-001** rights on the owner of a registered trade mark, the owner is given an incentive to promote the reputation of the mark and goods or services sold under the mark in the knowledge that others will not be able to exploit the mark's reputation.[1] Thus, as said by the Court of Justice of European Union ("CJEU") in *Arsenal FC v Reed*:

> "Trade mark rights constitute an essential element in the system of undistorted competition which the Treaty is intended to establish and maintain. In such a system, undertakings must be able to attract and retain customers by the quality of their goods or services, which is made possible only by distinctive signs allowing them to be identified."[2]

Therefore trade marks permit the public to distinguish between goods and **3-002** services of different trade origins. This is valuable both from the viewpoint of the consumer and the brand owner. The former can distinguish between goods and services on the market and, by being able to do so, gives the latter an incentive to produce high-quality goods or supply high-quality services sold under a mark. Of course, the consumer is primarily interested in the quality of goods or services rather than their trade origin. However, a uniform high quality will only be possible if the goods or services are produced or supplied under the control of a single undertaking to which responsibility for their quality can be attributed.[3] Although a trade mark

---

[1] *SA CNL-Sucal NV v HAG G.F. A.G. ("Hag II")* (C-10/89) [1990] E.C.R. I-3711; [1990] 3 C.M.L.R. 571, Jacobs AG's Opinion, at [19]. This statement has been oft-cited—see, e.g. *Lego Juris A/S v EUIPO* (C-48/09P) [2010] E.C.R. I-8403 at [38].

[2] *Arsenal FC v Reed* (C-206/01) [2003] E.C.R. I-10273 at [47]. See also (C-10/89) [1990] E.C.R. I-3711 at [13], and *Merz & Krell GmbH & Co v Deutsches Patent-und Markenamt* (C-517/99) [2001] E.C.R. I-6959 at [21].

[3] See R. Joliet, "Trade Mark law and the Free Movement of Goods: The Overruling of the Judgment

is not a legal guarantee of quality, the economic incentive of an undertaking to maintain a uniform high quality of products or services sold under a trade mark will normally be sufficient.[4]

3-003   From the above, it is clear that a registered trade mark has two roles, which complement each other. First, it enables a consumer to distinguish between goods from differing sources. Secondly, for a trade mark to be able to fulfil this role, the owner of the trade mark must have the exclusive right to market goods or services which are protected under the mark. The CJEU has recognised that trade marks have these two functions. In EU law, the first is called the "essential function" of the trade mark and the second is the "specific object" of the trade mark. These two functions should be seen as two sides of the same coin. As said by Tesauro AG:

> "The right to a trade mark, as an exclusive right, and protection against symbols which may be confused with it are substantially two sides of the same coin: to reduce (or extend) the scope of the protection against the risk of confusion means nothing other than to reduce (or extend) the scope of the right itself. Both aspects must accordingly be governed by a single, homogeneous source which, at present, is the internal legal order."[5]

3-004   This duality was recognised also by Jacobs AG in *HAG II*, who said:

> "Like patents, trade marks find their justification in a harmonious dovetailing between public and private interests. Whereas patents reward the creativity of the inventor and thus stimulate scientific progress, trade marks reward the manufacturer who consistently produces high-quality goods and they thus stimulate economic progress.
>
> Without trade mark protection there would be little incentive for manufacturers to develop new products or to maintain the quality of existing ones. Trade marks are able to achieve that effect because they act as a guarantee, to the consumer, that all goods bearing a particular mark have been produced by, or under the control of, the same manufacturer and are therefore likely to be of similar quality. The guarantee of quality offered by a trade mark is not of course absolute, for the manufacturer is at liberty to vary the quality however, he does so at his own risk and he—not his competitors—will suffer the consequences if he allows the quality to decline. Thus, although trade marks do not provide any form of legal guarantee of quality—the absence of which may have misled some to underestimate their significance—they do in economic terms provide such a guarantee, which is acted upon daily by consumers.
>
> A trade mark can only fulfil that role if it is exclusive. Once the proprietor is forced to share the mark with a competitor, he loses control over the goodwill associated with the mark. The reputation of his own goods will be harmed if the competitor sells inferior goods. From the consumer's point of view, equally undesirable consequences will ensue, because the clarity of the signal transmitted by the trade mark will be impaired. The consumer will be confused and misled."[6] [Emphasis supplied.]

3-005   The "clarity of signal" that Jacobs AG refers to in the passage above is a reference to the fact that each brand communicates a message about the products or services to which it is applied. In the past, a consumer made their choices very much on the basis of the characteristics of the goods or services to which the trade mark was attached and the quality of the undertaking supplying the goods or services. The trade mark enabled the consumer to choose the goods or services of a particular

---

in "HAG I" (1991) 2 I.I.C. 311.
[4]   See para.3-093 for more discussion about the function of a trade mark as a guarantee of quality.
[5]   *Deutsche Renault v Audi* (C-317/91) [1993] E.C.R. I-6227 at [21].
[6]   *CNL-Sucal NV SA v Hag GF AG ("Hag II")* (C-10/89) [1990] E.C.R. I-3711 at [18] and [19].

undertaking but did not influence per se their choice. However, in modern times, there is often little to differentiate between the characteristics of goods or services. In such circumstances, brand owners rely upon the brand image of the trade mark to affect consumer choice. Thus, there are two tiers of factors that affect a consumer in their purchasing decision of a product: the primary tier that are characteristics such as price, quality and availability of supply. These are product-related characteristics. The second tier of characteristics has nothing to do with the product but operate at a psychological level. These second tier characteristics can be collectively known as the brand image. Thus, an advertiser may decide to persuade consumers that a particular mobile telephone services provider is associated with a relaxed, youthful lifestyle whereas another may stress that its subscribers are demanding perfectionists. A beer brand may deliberately set out to persuade consumers that its beer is exclusive and for the aspirer.[7] These second tier factors will often not exist for a particular brand, e.g. a trade mark for a woodsaw. However, for luxury items such as cars, mobile telephones and alcoholic drinks, brand image will often be more important than the underlying product to today's image-conscious public. Where a trade mark has a very particular brand image, it is very important to the brand owner that its "signal" is not compromised by third party brands which undermine or alter this "signal". Because this signal works at a psychological level, it is much more sensitive to interference by uncontrolled third party use of a similar trade mark whose own signal causes "interference" in the psychological message broadcast by the first trade mark. Thus, the public may not actually be confused by two brands, but one may subtly interfere with the psychological message of the other brand.

This chapter considers how European trade mark law protects (or seeks to protect) these two functions of a modern trade mark, namely that as an indication of origin and its psychological message. As will be seen, these two functions are called the essential function and the communication function. However, in recent times, the CJEU has introduced two other functions: the investment function and the reputation function. Unfortunately, unlike the essential function and the communication function, the scope and effect of these functions are very unclear and indeed it is unclear whether they are truly functions of a trade mark at all.[8]   **3-006**

Supranational efforts to standardise trade mark law in Europe and to make the acquisition of trade marks cheaper and easier have come principally from two sources: the EU Commission and WIPO.[9] For a long period, their efforts went unrewarded. However, in the 1990s, their efforts came to fruition and there are now in force both EU measures and international treaties which have largely achieved the above aims.   **3-007**

On the international side, WIPO has secured the adherence of all EU countries to the Madrid Agreement and/or the Madrid Protocol, which are treaties designed to centralise and simplify the filing for trade marks worldwide and both of which are now in force. These procedural conventions supplement the original harmonis-   **3-008**

---

[7]   Thus, in an advertisement for *Stella Artois*, the strap line was "reassuringly expensive". This strap line takes a negative first tier factor of *Stella Artois* (price) and turn it into a positive second-tier factor (beer only drunk by the rich and discerning).

[8]   A more detailed discussion of these functions is discussed in the context of EU legislation, see para.3-069.

[9]   World Intellectual Property Organization.

ing convention, namely the Paris Convention, which in part, harmonises the substantive law of its contracting states.

3-009　　On the European side, the European Commission's efforts in the trade mark field have largely removed the barrier of territoriality that variation in the trade mark laws of Member States had historically caused so that there is a level playing field in the EU. To this end, there now exists a harmonising trade mark Directive ("TMD") which harmonises trade mark law throughout the Member States of the EU and a EU regulation ("EUTMR") for a EU Trade Mark ("EUTM") which has unitary effect throughout the EU. The substantive law of the TMD and EUTMR is virtually the same. The TMD has been fully implemented by all countries. Furthermore, there is now a very substantial body of case law from the Court of Justice and the General Court on the interpretation of the TMD and its counterpart, the EUTMR, which means that considerable flesh has been added to the skeleton of the TMD and the EUTMR.

3-010　　The EUTM has been an outstanding success. Year on year, there has been an increase in EUTM applications and registrations with 116,000 being filed and 126,000 being registered in 2016. Various trends can be identified from EUIPO's statistics.[10] First, whilst direct EUTM filings are up, international registrations designating the EU have dropped. Secondly, the increase in EUTM applications leading to registrations has increased proportionately much more (15 per cent) than the increase in applications (7 per cent). This may be due to the processing of a backlog of applications. Thirdly, oppositions were filed to 19,000 applications which suggest that broadly, one in five applications are opposed. This is again not surprising. Fourthly, most filed oppositions are eventually settled. Thus, in 2016, 16,500 oppositions were settled as against 19000 oppositions being filed in 2016. This suggests that EUIPO's standstill provisions for oppositions to encourage settlement work well. Fifthly, although there has been a drop in appeals filed to the Board of Appeals, there has been an 11 per cent increase in appeals filed to the General Court with 331 being filed in 2016. Perhaps more importantly, there has been a 26 per cent drop in appeals filed from the General Court to the Court of Justice. This no doubt reflects that the Court of Justice has become increasingly dismissive of appeals from the General Court. It is to be welcome as the Court of Justice represents the third appellate tribunal from first instance decisions of EUIPO and its resources are better deployed on other matters.

3-011　　Since the 4th edn was published, the substantive law of the EUTMR (formerly known as the Community Trade Mark Regulation) and TMD have been amended substantively for the first time since they were adopted. In summary, the main changes are the change in name of the Office of Harmonisation of the Internal Market ("OHIM") to European Union Intellectual Property Office ("EUIPO"); the change in name of Community Trade Marks to European Union Trade Marks ("EUTMs"); the abolition of the requirement that marks be represented graphically; the introduction of EU certification marks; the removal of the defence of use of a company name; and the right to seize "in transit" infringing goods. These changes were introduced in two stages: some came into force on 23 March 2016 and others on 1 October 2017. At the same time, the TMD has been amended to align it with the changes to the EUTMR. The new TMD repeals the old TMD with

---

[10]　Performance data over the years 2012-2016 is set out in Annex 3 of the Annual Report (see *https:// euipo.europa.eu/tunnel-web/secure/webdav/guest/document_library/contentPdfs/about_euipo/ annual_report/ar_2016_annex_03_en.pdf* [Accessed 18 August 2017]).

effect from 15 January 2019 and Member States must have implemented these changes by then. This means that for a period of time, the substantive law of the EUTMR and the trade mark laws of Member States will differ.

Finally, it is unclear how Brexit will affect EUTMs. All parties are aware that it will be unacceptable for any loss of rights in the UK for those who have EUTMs. It is likely that upon formal withdrawal of the UK from the EU, a EUTM will create a "cloned" identical UK trade mark for identical goods and services. However, as of April 2018 , negotiations on this are at an early stage.   **3-012**

STRUCTURE OF THIS CHAPTER

The structure of this chapter is as follows: **3-013**

(i)   A review of the international treaties including the Paris Convention, TRIPS (as they relate to trade marks), Madrid Agreement, Madrid Protocol and Trade Mark Registration Agreement.
(ii)   EU law of trade marks and a detailed examination of the substantive law of the TMD and EUTMR including the practice and procedure for applying for, revoking and seeking declarations of invalidity of EUTMs.
(iii)   Geographical Indications of Origin.
(iv)   The EEA Treaty.

INTERNATIONAL TREATIES

The Paris Convention for the Protection of Industrial Property was the result of the first international effort to standardise and simplify the protection of IPRs in Member States. It was concluded in Paris in 1883 and has been amended several times since. Its last amendment was in Stockholm in 1967.[11] Since then, the Agreement on Trade Related Aspects of IPRs (TRIPS) was concluded on 15 April 1994. This agreement binds all members of the WTO[12] and provides for minimum standards of protection for various IPRs in all contracting states. In relation to trade marks, TRIPS requires that each contracting state complies with the substantive obligations of the Paris Convention and provides a number of additional obligations over and above the protection required under the Paris Convention. In the field of procedural law, the Madrid Agreement and Protocol have provided a useful centralised procedure for applying for trade marks in many countries. These international agreements are now discussed in more detail.   **3-014**

Paris Convention

All European countries are contracting states of the Paris Convention.[13] Its fundamental principle is that contracting states are not allowed to discriminate between their nationals and nationals of other contracting states.[14] Thus, nationals of contracting states enjoy the same rights, advantages and protection as nationals of any other contracting state of the Convention.   **3-015**

The Paris Convention provides that the conditions for the filing and registration   **3-016**

---

[11]   Although that version was amended in minor ways in 1979.
[12]   World Trade Organization.
[13]   See *http://www.wipo.int* [Accessed 18 August 2017].
[14]   art.2.

of trade marks are determined by national laws.[15] It is thus concerned with the harmonisation of substantive and not procedural trade mark law. In relation to trade marks, the Convention makes the following provisions:

(a) Once a trade mark application has been filed in a contracting state, the applicant has a period of six months in which to file corresponding applications in other Member States without losing any rights. In effect, the subsequent filings are given a priority date of the first filing. This protects the applicant against third party rights acquired after the first filing but before subsequent convention filings.[16]

(b) An application for the registration of a mark filed by a national of a contracting state may not be refused nor its registration invalidated on the ground that filing or registration has not been effected in the country of origin.[17]

(c) Goods infringing a registered trade mark can be seized on importation.[18]

(d) A registered trade mark may only be cancelled after a reasonable period because of non-use of the mark and only if the person concerned cannot justify their inaction.[19]

(e) Use of a trade mark in a form differing in elements but which does not alter the distinctive character of the mark does not invalidate or diminish the protection granted by the mark.[20]

(f) Concurrent use of the same mark on identical or similar goods by industrial or commercial establishments considered as co-proprietors of the mark under domestic law may not prevent registration nor diminish the protection of the mark, provided that such use does not result in misleading the public and is not contrary to public interest.[21]

(g) No indication of the registered mark is required on the goods.[22]

(h) Marks which are "well known". These are protected by art.6*bis*. This provision is of considerable importance, as many countries have specifically provided in their trade mark legislation for protection for marks which are "well known" within the meaning of art.6*bis*. This Article states that the owners of a well-known mark are entitled to prevent the registration of a registered mark or the use of a trade mark which:

> "constitutes a reproduction, an imitation, or a translation, liable to create confusion, of a mark considered by the competent authority of the country of registration or use to be well known in that country as being already the mark of a person entitled to the benefits of this Convention and used for identical or similar goods. These provisions shall also apply when the essential part of the mark constitutes a reproduction of any such well known mark or an imitation liable to create confusion there with."

---

[15] art.6(1).

[16] art.4.

[17] art.6(2). "Country of origin" is defined as the country of the Union where the applicant has a real and effective industrial or commercial establishment, or, if they have no such establishment within the Union, the country of the Union of their domicile, or, if they have no domicile within the Union but they are a national of a country of the Union, the country of which they are a national—art.6*quinquies* (2).

[18] art.9.

[19] art.5(c)(1).

[20] art.5(c)(2).

[21] art.5(c)(3).

[22] art.5(c) (d).

The Paris Convention provides no assistance as to when a mark is well known. However, the following factors will be important in establishing that a mark is well known: degree of recognition of the mark, the extent to which the mark is used and the duration of use; the extent and duration of advertising and publicity accorded to the mark; the geographical extent of the above factors; the degree of inherent or acquired distinctiveness of the mark; the degree of exclusivity of the mark and the nature and extent of use of the same or similar marks by third parties; the nature of the goods or services and the channels of trade for the goods or services which bear the mark; and the degree to which the reputation of the mark symbolises quality goods and the extent of the commercial value attributed to the mark.[23] Further factors which, it has been suggested, should be taken into account by WIPO, are the record of successful enforcement of rights in the mark, the extent to which the mark is recognised as well known by competent authorities, and the value associated with the mark.[24] It should be noted that under art.16(2) of TRIPS, which concerns the ambit of art.6bis, members of the WTO must take account of the knowledge of the mark in the relevant sector of the public, including knowledge in the Member State concerned, which has been obtained as a result of the promotion of the trade mark.[25]

The protection afforded to marks which are well known is primarily for the purpose of jurisdictions which do not otherwise afford protection to unregistered marks. Two issues arise: (i) Is it necessary that the alleged well known mark has been used in the country for which protection is sought? (ii) Must the mark be well known in the country for which protection is sought?

On the first issue, in countries, such as the United Kingdom, where considerable protection is afforded to rights in an unregistered mark and, in particular, rights to oppose the registration of a mark where a person had priorly used the same or similar mark, art.6bis is of less importance. However, the critical difference between such common law protection and the protection afforded under art.6bis is that common law protection is generally based on the law of passing off, which requires use of the mark in the jurisdiction so as to give rise to goodwill in the mark.[26] In contrast, there is no requirement of goodwill under art.6bis. Thus, there is a strong body of opinion to support the position that a well-known mark need not actually have been used in the jurisdiction in which protection is sought and WIPO has recommended that such should not be a necessary condition for a well-known mark to be recognised in that jurisdiction.[27] Thus, in the UK,

---

[23] F. Mostert, *Famous and Well Known Marks—An International Analysis* (London: Butterworths, 1997), pp.11–17.

[24] WIPO Memorandum. *Joint Recommendation Concerning Provisions on the Protection of well known Marks* adopted by the Assembly of Paris Union and the General Assembly of WIPO at the 34th Series of Meetings of the Assemblies of the Member States of WIPO (20-29 September 1999), art.2.

[25] See para.3-029.

[26] The law of passing off in the UK is based upon the notion that it is a: "remedy for the invasion of a right of property not in the mark, name or get-up improperly used, but in the business or goodwill likely to be injured by the misrepresentation made by passing off one person's goods as the goods of another". per Lord Diplock in *Star Industrial Co Ltd v Yap Kwee Kor* [1976] F.S.R. 256 citing Lord Parker in *Spalding v Gamage* [1915] 32 R.P.C. 273.

[27] e.g. art.2 of the WIPO Memorandum, *Joint Recommendation concerning Provisions on the Protec-*

the protection afforded to marks which are well known within the meaning of art.6*bis* is expressly stated not to be dependent on the existence of goodwill in the mark in the UK.[28] However, it should be noted that at the 1958 Lisbon Revision Conference of the Paris Convention, a proposal that well-known marks should be protected without any requirement of use in the country in which protection was sought was defeated.[29]

On the second issue, there is a strong body of opinion and law that the mark must be well known in the country in which protection is sought in order for it to enjoy the benefit of art.6*bis*.[30] Thus, the fact that a mark is well known in the US but not in Europe will be of little assistance to an action under art.6*bis* in Europe. WIPO has recommended that it should be an irrelevant factor in determining whether a mark is protected by art.6*bis*, that it is also well known outside of the territory where the owner wishes to rely upon it but has said that Member States may require that the mark be well known in one or more jurisdictions other than the Member State concerned.[31]

The scope of protection afforded by a mark which is entitled to protection under art.6*bis* is to prevent the use or registration of marks that are confusingly similar which have been or are being used on the same or identical goods to those for which the well-known mark has been used. It will be noted that protection is not afforded to marks which are well known for services. This is a serious omission. However, in relation to WTO countries, art.16(2) of TRIPS extends protection for art.6*bis* marks which are well known for services. Indeed, art.16(3) of TRIPS extends protection for art.6*bis* marks to dissimilar goods or services where:

> "use of the offending mark would indicate a connection between the marks and such would be likely to damage the interests of the proprietor of the well-known mark."

The effect of this provision is discussed later in this chapter.[32]

Finally, it should be noted that there currently exists a Joint Recommendation in relation to well-known marks which proposes to extend their protection against "conflicting marks, business identifiers and domain names".[33] This proposes that protection be extended to use of the mark *irrespective of the goods and/or services for which a mark is used* which is the subject of an application for registration or is registered where at least *one* of the following conditions is fulfilled:

---

tion of well known Marks (see fn.24).

[28] Trade Marks Act 1994 s.56(1). A mark will not enjoy goodwill in a country unless there has been use on the market of that mark in a country.

[29] D. Gervais, *The TRIPS Agreement: Drafting History and Analysis*, 4th edn (London: Sweet & Maxwell, 2012).

[30] F. Mostert, *Famous and Well Known Marks—An International Analysis* (London: Butterworths, 1997), p.25. In the UK, it is a requirement that the mark be well known in the UK for protection to be afforded to the mark as a well known mark under art.6*bis*.

[31] art.2(3)(ii) of the WIPO Memorandum, Joint Recommendation concerning Provisions on the Protection of well-known Marks.

[32] See para.3-031.

[33] art.4(1)(b) of the *WIPO Memorandum, Joint Recommendation Concerning Provisions on the Protection of well known Marks*.

(i)   the use of that mark would indicate a connection between the goods and/or services for which the mark is used and the owner of the well-known mark and would be likely to damage their interests;

(ii)   the use of that mark is likely to impair or dilute in an unfair manner the distinctive character of the well-known mark; and

(iii)   the use of that mark would take unfair advantage of the distinctive character of the well-known mark.

It should be noted that the first condition is similar to art.16(3) TRIPS. The latter two conditions (in particular, taking unfair advantage or impairing the distinctive character of the mark) are very similar to provisions found in the TMD and EUTMR and have been the subject of considerable judicial discussion.[34]

Similar provisions are provided in relation to business identifiers. In relation to domain names which are similar or identical to a well-known mark, it is recommended that protection be afforded against domain names which have been registered in bad faith. Most domain name providers have a dispute resolution mechanism which will prevent the registration of domain names by third parties where the domain name is the same or similar to a well-known mark, the application was made in bad faith, and the applicant has no legitimate interest or rights in the domain name.[35]

(i)   Heraldic symbols, flats, armorial bearings, state emblems, etc. are not registrable.[36]

(j)   A trade mark registered in the country of origin of an applicant must be accepted for filing and registration "as is" in other Member States unless:

    (i)   it infringes third party rights;

    (ii)   it is devoid of distinctive character or consists exclusively of signs or indications which may serve, in trade, to designate the kind, quality, quantity, intended purpose, value, place of origin of the goods, or the time of production, or have become customary in the current language or in the bona fide and established practices of the trade of the country where protection is claimed; or

    (iii)   it is contrary to morality or public order or is liable to deceive the public.[37]

This provision is known as the *telle quelle* principle. In brief, it requires a Paris Union Country B to accept an application to register a mark if the home Country A accepted the same application. It does not work in reverse. If home Country A refused the application, such does not mean that Country B must refuse the application.[38] There is thus a curious asymmetry about it. It is a civil law concept which is not well known in Anglo-Saxon jurisdictions. The *telle quelle* principle plays no part in EU jurisprudence. Indeed, in *Füllkörper*,[39] the German Federal Court held that *telle quelle*

---

[34] See para.3-352.

[35] e.g. see *ICANN's Dispute Resolution Policy*. ICANN governs disputes for a number of top level domain names such as ".com". See *http://www.icann.org/en/help/dndr/udrp/policy* [Accessed 18 August 2017].

[36] art.6*ter*.

[37] art.6*quinquies*.

[38] See art.6(2).

[39] *Füllkörper* [1997] E.T.M.R. 431 (Bundespatentgericht).

registration is not available if the subject-matter of the registration is not recognised in the country of subsequent application.

In a WTO Panel Adjudication, which concerned the compliance of a provision of US law with the *telle quelle* principle, the Appellate Body concluded that art.6*quinquies* only applied to the "form" of the trade mark and not other matters such as ownership.[40]

(k) Service marks are to be protected.[41]

(l) Collective marks are to be protected.[42]

(m) Trade names are to be protected.[43]

(n) Contracting states are free to determine the conditions for filing and registration of trade marks.[44]

In addition, various provisions are made in the field of unfair competition.[45]

3-017   The Paris Convention is merely an international convention. In most contracting states, an international convention has no force of law until enacted in the appropriate way into domestic legislation. Thus, whilst all European countries have acceded to the Paris Convention (as amended), this does not mean that all its requirements have been made part of each country's domestic law. For instance, under English law, ratification of an international convention has no effect until it has been implemented by national legislation. Even in countries where an international convention forms part of domestic laws upon ratification, (as in France, Italy and Germany) the interpretation of such international law will differ. What is clear is that the Paris Convention laid down the cornerstone for harmonisation of trade mark law and has played an invaluable part over the last 100 years in enabling the standardisation of trade mark law in the world and preventing discrimination between nationals of different nations.

TRIPS

3-018   The WTO Agreement on Trade Related Intellectual Property matters (TRIPS) has been discussed in the introductory chapter of this book.[46] It makes a number of provisions in the field of trade marks. As discussed in the Introduction, the following are *minimum* requirements. Member States are free to provide more extensive protection.[47]

Registrability

3-019   Article 15 of TRIPS states the following:

"1.   Any sign, or any combination of signs, capable of distinguishing the goods or services of one undertaking from those of other undertakings, shall be capable of constituting a trade mark. Such signs, in particular words including personal names, letters, numerals, figurative elements and combinations of colours as well as any

---

[40]   Appellate Body Report. *Section 211 of the US Appropriations Act*, WT/DS176/AB/R 2 January 2002, (WTO), para.147.

[41]   art.6*sexies*.

[42]   art.7*bis*.

[43]   art.8.

[44]   art.6(1).

[45]   art.10*bis*. Discussed at para.7-259.

[46]   See para.1-167.

[47]   TRIPS art.1.

combination of such signs, must be eligible for registration as trade marks. Where signs are not inherently capable of distinguishing the relevant goods or services, Members may make registrability dependent upon distinctiveness acquired through use. Members may also require, as a condition of registration, that signs be visually perceptible.

2.   Paragraph 1 shall not be understood to prevent a Member from denying registration of a trade mark on other grounds, provided that they do not derogate from the provisions of the Paris Convention (1967).

3.   Members may make registrability depend on use. However, actual use of a trade mark shall not be a condition for filing an application for registration. An application shall not be refused solely on the ground that *intended* use has not taken place before the expiry of a period of three years from the date of application.

4.   The nature of the goods or services to which a trade mark is to be applied shall in no case form an obstacle to registration of the trade mark.

5.   Members shall publish each trade mark either before it is registered or promptly after it is registered and shall afford a reasonable opportunity for petitions to cancel the registration. In addition, Members may afford an opportunity for the registration of a trade mark to be opposed". [Emphasis supplied.]

Article 15 has a number of important elements to it. These can be described as: **3-020**

(1)   What signs can be a trade mark?
(2)   On what grounds can Member States refuse the registration of a trade mark?
(3)   What requirements regarding use or intention to use a trade mark can Member States impose on parties seeking registration of a mark?
(4)   What goods or services can a mark be registered for?
(5)   What procedural conditions must be satisfied prior to the registration of a mark?

What signs can be a trade mark?

Article 15 defines a trade mark as being any sign or combination of signs that is   **3-021** capable of distinguishing the goods of one undertaking from another. This definition of a trade mark is not found in WIPO-administered agreements. The focus is on the *capability* of a sign to distinguish and not whether it in fact does.[48] Thus, some descriptive signs may have an ability to distinguish but that ability will only be realised after use. In such cases, without use, the marks can be considered "immature" and must be used in the market in order to develop distinctive character in the eyes of the relevant public. Thus, a sign may possess distinctive character:

"if and when it is endowed by nature and/or nurture with the capacity to communicate the facts that the goods or services with reference to which it is used recurrently are those of one and the same undertakings".[49]

From a linguistic viewpoint, care must be exercised when considering the word   **3-022** "inherently" in the context of "not inherently capable of distinguishing the relevant goods or services". This is because "inherently" can be considered to mean marks which are incapable of distinguishing, even after considerable use. In the context of art.15, it clearly means marks which have the capability to distinguish but have

---

[48]   E.K. Meltzer, "TRIPS and Trade marks, or GATT, Got Your Tongue" [1993] 83 *The Trade Mark Reporter* 18 at 24.

[49]   See *AD2000 TM* [1997] R.P.C. 168 (Appointed Person, England) where the tribunal was concerned with analogous provisions in the TMD.

not been used sufficiently to realise that capability. It should be noted that under the Paris Convention, which art.15(2) expressly permits Member States to rely upon, marks can be refused registration if they are devoid of distinctive character or consist exclusively of signs or indications which may serve in trade to indicate a characteristic of the goods or services.[50] These provisions are found in the TMD and EUTMR.

3-023   Apart from the issue of distinctiveness and the requirement that signs have the ability to distinguish, art.15 is concerned with the issue of what type of signs can be trade marks. It mentions a number of things, such as letters, names, numerals, etc. that are eligible for registration as trade marks. However, it is clear from the fact that Member States *may* require as a condition of registration that the signs be visually perceptible, that art.15 envisages that non-visually perceptible signs can be registered. Thus, olfactory and sound signs would be capable of being registered. On a separate note, the Appellate Body of WTO has held that trade names are protected under TRIPS.[51]

On what other grounds can a trade mark be refused registration?

3-024   Article 15(1) is concerned with the criterion of distinctiveness of a trade mark as a condition for registrability. Article 15(2) permits Member States to deny registration of a mark on other grounds provided that "they do not derogate" from the provisions of Paris Convention. In the *Appellate Body Report on s.211 of the US Appropriations Act*, the Appellate Body of WTO had to consider whether Art.15 in the context of US legislation intended to disapply trade mark law to certain trade marks and trade names that were appropriated by the Cuban Government in or after 1959. In that context, the Appellate Body found that art.15 did not prohibit laws of Member States which would prevent the registration of a trade mark on grounds not mentioned in the Paris Convention provided that such grounds were not *inconsistent* with the grounds mentioned in the Paris Convention.[52] Thus, refusal of registration on the grounds of ownership was permissible even though not mentioned in art.15(1) TRIPS as art.15(1) was not concerned with ownership and the grounds for refusal in Paris Convention were not concerned with ownership. Such fell within art.6(1) of the Paris Convention which permitted Member States to determine the conditions of filing and registration.[53]

Requirements relating to use of a trade mark prior to registration?

3-025   Article 15(3) permits Member States to make registrability depend on use, but that actual use of a mark is not a condition for filing an application. This might be taken to mean that a Member State may provide that a trade mark has been used between filing and registration before it can be put on the register. However, the last sentence of art.15(3) makes it clear that an application cannot be refused solely on the ground that *intended* use has not taken place in a period expiring three years after the date of application. This qualifies the first sentence of art.15(3) in an

---

[50]   art.5*quinquies*(B).
[51]   Appellate Body Decision DS176—*Section 211 Omnibus Appropriations Act of 1998*. The primary reasoning was because art.8 of the Paris Convention which protects trade names is explicitly incorporated into art.2.1 of the TRIPS Agreement.
[52]   paras 153-156, 177
[53]   para.177.

important way. Because the application process, from filing to grant of registration, will normally take less than three years after the date of filing, it clearly demonstrates that Member States cannot require actual use of a mark between the date of filing and the date of registration. This neatly fits with art.19 of TRIPS, discussed below, which permits the revocation of a registered trade mark where there has been an uninterrupted period of three years of non-use. However, if a mark need not be used at the date of filing and Member States cannot require use of a mark between the date of application and registration, what is meant by the first sentence of art.15(3)—"Members may make registrability depend on use"? It is suggested that it means that a Member State may make registrability depend on actual use as of the date of application or an *intention* to use. This would explain the reference in the last sentence of art.15(3) to *intended* use. Moreover, other international instruments permit Member States to require a declaration of intention to use.[54] Thus, if an applicant has an intention to use a mark but has not done so within the first three years following the date of filing, a mark may not be refused registration. However, if an applicant does not intend to use the mark, then a Member State may refuse registration. However, this ill fits with the Paris Convention, which does not expressly permit a state to refuse registration based upon non-use (save in so far as such is relevant to the acquisition of distinctive character) or a lack of intention to use.[55] In brief, the Paris Convention does not expressly permit *registrability* (cf. the ability to revoke a registered mark) to depend on use (whether actual use or an intention to use) whereas TRIPS does.

The alternative interpretation of the first sentence of art.15(3) is that "registrability" is not intended to refer to the conditions of *grant* of registration but merely the *maintenance* of a registration once three years have expired from the date of application. However, it is not thought that this is correct. "Registrability" is a neologism of the "ability to register" which clearly indicates the process of applying and registering for a mark. Secondly, it is art.19 rather than art.15(3) which is concerned with the right of a person to revoke a mark after three years of uninterrupted non-use. Thirdly, in general, the right to revoke a mark for non-use will date from the date of registration and not the date of application.   **3-026**

What goods or services can a trade mark be registered for?

Article 15(4) makes it clear that trade mark protection is available for both services and goods, and must not depend on the nature of those goods or services. Thus, it has been said that the principle underlying this provision (and its equivalent in the Paris Convention, namely art.7) is that protection should not depend on whether the goods or services can legally be sold or provided within a country, e.g. where a pharmaceutical product has not yet received regulatory approval.[56]   **3-027**

Procedural requirements

Article 15(5) requires that each trade mark be published either before registration or promptly thereafter. Generally, Member States publish applications so that third parties may oppose such applications. Thus, the Office of Harmonisation for   **3-028**

---

[54] Common Regulations under the Madrid Agreement and Protocol r.7(2); Trade Mark Law Treaty art.3(1)(a)(xvii).
[55] art.6*quinquies*(2).
[56] D. Gervais, *The TRIPS Agreement*, 4th edn (London: Sweet & Maxwell, 2012), para.2.226.

the Internal Market (EUIPO) publishes EUTM applications. Publication of applications is required under art.3(4) of the Madrid Agreement and the Protocol.

Rights conferred by a mark

3-029   Article 16 of TRIPS states the following:

"1.   The owner of a registered trade mark shall have the exclusive right to prevent all third parties not having the owner's consent from using in the course of trade identical or similar signs for goods or services which are identical or similar to those in respect of which the trade mark is registered where such use would result in a likelihood of confusion. In case of the use of an identical sign for identical goods or services, a likelihood of confusion shall be presumed. The rights described above shall not prejudice any existing prior rights, nor shall they affect the possibility of Members making rights available on the basis of use.

2.   Article 6*bis* of the Paris Convention (1967) shall apply, mutatis mutandis, to services. In determining whether a trade mark is well known, Members shall take account of the knowledge of the trade mark in the relevant sector of the public, including knowledge in the Member concerned which has been obtained as a result of the promotion of the trade mark.

3.   Article 6*bis* of the Paris Convention (1967) shall apply, mutatis mutandis, to goods or services which are not similar to those in respect of which a trade mark is registered, provided that use of that trade mark in relation to those goods or services would indicate a connection between those goods or services and the owner of the registered trade mark and provided that the interests of the owner of the registered trade mark are likely to be damaged by such use."

3-030   Article 16(1) is self-explanatory. The last sentence makes it clear that a registered trade mark shall not prejudice any existing "prior rights". This should not be equated with "prior use". Indeed, the last sentence of art.16(1) makes it clear that rights are not to be equated with use. Prior use may give rise to rights but not necessarily always. Thus, under English law, the user of an unregistered mark will not have any rights in the mark per se. It must be shown that there exists sufficient reputation and goodwill in the trade mark to give rise to the ability to bring an action in passing off. As said above, it should be noted that TRIPS merely sets down a level of minimum of protection. More extensive protection may for example be provided, i.e. in relation to dissimilar goods. The CJEU has held that art.16(1) applies to trade names as well as to trade marks.[57]

Well-known marks

3-031   Article 16(2) and 16(3) seeks to extend the protection available to "well known" marks under art.6*bis* of the Paris Convention.[58] This is regardless of whether the "well known" mark has been registered. The Articles extend protection in two ways. First, the protection which is to be provided under art.6*bis* of the Paris Convention to well known trade marks is also given to service marks.[59] Secondly, in relation

---

[57]   See *Anheuser-Busch v Budějovický Budvar, národní podnik* (C-245/02) [2004] E.C.R. I-10989 at [85]. A trade name may also be a "prior right" within the meaning of art.16(1)—see [86]-[100].

[58]   See para.3-016.

[59]   art.16(2). Well known service marks are not protected under the Paris Convention—see para.3-016.

to well-known marks which are registered, protection for "well known" marks is extended to dissimilar goods and services.[60]

Article 16(2) sets out certain criteria for determining whether a mark is well **3-032** known or not within the meaning of art.6*bis*. In this regard, the test of "well known" under art.16(2) appears broader and the threshold lower than that under art.6*bis*. In particular, the wording of the last sentence of art.16(2) suggests that it is not necessary that goods have been sold or services supplied under the mark in the Member State. If the mark is well known by reason of promotion of the mark, such is sufficient. Indeed, the last sentence does not say that such promotion must have occurred in the Member State concerned. Thus, it would appear that there is no requirement in art.16(2) that the mark has been used at all (whether in relation to sales or marketing of products or services) in the Member State for which protection is sought. Thus, a court could take into account "spillover" advertising whereby extensive promotion in a number of countries will be deemed to have spilled over into other countries.[61]

Article 16(2) stipulates that "account shall be taken of the knowledge of the trade **3-033** mark in the relevant sector of the public". This means that a mark need not be known to the public at large but merely those who purchase relevant goods or services. This will have the effect of increasing the number of marks that are "well known". There may be marks which are very well known but only in a technical sector.[62]

Article 16(3) extends protection for "well known" marks to dissimilar goods or **3-034** services where use of the offending mark would indicate a connection between the marks and such would be likely to damage the interests of the proprietor of the well-known mark. Somewhat strangely, art.16(3) requires that the well-known mark is registered (presumably in the country where protection is sought). This is strange, because art.6*bis* is intended to protect the interests of well-known unregistered marks. Thus, art.16(3) appears to require that the mark is well known *and* registered in the country where protection under art.16(3) is sought. This puts it in conflict with art.6*bis* and yet at the same time art.16(3) is intended to implement art.6 *bis*. However, as art.16(3) TRIPS merely imposes a minimum requirement for protection of trade marks, countries which are members of both TRIPS and the Paris Convention are free under TRIPS to give greater protection than that provided under art.16(2) to owners of well-known marks which are not registered in the state for which protection is sought.

The requirement that use of the mark on dissimilar goods or services "would **3-035** indicate a connection" is somewhat unclear as to the nature of that connection. Must it be a connection in the course of trade between the owner of the well-known mark and the user of the offending mark? In other words, must it be shown that the public is confused as to trade origin? Or is it sufficient merely to show that the public will perceive some type of connection, i.e. a conceptual connection? In this regard, it should be noted that art.10.2(c) TMD, as interpreted by the CJEU, which confers protection for a registered trade mark which possesses a reputation in relation to dis-

---

[60] art.16(3).
[61] F.W. Mostert, *Famous and Well Known Marks—An International Analysis* (London: Butterworths, 1997), pp.28–29.
[62] F.W. Mostert, *Famous and Well Known Marks—An International Analysis* (London: Butterworths, 1997), p.26. Mr Mostert gives the example of "PURDEY" for shotguns. In the field of shotgun cognoscenti, this is exceptionally well known but the majority of the general public is unlikely to be aware of it.

similar goods where another mark which takes unfair advantage of or causes detriment to the distinctive character or repute of the mark, does not require confusion as to trade origin. There is a lower requirement that the mark of which complaint is made establishes a "link" with the registered mark and such takes unfair advantage of or is detrimental to the distinctive character or repute of the mark.[63]

3-036   In the author's opinion, unlike art.10.2(c) TMD, the necessary connection under art.16(3) is a connection *as to trade origin*. The wording used in art.16(3) is "a connection between those goods or services and the owner of the registered trade mark" and is thus not concerned with conceptual association between *two marks* but a connection between the *underlying goods* of the potential defendant and the *registered proprietor* of the well-known mark. It is difficult to conceive of a relevant connection except a connection as to trade origin. It should be emphasised that as TRIPS is simply intended to provide for a level of minimum protection for trade marks, art.10.2(c) of the TMD is not in conflict with this interpretation of art.16(3) of TRIPS as art.10.2(c) confers broader protection to trade marks with a reputation than art.16(3) does.[64]

3-037   Assuming that the requirement is that a connection in a course of trade be shown, then this will generally be easier to make out where the mark is well known and inherently distinctive. Thus, a member of the public who purchases a "Daimler-Benz" shoelace will probably assume some connection with Daimler-Benz cars, even if "Daimler-Benz" has never ventured into such a field. However, the purchaser of an "Ever Ready" condom may not assume such a connection, despite the fact that the mark "Ever Ready" is well known for batteries.[65] In relation to the requirement that there must be shown to be a likelihood of damage, this should not be too difficult to satisfy once it has been established that the public perceive a connection in trade between the goods bearing the offending mark and the registered proprietor of the "well known" mark. Damage could be done in a number of ways, including the possibility of injury to reputation, liability to law suits, damage to ability to merchandise marks, etc.[66]

Exceptions

3-038   Article 17 of TRIPS provides that:

"Members may provide limited exceptions to the rights conferred by a trade mark, such as fair use of descriptive terms, provided that such exceptions take account of the legitimate interests of the owner of the trade mark and of their parties."

3-039   This largely speaks for itself. Fair use of descriptive terms would include indications for the purpose of mere identification or information, such as bona fide use

---

[63] See para.3-352.
[64] TRIPS art.1.
[65] See *OASIS TM* [1998] R.P.C. 631, Trade Marks Registry, England where under an opposition based on s.5(3) of the Trade Mark Act 1994 (art.4(4)(a) of the TMD) it was held unlikely that the public would be confused into believing there to be a connection in the course of trade because of the fact that the mark "EVER READY" had a descriptive element.
[66] See, in UK, the passing off case of *Ewing v Buttercup* [1917] 2 Ch.1 per judgment of Warrington LJ. ("To induce the belief that my business is a branch of another man's business may do that other man damage in various ways. The quality of goods I sell, the kind of business I do, the credit or otherwise which I enjoy are all things which may injure the other man who is assumed wrongly to be associated with me.").

of a person's name, address or geographical name, etc.[67] Thus, this provision provides protection for third parties who are making use of a prima facie descriptive trade mark which has become distinctive by use in a descriptive manner. The CJEU has said the exceptions provided for in art.17 of the TRIPS Agreement are intended, inter alia, to enable a third party to use a sign which is identical or similar to a trade mark to indicate their trade name, provided that such use is in accordance with honest practices in industrial or commercial matters.[68]

It is of note that this provision does not apply merely to registered trade marks. It equally applies to unregistered trade marks.

3-040

Term of protection

Article 18 provides that:

3-041

"Initial registration, and each renewal of registration, of a trade mark shall be for a term of no less than seven years. The registration of a trade mark shall be renewable indefinitely."

This provision should be contrasted with the Madrid Protocol and the Trade Mark Law Treaty, which sets the initial period of protection at 10 years.

3-042

Requirements of use

Article 19 provides as follows:

3-043

"1.   If use is required to maintain a registration, the registration may be cancelled only after an uninterrupted period of at least three years of non-use, unless valid reasons based on the existence of obstacles to such use are shown by the trade mark owner. Circumstances arising independently of the will of the owner of the trade mark which constitute an obstacle to the use of the trade mark, such as import restrictions on or other government requirements for goods or services protected by the trade mark, shall be recognized as valid reasons for non-use.

2.   When subject to control of its owner, use of a trade mark by another person shall be recognized as use of the trade mark for the purpose of maintaining the registration."

This provision should be contrasted with art.5(c)(1) of the Paris Convention, which merely allows cancellation after a "reasonable period".[69] Valid reasons for non-use will only exist where they are outside the control of the owner of the trade mark. Thus, the need to obtain pharmaceutical approval may be considered an appropriate reason.

3-044

Article 19(2) is of interest because often use of a trade mark will be by a licensee of the registered proprietor. It should be noted that the requirement is that the use of a trade mark be "subject to the control of its owner". It is arguable that this would not include a bare licence where the licensee has been permitted to use the mark in any manner that they choose by the licensor. In such circumstances, the use of the mark is not under the control of the licensor. However, it is arguable that any licence which can be revoked or terminated does give the licensor *ultimate* control

3-045

---

[67]   See WIPO's *Model Law on Trade Marks* and D. Gervais, *The TRIPS Agreement Drafting History and Analysis*, 4th edn (London: Sweet & Maxwell, 2012), para.2.249.

[68]   *Anheuser-Busch Inc. v Budějovický Budvar, národní podnik* (C-245/02) [2004] E.C.R. I-10989 at [82] and [85].

[69]   See para.3-016.

over the use of the mark as it permits the licensor to revoke the licence if they are unhappy with the use of the mark by the licensee. This provision should be contrasted with art.16(6) of the TMD, which stipulates that use of the trade mark with the *consent* of the proprietor shall be deemed to be use by the proprietor. Thus, in the TMD, *consent* is the important criterion in the TMD whereas *control* is the important criterion in TRIPS. These are clearly different criteria.[70]

Unjustified requirements

3-046   Article 20 provides that:

> "The use of a trade mark in the course of trade shall not be unjustifiably encumbered by special requirements, such as use with another trade mark, use in a special form or use in a manner detrimental to its capability to distinguish the goods or services of one undertaking from those of other undertakings. This will not preclude a requirement prescribing the use of the trade mark identifying the undertaking producing the goods or services along with, but without linking it to, the trade mark distinguishing the specific goods or services in question of that undertaking."

3-047   This is self-explanatory. It was the subject of discussion in *Panel Report-Indonesian Autos*,[71] a decision of the WTO Panel. In that case, it was argued by the US that certain Indonesian legislation intended to penalise foreign car imports and foster domestic production was inter alia contrary to art.20 as it effectively amounted to an encumbrance on use. The Panel held that such legislation which was plainly intended to restrict sales of foreign cars amounted to the imposition of "special requirements" on the use of foreign (US) trade marks.

Licensing and assignment

3-048   Article 21 provides that:

> "Members may determine conditions on the licensing and assignment of trade marks, it being understood that the compulsory licensing of trade marks shall not be permitted and that the owner of a registered trade mark shall have the right to assign the trade mark with or without the transfer of the business to which the trade mark belongs."

3-049   This provision goes somewhat further than art.6 *quater* (1) of the Paris Convention, which implicitly allow contracting states to the Paris Convention to restrict the right of owners to assign trade marks without the underlying business. It has been said by certain commentators that it is noticeable that the expression "goodwill" has not been used in addition to "business" and that such must mean that countries can restrict the right of owners to assign trade marks without the goodwill.[72] Thus it has been said that a distinction should be drawn between the business which may be defined as the industrial or commercial establishment, i.e. the material basis of the activities, and the specific goodwill which can be described as the "customer

---

[70]   art.16(6) is discussed in the context of revocation for non-use—see para.3-674.
[71]   WTO Panel Report. Indonesia—Certain Measures Affecting the Automobile Industry, WT/DS54, 55, 59, 64R at 14.276–14.279 (see *http://www.worldtradelaw.net/reports/wtopanelsfull/indonesia-autos(panel)(full).pdf* [Accessed 18 August 2017]).
[72]   D. Gervais, *The TRIPS Agreement, Drafting History and Analysis*, 4th edn (London: Sweet & Maxwell, 2012).

base".[73] This view is somewhat supported by the draft of 23 July 1990, which included various proposals which distinguished between "goodwill" and the "undertaking". However, it is difficult to make a practical distinction between "the business *to which the trade mark belongs*" and the "goodwill" of the mark which has been said to represent "the attractive force that brings in custom".[74] Indeed, it has been said in an English case concerning the meaning of goodwill that:

"goodwill regarded as property has no meaning except in connection with some trade, business or calling. In that connection, I understand the word to include whatever adds value to a business by reason of situation, name and reputation, connection, introduction to old customers, and agreed absence from competition, or any of these things, and there may be others which do not occur to me. In this wide sense, goodwill is inseparable from the business to which it adds value, and in my opinion, exists where the business is carried on."[75]

In the author's opinion, this provision permits the bare assignment of a trade mark without any underlying goodwill or business.   **3-050**

Care must be applied in interpreting the provision that compulsory licensing is prohibited. Such should not be equated with prohibiting any general defence to the enforcement of trade mark rights.[76] However, it will be rare that such is the case as trade marks do not confer market power by themselves.   **3-051**

The Madrid System

Introduction

Under art.19 of the Paris Convention, Member States of the Paris Union are given the right to enter into treaties for the protection of IPRs provided that such does not contravene provisions of the Paris Convention itself. In 1891, shortly after the Paris Convention, the Madrid Arrangement for the International Registration of Marks ("the Madrid Agreement") was signed and ratified by four countries. The fundamental object of this Convention was to provide an international procedure for applicants who wished to acquire registered trade marks in countries that had ratified the Madrid Agreement. As such, it was essentially a procedural convention, as opposed to the Paris Convention, which sought to harmonise the substantive trade mark law of Member States. Since 1891, the number of Member States that have ratified the Madrid Agreement has increased considerably and the Madrid Agreement itself has been revised several times, the last three revisions being the 1957 Nice Revision and the Stockholm Revisions of 1967 and 1979. All states party to the Madrid Agreement are either subject to the Nice or the Stockholm Revisions. A single set of regulations governs the text of both revisions.   **3-052**

Some European countries have ratified the Madrid Agreement. However, its provisions were unacceptable to certain countries, including the UK, Denmark, Ireland and Greece in Europe and, elsewhere, the US, Australia and Japan. Accordingly, in the 1980s, and spurred on by the possibility of the EUTMR becoming a   **3-053**

---

[73] D. Gervais, *The TRIPS Agreement, Drafting History and Analysis*, 4th edn (London: Sweet & Maxwell, 2012) referring to G.H.C. Bodenhausen, *Guide to the Application of the Paris Convention for the Protection of Industrial Property* (Geneva: WIPO, 1968).

[74] Lord Macnaghten in *Inland Revenue Commissioners v Muller & Co* [1901] A.C. 217 HL at 223.

[75] per Lord Lindley in *Muller* [1901] A.C. 217 HL at 225.

[76] See TRIPS art.8(2), 40, which allows for defences based on, e.g. abuse of IPRs.

serious rival to the Madrid Agreement, the governing body of the Madrid Agreement, WIPO, made efforts to draw up a Protocol (in effect, an alternative Convention) to the Madrid Agreement, which made important changes to it so that the system would prove acceptable to the above countries. Their efforts culminated in a Diplomatic Conference in June 1989 which resulted in the adoption of the Protocol Relating to the Madrid Agreement Concerning the International Registration of Marks ("the Madrid Protocol").

3-054   On 31 July 2015, Algeria acceded to the Madrid Protocol. It was the last of the members of the Madrid Agreement who had not acceded to the Madrid Protocol. As under the Madrid Agreement, the Madrid Protocol alone applies to countries which have ratified both the Madrid Agreement and the Protocol,[77] the Madrid Agreement is no longer relevant and can be considered a "dead" treaty. This is because future applicants can only accede to the Madrid Protocol. Accordingly, all international registrations are governed solely and exclusively by the Madrid Protocol. This is welcome news as such simplifies enormously the filing and management of international registrations. As a result, WIPO now calls it the "Madrid System" and this book will adopt the same terminology. However, for "Madrid System", read "Madrid Protocol".

3-055   The Madrid System is administered by the International Bureau of WIPO. The legislative governing body consists of delegates of countries who have accepted or ratified it.[78] As of August 2017, there were 99 members covering 115 countries which represent 80 per cent of world trade. This includes the EU.

Fundamentals of the Madrid System

3-056   The Madrid System is an international procedural treaty which allows an applicant to file efficiently and economically for trade mark protection in all or some of the countries governed by the Madrid System. The following are the fundamentals:

- The Madrid System may only be used by a natural or legal entity established or domiciled in a Madrid System Member State.
- Before making an international application under the Madrid System, the applicant must have applied for an identical trade mark ("the home filing") in a Member State ("country of origin"). It is not necessary that the application has led to registration before making the international application.
- An international application is filed with the intellectual property office of the country of origin "office of origin"). It must designate those states (which must be members of the Madrid System) where protection is sought ("designated states") although the Madrid System allows for designation of states after filing the international registration. It must be filed in French, Spanish or English. Although the mark must be identical to the home filing, it is not necessary that the designated goods or services are the same. However, they must not be broader than the designated goods or services in the home filing.
- The EU is a member of the Madrid System. Accordingly, an applicant may select EU as a designated state. Where the EU is appointed, an international registration in the EU will lead to a EUTM rather than a basket of national trade marks in the Member States of the EU.

---

[77]   art.9*sexies* (1)(a) Madrid Protocol.
[78]   arts 10, 11.

- The fees payable for the international application are a composite of a basic fee, a fee for each designated state and a fee for each class of goods or services in excess of three.
- The office of origin will forward the application to WIPO who will examine it to ensure that the application including requirements as to the representation of the mark, the designation and classification of goods and services and other administrative formalities have been complied with.
- If the formalities are met, it will be published in the WIPO gazette and it becomes an international registration.
- An international registration has an initial period of protection of 10 years. It can then be renewed for further 10-year periods upon the payment of renewal fees.
- The effective date of international registration is the date on which the international application was received (or is deemed to have been received if there are irregularities) by the office of origin.
- As of the date of international registration, subject to any refusal by the intellectual property office of a designated state (see below), the international registration is treated as a registered trade mark as if it was a mark applied for directly to the office of the designated state.
- WIPO keeps and maintains a central register of the international registration. Thus, changes to the names of owners and licences are notified to and recorded by WIPO. The owner of the international registration does not need to notify the intellectual property offices of designated states of such changes. Furthermore, renewal fees are paid to WIPO. All of this greatly simplifies the administrative tasks of an owner and thus has very considerable benefits.
- WIPO will notify each designated state of the international registration and that state will then have the right to refuse protection for the international registration. Such refusal will be based on the substantive trade mark law of the designated state. The Madrid System is a procedural treaty and does not harmonise the substantive law of its Member States.
- Generally, the time limit for notification of a refusal is one year or 18 months if the designated state has so notified WIPO of its right to an extended period. If opposition proceedings are brought against the international registration in the designated state, then the period of refusal will be longer.
- For a period of five years from the date of international registration, the validity of it is dependent on the home filing ("central attack"). If the office of origin cancels the registered home mark or refuses the home filing, then such behaviour leads to cancellation of the international registration. However, the period of five years may be extended if proceedings (including appeals) to cancel the registered mark or application are pending as of the end of the five-year period, and subsequently the home filing is cancelled (or refused, if it is an application). This dependency also applies if the owner of the home filing withdraws the application or surrenders the registration.
- Where an international mark is cancelled by reason of the "home" cancellation proceedings described in the previous bullet point, the Madrid System allows the owner of the cancelled international registration to "transform" its international registration into a basket of national marks or applications in the designated states. A transformation application must be made within

three months of the date of cancellation of the international registration. Such applications are treated as they were filed on the date of the original international registration and can make the same claim to priority as the international registration. The procedure for doing so is a matter for designated states and is not governed by the Madrid System.

For those who wish to know more or understand in greater detail the procedural requirements, WIPO publishes a number of excellent guides to the Madrid System.[79]

The Trademark Law Treaty

3-057   The Trade Mark Law Treaty is an international treaty which seeks to harmonise national procedural provisions. It came into force for its contracting states in 1994. Its aim was to approximate and streamline national and regional trademark registration procedures via itself and its implementing regulations. The great majority of its provisions concern the procedure before national trademark offices and govern three phases: application for registration, changes after registration, and renewal. It differs from the Madrid Agreement and the Protocol because it is not concerned with a centralised procedure for applying for trademarks in countries which are contracting states to Madrid Agreement or the Protocol. It is administered by WIPO. All European countries bar Bulgaria and Norway are signatories to it.

EU LAW

Introduction

3-058   The trade mark law of Member States of the European Union has been harmonised via the Trade Mark Directive ("TMD").[80] Furthermore, a European Union Trade Mark Regulation ("EUTMR") provides for a European Union Trade Mark ("EUTM") (formerly known as a Community Trade Mark) which has unitary effect throughout the EU.[81] This is administered by the European Union Intellectual Property Office ("EUIPO") (formerly known as the Office of Harmonisation of the Internal Market) in Alicante. The substantive law of the TMD is, in essence, the same as the EUTMR. Both the TMD and EUTMR are considered later in this chapter. Although some of the TMD's provisions are optional and do not oblige Member States to implement them, they have been implemented by most Member States. The consequence of the implementation of the TMD means that the trade mark laws of Member States are now essentially the same. The substantive rationale for and the legislative mechanism used for both the TMD and EUTMR was to assist in the attainment of a single market in the EU by removing discrepancies in Member States' laws. However, barriers to inter-state trade will still exist

---

[79]   See *http://www.wipo.int/madrid/en/* [Accessed 18 August 2017].

[80]   Dir.2015/2436 [2015] OJ L336/1 which replaced Dir.2008/95/EC [2008] OJ L299/25 which in turn replaced the original trade mark directive (EC Dir.89/104 [1989] OJ L40/1 which was amended by Council Decision 92/10/EC [1992] OJ L6/35 (this latter decision merely extended the date for implementation of the TMD to 31 December 1992). Directive 2015/2436 aligns its substantive law with that of Reg.2017/1001 for EUTMs.

[81]   EC Reg.2017/1001 [2017] OJ L154/1. This codifies the changes made by Reg.2015/2424 [2015] OJ L341/21 which amended Reg.207/2009 [2009] OJ L78/1. This latter regulation replaced the original Community Trade Mark Regulation—EC Reg.40/94 [2004] OJ L11/1.

because undertakings may not have registered national trade marks in all Member States whether by choice or because of third party prior rights in one or more Member States.

The current EUTMR is Regulation 2017/1001. This is a codified version of **3-059** Regulation 207/2009 which was substantially amended by Regulation 2015/2424 in a number of important ways discussed below. Some of the changes came into effect on 23 March 2016 and others came into effect on 1 October 2017. The current Trade Mark Directive ("TMD") is 2015/2436. In broad terms, this Directive amends the former Directive (2008/95) so that the changes to the substantive law of the EUTMR are reflected in national laws of trade marks. This requires Member States to amend their national trade mark laws fully by latest 15 January 2019. Therefore, until January 2019, there will be a discrepancy between the substantive trade mark law of Member States and those under the EUTMR.

Since the introduction of the original TMD and EUTMR, a very large body of **3-060** case law has developed on the interpretation of the provisions of the TMD and the EUTMR and their predecessors. This has been primarily generated by rulings on preliminary references given by the CJEU from courts of Member States. However, on issues concerning the registrability of trade marks, a considerable amount of the case law has also been generated by the General Court and CJEU in relation to appeals from EUIPO. On any analysis, this case law can be considered not only to have clarified provisions of the TMD and EUTMR but also to have provided a further layer of conditions that need to be satisfied (and in certain circumstances, regrettably created uncertainty rather than clarity). Thus, it is now clear in an identical marks/identical goods or services action in infringement proceedings that the mere fact that acts fall within the literal wording of the TMD or EUTMR is not sufficient for liability to be established. It is necessary to show that one or more functions of a trade mark have been adversely interfered with for an infringement action to succeed.[82] This has made legal analysis difficult. Indeed, it could be said that the case law of the CJEU and General Court in the field of trade marks has demonstrated the wisdom of another well-known law—the law of unintended consequences. Whilst in the author's view, there is much to commend the CJEU's and General Court's desire to interpret provisions of the TMD or EUTMR by reference to the underlying economic rationale and justification for trade marks, it is regrettable that the EU courts have instead of *interpreting* the wording of the TMD and EUTMR by reference to such factors, superimposed "standalone" conditions which must be complied with such as the necessity to demonstrate that one or more of the functions of a trade mark have been adversely affected or not. Such has undermined certainty in the application of the law. The *means* (the reference to the underlying functions of a mark to interpret trade mark legislation) has become the *end* (the need to show the functions of a mark have been adversely affected). Furthermore, in relation to some of the functions, e.g. the investment and advertising function, it is unclear why they are "functions" of a trade mark or what precisely is meant by a "function". It is easy to understand the essential/origin function of a mark as the purpose of trade marks is to allow consumers to differentiate products and services in the marketplace. Thus, use of trade marks is reserved to their owner to prevent confusion as to trade origin. Equally, the communication function

---

[82] See *Interflora Inc v Marks and Spencer Plc* (C-323/09) [2011] E.C.R. I-8625 at [34]; *Google France* (C-236/238/08) [2010] E.C.R. I-2417 at [79]; *Bergspechte* (C-278/08) [2010] E.C.R. I-2517 at [21]; *L'Oréal v Bellure NV* (C-487/07) [2009] E.C.R. I-5185 at [60] and *Portakabin Ltd v Primakabin* (C-558/08) [2010] E.C.R. I-6963 at [29].

concerns the image that a trade mark projects. As the image of a brand is very important in the context of marketing, it is important that third parties cannot jeopardise the psychological message of a brand reflected in its image. However, the advertising and investment function are difficult to understand as functions of a mark. Registration of a trade mark does not guarantee the right to advertise the mark. Indeed, registration of a mark does not actually guarantee the right to use it on goods or services (let alone advertise it or promote it) but merely the right to exclude others from using it.[83] Similarly, registration of a trade mark does not guarantee that any investment in the promotion and advertising of the mark will be successful. A mark may be destroyed by fair competition from other brands or ultimately, the underlying good or service be of poor quality and not sell well.

3-061   Before considering the TMD, the EUTMR and the associated case law, it is useful to consider the approach of EU law to trade marks prior to their implementation in the late 1980s.

3-062   In the early days of the TFEU (then known as the Treaty of Rome), the CJEU appeared to consider trade marks as not being worthy of particular protection. Thus, in *Sirena Srl v Eda Srl*,[84] the CJEU held that:

> "The exercise of trade mark rights is particularly liable to contribute to the division of markets and therefore to prejudice the free movement of goods between States which is essential for the Common Market. Trade mark rights are distinguished from other industrial and commercial property rights in so far as the object of the latter is often more important and worthy of greater protection than the object of the former."[85]

3-063   A similar lacklustre approach to trade marks was taken in *HAG I*,[86] where the CJEU held that trade marks were merely useful for indicating the trade origin of a product, but stated that other means should be used so as not to affect the free movement of goods.[87] Such derisory treatment of trade marks was eventually rectified in *HAG II*,[88] where Jacobs AG said:

> "The truth is that at least in economic terms, and perhaps also 'from the human point of view', trade marks are no less important, and no less deserving of protection, than any other form of intellectual property. They are in the words of one author, 'nothing more nor less than the fundament of most market-place competition'."[89]

3-064   The CJEU supported this view and said that:

> "With regard to trade mark rights, it should be observed that such rights constitute an essential element of the system of undistorted competition which the Treaty aims to establish and maintain. In such a system enterprises must be able to gain customers by the quality

---

83   It is often forgotten that generally use of a registered trade mark is no defence to infringement of another registered trade mark. *Celaya Emparanza y Galdos Internacional SA v Proyectos Integrales de Balizamientos SL* (C-488/10) ECLI:EU:C:2012:88 (later Community registered design no defence to action based on earlier registered Community design).

84   *Sirena Srl v Eda Srl* (40/70) [1971] E.C.R. 69; [1975] C.M.L.R. 1.

85   (40/70) [1971] E.C.R. 69; [1975] C.M.L.R. 1 at [7]. The CJEU followed Dutheille de Lamothe AG, who observed that the debt owed to the inventor of the name "Prep Good Morning" is certainly not of the same nature as that which humanity owes to the discoverer of penicillin.

86   *Van Zuylen v HAG (HAG I)* (192/73) [1974] E.C.R. 731; [1974] 2 C.M.L.R. 127.

87   (192/73) [1974] E.C.R. 731 at [13] and [14]. This case is discussed in detail at para.7-210.

88   (C-10/89) [1990] E.C.R. I-3711; [1990] 3 C.M.L.R. 571. This case is discussed in detail at para.7-214.

89   *HAG II*, at [17] citing from W. Cornish, *Intellectual Property: Patents, Copyright, Trade Marks and Allied Rights*, 2nd edn (London: Sweet & Maxwell, 1989), p.393.

of their products or services, which can be done only by virtue of the existence of distinctive signs permitting identification of those products and services. For a trade mark to be able to play this part, it must constitute a guarantee that all the products bearing it have been manufactured under the supervision of a single enterprise to which responsibility for their quality may be attributed."[90]

Thus, trade marks are not to be treated as lesser forms of intellectual property.[91]

Pre-TMD and EUTMR, along with other unharmonised rights, EU law was that **3-065** Member States were free to provide for protection of trade marks in a manner they saw fit. However, when considering the exercise of trade marks in relation to products which were imported from one Member State to another, such invoked consideration of arts 34–36 TFEU (previously arts 28–30 EC Treaty and arts 30–36 Treaty of Rome). These provisions only permitted restrictions on imports and exports between Member States where it was justified for the protection of intellectual property rights and provided such did not amount to a disguised restriction on trade between Member States or artificially partitioned the EU (or common market as it was then known). This led to the development of the doctrine of exhaustion of rights whereby a trade mark proprietor could not exercise their rights to prevent trade in the EU in products bearing their trade mark where such had been put on the market in the EU by the proprietor or with their consent.

In the course of determining the relationship between trade mark rights and arts **3-066** 34–36, the CJEU had to consider carefully matters of policy including the purpose of trade marks in order to determine whether the exercise of exclusive rights by a trade mark proprietor was justified in preventing parallel imports or not. This led the CJEU to consider the economic justification for trade marks and thus in the 1970s it developed two important doctrines in the field of trade marks: the "specific object"[92] of a trade mark and the "essential function" of a trade mark. Following the adoption of harmonising EU legislation in the field of trade marks, these doctrines developed in relation to arts 34–36 have continued to be recited and refined in interpreting EUTM law. This is not surprising as the legislative basis for the TMD and EUTMR was the need to have a functioning single internal market where quantitative restrictions between Member States were eliminated—the very aim of arts 34–36. These two doctrines have been discussed at the start of this chapter and are considered in more detail below. Furthermore, the doctrine of exhaustion of rights as developed by the CJEU in the 1970s is still of significant relevance in the context of the interpretation of art.7 of the TMD and art.13 of EUTMR which is concerned with exhaustion of trade mark rights, and which were intended to codify this jurisprudence.

The reader who wishes to have a full understanding of the development of the **3-067** case law by the CJEU regarding the interaction of IPRs and the free movement of goods provisions of the TFEU is invited to read the introduction to this chapter and then read paras 7-001 to 7-068 before proceeding.

In the following section, the various functions of a trade mark are considered. **3-068**

---

90 (C-10/89) [1990] 3 C.M.L.R. 571 at [13].
91 The rehabilitation of trade marks by the CJEU in *HAG II* [1990] 3 C.M.L.R. 171 as being essential in a market economy is discussed in R. Joliet, "Trade Mark Law and the Free Movement of Goods: The Overruling of the Judgment in HAG I" (1991) 2 I.I.C. 303, 311.
92 Sometimes referred to as "the specific subject-matter".

Functions of a Trade Mark

Guarantee of trade origin

3-069   In its jurisprudence on the interaction of trade marks rights and arts 34–36, the CJEU developed the concept of the "essential function" of a trade mark. The essential function of a trade mark is to guarantee the identity of the trade origin of the trade-marked product to the consumer or ultimate user. The concept of "essential function" (as distinct from its elder brother, the doctrine of "specific object") was first discussed by the CJEU in *Hoffmann La-Roche v Centrafarm* in the late 1970s.[93] This was a case concerning the repackaging of pharmaceuticals by parallel importers. The CJEU said in considering the relationship between trade mark rights and arts 34–36 that:

> "…regard must be had to the essential function of the trade mark, which is to guarantee the identity of the origin of the trade-marked product to the consumer or ultimate user, by enabling him without any possibility of confusion to distinguish that product from products which have another origin. This guarantee of origin means that the consumer or ultimate user can be certain that a trade-marked product which is sold to him has not been subject at a previous stage of marketing to interference by a third person, without the authorisation of the proprietor of the trade mark, such as to affect the original condition of the product."[94]

3-070   Soon after that case, the CJEU said in *HAG II*:

> "the essential function of the mark would be compromised if the owner of the right could not exercise his option under national law to prevent the importation of the similar product under a name likely to be confused with his own mark because, in this situation, consumers would no longer be able to identify with certainty the origin of the marked product and the bad quality of a product for which he is in no way responsible could be attributed to the owner of the right."[95]

3-071   Following the enactment of the TMD and EUTMR, the doctrine of essential function has been relied upon for the purpose of interpreting provisions of this legislation and is oft cited in every single trade mark case.

3-072   Thus, as the CJEU said in *Arsenal FC v Reed*:

> "…the essential function of a trade mark is to guarantee the identity of origin of the marked goods or services to the consumer or end user by enabling him, without any possibility of confusion, to distinguish the goods or services from others which have another origin. For the trade mark to be able to fulfil its essential role in the system of undistorted competition which the Treaty seeks to establish and maintain, it must offer a guarantee that all the goods or services bearing it have been manufactured or supplied under the control of a single undertaking which is responsible for their quality."[96]

3-073   Although the function of a trade mark as an indication of origin is of primary importance to the end user or consumer, it will also be relevant to intermediaries

---

[93]   e.g. see *Hoffmann La-Roche v Centrafarm* (102/77) [1978] E.C.R. 1139.
[94]   See [7].
[95]   (C-10/89) [1990] E.C.R. I-3711; [1990] 3 C.M.L.R. 571 at [16]. This case is discussed at para.7-214, et seq.
[96]   (C-206/01) [2002] E.C.R. I-10273 at [48].

who deal with the product commercially. Such persons equally rely upon the function of the mark as an indication of trade origin.[97]

However, is the above analysis correct? In the modern world, consumers often **3-074** have little knowledge of who is the undertaking behind a well-known brand. This is best illustrated by a hypothetical example. Brand X, a well-known chocolate bar, is made by an English company A in a factory in England using specially sourced African cocoa beans. A US company, B, buys the English company, shuts down the English factory and moves production of Brand X to Brazil. Brazilian cocoa beans are used instead of African cocoa beans. The US company carries on selling Brand X as if nothing had changed. In such circumstances, what does Brand X mean to the consumer who carries on buying Brand X? The suggestion that Brand X is seen by the consumer as a guarantee of trade origin appears a rather weak old-fashioned suggestion. For all intents and purposes, there is no continuity *of trade origin*. For instance, during a transitional period, there could co-exist in the marketplace Brand X products manufactured and marketed by A as well as those manufactured and marketed by B. In this period, it is clear that Brand X is not used to indicate the trade origin of a single undertaking. Has the essential function of Brand X been hopelessly compromised? One is tempted to say that ultimately, the consumer of Brand X does not really care. As long as Brand X chocolate bars look and taste the same, the consumer is content. In short, the consumer wants *consistency of experience*. Whilst it must be recognised that the characteristics of Brand X may change over time as its proprietor decides to change its characteristics, it is very likely that such will be a carefully managed process often with considerable pre-launch publicity. Perhaps, it is better to say that a trade mark permits a *predictability of experience* for consumers.

Thus, it has been said that the notion that trade marks are guarantees of trade **3-075** origin is rather old-fashioned. As long ago as 1992, a well-known commentator on trade mark law said that the origin of a product is of no importance to consumers.[98] Rather, he said that a mark is a sign which enables consumers to identify a product or service—it facilitates the choice in the marketplace. In other words, goods bearing Trade Mark A can be distinguished from goods bearing Trade Mark B but that does not mean that all goods bearing Trade Mark A will ultimately come from the same trade origin. This view defines a trade mark in a negative way—"I don't know what Trade Mark A means but at least I can differentiate it from Trade Mark B".

In considering this view, Jacobs AG said in *Parfums Dior v Evora*[99]: **3-076**

> "[41] ... But the origin theory, understood more broadly, recognizes that marks deserve protection because they symbolize qualities associated by consumers with certain goods or services and guarantee that the goods or services measure up to expectations. It is in that broader sense that the origin function has been understood by the court. As it stated in *Hag GF* 'an undertaking must be in a position to keep its customers by virtue of the quality of its products and services, something which is possible only if there are distinctive marks which enable customers to identify those products and services. For the trade mark to be able to fulfil this role, it must offer a guarantee that all goods bearing it have been produced under the control of a single undertaking which is accountable for their quality.' It is apparent that that aspect of trade marks (sometimes referred to as the 'quality or guarantee function) can be regarded as part of the origin function'."

---

[97] *Björnekulla v Procordia Food AB* (C-371/02) [2004] E.C.R. I-5791; [2004] E.T.M.R. 69 at [23].
[98] C. Gielen, "Harmonisation of Trade Mark Law in Europe: The First Trade Mark Harmonisation Directive" [1992] E.I.P.R 262 at 264.
[99] (C-337/95) [1997] E.C.R. I-6013.

3-077   It will be appreciated from this carefully worded section that the highly respected Advocate-General is not jettisoning the trade origin function in favour of a guarantee of quality function. Rather, a trade mark still acts as a guarantee that goods have been produced under the control of a single undertaking that is *accountable* for their quality. The trade mark owner may market goods of varying quality under the trade mark but they are accountable for that variation in quality.

3-078   Thus, trade marks are not a guarantee of quality per se. Prior to the harmonisation of trade mark legislation in Member States, national courts had to consider the enforcement of trade marks rights where an undertaking had a policy of marketing products of differing quality in different countries under the same mark. In an early case pre-TMD, a German court held that the undertaking must suffer the consequences of its policy and accept the free movement of goods, although the importer may be required to conspicuously indicate that the product differs from the other same-branded product.[100] However, in England, the courts adopted a different approach in a case where EU law was not applicable. In *Colgate Palmolive v Markwell Finance*,[101] a US company owned trade marks in the UK and Brazil. These marks were licensed to Colgate-UK and Colgate-Brazil, subsidiaries of the US company. The products in each country looked the same but there were marked differences in quality between the products from the two countries. The Brazilian product was markedly inferior in composition and therapeutic benefit, principally because it contained no fluoride. Markwell, a parallel importer, imported Brazilian Colgate toothpaste into the UK. Colgate-US sued for trade mark infringement. The Court of Appeal held that the trade marks applied on the Brazilian imports were different trade marks, indicative of differing goods, although they were of the same name. The Brazilian trade mark COLGATE was different from the UK trade mark COLGATE, as each was a creature of national laws. Accordingly, the court held that there was no implied or express consent to their marketing in the UK. It was clear that the difference in quality of the goods and the possibility of consumer confusion of a therapeutic substance was of paramount importance in the court's mind.[102]

3-079   In the context of EU law, the CJEU has favoured the German and not the UK approach. In *Ideal Standard*,[103] a case which was principally concerned with examining the doctrine of exhaustion of rights within the context of a partial assignment of trade mark rights,[104] the CJEU refined the concept of "essential function". In the course of its judgment, the court said:

> "It must further be stressed that the *decisive factor is the possibility of control over the quality of goods, not the actual exercise of that control.* Accordingly, a national law allowing the licensor to oppose importation of the licensee's products on grounds of poor quality would be precluded as contrary to Articles [34] and [36]: if the licensor tolerates

---

[100] *Francesco Cinzano GmbH v Java Kaffeegeschafte GmbH* [1974] 2 C.M.L.R. 20, Bundesgerichtshof (importer of alcoholic drink of differing quality in differing Member States permitted to import trade-marked drink from French and Spanish subsidiary of Cinzano into Germany, provided conspicuous indication that product differed from product of plaintiff (the German subsidiary of Cinzano)).

[101] *Colgate Palmolive v Markwell Finance* [1989] R.P.C. 497 CA.

[102] In contrast, see *Champagne Heidsieck et Cie Monopole Sa v Buxton* (1930) 1 Ch. 330; [1929] R.P.C. 28, an English decision, a plaintiff who sold champagne which tasted differently and was marketed under slightly different labels in both France and England, sued a parallel importer in passing off and trade mark infringement. It was held that the plaintiff had exhausted his rights and that the consideration of free trade outweighed the protection of the public from confusion.

[103] *IHT Internationale Heiztechnik GmbH v Ideal Standard GmbH* (C-9/93) [1994] E.C.R. I-2789; [1994] 3 C.M.L.R. 857.

[104] This case is fully considered at paras 7-137 and 7-225.

the manufacture of poor quality products, despite having contractual means of preventing it, *he must bear the responsibility*. Similarly if the manufacture of products is decentralized within a group of companies and the subsidiaries in each of the Member States manufacture products whose quality is geared to the particularities of each national market, a national law which enabled one subsidiary of the group to oppose the marketing in the territory of that State of products manufactured by an affiliated company on grounds of those quality differences would also be precluded. *Articles [34] and [36] require the group to bear the consequences of its choice.*"[105] [Emphasis supplied.]

Thus, the essential function of a trade mark is merely as a guarantee of unitary **3-080** control and not a guarantee of quality. Trade marks do not provide a legal guarantee of quality but consumers rely upon the economic self-interest of trade mark proprietors to maintain the quality of products and services sold under a brand.[106] The decisive factor is the possibility of control over the quality of the goods and not its exercise. If a trade mark owner tolerates the manufacture of poor quality goods by a licensee, they must bear the responsibility.[107]

Here, the approach of the CJEU is simply to extend the approach under national **3-081** laws whereby if the trade mark proprietor had marketed products under the same brand but of differing qualities *in the same Member State*, the trade mark proprietor could do nothing about it to one applicable across the territories of Member States of the EU. The approach of the CJEU underscores the fact that the goal of attaining a single market without barriers in the EU is of paramount importance. Trade mark proprietors cannot adopt a marketing policy which would frustrate such a goal.

Thus, in *Dansk Supermarked v Imerco*, the CJEU held that once a party had **3-082** permitted sub-standard products to be placed on the market in the UK state, it could not rely upon trade marks or copyright to prevent their importation into another Member State even if there was an express agreement that the goods not be placed on the market in Scandinavia. However, it is not difficult to envisage that where factors such as public health are involved (health is specifically mentioned in art.36), such principles are likely to override the principles of free movement of goods.[108]

In an English case, *Scandecor*,[109] the House of Lords considered what a trade **3-083** mark means in the modern world where the public are often wholly ignorant of whom the trade mark proprietor is. Furthermore, it considered the position where a trade mark proprietor licenses a licensee to produce goods without any provision in the licence as to quality control (often called a "bare" licence). In such circumstances, the link between the trade mark proprietor and the goods is very tenuous and remote. Lord Nicholls said the following:

"[37] ... the public is now accustomed to goods or services being supplied under licence from the trade mark owner. For example there has been the growth of franchise operations. The potential for deception is therefore less. Moreover the strongest guarantee that a proprietor will maintain control over the way in which his trade

---

[105] (C-9/93) [1994] E.C.R. I-2789; [1994] 3 C.M.L.R. 857 at [38].
[106] See Jacob AG's Opinion in (C-10/89) [1990] E.C.R. I-3711; [1990] 3 C.M.L.R. 571. See also Mayra AG's Opinion in *Terrapin v Terranova* (119/75) [1976] E.C.R. 1039; [1976] 2 C.M.L.R. 482 at 358.
[107] *Schweppes SA v Red Parallel SL* (C-291/16) ECLI:EU:C:2017:990 at [45].
[108] *Dansk Supermarked A/S v Imerco A/S* (58/80) [1981] E.C.R. 181; [1981] 3 C.M.L.R. 590. See G. Tritton, "Articles 30 to 36 and Intellectual Property: Is the jurisprudence of the CJEU now of an Ideal Standard" [1994] E.I.P.R. 423. See as for public health, para.3-624 which discusses repackaging of pharmaceuticals.
[109] *Scandecor Development AB v Scandecor Marketing AB* [2001] UKHL 21; [2001] 2 C.M.L.R. 30.

mark is used is that it is in his own interest to do so. A trade mark is a valuable piece of property, in terms both of its power to attract customers and of the royalties which can be demanded from licensees. Its value is however ultimately dependent on its reputation with the public. If the proprietor tolerates uncontrolled use of his trade mark the value of this property will be diminished. In an extreme case the registration of the mark may become liable to be revoked if it has become deceptive or generic through such use. It is however the responsibility of the proprietor, not the Registrar, to prevent the devaluation of his own property.

[38]   Thus, the wider interpretation, according to which the source may be either the proprietor or an exclusive licensee, would not be at variance with customers' perceptions. Customers are well used to the practice of licensing of trade marks. When they see goods to which a mark has been affixed, they understand that the goods have been produced either by the owner of the mark or by someone else acting with his consent.

[39]   Nor does the wider interpretation undermine the protection which a trade mark is intended to afford customers. *For their quality assurance customers rely on the self-interest of the owner.* They assume that if a licence has been granted the owner can be expected to have chosen a suitable licensee and imposed suitable terms. They also assume that during the currency of any licence the licensee, as well as the owner, is likely to have an interest in maintaining the value of the brand name. Customers are not to be taken to rely on the protection supposedly afforded by a legal requirement that the proprietor must always retain and exercise an inherently imprecise degree of control over the licensee's activities." [Emphasis supplied.]

3-084   The criterion of "unitary control" does not require that the proprietor have legal control over the quality of the goods. It may simply be that the proprietor has de facto control over the goods, in particular because of co-operation between the parties. In *Doncaster v Bolton*,[110] a Spanish registered trade mark which had originally been in common ownership was assigned to a third party. Goods placed on the market in Spain were then imported by the defendant. In an action for trade mark infringement by a successor to the owner of the English trade mark, the Court of Appeal of England held that it was arguable that although there was no "conventional control" in the terms of licensing, franchising, etc. there was linkage or the possibility of other types of control such that the trade mark proprietor would be deemed to have exhausted their rights. Indeed, it is likely that de facto control over the quality of goods would be sufficient to qualify and thus if a trade mark proprietor was indeed able to exercise de facto control over trade marked goods imported into a Member State from another Member State, they would be deemed to have exhausted their rights. This approach was confirmed by the Court of Justice in *Schweppes v Red Paralela*[111] where the Court of Justice held that where trade marks for some Member States had been assigned to a third party but that the assignor and assignee maintained close links with each other, and actively and deliberately promoted the appearance of a single global trade mark, then the assignor could not exercise its trade marks rights to prevent parallel imports within the EEA.

3-085   However, as discussed at the start of this section, by reference to the hypothetical chocolate example, it is clear that a trade mark is a guarantee that *all* goods bearing the mark have been produced under the control (or the possibility of control)

---

[110] *Bolton Pharmaceutical Co 100 Ltd v Doncaster Pharmaceuticals Group Ltd* [2006] E.T.M.R. 65; [2007] F.S.R. 3.

[111] *Schweppes SA v Red Parallel SL* (C-291/16) ECLI:EU:C:2017:990.

of a single undertaking does not survive scrutiny. It fails to take into account that in the modern world, marks are trafficked, sold and dealt with as a commodity like the goods or services which they are used in connection with. They may or may not be sold with the underlying business.

From the above discussion, the reader may be forgiven for asking themselves— what is the essential function of a trade mark? If it can be dealt with like any other commodity (i.e. sold or transferred with or without the business), then the suggestion that it offers a guarantee that *all* goods bearing it have been produced under the control of a *single* undertaking bear little weight. Equally, if a trade mark proprietor can market under the same brand goods of widely differing quality, then it is clearly not a guarantee of quality (even if such is unlikely). **3-086**

Earlier in this section, we referred to the fact that in the modern world, it may be that a mark offers little more than a *predictability of experience* in relation to the goods or services for which it is used and that is best guaranteed by ensuring that at any given moment in time, the exclusive rights of the trade mark are vested in one natural or legal person only. Ultimately, it may be that the essential function of a trade mark amounts to little more than a guarantee that goods placed on the market under a brand (trade mark) are subject to the *potential* control of the undertaking who was the *registered proprietor at the time of marketing of* those *goods*. As the identity of the registered proprietor may change over time, this definition (unlike the definition in *Ideal Standard* cited above) does not require that *all* goods on the market have been produced under the control of a single undertaking. Whilst such is not particularly satisfactory, it is clear that consumers do get some assurance and peace of mind from such a limited guarantee. It excludes the marketing of goods bearing the trade mark by parties wholly independent of the proprietor which are not assigns or successors to the proprietor—the negative way of defining what a mark is as discussed earlier. Apart from the limited guarantee, the consumer relies upon the self-interest of the proprietor of the trade mark not to damage the reputation of the trade mark by inappropriate "self-harming" use of it. **3-087**

Guarantee against subsequent interference

A person may buy a product displaying a trade mark, alter it significantly and then sell it on. In such circumstances, the quality of the product when the consumer purchases it is not exclusively referable to the trade mark proprietor. Thus, in *Hoffmann La-Roche*,[112] a case concerning repackaging of genuine trade marked products, the CJEU said of the essential function: **3-088**

> "[7] ...the essential function is to guarantee the identity of the origin of the trade-marked product to the consumer or ultimate user, by enabling him without any possibility of confusion to distinguish that product from products which have another origin [and to] be certain that a trade-marked product...has not been subject at a previous stage of marketing to interference...such as to affect the original condition of the product... ."

This right to prevent interference in a stage of marketing which is liable to impair the guarantee of trade origin has been considered in a number of repackaging cases.[113] It is embodied in art.15(2) TMD/art.15(2) EUTMR which permits a trade mark proprietor to prevent further commercialisation of goods which have been **3-089**

---

[112] (102/77) [1978] E.C.R. 1139 at [7].
[113] See para.3-624.

placed on the market by them where there exist "legitimate reasons" to do so, which expressly include where the condition of the goods has been changed of impaired.

3-090   In *Parfums Dior v Evora*,[114] the CJEU had to consider the extent which a reseller of a luxury branded goods was entitled to make use of a trade mark in advertising and promotion to bring to the public's attention the further commercialisation of the goods. The CJEU held that the reseller was entitled to use the mark unless the use of the mark seriously damaged the reputation of the brand.

Internet keywords and adverse effect on the essential function

3-091   In the context of the use of a registered trade mark of a competitor as an Internet keyword by an advertiser for the purpose of advertising links to the advertiser's website, the CJEU[115] has said as follows:

> "[44]   The question whether a trade mark's function of indicating origin is adversely affected when internet users are shown, on the basis of a keyword identical with the mark, a third party's advertisement, such as that of a competitor of the trade mark proprietor, depends in particular on the manner in which that advertisement is presented. That function is adversely affected if the advertisement does not enable reasonably well-informed and reasonably observant internet users, or enables them only with difficulty, to ascertain whether the goods or services referred to by the advertisement originate from the proprietor of the trade mark or an undertaking economically connected to it or, on the contrary, originate from a third party (*Google France* and *Google*, paragraphs 83 and 84, and *Portakabin*, paragraph 34). In such a situation, which is, moreover, characterised by the fact that the advertisement appears immediately after the trade mark has been entered as a search term and is displayed at a point when the trade mark is, in its capacity as a search term, also displayed on the screen, the internet user may be mistaken as to the origin of the goods or services in question (*Google France* and *Google*, paragraph 85).
>
> [45]   Where a third party's advertisement suggests that there is an economic link between that third party and the proprietor of the trade mark, the conclusion must be that there is an adverse effect on that mark's function of indicating origin. Similarly, where the advertisement, while not suggesting the existence of an economic link, is vague to such an extent on the origin of the goods or services at issue that reasonably well-informed and reasonably observant internet users are unable to determine, on the basis of the advertising link and the commercial message attached thereto, whether the advertiser is a third party vis-à-vis the proprietor of the trade mark or whether, on the contrary, it is economically linked to that proprietor, the conclusion must be that there is an adverse effect on that function of the trade mark (*Google France* and *Google*, paragraphs 89 and 90, and *Portakabin*, paragraph 35)."

3-092   The need to view the matter from the aspect of the notional hypothetical internet user means that the fact that some Internet users have difficulty grasping that the

---

[114]   *Parfums Christian Dior SA v Evora BV* (C-337/95) [1997] E.C.R. I-6013. See para.3-169, et seq.

[115]   *Interflora v Marks and Spencer* (C-323/09) [2011] E.C.R. I-8265. See also, *Die Bergspechte Outdoor Reisden und Alpinschule Edi Koblmuller GmbH v Gunter Guni* (C-278/08) [2010] E.C.R. I-2517 at 35; *Portakabin Ltd v Primakabin BV* (C-558/08) [2010] E.C.R. I-6963; *Google France* (C-236/08) at [83]–[84].

service of the competitor is independent from that of the proprietor of the mark is irrelevant.[116]

Guarantee of quality function

For the reader who has read the previous section, they will understand that a trade mark does not act as a legal guarantee of quality per se. Rather, consumers rely upon the economic self-interest of trade mark proprietors to maintain the quality of products and services sold under a brand. A trade mark proprietor is free to vary the quality of products or services sold under a mark in a manner that it sees fit. However, a proprietor who fails to maintain any uniformity of quality of goods or services marketed under a trade mark risks endangering the economic message of the trade mark to consumers. A consumer who has widely varying experiences when consuming a chocolate bar bearing Brand X will cease to buy chocolate bars under that brand but that is all. **3-093**

Despite that, it is right to say that the Court of Justice has said a few times that one of the functions of a trade mark is to guarantee the quality of a product or service.[117] Such statements should be seen against the earlier jurisprudence of the CJEU which emphasises that the decisive factor is the possibility of control over the quality of goods and not the actual exercise of that control.[118] However, although a trade mark is not a legal guarantee of quality, a registered trade mark can be revoked if as a consequence of the use made of it by the proprietor of a trade mark or with their consent, the trade mark is liable to mislead the public as to the quality of the goods or services.[119] This might be thought to lend support to the notion that a trade mark is a guarantee of quality. However, as consumers generally know that goods sold under a trade mark may vary in quality, and indeed over time, normally do, they are not mislead by variation in quality even if this occurs. Rather, this provision is aimed at registered marks which have a descriptive element to them which denote *a* quality of goods (i.e. a *characteristic* of the goods)[120] but the trade mark proprietor uses the mark in a manner inconsistent with that, e.g. LUCO-SUGAR for a drink which does not contain sugar. **3-094**

Communication, advertising and investment functions

In the 1990s, Jacobs AG in *Parfums Dior v Evora*[121] referring to a well-respected English text book on intellectual property[122] mentioned the communication, investment and advertising functions of a trade mark. He said that those functions are said to arise from the fact that the investment in the promotion of a product **3-095**

---

[116] *Interflora v Marks and Spencer* [2013] EWHC 1291 at [49]. However, it should be noted that in the UK, the judge applying this decision has taken the view that under EU law, it is sufficient if a significant number of persons are confused—*Interflora v Marks and Spencer* [2013] EWHC 1291.

[117] See *W.F. Gözze Frottierweberei GmbH Wolfgang Gözze v Verein Bremer Baumwollbörse*, (C-689/15) ECLI:EU:C:2017:434 at [42]; *L'Oréal* (C-689/15 and C-487/07) EU:C:2009:378 at [58], and of 22 September 2011, *Interflora and Interflora British Unit* (C-323/09) EU:C:2011:604 at [38].

[118] See para.3-080.

[119] art.58.1(c) EUTMR; art 20(b) TMD.

[120] Although the French and English versions use the word "*qualité*","quality", the German version uses the word "*Beschaffenheit*" which translates as "composition" or "nature". See para.3-756, et seq.

[121] *Parfums Christian Dior SA v Evora BV* (C-337/95) [1997] E.C.R. I-6013.

[122] W. Cornish, *Intellectual Property: Patents, Copyright, Trade Marks and Allied Rights*, 3rd edn (London: Sweet & Maxwell, 1996).

is built around the mark and thus merit protection.[123] However, he considered that such were merely "derivatives of the origin function".[124] As he said, there would be little purpose in advertising a mark if it were not for the function of that mark as an indicator of origin. Thus, he held that the CJEU's emphasis on the origin function of trade marks was the appropriate starting point for the interpretation of European Union law relating to trade marks.[125] In the questions referred by the Hoge Raad in *Parfums Dior*, a case concerning whether a reseller of luxury branded goods could advertise such goods in a manner which damages the luxury and prestigious image of the brand, the Hoge Raad expressly used the phrase "advertising function". However, it is clear in that case that the Hoge Raad was using this expression to mean the image that that the brand conveys—what is now referred to as the "communication function".

3-096   Later in *Arsenal FC v Reed*,[126] the CJEU referred to the functions of a trade mark but did not elaborate on what those were other than the essential function.[127] However, foreshadowing this statement was the opinion of the late and highly esteemed Colomer AG in that case where he said that:

> "[46]   It seems to me to be simplistic reductionism to limit the function of the trade mark to an indication of trade origin. The Commission, moreover, took the same view in its oral submissions to the court. Experience teaches that, in most cases, the user is unaware of who produces the goods he consumes. *The trade mark acquires a life of its own, making a statement, as I have suggested, about quality, reputation and even, in certain cases, a way of seeing life.*
>
> [47]   The messages it sends out are, moreover, autonomous. A distinctive sign can indicate at the same time trade origin, the reputation of its proprietor and the quality of the goods it represents, but there is nothing to prevent the consumer, unaware of who manufactures the goods or provides the services which bear the trade mark—where the proprietor grants a licence to a third party to produce the goods covered by the trade mark, indication of trade origin becomes irrelevant and retreats into the background or may even disappear from view altogether—from acquiring them because he perceives the mark as an emblem of prestige or a guarantee of quality. When I examine the current functioning of the market and the behaviour of the average consumer, I see no reason whatever not to protect those other functions of the trade mark and to safeguard only the function of indicating the trade origin of the goods and services."

3-097   The reference to a trade mark acquiring a life of its own, making a statement about quality, reputation and even in certain cases, a way of seeing life is undoubtedly true. Indeed, it can be said that in the modern world, the trade mark rather than the underlying product or service *is* the traded commodity. Where through years of careful and prudent nurturing of a brand, it has come to connote certain abstract but positive values, the power of that brand becomes immense. A good example is the Virgin brand which has come to connote values of honesty, trustworthiness, coolness and innovation. As such, there is a strong desire of organisations to use the name "Virgin" in many different fields of business because consumers and end-users will associate these values with such a business. Without stating it expressly,

---

[123] This wording comes from Cornish and still exists in the 8th edn.
[124] See [42].
[125] See [42].
[126] *Arsenal Football Club v Reed* (C-260/01) [2002] E.C.R. I-10989; [2005] E.T.M.R. 27.
[127] See [54].

Colomer AG was clearly referring to the communication function of a mark, i.e. the *psychological signal* that a mark communicates to the public.

In *L'Oréal v Bellure*,[128] the CJEU had to consider what the functions of a trade **3-098** mark were other than its origin function (the essential function). The Advocate-General had referred to Jacobs AG's Opinion in *Parfums Dior* (discussed above) where he referred to the advertising, communication and investment function. The CJEU picked up on this in its judgment, commenting on these three functions without explaining them.[129] These three functions as well as the origin function are now firmly recognised by the CJEU.[130] It is an ironic truth that although these functions are much criticised by Anglo-Saxon commentators, the genesis of their inclusion into European Union law is from an English legal text book!

Despite Jacobs AG's view in *Parfums Dior* that the advertising, investment and **3-099** communication function were "derivatives" of the origin function, it is clear that such reasoning is no longer true. They are standalone independent functions which may be adversely affected even if there is no confusion as to trade origin.[131] It is thus necessary to consider these concepts. The communication function is reasonably well understood and is concerned with the *image* of a brand. The advertising and investment functions are poorly understood and one awaits further clarification as to whether these functions are truly separable from the essential or communication functions or indeed truly functions of a trade mark.

Communication function

As discussed in the introduction to this chapter, in *HAG II*, Jacobs AG referred **3-100** to the undesirable consequences if the "clarity of the signal" of a trade mark was impaired.[132] The idea that a trade mark with a reputation "broadcasts" a signal is at the heart of what is now known as the "communication function" of a trade mark. As again discussed in the introduction to this chapter, a trade mark may communicate a complex signal to the end-user about the product to which it is applied. A beer trade mark may have a psychological message that it will only be enjoyed by those with taste, culture and money. Thus, Stella Artois' "reassuringly expensive" advertising campaign turns a negative primary characteristic (price) into a positive secondary characteristic ("if you drink this beer, you are telling the world how successful you are").

In *SIGLA v OHIM*, the General Court said, in discussing the communication **3-101** function:

"[35]   In order to better define the risk referred to by Article 8(5) of No 40/94, it must be pointed out that the primary function of a mark is unquestionably that of an 'indication of origin' (see the seventh recital in the preamble to No 40/94). The fact remains that a mark also acts as a means of conveying other messages concerning, inter alia, the qualities or particular characteristics of the goods or services which it covers or the images and feelings which it conveys, such as, for example, luxury, lifestyle, exclusivity, adventure, youth. To that effect the mark

---

[128] *L'Oréal SA v Bellure NV* (C-487/07) [2009] E.C.R. I-5185 at [50]–[51] (AG Opinion).

[129] Judgment at [58].

[130] e.g. see *Google France Sarl v Louis Vuitton Malletier SA; Google France Sarl v Viaticum SA; Google France v Centre National de Recherche en Relation Humaines SARL* (C-236/08, C-237–08 and C-238/08) [2010] E.C.R. I-02417 at [77]; *Interflora Inc v Marks and Spencer Plc* (C-323/09) [2012] F.S.R. 3; [2011] E.C.R. 000 at [38].

[131] *L'Oréal SA v Bellure NV* (C-487/07) [2009] E.C.R. I-5185 at [65].

[132] See para.3-004.

has an inherent economic value which is independent of and separate from that of the goods and services for which it is registered. The messages in question which are conveyed inter alia by a mark with a reputation or which are associated with it confer on that mark a significant value which deserves protection, particularly because, in most cases, the reputation of a mark is the result of considerable effort and investment on the part of its proprietor. Consequently, Article 8(5) of No 40/94 ensures that a mark with a reputation is protected with regard to any application for an identical or similar mark which might adversely affect its image, even if the goods or services covered by the mark applied for are not similar to those for which the earlier mark with a reputation has been registered."[133]

3-102   The communication function has also been recognised by the CJEU in *L'Oréal v Bellure* although it did not explain it. Thus, the communication function is concerned with protection of the image of a brand.

3-103   By definition, an unused trade mark has no image. Thus, one would have thought that one is only concerned with a trade mark with a reputation. However, one may be concerned with protecting a specific brand image planned for the future.[134] In other words, a registered proprietor of a mark may have plans to market a brand in a particular mark. If a similar or identical mark is used by a third party and that adversely affects the *intended* image of the brand, such will damage the *intended* communication function of the brand. An obvious example is where the third party's mark is promoted so as to jeopardise the *intended* image of the other mark. In the context of the TMD and EUTMR, the communication function is of importance when considering whether a mark causes detriment to the distinctive character or repute of another trade mark.[135]

Advertising function

3-104   As said above, it would appear that originally the phrase "advertising function" was used in *Parfums Dior* to mean the communication function. However, in the *Google France* cases,[136] the CJEU held in a section entitled "adverse effect on the advertising function" that:

"[91]   Since the course of trade provides a varied offer of goods and services [sic], the proprietor of a trade mark may have not only the objective of indicating, by means of that mark, the origin of its goods or services, but also that of using its mark for advertising purposes designed to inform and persuade consumers.

[92]   Accordingly, the proprietor of a trade mark is entitled to prohibit a third party from using, without the proprietor's consent, a sign identical with its trade mark in relation to goods or services which are identical with those for which that trade mark is registered, in the case where that use adversely affects the proprietor's use of its mark as a factor in sales promotion or as an instrument of commercial strategy."

---

[133] *Sigla v EUIPO* (T-215/03) [2007] E.C.R. II-711.

[134] *Interflora Inc v Marks and Spencer Plc* (C-323/09) [2012] F.S.R. 3, ECLI:EU:C:2011:604 at [40]. There the CJEU said that a trade mark only performs the functions other than as an indication of trade origin if it has been used. However, in seeming contrast to that, it then said in the same paragraph that there are no grounds for holding that only trade marks with a reputation are capable of having functions other than that of indicating origin.

[135] See para.3-352.

[136] *Google France SARL v Louis Vuitton Malletier SA; Google France SARL v Viaticum SA; Google France v Centre National de Recherche en Relation Humaines SARL* (C-236/08, C-237–08 and C-238/08) [2010] E.C.R. I-02417.

In *Interflora v Marks & Spencer*, the CJEU said that the advertising function is not to protect its proprietor against "practices inherent in competition"[137]. Thus, in the context of a competitor using the registered trade mark of a proprietor (Interflora) as an Internet keyword to drive Internet traffic to the competitor's website as an alternative to the proprietor's business, it said that such is an inherent competitive practice.[138] Furthermore, it affirmed the approach taken in *Google France* that such does not deny the proprietor the opportunity of using its mark "effectively to inform and win over consumers".[139] In *Google France*, the CJEU held that the fact that an undertaking has successfully bid for a competitor trade mark as an Internet keyword did not affect the advertising function of that mark, as it was not in dispute that the competitor's links would appear in the natural results of the search when a search term used using Google and such was free of charge.   **3-105**

It would thus appear that the advertising function of a mark can only be damaged when use of a brand by a third party, prevents the trade mark proprietor from effectively advertising their own trade mark to win over consumers. It follows from *Google France* that the mere fact that a competitor is using the trade mark proprietor's own trade mark to divert business or that the proprietor's advertising costs must increase because of the competitor's use of the proprietor's mark is not sufficient to affect the advertising function of the mark. Therefore, one asks what is sufficient to affect the advertising function? It may be that in the future, an internet search engine becomes popular which *only* advertises sponsored links. In which case, a competitor's successful bid for a trade mark to be a sponsored mark will prevent the proprietor from using that search engine to advertise its mark. Yet, even on that basis, it is difficult to say that the proprietor cannot use its mark to inform and win over consumers—it could use other means including offline advertising.   **3-106**

Ultimately, the advertising function appears to serve little or no purpose. As said above, the original meaning of this phrase was the need to protect the image that a trade mark conveys (i.e. the communication function). As such an image is normally carefully promoted by advertising, it was known as the advertising function. It is unfortunate that the CJEU has introduced this notion with little real thought as to what it means. In the author's opinion, it should be jettisoned. Divorced from the communication function, it is a meaningless concept.   **3-107**

Investment function

Often for a trade mark to acquire a reputation, it is necessary that an investment is made in promoting and advertising the brand. However, a brand may become well known without any specific investment in advertising and promoting the brand. For instance, a patissier's pastries may become so well known that people flock to his patisserie from far and wide because his reputation has spread by word-of-mouth. In such circumstances, the patissier's reputation has developed without advertising or promotion. However, in the modern world, this is the exception rather than the rule. Generally, without any investment in promoting or advertising it, a brand will not become known to the public.   **3-108**

---

[137] Cf. *L'Oréal v Bellure NV* [2010] R.P.C. 23 CA at [57] where the Court of Appeal of England, in applying the *L'Oréal v Bellure* decision of the CJEU said that all advertisements for rival products will impinge on the owner's effort to promote his brand and affect the advertising function of the brand (see [30]).

[138] See [58].

[139] See [59].

3-109   The CJEU said in *Interflora v Marks and Spencer* that the investment function of a trade mark reflects the fact that a trade mark may be used by its proprietor to acquire or preserve a reputation capable of attracting consumers and retaining their loyalty.[140] Thus, as said by the CJEU, the investment function is adversely affected where "it substantially interferes with the proprietor's use of its trade mark to acquire or preserve a reputation capable of attracting consumers and retaining their loyalty".[141] However, in the same case, the CJEU said that such cannot mean that a competitor can prevent another competitor who, in conditions of fair competition that respects the trade mark's function as an indication of trade origin, uses an identical sign to that of the trade mark on identical goods for which the mark is registered if the *only* consequence is to oblige the proprietor of the trade mark to adapt its efforts to acquire or preserve its reputation.[142] Such was said in the context of a case where an undertaking was using the registered trade mark of a competitor as an Internet keyword which would cause the undertaking's website to be displayed as a sponsored link rather than the registered proprietor. It might be said that such was not fair competition but the CJEU did not say or suggest that such was the case. Indeed, the reference to "fair competition" appears to be related to simply respecting the trade mark's function as an indication of origin, i.e. avoiding causing confusion.

3-110   In a couple of UK cases following *Interflora v Marks & Spencer*, the court has considered the meaning of the investment function. In the High Court case applying the CJEU's judgment in *Interflora v Marks & Spencer*, the judge commented that it is not easy to understand what exactly the CJEU meant by the "investment function" and how it differed from the "advertising function". The judge said that it would appear that the CJEU was saying that if the third party's keyword advertising affected the reputation of a trade mark, as for example where the image that the trade mark conveyed is damaged, then there would be an adverse effect on the investment function.[143] Whilst the judge's reasoning based on a close contextual analysis of the CJEU's judgment in *Interflora v Marks & Spencer* seems correct, it rather highlights the confusion in the CJEU's mind. Damage to the image of a mark is a classic case where the *communication* function (i.e. the psychological signal) of a mark is damaged. In other words, damage to the *image* of a mark is best dealt with under the communication function. Perhaps much confusion arises from the ambiguous meaning of the English word "reputation" which tends to be used in two different ways: the *recognition* of the trade mark in the marketplace (which arises solely from exposure via use, marketing and advertising of the trade mark) and the *image* of the mark (what the trade mark "stands for") which is concerned with the psychological signal of the mark. It would be more helpful if this ambiguity is recognised. Indeed, the latter use is more concerned with the "repute" of the mark rather than the "reputation" (in the first sense). It is of note that under the EU, provisions dealing with marks with a reputation refers to "detriment to the distinctive

---

[140] *Interflora v Marks and Spencer* at [60]–[61].

[141] *Interflora*, at [66].

[142] See [64].

[143] *Interflora v Marks & Spencer* [2013] F.S.R. 33 at [270]–[274]. The judge was particularly influenced in his thinking by the rather "puzzling cross-reference" in the CJEU's judgment at [63]–[83] in *L'Oréal v eBay* which referred to the removal of packaging damaging the image of the product and hence the reputation of the trade mark.

character or repute of an earlier mark",[144] a distinction is drawn between "reputation" and "repute". "Reputation" is used to mean reputation in the first sense whereas "repute" is used to mean reputation in the second sense. Thus, damage to the "repute" of an earlier mark with a reputation is referred to as "tarnishment" and this is concerned with damage to the image of the mark.[145]

In a keyword advertising case in the UK, following the High Court decision in **3-111** *Interflora v Marks & Spencer*, namely *Cosmetic Warriors v Amazon*,[146] the court found that the investment function of the trade mark was damaged where Amazon, the well-known online retailer, used the registered trade mark "Lush", a well-known mark for cosmetics, in its internal search on the Amazon website to list goods that were not placed on the market by the proprietor but which were cosmetics. The judge found that the proprietor had built a successful image based on ethical trading. It had thus taken a decision not to allow its goods to be sold on the Amazon website. It considered that Amazon's standards did not comply with this.[147] He held that the use damaged the investment function of the trade mark.[148] However, in the author's view, this is, in substance, again a finding that the communication function of the mark was damaged by marketing of cosmetics in Amazon, which did not align with the image of the mark (here one of ethical trading). It is difficult to see how the investment function was damaged if the communication function was not damaged.

Therefore, as with the advertising function, it is difficult to understand what is **3-112** meant by the investment function and what it is intended to protect and whether it has any purpose where the origin or communication function of a mark is not damaged. The investment in a brand can be wholly destroyed by fair competition. Whilst clearly, if the investment in a brand is destroyed because of market confusion over two identical or similar brands, such is adequately catered for by the origin function. Equally, if, there is no risk of confusion but, as in *Interflora*, an undertaking can use a competitor's trade mark to drive business to its website and such is considered not to affect the investment function (but clearly will damage the investment in the trade mark), one is driven to ask in what circumstances, it can be relied upon where the origin function (i.e. the essential function) is not adversely affected.

An example of where the investment function is capable of being damaged could **3-113** be where a third party uses a mark which, although not liable to cause confusion in the marketplace, is liable to damage the distinctive character of the trade mark via dilution. Dilution of the reputation of a mark will affect its ability to attract custom and thus will affect the investment function. An example might be where the word "Champagne" is used for selling non-alcoholic drinks in a non-confusing get-up. In such circumstances, it is unlikely that consumers will be confused but it is inevitable that the use of the title "Champagne" for a variety of products will inevitable erode the distinctive nature of Champagne as the premier brand for sparkling wines coming from a region in France. As said by the Court of Appeal in an English case on passing off concerning the use of "Elderflower champagne" for a soft drink[149] when considering the issue of damage:

"The first plaintiffs' reputation and goodwill in the description Champagne derive not only

---

[144] e.g. see art.9.2(c) EUTMR and art.10.2(c) TMD.
[145] See para.3-386.
[146] *Cosmetic Warriors Ltd and Lush Ltd v Amazon.co.uk Ltd and Amazon EU SARL* [2014] EWHC 181.
[147] See [17], [70]–[76].
[148] See [69]–[71].
[149] *Taittinger v Allbev* [1993] F.S.R. 641 CA at 678.

from the quality of their wine and its glamorous associations, but also from the very singularity and exclusiveness of the description, the absence of qualifying epithets and imitative descriptions. Any product which is not Champagne but is allowed to describe itself as such must inevitably, in my view, erode the singularity and exclusiveness of the description Champagne and so cause the first plaintiffs damage of an insidious but serious kind. The amount of damage which the defendants' product would cause would of course depend on the size of the defendants' operation. That is not negligible now, and it could become much bigger. But I cannot see, despite the defendants' argument to the contrary, any rational basis upon which, if the defendants' product were allowed to be marketed under its present description, any other fruit cordial diluted with carbonated water could not be similarly marketed so as to incorporate the description champagne. The damage to the first plaintiffs would then be incalculable but severe."

3-114   Thus, in the author's opinion, the investment function is likely to be most relevant to arguments of dilution. Such is different to the detrimental effect on the investment into a trade mark caused by fair competition discussed in *Interflora*. In the latter case, the proprietor can adapt its effort to acquire or preserve its reputation. On the other hand, dilution cannot be effectively neutralised by greater investment. The effect of dilution is, as said above, insidious and, in the author's opinion, largely irreversible. The investment function is also clearly relevant to "tarnishment" arguments but in such circumstances, the communication function is also engaged as tarnishment affects the image of a brand.

3-115   It has been suggested that the investment function has no existence independent from other functions of a trade mark—particularly the communication function.[150] In other words, it is difficult to think of a situation where of all the other functions, only the investment function is affected other than as a result of legitimate competition. Thus, in the above "Champagne" example, it could be said that in reality, the diluting effects of using "Champagne" for non-alcoholic drinks is to impair the "clarity of the signal" of a premier brand as a premier exclusive brand, i.e. the use affects the communication function. In the author's opinion, there is much to be said for this view although there may be cases where use of a mark by a third party affects *neither* the image of the trade mark *nor* causes confusion but does cause dilution. For instance, the use of "Spanish Champagne" for sparkling wine of a high quality made in Spain will not confuse people nor is it likely to affect the *brand image* of Champagne if there is no suggestion that Spanish champagne is less good than sparkling wine made in the Champagne region of France.[151] However, it will undoubtedly dilute the goodwill vested in Champagne.[152]

Communication, advertising and investment function of unused marks

3-116   It might be questioned whether it is possible for these functions to be adversely affected where the registered mark has not been used. The CJEU in *Interflora v Marks & Spencer* appears to consider that it is possible to affect these functions

---

[150] D. Keeling, D. Llewelyn, J. Mellor, QC, T. Moody-Stuart, I. Berkeley, *Kerly's Law of Trade Marks and Trade Names*, 15th edn, (London: Sweet & Maxwell, 2011), para.2-020.

[151] Unless it is said that it undermines the exclusivity of the use of Champagne to mean sparkling wines from the Champagne region. However, such is not truly concerned with brand image. If it were, the communication function would be always affected by the mere use of an identical trade for identical goods by someone other than the proprietor who will have exclusive rights conferred on them by trade mark legislation. It then becomes what is called a "bootstraps" argument.

[152] See similar arguments accepted by the English courts in *Vine Products v Mackenzie & Co Ltd* [1969] R.P.C. 1; *Bollinger J v Costa Brava Wine Co Ltd* [1960] R.P.C. 16; [1961] R.P.C. 116.

even if the mark is not used although its reasoning is somewhat unsatisfactory.[153] As discussed above, one can envisage a situation where an *intended* brand image can be jeopardised by inappropriate use of the same or similar mark by a third party and thus the communication function be adversely affected. Equally, it could be said that unauthorised use of the same or similar mark could potentially adversely affect the ability of the proprietor in future to advertise the hitherto unused mark and thus affect the advertising function of the mark. It is more difficult to see how the investment function of an unused mark can be adversely affected by third party use of the same or similar mark.

Specific object/subject-matter of a trade mark

Although the above functions of trade marks have become the pre-eminent principle cited by the CJEU when considering the interpretation of EU legislative measures in the field of trade marks, in the early days of its jurisprudence when considering the interaction of arts 34–36 TFEU with the exercise of trade mark rights, reference was often made to the "specific object of a trade mark". This was defined as follows: **3-117**

> "The specific object of a trade mark right consists particularly in granting the owner the exclusive right to use the trade mark when first putting a product into circulation, and in thereby protecting him against competitors seeking to abuse the position and reputation of the trade mark by selling products which have been unlawfully furnished with the trade mark."[154]

It should be noted that "specific object" and "specific subject-matter" are used interchangeably in English.[155] Such a right provides protection against competitors wishing to take advantage of the status and reputation of the mark by selling products illegally bearing the trade mark.[156] The specific object of the trade mark means that once the goods have been lawfully placed on the market, the owner of the right has exhausted their rights in the trade-marked product. This principle is now cast iron and enshrined in art.15 TMD and art.15 EUTMR. There is thus no need to consider the underlying rationale for it, namely a balancing act between the goal of a single market and the exclusive rights of a registered trade mark.   **3-118**

As said in the introduction, the doctrine of "specific object" and the doctrine of "essential function" can be considered closely related and two sides of the same coin.[157] Nowadays, the doctrine plays little part in the jurisprudence of the CJEU. Moreover, often the phrases are used interchangeably.[158] Thus, the Advocate-   **3-119**

---

[153] See para.3-103 and fn.134.

[154] *Centrafarm BV v Sterling Drug Inc and Winthrop* (15 and 16/74) [1974] E.C.R. 1147, [1974] 2 C.M.L.R. 480. See also (102/77) [1978] E.C.R. 1139, [1978] 3 C.M.L.R. 217; *Pfizer Inc v Eurim-Pharm GmbH* (1/81) [1981] E.C.R. 2913, [1982] 1 C.M.L.R. 406; (119/75) [1976] E.C.R. 1039, [1976] 2 C.M.L.R. 482; *American Home Products Corp v Centrafarm* (3/78) [1978] E.C.R. 1823, [1979] 1 C.M.L.R. 326; (58/80) [1981] E.C.R. 181, [1981] 3 C.M.L.R. 590; (C-10/89) [1990] E.C.R. I-3711, [1990] 3 C.M.L.R. 571; (C-9/93) [1994] E.C.R. I-2789, [1994] 3 C.M.L.R. 857.

[155] "Specific subject-matter" is a translation of *objet spécifique*. Generally, see Ch.7 for discussion of the origin of this doctrine in the 1970s jurisprudence of the CJEU in relation to the free movement of goods provisions of the then Treaty of Rome.

[156] See (C-3/78) [1978] E.C.R. 1823; [1979] 1 C.M.L.R. 326 at [11]–[14].

[157] See the introduction to this chapter—para.3-001.

[158] e.g. see Sharpston AG's Opinion in *Boehringer Ingelheim KG v Swingward Ltd No.2* (C-348/04) [2007] E.C.R. I-3391; [2007] 2 C.M.L.R. 52 at [8]–[10].

General in *Boehringer v Swingward No.2*[159] said that the specific subject-matter of a trade mark has two components. First, there is the right to use the mark for the purpose of putting products protected by it into circulation for the first time in the EC, after which that right is exhausted. Secondly, there is the right to oppose any use of the trade mark which is liable to impair the guarantee of origin, which comprises both a guarantee of identity of origin and a guarantee of integrity of the trade-marked product. This second aspect is, as seen in the excerpt from *Hoffmann La-Roche* above, in essence, an element of the essential function of a mark.[160]

The Trade Mark Directive and European Trade Mark Regulation

Introduction

3-120   The original First Harmonisation Trade Marks Directive[161] resulted from the European Commission's decision to create a Community-wide unitary trade mark—the Community Trade Mark. In 1976, the Commission produced a Memorandum on the creation of a Community Trade Mark and made a comprehensive survey of the need for trade marks as facilitators of the process of identifying the choosing goods and services. In concluding that there was a need for a Community Trade Mark which covered the territory of the EU in order to facilitate the free movement of goods, the Commission realised that upon such happening, national trade mark laws would continue to exist. Differences in the application of such laws were perceived as being a potential obstacle to the free movement of goods. Accordingly, the Memorandum called for an approximation of national trade mark laws of Member States in order to complement the Community Trade Mark. It was intended that both should be implemented together, but with the political difficulties over the Community Trade Mark, especially the location of the Community office, the Commission pushed ahead first with the harmonisation of national laws.

3-121   The Commission chose to harmonise the trade mark laws of Member States by way of a Directive. The first draft was published in 1980 and, after a considerable degree of discussion between the Commission, the Parliament, Member States and other interest groups, the First Trade Mark Directive was adopted by the Council on 21 December 1988.[162]

3-122   The original Trade Mark Directive (89/104/EC) was replaced by a consolidating Trade Mark Directive (2008/95/EC)[163] which did not affect the substantive law. This in turn has been replaced a new Trade Mark Directive (Dir.2015/2436/EU[164]). This Directive is hereinafter called "TMD". The TMD requires Member States to amend their laws in accordance with the changes set out in the Directive by 15 January 2019. The changes in the TMD broadly reflect the changes that have been made to the law relating to EU trade marks. However, until those changes are implemented by Member States into their trade mark laws, there will be a divergence of substantive trade mark law provisions of Member States with that in the EUTMR.

---

[159] (C-348/04) [2007] E.C.R. I-3391; [2007] 2 C.M.L.R. 52 at [9].

[160] See para.3-069.

[161] First Council Directive 89/104/EEC to approximate the laws of the Member States relating to trade marks [1989] OJ L40/1.

[162] For more detail on the background to harmonisation and the drafting history of the Directive, see C. Gielen, "Harmonisation of Trade Mark Law in Europe: The First Trade Mark Harmonisation Directive" [1992] 14(8) E.I.P.R. 262.

[163] [2008] OJ L299/25.

[164] [2015] OJ L336/1.

With regards to EUTMs, the current Regulation is Regulation 2017/1001. This **3-123** is a codifying regulation which brings together the various amendments made to the predecessor regulation 207/2009[165] by Reg.2015/2424.[166] These changes came into force in two stages: the first came into force on 23 March 2016 followed by the second on 1 October 2017. Regulation 207/2009 itself replaced the first Community Trade Mark regulation (being Reg.40/94).[167] It is hereinafter referred to as the "EUTMR". There are also two new secondary regulations which govern the practice and procedure before EUIPO. These are Reg.2017/1431 (the Implementing Regulation) and Reg.2017/1430 (the Delegated Regulation). These set out the practice and procedure of EUIPO for examination of applications, dealings in EUTMs, oppositions, amendments of EUTM applications, cancellation and revocation applications, appeals, communications with EUIPO, calculation of time limits and representation before EUIPO and international registrations which designated the EU. These replace the previous implementing regulations of EUIPO.

As a result of these changes, a Community Trade Mark is known as a European **3-124** Union Trade Mark ("EUTM") and the Office of Harmonisation of the Internal Market ("OHIM") is now known as the European Union Intellectual Property Office ("EUIPO").

The following sets out the key changes made to Reg.207/2009 by Reg.2015/ **3-125** 2424 which are now codified in the EUTMR (Reg.2017/1001).

Changes in force from 23 March 2016

- The absolute grounds to the registration of shapes in art.7 has now been extended to "another characteristic". An example of a mark that will be objectionable under the "other characteristic" ground could be a sweet smelling fragrance which appeals to consumers to mask unpleasant smells. This would probably fall foul of the "gives substantial value" to the goods objection.
- Relative grounds objections based on protected geographical indications of origins (i.e. PDOs and PGIs) can now be made to applications for EUTMs.
- In relation to infringement, two specific rights, namely using the sign as a trade or company name or part of a trade or company name and using the sign in comparative advertising in a manner that is contrary to Dir.2006/114/EC (the comparative advertising directive) had been included. Whether these changes are intended to amend or merely codify existing case law in this area is unclear.
- A right to prevent goods bearing an EUTM which are "in transit" through the EU has been introduced. This is to permit seizure of counterfeit goods which are not intended to be placed on the market in the EU. However, this provision can only apply if the owner of the goods in transit can show that that the EUTM owner does have equivalent protection in the country of final destination.
- The "own name" defence is now limited to natural persons and does not apply to company names.
- A general right of "referential use" of another EUTM is introduced provided that such is in accordance with honest practices in industrial and commercial matters.

---

[165] [2009] OJ L78/1.
[166] [2015] OJ L341/21.
[167] Reg.40/94 [1994] OJ L11/1.

- A new defence of "use of a later EUTM" or use of a national trade mark is introduced unless that later EUTM is liable to be declared invalid by the earlier EUTM.
- Procedurally, there have also been some changes including:
  — the opposition period for international applications designating the EU now starts from one month after publication of the application and runs for three months (previously it was six months after publication);
  — one cannot now bring an invalidation action relating to the same subject-matter/cause of action that has already been the subject of an opposition or other earlier designs. This codifies the principle of res judicata;
  — the proof of use period for earlier EUTMs relied upon to invalidate later EUTMs now ends at the date of filing or if earlier the priority date of the contested mark rather than
  — from the publication date of the contested mark (in addition to proving genuine use for the five-year period preceding the date of the application in a declaration of invalidity); and
  — the IP Translator case and its effect have been formalised into the EUTM Regulation by making it clear that the use of NICE class headings will not extend beyond the literal interpretation of the wording of that heading.

Changes in force from 1 October 2017

- The requirement of graphical representation for an application for a EUTM is removed. Thus, a sound mark may be registered even if not capable of graphical musical notation. However, applications will need to comply with the *Sieckmann* criteria and indeed, such criteria must be considered as having been expressly included into the EUTMR by the new requirement that the public must be able *"to determine the clear and precise subject matter of the protection afforded to its proprietor"*.
- One will be able to file for EU certification marks.

3-126   There have been very many decisions about the provisions of the TMD and the EUTMR and its predecessors from the General Court and CJEU. Whilst many of these decisions are rulings on preliminary references under art.267 TFEU from courts of Member States, many decisions arise by reason of appeal from EUIPO to the General Court and thereafter on matters of law to the CJEU. The consequence of this is that national decisions of the courts of Member States have receded in importance and there is now considerable uniformity in Member States to the interpretation of the TMD and EUTMR. In any event, because the TMD is exhaustive in relation to substantial law, any differences that arise from decisions of national courts would arise from different interpretation of the same provisions of the TMD. Owing to the very substantial case law of the General Court and CJEU on all of the main substantive provisions of the TMD or EUTMR, there is little point in reviewing the national decisions of courts of Member States save where such assist in interpreting the CJEU's or General Court's decisions.

3-127   The TMD is not intended to harmonise trade mark laws of Member States in every respect but is intended to harmonise the substantive law of *registered* trade marks. Thus, the objective of the TMD is to foster and create a well-functioning internal market.[168] Moreover, the new TMD aims at providing a greater degree of harmonisation than the previous Directive (Dir.2008/95) and therefore seeks to approximate some procedural rules.[169] Consequently the new TMD seeks to harmonise the principal procedural rules and ensure that trade mark registration under the EUTMR and in Member States is aligned. The new TMD achieves that by setting out general principles leaving the Member States free to establish more specific rules.[170] Hence the TMD goes considerably further than Dir.2008/95 in harmonising both key procedural and substantive trade mark laws of Member States.

It has been said that the purpose of EU trade mark law is: **3-128**

"generally to strike a balance between the interests of the proprietor of a trade mark to safeguard its essential function, on the one hand, and the interests of economic operators in having signs capable of denoting their products and services."[171]

EU trade mark legislation and arts 34–36

In principle, the effect of the enactment of the TMD (and the EUTMR) is that **3-129** no recourse can be had to arts 34–36—the free movement of goods provisions to determine whether the exercise of rights under the TMD or EUTMR is legal. This is an application of the general principle that where EU legislation provides complete and exhaustive measures designed to guarantee protection of a particular interest set out in art.36 TFEU, then recourse to arts 34–36 is not permitted.[172]

Thus, in *Matratzen Concord A.G. v Hukla Germany SA*,[173] the mark **3-130** *MATRATZEN* was registered for mattresses. "*Matratzen*" is German for mattresses. In an action for invalidation of the mark, the Spanish court was concerned that it should take into account the fact that the monopolisation of the word "*Matratzen*" would have the effect of preventing imports from Germany of mattresses and thus be an impermissible restriction on the free movement of goods contrary to arts 34–36. The CJEU confirmed the general principle that where there has been exhaustive harmonisation at Community level, a national measure must be assessed in the light of that harmonising measure and not those of primary law such as arts 34–36.[174]

However, in the context of the *exercise* of trade mark rights (as opposed to the **3-131** *registrability* of trade marks), greater care must be taken in applying this doctrine. Thus, in *Pharmacia & Upjohn SA*,[175] a repackaging case concerning parallel imports, the CJEU held that where a pharmaceutical company used different marks in different Member States (*Dalacin* in Denmark *v Dalacin C* in Greece), that although art.15 TMD prevented the exercise of rights where goods had been placed on the market in the EU *under that trade mark,* it did not apply to where *a differ-*

---

[168] See Recitals 2,8 and 42 TMD.

[169] Recital 9 TMD.

[170] Recital 9 TMD.

[171] *Levi Strauss & Co v Casucci SpA* (C-145/05) [2006] E.C.R. I-3703; [2006] E.T.M.R. 71 at [29] (said in relation to a predecessor version of the TMD).

[172] See paras 7-059, 7-093.

[173] *Matratzen Concord A.G. v Hukla Germany SA* (C-421/04) [2006] E.C.R. I-2303; [2006] E.T.M.R. 48.

[174] (C-421/04) [2006] E.C.R. I-2303, [2006] E.T.M.R. 48 at [20]–[21], citing *Phytheron International SA v Jean Bourdon SA* (C-352) [1997] E.C.R. I-1729 at [17]; *Daimler Chrysler A.G. v Land Baden-Wurttemberg* (C-324/99) [2001] E.C.R. I-9287 at [32]; *R. (on the application of Swedish Match AB) v Secretary of State for Health* (C-210/03) [2004] E.C.R. I-11893 at [81].

[175] *Pharmacia & Upjohn SA v Paranova A/S* (C-379/97) [1999] E.C.R. I-6297.

ent mark was affixed by a repackager to allow the pharmaceutical to be marketed in the country of import. In such circumstances, the legitimacy of the exercise of rights under TMD had to be assessed by reference to arts 34–36 TFEU.[176]

3-132 In any event, the CJEU has said several times that it is legitimate to have recourse to the jurisprudence on arts 34–36 for *interpreting* art.15 TMD and art.15 EUTMR.[177] Indeed, in *Bristol Myers Squibb v Paranova*, the CJEU said that the TMD cannot justify obstacles to intra-Community trade save within the bounds set by the Treaty rules.[178] Such an approach would suggest that any exercise of rights to partition the internal market or prevent legitimate parallel imports would be illegal under the TMD because such is contrary to arts 34–36 TFEU.

3-133 However, in an English case, *Oracle v M-Tech*,[179] the Supreme Court of England and Wales had to consider the legitimacy of a defence under arts 34–36 regarding the exercise of trade mark rights granted pursuant to national legislation implementing the TMD and EUTMR. Oracle brought proceedings for infringement of its Sun registered trade marks in relation to genuine computer servers which M-Tech had imported into the UK and had been originally put on the market outside the EEA by Oracle or with its consent. As will be seen later in this chapter, a trade mark proprietor is entitled to bring infringement proceedings in relation to goods first placed on the market outside the EEA by the trade mark proprietor or with its consent unless it has given unequivocal consent to their importation into the EEA ("non–EEA Goods") but not where the goods were first placed on the market within the EEA ("EEA Goods") by the proprietor or with its consent.[180] However, on the facts of the case, M-Tech argued that it was impossible for independent resellers to determine whether goods were non-EEA Goods or EEA Goods. They were traded many times, the market was global and sellers were globally located. Indeed, M-Tech said that Oracle itself had said on its website that no comfort could be drawn from the fact that they had been bought in the EEA. Furthermore, M-Tech argued that Oracle was refusing to supply information which would permit independent resellers to determine such facts. It said that Oracle's actions of aggressive litigation and refusing to divulge such information was causing legitimate trade in EEA Goods to disappear and that indeed, such was the intention of Oracle. Thus, it said that independent resellers dare not trade at all in any Oracle computer servers and Oracle's actions were to reserve (and intended to reserve) the entire secondary market in Oracle servers for itself. It thus alleged that such was contrary to arts 34–36 as Oracle's actions had the object and effect of partitioning the internal market in EEA Goods. The above facts were assumed for the purpose of the application before the Supreme Court.[181]

3-134 In reversing the Court of Appeal's decision, the Supreme Court granted the summary judgment application in favour of Oracle. It held that the reconciliation between art.10 TMD and arts 34 and 36 of the TFEU was embodied in the relationship between art.10 and art.15 TMD. Thus, the Court held that M-Tech did not have a defence mainly because the goods of which complaint were made (i.e. the non-EEA Goods) had never been marketed in the EEA and such was clearly an

---

[176] See [27]–[30].
[177] e.g. see *Bristol Myers Squibb v Paranova A/S* (C-427/93) [1996] E.C.R. I-3457 at [27].
[178] See [36].
[179] [2012] UKSC 27.
[180] See paras 3-590 and 3-616.
[181] The application was for summary judgment and the first instance court proceeded on the basis as to whether such facts were proven in law at trial, M-Tech would have a defence in law.

infringement. In such circumstances, arts 34–36 were not engaged because the goods had not even entered the EEA and thus its free movement provisions which concerned trade between Member States was not engaged.[182]

The court continued by saying M-Tech may have a cause of action against Oracle **3-135** under arts 34–36 for damages in respect of Oracle's policy of withholding information about the history of its goods but that such was not a defence to Oracle's action for trade mark infringement. As said by the court:

> "It may well be that M-Tech has a perfectly good cause of action against Sun based on articles 34 to 36 of the Treaty for damages for preventing them from selling Sun products by their policy of withholding information about the previous history of the goods. I make no comment on that, because it is irrelevant to this appeal. We are not concerned in these proceedings with business that M-Tech have been prevented from doing, still less with business that other traders have been prevented from doing. We are concerned with business which M-Tech have done in infringement of Sun's trade marks. It is not a defence to proceedings brought on that basis that there is other business that M-Tech have been prevented from doing by Sun's arguably unlawful policy of withholding information."

Thus, the core of the Supreme Court's judgment was that the importation of non- **3-136** EEA Goods was undoubtedly an infringement and it was irrelevant that M-Tech was unable to trade in EEA Goods. There was clearly a justified concern in the Supreme Court that a freestanding Euro-defence which even industrial counterfeiters could rely upon as against Oracle was wrong in principle.[183] However, on the basis of the facts of the case, the effect of the Supreme Court's decision was to permit a trade mark proprietor to engage in conduct which has the object and effect of preventing trade in legitimate parallel imports. That conduct could only be achieved by, in part, exercising trade mark rights. One understands the Supreme Court's intuitive approach that Oracle should not be denied the basic right to exercise trade mark rights at all against non-EEA Goods.[184] Clearly, if M-Tech did have a legitimate counterclaim for injunctive relief and damages against Oracle for withholding provenance information of the goods then justice could be done as Oracle would be forced to disclose such information. If such information was provided, then independent resellers could differentiate between EEA and non-EEA Goods and enforcement of rights against non-EEA Goods would not affect trade in EEA Goods. However, it is highly dubious that arts 34–36 can act as a sword as opposed to a shield (i.e. give rise to a cause of action as opposed to merely a defence[185]). Thus, the effect of the Supreme Court's decision was that Oracle could enforce its rights even though such have the object and effect of preventing trade in EEA Goods as well as non-EEA Goods. Surprisingly, the Supreme Court held that the matter was acte clair and thus no reference to the CJEU was necessary.[186]

---

[182] Relying upon *EMI v CBS* (C-51/75) [1976] E.C.R. 811—see judgment at [18]–[19]. See para.7-104, et seq.

[183] M-Tech conceded in oral argument that industrial counterfeiters could rely upon the defence as well as independent resellers—see [28].

[184] Described by Lord Sumption as "pulling down the whole temple"—at [27].

[185] The Supreme Court held that it was irrelevant whether M-Tech had a perfectly good cause of action based on arts 34–36 TFEU for damages although said that it may well be that M-Tech did have such.

[186] Indeed, in *Van Doren + Q GmbH v Lifestyle Sports* (C-244/00) [2003] E.C.R. I-3051, a case concerning who carried the burden of proof of showing that goods were EEA Goods or non-EEA Goods, the Advocate General supported submissions of the German government and the European Com-

3-137   In an English case, *Doncaster Pharmaceuticals v Bolton Pharmaceutical*[187] which concerned parallel trade marks that been in common ownership but were no longer, the Court of Appeal refused to strike out a defence that continuing control between assignor and assignee meant the trade mark proprietor was prevented from exercising their rights under art.36. In the author's opinion, the better analysis would have been that art.15 of the TMD was arguably engaged. However, it is of note that the Court of Appeal had no hesitation in finding that one could have direct recourse to art.36. In a later case, *Flynn Pharma v Drugsrus*,[188] the Court of Appeal of England and Wales considered the application of art.36 and its reference to "disguised restriction" in the context of rebranded parallel imports between one Member State and another and whether there was unitary control between the goods placed on the market in the exporting Member State and the undertaking seeking to enforce its UK trade mark. The Court of Appeal considered the authorities of *HAG II* and *Ideal Standard* which are authorities decided prior to harmonisation of trade mark law by the TMD and EUTMR[189] and held that such involved a dual enquiry: (i) Were the imported goods placed on the market by the trade mark owner or with their consent? (ii) If no, does the party who did place the goods on the Member State of export also have "effective control" of the mark which is sought to be enforced? Again, in the author's view, this is an application of the provisions on exhaustion of rights codified in the EUTMR and TMD, which as said above, it is legitimate to rely upon the jurisprudence under arts 34–36 for the purpose of interpreting them.

TRIPS and the TMD

3-138   Although TRIPS is not of direct effect, the CJEU has said in a number of cases that EU trade mark legislation must be interpreted in the light of the wording and purpose of TRIPS.[190] Where a trade mark dispute occurred prior to the implementation of TRIPS, it will still apply if the dispute is after the date of application of TRIPS.[191]

Minutes of the Council meeting

3-139   At the Council meeting at which the TMD was adopted, a number of statements were made which could be considered relevant to the interpretation of the TMD. The CJEU has said that it is settled case law that declarations recorded in Council minutes in the course of preparatory work leading to the adoption of a TMD cannot be used for the purpose of interpreting the TMD where no reference is made to the content of the declaration in the wording of the provision in question, and that

---

mission that a duty be placed on the trade mark owner to take reasonable steps to permit parallel traders to determine whether or not the right conferred by the mark had been exhausted and the German government endorsed a proposal that the goods be marked whether they were EEA Goods or non-EEA Goods—see [86]–[100].

[187] *Doncaster Pharmaceuticals* [2006] E.T.M.R. 65; [2007] F.S.R. 3.
[188] [2017] EWCA Civ 226; [2017] E.T.M.R. 25.
[189] These are discussed in Ch.7 at paras 7-210 to 7-222, 7-225 to 7-227. See also paras 7-162 to 7-164.
[190] e.g. see *Anheuser-Busch Inc v Budĕjovický Budvar, národní podnik* (C-245/02) [2004] E.C.R. I-10989; [2005] E.T.M.R. 27 at [42]. Generally, see paras 1-179 to 1-181.
[191] (C-245/02) [2004] E.C.R. I-10989; [2005] E.T.M.R. 27 at [47]–[53].

such declarations have no legal significance.[192] Thus, in *Libertel*, which concerned the registrability of a single colour, the CJEU said that it could not take into account a statement in the Minutes that the Council considered that the TMD did not exclude the possibility of registering a single colour.[193] In *Präktiker*, the CJEU held that retail services were registrable despite the fact that Minutes of the Council meeting said that they were not.[194] In *Anheuser-Busch v Budějovický Budvar, národní podnik*,[195] the CJEU held that the "own name" defence applied to the name of companies as well as individuals even though the Minutes doubted its application to corporate names. In *Leno Merken v Hagelkruis*, the CJEU refused to follow the Minutes that genuine use in one Member State was sufficient to show genuine use of a EUTM.[196]

Substantive provisions of TMD and EUTMR

As discussed above, prior to the changes affected on Reg.207/2009 by Reg.2015/2424 and now codified in the EUTMR (Reg.2017/2001), the substantive law for national trade marks and EUTMs was essentially identical. Until the new TMD is implemented in Member States by the latest, January 2019, the substantive law will remain unaligned in a number of areas. Thereafter, assuming that the TMD is implemented by all Member States, by that date national mark and EUTM substantive trade mark law will become re-aligned as of January 2017. For the sake of analysis, the *substantive law* provisions of the EUTMR and TMD are considered as follows: **3-140**

- The EUTMR provision is the one considered. As of 1 October 2017, all of the changes are in force. The equivalent *new* TMD (Dir.2015/2436) provision is *not* identified unless it differs materially. Thus, the reader should assume that if reference is only made to the EUTMR, there are identical (or identical save in an immaterial manner) provisions in the TMD.
- Where the old Trade Mark Directive (Dir.2008/95) is *different* to the TMD, it is considered *briefly* at the end of the section. If a reader requires greater analysis of old TMD provisions which differ to the new TMD, they should consult the 4th edn of this book.
- For the sake of clarity, in the text of the book, a reference in an old case to a provision of an old version of the EUTMR or TMD is amended to refer to the equivalent provision in the new EUTMR or TMD.
- Where reference is in a verbatim quote to an article in an earlier now repealed trade mark Regulation or Directive, the new provision which corresponds to it (if there is one) is put in square brackets, i.e "[art.4]".

The EUIPO has published a helpful correlation table which maps the old and new provisions of the EUTMR and the implementing Regulations.[197]

---

[192] e.g. see *Leno Merken BV v Hagelkruis Beheer BV* (C-149/11) ECLI:EU:C:2012:816 at 46–48 (and cases cited therein); *Ministrio Publico and Fazenda Publica v Epson Europe BV* (C-375/98) [2000] E.C.R. I-4243 at 26.

[193] *Libertel v Benelux Markenbureau* (C-104/01) [2003] E.C.R. I-3793 at [24]–[26].

[194] See para.3-200.

[195] (C-245/02) [2004] E.C.R. I-10989.

[196] See para.3-718.

[197] See *https://euipo.europa.eu/ohimportal/en/eu-trade-mark-legal-texts* [Accessed on 9 October 2017].

Signs of which a trade mark may consist

3-141 Article 4 EUTMR[198] states that:

"An EU trade mark may consist of any signs, in particular words, including personal names, or designs, letters, numerals, colours, the shape of goods or of the packaging of goods, or sounds, provided that such signs are capable of:

(a) distinguishing the goods or services of one undertaking from those of other undertakings

(b) being represented on the Register of European Union trade marks, ('the Register'), in a manner which enables the competent authorities and the public to determine the clear and precise subject matter of the protection afforded to its proprietor."

3-142 This provision differs from the old EUTMR provision because it no longer requires an application for a EUTM to be capable of being graphically represented. Instead, the requirement will be that the sign which is the subject of the EUTM application must be capable of being represented on the Register in a manner which allows clarity as to the precise subject matter of protection sought. As explained at Recital 9 to Reg.2015/2424, this allows "more flexibility while also ensuring greater legal certainty with regard to the means of representation of trade marks" and thus, provided that a sign can be *"represented in any appropriate form using generally available technology,"* it is not necessary for it to be represented graphically. This will permit the registration of unusual marks, e.g. smell, taste marks and sound marks which are incapable of being identified graphically (e.g. for sound marks, by using musical notation). Thus, the implementing regulations will allow a sound trade mark to consist of a .MP3 file (max 2 MB).

3-143 However, the *Sieckmann* criteria (discussed in the next section) will still apply (as made clear in Recital 13 TMD which refers to the representation being *"clear, precise, self-contained, easily accessible, intelligible, durable and objective"*). These criteria may be difficult to satisfy. In particular, the public must be able to easily access the mark. However, in a digital age this is problematic if the mark is, e.g. a smell or taste mark.

Old TMD

3-144 The old TMD retains the requirement of graphical representation.

3-145 **Sieckmann criteria** In *Sieckmann*, the CJEU said that it is not necessary that a mark can be perceived visually provided it can be represented graphically.[199] However, the CJEU confirmed that it is important that the public should know the precise subject-matter and extent of the protection afforded by a registered trade mark monopoly and that the relevant authorities can fulfil their obligations to examine properly the applications. Accordingly, the CJEU said that a trade mark may consist of a sign which is not in itself capable of being perceived visually. This is provided that it can be represented graphically, particularly by means of images, lines or characters, and that the representation is *clear, precise, self-*

---

[198] art.3 TMD.
[199] *Sieckmann v Deutsche Patent und Markenamt* (C-273/00) [2002] E.C.R. I-11737; [2003] E.T.M.R. 37 at [45]. This decision was given when the EUTMR required a graphical representation.

contained, easily accessible, intelligible, durable and objective.[200] These criteria (often called the *Sieckmann* criteria) have been recited in a number of cases involving unusual trade marks which are looked at in the next section.

The *Sieckmann* criteria now appear in Recital 10 of the EUTMR.[201] Furthermore, **3-146** art.4 EUTMR now requires the application to allow the competent authorities and the public to determine "the clear and precise subject matter of the protection afforded to its proprietor." Again, this codifies the *Sieckmann* criteria. Consequently, although there is no longer an obligation for a graphical representation of the mark, the *Sieckmann* criteria must be considered equally relevant (indeed, more so) to the new EUTMR and TMD as to its predecessors.

Smell   In *Sieckmann*, the CJEU had to consider the registrability of a mark for the **3-147** smell of a chemical substance called cinnamic acid methyl ester. The application as lodged with the German Trade Mark Office consisted of the following:

"(i)   A scent whose chemical formula was C_6H_5-CH-CH-COOCH$_3$;
(ii)   A container containing a sample of the chemical was deposited;
(iii)   The applicant described the scent as "balsamically fruity with a hint of cinnamon.""

The CJEU said that such matters did not satisfy the requirements of intelligibil- **3-148** ity, precision, durability and objectivity as required under the predecessor regulation to EUTMR. A chemical formula did not represent the odour of a substance but merely a chemical formula. Furthermore, a description of the odour was not sufficiently clear, precise and objective. Finally, a deposit of an odour sample is not sufficiently durable as it is liable to change over time. In *Eden Sarl v EUIPO*,[202] the applicant sought to register with EUIPO a mark consisting of the smell of ripe strawberries for various goods. The sign was graphically represented by a picture of a red strawberry and the words "smell of ripe strawberries". The application was rejected by EUIPO. On appeal to the General Court, the General Court dismissed the appeal on the grounds that the "smell of ripe strawberries" was not sufficiently clear or precise. Indeed, a study conducted for the case showed that ripe strawberries could have a number of smells!

It might be wondered whether it would ever be possible to register a smell mark. **3-149** The short answer is that it is probably not possible until there is a generally accepted classification of smells (like the PANTONE classification for colours).[203]

Colours   In *Libertel*,[204] the CJEU considered the registrability of a single colour **3-150** per se. The court reiterated the requirements set out in *Sieckmann*, namely the need for clear, precision, accessibility, self-contained(ness), objectivity and durability. A sample of a colour attached to an application for a mark did not satisfy the requirement of durability as such could vary over time. It said that a description of the colour together with a sample was capable of fulfilling the requirement of registrability provided it satisfied the *Sieckmann* criteria. However, it did say that

---

[200]   See [55].
[201]   "A sign should be permitted to be represented in any appropriate form using generally available technology, and thus not necessarily by graphic means, as long as the representation is clear, precise, self-contained, easily accessible, intelligible, durable and objective".
[202]   *Eden Sarl v EUIPO* (T-305/04) [2005] E.C.R. II-4705; [2006] E.T.M.R. 14.
[203]   See comments by the General Court in (T-305/04) [2006] E.T.M.R. 14 at [34].
[204]   (C-104/01) [2003] E.C.R. I-3793; [2004] F.S.R. 4; [2003] E.T.M.R. 63.

reference to an international colour classification (e.g. PANTONE) would be precise and stable and thus likely to satisfy the criteria.

3-151   In *Heidelberger Bauchemie*,[205] the applicant applied for a mark which comprised a rectangular piece of paper which was blue and the lower half yellow. The following description of the mark accompanied the application:

> "The trade mark applied for consists of the applicant's corporate colours which are used in every conceivable form, in particular on packaging and labels. The specification of the colours is: RAL 5015/HKS 47-blue RAL 1016/HKS 3-yellow."

3-152   The CJEU held that such did not satisfy the *Sieckmann* criteria. It said:

> "[33]   Accordingly, a graphic representation consisting of two or more colours, designated in the abstract and without contours, must be systematically arranged by associating the colours concerned in a predetermined and uniform way.
>
> [34]   *The mere juxtaposition of two or more colours, without shape or contours, or a reference to two or more colours 'in every conceivable form,* as is the case with the trade mark which is the subject of the main proceedings, does not exhibit the qualities of precision and uniformity required by [Art.3] of the [TMD], as construed in paras [25] to [32] of this judgment.
>
> [35]   Such representations would allow numerous different combinations, which would not permit the consumer to perceive and recall a particular combination, thereby enabling him to repeat with certainty the experience of a purchase, any more than they would allow the competent authorities and economic operators to know the scope of the protection afforded to the proprietor of the trade mark."

3-153   *Heidelberger* was concerned with two colours and not one. Clearly, with two or more colours, there is a need to understand how those colours spatially relate to each other (i.e. are the colours painted side by side, are there two concentric circles of blue and yellow, etc.). A failure to make clear how these colours are used in relation to each other is liable to fail the *Sieckmann* criteria. *Heidelberger* makes it clear that in such circumstances, the applicant must set out spatially how the colours are to appear. Thus, the applicant would be advised to apply for different visual representations of the *use of the* colour(s), e.g. the way that it is used on letterheads, promotional items, etc. Provided that this is done, there should be no objection to the registrability of two-colour spatially delineated marks.[206]

3-154   It is less clear whether this requirement of "spatial arrangement" is necessary for a single colour. In *Libertel*, this did not form part of the CJEU's discussion (although the discussion was against a reference of the colour orange not spatially delimited).[207] It might be argued that the applicant cannot lay claim to a mark which consists of a very particular colour in any shape and form, as such does not have a distinct and unique appearance. However, care must be taken here. A person can apply for a word mark even though that word can appear visually in many different fonts and sizes. Thus, a *unique* visual appearance of the mark is clearly not necessary to satisfy the criteria of registrability. It is thus likely that at [35] of its judgment in *Heidelberger*, the CJEU is merely saying that with a non-spatially limited two-colour mark, it is capable of so many different appearances which if they were used, the consumer would not consider the different appearances as be-

---

[205] *Heidelberger Bauchemie GmbH's Trade Mark Application* (C-49/02) [2004] E.T.M.R. 99.
[206] e.g. see *Red Bull* EUIPO (Opposition Decision, B 794, 273).
[207] (C-104/01) [2003] E.C.R. I-3793; [2004] F.S.R. 4; [2003] E.T.M.R. 63 at [21].

ing manifestations of the same mark.[208] In relation to a single colour, this does not apply. A single very specific pantone colour could (with very considerable use and promotion) become so associated with a particular product or service of an undertakings that any use of it would be considered to be indicative of the trade origin of the product.

However, care must be taken when applying for a colour mark to be precise about what is being applied for. Thus, an application for "the colour purple (Panttone 2685C) applied to the whole visible surface or being the predominant colour applied to the whole visible surface" for chocolate combined with a colour swatch of the sample colour was held not to comply with the *Sieckmann* criteria because it was an attempt to register multiple signs with different permutations, presentations and appearances which were neither graphically represented nor described with an certainty or precision or at all. As said, such would be to allow a registration so lacking in specificity, clarity or precision of visual appearance that it would offend against the principle of certainty and fairness.[209]

3-155

Auditory marks In *Shield Mark v Joost Kist*,[210] the CJEU ruled on the registrability of auditory marks. Again, it reiterated the *Sieckmann* requirements. It said that in the case of sound signs, such requirements were not satisfied when the sign consisted of notes going to make up a musical work or the indication such as "cry of an animal" or a simple onomatopoiea. However, such was satisfied where the sign is represented by a stave divided into measures and showing musical notes, clefs and rests and other musical notations.[211] In *Metro-Goldwyn-Mayer (MGM) Lion Corp's Application*,[212] MGM applied to register the "sound of a lion". The application stated that the mark was constituted by the sound produced by the roar of a lion and was represented by a spectrogram. The Board of Appeal said that such was in principle registrable even though it was not music and that a form of graphic representation in the form of a sonogram fulfilled the requirements of registrability. However, it said that the sonogram was incomplete because it contained no representation of scale on the time axis and the frequency axis.[213]

3-156

Movement marks In *Lamborghini*,[214] the manufacturer applied for a mark for cars which contained the following description:

3-157

---

[208] i.e. if a consumer purchased a product bearing a mark which displayed a blue circle within a yellow circle and the next time purchased a product bearing a mark which was parallel stripes of blue and yellow, it is highly unlikely that the consumer would consider such to be the same mark.

[209] *Société des Produits Nestlé v Cadbury (UK) Ltd* [2013] EWCA Civ 1174 at [51]–[52]. See also *Glaxo Wellcome UK Ltd v Sandoz* [2017] EWCA Civ 335 (here the graphical image of an inhaler satisfied the *Sieckmann* criteria but the verbal description said that the mark consisted of dark purple applied to a significant proportion of the inhaler. The Court of Appeal of England and Wales held that it was wrong to ignore the verbal description and thus the Sieckmann criteria was not satisfied).

[210] *Shield Mark v Joost Kist* (C-283/01) [2003] E.C.R. I-14313; [2004] R.P.C. 17; [2004] E.T.M.R. 33.

[211] Shield Mark had registered various musical marks such as: (1) a sequence of musical notes being E, D#, E, D#, E, B, D, C, A (the first notes of *Für Elise*); (2) a musical stave representing the first nine notes of *Für Elise*; (3) the onomatopoiea "Kukelekuuuu" suggesting the sound made by a cockerel; and (4) the sound of a cockcrow.

[212] *Metro-Goldwyn-Mayer (MGM) Lion Corp's EUTM Application* [2004] E.T.M.R. 34, Fourth Board of Appeal, EUIPO. Care must be taken in applying this authority now that the graphical representation requirement has been removed.

[213] A sonogram is a species of spectrogram: *Metro-Goldwyn-Mayer* [2004] E.T.M.R. 34 at [26].

[214] *Automobili Lamborghini Holding SpA's EUTM Application* (R772/2001–1) [2005] E.T.M.R. 43, First Board of Appeal, EUIPO.

"The trade mark refers to a typical and characteristic arrangement of the doors of a vehicle. For opening the doors are turned upwardly namely around a swivelling axis which is essentially arranged horizontally and transverse to the driving direction."

3-158 The application was accompanied by a sequence of images of a typical gull-winged car opening its doors. A number of objections were taken including that it did not conform to the requirements of registrability set out in the predecessor provision to art.4 EUTMR[215] It is sufficient to note that this objection was eventually dropped. However, in the author's opinion, there are clear concerns based on *Sieckmann* about movement marks if the application fails to set out the length of time that the movement mark takes. Thus, in the *Lamborghini* case, there would appear to be no reference to the time taken for the doors to open. It may be that, in reality, the application was for a discrete series of three-dimensional marks each consisting of the various stages from the doors being fully closed to becoming fully open, rather than the images forming part of an animation.

3-159 **Design** Under the predecessor EUTM regulation, the Court of Justice held that shop layout may be a sign capable of graphic representation even if the "design" for which registration is sought includes no size or proportions.[216] The requirement of graphic representation no longer applies but it would still be necessary to satisfy the *Sieckmann* criteria.

3-160 **Concepts** In certain cases, an applicant may apply for registration of a concept. In *Dyson Ltd v Registrar of Trade Marks*,[217] Dyson applied for registration of a "transparent bin or collection chamber forming part of the external surface of a vacuum cleaner as shown in the representation". The representations consisted of two very different looking vacuum cleaners. At the time of application for the marks, Dyson had a de facto monopoly in bagless vacuum cleaners as a result of patents but the transparent collection chamber was not actively promoted as a trade mark by Dyson. The Trade Marks Registry refused to register the mark and the matter was ultimately referred to CJEU by High Court as to whether such was registrable under art.7(3) (acquisition of distinctive character).

3-161 The CJEU declined to answer the question referred but instead considered whether it was a sign within the meaning of the predecessor provision to art.4 EUTMR. It held that the subject-matter of the application was not a sign within the meaning of this provision as it was a concept which covered a multitude of appearances. The EUTMR was intended to prevent the abuse of trade mark law in order to obtain an unfair competitive advantage. Dyson was seeking to do just that. Thus the subject-matter of the application was a mere property of the product and not a sign.

3-162 In an English decision, concerning the well-known Scrabble® game, it was held that a registered trade mark for a three-dimensional ivory coloured tile on the top surface of which is shown a letter of the Roman alphabet and a numeral in the range of one to 10 was not a "sign" within the meaning of the predecessor provision to art.4 as such covered an infinite number of permutations of different sizes, posi-

---

[215] art.7.1(a) EUTMR provides that a mark cannot be registered if it does not conform to art.4.
[216] *Apple Inc v Deutsches Patent- und Markenamt* (C-421/13) ECLI:EU:C:2014:2070 at [19].
[217] *Dyson Ltd v Registrar of Trade Marks* (C-321/03) [2007] E.C.R. I-687.

tions and combinations of letter and number.[218] The judge held, applying *Dyson* that such amounted to an attempt to claim a perpetual monopoly on all conceivable ivory-coloured tile shapes and that such was a mere property of the goods and not a sign. The judge held that this would allow the registered proprietor to obtain an unfair competitive advantage.[219] Furthermore, it is irrelevant whether or not the mark is distinctive when considering whether the mark is a sign. A concept-type mark may be distinctive of the proprietor but still be unregistrable because it amounts to an attempt to obtain an unfair competitive advantage by claiming a multitude of appearances.[220]

Finally, it should be said that the inability to register a concept does not mean that **3-163** a concept cannot be protected if such is embodied in a mark that does satisfy the *Sieckmann* criteria. For instance, in *Sabel v Puma*,[221] the mark in issue consisted of a graphical representation of a "bounding puma". The issue in those proceedings was whether there was a likelihood of confusion with a cheetah on the grounds that they both embodied the concept of big cats. It is well established that where marks are conceptually similar, a likelihood of confusion may occur.[222]

Capable of distinguishing goods or services of one undertaking from another

Article 4 EUTMR requires that the sign is capable of distinguishing the goods **3-164** or services of one undertaking from another. It has been said by the CJEU in relation to this provision that it incorporates the "essential function" of a trade mark, which is to guarantee the identity of the origin of marked goods or services to the consumer, by enabling the consumer, without any possibility of confusion, to distinguish the goods or service from others which have another origin.[223] Thus, the recitals to the TMD state that the function of a trade mark is, in particular, to guarantee the trade mark as an indication of origin.[224] Article 7.1(a) EUTMR says that a sign shall not be registered if it does not comply with art.4.

There has been a degree of debate as to whether this requirement adds anything **3-165** to art.7.1(b) EUTMR which denies registration to a sign which is devoid of any distinctive character, or art.7.1(c), which also denies registration to a sign which consists exclusively of signs or indications which may serve in trade to designate a particular characteristic of the goods or services being registered. It might be thought that this is an arid academic debate as anything which does not satisfy the criteria set out in art.4 regarding capability to distinguish will a fortiori not satisfy

---

[218] *J.W. Spear and Sons LTd v Zynga Inc* [2012] EWHC 3345 (Ch).

[219] See [47].

[220] See [45]–[46], *J.W. Spear and Sons v Zynga Inc*, where the High Court held that the distinctive character of the mark is irrelevant to considering whether the mark is a sign under art.4 citing inter alia that in *Dyson*, the CJEU did not consider it necessary to consider whether the Dyson bagless vacuum cleaner had acquired distinctive character to determine whether the mark complied with art.4. Upheld on appeal, [2013] EWCA Civ 1175. It is of note that the Court of Appeal rejected an argument that when considering the *Sieckmann* criteria, one should have regard to the acquired distinctive character of the mark, saying that such was a "paella" approach not permissible under EU law.

[221] C-251/95 [1997] E.C.R I-6191.

[222] See para.3-350.

[223] *Merz & Krell GmbH* (C-517/99) [2001] E.C.R. I-6959 at [23], citing *Canon Kabushiki Kaisha v Metro Goldwyn Mayer Inc* (C-39/97) [1998] E.C.R. I-5507 at [28].

[224] Recital 16.

art.7.1(b).[225] However, it is worth noting that art.7.1(a) which prevents the registration of marks which do not satisfy art.4 cannot be overcome by evidence of acquired distinctive character.[226] It is also worth pointing out that art.4 mirrors the wording of art.15(1) of TRIPS.

3-166   Ultimately, the requirement under art.4 and art.7.1 EUTMR that the mark must be capable of distinguishing goods or services is very low. It must be simply shown that there is a *capability* of the sign to act as an indication of trade origin and thus distinguish the products of one undertaking from another. As said in *Libertel* in relation to the capability of colours to distinguish:

> "[39]   As to the question whether a colour per se is capable of distinguishing the goods or services of one undertaking from those of other undertakings, within the meaning of [Art.[3] TMD], it is necessary to determine whether or not colours per se are capable of conveying specific information, in particular as to the origin of a product or service.
>
> [40]   In that connection, it must be borne in mind that, whilst colours are capable of conveying certain associations of ideas, and of arousing feelings, they possess little inherent capacity for communicating specific information, especially since they are commonly and widely used, because of their appeal, in order to advertise and market goods or services, without any specific message.
>
> [41]   However, that factual finding would not justify the conclusion that colours per se cannot, as a matter of principle, be considered to be capable of distinguishing the goods or services of one undertaking from those of other undertakings. *The possibility* that a colour per se may in some circumstances *serve as a badge of origin* of the goods or services of an undertaking cannot be ruled out. It must therefore be accepted that colours per se may be capable of distinguishing the goods or services of one undertaking from those of other undertakings, within the meaning of Art.[3 TMD].
>
> [42]   It follows from the foregoing that, where the conditions described above apply, a colour per se is capable of constituting a trade mark within the meaning of [Art.3 TMD]." [Emphasis supplied.]

3-167   It will be a very rare case that something which fulfils the *Sieckmann* criteria is not capable of distinguishing the products or services of one undertaking from another within the meaning of art.4. There is some suggestion however that in the case of an application for a shop layout, such may not be capable of distinguishing the products or services of one undertaking from another unless the layout departs significantly from the norms or customs of the sector concerned.[227] However, in the author's view, the real analysis of distinctive character is under art.7.1(b), (c) and (d) EUTMR.

Definition of goods and services?

3-168   The *Sieckmann* criteria apply to the trade mark itself and not to the definition of the goods or services in a trade mark application. What degree of clarity is required

---

[225] If a mark is incapable of distinguishing the goods or services of one undertaking, it must follow that it is devoid of distinctive character under art.7.1(b)—the word "distinguishing" and "distinctive" are cognate. The converse does not follow. Even if a sign satisfies art.7.1(a) such does not mean it has distinctive character under art.7.1(b)—see *Apple v Deutsche Patent- und Markenamt* (C-421/13) ECLI:EU:C:2014:2070 at [21].

[226] Under art.7(3), a mark which is devoid of distinctive character under art.7.1(b) can be registered if as a result of its use as a trade mark it has acquired distinctive character. This does not apply to art.7.1(a).

[227] *Apple Inc v Deutsches Patent- und Markenamt* (C-421/13) ECLI:EU:C:2014:2070 at [20].

in relation to such? The concept of goods and services is clearly very far ranging and wide. The Nice Agreement concerning the International Classification of Goods and Services for the Registration of Marks shows a very wide variety of goods and services.[228] An application to register a mark must set out clearly the goods and services for which registration is sought and the relevant class. All European countries and EUIPO use the Nice system of classification.[229] In *IP Translator*,[230] an applicant applied for various services by reference only to general indications of the class heading of Class 41. In such circumstances, it had been the practice of both the UK Registry and EUIPO to consider the use of such general indications to cover all of the individual goods or services falling within the general indications.[231] Thus, the applicant applied for *education, providing of training, entertainment, sporting and cultural activities* which are all general indications under Class 41 of the Nice Classification. It was thus held to have applied for *translation services* as such falls under Class 41. The applicant denied that it had applied for translation services.[232]

On reference to the CJEU, it noted that there is no provision in the predecessor to the TMD which directly governed the question of the identification of the goods or services concerned. However, the CJEU held that such did not mean that it was not a matter which fell within the TMD. It held that the application of certain provisions of the TMD depended to a great extent on whether the goods or services covered by a registered trade mark were indicated with sufficient clarity and precision (e.g. grounds for refusal or invalidity).[233] It thus held that an applicant must set out with sufficient clarity and precision the goods and/or services for which protection is sought to enable the competent authorities and economic operators to determine the extent of the protection conferred by the trade mark.[234] The CJEU also said that where an applicant uses general indications of a particular class heading of the Nice classification, it should specify whether its application for registration is intended to cover all the goods or services included in the alphabetical list of the particular class concerned or only some of the goods or services and if the latter, which goods or services are intended to be covered.[235]   **3-169**

As a result of *IP Translator*, EUIPO amended its practice to align with the CJEU's decision in *IP Translator*. This is reflected in art.33.3 EUTMR. Thus, any use of class headings of the Nice Classification will no longer mean that all goods or services within that class are protected. Rather, the use of class headings will only include goods or services *literally* covered by the meaning of such terms.[236] As this could have caused considerable hardship to those who had obtained registrations under the old practice, art.33(8) EUTMR allowed owners of EUTMs applied for prior to 22 June 2012 who had used class headings to cover all goods and services   **3-170**

---

[228] See *http://www.wipo.int/treaties/en/classification/nice/index.html* [Accessed 9 October 2017].

[229] *http://www.wipo.int/classifications/fulltext/nice8/ennnot.htm* [Accessed 9 October 2017] sets out in detail all the classes of goods and services together with an Explanatory Note.

[230] *Chartered Institute of Patent Attorneys v Registrar of Trade Marks* (C-307/10) ECLI:EU:C:2012:361.

[231] e.g. see Communication 4/03 of President of EUIPO dated 16 June 2003 (now repealed).

[232] It could have simply expressly excluded such services in its application and thus avoided the need to go to the CJEU. It is perhaps such considerations that led EUIPO and the European Commission to suggest that the reference was rather artificial (see [30]–[34]).

[233] See [42]–[43].

[234] See [56], [64].

[235] See [61].

[236] art.33.5.

in that class a period of six months expiring on 24 September 2016 to declare that their intention had been to seek protection in respect of goods and services beyond those covered by the literal meaning of that heading.

3-171   Clearly, any good that can be traded in is capable of being the subject-matter of a registered trade mark. The notional reader of the specified goods and services will generally not have any difficulty in understanding a description of goods. However, the definition of services in trade mark applications is much more problematic. Thus, one could have specified services such as "business assistance", "environmental", "health", etc. The notional reader of a trade mark registration which claims such services will find it much more difficult to determine the precise scope of the monopoly. For instance, does "environmental" mean recycling, advising business clients about minimising the impact of their business activities on the environment, removing rubbish, etc?

3-172   It is hoped that the *IP Translator* case will impact upon the need for applicants to be precise on the services that they are applying for. In the author's view, there is no reason why the *Sieckmann* criteria should not apply to definition of goods or services. Clarity of the monopoly sought is a cornerstone of EU trade mark legislation. Thus, in *Sieckmann*, the findings of the Court of Justice concerning the need to be able to determine the precise subject matter of protection afforded by the registered trade mark and the need for economic operators to find out about registrations and its precise nature apply equally to the definition of goods of services as such defines as much the extent of monopoly as the representation of the mark. The issue of clarity of specification has now been referred to the Court of Justice by the English court in *Sky v Skykick*.[237]

3-173   The only argument against this is that the *Sieckmann* criteria were developed in the context of the proper interpretation of art.4 which is concerned with the depiction of the sign for which protection is sought, whereas there is no equivalent provision for the definition of goods and services. However, the Court of Justice in *IP Translator* considered that point but made it clear that such an observation was not sufficient to prevent it making its findings that there was a requirement of "clarity and precision" for the identification of goods and services and that the application of provisions of the EU trade mark law depend to a great extent on whether the goods or services are indicated with "sufficient clarity and precision".[238]

3-174   In *Präktiker*, the CJEU considered whether retail services were registrable. The Council of Minutes had indicated that retail services were not registrable.[239] There had been considerable debate regarding whether this was a real and distinct service rather than being merely concerned with the sale of goods. The CJEU held that retail services were registrable. It held that it was sufficient to use general wording such as "bringing together of a variety of goods, enabling customers to conveniently view and purchase those goods".[240] However, it said that it was necessary to specify the goods or types of goods to which those services related to by including particulars of such in the application for registration.[241]

---

[237] [2018] EWHC 155.
[238] See [39]–[49].
[239] As said above at para.3-139, such Minutes are not binding on the courts.
[240] (C-418/02) [2005] E.C.R. I-5873; [2005] E.T.M.R. 88 at [49]. This mirrored the description of retail services in the Explanatory Note to Class 35 of the Nice Classification.
[241] (C-418/02) [2005] E.C.R. I-5873; [2005] E.T.M.R. 88 at [50]. See also (C-420/13) *Netto Marken Discount AG & Co KG v Deutsches Patent- und Markenamt* ECLI:EU:C:2014:2069 where the CJEU

Absolute grounds for refusal

Article 7 EUTMR set out the absolute grounds of objection to the grant of a **3-175** EUTM. The absolute grounds in the TMD are essentially the same.[242] Absolute grounds of objection should be distinguished from relative grounds of objection. The latter are essentially concerned with the protection of earlier rights of a third party whereas the former are more concerned with the inherent registrability of the mark. Thus, public policy and the protection of the public plays an important part in relation to absolute grounds whereas relative grounds are concerned more with disputes between private undertakings which do not raise issues of public importance (whilst it could be said that it is important that the public is protected from confusingly similar trade marks being on the market, such is relevant to infringement rather than which marks are placed on the register).

Many of the absolute grounds in art.7 are derived from the Paris Convention. **3-176** Thus, art.7.1(b), (c), (d) and (f) EUTMR are virtually identical in wording to art.6*quinquies* of the Paris Convention.[243] These provisions are considered below.

Signs which do not comply with the definition of trade mark

Article 7.1(a) EUTMR prevents the registration of marks which do not comply **3-177** with the requirements of art.4 EUTMR.

The requirements of art.4 have already been discussed.[244] The CJEU has made **3-178** clear that there is no class of marks which have a distinctive character and are thus free from objection under art.7.1(b)–(d) but are nonetheless excluded from registration by art.7.1(a) on the grounds that the mark is incapable of distinguishing the goods of the proprietor of the mark from those of other undertakings.[245] Thus, the CJEU has said that a sign representing a shape falls among the signs which may constitute a trade mark provided that is capable of being represented graphically and capable of distinguishing the products or services of one undertaking from another.[246]

Objections on lack of distinctiveness

In broad terms, art.7.1(b)–(d) EUTMR prevents the registration of signs which **3-179** as of the date of filing, lack the necessary "character" to act as indications of trade origin. These grounds of objection are applicable to an application for a EUTM even if they relate only to part of the EU.[247]

The approach under art.7.1(b)–(d) is whether normal and fair use of the sign ap- **3-180** plied for would be likely to trigger perceptions and recollections in the mind of the

---

held that a retail mark for a variety of services was permissible provided they were "formulated with sufficient clarity and precision"—[53].

[242] The main differences are that the TMD allows Member States to provide for an objection based on the trade mark being for a sign of high symbolic value, in particular a religious symbol (art.4.3(b)). This has no counterpart in the EUTMR.

[243] See para.3-016.

[244] See para.3-164.

[245] *Koninklijke Philips Electronics NV v Remington Consumer Products Ltd* (C-299/99) [2002] E.C.R. I-5475; [2002] E.T.M.R. 81 at [40].

[246] *Pi-Design v Yoshida Metal Industry* (C-337/12P) ECLI:EU:C:2014:129 at [43] and cases cited there. The requirement that the mark be capable of being represented graphically no longer applies.

[247] art.7(2) EUTMR. This can comprise a single Member State—see *August Storck KG v EUIPO* (C-25/05P) [2006] E.C.R. I-5719 at [83].

average consumer that were "trade origin specific" rather than "trade origin neutral".[248]

3-181   There is now a substantial corpus of case law from the CJEU and General Court on the interpretation of art.7.1(b), (c) and (d). Although the case law is not entirely consistent,[249] one can now say with reasonable confidence what are the general principles to the interpretation of art.7.1(b)–(d):

(1)   It is not a valid consideration when considering art.7.1(b)–(d) to take into account the fact that both the TMD and the EUTMR afford defences where a defendant is using a sign in a descriptive way. Although *Procter & Gamble v EUIPO (BABY-DRY)*[250] appeared to suggest that such should be taken into account when considering these grounds, subsequent authorities have made it clear that this is not correct. Thus, in *Erpo Möbelwerk v EUIPO (Daz Prinzip der Bequemlichkeit)*,[251] the CJEU said that there can be no principle that, if in doubt, a quasi-descriptive mark should be registered simply because there are defences of descriptive use. As it said:

> "…examination of applications for registration must not be minimal but must be stringent and full in order to prevent trade marks from being improperly registered and to make sure that, for reasons of legal certainty and administration, trade marks whose use could be successfully challenged before the courts are not registered."[252]

Similarly, in *Nichols Plc v Registrar of Trade Marks*,[253] a case concerning the registrability of surnames, it was illegitimate to consider the availability of the "own name" defence when considering the registrability of an English surname. This approach must be correct. Indeed, in *Wrigley v EUIPO (Doublemint)*,[254] Jacobs AG who had given an Opinion in *BABY-DRY* recognised that a trade mark owner may threaten unmeritorious proceedings against a competitor who might capitulate rather than incur the costs of the litigation.[255]

(2)   The *legal* criteria to be applied under art.7.1(b)–(d) is the same regardless of the nature of the sign applied for.[256] However, certain signs are more likely to be perceived as trade marks than others. Thus, it may be that for the purpose of applying the criteria, the relevant public's perception is not necessarily the same in relation to different categories of mark and it would thus be more difficult to establish distinctiveness in relation to marks of

---

[248]   This is a term used in English courts, e.g. see *Telewest's Communication* [2003] R.P.C. 26.

[249]   The most important inconsistency is the difference of approach between the CJEU in *Procter & Gamble v EUIPO (BABY-DRY)* (C-383/99P) [2001] E.C.R. I-6251; [2002] E.T.M.R. 3, CJEU and the latter case—*Wrigley v EUIPO (Doublemint)* (C-191/01P) [2003] E.C.R. I-12447; [2004] E.T.M.R. 9. In general, *BABY-DRY* has not been followed where it is inconsistent with *DOUBLEMINT*. See para.3-183.

[250]   *Procter & Gamble v EUIPO (BABY-DRY)* (C-383/99P) [2001] E.C.R. I-6251; [2002] E.T.M.R. 3.

[251]   *Erpo Möbelwerk v EUIPO (Daz Prinzip der Bequemlichkeit)* (C-64/02P) [2005] E.T.M.R. 58; [2004] E.C.R. I-10031.

[252]   At [45] citing *Libertel Groep BV v Merkenbureau Benelux* (C-104/01) [2003] E.C.R. I-3793 at [58]–[59].

[253]   *Nichols Plc v Registrar of Trade Marks* (C-404/02) [2004] E.C.R. I-8449; [2005] E.T.M.R. 21.

[254]   *Wrigley v EUIPO (Doublemint)* (C-191/01P) [2003] E.C.R. I-12447; [2004] E.T.M.R. 9.

[255]   (C-191/01P) [2003] E.C.R. I-1244; [2004] E.T.M.R. 9 at [95], Opinion.

[256]   *Linde AG v Deutsche Patent-under Markenamt* (C-53/01) [2003] E.C.R. I-3161 at [42] and [46] (a case concerning a shape mark).

certain categories as compared with marks of other categories.[257] Thus, the public is accustomed to perceiving words and figurative marks as indications of trade origin. Conversely, in relation to colour, the public is not accustomed to perceiving colour as an indication of trade origin. That is because colour is not generally used as such.[258] Similarly, in the context of shape marks, the average consumer is not accustomed to making assumptions about the origin of products on the basis of their shape and it would thus be more difficult to establish distinctiveness in relation to a three-dimensional shape mark as opposed to a word or figurative mark.[259] As said in an English case, there is a spectrum of signs as regards the public's perception of them as candidates for trade marks. The most distinctive forms are those such as invented words and fancy devices. In the middle are things such as semi-descriptive words and devices. Towards the other end are shapes of containers. Finally, there is the very shape of goods.[260]

(3)   The distinctiveness of a trade mark must be assessed by reference to the goods and services for which protection is sought and by reference to the perception of them by the relevant public which consists of average consumers of the goods or services in question who are reasonably well informed and reasonably observant and circumspect.[261] All relevant facts and circumstances must be taken into account including the results of any study submitted by the applicant.[262] The level of attention of the relevant public is likely to vary according to the category of goods or services in question.[263]

(4)   The distinctiveness of a sign must be considered on a case-by-case basis. There is no category of signs which can be a priori refused. In a stark example of this, in relation to an application to register "α" (the Greek letter alpha) for alcoholic beverages, the application was rejected by EUIPO (on appeal) that as a matter of principle, without use, single letters could not have distinctive character. The General Court held that such was wrong in approach and EUIPO should have considered the application on its facts and the goods and services for which registration is sought and not by reference to general principles.[264] On appeal to the CJEU, it held that the General

---

[257]   *Borco-Marken-Import Matthiesen GmbH v EUIPO* (C-265/09P) [2011] E.T.M.R. 4 at [33]; *Procter & Gamble Co v Office for Harmonisation in the Internal Market (Trade Marks and Designs) (EUIPO) ("Three-dimensional geometrical shapes")* (C-473/01P) [2004] E.C.R. I-5173, [2004] E.T.M.R. 89 at [36]; *EUIPO v Erpo Möbelwerk (DAS PRINZIP DER BEQUEMLICHKEIT)* (C-64/02P) [2004] E.C.R. I-10031, [2005] E.T.M.R. 58 at [34]; *Henkel KGaA v EUIPO* (C-456/01P) [2004] E.C.R. I-5089, [2004] E.T.M.R. 87 at [36] and [38]; and *Audi AG v EUIPO* (C-398/08P) [2010] E.T.M.R. 18 at [37].

[258]   (C-104/01) [2003] E.C.R. I-3793 at [65].

[259]   *Henkel KGaA v EUIPO* (C-456/01 and 457/01) [2004] E.C.R. I-5089; [2005] E.T.M.R. 44 at [38].

[260]   *Bongrain SA's Trade Mark Application (No.2134604)* [2005] E.T.M.R. 47 CA at [25].

[261]   *Koninklijke v Benelux-Merkenbureau (Postkantoor)* (C-363/99) [2004] E.C.R. I-1619, [2004] E.T.M.R. 57 at [34]; *Gut Springenheide GmbH v Oberkreisdirektor des Kreises Steinfurt* (C-210/96) [1998] E.C.R. I-4657 at [31]; *Linde AG* (C-53/01 and C-55/01) [2003] E.C.R. I-3161 at [41], (C-104/01) [2003] E.C.R. I-3793 at [46] and [75]. This is settled law—see *Procter & Gamble v EUIPO (dishwasher tablet)* (C-474/01P) [2004] E.C.R. I-5173, [2004] E.T.M.R. 89 at [35].

[262]   (C-363/99) [2004] E.C.R. I-1619; [2004] E.T.M.R. 57 at [35].

[263]   *Ruiz-Picasso v EUIPO* (C-361/04P) [2006] E.C.R. I-643; *Nestlé Waters France v EUIPO* (T-305/02) [2003] E.C.R. II-5207.

[264]   *Borco-Marken-Import Matthiesen GmbH v EUIPO* (T-23/07) [2009] E.C.R. II-887. On appeal, (C-

Court's approach was correct. Indeed, even an application for a single let-ter "I" cannot be ruled unregistrable based on a rule that single letters are unregistrable.[265]

(5) Although each ground is concerned with whether the mark as applied is distinctive, it must be examined separately. The CJEU has said on a number of occasions that although there is a clear overlap between the scope of the respective provisions, each ground must be considered separately.[266]

(6) The court or tribunal must interpret each provision with regard to the underlying public interest.[267] The public interest of art.7.1(b) is not the same as that for art.7.1(c) or (d).

3-182   Objections under art.7.1(b), (c) and (d) can be overcome if the mark as applied for has acquired distinctive character by reason of their use in the market place under art.7.3. This is discussed later.[268]

Devoid of any distinctive character

3-183   Article 7.1(b) EUTMR prevents the registration of signs that "are devoid of any distinctive character". In addition to the principles set out in the previous section, the following principles apply to art.7.1(b):

(1) Under art.7.1(b), the fundamental inquiry is whether the sign applied for will be perceived as an indication of trade origin as of the date of filing without further education of the public. As said by the CJEU about this provision, it is intended to preclude registration of trade marks which are not capable of fulfilling the essential function of a trade mark.[269] The public interest underlying art.7.1(b) is "indissociable from the essential function of a trade mark".[270]

A secondary public interest under art.7.1(b) is the need not to unduly restrict the ability of operators to trade in goods or services. This considera-tion plays a much larger part in art.7.1(c) than art.7.1(b). However, in the context of colours and art.7.1(b), the CJEU has said that there is a public interest in not unduly restricting the availability of colours for traders.[271] Clearly, with word and figurative marks, there is an infinite choice of words. Thus, this public interest is unlikely to be engaged. However, in the context of descriptive words and promotional slogans, the public interest in traders not being unduly restricted in their ability to describe and promote their products or services does feature. Furthermore, the English Court of Ap-

---

265/09P) [2010] E.C.R. I-8265; [2011] E.T.M.R. 4.

[265] See *IVG Immobilien* (T-441/05) [2007] E.C.R. II-1937 at [42]. See also *Nichols Plc v Registrar of Trade Marks* (C-404/02) [2004] E.C.R. I-8499 at [29] (surnames); *Bang & Olufsen A/S v EUIPO* (T-460/05) [2007] E.C.R. II-4207, [2008] E.T.M.R. 46.

[266] *Koninklijke KPN Nederland* (C-363/99) [2004] E.C.R. I-1619, [2004] E.T.M.R. 57 at [67]; *Merz & Krell GmbH* (C-517/99) [2001] E.C.R. I-6959 at [35]–[36].

[267] *Pi-Design v Yoshida Metal Industry* (C-337/12P) ECLI:EU:C:2014:129 at [44]; *Libertel Groep BV v Benelux-Merkenbureau* (C-104/01) [2003] E.C.R. I-3793 at [51]–[52]; *Koninklijke KPN Nederland* (C-363/99) [2004] E.C.R. I-1619, [2004] E.T.M.R. 57 at [68].

[268] See para.3-277.

[269] *SAT.1 Satellitenfernsehen GmbH v EUIPO* (C-329/02) [2004] E.C.R. I-8317; [2005] 1 C.M.L.R. 57; [2005] E.T.M.R. 20 at [23].

[270] (C-329/02) [2004] E.C.R. I-8317; [2005] 1 C.M.L.R. 57; [2005] E.T.M.R. 20 at [27].

[271] *Libertel Groep BV v Benelux-Merkenbureau* (C-104/01) [2003] E.C.R. I-3793 at [60].

peal has said that this public interest, which it characterised as the "deple-tion" of public interest, should not be confined to colour marks.[272] However, when considering shape marks, the CJEU does not appear to have considered the "depletion" of public interest.

Finally, although it is tempting to consider the public interest to keep signs free for all in the inquiry under art.7.1(b), the CJEU has said that criterion is relevant to art.7.1(c) but not art.7.1(b). Thus, it is not relevant under art.7.1(b) to consider whether the sign is commonly used or capable of being commonly used in the trade.[273]

(2)   The essence of the inquiry under art.7.1(b) is whether the mark in question:

> "makes it possible to identify the product for which registration is sought as originating from a given undertaking and therefore to distinguish the product from those of other undertakings and therefore is able to fulfil the essential function of the trade mark."[274]

Thus, a sign is only distinctive for the purposes of art.7.1(b), if it may be perceived immediately as an indication of the commercial origin of the goods or services in question, so as to enable the relevant public to distinguish, without any possibility of confusion, the goods or services of the owner of the mark from those of a different commercial origin.[275]

(3)   When considering art.7.1(b), the CJEU has made it clear that it is not ap-propriate to consider whether the sign in issue is in current common use or capable of common usage.[276] It has said that considerations of usage are relevant to art.7.1(c) but not art.7.1(b). This is particularly relevant when considering slogans.[277] Thus, a sign may be objectionable as being devoid of distinctive character even if it is different from the usual way of designat-ing goods or services. This approach appears to be a departure from its posi-tion in *BABY-DRY* but must be correct. In that case, it said that the purpose of art.7.1(b) and (c) is to prevent registration of signs or indications which:

> "... because they are *no different from the usual way of designating the relevant goods or services or their characteristics*, could not fulfil the function of identify-ing the undertaking that markets them and are thus devoid of the distinctive character needed for that function."[278] [Emphasis supplied.]

Clearly, this approach, if such is taken literally to mean that marks which

---

[272] *Bongrain SA* [2005] E.T.M.R. 47 CA.

[273] *SAT.1 v EUIPO* (C-329/02) [2004] E.C.R. I-8317, [2005] 1 C.M.L.R. 57, [2005] E.T.M.R. 20 at [36]; (C-64/02P) [2005] E.T.M.R. 58, [2004] E.C.R. II-2837 at [46]; *BioID v EUIPO* (C-37/03P) [2005] E.C.R. I-7975, [2005] E.T.M.R. CN5 at [62].

[274] e.g. see *Borco-Marken-Import Matthiesen GmbH & Co KG v EUIPO* (C-265/09P) [2011] E.T.M.R. 4; *Erpo Möbelwerk v EUIPO* (C-64/02P) [2005] E.T.M.R. 58, [2004] E.C.R. I-10031 at [42]; (C-517/99) [2001] E.C.R. I-6959 at [37]; (C-53/01 and C-55/01) [2003] E.C.R. I-3161 at [40]; *SAT.1 v EUIPO* (C-329/02) [2004] E.C.R. I-8317, [2005] 1 C.M.L.R. 57, [2005] E.T.M.R. 20 at [23].

[275] *Best Buy Concepts Inc v EUIPO (BEST BUY)* (T-122/01) [2003] E.C.R. II-2235 at [20] and [21]. Cf. where the sign is too vague and determinate to confer a descriptive character—*Bank für Arbeit und Wirtschaft v EUIPO (EASYBANK)* (T-87/00) [2001] E.C.R. II-1259 at [31].

[276] *SAT.1 v EUIPO* (C-329/02) [2004] E.C.R. I-8317, [2005] 1 C.M.L.R. 57, [2005] E.T.M.R. 20 at [36]; *Erpo Möbelwerk GmbH v EUIPO*(C-64/02P) [2005] E.T.M.R. 58, [2004] E.C.R. I-10031 at [46].

[277] (C-37/03) [2005] E.C.R. I-7975; [2005] E.T.M.R. CN5 at [62]. See also the section on "Slogans" at para.3-188.

[278] (C-383/99P) [2001] E.C.R. I-6251; [2002] E.T.M.R. 3 at [37].

are different from the usual way of designating relevant goods or services or their characteristics are free from objection under art.7.1(b) is flawed. It conflates two different notions: the meaning of a sign and whether the sign has been used. In *Agencja Wydawnicza Technopol sp. z o.o. v EUIPO*,[279] the CJEU, said in referring to an argument of the appellant based on the above paragraph from *BABY-DRY* that such cannot be understood as defining a condition for refusing to register a sign as a EU trade mark.[280] Nevertheless, trade marks which *do* correspond to usual ways of designating goods or services or their characteristics will rarely be registrable. However, in such circumstances, the real objection is art.7.1(c).

However, if it can be shown that similar signs to the mark applied for are used in the market as *trade marks* in relation to relevant goods or services, this may show that an apparently non-distinctive sign is not devoid of any distinctive character. In such circumstances, it can be said that the public has been educated *in general* to perceive such signs as indications of trade origin. Thus, in *SAT.1*, which was concerned with the registrability of "SAT.1", the CJEU said that the fact that there was frequent use of trade marks consisting of a word and a number in the telecommunications sector means that "SAT.1" could not be considered to be devoid, in principle, of distinctive character.[281]

The CJEU also said in *BABY-DRY* that in determining whether a mark is "capable of distinctiveness", one should consider whether the mark "may be viewed as a normal way of referring to the goods or of representing their essential characteristics in common parlance".[282] It is clear that this approach is faulty because it conflates the requirements of art.7.1(b) and (c). Clearly, a very simple mark such as "?" or "A" for food does not describe food or a characteristic (let alone an essential characteristic) of food but is clearly devoid of distinctive character (without use) because the public would not, without education, perceive them as an indication of origin.[283]

(4)   Marks must be considered as a whole. The mere fact that elements, when considered separately, are devoid of distinctive character does not mean that their combination cannot present a distinctive character.[284]

---

[279]   (C-51/10P) [2011] E.C.R. 1541.

[280]   See [40].

[281]   See [44]. NB. This is a different argument to the one that the mark *in casu* has acquired distinctive character by reason of use in the marketplace. The above argument is concerned with the public's education to the use of particular type of quasi-descriptive brands in general in the relevant sector.

[282]   (C-383/99P) [2001] E.C.R. I-6251; [2002] E.T.M.R. 3 at [42]. This case was technically only concerned with an appeal against refusal to register under art.3(1)(c). However, the CJEU's comments at [42] appear, prima facie, to apply to both Articles.

[283]   Although, in *IVG Immobilien v EUIPO* (T-441/05) [2007] E.C.R. II-1937, the General Court upheld an appeal from EUIPO which rejected an application for the letter "I" in royal navy as the Board of Appeal had rejected the application on the basis that a single letter in a common font was per se unregistrable.

[284]   (C-329/02) [2004] E.C.R. I-8317, [2005] 1 C.M.L.R. 57, [2005] E.T.M.R. 20 at [28]; *Campina Melkunie BV v Benelux-Merkenbureau* (C-265/00) [2004] E.C.R. I-1699 at [40]-[41]; *Koninklijke KPN Nederland* (C-363/99) [2004] E.C.R. I-1619, [2004] E.T.M.R. 57 at [99]-[100].

Different genre of marks

Although as said above, the criteria applied under art.7.1(b) is the same regard- **3-184** less of the type of mark applied for, it is still informative to consider the approach of the CJEU and General Court to particular genre of marks.

Descriptive word or letter marks

In relation to descriptive word or letter marks, there is no requirement that a word **3-185** mark has a specific level of linguistic or artistic creativity for it to be registrable.[285] Thus, there is no per se rule that very simple words or letters are unregistrable. They must be examined on a case by case basis. Thus, the CJEU dismissed an appeal from the General Court where it held that EUIPO had erred in applying a per se rule that a single letter (the Greek letter α) was not registrable and that it should have considered the application on its facts.[286] Invented words and words which are allusive but not descriptive will not be devoid of any distinctive character. Words which are descriptive in relation to the goods or services for which registration is sought will generally not possess any distinctive character. Where a sign consists of elements which are individually devoid of distinctive character, it is necessary to consider the overall perception rather than the individual elements.[287] Regard can be had to practices in the relevant sector.[288] Ultimately, the matter is one of impression and each case turns on its facts. Generally, attempts to register normal, commonly used words are objected to unless such words have no relationship with the underlying goods or services. However, the following decisions will give the reader an idea of the level of distinctiveness required for word marks which have a large element of descriptiveness:

- *bestpartner* for insurance, internet and dataprocessing services was contrary to art.7.1(b) EUTMR. The two words "best" and "partner" were generic words which simply denoted the quality of services supplied and coupling them together did not "imbue them with any additional characteristic".[289]
- *Eurocool* for storage and keeping of frozen foods was not open to objection under art.7.1(b). Although "Euro" and "cool" were in everyday usage, such did not apply to the composite mark *Eurocool*.[290]
- *Companyline* for "insurance services" was devoid of any distinctive character.[291]
- *SAT.1* was registrable for telecommunication services.

---

[285] *SAT.1 V EUIPO* (C-329/02) [2004] E.C.R. I-8317; [2005] 1 C.M.L.R. 57; [2005] E.T.M.R. 20 at [41].
[286] *Borco-Marken-Import Matthiesen GmbH & Co KG v EUIPO* (C-265/09P) [2011] E.T.M.R. 4 at 38–40. See also *IVG Immobilien v EUIPO* (T-441/05) [2007] E.C.R. II-1937 (application for the letter "I").
[287] e.g. *SAT.1* (C-329/02) [2004] E.C.R. I-8317; [2005] 1 C.M.L.R. 57; [2005] E.T.M.R. 20, where the CJEU overturned a decision of the General Court which failed properly to consider the distinctiveness of *SAT.1* as a whole. See also, *Procter & Gamble v EUIPO (BABY DRY)* (C-383/99P) [2001] E.C.R. I-6251; [2002] E.T.M.R. 3 at [40].
[288] (C-329/02) [2004] E.C.R. I-8317; [2005] 1 C.M.L.R. 57; [2005] E.T.M.R. 20 at [44].
[289] *MLP Finanzdienstleistungen A.G. v EUIPO* (T-270/02) [2004] E.C.R. II-2837; [2006] E.T.M.R. 20.
[290] *Eurocool v EUIPO* (T-34/00) [2002] E.C.R. II-683; [2003] E.T.M.R. 4.
[291] *DKV v EUIPO* (T-19/99) [2000] E.C.R. II-1 upheld by CJEU in *DKV v EUIPO* (C-104/00) [2002] E.C.R. I-7561.

- *BABY-DRY* was registrable for disposal nappies.[292]

Laudatory word marks

3-186   Laudatory marks such as "super" are generally not registrable even though they do not describe a *characteristic* of the goods or services for which registration is sought. Thus, *TOP* for herbal supplements was held to be unregistrable under art.7.1(b).[293] As the CJEU said in discussing the registrability of "TOP":

> "[95]   Furthermore, although it is true that, due to its generic meaning which tends to exalt in an unspecified manner the nature, function, quality or one of the qualities of any product or service, the sign 'top' does not enable the consumer to imagine to what type of goods or services it refers, the fact nevertheless remains that, precisely because it is commonly used in everyday language, as well as in trade, as a generic laudatory term, that word sign cannot be regarded as appropriate for the purpose of identifying the commercial origin of the goods which it designates and, therefore, of performing the essential function of a trade mark."

3-187   However, *Ultraplus* was held to be "perceptibly different from a lexically correct construction" to be free from objection under art.7.1(b).[294] Also, following this decision, *Europremium* was held registrable for packaging goods and transport services.[295] However, in this case, the objection was art.7.1(c) and not art.7.1(b).[296] As laudatory marks are abstract in nature, generally art.7.1(b) will be the only relevant ground of objection.[297] Thus, words which are in common usage such as "top", "super", "best" are objectionable but laudatory marks which have an element of inventiveness about them are not.

Slogan word marks

3-188   A number of attempts have been made to register advertising slogans as trade marks. Generally, these have been unsuccessful and rejected under art.7.1(b) (or art.7.1(c)). Generally average consumers are not in the habit of making assumptions about the origin of products on the basis of advertising slogans.[298] In considering art.7.1(b), the court will consider whether a slogan would be perceived immediately as an indication of trade origin rather than as an advertising slogan. However, if the public does perceive the slogan as an indication of origin, the fact that the slogan is also understood (even primarily understood) as a promotional formula has no bearing on the assessment of distinctive character.[299]

3-189   It is not necessary that the slogan be in common use for it to be refused under

---

[292] However, as discussed, caution must be applied to this case because the underlying reasoning has not been followed in later cases.

[293] *Sunrider Corp v EUIPO* (T-242/02) [2005] E.C.R. II-2793. See also *Pioneer Hi-Bred v EUIPO* (T-424/07) [2009] E.C.R. II-00003 where the mark OPTIMUM was refused.

[294] *Dart Industries v EUIPO (Ultraplus)* (T-360/00) [2003] E.C.R. II-3867 at [47].

[295] *Deutsche Post Express v EUIPO (Europremium)*(T-334/03) [2005] E.C.R. II-65; [2006] E.T.M.R. 52. This can be thought of as a borderline laudatory/descriptive mark.

[296] As pointed out specifically by General Court, at [40]–[41].

[297] (T-334/03) [2005] E.C.R. II-65; [2006] E.T.M.R. 52 at [40].

[298] *Erpo Möbelwerk v EUIPO* (C-64/02P) [2004] E.C.R. I-10031; [2005] E.T.M.R. 58 at [35].

[299] *Audi AG v EUIPO* (C-398/08P) [2010] E.C.R. 535 at [44] (concerning the well-known Audi slogan "*Vorsprung durch Technik*"); *Delphi Technologies v EUIPO* (C-488/13P) EU:C:2014:1746 at [36]; *Juan Moreno Marin and ors v Abadia RetuertaSA* (C-139/16) ECLI:EU:C:2017:518 at [29].

art.7.1(b).[300] Conversely, it is not necessary that the slogan must have an additional element of imagination or originality to overcome an objection under art.7.1(b).[301] However, it is clear that the lack of such will often mean that the slogan will be objectionable under art.7.1(b) and conversely, if the slogan can be perceived as imaginative, surprising or unexpected, the presence of such characteristics is likely to endow the mark with distinctive character.[302]

Thus, a mark consisting of the words "BEST BUY" on a swingtag label for a broad range of services was held devoid of any distinctive character.[303] The slogan "LOOKS LIKE GRASS...FEELS LIKE GRASS...PLAYS LIKE GRASS" for synthetic surfacing was also held devoid of any distinctive character.[304] The slogan had no "particular rhetorical flourish, poetic character or rhythm" such as to confer distinctiveness upon it.[305] A mark *"MEHR FÜR IHR GELD"* ("more for your money") was held devoid of any distinctive character because it would be perceived immediately by the relevant public as a mere promotional formula or slogan. The fact that it did not tell the consumers about the content or nature of the goods did not mean that it was not devoid of any distinctive character.[306] The mark "Live Richly" for financial and monetary services was held not to be registrable.[307] The mark "TAME IT" was held unregistrable for soaps, perfumeries, essential oils, hair lotions and dentifrices as it would be seen as an advertising message rather than as an indication of trade origin.[308] The slogan "Real People, Real Solutions" was held unregistrable as there was nothing beyond its obvious promotional meaning that enabled the relevant public to memorise the sign easily and instantly as a distinctive trade mark for the designated services and without use of the mark, the relevant public would not perceive it other than in its promotional sense.[309] On the other hand, the General Court found that the Board of Appeal had been wrong to refuse to register slogan *"DAZ PRINZIP DER BEQUEMLICHKEIT"* ("the Principle of Comfort") for land vehicles, household and office furniture by reason of its lack of imagination or conceptual tension.[310]

3-190

Decorative patterns

Patterns such as stripes on clothing and shoes which are simple and ordinary are devoid of any distinctive character. Thus, in *Shoe Branding Europe BVBA v EUIPO*,[311] the General Court found that a mark consisting of two parallel stripes of equal width positioned on the sleeve of a shirt fell foul of art.7.1(b) EUTMR. To

3-191

---

[300] *Erpo Möbelwerk v EUIPO*, at [46].
[301] *Erpo Möbelwerk v EUIPO* (T-138/00) [2001] E.C.R. II-3739 at [43]–[44] (this part of the reasoning of the General Court was upheld on appeal, (C-64/02P) at [50]–[51]); *Fieldturf Inc v EUIPO* (T-216/02) [2004] E.C.R. II-3867, [2004] E.T.M.R. 86at [33].
[302] *Audi AG v EUIPO* (C-398/08P) [2010] E.C.R. I-535 at [47],
[303] *Best Buy Concepts v EUIPO* (T-122/01) [2003] E.C.R. II-02235; [2004] E.T.M.R. 226.
[304] *Fieldturf Inc v EUIPO* (T-216/02) [2004] E.C.R. II-3867; [2004] E.T.M.R. 86.
[305] *Fieldturf Inc v EUIPO* (T-216/02) [2004] E.C.R. II-3867; [2004] E.T.M.R. 86 at [31].
[306] *Norma Lebensmittelfilial Betrieb v EUIPO* (T-281/02) [2004] E.C.R. II-01915; [2005] E.T.M.R. 49.
[307] *Citicorp v EUIPO* (T-320/03) [2005] E.C.R. II-03411.
[308] *Wella AG v EUIPO* (T-471/07) [2009] E.C.R. II-3377; [2010] E.T.M.R. 27.
[309] *Sykes Enterprise v EUIPO* (T-130/01) [2002] E.C.R. II-5179 at [29].
[310] *Erpo Möbelwerk v EUIPO* (T-138/00), at [43]–[45]. This part of the General Court's decision was upheld by the CJEU. It would appear that as a result of this decision, EUIPO accepted the application—see EUTM 806620.
[311] (T-63/15 & T-64/15) EU:T:2015:97. See also *Adidas v OHIM* (T-145/14) ECLI:EU:T:2015:303. Upheld on appeal, (C-396/15P) ECLI:EU:C:2016:95.

permit registration of such would permit manufacturers to appropriate decorative patterns that should remain accessible to all except where the mark has acquired distinctive character through use.

Names

3-192   In *Nicholls Plc v Registrar of Trade Mark*,[312] the CJEU ruled on a preliminary ruling that the approach to registrability of surnames under the TMD equivalent to art.7.1(b) EUTMR was no different to that of other marks. It said that it was not right to take into account the fact that there is an "own name" defence.

Shapes

3-193   A review of the authorities shows inconsistencies in approach to the registrability of shape marks. It is helpful to consider the Court of Justice's landmark case of *Develey*,[313] where it set out the approach to the determination of the distinctiveness of shape marks:

> "[80]   According to equally consistent case law, the criteria for assessing the distinctive character of three-dimensional marks consisting of the appearance of the product itself are no different from those applicable to other categories of trade mark. Nonetheless, for the purpose of applying those criteria, the average consumer's perception is not necessarily the same in the case of a three-dimensional mark consisting of the appearance of the product itself as it is in the case of a word or figurative mark consisting of a sign which is independent of the appearance of the products it denotes. *Average consumers are not in the habit of making assumptions as to the origin of products on the basis of their shape or the shape of their packaging in the absence of any graphic or word element, and it may, therefore, prove more difficult to establish distinctiveness in relation to such a three-dimensional mark than in relation to a word or figurative mark (Mag Instrument Inc v Office for Harmonisation in the Internal Market (Trade Marks and Designs) (EUIPO) (C-136/02 P) [2004] E.C.R. I-9165 at [30], and Storck at [24] and [25]).*
>
> [81]   In those circumstances, *only* a mark which departs significantly from the norm or customs of the sector and *thereby* fulfils its essential function of indicating origin is not devoid of any distinctive character for the purposes of Art.7.1(b) of Regulation 40/94 (*Deutsche SiSi-Werke GmbH & Co Betriebs KG v Office for Harmonisation in the Internal Market (Trade Marks and Designs) (EUIPO) (C-173/04 P) [2006] E.C.R. I-551 at [31], and Storck at [26])." [Emphasis supplied.]*

3-194   In a subsequent *Henkel* case, the General Court upheld an appeal from the rejection of an application by EUIPO for a "truly individual" crystal-shaped bottle mark for soaps, detergents, etc. on the grounds that it did possess the necessary distinctive character.[314] It said that:

> "[40]   As regards, more particularly, the shape in question, it must be stated that, on examination of all the documents put before the Court by the parties, it appears that the *combination of the elements has a truly individual character and cannot be regarded as altogether common to all the products in question.* It should be pointed out that the container which it is sought to register possesses certain features which distinguish it from containers for washing and cleaning products

---

[312] (C-404/02) [2004] E.C.R. I-8499; [2005] E.T.M.R. 21.
[313] *Develey v EUIPO* (C-238/06P) [2007] E.C.R. I-9375; [2008] E.T.M.R. 20.
[314] *Henkel* (T-393/02) [2004] E.C.R. II-4115.

commonly used on the market. It must be observed in that regard that, as the applicant argues, the container in question is particularly angular, and that the angles, the edges and the surfaces make it resemble a crystal. Moreover, the container gives the impression of being a single object, as the stopper of the container forms an integral part of the overall image. Lastly, the container is particularly flat. That combination thus confers on the bottle in question a particular and unusual appearance which is likely to attract the attention of the relevant public and enable that public, once familiar with the shape of the packaging of the goods in question, to distinguish the goods covered by the registration application from those having a different commercial origin (see, to that effect, Case T–128/01 *Daimler Chrysler v EUIPO (Grille)* [2003] E.C.R. II-701, [46] and [48]; and *Shape of a bottle*, [41]).

[41]   Furthermore, having regard to the containers used for similar products, in the light, in particular, of the examples produced by the applicant, it must be held that the white and transparent nature of the bottle does not affect the distinctiveness of the sign which it is sought to register.

[42]   All in all, it must be noted that a minimum degree of distinctiveness is sufficient to render inapplicable the ground for refusal set out in Art.7.1(b) of Regulation No.40/94 (see Case T–34/00 *Eurocool Logistik v EUIPO (EUROCOOL)* [2002] E.C.R. II-683, [39]; and, to that effect, Grille, [49]). Accordingly, since, as stated above, the mark applied for is made up of a combination of elements, in a characteristic presentation, which distinguish it from other shapes available on the market for the products concerned, it *must* be held that the mark applied for, taken as a whole, possesses the minimum degree of distinctiveness required." [Emphasis supplied.]

In *Voss of Norway*,[315] the Court of Justice said that it is settled law that only a   **3-195**
mark which departs significantly from the norm or customs of the sector and thereby fulfils its essential function of indicating origin is not devoid of any distinctive character for the purposes of art.7.1(b) EUTMR.[316] All of these decisions (particularly *Develey*) suggest that it is a necessary *and* sufficient condition that the shape departs significantly from the norms or customs of the sector for it to overcome an objection under art.7.1(b).

Yet, other decisions emphasise the fundamental need for the consumer to   **3-196**
perceive the shape as an indication of origin. Thus, in *Voss*, the Court of Justice confirmed that the assessment of distinctive character is no different to other categories of mark and the average consumer is not in the habit of making assumptions about the origin of products from shapes.[317] In two decisions concerning odd-shaped sausages, the General Court rejected applications to register them on the grounds that consumers would not perceive them as indications of trade origin.[318] In another case which concerned the attempt to register four stripes on a shoe but which the court applied the principles established in relation to shapes, it held that whilst such a design may depart significantly from the norms or customs of a sector, such was a necessary but not sufficient condition for a finding that the sign is distinctive. As it said, the sign must also be independent of the appearance of the

---

[315]   (C-445/13) EU:C:2015:303.
[316]   See [81], [91]. See also *Jaguar Land Rover v OHIM* (T-629/14) where the General Court upheld the principles established in *Develey*.
[317]   See, in particular [92].
[318]   *Wim de Waele v EUIPO* (T-15/05) [2006] E.C.R. II-01511 (spiral sausage split into four sections); *Thomas Rotter v EUIPO* (T-449/07) [2009] E.C.R. II 1071 (pretzel-shaped sausage).

product it designates in order to be perceived by the relevant public not merely as a decorative element.[319]

3-197   The "necessary but not sufficient" approach is also that preferred by the English courts.[320]

3-198   In the author's view, there should be no presumption such as the "significantly depart" test to overcome an objection under art.7.1(b) when it comes to shapes (or indeed any genre of mark). Whether or not a shape mark has distinctive character must be fact-dependent. In particular, regard must be had to the goods to which the shape is affixed to (or is part of) and whether the relevant consumer is likely to see the shape mark as an indication of origin or a design or decorative feature of those goods. Consumers are more likely to see shapes when they form packaging (e.g. bottles) as indications of origin than the shape of the good itself. Furthermore, an oddly-shaped foodstuff which is a capricious design feature that plainly serves no functional or decorative purpose (e.g. a cheese shaped as a windmill) is more likely to be seen as an indication of origin than oddly-shaped electrical goods such as vacuum cleaners or electric fans where the odd shape is likely to be seen as a functional or design feature.

Packaging

3-199   In *Henkel KGAA v Deutsche Patent-und Markenamt*,[321] Henkel sought to register a three-dimensional trade mark consisting of a tall bottle which narrowed towards the top with an integral handle, a small pouring aperture and a two level stopper. On a preliminary reference, the CJEU took a similar approach to shape marks when considering art.7.1(b) EUTMR. It said that it must be shown that the packaging significantly departs from the norm or customs of the sector and thereby fulfils its essential function as a trade mark. The CJEU said that the average consumer is not in the habit of making assumptions about the origin of goods based on the shape of their packaging.[322] Thus, in dismissing an appeal from the General Court, the Court of Justice held that blue/white packaging for confectionery was devoid of distinctive character as consumers would not view such as an indication of origin but rather mere decorative patterns.[323] In *Deutsche SiSI-Werke GmbH v EUIPO* (drinking pouches),[324] the General Court dismissed an appeal from EUIPO that stand up "pouches" for packaging drinks were devoid of distinctive character under art.7.1(b). In particular, the General Court held that the Board of Appeal was entitled to mention the risk of a monopoly being created in stand-up pouches for the drinks concerned and that the risk of monopoly was appreciably higher since the trade mark applications covered a large number of conceivable variations on the standard form of stand-up pouch.[325] The CJEU dismissed the appeal from the General

---

[319] *K-Swiss Inc v EUIPO* (T-85/13) ECLI:EU:T:2014:509 at [40].

[320] *Bongrain SA* [2005] ETMR 47 CA (star-shaped cheese product); *London Taxi Corporation v Frazer-Nash Research Ltd* [2016] EWHC 52 (shape of taxi). On appeal, the Court of Appeal held that it was not acte clair—[2017] EWCA 1729 at [42].

[321] (C-218/01) [2004] E.C.R I-01725; [2005] E.T.M.R. 45.

[322] See [52].

[323] *August Storck KG v EUIPO* (C-417/16P) ECLI:EU:2017:340 at [42], dismissing an appeal from the General Court, *August Storck v EUIPO* (T-806/14) ECLI:EU:T:2016:284.

[324] *Deutsche SiSI-Werke GmbH & Co Betriebs KG v EUIPO* (T-146/02 and T-153/02) [2004] E.C.R. II-447; [2004] E.T.M.R. 72.

[325] See [54].

Court.[326] In general, the approach to registrability of packaging does not differ markedly from that of shapes where the shape of the packaging is largely dictated by the shape of the product. Thus, in *August Storck KG v EUIPO* (shape of sweet)[327] and *August Storck KG v EUIPO* (sweet wrapper),[328] the same approach was taken to the registrability of a 3D shape of a sweet and a figurative representation of a sweet wrapper which was wrapped around it.

Colour marks

As with other marks, there is no different test applied to the registrability of colours under art.7.1(b) than for other genre of marks. However, it will be an exceptional case that a single colour mark per se is not objectionable under art.7.1(b) unless it has acquired distinctive character via use.[329] In *Libertel*,[330] the CJEU said: **3-200**

> "[54] As regards the registration as trade marks of colours per se, not spatially delimited, the fact that the number of colours actually available is limited means that a small number of trade mark registrations for certain services or goods could exhaust the entire range of the colours available. Such an extensive monopoly would be incompatible with a system of undistorted competition, in particular because it could have the effect of creating an unjustified competitive advantage for a single trader. Nor would it be conducive to economic development or the fostering of the spirit of enterprise for established traders to be able to register the entire range of colours that is in fact available for their own benefit, to the detriment of new traders.
>
> [55] It must therefore be acknowledged that there is, in Community trade mark law, *a public interest in not unduly restricting the availability of colours for the other operators* who offer for sale goods or services of the same type as those in respect of which registration is sought.
>
> [56] The greater the number of the goods or services for which the trade mark is sought is to be registered, the more excessive the exclusive right which it may confer is likely to be, and, for that very reason, the more likely is that right to come into conflict with the maintenance of a system of undistorted competition, and with the public interest in not unduly restricting the availability of colours for the other traders who market goods or services of the same type as those in respect of which registration is sought." [Emphasis supplied.]

The CJEU continued by saying that the public was not accustomed to perceiving colour as indicative of trade origin. It said that it was "inconceivable" that without use, a colour per se was distinctive save in exceptional circumstances.[331] If the colour mark is spatially delimited (i.e. an orange coloured circle), then the public policy argument is less important because registration would not afford a monopoly on the colour. An application for two or more colours must be spatially limited.[332]   **3-201**

---

[326] *Deutsche SI-SI-Werke GmbH v EUIPO* (C-173/04P) [2006] E.C.R. I-551; [2006] E.T.M.R. 41 (drinking pouches).

[327] *Storck KG v EUIPO* (C-24/05P) [2006] E.C.R. I-5677 (shape of sweet).

[328] *August Storck KG v EUIPO* (C-25/05P) [2006] E.C.R. I-5719 (sweet wrapper).

[329] (C-49/02) [2004] E.T.M.R. 99.

[330] (C-104/01) [2003] E.C.R. I-3793.

[331] See [66].

[332] See para.3-150.

Sound marks

3-202   The General Court held that a sign consisting of two musical notes of the same tone (G sharp) was too banal to have distinctive character.[333] The court recognised that jingles and melodies are identified by consumers with a particular undertaking but that the mark which was of excessive simplicity and was not capable of being perceived as a trade mark.

EUTMs and disclaimers

3-203   At the request of EUIPO, an applicant for a EUTM can disclaim any exclusive rights in a descriptive element of a mark when applying for it.[334] The function of such disclaimers is to make apparent the fact that the exclusive rights of the proprietor of a mark do not extend to the non-distinctive elements of the mark.[335]

May serve in trade to designate characteristic of products or services

General principles

3-204   Article 7.1(c) EUTMR prevents registration of:

> "trade marks which consist exclusively of signs or indications which may serve, in trade, to designate the kind, quality, quantity, intended purpose, value, geographical origin, the time of production of goods or of rendering of services, other characteristics of the goods or services,"

are unregistrable.

3-205   The public interest underlying art.7.1(c) is that descriptive terms should be available for use by all. As said by the CJEU in *POSTKANTOOR*[336]:

> "[54]   As the Court has already held...[Art.4.1(c) TMD] pursues an aim which is in the public interest, namely that such signs or indications may be freely used by all. [Art.4(1)(c) TMD] therefore prevents such signs and indications from being reserved to one undertaking alone because they have been registered as trade marks.
>
> [55]   That public interest requires that all signs or indications which may serve to designate characteristics of the goods or services in respect of which registration is sought remain freely available to all undertakings in order that they may use them when describing the same characteristics of their own goods. Therefore, marks consisting exclusively of such signs or indications are not eligible for registration unless [Art.4(4)] of the [TMD] applies."

3-206   The following are general principles applicable to art.7.1(c) EUTMR:

(1)   It is not necessary that a sign is actually as of the date of application in the minds of the relevant class of persons, a description of the characteristic of the goods or services for art.7.1(c) to apply—it is sufficient that it is reason-

---

[333] *Global Comunicação e Participações S/A v EUIPO* (T-408/15) ECLI:EU:T:2016:468.
[334] art.37(2).
[335] *Agencja Wydawnicza Technopol sp. z o.o. v EUIPO* (T-425/07) and (T-426/07) [2009] E.C.R. II-4275 at [19] upheld on appeal (C-56/10P) [2011] E.C.R. I-89.
[336] *Koninklijke KPN Nederland NV v Benelux-Merkenbureau* (C-363/99) [2004] E.C.R. I-1619; [2004] E.T.M.R. 57.

able to assume that the sign may become descriptive in the future.[337] Thus, if the sign *could* be used to describe a characteristic of the goods or services concerned, such is sufficient to uphold an objection under art.7.1(c).[338] This principle follows from the public interest described above. Traders should not be inhibited from using signs which are descriptive regardless of whether they are actually being used.

On this topic, it is necessary to consider the *BABY-DRY* case which could be read as requiring a descriptive term is actually in use for art.7.1(c) to apply.[339] In the Advocate-General's Opinion in *Doublemint*, he said that he did not consider that *BABY-DRY* was intended to depart from the general principle that descriptive signs may be freely used by all.[340] In the CJEU's decision in *Doublemint*, the CJEU simply said without referring to *BABY-DRY* that it was not necessary that the sign actually be in use at the time of the application for art.7.1(c) to engage. It was simply sufficient that such signs *could* be used for such purposes and that one of the possible meanings designated a characteristic of the goods or services.[341] This approach was also taken in *POSTKANTOOR*,[342] another case that was decided after *BABY-DRY*. In *Agencja Wydawnicza Technopol sp. z o.o. v EUIPO*,[343] the CJEU, said in referring to an argument of the appellant based on the statement in *BABY-DRY* that the descriptive term must be in use for an objection under art.7.1(c) to be lawful, that *BABY-DRY* could not be understood as defining such a condition for refusing to register a sign as a Community trade mark.[344] The CJEU emphasised in that case that it is sufficient for an objection under art.7.1(c) that the sign applied for *could* be used in a descriptive way. It was deemed irrelevant whether the sign was actually in use and the "usual way" of designating the characteristic and equally that it was irrelevant whether there was a "real, current or serious need to leave a sign or indication free".[345] Thus, it must be concluded that *BABY-DRY* is no longer good law.

(2) It is irrelevant whether or not it is immediately obvious *which* characteristic of the goods or services the sign for which protection is sought is describing. Thus, in *Doublemint*, the General Court held that because "doublemint" could mean many things, e.g. the chewing gum had twice the mint or two flavours of mint, it did not immediately "and without further reflection" enable the public to detect the description of a characteristic in question.[346] On appeal, the CJEU held that such was the wrong approach and there was no basis in art.7.1(c) for such an approach. The test is whether the mark as ap-

---

[337] *POSTKANTOOR* (C-363/99) [2004] E.C.R. I-1619, [2004] E.T.M.R. 57 at [56]; (C-108/97) [1999] E.C.R. I-2779, [1999] E.T.M.R. 585 at [56].

[338] (C-363/99) [2004] E.C.R. I-1619; [2004] E.T.M.R. 57 at [97].

[339] *Procter & Gamble v EUIPO* (C-383/99P) [2001] E.C.R. I-6251; [2002] E.T.M.R. 3 at [37], [39] and [42].

[340] *Wrigley v EUIPO* (C-191/01P) at [97], Opinion.

[341] See [32].

[342] *Koninklijke KPN Nederland NV v Benelux-Merkenbureau* (C-363/99) [2004] E.C.R. I-1619; [2004] E.T.M.R. 57.

[343] (C-51/10P) [2011] E.C.R. 1541.

[344] See [40].

[345] See [38]–[39] and cases cited there.

[346] *Wrigley v EUIPO* (T-193/99) [2001] E.C.R. II-417.

plied for was *capable* of being used by other economic operators to designate a characteristic of the products or services applied for.[347] It said that the sign must be refused registration if at least one of its possible meanings designates a characteristic of the goods or services concerned.[348]

(3) It is somewhat unclear whether the characteristics of the goods or services need be "essential characteristics" for art.7.1(c) to engage. The authorities are in conflict. In *POSTKANTOOR*, the CJEU said:

> "[102] It is also irrelevant whether the characteristics of the goods or services which may be the subject of the description are commercially essential or merely ancillary. The wording of [Art.4(1)(c) of the TMD] does not draw any distinction by reference to the characteristics which may be designated by the signs or indications of which the mark consists. In fact, in the light of the public interest underlying the provision, any undertaking must be able freely to use such signs and indications to describe any characteristic whatsoever of its own goods, *irrespective of how significant the characteristic may be commercially*."[349] [Emphasis supplied.]

This conflicts with the decision in *BABY-DRY*, where the CJEU said that the signs referred to in art.7.1(c) EUTMR are thus *only* those which may serve in normal usage from a consumer's point of view to designate, either directly or by reference to one of their *essential* characteristics of the goods or services such as those in respect of which registration is sought.[350] This conflict is very unsatisfactory. However, it has been said that the influence of *BABY-DRY* has diminished very considerably and in recent times, the case is rarely cited by the CJEU or General Court.

The CJEU has not had to consider the conflict between *POSTKANTOOR* and *BABY-DRY* on this issue. In *NEW BORN BABY*,[351] (a case which settled after the handing down of the Advocate-General's Opinion), the Advocate-General referred to "essential characteristics" in the context of art.7.1(c) citing *BABY-DRY*. Furthermore, in General Court decisions following *BABY-DRY* there is repeated reference to "essential characteristics". Generally, nothing turns on the point as there is no real dispute that the characteristic relied upon is an essential characteristic. Thus, in *Nursery Room*,[352] it was argued that it was not necessary to show that the characteristics were essential (citing *POSTKANTOOR*). The General Court however did not decide the issue. Yet, in *EUROPREMIUM*,[353] the General Court said in the context of a submission that "Euro" was descriptive of geographical origin and thus unregistrable:

> "[36] In any event, the Court notes that *origin is not an essential characteristic of goods and services* relating to postal transport. The geographical origin

---

[347] *Wrigley v EUIPO* (C-191/01P) [2003] E.C.R. I-12477 at [35].

[348] *Wrigley v EUIPO* (C-191/01P) [2003] E.C.R. I-12477 at [32]. See also (C-363/99) [2004] E.C.R. I-1619; [2004] E.T.M.R. 57 at [56] and [97].

[349] *Koninklijke KPN Nederland NV v Benelux-Merkenbureau* (C-363/99) [2004] E.C.R. I-1619; [2004] E.T.M.R. 57 at [102].

[350] (C-383/99P) [2001] E.C.R. I-6251; [2002] E.T.M.R. 3 at [39].

[351] *Zapf v EUIPO (NEW BORN BABY)* (T-140/00) [2001] E.C.R. II-2927; [2001] E.T.M.R. 10.

[352] *Geddes v EUIPO* (T-171/03) [2004] E.C.R. II-4165.

[353] (T-334/03) [2005] E.C.R. II-65; [2006] E.T.M.R. 52.

of goods in Classes 16 and 20, which are, essentially, goods intended for packaging of items of all kinds, is manifestly not a characteristic *which determines the consumer's choice*, which will be made on the basis of factors such as the dimensions of the packaging or its durability. With regard to the services in Classes 35 and 39, there is again no reason to believe that *origin is a characteristic taken into account by the average consumer when making his choice.* Consequently the prefix 'euro' does not designate the goods and services at issue either directly or by reference to one of their *essential characteristic*s and is therefore not descriptive of them." [Emphasis supplied.]

The General Court did not refer to the relevant passage of *POSTKANTOOR* but did refer to *BABY-DRY*. It is submitted that this decision is wrong and contrary to *POSTKANTOOR*. In particular, it errs by focussing on the relevance of the characteristic to the consumer rather than the trader's freedom to describe any characteristic of goods or services, however commercially insignificant, as said by the CJEU in *POSTKANTOOR*. However, the General Court is still citing *BABY-DRY* as authority for the proposition that art.7.1(c) only applies to the essential characteristics of goods or services.[354]

(4) For an objection under art.7.1(c) to be valid, the sign or indication must designate a quality or characteristic of the goods or services applied for which the consumer is able to understand directly. Thus, the relevant public must be able to "immediately and without further reflection make a definite and direct association" between the mark and the goods or services applied for.[355] Where it is a case of evocation or allusion rather than a direct designation, art.7.1(c) is not engaged.[356] In the case of a neologism which consists of elements which are descriptive of characteristics of goods or services in respect of which registration is sought, its registration will be contrary to art.7.1(c) unless there is a perceptible difference between the neologism and the mere sum of its parts. Thus, the neologism must create an impression which:

> "is sufficiently far removed from that produced by the mere combination of meaning lent by the elements of which it is composed with the result that the word is more than sum of its parts."[357]

This should not be confused with the point discussed above that it is not necessary for art.7.1(c) to apply for the consumer to understand directly *which* characteristic is being referred to. In other words, *Doublemint* can be interpreted as meaning two mint flavours, twice as much mint, etc. but it is not evocative or allusive. Thus, the consumer understands directly that it is descriptive but does not understand directly *which* characteristic it is

---

[354] e.g. *Colgate-Palmolive v EUIPO (VISIBLE WHITE)* (T-136/07) [2008] E.C.R. II-304 at [32].

[355] *DKV v EUIPO (Eurohealth)* (T-359/99) [2001] E.C.R. II-1645 at [35]; *Sunrider v EUIPO (Vitalite)* (T-24/00) [2001] E.C.R. II-449 at [24]; (T-360/00) [2002] E.C.R. II-3867, [2003] E.T.M.R. 32.

[356] The *Sunrider Corporation v Office for Harmonisation in the Internal Market (Trade Marks and Designs) (EUIPO)* (T-24/00) [2001] E.C.R. II-449 at [24]; (T-360/00) [2003] E.C.R. II-3867 at [27].

[357] *Campina Melkunie BV v Benelux-Merkenburea (BIOMILD)* E.C.R. (C-265/00) [2004] I-01699; [2004] E.T.M.R. 58 at [43].

describing. The consumer does not have to make an intuitive jump to understand that it is descriptive.

(5) The fact that a word is descriptive of a characteristic of a product in one Member State is not a priori a reason for refusing to register it if applied for in another Member State where it is not so descriptive. Thus, in *Matratzen Concord AG v Hukla Germany SA*,[358] the applicant was the registered proprietor of *MATRATZEN* in Spain for bed items including mattresses. "*Matratzen*" means "mattress" in Germany. An action was brought in Spain to cancel the mark on the basis that it was descriptive of a characteristic of the products. The Provincial Court of Spain was concerned that a decision that the mark was valid would have the effect of restricting the import of mattresses from Germany and thus be contrary to arts 34–36.

The CJEU confirmed the general principle that no recourse should be made to arts 34–36 where there has been exhaustive harmonisation.[359] However, it did say that because of linguistic, cultural, social and economic differences between the Member States, a trade mark which is devoid of distinctive character of the goods or services in one Member State was not necessarily so in another Member State.[360]

(6) The characteristics referred to in art.7.1(c) TMD suggest that the characteristics concern characteristics of the *products* or *services* for which registration is sought as opposed to characteristics of the *uses* to which those product or services could be put to. However, in an English decision,[361] which concerned an attempt to register the name of a well-known rock group for posters and books in Class 16, it was said that a relevant characteristic would be the "subject-matter" of the mark. In that case, it was argued that to be a characteristic under art.7.1(c), it had to be measurable property of the goods rather than the information conveyed by the goods. This argument was not accepted. The tribunal found that art.7.1(c) covered the "subject matter" characteristic. Care must be exercised here as there is no Court of Justice or General Court authority on this issue. It would mean that any attempt to register a well-known name of a personality, pop group, fictional character, etc. could be prevented under art.7.1(c) for posters and books but not otherwise. This was the approach taken by the Board of Appeal.[362]

Individual decisions

3-207   There have been very many decisions by the General Court and CJEU about the registrability of signs which potentially engage art.7.1(c). A selection of these deci-

---

[358] (C-421/04) [2006] E.C.R. I-02303; [2006] E.T.M.R. 48.

[359] (C-421/04) [2006] E.C.R. I-2303; [2006] E.T.M.R. 48 at [20]. This principle is discussed elsewhere in this chapter—see para.3-129.

[360] See [25].

[361] *Linkin Park TM* [2006] E.T.M.R. 75, Appointed Person, England and Wales.

[362] See also *Yves Fostier v Disney Enterprises Inc* R1856/2013-2 where the 2nd Board of Appeal, EUIPO held, in relation to an application to register PINOCCHIO, the well-known name of the puppet whose nose grows as he tells lies, that it was registrable save in relation to various goods such as books, action figures, CDs on the grounds that consumers will simply think that the goods and services refer to the story of *Pinocchio*. The objection was under art.7.1(b) but could equally have been made under art.7.1(c).

sions will convey the approach. Care should be applied in taking any real comfort from decisions which predate *Postkantoor* and *Doublemint*.

The following were refused registration under art.7.1(c) EUTMR:

3-208

(a) *Universaltelefonbuch* for electronic media, directories, publishing services, and editing of written texts.[363]

(b) *Applied Molecular Evolution* for research activities directed towards molecular engineering of compounds.[364]

(c) *Streamserve* for data processing equipment and computers.[365]

(d) *TDI* (which stood for "turbo diesel injection") for vehicles and repair and maintenance of them.[366]

(e) *DigiFilm/DigiFilmmaker* for digital data and image data.[367]

(f) *MunichFinancialServices* for "financial services".[368]

(g) *Telepharmacy* for computer systems, dispensing systems and pharmacy services.[369]

(h) *Twist and Pour* for hand-held plastic containers.[370]

(i) *Lokthread* for bolts and nuts.[371]

(j) *Ellos* (the Spanish word for "them") for clothing, footwear and headgear for customers.[372]

(k) *Bioknowledge* for a variety of goods and services related to organisms.[373]

(l) *Instasite* for software and websites.[374]

The following signs were found not to be contrary to art.7.1(c) EUTMR:

3-209

(a) *Ultraplus* for plastic ovenware.[375]

(b) *Eurohealth* for financial services (but objection was upheld for insurance services).[376]

(c) *Celltech* for pharmaceutical, veterinary and sanitary preparations, compounds and substances; surgical, medical, dental and veterinary apparatus and instruments; research and development services; and consultancy services; all relating to the biological, medical and chemical sciences.[377]

---

[363] *Telefon & Buch v EUIPO* (C-326/01) [2004] I-1371; [2005] E.T.M.R. 50.

[364] *Applied Molecular Evolution Inc v EUIPO* (T-183/03) [2004] E.C.R. II-3113; [2005] E.T.M.R. 60.

[365] *Streamserve Inc v EUIPO* (T-106/00) [2002] E.C.R II-723; [2003] E.T.M.R. 59. Upheld on appeal, (C-152/02) [2004] E.C.R. I-1461; [2005] E.T.M.R. 57. The evidence established that the *Streamserve* referred to a technique for transferring digital data from a server, enabling it to be processed as a steady and continuous stream. However, the General Court held that the objection in relation to manuals and publications could not be maintained as there was no direct relationship between the two.

[366] *Audi A.G. v EUIPO* (T-16/02) [2003] E.C.R. II-5167; [2004] E.T.M.R. 59.

[367] *CeWe Color A.G. v EUIPO* (T-178/03 & C-179/03) [2005] E.C.R. II-3105; [2006] E.T.M.R. 34.

[368] *Münchener RG v EUIPO* (T-316/03) [2005] E.C.R. II-1951; [2006] E.T.M.R. 6.

[369] *Telepharmacy Solutions Inc v EUIPO* (T-289/02) [2004] E.C.R. II-2851; [2006] E.T.M.R. 10.

[370] *Sherwin-Williams Co v EUIPO* (T-190/05) ECLI:EU:T:2007:17.

[371] *MacLean-Fogg v EUIPO* E.C.R. (T-339/05) [2007] E.C.R. II-00061.

[372] *Ellos AB v EUIPO* (T-219/00) [2002] E.C.R. II-753; [2004] E.T.M.R. 7.

[373] *Proteome Inc's Application* (T-387/03) [2005] E.C.R. II-191.

[374] *Sabre GLBL, Inc v EUIPO* (T-375/16) ECLI:EU:T:2017:348. It was irrelevant that INSTASITE did not appear in a dictionary. See [54].

[375] (T-360/00) [2003] E.C.R. II-3867.

[376] (T-359/99) [2001] E.C.R. II-1645; [2001] E.T.M.R. 81.

[377] *Celltech R&D v EUIPO* (C-273/05P) [2007] E.C.R. I-09517; [2007] E.T.M.R. 52.

(d) *Europremium* for a variety of goods and services.[378]

(e) *Ellos* (the Spanish word for "them") for customer services for mail-order sales.[379]

Geographical names

3-210   There have been a number of decisions concerning the registrability of signs that are geographical names. In *Windsurfing Chiemsee*,[380] the case in which the CJEU first stated the public interest underlying art.7.1(c), namely that descriptive signs should be available for use by all, the CJEU ruled on a preliminary reference that where there is currently no association in the mind of the relevant class of persons between the geographical name and the category of goods in question, the competent authority must assess whether it is reasonable to assume that such a name is, in the mind of the relevant class of persons, capable of designating the geographical origin of that category of goods. The CJEU said that in making that assessment, particular consideration should be given to the degree of familiarity amongst the relevant class of persons with the geographical name in question, with the characteristics of the place designated by that name, and with the category of goods concerned. It also said that it was not necessary for the goods to be manufactured in the geographical location in order for them to be associated with it.

3-211   In *Nordmilch EG v EUIPO*,[381] a Germany dairy co-operative applied to register OLDENBURGER for dairy products, meat, fish and poultry. Oldenburg is the principal town of the region of Weser-Ems in Niedersachsen, Lower Saxony. Oldenburg is well known in Germany at a national level as the capital of a region which is essentially centred on agriculture, in particular in the dairy, livestock and meat-processing industries. A large amount of agricultural products carried the designation Oldenburger. The General Court concluded that the mark was contrary to art.7.1(c).[382] Interestingly, the General Court held that the objection was also valid in relation to the "fish" specification. It said that even though it had not been established that Oldenburg was well known for fish, it was reasonable to assume that fish would in future be associated with the town (applying the test in *Windsurfing Chiemsee*). In *Monaco*, the General Court held that "Monaco" could not be registered as a trade mark for magnetic tapes.[383]

3-212   In *Cloppenburg*,[384] the applicant sought to register *Cloppenburg* for retail trade services. Cloppenburg is a German town in Lower Saxony with a population of about 152,000 inhabitants. Towns and districts of the size of Cloppenburg were regularly referred to in weather reports. The Board of Appeal of EUIPO rejected the application. However, on appeal, the General Court held that it was not contrary to art.7.1(c). It would appear that the General Court considered that the Board of Appeal's reasoning was purely based on the fact that Cloppenburg is a town in Lower Saxony. The General Court considered that more needed to be done to uphold such an objection. Thus, it said it was a small town. Secondly, it said that

---

[378] (T-344/03) [2005] E.C.R. II-65; [2006] E.T.M.R. 52. The more appropriate objection would have been under art.7.1(b) where it might have been held to have been laudatory.

[379] (T-219/00) [2002] E.C.R II-753; [2004] E.T.M.R. 7. NB. The objection was upheld for clothing, footwear and headgear.

[380] (C-109/97) [1999] E.C.R. I-2779; [1999] E.T.M.R. 85.

[381] *Nordmilch EG v EUIPO* (T-295/01) [2003] E.C.R. II-4365; [2004] E.T.M.R. 70.

[382] The fact that the mark was *Oldenburger* was not sufficient to prevent the application of art.7.1(c).

[383] *Mem v OHIM (Monaco)* (T-197/13) ECLI:EU:T:2015:16.

[384] *Peek & Cloppenburg KG's Application* (T-379/03) [2005] E.C.R. II-4631; [2006] E.T.M.R. 33.

the Board of Appeal had not established that the town had a reputation as a place where goods or services are produced or rendered. Furthermore, it said that the Board of Appeal had not established that it was current practice in trade to indicate the geographical origin of retail trade services. In addition, it thus said that the geographical origin of retail services is not usually relevant when assessing the quality or characteristics of retail services. It therefore held that the town of Cloppenburg did not present any link with the category of services concerned and nor was it reasonable to assume that it might in the future designate the geographical origin of such services. In the author's opinion, the General Court erred in its approach in *Cloppenburg* and set the standard for a geographical objection under art.7.1(c) too highly. In particular, it failed to consider the public interest that shop traders from Cloppenburg should not be deterred from using the name "Cloppenburg" in the context of selling goods. The fact that the geographical origin of retail services is not usually regarded as relevant when considering the quality of retail services is irrelevant.[385] The registration of "Cloppenburg" for retail services means that any shop owners who lived in Cloppenburg must now think carefully of any use of the name "Cloppenburg" on its shop signage, letterheads, etc. That is contrary to the public interest underlying art.7.1(c)

A geographical name objection under art.7.1(c) must be based on an actual geographical place. Thus, an application to register *La Milla de Oro* (golden mile), a phrase often used in various languages to indicate a high-quality shopping area in a town or city but not specific to any town or city, is not an indication of geographical origin.[386] A geographical name can be registered as a EU collective mark. If such an application is made, then no objection can be taken by EUIPO under art.7.1(c).[387] **3-213**

Shape marks

In *Linde AG (3D car)*,[388] the Court of Justice confirmed that art.7.1(c) is relevant to the consideration of registrability of shape marks as much as it is to other type of marks. It said that when examining the ground for refusing registration in art.7.1(c) in a case concerning shapes, regard must be had to the public interest underlying that provision, which is that all three-dimensional shapes of product trade marks, which consist exclusively of signs or indications that may serve to designate the characteristics of the goods or service within the meaning of that provision, should be freely available to all and, subject always to proof of acquired distinctive character, cannot be registered.[389] **3-214**

It will often not be immediately apparent that a shape may serve to designate the characteristic of the goods or services in the way that a descriptive or quasi-descriptive word mark does. Thus, in relation to shape marks, often an objection under art.7.1(b) is more likely to succeed.[390] However, many shapes will have a relationship with the underlying product. Thus, a tribunal or office will need to consider the degree of functionality of the shape mark in relation to the underly- **3-215**

---

[385] Whether or not the characteristic is a relevant one from the viewpoint of the consumer is irrelevant—see para.3-206, point (3).
[386] *Juan Moreno Marin v Abadia Retuerta SA* (C-139/16) ECLI:EU:C:2017:518.
[387] art.74.2 EUTMR. For collective marks, see para.3-772.
[388] *Linde AG (3D car)* (C-53/01) [2003] E.C.R. I-3161; [2003] E.T.M.R. 78.
[389] See [77].
[390] See para.3-193.

ing product for which registration is sought. The shape of a cheese has little or no functional relationship with cheese. However, the shape of a car clearly does have a functional relationship with a car, as a car consists of wheels, an interior for carrying people, a container for the engine, etc. Clearly, the greater the relationship between the shape of the sign applied for and its functionality, the more likely that the 3D shape designates a characteristic of the product. It should be said that in such circumstances, the stronger objection will be under the sui generis shape objections.[391]

Subject matter

3-216   A mark may not describe a physical characteristic of the goods or services but instead describe the subject matter of the goods or services. Thus, the mark VIVALDI, the name of a well-known composer, when used for books, CDs, posters would most likely indicate to the average consumer the *content* or subject matter of such, i.e. a book on Vivaldi or the music of Vivaldi. In such circumstances, an objection under art.7.1(c) will succeed in relation to those goods or services where the average consumer would have a legitimate expectation that the mark describes the content or subject matter of the goods or services.[392] However, this would not prevent the use of a well-known character or name from acting as a trade mark in relation to goods or services where the average consumer would not assume that the name describes the content of them. Thus, in *Yves Fostier v Disney Enterprises Inc*,[393] the Board of Appeal of EUIPO considered the registrability of PINOCCHIO, the name of the well-known wooden puppet made famous by an Italian book in the 19th century, by Walt Disney, across a wide range of goods and services. It held that an objection under art.7.1(c) was well-founded in relation to CDs, printed matter and toys but said that there was nothing to say that PINOCCHIO was not capable of being distinctive for paint, clothing or pencils as the relationship between such goods was an indirect one.[394]

Signs which are customary in trade or bona fide established practices

3-217   Article 7.1(d) EUTMR prohibits the registration of:

"A trade mark which consists exclusively of signs or indications which have become customary in the current language or in the bona fide and established practices of the trade is not registrable."

3-218   As with art.7.1(b) and (c), art.7.1(d) is derived from art.6*quinquies* of the Paris Convention. A literal reading of art.7.1(d) gives rise to difficulties. This is because art.7.1(d) does not apparently relate to the goods or services for which registration is sought. Thus, it may be customary in English to use the word "Slipper" to mean a shoe worn in the bedroom, but in the context of a trade mark for semiconductor chips, it plainly has no relationship whatsoever to the item and is inherently distinctive.

---

[391] See para.3-247.
[392] EUIPO Guidelines, Part B, Section 4, Chapter 4, para 2.7. In the UK, see *Linkin Park* [2006] E.T.M.R. 74 (name of rock group).
[393] R-1856/2013-2, Board of Appeal.
[394] See [27].

In *Merz & Krell*,[395] the CJEU had to consider this very issue. The applicant **3-219** sought to register BRAVO for typewriters. The German Trade Mark Office rejected it on the basis that it was a term of praise or advertising slogan for the goods. A reference was made to the CJEU as to whether the provision in the Trade Mark Directive equivalent to art.7.1(d) should be interpreted as referring implicitly to signs or indications which have become customary in the current language or in the bona fide and established practice of the trade *to designate the goods or services for which the mark is sought to be registered.*

The CJEU held that the provision must be interpreted in the light of the es- **3-220** sential function of the mark. It thus said that the purpose of the article was to prevent the registration of signs or indications that are not capable of distinguishing the goods or services of one undertaking from those of other undertakings.[396] It said that such cannot be considered in the abstract and separately from the goods or services for which registration is sought. It thus held that the article must be interpreted as:

> "[31] ... precluding registration of a trade mark where the signs or indications of which the mark is exclusively composed have become customary in the current language or in the bona fide and established practices of the trade *to designate the goods or services in respect of which registration of that mark is sought.*" [Emphasis supplied.]

Thus, on the above example, SLIPPER for semiconductor chips would not be **3-221** objectionable under art.7.1(d).

Merz & Krell leaves unanswered two questions. First, does art.7.1(d) apply **3-222** merely to signs or indications which have become customary in the current language or in the bona fide and established practices of the trade to designate the actual goods or services themselves or does it also apply to *properties or characteristics* of the goods or services for which registration is sought? Secondly, does art.7.1(d) apply to signs or indications that are customarily used in a more general, laudatory way even though these do not describe the goods or services themselves or their characteristics?

On the first question, there is a hint in *Merz & Krell* that art.7.1(d) does apply to **3-223** words which are customarily used to describe properties or characteristics of the goods or services. In a paragraph dealing with the second question, the CJEU said:

> "[36] It follows that in order for [Art.4.1(d) TMD] to be effective, the scope of the provision in respect of which the Court's interpretation is sought should not be limited solely to trade marks which describe the properties or characteristics of the goods or services covered by them."

It is implicit in this passage that art.7.1(d) does indeed cover signs or indica- **3-224** tions that are customarily used to describe properties or characteristics of goods or services.

On the second question, the answer is probably that art.7.1(d) is not the ground **3-225** for objecting to mere laudatory marks. Ultimately, these may be academic questions because usually art.7.1(c) and/or art.7.1(b) will apply where art.7.1(d) applies. Thus, in *Merz & Krell*, clearly the use of BRAVO for typewriters was open to objection under art.7.1(b) being a laudatory mark.[397]

However, art.7.1(d) does have a role to play independent of art.7.1(b) and (c). **3-226**

---

[395] (C-517/99) [2001] E.C.R. I-6959; [2002] E.T.M.R. 21.
[396] See [28].
[397] See para.3-186.

Thus, there are words that are not descriptive (in the dictionary sense) but have become an alternative name for a product or characteristic of those goods. In the fast moving world of technology, new names are being invented on a regular basis. Examples of this are: "windsurfer" for a sailboard; a graphical sign which is commonly used to indicate the goods or services in question (e.g. the three-ball sign for pawnbrokers); "smartphone" for a mobile telephone with computer-like functionality; or where a particular phrase or set of initials has become shorthand for a product. A good example of this is in *Alcon Inc v EUIPO*,[398] where the applicant sought to register as a Community mark BSS for ophthalmic pharmaceutical preparations and sterile solutions for ophthalmic surgery. Evidence submitted before EUIPO showed that, as of the date of the application, BSS had become the generic term for "balanced salt solution" or "buffered saline solution". Accordingly, the application was refused under art.7.1(d).

Distinctive character acquired through use

3-227   As already discussed, certain signs have the capability to distinguish the goods or services of one undertaking from another but are not *inherently* distinctive. Such signs require use of the sign in the marketplace in such a manner that the public will be educated to perceive the sign as an indication of trade origin. Thus, these marks are not inherently distinctive but can acquire distinctive character through use.

The TMD and EUTMR permits marks that are de facto distinctive to be registered. Article 7.3 EUTMR states:

> "[Article 7.1(b)–(d)] shall not apply if the trade mark has become distinctive in relation to the goods or services for which registration is requested in consequence of the use which has been made of it."

Article 7.3 only relevant to overcome lack of distinctive grounds

3-228   Article 7.3 EUTMR only applies to objections taken under art.7.1(b)–(d). It does not apply to an objection under art.7.1(a)[399] and importantly, objections under art.7.1(e).[400] Thus a product may have a very distinctive shape which is instantly recognisable to the public but such may be necessary to obtain a technical result.[401] If so, it is unregistrable.

Relevant date

3-229   Under the EUTMR, it must be shown that the mark applied for has acquired distinctive character prior to the date of filing of the mark.[402] However, if a EUTM is registered in breach of art.7.1(b)–(d), it may not be declared invalid if it has acquired distinctive character after registration in relation to the goods or services

---

[398] *Alcon v EUIPO* (T-237/01) [2003] E.C.R. II-411, [2004] E.T.M.R. 6, General Court upheld on appeal by CJEU; *Alcon v EUIPO* (C-192/03P) [2004] E.C.R. I-8993, [2005] E.T.M.R 69.

[399] See para.3-177.

[400] See para.3-247.

[401] A shape which is necessary to obtain a technical result is incapable of being registered—see art.7.1(e)(ii). See para.3-257.

[402] *Imagination Technology v EUIPO* (C-542/07) [2009] E.C.R. I-4937; *BIC v EUIPO* (T-262/04) EU:T:2005:463 at [66].

for which it is registered.[403] Thus, a "lucky" applicant who applies for a mark which is not distinctive as of the date of filing (whether inherently or acquired) but no objection is taken prior to grant may be able to ex post facto validate that application if subsequently it acquires distinctive character. It was this oddity that an applicant sought to rely upon in adducing evidence at the application stage of acquired distinctive character after date of filing but the Court of Justice rejected this argument.[404] However, evidence of facts and matters which came into existence after the date of filing may be taken into account for the purpose of drawing conclusions regarding the acquired distinctiveness of the mark as of the filing date.[405]

All factors to be taken into account

In considering whether a mark has acquired distinctive character under art.7.3 EUTMR, the tribunal must take account of all the circumstances and in particular of any use which has been made of the mark.[406] In *Windsurfing Chiemsee Produktions v Huber*,[407] which has been discussed above, the CJEU considered what was required in order for a mark to acquire a distinctive character through use. It said that the following factors might be relevant when assessing the extent of the distinctive character acquired through use: **3-230**

> "[51] In assessing the distinctive character of a mark in respect of which registration has been applied for, the following may also be taken into account: the market share held by the mark; how intensive, geographically widespread and long-standing use of the mark has been; the amount invested by the undertaking in promoting the mark; the proportion of the relevant class of persons who, because, of the mark, identify goods as originating from a particular undertaking; and statements from chambers of commerce and industry or other trade and professional associations.
>
> [52] If, on the basis of such factors, the tribunal finds that the relevant class of persons, or at least a significant proportion of them, identify goods as originating from a particular undertaking because of the trade mark, it must hold that the requirement for registering the mark is satisfied. This assessment cannot simply be made by reference to general abstract data such a predetermined percentage."[408]

The CJEU has made it clear that the courts and tribunal should not consider whether art.7.3 is satisfied solely by reference to general, abstract data such as predetermined percentages.[409] A survey that showed that 22 per cent of interviewees in a survey associated the sign "*TDI*" (which stood for turbo diesel injection) with Audi was not sufficient to serve as a basis for any conclusions as to the degree of acceptance of the mark.[410]   **3-231**

It will be a rare case that mere evidence of use and sales under the mark will suffice under art.7.3. Such does not show that the relevant public perceive the mark   **3-232**

---

[403] art.52.2.
[404] *Imagination Technology v EUIPO* (C-542/07) [2009] E.C.R. I-4937.
[405] See *Mondelez v EUIPO* (T-112/13) ECLI:EU:T:2016:735 at [115] and the decisions cited therein.
[406] *Libertel Groep BV v Benelux-Merkenbureau* (C-104/01) [2003] E.C.R. I-3793 at [77].
[407] (C-108/97) [2003] E.C.R. I-3793 at [25].
[408] (C-108/97) [1999] E.C.R. I-2779; [1999] E.T.M.R. 585. See also (C-217/83) and (C-218/83) at [42].
[409] (C-108/97) [1999] E.C.R. I-2779, [1999] E.T.M.R. 585 at [52]; (C-299/99) [2002] E.C.R. I-5475, [2002] E.T.M.R. 81 at [63]. See also *Glaverbel SA v EUIPO* (T-151/06) [2007] E.C.R. II-114 at [32] and *Storck v EUIPO* (T-402/02) [2004] E.C.R. II-3849 at [77] (shape of a wrapper) and case law cited therein; see also (C-217/83) and (C-218/83) at [48].
[410] *Audi AG v Office for Harmonisation in the Internal Market (Trade Marks and Designs) (EUIPO)* (T-16/02) [2003] E.C.R. II-5167; [2004] E.T.M.R. 59 at [48].

as indicative of trade origin.[411] An applicant adducing evidence of acquired distinctive character must take great care to ensure that such evidence is cogent and probative of the issue. Readers are recommended to read *BIC v EUIPO (Shape of a lighter)*[412] where evidence of advertising, sales and surveys was dismissed by EUIPO as being unreliable or not cogent. The best type of evidence will be gained from trade associations and other persons knowledgeable of the relevant market sector. Witness evidence from representatives of the applicant are of little use.[413] Where the mark is a shape mark, because invariably such products are marketed with a work mark, level of sales are not helpful because it is unclear whether the shape or word mark is being promoted.[414]

Association, identification or reliance: what is the right approach?

3-233   In many cases, the determination of whether a mark has acquired distinctive character will cause little difficulty. Thus, a word mark may be prima facie descriptive but as a result of extensive use, become a highly recognisable trade mark. A good example would be British Airways. The assessment of that will be done in accordance with the paragraph above.

3-234   However, greater intellectual difficulties arise when the mark in issue is the shape of a product, often a foodstuff. A good example is the well-known "Toblerone" bar with its highly recognisable triangular "chunks" joined together in a line. Another example is the four-fingered "Kit Kat" bar. In both cases, the chocolate bars have been marketed extensively and for a long time under a distinctive word mark, here being TOBLERONE or KIT KAT. The public recognise them immediately. However, what would the public believe if an identical triangular chunky bar was marketed under another word mark, e.g. PYRAMID? Would the public believe that Toblerone were responsible for marketing PYRAMID? Or would they just think that the owners of the mark PYRAMID have taken the idea of the Toblerone shape but do not believe that Toblerone are responsible for its marketing? In such circumstances, what does an applicant for the foodstuff shape need to prove? That the public "associate" triangular chunky bars with Toblerone? That the public identify such bars in some manner with Toblerone? Or that they rely upon the shape of triangular chunky bars as telling them who is responsible for them being put on the market?

3-235   Often, following extensive marketing over a significant period of a foodstuff made in a particular shape but sold under a word mark, the owner of the product will seek to apply to register the shape as a trade mark. If it goes to registration then it will result in a perpetual monopoly in that shape for that foodstuff. Is that right? In *Nestlé v Unilever Plc*,[415] the High Court of England had to consider the registrability of a three-dimensional shape mark for ice cream dessert products. The shape was the appearance of an ice cream gateau that had been sold for many years under the word mark "Viennetta". A survey showed a high degree of recognition of the product as a product of the applicant (67 per cent). Jacob J said:

---

[411] (T-16/02) [2003] E.C.R. II-5167; [2004] E.T.M.R. 59 at [66]. See also *British Sugar* [1996] R.P.C. 281 (High Court of England) and *Bach Flower Remedies* [2000] R.P.C. 513 CA.

[412] *Bic v EUIPO (shape of a lighter)* (T-262/04) [2005] E.C.R. II-05959. However, see (C-217/83), at [43] where the CJEU said that national courts could resort to opinion polls in difficult cases.

[413] *Bacardi*, R666/2005 (Boards of Appeal, EUIPO).

[414] *Bacardi*, R666/2005.

[415] *Société des Produits Nestlé SA v Unilever Plc* [2003] E.T.M.R. 53 (Ch).

"[31] Putting the other products on one side for the moment, there can be no doubt that the product appearance has achieved considerable recognition on its own as denoting Walls' Viennetta-the product of a particular manufacturer. Is that enough to give it a 'distinctive character' within the meaning of [Art.4.3]? For what has not been proved is that any member of the public would rely upon the appearance alone to identify the goods. They recognise it but do not treat it as a trade mark.

[32] There is a bit of sleight of hand going on here and in other cases of this sort. The trick works like this. The manufacturer sells and advertises his product widely and under a well known trade mark. After some while the product appearance becomes well known. He then says the appearance alone will serve as a trade mark, even though he himself never relied on the appearance alone to designate origin and would not dare to do so. He then gets registration of the shape alone. Now he is in a position to stop other parties, using their own word trade marks, from selling the product, even though no-one is deceived or misled.

[33] I do not think that is what the European trade mark system is for. It is a system about trade marks, badges of trade origin. For that reason I think that in the case of marks consisting of product *shapes it is not enough to prove the public recognises them* as the *product of a particular manufacturer*. It must be proved that consumers regard the shape alone as a badge of trade origin in the sense that *they would rely upon that shape alone as an indication of trade origin*, particularly to buy the goods. If that cannot be proved, then the shape is not properly a trade mark, It does not have a "distinctive character" for the purposes of trade mark law." [Emphasis supplied.]

The conceptual distinction between on the one hand, the association of a shape with an undertaking and on the other hand, reliance upon that shape as an indication of trade origin was echoed by a decision of the English High Court prior to the TMD coming into force in the UK. In *Unilever Striped Toothpaste*[416] the judge said: **3-236**

"There is in my view a similar obstacle in the path of a trader who has enjoyed a de facto monopoly of a product with a relatively simple feature chosen not as a badge of origin but on the ground that it was likely to appeal to the public. The fact that members of the public now associate that feature with its product tells one nothing about what they would think if a product with a similar feature came upon the market."

The Court of Justice has now considered this issue in *Société des Produits Nestlé S.A. v Cadbury UK Ltd*[417] which concerned the registrability of the Kit Kat "four-fingered" shape discussed above. This was a reference from the UK. Survey evidence had established that 50 per cent of those polled *recognised* the four-fingered bar as being a Kit Kat. The core issue was precisely whether this proof of recognition was enough or whether something more needed to be proven and if so, what? The Court of Justice held in the declaratory part of its judgment as follows: **3-237**

"In order to obtain registration of a trade mark which has acquired a distinctive character following the use which has been made of it within the meaning of Article 3(3) of Directive 2008/95, regardless of whether that use is as part of another registered trade mark or in conjunction with such a mark, the trade mark applicant must prove that the relevant class of persons perceive the goods or services designated exclusively by the mark applied for, as opposed to any other mark which might also be present, as originating from a particular company."

It is clear from this decision that the Court of Justice was rejecting the **3-238**

---

[416] *Unilever Ltd's Striped Toothpaste* [1987] R.P.C. 19, High Ct.
[417] (C-215/14) ECLI:EU:C:2015:604.

"recognition/association" test as it drew a distinction between the "perception" test and this test.[418] As is often the case with judgments from the Court of Justice which are intended to "clarify" EU law, on return to the English courts, both sides argued that the decision favoured them. It went to the Court of Appeal[419] who, applying the Court of Justice decision, upheld the Hearing Officer's rejection of the application. It held that it was legitimate for a tribunal, when assessing whether a significant proportion of the relevant class of persons perceive the goods or services as originating from a particular undertaking, to consider whether such person would *rely* upon the sign as denoting the origin of the goods or services.[420] However, it said that the test was not one of reliance per se. The Court of Appeal held that the Hearing Officer was entitled to reject the application as the evidence merely showed recognition of the shape but not reliance on it to identify the origin of the goods.

3-239   It might be asked if survey evidence is not enough, what sort of evidence should be adduced to show that the public identify the shape as an indication of origin? A number of examples spring to mind:

-    Evidence of promotion of the shape of product in advertisements, etc.
-    Survery evidence where a "shop" is stocked with unbranded and differently shaped chocolate bars and potential customers are quizzed about what they had bought.
-    Combining the shape mark with another word mark (known or unknown) and asking what the reaction of the public was, i.e. did members of the public think that it was a new name for KITKAT or licensed by owners of KITKAT.[421]

3-240   Finally, it can be said that if proprietors wish the shape of a product to be identified as a trade mark, they may wish to consider marketing it without a word mark and have the courage of their convictions.

Acquired distinctive character and EU Trade Marks

3-241   In the case of EUTMs, it must be shown that the mark has distinctive character throughout the EU.[422] Thus, in those parts of the EU where the mark lacks distinctive character, it is necessary to show that the mark applied for has acquired distinctive character even if this is only one Member State.[423] Thus, where an applicant sought to register EUROPOLIS in the Benelux territories for financial and insurance services, the word "polis" in the Dutch-speaking part of Benelux meant "policy" and accordingly, was considered to lack distinctive character for that sector of the Benelux territory. However, the mark had been used in the Benelux territories. On reference to the CJEU, the court held that it must be shown that the mark has acquired distinctive character throughout the territory where there exists

---

[418]   See [58] of the judgment of the Court of Justice. See also the Court of Appeal's decision in *Société des Produits Nestlé SA v Cadbury UK Ltd* [2017] EWCA Civ 358 at [44] and [99] applying the Court of Justice's judgment where it makes this point.

[419]   *Société des Produits Nestlé SA v Cadbury UK Ltd* [2017] EWCA Civ 358.

[420]   See [84].

[421]   The first example was suggested in the Hearing Officer's decision—see [33] of the Court of Appeal's decision.

[422]   *August Storck KG v EUIPO* (C-25/05P) [2006] E.C.R I-5719 at [81].

[423]   *August Storck KG v EUIPO* (C-25/05P) at [83]. *Ford Motor Co v EUIPO* (T-91/99) [2004] E.C.R. II-9125 at [53]; *Audi AG v EUIPO* (T-16/02) [2003] E.C.R. II-5167, [2004] E.T.M.R. 59 at [52]. *Bic SA v EUIPO* (T-262/04) [2005] E.C.R. II-5959 at [62].

a ground of refusal.[424] Within that territory, it must be assessed whether the relevant public or a significant proportion of people identify the sign as indicative of trade origin.[425] This can be a very difficult hurdle to overcome and this is often known as the "Malta" torpedo, i.e. even if a prima facie descriptive mark has been extensively promoted, advertised and used throughout the EU such that it has acquired distinctive character in a significant part of the EU, if it has not acquired distinctive character in Malta, the application will fail.[426] Thus, in *Mondelez v EUIPO*,[427] where Mondelez sought to register the well-known chocolate "Kit Kat" bar, it adduced good survey evidence of recognition of the bar in 10 out of 15 Member States. As a result of these surveys and other evidence, the Board of Appeal held that acquired distinctive character had been shown and allowed the registration.

However, on appeal to the General Court, it said that the Board of Appeal appeared to consider that it was sufficient to show that a significant proportion of the relevant public of the EU perceived the mark as an indication of commercial origin for the purposes of art.7.3. The court said that such a criterion was incorrect and it was necessary to establish such *throughout* the EU, i.e. in every Member State.[428] Thus, the General Court annulled the decision of the Board of Appeal as there was no market survey evidence for Belgium, Ireland, Greece and Portugal and the Board of Appeal has failed to establish that the Kit Kat bar had acquired distinctive character in these countries. Such is an emphatic confirmation of the "Malta torpedo" principle. A similar approach was taken in *Coca Cola v EUIPO*[429] where the General Court rejected an application by Coca-Cola to register the Coca-Cola bottle shape minus the normal fluting on the grounds that it was inherently not distinctive and Coca-Cola had failed to adduce survey evidence in 17 Member States. **3-242**

By way of comment, the test that the mark must have acquired distinctive character in every Member State may seem harsh (particularly now that there are 28 Member States). For example, there is no requirement that a EUTM must have been put to genuine use in every Member State. Furthermore, it would go against the principle of treating the EU as a single territory. However, in mitigation, a EUTM applicant can always convert the application and obtain registration of the mark in those states where it has acquired distinctive character. **3-243**

Use as a trade mark

It must be shown that the acquisition of distinctive character has resulted from use of the mark as a trade mark. As the CJEU said: **3-244**

"[64] Finally, the identification by the relevant class of persons, of the product as originating from a given undertaking must be *as a result of the use of the mark as a trade mark* and thus as a result of the nature and effect of it, which make it

---

[424] *Bovemij v Benelux-Merkenbureau (Europolis)* (C-108/05) [2006] E.C.R. I-7605; [2007] E.T.M.R. 28 at [23].

[425] See [28].

[426] For the insuperable problems that this requirement can cause see *Liz Earle Beauty* (T-307/09) [2010] E.C.R. II-0000; *New Look v EUIPO* (T-435/07) [2008] E.C.R. II-296. See also G. Tritton, "Distinctiveness and Acquired Distinctiveness: The Approach and Territorial Aspects" [2012] ERA Forum 2–2012.

[427] *Mondelez UK Holdings v EUIPO* (T-112/13) ECLI:EU:T:2016:735.

[428] See [141]–[142].

[429] (T-411/14) ECLI:EU:T:2016:94.

> capable of distinguishing the product concerned from those of other undertakings."[430] [Emphasis supplied.]

3-245　　It was unclear from this excerpt whether it is a requirement that the applicant purposively and intentionally set out to use the mark as a trade mark or whether it is merely sufficient that the public has come to recognise the mark as a trade mark by reason of its use. This is important in relation to shape marks and other marks which are usually not intentionally marketed as a trade mark but by reason of extensive and often exclusive use become recognised by the public as being the product of a particular undertaking.

3-246　　In *Nestlé v Mars UK* ("HAVE A BREAK"),[431] Nestlé had used the phrase "HAVE A BREAK … HAVE A KIT KAT" for many years in the UK in relation to the advertisement and promotion of its Kit Kat chocolate bars. Indeed, the advertising phrase is extremely well known as the advertising strap line for these chocolate bars. Nestlé sought to register the mark "HAVE A BREAK". It accepted that it was inherently unregistrable and that it had to show that it had acquired distinctive character. However, it had never used the phrase "HAVE A BREAK" on its own but always with the registered trade mark KIT KAT. On a reference to the CJEU as to whether it had to be shown that there had been use of "HAVE A BREAK" on its own for the equivalent provision in the TMD to art.7.3 EUTMR to apply, the CJEU said:

> "[29]　The expression 'use of the mark as a trade mark' must therefore be understood as referring solely to use of the *mark for the purposes of the identification*, by the relevant class of persons, of the product or service as originating from a given undertaking.
>
> [30]　Yet, such identification, and thus acquisition of distinctive character, may be as a result both of the use, as part of a registered trade mark, of a component thereof and of the use of a separate mark in conjunction with a registered trade mark. In both cases it is sufficient that, in consequence of such use, the relevant class of persons actually perceive the product or service, designated exclusively by the mark applied for, as originating from a given undertaking." [Emphasis supplied.]

In this excerpt, it is unclear whether the CJEU is saying that it is or is not necessary that the registered proprietor promoted the sign applied for *as* a trade mark. This has led English courts to consider the matter to be unclear and refer this very question to the CJEU.[432] In the author's opinion, it would be strange if the subjective intention of the applicant is relevant to the registrability of a mark. Trade marks are about market perception and not the intention of the applicant (save perhaps in relation to bad faith and taking of unfair advantage). Thus if the public perceive the sign to be a trade mark, such should be sufficient under art.7.3 EUTMR. However, where the sign has not been promoted positively as a trade mark by the applicant, evidentially it may be very difficult to establish this. In any event, *Nestlé v Mars* makes it clear that it is not necessary that the sign has been used as a trade mark *on its own* for it to acquire distinctive character under art.7.3. The Court of Justice

---

[430]　*Koninklijke Philips Electronics NV v Remington Consumer Products Ltd* (C-299/99) [2002] E.C.R. I-5475; [2002] E.T.M.R. 81.

[431]　(C-353/03) [2005] E.C.R. I-6135; [2005] E.T.M.R. 96.

[432]　*Dysons Trade Mark Application* [2003] R.P.C. 47 (Ch). Although this question was referred, the CJEU did not answer it because they held that the sign applied for was not a sign within the meaning of art.4 TMD—see para.3-160. See also *Philips v Remington (No.2)* [2005] F.S.R. 17 (Ch) at 160–161.

in *Nestlé v Cadbury*[433] appears to suggest that it is sufficient if the public perceive the sign as indicative of trade origin and not that it was intentionally used as a trade mark.

Natural, functional and aesthetic marks

Article 7.1(e) EUTMR bans the registration of signs which consist exclusively of: **3-247**

(i) the shape or another characteristic which results from the nature of the goods themselves;

(ii) the shape or another characteristic of goods which is necessary to obtain a technical result; or

(iii) the shape or another characteristic which gives substantial value to the goods.

These grounds are not concerned with the issue of distinctiveness.[434] Thus, they   **3-248** cannot be overcome by proving acquired distinctive character. The policy reason for exclusion of registrability of such signs has been said to reflect "the legitimate concern to prevent individuals from resorting to trade marks in order to extend exclusive rights over technical developments."[435] This is certainly true of the second objection (technical result) but as will be seen, this provision is also concerned with prohibiting the monopolisation of aesthetic aspects which confer substantial value on goods.

With effect from 23 March 2016, this ground was amended so to extend the   **3-249** objection not only to shapes but also to "other characteristics". Thus, any mark which consists of a sound, taste, smell or colour where that sound, taste, smell or colour arises from the nature of the goods, is necessary to obtain a technical result or gives substantial value to the goods is not registrable. Examples could be an application for the sound of a motor engine being accelerated for cars; the taste of chocolate for chocolate; the smell of paint for paint; or an attractive colour for a car.

Mix of objections under art.7.1(e) not allowed

It is not permissible to combine the grounds under art.7.1(e) and each ground   **3-250** must be applied independently of each other.[436] In a reference from the High Court of England and Wales concerning whether the grounds for refusal laid down in the equivalent provisions to art.7.1(e) in the TMD, the referring court found that two of the essential features of the mark were necessary to obtain a technical result and one which resulted from the nature of the goods. The Court of Justice said that: (i) more than one ground under the Directive equivalent to art.7.1(e) can apply cumulatively; but (ii) it is not sufficient if one or more of three grounds is only partially established and each ground must be "fully applicable".[437] This might be thought odd. A shape mark could consist of three important design elements with two having a technical purpose and one having an aesthetic purpose and still be

---

[433] (C-215/14) ECLI:EU:C:2015:604 at [63]–[65].

[434] *The Procter & Gamble Co v EUIPO* (T-122/99) [2000] E.C.R. II-0265 at [43].

[435] Opinion of Ruiz-Colomer AG in (C-299/99) [2002] E.C.R. I-5475; [2002] E.T.M.R. 81 at [16].

[436] *Nestlé v Cadbury* (C-215/14) ECLI:EU:C:2015:604.

[437] *Nestlé v Cadbury*, at [49]–[50]. Accordingly, Nestlé accepted that no objection could made under these provisions—see *Nestlé v Cadbury UK* [2016] EWHC 50 at [6].

registrable. One would have thought that public policy should dictate that this is not registrable as it could permit the owner of such a mark to prevent use of the design elements (as a sign to infringe need not be identical).

Public policy

3-251   The rationale of the grounds for refusal of registration laid down in art.7.1(e) EUTMR is to prevent trade mark protection from granting its proprietor a monopoly on technical solutions or functional characteristics of goods which a user is likely to seek in the goods of competitor.[438] The aim is to prevent the exclusive and permanent right conferred by a trade mark from serving to extend indefinitely the life of other rights which the EU legislature has sought to make subject to limited periods.[439] Functional characteristics should not be interpreted as meaning just technical characteristics. It would also include characteristics which are aesthetic.[440]

TRIPS and art.7.1(e)

3-252   There is no equivalent provision to art.7.1(e) in TRIPS. In TRIPS, the touchstone of registrability is distinctiveness. If a sign is distinctive (whether inherently or by use), both conventions require signatory states to permit it to be registered. As said above, art.7.1(e) is not concerned with distinctiveness. Article 15(2) of TRIPS states that Member States cannot deny registration save on the grounds of art.15(1) (distinctiveness) and grounds contained in the Paris Convention. Yet, the Paris Convention also does not permit an objection based on the mark being a shape.

3-253   The illegality of art.7.1(e) under TRIPS is relevant to the interpretation of the former provision. It is settled law that since the EU is a party to the TRIPS Agreement, it is required to interpret its legislation on trade marks so far as possible in the light of the wording and purpose of that Agreement.[441] Whilst it might be argued that it is simply impossible to interpret art.7.1(e) in the light of TRIPS because it has no counterpart in that convention, it is equally arguable that art.7.1(e) should be narrowly construed.

Essential characteristics

3-254   Invariably, a shape mark will include aspects of it which are not intended to achieve a technical solution, give substantial value or result from the nature of the goods. If it was required that *all* aspects of a shape mark including immaterial elements had to be shown as satisfying the above, it would mean that art.7.1(e) would never be applicable. Therefore, the Court of Justice has developed the approach that it need only be shown that the essential characteristics of a shape are capable of objection under art.7.1(e).[442] As the Court of Justice said in *Lego Juris*, the presence of one or more "minor arbitrary elements" does not affect the application of

---

[438] *Philips* (C-299/99) EU:C:2002:377 at [78]; *Hauck* (C-205/13) EU:C:2014:2233 at [18]; *Nestlé v Cadbury* (C-215/44) at [44].

[439] *Hauck* (C-205/13) EU:C:2014:2233 at [19]; *Lego Juris v OHIM* (C-48/09 P) EU:C:2010:516 at [45]; *Nestle v Cadbury*, at [45].

[440] *Hauck*, at [30]–[32].

[441] e.g. *Hermes International v FHT Marketing Choice BV* (C-53/96) [1998] E.C.R. I-3603 at [28]; (C-49/02) [2004] E.T.M.R. 99 at [20]. See para.1-180.

[442] *Lego Juris v EUIPO* (C-48/09P), at [51]–[52]; *Philips v Remington*, at [79]. *Pi-Design v Yoshida Metal Industry* (C-337/12P) ECLI:EU:C:2014:129 at [46]; *Hauck GmbH v Stokke A/S* (C-205/13)

art.7.1(e)(ii).[443] The identification of the "essential characteristics" had to be done on a case-by-case basis. It said that the competent authority may either base its assessment directly on the overall impression produced by the sign or examine in turn each of the components of the sign concerned.[444] The Court of Justice said that once the essential characteristics had been identified, the competent authority still has to ascertain whether they all are capable of objection under one of the subparagraphs of art.7.1(e)[445] *Nestlé v Cadbury*, the Court of Justice held that this ground of objection only applies to the manner in which the goods at issue function and not the manner in which they are manufactured.[446]

Characteristics of the goods that results from the nature of the goods themselves

In *Hauck GmbH v Stokke A/S*,[447] the Court of Justice considered the registrability of a well-known children's chair called the "Tripp Trapp" chair which looked like this: **3-255**

The Gerechtshof sought guidance on the proper interpretation of the equivalent of art.7.1(e)(i) in the TMD for the well-known Tripp Trapp chair. The Court of Justice said that this provision pursued the same objective as art.7.1(e)(ii) and that one had to identify the essential characteristics of the sign. It then went on to say that this ground could not apply where the shape of goods included an element such as a decorative or imaginative detail which is not inherent "*to the generic function of the goods*" and that element plays an important or essential role.[448] However, it went on to say that it applies to a sign whose essential characteristics are inherent to the generic function or functions of the product which consumers may be looking for in the products of competitors. Such was not limited to natural products or regulated products (the shape of which is prescribed by legal standards).[449] Moreover, it rejected an interpretation of the provision whereby it was limited to signs which leave the manufacturer of the goods no leeway to make a personal es- **3-256**

ECLI:EU:C:2014:2233, at [21].

[443] See [52]. However, the presence of a major non-functional element such as a decorative or imaginative element would render art.7.1(e)(ii) inapplicable.

[444] See [70]. It is significant that the Court of Justice did not accept the submission of either parties on this point. Lego argued that the identification of the essential characteristics was synonymous with the dominant and distinctive elements and such had to be carried out from the perspective of the relevant public. EUIPO and Mega Brands contended that such was not correct. See also *Pi-Design v Yoshida Metal Industry* (C-337/12P) ECLI:EU:C:2014:129 at [47].

[445] See [72]. This was said in the context of the equivalent provision in the TMD to art.7.1(e)(ii) but is applicable to all three sub-paragraphs (see *Hauck*, [20]–[21]). See also *Yoshida Metal v EUIPO* (C-421/15) (irrelevant that there were ornamental elements which did not play an important role in the shape of the goods).

[446] (C-215/14) ECLI:EU:C:2015:604.

[447] (C-205/13) ECLI:EU:C:2014:2233.

[448] See [22].

[449] See [24]–[27].

sential contribution.[450] It is not wholly clear what is meant by "generic function" and how far this extends beyond characteristics that have a technical function (in which case, they would be objectionable under art.7.1(e)(ii)). The Advocate-General considered that the provision prevented the registration of a shape where essential characteristics resulted from the nature of the goods concerned and which are therefore determined by the practical function which those goods perform.[451] He gave examples such as the legs with a horizontal level in relation to a chair, an orthopaedic shaped sole with a V-shaped strap on flip-flops and the shape of a sailing boat hull or aircraft propeller.[452] One might have thought that all of these examples would also fall foul of art.7.1(e)(ii) (shape necessary to obtain a technical result).

Characteristic necessary to obtain a technical result

3-257   Of the three "shape" provisions, this has been the one most relied upon and adjudicated upon. In *Lego Juris v EUIPO*,[453] the CJEU stated, in relation to art.7.1(e)(ii):

> "[43]   ... it must be borne in mind that each of the grounds for refusal to register listed in [Article 7.1(e) EUTMR] must be interpreted in the light of the public interest underlying them (*Henkel v EUIPO*, paragraph 45, and Case C-173/04 *P Deutsche SiSi-Werke v EUIPO* [2006] ECR I-551, paragraph 59). The interest underlying [Article 7.1(e)(ii) EUTMR] is to prevent trade mark law granting an undertaking a monopoly on technical solutions or functional characteristics of a product (see by analogy, with regard to the [Article 4.1(e)(ii) TMD], *Philips*, paragraph 78, and *Linde and Others* Joined Cases C-53/01 to C-55/01 [2003] E.C.R. I-3161, paragraph 72).
>
> [44]   In that connection, the rules laid down by the legislature reflect the balancing of two considerations, both of which are likely to help establish a healthy and fair system of competition.
>
> [45]   First, the inclusion in [Article 7.1(e)(ii) EUTMR] of the prohibition on registration as a trade mark of any sign consisting of the shape of goods which is necessary to obtain a technical result ensures that undertakings may not use trade mark law in order to perpetuate, indefinitely, exclusive rights relating to technical solutions."[454]

3-258   However, the CJEU made it clear that the mere fact that the shape was functional did not trigger art.7.1(e)(ii) as any shape of goods is, to a certain extent, functional.[455] Thus, it was only shapes that incorporated a technical solution and thus whose registration would impede the use of that technical solution by other undertakings that were not to be registered.[456] However, as seen in the discussion under art.7.1(e)(iii), a functional characteristic may be objectionable for adding substantial value to the goods sold under the mark.

3-259   Furthermore, in *Lego Juris*, the CJEU made it clear, following *Philips v Remington*, that art.7.1(e)(ii) was not inapplicable merely because there were other

---

[450] See [23]. See also, the AG's Opinion which held that the fact that the product could take a different, alternative shape was irrelevant—see [65].

[451] See [55], Opinion.

[452] See [59].

[453] *Lego Juris v EUIPO* (C-48/09P) [2010] E.C.R. I-8403.

[454] See [45]. See also *Pi-Design v Yoshida Metal Industry* (C-337/12P) ECLI:EU:C:2014:129 at [45].

[455] See [48].

[456] See [48].

shapes that could achieve the same technical function.[457] As the CJEU said in *Lego Juris v EUIPO*, the proprietor of a shape trade mark could seek to prevent other undertakings not only from using the same shape but also similar shapes. Thus, a significant number of alternative shapes might therefore become unusable to the proprietor's competitors.[458] It is of note that the same approach is now taken under EU law relating to designs in relation to the "technical function" exclusion.[459] Indeed, as has been forcibly commented on in the field of Community design law, the alternative approach (called the multiplicity-of-forms theory) would permit an applicant to register all possible shapes necessary to achieve a technical result and thereby obtain a monopoly on a technical solution.[460]

When assessing whether the essential characteristics perform a technical function, it is legitimate to consider that by reference to the actual goods themselves that the shape mark embodies and not merely from the mark itself.[461] **3-260**

Characteristic that gives substantial value to the goods

In *Hauck GmbH v Stokke A/S*, the Court of Justice considered the meaning of this provision. The Gerechtshof was concerned whether it applied where the mark (being the TRIPP TRAPP chair) gave it significant aesthetic value but also had other characteristics (being safety, comfort and reliability) which gave it essential functional value. The Court of Justice held that the provision could not be limited purely to the shape of products having only artistic or ornamental value. It could also apply to products which had essential functional characteristics. In determining whether the essential characteristics gave substantial value to the goods, it said that the tribunal should take into account not only the perception of the average consumer but also the nature of the goods concerned, the artistic value of the shape in question, its dissimilarity from other shapes in common use, whether there exists a substantial price difference in relation to similar products, and the development of a promotion strategy which focuses on accentuating the aesthetic characteristics of the product in question. **3-261**

By referring to these criteria, the Court of Justice appears to blur the distinction between economic value arising from the inherent artistic or aesthetic nature of the shape and economic value arising from promotional or marketing strategies. The value of a brand will increase substantially by reason of its exposure to the marketplace but this has nothing to do with a policy based on preventing the registration of shapes indefinitely via the law of trade marks. **3-262**

In *Simba Toys GmbH v EUIPO*[462], the General Court held that for art.7.1(e)(iii) to apply, **3-263**

> "[87] ...it is necessary that the sign concerned consist exclusively of a shape and that the aesthetic characteristics of that shape, namely its external appearance, determine to a very large extent the consumer's choice and, therefore, the commercial value of the goods at issue. Where the shape thus gives substantial value to the goods at issue, it is irrelevant that other characteristics of those goods, such

---

[457] See *Lego*, at [53]; *Philips v Remington*, at [83].

[458] See [56].

[459] See para.5-144.

[460] See para.5-144.

[461] *Simba Toys GmbH v EUIPO* (C-30/15) ECLI:EU:C:2016:849.

[462] (T–450/09) EU:T:2014:982. Although this decision was appealed, the Court of Justice dismissed the appeal on other grounds—see *Simba Toys GmbH v EUIPO* (C-30/15P) ECLI:EU:C:2016:849.

as their technical qualities, may also confer on them considerable value (see, to that effect, judgment of 6 October 2011 in *Bang & Olufsen v EUIPO* (Representation of a loudspeaker), T–508/08, ECR, EU:T:2011:575, paragraphs 73 to 79)."

3-264   This brings the analysis of art.7.1(e)(iii) back to considerations of aesthetic value and whether such determine to a very large extent consumer choice. If they do, then it is irrelevant that the same characteristics also perform a technical function that also adds considerable value to the product. In short, if a characteristic of a mark adds substantial value to the goods (whether the value arises from aesthetic, technical or functional features), then art.7.1(e)(iii) applies. The General Court appears to be emphasising that "substantial value" is concerned with "commercial value". If so, the appropriate test must be to ask whether the essential characteristics of the sign, when applied to the goods for which registration is sought, allow the seller of the products to command a significantly greater price for goods bearing or incorporating the sign than goods which do not bear or incorporate the sign. To avoid any consideration of (and contamination by) the "reputation" value of the sign by reason of its promotion or advertisement in the marketplace, the tribunal should apply this test to a hypothetical situation where the sign has not been used on the goods.

Trade mark contrary to public policy or to accepted principles of morality

3-265   Article 7.1(f) EUTMR prevents the registration of trade marks which are contrary to public policy or to accepted principles of morality.

3-266   In considering this ground of objection, it is the intrinsic qualities of the mark applied for that is relevant and not whether use of the mark in a particular Member State by the registered proprietor or others would be illegal. Thus, in *Sportwetten GmbH v EUIPO (INTERTOPS)*,[463] which concerned an application for declaration of invalidity, it was held by the General Court that it was irrelevant whether the registered proprietor was permitted to provide such services in a Member State. The applicant had argued that as the registered proprietor was not licensed to supply betting services in Germany, the mark was registered contrary to art.7.1(f) of the EUTMR. It was held that the determination of whether the mark was inherently contrary to public policy or accepted principle of morality was to be carried out regardless of the applicant or its characteristics.

3-267   In applying this section, the courts and tribunals have drawn a distinction between marks that outrage sectors of the public and marks that are of dubious taste. Thus, in its guidelines, EUIPO distinguishes between words or images which are offensive, such as swear words or racially derogatory images or blasphemous image and those which are merely in poor taste. The latter do not offend art.7(1)(f). A review of marks refused by EUIPO under art.7.1(f) EUTMR include: *CLITORIS ALLSORTS, BIN LADIN, MAFIA, CASTRO, BILL CLINTON, JOHANNES PAUL II, FUCK OF THE YEAR, RASSISMUS (German word for racism), OPIUM, IPARRETARAK RECORDS*,[464] *BOLLOX*, and *BALLE* (German word for testicles).

3-268   In *DICK AND FANNY*,[465] EUIPO's Board of Appeal had to consider the mark which had been applied for clothing. In English slang, they refer to men and

---

[463] *Sportwetten GmbH v EUIPO (INTERTOPS)* (T-140/02) [2005] E.C.R. II-03247; [2006] E.T.M.R. 15.

[464] *"Iparretarak"* is an illegal organisation in Spain.

[465] (R-111/2002–4) [2005] E.T.M.R. 99, EUIPO (Fourth Board of Appeal).

women's sexual parts. However, they are also the diminutives for common English names, Richard and Francis. The Board overturned the objection under art.7.1(f) saying that it did:

"not proclaim an opinion, it contains no incitement, and conveys no insult."

In an English case, *Ghazilian's Trade Mark Application* ("TINY PENIS"),[466] the mark TINY PENIS was refused registration by the Trade Marks Registry. In upholding the Registry's objection, the Appointed Person said:

3-269

"The dividing line is to be drawn between offence which amounts only to distaste and offence which would justifiably cause outrage or would be the subject of justifiable censure as being likely significantly to undermine current religious, family or social values".

In *Basic Trade Mark Application*,[467] the mark JESUS for a wide variety of goods was refused registration by the English Trade Marks Registry. The objection was upheld on appeal by the Appointed Person. In the course of his decision, he referred to a US article which said that there are essentially seven categories of marks that are objectionable on the basis of scandalous or immoral marks. These are:

3-270

(a) those with a religious nexus;
(b) those consisting of or comprising racial slurs or epithets;
(c) those consisting of or comprising profane matter;
(d) those consisting of or comprising vulgar matter;
(e) those relating to sexuality;
(f) those involving innuendo; and
(g) those suggesting or promoting illegal activity.

In *CDW Graphic Design's Application*,[468] the English Registry refused an application for *www.standupifyouhatemanu.com*[469] in respect of bumper stickers, posters and door hangers. The Registry held that the connection between football and violence was well known and its use would be liable to incite violence. Thus, it was refused on the basis of public policy.

3-271

As the law of registered trade marks do not confer a right to use marks but rather, the right merely to exclude others from using marks, it might be thought strange that art.7.1(f) exists as the basis for the objection concerning the use of an offensive mark rather than the award of a monopoly. It might be that the real objection is giving an undertaking the right to control the commercial exploitation of offensive and culturally sensitive indications which is the real affront to public morality. Thus, giving a single undertaking the right to control the commercial use of JESUS in relation to goods or services is to treat a fundamental icon of Christianity as a commercial commodity. Such is the true offence.

3-272

Inherently deceptive marks

Article 7.1(g) prevents the registration of marks:

3-273

---

[466] *Ghazilian's Trade Mark Application* [2002] R.P.C. 33 at [30] ("TINY PENIS").
[467] *Basic Trade Mark Application* [2006] E.T.M.R. 24, Appointed Person (England).
[468] *CDW Graphic Design's Application* [2003] R.P.C. 30, Trade Marks Registry of England.
[469] For those not familiar with English football, this translates as "Stand up if you hate Manchester United"!

"which are of such a nature as to deceive the public, for instance as to the nature, quality of geographical origin of the goods or service".

3-274   This provision is concerned with marks which are likely to deceive when applied to the goods or services for which registration is sought. The provision will apply where the mark has a descriptive element to it and thus informs or alludes to an attribute of goods or services which is misleading as to the characteristic of the goods or services for which protection is sought. Thus, it must be established that the sign filed for the purposes of registration as a trade mark creates per se a risk of deception.[470] Put another way, the use of the sign must be deceptive *in every reasonably imaginable case*" when used in relation to the registered goods or services.[471]

3-275   For instance, "AllWool" registered for man-made textiles would be deceptive if used for such goods as plainly wool is not a man-made fibre. In many respects, it can be seen as the flipside of art.7.1(c) which prevents the registration of marks that *do* indicate a characteristic of goods. The requirement that the mark be deceitful per se means that the focus is on the mark and the specification of goods and not the use of the mark by its owner. For instance, if "AllWool" was registered for "clothing", it is plainly possible for such a mark to be used in a manner that does not deceive, i.e. by ensuring that the clothing sold under the mark is made from wool. Thus, no objection can be taken under art.7.1(g). If however, the owner uses the mark for clothing not made from wool for a long time, this may mean that the mark is liable to revoked for being used in a deceptive manner.[472]

3-276   Article 7.1(g) requires the existence of actual deceit or a sufficiently serious risk that the consumer will be deceived.[473]

3-277   A more difficult area is where the characteristic is more intangible, e.g. the mark is for a well-known person but that person has no connection with the registered proprietor. This issue was considered in the case of *Elizabeth Emanuel v Continental Shelf 128 Ltd*.[474] Elizabeth Emanuel is a well-known wedding dress designer who designed Princess Diana's wedding dress. She assigned her business including the goodwill to her name to another company. There then followed a series of assignments which resulted in an application by the ultimate assignee to apply to register "Elizabeth Emanuel" as a trade mark for clothing. Elizabeth Emanuel opposed this application on the basis that it was misleading under the equivalent in the TMD of art.7.1(g) as it suggested that she was still involved in the business. Although there is a public interest in misleading marks not being registered, there is an equal public interest in businesses being able to assign businesses including trade marks and assignors not being allowed to renege on such deals.

3-278   The CJEU held:

"[46]   However, in the case of a trade mark corresponding to the name of a person, the public interest ground which justifies the prohibition laid down by [Article 4.1(g)

---

[470] *W.F. Gözze Frottierweberei GmbH, Wolfgang Gözze v Verein Bremer Baumwollbörse* (C-689/15) ECLI:EU:C:2017:434 at [55].

[471] *Elizabeth Emanuel v Continental Shelf 128 Ltd* (C-259/04) [2006] E.C.R. I-3089; [2006] E.T.M.R. 56 at [57], AG's Opinion.

[472] See para.3-756.

[473] *W.F. Gözze Frottierweberei GmbH*, at [54].

[474] *Elizabeth Emanuel v Continental Shelf 128 Ltd* (C-259/04) [2006] E.C.R. I-3089; [2006] E.T.M.R. 56.

TMD] to register a trade mark which is liable to deceive the public, namely consumer protection, must raise the question of the risk of confusion which such a trade mark may engender in the mind of the average consumer, especially where the person to whose name the mark corresponds originally personified the goods bearing that mark.

[47] Nevertheless, the circumstances for refusing registration referred to in [Article 4.1(g) TMD] presuppose the existence of actual deceit or a sufficiently serious risk that the consumer will be deceived (*Consorzio per la tutela del formaggio Gorgonzola* Case C-87/97 [1999] E.C.R. I-1301, paragraph 41).

[48] In the present case, even if the average consumer might be influenced in his act of purchasing a garment bearing the trade mark 'ELIZABETH EMANUEL' by imagining that the appellant in the main proceedings was involved in the design of that garment, the characteristics and the qualities of that garment remain guaranteed by the undertaking which owns the trade mark.

[49] Consequently, the name Elizabeth Emanuel cannot be regarded in itself as being of such a nature as to deceive the public as to the nature, quality or geographical origin of the product it designates.

[50] On the other hand, it would be for the national court to determine whether or not, in the presentation of the trade mark 'ELIZABETH EMANUEL' there is an intention on the part of the undertaking which lodged the application to register that mark to make the consumer believe that Ms Emanuel is still the designer of the goods bearing the mark or that she is involved in their design. In that case there would be conduct which might be held to be fraudulent but which could not be analysed as deception for the purposes of [Article 4.1(g) TMD] and which, for that reason, would not affect the trade mark itself and, consequently, its prospects of being registered.

[51] Consequently the answer to the first two questions must be that a trade mark corresponding to the name of the designer and first manufacturer of the goods bearing that mark may not, by reason of that particular feature alone, be refused registration on the ground that it would deceive the public, within the meaning of [Article 4.1(g) TMD], in particular where the goodwill associated with that trade mark, previously registered in a different graphic form, has been assigned together with the business making the goods to which the mark relates."

The above reasoning is unsatisfactory and not easily understood. Paragraph 48 **3-279** appears to make it clear that even if the purchasing public was deceived into believing that Elizabeth Emmanuel was involved in the production of the wedding dress, such is irrelevant for the purpose of art.7.1(g). While it is true that the characteristics and quality of the product remain guaranteed by the trade mark proprietor, such is an argument which applies to *any registered trade mark*. Clearly, it would be a hopeless argument to say that "allwool" for "nylon clothing" is not deceptive because the characteristics and qualities of the product remain guaranteed by the registered proprietor. It is a clear non sequitur. Indeed, at [51], the CJEU is implicitly saying that *even if the goodwill had not been assigned*, the mere fact that the trade mark corresponds to the name of the designer is not by itself deceptive. This must be wrong. Plainly, in such circumstances, the mark would have been deceptive to the public.[475]

In truth, the CJEU would have done better to have acknowledged the public inter- **3-280** est that assignments of goodwill including trade marks should be respected by the

---

[475] Indeed, the reference to "in particular" where the business and goodwill is assigned is unconvincing. A very significant part of the public will be wholly unfamiliar with the assignment of the goodwill by Elizabeth Emanuel. If such is the case, then the public will be deceived because they will believe that Elizabeth Emanuel is still involved in the business.

assignor, and that such public interest takes priority over a potential for consumer confusion which can be dealt with in other ways rather than refusal to register a trade mark. Indeed, a refusal to register a misleading mark is not the same as preventing the use of a misleading mark. In the former case, such would simply mean that the registered proprietor had exclusive rights to prevent others from using a misleading mark. Registration does not confer a positive right on the proprietor to use a registered mark. There is a public interest in preventing the use of a misleading mark but it is difficult to identify the public interest in preventing the registration of a misleading mark.[476]

3-281   As an alternative approach, it is submitted that the CJEU could have interpreted art.7.1(g) in the TMD as only applying to marks which are *inherently* deceptive with regards to the goods or services for which it is registered, *regardless of the identity of the trade mark proprietor*. Support for this interpretation can be drawn from the words "of such a nature" in art.7.1(g). The focus is on the mark and the registered goods and services and not the owner of the mark. Thus, "all wool" is inherently deceptively if registered for "man-made fibres". However, "Elizabeth Emmanuel" is not inherently deceptive. Clearly, if the mark had been owned by Elizabeth Emanuel then it would not have been deceptive. In reality, Elizabeth Emanuel was claiming that because of her reputation as a wedding dress designer, an application for the mark by anyone else other than her would deceive the public. Characterised as such, it is more in the nature of a relative ground of objection under art.5(4)(b)(i) TMD (right to a name). The advantage of characterising her opposition as a relative rather than an absolute ground of opposition is that under art.5(5) TMD, such a ground may not be raised if the proprietor of the earlier right consents to the registration of the later trade mark. Thus, Ms Emanuel would have been deemed to have consented to the registration of the later mark because of the implicit consent contained within an assignment.

3-282   EUIPO distinguishes between on the one hand, applications where a list of goods/services is worded in a detailed way such that a non-deceptive use of the trade mark is impossible and on the other hand, where the list of goods/services is worded in such a broad way that a non-deceptive use is possible. Thus, if a trade mark KODAK VODKA was applied for vodka, gin, rum and whisky, an objection would be raised in relation to the goods "gin, rum and whisky" but if the application was KODAK VODKA for "alcoholic beverages", no objection would be raised as it would be assumed that the mark would be used in a non-deceptive manner.[477] EUIPO draws a distinction between marks which are merely suggestive about a characteristic of the goods or services for which registration is sought and a mark which is directly descriptive. Thus, *METALJACKET*,[478] for rustproofing preparations, was held not to be objectionable by the First Board of Appeal under art.7.1(g) because:

> "the mark is easily perceived as the fusion of two ordinary English words, 'Metal' and

---

[476] It has been suggested that the public interest lies in preserving the dignity of the registration system itself and not allowing the imprimatur of registration to accompany a mark which has become misleading—see D. Kitchin, D. Llewelyn, J. Mellor, R. Meade, T. Moody-Stuart, D. Keeling, and R. Jacob, *Kerly on Trade Marks and Trade Names*, 15th edn (London: Sweet & Maxwell, 2011), para.10–150 .

[477] EUIPO Guidelines, [1.2.2] at [18]. See *https://oami.europa.eu/tunnel-web/secure/webdav/guest/document_library/contentPdfs/law_and_practice/trade_marks_practice_manual/part%20_b_section_4_ag_manual_after_gl_en.pdf* [Accessed 13 April 2014].

[478] (R 314/2002–1) EUIPO (1st Board of Appeal).

'Jacket', nevertheless, it does not give any unambiguous indication as to the specific nature of the appellant's goods and services."

Heraldic symbols, flags, etc.

Under art.7.1(h) EUTMR, signs which are protected by Member States pursu- **3-283**
ant to art.6*ter* of the Paris Convention, such as national symbols, flags, heraldic symbols, coats of arms, etc. can be refused registration. Article 7.1(i) also prevents the registration of badges, emblems or escutcheons other than those covered by art.6*ter* and which are of particular public interest, unless the consent of the competent authority is given.

It should be noted that the protection provided under the TMD is slightly differ- **3-284**
ent to that of the EUTMR. First, the TMD expressly allows Member States to provide as an absolute ground, the prohibition of registration of signs "of high symbolic value, in particular, a religious symbol".[479] This has no counterpart in the EUTMR. Furthermore, the TMD refers to badges, emblems and escutcheons other than those covered by art.6 *ter* of the Paris Convention which are of "public interest". The EUTMR refers to "particular public interest".[480] It would be surprising if these textual differences were intended to create material differences.

The provisions of art.7.1(h) EUTMR extend to applications for trade marks for **3-285**
services as well as goods.[481]

Use of mark contrary to EU or national GIO or plant variety legislation

Article 7.1 EUTMR prevents the registration of marks if one of the following **3-286**
conditions are satisfied:

"(j)   trade marks which are excluded from registration, pursuant to Union legislation or national law or to international agreements to which the Union or the Member State concerned is party, providing for protection of designations of origin and geographical indications;

(k)   trade marks which are excluded from registration pursuant to Union legislation or international agreements to which the Union is party, providing for protection of traditional terms for wine;

(l)   trade marks which are excluded from registration pursuant to Union legislation or international agreements to which the Union is party, providing for protection of traditional specialities guaranteed;

(m)   trade marks which consist of, or reproduce in their essential elements, an earlier plant variety denomination registered in accordance with Union legislation or national law, or international agreements to which the Union or the Member State concerned is a party, providing for protection of plant variety rights, and which are in respect of plant varieties of the same or closely related species."

These grounds of objections were introduced into the EUTMR with effect from **3-287**
23 March 2016. As regards art.7.1(j)–(l), and as discussed later in this chapter, the EU provides protection for traditional names for foodstuffs and alcoholic bever-

---

[479]   art.4.3(b) TMD.

[480]   art.4.3(c) TMD, art.7.1(i).

[481]   *American Clothing SA v EUIPO* (C-202/08 & C-208/08) [2009] E.C.R. I-6933. The CJEU overturned a decision of the General Court who held that because art.6 *ter* of the Paris Convention did not extend to service marks, then art.7.1(h) did not apply to service marks. As held by the CJEU, art.6*ter* provides for a minimum level of protection and Member States are free to extend the scope of such protection (e.g. see [72]).

ages as geographical indications of origin ("GIOs") or Traditional Specialities Guaranteed ("TSG") through sui generis EU legislation.[482] The legislation itself regulates what names that are GIOs or TSGs can be registered as trade marks.[483] However, this ground was not reflected in Reg.207/2009 (the predecessor to the EUTMR). Accordingly, one had the odd and unsatisfactory position whereby Reg.207/2009 set out exhaustively absolute grounds of objection which did not include that the mark was a GIO or TSGs and yet, GIO legislation dealt with this. No doubt because of this, Reg.207/2009 was amended by Reg.2015/2424 (and thus such is reflected in the codifying EUTMR) to ensure that there was no lack of harmony between GIO legislation and EU trade mark legislation concerning the registrability of signs that would offend GIO legislation.

3-288   Although they are described as an absolute ground, they are more akin to a relative ground objection. This is because GIO legislation prevents the registration of a mark whose use in the marketplace for goods would infringe the exclusive right that a group of undertakings would have in a GIO. Those rights extend not just to use of a sign identical to a GIO but also to any sign that evokes, imitates or exploits the reputation of the GIO.[484]

Bad faith

3-289   Article 59.1(b) of the EUTMR states that a registered mark may be declared invalid if the applicant was acting in bad faith when they filed the application for a EUTM. It should be noted that unlike the corresponding provision in the TMD,[485] which permits Member States to make this a ground of opposition as well as cancellation, under the EUTMR, this ground cannot be relied upon as a ground of opposition (cf. cancellation). Although it is entitled as an absolute ground, in truth, the vast majority of bad faith cases are concerned with, at a very broad level, an allegation that the owner or applicant has misappropriated a trade mark which the honest and reasonable bystander would deem rightfully belongs to a third party or in appropriate cases, to no one.

3-290   Many people would say that the concept of "bad faith" should not be over-elaborated. It introduces a moral element into the registrability of trade marks. It requires consideration of current *mores* and what are considered acceptable practices in business and trade circles. Such people would say that where the issue of bad faith is raised, each application should be considered on its own facts.

3-291   However, there is always a difficulty with introducing a moral component into an area such as trade mark law. Whilst it may be clear to most people that stealing money is dishonest, the arcane area of trade mark law is less susceptible to moral analysis. For instance, where a person applies to register a mark in one country knowing that it is being used in another country by another person, is such dishonest? Indeed, in the UK, prior to the implementation of the Trade Marks Act 1994, the Court of Appeal held that it was irrelevant that the mark applied had been designed by the opponent, registered abroad in various countries, and that the op-

---

[482] See para.3-855.
[483] see para.3-904.
[484] See para.3-889.
[485] art.4.2.

ponent considered that they were the owners of the mark. The fact was that the opponent had no rights in the UK.[486]

Many business professionals would say that if an applicant is entitled under the law to apply for a mark, then the application cannot be dishonest. It will be readily appreciated that if such is indeed the case, then there is no room for a bad faith objection. If the relevant public's view is that the registrability of trade mark applications should be governed solely by whether the law permits them or not, then any argument that an application has been made in bad faith even though, in other respects, it complies with the law is logically circular and bound to fail. Whilst this might be thought rather Anglo-Saxon and hardnosed, it is of note that in *Budejovický Budvar, národní podnik v Anheuser-Busch Inc*,[487] the owner of one registered trade mark applied to have declared invalid another registered mark one day before the expiry of a relevant five-year period concerning acquiescence. The advantage of such tactics was that it meant that the other party could not apply to do the same to the first party in response as the relevant five-year period would have expired. Some would describe this as sharp practice—others would commend the party for astute legal tactics.[488] Indeed, it was suggested by some national governments that such amounted to an abuse of rights.[489] However, the Advocate-General considered that such was permissible conduct and that blurring the time limit in certain circumstances would undermine legal certainty and amount to a collateral attack on the validity of the legislation. In other words, undertakings are entitled to maximise to their full advantage the law of trade marks.[490]

3-292

Given the above metaphysical debate, it is perhaps not surprising that the concept of "bad faith" has indeed given rise to wide variances in approaches by Member States and EUIPO. To paraphrase a well-known English phrase, one man's clever tactics is another man's dishonest tactics.[491]

3-293

Leaving aside the metaphysical discussions above, it is clear that there are certain situations where instinctively, the application can be characterised as having been made in bad faith. For instance, an application for a trade mark which the applicant has only applied for in the sole hope of extorting monies from a brand owner who has used the mark in other jurisdictions is instinctively an application made in bad faith. It is ultimately an abuse of the trade mark system and use of the trade mark registration system for purposes which it was manifestly not intended.[492] However, other situations are less clear. For instance, what is the position where an applicant applies for marks for "defensive" purposes, i.e. the applicant has no intention of using the mark but wishes to use it as a "blocking" mark to prevent others from obtaining exclusive rights in it because they consider it commercially unac-

3-294

---

[486] *Al Bassam Trade Mark* [1995] R.P.C. 511 CA. It is fair to point out that there was no suggestion that the applicant had behaved other than in a bona fide way.

[487] (C-482/09) [2012] E.T.M.R. 12; [2011] E.C.R. I-8701.

[488] To use the colourful phrase of Jacob LJ in *Budejovický Budvar, národní podnik v Anheuser Busch* [2010] R.P.C. 7 when referring it to the CJEU—it is "to steal a march" defined in the Oxford English Dictionary as "to succeed in moving troops without the knowledge of the enemy; hence gen. to get a secret advantage over a rival or opponent".

[489] The abuse of rights doctrine based on civil law notions of *abus de droit* is discussed at para.14-055.

[490] The Advocate-General approved (see fn.79 of his Opinion) of a statement in an article that a right holder must be allowed to apply the rules of substantive and procedural law to his best advantage—J. Drew and H. Priestley, "Anheuser-Busch and Budvar march on to the ECJ" (2010) 5(2) *Journal of Intellectual Property Law & Practice*, 80.

[491] One man's meat is another man's poison.

[492] In this sense, it can be considered that the EU doctrine of *abus de droit* is relevant. This is discussed in Ch.14, para.14-055.

ceptable for someone else to use such a mark. Is that made in bad faith? Perhaps, more importantly, what is the situation where an applicant files for protection in all classes regardless of whether they wish to use the mark in those classes? Is that an application made in bad faith? Is it bad faith to repeatedly apply for the same trade mark for the same classes to avoid a registered mark being revoked for lack of genuine use in a five-year period? Is an application made for a trade mark in Member State A for goods X in bad faith where the applicant knows that the identical mark is being used by a competitor in Member State B for the same goods where such is not done for the overt purpose of extorting monies from the competitor? If the EU had deliberately adopted a first-to-file system, is that not perfectly legitimate provided that the applicant can show that such was done for the purpose of protecting the applicant's intended trade under the mark?

3-295   The meaning of "bad faith" was considered by the CJEU in *Chocoladefabriken Lindt & Sprüngli AG v Franz Hauswirth GmbH.*[493] The claimant was a Swiss company which had manufactured chocolate Easter bunnies wrapped in gold foil since the 1950s. In 2000, it applied to register and obtained as a three-dimensional Community trade mark an Easter bunny wrapped in gold coloured foil. The defendant was an Austrian company which had been producing similar looking chocolate bunnies wrapped in gold foil. They were not identical but similar—both also had a ribbon. The defendant claimed that the claimant had applied for the mark in bad faith as it was aware that there were competitors who have acquired a "valuable right" (*wertvollen Besitzstand*) in other Member States. In short, the claimant knew that producers in other Member States had been making and selling chocolate bunnies wrapped in gold foil for many years and the claimant sought to eliminate all its competitors. This was a difficult case. First, the EU trade mark system is fundamentally a first-to-file system which deliberately gives only limited protection to those persons who have used a mark prior to another undertaking filing for it. Secondly, the EU trade mark system permits undertakings to file for three-dimensional marks where such are not devoid of any distinctive character. Whilst this can be difficult with shape marks, it is not impossible. Thus, it would be a legitimate argument (as in *Budějovický Budvar*) to say that Lindt & Sprüngli were simply relying upon the EUTMR to their maximum advantage. On the other hand, it would be anathema to many that Lindt could have eliminated the competition in chocolate foil-wrapped bunnies throughout the EU by the use of trade mark law.

3-296   The CJEU first confirmed that the relevant time for determining whether there was bad faith was the time of filing the application for registration.[494] The CJEU said that the notion of "bad faith" requires an overall assessment taking into account all of the factors relevant to the particular case. So far, not very illuminating. However, it then considered the three factors referred to in the preliminary reference, namely: (i) the fact that the applicant knows or must know that a third party is using, in at least one Member State, an identical or similar sign for an identical or similar product capable of being confused with the sign for which registration is sought; (ii) the applicant's intention to prevent that third party from continuing to use such a sign; and (iii) the degree of legal protection enjoyed by the third party's sign and by the sign for which registration is sought. It said that these were

---

[493] (C-529/07) [2009] E.C.R. I-4893; [2009] E.T.M.R. 56.
[494] See [35].

relevant factors to be taken into account.[495] The CJEU made it clear that the fact that the applicant knew of third party use in a Member State of an identical or similar sign was not sufficient per se for a finding of bad faith.[496] This must be right because a fundamental aspect of the EU trade mark system is that it is first-to-file and not first-to-use.[497] The CJEU also said that consideration must be given to the applicant's intention at the time of filing. It said that such must be determined by reference to the objective circumstances of a particular case.[498] In applying this decision, the Austrian Supreme Court held that the application had not been made in bad faith.

3-297 It is a shame that the CJEU did not give guidance on the real issue raised by *Lindt & Sprüngli*—namely just how far can applicants for a trade mark take advantage of the rather strict and mechanistic provisions of the EUTMR (and TMD)? Was Lindt simply and legitimately "stealing a march" on its competitors like Anheuser-Busch sought to do in *Budejovický Budvar, národní podnik v Anheuser-Busch* discussed above? Thus, in two English cases, the judges have refused to condemn applications for trade marks as having been made in bad faith simply because they were made for "good tactical reasons" or "to strengthen their position".[499] A first-to-file system has always been viewed with suspicion by some countries (particularly Anglo-Saxon countries) because it means that a person who has not used a mark can injunct a person who has used a mark. The view is that registered marks are there to protect existing goodwill. However, the first-to-file system confers certainty. One can do a trade mark search and if it has not been applied for, know (under trade mark law) that one can apply for it without having to worry about whether someone has used it first.[500] Many "bad faith" arguments are based on the notion that it would be unfair to third parties who are using a trade mark for them to be denied the right to continue to do so by someone else applying to register that mark. Yet, the whole structure of the TMD and EUTMR is based upon first-to-file with some limited rights (both offensive and defensive) to prior users. When considering "bad faith" arguments, a court must take into account the inherent structure of the TMD and EUTMR even if such can, in certain factual circumstances, lead to (in the eyes of many) unfair consequences.

3-298 Thus, in *Lindt & Sprüngli*, it could be said that the fact that many other producers had been producing chocolate foil-wrapped bunnies for many years in various Member States was not relevant to bad faith but very relevant to the issue of distinctiveness. Indeed, in *Lindt & Sprüngli v EUIPO*,[501] the CJEU held that an application by Lindt & Sprüngli to register a chocolate bunny mark could not be registered because it was devoid of any distinctive character. In doing so, it relied upon the fact that chocolate foil-wrapped bunnies were ubiquitous—the very

---

[495] As said in *Peeters Landbouwmachines v EUIPO – Fors MW (BIGAB)* (T-33/11) ECLI:EU:T:2012:77 at [17], these are merely examples of factors to be taken into account. See also *pelicantravel.com s.r.o. v EUIPO* (T-136/11) ECLI:EU:T:2012:689 at [26].

[496] See [40].

[497] e.g. see *Hotel Cipriani Srl v Cipriani (Grosvenor Street)* [2009] R.P.C. 9, [178] (Arnold J); *Von Rossum v Heinrich Mack Nachf GmbH & Co* (CR366/207–2) (Second Board of Appeal, EUIPO)

[498] See [41] and [42].

[499] See *WHG (International) Ltd v 32 Red Plc* [2011] E.T.M.R. 21; [2011] R.P.C. 26 at [159] (upheld on this point on appeal); *Hotel Cipriani Srl v Cipriani (Grosvenor Street)* [2009] R.P.C. 9 (Arnold J, at [189]—upheld but for different reasons on appeal).

[500] Strictly, this is not true because the EUTMR does confer protection to prior users in certain circumstances.

[501] (C-98/11P) ECLI:EU:C:2012:307.

grounds relied upon by Hauswirth as being indicative of bad faith. It is submitted that courts should not use "bad faith" to deal with cases with difficult facts. The imputation of bad faith on behalf of an applicant is a serious one. It connotes disreputable behaviour and standards falling below honest businessmen. It is not a ground which should be relied upon merely because the application for the trade mark inconveniences third parties and may prevent use of marks they have been using for a substantial period.

3-299   Below are discussed various individual decisions. These decisions must be viewed with some caution as many of them pre-date *Lindt & Sprüngli*.

Manufacturer/distributor relationship—pre-emptive registrations

3-300   Where a distributor of products applies for a trade mark which is the trade mark used by a manufacturer or supplier of the products, such is likely to be found to have been applied for in bad faith. Thus, where an applicant intends through registration to obtain the trade mark of a third party with which it had contractual or pre-contractual relations, such will usually amount to bad faith.[502] In *R82 A/S V ATO Form*,[503] the Cancellation Division found that where applications by a distributor for six EUTMs which had been used by its suppliers on its products just before the distribution relationship was ended had been made in bad faith. It should be noted that art.8.3 EUTMR permits a proprietor of a mark to oppose the registration of a mark where the application has been made by an agent or representative of the proprietor of the trade mark without the proprietor's consent unless the agent or representative justifies their action. In *Poggio al Casone*,[504] the registered proprietor was the registered proprietor of marks essentially identical to an unregistered wine mark and wine labels used by a wine proprietor in Italy who was the applicant for a declaration of invalidity. The distributor had previously ordered wine from the applicant. Accordingly, the Cancellation Division found that the marks had been applied for in bad faith.

3-301   Similarly, where a person applies to register a mark in a country knowing that it is registered in other countries and knowing that the overseas proprietor intends to start trading under the mark in the country, then such will generally amount to bad faith. In *Daawat Trade Mark*, the Cancellation Division declared a EUTM invalid where an application to register the mark was made by a company who wished to do business with an Indian rice company who used the brand DAAWAT and knowing that the Indian company wished to enter the EU.[505] Indeed, although it is an optional provision in the TMD and does not appear in the trade mark laws of many Member States, support for this approach comes from art.4.4(c) TMD. This Article permits Member States to legislate that a trade mark should be refused if it is liable to be confused with a mark which was in use abroad as of the filing date, provided that the applicant was acting in bad faith.

3-302   In *Hotel Cipriani Srl v Cipriani (Grosvenor Street)*,[506] the English Court of Appeal, held applying *Lindt & Sprüngli* that an application had not been made in bad

---

[502] *BE NATURAL* C000479899/1 (Cancellation Division, EUIPO), at [10]. See also *Airhole Facemasks v EUIPO* (T-107/16) (application by distributor held to be in bad faith as it was applied contrary to agreement that the mark be registered in manufacturer's name).

[503] *R82 A/S v ATO FORM GmbH* [2006] E.T.M.R. 8, Cancellation Division.

[504] Filing No.301C Application No.001302306/1 *Poggio al Casone*, 25 August 2003.

[505] Application No.C-659037/1, *Daawat Trade Mark*, 28 June 2004.

[506] [2010] Bus. L.R. 1465.

faith because at the time of the application, there had been no significant use of the word "Cipriani" as a trade mark in relation to hotels or restaurants. The defendants had not had any right to use the word in a way which would have entitled it to local legal protection, and there was an agreement in place not to use the name. At first instance, Arnold J held that it did not constitute bad faith to apply to register a EUTM merely because the applicant is aware that third parties are using the same mark in relation to identical goods or services. As the judge said, the applicant may believe that they have a superior right to registration and use of the mark. These remarks are clearly right. A first-to-file system cannot be turned into a first-to-use system by the back door of "bad faith" arguments.

No intention to use mark is not bad faith

Unlike in certain Member States, EUIPO does not consider that a lack of intention to use a mark amounts to bad faith. Thus, in both *Trillium* and *Naked*, the Cancellation Division has made it clear that there is no need, on behalf of the applicant, to have an intention to use the mark.[507] In *Psytech International Ltd v EUIPO*,[508] the General Court held that EU trade mark law does not allow a court to make a finding of bad faith merely in view of the size of the list of goods and services in an application for registration.[509] Previous to this decision, the General Court had also said that the mere registration of a large variety of goods and services is a common practice of companies; it does not involve conduct that departs from accepted principles of ethical behaviour or honest commercial and business practices and that as a rule, it is legitimate for an undertaking to seek registration of a mark, not only for the categories of goods and services which it markets at the time of filing the application for but also for other categories of goods and services which it intends to market in the future.[510] **3-303**

It would appear that currently therefore, under EU law, undertakings are entitled to file for trade marks with as wide a specification as they see fit. It might be said that under the EUTMR and TMD, EU trade mark law considers that the protection against over-wide specification comes from the genuine use provisions. Namely, one can apply for a wide specification as one sees fit but if one has not used the mark for a period of five years or more, then such is vulnerable for revocation for non-use. However, as discussed below, this could itself be defeated by repeat filings for the same trade mark to avoid the consequence of revocation actions based on lack of genuine use. Whether such amounts to bad faith is discussed in the next section. **3-304**

In the UK there has been considerable debate and cases about the need (or lack of need) to show a bona fide intention to use the mark. This partly arises out of the home-grown provision of s.32(3) of the Trade Marks Act 1994 which requires applicants to declare that they have used the mark in relation to the goods or services applied for, or have a bona fide intention to use the mark. As a consequence of s.32(3), where an applicant knowingly makes a false statement pursuant to s.32(3) about their intention to use the mark in relation to the goods or services applied for **3-305**

---

[507] Application No.C-479899/1, *Trillium*, 28 March 2000; *Naked*, 813C, 14 February 2004.

[508] (T-507/08) [2011] E.C.R. II-165; ECLI:EU:C:2011:253.

[509] See [88]. This was held binding on a UK court, see *Jaguar Land Rover Ltd v Bombardier Recreational Products Inc* [2016] EWHC 3266. However, the English courts have now referred this issue to the Court of Justice—see *Sky v Skykick* [2018] EWHC 155.

[510] *Pelicantravel.com s.r.o.* (T-136/11) ECLI:EU:T:2012:689 at [54]–[55].

when they apply for the mark or with reckless disregard as to its truth, then the application will have been made in bad faith but not otherwise.[511]

Repeat filings

3-306   It is a common strategy to re-file the same trade mark for the same goods or services if an earlier mark is vulnerable to revocation for lack of genuine use. This could be done repeatedly. Such would plainly allow an undertaking to monopolise a trade mark indefinitely without ever using it. Such would defeat the policy of the EUTMR and TMD that unused marks are revoked.[512] The Board of Appeal has said the following concerning such a practice:

> "[17] To register a trade mark and then periodically to register an identical mark can serve to improperly and fraudulently extend the five-year grace period indefinitely to evade the legal obligation of genuine use and the corresponding sanctions, which are to be applied in their full effectiveness required by the equal and uniform application of Union law. These re-filings are made in fraudem legis (in fraud of the law), but they cannot be invoked to evade the corresponding sanctions according to the general principle of Union law by which fraud of law and abuse of rights are prohibited. Individuals must not improperly or fraudulently take advantage of Union law, that cannot cover abusive practices (see judgments of 5 of July 2007, C-321/05, '*Kofoed*', para. 38; and the case-law cited), carried out under the formal observance of the Union or national rules (in this case, rules governing the filing of trade marks) but infringing or circumventing actually a serious legislative purpose such as that pursued by the provisions imposing the obligation of genuine use of the trade marks, the full effectiveness of which cannot be avoided."[513]

3-307   However, whether or not such is bad faith is likely to be very fact-dependent on whether such a re-filing is made in bad faith. There may be all type of good reasons for a re-filing. For instance, it may be that the re-filing is necessary because an undertaking had been delayed in marketing goods under the mark so significantly that its earlier registration has become vulnerable for revocation for lack of genuine use. It thus wishes to preserve its position. The authorities suggest that there will be an intense focus on the reasons behind the re-filing. If it is for a genuine commercial purpose, it will be fine. However, if it is simply to preserve the rights of an undertaking so that it can bring infringement proceedings and thereby provoke the third party into buying the mark or paying substantial damages, then it is likely to be an application made in bad faith.[514] If the re-filings are made purely to avoid the effect of an application (or threatened application) to revoke for genuine use, then

---

[511] *McBride Trade Mark's Application* [2005] E.T.M.R. 85, Appointed Person (England). The issue of s.32(3) and whether it is compatible with EU law has now been referred to the Court of Justice in *Sky v Skykick* [2018] EWHC 155.

[512] e.g. see Recital 31, 32 TMD.

[513] *CANAL+* (R-1260/2013-2), at [17].

[514] See *pelicantravel v EUIPO* (T-136/11) ECLI:EU:T:2012:689 (no bad faith as mark applied for was an updated graphic design and the applicant wished to modernise the appearance of the mark in connection with the celebration of the 125th anniversary of the brand and not to stave off a successful revocation action); *NAVIGO* (R-2181/2012-2) (no bad faith); *PATHFINDER* (R-1785/2008-4), re-filed application was made in bad faith (registration was an identical repeat filing and done solely to avoid revocation; evidence of owner to sell mark to applicant for substantial sum); *CANAL+* (R-1260/2013-2). Here, the appellant argued that in substance, they were identical marks and thus, the owner should file evidence of use of the earlier marks. The Board of Appeal agreed with this approach (perhaps surprisingly). It is thought that the real attack should have been one that the re-filed marks had been made in bad faith.

it can truly be said (as the Board of Appeal suggests in its excerpt above) that such amounts to an *abus de droit*[515] If it is an *abus de droit*, it must be considered to have been done in bad faith.

Mental element in bad faith

In *Lindt & Sprüngli*, the CJEU said that in order to determine whether there was bad faith, consideration must be given to the applicant's intention at the time of filing the application for registration. It said that such is a subjective factor which must be determined by reference to the objective circumstances of the case.[516] Thus, the applicant's intention and motive in applying for the mark is clearly central to whether or not the application was made in bad faith. For instance, did the applicant apply for the mark to extort money from a third party or for the purpose of protecting an intended trade in the state where registration was sought? Did the applicant apply for a wide range of goods and services because they intended to trade at some time in all those goods and services by reference to the trade mark or because it wanted to exclude any use of the identical mark by third parties in relation to any goods or services? Indeed, it is suggested that ultimately, in the vast majority of cases, the applicant's intentions and motives are the critical and not just central factor. A person's state of mind at the time is a fact which can be evaluated like any other fact (albeit in some cases with difficulty).[517] The suggestion that evaluating such by reference to the objective circumstances of the case adds little—every fact must be determined by reference to the objective circumstances. However, the difficulty in evaluating a state of mind is that unlike many other facts, it is best done by live testimony (tested in cross examination) from the applicant. One can evaluate fairly easily whether products were on the market, it was dark at the time of the crime, etc. without live testimony but such is much more difficult with the state of mind of the applicant. Yet, the trade mark system (particularly EUIPO) does not permit cross examination. Therefore, it seeks to evaluate the intention of the applicant from circumstantial facts which is in many cases very difficult. Indeed, a person who files an application in bad faith is unlikely to admit what they did and indeed, if ex hypothesi, they are a person who has made the application with a dishonest or improper purpose, they are a person who is likely to lie or be dishonest in their evidence. **3-308**

There is a further discussion. Is it sufficient that the conduct to be regarded is that the application fell short of the standards of acceptable commercial behaviour as observed by reasonable people in the particular area of business being examined? Or must it be shown that the applicant personally appreciated that their conduct fell short of such standards? The position is somewhat unclear. It is unlikely that the "Robin Hood" defence[518] would succeed. In the UK, handed down prior to the CJEU's judgment in *Lindt & Sprüngli*, the test for bad faith was a "combined test" for dishonesty. It said that: **3-309**

---

[515] See Ch.14, para.14-055. *Kofoed* is a tax case concerned with *abus de droit*.

[516] See [41]–[42].

[517] In an English case, it has been said that the state of a man's mind is as much a fact as the state of his digestion (*Edgington v Fitzmaurice* [1885] 29 Ch D. 459, per Bowen LJ).

[518] Robin Hood saw nothing wrong in stealing from the rich and giving to the poor. However, that of course does not mean that theft is not an act of dishonesty.

"... the application fell short of the standards of acceptable commercial behaviour observed by reasonable and experienced men in the particular area being examined and that the applicant himself realised that by those standards his conduct fell short."[519]

3-310   As has been commented on, this test appears overly elaborate for the field of trade marks.[520] It is unlikely that Robin Hood who saw nothing wrong in stealing from the rich stood back, ever asked himself at any given time whether despite his view as to the need to rob the rich to feed the poor, that reasonable and experienced men would view his acts as theft and falling short of acceptable behaviour. Thus, the "Robin Hood" defence should not be a defence to a bad faith application. However, that does not mean that the applicant's state of mind is irrelevant. An applicant who applies for a mark with the intention of extorting money from a third party is clearly to be treated differently than one who does so with the intention of doing business under the mark. What is irrelevant is the applicant's *own* assessment of the morality of his conduct.

Relative grounds for refusal

3-311   Both the EUTMR and the TMD allow the owner of earlier rights, whether they are registered trade marks, unregistered trade marks, copyright, geographical indications of origins or indeed any type of earlier right which could prevent the use of a sign, to oppose the registration of the sign or have it cancelled if registered. These are described as relative grounds for refusal. In accordance with modern practice, the owner of the earlier right must oppose the application or cancel an existing registration—the examining office will not take the objection ex officio. Relative grounds are concerned with disputes between private undertakings and unlike absolute grounds, they do not engage the public interest.[521] Thus, trade mark offices rely upon the economic self-interest of undertakings to watch over their registered marks and prevent attempts by third parties to register signs that conflict with their registered marks. This means that many signs are allowed by EUIPO or national trade mark register that do give rise to a likelihood of confusion with a registered mark but the owner of the latter (if they know about the application) sees no reason to oppose it. This may be because they consider the legal basis weak or alternatively, they have no real commercial interest in enforcing this mark.

3-312   In the case of an application to register a sign which consists of letters or words and has no artwork in it, the only relevant earlier rights will be earlier trade marks (registered and unregistered), rights in names (if relevant) and in the case of foodstuffs and beverages, EU geographical indications of origin (PDOs/PGIs). If the sign goes beyond mere letters and words and, e.g. includes artwork, is a shape, uses a special font, etc. other IPRs may come into play and be relied upon. However, under the EUTMR, other than earlier trade marks or PDOs/PGIs, the owner of the right must wait until the sign becomes an EU registered mark before relying upon their earlier rights to cancel the same registration. With the TMD,

---

[519] *Chinawhite* [2005] F.S.R. 10 CA at [40].

[520] *McBride's TM Application* [2005] E.T.M.R. 85, Appointed Person where the decision was criticised. Indeed, in *Chinawhite*, the unchallenged evidence was that the applicant genuinely believed that his conduct in applying for the mark was honest and yet the Court of Appeal found that the application had been made in bad faith.

[521] Although it could be said that there is a public interest in not having confusingly similar marks in the marketplace, it seems difficult to see where the public interest is in not having confusingly similar marks on a trade mark register.

Member States may enact that all relative grounds provided for in the TMD be grounds of opposition as well as cancellation.

These relative grounds are now considered in detail. The following relative grounds exist under the EUTMR and TMD. They also state with regard to the EUTMR, whether such can only be a ground of cancellation: **3-313**

Opposition and Cancellation Proceedings: EUTMR and TMD

(1) the trade mark is identical to an earlier registered trade mark and is for identical goods or services (*"double identity"*);

(2) the trade mark is identical or similar to the earlier registered trade mark and is for identical or similar goods or services (but there is not "double identity") such that there exists a likelihood of confusion;

(3) the trade mark is identical or similar to an earlier registered mark with a reputation and will, without due cause, take unfair advantage of or be detrimental to the distinctive character or repute of the earlier mark;

(4) use of the trade mark would infringe non-registered trade mark rights including rights in unregistered trade marks or GIOs (geographical indications of origin); and

(5) the trade mark was applied for by an agent or representative of the proprietor of the earlier trade mark and such is not justified by the agent or representatives.

Opposition and Cancellation: TMD; Cancellation only: EUTMR

(6) The registered mark was applied for in bad faith.[522]

(7) The use of the registered mark would infringe the right to a name, right of personal portrayal, copyright, industrial property right or other right.

These are now discussed in more detail. These provisions mirror the infringement provisions. Thus, a registered trade mark confers on the proprietor the right to prevent the use of a sign which is identical or similar to a registered trade mark and is used for identical or similar goods as that protected by the registration such that there exists a likelihood of confusion. Similarly, a proprietor of registered marks which possess reputation can prevent the use of signs which are identical or similar to the mark and take unfair advantage of or are detrimental to the repute of the mark. **3-314**

Earlier trade marks

The vast majority of oppositions or cancellation proceedings are based on earlier registered trade marks. This means identifying: (i) Which trade marks are relevant? (ii) Are they "earlier"? In relation to the first question, the EUTMR identifies what are "earlier" marks. They are EU and national marks of Member States and international registrations registered under the Madrid Agreement or Protocol.[523] It also includes applications for the same subject to their registration.[524] **3-315**

As regards the second question, as the EUTMR and TMD operate a first to file system, "earlier" means a mark whose date of application is earlier than the date **3-316**

---

[522] Technically, this is an absolute ground of invalidity but almost invariably, it will be alleged that the sign was applied for in bad faith by a third party who has, in the broad sense, a legitimate interest or rights in use of the sign. See para.3-289.

[523] art.8.2 EUTMR.

[524] art.8.2(b) EUTMR.

of application for registration of the mark in issue, taking account, where appropriate, of priorities claimed in respect of those marks.[525]

3-317   When it comes to marks which have been used but not registered, the "first to file" basis of the EUTMR and TMD means that the *mere* fact that an undertaking has used a mark in a marketplace in the EU earlier than the date of application of the later mark is irrelevant. However, the EUTMR and TMD do give some protection to unregistered marks. First, if the mark is "well known" within the meaning of art.6*bis* of the Paris Convention, then it is deemed an earlier mark.[526] Secondly, if an undertaking has used a mark in the course of trade which is of more than mere local significance *and* EU or national law of a Member State confers rights on that undertaking to prevent the use of subsequent marks, then it is also deemed an earlier mark if such rights exist as of the date of filing of the opposed mark.[527] Regulation 2015/2424 introduced expressly into the EUTMR the ability of an owner of earlier Protected Geographical Indications ("PGI") or Protected Designations of Origin ("PDO") to oppose the registration of a mark. Here again, the owner of the PGI or PDO must have the right to prevent the use of the later trade mark. Whether or not it does have such a right will depend upon its right under EU law granted to GIOs or PDOs.[528]

Relative grounds and effect on functions of trade mark

3-318   As discussed earlier in this chapter,[529] the CJEU has developed a body of case law in its rulings on the interpretation of the equivalent infringement provisions of the TMD and EUTMR where there is "double identity" of goods and marks. The proprietor of the registered trade mark must also show that use of the defendant's sign has an adverse effect on the functions of the registered trade mark.[530] In *Budejovický Budvar, národní podnik v Anheuser-Busch*,[531] the CJEU had to consider whether such principles were also applicable to a declaration for invalidity of a later trade mark based on an earlier identical mark for identical goods. It held that they were.[532] Thus, where an opponent relies upon an earlier identical mark registered for identical goods, such in itself is not a sufficient condition. It must also be shown that the use of the later trade mark has or is liable to have an adverse effect on the essential function of the earlier trade mark.[533] In *Budejovický Budvar, národní podnik v Anheuser-Busch*, it held that where there had been a long period of hon-

---

[525]   art.8.2(a). In *Genesis Seguros v Boys Toys SA* (C-190/10) ECLI: EU:C:2012:157, the CJEU held in considering two applications made on the same day, whether the one filed earlier in time on that day was an "earlier mark" said that art.32 EUTMR (which stipulates the date of filing for EUTM applications) precludes taking into account the hour and minute of filing. Thus, in such circumstances, there is no "earlier mark".

[526]   art.8(2)(c).

[527]   art.8(4).

[528]   art.8(6). See para.3-855 for discussion of geographical indications of origin.

[529]   See para.3-069.

[530]   See para.3-439.

[531]   (C-482/09) [2011] E.C.R. I-8701. On application of this decision, the Court of Appeal of England held that despite some degree of confusion arising from the co-existence of the marks, there was no impairment of the guarantee of origin of either party's mark *Budejovický Budvar, národní podnik v Anheuser-Busch Inc* [2012] 3 All E.R. 1405; [2012] E.T.M.R. 48.

[532]   See [70]–[74].

[533]   See [74]. It is perhaps surprising that having considered that under the infringement provisions of the TMD, such were transposable to the invalidity/opposition grounds, that the Court of Justice held that under the latter, it must be shown that the essential function was affected rather than *any*

est concurrent use of two identical trade marks designating identical products, such use neither has nor is liable to have an adverse effect on the essential function of the trade mark.[534] It should be said *Budejovický Budvar* was an exceptional case.[535] Two beer brands had existed in the marketplace for 30 years without any real consumer confusion. In the vast majority of cases, there can be no dispute that use of an identical mark for identical goods would have an adverse effect on the essential function of the earlier mark or be *liable to do so*.

Where an opponent or cancellation applicant relies upon earlier rights where the double identity rule is not satisfied (i.e. similar mark/similar goods/likelihood of confusion or unfair advantage/detriment to repute or distinctive character), then it must prove this to be the case and the importance of showing any effect on the functions of the mark recedes into the background. **3-319**

For instance, proof of likelihood of confusion is concerned with confusion as to trade origin and accordingly, ipso facto, proof of such is proof that the later mark will have an adverse effect on the essential function of a mark. When it comes to reputation-based grounds, i.e. unfair advantage/detriment to distinctive character or repute of the mark, then there has been no suggestion in the CJEU judgments that the owner of the earlier right must also show an adverse effect on the functions of the mark other than in relation to the requirement of "without due cause".[536] Whilst there can be little doubt that where use of a later mark would cause detriment to the distinctive character (dilution) or repute of an earlier mark (tarnishment), that such would have an effect on the functions of the earlier mark, it is much more difficult to identify the adverse effect on a function of an earlier mark where it is shown that the later mark takes unfair advantage of the reputation of the earlier mark. Here, the focus is on the benefit to the later mark rather than the damage to the earlier mark. In truth, "unfair advantage" is concerned with unfair competition whereby a third party free-rides on the reputation of an earlier mark and thus reduce its marketing and promotional costs of the later mark. **3-320**

Thus, the reader should have a good understanding of the various functions of trade mark and read the relevant section in this chapter before proceeding.[537] **3-321**

Hypothetical marketplace—circumstances of notional use

When considering a relative ground, the tribunal or court, in essence, poses a hypothetical question. For instance, if it is considering whether there is a likelihood of confusion between the mark applied for and an earlier mark, it takes into account a hypothetical marketplace where an earlier trade mark is used in relation to the goods or services for which the earlier mark is registered. It assumes that the earlier trade mark has a reputation (even if it has never been used) in relation to the relevant goods or services for which it is registered. It then conducts the same exercise for the mark applied for, i.e. introduces into the hypothetical market place the mark applied for used in relation to the goods or services for which registra- **3-322**

---

function. It is suggested that the equivalent provisions be interpreted the same and thus, art.8.1(a) would be satisfied where any function of the earlier mark is or is liable to be affected.

[534] See [82].

[535] A point made by the Court of Justice, see [76].

[536] See para.3-391.

[537] See para.3-069.

tion is sought.[538] Having done that exercise, the tribunal or court asks itself whether there is a likelihood of confusion. In carrying out this exercise, it is irrelevant whether or not the later mark has been used and if so, for which goods. The comparison is of the goods or services covered by the marks at issue and not those for which the marks have been used.[539]

3-323   The CJEU has made it clear that when considering the likelihood of confusion, the tribunal or court should consider "all the circumstances in which the mark applied for might be used if it were to be registered".[540] However, this should not be taken too far and must be considered on a hypothetical marketplace and not the actual use made by the owner of the earlier or later mark in the marketplace. If, for instance, the later mark is being used in the marketplace by the owner with other marks or additional distinguishing material (e.g. if the issue is the likelihood of confusion of an earlier and later shape mark and the latter is used in the marketplace with a highly distinctive word mark which lessens the risk of confusion), such should not be taken into account. To take this into account would mean that the assessment of likelihood of confusion between two marks by a tribunal would vary depending on, at a particular time, the nature and extent of use of the marks in the marketplace by the owner of the earlier or later mark. In principle, this would be contrary to a system of registration whereby the monopoly afforded by registration should be deducible from the state of the register alone and not require third parties to investigate the marketplace.

Double identity of marks and goods

3-324   Article 8.1(a) EUTMR provides that a trade mark shall not be registered:

> "(a)   if it is identical to an earlier trade mark and the goods and the services for which registration is applied for are identical with the goods or services for which the earlier trade mark is protected."

3-325   The relationship between relative grounds and the need to show an adverse effect on the functions of a trade mark has been discussed already.[541] When it comes to double identity, the rationale for the automatic prohibition has been that, in these circumstances, the likelihood of confusion was so overwhelming that the EU legislators considered that such should be irrebuttably presumed. In many circumstances, such is indeed appropriate. However, there are a number of factual situations where despite identity of the mark and goods, in fact confusion is unlikely to occur. As said by the Court of Appeal in England and Wales in *Budejovický Budvar, národní podnik v Anheuser-Busch Inc*:[542]

> "[33] ... Those who framed the same mark/same goods rule were rather naïve. To say that confusion is necessarily so in such a case, is wrong. The apparently black and white rigid application of the rule which the hearing officer thought was compelled, has been

---

[538] e.g. see (in the context of infringement proceedings, the decision of the Court of Appeal of England and Wales in *Roger Maier and Assos of Switzerland SA v ASOS Plc* [2015] EWCA Civ 220 at [114]–[117]) where the court considered that the first instance judge had erred in not considering notional and fair use of the registered mark across the whole specification of goods

[539] *Massive Bionics SL v EUIPO* (T-223/16) ECLI:EU:T:2017:500 at [58] (unless proof of genuine use of the earlier mark has been requested pursuant to art.47.2 EUTMR).

[540] *O2 Holdings Ltd and O2 (UK) Ltd v Hutchison 3G UK Ltd* (C-533/06) [2008] E.C.R. I-4231 at [66].

[541] See para.3-318.

[542] [2012] E.T.M.R. 48 CA.

tempered to produce rational answers. The Court has steadily been recognising this in a series of cases, *O2 Holdings Ltd v Hutchison 3G UK Ltd* (C-533/06) [2008] E.C.R. I-4231; [2008] E.T.M.R. 55 (comparative advertising conforming with the Comparative Advertising Directive), *Hölterhoff v Freiesleben* (C-2/00) [2002] E.C.R. I-4187; [2002] E.T.M.R. 79 (purely descriptive use), *Bayerische Motorenwerke AG (BMW) v Deenik* (C-63/97) [1999] E.C.R. I-905; [1999] E.T.M.R. 339 (honestly stating that a garage repaired BMWs), *Adam Opel AG v Autec AG* (C-48/05) [2007] E.C.R. I-1017; [2007] E.T.M.R. 33 (use of mark on a toy car not infringing if no effect on essential function even though mark was registered for toys), *Céline Sarl v Céline SA* (C-17/06) [2007] E.C.R. I-7041; [2007] E.T.M.R. 80 (use as a business name for a clothes shop not affecting essential function of mark registered for clothing). The ruling here is another example of tempering the apparently inflexible same mark/same goods rule to produce a rational answer."

It is perhaps relevant to point out that the "naiveté" of the legislators of the same **3-326** mark/same goods rules primarily relates to the provisions of EU trade mark law to *infringement*. There are so many diverse uses that can be made of a mark which are not the paradigm situation clearly envisaged by the legislators whereby a defendant uses an identical mark in relation to identical goods or services without the permission of the trade mark proprietor, that the CJEU was ultimately bound to intervene. For instance, the earlier failure of the TMD or EUTMR to state that use of a registered trade mark to refer to the goods or services of its proprietor is not an infringement can be considered an obvious failing of the legislation.[543] However, in the context of an opposition or declaration of invalidity based on an earlier trade mark, the tribunal is concerned with hypothetical use of the marks in the marketplace to indicate the origin of goods or services marketed by the owners of the earlier and later marks. In such circumstances, the tribunal is concerned with the paradigm situation envisaged by the legislators as discussed above.

Identical marks

In *LTJ Diffusion SA v Sadas Vertbaudet SA*,[544] the CJEU had to consider, in the **3-327** context of an infringement action, whether the use of "Arthur et Felicie" for clothing infringed the registered mark "Arthur" for clothing. The CJEU was asked to rule on the meaning of "identical" in the provision in the trade mark directive equivalent to art.9.2(a) EUTMR (infringement where sign is identical to registered mark and goods are identical). In its judgment, the court ruled on the meaning of "identical". It held that because the provision did not require evidence of likelihood of confusion, the criterion of identity must be interpreted strictly. It thus said:

"... a sign is identical with the trade mark where it reproduces, without any modification or addition, all the elements constituting the trade mark or where, viewed as a whole, it contains differences so insignificant that they may go unnoticed by an average consumer".[545]

In some cases, when considering the issue of identity, it is necessary to identify **3-328** accurately the precise character of the registered mark. Thus, a sign which is applied for as a word mark by definition is not claiming any figurative element. A word mark will thus usually be depicted in the standard font of the Registry and dif-

---

[543] This has now been remedied by the introduction of a defence where a mark is used to identify or refer to the goods or services of the owner of the mark (art.14.1(c) EUTMR).

[544] (C-291/00) [2003] E.C.R. I-2799; [2003] E.T.M.R. 83.

[545] See [54].

ferences in font or cases will be irrelevant. However, where the mark is a figurative mark, then even where the word part is the same, there may not be identity if the figurative element is noticeable. Generally EUIPO applies the criterion of identity strictly. The following is from the EUIPO Guidelines which sets out the result of EUIPO decisions.[546]

Identical Word Marks

3-329

Earlier sign	Contested sign	Case no
MOMO	MoMo	B 1 802 233
BLUE MOON	Blue Moon	R 0835/2010–1
Global Campus	GLOBAL CAMPUS	R 0719/2008–2
Zeus	ZEUS	R 0760/2007–1
Jumbo	JUMBO	R 0353/2007–2
DOMINO	Domino	R 0523/2008–2
apetito	APETITO	T-129/09

Non-identical Word Marks

3-330

Earlier sign	Contested sign	Case no
She, SHE	S-HE	T-391/06
TELIA	Teeli	B 13 948
NOVALLOY	NOVALOY	B 29 290
HERBOFARM	HERBO-FARMA	R 1752/2010–1

Earlier sign	Contested sign	Case No
		B 2 031 741

IDENTICAL FIGURATIVE MARKS

---

[546] Other examples are given in EUIPO's Manual of Trade Mark Practice, Part C. See *https://euipo.europa.eu/ohimportal/en/trade-mark-guidelines* [Accessed 18 August 2017].

Earlier sign	Contested sign	Case No
N7	N°7	R 0558/2011-1
BASIC	basic	R 1440/2010-1
I 👍	I 👍	7078 C

NON-IDENTICAL FIGURATIVE MARKS

Identity of goods

When considering whether or not goods are identical, it will often be the case that there will be an overlap. In such cases, there will a partial identity of goods and the EUIPO will make findings to that effect. Where the earlier registration has a claim to a particular type of goods and the latter application is for a more general claim (e.g. the earlier registered mark is for jeans, the latter application is for clothing), the latter application will be treated as for identical goods unless the applicant restricts the list or EUIPO can split the list. EUIPO will not dissect the list itself.[547]   **3-331**

Likelihood of confusion: similar marks/similar goods—art.8.1(b)

Article 8.1(b) EUTMR prohibits the registration of a mark or if the mark is registered then it is liable to be declared invalid: **3-332**

> "if because of its identity with, or similarity to, the earlier trade mark and the identity or similarity of the goods or services covered by the trade marks there exists a likelihood of confusion on the part of the public in the territory in which the earlier trade mark is protected; the likelihood of confusion includes the likelihood of association with the earlier trade mark."

A number of preliminary points need to be made.

First, whilst it must be shown that there is a likelihood of confusion, it is not sufficient merely to show that such occurs. It must be shown that confusion arises *because* the marks are similar or identical and the goods or services are similar or identical. If *both* these "threshold" conditions do not exist then art.8.1(b) EUTMR does not apply. Therefore, an undertaking may apply for a mark for a highly distinctive and individual mark which is identical to an earlier registered mark but which is registered for goods that are not similar to the later mark. As discussed above, when considering an opposition based on relative rights, one considers a hypothetical marketplace with the marks being used for their respective goods or services. It may be that in doing so, a tribunal would conclude that there is a likelihood of   **3-333**

---

[547] *EUIPO Opposition Guidelines*, Part C, Chapter 2, section 2.3; *Pam-Pim's Baby Prop* (T-133/05) EU:T:2006:247 at [29].

confusion despite the goods not being similar. However, here, art.8.1(b) EUTMR would not apply as the goods are dissimilar. In such circumstances, the owner of the earlier mark must look to the "reputation-based" grounds, e.g. unfair advantage/detriment, if it wishes to oppose such an application. If it does not have the required reputation in the actual marketplace, then it is irrelevant that in the *hypothetical* marketplace, the tribunal assumes such a reputation.

3-334   Secondly, as will be seen, likelihood of confusion is concerned with confusion as to trade origin. It is sufficient if the average consumer would assume that the goods or services marketed under the marks are connected in the course of trade with each other. This connection could manifest itself in a number of ways. It could be legal, e.g. the owner of the earlier mark has licensed or authorised the use of the latter mark. It could be economic, e.g. the later mark is perceived as being a "sister" mark to the earlier mark. This will often be the case where the owner of the earlier mark has placed related products on the marketplace under brands which share a distinctive prefix and the later mark shares the same prefix. However, it is not sufficient for a finding of likelihood of confusion that the average consumer merely, wrongly "associates" the two marks, i.e. creates a mental link between the marks. The association must be such as to cause a likelihood of confusion as to trade origin.

Similarity of marks

3-335   In *Sabel v Puma*,[548] the CJEU said that that global appreciation of the visual, aural or conceptual similarity of the marks in question must be based on the overall impression given by the marks, bearing in mind, in particular, their distinctive and dominant components. The CJEU said that the perception of marks in the mind of the average consumer of the type of goods or services in question plays a decisive role in the global appreciation of the likelihood of confusion. The average consumer normally perceives a mark as a whole and does not proceed to analyse its various details.[549]

3-336   The jurisprudence of the CJEU suggests that the determination of the similarity of marks is a threshold test. Therefore, if the marks are not similar then one does not need to consider the reputation or recognition enjoyed by the earlier mark or other factors which would be relevant to the issue of likelihood of confusion.[550] However, this threshold test is very low. As said by the CJEU in *Ferrero*[551]:

"[65]   Although that global assessment implies some interdependence between the relevant factors, and a low degree of similarity between the marks may therefore be offset by the strong distinctive character of the earlier mark (see, to that effect, judgment of 7 May 2009 in Case C-398/07 P *Waterford Wedgwood v Assembled Investments (Proprietary) and EUIPO*, not published in the ECR, paragraph 33), the fact remains that where there is no similarity between the earlier mark and the challenged mark, the reputation or recognition enjoyed by the earlier mark and the fact that the goods or services respectively covered are identical or similar are not sufficient for it to be found that there is a likelihood of confusion between the marks at issue or that the relevant public makes a link between them (see, to that effect, Case C-254/09 P *Calvin Klein Trademark Trust v EUIPO* [2010] E.C.R. I-0000, paragraph 53 and the case-law cited).

---

[548]   *Sabel v Puma* (C-251/95) [1997] E.C.R. I-6191; [1998] E.T.M.R. 1.
[549]   See [23].
[550]   *Ferrero v EUIPO* (C-552/09P) ECLI:EU:C:2011:177 at [66]; *Vedial SA v EUIPO (SAINT HUBERT)* (T-110/01) [2002] E.C.R. II-5275, [2004] E.T.M.R. 102. Upheld on appeal, *Vedial SA v EUIPO* (C-106/03P) [2004] E.C.R. I-09573 at [54].
[551]   *Ferrero v EUIPO* (C-552/09P) ECLI:EU:C:2011:177.

[66]   As is apparent from paragraph 51 above, in order for [Article 8.1(b) or (5) EUTMR] to be applicable, the marks at issue must be identical or similar. Consequently, those provisions are manifestly inapplicable where the General Court has ruled out any similarity between the marks at issue (see, to that effect, *Calvin Klein Trademark Trust v EUIPO*, paragraph 68). *It is only if there is some similarity, even faint,* between the marks at issue that the General Court must carry out a global assessment in order to ascertain whether, notwithstanding the low degree of similarity between them, there is, on account of the presence of other relevant factors such as the reputation or recognition enjoyed by the earlier mark, a likelihood of confusion or a link made between those marks by the relevant public." [Emphasis supplied.]

The assessment of similarity of marks is a "gateway" condition to be assessed independently of the reputation of the mark or similarity of goods.[552] This is the same approach used for the assessment of similarity of goods, which is now considered.   **3-337**

Similarity of goods

In relation to the test for similarity of goods, the CJEU has provided guidance on whether goods are similar in *Canon v MGM*. As the court said: **3-338**

"[22]   It is, however, important to stress that, for the purposes of applying Article [5.1(b) TMD], even where a mark is identical to another with a highly distinctive character, it is still necessary to adduce evidence of similarity between the goods or services covered. In contrast to [Article 5.3(a) TMD][553], which expressly refers to the situation in which the goods or services are not similar, Article [5.1(b) TMD)] provides that the likelihood of confusion presupposes that the goods or services covered are identical or similar.

[23]   In assessing the similarity of the goods or services concerned, as the French and United Kingdom Governments and the Commission have pointed out, all the relevant factors relating to those goods or services themselves should be taken into account. Those factors include, inter alia, their nature, their end users [should read 'intended purpose'[554]] and their method of use and whether they are in competition with each other or are complementary."

The factors of nature, intended purpose, method of use, whether the goods are complementary to each other or in competition with each other have been described as the *Canon* factors. However, they are clearly not intended to be exhaustive. Thus, the General Court has held that the fact that the goods covered by the marks fell within the definition "cosmetic product" in cosmetic labelling regulation could constitute a relevant factor for the purpose of assessing the similarity of the goods.[555] EUIPO's Guidelines suggest that additional factors not mentioned in *Canon* would include distribution channels, relevant public and the "usual origin of the goods/   **3-339**

---

[552]   *Ferrero*, at [68]; *Gateway v EUIPO* (C-57/08) ECLI:EU:C:2008:718 at [55]–[57].

[553]   The reader should note that the article in the predecessor directive corresponding to art.4.4(a) TMD referred expressly to the goods being dissimilar. However, following the case law of the CJEU, art.4.4(a) has been changed so that it is irrelevant whether the goods of the two marks are similar or dissimilar.

[554]   The official judgment of this on the *http://www.curia.europa.eu* website says that "end users" should read "intended purpose". This is also reflected in the *EUIPO Guidelines for Opposition*, Part C, Chapter 2, para.3.1.1.

[555]   *Procter & Gamble v EUIPO* (T-366/07) [2010] E.C.R. II-194 at [56].

services".[556] EUIPO states that when considering similarity of goods and services the following are strong factors: "usual origin" (discussed below), purpose, nature, whether they are complementary to each other or in competition with each other, whereas the following are less important: method of use, distribution channels and relevant public (particularly where the "relevant" group is the general public).[557]

3-340   It is of note that these requirements do not necessitate the consideration of the likelihood of confusion. Therefore, it must be shown that the goods or services are similar regardless of whether there is a likelihood of confusion.[558] Thus, even if there are two highly distinctive and identical registered marks for very dissimilar goods (which the public may believe that such goods originate from the control of the same undertakings because of the improbability of usage of the same mark by two independent undertakings), it is necessary to establish that the goods are similar.[559] A striking example of this is in *Commercy AG v EUIPO*.[560] That case concerned whether services involving the supply of computer software for the purpose of setting up a travel agency/reservation website was similar to travel agency/reservation services. The General Court, applying the *Canon* criteria, held that the services were not in competition and that the relevant customer base was different. However, and strikingly, the marks were identical ("easyHotel"). Yet, if the average person was told that a company was providing a booking and reserva-tion computer programme called "easyHotel" to a travel agency called "easyHotel", it is difficult to believe that people would not be confused.

3-341   Thus, similarity of goods and services is a threshold requirement which must be determined purely by reference to the goods or services.

3-342   This threshold requirement should not be confused with the fact that *once it is established that the goods or services are similar*, then, as discussed later, the court is entitled to conclude that the *more* similar the goods or services, the *more* likely that confusion will occur.

3-343   **"Usual origin"**   Whilst helpful, the criteria in *Canon* are difficult to apply without reference to an underlying benchmark principle as to whether goods and services are similar or not. Where the issue is whether Good A is similar to Good B or Service A is similar to Service B, one is tempted to say that the benchmark principle should be that the relevant public would believe that an undertaking would be involved in making both Good A and Good B or supplying both Service A and Service B (or where it is alleged that Good A is similar to Service A, that an undertaking would be involved in both making Good A and supplying Service A). This test is particularly helpful when considering certain classes of goods or services. For instance, in *Vedial SA v EUIPO (SAINT HUBERT)*,[561] the General Court held that edible fats and vinegar sauces were similar goods because inter alia they were intended for human consumption and were everyday seasonings for foodstuffs. Secondly, they said such proximity between the goods in question could lead the targeted public to believe that, if the goods bear an identical or similar sign,

---

[556] Guidelines for Opposition, Part C, Section 3.
[557] Guidelines for Opposition, Part C, Section 3.
[558] See also *Vedial v EUIPO* (C-106/03P) [2004] E.C.R. I-09573 at [51]; See also *Intel v Sihra* [2004] E.T.M.R. 44 (Ch).
[559] *Assembled Investments (Proprietary) v OHMI—Waterford Wedgwood (WATERFORD STEL-LENBOSCH)* (T-105/05) [2007] E.C.R. II-00060 at [27].
[560] (T-316/07) [2009] E.C.R. II-43.
[561] (T-110/01) [2002] E.C.R. II-5275; [2004] E.T.M.R. 102.

they have originated under the control of a single undertaking which is responsible for their quality.[562] In contrast, in *Waterford TM*,[563] the General Court held that wine glasses and wine were not similar goods because even though complementary, such were not "sufficiently pronounced" to make them, from the consumer's viewpoint, similar goods. As part of that conclusion, the General Court considered it relevant that consumers would not perceive wine makers to be involved in manufacture or supply of wine glasses, i.e. consumers would not perceive that wine glasses and wine would come from the same undertaking.[564]

Above considerations have led EUIPO to consider that (despite not being stated in *Canon*) a strong factor in favour of determining similarity of goods or services is the principle of "usual origin".[565] This is concerned with asking who is the undertaking responsible for making the goods or providing the services in issue? Typically, would an undertaking make both or provide both? As EUIPO says, because the likelihood of confusion is concerned with whether the public might believe that the goods or services in question come from the same undertaking or economically linked undertakings, such is a strong indication of similarity when, in the minds of the relevant public, the goods or services would have the same origin.[566] However, EUIPO, acknowledging that there is a danger that by applying such a test to the exclusion of others, this would turn the examination of likelihood of confusion and similarity of similarity of goods/services "upside down", emphasises that the principle of "usual origin" is one (albeit strong) factor to be taken into account.   **3-344**

In the author's view, the "usual origin" test should indeed be a strong factor. Goods may ultimately appear to have many similarities by reason of their nature, quality, composition, etc. However, if the public would not believe that the same undertaking would make or both, then it is unlikely that they would conclude, by reason of the display of two brands, that the same undertaking would be responsible for both and thus be confused as to trade origin. The best way to apply the "usual origin" test should be to assume that the goods or services in issue are not marketed under a brand at all or alternatively under an unused brand of average distinctiveness.[567]   **3-345**

Complementarity   In *Boston Scientific Ltd v EUIPO*[568] the General Court said that goods are complementary if there is a close connection between them, in the sense that one is indispensable or important for the use of the other in such a way   **3-346**

---

[562] (T-110/01) [2002] E.C.R. II-5275; [2004] E.T.M.R. 102 at [46] referring to (C-39/97) [1998] E.C.R. I-5507 at [28].

[563] *Assembled Investments (Proprietary) v OHMI—Waterford Wedgwood (WATERFORD STEL-LENBOSCH)* (T-105/05) [2007] E.C.R. II-00060.

[564] See [34]. See also *Institut für Lernsysteme GmbH v EUIPO* (T-388/00) [2002] E.C.R. II-4301 where *educational textbooks* were held to have the same origin as *provision of correspondence courses* as "undertakings offering any kind of course often hand out these products to pupils as support learning materials"—see [55] and *Saul Zaentz v Bodegas Romero de Avila Salcedo SL* [2008] E.T.M.R. 49 (2nd Board of Appeal, EUIPO) where it was held that glassware and alcoholic beverages are distinct by their very nature and use, as being neither in competition with each other, substitutable for each other and not usually produced in the same geographical areas, and whilst complementary to each other, such was limited in nature.

[565] Guidelines for Opposition, Part C, section 3.2.8.

[566] Guidelines for Opposition, Part C, section 3.2.8.

[567] The latter test being proposed in *Kerly's Law of Trade Marks and Trade Names*, 15th edn (London: Sweet & Maxwell, 2011), para.9-072.

[568] (T-325/06) ECLI:EU:T:2008:338 at [82].

that customers may think that the responsibility lies with the same undertaking. This can be seen as an application of the "usual origin" principle.

Likelihood of confusion

3-347 **Relevant confusion**   Assuming that the goods are similar and the marks are similar, the essence of the investigation under art.8.1(b) EUTMR is whether there is a likelihood of confusion. In this regard, the relevant type of confusion is confusion as to trade origin. It must be shown that there a likelihood of the public assuming that the goods bearing one mark are from the same or an economically linked undertakings.[569] Thus, it is not sufficient to show a mere likelihood of association. The fact that art.8.1(b) refers to a "likelihood of association" does not mean that any type of association is sufficient. It refers to a likelihood of association as to trade origin, i.e. that a person will mistake goods bearing a particular mark as being connected or associated in the course of trade with the proprietor of the earlier trade mark.[570]

3-348   This was made clear in *Sabel v Puma*,[571] where the CJEU had to consider the meaning of "likelihood of association". As submitted by Member States' legal teams, the likelihood of association may arise in three sets of circumstances:

(1) where the public confuses the sign and the mark in question (likelihood of direct confusion);

(2) where the public makes a connection between the proprietors of the sign and those of the mark and confuses them (likelihood of indirect confusion or association); and

(3) where the public considers the sign to be similar to the mark and perception of the sign calls to mind the memory of the mark, although the two are not confused (likelihood of association in the strict sense).

3-349   The court concluded that the mere association which the public might make between two trade marks, as a result of their analogous semantic content, is not in itself a sufficient ground for concluding that there is a likelihood of confusion within the meaning of that provision. This was reinforced in *Canon v MGM*,[572] where the court made it clear that the relevant association was where the public was led to believe that products bearing the two marks came from the same or economically linked undertakings.[573]

Factors relevant to likelihood of confusion

3-350   The CJEU has considered the issue of likelihood of confusion in a number of cases. Generally, the court or tribunal has to consider whether there is a likelihood of confusion, assuming use of the registered mark in relation to the protected goods or services and use of the mark applied for in relation to goods or services for which protection is sought.[574] Thus, the tribunal must construct a hypothetical marketplace. However, it must disregard extraneous material.

---

[569] *Canon Kabushiki Kaisha v MGM* (C-39/97) [1998] E.C.R. I-5507 at [29]–[30].

[570] *Sabel v Puma* (C-251/95) [1997] E.C.R. I-6191; [1998] E.T.M.R. 1.

[571] *Sabel v Puma* (C-251/95) [1997] E.C.R. I-6191; [1998] E.T.M.R. 1.

[572] (C-39/97).

[573] See [28]–[29].

[574] See para.3-322.

The following represents a distillation of the principles applicable to consider-   **3-351** ing the issue of likelihood of confusion.[575] The reader is warned however that the General Court and CJEU have, by sheer reason of the number of cases they have considered on appeal from EUIPO, developed a host of principles concerning the determination of likelihood of confusion between two marks. It is impossible to address all of these principles in this textbook. Many of them are simply statements of common sense embodied as principles of law. The reader should also be aware that some of the cited cases concern likelihood of confusion in infringement cases and not opposition or cancellation proceedings. There is no difference in approach but in infringement proceedings, the comparison is "mark for sign" and not "mark for mark". Thus, in infringement proceedings, the court is concerned with the sign as used by the defendant, whereas in opposition or cancellation proceedings, the court is concerned with hypothetical normal and fair use of both marks in the marketplace. The most important ones are set out below:

(1) The likelihood of confusion must be appreciated globally, taking account of all relevant factors.[576] A global appraisal involves considering not just the registered marks but also the marks as used. Thus, where the earlier registered mark has been registered in black and white but has been used extensively in a particular colour with the result that it has become associated in the mind of a significant portion of the public with that colour, the fact that the later mark or sign uses the same or similar colour is relevant to the global assessment of the likelihood of confusion.[577] Equally, and perhaps more surprisingly, where, in an infringement action, the defendant uses a sign in a particular colour which is associated with the defendant, such too is relevant for the global assessment of the likelihood of confusion and could result in a reduction of the likelihood of confusion.[578]

(2) The matter must be judged through the eyes of the average consumer of the goods/services in question.[579] The average consumer is deemed to be reasonably well-informed and reasonably circumspect and observant. However, they rarely have the chance to make direct comparisons between marks and must instead rely upon the imperfect picture of them that they have kept in their mind.[580] The average consumer normally perceives a mark as a whole and does not proceed to analyse its various details.[581] However, the amount of attention the consumer pays to the goods will depend on the type of goods or services.[582] In certain goods, e.g. those which are expensive and technological, the average consumer displays a particularly high level of attention at the time of purchase of the goods.[583] In certain circumstances, the relevant public is not just the average

---

[575] Similar guidelines are used in UK courts, e.g. see *Roger Maier v ASOS Plc* [2015] EWCA Civ 220 at [75].

[576] *Sabel v Puma* [1997] E.C.R. I-6191, see [22].

[577] *Specsavers International Ltd v Asda Stores* (C-252/12) ECLI:EU:C:2013:497 at [41].

[578] *Specsavers International* (C-252/12), at [48]–[50].

[579] *Sabel*, at [23].

[580] *Lloyd Schuhfabrik Meyer v Klijsen BV* (C-342/97) [1999] E.C.R. I-3819 at [27].

[581] *Sabel* [1997] E.C.R. I-6191 at [23].

[582] Thus, in *Picasso v EUIPO* (C-361/04) [2006] E.C.R I-643; [2006] E.T.M.R. 29 on appeal from (T-185/02) [2004] E.C.R. II-1739, the General Court pointed out that in relation to cars, the amount of attention paid to purchasing of cars was high.

[583] (C-361/04) [2006] E.C.R I-643, [2006] E.T.M.R. 29 at [39]; (T-185/02) [2004] E.C.R. II-1739 at [59].

consumer but others in the market place. Thus, in the case of pharmaceutical preparations, the relevant public is composed of medical professionals and patients.[584]

In the UK courts, there has been considerable debate regarding whether the "average consumer" is to be considered a single hypothetical consumer who represents a consumer with characteristics that can be considered typical of those who buy the goods or services in issue or it is sufficient that a significant section of consumers in the relevant class would be confused even if the majority were not confused?[585]

(3)   In considering the similarity of the marks, the court must consider the visual, aural and conceptual similarities of the marks. In certain situations, there may be similarity in one area which is cancelled out by a dissimilarity in another area. Thus, in *Picasso v EUIPO*,[586] an opposition by the Picasso family who owned the registered mark "PICASSO" for motor vehicles against an application for "PICARO" for cars, it was held that the relevant public would inevitably see PICASSO as a reference to the world-renown painter and that such a:

> "rich conceptual reference is such as greatly to reduce the resonance with which, in this case, the sign is endowed as a mark, among others, of motor vehicles."[587]

As the General Court said in the appealed decision, it is not plausible to consider that the public will disregard the meaning of the mark as the name of the painter and just see it as a mark for cars.[588] Thus, it supported the decision by the General Court that the visual and aural similarities were outweighed by the conceptual differences. This is known as the "counteraction" theory and has been applied often.[589]

(4)   The issue of similarity of marks must be assessed by reference to the overall impressions created by the marks bearing in mind their distinctive and dominant components.[590] In general, the dominant and distinctive components of a mark are more easily remembered.[591] However, care must be taken in applying this principle. Thus, the dominant component should not be considered *in isolation* to the other components unless the impact of the other components is negligible.[592]

---

[584]   *Alcon v EUIPO (TRAVATAN)* (T-130/03) [2005] E.C.R. II-3859, dismissed on appeal (C-412/05) [2007] E.C.R. I-3569.

[585]   With the courts favouring the "significant proportion of consumers" test, see *SoulCycle v Matalan* [2017] EWHC 496 (Ch) and *Interflora v Marks & Spencer Plc* [2013] EWHC 1291 (Ch).

[586]   *Picasso v EUIPO* (C-361/04) [2006] E.C.R I-643; [2006] E.T.M.R. 29.

[587]   See [27].

[588]   (T-185/02) [2004] E.C.R. II-1739 at [57].

[589]   e.g. See *Les Editions Albert René SARL v EUIPO* (C-16/06P) [2008] E.C.R. I-10053 where the marks concerned were OBELIX and MOBILIX. The CJEU held that the General Court was right to find that there was no risk of confusion as OBELIX would be recognised as the famous character in the *Asterix* cartoon strip and therefore was conceptually different from MOBILIX. See also *Mülhens v EUIPO* (C–206/04 P) EU:C:2006:194 at [35]; *T.I.M.E. ART v EUIPO* (C–171/06 P) EU:C:2007:171 at [49]; *Pera-Grave–Sociedade Agricola, Unipesoal Lda v EUIPO* (C–249/14P) EU:C:2015:459 at [39].

[590]   *Sabel v Puma*, at [23].

[591]   *Oberhauser v EUIPO* (C-104/01) [2002] E.C.R. II-4359 at [47]–[48].

[592]   *Aceites del Sur-Coosure SA v EUIPO* (C-498/07P) [2009] E.C.R. I-7371 at [62]. See also *MEGA Brands International v EUIPO* (C–182/14P) EU:C:2015:187 at [32]. The Court of Justice also held

(5)   In the case of composite marks consisting of a number of signs, then in certain circumstances, it may be appropriate to consider the constituent elements if such have independent significance. Thus, in *Medion v Thompson Multimedia (THOMPSON LIFE)*,[593] the proprietor of a registered mark LIFE brought infringement proceedings against the defendant who was using the sign THOMPSON LIFE. THOMPSON was the company name of the defendant. In Germany, there existed a trade mark doctrine (*Prägetheorie*) which held that, in such circumstances, it must be shown that the common part (i.e. LIFE) was the dominant part otherwise infringement would not be found. On reference to the CJEU as to whether this was a permitted approach, the court held that such an approach was wrong. It said that provided the common part had "an independent distinctive role" in the composite mark, there may be a likelihood of confusion. In *Bimbo v EUIPO*[594] (which concerned with whether the sign BIMBO DOUGHNUTS could be confused with the earlier mark DOUGHNUTS which had been found to be the case by the Board of Appeal and the General Court), the Court of Justice clarified the approach to considering the likelihood of confusion between a later composite mark made up of several components where one of the components is an earlier mark. The Court of Justice emphasised again that there must be a global assessment of likelihood of confusion by comparing the marks as a whole. It then said that a composite mark may, in certain circumstances, be dominated by one or more of its components. However, only if the other components are *negligible* can the assessment of similarity be carried out *solely* on the basis of the dominant element. Where a component of a complex mark, being an earlier mark, retains "an independent distinctive role", there may be a likelihood of confusion if the public attributes the origin of the goods or services covered by the complex mark sign to the owner of the earlier mark. Nevertheless, this would not be the case if the component forms a unit having a different meaning as compared with the meaning of those components taken separately. In short, where the earlier mark consists of the sign A and the later mark consists of the sign "A+B", then there may well be a likelihood of confusion if the later mark is perceived as two independent signs rather than as a single sign (particularly if the later mark is seen as a brand variant or extension of the earlier mark). This makes sense. If the earlier mark is the well-known AMAZON brand and the later mark is AMAZON NESTLÉ, confusion is must more likely than if the later mark was AMAZON JUNGLE.

In the author's view, *Bimbo* confirms that *Medion* was primarily concerned with rejecting the German doctrine of *Prägetheorie* rather than introducing a new approach to the assessment of likelihood of confusion for complex marks with a dominant component element.[595]

(at [34]) that a descriptive element may be a dominant component of a mark ("magnet" was dominant component of MAGNET 4).

[593] *Medion v Thompson Multimedia (THOMPSON LIFE)* (C-120/04) [2005] E.C.R. I-8551; [2006] E.T.M.R. 13.

[594] *Bimbo v OHIM* (C-285/13P) ECLI:EU:C:2014:1751.

[595] See also *BGW Beratungs-Gesellschaft Wirtschaft mbH v Bodo Scholz* (C-20/14) EU:C:2015:714 which applies both *Medion* and *Bimbo*.

(6)   A lesser degree of similarity between the marks may be offset by a greater degree of similarity between the goods/services and vice versa.[596]

(7)   There is a greater likelihood of confusion where the earlier trade mark has a highly distinctive character either per se or because of the use that has been made of it.[597] This rule suggests that in relation to marks which are fancy marks and have no descriptive element, the public will not attribute any importance to small differences. This must be right. The difference between XANTAC and ZANTAK for pharmaceuticals is clearly less than between COMPUTER WORLD and COMPUTER WEEK for computer magazines. The public will attribute little trade mark significance to the latter marks and will be accustomed to small differences in the names of such magazines. However, where a descriptive mark has been used substantially, the likelihood of confusion will increase. Thus, in *L&D SA v EUIPO*,[598] in opposition proceedings, the earlier trade mark consisted of a shape mark of the silhouette of a fir tree. The opponent relied upon very extensive use of the mark as indicating that it had a very substantial reputation and thus it had become highly distinctive. In fact, the shape mark had been used in conjunction with a word mark "ARBRE MAGIQUE" (MAGIC TREE). The General Court said that it was legitimate to take such use into account where, because of its prolonged use and its being well known as part of another registered trade mark, it had come to be perceived as indicating the origin of the goods from a specific undertaking.[599]

However, where a mark has become *highly* distinctive because of the use made, this doctrine might be thought to be counterintuitive. If a trade mark is *very well known*, then it could be said that the public are more likely to notice another mark which differs in small ways from it. Thus, it might be said that the public is so familiar with VERSACE as a trade mark for fashion clothing that it is less likely to confuse that with a similar mark such as SERFACE but might have confused that with VERSACE if VERSACE was not very well known. In other words, the mark is so well-known that it can be considered "imprinted" on the mind of the average consumer so that there is no real danger of imperfect recollection. It is however stressed that this would be an exceptional finding.

(8)   The test for likelihood of confusion is assessed as of the date of application of the later mark.

(9)   Evidence of instances of confusion where the marks have been used side-by-side will often be a strong pointer to a finding of likelihood of confusion if it can be established that such confusion has arisen by reason of the marks. However, and conversely, a lack of evidence of confusion does not mean that there is not a likelihood of confusion. There are many reasons why two marks which are on the marketplace do not create evidence of confusion.[600] Indeed, it is often luck or happenstance that evidence of

---

[596] *Canon v MGM* (C-39/97) [1998] E.C.R. I-5507 at [17].

[597] *Sabel*, at [24].

[598] (T-168/04) [2005] E.C.R. II-2699. Upheld on appeal, (C-488/06P) [2008] E.C.R. I-5725.

[599] See [74]. This issue overlaps with the issue of registrability of shape marks where such are inherently devoid of distinctive character but have been used alongside a word mark for a substantial period of time. See para.3-233 for discussion of this.

[600] Generally, see *Aceites del Sur-Coosur SAS v EUIPO* (C-498/07P) [2009] E.C.R. I-7371 and also,

confusion comes to light. After all, a person who is confused by a trade mark is, ex hypothesi, unaware that they have been confused and only if some event occurs after the sale, e.g. the goods are faulty and need to be returned, will such possibly come to light. In the author's view, evidence of lack of confusion will only be relevant where:

(a)   there has been substantial use of the two marks in the marketplace for a considerable period in relation to the goods or services protected by the mark or for which protection is sought;

(b)   the *actual* use of the marks in relation to goods or services coincides or approximates to *normal and fair* use of the marks in relation to goods or services for which the mark is registered (or more pertinently, those goods or services on which the opponent relies upon); and

(c)   neither mark has been used in conjunction with additional distinguishing material (i.e. a house mark, a distinctive get-up, etc.) such as to reduce the likelihood of any confusion that may have arisen as a result of the use of the marks alone.

(10)   When considering the likelihood of confusion, the court or tribunal should consider all the circumstances in which the mark applied for might be used if it was to be registered.[601]

(11)   Where an argument is put forward that the mark applied for has an element in it which is common to a "family" of marks owned by the opponent and thus confusion is likely, it is necessary to show that there has been use of a sufficient number of the family of the marks which include the common element so as to educate the relevant public to associate that element with the opponent.[602] If such is substantiated, then the use of that common element in the mark applied for (whether by itself or as part of a composite mark), if such is sufficiently distinctive, will often result in what is called "stable" confusion, i.e. that the public will believe that the goods bearing the mark applied for is part of a family or stable of goods marketed by the opponent.

(12)   The risk of confusion must be more than hypothetical. Although not wholly clear, it seems that there must be a real risk of confusion and such must be genuine and properly substantiated.[603]

(13)   Although not expressly ruled upon, there is no requirement in either the EUTMR or TMD that the confusion must occur at the time of sale. Thus, in relation to pre-sale confusion, such confusion could be caused by an advertisement even though that particular confusion could be dispelled by the time the consumer actually buys the advertised goods or services.[604]

---

in England, *The European Ltd v Economist Newspaper Ltd* [1998] F.S.R. 283; *Compass Publishing BV v Compass Logistics Ltd* [2004] R.P.C. 41.

[601]   *O2 v Hutchison* (C-533/06) [2008] E.C.R. I-4231 at [66]. However, see para.3-323.

[602]   *Il Ponte Finanziaria SpA v EUIPO* (C-234/06) [2007] E.C.R. I-7333 at [63]–[66]. It is not sufficient merely to show that the opponent owns registrations of the marks. See also *Debonair Trading v EUIPO* (T-356/12) ECLI:EU:T:2014:178.

[603]   See *Marca Mode v Adidas* (C-425/98) [2000] E.C.R. I-4861. See also *Sabel v Puma*, Opinion of Jacobs AG, at [52]–[55].

[604]   In *Och-Ziff v Och Capital LLP* [2011] F.S.R. 11 at [101], the High Court of England concluded that pre-sale confusion (called "initial interest confusion") was actionable under art.9(1)(b) EUTMR. This was based in part on analysis of *Bergspechte* and *O2 Holdings*.

However, it is less clear that post-sales confusion can be considered relevant.[605]

(14) When considering the likelihood of confusion, the Court of Appeal of England and Wales has held that "wrong way around" confusion (i.e. where customers confused the goods of the owner of the trade mark which it seeks to enforce with those of the alleged infringer) was relevant to the assessment of likelihood of confusion (see *Comic Enterprises Ltd v Twentieth Century Fox*).[606]

Unfair advantage of/detriment to distinctive character or repute of mark

3-352   Article 8.5 EUTMR provides that:

"5.   Upon opposition by the proprietor of a registered earlier trade mark within the meaning of paragraph 2, the trade mark applied for shall not be registered where it is identical with, or similar to, an earlier trade mark, irrespective of whether the goods or services for which it is applied are identical with, similar to or not similar to those for which the earlier trade mark is registered, where, in the case of an earlier EU trade mark, the trade mark has a reputation in the Union or, in the case of an earlier national trade mark, the trade mark has a reputation in the Member State concerned, and where the use without due cause of the trade mark applied for would take unfair advantage of, or be detrimental to, the distinctive character or the repute of the earlier trade mark."

3-353   As with the likelihood of confusion grounds of opposition, these provisions have their counterpart in the infringement provisions of both the EUTMR and TMD.[607]

Functions of a trade mark and unfair advantage/detriment to distinctive character or repute of mark

3-354   Unlike the CJEU's analysis of the identical goods/identical marks provisions of the TMD and EUTMR, the CJEU has not sought to impose the requirement in these provisions that it must be shown that there is an adverse effect on one or more functions of a trade mark.[608] Unlike the identical goods/identical marks provisions, these provisions set out fairly clearly the requirements that must be established by the proprietor of the earlier mark. Indeed, in the case of taking unfair advantage, it is difficult to see what function of an earlier mark is adversely affected. In truth, the concept of taking unfair advantage, which involves the concept of "free riding" on the reputation of the earlier mark, is concerned more with the concept of unfair competition than the law of trade marks and the protection of the functions of a trade mark. In the case of detriment to distinctive character (dilution) and detri-

---

[605] There is some suggestion in *Ruiz-Picasso v EUIPO* (C-361/04P) [2006] E.C.R. I-643 that post-sales confusion is irrelevant (see [44]–[48])—see *Och-Ziff*, at [100].

[606] [2016] EWCA Civ 41.

[607] art.9.2(c) EUTMR; art.10..2(c) TMD.

[608] Although in *Interflora v Marks & Spencer* (C-323/09) ECLI:EU:C:2011:173, Jaaskinen AG said "For me it is also obvious that any of the uses covered by Article 5(2) of Directive 89/104 are likely to have an adverse effect on at least some of the trade mark functions mentioned above, especially since the widened protection provided by Article 5(2) of Directive 89/104 is usually motivated with reference to the communication, advertising and investment functions of trade marks"—at [61]. The author's view is that in the case of unfair advantage, it is anything but obvious! In the judgment, the CJEU did not refer to the functions of the mark when considering whether unfair advantage/ detriment to distinctive character or repute save in relation to "due cause".

ment to the repute (tarnishment), it is easier to see how the functions of a trade mark can be affected. Dilution ultimately erodes the attractive force that a mark with a reputation has and is, as discussed earlier in this chapter, the type of conduct to which the investment function is most relevant.[609] Tarnishment is concerned with damage to the image of a trade mark and this directly involves the communication function. However, it is stressed that the CJEU has not said these provisions require that it must be shown that the functions of the earlier mark are adversely affected.

Requirements

These provisions differ from the identical goods/identical marks and similar goods/similar marks provisions because they only apply to trade marks with a reputation. In the following sections, we look at the following requirements: **3-355**

(i)   similarity of marks and goods for services;
(ii)   reputation;
(iii)   the requirement that there be a "link";
(iv)   unfair advantage (free-riding);
(v)   detriment to distinctive character of mark (dilution); and
(vi)   detriment to repute of mark (tarnishment).

Similar marks

The issue of "similarity of marks" in the context of art.8.1(b) EUTMR has   **3-356**
already been discussed.[610] One might have thought that the test for similarity of marks under art.8.5 would be the same. In *Bitburger Brauerei v EUIPO*,[611] the General Court concluded that the marks were not visually, aurally or conceptually similar so that there was no likelihood of confusion under art.8.1(b) of the EUTMR. In going on to consider whether there was taking of unfair advantage of or detriment under art.8.5, it simply said that its finding of lack of similarity of the marks under art.8.1(b) was determinative of the matter. However, in *Intra-Presse— GOLDEN BALLS*,[612] the Court of Justice held, upholding an appeal from the General Court, that the degree of similarity of the marks required for art.8.5 differed from that for art.8.1(b) EUTMR and that for the purpose of art.8.5, the degree of similarity required is merely that sufficient for the relevant section of the public to establish a link between the two marks.[613] Nevertheless, if there is no similarity between the marks, however faint, then art.8.5 is inapplicable.[614]

Goods and services

In its earlier versions of the TMD and EUTMR, art.8.5 only referred to "dis-   **3-357**
similar goods". Historically, it was not thought that there was any room for application of this ground of objection to marks where the goods were similar. However, it struck many commentators as strange that in the absence of being able to prove a likelihood of confusion, a mark which had a reputation had greater protection

---

[609] See para.3-108.
[610] See para.3-338.
[611] *Bitburger Brauerei v EUIPO* (T-350/04 & T-352/04) [2006] E.C.R. II-04255.
[612] (C-581/13P) ECLI:EU:C:2014:2387.
[613] See [72], [76].
[614] *Ferrero v EUIPO* (C–552/09 P) EU:C:2011:177 at [53].

when a similar mark was used in relation to dissimilar goods than in relation to similar goods.

3-358   The CJEU dealt with this illogicality in *Davidoff & Cie v Gofkid Ltd*,[615] and *Adidas v Fitnessworld*,[616] by making it clear that these grounds applied to similar goods and services as well as dissimilar goods and services (contrary to the express). These decisions are now reflected in the new art.8.5 EUTMR which has replaced "*dissimilar goods or services*" with "*irrespective of whether the goods or services for which it is applied are identical with, similar to or not similar to those for which the earlier trade mark is registered*". Identical changes have been made to the new TMD. Thus, when considering the application of art.8.5, the specification of the earlier mark is ignored. Rather, one considers the reputation of the earlier mark and the goods or services for which it has a reputation. The only reason to consider the specification might be if the reputation of the earlier mark lies in relation to goods or services which are not covered by the earlier registration. It would be odd if art.8.5 EUTMR protected an earlier mark which has been used (and thus developed a reputation) in relation to goods disconnected with the goods for which the earlier mark is registered. The protection under art.8.5 is only afforded to registered EU and national marks and the specification of goods and services is an integral and fundamental aspect of a registered mark. In the same sense that the mark which has the relevant reputation in the marketplace must be identical to the registered mark, it is suggested that the reputation must lie in goods or services covered by the registration.[617]

Reputation

3-359   In *General Motors Corp v Yplon SA*,[618] the CJEU stated that, in order to take advantage of the predecessor provision to art.10.2(c) TMD (infringement), the test for "reputation" was whether it was known to a significant part of the public concerned by the products or services covered by the mark and that the reputation existed in a substantial part of a Member State. Whether this is the case depends on all of the circumstances including market share, intensity, geographical extent and duration of use and the size of the investment made by the undertaking in promoting it.[619]

Reputation and EU trade marks

3-360   Where the earlier mark relied upon is a EUTM, it must be shown that it has a reputation in the EU. In *Pago International GmbH v Tirolmilch Registrierte Genossenschaft mbH*,[620] the CJEU had to consider what was meant by this phrase. The CJEU said, in applying *General Motors* by way of analogy, that it meant that a EUTM must be known by a significant part of the public concerned by the products or services covered by the trade mark *and* in a substantial part of the territory of

615 *Davidoff & Cie v Gofkid Ltd* (C-292/00) [2003] E.C.R. I-389; [2003] E.T.M.R. 42.
616 (C-408/01) [2004] E.C.R. I-12537; [2004] E.T.M.R. 10.
617 This is the approach taken by EUIPO in its decisions, e.g. see R1033/2009-4 *PEP/bebe*, at [31]. Here, the Board of Appeal said that the reputation of the mark must lie in goods or services identical to that for which the earlier mark is registered. It should also be said that in *Intel v CPM* (C-252/07) [2008] E.C.R. I-8823, there are indications going both ways—see [50]–[52].
618 *General Motors Corp v Yplon SA* (C-375/97) [1999] E.C.R. I-5421 at [23]–[28].
619 See [27].
620 (C-301/07) [2009] E.C.R. I-9249; [2010] E.T.M.R. 5.

the EU. It said such a Member State *may* be considered to constitute a substantial part of the territory of the EU[621] Overall, it is clear that the intention of the CJEU is to treat the EU as one territory in much the same way as, for a national mark, one considers the national territory as a whole. However, it should be noted that the requirement that a EUTM is known to a significant number of the public in the EU is not sufficient. It must also be known in a substantial part of the territory of the EU. Whilst, these two concepts are clearly linked as whether a specific area is a substantial part of the territory of the EU will no doubt be evaluated in part by regard to the population in that area, they are legally separate requirements. Thus, it is feasible but unlikely that a mark may be known to a significant number of persons in the EU but the geographical spread of those persons is insufficient to mean that the mark has a reputation in a substantial part of the EU.

In *Iron & Smith kft v Unilever NV*,[622] the Court of Justice had to consider the posi- **3-361** tion where a mark was applied for in a Member State and an earlier EUTM was relied upon but its reputation lay outside the Member State. On reference from the Hungarian intellectual property office, the Court of Justice said that as a matter of law, it is sufficient if the earlier EUTM has a reputation in the EU but not in the Member State in which registration of a national mark is sought. However, recognising that it is difficult if not impossible to take unfair advantage or cause damage to a mark's reputation where that mark is not known by the relevant public, it said that even if the earlier EUTM is not known to a significant part of the relevant public in the Member State, it is conceivable that a commercially significant part of the latter may be familiar with it, and if so, then the tribunal should consider whether there is an actual or present risk of injury to the mark.[623] Conceptually, it is difficult to understand how a commercially significant part of the relevant public could be familiar with the earlier EUTM but at the same time, not know it. In the author's view, if the earlier EUTM has a reputation in the EU (regardless of whether it has a specific reputation in the Member State where the application is made for a national mark), then the only question is whether there is a risk of taking of unfair advantage of/detriment to distinctive character or repute or a serious risk that such may occur in the future. That may happen regardless of whether as of the date of application of the national mark, the EUTM is known or familiar to a significant proportion of the relevant public in the Member State where protection is sought for the later mark. If so, there is a serious risk that use of the later mark may indeed take unfair advantage of the reputation of the earlier EUTM or be detrimental to its distinctive character or repute.

---

[621] See [24] and [27]. The Member State under consideration was Austria. It should be said that in *Pago*, the Court of Justice was considering the meaning of the phrase "reputation in the Community" in art.9.2(c) EUTMR—an infringement provision. In *Iron & Smith kft v Unilever NV* (C–125/14) EU:C:2015: 539, the Court of Justice confirmed (in case it was in doubt) that the phrase has the same meaning as in art.5.3(a) TMD (relative grounds of opposition)—see [16]. Perhaps more importantly, the Court of Justice held that when considering an opposition by an earlier EUTM proprietor under art.5.3(a) TMD to an application in a Member State for a national trade mark, it was not necessary for the EUTM to have a reputation within the Member State of application for it to satisfy the requirement of reputation in the Community (See [21]).

[622] (C–125/14) EU:C:2015: 539 at [16]–[20].

[623] See [30]–[34].

"Link" but not confusion

3-362   The CJEU has made it clear that art.8.5 EUTMR does not require the existence of a likelihood of confusion but does require the existence of a link between the two marks.[624] Thus, in *Adidas-Salomon AG v Fitnessworld*,[625] the CJEU said concerning the infringement provisions in the TMD:

> "[29]   The infringements referred to in [Art.10.2(c) TMD], where they occur, are the consequence of a certain degree of similarity between the mark and the sign, by virtue of which the relevant section of the public makes a connection between the sign and the mark, that is to say, establishes a link between them even though it does not confuse them (see, to that effect, Case C-375/97 *General Motors* [1999] E.C.R. I-5421, para.23).
>
> [30]   The existence of such a link must, just like a likelihood of confusion in the context of [Art.10.2(b) TMD], be appreciated globally, taking into account all factors relevant to the circumstances of the case (see, in respect of the likelihood of confusion, *Sabel*, para.22, and *Marca Mode*, para.40).
>
> [31]   The answer to Question 2(a) must therefore be that the protection conferred by [Art.10.2(c) TMD] is not conditional on a finding of a degree of similarity between the mark with a reputation and the sign such that there exists a likelihood of confusion between them on the part of the relevant section of the public. It is sufficient for the degree of similarity between the mark with a reputation and the sign to have the effect that the relevant section of the public establishes a link between the sign and the mark."

3-363   In *Intel v CPM(UK)*,[626] the CJEU said that a link is established where the average consumer who is reasonably well informed, observant and circumspect, when he sees the later mark, calls the earlier mark to mind.[627] The court also gave guidance on how to assess whether a link was established. Thus, the CJEU emphasised that the test was a global one but pointed out that relevant factors would include: (i) the degree of similarity of the marks, (ii) the nature of the goods or services for which the conflicting marks were registered, (iii) the strength of the earlier mark's reputation, (iv) the distinctiveness of the earlier mark, and (v) the existence of likelihood of confusion.[628]

Unfair advantage or detriment to the distinctive character or repute of the mark

3-364   The CJEU has, in a number of cases on infringement (where there are parallel provisions), clarified that there are three situations to consider when considering whether a sign will "take unfair advantage of, or be detrimental to the, the distinctive character or the repute of the earlier national or EUTM". These are:

(a)   free-riding on the reputation of an earlier mark (taking unfair advantage),

(b)   dilution (detriment to the distinctive character of the earlier mark), and

(c)   tarnishment (detriment to the repute of the earlier mark).[629]

The decisions on infringement will have aspects that are irrelevant to a ground of opposition or cancellation based on an earlier registered mark. In particular, the

---

[624]   (C-425/98) [2000] E.C.R. I-4861; (C-292/00) [2003] E.C.R. I-289, [2003] E.T.M.R. 42 at [29].
[625]   (C-408/01) [2004] E.C.R. I-12537; [2004] E.T.M.R. 10 at [31].
[626]   *Intel Corp Inc v CPM United Kingdom* (C-252/07) [2008] E.C.R. I-8823; [2009] R.P.C. 15.
[627]   See [63].
[628]   See [42].
[629]   e.g. see *Interflora Inc v Marks and Spencer Plc* (C-323/09) [2011] E.C.R. 8625 at [72]–[75].

CJEU has considered unfair advantage in the context of Internet keywords and also comparative advertising.[630] When contemplating grounds of opposition or cancellation, one would not consider such types of use but more straightforward types of use. However, the CJEU's findings concerning the meaning of these three concepts is equally applicable to grounds of opposition or cancellation based on an earlier mark with a reputation as to infringement.

Unfair advantage

In *L'Oréal v Bellure*,[631] the CJEU said that: **3-365**

"[41]   As regards the concept of 'taking unfair advantage of the distinctive character or the repute of the trade mark', also referred to as 'parasitism' or 'free-riding', that concept relates not to the detriment caused to the mark but to the advantage taken by the third party as a result of the use of the identical or similar sign. *It covers, in particular, cases where, by reason of a transfer of the image of the mark or of the characteristics which it projects to the goods identified by the identical or similar sign, there is clear exploitation on the coat-tails of the mark with a reputation.*"[632]

Later in the judgment, the CJEU said:

"[49]   where a third party attempts, through the use of a sign similar to a mark with a reputation, *to ride on the coat-tails of that mark in order to benefit from its power of attraction, its reputation and its prestige, and to exploit, without paying any financial compensation and without being required to make efforts of his own* in that regard, the marketing effort expended by the proprietor of that mark in order to create and maintain the image of that mark, the advantage resulting from such use must be considered to be an advantage that has been unfairly taken of the distinctive character or the repute of that mark."

It will be appreciated from the above that unfair advantage is concerned less with   **3-366**
damage done to the earlier mark but rather the benefit accruing to the owner of the later mark. Therefore, unlike the situation where use of a later mark causes detriment to the distinctive character (dilution) or repute of the mark (tarnishment), which would have an adverse effect on the functions of the earlier mark, the concept of unfair advantage may involve no damage or adverse effect on the functions of the earlier mark. Indeed, it may not even cause economic damage to the owner of the earlier mark (for instance, where the owner of the earlier mark has no intention of entering the market covered by the goods or services of the later mark). Rather, it belongs more to the realm of unfair competition. In English law, it would amount to a specie of unjust enrichment, which is a principle recognised under the equity branch of English law.[633] Thus, even though in the context of art.8.5 EUTMR and its equivalent provisions in the TMD, the CJEU talks about assessing whether there is actual or present injury to the mark or a serious risk that such may oc-

---

[630]   See para.3-552 (Internet keywords) and para.3-562 (comparative advertising).

[631]   *L'Oréal SA v Bellure NV* (C-487/07) [2009] E.C.R. I-5185.

[632]   Cited in *Interflora v Marks and Spencer* (C-323/09) [2011] E.C.R. 8625 at [74]. This excerpt appears to have been derived from *Sigla v EUIPO* (T-215/03) [2007] E.C.R. II-711 at [40].

[633]   For a recent exposition of this principle by the UK Supreme Court, see *Benedetti v Sawiris* [2013] UKSC 50.

cur,[634] as said by EUIPO in its Guidelines, in the case of unfair advantage, there is not necessarily an injury whether to the mark or indeed more generally to its owner.[635]

3-367   Clearly, the paradigm example of free-riding or parasitism is where a competitor's mark causes confusion with another mark. However, as already discussed in relation to the requirement of "link", it is not necessary that the notional average consumer is likely to be confused—simply that one mark calls to mind the other mark.[636] Thus, a trader may choose to make use of the selling power of a brand for the purpose of launching their own product in a manner that does not actually deceive the consumer. Indeed, the trader may not wish the buyers of their branded products to be confused with the earlier mark but merely want them to be more likely to purchase its products as a result of the "transfer of image".

3-368   "Lookalike" products are a good example of free-riding in the 1990s whereby supermarkets sold "own brand" products using their own trade mark but mimicking the get up of the packaging of famous brands. This was done because it subtly reassured customers as to the quality of the "own brand" product but also conveyed information as to the nature of the goods. This was particularly done with breakfast cereals whereby use of "me too" get-up persuaded or induced buyers that the consumption of "own brand" supermarket cereal would lead to a similar experience to the consumption of the famous brand cereal (but at a cheaper price).

3-369   The concept of "unfair advantage" owes much to the law of unfair competition which is prevalent in continental Europe. Thus, in *DIMPLE*,[637] the Bundesgerichtshof said that it constitutes an act of unfair competition to associate the quality of one's goods or services with that of prestigious competitive goods for the purpose of exploiting the good reputation of a competitor's goods or services in order to enhance one's own promotional efforts. In *Adidas v Fitnessworld*, the Advocate-General suggested that Rolls Royce would be entitled to prevent a manufacturer of whisky from exploiting the reputation of the Rolls Royce mark in order to promote his brand.[638] In an Italian case, *Adidas-Salomon v Gruppo Coin*,[639] the Court of Rome referred to marks which imitate well known trade marks that, even where there is no deceit as regards the origin of the products:

> "[18]   ... guarantees to the infringing company the possibility of taking advantage, in a parasitic manner, of the said investments, in that the infringing company is enabled to participate in the economic competition without bearing the relevant costs and by virtue of its connection with the activity of a better known competitor, thereby taking undue advantage."

3-370   This is indubitably right. In *Ferrero v Kindercare*,[640] the First Board of Appeal said that:

> "[26]   The scenario of unjust enrichment or unfair advantage occurs when a third party exploits the reputation of the earlier mark to the benefit of its own marketing efforts. In practice, the third party 'hooks on to' the renowned mark and uses it as

---

[634]   e.g. see *Iron & Smith kft v Unilever* (C-125/14) ECLI:EU:C:2015:539 at [34].

[635]   Part C, para 3.4, Guidelines (fn.3).

[636]   See para.3-362.

[637]   *DIMPLE* [1985] G.R.U.R. 550.

[638]   See *Adidas-Saloman v Fitnessworld Trading Ltd* ECLI:EU:C:2003:404 at [39] citing a decision of the Bundesgerichtshof *Rolls-Royce I ZR* 133/80.

[639]   *Adidas-Salomon v Gruppo Coin* [2006] E.T.M.R. 39, Tribunale Roma.

[640]   *Ferrero v Kindercare* [2005] E.T.M.R. 6.

a vehicle to incite consumers' interest in its own, albeit different, products. The advantage for the third party is a substantial saving on investment in promotion and publicity for its own mark, since it benefits from that which has made the earlier mark highly famous, and it is unfair because it is done in a parasitic way (see Decisions of the First Board of Appeal of 8 February 2002 in Case R 472/2001–1-*BIBA/BIBA* (figurative mark) and of the Fourth Board of Appeal of 26 July 2001 in Case R 552/2000–4-*COSMOPOLITAN COSMETICS/COSMOPOLITAN*)."

As the First Board of Appeal said in *Ferrero*, the taking of unfair advantage is unlikely to occur unless there is a "sufficiently close" similarity between the two marks and in particular, a close visual similarity as such is associated with the image of the mark. In particular, the use of ancillary aspects of a mark such as patterns and figurative elements will often be necessary for a finding of detriment to be made. Indeed, in *Magefesa/Magefesa*,[641] the Board of Appeal said that a very high degree of similarity is a factor of particular importance in establishing that an unfair advantage has been taken of the registered mark. Where there is identity of marks and the earlier mark has a significant reputation and is distinctive, a finding of unfair advantage will readily be made. Thus, in *NASDAQ TM*,[642] the applicant filed for "NASDAQ + device" for sports equipment. The opponent was the well-known owner of the NASDAQ stock market indices. It had registrations for the mark for goods and services related to its business. Upholding the Boards of Appeal, the General Court held that taking account of the similarity of the marks, the importance of the reputation of the opponent and the highly distinctive character of the trade mark NASDAQ, the opponent had established prima facie the existence of a future risk which was not hypothetical of unfair advantage being taken by the applicant. However, such a finding will not automatically follow unless it can be shown that there is some advantage in using the earlier mark on the goods or services which have been applied for. Thus, in *NASDAQ TM*, it is not immediately apparent how the well-known stock market NASDAQ trade mark would benefit the sales of sports equipment. Rather unconvincingly, the General Court held that the image of modernity that the NASDAQ mark had would be transferred to the applicant's mark.[643]   **3-371**

In *L'Oréal v Bellure*, which has been discussed above, the CJEU gave guidance to courts to determine whether a mark has taken unfair advantage of the reputation of another mark. It said: **3-372**

"[44] In order to determine whether the use of a sign takes unfair advantage of the distinctive character or the repute of the mark, it is necessary to undertake a global assessment, taking into account all factors relevant to the circumstances of the case, which include the strength of the mark's reputation and the degree of distinctive character of the mark, the degree of similarity between the marks at issue and the nature and degree of proximity of the goods or services concerned. As regards the strength of the reputation and the degree of distinctive character of the mark, the Court has already held that, the stronger that mark's distinctive character and reputation are, the easier it will be to accept that detriment has been caused to it. It is also clear from the case-law that, the more immediately and strongly the mark

---

[641] R 303/2000.

[642] *Antartica srl v OHIM* (T-47/06) [2007] E.C.R. II-42.

[643] In fact, there was evidence in the documentation that the applicant had deliberately had in mind the NASDAQ index when it selected the mark. Thus, it would have been unattractive to deny that the earlier mark gave rise to any advantage.

is brought to mind by the sign, the greater the likelihood that the current or future use of the sign is taking, or will take, unfair advantage of the distinctive character or the repute of the mark or is, or will be, detrimental to them (see, to that effect, *Intel Corporation*, paragraphs 67 to 69)."

3-373 **Advantage must be "unfair"** It must be shown that the advantage is "unfair". Similar but perhaps not exactly the same concepts are conveyed in the French and German versions[644]. "Unfairness" is a concept that is very subjective and culturally-specific. For instance, many might say that in the context of business, which is normally competitive, there is little room for the notion of concept. If the law allows a practice, then such persons might say that the practice should be allowed and should be considered fair. Paradoxically, for a country known for its sense of "fairplay", this notion is prevalent in the UK which has always been resistant to the law of unfair competition being introduced into business practices.

3-374 In *L'Oréal v Bellure*, the CJEU did not distinguish between a situation where a trade mark takes fair advantage of another's reputation as opposed to unfair advantage. Rather, as seen at para.3-365, its view is that parasitism or free-riding was per se taking unfair advantage. It would be surprising if the concept of "unfairness" was to be determined by the state of mind of the applicant for the mark in applying for the mark and whether it intended to take advantage of the reputation of an earlier mark. Indeed, such would be artificial because the applicant applying for a mark is not per se seeking in doing so, to obtain permission to use the mark applied for, but rather to obtain a monopoly to assert against others. However, clearly if the evidence showed that the applicant was using the mark to take advantage of the reputation of an earlier mark and cut promotional costs, then such should be seen as a strong indication of unfair advantage.[645]

3-375 However, in *L'Oréal v Bellure*, the CJEU appeared to regard it as important that Bellure had intentionally sought to ride on the coat-tails of L'Oréal's well-known marks.[646] This emphasis led the English Court of Appeal in a case to conclude that that the *mere* taking of a commercial advantage was not sufficient. There had to be shown that there was an *intention* to take advantage or some other factor which rendered the advantage unfair.[647] However, such seems to have been based on a very literal and textual analysis of *L'Oréal*. In *Interflora v Marks and Spencer*, the CJEU said, in citing *L'Oréal* that where there is free-riding on the reputation of another trade mark such as to avoid the need to make marketing efforts of its own, the advantage obtained must be considered to be unfair.[648] There was no emphasis on the need to show intention. In the author's opinion, this is right. If a mark's similarity causes it to free-ride on the reputation of another mark, such is free-riding regardless whether the owner of the former mark intended such to occur. In *Enterprise Holdings Inc v Europcar Group UK Ltd*[649] the High Court of England held that there was nothing in the case law of the Court of Justice or England which

---

[644] In German, "*in unlauterer Weise*"; in French, the expression is "*indûment*". The author understands that *unlauterer* is a somewhat outdated word for "unfair" (with the English word "unfair" having crossed over into the German language in the late 19th century) and the French word being closest to the English word "*undeservedly*". In the author's view, these words are not perfect matches for the Anglo-Saxon word "unfair".

[645] A point made in EUIPO Guidelines, Part C, para 3.4.3.1.

[646] e.g. see [47] and [49].

[647] *Whirlpool v Kenwood* [2010] R.P.C. 2 at [136].

[648] See [89].

[649] [2015] EWHC 17.

precluded a court from concluding in an appropriate case that the use of a sign, the objective effect of which is to enable the defendant to benefit from the reputation and goodwill of the trade mark, amounts to unfair advantage even if it is not proved that the defendant subjectively intended to exploit that reputation and goodwill.

Detriment to reputation—dilution

In *Intel v CPM*, the CJEU stated that detriment to the distinctive character of a trade mark will occur: **3-376**

"[29]   As regards, in particular, detriment to the distinctive character of the earlier mark, often referred to as 'dilution', 'whittling away' or 'blurring', such detriment is caused when that mark's ability to identify the goods or services for which it is registered and used as coming from the proprietor of that mark is weakened, since use of the later mark leads to dispersion of the identity and hold upon the public mind of the earlier mark. That is notably the case when the earlier mark, which used to arouse immediate association with the goods and services for which it is registered, is no longer capable of doing so."

As said in the above excerpt, this damage is often called dilution. The above excerpt owes it origins to a famous article by Schechter, "The rational basis of trademark protection"[650] where he advocated protection against the whittling away or dispersion of the identity and hold upon the public mind of certain marks. As he said, if you allow Rolls Royce restaurants, Rolls Royce cafeterias, Rolls Royce pants and Rolls Royce candy, in 100 years, you will not have the Rolls Royce mark any more.[651] **3-377**

In making the assessment of whether there has been detriment to distinctive character, the CJEU said that the more immediately and strongly the earlier mark is brought to mind, the greater the likelihood that the later mark is or will take unfair advantage of or be detrimental to the repute of the mark. It also said that the stronger the reputation and/or distinctive character of the earlier mark; the easier it will be to prove detriment. It is not necessary for the earlier mark to be "unique" but the more "unique" it is, the greater the likelihood that the latter mark will be detrimental to its distinctive character. **3-378**

Importantly, the CJEU said that the proprietor of the earlier mark must provide proof that the use of the later mark is detrimental to the distinctive character of the earlier mark or there is a serious risk that such will occur in the future.[652] This requires evidence of a change in the economic behaviour of the average consumer of the goods or services *for which the earlier mark was registered* consequent on the use of the later mark or a serious likelihood that such a change will occur in the future.[653] **3-379**

The requirement of change in economic behaviour of the average consumer means that mere perfunctory arguments such as the marks are similar and thus dilution is inevitable will fail. However, it seems tolerably clear that if it can be established that the "selling power" of the earlier mark is reduced by normal and fair use of the later mark, then such arguments will succeed. It remains to be seen **3-380**

---

[650]   F.I. Schechter, "The rational basis of trademark protection" (1926) 40 *Harvard Law Review* 813.
[651]   This is cited by the Advocate-General in *Adidas v Fitnessworld* (C-408/01) [2003] E.C.R. I-12537 at [37].
[652]   See para.3-390 for further discussion of the standard and cogency of proof required.
[653]   See *Intel v CPM*, at [37], [39], [77].

exactly what type of evidence will be sufficient to establish this. Does it mean that one will need an expert in marketing to make a point which, in many cases, is obvious to all? The second important aspect is that one is concerned with the effect on the economic behaviour of the average consumer of the goods or services *for which the earlier mark is registered*. For instance, let us consider an application to register "Lego" for garden furniture and an objection taken by the owners of the "Lego" mark which is registered for "playthings". It would have to be shown that use of "Lego" for garden furniture will affect the decisions of consumers to buy Lego bricks. This may be difficult. Indeed, even though such is sufficient to establish a link, the fact that buyers of Lego garden furniture may believe that Lego is somehow connected in the course of trade with the company supplying the garden furniture would not be sufficient to show detriment (although it may be to establish unfair advantage). It is not the buyers of garden furniture that are relevant (assuming that Lego does not have a registration of Lego for garden furniture) but the purchasers of playthings.

3-381   The above detriment is often called dilution by blurring. The CJEU's statement in *Intel v CPM* owes much to the development of the concept by the Boards of Appeal of EUIPO which have given a fuller explanation of the concept of dilution by blurring. In *Hollywood*,[654] the Board of Appeal said this on the subject:

"[105] …This dilution occurs when consumers identify the trade mark used by a third party with different goods or services with different origins. This dilutes the trade mark's ability to identify a single originating undertaking without a likelihood of confusion as regards the origin of the goods or service or the existence of contractual or similar relationships between the holders of the right. This results in an association which weakens or reduces the trade mark's distinctive character.

[106] A trade mark's distinctive character is not a static fact, but may on the contrary evolve over time. Hence the distinctive character of a trade mark which is weak at the time of registration may be strengthened by the use made of it. Conversely, the distinctive character of a strong trade mark may be weakened by its misuse.

[107] The benefits bestowed by the exclusive right to the trade mark on its proprietor may include the trade mark's capacity to stimulate the desire to buy the kind of products for which it is registered. This capacity may also be detrimentally affected by the fact that persons other than the proprietor use the trade mark or a similar sign for products other than those for which it is registered. This detrimental effect may consist in the fact that owing to the loss of its exclusive character, the trade mark is no longer capable of evoking in the minds of the public an immediate association with the products for which it is registered and used. This other usage may therefore be detrimental to the trade mark's proprietor.

[108] The detrimental effect could be that use of the trade mark for another type of product would make the trade mark less attractive for the products for which it is registered. This would be the case when this other type of products, although not per se having a negative influence on the public's perception, nevertheless influences it in such a way that the trade mark is detrimentally affected in terms of its capacity to stimulate the desire to purchase the goods for which it was registered. This leads to an erosion of distinctive character caused by the proliferation of 'parasitic' trade marks which, although not debasing the original trade mark, are so numerous that they deprive the trade mark of its distinctive character and hence of its impact.

[109] The trade mark's ability to stimulate the desire to purchase normally depends on the degree of distinctive character and reputation it possesses. With regard to

---

[654] *Hollywood SAS v Souza Cruz* [2002] E.T.M.R. 64, Third Board of Appeal, EUIPO.

[Article 5.3(a) TMD] which is transposed into Article 8(5) EUTMR, the Court of Justice has ruled that 'the stronger the earlier trade mark's distinctive character and reputation the easier it will be to accept that detriment has been caused to it' (*Chevy* judgment, paragraph 30)."

Upon proper consideration, dilution by blurring can occur in three ways. First, **3-382** and most obviously, is where a third-party mark which is similar to the mark that has a substantial reputation has a "swamping" effect on the latter mark such that its use no longer evokes an immediate association with the products for which it is registered. As said above, the selling power of the mark is reduced. This is particularly damaging where a number of third parties use similar marks. For instance, substantial use of "big cat" car marques, Panther, Puma, Tiger, Cheetah by third party car manufacturers would inevitably reduce the selling power of the Jaguar car mark.

Secondly, and more subtly, dilution can occur where use of another similar mark **3-383** confuses or alters the "signal" that the mark with the reputation conveys to the public. In short, it modifies the "identity" of the mark and thereby affects the communication function of the mark. This does not need to be in a negative way.[655] In a UK case, *Taittinger v Allbev*,[656] which was a passing-off case, it was held that the use of champagne in the name of an elderflower fruit cordial (ELDERFLOWER CHAMPAGNE) was inevitably likely:

"to erode the singularity and exclusivity of the description Champagne and so cause the first plaintiff's damage of an insidious but serious kind".

This is undoubtedly correct because "Champagne" is a luxury brand (actually a **3-384** geographical indication of origin). It is wholly intuitive that if sweets, drinks, pens, cuddly toys, etc. were called "Champagne" and used extensively, that ultimately this would cheapen the image of champagne as an exclusive sparkling white wine from a particular area of France. This is because well known luxury brands inherently rely upon their exclusivity of use as their selling point. In an English case, it was held that use of INTEL-PLAY for children's puzzles would dilute the strength of the INTEL mark for semiconductor chips because such was founded on high quality, technologically based products with an international reputation.[657]

Thirdly, dilution can occur by reducing the actual distinctiveness of a trade mark **3-385** by inappropriate third party use, e.g. causing a mark to become a generic term for products or services or alternatively eroding the acquired distinctive character of an inherently non-distinctive mark. As with the "swamping" effect, the ultimate effect is to reduce the distinctive character of the mark but in a different way—by misuse of the mark itself rather than third party use. Good examples of this would be third party use of a mark such as HOOVER® as a name for vacuum cleaner.[658]

Detriment to repute—tarnishment

In *L'Oréal v Bellure*, the CJEU explained what is meant by detriment to the **3-386** repute of the mark which is often referred to as "tarnishment". It said:

---

[655] If it is negative, it is called "tarnishment" and is considered at para.3-386.
[656] [1993] F.S.R. 641. See also para.3-108 where this is discussed in the context of the investment function.
[657] *Intel Corp v Sihra* [2004] E.T.M.R. 44 (Ch).
[658] In the English speaking world, many refer to vacuum cleaners as "hoovers" because in the early days of vacuum cleaners, the Hoover® vacuum cleaner was so ubiquitous.

"[40]   As regards detriment to the repute of the mark, also referred to as 'tarnishment' or 'degradation', such detriment is caused when the goods or services for which the identical or similar sign is used by the third party may be perceived by the public in such a way that the trade mark's power of attraction is reduced. The likelihood of such detriment may arise in particular from the fact that the goods or services offered by the third party possess a characteristic or a quality which is liable to have a negative impact on the image of the mark."

3-387   Although the CJEU expressed tarnishment as occurring where the "power of attraction" of the trade mark is reduced, such could, if read widely, also apply to dilution by blurring. Tarnishment is generally used to apply to the case where the goods or services which the mark is used with have a negative impact on the image of the mark with the repute. Such requires investigation of the goods or services for which the sign is being used in connection with. In the case of oppositions, it requires investigation of the goods or services for which the applicant has applied. In the case of infringements, it requires investigation of the goods or services in connection with which the defendant has used the sign. If such goods or services have negative connotations, then such may be sufficient to make a finding of detriment by tarnishment. As said in *Elleni v Sigla*[659]:

"It must, therefore, be shown that the trade mark is sullied or debased by its association with something unseemly. This may happen when the applied for trade mark, to which the mark with reputation may be associated, is used, on the one hand, in an unpleasant, obscene or degrading context or, on the other hand, in a context which is not inherently unpleasant but which proves to be incompatible with the trade mark's image. In all cases, there is a comparison which is injurious to the trade mark's image and what is known in English as dilution by tarnishment. (see Decision of 25 April 2001, in Case R 283/1999–3, *HOLLYWOOD/HOLLYWOOD*, at [83])."

3-388   In *Hollywood v Souza Cruz*,[660] the Third Board of Appeal said on the subject of tarnishment:

"[86]   A trade mark is tarnished in this way when the consumer's ability to associate it with the goods or services for which it is registered by the fact that:
(a)   it is linked with goods of poor quality or which evoke undesirable or questionable mental associations which conflict with the associations or image generated by legitimate use of the trade mark by its proprietor;
(b)   it is linked with goods which are incompatible with the quality and prestige associated with the trade mark, even though it is not a matter of inappropriate use of the trade mark in itself;
(c)   its word or figurative element is amended or altered in a negative way.
[87]   Therefore the proprietor of the earlier trade mark must show that use of the applicant's trade mark would prompt inappropriate or at least negative mental associations with the opponent's trade mark, or associations conflicting with its image, which would be detrimental to it."

3-389   In that case, it was held that the use of HOLLYWOOD for tobacco and smoking articles was detrimental to the reputation of HOLLYWOOD which was a well-known chewing gum mark in France and which enjoyed a carefully nurtured brand image of health, youth and dynamism. The Board of Appeal held that tobacco has negative connotations which would be detrimental to the reputation of the registered

659   *Elleni Holding BV* (CR 1127/2000–3) [2005] E.T.M.R. 7, Third Board of Appeal.
660   *Hollywood v Souza Cruz* [2002] E.T.M.R. 64, Board of Appeal.

mark. In *Lucas Bols v Colgate-Palmolive*,[661] it was held by the Benelux Court of Justice that the use of KLAREIN for a detergent was detrimental to the reputation of a registered mark CLAERYN for gin as it impaired the capacity of the latter mark to stimulate the desire to buy. In the UK, it was held the use of VISA for condoms was detrimental to the reputation of VISA for financial services.[662] In contrast, in *SIGLA v EUIPO*, the General Court upheld the Boards of Appeal finding that VIPS for computer programming services for hotels and restaurants could not be considered to have any negative characteristics when considering an opposition by the owner of the mark VIPS for fast food.[663]

Standard of proof and quality of evidence

In *Intel v CPM*, the CJEU said, in considering the standard and burden of proof **3-390** in relation to proving dilution said that it must be shown that there is a clear and present injury to the mark or a serious risk that injury to the registered mark will occur in the future.[664] Such approach applies to unfair advantage and detriment to the repute of the mark. The General Court has said that it must be shown that the risk is non-hypothetical.[665] Such must be proven with cogent evidence and argument.[666] It will rarely be the case that unfair advantage or detriment is inferred, although it may be where the mark has an exceptionally high reputation.[667] The assessment as to whether there is a "serious risk" is based on logical deductions which are not the result of mere supposition and an analysis of probabilities taking account of normal practice in the relevant commercial sector.[668]

Without due cause

Historically, it was considered that "without due cause" should be construed very **3-391** narrowly. Thus, an old Dutch case which was concerned with the meaning of "without justifiable reason" in the Uniform Benelux Trade Mark Act[669] highlighted that it requires that the user of the mark be under such a compulsion to use the mark that they cannot honestly be asked to refrain from doing so, or that the user is entitled to the use of the mark in their own right and does not have to yield this right to the owner of the registered mark.[670] This approach was echoed by EUIPO in its earlier decisions, e.g. in *Hollywood*.[671]

However, in two landmark cases concerned with the interpretation of the **3-392** equivalent infringement provisions under the TMD, the CJEU has now made it clear

---

[661] *Lucas Bols* [1979] E.C.C. 419, Benelux Court of Justice.
[662] *CA Sheimer Trade Mark Application* [2000] R.P.C. 484, Appointed Person.
[663] *Sigla SA v EUIPO* (T-215/03) [2007] E.C.R. II-711 at [67]. Indeed, it could be said quite the opposite!
[664] See [38].
[665] (T-215/03), at [46]; *SPA-FINDERS* (C-67/04), at [34].
[666] *Creditmaster Trade Mark* [2005] R.P.C. 21, (Ch); *Elleni Holding (CR* 1127/2000–3) [2005] E.T.M.R. 7 Third Board of Appeal at [45].
[667] (T-215/03), at [48]. See also *Japan Tobacco Inc v EUIPO* (C-136/08P), at [42]; *Bimbo v EUIPO* (T-357/11), at [37]; *Nute Partecipazioni SpA and La Perla Srl v EUIPO* (T-59/08) [2010] E.R.C. II-05595 at [54].
[668] *Environmental Manufacturing LLP v OHIM* (C-383/12P) ECLI:EU:C:2013:741 at [42]–[43].
[669] Benelux law is generally considered to be the source for the unfair advantage/detriment provisions in the TMD and EUTMR.
[670] *Colgate Palmolive* [1979] E.C.C. 419. In the UK, see *Premier Brands v Typhoon* [2000] F.S.R. 767.
[671] *Hollywood v Souza Cruz* [2002] E.T.M.R. 64, Board of Appeal.

that a defence of "with due cause" to an allegation of infringement under art.10.2(c) TMD/art.9.2(c) EUTMR (reputation-based infringement provisions) is wider than was previously thought. These two cases are *Interflora v Marks and Spencer*[672] and *Leidseplein Beheer BV v Red Bull GmbH.*[673] *Interflora* is concerned with the use of the trade mark of a competitor as an Internet referencing keyword (Google Adword) to inform the Internet user who typed in the trade mark of the competing services that it provided (in that case, Marks and Spencer, a retailer, had successfully bid for INTERFLORA, the well-known flower delivery service mark, to advertise its own website which offered such services). Its relevance to an opposition based on relative rights is limited as a tribunal would not normally consider Internet keyword use when determining an opposition based on art.8.5 EUTMR (or art.5.3(a) TMD). Accordingly, it is considered later in this chapter when considering infringement.[674]

3-393   In *Leidseplein*, the CJEU was concerned with a defence of due cause based on "prior use" of the defendant's mark. Here, the defendant argued that it had been using its mark many years prior to the date of first use and registration of the claimant's mark asserted in the proceedings. In *Leidseplein* the CJEU was solely concerned with the proper interpretation of "due cause" under the TMD. It therefore took the opportunity to set out the principles underlying the concept. First, it said that the purpose of the TMD was generally to strike a balance between the interest which the proprietor of a trade mark has in safeguarding its essential function, on the one hand, and the interests of other economic operators in having signs capable of denoting their products and services.[675] The latter's interest can be taken account of when considering whether they have due cause to use the sign in issue.[676] Once the proprietor of a mark has established one of the three forms of injury (unfair advantage/tarnishment/dilution), the burden lies on the defendant to establish due cause for using the sign objected to.[677] The concept of "due cause" may include not only objectively overriding reasons to use the mark but also the subjective interest of the third party in using the sign.[678] A claim that there is due cause for using a sign similar to a mark with a reputation *"cannot lead to the recognition, for the benefit of that third party, the rights connected with a registered mark, but rather obliges the proprietor of the mark with a reputation to tolerate the use of the similar sign"*[679] The CJEU then said, when considering whether due cause could be established in the case where the defendant's sign had been used prior to the asserted registered mark being filed, that it was necessary for the national court to consider the degree of acceptance of the sign; the closeness between the goods and services for which the sign was originally used and the goods and services for which the asserted mark had a reputation; the economic and commercial significance of the use of that sign to the person using the sign; and the intention of the person using the sign and whether such use was in good faith.[680]

3-394   As said, *Leidseplein* is a case concerned with whether use of a sign which had been used prior to the date of filing of the asserted mark could amount to use with

---

[672] (C-323/09) ECLI:EU:C:2011:604, [2011] E.C.R. I-8625.
[673] (C-65/12) ECLI:EU:C:2014:49.
[674] See para.3-552.
[675] See [41].
[676] See [43].
[677] See [44].
[678] See [45].
[679] See [46].
[680] See [53]–[60].

due cause. It is clear from the Court of Justice's ruling in other areas[681] that despite the lack of an express defence of prior use in the TMD or EUTMR[682] that in the balancing act between the interests of a registered proprietor and third parties, that in certain circumstances, the interests of a third party will "trump" those of the registered proprietor, particularly where there has been a substantial period of bona fide prior use of a sign by that third party.

It should be noted that there is no defence of "due cause" where the registered proprietor asserts that the double identity rule has been infringed or because of use of an identical/similar mark in relation to identical/similar goods or services. As recognised by the CJEU in *Leidesplein*, the protection of trade marks with a reputation is more extensive than that for simple marks and will extend to situations where there may be no detriment to the distinctive character or repute of the mark (as in the case of unfair advantage).[683] Given such, it may be seen that the defence of "due cause" is a necessary counterweight to the wider protection that a trade mark proprietor can obtain for its mark under the reputation-based provisions and where there may be no risk of damage to the essential function of the registered mark.   **3-395**

It is less clear from *Interflora* and *Leidesplein* how relevant the defence of "due cause" is in opposition proceedings or cancellation proceedings. In such cases, the applicant for the later mark is not seeking to use the later mark but rather obtain rights in it. In *Leidesplein*, the CJEU said that the principle cannot lead to the recognition of rights connected with a registered mark but rather merely forces the proprietor of a trade mark to tolerate such use. Such an observation clearly is applicable only to infringement proceedings and not to a situation where an applicant does indeed seek rights of registration in a sign. In the decisions of the General Court, on appeal from EUIPO, the General Court has tended to dismiss any arguments based on due cause. It would appear from its decisions that for such a defence to be upheld, the applicant for the later mark must have a legitimate interest in using the later mark *and* a good and compelling reason to use it in order to defeat an otherwise good claim under art.8.5 EUTMR.[684] It might be added that there should be also be a good reason to register the sign (as opposed to merely use it). In its Guidelines, EUIPO takes the view that it is for the applicant to show that it has a *"legitimate justification that entitles it to use the mark"*.[685] However, such a formulation begs the question as to what is a legitimate justification that entitles the applicant to deny the otherwise proven rights of the earlier registered trade mark under art.8.5 EUTMR. EUIPO gives one example of legitimate justification being use of the sign for dissimilar goods prior to the opponent's mark being applied for or having acquired a reputation, especially where such coexistence has not affected the distinctiveness or repute of the earlier mark.[686]   **3-396**

In the author's view, the above authorities show that when considering due cause, a tribunal must weigh up on the one hand, the legitimate interests of a party being   **3-397**

---

[681] See para.3-537 where the Court of Justice has recognised a defence of "honest concurrent use".

[682] Other that the "particular locality" defence set out in art.14.3 TMD and art.138 EUTMR.

[683] See [39]–[40].

[684] e.g *Jackson International Trading Col. v EUIPO* (T-60/10) ECLI:EU:T:2012:348, in particular [68]; *L'Oreal SA v EUIPO* (T-21/07) ECLI:EU:T:2009:80, in particular [43]; *Kenzo Tsujimoto v EUIPO* (T-322/13) ECLI:EU:T:2015:47 (no due cause to register a surname or forename as a EUTM), see [47].

[685] Part C, para.3.5.

[686] The Guidelines give decisions of the Board of Appeal where due cause was found at para.3.5.1. In contrast, there would not appear to be any decisions of the General Court where such has been accepted.

able to continue to use a sign that has been used in good faith and which possesses its own reputation and goodwill and on the other hand, the harm or injury that will be caused to the owner of a registered mark with a reputation that ex hypothesi, has already established that the sign will take unfair advantage of or be detrimental to the distinctive character or repute of the its registered mark under art.8.5 EUTMR (or the equivalent in the TMD). If such favours the former, then a further check should be carried out as to whether the party has a legitimate interest in seeking to register the sign (as opposed to merely requiring the registered proprietor of the registered mark to tolerate such use). A good reason may be to protect the reputation and goodwill that the sign has.

Proof of use of earlier registered marks in opposition proceedings/cancellation proceedings

3-398   Under both the EUTMR and the TMD, where a registered mark is relied upon to oppose an application for a later mark, and more than five years has expired from the date of registration, the applicant may request that the owner of the earlier mark provide evidence that the earlier mark has been put to genuine use for the five-year period preceding the filing date or priority date of the later trade mark or that proper reasons for non-use existed.[687] If this particular request is made, the owner of the earlier mark must provide such evidence. In essence, the examining body then determines such as if an application has been made to revoke the earlier mark for lack of genuine use.[688] However, unlike a revocation for genuine use which, if successful would result in the earlier mark being revoked, the only effect is that the opposition is rejected (or if successful in relation to some of the goods or services, then the opposition proceeds on the basis of the earlier mark only being registered for the other goods or services).

3-399   A similar request also applies to cancellation proceedings where the owner of an earlier registered trade mark seeks to cancel a later national mark or EUTM based on the earlier mark.[689]

Unregistered trade marks and other rights

3-400   Both the EUTMR and the TMD provide for opposition to an application or cancellation of a registered mark on the basis that this conflicts with an earlier unregistered mark or "to another sign" where such give the owner the right to prohibit the use of the later mark.[690] Furthermore, the EUTMR and TMD also provide for relative grounds based on other earlier rights, and in particular, a right to a name, personal portrayal, copyright or industrial property right. However, in the case of the EUTMR, this is only a ground of cancellation and not a ground of opposition.[691] Finally, the EUTMR and TMD also provide for opposition or cancellation based on earlier GIOs (geographical indications of origin, being a PDO or PGI) where such would allow the person authorised under the relevant law to

---

[687] art.44.1 TMD; art.47.2 EUTMR.
[688] See para.3-674 for revocation proceedings for lack of genuine use.
[689] art 46.1 TMD; art 64.2, 64.3 EUTMR.
[690] art.8.4, 59 EUTMR; art.5.4(a), 45 TMD.
[691] art.5.4(b) TMD; art.60.2 EUTMR.

enforce such against the later mark.[692] These categories of rights are now considered.

Rights other than trade marks

Article 53.2 EUTMR allows the owner of "earlier rights" under the national law of Member States or EU law to seek to cancel existing registered EU marks. In particular, these rights are rights to a name, a right of personal portrayal, a copyright, or an industrial property right.[693] As said, the owner of such an earlier right cannot oppose an application but merely seek cancellation of an existing EUTM. There are two main requirements for such an action to succeed: (i) The right must be an earlier right. Although this is not defined, it seems clear that such a right must have existed as of the filing date or if earlier, the priority date of the EUTM.[694] (ii) The earlier right must entitle the owner to prohibit the use of the trade mark applied for.[695] Thus, a tribunal must consider the outcome of a hypothetical infringement action brought by the owner of the earlier right as of the date of filing (or priority if earlier) against the use of the later mark displayed on (or in the case of a shape mark, incorporated into) the goods covered by the specification or (in the case of services) used in relation to such services covered by the specification and whether the owner of the earlier right would be entitled to injunctive relief.

3-401

Unregistered marks

The EUTMR and TMD also provide some degree of protection for unregistered marks. The EUTMR allows the proprietor of a non-registered trade mark or sign which is more than mere local significance to oppose an application for a mark where the right to the mark or sign was acquired prior to the date of filing (or priority if earlier) for a later EUTM and such confers on the proprietor the right to prohibit the use of the EUTM applied for.[696] The TMD has a similar provision but there is no requirement that the non-registered mark be of more than mere local significance.

3-402

The ability to prevent use of a mark by reason of an earlier unregistered mark may arise by reason of the laws of unfair competition, laws relating to appellations of origins,[697] or in the case of the UK and Eire, by reason of the law of passing off.

3-403

The right of the owner of an unregistered mark to prevent the registration of a trade mark varies enormously from country to country. In certain countries, like the UK, under the law of passing off, a party who has a substantial reputation and goodwill in a trade mark can prevent the use of a confusingly similar mark in relation to goods or services where such would deceive the public. It is not necessary for the goods or services on which the defendant's mark is used to be the same or similar to that on which the unregistered mark has been used. However, it is easier to establish passing off where the mark has been used on the same or similar goods

3-404

---

[692] art.8.6, 59 EUTMR; art.5.3(c), 45 TMD.

[693] art.53.2(a)–(d).

[694] See by analogy, art.53.1(c) and last sentence of art.53.1.

[695] art.53.2.

[696] art.8.4 EUTMR.

[697] e.g. see *Budejovický Budvar v EUIPO* (T-225/06, T-255/06 & T-309/06) [2008] E.C.R. II-3555. See para.3-406.

or services. It is not within the ambit of this book to consider in detail the law of passing off.[698] In other countries, protection is afforded to unregistered marks only in limited circumstances, i.e. the mark is a well-known mark within the meaning of art.6*bis* of the Paris Convention. In some cases, the unregistered mark may be protected as an appellation of origin.[699]

3-405   It is not necessary that the unregistered mark act as an indication of origin of a single undertaking. In *Tilda Riceland Private Ltd v EUIPO (BASMATI)*[700] the opponent relied upon the UK "extended passing off" right. This is a right conferred on a sign which has come to indicate a definable set of characteristics in goods (usually foodstuffs). In this case it was argued that "Basmati" had come to indicate a certain type of rice. The General Court upheld an appeal from EUIPO who had held that art.8(4) EUTMR only protected unregistered marks which acted as an indication of origin. It held that no such limitation could be implied into art.8(4) which was widely drawn.

Geographical Indications of Origin

3-406   The EUTMR and TMD now provide for a ground of opposition based upon an earlier protected designation of origin ("PDO") or a protected geographical indication ("PGI").[701] These are creatures of EU law and are discussed at the end of this chapter.[702] Again, as with unregistered marks, it is necessary to consider whether the use of the later mark could be prohibited by exercise of the PDO or PGI. It is of note that there is no provision under the relative rights grounds for names which are Traditional Specialities Guaranteed ("TSG").[703] However, the name of a TSG is likely to be a right bestowed by EU law and thus is protectable under art.8.4 EUTMR if it is of more than mere local significance.

3-407   It might be thought that the introduction of protection for PDOs and PGIs would mean that signs which act as geographical indications of origin but which are not protected under EU law as PDOs or PGIs cannot be relied upon as a ground of opposition. However, it is submitted that this would be wrong. Article 8(6) EUTMR is a separate ground to art.8.4(a) EUTMR. The former protects unregistered signs that have been used in the course of trade and are of more than mere local significance. In contrast, art.8.4(a) protects geographical indications or "quality" marks protected under national laws of Member States regardless of whether they are protected under EU law as PDOs or PGIs. Thus, the General Court has said that a cancellation applicant can rely upon national laws of Member States that protect

---

[698] In the author's opinion, the seminal book is C. Wadlow, *The Law of Passing-Off: Unfair Competition by Misrepresentation*, 5th edn (London: Sweet & Maxwell, 2016). A simplistic approach to passing off when considering art.8(4) as amounting to a likelihood of confusion was criticised by the General Court in *Last Minute Network v EUIPO* (T-114/07 and T-115/07) [2009] E.C.R. II-1919.

[699] e.g. see *Budejovický Budvar v EUIPO* (T-53/04) [2004] E.C.R. II-57 where the earlier right relied upon was French law which gives protection to appellations of origin. Upon detailed consideration of that law including decisions of French court, the General Court held that the ground of opposition was not made out.

[700] (T-136/14) EU:T:2015:734

[701] art 8.6 EUTMR. This ground is discussed at para.3-907.

[702] See para.3-855.

[703] Although this can be an absolute ground for refusal. See para.3-286.

geographical indications of origin and that in this regard, it was irrelevant that there was also an EU system of protection for such.[704]

Proof of the earlier right

Often the reliance upon a right conferred by a Member State may require detailed **3-408** analysis of the national legislation, relevant national case law and indeed academic commentary. In the UK, proof of foreign national law is a matter for expert evidence and is considered a matter of fact to be proven in the same way as other facts. In relation to hearings before EUIPO and appeals, the CJEU has had to consider how such should be proved and whether the court or tribunal can make its own investigation. In *National Lottery Commission v EUIPO*,[705] an applicant for a declaration of invalidity of a figurative mark claimed that it infringed earlier Italian copyright in a figurative sign. In bitter dispute was the authenticity of an agreement to which the drawing on which copyright was claimed was attached. The registered proprietor claimed it was a forgery. This necessitated consideration of Italian law concerning the proof of documents and whether such could be challenged as forgeries. On appeal to the General Court, the General Court, without reference to the parties, examined a decision of the Italian Supreme Court of Cassation for the purpose of interpreting art.2704 of the Italian Civil Code and held that the Board of Appeal had misinterpreted its powers to conclude whether the document was genuine or not. On appeal to the Court of Justice, EUIPO argued that the General Court had exceeded its powers by investigating the scope of Italian law and furthermore had infringed the right to be heard by failing to ask EUIPO for its comments on the Italian Supreme Court of Cassation decision. On the first ground, the Court of Justice held that there was a positive duty on the General Court to investigate the scope and effect of national law.[706] However, this is not an excuse for the applicant relying upon national law under art.8.4(a) EUTMR to not adduce evidence of that law. It must adduce particulars establishing the content of that law.[707] On the second point, it held that the General Court had infringed the principle that a party should be heard by failing to give EUIPO the opportunity to comment on the Italian Supreme Court decision.[708]

---

[704] *IVDP v EUIPO* (T-659/14) EU:T:2015:863. Here, the General Court annulled the decision of the Board of the Appeal of EUIPO allowing registration of PORT CHARLOTTE for alcoholic beverages. The Cancellation Applicant, a Portuguese trade association for port producers, relied upon the well-known appellation of origin "porto" and "port". It claimed that such were protected by Portuguese law and EU Reg.491/2009 (EU GIO legislation now replaced). The General Court held that art.8.4 allowed a cancellation applicant to rely upon the laws of Member States which protected geographical indications of origin and that it was irrelevant that there was also a EU system of protection for wine appellations of origin under EU Reg.491/2009. In particular, it held that art.8.4 refers to earlier rights under EU legislation or national law. See also *Tilda Riceland* cited above at para.3-405 ("Basmati" quality mark protectable under art.8(4)(a)).

[705] (C-530/12P) ECLI:EU:C:2014:186.

[706] See [43]–[47].

[707] e.g. see *Staywell Universal Protein Supplements Corp v EUIPO* (T-727/14 and T-728/14) ECLI:EU:T:2016:372 (reference to EUIPO Guidelines on national laws protecting unregistered marks was not sufficient) at [30]. Rather, EUIPO's duty is to verify and check the accuracy of the particulars of national law put forward by the opponent or cancellation applicant.

[708] See [57]–[62].

Of more than mere local significance

3-409   Article 8.4 EUTMR requires that the earlier right must have more than mere local significance. This means that the right relied upon cannot be local. The provision should be read in conjunction with art.138 EUTMR which deals with "local"
earlier rights and their interaction with EUTMs. Thus, unregistered marks which
qualify as "local" rights under art.138 cannot prevent registration of EUTMs but
can be relied upon to prevent the use of EUTMs in the locality where the local mark
is known.[709] Conversely, a EUTM cannot be used to prevent the use of a "local"
right.[710]

3-410   Such being the case, it is a reasonable inference that the draughtsmen of the
EUTMR felt that there was no need to prevent the registration of a EUTM if the
right was merely "local". In other words, if the owner of the "local" right was suitably protected under art.138, it would be disproportionate to allow the owner of a
local right to prevent the registration of a EUTM which seeks protection throughout
the EU. It is tempting thus to conclude (as the wording would suggest) that in any
action for infringement of a EUTM against an undertaking which has used its mark
in a limited area in the EU, the owner of unregistered rights in a mark of a local
nature would be assured that, depending on the court's view of the extent of
geographical use, the EUTM will either be found invalid (if the use is of more than
mere local significance) or if use is merely local, give rise to a defence under
art.138.

3-411   The requirement that the mark must be of more than mere local significance in
art.8.4 was considered in *Anheuser-Busch Inc v Budějovický Budvar, národní
podnik*.[711] The CJEU had to consider whether this requirement meant that it must
be shown that the mark in which the territory was protected was of more than mere
local significance or that the mark had been used in a territory which was of more
than mere local significance. It held that the latter was applicable. Therefore, where
a mark has had limited use but under national law, the geographical extent of protection is wide, it may not be sufficient to satisfy the "more than mere local
significance" requirement. As the Court of Justice said, overturning the General
Court on this point, the right of opposition under art.8.4 must be reserved to signs
which actually have a real presence on the relevant market.[712]

3-412   Whether a mark has been used in a territory that does have more than mere local significance, the test is a multi-factorial one taking account of duration of use,
intensity of use, geographical extent of use and the population exposed to such a
mark.[713]

Acts of agents

3-413   In some cases, an agent or representative of the proprietor of a mark may apply
for registration in their own name without the consent of the proprietor. In such
circumstances, unless the agent or representative can justify their action, such would

---

[709] art.138.1.
[710] art.138.3. See para.3-513.
[711] (C-96/09P) [2011] E.C.R. 2131.
[712] See [155]–[160].
[713] *Anheuser-Busch Inc v Budějovický Budvar, národní podnik*, at [160]. See also *McCann Erickson
Advertising Ltd's Trade Mark Application* [2001] E.T.M.R. 52 at [32]–[35] (Board of Appeal).

amount to a valid ground of opposition.[714] This has its origins in art.6*septies* of the Paris Convention.[715] As said by the General Court[716]:

> "[83] It should be noted that Article 8(3) of Regulation No 40/94 is designed to prevent the misuse of a mark by the trade mark proprietor's agent, as the agent may exploit the knowledge and experience acquired during its business relationship with the proprietor and therefore improperly benefit from the effort and investment which the trade mark proprietor himself made."

The above suggests that art.8.3 requires the application to have been made in bad **3-414** faith. One might wonder therefore what the point of art.8.3 is if a EUTM registration can be declared invalid on the grounds that it was applied for in bad faith.[717] Certainly, EUIPO takes the view that the protection granted by art.8.3 is narrower than the right to cancel a granted EUTM for bad faith provided for by art.59.1(b) EUTMR and that the fact that the applicant filed the application in bad faith is not in itself sufficient for the purposes of art.8.3.[718] The only satisfactory answer is that art.8.3 is a ground of opposition whereas art.59.1(b) can only be invoked after registration of the mark and that the Paris Convention mandates such a ground.

The General Court has said that "agent" and "representative" must be interpreted **3-415** broadly[719]:

> "[64] … so as to cover all kinds of relationships based on a contractual arrangement under which one party is representing the interests of the other, regardless of how the contractual relationship between the proprietor or principal, on the one hand, and the applicant for the Community trade mark, on the other, is categorised. According to those guidelines, it is sufficient for the purposes of [Article 8.3 EUTMR] that there be some agreement of commercial co-operation between the parties of a kind that gives rise to a fiduciary relationship by imposing on the trade mark applicant – whether expressly or implicitly—a general duty of trust and loyalty as regards the interests of the trade mark proprietor. Nevertheless, some kind of agreement has to exist between the parties. If the applicant acts completely independently, without having entered into any kind of relationship with the proprietor, he cannot be treated as an agent for the purposes of [Article 8.3 EUTMR]. Thus, a mere purchaser or client of the proprietor cannot be regarded as an 'agent' or as a 'representative' for the purposes of that provision, since such persons are under no special obligation of trust to the trade mark proprietor."

If consent is alleged by the applicant, it would appear that such must be shown **3-416** as being clear, specific and unconditional.[720] This no doubt arises from the general approach of EU law that any consent to the use of a registered mark must be unequivocally demonstrated.[721] Bearing in mind that under art.8(3), the need to show consent will only arise if, bar consent, the agent or representative has acted in circumstances akin to bad faith, it is perhaps not surprising that courts or tribunals

---

[714] art.8.3 EUTMR.
[715] See para.3-015.
[716] *Safariland v EUIPO* (T-262/09) [2011] E.C.R. II-1629.
[717] art.59.(1)(b) EUTMR. See generally, para.3-289.
[718] *Opposition Guidelines*, Part 3, para.1.2.
[719] *Safariland LLC v EUIPO* (T-262/09) ECLI:EU:T:2011:171. The General Court found that such was not satisfied where the relationship was merely one of seller-customer—see [67]–[73].
[720] See *Def-Tec Defense Technology GmbH v EUIPO* (T-6/05) [2006] E.C.R. II-2671 at [39]–[40]. However, here the applicant did not challenge that it was an agent—see [39].
[721] See paras 3-526 and 3-418.

should be obliged to examine very carefully any argument by the applicant that the proprietor of the mark has consented.

Consent, acquiescence and honest concurrent usage

3-417   In certain circumstances, even though an undertaking has an earlier right which it wishes to invoke against an application for a mark, the undertaking may be prevented from doing so. This may be on the basis that the undertaking has either consented to the application or is debarred from objecting to its application because it has acquiesced in the application.

Consent

3-418   Under art.5.5 TMD, Member States can "in appropriate circumstances" permit registration of a trade mark where the proprietor of an earlier trade mark or earlier right consents to the registration of the earlier mark. Surprisingly, the EUTMR does not expressly permit the applicant for a EUTM to rely upon consent by an opponent to registration of a mark.[722] However, following registration, a EUTM cannot be declared invalid where the proprietor of the earlier mark or right consents expressly to the registration of the EUTM before submission of the application for a declaration of invalidity or the counterclaim.[723]

3-419   Thus, in a General Court case, the court considered that even if a co-existence agreement did amount to an agreement not to oppose registration of a mark, such was irrelevant to the assessment of the likelihood of confusion.[724] This very peculiar anomaly was considered by the High Court of England in *Omega Engineering*. In that case, the judge said that it would be "bizarre" to interpret the EUTMR in such a manner. As he said, why should an application be refused in opposition proceedings if it could not be invalidated once registered on precisely the same grounds.[725]

3-420   In *Dalsouple Société Saumuroise Du Caoutchouc v Dalsouple Direct Ltd*,[726] the High Court of England had to consider the approach to the determination of whether one party had consented to the application by another for a registered trade mark. In this case, the issue was whether a French manufacturer had orally consented to the application by its English distributor for a UK registered mark DALSOUPLE. Oral testimony was given in the Trade Mark Registry by the CEO of the English company that many years ago, the CEO of the French company had given his oral consent to the application being made by the English company. The latter died in 2000 and accordingly, it was the English CEO's testimony on oath which was tested in cross examination. Having heard the oral evidence, the Registry found that consent had been given although it might have been thought inherently improbable. On appeal, the French manufacturer argued that such a finding was not open to the

---

[722] Unless the objection is based on art.7.1(i) (objection based upon mark including badges, emblems or escutcheons) or art.8.3 (agent applying for registration in their own name).

[723] art.60.3 EUTMR.

[724] *Omega SA v EUIPO* (T- 90/05) ECLI:EU:T:2007:328 at [49]. However, there is no reasoning to this.

[725] *Omega Engineering v Omega SA* [2010] E.T.M.R. 49 at [118]. This oddity also influenced the decision of the Board of Appeal in *Sedea Electronique SA v Visionic* (R-946/2007) and (R-1151/2007–2) (2nd Board of Appeal, EUIPO) where the Board held that the proprietor of the earlier mark's consent to registration of a trade mark by another party is tantamount to the renunciation of the right to oppose the application for registration of the trade mark—cited at [116], *Omega Engineering*.

[726] [2014] EWHC 3963.

Registry because it needed to be shown, applying *Zino Davidoff v A&G Imports*[727] that consent had to be shown unequivocally. It said that the English CEO's evidence fell short of such a high standard.

The High Court accepted the legal point but dismissed the appeal. It held that **3-421** consent in the TMD should be given an autonomous and uniform interpretation and should be interpreted in the same way as consent in art.7.1 of the Directive (as interpreted by the CJEU in *Davidoff*). However, following that decision, it said that express consent was deemed by the CJEU as being unequivocal[728]. The High Court further said that it need not be in writing and that the determination of whether consent was express was to be determined by the national court in accordance with its own rules of evidence and procedure. The judge held that was exactly what the Hearing Officer in the Trade Marks Registry had so found and accordingly dismissed the appeal.

Acquiescence

In certain circumstances, the owner of the earlier right may be deemed to have **3-422** acquiesced in the registration for an earlier mark. Article 61.1 EUTMR says as follows:

"1. Where the proprietor of an EU trade mark has acquiesced, for a period of five successive years, in the use of a later EU trade mark in the Union while being aware of such use, he shall no longer be entitled on the basis of the earlier trade mark to apply for a declaration that the later trade mark is invalid in respect of the goods or services for which the later trade mark has been used, unless registration of the later EU trade mark was applied for in bad faith."

Article 61.2 EUTMR provides for a similar provision where the earlier mark is a national mark.[729]

The meaning of "acquiesce" has been interpreted by the CJEU.[730] The CJEU held **3-423** that "acquiesce" does not mean the same as "consent" which requires an unequivocal renunciation of the right.[731] It said:

"[44] As observed by the Advocate General in point 70 of her Opinion, referring in particular to the Danish and Swedish language versions of Article 9 of Directive 89/104, the characteristic of a person who acquiesces is that he is passive and declines to take measures open to him to remedy a situation of which he is aware and which is not necessarily as he wishes. To put that another way, the concept of 'acquiescence' implies that the person who acquiesces remains inactive when faced with a situation which he would be in a position to oppose.

[45] For the purposes of [Article 9.1 TMD], that concept of 'acquiescence' must therefore be interpreted as meaning that the proprietor of an earlier trade mark cannot be held to have acquiesced in the long and well-established honest use, of which he has long been aware, by a third party of a later trade mark which is identical with that of the proprietor if that proprietor was not in any position to oppose that use."

---

[727] (C-414/99) ECLI:EU:C:2001:617. See para.3-531.

[728] See *Dalsouple*, at [37]–[40], citing *Zino Davidoff*, at [46].

[729] See also equivalent provision in art.9.1 TMD. Article 9.2 TMD allows Member States to provide for a similar right of acquiescence for unregistered prior rights.

[730] *Budějovický Budvar, národní podnik v Anheuser-Busch Inc* (C-482/09) ECLI:EU:C:2011:605/ ECLI:EU:C:2011:46.

[731] *Budějovický Budvar, národní podnik v Anheuser-Busch Inc* (C-482/09) ECLI:EU:C:2011:605/ ECLI:EU:C:2011:46 at [43].

3-424   Thus, the proprietor of the earlier mark must have been in a position to have prevented the application of the earlier mark or (in the case of infringement), its use. The CJEU said in *Budweiser* that the five-year time limitation period ran from the date when the following four conditions have all been satisfied, namely:

(i)   the later trade mark has been registered,

(ii)   the application for that later trade mark was made in good faith,

(iii)   the later trade mark has been used in the Member State where it is registered, and

(iv)   the proprietor of the earlier trade mark knew that the later trade mark had been registered and used after its registration.[732]

3-425   It is important to note that the above four conditions must *all* be satisfied. For example, in the case of applications for declaration of invalidity, this provision has no application if the later registered mark has not been used. Therefore, the limitation period starts to run when the proprietor of the earlier trade mark becomes aware of the use of the later registered EUTM which must be a date later than that of registration of the later EUTM. It is at this point that the owner of the earlier EUTM has the option of not acquiescing and thus opposing it.[733] There is some suggestion in the EUIPO Guidelines that when considering awareness of the later EUTM, it is sufficient to show that the owner of the earlier EUTM could reasonably be presumed to be aware of it.[734] It would be surprising if this was the case. It would mean that if as a matter of fact, the owner of the earlier EUTM was not aware of the later registered mark but should have been, they can be deemed to have acquiesced. As this provision amounts to an extinction of an earlier right that would have otherwise existed, it is submitted that nothing other than actual awareness should suffice. Furthermore, there is nothing in the Court of Justice decision to show that awareness can be presumed. Of course, it may be that if the owner of the earlier EUTM could reasonably be presumed to have been aware of the later EUTM, the owner of the earlier EUTM has the evidential burden to show that they were not aware. However, that is all.

3-426   Finally, it should be said that the incorporation into the EUTMR and TMD of a EU concept of acquiescence means that there is no room for a defence of acquiescence or abusive exercise or other defences based on the laws of Member States.[735]

Honest concurrent usage

3-427   Even if the conditions for acquiescence are not satisfied, the CJEU said in *Budweiser* that a long period of honest concurrent use may defeat an objection based upon earlier rights if it is not established that use of the later mark has or is

---

[732]   (C-482/09), at [62].

[733]   e.g. see *Antonio Basile* (T-133/09) EU:T:2012:327 at [33]. It is the date of registration and not the date of filing of the later EUTM that is relevant, see *Antonio Basile*, at [33].

[734]   Part D, Cancellation, para.4.5.3.

[735]   e.g. see *Marussia Communications Ireland Ltd v Manor Grand Prix Racing Ltd* [2016] EWHC 809 (Ch.) (English concept of "estoppel by acquiescence" not allowed as a defence to action for trade mark infringement) citing *Zino Davidoff*, at [41], [58] and *Martin Y Paz SA v Depuydt* (C-661/11) ECLI:EU:C:2013:577 (no defence to trade mark infringement that enforcement of trade mark is abusive or unfair).

liable to have an adverse effect on the essential function of the trade mark.[736] It should be emphasised that honest concurrent usage is an exceptional defence to an opposition or infringement action. It will usually be raised as a defence to trade mark infringement and is discussed later in this chapter.[737]

Infringement

Both the EUTMR and the TMD exhaustively harmonise EU law on the rights of the owners of national marks registered in a Member State and EUTMs and the defences to the same.[738] Whilst EUIPO is responsible for granting a EUTM, they are enforced in Member States by EU Trade Mark Courts. Unlike national marks, the EUTM, being a unitary right, EU Trade Mark Courts can (and normally should) grant injunctions and damages for the whole of the EU.[739] The rights conferred by the TMD for national marks and the EUTMR for EUTMs are essentially the same save that, as said above, the EUTM covers the whole of the EU. Unlike the old TMD, the provisions of the new TMD concerning the rights of EUTM owners are all mandatory.   **3-428**

Rights mirror requirements of registrability

Not only are the rights granted to national marks and EUTMs the same but also they can be considered the mirror image of the provisions on registrability. For instance, the rights of a EUTM extend to the use of a sign which are the same or similar to the EUTM when used in relation to goods or services the same or similar to the goods or services protected by the EUTM. However, an application for a EUTM which is the same or similar to an earlier registration that protects goods or services the same or similar to that for which protection is sought in the application can be refused (or if registered, declared invalid). This is deliberate. It means that it will rarely be possible for an earlier mark or other right to infringe a later registered mark without it giving rise to grounds to invalidate the later registered mark. Thus, there is a symmetry between the grounds of registrability and infringement. It also permits "squeeze" arguments whereby a defendant can argue that either a later similar mark is invalidly registered by reason of the defendant's earlier mark or the defendant's earlier mark does not infringe.[740]   **3-429**

---

[736] See [74]. It might be thought odd that the CJEU only referred to the essential function of a mark but such would appear to be the case because the referring question only asked what the position is in relation to the essential function of the earlier mark-see *Budweiser*, at [26]. Thus, there is no reason to think that the tribunal considering the application should not reflect upon the effect on all the functions of the earlier mark. On application of the CJEU's decision in the UK, the Court of Appeal held that by reason of the long co-existence of the two marks, the application for a declaration of invalidity failed-[2013] R.P.C. 12.

[737] See para.3-537.

[738] e.g. see *Martin y Paz SA v Depuydt* (C-661/11) ECLI:EU:C:2013:577, at [54] and cases cited therein.

[739] art.1.2 EUTMR. See para.3-839.

[740] Although care must be taken in applying this provision because the relevant date for infringement is the date on which the defendant started using its mark, whereas for invalidity proceedings it is the date of application of the mark. It may be that the registered mark's scope of protection has increased over the period from filing by reason of its distinctive character being enhanced by use of the mark over the intervening period. Thus, a squeeze argument failed on this point in an English case-see *Hasbro Inc, Hasbro SA and Hasbro UK Ltd v 123 Nahrmittel GmbH and Marketing & Promotional Services Ltd* [2011] F.S.R. 21 at [82].

Infringement: abstracted marketplace

3-430   When a tribunal determines invalidity or opposition proceedings against a later mark based on an earlier mark, its approach is to consider the use of those marks in a hypothetical marketplace for the goods covered by the respective application or registration. For instance, where the owner of an earlier mark alleges that an application for a later mark would give rise to a likelihood of confusion with the earlier mark, the tribunal will consider use of both marks for their respective specifications in a hypothetical marketplace.[741] In infringement proceedings, the tribunal is concerned with actual use in the marketplace of the sign alleged to infringe rather than use of the later mark in the hypothetical marketplace. However, as will be seen, even in infringement proceedings, one cannot take account of every and all circumstances of use in the marketplace. Thus, a fake Rolex watch sold with a large disclaimer on it saying "fake" does not mean that it does not infringe the ROLEX trade mark. Thus, even in infringement proceedings, there is some degree of abstraction of the marketplace.

3-431   The assessment of infringement should follow the steps laid out below:

- First, the tribunal must identify the "sign" used by the defendant and the goods or services which it is used in relation to.
- The tribunal should then consider normal and fair use of the asserted mark for the goods and services for which it is registered
- Then, ignoring *extraneous material* but not the context of use, the tribunal should consider the use of the sign and the goods or services for which it is used in a hypothetical marketplace where the asserted mark has been used for the goods or services for which it is registered. In doing so, the tribunal may also take account of actual use in the marketplace of the asserted mark, e.g. for the purpose of establishing whether it has acquired distinctive character or established a reputation.
- Having done so, it should ask itself whether the alleged infringement (e.g. likelihood of confusion or unfair advantage) has been made out.[742]

Summary of exclusive rights

3-432   By reason of the symmetry discussed above, the exclusive rights of a national trade in a Member State or a EUTM extend to prohibiting the use of a sign in relation to goods or services where: (i) both the sign and goods/services are identical to the asserted registered mark, (ii) the sign is identical or similar to the earlier mark and is used for identical or similar goods or services to those protected by the earlier mark such as to give rise to a likelihood of confusion, and (iii) the sign is identical or similar to the earlier mark and its use would take unfair advantage of or be detrimental to the distinctive character or repute of the earlier mark.[743]

3-433   As discussed, these mirror the grounds of opposition or invalidity of applications or registered marks. Accordingly, many of the principles have already been discussed, namely the meaning of:

---

[741] See para.3-322.

[742] Where the infringement action is based on the reputation of the earlier mark, the specification of goods or services of the earlier mark is largely (but not wholly) irrelevant. See para.3-357. See also para.3-448 (context of use).

[743] art.10 TMD; art.9 EUTMR.

(a) identical and similar marks[744];
(b) identical and similar goods or services[745];
(c) likelihood of confusion[746];
(d)
-   unfair advantage:
-   detriment to the reputation of a mark; and
-   detriment to the repute of a mark.[747]

Furthermore, many of the principles established by the Court of Justice and **3-434** General Court in interpreting these provisions have been applied to both infringement and validity of marks. Thus, the courts have applied the same principles for likelihood of confusion to both infringement and validity. Therefore, it would be an exercise in repetition to set those principles out in this section on infringement.

Issues peculiar to infringement

The following issues thus arise when considering infringement regardless of **3-435** whether the mark is national mark or a EUTM and are peculiar to the issue of infringement. They thus have not been discussed already in the context of relative grounds of opposition. They are:

- Does the *use* adversely affect one or more functions of the registered trade mark? This is discussed at para.3-439.
- Identifying the "sign". Is the context of use of the sign relevant? Can one take into account, e.g. disclaimers? This is discussed at para.3-446.
- Who is liable for proven acts of infringement? Intermediaries such as ISPs; sub-contractors, accessories, directors? This is discussed at para.3-454.
- Is the sign used "in the course of trade"? E.g. would use of a sign by a charity infringe? This is discussed at para.3-477.
- Is the sign being used "in relation to" goods or services? Does this require that it be shown that the sign is being used as an indication of origin of the goods or services? This is discussed at para.3-478.
- What types of use infringe? E.g. advertising, packaging, etc. This is discussed at para.3-483.
- Is the infringing act occuring in the territory protected by the mark? As this is relevant primarily to Internet use, it is discussed in the section on Internet use (see para.3-549).

Defences

- It is also necessary to consider the defences. These are a mixture of express **3-436** defences in the EUTMR/TMD and also "case law defences. This is discussed at para.3-488.

Express defences

- Honest use of own name. This is discussed at para.3-491. **3-437**

---

744 See paras 3-335 and 3-356.
745 See para.3-338.
746 See para.3-347.
747 See para.3-352.

- Honest use of signs or indications to refer to characteristics of goods or services. This is discussed at para.3-495.
- Honest "referential" use (use of sign to refer to goods or services of the proprietor). This is discussed at para.3-502.
- Local prior use. This is discussed at para.3-573.
- Use of a later registered mark. This is discussed at para.3-515.
- Acquiescence in use of sign. This is discussed at para.3-522.
- Consent to use of sign. This is discussed at para.3-526.

Special situations

3-438   It is also necessary to consider infringement in special situations. These are:

- Honest concurrent use/co-existing marks. This is discussed at para.3-537.
- Internet use. This is discussed at para.3-544.
- Comparative advertisements. This is discussed at para.3-562.
- "In transit" infringement where goods are passing through the EU. This is discussed at para.3-584.
- Exhaustion of rights in a trade mark or EUTM. Technically, this is a defence but it is a topic in itself and is thus considered separately. This is discussed at para.3-590.
- Sales by a licensee in breach of a licence. This is discussed at para.3-664.

Adversely affects one or more functions of a trade mark

Double identity of marks and goods/services

3-439   It is now firmly established for infringement to be made out under the "double identity" provisions (i.e identical mark/sign, identical goods or services) of the TMD and EUTMR, it must be shown that the defendant's use must adversely affect or be liable to affect one or more of the functions of a trade mark which includes not only the essential function of a mark but also its other functions, in particular, those of communication, investment or advertising.[748] Indeed, it is in infringement cases that the court has primarily developed this doctrine and discussed the nature and extent of these functions. Earlier in this chapter, we considered in detail these functions and the reader is invited to read this section.[749] The CJEU has referred to the need that the functions of a mark be adversely affected in the following infringement cases:

(a)   The sale of unauthorised football club scarves and other shirts which displayed registered trade marks of a football club where it was argued by

---

[748] *Céline v Céline SARL* (C-17/06) [2007] E.C.R. I-07041 at [16]. See also *Arsenal Football Club v Reed* (C-206/01) [2002] E.C.R. I-10273 at [51]; *Anheuser-Busch Inc v Budějovický Budvar, národní podnik* (C-254/02) [2004] E.C.R. I-10989 at [59]; *Adam Opel AG v Autec AG (Deutscher Verband der Spielwaren-Industrie eV intervening)* (C-48/05) [2007] E.C.R. I-1017 at [21]; *O2 Holdings Ltd v Hutchison 3G UK Ltd* (C-533/06) [2008] E.C.R. I-4231, [2008] E.T.M.R. 55 at [57]; *L'Oréal v Bellure* (C-487/07) [2009] E.C.R. I-5185 at [63]–[65]; *UDV North America Inc v Brandtraders NV* (C-62/08) [2009] E.C.R. I-1279, [2010] E.T.M.R. 25 at [42]; *Google France* (C-236/08) [2010] E.C.R. I-2417 at [75]); *Interflora v Marks and Spencer* (C-323/09) [2011] E.C.R. I-8625 at [37].
[749] See para.3-069.

the defendant that purchasers bought them as badges of allegiance and not because they saw them as indications of trade origin.[750]

(b) The use of a car marque on model cars where it was argued that such was necessary for the purpose of making realistic model cars and such was not being used as an indication of origin of the model cars.[751]

(c) In comparative advertisements where the advertiser refers to the registered mark of a competitor.[752]

(d) Where the registered mark is used as an Internet keyword by a competitor to attract Internet traffic to the competitor's website.[753]

(e) Where the registered mark was used in comparison lists for perfumes so as to inform the reader what the imitation perfume smelt like.[754]

(f) Where a registered mark is used as a shop name.[755]

(g) Where a registered mark is used as a company name or trading name.[756]

Unused marks and functions of a mark

One aspect which was considered in *Interflora v Marks & Spencer* was whether **3-440** the tribunal must consider the functions of a mark in a double identity case other than the essential function if the mark has not been used. There is, of course, no requirement that a mark be used prior to bringing proceedings for infringement. It is difficult to see how the functions of a mark such as, e.g. its communication function can be affected by use by a third party if, in fact, the mark has not been used. In such circumstances, it does not communicate any "psychological signal" capable of protection. Equally, it is difficult to see how use of a sign by a defendant affects the investment function of a mark if it has not actually been used.

Such considerations led to, in *Interflora v Marks and Spencer*, the European **3-441** Commission suggested that when considering the issue of infringement under the double identity provisions, one should only consider the essential function of the trade mark.[757] In relation to this submission, the CJEU said:

"[40] Admittedly, a trade mark is always supposed to fulfil its function of indicating origin, whereas it performs its other functions only in so far as its proprietor uses it to that end, in particular for the purposes of advertising or investment. However, that difference between the essential function of the trade mark and its other functions can in no way justify-when a trade mark fulfils one or more of those other functions-excluding from the scope of Article 5(1)(a) of Directive 89/104 and Article 9(1)(a) of Regulation No 40/94 acts adversely affecting those functions. Likewise, there are no grounds for holding that only trade marks with a reputation are capable of having functions other than that of indicating origin." [Emphasis supplied.]

---

[750] *Arsenal Football Club v Reed* (C-206/01) [2002] E.C.R. I-10273.

[751] *Adam Opel AG v Autec AG (Deutscher Verband der Spielwaren-Industrie eV intervening)* (C-48/05) [2007] E.C.R. I-1017.

[752] *O2 Holdings Ltd v Hutchison 3G UK Ltd* (C-533/06) [2008] E.C.R. I-4231 (this was strictly not an identical goods/identical marks case).

[753] *Google France* (C-236/08) [2010] E.C.R. I-2417; *Interflora v Marks and Spencer* (C-323/09) [2011] E.C.R. I-8625.

[754] *L'Oréal v Bellure* (C-487/07) [2009] E.C.R. I-5185.

[755] *Céline v Céline SARL* (C-17/06) [2007] E.C.R. I-07041.

[756] *Anheuser-Busch Inc v Budějovický Budvar, národní podnik* (C-254/02) [2004] E.C.R. I-10989; *Céline v Céline SARL* (C-17/06) [2007] E.C.R. I-07041.

[757] See [35].

3-442   Whilst it might be thought that the CJEU's reasoning has gone awry, it should be remembered that unused trade marks will eventually be used (or otherwise revoked for lack of genuine use). Thus, an entity may be about to embark upon a substantial advertising campaign for a trade mark which is intended to communicate a particular image of the brand to the public. The defendant's use of an identical sign might jeopardise such a campaign. In such circumstances, one can see that the defendant's use would be *liable to* adversely affect the communication function of a trade mark (and possibly the advertising function). In other words, the trade mark proprietor has the right to control the image by preventing others from using a sign which adversely affects the functions of a used mark or the image that the proprietor intends to adopt for the mark. Thus, in relation to the advertising function, if the defendant's sign substantially affects the ability of the registered proprietor to carry out an advertising campaign for the trade mark *in the future*, then there is no special reason why the latter should not be entitled to argue that the advertising function of the mark has been adversely impaired. Further discussion on the ability of the functions of an unused mark to be adversely affected can be found earlier in this chapter.[758]

Similar marks/similar goods or services

3-443   Where infringement is based on the similar mark/similar goods provisions of the TMD or EUTMR,[759] it must be shown that there is a likelihood of confusion. Where a likelihood of confusion exists, it must follow that there is a risk of an adverse effect on the essential function of the asserted registered mark. However, as discussed above, where the double identity rule is satisfied, it is sufficient if a function of the asserted mark is liable to be adversely affected. This is odd as it would mean that if the two marks are very similar but not identical, then proving an adverse effect on functions other than the essential function of the mark is irrelevant. A likelihood of confusion must be proven which requires consideration of the essential function but not other functions of the mark.

3-444   Indeed, in *O2 v Hutchison 3G*, this occurred.[760] In a comparative advertising case, Hutchison 3G had used a sign which was similar to a "bubbles" registered trade mark owned by O2. The CJEU said that art.10.2(b) TMD was to be interpreted as meaning that the proprietor of a registered trade mark was not entitled to prevent the use by a third party in a comparative advertisement of a sign similar to the mark in relation to goods or services identical with or similar to those for which the mark is registered where such use does not give rise to a likelihood of confusion.[761] Yet, in the context of a comparative advertisement, it is highly unlikely that there will ever be a likelihood of confusion.[762] However, if the bubbles used had been identical, then O2 would not have had to shown a likelihood of confusion if it could have shown that use by Hutchison was liable to affect the communication, investment or advertising function of its bubbles mark. It does not make sense to have a very different approach to an identical mark as opposed to a very similar mark. Such suggests a real fault line in the jurisprudence of the CJEU.

---

[758] See paras 3-103 and 3-116.

[759] art.10.2(b) TMD; art.9.2(b) EUTMR.

[760] *O2 Holdings Ltd and O2 (UK) Ltd v Hutchison 3G UK Ltd* (C-533/06) [2008] E.C.R. I-4231.

[761] See [69].

[762] See paras 3-446 and 3-453 concerning the context of use.

Reputation-based infringement

It is also less clear whether an action for infringement based on the reputation-based infringement grounds of the TMD or EUTMR (unfair advantage/detriment to distinctive character or repute) requires it to be shown that there is an adverse effect on one or more of the functions of the registered trade mark. This issue has already been discussed in the context of oppositions based on earlier marks with a reputation and the reader is referred to that discussion.[763]   **3-445**

Identifying the sign and relevance of context

Identification of the "sign" complained of

In the case of an opposition to an application for a registered trade mark or   **3-446**
proceedings for a declaration of invalidity of a registered trade mark, the identification of the mark opposed or the registered mark is unproblematic. It is that depicted or identified in the application. However, in the case of infringement proceedings, the TMD and EUTMR refer to the exclusive rights of the proprietor to prevent the use in the course of trade of signs which are identical or similar to the registered trade marks. Thus, the comparison is the mark for the sign. Therefore, it is important to identify the relevant "sign". Three examples suffice that highlight some difficulties that may arise:

- A defendant uses a logo which consists of a word plus decorative artwork. The asserted registered mark is a word only mark. Is the sign the word or the word+artwork?
- The defendant markets a foodstuff which is shaped in a distinctive manner, packaged in another distinctive manner and which displays a distinctive word mark. The asserted registered mark is a shape mark. Is the sign merely the shape of the foodstuff, shape+package or shape+package+word?
- A supermarket defendant displays a mark X next to Y where X is a word sign similar to the asserted registered mark but Y is the supermarket's name. Is the sign X or X + Y?

There are two options: (i) the sign is that which the proprietor of the asserted   **3-447**
mark (i.e. the claimant in the proceedings) identifies as the mark of which complaint is made; or (ii) the sign used by the defendant is to be determined objectively by a court or tribunal. It is submitted that there can be little question that it is the latter. If it were the former, a claimant could isolate in a wholly artificial manner some aspect of the sign used by the defendant, i.e. if the defendant was using a sign consisting of a first name and surname, e.g. ROBERT H TRYON as a trade mark for chocolates, it would be artificial and self-serving for the claimant to assert that the defendant was using the sign "H" or 'ROBERT H" in order to improve their prospect of infringement based on a registered mark for H or ROBERT. On any objective basis, the sign is the whole name. Nevertheless, how should a tribunal assess what is the sign being used by the defendant? For instance, in the case of the second example above, it could well be said that the defendant is using three signs: the shape, the packaging and the word mark and each of those should be considered a relevant sign for the purpose of infringement. First, it is tempting to say that the comparison should be "like for like", i.e. taking the second example, if the

---

[763] See para.3-354.

registered mark is a shape mark, then one considers only the shape of the foodstuff and not e.g. shape+packaging+word. However, in the case of the first example, is it right to identify the sign being used as merely the word or is it the word+decorative logo where a word mark is asserted? Here, it is suggested that the relevant test should be whether, when viewed from the eyes of the average consumer, the sign of which complaint is made would be seen in a normal way as an indication of origin *by itself*. Thus, if the aesthetics/artwork is an integral part of the word and always appears with the word, it would be artificial to say that the sign is the word. Nonetheless, if as a variant, the decorative artwork would be seen as mere background to the word sign by the average consumer, then it would not be so artificial to consider the sign (or one of the signs) as the word. In the third example, if the average consumer would recognise that two signs were being used- as one, the supermarket name (often called the house mark) to identify the retailer and the other, the product name as a product mark—then it would be wrong in principle to find that the sign is a single composite sign for the purpose of infringement.

Context of use of sign

3-448   Should the context of the use of a mark be taken into account? Infringement actions require a comparison of "mark for sign" and not broader considerations of whether the public will be deceived *in fact* taking account of disclaimers, knowledge of consumer, use of additional distinguishing matter, etc. Such is the province of unfair competition laws, consumer protection laws and (in the UK), the law of passing off. Thus, a counterfeiter who uses the mark ROLEX for watches, should not be able to avoid liability for trade mark infringement by saying that the public who buy his watches know perfectly well they are not genuine ROLEX watches from, for example, the fact that they are very cheap, sold in street markets, and he has a sign which says "COUNTERFEIT ROLEX watches".

3-449   Surprisingly, this issue has not been considered in much depth by the EU courts. In *O2 v Hutchison 3G*,[764] the CJEU had to consider a comparative advertising case where a competitor had used a very similar mark to that of the registered proprietor for the purpose of advertising its telecommunication services. The nature of comparative advertising is that the consumer is unlikely to confuse the two marks as the whole object is to contrast the quality of the goods or services being provided. The CJEU held in contrasting the position relating to the validity of a registered trade mark and infringement proceedings:

> "[63]   By contrast, in accordance with the referring court's own findings, the use by H3G, in the advertisement in question, of bubble images similar to the bubbles trade marks did not give rise to a likelihood of confusion on the part of consumers. *The advertisement, as a whole*, was not misleading and, in particular, did not suggest that there was any form of commercial link between O2 and O2 (UK) on the one hand, and H3G, on the other.
>
> [64]   In that regard, contrary to the submission of O2 and O2 (UK), the referring court *was right to limit its analysis to the context in which the sign similar to the bubbles trade marks was used by H3G*, for the purpose of assessing the existence of a likelihood of confusion.
>
> [66]   [Article 5 TMD] however, concerns the application for registration of a mark. Once a mark has been registered its proprietor has the right to use it as he sees fit

---

[764]   *O2 Holdings Ltd and O2 (UK) Ltd v Hutchison 3G UK Ltd* (C-533/06) [2008] E.C.R. I-4231.

so that, for the purposes of assessing whether the application for registration falls within the ground for refusal laid down in that provision, it is necessary to ascertain whether there is a likelihood of confusion with the opponent's earlier mark in all the circumstances in which the mark applied for might be used if it were to be registered.

[67] By contrast, in the case provided for in [Article 10 TMD], the third-party user of a sign identical with, or similar to, a registered mark does not assert any trade mark rights over that sign but is using it on an ad hoc basis. In those circumstances, in order to assess whether the proprietor of the registered mark is entitled to oppose that specific use, *the assessment must be limited to the circumstances characterising that use*, without there being any need to investigate whether another use of the same sign in different circumstances would also be likely to give rise to a likelihood of confusion." [Emphasis supplied.]

In an English case,[765] the court interpreted *O2* and said as follows:

3-450

"[78] In my judgment the context and circumstances are limited *to the actual context and circumstances of the use of the sign itself.* The Court of Justice explicitly said at [64] that the referring court was right to 'limit its analysis to the context in which the sign was used.' *Furthermore, it referred at [67] to the circumstances 'characterising the use', not to the circumstances more generally.* Thus circumstances prior to, simultaneous with and subsequent to the use of the sign may be relevant to a claim for passing off (or, under other legal systems, unfair competition), but they are not generally relevant to a claim for trademark infringement under [Art. 10.2(b)]. In saying this, I do not intend to express any view on the question of post-sale confusion referred to below." [Emphasis supplied.]

Since *02 v Hutchison*, the Court of Justice has revisited the issue of context of use in *Specsavers*.[766] On reference from the English courts, the issue was whether, in an infringement action, a court should take into account the colours which the registered trade mark and the third party sign were using when deciding likelihood of confusion or unfair advantage. The Court of Justice said that where a EUTM owner had used the EUTM in a particular colour, such was a factor to be taken into account even though the EUTM was itself not registered in colour. It also said that where the third party used a colour for the representation of the sign, where that colour was associated with the third party, it was also a relevant factor to be taken into account. The Court of Justice stated that the fact that the relevant public associated the defendant with the colour green, which was being used for the signs alleged to infringe certain registered mark, could result in a reduction of the likelihood of confusion between the signs. In doing so, the Court of Justice said that "*assessments must take account of the precise context in which the sign which is alleged similar to the registered trade mark was used*".[767] It will be appreciated from this decision that the Court of Justice is allowing the taking of account of factors both *intrinsic* and *extrinsic* to the actual sign itself. The intrinsic aspect is that the sign was in green-so far so good; however, the extrinsic aspect is that this colour was associated with the third party.

3-451

Whilst the Court of Justice's decision is understandable, there is a danger of "mis-

3-452

[765] *Och-Ziff Management Europe Ltd and Oz Management LP v Och Capital LLP, Union Investment Management Ltd and Ochocki* [2011] F.S.R. 11, [2011] E.T.M.R. 1; see also *Specsavers International Healthcare Ltd, Specsavers BV, Specsavers Optical Group Ltd and Specsavers Optical Superstores Ltd v Asda Stores Ltd* [2012] F.S.R. 19 at [67].
[766] *Specsavers International Healthcare Ltd v Asda Stores* (C-252/12) ECLI:EU:C:2013:497.
[767] Citing *02 Holdings* (C-533/06), at [64].

sion creep" whereby all relevant factors are taken into account concerning the alleged infringing sign in trade mark infringement proceedings. It remains to be seen what other *extrinsic* circumstances will be taken into account which may lessen or increase a finding of infringement. For instance, let us take a case where a defendant, who is a very large and well-known undertaking, has used a sign for an extensive period of time which is very similar to a small undertaking's registered trade mark which has not been used at all. In such circumstances, is it a legitimate argument to say that the defendant has educated the relevant public to see the sign as an indication of origin of the defendant and consequently, by analogy with *Specsavers*, lessen the likelihood of confusion?

3-453   It would be unfortunate if such arguments were allowed to prevail. It is important that trade mark infringement actions do not become proceedings that are merely concerned with whether, when taking into account all the circumstances, consumers are confused. In trade mark infringement proceedings, there is a degree of *abstraction* from the actual marketplace-the comparison should be principally whether to the average consumer, the use of the sign *by itself* when used with the defendant's goods or services would give rise to a likelihood of confusion with the registered mark. This allows the proper degree of protection for a registered trade mark. Historically, in the UK the approach has been to disregard additional distinguishing matter, i.e. matter intended to reduce confusion but which does not form part of the sign, e.g. a disclaimer or the get-up of packaging on which the sign is used.[768] It also allows a court to ignore disclaimers of trade connection and indeed, arguments as canvassed earlier in this section that buyers at a counterfeit street market know fully that they are not buying genuine ROLEX watches.

Who is liable for infringing acts?

3-454   In opposition proceedings or a declaration for invalidity, the tribunal proceeds on the assumption that the applicant or registered proprietor of the later mark will use the later mark as an indication of origin for its goods or services. However, in infringement proceedings, it is necessary to determine who is the person using the sign and thus liable. In most cases, this will not be difficult. Indeed, by reason of the various categories of what amounts to types of use is prohibited under the EUTMR and TMD,[769] it may be that there are a number of people who are liable. For instance, the manufacturer who affixes the mark to products, the distributor who supplies products bearing the mark and the retailer who sell the same products to the relevant public. By definition of use, all of the aforementioned will be liable.

3-455   However, what about the sub-contractor who affixes the mark and is bound to return the goods to its principal? Technically, that undertaking has affixed the mark. Is such sufficient? What about where an undertaking provides a facility, e.g. a website portal or a marketplace to allow undertakings to sell their goods using that website or marketplace? Are such persons (often called "intermediaries") liable for infringement? Here there is a complex overlay of national and EU law. For instance, many Member States have a law on accessory liability relevant to all torts including IP infringement. These laws differ markedly. Thus, in Germany, accessory liability extends to those who assist a third party knowing that the third party is or there is a high risk that they will carry out an infringing act. In contrast, in the UK,

---

[768] e.g. See *Origins* [1995] F.S.R. 280; *Decon Laboratories v Fred Baker* [2001] R.P.C. 17.
[769] See para.3-483.

generally, assistors are not liable even if they know that there is a high risk of infringement unless they act pursuant to a "common design" to infringe.[770] Neither the EUTMR, TMD nor EU law harmonise exhaustively accessory law for wrongs. Yet, as will be seen, the Court of Justice has interpreted provisions in the EUTMR and TMD to accessory-type situations. Therefore, when advising in this area, one must take account of both national and EU law. In this section, we look at EU law on the issue of who is liable for acts of infringement of a trade mark.

Broadly, in the author's submission, and this reflects EU case law, the key distinction to be drawn is whether or not, the alleged infringer is itself involved in the acts of advertising, promotion, sale or supply of the alleged infringing goods or services or merely providing services which enable a third party to carry out such acts. A key factor to help determine this will be whether or not the alleged infringer has a commercial or vested interest in the sale or supply of the alleged infringing goods or services actually happening. If their remuneration is not dependent on such sales or supply, it is a key pointer that they are not themselves using the sign in the course of trade so as to render themselves liable for infringement under EU trade mark law. Nevertheless, they may be liable under the laws of Member States as to accessory liability. **3-456**

Use of infringing mark outside control of defendant

In *Daimler AG v Együd Garage Gépjármujavító és Értékesítö Kft*,[771] the Court of Justice had to consider whether a defendant was liable for use of a registered trade mark on the Internet which they were originally responsible for but which was now outside their control. In this case, the defendant had been an authorised Mercedes-Benz dealer in Hungary. Whilst the dealership was in place, it ordered online advertising services from a Hungarian company, MTT, whereby it advertised that it was an authorised Mercedes-Benz dealer. Its dealership was then ended and Daimler required Együd to cease advertising itself as an authorised Mercedes-Benz dealer. Együd asked MTT to change its advertisement to remove the reference to it being authorised as such. It also wrote to other websites which had advertised Együd as an authorised Mercedes-Benz dealer without Együd having ordered any advertising from these websites. Despite taking such steps, these advertisements continued and when "Együd Garage" was inserted into the Google search engine, advertisements appeared showing it to be an authorised Mercedes-Benz dealer. Daimler brought an action for trade mark infringement. The Hungarian Court referred to the Court of Justice whether, in essence, Együd Garage was liable for trade mark infringement. **3-457**

The Court of Justice considered whether such use was use *by* Együd Garage. It considered the different language versions of art.10 TMD for "use" and held that this involves *"active behaviours and direct or indirect control of the act constituting the use"*. It said that it is clear that only a third party *"who has direct or indirect control of the act constituting the use is effectively able to stop that use and therefore comply with that prohibition"*.[772] The Court of Justice held that it was not sufficient that such use could provide a financial benefit to the third party as this would conflict with the principle that no one can be legally obliged to do the impossible **3-458**

---

[770] See in the UK, *CBS v Amstrad* [1987] R.P.C. 42 (HL); *Sea Shepherd v Fish & Fish Ltd* [2015] UKSC 10; In Germany, see s.830 *Burgerliches Gesetzbuch* (BGB); *Solarinitiative* BGH, GRUR 2013, 301.
[771] (C-179/15) ECLI:EU:C:2016:134.
[772] See [41].

(*impossibilium nulla obligation est*).[773] Accordingly, it concluded that a third party does not make use of a sign where they have expressly requested the operator of the website to remove the advertisement or the reference to the mark contained therein.

Intermediaries: ISPs, OMO and marketplace owners

3-459   In *Google France*,[774] the CJEU had to consider whether an Internet search provider (in this case, the well-known Google company) was liable for trade mark infringement where an undertaking purchased via its recognised Google Adwords service a keyword which was the same as that of a registered trade mark of a competitor. The CJEU held that Google itself had not used the sign within the meaning of art.10 TMD and art.9 EUTMR. It said that "use" implies "at the very least", that that third party uses the sign in "its own commercial communication". It held that a referencing service provider does not use the sign as an Internet reference keyword but allows its clients to use such.[775] It held that such a conclusion was not affected by the fact that Google had been paid by its clients for the use of the keywords. It said that the fact of creating the technical conditions necessary for the use of a sign and being paid for that service does not mean that the party offering the service itself uses the sign.[776]

3-460   In contrast, the CJEU held that the advertiser (i.e. the person who successfully bid for the sign) has used the sign.[777] Such is regardless of whether the sign selected as the keyword appears in the advertisement itself or not.[778]

3-461   In *L'Oréal v eBay*,[779] the CJEU had to consider the liability of an online market operator (OMO), the well-known eBay, where its online site was being used to sell counterfeit perfume by individuals. There were two types of trade mark use to consider. First, eBay had itself bought various keywords for well-known trade marks as sponsored links to lead directly to the eBay online market. Secondly, there was use by "customer-sellers" on eBay's website.

3-462   In relation to the first type of use, the CJEU held, following *Google France*, that where the online market operator advertises using keywords which it has successfully bid for and which are identical to the registered mark of a third party, that they are liable as infringers where the advertising does not enable reasonably well informed and observant internet users or enables them to ascertain with difficulty whether the goods concerned originate from the proprietor of the trade mark or from third parties. The CJEU said that the fact that an economic operator uses a sign corresponding to a trade mark in relation to goods which are not their own goods-in the sense that the operator does not have title to them-does not in itself prevent that

---

[773] See [43].

[774] *Google France and Google* (C-236/08 to C-238/08) [2010] E.C.R. I-2417 at [49]–[52].

[775] Cf. *North Face Apparel Corp v Backman* [2009] E.T.M.R. 23 at [56] (Hogsta Domstolen, Sweden) where the Swedish court held that a father who purchased jackets bearing trade marks from a contact in China for use by his daughter's business was liable for trade mark infringement because the EUTMR had no requirement that the defendant be carrying out the business himself.

[776] See [57].

[777] *Google France and Google* (C-236/08 to C-238/08) [2010] E.C.R. I-2417 at [49]–[52]; *BergSpechte* (C-278/08) [2010] E.C.R. I-2517 at [18]; *Interflora Inc v Marks & Spencer Plc* (C-323/09) ECLI:EU:C:2011:173.

[778] *BergSpechte*, at [30]; *Interflora v Marks & Spencer*, at [31].

[779] *L'Oréal SA v eBay International AG* (C-324/09) ECLI:EU:C:2011:474.

use from being an infringement.[780] In contrast, the CJEU held that where a customer-seller of that online market operator uses the registered trade mark of a third party to sell products, the online market operator is not liable for its display on its website because it does not "use" the sign.[781] Here, eBay was merely providing an electronic framework as a mechanism for its customer-sellers to sell products under the sign. It was not involved in the act of marketing those goods.[782] In contrast, an undertaking which ran an online market website which matched vendors with purchasers but once an agreement had been reached, would act as the vendor's broker and conclude with the purchaser a contract of sale for commission, was held to be "using" a registered trade mark where the vendor's goods were infringing goods.[783]

The above reasoning applies equally to physical marketplaces. Thus, a landowner who leases market stalls to persons who then sell infringing goods would not be liable for trade mark infringement if all they do is provide the means for customer-sellers to sell infringing goods.   **3-463**

It should be said that intermediaries, even if not themselves liable for trade mark infringement, may be liable to be injuncted under the Enforcement Directive as intermediaries to prevent the provision of facilities to third party infringers. This is discussed further in another chapter in this book.[784]   **3-464**

Sub-contractors

In *Frisdranken Industrie Winters BV v Red Bull GmbH*,[785] the issue was whether an undertaking which filled empty cans with a beverage for a third party bearing various registered trade marks was liable for trade mark infringement. On reference from the Dutch courts, the CJEU had to consider whether the undertaking was liable for trade mark infringement. It held, by analogy with *Google France*, that the undertaking was not itself using the sign. The CJEU said that the undertaking which merely executes a technical part of the production process of the final product without having any interest in the external presentation of those cans and in the signs, does not itself use the signs within the meaning of art.10 TMD but "only creates the technical condition necessary for the other person to use them".[786] Interestingly, it also held that the undertaking's service was filling cans and not selling non-alcoholic drinks. Accordingly, it held that there was no similarity between the services provided by the undertaking and the products for which the trade mark was registered.[787]   **3-465**

However, with the introduction by the new EUTM Regulation and the new TMD of provisions allowing trade mark owners to prevent affixing of signs on labels, packaging, etc. and dealings in such,[788] sub-contractors may become liable in certain cases. Thus, a sub-contractor who makes labels or packaging whereby a sign is af-   **3-466**

---

[780] See [91] citing *UDV North America Inc v Brandtraders NV* (C-62/08) [2009] E.C.R. I-1279 at [43].

[781] *L'Oréal v eBay*, at [105].

[782] eBay charges an insertion fee and a final value which is a commission on the item's final selling price. However, properly construed, such is merely a mechanism for payment of its platform services rather than because it has been actively involved in the selling of the products of the customer-seller.

[783] *UDV North America Inc v Brandtraders*.

[784] See para.15-035.

[785] (C-119/10) ECLI:EU:C:2011:837.

[786] See [30].

[787] See [31].

[788] See para.3-471.

fixed or stocks such labels or packaging will now become liable if a "risk exists" that these could be used to infringe.

Warehouses

3-467   The provision of a warehouse service for goods bearing another trade's trade mark does not constitute use of a sign under the Trade Mark Directive.[789]

Accessory liability

3-468   A big unanswered question is whether the issue of accessory liability for trade mark infringement is a matter of EU law or national law and if the former, what is the appropriate test? For instance, where one undertaking authorises, procures or directs the carrying out of acts of trade mark infringement by another, is the former liable as an accessory as well as the latter? Both the TMD and EUTMR are silent on these issues. In *L'Oréal v Ebay*, the High Court of England said that it might be argued that the TMD and EUTMR did approximate national laws on accessory liability but that his view was that the question of accessory liability was primarily a matter for national law.[790] Article 17(1) EUTMR states that the "effects of EU trade marks" shall be governed solely by the provisions of the EUTMR but that in other respects, national law shall apply relating to infringement of a national trade mark. It is difficult to say that the question of who is liable falls within the "effects" of EUTMs.

3-469   Moreover, with the new EUTMR and TMD, there are some limited provisions which extend into the field of accessory liability. So, as discussed below,[791] the owner of a EUTM can bring proceedings to prohibit the affixing of signs on packaging, labels, tags, security or authenticity features or offering or placing on the market the same to which the mark if affixed where there exists a risk that such could be used in relation to goods or services and such use would constitute an infringement of the rights of the EUTM owner.[792] Given that such is the extent of the inroads of EU law into accessory liability, it seems fairly clear that the EU legislature has not sought to harmonise exhaustively EU law on accessory liability for trade mark infringement but has left the same for Member States to provide as they see fit.

3-470   However, it should be said that under the Enforcement Directive, Member States are required to ensure that the "measures, procedures and remedies" that they provide for the purpose of enforcement of IPRs are "effective, proportionate and dissuasive".[793] Accessory liability often arises where an individual uses a company to carry out infringing acts. In the UK and other countries, where such acts are procured or directed by an individual including a director, the individual is jointly liable for the infringing acts even if that individual is a director of the company.[794] Without such accessory liability, enforcement of IPRs would be very difficult because it is all too easy for a director to use a successive number of corporate vehicles to infringe knowing that they are not liable. In the author's view, in the

---

[789] *Top Logistics BV and Van Caem International BV v Bacardi & Co Ltd* (C-379/14) EU:C:2015:497 at [45] applying *Frisdranken Industrie Winters BV* discussed at para.3-485.

[790] *L'Oréal v Ebay* [2009] EWHC 1094 (Ch) at [343]-[345].

[791] See para.3-471.

[792] art.10 EUTMR; art.11 TMD.

[793] art.3(2) Directive 2004/48. See para.15-009.

[794] e.g. see *L'Oréal v eBay* [2009] R.P.C. 21 at 346. In Germany, director's liability can arise under s.830 BGB as an accessory. See also *Geschaftsfuhrerhaftung* BGH, GRUR 2014, 883.

absence of accessory liability, the enforcement of IPRs would not be effective, proportionate and dissuasive as required by the Enforcement Directive. Thus, in the author's view, there is an obligation to provide for some degree of accessory liability (at least director liability) but it derives from the Enforcement Directive and not the TMD or EUTMR. However, the modality of how such is provided is very much a matter for the Member State.

Packaging, labels, etc.

Article 10 of the EUTM Regulation and art.11 TMD have introduced a right to prevent certain preparatory acts such as affixing a sign identical to or similar to a EU or national trade mark on packaging, labels, tags, security or authenticity features, etc. or dealing in such items to which these signs are affixed if there exists a risk that the items *could* be used in relation to goods or services and such use *would* constitute an infringement.[795] As a preliminary point, it should be noted that it is not said that such an act falls within the exclusive rights of, e.g. a EUTM owner. Article 9, rather than art.10, deals with the rights conferred by a EUTM. Article 10 is concerned with injunctive relief as opposed to entitling the EUTM owner to seek the usual remedies for trade mark infringement. To this extent, art.10 can be likened to the right granted in the Enforcement Directive to injunct intermediaries to prevent infringements by third parties.[796] **3-471**

There are three requirements to trigger the right of a EUTM owner to obtain injunctive relief under art.10 EUTMR: **3-472**

- A sign identical or similar to EU or national marks has been affixed on labels, packaging, tags, security, authenticity features, devices, etc..
- There is a risk that the labels, packaging, etc. bearing the affixed mark *could* be used "in relation to goods or services".
- This use *would* constitute an infringement of the EUTM owner under art.9.

In relation to the second requirement, the phrase "*where the risk exists... the [packaging, etc] could be used in relation to goods or services*" sets a low threshold. First the combination of the words "risk" and "could" suggest that a probability above merely speculative would suffice. Secondly, it should be noted that one need only show a risk of use of the packaging in relation to *any* goods. As packaging, labels, tags, etc. are intended to be used with goods, this should be easy to prove. **3-473**

Accordingly, the focus is on the third requirement. There are two possible interpretations. The first interpretation is that the EUTM owner must show that the labels, packaging with the affixed mark *will* be or *are intended to be* used on goods or in relation to services which, if so used, would infringe the rights of the EUTM owner. The second interpretation is that the court or tribunal need only consider whether *if* the affixed mark was used on *any type of* goods, such goods would infringe the rights of the EUTM owner. The first interpretation would require a court to consider what is likely to happen to the labels, packaging, etc. with the marks affixed on them. For instance, are they likely to be used on goods that if so used, would infringe the rights of the EUTM owner? Thus, it may be that the labels are intended to be used on goods that fall far outside the specification of goods of the EUTM and therefore do not infringe. The second interpretation is more hypotheti- **3-474**

---

[795] art.10 EUTMR; art.11 TMD.
[796] See para.15-035.

cal and would ignore possible non-infringing uses if a possible use is infringing. This interpretation is not concerned with the likely destination of the labels.

3-475   On the literal wording of art.10, the second interpretation would appear to be the correct one. First, the second requirement merely requires that the labels, etc. with the affixed mark *could* be used on goods which if used, *would* infringe. It does not say that the labels *would* be used in relation to goods or services that *would* constitute an infringement of the rights of the EUTM owner. Secondly, it must be remembered that art.10 EUTMR is only concerned with injunctive relief and does not expose the labeller or packager to liability for trade mark infringement.

3-476   However, it can be seen that the second interpretation could work injustice. If it is clear that the labels with the affixed mark are intended and will be used for, e.g. clothing which, if it happens, will not infringe the rights of a EUTM owner registered for, e.g. cosmetics, it is an unattractive argument for art.10 EUTMR to be triggered merely because the labels *could* be affixed to cosmetics which, if such occured, *would* infringe. Given such an unattractive scenario, the Court of Justice may decide that the first interpretation is right despite the width of the wording of art.10 EUTMR.

Use in the course of trade

3-477   For infringement to be proven, the defendant's use must be in the course of trade. This has been interpreted as meaning that it must be in the context of commercial activity with a view to economic advantage and not as a private matter.[797] Interestingly, in *Silberquelle*,[798] it was held that the handing out of promotional items (alcohol-free drinks) as a reward for the purchase of other goods (clothes) and to encourage the sale of the latter, did not amount to "genuine use" of a registered trade mark for alcohol-free drinks.[799] Conversely, there is genuine use by a non-profit-making organisation where it uses a trade mark on business papers, etc.[800] Thus it is likely that such use would also amount to use in the course of trade. After all, substantial use of a sign by a defendant charity is as capable of affecting the functions of a trade mark as use by a profit-making organisation. Therefore, it is likely that economic advantage would be interpreted to cover the same.

Is use "in relation to" goods or services? Use as a trade mark?

3-478   Both the TMD and EUTMR require that use of the sign by the defendant be "in relation to goods or services". How should this requirement be interpreted? For instance, does the mere *existence* of a mark on the packaging of a product mean that it is being used "in relation to" that product? A number of commentators considered that there was a threshold requirement that the sign must be used for the purpose of distinguishing the goods or services, i.e. as trade mark use referring to art.10(6) Dir.89/104 (the first trade mark directive).[801]

---

[797] e.g. *Google France*, at [50]; *Arsenal Football Club* (C-206/01) [2002] E.C.R. I-10273, at [40]; *Céline v Céline Sarl*, at [17].

[798] *Silberquelle GmbH v Maselli-Strickmode GmbH* (C-495/07) [2009] E.C.R. I-317.

[799] A registered trade mark is liable to be revoked if it has not been put to genuine use within a five-year period following its registration.

[800] *Verein Radetzky-Orden v Bundesvereinigung Karmeradschaft "Feldmarschall Radetzky"* (C-422/07) [2008] I-09223.

[801] art.5(5) Dir.89/104 suggested that it was not intended to harmonise provisions of national law which

In earlier versions of this book, there was considerable discussion as to whether the case law of the Court of Justice endorsed such approach.[802] **3-479**

However, it appears clear from the new EUTMR and TMD that use to indicate trade origin, i.e. trade mark use is a necessary requirement under EU trade mark law for infringement to be made out. Thus, Recital 18 TMD says that "*It is appropriate to provide that an infringement of a trade mark can only be established if there is a finding that the infringing mark or sign is used in the course of trade for the purposes of distinguishing goods or series. Use of the sign for purposes other than for distinguishing goods or services should be subject to the provisions of national law*". Although less clear, the same can be taken from Recital 13 EUTMR.[803] **3-480**

It might be thought that if a sign is not used as an indication of origin, then there will always be a defence under art.14.1(b) EUTMR/art.14.1(b) TMD (signs or indications concerning the characteristics of a product). In the previous edition of this book, reference was made to the typical example much beloved by trade mark practitioners, namely where the trade mark "?" is registered for magazines and a defendant uses the symbol "?" on a magazine title in a grammatical sense.[804] It was said that it is difficult to say that "?" describes any characteristic of a product but equally its use will not be taken as an indication of trade origin.[805] However, in the new EUTMR and TMD, these provisions have been widened to include any use by a third party in the course of trade of "*signs or indications which are not distinctive…*". As said in the recitals to the new TMD, "*such use should further permit the use of descriptive or non-distinctive signs or indications in general.*"[806] Such suggests that not only is use of a sign as an indication of origin a necessary element for infringement but a lack of such use is also a defence (to put the matter beyond doubt). This is because if a sign is not being used as an indication of origin, then it must be being used as an indication "in general", i.e. not as an indication of trade origin. **3-481**

Therefore, it is considered that use of a sign can only be "in relation to" goods or services if it is being used as an indication of trade origin. **3-482**

What types of use infringes?

A registered trade mark confers exclusive rights on its owner to prevent third parties not having its consent from using a sign in the course of trade in relation to goods or services that infringes the right of the registered owner. Earlier on in this chapter we considered whether a sign would infringe the exclusive rights, e.g. where it is identical to the registered trade mark and used in relation to identical goods or services to those covered by the registration. The EUTMR and TMD both state that **3-483**

---

related to the "protection against the use of a sign *other* than for the purpose of distinguishing goods or services." However, this provision is not in the current TMD.

[802] See paras 3-202 to 3-204 of the 4th edn of this book.

[803] "Infringement of an EU trade mark should therefore also comprise the use of the sign as a trade name or similar designation as long as the use is made for the purposes of distinguishing goods or services". Although said in the context of trade names there is no reason to suppose that such a requirement is limited only to use of trade name and such would make no sense.

[804] For instance, the use of a "?" by itself on a front cover of a current news magazine as a dramatic way of indicating some fundamental question which remained unanswered in relation to a current news item.

[805] This example is referred to in *R v Johnstone* [2003] UKHL 28 HL at [13] per Lord Walker of Gestingthorpe.

[806] Recital 27. See also Recital 21, EUTMR which has the same wording.

the owner of a EUTMR or national mark may prevent the use of a sign in the course of trade in relation to goods or services that infringes the exclusive rights. We have already discussed the meaning of "in the course of trade" and "in relation to goods or services". Here, we discuss the *types* of *use* that infringe a trade mark.

3-484 The paradigm situation is where the sign is affixed to the packaging of goods and those goods are traded in. The overarching requirement is that there is use in the course of trade. However, the EUTMR and TMD give examples of what that means. These include: affixing the sign to the goods or to the packaging, offering the goods or putting them on the market or stocking them for these purposes under the sign, or offering or supplying services under a mark, importing or exporting goods under the sign, and using the sign on business papers and in advertising.[807] It is worth noting that some of these types of use would not by themselves affect adversely the functions of a trade mark. For instance, the mere affixing of a mark onto goods in a factory does not mean that such goods are placed on the market or otherwise exposed to consumers or traders. Equally, the export of goods bearing an infringing sign will not come to the attention of consumers or traders. A manufacturer based in the EU could export goods to the USA with such goods remaining inside containers from the factory site to the USA and never see a single consumer in the EU. Therefore, an astute lawyer might argue that even though this is a prohibited use under the EUTMR and TMD (export under a mark is an infringment), the case law of the Court of Justice requires, at least in the case of infringement not dependent on the market having a reputation, that there be an adverse effect on a function of the mark and that in the case of export or mere affixing of a mark, this will not happen as in such circumstances, the relevant public will not be exposed to such goods within the EU (i.e. the protected territory).

3-485 It is unlikely that the CJEU would be seduced by such arguments. It is clear that as a matter of policy, the EUTMR and TMD are intended to confer the right of owners of EUTMs and national trade marks to *control* the use in the course of trade of any infringing sign with the territory protected by the registration. Thus, it may be that there are steps taken by a third party, which whilst they do not themselves affect adversely the functions of a trade mark, give rise to a high risk that they will do so. For instance, there is a high risk that goods sitting in a factory warehouse in the EU bearing an infringing sign will be traded within the EU. Equally, goods waiting to be exported out of the EU bearing an infringing sign could instead easily be placed on the market in the EU by the owner of the goods. Therefore, it is clear that the EU lawmakers have chosen a policy whereby EUTM and national trade mark owners should be able to exercise control over infringing sign all the way down the supply chain from manufacture to final disposal. Indeed, recently, this policy of control has meant that the EU lawmakers have extended the types of infringing use to goods bearing an infringing sign that are merely in transit throughout the EU.[808] This is further discussed later in the chapter.[809] Further support for this policy of control arises from the fact that the Court of Justice has held that subcontractors who affix a trade mark onto bottles (e.g. a bottling plant) but do not have the right to market the goods themselves do not themselves infringe a registered trade mark even though, technically, they may have affixed an infringing sign.[810] Here, there cannot be said to be a high risk that the subcontractor will place goods bearing the infringing sign on the market.

---

[807] art.10.3(a)–(c), (e) TMD; art.9.2(a)–(c),(e) EUTMR.
[808] art.9.4 EUTMR; art.10.4 TMD.
[809] See para.3-584.
[810] See para.3-464.

As well as introducing an "in transit" right, the new EUTMR now establishes **3-486**
examples of infringement being:

- Use of a sign as a trade or company name or part of a trade or company name. This is discussed below.
- Use of a sign in comparative advertising that is contrary to Dir.2006/114/EC. The interaction of the EUTMR and TMD and Dir.2006/114/EC is discussed at para.3-562.
- Dealings in packaging, labels, etc. that bear an infringing sign. Here, the EUTM or national trade mark owner can bring injunctive relief regardless of whether the packager or labeller is carrying out an act of infringement. This is discussed at para.3-471.

Use of the sign as a trade or company name

As part of the exclusive right, art.9.3(d) EUTMR says that using the sign as a **3-487**
company name or trading name (or part thereof) may be prohibited. In the author's
opinion, this is not conferring a "standalone" right to prevent the use of a sign as a
company name. Rather, insofar as the company or trading name is used in relation
to goods or services which would give the EUTM owner a right to prevent under
art.9.2, it is not an absolute defence to that cause of action that such is use of a
company or trading name. In *Céline v Céline Sarl*[811] the Court of Justice held that
a third party's use of a company or trading name may infringe a EUTM or national
trademark where there is use in relation to goods or services and such occurs where
the third party uses that sign in such a way that a link is established between the
sign which constitutes the company, trade or shop name of the third party and the
goods marketed or the services provided by the third party.[812]. This is reflected in
the recitals of the TMD and EUTMR which state that "the concept of infringement of a trade mark should also comprise the use of the sign as a trade name or
similar designation, *as long as such use is made for the purposes of distinguishing
goods or services*."[813] In the author's view, this embodies the principle of law
established in *Celine*.

Defences to infringement

Introduction

The EUTMR and TMD provide a number of express defences to an action. These **3-488**
are:

- Use of the name or address of a natural person.[814]
- Use of signs or indications which are not distinctive or which concern a characteristic of the goods or services.[815]

---

[811] (C-17/06) EU:C:2007:497.
[812] See [23].
[813] e.g. Recital 19, TMD.
[814] art.14.1(a) EUTMR.
[815] art.14.1(b) EUTMR.

- "Referential use", i.e. use of a mark for the purpose of identifying the goods or services of the owner of the mark.[816]
- Use of a later EUTM or national registered mark.[817]
- Use which the owner of the registered mark has acquiesced in.[818]
- Use of a sign with the consent of the proprietor.[819]
- Dealing in goods placed on the market by the owner of the EUTM or national mark.[820] This is often called "exhaustion of rights" and is a topic in itself. It is discussed at para.3-590.

3-489   The reader should note that some of these defences in Reg.2017/1001 were introduced or modified by Reg.2015/2424 with effect from 23 March 2016. First, this removed the defence of use of own name where such is not the name of a person but a company. Secondly, it introduced a defence of use of "signs or indications which are not distinctive" into the old defence which merely provided for a defence of use of a sign to indicate a characteristic of goods or services. Thirdly, the referential use defence (i.e. use of a sign to indicate the goods or services of the trade mark owner) was extended from a narrow one limited to "accessory or spare parts" to any type of referential use. Finally, the use of a later EUTM or national registered trade mark was also introduced as a defence.

3-490   The reader should also be aware that there are other "defences" in existence which are not said to be expressly defences. These include:

- Use of a sign in the context of a comparative advertisement where such use complies with the Comparative Advertising Directive ("CAD"). This is a type of referential use of a trade mark. However, the interaction of CAD and the EUTMR and TMD is a topic in its own right. This is discussed below at para.3-562.
- Honest concurrent use. This is discussed at para.3-537.

Use of own name or address

3-491   The EUTMR and TMD provide for a defence of the use of the name or address of a "third party" where that third party is a natural person, i.e. a human being.[821] "Third party" would include use of the name of a defendant in infringement proceedings.[822] By Reg.2015/2424 the availability of this defence for company names and other legal persons was removed with effect from 23 March 2016. The removal of this is explained in the recitals to the TMD as to provide equal conditions between the protection granted for trade names and trade marks and whereby trade names are regularly granted unrestricted protection against later trade marks.[823] This statement appears to reflect the fact that in a number of Member States, there is sui generis protection for trade names. It might be said that a more fundamental distinction is that company names are chosen and can be changed by directors whereas natural names are chosen at birth. Thus, there cannot be said to be any compelling reason to use a company name which infringes a registered trade mark

---

[816] art.14.1(c) EUTMR.
[817] art.16 EUTMR.
[818] art.61 EUTMR.
[819] art.10.2 EUTMR.
[820] art.15 EUTMR; art.15 TMD.
[821] art.14.1(a) EUTMR; art.14.1(a) TMD.
[822] See use of "third party" in art.9.2 (rights conferred by a EU trade mark) and art.12.1 EUTMR.
[823] e.g. Recital 27, TMD.

whereas it would be oppressive in many circumstances to prevent a human being from using their name which might be said to breach fundamental rights of identity.

Where a company has been trading under its own name prior to 23 March 2016, **3-492** it is considered that the effect of the change is to remove the defence for use of the name on or after 23 March 2016 but not to render it liable for such use prior to 23 March 2016. This would be in accordance with general principles of EU law whereby accrued rights of defence (i.e. what was not an infringement cannot be made into an act of infringement) cannot be removed but equally, no undertaking can assume that the law will not change.

With regard to an address, this would cover the domestic or business address of **3-493** a natural person. It is unlikely that such would be invoked. However, there is clearly argument for the proposition that it covers the domain name of a natural person, e.g. *www.guytritton.com.*

As with other defences under art.14 EUTMR, the use must be in accordance with **3-494** honest practices in industrial and commercial matters. This is discussed later at para.3-507.

Use of non-distinctive signs or indications or which indicate characteristic of goods or services

The EUTMR and TMD provide that "signs or indications *which are not distinc-* **3-495** *tive* or which concern the kind, quality, quantity, intended purpose, value, geographical origin, the time of production of goods or of rendering of the services, or other characteristic of goods or services" is a defence.[824] The words in italics above were introduced with effect from 23 March 2016 by Reg.2015/2424. This is explained in the EUTMR as being to "...*permit the use of descriptive or non-distinctive signs or indications in general.*"[825] Whether this adds much to the already existing defence is discussed below. As with the own name defence, such use must be in accordance with honest practices in industrial and commercial matters.

It should be noted that the wording of this defence closely mirrors a ground of **3-496** objection to the registration of a mark, namely that one cannot register a mark which consists exclusively of signs or indications which may serve in trade to designate characteristics of the goods or services.[826] However, it would be a mistake to assume that if a sign which is identical to a registered trade mark is being used to indicate a characteristic of goods or services covered by the registration, then the registered mark must be considered invalidly registered. This is because a mark may overcome such an objection by having acquired distinctive character by reason of its use in the marketplace. Thus, this defence does have an important role.

Use of sign as a trade mark?

It might be thought that this defence does not cover use of the defendant's sign **3-497** where such is used as an indication of trade origin, i.e. as a trade mark. However, such is not the case. In *Gerolsteiner Brunnen & Co GmBH v Putsch GmbH*,[827] the CJEU confirmed that for the purpose of this defence, it was irrelevant whether use

---

[824] art.14.1(b) EUTMR; art.14.1(b) TMD.
[825] Recital 21, EUTMR.
[826] See para.3-204.
[827] *Gerolsteiner Brunnen GmbH & Co v Putsch GmbH* (C-100/02) [2004] E.C.R. I-691; [2004] E.T.M.R. 40.

of the defendant's sign was as a trade mark or not.[828] In particular, the CJEU noted that in the *travaux préparatoires*, the requirement that the use of the sign must be "in accordance with honest industrial or commercial practice" replaced the requirement "as a trade mark".[829] Thus, in *Gerolsteiner*, which is discussed later, a geographical name KERRY SPRING was being used as a trade mark for mineral water which came from a spring called Kerry Spring. It was argued that such infringed the mark GERRI for mineral water. The CJEU held that there was a defence under this section even though KERRY SPRING was being used as both a trade mark and a geographical indication of origin, provided such was in accordance with honest industrial or commercial practice. In particular, it said:

> "[19]   It should be noted that that provision draws no distinction between the possible uses of the indications referred to in [Article 14.1(b) TMD]. For such an indication to fall within the scope of that article, it suffices that it is an indication concerning one of the characteristics set out therein, like geographical origin."

3-498   Thus, provided that one of the functions of the sign is to indicate a characteristic of the goods, the fact that it *also* acts as a trade mark (whether this is because it is the intention of the defendant or because it is perceived to be so by the public by reason of an identical or similar registered mark's reputation) does not render art.14.1(b) TMD/art.14.1(b) EUTMR inapplicable. It is not thought that the changes to this defence introduced by Reg.2015/2424 affect the validity of this decision.

Use of signs or indications which are not distinctive

3-499   This wording which was, as said above, introduced with effect from 23 March 2016, by Reg.2015/2424 is somewhat odd. It might be thought that it introduces a requirement that the sign must be used as an indication of trade origin. There is little doubt that there is no infringement of the exclusive rights of a EUTM or national mark unless a sign is used as an indication of trade origin. Such use would not be use "in relation to" goods or services.[830] Leaving this aside, it might be asked what this new wording covers which is not already covered by the previous wording in this defence. The answer is that there are some signs which it is difficult to say describe a characteristic of a good or service but which are plainly not being used as an indication of origin. For instance, a grammatical symbol such as "?" or "!". With the ever increasing ease that exists for registering signs as trade marks that are not obvious candidates for trade marks,[831] this provision can be seen as a further reminder that use of a sign must be as an indication of origin (and not thus merely descriptive) for it to infringe the rights of a registered trade mark in the EU (EUTM or national).

Other characteristics

3-500   The wording of this provision suggests a wide interpretation of "other characteristics". Therefore, in the UK, when considering whether the registration

---

[828] See [15]. Accordingly, Jacob J's remarks in *British Sugar v James Robertson* [1996] R.P.C. 281 (Ch D) that the predecessor provision to art.14.1(b) TMD has no relevance where the sign is used as a trade mark for the defendant's goods must be considered bad law.

[829] See [14].

[830] See para.3-478 for discussion of this.

[831] Thus, "WHICH?" is a UK-registered mark of a well-known consumer organisation in the UK.

of a mark consisting of the name of a pop group, LINKIN PARK, applied for was contrary to the absolute grounds in art.4.1(c) TMD (trade marks which consist exclusively of signs or indications which may serve to designate characteristics of goods or services), it was held that such was not registrable for posters and other material in Class 16 because such was the "subject matter" of the posters.[832] The tribunal held that it was not the case that characteristic meant a *measurable* property of the goods rather than information content concerning the goods. The tribunal held that the fact there was no better way of describing a poster of the rock group as a LINKIN PARK poster meant that the application of art.4.1(c) could not be avoided and that by so describing it as such, LINKIN PARK was being used to describe a characteristic of the goods being sought, namely their subject matter.

EUIPO take a similar approach. In its Guidelines, it considers that terms describ-   **3-501**
ing subject matter or content of goods or services are objectionable under art.7.1(c) EUTMR. Thus, it says that a widely known name such as "Vivaldi" will immediately create a link to the famous composer and thus indicate that the content of, e.g. a book or CD is to the life or music of Vivaldi. However, as the EUIPO makes clear, this would only apply to goods that would be expected to have content linked to relevant items, e.g books, CDs, photographs, etc.[833] There is no reason why this logic should not apply to a defence against a trade mark infringement action, i.e. the use of the name of a rock band on a poster consisting of photographs of members of the rock band.

Referential use

Both the new TMD and EUTMR provide for a defence of "referential use", i.e.   **3-502**
use of a registered trade mark *"for the purpose of identifying or referring"* to goods or services as those of the owner of the registered trade mark.[834] Prior to the amendments introduced by Reg.2015/2424, there was no free-standing defence of referential use. However, there was a defence of use of a trade mark where it was necessary to indicate the intended purpose of a product or services in particular as accessories or spare parts. Such is a type of referential use and thus in the new EUTMR and TMD, this now survives as an example of referential use. Again, as with the above defences, this defence can only apply if the use is in accordance with honest practices in industrial or commercial matters.[835]

This defence is long overdue. There are many situations where a trader must use   **3-503**
a registered trade mark of another for the purpose of providing information to the public. Thus, a trader may wish to inform the public that it is offering for sale or dealing in goods bearing a registered trade mark of a third party in advertisements, circulars and other promotional material. An independent garage may wish to inform the public that it will repair and service a certain manufacturer's car by reference to their brands, e.g. BMW, Mercedes, Volvo, etc. These will almost always be registered trade marks. An independent manufacturer may wish to inform the public that its tyres and wheels can be installed in BMW cars. All of this type of use can be considered "informational" use of a registered trade mark.

Under the old wording *"the trade mark where it is necessary to indicate the*   **3-504**

---

[832] *LINKIN PARK* [2006] E.T.M.R. 74, Appointed Person (UK).
[833] Part B, Section 4, Chapter 4, para.2.7, EUIPO Guidelines. See also *Yves Fostier v Walt Disney* R 1856/2013-2 (2nd Board of Appeal, EUIPO) and para.3-216.
[834] art.14.1(c) EUTMR; art.14.1(c) TMD.
[835] art.14.2.

intended purpose of a product or service, in particular as accessories or spare parts" which represented the law for EUTMs prior to 22 March 2016, there were a number of references concerning the gist of this provision including the meaning of the word "necessary".[836] However, whilst this wording remains in the new defence in the EUTMR for this particular type of use, there is now no general requirement of necessity. Therefore, it is irrelevant if there are other means of referring to the goods or services of a third party without using a registered trade mark.[837]

3-505   Nevertheless, the reader should be aware and astute to distinguish between genuine informational use of a third party and use of a third party's mark which may suggest a commercial connection between the user and the registered proprietor. For instance, "our garage services BMW cars" is informational use but "BMW garage" could suggest an authorised or franchised BMW dealer and garage which would be misleading if not true. The latter is not allowed. Thus, in *BMW v Deenik*,[838] the CJEU had to consider in what circumstances a second-hand car dealer who provided repair services could make use of a registered trade mark. It said that in relation to the old TMD:

> "[64]   [the TMD] does not entitle the proprietor of a trade mark to prohibit a third party from using the mark *for the purpose of informing the public* that he carries out the repair and maintenance of goods covered by that trade mark and put on the market under that mark by the proprietor or with his consent, or that he has specialised or is a specialist in the sale or the repair and maintenance of such goods, unless the mark is used in a way that may create the impression that there is a commercial connection between the other undertaking and the trade mark proprietor, and in particular that the reseller's business is affiliated to the trade mark proprietor's distribution network or that there is a special relationship between the two undertakings."[839] [Emphasis supplied.]

The new EUTMR and TMD does not change this approach. It would plainly be contrary to honest practices in industrial or commercial matters to create such an impression contrary to the truth.

No "original appearance" defence

3-506   In *Ford Motor Co v Wheeltrims srl*[840] (which is discussed in Ch.5, "Design Protection in Europe"[841]), the Court of Justice held that where an undertaking marketed wheel covers that were intended to repair car wheels back to their original appearance (including adding the Ford marque), so that such activity would be covered by the "repairs" defence under the EU Design Regulation and Directive, this defence did not also provide a defence to an action for trade mark infringement per se. In a Reasoned Order, the Court of Justice held that the "repairs"

---

[836] *Gillette v LA-Laboratories* (C-228/03) [2005] E.C.R. I-2337; [2005] E.T.M.R. 67.

[837] It might be asked whether it is still the law that when using a EUTM for the purpose of indicating the intended purpose of accessories or spare parts, that it must be shown that such use is necessary. This would be strange if there is no such general requirement. It is submitted that the proper interpretation is that if the use of the EUTM is necessary, then such is a paradigm application of the referential use defence but it is not *necessary* to show that the use of the EUTM is *necessary* to indicate the intended purpose of accessories or spare parts for the defence to apply!

[838] (C-63/97) [1999] E.C.R. I-905.

[839] See [64]. See also *BMW v Technosport* [2017] EWCA Civ 779 applying *BMW v Deenik* (Court of Appeal, England and Wales).

[840] *Ford Motor Co v Wheeltrims* (C-500/14) EU:C:2015:680.

[841] See para.5-185.

defence in EU design law could not be relied upon as a defence to a trade mark infringement action, even though the affixing of the Ford marque was the only way of restoring the vehicle to its original appearance. It should be said that the Court of Justice did not rule on whether there was such a defence *within* the TMD and EUTMR. If trade mark infringement proceedings had been brought, it seems fairly clear that Ford would have won unless Wheeltrims could have argued similarly to *Adam Opel v Autec AG* (use of marque on model cars) that the use did not adversely affect one or more of the functions of a trade mark.[842] In the case of real cars, this seems highly unlikely. The appearance of a Ford marque on a wheel cover would suggest to the average consumer that the wheel cover was manufactured by Ford.

Use in accordance with honest practices in industrial and commercial matters

The above defences all require that the use of the sign be in accordance with honest practices in industrial or commercial matters.[843] The CJEU has said that this imposes on the user a duty to act fairly in relation to the legitimate interests of the trade mark owner.[844] This reflects art.17 of TRIPS which requires that exceptions to the exclusive rights of trade marks take account of the legitimate interests of the owner of the trade mark and of third parties.[845] In *Gerolsteiner*, the CJEU said that the mere fact that some confusion occurred was not sufficient to conclude that the use of the sign was not in accordance with honest practices.[846] Otherwise, such would be to render the defence wholly ineffective in an infringement action brought on the grounds of likelihood of confusion. Equally, for the same reasons, it is the author's view that the mere fact that there may be some detriment to the distinctive character of the mark (i.e. dilution) should not be fatal.[847] However, if unfair advantage is taken of the reputation of a mark (whether intended or not), it is difficult to characterise such use as ever being honest use.

3-507

In *Gillette v LA-Laboratories*, the CJEU gave further guidance on the requirement of "honest practices" in the context of the "accessories/spare parts" defence discussed in the previous section. It said that this is not the case where use of the sign is such that:

3-508

"(i)   it is done in such a manner as to give the impression that there is a commercial connection between the third party and the trade mark owner;
(ii)   it affects the value of the trade mark by taking unfair advantage of its distinctive character or repute;
(iii)   it entails the discrediting or denigration of that mark;
(iv)   or where it presents its product as an imitation or replica of the product bearing

---

[842] See para.3-439.
[843] art.14.2 EUTMR; art.14.2 TMD.
[844] See *BMW v Deenik* (C-63/97) [1999] E.C.R. I-905, [1999] E.T.M.R. 339 at [61]; *Gerolsteiner Brunnen GmbH v Putsch GmbH* (C-100/02) [2003] E.C.R. I-691, [2004] E.T.M.R. 40 at [24]; *Gillette v LA-Laboratories* (C-228/03) [2005] E.C.R. I-2337, [2005] E.T.M.R. 67 at [41]; *Anheuser-Busch Inc v Budějovický Budvar, národní podnik* (C-245/02) [2004] E.C.R. I-10989, [2005] E.T.M.R. 27 at [82].
[845] (C-245/02) [2004] E.C.R. I-10989; [2005] E.T.M.R. 27 at [82].
[846] *Gerolsteiner Brunnen v Putsch* (C-100/02) [2003] E.C.R. I-691 at [24]–[25].
[847] Although see *Hotel Cipriani v Cipriani (Grosvenor Street)* [2009] R.P.C. 9 (Ch) per Arnold J where he considers that if such was shown, it was unlikely to qualify as being in accordance with honest or commercial practices.

the trade mark of which it is not the owner (in particular in terms of having the same quality or having equivalent properties)."[848]

3-509   It will be apparent to the careful reader that these criteria owe much to the criteria in the Comparative Advertising Directive that determine the legality of a comparative advertisement. Indeed, the CAD was mentioned in *Gillette*. The court also said that the following matters should be inter alia taken into account when determining whether there has been honest use:

"(i)   account should be taken of the overall presentation of the product marketed by the third party, particularly the circumstances in which the mark of which the third party is not the owner is displayed in that presentation,

(ii)   the circumstances in which a distinction is made between that mark and the mark or sign of the third party,

(iii)   the effort made by that third party to ensure that consumers distinguish its products from those of which it is not the trade mark owner."[849]

With regard to the first condition (impression of commercial connection), in *Gerolsteiner*, the CJEU held, as discussed above, that it is not sufficient that there is a mere likelihood of confusion.[850] This judgment was interpreted in an English case in the context of the "own name" defence. The Court of Appeal held it was not dishonest use where a man uses his own name even if there is some actual confusion with a registered trade mark but not if objectively considered, the amount of confusion amounts to unfair competition.[851] Thus, the Court of Appeal said that in practice there would have to be significant actual deception such as to amount to unfair competition before a finding that such use was not in accordance with honest commercial practice.[852] The Court of Appeal said that where use of the sign gave rise to an action in passing off, such would not be in accordance with honest commercial practices.[853]

3-510   In *Roger Maier of England and Wales and Assos of Switzerland SA v ASOS Plc*[854], the Court of Appeal of England and Wales upheld, in the context of an "own name" defence, that the defendant had not conducted its business so as to compete unfairly with the business of the registered proprietor and therefore its use of its own name was in accordance with honest practices in industrial or commercial matters. The factors that the majority of the Court took into account when upholding the defence were that:

(i)   the marks had been adopted independently,

(ii)   the defendant had taken the view that the registered proprietor's business was specialised in the field of specialist cycling wear and not fashion wear,

(iii)   there had been no confusion in practice and no real likelihood of it occurring in the future,

(iv)   the finding of infringement was based upon hypothetical and notional use

---

[848]   (C-228/03) [2005] E.C.R. I-2337; [2005] E.T.M.R. 67 at [49].

[849]   (C-228/03) [2005] E.C.R. I-2337; [2005] E.T.M.R. 67 at [46].

[850]   (C-100/02) [2003] E.C.R. I-691; [2004] E.T.M.R. 40 at [25].

[851]   *Reed Elsevier v Reed Business Information* [2004] R.P.C. 40 at [129].

[852]   *Reed Elsevier* [2004] R.P.C. 40 at [129].

[853]   *Scandecor Development v Scandecor Marketing* [1999] F.S.R. 26 CA; *Asprey & Garrard Ltd v WRA (Guns) Ltd* [2002] F.S.R. 310 CA. An action of passing off requires inter alia the claimant to prove that a substantial number of persons have been deceived as to the trade origin of a product (or in quia timet action, would be deceived). A mere likelihood of confusion is not sufficient.

[854]   [2015] EWCA Civ 220.

of the mark for certain of the protected goods in the specification which, on the evidence, the registered proprietor had no intention of making, and

(v)   the defendant had conducted its business in a way so as not to cause confusion and avoid the selling of cycling inspired fashion.

In the dissenting judgment, the judge considered that greater weight should be given to the interests of the EUTM proprietor and the relevant public in the application of the "honest practices" standard than the majority judgment had given. In particular, at the heart of the dissenting judgment, was the weight to be given to a failure of the defendant to carry out checks regarding the existence of registered trade marks. The judge considered that as of the date of commencement of use of the mark ASOS by the defendant, the registered proprietor had already obtained an international registration and was using the mark for specialist cycling clothing. Thus, it was incumbent on the defendant to have carried out checks for competing marks and what competing marks were being used in the relevant market.   **3-511**

The authors have some sympathy with the dissenting judgment. In a perfect world, every business would carry out a trade mark check prior to using its mark (whether such is its own name or not). If it found an earlier mark on the trade mark register (or indeed, in the marketplace) and went on to use its own name as its brand, one can see a powerful argument that the adoption of its own name would not be consistent with honest commercial practices. Equally, if it did carry out a trade mark check but not find any conflicting earlier mark, this discovery would be of powerful assistance to the defendant. The difficulty is whether it is dishonest for an undertaking to use its own name in circumstances where if it had done a trade mark check, it would have found the claimant's conflicting trade mark but in fact, did not do such a search. The authors have their doubts that such conduct can be described as dishonest. It may be negligent but is it dishonest? In our view, dishonesty requires some knowledge on behalf of the defendant that would mean that its actions could be viewed as falling below the acceptable mores of industry. Thus, if the defendant deliberately did not do a search, it would be no better off than the defendant who found the mark, having done the search. However, if the defendant did not think of doing such a search or did a cursory but incompetent check, then it is difficult to describe its conduct as being dishonest.   **3-512**

Local "prior right" use

Both the TMD and EUTMR provide some degree of defence to owners of prior rights which only apply to a particular locality.[855] There are three elements to this defence: (i) the defendant must have a "right" to a sign, (ii) it must be an earlier right, and (iii) it must apply only to a particular locality. On the second point, it is clear that "earlier" means that the "right" existed as of the date of filing (or priority date if applicable) of the EUTM or the national mark which is asserted in the proceedings.[856] More difficult is the meaning of "right"? Does this mean that the defendant must have merely used the alleged infringing sign or that by reason of such use, it has acquired rights to prevent the use of the *asserted* registered mark in the locality? It seems fairly clear that it is the latter. First, in essence, EU trade mark legislation is a "first to file" and not a "first to use" system. Secondly, both the TMD and EUTMR refer to a "prior right" and not a prior use. Thirdly, art.138.1   **3-513**

---

[855] art.14.3 TMD; art.138.3 EUTMR ("particular locality" is used in art.138.1 to which art.138.1 refers).
[856] For by way of analogy, art.8.2, art.8.4 EUTMR.

EUTMR refers to the owner of the "earlier right" opposing the use of a EUTM where "his right is protected". Article 138.3 EUTMR which provides the defence of use of an earlier right refers to art.138.1 EUTMR. Thus, in the EUTMR, it is clear that the "earlier right" must be able to act as a sword against the asserted mark and not merely a shield. In the TMD, it is less clear but there is no reason to interpret the same phrase differently in the TMD.

3-514   Finally, in the EUTMR, the owner of an earlier non-registered right can invalidate a later EUTM provided that it is of "more than mere local significance".[857] It seems clear and such gives rise to a logically satisfying outcome that owners of rights which are of more than mere local significance may invalidate a later registered mark whereas owners of rights which are merely local are simply granted a defence to infringement proceedings based on the later registered mark. If this logic is right, then the meaning of "particular locality" clearly means all those marks which are *not* of "more than mere local significance". In other words, rights which arise under the national law of Member States from the use of a mark prior to the date of filing or priority of a registered mark will give the owner of that earlier right *either* a defence to infringement proceedings based on that later mark *or* a right to invalidate the same depending on whether such right is limited to a "particular locality" or not.

Defence of use of later EUTM or national registered mark

3-515   Regulation 2015/2424 introduced a defence of use of a later registered EU trade mark or national registered mark into the EUTMR.[858] This defence is rather odd because a registered mark is exclusionary in nature. By itself it confers no right to use the mark but rather the right to exclude others. A similar defence is provided in the TMD of use of a later national mark or EUTM in proceedings concerning enforcement of a national trade mark.[859]

3-516   However, for this defence to apply, it must be shown that the later mark is *not* liable to be declared invalid under certain stipulated grounds expressed in the alternative.

3-517   There is some logical complexity here. Thus, if one takes art.16.1 EUTMR, it provides that:

> "1.   In infringement proceedings, the proprietor of an EU trade mark shall not be entitled to prohibit the use of a later registered EU trade mark where that later trade mark would not be declared invalid pursuant to Article 60(1), (3) or (4), Article 61(1) or (2), or Article 64(2) of this Regulation."

3-518   The named grounds are:

- art.60(1)—Relative grounds for invalidity based on earlier marks or rights;
- art.60(3)—EUTM *cannot* be declared invalid if owner of earlier mark or right consents;
- art.60(4)—No right to apply for invalidity if one could have claimed the right in an earlier application or counterclaim;
- art.61(1)/(2)—No right to apply for declaration of invalidity if owner of earlier EUTM or national mark has acquiesced for five years in use of later EUTM; and

---

[857]   art.8.4 EUTMR. See para.3-400.
[858]   art.16 EUTMR.
[859]   art.18 TMD.

- art.64(2)—No right to seek declaration of invalidity if earlier EUTM not used for five-year period prior to date of application for declaration of invalidity.

A number of comments need to be made. First, the wording is complicated and unclear. It would seem that the purpose of such provisions is to give a right of defence to the owner of a later EUTM in infringement proceedings brought by the owner of an earlier EUTM if the owner of an earlier registered mark *could not* have invalidated the later mark on certain specified grounds (in cancellation proceedings). Secondly, if there are grounds for invalidating the later EUTM which are not set out above, then the defence does not apply at all. For instance, if a ground of validity was asserted that the later trade mark had been registered in bad faith (art.59.1(b)), then it does not apply. The owner of the later EUTM cannot say that the defence applies (i.e. it was *not* registered in bad faith) as art.59.1(b) is not referred to in art.16. However, what happens here? Does the owner of the earlier mark merely need to assert a prima facie case that the later mark was applied for in bad faith? Is that enough to deprive the owner of the later EUTM the defence under art.16.1 EUTMR? Thirdly, the grounds are a somewhat curious mixture of reasons for seeking a declaration of invalidity and defences to such applications (e.g. consent/acquiescence). Thus, the owner of the later EUTM may rely upon an acquiescence defence to a hypothetical application by the owner of the earlier EUTM to cancel the later EUTM on some ground (e.g. relative rights) to defeat an allegation of trade mark infringement by an earlier EUTM owner. Such would require a court to consider three "trials within trials". First, does the later EUTM infringe an exclusive right of the earlier EUTM? Secondly, is the later EUTM liable to be declared invalid on some ground, e.g. relative grounds based on the earlier EUTM under art.8 EUTMR? Thirdly, would the owner of the later EUTM have a defence to the hypothetical cancellation action on the grounds of acquiescence? All in all, it is very confusing. **3-519**

It should be noted that where the later mark is not a EUTM but a national mark, then the defence of use of a later national mark does not apply if it is liable to be declared invalid under arts 8, 9(1), 9(2) or 46(3) of Dir.2015/2436.[860] These broadly correspond to arts 53(1), (3), (4), 54(1), (2) or 57(2) of the EUTMR but not exactly. Thus, art.8 TMD does not correspond to art.60.1 EUTMR (declaration of invalidity based on earlier rights) but rather provides a defence to a declaration of invalidity based on absolute or relative grounds where the necessary conditions would not have been satisfied as of the date of filing or priority date of the later trade mark. This suggests that the defence of use of a later national mark would not apply if the later mark *was liable* to be declared invalid on absolute grounds, whereas no such ground appears in art.16.1 EUTMR. It should be said that the drafting is not that clear. **3-520**

The author cannot help mentioning that all of the above is unnecessarily complicated arising from what appears to be a desire that a registered trade mark should be seen as giving some right to *use* rather than merely to *exclude* others from using the trade mark. Whilst this is a common misunderstanding of laymen, it is well understood amongst trade mark lawyers that a registered trade mark gives no right to use (and indeed patent practitioners are also very familiar with the concept that a patent does not give the right to work the patented invention, e.g. where it **3-521**

---

[860] art.16.2.

patents an innovative development of a basic invention for which the patent is owned by a third party).

Acquiescence

3-522   Earlier in this chapter, we considered where the owner of an earlier right may not oppose an application for a later mark because they are deemed to have acquiesced in the application for the later mark. In essence, both the TMD and EUTMR provide a five-year limitation period for owners of earlier marks in which they can declare invalid a later EUTM or national mark. The five-year period begins when the following three conditions have been satisfied: (i) the date of registration of the later trade mark, (ii) use of the later trade mark, and (iii) the owner of the earlier mark is aware of such use. However, the owner of the earlier right is not deemed to have acquiesced if registration of the later mark was applied for in bad faith.[861]

3-523   However, is there a similar defence of acquiescence to infringement proceedings? In other words, what is the position if the owner of the earlier EUTM or national trade mark has known for at least five years following its registration about the use of the later registered mark and done nothing to prevent it? Under the old TMD and EUTMR, in the acquiescence provisions, it was expressly said that the owner of the later mark could rely upon a defence of acquiescence in infringing proceedings. However, in the new TMD and EUTMR such wording is absent in the provisions dealing specifically with acquiescence. Neither say that in such circumstances the owner of the earlier EUTM or national mark may not enforce its rights against the user of the later mark (even though they could not have the later mark declared invalid).[862]

3-524   However, as discussed in the previous section, art.16 EUTMR and art.18 TMD provide for a defence of use of a later registered mark but not if (inter alia) the later mark is liable to be declared invalid on the basis of an earlier mark or rights. One of the defences to a declaration of invalidity is if the proprietor of the earlier mark has acquiesced in the use of the later mark as set out above. Thus, where the owner of an earlier trade mark could have brought proceedings to declare the later mark invalid on the grounds of the earlier trade mark but has acquiesced in its use for a period of five years, then the defence under art.16 EUTMR/art.18 TMD apply. Accordingly, in a logically rather convoluted manner, the defence of acquiescence for the use of a later EUTM or national mark still applies although it requires some digging around the EUTMR and TMD.

3-525   Finally, it should be said that if the owner of the earlier EUTM or national mark cannot oppose the use of the later EUTM or national mark because of the acquiescence defence, the owner of the later EUTM or national mark cannot oppose the use of the earlier mark.[863] In short, both owners must live with the use of the mark by the other owner.

---

[861] See para.3-422.

[862] Thus art.9.1 Dir.2008/95, the predecessor to the TMD, refers to the owner of the earlier mark not being "entitled on the basis of the earlier trade mark either to apply for a declaration that the later trade mark is invalid *or to oppose the use of the later trade mark* ...". Article 9 Dir.2015/2436 does not contain the aforesaid underlined words. The same underlined wording is also missing in art.61 EUTMR.

[863] e.g. art.61.3 EUTMR.

Has the sign been used with the consent of the proprietor?

Both art.10 TMD and art.9 EUTMR provide that there is only infringement if the **3-526** acts of which complaint is made were not done with the consent of the proprietor of the registered mark. Thus, even if the marketing of goods do adversely affect the functions of a trade mark and otherwise fall within art.10 TMD/art.9 EUTMR, the registered proprietor has no cause of action. Consent is also mentioned in the exhaustion of rights provisions. Therefore, art.15 EUTMR says that a trade mark proprietor cannot exercise their rights where goods have been put on the market in the European Economic Area ("EEA") by the proprietor or *with its consent*.

Confusion can sometimes arise as to the relationship of consent in, e.g. art.9 **3-527** EUTMR and art.15. The best way to understand this is to see that art.15 EUTMR (exhaustion of rights) provision effectively *deems* the EUTM owner to have consented to *all acts* of marketing of goods under the trade *subsequent* to the placing of the goods under the mark in the EEA by the EUTM owner or with its consent.

This is starkly illustrated by the fact that even where a trade mark owner **3-528** expressly prohibits the onward marketing of goods bearing the trade mark to other Member States via contractual restraints, its rights are deemed exhausted if its owner has consented to the act placing of goods bearing the trade mark in *any* Member State.[864] However, if the exhaustion provisions do not apply (i.e. the act of first marketing was outside the EEA), then if the act of marketing of goods under a mark would be an infringement aside from the issue of consent, it must be shown that the EUTM owner has consented to each act of marketing of which complaint is made. Exhaustion of rights is considered later in this chapter.[865]

Express consent

In both situations (discussed two paragraphs above), the CJEU has now made it **3-529** clear that consent can either be expressed or implied. In the case where it is argued that there is express consent, this is unproblematic. Such consent can be express, e.g. under a licence or where despite the goods having no connection with the trade mark proprietor, they grant permission for such goods to be marketed in the EU (e.g. pursuant to a non-aggression settlement agreement). If there is an evidential issue as to whether consent has been *expressly* given, this would be decided in accordance with the evidential law of the court seized with the infringement action. Therefore, where the issue was whether consent was given orally, in an English case, the court held that such would be determined on the balance of probability.[866]

However, what is the position where a trade mark owner does not *expressly* give **3-530** their consent to the marketing of goods in the EEA bearing their trade mark? Can a defendant argue that consent should be *implied* by reason of all the circumstances?

Implied consent: goods first placed on the market outside the EEA

The issue of implied consent first came before the CJEU in the context of genuine **3-531** goods of the trade mark proprietor being first marketed outside the EEA and the

---

[864] *Peak Holdings v Axolin-Elinor AB* (C-16/03) [2004] E.C.R. I-11313.

[865] See para.3-590.

[866] See *Dalsouple Societe Saumuroise du Caoutchouc v Dalsouple Direct Ltd* [2014] EWHC 3963. It should be remembered that in English proceedings, there will generally be cross examination of witnesses and disclosure of relevant documents (whether favourable or adverse) giving evidence which will allow the court or tribunal to evaluate carefully the truthfulness and strength of the testimony of witnesses that oral consent was given.

defendant importing them into the EEA to market. As discussed below, the doctrine of exhaustion of rights does not extend to such goods and thus there is no issue of *deemed consent*. The astute reader will immediately realise that if consent was too readily implied, such would become perilously close to introducing the doctrine of international exhaustion of rights principle through the back door.

3-532   This issue was first considered by the CJEU in the joined cases of *Zino Davidoff SA v A&G Imports; Levi Strauss v Tesco and Levi Strauss v Costco*.[867] In a short and clear judgment, it held that:

> "(1) the consent of a trade mark proprietor to the marketing within the EEA of products bearing its mark, such products having previously been placed on the market outside the EEA by that proprietor or with his consent, could be implied where the facts and circumstances prior to, simultaneous with, or subsequent to the placing of the goods on the market outside the EEA, *unequivocally demonstrated* that the proprietor had renounced his right to oppose the placing of the goods on the market within the EEA;
> (2) implied consent could not be inferred from the fact that;
>> (a) the trade mark proprietor had not communicated to all subsequent purchasers outside the EEA his continued opposition to marketing within the EEA,
>> (b) the goods carried no warning of the prohibition,
>> (c) ownership was transferred without a contractual reservation prohibiting resale within the EEA, and
> (3) with regard to the exhaustion of the proprietor's exclusive right, it was not relevant that the importer was ignorant of the objections to resale in the EEA or that the authorised retailers had failed to impose a contractual reservation on subsequent purchasers setting out such opposition." [Emphasis supplied.]

3-533   The requirement that consent be "unequivocally demonstrated" means that parallel importers from products bearing registered marks placed outside the EEA will hardly ever be able to convince a court or tribunal that the proprietor has *impliedly* consented. However, it is clear from the judgment that the court envisaged circumstances stopping short of actual and express consent where consent can be implied. In an English case, *Mastercigars*,[868] it was held that this phrase meant that in English proceedings, the evidence must establish that, on the balance of probability, the facts were only consistent with consent. Thus if two alternative interpretations of the determined facts could be drawn, then consent was not unequivocally demonstrated. The burden and standard of proof in exhaustion cases is discussed in more detail in Ch.7.[869]

Implied consent: goods first placed on the market inside the EEA by a third party

3-534   It might have been thought that the need to unequivocally demonstrate that the proprietor has impliedly consented to the importation of non-EEA goods into the EEA would not apply where the goods were first marketed in the EEA. This reasoning would be based on the fact that there was no need for such a high standard where there was no danger of introducing an international exhaustion of rights

---

[867] Joined cases of *Zino Davidoff v A&G Imports* (C-414/99), *Levi Strauss v Costco Wholesale* (C-416/99) and *Levi Strauss v Tesco Stores* (C-415/99) [2001] E.C.R. I-08691.
[868] *Mastercigars* [2007] E.T.M.R. 44; [2007] R.P.C. 24 CA.
[869] See para.7-114, et seq.

doctrine through the back door. However, in *Makro v Diesel*,[870] the CJEU rejected such arguments and held that the requirement of "unequivocal demonstration" of consent applies even where the issue is whether the trade mark proprietor consented to the *first* marketing of goods in the EEA.[871] In that case, the registered proprietor had entered into a distribution agreement with an Italian distributor for Spain, Portugal and Andorra for its "Diesel" clothing. The Italian distributor entered into an exclusive distribution agreement with a Spanish distributor under which it was granted exclusive selling rights in relation to a number of goods including shoes for Spain, Portugal and Andorra for the purpose of conducting market tests of shoes bearing the mark "Diesel". The Spanish distributor then entered into a contract with another business for it to manufacture and sell shoes, bags and belts bearing the "Diesel" trade mark. Such was done without the express approval of the Italian distributor or the registered proprietor. This business sold them to two Spanish undertakings who then sold them to a Dutch supermarket chain, Makro, who placed them on the market. The registered proprietor brought proceedings against Makro for trade mark infringement in the Netherlands. On reference to the CJEU as to whether the *Davidoff* approach applied to goods first put on the market in the EEA and which had not been previously marketed outside the EEA, the CJEU held that no distinction could be drawn and thus it was necessary for the defendant who had no economic link with the proprietor to demonstrate unequivocally that the proprietor had renounced his exclusive rights.[872]

3-535 Consent to a batch of trade marked goods being imported into the EEA does not amount to consent to other batches bearing the same mark which had been placed on the market in similar conditions. In *Sebago Inc v GB-UNIC SA*,[873] a parallel importer sought to market genuine shoes bearing the "Sebago" and "Docksides" marks which had been put on the market in El Salvador with the consent of the proprietor. It was argued that, in order to prove consent, it was only necessary to show that goods of the same type bearing the same marks had been marketed with the consent of the proprietor in the EEA. This was rejected by the CJEU, since it would, in practice, have effectively imposed the doctrine of international exhaustion which it had rejected in *Silhouette* by imposing a "once and for all" doctrine of consent. It should also be noted that this judgment preceded *Zino Davidoff*.

3-536 The burden of proving consent lies on the trader asserting consent.[874]

SPECIAL SITUATIONS

Honest concurrent usage

3-537 Neither the TMD nor the EUTMR provide for an express defence whereby if two trade marks have been used alongside each other for many years with no substantial confusion in the marketplace, the owner of the earlier mark cannot enforce it against

---

[870] (C-324/08) [2009] E.C.R. I-10019.

[871] See also *Coty Prestige Group GmbH v Simex Trading AG* (C-127/09) [2010] E.C.R. I-4954 at [30], [35]–[38].

[872] See [35].

[873] *Sebago Inc v GB-UNIC SA* [1999] E.C.R. I-4103; [2000] R.P.C. 63.

[874] e.g. see *Class International v Colgate-Palmolive* (C-405/03) [2005] E.C.R. I-8735 at [74].

the later mark. The nearest that the TMD and EUTMR get to such a defence of "honest concurrent use" is the defence of acquiescence discussed earlier.[875]

3-538   However, in *Budweiser/Budvar*,[876] the Court of Justice considered whether such a defence existed outside the express defence of acquiescence. In that case, the English Court of Appeal had referred by way of preliminary reference to the Court of Justice whether Dir.89/104 (the predecessor to the current TMD) permitted the owner of an earlier trade mark to cancel an identical later trade mark designating identical goods if there had been a long period of honest concurrent use. Thus, strictly speaking the question was not concerned with infringement but cancellation proceedings.[877] However, the Court of Justice considered that the conditions of application for cancellation based on an earlier identical mark for identical goods were the same as those for infringement based on "double identity". The Court of Justice emphasised that the exclusive right under Dir.89/104 existed to protect the specific interests of the trade mark owner, i.e. where use by the defendant did or was liable to affect the functions of the earlier trade mark. The Court of Justice held that where there had been a long period of honest concurrent use, the owner of the earlier trade mark could not obtain the cancellation of the later mark in circumstances where such use neither had nor was liable to have an adverse effect on the essential function of the trade mark.[878] The Court of Justice stressed that this was an exceptional case relying upon the fact that: both companies had been marketing their beer under the sign BUDWEISER for 30 years prior to the registration of the marks concerned; both had been using their Budweiser marks in good faith; and UK consumers were well aware of the difference between the two beers and both were clearly identifiable as being produced by different companies.

3-539   As said, strictly, the Court of Justice's judgment concerned cancellation proceedings. Yet, equally, the court made no distinction between infringement and cancellation proceedings. If there had been a period of long honest concurrent use such that the later mark cannot be said to have had an effect on the functions of the earlier mark, then this is a defence to both cancellation and infringement proceedings. Accordingly, on return to the Court of Appeal, it found the defence of honest concurrent use made out in the infringement action.[879]

3-540   The defence of honest concurrent use is firmly based on the principle that in double identity infringement actions, the claimant must show that the use of the alleged infringing sign by the defendant has or is liable to have an adverse effect on the functions of the claimant's mark. Thus, whilst it is common to refer to an "honest concurrent use" defence, in truth, such a defence is employed because in circumstances of honest concurrent use over a long period of two identical marks, it can often be safely presumed and found that the later mark has not affected the functions of the earlier mark.

3-541   By the above reasoning, it might be thought that if confusion was more than de minimis, there is an adverse effect on the essential function of the earlier mark and the defence cannot be made out. However, as held by the English Court of Appeal, where there was indeed more than de minimis confusion, in the case of honest concurrent use, the earlier mark does not solely indicate the goods of services

---

[875] See para.3-522.
[876] (C-482/06) ECLI:EU:C:2011:605.
[877] See para.3-418 where this is discussed.
[878] See [70]–[84].
[879] [2012] EWCA Civ 880; [2013] R.P.C. 12.

of the owner of the earlier mark. There never was a guarantee of *exclusive trade origin* conferred by the earlier mark.[880]

Moreover, the Court of Justice's judgment in *Budweiser/Budvar* assumed (as **3-542** such was within the question referred to it) that the concurrent use had been "honest". Thus, one can envisage a situation where the longstanding concurrent use could be said not to have affected the functions of the earlier mark but on the facts, the use cannot be considered as "honest". In an English decision, the court has said that when considering whether longstanding concurrent use has been honest, there were a number of matters to take account of including: whether the defendant had acted fairly in relation to the legitimate interests of the trade mark owner; whether it was unfairly competing with the trade mark owner; and whether the defendant had taken steps to increase the level of confusion beyond that which is inevitable.[881]

In summary, it must be considered that there is now a defence of honest concur- **3-543** rent use which is a standalone one. However, when considering whether it applies to a set of facts, there are three main issues: (a) Has there been a period of long concurrent use of two marks alongside each other in the marketplace? (b) Is the use of the defendant's mark honest? (c) Has the use of the defendant's mark materially and significantly adversely affected the functions of the asserted earlier mark or not, bearing in mind that for a long period, the asserted mark has not acted as an exclusive indication of origin?

Internet use

In the 21st century, it can be fairly said that the Internet has become a very **3-544** important if not the most important method of advertising, promoting and selling goods and services. It is used in a number of ways. First, the website of a trader will allow customers to buy goods from that trader with the whole cycle of ordering to fulfilment of that order being conducted through the website. Secondly, traders will use the Internet to promote and advertise their goods or services. In particular, it is now recognised that a large number of people use search engines like Google to find goods and services. This has led to the widespread use of keywords whereby traders will bid for keywords which could be merely descriptive, e.g. leather shoes or often will be a trade mark for such shoes, e.g. Louboutin. If a trader's bid for a keyword is successful, then search engines like Google will cause searches by consumers against those keywords to display advertisements for the successful keyword bidder to be displayed on the first page of the search as a "sponsored" or "paid for" search. Clicking on that will usually take the consumer to a website of the successful keyword bidder. Such results should be distinguished from "natural" results. Thus, the first page generated by a keyword search will contain a mix of sponsored/paid-for and natural results. The latter arises by reason of algorithms used by search engines based on a large number of factors which the search engines seek to keep secret from the public but will be based on factors such as Internet traffic to a website, links to that website, etc.

The original EUTMR and TMD were crafted in a pre-Internet era. Their **3-545** predecessors came into existence in the late 1980s when the Internet did not exist.

---

[880] [2012] EWCA Civ 880; [2013] R.P.C. 12 at [51] per Kitchin LJ. See also *Victoria Plum Ltd and Victorian Plumbing Ltd* [2016] EWHC 2911 (Ch) at [71]–[74].
[881] *Victoria Plum Ltd*, at [79]. In that case, Carr J held that the defence was not available to the defendant bidding on the claimant's trade marks as keywords, see [81]–[87]. However, in this case the defendant and claimant's marks were not identical but closely similar.

Even the current EUTMR and TMD do not seek to provide any rules relating specifically to the issue of trade mark infringement and the Internet.[882] Instead, the EU lawmakers are happy to allow the Court of Justice to mould or shape EU trade mark law so that it is fit for purpose for the digital Internet era.

3-546   It is a feature of the Internet that unlike a shop, a live website is immediately accessible to consumers in any part of the world if they have access to the Internet. Indeed, the Internet is truly global in many ways. Thus, a Russian trader may offer for sale shoes of a well-known French brand X which are made in Vietnam on a website hosted on a server in Panama. This website may be in the Spanish language, use a Brazilian top level URL (e.g. *www.xbrand.br*) and targets nationals or residents throughout South America in the Spanish and Portuguese language. The Russian trader bids successfully for "X" and "shoes" as a Google Adword on various Spanish language Google search engines. An astute and Internet-knowledgeable German national resident in Germany discovers this website and finds that the X-branded shoes are much cheaper here than websites offering such X-branded shoes which target Germany and a German speaking audience. He thus places an order via that website and the Russian website fulfils and ships his shoes from a warehouse in Vietnam to him in Germany.

3-547   In such circumstances, can the French owner of a EUTM X for shoes sue the Russian trader on the grounds that its website infringes its EUTM (assume that the shoes are counterfeit or unlawful parallel imports)? For bidding for a keyword that consists of the brand "X"?

3-548   In this section, we consider two factual situations which are peculiar to the Internet.

- In what countries will there be use of a sign under EU trade mark law when that sign is displayed on a website?
- Is it allowed under EU trade mark law for a trader to apply for and obtain as a keyword to be used by search engines the registered trade mark of a third party to drive custom or traffic to the trader's website?

Internet use—targeting of consumer

3-549   A trade mark is territorial and thus only has effects in the country (or in the case of a EUTM, the EU) of registration. Thus, for infringement to occur, there must be use of a sign within the relevant territory.

3-550   In *L'Oréal v eBay*[883] the CJEU said that if defendants who advertise infringing goods on the Internet could avoid liability by using a server situated outside the EEA, such would render the TMD and EUTMR ineffective. The CJEU therefore concluded that it must be shown that the website "targets" consumers within the EU (the case concerned EUTMs). It said, however, that the mere fact that a website could be viewed by consumers in the EU did not mean that it only targeted consumers within the EU. The CJEU stated that it falls to the national courts to assess on a case-by-case basis whether there are any relevant factors on the basis of which it may be concluded that an offer for sale, displayed on an online marketplace accessible from the territory covered by the trade mark, was targeted at consumers in that territory. In particular, it said that when the offer for sale is accompanied by details

---

[882] The TMD only mentions "Internet" once and that instance is merely in the context of a Commission communication in the recitals. The EUTMR makes no mention of it at all.
[883] *L'Oréal SA v eBay International* (C-324/09) [2011] E.C.R. 6011.

of the geographic areas to which the seller is willing to dispatch the product, that type of detail is of particular importance in the said assessment.[884] In English proceedings, applying *L'Oréal*, it has been said that the approach is an objective one—whether the average consumer would consider that the website is directed at them in the territory protected by the trade mark. If so, the fact that the trader did not intend this to be the case is irrelevant.[885]

The approach in *L'Oréal* was considered in *Blomqvist* where a consumer bought **3-551** a counterfeit Rolex watch from a Chinese website and imported it into the EU for his own personal use. The watch was seized by Danish customs but the purchaser did not agree to its destruction. The Danish Supreme Court referred a number of matters to the CJEU including whether any acts of infringement had occurred in the EU. The difficulty was that the purchaser had bought the watch for personal use and therefore (as was common ground in the proceedings) had not himself infringed the registered trade marks. Thus, the issue was whether the owners of the Chinese website had infringed the trade mark rights of "Rolex" in the EU. The Danish Supreme Court was concerned that it was necessary to show that the Chinese website had targeted EU purchasers prior to the sale. The CJEU dealt with the preliminary reference summarily and dispensed with the need for an opinion from the Advocate-General. It said that the watch could be considered counterfeit goods (i.e. infringing goods) under the relevant customs legislation where it is proven that they are intended to be put on sale in the EU and such proof was provided inter alia where the goods have been sold to a customer in the EU. The CJEU stated that in these circumstances there was no need to prove that the Chinese website targeted EU consumers.[886] In brief, it is difficult to deny that a website targets EU customers if, following an order for goods being placed on the website, the website owner ships (or arranges to ship) the goods to an address in the EU.

Keywords

As said above, the use of keywords to advertise goods and services is com- **3-552** monplace these days. However, can a trader bid for a keyword which is the registered trade mark of another undertaking (often a competitor)? There are a number of reasons why a trader might want to do this. First, if the other undertaking is a market brand leader it is tempting and will save advertising and promotion costs to use the brand of a market leader to drive Internet users to one's own website. Thus, if an Internet user types in "Samsung mobile phones" and a start-up mobile phone company wishes to save promotional costs, then if that company has bid successfully for the keyword "Samsung", then an advertisement may pop up declaring "Try a cheap alternative—use Brand Y mobiles". Many would see this as freeriding on the reputation of a market leader. However, others will see this as fair competition—drawing the attention of consumers to the fact that there is an alternative to the market leader—a type of comparative advertising. For instance, if there were two well-known brands on the marketplace, e.g. Samsung and Apple, many would say there is nothing wrong in Samsung bidding successfully for "Apple" as a keyword so that an advertisement is displayed saying, e.g. Samsung

---

[884] See [62]–[65].
[885] See *Argos Ltd v Argos Systems Inc* [2017] EWHC 231 at [177]–[180], [186].
[886] *Martin Blomqvist v Rolex SA, Manufacture des Montres Rolex SA* (C-98/13) ECLI:EU:C:2014:55 at [31]–[35].

Galaxy 10 now has similar features to an Apple iPhone[887]. They would see this as honest use.

3-553   The lawfulness of this practice was first considered in *Interflora v Marks and Spencer*,[888] a case concerning the use of a well-known registered trade mark (Interflora for flower delivery services) as an Internet keyword by a competitor (Marks & Spencer, an upmarket supermarket which had a flower delivery service) to inform internet users of the latter's services.[889] When a user entered the word "Interflora", an advertisement appeared saying "M&S Flowers Online *www.marksandspencer.com/flowers* Gorgeous fresh flowers & plants. Order by 5pm for next day delivery". Interflora brought proceedings saying that this amounted to trade mark infringement both under the "double identity" basis (identical mark/identical goods[890]) and also that it took unfair advantage/diluted the Interflora mark. The High Court of England referred a number of questions to the Court of Justice as to whether this amounted to infringement. It further asked whether it made any difference if some members of the public believed that Marks & Spencer was a member of Interflora's commercial network (when they were not). This was particularly relevant as Interflora franchised the use of its trade mark to independent flower sellers.

3-554   In its judgment, the Court of Justice made a number of findings in respect of keywords:

- A keyword amounts to use of a sign in the course of trade in relation to the advertiser's goods or services even where the sign does not appear in the advertisement.[891]
- In the case of double identity infringement, the trade mark proprietor must show that the keyword adversely affects or is liable to adversely affect a function of the trade mark, being the essential function, the advertising function and the investment function.[892]
- In the case of keywords, it held that the essential function is adversely affected if the advertisement displayed by the search result does not enable reasonably well-informed and reasonably observant internet users, or enables them only with difficulty, to ascertain whether the goods or services referred to by the advertisement originate from the proprietor of the trade mark or an undertaking economically connected to it or, on the contrary, originate from a third party.[893] Such was a matter for the national court to determine. Thus, it said that the national court would have to determine whether or not the use of "M&S Flowers" in the advertisement would al-

---

[887] Samsung has actually done something similar. It bid successfully for "iPhone 6s" as a Google Adword so that when a user typed such into Google, an advertisement was displayed "*Awkward You Obviously – Mean S6 – samsung.com*" combined with text that said "Our battery lasts up to 4 Hours from Only 10 Minutes Charge!)—see *http://blog.thetrademarkhub.com/intellectual-property/trademark-infringement-google-adwords/* [Accessed 19 September 2017]. NB. The advertisement itself did not display the mark "iPhone".

[888] (C-323/09) ECLI:EU:C:2011:604.

[889] e.g. a Google Adword.

[890] The mark INTERFLORA was registered for flower delivery services so there was no issue that prima facie, the double identity rule applied, e.g. art.10.1(a) TMD.

[891] See [30]–[31] citing *Google France and Google* (C-236/08 to C-238/08) [2010] E.C.R. I-2417 at [49]–[52], and *BergSpechte* (C-278/08) [2010] E.C.R. I-2517 at [18]; *Eis.de* (C-91/09) at 18.

[892] See [33]–[43]. These functions are discussed earlier in this chapter at para.3-069.

[893] See [44].

low such users who have entered the "Interflora" search term to tell that the flower delivery service did not originate from Interflora.[894]

- In the case of keywords, the use of a competitor's trade mark to win over consumers did not affect the advertising function. As a general rule, where such was merely to offer Internet user alternatives to the goods or services of the trade mark owner, it was allowable as the purpose of the advertising function was not protect the owner of a trade mark against practices inherent in competition. This was the case even if it caused the owner to intensify its own advertising.[895]

- In the case of keywords and their effect on the investment function, the use of a competitor's trade mark—in conditions of fair competition that respected the trade mark's function as an indication of origin—could not be prevented if the only consequence was to oblige the owner of the trade mark to adapt its efforts to acquire or maintain the reputation of the mark. The fact that such use may cause consumers to switch away from goods or services sold under the trade mark was not sufficient per se to damage the investment function. However, if it substantially interfered with the trade mark owner's use of its trade mark to acquire or preserve its reputation, then the use would adversely affect the investment function.[896]

- In the case of keywords and whether or not such causes detriment to the distinctive character of a trade mark (dilution), the Court of Justice said that this would not be the case if the reasonably well informed and observant Internet user was able to distinguish the service promoted by the advertiser (Marks & Spencer) from that of the trade mark owner (Interflora). In these circumstances, the trade mark owner could not argue that its trade mark had contributed to turning itself into a generic term (i.e. for flower delivery services).[897]

- In the case of keywords and whether or not such resulted in taking unfair advantage of the reputation of the registered trade mark without due cause, it said as follows:

> "[89] It is clear from those particular aspects of the selection as internet keywords of signs corresponding to trade marks with a reputation which belong to other persons that such a selection can, in the absence of any 'due cause' as referred to in [Article 10.2(c) TMD; Article 9.2)(c) EUTMR], be construed as a use whereby the advertiser rides on the coat-tails of a trade mark with a reputation in order to benefit from its power of attraction, its reputation and its prestige, and to exploit, without paying any financial compensation and without being required to make efforts of its own in that

---

[894] On its return to the English courts, the High Court held (*Interflora Inc v Marks and Spencer Plc* [2013] EWHC 1291) that in a case of double identity infringement (art.10.2(a) TMD) (as opposed to a "likelihood of confusion" case (art.10.2(b) TMD)), the Court of Justice had placed the burden of proof on the defendant advertiser to show that a reasonably well-informed and observant user *would not be* confused. However, on appeal, *Interflora Inc v Marks and Spencer Plc* [2014] EWCA Civ 1403, the Court of Appeal of England held that that this was wrong and the burden lay on the trade mark owner to show that they *would be confused*. ([151]). The Court of Appeal remitted it back for a further trial. By this time, both parties had had enough (the case had gone on for six years) and the case was settled.

[895] See [54]–[59].

[896] See [60]–[65].

[897] See [76]–[83].

regard, the marketing effort expended by the proprietor of that mark in order to create and maintain the image of that mark. If that is the case, the advantage thus obtained by the third party must be considered to be *unfair* (Case C-487/07 *L'Oréal and Others*, paragraph 49).

[90] As the Court has already stated, that is particularly likely to be the conclusion in cases in which internet advertisers offer for sale, by means of the selection of keywords corresponding to trade marks with a reputation, goods which are imitations of the goods of the proprietor of those marks (*Google France and Google*, paragraphs 102 and 103).

[91] By contrast, where the advertisement displayed on the internet on the basis of a keyword corresponding to a trade mark with a reputation puts forward—without offering a mere imitation of the goods or services of the proprietor of that trade mark, without causing dilution or tarnishment and without, moreover, adversely affecting the functions of the trade mark concerned—an alternative to the goods or services of the proprietor of the trade mark with a reputation, it must be concluded that such use falls, as a rule, *within the ambit of fair competition* in the sector for the goods or services concerned and is thus not without 'due cause' for the purposes of [Article 10.2(c) TMD; Article 9.2)(c) EUTMR]." [Emphasis supplied.]

3-555 It will be appreciated from this excerpt that the Court of Justice considered even though prima facie there would be a taking of unfair advantage, there was due cause to do so where the advertiser was offering an alternative to the goods or services of proprietor provided that the goods or services offered were not (i) mere imitations, (ii) there was no dilution or tarnishment, and (iii) there would be no adverse effect on the functions of the trade mark.

Commentary

3-556 Insofar as the use of a keyword gives rise to confusion as to trade origin, the Court of Justice's ruling is unproblematic.[898] The advertiser must exercise care here. A user who searches by reference to a brand name is likely to be looking for that brand and thus there is a need to ensure that it is "transparent" that the advertisement found by the keyword search is not offering the goods or services of the brand owner.[899] A lack of transparency would plainly adversely affect the essential function of the registered trade mark. However, assuming that there is no finding that this will happen, has the Court of Justice reached the right result? For example, when considering its findings on unfair advantage, *it is difficult to see how behaviour which takes unfair advantage of the reputation of a mark can ever be described as fair competition* (and thus there is due cause to use). The concept of unfair advantage explicitly and implicitly connotes unfair competition.

3-557 It is clear that the Advocate-General and the court considered that the use of a competitor's trade mark in Internet keywords was not only permissible but to be encouraged in the modern world and that therefore there was due cause to use, even though it was clear that Marks & Spencer had clearly intended to take advantage of the reputation of the Interflora mark.[900] The Advocate-General's view appears to have influenced the court. He said:

---

[898] For a finding that there such confusion would occur, see *Victoria Plum Ltd (t/a VictoriaPlum.com) v Victorian Plumbing Ltd* [2016] EWHC 2911 (Ch).

[899] See *Google France Sarl v Louis Vuitton Malletier SA* (C-236/08) at [85]–[86]. See also *Victorian Plum*, at [51].

[900] See AG's Opinion, [96].

"[99] In the case of identical or similar goods or services, the purpose of presenting a commercial alternative to the goods or services protected by a trade mark with a reputation should count as due cause in the context of modern marketing relying on keyword advertising on the internet. Otherwise keyword advertising using well known third party trade marks would be as such prohibited free-riding. Such a conclusion cannot be justified in view of the need to promote undistorted competition and the possibilities of consumers to seek information about goods and services. The point with market economy is, after all, that well-informed consumers can make choices in accordance with their preferences. I would find it inappropriate that the trade mark proprietor could prohibit such use unless he has reasons to object [to] the ad resulting from typing of a search term corresponding to a keyword."

As a matter of EU economic and competition policy, the Advocate-General may be right—namely that the use of well-known trade marks should be open for use by competitors as Internet keywords. Outside the field of Internet keywords (and discussed further below), it is in the nature of comparative advertisements that an advertiser will refer to a well-known brand of a competitor for the purpose of selling its own goods. It might be said that the use of keywords is an online version of the same. **3-558**

However, that does not mean such use is not taking unfair advantage or indeed that there is due cause to do so. As will be seen below, even in the case of comparative advertisements, this behaviour is forbidden if the use of a registered trade mark in a comparative advertisement takes unfair advantage of the reputation of a competitor's trade mark. **3-559**

The emphasis by the Advocate-General on well informed consumers making choices in accordance with their preferences is to focus on the *consumer's interests* but the whole notion of "unfair advantage" (and indeed unfair competition) is concerned not so much with the consumer's interests but the legitimate and fair *interests of businesses*. The free-rider who uses a competitor's well known mark to steer customers to their website is ultimately reliant on the investment made by the competitor in promoting and advertising the well-known mark. That competitor will be much less incentivised to promote their mark if they know that another person can, for the fraction of the cost of that promotion, appropriate that investment. Competition law is very familiar with the concept of free-riding. Thus, as discussed elsewhere in this book, competition law will permit the grant of exclusivity in a particular territory to a distributor of branded goods for a period of time as it is recognised that this encourages the distributor to invest in promoting and advertising those goods in the territory without running the risk of subsequent distributors free-riding on that investment. Without exclusivity, the distributor would be discouraged from such investments and competition would suffer overall.[901] **3-560**

It is right to point out that the CJEU's finding of "due cause" is subject to a number of caveats—i.e. the goods or services offered must not be imitations, not cause dilution or tarnishment, and not affect adversely the functions of the trade mark concerned. However, these caveats are illusory. It will be a rare case that the advertising is offering imitation goods; the requirement of lack of dilution or tarnishment is referring to the other two heads of complaint under art.4(4)(a) and in the case of unfair advantage, it is difficult to see how the functions of a mark are adversely affected by a sign which *only* takes unfair advantage. Assuming that there **3-561**

---

[901] Generally, see para.8-213, et seq.

is no likelihood of confusion, it is difficult to see how the communication or advertising function is engaged.[902] The investment function is a more promising candidate. One is tempted to say that it is inevitable that widespread use of a trade mark with a reputation by competitors as Internet keywords is bound to affect the investment function of that mark, i.e. it substantially interferes with the proprietor's use of its trade mark to acquire or preserve a reputation capable of attracting consumers and retaining their loyalty.[903] However, the CJEU has made it clear that the investment function is not affected in circumstances of fair competition where there is no likelihood of confusion.[904]

Comparative advertisements

Introduction

3-562 In comparative advertisements, an undertaking seeks to compare characteristics of its goods or services in a favourable light to those of its competitors. Often, it requires that the undertaking use a registered trade mark of another for the purpose of identifying the particular goods or services of its competitors.

3-563 In the 1980s the EU legislated in the field of misleading advertisements by enacting EC Dir.84/450.[905] In the 1990s and early 2000s, this Directive was amended several times (in particular by EC Dir.97/55) to introduce a Directive on comparative advertising. These various amendments were codified into a consolidating Directive—EC Dir.2006/114.[906] The purpose of this Directive (hereinafter referred to as "CAD") is to inter alia set out the rules governing what is and what is not allowed in comparative advertisements. The policy behind CAD and the approach to be taken has been said by the CJEU to be as follows:

> "[21] Furthermore, according to settled case-law of the Court, since comparative advertising contributes to demonstrating, in an objective manner, the advantages of various comparable goods and thus to stimulating competition between suppliers of goods and services to the consumer's advantage, the conditions to be met for such advertising must be interpreted in the sense most favourable to that advertising, while ensuring at the same time that comparative advertising is not used anticompetitively and unfairly or in a manner which affects adversely the interests of consumers... ."[907]

---

[902] As made clear in *Google France*, the advertising function will not be engaged if the website of the proprietor of the registered trade mark appears in the natural searches where (if the mark is not a common word and well known), such is likely to occur.

[903] See para.3-108 for discussion of investment function.

[904] *Interflora*, at [60]. Although for a case where the investment function was found to have been adversely affected by the use of a keyword of a well-known brand by Amazon, the recognised online marketplace, see *Cosmetic Warriors Ltd and Lush Ltd v Amazon.co.uk Ltd and Amazon EU SARL* [2014] EWHC 181 (Ch). Here, the High Court found that the trade mark owner had built up an image of ethical trading for its mark (LUSH) and thus had chosen not to sell its goods on Amazon. Thus, the use of its trade mark as a keyword by Amazon did affect the investment function of the mark.

[905] EC/84/450/EEC concerning misleading advertisements [1984] OJ L250/17.

[906] OJ [2006] L376/21.

[907] *Carrefour Hypermarchés SAS v ITM Alimentaire International SASU* (C-562/15) ECLI:EU:C:2017:95.

"Comparative advertising" is defined widely as meaning "any advertising which explicitly or by implication identifies a competitor or goods or services offered by a competitor".[908] **3-564**

Article 4 sets out the conditions that must be met for comparative advertising to be allowed ("*the CAD Conditions*"): **3-565**

"(a) It is not misleading within the meaning of Articles 2(b), 3 and 8(1) of this Directive or Articles 6 and 7 of Directive 2005/29/EC of the European Parliament and of the Council of 11 May 2005 concerning unfair business-to-consumer commercial practices in the internal market ('Unfair Commercial Practices Directive');

(b) it compares goods or services meeting the same needs or intended for the same purpose;

(c) it objectively compares one or more material, relevant, verifiable and representative features of those goods and services, which may include price;

(d) it does not discredit or denigrate the trade marks, trade names, other distinguishing marks, goods, services, activities or circumstances of a competitor;

(e) for products with designation of origin, it relates in each case to products with the same designation;

(f) it does not take unfair advantage of the reputation of a trade mark, trade name or other distinguishing marks of a competitor or of the designation of origin of competing products;

(g) it does not present goods or services as imitations or replicas of goods or services bearing a protected trade mark or trade name;

(h) it does not create confusion among traders, between the advertiser and a competitor or between the advertiser's trade marks, trade names, other distinguishing marks, goods or services and those of a competitor."

These provisions are cumulative and therefore all must be complied with.[909] They are considered in detail below.

CAD is exhaustive

In *Pippig v Hartlauer*,[910] the case concerned a comparative advertisement for spectacles. In preparation for the advertisement the advertiser underwent a test purchase of a pair of spectacles. The subsequent advertisement not only compared the prices of spectacles but also contained a photograph of the comparator's logo and shop front, and, according to the complainant, showed the advertiser "standing triumphantly" outside it. The CJEU said (at [44]) that: **3-566**

"Directive 84/450 carried out an *exhaustive harmonisation* of the conditions under which comparative advertising in Member States might be lawful. Such a harmonisation implies by its nature that the lawfulness of comparative advertising throughout the Community is to be assessed solely in the light of the criteria laid down by the Community legislature. Therefore, stricter national provisions on protection against misleading advertising cannot be applied to comparative advertising as regards the form and content of the comparison." [Emphasis added.]

Thus, Dir.2006/114 is an exhaustive harmonisation of the conditions in which

---

[908] art.2(c).

[909] *L'Oréal v Bellure NV* (C-487/07) [2009] E.C.R. I-5185 at [67]; *Lidl SNC v Vierzon Distribution SA* (C-159/09) [2010] I-11761.

[910] *Pippig Augenoptik GmbH & Co KG v Hartlauer Handelsgesellschaft mbH* (C-44/01) [2003] E.C.R. I-3095.

Member States may permit comparative advertising and thus the lawfulness of comparative advertising can only be assessed by EU law and there is no room for the laws of Member States.[911]

Interaction of CAD and Trade Mark Law

3-567   Prior to the new EUTMR and TMD there was no mention of the CAD in EU trade mark law. Was there infringement where the advertiser used the registered trade mark of another in a comparative advertisement? Such is plainly "referential use", i.e. use to indicate the goods or services of the trade mark proprietor. However, until the new EUTMR and TMD came into force, there was no general "referential use" defence. Two issues arose for determination under the old EU law:

- Did such amount to use of a sign in the course of trade in relation to goods or services?
- If it did, was there a defence to an action for trade mark infringement that the advertisement complied with CAD?

In *O2 v Hutchison*,[912] the CJEU answered "yes" to both questions.

3-568   The new EUTMR and TMD now codifies the Court of Juctice's decision in *O2 v Hutchison*. In consequence, art.9.3(f) EUTMR states that the use of a sign in comparative advertising in a manner that is contrary to Dir.2006/114/EC may be prohibited as a type of use that infringes the trade mark rights of a EUTM. A similar provision is art.10.3(f) TMD —for national trade marks. In general, in a comparative advertisement, the advertiser will refer to the actual trade mark of its competitor to sell competitive goods which fall within the specification of the earlier registered trade mark. Thus, it is highly likely that the "double identity" rule will be satisfied.

3-569   It might be argued that under the Court of Justice case law applicable to "double identity" infringement actions that it must still be shown, even in a comparative advertisement, that the use would affect adversely one of the functions of a trade mark. It may be difficult to identify a function of a trade mark which is affected adversely in a comparative advertisement. It is in the nature of comparative advertising that the essential function will not be adversely affected. A better candidate is the investment function if the comparative advertisement breaches CAD. In the author's view, plainly the intention of the EU lawmaker in the new EUTMR and TMD was to prohibit the use of a registered trade mark in a comparative advertisement which is contrary to the CAD. Thus, there should be no room for the application of such case law as otherwise it might make it very difficult for a trade mark owner to enforce its trade mark against the user of its mark in a manner that contravenes the CAD.

3-570   Equally, it is argued that even if the sign used is not identical to the registered trade mark but is clearly intended to refer to the mark (i.e. the registered trade mark is a word+decorative device and the sign used is only the word), that it is not necessary to show a likelihood of confusion (as plainly, in a comparative advertisement, the average consumer will rarely be confused as the nature of such advertisements is to compare and contrast two brands). Whilst it is accepted that art.9.3(f) of the new EUTMR is not in itself a deeming provision of infringement but rather

---

[911] *Carrefour Hypermarchés SAS v ITM Alimentaire International SASU* (C-562/15) ECLI:EU:C:2017:95 at [20].
[912] *O2 Holdings Ltd and O2 (UK) Ltd v Hutchison 3G UK Ltd* (C-533/06) [2008] E.C.R. I-4231.

merely sets out a *specie* of use that may be prohibited if art.10.2 is otherwise infringed, it would plainly be contrary to the EU lawmakers' intention that such use be prohibited. It would be a rogue's charter to find otherwise.

However, can a EUTM owner prevent use of its registered trade mark by an **3-571** advertiser in a comparative advertisement even though the comparative advertisement is CAD-compliant, e.g. where it *does comply* with Dir.2006/114/EC? It is not thought that the EUTMR or TMD is intended to change the earlier law as set out by the Court of Justice in *O2 v Hutchinson* that the lawfulness of comparative advertisements is to be assessed solely by reference to Dir.2006/114 even where a registered trade mark is used in such an advertisement.[913] As said by the Court of Justice in *O2 v Hutchison*, a proprietor of a trade mark cannot prevent the use of a sign under EU trade mark law which is compliant with CAD.[914]

Vice versa, it might be argued that the introduction of the new "honest referential **3-572** use" defence in the EUTMR and TMD[915] could provide a defence where the advertisement is *not* CAD-compliant. Strictly speaking, on the structure of the (new) TMD and EUTMR, this defence is applicable even where the use of a trade mark has been found to infringe by reason of such use not being CAD-compliant. However, it is not thought that here this defence would be available. First, it would offend against the Court of Justice's judgments in *Pippig v Hartlauer* and *O2 v Hutchison* that the issue of lawfulness of use of a registered trade mark in a comparative advertisement is governed exclusively by the CAD. Secondly, it seems unlikely that it could ever be said that use of a registered trade mark which is *not* CAD-compliant can be considered in accordance with honest practices in industrial or commercial matters. An advertiser who breaches the rules set out in the CAD would contravene EU law and a lawbreaker cannot be considered honest.

Accordingly, it is submitted that where there is use of a sign by a defendant which **3-573** is intended to be a reference to the registered trade mark of a third party in a comparative advertisement (whether by reason of the sign being an identical or very similar to the third party's trade mark), the lawfulness of such use is determined exclusively by Dir.2006/114.

It is therefore necessary to consider the CAD and the Court of Justice's case law **3-574** on it.

Is the advertisement CAD-compliant?

In general terms, the CJEU has said a number of times that comparative advertis- **3-575** ing is good for competition and consumers' interests and thus interpretation of the CAD conditions must be explained in the sense most favourable to it.[916]

The CJEU has considered some of the CAD Conditions. Some of the condi- **3-576** tions have parallel provisions in the TMD or EUTMR, e.g. an advertisement must not take unfair advantage of a competitor's trade mark or cause confusion with that

---

[913] See Recital 20 TMD which refers to the right of a trade mark owner to prevent the use of a sign in comparative advertisements where such is contrary to Dir.2006/114. It notably does not say that it can do so even where it is *not* contrary to the directive.

[914] *O2 v Hutchinson*, at [45]. However, it should be acknowledged that this was made in the context of whether national laws of Member States could legislate in the field of comparative advertisements and not whether other *EU law* could so affect the lawfulness of such advertisements.

[915] See para.3-502.

[916] See *Pippig*, at [37].

mark. These conditions are interpreted in the same manner.[917] Below are considered those provisions which do not have exact parallels in the TMD or EUTMR.

Misleading—art.4(a)

3-577   Whether a comparative advertisement is misleading will generally be a matter of fact. The court must take into account the reaction of the average consumer who is reasonably well-informed and circumspect.[918] Article 2(b) CAD gives a definition of "misleading advertising". It includes any advertisement which "deceives or is likely to deceive" the persons to whom it is addressed. It is necessary that the deceptive nature of the advertisement is "likely to affect their economic behaviour" *or* "injures or is likely to injure a competitor". This is very broad in its definition. Also, art.4(a) refers to arts 6 and 7 of the Unfair Commercial Practices Directive ("UCPD").[919] If the advertisement is misleading within the definition of those articles, then it is misleading for the purposes of CAD. Article 6 of UCPD makes it clear that even if the information is factually correct, the advertisement can be misleading if it is likely to deceive the average consumer. Thus, in *Lidl v Vierzon*, which was a case concerning an advertisement where the price of an "average basket" of foodstuffs in one supermarket was less than the equivalent in other supermarkets, the CJEU said that it would be misleading to omit reference to the brand name of the better known product if the consumer's knowledge of the brand names of rival products differs considerably.[920] Article 7 UCPD goes further by deeming an advertisement misleading if it omits material information that the average consumer needs in order to take an informed transactional decision, if such omission causes or is likely to cause the average consumer to take a transactional decision that they would not have done otherwise. This is a very wide definition of "misleading". For instance, consider a comparative advertisement for crisps which highlights the fact that the advertiser's crisps are the only crisps made exclusively from organically grown potatoes in Third World countries where the farmers receive a share of revenue but omits to say that the salt content in its crisps is higher than the crisps of its competitors. As the salt content of crisps are likely to affect the decision making process of consumers (or some of them), such an omission of information would make the advertisment misleading even though it is factually correct.[921]

Meeting same needs or purposes—art.4(b)

3-578   The essence of comparative advertising is to contrast characteristics of goods or services of the advertiser and the competitors. The advertiser will seek to show to the consumer that the characteristics of its goods are better than those of its

---

[917] e.g. see *O2 Holdings Ltd v Hutchison 3G* (C-533/06) at [49]–[51].

[918] See *Pippig*, at [55].

[919] Dir.2005/29/EC [2005] OJ L149/22–39.

[920] See *Pippig*, at [53]; *Lidl v Vierzon*, at [53].

[921] See also *Lidl v Colruyt* (C-356/04) [2006] I-08501 at [80] (advertisement which conceals a material fact which, if known, would have deterred a significant number of consumers from making a purchase would be misleading within the meaning of CAD); *Lidl v Vierzon* (C-159/09) [2010] E.C.R. I-11761 at [54] (advertisement comparing prices of baskets of foodstuffs may be misleading if such omits to refer to features of foodstuffs such as method or place of production if such would have a significant effect on the buyer's choice). See also *Carrefour Hypermarché SA v ITM Alimentaire Int'l* (C-565/15) ECLI:EU:C:2017:95 (supermarket price comparison misleading if price comparison was not between like-for-like shops (high street minimarket shops v supermarket).

competitors. In doing so, the CJEU has said that the purpose of the CAD Conditions is to:

> "[20] ...stimulate competition between suppliers of goods and services to the consumer's advantage, by allowing competitors to highlight objectively the merits of various comparable products while, at the same time, prohibiting practices which may distort competition, be detrimental to competitors and have an adverse effect on consumer choice."[922]

A comparative advertisement which does not compare goods of sufficient similarity will inevitably be misleading or unfair. Thus, the CAD Conditions require that the comparison must relate to goods or services which meet the same needs or are intended for the same purposes. The CJEU has said that such means that the goods must display a "sufficient degree of interchangeability" for consumers.[923] Thus, it is not necessary that the goods are identical. An individual and specific assessment as to whether there is a sufficient degree of interchangeability is to be conducted by the national court.[924] However, care must be exercised here because if the goods are not identical, the comparison may be misleading if material differences are not communicated to the addressee of the advertisement.   **3-579**

Objective comparison of material, relevant, verifiable and representative features—art.4(c)

Article 4(c) requires that the comparison be of material, relevant, verifiable and representative features of products or services. It might be thought that this provision would rule out comparison based on highly subjective phenomena such as taste, smell, etc. which very much depends on individual users. However, an advertisement which says that in a blind tasting, 98 out of 100 tasters preferred the taste of Brand A over Brand B champagne is an objective comparison of the tastes of the public and clearly taste is material and relevant to the purchase of champagne. However, an advertisement which simply said that Brand A tastes better than Brand B would not be objective and in any event, would be incapable of being verified. With regards to the requirement of verifiability, the CJEU has said that such requires the addressees of the advertisement to be in a position to satisfy themselves that they have been correctly informed with regard to the purchases of basic consumables which they are prompted to make.[925] This must be on the basis of information in the advertisement.[926]   **3-580**

Does not discredit or denigrate trade marks of competition

A comparative advertisement does not comply with CAD if it discredits or denigrates the trade marks of competitors. Care must be taken in applying this provision because it is in the nature of comparative advertisements that the advertisement will be saying that Brand A is better than Brand B. If this is by reference to a particular characteristic, then it must be permissible under CAD even if the side-effect is that the reputation of the competitor's brand suffers as a   **3-581**

---

[922] *Lidl v Vierzon* (C-159/09) [2010] E.C.R. I-11761.
[923] *Lidl v Vierzon*, at [25]; *De Landtsheer Emmanuel SA v Comite Interprofessional du Vin de Champagne* (C-381/05) [2007] E.C.R. I-3115 at [27]–[29]; *Lidl v Colruyt* (C-356/04), at [26].
[924] e.g. *Lidl v Vierzon*, at [33].
[925] *Lidl v Vierzon*, at [61].
[926] *Lidl v Colruyt*, at [61]; *Lidl v Vierzon*, at [60].

consequence. It is likely that this provision is intended to prevent slurs of a general nature and personal attacks against another brand. The language used must be impersonal and based on provable facts.

Does not take unfair advantage—art.4(f)

3-582   This provision is similar to the "unfair advantage" provisions in the EUTMR and TMD. This provision may be relevant where there is a very substantial disparity between the reputations of the two brands. For example, if a battery manufacturer decides to launch a new battery on the market under Brand X and promotes it via a comparative advertisement which states "Better than Duracell® batteries[927] for length of life, recyclability and defects", Duracell could legitimately say that this statement is taking unfair advantage of its reputation established by extensive marketing over decades, even if the statement is true. It would say that the defendant was free-riding on its reputation rather than investing in its own advertising. Clearly, this raises difficult issues because many would consider this to be fair competition and that such advertising should be permissible. It should be noted in the TMD and EUTMR that such could be dealt with by saying that there was "due cause" in a similar fashion to *Interflora v Marks & Spencer*,[928] where although the use of "Interflora" as a key-word by Marks and Spencer to attract Internet customers to their website was considered to be taking unfair advantage, it was held that there was due cause for this as it was fair competition. However, this type of approach is not available under the CAD due to the absence of the wording "without due cause". This could lead to an extraordinary situation, where in a comparative advertisement the use of a competitor's trade mark does not infringe that mark but also offends CAD. The approach of the CJEU to take a favourable approach to comparative advertising may mean that the CJEU would permit such advertising even though, objectively viewed, it would be difficult to deny that the battery manufacturer has not taken unfair advantage of Duracell®'s reputation.

Does not present goods or services as imitations or replicas of goods or services bearing a protected trade mark or trade name—art.4(g)

3-583   This provision has caused considerable controversy. In *L'Oréal v Bellure*,[929] the CJEU made it clear that this condition applies not only to counterfeit goods but also to any imitation or replica. It also made it clear that it is not only advertisements which explicitly evoke the idea of imitation or reproduction but also those which are capable of implicitly communicating such an idea. Thus, in *L'Oréal v Bellure*, which concerned "smell alike" perfumes, Bellure used "comparison lists" to draw the attention of the relevant public to the original fragrance which they said that the perfumes smelt like. The CJEU thus said that Bellure was presenting its goods as being imitations of goods protected by registered trade marks.[930] The CJEU also said that it was irrelevant whether the imitation was of the product or merely the imitation of an essential characteristic of the product, e.g. the smell of the goods in

---

[927] Assume that such is the market leader.
[928] See paras 3-391 and 3-553.
[929] (C-487/97) [2009] E.C.R. I-5185.
[930] *L'Oréal v Bellure*, at [76].

question.[931] In applying this decision, the Court of Appeal of England and Wales attacked this decision on the basis that it cannot be wrong to prevent traders from making honest statements about their products and that such was protected by human rights.[932] Certainly, as commented on by the Court of Appeal, the decision appears to go against previous pronouncements of the CJEU that CAD should be interpreted in a light most favourable to comparative advertising.[933] "Imitation" suggests a conscious copying of a characteristic of the goods protected by the trade mark. The mere fact that reference is made in the advertisement that a characteristic of the advertised goods is the same as the goods sold under the registered mark is not, it is considered, sufficient. After all, it is in the nature of comparative advertising that the goods and their characteristics are "comparable".

Goods in transit through the EU

Prior to the current EUTMR coming into force, there had been considerable debate as to whether goods that were in transit through the EU but which were not intended to be marketed in the EU or which were in customs warehouses physically located in the EU but which were not free to circulate within the EU, infringed EUTMs or national trade marks in Member States.   **3-584**

On this issue, the Court of Justice handed down a number of decisions when considering the lawfulness of customs seizures of such goods. This case law is discussed in the 4th edn of this book in the context of the Customs Regulation.[934] It suffices to say that the Court of Justice held that the mere physical presence of goods in the EU was not sufficient for infringement proceedings or customs seizure. It had to be shown that there was concrete evidence that the goods would be placed on the market in the EU.[935]   **3-585**

With effect from 23 March 2016, Reg.207/2009 (the old EUTMR) was amended by Reg.2015/2424. This means that trade mark owners can enforce EUTMs against the bringing into the EU of goods bearing an EU trade mark or a sign "which cannot be distinguished in its essential aspects from that trade mark", even if the goods are not intended to be put on the market in the EU.[936] The recitals explain that this is to ensure trade mark protection, to combat counterfeiting effectively, and also to implement international obligations under the WTO.[937] The emphasis on fighting counterfeiting is reflected by the fact that the criteria for seizure of "in transit" goods is not merely that they infringe as it does not include goods bearing a similar mark. The Recitals make it clear that customs authorities are also entitled to seize infringing goods which are physically in the EU but are in customs free zones, warehouses, etc.[938]   **3-586**

By way of counterbalance, this right lapses if evidence is provided by the holder or declarant of the goods that the EUTM owner could not prohibit the placing of   **3-587**

---

931 *L'Oréal v Bellure*, at [76].
932 *L'Oréal v Bellure* [2010] R.P.C. 23 at [9]–[19].
933 See [36]–[37].
934 para.15-025 of the 4th edn of this book.
935 *Class International BV v Colgate-Palmolive* (C-405/03) ECLI:EU:C:2005:616; *Koninklijke Philip Electronics NV v Lucheng* (C-446/09); *HMRC v Nokia Corporation* (C-495/09) ECLI:EU:C:2011:796.
936 art.9.4 EUTMR.
937 Recitals 15, 16.
938 Recital 16.

the goods on the market in the country of final destination.[939] In other words, the goods must infringe rights of the EUTM owner in the country of final destination. Normally, this would require that the EUTM owner has parallel trade mark protection in such a country. However, it may have other rights in the country of final destination which would allow it to prohibit the placing of the goods on the marketplace of that country. This "carve out" is intended to strike a balance between fighting counterfeiting and the need to allow free trade of lawful goods.[940]

3-588   Oddly, this "carve out" is said to apply only in the context of customs seizures "initiated in accordance" with Reg.608/2013 (the "Customs Regulation"). This jars with Recital 17 which refers to proceedings initiated before a EU Trade Mark Court competent to take a substantive decision on whether a EU trade mark has been infringed. The conflict between the Recital and the operative provision is unfortunate. In the author's opinion, a robust interpretation is required that regardless of the *mechanism* used to seize the "in transit" goods, i.e. customs seizure or court orders, it must be shown that the goods would infringe a right of the EUTM owner in the country of the final destination which would entitle the owner to prohibit the placing on the market of such goods in that country.

3-589   Finally, it should be said that the "in transit" provision does not expressly distinguish between counterfeit and unlawful parallel imports. It is suggested that this provision is not in any way intended to allow the seizure of genuine products bearing the EUTM which are "in transit" through the EU but which if placed on the market in the EU, would be an unlawful act because the EUTM has not consented to the parallel imports being placed on the market in the EU. Recital 15 makes it clear that this provision is about combating counterfeiting and art.9.4 EUTMR refers to where the goods "bear without authorisation a trade mark". Clearly, in the case of unlawful parallel imports, the goods bear (i.e. display) the mark *with* the authorisation of the EUTM owner.

Exhaustion of the rights conferred by a trade mark

Introduction

3-590   Article 15 EUTMR provides that:

> "*Exhaustion of the rights conferred by an EU trade mark*
>
> 1.   An EU trade mark shall not entitle the proprietor to prohibit its use in relation to goods which have been put on the market in the European Economic Area under that trade mark by the proprietor or with his consent.
> 2.   Paragraph 1 shall not apply where there exist legitimate reasons for the proprietor to oppose further commercialisation of the goods, especially where the condition of the goods is changed or impaired after they have been put on the market."

3-591   Prior to 23 March 2016, this provision referred to the European Community (the "EC") (the old name for the EU).[941]

3-592   Article 15 TMD contains a similar provision but instead of reference to the "European Economic Area" (the "EEA"), it refers to "the Union". However, the EEA Agreement amends this so that "Union" is replaced by "the European

---

[939] art.9.4, second paragraph EUTMR.
[940] Recital 17.
[941] art.13 Reg.207/2009 (prior to amendment by Reg.2015/2424).

Economic Area".[942] Thus, the change to the EUTMR aligns the exhaustion provisions of the TMD and EUTMR so that the rights of an owner of a national trade mark registered in a EU country and also a EUTM are exhausted where the goods which are the subject of infringement proceedings have been placed on the market in the EEA by the owner or with their consent. This is welcomed.

The above provisions owe their origins to the jurisprudence of the CJEU which was developed in connection with arts 34–36 TFEU (ex-arts 28–30 EC Treaty; arts 30–36 Treaty of Rome) and the enforcement of IPRs. This case law is discussed in another chapter.[943] In particular, prior to the enactment of the TMD, the CJEU considered the issue of enforcement of IPRs including national registered trade marks where such were used to prevent the marketing of trade-marked goods, and where the goods had been placed on the market in the European Economic Community (the "EEC") (as the EU was then called) by the registered owner or with their consent.　**3-593**

In this regard, the CJEU developed the doctrine of exhaustion of rights whereby a trade mark owner's rights are deemed to have been exhausted once a product bearing the mark has been placed on the market within the EEC by the owner or with their consent.[944] It was developed to reconcile the principle of free movement of goods with the protection of IPRs. In this regard, it expanded Member States' laws as to national exhaustion of rights to an EEC-wide concept. As part of its justification for the doctrine of exhaustion of rights in connection with trade marks, it developed the doctrine of the "specific object" of a trade mark[945] and the "essential function" of a trade mark.[946]　**3-594**

Article 15.1 EUTMR is often described as an exception to the rights conferred under art.10.1 EUTMR.[947] However, as commented by Sharpston AG in *Boehringer No.2*,[948] it is more helpful to consider these articles as the counterparts of arts 34 and 36 TFEU, with art.15.1 representing the basic principle of free movement of goods enshrined in art.34, and art.10.1 representing the exception in art.36 which permits restrictions on the free movement of goods for the protection of IPRs.[949] In this sense, art.15.2 is also an exception to the basic principle of free movement of goods and should also be construed narrowly.[950]　**3-595**

Consent and exhaustion—the same thing?

It is tempting to equate the exhaustion of rights with the issue of consent. In other words, it is tempting to consider that art.15 EUTMR is merely an embodiment of the general principle that a person who consents to an action cannot object to that action. Such is a fundamental principle of most legal systems encapsulated in the principle *quod approbo no reprobo*. Thus, art.15 only applies where the products　**3-596**

---

[942] See para.3-929.

[943] See Ch.7.

[944] See Ch.7.

[945] See Ch.7, in particular, para.7-025.

[946] See para.3-069.

[947] *Peak Holding AB v Axolin-Elinor AB* (C-16/03) [2004] E.C.R. I-11313 at [34] and case law cited.

[948] *Boehringer, Glaxo Group v Swingward & Boehringer, Glaxo, Smith Kline v Dowelhurst (Boehringer No.2)* (C-348/04) [2007] E.C.R. I-3391; [2007] 2 C.M.L.R. 52.

[949] See [12], Opinion.

[950] See [13], Opinion. It should be noted that art.15(2) does not provide a stand-alone right of action. The right of action where art.15(2) applies is art.5. The effect of art.15(2) is to negate the "defence" of art.15(1) in certain situations. It is thus often called a "clawback".

bearing the trade mark have been marketed by the proprietor or with their consent. In such circumstances it could well be said that they have consented to the goods bearing the trade mark being traded in any manner the purchaser sees fit. However, this would be wrong for a number of reasons. First, the exclusive rights conferred by a registered trade mark do not extend merely to the act of *first* marketing. The exclusive rights extend to all acts of commercialisation of products bearing a registered trade mark regardless of whether they occur before or after the act of first marketing. Thus, the proprietor might expressly consent to the sale of a product bearing their registered trade mark in France but expressly forbid its subsequent importation in Spain (e.g. by a notice on the goods themselves). Yet, art.15 means that in such circumstances, the proprietor has exhausted their rights. Secondly, and conversely, if the proprietor consents to the marketing of a product bearing their registered trade mark *outside* of the EEA, they *can* object to its commercialisation *within* the EEA as art.15 does not extend to acts of first marketing outside the EEA. Thirdly, a licensee may market a product in contravention of a licence (and thus without the consent of the proprietor) and yet be deemed to have exhausted their rights. Thus, in *Copad SA v Christian Dior Couture SA*,[951] the CJEU held that where a licensee puts goods bearing the mark on the market, they must, as a rule, be considered to have done so with the consent of the proprietor for the purpose of art.15 TMD regardless of the exact terms of the licence. This is the case unless the marketing of the goods was in breach of: provisions relating to form covered by the registration in which the trade mark is used, the scope of the goods or services for which it was granted, the territory in which the trade mark may be affixed, or the quality of the goods manufactured of or of the services provided by the licensee.[952] It is only marketing of the licensee's goods in contravention of such obligations which will mean that the proprietor has not exhausted its rights in respect of such goods.[953] Thus, the marketing of goods to a category of customers in breach of a provision of a licence which bans sales to those customers may amount to a breach of the licence. However, any dealings in those goods by third parties will not amount to an act of trade mark infringement.[954]

3-597   In truth, the doctrine of exhaustion of rights, as said above, does not owe its origins to the concept of consent but rather to the goal of attainment of a single market being a fundamental objective of the EU and the desire for free movement of goals within the EU (and EEA).

Article 15.2 —legitimate reasons to prevent subsequent dealings

3-598   A person may buy a product, alter it significantly and then sell it on. In such circumstances, the quality of the product when a subsequent consumer purchases it is not exclusively referable to the trade mark proprietor. In *Hoffmann La-Roche*,[955] a case concerning repackaging of genuine trade marked products, the CJEU said of the essential function:

> "[7] ... the essential function is to guarantee the identity of the origin of the trade-

---

[951] (C-59/08) [2009] E.C.R. I-3421 at [46].

[952] These provisions are set out in art.8(2) TMD. Generally, see para.3-664.

[953] *Copad*, at [50].

[954] See, e.g. *Peak Holdings v Axolin-Elinor AB* (C-16/03) [2004] E.C.R. I-11313, thereby give rise to a claim for breach of contract (although such may be unenforceable as being an unlawful customer restriction under art.101 TFEU).

[955] (102/77) [1978] E.C.R. 1139 at [7].

marked product to the consumer or ultimate user, by enabling him without any possibility of confusion to distinguish that product from products which have another
origin [and to] be certain that a trade-marked product ... has not been subject at a
previous stage of marketing to interference ... such as to affect the original condition of the product... ."

This right to prevent interference in goods bearing a registered trade mark at any **3-599**
stage of marketing after the act of first marketing is embodied in art.15.2 EUTMR/
TMD which allows the EUTM owner to prevent further circulation of goods where
there exists "legitimate reasons" to do so, such as the impairment of the goods bearing the mark. It is intimately connected with the essential function of a trade
mark.[956] Hence, when interpreting "legitimate reasons", one must have regard to the
functions of a trade mark and in particular, its essential and communication
functions. Thus, the example given in art.15.2 of change or impairment to the condition of the goods would clearly adversely affect the essential function of a trade
mark. Furthermore, inappropriate marketing of goods placed on the market by the
trade mark proprietor or with their consent—particularly luxury goods—may damage the image of a trade mark and thus its communication function. In such
circumstances, a proprietor may invoke art.15.2.[957]

Issues arising under the doctrine of exhaustion of rights

The doctrine of exhaustion of rights has given rise to a number of difficult areas **3-600**
of application which the CJEU has ruled upon which, in some cases, are relevant
to all types of intellectual property. In particular these are as follows:

Division of marks, common ownership and unitary control

In the modern world, brands are dealt with as commodities. A worldwide **3-601**
undertaking which owns a well-known brand may decide to sell the rights to that
brand in a region or country to a third party so that the rights to that brand become
divided between two independent undertakings. In other cases, the rights to a brand
in a particular country may be expropriated without the consent of the original
owner of the brand, e.g. due to wartime laws. Often, the public is unaware that the
brand is owned by different undertakings—this may often be the case where the
goods and their qualities sold under the brand are the same and the brand image is
the same. Often a parallel importer will see to take advantage of price differences
and import goods bearing the brand from one set of countries where the brand is
owned by Undertaking A into another set of countries where the brand is owned by
Undertaking B. In such circumstances, can Undertaking B bring trade mark
infringement proceedings? Or are its rights deemed to be exhausted by reason of
the fact that the trade marks were once in common ownership? What is the position if they are no longer in common ownership but Undertaking A and B co-

---

[956] See para.3-088 where this aspect of the essential function is discussed.
[957] *Parfums Christian Dior SA v Evora BV* (C-337/95) [1997] E.C.R. I-6013; *BMW AG v Deenik* (C-
63/97) [1999] E.C.R. I-905; *Copad SA v Christian Dior Couture SA* (C-59/08) [2009] E.C.R. I-3421.
It should also be noted that the need to preserve a luxury image of goods may justify a selective
distribution system which prohibits sales on third party Internet platforms under art.101 TFEU, e.g.
see *Coty Germany GmbH v Parfümerie Akzente GmbH* (C-230/16) ECLI:EU:C:2017:941. Selective distribution systems for luxury goods and Internet sales bans are discussed in the context of
art.101 at para.11-074.

operate as to the marketing of the brand or Undertaking A has some degree of control over the use of the brand by Undertaking B?[958] This issue is common to all forms of intellectual property and is discussed further in Ch.7.[959]

International exhaustion of rights?

3-602   Does the expression "put on the market in the [European Economic Area]" in art.15 EUTMR/TMD mean that the trade mark proprietor does not exhaust their rights if they place a product bearing the trade mark on the market outside the EEA. This discussion concerns the meaning of art.15 EUTMR/TMD and is discussed below.[960]

Consent

3-603   What is the meaning of "consent" in art.15? Can consent be implied by reason of all the circumstances, i.e. a failure to contractually ban purchasers from onward selling? Although the issue of consent is common to all IPRs involving exhaustion of rights, a specific body of case law has developed about the meaning of consent in arts 9 and 15 EUTMR (and their equivalent provisions in the TMD). This is discussed above.[961]

Advertising and promotion of parallel imported goods

3-604   Often, an undertaking will wish to advertise the sale of genuine parallel imported goods by use of the registered mark. The extent to which an undertaking can do so is discussed in this chapter.[962]

Repackaging

3-605   What is the nature and extent of the rights of the owner of a registered trade mark to prevent the repackaging of branded goods, particularly pharmaceuticals? This subject has seen very considerable case law both before and after the coming into force of the EUTMR and TMD. It is peculiar to trade mark law and is thus discussed in this chapter.[963]

---

[958] As was the case in *Schweppes v Red Parallel SL* (C-291/16) ECLI:EU:C:2017:990.

[959] See para.7-029.

[960] See para.3-616. However, it is right to point out that similar provisions appear in other Directives seeking to harmonise intellectual property legislation and have been interpreted in a consistent fashion. Nevertheless, because the issue is one essentially of interpretation of a provision of the EUTMR/TMD and not arts 34–36, it is not right to treat each provision as equivalent as different considerations may apply to different IPRs.

[961] See para.3-526. However, the reader is invited to read paras 7-025 to 7-026 for a full exploration of the doctrine of consent in the context of the free movement of goods provisions of the TFEU.

[962] See para.3-619.

[963] See para.3-624.

Burden of proof

Who bears the burden of proof in exhaustion cases? Although this is an issue **3-606** common to all IPRs, it has loomed large in trade mark cases. Therefore, it is discussed in this chapter.[964]

Placed on the market

When and where are goods bearing a trade mark "put on the market" within the **3-607** context of art.15? The doctrine of exhaustion of rights only applies if the goods have been placed on the market by the IPR owner or with their consent within the EEA (or in the case of a EUTM, within the EU). This issue which is common to all IPRs is discussed in Ch.7.[965]

Background reading

The reader who wishes to obtain a full and exhaustive understanding of this area **3-608** of the law is invited to read Ch.7 before embarking on reading this section. In particular, this is because, as discussed, art.15 EUTMR and art.15 TMD owes its origins to the jurisprudence of the court in relation to arts 34–36 TFEU. Furthermore, although the CJEU has said that art.15 comprehensively regulates the issue of exhaustion of rights, it has qualified such a statement by saying that it is to be interpreted in the light of arts 34–36 TFEU and its jurisprudence.[966]

Historical background

As discussed in Ch.7, prior to the enactment of the TMD and EUTMR, histori- **3-609** cally, the CJEU had consistently held that once the owner of an IPR had placed a product protected by the IPR on the market in the EEC, they had exhausted their rights in that product and could not prevent further circulation of such goods within the EEC by the exercise of such an IPR. The justification for such a legal doctrine was explained in *Centrafarm v Winthrop*,[967] where it was discussed that the specific subject-matter of a trade mark is to guarantee to the owner of that mark the exclusive right to use it for putting products protected by the trade mark into circulation for the first time. This was further elaborated in other decisions of the CJEU.[968]

This doctrine was derived from the free movement of goods provisions (arts **3-610** 34–36 TFEU), which prevented quantitative restrictions between Member States. Thus, the CJEU held that this principle of exhaustion of rights did not apply where the trade-marked goods were initially placed in the market outside the EEC and were imported into the EEC, as such did not concern trade between Member

---

[964] See para.3-662. However, see also para.7-114, et seq.

[965] See para.7-165.

[966] *Bristol-Myers Squibb v Paranova A/S* (C-427/93); *C.H. Boehringer Sohn, Boehringer Ingelheim KG and Boehringer Ingelheim A/S v Paranova A/S and Bayer Aktiengesellschaft and Bayer Danmark A/S v Paranova A/S* (C-436/93) [1996] E.C.R. I-3457 (hereinafter known as *Paranova*) at [26]–[28]; see also *Peak Holding v Elinor* (C-16/03) [2004] E.C.R. I-11313 at [34]. NB. *Boehringer No.2* (C-348/04) where Sharpston AG said that it is time to move on from considering the matter in the context of arts 34–36 (see [15]). The issue of whether direct recourse can be had to arts 34–36 is dealt with at para.3-129 and more generally at para.7-093.

[967] *Centrafarm v Winthrop* (16/4) [1974] E.C.R. 1183.

[968] See para.7-025, et seq.

States.[969] However, whilst Community law did not concern itself with the importation of branded goods from outside the EEC, national trade mark laws of certain Member States generally did prevent the owner of a trade mark exercising their rights to prevent the importation of branded goods placed on the market anywhere in the world by the owner or with their consent.[970] Only where the trade mark had been used for products of differing qualities in various countries did the courts of Member States permit the trade mark owner to exercise their rights. Thus, where a trade mark had been used for toothpaste which did not include fluoride in Brazil but the same mark had been used for toothpaste in Britain, the English courts held that the trade mark owner was entitled to prevent the importation of the Brazilian branded toothpaste into the UK because such would cause confusion amongst the UK public.[971] Other countries, such as Germany, the Benelux Countries, Austria, Denmark, Sweden and Norway, also had in their trade mark laws an international exhaustion of rights doctrine.[972] Thus, national laws on international exhaustion of rights sat side by side with Community laws on exhaustion of rights in the EEC.

3-611   In 1980, the Commission put forward a proposal for a EUTM and a Directive for harmonising trade mark law in Member States which led to the TMD.[973] Included within the draft directive was a provision that was intended to codify the CJEU's jurisprudence on exhaustion of rights. The substantive proposals, including the exhaustion provisions, were treated as one during the legislative process. This first draft stated (art.6(1) of the draft Directive and art.11(1) of the draft Community Trade Mark Regulation) that:

> "The trade mark shall not entitle the proprietor thereof to prohibit its use in relation to goods which have been put on the market under that trade mark by the proprietor or with his consent." [Author's emphasis.]

3-612   Such wording essentially replicates the court's ruling in *Centrafarm v Sterling & Winthrop* which is discussed in Ch.7.[974]

3-613   Initially, it was clear that the Commission's intent was to provide for an international exhaustion of rights.[975] However, the Economic and Social Committee proposed that the words "in the Community" were put in art.6 after "on the market". Their reasoning was as follows:

> "The Committee is of the opinion that an approach based solely on principles of trade

---

[969] See *EMI v CBS* (51/75) [1976] E.C.R. 811; [1976] 2 C.M.L.R. 235. See also para.7-104.

[970] e.g. in the UK see Trade Marks Act 1938 s.4(3)(a); *Revlon v Cripps* [1980] F.S.R. 85; *Castrol Ltd v Automotive Oil Supplies Ltd* [1983] R.P.C. 315; and *Colgate Palmolive v Markwell Finance* [1990] R.P.C. 197.

[971] *Colgate Palmolive* [1990] R.P.C. 197. The court's reasoning was that, in effect, the two marks were different, even though they shared the same name because trade marks are, in essence, territorial in nature, cf. *Dansk Supermarked v Imerco* (58/80) [1981] E.C.R. 181, a pre-TMD case where the CJEU held in relation to a similar case where substandard goods were placed on the market in one Member State that the trade mark owner could not exercise his rights to prevent their importation into and sale in a Member State where goods of such quality had not been permitted to be marketed under the mark—see para.3-082.

[972] J. Rasmussen, "The Principle of Exhaustion of Trade Mark Rights pursuant to Directive 89/104 (and Regulation 40/94)" [1995] 4 E.I.P.R. 174. See also C. Stothers, *Parallel Trade in Europe* (Oxford: Hart Publishing, 2007).

[973] COM (80) 635 [1980] OJ C351/1.

[974] See Ch.7, para.7-031 in particular, (16/74) [1974] E.C.R. 1183; [1974] 2 C.M.L.R. 480 at [10].

[975] e.g. see Recital 8 and the commentary in the Explanatory Memorandum to art.11 in the draft EUTMEUTMR.

mark law would lead to undesirable commercial consequences. In so far as third countries do not acknowledge the principle of international exhaustion the Commission proposal would result in discrimination of the industry in the Community."

This led to a proposal by the European Parliament's Committee on Economic and **3-614** Monetary Affairs proposing that the exhaustion of rights principle be limited only to goods placed on the market in the Community. Despite objections from the Socialist Group that this was trade protectionism, the European Parliament maintained such a limitation. As a result, when the Commission put forward its amended proposal for a EUTM, this limitation was included.[976] The Commission explained that this was intended to delete international exhaustion. It said in the Explanatory Memorandum:

"Paragraphs 1 and 2 of this article correspond to Parliament's opinion. On the question of international exhaustion of the rights conferred by a Community trade mark, the Commission has formed the opinion that the Community legislator should refrain from introducing this principle and make do with the rule of Community-wide exhaustion. The Community must, however, be empowered to conclude, at some future time with important trading partners, bilateral or multilateral agreements, whereby international exhaustion is introduced by the contracting parties. The restriction to Community-wide exhaustion, however, does not prevent the national courts from extending this principle, in cases of a special nature, in particular where, even in the absence of a formal agreement, reciprocity is guaranteed."[977]

Similar reasoning was used in relation to the corresponding provisions in the **3-615** amended draft TMD, where the Commission said that it had been decided not to introduce an international exhaustion of rights principle.[978] However, an attempt to clarify by way of Council minutes the ability of national courts to grant in specific cases, the right to prohibit or not the exercise of trade mark rights where goods were put on the market for the first time outside the Community[979] was rejected by other Member States.[980] Such wording subsequently remained unchanged and these provisions became what is now art.15 of the EUTMR and the TMD.

Abolition of international exhaustion of rights principle

By reason of the above, it is an inescapable conclusion that the EU lawmakers **3-616** intentionally did not adopt an international exhaustion of rights principle. Furthermore, it is clear that the reasoning for not having an international exhaustion of rights principle was economic and political and not to protect the essential function of the trade mark, namely as an indication of origin. Thus, to construe art.15 EUTMR/TMD in the light of the essential function of trade mark would clearly be wrong, as a purposive construction of the TMD based on the *travaux*

---

[976] COM (84) 470 [1985] OJ C351/4. Generally, see C. Stothers, *Parallel Trade in Europe* (Oxford: Hart Publishing, 2007), pp.335–338, where the author sets out in detail the legislative history leading to the rejection of an international exhaustion of rights principle.

[977] Explanatory Memorandum, Clause VI.

[978] J. Rasmussen, "The Principle of Exhaustion of Trade Mark Rights pursuant to Directive 89/104 (and Regulation 40/94)" [1995] 4 E.I.P.R. 174. See also C. Stothers, *Parallel Trade in Europe* (Oxford: Hart Publishing, 2007).

[979] At the urging of Germany.

[980] Summary of conclusions of the 52nd meeting of the Working Party on Intellectual Property (Trade Mark) on July 30–31, 1987, Council doc. 8117/87, at 6. Generally, see C. Stothers, *Parallel Trade in Europe* (Oxford: Hart Publishing, 2007).

préparatoires makes it quite clear what the intention of the legislature was.[981] Any doubts that Member States could maintain a discretion to retain an international exhaustion of rights principle after the implementation of the TMD into national laws were put to rest in *Silhouette International Schmied GmbH & Co v Handelgesellschaft mbH*.[982] The case concerned out-of-fashion glasses sold under the "SILHOUETTE" brand. They had been put on the market in Bulgaria with the consent of the brand owner. The proprietor instructed its agent in Bulgaria that they were to be sold on the condition that they would only be sold in Bulgaria and the former USSR. Since it was not established by the evidence that the purchaser was informed of this prohibition, the CJEU proceeded on the assumption that no consent had been given for the sunglasses to be sold in Austria. Thus the re-importation and sale of these sunglasses in Austria were liable to be prevented as an infringement of SILHOUETTE's trade mark rights, unless the brand owner was deemed to have exhausted their rights. The CJEU held that a doctrine of international exhaustion was contrary to what is now art.15 TMD, and individual Member States had no discretion to apply such a doctrine. It held that the TMD provides for exhaustive codification of the law.[983]

3-617   The CJEU said that a situation in which some Member States could provide for international exhaustion while others provided Community-wide exhaustion would inevitably give rise to barriers to the free movement of goods within the EEA. It should be noted that the CJEU rejected the approach taken by the EFTA Court in *Mag Instrument Inc v California Trading Co*,[984] where the court interpreted the equivalent provision in relation to the EFTA states and held that EFTA states had a discretion to decide whether to introduce or maintain the principle of international exhaustion of rights. Primarily, this was because the European Community Treaty (as it was then known), unlike the European Free Trade Agreement (EFTA), is a genuine customs union whose aim is to attain a single market. Thus, different principles underlie the interpretation of the EU Treaty and EFTA.[985] The reader should note now that the EFTA Court has itself reversed its decision in *Mag Instrument*.[986]

3-618   Thus, the placing of a branded product outside the EEA by the brand owner or with their consent does not give rise to an exhaustion of rights. The owner of a EUTM or national trade mark can exercise its rights to prevent the importation of the product into the EEA unless they have consented to its importation into the EEA. The meaning of "consent" is considered below.

Use of mark by resellers in advertisement and promotions

3-619   Prior to the changes brought in on 23 March 2016, there was no freestanding "referential use" defence, i.e. use of a mark to refer to the goods or services of the

---

[981] The principle that one can consider the *travaux préparatoires* in interpreting a EU legislative act has been upheld several times by the CJEU, see *Stauder* (29/69) [1969] E.C.R. 425 at [5]; *Pigs Marketing Board* (83/78) [1978] E.C.R. 2372 at [54]; *Padovani* (69/84) [1985] E.C.R. 1868 at [12]; *Bakels* (14/70) [1970] E.C.R. 1009; and *Siemens* (30/71) [1971] E.C.R. 927 at [5].

[982] *Silhouette International Schmied GmbH & Co v Handelgesellschaft mbH* (C-355/96) [1998] E.C.R. I-4799; [1998] F.S.R. 729.

[983] See also (C-352/95) [1997] E.C.R. I-1729.

[984] *Mag Instrument Inc v California Trading Co* [1998] E.T.M.R. 85; [1998] 1 C.M.L.R. 331 at [17].

[985] See analysis in *Mag Instrument Inc v California Trading Co* [1998] E.T.M.R. 85; [1998] 1 C.M.L.R. 331 by EFTA Court.

[986] See para.3-931.

owner of a EUTM or national mark.[987] Thus, an issue arose whether resellers of branded goods could advertise such goods by reference to a registered trade mark.

In *Parfums Christian Dior v Evora*[988] a parallel importer of Christian Dior **3-620** perfume placed on the market by Christian Dior, a luxury and prestigious brand, and placed advertisements in the media where the mark was used. The issue was whether and how the importer was entitled to advertise and promote the perfumes using the mark CHRISTIAN DIOR. The CJEU said:

"[36]   If the right to prohibit the use of his trade mark in relation to goods, conferred on the proprietor of a trade mark under [Article 10 of the TMD], is exhausted once the goods have been put on the market by himself or with his consent, the same applies as regards the right to use the trade mark for the purpose of bringing to the public's attention the further commercialization of those goods.

[37]   It follows from the case law of the Court that [Article 15 of the TMD] is to be interpreted in the light of the rules of the Treaty relating to the free movement of goods, in particular Article [36] (Joined Cases C-427/93, C-429/93 and C-436/93 *Bristol-Myers Squibb and Others v Paranova* [1996] E.C.R. I-3457, paragraph 27) and that the purpose of the exhaustion of rights' rule is to prevent owners of trade marks from being allowed to partition national markets and thus facilitate the maintenance of price differences which may exist between Member States (see *Bristol-Myers Squibb*, cited above, paragraph 46). If the right to make use of a trade mark in order to attract attention to further commercialization were not exhausted in the same way as the right of resale, the latter would be made considerably more difficult and the purpose of the exhaustion of rights' rule laid down in Article 7 would thus be undermined".

However, it is clear that certain types of advertising can damage the reputation **3-621** of a trade mark. If the trade mark proprietor does not have exclusive rights over the use of its trade mark, the communication function of the trade mark can be damaged. On this issue, the CJEU said:

"[44]   It follows that, where a reseller makes use of a trade mark in order to bring the public's attention to further commercialization of trade-marked goods, *a balance must be struck between the legitimate interest of the trade mark owner in being protected against resellers using his trade mark for advertising in a manner which could damage the reputation of the trade mark and the reseller's legitimate interest in being able to resell the goods in question by using advertising methods which are customary in his sector of trade.*

[45]   As regards the instant case, which concerns prestigious, luxury goods, *the reseller must not act unfairly in relation to the legitimate interests of the trade mark owner.* He must therefore endeavour to prevent his advertising from affecting the value of the trade mark by detracting from the allure and prestigious image of the goods in question and from their aura of luxury.

[46]   However, the fact that a reseller, who habitually markets articles of the same kind but not necessarily of the same quality, uses for trade-marked goods the modes of advertising which are customary in his trade sector, even if they are not the same as those used by the trade mark owner himself or by his approved retailers, does not constitute a legitimate reason, within the meaning of Article 7(2) of the TMD, allowing the owner to oppose that advertising, *unless it is established that, given the specific circumstances of the case, the use of the trade mark in the reseller's advertising seriously damages the reputation of the trade mark.*" [Emphasis supplied.]

---

[987] See para.3-502.
[988] *Parfums Christian Dior v Evora* (C-337/95) [1997] E.C.R. I-6013.

3-622   Another legitimate reason for opposing use of the mark would be where use of the trade mark gives the impression that the reseller's business is affiliated to the proprietor's distribution network or there is a special relationship between the proprietor and the reseller.[989]

3-623   With the introduction of the freestanding defence of "referential use" in both the new EUTMR and TMD, is this good law? Strictly speaking, the exhaustion defence is a separate defence to that of referential use. Hence, whether or not there is *also* a referential use defence could be said to be irrelevant. However, is the new freestanding referential defence intended to subtly change the nature and extent of any defence of use of a mark by resellers in advertisements or promotions to bring to the attention of consumers that such branded goods are on sale? It is not thought so. Indeed, as seen in the excerpt above from *Parfums Christian Dior*, the CJEU's decision is based on a balancing of the legitimate interests of reseller and trade mark owner. Equally, when applying the referential use defence, a court would have to be satisfied that the use by the reseller of the trade mark was in accordance with honest practices in industrial or commercial matters. The CJEU has interpreted that as meaning that the reseller must have proper regard to the legitimate interests of the trade mark owner.[990] Therefore, both roads lead to Rome.

Repackaging of trade-marked products

Pre-TMD/EUTMR

3-624   Parallel importers who wish to import trade-marked products from one Member State into another are normally motivated by large price differences between countries. In particular, this often arises with pharmaceuticals because of state intervention in prices. However, because of legal or cultural variations between Member States, in particular as to packaging and labelling laws and consumer preferences, often a parallel importer will wish to repackage the goods and maybe re-affix the mark in order to ensure that they can legally and effectively sell the goods in the country of importation. Sometimes, they may even re-affix a different mark where the proprietor has used different variants in Member States for the identical product.

3-625   In the 1970s, the CJEU first had to consider the extent to which repackaging of pharmaceuticals was allowable under the predecessor free movement of goods provisions to arts 34–36 in the Treaty of Rome in *Hoffman-La Roche & Co v Centrafarm*.[991]

3-626   In this case, Hoffman-La Roche, who owned the trade mark VALIUM, licensed a British and a German company to market Valium tablets in their respective countries. The price of Valium in the UK was considerably lower than in Germany. Centrafarm imported the British Valium tablets into Holland, repackaged the tablets, re-affixed the mark VALIUM and exported them to Germany. A notice was inserted that the drug had been "marketed by Centrafarm GmbH". Hoffmann-La Roche and its German company brought infringement proceedings against Centrafarm in Germany. The matter was referred to the CJEU as to whether the exercise of their trade mark rights was, inter alia, contrary to arts 30–36 of the Treaty of Rome (now arts 34–36 TFEU).

---

[989] *Portakabin v Primakabin* (C-558/08) at [80]; *Boehringer Ingelheim* (C-348/04) [2007] E.C.R. I-3391 at [46].

[990] See para.3-507.

[991] (102/77) [1978] E.C.R. 1139; [1978] 3 C.M.L.R. 217.

The CJEU states that, as the trade mark was primarily a guarantee of origin, the **3-627** consumer was entitled to know that the product that they were buying, which bore a trade mark, had not been interfered with such as to affect the original condition of the product.[992] Thus, the CJEU held that the owner was justified under art.36 in preventing the importer of a trade-marked product from affixing the trade mark after repackaging without authorisation of the trade mark owner.

However, the CJEU felt it was necessary to consider the second sentence of **3-628** art.36. Did the exercise of the trade mark owner's rights amount to a "disguised restriction on trade between Member States"? The court decided that it did if the following conditions were fulfilled, namely:

(1) That it is established that the use of the trade mark right by the proprietor, having regard to the marketing system which the proprietor has adopted, will amount to an artificial partition of the markets between the Member States.

(2) The repackaging cannot adversely interfere with the original condition of the product.

(3) The proprietor of the mark receives prior notice of the repackaging.

(4) It is stated on the new packaging that the product has been repackaged.

Despite their antiquity, these "*Hoffmann*" guidelines have withstood the test of **3-629** time and represent the approach to repackaging under the exhaustion of rights principles enshrined in art.15 TMD/EUTMR. There then followed two further decisions of the CJEU shortly thereafter. In *Centrafarm BV v American Home Products Corp*,[993] American Home Products (AHP) sold a tranquilliser under the SERESTA mark in Holland, France and Belgium and under SERENID D in the UK. The only difference between the Seresta and Serenid D drugs was one of taste. The therapeutic effect was the same. Centrafram imported Serenid D into Holland and repackaged it so that it bore the mark SERESTA and "marketed by Centrafarm BV". The CJEU held that this was going too far. Rather than over-refine its previous decision, it returned to first principles and said that a trade mark owner must have the right to prevent an unauthorised third party from usurping the right to *first* affix one or other marks to any part whatsoever of the production or to change the marks affixed by the proprietor to different parts of the production. Thus, it held that the proprietor of a trade mark which is protected in one Member State is accordingly justified by art.36 in exercising its rights to prevent the import of a product bearing the mark. This is the case even if the product had been lawfully marketed in another Member State under another mark in the latter state by the same proprietor.[994] However, it said that such a practice may fall within art.36 (second sentence) and that it was for the national court to settle in each particular case whether the proprietor had followed the practice of using different marks for the same product for the purpose of partitioning the markets.[995]

Later, in *Pfizer Inc v Eurim-Pharm GmbH*,[996] the court was concerned with a **3-630** parallel importer who had merely replaced the outer covering of packaging of pharmaceuticals with its own smaller pack without touching the inner packing and, by using a transparent window on the outer packing, had permitted the trade mark

---

[992] See [7].
[993] (3/78) [1978] E.C.R. 1823; [1979] 1 C.M.L.R. 326.
[994] (3/78) [1978] E.C.R. 1823; [1979] 1 C.M.L.R. 326 at [18].
[995] (3/78) [1978] E.C.R. 1823; [1979] 1 C.M.L.R. 326 at [23].
[996] (1/81) [1981] E.C.R. 2913; [1982] 1 C.M.L.R. 406.

affixed by the manufacturer to be visible. Thus, the only material difference in fact to the *Hoffman-La Roche* case was that, in the latter, the parallel importer had actually re-affixed the mark VALIUM on the packaging. The court held that where repackaging does not affect the condition of the product and does not misrepresent the origin of the product, then Art.36 cannot be invoked by the trade mark owner.

Decisions under TMD/EUTMR

3-631   The issue of the legitimacy of trade mark proprietors objecting to repackaging of products bearing their mark was in the *travaux préparatoires* for the TMD and EUTMR. Initially, it was proposed by the Commission that there be a general right to prevent repackaging. However, such proposals met resistance from the Council and the European Parliament. In the amended proposals, the Commission deleted the reference to repackaging and the Council Presidency indicated that art.7 (the predecessor to art.15) reflected the jurisprudence of the CJEU whereby in a particular case, the exercise of trade mark could be justified under art.36.[997]

3-632   The exhaustion of rights provisions in the EUTMR and TMD were first considered in *Bristol-Myers Squibb v Paranova*[998] where the CJEU revisited the problem of repackaging in the context of harmonised EU trade mark laws. This case raised very similar issues as in *Eurim-Pharm v Beiersdorf*[999] and *MPA Pharm GmbH v Rhône-Poulenc Pharma GmbH*,[1000] in which judgment was handed down on the same day. For the purposes of this book, reference is made only to *Bristol-Myers Squibb v Paranova*.

3-633   The court in *Bristol-Myers Squibb v Paranova* said that the predecessor to art.15 TMD, like arts 34–36 TFEU, is intended to reconcile the fundamental interest in protecting trade mark rights with the fundamental interest in the free movement of goods within the EU, so that the court's case law under arts 34–36 must be taken as the basis for determining whether, under art.7(2) of the TMD (now art.15(2), a trade mark owner has legitimate reasons in opposing the further commercialisation of products which have been put on the market in the Community by the trade mark proprietor or with their consent.[1001] Thus, the Advocate-General has said that, in considering the applicability of art.7(2), the registered proprietor must show that further commercialisation would affect the essential function of the trade mark in a way which the trade mark proprietor could not be expected to tolerate.[1002] She also saw no reason to distinguish between situations where the mark is re-affixed to packaging and where such did not occur.[1003]

3-634   The court in *Bristol-Myers Squibb v Paranova* took the opportunity to clarify the four *Hoffmann* principles and add an extra one.[1004] These conditions are often called the *Bristol-Myers* or *Paranova* guidelines and are frequently referred to. Thus, a trade mark owner may legitimately oppose the further marketing of a repackaged

---

[997] See C. Stothers, *Parallel Trade in Europe: Intellectual Property, Competition and Regulatory Law* (Oxford: Hart Publishing, 2007), pp.79–80.

[998] (C-427/93) (C-429/93), (C-436/93) [1996] E.C.R. I-3457.

[999] *Eurim-Pharm Arzneimittel GmbH v Beiersdorf A.G.; Boehringer, Ingelheim KG and Farmitalia Carlo Erba GmbH* (C-71–73/94) [1996] E.C.R. I-3603.

[1000] *MPA Pharma GmbH v Rhône-Poulenc Pharma GmbH* (C-232/94) [1996] E.C.R. I-3671.

[1001] See [40]–[41].

[1002] per Stix-Hackl AG in *Zino Davidoff v A&G Imports Ltd* (C-414/99) at [105].

[1003] See [39]. In other words, she saw no reason to distinguish between the facts in *Hoffmann-La Roche* and *Pfizer v Eurim-Pharm*.

[1004] See [79].

pharmaceutical product unless:

(a) that would contribute to the artificial partitioning of the markets between Member States. This is the case, in particular, where the repackaging is *necessary* in order to market the product in the Member State of importation;

(b) the repackaging cannot affect the original condition of the product inside the packaging;

(c) the new packaging clearly states who repackaged the product and the name of the manufacturer;

(d) the presentation of the repackaged product is not such as to be liable to damage the reputation of the trade mark and of its owner; thus, the packaging must not be defective, of poor quality, or untidy [*the new guideline*]; and

(e) the importer gives notice to the trade mark owner before the repackaged product is put on sale, and, on demand, supplies them with a specimen of the repackaged product.

The conditions must be seen as a balance between the need to attain a single market and protection of the essential function of a trade mark. The CJEU said: **3-635**

> "The change brought about by any new carton or relabelling of a trade-marked medicinal product creates by its very nature real risks for the guarantee of origin which the mark seeks to protect. Such a change may thus be prohibited by the trade mark proprietor unless the new carton or relabelling is necessary in order to enable the marketing of the products imported in parallel and the legitimate interests of the proprietor are also safeguarded".[1005]

These conditions are cumulative and must all be satisfied for the trade mark owner to be deprived of their rights. Thus, a failure to comply with any one measure will mean that the repackaged goods are infringing goods.[1006] These five requirements are now considered in detail. **3-636**

Artificial partitioning of the market between Member States (Paranova No.1)

Prior to *Bristol-Myers*, there had been some uncertainty in the CJEU case law as to whether the owner had to have intended to artificially partition the markets or merely that as a result of the exercise of the right, such would occur. Thus, in *Centrafarm v American Home Products*,[1007] the court had said that the national courts should determine whether the proprietor had used different marks for the purpose of partitioning the markets.[1008] This had been interpreted by the Bundesgerichtshof when applying the preliminary ruling of the CJEU in *Hoffmann-La Roche v Centrafarm* as requiring a deliberate intention to partition.[1009] Other national courts had construed such a requirement restrictively against the parallel importer.[1010] In contrast, Capotorti AG in *Pfizer Inc v Eurim-Pharm* had held that it was not necessary to show a subjective intention to partition the market, **3-637**

[1005] See [30]–[31].

[1006] *Boehringer (No.2)*, at [60].

[1007] (3/78) [1978] E.C.R. 1823; [1979] 1 C.M.L.R. 326.

[1008] (3/78) [1978] E.C.R. 1823; [1979] 1 C.M.L.R. 326 at [23].

[1009] *Hoffmann-La Roche v Centrafarm* [1984] 2 C.M.L.R. 561.

[1010] See, e.g. *Hoechst AG v Centrafarm BV* [1980] 1 C.M.L.R. 650; *The Boots Co Ltd v Centrafarm* [1979] 2 C.M.L.R. 495 (both cases were in the District Court Rotterdam).

merely because as a result of the exercise of trade mark rights, an artificial partitioning of the market occurred.[1011]

3-638   In *Bristol Myers v Paranova*, the court made it clear that a deliberate intention to partition the markets was not necessary.[1012] Thus, the test is an objective one. In substance, the inquiry under the first condition turns to the issue of whether the repackaging is necessary to market the product in the Member State of importation, although such is stated simply to be an example of where enforcement of trade mark rights would amount to artificial partitioning of the EC.

3-639   **Necessary to market the product in the Member States of importation**   The first *Paranova* guideline is satisfied if the repackager can show that repackaging is *necessary* in order to market the product in the Member State of importation. This requirement of "necessity" raises the question of whether such means a *marketing* necessity (e.g. consumers will not buy the product if it is in original packaging), a *technical* necessity (e.g. transport companies will only handle pharmaceutical boxes of a particular size), or *legal* necessity (e.g. legislative measures requires that pharmaceuticals are packaged and labelled in a particular way). There is no doubt that legislative requirements of the country of importation which desire the addition, amendment or deletion of information to the packaging or translation fall within the meaning of "necessary". Thus, shortly after that decision, in *Phytheron*,[1013] the CJEU held that where the importer had merely added labelling to packaging so as to ensure that the product complied with legislative requirements in the country of importation, it would be unlawful of the trade mark owner to exercise their rights to prevent the importation of trade-marked products into that Member State.

3-640   The more difficult issue is where it is argued by the parallel importer that although not technically or legally necessary, repackaging in a particular way is necessary to achieve effective market penetration. This may be because consumers are resistant to buying pharmaceuticals which are repackaged in a particular manner, e.g. where the boxes are over-stickered as opposed to re-boxed.

3-641   The issue of "necessity" was considered in a UK case which involved two references to the CJEU. In *Boehringer No.1*,[1014] the UK courts were concerned with the practice of re-boxing products in new exterior cartons designed by the parallel importer and bearing some or all of parallel importer's own logo, trade mark or house style or get up. This can occur in a number of ways. In "co-branding" cases, the parallel importer reaffixes the original trade mark to the new exterior carton in conjunction with its own mark/get-up. In "debranding" cases, the original trade mark is not reaffixed. It is simply removed from the packaging although it will remain on the pharmaceuticals, their blister packs and other products.[1015] Instead, the generic name of the drug is indicated. Finally, there can be a change in packaging without any re-affixing of the trade mark.

[1011] See, e.g. *Hoechst AG v Centrafarm BV* [1980] 1 C.M.L.R. 650; *The Boots Co Ltd v Centrafarm* [1979] 2 C.M.L.R. 495.

[1012] See [79], first indent. See also *Pharmacia & Upjohn v Paranova*, at [39]–[41].

[1013] (C-352/95) [1997] E.C.R. I-1729.

[1014] *Boehringer Ingelheim KG, Boehringer Ingelheim Pharma KG, Glaxo Group Ltd, The Wellcome Foundation Ltd, SmithKline Beecham Plc, Beecham Group plc, SmithKline & French Laboratories Ltd and Eli Lilly and Co v Swingward Ltd and Dowelhurst Ltd* (C-143/00) [2002] I-03759 (hereinafter referred to as "*Boehringer No.1*").

[1015] Thus, the parallel importers were still importing products bearing the mark. If the trade marks had been removed from all the products and packaging, then no act of trade mark infringement would have occurred. See Court of Appeal in *Glaxo v Dowelhurst* where the court said that a trade mark

Boehringer has a complicated history. Initially, in High Court proceedings, a **3-642** reference was made to the CJEU concerning the scope of art.7(2) TMD (now art.15.2).[1016] This resulted in a judgment from CJEU (here called *Boehringer No.1*[1017]). This was then applied by the High Court which held that both debranding and co-branding infringed the claimants' trade marks.[1018] Both parties then appealed to the Court of Appeal.[1019] However, the Court of Appeal was concerned about interpretation of certain parts of *Boehringer No.1* in relation to the meaning of "necessary", the burden of proof and the consequence of failure to give notice. It accordingly referred another further *13* questions to the CJEU.

In *Boehringer No.1*, the CJEU held that repackaging is "objectively necessary" **3-643** if without such repackaging:

> "... effective access to the market concerned, or to a substantial part of that market, must be considered to be hindered as the result of strong resistance from a significant proportion of consumers to relabelled pharmaceutical products."[1020]

In applying this part of the judgment, the High Court of England held in **3-644** *Boehringer (No.1)* that the necessity test applied not only to whether the importers could repackage at all but also to determine the *type* of repackaging which was permissible. The only permissible repackaging was that which represented the *minimum change* necessary to achieve effective access to the market of the country of importation. It accordingly concluded that both debranding and co-branding infringed the claimants' trade mark rights.

On appeal to the Court of Appeal, the Court of Appeal considered that there was **3-645** an ambiguity about the requirement of "necessity" in *Boehringer (No.1)*. They thus asked the CJEU to rule on whether it must simply be shown that it is necessary to repackage the product in order that effective market access is not hindered, or whether it also must be shown that the precise manner and style of the re-boxing carried out by the parallel importer was necessary as well. In other words, was the High Court right to conclude that the parallel importer had to choose the most unobtrusive form of packaging necessary to achieve effective market access? On this reference, in *Boehringer No.2*,[1021] the CJEU held that the requirement of necessity applied only to the fact of repackaging rather than the manner or style in which it was to be repackaged.[1022] Thus, once it is shown that it is necessary to repackage, the manner or style of repackaging is only relevant to the issue as to whether such is liable to damage the reputation of the trade mark or that of its proprietor.[1023] Although the reasoning at reaching this conclusion is very cursory, this finding is welcome. It avoids courts having to consider whether a repackager could have used less extensive repackaging/relabelling (inevitably there will always be some lesser form of repackaging/relabelling) and thus making parallel imports of repackaged products very difficult.

---

owner has no right to require subsequent dealers to keep their trade mark on the product.

[1016] *Boehringer* [2000] 2 C.M.L.R. 571; [2000] E.T.M.R. 415, High Ct.

[1017] (C-143/00) [2002] E.C.R. I-3759.

[1018] [2003] E.T.M.R. 89; [2003] 2 C.M.L.R. 8, High Ct.

[1019] [2004] E.T.M.R. 65 CA.

[1020] See declaratory part of judgment.

[1021] (C-348/04) [2007] E.C.R. I-3391.

[1022] See [38].

[1023] *Wellcome Foundation Ltd v Paranova Pharmazeutika Handels GmbH* (C-276/05) [2008] E.C.R. I-10479 at [26].

3-646   The parallel importer has an obligation to furnish the trade mark proprietor with information which is necessary and sufficient to enable the latter to determine whether the repackaging was necessary in order to market the product in the Member State of importation.[1024]

3-647   More recently, the Court of Justice has given further guidance as to the meaning of "effective access". In *Ferring Laegemidler A/S v Orifarm A/S*,[1025] a pharmaceutical company, Ferring, marketed a medicinal product in Denmark, Finland, Sweden and Norway under the brand KLYX and in packaging of containers of 120ml, 240ml as well as in packets containing one or 10 such containers. A parallel importer, Orifarm, imported Klyx in packets of 10 in Norway and sold them in Denmark in individual packets, reaffixing the KLYX mark on the outer packaging. Ferring said that such repackaging was not necessary as it sold Klyx in packets of 10 in Denmark and Orifarm only repackaged packets of Klyx to obtain a commercial advantage. Orifarm said that it was necessary to repackage to gain access to those persons in the Danish market who wanted individually packaged Klyx. On reference to the Court of Justice, the court repeated its case law on the need for a parallel importer to have effective access and said that partitioning of the markets would exist if an importer was able to sell the pharmaceutical to part of the market (i.e. the market for individual packets). Such was for the parallel importer to prove.[1026]

3-648   **Changing trade marks**   In some cases, a pharmaceutical manufacturer will use different marks in Member States. This may be because of its inability to register the same mark throughout all Member States, consumer sensitivities to a particular mark, or possibly to make it more difficult for parallel importers. In *Pharmacia & Upjohn v Paranova*,[1027] the trade mark proprietor used variants of the mark DALACIN in Member States. Thus, DALACIN was used in Germany, Denmark and Spain, DALACINE in France and DALACIN C in the other Member State. The importer sought to change the marks to the one used in the country of importation. The matter was referred to the CJEU.

3-649   It might be thought that in such circumstances, art.15 TMD/EUTMR has no application because on its wording, it only applies where goods have been put on the market in the EEA "under *that* trade mark by the proprietor or with his consent". Here, a different trade mark is being applied to the one originally applied. Indeed, the CJEU held that art.7 TMD (predecessor to art.15 TMD) did not apply where the parallel importer replaces the original trade mark with a different one. However, it said that the respective rights of the proprietor of the trade marks and of the parallel importer are determined by the interaction of art.5 TMD (rights of trade mark owner—now art.9 TMD) and arts 34–36 of the TFEU.[1028] However, the CJEU did not consider that such would lead to a different result because both art.7 of the old TMD and art.36 TFEU were intended to reconcile the fundamental interest of protecting trade mark rights with that of free movement of goods within the com-

---

[1024] *Wellcome Foundation Ltd v Paranova Pharmazeutika Handels GmbH* (C-276/05) [2008] E.C.R. I-10479 at [37].

[1025] (C-297/15) ECLI:EU:C:2016:857.

[1026] See [22]–[29].

[1027] *Pharmacia & Upjohn SA v Paranova A/S* (C-379/97) [1999] E.C.R. I-6927.

[1028] *Pharmacia & Upjohn SA v Paranova A/S* (C-379/97) [1999] E.C.R. I-6927 at [28]. This finding is of interest because the CJEU has said that where there is exhaustive harmonising secondary legislation in a particular field, no reference can be had to the primary Articles of the Treaty—see paras 7-093 and 3-129.

mon market.[1029] Accordingly, the court held that this condition of necessity was satisfied if the prohibition imposed on the importer against replacing the trade mark hindered "effective access to the markets of the importing Member State".[1030] The court said that this condition was satisfied where use of the trade mark was illegal in the importing Member State because it was liable to cause confusion, but not so where the replacement of the mark was solely to secure a commercial advantage (to ride on the reputation of the mark in the importing Member State).[1031] There is a fine line between requiring "effective access" to a market and doing so, solely to secure a commercial advantage. In *Pharmacia*, one can understand that consumers would be confused between DALACIN and DALACIN C, believing one maybe to have a slightly different therapeutic quality to the other. However, if the marks were very different, e.g. DALACIN and THRIX, then the rebranding by importer from one brand to the other is likely to be to make marketing in the country of importation much easier rather than to gain effective access. Nevertheless, here it would be legitimate to ask whether the fact that the trade mark owner used very different marks in each Member State was itself contrary to arts 34-36 (and thus prevent the owner from exercising its rights) as such in itself would lead to artificial partitioning of the markets between Member States.

Removal of identification numbers by the parallel importer In *Frits Loendersloot v George Ballantine*,[1032] a parallel importer sought to remove identification numbers of Scotch whisky which were used for the purpose of identifying the parallel imports, and then re-affix labels which were similar in nature. The CJEU reaffirmed the principles set out in *Hoffmann-La Roche v Centrafarm*, and said that it was for the international court to assess whether those conditions had been satisfied. In particular, it said that the national court should ascertain whether, on the one hand, the identification system was meant to hinder parallel imports, or on the other hand, comply with national or Community legislation. If it was the former, such would lead to artificial market partitioning and entitle the parallel importer to remove the labels.[1033] Where, as will often be the case, the identification codes are used both to prevent parallel imports and for legitimate purposes such as prevention of counterfeiting and quality control, the CJEU said in *Loendersloot* that: **3-650**

> "it is under the Treaty provisions on competition that those engaged in parallel trade should seek protection against action of the latter type."[1034]

In general, it will be rare not to be able to justify the use of identification codes to combat counterfeiting. Thus, this decision would suggest that a trade mark proprietor cannot exercise its rights to prevent such from happening but must put forward a claim of infringement of art.101 TFEU or art.102 TFEU. In *Sportswear*   **3-651**

[1029] See [30].

[1030] See [43]. For legislative historians, it should be noted that this decision pre-dated *Boehringer No.1* and thus was the first case to introduce the concept of "effective access" when considering the meaning of "necessity" in the context of the *Paranova* guidelines.

[1031] See [44]. The CJEU emphasised this principle in *Boehringer No.2*, at [37].

[1032] *Frits Loendersloot v George Ballantine* (C-349/95) [1997] E.C.R. I-6227; [1998] E.T.M.R. 10; [1998] 1 C.M.L.R. 993.

[1033] See [40].

[1034] See [43].

v Stonestyle,[1035] an English case, the claimant, a premier brand owner, brought proceedings against an importer and wholesaler who had removed identification codes from labels and swing tags of clothing. The claimant argued that such was detrimental to the image and reputation of the brand. The defendant argued that such was necessary because the claimant was intent on preventing parallel imports. In this regard, it relied upon distribution agreements between the claimant and its UK distributor which contained a hard-core parallel imports ban. The defendant pleaded that the agreements were contrary to art.102 TFEU and that the identification codes were used for the purpose of implementing the agreements. The claimant applied to strike out the defence on the ground that such was not a defence to a claim under art.7(2) (now art.15.2). In particular there was not sufficient nexus.[1036] The claimant relied upon the above passage in *Loendersloot* as indicating that in such circumstances, art.101 TFEU provided a sword but not a shield (i.e. it gave rise to a counterclaim but not a defence). On appeal, the Court of Appeal of England held that it was arguable that it gave rise to a defence and not merely a counterclaim.

3-652   However, it should be noted that the CJEU's analysis in *Loendersloot* concerned whether the exercise of rights would amount to artificial partitioning of the internal market.[1037] As discussed, such is only one of the *Paranova* conditions that a parallel importer must establish in order to permit interference with goods or their packaging which bear a registered trade mark. Another is the requirement that the original condition of the goods must not be interfered with. In *Zino Davidoff v A&G Imports,*[1038] although the CJEU did not consider the issue, the Advocate-General said that the removal or obliteration of such numbers may be relevant for purposes of trade mark rights only if such had a "disproportionately adverse effect on the specific subject matter of the trade mark right".[1039]

Whether the original condition of the product is adversely affected (Paranova No.2)

3-653   The second condition of *Hoffmann* was considered carefully by the court in *Bristol-Myers Squibb v Paranova*. The court emphasised that the purpose of this provision was to ensure that the essential function of the mark as an indication of origin was not compromised and that the public received goods which had been under the sole supervision of the brand proprietor.[1040] The court clarified that it was the condition of the product inside the packaging that was relevant.[1041] The test to be applied is whether repackaging involves "a risk of the product inside the package being exposed to tampering or to influences affecting its original condition". In determining such a risk, regard should be had to the nature of the product and the method of repackaging. It is rare that such a direct risk will occur.

3-654   In the declaratory part, the CJEU in *Bristol Myers v Squibb* in relation to this condition gave surprisingly detailed advice as to whether this is satisfied:

"that the repackaging cannot affect the original condition of the product inside the packag-

---

[1035] *Sportswear v Stonestyle* [2006] E.T.M.R. 66 CA.
[1036] For the requirement of a sufficient nexus between a plea of art.101 and an action for IPR infringement, see para.14-013.
[1037] e.g. see [42].
[1038] (C-414/99) [2001] E.C.R. I-08691.
[1039] See [120].
[1040] See [67]. See also discussion of essential function at para.3-069.
[1041] See [58].

ing such is the case, in particular, where the importer has merely carried out operations involving no risk of the product being affected, such as, for example, the removal of blister packs, flasks, phials, ampoules or inhalers from their original external packaging and their replacement in new external packaging, the fixing of self-stick labels on the inner packaging of the product, the addition to the packaging of new user instructions or information, or the insertion of an extra article; it is for the national court to verify that the original condition of the product inside the packaging is not indirectly affected, for example, by the fact that the external or inner packaging of the repackaged product or new user instructions or information omits certain important information or gives inaccurate information, or the fact that an extra article inserted in the packaging by the importer and designed for the ingestion and dosage of the product does not comply with the method of use and the doses envisaged by the manufacturer."

As said by the Advocate-General in *Boehringer No.2*, it is somewhat surprising that the CJEU said that the provision of inadequate information could be considered to affect the original condition of the product. Whilst it could plainly mislead the consumer as to the condition of the product, such is a different matter. In fact, in *Bristol Myers Squibb v Paranova*, the court merely said that the original condition of the product might be "indirectly affected" by misleading or incomplete information.[1042] It will be rare that the parallel importer will allow themselves to achieve such an "own goal" as misleading or incomplete information would render them liable to consumer protection laws as well as trade mark laws. However, it is clear that the essential function of the mark would be compromised if the public were being informed that the products sold under the mark were different in composition to what was the real position. **3-655**

Notice on goods that they had been repackaged (Paranova No.3)

The CJEU has repeatedly said that an indication must be clearly shown on the external packaging of the repackaged products that they have been repackaged and who has done the repackaging.[1043] It is not necessary that the repackaged products display the undertaking which has *actually* done the repackaging but only the entity who assumes responsibility for the repackaging.[1044] The national court must assess whether it is printed in such a way as to be understood by a person with normal eyesight, exercising a normal degree of attentiveness.[1045] However, it is not necessary to say in the statement on the packaging that the repackaging was carried out without the authorisation of the trade mark owner.[1046] Where the parallel importer has added to the packaging an extra article from a source other than the trade mark owner, they must ensure that the origin of the extra article is indicated in such a way as to dispel any impression that the trade mark owner is responsible for it.[1047] Furthermore, a clear indication will usually be required on the external packaging **3-656**

[1042] See [65].

[1043] (C-102/77) [1978] E.C.R. 1139 at [12]; *Pfizer v Eurim-Pharm GmbH* (1/81) [1981] E.C.R. 2913, [1982] 1 C.M.L.R. 406 at [11]; *Bristol-Myers* (C-427/93) at [71]. *Boehringer No.2*, at [21] and *Orifarm A/S v Merck Sharp & Dohme Corp* (C-400/09 & C-207/10) [2011] E.C.R. I-0000, [2012] C.M.L.R. 10.

[1044] *Orifarm A/S v Merck Sharp & Dohme Corp* (C-400/09 & C-207/10) [2011] E.C.R. I-0000, [2012] C.M.L.R. 10 at [34].

[1045] *Bristol-Myers* (C-427/93), at [71].

[1046] *Bristol-Myers* (C-427/93), at [72]. This is because such would suggest that the goods were "not entirely legitimate".

[1047] *Bristol-Myers* (C-427/93), at [72].

as to who manufactured the product, since it may be in the manufacturer's interest that the consumer or end user should not be led to believe that the importer is the owner of the trade mark, and that the product was manufactured under their supervision.[1048]

Presentation of repackaged product is liable to damage the reputation of the trade mark and of its owner (Paranova No.4)

3-657 The parallel importer must ensure that the repackaged product is presented in a manner which will not damage the reputation of the trade mark. In such a case, the trade mark owner has a legitimate interest, in being able to oppose the marketing of the product. In assessing whether the presentation of the repackaged product is liable to damage the reputation of the trade mark, account must be taken of the nature of the product and the market for which it is intended.[1049] This will normally occur with defective, untidy or poor-quality packaging.[1050]

3-658 In *Boehringer No.2*, the Court of Appeal of England and Wales referred the issue as to whether this condition is limited to defective, poor quality or untidy packaging or whether it applies whenever there is a risk that the reputation of the trade mark will be damaged. In answer to that reference, the CJEU said the court is not so limited but also to consider whether the repackaged pharmaceutical product was "presented inappropriately" so that it damaged the trade mark's reputation by "detracting from the image of reliability and quality attaching to such a product and the confidence it is capable of inspiring in the public concerned".[1051] It should be noted that the Advocate-General said, following the court in *Parfums Christian Dior*[1052] this condition will only apply where there is "serious risk that the reputation of the trade mark will be damaged".[1053] The CJEU did not specifically deal with the degree of damage to the reputation of the mark that must be shown for this condition to be satisfied but it is considered that the approach in *Parfums Christian Dior* should be followed.

3-659 The Court of Appeal also referred the issue as to whether "debranding" and "co-branding" should be considered damaging to the reputation of the trade mark. The CJEU in *Boehringer No.2* had said that the question of whether the fact that a parallel importer fails to: (i) affix the trade mark to the new exterior carton ("debranding"), (ii) applies either their own logo, a house-style, or a get-up used for a number of different products ("co-branding"), (iii) positions the additional label so as to wholly or partially obscure the proprietor's trade mark, (iv) fails to state on the additional label that the trade mark in question belongs to the proprietor, or (v) prints the name of the parallel importer in capital letters, is liable to damage the trade mark's reputation is a question of fact for the national court to decide in the light of the circumstances of each case.[1054] Following the reference, the Court of Appeal held that total debranding was not an infringement of a trade mark and thus

---

[1048] (1/81) [1981] E.C.R. 2913; [1982] 1 C.M.L.R. 406 at [11]; *Bristol-Myers* (C-427/93), at [74].

[1049] *Bristol-Myers* (C-427/93), at [75].

[1050] *Bristol-Myers* (C-427/93), at [75]. See also Stix-Hackl AG's Opinion in *Zino Davidoff v A&G Imports* (C-414/99), at [112]. The CJEU did not answer this question.

[1051] See [43].

[1052] This is discussed at para.3-619.

[1053] See [61].

[1054] See [47].

no defence was needed. In relation to partial debranding, it held that such could be damaging to the reputation but such was not found proven on the facts.[1055]

Advance notice of repackaging (Paranova No.5)

The trade mark owner must be given advance notice of the repackaged product being put on sale. The owner may also require the importer to supply them with a specimen of the repackaged product before it goes on sale, to enable the owner to check that the repackaging is not carried out in such a way as to directly or indirectly affect the original condition of the product, and that the presentation after repackaging is not likely to damage the reputation of the trade mark.[1056] This requirement was criticised in *Boehringer* by the High Court of England.[1057] However, in *Boehringer No.1*, the requirement of advance notice was confirmed. The CJEU indicated that reasonable notice must be given and indicated that where the packaging was included with the notice, a period of 15 days was likely to be sufficient.[1058] Furthermore, they said that the trade mark proprietor may oppose the marketing of the repackaged product if such is not done.[1059]

3-660

In *Boehringer No.2*, the Court of Appeal referred to the CJEU various questions relating to the consequences of failing to give notice. In particular, the Court of Appeal was concerned to know whether the failure to give adequate notice meant that the goods had been infringed. In her Opinion, the Advocate-General said that in contrast to the other four *Paranova* conditions, this requirement was a procedural requirement. She thus said that breach of it should attract a sanction distinct from the sanction applicable to breaches of the other conditions.[1060] The Advocate-General distinguished between the situation where no or inadequate notice had been given but there was compliance with the other four conditions and when there was not compliance with one or more of the other four conditions. In her opinion, in the former situation, the sanction should be effective and dissuasive but not equal to a breach of a substantive condition. The CJEU held that a failure to comply with the requirement to give prior notice meant that the goods should be treated as equivalent to spurious goods, i.e. goods where the mark is first affixed to the pharmaceutical without the consent of the registered proprietor. Thus, the CJEU did not follow the Advocate-General's opinion. The CJEU held that the issue of financial relief is a matter for the national court but must take into account the extent of damage caused by the infringement and in accordance with the principle of proportionality.[1061] However, where notice has not been given of repackaged goods, courts of Member States have treated the issue of compensation no differently from normal infringing goods.[1062]

3-661

[1055] *Boehringer Ingelheim v Swingward* [2008] 2 C.M.L.R. 22 CA.

[1056] *Bristol-Myers* (C-427/93), at [78]. The court also said that this gave better protection against counterfeiting.

[1057] *Boehringer* [2000] 2 C.M.L.R. 571; [2000] E.T.M.R. 415, High Ct.

[1058] See [67].

[1059] See [68].

[1060] See [72].

[1061] See [63].

[1062] In an English case, *Hollister Inc and Dansac A/S v Medik Ostomy Supplies* [2013] E.T.M.R. 10, the Court of Appeal held that where no notice was given, the trade mark proprietor was entitled to recover the profit made on the sales of the repackaged pharmaceuticals (an account of profit made by the infringer is a standard remedy in UK infringement proceedings). See also the German deci-

Burden of proof in exhaustion and repackaging cases

3-662   In *Van Doren + Q*, the CJEU said that a national rule of evidence which places the burden on a defendant of proving that goods were placed on the market in the EEA by the trade mark owner or with its consent was consistent with the predecessor to the TMD and EUTMR.[1063] However, in certain cases, it may be difficult for the parallel importer to prove that the goods were *first* placed on the market by the trade mark proprietor or with his consent inside the EEA as opposed to outside the EEA. This is, of course, of vital importance to the parallel importer because they cannot be prevented from dealing in goods in the former case but in the latter case, the parallel importer must show unequivocal consent of the trade mark proprietor to them dealing in such goods.[1064] In *Van Doren + Q*, the CJEU recognised that in such circumstances, if the burden of proof was on the parallel importer, it could lead to market partitioning within the EEA. It thus said that where the defendant succeeds in establishing a real risk of partitioning of national markets if the defendant bears the burden of proof of showing that the goods were placed on the market in the EEA, then arts 34–36 TFEU required that the trade mark proprietor should bear the burden of proof to show that the goods were initially placed on the market outside the EEA.[1065]

3-663   The CJEU in *Boehringer (No.2)* has held that the burden lay on the parallel importer to prove the *Bristol Myers* conditions save that in relation to the condition that the repackaging does not affect the original condition of the product or does not damage the reputation of the mark, it is sufficient that the parallel importer furnishes evidence that leads to a reasonable presumption that such conditions are fulfilled.[1066] This then shifts the burden to the registered proprietor to prove that in fact, these two conditions are not fulfilled.

Infringement and breach of licence

3-664   Article 25.1 EUTMR stipulates that a trade mark may be licensed for some or all of the goods or services for which it is registered and for the whole or part of the EU and may be exclusive or non-exclusive. Article 25.2 also permits a proprietor of a trade mark to invoke the rights of a EUTM against a licensee if they contravene any provision in the licence with regard to: *the duration; the form of the trade mark; the scope of goods or services for which the licence is granted; the territory in which the trade mark may be affixed; or the quality of the goods manufactured or the services provided by the licensee*—hereinafter referred to as "art.25.2 conditions". Article 25 TMD is similarly worded. These provisions are exhaustive.[1067] Thus, a breach of any other licence condition does not give the proprietor the right to sue for trade mark infringement although of course it will give

---

sion *Zoladex* I ZR 87/07 (Bundesgerichtshof) where the court held that the trade mark proprietor was entitled to the whole of the repackager's profits (see [19]).

[1063] *Van Doren + Q GmbH v Lifestyle Sports* (C-244/00) [2003] E.C.R. I-3051; [2003] E.T.M.R. 75 at [36].

[1064] See para.3-526. Generally, the burden and standard of proof in exhaustion cases is also discussed in the context of the relationship of arts 34–36 and IPRs at para.7-114.

[1065] See [37]–[42].

[1066] See [54].

[1067] *Copad SA v Christian Dior SA* (C-59/08) [2009] E.C.R. I-0342 at [21].

rise to a cause of action for breach of contract.[1068] The CJEU has made it clear in *Copad v Christian Dior* that if goods are marketed in breach of a term of the licence, a trade mark can only be enforced where the breach is of an art.25.2 condition.[1069]

Upon proper analysis, the art.25.2 conditions either relate to matters which could **3-665** affect the functions of a trade mark (e.g. quality of the goods, the representation of the mark or the type of goods that the marks can be affixed to) or can be considered terms which define the market (territory or duration restrictions) which the licensor is prepared to allow the licensee to exploit the mark. In relation to the former, this would adversely affect the functions of a mark, e.g. that the quality was guaranteed by the EUTM owner. The same point can be made as to the representation of the mark or the type of goods which the mark is affixed to. In relation to the latter, it is clear that marketing of trade-marked goods outside the defined market could adversely affect the markets reserved to the licensor or other licensees. However, it is less clear that such a breach could adversely affect any function of the mark. Plainly if the goods had been placed on the licensed market and then parallel imported into a reserved territory, such would be permissible as the rights of the EUTM owner would be deemed exhausted. Yet, the effect in the marketplace of direct marketing the goods into another territory and them being parallel imported into that territory is exactly the same. The same point can be made as regards marketing of goods after the expiry of the licence.

One is driven to the conclusion that the public policy behind treating a breach **3-666** of the licensing terms relating to territory and duration is one of competition rather than preventing damage to the functions of a mark. If a EUTM owner could not control the territories and the period of licence in which it allows a licensee to market goods bearing a EUTM to be placed on the market and therefore treat these goods as infringing goods, he may be deterred from granting such licences in the first place. After all, it is easy for a licensee company to sell goods outside the territories or beyond the duration of the licence and then go into liquidation. Here a mere right to bring proceedings against the licensee is illusory. Another view is that treating marketing of goods bearing a trade mark outside the licensed territory or after the duration of a licence is more concerned with respecting the specific object of a trade mark, which is the right to first market goods in the EEA under the mark than any functions of the mark.[1070]

In *Copad v Christian Dior*, the CJEU had to consider whether the sale of luxury **3-667** goods by a licensee to discount stores in breach of an express restriction against such sales permitted the trade mark proprietor to sue the discount store for trade mark infringement. This, in turn, turned on the question of whether the term of the licence was an art.25.2 condition—in particular, whether it related to the quality of the goods. The CJEU held, with a certain degree of judicial creativity, that the quality of luxury goods is in part attributable to not only to their physical characteristics but also the aura of luxury that they have.[1071] Thus, it held that impairment to this aura of luxury would affect the quality of goods sold under the brand. Accordingly, it held that the trade mark proprietor was entitled to bring proceedings for trade mark infringement where a licensee sold goods to a discount store in breach of the licence if such damages the allure and prestigious image of the brand.

[1068] *Copad SA v Christian Dior SA* (C-59/08) [2009] E.C.R. I-03421.

[1069] *Copad SA v Christian Dior SA* (C-59/08) [2009] E.C.R. I-03421 at [50]–[51].

[1070] For discussion of the specific object of a trade mark, see paras 3-117 and 7-044.

[1071] The remark as to judicial creativity stems from the fact that the image of a mark is certainly attributable to the aura of luxury but it is difficult to say that the physical characteristics (i.e. the quality of the goods manufactured) of the goods bearing the mark depend on which shops they are sold to!

3-668   Finally, it should be noted that even if the goods were marketed in breach of a condition which was not an art.25.2 condition (and thus deemed exhausted), such is not intended to affect the rights of the proprietor under art.15.2 EUTMR to prevent further circulation of the goods where legitimate reasons exist. This will be the case where the circumstances of the resale would be such as to affect the reputation of the mark.[1072] The keen reader will see that in *Copad*, the Court of Justice held that a trade mark owner can bring proceedings for infringement of a trade mark where either (i) there is a breach of an art.25(2) condition where goods are sold to a discount such as to damage "*the allure and prestigious image of the brand*"; or (ii) where if goods are deemed to have been placed on the market by the licensee with the consent of the trade mark owner (i.e. no breach of art.25(2) conditions), the further resale damages "*the reputation of the trade mark*". Hence, the Court of Justice said in *Copad v Dior* when considering art.25(2) TMD (equivalent to art.25 EUTMR):

> "[57]   Therefore, should the national court find that sale by the licensee to a third *party is unlikely to undermine the quality of the luxury goods* bearing the trade mark, so that it must be considered that they were put on the market with the consent of the proprietor of the trade mark, it will be for that court to assess, taking into account the particular circumstances of each case, whether further commercialisation of the luxury goods bearing the trade mark by the third party, using methods which are customary in its sector of trade, *damages the reputation of that trade mark.*"

3-669   The above suggests that there may be circumstances where there is no damage to the allure and prestigious image of a trade mark but there is damage to the reputation of a trade mark. It is difficult to understand what these circumstances might be. It should be noted that in *Parfums Christian Dior* (which the Court of Justice referred to in this part of its judgment), the Court of Justice refers to "seriously" damaging the reputation and that the expression "allure and prestigious image" when considering that art.25 is derived from *Parfums Christian Dior* which was, as said above, concerned with legitimate reasons under art.15.2. Such suggests that they mean the same. It also means that where a court find that the sale by a licensee of goods bearing the trade mark outside a selective distribution network is not damaging to the allure and prestigious image of the mark (and thus not a breach of art.25.2), a court would be and should be highly unlikely to find that there are "legitimate reasons" to prevent the circulation of goods under art.15.2 on the grounds of serious damage to reputation of the mark.[1073]

Grounds for invalidity of registered trade marks

3-670   Both the EUTMR and TMD allow for an applicant to seek to declare a registered trade mark as invalid if when it was filed, there existed absolute or relative grounds for its refusal. Thus, it is not fatal that an applicant missed the opportunity to file

---

[1072] *Copad*, at [52]–[59] citing *Parfums Christian Dior* (C-337/95) [1997] E.C.R. I-6013. This is discussed at para.3-619.

[1073] See also *Coty Germany GmbH v Parfümerie Akzente GmbH* (C-230/16) ECLI:EU:C:2017:941 (where a selective distribution system for luxury goods designed to preserve the luxury image of those goods and which banned distributors from selling to third party Internet platforms was compatible with art.101 TFEU if such had the objective of preserving the luxury image of those goods). For discussion of this, see para.11-074.

an opposition to an application for a registered mark.[1074] In both opposition and cancellation proceedings, the issue will be whether as of the date of filing, there existed absolute or relative grounds for refusal of the mark applied for.

However, there are some points of difference to opposition proceedings. These are:

3-671

- If the mark has acquired distinctive character after its registration as a consequence of its use, then it may not be declared invalid on absolute grounds relating to lack of distinctive character.[1075]
- Under the EUTMR, an applicant may not oppose the filing of a EUTM on the grounds of bad faith but may seek cancellation of it on such grounds.[1076]

Grounds for revocation of registered trade marks

There are three main grounds for revocation of a registered trade mark. Revocation differs from cancellation proceedings for a declaration of invalidity as the mark is not declared invalid ab initio but from the relevant date. Thus, a revoked mark may be relied upon in infringement proceedings if the acts of infringment predate the relevant date of revocation.[1077]The relevant date for revocation may be the date of the application for revocation or an earlier date on which one of the grounds for revocation occurred, if requested by the application for revocation.[1078]

3-672

The three main grounds are:

3-673

- Lack of genuine use of the trade mark in a five-year period.
- As a consequence of the acts or inactivity of the proprietor, the trade mark has become the common name for a product or service in respect of which it is registered.
- In consequence of the use of the trade mark by the proprietor or with their consent, the mark is liable to mislead the public.

These three grounds are now considered.

Non-use of registered trade mark

Under both the TMD and EUTMR, there is consquently no requirement that when filing an application for registration, the applicant has used the mark or has an intention to use the mark.[1079] However, it will be readily understood that if there was no requirement that a registered trade mark be used for its lifetime, national registers of EU Member States and the EUIPO Register of EUTMs could (and most likely would) become full of unused registered marks which would prevent other

3-674

[1074] arts 4, 5 TMD; arts 59, 60 EUTMR.

[1075] art.59.2 EUTMR; art.4.4 TMD. The wording of these two provisions subtly differs as in the case of art 59.2 EUTMR, it refers to the acquisition of distinctive character "after registration" whereas art 4.4 TMD omits such wording. Thus, it might be arguable that for a EUTM, distinctive character acquired between filing and the date of registration should be ignored. It is not believed that this was intended and ultimately, if as of the date of the filing of the cancellation proceedings, the mark is able to act as an indication of origin, such is sufficient.

[1076] art.59.1.(b) EUTMR. Under the TMD, a Member State may allow for opposition based on such a ground—see art.5.4(c).

[1077] art.62.1, 62.2 EUTMR.

[1078] art 62.2 EUTMR, art.47 TMD.

[1079] This has already been discussed in the context of "bad faith". See para.3-303.

traders from using or protecting their own used marks.[1080] This is contrary to the public interest that businesses and undertakings who do wish to use marks are not prevented by registered marks which have not been used for many years. Thus, the Recitals to the EUTMR refer to there being no "justification for protecting EU trade marks ... except where the trade marks are actually used".[1081] The Recitals to the TMD also emphasise that trade marks fulfil their purpose of distinguishing goods or services and allowing consumers to make informed choices only when they are actually used on the market. Furthermore, they underscore that it is necessary for marks to be used to reduce the number of conflicts which arise between marks.[1082]

3-675 To strike the right balance, both the TMD and EUTMR give the owner of a EUTM or national trade mark in a Member State a "grace period" of five years from the date of registration to begin to make "genuine use" of the mark in relation to the goods or services for which it is registered. If there is no use of the mark for all or some of the registered goods or services, it becomes vulnerable to be revoked for non-use for those goods or services for which there has been no genuine use.[1083]

3-676 In more detail, the revocation provisions based on lack of use of both the EUTMR and TMD work as follows[1084]:

- Once the grace period of five years from the "date of completion of the registration procedure" has expired, a registered trade mark is vulnerable to revocation for lack of use.
- After the grace period, a third party can bring proceedings before EUIPO or a national intellectual property office to revoke, respectively, a EUTM or national registered mark on the grounds of lack of use. In infringement proceedings, a defendant can also by way of counterclaim seek to revoke the registered mark relied upon in the infringement proceedings.
- If in the five-year period prior to the date of the bringing of those proceedings, the EUTM or national trade mark owner has started or resumed genuine use of the registered mark, then the mark is not liable to be revoked even if there was an earlier five-year period of non-use.
- Use of a trade mark in a form which does not alter the distinctive character of the registered mark is deemed use of the latter.
- Use of a registered trade mark with the consent of the owner is deemed use by the owner.
- Mere use of a mark in relation to goods or services for which the mark is registered during the relevant five-year period is not sufficient. It must be shown that the use is:
  — genuine use; and
  — the mark has been used as an indication of trade origin for the registered goods or services, i.e. as a trade mark.
- If the owner shows genuine use of the mark for some of the goods or services but not others, then in revocation proceedings the scope of goods and services will be restricted accordingly.
- If grounds for revocation exist, such does not mean that the mark is declared

---

[1080] In a colourful phrase, Jacob J described such marks as abandoned vessels in the shipping lanes of trade—see *Laboratoire de la Mer (Reference to CJEU)* [2002] E.T.M.R. 34; [2002] F.S.R. 51, High Ct at [19].

[1081] Recital 24, EUTMR.

[1082] Recitals 31, 32 TMD.

[1083] *Länsförsäkringar AB v Matek A/S* (C-654/15) ECLI:EU:C:2016:998 at [25]–[26].

[1084] For the EUTMR, the relevant provisions are art.18, art.58.1(a), (b). For the TMD, it is art.16, art.45.

invalid ab initio. Rather, the effect is that the registered mark is deemed not to have any rights as from the date of the application for revocation or if grounds for revocation existed prior to the date of the application, from that date. Thus, if an application to revoke is brought against a registered mark on the anniversary of the 12th year of the date of registration and the mark was never used, then the mark is deemed not to have any protection from the 5th anniversary of registration.[1085]

It is now necessary to consider in detail some of the above concepts.

Date of completion of registration procedure

The date of completion of the registration procedure means the date of registration. However, in the case of international registrations under the Madrid Agreement or Protocol, the matter is somewhat more complicated. **3-677**

In *Häupl v Lidl*,[1086] the Austrian courts were concerned with what was the relevant date of completion of the registration procedure where the mark has been applied for and registration obtained via the Madrid Agreement.[1087] Under art.3(4) of the Madrid Agreement, the International Bureau registers a mark which has been filed pursuant to an international application. The registration bears the date of the application for international registration provided such is received within two months from the date of filing. **3-678**

However, under the Madrid Agreement, at a subsequent date, contracting states which have been designated can either refuse or confirm protection. **3-679**

Thus the critical question was whether "date of completion of the registration procedure" meant the date of international registration or the later date of confirmation by the national registry. In the Austrian proceedings, there had not been use in the five-year period from the date of filing of the international application but there had been if that period started from the date of acceptance of the international registration by the Austrian trade mark office. **3-680**

On reference, the CJEU held that such law was procedural and thus not harmonised by EU law and was to be determined by Member States in accordance with the procedural rules on registration in force.[1088] **3-681**

Under the EUTMR, the relevant date for a Madrid application designating the EU is the date of the international application.[1089] **3-682**

Genuine use

Considerable debate has been generated as to the meaning of "genuine" use. In part, this is because subtly different words appear in the different language versions of the TMD. In normal English usage, "genuine" means "bona fide", i.e. not sham or artificial. However, in French, the word is *"serieux"*, in German, *"ernsthaft"*, in Italian, *"effettivo"*, in Spanish, *"efectivo"*, in Portuguese, *"serio"*, in Dutch, *"normaal"*, in Danish, *"reel"*, and in Swedish, *"verkligt"*. Although the author does not profess to be a linguistic expert, such words do not correspond with **3-683**

[1085] art.62.1 EUTMR; art.47.1 TMD.
[1086] *Häupl v Lidl* (C-246/05) [2007] E.C.R. I-4673.
[1087] Generally, see para.3-056 for the procedure for applying for a registered mark via the Madrid System.
[1088] See also *Lancome parfums et beaute & Cie v EUIPO* (T-466/08) [2011] E.C.R. II-1831.
[1089] art.189(2) EUTMR.

the meaning of "genuine" in English.[1090] Rather, they imply that the use of the registered mark should be more than minimal (taking account of all the circumstances of the relevant market).

3-684   The debate has focussed on whether "genuine" means that the registered proprietor need simply show that use of the mark has not been sham or artificial (i.e. simply intended to maintain the registration) or whether they must show more. In particular, does any level of use suffice including minimal use in the five-year period?

3-685   Because of the importance of this issue,[1091] it is necessary to consider the *travaux préparatoires*, the decision of the CJEU in *Ansul v Ajax*, the Reasoned Order in *Laboratoire de la Mer* and *Reber* as well as certain decisions of the General Court.

3-686   **Travaux Préparatoires**   In 1976, the European Commission published a proposal for a EUTM.[1092] This said:

> "[127]   It is also essential that a 'genuine', and not merely a token use of the trade mark should be take to comply with the user requirements. The trade mark need not necessarily be used on the goods themselves, but it must be used in relation to the goods (for example, if it is impossible to affix the trade marks to the goods in question). Individual questions must be left to the Courts, which should apply strict, rather than liberal standards. This applies also to the interpretation of the exception envisaged in the Paris Convention according to which non-user may be excused for good reason." [Emphasis supplied.]

3-687   In 1980, the Commission published a paper entitled as "New trade-mark system for the Community: Proposed TMD and EUTMR".[1093] This paper contained both a draft TMD and a draft EUTMR for a EUTM. Article 11(1) of the English version of the draft TMD provided that:

> "(1)   A trade mark shall be put to *serious* use in the Member State concerned, consistently with the terms of this TMD, in connection with the goods or services in respect of which it is registered, unless there exist legitimate reasons for not doing so."[1094]

3-688   Article 14 of the draft TMD provided that:

> "(1)   A trade mark shall be invalidated if it has not been used in manner required by Article 11 for an unbroken period of five years; but a trade mark is not to be invalidated where, between the expiry of that period and the date on which the validity of the trade-mark is contested, it has been used in good faith and in a manner required by Article 11."

3-689   Similarly, art.13 of the draft EUTMR provided that:

> "(1)   A Community trade-mark shall be put to serious use in the common market, consistently with the terms of this EUTMR, in connection with the goods or services in

---

[1090] See *Laboratoire de la Mer* [2002] F.S.R. 51 High Ct at [28].

[1091] Where an earlier national or Community trade mark is relied upon in opposition proceedings to a EUTM and is more than five years old, the applicant for a mark can call upon the opponent to show that genuine use has been made of the registered mark. See para.3-398.

[1092] Supplement 8/76 to the Bulletin of the European Communities.

[1093] Supplement 5/80 to the Bulletin of the European Communities.

[1094] p.11. Thus, it can be seen that "serious" replaced the original recommendation of "genuine".

respect of which it is registered, unless there exist legitimate reasons for not doing so.[1095]

Article 39 of the draft EUTMR provided that: **3-690**

"(1) The rights of the proprietor of a Community trade-mark shall be revoked:
      (a) if the trade mark has not been used in a manner required by Article 13 during
           an unbroken period of five years; but no person may claim that the proprietor's
           rights in a Community trade-mark should be revoked where, during the interval
           between expiry of the five-year period and filing of the application for revoca-
           tion, the trader-mark has been used in manner required by Article 13 and this
           use was made in good faith."[1096]

In the Explanatory Memorandum to art.39, it said as follows: **3-691**

"... The five year period commences not earlier than the date of registration but it may
start to run at any subsequent date. A single instance of use which nevertheless must fulfil
the conditions laid down in Article 13, is enough to cause a new five-year period to
run...".[1097]

However, when the second draft TMD and EUTMR came out in 1984, "seri-   **3-692**
ous" had been replaced with the original "genuine". Thus, art.13(1) of the draft
EUTMR provided that:

"If, within a period of five years, following registration, the proprietor has not put the
Community trade mark to genuine use in the Community in connection with the goods
or services in respect of which it is registered, or if such use has been suspended during
an uninterrupted period of five years, the Community trade mark shall be subject to the
sanctions provided for in this EUTMR, unless there exist legitimate reasons for non-
use".

Similarly, art.11(1) of the draft TMD[1098] also replaced the requirement of "serious" use with "genuine".

Although open to doubt, it is suggested that such makes it clear that it was the   **3-693**
intention of the legislator that "genuine" use meant use which was not token or
sham use but otherwise did not import any threshold of use, below which there was
deemed not be "genuine use".

However, as will be seen, the CJEU now appears to endorse a requirement of   **3-694**
some undefined "threshold" of use, below which, there will not be deemed to be
genuine use. Three landmark cases in this area are now considered.

Ansul v Ajax In *Ansul BV v Ajax Brandbeveiling BV*,[1099] the CJEU had to   **3-695**
consider the meaning of "genuine use" on a reference from the Hoge Raad
("*normaal* use" in Dutch). The facts were that Ansul was the registered proprietor
of MINIMAX for fire extinguishers and associated products. In 1988, authorities
to sell these expired. From 1989, *Ansul* ceased selling fire extinguishers. However,
from 1989 to 1994, it sold component parts and extinguishing substances for fire
extinguishers to undertakings responsible for maintaining existing fire

---

[1095] p.24.
[1096] p.30.
[1097] p.69.
[1098] COM/85/793 [1985] OJ C351/4.
[1099] *Ansul BV v Ajax Brandbeveiling BV* (C-40/01) [2003] E.C.R. I-2439.

extinguishers. It also maintained, checked and repaired equipment bearing the mark MINIMAX using the mark on invoices and affixing stickers to fire extinguishers which said "Gebruiksklaar Minimax" (Ready for Use Minimax). Ajax brought proceedings to revoke the mark on the basis of non-use. The central issue was whether in the period 1989 to 1994, there had been genuine use of the mark in relation to the protected goods. There was no evidential dispute that there had been use of the mark in the manner described above.

3-696   The Regional Court of Appeal of the Hague held that Ansul had not been putting the Minimax trade mark to *normaal* use since 1989. It found, inter alia, that Ansul had not been releasing new products onto the market since that time but had merely maintained, checked and repaired used equipment. The court stated that the use of stickers and strips bearing the mark was not distinctive of the extinguishers and that, even if it were to be regarded as amounting to use of the mark, it could not amount to *normaal* because the object was not to create or preserve an outlet for fire extinguishers. On appeal, the Hoge Raad said that:

> "in assessing whether the use to which a trade mark is put is normal, regard must be had to all the facts and circumstances specific to the case and those facts and circumstances must demonstrate that having regard to what is considered to be usual and commercially justified in the business sector concerned, the object of use is to create or preserve an outlet for trade marked goods and services and not simply to maintain the rights in the trade mark... that so far as those facts and circumstances are concerned, account must, as a rule, be taken of the kind, extent, frequency, regularity and duration of the use in conjunction with the kind of goods or service and the kind and size of the undertaking."[1100]

3-697   However, it was unclear whether such was the correct view. Accordingly, it referred the issue of the meaning of "genuine use" to the CJEU. Because two very differing views about the meaning of the CJEU's judgment in *Ansul* have been adopted, it is necessary to set out the relevant part of the CJEU's judgment in full. The CJEU said:

> "[34]   As the provisions of the Paris Convention thus contain no guidance for defining the concept of genuine use, the scope of that expression must be determined solely on the basis of an analysis of the provisions of the TMD itself.
>
> [35]   Next, as Ansul argued, the eighth recital in the preamble to the TMD states that trade marks must actually be used or, if not used, be subject to revocation. Genuine use therefore means actual use of the mark. That approach is confirmed, inter alia, by the Dutch version of the TMD, which uses in the eighth recital the words *werkelijk wordt gebruikt*, and by other language versions such as the Spanish (*uso efectivo*), Italian (*uso effettivo*) and English (genuine use).
>
> [36]   Genuine use must therefore be understood to denote use that is not merely token, serving solely to preserve the rights conferred by the mark. Such use must be consistent with the essential function of a trade mark, which is to guarantee the identity of the origin of goods or services to the consumer or end user by enabling him, without any possibility of confusion, to distinguish the product or service from others which have another origin.
>
> [37]   It follows that genuine use of the mark entails use of the mark on the market for the goods or services protected by that mark and not just internal use by the undertaking concerned. The protection the mark confers and the consequences of registering it in terms of enforceability vis-à-vis third parties cannot continue to operate if the mark loses its commercial raison d'être, which is to create or preserve an outlet for the goods or services that bear the sign of which it is

---

[1100] See [21].

composed, as distinct from the goods or services of other undertakings. Use of the mark must therefore relate to goods or services already marketed or about to be marketed and for which preparations to secure customers by the undertaking are under way, particularly in the form of advertising campaigns. Such use may be either by the trade mark proprietor or, as envisaged in [Article 16.6 TMD], by a third party with authority to use the mark.

[38] Finally, when assessing whether there has been genuine use of the trade mark, regard must be had to all the facts and circumstances relevant to establishing whether the commercial exploitation of the mark is real, in particular whether such use is viewed as warranted in the economic sector concerned to maintain or create a share in the market for the goods or services protected by the mark.

[39] Assessing the circumstances of the case may thus include giving consideration, inter alia, to the nature of the goods or service at issue, the characteristics of the market concerned and the scale and frequency of use of the mark. Use of the mark need not, therefore, always be quantitatively significant for it to be deemed genuine, as that depends on the characteristics of the goods or service concerned on the corresponding market.

[40] Use of the mark may also in certain circumstances be genuine for goods in respect of which it is registered that were sold at one time but are no longer available.

[41] That applies, inter alia, where the proprietor of the trade mark under which such goods were put on the market sells parts which are integral to the make-up or structure of the goods previously sold, and for which he makes actual use of the same mark under the conditions described in paragraphs 35 to 39 of this judgment. Since the parts are integral to those goods and are sold under the same mark, genuine use of the mark for those parts must be considered to relate to the goods previously sold and to serve to preserve the proprietor's rights in respect of those goods.

[42] The same may be true where the trade mark proprietor makes actual use of the mark, under the same conditions, for goods and services which, though not integral to the make-up or structure of the goods previously sold, are directly related to those goods and intended to meet the needs of customers of those goods. That may apply to after-sales services, such as the sale of accessories or related parts, or the supply of maintenance and repair services.

[43] In the light of the foregoing considerations the reply to the first question must be that [Article 16.1 TMD] must be interpreted as meaning that there is genuine use of a trade mark where the mark is used in accordance with its essential function, which is to guarantee the identity of the origin of the goods or services for which it is registered, in order to create or preserve an outlet for those goods or services; genuine use does not include token use for the sole purpose of preserving the rights conferred by the mark. When assessing whether use of the trade mark is genuine, regard must be had to all the facts and circumstances relevant to establishing whether the commercial exploitation of the mark is real, particularly whether such use is viewed as warranted in the economic sector concerned to maintain or create a share in the market for the goods or services protected by the mark, the nature of those goods or services, the characteristics of the market and the scale and frequency of use of the mark. The fact that a mark is not used for goods newly available on the market but for goods that were sold in the past does not mean that its use is not genuine, if the proprietor makes actual use of the same mark for component parts that are integral to the make-up or structure of such goods, or for goods or services directly connected with the goods previously sold and intended to meet the needs of customers of those goods."

Ansul makes it clear that token or sham use of a registered mark purely to **3-698** preserve the registration does not fall within "genuine use". That has never been doubted. *Ansul* also makes it clear that "internal" use is not "genuine use". The use of the mark must be use on the market. Thus, the fact that the mark has been used on internal memoranda of the registered proprietor or on advertising and promotional material which has been printed but not placed on the market is not sufficient.

3-699   However, there has been a keen debate as to whether *Ansul* imposes a further requirement, namely that the registered proprietor must establish that it has made substantial or significant use of the market for the goods or services protected by the mark. If this view is correct, it would suggest that there is a threshold of use, i.e. in certain cases, there may have been bona fide and external use of the mark but such use was not quantitatively sufficient to create or maintain a share in the relevant market and thus prevent revocation of the mark.

3-700   **Laboratoire de la Mer**   This issue came up in *Laboratoire de la Mer*.[1101] In the aforementioned case, an importer had imported very small quantities of health products bearing the registered mark into the UK from France during the relevant period. However, there was no evidence that these goods had been then onwardly sold or advertised. Thus, the only use was the act of importation. The High Court of England referred to the CJEU a number of issues as to whether there had been a "genuine use" of the mark. In particular, the national court was concerned to know whether any amount of use, however small, was sufficient if it was not sham use. The reference pre-dated the handing down of the judgment in *Ansul*. The CJEU issued a Reasoned Order saying that the answers to the questions referred could be clearly deduced from *Ansul*. However, in many respects, the Order reads as a judgment. Moreover, this case has been cited often enough to suggest that it did indeed break new ground in the law.

3-701   The CJEU quoted [35]–[39] of *Ansul* and said:

> "[20]   It follows from those considerations that the preservation by a trade mark proprietor of his rights is predicated on the mark being put to genuine use in the course of trade, on the market for the goods or services for which it was registered in the Member State concerned.
>
> [21]   Moreover, it is clear from paragraph 39 of *Ansul* that use of the mark may in some cases be sufficient to establish genuine use within the meaning of the TMD, even if that use is not quantitatively significant. Even minimal use can therefore be sufficient to qualify as genuine, on condition that it is deemed to be justified, in the economic sector concerned, for the purpose of preserving or creating market share for the goods or services protected by the mark.
>
> [22]   The question whether use is sufficient to preserve or create market share for those products or services depends on several factors and on a case-by-case assessment which is for the national court to carry out. The characteristics of those products and services, the frequency or regularity of the use of the mark, whether the mark is used for the purpose of marketing all the identical products or services of the proprietor or merely some of them, or evidence which the proprietor is able to provide, are among the factors which may be taken into account.
>
> [23]   Similarly, as emerges from paragraphs 35 to 39 of *Ansul* set out above, the characteristics of the market concerned, which directly affect the marketing strategy of the proprietor of the mark, may also be taken into account in assessing genuine use of the mark.
>
> [24]   In addition, use of the mark by a single client which imports the products for which the mark is registered can be sufficient to demonstrate that such use is genuine, if it appears that the import operation has a genuine commercial justification for the proprietor of the mark.

[1101] (C-259/02) [2004] E.C.R. I-1159.

[25]   In those circumstances, it is not possible to determine a priori, and in the abstract, what quantitative threshold should be chosen in order to determine whether use is genuine or not. A 'de minimis' rule, which would not allow the national court to appraise all the circumstances of the dispute before it, cannot therefore be laid down.

[26]   Finally, it can clearly be inferred from paragraph 36 of *Ansul* that, where use of the mark does not have as its essential aim the preservation or creation of market share for the goods or services which it protects, such use must be considered in fact to be intended to defeat any request for revocation. Such use cannot be characterised as 'genuine' within the meaning of the TMD.

[27]   In the light of the foregoing, the answer to the first, secondly, third, fourth and sixth questions must be that [Article 16 TMD] must be interpreted as meaning that there is 'genuine use' of a trade mark where it is used in accordance with its essential function, which is to guarantee the identity of the origin of the goods or services for which it is registered, in order to create or preserve an outlet for those goods or services; genuine use does not include token use for the sole purpose of preserving the rights conferred by that mark. When assessing whether use of the trade mark is genuine, regard must be had to all the facts and circumstances relevant to establishing whether the commercial use of the mark is real in the course of trade, particularly whether such use is viewed as warranted in the economic sector concerned to maintain or create a share in the market for the goods or services protected by the mark, the nature of those goods or services, the characteristics of the market and the scale and frequency of use of the mark. When it serves a real commercial purpose, in the circumstances cited above, even minimal use of the mark or use by only a single importer in the Member State concerned can be sufficient to establish genuine use within the meaning of the [TMD]."

In the author's opinion, this Order (particularly, at [24]) makes it clear that   **3-702** minimal non-sham, non-internal use would qualify as "genuine use". However, the application of this Order in the UK gave rise to further interpretational difficulties. In short, the applicant for revocation argued that *Ansul* required the registered proprietor to show that it had maintained or created a share in the market for the goods or services protected by the mark. The High Court agreed with the applicant and held that the use was not sufficient to qualify as "genuine use". However, on appeal, the Court of Appeal held that such was a wrong interpretation of *Ansul* and *La Mer*.[1102] In short, it held that *Ansul* and *La Mer* merely require the registered proprietor to establish that there has been some use, however small, of the mark in the Member State concerned which is not sham and which is not internal. The Court of Appeal did not accept that *Ansul* imposes a requirement on the registered proprietor to show that it had created or maintained a relevant market share. As said by the Court of Appeal:

"[46]   Secondly, once one imposes a requirement of significance or substantiality, it becomes potentially difficult, time-consuming, and expensive to decide whether, in any particular case, that requirement is satisfied. In this connection, Mr Tritton made a fair point when he suggested that the introduction of a test of significant use could lead to detailed arguments about the precise nature and extent of the market in which a particular trade mark is to be used, as well as a detailed enquiry in many cases as to the precise nature and extent of the use of the particular mark over the relevant five-year period. I do not regard that as a particularly desirable outcome."

The Court of Appeal provides its explanation of *Ansul*. It said that at [38], and   **3-703**

[1102] [2006] F.S.R 6 CA.

the first sentence of [39] the Court of Justice were concerned with giving guidance to domestic tribunals when they are called upon to decide, in a particular case, whether the use of a trade mark is genuine or whether it is internal or token. They did not impose an additional requirement of substantial, or even significant, use.[1103] Furthermore, it held that the words "sufficient to preserve or create market share" which can be found in *Ansul* and *La Mer* meant "sufficient *for the purpose of* preserving or creating market share" and that such was a correct reading of the words.[1104]

3-704   In the author's opinion,[1105] the Court of Appeal was right and such is the correct interpretation of *Ansul*. There is no quantitative threshold that must be overcome before small use of the mark becomes "genuine use".

3-705   Thus, in each case, the registered proprietor must provide evidence of use of the mark on the market in the Member State concerned. Once this is done, the court or tribunal must determine whether on the one hand, such use is sham or token or, on the other hand, genuine in the sense of being use which was *for the purpose* of creating or preserving a market outlet for the goods or services bearing the mark. If this is in dispute, the court or tribunal should have regard to all the circumstances and facts of the case including the size of the market, the nature of the goods, etc. *for the purpose of determining on the evidence whether such use was sham or not.* This makes sense. Clearly, if a multinational confectionery company adduces evidence of 10 sales of sweets in a small shop over a five-year period, this immediately raises suspicions that such sales were sham as such is odd economic behaviour. However, if a registered proprietor owns a small shop and only starts using the mark towards the end of the relevant period, then 10 sales of sweets do not necessarily raise a suspicion. A good example of the correct approach is in *Sonia Rykiel v EUIPO*.[1106] In that case, the evidence of use were nine invoices for clothing amounting to €324. The General Court considered the size of the market and the size of the registered proprietor against such very small use. It held that:

"[58]   However, the fact remains that such an explanation *is not sufficient to dispel the doubts as to the genuine use* of the earlier word mark arising from the extremely limited commercial volume of its exploitation.

[59]   The contested decision does not include either any concrete information on or an adequate analysis of the relevant factors, referred to in the previously cited case-law, enabling the minimal turnover (EUR 432) and the very small quantity of goods sold under the earlier word mark (85 units) over a relatively long period (13 months) to be placed in context.

[60]   In addition, the total amount of transactions over the relevant period seems to be so token as to suggest that, in the absence of supporting documents or convincing explanations to demonstrate otherwise, the use by Cuadrado of the earlier word mark cannot be held to be warranted, in the economic sector concerned and taking account of the nature of the goods concerned, *for the purpose of maintaining or creating market shares* for the goods protected by the earlier word mark." [Emphasis supplied.]

3-706   In the author's view, the General Court is confirming the interpretation of *La Mer* and *Ansul* by the Court of Appeal that in deciding whether there is genuine use, the court or tribunal must consider all the circumstances of the use to determine whether

---

[1103] See [42] per Neuberger LJ.
[1104] See [44] per Neuberger LJ.
[1105] The author must profess some partiality here as he was Counsel for the registered proprietor.
[1106] *Rykiel creation and diffusion de modeles v OHIM* (T-131/06) [2008] E.C.R. II-67.

the use was either token or *for the purpose of* maintaining or creating a market share. The fact that such use may not have been successful in creating or maintaining a market share is irrelevant provided that it was for such a purpose.

Reber v EUIPO   The above line of authorities must be read in the light of the important case of *Reber Holding GmbH & Co v EUIPO*.[1107] In this case, the owner of an Austrian registered mark had made very small but bona fide use of the mark in a boutique shop selling chocolates. It relied upon the registered mark to oppose a later mark. The applicant requested that the owner of the earlier Austrian mark prove genuine use of the earlier mark in the five-year period prior to the date of application of the later mark. The Board of Appeal upheld an appeal that the evidence provided did not show genuine use of the mark. It held that the use was "*narrow and local*" and thus could not be considered as genuine use. On appeal, the General Court dismissed the appeal upholding the Board of Appeal and its finding that the use was to be regarded as narrow and local and thus not to be regarded as genuine use. Interestingly, the General Court rejected an argument of infringement of the principle of equal treatment between small undertakings and large multinationals. It said that the appreciation of the use of a mark cannot lead to a difference in treatment between SMEs and large groups. In short, the size of the owner of the mark is irrelevant. On further appeal, and dispensing with the need for an opinion from the Advocate-General, the Court of Justice said that contrary to the submissions of the owner of the mark, the test of genuine use cannot be reduced to mere finding of a use of the mark in the course of trade since it is required that there be shown "genuine use" and thus the mere proof of commercial exploitation of the mark cannot be automatically regarded as genuine use of the mark in question (in the original German "*Daher kann nicht jede nachgewiesene geschäftliche Verwertung automatisch als ernsthafte Benutzung der fraglichen Marke eingestuft werden.*"[1108]). It therefore dismissed the appeal. Disappointingly, it did not consider *La Mer*.   **3-707**

It is clear from the judgment that this amounts to the death-knell for the approach that even minimal use of a trade mark which is bona fide and outward facing commercial use of the mark for the goods or services of the registered mark will amount to genuine use. The approach in the Order of *La Mer* (which because it was a Reasoned Order, would suggest that the matter was clear), now appears wrong. There was no attempt by the Court of Justice to reconcile *La Mer* with its judgment in *Reber*. In a UK case (*Memory Opticians Ltd*[1109] cited with approval in *London Taxi Corporation v Frazer Nash Research Ltd*[1110] by Arnold J), the Appointed Person held that Reber rejected the view that non-internal, non-token use was genuine use.   **3-708**

In the author's view, the law on genuine use is now in a real mess. On the one hand, one is told that minimal use may suffice where "it serves a real commercial purpose" (*La Mer* at [27]) but on the other hand, it is clear that the Court of Justice and General Court's view in *Reber* is that minimal outward use for the purpose of creating a market does not suffice to amount to genuine use. Owners of registered   **3-709**

[1107] (C-141/13P) ECLI:EU:C:2014:2089, on appeal from *Reber v OHIM* (T-355/09) ECLI:EU:C:2013:22.
[1108] Last sentence, at [32].
[1109] [2016] ETMR 8.
[1110] [2016] EHWC 52. On appeal, the Court of Appeal did not disturb this finding ([2017] EWCA Civ 1729).

trade marks now can have no comfort that if they use a mark for the purpose of creating a market under the mark that they will keep their registered trade mark. It is all guesswork. Furthermore, it is clear that the law is now tilted in favour of large companies against small companies precisely because the size of the undertaking is irrelevant to the assessment of genuine use. Yet, it is precisely the small companies that need the protection of a trade mark. One gets the impression that there is some type of "value" judgment to be carried out by a court when assessing genuine use. For instance, for national marks, it would appear that the court should ask itself whether the use by the owner of a national trade mark in a Member State is sufficient to *justify protection as a registered trade mark* which confers monopoly rights for the mark in the whole territory of a Member State (as opposed to merely being a local right which would give the owner of the mark a defence in any third party infringement proceedings but not a monopoly in the mark in the Member State[1111])? The finding by the Board of Appeal and the General Court that the use was narrow and local would support such a conclusion. There is some support in the TMD and EUTMR for the view that a mark which is not of more than mere local significance should not confer rights at a national or EU level.[1112] However, this is concerned with unregistered rights. It is also arguable that the CJEU's decision is not consistent with TRIPS.[1113] Article 15(3) TRIPS states that members may make registrability depend on use. If it does, art.19 says that the registration may *only* be cancelled after an uninterrupted period of at least three years of non-use. There is nothing in TRIPS which says that a Member (the EU is a member of TRIPS) may impose a *further* condition which requires use to be nationwide or of such a level as to merit protection as a national trade mark. Indeed, art.20 says that the "*use of a trademark in the course of trade shall not be unjustifiably encumbered by special requirements*". Finally, it should be said that the Court of Justice has yet to grapple with the significance of art.18.1(b) EUTMR. This deems the export of a EU mark solely for the purpose of export as being genuine use of the mark. The equivalent provision in the TMD is art.16.5(b). Thus, the affixing of a mark in the UK solely for the purpose of exporting products bearing the mark to France is considered genuine use in the UK. Yet, plainly such was not done to create or maintain a market in the UK. There was discussion of this provision in the Court of Appeal in *La Mer* but the court declined to express any comment on it.

3-710   The requirement that the use of the mark must be for the purpose of creating or maintaining a market share in the goods bearing the mark means that the handing out of promotional items (alcohol-free drink) as gifts to those purchasing clothing was held not to be genuine use of the mark in relation to the promotional items. The proprietor was not seeking to create or maintain a market share in the promotional items.[1114] This is an understandable application on the criteria in *Ansul* and *La Mer*. However, it leads to the paradoxical conclusion that actual use of a mark in relation to the goods or services protected by a registered trade mark does not necessarily amount to genuine use. Thus, the public may have become extremely familiarised with the use of the mark in relation to the promotional items but yet there has been no genuine use within the meaning of the TMD and EUTMR such that the mark is vulnerable to revocation.

[1111] See art.14.3 TMD (defence of use of an earlier right in a particular locality).
[1112] See para.3-513.
[1113] For discussion of TRIPs and trade marks, see para.3-025.
[1114] *Silberquelle GmbH v Maselli-Strickmode* (C-495/07) [2009] E.C.R. I-397.

Relevant market: wholesale or retail?   As said above, it is necessary to show use   **3-711**
of the registered mark on the market. This raises the question as to which market?
In the case of normal goods, does this mean the retail or end-user market or can it
include wholesale and other intermediate markets? This was an issue in *Laboratoire
de la Mer*. The only evidence was of goods being imported under the mark.
However, there was no evidence of such goods being marketed to consumers or
end-users. Paragraph 22 of *Laboratoire de la Mer* (CJEU) makes it clear that
importation by a single client can be sufficient to qualify as "genuine use" provided
there was a genuine commercial justification for the act of importation. This was
given in answer to a question from the national court as to whether importation
alone was sufficient to qualify as "genuine use".

However, in the High Court, and despite this paragraph, it was argued that such   **3-712**
use was akin to internal use and therefore did not qualify. Moreover, it was further
argued that [36] of *Ansul* required that use be on the consumer or end-user market.
This argument was accepted by the High Court. However, on appeal, the Court of
Appeal disagreed. It held that the act of importation resulted in ownership of the
goods changing hand and was external to the registered proprietor. Accordingly,
there had been use of the mark on the market. Furthermore, there still had been use
of the mark on the market even if such was not the consumer or end-user market.
As said by Neuberger LJ in *Laboratoire de la Mer*:

> "[49]   A wholesale purchaser of goods bearing a particular trade mark will, at least on
> the face of it, be relying upon the mark as a badge of origin just as much as a
> consumer who purchases such goods from a wholesaler. The fact that the
> wholesaler may be attracted by the mark because he believes that the consumer
> will be attracted by the mark does not call into question the fact that the mark is
> performing its essential function as between the producer and the wholesaler."[1115]

In the author's view, it is clear that genuine use does not require exposure of the   **3-713**
trade mark to end users or consumers. Indeed, art.18.1(b) EUTMR states that affixing a mark solely for export purposes in a Member State is deemed to qualify
as "use" for the purpose of determining whether a EUTM has been put to genuine
use or not. Ex hypothesi, exported goods bearing the mark will not be placed on
the consumer or end-user market in the Member State of export. Thus, if "genuine"
meant that the creation of a market share in the Member State of export was a necessary condition, it would give rise to a logical impasse as it would mean export use
could never qualify as "genuine use".[1116] It is disappointing that in *Reber* and other
judgments, this provision and its impact has not been taken account of when
considering whether there has been genuine use of a mark in a Member State.

The General Court also takes the view that the mere fact that acts of use of a trade   **3-714**
mark were not aimed at end users or final consumers is not enough for a finding of
lack of genuine use.[1117]

Use as a trade mark   For a court or tribunal to find that there is genuine use of a   **3-715**
trade mark, it is necessary that the mark be used in accordance with its essential

---

[1115] This observation is consistent with the CJEU's approach in (C-371/02) [2004] E.T.M.R. 69 which
emphasised the fact that the essential function of a mark is to act as a guarantee of origin to wholesalers and others in the supply chain as well as to end-users and consumers—see [23].
[1116] This argument was raised in the Court of Appeal in *Laboratoire de la Mer* but not adjudicated upon.
[1117] *Fruit of the Loom, Inc v EUIPO* (T-431/15) ECLI:EU:T:2016:395 at [64].

function, i.e. as an indication of trade origin.[1118] Thus, where a registered trade mark was used as a label of quality (in essence, as a certification mark) by a number of unconnected undertakings but not as an indication of trade origin of one undertaking, this did not amount to genuine use of a trade mark.[1119]

3-716 **Genuine use of mark when used with other marks** In some cases, a registered mark may be used in conjunction or juxtaposed with other marks. Two issues will arise here. What is the mark that has been used—is it a composite of the two marks or have two distinct marks been used? Secondly, if the mark used is considered a composite mark consisting of the two marks, does such alter the distinctive character of the registered mark? In some circumstances, it is fairly easy to say that there has been use of two marks. Thus, in *Castellblanch SA v EUIPO*,[1120] there was an issue as to whether there had been genuine use of the registered mark CRYSTAL. The mark "cristal" had been used with "Louis Roederer" on champagne bottles. It was argued by the party alleging lack of genuine use that such altered the identity of the earlier mark and thus did not constitute genuine use. The General Court held that there was no obligation on the registered proprietor to prove that the mark had been used on its own independently of another mark. The General Court said that in *Castellblanch* that the fact that several signs were being used simultaneously without altering the distinctive character of the registered sign. It thus held that the fact that the word mark CRISTAL was used with other indications was irrelevant.[1121] In *Colloseum Holding AG v Levi Strauss*,[1122] the CJEU had to consider whether a registered mark for the well-known red tab for Levi jeans (Red Tab Only Mark) had been put to genuine use where it was used only with the word "Levi" superimposed on it (Red Tab+Levi Mark). The referring court considered that these two marks differed in ways that did alter the distinctive character and thus Red Tab+Levi Mark could not be considered as use of Red Tab Only Mark.[1123] However, that left the question of whether there actually been use of Red Tab Only Mark by use of the composite mark, Red Tab+Levi Mark. In a short judgment, the CJEU noted that under its case law, it was possible for a mark which formed part of a composite mark to acquire distinctive character itself such as to permit it to be registered.[1124] It said that such an approach must be applied to the issue of genuine use provided that the registered mark is perceived as indicative of the origin of the goods despite being used in a composite mark.[1125] Accordingly, it held that where a registered trade mark has become distinctive as a result of its use in a composite mark of which it forms an element such use may amount to genuine use of the registered trade mark.

3-717 In *Specsavers v Asda*,[1126] which purported to follow *Colloseum*, the facts were similar. A figurative mark (an image of spectacles) was used with the word mark SPECSAVERS overlaid on it (i.e. appearing within the outline of the spectacles).

[1118] *W.F. Gözze Frottierweberei GmbH, Wolfgang Gözze v Verein Bremer Baumwollbörse* (C-689/15) ECLI:EU:C:201:434 at [37]–[42].

[1119] *W.F. Gözze Frottierweberei GmbH, Wolfgang Gözze v Verein Bremer Baumwollbörse* at [43]–[51].

[1120] *Castellblanch SA v EUIPO* (T-29/04) [2005] E.C.R. II-5309.

[1121] See [38].

[1122] (C-12/12) ECLI:EU:C:2013:253.

[1123] art.18.1(a) EUTMR states that use of the EUTM in a form differing in elements which do not alter the distinctive character of the mark in the form in which it is registered can be considered use of the EUTM. See also art.16.5(a) TMD.

[1124] See [27] applying *Nestlé* (C-353/02) [2005] E.C.R. I-6135. This is discussed at para.3-246.

[1125] See [30]–[35].

[1126] (C-252/12) ECLI:EU:C:2012:653.

It was alleged that such was not genuine use of the figurative mark. The CJEU held that in such circumstances, there was no use of the figurative mark on its own. It said that in such a case, it was not a mere juxtaposition of two marks—in part, because certain elements of the wordless logo mark were hidden by the word sign. It thus held that for genuine use to be established, it had to be shown that there had been use of a mark in a form differing in elements but which did not alter the distinctive character of the mark.[1127]

Genuine use of EUTMs Unlike national marks, EUTMs must be put to genuine use "in the Union" in connection with the goods or services in respect of which it is registered.[1128] This raises the issue as to whether, in the case of EUTMs, a higher level of use than for national marks is required both in terms of geographical extent or level of use. Thus, could a situation arise when the proven use of the mark is sufficient to prevent revocation of a national registered trade mark but not of a corresponding EUTM? Clearly, if there was a different test, this would be a real deterrent to applying for a EUTM, and in particular would discriminate against small or medium-sized enterprises. This would be contrary to the whole rationale of the EUTM which is intended to be for all. In the Joint Minutes, it was said that use in a single Member State would be sufficient. However, such minutes cannot be relied upon in interpreting the EUTMR.[1129]   **3-718**

In *Leno Merken BV v Hagelkruis Beheer BV*,[1130] the CJEU had to consider this issue in the context of opposition proceedings where the applicant asked the opponent to provide proof of genuine use of a EU trade mark relied upon in an opposition. The opponent proved genuine use of the EUTM in the Netherlands but not in the rest of the EU. Thus, the Dutch court wished to know whether use of a EUTM in a single Member State constituted genuine use of a EUTM "in the Community" (as it was then called). The CJEU held that the purpose of the EUTMs is to offer on the internal market conditions which are similar to those obtained in a national market. It thus held that the territorial borders of the Member States should be disregarded in the assessment of genuine use of a EUTM.[1131] In doing so, it disregarded the Joint Statement in the Council minutes.[1132] It also did not consider that the provisions of the predecessor provision of art.139.2(a) EUTMR which permits conversion of a EUTM into a series of national trade marks where the "rights of the proprietor of the EUTM have been revoked on the grounds of non-use unless in the Member State for which conversion is requested the EUTM has been put to use which would be considered to be genuine use under the laws of that Member State" to be of any assistance. Such a provision suggests that genuine use of a EUTM could not be limited to merely one Member State. The CJEU also held that there was no requirement that the EUTM be used in a substantial part of the EU.[1133] However, the CJEU did say that "*it is reasonable to expect that a Community trade mark should be used in a larger area than a national mark*" although   **3-719**

[1127] See [21]. Article 16.5(a) TMD states that use of a trade mark in a form differing in elements which do not alter the distinctive character of the mark in the form in which it is registered is to be considered use of the registered mark—see para.3-729.

[1128] art.18.1(a).

[1129] See para.3-139.

[1130] (C-149/11) ECLI:EU:C:2012:816.

[1131] See [44].

[1132] See [45]–[48].

[1133] See [52] (by analogy with *General Motors* (C-375/87) [1999] E.C.R. I-5241 and *Pago International* (C-301/07) [2009] E.C.R. I-9429 at [27]).

they said that "*it is not necessary that the mark should be used in an extensive geographic area for the use to be deemed genuine, since such a qualification will depend on the characteristics of the product or service concerning on the corresponding market*".[1134] In summary, the CJEU held that a EUTM is put to genuine use in the Community when it is used in accordance with its essential function and "*for the purpose of maintaining or creating market share within the European Community for the goods or services covered by it*". The CJEU said that it is for the referring court to assess whether such conditions are met, taking account of all the relevant facts including the characteristics of the market concerned, the nature of the goods or services protected by the trade mark, and the territorial extent and the scale of the use as well as its frequency and regularity.[1135]

3-720   Following *Leno Merken*, the General Court held that use of a EUTM in London and the Thames valley constituted genuine use of a EUTM.[1136] However, there is some suggestion in *Leno Merken*, that use in one Member State would normally not be enough to qualify as use throughout the EU. Thus, the CJEU in *Leno Merken*, having said that national borders of Member States should be ignored, made the following two statements which suggest that use in one Member State would not normally be considered enough:

> "[50]   Whilst there is admittedly some justification for thinking that a Community trade mark should—because it enjoys more extensive territorial protection than a national trade mark—*be used in a larger area than the territory of a single Member State* in order for the use to be regarded as 'genuine use', it cannot be ruled out that, in certain circumstances, *the market for the goods or services for which a Community trade mark has been registered is in fact restricted to the territory of a single Member State*. In such a case, use of the Community trade mark on that territory might satisfy the conditions both for genuine use of a Community trade mark and for genuine use of a national trade mark."

And

> "[54]   Secondly, whilst it is reasonable to expect that *a Community trade mark should be used in a larger area than a national mark*, it is not necessary that the mark should be used in an extensive geographic area for the use to be deemed genuine, since such a qualification will depend on the characteristics of the product or service concerned on the corresponding market. (see, by analogy, with regard to the scale of the use, *Ansul* [2003] E.T.M.R. 85 at [39])." [Emphasis supplied.]

3-721   These two passages were critical to a finding in an English case that use in the UK alone was not enough to amount to genuine use in the EU. In *Sofa Workshop Ltd v Sofaworks Ltd*,[1137] the English court concluded that these two passages meant that genuine use in the Union would in general require use in more than one Member State unless the market for the relevant goods or services is limited to the

---

[1134] See [54].

[1135] See [58] and declaratory part of judgment.

[1136] *Now Wireless Ltd v OHIM* (T-278/13) ECLI:EU:T:2015:57 (although the grounds of appeal were not aimed directly at such use not being sufficiently geographically widespread so as to amount to "use in the Union"). See also *TVR Automotive Ltd v OHIM* (T-398/13) ECLI:EU:T:2015:503 at [57] where the General Court held that use of a mark in the UK was enough to amount to use in the EU, applying *Leno Merken*.

[1137] [2015] EWHC 1773 (IPEC).

territory of a single Member State.[1138] There can be no doubt that based on a close textual analysis of *Leno Merken*, this English judgment is logical.[1139] However, in the author's view, it is difficult to reconcile this finding with the statement in *Leno Merken* that territorial borders should be disregarded when considering whether or not there has been genuine use in the EU. It would be most odd if use in London and the Thames Valley (population of around 14 million) is deemed not to be genuine use in the EU but use of a EUTM in the Netherlands and Luxembourg is deemed genuine use because it involved two Member States. Clearly, as seen above, such an approach has not been taken by the General Court. The better approach is a multi-factorial method whereby the EU is considered one large single territory and against that fact, a court or tribunal assesses the issue of genuine use. Thus, it may well be that the nature and extent of use of a trade mark is such as not to qualify as genuine use of a EUTM in the EU but is suitable to qualify as genuine use of a national mark in a Member State. However, such a finding would not depend on whether the mark is used in one or more of the Member States. Rather, it would merely reflect the fact that the EU is a much larger territory than any single Member State.[1140]

Proper reasons for non-use

Where there has been no genuine use of a mark in the relevant period, it will not be revoked if there are "proper reasons for non-use".[1141] It is necessary to interpret this provision in the light of art.19(1) of TRIPS which provides for revocation: **3-722**

> "… unless valid reasons based on the existence of obstacles to such use are shown by the trade mark owner. Circumstances arising independently of the will of the owner of the trade mark which constitute an obstacle to the use of the trade mark, such as import restrictions on or other government requirements for goods or services protected by the trade mark, shall be recognized as valid reasons for non-use."

Each case will turn on its facts. However, should "proper reasons" for non-use be given a wide interpretation? For instance, should it cover a situation where a proprietor has experienced commercial difficulties in finding a licensee? Or is it confined to more extreme situations such as where use of the mark would be illegal as envisaged in art.19 of TRIPS?   **3-723**

It is likely that "proper reasons" means reasons which are unusual or abnormal and not mere business difficulties. It has been suggested that the term "proper" was not intended to cover normal situations or routine difficulties. Thus, it is intended to cover abnormal situations in the industry or the market, or perhaps some temporary but serious disruption affecting the registered proprietor's business. Thus, a delay caused by some unavoidable regulatory requirement, such as the approval   **3-724**

[1138] See [25]. It will be an exceptional case where a market for goods or services is confined to one Member State.

[1139] In *The London Taxi Corporate v Frazer-Nash Research* [2016] EWHC 52 at [230], Arnold J said in commenting on *Sofa Workshop*, that whilst he found the thrust of the judge's analysis in *Sofa Workshop* "persuasive", he preferred to say that the assessment was a multi-factorial one which included the geographical extent of the use.

[1140] This appears to be the thrust of Arnold J's finding in *The London Taxi Corporation* (see previous footnote).

[1141] art.18.1 EUTMR; art.16.1 TMD.

of a medicine, might be acceptable, but not normal delays found in marketing the product which are matters within the businessman's own control.[1142]

3-725 This approach has been adopted by the General Court in *Giorgio/Giorgi*,[1143] the General Court said:

> "[41] In any event, the concept of proper reasons in that article must be considered to refer essentially to circumstances unconnected with the trade mark owner which prohibit him from using the mark, rather than to circumstances associated with the commercial difficulties he is experiencing".

3-726 Interestingly, EUIPO has considered in a number of decisions whether court proceedings against the registered proprietor for use of the registered trade mark could constitute proper reasons for non-use. It thus has said that the mere threat of litigation or a pending cancellation action against the earlier mark should not exempt the opponent from the obligation to use its trade mark.[1144] Rather more controversially, it said that a person who refrains from using a registered trade mark by reason of such infringing a third party mark is not for proper reasons but that an interim injunction or a restraining court order in insolvency proceedings imposing a general prohibition of transfers or disposals on the trade mark owner could amount to proper reasons for non-use.[1145]

3-727 In *Häupl v Lidl*,[1146] an Austrian court referred to the CJEU the question of whether there were "proper reasons" for non-use if the implementation of a corporate strategy is delayed for reasons outside the control of the undertaking or whether the undertaking was obliged to change its strategy. The CJEU held that art.19(1) of TRIPS should be applied. The court also held that bureaucratic obstacles were not sufficient and that it must be shown that the obstacles have a:

> "sufficiently direct relationship with a trade mark making its use impossible or unreasonable and which arise independently of the will of the proprietor of that mark"

before proper reasons will be made out. This reinforces the General Court's ruling in *Giorgio/Giorgi* that the proper reason must be a reason that *any* undertaking who owned the registered mark would have experienced, i.e. they must be circumstances unconnected with the trade mark owner.

3-728 In the author's opinion, "proper reasons" should be construed narrowly for the following reasons:

(1) The absence of a requirement of intention to use when applying for a mark means that there is no initial filter to applications for marks. Thus, a register can quickly fill up with registered marks which do not reflect current or anticipated use of the mark.

(2) The period of five years is generous. Indeed, as the relevant date for an ap-

---

[1142] *Invermont* [1997] R.P.C. 125.

[1143] *Laboratories RTB v EUIPO* (T-156/01) [2003] E.C.R. II-2789.

[1144] EUIPO *Opposition Guidelines*, Part C, section 2.11.2 and cases cited thereto.

[1145] It is difficult to understand EUIPO's approach. Thus, it says that use of a mark contrary to a court order would make the trade mark owner liable to damage claims but so of course would using a trade mark which infringes a third party mark. If a third party claim is very strong, it is odd that a distinction should be drawn between capitulating and one where a court order is granted. Indeed, it is odd that a trade mark proprietor who is prevented from using their mark by reason of the assertion in court of third party trade mark rights is better off than the proprietor who acts reasonably and recognises the strength of the third party's claim.

[1146] (C-246/05) [2007] E.C.R. I-4763.

plication to revoke for non-use is the date of registration, it means that the effective period will usually be considerably in excess of five years. This is particularly the case where there has been extensive delay between filing and registration, e.g. lengthy opposition proceedings.

(3) A mark which is not used serves no purpose in the marketplace.

(4) The Recitals of the TMD make it clear that it is "essential" that marks are used to reduce the number of conflicts by requiring that a registered mark is actually used.

Use of variants of the registered mark

Article 18.1 (a) EUTMR deems use of a trade mark in a form "differing in elements which do not alter the distinctive character of the mark in the form in which it is registered" to be use of a registered mark. The TMD contains an identical provision.[1147]   **3-729**

In an English case, *Budweiser Budvar TM*,[1148] the Court of Appeal said that it involves a two-stage test. First, the court or tribunal must identify what points of difference exist between the mark as used and the mark as registered. Once those differences have been identified, the second part of the inquiry is to discover whether they alter the distinctive character of the mark as registered.[1149] The Court of Appeal said that the distinctive character of a trade mark (what makes it in some degree striking and memorable) is not likely to be analysed by the average consumer, but is nevertheless capable of analysis.[1150] Ultimately, this is a matter of impression. In a number of decisions of the General Court, they have emphasised that one must have regard to the dominant and distinctive components of the mark.[1151] Thus, in *J&F Participacoes (FRIBO)*, it held that the Board of Appeal was entitled to determine that the use of a figurative mark containing the word mark FRIBO amounted to genuine use of the word mark since the dominant and distinctive element of the figurative mark was FRIBO and the "other elements would not be regarded by consumers as fulfilling the function of distinguishing the goods concerned from those of other undertakings".[1152]   **3-730**

However, what is the position where the registered mark is used in a composite mark where the other elements are also themselves distinctive. *J&F Participacoes* suggests that if the other element also acts as a trade mark, then art.18.1(a) is inapplicable. Nevertheless, it may be that there is use of the registered mark despite such being used in a composite mark. This has been discussed above.[1153] In *Specsavers v Asda*,[1154] the Court of Justice considered whether a composite mark consisting of   **3-731**

[1147] art.16.5(a) TMD.

[1148] *Budweiser Budvar TM* [2003] R.P.C. 25 CA.

[1149] See [43].

[1150] In doing so, Lord Walker of Gestingthorpe referred to the line of poetry "Bare ruin'd choirs, where late the sweet birds sang" (this comes from Shakespeare's Sonnet 73) saying that such is effective whether or not the reader is familiar with Empson's commentary pointing out its rich associations (including early music, vault-like trees in winter, and the dissolution of the monasteries—see [44]).

[1151] e.g. see *Gfk AG v EUIPO* (T-135/04) [2005] E.C.R. II-4865; *J&F Participacoes SA v EUIPO* (T-324/09) [2009] E.C.R. I-000; *Laboratorios RTB v EUIPO* (T-156/01) [2003] E.C.R. II-2789.

[1152] (T-324/09), at [36].

[1153] See para.3-716.

[1154] (C–252/12) EU:C:2013:497.

(the Specsavers Mark)

could amount to genuine use of a EUTM for

(the Spectacles Mark)

under the predecessor provision to art.18(1)(a) EUTMR.

3-732 In its judgment, the Court of Justice made it clear that the Specsavers Mark was not use of the Spectacles Mark per se as the word Specsavers was not a mere juxtaposition to the Spectacles Mark. Certain parts of the Spectacles Mark were hidden by the word "Spectacles". Thus, for there to be genuine use, art.18(1)(a) had to apply.

3-733 At first blush, it would appear an unpromising argument that this was the case. The word "Specsavers" plays a dominant role in the Specsavers Mark and one might have thought that the Spectacles Mark played a subsidiary role. However, the Court of Justice said, adopting its approach to the determination of whether a mark has acquired distinctive character when used as a component of a composite mark,[1155] that the composite mark ("Specsavers Mark") could be considered genuine use of the component mark ("Spectacles Mark") if the latter was distinctive of the goods of the registered proprietor. In other words, did the relevant public perceive the Spectacles Mark as a distinct and separate mark to the Specsavers Mark or an integral composite element of the Specsavers Mark? If the former, then use of the Specsavers Mark amounted to use of the Spectacles Mark.

3-734 When the action came back to the English courts,[1156] the parties had settled. However, the Spectacles Mark had been revoked (there having been no use of it as opposed to the Specsavers Mark in the relevant period) and Specsavers thus pursued the appeal to have the mark reinstated on the Registry. Therefore, the question was whether this was a valid revocation in the light of the Court of Justice's judgment.

[1155] See para.3-246.
[1156] [2014] EWCA Civ 1294.

The Court of Appeal also considered that at first blush, it was an unpromising argument. However, it held that, applying the guidance of the CJEU in *Specsavers*, the conditions of art.18.1(a) were satisfied:

- there had been very considerable use of the Specsavers Mark;
- none of the competitors had used a mark remotely similar;
- Asda's own internal memorandum whereby it had used a mark similar to the Specsavers Mark but with Asda Optician in it and had called it the "Asda version of Specsavers—rip off"; and
- green ellipses catch the eye in the Specsavers Mark (particularly from a distance).

Thus, the Court of Appeal found that "in the rather unusual circumstances", use **3-735** of the "Specsavers" mark amounted to use of the "Spectacles Mark".

One cannot help thinking that something has gone wrong here. In effect, the **3-736** Court of Justice has held that where there exists a composite mark which composes of two distinctive elements both recognised by the public (but which are not a mere juxtaposition), then there has been genuine use of both elements. Therefore, in *Asda v Specsavers*, the "Specsavers" word was the dominant distinctive element of the "Specsavers Mark", with the "Spectacles Mark" being the subservient element and yet this fact is ignored when considering art.18(1)(a) solely on the grounds that the subservient element also has distinctive character. Instinctively and as a matter of logic, it is, as the Court of Appeal said, an unpromising argument.

Variant is itself a registered mark—irrelevant

Prior to the amendments to the EUTMR and TMD, the Court of Justice held that **3-737** it was irrelevant if the mark used in the marketplace was itself a registered mark when considering whether the used mark satisfied art.18.1(a).[1157] This case law has now been expressly incorporated into the EUTMR and TMD.[1158]

Use with consent of registered trade mark proprietor

Under both the TMD and EUTMR, use with the consent of the proprietor of a **3-738** registered trade mark amounts to relevant use for the purpose of any determination of genuine use.[1159] However, as discussed above, if a mark is not used in accordance with the essential function, namely as a guarantee that the goods marketed under the mark come from a single undertaking under the control of which they are manufactured and which is responsible for their quality, then there is no genuine use of the mark.[1160] Thus, where a trade mark owner consents to the use of a registered trade mark without any possibility of control over the quality of goods

---

[1157] See *Rintisch* (C-553/11) ECLI:EU:C:2012:672. Followed in *Specsavers* (see [27]). NB. The CJEU in *Rintisch* distinguished *Il Ponte Finanziaria SpA v EUIPO* (C-234/06P) [2007] E.C.R. I-7333 which the CJEU said in *Rintisch* was concerned specifically with a family of marks and that it was not possible to claim that a family of registered marks had been used where only one mark had been used on the grounds that one mark was a slight variation of the other (see [29]).

[1158] art.16.5(a) TMD; art.18.1(a) EUTMR.

[1159] art.18.2 EUTMR; art.16.6 TMD.

[1160] See *W.F. Gözze Frottierweberei GmbH, Wolfgang Gözze v Verein Bremer Baumwollbörse*, at [46].

(what is often called a "bare licence") marketed under the mark, it is considered that this does not amount to genuine use.[1161]

Partial revocation

3-739 Article 58.2 EUTMR permits partial revocation of the specification of goods or services where there has been genuine use of the mark only in relation to part of the goods or services.[1162] It raises the issue as to whether the court or tribunal must only consider the specification as written or can rewrite it. For instance, if someone registers a mark for motor vehicles and it is shown that the mark has only been used for motorcycles, can a court rewrite the specification and limit it to motorcycles?

3-740 The General Court has considered the issue of partial revocation in *Reckitt-Benkiser v EUIPO*.[1163] In opposition proceedings, the opponent was requested to provide evidence of use of the mark.[1164] The earlier mark was registered for "polish for metals". However, the Board of Appeal found that use had only been on "product for polishing metals consisting of cotton impregnated with a polishing agent (magic cotton)". On appeal to the General Court, the General Court held that such was too fine a distinction. It said:

> "[45] It follows from the provisions cited above that, if a trade mark has been registered for a category of goods or services which is sufficiently broad for it to be possible to identify within it a number of sub-categories capable of being viewed independently, proof that the mark has been put to genuine use in relation to a part of those goods or services affords protection, in opposition proceedings, only for the sub-category or sub-categories relating to which the goods or services for which the trade mark has actually been used actually belong. However, if a trade mark has been registered for goods or services defined so precisely and narrowly that it is not possible to make any significant sub-divisions within the category concerned, then the proof of genuine use of the mark for the goods or services necessarily covers the entire category for the purposes of the opposition.
>
> [46] Although the principle of partial use operates to ensure that trade marks which have not been used for a given category of goods are not rendered unavailable, it must not, however, result in the proprietor of the earlier trade mark being stripped of all protection for goods which, although not strictly identical to those in respect of which he has succeeded in proving genuine use, are not in essence different from them and belong to a single group which cannot be divided other than in an arbitrary manner. The Court observes in that regard that in practice it is impossible for the proprietor of a trade mark to prove that the mark has been used for all conceivable variations of the goods concerned by the registration. Consequently, the concept of 'part of the goods or services' cannot be taken to mean all the commercial variations of similar goods or services but merely goods or services which *are sufficiently distinct* to constitute coherent categories or sub-categories."[1165] [Emphasis supplied.]

3-741 This passage suggests that the correct approach is not to restrict specifications too narrowly. However, the test is easier to state than to apply. When are goods or

---

[1161] It might be said that the reasoning of the Court of Justice in *Gözze Frottierweberei GmbH* at [52]–[61] is contrary to this. However, the Court of Justice's reasoning was confined to a very specific question which involved consideration of art.7.1(g) (deceptive marks).

[1162] See also art.21 TMD.

[1163] *Reckitt Benckiser v EUIPO (ALADIN)* (T-126/03) [2005] E.C.R. II-2861.

[1164] See para.3-398.

[1165] See [45]–[46].

services "sufficiently distinct" to constitute coherent categories or sub-categories? Ultimately, each case must turn on its facts. Thus, in *Armour Pharmaceutical Co v EUIPO (GALZIN)*,[1166] a registration for "pharmaceutical and medical preparations, more specifically calcium-based preparations", use was only of calcium-based preparations. The General Court held that in considering an opposition based on that mark, only calcium-based preparations should be taken into account. "Pharmaceutical preparations" was sufficiently broad a term for it to be possible to identify within it various sub-categories in general. The General Court said that "pharmaceutical preparations" covered goods which are suitably different in their intended purposes and end consumers, according to their specific therapeutic indications and in their channels of distribution, depending on whether they are available on medical prescription or over the counter.

If one considers the matter in terms of policy, it is clear that the Recitals of the EUTMR and TMD require and consider it essential that marks must be used, or if not used they should be subject to revocation so as to avoid the number of conflicts which arise between them. Conflicts will arise between identical or similar marks and marks and signs where use is on identical or similar goods.[1167] Such an approach favours a narrowing of the specification where the wording of the specification encompasses goods or services that are not similar and there has only been use on one type of good or service. Thus, a specification for "computer software" in reality encompasses many different types of computer software from financial software to embedded electrical control mechanisms. Such software cannot be regarded as similar within the meaning of arts 4 and 5 of the TMD.[1168] Thus, if a registered proprietor was entitled to retain a specification of "computer software" per se when they have only used it for embedded electrical control mechanisms, in reality, the proprietor obtains protection for goods or services dissimilar to those which they trade in.[1169] If the purpose of art.58.2 EUTMR is to align the goods or services protected by a registered mark with those goods or services in relation to which the proprietor has used the mark, then a failure to rewrite the "computer software" specification results in unduly wide protection to dissimilar goods which the TMD has seen fit only to grant in very particular circumstances.[1170]   **3-742**

In an English case, *Roger Maier and Assos of Switzerland SA v ASOS Plc*,[1171] the majority of the Court of Appeal of England and Wales held that the cutting down of a specification of "clothing, footwear and headgear" to "specialist clothing for racing cyclists; jackets, t-shirts, polo shirts, track-suit tops, track-suit bottoms, casual shorts, caps" by the first instance court was permissible. The dissenting judgment held that the appropriate formulation was "specialist clothing for racing cyclists and casual wear" and that it was not sensible and indeed arbitrary to divide the sort of leisurewear which the registered proprietor had sold and casual wear generally. In the authors' view, the dissenting judge was correct. As said in *Reckitt-Benkiser*, the principle of partial use must not result in the proprietor being stripped of all protection for goods which although not strictly identical to those in respect   **3-743**

[1166] *Armour Pharmaceutical Co v EUIPO (GALZIN)* (T-483/04) [2006] E.C.R. II-4109.

[1167] Where the mark has no reputation.

[1168] For the meaning of "similar goods", see para.3-338.

[1169] Of course, it might be that the mark has a substantial reputation. However, as art.10 and art.12 do not require the registered proprietor to establish a reputation but mere use, such will often not be the case.

[1170] i.e. when the mark has a reputation and the sign or mark takes unfair advantage or causes detriment to the repute of the mark.

[1171] [2015] EWCA Civ 1101.

of which they have succeeded in proving genuine use, are not in essence different from them and belong to a single group which cannot be divided other than in an arbitrary manner.

3-744   It is not possible to rewrite a specification of goods by a negative limitation of goods with a particular characteristic.[1172]

International trade marks and genuine use

3-745   In *Rivella v EUIPO*,[1173] the opponent in opposition proceedings was required to prove genuine use of its trade mark.[1174] The opposition was based on an international figurative mark which had been designated for a number of Member States pursuant to the Madrid Agreement.[1175] The effect of an international application under the Madrid Agreement is to give rise to a basket of national trade marks in the designated states. The opponent only relied upon the designated German registration. It had not used the mark in Germany but only in Switzerland. However, it relied upon an 1892 bilateral convention between Switzerland and Germany whereby if the mark had been used in one territory, such amounted to use by the other territory. The CJEU said that marks which are the subject of international registrations should not be treated differently to national marks.[1176] This must be right as that was precisely the intention of the Madrid Agreement. More interestingly, Rivella argued that the question of whether there had been use of a mark in a Member State should be governed by national law and thus the 1892 Convention was applicable. The CJEU disagreed and held that the question of whether there has been use of a trade mark in a Member State is governed exclusively by European Union law and therefore the 1892 Convention had no applicability in the EU trade mark system.[1177] Again, this must be right.

Mark has become generic

3-746   Article 58.1(b) EUTMR permits the revocation of a mark where, after the date on which it was registered:

> "(b)   in consequence of acts or inactivity of the proprietor, it has become the common name in the trade for a product or service in respect of which it is registered".

3-747   This ground should be compared with the absolute grounds under the EUTMR whereby signs which are devoid of distinctive character or are customary terms in the trade cannot be registered. Under art.58.1(b), the primary focus is on marks which were distinctive as of the date of filing but which have become generic names for a product. For instance, ASPIRIN for a pharmaceutical made from acetylsalicyclic acid which although a Bayer trade mark in many countries is considered generic in others. Other examples are YO-YO for the well-known children's toy;

[1172] *POSTKANTOOR* (C-363/99) [2004] E.C.R. I-1619 at [117]. In UK, see *Croom's Application* [2005] R.P.C. 2 where it was held that a limitation of "not haute couture" was not permissible.

[1173] (C-445/12P) ECLI:EU:C:2013:826.

[1174] In opposition proceedings, the proprietors of earlier trade marks can be required to prove genuine use of their marks in the five-year period preceding the date of publication of the EUTM application—art.47(2). See para.3-398 for further discussion.

[1175] For further discussion of international applications under the Madrid Agreement or Madrid Protocol, see para.3-052.

[1176] See [36]–[41].

[1177] See [48]–[53].

TRAMPOLINE for trampolines; DAIQUIRI for an alcoholic drink; PINA COLADA for a new cocktail[1178]; and SHREDDED WHEAT for a breakfast cereal.[1179] Often, the problem is that the mark is used for a groundbreaking product of which, prior to its invention, there was no similar good. In a wholly foreseeable manner, the public starts to use the mark as the name for the product. A number of issues arise under art.58.1(b) which are now discussed.

Acts or inactivity of the proprietor

The cause of the mark becoming a common name must arise because of the acts **3-748** or inactivity of the proprietor. This will be the case where the proprietor uses the mark in a generic way or where the proprietor fails to police use of the mark by third parties in a generic sense. In *Levi Strauss v Casucci*,[1180] the court explained that there was a necessity for vigilant conduct in relation to infringements since the purpose of the TMD is to strike a balance between the interest of the proprietor to safeguard the essential function of a trade mark and the interests of other economic operators to be able to use signs capable of denoting their products and services. In *Backaldrin Österreich The Kornspitz Company GmbH v Pfahnl Backmittel GmbH*,[1181] an issue was whether the registered proprietor had been guilty of "inactivity" where it had not encouraged sellers to make more use of the trade mark in marketing the bread rolls. The CJEU gave a wide interpretation of the meaning of "inactivity" by saying that it *"includes all those [acts or omissions] by which the proprietor of a trade mark shows that he is not sufficiently vigilant as regards the preservation of the distinctive character of his trade mark"*.[1182] Thus, it held that a failure by the proprietor to take an initiative to encourage its sellers to make more use of the mark could be classified as relevant inactivity.[1183]

Where the trade mark is the name of a groundbreaking innovative product, the **3-749** proprietor is best advised to come up with a descriptive name for a new product as well as a registered mark. Other steps would include use of the ® symbol and ensuring that its use of the mark is never descriptive and that licensees and distributors do not use the mark in a descriptive way. A failure to take these steps could result in a finding that a mark has become a common name through the fault of the proprietor. The *Kornspitz* case highlighted that there are some steps that the proprietor could have taken to prevent the mark becoming the common name for the product. Otherwise art.58.1(b) would be applicable if the mark does become the common name.

Article 12 EUTMR permits a EUTM owner to take action to prevent descrip- **3-750** tive use of a EUTM in dictionaries by requiring the publisher of a dictionary to state that it is a registered trade mark. Article 12 TMD functions similarly.

[1178] See *Daiquiri Rum Trade Mark* [1969] F.S.R 89 (House of Lords, England); *Bardinet SA v Ego-Fruits SCP* [2002] E.T.M.R. 85 (Cour d'Appel de Paris).
[1179] *The Shredded Wheat Co Ltd v Kellogg Co of Great Britain* [1940] R.P.C. 137.
[1180] (C-145/05) [2006] E.C.R. I-3703; [2006] E.T.M.R. 71.
[1181] (C-409/12) ECLI:EU:C:2014:130.
[1182] See [34].
[1183] See [23].

Common name to wholesalers or consumers?

3-751 This provision was considered in *Björnekulla*.[1184] In that case, an application was brought under Swedish trade mark law to revoke the mark BOSTONGURKA on the grounds that it had become the common name for chopped pickled gherkins. Two consumer surveys were relied upon. The registered proprietor relied upon surveys amongst wholesalers and intermediaries who were aware that it was the registered mark of the proprietor. The Swedish court referred to the CJEU the issue as to who was the relevant public. It held that generally, the relevant classes of persons comprised consumers and end users but that depending on the features of the product market concerned, the influence of intermediaries on decisions to purchase and thus their perception of the trade mark had also to be taken into consideration. This decision was clarified in *Kornspitz*, which is discussed in the foregoing section.[1185] The case concerned the KORNSPITZ mark which was registered for flour and preparations as well as for bakery goods and pastry confectionery. The mark was used in relation to a baking mix supplied primarily to bakers which was then turned into an oblong bread roll and also marketed under the mark KORNSPITZ. The evidence suggested that end users perceived the mark as the common name for an oblong bread roll (with two points at both ends) even though the bakers were aware that it was a registered mark for a baking mix. Revocation proceedings were brought by a competitor to the registered proprietor who argued that it had become a common name for a bakery product. The Austrian Supreme Patent and Trade Mark Court (on appeal from the Austrian Patent Office) dismissed the application in relation to the baking mix (flour and preparations) but was less sure in relation to finished goods (e.g. bakery goods and pastry confectionery) and thus referred the matter to the CJEU. It was unsure whether it should take into account the views of the end-users, the bakers or both. The CJEU said that whilst in *Björnekulla*, the CJEU did say that the perception of intermediaries who participate in the distribution should be taken into account, in general, the perception of consumers or end users "will play a decisive role" and the fact that the sellers are aware of the existence of the trade mark cannot, preclude such a revocation.[1186]

More than one common name

3-752 It might be thought that the reference to "the common name" means that this provision does not apply if there is more than one common name for a product. In *Kornspitz* the CJEU said that it is irrelevant whether there are other names (common or not) for the product for which the trade mark has become the common name.[1187]

Common name and indication of origin

3-753 What is the position where the trade mark has become the common name for the products yet is still recognised as an indication of origin. Whilst it might be thought that the above is a contradiction—a common name cannot act also as an indica-

---

[1184] (C-371/02) [2004] E.C.R. I-5791; [2004] E.T.M.R. 69.
[1185] (C-409/12) ECLI:EU:C:2014:130.
[1186] See [27]–[30].
[1187] See [37]–[40].

tion of origin—it is not. As said above, many trade marks are vulnerable to becoming generic because they are used as a trade mark for a groundbreaking innovative product which has enjoyed a long period of monopoly as a result of a patent or market forces. By reason of such, the trade mark becomes a *descriptor* for a product with a particular set of characteristics but is also perceived as a trade mark. For instance, let us take "Aspirin". A person may recognise it as a trade mark of Bayer for a pharmaceutical made from acetylsalicylic acid yet also will use it to describe a pharmaceutical made from the same active ingredient. One might say, by analogy to the reasoning of the CJEU in *Kornspitz* considered in the foregoing paragraph, that it is irrelevant whether it is also perceived as an indication of origin. This also has parallels with the CJEU's finding in *Gerolsteiner* that use of a geographical name is a defence to trade mark infringement proceedings even though the geographical name is also used as a trade mark.[1188]

Loss of distinctive character

One real lacuna in the EU trade mark law is that there is no express provision which allows the revocation of a trade mark which has ceased to have distinctive character. Article 58.1(b) appears limited to situations where the mark has become the common name for a product and not merely ceased to have distinctive character. A mark may simply lose its distinctiveness over time. For instance, whether due to use of the sign by third parties or lack of appropriate promotion by the trade mark owner, the mark loses its ability to act as an indication of origin. This may often be the case for non-word marks, e.g. colours, packaging and shape marks. These may have been distinctive as of the date of application but subsequently become so widely used by third parties (or not used enough by the trade mark owner) that they cease to have distinctive character. However, equally, one could not say without considerable distortion to the meaning of "common name" that they have become the common name for goods. Packaging and shapes are not names. **3-754**

The answer may lie in an argument based on fundamental principles, namely that the essential function of such a registered mark has ceased to exist and that on a purposive construction of EU trade mark law, where a mark has ceased to act as an indication of trade origin, it should be revoked—in particular, as other economic operators may have an interest in using such a trade mark to denote products and services (or their characteristics).[1189] This could be done by the CJEU interpreting art.58.1(b) EUTMR by holding that "common name" includes any mark which no longer serves as an indication of origin.[1190] **3-755**

Mark liable to mislead

Article 58.1(c) EUTMR permits the revocation of a registered trade mark: **3-756**

"(c)   *if, in consequence of the use made of it by the proprietor of the trade mark or with his consent in respect of the goods or services for which it is registered, the trade*

[1188] See para.3-497.

[1189] (C-145/05) [2006] E.C.R. I-3703; [2006] E.T.M.R. 71 at [29].

[1190] In other cases, the CJEU has not shown much reluctance to interpret the literal meaning of provisions in EU trade mark law in a manner that does considerable violence to the language but is consistent with the underlying policy of EU trade mark law. For instance, see its interpretation of art.10.1(c) TMD (dissimilar goods = similar goods) at para.3-357 and also see the interpretation of art.4.1(d) (customary name). See para.3-217.

mark is liable to mislead the public, particularly as to the nature, quality or geographical origin of those goods or services."

Its counterpart in the TMD is art.20(b).

3-757   Article 58.1(c) EUTMR has a parallel in the absolute ground for refusal, art.7.1(g) (marks which are of such a nature as to deceive the public). This has been discussed already.[1191] In *Emanuel v Continental Shelf 128*,[1192] the CJEU considered the equivalent provisions in the TMD. It said that the conditions for revocation under the identical predecessor provision to art.20(b) TMD are the same as art.4(1)(g) TMD (counterpart in the TMD to art.7.1(g) EUTMR).[1193] Literally read, this is plainly wrong as art.20(b) has a requirement that it must be shown that is a consequence of the proprietor's use or use with the proprietor's consent that it has become misleading.

3-758   This provision has not been the subject of much judicial comment. What little there has been suggests that it is concerned with use of a trade mark which conflicts with the meaning of a trade mark. Thus, the mark MÖVENPICK OF SWITZERLAND was revoked because the goods in question (biscuits) had been made in Germany and not Switzerland.[1194]

3-759   For the legal theorist, there is a conceptual difficulty here. This is that where the owner of a trade mark uses it in a manner that conflicts with the meaning of the trade mark, it is not the *trade mark* that becomes misleading but rather it is that *the goods or services* marketed under that trade mark deceive the customer. For instance, let us take a geographic mark, e.g. IRISH SPRING for mineral water. Such suggests that the mineral water comes from County Kerry in Ireland. Let us assume that after many years, it is discovered that the registered proprietor has used IRISH SPRING for mineral water that comes from Spain and that the public have been deceived. Such does not mean that the trade mark IRISH SPRING is liable to mislead the public in respect of a characteristic of mineral water, namely its geographical origin. It simply means that the trade mark has been used by the registered proprietor in a misleading manner (and it is likely that consumer protection laws could prevent such use). It is the *use of the mark* and not the *mark* itself which is misleading. Thus, no doubt the public would still assume that the trade mark IRISH SPRING when used for mineral water means water sourced or drawn from Eire (the Republic of Ireland). Indeed, if they did not, there would be no confusion.

3-760   In short, art.58.1(c) EUTMR strays into the field of consumer protection. There is nothing particularly wrong with this. The *ordre public* provision of the EUTMR and TMD prevent the registration of marks which are offensive and yet of course, in doing so, they ensure that *anyone* can use an offensive word as a trade mark

Deception as to trade origin

3-761   One of the ways in which a mark may become deceptive is because it is liable to mislead the public as to trade origin. This could occur, for instance, if the mark is assigned without goodwill or is licensed under a bare licence for a substantial

---

[1191] See para.3-273.

[1192] (C-259/04) [2006] E.C.R. I-3089; [2006] E.T.M.R. 56.

[1193] See [52]–[53].

[1194] *Biscosuisse and Chocosuisse v Mövenpick Holding* R 697/2008-1 (EUIPO, 1st Board of Appeal). See also para.3-094 and fn.120 concerning the meaning of "quality".

period of time with no possibility of control. In such situations, the tribunal must ask whether the public is deceived. This requires a consideration of how the public perceives a mark. Nowadays, with multinational restructuring, mergers and acquisitions, sales of marks, etc. the public often knows little about the actual entity behind the mark. These matters came up in an English case, *Scandecor Development v Scandecor Marketing*,[1195] which concerned the ownership of marks where there had been a considerable amount of assignment of marks and restructuring of companies. The English provision that enacted the predecessor obligation to art.20(b) of the TMD was considered. The House of Lords considered what a mark meant to the general public in modern times. Lord Nicholls of Birkenhead said:

> "[28] Customers are well used to the practice of licensing of trade marks. When they see goods to which a mark has been affixed, they understand that the goods have been produced either by the owner of the mark or by someone else acting with his consent.
>
> [39] Nor does the wider interpretation undermine the protection which a trade mark is intended to afford customers. For their quality assurance customers rely on the self-interest of the owner. They assume that if a licence has been granted the owner can be expected to have chosen a suitable licensee and imposed suitable terms. They also assume that during the currency of any licence, the licensee, as well as the owner, is likely to have an interest in maintaining the value of the brand name. Customers are not to be taken to rely on the protection supposedly afforded by a legal requirement that the proprietor must always retain and exercise an inherently imprecise degree of control over the licensee's activities."[1196]

Thus, the public is used to licensing and franchising of the mark, even where there are no quality control provisions. However, the House of Lords did not consider the matter to be acte clair. Accordingly, it referred to the CJEU the issue as to whether a mark was liable to mislead the public if it had only been used by a bare exclusive licensee. However, this case was settled before the CJEU ruled on it.   **3-762**

It is submitted that there is no reason why art.58.1(c) EUTMR/art.20(b) TMD should not apply to marks which have become misleading as to trade origin. However, it will be rare that such a case is made out for the reasons set out in *Scandecor*. In short, where a mark is not a personal name or well-known company name, the public are plainly familiar with the fact that marks are bought and sold. They rely upon the self-interest of the *current* owner to preserve the reputation of the mark but will not normally concern themselves about the *identity* of that owner. However, where the mark is the name of a known personality or company name, then it not only serves as an indication of origin but also as an indication of the *identity* of that trade origin. In such circumstances, where that connection no longer exists, the mark may well be misleading. This connection may be severed as a result of an assignment and this is now considered.   **3-763**

Misleading assignments of marks

In *Emanuel v Continental Shelf 128*,[1197] the CJEU had to consider whether the assignment of a registered mark together with the goodwill of a well-known name of a wedding designer meant that the mark had become misleading because the   **3-764**

[1195] *Scandecor Development v Scandecor Marketing* [2001] 2 C.M.L.R. 30; [2002] F.S.R. 7 HL.
[1196] See [38]–[39], Lord Nicholls of Birkenhead.
[1197] (C-259/04) [2006] E.T.M.R. 56.

goods no longer had any connection with the wedding designer. This case has already been considered in the context of the absolute grounds of inherently deceptive marks.[1198]

3-765   The CJEU applied its reasoning in relation to inherently deceptive absolute grounds for refusal to the identical predecessor provision to art.20(b) TMD. The CJEU thus said that a trade mark corresponding to the name of the designer and first manufacturer of the goods bearing that mark is not, by reason of that particular feature alone, liable to revocation on the ground that that mark would mislead the public, in particular where the goodwill associated with that mark has been assigned together with the business making the goods to which the mark relates.[1199]

3-766   The reasoning of this judgment has already been criticised in this chapter in relation to its findings under inherent deceptiveness[1200] and thus this criticism equally applies to the application of such reasoning to art.20(b).[1201] It is stressed that the criticism is of the CJEU's reasoning but not the result. It would be most surprising if a voluntary assignment of the goodwill in a brand consisting of the assignor's personal name could be negated by the assignor by relying upon art.20(b) TMD. Ultimately, as discussed earlier, there is a clear conflict of two principles, namely the right of persons to buy and sell trade marks with or without the goodwill and the need to ensure that misleading marks are not registered. In the author's opinion, the latter should yield to the former. If *use* of the mark is misleading, this can be dealt with under consumer protection laws. Preventing the *registration* of a misleading mark is not detrimental to the public and thus, there is no real public interest, whereas there is the public interest that commercial bargains are honoured by all parties. Moreover, art.20(b) TMD/art.58.1(c) EUTMR must be interpreted in the light of art.21 of TRIPS which states that owners of registered marks must be permitted to assign these marks without the goodwill. It would be odd and contrary to the nature and spirit of art.21 TRIPS if assignments of marks which were names, in particular of personal names, resulted in an almost automatic finding that the mark was misleading because the selling power of the mark was directly linked to the fact that it was the name of a well-known person.[1202]

Collective and certification marks

3-767   Trade marks are ultimately concerned about conveying *information* to consumers and traders or anyone else in the supply chain from manufacture (or in the case of services, supply) to the end user. A "classical" trade mark provides information that goods or services which are marketed under that mark have a connection in the course of trade with the owner of that trade mark. However, some trade marks convey a different type of information. These are collective marks and certification marks. Collective marks act as a guarantee not of one undertaking but of members of an association. Thus, an association of manufacturers which is governed by its own contractual rules may register a collective mark to identify the association. Members will also use the collective mark to identify themselves as members of the association. Those manufacturers will usually have no economic

---

[1198] See para.3-274.
[1199] See [53].
[1200] art.4.1(g).
[1201] See para.3-277.
[1202] As the EU is a signatory to TRIPS, it is requested to interpret the TMD in accordance with the spirit and purpose of TRIPS—see para.1-180, et seq.

links with each other. Collective marks are often owned by non-incorporated associations on behalf of all its members, e.g. trustees.

A certification mark is a mark that indicates that a product or service displaying **3-768** the mark has certain technical or quality standards certified by its proprietors. They are used extensively throughout the world. Unlike collective marks, certification marks are available to be used by any undertaking that can satisfy that its products or services meet certain standards. Generally, certification marks are administered by organisations independent of the undertakings that may wish to use the certification mark, e.g. a not-for-profit technical testing body. By definition, certification marks do not act as guarantees of trade origin. Thus, they are different to normal trade marks or collective marks but are intended to confer exclusive rights on the proprietors of the marks to use such marks in the course of trade (and to license those who they consider are entitled to use them). In the 21st century, certification marks have come to the fore as consumers are increasingly aware and place emphasis on the adherence of manufacturers to a set of social and environmental standards. Thus, the FAIRTRADE movement and suppliers allows food suppliers to use the FAIRTRADE® mark in return for agreeing to a set of standards, e.g. only buying food from farms which practise sustainable farming and where workers are paid a proper living wage that gives them a good livelihood.

In some cases, the distinction between traditional marks and collective and **3-769** certification marks can be fairly thin. Thus, a franchise mark like Interflora® acts similarly to a collective mark—the owner of the mark is a commercial organisation that licenses the mark to florists to use in their shops to indicate they are part of the Interflora flower delivery network. The undertakings have no economic connection with each other or indeed the trade mark proprietor but as is common, have legal agreements with the registered proprietor which will normally include quality control provisions. Thus, in appropriate circumstances, there is no reason why a normal trade mark cannot be treated as if it were a collective or certification mark. Similarly, the contractual rules relating to the use of a collective mark will often have many similarities to a certification mark by imposing a set of standards that members must adhere to in order to use the mark.

As from 1 October 2017, the EUTM regulation now allows the registration of **3-770** certification marks. This brings it into line with the Trade Mark Directive which has always enabled Member States to allow such marks. The failure to allow for EU certification marks meant that many undertakings applied for a "classical" EUTM but in practice, used it and licensed it, as if it were a certification mark. The dangers of doing this were highlighted in the CJEU decision of *W.F. Gözze Frottierweberei GmbH v Verein Bremer Baumwollbörse*.[1203] In that case, VBB, a cotton trading association owned a EUTM being a device mark representing a cotton flower. It was used by manufacturers of textiles made from cotton to certify the composition and quality of their goods. VBB concluded licence agreements of this mark with undertakings affiliated to VBB. These undertakings agreed to use the mark only for goods made from good quality cotton fibres. Compliance with this was checked by VBB. A non-affiliated undertaking, *Gözze*, used the cotton flower sign without having agreed a licence with VBB. Infringement proceedings were brought in the Landgericht, Düsseldorf. *Gözze* brought a counterclaim seeking to invalidate the mark and to revoke it for lack of genuine use. At the heart of the counterclaim was whether a "classical" EUTM used as if it were a certification or quality mark was

---

[1203] (C-689/15) ECLI:EU:C:2017:434.

contrary to the EUTMR. On reference to the Court of Justice, the court held that for there to be genuine use of a "classical" EUTM, it had to be shown that the goods marketed under the mark came from a single undertaking under the control of which the goods are manufactured and which is responsible for their quality.[1204] As said by the Court of Justice, the essential function of a classic (individual) trade mark is to guarantee the origin of the marked goods or services to the consumer or end user, by enabling them, without the possibility of confusion, to distinguish the goods or services from others which have another origin. Thus, the mark must offer a guarantee that the goods or services bearing the mark have been manufactured or supplied under the control of a single undertaking which is responsible for their quality. With a "quality" mark, this was not the case.[1205] VBB's mark only served to guarantee the quality of the raw cotton used. Such was sufficient for a certification mark but not a classic trade mark.[1206] In response to a second question referred to it, the CJEU emphasised that the quality control provisions for collective marks did not apply to classical trade marks.[1207] The two regimes were distinct.

3-771   We now consider collective marks and certification marks.

Collective marks

3-772   The EUTMR defines a collective mark as a EUTM which is capable of distinguishing the goods or services of the members of an association which is the proprietor of the mark from other undertakings.[1208] An applicant for a collective EUTM must apply for it as such. The EUTMR envisages that a wide variety of persons can apply for a collective EUTM being associations of manufacturers, producers, suppliers of services, traders and legal persons governed by public law.[1209] The applicant must submit regulations governing the use of the collective mark to EUIPO.[1210] Those regulations must specify the persons authorised to use the mark, the conditions of membership of the association, the conditions of use of the mark, and sanctions.[1211] An application for a collective mark may be refused if it is liable to mislead the public as regards the character or the significance of the mark. In particular, that it is likely to be taken as something other than a collective mark.[1212] It would appear that this objection would be primarily based upon the fact that the regulations for use of the collective EUTM submitted to EUIPO do not comply with the requirements in the EUTMR for a mark to be a collective EUTM.[1213]

3-773   A collective mark is often typically used by members who lie within a geographical area, e.g. a collective mark for food or drinks. Thus, a collective mark may be the name of a geographical region. If "geographical" collective marks were classical individual trade marks, an objection would lie against them on the grounds of such being an indication or sign that may serve to indicate a characteristic of the

---

[1204] See [51].
[1205] See [41]–[46].
[1206] See [50].
[1207] See [52]–[61].
[1208] art.74 EUTMR. The corresponding provision in the TMD is art.27(b).
[1209] art.74.2.
[1210] art.75.1.
[1211] art.75.2.
[1212] art.76.2.
[1213] See art.75.2; art.76.3.

goods.[1214] Accordingly, the EUTMR states that such an objection does not lie against collective marks. However, to act as a counterbalance, unlicensed users of collective signs who use them in accordance with honest practices in industrial or commercial matters will have a defence.[1215] Furthermore, so will parties who are "entitled to use a geographical name". This is most likely intended to mean parties who are entitled under EU or national legislation to use a geographical indication of origin. This is further discussed later in this chapter.[1216]

Geographic name collective marks and GIOs

Where a collective mark is the name of a geographical region, it is tempting to see the collective mark as equivalent in protection to a geographical indication of origin ("GIO"). These are protected by EU law and discussed at the end of this chapter. It is much easier to register a collective mark than to register a GIO. Furthermore, where a collective mark is a geographical name, the regulations submitted to EUIPO must authorise any person whose goods or services originate in the geographical area to be entitled to use the collective mark.[1217] Thus, like GIOs, geographical name collective marks are open for use by anyone whose goods or foodstuffs originate within the geographical region. However, as has been said by the Court of Justice, GIOs and "geographical name" collective marks are governed by distinct legal regimes and pursue different aims.[1218] Therefore, as said by the General Court, the essential function of a GIO is to guarantee to consumers the geographical origin of goods and the qualities inherent in them. Whereas, the essential function of a collective mark is to distinguish the goods or services of members of the association who are the owners of the mark from that of other association or undertakings.[1219] Undoubtedly, this is true. However, it fails to take into account art.75.2 EUTMR which, as said above, requires the owner of a geographical name collective mark to authorise anyone whose goods or services originate in the geographical area to use the collective mark. That makes the distinction between the essential functions of the two types of mark much finer. In essence, by reason of art. 75.2, the "members of the association" who have no connection to each other except making goods or supplying services that originate in the protected geographical area may use the collective mark. In substance, that is the class of persons who are entitled to use a GIO.

3-774

Under the EUTMR, the rights of a EU collective mark are the same as for individual trade marks and indeed, generally EU collective marks and EU individual marks are treated the same under the EUTMR.[1220] In the case of geographical name collective marks, whilst there is some overlap with the rights of GIOs conferred by EU GIO legislation, the wording is different and, as said above, they pursue different aims.[1221] The Court of Justice and General Court have considered the scope of

3-775

[1214] See para.3-240.
[1215] art.74.2.
[1216] See para.3-855.
[1217] art.75.2 EUTMR.
[1218] *The Tea Board v EUIPO* (C-673/15P to C-676/15P) ECLI:EU:C:2017:702 at [62].
[1219] *The Tea Board v OHIM ("Darjeeling")* (T-625/13) ECLI:EU:T:2015:742 at [41].
[1220] art.74.3.
[1221] See generally *The Tea Board* case which concerned an application to register DARJEELING for lingerie and clothing which was opposed by the Tea Board of India based on a collective mark DARJEELING for tea. For the rights conferred by EU law for a GIO, see para.3-889.

protection of collective marks for a geographical name in the *Darjeeling* cases.[1222] DARJEELING is a well-known GIO for tea from the Darjeeling region of India. It was registered as a collective EU mark for tea. An application was made by a third party to register DARJEELING as a trade mark at EUIPO for a variety of goods and services including ladies clothing and underwear, business consultancy services and telecommunication services. On appeal, the General Court dismissed the case based under art.8(5) because of dilution but found that there was an unfair advantage as the use of Darjeeling for lingerie would benefit from the positive qualities conveyed by the earlier trade marks and the image of sophistication or exotic sensuality conveyed by the word element "Darjeeling".[1223] Here, it is debatable that such a finding is right. Darjeeling tea has a reputation as a fine, aromatic tea from the Darjeeling region but the General Court's finding is based on the idea of the mysterious Orient rather than the qualities of tea associated with the GIO Darjeeling. Thus, as said by the General Court, the element "Darjeeling" is likely to evoke images of exoticism, sensuality and mystery associated with the Orient.[1224] This has nothing to do with the reputation and qualities of tea from the Darjeeling region but merely the mental imagery evoked by India and its regions (including Darjeeling).

Certification marks

3-776   With effect from 1 October 2017, the EUTMR allowed the registration of certificate marks. This brought it in line with the TMD which has always allowed Member States to provide for certification marks. A EU certification mark is described as a mark that is capable of distinguishing goods or services which are certified by the proprietor of the mark in respect of material, mode of manufacture of goods or performance of services, quality, accuracy or other characteristics from those which are not certified. However, a EU certification mark cannot be granted where that characteristic is geographical origin .[1225] The exclusion of geographical origin as a relevant characteristic for a EU certification mark would appear because the EU lawmakers see collective marks or geographical indications of origin as being the more apt type of mark. Importantly, the owner of a certification EU mark may not themselves carry on a business involving the supply of goods or services of the kind certified.[1226] This rule no doubt applies to ensure that the owner of a certification mark has no vested interest in which undertakings can use the certified mark. The applicant must, as with collective marks, submit regulations concerning the use of the EU certification mark.[1227]

3-777   The essence of a certification mark is that any undertaking may use it provided they "have authority to use it pursuant to the regulations governing [its] use".[1228] In infringement proceedings, the focus will thus be on whether the defendant has complied with the regulations. It might be arguable that it must *also* be shown also that the undertaking has obtained express consent to use the EU certification mark, i.e. the mere fact of compliance with the regulations governing the use of the EU

[1222] *The Tea Board v OHIM* (T-625/13) ECLI:EU:C:2015:742, appeal dismissed—(C-673/15P and C-676/15P) ECLI:EU:2017:702.
[1223] At [143].
[1224] At [140].
[1225] art.83.1.
[1226] art.83.2.
[1227] art.84.1.
[1228] art.87.

certification mark is not enough. Such gains support from the definition of an EU certification mark which refers to distinguishing goods or services "certified by the proprietor of the mark in respect of material, mode of manufacture ...". This suggests that the owner of the EU certification mark must have actively "certified" that the goods or services sold or supplied under the mark comply with the regulations and not merely that they do. Interestingly, in the original Trade Mark Directive (EC/89/104), art.10.3 said that use of the trade mark with the consent *or* by any person who has authority to use a collective mark or a guarantee or certification mark is deemed to constitute use by the proprietor. This would suggest that authority is not to be equated with consent (and thus presumably simply means compliance with the regulations). This provision is no longer found in either the EUTMR or the TMD but it is not clear whether that was intended to change the law. It is also of note that there is no obligation in the EUTMR or the implementing regulations to publish the regulations governing the use of the EU certification mark.[1229] This would mean that it would be difficult for a third party to satisfy itself that it complies with the regulations. It is surprising that this fundamental point is not settled definitively in the EUTMR or the TMD. In the author's view, express consent from the owner of the EU certification mark is not required as otherwise it would in effect require a certification mark to be a collective mark or indeed an individual classic mark, i.e. a mark which can only be used by a group of undertakings or indeed a single undertaking. In essence, a certification mark is a quality mark and there should be no requirement that the use of it be under the unitary control of a single undertaking, i.e. in accordance with the essential function of a classic trade mark. As stated by the Court of Justice in *Frottierweberei*, the essential function of a classic trade mark should not be confused with that of guaranteeing quality.[1230] To require the consent of the owner of the EU certification mark would mean that the use of the EU certification mark was indeed under the control of a single undertaking.

A certification mark may be revoked on a number of grounds. This includes revocation for lack of genuine use.[1231] However, the case law under that provision must be modified to take account of the different nature of certification marks. Therefore, unlike with individual classic trade marks, there would be no need to show that use has been in accordance with the essential function of a classic trade mark.[1232] This is because the essential function of a certification mark is not to act as a guarantee of trade origin but rather to act as a guarantee that goods or services sold or supplied under the mark meet a set of defined characteristics, being those set out in the regulations. Other grounds for revocation include inter alia that the owner of the EU certification mark has not taken reasonable steps to prevent the mark from used in a manner that is incompatible with the regulations laying down the conditions of use.

3-778

Practice, procedure and remedies

EU trade mark law is primarily concerned with the harmonisation of the substantive law of trade marks in the EU. Thus, the procedural rules governing the applica-

3-779

[1229] art.7, Reg.2017/1431 which gives an exhaustive list of what must be published.
[1230] *W.F. Gözze Frottierweberei GmbH v VBB* (C-689/15) ECLI:EU:C:2017:434[44]. See para.3-770 for discussion of this case.
[1231] arts 58, 91.
[1232] See para.3-715.

tion for trade marks and proceedings for infringement of them is a matter for Member States. However, the latest TMD has sought to align the principal procedural rules for applications for trade marks by setting out general principles but leaving the detail to Member States.[1233]

3-780   As regards the EUTM, the procedural rules for applying for a EUTM are exhaustively set out in the EUTMR and the implementing regulations.[1234] EUIPO has sole control over this. Nevertheless, infringement proceedings based on the EUTMR are brought and can only be brought in the courts of Member States. The procedural rules governing this are a matter for Member States but the EUTMR sets out the remedies available for infringement of a EUTM. The reader should also be aware of the Enforcement Directive which sets out a number of principles and also detailed provisions governing the remedies available to owners of national and unitary intellectual property rights in the EU. This is discussed later in this book.[1235]

3-781   As regards revocation or cancellation proceedings for EUTMs, there is an overlap of jurisdiction as not only can EUIPO cancel or revoke marks but so can courts of a Member States where such is raised by way of counterclaim to infringement proceedings. The procedure for the latter is governed by the litigation rules of Member States but the former is exhaustively governed by the EUTMR and its implementing regulations.

3-782   The following section considers the practice and procedure for applying for EUTMs, opposing them and also cancellation and revocation proceedings. It also considers the remedies available. As this book is not intended to be a practitioner's guide to procedure before EUIPO, it is necessarily at a high level. For the reader who wishes to know more, EUIPO publishes detailed guidelines as to the practice and procedure on its website.

EUROPEAN UNION TRADE MARK: PRACTICE AND PROCEDURE BEFORE EUIPO AND NATIONAL COURTS

Introduction

3-783   Applications for EUTMs are administered by the European Union Intellectual Property Office ("EUIPO"). The seat of EUIPO is in Alicante, Spain. The procedure is entirely written (although in exceptional cases, an oral hearing can be requested).

3-784   EUTMs and national trade marks can sit alongside each other. Therefore, an undertaking may have EUTMs and national marks which are for the same mark and registered for the same goods and services. Whilst the EUTMR provides an incentive to owners of national marks to abandon them in favour of corresponding EUTMs by the mechanism of "seniority", there are some advantages to retaining national marks. In particular, a EUTM may be liable to be revoked for lack of genuine use if the use has not been in the EU, whereas there is no requirement of use in the EU for national marks.[1236] Similarly, in infringement proceedings, where the owner of a EUTM wishes to rely upon the provisions for marks that have a

---

[1233] Recital 9, TMD and Section 2, TMD.
[1234] Reg.2017/1431.
[1235] See Ch.15.
[1236] See para.3-718.

reputation, e.g. unfair advantage, it must also show that the reputation of the EUTM is in the Union.[1237] Against this is, of course, the cost of maintaining dual protection.

The practice and procedure of applying for and obtaining a registered EUTM is   **3-785**
not substantially different to a typical national trade mark office. The following stages occur:

(i)   An application containing a representation of the mark and the goods or services for which protection is sought is filed with EUIPO or via national intellectual property offices.

(ii)   A search report is drawn up citing EUTMs or EUTM applications which are similar earlier marks potentially citable against the application.

(iii)   The application is examined for absolute grounds by EUIPO but not relative grounds.

(iv)   The application is published.

(v)   The application enters the opposition phase when third parties can oppose it on the basis of absolute or relative grounds. In the latter case, it must own the earlier rights relied upon. If opposition proceedings are initiated, then EUIPO will decide whether the application should proceed to grant.

(vi)   Assuming no, or no successful opposition proceedings, the application is then registered and published.

(vii)   The EUTM registration will then remain on the register for an unlimited period provided all renewal fees are paid and it is not surrendered, declared invalid or revoked.

(viii) Undertakings may bring cancellation or revocation proceedings after grant of the EUTM.

(ix)   Appeals lie to the Boards of Appeal and thereafter to General Court and ultimately to the Court of Justice.

Where an application for a EUTM is refused, revoked or invalidated, the ap-   **3-786**
plicant may request the conversion of their application into one or more national applications.[1238] Thus, where there are earlier rights in certain Member States which prevent the registration of a EUTM or because of linguistic differences in the Union, absolute grounds exist for objecting to the regsitraiton of the EUTM in some Member States, the applicant can obtain national registrations in the Member States unaffected by those earlier rights without losing the priority date for the EUTM application.

EUTMs and national trade marks can sit alongside each other. Thus, an undertak-   **3-787**
ing may have EUTMs and national marks which are for the same mark and registered for the same goods and services. Whilst the EUTMR provides an incentive to owners of national marks to abandon them in favour of corresponding EUTMs by the mechanism of "seniority", there are some advantages to retaining national marks. In particular, a EUTM may be liable to be revoked for lack of genuine use if the use has not been in the EU, whereas there is no requirement of use in the EU for national marks.[1239] Similarly, in infringement proceedings, where the owner of a EUTM wishes to rely upon the provisions for marks that have a

---

[1237] See para.3-360.
[1238] Conversion is discussed below at para.3-801.
[1239] See para.3-718.

reputation, e.g. unfair advantage, it must also show that the reputation of the EUTM is in the Union.[1240] Against this is of course the cost of maintaining dual protection.

3-788   It is beyond the scope of this book to provide a detailed guide to the practice and procedure before EUIPO. In previous editions of this book, an attempt was made to do so. However, in this edition, the authors have taken the view that this book can never be a proper substitute for EUIPO's Guidelines which are very good and comprehensive.[1241]

3-789   Thus, in the following sections, the book focusses not on the mechanics of applying for a mark which do not differ that dramatically from that in national intellectual property offices but rather highlights peculiarities relating to EUTMs. Furthermore, it looks at the enforcement of EUTMs in the courts of Member States.

Seniority

3-790   In order to persuade proprietors of national marks to register their marks as EUTMs, a EUTM application which is identical to an earlier national mark and whose goods or services are identical with or contained within those for the earlier mark, can claim the seniority of the earlier trade mark in respect of the Member State for which it is registered.[1242] A claim to seniority requires a triple identity of applicant, mark and goods and services.[1243] Seniority has the sole effect of conferring on the EUTM the same rights as those granted under the earlier national trade mark if the latter is surrendered or lapses.[1244] This means that a EUTM owner can surrender or allow the "senior" national mark to lapse (by not renewing it) thereby avoiding the cost of maintaining a national and EUTM registration. It is important to note that there is no increase in rights. Thus, a EUTM which has a valid claim of seniority to an earlier identical mark for identical products in a Member State will not obtain increased rights in other Member States. Rather, as said by the Court of Justice, the provision in the EUTMR which allows the claim of seniority "creates a fiction intended to enable the proprietor of the EU mark to continue to enjoy, in that Member State, the protection enjoyed by the earlier national mark which was cancelled and not to enable that mark to continue to exist in the same form".[1245]

3-791   The proprietor of an already registered EUTM can claim seniority as well as an applicant for a EUTM.[1246]

3-792   However, in certain cases, this could cause an injustice. For instance, the national mark that is allowed to lapse may itself be vulnerable for revocation or be declared invalid. If the owner of a EUTM can claim the same rights as the senior national mark but at the same time, a third party cannot revoke or invalidate the now lapsed

---

[1240] See para.3-360.

[1241] See *https://euipo.europa.eu/ohimportal/en/trade-mark-guidelines* [Accessed 8 October 2017].

[1242] art.39 EUTMR.

[1243] In determining whether there is identity of applicant, the Boards of Appeal have said that actual ownership of the mark rather than recorded ownership is the test. Thus, where earlier trade marks were in the process of being transferred to the EUTM applicant but not recorded on the relevant national registers, such was not fatal to a claim for seniority—*BatMark* [1998] E.T.M.R. 448, First Board of Appeal.

[1244] art.39(3). See also *Peek & Cloppenburg KG, Hamburg v Peek & Cloppenburg KG, Düsseldorf* (C-148/17) ECLI:EU:C:2018:271 at [24].

[1245] *Peek & Cloppenburg KG*, at [30]. Thus, in *a posteriori* proceedings under art.6 TMD, use of the mark after surrender or lapse of the national mark cannot be taken into account to "cure" the lack of use prior to the date of surrender or lapse. As said by the Court of Justice, such use must be considered of the EUTM and not the cancelled national mark on which the EUTM claimed seniority.

[1246] art.40.

senior national mark, the owner of a EUTM would have rights predating the application date for the EUTM which could not be attacked.

Article 39(4) of EUTMR party seeks to deal with this problem. It states that: **3-793**

"The seniority claimed for the EU trade mark shall lapse where the earlier trade mark the seniority of which is claimed is declared to have been revoked or to be invalid. Where the earlier trade mark is revoked, the seniority shall lapse provided that the revocation takes effect prior to the filing date or priority date of that EU Trade mark."

However, this provision only works if the national mark remains on the national **3-794**
register. As the whole purpose of seniority is to encourage owners of EUTMs to allow national marks to lapse, it does not deal with the problem if the senior mark has indeed been allowed to lapse as intended by the EUTMR.

This problem was foreseen in the TMD, where art.6 says: **3-795**

"Where the seniority of a national trade mark or of a trade mark registered under international arrangements having effect in the Member State, which has been surrendered or allowed to lapse, is claimed for an EU trade mark, the invalidity or revocation of the trade mark providing the basis for the seniority claim may be established *a posteriori*, provided that the invalidity or revocation could have been declared at the time the mark was surrendered or allowed to lapse. In such a case, the seniority shall cease to produce its effects."

Although the phrase *a posteriori* is probably not the right expression,[1247] art.6 al- **3-796**
lows a party to establish that a lapsed or surrendered earlier mark which is relied upon for the purpose of seniority *would* have been declared invalid or revoked *if still on the register* so as to defeat any claim to seniority. Although art.6 does not state the date which should be used to examine whether the conditions for invalidity or revocation have been met, the Court of Justice has said that it is clear from the wording and purpose of the predecessor provision to art.6 that it is the date on which the earlier national mark was surrendered or allowed to lapse, and not the date on which a ruling is made on an application seeking to establish *a posteriori* that the national mark should be declared invalid or revoked.[1248]

Proof of use of earlier registered right in opposition proceedings

In opposition proceedings where an earlier EUTM or national mark is relied **3-797**
upon, the applicant for a EUTM can request that the opponent furnish proof that during the period of five years preceding the date of filing or the date of priority of the EUTM application, the earlier mark has been put to genuine use in the EU in connection with the goods or services for which it is registered or that there are proper reasons for non-use if the earlier mark has been registered for not less than five years. If proof is not provided, the opposition is rejected. If the earlier mark has only been used for part of the goods or services for which it is registered, for the purposes of the opposition, it is deemed to be registered only in respect of those goods or services.[1249]

[1247] It means "derived by or designating the process of reasoning from facts or particulars to general principles or from effects to causes; inductive; empirical". It is thought that the correct expression should have been "ex post facto".
[1248] *Peek & Cloppenburg*, at [26].
[1249] art.47(2).

Res judicata between Opposition and Cancellation Divisions and decisions of national courts and intellectual property offices

3-798   It will be appreciated that a third party could seek to oppose an application based on an earlier right, fail and then after the mark has become registered, seek to cancel the mark based on the earlier right. To avoid such abuse, art.63(3) EUTMR states that cancellation or revocation proceedings are inadmissible where the proceedings relate *"to the same subject matter and cause of action, and involving the same parties"* and either EUIPO or an EU Trade Mark Court has *"adjudicated on its merits"*.[1250] This codified the well-known doctrine of res judicata. However, it should be noted that there must be strict identity of subject matter. Thus, in *Apple and Pear Australia Ltd v EUIPO*,[1251] in a case concerning whether a Belgian decision meant that there was res judicata whereby the Belgian court had annulled the mark ENGLISH PINK by reason of the earlier mark PINK LADY and injuncted the defendant from using ENGLISH PINK for fruit throughout the EU. In EUIPO proceedings, the Opposition Division had rejected an opposition founded on PINK LADY against the registration of ENGLISH PINK (both for inter alia fruit).

3-799   The issue before the Court of Justice was whether the issue was res judicata and the scope of that doctrine in EUIPO proceedings. The Court of Justice held that:

> "[52] In that regard, it should be noted that, although Regulation No 207/2009 does not explicitly define the concept of 'res judicata', it follows, in particular, from Article 56(3) and Article 100(2) of that regulation that, in order that decisions of a court of a Member State or EUIPO which have become final are res judicata and can therefore be binding on such a court or EUIPO, it is required that parallel proceedings before them have the same parties, the same subject matter and the same cause of action."

It then held that although the action was between the same parties, it did not concern the same subject matter. One concerned the validity of a Benelux mark whereas the other concerned the registration of a EUTM. Strictly speaking that is correct but plainly the *issue* was the same, namely whether or not use of ENGLISH PINK gave rise to a likelihood of confusion with PINK LADY, the earlier mark. However, in the author's view, it is a correct application of the doctrine of res judicata.

3-800   It would be unfortunate if the doctrine of res judicata did not bind successors of the unsuccessful party or assignees of the mark relied upon as that would be a clear "cheat's charter"—particularly, if the intention behind the succession or assignment was to circumvent this provision. More difficult will be where the unsuccessful opponent relies upon one ground in the opposition and another ground in the invalidity (e.g. likelihood of confusion vs. taking unfair advantage of the reputation of the earlier mark). As it is necessary for an adjudication on its merits, an opponent may decide not to risk a decision on one ground, holding it back for cancellation proceedings. However, this seems an unlikely scenario as there would be little reason to do so. In the UK, it is a general point of procedural law that a party must seek to litigate all relevant matters with another party in one go. Thus, where a party *could* have put forward a ground of objection in earlier proceedings and the court considers that it *should* have put forward that ground, it would be an abuse of

---

[1250] Thereby disapplying the law predating this provision—see *Ferrero Spa v EUIPO* (T-140/08) [2009] E.C.R. II-3941.

[1251] (C–226/15P) EU:C:2016:582. This case was concerned with the interpretation of the predecessor regulation to the EUTMR, Reg.207/2009. There was no provision that corresponded to art.63(3).

process for it to seek to litigate that point in subsequent proceedings (e.g. see *Johnson v Gore-Wood*[1252]). However, it seems tolerably clear that this would not be the same subject matter and thus by reason of *Apple and Pear Australia*, there is no res judicata.

Conversion of a EU Trade Mark

The strength of a EUTM is that it has unitary effect throughout the EU. However, this fact also makes it often very hard to register a EUTM. If a third party has prior rights in any of the 28 Member States, such can give rise to an objection to the registration of a EUTM. Equally, the current jurisprudence of the CJEU is that where there are objections based on absolute grounds (e.g. lack of distinctive character), such objections are valid if those absolute grounds pertain only to one Member State. Thus, if the mark applied for has distinctive character in all Member States bar Malta, this means that it cannot be registered as a EUTM.[1253] Equally, it may be that a EUTM can be revoked for lack of genuine use in the EU whereas a national mark would not be. For instance, it might that a mark is put to genuine use in Latvia but such use would not amount to "use" in the EU.   **3-801**

Because of these issues, in order to make the EUTM system more attractive, the EUTMR provides for a conversion procedure whereby an application for a EUTM or a registered EUTM can be converted into a basket of national registration in one, some or all of the Member States.[1254] National registration will benefit from the filing or priority date of the EUTM and indeed, if it has a claim to seniority, the seniority claim.[1255] The right to conversion applies not only to decisions of EUIPO but also to decisions of EU Trade Mark courts. Thus, if in national proceedings, where the validity of a EUTM is raised by way of counterclaim and the court finds the EUTM to be invalid, the owner of the EUTM can request conversion through EUIPO.[1256]   **3-802**

In general, the owner of a EUTM or the applicant for a EUTM has three months to apply for conversion from the date of the decision giving rise to the refusal, revocation or cancellation (or if appealed, the date of the decision of the appeal court or tribunal).[1257] EUIPO will then decide whether conversion can happen.   **3-803**

Importantly, the EUTM or application for a EUTM will not be converted into a national trade mark of a Member State if grounds for objection exist in that Member State.[1258]   **3-804**

The procedure for conversion is in two stages. The first formal stage is carried out by EUIPO and the second stage (the substantive stage) is carried out the national intellectual property offices. Depending on national law, the converted trade mark will either be registered immediately or enter a national phase of examination, opposition and registration as if it were a normal national trade mark application.[1259]   **3-805**

It should be noted that EUIPO is not obliged to set out in its decisions in opposition proceedings those Member States that the opponent has made out their objection for the purpose of assisting the applicant to determine which Member States   **3-806**

[1252] [2002] A.C. 1, House of Lords.
[1253] See para.3-241.
[1254] arts 139–141 EUTMR.
[1255] For an explanation of seniority, see para.3-790.
[1256] art.139(6).
[1257] art.139(4)–(6).
[1258] art.139(2).
[1259] See EUIPO Guidelines, Part E, Section 2

they can designate when converting the refused application. Thus, in proceedings where EUIPO upheld an opposition between two marks based on the fact that there would be a likelihood of confusion in the non-English speaking public, the CJEU held that EUIPO was not obliged to rule on whether there was a likelihood of confusion in the English speaking public for the purpose of resolving in advance any possible conflicts at national level.[1260] However, the failure to do so meant that the applicant could convert the application to national trade marks for those Member States which were English-speaking countries.[1261]

Enforcement of a EUTM in EU Trade Mark Courts

Introduction

3-807   This section considers the enforcement of EUTMs. EUIPO has no jurisdiction to enforce EUTMs. In general, their enforcement is a matter for the courts of Member States and national procedural rules applicable to enforcement of intellectual property rights will apply. However, the EUTMR does set out various rules that apply to enforcement of EUTMs to EU Trade Mark Courts. These are as follows:

- Which national courts have jurisdiction to enforce EUTMs?
- Which persons other than the EUTM owner has the right to enforce a EUTM in infringement proceedings in a Member State?
- Which Member States have jurisdiction to hear infringement proceedings of a EUTM?
- Allocation of jurisdiction where there are parallel proceedings for revocation or invalidity of a EUTM in Member States or EUIPO?
- What is the applicable law to enforcement of EUTMs in Member States?
- What are the remedies available for infringement of a EUTM?

There is a hierarchy of rules relating to proceedings before the courts of Member States. First, if provided for in the EUTMR, those provisions will apply. If it not provided, then national law shall apply.[1262] To take an example, when it comes to which Member States have jurisdiction to hear EUTM infringement proceedings, there are a set of rules in the EUTMR. However, if those rules do not deal with an issue, then the Recast Jurisdiction Regulation applies if it would apply otherwise (i.e. the defendant is domiciled in a Member State).[1263] If that regulation does not apply, then the domestic jurisdictional rules of Member States will apply. The reader should also be aware that the Enforcement Directive, which governs all IP litigation in Member States will also apply to enforcement of EUTMs in Member States. This is discussed in another chapter.[1264]

Exclusive jurisdiction of EUTM Courts

3-808   The enforcement of EUTMs is carried out in European Union Trade Mark Courts ("EUTM Courts") of Member States. Member States are required to designate

---

[1260] *Armacell Enterprise GmbH v EUIPO* (C-514/06 P) [2008] E.C.R. I-128 at [61].
[1261] See [62].
[1262] art.129.
[1263] The Recast Brussels Regulation is discussed at Ch.17.
[1264] See Ch.15.

EUTM Courts at both first and second instance.[1265] EUTMs are not enforceable by proceedings before EUIPO. This reflects the administrative nature of EUIPO.

EUTM Courts have exclusive jurisdiction for all infringement proceedings, actions for declarations of non-infringement and counterclaims for revocations or a declaration of invalidity in infringement proceedings.[1266]   **3-809**

Who may enforce a EUTM?

In general, actions must be brought by the registered owner of a EUTM. However, in certain situations, the EUTMR also allows licensees to bring proceedings. A licensee may bring proceedings for infringement of a EUTM. The situations are as follows: **3-810**

- A licensee may bring proceedings if the proprietor consents.[1267]
- An exclusive licensee may bring proceedings if the proprietor does not, after formal notice, bring infringement proceedings within an appropriate period.[1268]
- A licensee may intervene in proceedings for infringement of a EUTM for the purpose of obtaining compensation for damage suffered by it.[1269]

In *Hassan v Breidung Vertriebsgesellschaft*,[1270] the Court of Justice held that it was not necessary that a licence be registered with EUIPO for a licensee to bring proceedings alleging infringement of a EUTM. Furthermore, where a licensee brings proceedings in its own right (as opposed to intervening in proceedings for infringement of a EUTM brought by another, e.g. the owner), the licensee can recover damages suffered by it.[1271]   **3-811**

Jurisdiction between EUTM Courts and EUIPO

The EUTMR contains special rules governing jurisdiction between Member States and also where there are parallel proceedings for revocation or invalidity of a EUTM before Member States and EUIPO. The jurisdiction rules of the EUTMR can be considered a *lex specialis* and where there are no specific provisions, then the Recast Brussels Regulation (Reg.1215/2012) will determine the jurisdictional dispute.[1272]   **3-812**

Infringement

The specific rules under the EUTMR governing infringement proceedings for EUTMs are as follows (in descending order):   **3-813**

(a) in the courts of the Member State where the defendant is domiciled;

[1265] art.123(2).
[1266] art.124.
[1267] art.25(3).
[1268] art.25(3).
[1269] art.25(4).
[1270] (C–163/15) EU:C:2016:17.
[1271] By analogy, *Thomas Phillips GmbH v Grüne Welle Vertriebs GmbH* (C-419/15) ECLI:EU:C:2016:468 at [26]–[32] (this concerned similar provisions in the EU Design Regulation, Reg.6/2002).
[1272] art.122. See Ch.17.

(b) in the courts of the Member State where the defendant has an establishment[1273];

(c) in the court of the Member State in which the claimant is domiciled;

(d) in the court of the Member State in which the claimant has an establishment; and

(e) in Spain.[1274]

3-814 Where jurisdiction is based on any of these grounds, then a EUTM Court has jurisdiction in respect of all acts of infringement committed or threatened throughout the EU.[1275] There are three main exceptions to the above "waterfall" rules. First, they can be ousted by agreement that another EUTM court has exclusive jurisdiction pursuant to a written agreement.[1276] Secondly, the defendant submits to the jurisdiction of another EUTM Court.[1277]

3-815 Thirdly, under art.125.5 EUTMR, there is a parallel jurisdiction to bring the proceedings in the courts of the state where the infringement "has been committed or threatened". If jurisdiction is based on art.125(5), then under art.126(2), the court only has jurisdiction in respect of acts committed or threatened within the territory of the Member State in which the court is situated.[1278]

3-816 Article 125.5 EUTMR might be thought analogous to the supplemental ground of jurisdiction, being art.7(2) Recast Brussels Regulation, whereby a claimant may sue a defendant for wrongful acts in the courts of the Member State where "the harmful event occurred".[1279] As can be read in the chapter on Jurisdiction, there has been a line of CJEU on the proper interpretation of this provision in the Recast Jurisdiction Regulation (and its predecessors). In particular, the CJEU has interpreted this provision as conferring jurisdiction on the courts of both the Member State where the event giving rise to the damage as well as where the damage occurred. In the context of online IP infringements, its interpretation has given rise to a series of jurisdictional rules for determining infringement.[1280]

3-817 In the 3rd edn of this book, it was suggested that the wording "committed" in art.125(5) suggested active conduct giving rise to the infringement and therefore it should not be interpreted in the same way as art.7(2) Recast Brussels Regulation. In particular, it was suggested that the mere fact that damage happened in a Member State was not, by itself, enough to confer jurisdiction on the court of that Member State under the EUTMR. This approach was adopted in *Coty v Germany*[1281] relying upon the Advocate-General's Opinion which itself referred to the 3rd edn of this book. Thus, the court said that art.125(5) did not have the same meaning as art.7(2) Recast Brussels Regulation.

3-818 In an English case,[1282] an English court had to consider whether it had jurisdiction under art.125(5) to hear an action which concerned whether a EUTM was infringed by a website controlled and operated by a Spanish company, domiciled

---

[1273] See *Hummel Holding A/S v Nice Inc* (C-617/15) ECLI:EU:C:2017:390 for meaning of "establishment" in the context of a multinational company where proceedings were brought against the company in Germany based on a second tier subsidiary having an establishment in Germany.

[1274] art.125. Spain qualifies as the Member State where EUIPO is situated.

[1275] art.126.1(a).

[1276] art.125.4(a); art.25 Reg.1215/2012.

[1277] art.125.4(b); art.26 Reg.1215/2012.

[1278] art.126(2).

[1279] art.7.2 Reg.1215/2012.

[1280] art.7(2) and its interpretation is discussed at Ch.17 at para.17-044.

[1281] (C-360/12) ECLI:EU:C:2014:1318 at [34].

[1282] *AMS Neve v Heritage Audio S.L.* [2016] EWHC 2563 (IPEC).

in Spain, that targeted the UK. It held, in applying the Court of Justice's cases on online infringement and art.7(2) Recast Brussels Regulation, that art.125(5) EUTMR should be interpreted to mean that it conferred jurisdiction on the Member State of the centre of the advertiser's interests despite it being arguable that the website did indeed target the UK. This was based on case law concerning the interpretation of art.7(2) to online IPR infringements.[1283] Accordingly, it held that the UK court had no jurisdiction to hear the EUTM infringement action.

However, on appeal, the Court of Appeal of England considered that it was not **3-819** acte clair and referred the matter to the Court of Justice.[1284] It made three points. First, that it was inherent in the legislative scheme of the EUTMR that a defendant who has carried out infringements in several Member States could be sued in those states in respect of those particular infringements. Secondly, the Court of Justice had said in *Coty* that the predecessor to art.125(5) EUTMR should be interpreted independently of the predecessor to art.7(2) Recast Brussels. Thirdly, as the predecessor provision to art.125(5) should be read together with the predecessor to art.126(2), it would mean that where a defendant in Member State A targeted an advertisement at consumers in Member State B, it would end up with neither state having jurisdiction under art.125(5) which would be a surprising result.[1285]

In the author's view, the Court of Appeal's doubts about the lower court's **3-820** interpretation of art.125(5) to infringements which target a Member State are right. It makes little sense to interpret art.125(5) in the context of case law decided under art.7(2) Recast Brussels Regulation where the Court of Justice has said that the two provisions should be interpreted differently. Furthermore, a proper interpretation of art.125(5) should provide for a meaningful alternative ground of jurisdiction to that set out in art.125(1)–(4). If a website, in actively targeting consumers of a Member State, uses an infringing sign, then art.125(5) should permit a EUTM owner to bring proceedings in the court of that Member State.

Revocation or declarations of invalidity

In general, a EUTM Court must treat a EUTM as valid but in infringement **3-821** proceedings, a defendant may by way of counterclaim seek a declaration of invalidity or seek to revoke it.[1286] Standalone applications for revocation or declaration of invalidity must be brought at EUIPO. The validity of a EUTM cannot be put in issue in proceedings for a declaration of non-infringement.[1287]

Article 127.3 EUTMR provides that in infringement proceedings, "… a plea **3-822** relating to revocation of the EU trade mark submitted otherwise than by way of a counterclaim shall be admissible where the defendant claims that the EU trade mark could be revoked for lack of genuine use at the time the infringement action was brought." This somewhat strange provision is probably intended to deal with a scenario whereby the owner of a EUTM which has been allowed to lapse but which has rights prior to the date of lapse sues a defendant for infringement for acts prior to the date of lapse. In such circumstances, a defendant could not counterclaim for revocation of the EUTM as it is no longer registered. Thus it has parallels with the provision in the TMD whereby a defendant can *a posteriori* challenge a claim of a

---

[1283] See para.17-072.
[1284] *AMS Neve Ltd v Heritage Audio S.L.* [2018] EWCA Civ 86.
[1285] See [57]–[59].
[1286] art.127.1.
[1287] art.127.2.

EUTM to the seniority of a national mark which has been surrendered or allowed to lapse, on the grounds that that it was invalidly registered or liable to be revoked as of the date of surrender or lapse.[1288]

3-823   If a EUTM court is validly seized of a counterclaim for invalidity or revocation, then a number of steps must be taken by the court or an interested party. First, if a proprietor of a EUTM is not a party to the proceedings, they must be informed and may be joined as a party in accordance with national law.[1289] Secondly, the interested party or the court must inform EUIPO of the counterclaim before proceeding to examine the counterclaim.[1290] This procedure is important because a standalone application for revocation or invalidity may already have been filed with EUIPO. If such has happened, then the EUTM court must stay the proceedings pending the outcome of EUIPO proceedings.[1291] Thirdly, a EUTM court may stay proceedings on a counterclaim on application by the proprietor that the defendant submits an application for revocation or a declaration of invalidity before EUIPO within a specified time limit.[1292] Fourthly, if the counterclaim is successful, the court must notify EUIPO, who will revoke or declare invalid the EUTM.[1293]

Lis alibi pendens: parallel and successive infringement proceedings of "double identity" EUTMs and national marks

3-824   The EUTMR has limited provisions concerning pending proceedings for infringements of EUTMs and national trade marks in different Member States. The focus in the EUTMR is on the peculiarities caused by EUTMs and national trade marks that are for the same mark and the same goods or services. As the substantive law of the EUTM is the same as that of national trade marks in Member States, there is plainly a real danger of conflicting decisions. Thus, in proceedings as to whether EUTM XYZ and national mark XYZ for pharmaceuticals is infringed by YYZ branded pharmaceutical on the grounds of likelihood of confusion, the outcome should be the same in 99 per cent of cases.[1294] Outside this area of conflict peculiar to EUTMs, the Recast Brussels Regulation applies, in particular its *lis alibi pendens* rules.[1295]

3-825   Where proceedings involving the "same cause of action and between the same parties" are brought in the courts of different Member States, one based upon a EUTM and the other based on a national mark, the court other than the first seized must decline jurisdiction where the trade marks concerned are "identical and valid for identical goods or services".[1296] This could work an injustice if the second action is based on a EUTM which seeks pan-EU relief but the first action (by necessity) is limited to the territory of the national mark. In such circumstances, if this

---

[1288] See art.6 TMD and para.3-790.
[1289] art.128(3). This provision exists because a licensee may bring proceedings for infringement of a EUTM—art.22(3).
[1290] art.128.4.
[1291] art.128.4.
[1292] art.128(7).
[1293] art.128(6).
[1294] Different outcomes may arise lawfully on the facts, e.g. if the mark is not particularly distinctive in a Member State because of linguistic reasons and/or the EUTM has acquired distinctive character but not in the Member State of the national mark.
[1295] art.122 EUTMR. See also AG Szpunar's Opinion in *Merck KGaA v Merck & Co* (C-231/16) ECLI:EU:C:2017:330 at [24]–[31]. See Ch.17 on the Recast Brussels Regulation and para.17-184 on its *lis alibi pendens* rules.
[1296] art.136.1.

provision were to apply with full force, the result would be that the EUTM owner would be prevented from obtaining relief in all and any Member States. One answer may be to say that in such circumstances, the EUTM owner should ensure that it issues the action based on the EUTM first. However, in *Merck KGaA v Merck & Co Inc*,[1297] the Court of Justice took a more pragmatic view. It held that "cause of action" should be interpreted in the same manner as "cause of action" in the *lis pendens* provisions of the Recast Brussels Regulation.[1298] Accordingly, in the case of parallel proceedings based on identical national and EU trade marks, there was only the same cause of action where the territories overlapped.[1299]

In this case, the claimant issued proceedings in the UK alleging infringement of a UK trade mark. Three days later, the claimant brought an action in Germany against inter alia the same defendants alleging infringement of the identical EUTM seeking pan-European relief. The acts of which this complaint was made concerned the websites of the defendants who were not targeting any particular Member State. Realising the difficulties caused by the predecessor provision to art.136.1, the claimant withdrew the UK action. The German courts referred a number of questions to the Court of Justice. Having set out what is meant by "cause of action", it held that in such circumstances, there was no jurisdictional bar to the German (second seized) court hearing the EUTM infringement action, save in respect of acts of infringement of the EUTM carried out in the UK. **3-826**

It is likely that "same parties" will be interpreted to include different companies in a corporate group, e.g. parallel proceedings brought against respectively, a parent and subsidiary, so there is no risk of irreconcilable judgments.[1300] **3-827**

Where there is an overlap in the specification of the national and EUTM marks, the court other than the first seized need only decline jurisdiction in favour of the court first seized only in so far as the trade marks are registered (valid) for identical goods or services.[1301] **3-828**

Instead of declining jurisdiction, the second seized court may stay the proceedings if jurisdiction of the first seized court is disputed.[1302] The expression "identical and valid for identical goods or services" is somewhat strange. Does this provision apply if the validity of the mark is disputed? One rather suspects that the legislator simply meant that the marks are identical and registered for the same goods or services.[1303] Where the double identity rules does not apply (i.e. either the marks are similar but not identical or the goods are similar but not identical), then the court other than court first seized may stay its proceedings.[1304] **3-829**

Successive infringement proceedings

If final judgment has already been given on the same "cause of action" and between the same parties on the basis of an identical national trade mark valid for **3-830**

[1297] (C-231/16) ECLI:EU:C:2017:771.

[1298] *Merck KGaA v Merck* , [33] to [36] . See Ch.17, "Jurisdiction" at para.17-184.

[1299] See [42].

[1300] Szpunar AG's Opinion in *Merck KGaA v Merck & Co* (C-231/16) ECLI:EU:C:2017:330 at [37]–[46]. The Court of Justice did not rule on this point (as it was not being a question referred by the Landgericht Hamburg).

[1301] See [59]–[62].

[1302] art.136.1(a).

[1303] Thus, in *Prudential Assurance v Prudential Insurance* [2002] E.T.M.R. 1013, the High Ct of England and Wales read "valid" in the predecessor provision to art.136.1 as meaning "registered" or "in force".

[1304] art.136.1(b).

identical goods or services, then pursuant to art.136.2 EUTMR, the court must reject a later action for infringement based on the EUTM.[1305] Vice versa, the same result happens if it was the EUTM on which an earlier judgment had been handed down. A later action based on an identical mark for identical goods must be rejected where it was between the same parties.[1306]

3-831   Article 136.2 was considered in an English case, *Prudential Assurance Co Ltd v Prudential Insurance Co of America*.[1307] In that case, the Court of Appeal had to decide whether art.136.2 applied to infringement proceedings in the UK based upon a EUTM where a court in France in opposition proceedings had rejected a finding of confusion between the EUTM and an earlier mark which was identical to the infringing mark and was being used for identical services. The High Court judge had held that art.136.2 was only intended to apply to successive actions for infringement and in any event there was not double identity. The Court of Appeal dismissed the appeal, finding that there was not "double identity" as required by art.136.2. However, on the alternative ground, the Court of Appeal held that it was not certain that art.136.2 should only apply to successive infringement actions. It is submitted that the High Court was manifestly correct. The whole sense of art.136 is that art.136.1 applies to simultaneous infringement actions and art.136.2 applies to successive infringement actions. Article 136.1 refers specifically to "actions for infringement". Thus, it cannot apply to successive opposition/infringement proceedings. It would be most odd if such did apply to successive opposition/infringement proceedings. In any event, it is difficult to describe opposition proceedings and infringement proceedings as involving the "same cause of action".[1308]

3-832   In truth, there is a legal fiction here because a cause of action based on infringement of a EUTM is different per se to one based on infringement of a national mark. Therefore, care should be taken to avoid interpreting it without regard to the justice of the case. For instance, an action for an identical EUTM for infringement of the EUTM on the grounds of unfair advantage may have been dismissed by a court of Member State A on the grounds that the EUTM did not have a reputation "within the EU". In a following action in Member State B based on an identical national mark for identical goods, a national court may consider that the action is well-founded because the owner of the national mark did have a reputation within the Member State. Would art.136 prevent the court of Member State B hearing the action on the basis of the earlier action in Member State A? It is submitted that this would cause injustice and that in such circumstances, there is a different "cause of action".

Lis alibi pendens: infringement proceedings and invalidity proceedings in EUIPO or Member States

3-833   Where the validity of a EUTM is already in issue before another EUTM court or EUIPO, then the EUTM court seized of infringement proceedings must stay those proceedings pending the outcome of the other proceedings "unless there are

---

[1305] art.136.2.

[1306] art.136.3.

[1307] *Prudential Assurance Co Ltd v Prudential Insurance Co of America* [2003] E.T.M.R. 69 CA.

[1308] The meaning of "cause of action" is discussed in the context of *lis alibi pendens* in Ch.17 at para.17-192. Whilst the issue of "likelihood of confusion" may be *an identical issue* in opposition proceedings and infringement proceedings, this does not mean that they involve the same "cause of action".

special reasons for continuing the hearing".[1309] This has resulted in tactical applications to revoke a EUTM or have it declared invalid being lodged at EUIPO when infringement proceedings are threatened but no proceedings have been issued. Applications to revoke or have a mark declared invalid before EUIPO can take years if one takes account of appeals and the fact that appeals have suspensive effect. So this has been termed the "EUIPO Torpedo".

This provision has been the subject of a number of decisions in England where **3-834** invalidity or revocation proceedings have been brought before EUIPO in circumstances where infringement proceedings have been threatened. The Court of Appeal has said that "special reasons" means reasons which are peculiar to the facts of the case and not systemic differences between EUTM courts and EUIPO, e.g. the substantial delay in resolving EUIPO applications (including appeals).[1310] It held that a reactive application to EUIPO as a result of threatened proceedings was not a relevant consideration. A special reason could be one of urgency if the interests of the trade mark proprietor could not be adequately protected by provisional and protective measures.[1311]

Vice versa, EUIPO must stay proceedings for revocation or invalidity, unless **3-835** there are special grounds for continuing the hearing, where the validity of the EUTM is already an issue before a EUTM Court on account of a counterclaim.[1312]

Issuing EUIPO proceedings after issue of national proceedings

What is the position where, in infringement proceedings before a EUTM court, **3-836** a defendant deliberately refrains from issuing a counterclaim to revoke or have the EUTM declared invalid and then issues an application seeking the same before EUIPO? Could it then seek a stay of the infringement proceedings before the EUTM court on the grounds that an application for revocation or invalidity *"has already been filed at the Office"*? Such would be a naked tactical ploy to take advantage of the long delays (including appeals) in EUIPO proceedings compared to proceedings in some Member States.[1313] In modern wording, this is called "gaming the system". A EUTM court would clearly be reluctant to stay the proceedings for infringement. It could justify such reluctance by holding that "already been filed at the Office" means as of the date of issue of proceedings, i.e. "the action". However, this is to imply wording which is not there. Moreover, art.132.2 does not allow EUIPO to stay proceedings before it unless there the validity of the EUTM is already in issue on account of a counterclaim before a EUTM court. Thus, EUIPO would be bound to adjudicate on the revocation or invalidity proceedings before it[1314] and then there would be two parallel proceedings seeking to invalidate or revoke it which is undesirable. Alternatively, a EUTM court could hold that there

---

[1309] art.132.1.

[1310] *Starbucks (HK) Ltd v British Sky Broadcasting Group Plc; EMI(IP) Ltd v British Sky Broadcasting Group Plc* [2012] EWCA Civ 1201. In this regard, the Court of Appeal followed the CJEU's approach to "special reasons" for not granting an injunction as set out in *Nokia v Wardell*—see para.3-839.

[1311] See art.131 EUTMR.

[1312] art.132.2.

[1313] Thus, in the UK, proceedings for infringement of a EUTM will nowadays take normally less than 18 months.

[1314] It is of note that art.132.2 allows the EUTM Court to stay the proceedings before it on request of the parties but there is no corresponding provision regarding the request for stay of proceedings before the EUIPO.

are special reasons for continuing with the infringement proceedings on the grounds that such was a naked ploy. Despite the attractiveness of such, there are considerable counterarguments against it. First, the issue of EUIPO revocation or invalidity proceedings *prior* to the issue of infringement proceedings could also be a naked tactical ploy yet, wholly permissible (as discussed above by the Court of Appeal in England and Wales). Secondly, it could lead to the EUTM court granting injunctive relief, etc. in infringement proceedings whilst proceedings before EUIPO are ongoing which could lead to EUIPO revoking the EUTM or declaring it invalid. This is plainly undesirable. In the authors' view, the arguments are finally balanced. Their strong preference is that once infringement proceedings are brought, all issues of infringement and validity should be heard by the EUTM court. Yet, they recognise that the EUTMR plainly envisages split proceedings of infringement and validity/revocation before EUTM courts and EUIPO with all the inconvenience, delay and possible injustice that this could cause.[1315] In such circumstances, EUIPO proceedings must have exhausted themselves before any judgment on infringement can be given.

3-837   Finally, it should be noted that nothing would stop the EUTM court from granting provisional or protective measures.[1316]

Remedies

3-838   In general, the EUTMR leaves the question of what remedies should be granted, following a finding of infringement, to EUTM courts. Whilst this is a matter of national law, the Enforcement Directive requires Member States to grant remedies that are effective, proportionate and dissuasive and sets out broad principles as to the award of injunctions and damages for infringement of intellectual property rights.[1317] However, the EUTMR makes limited provisions concerning the remedies for infringement of EUTM. These are now discussed.

Injunctions

3-839   If the court finds that infringement has occurred, it must issue an order prohibiting the defendant from proceeding with the infringing acts unless there are special reasons for not doing so.[1318] "Special reasons" mean factual circumstances specific to a given case.[1319] Thus the mere fact that the risk of further infringement or threatened infringement of a EUTM is not obvious or is otherwise merely limited does not constitute a special reason for a EUTM court not to issue an injunction restraining further acts of infringement.[1320]

3-840   The CJEU has said in *DHL v Chronopost* that "as a rule", a prohibition against further infringement or threatened infringement issued by a competent EUTM court must extend to the entire area of the EU.[1321] The CJEU said that such flows from the unitary nature of a EUTM. However, the CJEU qualified this by saying that the

---

[1315] Often, there is no bright line between infringement and validity of a mark—e.g. in "squeeze" arguments.
[1316] art.131.
[1317] The Enforcement Directive is discussed in Ch.15.
[1318] art.130.1.
[1319] *Nokia Corp v Wardell* (C-316/05) [2006] E.C.R. I-12083.
[1320] *Nokia Corp v Wardell* (C-316/05) [2006] E.C.R. I-12083 at [36].
[1321] *DHL v Chronopost* (C-235/09) [2011] E.C.R. 2801 at [44]. See also *combit Software GmbH v Commit Business Solutions* (C-223/15) ECLI:EU:C:2016:719 and *Ornua Cooperative Limited v Tindale*

exclusive right of a EUTM proprietor and hence its territorial scope may not extend beyond those uses which are liable to affect the functions of the trade mark. The CJEU said that acts or further acts of a defendant which do not affect the functions of a EUTM cannot therefore be prohibited.[1322] Thus, if a defendant proves that the use of a sign at issue does not affect or is not liable to affect the functions of a trade mark, for example on linguistic grounds, the court must limit the territorial scope of the injunction which it issues to those countries where there is an adverse effect on the functions of a mark.[1323] Thus, where a German court found for linguistic reasons that German-speaking Member States would be confused but not English-speaking Member States, then an injunction for infringement of the EUTM should not lie against English-speaking Member States.[1324]

This approach is welcome. For instance, it would be most odd if an SME who is the registered proprietor of a EUTM seeking to enforce the EUTM in Latvia, based on a localised reputation of the EUTM where he is claiming taking unfair advantage, should get injunctive relief in all Member States of the EU to which the localised reputation does not extend. **3-841**

A EUTM court may grant such provisional relief in respect of a EUTM as is available under its laws in respect of a national trade mark, even where another court has jurisdiction as to the substance of the matter.[1325] Furthermore, a EUTM court whose jurisdiction is based on any ground other than being the EUTM court of the Member State where the infringement took place, may grant provisional measures which, subject to any necessary procedure for recognition and enforcement under the Recast Brussels Regulations, are applicable in the territory of any Member State.[1326] **3-842**

Damages and other relief

Aside from injunctions, the EUTMR does not set out the relief available to a EUTM owner who wins in infringement proceedings. They are thus governed by national law.[1327] However, as discussed in another chapter, the Enforcement Directive is applicable to the determination of damages in a trade mark infringement action.[1328] **3-843**

However, there are a number of provisions in the EUTMR that, although not relevant to the determination of damages, set out where damages should be awarded. First, art.11(2) EUTMR states that reasonable compensation may be claimed in respect of acts of infringement occurring after the date of publication of **3-844**

& *Stanton Ltd Espana SL* (C-93/16) ECLI:EU:C:2017:571. See also *Merck KGaA v Merck & Co* (C-231/16) ECLI:EU:C:2017:771 at [50] ("prohibition .... must therefore, as a rule, extend to the entire area of the European Union"). NB. Article 1(2) EUTMR says that use of a EUTM shall not be prohibited save in respect of the whole EU and *not* that the owner of a EUTM is entitled to prohibit use of an infringing sign throughout the EU.

[1322] See [47]. The burden lies on the defendant—see *combit*, at [32].

[1323] See [48]. The wording of this paragraph suggests that the onus lies on the defendant to prove that its use of the sign would not affect the functions of the registered mark which is sought to be enforced.

[1324] See *combit Software* (C-223/15) ECLI:EU:C:2016:719.

[1325] art.131.

[1326] art.131(2). For recognition of ex parte orders under the Recast Brussels Regulation, see para.17-248.

[1327] art.130(2).

[1328] See Ch.15.

a EUTM application if such acts would infringe the EUTM once granted.[1329] However, the EUTMR makes it clear that a court cannot grant such relief until the registration has been published.[1330] In *Irina Nikolajeva v Multi Protect OÜ*[1331] the Court of Justice considered a number of questions referred to it by Estonian courts on the meaning of the predecessor provision to art.11(2), namely the right to recover reasonable compensation in respect of acts of third parties occurring before the publication of the application for registration. Unsurprisingly, given its wording, the Court of Justice held that there was no such right. More interestingly, in relation to acts occurring after publication of the application but before the registration of the mark, it held that "reasonable compensation" must be smaller in scope than the damages which the proprietor of a EUTM could claim in respect of harm caused by an act of infringement after publication of the registration of the mark. It thus held that compensation does not extend to redress for the *"wider harm that the proprietor of the trade mark concerned may have suffered on accounts of its use, which may include, in particular, moral prejudice"*.[1332] However, it did extend to the recovery of profits unfairly derived by third parties from the use of the trademark after publication of the application.[1333]

3-845   In the case of collective and certification marks, compensation is available against persons who have authority to use the mark but use it in an unauthorised manner.[1334]

Appeals within and from EUIPO

3-846   In proceedings before EUIPO, appeals from the various divisions of EUIPO lie to the Boards of Appeal.[1335] Appeals from the Boards of Appeal lie to the General Court and on narrow grounds to the Court of Justice. Notices of appeal must be filed within two months after the date of notification of the decision appealed from.[1336]

3-847   The nature of appeals to the Boards of Appeal is fairly flexible. Thus, the Boards of Appeal will invite the parties as often as necessary to file observations within a fixed time limit. Although the Board of Appeal must limit its examination of facts to that presented to it, the Board can consider matters of law even if not raised by the parties, if it is necessary to resolve that matter in order to ensure a correct application of EUTMR (see *Linex*[1337] and *Hooligan*[1338]).

3-848   An appeal from the Board of Appeal lies to the General Court on the grounds of lack of competence, infringement of an essential procedural requirement, infringement of the Treaty, and infringement of the EUTMR or any rule of law relating to their application or misuse of power.[1339] An appeal must be filed within two months of the date of notification of the decision.[1340] This appeal will be limited to

---

[1329] art.11(2).
[1330] art.11(3).
[1331] (C–280/15) EU:C:2016:467.
[1332] See [57].
[1333] See [58].
[1334] arts 80(2), 90(2).
[1335] arts 66–73.
[1336] art.68.
[1337] (T-444/12) EU:T:2014:886.
[1338] (T-57/03) EU:T:2005:29.
[1339] art.72. These grounds mirror those laid down in art.263 TFEU which permits the CJEU to review the legality of acts of the Council and Commission (which includes decisions of the Commission). See para.1-081.
[1340] art.65(5).

consideration of the facts and arguments raised in EUIPO.[1341] This reflects the difference between appeals within EUIPO and from EUIPO. The former is more like an internal review of an administrative decision whereas the latter is more akin to an external appeal. However, despite the apparent limits on the General Court's jurisdiction, in practice, the General Court tends to review the totality of the Board of Appeal's decision and will often simply replace the Board of Appeal's view on multifactorial issues such as likelihood of confusion with its own. If the appeal is allowed, the matter is generally remitted back to EUIPO for reconsideration although the General Court does have the right to alter the contested decision.[1342]

A further appeal lies on a point of law to the Court of Justice. In such circumstances, its jurisdiction is confined to reviews of the findings of law argued by the parties before the General Court.[1343] Thus, the General Court has exclusive jurisdiction to find and appraise the relevant facts and to assess the evidence. Only where that appraisal "distorts the evidence" does such amount to a point of law which is reviewable as a point of law by the CJEU.[1344]

3-849

International registrations and EUTMs

As mentioned earlier, the EU is a party to the Madrid Protocol.[1345] Accordingly, an applicant for an international registration can designate the EU instead of designating individual Member States. Such applications are processed by EUIPO. Furthermore, such will have the same effect as an application for a EUTM.[1346] Thereafter, in essence, the application will be processed as an application for a EUTM. Thus, the applicant may claim seniority of an earlier trade mark registered in a Member State of the EU[1347]; the application will be examined for absolute grounds of refusal[1348]; a search will be carried out[1349]; and as WIPO will have already published the international application, EUIPO publishes the date of registration of the mark under WIPO.[1350] This starts the period for opposing the designation of the EU under the international registration; and it can be the subject of opposition proceedings.[1351] Furthermore, it can be converted into national trade marks or into a designation of a Member State party to the Protocol.[1352]

3-850

[1341] *Hammarplast AB v EUIPO* (T-499/04) [2006] E.C.R. II-84.

[1342] art.72.3.

[1343] e.g. *August Storck AG v EUIPO* (C-24/05P) [2006] E.C.R. I-5677 at [45]. Due to the many appeals from the General Court, the court has applied the criteria strictly—no doubt to deter appeals.

[1344] *Sergio Rossi SPA v EUIPO* (C-214/05P) [2006] E.C.R. I-7057 at [26]; (C-104/00) [2002] E.C.R. I-7561 at [22]. See also *Sunrider Corporation* (C–142/14) EU:C:2015:371, where the Court of Justice gives guidance as to the jurisdiction of the General Court and European Court of Justice to review decisions of EUIPO on facts and law. In *Sunrider* the Court of Justice said that there is a distortion of the evidence where the "assessment of the existing evidence appears to be clearly incorrect" (at [47]–[61]).

[1345] See para.3-052. The EU is not a party to the Madrid Agreement.

[1346] art.189.1.

[1347] art.191.

[1348] art.193.

[1349] art.195.

[1350] art.190. Under the Madrid Protocol, international applications are registered but can be opposed post-registration. EUIPO has such a procedure.

[1351] art.196.

[1352] art.159.

EUTM, National Trade Marks and Madrid System

3-851   Obtaining protection for trade marks in Europe can now be made via several routes:

(a) One could apply for registration for a mark in all Member States.
(b) One can apply for a EUTM.
(c) One can make an international application under the Madrid System designating all Member States.
(d) One can make an international application designating the EU which will result in a EUTM.

3-852   Which route to take will depend on a number of factors. If it is not expected that there will be earlier rights which will be cited against it (e.g. the mark applied for is highly unusual), then applying for a EUTM is much cheaper and quicker. If it is likely that there will be earlier rights in some Member States which could be cited against it, the EUTM will be refused whereas an international application will only experience difficulties in that state. Although a refused EUTM can be converted into national trade mark applications, this will be slower than making an international application designating individually the Member States. Thus, in such circumstances, an international application makes more sense than a EUTM application.

3-853   If the owner of the mark is concerned about infringement rather than validity, then the uniform nature of the EUTM makes it easy for one set of proceedings to be brought in respect of infringement through the EU. Indeed, bringing proceedings in the defendant's state of domicile will mean getting effective pan-European relief. Relief in proceedings under national trade mark will be limited to the relevant Member State.

3-854   Since the adherence of EU to the Madrid Protocol, there is considerable flexibility. For an undertaking seeking worldwide protection, designating the EU so as to obtain a EUTM in Europe clearly has its attractions rather than pursuing parallel applications in 28 Member States. With the knowledge that one can convert a EUTM application which is refused because of earlier rights in certain Member States, this route must be considered one of the most attractive.

Geographical Indications of Origin

Introduction

3-855   Since time immemorial, foodstuffs or beverages have been marketed under geographical names. Originally, the geographical name would have been used merely to indicate the region or locality whence the product came from. However, over a substantial period of time, for foodstuffs from a region or locality which was highly regarded by consumers, the geographical name helped consumers in their purchasing choice. For example, wines from the Burgundy region have, over many centuries, gained a reputation for excellence. As a result, purchasers actively seek out bottles bearing the label "Burgundy wine" or "*vins de Bourgogne*". Unsurprisingly, in order to prevent abuse of the use of such names, over the centuries, countries developed sui generis legal protection for such names. Thus, in France, "*Bourgogne*" is an "*appellation d'origine contrôlé*". Furthermore, often countries have developed laws to ensure that the reputation of "the appellation" is maintained by rigorous quality control procedures and emphasis on particular methods of making such wines or foodstuffs. Whilst in some circumstances, the characteristics of the wine or foodstuff is attributable to particular characteristics of the soil, climate, etc. found in the area, more often, it is often simply the case that the area has become known for producing good-quality wines or foodstuffs. Thus, one can buy many excellent *methode champenoise* sparkling wines which are made from grapes grown outside the Champagne region of France.[1353] However, to the consumer, "champagne" has come to mean sparkling white wines from the Champagne region.

Protection for geographical indications can be found in the Paris Convention, the Madrid Arrangement for the Repression of False or Misleading Indications of Origin 1891, the Lisbon Agreement for the Protection of Appellations, the TRIPS Agreement, and in bilateral treaties.[1354] **3-856**

The Lisbon Agreement is an international agreement in the area of geographical indications of origin ("GIOs"). It was adopted in 1958 and revised at Stockholm in 1967 and Geneva in May 2015. The Geneva Act is a radical revision of the Lisbon Agreement expanding the current protection only for "appellations of origin" to GIOs and bringing it into line with art.22 TRIPS.[1355] Appellations of origin are a special kind of GIO for products which have a specific quality or characteristics that are essentially due to the geographic environment in which they are produced.[1356] **3-857**

It is fair to say that the Lisbon Act has met substantial resistance from many countries, particularly in the New World where many names that are protected as GIOs in Europe are used in a generic manner to indicate a type of product. Thus, there are only 27 Contracting Parties to the Stockholm revision and the Geneva revision has only been ratified by one country (May 2018) and is a long way from coming into force. However, the EU is eager to accede to the Geneva Revision and is currently taking soundings from relevant sectors. In particular, this is because, as determined by the Court of Justice,[1357] the EU has exclusive competency (and thus not Member States) to adhere to the Geneva Act as it is concerned with the common commercial policy of the EU.[1358] **3-858**

It is a WIPO-administered agreement. It keeps an international register of appellations of origin. It is also supplemented by regulations which are regularly updated. An up-to-date copy of the Lisbon Treaty and regulations can be found at the WIPO website.[1359] The Lisbon Agreement is similar in nature to the Madrid System for trade marks which has been discussed earlier in this chapter.[1360] It is an international procedural convention for protecting appellations of origin which have been first protected in the country of origin. Contracting states have a right to refuse such protection, for example, on the grounds that, in their territory, the appellation of origin is generic. **3-859**

[1353] Including nowadays in England (thanks to global warming)!

[1354] See C. Heath, "Parmigiano Reggiano by another name—on the Court of Justice's Parmesan Decision" [2008] *International Review of Industrial Property and Copyright Law* 39(8), 951–962. See also D. Marie-Vivien, "The protection of geographical indications for handicrafts or how to apply the concepts of natural and human factors to all products" [2013] OJ WIPO 4(2).

[1355] For a good overview of the Lisbon Agreement and the Geneva Act, see Ch.5, "A look at the Geneva Act of the Lisbon Agreement: a Missed Opportunity?" in D. Gervais, *Geographical Indications at the Crossroads of Trade, Development and Culture*, (Cambridge: Cambridge University Press, 2017).

[1356] art.2 Lisbon Agreement.

[1357] *European Commission and Parliament v Council of the European Union* (C-389/15) ECLI:EU:C:2017:798.

[1358] See para.1-115.

[1359] *http://www.wipo.int/lisbon/en/legal_texts/* [Accessed 6 June 2018].

[1360] See para.3-052.

3-860 Article 22 TRIPS stipulates:

> "1. Geographical indications are, for the purposes of this Agreement, indications which identify a good as originating in the territory of a Member, or a region or locality in that territory, where a given quality, reputation or other characteristic of the good is essentially attributable to its geographical origin."

3-861 This requires that contracting states protects not only GIOs where the products that use them owe their quality to the geographical origin but also products where the reputation of the products (but not the physical characteristics) are associated with a particular geographical area. This distinction is reflected in GIO legislation within the EU which permits protection of both types of GIOs as "designations of origin" ("PDO") and "geographical indications" ("PGI").

3-862 Historically, GIOs have been protected by a national patchwork of laws, bilateral agreements, etc. in the EU. Generally, such laws were exercisable by private individuals without contravening the EU provisions on free movement of goods, because they were held justified under art.36 TFEU on the grounds of protection of industrial and commercial property.[1361]

3-863 However, such piecemeal national legislation hindered the attainment of a single market. Accordingly, the EU introduced (in its own patchwork way) EU legislation (by way of regulations) which sought to set up an EU-wide regime for GIOs. Eventually, the European Commission sought to bring some order to the whole EU regime of GIOs and what is called Traditional Speciality Guaranteed ("TSG") which seek to protect traditional methods of production by rationalising and consolidating previous legislation.

3-864 The current position is that there are two main regulations. In the field of wine and alcoholic beverages, there is EU Reg.1308/2013.[1362] Outside the field of wine, the primary current regulation protecting GIOs and TSGs is EU Reg.1151/2012.[1363] The regulation which will be considered in detail is the latter which covers a wide range of agricultural products and foodstuffs. However, the two regulations are similar in nature. Regulation 1151/2012's predecessors are Regs 509/2006 and 510/2006.[1364] They have been the subject of a number of decisions of the CJEU. Under this regime, there are three types of protection:

(a) Protected Designations of Origins ("PDO"). These cover agricultural products and foodstuffs which are produced, processed and prepared in a given geographical area using recognised know-how.

(b) Protected Geographical Indications ("PGI"). This covers agricultural products and foodstuffs closely linked to the geographical area and at least one of the stages of production, processing or preparation takes place in the area.

[1361] e.g. *Exportur SA v LOR SA and Confiserie du Tech SA* (C-3/91) [1992] E.C.R. I-5529. See paras 7-293 and 7-296.

[1362] [2013] OJ L347/71. This replaced Reg.1234/2007 [2007] OJ L299/1.

[1363] [2012] OJ L343/1. This replaced Regs 509/2006 and 510/2006.

[1364] PDOs and PGIs were protected by Council Regulation 510/2006 of 20 March 2006 on the protection of geographical indications and designations of origin for agricultural products and foodstuffs [2006] OJ L93/12, which replaced Council Reg.2081/92 of 14 July 1992 on the protection of geographical indications and designations of origin for agricultural products and foodstuffs [1992] OJ L208/1. TSGs were previously protected by Reg.509/2006 [2006] OJ L93/1. This in turn replaced Reg.2082/92 (which introduced certificates of special character for agricultural products and foodstuffs) [1992] OJ L208/9 and Reg.1848/93 (which introduced the term "traditional speciality guaranteed") [1993] OJ L168/35.

(c) Traditional Speciality Guaranteed ("TSG"). These cover foodstuffs composed of or made in a traditional manner but which are not geographical specific.

It is a useful exercise to summarise current EU legislation for PDOs, PGIs and TSGs as the legislative landscape is somewhat complex: **3-865**

Agricultural products and foodstuffs

Regulation 1151/2012 (PDOs, PGIs, TSGs) is concerned with agricultural **3-866** products for human consumption and includes a wide range of products including inter alia meat, meat products, eggs, honey, dairy products (but not butter), oils, cheeses, fruit, vegetables, cereals, fish, spices, beer, chocolate, bread, pastry, cakes, biscuits, pasta, salt, gums, mustard, hay, oils, cork, flowers, cotton, wool, leather, fur and feathers. Under this regulation, the European Commission may adopt delegated acts in certain areas. Thus, the European Commission has adopted Reg.665/2014 which regulates the use of the term "mountain product".

Wines

Regulation 1308/2013 is concerned with PDO and PGI for wines.[1365] **3-867**

Spirit drinks

Regulation 110/2008[1366] is concerned with PGIs for spirit drinks. **3-868**

Aromatised wines

Regulation 251/2014[1367] is concerned with PGIs for aromatised wines. **3-869**

The structure of these regulations are similar. They provide for the examination **3-870** of candidates of names to be protected as GIO (and whether such should be a PDO, PGI or TSG). Once protected, they confer sui generis protection against unauthorised use of names for foodstuffs and alcoholic beverages which can be considered, in broad terms, to lead to deception of consumers or amount to unfair competition.

The EUIPO has published a useful study on the infringement of PDOs and PGIs **3-871** in the EU dated April 2016.[1368] Highlighted facts in this report are:

- There are nearly 3400 GIOs.
- The premium that a GIO allows its producer to charge varies from 2.75 (wines) to 1.16 (fresh meat).
- The value of agricultural products protected by EU GIOs in 2010 was €54.3 billion.
- The top GIOs were (in alphabetic order) Bayerisches Bier, Cava, Cham-

---

[1365] This replaces Regs 922/72; 234/79; 1037/2001 and 1234/2007. Regulation 1308/2013 is very large as it deals with the EU common agricultural policy. The provisions on PDO and PGI are at Section 2, arts 92–116.
[1366] This replaces Reg.1576/89.
[1367] This replaces Reg.251/2014.
[1368] See *https://euipo.europa.eu/tunnel-web/secure/webdav/guest/document_library/observatory/documents/Geographical_indications_report/geographical_indications_report_en.pdf* [Accessed 8 October 2017].

pagne, Cognac, Grana Padano, Parmigiano, Pays d'Oc, Prosciutto di Parma, Rioja, and Scotch Whisky. These represent 28 per cent of all sales of GIO products in the EU.

- In 2014, the estimated infringements of GIOs amounted to €4.3 billion, corresponding to 9.0 per cent of total EU GIO product market.
- Consumer loss is c.€2.3 billion.[1369]
- The infringements are split as follows: 42 per cent—imitation or evocation of GIO; 38 per cent—misleading information about origin of non-GIO products; 21 per cent—non-conformity of GIO products with specifications.

3-872   In the following sections, Reg.1151/2012 is considered. However, as said above, all GIO EU legislation has a similar structure.

Regulation 1151/2012

Introduction

3-873   This regulation lays down rules on PDOs, PGIs and TSGs. It covers a wide variety of foodstuffs, such as cheese, mineral water, meat, vegetables, etc. For ease of reference, it is referred to hereinafter as the "2012 Regulation". It is intended to provide a uniform and exhaustive system for the protection of PDOs, PGIs and TSGs within the EU for foodstuffs.[1370] Thus, national laws protecting such are not permissible.[1371] The 2012 Regulation provides for a register of PDOs, PGIs and TSGs that is EU-wide. Interestingly, the 2012 Regulation sets out in the articles as opposed to the recitals the objectives of the Regulation. These are: (a) fair competition for farmers and producers, (b) the availability to consumers of reliable information, (c) respect for intellectual property rights, and (d) the integrity of the internal market.[1372]

Definition of PDOs PGIs and TSGs

Designation of origin ("PDOs")

3-874   A PDO is defined as a name which identifies a product:

"(a)   originating in a specific place, region or, in exceptional cases, a country;
(b)   whose quality or characteristics are essentially or exclusively due to a particular geographical environment with its inherent natural and human factors; and
(c)   the production steps of which all take place in the defined geographical area."[1373]

3-875   No doubt as a result of lobbying by some Member States whose PDOs would not have fallen within such a definition, the Regulation also provides:

"3.   Notwithstanding paragraph 1(a), certain geographical designations shall be treated as designations of origin even though the raw materials for the products concerned come from a geographical area larger than, or different from, the defined geographical area, provided that:

[1369] Defined as the price premium paid by consumers in the belief that they are buying a genuine GI product.
[1370] Recital 17.
[1371] See para.3-914.
[1372] art.1 (see also art.4).
[1373] art.5(1).

(a)   the production area of the raw materials[1374] is defined;
(b)   special conditions for the production of the raw materials exist; and
(c)   there are control arrangements to ensure that the conditions referred to in point (b) are adhered to; and
(d)   the designations of origin in question were recognized as designations of origin in the country of origin before 1 May 2004."

By reason of the above definitions, it is necessary for a geographical name to qualify as a PDO and that there is a clear link between the physical characteristics of the product with which the geographical name has been used and the geographical area.   **3-876**

Geographical indications ("PGIs")

A PGI is defined as a name which identifies a product: **3-877**

"(a)   as originating in a specific place, region or country;
(b)   whose given quality, reputation or other characteristic is essentially attributable to its geographical origin; and
(c)   at least one of the production steps of which take place in the defined geographical area."[1375]

PGIs can be considered a form of protection where there is not a strong connection between the terroir and the qualities of the foodstuffs as for PDOs. Thus, the distinction has been explained as being that the causal link between the place of origin and the quality of the product may be a matter of reputation in PGIs rather than verifiable fact, which is the case in PDOs.[1376] This is reflected in the definition above which makes it clear under condition (b) that it would be sufficient for the reputation alone to be linked to a geographical area. Furthermore, it is clear from condition (c) that it is not necessary that the raw materials for the foodstuffs emanate from the region, provided that a step of production or processing occurs there.[1377]   **3-878**

In the early 1990s, it was argued that the enforcement of national laws that protected PGIs were incompatible with the articles of the European Economic Community ("EEC") relating to free movement of goods. Thus in *Exportur*,[1378] the European Commission argued that the enforcement of geographical names protected by national laws of Member States were only enforceable if the products to which the protected name is applied possessed qualities and characteristics which were due to the geographical place of origin and gave the products their individual character. However, the CJEU rejected this. They said that the Commission's position: **3-879**

"[28]   ... would have the effect of depriving of all protection geographical names used for products which cannot be shown to derive a particular flavour from the land and which have not been produced in accordance with quality requirements and manufacturing standards laid down by an act of public authority, such names be-

---

[1374] Which can only be live animals, meat and milk (art.5(3)).
[1375] art.5(2).
[1376] per Lord Hoffmann in *Consorzio del Prosciutto di Parma v Asda Stores Ltd* [2001] 1 C.M.L.R. 43 at [8].
[1377] See also *Carl Kuhne GmbH & Co KG v Jutro Konservenfabrik GmbH & Co, KG* (C-269/99) [2001] E.C.R. I-9563 at [61] (interpreting art.2(2)(b) Reg.2081/92, predecessor to the 2012 Regulation).
[1378] *Exportur SA v LOR SA and Confiserie du Tech SA* (C-3/91) [1992] E.C.R. I-5529. Generally, see paras 7-293 to 7-296.

ing commonly known as indications of provenance. Such names may nevertheless enjoy a high reputation amongst consumers and constitute for producers established in the places to which they refer an essential means of attracting custom. Therefore they are entitled to protection."

Traditional Specialities Guaranteed ("TSGs")

3-880 A TSG is defined a name which describes a specific product or foodstuff that:

"(a) results from a mode of production, processing or composition corresponding to traditional practice for that product or foodstuff; or

(b) is produced from raw materials or ingredients that are those traditionally used."[1379]

3-881 The qualities of a TSG do not need to be attributable to a specific geographical region. Thus, a TSG is different in nature to a PDO or PGI. However, that does not mean that the name of a TSG cannot include a geographical name. Therefore, the name "Gloucestershire Old Spot Pork" is a TSG reserved for pork which emanates from pedigree Gloucestershire Old Spots pigs registered as purebred by a recognised pig breeders' association, where the pigs have been reared from birth to slaughter in a natural environment, fed with a prescribed diet of vegetables, etc.[1380] The objective of protection for TSGs is to help the producers of traditional products to communicate to consumers the value-adding attributes of their product.[1381] It would appear that Reg.510/2006 did not result in many TSGs being registered and thus the TSG provisions in the 2012 Regulation have been improved, clarified and sharpened in order to make the TSG scheme more understandable, operational and attractive to potential applicants.[1382]

Grounds for objection to PDOs/PGIs

3-882 Aside from a name not fulfilling the above requirements for a PDO, PGI or TSG, there are a number of other grounds for objecting to the registration of a geographical name for a PDO or PGI. These are now discussed.

Generic names

3-883 The Regulation prohibits the registration of names that have become generic.[1383] This is defined as "names of products which, although relating to the place, region or country where the product was originally produced or marketed, have become the common name of a product in the Union".[1384]

3-884 A predecessor provision (art.2 Reg.2081/92) was considered by the CJEU in relation to whether the Commission had properly decided that *Feta* cheese should be treated as a PDO.[1385] The court annulled the Commission's decision that *Feta* was a PDO because the Commission had not taken into account the fact that *Feta* had been used for a considerable time in certain Member States other than Greece.

[1379] art.18(1).
[1380] [2009] OJ C238/8. "Gloucestershire" is a county (geographical region) in England.
[1381] Recital 34.
[1382] Recital 34.
[1383] art.6(1).
[1384] art.1(6).
[1385] *Kingdom of Denmark, Federal Republic of Germany and French Republic v EU Commission* (C-289, 293 & 299/96) [1999] E.C.R. I-1541; [1999] E.T.M.R. 478.

The Commission then carried out a market research exercise to establish that this was not the case and the PDO was ultimately re-registered.[1386] In *Germany and Denmark v Commission*,[1387] Germany and Denmark sought to challenge the re-registration of *Feta* as a PDO. The states submitted that *Feta* comes from the Italian language and means "slice". They declared that it was generic and did not qualify under art.2(3) of Reg.2081/92. The CJEU held that there were a number of factors which suggested that *Feta* was not generic. They were: (i) the production of *Feta* remained concentrated in Greece; (ii) 85 per cent of consumption of *Feta* takes places in Greece; (iii) the majority of consumers in Greece consider that the *Feta* carries a geographical and not generic connotation; (iv) in Member States other than Greece, the marketing of *Feta* is commonly by reference to Greek cultural traditions and civilisation and thus it was legitimate to infer that consumers in those Member States perceive *Feta* as a cheese associated with Greece even if this was not in reality the case; (v) only Denmark and Greece had legislation specifically relating to *Feta* and in the case of Denmark, the legislation referred to Danish *Feta* which tended to suggest that *Feta* by itself retained a Greek connotation; and (vi) in a bilateral convention between Austria and Greece, the use of the name *Feta* in Austria had been reserved exclusively for Greek products. It accordingly held that the Commission could lawfully decide that *Feta* was not generic.

3-885

Plant variety and animal breeds

The Regulation also prohibits the registration of PDOs or PGIs which conflict with the name of a plant variety or animal breed and as a result would be likely to mislead the public as to the true origin of the product.[1388]

3-886

Homonyms

A name proposed for registration that is wholly or partially homonymous[1389] with a name already entered on the register may not be registered unless there is sufficient distinction in practice between the conditions of local and traditional usage and presentation of the homonym registered subsequently and the name already entered in the register, taking into account the need to ensure equitable treatment of the producers concerned and that consumers are not misled.[1390] The 2012 Regulation says that a homonymous name which misleads the consumers into believing that products come from another territory may not be registered even if the name is accurate as far as the actual territory, region or place of origin of the products in question is concerned.[1391]

3-887

[1386] See (C-289, 293 & 299/96) [1999] E.C.R. I-1541; [2001] 1 C.M.L.R. 379; [1999] E.T.M.R. 478 for the annulment decision and Reg.1829/2002 [2002] OJ L277, p.10 for the second attempt at registration.

[1387] *Federal Republic of Germany and Kingdom of Denmark v Commission* (C-465/02 & C-466/02) [2005] E.C.R 9115.

[1388] art.6(2).

[1389] A homonym is a word that has the same sound and often the same spelling as another word but which differs in meaning, e.g. in English, the word "bank" can mean elevated land next to a river and also a building where money is kept.

[1390] art.6(3).

[1391] art.6(3), second paragraph.

Trade marks of reputation or renown

3-888   A PDO or PGI cannot be registered where in the light of a trade mark's reputation or renown and the length of time it has been used, registration is liable to mislead the consumer as to the true identity of the product.[1392] It should be noted that it does not appear that it is required that the trade mark is registered. Indeed, as discussed below, there is no per se ground of objection to the registration of a PDO or PGI that there is an earlier registered trade mark.[1393]

Rights afforded by a PDO or PGI

3-889   Once a PDO or PGI is registered, art.13(1) affords the following protection:

"(a)   any direct or indirect commercial use of a registered name in respect of products not covered by the registration in so far as those products are comparable to the products registered under that name or where using the name exploits the reputation of the protected name, including when those products are used as an ingredient;

(b)   any misuse, imitation or evocation, even if the true origin of the product is indicated or if the protected name is translated or accompanied by an expression such as 'style', 'type', 'method', 'as produced in', 'imitation' or similar, including when those products are used as an ingredient;

(c)   any other false or misleading indication as to the provenance, origin, nature or essential qualities of the product, on the inner or outer packaging, advertising material or documents relating to the product concerned, and the packing of the product in a container liable to convey a false impression as to its origin;

(d)   any other practice liable to mislead the consumer as to the true origin of the product."[1394]

3-890   Article 13.1(a) is concerned with use of the registered name itself, i.e. a sign identical to the protected GIO. Liability for use of the GIO on products the same or comparable goods to that protected by the GIO is absolute. No evidence is required (other than perhaps to demonstrate that the goods are comparable[1395]). Even if the goods are not comparable, then there is infringement if the name exploits the reputation of the protected name. Article 13.1(b) is more concerned with use of similar signs to the registered name. Article 13.1(c) would suggest by the wording "*any other* false or misleading indication" that art.13 is overall concerned with consumers being misled as to the nature or essential qualities *or* geographical origin of goods.[1396] However, as seen in the next section, the Court of Justice has held that there is no need when considering the concept of "evocation", to show a likelihood of confusion. Despite this, as discussed in the section on protection of GIOs to dissimilar goods, a purposive approach of art.13 would suggest that the rights of owners of GIOs should not be allowed to be construed too far so as to extend to any use of a GIO or similar sign to a GIO for any product (however dissimilar) merely because they call to mind the GIO. The Recitals and art. 4 suggest that the

---

[1392] art.6(4).

[1393] See paras 3-904 and 3-911.

[1394] art.13(1).

[1395] It might be thought that "comparable to the products" should have the same meaning as "similar goods" in EU trade mark law.

[1396] *Comité Interprofessionnel du Vin de Champagne v Aldi Süd Dienstleistungs-GmbH & Co OHG* (C-393/16) ECLI:EU:C:2017:991 at [60]–[64] (false or misleading indications applies to both false impression as to geographical origin and nature or essential qualities of the product).

rights of a GIO owner extend to protecting consumers from being misled and in the absence of confusion, ensuring that third parties use them "fairly".[1397] It is considered that this is consistent with the Geneva Act of the Lisbon Agreement to which the EU has yet to accede.[1398] Article 11(1)(a) of the Geneva Act of the Lisbon Agreement extends protection to GIOs to goods or services that are not of the same kind if such use would be likely to impair or dilute in an unfair manner or take unfair advantage of that reputation.[1399]

Exploitation of reputation

There is exploitation of the reputation of a GIO where the use of a GIO takes   **3-891**
unfair advantage of the reputation of the GIO.[1400] Where a supermarket sold a sorbet as CHAMPAGNER SORBET which had 12 per cent Champagne and the taste of the product was primarily due to the presence of champagne in the product, there was no unfair advantage taken of the GIO Champagne.

Evocation

Article 13 is very similar to the predecessor regulation.[1401] In *Gorgonzola/*   **3-892**
Cambozola[1402] the CJEU considered the meaning of "evocation" in art.13(1)(b). It said that it is possible for a protected designation to be evoked where there is no likelihood of confusion between the products concerned and even where no EU protection extends to the parts of that designation which are echoed in the term or terms at issue. In that case, the consortium of manufacturers of *Gorgonzola* complained of the use of the name CAMBOZOLA in relation to another soft, blue cheese which was not dissimilar in appearance to *Gorgonzola*. The CJEU said that it would seem reasonable to conclude that a protected name is indeed evoked where the term used to designate that product ends in the same two syllables and contains the same number of syllables, with the result that the phonetic and visual similarity between the two terms is obvious. Also the CJEU noted that the fact that the packaging for Cambozola indicated the product's true origin did not prevent the protected designation from being evoked.

In the *Parmigiano* decision,[1403] the Commission brought an action against   **3-893**
Germany for its failure to give clear instructions to governmental bodies that the

---

[1397] See Recitals 3, 4, 5, 29. See also *Comité Interprofessionnel du Vin de Champagne v Aldi Süd Dienstleistungs-GmbH & Co OHG* (C-393/16) ECLI:EU:C:2017:991 at [39].

[1398] See para.3-857. The EU is proposing acceding to the Geneva Act of the Lisbon Agreement (the Revised Lisbon Agreement). However, as of May 2018, it has not acceded to it. See para.3-858.

[1399] "Geographical Indications and the Principles of Trade Mark Law—A Distinctly European Perspective" *Heath and Marie-Vivien* IIC (2015) 46:819-842, 832. If the EU accedes to the Revised Lisbon Agreement, then EU GIO legislation will have to be interpreted in the light of the Revised Lisbon Agreement (see Ch.1, paras 1-158 to 1-166). It will be noted that this "extended protection" to dissimilar goods is similar to the extended protection afforded to EU trade marks with a reputation.

[1400] *Comité Interprofessionnel du Vin de Champagne v Aldi Süd Dienstleistungs-GmbH & Co OHG* (C-393/16) ECLI:EU:C:2017:991 at [37]–[53]. For "Unfair advantage" in the context of trade marks, see para.3-365.

[1401] art.13 Reg.510/2006. The main difference is that art.13(1)(a) and (b) introduce the wording of "including when those products are used as an ingredient". However, it is difficult to see how the use of a PDO or PGI in a list of ingredients should be objectionable if true.

[1402] *Consorzio per la tutela del formaggio Gorgonzola v Käserei Champignon Hofmeister GmbH & a; Co KG and Eduard Bracharz GmbH* (C-87/97) [1999] E.C.R. I-1301; [1999] E.T.M.R. 455.

[1403] *Commission of European Communities v Federal Republic of Germany* (C-132/05) [2008] E.C.R. I-957.

marketing in Germany of cheese designated as "Parmesan" infringed the PDO *Parmigiano Reggiano*. The German Government held that "Parmesan" had become a generic name for hard cheeses of diverse origin which was distinct from the PDO *Parmigiano Reggiano*. Accordingly, the Commission brought proceedings against Germany. At the heart of the dispute was whether "Parmesan" fell within art.13 Reg.2081/92 (the predecessor to Reg.510/2006). The CJEU rejected the submission that a PDO only enjoys protection under art.13 in the exact form in which it is registered and thus not in its components. Indeed, such argument had been rejected in an earlier case.[1404] The Commission argued that "Parmesan" was a translation of *Parmigiano Reggiano* and furthermore evoked that PDO. The CJEU held, in applying *Gorgonzola/Cambozola* that art.13(1)(b) applied where the consumer is confronted with the name of a product and it brings to mind an image of the PDO.[1405] It held that when applying that test that the conceptual proximity between the two terms must also be taken into account. It also held that by reason of the conceptual proximity and the phonetic and visual similarities, "Parmesan" must be regarded as an evocation of the PDO *Parmigiano Reggiano*.[1406] It said that it was irrelevant whether or not "Parmesan" was a translation of the PDO *Parmigiano Reggiano*.[1407] As has been pointed out, the use of translations of PDOs is not infringing per se.[1408]

3-894   The German Government finally argued that "Parmesan" was a generic name and thus its use could not amount to an unlawful evocation of the PDO "*Parmigiano Reggiano*". This is an interesting argument. It could not argue that "*Parmigiano Reggiano*" was generic as it was a registered PDO.[1409] However, art.13(1) provides a defence that where a registered name contains within it the name of an agricultural product or foodstuff which is considered generic, the use of that generic name on the appropriate agricultural product or foodstuff is not contrary to art.13(1)(a) or (b). Applying the case law it had developed in relation to art.6(1),[1410] the CJEU held that such had not been proven on the facts.[1411]

3-895   In *Viiniverla Oy v Sosiaali- ja terveysalan lupa- ja valvontavirasto*,[1412] the Court of Justice had to consider whether VERLADO for an apple spirit evoked "*Calvados*" (the well-known French apple spirit) in the context of Reg.110/2008 (legislation relating to the protection of GIOs for spirit drink). The wording of art.16(b) of Reg.110/2008 is essentially the same as art.13(1)(b) of Reg.1151/2012. On a

---

[1404] *Chiciak/Fol* (C-129/07 & C-130/07) [1998] E.C.R. I-3315. See *Parmigiano*, at [31]. It is however of note, as pointed out by the German government, that Italy expressly and purposely did not apply to register *Parmigiano* (solus) as a PDO—*Parmigiano*, at [26].

[1405] See [44].

[1406] See [46]–[49].

[1407] See [50].

[1408] C. Heath, "Parmigiano Reggiano by Another Name—The Court of Justice's Parmesan Decision" (2008) *International Review of Industrial Property and Copyright Law* 39(8), 951 at 960.

[1409] art.13(2). Generic names cannot be registered as PDOs but if they are registered as PDOs, it cannot be argued in infringement proceedings that they are generic. The method of attack would be to annul the registration (as was done in the *Feta* case—see para.3-883).

[1410] See para.3-883.

[1411] A difficulty for Germany arose in *Bigi v Consorzio del Formaggio Parmigiano Reggiano* (C-66/00) ECLI:EU:C:2002:397. This case was a reference from an Italian court concerning criminal proceedings brought against Mr Bigi for selling dried grated pasteurised cheese as "Parmesan" in France which did not comply with the *Parmigiano Reggiano* PDO. The Court of Justice held that it was far from clear that the designation "parmesan" was generic. Indeed, it noted that all governments which had submitted written observations had, apart from Germany, said that "parmesan" was a correct translation of the PDO *Parmigiano Reggiano*—[20]–[21].

[1412] (C–75/15) EU:C:2016:35.

preliminary reference from the Finnish court, it advised that the assessment of evocation requires consideration of the perception of the average consumer who is reasonably well informed and reasonably observant and circumspect, and that concept covered European consumers as well as consumers of the Member State in which the product giving rise to the (alleged) evocation of the PGI was manufactured. It also elaborated on the notion of "evocation" as meaning that:

> "[48] ... the referring court must take into consideration the phonetic and visual relationship between those names and any evidence that may show that such a relationship is not fortuitous, so as to ascertain whether, when the average European consumer, reasonably well informed and reasonably observant and circumspect, is confronted with the name of a product, *the image triggered in his mind is that of the product whose geographical indication is protected.*"

In an appeal from EUIPO to the General Court (*IVDP v EUIPO*[1413]), the latter held that the Board of Appeal had not been wrong to conclude that PORT CHARLOTTE did not evoke the designation of origin "porto" or "port" as PORT CHARLOTTE would be read as a "logical and conceptual unit" and thus would be designating a harbour named after a person called Charlotte and no direct link would be made with the designation of origin "porto".[1414]   **3-896**

In *Champagner Sorbet*, the Court of Justice held that there was no "misuse, imitation or evocation" where the PDO was used as part of the name of a sorbet in circumstances where the sorbet included an ingredient that did correspond to the specification of the PDO (the sorbet contained 14 per cent Champagne).[1415] Interestingly, the Court of Justice said that whilst the concept of "evocation" was settled (citing *Viiniverla*), the incorporation of the name of the PDO in its entirety in the foodstuff concerned, to indicate the taste of that food, does not correspond to that situation.[1416] This suggests that there are limits to the protection afforded by a GIO under the principle of "evocation". After all, CHAMPAGNER SORBET triggers in the mind of consumers the drink Champagne but it does so to *inform* the consumer in a fair and truthful manner.   **3-897**

Use of GIOs for dissimilar goods

Under EU trade mark law, a registered trade mark with a reputation can be infringed by use of a sign on dissimilar goods where such takes unfair advantage of or is detrimental to the distinctive character or repute of the registered trade mark.[1417] What is the law with regards to use of GIOs for goods dissimilar to which it is protected?   **3-898**

Let us consider an example. A mass motor vehicle manufacturer markets an upmarket version of a range under the marque CHAMPAGNE. Here, there is plainly an "evocation"—indeed the sign is the same as the protected GIO. Equally, it could be said that the marque exploits the aura of exclusivity and class which is associated with champagne. Yet, the public will be unlikely to misled, e.g. into believing that somehow a Champagne house is behind this. Equally, it stretches   **3-899**

[1413] (T-659/14) EU:T:2015:863

[1414] See [71].

[1415] *Comité Interprofessionnel du Vin de Champagne v Aldi Süd Dienstleistungs-GmbH & Co OHG* (C-393/16) ECLI:EU:C:2017:991 at [54]–[59].

[1416] See [58].

[1417] Generally, see para.3-433.

credulity to say that such use is somehow unfair to makers of Champagne.[1418] Whilst undoubtedly, the use of CHAMPAGNE as a marque for a car is intended to evoke the aura of exclusivity and class that "Champagne" also evokes, it goes no further. For instance, the public would not believe that somehow a Ford car marketed under the marque CHAMPAGNE would be made in the Champagne region of France or has the physical characteristics of sparkling white wine made in that region. As with "Champagner Sorbet", it could be said that it is merely informing the consumer that the car is stylish and exclusive and whilst it "evokes" the GIO, it does not do so in a manner that infringes art.13.

3-900   Yet, there can be little doubt that extensive use of CHAMPAGNE for a wide range of goods would ultimately result in the dilution of the mark and weaken and dilute its attractiveness. Courts of Member States have found this to be the case when considering the use of "Champagne" for products other than sparkling white wines.

3-901   Therefore, as said in an English passing off action[1419] concerning the use of the sign ELDERFLOWER CHAMPAGNE for a non-alcoholic fruit drink made with elderflower upholding a finding of passing off:

> "Like the judge, I do not think the defendants' product would reduce the first plaintiffs' sales in any significant and direct way. But that is not, as it seems to me, the end of the matter. The first plaintiffs' reputation and goodwill in the description Champagne derive not only from the quality of their wine and its glamorous associations, but also from the very singularity and exclusiveness of the description, the absence of any qualifying epithets and imitative descriptions. *Any product which is not Champagne but is allowed to describe itself as such must inevitably, in my view, erode the singularity and exclusiveness of the description Champagne and so cause the first plaintiffs damage of an insidious but serious kind.* The amount of damage which the defendants' product would cause would of course depend on the size of the defendants' operation. That is not negligible now, and it could become much bigger. But I cannot see, despite the defendants' argument to the contrary, any rational basis upon which, if the defendants' product were allowed to be marketed under its present description, any other fruit cordial diluted with carbonated water could not be similarly marketed so as to incorporate the description champagne. The damage to the first plaintiffs would then be incalculable but severe." [Emphasis supplied.]

3-902   Equally, in applying national laws on geographical indications of origin, French courts have not been slow to find that the use of signs the same or similar to well-known GIOs on dissimilar goods can be prevented where such leads to a weakening of the value of reputation and attractiveness of a GIO.[1420] However, EU law is more limited and the Court of Justice has yet to rule on the principles to be applied to EU GIOs when used for dissimilar goods.[1421]

3-903   In the authors' view, whilst there can be no doubt that the rights of PDOs and

---

[1418] As said above, protection of GIOs is aimed at preventing consumers from being misled and also ensuring that GIOs are used "fairly"—see para.3-890.

[1419] *Taittinger v Allbev Ltd* [1993] F.S.R. 641 CA.

[1420] e.g. *Tribunal de Grande Instance*, 5 March 1984 [1984] RIPIA, p.40 ("Champagne" used to designate tobacco and matches); Supreme Court (18 February 2004) [2004] PIBD 787-III, p.331 ("*Bain Champagne*" for perfume). These cases and other are discussed in C. Heath and D. Marie-Vivien, "Geographical Indications and the Principles of Trade Mark Law—A Distinctly European Perspective" IIC (2015) 46:819–842, 829. The concept of "dilution" is familiar to trade mark lawyers and is discussed at para.3-393.

[1421] C. Heath and D. Marie-Vivien, "Geographical Indications and the Principles of Trade Mark Law—A Distinctly European Perspective" IIC (2015) 46:819–842, at 831.

PGIs extend and should extend beyond the goods or comparable goods for which they are registered, real care should be taken in extending the rights to identical or similar signs used on very different goods. In particular, GIOs will be, by their very nature, names of geographical regions. Yet, a geographical region may produce many different types of goods and it would be oppressive to find that the name of that region cannot be used for such goods, merely because a GIO is "evoked". The essential function of GIOs is to guarantee to consumers the geographical origin of goods and the special qualities inherent in them.[1422] Use of a GIO for very dissimilar goods will rarely affect that function. In particular, when considering the concepts of "evocation", care must be taken by a court or tribunal to distinguish between whether the sign evokes the GIO itself or merely qualities associated with the geographical region.[1423] Furthermore, whilst the Court of Justice has said that "evocation" means a triggering in the mind of the product with which the GIO is protected, its interpretation, as seen in *Champagner Sorbet*, has been not to interpret "evocation" too literally but rather to consider the context of the use of the GIO—and in particular, whether it is being used to convey information fairly or unfairly regarding a product. As said earlier,[1424] it is considered that art.11.1(a)(ii) of the Geneva Act of the Lisbon Agreement which confers the right on owners of GIOs to prevent "because of the reputation of the appellation of origin or geographical indication in the Contracting Party concerned, such use would be likely to impair or dilute in an unfair manner, or take unfair advantage of, that reputation" provides useful guidelines. Whilst not yet in force in the EU, there is no reason not to interpret the 2012 Regulation in a manner that gives effect to the above wording.

Interrelationship of the law of registered trade marks and GIOs

GIOs have similarities and differences with trade marks, particularly collective marks where the mark is the name of a geographic region. This has been discussed earlier in this chapter.[1425] The similarity is such that the 2012 Regulations and EU trade mark law have provisions to avoid conflict. These are now considered.

3-904

Application for EUTM or national trade mark which is a protected GIO: absolute grounds

Once a PDO or PGI has been registered, art.14 of the 2012 Regulation stipulates that an application for registration of a trade mark "the use of which would contravene Article 13(1) and which relates to a product of the same type" must be refused if submitted after the date of submission to the Commission for the grant of a PDO or PGI.[1426] The 2012 Regulation stipulates that where trade marks have

3-905

[1422] *The Tea Board v OHIM* (T-625/13) ECLI:EU:C:2015:742 at [41] citing *Anheuser-Busch v Budějovický Budvar* (C-96/09) EU:C:2011:189 at [147].

[1423] In *The Tea Board* (T-625/13) which concerned a collective EU mark for "Darjeeling" for tea, the General Court held that use of "Darjeeling" for lingerie would take unfair advantage of the reputation of Darjeeling as it would "evoke" images of exoticism, sensuality and mystery (see [140]). Yet, as said earlier in this chapter (para.3-775), those are qualities associated with India and the Darjeeling region rather than Darjeeling tea itself.

[1424] See para.3-890.

[1425] See para.3-774 concerning protection for collective marks under EU trade mark law and the similarities and differences between EU collective marks and GIOs.

[1426] art.14(1).

been registered in breach of this condition, they must be declared invalid.[1427] Article 13(1) refers to the scope of protection of a PDO or PGI and has been discussed above.[1428] Therefore, art. 14 envisages use of the mark applied on a hypothetical marketplace for the goods for which protection is sought and then considering whether: (i) the goods are of the same type, and (ii) if so, whether such would infringe the art.13 rights of the owner of a GIO.

3-906　　What does "product of the same type" mean? Article 13 is not restricted to use of a GIO on goods covered by the registration. Thus, it would prohibit elderflower sparkling juice called "Elderflower Champagne" or "*Methode champenoise* Elderflower Juice" even though elderflower juice is not an alcoholic beverage, let alone sparkling white wine. Yet plainly these are not products of the same type. Alcoholic sparkling wine and non-alcoholic sparkling juices are very different in many ways other than they are both drunk. In the author's view, "product of the same type" should be construed narrowly and indeed, interpreted as "comparable" goods within the meaning of art.13.1(a) 2012 Regulation. It should be noted that both the EUTMR and TMD provide as an absolute ground of objection, the registration of trade marks which are "excluded from registration" under EU legislation relating to GIOs.[1429]

Application for EUTM or national trade mark which is a protected GIO: relative grounds

3-907　　Article 8(4) EUTMR provides for a relative ground of opposition based on an earlier non-registered trade mark or other sign of more than mere local significance which confers on its proprietor the right to prohibit the use of a subsequent trade mark. Article 8(6) EUTMR provides a similar ground of opposition based on earlier EU or national PDOs and PGIs.

3-908　　In *IVDP v EUIPO*,[1430] in a cancellation application based on the predecessor provision to art.8(4), the General Court held that the Board of Appeal erred in not considering national laws protecting GIOs for wines as well as EU laws (in that case, Reg.491/2009 which amended Reg.1234/2007 (now replaced by Reg.1308/ 2013). In the case, the Cancellation Applicant argued that the registered mark PORT CHARLOTTE should be struck off the register because inter alia "porto" and "port" were protected under Portuguese law as geographic indications of origin. The Board of Appeal had found that the protection of designations of origin for wines was governed exclusively by Reg.491/2009 and rejected the argument that PORT CHARLOTTE evoked "porto" or "port". The General Court held that as regards the allegedly exhaustive nature of protection conferred by Reg.491/2009, this regulation could not be construed as being exhaustive in the sense that that protection could not be supplemented by another system of protection.[1431] It held that art.8(4) of Reg.207/2009 (the EUTMR) permitted reliance on national earlier rights and that a clear distinction could be drawn between rights protected under EU legislation and that under national law.[1432]

3-909　　In the author's view, the real point here is whether Portuguese GIO law protect-

---

[1427] art.14(1), second paragraph.
[1428] See para.3-889.
[1429] art.7.1(j)–(l) EUTMR. Article 4.1(i)–(k) TMD. See para.3-286.
[1430] (T–659/14) EU:T:2015:863.
[1431] See [44].
[1432] See [45].

ing "port" was unenforceable because Reg.491/2009 (the EU GIO wine legislation) exhaustively harmonised the law on protection of GIOs for wine. Whether EU GIO legislation is exhaustive is considered below.[1433] In *IVDP*, the General Court held that Reg.491/2009 was not exhaustive and permitted GIO national legislation.[1434] However, it did so by referring to Reg.207/2009 (the predecessor EUTMR) by saying that art.8(4) permits opposition based on earlier national rights.

However, this seems false logic. Whether or not Reg.491/2009 exhaustively harmonises GIOs for wine and thus excludes the protection of such GIOs via national legislation is a matter to be considered solely by reference to Reg.491/2009 and not EU trade mark legislation. Therefore, for the 2012 Regulation, the Court of Justice has found that it does exhaustively harmonise the law for PDOs, PGIs and TSGs and thus excludes the enforcement of national legislation which seeks to protect analogous GIOs.[1435] The real question should have been whether Reg.491/2009 was exhaustive so that analogous Portuguese GIO wine legislation was unenforceable. It is a false argument and a non sequitur to suggest that as the EUTMR protects enforceable national rights therefore Reg.491/2009 is not exhaustive. **3-910**

Earlier trade mark/later GIO

Finally, it should be noted that for a trade mark to be refused registration on absolute or relative grounds based on a GIO, the application for the trade mark must have been filed after the date of filing for the PDO or PGI.[1436] However, such does not apply vice versa, i.e. if the trade mark was applied for prior to the GIO being applied for. As discussed above, the only ground where a GIO can be objected to on the grounds of an earlier mark is if the earlier mark, by reason of the reputation, renown and length of time that the mark has been used, would mean that use of the GIO would be liable to be misled as to the true identity of the product.[1437] The focus is on the reputation of the earlier mark. Whether or not such is registered is irrelevant. Thus, there is an asymmetry between the 2012 Regulation and the EUTMR and TMD with registered trade marks being treated as the junior relation. **3-911**

However, to mitigate the impact of the above, the 2012 Regulation provides a defence against the enforcement of a PDO or PGI where the defendant uses a trade mark which was applied for, registered or established by use (i.e. an unregistered mark) prior to the date of application of the PDO or PGI. Nevertheless, for this defence to apply, the application, registration or use must have been made in good faith within the territory of the EU and there must be no grounds for invalidity or revocation of the trade mark under the TMD or EUTMR.[1438] If such conditions apply, then the PDO/PGI and trade mark will be allowed to co-exist in the marketplace.[1439] **3-912**

In *Gorgonzola/Cambozola*, discussed above, the CJEU considered the meaning of "good faith" in the context of the predecessor to art.14(2). It said that such a **3-913**

[1433] See para.3-914.
[1434] See [44].
[1435] See para.3-914.
[1436] arts 7, 8(6) EUTMR; art.14 2012 Regulation.
[1437] See para.3-888.
[1438] art.14(2) 2012 Regulation.
[1439] art.14(2), last sentence.

concept must be viewed in the light of both national and international law in force at the date of the application for the trade mark registration.

Interrelationship of EU and national legislation for GIOs

3-914   Member States have sought historically to protect GIOs via their own legislation. However, insofar as the subject-matter of such legislation falls within the subject-matter of the 2012 Regulation, it is unlawful as the latter is intended to be exhaustive and thus intended to exclude the continued existence of national legislation whose requirements might be less strict for such products.[1440]

3-915   An issue which has arisen in a number of cases is what geographical names and indications does the 2012 Regulation cover? This arose in the context of a predecessor of it, Reg.2081/92. In *Monts de Lacaune*[1441] the CJEU was concerned with a reference from the French criminal court where proceedings had been brought against individuals who managed salted meat manufacturing companies in the Tarn region of France for applying the words "*montagne*" and "*Monts de Lacaune*" to cooked meats without obtaining permission to use such "*appellations*" as required pursuant to French law. One of the questions referred to the court was whether French law was compatible with the predecessor regulation to Reg.510/2006 (Reg.2081/92). Article 13(2) of that regulation only permitted Member States to maintain their own equivalent national measures for a limited transitional period. After such a period, protection of "names of origin" and "indications of geographical origin" had to comply with the definitions as laid down in the regulation.

3-916   The CJEU held that there was no conflict between the French law which required "*montagne*" to be used only for produce from mountain areas (which was specifically defined) and Reg.2081/92, because the definition for "*montagne*" transcended national boundaries and did not denote a specific regional area. Thus, the national law limited itself to giving general protection to a name evoking in consumers qualities abstractly linked to the origin of products from mountain areas. This was held to be too far removed from the material objective of Reg.2081/92 for it to conflict with. Similarly, in *Warsteiner*, the CJEU held that Reg.2081/92 did not preclude the application of national legislation which prohibits the potentially misleading use of a geographical indication of source in the case of which there is no link between the characteristics of the produce and its geographical provenance.[1442] Importantly, the CJEU went on to say that the purpose of Reg.2081/92 could not be undermined by the application of national rules for the protection of geographical indications which did not fall within its scope.[1443] Thus, it seems tolerably clear that although in the declaratory part of its judgment the CJEU said that Reg.2081/92 did not prevent the application of national legislation which prohibited the potentially misleading use of a geographical indication of source where there was no link between the characteristics of the product and its geographical provenance, such

---

[1440] *Budejovický Budvar, národní podnik v Rudolf Ammersin* (C-478/07) [2009] E.C.R. I-7721 at [114]–[129] relating to a bilateral instrument between Austria and the former Czechoslovakia which sought to protect "Bud" as a protected designation for beer. See also *Fietje* (27/80) [1980] E.C.R. 3839 at [7] referred to in *Schutzverband gegen Unwesen in der Wirtschaft eV v Warsteiner Brauerei Haus Cramer GmbH & Co KG* (C-312/98) [2000] E.C.R. I-9187 at [41].

[1441] *Criminal proceedings against Jacques Pistre, Michle Barthes, Yves Milhau and Didier Oberti* (C-321–324/94) [1997] E.C.R. I-2343; [1998] E.T.M.R. 457.

[1442] *Schutzverband gegen Unwesen in der Wirtschaft eV v Warsteiner Brauerei Haus Cramer GmbH & Co KG* (C-312/98) [2000] E.C.R. I-9187 at [46] citing the 9th recital of Reg.2081/92.

[1443] See [49]–[50].

was merely an application of the general principle that geographical indications of origin that do not fall within the scope of EU PDO/PGI legislation can be protected by national legislation. Therefore, in *Budejovický Budvar, národní podnik v Rudolf Ammersin GmbH*,[1444] the CJEU held, following *Warsteiner*, that Reg.2081/92 did not preclude the protection of simple indications of geographical origin under national laws where those designations did not meet the conditions for registration under Reg.2081/92.[1445]

In a UK case, *Fage UK v Chobani UK*[1446] an action was brought for extended **3-917** passing off against a yoghurt manufacturer who sold yoghurt under the name "Greek yoghurt" but which had been made in the US. The claimant had sold yoghurt in UK which it imported from Greece under its trade mark FAGE and which it called Greek yoghurt. Extended passing off is a species of unfair competition law peculiar to the UK whereby a trader can bring an action that the defendant's use of a sign is liable to mislead a significant proportion of the public by use of a name or mark as to the quality or characteristics of the product. An argument was run that there was no room for the law of extended passing off in relation to geographical indications as the 2012 Regulation was exhaustive. The Court of Appeal of England and Wales said that the critical aspect was whether the geographical denomination in issue (i.e. Greek yoghurt) fell within the definition of PDO or PGI under the 2012 Regulation. The Court of Appeal said that there was no suggestion that Greek yoghurt met the requirement that its quality or characteristics were essentially due to any aspect of the environment in Greece. It thus was not a PDO. It then went on to consider whether it fell within the definition of PGI. The defendant argued that "Greek yoghurt" fell within the definition of PGI: it originated from Greece, its reputation of Greek yoghurt was essentially attributable to its Greek origin and at least one of the production steps was in Greece. However, the claimant held that the argument must fail because in order for a PGI to be registrable under the 2012 Regulation, the PGI must be used in the geographical area of origin and it must be registered in the languages which are or were historically used to describe the product in the area. It was common ground that the phrase "Greek yoghurt" had never been used in Greece and had no reputation there. The product was described in Greece by a term which meant "strained yoghurt". The Court of Appeal accepted this argument.

It will be noted that in *Fage v Chobani*, the real argument concerned the "scope" **3-918** of the 2012 Regulation. Did it mean that a product that satisfies the definition of PGI in art.5(2) falls within the scope of the Regulation even though it could not actually be registered because it failed to meet other registration requirements or was it sufficient that a product will not fall within the scope of the 2012 Regulation if it could not in fact be registered as a PGI. The Court of Appeal, applying *Warsteiner* and *Budejovický Budvar, národní podnik v Rudolf Ammersin GmbH*, held that the latter was the correct approach.[1447]

It might be thought that the above is somewhat surprising[1448]. After all, if one **3-919** takes the law of trade marks (where the Trade Marks Directive is intended to be an

---

[1444] (C-216/01) [2003] E.C.R. I-13617.

[1445] See [74].

[1446] *Fage UK Ltd v Chobani UK Ltd* [2014] E.T.M.R. 26 CA.

[1447] See, in particular, judgment of Lewison LJ, at [169]. In particular, the court relied upon *Warsteiner* at [49]–[51]: "... do not meet the conditions for registration under Reg.2081/92... ."

[1448] See C. Heath and D. Marie-Vivien, "Geographical Indications and the Principles of Trade Mark Law—A Distinctly European Perspective" IIC (2015) 46:819–842, at 839 ("the Court of Justice deci-

exhaustive harmonisation of the substantive law of trade marks within the EU), it would be a plainly hopeless argument to say that because a sign is unregistrable under the Trade Mark Directive, a national law which permits the registration of that sign as a trade mark (and its enforcement) is permissible. Therefore, one might ask why, as a matter of principle, is the fact that "Greek yoghurt" is not registrable under the 2012 Regulation (or its predecessors) means it can be protected under national laws when plainly is intended to be a PGI?

3-920   However, even the Trade Mark Directive permits the enforcement of laws similar to trade marks against signs used in course of trade, e.g. unfair competition or consumer protection laws regardless whether those signs are or are not registrable.[1449] Indeed, as stated by Lewison LJ in *Fage v Chobani*, it would be surprising if EU law were to prevent Member States for taking action against deceptive marketing.[1450] The law of extended passing off in the UK is a *specie* of unfair competition law. Thus, at a broad level, the distinction is that the law of extended passing off and other unfair competition laws are not sui generis national GIO legislation (which should be impermissible) but laws of broad application which are applicable as much to misleading geographical indications of origin as they are to wholly unrelated fields.

3-921   Finally, it should be noted that in late 2017, the Court of Justice held that the EU and not Member States has exclusive competency to accede to the Geneva Act of the Lisbon Agreement on GIOs.[1451] It accordingly annulled a Council Decision authorising the opening of negotiations on the Geneva Act. The Council said that its decision was based on Member States having shared competency with the EU.

Enforcement of PDOs and PGIs

3-922   Although the CJEU in the *Gorgonzola* case (discussed above) appeared to proceed on the basis that Reg.2081/92 (a predecessor to the 2012 Regulation) was directly enforceable, this was questioned in a decision of the House of Lords of England and Wales, *Consorzio Del Prosciutto di Parma v Asda Stores Ltd*,[1452] and a reference on this issue has been made to the CJEU. The facts of the case were unusual. The consortium of producers of Parma ham objected to the sale by Asda of sliced Parma ham. The term *"Prosciutto di Parma"* was registered as a PDO. The product specification (which detailed inter alia the manner in which the ham was to be sliced and packaged) was in Italian and was not published in any official community journal. By reason of this, the House of Lords could not agree on the issue as to whether the "Parma Ham" PDO meant that retailers were infringing the rights of the PDO owner by slicing and packaging the ham. However, it seems tolerably clear from the judgments of the House of Lords that if the PDO had been clear about the ambit of its monopoly, Reg.2082/91 would have been enforceable.[1453] The House of Lords referred the issue to the CJEU. In *Consorzio del Prosciutto di*

---

sions leads to arbitrary results in that subject matter than cannot be protected under Regulation 1151/2012 may fare better than subject matter that could".)

[1449] Recital 40 TMD.

[1450] See [173].

[1451] *European Commission and Parliament v Council of the European Union* (C-389/15) ECLI:EU:C:2017:798. For discussion of the competencies of Member States and EU and whether this is shared or not, see the Ch.1, para.1-115.

[1452] *Consorzio Del Prosciutto di Parma v Asda Stores Ltd* [2001] E.T.M.R. 53.

[1453] In particular, see [20]–[25] of Lord Hoffmann's judgment. Previously, claimants have relied upon labelling and name regulations as giving a directly enforceable right—e.g. *Taittinger SA v Allbev Ltd*

Parma v Asda Stores Ltd,[1454] the issue of direct enforceability was not part of the reference. The CJEU held that there was nothing to prevent technical characteristics such as slicing and dicing from being part of the PDO. Furthermore, it held that although such measures fell within art.34, they were justified under art.36. However, the CJEU held that as the requirement of slicing and dicing had not been given "adequate publicity" in EU legislation, it was unenforceable.[1455]

In the *Parmigiano* case, the CJEU said that the possibility of taking action for infringement of a PDO or PGI is not reserved to the holder of the PDO or PGI but is open to competitors, business associations and consumer organisations.[1456] The 2012 Regulation requires Member States to set up enforcement authorities to enforce it.[1457]   **3-923**

Practice and procedure for applying for PDOs/PGIs/TSGs

The 2012 Regulation sets out the procedure to be applied in applying for a PDO/PGI/TSG. The applicant needs to be made by a group of producers or processors (save in exceptional cases, a natural or legal person may apply).[1458]   **3-924**

In the case of PDOs and PGIs, the application form must set out a number of matters including: the name to be protected as a PDO or PGI; a description of the product including the raw materials and the principal physical, chemical, microbiological or organoleptic characteristics of the product; the definition of the relevant geographical area/evidence that the produce originates from the defined geographical area; a description of the method of obtaining the product; and details establishing the link between the quality or characteristics of the product, and where appropriate, the link between the given quality, reputation of other characteristics of the product and any specific labelling rules.[1459]   **3-925**

In the case of TSGs, the product specification is rather more limited. It must include: the name, a description of the product including its main physical, chemical, microbiological or organoleptic characteristics, showing the product's specific character and a description of the production method that the producers must follow, and the key elements establishing the product's traditional character.[1460]   **3-926**

The 2012 Regulation sets out a two-stage procedure whereby first, the application is made to a Member State and then if accepted, it is further scrutinised by the European Commission.[1461] An application may be made by groups "who works the   **3-927**

"*Elderflower Champagne*" [1993] F.S.R. 64 CA at 673 (right to use name "Champagne" as part of a non-alcoholic cordial made from elderflower).

[1454] *Consorzio del Prosciutto di Parma* [2003] E.C.R. I-5121; [2003] 2 C.M.L.R. 21; [2004] E.T.M.R. 23.

[1455] See also *Abadia Retuerta v EUIPO* (T-237/08) [2010] E.C.R. II-1583 where the General Court held that the fact that the geographical indication "*el Palomar*" for wines had not been published in the Official Journal in accordance with art.54(5) Reg.1493/99 (quality wines psr), was not fatal because the Spanish law designating *el Palomar* as a Spanish quality wine psr had been published in the Official Journal (even though the General Court accepted that such publication was hardly effective to ensure that the public was fully and completely informed of designated quality wines psr—see [102]).

[1456] See [64].

[1457] See art.13(2).

[1458] art.49.

[1459] art.7.

[1460] art.19.

[1461] arts 49–54.

products with the name to be registered".[1462] Where the PDO/PGI/TSG relates to a specific Member State, the application is made to the authorities of that Member State. The Member State then examines it and initiates a national objection procedure ensuring that the application is sufficiently publicised and allowing a reasonable period for objections from persons with a legitimate interest. If the application is then deemed acceptable, it is forwarded to the European Commission. If the application relates to a geographical area outside the EU, the Commission deals with it directly or through the authorities of that country. The Commission will then examine the application and if those conditions are met, publish it in the Official Journal or otherwise reject it. Within three months from the date of publication, any Member State, third countries or natural or legal persons with a legitimate interest may object to the registration. If there is opposition, the matter then proceeds to an adversarial stage with the Commission assisted by the Agricultural Product Quality Policy Committee. If successful, the name is entered on the register. The Commission or natural or legal persons with a legitimate interest may apply to cancel registrations.[1463]

3-928   EU Reg.664/2014 is the implementing regulation for the application for PDOs PGIs and TSGs.[1464]

EEA LEGISLATION

3-929   EFTA has adopted Dir.2008/95—the predecessor directive to the current TMD, being Dir.2015/2436—and such is in force.[1465] Thus Annex 17 of the EEA Agreement (the Intellectual Property Annex) has been amended accordingly.[1466] Directive 2015/2436 is under scrutiny[1467] and there is little reason to believe it will not be adopted. Because EUTMs do not extend to EFTA countries, the EU Trade Mark Regulation has not been adopted by EFTA.[1468] As regards the patchwork of EU GIO legislation, with the exception of Reg.1151/2012, these have been adopted by EFTA.[1469]

3-930   As EFTA has adopted Dir.2008/95, this means that there is an EEA-wide exhaustion of principle.[1470] This is important because the TMD does not itself (unlike the EUTMR) provide for an exhaustion of rights principle in the EEA. Thus, where trade-marked goods are marketed in a contracting state (i.e. an EU or EFTA state)

[1462] art.49.1. In exceptional circumstances, it may be made by a single person (art.49.2).

[1463] art.54.

[1464] [2014] OJ L179/17-22.

[1465] Joint Committee Decision 146/2009. This decision also simultaneously deleted para.4 of Annex XVII which related to Dir.89/104).

[1466] See para.9h Annex XVII, EEA Agreement amended pursuant to Decision 146/2009. This provides that Dir.2008/95 applies to EFTA but excludes the provisions relating to the EUTM as and until the EUTM extends to EFTA countries which currently it does not.

[1467] As of 5 May 2018 (see *http://www.efta.int/eea-lex/32015L2436* [Accessed 5 May 2018]).

[1468] However, the EUTMR now expressly provides for an EEA-wide exhaustion of rights principle. See para.3-590.

[1469] EFTA runs an online legal database at *http://www.efta.int/eea-lex* [Accessed 9 October 2017] which allows the user to check whether EFTA has adopted a EU legislative measure. The easiest way of doing so is by entering the EUR-LEX number of the EU legislative measure (see *http://eur-lex.europa.eu/homepage.html*).

[1470] Under Protocol 1 of the EEA Agreement, references to EU are deemed to be references to territories of the Contracting Parties of the EEA Agreement. Accordingly, the EU-wide exhaustion of rights principle in Dir.2008/95 becomes a EEA-wide exhaustion of rights principle by reason of Joint Committee Decision 146/2009. See also Art.2 Protocol 28, EEA Agreement.

by the proprietor or with their consent, the proprietor cannot enforce their national marks or EUTMs to prevent further movement of the goods in the EEA.[1471]

Initially, as held by the EFTA Court in *Mag Instrument*, EFTA states were free to introduce or retain a doctrine of international exhaustion of rights.[1472] However, 10 years later in *L'Oréal Norge* the EFTA Court changed its mind.[1473] Accordingly, there now exists as much a Fortress-EEA as there is a Fortress-EU when it comes to the lawfulness of importation of parallel imports of goods placed on the market outside the EEA.

3-931

[1471] See EEA section on Enforcement of Intellectual Property, at para.7-335, et seq.
[1472] See para.3-617.
[1473] See para.7-344.

CHAPTER 4

COPYRIGHT IN EUROPE

INTRODUCTION

Copyright restricts the use that can be made of a variety of protected works. As **4-001** indicated by the word "copyright" itself, one such restriction is the right to copy such works.[1] For any infringement to be established, it must be shown that the use complained of is derived either directly or indirectly from the copyright work alleged to be infringed. Independent origin is therefore a complete defence to any type of copyright infringement. Because of this, copyright is often described as a "qualified" monopoly[2] rather than an "absolute" monopoly such as a patent, registered design, trade mark or plant breeders' right.

Copyright arises automatically and without formality upon creation of an eligible[3] **4-002** work, generally once it is fixed in some material, reproducible form.[4] Therefore, while there may be considerable sums invested in the creation of a copyright work such as a film, no cost is associated with "copyrighting" it.

It is often argued that copyright rewards, and therefore stimulates, the creativity **4-003** of authors whilst protecting the investment made by entrepreneurs in works. These or similar justifications—which generally underpin the common law approach to copyright—are frequently deployed in relation to other intellectual property rights such as patents. Perhaps more distinctive of the copyright field, however, are personality-based or natural rights-based justifications. These emphasise the individuality of the copyright work as the manifest expression of the unique nature of its creator and thus the property of the creator. There is a tendency for this latter

---

[1] Reproduction of the copyright work without permission is one form of infringing act. Other acts that the owner of the copyright or related right may be able to restrict include the following: issuing copies to the public; communicating the work to the public; renting the work; lending the work; performing the work in public; or communicating the work to the public.

[2] Or not a "monopoly" at all: see K. Garnett, QC, G. Davies, and G. Harbottle, *Copinger and Skone James on Copyright*, 16th edn (London: Sweet & Maxwell, 2010), para.1–34.

[3] The requirements for eligibility, such as a requirement that a work be "original" in EU law, are discussed below at para.4-089.

[4] "It shall, however, be a matter for legislation in the countries of the Union to prescribe that works in general or any specified categories of works shall not be protected unless they have been fixed in some material form."—art.2(2) Berne Convention. For example, there may be a right to authorise or prohibit the recording of an unfixed performance.

variety of justification to provide the theoretical underpinnings for the award of strong rights over prolonged periods.

4-004   The nature and extent of copyright is complex and the potential subject-matter covered is vast. Copyright and its related rights encompass, for example, highly "authorial" works such as novels, plays, symphonies, paintings, and films, as well as less lofty subject-matter such as computer programs, sound recordings, performances, broadcasts, cable transmissions, typographical arrangements, and databases. A single product such as a video game will usually be subject to a complex array of copyrights and related rights, each of which may, in turn, be owned by different people or companies. Moreover, there will often be a plethora of licensing arrangements in place conferring various permissions upon various entities so that they may do particular things for certain periods within certain territories. Accordingly, exploitation can be extremely cumbersome. In addition, if the nature and scope of the relevant rights differ substantially from country to country, market partitioning (whether intentional or not) can easily occur.

4-005   Even prior to the coming into force of the harmonising measures described below, copyright protection existed in some form in all European countries. Harmonisation of a sort had been achieved by adherence to many of the minimum standards set out in the Berne Convention over its various revisions. In addition, the principle of national treatment set out in that Convention has mitigated some of the worst effects of international divergence over the nature and scope of copyright.[5]

4-006   Within the EU, the 1990s saw the Commission embark upon an active, though piecemeal, programme of harmonisation of Member States' laws in the area of copyright and related rights. The so-called "first generation"[6] of harmonisation measures of Member States' laws comprised six Directives covering a range of miscellaneous subject-matter such as computer programs, the duration of rights, rental rights (which also harmonised some forms of infringement, such as the distribution of phonograms, fixations of performances, films, and broadcasts[7]), satellite broadcasting, and databases. Significantly, this first generation were enacted in a substantially pre-Internet era. In the early 21st century, the EU Commission embarked upon a "second generation" of EU copyright harmonisation measures. In particular, it enacted the Information Society Directive,[8] which can be regarded as the first real step towards an EU copyright code. Other second-generation directives include the Artists Resale Directive and the Collective Rights Management Directive.

4-007   Although the second-generation measures were alive and took account of the Internet—in particular, by introducing a "making available" a copyright work on the Internet—the measures were still grounded in an analogue and not digital era.

4-008   The European Commission is now firmly alive to the digital era. It has adopted the Digital Single Market Strategy. The purpose of this strategy is to open up digital opportunities for people and businesses in the EU. There are three pillars to this strategy: (1) better access for consumers and businesses to digital goods and

---

5   For an analysis of the Berne Convention, see para.4-012.
6   J. Reinbothe, *"Recent Intellectual Property Legislative Developments in the European Union: Copyright and Related Rights"*, 9th Annual Conference on Intellectual Property Law and Policy, Fordham University, 19 April 2001.
7   art.9 of that Directive.
8   See para.4-264.

services across the EU, (2) creation of the right conditions and a level playing field for digital networks and innovative services to flourish, and (3) maximisation of the growth potential of the digital economy.[9]

As part of the Digital Single Market reforms, the European Commission has in 2015 and 2016, made a number of proposals which are intended to modernise EU copyright law so that it is fit for purpose for the digital online era. On 14 September 2016, it proposed two directives and two regulations to adapt EU copyright law to the realities of the Digital Single Market.[10] These proposals are somewhat of a "smorgasbord" of piecemeal changes to copyright law including:

4-009

- harmonising the "country of origin" principle for the provision of simulcasting and "catchup" online radio and TV programmes which have been (or in the case of simulcasting), are being broadcast;
- requiring holders of copyrights and related rights other than broadcasting organisations to exercise their rights as regards the "retransmission" right of television and radio programmes through a collective rights organisation;
- giving enhanced rights to news publishers as against news aggregators and online operators;
- laws relating to ISPs that host copyright works;
- allowing research organisations to carry out text and data mining for the purposes of scientific research;
- providing an exception for digital and cross border teaching activities;
- allowing cultural heritage institutions to make copies for the purpose of the preservation of works;
- making it easier for cultural heritage institutions to obtain licences for all rights in out-of-commerce works for the purpose of giving the public access to such works;
- ensuring that publishers of press publications are protected against digital use of their publications;
- authors and performers receive regular reports on the exploitation of their works from their licensees (including collective rights organisations); and
- mandatory exceptions allowing access to published works for persons who are blind, visually impaired or otherwise print disabled (pursuant to EU obligations under the Marrakesh Treaty).

These proposals cut across a number of differing areas of EU law not only copyright. Thus, they sit in a complex legal ecosystem which includes distance selling EU law and the Enforcement Directive. Indeed, as of October 2017, these proposals are being discussed by the European Parliament. In order to achieve their aims, these proposals envisage changes to existing directives. Whilst it is likely that these proposals will be enacted, it remains to be seen what amendments will be made to them as they go through the European Parliament. Rather than deal with these proposals which are likely to involve considerable amendment, it is thought better to deal with them once their wording is settled and the European Council approves them. Thus, it is likely that they will be discussed further in a supplement to this edition.

4-010

---

[9] *https://ec.europa.eu/digital-single-market/en/policies/shaping-digital-single-market* [Accessed 22 October 2017].

[10] *https://ec.europa.eu/digital-single-market/en/modernisation-eu-copyright-rules* [Accessed 22 October 2017].

4-011   This chapter begins by examining the various international conventions and the way they affect European copyright. It then goes on to analyse more EU-specific harmonisation measures.

INTERNATIONAL LEGISLATION

The Berne Convention

4-012   During the 19th century, the major industrial powers entered into a large number of bilateral agreements with each other and with third countries for the protection in those other countries of copyright in artistic and literary works of their nationals. However, such "bilateralism" led to undue complexity and uneven protection. It was apparent to most that a better solution was for a group of countries to ensure protection by way of a multilateral, international convention. On 5 December 1887, therefore, several countries[11] ratified the Berne Convention for the Protection of Literary and Artistic Works of 1886. Those countries to which the Berne Convention applies, the contracting states, were constituted into the Berne Union.[12] The fundamental principle of the Berne Convention was that contracting states would not discriminate between domestic authors and authors of other contracting states in respect of the level of protection they conferred on qualifying artistic and literary works. This is known as the principle of "national treatment". It provided, if not a substitute for harmonisation, then at least some mitigation of the worst effects of the divergence in national approaches to copyright. As a consequence, at least some protection was usually available, even if it differed in certain respects from that which the author might be able to obtain in their home country. Other essential objectives of the Berne Convention throughout its revisions have been to harmonise copyright laws in contracting states to some extent while allowing their protection and enforcement to remain a matter of national law, and to remove the need for formalities.

4-013   The Berne Convention has been revised several times since 1886. A full account of the legislative history of the Berne Convention is outside the scope of this book.[13] The following is a brief summary. The Convention was shortly followed by the Additional Act of Paris 1896, which was, in turn, followed by the revised Berne Convention of Berlin 1908 and further revisions at Rome in 1928, at Brussels in 1948, at Stockholm in 1967, and at Paris in 1971.[14] The Berlin revision was significant in its articulation of the principles of national treatment, national protection of rights and the principle of the absence of formalities. The Rome revision embodied the first recognition of moral rights as well as broadcasting rights. The Brussels revision introduced the *"droit de suite"* or artist's resale right.[15] The Stockholm revision introduced a Protocol Regarding Developing Countries pursuant to which those countries would be able to join the Berne Union but derogate from some of the major forms of protection if their domestic circumstances warranted it. These provisions were substantially altered in the Paris Act, which meant that the Paris revision became acceptable to most industrial countries. Accord-

---

11 Belgium, France, Haiti, Germany, Italy, Spain, Switzerland, Tunisia, and the UK.
12 art.1 Berne Convention.
13 See S. Ricketson and J. Ginsburg, *International Copyright and Neighbouring Rights: The Berne Convention and Beyond*, 2nd edn (New York: Oxford University Press, 2006).
14 Minor amendments to the Administrative Sections of the Paris version were made in 1979.
15 See para.4-362 on the Artists' Resale Right Directive.

ingly, many countries have now signed and ratified the Paris Act, including all EU countries and the US.

The essential provisions of the Berne Copyright Convention (Paris revision 1971) are set out as follows. **4-014**

Literary and artistic works

The Berne Convention provides that the rights of authors in literary and artistic works are to be protected in the countries which adhere to the convention.[16] "Literary and artistic works" include every production in the literary, scientific and artistic domain, whatever may be the mode or form of its expression.[17] Thus, the expression includes written material, lectures, dramatic work, choreographic works, musical compositions, cinematographic works, works of drawing, painting, architecture, sculpture, and photographic works.[18] It is, however, a matter for contracting states to decide whether all or any such works are protected only if they have been fixed in some material form.[19] **4-015**

Qualifying works

The protection of literary and artistic works under the Berne Convention is only extended to the works of those authors who are nationals of one of the countries which belong to the Berne Union (whether those works have been published or not) or to works which were either first published in a country of the Berne Union or simultaneously published in a country outside the Union and in a country of the Union (whether or not the author is a national of one of the contracting states).[20] Authors who are in habitual residence in a country of the Berne Union are, for the purposes of the Berne Convention, deemed to be nationals of that country.[21] With regard to the criteria of simultaneous publication, a work is considered to have been published simultaneously if it is published in two or more countries within 30 days of its first publication.[22] **4-016**

Principle of national treatment

The Berne Convention provides that works qualifying for protection under the Convention receive the same protection in each contracting state as works of authors from that contracting state.[23] Thus, the Convention prevents contracting states from discriminating against foreign authors of qualifying works. Furthermore, such a state may not make this protection dependent on the existence of protection in the country of origin of the work.[24] Protection in the country of origin is governed by domestic law.[25] "Country of origin" is deemed to be the country where the work was first published if the country is a contracting state, or if first published outside **4-017**

---

[16] arts 1, 2(6), 3, and 5(1).
[17] art.2(1).
[18] art.2(1).
[19] art.2(2).
[20] art.3(1).
[21] art.3(2).
[22] art.3(4).
[23] art.5(1) and art.5(3).
[24] art.5(2).
[25] art.5(3).

the Berne Union, the contracting state where the author is a national or habitually resident.[26] The cumulative effect of the above principles being applicable in all countries of the Berne Union is that the protection afforded to a qualifying work will depend on the domestic copyright law of the contracting state where protection is sought, provided that the author is a national of a country adhering to the Berne Convention or the work was first published in such a country.

4-018   There are four important derogations from the above principle. First, the protection of works of applied art and industrial designs can be limited to that available in the country of origin.[27] Secondly, where a non-contracting state fails to provide adequate protection for the works of an author of a contracting state, the latter may restrict protection conferred under the Berne Convention to the works of authors who are nationals of that non-contracting state and not habitually resident in a Berne Union state. For instance, where an author of a non-contracting state first publishes their work in a contracting state, such a work would normally qualify for protection under the Convention. However, any contracting state may restrict protection to such work if the non-contracting state does not confer reciprocal protection for works of that contracting state. Furthermore, if the contracting state where the work was first published avails itself of this right, then other contracting states can similarly restrict protection to such a work, regardless of whether works of their own nationals are protected adequately in the non-contracting state.[28] Thirdly, the length of protection in a Berne Union country need not exceed that available in the country of origin.[29] Fourthly, the inalienable right of authors (or, if they are dead, their personal representatives) to enjoy an interest in any subsequent sale of original works of art or manuscripts granted by the Berne Convention (commonly known by the French "*droite de suite*") may be limited to that available in the country to which the author belongs.[30] Such derogations are problematic within the EU, as they potentially discriminate between nationals of different Member States.[31]

---

[26] If neither of these conditions applies, then the work is not a work which qualifies for protection under the Berne Convention—see Qualifying Works at para.4-016.

[27] art.2(7).

[28] art.6. This derogation was only used by Canada and is not practically without importance.

[29] art.7(8).

[30] art.14*ter*. Accordingly, prior to the Artists' Resale Right Directive (see para.4-362) which imposes a resale right throughout the EU, a UK artist could not claim a resale right in respect of a sale of their work in France because the UK had no resale right.

[31] *Phil Collins v Imtrat Handelsgesellschaft GmbH* (C-92/92) [1993] E.C.R. I-5145, [1993] 3 C.M.L.R. 773, though see the discussion by Mout-Bouwman concerning the Netherlands Hoge Raad ruling in *Cassina v Sedeti* [2000] Rvd.W. 141 (HR (NL)) in "Netherlands: Copyright-Phil Collins Revisited" [2001] E.I.P.R. N84–86. See also I.W. VerLoren van Themaat and H.W. Wefers Bettink, "Another Side of the Story" [1995] 17 E.I.P.R. 307, where the authors argue that art.307 (ex-art.234) of the TFEU (which protects and upholds rights and obligations arising from treaties entered into prior to the Treaty of Rome coming into force between one or more Member States and one or more third countries) should apply, and that therefore the Berne Convention should take precedence where the relevant Article predates the Member State's accession and ratification of the EC Treaty. See also *Land Hessen v G. Ricordi & Co Bühnen- und Musikverlag GmbH* (C-360/00) [2002] E.C.R. I-5089 (art.6 EC Treaty (prohibition of discrimination) precluded a legislative measure of a Member State whereby the term of protection depended on whether the author of artistic works was a German national or not).

Term of protection

The Berne Convention provides that the minimum term of copyright is the life **4-019** of the author and 50 years after their death.[32] Contracting states may grant a term of protection in excess of such a period.[33] For various specific types of works, there are derogations from this general principle. For a cinematographic work (meaning, in the context of the Berne Convention[34] the work that accrues to an author as a consequence of their creation of an original work, not the work that arises through the first fixation of a film), the Berne Convention permits Member States to provide that the term of protection shall expire 50 years after the work has been made available to the public with the consent of the author or, if the cinematographic work is not made available within 50 years from its making, then the term of protection is 50 years after the making.[35] For photographic works and works of applied art, the Berne Convention allows Member States to provide for a minimum of 25 years' protection but leaves it to national law to fix an upper limit.[36] Time runs from the first of January of the year following the author's death or other relevant event.[37] In relation to every type of work, the Convention permits signatories to grant longer terms of protection than the minimum it requires.[38]

Translations

Translations, adaptations, arrangements of music and other alterations of a liter- **4-020** ary or artistic work are protected under the Berne Convention as original works but this is without prejudice to the copyright in the original work.[39] Given the international dimensions of the Convention, this is an important right.

Collections

Collections of literary or artistic works such as encyclopaedias, anthologies, **4-021** which "by reason of the selection and arrangement of their contents constitute intellectual creations"[40] are protected per se under the Berne Convention but, again, are protected without prejudice to the copyright in the works forming part of such collections.[41] Moreover, it is of interest that WIPO's view is that products of the original selection of data and/or other material not protected by copyright are protected under art.2(1) as original works.[42]

---

[32] art.7(1). In the case of joint authorship, the relevant date is 50 years from the death of the last surviving author—art.7bis.
[33] art.7(6). In the EU this is now life of the author and 70 years after their death: see the Term Directive at para.4-203.
[34] art.14bis.
[35] art.7(2).
[36] art.7(4).
[37] art.7(5).
[38] art.7(6).
[39] art.2(3).
[40] This originality standard has now been adopted by the Court of Justice for all copyright works: see para.4-089.
[41] art.2(5).
[42] *Industrial Property and Copyright* (WIPO, May 1996), p.69, para.40.

Cinematographic works

4-022   Cinematographic works are protected under the Berne Convention as original works.[43] Such a right is separate from the copyright in any underlying work from which a film is derived, for example a novel, play, treatment or script, and also separate from any of the other copyrights which may be embodied in a film, such as the rights in the music. The issue of ownership of copyright in such a work is a matter of domestic legislation in the country where protection is claimed.[44] The Berne Convention also provides that in countries where authorship is attributed to those who have contributed to the cinematographic work, such authors may not object, in the absence of any contrary or special stipulation, to the exploitation of the work.[45]

Exclusive rights

4-023   The Convention provides authors of qualifying works with a number of exclusive rights relating to works protected by the Convention.

Reproductive translation and adaptation right

4-024   The Berne Convention confers on authors, in relation to literary and artistic works, an exclusive right to authorise the reproduction of their works in any manner and form, and to authorise the translation of their works throughout the term of protection of their rights in the original works.[46] This expressly includes the right to make a visual or sound recording.[47] Importantly, the Berne Convention permits reproduction in certain special cases provided that such reproduction does not "conflict with a normal exploitation of the work and does not unreasonably prejudice the legitimate interests of the author".[48] The expression "literary and artistic works" is defined very widely and in particular includes musical works.[49] It should be noted that there is no distribution right specifically provided for of copies of literary and artistic works. This is contrast with other treaties, e.g. the WIPO Copyright Treaty.[50]

Cinematographic rights

4-025   As well as the basic reproduction right, authors of literary and artistic works that qualify for protection under the Berne Convention enjoy exclusive rights to authorise the cinematographic adaptation and reproduction of their works; the

---

[43]   art.14*bis*.
[44]   art.14*bis*(2)(a).
[45]   art.14*bis*(2)(b).
[46]   arts 8 and 9 and in relation to adaptation right, art.12.
[47]   art.9(3). However, art.13 permits contracting states to impose reservation on the right of an author of a musical work to authorise the recording of that work, provided such does not prevent the author from receiving equitable remuneration.
[48]   art.9(2).
[49]   art.2(1). See Literary and artistic works at para.4-015.
[50]   See para.4-064.

distribution of such works and the public performance and communication to the public by wire (e.g. cable transmission) of such works thus adapted or produced.[51]

Public performance of dramatic, dramatico-musical and musical works

Authors of dramatic, dramatico-musical and musical works enjoy the exclusive right of authorising any public performance of their works and any communication to the public of such performances of their works.[52]

4-026

Broadcasting rights

Authors of literary and artistic works enjoy the exclusive right to authorise any broadcast of their protected works.[53] This includes the communication by wire (e.g. cable transmission) of any broadcast and the public performance of a broadcast over speakers or an analogous means that displays images (e.g. a TV screen).[54] It should be mentioned that countries have a right to determine the conditions under which the broadcasting rights are exercised, but such must not prevent the author of the work obtaining equitable remuneration.[55]

4-027

Recitation right

Authors of literary works enjoy the exclusive right of authorising any public recitation of their works or any communication to the public of the recitation of their works.[56]

4-028

Moral rights

The Berne Convention provides that, independently of the "economic" rights mentioned above, the author of literary or artistic work has certain "moral" rights, namely the right to claim authorship of their works and to object to any distortion, mutilation, modification or other derogatory action in relation to their works which will be prejudicial to the author's honour or reputation.[57] Furthermore, the Berne Convention provides that such moral rights can be enforced after the death of the author by those responsible under local laws for the enforcement of copyright protection.[58] The means of safeguarding such rights is left to the legislation of contracting states.[59]

4-029

Exceptions and the "three-step" test

The Berne Convention provides that contracting states may permit certain exceptions to the exclusive right of reproduction conferred on the author, but they may

4-030

---

[51] art.14.
[52] art.11.
[53] art.11*bis*.
[54] art.11*bis*.
[55] art.11*bis*(2).
[56] art.11*ter*.
[57] art.6*bis*(1).
[58] art.6*bis*(2).
[59] art.6*bis*(3). In the UK, prior to ss.77–83 of the CDPA 1988, this was sought to be achieved mainly through the law of passing off and defamation as well as the limited protection for artistic works under Copyright Act 1956 s.43.

only do so subject to what has become known as the "three-step" test. Under the test, exceptions (i.e. defences) to liability are permissible only if: (Step 1) they are confined to "certain special cases"; (Step 2) they do not conflict with a normal exploitation of the work; and (Step 3) they do not unreasonably prejudice the legitimate interest of the author.[60] The "three-step" test has gained increasing currency in both international and European copyright legislation over recent years.[61]

4-031   The Convention makes particular provision for the making of quotations for newspaper articles and press summaries from a work which has been already published, providing such is compatible with fair practice, does not exceed that justified by its purposes, and provided the source and original author are identified.[62] This should be distinguished from "news of the day" or "miscellaneous facts having the character of mere items of press information", which do not attract copyright in the first place.[63] The Convention also provides for the use of literary or artistic works for teaching purposes, provided such use is compatible with fair practice.[64] Finally, the Convention permits contracting states to allow the reproduction, the broadcasting or the communication to the public of literary and artistic works in the press or in periodicals where they relate to current economic, political or religious topics.[65] In such a case, the source of the article must always be clearly indicated.

"Droit de suite" in works of art and manuscripts

4-032   The Berne Convention also provides that, in respect of original works of art and manuscripts of writers and composers, the creator, or after the creator's death, those specified by the law of contracting states, shall enjoy the inalienable right to an "interest" (that is, a pecuniary interest rather than the right to prevent the sale or any "moral"-type right) in any resale of the work subsequent to the first transfer by the creator.[66] The amounts recoupable and the procedure for collecting them is left to the law of contracting states.[67] The right depends on reciprocity under the Convention. Authors who belong to a country where there is no such right are not permitted to claim it in a country which has introduced it.[68]

---

[60] art.9(2). For a discussion of the three-step test and the WTO Panel ruling in *Re United States (Music Licensing)* WT/DS160/R see P. Johnson, "One Small Step or a Giant Leap" 2004 E.I.P.R. 26(6), 265–272, and D. Brennan, "The Three-Step Test Frenzy-Why the TRIPS Panel Decision Might be Considered per incuriam" (2002) 2 I.P.Q. 212.

[61] For example, art.13 TRIPS, art.10 WIPO Copyright Treaty ("WCT"), art.16 WIPO Performances and Phonograms Treaty ("WPPT"), art.6(3) Computer Programs Directive, art.6(3) Database Directive, and art.5(5) Information Society Directive.

[62] art.10.

[63] art.2(8).

[64] art.10(2).

[65] art.10*bis*.

[66] art.14*ter*(1). See the Artists' Resale Right Directive, below at para.4-362, which draws the right more narrowly than the Berne Convention. The Directive only covers art works and there is a notable exception in relation to private sales.

[67] art.14*ter*(3).

[68] art.14*ter*(2).

Presumption of authorship and infringement proceedings

The Berne Convention provides for a presumption that the author of a literary **4-033** or artistic work is the person whose name appears on the work in the usual manner.[69] Similarly, in relation to cinematographic works, the person or body corporate whose name appears on such a work is, unless otherwise proved, presumed to be the maker of the said work.[70] The above is only a presumption and evidence can be adduced to prove the contrary. The Berne Convention provides specifically that infringing copies of the work shall be liable to seizure in any country of the Union.[71]

Retrospective effect of the Berne Convention

The Berne Convention applies to all works which at the moment of the Conven- **4-034** tion coming into force in a contracting state have not fallen into the public domain in the country of origin through the expiry of the term of protection.[72]

Minimum protection under the Berne Convention

The Berne Convention focuses on minimum, rather than maximum, standards of **4-035** protection. Accordingly, it is left open to contracting states to legislate in order that a certain right or certain subject-matter is given greater protection than the Convention requires.[73] This is complemented by the provision that allows contracting states to enter into "special agreements" among themselves in order to grant such greater protection.[74] Within the EU, the harmonising copyright Directives are examples of such agreements. The WIPO Copyright Treaty (WCT)[75] is another example of a special agreement.

Miscellaneous provisions

The Berne Convention provides for an assembly, executive committee and a **4-036** financial budget. Such administrative functions are generally performed by the International Bureau of WIPO. There are also various provisions as to ratification of the Berne Convention.[76]

The Universal Copyright Convention

The Universal Copyright Convention was signed at Geneva on 6 September **4-037** 1952, came into force on 16 September 1955, and was further revised at Paris in 1971. It is administered by UNESCO. Its original purpose was to provide a bridge between the Berne Convention countries and the Pan-American Convention countries. In particular, it permitted the US and Berne Members to be parties to a common instrument, whilst permitting the US to keep its (then subsisting) formality provisions regarding copyright. In recent years, the accession to the Berne

---

[69] art.15(1).
[70] art.15(2).
[71] art.16.
[72] art.18(1).
[73] art.19.
[74] art.20.
[75] See commentary on the WCT at para.4-061.
[76] art.22, et seq.

Convention of the US, the Russian Federation and many Latin-American countries has reduced the importance of the Universal Copyright Convention. Its applicability in Europe was, in any event, always limited because it is expressed not to affect the provisions of the Berne Convention.[77] In particular, it is expressed not to apply to relationships among countries of the Berne Union in so far as it relates to the protection of works having as their country of origin, within the meaning of the Berne Convention, a country of the Berne Union.[78] It is thus only relevant to works which have not been published in a Berne Union country and whose authors are not nationals or resident in a Berne Union state. It provides less protection than the Berne Convention as regards duration of copyright, the subject-matter protected and the extent of protection. Its most notable contribution was to provide that works of authors of another contracting state were to be afforded protection without formality, provided that all copies bore the copyright symbol © accompanied by the name of the copyright proprietor and the year of first publication placed in such a manner and location so as to give reasonable notice of claim of copyright.[79]

The Rome Convention and the Phonograms Convention

4-038   The Berne Convention covered literary and artistic works[80] but did not make any provision for performers, producers of phonograms or broadcasters. With the development of sound recording, cinematographic and broadcasting technology during the 20th century, performers in particular had grown increasingly wary that their live performances were being replaced by fixations of their earlier performances which could be played repeatedly in public places such as bars, cafes and dance halls without further remuneration being paid to them. Accordingly, and in the face of some resistance from authors (who were concerned that the introduction of such rights might make the exercise of their own rights unwieldy or less profitable) the Convention for the Protection of Performers, Producers of Phonograms and Broadcasting Organisations was signed at Rome on 26 October 1961. As of 1st May 2018, the Rome Convention had 93 Contracting Parties.[81] The US is not a signatory.

4-039   The Rome Convention was, in a sense, more ambitious than the Berne Convention in that it attempted to introduce new rights in a wholesale manner, rather than simply to reflect the pre-existing legislation of contracting states. The rights introduced by the Rome Convention are generally termed "neighbouring rights" ("*droits voisins*") or "related rights"[82] in that the relevant works will normally incorporate artistic or literary works which may be protected under copyright proper, and for which the performer, producer, etc. will require permission from the author. To ensure that there is no ambiguity in this regard, the Rome Convention is expressed so as to be without prejudice to the protection of copyright in literary

---

[77]   art.XVII Universal Copyright Convention.
[78]   Appendix Declaration concerning art.XVII.
[79]   art.III.
[80]   See para.4-012 for the Berne Convention definition of such works.
[81]   See *http://www.wipo.int/treaties/en/* [Accessed 1 May 2018] for a current list. For a thorough review of the origins of the Rome Convention, see Professor G. Davies, "The Origins of the Rome Convention" *Zeitschrift für Geistiges Eigentum* Bard 9, 2017, 125–134.
[82]   The latter term is preferred by the European Commission and finds its way into various EU Directives. Accordingly it is the term used throughout this chapter.

and artistic works.[83] Thus, the Rome Convention introduced a new "layer" of rights which will often "sit" on top of rights in literary and artistic works. However, this is not true in all cases. Thus, a performer will have a performance right in an improvised live performance which is not itself a performance of, e.g. a dramatic work. Similarly, a broadcast may be of a live or current event as opposed to, e.g. a broadcast of a performance of a dramatic work or cinematographic work. The Rome Convention not only obliges contracting states to protect performers, producers of phonograms and broadcasters but art.2 also requires each contracting state to confer the same rights to nationals of other contracting states as it does to its own—this is called "national treatment".

Though there was a broad consensus on the need to confer protection on sound recordings, initially many countries had misgivings over the introduction of performers' and broadcasting rights and thus refused to sign up to the Rome Convention. Indeed, by 1970, nine years after its creation, the number of signatories to the Rome Convention was a mere 10.[84] The need to protect phonograms was paramount. Accordingly a second Convention, devoted only to phonograms, came into being. The Phonograms Convention (as it is commonly known) was signed at Geneva on 29 October 1971. Ironically, after its introduction, the resistance to the introduction to performers' rights and broadcasting rights disappeared such that there are now less signatories to the Phonograms Convention than there are to the Rome Convention.[85] However, importantly, the US is a signatory to the Phonograms Convention. The Phonograms Convention broadly incorporates the provisions of the Rome Convention for sound recordings.[86]   **4-040**

Performers' rights

Protection for performers[87] under the Rome Convention focuses on "bootlegging"-type activities, i.e. the fixation of performances without their consent; the broadcasting and communication to the public of "live" performances made without their consent and the reproduction of fixations of their performance, without their consent, if the original fixation was made without their consent or the reproduction was made for purposes different from those for which the performers gave consent.[88] Thus, apart from this final provision ("different purposes"), performers have no secondary rights to control the exploitation of fixations of their performances which were made with their consent. Indeed, in partial derogation from the "different purposes" provision, the Rome Convention expressly stipulates that once a performer has consented to the incorporation of their performance in a visual or audio-visual medium (i.e. films), they cannot prevent any further use of that performance.[89]   **4-041**

Contracting states must grant "national treatment" to a performance which took   **4-042**

---

[83] art.1 Rome Convention.

[84] See *http://www.wipo.int/treaties/en/StatsResults.jsp?treaty_id=17&lang=en* [Accessed 22 July 2014].

[85] As of 1 May 2018, there were 79 signatories to the Phonograms Convention and 93 to the Rome Convention. By 2000, there were more signatories to the Rome Convention than for the Phonograms Convention (67 vs. 64)—cf. in 1990, this figure was 34 vs. 42.

[86] There are some differences discussed below at para.4-048.

[87] art.2(1)(a). "Performers" is widely defined as including any one who performs an artistic or literary work—art.3(a). However, contracting states may extend performers' rights to artistes who do not perform literary or artistic works (i.e. impromptu performances)—art.9.

[88] art.7.

[89] art.19. This provision is entitled "Performers' Rights in Films" and is expressed to be "notwithstand-

place in another contracting state,[90] to performances incorporated in a phonogram which is protected under the Convention,[91] and unfixed performances which are carried by a broadcast which is protected under the Convention.[92]

4-043   The term of protection lasts for 20 years from the date of the performance, or, if fixed in a phonogram, 20 years from the date of fixation.[93]

Rights of producers of phonograms

4-044   Under the Rome Convention, each contracting state must give "national treatment" to phonograms[94] which fulfil any of the following conditions:

    (a)   were produced by the national of another contracting state;

    (b)   were first fixed in another contracting state (criterion of fixation); or

    (c)   were first published in another contracting state (criterion of publication) in the same manner as phonograms made by its own nationals and first fixed or published in its own territory.[95]

4-045   Producers of phonograms (who are defined as the legal entity or person who first fixes the sound of a performance or other sound[96]) have the exclusive right to authorise or prohibit the direct or indirect reproduction of their phonograms.[97]

4-046   The Rome Convention deems any national legislative measure relating to formality of protection of phonograms to be complied with where the sound recording bears the phonogram symbol (P) accompanied by the year of the first publication placed in such manner as to give reasonable notice of a claim of protection, and must also bear the names of the producer or owners of the phonogram rights together with the names of the principal performers or the owner of their rights.[98]

Equitable remuneration for performers and phonogram producers

4-047   Importantly, the Rome Convention provides that where the phonogram is used directly for broadcasting or for any communication to the public, contracting parties may permit for the payment by the user of a single equitable remuneration to the performers or to the producers of the phonogram or both.[99] The term of protection is a minimum of 20 years from the date of fixation of the phonogram.[100]

---

ing anything in this Convention". Thus, it would override art.7.1(c)(ii) ("the different purposes" provision). In other words, art.7.1(c)(ii) will apply only to mere audio fixations of performances (i.e. sound recordings).

[90]   art.4(a). For "national treatment", see para.4-039.

[91]   art.4(b).

[92]   art.4(c).

[93]   art.14(b).

[94]   Defined as any exclusively aural fixation of sounds: art.3(b). For "national treatment", see para.4-039.

[95]   arts 2 and 5. A phonogram is deemed first published in a contracting state if it is published within 30 days of first publication in a non-contracting state—art.5(2). Contracting states may declare that either the criterion of fixation or the criterion of publication do not apply (but not both)—art.5(3).

[96]   art.3(c).

[97]   art.10.

[98]   art.11.

[99]   art.12. NB. contracting states can derogate from this provision—art.16.

[100]   art.14(a).

Rome Convention and Phonogram Conventions: differences

The provisions of the Phonograms Convention are less ambitious than the Rome **4-048**
Convention. The notable differences are as follows. First, the Phonograms Convention provides for an importation and distribution right of phonograms whereas the Rome Convention does not.[101] Secondly, it allows the contracting state to decide how such protection should be afforded under national law; such protection does not necessarily have to be by way of copyright.[102] Thirdly, under the Phonograms Convention, contracting parties can determine that the length of protection, whilst being a minimum of 20 years, can be calculated from either the date of fixation or the year in which the phonogram was first published.[103] Fourthly, there is no equivalent provision to the "single equitable remuneration" right.[104]

Rights of broadcasting organisations

In relation to broadcasts,[105] the Rome Convention provides that each contract- **4-049**
ing state is to provide "national treatment" under its laws to broadcasting organisations, situated in another contracting state or broadcast from a transmitter in another contracting state, as it would to domestic broadcasts by domestic organisations.[106] Contracting states can provide that such protection is only to be given where the transmitter and broadcasting organisation are situated in the same contracting state.[107] Broadcasting organisations have the right to authorise or prohibit the re-broadcasting of their broadcasts; the fixation of their broadcasts or the reproduction of unauthorised fixations of their broadcasts or the communication to public of their broadcasts if such communication is made in places accessible to the public against payment of an entrance fee.[108] The term of protection is (as with phonograms) fixed for a minimum period of 20 years from the date that the broadcast took place.[109]

Defences

Contracting states may make the rights introduced by the Rome Convention **4-050**
subject to exceptions on the grounds of, among other things, private use, reporting current events, teaching and research.[110] In addition, any other "fair dealing"—or "fair use"—type defences already applicable to the literary and artistic works in the law of contracting states are permitted to be applied to the rights introduced by the Rome Convention, provided that they are compatible with it.[111]

---

[101] art.2 Phonograms Convention.
[102] art.3.
[103] art.4 Phonograms Convention (cf. the Rome Convention, where it is only from the date of fixation).
[104] Although this has less effect because of the ability, exercised by many states, to derogate from this provision pursuant to art.16 Rome Convention—see fn.99.
[105] art.3(f) Rome Convention. The relevant definition, "the transmission by wireless means for public reception of sound or of images and sounds" excludes cable—though probably not satellite—transmission.
[106] arts 2 and 6(1).
[107] art.6(2).
[108] art.13.
[109] art.14(c).
[110] art.15.
[111] art.15(2).

The TRIPS Agreement

4-051   In 1986, at the prompting of the US, intellectual property was brought within the realm of the General Agreement on Tariffs and Trade (GATT) system and negotiations commenced concerning international "trade-related aspects of intellectual property rights". On 15 April 1994 the Uruguay Round of negotiations concluded with the signing, in Marrakesh, of the Final Act Embodying the Results of the Uruguay Round of Multilateral Trade Negotiations, which contained a number of agreements, including both the World Trade Organization Agreement (establishing the WTO) and the Agreement on Trade-Related Aspects of Intellectual Property Rights (known as the TRIPS agreement).

Substantive rights

4-052   TRIPS covers many areas of intellectual property, including trade marks, geographical indications, patents, designs and undisclosed information, as well as related areas such as the control of anti-competitive practices in licences.[112] It also covers copyright and related rights. Fundamentally, in the field of copyright it requires WTO members to comply with arts 1–21 of the Berne Convention (Paris Act of 1971) and the Appendix thereto, with the exception of the Berne provisions relating to moral rights.[113] The EU is itself a member of TRIPS and as a result, in accordance with EU law, as TRIPS legislates in the field of copyright, it is necessary to interpret EU copyright legislation in the light and purpose of the Berne Convention.[114] Member States are not required to comply with the Rome Convention,[115] though there are quite similar provisions concerning performances, sound recordings and broadcasts.[116]

4-053   TRIPS sets basic standards which WTO Member States are required to implement into their domestic law according to their own legal systems. TRIPS also embodies the familiar Berne concept of "national treatment"[117] (that is, the principle according to which the same rights are granted to nationals of other Member States as are granted to one's own nationals) except with respect to the Rome Convention rights.[118] In addition, TRIPS embodies the concept of "most-favoured-nation treatment". Under this provision, subject to certain exceptions, any advantage, favour, privilege or immunity granted to one Member State to any other country must be granted to all other WTO Member States.[119] Because the Berne Convention is comprehensive in relation to "traditional" copyright (e.g. protection for literary, artistic and musical works), TRIPS, having incorporated the Berne Convention into it, effectively "fine-tunes" it by updating it to take account of new technology (e.g. computer programs and databases) and also to emphasise certain well established legal principles.

4-054   Thus, the idea/expression dichotomy, a familiar notion to common law copyright lawyers, is enshrined in art.9(2) of TRIPS, which states:

---

[112] art.40. For discussion of TRIPS, see the Ch.1, para.1-167
[113] art.9 TRIPS.
[114] See para.1-180. See also *SGAE v Rafael Hoteles SA* (C-306/05) [2006] E.C.R. I-11519; [2007] E.C.D.R. 2 at [3]–[10].
[115] Without prejudice to the existing obligations they may have under it: art.2(2).
[116] art.14.
[117] art.3. See para.4-017.
[118] For these, national treatment only applies in so far as such rights exist within TRIPS itself.
[119] art.4.

"Copyright protection shall extend to expressions and not to ideas, procedures, methods of operation or mathematical concepts as such."

In addition to the Berne rights, TRIPS makes provision for the protection of computer programs as literary works within the meaning of the Berne Convention, and for compilations of data or other material which "by reason of the selection of arrangement of their contents constitute intellectual creations."[120] There is also a qualified rental right in relation to computer programs, films and sound recordings.[121]   **4-055**

TRIPS provides that the duration of any rights in the copyright field not measured by reference to a natural person's life should be 50 years from the end of the calendar year of authorised publication, or, failing such authorised publication within 50 years from the making of the work, 50 years from the end of the calendar year in which the work was made.[122]   **4-056**

In contrast to the Berne Convention, TRIPS also contains detailed standards concerning civil procedure and remedies. It includes, in particular, provisions relating to evidence, injunctions, damages, disposal, obliteration, and obtaining information concerning the identities of third party infringers.[123]   **4-057**

Any Member State can complain to the WTO concerning the failure by another Member State to comply with its TRIPS obligations.[124] The WTO's dispute resolution procedure can lead, ultimately, to trade sanctions.[125] Under the Berne Convention, by contrast, there were no sanctions for non-compliance and the only remedy lay in an adverse ruling from the International Court of Justice as to the legality or otherwise of the compliance.   **4-058**

All WTO Member States are automatically Member States for the purposes of the TRIPS Agreement.   **4-059**

Defences and exceptions

All limitations and exceptions to the rights conferred under TRIPS are required to satisfy the Berne Convention "three-step" test,[126] that is, that they be: (1) "special cases", which (2) "do not conflict with a normal exploitation of the work in question", and (3) "do not unreasonably prejudice the legitimate interests of the right holder."[127] This extends the three-step test under the Berne Convention, under which only exceptions to the reproduction right are subject to such requirements.[128]   **4-060**

The WIPO Copyright Treaty and the WIPO Performances and Phonograms Treaty

By the mid-1990s, internet use had become more widespread and its potential as a means of copying and disseminating copyright works became more of a concern   **4-061**

---

[120] art.10.

[121] art.11, art.14(4).

[122] art.12.

[123] arts 42–61.

[124] For the position concerning the place of TRIPS in EU law, see para.1-180.

[125] Some might view such sanctions as disproportionate in circumstances where international institutions are less democratic than domestic ones: see, e.g. P. Gerhart, "Why Lawmaking for Global Intellectual Property is Unbalanced" [2000] E.I.P.R. 309.

[126] See para.4-030.

[127] art.13.

[128] art.9 Berne Convention.

to right holders. Accordingly, pressure grew for international regulation covering the exploitation of works in the online and digital environments.[129] On 20 December 1996, two new international treaties were adopted through the World Intellectual Property Organization (WIPO), namely, the WIPO Copyright Treaty ("WCT") and the WIPO Performances and Phonograms Treaty ("WPPT"). As of 1 May 2018, there were 96 contracting parties to both the WCT and WPPT.[130]

4-062   Importantly, unlike the Berne Convention, which does not permit any entity other than a country to sign it, the WCT and WPPT do. Accordingly, in 1996, the EU became a contracting party of the WCT and WPPT. Under the WCT, contracting parties are required to comply with arts 1–21 and the Appendix of the Berne Convention.[131] Thus, by an indirect route, the EU must apply the Berne Convention. This means that EU legislation in the field of the WCT and WPPT must be interpreted in the light of the purpose and objectives of the Berne Convention.[132]

The WCT

4-063   The WCT is a "special agreement" within the meaning of art.21 of the Berne Convention. In some respects, the WCT follows closely the provisions of TRIPS. For example, there are similar provisions concerning the idea/expression dichotomy,[133] the protection of computer programs as literary works within art.2 of the Berne Convention,[134] and compilations of data.[135] The permissible limitations and exceptions to the rights in the WCT follow the familiar "three-step" requirement in art.9(2) of the Berne Convention and art.13 of TRIPS, i.e. they are confined to:

> "certain special cases that do not conflict with a normal exploitation of the work and do not unreasonably prejudice the legitimate interests of the author."[136]

The detailed TRIPS provisions concerning civil procedure and remedies (arts 42–61) are not carried over into the WCT.

4-064   However, there are important extensions to the rights set out in TRIPS. For example, there is a distribution right which is defined as an exclusive right given to authors of literary and artistic works to authorise the making available to the public of the original and copies of their works as tangible objects.[137] There is also a (heavily qualified) rental right covering computer programs, films and works embodied in sound recordings.[138]

4-065   In addition, there are the new provisions aimed at the online environment. First, there is a right of "communication to the public", which is defined as the right of authorising any communication to the public of works, by wire or wireless means.

---

[129] See WCT Recital 2 and WPPT Recital 2.
[130] For a current list, see *http://www.wipo.int/treaties/en/* [Accessed 1 May 2018].
[131] art.1(4).
[132] Generally, see Ch.1 which discusses the position where the EU is a member of an international treaty at para.1-158. TRIPS also requires compliance with arts 1–21 of Berne Convention, see para.4-052.
[133] WCT art.2.
[134] art.4.
[135] art.5. The question of sui generis protection for databases was not dealt with.
[136] art.10.
[137] art.6. See also the agreed statements adopted by the Diplomatic Conference on 20 December 1996. These statements were adopted on the same day as the Treaty and are an aid to its interpretation.
[138] art.7.

This includes the making available to the public of works in such a way that members of the public may access these works from a place and at a time individually chosen by them.[139] Such a definition would accordingly cover placing a work on a website, broadcasts and "web-casts" as well as the downloading of web content on demand and interactive services. The relevant Agreed Statement implies that there is a defence for internet service providers who merely engage in the "provision of physical facilities for enabling or making a communication".[140] Secondly, Contracting Parties must provide against the "circumvention of effective technological measures" that restrict unauthorised acts in relation to protected works.[141] Thirdly, contracting states must provide remedies against those who remove or alter any "electronic rights management information"[142] without authority, or who distribute, broadcast or communicate to the public, such altered works. The Agreed Statement contains a warning to Member States not to use the latter provision to introduce impermissible formalities by a side-wind.[143]

The WPPT

Like the Rome Convention, the WPPT contains provisions concerning performers and phonogram producers. However, unlike that Convention, it has no provisions relating to broadcasters. **4-066**

Performers

Perhaps the most striking aspect of the WPPT is that it confers the moral rights of attribution and integrity to performers in respect of "live aural performances or performances fixed in phonograms."[144] Contracting states are given a certain amount of latitude as to the duration of such rights after the death of the performer. **4-067**

The economic rights granted to performers are wide ranging. Performers can control: the fixation of their unfixed performances; the broadcasting and communication to the public of their unfixed performances;[145] the direct or indirect reproduction of their performance fixed in a phonogram;[146] and the distribution, rental and making available to the public by wire or wireless means in such a way that members of the public may access them from a place and a time individually chosen by them (the Internet right), of their performances fixed in phonograms.[147] These rights extend beyond that of the Rome Convention which is, as discussed above, does not provide performers with the right to control the downstream market in relation to performances which were fixed with the consent of the performer. As said, the Rome Convention was primarily aimed at preventing the commercial **4-068**

---

[139] art.8.
[140] Agreed Statement Concerning art.8.
[141] art.11.
[142] This means: information which identifies the work, the author of the work, the owner of any right in the work, or information about the terms and conditions of use of the work, and any numbers or codes that represent such information, when any of these items of information is attached to a copy of a work or appears in connection with the communication of a work to the public". See art.12(2).
[143] Agreed Statement Concerning art.12.
[144] WPPT art.5.
[145] art.6.
[146] art.7.
[147] arts 8–10.

exploitation of "bootleg" recordings of performances[148] and the downstream market in fixations of their performances made with the consent of the performer.

4-069   However, the WPPT does not give the performer complete control over the downstream market in recordings of their performances. First, there are no downstream rights in relation to performances which are incorporated in cinematographic or other audiovisual works.[149] Secondly, a performer does not have the right to prevent broadcasts of their performance save in relation to unfixed performances (i.e. live events).

Phonogram producers

4-070   Phonogram producers are permitted exclusive rights to authorise the direct or indirect reproduction of their phonograms; the right of distribution to the public of their phonograms; the rental of their phonograms and making available to the public of their phonograms, by wire or wireless means, in such a way that members of the public may access them from a place and at a time individually chosen by them (the last being in effect the Internet right).[150] Again, these rights extend substantially beyond the rights for phonogram producers conferred by the Rome Convention and the Phonograms Convention.

Common provisions

4-071   There are also provisions common to both performers and producers. First, as under the Rome Convention, there is the right to "single equitable remuneration" payable by the user to either the performers or to the producers of the phonograms for the direct or indirect use of phonograms published for commercial purposes for broadcasting or for any communication to the public.[151] Secondly, the limitations and exceptions are subject to the "three-step" requirement set out in art.9(2) of the Berne Convention and art.13 of TRIPS, i.e. they are confined to:

> "certain special cases that do not conflict with a normal exploitation of the performance or phonogram and do not unreasonably prejudice the legitimate interests of the author."[152]

4-072   Thirdly, the WPPT's provisions mirror the new "digital agenda" remedies set out in the WCT: that is those aimed at preventing circumvention of anti-copying technology and the removal of electronic rights management information.[153] Finally, the term of protection is 50 years, calculated, in respect of performers, from the end of the year in which the performance was fixed, and in the case of producers, the end of the year in which the phonogram was published.[154]

---

[148] "Bootleg" means recordings of performances made without the consent of the performer. See para.4-041.

[149] see art.2(b) (definition of "phonogram").

[150] arts 11–14.

[151] art.15. Domestic law may lay down rules as to how such remuneration is to be shared between producers of phonograms and performers—art.15(2). The equivalent provision in the Rome Convention is art.12: see para.4-047. There are some subtle differences in wording, e.g. art.15 applies to indirect use of phonograms whereas art.12 refers only to direct use. However, it is not considered these differences are substantial.

[152] art.16.

[153] arts 18–19.

[154] art.17.

The Beijing Treaty on Audiovisual Performances

As a consequence of the limited protection granted to performers of their audiovisual performances under the WPPT, WIPO made a number of attempts to provide further protection to performers. This culminated in the agreement to a new treaty at the Diplomatic Conference that took place in Beijing from 20–26 June 2012. That treaty is entitled "the Beijing Treaty on Audiovisual Performances". We shall therefore refer to it as the BTAP. The BTAP is not yet, as of May 2014, in force. It will come into force three months after 30 eligible parties have deposited their instruments of ratification or accession.[155] As of 24 May 2014, there were 72 signatories to the BTAP, but only two of these signatories (Botswana and Syria) had deposited their instruments of ratification.[156] **4-073**

This new treaty provides performers with moral rights of attribution and the ability: to object to derogatory treatment,[157] to control the fixation of their unfixed performances, and to control broadcasts of those unfixed broadcasts.[158] Also, in relation to audiovisual fixations of those performances the treaty provides: a reproduction right,[159] a distribution right,[160] a rental right,[161] a right for making available in relation to fixations of their performances,[162] and a right of broadcasting and communication to the public of those fixations.[163] **4-074**

The BTAP also adds that the national laws of a contracting party can provide for the rights in the fixation to be exercised by a party to whom the performer has granted permission to make a fixation of their performance.[164] **4-075**

The BTAP also allows for contracting parties to provide limitations and exceptions to these rights. These must be "the same kinds of limitations or exceptions with regard to the protection of performers as they provide for, in their national legislation, in connection with the protection of copyright in literary and artistic works" and, as with the treaties mentioned in the earlier paragraphs of this chapter, must comply with the same "three-step" requirement set out in art.9(2) of the Berne Convention and art.13 of TRIPS, i.e. they are confined to: **4-076**

"certain special cases that do not conflict with a normal exploitation of the performance or phonogram and do not unreasonably prejudice the legitimate interests of the performer."[165]

Further, the contracting parties must provide against the "circumvention of effective technological measures" that restrict unauthorised acts in relation to protected works.[166] In addition, contracting parties must provide remedies against those who remove or alter any "electronic rights management information"[167] **4-077**

---

[155] art.26.
[156] For the current position, see *http://www.wipo.int/treaties/en/* [Accessed 7 June 2018].
[157] art.5.
[158] art.6.
[159] art.7.
[160] art.8.
[161] art.9.
[162] art.10.
[163] art.11.
[164] art.12.
[165] art.13.
[166] art.15.
[167] art.16.

without authority, or who knowingly distribute, broadcast or communicate to the public, such altered fixations.[168]

4-078   The minimum term of protection for the rights specified under the BTAP is 50 years computed from the end of the year in which the performance was fixed.[169]

EU LAW

Introduction

4-079   European Union involvement in the field of copyright and neighbouring rights was relatively late in the day compared to the other IPRs. As early as the 1970s, the Commission had already focused on the creation of a Community patent system.[170] The law of trade marks was next. The end of the 1980s and early 1990s culminated in the harmonisation of Member States' domestic trade mark laws by way of the Trade Marks Directive and the introduction of a new unitary, Community-wide trade mark right.[171] The 1990s saw the Commission turn its hand to plant varieties[172] and registered and unregistered designs[173] as well as introducing its first copyright directive—the Computer Software Directive.

4-080   The background to the Commission's first foray into the copyright field was set out in the Green Paper entitled Copyright and the Challenge of Technology.[174] In it, the Commission argued that the protection of artistic, literary and other works was of growing importance in that a general shift had occurred in the economic activities of industrialised countries, away from the production of "basic" goods to the production of goods to which there had been added considerable value by way of technology, skill and creativity. The Commission regarded such industries as particularly vulnerable to damage through unauthorised copying. Lack of protection favoured third parties who had not had to incur the often large research and development expenditure undertaken by the original author or entrepreneur.

4-081   The Green Paper's concerns were, essentially, fourfold. First, the requirement of a single internal market meant that it was necessary to eliminate obstacles and divergences of approach in copyright laws at a national level. Secondly, the EU had to develop policies that would improve the competitiveness of its economy in relation to its global trade partners and, in order to achieve this it was perceived that it was necessary to set a high level of protection in relation to copyright. Thirdly, it was important that intellectual property resulting from the creative effort of substantial investment within the EU should not be misappropriated by others outside the EU. Fourthly, it was noted that in some areas, notably industrial design and computer software, copyright protection could in some circumstances have a restrictive, rather than an enhancing effect on competition.

4-082   The Commission accordingly identified certain issues which it regarded as requiring urgent attention at EU level. These were the following: piracy; home copying of sound and audio-visual material; distribution and rental rights for certain classes

---

[168] art.16.
[169] art.14.
[170] See para.2-506.
[171] See the Trade Marks Directive and the EU Trade Mark Regulation in Ch.3.
[172] See the Community Plant Variety Regulation in Ch.6.
[173] See the Designs Directive and the Design Regulation in Ch.5.
[174] Commission of the European Communities. *Green Paper on Copyright and the Challenge of Technology-Copyright Issues Requiring Immediate Action* COM (88) 172 final.

of work (in particular, sound and video recordings); the protection of computer programs and databases; and finally, the limitations on the protection available to European Union right holders in non-Member States. The Commission left the question of the protection of industrial designs for a later consultation paper.[175]

The approach was not to be one of wholesale harmonisation. The Commission stated that EU legislation should be restricted to that which was necessary for the proper functioning of the EU and that it regarded many issues of copyright law as not requiring any specific action at EU level. It said that since all Member States belonged to the Berne Union,[176] a certain basic convergence of their laws had already been achieved, and, in any event, many of the differences that remained had no significant impact on the function of the internal market or upon the EU's global economic competitiveness. The Commission gave as an example the issue of authors' moral rights. The Green Paper therefore proposed the issuing of various directives on copyright law under art.114 of TFEU (then art.100a of the Treaty of Rome, thereafter art.95 of the EC Treaty), which permits action in relation to matters that directly affect the functioning of the internal market. **4-083**

As a result of this rather tentative approach, the "first generation"[177] of EU copyright and related rights Directives is a patchwork of measures covering seemingly unrelated (and, in some cases, apparently unimportant) areas of the law. Some subject-matter is the target of detailed treatment[178] whilst other areas are dealt with in a cursory manner. Sometimes, completely different areas of the law are cobbled together to be dealt with in the same Directive.[179] The central areas of harmonisation, such as the very subsistence of copyright, the main infringing acts, the possibility of "fair use"-type exceptions, etc. were largely left for another day.[180] Whilst such a piecemeal approach was no doubt easier to agree upon than the sort of fundamental harmonisation seen in the sphere of trade marks, it was also bound to lead to uneven protection and considerable complexity, as the following sections illustrate. **4-084**

The first generation was comprised of six Directives covering, in chronological order, computer programs,[181] rental, lending and neighbouring rights,[182] satellite broadcasting and cable retransmission rights,[183] the duration of copyright and related rights,[184] and the protection of databases.[185] **4-085**

The "second generation" of EU harmonisation then took place with the entry into force of the Information Society Directive.[186] This is sometimes called the Copyright Directive. This too has been implemented throughout the EU. With its far-reaching effects upon matters such as the reproduction right, the communication to the public right and the range of permissible defences, the Information **4-086**

---

[175] See para.5-030.
[176] See para.4-012 in relation to the Berne Union.
[177] J. Reinbothe, "Recent Intellectual Property Legislative Developments in the European Union: Copyright and Related Rights", 9th Annual Conference on Intellectual Property Law and Policy, Fordham University, 19 April 2001.
[178] For example, see the Computer Programs Directive.
[179] For example, see the Rental Right Directive, a name only apt for part of its contents.
[180] See the Information Society Directive, para.4-264.
[181] See para.4-092.
[182] See para.4-145.
[183] See para.4-186.
[184] See the Term Directive, at para.4-203.
[185] See the Database Directive, at para.4-234.
[186] See the Information Society Directive, para.4-264.

Society Directive probably ought to be regarded as the true precursor to a EU copyright code. In the same year (2001), the Commission introduced a Directive which provided for a right of royalties to artists from the resale of their works.[187] Twelve years later, the Commission's attention then turned to the question of orphan works and the question of cross-border collective management of rights and enacted directives to harmonise the law here.[188]

4-087   The European Commission has now turned its approach to modernising copyright in the digital world. This has been discussed at the introduction to this chapter.[189]

4-088   It will be observed at certain points in the sections that follow that the Commission's approach evinces a general desire to harmonise "up" (that is, towards the build-up or extension of protection) rather than "down". If harmonisation were the only goal, it could have been achieved by either route, though, of course, the latter has the disadvantage of potentially stripping away pre-existing property rights.[190] However, harmonisation was never the only goal. As illustrated in the recitals to many of the copyright Directives, the Commission has consistently repeated the principle that more copyright is self-evidently a better thing, arguing that a "high level of protection" rewards authors and stimulates their creativity.[191] Nevertheless, it is argued below that, in relation to the Term Directive and the Artists' Resale Right Directive, the case for such a stance appears to have been either superficially considered or simply assumed.

Author's own intellectual creation—test for subsistence of copyright

4-089   A further point to note about EU harmonisation measures is the systematic adoption, wherever possible, of the "author's own intellectual creation" standard for the determination of whether a work is "original" and then entitled to copyright, and the gradual falling away and demise of the "sweat of the brow" approach previously favoured by some Member States, notably the UK.[192] As said by Mengozzi AG in *Football Dataco Ltd v Yahoo! UK Ltd*[193]:

> "[36] It is common knowledge that, within the European Union, various standards apply as regards the level of originality generally required for copyright protection to be granted. In particular, in some EU countries which have common law traditions, the decisive criterion is traditionally the application of 'labour, skills or effort'. For that reason, in the United Kingdom for example, databases were generally protected by copyright before the entry into force of the Directive. A database

---

[187] See para.4-362.

[188] See paras 4-385 and 4-399.

[189] See para.4-008.

[190] "It is much easier to harmonise intellectual property rights up than down. No one minds being given more rights than they had before, whereas people are apt to complain very seriously-raising cries of destruction of property without compensation-if their rights are cut down": Jacob LJ (an English Court of Appeal judge), "Industrial Property-Industry's Enemy" at 1997 I.P.Q. 1, 3–15.

[191] See, for example, Satellite and Cable Directive Recital 24; Term Directive Recitals 10 and 11; Information Society Directive Recitals 4 and 9.

[192] However, it is to be noted that in *Newspaper Licensing Agency v Meltwater* [2012] R.P.C. 1 at [20], the English Court of Appeal held that the author's own intellectual creation standard is no different (other than, presumably, in its form of expression) from the pre-existing UK standard of originality of copyright works. However, this has been doubted subsequently in the Court of Appeal subsequently—see *SAS Institute Inc v World Programming Limited* [2013] EWCA Civ 1482 at [36]–[37] per Lewison LJ. In the author's view, the Court was right to so doubt.

[193] (C-604/10) ECLI:EU:C:2012:155.

was protected by copyright if its creator had had to expend a certain effort, or employ a certain skill, in order to create it. On the other hand, in countries of the continental tradition, for a work to be protected by copyright it must generally possess a creative element, or in some way express its creator's personality, even though any assessment as to the quality or the 'artistic' nature of the work is always excluded.

[37]   Now, on this point there is no doubt that, as regards copyright protection, the Directive espouses a concept of originality which requires more than the mere 'mechanical' effort needed to collect the data and enter them in the database. To be protected by the copyright, a database must—as art.3 of the Directive explicitly states—be the 'intellectual creation' of the person who has set it up. That expression leaves no room for doubt, and echoes a formula which is typical of the continental copyright tradition."

This opinion was followed by the CJEU.[194] The Computer Programs Direc-   **4-090**
tive[195] is an example. The relevant test is that the software must be the author's own intellectual creation. Under a common law approach, to attract copyright the work only had to be original in the sense of it not having been copied from another. Such can no longer be regarded as the proper test in respect of computer software. A further example is the Database Directive in relation to copyright protection of original databases.[196] In *Infopaq A/S v Danske dagblades*,[197] the CJEU indicated that this was a standard to be applied across all types of copyright and related rights, regardless of whether or not (as in the case of the Information Society Directive) that term appeared in the directive under analysis.[198]

It is suggested that this higher[199] originality standard at least has the merit of   **4-091**
counter-balancing the general drift "up" of harmonisation just referred to and, accordingly, of containing copyright's otherwise unchecked expansion into new fields and new types of works. To have combined the harmonisation "up" approach with a very low originality requirement such as that of the UK would, it is suggested, have resulted in the worst of both worlds. A higher originality requirement can cut down on the number of works that can actually—rather than just potentially— obtain copyright's favourable treatment (for example, as regards matters such as formality, novelty and duration) when compared to other intellectual property rights.

The Computer Programs Directive

Introduction

Prior to the enactment of specific legislation at a EU level, there was a significant   **4-092**
divergence in the approach of Member States in the protection given to computer

---

[194]   *Football Dataco v Yahoo! UK* (C-604/10) ECLI:EU:C:2012:155; [2012] E.C.D.R. 10 at [37]–[39]. See also *Bezpečnostní softwarová asociace v. Svaz softwarové ochrany v Ministerstvo kultury* (C-393/09), ECLI:EU:C:2010:816 at [45]–[46]; *Painer v Standard Verlags GmbH* (C-145/10) ECLI:EU:2013:138 at [89] (author must be able to express "his creative abilities in the production of the work by making free and creative choices").

[195]   art.1.3. See para.4-092. See also art.2(5) Berne Convention and art.10 TRIPS.

[196]   Though databases falling short of this standard may attain sui generis database right protection: see para.4-255. See also art.2(5) Berne Convention and art.10 TRIPS.

[197]   (C-5/08) [2009] E.C.R. I-6569, [2009] E.C.D.R. 16 at [33]–[37].

[198]   For a full review of the UK, EU and civil law countries to the issue of originality in copyright, see A. Rahmatian, "Originality in UK Copyright Law: The Old 'Skill and Labour' Doctrine under Pressure" (2013) 44(1) *International Review of Intellectual Property and Competition Law*, 4-34.

[199]   If, indeed, it is higher—see fn.192.

programs.[200] There was no copyright protection in seven of the (then) 12 Member States, and where there was, standards varied widely. Germany, for instance, had a very high originality threshold.[201] In addition, though many Member States allowed the laws of contract and/or confidentiality to do the work of protecting programs, such an approach was obviously powerless against those who were not parties to the contract or confidential relationship.

4-093   Though the idea of using copyright to protect computer programs was not without its critics,[202] its popularity as a means of software protection arose because a sui generis approach would have required the creation of a new instrument for international protection, whereas copyright had the advantage of integrating computer program protection into an established international system embodying principles of national treatment and the absence of formalities. Moreover, these principles (and some minimum standards of harmonisation) had been the subject of considerable international co-operation and harmonisation since the Berne Convention of 1886. In addition, it was thought that copyright could be used to strike the appropriate balance between protection and fair competition, through the imposition of precisely defined conditions concerning acts such as reverse engineering.

4-094   The essential effect of the Directive is to confer copyright protection to computer programs as literary works within the meaning of the Berne Convention, and to harmonise the standard of originality. That standard is that the work must be the "own intellectual creation of the author"—no more and no less. Other features of the Directive are that there are a number of restricted acts and a number of reverse engineering defences. Ownership questions are left to Member States. Moral rights for computer programs are excluded. There are also a number of important provisions affecting software licensing.

History of the Directive

4-095   In 1985 the Commission published its White Paper which was followed, in June 1988, by the publication of its Green Paper entitled Copyright and the Challenge of Technology.[203] The Commission's draft proposal for a Directive was presented to the Council in January 1989. It was also submitted to the European Parliament for its opinion, which was delivered in July 1990. In October 1990 the Commission published the Amended proposal for a Council Directive on the legal protection of computer programs, taking into account the European Parliament's proposals, including the addition of an Article expressly allowing reverse engineering/decompilation of programs to achieve interoperability. Within two months, the Council was able to adopt the Common Position, which was approved without amendment by the Parliament in April 1991. The Council then enacted the common position and the Directive was published in May 1991 as Dir.91/250. That Directive was repealed and replaced by a codified version as Dir.2009/24/EC in

---

[200] Recital 1 Computer Programs Directive.

[201] See the *Inkassoprogramm* case law of its Supreme Court, which required a high level of creativity ("Schöpfungshöhe"): B.G.H.Z. 94, at 276.

[202] For example, A. Christie, "Designing Appropriate Protection for Computer Programs" [1994] 11 E.I.P.R. 486.

[203] Green Paper on Copyright and the Challenge of Technology COM (88) 172 Final. The Green Paper is dealt with more fully above at para.4-080.

May 2009.[204] Where the numbering of Recitals and Articles has changed, the new numbering is used herein. The effect of the Directive remains unchanged. The CJEU has indicated in *UsedSoft v Oracle*[205] that the protection of computer programs under this directive is a lex specialis in relation to the Information Society Directive, and so this Directive, rather than the Information Society Directive, specifically governs the protection of computer programs by copyright.

Protection of computer programs by copyright

Computer games and multimedia programs

The Computer Software Directive is concerned specifically with computer **4-096** programs. For instance, computer games normally consist of a large array of video, graphical and sound elements which will be ultimately compiled to binary machine code. However, although the Computer Software Directive is a lex specialis in relation to the Information Society Directive,[206] such does not mean that it governs exhaustively the issue of protection by copyright of electronic graphic and sound elements even though they are compiled into machine code to be executed by a computer. As said in *Nintendo v PC Box Srl*[207] by the CJEU:

> "[23] ... As is apparent from the order for reference, videogames, such as those at issue in the main proceedings, constitute complex matter comprising not only a computer program but also graphic and sound elements, which, although encrypted in computer language, have a unique creative value which cannot be reduced to that encryption. In so far as the parts of a videogame, in this case, the graphic and sound elements, are part of its originality, they are protected, together with the entire work, by copyright in the context of the system established by Directive 2001/29 [Information Society Directive]."

This follows the decision in *BSA* (discussed below) whereby it held that although **4-097** a graphical user interface was not protectable under the Computer Software Directive, it was capable of protection under the Information Society Directive.[208]

Expression in any form of a computer program

The Directive requires Member States to protect computer programs by copyright **4-098** as literary works under the Berne Convention.[209] "Preparatory design material" (PDM) for programs is also protected.[210] The Directive specifically states that protection applies to the "expression in any form of a computer program".[211] Thus, it does not extend to ideas and principles which underlie any element of a computer program including those which underlie its interfaces.[212] Thus, to the extent that logic, algorithms and programming languages comprise ideas and principles, they

---

[204] [2009] OJ L111/16..
[205] *UsedSoft GmbH v Oracle International Corp* (C-128/11), ECLI:EU:C:2012:407, [51] and [56].
[206] See para.4-264.
[207] (C-355/12) ECLI:EU:C:2014:25.
[208] *Bezpečnostní softwarová asociace – Svaz softwarové ochrany v Ministerstvo kultury* (C-393/09) [2010] E.C.R. I-3971.
[209] art.1(1).
[210] art.1(1).
[211] art.1(2).
[212] art.1(2), Recital 11.

are not protected by the Directive.[213] The reference to "any form" means that protection extends to programs incorporated into hardware, e.g. firmware.[214]

4-099   The dichotomy between expression and ideas is familiar to copyright lawyers. Copyright does not protect ideas but merely the expression of these ideas in some material form.[215] The CJEU has had to consider the requirement of "expression in any form of a computer program" in two cases. In *BSA*,[216] an issue arose in the Czech Republic as to whether a graphical user interface (GUI) of a computer program was protected by the Computer Software Directive. BSA was an association that applied to the Czech authorities for authorisation to administer collectively copyrights to computer programs. The application was rejected, in part, because BSA wished to collect levies where the GUI was transmitted via television broadcasts or cable television. The Czech courts took the view that object and source code was protected by Czech copyright law but not the GUI (which in their view, was only protected against unfair competition). The issue as to whether a GUI was protected under the Computer Software Directive was thus referred to the CJEU. The CJEU took the view that it was not. Having stated that source code and object code were protected by the Directive, it commented on the fact that so was preparatory design work. It thus endorsed the AG's Opinion that any form of expression of a computer program must be protected from the "moment when its reproduction would engender the reproduction of the computer program itself, thus enabling the computer to perform its task."[217] It thus held that a GUI did not enable the reproduction of the computer program and thus was not protected by copyright under the Directive.[218]

4-100   As discussed above, the CJEU followed the AG's Opinion. It is thus helpful to consider the AG's Opinion on this point. He considered that not only was the source and object code protected under the Directive but so was the PDM. He said that the PDM could include, for example, a structure or organisational chart developed by the programmer which could be transcribed into source code and object code thus enabling the machine to execute the computer program.[219] He said that such an organisational chart could be compared to the scenario of a film.[220] He accordingly held that a GUI did not enable the computer program to perform the task for which it was created as it did not entail reproduction of the computer program itself and it was possible for computer programs having different sources and object codes to share the same interface. Thus, he said that the GUI did not "divulge" the computer program—it merely made its use easier and more user-friendly.[221]

4-101   In *SAS v WPL*,[222] WPL had reproduced the functionality of SAS's substantial and complex statistical analysis software. In doing so, WPL had reproduced the syntax

---

[213] Recital 11.
[214] Recital 7.
[215] Such is acknowledged at Recital 11 which refers to this being recognised in international copyright conventions. Thus, art.2(1) of the Berne Convention makes this distinction. See also art.2 of the WIPO Copyright Treaty which states that "copyright protection extends to expressions and not to ideas, procedures, methods of operation or mathematical concepts".
[216] *Bezpečnostní softwarová asociace – Svaz softwarové ochrany v Ministerstvo kultury* (C-393/09) [2010] E.C.R. I-3971.
[217] See [38].
[218] See [42].
[219] See [63].
[220] See [63]. This is the official English translation of the French word "*scénario*". It is better translated as script or screenplay.
[221] See [65].
[222] *SAS Institute Inc v World Programming Ltd* (C-406/10) ECLI:EU:C:2012:259.

of numerous functions to enable scripts written to direct the operation of SAS's software to be reused to direct the operation of the WPL software, and had copied printed manuals that described the operation of SAS's statistical algorithms (both in the production of WPL's rival software and in the production of the manuals for it). The CJEU was asked, in essence, whether art.1(2) of the Computer Programs Directive must be interpreted as meaning that the functionality of a computer program, its programming language and the format of data files used with it constitute a form of expression of that program, such that they are protected by copyright under that Directive. The CJEU held that none of those elements constituted a form of expression of SAS's program.[223] To hold to the contrary, it held would permit the monopolisation of ideas to the detriment of technological progress and industrial development.[224] It further continued by saying the main advantage of protection of computer programs by copyright is that such protection covers only the individual expression of the work and thus leaves other authors the "desired latitude" to create similar or even identical programs, provided that they refrain from copying.[225] In relation to the functionality of a computer program, it is useful to consider the AG's Opinion who said that:

> "[52] The functionality of a computer program can be defined as the set of possibilities offered by a computer system, the actions specific to that program. In other words, the functionality of a computer program is the service which the user expects from it ...
>
> [54] Let me give a specific example. Where a programmer decides to develop a computer program for airline ticket reservations, that software will contain a multitude of functionalities needed to make a booking. The computer program will have to be able, in turn, to find the flight requested by the user, check availability, book the seat, register the user's details, take online payment details and, finally, edit the user's electronic ticket. All of those functionalities, those actions, are dictated by a specific and limited purpose. In this, therefore, they are similar to an idea. It is therefore legitimate for computer programs to exist which offer the same functionalities.
>
> [55] There are, however, many means of achieving the concrete expression of those functionalities and it is those means which will be eligible for copyright protection under [the Software Directive]. As we have seen, creativity, skill and inventiveness manifest themselves in the way in which the program is drawn up, in its writing. The programmer uses formulae, algorithms which, as such, are excluded from copyright protection because they are the equivalent of the words by which the poet or the novelist creates his work of literature. However, the way in which all of these elements are arranged, like the style in which the computer program is written, will be likely to reflect the author's own intellectual creation and therefore be eligible for protection."

However, although the CJEU held the SAS language and format of SAS's data **4-102** files was not protected under the Computer Software Directive, it held that there was a possibility that such "might be protected, as works, under Dir.2001/29 [the Information Society Directive] if they are their author's own intellectual creation".[226] This led to argument when the matter returned to the English court that indeed, such was protected by the Information Society Directive. However, such

---

[223] See [39].
[224] See [40].
[225] See [41].
[226] Applying *BSA*, at [44]–[46].

was dismissed by the English Court of Appeal who held that the same approach should be taken under the Information Society Directive as what is capable of protection (i.e. form of expression rather than as an idea) as under the Computer Software Directive, in particular because European legislation was enacted against the background of many international treaties and well-established principles of copyright law and the Directives had to be interpreted against such a background.[227]

Dividing line: preparatory design material

4-103   The decisions of the CJEU in *BSA* and *SAS* clearly assist in determining the dividing line between what is protected under the Directive and what is not. The functionality of a computer program is not protected. A person can set out to replicate *what* a computer program does (i.e. its functionality) without infringing the copyright in that program provided that they do not copy the source code or object code (or the preparatory design material).[228] On the other hand, clearly protection extends beyond mere copying of the source or object code as preparatory design material (PDM) is protected as well. But how detailed and developed must a document be for it to qualify for protection under the Directive as a PDM? When creating a program, there will normally be a number of steps including system analysis, functional specification (*what* the program is to do) and then a series of documents setting out the architecture and structure of the program (*how* the program is to fulfil the functional specification), coding, testing and debugging and beta-testing with the client. Recital 7 of the Directive states that the "nature of the preparatory work is such that a computer program can result from it at a later stage". This is so general as to be of little assistance. A computer program can result from a functional specification but such does not set out the structure or architecture of a program. The judgment and Opinion in *BSA* (discussed above at para.4-099) appear to suggest that for such a document to quality as a PDM, it must consist of or be analogous to an organisational or structure chart and should be considered analogous to a screenplay for a film. Clearly, this means that it is possible to write a number of different programs to implement a PDM (in the same sense that one could have a number of different films that implement a screenplay). In the author's view, a correct approach is that for a document or work to amount to a PDM, it must sufficiently circumscribe the freedom of the coder seeking to write a program to implement the PDM, so that *each and any* program written to implement the PDM can be considered, in substance, a reproduction of each other.

Originality

4-104   The Directive states that a computer program shall be protected if it is original in the sense that it is the "author's own intellectual creation".[229] This is a similar test to that contained in the Database Directive in relation to databases attracting

---

[227] *SAS Institute Inc v World Programming Limited* [2013] EWCA Civ 1482 at [69]–[70].

[228] Normally that person will not have access to the source code or the preparatory design material. In relation to the object code, it is essentially impossible to adapt or alter this as it is simply a series of 1s and 0s and it is very difficult to determine any structure in such. Thus, copying of object code will either be a facsimile copy (identical) or not occur.

[229] art.1(3). See also art.10 TRIPS.

copyright protection[230] and has been held by the CJEU to apply to any EU copyright law which has a requirement of originality.[231] Such a test implies, not just a quantitatively higher amount of input than the traditional "sweat of the brow" threshold of common law countries such as the UK, but qualitatively a different kind of input by the author. Merely expending more effort or resources therefore will not suffice. There has to be something personal and intellectual that results in the creation. The originality standard does not mean, however, that the creation itself—the computer program—has to be particularly inventive, novel, sophisticated or efficacious. The recitals state that, in considering the issue of originality, no tests as to the qualitative or aesthetic merits of the program should be applied.[232] The adoption of this standard apparently required 12 Member States to lower their threshold of originality and three to raise it.[233] That said, it will be very rare that any program which is not a slavish copy of another program will not be the result of the intellectual creation of a programmer. Even the coding of very simple scripts (e.g. move cursor to top of screen) can be coded in enough differing ways so that the way chosen by the coder is an intellectual task requiring creativity, choice and not merely the expenditure of labour and effort.

Authorship and ownership

The copyright in a computer program belongs to the author. The author of the program is defined as the natural person or group of persons who created the program.[234] The Directive permits derogation from these provisions if Member States' national legislation otherwise so provides. Thus, the author of the program may be deemed to be the legal person designated as the right holder by that legislation.[235] In effect, this means that Member States have considerable freedom to decide who owns the copyright in a computer program.   **4-105**

Where a computer program is created by an employee in the execution of their duties or following instructions given by an employer, the employer is exclusively entitled to exercise all economic rights unless otherwise provided by contract.[236] The Directive is silent on whether the employer has an exclusive licence from the employee or, in fact, owns the copyright. In practice, there should be little distinction because in most Member States' laws, an exclusive licensee can sue third parties for infringement of copyright.   **4-106**

The Directive does not specifically regulate ownership of copyright in commissioned programs. Consequently, in the absence of special provision under national legislation, the author will own the copyright in the program. The position may be controlled by the application of the contract law of the relevant Member State.   **4-107**

The question of whether copyright is to be owned by a company or an individual   **4-108**

---

[230] Though databases falling short of this standard may attain sui generis database right protection: see para.4-255.
[231] See the discussion of *Infopaq* (C-5/08) [2009] E.C.R. I-6569, and later cases, in the context of the Information Society Directive, para.4-264. See also above a general discussion as to the requirement of "author's own intellectual creation" at para.4-089.
[232] Recital 8.
[233] Commission of the European Communities. *Report on the implementation and effects of Directive 91/250/EEC on the legal protection of computer programs*, 10 April 2000, COM (2000) 199 final.
[234] art.2(1). Where the program is created by a group of persons jointly, the exclusive rights are owned jointly—art.2(2).
[235] art.2(1).
[236] art.2(3).

is left to Member States. The Directive provides that protection shall be granted to all natural or legal persons eligible under national copyright legislation as applied to literary works.[237]

Infringement

4-109   Under art.4 of the Directive, the owner of copyright is granted the exclusive right to do or authorise:

(a)   the permanent or temporary reproduction of a computer program by any means and in any form in part or in whole. In so far as loading, displaying, running, transmission or storage of the computer program necessitate such reproduction such acts shall be subject to authorisation by the right holder[238];

(b)   the translation, adaptation,[239] arrangement and any other alteration of a computer program and the reproduction of the results thereof, without prejudice to the rights of the person who alters the program; and

(c)   any form of distribution to the public, including the rental of the original of the program or of copies thereof.[240]

4-110   These provisions are self-explanatory. In *SAS v WPL*, the CJEU held that, if WPL had access to parts of the source code or object code relating to the programming language, data files format and created similar elements in its own computer program, such would amount to copyright infringement.[241] However, it should be remembered that the definition of computer program includes the preparatory design material.[242] Thus, art.4 is not merely concerned with the copying of source code or object code. The coding of a program which implements the logical structure of the preparatory design material will be an infringement. However, the ideas and principles embodied in the preparatory design material is not protected and accordingly, the creation of a program which implements those principles and ideas within the preparatory design material, even if sourced from the preparatory design material, will not be an infringement.[243] In relation to the meaning of "part" of program and how much needs to be taken, there is no reason why this should be interpreted any differently than the reproduction right conferred by the Information Society Directive and the reader is referred to the section on this.[244]

---

[237] art.3.

[238] art.4(1)(a). See also art.5(1) discussed at para.4-116 which provides a defence of "intended purpose".

[239] art.4(1)(b). "Adaptation" is not defined but in the context of computer software, is normally understood as meaning compilation from high level source code to low level machine code or de-compilation from the latter to the former.

[240] art.4(1)(c). Recital 12 states that "renting" does not include public lending. However, a lending right was introduced under the Rental Right Directive for all literary works including computer programs: see para.4-145. It is somewhat surprising that in the consolidated Rental Right Directive which postdates the original Rental Right Directive that this was not dealt with explicitly.

[241] See [43].

[242] art.1(1).

[243] Generally, see para.4-098 for discussion of the ideas/expression dichotomy.

[244] See paras 4-264 and 4-282.

Exhaustion of rights

In accordance with established EU jurisprudence on intellectual property and the **4-111** free movement provisions of the TFEU,[245] the Directive provides that once a copy of a program has been sold in the EU by the rights holder or with their consent, their distribution rights in relation to that copy are exhausted within the EU with the exception of the right to control its further rental.[246]

In *UsedSoft v Oracle*,[247] UsedSoft (as its name implies) marketed previously used **4-112** software licences. In particular, UsedSoft sold licences or parts of bulk user licences to Oracle's client-server database software where those licences had previously been used to permit the installation (by downloading from Oracle's servers) and subsequent use of Oracle's software on the computers of a third party. Oracle's user licences were expressly "non-transferrable". The CJEU was asked whether the entry into a licence agreement and the provision of a copy of Oracle's software via a download was a "sale" within the meaning of art.4(2) of the Directive. Oracle argued that it made no "sales" of its software, but instead it made free copies available to download and, separately, it entered into licence agreements. This argument was dismissed, the court holding that the downloading and the subsequent conclusion of a licence agreement to permit its use were two aspects of an indivisible whole, and that the original purchaser received a right, in return for a fee, to use the software for an unlimited period. These circumstances involved a transfer of the right of ownership of a copy of the software, and therefore amounted to a sale. This was not affected by the fact that the software was provided via a download, rather than in a material form, e.g. a CD: the reference to "sale... of a copy of a program" in art.4(2) was not limited according to whether the copy in question was in tangible or intangible form.[248] However, the original recipient of a multi-user licence is not authorised by the exhaustion principle to subdivide their licence and sell on some licences. This is because, in order to sell on the copy of the software, the original recipient must make their own copy unusable.

Moreover, in a case following *UsedSoft*, the Court of Justice has said, in a **4-113** somewhat confusing judgment, that the exhaustion right does not extend to the sale of a backup copy of the programme provided to the first buyer, even if the original medium on which the programme was provided to the first buyer is damaged, destroyed or lost.[249] The reason for saying that it is confusing is that the Court of Justice rejected an argument that there is only exhaustion of the distribution right for the original material medium, acquired by the first buyer.[250] As the Court of Justice said, the exhaustion of the distribution right concerns the copy of the computer programme and the accompanying user licence and not the material medium on which that copy was first offered for sale as art.4(c) of the Software Directive makes no distinction between the tangible or intangible form of the copy in question, relying upon *UsedSoft*.[251] It then held that a backup copy can only be

---

[245] arts 34–36.

[246] art.4(2). See *Laserdisken ApS v Kulturministeriet* (C-479/04) [2006] E.C.R. I-8089 and *Micro Leader Business v Commission* (T-198/98) [1999] E.C.R. II-3989.

[247] *UsedSoft GmbH v Oracle International Corp* (C-128/11) ECLI:EU:C:2012:407.

[248] See [55].

[249] *Aleksandrs Ranks,Jurijs Vasiļevičs v Finanšu un ekonomisko noziegumu izmeklēšanas prokoratūra, Microsoft Corp* (C-166/15) ECLI:EU:C:2016:762.

[250] See [32]–[33].

[251] See [34]–[36].

used to meet the sole needs of the first buyer.[252] It then said that a lawful acquirer of a copy of a computer program who no longer has the original CD or DVD on which the copy of the software was originally delivered to him, as he has destroyed, damaged or lost it, cannot be deprived by that reason of the possibility of reselling "that copy" to a third party since that would render ineffective the exhaustion of the distribution right.[253] One might have thought that such an observation would mean that in such circumstances, it could supply a copy on a non-original medium (this clearly being the only way of supplying a physical copy). Moreover, the Court of Justice appeared to hold that the second buyer ("new acquirer") could download a copy from the copyright owner if the original disk was damaged or lost.[254] Therefore, one has the rather strange situation that where the original medium is damaged, lost or destroyed, the second buyer can download a copy from the software publisher but not buy a back up copy. This makes little sense. One cannot help thinking that the facts of the case (which appeared to involve large scale counterfeiting activities) influenced the decision.

4-114   The CJEU's decision in *UsedSoft* was, to many, controversial. It has to a large extent, destroyed the concept of a non-transferable "shrink wrap" licence whereby the purchaser of software is the only person entitled to use the software. Thus, in *UsedSoft*, the licence agreement stated that the licence granted was exclusively for internal business purposes, non-exclusive and non-transferable. Despite such, the CJEU held that the purchaser was entitled to sell on the user licence.[255] This may sound dramatic but it is not. The CJEU has made it clear that a contract to sell goods which seeks to restrict the sale of those goods in one Member State (or indeed, outside the EU) does not prevent the exhaustion doctrine from applying.[256] The CJEU's decision in *UsedSoft* is an extension of that doctrine into a new area of technology. However, it is of note that the CJEU did not follow the AG's Opinion. Moreover, it has not been followed in the US.[257] It has resulted in advice to legal advisors advising their clients to switch to subscription or cloud-based business models which avoid the transfer of ownership as a result of sale and are more akin to the rental of computer programs.[258] The Computer Software Directive specifically excludes the application of the exhaustion right to the rental of computer programs.[259] In short, technology will often develop quicker than the development of the law which by necessity, must deal with historical events, often many years ago.[260]

Exceptions to exclusive rights: generally

4-115   The restricted acts are so broadly defined in the Directive that exceptions were required to allow normal licensed users to: (a) use the program; (b) carry out error

---

[252] See [43] interpreting art.5(1) Software Directive. This is discussed below—see para.4-116.
[253] See [53]. "That copy" clearly does not mean the copy on the original medium and thus mean a copy made on another medium.
[254] See [55]–[56].
[255] See [84].
[256] See para.7-111.
[257] *Capital Records v ReDigi In* No. 12 CXiv. 95, Memorandum and Order, March 30, 2013 (US District Court). A useful article reviewing the differences is A. Nicholson, "Old Habits Die Hard: Usedsoft v Oracle" *Scripted* 10(3) October 2013 (see *http://script-ed.org/wp-content/uploads/2013/10/nicholson.pdf* [Accessed 1st May 2018].
[258] See para.4.4. A. Nicholson, "Old Habits Die Hard: Usedsoft v Oracle" *Scripted* 10(3) October 2013
[259] art.4(2).
[260] As said by Nicholson, the events which gave rise to the *UsedSoft* litigation took place in 2005 and the case was decided in 2012. By then, cloud-based subscription models were common (para.4.4).

correction; (c) make back-up copies; (d) observe and study the program in order to understand how it works; and (e) decompile it in order to obtain interface information. These will be dealt with in turn.

Using the program and error correction

Article 5(1) provides that: **4-116**

> "in the absence of specific contractual provisions, the acts referred to in Article 4(a) and (b) shall not require authorisation by the rightholder where they are necessary for the use of the computer program by the lawful acquirer in accordance with its intended purpose including for error correction."

These provisions are self-explanatory. However, they give rise to three questions: **4-117** (a) who is a lawful acquirer, (b) what is meant by "intended purpose", (c) error correction, and (d) can the supplier contract out of art.5(1)?

Lawful acquirer/intended purpose

Article 5(1) refers to the lawful acquirer. Such must mean that the user has a **4-118** legitimate right to use the program. Thus, the copy of the computer program that the user is using must be a licensed copy (and not an infringing copy). However, such does not mean that the right holder must have acquired a licence *direct* from the right holder. As seen above, they may have acquired it from a licensee in circumstances whereby it can be said that the right holder's rights are exhausted.[261]

What is meant by "intended purpose"? In *SAS v WPL*, the CJEU was asked **4-119** whether reliance on the exception in art.5(2) and art.5(3) whereby only a person having a right to use the computer program may make a back-up copy or observe, study or test the functioning of the program was affected by the purpose for which such was done. On the facts of that case, the tasks undertaken by WPL in order to observe the operation of SAS's program fell outside the permitted purpose of their activities under their licence (which was a "learning edition" licence restricted to non-production purposes). The CJEU held that this restriction as regards the purpose for which a licence was granted was irrelevant: in effect, as indicated by the CJEU's conclusion at [59], once the user was permitted to perform certain acts (loading, displaying, etc.) it was not relevant that the purpose for which permission to perform those acts was granted was limited. As said by the Court of Appeal when the matter returned to England,[262] on a proper interpretation of the decision of the CJEU:

> "[101] ... the [CJEU] distinguished between *acts* permitted by the licence, and the *purpose* for which those permitted acts were carried out. Once you have crossed the threshold of being entitled to perform acts for any purpose specified in the licence, article 5 (3) permits you to perform those same acts for a purpose that falls within article 5(3)."[263]

However, the wording in art.5(1) is different—unlike art.5(2) and 5(3), it expressly

---

[261] See para.4-111.

[262] [2013] EWCA Civ 1482.

[263] It is important to note that the question referred to the CJEU by the English court was whether WPL's use of the Learning Edition for a purpose that was not permitted by the licence was nevertheless permitted by art.5(3) rather than whether, if WPLD's acts fell within art.5(3), the right holder could contract out. Thus, it was concerned with the scope of art.5(3).

states that the use must be "in accordance with its intended purpose". It has been suggested that the intended purpose of the program must be determined objectively, having regard to the interests of both parties.[264] Presumably, the licensor can stipulate what field of use the licensee is allowed to use this software. It would be an unattractive argument for a licensee to say that their interests lie outside the stipulated field of use in the licence. Thus, if the use is outside the licensed field-of-use, the acts of running and loading would be an infringement. For instance, a licence may stipulate that a computer 3D graphics program can only be used for computer games and not for creating 3D models for ships or buildings. If such is the case, the use for the latter would be an act of infringement.

Error correction

4-120   "Error correction" would mean fixing bugs and other glitches which prevent or hinder the program from working (e.g. crashes), and it is considered, where the program does not have the functionality as promised or represented by the software owner. It would also allow a licensee of software to download patches or fixes made available by the software owner regardless of whether a licence has been granted to the licensee to download or install the fix or patch.

Contracting out of art.5(1)

4-121   The first seven words of this Article implies that the rights holder can exclude the right to do the acts in art.5(1) by contract. However, Recital 13 provides that:

> "The exclusive rights of the author to prevent the unauthorised reproduction of his work should be subject to a limited exception in the case of a computer program to allow the reproduction technically necessary for the use of that program by the lawful acquirer. This means that the acts of loading and running necessary for the use of a copy of a program which has been lawfully acquired, and the act of correction of its errors, *may not be prohibited by contract* In the absence of specific contractual provisions, including when a copy of the program has been sold, any other act necessary for the use of the copy of a program may be performed in accordance with its intended purpose by a lawful acquirer of that copy." [Emphasis supplied.]

4-122   Furthermore, art.8 (previously art.9(1) of Dir.91/250) provides that:

> "The provisions of this Directive shall be without prejudice to any other legal provisions such as…the law of contract.
>   Any contractual provisions contrary to Article 6 or to the exceptions provided for in Article 5(2) and (3) shall be null and void."

4-123   These provisions are somewhat difficult to interpret. For instance, on the principle of *inclusio unum est exclusio alterum*, art.8 would specifically permit contractual derogations to art.5(1). This is supported by the wording of art.5(1). Yet, Recital 13 suggests that the act of using a program (and loading) and error correction cannot be excluded by contract although other acts can be. The reason for the unfortunate wording in the recitals and articles of the Directive stem directly from

---

[264] G. Smith, "EC software protection directive-an attempt to understand Art.5(1)" [1990–91] 7 *Computer Law and Security Report* 148, 150.

the Commission's proposal for the Directive.[265] The Commission's view was that when a program was sold, there should be no need to obtain authorisation to carry out acts necessary to use the program. Moreover, it is clear that it was concerned about the practice of "shrink wrap" licensing and the terms and conditions being used to impose conditions on the use of programs which have in reality been sold to the consumer. Thus, it took the view that right holders should be able to control through contract the acts licensed to the user where a written licence was signed but not in the case of shrink wrap licences. In the latter, it saw a need for art.5(1) to over-ride terms in shrink wrap licences which had not truly been agreed. It said that such was a necessary compromise between the interests of suppliers and consumers of computer programs. It said that the restricted acts in art.4 gave wide power to right holders to control the acts of reproduction, adaptation and distribution but:

> "these powers should not in fairness be used to circumscribe the normal enjoyment of property by a person who legally acquires a program by purchase. If program producers wish to ensure the greater degree of control over the reproduction, adaptation and distribution of their programs which the system of licences permits, the would-be purchaser of a program should be required to read and sign a legally binding licence agreement at the point of sale."[266]

The distinction between shrink wrap licences and written signed existed in the **4-124** original draft art.5(1). However, this was removed in the amended proposal during its passage and eventually the wording in art.5(1) was adopted. Although the distinction between written signed licences and shrink wrap licences disappeared, the intention remained, namely that purchasers of software should not be prevented from the normal enjoyment of their software unless they conciously read and sign a licence which specifically contracts out of art.5(1). As part of determining what is "normal enjoyment", the right holder should be entitled to make clear the purpose (and thus the scope) of the licence, i.e. student use or professional use and the field-of-use (home accountancy). The real explanation for art.5(1) is that it was intended to be a consumer protection measure and indeed it would have been preferable to have been dealt with under EU consumer protection law.[267] It would thus be a reasonable conclusion that "specific contractual provisions" means business-to-business negotiation agreements rather than shrink wrap or standard forms between business and consumer.

The making of a back-up copy

Article 5(2) allows the making of a back-up copy by a person having the right **4-125** to use the computer program cannot be prevented by contract in so far as it is necessary for that use.[268]

This short provision is puzzling. Prima facie, the unauthorised making of a **4-126** back-up copy is an infringement in as much as any reproduction of a computer program is an infringement of copyright in the program. Thus, there would be no need to prevent its use by contract as making a back-up is an infringement of

---

[265] Proposal for a Council Directive on the legal protection of computer programs (COM(88) 816 final) [1989] OJ C91/4 (accessible at *http://eur-lex.europa.eu/legal-content/EN/HIS/?uri=celex:31991L0250* [Accessed 24 July 2014].

[266] p.12.

[267] e.g. the Unfair Business-to-Consumer Commercial Practices Directive (2005/29/EC).

[268] art.5(2). See also art.9(2).

copyright. A proper interpretation of this provision must be therefore that it is not an infringement of copyright to make a back-up copy of a software program regardless of the terms of the software licence (see also art.8).

4-127   In relation to the copy being "necessary for that use", making a back-up is invariably necessary because it is the nature of computers and programs to break down or degrade occasionally.[269] Thus, a person who does not make a back-up is probably imprudent, and any mildly sophisticated organisation is likely to employ a strategy of frequently backing up important elements of its computers' hard drives.

Observing, studying and testing

4-128   Article 5(3) permits a lawful user, without the authorisation of the right holder:

> "to observe study or test the functioning of the program in order to determine the ideas and principles which underlie any element of the program if he does so while performing any of the acts of loading, displaying, running, transmitting or storing the program which he is entitled to do."

4-129   Parties are not allowed to contract out of this provision.[270] Recital 14 explains the purpose behind this by saying:

> "A person having a right to use a computer program should not be prevented from performing acts necessary to observe, study or test the functioning of the program, provided that those acts do not infringe the copyright in the program."

4-130   The expression "provided that *those* acts do not infringe the copyright in the program" must be referring to the acts of loading, displaying, running, etc. In other words, provided that the lawful user is entitled to run, load, display, transmit, etc. the program in accordance with the licence, then they are free to observe study or test the functioning of the program to determine the ideas and principles. However, as the acts of observation, study or testing (or at least observations and studying) are not per se restricted acts, what precisely is the purpose of art.5(3)? A literal interpretation of art.5(3) (as explained by Recital 14) might conclude that it provides no defence at all on the basis that it amounts to little more than saying that the right holder cannot prevent the lawful user from doing any restricted act that he is entitled to do—which is wholly circular. Yet, clearly, it must be interpreted as meaning something more than that. It was this issue of interpretation which led to a reference in *SAS v WPL*. The case has been discussed above.[271] In short, the national courts were concerned that although the defendants were licensed to use the program for educational purposes, they were not licensed to observe, study and test it for working out its functionality for commercial purposes. However, in essence, it was held that if the *acts* of loading, running, reproduction, etc. have been permitted *for a licensed purpose*, a party is entitled under art.5(3) to observe, study or test the functioning of the program even if such is for an *unlicensed* purpose.

4-131   Finally, it is of note that unlike the decompilation defence discussed next, the Directive does not provide that the Berne three-step test must be satisfied.[272]

---

[269] Certainly in the authors' experience!
[270] art.8, second paragraph.
[271] See paras 4-101 and 4-119.
[272] For discussion of this, see para.4-030.

Decompilation/reverse engineering

Article 6 of the Directive introduces a decompilation defence where such is **4-132** "indispensable to obtain the information necessary to achieve the interoperability of an independently created program with other programs."[273] The right to decompile cannot be excluded by contract.[274]

Software firms often wish to ensure that their programs are compatible (or **4-133** "interoperable") with others. Interoperability is, in essence, the ability to connect computer systems together where the software is made by different firms. For example, software for word processing might be made by one firm and a software application for the bulk creation of documents from a mailing list by another. For the bulk mailing software to work, the two programs will need to be able to communicate ("interface") with each other. The first step in achieving interoperability often consists of a computer programmer "decompiling" the target program, that is, converting its machine-readable "object code" into something resembling "source code", or code that is in a human-readable form. The computer programmer does this by obtaining a copy of the target software, loading it onto a computer and converting it using decompilation software. Once it is thus decompiled, the target program usually contains sufficient information to allow a programmer to understand the nature of the parts relevant to interoperability. They will then use this information to write the new code for the program that is to be interoperable with the decompiled software. The problem, of course, is that many of the acts in this process are prima facie an infringement of copyright (in particular the reproduction right) in the decompiled software.

Initial drafts of the Directive were silent on the question of interoperability. Two **4-134** powerful lobby groups developed rival stances on the issue. The first, the ECIS (European Committee for Interoperable Systems, consisting of smaller firms: ICL, Bull, etc.) argued that the Directive should permit reverse engineering on the basis that such would facilitate competition and promote innovation. The other main group, SAGE (the Software Action Group for Europe comprising large firms such as IBM, Microsoft, etc.) took the opposite view, emphasising the need for protection of right holders. Though reverse engineering provisions were eventually included in the Directive, the way that they were drafted represents a compromise between these stances.

Under art.6 of the Directive, the copyright owner's permission is not required **4-135** where reproduction of the code and translation of its form are "*indispensable* to obtain the information *necessary* to achieve the interoperability of an independently created computer program with other programs" (emphasis added), provided that the following conditions are met:

(a) the acts are performed by the licensee or by another person having a right to use a copy of a program, or on their behalf by a person authorised to do so[275];

(b) the information necessary to achieve interoperability has not previously been readily available to the above persons[276]; and

---

[273] art.6(1).
[274] art.8(1).
[275] art.6(1)(a).
[276] art.6(1)(b). Quaere whether a right holder can make the information available but subject to the pay-

(c)   these acts are confined to the parts of the original program which are necessary to achieve interoperability.[277]

4-136   The right holder's rights are further bolstered in that the Directive provides that any information obtained in such a way cannot:

(a)   be used for goals other than to achieve interoperability of the independently created program;

(b)   be given to others, except when necessary for the interoperability of the independently created computer program; or

(c)   be used for the development, production or marketing, of a computer program substantially similar in its expression, or for any other act which infringes copyright.[278]

4-137   A further control on the right to decompile is provided by art.6(3) of the Directive, which incorporates the familiar Berne Convention "three-step" test that is found in several international instruments as well as other EU Directives.[279]

4-138   It should be noted that the above provisions are exhaustive and comprehensive in nature. Accordingly, a defendant may not resort to "fair dealing" or "fair use" provisions in national copyright laws (in so far as they exist) to justify the carrying out of restricted acts in the course of decompilation.[280]

4-139   Article 6 of the Directive raises a number of questions. First, what is meant by "indispensable" and "necessary" in art.6(1)? Does it mean that if another (however time-consuming or expensive) method of achieving interoperability can be found, that route should be taken? Secondly, does "readily available" include availability at a very high price but nonetheless one that the potential decompiler could afford? Furthermore, whilst art.6(1)(c) seems aimed at preventing "wholesale" decompiling, those who invoke its provisions are not always going to know which parts of the right holder's program contains the elements "necessary to achieve interoperability". Are they liable if they decompile the whole program to find the relevant part? It is unlikely that the CJEU will adopt an approach which is uncommercial. Thus, in the context of trade marks and whether repackaging of pharmaceuticals is "necessary" to market the product in the Member State of

---

ment of a royalty. In such circumstances, is the information "readily" available?

[277]   art.6(1)(c).

[278]   art.6(2)(a)–(c).

[279]   For example, art.13 TRIPS, art.10 WCT, art.16 WPPT, art.6(3) Computer Programs Directive, art.6(3) Database Directive, and art.5(5) Information Society Directive. See para.4-030 for discussion of this in the section on the Berne Convention. The first step of the Berne three-step test is that it should only apply in special cases and clearly decompilation to discover interoperability information satisfies this condition.

[280]   In the US, the copying of a computer program in the context of reverse engineering is permissible under the doctrine of fair use so long as the reproduction "is strictly necessary to ascertain the balance of protected information within the work"—*Atari v Nintendo*, Court of Appeals for the Federal Circuit, 10 September 1992. It held that the peeling of a semiconductor chip to examine the object code and further disassembly of the object code to determine the functioning of the Nintendo locking system was "fair use" (reversing *Sega Enterprises v Accolade*, District Court). However, copying of source code was not permitted in the context of reverse engineering because copy was obtained under false pretences and fair use required that the user have "clean hands". Also, note that in *Bowers v Baystate Technologies* (320 F.3d 1317), the United States Court of Appeals (Federal Circuit) held that the right to reverse engineer could be prevented by a shrink wrap licence. Note that under Recital 15, the decompilation right in the Directive is deemed to be compatible with fair practice quaere whether the obtaining of source code under false pretences would prevent the application of art.6.

importation, the CJEU has adopted an approach whereby it must be shown that the repackaging is objectively necessary to ensure effective access to the market.[281] Following this lead, it is submitted that the requirements of "indispensability" and "necessary" and "readily available" should be interpreted purposively to mean that that the decompilation defence is available where there are no other economically feasible means to discover the interoperability information. The criterion of "economically feasible" would relate as much to researching the marketplace to discover whether the information is readily available as to technical examination or analysis of the software to determine the interface information other than via decompilation.

Remedies

The Directive states that Member States must provide, in accordance with their national legislation, appropriate remedies against persons committing any of the following acts: **4-140**

    (a) putting into circulation a copy knowing or having reason to believe that it is an infringing copy;

    (b) possessing a copy for commercial purposes knowing or having reason to believe that it is an infringing copy; and

    (c) putting into circulation or the possession for commercial purpose of devices designed to facilitate the unauthorised removal or circumvention of any copy protection device.[282]

Furthermore, the Directive provides that infringing copies must be liable to seizure.[283]

The requirement of knowing or having reason to believe is a concept very familiar in UK copyright and design right law which includes such requirements where the defendant deals commercially in infringing copies.[284] Correspondence to a potential defendant that they are dealing in infringing copies will normally suffice to give them reason to believe that they are dealing in infringing copies. Finally, it should be noted that, although innocent possession of an infringing copy is not an infringement, such copies are subject to seizure. **4-141**

Term of protection

Copyright protection in a computer program extends for 70 years after the author's death.[285] **4-142**

---

[281] See para.3-639.

[282] art.7(1).

[283] art.7(2).

[284] See Copyright Designs and Patents Act 1988. See also *LA Gear Inc v Hi-Tec Sports plc* [1992] F.S.R. 121 ("reason to believe" involves the concept of "knowledge of facts from which a reasonable man would arrive at the relevant belief. Facts from which a reasonable man might suspect the relevant conclusion cannot be enough. Moreover, as it seems to me, the phrase does connote the allowance of a period of time to enable the reasonable man to evaluate those facts so as to convert the facts into a reasonable belief"). See also art.13 Enforcement Directive—para.15-041.

[285] art.11 Term Directive, which repealed art.8 Computer Programs Directive. See para.4-203, et seq.

Miscellaneous

4-143   The Directive leaves untouched other legal provisions governing computer programs, such as the laws of patents,[286] trade marks, unfair competition, trade secrets, semiconductor product protection or the law of contract.[287]

4-144   According to the 10 April 2000 Commission Report, the effect of the Directive on the software industry was beneficial[288] and there has been no serious pressure from interested circles to amend the Directive in any way.

The Rental Right and Neighbouring Rights Directive

Introduction

4-145   Like the Computer Programs Directive, the initial Rental Right Directive (92/100/EEC) has been repealed and a codified version (2006/115/EC) brought into force. The codified version renumbers many of the Recitals and Articles but does not seek to alter their meaning or effect. Where references are made to Recital and Article numbers, they are to the recitals and articles of the codified version.

4-146   The Rental Right Directive contains two very different parts. Chapter I confers rental and lending rights upon authors of works (in the Berne Convention sense), as well as upon performers and producers of phonograms and films. Chapter II goes well beyond rental and lending rights to confer rights for performers, phonogram producers and broadcasters. In these areas, the Directive deals with matters covered under the Rome and Phonograms Conventions.[289]

4-147   In the 1970s, the advent of certain technologies that made home copying easier, such as tape-to-tape audio-cassette recorders, VCRs and so on, had begun to lead to increasing concern that those who obtained copyright works could be copying them in private and disseminating them to others. Meanwhile, there was also a sharp increase in rental—in particular video cassette rental—as a means of exploiting copyright works.[290] Accordingly, and to the extent that a separate economic justification was necessary in respect of a right to proceeds from rental, it was considered that providing rental income to copyright owners might go some way towards offsetting the loss of income to rights holders as a result of the increased threat of piracy.[291]

4-148   It was not immediately obvious that the law of copyright could or should step into the breach. In some Member States, once the product embodying the copyright work (say, a CD) was sold, the copyright owner lost control over it as an economic object. If there was no subsequent copying of the CD, there was little the copyright owner could do.

---

[286] See the *Promoting innovation through patents-the follow-up to the Green Paper on the Community patent and the patent system in Europe* COM (1999) 42 final.

[287] With the exception of the particular prohibitions on certain licensing provisions that are contained in the Computer Program Directive itself.

[288] According to the Report's statistics, piracy had declined from 78 per cent in 1990 to 36 per cent in 1998, whilst the value of the software industry has increased from €19 billion in 1992 to €31 billion in 1997.

[289] See para.4-038. The adoption of the Directive coincided with a resolution that Member States should become, by 1 January 1995, parties to the Paris Act of the Berne Convention and the Rome Convention: *Council Resolution on increased protection for copyright and neighbouring rights* [1992] OJ C138/1.

[290] See Rental Right Directive Recital 2.

[291] Rental Right Directive Recitals 2, 3 and 5, and *Metronome Musik v Musik Point Hokamp* (C-200/96) [1998] E.C.R. I-1953 at [24] (this case concerned the validity of the Rental Directive).

Initially, the proposal had been for relatively unambitious harmonisation legislation confined to rental rights alone. However, the Commission's proposals were considerably altered during a series of debates which involved rounds of discussions with interested parties and a two-day hearing.[292] This finally resulted in the issue of the Rental Right Directive.[293] Owing to strenuous lobbying by those who advocated the similarity of rental and lending rights, the Commission decided, in addition, to include a lending right in the Directive. This had been contrary to the original proposal of the Green Paper.

4-149

The Rental Right Directive is in conformity with arts 11 and 14 of TRIPS.[294] Article 11 of TRIPS provides that:

4-150

> "in respect of at least computer programs[295] and cinematographic works, a Member shall provide authors and their successors in title the right to authorise or to prohibit the commercial rental to the public of originals or copies of their copyright works."

Article 14 of TRIPS provides that the provisions of art.11 are to:

4-151

> "apply mutatis mutandis to producers of phonograms and any other right holders in phonograms as determined in a Member's law. If on April 15, 1994 a Member has in force a system of equitable remuneration of right holders in respect of the rental of phonograms, it may maintain such system provided that the commercial rental of phonograms is not giving rise to the material impairment of the exclusive rights of reproduction of right holders."

Member States were obliged to bring into force the necessary legislation for the implementation of the Rental Right Directive by 1 July 1994.[296] The following sections examine the provisions of the codifying directive—Dir.2006/115.

4-152

Rental and lending rights: definitions

Article 1 of the Directive requires Member States to provide a right to authorise or prohibit the rental and lending of originals and copies of copyright works. This applies to all works other than buildings and works of applied art.[297] The rental and lending right extends to performances, phonograms and films.[298] "Rental" is broadly defined as "making available for use for a limited period of time and for direct or indirect economic or commercial advantage."[299] Lending is defined as:

4-153

---

[292] To see how much the finally adopted Directive differs from proposal, see S. von Lewinski, "Rental Right, Lending Right and Certain Neighbouring Rights: The E.C. Commission's Proposal for a Council Directive" [1991] 13(4) E.I.P.R. 117–123. The second proposal of the Commission as set out therein bears little resemblance to the final Directive.

[293] Directive 92/100/EEC on rental right and lending right and on certain rights related to copyright in the field of intellectual property [1992] OJ L346/61.

[294] See para.4-051.

[295] A rental right had already been introduced in respect of software through the Computer Programs Directive art.4(c): see para.4-109. The Rental Right Directive is expressed to be without prejudice to that: see art.4 Rental Right Directive.

[296] art.15.

[297] art.3(2).

[298] arts 1(1) and 3(1).

[299] art.2(1), introductory words and art.2(1)(a).

"making available for use, for a limited period of time and not for direct or indirect economic or commercial advantage, when it is made through establishments which are accessible to the public."[300]

4-154   It is made clear that certain acts which might be considered rental or lending are not covered by the new right. These are the showing of films or playing of music in public, and the exhibiting of works and making them available for on-the-spot reference use.[301] This gap was remedied in the later Information Society Directive by the "communication to the public" right.[302]

Exhaustion of rental and lending rights

4-155   In accordance with a considerable amount of CJEU jurisprudence[303] on the point, the Directive provides that rental and lending rights are not exhausted by the sale or other act of distribution of the object embodying the copyright work within the EU.[304]

4-156   Similarly, the rental right is not exhausted by the prior, consensual rental of the work in another Member State. In *Foreningen AF Danske Videogramdistributorer v Laserdisken*[305] the claimant, the Association of Danish Video Distributors, sued the defendant who had imported videodisks from the UK into Denmark and sought to offer them for rental in circumstances where the UK copyright owner had earlier consented to their rental on the UK market only. The Danish court referred to the CJEU two questions as to whether it was contrary to the EC Treaty or the Rental Right Directive for the holder of the rental right to prohibit copies of a film being rented in a Member State, where offering those copies for rental had been authorised in another Member State. The Commission and several Member States submitted that the rental right in a film is analogous to the right of public performance, which, unlike the right of distribution, is not exhausted as soon as it has first been exercised.[306] The CJEU held that there was no exhaustion of the Danish rental right, observing that the rental right in a video film was, by its very nature, to be exploited by repeated and potentially unlimited transactions, each of which gave a right to remuneration. The right would accordingly be rendered meaningless and worthless if it were held to be exhausted as soon as the object was first offered for rental.

Ownership of rental and lending rights

4-157   The exclusive rental and lending right is deemed to belong to the following: the author in respect of the original and copies of their work; the performer in respect of fixations of their performance; the phonogram producer in respect of their phonograms; and the producer of the first fixation of the film in respect of the original and copies of their film.[307]

---

[300] art.2(1)(b).
[301] Recital 10.
[302] See paras 4-264 and 4-293.
[303] See *Warner Brothers v Christiansen* (158/86) [1988] E.C.R. 2605; and *Ministère Public v Tournier* (395/87) [1989] E.C.R. 2521. See also *Metronome* (C-200/96) [1998] E.C.R. I-1953, [1999] E.M.L.R. 93.
[304] art.1(2).
[305] *Foreningen af Danske Videogramdistributorer v Laserdisken* (C-61/97) [1998] E.C.R. I-5171.
[306] See *Warner Brothers* (158/86) [1988] E.C.R. 2605 and discussion at para.7-251.
[307] art.3(1).

Cinematographic works, audiovisual works and the rental right

The Directive contains various provisions concerning the rental and lending of cinematographic works. The principal director of a cinematographic work or audiovisual work is deemed to be the author, but Member States can provide that others, too, shall be considered authors.[308] As a cinematographic work often consists of several protected works in addition to the exclusive rights in the cinematographic work per se, (e.g. the book on which the film was based, the theme music or lyrics, the performances of the actors, etc.), each of which would potentially give rise to a separate rental right, the Directive seeks to simplify matters. Thus, a performer is to be presumed in a contract, subject to express contractual stipulations to the contrary, to have transferred their rental right to the film producer.[309] Member States may also compel performers to authorise the rental of a film when they conclude a contract with a film producer but must ensure that the performer is equitably remunerated.[310] The right of an author or performer to equitable remuneration is always retained and cannot be waived.[311] This is intended to protect such persons who may be in a weak bargaining position, though their position may be considerably strengthened given that the administration of this right may be assigned to the appropriate collecting societies within Member States.[312]

4-158

Compulsory licence of lending rights

Article 6(1) of the Directive permits Member States to provide for the compulsory licensing of the lending right in respect of public lending of copyright works and their copies, provided that authors are remunerated, taking account of their cultural promotion objectives.[313] In respect of the public lending of phonograms, films and computer programs, Member States need only provide remuneration for authors.[314] For instance, a Member State need not remunerate a phonogram producer where their phonogram is publicly lent, but must provide for remuneration for the writer of the song. Member States may also exempt certain categories of establishments from the payment of such remuneration.[315] In *Vereniging van Educatieve en Wetenschappelijke Auteurs (VEWA) v Belgische Staat*,[316] the CJEU concluded that art.6(1) of the Directive precluded a national provision which set an annual remuneration at a flat rate based on the number of borrowers registered

4-159

---

[308] art.2(2). Member States did not need to enact this provision until 1 July 1997: see art.13(5) of Directive 92/100/EEC. In *Luksan v van der Let* (C-277/10) ECLI:EU:C:2012:65, [2013] E.C.D.R. 5 it was held at [72] that this provision precluded national legislation which allocated those rights by operation of law to persons not including the principal director. Further, it was held at [47], the first ownership of copyright by at least the principal director also applied to rights in that director's works under the Information Society Directive. However, it was permissible for the Member State to create a rebuttable presumption of the transfer of those and other rights to the producer when a contract concerning film production is concluded between the director and the producer (see [87]).

[309] art.3(4). Member States may provide for a similar presumption in respect of authors: see art.3(5). The purpose of this is to enable the producer to recoup their investment in the making of the film, as indicated in Recital 5 and confirmed in *Luksan v van der Let* [2012] E.C.R. 0000; [2013] E.C.D.R. 5 at [79].

[310] art.3(6).

[311] art.5(1), (2). This was also confirmed in *Luksan v van der Let* (C-277/10).

[312] art.5(3), (4).

[313] art.6(1).

[314] art.6(2).

[315] art.6(3).

[316] (C-271/10) [2011] E.C.R. I-5815.

with public establishments and a low fixed flat-rate amount per borrower. While the CJEU stated that public lending does not have a direct or indirect economic or commercial character, such that the amount of remuneration will necessarily be less than the amount of "equitable remuneration" required for commercial rental and might even be a fixed rate, that remuneration, as required by Recital 5 to the Directive, must be capable of allowing authors to receive an "adequate income". The Belgian scheme did not take into account the extent to which works were made available to the public under the lending right. Thus, while the setting of the adequate income was within the Belgian state's discretion, the national provisions did not have sufficient regard for the extent of the harm suffered by authors, nor for the principle that those authors must receive remuneration that is equivalent to an adequate income.[317]

4-160   In the digital era, what is the legal position concerning the lending of digital copies whereby the server of a public library allows a user to download such a copy onto his computer in circumstances that only one copy may be downloaded and after the lending period, the downloaded copy is rendered unreadable? Is such covered by art.6(1) of the Directive or must consent be obtained from the right holders? The Court of Justice considered this in *Vereniging Openbare Bibliotheken v Stichting Leenrecht*[318] where they held that this did fall within the public library exception in art.6(1) but that Member States could make such a scheme dependent on the right holder having published a digital version of the book. Moreover, it did not extend to digital copies where that copy was obtained from an unlawful source.

Duration of rental and lending rights and miscellaneous

4-161   Article 11 of Dir.92/100 originally provided that the rental and lending rights were to run for the duration of the primary rights provided for by the Berne Convention, and to expire simultaneously with them. This was originally expressed to be without prejudice to further harmonisation. The first Term Directive repealed these provisions.[319] Accordingly, the duration of the rental right must be calculated by reference to the period of protection provided by that Directive.[320] Transitional provisions permitted Member States to deem that a rights holder had authorised the rental or lending of a work which has been made available to third parties for such purposes or had been acquired prior to 1 July 1994.[321]

Neighbouring rights

4-162   In addition to the rental and lending rights, the Directive provides for performers' rights, phonogram producers' rights, cinematographic producers' rights and broadcasting rights. Apart from the cinematographic producers' rights, the rights provided coincide with those provided under the Rome Convention.[322] Since the Rental Right Directive was issued, the Satellite and Cable Directive has been adopted. This latter Directive extends the protection given to phonogram produc-

---

[317] For a further discussion of this judgment, see N. Caddick QC, G. Davies, and G. Harbottle, *Copinger and Skone James on Copyright*, 2nd Supplement to the 16th edn (London: Sweet & Maxwell, 2013), para.19–02.

[318] (C-174/15) ECLI:EU:C:2016:856.

[319] art.11(2) of Dir.93/98/EEC.

[320] See the Term Directive at para.4-203.

[321] art.11(3).

[322] See Rome Convention, para.4-038.

ers, performers and broadcasting organisations in the Rental Right Directive to include communication to the public by satellite.[323] For ease of reference, the provisions of the Satellite and Cable Directive which apply to the above persons are discussed in the commentary below.

Performers' rights

The Directive with the Information Society Directive compels Member States to provide that performers are given the exclusive right to authorise or prohibit the fixation of their performances[324]; the exclusive right to prevent temporary or permanent reproduction by any means and in any form, in whole or in part of such fixations[325]; the right to a share with phonogram producers in a single equitable remuneration paid for the broadcasting (whether by wireless means or satellite) or communication to the public of phonograms incorporating their performances[326]; and the right to prevent the broadcasting or communication to the public of their performances themselves unless such is already a broadcast performance or is made from a fixation.[327] Thus, performers have the right to prevent live broadcasts but not broadcasts of recorded material. Performers also have the exclusive right to distribute fixations of their performances until any such fixation is sold with the consent of the rights holder, after which the distribution right is exhausted.[328]   **4-163**

The duration of performers' rights are set out in the Term Directive.   **4-164**

Phonogram producers' rights

Phonogram producers are granted the exclusive right to prevent the temporary or permanent reproduction by any means and in any form, in whole or in part of their phonograms[329]; the right to a single equitable remuneration for the broadcast (whether by wireless means or via satellite) or for any communication to the public of their phonograms (such remuneration to be shared with the performers whose performance is incorporated in the phonogram)[330]; and the right to distribute their phonograms until any such phonogram is sold with their consent, after which the distribution right is exhausted.[331] A phonogram right runs for a period of 50 years from the date of fixation or, if lawfully published or communicated to the public   **4-165**

---

[323] arts 4–7 Satellite and Cable Directive: see para.4-186.

[324] art.7(1).

[325] art.2(b) Information Society Directive, which, by art.11, repeals what was art.7(1) of the Rental Right Dir.92/100. The original provision had defined the reproduction right as "the exclusive right to authorize or prohibit the direct or indirect reproduction of...", etc.

[326] art.8(2) Rental Right Directive and Satellite and art.4(2) Cable Directive (in relation to broadcasting by satellite). Member States are free to provide more far-reaching protection for performers in this area: see Recital 16 of the Rental Right Directive and art.6(1) Satellite and Cable Directive.

[327] arts 8(1) and 4(2) Satellite and Cable Directive (with regard to satellite broadcasting). Member States are free to provide more protection than that provided under these Articles.

[328] art.9(1) and (2).

[329] art.2(b) Information Society Directive, which, by art.11, repeals what was art.7(1) of the Rental Right Dir.92/100. The original provision had defined the reproduction right as "the exclusive right to authorise or prohibit the direct or indirect reproduction of...", etc.

[330] art.8(2). Member States are free to provide more protection for phonogram producers in this area—see Recital 16 and art.6(1) Satellite and Cable Directive.

[331] art.9(1), (2).

in this period, 70 years from the date of publication or communication to the public.[332]

Equitable remuneration for broadcast and communication to the public of phonograms: performers and phonogram producers

4-166   Article 8(2) of the Rental Rights Directive makes provision for a "single equitable remuneration" to be paid by the user if a phonogram published for commercial purposes, or a reproduction of such phonogram, is used, broadcasted or communicated to the public, and requires Member States to ensure that this equitable remuneration is shared between the relevant performers and phonogram producers. This provision implements art.12 of the Rome Convention.[333] The Article is silent on the meaning of "equitable remuneration" but does say that Member States may, in the absence of agreement between the relevant performers and phonogram producers, lay down conditions as to how the remuneration is to be shared. In the *SENA* case,[334] the CJEU confirmed that "equitable remuneration" was a EU concept that had to be interpreted uniformly in all Member States, but that Member States had to determine within their own territory the relevant criteria in each individual case. Regard could be to factors such as the number of hours broadcast, the viewing and listening figures, equivalent tariffs for music copyright, and the tariffs set by public broadcasters and commercial stations.[335]

4-167   In *SCF v Del Corso*[336] and in *Phonographic Performance Ireland*,[337] two cases handed down by the Third Chamber of the CJEU on the same day, the CJEU considered whether the playing of a phonogram in a dentist waiting room (*SCF*) and a private room in a hotel (*PPI*) amounted to a communication to the public of the phonogram. As the CJEU has now confirmed that the interpretation of "communication to the public" right in the Rental Directive is the same as for the Information Society Directive, this is discussed later in this chapter.[338]

Cinematographic producers' rights

4-168   Producers of the first fixations of films have the exclusive right to prevent the temporary or permanent reproduction by any means and in any form, in whole or in part of the original and any copies of their films,[339] as well as the exclusive right to make available to the public the original or copies until they are sold with their consent, after which the distribution right is exhausted.[340] Where the film incorporates literary or artistic works, the duration of protection for these people

---

[332] See para.4-220.

[333] See para.4-047.

[334] *Stichting ter Exploitatie van Naburige Rechten (SENA) v Nederlandse Omroep Stichting (NOS)* (C-245/00) [2003] E.C.R. I-1251. See also *Lagardère Active Broadcast v Société pour la perception de la rémunération équitable (SPRE)* (C-192/04) [2005] E.C.R. I-7199.

[335] See [46].

[336] *Societa Consortile Fonografici (SCF) v Del Corso* (C-135/10) ECLI:EU:C:2012:140, [2012] E.C.D.R. 16.

[337] *Phonographic Performance (Ireland) Ltd v Ireland* (C-162/10) ECLI:EU:C:2012:141, [2012] E.C.D.R. 15.

[338] See para.4-293.

[339] art.2(d) Information Society Directive, which, by art.11, repealed art.7(1) of the original Rental Right Directive 92/100. The original provision had defined the reproduction right as "the exclusive right to authorise or prohibit the direct or indirect reproduction of...", etc.

[340] art.9(1), (2).

in the cinematographic work is 70 years after the last death of the principal director, the author of the screenplay, the author of the dialogue, and the composer of music specifically created for use in the work.[341] As regards producers of a cinematographic or audiovisual work, the Directive originally provided that the period of protection was for 20 years after the date of fixation.[342] However, this was increased for producers by the Term Directive to 50 years from date of first fixation.[343]

Broadcasting organisations' rights

Under the Directive, broadcasters have the exclusive right to authorise or prohibit the fixation of their broadcasts, whether these are transmitted by wire or over the air, including by cable and by satellite[344]; the exclusive right to prevent the temporary or permanent reproduction by any means and in any form, in whole or in part of such fixations[345]; the exclusive right of distribution of fixations of their broadcasts[346]; and the exclusive right to prevent re-broadcasts by wireless means or via satellite or communication to the public of their broadcasts where such communication is made in places accessible to the public against payment of an entrance fee.[347] These broadcasting rights expire 50 years from the date of the first transmission.[348]   **4-169**

Communication to the public

The concept of "communication to the public" has been the subject of many decisions of the Court of Justice when considering the equivalent provision in the Information Society Directive which protects the communication to the public of copyright works.[349] The Court of Justice has said that the concepts have the same meaning and accordingly, the reader is referred to that case law.[350]   **4-170**

Payment of an entrance fee

As said above, unlike the communication to the public right for authors of copyright works and public performers and phonogram producers,[351] the communication to the public right for broadcasters is only where the broadcast is in a   **4-171**

---

[341] art.2(2) Term Directive.

[342] art.12 Rental Right Directive.

[343] art.3(3) Term Directive, which replaced art.12(2) of the original Rental Right Directive 92/100 (the repealing provision is art.11(2) Term Directive).

[344] art.7(2). This right does not extend to cable distributors who merely retransmit the broadcasts of another: see art.7(3).

[345] art.2(e) Information Society Directive, which, by its art.11, repeals art.7(1) of the original Rental Right Directive 92/100. The original provision had defined the reproduction right as "the exclusive right to authorize or prohibit the direct or indirect reproduction of…", etc.

[346] art.9(1)(d).

[347] art.8(3). Member States are free to provide more far-reaching protection in this area for broadcasting organisations: see Recital 16.

[348] art.3(4) Term Directive. Article 11(2) repealed art.12 of the original Rental Right Directive 92/100, which provided for 20 years from the date of the first transmission.

[349] See paras 4-264 and 4-293.

[350] See *Verwetungsgesellschaft GmbH v Hettegger Hotel Edelweiss GmbH* (C-641/15) ECLI:EU:C:2017:131 at [19]. For discussion of communication to the public under the Information Society Directive, see para.4-293.

[351] For performers and phonogram producers, see paras 4-163 and 4-165.

place accessible to the public against payment of an entrance fee. The reason for this somewhat odd condition is that art.13(d) of the Rome Convention uses the same wording.[352] In *Verwertungsgesellschaft Rundfunk GmbH v Hettegger Hotel Edelweiss*,[353] the Court of Justice had to consider whether the transmission of broadcasted television and radio programmes by a hotel to televisions in hotel rooms of broadcasts for the benefit of guests who paid for their rooms amounted to communication to the public of broadcasts against payment of an entrance fee. The Court of Justice held, having considered WIPO guidance material on art.13(d) Rome Convention that the condition presupposed a payment "specifically requested in return for the communication to the public of a TV broadcast" and thus the mere fact of payment for a meal or drinks in a restaurant or in a bar where TV broadcasts are aired was not to be regarded as payment of an entrance fee within the meaning of art.8(3) of the Rental Directive. The court held that the same reasoning applied to the price of a hotel room and therefore whilst there was a communication to the public, it was not against the payment of an entrance fee.[354]

On demand/live streaming of broadcasts

4-172   In considering the rights of broadcasting organisations in their broadcast to prevent access of broadcasts through the Internet, the reader should be aware of two provisions. First, art.3(2)(d) of the Information Society Directive provides for a "making available" (Internet) right but not a more general "communication to the public" right to the owners of neighbouring rights, including for broadcasting organisations, the fixations of their broadcasts whether transmitted by wire or over the air and whether by satellite or cable.[355] Manifestly, art.3(2)(d) of the Information Society Directive does not apply to "live" Internet broadcasts, as the "making available" right is defined as a right that permits members of the public to choose the time that they view the work.

4-173   The other provision is art.8(3) of the Rental and Neighbouring Rights Directive. This confers on broadcasting organisations the exclusive right to authorise or prohibit the rebroadcasting of their broadcasts by wireless means as well as the communication to the public of their broadcasts if such communication is made in places accessible to the public against payment of an entrance fee. This provision is also not aimed or focussed at online "live" streaming of broadcasts but rather broadcasts shown in theatres, pubs, bars, etc. This might be thought surprising but in truth the current Rental and Neighbouring Rights Directive is little more than a codified version of a pre-Internet era Directive, being Dir.92/100.[356]

4-174   Such subtleties came to light when a Swedish court referred a question to the Court of Justice concerning the interpretation of art.3(2)(d) of the Information Society Directive in *C More Entertainment v Linus Sandberg*.[357] In that case, the defendant provided links on an Internet site which enabled Internet users to access live streaming broadcasts of ice hockey matches without paying a fee. Swedish law provided greater protection than art.3(2)(d) as it was not limited to "on demand" viewing as it applied to live broadcasts which are clearly, not "on demand".

---

[352] See para.4-038. See also Recital 7 Dir.2006/115 which says that the Directive is not intended to conflict with the international conventions on which the copyright and related laws of many Member States are based.

[353] (C-641/15) ECLI:EU:C:2017:131.

[354] See [23]–[27].

[355] See para.4-293.

[356] See para.4-149.

[357] (C-279/13) ECLI:EU:C:2015:199.

The Swedish court asked whether a Member State could give wider protection **4-175** than provided for in art.3(2) Information Society Directive. The Court of Justice considered that art.3(2)(d) was not applicable as it did not cover live streaming.[358] So far no surprise. However, it then went on to find that art.3(2) was not intended to be exhaustive and was not intended thus to harmonise laws (by excluding them) relating to the extension of the rights of broadcasters to prevent unauthorised live streaming of their broadcasts on the Internet.[359] The Court of Justice then considered art.8(3) of the Rental and Neighbouring Rights Directive. As said above, it does not cover the acts of online free live streaming of broadcasts. However, the Court of Justice said that it was apparent from the recitals to the Rental and Neighbouring Rights Directive that Member States could provide for greater protection to broadcasting organisations than that provided for in that Directive.[360]

The significance of the above is that whilst the Information Society Directive and **4-176** the Rental and Neighbouring Rights Directive does protect broadcasters as regards the unauthorised on-demand access of their broadcasts and broadcasts in pubs, bars, etc. they do not provide wider protection for broadcasting organisations more apt and suitable for the Internet era. As made clear by the Court of Justice, Member States are free to provide greater protection, e.g. to prevent unauthorised live streaming of broadcasts on the Internet. It may be that Member States who have merely transcribed the provisions of these Directives into their domestic law should ask themselves whether they should be providing more protection.

Infringement of "signal" rights: what is the right test?

Films, broadcasts and sound recordings are often known as "signal" rights. Ac- **4-177** cordingly, they are not concerned with the protection of the creativity of an author in creating a literary, dramatic or artistic work. The right arises automatically upon the act of recording on audiovisual media or in the case of broadcast, converting an event into an electronic feed. Therefore, it might be thought that the test of infringement of such works, being whether a defendant has taken the "intellectual creation" of the author is inapplicable.[361] However, if this is not applicable, what is the test? Does a one-second sample of a sound recording amount to infringement on the basis that even though it is very short, that single second will be exactly the same as the equivalent in the original recording?

In an English case, concerning a software app that allowed the playing of short **4-178** clips (lasting up to eight seconds) of highlights of cricket matches which had been broadcast by a sporting broadcasting company, the High Court considered whether there had been an infringement of the right granted under the Information Society Directive to protect the reproduction and making available to the public rights for fixation of films and fixations of broadcasts.[362] It held that the decisions of the Court of Justice which set down the "intellectual creation" test for infringement of liter- ary and artistic works under the Information Society Directive were inapplicable to signal rights.[363] However, it held that an analogous approach should be applied.[364] Thus, the court held that parts of broadcasts and first fixations of films enjoyed

---

[358] See [27].
[359] See [31].
[360] See [33], citing Recital 16 to Dir.2006/115.
[361] See para.4-089 for discussion of this.
[362] arts 2(d), (e); 3.2(c), (d) Information Society Directive. See para.4-264.
[363] *England and Wales Cricket Board Ltd v Tixdaq Ltd* [2016] EWHC 575 (Ch.) at [61].

protection under the Information Society Directive "provided that they contain elements which reflect the rationale for protecting broadcasts and first fixations, that is to say, the investment made by the broadcaster or producer".[365] It went onto say that the correct test was to consider the degree of reproduction both quantitatively and qualitatively, having regard to the extent to which the reproduction exploits the investment made by the broadcaster or producer.[366] The court held that each clip, being of highlights and thus of interest and value to the public, exploited the claimant's investment in producing the relevant broadcast and films.[367]

4-179   The approach of the English court has echoes of the test for infringement of database rights, namely whether there has been appropriation of the investment made by undertakings in the creation of databases.[368] Moreover, in both the Rental Directive and the Information Society Directive, the recitals refer to the investment that producers put into the production of phonograms and films and that such are especially high and risky.[369] However, the court's approach was in part coloured by the fact that it was considering clips of sporting highlights. As is well known, and the judge noted, broadcasters and producers will carry out careful editing of footage from multiple camera angles, close ups, slow motion and the like to make them as appealing as they can to watchers.[370] Indeed, as the judge said, such acts of editing may have allowed the claimant to claim that they were dramatic works by the same reasoning.[371] Therefore, the court considered that short clips which were not of highlights were not infringements.[372]

4-180   However, what would have been the position if there had been no such editing and the highlight clips marketed by the defendant were merely clips of a raw video feed recorded or broadcast by one camera on the edge of the cricket pitch? It cannot be said that the *investment* in producing an eight-second raw unedited feed of a catch, taking of a wicket, etc.[373] is any different than that of a raw unedited feed of any other eight-second part of a game.

4-181   Of course, what is different is the *value* of the clip to the watcher or viewer. Is it fair to consider the value of a clip when considering whether there is infringement of a signal right? Clearly, the public are not interested in looking at eight seconds of a video feed of the grass on a football pitch. A value approach would permit the protection of the copying of "human interest" homemade films even where no investment has been made into them but they are of real commercial value.[374] However, there is a danger in this approach in that one might say that anything that someone wants to copy has value and thus, it becomes self-fulfilling.

4-182   One is tempted to say that as the EU lawmakers and indeed international conventions have chosen to protect signal rights which do not require any creativity, originality and often involve no investment, then the copying or showing of any part of a protected signal regardless of its content should be an infringement unless it

---

[364] See [66].
[365] See [66].
[366] See [66].
[367] See [99].
[368] See para.4-255.
[369] Recital 5, Dir.2006/115; Recital 10, Dir.2001/29.
[370] See [66]. The claimant did not make such a claim.
[371] See [59].
[372] See [102].
[373] For those not familiar with cricket, this is the equivalent to the scoring of goals, penalty shots, etc.
[374] There is a big market in such, e.g. home videos on mobile phones of a child trying out some trick filmed by his father or mother.

is de minimis and leave the defendant to look for "fair use" defences, e.g. if the clip is very short, that its use is incidental. The alternative approach is for a radical decision of the Court of Justice that recordings and films where no or minimal investment has been made do not qualify for protection. However, this would be a radical departure from the understanding of the marketplace that such are protectable.

Limitations to the related rights

The Directive permits Member States to provide for limitations to the related rights in respect of private use; use of short excerpts in connection with the reporting of current events; ephemeral fixation by a broadcasting organisation by means of its own facilities and for its own broadcasts; and for use solely for the purposes of teaching or scientific research.[375] The Directive reserves the right to enact future legislation providing remuneration for reproduction for private use.[376]   **4-183**

Member States may provide for the same kind of limitations with regard to the protection of performers, producers of phonograms, broadcasting organisations, and producers of the first fixations of films as they provide in respect of artistic or literary works. However, compulsory licences may be provided only to the extent to which they are compatible with the Rome Convention.[377]   **4-184**

Finally, where the Directive provides for a distribution right,[378] this right is exhausted in relation to a particular work—unlike the rental right[379]—once that work has been put on sale on the EU by the rights holder or with the right holder's consent.[380]   **4-185**

The Satellite and Cable Directive

Introduction

In December 1990, the Commission issued a Discussion Paper entitled *Broadcasting and Copyright in the Internal Market*, in which it suggested various harmonisation measures related to satellite broadcasting and cable re-transmission. It had become apparent that communication to the public of copyright works via these media had increased immensely in the 1980s and was expected to carry on increasing. However, the trans-national nature of satellite broadcasting meant that there was debate over the applicable copyright law. Possible candidates appeared to be the following: (a) the country where the broadcaster was situated; (b) the country where the broadcast signal was transmitted to the satellite, that is, the "uplink" country; or (c) the country where the signal was received, that is the "footprint" country. This issue was important because there was much disparity in Member States' laws over the protection awarded to performers, phonogram producers and film producers in relation to broadcasting, whether by wireless or satellite. Moreover, there was a potential problem of split ownership of rights   **4-186**

---

[375] art.10(1) Rental Right Directive.
[376] art.10(3).
[377] art.10(2). In this regard, the most important provision is art.12 of the Rome Convention, which provides that phonogram producers and performers are only entitled to a single equitable remuneration (which may be payable to either or both) where a phonogram is broadcast or communicated to the public.
[378] art.9(1).
[379] See para.4-115.
[380] art.9(2).

between the emitting and receiving country if such countries took a different approach to the issue of ownership. For example, some countries merely provided a right to equitable remuneration to performers and phonogram producers when their works were broadcast, while others provided for an exclusive right to authorise or prohibit. Furthermore, it was clear that a minimum level of legal harmonisation should be secured to protect rights holders with regard to satellite broadcasting.

4-187   On the issue of cable re-transmissions, the Commission noted that legal certainty was missing where programmes were transmitted across borders and were fed into and retransmitted through cable networks. Cable operators were often unsure whether they had acquired all the programme rights covered by an agreement.[381]

4-188   On 22 July 1991, the Commission submitted to the Council a Proposal for a Council Directive on the co-ordination of certain rules concerning copyright and neighbouring rights applicable to satellite broadcasting and cable retransmissions. After amendments by the European Parliament, this led to the Satellite and Cable Directive.[382]

4-189   The main feature of the Satellite and Cable Directive is that, subject to certain exceptions, the act of communication to the public by satellite is deemed to be solely that of the Member State where the programme-carrying signals are introduced into an uninterrupted chain of communication leading to the satellite and down towards the earth.[383] Member States are required to provide an exclusive right for the author (of a copyright work) to authorise satellite transmission.[384] With regard to cable retransmission rights, the Directive provides that copyright and related rights holders have the right to authorise (through a collecting society) retransmission of broadcasts.

4-190   The European Commission is currently evaluating whether the Satellite and Cable Directive is fit for purpose in the modern world. When the Directive was enacted in 1993, there were two forms of transmission of television and radio programmes other than terrestrial broadcasts, namely satellite broadcasts and cable retransmission. In the 21st century, broadcasters are increasingly using other technological means to transmit their programmes including: (i) simulcasting over the Internet; and (ii) "catch up TV/radio" via the Internet. This means that broadcasters often need a different set of rights than those required for the initial broadcast, namely the reproduction right and the making available right. This has inhibited broadcasters from offering their services on a multiterritorial basis. Furthermore, the report has identified the need for a more transparent, collective licensing approach to the clearance of rights to ensure an effective single market approach. This has led to a draft regulation to extend the "country of origin" rule to simulcasts and "catch up" online television and radio programmes.[385] This is currently before the European Parliament.

---

[381] Recital 10, Satellite and Cable Directive.
[382] Dir.93/83. [1993] OJ L148/15.
[383] art.1(2)(b).
[384] art.2.
[385] COM (2016) 594 14.9.2016.

Satellite broadcasting

The Directive requires Member States to provide an exclusive right for the author **4-191** to authorise the communication to the public by satellite of copyright works.[386] Member States are not permitted to enact a compulsory licensing scheme and must ensure that authorisation is only acquired by agreement.[387] Member States may provide that a collective agreement between a collecting society and a broadcasting organisation regarding a given category of works (but not cinematographic works) extends to the satellite broadcasting provided that the satellite broadcast is simultaneous with the terrestrial broadcast and the unrepresented rights holder has the possibility of excluding such an automatic extension of the agreement to include satellite broadcasting.[388]

"Satellite" is defined as: **4-192**

> "any satellite operating on frequency bands which, under telecommunications law, are reserved for the broadcast of signals for reception by the public or which are reserved for closed point-to-point communication."[389]

"Communication to the public by satellite" is the act of emitting the signals into **4-193** a chain of communication for eventual reception by the public,[390] whether such are encrypted or not.[391] However, the question of whether a particular reception amounts to a "public" reception—for example, whether the reception by a hotel of satellite or terrestrial television signals and their distribution by cable to the rooms of the hotel was an "act of communication to the public" or "reception by the public"—is not provided for by the Directive.[392] These terms have since been interpreted by the CJEU in a number of cases dealing with communication to the public, primarily but not exclusively in the context of the Information Society Directive. The joined *Airfield*[393] cases do specifically address the communication to the public right under the Satellite and Cable Directive. In those cases, Airfield, a satellite channel package provider, offered a bouquet of channels to its customers. Some channels were included in that bouquet of channels in such a way that Airfield's customers received them directly from their original broadcaster. Other channels were received by Airfield off-air from their original broadcasters, and rebroadcast by Airfield to be received by its customers. Airfield contended that it did not require consent for that rebroadcasting, as it was indivisible from and formed part of a single act of communication to the public commenced by the original broadcaster, which had relevant consent from the rights holders. The CJEU

---

[386] art.2.

[387] art.3(2).

[388] arts 3(2), (3).

[389] art.1(1).

[390] See *Mediakabel BV v Commissariaat voor de Media* (C-89/04) [2005] E.C.R. I-4891.

[391] art.1(2)(a), (c). See *Lagardère* (C-192/04) [2005] E.C.R. I-7199 for a rare case where the transmission did not fall within the definition. Lagardère transmitted its programming from France via satellite to FM repeater stations. As FM did not cover the whole of France, the satellite also sent signals to a powerful transmitter in Saarland (Germany) which then broadcast to the whole of France on long wave.

[392] *Entidad Gestion de Derechos de los Productores Audiovisuales (Collecting Society for Audio-visual Producers) ("Egeda") v Hosteleria Asturiana SA* (C-293/98) [2000] E.C.R. I-629; [2000] E.M.L.R. 523. Egeda was decided before the passage of the Information Society Directive, which enacted a "communication to the public" right. See, in relation to that right under the Information Society Directive, the discussion at para.4-293.

[393] *Airfield v SABAM; Airfield v AGICOA* (C-431/09 and C-432/09) [2011] E.C.R. I-9363.

held that Airfield did need further authorisation for its rebroadcasting because it reached an audience not contemplated by the rights holders when giving their authorisation to the original broadcasters and which, without Airfield's intervention, would not be able to enjoy the works broadcast.[394]

4-194   A central feature of the Satellite and Cable Directive is its introduction of the "country of origin" principle. The act of communication to the public by satellite is deemed to occur *solely* in the Member State where:

> "under the control and responsibility of the broadcasting organisation, the programme-carrying signals are introduced into an uninterrupted chain of communication leading to the satellite and down towards the earth."[395]

4-195   It is thus the law of this Member State which is relevant in considering whether the exclusive right of communication to the public by satellite has been infringed.[396] If the programme-signals are introduced in a non-Member State which does not provide the same level of protection as that provided under the Directive, then, if the programme carrying signals are transmitted to the satellite via an uplink station situated in a Member State, the act of communication to the public via satellite is deemed to have occurred in the latter Member State and to have been carried out by the person operating the uplink station. The relevant law will thus be the law of that Member State.[397] If both the introduction of the programme-carrying signals and the uplink occur in non-Member States, then if the broadcasting organisation which commissioned the act of communication to the public by satellite has its principal place of establishment in a Member State, the exclusive satellite broadcasting rights may be exercised against the broadcasting organisation.[398]

4-196   Accordingly, the Directive does not provide effective and enforceable protection for rights holders where: (a) the satellite broadcast is beamed direct to a satellite from outside the EU or via an uplink not in the EU; and (b) where the broadcasting organisation's principal place of establishment is outside the EU. The Commission recognised that in such circumstances Member States would be free to treat these broadcasts differently.[399] It has been noted that this may have the effect of encouraging satellite broadcasters to relocate outside the EU to countries where rights holder's satellite broadcasting rights are not so well protected.[400]

4-197   The European Commission has launched a review of the "country of origin"

---

[394] At [79]. The "new public" approach has been followed in relation to the "communication to the public" provision of the Information Society Directive. See para.4-293.

[395] art.1(2)(b).

[396] The private international law of the *lex emissionis* may take into account the laws of the countries where the broadcast is received (the "footprint" countries). In a French/Austrian case, the courts of both countries held that broadcasters must comply with the laws of the footprint countries, either because they created damage or because they were intended to be received by the audience of that country: see P. Kern, "The EC Common Position on Copyright Applicable to Satellite Broadcasting and Cable Retransmission" [1993] 8 E.I.P.R. 276, 280. See also J.A.L. Sterling, "*Intellectual Property Rights in Sound Recordings, Film and Video*" (London: Sweet & Maxwell, 1992).

[397] art.1(2)(d)(i).

[398] art.1(2)(d)(ii).

[399] See Proposal submitted on 2 July 1991 and P. Kern, "The EC Common Position on Copyright Applicable to Satellite Broadcasting and Cable Retransmission" [1993] 8 E.I.P.R. 276, 277.

[400] See P. Kern, "The EC Common Position on Copyright Applicable to Satellite Broadcasting and Cable Retransmission" [1993] 8 E.I.P.R. 276, 277.

rule.[401] In particular, there is a new proposed regulation (COM(2016) 594) which proposes that the "country of origin" principle be extended to simulcasting (simultaneous broadcast of TV and radio programmes over the Internet) and "catch up" television and radio programmes (where a viewer can access online a programme that has already been broadcast). This proposal makes sense in the 21st century where such practices are now widespread.

Harmonisation of neighbouring rights with respect to satellite broadcasting

The Commission recognised that if legal protection for rights holders differed in Member States, satellite broadcasters would be encouraged to relocate their transmitters and uplink stations so as to take advantage of such differences. Accordingly, the Directive provides a certain level of harmonisation of copyright and related rights with regard to satellite broadcasting. As mentioned above, authors are granted the exclusive right to authorise the communication to the public by satellite of copyright works. This was a relatively uncontroversial proposal as most countries already protected such rights.   **4-198**

With regard to performers, phonogram producers and broadcasting organisations, the Directive integrates the satellite broadcasting right of such persons with the exclusive right of communication to the public provided for in the Rental Right Directive (which inter alia harmonises the level of protection in the EU for performers, etc.[402]). For ease of reference, the reader is referred to the discussion on the Rental Right Directive, which includes a detailed analysis of the application of this Directive to such rights.[403]   **4-199**

Cable retransmission right

The Commission realised that legal certainty, which was a prerequisite for the free movement of broadcasts, was missing where programmes were transmitted via cable networks.[404] Cable operators were not sure whether they had the rights to retransmit broadcasts via cable networks. Initially, the Commission proposed a compulsory licensing scheme for cable retransmission. However, after intensive lobbying, it dropped this idea. Under Ch.III of the Directive, Member States must now ensure that when programmes from other Member States are retransmitted via cable in their territory, the applicable copyright and related rights are observed.[405] However, the "cable retransmission right" to grant or refuse authorisation may only be exercised through a collecting society.[406] If the right holder has not actually transferred their rights to a collecting society, then they are deemed to have transferred their rights to a collecting society which manages rights of the same category.[407] In such circumstances, the rights holder may claim any royalties within a period not shorter than three years from the date of the cable retransmission of   **4-200**

---

[401] See para.4-009.
[402] art.4, et seq.
[403] See para.4-145.
[404] See Recital 8.
[405] art.8.
[406] art.9(1). "Collecting society" is defined as any organisation which manages or administers copyright or rights related to copyright as its sole purpose or as one of its main purposes: art.1(4).
[407] art.9(2).

their works.[408] Where a collecting society is deemed to be mandated to manage the rights of the rights holder, (i.e. in cases where management of the rights has not actually been transferred) the collecting society has the right to grant or refuse authorisation to a cable operator of the cable retransmission right. Its mandate is not limited to management of the royalties.[409]

4-201 Two important exceptions apply to the compulsory "collectivisation" of the cable retransmission right. First, where the cable retransmission right is owned by a broadcasting organisation in respect of its own transmission, there is no obligation to transfer such rights to a collecting society.[410] Secondly, where a Member State does not provide for a right to authorise, but merely a right to a single equitable remuneration, such rights holders are free to decide whether to act collectively or individually.[411]

4-202 The Directive contains certain provisions aimed at helping such negotiations to bear fruit. First, parties are entitled to call upon the assistance of mediators whose task is to provide assistance with negotiation and to submit proposals.[412] Secondly, Member States must ensure that parties enter and conduct negotiations regarding authorisation for cable retransmission in good faith and do not prevent or hinder such negotiations without valid justification.[413]

The Term Directive

Introduction

4-203 Prior to harmonisation, the duration (or "term") of copyright and related rights in Member States' laws varied widely. In Germany, Austria and Spain the term was 70 years post mortem auctoris ("pma"), i.e. from the death of the author. In the UK it was 50 years. In Portugal, copyright was at one time perpetual.

4-204 The issue of how long copyright and related rights should last is important. Divergent approaches on the issue among Member States can lead to obstacles to the creation of the single internal market. Such difficulties were exemplified by the *Patricia* case[414] in which the defendant attempted to import into Germany from Denmark certain Cliff Richard recordings in which the Danish sound recording rights (25 years from the date of original recording) had expired. In Germany the sound recordings were still protected (25 years, but initially calculated from the date of the statute and so not yet expired). The defendant argued that the recordings should be allowed in under free movement principles pursuant to arts 34 and 36 TFEU. The CJEU upheld the right of the German right holder, observing that:

"... the problem arises from the disparity between legislation of different countries regarding the protection period given by copyright and by similar rights. The disparity lies either

---

[408] art.9(2).
[409] *Uradex SCRL v Union Professionnelle de la Radio et de la Télédistribution (RTD), Société Intercommunale pour la Diffusion de la Télévision (BRUTELE)* (C-169/05) [2006] E.C.R. I-4973.
[410] art.10.
[411] See P. Kern, "The EC Common Position on Copyright Applicable to Satellite Broadcasting and Cable Retransmission" [1993] 8 E.I.P.R. 276, 281.
[412] art.11.
[413] art.12.
[414] *EMI Electrola GmbH v Patricia Im-und Export Verwaltungsgesellschaft GmbH* (C-341/87) [1989] E.C.R. 79. See also (C-360/00) [2002] E.C.R. I-5089 concerning discrimination on grounds of nationality between copyright terms of German authors and foreign authors.

in the duration of protection itself or the details of protection, such as the time when the protection period begins to run. In this connection it should be observed that, in the present state of European Union law, which is characterized by the absence of harmonisation or approximation of legislation on the protection of literary and artistic property, it is for national legislatures to specify the conditions and rules for such protection."[415]

The essence of the Term Directive[416] is to extend the term of protection for copyright works protected by the Berne Convention (which was 50 years pma) to a uniform standard of 70 years pma. It should be noted that there is no conflict between the Term Directive and the Berne Convention or TRIPS, as those instruments provide only for minimum periods of protection.[417] **4-205**

Member States with longer terms than 70 years are allowed, under the Term Directive, to let those terms run their course in relation to existing works but must confer a 70-year term on all new works following the cut-off date. For Member States with shorter terms, the effect of the Term Directive is that copyright "revives" for certain works in which it had expired. **4-206**

The Term Directive should be read in conjunction with the Rental Right Directive.[418] **4-207**

Of course, in order to achieve harmonisation, the duration bar could have been lowered for some Member States (for example, to the 50 years pma level of the UK) rather than raised. In other words, it was possible to harmonise "down" rather than "up". However, the Term Directive arose out of the Green Paper's statement[419] that there was a need to harmonise copyright and neighbouring rights at a "high level of protection", since such rights were said to be fundamental to intellectual creation. This policy is expressly mentioned in Recital 11 of the Term Directive.[420] Further express justifications for the higher term are provided by other recitals to the Term Directive. It is stated, for instance, that the Berne Convention had intended to provide protection to the author plus two generations of descendants and that life spans had grown longer.[421] In addition, it was noted that a longer term than 50 years had been granted by some Member States to offset the effects of the two World Wars on lifespans of authors who had died in their youth.[422] **4-208**

This drive to harmonise "up" continues to pervade EU legislation. The more recent amending Directive 2011/77/EU which amends the Term Directive (and which Member States were required to bring into force in their national legislation by 1 November 2013) does so in the following ways, each of which serves to **4-209**

---

[415] See also Ch.7 at paras 7-070, 7-074.

[416] Initially, Council Directive 93/98/EEC of 29 October 1993 harmonizing the term of protection of copyright and certain related rights [1993] OJ L209/0. This has since been repealed and replaced by a codified version, Directive 2006/116/EC of the European Parliament and of the Council of 12 December 2006 on the term of protection of copyright and certain related rights (codified version). References in this chapter to the Term Directive are to that codified version. The Term Directive has since been amended by Directive 2011/77/EU of the European Parliament and of the Council of 27 September 2011 amending Directive 2006/116/EC on the term of protection of copyright and certain related rights. Member States were required to transpose that amending Dir.2011/77/EU into their national laws by 1 November 2013.

[417] art.7(6) Berne Convention, art.12 TRIPS. See paras 4-012 and 4-015.

[418] See para.4-145.

[419] Commission of the European Communities, *"Working programme of the Commission in the field of copyright and neighbouring rights"*. Follow-up to the Green Paper COM (90) 584.

[420] See also Recital 24 of the Satellite and Cable Directive and Recitals 4 and 9 of the Information Society Directive.

[421] Recital 6, Term Directive.

[422] Recital 7, Term Directive.

increase the term of protection. First, the protection of a musical composition with words shall last for 70 years after the last surviving creator of any copyright in the words or in the musical composition dies. Secondly, performers' rights in a performance that is fixed in a phonogram shall last for 70 years from the date of the first publication or communication to the public of that phonogram. Thirdly, for producers of phonograms, the term of protection is increased from 50 years to 70 years from date of first publication.

4-210   This amending Directive also provides for "use it or lose it" provisions, who have assigned their rights to phonogram producers and other measures to ensure that this extended term is of benefit to performers who have assigned their rights to phonogram producers. These are discussed further below.[423]

4-211   The recitals to this amending Directive indicate that the motivations for these extensions are as follows. For the modification in relation to musical compositions with words, the logic explained in the recitals is that musical compositions with words are "overwhelmingly co-written",[424] but some Member States protect the lyrics and the music separately, while others consider them to be a single work. As such, the term for one may expire before the other in some Member States, creating obstacles to free movement. For the extension of term for performers recorded on phonograms, the amending Directive talks of "the socially recognised importance of the creative contribution of performers", and that this "should be reflected in a level of protection that acknowledges their creative and artistic contribution."[425] The recitals go on to state that "performers generally start their careers young and the current term of protection of 50 years applicable to fixations of performances often does not protect their performances for their entire lifetime",[426] before concluding that they should have protection for their lifetime, and that therefore the term for the protection of fixations of their performances should be extended to 70 years.[427] In addition (although without any obvious support from the foregoing recitals), the term of protection for phonograms is also said in Recital 7 to be justified on the same basis.

4-212   It is suggested that the foregoing policy considerations are suspect. First, the question of how long copyright protection should last is generally a remote one to any person creating a copyright work; it is unlikely to be a stimulus for greater creativity.[428] The analysis is particularly strained in respect of less "authorial" works, such as computer programs, in which the copyright is often shared among many or owned by a corporation. Secondly, the arguments based on life spans seem odd. There is no good reason, for example, why two (rather than one, or three) generations of descendants should benefit.[429] It is also disproportionate that the term of all copyright works being created now and into the future, should be based on a loss of life which took place 50–75 years ago.

4-213   The choice of the 70-year term represents, it is suggested, part of an overall ap-

---

[423] See para.4-222.
[424] Recital 18, Dir.2011/77.
[425] Recital 4, Dir.2011/77.
[426] Recital 5.
[427] Recital 7.
[428] "No one is going to be more inclined to write computer programs or speeches, compose music or design buildings because 50, 60 or 70 years after his death a distant relative whom he has never met might still be getting royalties": see Laddie J (an English High Court judge), "Copyright: Over-Strength, Over-Regulated, Over-Rated" [1996] 18(5) E.I.P.R. 253–260.
[429] The fact that some authors donate works to be held in trust for social purposes is an argument for longer, even permanent, monopolies.

proach by the part of the Commission to harmonise "up" rather than "down" in the copyright and related rights field, as pointed out elsewhere in this chapter.[430] There is a legal basis for such "due regard for established rights"[431] in the principles (at least) of legitimate expectation and the non-expropriation of property without compensation.[432] However, whether such high levels of protection are actually warranted is a question that is never addressed. It is simply assumed that a longer term stimulates creativity. So far as rewarding such creativity is concerned, it has been said that it is odd to award long monopolies (even qualified ones) to copyright works when such works are generally exploited to the full extent of their economic value in the first few months or years of their term.[433] The justifications for extending the term of protection for fixations of performances and for phonograms also do not stand scrutiny. The sole stated basis for such extension is that performers should have protection throughout their lifetime. There is no attempt to provide any support for that proposition. Why, one could fairly ask, should a performer continue to receive remuneration for a single piece of work for the rest of their life? No answer is offered by the recitals. Finally, if protection for the life of a performer were the objective, why is the term not set according to their lifespan, rather than a fixed number of years?

Duration of copyright for literary and artistic works

The central provision of the Term Directive is that the rights of an author of a   **4-214** literary or artistic work within the meaning of art.2 of the Berne Convention now run for the life of the author and to 70 years after their death, irrespective of the date when the work was lawfully made available to the public.[434] In the case of joint authorship, the 70-year period is calculated from the death of the last surviving author.[435] In the case of anonymous or pseudonymous works, the period of protection is 70 years after the work was lawfully made available to the public.[436] This latter period of protection also applies to collective works or where a legal person is designated as the rights holder, unless the author of the collective work itself is identified in the published versions.[437] This "collective" right is expressed to be without prejudice to the rights of identified authors of identifiable contributions in the collection.[438] Under the amending Dir.2011/77/EU,[439] the term of protection for a musical composition with words, where the music was composed and the lyrics written specifically for the purpose of their use together in a musical composition with words has, from 1 November 2013, been calculated by reference to the death of the last to die of the author of the lyrics and the composer of the musical work, irrespective of whether or not they were joint authors. Presumably, if either the lyrics or music was itself a work of co-authors, then the term will be calculated from the date of death of the last co-author to die.

---

[430] See, for example, the Artists' Resale Right Directive, at para.4-362.
[431] Recital 9.
[432] Jacob LJ (an English Court of Appeal judge), "Industrial Property-Industry's Enemy" [1997] 1 I.P.Q. 3–15.
[433] See fn.430.
[434] art.1(1).
[435] art.1(2).
[436] art.1(3).
[437] art.1(4).
[438] art.1(4).
[439] As a consequence of its art.1(1), adding a new art.1(7) to the Term Directive.

4-215   If a work is published in volumes, parts, instalments, issues or episodes and the term of protection runs from the time when the work was lawfully made available to the public, the term of protection runs for each item separately.[440]

4-216   Finally, in the case of works for which the term of protection is not calculated from the death of the author(s) and which have not been lawfully made available to the public within 70 years from their creation, protection for such works ceases.[441]

Duration of copyright for cinematographic or audiovisual works

4-217   The principal director of a cinematographic or audiovisual work is deemed to be the author or one of its authors.[442] Member States can designate other co-authors.[443] The term of protection for such works expires 70 years after the death of the last of the following persons to survive, whether or not these persons are designated as co-authors: the principal director, the author of the screenplay, the author of the dialogue, and the composer of music specifically created for use in the cinematographic or audiovisual works.[444]

Duration of neighbouring rights

4-218   As noted, many provisions of the Term Directive were, as of 1 November 2013 amended by Dir.2011/77/EU such that certain rights last for 70 years, not 50. As a consequence, the rights of performers run for 50 years from the date of the performance.[445] However, if a fixation of the performance in a phonogram is law-fully published or communicated to the public within this period, the rights will expire 70 years from the date of the first such publication or communication (whichever is the earliest) or, if a fixation of the performance otherwise than in a phonogram is lawfully published or communicated to the public within this period, the rights expire 50 years from the date of the first such publication or communica-tion (whichever is the earliest).[446]

4-219   The rights of broadcasting organisations expire 50 years from the first transmis-sion of a broadcast.[447]

4-220   The period of protection for the producer of a phonogram, as originally enacted by the Term Directive, was 50 years from the date of fixation. However, if the phonogram was lawfully published or lawfully communicated to the public dur-ing this period, the period of protection was 50 years after the date of first publica-tion or first communication to the public (whichever was the earliest).[448] However, art.3(2) of the original Term Directive was amended by art.11(2) of the Informa-tion Society Directive, and later by Dir.2011/77/EU, so that it now states as follows:

"The rights of producers of phonograms shall expire 50 years after the fixation is made.

---

[440] art.1(5).

[441] art.1(6).

[442] art.2(1). Member States were not required to apply this provision to works created before 1 July 1994 (see art.10) and could determine the date from which this provision applied, provided that date was no later than 1 July 1997: see art.10(5).

[443] art.2(1).

[444] art.2(2).

[445] New art.3(1).

[446] New art.3(1). See para.4-163 for performers' rights in the Rental Directive.

[447] art.3(4). See also Recital 19. See para.4-169 for broadcasting organisations' rights in the Rental Directive.

[448] art.3(2). See also para.4-165 for phonogram producers' rights in the Rental Directive.

However, if the phonogram has been lawfully published within this period, the said rights shall expire 70 years from the date of the first lawful publication. If no lawful publication has taken place within the period mentioned in the first sentence, and if the phonogram has been lawfully communicated to the public within this period, the said rights shall expire 70 years from the date of the first lawful communication to the public. However, this paragraph shall not have the effect of protecting anew the rights of the producers of phonograms where, through the expiry of the term of protection granted pursuant to Article 3(2) of Directive 93/98/EEC in its version before amendment by [the Information Society Directive] the rights of producers of phonograms are no longer protected on 22 December 2002."

The length of protection for the rights of producers of the first fixation of film is 50 years from the date of first fixation.[449] A "film" is defined as a cinematographic or audiovisual work or moving image, whether or not it is accompanied by sound.[450] **4-221**

In addition to the amendments by Dir.2011/77/EU,[451] such that certain rights last for 70 years, not 50, that amending Directive introduced a series of measures to accompany the term extension in relation to performers' rights and in relation to phonograms which are designed[452] to benefit performers who have assigned their exclusive rights to phonogram producers. There are three measures,[453] each of which arises 50 years after a phonogram has been first published or first made available to the public. They are as follows: **4-222**

- The first measure, which has become art.3(2a) of the Term Directive, provides for a "use it or lose it" provision. This right applies where the rights in a performance recorded in a phonogram have been assigned by the performer to the phonogram producer, where that producer is not exploiting that phonogram by offering copies for sale in sufficient quantity or by making it availably by wire or wireless means. The measure provides that if, within one year of receiving notification from the performer of their intention to terminate the assignment to the producer of those performing rights, the phonogram is not exploited by both sale *and* by being made available by wire or wireless means, then the producer's rights in the phonogram shall expire. This right to revoke an assignment may not be waived by the performer.

- The second measure, which is set out in arts 3(2b)–3(2d) of the Term Directive, provides for additional remuneration for performers where a contract they entered into on transfer or assignment of a performer's rights gives the performer a right to claim a non-recurring remuneration. In such circumstances, the performer has the right to obtain an annual supplementary remuneration from the phonogram producer. That remuneration is 20 per cent of the revenue derived from exploitation of the phonogram by the phonogram producer in the previous year. The right must be administered by a collecting society. The right to obtain such annual supplementary remuneration cannot be waived by the performer.

- The third measure, which has become art.3(2e) of the Term Directive, provides that, where a performer is entitled to recurring payments, neither

---

[449] art.3(3). However, for the authors of a film, see para.4-217 for audiovisiual works. See also para.4-168.
[450] art.3(3).
[451] art.1(2) of that amending Directive, amending art.3(1) of the Term Directive.
[452] According to recital (10) of that amending Dir.2011/77/EC.
[453] art.1(2)(c) of that amending Directive, adding new arts 3(2a)–3(2e) of the Term Directive.

advance payments nor any contractually defined deductions shall be deducted from the payments made to the performer.

Duration in unpublished works whose copyright has expired

4-223   If a person publishes or communicates to the public an unpublished work in which copyright has expired, then that person is entitled to economic rights equivalent to those of an author. The term is 25 years from the time when the work was first published or communicated.[454]

Duration in critical and scientific publications

4-224   The Term Directive also permits Member States to protect critical and scientific publications which have come into the public domain for a period of 30 years from the time when the publication was first lawfully published.[455]

Subsistence and duration of copyright in photographs

4-225   Photographs which are original in the sense that they are the author's own intellectual creation are protected for a period equivalent to any other artistic or literary work.[456] Recital 17 elaborates on this:

> "... the protection of photographs in the Member States is the subject of varying regimes; ... in order to achieve a sufficient harmonisation of the term of protection of photographic works, in particular of those which, due to their artistic or professional character, are of importance within the internal market, it is necessary to define the level of originality required in this Directive; ... a photographic work within the meaning of the Berne Convention is to be considered original if it is the author's own intellectual creation reflecting his personality, no other criteria such as merit or purpose being taken into account; ... the protection of other photographs should be left to national law."

4-226   In *Painer v Standard Verlags GMBH*,[457] a portrait photograph had been taken of an Austrian school girl who had then been kidnapped and held captive for many years before her escape. That photograph and versions of it which had been manipulated to predict the appearance of its subject after her years in captivity were widely published in the Austrian press after her escape but before any public appearance had been made. The Austrian courts referred inter alia whether a portrait photograph was entitled to copyright protection under the Term Directive. The CJEU held that a portrait photograph can, under art.6 of the Term Directive, be protected by copyright if it is an intellectual creation of the author reflecting their personality and expressing their free and creative choices in the production of that photograph. It said that by making these choices, the photographer can stamp the work with their "personal touch."[458]

4-227   Such suggests that many photographs will not qualify under art.6. Thus, in *Painer*, if a passerby had taken a photograph of the school girl quickly as she appeared at a window, it would be difficult to say that such a photograph had a

---

[454] art.4.

[455] art.5.

[456] art.6. See para.4-089 for a discussion of how this test differs from a "sweat of the brow" approach to originality which is prevalent in countries such as the UK. See also para.4-282.

[457] (C-145/10) ECLI:EU:C:2011:798; [2012] E.C.D.R. 6 at [89].

[458] See [92].

"personal touch" although it may have been very valuable to newspapers and security services. Thus the economic value of a photograph is irrelevant under art.6. However, no doubt precisely because of this, and the important of such photographs, e.g. the paparazzi pursuit of celebrities, art.6 permits Member States to protect other photographs. Thus, in many countries, *any* photograph will enjoy copyright.

Protection vis-à-vis third countries

The Term Directive also provides that: 4-228

> "Where the country of origin of a work, within the meaning of the Berne Convention, is a third country and the author of the work is not a [European Union] national, the term of protection granted by Member States shall expire on the date of the expiry of the protection granted in the country of origin"

but may not exceed the lifetime of the author plus 70 years.[459] In the case of neighbouring rights under art.3, where the rights holder is not a EU national,[460] the term of protection of such rights must not exceed the term of protection in the country of which the rights holder is a national without prejudice to the international obligations of Member States.[461]

Calculation of terms

The terms referred to in the Term Directive are calculated from the first day of 4-229 January of the year following the event which gave rise to them.[462]

Transitional provisions and revived rights

Where the term of protection was already running as of 1 July 1995, the Term 4-230 Directive does not have the effect of shortening the period of protection.[463] Therefore, Member States with terms longer than 70 years are permitted to let them expire, but must apply the new uniform standard to all new works coming into existence after the cut-off date.

Provision is also made for expired copyright to revive in certain circumstances. 4-231 The term of protection provided for in the Term Directive applies immediately to

---

[459] art.7(1). The expression "country of origin" in the Berne Convention means essentially the country of publication—see para.4-107. There is some ambiguity about the meaning of the phrase "third country". In the 1st edn of this book, it was submitted that it meant a non-Berne Union country as opposed to a non-EU country, otherwise such would result in discriminatory treatment contrary to art.5(1) of the Berne Convention. However, it has been pointed out by Professor Sterling that art.7(8) of the Berne Convention permits comparison of terms between the country where protection is claimed and the country of origin and, in effect, permits the former country to level down the period of protection to that available in the country of origin. After careful consideration, it is considered that Professor Sterling's views are indeed correct. If "third country" was intended to mean a non-Berne Union country, one would expect that the criterion of nationality would equally have been that of a Berne country. Instead, it would appear that the EU has again chosen a "Fortress Europe" approach, and denying protection to nationals of non-EU countries which do not match the 70-year pma period imposed in the EU.

[460] art.7(2). i.e. performer's rights, phonogram producer's rights and broadcasting organisation's rights.

[461] art.7(2).

[462] art.8.

[463] art.10(1).

all works which, as of 1 July 1995, were protected in at least one Member State.[464] This means that, where copyright in a work had expired in one Member State, it may have revived if it was still protected in another Member State on that date.[465] In order to ameliorate the effect of this provision on those who had acquired rights or who had been exploiting public domain works, the Term Directive is expressed to be without prejudice to acts of exploitation performed before 1 July 1995.[466] Member States are also required to protect the acquired rights of third parties and the principle of legitimate expectation.[467]

4-232   The transitional provisions were examined in some detail by the CJEU in *Butterfly Music Srl v Carosello Edizioni Musicali E Discografiche Srl*.[468] In that case, the Italian law implementing the Term Directive (Italian Law 52/96) extended the term of sound recordings from 30 to 50 years, also applying the term to works in which protection had expired in Italy but which were protected in another Member State. However, these provisions were expressed to be without prejudice to the right that records and similar media in which protection under the previous Italian law had expired could be distributed for up to three months following the entry into force of the new law. The CJEU took the opportunity to clarify the position in respect of revived rights generally. It observed, first, that the effect of the Term Directive was to bring some works back into copyright. Secondly, it said, though it was a matter for national law precisely how and to what extent the acquired rights of third parties under art.10(3) were protected, it was not permissible to allow such rules to have the overall effect of preventing the application of the new terms of protection on the date laid down by the Term Directive. Thirdly, said the CJEU, preventing a party from continuing to exploit works in the future did not offend against the principle against retroactive legislation, since past acts were not made illegal. Fourthly, though the principle of legitimate expectation was important, it was not aimed at preventing new rules from applying to the future consequences of situations which arose under previous legislation. In the event, the CJEU did not consider that the three-month period was unreasonable, having regard to the objective pursued. Note, however, that though the Italian law was expressed to be "without prejudice to instruments and contracts predating June 29, 1995", the CJEU did not embark upon any analysis of the position of those acquiring rights under contracts entered into before the cut-off date. Recitals 26 and 27 of the Term Directive appear to leave the details of such protection entirely in the hands of national law subject to the principle in art.10(3).

---

[464] art.10(2). Thus, if the work was not protected as of 1 July 1995, the Directive is inapplicable to extend protection—see *Montis Design BV v Goossens Meubelen BV* (C-169/15) ECLI:EU:C:2016:790 (copyright owner had failed to comply with Benelux procedural law concerning the filing of a maintenance declaration and thus copyright had expired on 18 April 1993).

[465] See K. Jorna and M. Martin-Prat, "New Rules in European Copyright" [1994] 4 E.I.P.R. 145, for some useful hypothetical examples.

[466] art.10(3).

[467] art.10(3). See also Recital 27, which rehearses the principle of legitimate expectation and permits Member States to protect the position of persons who "undertook in good faith the exploitation of the works at the time when such works were in the public domain". See also, K. Jorna and M. Martin-Prat, "New Rules in European Copyright" [1994] 4 E.I.P.R. 145.

[468] *Butterfly Music Srl v Carosello Edizioni Musicali e Discografiche Srl (CEMED)* (C-60/98) [1999] E.C.R. I-3939.

Date for implementation of the Term Directive

Member States were required to bring the Directive into force by 1 July 1995.[469]   **4-233**
All have now done so. As noted above, Member States were required to bring the
amendments of Directive 2011/77/EU into force by 1 November 2013.[470]

Database Directive

Introduction

The Database Directive[471] potentially covers a very wide field of subject-matter.   **4-234**
This is because the Directive's definition of what amounts to a "database" goes
much further than what is meant by that word in common parlance. When people
speak of a "database", they generally mean a collection of data held in the electronic
memory of a computer—for example, the names and email addresses of the customers of a business. However, the Database Directive is not confined to electronic
databases. It potentially bites where there is any collection of "works, data, or
materials", provided certain stipulated requirements are met. In relation to this vast
array of potential subject-matter, the Directive provides a two-tier system of
protection. First, there is the possibility of ordinary copyright protection for that
aspect of the database that is the result of personal intellectual creativity in the selection and arrangement of content. In addition, or alternatively, there may be a sui
generis "database right" protecting the content (irrespective of whether there has
been creativity in its arrangement), provided that there has been substantial investment in obtaining, verifying or presenting the material.

In 1988, the global electronic database industry was estimated to be $5 billion,   **4-235**
of which the US was responsible for four-fifths and the EU about $350 million. In
an effort to foster the growth of the EU database industry, the Commission decided
that it would examine whether some form of protection against unauthorised copying of databases was necessary. In the resulting Green Paper on Copyright,[472] the
Commission noted that the storage in databases of copyright works required the
permission of the right holders and that the retrieval of such works was also a
restricted act if reproduction was involved. In these respects, the Commission
observed, the laws of Member States did not vary greatly.

However, there was considerable divergence among the laws of Member States   **4-236**
as regards the protection of the database itself. The majority of Member States
protected original collections and compilations of copyrightable works in accordance with art.2(5) of the Berne Convention.[473] However, some Member States had
gone further by providing protection for collections of non-copyright works.
Throughout the Member States there was a marked divergence of approach on the
question of originality. For example, the approach of the UK was to protect virtually any collection of works, provided the work had originated from the author (in
the sense of not having been copied from another) and provided they had expended

---

[469] art.13.

[470] art.2 of Dir.2011/77/EU.

[471] Dir.96/9/EC on the legal protection of databases [1996] OJ L77/20.

[472] See para.4-081.

[473] That is: "collections of literary and artistic works, such as encyclopaedias and anthologies which,
by reason of the selection and arrangement of their contents, constitute intellectual creations shall
be protected as such, without prejudice on the copyright in each of the works forming part of such
collections."— art.2(5) Berne Convention. See para.4-012.

a modicum of effort in compiling it. In other Member States, a higher threshold of originality in the process of selecting and arranging the database was required. In Germany, for example, copyright only subsisted in a database if the selection, accumulation, arrangement and organisation thereof had been the subject of know-how beyond that possessed by the average programmer.[474] In addition, some Member States, such as Denmark, had enacted sui generis rights to prevent the copying of works like catalogues, tables and similar works which did not attract genuine copyright protection because the works were not sufficiently original.[475]

4-237   Accordingly, the Commission proposed that protection for the compilation of copyright works in databases should be provided in the EU. It also invited comments on whether such protection should be extended to databases where the material was not in itself protectable by copyright and, if so, whether such protection should be by way of copyright or some sort of sui generis right.

4-238   In May 1992, the Commission issued its first proposal for a directive on the Legal Protection of Databases, which was accompanied by an Explanatory Memorandum.[476] The Draft Directive proposed that those databases which did not qualify for copyright because they did not meet the criterion of creativity should be subject to a sui generis unfair extraction right (the "database right"). The proposal was discussed by the Economic and Social Committee and by the European Parliament which voted in support of the proposals subject to a number of detailed amendments. The Commission considered the Parliament's amendments and, on 4 October 1993, presented its amended proposal along with an explanatory memorandum.[477] The Database Directive was finally adopted by the European Council on 11 March 1996, and it has since been implemented in all Member States.

4-239   The Database Directive is organised into 60 Recitals, followed by four chapters. Chapter I contains the relevant definitions. Chapter II sets out the copyright protection regime for databases. Chapter III deals with the sui generis right (hereafter referred to as the "database right"). Chapter IV sets out some provisions that are common to both copyright and database right protection.

Definition of a database

4-240   A "database", for the purposes of either the copyright or the database right regime, is defined by the Database Directive as:

> "a collection of independent works, data or other material arranged in a systematic or methodical way and individually accessible by electronic or other means."[478]

This is intended to be a very wide definition.[479] It potentially covers not only electronic subject matter such as online databases, websites, customer lists, etc. but might also cover any or all of the following: encyclopaedias, dictionaries, scientific

---

[474] *Inkassaprogram*—Bundesgerichtshof, 9 May 1985.

[475] art.49 Danish Copyright Act, which provided for an exclusive right to the creator of the work for 10 years: see s.6.4.5 of the Commission's Green Paper.

[476] Commission of the European Communities. *Draft Directive on the Legal Protection of Databases* COM (92) 24 Final.

[477] Commission of the European Communities. *Amended proposal for a Council Directive on the Legal Protection of Databases* COM (93) 464; [1993] OJ C308/1.

[478] art.1(2).

[479] Recital 17: "Whereas the term 'database' should be understood to include literary, artistic, musical or other collections of works or collections of other material such as texts, sound, images, numbers, facts, and data".

or technical reference works, public registers, anthologies of poems, collections of recipes, street directories, atlases, address books, business records, lists of purchase orders or invoices, timetables, catalogues, price lists, parts lists, newspapers, and magazines. Indexation and other systems necessary for the operation or consultation of the database are included.[480] The definition excludes any computer program used in the making or operation of databases accessible by electronic means.[481] Databases stored on CD-ROMs, DVDs and other such media may be included.[482] *In Freistaat Bayern v Verlag Esterbauer GmbH*[483] on a reference from the German court, the Court of Justice had to consider whether the Database Directive extended to topographical maps covering the state of Bavaria. An Austrian publisher had used these maps and underlying data to produce its own maps. It would appear that the Austrian publisher had taken: (i) a set of geographical co-ordinates; and (ii) the features associated with those co-ordinates, e.g. a church, landmark, tracks appropriate for cyclists, mountain bikers, etc. Verlag, the publisher, and the European Commission argued that the "*informative value*" of such information was reduced almost to zero once extracted from the map since, to take the example of a church, this did not show whether the church was located in a town or village. Against such its arguments, the Bundesgerichtshof had its doubts as to whether such information contained in topographic maps fell within the meaning of "database" within art.1(2) of the Database Directive.

Thus, the real issue, as identified by the Court of Justice, was whether such data as extracted from a topographic map constituted "independent materials" within the definition. The Court of Justice emphasised that the concept of "database" within the meaning of the Directive was a broad one and was defined in terms of its function. It also emphasised that the legal protection was introduced to stimulate investment in data storage and processing systems. Perhaps unsurprisingly, as the information extracted was clearly of value, the Court of Justice held that such data could be classified as independent materials of a database. **4-241**

One wonders whether the Bundesgerichtshof asked the real question. It seems that there was little doubt that the topographic maps *as a whole* possessed database right. The maps and their associated data (like the location of a church) would plainly qualify as a database because such was a collection of data gathered from pre-existing data (e.g. the location of a church), gathered and presented in a meaningful, systematic way. Thus, the real question was whether the *extraction* of some of that information rather than all of it amounted to an *infringement* of the database right. The owner of a database right has the privilege to prevent extraction and/or re-utilisation of the whole or a substantial part of the database, evaluated qualitatively and/or quantitatively. There seems little doubt that the extraction of data relating to the location of churches, cycle paths, etc. on a systematic basis from a topographical map would satisfy this requirement. Overall, the Court of Justice's judgment very much emphasises that where significant investment has gone into gathering pre-existing data (of whatever kind, including geographical data) so that it is arranged and presented in a systematic and methodical way, the end-result will be protected as a database under the Directive. Here, Verlag, instead of gathering data on cycle paths, mountain biker paths, etc. itself, had chosen, no doubt to avoid the cost of doing so, to take such information from the Bavarian State **4-242**

---

[480] Recital 20.
[481] art.1(3). This is intended to avoid overlap with the Computer Programs Directive.
[482] Contrast Recital 19 and Recital 22.
[483] (C–490/14) ECI:EU:C:2015:735.

topographical maps. The prevention of such misappropriation of another's investment is precisely why the Database Directive was introduced.

4-243   It is suggested that arrangement in a "systematic or methodical way" does not imply a very high standard of organisation. The materials do not have to have been physically stored in an organized manner, provided that they are accessible.[484] In particular, such terminology should be contrasted with the test as to whether a database possesses copyright—namely the "selection and arrangement" test. The only real limiting factors in the definition are those of "independence" and "individual accessibility". However, there must be some "coherence" to the data or works such it is not merely a collection of random data.

4-244   By way of example, in the *Fixtures Marketing*[485] case, the CJEU held that a football league fixture list constitutes a "database" within the meaning of art.1(2) of the Database Directive. The court essentially held that the combination of the date, the time and the identity of the two teams playing in both home and away matches has autonomous informative value which renders them "independent materials" within the meaning of art.1(2) of the Directive and that the arrangement, in the form of a fixture list, of the dates, times and names of teams in the various fixtures of a football league met the conditions set out in art.1(2) of the Directive as to the systematic or methodical arrangement and individual accessibility of the data contained in the database.

4-245   The Database Directive's recitals state that a recording or an audiovisual, cinematographic, literary or musical work as such does not fall within its scope as such are not considered systematically or methodically arranged or capable of individual access.[486] This restriction would apply to prevent, for example, an undivided recording of a person reading out, methodically, a list of names and addresses, but, it is suggested, would not apply to prevent a commercially sold DVD of a film from falling within the definition of a database. Such a DVD normally allows individual access to different segments of a film work, and to different independent recordings (say, an interview with the film's director) which no doubt are intended to be accessed and viewed separately from other parts of the DVD's contents. However, merely because the arrangement and accessibility of the contents of a DVD mean that it could fall within the definition of a database, it may still lack protection because the database fails to meet either the requirements of originality (for copyright protection) or substantial investment (for database right), rather than because it does not fall within the definition of a database in the first place.[487]

"Authors" vs. "makers" of databases

4-246   The owner of the copyright in a database is its author.[488] The author is:

---

[484] Recital 21.
[485] *Fixtures Marketing Ltd v Organismos Prognostikon Agonon Podosfairou (OPAP)* (C-444/02) [2004] E.C.R. I-8961; [2005] E.C.D.R. 3 at [33]–[36].
[486] Recital 17.
[487] Recital 19.
[488] art.4 read together with art.5.

"the natural person or group of natural persons who created the base [sic] or, where the legislation of the Member States so permits, the legal person designated as the right holder by that legislation."[489]

The author has the right to prevent others from doing any of the "restricted acts"[490] in relation to the author's database. **4-247**

The database right, by contrast, is owned by the "maker" of the database. The "maker" is left largely undefined by the Database Directive, with Recital 41 merely suggesting that the maker is "the person who takes the initiative and the risk of investing", and that such excludes those who are acting upon that person's instructions, such as sub-contractors. Such makers must be nationals of a Member State or have their habitual residence in the EU, or in the case of corporations, have their central administration, principal place of business or genuine operations within the EU.[491] The maker has the right to prevent extraction and/or re-utilisation of the whole or a substantial part of the database.[492] **4-248**

Copyright protection: originality

Copyright protection of a database concerns the "structure" of the database, not its "contents";[493] consequently, copyright protection can be accorded to a database irrespective of any copyrights that individual works contained in it may attract. Indeed, any creativity exerted in the creation of the contents of a database is not relevant when considering whether the database itself will be protected by copyright. In order to obtain copyright protection, the database must satisfy the originality requirement within the Database Directive. Databases are only original for the purposes of copyright protection if "by reason of the selection or arrangement of their contents, [they] constitute the author's own intellectual creation".[494] The concepts of "selection" and of "arrangement" within the meaning of art.3(1) of the Database Directive refer respectively to the selection and the arrangement of data, through which the author of the database gives the database its structure. By contrast, those concepts do not extend to the creation of the data contained in that database.[495] This test of originality, which has gained almost universal currency in European and international copyright instruments, should be regarded as more stringent than—and qualitatively different from—the "sweat of the brow" approach applicable in some Member States, notably the UK, prior to harmonisation.[496] As a consequence, the author of the database must have some personal creative input in deciding what data to include and how that data should be organised. As described by the CJEU in *Football Dataco v Yahoo! UK*, citing a number of earlier decisions, in the context of "the setting up of a database, that criterion of originality is satisfied when, through the selection or arrangement of the data which it contains, its author expresses their creative ability in an original man- **4-249**

---

[489] art.4(1). This allows Member States to specify that copyright can vest in employers: see Recital 29.
[490] art.5.
[491] art.11.
[492] art.7.
[493] See the decision of the CJEU in *Football Dataco v Yahoo! UK* (C-604/10) ECLI:EU:C:2012:115; [2012] E.C.D.R. 10 at [30].
[494] art.3(1). The test of "author's own intellectual creation" is applied to the test for originality in all areas of copyright: see paras 4-089, 4-282.
[495] *Football Dataco v Yahoo! UK* (C-604/10) ECLI:EU:C:2012:115, [2012] E.C.D.R. 10 at [32].
[496] Note the comment in relation to the UK case of *Newspaper Licensing Agency v Meltwater*, at fn.192.

ner by making free and creative choices and thus stamps their "personal touch" [on the structure of the database]".[497] Note that such effort and input must be directed towards the selection and arrangement of the information rather than merely obtaining it or verifying it (as would be relevant for the sui generis database right, considered below). This does not mean, however, that the actual product of that input—the database itself—has to be particularly inventive, sophisticated or efficacious (still less, aesthetically pleasing) since Recital 16 makes it clear that no other criteria should be applied in considering the issue of originality.

4-250   If this is a higher threshold of originality, its combination with the very wide definition of what amounts to a database, may lead to a loss of copyright protection for some works which might formerly have been protected under the "sweat of the brow" approach in some Member States. Moreover, if there has been an insufficiently substantial investment by the maker of the database in the obtaining, verification or presentation of the contents of the database, then that database will not attract the sui generis database right either. Accordingly, it is observed in passing that the Database Directive is a rare example of an EU copyright harmonisation measure which might result in the loss of protection rather than the accretion or extension of rights.[498] However, this is offset by the introduction of the sui generis database right which plainly does protect "sweat of brow" databases.

Copyright protection: restricted acts

4-251   The author of the database has the right to carry out or authorise the following acts:

   (a)   temporary or permanent reproduction by any means and in any form, in whole or in part;
   (b)   translation, adaptation, arrangement and any other alteration;
   (c)   any form of distribution to the public of the database or of copies thereof. The first sale in the EU of a copy of the database by the right holder or with the right holder's consent exhausts the right to control resale of that copy within the EU;
   (d)   any communication, display or performance to the public; and
   (e)   any reproduction, distribution, communication, display or performance to the public of the results of the acts referred to in (b).[499]

4-252   It should be noted that, in relation to the right of reproduction, the act may be in relation to either the whole of the author's database or merely part of it. There is no overt "substantiality" requirement under the copyright protection regime for databases, in contrast to the position under the sui generis database right.[500] It might seem arguable, therefore, that an act of reproduction in relation to any part of an original database—however small or inconsequential—potentially infringes copyright, perhaps subject only to the principle of *de minimis non curat lex*, i.e. that

---

[497]   *Football Dataco v Yahoo! UK* (C-604/10), [32] and [38]. The earlier cases relied upon, by analogy, were *Infopaq International v Danske Dagblades Forening* (C-5/08) [2009] E.C.D.R. 16 at [45]; *Bezpečnostní softwarová asociace v Ministerstvo Kultury* (C-393/09) [2011] E.C.D.R. 3 at [50]; *FAPL v QC Leisure* (C-403/08 and C-429/08) [2012] E.C.R. I-9083; and *Painer v Standard Verlags GMBH* (C-145/10) ECLI:EU:C:2011:798 at [89]).

[498]   See para.4-088 for a discussion of the general approach of harmonisation "up" rather than "down" in the copyright and related rights field.

[499]   art.5.

[500]   art.7(1): see para.4-255.

the law does not concern itself with trivialities. However, it is suggested that such a construction of the Database Directive's infringement provisions would be strained. Given the stringent originality threshold for copyright protection of databases,[501] the courts are likely to approach this provision as requiring some part of the personal creative input to have been appropriated. It is difficult to imagine that small or inconsequential takings can be said to do so.[502]

Copyright protection: defences

The Database Directive provides a number of "lawful user" provisions which are necessary for the ordinary licensed use of a database and for access to its contents.[503] These are reminiscent of those found in the Computer Software Directive.[504]   **4-253**

In addition, Member States have the option of implementing a number of limita-   **4-254** tions and defences relating to reproduction for private purposes of a non-electronic database; use of illustrations for teaching or scientific research and use in administrative or judicial procedures. Member States may also extend any existing defences (for example, fair dealing or fair use provisions) to databases provided that such defences satisfy the "three-step" test contained in art.9(2) of the Berne Convention.[505]

Sui generis database right: substantial investment

For a database right to subsist in a database, art.7(1) requires there to have been   **4-255** "qualitatively and/or quantitatively a substantial investment in either the obtaining, verification or presentation of the database's contents." This provision was analysed at some length by the CJEU in *British Horseracing Board* ("BHB").[506] In that case, BHB contended that there had been a substantial investment in the creation of its database of horses and jockeys for race meetings. The evidence was that the BHB ran a call centre with about 30 employees who took calls from those entering horses in each race. The identity and status of each person entering the horse was checked, as were the characteristics of the horse itself. A central computer allocated the horse a number and determined its starting stall position. The final list of runners and riders was published the day before each race. The CJEU did not consider this to be a relevant investment primarily because it amounted to investment in the "creation" of data rather than an independent investment in the "obtain-

---

[501] See para.4-249.
[502] See para.4-282.
[503] See art.6.1. In *Ryanair Ltd v PR Aviation BV* (C–30/14) ECLI:EU:C:2012:115, a Dutch case concerning screen-scraping by third party automated systems of price data of low cost flights on the website of Ryanair, a budget flight operator, the Court of Justice held that these defences have no applicability to a breach of contract action (the contract governed access to Ryanair's website) where the database did not qualify for copyright protection under Dir.96/9 as the purpose and structure of the Directive was to provide defences to assertions of copyright provided for under Dir.96/9.
[504] See para.4-092.
[505] art.6(3). The "three-step" test is also found in art.13 TRIPS, art.10 WCT, art.16 WPPT, art.6(3) Computer Programs Directive, and art.5(5) Information Society Directive. For discussion of art.9(2) of the Berne Convention, see para.4-030.
[506] *Fixtures Marketing Ltd v Oy Veikkaus Ab* (C-46/02) [2004] E.C.R. I-10365; *The British Horseracing Board Ltd v William Hill Organisation Ltd* (C-203/02) [2004] E.C.R. I-10415, [2005] 1 C.M.L.R. 15; *Fixtures Marketing Ltd v AB Svenska Spel* (C-338/02) [2004] E.C.R. I-10497; and *Fixtures Marketing Ltd v Organismos prognostikon agonon podosfairou AE "OPAP"* (C-444/02) [2004] E.C.R. I-10549.

ing" or "verification" of the data itself. Whilst it was possible that a separate investment in the obtaining and verification of data could be made at the same time as the investment made in creating the data, that did not appear to have occurred in this case because the investment was not independently directed.

Database right: the right to prevent extraction and/or re-utilisation

4-256   The owner of the database right has the right to prevent "extraction and/or re-utilization of the whole or of a substantial part of the database, evaluated qualitatively and/or quantitatively."[507] "Extraction" is defined as the permanent or temporary transfer of all or a substantial part of the contents of a database to another medium by any means or in any form.[508] "Re-utilisation" means "any form of making available to the public all or a substantial part of the contents of a database by the distribution of copies, by renting, by online or other forms of transmission."[509] In the *British Horseracing Board* case,[510] the CJEU held that indirect extraction or re-utilisation would also infringe. Therefore, even if a defendant does not himself take data from the claimant's database, if they take it from a third party source which was in part derived from the right holder's database, that may infringe, provided sufficient material is taken.

4-257   In a second *Football Dataco* case, *Football Dataco v Sportradar*,[511] a question was referred to the CJEU by the UK Court of Appeal asking whether a party who uploads data from a database protected by sui generis right under the Directive onto that party's web server located in Member State A and in response to requests from a user in Member State B, the web server sends such data to the user's computer so that the data is stored in the memory of that computer and displayed on its screen has committed an act of "extraction" or "re-utilisation" and, if so, whether that act takes place in state A, state B, or both. The CJEU concluded that an act of making available took place *at least* in state B, if evidence permits a conclusion that the operator of the server targeted members of the public in state B. This seems to be an eminently sensible conclusion. On the one hand, if making available was held *only* to take place at the location of the server, this would lead to infringers (of all types of copyright and related rights, not simply the database right) setting up infringing servers in jurisdictions where the laws did not provide protection against making available, or where enforcement was difficult if not impossible. On the other hand, if making available was held to arise in any place from which access to the database was possible, then operators of databases accessible over the internet would face the unnecessary burden of being sued in Member States in which they had no interest.[512] The reference to "at least" in State B suggests that the CJEU may decide in a different case that the act of making available also occurs in State A, the state where the server is located. In the author's view, this would be wrong as the location of the server has no economic relevance[513].

4-258   As in the case of copyright protection, in order to infringe, the defendant must

---

[507] art.7(1).

[508] art.7(2)(a).

[509] art.7(2)(b).

[510] (C-203/02) cited above.

[511] *Football Dataco Ltd v Sportradar GmbH* (C-173/11) ECLI:EU:C:2012:642.

[512] For the separate question as to whether the court of the Member State of reception has jurisdiction, see para.17-086.

[513] When determining jurisdiction under art.7(2) Recast Brussels Regulation, the Court of Justice has ignored the location of the server. See Ch.17, "Jurisdiction and Intellectual Property" at para.17-

derive the data from the maker's database rather than devise it independently.[514] The database right also has an express "substantiality" requirement in relation to infringement. As mentioned above, this is missing from the provisions concerning copyright protection for databases.[515] Under the database right, such substantiality is assessed by reference to qualitative as well as quantitative factors. Therefore, the importance of what is taken or re-utilised can offset the fact that it may represent a relatively small part of the maker's database. The taking of insubstantial and unimportant parts of the maker's database will not normally result in liability.[516] However, the Database Directive provides that if the repeated taking of small helpings "conflicts with a normal exploitation of that database or unreasonably prejudices the legitimate interests of the maker of the database", they are not permitted.[517]

In *Innoweb v Wegener*[518] questions were asked of the CJEU in a case concerning a dedicated meta-search engine which allowed internet users to make a single query of numerous websites listing second-hand cars for sale and returned to those users (after a real-time query of the underlying listings websites) an amalgamated collection of results. The referring court proceeded on the basis that the underlying car listing websites did attract the sui generis database right, but held that the results returned from the individual queries on the metasearch engine, even taken cumulatively, did not extract the whole or any substantial part of those underlying databases. The question for the court was, therefore, whether or not this method that made it possible for an internet user to search the whole of another website was a re-utilisation of the whole or a substantial part of the underlying databases contrary to art.7(1)? The CJEU held that it was. Following a number of earlier cases, the court held that "re-utilisation" referred to any unauthorised act of distribution to the public of the contents of a protected database or a substantial part of such contents, and that nature and form of the process used are of no relevance in this respect.[519] The reason for this broad interpretation was the protection of the database owner's ability to redeem their investment in the creation of the database. Particular factors which were mentioned as relevant were the alteration of the means of access to the database from that intended by its maker, the loss of collateral advertising revenue and the potential diminution in the number of car sellers paying for listings.[520]   **4-259**

Database right: defences

Articles 7 and 8 of the Database Directive contain provisions aimed at lawful, (i.e. licensed) users of databases. These appear to be more extensive than those   **4-260**

068, et seq.

[514] See *The British Horseracing Board Ltd v William Hill Organisation* (C-203/02).

[515] See para.4-251.

[516] In the *British Horseracing Board* case, the CJEU regarded the defendant's extraction and re-utilisation to have amounted to an insubstantial part. Only the names of the horses and the dates and times of the races had been used.

[517] art.7(5).

[518] *Innoweb BV v Wegener ICT Media BV* (C-202/12) ECLI:EU:C:2013:850.

[519] At [37], citing *British Horseracing Board* (C-545/07) at [67]; *Apis-Hristovich* (C-547/07) [2009] E.C.R. I-1627 at [49]; and *Football Dataco v Yahoo!* (C-173/11) at [20].

[520] See [40]–[43].

relating to users of copyrightable databases.[521] A lawful user may extract or re-utilise the database or parts of it for "any purposes whatsoever."[522] However any acts by a lawful user must not conflict with normal exploitation of the database, unreasonably prejudice the legitimate interests of the maker of the database, or cause prejudice to the holder of a copyright or related right in respect of the works or subject-matter contained in the database.[523] Moreover, a lawful user may extract for private purposes the contents of a non-electronic database,[524] or obtain the contents for the purposes of illustration for teaching or scientific research, as long as the source is indicated and such use is only to the extent justified by the non-commercial purpose to be achieved.[525] A lawful user may also extract or re-utilise the data for the purposes of public security or an administrative or judicial procedure.[526] A contractual provision which is contrary to the defences in art.8 is null and void.[527]

Term of protection: copyright and database right

4-261 The duration of copyright protection of an original database is the same for other copyright works, namely 70 years pma.

4-262 The duration provisions for the database right are, like the right itself, sui generis in nature. If the database is made available to the public, its term of protection runs for 15 years from the first of January of the year following the date when it was first made available. If it was not made available to the public, protection expires 15 years from the first of January of the year following the date of completion.[528] There are special provisions that take account of the fact that databases rarely remain in a permanently fixed form. Indeed, a good database is likely to be one that is frequently updated and altered. Accordingly, art.10(3) of the Database Directive provides that:

> "any substantial change, evaluated qualitatively or quantitatively, to the contents of a database, including any substantial change resulting from the accumulation of successive additions, deletions or alterations, which would result in the database being considered to be a new investment, evaluated qualitatively and quantitatively, shall qualify the database resulting from that investment for its own term of protection."

Implementation

4-263 The Commission produced a lengthy report on implementation of the Database Directive dated 12 December 2005. All Member States have now implemented the Directive, though a number were late. Of more significance were the Commis-

---

[521] art.8. In *Ryanair Ltd v PR Aviation BV*, discussed in relation to copyright defences at fn.505 at para.4-253, the Court of Justice held that art.8 had no applicability to a database which did not qualify for sui generis protection.

[522] art.8(1).

[523] art.8(2), (3).

[524] art.9(a).

[525] art.9(b).

[526] art.9(c).

[527] art.15. However, where the database is not protected by the sui generis right, art.15 is inapplicable and thus a party may adopt contractual clauses which concern the conditions of use of such a database without regard to the defences in the Database Directive (*Ryanair Ltd v PR Aviation BV*, at [39]).

[528] art.10.

sion's conclusions regarding the effect of the *BHB* and *Fixtures Marketing* cases. In summary, the Commission considered that those cases have resulted in a significant narrowing of the scope of sui generis database right protection and that this may go some way to meeting concerns about unfair competition. Interestingly, the Commission also conducted an empirical study of database creation before and after the Directive, concluding that EU database production had fallen back to pre-Directive levels and that its economic impact was "unproven."[529] A second 2018 Commission Report has found the same and indeed said that the European Commission "should not overlook its abolition."

Information Society Directive

Introduction

The name of "the Information Society Directive", which is reflected in the full title of Dir.2001/29,[530] recognises that it was originally aimed at dealing with the copyright implications of the internet. Certainly, this Information Society Directive does cover some important online issues, such as the responsibility of internet service providers, access to works on-demand, circumvention of copy protection devices and interference with rights management information, but it also goes much further. Its definition of the reproduction right, for instance, is of general application. Perhaps its most striking feature, however, is its exhaustive list of optional exceptions to liability. These are not confined to "the information society" nor to digital or even electronic material. As such, it may be proper to regard the Information Society Directive as the first proper step towards an eventual EU copyright code.[531]   **4-264**

The Information Society Directive contains 61 Recitals. Its Chapter I sets out how the Directive interacts with previous EU legislation in the copyright and related rights field. Chapter II sets out the reproduction; communication to the public and distribution right. Chapter II also sets out the exceptions (defences). These comprise a mandatory defence that Member States must implement concerning online service providers, followed by a long and exhaustive list of the optional defences that Member States are entitled to implement. In keeping with the general accretion of rights that result from the Directives discussed in this chapter, any further defences that were previously available in Member States are not permitted.[532] Chapter III deals with devices aimed at circumventing copy protection and interference with rights management information. The provisions of Chapter IV deal with matters   **4-265**

---

[529] Commission of the European Communities, "*DG Internal Market Working Paper: First evaluation of Directive 96/9/EC on the legal protection of databases*" 12 December 2005, available at: *http://ec.europa.eu/internal_market/copyright/docs/databases/evaluation_report_en.pdf* [Accessed 1st May 2018].

[530] Directive 2001/29/EC on the harmonisation of certain aspects of copyright and related rights in the information society [2001] OJ L167/10–19.

[531] The Directive is, in the recent CJEU cases that examine it and which are discussed in this chapter, invariably referred to as the "Copyright Directive". In this chapter, however, it is called the Information Society Directive both to distinguish it from the other Directives that also deal with copyright issues and because there will be future EU legislation in this area which might include a Directive that is even more deserving of so grand a title.

[532] It should be noted, of course, that the Information Society Directive, like other Directives, does not have horizontal effect. If a defence that falls outside of the exhaustive list in the Information Society Directive has survived in any national legislation, that defence will still be a good defence in proceedings between private persons. The claimant would, however, if their action failed because of such a defence, have a cause of action against the state in question. See para.1-051, et seq.

such as remedies, amendments to other Information Society Directives, and implementation.

4-266   The Information Society Directive was aimed at further implementing the two 1996 WIPO "Internet Treaties", the WCT, and WPPT, which the EU had become a party to in 1996.[533] Many of the Member States had already signed those Treaties at the time and they have now entered into force. The WCT and WPPT obligations had already been partly implemented by certain Directives already dealt with in this chapter. For example, the Computer Programs Directive had implemented art.4 of the WCT regarding protection of software as a literary work.[534] The Database Directive had implemented art.5 of the WCT as regards copyright protection for databases.[535] The Rental Right Directive had dealt with a number of WCT/ WPPT issues. For example, the rental rights in relation to phonograms and performances fixed in phonograms set out in Chapter I of the Rental Right Directive[536] was an implementation of art.7 of the WCT and art.9 of the WPPT. Chapter II of the Rental Right Directive[537] had also implemented the provisions concerning economic rights of performers in their unfixed performances, their right of distribution, and their rental right as set out in arts 6, 8 and 9 of the WPPT. The same chapter had also dealt with the distribution rights and rental rights for producers of phonograms that are set out in arts 12 and 13 of the WPPT, as well as the single equitable remuneration contained in art.15 of the WPPT.[538]

4-267   Nevertheless, there were a number of outstanding WCT/WPPT issues. In particular there were the distribution and "making available" rights (the latter often is called the Internet right) for authors in arts 6 and 8 of the WCT.[539] As regards performers and the producers of phonograms, the "making available" right also remained to be implemented. In addition, the provisions concerning the circumvention of copy protection devices and interference with rights management information that are contained in arts 11–12 of the WCT and arts 18–19 of the WPPT remained to be dealt with.[540]

4-268   The Information Society Directive is expressed to be without prejudice to earlier EU Directives in the area of copyright and related rights unless otherwise specified.[541] However, there are some express amendments. The reproduction right in art.2 of the Information Society Directive is of broad application and thus, narrower definitions of reproduction in preceding directives were repealed.[542] In addition, the Information Society Directive amended the provisions relating to the term of phonogram producers' rights that were contained in art.3(2) of the original Term Directive.[543]

4-269   The provisions of the E-Commerce Directive[544] are also relevant to a consideration of the Information Society Directive. The E-Commerce Directive concerns

---

[533] See Recital 15. These treaties are discussed at para.4-061.
[534] See para.4-255.
[535] See para.4-234.
[536] See paras 4-163 to 4-165.
[537] See para.4-163.
[538] See para.4-166.
[539] See para.4-065.
[540] See paras 4-065 and 4-072.
[541] Recital 20 and art.1(2).
[542] e.g. the reproduction right for performers, phonogram producers and cinematographic producers' rights: see art.11.
[543] art.11(2) Information Society Directive. See also the Term Directive at para.4-203.
[544] Directive 2000/31/EC on certain legal aspects of information society services, in particular electronic

many matters relating to online business that are either outside the scope of this book, (e.g. electronic contracts, unsolicited goods, etc.). However, it also exempts internet service providers and other intermediaries in relation to internet content where they are "mere conduits" or where they engage in hosting or caching of information. The conduit, caching, hosting defences are general defences not specific to copyright. Thus, although they relate to the information society, they are discussed elsewhere in this book.[545] These provisions should be read together with the mandatory defence in relation to transient or incidental reproduction that is contained in the Information Society Directive and are specific to copyright.[546] The short implementation timescale for the Information Society Directive was attributable to the desire to bring about implementation of the two Directives together.[547]

The Information Society Directive was the result of years of preparatory work, **4-270** consultation and debate. Those interested in its legislative background should consult the 1995 and 1996 Green Papers on Copyright and Related Issues in the Information Society[548] as well as the Commission's first proposal in 1997[549] and the amended proposal in 1999.[550]

The Information Society Directive survived an attack on its validity in the **4-271** *Laserdisken* case.[551] The challenge was brought on the basis of arts 47(2), 55, 95, 151 and 153 of the EC Treaty, and arts 1(c) and 2(a) of the OECD Convention, competition principles, proportionality and breach of the principle of freedom of expression. The CJEU dismissed all of these grounds.

Exclusive rights, express and implied consent

The Information Society Directive grants a number of rights to authors of works **4-272** including the right to prevent reproduction of their works and the right to authorise or prevent the communication to the public of their works. These are discussed below. As stated by the CJEU, the protection conferred by these rights must be given a broad interpretation and extends not only to the enjoyment of such rights but also the exercise of such rights.[552]

Therefore, any reproduction or communication to the public of a work without **4-273** the prior written consent of the copyright owner infringes the copyright in that work unless it falls within the exceptions discussed below in art.5 of the Directive[553]

An issue that often arises in the context of intellectual property cases is whether **4-274** a copyright owner can be considered to have implicitly consented to the use of a copyright work. For instance, what is the position where a copyright owner has failed to object to longstanding use of an otherwise infringing copy of his work? In the context of trade marks, the CJEU has been astute to make it clear that in the

---

commerce, in the Internal Market ("Directive on electronic commerce") [2000] OJ L178/1–16.
[545] arts 12–14 E-Commerce Directive. See para.14-073.
[546] art.5(1) Information Society Directive. See para.4-327.
[547] Recital 16, Information Society Directive.
[548] Commission of the European Communities, *Green Paper on Copyright and Related Rights in the Information Society* COM (95) 382 final; and Commission of the European Communities, *Follow-up to the Green Paper on copyright and related rights in the Information Society* COM (96) 586 final.
[549] Commission of the European Communities, *Proposal for a Directive on the Harmonisation of Certain Aspects of Copyright and Related Rights in the Information Society* COM (97) 628 final.
[550] *Amended Proposal for a Directive on the Harmonisation of Certain Aspects of Copyright and Related Rights in the Information Society* COM (1999) 250 final.
[551] (C-479/04) [2006] E.C.R. I-8089.
[552] *Soulier and Doke* (C-301/15) ECLI:EU:C:2016:878 at [30]–[31].
[553] *Soulier and Doke*, at [34].

absence of express consent, a court can only imply consent where such is unequivocally demonstrated.[554] In the context of the Information Society Directive and the exclusive rights that it confers on copyright owner, the CJEU has said that whilst prior express consent of the author is not required, the circumstances in which "implicit consent can be admitted must be strictly defined in order not to deprive of effect the very principle of the author's prior consent."[555] Thus, national legislation which deemed an author to have given consent to publication of "out of print works" if he did not oppose within six months after their registration in a database was contrary to the Information Society Directive as "every author must actually be informed of the future of his work by a third party and the means at his disposal to prohibit if he so wishes".[556] The CJEU went on to say that "the lack of opposition of a given author within the prescribed period cannot be construed ... as the expression of his implicit consent to that use."[557]

Reproduction right

4-275   The Information Society Directive introduced a harmonised reproduction right. The right is defined in the Directive as:

> "the exclusive right to authorise or prohibit, direct or indirect, temporary or permanent reproduction by any means and in any form, in whole or in part."[558]

4-276   The right is applicable to authors in respect of copyright protection for their "works" (discussed below), as well as performers, phonogram producers, film producers, and broadcasters as regards, respectively, fixations of performances, phonograms, first fixations of films, and fixations of broadcasts. A fortiori, there can be no reproduction right if such works, etc. did not enjoy copyright. Thus, although art.2 is described as the reproduction right, it is also concerned with subsistence of copyright in such works.

Works

4-277   There is no definition in the Information Society Directive of what constitutes a "work". As discussed earlier, because the EU is a signatory to both the WIPO Copyright Treaty and TRIPS, then EU legislation must be interpreted in the light of both international treaties.[559] Both these conventions require compliance with the Berne Convention. In its turn, the Berne Convention refers to works including every production in the literary, scientific and artistic domain whatever may be the mode or form of its expression but that it is a matter for contracting states to prescribe that works in general shall not be protected unless they have been fixed in some mate-

---

[554]   See Ch.3. para.3-526.
[555]   *Soulier*, at [35].
[556]   *Soulier*, at [38].
[557]   *Soulier*, at [43].
[558]   art.2.
[559]   For TRIPS, see para.4-015 and for WCT, see para.4-061. For the obligation that EU legislation must be interpreted in the light and purpose of international conventions to which the EU is a signatory, see para.1-165.

rial form.[560] The Directive does not stipulate that the work must be fixed in material form. Accordingly, it is suggested that such is not a requirement.[561]

However, if it is not a requirement that the works be fixed in a material form, **4-278** what does "works" mean in the Information Society Directive? The definition of works was considered by the CJEU in *Football Association Premier League Ltd v QC Leisure ("FAPL")*.[562] There it said that sporting events cannot be classified as works as to so classify, the subject matter would have to be original in the sense that it was the author's own intellectual creation.[563] It thus said that sporting events cannot be regarded as intellectual creations classifiable as works within the meaning of the Information Society Directive.[564] In particular in the case of football matches, the control imposed by the rules of the game left no room for creative freedom for the purposes of copyright.[565] There is a lack of clarity here. For instance, let us imagine a talented footballer who goes around cities displaying his "keepy-uppy" skills.[566] It is difficult to describe his various displays of skill in keeping the football from not touching the ground as not being the footballer's own intellectual creation. The only rule is that he keeps the football from touching the ground. Whilst his performance would be protectable as a performer's right, that protection will generally be more limited than for literary or artistic works. Yet, if such enjoys copyright as a "work", it is difficult to say that a football match which will consist of 22 players displaying their own creative talents as not being the collective creation of those 22 players. In the author's view, the better approach is to consider art.2 of the Berne Convention which sets out the meaning of literary and artistic works and gives examples of such.[567] Upon considering those examples, on a proper interpretation,[568] it is difficult to describe sporting events as being a literary or artistic work. Finally, it should be noted that the CJEU's comment in *FAPL v QC Leisure* would not extend to fixations of films of the sporting event, as made clear, for example, at [151] of that judgment.

Electronic and transient copying/streaming

Prior to the Information Society Directive, there was a divergence in the approach of Member States on the question of whether electronic, transient copying **4-279** would amount to an infringement of the reproduction right. This led to inconsistencies in the approach by Member States. The Computer Programs Directive and Database Directive had provided that such did amount to an infringement in relation to the works covered by those Directives. Article 2 of the Information Society Directive harmonises such inconsistencies and it is now clear that electronic copying, i.e. copying an electronic work onto a durable media (e.g. hard disk) or

---

[560] art.2(1), 2(2).

[561] See also Recital 29 which discusses the exclusive right to control distribution and where it refers to "distribution of the work incorporated in a tangible article" which would suggest that "work" should be construed more widely. This was a point accepted by the English High Court of Justice in *ITV Broadcasting Ltd v TVCatchup Ltd* [2011] EWHC 1874 (Pat) at [24].

[562] (C-403/08) [2011] E.C.R. I-9083.

[563] See [96]–[97]. This appears to conflate the requirement of "originality" and the definition of "works".

[564] See [98].

[565] An observation that may upset many a professional footballer!

[566] This is a rather ugly English phrase to describe those persons who can repeatedly kick a football up in the air so as to ensure that it does not touch the ground and thus can "keep up" the football.

[567] See para.4-015.

[568] Particularly applying the ejusdem generis principle of construction.

temporarily into a computer's memory, e.g. loading a program or part of it into the Random Access Memory (RAM) part of a computer for the purpose of running it will fall within the reproduction right. This is important because in the modern world, the user will often not have in his possession a hard copy of the work but will need to load up electronic transient copies of the work to run a program. Although the approach is no different with regards to computer programs (as opposed to other electronic works, e.g. audio and video files), readers should be aware that the Computer Software Directive is considered a *lex specialis* of the Information Society Directive and thus readers should consult that first.

4-280   In *FAPL v QC Leisure*, the CJEU had to consider whether the creation of transient sequential fragments of a broadcast within the memory of a satellite decoder and on a television screen which are immediately effaced and replaced by the next fragment fell within art.2. In particular, the referring court was uncertain whether it must conduct its appraisal by reference to all the fragments as a whole or only be reference to those which exist at a given moment. The CJEU rejected the successive "aggregate" approach but said that the reproduction right extends to simultaneous transient fragments within the memory of a satellite decoder and on a television screen provided that such fragments "contain elements which are the expression of the author's own intellectual creation."[569]

4-281   However, even if such is established, it is necessary to consider whether there is a defence under art.5(1). As will be seen, this defence applies to acts of reproduction which are temporary, transient, form part of a technological process, whose sole purpose is to enable a transmission in a network between third parties by an intermediary or a lawful use, and finally, have no independent economic significance. These provisions have been interpreted widely.[570]

Reproduction in part, subsistence of copyright and author's own intellectual creation

4-282   The reproduction right can be described, without controversy, as one of the fundamental rights conferred by copyright. Accordingly, its introduction via the Information Society Directive would not, in itself, have changed the laws of Member States. However, more difficult has been that the Directive provides that the reproduction right extends to reproduction of *part* of the work. There is no overt "substantiality" threshold within the reproduction right as set out in the Information Society Directive, as there is, for example, in relation to the sui generis database right under the Database Directive.[571] Thus, the issue is just how small could such a part of the copyright work be for its reproduction to amount to an infringing act?

4-283   This issue was addressed by the decision of the CJEU in *Infopaq International v Danske Dagblades Forening*.[572] *Infopaq* concerned the reproduction of small extracts from newspaper reports that were sent to the clients of Infopaq's media monitoring and analysis service. Those small extracts each consisted of a search word in which Infopaq's client was interested and the five words either side of it (therefore totalling 11 words). The court was asked (in the first question) whether those 11-word extracts could be regarded as acts of reproduction under art.2 of the Information Society Directive.

---

[569] See [153]–[159].
[570] This is discussed at para.4-327.
[571] art.7(1) Database Directive. And as there is under the UK law of copyright: CDPA 1988 s.16(3), and in the US under the fair use defence: US Copyright Act 1976 s.7.
[572] *Infopaq International v Danske Dagblades Forening* (C-5/08) [2009] E.C.R. I-6569.

In reaching its conclusion, the CJEU made the following three important **4-284** statements. First,[573] the court stated that the need for uniform application of EU law meant that the meaning of "reproduction in part" had to be given an autonomous and uniform interpretation throughout the EU. Secondly, by reason of the need to give a high level of protection to copyright, it was necessary to give a broad interpretation of art.2.[574] Thirdly,[575] that as part of its role in establishing a harmonised legal framework for copyright, the Information Society Directive is based on the same principle of originality, in the sense that works are only original if they are their author's own intellectual creation, as is set out in art.1(3) of the Computer Programs Directive; art.3(1) of the Database Directive; and in art.6 of the Rental Directive.[576] This common basis was evidenced, held the CJEU, by Recitals 4, 9–11 and 20 of the Information Society Directive. Recital 20, in which the principle is most clearly expressed, reads as follows:

> "(20) This Directive is based on principles and rules already laid down in the Directives currently in force in this area, in particular [the Computer Programs Directive and the Database Directive] and it develops those principles and rules and places them in the context of the information society. The provisions of this Directive should be without prejudice to the provisions of those Directives, unless otherwise provided in this Directive."

As a consequence, the CJEU held[577] that art.2 of the Information Society Direc- **4-285** tive only applied to subject-matter which is original in the sense that it is its author's own intellectual creation. To add some flesh to this remark, the CJEU said that given the requirement for broad protection, the possibility could not be ruled out that certain isolated sentences, or certain parts of sentences in the text in question, may amount to the author's own intellectual creation although it ruled out words themselves. As it said:

> "[45] Regarding the elements of such works covered by the protection, it should be observed that they consist of words which, considered in isolation, are not as such an intellectual creation of the author who employs them. It is only through the choice, sequence and combination of those words that the author may express *his creativity in an original manner* and achieve a result which is an intellectual creation." [Emphasis supplied.]

It is clear that this test is very wide. There is no threshold applicable to determin- **4-286** ing whether "a part" has been reproduced provided that part amounts to the author's own intellectual creation. More difficult issues arise where the part taken is very mundane and factual. A news reporter who reports that "An airplane has been shot down in Ukraine" can hardly be said to have "expressed his creativity in an original manner." Thus, a webscraping service which "scrapes" such a sentence from a third-party news website may have benefitted economically from obtaining such a news snippet and disclosing it to its subscribers. However, it is doubtful that such a sentence can be described as the author's own intellectual creation. In other words, economic value and intellectual creation are two very different concepts.

---

[573] At [27].
[574] At [43].
[575] At [31]–[36].
[576] Although, note that the definition of the reproduction right in relation to fixations of performances, phonograms, first fixations of films, and fixations of broadcasts, as originally enacted by the Rental Right Directive was replaced by the Information Society Directive.
[577] At [37].

4-287   It should be noted that the CJEU is treating the issue of "reproduction in part" and subsistence of copyright as one and the same. In other words, what gives rise to protection under the law of copyright cannot be appropriated by another. There is thus a symmetry between the test for subsistence of copyright and that for infringement. The approach in *Infopaq* of "author's own intellectual creation" has been applied to the issue of subsistence in copyright in a number of cases, some not specifically concerned with the reproduction right under the Information Society Directive.

4-288   In *Painer v Standard Verlags GMBH*,[578] the CJEU considered the question of whether copyright existed in a portrait photograph taken of an Austrian school girl who had then been kidnapped and held captive for many years before her escape. The CJEU held that a portrait photograph can be protected by copyright if it is an intellectual creation of the author reflecting their personality and expressing their free and creative choices in the production of that photograph. In reaching this conclusion, the court referred to Recital 17 of the Term Directive, which expressly states that a photograph is to be considered original within the meaning of the Berne Convention "if it is the author's own intellectual creation reflecting his personality."[579]

4-289   In *FAPL*, the CJEU considered whether the reproduction right extended to prohibit the creation of transient fragments of the works within the memory of a satellite decoder and on a television screen where such is immediately replaced by other transient fragments. Applying the decision in *Infopaq*, the CJEU held[580] that the creation of such fragments could be controlled by the reproduction right if such fragments, considered individually, contained elements which were the expression of the author's own intellectual creation. It was for the national court to determine whether or not they did.

4-290   In *Bezpečnostní softwarová asociace—Svaz softwarové ochrany v Ministerstvo Kultury*[581] the court was asked a question that was limited to a consideration of the Software Directive, but deemed that the national court would need further guidance as to the applicability of the Information Society Directive. The CJEU held that a graphical user interface was not protected by the copyright in a computer program but might be protectable as a work under the Information Society Directive. In order for it to attract that protection, it was held that it can be protected if it is the author's own intellectual creation. While the applicability of that criterion was clear from earlier decisions, *BSA* gave further guidance[582] as to factors relevant to the consideration of whether or not it had been satisfied: mere inclusion of components dictated by their technical function cannot suffice, because by doing so the author is unable to express their creativity in an original manner. In contrast, it would seem that a creation that does permit the original expression of the author's creativity would be capable of satisfying the criterion.

---

[578] (C-145/10) ECLI:EU:C:2013:138; [2012] E.C.D.R. 6 at [89].

[579] That recital goes on to state that "no other criteria such as merit or purpose being taken into account" but that "the protection of other photographs" (i.e. those that are not original within the meaning of the Berne Convention) should be left to national law. It is therefore open to national laws to provide protection for photographs that do not reach that level of originality, for example those taken by automated security apparatus or taken by accident. See para.4-225.

[580] See [157]–[159].

[581] (C-393/09) [2011] E.C.R. 6497; [2011] E.C.D.R. 3; [2011] F.S.R. 18 at [45].

[582] See [48]–[50].

In *Football Dataco v Yahoo! UK*[583] the CJEU was asked (in the context of a 4-291 copyright database and the consideration of the Database Directive) whether the author's own intellectual creation criterion required more than significant labour and skill from the author, and if so, what? It concluded that "the fact that the setting up of the database required, irrespective of the creation of the data which it contains, significant labour and skill of its author, cannot as such justify the protection of it by copyright under Dir.96/9, if that labour and that skill do not express any originality in the selection or arrangement of that data."

In an interesting case, *BVR* 1585/13, the German Constitutional Court—the 4-292 Bundesverfassungsgericht—held that the Bundesgerichtshof should have taken into account the "freedom of art" when considering whether the use of a two-second sequence of a musical piece protected by copyright as a "sample" infringed the phonogram producers' rights. It said that if there was doubt about the interpretation of the Information Society Directive and its interaction with the Charter of Fundamental Rights, the Bundesgerichtshof should refer the matter to the Court of Justice.

Communication to the public/right of making available

Article 3 of the Information Society Directive provides for a right of communica- 4-293 tion to the public and a right of making available to the public of works of authors. It also provides for a right of making available performances, phonograms, films and fixations of broadcasts but not communication to the public of the same. This is because the Rental and Neighbouring Rights Directive provides for this right.[584] For present purposes, the reader need only know that the protection is not the same. Thus, for phonograms, the producer only has a right to equitable remuneration (shared with performers whose performances are on the phonogram) and the communication right for broadcasts is restricted to where the communication is made in places accessible to the public upon payment of an entrance fee.[585] The "making available" right applies where a work is made available to the public "*in such a way that members of the public may access them from a place and at a time individually chosen by them*".[586] This is often called the Internet right as it is the hallmark of the Internet that members of the public can access such works in such a manner. However, it does not cover "live streaming" of works through the Internet.[587] Member States can provide protection against this but the legislative "home" for this topic is the Rental and Neighbouring Rights Directive.[588]

The Information Society Directive does not seek to define the expression "com- 4-294 munication to the public", and has instead left the scope of the right to be determined through interpretation by the CJEU. The first important case to address the meaning of this section was the *SGAE* case.[589] In that case, the CJEU held

---

[583] (C-604/10) ECLI:EU:C:2012:115, [2012] E.C.D.R. 10 at [38].
[584] See para.4-162, et seq.
[585] See para.4-166.
[586] art.3.1.
[587] See para.4-172.
[588] See para.4-172.
[589] *Sociedad General de Autores y Editores de España (SGAE) v Rafael Hoteles SA* (C-306/05) [2006] E.C.R. I-11519.

that the expression "communication to the public" was a European Union concept[590] that is to be interpreted broadly pursuant to the Recital 23 of the Directive.[591]

4-295   In *SGAE*, and then in number of subsequent cases discussed below— *Organismos*,[592] *FAPL*,[593] *ITV Broadcasting*,[594] *BSA*,[595] *Svensson*,[596] and *OSA*[597]; in two cases that primarily concern the Rental and Neighbouring Rights Directive: *SCF*[598] and *Phonographic Performance Ireland*, and in a case primarily concerning the Satellite and Cable Directive, *Airfield*[599] the CJEU has sought to explain the concepts of "communication" and the characteristics of "the public" to which that communication must be made for this right to be infringed. The reasons given by the CJEU to support findings that there has been a communication to the public in some cases are, however, difficult to reconcile on any principled basis with the reasons given to support a finding that there has not been a communication to the public in other cases. Notwithstanding that difficulty (which leaves some uncertainty about exactly which acts will be held to infringe this right), it is now possible at least to say the following with some confidence:

(1)   There will be a "communication" when a work is made available by a transmission in such a way that persons may access it: *SGAE*, at [43]; *FAPL*, at [193]; and *OSA*, at [25].

(2)   It is not necessary for any person actually to take advantage of the opportunity to access the work: *SGAE*, at [43].

(3)   Any act of transmission which either constitutes the whole act of communication[600] or takes place between the point at which a communication originates and the final point of potential reception is itself a communication: *SGAE*, at [46], *FAPL*, at [203]; unless it is only a technical means to ensure or improve reception: *FAPL*, at [194], *ITV Broadcasting*, at [28], *Airfield*, at [74].

(4)   However, if there is no physical separation between the point of interpretation of a work and the reception of that interpretation then there is no communication: *FAPL*, at [201], *Circul Globus*,[601] at [33]–[37].

(5)   The communication will be to a "public" when it is made to an indeterminate number of potential recipients who constitute a fairly large number of persons: *SGAE*, at [37] and [38], *ITV Broadcasting*, at [32], *OSA*, at [27].

(6)   The requirement for a fairly large number of persons indicates that the

---

[590]   *SGAE*, at [31].

[591]   *SGAE*, at [36].

[592]   *Organismos Sillogikis Diacheirisis Dimiourgon Theatrikon kai Optikoakoustikon Ergon v Divani Akropolis Anonimi Xenodocheiaki kai Touristiki Etaireai* (C-136/09) [2010] E.C.R. I-0037.

[593]   (C-403/08) and (C-429/08) ECLI:EU:C:2011:631.

[594]   *ITV Broadcasting Ltd v TV Catchup Ltd* (C-607/11) ECLI:EU:C:2013:147.

[595]   *Bezpecnostni Softwarova Asociace – Svaz Softwarove Ochrany v Ministerstvo Kultury* (C-393/09) [2011] E.C.R. 102.

[596]   *Svensson v Retriever Sverige AB* (C-466/12) ECLI:EU:C:2014:76.

[597]   *Ochranný svaz autorský pro práva k dílum hudebním o.s. v Léčebné lázně Mariánské Lázně a.s.* (C-351/12) ECLI:EU:C:2014:110.

[598]   See para.4-167.

[599]   *Airfield v SABAM*; *Airfield v AGICOA* (C-431/09 and C-432/09) [2011] E.C.R. I-9363.

[600]   And includes making the sounds or representations of sounds fixed in a phonogram audible to the public, such as by providing phonograms and playing equipment to the public: see *Phonographic Performance (Ireland) Ltd v Ireland* (C-162/10) [2012] E.C.D.R. 15 at [58]–[63].

[601]   *Circul Globus Bucureşti v Uniunea Compozitorilor şi Muzicologilor din România – Asociatia pentru Drepturi de Autor (UCMR – ADA)* (283/10) [2011] E.C.R. I-12031.

concept of "public" has a de minimis threshold, and that groups of persons which are too small, or insignificant are excluded: *SCF*, at [86].

(7) In determining whether the number of persons is fairly large, all potential recipients of the alleged infringer's acts of transmission including those with successive access to those acts of transmission must be considered cumulatively: *SGAE*, at [39], *ITV Broadcasting*, at [33], *OSA*, at [28].

(8) However, in determining whether a fairly large number of persons have had successive access to the alleged infringer's acts of transmission, it is necessary to consider whether or not those persons will or will not have access to the particular work or works alleged to be infringed: *SCF*, at [96].[602]

(9) Communications will be infringing acts of communication to the public if either: (a) the original act of communication was not authorised by the copyright owner[603], or (b) if the public reached by the alleged infringer's acts of communication are to a "new public": *SGAE*, at [41]; *FAPL*, at [198]; *Svensson*, at [24].

(10) There will be a "new public" if there is a public (i.e. an indeterminate number of potential recipients who constitute a fairly large number of persons) that was not taken into account by the copyright owner when giving their authorisation for the original communication.

    (a) Examples of a "new public" arise where:
        (i) the recipients are neither the owners of ordinary reception equipment nor within that equipment owner's private or family circles: *SGAE*, [41]; *FAPL*, at [198]; or
        (ii) the public reached by the alleged infringer's acts of communication are reached by a transmission made by different specific technical conditions: *ITV Broadcasting*, at [39]; explained as relating to a "new public" in *Svensson*, at [24].

    (b) It is relevant to consider whether an alleged infringer intends to make a profit when they undertake a transmission that provides traditional television broadcasts to a group of people: *FAPL*, at [204]; *ITV Broadcasting*, at [42].

    (c) The fact that the alleged infringer, by bringing together a number of sources, provides a new audiovisual product may also be relevant: *Airfield*, at [81].

    (d) But there is no "new public" if the initial communication is unrestricted to users of the internet, and the further acts of transmission relies on the original communication, even where that is not apparent to the internet user, and/or is done for profit: *Svensson*, at [27]–[30].

(11) In the context of websites, there is an act of communication to the public in a Member State if the website targets a specific audience in that Member State.[604]

Although the principles are fairly easy to state, the Court of Justice has strug-   **4-296**

---

[602] But see also the discussion below at para.4-297.

[603] This is not expressly stated in any decision, but is the only realistic interpretation of the need for a "new public": plainly, for there to be a "new public", there must have been an authorised original public. If there is no authorised original public then all acts of communication to a public must be infringements.

[604] See *L'Oréal v eBay* (where the CJEU, held in the context of trade mark infringement and Community Trade Marks, that a website must target consumers within the EU for a CTM to be

gled to give coherent guidance to their application to common factual situations where there have been a number of references from the courts of Member States to it. Any attempt to establish a "grand unified theory" from the cases is doomed to fail. It is thus better to consider the approach of the CJEU to different "cluster" of facts. Thus, its approach to the communication to the public on the Internet is very different to that of broadcasting of music or programmes in hotels, dentist waiting rooms, etc.

Hotels, dentists' waiting rooms, pubs, clinics

4-297   There have been a number of references from Member States as to whether the playing of music in hotel rooms, pubs, waiting rooms for dentists, clinics, etc. amounts to a "communication to the public". The central issue is whether the persons in the waiting room, clinics, etc. can be considered "the public" such that there is a communication to the public. In *SCF*, the CJEU considered that there was no communication to the public where music was played in a waiting room of a dentist. In *SGAE* and in *Phonographic Performance Ireland*,[605] it was held that the distribution of television signals and the transmission of music from sound recordings into private hotel rooms was a "communication to the public". In *FAPL*, it was held that there was a communication to the public where broadcasts were played in pubs.

4-298   In *Reha Training v GEMA*,[606] the issue was whether there was a communication to the public where television programmes were played to patients in waiting rooms and a training room of a rehabilitation clinic. The CJEU was given the task of reconciling its decisions in *SCF*, *FAPL*, *Phonographic Performance Ireland* and *SGAE*. To do so, it decided the case as a Grand Chamber (13 judges). This was so as to clarify the law about "communication to the public".

4-299   The CJEU held that the following facts meant that there was a communication to the public: the patients were "persons in general" (i.e. not a private club); the patients could not watch television without the "targeted intervention" of the clinic owner and were not taken into account when the original authorisation for the work was given; the supply of television programmes had no medical benefit but could be seen as an additional service increasing the competitiveness of the clinic; and the broadcasts of the works could be considered for profit as the user was likely to make the clinic more attractive to patients. In contrast, it said that in *SCF*, patients of dentists did not as a general rule, place any importance on the playing of music in a waiting room and their numbers would not be increased as a result.

4-300   The CJEU's decision in *Reha Training* goes a long way to clarifying what can be considered a "communication to the public" when television or music is played to members of the public in the rooms of offices, clinics, pubs, health centres, etc. With some hesitation, it can be said that the test is a multi-factorial one with the fol-

---

infringed)—discussed in the main text at para.3-549. This approach has been applied to the act of "communication to the public" under the InfoSoc Directive in English courts. In *EMI v BskyB* [2013] EWHC 379 and *Omnibill (Pty) Ltd v Egpsxxx Ltd* [2014] EHWC 3762 (IPEC), the English courts have applied the "targeting" test to a server that was located outside the UK and hosted an infringing work specifically targeting UK consumers. It held that the websites, although located outside the UK, targeted UK consumers (amongst other countries), and accordingly there was an act of "communication to the public" of an infringing work hosted on servers outside the UK.

[605] *Phonographic Performance (Ireland) Ltd v Ireland* (C-162/10) [2011] E.C.R. I-10923; [2012] E.C.D.R. 15.

[606] (C-117/15) EU:C:2016:379.

lowing facts being particularly relevant:

- Whether or not the film, broadcast or music is deliberately made available to users through the intended intervention of the operator of the premises or is accidental in nature.
- Whether or not the copyright works would have been available to the users but for that intervention.[607]
- Whether or not the users were taken into account when the original authorisation for the work was given.[608]
- Whether or not the works are likely to increase in a material manner the attractiveness and increase the competitiveness of the business (and thus its profits) rather than being incidental.
- Whether or not the transmission of the copyright works is restricted to a closed private group of persons or an indeterminate number of persons.
- The number of people who will hear or see the audiovisual work whether at the same time (simultaneously) or over a period of time (successively).

New technical means

In the 21st century a broadcast may be retransmitted to the user in many ways. **4-301**
Thus, an undertaking might seek to transmit the broadcast through cables to viewers where a signal is weak. Alternatively, an undertaking may "live stream" a broadcast through an Internet platform so that it can be viewed on computers or smartphones rather than on a television.

In principle, one would have thought that merely providing a different way for **4-302**
viewers to watch a broadcast would not give rise to a communication to a "new" public. Thus, if the broadcast "footprint" of a national broadcasting company is a Member State so that any resident of that Member State with a television can watch that broadcast, one can reasonably say that the intended recipients of the original broadcast are all residents of that Member State. This would suggest that the transmission of a broadcast to a resident within that "footprint" via cable or a smartphone would not infringe the "communication to the public" right as there is no "new public". In other words, it cannot be reasonably said that there is a "new" public merely because of the technical means that the "old" public decides to watch the broadcasts. However, as discussed hereinbelow, the CJEU's approach to whether

---

[607] This appears to amount to little more than the operator providing televisions in the rooms—see *FAPL*, at [195]; *SGAE*, at [42]; *Reha Training*, at [51].

[608] This is a difficult concept. In the case of a terrestrial broadcast of television programmes, it is difficult to say that the public at large was not taken into account as anyone in the broadcast "footprint" with a television set would have had access to such. In the case of "pay" TV, e.g. satellite broadcasts, it is plainly an easier concept as users will tend to be paid subscribers. In *Reha Training*, it is not clear whether the programmes were terrestrial "free" TV or satellite "pay" TV. The CJEU said that it is clear that the patients were clearly not taken into account when the original authorisation was given. It would seem that the CJEU had in mind previous statements that when an author authorises a broadcast of his work, he considers, in principle, only the owners of television sets, who, either personally or within their own private or family circles, receive the signal and follow the broadcasts (see [62], AG Opinion, *Reha Training* citing *FAPL*, at [198]). In the author's view, this is somewhat of a "legal fiction". For instance, in *AKM v Zürs.net Betriebs GmbH* (C-138/16) ECLI:EU:C:2017:218, in a Reasoned Order, the CJEU held that that right holders are aware that when they grant permission to national broadcasting organisations, their broadcasts may be received by all persons within a country—at [28]. It thus held that the transmission of broadcasts by cable transmission was not a communication to a new public. This case is discussed in the "new technical means" section at para.4-301.

retransmission of a broadcast by a "new" technical means amounts to an infringement of this right has been inconsistent.

4-303   Before doing so, it is necessary to remind the reader that under the Information Society Directive, there is no communication to the public right for broadcasts, films, sound recordings and performances per se. Whilst the Rental and Neighbouring Rights Directive does provide for some protection for the communication to the public of such, they are limited in nature.[609] For instance, the communication to the public of a broadcasts is only protected if access is to the public upon payment of an entrance fee. This does not apply often to livestreaming of broadcasts onto a mobile phone.[610]

4-304   However, films, broadcasts and sound recordings will include literary, artistic, dramatic and/or musical works. It is only in the cases where such does not exist (e.g. a broadcast of a sporting event) that this gives rise to an issue. Moreover, broadcasts of live events will often include artistic, literary or musical works, e.g. words or graphics on the TV screen or accompanying music. These are called "ransom strips" by copyright lawyers because whilst they are of little or no interest to the public (as compared to the sporting event), as they are literary or musical works, they are protected by the communication to the public right in art.3.1 Information Society Directive.

4-305   In a number of authorities, the CJEU has said that a mere technical means to ensure or improve reception of the original transmission does not constitute a communication to the public.[611] But what is the position if the technical means does not merely boost the signal? In *ITV Broadcasting v TVCatchup*,[612] the CJEU held that the live streaming of free-for-all broadcasts of sporting events via the Internet did not amount to such "mere" technical means and indeed amounted to a communication to the public.[613] In doing so, it rejected a submission that because the users receiving it could have received the broadcast on their television sets, there was no transmission to a "new public". The CJEU instead said that the "new public" principle did not apply where the transmission of the broadcast was under "*specific technical conditions, using a different means of transmission for the protected works*" and that the EU legislature intended that each transmission or retransmission using a specific technical means was different to that original authorised by the author.[614] This approach was followed in *VCAST v RTI*.[615] Here the Court of Justice held that where a company made available to its customers via the Internet, a video recording system, in the cloud, for terrestrial programs of Italian television companies, this was an infringement of the "communication to the public right" as the provision of such was using a different means of transmission than that used by the Italian television companies.[616] It held, following *FAPL*, that it was not necessary to consider whether there was a "new public."[617]

---

[609] See paras 4-162 and 4-176.

[610] Although Member States can provide greater protection under the Rental Directive as that merely sets out a minimum level of protection, see para.4-171.

[611] *FAPL*, at [194], *Airfield*, at [74], [70], and *ITV*, at [28].

[612] (C-607/11) ECLI:EU:C:2013:147.

[613] Here, the "ransom strip" musical and literary copyright were relied upon.

[614] See [28]–[30], [39].

[615] (C-265/16) ECLI:EU:C:2017:913.

[616] See [47]–[49].

[617] See [50] applying *ITV Broadcasting*, at [39].

However, in another case, *AKM v Zürs.net Betriebs GmbH*,[618] which was heard **4-306** by the CJEU in between *ITV Broadcasting* and *VCAST*, the CJEU adopted an approach which is very difficult to reconcile with *ITV Broadcasting* and *VCAST*. Zürs.net operated a cable network in a town in Austria. It used this to transmit television and radio broadcasts which were broadcast by an Austrian national broadcasting organisation. It had only 130 subscribers. AKM, a copyright collecting society, claimed that this amounted to a "communication to the public" within the meaning of art.3.1 Information Society Directive. The CJEU, in a Reasoned Order, held that as different technical means were used than that for the initial broadcast transmission, there was a "communication" but such left for determination whether the communication was intended for a "new public".[619] It held that as the subscribers to Zürs.net were persons taken into account by the right holders when they granted the original authorisation to the national broadcaster, the subscribers could not be considered a "new public" and therefore there was no communication to the public. This was because right holders when they grant consent, are aware that the broadcasts made by the national broadcasting corporation may be received by all persons in Austria.[620] There was no mention of *ITV Broadcasting* in the judgment which is unfortunate. Exactly the same argument was made in *ITV Broadcasting* but rejected. Indeed, in both *ITV* and *VCAST*, the Court of Justice has twice stated that if new technical means are used, there is no need to consider whether the communication is to a new public.

Clearly, there is a need for a coherent approach as to when a "new technical **4-307** means" is sufficiently groundbreaking that the requirement to consider whether the transmission is to a new public is unnecessary. To be fair to the CJEU, there is a material difference between on the one hand, users who have televisions who receive a broadcasted signal through cables rather than directly through a television aerial and on the other hand, users who receive the signal through, e.g. smartphones and/or (in the case of VCAST), recordings watched at the watcher's convenience rather than live. In the latter cases, the "technical means" allows watchers to watch the broadcast on a very different *device* or *manner* to that originally envisaged by the broadcaster. In the former case, they watch it on the same device to that originally intended. Thus, a right holder may wish to license the "home television" viewing market differently to the "smartphone" on-the-move viewing market. In contrast, it is a commercially meaningless distinction to subdivide the "home television" viewing market into segments which depend on the technical means as to how the film is transmitted to the "home television" viewing market. With such in mind, the CJEU's approach in *ITV*, *VCAST* and *AKM* makes sense. It would be a nonsense if the live streaming of sporting events onto a computer in a home is an infringement of the communication of public right if such could be watched on a television in a home via cable or a TV aerial. This is particularly the case where the distinction between computers and televisions is becoming blurred and indeed, in many cases, one device performs the role of both. Yet, a material distinction can be made between those who watch it on smartphones who are moving around and televisions in a home. There is a need for the CJEU to take a holistic, multifactorial approach to the issue of "new technical means" as it has in *Reha Training* when considering the playing of music or films in pubs, clinics, etc. In the

---

[618] (C-138/16) ECLI:EU:C:2017:218.
[619] See [26]–[27].
[620] See [28].

authors' view, of primary importance must be the commercial realities of the marketplace (i.e. home viewing, mobile viewing, live and "catch-up", etc.) and the need to ensure a high level of protection for authors and for them to obtain an appropriate reward for the use of their works.[621]

Liability of intermediaries

4-308   In *SBS Belgium NV v SABAM*[622] the Court of Justice had to consider whether a process of transmitting programmes exclusively to signal distributors via "direct injection" amounted to an act of "communication to the public". In this case, SBS, a Dutch broadcasting company, transmitted programmes via a two-step process. The first step involved SBS transmitting the programme—carrying signals via a private line to its distributors in Belgium. At that point, the signals could not be received by the general public. The second step involved the distributors sending the programme to their subscribers so that the latter could view the programmes on their television sets. Sometimes, they were transmitted by satellite or sometimes by cable. SABAM, the Belgian collecting society, took the view that SBS was making a communication to the public by using the first step, called the "direct injection" method. SBS denied this by saying that it was their distributors who were making the communication to the public, i.e at the second step.

4-309   The real issue in this case was whether the distributors were merely acting as a technical means for communicating the programmes to the end user or not. It was not disputed that the distributors themselves were not "the public" for the purpose of art.3(1) Information Society Directive. However, applying *Airfield* and *FAPL*, if the distributor was not independent in relation to the broadcasting organisation and its distribution service was purely technical in nature, then the subscribers of the distributors could be considered to be the public for the purpose of the communication by the broadcasting organisation with the result that the latter was making a communication to the public of the programmes. Accordingly, the Court of Justice held that the broadcasting organisation did not carry out the act of communication to the public unless the "intervention of the distributors in question is just a technical means" which it said was for the national court to ascertain.

Making available right/Internet use/hyperlinks

4-310   The "making available" right is aimed at preventing the "posting" of literary, dramatic, artistic, musical works, sound recordings, films and fixation of broadcasts or performances onto the Internet without the consent of the owner of those rights. The "making available" right does not apply to live streams as they are not made available to member of the public "at a time individually chosen by them".[623] It should be noted that the "making available" right is considered a type of "communication to the public" right.[624] Generally, the application of this right is unproblematic. If copyright work is posted on the Internet without consent of the copyright owner, then it is an infringement.

---

[621] *ITV Broadcasting*, at [20].
[622] (C-325/14) ECLI:EU:C:2015:764.
[623] arts 3.1, 3.2 Information Society Directive. See (C-279/13) *C More Entertainment AB v Linus Sandberg* ECLI:EU:C:2015:199 at [26]–[27] and para.4-172.
[624] See art.3.1 which refers to the communication to the public right including the "making available" right.

However, in a number of cases, the CJEU has had to consider whether the post- **4-311**
ing of hyperlinks on Website A linking to copyright works on Website B was a
"communication to the public". See for example: *Svensson*,[625] *BestWater*
International GmbH v Mebes/Potsch[626] and *GS Media BV v Sanoma Media*
Netherlands BV.[627] These decisions show that a number of factors need to be taken
into account to determine whether the posting of the hyperlink on Website A which
links to Website B where the copyright work can be viewed or downloaded
infringes the communication to the public right. These are:

- Was the work on Website B posted with the consent of the right holder?
- Is Website B able to be viewed by all or behind a paywall?
- If the work on Website B has been posted without the consent of the right
  holder, did the poster of the hyperlink on Website A know that or have
  reason to believe that it was unauthorised?
- Was the hyperlink posted to allow the owner of Website A to make a profit
  or not?

Svensson concerned the provision of links to freely available internet sites. The **4-312**
CJEU held that the provision of such links did not make a communication to the
public because there was no communication to a "new public". The astute reader
might wonder how this is different to an operator providing a television in a
rehabilitation clinic (*Reha Training*) to access a free-for-all television broadcast
which could be accessed by anyone with a television. The answer is probably that
in *Svensson*, the user would have had a computer and thus, he was, literally, always
a "click away" from finding the work on Website B whereas in *Reha Training*, it
required the intervention of the operator to provide a technical means (the television) to allow access to the broadcast in the clinic. However, the CJEU in *Svens-*
son said that it would be different if the hyperlink allowed a user to access a website
behind a paywall that was otherwise not available to be viewed by the general
public.[628]

In *BestWater International GmbH v Mebes/Potsch*, by Reasoned Order, the Court **4-313**
of Justice confirmed that *Svensson* applies to content which is made freely available to the public on a website and then a third party displays that content in its own
website by "framing" (such that it appears to be an integral part of the third party's
website). In that case, the facts were that a competitor of a water filter company,
where the latter had produced a film available to be viewed on the Internet on the
subject of water pollution and in where it owned the rights, "framed" the film available to be viewed on the Internet on their own website. The Court of Justice held,
applying *Svensson*, that this did not by itself amount to a communication to the
public within the meaning of art.3(1) of the InfoSoc Directive. It is clear here that
the CJEU did not see any difference in principle between a hyperlink to a website
and a framing of that website. In both cases, the copyright work was available for
viewing by all and thus there was no communication to a "new public". Hence, it
being a Reasoned Order. However, from the perspective of the owner of the
copyright work, they may be deprived of digital advertising revenue from advertisements appearing on Website B as that is not in their control.

In *GS Media BV*, the Court of Justice had to consider the application of *Svens-* **4-314**

---

[625] *Svensson v Retriever Sverige AB* (C-466/12) EU:C:2014:76
[626] (C–348/13) EU:C:2014:2315.
[627] (C–160/15) EU:C:2016:644.
[628] *Svensson*, at [31].

son and *BestWater* where an undertaking provided a hyperlink to infringing copyright works which were freely available on another website. In this case, a well-known Dutch website provided hyperlinks to unauthorised photographs which could be viewed on another website and which had been posted by a third party. The latter website was not well known so the Dutch website was, in effect, publicising it to an audience which in large part, would not have known about the website with the infringing material. The Court of Justice was clearly conflicted here. On the one hand, encouraging people to view infringing copyright works which they might not have seen otherwise would plainly encourage viewings of an unlawful work to the detriment of the copyright owner. On the other hand, it is very difficult for undertakings posting hyperlinks to other websites to know whether or not the copyright work is an unauthorised one. As submitted by the European Commission and several Member States, automatically restricting the posting of hyperlinks to other websites could have highly restrictive consequences for freedom of expression and information as the poster would often not know and it would be difficult to find out, whether such copyright works have been posted on the Internet with the consent of the copyright owner. To resolve that conflict, the Court of Justice held that there was a "communication to the public" unless the undertaking which provided the hyperlink did so without the pursuit of financial gain and did not know and could not reasonably have known the illegal nature of the publication. As for undertakings who posted hyperlinks for profit, it held that there was a "rebuttable presumption" that the poster would know whether or not the copyright work had been posted with the authorisation of the copyright owner.[629] In the Dutch case, this did not help GS Media BV as it had provided the hyperlinks for profit and they were aware that the photographs had not been posted with the consent of the copyright owner.

4-315   It can be appreciated that the "rebuttable presumption" that profit-making undertakings knew whether a work which the undertaking provides a hyperlink to is authorised is artificial in many cases. Thus, it would be fanciful to suggest that owners or operators of search engines which automatically provide hyperlinks through using webcrawlers knew whether content which is accessed by the hyperlinks is unauthorised or not. This has led to a German decision which has said that the presumption in *GS Media* is not applicable to search engines.[630] In the author's view, there is some confusion here. The CJEU merely said that there was a rebuttable presumption. Clearly, in the case of search engines which automatically generate hyperlinks, this presumption is rebutted easily forcefully. A rebuttable presumption simply means that the burden of proof lies on the defendant to show that they did not know. It is a burden very easily discharged. It should not be confused with a *duty* being imposed on the defendant to show that, e.g. they took reasonable care not to provide a hyperlink to unauthorised works.

Accessory liability

4-316   The CJEU has held that the mere provision of physical facilities that allow the communication to the public of copyright works does not in itself amount to communication within the meaning of the Information Society Directive.[631] However, the CJEU has been astute to find that devices which are specifically targeted at al-

---

[629] See [51].
[630] *I ZR* 11/16 Preview III, BGH.
[631] *Stichting Brein v Jack Frederik Willems* (C-527/15) ECLI:EU:C:2017:300 at [39] citing Recital 27.

lowing consumers to have access to works on the Internet which have been uploaded without the consent of copyright owners amounts to an act of communication to the public. In *Stichting Brein v Willems*, the latter advertised and sold a multimedia player which included open source software which made it possible, through pre-installed add-ons that contained hyperlinks to websites which had uploaded audiovisual files without the consent of copyright owners. Mr Willems indeed advertised such a fact. The CJEU held that the sale of these multimedia players amounted to a communication to the public. It is questionable whether the mere sale of a device that enables a user to access unauthorised audiovisual files is itself a communication to the public of unauthorised copyright works. Manifestly, by itself, it is not. The seller of the device is not itself hosting the third party website that has infringing audiovisual works. He merely enables users to easily find such websites. It may have been more intellectually honest if the CJEU had said that Mr Willems was liable under general principles of accessory law, i.e. he had assisted others to infringe copyright knowing that such did indeed infringe copyright. However, it is generally considered that the law on accessory liability to wrongs (torts) is a matter for the national law of Member States and not EU law.

The CJEU took the same approach in *Stichting Brein v Ziggo BV*[632] where two **4-317** ISPs (Internet Service Providers) had a significant number of subscribers who accessed the well-known online sharing platform "The Pirate Bay". This platform allowed users to download unauthorised copyright works using the BitTorrent protocol. It is a protocol which allows users (known as "peers") to share files. Files are divided into segments and then distributed across users. A person who wishes to download a file would then, using an application known as BitTorrent Client, aggregate all of these segments into a complete file. The indexation of these segments was done by The Pirate Bay platform. The Pirate Bay platform was thus an essential "gateway" as it identified the users with segments of a particular file and allowed their aggregation. The Hoge Raad was not sure whether The Pirate Bay platform was communicating to the public the copyright works. The Court of Justice held that it was doing so. Here, The Pirate Bay platform played a central role. Without its intervention, users could not have watched or downloaded the infringing works. Its role went far beyond mere facilitation as was the case in *Stichting Brein v Willems* and it can be considered an "instigator" rather than a mere accessory.

However, there can be little doubt from both of these cases that the CJEU's view **4-318** is that undertakings who play an important role in allowing users to watch or download unauthorised works on the Internet and know that this will happen are to be considered infringers as much as an undertaking who hosts a website that contains unauthorised copyright works. In truth, the Court of Justice has introduced accessory liability as EU law into the "communication to the public" right.

Same approach under the InfoSoc and Rental Directives

It should be said that the above decisions are concerned with the meaning of **4-319** "communication to the public" in two directives: the Rental Directive and the Information Directive. Thus, *SCF* was concerned with the Rental Directive. As discussed already, the nature of the "communication to the public" right is different, e.g. under the Rental Directive, phonogram producers and performers only have

---

[632] (C-610/15) ECLI:EU:C:2017:456.

a right to equitable remuneration for the communication to the public of their recordings or performances. Despite this, and indeed, in an early case, *SCF*, the CJEU saying that such meant that the interpretation of "communication to the public" should be "individual",[633] it is clear that now, the CJEU takes the view that the interpretation of the concept is and should be the same in both Directives.[634]

Distribution right and exhaustion

4-320   The distribution right contained in the Information Society Directive is confined to authors' works. This is because for phonograms, films, fixations of broadcasts and performances, the Rental and Neighbouring Rights provide for a distribution right.[635]

4-321   It provides that authors shall have, in respect of the original of their works or copies thereof, the exclusive right to authorise or prohibit any form of distribution to the public by sale or otherwise.[636] As with other EU IP Directives, it provides for exhaustion of the distribution right where transfer of ownership by "first sale or other transfer of ownership" in the original or copy is made by the right holder or with their consent.[637] The CJEU has confirmed that it is not open to Member States to retain a rule of exhaustion other than EU-wide exhaustion,[638] and in this regard the position is the same as that in respect of registered trade marks.[639]

4-322   In *Peek & Cloppenburg*,[640] the CJEU held that the fact that distribution right referred to "by sale or otherwise" did not mean that "otherwise" did not require a transfer of ownership.[641] Thus, a clothing shop which had armchairs in its restrooms for use by customers made to a design without the consent of the copyright owner in that design did not infringe the distribution right. It is also of note that the CJEU has also ruled that the act of distribution, while limited to circumstances that result in the transfer of ownership, is a continuing set of activities that involve not only the conclusion of a contract of sale but also the delivery of the goods to the purchaser.[642]

4-323   In *Art & Allposters International BV v Stichting Pictoright*,[643] the Court of Justice had to consider the application of the Information Society Directive to the "transfer"

---

[633] *SCF*, at [76].

[634] *Verwertungsgesellschaft Rundfunk GmbH v Hettegger Hotel Edelweiss GmBH* (C-641/15) ECLI:EU:C:2017:131 at [19]; See in particular *Reha Training*, at [28]–[33].

[635] art.9 Dir.2006/115. See para.4-162, et seq.

[636] art.4(1).

[637] art.4(2).

[638] See *Laserdisken ApS v Kulturministeriet* (C-479/04) [2006] E.C.R. I-8089 and *Micro Leader Business v Commission* (T-198/98) [1999] E.C.R. II-3989.

[639] See Ch.3, "Trade Marks in Europe" at para.3-590, and *Silhouette International Schmied GmbH & Co KG v Hartlauer Handelsgesellschaft mbH* (C-355/96) [1998] E.C.R. I-4799; *Sebago and Maison Dubois* (C-173/98) [1999] E.C.R. I-4103; and *Zino Davidoff v A&G Imports Ltd* (C-414/99) [2001] E.C.R. I-8691; [2002] 1 C.M.L.R. 1, all of which indicate that the principle of "Fortress Europe" has found favour over the principle of international exhaustion.

[640] See *Peek & Cloppenburg KG v Cassina SpA* (C-456/06) [2008] E.C.R. I-2731 at [36].

[641] See [35] relying upon art.6(1) WIPO Copyright Treaty which referred to the "making available to the public" right whether "through sale or other transfer of ownership" and holding that art.4 Dir.2001/29 should be interpreted in accordance with the WIPO Copyright Treaty.

[642] *Criminal Proceedings Against Titus Donner* (C-5/11) ECLI:EU:C:2012:370 at, [26]–[28]. The same principle was applied in the context of the Customs Regulation 1383/03 in *Blomqvist v Rolex* (C-98/13), where a contract for the sale of goods subject to copyright protection was concluded in China and the goods then sent by the seller to a recipient in Denmark.

[643] (C-419/13) ECLI:EU:C:2015:27.

of an artwork printed on a poster to a canvas without the consent of the copyright owner. Allposters, a poster company, offered a service to its client whereby, artwork on a poster could be chemically "lifted" from the poster and placed onto a canvas. The result was that the image of the artwork disappeared from the poster and was transferred to the canvas. Pictoright, a Dutch copyright collecting society, brought proceedings based on Dutch copyright law based on the InfoSoc Directive (*Auteurswet*). It claims that the sale of the canvas works infringed the copyright in the artwork.

At the heart of the dispute was whether the subsequent distribution of the canvas **4-324** displaying the artwork infringed the distribution right or such was exhausted. This led to a focus on whether the canvas was the same "object" as the poster, so as to trigger the exhaustion provisions of art.4(2).[644]

The Court of Justice held that art.4(2) meant (and in doing so, it considered that **4-325** the InfoSoc Directive had to be interpreted in the light of the WIPO Copyright Treaty and its *travaux préparatoires*) that "copy" had to be a fixed copy that could be put into circulation as a tangible object. It then went on to consider whether the fact that the copy had been altered had an impact on the exhaustion of distribution right within art.4(2). It held that in fact there had been a new reproduction of the copyright work within the meaning of art.2. It rejected the argument of Allposters that there was no reproduction because there was no multiplication of copies. It said what was important was whether the altered object, taken as a whole, was physically the object that had been placed on the market with the consent of the right holder.[645] Clearly, this was not the case. Accordingly, it held that art.4(2) was not applicable and therefore there was an infringement.

The decision was a controversial one. Part of the problem was that the Dutch courts referred a question under the distribution rights (art.4) and not the reproduction right (art.2). This was picked up by the Advocate-General. He said the Dutch court could have asked whether Allposters had acquired the right to reproduce the work in canvas. He however did not consider the issue. The Court of Justice had no sensitivities on this score. It said, ignoring the terms of the reference, that there was a reproduction of the work within the meaning of Information Society Directive.[646] In the authors' view, this is manifestly right. A reproduction right is plainly infringed when a person reproduces an artistic work onto another medium even if they destroy the original. Whether the destruction of the original arises from the reproduction process itself or by the person destroying the original by other means must be irrelevant.

The exceptions: temporary reproduction

The basic structure of the defences under the Information Society Directive is as **4-326** follows. There is one compulsory exception under art.5(1) and a large and exhaustive list of optional exceptions, with a saving for existing national analogue defences, under art.5(2). All of the foregoing defences are subject to the Berne

---

[644] art.4(2) says "The distribution right shall not be exhausted within the Community in respect of the original or copies of the work, except where the first sale or other transfer of ownership in the Community of that object is made by the rightholder or with his consent".
[645] See [45].
[646] See [43].

"three-step" test[647] introduced for the first time by the Information Society Directive itself.

The compulsory exception: transient, temporary electronic copies

4-327   The Information Society Directive provides that Member States must implement a special defence aimed at preventing copyright actions against makers of temporary copies where the making of those copies are an integral and essential part of a technological process. Primarily this defence will avail online service providers and other similar intermediaries who may cache, host or transmit material in a way that would otherwise infringe the reproduction right. However, it is not just available to intermediaries but also end-users. Thus, the defence is relevant to an end-user who lawfully receives a satellite broadcast but in the process makes transient copies of copyright works as part of the internal operation of a digital satellite television receiver and on the television screen.

4-328   As is apparent from the text of art.5(1), the ambit of the defence is narrow. It is only available as a defence to the reproduction right which meet all of the following five conditions. The acts must:

  (a)   be temporary;
  (b)   be transient or incidental;
  (c)   be an integral and essential part of a technological process;
  (d)   have as their sole purpose to enable either a transmission in a network between third parties by an intermediary, or a lawful use to be made of a work or other subject-matter; and
  (e)   have no independent economic significance.[648]

4-329   The scope of the mandatory defence is further narrowed by the application of the Berne Convention "three-step" test,[649] which must be satisfied by all defences in the Information Society Directive. The test requires that:

> "the exceptions and limitations provided for shall only be applied (i) in certain special cases (ii) which do not conflict with a normal exploitation of the work or other subject-matter and (iii) do not unreasonably prejudice the legitimate interests of the rightholder."[650]

4-330   The scope of the temporary electronic copy defence was first dealt with by the CJEU in *Infopaq* (above). In that case, the CJEU held the following.

  (i)   Unsurprisingly, that the five conditions set out above are cumulative.
  (ii)   As the defence is a derogation from a general principle, the provisions giving rise to it must be interpreted strictly, particularly in light of the control exercised by the Berne "three-step test", which is made expressly applicable by art.5(5).[651]
  (iii) The acts of reproduction protected by the defence cannot exceed what is

---

[647] See para.4-030.
[648] art.5(1).
[649] The test has its origins in the art.9(2) Berne Convention, and is also found in art.13 TRIPS, art.10 WCT, art.16 WPPT, art.6(3) Computer Programs Directive, and a art.6(3) Database Directive. See para.4-030.
[650] art.5(5).
[651] See [56]–[58].

necessary for the proper completion of the technological process for which the reproduction is an integral and essential part.[652]

(iv)   The storage of the temporary and transient reproduction must be deleted as soon as the justification for the storage by the function of enabling the completion of the technological process ceases.[653]

(v)   The deletion of the stored reproduction must be automatic and not be dependent on discretionary human intervention.[654]

In *FAPL v QC Leisure*,[655] the CJEU was concerned with the reception via a satellite decoder onto a television screen of football events beamed from abroad. It was common ground that the technical process meant that any acts of reproduction in the satellite decoder or television screen were temporary, transient and formed an integral part of a technological process. Thus, the issue was whether such was for lawful use and whether it had independent economic significance. The reproduction was found to be lawful as the picking up of broadcasts in private circles was not an act restricted by EU legislation.[656] Most important was the CJEU's discussion of the fifth condition, namely that the acts of temporary reproduction had no independent economic significance. In this regard, the court explained[657] that the economic significance of the transient reproduction must go beyond the economic advantage derived from the mere reception of a broadcast containing protected works. In other words, it must go beyond the mere advantage derived from the lawful use.[658] The CJEU said that the temporary acts of reproduction formed an inseparable and non-autonomous part of the process of reception and are performed without influence, or even awareness on the part of the persons thereby having access to the protected works.[659] Thus, it held that the fifth condition was satisfied. **4-331**

In *Infopaq II*[660] a second reference to the CJEU in the same *Infopaq* case was made. This second reference concerned the third to fifth conditions set out in *Infopaq* (above) and specifically asked whether or not a process satisfied these conditions if it had been manually initiated. The CJEU noted in its Reasoned Order[661] that in *Infopaq* it had emphasised that the *deletion* of a temporary copy had to be performed without discretionary human intervention. It was not a requirement that the *initiation* of a process had to be automatic. The CJEU also expanded upon the requirement that copying permitted by the defence should be an integral and essential part of a technological process. It held that this requirement meant that the acts of temporary reproduction had to be carried out entirely within the implementation of the technological process, although the requirement for the act to be "essential" only meant that the act had to be necessary for the process to function "correctly and efficiently".[662] It appears therefore that, even if a process can in fact function without an act of temporary reproduction that act of temporary **4-332**

---

[652] See [61].

[653] See [62] and [64].

[654] See [62].

[655] (C-403/08) ECLI:EU:C:2011:631.

[656] See [172]. Of course, if the use was not lawful, the question whether transient electronic reproduction was unlawful becomes academic.

[657] See [177].

[658] See [175].

[659] See [176].

[660] *Infopaq International A/S v Danske Dagblades Forening* (C-302/10), Reasoned Order ECLI:EU:C:2012:16.

[661] See [32].

[662] See [30].

reproduction will remain essential to the process if it cannot function efficiently without it.

4-333   In *Public Relations Consultants Association ("PRCA")*,[663] questions were referred to the CJEU in respect of the applicability of defence to internet browsing. The reference arose because, when a user browses the internet, a copy of a webpage will remain on the user's screen until such time as the user makes a discretionary decision to navigate to another page. Further, copies of webpages or elements of webpages are stored in a cache on a user's local computer after the user navigates away, enabling that page to be efficiently reloaded if the user returns to it. Cached copies remain stored until eventually overwritten by pages subsequently visited. The on-screen copy is only deleted if and when a user decides to navigate to another page. The cached copies are only deleted once the user has decided to visit a certain number of other pages; that number depends upon the settings of the user's computer. The question posed largely concerned the fifth *Infopaq* criterion: was the deletion of the on-screen and cached copies automatic, or did it depend upon discretionary human intervention? While the national court thought that the answer was clear, the obvious importance of the question to users of the World Wide Web led to the referral of a question so that a decisive answer could be given to enable uniform application throughout the EU.

4-334   The CJEU held that the on-screen and cached copies were covered by the temporary copies defence, despite those elements of human intervention. This was because the technological process in question—the process of internet browsing—was not itself completed until the user had finished viewing a particular page and moved onto the next. In an extension of its statement in *Infopaq II*, the CJEU stated[664] that a technological process the subject of this defence can be both initiated and terminated manually. Therefore, upon the termination of the process by navigating away from a page, the on-screen copy of that page was automatically deleted.[665] There was therefore no discretionary intervention in the deletion of the copy, merely a discretionary decision to complete the process, which was permissible.[666] Further, the cached copies were subject to the defence because they were incidental to the technological process of internet browsing[667] and are deleted without human intervention. It was not relevant that, because they are not deleted immediately upon the termination of the technological process, they might not also be "transient": the requirements for a copy to be either "transient" or "incidental" are alternatives, not cumulative.[668] Finally, the CJEU held[669] that the creation of temporary copies during the process of internet browsing was a special case which did not conflict with a normal exploitation of the work and does not unreasonably prejudice the legitimate interests of the right holders, within the requirements of art.5(5) of the Directive. In this regard, the CJEU considered that it was significant that the publicity material scraped from newspaper websites was licenced by copyright holders since making available the publicity material constituted a com-

---

[663] *Public Relations Consultants Association Ltd v The Newspaper Licensing Agency Ltd* (C-360/13) ECLI:EU:C:2014:1195.
[664] See [32].
[665] See [44]–[46].
[666] See [41].
[667] See [34]–[48].
[668] See [48].
[669] See [54]–[62].

munication to the public.[670] Thus, as the CJEU said, there was no need for requiring internet users to obtain a further authorisation allowing them to avail themselves of the same communication as that already had been authorised by the copyright holder in question.[671] The CJEU also held that such represented a normal exploitation of the works.[672]

In contrast, where a person provides a multimedia player which is intended to allow easy user-friendly access to unauthorised works on the Internet deliberately and in the full knowledge of such, the temporary acts of reproduction on that multimedia player of copyright-protected works falls outside the exception in art.5 of the Information Society Directive.[673]   **4-335**

A fourth step in the Berne three-step test?

The Information Society Directive appears to go even further than the "three-step" test in relation to any defence invoked specifically in the context of the internet. Recital 44 sets out the Berne "three-step" test then goes on to state as follows: **4-336**

> "The provision of such exceptions or limitations by Member States should, in particular, duly reflect the increased economic impact that such exceptions or limitations may have in the context of the new electronic environment. Therefore, the scope of certain exceptions or limitations may have to be *even more limited* when it comes to certain new uses of copyright works and other subject-matter." [Emphasis supplied.]

In previous editions of this work, it was suggested that this Recital meant that, when considering the application of the Berne "three-step" test in an internet-based or digital context, the court was obliged to be alive to the fact that technology in these fields makes for faithful reproduction and rapid dissemination and, accordingly, the scope for economic harm can be greater than in the analogue context. As such, it was suggested that when dealing with a "new electronic environment" type of case, the court might well regard this as a fourth step in the analysis, thereby narrowing the relevant exception to liability yet further. However, there was no mention of Recital 44 or of the principle it encapsulates either in *Infopaq* or in *FAPL*, which each discussed the application of the defence under art.5(1). On the contrary, in *FAPL* it was made clear by the court that one purpose of the defence under art.5(1) was to "allow and ensure the development and operation of new technologies and safeguard a fair balance between the rights and interests of right holders, on the one hand, and of users of protected works who wish to avail themselves of those new technologies, on the other".[674] It is therefore suggested that the presence of Recital 44 does not lead to any further narrowing of the defences.   **4-337**

The optional exceptions: defences

The Information Society Directive contains a long list of permissible defences that Member States may implement if they choose. Some are exceptions to the   **4-338**

---

[670] See [57].
[671] See [59].
[672] See [61].
[673] *Stichting Brein v Jack Frederik Willems* (C-527/15) ECLI:EU:C:300 at [59]–[72]. See para.4-317.
[674] See [164].

reproduction right only.[675] Others are exceptions to both the reproduction right and the communication to the public right.[676] There is also the ability for Member States to provide defences to the distribution right where they provide an equivalent optional defence to the reproduction right.[677] These defences are exhaustive. Member States may not enact any other new defences.[678] There is a saving in relation to pre-existing analogue defences which is dealt with further below.

4-339   The list of defences in relation to the reproduction right covers the following: photocopying (except of sheet music); private and non-commercial copying by individuals provided fair compensation is paid; copying by libraries, educational establishments, or museums which are not for direct or indirect economic or commercial advantage; ephemeral recordings of works made by broadcasting organisations by means of their own facilities and for their own broadcasts; and reproductions of broadcasts by non-commercial institutions such as hospitals or prisons provided that rights holders receive fair compensation.[679] These defences are specifically concerned with acts of reproductions.

4-340   In contrast, other defences of wide applicability are defined by reference to the *use* to which the copies of the works are put to. In summary, the defences cover the following areas: use for the sole purpose of illustration for teaching or scientific research; use for the benefit of people with a disability; use for the reporting of current economic, political or religious topics; quotations for purposes such as criticism or review of published works; use for public security purposes or the reporting of administrative, parliamentary or judicial proceedings; use of political speeches and public lectures; use during religious celebrations or official celebrations organised by a public authority; use of works such as architecture or sculpture made to be permanently located in public places; incidental inclusion in other material; use for advertising the public exhibition or sale of artistic works to the extent necessary to promote the event; use for the purpose of caricature, parody or pastiche; use in connection with the demonstration or repair of equipment; and use of an artistic work in the form of a building or a drawing or plan of a building for the purposes of reconstructing the building or use for the purpose of research or private study to individual members of the public by dedicated terminals of libraries, educational establishments.

4-341   As with the mandatory defence of temporary reproductions, all of the optional defences are required to pass the Berne Convention "three-step" test.[680] The Swedish Supreme Court (*Hogsta domstolen*) in *Bildupphrovsratt v Wikimedia* considered the interpretation of Swedish law which sought to implement the optional defence in art.5(3)(h) of the Information Society Directive ("use of works, such as works of architecture or sculpture, made to be located permanently in public places"). Sweden implemented that defence in the Swedish Copyright Act by allowing photography of public works of arts if they were to advertise an exhibition or to form part of a collection or catalogue not in digital form (s.24(1) SCA). Here, Wikimedia had made available on its online database photographs of three public

---

[675] art.5(2).

[676] art.5(3).

[677] art.5(4).

[678] It has been suggested that the fact that the list is exhaustive leaves no room for the development of defences in the future in line with new technologies as they arise: T. Heide, "The Berne Three-Step Test and the Proposed Copyright Directive" [1999] 21(3) E.I.P.R., 105–109.

[679] art.5(2).

[680] art.5(5). See para.4-030.

sculptures. The Swedish Supreme Court held that they had to apply the Berne Convention three-step test embodied in art.5(5) of the Information Society Directive. It concluded that making available images of artworks through publicly accessible online database would unreasonably prejudice the right holder's legitimate interests in that it would deprive them of potential commercial revenue arising from online exploitation. The public interest underlying the non-profit and open nature of Wikimedia's database did not offset the prejudice caused to right holders.

A body of CJEU case law interpreting the provisions that provide for these optional exceptions is beginning to build. A comprehensive review of that case law is beyond the scope of this book.[681] However, it is relevant to consider the important decision in *ACI Adam*[682] because of its general importance in respect of the defences under art.5 of the Directive. *ACI Adam* was a reference from the Supreme Court of the Netherlands in respect of the private copying defence and associated levy under art.5(2)(b) of the Directive. Under a Dutch law, the defence and the levy applied both to copies made from lawful sources (such as legitimately purchased CDs) and from unlawful sources (such as copies unlawfully made available for download from the internet). The questions referred to concerned, in essence, whether the defence (and therefore the entitlement to a levy) applied to the private copying of unlawful copies. **4-342**

The CJEU noted[683] that, because the Directive did not expressly address the lawful or unlawful nature of the source from which a reproduction of the work may be made, it was necessary to employ the strict interpretation applied to derogations **4-343**

---

[681] A list of such cases (and others interpreting the Information Society Directive) can be found at *http://eur-lex.europa.eu/legal-content/EN/LKD/?uri=CELEX:32001L0029* [Accessed 2 November 2017]. The relevant cases on these exceptions appear under the rubric "AO5P2XX". There are a number of cases on the principles to be applied in relation to the private copying exception, in determining who is liable, in what circumstances and what is fair compensation. This is because in many countries, a collecting society is responsible for collecting such and this is often done by the enforcement of a private copying levy against the suppliers of blank recordable media. See *Padawan SL v SGAE* (C-467/08) [2010] E.C.R. I-10055 (approach to "fair compensation" in relation to the private copying); *Stiching de Thuikopie v Opus Supplies Deutschland GmbH* (C-462/09) [2011] E.C.R. I-5331 and *Amazon.com International Sales Inc v Austro-Mechana Gesellschaft zur Wahrnehmung mechanisch-musikalischer Urheberrechte Gesellschaft mbH* (C-521/11) ECLI:EU:C:2013:515 (whether companies that made blank electronic media could be liable to pay the fair compensation for private copying); *R and TV2 Danmark A/S v NCB – Nordisk Copyright Bureau* (C-510/10) ECLI:EU:C:2012:244 (the preservation of ephemeral recordings in official archives made by broadcasting organisations by means of their own facilities); *Eva-Maria Painer v Standard VerlagsGmbH* (C-145/10) ECLI:EU:C:2013:138 (use of work in press report and use of work for security purposes); *Technische Universität Darmstadt v Eugen Ulmer* (C-117/13) ECLI:EU:C:2014:2196 (extent of library rights). *Copydan Bandkopi v Nokia* (C-463/12) EU:C:2015:144 (determination of fair compensation in relation to the private copying exception in the InfoSoc Directive); *Microsoft Mobile Sales International Oy v and ors v MIBAC* (C-110/15) ECLI:EU:C:2016:717 (Italian law which determined fair compensation under private copying exception was unlawful); see also *BACSA v the Secretary of State for Business, Innovation and Skills* [2015] EWHC 1723, where the Administrative Court of England and Wales struck down legislation which permitted a very narrow private copying by a purchaser of content but which did not provide for fair compensation as required under art.5(2)(b); *EGEDA v AMETIC* (C-470/14) EU:C:2016:418 (compensation for private copying provided by state finance was illegal as it did not ensure that the cost of that compensation is borne by the users of private copies); *Hewlett-Packard Belgium SPRL v Reprobel* (C-572/13) EU:C:2015:730 (complicated Belgium legislative scheme for payment involving a flat levy of €49 for sale of printer/photocopiers was unlawful).

[682] *ACI Adam BV v Stichting de Thuiskopie, Stichting Onderhandelingen Thuiskopie vergoeding* (C-435/12) ECLI:EU:C:2014:254.

[683] See [29]–[30].

from the general principle of a Directive. As a consequence, the exception was held[684] only to apply to the copying of lawfully made copies. There is no reason to think that any different conclusion would be reached in respect of other optional defences where the source material was unlawful.

4-344 The CJEU also took the opportunity to set out the ways in which the underlying objectives of the Directive have a bearing on the optional defences. First, it noted[685] that the purpose of the list of exceptions in art.5 was to ensure a balance between the different legal traditions of Member States so as to ensure the proper functioning of the internal market. While Member States were given discretion as to whether or not they implemented a particular exception, where they did so it was essential that the exception was applied coherently by each of them. Secondly, it noted[686] that national legislation that did not distinguish between private copies made from lawful sources and those made from unlawful sources could not be tolerated. Thirdly, it noted[687] that such national legislation may be contrary to the requirements of art.5(5). Fourthly, it noted[688] that the existence or absence of technological measures to control unlawful copying was not relevant to the application of art.5(2)(b). Finally, the CJEU noted[689] that the requirement for "fair compensation" under that article did not call into question the conclusion that the exception applied only to private copying from lawful copies: it would not be fair to impose the burden of compensation in respect of copies made from unlawful sources on every person making private copies.

4-345 Another case also worthy of not being demoted to the footnotes because of its general importance is *Johan Deckmyn v Helena Vandersteen*.[690] In this case, the Court of Justice had to interpret the parody defence at art.5(3)(k) of the Information Society Directive which allows Member States to provide for a defence of "use for the purpose of caricature, parody or pastiche". A far-right political party had taken a drawing on the cover of a 1961 comic book of a generous character throwing coins to people and replaced it with the Mayor of Ghent throwing coins to veiled persons and people of colours. The copyright owner in the comic book took exception to this and brought infringement proceedings. The issue was whether this was a work of parody.

4-346 Having found, unsurprisingly, that the concept of parody in the InfoSoc Directive was an autonomous concept of EU law, the Court of Justice then discussed what it meant. The Court of Justice held that the essential characteristics of parody are first to evoke an existing work whilst being noticeably different from it and secondly to constitute an expression of humour or mockery. It was not necessary that it should display an original character of its own other than displaying noticeable differences with the respect to the original work. The Court of Justice held that the exception must strike a fair balance between the interests of the copyright owner and the freedom of expression of the person relying on the parody defence.

4-347 The Court of Justice said that the copyright owner had a legitimate interest in ensuring that a work protected by copyright is not associated with a discriminatory message. This might appear to be a "steer" from the Court of Justice to find in

---

[684] See [31].
[685] See [33].
[686] See [3]–[37].
[687] See [38]–[40].
[688] See [42]–[46].
[689] See [47]–[57].
[690] (C–201/13) EU:C:2014:2132.

favour of the copyright owner. Yet, it could be said that freedom of expression is very important in the political field however distasteful the views of a political party are. Parody and satire play a very important role in the political arena and national courts must be careful of muzzling the right of political parties to express their views merely on the grounds of sensitivity.

Some commentators have considered that the reference to "legitimate interests" **4-348** is, in truth, a reference to the moral rights of the author in the work and that moral rights are not covered by the InfoSoc Directive (see Recital 19 cited by Villalon AG, at [28]). This is an interesting observation. However, in the authors' view, it is difficult to say that, in substance, *Deckmyn* is a case of moral rights. Parody of an artistic work will often involve alteration to a work in a manner that the author may not like. The nearest relevant moral right must be the right of integrity (the right of an author to prevent distortion of their work). Yet, that is precisely what a parody of an artistic work will do. The Court of Justice's point must surely be that the unauthorised copying or adaptation of a work can have various consequences from the trivial to the serious and that the adaptation of a comic cartoon for the purpose of discriminatory political imagery must fall towards the latter. There is no reason why, as said in the previous paragraph, that this cannot be taken into account. A political party has no need to use someone else's artistic work unless it is that type of parody where the parodic work is intended to mock or poke fun at the original work, i.e. where one political party alters a poster of another political party. Such was not the case in *Deckmyn*.

National analogue defences

There is also a saving provision in relation to any existing defence in the national **4-349** law of any Member State that is not contained in the above list of defences.[691] However, there are four prerequisites if any such defence is to remain in being following implementation of the Information Society Directive. First, it must be confined to cases "of minor importance."[692] Secondly, it must be confined to "analogue" (i.e. non-digital) uses. Thirdly, it must not interfere with the free movement provisions of the TFEU. Finally, it must also satisfy the Berne "three-step" test.[693] It is suggested that very few, if any, defences will satisfy such a narrow definition. An example might be the provision in Belgian copyright law protecting the use of selected readings from a deceased author.[694]

Copy protection circumvention

The Information Society Directive's provisions concerning the circumvention of **4-350** copy protection devices are intended to implement the provisions of art.11 of the WCT and art.18 of the WPPT. They provide, in essence, that Member States are to provide adequate legal protection against the circumvention of any "effective

---

[691] art.5(3)(o).

[692] *AKM v Zürs.net Betriebs GmbH* (C-138/16) ECLI:EU:C:2017:218 (Austrian legislation which excluded communication to the public right from applying where the number of subscribers was no more than 500 was not of "minor importance") because of the cumulative effect of many economic operators relying upon this provision.

[693] art.5(5) cross-refers the analogue defences in art.5(4).

[694] art.21 Belgian Copyright Act of 30 June 1994. This example was suggested in an EU-wide review of the impact on Information Society Directive by Linklaters & Alliance, entitled *IP Special Report* (July 2001).

technological measures" which the person concerned carries out in the knowledge, or with reasonable grounds to know, that they are pursuing that objective.[695] The words "technological measures" mean any technology designed to prevent acts (e.g. copying) in respect of works which are subject to copyright or related rights protection.[696] Such measures are "effective" when the subject-matter is sought to be controlled by the rights holders through processes such as encryption, scrambling, or other transformation or copy control mechanisms which achieve same results.

4-351   However, the Information Society Directive also goes further than the WCT/ WPPT to restrict not just the actual acts of circumvention but also secondary acts of:

> "the manufacture, import, distribution, sale, rental, advertisement for sale or rental, or possession for commercial purposes of devices, products or components or the provision of services which are promoted, advertised or marketed for the purpose of circumvention of, or have only a limited commercially significant purpose or use other than to circumvent, or are primarily designed, produced, adapted or performed for the purpose of enabling or facilitating the circumvention of, any effective technological measures."[697]

Note that these acts do not have a requirement of knowledge or reasonable belief, unlike the "primary" acts of circumvention referred to earlier in the previous paragraph.

4-352   These provisions were apparently among the most hotly contested during the Information Society Directive's preparatory process.[698] The problem was how to allow a defence to operate (for example, the defence of copying for the purposes of illustration for teaching under art.5) where a right holder also has in place an anti-copying measure, such as a digital tracker. The Directive attempts to rectify this potential difficulty by providing that rights holders make available for the beneficiary any exception, (i.e. defence) under art.5(2)(a), art.5(2)(c)–(e) inclusive, art.5(3)(a)–(b) inclusive, and art.5(3)(e) the means of benefiting from that exception to its necessary extent where that beneficiary has legal access to the protected work.[699] The fact remains, however, that the vast majority of defences can be rendered ineffective by copy protection technology since most of them are not mentioned by art.6(4).

4-353   In *Nintendo v PC Box*,[700] the CJEU was asked questions in respect of a protection system employed in Nintendo gaming consoles which depended upon an interaction between the console and an encrypted code stored in the physical housing of the protected works (e.g. in the DVD on which the game is stored). The effect of this protection measure was not merely to prevent the use of unlawfully copied games in which the copyright[701] was owned by Nintendo or its affiliates, but also prevented the use of games not authorised by Nintendo (so called "homebrew"

---

[695] art.6(1).

[696] art.6(3).

[697] art.6(2).

[698] See Commission press release, "Commission welcomes adoption of the Directive on copyright in the information society by the Council" (9 April 2001), available online at *http://europa.eu/rapid/ press-release_IP-01-528_en.pdf* [Accessed 30 May 2014].

[699] art.6(4).

[700] *Nintendo Co Ltd v PC Box Srl* (C-355/12) ECLI:EU:C:2014:25.

[701] The CJEU held, consistently with the view of the referring court, that a computer game was not merely a computer program protected by the Software Directive, but also contained graphic and sound elements with a unique creative value which were protected by the Information Society

games). The defendant, PC Box, marketed modified consoles which were capable of use with such "homebrew" games, but which as a consequence also enabled the use of unlawful copies of Nintendo games. The referring court asked, in essence, whether or not the protection afforded to effective technological measures extended to such a system and also questioned what factors (such as Nintendo's intention and the predominant use to which the PC Box equipment was put) should be considered when answering that question.

The CJEU held that the sort of technological measures employed by Nintendo **4-354** were capable of falling within the meaning of "effective technological measures" in art.6(3) of the Directive if their objective was to prevent or to limit infringing acts. In assessing whether or not that was the objective of the technological measures, the CJEU held that technological measures should not prohibit devices or activities which have a commercially significant purpose other than the circumvention of the protection measures and must not go beyond what is necessary for that purpose.[702] In determining whether or not that was the case, the national court must make a multifactorial assessment, considering the costs, efficacy, practicality and effect of the protection measure employed and its alternatives. The court must also consider the use to which the devices or activities which may have a purpose other than enabling infringement of copyright are actually put.

Interference with rights management information

The Information Society Directive's provisions concerning interference with **4-355** rights management information closely mirror those contained in art.2 of the WCT and art.19 of the WPPT. They provide, in essence, that Member States are to implement adequate legal protection against any person knowingly performing any of the following acts: (a) The removal or alteration of any electronic rights management information. (b) The distribution, importation for distribution, broadcasting, communication or making available to the public of works or other subject-matter protected under the Information Society Directive or the databases protected by the sui generis database right under the Database Directive from which electronic rights management information has been removed or altered (provided the person knows, or has reasonable grounds to believe that they are thereby inducing, enabling, facilitating or concealing an infringement of copyright or related rights).[703]

The expression "rights management information" means any information which **4-356** identifies any of the following: the work (or phonogram, fixation of performance or broadcast, non-original database, etc.); the author or any other rights holder; information about the terms and conditions of use of the work or other subject-matter; and any numbers or codes that represent such information.[704]

Remedies

Under the Information Society Directive, Member States must provide "appropri- **4-357** ate sanctions and remedies" (including damage, injunctions, and seizure) in respect

---

Directive.
[702] See [28]–[31].
[703] art.7(1).
[704] art.7(2).

of infringements of rights set out in the Directive. Such sanctions must be "effective, proportionate and dissuasive."[705]

4-358   The provisions concerning remedies are rather elliptical. They fall well short of the provisions set out in Ch.III of TRIPS,[706] for example. The reference to "dissuasive" sanctions may mark a departure for those Member States (for example, the UK) whose copyright damages are awarded primarily on a compensatory, rather than punitive or deterrent, basis.[707] However, it is submitted that better guidance as to the approach to what remedies are effective, proportionate and dissuasive can be obtained from the Enforcement Directive which contains the same wording.[708]

Cumulative protection

4-359   Article 9 of the Information Society Directive states that the Information Society Directive is without prejudice to provisions concerning in particular: patent rights, trade marks, design rights, utility models, topographies of semi-conductor products, typefaces, conditional access, access to cable of broadcasting services, protection of national treasures, legal deposit requirements, laws on restrictive practices and unfair competition, trade secrets, security, confidentiality, data protection and privacy, access to public documents, and the law of contract.

4-360   This is a long list and is intended to make it clear that cumulative protection may apply to works in many ways. This is consistent with the general approach of intellectual property whereby differing IPR laws protect differing aspects of a work.

Exhaustive nature of Information Society Directive

4-361   In *ITV Broadcasting Ltd v TV Catchup (No.2)*,[709] the CJEU had to consider the meaning of "access to cable of broadcasting services" in art.9. UK legislation deemed copyright not to be infringed where works broadcast on television channels subject to public service obligations (i.e. BBC) were immediately retransmitted by cable (or the Internet) in the area of initial broadcast. The CJEU held that this was not permitted as the Information Society Directive harmonised the concept of communication to the public and such governed retransmission by means of an Internet stream.[710] The CJEU held that art.9 was intended to maintain provisions applicable in areas other than that harmonised by the Information Society Directive.[711] Accordingly, it held that the Directive precluded the UK legislative measure.

Artist's Resale Right Directive

Introduction

4-362   The Artist's Resale Right Directive[712] is a measure which has attracted considerable attention and comment in spite of its relatively limited scope. The Resale Right

---

[705] art.8(1). This provision also appears in the Enforcement Directive discussed in Ch.15, para.15-009.
[706] See para.1-172.
[707] Under CDPA 1988 s.97(2), additional damages can be awarded in the UK, but their rationale and scope is uncertain. It may be that the "dissuasive" aspects become more prominent.
[708] The Enforcement Directive is discussed at para.15-009.
[709] (C-275/15) ECLI:EU:C:2017:144.
[710] See [23] citing *ITV Broadcasting* (C-607/11), at [20], [40].
[711] *ITV*, at [26].
[712] Dir.2001/84/EC on the resale right for the benefit of the author of an original work of art [2001] OJ

Directive aims, in essence, to give contemporary artists who have already sold their creations the right to claim a portion of the proceeds of any subsequent sales for the term of the copyright. There is a sliding scale of payable rates based on the value of the subsequent sale.

The resale right is not really a "copyright" or "related right" in the same sense as the other rights dealt with in this chapter. It has moral rights overtones—it is said to be "inalienable" and "integral to copyright" in its recitals, for example—yet it is fundamentally economic in nature. It is perhaps best regarded as a sui generis right which, though linked to term of copyright for an artistic work, is in all other respects entirely divorced from the copyright regime.   **4-363**

The origins of the resale right lie in the French "*droit de suite*" (the right of "following" the work). *The droit de suite* arose as a result of the decline of the Salon system of state arts patronage in France at the end of the 19th century. For the first time, artists had to compete with each other in the search for patrons in an open market. The perception grew that art dealers were flourishing whilst the artists themselves and their heirs struggled. *The droit de suite* was introduced as a way of redressing this imbalance.[713]   **4-364**

In European copyright law terms, the resale right has its origins in art.14 *ter* of the Berne Convention.[714] It should be noted, however, that the Resale Right Directive differs from the Berne Convention in a number of fundamental respects. First, the subject-matter is narrower in that "original manuscripts of writers and composers" are excluded. Secondly, unlike the Convention, the Directive contains an exception in relation to private sales. Finally, the Directive imposes a sliding scale of payable amounts whereas the Convention states that "… the amounts shall be matters for determination by national legislation."   **4-365**

The Resale Right Directive has always been controversial. Its proponents argue that the inequalities of bargaining power between artist and dealer when a work is first sold justify the artist obtaining a windfall if the work is later sold for a substantially greater sum. Moreover, they argue, painters and sculptors are denied the profits awarded to other copyright owners, such as musicians, who are able repeatedly to claim royalties whenever their works are reproduced or enjoyed in public. There is also the broader economic point that the resale right serves as a convenient supplement to state funding of the arts paid for by those interested in the arts.   **4-366**

The Resale Right Directive's detractors respond by claiming that the historical conditions that created the right in the 1880s no longer exist in the 21st century. The inequalities are no longer as acute and, in any case, once an artist is in a position to make money from a resale right, the artist is (if they are still alive) usually in a position to sell new work for a high price in any event. So far as musicians and other creators are concerned, they too are often in unequal bargaining positions when they sign agreements with record companies, film companies, etc. for the exploitation of their works. Why should painters and sculptors obtain special treatment? The Directive's detractors also add that, like musicians, artists maintain reproduction rights over their work via copyright. So far as the state sponsorship point is concerned, the Directive's detractors argue that arts funding actually appears to be   **4-367**

L272/32.

[713] For an account of the background to the "*droit de suite*", see D.L. Booton, "A Critical Analysis of the European Commission's Proposal for a Directive Harmonising the Droit De Suite" (1998) I.P.Q. 2, 165–191.

[714] See para.4-032.

higher in those countries where there is a resale right than those where there is not (compare, for example, France and the UK).

4-368   It is suggested, however, that the above arguments serve ultimately only to cloud the real areas of dispute, which are: (a) whether harmonisation in this area was really necessary in the first place, and, (b) if so, whether such harmonisation should have been "up" or "down", i.e. whether the right should have been imposed on all Member States or whether it should have been repealed by any Member State that had it. A brief consideration of these questions follows.

4-369   Prior to the Resale Right Directive, Belgium, Denmark, France, Germany, Italy, Luxembourg, Portugal, Spain and Sweden all formally had the right but few of them actually applied it with any rigour. Austria, Ireland, the Netherlands and the UK did not have a resale right at all. The Directive proceeds on the assumption that such a divergence of approach leads to a distortion of competition within the EU through the displacement of art sales and, accordingly, that there is interference with the single market principle. Note that the legal basis of the Directive is expressed to be art.114 of TFEU (originally art.100a of the Treaty of Rome, thereafter art.95 of the EC Treaty), which is aimed at promoting the single market. Such a goal is mentioned by no less than seven of the Directive's recitals.[715]

4-370   However, it is suggested that the single-market argument is problematic in this context. It fails to take into account a much greater divergence between Member States concerning the actual relevance of the right to their respective economies. Put simply, the London art market dwarfs that of any other Member State, accounting for 60–70 per cent of the total EU turnover.[716] There is no true EU "internal market" when it comes to art sales. Furthermore, London's dominance in this area is not attributable solely—or even mainly—to the absence of a resale right. Other factors such as the reputation and expertise of London dealers must come into account.[717] Finally, the logical conclusion of the single-market argument is bizarre, because if London's success was in fact a direct consequence of the absence of an artist's resale right, then the imposition of a resale right throughout the EU would result in the displacement of art business to places outside the EU where there is no resale right, such as to the US or to Switzerland.[718]

4-371   Accordingly, if harmonisation was necessary in this area, perhaps it should have been by way of abolition of the resale right throughout the EU. It has been observed elsewhere in this chapter, however, that harmonisation in a downwards direction runs contrary to the general drift towards increased protection favoured by the Commission and Parliament in the area of copyright and allied areas.[719]

4-372   The structure of the Resale Right Directive is as follows. There are 30 Recitals.

---

[715] Artist's Resale Right Directive Recitals 9–15 inclusive.

[716] C. Michalos, "Artists gain but markets lose" *The Times*, 17 July 2001. Note also that 70 per cent of the global art market is shared by London and New York: see D.L. Booton, "A Critical Analysis of the European Commission's Proposal for a Directive Harmonising the Droit De Suite" (1998) I.P.Q. 2, 165–191. Geneva is the third largest art centre. Like the UK, neither Swiss nor New York State law contain a resale right.

[717] D.L. Booton, "A Critical Analysis of the European Commission's Proposal for a Directive Harmonising the Droit De Suite" (1998) I.P.Q. 2, 165–191 who concludes that there is no evidence that differences amongst the resale right law of the Member States distort the internal market in works of art.

[718] Booton gives the example of a Sotheby's auction house in California that was terminated following the introduction of the resale right there in 1976, observing, however, that the decision may have been as much strategic as economic. See D.L. Booton, "A Critical Analysis of the European Commission's Proposal for a Directive Harmonising the Droit De Suite" (1998) I.P.Q. 2, 165–191.

[719] See para.4-088 and fn.190.

Chapter I contains provisions concerning the basic right and its exceptions, as well as the nature of the works covered. Chapter II contains provisions relating to the minimum sale price; the sliding scale of rates; the persons entitled to receive the payment; various reciprocal arrangements with non-EU countries; the term of protection; and the right to obtain information from art dealers concerning relevant sales. Chapter III contains provisions concerning implementation and reporting.

Works of art to which the Resale Right Directive applies

The Resale Right Directive only applies to a works which are "original works of art", which it defines as works of graphic or plastic art such as pictures, collages, paintings, drawings, engravings, prints, lithographs, sculptures, tapestries, ceramics, glassware and photographs, provided they are made by the artist personally or are copies considered to be original works of art.[720] Limited edition copies also fall within its ambit.[721] Note that, unlike art.14*ter* of the Berne Convention, writers' and composers' manuscripts are excluded.   **4-373**

For a Directive aimed at providing a windfall for contemporary artists, the above definition appears unduly restrictive. The proviso that such works be "made by the artist himself"—unless it is construed very liberally—potentially excludes a great many works that form the staple of contemporary art exhibitions. Take for example "ready-made" or "found" objects. Contemporary artists have used industrial, prefabricated products, waste and even organic material as art works in recent years. These can only be characterised as having been "made by the artist himself" in the sense that it is the artist who has actually taken the decision to make an artwork of them. Often the artist has not further manipulated the material in any way. Such works have won plaudits and changed hands for large sums of money in recent years yet, under the Resale Right Directive, may not be covered. Similarly, unless one regards "making" as "making the arrangements for,"[722] it is possible that computer-generated art work is excluded. In addition, many of today's artists, like those before them, employ teams of assistants to help them create large and complicated works. Yet such works are attributed to the artist, not the artist's helpers. Can such works be said to be "made by the artist himself"? Note that, despite the potential exclusion of such art, the Directive's definition includes things that most people would not regard as fine art but rather as *objets*, such as ceramics and glassware.   **4-374**

It is suggested that, in order to cope with such anomalies, the definition of "original work of art" in the Resale Right Directive ought to have contained an additional provision extending the right to any other work which is regarded by artists, by the art trade, or by the public at large as an original art work. Whilst such a provision may have been difficult to apply, it would at least have allowed the court to reach a decision with the assistance of expert and/or survey evidence.   **4-375**

The nature of the right

The Resale Right Directive provides that Member States should provide, for the benefit of the author of an original work of art, a resale right (to be defined as an   **4-376**

---

[720] art.2.
[721] art.2(1).
[722] See, for example, the definitions of author in the UK copyright legislation, CDPA 1988 s.9.

inalienable[723] right which cannot be waived, even in advance) to receive a royalty based on the price obtained for any resale of the work, subsequent to the first transfer of the work by the author.[724] The right only applies where such sales involve—as sellers, buyers or intermediaries—art market professionals, such as salesrooms,[725] art galleries or art dealers. The royalty is payable by the seller.[726]

4-377 In addition, even where there has been the involvement of an art market professional, there is an optional exclusion in respect of any resales within three years of the direct acquisition of the work from the artist, provided the resale price does not exceed €10,000.

4-378 Sums payable under the resale right should be paid to the artist directly, or, after the artist's death, to "those entitled under him/her".[727] In relation to the identification of those who are entitled under the artist, Recital 27 to the Resale Right Directive provides that:

> "The persons entitled to receive royalties must be specified, due regard being had to the principle of subsidiarity. It is not appropriate to take action through this Directive in relation to Member States' laws of succession. However, those entitled under the author must be able to benefit fully from the resale right after his death…".

4-379 In *Fundación Gala-Salvador Dalí, v ADAGP*,[728] the CJEU considered the implementation of the Directive in France. Under French law, the resale right accrued exclusively to an artist's natural heirs, regardless of any testamentary disposition to others. However, under Dali's will, and according to Spanish law, the resale right was transferred to the Spanish state. The provision under French law was held not to have any effect on the functioning of the internal market and so was not precluded by the Directive. Member States may make provision for the collection societies to administer the right.[729]

4-380 The right is complemented by a further "right of information". This right entitles the artist (or, as appropriate, the artist's heirs) for a period of three years after any resale, to request the relevant art market professional to furnish "any information that may be necessary in order to secure payment of royalties in respect of the resale."[730] Accordingly, the artist need not have any reasonable grounds for believing that there has been a sale by a gallery. A possible implication of this widely drafted right may be a certain number of "busybody" requests for information by artists concerning possible sales by a number of galleries.

---

[723] Rather like moral rights. The moral rights analogy is echoed in Recitals 1 (inalienable) and 4 (integral part of copyright) though some commentators regard the Directive as begging the question in issue: see Jacob J (an English High Court judge), "Industrial Property-Industry's Enemy" (1997) I.P.Q. 1, 3–15.

[724] art.1(1).

[725] art.1(2).

[726] art.1(4). Although the liability to pay the royalty rests on the reseller, the Directive does not preclude that liability being discharged pursuant to contractual terms and conditions by the buyer—see *Christie's France SNC v Syndicat des Antiquaires* (C–41/14) ECLI:EU: C:2015:119, where the Court of Justice held that it was not contrary to the Directive for the contract of an auction house to oblige the buyer to pay the amount equal to the royalty due to the author under the Directive.

[727] art.6(1).

[728] (C-518/08) [2010] E.C.R. I-3091; [2010] E.C.D.R. 2010.

[729] art.6(2).

[730] art.9.

Applicable rates

The Resale Right Directive bases the resale royalty on the actual value of the **4-381** resale rather than on the amount of increase from any prior sale. The total royalty payable on any single transaction is capped at €12,500.[731] Member States have the option of providing for a minimum threshold before any resale right is payable, provided such does not exceed €3,000.[732] This is said to be aimed at avoiding disproportionate collection costs for trivial sums.[733] The sale price is calculated net of tax.[734] The sliding scale of rates is as follows:

(a) 4 per cent for the portion of the sale price up to €50,000;

(b) 3 per cent for the portion of the sale price from €50,000,01 to €200,000;

(c) 1 per cent for the portion of the sale price from €200,000,01 to €350,000;

(d) 0.5 per cent for the portion of the sale price from €350,000,01 to €500,000; and

(e) 0.25 per cent for the portion of the sale price exceeding €500,000.

Term and implementation

The term of the right is the same as the copyright in the underlying work, namely **4-382** 70 years pma.[735] Normally, this will mean that there will be a resale right in respect of any art work which was in copyright on the day that the Resale Right Directive came into force and that such right will run for the remainder of the copyright term.[736]

The time limits for implementation were at the heart of the dispute between the **4-383** Commission and Council over the adoption of the Resale Right Directive.[737] The Council was originally contemplating a 15-year implementation period. In the event, Member States were required to implement the Directive by 1 January 2006.[738] Any Member State which did not already have a resale right, (i.e. Austria, Ireland, the Netherlands and the UK) was entitled to wait at least until 1 January 2010 before applying it for the benefit of an artist's heirs.[739] If the Member State requests an extension, that period could be extended for a further two years, subject to consultation with the Commission. The four Member States that did not have a resale right in their national law at the time of the Directive, and Malta, all applied for such an extension, each of which came to an end on 1 January 2012.

The Resale Right Directive contains monitoring provisions which required the **4-384** Commission to report by 1 January 2009, and regularly thereafter, upon its economic impact with particular regard to the competitiveness of EU art market as compared to other markets that do not operate the *droit de suite*.[740] The first report

---

[731] art.4.

[732] art.3.

[733] Recital 22.

[734] art.5.

[735] See art.8(1) and art.1 of the Term Directive.

[736] art.10.

[737] See Commission press release, " (19 July 2001), available online at: *http://europa.eu/rapid/press-release_IP-01-1036_en.htm* [Accessed 6 May 2018].

[738] art.12.

[739] art.8(2).

[740] art.11.

on the implementation and effects of the Resale Right Directive[741] was published on 14 December 2011. While that report noted a significant decrease in the EU's share of the market in works of living artists since the date of the Resale Right Directive, this coincided with global changes in that market (principally the substantial growth of the market in China) such that there was insufficient evidence to link any change in the market to the effect of the Directive. There was no evidence of a shift of sales within the EU in favour of countries that had delayed implementation. A significant problem was identified in the poor administration of the Resale Right, which was led to substantial deductions from the distributions to artists and was particularly damaging to traders at the lower end of the market. The Commission promised action on this poor administration and the Parliament concurred in this objective by its resolution of 20 November 2012.[742] On 17 February 2014, following consultation with "stakeholders", representatives of collecting management organisations, authors and art market professionals signed up to a document containing "Key Principles and Recommendations on the Management of the Author Resale Right"[743] which made recommendations as to the practice of administration, the provision of information as to the various collecting bodies members and policies, and mutual sharing of knowledge.

Orphan works

Introduction

4-385   Directive 2012/28/EU sets out common rules on the digitisation and online display of so-called "orphan works". Orphan works are works such as books, newspaper and magazine articles and films that are still protected by copyright but whose authors or other right holders are not known or cannot be located or contacted to obtain copyright permissions. The purpose of this Directive is the creation of rules to permit the inclusion of such orphan works from the collections of libraries and other cultural institutions in digitisation projects, where the author or other right holder cannot be found in order to seek permissions.

4-386   According to the Commission's proposal for the Directive, the initiative for the Directive stems from the Commission's 2006 Recommendation on the digitisation and online accessibility of cultural content and digital preservation.[744] Also, the creation of a legal framework to facilitate the cross-border digitisation and dissemination of orphan works in the single market is one of the key actions identified in the Digital Agenda for Europe[745] which is part of the "Europe 2020 Strategy".[746] The need for a Directive of this nature in pursuing those objectives is made obvious by a consideration of the proportion of the collections of Europe's cultural institutions that are thought to be orphan works. For example, according to an answer in a list of "frequently asked questions" published by the Commis-

---

[741] *Report on the Implementation and Effect of the Resale Right Directive (2001/84/EC)* COM(2011) 878 final.

[742] A7-0326/2012.

[743] See *http://ec.europa.eu/internal_market/copyright/resale-right/index_en.htm* [Accessed 6 May 2018].

[744] Commission Recommendation 2006/585/EC of 24 August 2006 on the digitisation and online accessibility of cultural content and digital preservation (OJ L 236, 31 August 2006, pp.28–30).

[745] *A Digital Agenda for Europe—COM*(2010) 245.

[746] *Europe 2020: A strategy for smart, sustainable and inclusive growth: COM* (2010) 2020.

sion, the British Library estimates that 40 per cent of its copyrighted collections—150 million works in total—are orphan works.[747]

There does not appear to have been any serious opposition to the Directive, **4-387** perhaps because those authors or copyright owners who are likely to be associated with orphan works are no longer interested in their works, or are not sufficiently organised to raise any objection or to group together to present a united front in opposition. Or, perhaps simply this is because they do not believe that their works are orphan works. Alternatively, it may just be the case that any potentially interested party concluded that the Directive provided them adequate protection (as it appears that it does) through mechanisms of diligent search and the cessation of orphan work status if the relevant rights holder is identified or if they come forward.

The legal basis for the Directive is stated to be art.114 of TFEU, which is aimed **4-388** at promoting the single market.[748]

Works to which the Directive applies

Article 1 of the Directive sets out the types of copyright work to which the Direc- **4-389** tive applies. First, it applies to works (i.e. Berne convention works) published in the form of books, journals, newspapers, magazines or other writings held in the collections of various cultural bodies[749]; secondly it applies to cinematographic or audiovisual works and phonograms in the collections of various cultural bodies or in the archives of public service broadcasters.[750] In each case, the protected work must be subject to copyright and must have been first published or broadcast in a Member State, or, if not published or broadcast, must have been made accessible by the cultural body with the owner's consent and it is reasonable to assume that the right holder would not oppose it being made available (and associated digital reproduction) in pursuit of the public purposes of that cultural body.[751] Finally, the Directive applies to works and other protected subject matter incorporated within a work or phonogram that is otherwise subject to the Directive.[752]

The exceptions of the Directive only apply to such works if they are orphan **4-390** works. What amounts to an orphan work is defined in art.2. A work or a phonogram within art.1 is an orphan work, "if none of the right holders in that work or phonogram is identified or, even if one or more of them is identified, none is located despite a diligent search for the right holders having been carried out".[753] Alternatively, if some but not all of the rights holders are located, and if those that are located give their consent for the use intended under the Directive, then the work is an orphan work.[754] The requirements of the "diligent search" are set out in art.3. The organisation (from an exhaustive list in art.1(1): publicly accessible libraries, educational establishments and museums, archives, film or audio heritage institutions, and public-service broadcasting organisations, established in the Member States, in order to achieve aims related to their public-interest missions) that wishes to make a use of the orphan work must "ensure that a diligent search is carried out

---

[747] European Commission MEMO/12/743 of 4 October 2012. Recital 10.
[748] See para.1-100.
[749] art.1(2)(a).
[750] art.1(2)(b) and (c).
[751] art.1(3).
[752] art.1(4).
[753] art.2(1).
[754] art.2(2).

in good faith in respect of each work or other protected subject-matter, by consulting the appropriate sources for the category of works and other protected subject-matter in question. The diligent search shall be carried out prior to the use of the work or phonogram."[755]

Duty of diligent search

4-391   As is clear from the foregoing, the conduct of a diligent search is necessary before advantage of the permissions given by the Directive can be taken. The "appropriate sources" to be investigated are to be specified[756] by each Member State as part of its implementation of the Directive, and must include the sources identified in the annex to the Directive (which include sources such as public library catalogues and the records of authors' associations). The diligent search must be carried out in the country of first publication or (if there has been no publication) first broadcast, or, in the case of cinematographic or audiovisual works for which the producer has headquarters or habitual residence in a Member State, in that Member State, unless the work falls within the scope of the Directive only because it has been made publicly accessible by a cultural body, in which case the diligent search is to be carried out in the Member State where that access was provided.[757] If there is evidence to suggest that relevant information on right holders is to be found in other countries (note: not limited to Member States), sources of information available in those other countries shall also be consulted.[758] Finally, arts 3(5) and 3(6) provide that records of the diligent searches, their results, and other associated information must be kept and, in accordance with measures to be imposed by Member States, communicated to OHIM in order for it to record that information in a single publicly accessible database.

4-392   The Directive does not give further elaboration of the level of "diligence" necessary. Recital 14 records that "[i]t is appropriate to provide for a harmonised approach concerning such diligent search in order to ensure a high level of protection of copyright and related rights in the Union", indicating that the search will have to be sufficiently thorough to provide the oft-stated high level of protection to authors, but also refers to guidelines that Member States may wish to refer to when specifying the various sources that cultural bodies will be obliged to search. That guidance not only suggests that relevant sources be searched, but also suggests that publications of announcements to seek to identify relevant persons may also be appropriate. While undoubtedly labourious, it is submitted that complying with this duty of diligent search is unlikely to cause any particular problems for the cultural bodies covered by this Directive: provided that they make a competent search of all the designated sources, pay attention to evidence that comes to their awareness (whether as a result of those searches or otherwise) and take reasonable steps to pursue any promising avenues of further investigation, document their search, and maintain a published list of works for which they are seeking authors and rights holders, then the standard is likely to be met.

4-393   In order to avoid duplication of search across the EU, art.4 of the Directive provides that, if a work or phonogram is classified as an orphan work in one Member State, then it shall be considered as such in all Member States.

---

[755] art.3(1).
[756] art.3(2).
[757] art.3(3).
[758] art.3(4).

Article 5 ensures that any right holder has the ability to put an end to the orphan **4-394** work status of their works. No doubt, notification procedures that allow right holders to identify themselves and their rights will have to be put in place.

The permitted uses

If a work falls within the scope of the Directive and is classified as an orphan **4-395** work, then art.6 provides that Member States shall provide, for the benefit only of cultural bodies identified in art.1(1) of the Orphan Works Directive and in pursuit only of their public interest missions,[759] an exception or limitation to the rights of making available and reproduction that arise under arts 2 and 3 of the Information Society Directive. The exception to the reproduction right is only permitted to extend to acts undertaken for the purposes of for the purposes of digitisation, making available, indexing, cataloguing, preservation or restoration of the orphan work.[760] The cultural bodies are to be placed under an obligation to identify the names of any identified rights holders when performing a permitted act.[761] If a right holder is identified or otherwise comes forward so that the orphan work status of their works is put at an end, then the Member States shall provide for fair compensation for the permitted use that has been made of their works while they were classified as orphan works. It is for the Member State to determine the level of compensation, within the limits of union law.[762] This would prohibit any discriminatory acts in the setting of the level of compensation. Recital 18 gives guidance as to some factors that may be taken into account when determining fair compensation: these are the Member States' cultural promotion objectives, the non-commercial nature of the use made by the organisations in question in order to achieve aims related to their public-interest missions, such as promoting learning and disseminating culture, and of the possible harm to right holders. In the context of orphan works, it is highly unlikely that a right holder will be actively exploiting or seeking to exploit the works or phonograms in question, so circumstances in which there is any more than negligible possible harm to right holders will be rare. It is therefore likely, it is submitted, that any sums paid as fair compensation under these provisions are likely to be small.

Term and implementation

The permitted uses under the Orphan Works Directive are not appropriately **4-396** described as having a "term". Instead, the right will exist while the qualifying conditions exist—in the main, those will remain for the duration of the copyright in the work or phonogram unless its status as an orphan work comes to an end.

The time limit for the implementation of the Directive is 29 October 2014[763] and **4-397** only acts conducted after that date can be permitted by it.[764]

Review

The Commission is obliged by art.10 to keep the development of rights informa- **4-398** tion sources (to be consulted as part of the diligent search) under constant review,

---

[759] art.6(2).
[760] art.6(1)(b).
[761] art.6(3).
[762] art.6(5).
[763] art.9.
[764] art.8.

and shall annually submit a report concerning the possible inclusion of addition categories of works (particularly such as stand-alone photographs) within the scope of the Directive.

The Collective Rights Management Directive

Introduction

4-399 Having dealt with the substantive rights and enforcement of copyright, the Commission began to look at what it called the "third pillar" of copyright,[765] namely collective rights management. Various problems had been identified. The large number of national collecting societies meant that administrative inefficiency was encountered when dealing with content that was to be exploited throughout Europe. In addition, there was a perception that some collecting societies were not running their affairs in a transparent or equitable way. Ultimately this led to the Collective Rights Management Directive.[766] The transposition date for the Directive is 10 April 2016.[767]

The history of the Directive

4-400 In April 2005, the Commission set out[768] three options that it would shortly consult upon. The first option was to do nothing. The second option was to issue guidelines that could be transformed into a code of conduct for collective rights managers. The third option was a "light touch regulatory framework" that is to say, a framework Directive that would oblige collective rights managers to set up minimum rules on how they account for revenue collected, how they distributed the revenues, and how they themselves were organised.

4-401 Following the July 2005 consultation there was broad consensus that Option 1 was not an option. Opinions were divided between Options 2 and 3, with commercial users favouring Option 2, the majority of collective rights managers favouring modified versions of Option 2, and the music publishers' EU, the independent record labels and certain collective rights managers favouring Option 3.

4-402 On 12 October 2005 the Commission adopted the "Commission Recommendation on collective cross-border management of copyright and related rights for legitimate online music services."[769]

4-403 That Recommendation takes the form of a series of non-binding guidelines addressed to Member States. It is a short document that contains general principles rather than detailed provisions. The Recitals acknowledge that in the era of online

---

[765] J. Reinbothe, speech at Fordham University, 10th Annual Conference on International IP Law and Policy, 4 April 2002.

[766] Dir.2014/26/EU of 26 February 2014 on collective management of copyright and related rights and multi-territorial licensing of rights in musical works for online use in the internal market [2014] OJ L84/72.

[767] art.43.

[768] T. Lueder, Acting Head of the Copyright Unit, DG Internal Market and Services, speech at Fordham University, 13th Annual Conference on International IP Law and Policy, April 2005.

[769] Commission Recommendation of 18 May 2005 on collective cross-border management of copyright and related rights for legitimate online music services [2005] OJ L276/54. Note that the date on the recommendation is 18 May 2005, which is an error. See the corrigendum: Corrigendum to Commission Recommendation 2005/737/EC of 18 May 2005 on collective cross-border management of copyright and related rights for legitimate online music services (OJ L 276, 21 October 2005) [2005] OJ L284/10.

exploitation, commercial users need a licensing policy that corresponds to the multi-territorial nature of the internet, and that this will lead to an increased revenue stream for right holders.[770] In addition, there is acknowledgement that greater transparency is required for the purposes of competition law.[771] Member States are encouraged to promote a regulatory environment that is consistent with the recommendation.[772]

The key recommendation is that right holders should have the right to entrust the management of any of the online rights to a collecting society of their choice, irrespective of the residence or nationality of either the right holder or the collecting society.[773] In addition right holders should be able to dictate what rights are entrusted to that collecting society, including the territorial scope of such rights.[774] Right holders should be able to transfer the management of their rights from one collecting society to another.[775]   **4-404**

There are various guidelines concerning the management and procedures of collecting societies. They must run their affairs transparently, treat rights holders equitably and make it clear what deductions are being made from royalties.[776] They must also report regularly to rights holders.   **4-405**

Thereafter public hearings took place on 23 April 2010, and monitoring of Europe's online music sector, (which included a call for comments launched on 17 January 2007 concluded by a summary report published on 7 February 2008) took place. A draft Directive was published on 11 July 2012.   **4-406**

The reader should be aware that the consideration of how collective rights societies enforce rights themselves and between themselves across the EU may involve considerations of competition law. This is discussed elsewhere in this book.[777]   **4-407**

To whom does the Collective Rights Management Directive apply?

Article 2 of the Directive, which sets out its scope, states that the Directive applies to "collective management organisations" established in the EU. Those organisations are defined in art.3(a) to mean any organisation which is authorised by law or by way of assignment, licence or any other contractual arrangement to manage copyright or rights related to copyright on behalf of more than one right holder, for the collective benefit of those right holders, as its sole or main purpose, and which is owned or controlled by its members and/or is organised on a not-for-profit basis. Some of the requirements of the Directive only apply to collective management organisations whose activities include the management of authors' rights in musical works for online use on a multi-territorial basis. Further, some of the provisions of the Directive apply to independent management entities established in the EU, defined in art.3(b) to be much like collective management organisations, save that they are organised on a for-profit basis and are neither owned nor controlled, directly or indirectly, wholly or in part, by right holders. The obligations placed on such independent management entities are limited to obliga-   **4-408**

---

[770] Recital 8.
[771] Recital 10.
[772] art.2.
[773] art.3.
[774] art.5.
[775] art.5.
[776] arts 10 and 11.
[777] See para.8-409 and para.12-290.

tions to license rights in good faith,[778] to provide information to rights holders explaining certain aspects of the management of their rights,[779] to provide information as to the identity of the works it manages or, where the specific identity of the rights it manages cannot be determined, the types of works it manages,[780] and to provide general information about its constitution and terms.[781]

The objectives and provisions of the Collective Rights Management Directive

4-409   The Directive is divided into different titles which each set out provisions aimed at achieving a particular objective.

4-410   Title II has a general principle, as set out in art.4, to "ensure that collective management organisations act in the best interests of the right holders whose rights they represent and that they do not impose on them any obligations which are not objectively necessary for the protection of their rights and interests or for the effective management of their rights." This is achieved by requirements that Member States ensure the provision of a variety of rights to rights holders,[782] controls on membership rules,[783] a requirement for an annual (or more frequent) general assembly,[784] the putting in place of a supervisory function,[785] and the imposition of requirements on the persons who manage the organisation.[786] Further, there are controls on the collection and use of revenues,[787] on deductions,[788] on distributions to right holders,[789] on the relationship with users of rights,[790] and requirements in respect of reporting and the provision of information.[791]

4-411   Title III addresses the grant of multi-territorial licences for online rights in musical works.[792] The title does not apply to multi-territorial licences granted to radio or television providers who make traditional broadcasts that are simultaneous with an online offering.[793] It contains provisions obliging collective management organisations to have the necessary facilities to process multi-territorial licences[794] and for identifying their repertoire of musical works.[795] There are also provisions that will impose obligations on collective management organisations to provide transparent and accurate information about their repertoires,[796] to make accurate and timely reports of the use of their repertoire by service providers[797] and to make ac-

---

[778] Under art.16(1).
[779] Under art.18.
[780] Under art.20.
[781] Under art.21(1).
[782] art.5.
[783] art.6.
[784] art.8.
[785] art.9.
[786] art.10.
[787] art.11.
[788] art.12.
[789] art.13.
[790] arts 16 and 17.
[791] arts 18–22.
[792] art.23.
[793] art.32.
[794] art.24.
[795] art.25.
[796] art.26.
[797] art.27.

curate and timely payments to rights holders.[798] Finally, this title of the Directive prohibits exclusive agreements between collective management organisations for multi-territorial licensing,[799] places an obligation on a collective management organisation that already offers management on behalf of one or more other organisations, to agree to manage the rights of any further organisation that approaches it,[800] and allows rights holders to remove their rights from a collective management organisation that is not, by 10 April 2017, offering access to multi-territorial licensing either directly or through agreement with another organisation.[801]

Title IV provides for enforcement measures to be taken against non-compliant collective management organisations and Title V provides for reporting on and analysis of the effect of the Directive, as well as for various general provisions. **4-412**

EEA LEGISLATION

The only legislation that was adopted in the copyright field by the cut-off date of 31 July 1991 for the purposes of the EEA Agreement was the Computer Programs Directive. That Directive forms part of the *acquis communautaire* of the EEA Agreement.[802] The only material amendment to this directive for the EEA Agreement is that the exhaustion principle set out in art.4(c) applies to the territories of the Contracting Parties. Accordingly, the sale of a copy of a programme in the EEA exhausts the rights of the copyright owner in that programme to prevent further movement within the EEA of that copy. However, it does not affect the right to control further rental of the program or the copy.[803] The codified version of the Computer Programs Directive was adopted by the Decision of the EEA Joint Committee in 2011.[804] **4-413**

Since the cut-off date, the Rental Right Directive, the Term Directive and the Satellite and Cable Directive were adopted into the EEA Agreement by the Decision of the EEA Joint Committee No.7/94.[805] Subsequently, the Database Directive was adopted by the Decision of the EEA Joint Committee No.59/96;[806] the Resale Right Directive was adopted by the Decision of the EEA Joint Committee No.171/2002;[807] the Information Society Directive was adopted by the Decision of the EEA Joint Committee No. 110/2004[808] and the codified versions of the Rental Right Directive and the Term Directive were adopted by the Decision of the EEA **4-414**

---

[798] art.28.
[799] art.29.
[800] art.30.
[801] art.31.
[802] EEA agreement Annex XVII.5.
[803] EEA agreement Annex XVII.5.
[804] Decision of the EEA Joint Committee No. 39/2011 amending Protocol 17 (intellectual property) and certain Annexes to the EEA Agreement [2011] O L171/40.
[805] Decision of the EEA Joint Committee No.7/94 amending Protocol 47 and certain Annexes to the EEA Agreement [1994] OJ L160/1.
[806] Decision of the EEA Joint Committee No.59/96 amending Annex 17 (intellectual property) to the EEA Agreement [1997] OJ L021/11.
[807] Decision of the EEA Joint Committee No.171/2002 amending Annex 17 (intellectual property) to the EEA Agreement [2003] OJ L038/36.
[808] Decision of the EEA Joint Committee No.110/2004 amending Annex 17 (intellectual property) to the EEA Agreement [2004] OJ L376/45.

Joint Committee No.56/2007.[809] More recently, the Orphan Works Directive was adopted by the Decision of the Joint Committee No.29/2015[810] and the Collective Rights Management Directive was adopted by the Decision of the Joint Committee No.186/2017.[811]

4-415   In *L'Oréal Norge AS v Smart Club AS*[812] the EFTA Court, reversing its earlier decision in *Mag Instrument Inc v California Trading Company*[813] held that the exhaustion of rights provisions in the Trade Mark Directive (which formed part of the *acquis communautaire*) precluded contracting states to the EEA from introducing an international exhaustion of rights principle for trade marks. As discussed in Ch.3, the CJEU had interpreted this provision to preclude Member States from unilaterally providing for an international exhaustion of rights principle.[814] There seems no reason why the reasoning of the EFTA Court, which was based upon the fact that the differences between the EEA Agreement and the EC Treaty (the predecessor to the TFEU) did not constitute compelling grounds for divergent interpretations of art.7(1), should not be applicable to copyright Directives which have become part of the *acquis communautaire* of the EEA. Thus, insofar as a copyright Directive creates an EU-wide exhaustion of rights principle and which has been incorporated into the EEA by reason of its adoption by the EEA Joint Committee (thereby leading to an EEA-wide exhaustion of rights principle), it is submitted that EEA countries cannot unilaterally provide for an international exhaustion of principle.

---

[809]   Decision of the EEA Joint Committee No.56/2007 amending Annex 17 (intellectual property) to the EEA Agreement [2007] OJ L266/17. The codified version of the Term Directive (2011/77) was adopted in 2013—[2013] OJ L291/60.

[810]   Decision of the EEA Joint Committee No.29/2015 amending Annex 17 (intellectual property) to the EEA Agreement [2016] OJ L63/44].

[811]   Decision of the EEA Joint Committee No.29/2015 amending Annex 17 (intellectual property) to the EEA Agreement [2017] OJ (yet to be published).

[812]   E-9 & 10/07 [2008] EFTA Ct. Rep. 259.

[813]   E-2/97 [1997] EFTA Ct. Rep. 129.

[814]   See para.3-616.

DESIGN PROTECTION IN EUROPE

INTRODUCTION

Design rights, in general, divide into two categories: a registered right, often **5-001** limited to industrial designs which confer a true monopoly and an unregistered right similar to copyright which does not require registration and entitles the owner to prevent copying of their design. Although the Paris Convention effected some small uniformity in the field of designs, historically, the nature and extent of protection varied greatly. Such variation was even more marked in the field of unregistered designs.

Much of the reason for the variation in protection of designs arose from the dif- **5-002** ficulty of defining what "design" meant. In earlier days, designs were regarded as merely cosmetic and applied to an article for decorative effect. A clear distinction was made between the functional article and decorative design. More recently, with increasing sophistication in technology, such an approach is outdated. Thus, it has been said that the design of an article be seen as extending from colour through to the patentable basis of the article.[1] In the cases of many industrial items, e.g. a car, the design of the shape of a car is usually an intimate combination of function (aerodynamics) and aesthetics (sleek lines). Thus the following definitions have been put forward as to what design means:

- "the arrangement or layout of a product"[2];
- "the visual appearance of a product, whether that appearance is created by a choice of a particular shape or by surface ornamentation, or by a combination of shape and ornamentation"[3];
- "the design of any aspect of the shape or configuration (whether internal or external) of the whole or part of an article"[4];
- "a product of design is what it should be at the moment when it should be and in the place where it should be. It is not fanciful nor oriented to flatter

---

[1] Australian Discussion Paper, August 1994, on Designs, para.3.3.
[2] *Oxford English Dictionary.*
[3] C. Tootal, *The Law of Industrial Designs* (Surrey: C.C.H. Wolters Kluwer, 1990).
[4] Copyright Designs and Patents Act 1988 s.213(2), in relation to the unregistered design right created under that Act in UK law.

or capture the wishes of the public. It results from logical design and engineering"[5]; and

- "the enhanced functionality of a product by way of its design."[6]

5-003   Such definitions or explanations demonstrate that there was little consensus as to what design meant. Indeed, it could be said that the design of a product is merely the sum of every aspect of that which is visible about a product.

5-004   The main reason for variation was a reflection of the different cultures and philosophies of Member States.[7] Most countries had registered design laws. However, prior to harmonisation, the type of designs that were registrable varied considerably.[8] Outside the laws of registered designs, certain countries with civil law backgrounds emphasised the protection of design as a form of applied art and afforded protection to designs by way of copyright, whilst other countries like the UK denied (and still deny) copyright protection to industrial designs and provide a special scheme of protection for the protection of aspects of shape and configuration of industrial designs.

PLAN OF CHAPTER

5-005   This chapter first considers the international conventions in the field of designs. It then gives an overview of EU legislation which includes matters peculiar to one or the other rights. Following is a detailed analysis of the common provisions under the Directive and the Regulation, basically the substantive law. The chapter then details the relatively small number of provisions peculiar to the Directive or the Regulation. Finally, it considers the differences in national laws of Member States relating to industrial designs outside the harmonised areas.

INTERNATIONAL LEGISLATION

Paris Convention[9]

5-006   The Paris Convention for the Protection of Industrial Property requires that industrial designs be protected in all countries who are members of the Paris Convention.[10] Although it is not explicit, it is fairly clear that this is referring to protection via a system of registration.[11]

5-007   The Paris Convention stipulates a number of requirements regarding the protec-

---

5   M. Franzosi, "The Legal Protection of Industrial Design: Unfair Competition as a Basis of Protection" [1990] 12(5) E.I.P.R. 154, 156.
6   European Commission, *"Introduction to the Green Paper on the Legal Protection of Industrial Design Commission"* III/F/5131/91-EN, June 1991.
7   M. Franzosi, "The Legal Protection of Industrial Design" [1990] 5 E.I.P.R. 154, fn.5.
8   Thus, the UK, Spain, Italy and Germany required an aesthetic element to the design for it to be registrable whereas Benelux and France permitted the registration of the appearance of functional items.
9   Paris Convention for the Protection of Industrial Property. The most up-to-date version can be obtained from WIPO's web site at: *http://www.wipo.int/treaties/en/ip/paris/* [Accessed 14 December 2017]. All European countries are signatories to it.
10   Paris Convention art.5*quinquies*.
11   This can be deduced from the following provisions: arts 4A–4E (which refer to the filing of an industrial design and its entitlement of priority from earlier filings); art.5D which prohibits the requirement that products be marked with details concerning "the deposit of the industrial design"; and art.12 (countries to provide for a central office for the publication of industrial designs). However, it should be noted that at least one commentator considers that art.5*quinquies* would be

tion of industrial designs. These are:

(a) industrial designs shall not, under any circumstance, be subject to any forfeiture, either by reason of failure to work or by reason of the importation of Articles corresponding to the protected design[12];

(b) the protection of industrial designs shall not be dependent on the marking of goods with a "deposit" of the industrial design[13];

(c) that industrial designs shall benefit from a six-month priority period[14];

(d) a minimum six-month grace period for the payment of renewal fees shall apply[15]; and

(e) a degree of protection for prior disclosure if such disclosure of the industrial design was at an official exhibition.[16]

Berne Convention[17]

The Berne Convention for the Protection of Literary and Artistic Works is not primarily concerned with industrial designs. However, as mentioned in the introduction, industrial designs may be capable of protection as works of applied art and thus there is a degree of overlap. Article 2(7) of the Berne Convention leaves the extent and conditions of protection of industrial designs and works of applied art to the countries of the Union. However, it does provide for a degree of reciprocity of protection. Thus, art.2(7) requires that a work which is protected solely as a design shall be entitled to protection as a design in other countries of the Union or if no specific protection exists for designs, it shall be entitled to protection as an artistic work. In-so-far as the design is protected as work of applied art, protection is for a minimum term of protection of at least 25 years from the making of the work.[18] Thus, the Berne Convention envisages the protection of industrial designs by both sui generis laws, which it does not attempt to harmonise, and the law of copyright, by being a work of applied art.

5-008

WTO Agreement (TRIPS)

Articles 25 and 26 of TRIPS are relevant to industrial designs and provide for a degree of protection for industrial designs. Article 25(1) provides that:

5-009

"Members *shall* provide for the protection of independently created industrial designs that are new or original. Members *may* provide that designs are not new or original if they do not significantly differ from known designs or combination of design features. Members

---

satisfied if designs were protected under the laws of copyright or unfair competition: see G.H.C. Bodenhausen, et al., *Guide to the Application of the Paris Convention for the Protection of Industrial Property* (Geneva: WIPO, 1969). This can be viewed at *http://www.wipo.int/publications/en/details.jsp ?id=239* [Accessed 14 December 2017].

[12] art.5B.
[13] art.5D Paris Convention.
[14] art.4 Paris Convention.
[15] art.5*bis* Paris Convention.
[16] art.11.
[17] Berne Convention for the Protection of Literary and Artistic Works. (An up-to-date version is available from:
    http://www.wipo.int/treaties/en/ip/berne/ [Accessed 14 December 2017]). All European countries are members.
[18] art.7(4).

may provide that such protection shall not extend to designs dictated essentially by technical function or functional considerations."[19]

5-010   As emphasised above, the first sentence of the Article is mandatory whereas the second and third sentences are optional. It has been said that the first sentence applies a "subjective novelty" test in that the design must not have been copied from another design whilst the second sentence provides for an objective test.[20] Thus, it has been said that the first sentence is closer to a copyright-type test for subsistence whereas the second sentence resembles the "prior art" novelty test in patents.[21] Certainly, the requirement that designs must be new *or* original does give rise to interpretational difficulties. In the UK, originality is a different concept from novelty. Originality merely requires that the work is the author's work and has not been copied from another's work. Copyright will subsist in any original literary, dramatic or work and it does not matter that there exists an identical prior work which the designer was unaware of. By way of contrast, novelty or newness requires that there does not exist an identical work in the world, regardless of the designer's knowledge of such a work. The requirement of absolute novelty over existing prior art (regardless whether the designer copied the prior art or indeed was aware of it) is a feature of all intellectual property rights which require registration. However, in general, it is not a feature of unregistered rights like copyright or for instance, the unregistered design right law of the UK.[22] It is of note that the phrase "independently created" was added towards the end of the negotiation, as if to emphasise that independent creation is the important criterion and not absolute novelty.[23]

5-011   The effect of the above is that Member States are permitted a considerable degree of latitude as to the requirements of novelty and originality for protection of industrial designs.[24] Indeed, art.25 does not make it clear whether protection should be via a registration system or via an unregistered system akin to copyright. Registration systems normally require that the right applied for is in respect of a novel item,[25] but it is clear that art.25 would permit an "originality"-only system which is more the province of copyright, an unregistered IPR.

---

[19]   art.25(2) is particular to textile designs and requires Members not to make registration of textile designs too onerous in time, money or effort.

[20]   See D. Gervais, *The TRIPS Agreement: Drafting History and Analysis*, 4th edn (London: Sweet & Maxwell, 2012), p.411.

[21]   D. Gervais, *The TRIPS Agreement: Drafting History and Analysis*, 4th edn (London: Sweet & Maxwell, 2012), p.411.

[22]   e.g. see *Bailey (t/a Elite) v Haynes* [2007] F.S.R. 10 at [46]. However, if the design is "commonplace", it will not benefit from UK unregistered design right even if not copied from an earlier design—s.213 of the Copyright Designs Patents Act 1988.

[23]   It is of note that in the drafting of this section, many lobbied for the phrase "new *and* original" precisely because they were concerned that a design that was not "new" could still be original (as is the case in copyright)—D. Gervais, The TRIPS Agreement, 4th edn (London: Sweet & Maxwell, 2012), pp.411–412. The fact that such an amendment was not permitted suggests clearly that a proper interpretation of "new or original" is that the two words are not synonymous and have different markings.

[24]   See Opinion of Wathelet AG, *Karen Millen Fashions Ltd v Dunnes Stores* (C-345/13) ECLI: EU:C:2014:2013 at [37] whereby he said that art.25 merely sets out an *option* which is left to the discretion of the parties to TRIPS to decide whether a design is novel if it *combines* known features in the prior art (citing the 3rd edn of this book). See also the judgment, at [34].

[25]   Generally, the rationale for registration is that in return for communicating a technological or other advantage to the world via a public register of the advantage, one is conferred an absolute monopoly for that advantage for a limited period. Clearly, that rationale does not apply if the world is already

The third sentence of art.25(1) permits Member States to exclude design protec- **5-012**
tion for designs dictated by technical or functional considerations. In the Design
Directive and the Design Regulation, the EU has enacted a similarly-worded
provision. The current interpretation of this provision in the Regulation and Directive is that it includes designs where the only considerations in the creation of the
design were technical or functional rather than aesthetic. The multiplicity-of-
forms approach (whereby protection was permitted if it could be shown that a different design could achieve the same technical function), has been rejected.[26]

Article 26, which is concerned with the scope of protection, provides: **5-013**

> "1. The owner of a protected industrial design shall have the right to prevent third par-
> ties not having the owner's consent from making, selling or importing articles bear-
> ing or embodying a design which is a copy, or substantially a copy, of the protected
> design, when such acts are undertaken for commercial purposes.
> 2. Members may provide limited exceptions to the protection of industrial designs,
> provided that such exceptions do not unreasonably conflict with the normal
> exploitation of protected industrial designs and do not unreasonably prejudice the
> legitimate interests of the owner of the protected design, taking account of the
> legitimate interests of third parties.
> 3. The duration of protection available shall amount to at least 10 years."

The main issue under art.26(1) is whether the phrase "copy" requires not merely **5-014**
a correspondence between the designs but that the infringing design was derived
from the protected design.[27] In other words, would a design that has been
independently created in a closed room by a designer with no knowledge of other
designs, but which is identical to the protected design, be an infringing design? As
there is a degree of latitude over whether Member States provide for an unregistered
copyright system, or a registered system which requires absolute novelty, it is probable that there is some latitude here. A copyright system requires an actual act of
derivation whilst such is not required in a registration system.

Article 25 contains both mandatory and optional provisions. TRIPS is intended **5-015**
to provide for a minimum level of protection for IPRs.[28] In relation to the optional
provisions, it is not clear whether contracting states have latitude to enact different provisions in the field to which the optional provisions relate.[29] There is some
doubt as to whether EU legislation in this field complies with arts 25 and 26. In
particular, is the requirement in EU law that designs have "individual character"
over known designs equivalent to "do not significantly differ from known designs"
in the second sentence of art.25?[30] As the EU is a signatory to TRIPS, national
courts of Member States are required to interpret national provisions as far as possible in the light of the wording and purpose of the relevant provisions of TRIPS.[31]
Perhaps, more importantly, is the EU requirement that the prior art be known to
business circles in the sector concerned in the EU, an impermissible qualification

---

aware of that advantage.
[26] See para.5-144, et seq.
[27] In the UK, the word "copy" in "copyright" reflects the legal principle that there is no infringement
of copyright unless the alleged infringing work is derived (copied) from the copyright work (regardless how similar the two may appear). NB. in the French version, the word is "*copie*".
[28] art.1 TRIPS.
[29] art.1(1) TRIPS provides that contracting states may provide more extensive protection than is
required by TRIPS "provided that such protection does not contravene the provisions of this
Agreement".
[30] See para.1-167.
[31] See para.1-180.

of the test of novelty set out in the second sentence of art.25. This would lead to discrimination against designs only known outside the EU and would thus appear to be contrary to the requirement of non-discrimination in art.3 of TRIPS.[32] Furthermore, the EU scheme permits a "grace period" whereby commercialisation by the designer in a period of 12 months prior to filing is not to be taken into account for the purpose of novelty. Again, there seems no scope for such a qualification on novelty in TRIPS. However, as this strengthens rather than weakens IPR protection for the designer, it is unlikely to offend TRIPS.

The Hague Agreement

Introduction

5-016   The Hague Agreement[33] is a very different creature from those discussed above. Whilst the Paris Convention and the WTO Agreement set out a certain minimal harmonisation threshold, the Hague Agreement is a procedural convention administered by WIPO. It provides for an international procedure for applying for the registration of industrial designs, similar to the Madrid System in respect of trade marks. Substantive examination of the application is left to Contracting States. There are (at present) 68 contracting parties to the Agreement.[34] Importantly, the US and the Russian Federation have now joined.

5-017   In 2006, the EU acceded to the Hague Agreement thereby permitting applicants to obtain a Community Design.[35]

5-018   In summary, the Agreement allows an applicant to file (described in the Agreement as a "deposit") a single application at WIPO which, after formalities examination, is passed on to those Member States designated in the application. Those states have a limited time period (generally six months from date of publication of the international registration) in which to refuse protection. The absence of any notified refusal leads to automatic grant. Hence, an applicant may achieve granted registrations in several contracting states. Assignment and/or renunciation of a granted registration is effected at WIPO, although matters concerning the infringement of a registration are dealt with on a national basis under the law of an individual state.

5-019   Use of the Agreement fell very significantly in the period 2000–2007 from a high of over 4000 registrations to just over 1000 (registrations does not equal designs since multiple designs can be protected in a single registration). This was largely due to the introduction of the Community Design. However, with the EU and USA's accession to the Hague Agreement, registrations have grown again numbering 5562 in 2016.

---

[32]   art.3 requires that Members of WTO shall not accord to nationals of other Members less favourable treatment than it accords to its own. Whilst such a criterion is directed at nationals rather than novelty, it is clear that indirectly such is likely to prejudice nationals of non-EU countries as it is likely that overall designs will be first commercialised in the country of nationality of the designer.

[33]   Its full title is The Hague Agreement concerning the International Registration of Industrial Designs. The various legal texts can be downloaded from: *http://www.wipo.int/treaties/en/registration/ hague/* [Accessed 14 December 2017].

[34]   The current members can be found at: *http://www.wipo.int/hague/en/members/* [Accessed 6 May 2018]. The UK acceded to the Hague Agreement in April 2018.

[35]   Council Decision 954/2006. This led to Council Regulation 1891/2006 [2006] OJ L386/14 amending the Design Regulation and Design Directive to give effect to the accession including permitting an applicant under the Hague Agreement to designate the EU and thereby obtain a Community Design—arts 106a–106f of Reg.6/2002.

The Agreement is complicated by the fact that there are, in effect, three differ- **5-020** ent forms following various revisions. These are:

(i)   the 1934 revision at London;
(ii)   the 1960 revision at The Hague; and
(iii)   the Geneva Act of 1999.

If the subsequent form of the Agreement has not been acceded to by a particular **5-021** contracting state then the earlier form of the Agreement must be followed. However, this rather complex situation is perhaps less difficult in practice. First, on 18 October 2016, the London Act of 1934 was terminated and no longer applies. Secondly, there are common regulations for both the 1960 and 1999 Acts.[36] For this reason only the most recent, the Geneva Act will be outlined in any detail below and all references are to this version of the Agreement unless otherwise stated.

Principal features of the system

Deposit

A single application only need be deposited (i.e. filed[37]) with the International **5-022** Bureau of WIPO in Geneva or (if permitted by the applicable national law) at the national intellectual property office of the contracting state.[38] Priority of up to six months may be claimed from an earlier application in any state subject either to the Paris Convention or WTO Agreement.

Importantly (like the Patent Cooperation Treaty) a filing can only be made by a **5-023** national of a contracting state. The applicable test here is whether the undertaking is "domiciled or [has] a real and effective industrial or commercial establishment in the territory of a contracting state".[39] Each application may contain up to 100 different designs although they must all fall within the same single class of the International Classification of Industrial Designs (Locarno classification). A graphic representation or photograph of each design must be included. The application may be in either English, French or Spanish.[40] The application must designate the states for which protection is sought.[41]

The application may also contain, on a voluntary basis, a short (not exceeding **5-024** 100 words) description of the "characteristic features" of the design,[42] the legal significance of which, if any, is unclear.

Subsequent procedure

If the application meets the filing requirements referred to above, it is published **5-025** in the International Designs Bulletin, although the applicant may, if they wish, defer such publication until one year from priority at the latest.

---

[36]   The current Common Regulations are those as in force on 1 January 2017. An English version can be found at: *http://www.wipo.int/wipolex/en/treaties/text.jsp?file_id=429512* [Accessed 14 December 2017].

[37]   The 1960 version of the agreement uses the term "deposited", although the 1999 Act uses the more conventional term "filed".

[38]   art.4 Hague Agreement.

[39]   art.3 Hague Agreement.

[40]   r.6(1) Common Regulations.

[41]   art.5(1)(v) Hague Agreement.

[42]   art.5(2) Hague Agreement.

5-026   The International Bureau of WIPO does not operate any examination system, but refusal in any contracting state is possible within a limited time period. Only contracting states which themselves operate either a novelty examination process or an opposition system may take advantage of this refusal provision. In such cases, the national office may refuse the design[43] for that state on any grounds which are available under its national law (not being formal or administrative grounds which are the province of WIPO).[44] Such refusal must generally be communicated to WIPO within six months of publication of the international registration.[45] WIPO statistics indicate that cases of refusal are very rare, only occurring in relation to about a dozen deposits each year. This is because in general, there is no opposition procedure (unlike trade marks) for applications for designs.

5-027   There is no formal grant process under the Agreement, the design merely becomes ineligible for refusal after the period discussed above. The design is, in effect, registered upon its filing[46] (provided that the formal requirements have been complied with) and thereafter has the same effect in a contracting state as a national registration.[47]

Term and post-registration matters

5-028   The initial period of registration is for five years from the date of deposit. This is renewable (upon payment of a fee) at five-yearly intervals up to a period of 15 years.[48] In respect of states which provide national protection for in excess of this period, the Hague deposit may be renewed for further periods of five years up to the maximum protection period provided for under national law.[49] All renewal fees are payable centrally to WIPO.

5-029   Changes in the ownership of the registration may be centrally recorded at WIPO and the registration may also be renounced centrally.

EU LEGISLATION

Introduction

5-030   In 1991, the European Commission published a *Green Paper on the Legal Protection of Industrial Design*. The Commission had long recognised that national laws on design in the Member States were unsatisfactory. First, they failed to provide adequate protection for designs as they only effectively protected the ornamental features of a design rather than the salient features of a contemporary industrial design which, it described as "the enhanced functionality of a product by way of its design."[50] Secondly, the Commission was concerned about the disparate protection of designs in Member States and the effect that had on the creation of

---

[43] art.12(1) Hague Agreement.
[44] art.8 Hague Agreement.
[45] art.12 Hague Agreement; r.18(1)(a) Common Regulations, although a Geneva Act state can give notice to extend this to 12 months (r.18(1)(b) Common Regulations).
[46] art.10 Hague Agreement.
[47] art.14 Hague Agreement.
[48] art.17 Hague Agreement.
[49] art.17(2) Hague Agreement.
[50] *Green Paper on the Legal Protection of Industrial Design*, Commission III/F/5131/91-EN, June 1991, p.2.

an internal market.[51] Accordingly, it proposed in the Green Paper the introduction of a Community Design Regulation accompanied with a harmonisation directive of Member States' registered designs laws. The first proposal drew heavily on a proposal for a Community Design by the Max Planck Institute for Foreign and International Patent, Copyright and Competition Law.

As a result of this, in December 1993, the Commission put forward a draft Com-   **5-031**
munity Design Regulation and a Design Directive. Whilst the Design Directive could use the legislative mechanism set out of what is now art.114 TFEU,[52] such a mechanism was not available for the Design Regulation and this had to be legislated for pursuant to what is now art.352 TFEU.[53] Accordingly, the Design Directive was "fast tracked" and was adopted on 13 October 1998. The corresponding Regulation was adopted by the EU Council on 12 December 2001. The Community Design is similar in nature to the EU Trade Mark. It should be called the EU Design but Reg.6/2002 was adopted before the name of the European Community changed its name to the European Union by the 2009 Treaty of Lisbon.

The Directive harmonises the laws of Member States in the field of registered   **5-032**
designs. However, the Regulation not only provides for a unitary EU-wide Design capable of protection for 25 years but also creates a new Unregistered Community Design ("UCD") although this is relatively short lived with a protection term of three years. Unlike the Community Design, this merely protects the owner of the UCD against copying of its design. The substantive law under the Directive and the Regulation is virtually the same.

The Community Design is administered by the European Union Intellectual   **5-033**
Property Office ("EUIPO") in Alicante and filings have been accepted since 1 April 2003. It is important to emphasise that whilst the Regulation harmonises the law as to registered designs, the Directive and the Regulation do not harmonise *all* laws applicable to industrial designs. This is because it is expressly stated that these do not affect the applicability of other laws to industrial designs outside the field of registered designs. Thus, there will still remain considerable diversity in the applicability of copyright, utility models, unfair competition and national unregistered design rights to industrial designs throughout the EU.[54]

The Community Design Regulation has been a great success. In 2016, 105,597   **5-034**
filings for a Community Design were made. However, it must be recognised that a fundamental failing of the Community Design is that there is no substantive examination of applications. Provided formalities are complied with, grant of an application is automatic. Applicants are not bound to declare that to their knowledge, the design applied for is novel and has individual character over prior art or indeed indicate to their knowledge what the closest prior art is. Nor is there any requirement that the applications can be invalidated for having been made in bad faith (i.e. no intention to use the design). Thus, an applicant can apply for a registered design knowing that the design applied for is wholly invalid and yet obtain a 25-year monopoly (if renewal fees are paid). At least, in the case of the EU Trade Mark Regulation, there is a provision whereby a EU Trade Mark can be declared invalid

---

[51] See s.3.2, et seq.
[52] Previously art.95 ECT. See para.1-100.
[53] Previously art.308 ECT. NB. There is now a sui generis provision for the enactment of unitary EU rights, art.118 TFEU. This was introduced in the 2009 Lisbon Treaty. See para.1-106.
[54] arts 16, 17. For example, in the UK, industrial designs are protected by an unregistered design right under the Copyright Designs and Patents Act 1988 but in general, are not protected by copyright (see s.51 of the CDPA 1988). Generally, see paras 5-206 to 5-211.

if applied for in bad faith. A perusal of the registry of Community Designs demonstrates that many designs are for very mundane and trivial designs. Whilst it is plainly unrealistic to expect ex officio substantive examination of designs applied for as against prior published applications or registrations, there is no reason why a "full and frank" disclosure approach, similar to that adopted by the US Patent Office, should not be adopted by EUIPO whereby the applicant: (i) is obliged to identify the closest prior art known to them (which would be made available to the public); and (ii) declares that they are entitled to apply for the design because they are the designer or entitled to the design by operation of law (e.g. that of employment).[55] Furthermore, there is no requirement that the registered proprietor need use the design or lose it (as with registered trade marks). Thus, an applicant could obtain a monopoly for a design for 25 years and yet that design may never be used by the proprietor or any third party but used to prevent designs on the market. In the authors' view, these are serious deficiencies which should be remedied. The CJEU may consider in an extreme case application of the "*abus de droit*" doctrine discussed in Ch.14.

The Design Directive[56]

5-035   Directive 98/71/EC provides for the harmonisation of the law of registered designs in the Member States of the EU. It has now been implemented in all EU states.

5-036   Before examining the scheme of protection in detail, it is important to emphasise two important areas which the Directive does not seek to harmonise. First, the Directive only harmonises the law of registered designs. Thus, it expressly states that it is not intended to harmonise the laws of Member States relating to copyright, unregistered design rights, trade marks, patents and utility models, typefaces, civil liability or unfair competition, in-so-far as they are relevant to industrial designs.[57] As seen in the last section of this chapter, many countries also provide additional protection for designs without requiring registration.

5-037   Secondly, it does not harmonise the law relating to the use of spare parts to repair or renovate complex products, e.g. cars. This was as a result of the substantial lobbying of the motor car industry and caused considerable friction between the Commission and Parliament in the drafting of the Directive. The compromise that was reached was the so-called "freeze-plus" position, which can only be described as far from satisfactory. In 2004, the Commission published a proposal for amending the Directive[58] to allow designs for visible spare parts to be freely reproduced and marketed in the EU by independent parts manufactures for repair purposes. However, despite approval by the European Parliament, it was never adopted by the Council.[59] Indeed, that proposal has now been withdrawn and thus efforts to

---

[55] It is of note that art.36 of the Regulation which sets out the formal conditions which the applicant must comply with does not expressly require the applicant to state that they are so entitled. Thus, whilst art.14 of the Regulation states that the right to the Community design vests in the designer, there is no formal examination of this requirement and indeed, under art.25(1)(c), this ground can only be invoked where there has been a court decision declaring that the right holder is not entitled to the design. This can provide little comfort.

[56] Dir.98/71/EC on the legal protection of designs [1998] OJ L289/28.

[57] Dir.98/71/EC arts 16, 17.

[58] COM(2004) 852.

[59] It is well known that the major car-manufacturing countries in the EU, notably Germany and France,

harmonise European design law to establish a Europe-wide "repair clause" have been terminated.[60]

Procedural requirements

The Directive does not impose any procedural provisions regarding registration, renewal or invalidity.[61] Thus, it imposes no requirement of examination upon the industrial property offices of the Member States between filing of the design and grant. At present, many of the offices of the Member States do not conduct any examination and to the author's knowledge, none conduct any sort of prior art searching.

5-038

Community Design Regulation

On 12 December 2001, the European Council adopted Reg.6/2002 on the Community Design. The Regulation was published on 5 January 2002[62] and accordingly came into force on 6 March 2002.[63] As previously stated, the Regulation provides for both a registered and a short-lived Community unregistered right. Although the European Community is now called the European Union, there have been no changes to the name of the Community Design Regulation.

5-039

As with the Directive, the Regulation is not intended to affect other intellectual property laws applicable to designs that Member States have, e.g. unregistered designs, trade marks or other distinctive signs, patents and utility models, typefaces, civil liability or unfair competition.[64] The UK unregistered design right is rather different to the Community Unregistered Design right and protects both internal and external features, whether visible or not, and is concerned with the shape and configuration of a product but does not protect surface decoration on a product (which is seen as the concern of copyright law). Thus, one may still obtain greater protection for an industrial design under UK law than under the Regulation. In particular, the UK unregistered design right lasts for 10 years.

5-040

Unlike the Design Directive, which did not harmonise the laws relating to the supply of spare parts, the Regulation does provide for a specific "spare parts" defence where such are supplied for the purpose of repair of a complex part so as to restore its original appearance.[65] This was intended to be a transitional provision pending a Commission proposal but as discussed above in relation to the Directive, the Commission proposal has now been withdrawn and thus 13 years later, this "transitional" provision remains.

5-041

Registered Community Design

The Community Design is a unitary right effective throughout the entire EU. In this respect, it is similar to the CTM. The substantive conditions for validity and

5-042

---

were opposed to the proposal. It has been said that the proposal is not compliant with art.26(2) TRIPS—see A.G. de Borja, "Exceptions to design rights: the potential impact of Article 26(2) TRIPS" (2008) 30(12) EIPR, 500–508.

[60] Withdrawal of obsolete Commission Proposals [2014] OJ C153/6.

[61] Directive 98/71/EC Recital 6.

[62] Reg.6/2002 on Community Designs [2002] OJ L3/1 amended to give effect to the accession of the EU to the Geneva Act of the Hague Agreement (Council Regulation 1891/2006 of 18 December 2006 OJ EC No L386 of 29 December 2006, p.14)—see para.5-017.

[63] Reg.6/2002 art.111.

[64] art.96.

[65] This is discussed at para.5-177.

infringement are essentially the same and are intended to be the same as that in the Design Directive.[66] It is therefore convenient to deal with them together.[67] If there are any differences, these are highlighted. There are some provisions unique to the Community Design and these are dealt with at the end of this chapter.

5-043   The Community Design is administered by EUIPO in a broadly similar manner to the EU Trade Mark. There is little substantive examination (none on novelty or individual character) although a limited number of procedural objections can be raised.[68] Moreover, the Regulation does not provide for a pre-grant opposition unlike an application for a EU Trade Mark. The Community Design has a maximum protection period of 25 years subject to the payment of renewal fees every five years.

5-044   EUIPO also administers an Invalidity Section (together with Boards of Appeal) permitting a third party to challenge the validity of the right and there is now a small but growing body of case law. A further appeal lies to the General Court and, ultimately, there is a yet further tier of appeal to the Court of Justice of the European Union.

Unregistered Community Design

5-045   As noted in the recitals to the Regulation, certain sectors produce a large number of designs which have a short market life. In such circumstances, it was felt that there was a need for protection without the burden of registration formalities.[69] Accordingly, the Regulation also provides for an Unregistered Community Design ("UCD") which confers protection for designs for three years as from the date on which they were first made available in the EU to the public without the need for registration.[70] In contrast to the Community Design, the right only extends to preventing the *copying* of the design. Independently created designs will not infringe the UCD.[71]

Common provisions under the Directive/Regulation

Fundamental requirements

5-046   The basic (cumulative) requirements for a Community Design or national registered design of a Member State are set out over a number of Articles. They are expressed in both positive and negative terms. They are:

   (a)   the application is for a "design" with the meaning of the Directive/Regulation[72];
   (b)   the design is novel[73];

---

[66]   Reg.6/2002, Recital 9.
[67]   See next section.
[68]   See para.5-192.
[69]   Recital 16.
[70]   Reg.6/2002 arts 1(2) and 11. It should be noted that the right only starts from the date when it was made publicly available within the Community. In this respect it is different to, for example, most systems of copyright protection and the UK unregistered right, where protection begins automatically upon creation.
[71]   Dir.98/71/EC art.19(2).
[72]   Dir.98/71/EC art.11(1)(a); Reg.6/2002 art.25(1)(a).
[73]   Dir.98/71/EC arts 11(2)(b), 3(2), 4; Reg.6/2002 arts 25(1)(b), 4(1), 5.

(c)   the design possesses individual character[74];

(d)   the design does not consist of features dictated solely by their technical function[75];

(e)   the design is not a mechanical interface[76];

(f)   the design is not contrary to public policy or morality[77]; and

(g)   the applicant for the design is entitled to it (under the law of the Member State concerned).[78]

Furthermore, it is necessary to consider the requirements for a UCD (insofar as they are different). These requirements are now considered in more detail.

5-047

"Design" within the meaning of the Directive/Regulation

Provision

Article 1 Directive/art.3 Regulation
A "design" is defined as:

5-048

"... the appearance of the whole or a part of a *product* resulting from the features of, in particular, the lines, contours, colours, shape, texture and/or materials of the product itself and/or its ornamentation."[79]

"Product" is defined as:

"... any industrial or handicraft item, including inter alia parts intended to be assembled into a complex product, packaging, get-up, graphic symbols and typographic typefaces, but excluding computer programs."[80]

Commentary

It can be seen from the above that the definition of what is registrable as a design is extremely wide. No distinction is drawn between aesthetic or functional items.[81] The decisive factor for a design under the Regulation is its appearance.[82] As regards what products may be the subject of a Community Design, this is plainly very wide. Indeed, the exclusion of "computer programs" says much about what is a product and thus what is a protectable design. A computer program cannot be seen whereas the other items listed in the definition of "product" can be seen. The primary thrust of the definitions is that anything which is capable of having an "appearance" can be registered, however abstract or concrete it is. Indeed the only real suggestion of what might not be registrable in EUIPO's Invalidity Manual[83] is where the design displays inconsistent products or "mere representations of nature (landscapes, fruits,

5-049

[74]   Dir.98/71/EC arts 11(2)(b), 3(2), 5; Reg.6/2002 arts 25(1)(b), 4(1), 6.

[75]   Dir.98/71/EC arts 11(2)(b), 7(1); Reg.6/2002 arts 25(1)(b), 8(1).

[76]   Dir.98/71/EC arts 11(2)(b), 7(2); Reg.6/2002 arts 25(1)(b), 8(2).

[77]   Dir.98/71/EC arts 11(2)(b), 8; Reg.6/2002 arts 25(1)(b).

[78]   Reg.6/2002 art.25(1)(c).

[79]   Dir.98/71/EC art.1(a); Reg.6/2002 art.3(a).

[80]   Dir.98/71/EC art.1(b); Reg.6/2002 art.3(b).

[81]   Recital 10, Reg.6/2002; Recital 14, Dir.98/71/EC Recital 14.

[82]   *DOCERAM GmbH v CeraTec GmbH* (C-395/16) ECLI:EU:C:2018:172 at [25].

[83]   The *Manual concerning the Examination of Design Invalidity Applications* (can be found at:// https :euipo.europa.eu [Accessed 14 December 2017]).

animals, etc.)".[84] This is even where the design of, e.g. a fruit is very unusual. Thus, an application to register a heart-shaped tomato failed as it was not the result of a manual or industrial process.[85]

Trade marks and designs

5-050   Legal advisors will realise that the inclusion in the definition of a product of get-up and graphic symbols means that many trade marks will be capable of being registered as registered designs. It is an interesting point as to whether a word per se falls within the definition of "product". It might be said that a word is a concept (even if capable of being visibly displayed) which is not the product of creative hands rather than a product to which a design has been applied for (which is finally the work of creative hands). Therefore, a device mark or a special typographical arrangement of a word is the work of creative hands but a word mark is not the work of creative hands, thus no "appearance". Furthermore, it is difficult to define a word mark per se as an industrial or handicraft item (although the same could be said of graphic symbols and get-up). If a word mark per se is registrable, the protection will lie in the visual representation of the word and not its aural or conceptual connotations.[86] It should be noted that the word mark would have to be a nonsense word as otherwise the requirements of novelty would not be made out (see below).[87]

Literary and artistic works and designs

5-051   Clearly, under the scheme, one could obtain a Community design for an artistic painting. This would prevent people from replicating the painting even if they did not copy it. More interesting, a literary work may be registrable as a registered design. Whilst it is unlikely that this would be done, because copyright protection generally affords considerably longer protection than a registered design, there is no reason why the appearance of a book could not include the appearance and layout of words in that book. A designer may come up with a novel way of structuring the layout of words in books (i.e. using indentation, bullet points, justification, etc.) which would be capable of registration.

Character merchandising and designs

5-052   Again under the scheme, there would seem no reason why one could not register the picture of a cartoon character, e.g. for the purpose of character merchandising. It is clear that two-dimensional objects are registerable under the scheme and such is analogous to get-up and graphic symbol. This is important to advisors because there may be difficulties in registering cartoon characters as trade marks because the public do not necessarily see them as badges of origin and, thus, they are inher-

---

[84]   s.C.1. Clearly here the objection is that representations of nature are not industrial or handicraft items which envisage some degree of human intervention and/or creation.
[85]   R-595/2012-3 *Groente en fruit*, at [11]. Plant breeders would disagree with this analysis as the creation of new breeds or varieties of plants is very much the result of breeders deliberately crossing one variety with another by cross-pollination.
[86]   This is different from the protection afforded to trade marks under trade mark legislation—see Ch.3.
[87]   Alternatively, it could be a word in a language which is not European or familiar to Europeans–see the section on novelty at para.5-059.

ently undistinctive.[88] Moreover, the advantage of registering a cartoon character as a registered design is that it gives protection to the application of the design on any product. In trade marks, one must specify the goods or services for which one is seeking protection. However, the protection afforded may be limited if the decision in *Baena Grupo v OHIM* is followed since in that case similar cartoon characters were found to have different individual characteristics.[89] Registered designs are not as good for protecting concepts.

Buildings, cities and other large items and designs

It is somewhat unclear whether the definition of a product would cover large   **5-053**
constructions like the design of the fascia of a building. It is difficult to say that a building is an industrial or handicraft item without doing violence to these words. Thus, the design of the layout of a park might be registrable but again, it is difficult to say that such is an industrial item or handicraft item despite its wide definition.

Parts and component parts

The scheme permits the registration of the appearance of the whole or part of a   **5-054**
product. However, if the design is applied to or incorporated in a product which constitutes a component part of a complex product,[90] it is only considered to be new and have individual character if the component part, once incorporated into the complex product, remains visible during normal use of the complex product (which means use by the end user excluding maintenance, servicing or repair work).[91] The practical effect of this can be considered in relation to a car. It permits the registration of the design of the whole car, the design of any part of the car (i.e. the bonnet plus bumper plus front wheel arch of the car), the front door, the wing mirror, the steering wheel, or the gear stick. It would not permit the registration of oil filters, fan belts and engine parts.[92]

The cases indicate that component part is being given a fairly broad meaning taking   **5-055**
little regard of the definition of "complex product" relating to replacement, disassembly and reassembly. Some scope has been allowed for argument as to the visibility requirement. For example in *Kwang Yang Motor v OHIM*,[93] the General Court held that the engine of a lawnmower was visible in ordinary use (such use consisting of the user pushing the mower from behind). Moreover, the court held that the features most easily visible (the top) chiefly contributed to the assessment of individual character. However, in *Electrical Contactors*[94] the Board of Appeal invalidated the registration of an electrical component since it would have to be

---

[88] See Ch.3. See also, J. Adams, J. Hickey and G. Tritton, *Merchandising Intellectual Property*, 3rd edn (London: Tottel/Bloomsbury Publishing, 2007).

[89] *Baena Grupo v OHIM* (T-513/09) [2010] E.C.R. II-239 upheld on appeal *Neuman and Galdeano del Sel v Jose Manuel Baena* (C-101/11P) ECLI:EU:C:2012:641. This case concerned a comparison of an earlier EU trade mark with an application for a registered design.

[90] Complex product is defined as "a product which is composed of multiple components which can be replaced permitting disassembly and reassembly of the product." (Dir.98/71/EC art.1(c), art.3(c) Regulation).

[91] Dir.98/71/EC art.3(3), (4).

[92] See Press Announcement by Mario Monti, Single Market Commissioner, 13 March 1997.

[93] *Kwang Yang Motor v OHIM* (T-10/08) [2011] E.C.R. II-265.

[94] *Albright France (SARL) v Schaltbau GmbH* R1052.2008–3.

within a housing for safety reasons, dismissing the argument that such housing could be transparent as hypothetical. It should be noted that that even where the component could be visible during normal use, if aesthetic considerations played no part in the design of the component part, then based upon the current law, a "technical function" objection may be applicable to the registration of the design.[95] The reason for exclusion of protection of component parts which are not visible during normal use has been explained that in such circumstances, no aesthetic considerations would have played a part in their design.[96]

Subsistence of Community unregistered design right

Provision

5-056
Article 85(2)
"**2.** In proceedings in respect of an infringement action or an action for threatened infringement of an unregistered Community design, the Community design court shall treat the Community design as valid if the right holder produces proof that the conditions laid down in Article 11 have been met and indicates what constitutes the individual character of his Community design. However, the defendant may contest its validity by way of a plea or with a counterclaim for a declaration of invalidity."

Commentary

5-057   In the case of registered designs, the certificate of registration is all that is required to prove that the right subsists. However, in the case of Community unregistered design right, is it sufficient merely to assert that one has such a right? This was considered by the CJEU in *Karen Millen*.[97] The Irish courts referred to the CJEU the question as to the meaning of art.85(2). For completeness' sake, art.11 which is referred to in art.85(2), states that a design which meets the requirements of s.1 (i.e. novelty and distinctive character) is protected as an unregistered design for a period of three years from the date on which the design was first made available to the public within the Community.

5-058   The CJEU held that it is not necessary for the right holder of the design to prove that the design has individual character but need only indicate what constitutes the individual character of the design, i.e. what, in right holder's view, are the element or elements of the design concerned with which gives it its individual character.[98] In the authors' view, this is right. It is impossible to prove a negative, i.e. that the design in issue has distinctive character over *all* prior art which will very rarely be known to the designer. Thus, provided that the designer of the design indicates in their view what are the elements which confer individual character over the prior art, then the defendant may focus on those in seeking to determine whether there is prior art that invalidates the claim of unregistered Community design. This requirement is fair because in the case of registered designs, the applicant will apply for a graphic representation of the design for which it is seeking protection. This representation will determine whether the applicant is seeking protection for the whole or part of a product and whether it is purely the shape of the design or also

---

[95] See para.5-114.
[96] See para.5-123 and *Lindner Recycling*, at [34].
[97] (C-345/13) ECLI:EU:C:2014:2013.
[98] See [47].

includes colour, ornamentation, etc.[99] Thus, it is only fair that the designer who asserts Community unregistered design right identifies the design features for which they seek protection. It is of course possible that if prior art is identified by the defendant that suggests that the chosen elements do not confer individual character on the design, the designer may choose to identify other elements to overcome such an attack (in other words, change their initial view as to what elements of the design confer individual character). Whether such is permissible is probably a matter for the procedural laws of the Member State of the Community Design Court.

Novelty

Provision

Article 4 Directive

"A design shall be considered new if no identical design has been made available to the public before the date of filing of the application for registration or, if priority is claimed, the date of priority. Designs shall be deemed to be identical if their features differ only in immaterial details.

2. Designs shall be deemed to be identical if their features differ only in immaterial details." **5-059**

Article 5 Regulation

"**1.** A design shall be considered to be new if no identical design has been made available to the public: **5-060**

    (a)   in the case of an unregistered Community design, before the date on which the design for which protection is claimed has first been made available to the public;

    (b)   in the case of a registered Community design, before the date of filing of the application for registration of the design for which protection is claimed, or, if priority is claimed, the date of priority."

Commentary

It is not considered that such a requirement of novelty will give rise to particular difficulty, as most Member States are familiar to a similar requirement in their domestic laws. Significantly, however, the definition of "novel" is extended beyond its usual meaning (or at least its meaning in the law of patents) as designs are deemed to be "identical" in the event that their features differ only in immaterial details (although this would seem to encroach on the territory of individual character). As the requirements of novelty and individual character both need to be satisfied and the latter is more difficult to satisfy than novelty, the exact meaning of novelty is likely to be of little legal significance[100] although in *Nail Files* the Board of Appeal used the rider to invalidate a design on the basis of novelty where there was "a hardly noticeable difference in detail."[101] Finally it should be noted that **5-061**

---

[99] See para.5-192 as to the requirements of graphic representation in an application for a Community design.

[100] Indeed the Board of Appeal noted as much on R0887/2008–3 *Normann Copenhagen ApS v Paton Calvert Housewares Ltd ("Colanders")* at s.24. NB. Here the prior art was a published European patent application.

[101] *Vera Sindelarova v Blazek Glass s.r.o.* R0921/2008–3.

features of component parts of complex products which are not normally visible in normal use are deemed not to be novel and have individual character.[102]

Community Unregistered Design Right and prior use outside the EU

5-062   In respect of the Community unregistered right, the German courts have identified an interesting discrepancy between provisions concerning commencement of the protection term (first availability within the Community) and the assessment of novelty (assessed in relation to availability anywhere). In this case, the design in question (the "Ab Swing") in which UCD was claimed, had been sold and advertised in the USA (June 2002) prior to the date when the design was made available in the EU for the first time (October 2002). The court held (rightly) that a design is deemed to have been made available to the public if it has been made public under art.7 of the Regulation and that it is irrelevant where the disclosure occurred.[103] However, it then held that the Community design lacked novelty within the meaning of art.5. It said that prior to the date when the design had for the first time been made available to the public; an "identical design" had already been made available to the public in the USA.[104] It would appear that the claimant argued that their own prior use in USA did not destroy novelty but merely shifted the commencement period to an earlier date, e.g. June 2002. However, this argument was rejected.[105]

5-063   Is this decision right? It would clearly be problematic for non-European companies who are more likely to first disclose in a non-EU country and potentially discriminatory. Article 5 stipulates that a design shall be considered new if no identical design, in the case of a UCD, "before the date on which the design for which protection is claimed has been first made available to the public". This is also the relevant date for determining whether there has been prior disclosure of the design under art.7. In both cases, neither provision differentiates between the EU and other parts of the world. Thus, there is symmetry between these two provisions. On the other hand, the *commencement of the term of protection of a UCD* starts from the date on which the design was first made available to the public within the Community (art.11). The error of the German court appears to be that it held that the date for determining novelty was October 2002, i.e. the date when protection was alleged to have commenced.[106] There appears to be have no argument that the date for determining the novelty of the design is a *different* date to the determination of the date when protection under the Regulation starts. In the authors' view, there is no reason why the determination of the date for novelty of an unregistered design should not be a different date to the date for determining the commencement of the three-year period for protection of the alleged UCD. Indeed the wording of art.11 makes it clear that the conditions for subsistence of UCD are to be found in Section 1 of the Regulation whereas art.11 is found in Section 2. Thus, applying normal principles of interpretation, the issue of subsistence is not to be

---

[102] See para.5-054.

[103] *Re Thane International Group's Application* O 5/04, Landgericht (Germany) (3/12) [2006] E.C.D.R. 8 at [12]. See however para.5-092.

[104] See [14].

[105] See [17].

[106] e.g. see [9] of the decision where the court appears not to distinguish between when the design was made available to the public and when it was first advertised and sold within the EU. This may be because of how the "Ab Swing" party put its argument.

determined by reference to art.11 itself which is only concerned with the period of protection and not subsistence.[107]

Individual character

Provision

Article 5 Directive

"**1.** A design shall be considered to have individual character if the overall impression it produces on the informed user differs from the overall impression produced on such a user by any design which has been made available to the public before the date of filing of the application for registration or, if priority is claimed, the date of priority.

2. In assessing individual character, the degree of freedom of the designer in developing the design shall be taken into consideration."

5-064

Article 6 Regulation

"A design shall be considered to have individual character if the overall impression it produces on the informed user differs from the overall impression produced on such a user by any design which has been made available to the public:

    (a)   in the case of an unregistered Community design, before the date on which the design for which protection is claimed has first been made available to the public;

    (b)   in the case of a registered Community design, before the date of filing the application for registration or, if a priority is claimed, the date of priority.

2. In assessing individual character, the degree of freedom of the designer in developing the design shall be taken into consideration."

5-065

Commentary

This requirement breaks new territory and would seem to have no basis in the laws of any of the Member States. Whilst "overall impression" is a nebulous concept, courts are familiar with applying such concepts in a robust manner.[108] There is already a body of (somewhat contradictory) first instance case law before EUIPO as to ambit of individual character, but the overall theme is that it is not a particularly high hurdle to satisfy. The requirement of individual character is also referred to in the recitals to the Regulation. Recital 14 states:

5-066

"The assessment as to whether a design has individual character should be based on whether the overall impression produced on an *informed user* viewing the design clearly differs from that produced on him by the *existing design corpus*, taking into consideration the nature of the product to which the design is applied or in which it is incorporated, and in particular the industrial sector to which it belongs and the degree of freedom of the designer in developing the design." [Emphasis supplied.]

It is necessary to consider a number of concepts. What is meant by the "informed user"? What is the approach to the determination of individual character? What is

5-067

---

[107] Another point in favour of this approach is that it should be noted that art.11(2) which sets out when a design has been made available to the public within the Community for the purpose of art.11(1) in essence replicates art.7(1). Such would be unnecessary if art.11 is concerned with the issue of prior art as well as duration of protection.

[108] Thus, it could be said to be no more difficult to apply than the test of "likelihood of confusion" in trade marks.

the meaning of design corpus? How should the degree of freedom of the designer be taken into account? These are now considered.

Informed user

5-068   It is important to emphasise that it is not the judge's personal overall impression but the impression on the "informed user". Thus, hypothetically, courts should always come to the same conclusion. It is possible that an expert will be required to give evidence in this area, since the "informed user" will often not be the everyday public. Thus, in esoteric fields, expert evidence would need to be established.[109] However, even in everyday fields such as cars, an informed user will a fortiori know more about the subject than the everyday uninformed user. Thus, it may not be sufficient to show mere confusion in the marketplace because it could be argued that the informed user would be more astute to notice differences.

5-069   The CJEU said in *PepsiCo*[110]:

> "[53]   It should be noted, first, that Regulation No 6/2002 does not define the concept of the 'informed user'. However, as the Advocate General correctly observed in points 43 and 44 of his Opinion, that concept must be understood as lying somewhere between that of the average consumer, applicable in trade mark matters, who need not have any specific knowledge and who, as a rule, makes no direct comparison between the trade marks in conflict, and the sectorial expert, who is an expert with detailed technical expertise. Thus, the concept of the informed user may be understood as referring, not to a user of average attention, but to a particularly observant one, either because of his personal experience or his extensive knowledge of the sector in question[111]
>
> ...
>
> [57]   Thirdly, as regards the informed user's level of attention, it should be noted that, although the informed user is not the well-informed and reasonably observant and circumspect average consumer who normally perceives a design as a whole and does not proceed to analyse its various details (see, by analogy, Case C-342/97 *Lloyd Schuhfabrik Meyer* [1999] ECR I-3819, paragraphs 25 and 26), he is also not an expert or specialist capable of observing in detail the minimal differences that may exist between the designs in conflict."

5-070   The court in *PepsiCo* also stated that although the informed user will normally make a direct comparison between the designs at issue (unlike the average consumer in trade mark law), they may not where such is impracticable or uncommon, thereby hinting that the concept of imperfect recollection (familiar from trademark law) might be applicable.[112] It gave no guidance as to which test might be more appropriate or the extent to which it would depend on the overall circumstances pertaining to the use of the design.

5-071   Following this decision, the General Court has considered the concept of "informed user" in a number of cases. It has said that it is settled law that an informed user is a person who is particularly observant and who has some awareness of the prior art. That is to say, the corpus of previous designs relating to the product in question that had been made available to the public as of the date of fil-

---

[109] For example, the UK case of *Woodhouse v Architectural Lighting Systems (t/a Aquila Designs)* [2006] E.C.D.R. 11; [2006] R.P.C. 1 concerned street lamps and evidence was heard from designers in the field.

[110] *PepsiCo v Grupo Promer Mon Graphic* (C-281/10P) [2011] E.C.R. I-10153.

[111] See [53].

[112] See [55].

ing of the contested design.[113] Thus, in *Antrax*, which concerned radiators, the Board of Appeal defined the informed user as being someone who buys radiators for heating in order to install them in their home and who, "without being an expert in industrial design (as an architect or an interior decorator would be), is aware of what the market offers, fashion trends and the basic features of the product".[114]

In *Sphere Time v OHIM*,[115] the General Court held that there could be more than one category of informed user. That case concerned a lanyard and the court found that the informed users were both the "average consumer" and the professional buyer. Somewhat fortuitously, the court held that the overall impression to both groups would be the same, permitting it to give no guidance whatsoever as to the consequences had this not been the case.   **5-072**

If a design has been determined in accordance with the Design Regulation, as having been made available to the public and is thus relevant prior art, it is irrelevant that the informed user would not have known of that design when assessing individual character.[116] Thus, as said by the CJEU, when a design has been made available to the public within the meaning of art.7(1) Design Regulation, that disclosure is valid for the assessment of both novelty and individual character.[117]   **5-073**

Individual character

The test for individual character requires as a starting point a single individual design, it being impermissible to draw on a number of earlier designs in order to combine features.[118] The comparison is design for design.   **5-074**

The General Court has said that individual character of a design: **5-075**

> "[52] ... results from an overall impression of difference or lack of 'déjà vu', from the point of view of an informed user, in relation to any previous presence in the design corpus, without taking account of any differences that are insufficiently significant to affect that overall impression, even though they may be more than insignificant details, but taking account of differences that are sufficiently marked so as to produce dissimilar overall impressions."[119]

In assessing individual character it seems that all features of the design are not treated equally. In *Shenzhen Taiden*[120] the General Court held that the informed user should be assumed to be using the product in accordance with the purpose for which that product was intended. Perhaps following similar reasoning in *Kwang Yang/*   **5-076**

---

[113] *Antrax It Srl v EUIPO* (T-828/14 & T-829/14) ECLI:EU:T:2017:87 at 53 and case law cited therein.

[114] *Antrax*, at [57]. This definition was not contested on appeal.

[115] (T-68/10) [2011] E.C.R. II-2775.

[116] *Easy Sanitary Solutions BV v EUIPO* (C-361/15P and C-405/15P) ECLI:EU:C:2017:720 at [125]–[134].

[117] *Easy Sanitary Solutions BV v EUIPO* (C-361/15P and C-405/15P) ECLI:EU:C:2017:720 at [128].

[118] *Karen Millen Fashions v Dunnes Stores* (C-345/13) ECLI:EU:C:2014:2013 at [35]. It should be noted that under art.25(1) TRIPS, it is an optional feature as to whether combinations of prior art should be considered when considering the registration of a design—see para.5-011 and fn.24. See also *Easy Sanitary Solutions BV v EUIPO* (C-361/15P and C-405/15P), at [61] (assessment must be by reference to "one or more specific, individualised, defined and identified designs from among all the designs which have been made available to the public previously...".).

[119] *Budziewska v OHIM – Puma SE (Bounding Feline)* (T-666/11) EU:T:2013:584 at [29] and case law cited thereto. This case has been cited several times in other General Court cases, e.g. *Antrax*, at [53]; *Ball Beverage Packaging Europe Ltd v EUIPO* (T-9/15), at [78]; *Thomas Murphy v EUIPO* (T-90/16), at [43].

[120] (T-153/08) [2010] E.C.R. II-2517.

Internal Combustion Engine,[121] the General Court held that it was legitimate to give more emphasis to the top of the engine since this was the part most easily visible to the user in ordinary use (pushing from behind). *Baena Group*[122] concerned two cartoon characters which were remarkably similar save in their facial expressions one of which was angry and the other non-committal. The General Court held that the informed user (young people and children) would see the differences as especially important (e.g. when customising objects) leading to a finding of different overall impression. Also, in *Grupo Promer*, the CJEU said that as regards the assessment of the overall impression produced by the designs at issue on the informed user, the latter will automatically disregard elements that are totally banal and common to all examples of the type of product in issue and will concentrate on features that are arbitrary or different from the norm.[123] Conversely, as said by the English court, the greater the difference that the design feature has from the norm, the more weight to be attached to it.[124]

5-077   It should be noted that the scope of protection afforded by a registered design extends to designs which do not give an overall different impression. Thus, the registrability requirement is the same as the scope of protection.[125] This symmetry means that a design which constitutes prior art for the purpose of the Directive should not be able to infringe a registered design without at the same time, invalidating the registration.

Design corpus

5-078   The familiarity of the informed user with the designs of products on the marketplace as of the relevant date—often called the design corpus—is also relevant. The design corpus is referred to in Recital 14 of the Regulation as being a matter to be taken into account when considering individual character. In *Grupo Promer*, the CJEU said that the informed user is particularly observant and has some awareness of the prior art, that is to say the previous designs relating to the product in question that have been disclosed on the date of filing of the contested design.[126] The CJEU continued by saying that the informed user had a certain degree of knowledge with regards to features which the designs normally include and as a result of the informed user's interest in the products concerned, shows a relatively high degree of attention when they use them.[127] The reference to the products in questions means those of the products that the design relates to. Generally, in most cases, there will be no difficulty in identifying the products to which the design relates to. However, in certain cases, where this is not obvious, e.g. where the design is ornamental and capable of being used on a wide variety of products, this is more problematic. It might be thought that the indication in the application for the registration of design is relevant but such does not affect the scope of protection of the design.[128] In English proceedings, it has been said that whilst prior art in a different field to that for which the design is registered is still prior art, conversely,

---

[121] *Kwang Yang Motor v OHIM* (T-10/08) [2011] E.C.R. II-265.
[122] (T-513/09) [2011] E.C.R. II-289.
[123] See [74].
[124] See [52], *Apple v Samsung* [2013] E.C.D.R. 1.
[125] See para.5-155 on infringement.
[126] See [62].
[127] At [59]. See also *Shenzhen* (T-153/08) [2010] E.C.R. II-2517.
[128] art.36(6) of the Regulation. In *Grupo Promer*, the General Court held that the indication of goods should be taken into account but also the design itself insofar as it makes clear the nature of the

when considering what designs the informed user is aware of (the design corpus), the user will not be aware of products different in nature to that for which the design is registered.[129]

What is the effect of the design corpus on the informed user when determining individual character? Care must be taken here when considering whether one design has individual character over another design. The comparison is as said above, one design to another design. Therefore, it is not possible to mix up various features of the prior art design with other design features in the design corpus. For instance, if a registered design consists of a coat with a striking design combined with an unusual upturned collar and the cited prior art design was of a coat with the same striking design but without the unusual upturned collar, it would not be legitimate to say that in the design corpus that there were many instances of upturned collars on coats of different designs and thus the later design lacked individual character.[130] Rather, the design corpus is merely a "background" factor taken into account by the informed user when comparing two designs.

5-079

However, in the clothing/fashion world, it may be that the latest trend is to have backless blue dresses with an asymmetrical curving hemline. This would mean that there may be many dresses in the design corpus which, whilst all subscribing to this trend, differ in more minor ways. For example, the shade of blue, the degree of backlessness and the precise design of the hemline. The informed user would know of this trend and these dresses and would therefore attribute more importance to minor design variations between a registered design and a prior art design which both follow this trend. They would be more ready to see the two designs as having a different overall impression. Conversely, if there was no such trend, then the informed user may consider that two backless blue dresses with asymmetrical hemlines create an overall impression which is the same.

5-080

In *Antrax IT Srl v EUIPO*[131] the General Court said:

5-081

> "[54] In the assessment of the individual character of a design in relation to any previous presence in the design corpus, account must be taken of the nature of the product to which the design is applied or in which it is incorporated, in particular the industrial sector to which it belongs (recital 14 of Regulation No 6/2002), *the degree of freedom of the designer in developing the design, whether there is saturation of the state of the art, which could be capable of making the informed user more attentive to the differences in the designs compared*, and also the manner in which the product at issue is used, in particular according to the manner in which it is normally handled when used (see judgment of 7 November 2013, *Bounding feline*, T-666/11, not published, EU:T:2013:584, paragraph 31 and the case-law cited).
>
> [55] Although saturation of the state of the art cannot be said to limit the freedom of the designer, it may, once proven, make the user more attentive to the differences

---

product, its intended purpose or function. The English courts have interpreted this as meaning that the product in question could belong to a narrower category than the indication of goods (*Dyson* [2011] EWCA Civ 1206 at [55]; *Gimex International Groupe Imports Export v Chill Bag Company Ltd* [2012] E.C.D.R. 31 at [63]).

[129] *Gimex*, at [65]. In that case, the registered design was for an ice bucket bag whereas the prior art was a bag used to carry wine bottles. The prior art was considered in relation to an attack based on lack of individual character but it was not considered to form part of the design corpus that the informed user would be aware of. The fact that the prior art was a bag and not a bottle chiller seems to have caused the judge to attribute more significance to the visual differences than if both had been for a bottle chiller —see [115].

[130] See para.5-074.

[131] (T-828/14 & T-829/14) ECLI:EU:T:2017:87.

of detail between the conflicting designs. Consequently, a design may, *due to saturation of the state of the art*, have individual character resulting from features which, *in the absence of saturation*, would not tend to give rise to a different overall impression for an informed user (see, to that effect, judgments of 12 March 2014, *Tubes Radiatori v OHIM —Antrax It (Radiator)*, T-315/12, not published, EU:T:2014:115, paragraph 87 and the case-law cited, and 29 October 2015, *Roca Sanitario v OHIM —Villeroy & Boch (Single control handle faucet)*, T-334/14, not published, EU:T:2015:817, paragraph 83)." [Emphasis supplied.]

5-082   As made clear in this decision, the issue of whether the designer's freedom is restricted (which is considered in the next section) is a separate issue to what is often called the "saturation"/"crowded field" argument set out above. Thus, in *Antrax*, there was no suggestion that the designer's freedom was restricted by technical or legal constraints—the designs were for radiators which can take many shapes. However, whilst the "crowded field" issue and the freedom of the designer are two separate issues—both of which must be considered independent of each other when considering whether the design has individual character over the prior art—it is often the case that a "crowded field" prior art will have been caused by a lack of freedom of the designer caused by technical or legal constraints.

5-083   Rather, a crowded field is caused by an aesthetic or commercial straitjacket, e.g. the need to follow a particular fashion trend. After all, if one looks at the history of fashion from Greek times, one can see that there are very many ways of clothing the human form. Compared to such, Western 21st century fashion can be seen as very narrow in the scope and variety of its designs. Yet, when it comes to comparing two modern Western clothing designs to determine whether one has individual character over the other, the design corpus will clearly be that of Western 21st century fashion rather than all designs of clothing since ancient times. In doing so, the informed user will attribute significance to design variants which would be insignificant when considered against all designs of clothing since olden times.

5-084   In order to support conclusions drawn from the assessment of the designs, when considering the issue of individual character, it is legitimate for a court or tribunal to take into account (in order to compare designs), products marketed which correspond to the designs, for illustrative purposes.[132] However, care must be taken to ensure that the product does correspond to the design and that this information is provided to the tribunal.[133] It may also be legitimate to take account of how a product represented by the design is used. Thus, in the case of lever-action corkscrews which were designed to fold up, the General Court held that the Board of Appeal could not be criticised for having taken account of the impression produced by the designs on the informed user when the corkscrews in question were closed.[134]

Freedom of designer

5-085   The freedom of the designer is a factor to be taken into account when determining individual character. The greater the freedom of the designer, the less likely that

---

[132] *PepsiCo v Grupo Promer Mon Graphic* (C-281/10P) EU:C:2011:679 at [73]–[74].
[133] *Thomas Murphy v EUIPO* (T-90/16) ECLI:EU:T:2017:464 at [53]–[54].
[134] *El Hogar Perfecto del Siglo XXI, SL v OHIM* (T-337/12) ECLI:EU:T:2013:601 at [46] and cases cited there.

minor differences will suffice to create a different overall impression. As said by the General Court in *H&M Hennes & Mauritz v OHIM*[135]:

> "[28] As regards the degree of freedom of the designer of a design, it is apparent from the case-law that that is determined, inter alia, *by the constraints of the features imposed by the technical function of the product or an element thereof, or by statutory requirements applicable to the product.* Those constraints result in a standardisation of certain features, which will thus be common to the designs applied to the product concerned (judgment of 9 September 2011 in *Kwang Yang Motor v OHIM — Honda Giken Kogyo (Internal combustion engine)*, T-11/08, EU:T:2011:447, paragraph 32, and judgment in *Wristwatch* case, cited in paragraph 15 above, EU:T:2013:214, paragraph 112).
>
> [29] Therefore, the greater the designer's freedom in developing a design, the less likely it is that minor differences between the designs at issue will be sufficient to produce different overall impressions on an informed user. Conversely, the more the designer's freedom in developing a design is restricted, the more likely it is that minor differences between the designs at issue will be sufficient to produce different overall impressions on an informed user. *Consequently, if the designer enjoys a high degree of freedom in developing a design, that reinforces the conclusion that designs that do not have significant differences produce the same overall impression on an informed user* (judgments in *Internal combustion engine*, cited in paragraph 28 above, EU:T:2011:447, paragraph 33, and *Wristwatch* case, cited in paragraph 15 above, EU:T:2013:214, paragraph 113)." [Emphasis supplied.]

In the previous section on design corpus, it was said that in a saturated market **5-086** where there were many fashion designs which were close to each other, this was a factor that would be taken account of by the informed user. It will be appreciated that fashion trends do not fall within technical or statutory requirements. Yet indisputably, fashion trends de facto restrict the freedom of a designer. It can hardly be said that a clothes designer in the 21st century has a limitless freedom to design clothing as the history of fashion shows that clothing can take almost any form. The 21st clothes designer will not sell much clothing if they design clothing in a 13th Century style. De facto, the designer is clearly constrained. Thus, in a field where fashion and consumer preference is very marked (e.g. clothing), one might have thought that such arguments should carry weight. For instance, when considering men's clothing, generally men will not wear anything on their legs other than trousers.[136] However, this is clearly a cultural and fashion preference and nothing to do with technical or statutory restraints.

EUIPO take the view that the degree of freedom of the designer is not affected **5-087** by the fact that similar designs co-exist on the market and form a general trend.[137] In a strict sense, this is of course correct. However, as said above, a saturated market whose design corpus is full of similar looking designs is relevant when assessing the overall impression of two designs to the informed user.

Exclusion of unprotected features

As discussed below, certain features are excluded from protection. For instance, **5-088** any feature of a product that is dictated solely by technical function is excluded

---

[135] (T-525/13) ECLI:EU:T:2015:617.
[136] Scotland excepted!
[137] See section 5.5 of the EUIPO Guidelines (Examination of Design Invalidity Applications) citing *Shenzhen Taiden Industrial Co Ltd v OHIM* (T-153/08) [2010] E.C.R. II-2517 at [58].

from protection. Equally, features which are not visible during normal use are excluded from protection.

5-089   Recital 10 of the Regulation makes it clear that such features should not be taken into consideration for the purpose of assessing whether other features of a design fulfil the requirements for protection. Thus, when assessing overall impression of one design over another, the correct approach is to consider only those features of both the registered design and the prior art design which are not excluded from protection.[138]

Prior art

Provision

Article 6 Directive

5-090   Disclosure

"(1)   For the purpose of [novelty and individual character], a design shall be deemed to have been made available to the public if it has been published following registration or otherwise, or exhibited, used in trade or otherwise disclosed, except where these events could not reasonably have become known in the normal course of business to the circles specialised in the sector concerned, operating within the Community, before the date of filing of the application for registration or, if priority is claimed, the date of priority. The design shall not, however, be deemed to have been made available to the public for the sole reason that it has been disclosed to a third person under explicit or implicit conditions of confidentiality.

(2)   A disclosure shall not be taken into consideration for the purpose of applying [the criteria of novelty and distinctive character] if a design for which protection is claimed under a registered design right of a Member State has been made available to the public:

(a)   by the designer, his successor in title, or a third person as a result of information provided or action taken by the designer, or his successor in title; and

(b)   during the 12-month period preceding the date of filing of the application or, if priority is claimed, the date of priority.

(3)   Paragraph 2 shall also apply if the design has been made available to the public as a consequence of an abuse in relation to the designer or his successor in title."

The substantive provisions of art.7 of the Regulation are the same.[139]

Commentary

5-091   This provision identifies what is the prior art for the purpose of determining novelty and individual character. It should be noted that the emphasis is on whether the design has been made available and not a product incorporating the design.

---

[138]   e.g. see *Easy Sanitary Solutions BV v EUIPO* (C-361/15P) ECLI:EU:C:2017:720, at [25] where EUIPO, when considering whether a design for a a shower drain consisting of a plate, collector and a siphon was validly registered over cited prior art, declared that the only visible feature during normal use was the top of the plate and thus, the only feature to be taken into account when determining the validity of the design over the prior art. See also *Single control handle faucet* (T-334/14) EU:T:2015:817 at [58]; *Thomas Murphy v EUIPO* (T-90/16), at [55].

[139]   art.7 identifies the relevant dates and that such are different in the case of registered and unregistered Community design.

Thus, the comparison is design to design. It is debatable whether art.6(1) is compatible with TRIPS—see para.5-015.

Known to circles specialised in the sector concerned operating within the Community

Article 6(1) excludes prior art which could not have reasonably have become known in the normal course of business to the circles specialised in the sector concerned, operating within the EU. This exception makes it clear that the test of novelty is not akin to the test for novelty under European patent law where any worldwide disclosure is relevant regardless of the degree of public knowledge of that disclosure. The *travaux préparatoires* say that the intention is to avoid the situation where design rights can be invalidated by infringers claiming that antecedent designs can be found in remote places or museums.[140] As said by the Board of Appeal in commenting on this provision:

> "[38] The Board notes first of all that the definition of prior art in patent law and of a prior design are not the same. Absolute novelty in patent law is far-reaching. However, as to designs, the intention of the legislator was to introduce a 'common sense' limitation to temper the harshness of absolute novelty, in the form of a safeguard clause.[141]"

It is debateable why the test for novelty should be less stringent for registered designs than for patents. The general principle behind absolute novelty for patents is that one should not get a 20-year monopoly in a technical innovation by merely discovering something that already exists. This approach has much to commend itself in relation to registered designs where the 25-year period of protection actually exceeds that of patents and indeed, the grant of a registered design is a virtual formality. Against this, a registered design does not protect something as fundamental as a technical innovation (and is thus easier to work-around).

Could have become reasonably known

It is important to emphasise that the requirement is not that: (i) the prior art *was* known, or (ii) that it *would* have become known, but whether (iii) it *could* have become *reasonably* known to the specialised circles. Moreover, as said by an English judge, who accepted this argument, such must be in the context of the normal course of business.[142] There could be said to be some difficulty in interpreting this requirement. Technically, any obscure disclosure *could* come to the attention of the specialised circles if sufficient publicity is given to it. Indeed, there is some suggestion in the approach by the General Court and EUIPO that patent and trade mark applications which are published in worldwide official bulletins should, as a matter of default, be considered relevant prior art and are not excluded by this provision.[143] Yet, it is difficult to see why designs in remote places and museums are any more obscure than, e.g. a drawing in a patent application which is published in a Kazakhstani official bulletin for patent applications. Indeed, a person interested

5-092

5-093

5-094

---

140 Explanatory Memorandum to the second draft of the Directive.
141 *Termo Organikia Sp. Z.o.o. v Austrothemr GmbH* (R 1482/2009–3), Third Board of Appeal citing D. Musker, *Community Design Law, Principles and Practice* (London: Sweet & Maxwell, 2002).
142 *Magmatic v PMS International Ltd* [2013] EWHC 1925 at [39], overturned on appeal but on different grounds, *Magmatic v PMS International* [2014] EWCA Civ 181.
143 See para.5-101.

in a design field is more likely to search out designs in Kazakhstani museums than Kazakhstani patent official bulletins. In the author's view, the correct approach is whether it can be said *with reasonable probability* that a person within the specialised circle within the EU *would* have discovered the design in the normal course of business. Thus, if it is normal for a person in circles specialised in a particular field to monitor patent applications published in Kazakhstan as part of their normal business, then the fact that no person had *actually* found the cited design in the Kazakhstan official bulletin would be irrelevant. Conversely, if such monitoring activity was not usual for the specialised circles, then it can be said with reasonable probability that a person within the specialised circle would not have discovered the relevant Kazakhstani patent application cited by a cancellation applicant and the cited patent application would be excluded from consideration as prior art.

Sector concerned?

5-095　The meaning of "sector concerned" in art.6(1) is rather ambiguous. Does it mean the sector from which comes the prior art design relied upon or does it mean the sector from which comes the design applied for? The answer, according to the English court is that it is the sector which consists of or includes the prior art.[144] This would appear to be logical, since the scope of protection is not limited by sector and if the "sector" was the sector that the design was applied for, well known (in at least one sector) prior art would be capable of infringing a subsequent filed Community design—which would be illogical and unfair. Thus, an infringer who sells a product does not restrict what he sells for a particular purpose or to a limited field.[145] Furthermore, as the English Court of Appeal said, such is confirmed in the *travaux préparatoires*. It referred to the fact that the Economic and Social Committee Opinion in 1994 when considering the novelty provision, referred to the problem of sellers of counterfeit textile products often obtaining false certification that the disputed design had already been created in a third country. It accepted an argument that if the application was for teapots and the alleged prior art was for Columbian textiles, it would be the textiles circles in Europe who would be in a position to know whether the certification was genuine and not the teapot circles.[146] However, the Board of Appeal in *Crocs Inc v Holey Sole Holdings* has held that the sector concerned is the one concerned by the challenged design.[147] This observation appears to have been made without any real argument and in that case, both the prior art and the challenged design were the same (in fact, the holder of the design was held to have self-anticipated its own design).

5-096　In September 2017, the Court of Justice in *Easy Sanitary Solutions BV v EUIPO*,[148] on an appeal from the General Court, the Court of Justice held that the "sector concerned" was not limited to that of the product in which the contested design was intended to be incorporated or applied. In doing so, it very much followed the arguments set out above that as protection for a design is not limited to the products in which it is intended to be incorporated in, so the assessment of

---

[144] *Green Lane Products v PMS International Group Ltd* [2007] EWHC 1712 (Pat Ct). This was upheld on appeal, see *Green Lane Products v PMS International Group* [2008] F.S.R. 28.
[145] See *Green Lane*, at [54] (CA).
[146] See [69].
[147] See *Crocs Inc v Holey Sole Holdings Ltd* (R 9/2008–3) [2010] E.C.D.R. 11 at [62].
[148] (C-361/15P & C-405/15P) ECLI:EU:C:2017:720.

novelty of a design must also not be so limited as otherwise, an absurd result would follow.[149]

The effect of this is that a prior art design may be in a different product field to that of the registered design but still be relevant prior art. Of course, it will be rare that a design in the field (other than an ornamental design, e.g. decoration) will be relevant to a different field. For instance, designs for cars are very different to designs for, e.g. tractors. In *Easy Sanitary Solutions*, the facts were somewhat unusual: the design in issue was limited to the design of the top of a plate for a shower drain (the rest being considered irrelevant as it was not visible during normal use) whereas the prior art was a top plate used for drainage of liquid waste.[150]

5-097

Specialised circles

In *H. Gautzch Großhandel GmbH v Munchener Boulevard Mobel Joseph Duna GmbH*,[151] the court had to consider the meaning of "specialised circles". It was considered by the referring court that many people had assumed that the specialised circles did not include traders as a body but rather those involved in creating designs and developing or manufacturing products based on designs.[152] The CJEU rejected this view. It held that no such interpretation could be taken from the concept of "the circles specialised". However, and rather unhelpfully, it said that it is a matter of fact whether the distribution of an unregistered design to traders was sufficient grounds for considering that the design could reasonably have become known in the normal course of business to the circles specialised in the sector.[153] It is tempting, although art.11(2) of the Regulation does not refer to it, to assume that the circles specialised in the sector should be assimilated to the concept of the informed user. However, this is probably wrong. The real question is, as identified by the Advocate-General, is "who is in the circle?"[154] There is no reason why a trader should not be in the circle if that trader is knowledgeable about designs in the sector. Thus, in *Harron SA v THD Acoustics Ltd*, the Board of Appeal held that the circles included experts and all business involved in the trade including importers.[155] In the UK, it was held that it comprised all individuals who conducted trade in relation to products in a sector including those who designed, made, advertised, marketed, distributed and sold such products in the Community.[156]

5-098

Disclosure in the EU

Although arts 7(1) and 11(2) of the Regulation refer to specialised circles "within the Community", such does not mean that the disclosure must have been in the Community. In *H. Gautzch Großhandel GmbH*, the referring court was concerned as to whether a prior art design presented in showrooms in China and sent to a

5-099

---

[149] See [96].
[150] Thus both designs were concerned with drainage but draining in different fields (liquid waste vs. shower water)
[151] (C-479/12) ECLI:EU:C:2014:75.
[152] At [25].
[153] At [39].
[154] AG Opinion citing *Green Lane Products Ltd v PMS International Group Ltd* [2007] EWHC 1712 at 38.
[155] R-552/2008-3 *Harron S.A. v THD Acoustics Ltd*, at [21] cited in *Magmatic v PMS International Group* [2013] E.C.C. 29.
[156] *Green Lane* [2007] EWHC 1712 at [34]–[35] approved in *Magmatic*, at [38].

Belgium company meant that such should be treated as prior art or not. The CJEU held, unsurprisingly, that it was a matter of fact which depended on the particular circumstances of the individual case. Thus, the German court has indicated, for example, that publication in a journal in Taiwan would qualify because:

"the foreign market can also be part of the cultural circle that German specialist circles can be expected to include in their observations of the forms of designs."[157]

5-100   In *Crocs*,[158] the Board of Appeal held, in relation to designs concerning footwear, that exhibition at the Fort Lauderdale Boat Show in the US of footwear incorporating the registered designs (prior to the relevant priority date) amounted to disclosure to the specialised circles in the Community. The holder of the design said that as the subject of the show was boats and not footwear, the disclosure of the clogs would not have become known to the specialised circles in the Community. The Board disagreed saying that such shows attracted exhibitors of boat-related products including footwear sellers. Likewise it held that publication on the right holder's website and sales (which were apparently modest in the context of the US market) were both individually sufficient for the design to become known. Indeed it stated that these were "precisely the sort of activities" which would make the design known.[159]

Publication in patent or trade mark bulletins

5-101   It is generally assumed that publication by an intellectual property office will be sufficient for a prior design to become prior art.[160] Thus, EUIPO's view is that once proof of publication of a design in the bulletin of any industrial property office worldwide has been provided by the applicant, disclosure is assumed to have taken place and it is incumbent on the holder to provide facts, arguments or evidence to the contrary that the publication would not have become known the circles specialised in the EU. In relation to trade mark and patent bulletins, its view is that such also amounts to a disclosure but not if a patent office holds a document which is not published but can be inspected.[161] Thus, it has been held that a registered but not yet published German utility model (which was publicly accessible had anyone requested it) is not relevant prior art.[162] It is highly debateable that specialised circles in the EU spend their time reviewing the official journal publications of, e.g. the European Patent Office or national intellectual property offices. EUIPO's view amounts to a legal fiction which bears little relationship to the wider world. The idea that there should be a rebuttable presumption that *specialised circles within the Community* monitor the drawings of every Taiwanese patent publications is, with respect to EUIPO, fanciful and unlikely to survive scrutiny by the General Court or CJEU. Indeed, such an observation jars with the Third Board of Appeal's observation that there should be a "common sense" limitation to temper the harsh-

---

[157] *Computergehause* (I ZR 163/01). See [2005] IIC 260.
[158] *Crocs, Inc v Holey Soles Holdings Ltd and Partenaire Hospitalier International (PHI)* R9/2008–3.
[159] See [60].
[160] Such was assumed for example in the case of a granted trade mark in *Jose Manuel Baena Grupo SA v OHIM* (T-513/09) [2010] E.C.R. II-289. Furthermore, see R0887/2008–3 *Normann Copenhagen ApS v Paton Calvert Housewares Ltd* ("Colanders") where the prior art was a published European patent application.
[161] EUIPO Guidelines, 5.5.1.2.
[162] *Termo Organika Sp. Z.o.o. v Austrotherm GmbH* R-1482/2009–3.

ness of the test of absolute novelty as discussed above.[163] Even though the test is not one of "would" but "could",[164] it is suggested (as discussed above) that only if it could be shown as a matter of evidence that persons in the specialised circles are accustomed to reviewing patent bulletin applications of a particular patent office should designs disclosed in that bulletin be deemed to fall outside art.6(2).

Design corpus and prior art

A prior art design may constitute relevant prior art but not form part of the design corpus. Thus, in *Magmatic v PMS International*, a prior art design was held not to form part of the design corpus but to be a prior art design.[165]   **5-102**

12-month grace period

Article 6(2) of the Directive (art.7(2) of the Regulation) introduces a so-called grace period, allowing the designer, their successor in title or a third person as a result of information provided or action taken by the designer or their successor in title to make the design public without destroying the novelty of the design by so doing. This grace period is for 12 months prior to the filing, or, if earlier, the priority date.[166] In *Sphere Time v OHIM*,[167] the General Court said that for the provision to be applicable, the holder of the registered design must show where a design is relied upon as prior art, that it is the *creator* of the *disclosed* prior art design or the successor in title to that creator.[168] Thus, where a third party made public a design copied from a design which was previously disclosed within the grace period by the holder, this provision is applicable.[169] It has also been said that it is not necessary for the previously disclosed design to be identical to the registered design on the grounds that art.7(2) of the Community Design Regulation also provides for immunity against the loss of individual character.[170] However, this can only apply if the prior art design was a copy of the registered design. It would obviously be contrary to the purpose of art.7(2) if a determined opponent copied the design disclosed during the grace period, altered it slightly (but not so much as to make it irrelevant prior art) and then claimed it as prior art not covered by art.7(2) on the grounds that the altered design was not identical to the registered design. In the author's view, the correct approach is to ask whether the prior art design has been derived from the applied-for design which is marketed in the grace period. If so, then it is not relevant prior art. Otherwise, an unscrupulous third party can undermine the policy behind the grant of a grace period by deliberately making available to the public the same or similar design reproduced from the registrar's design.   **5-103**

This grace period permits a designer to evaluate the market's reaction to the design for 12 months prior to incurring the expense of registering it. However, there are risks involved. Whilst products incorporating the designer's design cannot be   **5-104**

---

[163] See para.5-092.
[164] See para.5-094.
[165] *Magmatic v PMS International Ltd* [2013] EWHC 1925. This finding was not disturbed on appeal.
[166] art.6(2) of the Directive; art.7(2) of the Regulation.
[167] (T-68/10) [2011] E.C.R. II-2775.
[168] See [26].
[169] *Guiyuan Zhang v Aerospace Science & Industrie (Light Emitting Devices)* (R-658/2010–3), Third Board of Appeal; EUIPO Guidelines, at 5.5.1.9.
[170] EUIPO Guidelines, at 5.5.1.9 relying on *Guiyuan Zhang*, at [40].

relied upon to invalidate the subsequently applied for design, it provides no protection against disclosures during this period by third parties. Only if it can be shown that the third party design was derived from the designer's products, will such third party prior art be disregarded. Indeed, this occurred in *Sphere Time* when there was a third party prior art disclosure during the grace period (which may well have been a copy but the registered proprietor did not argue such). Thus, the wise step is to file first and exploit afterwards.

5-105   Whilst the introduction of a grace period would seem advantageous for the right holder, it is clearly not in the interests of third parties. This is because a design could be in the public domain for up to 18 months (if there is a priority application) before a registration in the EU needs to be applied for, such third parties will be unsure whether they can legally exploit the design themselves until the expiry of this period.

Abuse in relation to the designer

5-106   Article 6(3) of the Directive/art.7(3) of the Regulation states that the "grace period" provision discussed above also applies if the design was made available to the public as a consequence of an abuse in relation to the designer or their successor in title. In the previous section, we discussed that the disclosure by a third party of a copy of the design placed on the market by the registered proprietor did not amount to prior art capable of citation against the registered design. Bearing in mind the interpretation of art.7(2) that any disclosure of a copy of the registered design in the 12-month period should be ignored, it might be thought that art.7(3) was unnecessary as by definition, such is a copy of the design. However, art.7(3) would cover a situation where the abusive disclosure did not arise from copying a product incorporating the design placed on the market during the grace period by the registered proprietor.

5-107   In *Light Emitting Devices*,[171] such abuse was shown where copying (despite the designs not being identical) was found to have stemmed from a trade show at which both parties had taken booths. The question whether there has been an abusive disclosure must be assessed on a case by case basis on the basis of the facts, arguments and evidence submitted by the parties.[172] In *MP3 Player*,[173] abuse was not found to have occurred despite surrounding circumstances suggesting access and the almost identical nature of the designs.

Prior protected design published after filing/protected before priority date

Provision

5-108   The Regulation allows a Community design to be invalidated if "in conflict" with a prior design which was made available to the public *after* the date of filing of the Community design but which was protected from a date *prior* to the date of application or priority (if earlier). The prior design must be a registered Community design or application for a design; a registered design right of a Member State or

---

[171] R-658/2010–3 cited above.
[172] R-0552/2008–3 *Harron S.A. v THD Acoustics Ltd (MP3 Player Recorder)*, 3rd Board of Appeal, at [24]–[27].
[173] R-552/2008.

application for such a right; or a design right registered under the Geneva Act of the Hague Agreement with effect in the EU or an application for such.[174]

The Directive has a similar provision but no mention is made of the Geneva Act   **5-109**
of the Hague Agreement.[175]

Commentary

There are a number of comments to be made about this. First, the Regulation was   **5-110**
amended to refer to the Geneva Act of the Hague Agreement as a result of the EU acceding to the Geneva Act of the Hague Agreement.[176]

Secondly, the earlier design will be "in conflict" with the later design if the later   **5-111**
design lacks individual character over the earlier design.[177] As explained by the General Court in *Grupo Promer*, such an interpretation is the only one which can ensure that the proprietor of the prior design is protected against infringing the later design and also that he is not deprived of the exclusive rights conferred by the prior design.[178]

Thirdly, what is the relevant date for determining whether the prior design is   **5-112**
indeed a "protected" design? Thus, art.25(1)(d) refers to it being "protected from a date prior to" the date of filing or priority (if claimed). Does this mean the date of filing or the date of registration of the prior design? This is answered by art.12 which states that the initial period of protection is five years from the date of filing of the application. This also accords with common sense as the date of registration is arbitrary.

Fourthly, it should be noted that this ground may only be raised by the owner of   **5-113**
the earlier right or the appropriate authority of the Member State in question.[179]

The technical function exclusion

Provision

Article 7(1) Directive; art.8(1) Regulation   **5-114**

"A [Community design/design right] shall not subsist in features of appearance of a product which are solely dictated by its technical function."

Commentary

The previous laws of most Member States included an exclusion from design   **5-115**
protection of the technical aspects of a design, these being considered solely fit for patent protection. The nature and extent of such exclusions were, however, very different. Both the Directive and Regulation deal with the issue shortly as set out above. Although such an exclusion may at first seem clear, by reason of its very

---

[174] art.25.1(d) reg.6/2002.
[175] art.11(1)(d).
[176] Council Decision 954/2006.
[177] *Grupo Promer Mon Graphic SA v OHIM* (T-9/07) ECLI:EU:T:2010:96 at [52].
[178] See [53]. Whilst this is undoubtedly the right decision, the second explanation that the owner of the prior design would be deprived of the exclusive rights is not understood. The owner of the later design would not be able to rely upon the ownership of this design as a defence to an action for infringement brought by the owner of the earlier design. Exploitation of a later registered design is no defence to an action for infringement of a prior design—see para.5-174.
[179] Dir.98/71/EC art.11(4), (6); art.25(3) of the Regulation.

brevity, it leaves as many questions unanswered. In particular, this provision is capable of being interpreted in two ways:

(a) the exclusion is only effective if the design feature in question can not take any other appearance whatsoever[180]; (this is called the "multiplicity-of-forms" approach); and

(b) the exclusion depends upon whether solely technical considerations applied to the creation of the design feature.[181]

5-116   Furthermore, if the interpretation in (b) is correct, does that mean that the design must be aesthetically appealing or is there an intermediate category of functional design which is neither aesthetic nor is intended to achieve a technical result but which is still registrable?

5-117   Difficulties arise with both (a) and (b). The first interpretation seems so narrow as to be worthless, it being difficult to conceive of features which could only take a single appearance.[182] Moreover, it potentially permits an absolute monopoly by the filing of several applications in the case where there are finite solutions to a particular technical problem. However, the second interpretation might be said to exclude purely functional designs. This is in conflict with the object of the legislation, which makes no distinction between aesthetics and functional designs. Indeed, the Recitals make it clear when discussing this provision that the provision does not mean that a design must have an aesthetic quality.[183] Clearly, the opposite of aesthetic is functional.

5-118   The Court of Justice has considered the scope of the technical function exclusion in *DOCERAM GmbH v CeramTec GmbH*[184] in 2018. It has endorsed the approach set out in (b) above.

Early views

5-119   It initially seemed likely that the first interpretation would be adopted. Thus, in the Explanatory Memorandum to the Amended Proposal,[185] the Commission stated that whether a design did or did not have an aesthetic element was irrelevant, but there was a need for a provision indicating that protection should not be available in those extremely rare cases where "form necessarily follows function". Such clearly favours the first interpretation.

5-120   An early but obiter indication that the multiplicity-of-forms interpretation was likely and intended appears from remarks made in the Advocate-General's opinion in the trade mark case of *Phillips v Remington*.[186] This case concerned exclusion under the law of trade marks for shapes "necessary to obtain a technical result".[187] The Advocate-General contrasted with this the provision under the Design Directive concluding:

---

[180] The position previously in Benelux law.
[181] The position previously in Italian, Spanish and UK law.
[182] As pointed out by the House of Lords in *Amp v Utilux* [1972] R.P.C. 103. Generally, care should be applied before relying upon this case (which considered a similar provision in the Registered Design Act 1949), as the Registered Design Act generally did not permit the registration of functional items. Thus, the context of the exclusion of features dictated by function was very different.
[183] Recital 14.
[184] *Doceram GmbH v CeramTec GmbH* (C-395/14)—see para.5-124.
[185] Explanatory Memorandum to the Amended Proposal [1996] OJ C142/7.
[186] *Philips v Remington* (C-299/99) [2001] E.C.R. I-5475; [2002] 2 C.M.L.R. 52; [2001] E.T.M.R. 509.
[187] See para.3-257.

"The wording used in the Designs Directive for expressing that ground for refusal does not entirely coincide with that used in the Trade Marks Directive. That discrepancy is not capricious. Whereas the former refuses to recognise external features 'which are solely dictated by its technical function', the latter excludes from its protection 'signs which consist exclusively of the shape of goods which is necessary to obtain a technical result'. In other words, the level of functionality must be greater in order to be able to assess the ground for refusal in the context of designs; the feature concerned must not only be necessary but essential in order to achieve a particular technical result: form follows function. *This means that a functional design may, none the less, be eligible for protection if it can be shown that the same technical function could be achieved by another different form.*"[188] [Author's emphasis.]

Again, initially the English Court of Appeal appears to have followed the route of the exclusion being narrow. Indeed the court went so far as to say that the exclusion would not apply unless it could be shown that that purpose could not be achieved by any other means.[189] The Spanish Court also seem to have adopted the narrow approach.[190]   **5-121**

Rejection of multiplicity-of-forms theory

The Board of Appeal rejected the multiplicity-of-forms theory in *Lindner Recyclingtech GmbH v Franssons Verkstader AB* ("Chaff Cutter").[191] This decision concerned a registered design for a "chaff cutter". This was a design for a component part for use in a machine for shredding used paper, cardboard, etc. It was a metal cylinder, with knives attached, which rotated and cut up material that was fed into the shredder.[192] An argument that it was a component part which was not visible during normal use failed on the facts. The main argument of the cancellation applicant was that the design of the chaff cutter was excluded from protection as its appearance was solely dictated by the product's technical function. On the face of it, there was nothing aesthetic about the design. The design was wholly functional in the sense that it was an industrial part that formed part of an industrial product and was not intended to have any "eye appeal". Although evidence was put forward by an employee of the registered proprietor that the "knives" on the design were chosen for aesthetical reasons, such seemed highly doubtful. The main argument of the proprietor was that there were alternative technical designs that could also achieve the same cutting effect of the registered design.   **5-122**

The Board of Appeal reviewed the two different approaches to art.8(1) of the Regulation which have been discussed above. It noted that the first approach (which was described as the "multiplicity-of-forms" theory) had been supported by German authors, followed in the English, Spanish, French courts and also by the Advocate-General in *Philips v Remington* (discussed above).[193] However, the Board considered: that there was "a major flaw" to the approach namely that it would only   **5-123**

---

[188] See [34]. The Advocate-General says that this is particularly telling in the German language version which uses the words "*erforderlich*" and "*bedingt*".

[189] *Landor v Azure* [2006] E.C.D.R. 31; [2007] F.S.R. 9.

[190] *Juzgado de lo Mercantil PTO Número Uno de Alicante*, Auto No 267/07, 20 November 2007, in *Silverlit Toys Manufactory Ltd v Ditro Ocio 2000 SL*.

[191] R 690/2007–3, Decision of Third Board of Appeal. It would appear that an appeal was made to the General Court but it was out of time (*Franssons Verkstader AB v OHIM* (T-98/10)), Order of General Court, 10 May 2010.

[192] The decision includes pictures of the chaff cutter and the machine that it was to be used in.

[193] See [28]–[29]. The cases cited *were Landor & Hawa International Ltd v Azure Designs Ltd* [2006]

be applicable in "highly exceptional circumstances and its very purpose will be in danger of being frustrated." Furthermore, where there were a finite number of technical solutions, the Board pointed out that a rights holder could secure an absolute monopoly to a technical solution by the filing of multiple designs for each of those technical solutions. Turning to the alternative approach, the Board noted its origin in the British case of *Amp v Utilux* and the rejection in the 21st century by the French courts of the previous "multiplicity-of-forms" theory.[194] The Board said that the assumption for the "technical function" exception had always "been to prevent design rights from being used to obtain monopolies over technical solutions without meeting the relatively stringent conditions laid down in patent law".[195] Thus, the Board said that the second approach was not only supported by a teleological interpretation but also by the wording of the article.[196] The Board then said in an excerpt which bears being quoted in full:

"[33] Good design involves two fundamental elements: the product must perform its function and it should be pleasant to look at. In the case of some products, such as pictures and ornaments, their very function is to please the eye. In the case of other products, such as the internal working parts of a machine, the visual appearance is irrelevant. That is why the Community design legislation denies protection to component parts that are not visible in normal use. In the case of most products the designer will be concerned with both the functional and the aesthetic elements. That applies also to large items of industrial equipment, such as shredders for use in recycling plants. The shredder must, in the first place, perform its function effectively and safely and without creating excessive noise, but it is also desirable that the shredder should be pleasing to the eye and thus enhance the working environment of the people who operate it and see it in use. For that reason there is no objection in principle to granting design protection to industrial products whose overall appearance is determined largely, but not exclusively, by functional considerations.

[34] It is often pointed out that the Community design legislation, unlike the old laws of some Member States, does not lay down any requirement of aesthetic merit, artistic creativity or eye appeal. The absence of such a requirement is expressly mentioned in the 10th recital in the preamble of Regulation 6/2002 and in the 14th recital in the preamble to Directive 98/71. Some authors infer from this that purely functional designs are protectable. That is a false analysis. Community design law is concerned with the visual appearance of products. That is clear from the definition of "design in art.3(a) CDR and from the requirement of visibility in normal use for component parts in art.4(2)(b) CDR. Those parts of a product that cannot be seen are of no concern to the Community law of design because no one cares what they look like. All that matters is that such parts perform their function. If the law were intended to protect purely functional designs it would not be logical to exclude the non-visible aspects of design from protection.

[35] The significance of limiting protection to the visual appearance of products is that aesthetic considerations are in principle capable of being relevant only when the designer is developing a product's visual appearance. Most of the time the designer will be concerned with both elements of good design: functionality and eye appeal.

EWCA Civ 1285 (England); *Silverlit Toys Manufactory Ltd v Ditro Ocio* 2000 SL (Spain). In relation to France, the board relied upon commentary in a French book (D. Cohen, *Le droit des dessins et modeles: droit communautaire, droit international, droit français et autres droits étrangers*, 2nd edn (Paris: Economica, 2004)).

[194] Again citing D. Cohen, *Le droit des dessins et modeles: droit communautaire, droit international, droit français et autres droits étrangers*, 2nd edn (Paris: Economica, 2004).

[195] See [28].

[196] This particular argument was rather less convincing.

In some cases functionality will be the dominant preoccupation of the designer. The need to make a product that works will be uppermost in the designer's mind and will largely determine the appearance of the product. As long as functionality is not the only relevant factor, the design is in principle eligible for protection. It is only when aesthetic considerations are completely irrelevant that the features of the design are solely dictated by the need to achieve a technical solution. This is not, it must be stressed, tantamount to introducing a requirement of aesthetic merit into the legislation. It is simply recognition of the obvious fact that when aesthetics are totally irrelevant, in the sense that no one cares whether the product looks good, bad, ugly or pretty, and all that matters is that the product functions well, there is nothing to protect under the law of designs.

[36]   It follows from the above that art.8(1) CDR denies protection to those features of a product's appearance that were chosen exclusively for the purpose of designing a product that performs its function, as opposed to features that were chosen, at least to some degree, for the purpose of enhancing the product's visual appearance. It goes without saying that these matters must be assessed objectively: it is not necessary to determine what actually went on in the designer's mind when the design was being developed. The matter must be assessed from the standpoint of a reasonable observer who looks at the design and asks himself whether anything other than purely functional considerations could have been relevant when a specific feature was chosen.

[37]   The fact that a particular feature of a product's appearance is denied protection by art.8(1) CDR does not mean that the whole design must be declared invalid, pursuant to art.25(1)(b) CDR, on the ground that it does not, 'fulfil [one of] the requirements of Articles 4 to 9'. The last sentence of the 10th recital in the preamble to the Regulation makes it clear that the design as a whole may be valid even though certain features of the design are denied protection. The design as a whole will be invalid only if all the essential features of the appearance of the product in question were solely dictated by its technical function."

The above issue came to be decided by the Court of Justice in March 2018 in **5-124** *DOCERAM GmbH v CeramTech GmbH*.[197] Following the Advocate-General's Opinion, it rejected the multiplicity-of-forms argument for the same reasons as set out by the EUIPO in the above decisions. It said that art.8(1) "intends to prevent technological innovation from being hampered by granting design protection to features dictated solely by a technical function of a product."[198] It thus said that art.8(1) excludes protection under the law on Community designs for features of appearance of a product "where considerations other than the need for that product to fulfil its technical function, in particular those related to the visual aspect, have not played any role in the choice of those features, even if other designs fulfilling the same function exist",[199] Therefore, in the declaratory part of the judgment, it stated:

"1.   Article 8(1) of Council Regulation (EC) No 6/2002 of 12 December 2001 on Community designs must be interpreted as meaning that in order to determine whether the features of appearance of a product are exclusively dictated by its technical function, it must be established that the technical function is the only factor which determined those features, the existence of alternative designs not being decisive in that regard.

2.   Article 8(1) of Regulation No 6/2002 must be interpreted as meaning that, in order

---

[197] (C-395/16) ECLI:EU:C:2018:172.
[198] See [29]. This wording comes from Recital 10 of the Regulation.
[199] See [31].

to determine whether the relevant features of appearance of a product are solely dictated by its technical function, within the meaning of that provision, the national court must take account of all the objective circumstances relevant to each individual case. In that regard, there is no need to base those findings on the perception of an 'objective observer."

5-125 The emphasis that protection for a feature is only excluded where technical function is the "only factor" which determined the appearance of that feature is welcome. It makes it clear that the law of registered designs in the EU cannot be used to monopolise technical innovations which have always belonged to the field of patent law. Yet, in fact, the exclusion under art.8.1 goes further than removing technical innovations from the scope of protection under Community design law. It appears to exclude from protection a wider range of technical and functional, every day, mundane, non-innovative features of a product where aesthetic, ornamental or decorative considerations have played no part in their design. Still, how is the Court of Justice's judgment reconciled with the statement in Recital 10 that it is not necessary that the design have an aesthetic quality? Must it not follow that a design of a feature where technical function is not the only factor guiding the designer, must have an aesthetic quality? Unlike the Court of Justice, the Advocate-General whose opinion was followed by the Court of Justice grappled with this issue. He said, that art.8(1) only applies where "it appears that other kinds of considerations, in particular, visual ones, played no part in the adoption of the design concerned."[200] He said that the key question is where the formal constraints connected with the product's technical function stop and where its designer's freedom of choice starts.[201] By itself, this statement should not be interpreted too literally. A designer may have a freedom of choice of alternative designs, which are all technical in nature. If this were the test, the multiplicity of forms approach would be the correct one. Yet it was emphatically rejected.

5-126 *DOCERAM* makes clear that a court or tribunal must be satisfied that the designer did not have *only* technical considerations when creating the design of the contested feature. This is not easy to reconcile with the statement in Recital 10 that the design need not have an aesthetic quality. In the authors' mind, it means that a court or tribunal does not need to consider whether the design appeals aesthetically to the relevant public. In other words, the design may in fact be (viewed objectively) very unattractive yet plainly not solely dictated by technical considerations. The test is a negative one. Provided that it can be said that the appearance of the feature was *not* solely dictated by technical functional considerations, it does not matter whether it is aesthetically appealing. In brief, if aesthetic *considerations* can be said to have played a role in the design of the feature, art.8(1) does not apply even if the design of the feature has no aesthetic *appeal* (i.e. quality). Ugly, boring and commonplace designs are protected as much as designs which appeal to the eye and mind. The intention and not the result in the test. Moreover, art.8(1) would not apply to a feature whose design is based on an intimate indivisible mixture of technical and aesthetic considerations. Such is of course the hallmark of 21st century design. However, in *DOCERAM*, the registered design was for weld centring pins in the automotive, textile machinery and machinery industries. For sitems such as these, it will be rare that the design of them will have been dictated by anything other than the technical role that pins must play. Equally, from the buyer's perspec-

---

[200] See [29], Opinion.
[201] [29]

tive, they would not care what they look like. Weld centring pins are bought to carry out a technical role rather than because their appearance appeals to their purchasers. Thus, an important factor in determining whether art.8(1) applies must be whether the buyer or consumer would care what the product looks like. If not, it is likely that the designer has only taken technical considerations into account when draughting the product.

"Interface" exception

Provision

Article 7(2) Directive; art.8(2) Regulation

"A [design right/Community design] shall not subsist in features of appearance of a **5-127** product which must necessarily be reproduced in their exact form and dimensions in order to permit the product in which the design is incorporated or to which it is applied to be mechanically connected to or placed in, around or against another product so that either product may perform its function."[202]

Commentary

This wording is narrower than the superficially similar "must fit" exception in **5-128** the UK law of unregistered design since it is limited to mechanical connections.[203] The Recitals explain the rationale behind this exception which is to permit the interoperability of products of different makes by not extending protection to the design of mechanical fittings.[204] The classic example would be the mechanical fittings between exhaust pipe and manifold.

At present there seems to be no real guidance from EUIPO or the courts as to **5-129** how this provision might be interpreted. It has been said that the provision is relevant if it applies to all the essential features of the registered design.[205]

Modular designs clawback

Provision

Article 7(3) Directive; art.8(3) Regulation   **5-130**

"Notwithstanding paragraph 2, a [design right/Community design] shall, under the conditions set out in Articles 4 and 5, subsist in a design serving the purpose of allowing multiple assembly or connection of mutually interchangeable products within a modular system."

Commentary

This provision is as a result of intensive lobbying. In effect, where the mechani- **5-131** cal fittings of modular products represent an "important element of the innovative

---

[202] art.7(2) Dir.98/71/EC.
[203] Copyright Designs and Patents Act 1988 s.213(3)(b)(i).
[204] Recital 14.
[205] EUIPO Guidelines, at 5.4.

characteristics of modular products and present a major marketing asset",[206] such will be registrable. Obvious examples are the well known Lego bricks which are modular in form.

Public policy or morality

Provision

5-132   Art.8 Directive/art.9 Regulation

> "A [design right/Community design] shall not subsist in a design which is contrary to public policy or to accepted principles of morality."

Commentary

5-133   This exclusion, which appears in the law of both patents[207] and trade marks,[208] is again mirrored in that of designs. The recitals make it clear that the legislation does not purport to harmonise national concepts of what is or is not acceptable, hence it may well be the case that decisions (which are fairly infrequent in any event) can and will differ from state to state.

5-134   As stated, decisions on acceptable morality are few and far between. An oft repeated case under a similar provision of the old UK law, is that of *Masterman's Design*[209] in which it was held that an anatomically correct model doll of a Scotsman in a kilt did not breach the provision. The German court (under their old law) have held that key rings bearing reduced sized pictures of Euro banknotes would also not breach the provision.[210]

Entitlement to apply for design

5-135   The Design Directive and Regulation are not harmonised on the issue of proprietorship of a national registered and Community registered design. The Regulation provides that the right to a Community design vests in the designer or the designer's successor in title.[211] If done by an employee in the execution of their duties or pursuant to instructions given by their employer, the right is vested in their employer.[212] However, only the person so entitled can apply to invalidate a Community Design on the grounds that the registered proprietor is not so entitled.[213] However, to do so, the right holder must have a court decision in their favour that they are not entitled to the Community design.[214]

5-136   In contrast, the Directive provides that the applicant or the holder of the right must be entitled to apply for it under the laws of the Member State concerned.[215] However, as with the Regulation, this ground of objection or invalidity can only be

---

[206] Recital 15 Dir.98/71/EC.
[207] art.53(a) EPC.
[208] art.3(1)(f) Dir.98/71/EC; art.7(1)(f) Reg.6/2002.
[209] *Masterman's Design* [1991] R.P.C. 89.
[210] *Key Ring Designs* (I ZB 1/02) [2004] E.C.D.R. 29.
[211] art.14(1).
[212] art.14(3).
[213] art.25(2).
[214] art.25(1)(c).
[215] art.11(1)(c) Dir.98/71/EC.

taken by the person who is so entitled under the laws of the relevant Member State.[216]

The effect of these provisions is that anyone can apply to register a new design as either a national or Community registered design and enforce it against third parties. As discussed earlier, this is one of the defects of the Community design regime.[217] Indeed, one could have the strange situation whereby a number of persons, none of whom are the designers, apply to register the same design and enforce it against the same third party. If the original designer does not seek to invalidate the registered design, the third party could find itself being found liable for the same acts of infringement to a number of persons.   **5-137**

The fact that there is freedom on Member States to determine who is entitled to apply for a national registered design means that different people may be entitled to apply for a national registered design as for the corresponding Community registered design. Thus, the UK has chosen to treat the issue of entitlement to a registered design in the same manner as that pertaining to the law of unregistered designs. Thus, if a design has been made subject to a commission for money, the commissioner, rather than the designer, is entitled to apply for the design.[218] However, in contrast, the designer will be entitled to apply for the Community Registered Design. Clearly, this is bound to cause difficulties. Furthermore, it is clear that there is considerable scope here for ownership of a design by different entities depending on how Member States enact this provision. Thus, one could have a situation whereby the employer is entitled to the registered design in Germany, the employee in UK and the commissioner in France. Undoubtedly, this will not further integration of the internal market.   **5-138**

Other grounds for refusal/invalidity

The grounds which follow are optional for implementation by Member States under the Directive. All have been implemented under the Regulation.   **5-139**

Prior rights: trade marks

Provision

Article 11(2)(a) Directive; art.25(1)(e) Regulation   **5-140**

"[Any Member State *may* provide that a design shall be refused registration, or, if the design has been registered, that the design right shall be declared invalid/A Community design may be declared invalid ....]:

(a) if a distinctive sign is used in a subsequent design, and Community law or the law of the Member State concerned governing that sign confers on the right holder of the sign the right to prohibit such use."

---

[216] art.11(3) Dir.98/71/EC.
[217] See para.5-034.
[218] Registered Designs Act 1949 (as amended) s.2(1A).

Commentary

5-141   As can be seen from the above, this provision is optional in the Directive. Only the owner of this right can invoke this ground.[219] Many designs (even designs which are an integral part of a product) will be capable of registration as trade marks. Alternatively they may as a result of use in the market place give rise to a right in passing off or unfair competition.[220] In the authors' view, the policy here is to give the owner of an earlier registered or unregistered trade mark the right to prevent registration of a subsequent design which, if used, would give rise to a cause of action under trade mark law (or equivalent law) which if successful, the owner would be entitled to injunctive relief. Thus, if the applicant for cancellation sought to rely upon an earlier registered trade mark, the tribunal should consider the outcome of a hypothetical trade mark infringement action brought as of the date of application of the later design assuming that the design was used in the marketplace. This may involve consideration of a multitude of matters which are often considered in trade mark infringement actions, e.g. the distinctive nature of the earlier trade mark, the similarity of the mark and the design, and the reputation of the earlier mark[221]. By reason of the nature of designs, the tribunal will generally be considering shape marks, i.e. three-dimensional trade marks (unless the design in issue is for, e.g. a logo). Indeed, the owner of the registered design may consider that the earlier 3D mark lacks distinctive character and was invalidly registered and bring its own cancellation proceedings against the registered mark. If it does not, the tribunal will consider the earlier mark to be validly registered and thus the primary issue for the tribunal will be whether there is a likelihood of confusion (or possibly whether there is a taking of unfair advantage/dilution).[222] The applicant for cancellation of the registered design is advised not only to rely upon its earlier registered trade mark but also if it has used the mark on the marketplace prior to the date of application of the registered design, the product which displays or incorporates the trade mark. This is because in such circumstances, it will be able to argue both likelihood of confusion (trade mark law) and that the later design does not create an overall impression to the informed user which is different to the earlier design (design law).

5-142   This provision was considered by the General Court.[223] In that case, the registered design was a highlighter marker pen. Stabilo, a German company, brought an application to annul the registered design based upon an earlier German registered mark for a marker pen.[224] The Board of Appeal held, in upholding the Cancellation Division's annulment of the design, that use of the registered design would breach the exclusive rights granted on Stabilo by German trade mark law (which was based upon the Trade Mark Directive). A number of arguments were put forward by the registered proprietor on appeal to the General Court. First, it was said that the provision only applied where the earlier sign was identical to the

---

[219] art.11(4) Directive 98/71/EC; art.25.3 of the Regulation.

[220] See Ch.3.

[221] A good example of this can be seen in *BMB sp.z o.o. v EUIPO* (T-695/15) ECLI:EU:T:2017:684 where the General Court, dismissing an appeal from the Board of Appeal, held that the latter had been right to find that there was a likelihood of confusion between the Community registered design and an earlier international registered mark which designated France.

[222] See *Beifa Group v OHIM (Writing Instrument)* (T-148/08) [2010] E.C.R. II-1681 at [73].

[223] See *Beifa Group v OHIM (Writing Instruments)* (T-148/08) [2010] E.C.R. II-1681.

[224] In fact, the earlier mark was a figurative representation of a Stabilo pen and not a 3D shape mark. This led to the General Court annulling the decision of the Board of Appeal as the latter treated it as a 3D mark when it was not, see [121].

registered design. Unsurprisingly, this was rejected. The court held that it applied where the design was so similar that there would be a likelihood of confusion.[225] This must be right if the authors are correct that one must consider a hypothetical trade mark infringement action. Secondly, the proprietor submitted that as Stabilo was relying upon a registered mark, it should have adduced proof of genuine use of the earlier mark in the same way that if it had relied upon the mark in trade mark opposition proceedings in EUIPO, it would have been required to do so.[226] The court accepted this argument but held that such a request should have been made before the Cancellation Division and it failed to do so.[227] Thirdly, the General Court also held that it was necessary for the tribunal to determine whether the relevant public would form the impression that the Community design has made use of the earlier distinctive sign. If it did not find such was the case, then any likelihood of confusion could be ruled out.[228] This seems a useful "threshold" test but is of course not a substitute for deciding whether a hypothetical trade mark infringement action would have succeeded. Finally, the court held that it was not necessary to determine whether the relevant public would perceive the Community design itself as a distinctive sign.[229] This argument is more dubious because if the public did not perceive the Community design as a trade mark, i.e. an indication of trade origin, then it seems difficult to see how it could be said that such would affect adversely the functions of a trade mark (at least, the essential function) which is a requirement of trade mark law.[230]

The question as to what type of use of the design is to be assumed when considering whether identical, similar or dissimilar goods or services are involved (and so the requisite test for trade mark infringement) has so far been avoided by the Boards and the Courts. Registration of design is not specific to goods or services although the Locarno classification is used for searching purposes. In most cases, it is fairly obvious what goods or services the registered design relates to. Thus, in *Beifa Group v OHIM (Writing Instruments)*, it was clear that the registered design was for writing instruments. The earlier registered mark was registered for writing instruments and accordingly, there was little difficulty when considering the notional trade mark infringement case that the goods were identical. However, in other cases, particularly ornamental designs which can be applied to a wide variety of products, this may be more problematic. In the author's view, if the ornamental registered design is capable of being applied to the goods for which the earlier mark is registered, then for the purpose of determining the hypothetical trade mark infringement action under this provision, the tribunal should consider that it is a trade mark action where the design is used on goods identical to those protected by the registered mark. Whilst this may seem harsh to the registered proprietor of the design, it should be remembered that the registered design gives protection in relation to the ornamental design regardless of the goods to which it is applied. Thus, a failure to cancel the later registered design would mean that the proprietor of the registered design could bring an action for infringement against use of the earlier

5-143

---

[225] See [55].

[226] Generally, see para.3-398.

[227] See [71]–[78].

[228] See [105]–[106]. For application of this principle, see also *Su-Shan Chen v OHIM* (T-55/12) ECLI:EU:T:2013:219 where the General Court held that the features of the earlier mark were discernible in the registered design and it was irrelevant that there were other additions or differences, at [28].

[229] See [107].

[230] Generally, see para.3-439.

registered mark if the latter did not create an overall impression to the informed user which was different to that of the registered design.[231]

Prior rights: copyright

5-144   A similar ground for refusal is if the registered design constitutes an unauthorised use of a work protected under the copyright law of the Member State concerned.[232] Thus, in countries where a third party owns copyright in the design as a work of applied art, the third party will be able to prevent the application going on the register. The incorporation of a painting in a design will therefore give grounds for objection. However, as copyright is only a right against copying, it would have to be shown that the design was derived from the copyright work.

Prior rights: other rights

5-145   Apart from prior trade marks and copyrights, the only other prior rights that can be relied upon under the Directive and the Regulation are where the design constitutes improper use of badges, emblems, etc. protected under art.6*ter* of the Paris Convention or emblems of particular public interest in the Member State concerned.[233] Thus, the Directive does not provide for refusal of registration where other rights exist. In particular, of interest to UK practitioners is that it does not confer a right of refusal where there is an earlier national unregistered design right and use of the design applied could be prevented by the owner of the unregistered design right. It has been already stated that neither the Directive nor the Regulation are intended to affect other rights such as the laws of the unregistered design right.[234] Thus, a person may be able to obtain a registered design but be unable to exploit it because it conflicts with a prior right such as UK unregistered design right. This is a familiar concept with patent lawyers where an improvement patent may be granted but the invention described in it cannot be exploited without the permission of the owner of the basic patent.

Rights conferred by a Registered Design

Provision

5-146   Article 12 Directive; art.19 Regulation

> "[A registered Community design/The registration of a design] shall confer on its holder the exclusive right to use it and to prevent any third party not having his consent from using it. The aforementioned use shall cover, in particular, the making, offering, putting on the market, importing, exporting or using of a product in which the design is incorporated or to which it is applied, or stocking such a product for those purposes."

---

[231] It is of note that whilst there is a "prior use" defence in the Regulation (art.22), there is no corresponding defence in the Directive. The nearest it gets to is a transitional provision where there was use prior to the coming into force of the Directive (art.12(2)).

[232] art.11(2)(b) Dir.98/71/EC; art.25(1)(f) Reg.6/2002.

[233] art.11(2)(c) Dir.98/71/EC; art.25(1)(g) Reg.6/2002.

[234] art.16 Dir.98/71/EC.

Commentary

The scope of the rights must be determined objectively and does not vary according to the intention or conduct of the defendant.[235] It should be appreciated that a registration gives no positive right to use. That registration may itself infringe another party's earlier registration. Thus, where a defendant has a registration for the design that it is using, such is no defence to an action for infringement of another registration.[236]   **5-147**

Rights conferred by an Unregistered Community Design

In relation to the Unregistered Community Design ("UCD"), the scope of protection and the rights afforded by it are the same as that for a Community Registered Design (Community Design) but subject to the additional condition that it must be shown that the infringing Article has been copied from the protected design.[237] Article 19(2) states that: **5-148**

> "An unregistered Community design shall, however, confer on its holder the right to prevent the acts referred to in paragraph 1 [ie acts of making, offering, putting on the market, etc.] only if the contested use results from copying the protected design.
> The contested use shall not be deemed to result from copying the protected design if it results from an independent work of creation by a designer who may be reasonably thought not to be familiar with the design made available to the public by the holder."

The inclusion of the phrase "a designer who may reasonably thought not to be familiar with the design made available to the public by the holder" complicates the issue. Does that mean that a defendant who can be reasonably thought to be familiar with the claimant's design will not be able to plead independent design by way of defence even if *in fact* the defendant did not know of the design? Does the fact that a defendant who may reasonably be thought to be familiar with the claimant's design merely raise a rebuttable presumption that the defendant has consciously or subconsciously copied the design of the claimant? The Recitals emphasise that the UCD only gives rise to a right to prevent copying and cannot extend to design products which are independently designed by a second designer.[238] Accordingly, in the authors' view, the second approach is correct. The first approach not only would be contrary to the Recitals but ignores the fact that the second paragraph of art.19(2) is a deeming provision of non-infringement and is not decisive of the issue of infringement where its conditions are *not* satisfied.   **5-149**

---

[235] *Celaya Emparanza y Galdos Internacional SA v Proyectos Integrales de Balizamiento SL* (C-488/10) ECI:EU:C:2012:88 at [55]–[58]. It is fair to point out that this observation was in the context of where the third party had itself obtained a later Community registered design. However, the observation appears to be equally applicable even if the third party had not applied for a later registered design but was, e.g. claiming that it did not know of the Community registered design. In any event, it is clear that in the case of a Community registered design, there is no requirement of knowledge of the registered design.

[236] *Celaya Emparanza y Galdos Internacional SA v Proyectos Integrales de Balizamiento SL* (C-488/10). In this case, the defendant's registered design was later than the registered design which was sought to be enforced. However, there is no reason why such should not apply where the registered design is an earlier registered design than the registered design which is sought to be enforced. Of course, in such circumstances, the obvious thing to do is counterclaim to invalidate the later registered design.

[237] art.19(2) Reg.6/2002.

[238] Recital 21 Reg.6/2002.

5-150   This provision was considered by the CJEU in *Gautzsch Großhandel GmbH v Münchener Boulevard Mobel Joseph Duna GmbH.*[239] In this case, the referring court was unclear whether the holder of an unregistered Community design bore the burden of proving copying and if so, whether the burden of proof was reversed or "lightened" if there were material similarities between the design and another design. The CJEU held as follows:

> "[41] In view of that objective and in view of the structure and broad logic of Article 19(2) of Regulation No 6/2002, it should be held that, where the holder of a protected design is relying on the right set out in the first subparagraph of that provision, the onus of proving that the contested use results from copying that design rests with that holder, whereas, in the second subparagraph of that provision, the onus of proving that the contested use results from an independent work of creation rests with the opposing party."

5-151   It then said that the matter of determination of such "rules" is a matter for the laws of Member States but that in applying those rules, Member States must apply the principles of equivalence and effectiveness and ensure that such rules are not less favourable than those applicable to similar domestic actions and do not make it in practice impossible or excessively difficult for individuals to exercise rights conferred by EU law.[240] Thus, it said that if it was difficult for the holder of the protected design to prove that the contested use resulted from copying, the court is required to counter that difficulty and if necessary, adjust or lighten the burden of proof.[241]

5-152   There are conceptual difficulties here. The CJEU appears to be putting forward two "rules" based upon the two subparagraphs of art.19(2). The first rule is that the burden of proof lies on the holder of the design to prove copying. The second rule is that the burden of proof rests on the defendant to prove that the work was independently created. However, the issues of copying and independent creation are obviously two sides of the same coin. Ex hypothesi, a work is not copied if it is independently created and equally a copied work is not independently created.

5-153   In the authors' view, some assistance can be obtained from the approach in English courts in relation to copyright infringement actions when deciding whether copying has taken place. In the House of Lords in *Designers Guild Ltd v Russell Williams (Textiles) Ltd*,[242] Lord Foscott said as follows (this approach has been applied in many cases):

> "The first step in an action for infringement of artistic copyright is to identify those features of the defendant's design which the plaintiff alleges have been copied from the copyright work. The court undertakes a visual comparison of the two designs, noting the similarities and the differences. The purpose of the examination is not to see whether the overall appearance of the two designs is similar, but to judge whether the particular similarities relied on are sufficiently close, numerous or extensive to be more likely to be the result of copying than of coincidence. It is at this stage that similarities may be disregarded because they are commonplace, unoriginal, or consist of general ideas. If the plaintiff demonstrates sufficient similarity, not in the works as a whole but in the features which he alleges have been copied, and establishes that the defendant had prior access to

---

[239] (C-479/12) ECLI:EU:C:2014:75.
[240] See [42].
[241] See [43].
[242] [2000] 1 W.L.R. 2416.

the copyright work, the burden passes to the defendant to satisfy the judge that, despite the similarities, they did not result from copying."[243]

In other words, in the language of English procedural law, the *legal* burden of proving copying lies on the owner of the design right but if there is *sufficient similarity* that it gives rise to an *inference* of copying rather than of coincidence, then the *evidential* burden lies on the defendant to prove that the design arose from independent design. In the authors' view, this approach would accord with the principles set out in the CJEU's judgment in *Gautzsch Großhandel*.

5-154

Scope of protection of a Community Design

Provision

Article 9 Directive; art.10 Regulation

5-155

"The scope of the protection conferred by a [Community design/design right] shall include any design which does not produce on the informed user a different overall impression.
  In assessing the scope of protection, the degree of freedom of the designer in developing his design shall be taken into consideration."

Commentary

This provision uses identical wording to the registrability requirements. Thus, a prior art design could never infringe a registered design without invalidating it.[244] The one exception to this rule is if the prior art was not known to Community circles in the sector concerned.[245] This could give rise to an unfortunate set of circumstances whereby a prior art design, if unknown in the relevant Community circles, would infringe a registration applied for at a later date.[246]

5-156

As the provisions in the Directive and Regulation for infringement (namely whether the alleged infringing design creates a different overall impression to the informed user over the registered design) is the same as that for determining whether the registered design is validly registered over cited prior art, the authors' view is that the approach should be the same and the reader is referred to the earlier sections on individual character and novelty.[247]

5-157

However, is it possible that some different approach should be taken to determining individual character when considering infringement than when considering validity? In *Procter & Gamble Co v Reckitt Benckiser*[248] the Court of Appeal of England and Wales considered Recital 14 of the Regulation which states as follows:

5-158

"(14) The assessment as to whether a design has individual character should be based on whether the overall impression produced on an informed user viewing the design *clearly differs* from that produced on him by the existing design corpus, taking into consideration the nature of the product to which the design is applied or in which it is incorporated, and in particular the industrial sector to which it belongs and the degree of freedom of the designer in developing the design." [Emphasis supplied.]

---

[243] p.2425.
[244] Such "squeeze" arguments are familiar to patent practitioners.
[245] See para.5-092.
[246] Unless the defendant can rely upon the "prior use" defence discussed at para.5-191.
[247] See para.5-064, et seq.
[248] *Procter & Gamble Co* [2007] EWCA Civ. 936.

5-159   This recital applies to the assessment of individual character when determining the validity of a registered design over prior art. In *Procter & Gamble*, the Court of Appeal considered that such meant that a different approach should be taken to determining individual character for infringement (where there is no equivalent recital). The Court considered that meant that when considering registrability, it was necessary to show that the overall impression on the informed user had to clearly differ (between the registered design and the prior art) whereas such did not apply when considering infringement. The Court said that different policies applied to validity and infringement because there was a real risk that design monopolies may interfere with routine, ordinary, minor, everyday design modifications but no such policy applied to the scope of protection.[249] Whilst there is some force to this observation, in the authors' view, the fact is that the wording in the articles of the Directive and Regulation are identical. This cannot be a coincidence and it would be very odd to interpret the identical wording in the provisions relating to validity and scope of protection differently. In fact, in a later case, Jacob LJ, who gave the leading judgment in *Procter & Gamble*, said that in fact his conclusion was wrong. As he said, the difference in wording was merely the result of sloppy drafting of the recitals of the Regulation and Directive.[250]

5-160   Despite this, it is the authors' view that *Procter & Gamble* provides useful assistance to the *approach* in determining whether the alleged infringing design does create an overall impression different to the informed user over the registered design. The Court said that:

- The court must identify the overall impression of the registered design with care.
- The level of generality which the court must descend to is important. The appropriate level of generality is that which would be taken by the notional informed user.
- The court should then do the same exercise for the alleged infringement.
- The court should then ask whether the overall impression of each is different. This is almost the equivalent to asking whether they are the same: the difference in nuance probably involving a question of onus and no more.[251]

Level of generality of protection

5-161   Many registered designs may not contain colour, texture or other matters. Thus, an applicant could choose to depict a three dimensional design by reference to: (i) a three dimensional wire-frame image of the design; (ii) a "block" image of the design; (iii) a block image of the design with colour added; and (iv) a block image of the design with colour and graphics, labelling, etc. In such circumstances, as said by EUIPO:

"The registration holder is entitled to choose the level of generality at which his design is to be considered. If he chooses too general a level, his design may be invalidated by

---

[249] See [19].
[250] Referring to A. von Mühlendahl, *Design Protection In Europe* (Cologne: Carl Heymanns Verlag, 2009) 3rd edn, pp.232–233 (Mühlendahl was once the President of EUIPO).
[251] *Procter & Gamble Co* [2007] EWCA Civ. 936 at [35]. See also para.5-173.

prior art. If he chooses too specific a level he may not be protected against similar designs."[252]

Thus, if a registered design is a wire-frame image of a three dimensional shape, **5-162** the comparison will be purely of the shape of the infringing item with the shape depicted in the registered design and extraneous matters such as graphics, colour, etc. will be ignored.[253] Conversely if the representations show a solid surface it may be that the lack of adornment of that surface will be taken into account when assessing the scope of protection.[254] The scope of protection of a "grayscale" Community registered design was considered by the UK Supreme Court in *PMS International Group plc v Magmatic Ltd*.[255]

In this case, the owner of the Community Design had applied for a CRD for six **5-163** images of a child's wheeled suitcase prepared by a 3D computer assisted design in monochrome with greyscale shading and distinct tonal contrasts. Unfortunately, for the owner, the design was not purely grayscale with the wheels, straps and strips on the front and rear shaded in black as opposed to grey. This is shown below:

The Supreme Court held that the difference in shading meant that such ele- **5-164** ments were for colours which contrasted with that of the remainder of the product. A further issue in the case was whether it was a design with an absence of ornamentation as opposed to merely the shape. The Supreme Court said absence of decoration could be a feature of a design. As it said "Simplicity or minimalism can notoriously be an aspect of a design and it would be very curious if a design right registration system did not cater for it."[256] The difficulty (as recognised by the Supreme Court) is that EUIPO does not allow any wording to define the protection of a Community Design to affect the scope of protection.[257] It is difficult to convey that absence of ornamentation is a feature of a design (as opposed to that one is merely seeking to protect the shape).

This judgment emphasises the importance of the depiction of the design when **5-165** applying for a registered design. The application is advised to file different depictions of the design in wire frame, grey scale and full colour with ornamentation. The cost of doing so is hardly more than merely applying for one depiction of the design.

If the applicant wishes to protect a design with no ornamentation (as opposed to **5-166** the mere shape), they are best advised to file various designs in a plain colour. As this might be said to introduce colour into a product as part of the design, then one may use line drawings with shading.

Parts of designs

The definition of "design" is to the appearance of "of the whole or a part of a **5-167** product". This definition for "design" is applicable throughout the Directive and the

---

[252] *Eredu v Armet (EUIPO Invalidity Division)*, ICD000000024, Unreported 27 April 2004. EUIPO approach in *Eredu* was endorsed by the UK High Court in *Procter & Gamble v Reckitt Benckiser (UK) Ltd* [2007] E.C.D.R 4.

[253] e.g. see *Procter & Gamble* [2007] E.C.D.R. 4 at [48].

[254] As happened in *Magmatic v PMS International* [2014] EWCA 181 before the UK Court of Appeal. Upheld on appeal, *PMS International Group Plc v Magmatic Ltd* [2016] UKSC 12.

[255] [2016] UKSC 12.

[256] See the judgment at [45]. See also *H&M Hennes v OHIM* (T-525/13, T-526/13) ECLI:EU:T:2015:617 at [37] where the General Court, noted that the Board of Appeal held that one bag design was of "formal simplicity" whereas the other was of a "more 'worked' bag...which is adorned with ornamental motifs."

[257] See art.36(6).

Regulation. Musker[258] suggests that this leads to three possibilities for the protection of parts of design as follows:

- register the whole product assuming that it will automatically cover parts thereof;
- as above, but specifically indicate for which part protection is sought; or
- just apply to register the part concerned.

5-168   In a previous edition of this book, we submitted that it would be impermissible to compare part of the registered design with the whole or part of the infringing product, in other words possibility (i), above, was wrong. This is because the registration document defines what the design is for which protection is sought.[259] The English court in *Woodhouse*[260] came to the same conclusion. In that case, the rights holder had registered and the representations showed a distinctive street lantern in combination with a (fairly ordinary) mounting bracket. The court held that the mounting bracket was a part of the design and needed to be taken into account for the purposes of assessing the scope of protection. Hence it held that lanterns (the lantern part of which made the same overall impression) but which were mounted on different brackets, and indeed lanterns sold on their own did not infringe the registration.

5-169   Also, in the previous edition of this book we submitted that it would however be possible to compare the whole of the appearance of the registered design with only part of the design of the alleged infringing product. In other words options (ii) and (iii) above are viable protection strategies. It should be noted that in the case of a Community registered design, the applicant for a registered design can specifically disclaim features of a design.[261]

Example 1
A registered design contains a representation which shows a spoon which has a distinctive handle. An alleged infringer takes the distinctive handle and incorporates it into a fork.

Analysis

When considering the alleged infringing design, the court compares the whole of the registered design, namely the spoon with distinctive handle, with the whole of the fork. It is likely therefore that it will conclude that there is a different overall impression.

Example 2

A registered design contains a representation which shows a spoon which has a distinctive handle but this time the spoon portion is indicated in dotted lines and the registration includes a disclaimer that no protection is sought for this portion. Again an alleged infringer takes the distinctive handle and incorporates it into a fork.

Analysis

When considering the alleged infringing design, now the court compares the only operative part of the registered design, namely the distinctive handle, with the corresponding part of the fork. It should therefore conclude that there is the same overall impression.

---

[258] D. Musker, *Community Design Law: Principles and Practice* (London: Sweet & Maxwell: 2002), p.20.
[259] Thus, whilst one could apply to register for "part" of a design, once one has registered either part or whole of the design, that defines the design right.
[260] *Woodhouse* [2006] R.P.C. 1.
[261] See para.5-192.

Where a design has more than one distinctive feature, the legal advisor is recom- **5-170**
mended to register multiple applications each containing a single distinctive feature.
Otherwise, if only one of the distinctive features is taken, this could mean that a different overall impression is caused. EUIPO and many Member States permit the filing of multiple representations under one application in order to permit such a
strategy.

Reliance upon prior art design corpus to interpret scope of protection

As discussed earlier in this chapter, the informed user is deemed aware of the **5-171**
design corpus when considering whether a registered design is invalidated by a prior
art design. Thus, as discussed above, the courts have held that in a "crowded field",
small difference will suffice to confer individual character on a design.[262] It must
thus also follow that in a crowded field, small differences will suffice to prevent a
design from infringing the registered design. Conversely, a design should receive
a broader scope of protection where it is markedly different to the design corpus.[263]
It should be emphasised that this approach only applies to the design corpus and
not specific prior art. Thus, the consideration of whether the alleged infringing
article creates an overall impression on the informed user which is the same or different to the registered design is not influenced by the fact that the closest prior art
identified by the defendant to the registered design is quite different. The informed
user is not deemed aware of all prior art but only the design corpus and clearly there
may be other prior art not identified by the defendant. It is quite possible for the
prior art not to form part of the design corpus.[264] Conversely though, any design in
the design corpus must by definition, be a prior art design. Thus, if the cited closest prior art is quite different to the registered design, it must follow that (assuming competent legal representation) any design in the design corpus is no closer.

Excluded features

As discussed above, when considering whether a design has individual character **5-172**
over prior art, one must disregard features which are excluded from protection.[265]
It follows that when considering the scope of protection, features excluded from
protection, e.g. those dictated by technical function must be disregarded. The
comparison must be of each feature not exclusively dictated by functional
considerations in the registered design as against equivalent non-functional features
in the alleged infringing design. It is not obvious in some of the EUIPO decisions
that this approach has been taken.

Practical guide to determining infringement

Guidance as to the correct approach for determining infringement has been given **5-173**
in a number of cases. In the authors' view, in *Samsung v Apple*, the English court
set out a helpful step-by-step approach. It involves the following steps (somewhat
paraphrased by the authors):

---

[262] See para.5-078.
[263] See in *England, Dyson v Vax* [2010] E.C.D.R. 18 at [39]–[40] applying *Grupo Promer; Samsung Electronics (UK) v Apple* [2013] E.C.D.R. 1.
[264] As in *Magmatic v PMS International* where it was held that a specific item of prior art did not form part of the design corpus but was relevant prior art as it was known to specialised circles in the Community.
[265] See para.5-088.

- Identify the informed user.
- Identify the existing design corpus.
- Break down the registered design into features and consider in relation to each essential feature whether: (i) it is dictated solely by technical function, (ii) it is dictated by a lack of design freedom, (iii) the extent of its inherent originality or triviality, and (iv) the extent as to how far the feature differentiates itself from equivalent features in the design corpus. One can then either exclude the feature or if it is not excluded, give it a certain "weight" which will determine its significance when determining overall impression.
- Compile a list of similarities of features of the designs.
- Having done the above:
  - attributing the appropriate "weight" to each feature and whether the same or similar feature appears in the alleged infringing design[266], and
  - considering that the informed user is particularly observant and pays attention to detail decide whether or not the similarities are sufficient to mean that the overall impression to the informed user of the alleged infringing design is the same as that of the registered design.

Defences

5-174   A number of "fair dealing" acts are excluded from infringement. These are acts done privately and for non-commercial purposes; acts done for experimental purposes; acts of reproduction for the purposes of making citations or of teaching, provided that such acts are compatible with fair trade practice and do not unduly prejudice the normal exploitation of the design, and that mention is made of the source.[267] In the case of Community designs, there is a protection of "prior use" which is considered below.[268]

Period of protection

5-175   In the case of national registered designs under the Directive and Registered Community Designs, the period of protection is for a period of five years from the date of filing extendable by renewal up to a total term of 25 years from the date of filing.[269]

5-176   For the UCD, the period of protection is three years from the date on which the design was first made available to the public within the Community.[270]

Spare parts for repair

5-177   The principal reason for the delay in adopting the Directive and Regulation was the question of protection for spare parts. This was due to extensive lobbying by the motor vehicle manufacturers in relation to spare parts. No actual agreement could be reached and so the Directive provides what is known as the "freeze-plus" compromise. Thus, art.14 of the Directive says:

---

[266] i.e. if a significant (heavily weighted) feature is replicated in the alleged infringing design, then such will be a strong factor in determining that there is the same overall impression. Conversely, the absence of a significant feature of the registered design in the alleged infringing design will be a strong factor in finding no infringement.

[267] art.13(1) Dir.98/71/EC. art.20 Reg.6/2002.

[268] See para.5-191.

[269] art.12 Reg.6/2002.

[270] art.11(1) Reg.6/2002.

"Until such time as amendments to this Directive are adopted on a proposal from the Commission in accordance with the provisions of Article 18, Member States shall maintain in force their existing provisions relating to the use of the design of a component part used for the purpose of the repair of a complex product so as to restore its original appearance and introduce changes to those provisions only if the purpose is to liberalise the market for such parts."

It is important to emphasise that art.14 does not harmonise the law of Member **5-178** States as "spare parts" but fetters the rights of Member States to change their laws adversely to spare parts providers.

Article 110 of the Regulation provides that: **5-179**

"1.　Until such time as amendments to this Regulation enter into force on a proposal from the Commission on this subject, protection as a Community design shall not exist for a design which constitutes a component part of a complex product used within the meaning of Article 19(1) for the purpose of the repair of that complex product so as to restore its original appearance."

The provisions are not concerned with the requirements of registrability but what **5-180** acts involving spare parts constitute acts of infringement. Thus, this provision should be kept conceptually distinct from which component parts are registrable and which are not.[271]

In Joined Cases *Acacia Srl v Pneusgarda Srl and Audi AG* and *Rolando D'Amato* **5-181** *v Porsche AG*,[272] the Court of Justice had to consider the extent of the spare parts defence to the manufacturers of alloy wheels for cars. Alloy wheels are big business. Many car owners like to replace the original set of alloy wheels with further sets of different designs. Therefore, there is a thriving market for alloy wheels of differing designs. Other car owners may wish to replace their original sets with alloy wheels of an identical design (as alloy wheels are often stolen). In contrast, car doors have to match other car doors and thus practically, can only be one design. The Court of Justice had to consider a number of questions in a dispute between Porsche and Audi, who have many registered designs for alloy wheels and an Italian manufacturer of various alloy wheels which Porsche and Audi owners bought, sometimes through an Internet site.

The first issue was whether the "repair" clause applied only to component parts **5-182** such as car doors or bonnets whose shape and appearance is dictated by or dependent upon the complex product (so that realistically they can only be made to one design) or extended wider to cover any component part, e.g. alloy wheels whose design was not dependent on the rest of the car.[273] The Court of Justice held that the literal wording of art.110 was not so restricted and the *travaux préparatoires* showed that wording "upon whose appearance the design is dependent" was omitted from the final provision adopted by the EU Council. Accordingly, it held that such a requirement could not be read into art.110.[274]

The second issue was how narrowly should the wording "*to restore its original* **5-183**

---

[271]　See para.5-054.

[272]　(C-397/16 & C-435/16) ECLI:EU:C:2017:992.

[273]　Although it might be said that the design of one alloy wheel is dependent on the design of the other three alloy wheels. However, one can plainly replace a set of alloy wheels with those of a different design whereas even if all the car doors were replaced with another set of car doors, the need to integrate their design with the rest of the car mean that they would still have to be of the same design.

[274]　See [29]–[54]. In doing so, they acknowledged but did not follow Recital 13 which has the wording "which constitutes a component part of a complex product upon whose appearance the design

appearance" be interpreted? The Court of Justice held that this meant that the spare part must be "visually identical to original parts".[275] That includes colour and dimensions.[276]

5-184   The third issue concerned what steps a manufacturer or seller of a component part must take to ensure that the component part it sells is purchased exclusively for repair purposes. Thus, alloy wheels can be bought online and not just from repair garages. Whether a replacement alloy wheel is used for the purpose of repair or merely as a fashion item is a matter for the end user and not manufacturer. The Court of Justice held that the manufacturer and seller are under a duty of diligence as regards compliance with the requirement of repair. This includes informing the downstream user through a clear and visible indication on the product, its packaging, catalogues and sales document that the component part is for repair purposes only and also through contractual means. The manufacturer and seller must also refrain from selling a component part where they know or ought reasonably to know that the part in question in will not be used for repair purposes.[277]

5-185   In *Ford Motor Co v Wheeltrims srl*[278] the Court of Justice had to consider whether the "spare parts" defences at art.14 of the Design Directive and art.100 of the Design Regulation overrode the provisions of the Trade Mark Directive and EU Trade Mark Regulation. In the case, Wheeltrims marketed wheel covers which faithfully reproduced the trade mark of various motor vehicle motor manufacturers when repairing cars. This including Ford, who brought an action against Wheeltrims relying upon its trade mark rights under national legislation implementing the Trade Mark Directive and the EUTMR. Wheeltrims argued that the use of the mark was purely descriptive and relied upon the "spare parts" defence in the Design Directive and Design Regulation. By a Reasoned Order, the Court of Justice held that the "spare parts" defence did not "trump" (override) the Trade Mark Directive and Regulation even if the use made of the trade mark was the only way of repairing the vehicle concerned to restore the complex product to its original appearance.

Review

5-186   Article 18 of the Directive provides for review of the working of the spare parts provision, three years after it enters into force. The review is stated, in particular, to address the needs of manufacturers of complex products and component parts. One year after such review the Commission is obliged to propose amendments to the Directive in response to the review. Under art.110(2) of the Regulation, the Commission is obliged to take such a review into account for the purposes of Community designs also.

5-187   In fact, the Commission conducted the review early and published its report on 14 September 2004.[279] It summarised these conclusions in a press release as follows:

"The Commission believes this is the right time to introduce a 'repairs clause', in other

---

is dependent...". It should be said that there were a number of decisions of Member State courts which went both ways on this point. In England, see *BMW v Round & Metal* [2012] EWHC 2099 (which must now be considered overruled). See also cases cited at fn.9 and fn.10 to the Opinion of the Advocate-General.

[275] See [75].
[276] See [77].
[277] See [79]–[89].
[278] (C-500/14) ECLI:EU:C:2015:680.
[279] Proposal for a Directive amending Directive 98/71/EC on the legal protection of designs (SEC (2004)

words a provision that suppliers, other than those who supply and hold design rights over a part for a new car, should be able to supply, as a replacement part, a component using an identical design. This is the right time because it has proved impossible to reach a voluntary agreement within the industry itself.

Change will benefit consumers. It is also a logical consequence of the 'Monti package' of changes to the competition rules (Block Exemption Regulation) for car dealerships (see IP/02/1073 and MEMO/02/174), which has opened up competition in the retail market for new cars and is leading to reductions in the differences between new car prices in different Member States.

The Commission is not bound by the timetable for possible revisions mentioned in Article 18 of the 1998 Directive. It can propose a modification of any Directive at any time and is making this proposal after a full consultation exercise."

Since the review, however, there appears to have been little further progress.[280] **5-188**
In fact, recently, the Commission has abandoned its attempts to find a solution.[281]

Exhaustion of design right

The legislation provides that there is exhaustion where the product has been put **5-189**
on the market in the Community by the holder of the design right or with their consent.[282] This Directive has been adopted by the EEA, so in fact it is an EEA-wide exhaustion of rights. It is likely that this would prevent any Member State from maintaining a domestic international exhaustion of rights principle in line with the reasoning in *Silhouette v Hartlauer*[283] and *Laserdisken*[284] as such could contribute to the partitioning of the internal market.[285]

Provisions peculiar to the Regulation

Disputes over ownership of Community Design

The law regarding the ownership of a Community Design has already been **5-190**
discussed.[286] Jurisdiction in disputes over ownership of Community Designs will be decided in accordance with the Brussels Convention.[287] Where there are disputes as to the entitlement of a Community Design, the person claiming rightful ownership may issue legal proceedings.[288] Importantly, these legal proceedings can only be issued within three years after the date of publication of the Community Design or the date of disclosure of an UCD unless the registered owner of the Community

---

1097), COM/2004/0582 final-COD 2004/0203.

[280] The legislative history was reviewed extensively by the UK Court in *BMW v Round & Metal* [2012] EWHC 2099 (Pat).

[281] See para.5-037.

[282] art.15 Dir.98/71/EC.

[283] *Silhouette v Hartlauer* [1998] E.C.R. I-4799; [1999] Ch. 77; [1998] 3 W.L.R. 1218. See para.3-616.

[284] *Laserdisken v Aps v Kulturministeriet* (C-479/04) [2007] 1 C.M.L.R. 6; [2006] E.C.D.R. 30. See para.4-320.

[285] However, it would not appear that this provision was intensely discussed whilst in the legislative pipeline from the *travaux préparatoires*.

[286] See para.5-135.

[287] Reg.6/2002 art.76. See Ch.16.

[288] arts 15–16.

Design or claimant to the UCD was acting in bad faith.[289] All designers have a quasi-moral right to be cited on the EUIPO Register as the designers of a Community Design regardless as their entitlement to the Community Design.[290]

Prior use defence

5-191   In the Regulation but not the Directive, there is a "prior use" defence for any person who can establish that before the date of filing of the application, or, if a priority is claimed, before the date of priority, the person can establish that they have in good faith commenced use within the Community, or have made serious and effective preparations to that end, of a design included within the scope of protection of the Community Design, which has not been copied from the Community Design.[291] However, this right of prior use does not extend to granting a licence to other persons to exploit the design.[292]

Application for a Community Design

5-192   Applications for Community Design are very similar to applications for a EU Trade Mark but simpler. An application can be made directly to EUIPO or via the intellectual property offices of Member States.[293] The application must identify the applicant and a representation of the design suitable for registration. The applicant may use dotted lines to indicate elements for which no protection is sought.[294] EUIPO must satisfy itself that the representation permits a third party to determine with clarity and precision all the details of the design for which protection is sought.[295] The application must contain an indication of the products in which the design is intended to be incorporated or to which it is intended to be applied and may contain a written description explaining the design or the specimen.[296] However, neither the indication nor the description affects the scope of protection of the design.[297]

5-193   The application can contain multiple designs provided that such designs all belong to the same class of the International Classification for Industrial Designs.[298] The relevant date for the purpose of novelty is that of the date of filing unless priority is claimed from an earlier filing made within the previous period of six months

---

[289]   art.15(3). In relation to the UCD, this provision can give rise to difficulties as the rightful owner may be wholly unaware of a disclosure in the Community of their design. Of course, there is nothing to prevent the rightful owner issuing their own proceedings for infringement of UCD. However, art.15(3) is relevant if the rightful owner wishes to enjoy the fruits of protection that the wrongful claimant of a UCD is seeking or has obtained. It is assumed that "disclosure" in art.15 should be equated with making "available to the public" in art.11(2).

[290]   art.18.

[291]   art.22 Reg.6/2002.

[292]   art.22(3) Reg.6/2002.

[293]   art.35.

[294]   Decision EX-03-9 of the President of EUIPO, 9 December 2003. This approach was endorsed in *Sphere Time v OHIM* (Watch attached to a lanyard) (T-68/10) ECLI:EU:T:2011:269 at [59]–[64]. See also *Thomas Murphy v EUIPO* (T-90/16) ECLI:EU:T:2017:464 at [57].

[295]   *Mast-Jägermeister SE v EUIPO* (T-16/16) ECLI:EU:T:2017:68, at [35] and [45] applying the *Sieckmann* criteria used by EUIPO when examining applications for EU trade marks—discussed at para.3-145.

[296]   arts 36.2, 36.3(a).

[297]   art.36.6; *Ball Beverage Packaging Europe Ltd v EUIPO*, (T-9/15) ECLI:EU:T:2017:386 at [66].

[298]   art.37.

in a Paris Convention country.[299] There is very limited examination by EUIPO limited to satisfying itself that the formalities have been complied with, that the design falls within the definition of "design" and is not contrary to accepted principle of public morality.[300] If such formalities are found to have been complied with, it is then registered and published.[301]

Dealings in and licensing of a Community Design

A Community design can only be dealt with in its entirety. Thus the area of protection of a Community Design or Unregistered Community Design cannot be divided.[302] However, a Community design can be licensed for the whole or part of the Community.[303] As with the EUTM licensing provisions, the holder of a Community Design may invoke the rights conferred by the Community design against a licensee who contravenes any provision in his licensing contract with regard to its duration, the form in which the design may be used, the range of products for which the licence is granted and the quality of the products manufactured by the licensee.[304] This has the advantage of permitting the holder to bring proceedings for infringement of a Community Design against third parties who are in possession of goods bearing the design which do not comply in the above manner with the licence as such goods will be infringing products.[305] A licensee may bring proceedings for infringement of a Community design if the right holder consents. An exclusive licensee may bring proceedings for infringement if the rights holder has been given notice of such and has declined to take any action within an appropriate period.[306] In *Thomas Philipps GmbH v Grüne Welle Vertriebs GmbH*[307] the Court of Justice held, following its approach in *Hassan* under the EUTMR, that a licensee can bring proceedings for infringement of a Community Design even if the licence has not been entered on the Register. Furthermore, on a proper interpretation of art.32(3) of Reg.6/2002, it held that a licensee can recover damages for its own loss.

5-194

Jurisdiction and procedure in legal actions relating to Community Designs

As with the Community Trade Mark Regulation, the Community Design Regulation provides its own sui generis provisions relating to the jurisdiction of courts and EUIPO over proceedings relating to Community designs.[308] Thus, although nominally, the Brussels Convention is stated to apply to such proceedings, in fact the majority of the relevant provisions of the Convention are specifically expressed not to apply.[309] The Regulation envisages the setting up of a Community Design Courts which is a similar concept to the setting up of EU Trade Mark Courts under

5-195

---

[299] art.41.
[300] arts 45–47. See *Mast-Jägermeister SE v EUIPO* (T-16/16) ECLI:EU:T:2017:68 at [35].
[301] arts 48–49.
[302] art.27. For transfers of CRD, see art.28.
[303] art.32(1).
[304] art.32(2).
[305] Although see art.33 which states that the effects vis-à-vis third parties of legal acts referred to in art.32 is governed by the law of the Member State determined in accordance with art.27.
[306] art.32(3) Reg.6/2002.
[307] (C–419/15) EU:C:2016:468.
[308] arts 79–95 Reg.6/2002.
[309] art.79(3) Reg.6/2002. Pursuant to art.57 of the Brussels Convention, the convention does not apply where Member States have agreed specific jurisdictional provisions in relation to a particular matter.

the EU Trade Mark Regulation.[310] Under art.81, Community Design Courts have jurisdiction to hear proceedings relating to:

- infringement actions and threatened infringement actions;
- actions for declaration of non-infringement (if permitted under national law);
- actions for a declaration of invalidity of an unregistered Community design; and
- counterclaims for a declaration of invalidity of a Community design raised in connection with infringement proceedings.

5-196   It can be seen from the above that Community Design Courts do not have jurisdiction to hear actions for declaration of invalidity of registered Community designs other than by way of counterclaim. Further, the validity of a Community Design cannot be put in issue in an action for a declaration of non-infringement.[311] Where a party wishes to bring proceedings for invalidity of a registered Community design other than by way of counterclaim, such proceedings must be brought at EUIPO.[312]

Jurisdiction of Community Design Courts

5-197   Article 81 proceedings must be brought (in descending order of priority) in:

- the Community Design Courts of the Member State in which the defendant is domiciled or if the defendant is not domiciled in any Member State, in any Member State in which they have an establishment;
- the Community Design Courts of the Member State in which the claimant (plaintiff) is domiciled or if the claimant is not domiciled in any Member State, in any Member State in which they have an establishment; and
- in the courts of the Member State where EUIPO has its seat (Spain).[313]

5-198   The above provisions will not apply if the parties agree in writing that a different Community Design Court shall have jurisdiction[314] or if the defendant submits to the jurisdiction of a different Community Design Court.[315] In all cases where the court's jurisdiction is based upon the above grounds, the Community Design Court shall have jurisdiction in relation to all acts of infringement committed or threatened within the territory of any Member State.[316]

5-199   Finally, as an alternative ground of jurisdiction to the above grounds, the claimant can bring proceedings in the courts of a Member State where the act of infringement has occurred or been threatened.[317] However, in such a case, the Member State

---

[310] art.80 Reg.6/2002. Until such have been set up, then the national courts of Member States which would have jurisdiction over proceedings relating to equivalent national design rights will have jurisdiction over proceedings relating to Community Designs—art.80(5).

[311] art.84(4) Reg.6/2002. However, if the right relied upon is unregistered, the applicant can issue separate proceedings for a declaration of invalidity of an unregistered Community design— art.81(d).

[312] art.52 Reg.6/2002.

[313] art.82 Reg.6/2002.

[314] art.82(4)(a) Reg.6/2002; art.17 Brussels Convention.

[315] art.82(4)(b) Reg.6/2002.

[316] art.83(1) Reg.6/2002.

[317] art.82(5) Reg.6/2002.

only has jurisdiction in relation to acts committed or threatened in that state.[318] This alternative ground of jurisdiction is mirrored in the EU Trade Mark Regulation and has been the subject of interpretation by the Court of Justice. The reader is referred to Ch.3, "Trade Marks in Europe."[319]

Related proceedings: Community Design Courts and EUIPO

As can be seen from the above, there will often exist more than one Community **5-200** Design Court in which proceedings can be brought for infringement of a Community Design Court. Furthermore, invalidity proceedings of a Community design can be brought in EUIPO or, by way of counterclaim, in the Community Design Court which has been seized of infringement proceedings. As with the Community Trade Mark Regulation, the Community Design Regulation includes provisions where proceedings have been brought in more than one jurisdiction. Thus, a Community Design Court cannot hear an application for a declaration of invalidity of a Community Design if EUIPO has already determined such an application relating to the same subject-matter and cause of action and involving the same parties.[320] A Community Design Court hearing a counterclaim for a declaration of invalidity can request the defendant to submit such an application to EUIPO.[321]

Furthermore, a Community Design Court must, unless there are grounds, stay any **5-201** proceedings other than a declaration for non-infringement where the validity of the Community Design is already in issue before another Community Design Court or where an application for a declaration of invalidity has already been filed at EUIPO.[322] Similarly, EUIPO must, save where there are special circumstances, stay its proceedings if there are prior proceedings relating to the validity of the Community Design in a Community Design Court.[323] These provisions are essentially identical to those in the EU Trade Mark regulation and the reader is referred to the commentary on these provisions.[324]

In relation to parallel proceedings in different Member States for infringement **5-202** of a Community Design, such actions may be considered related actions under arts 21 and 22 of the Brussels Convention. As such provisions have not been excluded by the Community Design Regulation,[325] then a Community Design Court other than the Community Design Court first seized may be compelled or alternatively

---

[318] art.83(2) Reg.6/2002.
[319] See at para.3-813, et seq.
[320] art.86(5) Reg.6/2002.
[321] art.86(3) Reg.6/2002.
[322] art.91(1) Reg.6/2002.
[323] art.91(2) Reg.6/2002. However, in such circumstances, the Community Design Court can stay its proceedings and permit the proceedings to continue at EUIPO.
[324] See para.3-833. See also *Samsung Electronics (UK) Ltd v Apple Inc* [2013] F.S.R. 8, Court of Appeal of England and Wales, where the court said that the purpose of art.91 was to prevent the validity of a registered Community design being considered in parallel proceedings save where there were special grounds for permitting the proceedings to continue or where one action was for a declaration of non-infringement. In relation to the latter, it said that where there were proceedings in EUIPO concerning the validity of a registered Community design and a claim in English courts for a declaration of non-infringement of that design, the stay required under art.91, absent special grounds, was of the counterclaim (i.e. that of infringement) and not the claim (for a declaration of non-infringement). The circumstances where "special grounds" apply have been considered in the context of the EU Trade Mark Regulation by the English courts—see para.3-833.
[325] See art.79 Reg.6/2002.

choose to decline jurisdiction in favour of the Community Design Court first seized if the conditions in arts 21 and 22 are satisfied.[326]

5-203   Where there are parallel actions on the basis of Community design and equivalent national design rights in the courts of different Member States, the courts other than the court first seized must decline jurisdiction.[327] Where a Community Design Court is hearing an action for infringement or threatened infringement of a Community Design and a court has already given judgment on the same cause of action and between the same parties on the basis of a design right providing simultaneous protection, then the Community Design Court must reject the action.[328] The same principle applies where a court is hearing an action for infringement of a national design right and a Community Design Court has already given judgment on the equivalent Community Design.[329] Again, these rules are identical to those in the EU Trade Mark Regulation.[330]

Relationship to other forms of IPRs

5-204   The Regulation makes it clear that cumulative protection is permissible. Thus, it is stated to be without prejudice to other Community or national provisions relating to unregistered design rights, copyright, trade marks or other distinctive signs, patents and utility models, typefaces, civil liability or unfair competition.[331]

NATIONAL DESIGN PROTECTION LAWS

5-205   At present, protection of designs in Europe greatly varies. Protection is afforded by means of registered designs, unregistered design rights, copyright, trade mark and unfair competition law.[332] As mentioned above, the Design Directive harmonises the law for registered designs. Furthermore, the Trade Mark Directive has harmonised the laws for registered trade marks. Accordingly, in this section, one examines the other laws applicable to designs.

Copyright

5-206   All European countries belong to the Berne Convention. Thus protection is afforded under copyright to design and products incorporating designs that amount to works of applied art. Germany, Portugal, Spain and Benelux require that there is a high or marked degree of artistic merit in the work.[333] Furthermore, since the passing of the Information Society Directive, the test for determining whether a literary or artistic work is protected, the test of author's own intellectual creation

---

[326] The Brussels Convention has been superseded in the EU by the Recast Brussels Regulation. However, when the Community Design Regulation came into force, neither the Recast Brussels Regulation nor its predecessor were in force. For the lis pendens rules of the Recast Brussels Regulation (which are in substance the same as that of the Brussels Convention), see para.17-184.

[327] art.95(1) Reg.6/2002.

[328] art.95(2) Reg.6/2002.

[329] art.95(3) Reg.6/2002.

[330] See para.3-830.

[331] art.96 Reg.6/2002. See also Recitals 31 and 32.

[332] A very useful resumé of the variety of national protection afforded to industrial designs in Benelux, France, Spain, Germany, Italy and the UK is set out in A. Firth, "Aspects of Design Protection in Europe" [1993] 2 E.I.P.R. 45. See also Chs 2 and 4, Green Paper.

[333] However, case law in Benelux has given a broad interpretation to this requirement, *Screenprints Ltd v Citroën Nederland, Benelux Court of Justice*, 22 May 1987.

must be applied and protection cannot be excluded on the grounds that the design is a registered design.[334]

The CJEU have ruled that it is impermissible to deprive works of any copyright protection on the basis that the work has additionally been protected as a design.[335] This has led to a change in the change in Italian law which formerly deprived a copyright owner of such protection in the event of a design being registered. This CJEU judgment has also led to the repeal of a UK provision which limits protection to 25 years in the event of industrial exploitation of a copyright work.[336]   **5-207**

In the UK, copyright vests in designs but this protection is largely negated (and the work protected by the "parallel" unregistered design right) by the fact that it is not an infringement of any copyright in a design document or model recording or embodying a design for anything other than an artistic work or a typeface to make an article to the design or to copy an article made to the design.[337] Of course, copyright in the UK applies to artistic works.   **5-208**

Utility models

Many countries have introduced specific legal instruments to cater for functional designs which have an exclusive technical function but are not sufficiently inventive to be protected under patent law. This is available in Germany, Greece, Italy, Spain and Portugal, although the degree of inventive step differs. The usefulness of the utility patents is that examination only takes place if challenged by a potential infringer.[338]   **5-209**

Unfair competition

It is possible in most European countries (or under the law of passing-off in the UK) to invoke unfair competition laws where consumers are confused as to the trade origin of two products. Most continental countries recognise slavish imitation or exploitation of another's reputation as actionable. In France, arguments of exploitation of a design have succeeded even where confusion has been absent. The limitation of unfair competition protection for industrially designed products is that normally they will require an element of capricious distinctiveness readily recognisable to the public. In a typical well designed but commonplace functional object, this will often not be the case.[339]   **5-210**

Sui generis unregistered design right laws

The UK provides sui generis copyright-type protection for aspects of shape and configuration of industrial designs.[340] The period of protection lasts for 10 years from the date of commercialisation of the design. For the last five years licence of rights have been available. The criteria for subsistence of design right is that the   **5-211**

---

[334] Generally, see Ch.4, "Copyright in Europe".

[335] *Flos v Semeraro* (C-168/09) ECLI:EU:C:2011:29 [2011] E.C.D.R. 8; [2011] R.P.C. 9.

[336] s.52 of the Copyright Designs and Patents Act 1988 by the Regulatory Reform Act 2013.

[337] CDPA 1988 s.51.

[338] See a review of utility models by Dr Haertel, meeting on Union of European Practitioners in Industrial Property, Brussels summarised in Union Bulletin, 3 March 1992.

[339] e.g. see *Hodgkinson & Corby Ltd v Wards* [1995] F.S.R. 189 HC where a passing-off action based on a slavish imitation of a functional object (an invalidity cushion) failed.

[340] Copyright Designs Patents Act 1988 s.213, et seq.

design is original (in the sense of not being copied from another design as opposed to absolutely novel) and is not commonplace. Protection is provided against copying of the design not mere similarity of design. Thus, independent design of an identical or similar design is a defence. Design right is not conferred on features that "must fit" with other products (i.e. features that "must match" with other products (i.e. car doors)).

CHAPTER 6

PLANT VARIETY RIGHTS IN EUROPE

INTRODUCTION

What is a plant variety?

Plants are hierarchically classified according to the number of shared character- **6-001**
istics that they possess with other plants. From most general to specific, the levels
(referred to in Latin) are:

- *divisio*;
- *classis*;
- *ordo*;
- *familia*;
- *genus*;
- *species*;
- *subspecies*;
- variety; and
- form.

Generally speaking, "species" denotes a group of organisms which share: a large **6-002**
number of heritable characteristics; an ability to interbreed; and which are genetically isolated from other species by "sterility barriers". However, it should be
emphasised that what is or is not a species is open to constant revision. For example,
elephants have been divided since early times into two species, namely African and
Indian. However, it now appears that the African elephant, in fact, includes two
distinct species, namely the forest and savannah-dwelling elephants, which are as
genetically distinct as lions are from tigers (*Loxodonta cyclotis* and *Loxodonta
africana*, respectively). The former forest-dwelling species is smaller, has straighter
tusks and round, rather than pointed ears. Moreover, the "sterility barrier" is not an
absolute characteristic. For instance, a lion and a tiger are distinct species and yet
may interbreed to give a liger or a tigon.

Certain species, particularly cultivated ones, comprise distinct types. These may **6-003**
be taken into account in nomenclature through various intraspecific levels: subspecies, variety, form (from general to specific). The meanings of these terms are not
precise and there is no general agreement as to when one should use subspecific or
varietal designation to indicate a unique population of plants. A common perspective though, is that "subspecies" should be used to describe populations that do not

live in the same place, whereas "variety" is used to differentiate between different subtypes of a species in the same area. However, the precise nature of the group of plants that may comprise a variety within any particular species depends upon a number of factors, such as the mode of propagation of the plants, their floral biology and the plant breeding techniques that have been used. Form is usually a reference to very small variation.

6-004   The easiest way to consider what these terms mean in practice is to consider carnivorous plants:

Example
The carnivorous pitcher plant *Sarracenia purpurea* grows in Canada and all along the eastern edge of the US. Yet, the plants in Canada and the north-eastern US are different from the plants in the south-eastern US. Hence, the south-eastern plant is named *Sarracenia purpurea* subsp. *Venosa* ("subsp." is the contraction for subspecies); while, the ones in Canada and the north-eastern US are given the name *Sarracenia purpurea* subsp. *Purpurea*.

Another carnivorous plant, *Drosera binata* ("binata" means fork-leafed) has a variety that produces leaves with many (multi) branches, hence *D. binata* var. *multifida*. There exists a rare form of *D. binata* var. *multifida* which has a great number (more than around 16) leaf tips. It is called *D. binata* var. *multifida f. extrema*. For more information see: *http://www.sarracenia.com* [Accessed 20 February 2014].

6-005   Owing to the lack of clear definition as to the scientific meaning of "variety", art.1 of the 1991 Act of the UPOV Convention, the current international convention in the field of plant breeders' rights, defines "plant variety" for the purpose of the Act. This is considered later. It suffices to say two things at this stage about the classification of animals and plants according to the Linnaean system of classification[1]: first, it arises out of man's innate desire to impose order upon what is ultimately the chaotic result of evolution—nature does not always behave in a nice, tidy way; secondly, the classification system is primarily based on classifying the mainly outwardly expressed visual characteristics of plants and animals. These characteristics are called phenotypic characteristics or sometimes morphological characteristics which can be sensed (primarily visually) by humans. However, since the 20th century, it is now known that these phenotypic characteristics are expressed by the particular genetic sequences of plants and animals, i.e. their DNA. In general, although there is not an exact correlation, the more similar the phenotypic characteristics of two plants or animals, the more similar is the genetic sequence of those two plants or animals—the latter are called the genotypic characteristics of the plant or animal. However, often the phenotypic characteristics are not caused by a particular genetic sequence but a complex interaction of various discrete and separate genetic sequences of the DNA code of that plant or animal. Thus, the high yield characteristics of a particular wheat variety is not due to a particular genetic sequence but a complex interplay of the genes.[2]

---

[1]   Linnaeus was a Swedish botanist and zoologist. He did not invent the classification of plant and animals (taxonomy) which has existed since ancient times but introduced a binominal nomenclature system for all plants and animals and is credited in bringing order to taxonomy when before there was chaos.
[2]   It is a little known fact that the DNA sequence of wheat consists of 17 billion base pairs of nucleotides. This is *five times* that of humans!

Background to plant variety rights

Since the earliest times, farmers and herdsmen have sought to improve the **6-006** productivity and other useful or desired characteristics of their crops and livestock.[3] By the end of the 18th century, when systematic plant breeding by selection began, the plants grown by farmers were the result of several thousand years of partly conscious, partly unconscious, selection. The art of plant breeding resulted from the realisation by innovative farmers that considerable further progress was possible by systematic selection. In the 20th century, the rediscovery of Mendel's laws of heredity meant that plant breeding could proceed on a scientific basis.

The essence of plant breeding is the discovery or creation of genetic variation in **6-007** a plant species and the selection from within that variation of plant of those with desirable phenotypic traits that can be inherited. Plant varieties are important in the areas of food, fuel, fibre, raw materials for industry such as vegetable oils, rubber and pharmaceutical materials. However, it is the area of food where they are most important. It is estimated that by the year 2020, the Earth's population will be eight billion with 83 per cent living in developing countries. Annual food production will have to increase to 3,000 million metric tonnes from the current 1,800 million metric tonnes. At the same time, productive farm land is being swallowed up into urban centres and other non-farm uses. Thus, the imperative to be able to develop cereal plant varieties which provided for greater yields or which have other qualities such as lower water requirement, greater winter-hardiness or pest-resistance is clear. At the same time, there is an increasing leisure demand for specimen flowers and other ornamental plants.

However, developing new, commercially successful varieties is usually a very **6-008** time-consuming and expensive process. It may often have taken between 10 and 20 years to develop a new variety in a species. Often, the development does not work and the investment is wasted. Furthermore, because a breeder is developing a living material, the breeder can release a new variety to a grower who can then, without recourse to the breeder, reproduce the variety. In such circumstances, it became clear in the 20th century that there was a need to provide protection for work of plant breeders, so as to reward their efforts and provide them with sufficient incentive to continue developing new varieties. Moreover, an equal need for protection existed because breeders needed to control the reproduction of varieties that they had created. Thus, many plant breeding institutions are more concerned with the improvement of existing stock through the advancement of knowledge. For these bodies, the legal ability to control exclusively the use of reproductive and propagating material of varieties that they have bred was paramount in order to maintain the variety.

Initially, breeders sought protection under the patent system but the patent system **6-009** was not directed to protecting plant varieties and, thus, there were a number of legal and technical hurdles. As said by Rozès AG in *Nungesser v Commission ("Maize Seeds")*,[4] a protection system devised for live organisms which are subject to change raises very different problems from those relating to a technical invention.[5] Gradually, countries began creating sui generis plant breeders' rights which

---

[3] Genesis: vv, 31–43: even though the methodology described therein reveals a more Lamarckian (i.e. teleological), than Darwinian, approach to the introduction of certain desired traits.
[4] *Nungesser v Commission ("Maize Seeds")* (C-258/78) [1982] E.C.R. 2015, 2081, et seq.
[5] Quoted by Colomer AG in *STV v Schulin* (C-305/00) [2003] E.C.R. I-3525 at [8].

conferred certain exclusive rights in respect of certain varieties.[6] However, it was not until 1961, when the Act of the International Convention for the Protection of New Varieties of Plants 1961 was adopted that plant breeders' rights were recognised on an international basis.

Current plant variety legislation

6-010   At present, the relevant international and European legislation in the field of plant varieties is:

(a) TRIPS;
(b) UPOV; and
(c) Community Plant Variety Right (CPVR) Regulation.

6-011   These are all considered in detail below. Mention is also made of the Convention on Biological Diversity ("The Rio Convention"). However, before considering these treaties, it is useful to review the interaction between plant variety rights and patents.

Plant varieties, biotechnology and patents

6-012   The discovery of the structure of the DNA molecule, and the fact that it constitutes the genetic code governing the inheritance of the features of almost all living organisms, means that plant breeders can now transfer directly into a plant a genetic sequence which exhibits a particularly useful feature, without the need to search laboriously in the progeny of cross-fertilised varieties for a plant with the desired characteristic. Accordingly, the ability of the plant breeder to create variation has been immeasurably increased by modern biotechnology. However, it would be wrong to consider that biotechnology renders traditional plant breeding redundant. Many of the most important features of crop plants, such as yield, are the result of the complex interplay of a vast number of genes. These features are not directly attributable to a particular genetic sequence, and so cannot be achieved by the insertion of a genetic sequence into any cereal crop. Thus, the two are complementary and their benefits are cumulative. For instance, one could take a cereal crop which has a high yield created by traditional plant breeding rights, and then transgenically introduce a pest-resistant genetic sequence to give a high-yielding, pest-resistant strain but it may be very difficult to isolate the high-yielding genetic sequence.

6-013   Under art.53(b) of the European Patent Convention (the "EPC"), patents cannot be obtained for plant varieties. The legislative reason for this exclusion was examined fully in *Transgenic Plant/Novartis II*.[7] In a full judgment, which is considered in Ch.2, "Patents in Europe", the Enlarged Board of Appeal (the "EBA") determined that the reason for exclusion was because art.2(1) of UPOV 1961 did not permit the simultaneous protection of a plant via plant breeders' rights and patents. This ban was abandoned in the UPOV Act 1991 but the EPC has not been amended to take this into account.

6-014   However, whilst plant varieties per se are not patentable, biotechnological inven-

---

[6]   e.g. in the Netherlands, Breeders' Ordinance of 1941; in Germany, the Law on Protection of Varieties and Seeds of Cultivated Plants and in 1930, the US created a particular "plant patent" for asexually reproduced plant varieties.

[7]   *NOVARTIS/Transgenic Plant* (G1/98) [2000] E.P.O.R. 303 See para.2-291.

tions for plants are patentable. Indeed, the EU has enacted a Biotechnological Directive which sets out the principles for the patenting of biotechnological inventions. The reader is referred to Ch.2, "Patents in Europe" for more information.[8] The matter is also complicated by the implementation of the Community Plant Variety Right Regulation. It specifically prohibits parallel enforcement of patent protection or national plant variety rights protection in a plant variety where a Community Plant Variety Rights has been granted.[9]

THE TRIPS AGREEMENT

The Uruguay round of the General Agreement on Tariffs and Trade ("GATT") **6-015** resulted in the Trade-Related Aspects of Intellectual Property Rights ("TRIPS") Agreement being concluded. The TRIPS Agreement forms Annex 1C of the Marrakech Agreement Establishing the World Trade Organization,[10] which was signed in Marrakech, Morocco on 15 April 1994. It came into force on 1 January 1995. Articles 27 to 34 inclusive are concerned with patents and in passing plant varieties. Article 27(3) reads:

"Members may also exclude from patentability:

'… plants and animals other than micro-organisms, and essentially biological processes for the production of plants or animals other than non-biological and microbiological processes. However, Members shall provide for the protection of plant varieties either by patents or by an effective sui generis system or by any combination thereof. The provisions of this subparagraph shall be reviewed four years after the date of entry into force of the WTO Agreement.'"

This provision requires that protection be afforded to plant varieties either by **6-016** patents or sui generis protection or *by a combination thereof*. However, in Europe, cumulative protection is not permitted under both the European Patent Convention and the Community Plant Variety Regulation ("CPVR"). Thus, patent protection for plant varieties is prohibited by art.53(b) EPC. Furthermore, upon grant of the Community Plant Variety Right, the holder of the CPVR for a plant variety cannot enforce parallel patent protection for a national plant variety and cannot enforce that patent.[11] Accordingly, European members of WTO are obliged to provide for sui generis protection. In this regard, commentators are agreed that protection in accordance with UPOV would be sufficient to satisfy this condition.[12]

In the negotiations leading to TRIPS, there was much debate and discussion **6-017** concerning the exceptions to patentability. Accordingly, provision was made for a review of the exceptions to be held within four years, namely by 1999. This was within the five years that had been allowed for developing countries to implement the Agreement as a whole. This was the only provision that provided for a review

---

[8] See para.2-577.
[9] See para.6-139 for further discussion.
[10] Its website may be found at *http://www.wto.org* [Accessed 21 January 2018]. For a detailed discussion of TRIPS, see Ch.1, para.1-167.
[11] art.92 CPV Regulation. See para.6-139.
[12] See, for example, R.S. Crespi, "Patents and Plant Variety Rights: Is There an Interface Problem?" [1992] 2 I.I.C. 168; S.K. Verma, "TRIPS and Plant Variety Protection in Developing Countries" [1995] E.I.P.R. 281; D. Gervais, *The TRIPS Agreement: Drafting History and Analysis*, 4th edn (London: Sweet & Maxwell, 2012).

within this time-frame.[13] Apparently, the review that occurred in 1999 did not alter this Article.

THE CONVENTION ON BIOLOGICAL DIVERSITY

6-018   The political community as a whole is becoming more aware of issues that relate to the environment. One aspect of this resulted in the Convention on Biological Diversity that was opened for signature at Rio de Janeiro on 5 June 1992[14] (the "Rio de Janeiro Convention"). This Convention is phrased in the most general way. For example, the first two recitals read:

> "Conscious of the intrinsic value of biological diversity and of the ecological, genetic, social, economic, scientific, educational, cultural, recreational and aesthetic values of biological diversity and its components...
> Conscious also of the importance of biological diversity for evolution and for maintaining life sustaining systems of the biosphere."

6-019   The essence of the Rio de Janeiro Convention is contained in arts 1 and 3, which state:

> "1.   The objectives of this Convention, to be pursued in accordance with its relevant provisions, are the conservation of biological diversity, the sustainable use of its components and the fair and equitable sharing of the benefits arising out of the utilization of genetic resources, including by appropriate access to genetic resources and by appropriate transfer of relevant technologies, taking into account all rights over those resources and to technologies, and by appropriate funding.
> 2.   ...
> 3.   States have, in accordance with the Charter of the United Nations and the principles of international law, the sovereign right to exploit their own resources pursuant to their own environmental policies, and the responsibility to ensure that activities within their jurisdiction or control do not cause damage to the environment of other States or of areas beyond the limits of national jurisdiction."

6-020   Part of the genesis of the Rio de Janeiro Convention lay in the concern that some countries, and, in particular, a few large multi-national companies, were obtaining novel chemicals from natural plant material in developing countries that could be used in the pharmaceutical industry, or were obtaining genetic material that could be used for profitable (mainly) plant breeding programmes. In particular, there was a concern that once these chemicals or plants had been discovered by these companies, that patent protection or the like would be sought such that the originating country would then have to pay a royalty to the rights holder in order to secure the benefit of what had originated from that country.

6-021   These concerns also formed part of a wider political concern, namely that it appeared that the developed countries were exploiting the natural resources of less well developed countries.[15] These natural resources included not only the genetic, but also the cultural, (e.g. by identifying the active component in traditional folk

---

[13] M. Blakeney, *Trade Related Aspects of Intellectual Property Rights: A Concise Guide to the TRIPS Agreement* (London: Sweet & Maxwell, 1996), p.83, para.8.04. The matter has been complicated by the 2001 Doha Declaration which mandated the TRIPS Council to work on the relationship between TRIPS and the UN Convention on Biological Diversity.

[14] See *http://www.cbd.int/convention/text* [Accessed 21 January 2018].

[15] This concern was manifested in 2001 by the Doha Declaration on TRIPS discussed in the introductory chapter to this book at para.1-177.

lore cures and the like) and then reaping the profits without any financial compensation to the original country.[16] This was felt to be inequitable, and was vividly referred to as "bio-piracy".

To date, this Convention has had little impact on plant variety rights. However, **6-022** it is likely that its importance will increase with time and may result in a duty to compensate countries from which rare genetic material has originated and which has resulted in plant variety rights and, possibly, the granting of state-wide compulsory licences for developing countries. Furthermore, it is important to note that the Convention covers not only the land masses and continental shelf that forms the natural jurisdictions of the respective countries, but also "areas beyond the limits of national jurisdiction", e.g. the 60 per cent of the surface of the Earth where the sea bed is more than one mile deep.[17]

THE UPOV CONVENTION

Introduction

The International Union for the Protection of New Varieties of Plants ("UPOV")[18] **6-023** is an intergovernmental organisation with its headquarters in Geneva, Switzerland.[19] The first Convention was concluded in Paris in 1961 and came into force in 1968 (the "1961 Act"). It was signed by most European countries.[20] This Act was revised in Geneva in 1972. A further revision occurred in 1978 (the "1978 Act"), which came into force on 8 November 1981. This was revised again in 1991 (the "1991 Act"), which came into force on 24 April 1998. Thus, the current membership of the Union comprises those bound by the 1961 Act as revised in 1972; those bound by the 1978 Act; and, those bound by the 1991 Act. This last revision incorporated some considerable changes, and was the result of extensive discussions amongst interested bodies.[21]

Since the last edition of this book and driven by the accession of the EU to the **6-024** 1991 Act, all European countries have signed and ratified the 1991 Act other than Italy, Norway, Portugal and Belgium[22] who are signatories to earlier UPOV Acts.[23] The 1991 Act provides for the possibility of accession by any intergovernmental organisation that has competence in the field of plant breeders' rights and that has its own legislation providing for the grant and protection of plant variety rights. On 29 June 2005, the EU became the first intergovernmental organisation to become a member of the 1991 Act.[24] This lays the legal foundation for the CPVR which is an EU-wide, unitary right like the European Union Trade Mark and the Com-

---

[16] For a series of articles on this topic, see M. Blakeney, "Perspectives on Intellectual Property" in *Intellectual Property Aspects of Ethno-biology* (London: Sweet & Maxwell, 1999), Vol.6.

[17] About 1.6 km.

[18] *Union internationale pour la protection des obtentions végétales.*

[19] Its website may be found at: *http://www.upov.int* [Accessed 18 January 2018].

[20] Belgium, France, Federal Republic of Germany, Italy and Holland adopted it in 1961; the UK and Sweden in 1962; and Ireland, Hungary, Spain and Switzerland in 1969.

[21] See B. Greengrass, "The 1991 Act of the UPOV Convention" [1991] 12 E.I.P.R. 466-472.

[22] Italy, Norway and Portugal are signatories to the 1978 Act and Belgium is a signatory to the 1961/1972 Act.

[23] See *http://www.upov.int/export/sites/upov/members/en/pdf/pub423.pdf* [Accessed 18 January 2018].

[24] Council Decision 2005/523 approving the accession of the European Community to the International Convention for the Protection of New Varieties of Plants, as revised at Geneva on 19 March 1991 [2005] OJ L192/63–77.

munity Registered Design. The failure of Italy, Portugal and Belgium to sign and ratify the 1991 Act is thus mitigated by the fact that an applicant can obtain a CPVR which is based on the 1991 Act for the EU.

6-025   The objective of the Convention is to provide sui generis protection for plant varieties for a limited period so long as certain criteria are met. Interestingly, it was felt to be imperative to adopt a system different from the patent system. Thus, the UPOV Convention does not provide for a single "central application" system like the EPC. Rather, it simply sets out the requirements to which the countries wishing to set up national plant variety rights must adhere. Furthermore, it provides for different periods of protection for different species of plants. This was justified on the grounds that the protection that was thereby conferred could be tailored to suit the specific biological and commercial requirements of the different plant varieties.

6-026   As plant breeders' rights are of relatively recent invention and very much sui generis, countries that have acceded to the UPOV Convention have generally not inherited any corpus of law relating to plant breeders' rights. Countries and now intergovernmental organisations (under the 1991 Act), may become a member of the UPOV by depositing an instrument of accession. No country or intergovernmental organisation may accede to any Act other than the 1991 Act. Furthermore, under the UPOV Convention, countries that ratify the UPOV Convention are required, before depositing an instrument of ratification, to ask the UPOV Council to advise them in respect of the conformity of their laws with the provisions of the Convention.[25] This has resulted in a very high degree of similarity between Member States' laws of those who have acceded to the 1991 Act.[26] Moreover, litigation is rare, and so no substantial case law has developed.[27] The main reason for this is that the system was set up by plant breeders for plant breeders, and the tribunals set up by national systems that hear disputes comprise scientists as well as lawyers and, typically, this leads to resolution of potential problems without recourse to full trial. Thus, there is little to be gained from carrying out a comparison of the law of plant breeders' rights in European countries. Of course, the precise application and interpretation of the UPOV Convention, as enacted nationally by national tribunals and states, has and shall vary.[28]

The 1991 Act

6-027   The 1991 Act is the most recent revision of the UPOV Convention. As of January 2018, 75 countries and the EU itself were parties to one of the three versions of the Convention, namely the 1961 Act, the 1978 Act or the 1991 Act. A complete

---

[25]   e.g. see art.34(3) of the 1991 Act.
[26]   For the UK, see Plant Varieties and Seeds Act 1997.
[27]   Although a small of body of Boards of Appeal decision of the CPVO is beginning to develop.
[28]   There will often be considerable variation in the extent of ex officio testing of varieties by national offices prior to the grant of rights. Thus, in *Daehnfeldt v Controller of Plant Varieties* [1976] F.S.R. 94, an appeal from a decision of the Controller to the Plant Variety Rights Tribunal, the issue was whether the Italian ryegrass variety named PREGO was sufficiently distinct from TIARA and VEJRUP. The British examiners had been unable to distinguish clearly between these varieties and had refused registration. In contrast, plant breeders' rights had been granted in Germany and Denmark, because in the former, the German authority had not compared PREGO against VEJRUP, and the tests in Denmark had been very bare and uninformative. The appeal was unsuccessful and it is believed that the German authorities then revoked the rights-an example of co-operation between the national authorities. See N.J. Byrne, "The Agritechnical Criteria in Plant Breeders' Rights Law" [1983] I.P. 293, 299.

list of European countries that are members and the Act which they have ratified can be viewed on UPOV's website.[29]

As discussed earlier in this chapter, art.27(3) GATT/TRIPS Agreement which was established in 1994, requires members of WTO to provide patent or plant variety rights protection for plant varieties or a combination of both.[30] In Europe, the ban on patenting plant varieties under art.53(b) of the EPC means that contracting states to the EPC must provide for the obtaining and registration of plant variety rights. This has led to a substantial number of new countries signing up to the 1991 Act to comply with their GATT/TRIPS obligations (UPOV does not permit ratification of earlier texts of the UPOV Convention). Prior to the GATT/TRIPS Agreement, the UPOV Convention was seen as essentially European in content and application. Thus, by 2014, the vast majority of European and non-European countries have now ratified the 1991 Act. Accordingly, this book only examines the 1991 Act. Usefully, the UPOV website has a webpage which sets out the national legislation of UPOV members which implements their UPOV obligations.[31]

6-028

Fundamental principles of the 1991 Act

The 1991 Act does not alter the fundamental principles of the previous Acts, namely that contracting parties are to grant and protect breeders' rights in the reproductive and propagating material of plant varieties.[32] Under the 1991 Act, breeders who have produced a variety that is new, distinct from the prior art, uniform and stable may apply for registration of its variety at a national level. If registration is obtained, the proprietor has the exclusive right to exploit commercially the reproductive or propagative material of variety. The Convention lays down that such protection shall last for a minimum of 20 years, but shall not be shorter than 25 years for trees and vines. In some cases, like potatoes, the rights can last up to 30 years. It is important to emphasise that the Convention primarily protects the reproductive material of a variety, rather than the variety itself. This is often why many refer to the system as plant breeders' rights rather than plant variety rights.

6-029

Equality of treatment

The 1991 Act, as with the previous Acts, provides that contracting states must not discriminate in the grant of plant variety rights between their own nationals and nationals of another contracting state.[33]

6-030

Cumulative protection

The 1991 Act abolishes the ban on double protection under both patent and plant variety law that had existed in the 1978 Act.[34] Applicants now will be able to obtain both patent protection and plant variety rights for a plant variety. However, in

6-031

---

[29] *http://upov.int/export/sites/upov/members/en/pdf/pub423.pdf* [Accessed 18 January 2018].

[30] See para.6-015.

[31] See *http://www.upov.int/upovlex/en/* [Accessed 18 January 2018] although this is far from complete.

[32] art.2.

[33] art.4. Where the state is an intergovernmental organisation, "nationals" means nationals of the states belonging to that organisation—art.4(2).

[34] See art.2(1) of the 1978 Act. B. Greengrass, "The 1991 Act of the UPOV Convention" [1991] 12 E.I.P.R. 466, 467 states that Member States are free to enact legislation that an applicant must decide

Europe, this has no effect as both the EPC and CPV Regulation do not allow double protection.[35]

Protection of plant genera and species

6-032   Under the 1978 Act, no requirement was placed on contracting states to protect varieties in all plant genera and species. It merely required that acceding states protect five genera or species on accession and that they should protect a minimum of 24 *genera* or species within eight years.[36] The 1991 Act distinguishes between states that have already ratified the UPOV Convention and new members of UPOV. In the former case, such states must extend protection to all genera and species by the end of five years from the date that the state is bound by the 1991 Act. In the latter case, new members must initially protect a minimum of 15 plant *genera* and species and, within 10 years from being bound by the Convention, all plant genera and species.[37] A consequence of this requirement is that a contracting state must eventually confer protection even on those species that cannot be grown in that country. This could present practicable problems related to the testing of the variety. However, these could be overcome by co-operation between the different national offices.

Conditions for protection for plant varieties

6-033   Protection is only granted to plant "varieties". The scientific meaning of "varieties" has already been considered.[38] The legal definition of variety is considered below. The main legal requirement for a variety to be protected is that it must be new, distinct, uniform and stable.[39] Apart from this requirement, the grant of a plant variety right can only be subject to the requirement that it is designated by a denomination and that the application complies with the formalities provided for by the law of the state where the application has been filed.[40] The aim of the 1991 Act is that protection is granted to plant varieties of all genera and species. However, for acceding states, there are transitional provisions in the 1991 Act which provide for a transitional period of up to 10 years, whereby contracting states need not provide protection for all plant *genera* and species.[41]

Examination

6-034   Each variety must be examined prior to the grant of plant variety rights in order to demonstrate that it fulfils the above requirements of novelty, distinctness, uniformity and stability. In comparing varieties for the purposes of whether such criteria are met, UPOV at Geneva provides guidelines that are intended to provide

---

between patent or plant variety rights. This seems to conflict with art.2 which boldly states that contracting states shall grant plant variety rights to those varieties protectable under the Convention. However, this statement is correct in the case of art.27(3) of TRIPS.
[35] See paras 6-139 and 2-291.
[36] art.4 of the 1978 Act. There is a provision in art.4 that contracting states should progressively expand protection to as many genera and species as possible, although it is not a binding provision.
[37] art.3 of the 1991 Act.
[38] See para.6-001, et seq.
[39] art.5.
[40] art.5(2).
[41] art.3(2).

contracting states with a common basis for testing varieties and establishing varietal descriptions in a standardised form.[42] These guidelines are prepared for each plant species and are regularly updated to take account of technical progress and new insights on species. Furthermore, they provide information on the relevant characteristics for each species that should be taken into account in deciding whether plant breeders' rights should be granted. For instance, relevant characteristics for a flower could include plant height, colour of stem, leaf width, thickness, and type of flower head. Clearly, relevant characteristics for flowers will be different from those for crop varieties.

Variety

In the 1991 Act, "variety" is defined as meaning: **6-035**

"A plant grouping within a single botanical taxon of the lowest known rank, which grouping irrespective of whether the conditions for the grant of a breeder's rights are fully met, can be:

- defined by the expression of the characteristics resulting from a given genotype or combination of genotypes;
- distinguished from any other plant grouping by the expression of at least one of the said characteristics and;
- considered as a unit with regard to its suitability for being propagated unchanged."[43]

Previously, in the 1978 Act, there was no definition of "variety" despite the fact   **6-036**
that the 1961 Act defined "variety" as "any cultivar, clone, line, stock or hybrid which is capable of cultivation" and which is homogeneous and stable.[44] When it came to drafting the 1991 Act, there was much discussion as to whether a definition of "variety" was required or even desirable. This was because under art.53(b) of the EPC, patents cannot be granted for "plant or animal varieties or essentially biological processes for the production of plants or animals".[45] Thus, any definition of "variety" by UPOV was likely to affect the patentability of a plant invention. Indeed, in *Ciba-Geigy*,[46] the Technical Board of Appeal ("TBA") of the EPO interpreted the meaning of "plant variety" by reference to the UPOV 1961 Act.[47] Thus, it was realised that a definition of "plant variety" would be used for the purpose of the EPC and this could adversely affect the patentability of plant innovations.[48] Despite these fears, it was decided to define "variety" as above.

---

[42] General Introduction to the Examination of Distinctness, Uniformity and Stability and the Development of Harmonised Descriptions of New Varieties of Plants TG/1/3 (April 2002). This can be accessed at [*http://www.upov.int/test_guidelines/en/introduction.html*] [Accessed 6 May 2018]
[43] art.1(vi).
[44] "Homogeneous" tends to be interchanged with "uniform". For the purposes of plant variety rights, the two mean the same.
[45] See para.2-291, et seq.
[46] *CIBA-GEIGY* (T-49/83) [1984] OJ EPO 112; [1979–85] E.P.O.R. C 758.
[47] The TBA's approach in *Ciba-Geigy* was confirmed in *Lubrizol I* [1990] E.P.O.R. 177.
[48] Thus, patent circles were concerned that the definition of "variety" in the UPOV 1991 Act might embrace a plant cell line—see B. Greengrass, "The 1991 Act of the UPOV Convention" [1991] 12 E.I.P.R. 466, 467.

Subsequently, in a latter EPO case, in fulfilment of the above fears, the EPO used this definition for the purposes of re-defining "plant variety" in art.53(b).[49]

6-037   It will be noted that the definition of "variety" is expressly stated to be irrespective of whether conditions for protection as a plant variety right are "fully met". This differs from the previous Acts of the UPOV Convention, in which the definition of "variety" was the same as what was a protectable variety. In framing a definition for the 1991 Act, it was considered that the definition of "variety" should be less stringent than the requirements for a variety to be protected.[50]

6-038   Thus, the three indents in the definition correspond approximately to three out of four of the requirements for protection, namely uniformity, distinctness and stability but are considered to set these requirements at a lower level than that necessary for protection.[51] The effect of this is that when considering whether a plant variety satisfies the requirements under the 1991 Act, due regard can be taken of "prior art" varieties which themselves do not qualify or could not have qualified for protection. For example, a variety will only qualify for protection under the 1991 Act if it is clearly distinguishable from any other variety whose existence is a matter of common knowledge at the time of filing of the application (the requirement of distinctness). If the variety in issue is not distinguishable from a "prior art" variety then it does not qualify for protection, even if the prior art variety does not itself qualify for protection.

6-039   It may be that this distinction makes little difference in practice. For instance, in relation to agricultural and some vegetable varieties, in the UK, a variety can only be commercialised if it is entered on a national list. The requirements for registration on the national list of a variety (which normally takes place at the same time as assessment for the purposes of plant variety rights) is similar to that for the conferring of plant variety rights.[52] Thus, a prior variety is unlikely to be commercially exploited unless it is also capable of protection by way of plant variety rights. However, in relation to other types of plants (i.e. horticultural varieties), there is no requirement of national registration.

Novelty

6-040   The 1991 UPOV Act states:

"The variety shall be deemed to be new if, at the date of filing of the application for a breeder's right, propagating or harvested material of the variety has not been sold or otherwise disposed of to others, by or with the consent of the breeder, for the purposes of exploitation of the variety:

(i)   in the territory of the Contracting Party in which the application has been filed earlier than one year before that date and

(ii)   in a territory other than that of the Contracting Party in which the application has

---

[49]   *PLANT GENETIC SYSTEM/Glutamine Synthetase Inhibitors* (T-356/93) [1995] E.P.O.R. 357 at [23].
[50]   See B. Greengrass, "The 1991 Act of the UPOV Convention" [1991] 12 E.I.P.R. 466, 467.
[51]   See B. Greengrass, "The 1991 Act of the UPOV Convention" [1991] 12 E.I.P.R. 466.
[52]   And in some respects, the requirement to get on the National List is higher than that to obtain PVRs, see *Moulin Winter Wheat* [1985] F.S.R. 283 (Plant Variety Tribunal, UK) where it was noted that the requirement of "sufficient uniformity" was applied more strictly for the National List than for the purpose of obtaining national PVRs.

been filed earlier than four years or, in the case of trees or of vines, earlier than six years before the said date."[53]

It can be seen from the above definition that this condition is concerned with whether there has been prior commercialisation of the variety applied for by the applicant for protection of that plant variety. In patent-speak, it is concerned with "prior user by self-anticipation". It is not concerned with whether there exists an identical "prior art" variety created by a third party which is identical in all respects to the variety applied for. Such a variety would not have been sold "by or with the consent of the breeder". Thus, the novelty test is different from that in patent law, which is concerned about absolute novelty and not mere "prior user". This does not, in practice, make much difference because the applicant must still satisfy the test of distinctness, i.e. that the variety right is distinguishable from other varieties which is indeed akin to the patent novelty test.[54]   **6-041**

The test also requires that the propagating or harvested material was disposed of "for the purposes of exploitation of the variety". This was absent in the 1978 Act. This additional requirement relaxes the test of novelty. If the applicant can show that a first variety has been sold or disposed of as propagating material for the purposes of creating a second variety, then it is difficult to say that the first variety has been sold for exploitation of the first variety. For instance, an inbred-line parent "variety" that has only been sold or disposed for the purposes of producing an F1 hybrid[55] has not itself been sold or disposed of for the purpose of exploitation of the parent variety. Thus, where the applicant wishes now to exploit commercially the parent inbred-line variety itself, an application for such will not be defeated on the basis of lack of novelty, even if they have for many years been selling the parent variety as propagating material to produce the F1 hybrid. Equally, if the inbred-line parent variety has been sold as propagating material to produce another variety, then the fact that it could have been used to create the F1 hybrid will not result in a loss of novelty for an application for the F1 hybrid as the parent variety was not sold for the purpose of exploiting the F1 hybrid.   **6-042**

In contrast, the addition of the words "propagating or harvested material of the variety" in the 1991 Act as against just "variety" in the 1978 Acts tightens the test of novelty. Novelty will not exist if the material for propagating the variety or harvested material from that variety has been commercialised. For instance, if a breeder has marketed parent inbred lines for the purposes of production and subsequent exploitation of an F1 variety, then the breeder has provided propagating material for the F1 variety and they will not be able to obtain plant variety rights for the F1 variety under the 1991 Act. Under the 1978 Act, the breeder could have obtained plant variety rights, provided that the F1 variety itself had not been commercially exploited.   **6-043**

---

[53] art.6(2).

[54] See para.6-046.

[55] An F1 hybrid is the direct progeny of two different parent varieties, which in turn are often inbred lines so that the characteristics of the F1 hybrid are predictable—see N.J. Byrne, "The Agritechnical Criteria in Plant Breeders' Rights Laws" [1983] I.P. 293, 296. Often the F1 hybrid is sterile and cannot reproduce itself. For example (from the animal kingdom), the cross between a male donkey and a female horse results in a sterile mule (cf. hinney, a cross between a female donkey and a male horse, and which is not usually sterile). Accordingly, breeders must always use the parent varieties to produce it. For instance, many wheat varieties are sterile hybrids. Hybrids are often commercially popular, because commonly they produce strong plants; this is called "F1 vigour".

6-044   The application will not fail for want of novelty if the propagating or harvested material of the variety was marketed later than one year before the date of application in the applicant's territory or a maximum of six years in other territories. This "grace period" is similar to the one-year grace period for Community Registered Designs where the applicant has a one-year period of protection prior to the date of filing from disclosures of the design applied.[56] This permits the breeder to place the variety on the market in order to ascertain its commercial worth before applying for plant breeders' rights.

6-045   Where a Contracting Party applies the 1991 Act to a plant genus or species to which it had not previously applied it, it may extend the grace periods referred to above for the purposes of novelty.[57]

Distinctness

6-046   Under the 1991 Act, a variety is distinct if:

"if it is clearly distinguishable from any other variety whose existence is a matter of common knowledge at the time of the filing of the application. In particular, the filing of an application for the granting of a breeder's right or for the entering of another variety in an official register of varieties, in any country, shall be deemed to render that other variety a matter of common knowledge from the date of the application, provided that the application leads to the granting of a breeder's right or to the entering of the said other variety in the official register of varieties, as the case may be."[58]

6-047   This provision is thus not concerned with prior exploitation of the variety itself (such is governed by the novelty test) but is concerned with third party prior art varieties. The 1991 Act differs from the 1978 Act in that the requirement that the variety be distinguishable by one or more *important* characteristics from any other variety has been abandoned since this condition was thought to be needlessly ambiguous. The word "important" suggested that a variety must, to be protectable, be distinct from existing varieties by some feature related to merit.[59]

6-048   The notion of common knowledge is not refined further in the 1991 Act, but it deems that the filing of an application for the grant of plant variety rights or the entering of a variety in an official register shall make such a variety a matter of common knowledge from the date of application or filing, provided that this leads to the grant of plant variety rights. In considering the issue of distinctness, the national office will examine the claimed characteristics of the variety as against other "commonly known" varieties. National plant variety offices will not seek to examine the actual genetic structure of the variety in order to determine whether it differs from other varieties, but merely whether the variety expresses differing characteristics from other varieties, i.e. the phenotype rather than the genotype is examined.[60] This approach to distinctness now closely accords with the definition of "variety" in the 1991 Act, whereby the important criterion is the exhibition of at least one distinctive characteristic (see second indent) from other plants. However, as previously

---

[56]   See para.5-103.
[57]   art.6(2).
[58]   art.7.
[59]   See B. Greengrass, "The 1991 Act of the UPOV Convention" [1991] 12 E.I.P.R. 466, 468.
[60]   For the meaning of "phenotype" and "genotype", see para.6-005.

mentioned,[61] the intention was that the definition of variety in the 1991 Act be less demanding than the requirement for a plant variety to be registrable.

Uniformity

The variety must be uniform for protection to be granted. The 1991 Act deems this to be so if: **6-049**

> "subject to the variation that may be expected from the particular features of its propagation, it is sufficiently uniform in its relevant characteristics."[62]

The wording is somewhat different from the 1978 Act, but it is not intended that there should be any change in substance.[63] The above wording emphasises that absolute uniformity is not required. Clearly, the criteria of uniformity is linked with that of distinctness and stability. Without a sufficiently homogeneous variety, it may be difficult to satisfy the distinctness criteria between similar varieties of plants. **6-050**

Equally, if a variety is unstable, uniformity will not be shown over the generations. Thus, a uniform first-generation cross-pollinating variety may produce a heterogeneous second-generation variety, i.e. the F2 generation. Similarly, a non-sterile F1 hybrid that contains both a dominant and recessive gene (i.e. it is a heterogeneous genotype) for a particular feature may be homogeneous phenotypically, because of the dominant gene, but when it self-pollinates, the second generation (i.e. the F2 generation) will produce 25 per cent double recessive gene plants that will exhibit the recessive gene characteristics as opposed to the 75 per cent that will exhibit the dominant characteristics. In such cases, an apparently uniform variety is not truly so when measured across the generations because it is unstable.[64] This reflects the difference between a homogeneous phenotype and genotype.[65] **6-051**

---

[61] See para.6-038.

[62] art.8. See *Moulin Winter Wheat* [1985] F.S.R. 283 (Plant Varieties and Seed Tribunal) where it was held that "sufficiently uniform" meant:

> "the degree of uniformity a capable breeder skilled in the art could reasonably be expected to achieve having regard generally to the nature of plant material and particularly to the biological possibilities of the species in question, including its mode of reproduction, and to any special features of the variety in consideration. The best test for this was to determine what breeders skilled in the art have achieved and are achieving in the particular species, and to make suitable allowance for any special difficulties arising in the case of particular varieties". (At 283–284.)

[63] See B. Greengrass, "The 1991 Act of the UPOV Convention" [1991] 12 E.I.P.R. 466, 469.

[64] In *Zephyr* [1967] F.S.R. 576, the Controller of the Plant Variety Tribunal emphasised that, in such matters, the real criteria to consider is that of stability, because essentially it is a condition precedent to the issue of uniformity.

[65] The phenotype refers to the characteristic as manifested in the actual organism, while the genotype refers to the genetic composition, regardless of whether or not it is actually manifested. The gene for blue eyes (Bu) is recessive, while that for brown eyes (Br) is dominant. Accordingly, a person who has blue eyes (i.e. who is phenotypically "blue-eyed"), must be genotypically homogeneous with the genetic composition BuBu. In contrast, a person who has brown eyes (i.e. one who is phenotypically "brown-eyed"), may be genotypically homogeneous with the genetic composition BrBr, or else be genotypically heterogeneous, with the genetic composition BuBr. An F1 cross between genotypically pure brown or blue-eyed parents (i.e. BrBr and BuBu), will result in an F1 generation of only heterogeneous genotypes (BuBr), all of whom will be brown-eyed. However, the F2 generation from two mated F1 hybrids will result in one homogeneous genotypical (and hence phenotypical) blue-eyed off-spring, and three phenotypical brown-eyed off-spring, two of whom will be genotypically heterogeneous (BuBr), and one of whom will be genotypically homogeneous (BrBr).

Stability

6-052   The 1991 Act deems a variety to be stable if its relevant characteristics remain unchanged after repeated propagation or, in the case of a particular cycle of propagation, at the end of each such cycle.[66] Again, there is a change of wording from the 1978 Act, but no substantive change was intended.[67] The UPOV Guidelines says that experience shows where a sample of the variety proves uniform, the variety can be considered stable.[68] However, as seen above, this may not be the case, and so, where there is reason to doubt it, stability must be tested by growing a further generation or new seed stock to verify that it exhibits the same characteristics as those shown by the previous sample of the variety.[69]

Scope of plant variety rights

6-053   Article 14 states that the owner of plant variety rights under the 1991 Act has the exclusive right in respect of propagating material to produce or reproduce [multiply]; condition for the purposes of propagation; offer for sale, market, export, import; and, finally, to stock for any of these purposes.[70] This differs from the 1978 Act, which included the condition "for the purposes of commercial marketing."[71] The 1978 Act had the effect of implicitly creating "farmers' rights" to re-plant on their farms propagating material from the previous year's harvest.

Farmer's privilege

6-054   The 1991 Act deals with the issue of such farmer's privileges in a different way. It imposes no mandatory provisions, but permits Contracting Parties "within reasonable limits and subject to the safeguarding of the legitimate interests of the breeder" restrict breeder rights *"in order to permit farmers to use for propagating purposes, on their own holdings, the product of the harvest which they have obtained by planting, on their own holdings"*.[72] This is commonly known as "the farmer's privilege". The Diplomatic Conference formally recommended that such a provision:

> "should not be read so as to be intended to open the possibility of extending the practice commonly called 'farmer's privilege' to sectors of agricultural or horticultural production in which such a privilege is not a common place."[73]

---

[66] art.9.

[67] B. Greengrass, "The 1991 Act of the UPOV Convention" [1991] 12 E.I.P.R. 466, 469.

[68] UPOV TG/1/3 *General Introduction to Guidelines*, para.7.3.1.1. [*http://www.upov.int/export/sites/ upov/publications/en/tg_rom/pdf/tg_1_3.pdf* [Accessed 18 January 2018]]. However, in fact, logically, uniformity needs to be considered at two levels: *intra-generational* and *cross-generational*. As said by the UK Plant Variety Tribunal (see fn.64), logically stability should be considered prior to uniformity.

[69] UPOV TG/1/3 *General Introduction to Guidelines*, para.7.3.1.2.

[70] art.14(1). Contracting parties may extend this list of rights to cover other acts—art.14(4).

[71] art.5 of the 1978 Act.

[72] art.15(2).

[73] See B. Greengrass, "The 1991 Act of the UPOV Convention" [1991] 12 E.I.P.R. 466, 469. This provision can be implemented in many ways. In the CPVR Regulation, detailed provisions have been enacted in relation to the exact nature and scope of the farmers' exemption. In the UK, Plant Varieties and Seeds Act 1997 s.9 provides for a farmer's exemption similar to that adopted in the CPVR.

The 1991 Act makes it clear that the plant variety right does not extend to: acts **6-055** done privately and for non-commercial purposes, acts done for experimental purpose, and importantly, it retains the right of plant breeders to use a protected variety to produce other varieties without infringing plant variety rights.[74] However, as will be seen, this exemption does not apply to the creation of varieties that are "essentially derived" from the protected variety.[75]

Second and third generation material

The 1991 Act makes provision for the protection of harvested material ("second **6-056** generation material") including entire plants and parts of plants derived from the protected variety, and also for products made directly from the harvested material ("third generation material"). Such protection was seen as necessary, because often the plant breeder would not have had an opportunity to exercise their rights in relation to the initial propagating material.[76] In both cases, the extension of plant variety rights is dependent on the breeder not having had "reasonable opportunity to exercise his right" in relation to material of an earlier generation.[77] Thus, the 1991 Act provides for a "cascade" of rights in relation to a variety, namely propagating material, harvested material of propagating material, and products directly derived from such harvested material whereby the exercise of rights against one type is dependent on the rights owner not being able to exercise their rights against the breeder or user of the previous generation. Clearly, the rights owner must have had an opportunity to exercise their rights against the propagating material actually used for making the harvested material in casu rather than any propagating material. A similar argument applies to products that have been directly derived from the harvested material.

Derived varieties

The 1991 Act also extends a plant breeder's exclusive rights to "essentially **6-057** derived varieties" ("EDVs"), varieties that are not clearly distinguishable from the protected variety and "varieties whose production requires the repeated use of the protected variety."[78] EDVs are discussed in the next section.

Protection starts from the date of grant of plant variety rights, although contract- **6-058** ing parties must enact that the holder of such rights is entitled to at least equitable remuneration for acts that would otherwise infringe the owner's rights but are carried out between the date of application and that of grant.[79]

Essentially derived varieties ("EDVs")

A breeder cannot prevent another breeder from using the former's protected **6-059** variety to breed another variety. This exception is contained in both the 1978 and

---

[74] art.15(1)(i)–(ii).
[75] art.15(1)(ii) and see para.6-059.
[76] i.e. where harvested material of a protected variety is imported from a country where there is no plant variety protection or where the owner of the rights was unaware of the existence of the propagating material used to make the harvested product.
[77] art.14(2), (3).
[78] art.14(5)(a)(i)–(iii).
[79] art.13.

1991 Acts.[80] However, in drafting the 1991 Act, it was felt that, as the test for distinctness was so low, a breeder could easily introduce a minor variant into a competitor's protected variety and so produce a new variety and thereby take advantage of this provision, and that this unfairly prejudiced owners of the parent variety right. Accordingly, the 1991 Act introduced an extension of the scope of protection of plant variety rights to cover varieties that are "essentially derived" from the protected variety where the protected variety is not itself an essentially derived variety.[81] Article 14(5)(b) of the 1991 Act defines an "essentially derived variety" as meaning:

"(i)   it is predominantly derived from the initial variety, or from a variety that is itself predominantly derived from the initial variety, while retaining the expression of the essential characteristics that result from the genotype or combination of genotypes of the initial variety

(ii)   it is clearly distinguishable from the initial variety and

(iii)   except for the differences which result from the act of derivation, it conforms to the initial variety in the expression of the essential characteristics that result from the genotype or combination of genotypes of the initial variety."[82]

6-060   Article 14(5)(c) provides that essentially derived varieties may be obtained, for example, by the selection of a natural or induced mutant, or of a somaclonal variant, the selection of a variant individual from plants of the initial variety, backcrossing or transformation by genetic engineering. When introduced, it was felt that there were aspects of this legislation which unclear. Thus, there was a resolution on art.14(5) which called for the immediate establishment of draft standard guidelines for adoption by the Council of UPOV on essentially derived varieties. This has now been provided.[83] It will be observed that the second requirement at art.14(5)(b)(ii) set out above states that a variety is only deemed an essentially derived variety if it is clearly distinguishable from the initial variety. Thus, if the derived variety is not clearly distinguishable, then it is not an essentially derived variety but will infringe the exclusive rights of the initial variety.[84] An essentially derived variety is capable of being subject to plant variety rights if it satisfies the distinctness test. However, the owner of such a right will require the permission of the initial variety rights' owner in order to exploit it.[85] Thus, the situation is analogous to that of the proprietor of a patent for an improvement invention under patent law whereby the proprietor of an improvement patent cannot exploit the invention without the permission of the owner of the patent for the underlying invention. Thus, where there is a plant breeder's rights on both the initial variety (A) and an essentially

---

[80]   art.5(3) of the 1978 Act; art.15(1)(iii) of the 1991 Act.

[81]   art.14(5)(a)(i).

[82]   art.14(5)(b).

[83]   The latest version is 6 April 2017 [*http://www.upov.int/edocs/expndocs/en/upov_exn_edv.pdf* [Accessed 18 January 2018].

[84]   art.14(5)(a)(ii), art.14(5)(a)(iii).

[85]   During discussions of the 1991 Act, it was suggested that the breeder of an essentially derived variety should be able to force the breeder of the initial variety to grant a licence. However, no such provision appears in the 1991 Act. In the Community Plant Variety Regulation, a compulsory exploitation licence of the initial variety may be available for the breeder of an essentially derived variety if in the public interest—see para.6-109.

derived variety (B), the authorisation of both the breeder of Variety A and Variety B is required for the commercialisation of Variety B.[86]

Article 14(5)(a)(i) states that protection does not exist for essentially derived **6-061** varieties where the protected variety is itself an essentially derived variety. Such a provision prevents a proliferation of claimants representing first, second, third and subsequent generation breeders suing, for example, a breeder of an F3 variety essentially derived via several generations from an initial protected variety.[87] It is important to point out that such does not stop the owner of the original protected variety "reaching through" a number of generations to prevent the marketing of an essentially derived variety. Thus, the owner of the right in the *original* protected variety may bring proceedings against the F3 variety but not the owners of any variety rights in the intermediate essentially derived varieties.[88]

The requirement under art.14(5)(b)(i) means that it must have been causally **6-062** derived from the original protected variety, i.e. it shares the genotype or combination of genotypes of the initial variety. This means that a variety that has been arrived at independently of the protected variety will not be considered an essentially derived variety, even if it shares essential characteristics with the initial variety. Thus, such a right is similar to copyright where there is the dual requirement of copying and a substantial similarity for an infringement action to be successful.[89] The specific mention of "genotype" means that the mere coincidence of observable features is not sufficient even where there has been a causal derivation—the features must be derived from the particular genotype.[90]

Exhaustion of the plant variety rights

The 1991 Act deems the plant variety rights to have been exhausted in relation **6-063** to any material of the protected variety or any material derived from such material or an essentially derived variety once it has been sold or otherwise marketed by the breeder or with their consent in the territory of the Contracting Party concerned.[91] This provision mirrors the jurisprudence of the CJEU in relation to the free movement of goods and intellectual property rights.[92] The CJEU has held that competition law must be applied to the marketing of the seeds of protected varieties.[93] Interestingly, the CJEU's jurisprudence deems a rights owner to have exhausted their rights even if they have marketed it in a Member State where the owner has

---

[86] See *Guidance for the Preparation of Laws Based on the 1991 Act of the UPOV Convention* (UPOV/ INF/6/3), 24 October 2013, p.62. This is accessible at: *http://www.upov.int/edocs/infdocs/en/upov_ inf_6_3.pdf* [Accessed 18 January 2018].

[87] F3 means a third-generation variety.

[88] This is made clear in the *Guidance for the Preparation of Laws*, above, pp.60–67.

[89] art.14(5)(b)(i) and (iii) are similar to the requirements of copying and substantial similarity in copyright.

[90] "Genotype" means a particular version ("allele") of a gene. A genotype will often produce observable characteristics (a phenotype) that result from the interaction between the genotype and its environment.

[91] art.16.

[92] See Ch.7.

[93] See *L.C. Nungesser K.G. & Eisele v EC Commission* (C-258/78/) [1982] E.C.R. 2015; [1983] 1 C.M.L.R. 278 at [41], et seq. The CJEU takes a more lenient view as to the application of competition law to the distribution of basic seeds merely used to produce first- and second-generation seeds—*Louis Erauw-Jacquery v La Hesbignonne* (C-27/87) [1988] E.C.R. 1919; [1988] 4 C.M.L.R. 576. See Ch.8 and para.8-170.

no protection.[94] The 1991 Act merely deems a plant variety rights owner to have exhausted their rights if they have marketed it in the country where the rights owner seeks to exercise their rights. Thus, the 1991 Act does not provide a Convention-wide exhaustion of rights doctrine whereby a plant breeder who markets material of a protected variety in Contracting State A is deemed to have exhausted his rights in that material so as to be able to prevent its import into Contracting State B. However, art.16(3) allows for a regional exhaustion of rights principle for contracting states who belong to the same intergovernmental organisation. Such has led to thus, an EU-wide exhaustion of rights principle for contracting states who are also Member States of the EU.

6-064   The 1991 Act provides that no exhaustion of rights shall be deemed to have taken place in relation to acts that involve further propagation of the variety in question or involve an export of material of the variety, that enables the propagation of the variety, into a country that does not protect varieties of the plant genus or species to which the variety belongs, except where the exported material is for final consumption purposes.[95] This prevents third parties from corrupting a variety by further breeding and emphasises the importance of the fact that a plant breeder has control over a variety so that it does not degenerate.[96] In relation to the export of a variety, the measure is aimed at preventing propagation of a variety in a country where the breeder is not able to own rights.

Procedure

6-065   The 1991 Act provides for a procedure whereby a qualifying person under the Convention applies to the appropriate office of a Contracting Party.[97] The Convention provides for a 12-month priority period whereby an applicant can claim a priority date that equates to the date of filing of the first application.[98] The relevant authority must examine the application for compliance with the requirements of the UPOV Convention and must grow the variety, carry out other necessary tests, or take into account results of trials in order to ascertain whether such requirements have been met.[99] The rights may be revoked if the requirements of novelty, distinctness, uniformity or stability have been proved not to have been satisfied.[100]

Miscellaneous

6-066   The 1991 Act contains the usual administrative provisions.[101] It does not permit contracting states to make any reservations except where states provide for protec-

---

[94] See *Merck v Stephar* (C-187/80) [1981] E.C.R. 2063; [1981] 3 C.M.L.R. 463 and Ch.7, para.7-184, et seq. In relation to exhaustion of rights under the CPVR regime, see para.6-114.
[95] art.16(2).
[96] See *Louis Erauw-Jacquery v La Hesbignonne* (C-27/87) [1988] E.C.R. 1919; [1988] 4 C.M.L.R. 576 at [10], where the CJEU emphasises that a breeder must have the right to prevent improper handling of a variety—see para.8-170.
[97] art.10.
[98] art.11.
[99] art.12.
[100] arts 21, 22.
[101] art.21, et seq.

tion for varieties that reproduce asexually via rights other than the plant variety right, they may continue to do so and need not apply the 1991 Act.[102]

EU Regulation on Plant Rights[103]

Introduction

At a EU level, the European Commission has been active in seeking to harmonise plant variety protection within the EU. After four years of consultation, on 27 July 1994, the European Council adopted the Regulation on Community Plant Variety Rights,[104] which came into force on 1 September 1994 but whose principal provisions were not effective until 27 April 1995.[105] This Regulation has affected the whole structure of plant variety rights within the EU. The object of the Regulation is to create an EU regime that, although co-existing with national regimes,[106] allows for the grant of a Community Plant Variety Right ("CPVR") that is valid and has unitary effect throughout the EU.

6-067

The effect of the Regulation and the 1991 Act is that the legislatures of most European countries have amended their existing PVR legislation in order to comply with their international obligations.

6-068

The Regulation establishes a CPV Office ("CPVO") with a legal personality that is responsible for the administration of the granting of CPVRs. The office's seat is at Angers, France.

6-069

The substantive law of the Regulation closely mirrors the 1991 Act, to which the EU is a signatory and which it expressly refers to and it will be re-examined if there are future developments in the 1991 Act.[107]

6-070

The CPVO has proved popular with plant breeders. In 2017, it received 3,391 applications—1605 for ornamental, 660 for vegetable, 817 for agricultural and 308 for fruit. Two thousand, eight hundred and sixty-five CPVR registrations were granted. Most applications come from a limited number of undertakings and countries. The Netherlands is responsible for around 50 per cent of all CPVR applications with France, Germany, the US and Switzerland some distance behind.[108] Technical examination is carried out by a number of national organisations which are delegated the task.

6-071

An implementing regulation, Reg.874/2009 provides detailed rules as to the practice and procedure in applying for a CPVR. The structure of these rules is very similar to that used by EUIPO and will be familiar to trade mark practitioners who apply for EU trade marks and Community Designs.[109]

6-072

---

[102] This provision was specifically designed for the US which provides a type of plant patent protection for such varieties—see B. Greengrass, "The 1991 Act of the UPOV Convention" [1991] 12 E.I.P.R. 466. Indeed, the US has adopted the 1991 Act with this reservation. It is not thought to affect European countries.

[103] Reg.2100/94 [1994] OJ L227/1.

[104] Reg.2100/94 [1994] OJ L227/1. This has been amended a number of times-an unofficial consolidated text can be obtained at *http://cpvo.europa.eu/sites/default/files/documents/en2100consolide.pdf* [Accessed 18 January 2018].

[105] art.118.2.

[106] It should be noted that the grant of a CPVR for a variety prevents the exercise of a national PVR for the same variety—see para.6-139.

[107] See Recitals. See also para.1-158 (status of international conventions in EU law).

[108] The CPVO publishes annual reports which provide insightful statistics.

[109] [2009] OJ L251/3. This can be found at the CPVO website.

Definition of "variety"

6-073   The definition of "variety" is virtually the same as that under the UPOV 1991 Act.[110] As the meaning of terms contained in the Regulation is ultimately determined by the CJEU, this means that this definition is now subject to the jurisprudence of that court. Further, as this definition has been adopted by the EPO in determining the meaning of the exclusion of patents for plant varieties, it means that, indirectly, the CJEU may have some influence on the jurisprudence of the EPO on this particular issue.[111] However, as yet, the CJEU has not opined on the precise meaning of plant variety in the Regulation.

6-074   However, the CPVR provides two important additions to the UPOV definition. First, the expression "plant grouping" in the UPOV definition is clarified as applying to either entire plants or to parts of plants "as far as such parts are capable of producing entire plants".[112] The Regulation refers to both as "variety constituents".

6-075   Secondly, the Regulation states that the requirement that the characteristics that result from a genotype or combination of genotypes may be invariable or variable "between variety constituents of the same kind" provided that such variation arises from the genotype or combination of genotypes.[113] However, this does not affect the rule that the "variety" must distinguish itself from any other plant grouping by at least one characteristic. Thus, a "variety" may demonstrate *genotypic* variability in one or more characteristics but it must still be distinguishable in at least *one* characteristic from other plants.

6-076   It is important to emphasise, as in the 1991 Act, that the definition of "variety" in the CPVR is not dependent on whether the "variety" is protectable under the CPVR. Thus, there is no requirement for a variety to be distinct, uniform and stable ("DUS") to be considered a variety under the CPVR but such will not be protectable as a CPVR.

Requirements for protection

6-077   Varieties of all botanical genera and species including hybrids between genera and species may form the object of CPVRs.[114] The substantive requirements for a plant variety to qualify for registration are similar to those under the 1991 Act. Thus, the variety must be distinct, uniform, stable and new, and moreover it must be designated by a denomination.[115]

Distinctness

6-078   This test is the same as under the 1991 Act.[116] It specifically provides that the "prior art" includes a prior application for a CPVR that results in the grant of a CPVR.[117] The Regulation permits the implementation of rules that would specify

---

[110] art.5(2). See para.6-035.
[111] See para.2-291. However, see para.2-115 (EU and EPC).
[112] art.5(3).
[113] art.5(4).
[114] art.5(1).
[115] art.6. Article 17 compels persons offering or disposing variety constituents of a protected variety to use the variety denomination even after termination of the CPVR.
[116] See para.6-046.
[117] art.7.

further cases as examples that would be deemed to be a matter of common knowledge.[118]

Uniformity

The definition of uniformity in the Regulation is very similar to that in the 1991 **6-079** Act.[119] Under both, the applicant must show that the plant's characteristics are "sufficiently uniform" subject to the variation that may be expected from the particular features of its propagation.[120] The requirement of "sufficiently uniform" echoes the definition of "variety" in the CPVR which permits some degree of variation in its characteristics, provided that the variation results from the genotype or combination of genotypes of the plant.[121]

The difference between the 1991 Act and the Regulation is that the 1991 Act **6-080** merely requires the "relevant characteristics" to be sufficiently uniform whereas the Regulation requires:

> "the expression of those characteristics which are included in the examination for distinctness, as well as any others used for the variety description"

to be sufficiently uniform. In essence, the Regulation spells out which characteristics are relevant, i.e. they must be the ones who are submitted for examination and referred to in the variety description. In case there was any doubt, the Regulation makes it clear by the reference to "expression of those characteristics" that the CPVO is interested in tangible, observable features, in considering the issue of uniformity, and not uniformity in relation to the underlying genetic structure or other unobservable characteristics.

Stability

The definition of stability in the Regulation is also very similar to that contained **6-081** in the 1991 Act.[122] The applicant must show that the expression of the characteristics that are included in the examination for distinctness, as well as any others used for the variety description, remains unchanged after repeated propagation, or, in the case of a particular cycle of propagation, at the end of each such cycle.[123]

Novelty

The Regulation provides the same test of novelty as under the 1991 Act, includ- **6-082** ing the same "grace periods" whereby the applicant may test the commercial value of the variety prior to the date of application.[124] Thus, a variety is deemed to be new if, at the date of application[125]:

> "...variety constituents or harvested material of the variety have not been sold or otherwise

---

[118] For an assessment of distinctness and whether a variety was a matter of common knowledge, see *Schräder v CPVO* (T-187/06) [2008] E.C.R. II-3151.
[119] See para.6-049 for the approach to uniformity under the 1991 Act.
[120] art.8 CPVR Regulation; art.8 of the UPOV 1991 Act.
[121] See para.6-035.
[122] See para.6-052 for the approach to stability under the 1991 Act.
[123] art.9.
[124] See para.6-044 for the approach to novelty under the 1991 Act.
[125] For the determination of "date of application", see art.51.

disposed of to others, by or with the consent of the breeder ... for purposes of exploitation of the variety

    (a)   earlier than one year before [the date of application] within the territory of the Community;

    (b)   earlier than four years, or in the case of trees or of vines, earlier than six years before [the date of application] outside the territory of the Community."[126]

6-083   As with the 1991 Act, when considering novelty, the emphasis is on whether or not there has been any commercial exploitation prior to the date of application by the applicant or with their consent and not the novelty test applied in patent law.[127] The expression "sold" gives no difficulties but the drafters of the Regulation anticipated problems with whether a variety has been "disposed of to others", and so art.10 of the Regulation clarifies the position in relation to certain cases, whereas the 1991 Act is silent on this issue. The exemptions listed below in relation to whether or not a disposal is deemed to be a novelty-destroying disposal reflects the broad emphasis that a disposal is only relevant if it is a disposal for commercial gain.

6-084   First, where the breeder gives variety constituents to a statutory body or other bodies solely for production, reproduction, multiplication, conditioning or storage, this is not deemed to be a disposal provided that the breeder preserves the exclusive right of disposal of these and other variety constituents and no further disposal is made.[128] Accordingly, where a breeder sub-contracts the growing and testing of the variety to a third party, this will not constitute a disposal. However, the breeder must maintain legal control over the variety and the subcontractor or other third party must not be able to sell or dispose the variety (whether variety constituents or harvested material) to third parties. In this regard, the Regulation makes it clear that if the third party repeatedly uses the variety constituents of a parent variety to make a hybrid variety and then sells or disposes the variety constituents or the harvested material of the hybrid variety, then that will destroy novelty in the parent variety.

6-085   Secondly, a disposal of variety constituents by one company or firm to another company or firm that belongs to the same economic unit is not deemed a disposal.[129]

6-086   Thirdly, where variety constituents or harvested material are produced from plants grown for experimental purposes or for the purposes of breeding or discovering other varieties, then their disposal will not be deemed to be for the purposes of exploitation of the variety, provided that they are not used for further reproduction or multiplication.[130] For instance, where grain is produced by a new cereal plant pursuant to experimental research, the disposal of that grain to a farmer for use as animal feed would not constitute a novelty-destroying disposal. However, if the farmer used that grain to produce further grain, it would be a novelty-destroying disposal, as the grain is then used for further reproduction or multiplication. The exception to the general rule is that if reference is made to the variety for the purposes of disposal, then that will constitute a novelty-destroying-disclosure.[131]

---

[126] art.10(1).

[127] See para.6-040.

[128] art.10(2).

[129] art.10(2).

[130] art.10(3).

[131] art.10(3), last sentence.

The three exceptions operate by deeming that the aforementioned disposals are **6-087** not to be a "disposal" for the purposes of art.10(1). Where the plant varieties are sold, do the three exceptions apply? The reference in art.10(1) to "sold or otherwise disposed of to others" suggests that a sale is considered an example of a disposal. Therefore, it is submitted that the three above exceptions apply where the disposal is by way of sale.

Entitlement to CPVR

The person who bred or discovered and developed the variety is entitled to the **6-088** CPVR for that variety.[132] As with other rights, if the above activities were carried out by more than one person, they are jointly entitled to the CPVR. If one person discovered the variety and the other developed it, then the CPVR vests jointly in the discoverer and developer.[133] The Regulation permits persons declared in writing to be entitled to a CPVR, to apply for a CPVR. If the breeder is an employee, the entitlement to the CPVR is determined in accordance with the national law applicable to the employment relationship in the context of which the variety was bred or discovered and developed. A court seized of an employer-employee dispute will have to resort to its private international laws in order to determine the relevant domestic law.[134]

Prior to 2008, only persons or legal persons who were nationals of an EU state, **6-089** nationals of a UPOV Convention country, or who were domiciled or had their seat or establishment within such a country could apply for a CPVR.[135] However, in 2008, the Regulation was amended to permit any natural or legal person to apply for a CPVR.[136]

Scope of CPVR

Infringing acts

The exclusive rights of the owner of a CPVR extend to the following organic **6-090** material:

- The variety itself.
- The seeds and other propagating material of the variety.
- Harvested material insofar as it comes from unauthorised use of the variety.[137]
- First generation "essentially derived" varieties.[138]
- Varieties which are not "distinct" from the protected variety.[139]
- Varieties whose production requires the repeated use of the protected variety.[140]

---

[132] art.11.
[133] art.11(2).
[134] Cf. the approach under the EPC to choice of law issues regarding entitlement to a European patent.
[135] art.12.
[136] Reg.15/2008 [2008] OJ L8/2.
[137] art.13.
[138] art.13.5(a). "Essentially derived" varieties are discussed in the next section.
[139] art.13.5(b).
[140] art.13.5(c).

6-091   As regards what acts a CPVR holder can prevent in relation to infringing material, it has the right to prevent the production or reproduction (multiplication), conditioning for the purpose of propagation, offering for sale, selling or other marketing, exporting from the EU, importing to the EU, or stocking for any of the above purposes.[141] This is identical to the 1991 Act.

Harvested material

6-092   The Regulation only permits the exercise of the above rights in relation to the harvested material if the holder has not had reasonable opportunity to exercise their rights in relation to the unauthorised use of the parent variety constituents.[142] In this respect, the Regulation is identical to the 1991 Act. In a German decision, the Bundesgerichtshof held that where the defendant purchased ornamental plants (*Calluna Vulgaris*) from a Dutch company who themselves had purchased them from a plant grower in France and the claimant owned a CPVR for a *Calluna Vulgaris* variety, the plant was not to be seen as "harvested material" within the meaning of art.13 Regulation as "no act of a harvest" occurred in their production.[143]

Products directly obtained from material of the protected variety

6-093   The Regulation permits the implementation of rules that, in specific cases, the CPVR holder may enforce their rights in respect of products directly obtained from material of the protected variety. However, as of January 2018, such have not been implemented.[144] For the avoidance of doubt, this is a separate right to the exclusive rights that a CPVR holder enjoys in the material identified in the bullet points above.

6-094   As provided for in the 1991 Act, the Regulation also permits the exercise of rights against any essentially derived variety; any variety which is not distinct from the protected variety; and varieties whose production requires the repeated use of the protected variety.[145] The issue of what is an essentially derived variety is considered in the next section.

Essentially derived varieties

6-095   The CPVR holder's rights extend to "essentially derived" varieties. Thus, art.13(5) states that the exclusive rights extend to:

> "(a)   varieties which are essentially derived from the variety in respect of which the Community plant variety right has been granted, where this variety is not itself an essentially derived variety;"

6-096   Article 13(6) states that a variety shall be deemed to be essentially derived from another variety (defined as the "initial variety") where:

> "(a)   it is predominantly derived from the initial variety, or from a variety that is itself predominantly derived from the initial variety;
> (b)   it is distinct in accordance with the provisions of Article 7 from the initial variety; and

---

[141] art.13.
[142] art.13(3).
[143] *X ZR 93/04 Melanie/Amethyst* Decision of Bundesgerichtshof dated 24 February 2006.
[144] art.13(4).
[145] art.13(5)(a)–(c).

(c) except for the differences which result from the act of derivation, it conforms essentially to the initial variety in the expression of the characteristics that results from the genotype or combination of genotypes of the initial variety."

These provisions are virtually identical to those in the 1991 Act.[146]

In *Blancanieves/Dangypmini*,[147] the Court of Appeal of the Hague, the Netherlands considered the issue whether two varieties, "Blancanieves" and "Summer Snow" were essentially derived varieties ("EDV") of the protected variety "Dangypmini" within the meaning of art.13 of CPVR. In the previous edition of this book, we commented on the first instance decision. On appeal, the Court of Appeal said that despite textual differences between art.13(5) and (6) of the Regulation and art.14(5) of the 1991 Act, there was no reason to assume that the intention was for the Regulation to set out a different test to that in the 1991 Act. It said that the tests laid down in art.13(6) had to be applied cumulatively. It said that a logical order in the assessment of the requirements was that first, one must ask whether the putative EDV could be distinguished from the initial variety. This was easily answered in the case as the putative EDV had been granted plant variety rights and thus satisfied the test of distinctness. The second question was whether there was predominant derivation from the initial variety. It said that this meant "genetic conformity" which could be proved in a number of ways, not only by means of a DNA test. Thus, it said that phenotypic similarity can be taken into account. The final test was whether the putative EDV was "essentially similar" to the initial variety in terms of characteristics, resulting from the genotype or combination of genotypes. It said that any differences arising from the act of derivation must be left out of consideration. Thus, it said that what is at issue in relation to this question is the degree of phenotypic similarity.[148]   **6-097**

In relation to the requirement in the 1991 Act (but not expressly referred to in art.13(6)) that for a variety to be an EDV, it must retain "the expression of the essential characteristics, which is the result of genotype or combination of genotypes of the initial variety", the court said that it was reasonable to assume that those characteristics which are unique in the initial variety and recurred in the putative EDV, find their basis in the genotype of the initial variety but that any similarity in characteristics that are not typical of the initial variety, such must be left out of consideration.[149] In other words, observable similarities (phenotypic similarities) relating to the essential characteristics may be prima facie evidence of genotypic similarities.   **6-098**

The Court of Appeal held, in finding no infringement, that in view of the "morphological differences" (i.e. phenotypical differences) that Blancanieves was not an EDV as it differed from the initial variety in more than one or two inheritable characteristics and accordingly, art.13(6)(c) was not satisfied.[150] In doing so, it rejected an argument of the CPVR holder that a variety could be an EDV, even if there was a relatively large number of phenotypic differences between the putative EDV and the initial variety if there was substantial *genotypical* similarity.[151]   **6-099**

---

[146] See para.6-059.

[147] *Blancanieves/Dangypmini (Danzinger "Dan" Flower Farm v Astee Flowers BV*, 29 December 2009).

[148] See [11].

[149] See judgment at [11].

[150] See [22].

[151] See [20].

Miscellaneous provisions

6-100   The exclusive rights of a CPVR does not extend to acts done privately and for non-commercial purposes, acts done for experimental purposes, nor acts done for the purpose of breeding or discovering and developing other varieties.[152]

6-101   The Regulation also prohibits the exercise of rights that would violate any provisions adopted on the grounds of public morality, public policy or public security, the protection of health and life of humans, animals or plants, the protection of the environment, the protection of industrial or commercial property, or the safeguarding of competition, of trade or of agricultural production.[153] This provision has no counterpart in the 1991 Act. It should be contrasted with the EPC that prevents the grant of a European patent that is contrary to ordre public or morality, which is much wider in scope.[154] The Regulation prohibits the exercise of a CPVR and not the granting of such a right in the first place. This shifts the emphasis from whether the right in itself is contrary to public policy, to whether, in certain circumstances, its exercise is contrary to provisions adopted on the grounds of public policy.

6-102   Furthermore, it should be noted that the prohibition only applies where EU or national provisions have been adopted on the above grounds. This means that the exercise of rights must violate legislative measures. It is not a defence merely to allege that the exercise of the CPVR is contrary to public policy per se. It should be noted that a person may apply to the CPVO to exploit a CPVR on the grounds of public interest[155] but that a Member State may not grant a compulsory licence of a CPVR. It is an interesting point whether a national legislative defence which is ostensibly on the grounds of public policy or the other grounds listed above could be considered to be the grant of a compulsory licence by a Member State and thus be illegal. There is clearly a fine line between Member State legislation which purports to prevent the exercise of rights on the grounds of, e.g. public policy or agricultural production and such being, in substance, the grant of a compulsory licence.

Farmers' privilege

6-103   The Regulation provides a "farmers' privilege" that permits farmers to use the product of the harvest of a protected variety for re-planting. The provisions relating to farmers' privilege should be contrasted with the corresponding and far less detailed and optional provision contained in the UPOV 1991 Act.[156]

6-104   Article 14(1) authorises farmers to use, for propagating purposes in the field, and on their own holding, the product of the harvest that they have obtained by planting on their own holding, propagating material of a variety other than a hybrid or synthetic variety that is covered by a CPVR. However, this privilege only applies to certain agricultural plant species specified in art.14(2).[157] The Regulation distinguishes between small and large farmholdings. Farmers who grow plants on

---

[152] art.15.

[153] art.13(8).

[154] art.53(a) EPC. See para.2-269.

[155] See para.6-109.

[156] See para.6-054.

[157] These are fodder plants (chickpea milkvetch, yellow lupin, lucerne, field pea, Berseem/Egyptian clover, Persian clover, field bean, common vetch, and Italian ryegrass); cereals (oats, barley, rice, canary grass, rye, triticale, wheat, durum wheat, and spelt wheat); oil and fibre plants (swede rape, turnip rape and linseed (but not flax)) and potatoes. These plants are considered to be the most

an area less than the area required to produce 92 tonnes of cereals are not required to pay any remuneration to the CPVR holder.[158] Other farmers are required to pay an equitable remuneration to the CPVR holder which shall be "sensibly lower than the amount charged for the licensed production of propagating material of the same variety in the same area".[159]

A regulation has been introduced pursuant to art.14 CPVR which define the exact nature and scope of the farmers' privilege based on the above criteria and the level of remuneration to be provided.[160] These regulations provide rules as to the method of calculation of equitable remuneration, the exact meaning of "small farmers", etc.   **6-105**

In particular, farmers may be required to give information regarding use of a protected variety. This has given rise to a number of references to the CJEU as to when a farmer is required to give information[161] In general, the "sensibly lower" figure of equitable remuneration has been set at 50 per cent but where the farmer's use of the plant variety for propagating is inordinately high compared to that which the farmer sells on, the level will be higher.[162]   **6-106**

The onus is on the farmer to inform accurately the CPVR holder of the quantity of the product of the harvest which would fall within the CPVR and pay equitable remuneration. A failure by a farmer to do such will disentitle it from relying upon art.14 and mean that they shall be treated like any other infringer of a CPVR.[163]   **6-107**

Compulsory exploitation right

The CPVR Regulation permits persons to apply to the CPVO for compulsory licences to exploit a protected variety on the grounds of public interest.[164] The CPVR Regulation has also been amended to permit the holder of a patent for a biotechnological invention to apply for a compulsory licence where a CPVR is blocking exploitation of the patent. No application for a compulsory licence can be applied to Member States.[165]   **6-108**

---

important agricultural crops (see report of Kiewiet, President of CPVO, in report presented at Einbeck on 26 January 2001 (*Modern Plant Breeding and IPR*).

[158] art.14(3). Comparable criteria will apply to farmers who grow other plant species. Thus art.7(3)(b) Reg.1768/95 [1995] OJ L173/14 provides that in the case of potatoes, it is 185 tonnes.

[159] art.14(3).

[160] art.14(3). Regulation 1768/95 Implementing Rules on Agricultural Exemption [1995] OJ L173/14 as amended by Reg.2605/98 [1998] OJ L328/6. A consolidated version is available at *www.cpvo.europa.eu*.

[161] art.8 Reg.1768/95. Thus, a holder of a plant variety right cannot require a farmer to provide information regarding use that he has made (if any) of the farmer's privilege where there is no indication that the farmer has otherwise, but for the farmer's privilege, infringed the relevant right. *Schulin v Saatgut-Treuhandverwaltungs GmbH* (C-305/00) [2003] E.C.R I-3525 and *Jäger v Saatgut-Treuhandverwaltungs GmbH* (C-182/01) ECLI:EU:C:2004:135. See also *Raiffeisen-Waren-Zentralen Rhein-Main eG v Saatgut-Treuhandverwaltungs GmbH* (C-56/11) ECLI:EU:C:2012:713.

[162] art.5 Reg.1768/95 as amended by art.1 Reg.2605/98. See *Saatgut-Treuhandverwaltungs GmbH v Deppe* (C-7–9/05) [2006] E.C.R. I-5045 where the court held that 80 per cent was not a "sensibly lower" figure and that for a negotiated agreement between farmers and rights holders to act as a guideline pursuant to art.5(4) Reg.1768/95, such must have been notified to the Commission and published in the Official Journal.

[163] *Schulin* (C-305/00), at [71]; *Geistbeck v Saatgut-Treuhandverwaltungs GmbH* (C-509/10) ECLI:EU:C:2012:416 at [23]–[35]—a farmer who substantially under-declared an amount of seed to a CPVR holder should be regarded as third party infringer.

[164] art.29.

[165] art.29(7).

Public interest

6-109   This provision mirrors art.17 of the UPOV 1991 Act, which permits Contracting Parties to grant compulsory licences on the basis of public interest. The Recitals state that public interest may include the need to supply the market with material offering specified features, or to maintain the incentive for continued breeding of improved varieties. The former reason is analogous to a compulsory licence granted under patent law where the patentee fails to adequately work the invention. Clearly, if the CPVR holder grew sufficient quantities (whether the CPVR holder or via their licensees) to satisfy market demand, this would not constitute a ground. However, the CPVO would probably consider other factors such as whether the plant variety was supplied at a reasonable price, whether the variety was widely distributed, and whether the produced variety was of a proper quality.[166] The latter reason would appear to relate to the situation where a breeder wished to improve a protected variety for the purposes of commercial exploitation. If the improved variety was an "essentially derived" variety of a protected variety, then the breeder of the EDV would need a licence to exploit commercially their variety from the holder of the CPVR in the initial variety.[167] The breeder would be entitled to one if they could show that there was a public interest.[168]

6-110   If the CPVO grants a compulsory licence, then it must stipulate the type of acts covered and impose reasonable conditions. This may provide for the payment of an appropriate royalty. If the compulsory licence is applied for in relation to the holder of an "essentially derived" variety and that person can show that there is a public interest in the grant of such a licence, the licence *must* provide for payment of an appropriate royalty as equitable remuneration to the holder of the initial variety.[169]

CPVR blocking exploitation of patent and vice versa

6-111   Article 12 of the Biotechnological Directive[170] lays down rules for the grant of non-exclusive compulsory licences where protected plant varieties including Community plant varieties incorporate patented inventions and vice versa. To reflect the provisions of art.12(2) of the Biotechnological Directive which stipulates that patent holders can apply for compulsory licences of national plant variety rights provisions, the Regulation was amended[171] to permit holders of patents for biotechnological inventions to apply for a compulsory licence of a CPVR upon payment of an appropriate royalty as equitable remuneration. The applicant must show that:

---

[166] In the UK, under Plants Varieties and Seeds Act 1997 s.17(2), one of these conditions need to be satisfied before one can apply for a compulsory licence.

[167] See para.6-095.

[168] art.29(5). Clearly, this can be abused if the essentially derived variety was little improvement on the basic variety. In these circumstances, it is likely that the CPVO will take a similar line to that taken under art.31(g) TRIPS in relation to compulsory licences of an improvement patent. See para.2-026. Indeed, it might be said that the holder of the EDV would need to satisfy the conditions mutatis mutandis set out in art.29(5a) which apply to the grant of a compulsory licence of a CPVR to the holder of a biotechnology patent (discussed in the next section).

[169] art.29(5). In contrast a compulsory licence granted on other grounds does not have to include the payment of an appropriate royalty although it is difficult to envisage circumstances where such would not be applicable.

[170] Dir.98/44/EC on the legal protection of biotechnological inventions [1998] OJ 213/13. This is discussed at para.2-598.

[171] EC Reg.873/2004 [2004] OJ L162/38. This has been inserted as art.29(5a).

(i)   they have applied unsuccessfully to the holder of the CPVR to obtain a contractual licence; and

(ii)   the invention constitutes significant technical progress of considerable economic interest compared with the protected plant variety.[172]

The requirement of "significant technical progress of considerable economic significance compared with the protected plant variety" echoes the test in art.31 TRIPS. This permits contracting states to grant compulsory licences of a basic patent which blocks the development of an invention protected by an improvement patent, where the invention involves an important technical advance of considerable economic significance in relation to the invention claimed in the basic patent.[173] Furthermore, although not explicitly set out, there seems little doubt that the compulsory licence is only available where the holder of the patent cannot exploit the patent without infringing the CPVR.[174] **6-112**

A compulsory cross-licence of a CPVR is also available to the holder of a patent for a biotechnology invention where the CPVR holder has successfully obtained a compulsory licence of the patent pursuant to the provisions of domestic legislation implemented pursuant to art.12 of the Biotechnology Directive. As discussed in Ch.2,[175] under that Directive, the owner of a national plant variety right can apply for a compulsory licence of a biotechnology patent where they cannot acquire or exploit a plant variety right without infringing a prior patent subject to payment of an appropriate royalty.[176] However, as with the Regulation, it must be shown that they have applied unsuccessfully to the holder of the patent and the plant variety right constitutes significant technical progress of considerable economic interest compared with the invention. It should be said that the reverse cross-licence provisions apply to the CPVR holder where the holder of the biotechnology patent has acquired a compulsory licence of the CPVR. In such circumstances, the CPVR holder can apply for a cross-licence of the patent.[177] Thus, in both cases, a successful application for a compulsory licence against a "blocking" patent or CPVR will result in the grant of a cross-licence to the owner of the "blocking" right in relation to the "blocked" patent or CPVR. Such a cross-licence will be granted "on reasonable terms". **6-113**

Exhaustion of CPVR

As with other EU intellectual property rights, the Regulation contains provisions regarding the exhaustion of rights, i.e. that the owner of the CPVR is not entitled to exercise its rights once they have disposed of material of the protected variety or such have been disposed of with their consent. However, in the case of plant variety rights, the matter is complicated by the fact that unlike other products, **6-114**

---

[172] art.29(5a)(i)–(ii). The second test is similarly worded to that applicable under art.31(a) of TRIPS where a basic patent blocks the exploitation of an improvement invention—see para.2-026.

[173] art.31(l)(i) TRIPS.

[174] This would appear to follow from the express reference in art.29(5a) of the Regulation to art.12(2) Biotechnology Directive—the latter only permits the grant of a compulsory licence for national plant variety rights where the holder of the patent could not exploit the right without infringing the national plant variety right. Whilst art.12(2) was only concerned with the grant of compulsory licence of national plant variety rights, it is to be assumed that art.29(5a) would also apply where the same conditions were satisfied in relation to a "blocking" CPVR.

[175] See para.2-598

[176] art.12(1).

[177] art.12(2) Biotechnology Directive.

plant material can be used both to create more material and also as foodstuff. To deal with this, art.16 of the Regulation states as follows:

> *"Exhaustion of Community plant variety rights*
> The Community plant variety right shall not extend to acts concerning any material of the protected variety, or of a variety covered by the provisions of Article 13 (5), which has been disposed of to others by the holder or with his consent, in any part of the Community, or any material derived from the said material, unless such acts:
>
> (a)   involve further propagation of the variety in question, except where such propagation was intended when the material was disposed of; or
> (b)   involve an export of variety constituents into a third country which does not protect varieties of the plant genus or species to which the variety belongs, except where the exported materials is for final consumption purposes."

6-115   Thus, once material of the protected variety (which includes EDVs[178]) has been disposed of in the EU, art.16 provides that the CPVR holder is deemed to have exhausted their rights in such material.[179] Moreover, their rights are exhausted as against "any material derived from the said material". Thus, the CPVR holder has no rights against harvested material derived from propagating material placed on the market in the Community by themselves or with their consent. However, harvested material can be used itself to propagate further harvested material (e.g. wheat).

6-116   Consequently, art.16 provides for an exception from the exhaustion of rights if such acts would involve further propagation unless such propagation was intended when the material was disposed of. This exception is concerned with not only actual acts of propagation but also the intention of the person with regards to material of the protected variety that they have purchased legitimately on the market. Thus, by itself, harvested material does not have to be used for propagation—it can be eaten instead. In contrast, the sale of propagating material (i.e. seeds) is plainly intended for propagation. If a person sought to sell harvested material for propagating purposes, then it raises the question whether the harvested material is infringing per se (and thus, can be seized as infringing goods) or merely that an injunction can be obtained from such material being sold for propagating purposes. Ultimately, this may be a matter of discretion for courts enforcing CPVRs and be fact-sensitive. Thus, the precise remedy may depend on the likelihood that the harvested material would be used for propagating purposes.

6-117   Article 16(b) permits the exercise of CPVRs against exports of variety constituents into a third country which does not protect the variety constituents even where those variety constituents have been placed on the market by the holder of the CPVR or with their consent. However, if such material is to be used for "final consumption purposes", then they cannot exercise their rights. It is not clear whether this means that the exported materials themselves must be intended to be eaten or whether such extends to the harvested material of the exported materials. It seems that the latter is more likely because art.16(b) extends not just to harvested material but also to propagating material (both would be covered by the expression "variety constituents") and much propagating material is in itself inedible. However,

---

[178]   The reference to art.13(5) is to the right of the holder of an initial variety to control the marketing of EDVs (essentially derived varieties). This is discussed at para.6-095.
[179]   art.16.

clearly a practical problem arises here because once the variety constituents have left the EU, what may have been intended for final consumption may be used for propagating purposes.

In *Greenstar-Kanzi Europe NV v Hustin and Goossens*,[180] the CJEU had to **6-118** consider whether the rights of a CPVR holder were exhausted where protected material had been sold by a licensee to a third party in contravention of the licence. In other EU rights (e.g. EU Trade Mark), the regulation is specific as to which type of clauses in a licence can, if breached, entitle the EUTM owner to bring an action for trade mark infringement against third parties who buy from the licensee.[181] However, the CPVR is much less specific. Article 27 of the Regulation simply provides that the CPVR holder may invoke the rights of a CPVR against a person enjoying the right of exploitation who contravenes any of the conditions or limitations attached to the exploitation right in the licence.

In *Greenstar-Kanzi*, the licence stipulated that the licensee could not sell or **6-119** dispose of any product to a buyer unless the buyer signed in advance a grower's licence or marketing licence annexed to the licence. This was not complied with and a Mr Goossens acquired apples protected by the CPVR and started selling them. An action was brought against him in the Netherlands for infringement of the CPVR. Arguing by way of analogy with the European Union Trade Mark Regulation, the CJEU held that the rights are not exhausted where the term or condition of the licence which was breached related "directly to the essential features of the Community plant variety right".[182] It is not clear what those terms would be. However, art.25(2) EUTMR sets out the terms that if breached, the EUTM proprietor can bring an action for trade mark infringement against the licensee. They are duration, form covered by the registration, scope of the goods or services for which the licence is granted, the territory of the licence, and quality of the goods. By way of analogy, it is thought that terms relating to duration, territory, and field of use would be essential features. The CPVR holder is entitled to determine the amount of competition it is prepared to permit and clearly the grant of a limited licence should not be made, via the rule on exhaustion, into a blanket licence to carry out all and any acts that infringe the CPVR. However, in the case of plant variety rights, a key concern of the CPVR holder is to protect against the deterioration of the quality of the variety. Thus, it is not unreasonable for the CPVR holder to require a purchaser of the fruit or the seeds of a plant variety right to agree to conditions which are intended to safeguard against such deterioration. Finally, it should be noted that when considering whether there is exhaustion, it is immaterial whether the buyer of the fruit or seed is aware that such has been sold in breach of the conditions of the licence.[183]

Duration and termination of CPVR

A CPVR lasts for 25 years or, in the case of varieties of vine and tree species, **6-120** 30 years,[184] and 30 years for potatoes.[185] The EC Council may extend these terms

---

[180] *Greenstar-Kanzi Europe NV v Jean Hustin and Jo Goossens* (C-140/10) [2011] E.C.R. 10075.
[181] See para.3-664.
[182] *Greenstar-Kanzi Europe NV v Jean Hustin and Jo Goossens* (C-140/10) [2011] E.C.R. 10075 at [43].
[183] *Greenstar-Kanzi Europe NV v Jean Hustin and Jo Goossens* (C-140/10) [2011] E.C.R. 10075 at [49].
[184] art.19.
[185] art.1(1) Reg.2470/96, 17 December 1996.

up to a period of five years for specific genera or species. The CPVO can cancel CPVRs if, after grant, it is established that the variety has ceased to remain uniform or stable.[186] Where a CPVR is granted under art.116,[187] the duration of the CPVR is reduced by the longest period during which variety constituents or harvested material thereof has been sold or otherwise disposed of to others by or with the consent of the breeder within the territory of the Community for the purposes of exploitation of the variety, or for the period in which national PVRs have been effective but for not more than five years.[188]

Practice and procedure: CPVO

6-121   Proceedings before the CPVO are governed by the Regulation and implementing regulations.[189] An outline of the relevant provisions is given below.

General principles applicable to CPVO

6-122   The Court of Justice has emphasised several times that the CPVO's task is one of scientific and technical complexity when determining whether an application for a CPVR satisfies the DUS criteria and thus, the CPVO is accorded a "broad discretion" in carrying out its functions.[190] Moreover, the CPVO, is subject to the principle of "sound administration" which means that it must examine an application for a CPVR "with care and impartiality" and gather all the factual and legal information necessary to exercise its discretion. Furthermore, it must ensure the proper conduct and effectiveness of proceedings which it sets in motion.[191]

Applications

6-123   Applications for a CPVR can be filed directly with the CPVO or a designated national office.[192] The application must contain a request for the grant of a CPVR, identification of the botanical taxon, information identifying the applicant(s), the name of the breeder and an assurance regarding entitlement to the CPVR, provisional designation of the variety, technical description of the variety, geographic origin of the variety, the credentials of the procedural representative, details of any previous commercialisation of the variety, and of any other application made in respect of the variety.[193] The date of application is deemed to be the date which a valid application was received by the CPVO subject to payment of the relevant fees.[194]

6-124   An application that is filed within 12 months of the filing of an earlier application for the same variety in any state will enjoy a right of priority based on the date

---

[186] art.21.
[187] These are transitional provisions.
[188] art.116(4), 4th indent.
[189] Reg.1239/85 [1995] OJ L121/37 as amended. A consolidated text is available at *www.cpvo.europa.eu* [Accessed 9 April 2018].
[190] *Schniga GmbH v CPVO* (C-625/15P) ECLI:EU:C:2017:435 at [46] and the case law cited thereto.
[191] *Schniga*, at [47].
[192] art.49 of the Regulation.
[193] art.50.
[194] art.51.

of the earlier application.[195] The claim for priority is dependent on the applicant filing within three months of the date of application copies of the earlier application being certified by the authority responsible for such an application.[196]

The application then undergoes a three-part examination test.　　　　　6-125

- the first examination is purely formal;
- in the second part, which is called the "substantive examination", the CPVO examines for novelty; whether the variety applied for is a "variety" for the purposes of the CPVR Regulation; for entitlement; and whether the denomination is suitable[197]; and
- the final examination is the technical examination to see if the variety meets the DUS requirements (distinctness, uniformity and stability).[198]

The technical examination is conducted in accordance with test guidelines is-　6-126
sued by the Administrative Council and the CPVO.[199] Following these guidelines is important and a failure to do so may render any subsequent registration as null and void.[200] The President of the CPVO may provide their own guidelines where there are no guidelines adopted by the Administrative Council or where there are guidelines, insert additional characteristics.[201]

This examination is carried out by national offices designated by the CPVO　6-127
called "Examination Offices". These offices must grow the variety or carry out any other investigations that are required. However, where there are available findings resulting from proceedings for the grant of national PVRs, the technical examination may be carried out by the CPVO on the basis of such findings with the agreement of the relevant authority.[202] Care must be taken by the examination office. Thus, an appeal to the Board of Appeal against a refusal to grant a CPVR based on lack of uniformity because of a sickly row of plants was upheld on the basis that the cause was likely to be nothing to do with genetic lack of uniformity but rather pests, diseases or compactness of the soil.[203] The CPVO is not bound to rely on the results of any testing authority but must consider all relevant and reliable facts and come to its own conclusion.[204] Ultimately, the burden is on the applicant to convince the CPVO that the variety is worthy of exclusive rights. Thus, if the CPVO points to a similar variety, the applicant must show that their variety is distinct from it.[205]

Third parties may file written objections, but only on the grounds that either　6-128
novelty or the DUS criteria are not satisfied or that there is an impediment under

---

[195] art.52. Following the relaxation of the rules regarding who could apply for a CPVR, (see para.6-088), the Regulation was amended so that a claim could be made for priority regardless of whether the application was filed in a Member State or UPOV state—see Reg.15/2008 [2008] L8/2 amending art.52 of Reg.2100/94.

[196] art.52(5).

[197] art.54. As to whether the denomination is suitable, see art.63.

[198] arts 55, 56.

[199] art.56(2); art.22 Reg.1239/95 (implementing regulation); *Schniga*, at [49].

[200] See Guidelines.

[201] *Schniga*, at [50]–[51].

[202] art.116(3).

[203] *Tristam/Walfrasun* (A5/2004). Decisions of the CPVO can be found at the CPVO's website—*http ://www.cpvo.europa.eu/main/* [Accessed 18 January 2018].

[204] *Svalof Weibull/Estrade* (A002/2000).

[205] *Svalof Weibull/Estrade* (A002/2000), at 4.

art.63(3) or (4) to the proposed variety denomination.[206] It should be noted that a third party cannot object on the basis of entitlement.[207]

6-129   Subject to the principle of sound administration, the CPVO has considerable discretion as to how it examines the application.[208]

Variety denominations

6-130   Under art.63, the CPVO must approve the variety denomination for the CPVR. Such a denomination must be suitable. It is not suitable if:

(a)   a third party has a prior right over the name;

(b)   it may commonly cause its users difficulties as regards recognition or reproduction;

(c)   it is identical or may be confused with a variety denomination under:

    (i)   which another variety of the same or of a closely related species is entered in an official register of plant varieties; or

    (ii)   which material of another variety has been marketed in a Member State, or in a Member of the International Unit for the Protection of New Varieties of Plants unless the other variety no longer remains in existence and its denomination has acquired no special significance;

(d)   if it is identical or may be confused with other designations that are commonly used for the marketing of goods or that have to be kept free under other legislation; or

(e)   if it is liable to give offence in one of the Member States or is contrary to public policy.[209]

6-131   These provisions were considered in *Ginpent/Gynosemma Pentaphyllum*.[210] In that case, a person was granted the CPVR for a variety for the species *Gynostemma pentaphyllum*. The CPVO approved the name GINPENT for it. A third party objected on the basis that GINPENT was derived from *Gynosemma Pentaphyllum* being merely an abbreviation of the name. The Board of Appeal held that a species denomination should not be equated with a variety denomination. Thus, it rejected the argument under art.63(3)(c). It also rejected the argument under art.63(3)(d) as it was not established that GINPENT was being used as a common abbreviation for *Gynostemma pentaphyllum*.

6-132   Interestingly, the unsuccessful appellant pointed out that the holder of the CPVR was using the variety denomination to indicate it was a registered trade mark by the use of GINPENT®. The Board of Appeal held that although such was true, it did not give grounds to require an amendment to the name of the variety denomination. It said that pursuant to art.17 of the Regulation, the holder of the variety right is obliged to use the variety denomination in a readily distinguishable manner and this meant that it could not be used as a trade mark. However, it said that a breach of this obligation could not be a ground for challenge under art.63.

---

[206] art.63(3) and (4) are discussed below.

[207] See para.6-147.

[208] *Brookfield New Zealand v CPVO* (C-534/10P) ECLI:EU:C:2012:813 at [51]–[53].

[209] art.63(3). Reg.930/2000 [2000] OJ L108/3 establishes detailed rules as to permissible denominations based on art.63. This is periodically updated, e.g. see Reg.920/2007 [2007] OJ L201/3–5.

[210] *Vegetal-Progress SRL v Giovanni Ambrogio* (A4/2004) (18 July 2005).

Cancellation proceedings

Proceedings to declare a CPVR null and void can be brought before the CPVO. **6-133**
The grounds are: (a) that the plant variety is not distinct or novel, (b) the requirement of uniformity and stability were not met where the grant of the CPVR "*has
been essentially based upon information and documents furnished by the applicant*", and (c) the right has been granted to a person who is not entitled to it.[211]
The CPVO has a "broad discretion" to cancel a CPVR. Thus, only where there are
serious doubts that the requirement of distinctness or novelty have not been met
when an application for a CPVR was examined, is the CPVO required to re-
examine these requirements in cancellation proceedings.[212] Thus, a cancellation applicant must adduce evidence and facts of sufficient substance to raise serious
doubts on such grounds.[213] However, where the CPVO does not follow its own
guidelines on examination, such is a ground for re-examination.[214]

Fees

Applicants for CPVRs are required to pay fees for the various stages in the **6-134**
application. CPVR holders must also pay annual renewal fees.[215]

Appeal

In relation to most decisions of the CPVO, an appeal lies to the Board of Appeal. **6-135**
Such an appeal has a suspensory effect on proceedings. The Board of Appeal is
required of its own motion to examine carefully and impartially all the relevant
factual and legal information in the case before it.[216]

A further appeal to the CJEU lies from the decisions of the Boards of Appeal on **6-136**
grounds of lack of competence, infringement of an essential procedural requirement, infringement of the Treaty, of the Regulation or of any rule of law relating
to their application, or misuse of power.[217] The latter grounds are the same as under
art.63 of the EU Trade Mark Regulation. Thus, the CJEU has held that the General
Court is entitled to carry out a full review of the legality of the decisions of the
CPVO.[218] The General Court has made it clear that in relation to the assessment of
complex technical issues such as distinctness, the CPVO has a wide measure of
discretion and that such is subject to limited judicial review. Thus, the General Court
will restrict itself to examining the accuracy of the findings of fact and law made
by the authority concerned and the action taken by the authority to ensure that it is
not vitiated by manifest error or misuse of powers.[219] However, such does not
prevent the court from reviewing the CPVO's interpretation of economic or techni-

---

[211] art.20.
[212] *Schräder v CPVO* (C-546/12P) EU:C:2015:332 at [56]; *Aurora Srl v CPVO* (T-140/15)
ECLI:EU:T:2017:830 at [57].
[213] *Aurora*, at [58].
[214] *Aurora, Srl v CPVO* (guidelines setting out test guidelines for technical analysis of sugar beet species not followed by CPVO).
[215] art.83. The fees are set out periodically by implementing regulations.
[216] *Aurora Srl v CPVO* at [74]; *Schräder v CPVO* at [46].
[217] arts 67–75.
[218] *Schrader v CPVO* (C-38/09P) [2010] E.C.R. I-3209 at 69; *Brookfield New Zealand v CPVO* (C-534/
10P) ECLI:EU:C:2012:813 at [40].
[219] *Ralf Schräder v CPVO* (T-187/06) [2008] E.C.R. II-3151 at 59–60 (upheld on appeal *Schrader v
CPVO* (C-38/09P) [2010] E.C.R. I-3209). See also in the fight between Herr Schräder and the CPVO

cal data although it is not entitled to substitute its own assessment for that of the CPVO.[220]

6-137   An appeal direct to the CJEU lies from a decision of the CPVO in relation to applications for compulsory licences.[221]

Conditions governing proceedings

6-138   The Regulation makes the usual provisions regarding the need for reasoned decisions, oral proceedings, taking of evidence, and the award of costs.[222] These provisions are virtually identical to that for the EU Trade Mark and the Community Registered Design.[223]

Prohibition on cumulative protection

6-139   Whilst the CPVR is designed to co-exist with national plant variety rights,[224] the holder of a CPVR is not permitted to enforce national plant variety rights or patent rights for the same variety.[225] Once a CPVR has been granted, such national rights become ineffective. Accordingly, an applicant must choose whether they require national PVR or patent protection or CPVR protection. There is nothing to stop the applicant from initially pursuing both or indeed all three routes. It is only upon grant of the CPVR that the national PVR and/or patent becomes ineffective. The prohibition on the exercise of patent or national PVR rights following grant of a CPVR may seem rather draconian and extreme. However, under the EPC, patents cannot be granted for plant varieties. Thus, as all EU states are members of the EPC, the ban on enforcement of a patent for a plant variety is of academic significance only. The ban on double protection of national PVRs and CPVRs is more substantial as there is no directive harmonising national plant variety right law.

Remedies

Remedies

6-140   Where infringement of a CPVR is proven, the owner of a CPVR is entitled to an injunction or compensation.[226] The default position is that under art 94.1, the owner is entitled to reasonable compensation. This means the remuneration payable for licensed production.[227] However, if the acts of infringement were carried out intentionally or negligently, then under art.94.2, the owner of the infringed CPVR is entitled to compensation representing "further damage resulting from the act in

---

(*Ralf Schräder v CPVO* (C–546/12) EU:C:2014:2348) where the Court of Justice dismissed an appeal from various decisions of the General Court which in turn were appeals from the CPVO, where the appeals were based on various procedural allegations of: infringement of principle of good administration, right to an effective remedy, distortion of facts, or evidence adduced by appellant.

[220]   *Ralf Schräder v CPVO* (T-187/06) [2008] E.C.R. II-3151 at 61.

[221]   art.74.

[222]   arts 75–86.

[223]   See para.3-783.

[224]   See Recitals.

[225]   art.92.

[226]   art.94.1.

[227]   *Geistbeck v Saatgut-Treuhandverwaltungs GmbH* (C-509/10) ECLI:EU:C:2012:416 at [37].

question."[228] In other words, this would suggest that the owner is entitled to compensation for all damage done. However, in the case of slight negligence,[229] such a claim (i.e. a claim based on negligence) may be reduced but not to the extent that the compensation is less than the advantage derived therefrom by the person who committed the infringement, i.e. the profit made by the infringer.[230] Bearing in mind that an innocent infringer is obliged to pay reasonable compensation, it would be surprising if the level of compensation for slight negligence would, in any event, be lower than what would be reasonable compensation to the CPVR owner. Therefore, there is a sliding scale of infringement from innocent infringement (reasonable compensation) to full compensation (intentional or negligence). To this, must be added art.97 which allows Member States to provide a remedy of restitution where the infringer has gained at the expense of the CPRV owner or licensee.

In *Jørn Hansson v Jungpflanzen Grünewald GmbH*,[231] the Court of Justice had **6-141** to consider the approach to the assessment of damages for infringement of a CPVR. In that case, infringement of a CPVR was established before the German courts. The CPVR owner sought compensation on a number of grounds including punitive damages. The court determined compensation by reference to licence fees that the CPVR owner charged. However, it refused to grant any punitive damages. The CPVR owner sought an uplift of half the licence fee by way of punitive damages. The Court of Justice took the opportunity to set out a number of principles:

- Compensation under art.94 must reflect "as accurately as possible, the actual and certain damage suffered by the CPVR holder".[232]
- Article 94 does not allow for damages to be awarded on a punitive basis.[233]
- Article 94 does not serve as a basis for restitution of profits or gains made by the infringer.[234]
- "Reasonable compensation" (under art.94.1) means that it covers not only the fee that would normally be payable for licensed production (citing *Geistbeck*) but also "all damage that is closely connected to the failure to pay that fee", e.g. default interest.[235]
- Compensation under art.94.2 should be determined by the evidence put forward by the CPVR holder but can be determined by a lump sum where it is difficult to quantify precisely the damage suffered.[236]
- Article 94 allows the courts of Member States to award legal costs.[237]

---

[228] art 94.2.

[229] In French, "*en cas de faute légère*".

[230] art.94.2.

[231] (C–481/14) EU:C:2016:419.

[232] See [35].

[233] See [34], [38] citing Recital 13.

[234] See [41], [43]. However, as discussed above, in the case of slight negligence, compensation cannot be less than the "advantage derived" from the infringement by the infringer (art 94.2). This must mean the profit made by the infringer. Such suggests that in the case of intentional or negligent infringement, the profits made by the infringer amount to a "floor" to any award of damages. The Court of Justice does not appear to have discussed this aspect of art.94.2, e.g. see [41].

[235] See [54].

[236] See [64].

[237] See [64].

Farmer's privilege

6-142 Farmers who seek to rely upon the "farmer's privilege" to use the product of the harvest of a protected variety for re-planting but fail to comply with the provisions set out in the Regulation and its implementing regulations are treated as infringers and thus must pay reasonable compensation as opposed to the substantially lower remuneration envisaged for such persons.[238]

Incorrect usage of denomination

6-143 The owner of a CPVR may seek similar relief in respect of incorrect usage of the variety denomination or use by a third party of an identical or confusingly similar denomination on another variety of the same botanical species or a species regarded as related pursuant to a CPVO publication.[239]

6-144 For infringing acts between the publication date of the application for the CPVR and the grant, the holder is entitled to reasonable compensation.[240]

Limitation periods

6-145 The holder of a CPVR must sue for infringement within three years of the following three events (whichever occurs latest):

(a) grant of the CPVR;
(b) knowledge of the infringing acts; and
(c) knowledge of the party liable for the acts.[241]

6-146 In any event, there is an absolute bar on proceedings brought after 30 years from the termination of the offending acts.

Disputes on entitlement to CPVR

6-147 Where a person considers that they are entitled to be the holder (whether jointly or not) or be named as an applicant for the grant of a CPVR, they must make a claim in the court of the appropriate Member State.[242] Such a claim must be made within five years from the publication of the grant of the CPVR, unless the holder knew that they were not entitled to the CPVR whether solely or at all.[243] If the appropriate court adjudicates that there should be a complete change in the ownership of the CPVR, any exploitation or other rights which arose from the previous holder lapse upon entry of the person on to the CPVR Register.[244] However, persons owning such rights (including the previous holder) can apply for non-exclusive exploitation

---

[238] See *Geistbeck v Saatgut-Treuhandverwaltungs GmbH* (C-509/10) ECLI:EU:C:2012:416 at [43]. However, the costs of monitoring compliance with the rights of a plant variety right holder cannot be taken into account when assessing the calculation of reasonable compensation.
[239] art.94.
[240] art.95.
[241] art.96.
[242] art.98. See para 6-148.
[243] art.98(3).
[244] art.100(1).

rights from the new holder or, in the absence of agreement, from the CPVO where they have effected any prohibited acts or made "effective and genuine arrangements" to do so prior to the commencement of "the proceedings", unless the previous or other persons enjoying exploitation rights acted in bad faith.[245]

Jurisdiction in infringement or entitlement disputes

The Regulation sets out jurisdictional rules as to where actions for infringement **6-148** of CPVRs or disputes as to the entitlement to a CPVR are to be brought. The general rule is that the Lugano Convention applies.[246] However, the Regulation also sets out complementary jurisdictional provisions which apply as well.[247] Thus, the Regulation provides that proceedings must be brought:

(a) in the court of the Member State or other Contracting Party of the Lugano Convention in which the defendant is domiciled or has their seat[248] or in the absence of such, has an establishment; failing which,

(b) in the court of the Member State where the claimant is domiciled or has their seat or in the absence of such, has an establishment; failing which,

(c) in the court of the Member State where the CPVO is located, i.e. France.[249]

This allocation is very similar to the EU Trade Mark Regulation and Design **6-149** Regulation. Unlike the EU Trade Mark Regulation, the CPVR Regulation does not designate specific courts but merely refers to the "competent courts". It is assumed that these will be the same courts as would deal with the infringement of national PVRs. A competent court that is seized of an infringement action under the above rules has jurisdiction in respect of infringements committed in all Member States.[250]

A CPVR holder can also bring an action for infringement in the Member State **6-150** where the harmful event occurred. However, the competent court in that state will only have jurisdiction in respect of acts of infringement committed in that state.[251]

The above jurisdictional rules can be waived if the parties have agreed in writ- **6-151** ing to try the dispute in a particular jurisdiction or the defendant submits to the jurisdiction of a court in a particular state.[252]

National courts seized of disputes relating to CPVRs must apply the same rules **6-152**

---

[245] art.100(2). The Regulation is unclear as to whether "the proceedings" referred to are the proceedings relating to entitlement or proceedings for infringement following change in ownership for infringement. It is submitted that it is the former, as clearly everyone is on notice once proceedings for entitlement are brought that there is a genuine dispute over ownership and also the use of the definite article in "the proceedings" suggests an implicit reference to the proceedings concerning entitlement, rather than possible future proceedings for infringement.

[246] art.101. For commentary on the Lugano Convention, see para.17-007.

[247] The wording of art.101 suggests that, unless expressly excluded, both the Lugano Convention and the Regulation's jurisdictional provisions apply.

[248] For definition of domicile or seat, art.102 states that the definition in arts 52 and 53 of the Lugano Convention shall apply. See para.17-030.

[249] art.101(2).

[250] art.101(2).

[251] art.101(3). This ground is similarly but not identically worded to art.125(5) EUTMR—the equivalent provision in the EUTMR—see para.3-813. It is not thought that the difference in wording is intended to give rise to a different meaning.

[252] art.102(2).

of procedure as applicable to corresponding national property rights.[253] In the case of employer/employee disputes, the relevant national law is that applicable to the relationship in the context of which the variety was bred, or discovered and developed.[254]

6-153 Where the validity of the CPVR is challenged in national proceedings, this is dealt with below.

Entitlement to sue

6-154 Actions for infringement may be brought by the holder of the CPVR. Under art.104, persons enjoying exploitation rights may also bring such actions:

> "unless that has been expressly excluded by agreement with the holder in the case of an exclusive exploitation right or by the Office pursuant to Articles 29 or 100(2)."[255]

6-155 It means that anyone who has any authorisation (whether via permission of the holder or via a compulsory exploitation right) to exploit the variety may sue for infringement.[256] This could lead to a multiplicity of claimants, and a situation in which a defendant is sued twice over the same wrong, i.e. suffers double jeopardy. However, it is presumed that in such a situation, the defendant could contend that there has been an abuse of process and that the second claimant ought to account to the first claimant if that were just and equitable in all the circumstances. Even where the holder has initiated an action for infringement, any person enjoying exploitation rights is entitled to intervene in such an action for the purpose of obtaining compensation for damage they have suffered.[257]

Validity of CPVR in national proceedings and stays

6-156 In actions for infringement of a CPVR, national courts are obliged to treat the CPVR as valid.[258] Only the CPVO may revoke the right once granted. Thus, the Regulation differs from the EU Trade Mark Regulation and Community Design Regulation as in infringement proceedings, the defendant can bring a counterclaim for revocation or cancellation of the EU Trade Mark or Community Design where infringement proceedings are brought in the courts of a Member State.

6-157 The inability to raise validity of a CPVR before the courts of Member States whether by way of direct action or counterclaim in infringement proceedings reflects the fact that unlike Community Designs or EU Trade Marks, the determination of the validity of grant of a CPVR is a complex technical matter which requires special expertise.

6-158 If proceedings for revocation or cancellation of the CPVR have been "initiated" before the CPVO, then under art.106(2), an action for infringement of a CPVR

---

[253] art.103.
[254] art.11(4).
[255] art.104. Article 29 concerns the grant of compulsory exploitation rights by the CPVO—see para.6-108—and art.100(2) concerns the grant of a non-exclusive exploitation right to the former holder of a CPVR where it has been transferred to the new holder following judgment in a dispute over entitlement to a CPVR. In both cases, the CPVO could restrict the right of the compulsory licensee or of the art.100(2) licensee to bring proceedings for infringement of the CPVR.
[256] This provision is similar to that in the EU Trade Mark Regulation and the Community Design Regulation.
[257] art.104(2).
[258] art.105.

should be stayed if it is dependent on the validity of the CPVR.[259] There is no suggestion in art.106(2) that the proceedings for revocation or cancellation should have commenced prior to the initiation of infringement proceedings in a Member State.

If there is a dispute over the entitlement to be named as an applicant for an application for a CPVR, then the national court must stay proceedings until the CPVO has decided on the merits of the application.[260]

6-159

---

[259] art.106(2).
[260] art.106(1); art.98(4).

CHAPTER 7

INTELLECTUAL PROPERTY AND FREE MOVEMENT OF GOODS

TABLE OF CONTENTS

INTRODUCTION

Since the founding Treaty of Rome, a cornerstone of the various EC and EU   **7-001**
Treaties has been the attainment of a unitary internal market within the European
Union (formerly the European Community). In other words, manufacturers, traders, businessmen and consumers should be able to market and buy goods and
services throughout the EU with no more difficulty than in their home state. Whilst
of course, such is a utopia (for instance, the various languages of Member States
in themselves impose translational costs), the aim was to eliminate artificial barriers to trade rather than the inherent cultural, societal and linguistic barriers. In
particular, the aim was to eliminate legal and financial barriers such as custom duties and laws of Member States which applied to imports or exports from one
Member State to another.

Thus, art.26 of the TFEU requires the EU to adopt measures with the aim of   **7-002**
establishing or ensuring the functioning of the internal market. This is defined by
art.26(2) as "an area without internal frontiers in which the free movement of goods,
persons, services and capital is ensured in accordance with the provisions of the
Treaties". These measures are mirrored in art.3 of its sister treaty, the Treaty of the
European Union which requires Union to establish an internal market.

With such lofty goals in mind, it was inevitable that the exercise of national intel-   **7-003**
lectual property rights to prevent imports of products from one Member State to
another would give rise to concern from EU institutions, especially, the EC and the
Court of Justice of the European Union (the "CJEU"). In particular, a substantial
corpus of law has been developed by the CJEU which is designed to balance the
need to attain a single market, where goods and services can flow freely between
Member States, and the need to ensure that the social, artistic, economic and
technological benefits which flow from intellectual property laws are not
substantially damaged.

[783]

7-004   The founding members of the original Treaty of Rome in 1958 were well aware that it would take time to achieve a single market whereby goods legitimately placed on the market in what was then known as the European Economic Community (the "EEC") would experience no actual or legal barrier to their subsequent circulation throughout the Community. However, Member States were not prepared entirely to surrender their sovereignty over the flow of goods and services. Thus, art.36 of the Treaty of Rome[1] ensured that in the fields of public morality, public policy or public security; the protection of health and life of humans, animals or plants; the protection of national treasures possessing artistic, historic or archaeological value or the protection of industrial and commercial property, Member States still had the right to prevent imports and exports between Member States. This was a derogation from the main provisions concerning free movement of goods that abolished quantitative restrictions between Member States. Clearly of interest to this book is the provision relating to the protection of industrial and commercial property (which has been interpreted by the CJEU as applying to intellectual property). However, neither the Treaty of Rome nor its successor treaties have ever stated unequivocally that the exercise of intellectual property rights by undertakings is exempt from the free movement of goods provisions of those Treaties. Thus, art.36 and its successor Treaties require that such exercise is "justified" for the protection of industrial and commercial property. Furthermore, art.36 requires that their exercise not be used as a means of arbitrary discrimination or a disguised restriction on trade between Member States.

7-005   In seeking to interpret the Treaty provisions above, it is perhaps not surprising that the European Commission and CJEU have sought to examine the rationale for the existence of patents, copyright, trade marks, etc. In doing so, they have sought to ensure that a fair balance is achieved between on the one hand, the need to attain a single internal market and on the other hand, the need to respect IPRs and ensure that the undoubted benefits that such brings to the marketplace and that technological and artistic progress are not hindered or compromised. An internal market is one goal of the EU but another goal is that where inter-brand competition flourishes, innovation and invention thrives and the EU's artistic and musical talents are encouraged. None of this is possible without IPRs.

7-006   There are essentially two reasons for the creation of IPRs. First, there is the doctrine of private justification. This rationalises the existence of intellectual property as being a reward for the endeavours of the inventor (in the case of patents), the author or artist (in the case of copyright), the designer (in the case of industrial design), the plant breeder (in the case of plant breeder's rights), and the owner of branded goods with a reputation (in the case of trade marks). Secondly, there is the doctrine of public justification. This justifies the existence of intellectual property as necessary to encourage technical and artistic progress in society, i.e. the grant of the IPR is in the public interest. Thus, the lure of a 20-year patent monopoly will encourage companies to invest in research and development which may lead to an invention. Similarly, plant breeders need a considerable time for propagating before seeds can be brought to the market. Without a monopoly, there would be little incentive to develop new strains. Trade marks can also be publicly justified as being necessary to prevent confusion in the marketplace and encourage competition between rival concerns. In most examples of intellectual property,

---

[1]   Now art.36 TFEU.

both doctrines are capable of applying, though on particular facts, only one may apply. For instance, the person who invented the wheel probably did not do a large amount of research and development into circular dynamics but had a brainwave. In such circumstances, there is no public justification for granting a 20-year patent, merely the private justification. Conversely, the financial ability to conduct research into an inventive biotechnological cure for cancer will probably only exist in large undertakings. Such undertakings have to justify their activities to shareholders by demonstrating that such research will lead to financial rewards. In such circumstances, clearly the carrot of a 20-year monopoly is required. Thus, in such circumstances, the public justification for the grant of a patent is manifestly demonstrated.

In certain cases, both private and public justification may exist. Thus, the grant **7-007** of exclusion rights in a trade mark for a well-known and respected brand both rewards the brand owner for the development of a well-known reputable brand (the private justification) and ensures that the public are able to differentiate their products from other competing products on the market by the prevention of use by third parties of confusingly similar brands (the public justification).

In considering the relationship between intellectual property and competition law, **7-008** there has been much emphasis on the public justification theory. Thus, intellectual property monopolies are often defended in a competition context as encouraging technological and artistic progress and increasing consumer choice.[2] In contrast, in relation to arts 34-46 of the TFEU and the exercise of intellectual property rights, the Commission and the CJEU have emphasised the private justification theory, and the public justification theory has played little part in the jurisprudence of arts 34-36 in relation to intellectual property.

Thus, the CJEU has developed the doctrine of exhaustion of rights whereby IPRs **7-009** cannot be exercised in relation to goods placed on the market in the EU by the IPR owner or with their consent. The original rationale is that once the IPR owner has received their reward by marketing a product protected by the IPR in the EU and for which they have exclusive rights, their rights are exhausted. They cannot prevent the further circulation of that product from one Member State to another Member State. This approach is intended to balance the right of the IPR owner to benefit from the exclusive rights that they have in their IPR and the need to achieve a single internal market in the EU free of barriers.

Over a period of time, this doctrine of exhaustion of rights has become a cast- **7-010** iron doctrine and has become detached from its raison d'être, namely that of reward to the owner of the IPR. In short, the servant has forgotten his master and become the master itself. Rather, it is for the IPR owner to decide in what circumstances they shall market their goods or services in the EU, and they must always accept the consequences of a decision to market goods in the EU. Thus, as will be seen, even where the IPR owner places the product on the market in a Member State where no such right existed, the IPR owner cannot prevent the subsequent importation of those goods into a Member State where the IPR owner had IPRs. Arguably, it could be said that, in such circumstances, the IPR owner has not been rewarded, because they have not placed the product into circulation in a market where they have been able to reap the benefits of the monopoly-right afforded by the IPR.

Since the enactment of the Trade Mark Directive in the late 1980s, the doctrine **7-011**

---

[2] See paras 8-001 to 8-025.

of exhaustion of rights has been codified into the Trade Mark Directive and European Union Trade Mark Regulation (the "EUTM Regulation"); the Design Directive and Community Design Regulation; the Rental Directive (recordings of performances, broadcasts and sound recording rights); the Computer Software Directive (distribution of software); the Copyright Directive (distribution of copyright works); and the Community Plant Variety Regulation. In each case, the intention has been to codify the jurisprudence of the CJEU under arts 34-36 TFEU. The principles that were developed by the CJEU prior to adoption of the harmonising legislation to reconcile the exercise of IPRS with the aim of an internal market have been imported wholesale into the interpretation of the codifying provisions in the harmonising legislation. A good example of this is in the field of re-packaging of pharmaceuticals. Prior to the adoption of the Trade Mark Directive (the "TMD") and EU Trade Mark Regulation (the "EUTMR"), the CJEU gave a "shopping list" of requirements that re-packagers must comply with when re-packaging pharmaceuticals whose packaging bore by registered trade marks in order to have a defence to a trade mark infringement action by reason of the free movement of goods provisions of the predecessor treaties to the TFEU. Following the implementation of the TMD and the EUTMR, that shopping list was adopted wholesale by the CJEU when determining whether re-packagers had a defence of exhaustion under the relevant provisions of the TMD or EUTMR. Thus, even when considering the exhaustion provisions of harmonising secondary legislation, the legal researcher needs to understand the origin of such provisions in the primary Articles of the TFEU and its predecessors as interpreted by the CJEU.

7-012   In this chapter, the CJEU's jurisprudence on arts 34-36 TFEU is considered rather than particular clauses in Directives or Regulations which provide for EEA-wide or EU-wide exhaustion of rights and are intended to codify the earlier jurisprudence of the CJEU. Thus, the reader who wishes to have a deep understanding of the relationship between free movement of goods and intellectual property is advised to first read this chapter to understand fully the CJEU's approach to parallel imports from within and outside the EU and then against this early jurisprudence, consider analogous provisions in a Directive or Regulation. Where jurisprudence on a particular provision concerning parallel imports is of general application to all IPRs, it is discussed in this chapter.

PLAN OF CHAPTER

7-013   This chapter is concerned with whether or not the enforcement of intellectual property rights is contrary to the free movement of goods provisions of the TFEU. The chapter examines the application of arts 34–36 TFEU to intellectual property, unfair competition law and consumer protection laws. At the end, it examines the effect of art.101 on parallel imports. The reader should be aware that the enforcement of intellectual property rights may also amount to an infringement of art.101 and/or an abuse of a dominant position contrary to art.102. This is discussed later in this book.[3]

7-014   As with other chapters, for the sake of consistency and clarity, reference is made to provisions of the TFEU even if a predecessor Treaty was in force at the time of a judgment.

---

[3]   See Chs 8 and 12.

FREE MOVEMENT OF GOODS—TFEU PROVISIONS

Article 3 of the TFEU provides that the EU has exclusive competence in (inter **7-015** alia) the areas of customs union and the establishing of competition rules necessary for the functioning of the internal market. In contrast, the EU shares competence with Member States in relation to the internal market. This in itself is significant because IPRs do affect the functioning of the internal market but are not competition rules. As IPRs can be granted by Member States, clearly their exercise does affect the attainment of the internal market if exercised against imports from other Member States. Hence, the need for shared competency in this field. However, in certain circumstances, the exercise of IPRs may give rise to competition issues (e.g. exercise of IPRs where such protect a technological standard). If such exercise does affect the internal market, then European Union law has exclusive competence to prohibit the exercise of such rights if they contravene either arts 101 or 102 TFEU (which by definition, requires that they affect trade between Member States).

More specifically on the internal market, Title I of Pt III of the TFEU is **7-016** concerned with the internal market. Article 26 TFEU states:

"1.   The Union shall adopt measures with the aim of establishing or ensuring the functioning of the internal market, in accordance with the relevant provisions of the Treaties.
2.   The internal market shall comprise an area without internal frontiers in which the free movement of goods, persons, services and capital is ensured in accordance with the provisions of the Treaties.
3.   The Council, on a proposal from the Commission, shall determine the guidelines and conditions necessary to ensure balanced progress in all the sectors concerned."

Article 34 states that: **7-017**

"Quantitative restrictions on imports and all measures having equivalent effect shall be prohibited between Member States."

Article 35 states very much the same with regard to exports: **7-018**

"Quantitative restrictions on exports, and all measures having equivalent effect shall be prohibited between Member States."

Article 36 provides that: **7-019**

"The provisions of Articles 34 and 35 shall not preclude prohibitions or restrictions on imports, exports or goods in transit justified on grounds of public morality, public policy or public security; the protection of health and life of humans, animals or plants; the protection of national treasures possessing artistic, historic or archaeological value; or the protection of industrial and commercial property. Such prohibitions shall not however constitute a means of arbitrary discrimination or a disguised restriction on trade between Member States.[4]"

Unlike arts 101 and 102 TFEU, there is no "appreciable effect" rule for art.34.[5]   **7-020**

---

[4]   For convenience's sake, the two sentences will hereafter be referred to as art.36(1) and art.36(2).
[5]   See *Van de Haar and Kaveka de Meern* (177-178/82) [1984] E.C.R. 1797; *Criminal Proceedings against Karl Prantl* (16/83) [1984] E.C.R. 1299, [1985] 2 C.M.L.R. 238, Point 20; *Criminal proceedings against Jan van der Haar and Kavekia de Meern BV* (177-178/82) [1984] E.C.R. 1797 at [14]; *Schutzverband gegen Unwesen in der Wirtschaft e.V. v Yves Rocher GmbH* (C-126/91) [1993] E.C.R.

It is thus applicable to any imports or exports between Member States regardless of the level of such.

7-021 Also of importance for the purposes of discussion below is art.345 TFEU, which provides that:

"The Treaty shall in no way prejudice the rules in Member States governing the system of property ownership."

7-022 The CJEU has, on several occasions, repeated that art.34, as it constitutes a derogation from the basic rule that all obstacles to the free movement of goods between Member States shall be eliminated, must be interpreted strictly.[6] However, in contrast, the CJEU has interpreted the expression "industrial and commercial property" widely. The expression is one more familiar to continental lawyers and has been held to apply to patents, trade marks, industrial designs, copyright and plant variety rights. However, it does not apply to unfair competition and fair trading laws, which are to be considered under art.34 (save where such is concerned with protection of geographical indications).[7] Service marks probably fall within the expression "industrial property" but are not used in relation to goods and are thus not affected by arts 34-36.[8]

7-023 The phrase "justified" in art.36(1) means that the mere exercise of intellectual property rights ("IPRs") so as to prevent imports or exports is not sufficient to bring such a prohibition within art.36(1). It must be justified on grounds of the protection of industrial and commercial property. Secondly, the phrase "such prohibitions" in art.36(2) refers to the prohibitions in the first sentence. Thus, on a strict literal analysis of art.36, even if the prohibitions or restrictions are justified for the protection of industrial and commercial property, they must not constitute a means of arbitrary discrimination or a disguised restriction on trade between Member States.[9]

7-024 The CJEU has issued numerous judgments on the meaning of arts 34-36 in relation to the use of intellectual property rights to prevent inter-Member State trade. These judgments tend to be old judgments because, once the relevant IPR has been harmonised, the validity of the exercise of those IPRs is considered within the

---

I-2361 at [21]. See also, A. Reindl, "The Magic of Magill: TV Program Guides as a Limit of Copyright Law?" (1993) 1 I.I.C. 60, 70 and Fennelly AG's Opinion in *Germany v Parliament and Council* (C-74/99) [2000] E.C.R. 2000 I-8419, cf. Jacob AG's Opinion in *Preussen Elecktra AG v Schleswag AG* (C-379/987) [2001] E.C.R. I-2099 at [204], where he says that there is some doubt as to whether there is a de minimis rule in relation to art.34 and cites various authorities to that effect. See also, 3.1.6 of *Free movement of goods Guide to the application of Treaty provisions governing the free movement of goods* (published in 2010) by European Commission. This is accessible as an online EU publication at *www.ec.europa.eu* [Accessed 18 January 2018].

[6] *Bauhuis v Netherlands* (46/76) [1977] E.C.R. 5; *EC Commission v Italy* (95/81) [1980] E.C.R. 2187; and *EC Commission v Italy* (103/84) [1986] E.C.R. 1759.

[7] See *Rewe-Zentral A.G. v Bundesmonopolverwetung für Branntwein* (120/78) [1979] E.C.R. 649; [1979] 3 C.M.L.R. 494 (commonly known as the *Cassis de Dijon* case). See also, F.K. Beier, "Industrial Property and Internal Market" (1990) 2 I.I.C. 131, 145, for criticism of the exclusion of such laws from art.36. The application of art.34 to national laws relating to unfair competition and geographical indications of origin is considered at para.7-259, et seq.

[8] See F.K. Beier, "Industrial Property and Internal Market" (1990) 2 I.I.C. 131, 145, fn.33.

[9] See *Terrapin v Terranova* (119/75) [1976] E.C.R. 1039; [1976] 2 C.M.L.R. 482, Point 4 of the CJEU's judgment, where it was stressed that the national court should concern itself as to whether the rights in question are exercised with the same strictness against all, whatever the national origin of any possible infringer. See para.7-086.

framework of the harmonising legislation. Certain doctrines have developed from such case law and these are discussed below.

ARTICLES 34–36 AND INTELLECTUAL PROPERTY RIGHTS

Early cases on the application of arts 34–36 to the import and export of goods which were alleged to infringe intellectual property rights under national law were few, and alluded to the free movement provisions rather than directly applying them.[10] This is despite the fact that, nowadays, the facts of the cases would be recognised as falling within arts 34–36. It seems that the parties involved in these early disputes were slow to realise that their facts came within the free movement provisions. Most defendants tried to argue that the exercise of property rights was prohibited by virtue of art.101.[11] When these cases were referred under art.267 TFEU to the CJEU, it only concerned itself with resolving the specific questions that had been referred. The CJEU often strained the meaning of art.101 so as to find the practice contrary to the Article. In relation to the interaction between the free movement of goods provisions of the Treaty of Rome and IPRs, this was first mentioned obiter dicta in *Parke Davis*,[12] a patent case, where the CJEU said that:

> "As regards the provisions relating to the free movement of products, prohibitions and restrictions on imports may be justified under Article [36] on grounds of the protection of industrial property, but subject to the expressly stated reservation that these 'shall not, however, constitute a means of arbitrary discrimination or a disguised restriction on trade between Member States'. For similar reasons, the exercise of the rights arising under a patent granted in accordance with the legislation of a Member State does not, of itself, constitute an infringement of the rules on competition laid down by the Treaty.[13]"

7-025

In the early 1970s, the CJEU gave a series of landmark judgments on arts 34-36 in relation to intellectual property. These judgments established certain doctrines and laid the foundations for the reconciliation of intellectual property with the free movement of goods. To facilitate the discussion of such doctrines, three landmark cases are set out in detail below. These cases established three important doctrines.

7-026

Deutsche Grammophon

The first landmark judgment of the CJEU which directly ruled on the application of arts 34-36 was *Deutsche Grammophon*.[14] In this case, the reference was from the Hanseatische Oberlandesgericht. Deutsche Grammophon was a German company which produced gramophone records. In Germany, it supplied records under the "Polydor" mark directly to retailers. The retail prices of the records were controlled. Retailers contracted, inter alia, that they would only import Deutsche Grammophon records from abroad with the authorisation of Deutsche. This was given if the retailer undertook to observe the resale price maintenance scheme with

7-027

---

[10] *Etablissements Consten SA and Grundig-Verkaufs-GmbH v EC Commission* (56/64) [1966] E.C.R. 299, [1966] C.M.L.R. 418, 476; *Parke-Davis v Probel* (24/67) [1968] E.C.R. 55, [1968] C.M.L.R. 47 at 59; *Sirena SRL v Eda SRL* (40/70) [1971] E.C.R. 64, [1971] C.M.L.R. 260 at 273.

[11] For the success of such arguments, see paras 7-308, 8-435 and Ch.14.

[12] See fn.10.

[13] See [4] and [5]. Referred to in Fennelly AG's Opinion in *Merck v Primecrown*; *Beecham v Europharm* (267-268/95) [1996] E.C.R. I-6285 at [92].

[14] *Deutsche Grammophon GmbH v Metro-SB-Grossmarkte GmbH & Co, KG* (78/70) [1971] E.C.R. 487; [1971] 1 C.M.L.R. 631.

respect to these imported goods as well. Deutsche Grammophon in Germany exported records to its Paris subsidiary in France. These were then re-exported back to Germany where Metro, a German wholesaler and not part of the Deutsche Grammophon network, purchased them. These records were then sold by Metro to retail customers at a price below that fixed by Deutsche Grammophon in Germany.

7-028   Deutsche Grammophon obtained an injunction in Germany for infringement of its exclusive right under German law, as manufacturer of the sound recording, to distribute the recording in Germany. The matter went on appeal to the Hanseatische Oberlandesgericht, who referred the matter under art.267 to the CJEU on questions concerning the interpretation of arts 101 and 102.

7-029   Although it had not been asked to rule on the compatibility of arts 34-36 with the legality of the German action, the CJEU held that the enforcement of such a right was incompatible with these provisions.

7-030   The CJEU said that:

> "[11]   Amongst the prohibitions or restrictions on the free movement of goods which it concedes Article [36] refers to industrial and commercial property. On the assumption that those provisions may be relevant to a right related to copyright, it is nevertheless clear from that Article that, although the Treaty does not affect the existence of rights recognized by the legislation of a Member State with regard to industrial and commercial property, the exercise of such rights may nevertheless fall within the prohibitions laid down by the Treaty. Although it permits prohibitions or restrictions on the free movement of products, which are justified for the purpose of protecting industrial and commercial property, Article [36] *only admits derogations from that freedom to the extent to which they are justified for the purpose of safeguarding rights which constitute the specific subject-matter of such property.*
>
> [12]   If a right related to copyright is relied upon to prevent the marketing in a Member State of products distributed by the holder of the right or with his consent on the territory of another Member State on the sole ground that such distribution did not take place on the national territory, such a prohibition which would legitimize the isolation of national markets, would be repugnant to the essential purpose of the Treaty, which is to unite national markets into a single market.
>
> That purpose could not be attained if, under the various legal systems of the Member States, nationals of those States were able to partition the market and bring about arbitrary discriminations or disguised restrictions on trade between Member States.
>
> [13]   Consequently, it would be in conflict with the provisions regarding the free movement of products within the common market for a manufacturer of sound recordings to exercise the exclusive right to distribute the protected articles conferred upon him by the legislation of a Member State, *in such a way as to prohibit the sale in that State of products placed on the market by him or with his consent in another Member State solely because such distribution did not occur within the territory of the first Member State.*" [Emphasis added.]

Centrafarm v Sterling & Winthrop

7-031   The next landmark decisions in this area were in the joined cases of *Centrafarm BV v Sterling Drug Inc*[15] and *Centrafarm BV v Winthrop BV.*[16] In these cases, Sterling Drug Inc held parallel national patents for a drug for urinary tract infec-

---

[15]   *Centrafarm BV v Sterling Drug Inc* (15/74) [1974] E.C.R. 1147.
[16]   *Centrafarm BV v Winthrop BV* (16/74) [1974] E.C.R. 1183; [1974] 2 C.M.L.R. 480.

tions in, inter alia, Holland and Great Britain. Furthermore, Sterling-Winthrop Group Ltd held the trade mark "Negram" for the drug in the UK and its wholly-owned subsidiary Winthrop BV held it in Holland. Centrafarm imported into Holland, without the consent of Sterling Drug Inc, the drug from the UK, where it had been properly put on the market by subsidiaries of Sterling Drug Inc (whom were licensed by Sterling Drug Inc), thus benefitting from a considerable price difference for the drug in the two countries. Some of the drug packaging bore the mark "Negram".

Sterling Drug Inc and Winthrop BV brought patent and trade mark infringe-   **7-032** ment proceedings in Holland against Centrafarm. Proceedings eventually went to the Hoge Raad (the Dutch Supreme Court), who referred to the CJEU (inter alia) the question of whether the use of the trade mark and patent rights was contrary to arts 34-36.

The CJEU stated that such an exercise of rights was incompatible with arts 34-   **7-033** 36. It said that:

"[8]   Inasmuch as it provides an exception to one of the fundamental principles of the common market, Article [36] in fact only admits of derogations from the free movement of goods where such derogations are justified for the purpose of safeguarding rights which constitute the specific subject-matter of this property.

[9]   In relation to patents, *the specific subject-matter of the industrial property is the guarantee that the patentee, to reward the creative effort of the inventor, has the exclusive right to use an invention with a view to manufacturing industrial products and putting them into circulation for the first time, either directly or by the grant of licences to third parties, as well as the right to oppose infringements.*

[10]   An obstacle to the free movement of goods may arise out of the existence, within a national legislation concerning industrial and commercial property, of provisions laying down that a patentee's right is not exhausted when the product protected by the patent is marketed in another Member State, with the result that the patentee can prevent importation of the product into his own Member State when it has been marketed in another state.

[11]   Whereas an obstacle to the free movement of goods of this kind may be justified on the ground of protection of industrial property where such protection is invoked against a product coming from a Member State where it is not patentable and has been manufactured by third parties without the consent of the patentee and in cases where there exist patents, *the original proprietors of which are legally and economically independent,* a derogation from the principle of the free movement of goods is not, however, justified where the product has been put onto the market in a legal manner, *by the patentee himself or with his consent,* in the Member State from which it has been imported, in particular in the case of a proprietor of parallel patents.

[12]   In fact, if a patentee could prevent the import of protected products marketed by him or with his consent in another Member State, he would be able to partition off national markets and thereby restrict trade between Member States, in a situation where no such restriction was necessary to guarantee the essence of the exclusive rights flowing from the parallel patents." [Emphasis added.]

In relation to the trade mark action, the court came to the same conclusion and   **7-034** said:

"[7]   Inasmuch as it provides an exception to one of the fundamental principles of the common market, Article [36] in fact only admits of derogations from the free movement of goods where such derogations are justified for the purpose of safeguarding rights which constitute the specific subject-matter of this property.

[8]   In relation to trade marks, *the specific subject-matter of the industrial property is*

the guarantee that the owner of the trade mark has the exclusive right to use that trade mark, for the purpose of putting products protected by the trade mark into circulation for the first time, and is therefore intended to protect him against competitors wishing to take advantage of the status and reputation of the trade mark by selling products illegally bearing that trade mark.

[9] An obstacle to the free movement of goods may arise out of the existence, within a national legislation concerning industrial and commercial property, of provisions laying down that a trade mark owner's right is not exhausted when the product protected by the trade mark is marketed in another Member State, with the result that the trade mark owner can prevent importation of the product into his own Member State when it has been marketed in another Member State.

[10] Such an obstacle is not justified when the product has been put onto the market in a legal manner in the Member State from which it has been imported, by the trade mark owner himself or with his consent, so that there can be no question of abuse or infringement of the trade mark." [Emphasis supplied.]

King, Queen and Knave

7-035   The above cases introduced or clarified three doctrines (as can be seen from the emboldened wording) in regard to intellectual property and arts 34-36 which are generally described as:

    (a)   the "existence vs. exercise" doctrine;
    (b)   the "specific subject-matter" doctrine; and
    (c)   the "exhaustion" doctrine.

7-036   In broad and colourful terms, the "exhaustion" doctrine has become the king of doctrines when considering the interrelationship of IPRs and arts 34-36. The doctrine of specific subject-matter is the queen, similar and closely linked with her husband but never being allowed to veto him, and the "existence vs. exercise" doctrine is the knave, which is now considered to have little or anything to contribute.[17] These are now considered below.

Existence vs. exercise

7-037   As discussed above, the "existence vs. exercise" doctrine mentioned in *Deutsche Grammophon* had been mentioned previously by the court in relation to art.101.[18] It was, however, the first time that it had been applied by the court in relation to an arts 34-36 ruling. This doctrine distinguishes between two aspects—the existence and the exercise-of an IPR. The former is unaffected by the EC Treaty, whereas the latter may come within the prohibitions of the Treaty.

7-038   Such a distinction has been forcefully criticised by several authors.[19] The origin of the "existence vs. exercise" doctrine comes from the CJEU's judgment in *Consten & Grundig v EC Commission*[20] in response to Consten's argument that applying art.101 to a particular use of a trade mark would violate art.345 TFEU which states that the Treaties shall in no way prejudice the rules in Member States govern-

---

[17]   With all the negative connotations that "knave" means.
[18]   *Etablissements Consten SA and Grundig-Verkaufs-GmbH v EC Commission* (56/64) [1966] E.C.R. 299, [1966] C.M.L.R. 418; *Parke Davis Probel* (24/67) [1968] E.C.R. 55, [1968] C.M.L.R. 47.
[19]   F.K. Beier, "Industrial Property and Internal Market" (1990) 2 I.I.C. 131; A. Reindl, "The Magic of Magill: TV Program Guides as a Limit of Copyright Law?" (1993) 1 I.I.C. 60; V. Korah, *An Introductory Guide to EEC Competition Law*, 4th edn (London: Sweet & Maxwell, 1990).
[20]   (56/64) [1966] E.C.R. 299; [1966] C.M.L.R. 418.

ing the system of property ownership. The CJEU responded by saying that the challenged decision of the Commission did not affect the grant of the right, but only limited its exercise to the extent necessary to give effect to the prohibition under art.101.

However, legal commentators have noted that art.345 was derived from art.83 **7-039** of the ECSC Treaty, which was intended only to ensure that Member States would be free to determine whether enterprises subject to the ECSC Treaty were publicly or privately owned.[21] Thus, critics argue that art.345 provides no basis for the "existence vs. exercise" doctrine.[22]

If the "existence vs. exercise" doctrine owes its origin to art.345, then "system **7-040** of property ownership" in that Article would have to be construed narrowly as not including the crucial aspect of IPR legislation which is the conferring of private rights on individuals. Such analysis is unhelpful and contributes little to resolving the conflict between the principle of the free movement of goods and the protection of industrial property.[23] The conferring of private rights on individuals by intellectual property statutes is the essential part of intellectual property law. A prohibition on the exercise of such rights means that the essential part of the relevant law is unenforceable and as such, the prohibition constitutes an attack on the very existence of such laws. Moreover, arts 34-36 are concerned with obstacles to the free movement of goods caused by state measures and the enforcement of those measures. If a state measure constitutes a quantitative restriction and is not justifiable under art.36, it is prohibited and has no effect. Thus, in reality, arts 34-36 are concerned with the validity of a Member State's legislative measures. As one commentator has said, it is not the exercise of the right, that constitutes the obstacle to free movement; it is the national legislation making it possible to exercise the right in such circumstances by instituting infringement proceedings.[24] If a law is found to be prohibited under arts 34-36, it no longer has any valid existence at a EU level. Accordingly, to introduce a distinction between the existence and exercise of rights for the purposes of arts 34-36 is illogical and wrong. On a more pragmatic basis, the existence of intellectual property rights is valueless unless the owner is prepared to exercise them. At best, the "existence" of rights may have a deterrent value on potential infringers. However, the moment they are used to found a cause of action against another (or even where the other party is threatened with court action), they are being exercised. Accordingly, from a private party's viewpoint (and hence their legal advisers), the distinction serves no purpose.

Accordingly, it is submitted that the application of the "existence vs. exercise" **7-041** doctrine is of little value.[25] In recent times, the doctrine has not been invoked in the analysis of intellectual property cases under arts 34-36 save in one case discussed below. Thus, in an important case on the application of art.102 to a refusal to license, the General Court stated that the exercise of an exclusive right in principle

---

[21] See T.C. Vinje, "Magill: Its Impact on the Information Technology Industry" [1992] 11 E.I.P.R. 397, 398. See also, G. Marenco and K. Banks, "Intellectual Property and the Community Rules on Free Movement: Discrimination Unearthed" [1990] 15 Eu. L.R., 224 and 226; M.E. Myrick, "Will IP on Technology Still be Viable in a Unitary Market?" [1992] 9 E.I.P.R. 298, 299.

[22] e.g. see T.C. Vinje, "Magill: Its Impact on the Information Technology Industry" [1992] 11 E.I.P.R. 397, 398.

[23] F.K. Beier, "Industrial Property and Internal Market" (1990) 2 I.I.C. 131, 147.

[24] See R. Joliet, "Trade Mark Law and the Free Movement of Goods: the overruling of HAG I" (1992) 3 I.I.C. 317, 313.

[25] See A. Reindl, "The Magic of Magill: TV Program Guides as a Limit of Copyright Law?" (1993) 1 I.I.C. 60, 68, fn.30.

corresponds to the substance of the relevant intellectual property.[26] Such suggests that it is implicitly recognised that it serves little purpose to talk of the existence of rights as opposed to their exercise. In *Merck v Primecrown*,[27] Fennelly AG said in his Opinion that:

> "the distinction between the existence and the exercise of rights can, at times, be quite unreal. It has not been referred to in recent case law, such as HAG II, and may now, at least in so far as the interpretation of [Articles 34 to 36] is concerned, be discarded.[28]"

7-042   Similarly, in *TV Listings*, Gulman AG said that:

> "an exercise of rights that falls within the specific subject-matter of an intellectual property right will relate to its existence. In other words, the distinction between the existence and the exercise of rights and the application of the concept of the specific subject-matter are basically expressions of the same conceptual approach [and that] the distinction between the existence and exercise of rights has no independent significance for resolving specific questions of delimitation.[29]"

7-043   The one case referred to above where in recent times, the principle has been invoked is that of *Matratzen*.[30] The CJEU had to consider a preliminary reference from a Spanish court as to whether the validity of registration of a trade mark in one Member State which was wholly descriptive in another Member State ("*matratzen*" means "mattress" in German) constituted a disguised restriction on trade between Member States contrary to arts 34-36 TFEU. The CJEU held that no resort could be had to art.36 TFEU but that in any event, such a rule did comply with arts 34-36 TFEU because the TFEU (or its predecessor) did not affect the existence of rights but only their exercise.[31] Importantly, the case was solely concerned with registrability or validity of marks and was not an infringement action and thus was not concerned with the compatibility of the exercise of rights with the EU Treaties. However, if the validity of a mark had been raised by way of a counterclaim in an action for infringement, the difference between the existence (i.e. validity) and its exercise would have been less obvious. After all, one cannot bring an infringement action if a registered mark is declared invalid. Despite *Matratzen*, it is not considered that the doctrine of "existence vs. exercise" has been resurrected. It is perhaps best if *Matratzen* is seen as authority for the narrow principle that the conditions determining the grant of an IPR are not affected by the free movement of goods provisions of the TFEU.

---

[26] *Radio Telefis Eireann (RTE) v EC Commission* (T-69/89) [1991] E.C.R. II-485, [1991] 4 C.M.L.R. 586; *BBC v EC Commission* (T-70/89) [1992] E.C.R. II-535, [1991] C.M.L.R. 669; *Independent Television Publication Ltd v EC Commission* (T-76/89) [1992] E.C.R. II-575, [1991] C.M.L.R. 745 (the TV Listingscases); *RTE*, at [72].

[27] (267-268/95) [1996] E.C.R. I-6285.

[28] (267-268/95) [1996] E.C.R. I-6285 at [93].

[29] *TV Listings* (C-241/91P and C-10/89) [1995] E.C.R. I-743, AG's Opinion, at [31]. However, as said by C. Stothers in *Parallel Trade in Europe: Intellectual Property, Competition and Regulatory Law* (Oxford: Hart Publishing, 2007), intellectual property rights are not single indivisible rights. They will normally include the exclusive right to manufacture, import, distribute, perform in public (in the case of copyright), etc. Thus, a prohibition on the exercise of certain rights does not affect the existence of the whole IPR but merely those sub-rights (see p.29).

[30] *Matratzen Concord AG v Hukla Germany SA* (C-421/04) [200] E.C.R. I-2303. This did not cite the above cases.

[31] (267-268/95) [1996] E.C.R. I-6285 citing *Terrapin* (C-119/75) [1976] E.C.R. 1039 and *Dansk Supermarked* (C-58/50) [1981] E.C.R. 181 at 11.

Specific subject-matter

In *Deutsche Grammophon v Metro-Grössmarkte*,[32] the CJEU stated that art.36   **7-044**
only permits prohibitions or restrictions on the free movement of goods in the
European Union to the extent that they are justified for the protection of the rights
that form the "specific subject-matter" of the industrial or commercial property.[33]
This statement has been repeated many times by the CJEU in relation to a number
of different types of intellectual property.[34] The original language of this case was
French. In the translation into the English language, the phrase "specific subject-
matter" and "specific object" appear to be used interchangeably by translators. In
fact, as pointed out by several commentators, the French phrase *objet spécifique* has
a subtlety about it which is not captured by the English phrase "specific subject-
matter" or "specific object". In effect, the phrase describes both the *essence* of the
right and the *policy* reason behind the right.[35] In a judgment handed down in 2018,
the Court of Justice referred to it as "the specific purpose".[36] In this chapter the
phrase "specific subject-matter" is used.

The reference in *Deutsche Grammophon* begged the question as to what is the   **7-045**
specific subject-matter of a particular IPR. The answer for patents and trade marks
was provided in the joined cases of *Centrafarm BV v Sterling Drug Inc* and
Centrafarm v Winthrop.[37] The CJEU said that the specific subject-matter of a patent is inter alia to ensure to the holder, so as to recompense the creative effort of
the inventor, the exclusive right to utilise an invention with a view to the
manufacture and first putting into circulation of industrial products either directly
or through licensees. This principle has been re-iterated many times.[38] Similarly, for
trade marks, the specific subject-matter was the exclusive right to utilise the mark
for the first putting into circulation of a product and to protect the trade mark owner
against competitors who would take advantage of the position and reputation of the
mark by selling goods improperly bearing the mark. Again, this principle has been
re-iterated many times up to 2018.[39]

In relation to designs, it has been said that the right to prevent third parties from   **7-046**

---

[32] (78/70) [1971] E.C.R. 487; [1971] C.M.L.R. 631.
[33] See [11].
[34] e.g. *Merck v Stephar* (187/80) [1981] E.C.R. 2063 (patent); *Allen and Hanburys v Generics (UK) Ltd* (434/85) [1988] E.C.R. 1245, [1988] 4 C.M.L.R. 701 (patent); *SA CNL-Sucal NV v HAG G.F. AG ("HAG II")* (C-10/89) [1990] E.C.R. I-3711 at [23] (patent); *FDV v Laserdisken* (C-61/97) [1998] E.C.R. I-5171 at [13] (video rental right); *UsedSoft GmbH v Oracle International Corp* (C-128/11) ECLI:EU:C:2012:407 at [62] (copyright in computer programs); *EC Commission v France* (C-23/99) [2000] E.C.R. I-7653 at [37] (design); *ADDI v Rioglass* (C-115/02) [2003] E.C.R I-12705 at [36] (trade mark).
[35] V. Korah, "National Patents and the Free Movement of Goods within the Common Market" [1975] 38 M.L.R. 333, 335; D.T. Keeling, "Intellectual Property Rights in the EU", Vol.1 (Oxford: Oxford University Press, 2004), p.63.
[36] *Schweppes SA v Red Paralela SL* (C-291/16) ECLI:EUI:C:2017:990 at [37].
[37] *Centrafarm BV v Sterling Drug Inc* and *Centrafarm v Winthrop* (15-16/74) [1974] E.C.R. 1147; [1974] 2 C.M.L.R. 480.
[38] For re-iteration of this principle, see *Merck v Stephar and Exler* (187/80) [1981] E.C.R. 2063; *Pharmon v Hoechst* (19/84) [1985] E.C.R. 2281; (434/85) [1988] E.C.R. 1245; *Thetford v Fiamma* (35/87) [1988] E.C.R. 3585, [1988] 3 C.M.L.R. 549; *Commission v Italy* (C-235/89) [1992] E.C.R. I-777; *Commission v United Kingdom* (C-30/90) [1992] E.C.R. I-829; *Generics v Smith Kline & French Laboratories Ltd* (C-191/90) [1992] E.C.R. I-5335; and (267-268/95) [1996] E.C.R. I-6285.
[39] e.g. (C-10/89) [1990] E.C.R. I-3711 at [14]; *Ideal Standard* (C-9/93) [1994] E.C.R. I-2789 at [33]; *Loendersloot v George Ballantine & Son Ltd* (C-349/95) [1997] E.C.R. I-6227 at [22]; *ADDI v Rioglass* (C-115/02) [2003] E.C.R. I-12705, [2004] E.T.M.R. 38 at [25]; *Bristol-Myers Squibb* (C-

manufacturing, selling or importing without their consent products incorporating the design forms part of the specific subject-matter of the design right.[40] However, it was not the specific subject-matter of the right to prevent the transit of a product bearing the design through the territory of a Member State as such involved no use of the appearance of the protected design.[41]

7-047   In relation to copyright, the CJEU has said that the specific subject-matter of those rights, as governed by national legislation, is to ensure the protection of the moral and economic rights of their holders. The protection of moral rights enables authors and performers, in particular, to object to any distortion, mutilation or other modification of a work which would be prejudicial to their honour or reputation. Copyright and related rights are also economic in nature, in that they confer the right to exploit commercially the marketing of the protected work, particularly in the form of licences granted in return for payment of royalties.[42] Thus, in *UsedSoft GmbH v Oracle International Corp*,[43] a case concerning whether a buyer of a computer software licence could sell on the licence on the grounds that the rights of the copyright owner in the computer software was exhausted, the CJEU said that:

> "[62] ... it must be recalled that the objective of the principle of the exhaustion of the right of distribution of works protected by copyright is, in order to avoid partitioning of markets, to limit restrictions of the distribution of those works to what is necessary to safeguard the specific subject-matter of the intellectual property concerned."[44]

7-048   It will be appreciated from the above that the specific subject-matter of an IPR is not a mere re-statement of the rights conferred on the owner of the IPR by national laws. In one sense, this is obvious because in the case of parallel rights, *national laws* confer on the IPR owner the right to control marketing of goods subject to IPR in all Member States. The introduction of the doctrine obliges a court to consider whether the exercise of IPRs as conferred by national laws is consistent with the policy and rationale behind the right.

7-049   In *Allen & Hanbury v Generics (UK) Ltd*,[45] the CJEU provided a general statement as to what was the specific subject-matter of industrial property. It said that:

> "In general terms the specific subject-matter of industrial and commercial property includes the exclusive right for the patent proprietor to use an invention with a view to manufacturing industrial products and putting them into circulation for the first time, either directly or by the grant of licences to third parties, as well as the right to oppose infringements."[46]

7-050   However, in that case, which involved compulsory "licence of rights", the CJEU

427/93) EU:C:1996:282 at [44]; C-291/16 *Schweppes SA v Red Paralela SL* ECLI:EUI:C:2017:990 at [37].

[40]   *Volvo v Veng* (C-238/87) [1988] E.C.R. 6211 at [8]; *Commission v France* (C-23/99) [2000] E.C.R. I-7653 at [39].

[41]   (C-23/99) [2000] E.C.R. I-7653 at [33]–[35].

[42]   *Phil Collins v IMTRAT* (C-92/92) [1993] E.C.R. I-5415 at [20]. *Musik-Vertrieb membran v GEMA* (55/80 and 57/80) [1981] E.C.R. 147 at [12].

[43]   *UsedSoft GmbH v Oracle International Corp* (C-128/11) ECLI:EU:C:2012:407.

[44]   Citing *Metronome Musik GmbH v Music Point Hokamp GmbH* (C-200/96) [1998] E.C.R. I-1953, [1998] 3 C.M.L.R. 919 at [14]; *Foreningen af Danske Videogramdistributorer v Laserdisken* (C-61/97) [1998] E.C.R. I-5171, [1999] 1 C.M.L.R. 1297 at [13]; and *Football Association Premier League* (C-403/08) [2012] 1 C.M.L.R. 29 at [106]).

[45]   (434/85) [1988] E.C.R. 1245; [1988] 4 C.M.L.R. 701.

[46]   See [11].

said that where a patent is endorsed "licences of right", the substance of the exclusive rights of the patent proprietor is appreciably altered. In such circumstances, the CJEU said that the patentee merely retains the right to obtain a fair return. Thus, the CJEU said the exercise of patent rights would only be justified under art.36 in order to ensure a fair return for the patentee.[47]

From the above analysis, it can be seen that the specific subject-matter of an IPR is essentially the exclusive right for the IPR owner to first place a product on the market. Furthermore, such is for the purpose of rewarding the IPR owner. However, each IPR may have other considerations. Thus, the specific subject-matter of copyright requires consideration of the moral rights of the author. The specific subject-matter of trade mark requires consideration of the protection of third parties taking unfair advantage of the reputation of the mark. In the case of patents, there is no such gloss. The specific subject-matter is simply the right of first marketing in the Community. **7-051**

The fact that the common feature of the specific subject-matter of all IPRs is the right of first marketing means that there is a clear relationship with the principle of exhaustion of rights. By placing a product protected by an IPR on the market or permitting another to place such a product on the market, the IPR owner has gained their legitimate reward. Thereafter, generally, the IPR owner is no longer entitled to exercise their rights because such use would be outside the specific subject-matter of the right. Accordingly, the IPR owner's rights are exhausted. Thus, the principle of exhaustion of rights and the specific subject-matter are, in essence, two sides of the same coin and emanate from the same landmark cases. **7-052**

Although the specific subject-matter of an IPR is closely associated with the right to first market, it would be wrong to equate the two and such an analysis is over simplistic when one reviews the case law of the CJEU. In *Windsurfing*,[48] quality-control clauses relating to products covered by the patent were held to fall within the specific subject-matter of a patent.[49] Similarly, a contractual clause, stipulating that a notice stating that licensed products had been licensed by Windsurfing International, was held to fall within the specific subject-matter of a patent.[50] Also in cases concerning compulsory licences of patents, the CJEU has held that the specific subject-matter of a patent had been altered from the exclusive right to first place on the market to a right to a fair return for the patentee, i.e. normally the specific subject-matter of a patent is more than a fair and just reward for the patentee.[51] **7-053**

Such cases demonstrate that the specific subject-matter of an IPR is a fluid concept, which is defined and refined on a case-by-case basis. As has been commented, the main advantage of this formula is that it allows subtle distinctions to be made, depending on the type of intellectual property in issue, as to whether exercise of an IPR is compatible with arts 34–36.[52] The disadvantage of this flexibility is that its application to a set of facts different from that of a decided case **7-054**

---

[47] See [13].

[48] *Windsurfing International v EC Commission* (193/83) [1986] E.C.R. 611; [1986] 3 C.M.L.R. 489. This case concerned the application of art.101 to a patent licence and is discussed in detail at para.8-183, et seq.

[49] See [45].

[50] See [72].

[51] See *Pharmon v Hoechst* (19/84) [1985] E.C.R. 2281; [1985] 3 C.M.L.R. 775 and *Allen and Hanburys Ltd v Generics (UK) Ltd* (434/85) [1988] E.C.R. 1245; [1988] 1 C.M.L.R. 701.

[52] Jacobs A.G. in *SA CNL-Sucal NV v HAG G.F. A.G. ("HAG II")* (C-10/89) [1990] E.C.R. I-3711; [1990] 3 C.M.L.R. 571 at [11].

may be uncertain. Indeed, in a patent case, Jacobs AG said, the "specific subject-matter" test is not intended to be used to solve all detailed aspects of the scope of patent protection and that the formulation itself had no "vocation to be exhaustive".[53] Indeed, commentators have said that the "CJEU defines the specific subject matter so as to exclude the restrictions the CJEU wishes to exclude".[54]

7-055   As said above, at the heart of the doctrine of specific subject-matter is the right of reward. That comes clearly from *Centrafarm v Sterling*. However, as is discussed later,[55] the CJEU's application of the principle of exhaustion of rights is done without regard to the right of an IPR owner to be rewarded by appropriation of the inherent value of a monopoly that an IPR confers on its owner. Indeed, the failure of the CJEU to recognise the intimate link between the specific subject-matter, and, in particular, its emphasis on the right of compensation, and the principle of exhaustion of rights, has resulted in quixotic judgments and those which are, from a businessman's viewpoint, commercially bizarre. Such is normally an indication that there is an underlying fault in the jurisprudence.

7-056   Unlike the existence vs. exercise doctrine (save the isolated instance of *Matratzen* already discussed), reference is still made by the CJEU to the specific subject-matter of a right when considering the interrelationship between IPRs and arts 34–36.[56] However, modern references to it show the fluidity of the concept. Thus, in *Rioglass*, it was said that the specific subject-matter of a trade mark was the right to put a product on market under the mark for the first time so as to protect him against competitors wishing to take unfair advantage of status and reputation of trade mark.[57] In *Boehringer v Swingward (No.2)*, it was said that that specific subject-matter of a trade mark is to guarantee the origin of the product bearing the mark.[58] In the first case which concerned whether goods in transit through a Member State are placed on the market in that Member State, such is to equate the specific subject-matter with the doctrine of exhaustion of rights. In the second case, which concerned re-packaging of pharmaceutical products, such is to equate the specific subject-matter with the essential function of a trade mark.[59] Thus, it is not so much used as an analytical tool but rather to indicate in a particular area (e.g. pharmaceutical re-packaging), the underlying policy to be applied. In *FAPL v QC Leisure*,[60] a case discussed elsewhere in this chapter,[61] a central issue was whether owners of public houses in England were entitled to buy decoder cards to satellite broadcasts which had been put on the market in Greece so that the public in England could watch English premier league football matches. UK legislation prohibited dealing in such devices. FAPL, the owner of rights in football matches argued that it was entitled to grant territorial licences and that the use of decoders undermined

---

[53]   *Generics v Smith Kline & French* (C-316/95) [1997] E.C.R. I-3929; [1998] 1 C.M.L.R. 1 at [30].
[54]   N. McFarlane, C. Wardle and J. Wilkinson, "The Tension between National Intellectual Property Rights and Certain Provisions of E.C. Law" [1994] E.I.P.R. 525, 527.
[55]   See para.7-184, et seq.
[56]   e.g. see *ADDI v Rioglass SA and Transremar SL* (C-115/02) [2003] E.C.R. I-12705, [2004] E.T.M.R. 38; *Boehringer Ingelheim KG v Swingward Ltd and Dowelhurst Ltd* (C-348/04) [2007] E.C.R. I-3391 at [14]; *Schweppes SA v Red Paralela SL* (C-291/16) ECLI:EUI:C:2017:990 at [34]–[37].
[57]   *ADDI v Rioglass SA and Transremar SL* (C-115/02) [2003] E.C.R. I-12705, [2004] E.T.M.R. 38 at [25].
[58]   *Boehringer Ingelheim KG v Swingward Ltd and Dowelhurst Ltd* (C-348/04) [2007] E.C.R. I-3391 at [14].
[59]   For discussion of "essential function", generally see para.3-068.
[60]   *Football Association Premier League Ltd v QC Leisure; Murphy v Media Protection Services Ltd* (C-403/08 & C-429/08) [2011] E.C.R. 9083.
[61]   See para.7-250.

such a policy. If the practice of the English public houses was allowed, it would effectively "level down" the amount chargeable to the lowest rate charged in Europe and prevent allocative efficiencies being achieved.[62] The CJEU said that the specific subject matter of intellectual property is intended to ensure for rights holders the right to market or make available the protected subject matter, by the grant of licences, in return for payment of remuneration.[63] However, in order to refute the arguments of FAPL, it said that the specific subject matter does not guarantee the right holders concerned the opportunity to demand "the highest possible remuneration" but "only appropriate remuneration for each use of the protected subject-matter".[64] In particular, it said that such remuneration must be reasonable in relation to the economic value of the service provided and it must be reasonable "in relation to the actual or potential number of persons who enjoy or wish to enjoy the service". It might be thought that such arguments would have favoured FAPL because the remuneration for the Greek licence was clearly granted on the basis of the number of persons who would wish to watch English premier league football matches. However, the CJEU said that there had been nothing to prevent FAPL from asking at the time for an amount which took account of the actual audience and the potential audience both in the Member State of broadcast and in any other Member State in which the broadcasts would be received.[65] It said that it was possible to determine with a very high degree of precision the total number of viewers who form part of the actual and potential audience of the broadcast. The CJEU said that whilst premiums paid by broadcasters to be granted absolute territorial exclusivity reflected the territory granted, such resulted in artificial price differences and in the partitioning of national markets. It said that such was irreconcilable with the fundamental aim of the Treaty which was completion of the internal market and resulted in artificial price differences.[66] Accordingly, it held that such was not permissible. This authority is a good example of the flexibility of the doctrine of specific subject matter. Here, the CJEU introduces the notion that a rights holder is only entitled to "appropriate remuneration" for use of the protected subject matter. Yet, does a right holder have to consider every time it places a protected product on the market whether the price that it is charging represents "appropriate remuneration"? Historically, IPR holders have only had to been sensitive to such pricing issues when in dominant positions.[67] Competition regulates prices and it is submitted that it is to competition law that the law should look if there are concerns about excessive pricing and not nebulous doctrines such as specific subject matter. It is hoped that *FAPL v QC Leisure* is restricted very much to its facts.[68]

In *UsedSoft GmbH v Oracle International Corp*,[69] an important copyright case concerning whether a purchaser of a licence for a copyright-protected program downloaded from the Internet was entitled to sell on the licence (which he would **7-057**

---

[62] The rate charged in Greece was, because of economic factors, much less than in UK. This argument is a familiar one and is in essence an example of Ramsey pricing—charge more to those who can afford to pay more. See para.8-046.

[63] See [107] citing *Musik-Vertrieb Membran*, at [12], and *Collins v Imtrat Handelsgesellschaft mbH*, at [20].

[64] See [108].

[65] See [112].

[66] See [115].

[67] See Ch.12.

[68] It would be unfortunate if, for instance, an exclusive distributor of protected goods in a Member State had to consider what was appropriate remuneration before pricing goods.

[69] *UsedSoft GmbH v Oracle International Corp* (C-128/11) [2012] ECLI :EU:C:2012:407.

have been able to do if he had purchased the program on a enduring medium such as a DVD), the CJEU, in considering the interpretation of the exhaustion provisions of the Computer Software Directive, held that the objective of the principle of the exhaustion of the right of distribution of works protected by copyright was, in order to avoid partitioning of markets, to limit restrictions of the distribution of those works to what was necessary to safeguard the specific subject matter of the intellectual property.[70] Relying upon this principle, the CJEU said that it was not permissible to allow the copyright holder to control the resale of copies downloaded from the Internet and to demand further remuneration on the occasion of each new sale, as the first sale of the copy had already enabled the right holder to obtain an appropriate remuneration. This statement very much reiterates the early statements of the CJEU that the specific subject matter of an IPR was the right to remuneration by *first* marketing a product protected by the IPR.

Consent/exhaustion

7-058   Both *Deutsche Grammophon* and *Centrafarm v Sterling & Winthrop* emphasise that, where a product protected by an IPR has been placed on the market by the rights owner or with their consent in a Member State, then art.36 cannot be invoked and, thus, the owner cannot use their rights to prevent further dealings in the product in the EU. This is known as the doctrine of consent. The doctrine of consent is sometimes referred to as the doctrine of exhaustion in that it is said that the owner of the right has "exhausted" their rights in the intellectual property once the protected product had been placed on the market in the EU by the owner or with their consent.[71] The doctrine of consent or exhaustion of rights has been consistently applied and refined by the CJEU since the *Deutsche Grammophon* and *Sterling* cases.[72]

Internalisation of doctrine of exhaustion into harmonising IPR Directives

7-059   The principle of exhaustion of rights has been internalised into harmonising EU legislation in the field of IPRs. Thus, the Trade Mark Directive, the Design Directive, the Computer Copyright Directive, the Rental Directive, and the Copyright Directive all have provisions which confer an EEA-wide exhaustion of rights

---

[70] See [62], citing *Metronome Musik GmbH v Music Point Hokamp GmbH* (C-200/96) [1998] E.C.R. I-1953, [1998] 3 C.M.L.R. 919 at [14]; *Foreningen af Danske Videogramdistributorer v Laserdisken* (C-61/97) [1998] E.C.R. I-5171, [1999] 1 C.M.L.R. 1297 at [13]; and *Football Association Premier League v QC Leisure* (C-403/08) and (C-429/08) [2011] E.C.R. 9083 at [106].

[71] That the two concepts are essentially the same has been recognised by the court. For instance see *Pharmon v Hoechst* (19/84) [1985] E.C.R. 2281; [1985] 3 C.M.L.R. 775 at Point 20. The principle of exhaustion is recognised in the national laws of most Member States—see F.K. Beier, "Industrial Property and Internal Market" [1990] 2 I.I.C. 131, 151–152.

[72] See (119/75) [1976] E.C.R. 1039, [1976] 2 C.M.L.R. 482; *MEMBRAN & K-TEL v GEMA* (55 and 57/80) [1981] E.C.R. 147, [1981] 2 C.M.L.R. 44; *Merck v Stephar* (187/80) [1981] E.C.R. 2063, [1981] 3 C.M.L.R. 463; *Dansk Supermarked A/S v Imerco A/S* (58/80) [1981] E.C.R. 181, [1981] 3 C.M.L.R. 590; *Keurkoop v Nancy Kean Gifts BV* (144/81) [1982] E.C.R. 2853, [1983] 2 C.M.L.R. 47; *Pharmon v Hoechst* (19/84) [1985] E.C.R. 2281, [1985] 3 C.M.L.R. 775; *SA CNL-SUCAL NV v HAG GF AG ("HAG II")* (C-10/89) [1990] 3 C.M.L.R. 571; *IHT Internationale Heiztechnik GmbH v Ideal-Standard GmbH* (C-9/93) [1994] E.C.R. I-2789, [1994] 3 C.M.L.R. 857; *Merck v Primecrown Ltd* (267–268/95) [1996] E.C.R. I-6285.

principle.[73] Moreover, the EU Trade Mark Regulation, Community Design Regulation and Community Plant Variety Regulation all provide for a EEA-wide or EU-wide exhaustion of rights principle. Where an IPR Directive exhaustively provides for measures designed to provide a balance between the interests of the right holder and the free movement of goods, the legitimacy of any exercise of rights under the law of a Member State designed to implement the IPR Directive prima facie is to be assessed by reference to the provisions of the directive and not arts 34–36 TFEU. However, the Directive (and thus the national law) must be interpreted in light of the TFEU rules on free movement of goods.[74] Furthermore, the Court of Justice has not been wholly consistent on whether arts 34–36 can be relied upon *directly* by a defendant to any IPR infringment action. This is discussed at para.7-093.

Specific subject-matter and the doctrine of consent

Prior to the entry into force of the TFEU or its predecessors, virtually all of the national patent laws of Member States limited the patentee's monopoly to the first sale of the patented product in the territory of the Member State.[75] In the case of the UK and Ireland, this was under the legal fiction of an implied licence. Thus, unlike other countries, the implied licence could be restricted by contract. However, there was no exhaustion of rights in the original Member States if the product was marketed outside the relevant Member States with the patentee's consent. Such did not negate the right of the patentee to oppose imports.[76] However, it became apparent that such a principle could conflict with the provisions on the free movement of goods where the patentee had put the product on the market in the EU.   **7-060**

In *Centrafarm v Sterling*, the CJEU emphasised the right of the patentee to be rewarded by having the exclusive right to put the patented product into circulation for the first time. The court continued by saying that where a product had been placed on the Community by the patentee or with the patentee's consent, a restriction on its further circulation would not be necessary to guarantee the essence of the exclusive rights flowing from the parallel patents. As discussed earlier, such suggests that the doctrine of specific subject-matter and the doctrine of consent are closely related.[77]   **7-061**

Furthermore, it suggests that, if the patentee does not have exclusive rights in the territory where they market the product, then they have not exhausted their rights and would be able to prevent further circulation of the patented product in the Community. Thus, if the patentee were to place the product on the market in a country where they had no patent protection, they would not have exhausted their rights. Thus, Fennelly AG in *Merck v Primecrown* said, in considering *Centrafarm v Sterling*, that: **7-062**

---

[73] These have been extended to a EEA-wide exhaustion of rights principle following accession of EU states to the EEA. See para.7-335.

[74] For a recent restatement of this principle, see *Schweppes SA v Red Paralela SL* (C-291/16) ECLI:EU:C:2017:990 at [30].

[75] See AG's Opinion in *Merck v Primecrown Ltd* (267–268/95) [1996] E.C.R. I-6285 at [91].

[76] See AG's Opinion in *Merck v Primecrown Ltd* (267–268/95) [1996] E.C.R. I-6285 at [91].

[77] See para.7-058.

"It follows in my view that once the patentee has enjoyed *guaranteed* exclusivity at the point of first marketing, which is not a guarantee of monopoly profits, the specific subject-matter of its patent is exhausted."[78] [Emphasis supplied.]

7-063   Clearly, the Advocate-General considered that there was no exhaustion of rights where a patentee markets a product in a country where they have no protection. In *Centrafarm v Sterling*, there was parallel protection. At [11] of the judgment in *Centrafarm v Sterling*, the court said that it would be permissible to exercise the rights where it came from a Member State "where it is not patentable and has been manufactured by third parties without the consent of the patentee". However, as noted by Fenelly AG, it does not deal with the situation where only one of those conditions is satisfied. It could be said that, as, plainly, the rights could always be exercised where the product was put on the market by a third party without the consent of the patentee, that some significance should be given solus to whether it was patentable in the country of origin.

7-064   In the author's opinion, Fennelly AG's view has much to commend itself. In *Centrafarm v Sterling*, the specific subject-matter of a patent was to confer the exclusive right to first place a patented product in a market in order to recompense the patentee. Clearly, if the patentee has no patent in a particular country, they do not have the opportunity to obtain extraordinary profits in comparison to other manufacturers. The patentee thus has no opportunity of recompense. The doctrine of exhaustion clearly only makes sense if the patentee has exclusive rights in the Member State where they have marketed their products. Fennelly AG's view neatly and attractively combines the two doctrines of exhaustion and specific subject-matter. The latter provides the rationale for the existence of the former rule. To dissociate the former from the latter is to risk interpreting a principle without due regard to the policy for that principle. Put another way, it is to risk trying to understand an effect without due regard to its cause.

7-065   However, the CJEU has not chosen to apply the principle of exhaustion of rights by reference to the patentee's right to reward by having guaranteed exclusivity at the point of first marketing. Thus, it has held that the marketing of a product in a Member State by an undertaking in a Member State where the patentee has no patent protection means that the patentee cannot prevent subsequent circulation of the product, even in countries where they have patent protection.[79] Rather, it has elevated the principle of consent to a cast-iron hard principle without due regard to its origins and has applied it in all circumstances, regardless of the consequences. In particular, as will be seen throughout this chapter, the failure of the CJEU to adopt the approach of Fennelly AG has led to a number of somewhat bizarre decisions where it has blindly applied the consent test without regard to its rationale. Specifically, this can be seen in the case where a product is marketed pursuant to a compulsory licence for reasonable remuneration of a patent (patentee rewarded but can prevent further circulation) and where the patentee markets a pharmaceutical in a Member State where pharmaceutical patents are not allowed and it is imported into another Member State where a patentee does have protection (patentee not rewarded but cannot prevent importation into latter state).[80] In all cases, where there is a conflict, the CJEU has ruled that the issue of consent is the key and only criterion.

---

[78] See [97].
[79] *Merck v Stephar* (C-187/80) [1981] E.C.R. 2063, confirmed in *Merck v Primecrown* (267–268/95) [1996] E.C.R. I-6285.
[80] See paras 7-184 and 7-198.

Ultimately, it is submitted that an attempt to reconcile the doctrine of specific subject matter with that of exhaustion of rights is doomed to fail. This is best illustrated by reference to *Allen & Hanbury v Generics (UK) Ltd*[81] and *Pharmon v Hoechst*.[82] In the former case, the court was also concerned with "old" UK patents which were subject to "licences of right" in the last four years of their life. The case was primarily concerned with a UK legal measure which permitted an injunction to be granted against an importer of products which had been manufactured in another Member State who had undertaken to take a "licence of right" but did not permit an injunction to be granted where the products had been manufactured in the UK. In this regard, it is essentially concerned with an issue of discrimination and not exhaustion of rights, and is discussed elsewhere in this chapter.[83] However, the CJEU noted that where patents are endorsed "licence of right", the specific subject-matter of the patent is altered from the exclusive right to first put on the market to a right of fair return for the patent.[84] Such would appear to suggest that if the patentee had received a fair return for the marketing of goods under the patent, the patentee's rights were exhausted. However, in *Pharmon v Hoechst*, the CJEU held that a patentee was entitled to prevent the circulation of goods marketed under a compulsory licence despite the patentee receiving a fair return under the licence. This suggests that, by the late 1980s, the jurisprudential "divorce" between the application of the doctrine of specific subject-matter and that of the principle of consent was complete. The application of the two principles to a compulsory licence leads to diametrically opposing results.

7-066

Further principles applicable to arts 34–36

As seen above, the "existence vs. exercise", "specific subject-matter" and "exhaustion of rights" principles are derived from the landmark cases of *Deutsche Grammophon*, *Centrafarm v Sterling*, and *Centrafarm v Winthrop*. As said above, the exhaustion of rights principle has become the dominant principle and the other two play little part in the jurisprudence of the CJEU. It is considered in depth later in this chapter. However, other principles have also played their part in the relationship of arts 34–36 with IPRs. These are:

7-067

(i)　the purpose of the TFEU is to achieve a single unified market;

(ii)　in the absence of harmonisation, the scope and nature of protection of IPRs is a matter of national law;

(iii)　the exercise of rights must not be improper so as to cause artificial partioning within the common market or a disguised restriction on trade between Member State;

(iv)　where there has been exhaustive harmonisation designed to legislate in a particular area, recourse to arts 34–36 is not permitted;

(v)　arts 34–36 is concerned with trade between Member States and not imports into the EC; and

(vi)　consent to marketing cannot be limited to one Member State.

These principles are discussed as follows.

---

[81]　(434/85) [1988] E.C.R. 1245; [1988] 4 C.M.LR. 701.
[82]　(19/84) [1985] E.C.R. 2281; [1985] 3 C.M.L.R. 775.
[83]　See para.7-079.
[84]　See [13].

Attainment of a single market

7-068   In *Polydor v Harlequin Records*,[85] (a case which concerned the importation of copyright goods from Portugal, which at that time was not a member of the European Community, and is discussed later[86]) the CJEU was concerned with whether identical provisions in the Portugal-EEC Free Trade Agreement to arts 34–36 meant that, where a product had been placed on the market by the IPR owner or with their consent, the IPR owner cannot prevent importation into a Member State. The CJEU rejected such an approach and said:

> "[15]   However, such similarity of terms is not a sufficient reason for transposing to the provisions of the agreement the above-mentioned case law, which determines in the context of the European Union the relationship between the protection of industrial and commercial property rights and the rules on the free movement of goods.
>
> [16]   The scope of that case law must indeed be determined in the light of the Community's objectives and activities as defined by Arts 2 and 3 of the EEC Treaty. As the court has had occasion to emphasize in various contexts, the Treaty, by establishing a common market and progressively approximating the economic policies of the Member States, seeks to unite national markets into a single market having the characteristics of a domestic market.
>
> [17]   The considerations which led to that interpretation of Articles [34] and [36] of the Treaty do not apply in the context of the relations between the Community and Portugal as defined by the agreement. It is apparent from an examination of the agreement that although it makes provision for the unconditional abolition of certain restrictions on trade between the Community and Portugal, such as quantitative restrictions and measures having equivalent effect, it does not have the same purpose as the EEC Treaty, inasmuch as the latter, as has been stated above, *seeks to create a single market reproducing as closely as possible the conditions of a domestic market.*
>
> [18]   It follows that in the context of the agreement restrictions on trade in goods may be considered to be justified on the ground of the protection of industrial and commercial property in a situation in which their justification would not be possible within the Community." [Emphasis added.]

7-069   It can be seen from the above excerpt that the CJEU considers that the purpose of the TFEU Treaty is to replicate the market of a Member State across the entirety of the EU. As Member States have always had internal domestic exhaustion of rights principle (i.e. once a person markets a product in a Member State, they cannot prevent the subsequent circulation of that product in that Member State), then the effect of arts 34–36 TFEU is to expand the domestic exhaustion of rights principle to a EU-wide exhaustion of rights principle.

Scope and nature of protection is a matter of national law

7-070   The CJEU has stated quite clearly that, in the absence of EU standardisation or harmonisation of laws, the determination of the conditions and procedure under which protection for intellectual property rights is granted is a matter for national rules.[87] Such an approach recognises the importance of art.345, which prevents the TFEU from prejudicing the rules in Member States governing the system of

---

[85]   (270/80) [1982] E.C.R. 329; [1982] 1 C.M.L.R. 677.
[86]   See para.7-322.
[87]   In relation to patents, see *Thetford v Fiamma* (35/87) [1988] E.C.R. 3585; [1988] 3 C.M.L.R. 549,

property ownership. Owing to the extensive level of harmonisation, this principle is of little relevance nowadays. However, it is still relevant in the fields of patents[88] and laws protecting designs other than the law of registered designs.[89] Furthermore, for the sake of completeness, the position regarding trademarks or copyright pre-harmonisation is set out.

Designs

The CJEU first stated this principle in *Keurkoop v Nancy Kean*.[90] Under Dutch law, a person could apply for a registered design even if they were not the creator of the design. Although the creator of the design could challenge the grant of a registered design, third parties could not. Third parties could seek to invalidate the design on the basis that it was not a novel design. In that regard, it had to be shown that the design was not commonly known in the industrial or commercial circles concerned in the Benelux territory during the 50 years prior to the filing of the design. The rationale for the rule appears to be that traders should have the right to monopolise a design for a limited period where such a design is not known to the public. This is to ensure that other products are not put on the market bearing the same design and are thus mistaken for the protected design and also for the sake of simplicity.[91] In *Keurkoop*, Nancy Kean had registered a design for handbags and had not obtained the consent of the author. Keurkoop sought to market a handbag in the Netherlands whose design was very similar. It considered that the law was a bad law and its enforcement contrary to arts 34–36. The CJEU said that in the present state of EU law and in the absence of EU standardisation or of a harmonisation of laws, the determination of the conditions and procedures under which protection of designs was granted was a matter for national rules.[92]

7-071

Patents

This approach was followed in *Thetford v Fiamma*.[93] In that case, UK patent laws (unlike other Member States' laws) did not treat patent specifications that had been published more than 50 years earlier than the filing date for a patent application as prior art when considering the prior art for that patent application. The court re-stated the principle that it was for national law to determine the conditions governing the protection of intellectual property rights. This was despite the fact that unlike *Keurkoop*, there was some degree of harmonisation at an international level (if not at EU level). However, the court then went on to consider whether the 50-year

7-072

---

discussed in detail at para.7-072 and *EC Commission v United Kingdom & Italy* (C-30/90 and (C-235/89) [1992] E.C.R. I-829; [1992] 2 C.M.L.R. 709 at [17]. In relation to copyright, see *EMI Electrola GmbH v Patricia Im und Export* (C-341/87) [1989] E.C.R. 79; [1989] 2 C.M.L.R. 413 at [11], discussed later at para.7-074 and *Phil Collins v Imtrat and EMI Electrola* (C-92/92) [1993] E.C.R. I-5145 at [19]. In relation to industrial design, see *Keurkoop v Nancy Kean* (144/81) [1982] E.C.R. 2853; [1983] 2 C.M.L.R. 47 at [18]. In relation to trade marks, see *Deutsche Renault v Audi* (C-317/91) [1993] E.C.R. I-6277 at [20].

88 Although harmonised by the EPC, it is not harmonised by reason of EU law. The EPC is a regional Treaty and not a EU legislative measure.

89 The Design Directive does harmonise the law of registered designs but is not intended to harmonise unregistered design rights (art.16 Dir.98/71).

90 *Keurkoop v Nancy Kean* (144/81) [1982] E.C.R. 2853.

91 See [11] and [15].

92 At [18].

93 (35/87) [1988] E.C.R. 3585; [1988] 3 C.M.L.R. 549.

rule amounted to a means of arbitrary discrimination or disguised restriction on trade between Member States within the meaning of the latter part of art.36. However, it said there were none.

Trade marks

7-073   Similarly, in the field of trade marks prior to it being harmonised, a German company brought an action for infringement of its trade mark "QUATTRO" against a German subsidiary of a French company for importing cars with the mark "QUADRA". The defendant claimed that it was contrary to arts 34–36 to permit the registration of a representation of a number (i.e. the number four), which has a significant meaning in the automobile trade (i.e. four-cylinder engine). The CJEU held, following its line of reasoning adopted in previous decisions for other types of intellectual property, that Member States are not prevented from relying on their own criteria to determine what marks were registrable, provided that the measures adopted do not lead to arbitrary discrimination or a disguised restriction on trade between Member States.[94]

Copyright

7-074   In the field of copyright, in *EMI Electrola v Patricia Im und Export*,[95] sound recordings were subject to differing periods of copyright protection in Germany and Denmark (which had a shorter period). Sound recordings were placed on the market in Denmark after the expiry of the right in Denmark without the consent of the proprietor of rights in Germany and then exported to Germany where the right had yet to expire. The importer argued that enforcement of the sound recording rights in Germany was contrary to arts 34–36. On reference to the CJEU, the court reiterated the principle that in the absence of harmonisation, it is for Member States to determine the conditions and detailed rules for protection.

Article 36(2) and disparity in Member States' laws

7-075   In *EMI Electrola*, the court said:

> "[12]   In so far as the disparity between national laws may give rise to restrictions on intra-Community trade in sound recordings, such restrictions are justified under Article [36] of the Treaty if they are the result of differences between the rules governing the period of protection and *this is inseparably linked to the very existence of the exclusive rights.*
>
> [13]   *No such justification* would exist if the restrictions on trade imposed or accepted by the national legislation relied on by the owner of the exclusive rights or his *licensee were of such a nature as to constitute a means of arbitrary discrimination or a disguised measure to restrict trade.* However, there is nothing in the documents before the Court to suggest that such a situation might exist in a case such as the present one.[96]" [Author's emphasis.]

7-076   Such suggests that EU law will not wholly disregard differences of the intel-

---

[94]   See *Deutsche Renault AG v Audi AG* (C-317/91) [1993] E.C.R. I-6277.

[95]   (C-341/87) [1989] E.C.R. 79.

[96]   (341/87) [1989] E.C.R. 79; [1989] 2 C.M.L.R. 413 at [12] and [13]. Followed in *Sarl Arioso v La Bibliotheque National* [1998] E.C.C. 131, Cour d'Appel de Paris, 17 January 1998 (French copyright owner entitled to exercise rights against imports from England of Fauré music sheets where copyright had expired).

lectual property laws of Member States where there is no harmonisation but instead will consider whether such differences are contrary to art.36(2). Thus, differences concerning the subsistence, extent of protection and duration of the rights would be inseparably linked to the very existence of the exclusive right. However, in both *Thetford v Fiamma* and *EMI Electrola*, the CJEU showed that it will examine the conditions of protection of an IPR to determine whether there is "arbitrary discrimination or a disguised measure to restrict trade" contrary to art.36(2). Clearly, this must require proof of something more than a mere discrepancy between the intellectual property laws of Member States, as otherwise this exception would overwhelm the primary rule. The requirement that the restriction caused by the discrepancy of laws of Member States must be inseparably linked to the very existence of the exclusive right suggests that only a national rule that is far removed from the essence of the right may be objectionable.

Discrimination

The most obvious example of arbitrary discrimination is where the laws of a **7-077** Member State discriminate between nationals of one Member State and another. In particular, art.18 TFEU does not permit discrimination on the grounds of nationality. The CJEU has made it quite clear that in *Phil Collins* there can be no justification for discrimination on the grounds of nationality even where there is a lack of harmonisation and the laws of Member States do not provide the same degree of protection.[97] In *Phil Collins*, German law did not afford protection to recordings of performances that had taken place in a country which was not a party to the Rome Convention for the Protection of Performers, Producers of Phonograms and Broadcasting Organisations.[98] In this case, the relevant performance was a concert by Phil Collins in the USA. However, the above rule did not apply if the performer was a German national. The German national enjoyed performers' rights regardless of the place of performance. Such clearly discriminated against nationals of other Member States (Phil Collins is British[99]). An attempt was made to justify the discrimination on the grounds that national differences in protection of performances existed and that not all Member States had acceded to the Rome Convention. However, the court said that such matters could not justify a breach of art.18.

On the other hand, in *Thetford v Fiamma*,[100] the court was concerned with a UK **7-078** patent measure that disregarded, for the purpose of novelty, any disclosure in a UK patent specification which was more than 50 years old. The court held that such a measure did not amount to an arbitrary discrimination, because it applied equally to both English and foreign specifications and because under English law, foreign nationals had the same rights as UK nationals. Similarly, in *CICRA v Renault*,[101] a design law that protected the manufacture of spare parts for cars without the permission of the owner of the design right in the overall car was held not to amount to

---

[97] (C-92/92) [1993] 3 C.M.L.R. 773 at [31]. However, see W. Verloren van Themaat and W. Wefers Beltink, "Another side of the story: why the Phil Collins judgment does not necessarily mean the end of the reciprocity principle" [1995] E.I.P.R. 307.

[98] See para.4-038.

[99] For the cognoscenti, he used to be the lead singer in the UK rock group, Genesis.

[100] (35/87) [1988] E.C.R. 3585; [1988] 3 C.M.L.R. 549.

[101] *CICRA v Renault* (53/87) [1988] E.C.R. 6039.

arbitrary discrimination because it applied equally to domestic and imported products.

Discrimination and compulsory patent licences

7-079   The CJEU has adjudicated on several cases concerning the compatibility of Member States' laws on compulsory licensing for patents with arts 34–36. In doing so, the CJEU has said that compulsory licensing laws cannot be justified by art.36 because the object of the rules is not to ensure the protection of industrial and commercial property but, on the contrary, to limit the rights conferred by such property.[102]

7-080   Thus, in *Commission v United Kingdom & Italy*,[103] the CJEU held that provisions in UK and Italian law that permitted a third party to obtain a licence on payment of a reasonable royalty where the patentee failed to work the patent in the UK and Italy fell to be considered under art.34. The CJEU held that such law was contrary to art.34 as they encouraged the patentee to manufacture in the UK and Italy rather than in other Member States. Consequently, they discriminated against foreign manufacturers from other Member States.[104]

7-081   The CJEU has also held that other provisions in the compulsory licensing laws of Member States, which have the effect of indirectly discriminating between manufacturers of different Member States, are contrary to arts 34–36. In *Allen & Hanburys Ltd v Generics (UK) Ltd*,[105] a person was entitled to a licence of right for "old" patents after 16 years of the patent had expired.[106] The law further provided that, where the article was made in the UK, an injunction would not be granted for infringement of the patent if the defendant undertook to enter into a licence by right. In contrast, an injunction could be granted against an importer of an infringing article and the licence of right could be endorsed with a ban on importation of the patented product. On reference to the CJEU, it was held that such provisions discriminated against manufacturers in other Member States and was contrary to arts 34–36. A more subtle form of discrimination was highlighted in *Generics (UK) Ltd v Smith Kline and French Laboratories Ltd*.[107] In that case, the patent office of the UK, which granted the terms of licences of right for "old" patents, had a practice of refusing authorisation to a licensee of right to import the patented product from non-Member States, where the proprietor of the patent manufactured the product within the UK, but granting authorisation to imports from non-Member States where the proprietor of the patent worked his patent by importing the product from other Member States of the Community. The CJEU held that such a practice was discriminatory because it encouraged proprietors of patents to manufacture patented products within the UK rather than to import them from other Member States. These

---

[102] *EC Commission v United Kingdom & Italy* (C-30/90 & C-235/89) [1992] E.C.R. I-777; [1992] 2 C.M.L.R. 709 at [14].

[103] *EC Commission v United Kingdom & Italy* (C-30/90 & C-235/89) [1992] E.C.R. I-777; [1992] 2 C.M.L.R. 709 at [14].

[104] See also P. Demaret, "Compulsory Licence and the Free Movement of Goods under Community Law" 18 I.I.C. 161, where he analysed the compatibility of a domestic manufacturing requirement with arts 34–36, and predicted accurately that such a requirement was prohibited by the same.

[105] (434/85) [1988] E.C.R. 1245; [1988] 4 C.M.L.R. 701.

[106] Under the Patents Act 1949, the term of a patent was 16 years. This was extended to 20 years by the Patents Act 1977, which, however, permitted third parties to apply for a licence of right for the last four years of patents granted under the 1949 Act.

[107] (C-191/90) [1992] E.C.R. I-5335; [1993] 1 C.M.L.R. 89.

cases must be seen as an application of the general principle in the TFEU that national laws must not discriminate against nationals or goods of other Member States. Where transitional provisions for acceding states derogate from the Treaty's provisions on free movement of goods, such discriminatory legislation is permissible in relation to imports from the acceding states.[108]

Thus, in the English courts, it has been said that there may exist covert **7-082** discrimination, where procedural obstacles are put in the way of non-residents, who will generally be nationals of another country.[109] Indeed, an important question is whether arbitrary discrimination can arise indirectly in that a domestic provision, although it applies equally to foreign and domestic products and equally to nationals of any Member State, is, because of background factual circumstances, likely to be more often applicable to foreign rather than domestic products.[110] This is often called indirect indiscrimination.

However, care must be taken in extending this concept of indirect discrimina- **7-083** tion too far as such would undermine the principle that the determination of the conditions for protection is, in the absence of harmonisation, a matter of national law. For instance, in *Keurkoop*, it could have been argued that the principle of Dutch law that permitted an applicant to apply for a registered design, regardless of whether the design had been created by the applicant or not, would have encouraged design houses to locate in the Netherlands where they could get better protection. Similarly, in *EMI Electrola*, it could have been argued that the longer period of protection in Germany for sound recording rights over Denmark would encourage sound recording studios to move to Germany to benefit from better protection.[111] Clearly, these arguments are somewhat fanciful but illustrate the point.

Accordingly, it is considered that before a provision of national intellectual **7-084** property law is prohibited under art.36(2) on the grounds that such amounts to indirect discrimination, it is necessary to show that the alleged indirect discriminatory effect has a direct and prejudicial effect on inter-state trade between Member States and is not capable of objective justification, e.g. because it is inseparably linked to the existence of the intellectual property right.

---

[108] See (C-191/90) [1992] E.C.R. I-5335; [1993] 1 C.M.L.R. 89 and *Merck v Primecrown* (267–268/ 95) [1996] E.C.R. I-6285. See also a decision of the English Patents County Court in *The Wellcome Foundation Ltd v Discpharm Ltd* [1993] F.S.R. 433 (Pat) and an article on that decision by J. Jones, "Exhaustion of Rights: Pharmaceuticals Marketed in Spain—A Wellcome Exception" [1993] 3 E.I.P.R. 107.

[109] *Biotrading v Biohit* [1996] F.S.R. 393 unreported (on this point). See also *Berkeley Administration v McClelland* [1990] 2 Q.B. 407.

[110] For instance, see *Hagen v Moretti* [1980] 3 C.M.L.R. 253; [1980] F.S.R 517, where the Court of Appeal held that a rule of English patent law (now abolished), where prior use in England invalidated a patent, but not prior use in other Member States, was arguably contrary to arts 34–36 and permitted the defendant to amend his pleadings to that effect. Although the matter was not finally adjudicated, it might be said that, despite such a rule being applicable to foreign patentees as well as domestic patentees, it is likely to have a discriminatory effect, because foreign manufacturers in other Member States are more likely to have used the invention before the priority date in their Member States rather than in the UK.

[111] Whilst a company established in another Member State would still benefit from the Dutch or German law, it is well established that generous intellectual property laws encourage domestic enterprise.

Disguised restriction

7-085   In *Thetford v Fiamma*,[112] the court held that the 50-year rule did not amount to a disguised restriction because the purpose of the rule was to foster creativity. However, it does suggest that, if there is little objective justification for a national rule, it might be considered to be a disguised restriction on trade between Member States even if there is no discrimination in the application of this law. Clearly there is a tension between this approach and the principle that the scope and nature of protection is, in the absence of harmonisation, a matter for national laws. It is submitted that in general, there must be some justification for the rule on which there are national differences but the burden of establishing this is a light one.

Article 36(2) and exercise of rights

7-086   In the previous section, consideration was given to whether a *provision* of intellectual property law of a Member State could be considered contrary to arts 34–36. In particular, it was discussed whether such a provision could amount to arbitrary discrimination or a disguised restriction on trade between Member States.

7-087   This section considers whether the *exercise* of the rights may be prevented under art.36(2) in circumstances where there is no suggestion that the underlying law is contrary to art.36(2).

7-088   The court has said in relation to art.36 that:

> "Article [36] is thus intended to emphasise that the reconciliation between the requirements of the free movement of goods and the respect to which industrial and commercial property rights are entitled must be achieved in such a way that protection is ensured for the legitimate exercise, in the form or prohibitions on imports which are 'justified' within the meaning of that Article, of the rights conferred by national legislation, but is refused, on the other hand, in respect of any improper exercise of the same rights which is of such a nature as to maintain or establish artificial partitions within the Common Market. The exercise of industrial and commercial property rights conferred by national legislation must consequently be restricted as far as is necessary for that reconciliation."[113]

7-089   Thus, the first and second sentences of art.36(2) represent the demarcation between legitimate and improper use.[114] However, as has been pointed out, the CJEU has not provided any objective criterion for determining what is legitimate or improper and that classification of some use of an intellectual property right as improper or legitimate may be "the result of an analysis but it cannot be the instrument of the analysis".[115]

7-090   As a fundamental principle, if national laws must not directly or indirectly discriminate against goods or nationals from different Member States, then it must follow that, equally, the exercise of IPRs should also not discriminate against such goods or persons. The court in *Terrapin v Terranova*[116] (in which none of the above doctrines were held to prevent the exercise of the right *in casu*) stated that it was for the national court, with regard to art.36(2), to consider whether the rights in

---

[112] *Thetford v Fiamma* (35/87) [1988] E.C.R. 3585, [1988] 3 C.M.L.R. 549.

[113] *Keurkoop BV v Nancy Kean Gifts BV* (144/81) [1982] E.C.R. 2853 at [24]. See also (119/75) [1976] E.C.R. 1039; [1976] 2 C.M.L.R. 482 at [7].

[114] See F.K. Beier, "Industrial Property and Internal Market" (1990) 2 I.I.C. 131, 149–150.

[115] R. Joliet, "Trade Mark Law and the Free Movement of Goods: The Overruling of the Judgment in HAG I" (1991) 2 I.I.C., 315.

[116] (119/75) [1976] E.C.R. 1039; [1976] 2 C.M.L.R. 482 at [7], point 4.

question are in fact exercised by the proprietor with the same strictness, whatever the national origin of any possible infringer. In this respect, as the court is concerned with the free movement of goods, it is submitted that this principle applies in relation to the national origin of the infringing product as well as the infringer.[117]

A potential application of art.36(2) is where a trade mark proprietor divests itself **7-091** of a registered trade mark to avoid the effects of parallel imports. In *Doncaster v Bolton Pharmaceuticals*, where a UK pharmaceutical company had assigned its Spanish trade mark to a foreign company, it was argued that such may have been part of a planned process for deliberately and artificially partitioning and manipulating the EU market for the brand so as to amount to a disguised restriction on trade between Member States.[118] Evidence established that parallel imports from Spain to the UK had been very substantial.[119] The Court of Appeal of England held that there was a triable issue as to whether the enforcement of trade mark rights against the importer was contrary to arts 34–36 TFEU. However, in *Schweppes SA v Red Paralela SL*,[120] on similar facts, where, after assignment, the two parties maintained close links with each other and adopted a common marketing policy to ensure that the brand was marketed in the same way, the Court of Justice has preferred to consider this in the context of the exhaustion of rights provisions in the Trade Mark Directive, read in the light of art.36 TFEU. Thus, it held that where such facts are made out, the exhaustion provisions in the Trade Mark Directive precluded the owner of a national trade mark from exercising its rights against goods bearing a trade mark which had been put on the market in a Member State by a third party who had acquired the rights by assignment from the owner.

The CJEU has also dealt with the relationship of art.36(2) to the exercise of IPRs **7-092** in relation to repackagers of pharmaceutical goods. The reader is referred to the chapter on Trade Marks, where the application of art.15 (the provision which incorporates the doctrine of EEA-wide exhaustion of rights into the Trade Mark Directive) is discussed in relation to the exercise of trade-mark rights against repackagers being permissible only if such exercise does not lead to a disguised restriction or arbitrary discrimination.[121] In particular, in the context of the repackaging cases, the CJEU has favoured an objective approach to art.36(2). Thus, art.36(2) applies even if it is not the intention of the parties when exercising their rights arbitrarily to discriminate or create a disguised restriction.[122]

EU secondary legislation and arts 34–36

Where harmonising legislation is exhaustive in a particular field of IPR, Member **7-093** States are not free to adopt any measures which might undermine or create exceptions to that legislation. For instance, art.15(1) of the Trade Mark Directive enacts an EEA-wide doctrine of exhaustion of rights. As a result, it was held in *Silhouette v Hartlauer* that Member States were not free to retain an international exhaustion

---

[117] art.18 TFEU prohibits discrimination on the grounds of nationality.
[118] *Bolton Pharmaceutical Co 100 Ltd v Doncaster Pharmaceuticals Group Ltd* [2006] E.T.M.R 65; [2007] F.S.R 3 (Court of Appeal, England and Wales) at [79].
[119] See [75].
[120] *Schweppes SA v Red Paralela SL* (C-291/16) ECLI:EUI:C:2017:990. See also para.7-162.
[121] See para.3-624, et seq.
[122] See para.3-637.

of rights principle.[123] A good example of the application of the above principle is considered in the *Prantl* case.[124] This case concerned inter alia, the validity of a provision of German law which reserved the use of a particular shape of bottle (called the *Bocksbeutel*) to producers of Franconia and Baden in Germany. Mr Prantl imported wine from Italy bottled in a similar shape. The Commission argued that the German provision of the law was invalid, as there was existing European Union legislation on the marketing of wines and such was exhaustive and complete. The CJEU held that the legislation was exhaustive with regard to prices, regulation of production and of technical methods, naming and labelling, but could not be regarded as exhaustive in relation to the shape of bottle as such was ancillary to the main objects of a common organisation. Therefore, Member States were free to legislate in this area unless such legislation contravened arts 34–36.[125] However, if the Commission had exhaustively legislated for the shape of bottles for wines, then the relevant provision of German law would have been void.

7-094   Separate from the above principle, it has also been said in a number of CJEU cases that where European Union secondary legislation provides complete and exhaustive measures designed to guarantee protection of a particular interest set out in art.36, then recourse to arts 34–36 is not permitted.[126] Such has been explained by the Supreme Court of the UK, namely that in such circumstances, the rationale is not that the EU legislator is at liberty to override or displace the provisions of the Treaty but rather that the harmonisation measures are directed to the achievement of the single market and thus such measures must be treated, assuming they are valid, as giving effect in the relevant commercial context both to the principle of free movement of goods and to the limitations contained within art.36.[127] In the *Guide to the Application of Treaty Provisions governing the Free Movement of Goods* (2010), at para.3.1.1, the European Commission, put the point in this way:

"This is due to the fact that harmonising legislation can be understood as substantiating the free movement of goods principle by establishing actual rights and duties to be observed in the case of specific products. Therefore, any problem that is covered by harmonising legislation would have to be analysed in the light of such concrete terms and not according to the broad principles enshrined in the treaty."

7-095   Thus, art.15(1) Trade Mark Directive (exhaustion of the trade mark right where goods bearing a trade mark are placed on the market in the EU by a proprietor or with their consent) and the clawback in art.15(2) of the Trade Mark Directive

---

[123] *Silhouette v Hartlauer* (C-355/96) [1998] E.C.R. I-4799. See para.3-590 for further discussion of art.15(1) of the Trade Mark Directive.

[124] (16/83) [1984] E.C.R. 1299; [1985] 2 C.M.L.R. 238.

[125] The finding that there was not exhaustive legislation was despite the fact that art.18 of Reg.997/81 protected the use of the traditional *Flute d'Alsace* but no other shape of bottle. For a case comment, see J.D.C. Turner, "The Prosecution of Karl Prantl Bottles on the Incoming Tide" [1985] 4 E.I.P.R. 113.

[126] See *Simmenthal v Ministero delle Finanze* (35/76) [1976] E.C.R. 1871, [1977] 2 C.M.L.R. 1; *Tedeschi v Denkavit Commerciale Srl* (5/77) [1977] E.C.R. 1555, [1978] 1 C.M.L.R. 1; *Campus Oil Ltd v Minister for Industry and Energy* (72/83) [1984] E.C.R. 2727, [1984] 3 C.M.L.R. 544; *Bavaria v Eurim-Pharm GmbH* (C-347/89) [1991] E.C.R. 1747, [1993] 1 C.M.L.R. 616 at [26]; *Bristol-Myers Squibb Co v Paranova A/S* (C-427/93, C-429/93 and C-436/93) [2003] Ch. 75, [1996] E.C.R. I-3457, [1997] F.S.R. 102 at [25]–[26]; *Phytheron International SA v Jean Bourdon SA* (C-352/95) [1997] E.C.R. I-1729, [1997] F.S.R. 936 at [17]; *Matratzen Concord AG v Hukla Germany SA* (C-421/04) [2006] E.C.R. I-2303 at [20]. See also in the UK, *Oracle America Inc v M-Tech* [2013] F.S.R. 14, Supreme Court at [13].

[127] *Oracle America Inc v M-Tech* [2013] F.S.R. 14, Supreme Court, England and Wales at [13].

(art.15(1) does not apply where legitimate reasons to prevent commercialisation of such goods) is intended to reconcile the fundamental interest of trade mark rights with the free movement of goods provisions of the TFEU.[128] Indeed, it is clear that art.15 is intended to codify the case law of the CJEU on exhaustion of rights.[129]

In general, the principle assists with legal certainty and avoids the need for courts **7-096** always to consider the validity of an act by reference to both secondary and primary European Union legislation. A good example of this was in *Matratzen Concord AG v Hukla Germany SA*.[130] In that case, the registered proprietor of the word MATRATZEN sought to oppose the registration of a word mark which included the term MATRATZEN for various products such as beds. The complicating factor was that the word *matratzen* means "mattress" in German. The Spanish court was concerned that the registered mark permitted its owner to limit or restrict the import of mattresses from German-speaking Member States and thus offended arts 34–36. The CJEU held that resorting to arts 34–36 was not permissible as in the field of trade marks there had been exhaustive harmonisation.[131] It held that the TMD did not prevent the registration in a Member State of a word borrowed from the language of another Member State. Here, it is submitted, the CJEU was entirely right to take such an approach. Provisions concerning the registrability of words as trade marks under the TMD were adopted pursuant to EU enabling legislation which permits the adoption of harmonising directives where such is necessary for the attainment of the single market.[132] It would thus be odd if the provisions of the TMD concerning the registrability of a mark were not sufficient by themselves for the purpose of determining registrability.

However, notwithstanding the above, despite harmonising provisions, the CJEU **7-097** has resorted directly to the free movement provisions of the Treaties where a direct application of the harmonising legislation would have led to an undesirable result contrary to the policy of a single market. Thus, in *Pharmacia & Upjohn v Paranova*,[133] a repackaging case where the repackager changed the trade mark from Dalacin C to Dalacin (the mark used by the pharmaceutical manufacturer in the Member State of importation), it was argued that the predecessor article to art.15 TMD did not apply where after repackaging, a different trade mark is affixed to the trade mark originally on. The CJEU had to accept this submission.[134] However, this led to difficulties because it would have meant that the trade mark proprietor could exercise his rights in circumstances where it was difficult to justify such behaviour.[135] Thus, the CJEU said:

"[28] It follows, as the Commission has pointed out, *that article [15] of the Directive is applicable* where, after repackaging of the product, *the original trade mark is reaffixed*. In contrast, that article does not apply where the parallel importer

---

[128] e.g. see *Bristol-Myers Squibb Co v Paranova A/S* (C-427/93, C-429/93 and C-436/93) [2003] Ch. 75, [1996] E.C.R. I-3457, [1997] F.S.R. 102 at [40]; *Oracle America Inc v M-Tech* [2013] F.S.R. 14, Supreme Court at [15].

[129] e.g. see *Schweppes SA v Red Paralela SL* (C-291/16) ECLI:EUI:C:2017:990 at [30].

[130] (C-421/04) [2006] E.C.R. I-2303.

[131] See [20].

[132] See para.1-100.

[133] (C-379/97) [1999] E.C.R. I-6927.

[134] art.15 TMD was previously art.7 in Dir.2008/95. It only applies to goods placed on the market in the EU "*under the mark*". Thus, without doing very considerable violence to the wording of the article, art.15 had no application.

[135] Both marks were used for the same pharmaceutical and thus it is difficult to see how any consumer confusion would have occurred.

replaces the original trade mark with a different one. *In the latter case, the respective rights of the proprietor of the trade marks and of the parallel importer are determined by articles [34] and [36] of the Treaty.*

[29] In the present case, it is clear from the order for reference, and in particular from the wording of the questions, that the national court is proceeding on the assumption that the Upjohn group has used different trade marks in Denmark, France and Greece for the marketing of clindamycin-based pharmaceutical products. It is thus in the light of article [36] of the Treaty that the legality of the trade mark proprietor's opposition to the replacement of the trade mark falls to be assessed.

[30] Moreover, according to the court's case law, article [15] of the Directive, like article [36] of the Treaty, is intended to reconcile the fundamental interest in protecting trade mark rights with the fundamental interest in the free movement of goods within the common market. It follows that those two provisions, which pursue the same result, must be interpreted in the same way: see *Bristol-Myers Squibb* [1996] E.C.R. I-3457, 3531, para.40." [Emphasis supplied.]

7-098   Here, the CJEU is explicitly recognising that even where art.15 TMD does not apply, such does not mean that the trade mark proprietor is bound to succeed on the basis of art.10 (the right to prevent affixing of a registered mark). Rather, the court must consider whether the exercise of rights contravene arts 34–36. This is a good example of the importance that the CJEU places on the fundamental principle of a single market implemented via arts 34–36. In *Van Doren + Q*, the CJEU had to consider the legality of a German rule that the burden of proof lay on the parallel importer to show that trade-marked goods were first marketed in the EU. The CJEU held that such a rule was consistent with the TMD but this may need to be qualified by reason of the free movement of goods provisions in arts 34–36.[136] It held that where there was a real risk of partitioning of national markets if the parallel importer bore the burden of proof, then the proprietor should bear the burden of proof.[137]

7-099   Thus, prima facie, the CJEU's approach to whether recourse can be had to arts 34–36 appears to be inconsistent. Is there a way of reconciling its various decisions? In considering this, it is important to point out by way of preliminary remark that that there is no dispute that even if recourse cannot be had directly to arts 34–36, if the case law of the CJEU has been codified into a Directive (as was the case with art.15(1) TMD), then the court must consider the previous case law in order to interpret the provision.[138] Indeed, the CJEU has said in *Bristol-Myers Squibb* that a Directive cannot justify obstacles to intra-EU trade except within the bounds set by the Treaty rules.[139] Such suggests that when considering a provision of, e.g. the Trade Mark Directive, one must ensure that any interpretation of its provision is not contrary to the primary Treaty and its objectives. Whilst, in most cases, it can be safely assumed that the provisions of the Directive are intended to achieve the

---

[136] *Van Doren + Q GmbH v Lifestyle Sports & Sportswear Handelsgesellschaft mbH* (C-244/00) [2003] E.C.R. I-3051.

[137] See [37]–[41]. See also *Schweppes SA v Red Paralela SL* (C-291/16) ECLI:EUI:C:2017:990 at [52] (burden of proof lies on owner of trade mark to prove exhaustion where there has been voluntary division of marks in the EU and there is a risk of partitioning national marks citing *Van Doren+Q*).

[138] e.g. see *Bristol-Myers Squibb Co v Paranova A/S* (C-427/93, C-429/93 & C-436/93) [2003] Ch. 75, [1996] E.C.R. I-3457; [1997] F.S.R. 102 at [41] (court's case law under art.36 must be used for determining whether art.7(2) entitles trade mark owner to oppose marketing of repackaged products). See also *Oracle America Inc v M-Tech* [2013] F.S.R. 14, Supreme Court at [14]; *Schweppes SA v Red Paralela SL* (C-291/16) ECLI:EUI:C:2017:990 at [30], [34].

[139] *Bristol-Myers Squibb Co v Paranova A/S* (C-427/93, C-429/93 and C-436/93) [2003] Ch. 75, [1996] E.C.R. I-3457, [1997] F.S.R. 102 at [36].

objectives of the primary Treaty, it would be dangerous to assume that such is always the case.

In the author's view, a distinction can be drawn between the law pertaining to **7-100** registrability and validity of harmonised IPR measures and the exercise of rights. In the case of the former, the EU legislature has adopted a series of measures, checks and balances following extensive consultation to determine what marks are registrable or not. It would be wrong to require tribunals or courts, when considering the registrability of marks (i.e. distinctiveness of marks), to consider whether their decision complies with arts 34–36. However, in the case of the exercise of rights, such are capable of being exercised in countless myriad of ways that it is impossible to say that the EU legislature must have all such ways in mind. For instance, a trade mark proprietor could choose to exercise its rights in such a manner as blatantly to discriminate against third party goods from a particular Member State or where the owner of such goods are owned by persons of a particular nationality. It is a fundamental principle of the TFEU that discrimination on grounds of nationality is prohibited. Such being the case, to say that the discriminatory exercise of rights under the Trade Mark Directive is permissible because the Directive says nothing about discriminatory conduct being impermissible and no resort can be had to the Articles of TFEU must be wrong. Indeed, as said above, a Directive cannot justify obstacles to intra-EU trade save within the bounds of the Treaty.

The above issues were considered by the Supreme Court of England and Wales. **7-101** In *Oracle v M-Tech*,[140] the issue was whether the trade mark proprietor was entitled to exercise its rights against genuine goods (computer servers) bearing the proprietor's mark where such had first been placed on the market outside the EEA (and thus under the Trade Mark Directive were infringing goods). It was accepted by M-Tech that the goods which were the subject of the action had first been placed on the market outside the EEA. However, M-Tech ran a defence that it was impossible to distinguish between genuine goods first placed on the market outside the EEA (non-EEA Goods) by Oracle or with its consent and those first placed on the market in the EEA by Oracle or with its consent (EEA Goods)—the latter being goods in which Oracle's rights were exhausted. Thus, M-Tech said that the enforcement of rights by Oracle had the effect of eliminating trade in both EEA and non-EEA Goods (as traders could not run the risk of being sued every time they purchased Oracle goods). Oracle had an internal database which permitted it to identify by reference to serial numbers whether the goods were EEA Goods or non-EEA Goods. M-Tech alleged (and such was assumed for the purpose of the hearing) that the object and effect of Oracle's actions was to eliminate trade in genuine EEA goods as well as non-EEA Goods and thus to eliminate the independent sector in its genuine goods (regardless of whether such were EEA or non-EEA Goods). It thus argued that such was contrary to arts 34–36. The Supreme Court of England and Wales disagreed holding that as Oracle was entitled to enforce its rights in relation to the non-EEA Goods and that the defence was too collateral to such an action. It also held that no resort could be made to arts 34–36.[141]

Whilst understanding the Supreme Court's approach, it would be surprising if a **7-102** trade mark proprietor was permitted to exercise its trade mark rights in a manner which permits it to eliminate trade in EEA Goods. The attainment of a single market has always been a fundamental objective of the EU Treaties and is embodied in the

---

[140] *Oracle America Inc v M-Tech* [2013] F.S.R. 14, Supreme Court.
[141] This case is also considered at para.14-022 in relation to an art.101 defence.

free movement of goods provisions. The exercise of rights under a Directive which has the object and effect of eliminating genuine and legitimate parallel imports is plainly antithetical to the single market objective. It is difficult to see why a Directive can justify obstacles to intra-EU trade which would not be permitted under the Articles of the TFEU. In the author's opinion,[142] any exercise of trade mark rights or other IPRs under secondary EU legislation cannot be considered in isolation to the Articles of the TFEU and the principles that they embody. Whilst in most cases, the provisions of an IPR Directive will, as the Supreme Court said, be intended to achieve the objectives of the TFEU and thus, it will be rare that one will need to consider the primary Treaties (whether by way of direct application or for the purpose of interpreting secondary EU legislation), inevitably there will be circumstances where such is necessary to avoid a judicial result which is at odds with the primary Treaties and their objectives and policies. If such cannot be obtained by proper interpretation of the secondary IP legislation in the light of the Treaty provisions, then resort should be allowed to the primary rules of the TFEU to prevent an outcome contrary to the fundamental provisions of EU law.

7-103   Finally, it is of note that in *Matratzen*, some support for a distinction being made between on the one hand, the conditions pertaining to the registrability of IPRs and on the other hand, the conditions pertaining to the exercise of IPRs can be obtained. In that case, the CJEU held the registrability provisions in the TMD were compatible with arts 34–36 TFEU because arts 34–36 are only concerned with the *exercise* of rights and not their *existence*.[143] Whilst such can be considered a throwaway remark (i.e. said without in-depth consideration of the law), it is clearly authority for the proposition that resort can be had to arts 34–36 when considering the legality of *exercise* of IPRs.

Imports from outside the EU

7-104   The free movement of goods provisions under the TFEU are only concerned with quantitative restrictions which affect trade between Member States. This was highlighted in the case of *EMI Records v CBS*.[144]

7-105   In this case, the mark "Columbia" was held by EMI Records Ltd in various Member States, whilst CBS held the rights to the mark in the US and other non-Member States. The mark had once been in common ownership, a long time before the Common Market was established. CBS sought to import goods bearing the Columbia mark into the EU. Furthermore, they sought to manufacture goods, and subsequently affix the mark on them, in the EU. EMI sued for infringement of its registered trade mark in various Member States.

7-106   Upon reference under art.267 from various Member States' courts, the CJEU held that the exercise of a trade mark right in order to prevent the import of goods from a non-Member State bearing an identical mark could not come within the free movement of goods provisions, as such exercise of rights did not apply "between Member States" as required under art.34 and art.36(2). It said as follows:

> "[9]   Article 36, in particular, after stipulating that articles [34 and 35] shall not preclude restrictions on imports, exports or goods in transit justified inter alia on grounds

---

[142] It is only fair to say that the author acted on behalf of M-Tech.
[143] See [28]. For discussion on the "existence vs. exercise" doctrine, see para.7-037.
[144] *EMI Records Ltd v CBS United Kingdom Ltd* (51/75) [1976] E.C.R. 811; [1976] 2 C.M.L.R. 235. The doctrine was repeated in *Generics (UK) and Harris Pharmaceuticals v Smith Kline French Laboratories Ltd* (C-191/90) [1992] E.C.R. I-5335; [1993] 1 C.M.L.R. 89.

of the protection of industrial and commercial property, states that such restrictions shall in no instance constitute a means of arbitrary discrimination or disguised restriction on trade 'between member states'.

[10] Consequently the exercise of a trade mark right in order to prevent the marketing of products coming from a third country under an identical mark, even if this constitutes a measure having an effect equivalent to a quantitative restriction, does not affect the free movement of goods between member states and thus does not come under the prohibitions set out in article [34] et seq of the Treaty.

[11] In such circumstances the exercise of a trade mark right does not in fact jeopardise the unity of the common market which article [34] et seq are intended to ensure.

...

[21] It follows that neither the rules of the Treaty on the free movement of goods nor those on the putting into free circulation of products coming from third countries nor, finally, the principles governing the common commercial policy, prohibit the proprietor of a mark in all the member states of the Community from exercising his right in order to prevent the importation of similar products bearing the same mark and coming from a third country."

This principle has been affirmed in a number of cases.[145] German courts have held that the principle in *EMI v CBS* applies even if the rights owner seeks to exercise their rights against imports from another Member State if such imports originally came from outside the EU and were marketed by the patentee or with their consent. Thus, where a patentee had put protected products onto the market in a country outside the EU, and these were then exported to Holland and then further exported to Germany, a German court has interpreted this as meaning that the patentee has not exhausted its rights and can sue for infringement.[146] Furthermore, on a variation of the above situation, a German court has held that the patentee has not exhausted its rights where the patentee does not possess a parallel patent in the intermediate Member State.[147]   **7-107**

In the author's opinion, in the absence of harmonisation of an IPR, care must be taken in applying *EMI v CBS*. The premise of *EMI v CBS* is that imports from outside the EU into the EU are not governed by arts 34–36 because the exercise of rights by the IPR owner will not affect trade between Member States. However, in the German cases, it is plain that the exercise of rights by the patentee did affect trade between Member States. In the first case, it meant that goods in Holland could not be imported into Germany. In the second case, it meant that goods could not be imported from the intermediate Member State. In the author's submission, the critical fact in *EMI v CBS* was that EMI had protection in all Member States and was taking action to prevent the importation of Columbia-marked goods into the whole of the EU. Clearly, if EMI could exercise its rights, then no goods could not have lawfully entered *any* Member State. In such circumstances, the exercise of rights could not have affected trade between Member States. Thus, where an IPR owner relies on a EU-wide unitary right, such as a Community Trade Mark, the EU   **7-108**

---

[145] e.g see *Generics (UK) Ltd v Smith Kline and French Laboratories* (C-191/90) [1992] E.C.R. I-4621 at [17]. See also, in the UK, *Oracle v M-Tech* [2012] 1 W.L.R. 2026 at [19] (Supreme Court).

[146] See *Re Tylosin* [1977] 1 C.M.L.R. 460, Bundesgerichtshof.

[147] See *Re Patented Bandages Material* [1988] 2 C.M.L.R. 359; [1988] F.S.R. 505, Hanseatisches Oberlandesgericht Hamburg. See also, *Re Tylosin* [1977] 1 C.M.L.R. 460, Bundesgerichtshof, where the Bundesgerichtshof held that unsanctioned imports from Italy (where patents for veterinary medicines were not permissible) infringed German patent rights in the veterinary medicine. See reference to these cases by Fennelly AG in *Merck v Primecrown* (C-267–268/95) [1996] E.C.R. I-6285 at [92].

is, in effect, one territory. In contrast, where an IPR owner places products on the market outside the EU and these are lawfully imported into a Member State of the EU, and the IPR owner then seeks to prevent their importation into another Member State, it is submitted that, because the exercise of rights will manifestly affect trade between Member States, arts 34–36 are applicable. Such does not mean by itself that the proprietor of the right has exhausted its rights because the doctrine of exhaustion of rights under arts 34–36 as developed by the CJEU has been confined to where the first marketing was in the EU. Thus, in such circumstances, the correct analysis would be that arts 34–36 is engaged but there is no exhaustion at a EU level (although there may be at a domestic level where the right is unharmonised).

7-109   The effect of *EMI v CBS* is much reduced by the fact that in many areas of intellectual property laws, EU law has created an EU-wide or EEA-wide exhaustion of rights principle which has had the effect, as decided by the CJEU, of preventing Member States from maintaining or introducing an international exhaustion of rights principle. Thus, goods which have been placed on the market by the IPR owner or with their consent outside the EU cannot be imported into the EU without the consent of the IPR owner. However, until the Unitary Patent comes into force, in the field of patents there has been no harmonisation. *EMI v CBS* is thus relevant to patented products placed on the market outside the EU by the patentee or with their consent. In short, the mere fact that a patentee has placed a patented product on the market outside the EU does not mean that the free movement of goods provisions of the TFEU prohibit the exercise of their parallel EU patents to prevent the importation of such products into the EU by a third party. Articles 34–36 TFEU are not engaged at all. In the field of unharmonised IPR, the TFEU does not impose an international exhaustion of rights principle and Member States are free to determine whether or not to have such a doctrine as part of their domestic law.

7-110   On a separate matter, trade between Member States can be affected even though the ostensible nature of IPR legislation is aimed against non-Member States. Thus, in a case concerning the settlement of conditions for compulsory licences by the UK authorities, it was the practice of the UK Patent Office to permit in a compulsory licence a term which permitted the importation of the patented product from non-Member States where the proprietor of the patent did not manufacture the product within the UK but imported from other Member States.[148] The CJEU confirmed the authority of *EMI v CBS* but held that that national authorities were not entitled, in exercising their powers with respect to imports from non-Member countries, to apply criteria which, by their discriminatory nature, affected trade between Member States in contravention of arts 34–36 of the TFEU.

Cannot limit consent to one Member State

7-111   An IPR owner cannot limit their consent to the marketing of a product to a particular Member State (e.g. by the imposition of a notice on goods that the goods are not for sale outside a particular Member State). The application of the principle of consent is only relevant to the act of first marketing of the product in the Community. If consent to that act has occurred, it is not possible to limit the circulation of that product throughout the EU by contractual restraints.[149] Such restraints are only relevant as between the parties.[150]

---

[148] *Generics (UK) and Harris Pharmaceuticals v Smith Kline & French Laboratories Ltd* (C-191/90)

Application of the principle of exhaustion of rights

In the previous section, we discussed the differing doctrines that have developed **7-112** in relation to intellectual property and arts 34–36. As stated, the CJEU has given primacy to the principle of exhaustion of rights, i.e. a person has exhausted their rights when a product is placed on the market in the EU by the person or with their consent.[151] In the following sections, this book considers aspects of the principle of consent (exhaustion of rights) and its application to particular sets of facts. In particular, the chapter considers the following aspects:

(a) Who has the burden and what is the standard of proof in exhaustion cases?

(b) Other than the owner of the IPR, which categories of persons who market products which are subject to IPR will exhaust the rights of the IPR owner? In particular, this section looks at marketing by licensees; undertakings which are economically linked to the IPR owner and where the rights were originally in common ownership but have now been assigned to independent undertakings.

(c) When and where is a product first placed on the market? This is important as only if the product is placed on the market in the EU (or in certain cases, the European Economic Area (the "EEA")) does the principle of exhaustion apply.

(d) Where there are differing levels of protection in Member States. In such circumstances, has an IPR owner exhausted their rights to prevent importation of products into Member State B where the products are protected by IPRs when it first marketed a product in Member State A where there exists no protection or less than in Member State B?

(e) When will a person be *deemed* to have consented to the marketing of a product? This section considers the position where an IPR owner has not expressly consented to the marketing of a product but it is argued by the parallel importer that they must be deemed to have consented, e.g. because the product has been marketed pursuant to a compulsory licence pursuant to the laws of a Member State for failure to work the patent.

(f) Does the TEFU preclude an international exhaustion of rights principle in Member States' laws?

In certain respects, the above topics overlap. Thus, in relation to the last two top-   **7-113** ics, considerable argument has been made by parallel importers that a person who markets a product outside the EEA must be deemed to have consented to its marketing in the EEA. Thus, the reader is advised to read the entirety of the above sections. Furthermore, in relation to intellectual property which is the subject of a harmonising directive, e.g. trade marks, there has been considerable case law of the CJEU

[1992] E.C.R. I-5335; [1993] 1 C.M.L.R. 89; [1993] F.S.R. 592 at 612.

[149] *Dansk Supermarked v Imerco* (58/80) [1981] E.C.R. 181, [1981] 3 C.M.L.R. 590; *Peak Holding v Axolin-Elinor AB* (C-16/03) [2004] E.C.R. I-11313, [2005] E.T.M.R. 28.

[150] (C-16/03) [2004] E.C.R. I-11313, [2005] E.T.M.R. 28; (C-115/02) [2004] E.T.M.R. 38 and *Consten and Grundig v Commission* (56/64) [1966] E.C.R. 299.

[151] In the case of harmonised IPRs, the exhaustion of rights principle has been extended to the EEA where the harmonising directive has been adopted by the EEA Joint Committee—see paras 1-133, 1-144 and 7-335. Thus, in the field of trade marks, art.15 stipulates a EU-wide exhaustion of rights. However, Member States are required by being members of the EEA to extend this to the EEA. In the case of the EU Trade Mark, the exhaustion principle now also extends to the EEA but not as of May 2018, for other unitary rights.

on the provisions of the harmonising directive which "internalise" the principle of exhaustion of rights. Thus, the reader is also advised to read the relevant sections in the relevant chapter. What is discussed below is common to all forms of IPRs.

Burden and standard of proof and exhaustion of rights

7-114   In a case where it is alleged that the owner of an IPR has exhausted their rights in goods because they have placed the goods on the market in a Member State or have consented to such goods being marketed in the EU, it may often be difficult for the parallel importer to establish that: (i) the goods in question have been *first* placed on the market in the EU by the IPR owner or with their consent; or (ii) the IPR owner has consented to the goods being imported into the EU from outside the EU. As discussed earlier, in general terms, whether the IPR has been harmonised or not, the mere placing of products on the market by the IPR owner outside the EU does not exhaust the rights of the IPR owner according to EU law.[152]

7-115   In any case, where it is alleged that there has been exhaustion of rights, a number of factual issues may arise, e.g.:

(a)   Where were the goods protected by the IPR *first* marketed? Within the EU or outside of it?

(b)   Who was the person who carried out the act of first marketing? The registered proprietor or someone else?

(c)   If someone other than the registered proprietor first marketed the goods, did the registered proprietor unequivocally consent to their marketing into the EU?

7-116   In relation to each of these issues, it is necessary to consider who has the burden of proving such and what the standard of proof is. As said above, difficulties may arise if such falls on the parallel importer and they are unable to determine whether the goods are genuine or counterfeit and whether they were first marketed inside or outside the EU.

Burden of proof in exhaustion cases

7-117   Because in relation to harmonised IPRs, there is exhaustion of rights if goods protected by the harmonised right were marketed by the owner of the right in the EEA but not if outside the EEA, the issue of burden of proof is very important. Invariably, the registered proprietor will know whether they marketed the goods in or outside the EEA and/or consented to their marketing in the EEA. In contrast, (unless the parallel importer buys directly from the registered proprietor), the parallel importer will not. In such circumstances, to impose the burden of proof on the parallel importer to prove that the registered proprietor has marketed the goods in the EEA may be an impossible burden to discharge and may result in the registered proprietor winning by default. This would have an adverse effect on legitimate parallel trade to the detriment of consumers in the EEA.

7-118   This issue arose in *Van Doren+Q*.[153] Van Doren, who had exclusive distribution rights from the trade mark proprietor, maintained that the parallel importer, Lifestyle, had marketed products originally put on the market by the registered

---

[152] See para.7-104.
[153] *Van Doren + Q GmbH v Lifestyle Sports Sportswear Handelsgesellschaft mbH* (C-244/00) [2003] E.C.R. I-3051; [2003] E.T.M.R. 75.

proprietor in the US. Lifestyle maintained that they had sourced the products in the EEA from an intermediary who they assumed had purchased it from an authorised distributor. However, they were not prepared to name the intermediary for fear of their source drying up. The German courts referred to the CJEU whether, in a trade mark infringement action against a parallel importer, a national rule that the full burden of proof of proving the factual conditions for exhaustion of rights conferred by a trade mark lay on the parallel importer was contrary to arts 34–36. As noted by the German court, such a rule could permit the partitioning of the internal market by the trade mark proprietor because although a dealer may be readily able to show that they have purchased goods, they will not be able to make their suppliers reveal the suppliers further up the supply chain and even if they were able to trace the distribution channel back to the trade mark proprietor, the supply source would be liable to dry up immediately.

The CJEU held that such a rule of evidence was consistent with EU law and in **7-119** particular arts 5–7 of the the then Trade Mark Directive. However, it held the requirements of free movement of goods flowing from arts 34–36 meant that such a rule of evidence needed to be qualified. It said that where there was a real risk of partitioning of national markets if the burden of proof lay on the parallel importer, then the burden of proof would lie on the proprietor to establish that the goods were initially placed on the market outside the EEA by them or with their consent.[154] It said that if such was done, then the burden lay on the third party to prove the consent of the trade mark proprietor to subsequent marketing of those products in the EEA.[155]

It will be noted that nothing was said by the CJEU that the standard and burden **7-120** of proof of showing first marketing in the EEA was a matter for the Trade Mark Directive and not a matter for German procedural law. Indeed, the clear implication was that it was not and such is supported by the recitals of the Trade Mark Directive.[156] However, in *Class International BV v Colgate-Palmolive*,[157] the CJEU said in a case involving whether genuine goods bearing a registered trade mark seized at Rotterdam had entered the EU (and thus infringed the rights of the registered proprietors):

"[73] In respect of the issue of the onus of proving that interference, it must be pointed out, first, that if it were a matter for the national laws of the Member States, the consequence for trade mark proprietors could be that protection would vary according to the legal system concerned. The objective of 'the same protection under the legal systems of all the Member States' set out in the ninth recital in the preamble to the Directive, where it is described as fundamental, would not be attained (see, on the subject of the Directive, *Zino Davidoff* and *Levi Strauss*, cited above, paragraphs 41 and 42).

[74] It must then be stated that, in a situation such as the one in the main proceedings, the onus of proving interference must lie with the trade mark proprietor who alleges it. If that is proven, it is then for the trader sued to prove the existence of the

---

[154] See [41]–[42]. See also *Schweppes SA v Red Paralela SL* (C-291/16) ECLI:EUI:C:2017:990 at [52]–[54].

[155] See [42].

[156] Recital 11, Dir.2008/95; See also Recital 16, Dir.2015/2436. This refers to the burden of proof to prove that likelihood of confusion is a matter for national law. Whilst it is right to acknowledge that this does not refer to the burden of proof in other situations where such is not an issue, it is a clear indicator that the Directive was not intending to harmonise rules of evidence. See also *Interflora v Marks & Spencer* [2013] EWHC Civ 1291 (Ch) at [235].

[157] (C-405/03) [2005] E.C.R. I-8735.

consent of the proprietor to the marketing of the goods in the Community (see, on the subject of the Directive, *Zino Davidoff* and *Levi Strauss*, cited above, paragraph 54)."

7-121   Such suggest that the burden of proof in exhaustion cases, whilst ostensibly a matter of national procedure, is indeed harmonised via the Trade Mark Directive. Whilst it might be said that in *Class International*, the CJEU was considering the specific issue of burden of proof on the specific issue as to whether or not the proprietor had consented to the importation of goods into the EU, the above excerpt is broad and general in its scope and would apply to the act of first marketing. Furthermore, in *Makro Diesel*, discussed at para.7-127, the CJEU has held that the approach to the determination of the issue of consent by the registered proprietor to first marketing does not depend on whether the goods were first marketed in the EEA or outside it. Equally, it might be argued that a distinction should be drawn between the matters of burden of proof regarding the issue of where goods were first marketed as opposed to whether the registered proprietor had consented to such marketing. However, this seems to take a narrow approach to such issues and does not appear justified by the authorities. Thus, in the excerpt above in *Class International*, the distinction is between interference in trade mark rights (burden on trade mark proprietor) and consent exhaustion of rights (burden on defendant).

7-122   The above cases, although ostensibly based on provisions in the Trade Mark Directive, are common to all harmonised IPRs in EU. Thus, in the author's view, the current position is that under EU law, the burden of proof lies on the parallel importer to prove exhaustion of rights. That would include proving if relevant, that the goods were first placed on the market in the EEA by the registered proprietor or with their consent, or alternatively that the registered proprietor consented to the importation of the goods into the EEA. However, where the imposition of such a burden gives rise to a real risk of partitioning national markets, then the burden of proof on the issue of whether the goods were first marketed in the EEA or outside by the proprietor will shift to the registered proprietor. If the latter is established, the burden lies on the parallel importer to show consent to their marketing into the EEA.

Standard of proof in exhaustion cases

7-123   In general, the standard of proof on any legal or factual issue in a civil case is on the balance of probabilities. In *Davidoff*,[158] the CJEU had to consider to what standard consent needed to be shown when the registered proprietor had marketed its goods outside the EEA and the parallel importer was alleging that it had consented to their importation into the EEA. The facts were that Davidoff, the proprietor of two trade marks for toiletries, had entered into an exclusive distribution contract with a trader in Singapore whereby the trader undertook to sell Davidoff products solely within a defined territory outside the EEA to sub-distributors and retailers. It was part of the contract that the trader impose on those persons a prohibition on resale outside the territory. A trader acquired the products in Singapore and imported them into the UK and removed the batch code numbers on them.

7-124   The CJEU held:

---

[158] *Zino Davidoff v A&G Imports; Levi Strauss v Tesco Stores Ltd; Levi Strauss v Costco Wholesale UK Ltd* (C-414–416/99) [2001] E.C.R. I-8691.

"[45]   In view of its serious effect in extinguishing the exclusive rights of the proprietors of the trade marks in issue in the main proceedings (rights which enable them to control the initial marketing in the EEA), *consent must be expressed that an intention to renounce those rights is unequivocally demonstrated.*

[46]   Such intention will normally be gathered from an *express statement of consent.* Nevertheless, it is conceivable that consent may, in some cases, be inferred from facts and circumstances prior to, simultaneous with or subsequent to the placing of the goods on the market outside the EEA which has renounced his rights." [Emphasis supplied.]

The CJEU said that it is for the trader alleging consent to prove it, and that consent will not be inferred from the mere silence of the trade mark proprietor.[159] Furthermore, consent would not be inferred from the failure of a trade-mark proprietor to communicate their opposition to marketing within the EEA via the absence of contractual restraints or a notice on the products or by operation of national law.[160]   **7-125**

The phrase "unequivocally demonstrated" might be interpreted as meaning that there can be no reasonable doubt in the court or tribunal's mind that the registered proprietor has consented. However, in an English case, *Mastercigars*, the Court of Appeal rejected a submission that "unequivocal" meant that it must be proven to the criminal standard, i.e. beyond reasonable doubt. Jacob LJ said that "unequivocal" simply meant that the proven facts must be consistent only with consent and not also a lack of consent. Such facts are to be proven on the balance of probability (the standard of proof for proving facts in civil cases in England).[161] In other words, when determining the relevant facts, such must be determined in accordance with the rules of evidence of the Member State (normally such is on the balance of probability). Once those facts have been determined by the court or tribunal, it must then ask itself whether such proven facts are consistent only with consent. This is best illustrated by two examples: **7-126**

Example 1

There is a dispute about the authenticity of a document wherein overtly, the IPR owner states their consent to importation of goods placed on the market outside the EEA. The court of a Member State would determine whether the document was a forgery according to its domestic standard of proof. If the document is established as being authentic, then it is unequivocal that the IPR owner has consented to the importation of such goods. It would not be sufficient for the registered proprietor to say that there is a reasonable doubt whether the document was a forgery and thus, the parallel importer had failed to show consent.

Example 2

Trade-marked electrical goods are sold to a purchaser based outside the EEA by the registered proprietor of the trade mark. Accompanying documentation is in many

---

[159] See [54]–[55].

[160] See [58], et seq. See also *Coty Prestige Lancaster Group v Simex Trading AG* (C-127/09) [2010] E.C.R. 4965 (sale of perfume testers without transfer of ownership to intermediaries for marketing purposes did not amount to implied consent to marketing in EEA).

[161] *Mastercigars Direct Ltd v Hunters & Frankau Ltd* [2007] R.P.C. 24; [2007] E.T.M.R. 44. See also *Dalsouple Société Saumuroise du Caoutchouc v Dalsouple Direct* [2014] EWHC 3963 (Ch) where the court said that evidentially, express or implied consent must be proven on the balance of probability (the issue was whether an undertaking had given oral express consent to registration of a mark). See also para.3-529.

languages including Flemish, a language only spoken in the EEA and the documentation also contains reference to Flemish certificates confirming compliance of the goods with Belgian electrical safety laws. One inference from this is that the proprietor meant for such goods to be marketed in Belgium.[162] However, an alternative inference is that the manufacturer simply prints all his documentation in all relevant languages because he does not wish to have the extra costs of printing different instruction leaflets, etc. On the strength of *Mastercigars* and *Davidoff*, these facts are not consistent only with consent. Thus, there is no unequivocal demonstration of consent.

In general, it will be very difficult to show implied consent.[163]

7-127   In the 3rd edn of this book, it was queried whether the CJEU would take the same approach in *Davidoff* to the issue of consent where there is no dispute that the goods were first marketed in the EEA but the issue is whether the registered proprietor consented to their marketing. As said in that edition, the background to *Davidoff* was that the CJEU had made it clear in previous cases that the TMD did not permit an international exhaustion of rights principle. As said in the book, if the CJEU had allowed too lax a test to the determination of consent to importation into the EEA of goods first placed on the market outside the EEA, such would risk bringing the doctrine of international exhaustion of rights through the "back door" of consent. Such is clearly not a concern when the goods were first marketed in the EEA. However, in *Makro v Diesel*,[164] the CJEU held that the approach in *Davidoff* to the determination of implied consent applied equally where the goods were first marketed in the EEA.[165] In *Makro*, an authorised Spanish distributor of *Diesel* clothing entered into a limited distribution agreement with another Spanish company to conduct market tests on *Diesel* shoes. This company in turn sought to grant a sublicence to Cosmos to manufacture and sell *Diesel* shoes. They in turn sold these shoes which eventually Makro bought. Makro argued that Diesel had exhausted its rights because Cosmos had marketed the shoes with Diesel's consent. The CJEU held that there was no reason to apply a different approach to the determination of consent where goods were first placed on the market inside as opposed to outside the EEA.[166]

7-128   Although the cases above specifically concerned the meaning of consent in the predecessor articles to arts 10 and 15 of the Trade Mark Directive, the principles (also stated above) are capable of general application when considering the doctrine of exhaustion of rights. In particular, this is because art.15 owes its origin to the case law of the CJEU under arts 34–36.[167] Whilst it might be argued that the Trade Mark Directive legislated for a EU-wide only exhaustion of rights principle and that the CJEU's requirement of "unequivocal demonstration" is in part, caused by the need to prevent a worldwide exhaustion of rights principle being brought in via the "back door" (i.e. through too liberal an interpretation of consent to importation into the EEA), the CJEU's approach in *Makro*, whereby it says that the same approach applies where the goods were first marketed in the EEA, means that such is not correct and that the requirement of unequivocal demonstration is, as said in *Davidoff*,

---

[162] To the author's knowledge, no country other than Belgium has Flemish as its national language.

[163] An example where it was shown was in a very unusual case *Honda v Neesam* [2008] EHWC 338 (Ch).

[164] *Makro Zelfbedieningsgroothandel CV v Diesel SpA* (C-324/08) [2009] E.C.R. I-10019.

[165] See [28]–[35].

[166] See also para.3-354.

[167] See para.3-609.

simply a consequence of the "serious effect" of finding that a trade mark proprietor has extinguished its rights by consenting to the marketing of goods in the EEA.

IPR products marketed in the EEA by licensees, economically-linked persons and assignees

In seeking to determine whether the IPR owner has exhausted their rights, the doctrine of exhaustion stipulates that such rights are exhausted where the product has been first placed on the market in the EU by the IPR owner or with their consent. Clearly, the determination whether or not the IPR owner has *itself* first placed the product on the market in the EU is a relatively easy factual issue.[168] Such must be considered the paradigm case of consent.

7-129

This section is concerned with determining when an IPR owner has exhausted their rights where a product is placed on the market by a person (natural or legal) who is neither the IPR owner nor someone who is wholly independent of the IPR owner, i.e. a counterfeiter or independent undertaking. In particular, it is concerned with three situations:

7-130

(a) the product is marketed by persons who have a *legal* connection with the IPR owner, e.g. a licensee;
(b) the product is marketed by persons who have an *economic* connection with the IPR owner, e.g. a parent, subsidiary or parent company; and
(c) the product is marketed by a person who has been *assigned* rights by the IPR owner (in the case of parallel rights).

In each case, the over-arching inquiry is whether the IPR owner has consented to the product being placed on the market. However, in certain situations, this can be a difficult question to answer. For instance, does an IPR owner "consent" to marketing of products by a subsidiary company? Does a subsidiary consent to marketing by its parent? Does a company consent to marketing by an associate company with which he has a minority shareholding? Does an assignor consent to marketing of all goods forever by an assignee?

7-131

Somewhat surprisingly, a review of the CJEU's authorities demonstrate some difficulties in determining this. The problem is that the CJEU has, as discussed above, introduced the notion that it must be shown unequivocally that the registered proprietor of a right has consented to the marketing of goods within the EU (or EEA). Yet, as will be seen below, a review of the authorities is that exhaustion of rights will be deemed to have occurred where the goods have been marketed by persons with a legal or economic connection with the IPR owner. If the latter condition is satisfied, e.g. it is shown that the protected goods have been marketed by an associate company to the IPR company (i.e. where there are common shareholdings), does that mean that there is exhaustion of rights even where it cannot be said that consent has been unequivocally demonstrated (e.g. that the IPR owner has unequivocally consented to the marketing of the goods by the associate company)?

7-132

Put another way, are issues such as whether the undertaking of marketing the goods is economically connected with the IPR owner part of the factual inquiry to the ultimate question: has the IPR owner *unequivocally consented* to the marketing of the protected goods or alternatively, determine conclusively the very issue as to whether the IPR owner has exhausted their rights? This issue is now considered.

7-133

---

[168] What is meant by "placed on the market" is considered below at para.7-165.

7-134   Historically, the CJEU has held that there is exhaustion of rights where a person legally or economically dependent on the proprietor has marketed the protected product. Thus, in the landmark case of *Deutsche Grammophon*, Roemer AG considered that the right to prevent circulation of goods in the European Union was exhausted where the IPR owner or *an undertaking dependent on the holder* had placed the product on the market in a Member State. However, the CJEU in that case replaced the criterion of dependency with the criterion of consent. In *Keurkoop v Nancy Kean*,[169] the CJEU said an IPR owner may not oppose the importation of a product which has lawfully been marketed in another Member State: "by, or with the consent of, the proprietor of the right himself or a person *legally or economically dependent on him*".

7-135   In the late 1980s, the court re-emphasised this. In *HAG II*,[170] where the CJEU rejected the doctrine of common origin[171] and reversed its decision in *HAG I*, the court said in considering the issue of who could give consent on behalf of the IPR owner:

> "[12]   As the Court has consistently held, Article [36] only admits derogations from the fundamental principle of the free movement of goods within the common market to the extent to which such derogations are justified for the purpose of safeguarding rights which constitute the specific subject-matter of such property consequently, the owner of an industrial property right protected by the legislation of a Member State cannot rely on that legislation to prevent the importation or marketing of a product which has been lawfully marketed in another Member State *by the owner of the right himself, with his consent, or by a person economically or legally dependent on him* (see, in particular, the judgments in Case 78/70 *Deutsche Grammophon v Metro* [1971] E.C.R. 487, in Case 16/74 *Centrafarm v Winthrop* [1974] E.C.R. 1183 and in Case 19/84 *Pharmon v Hoechst* [1985] E.C.R. 2281).
>
> [13]   Trade mark rights are, it should be noted, an essential element in the system of undistorted competition which the Treaty seeks to establish and maintain. Under such a system, an undertaking must be in a position to keep its customers by virtue of the quality of its products and services, something which is possible only if there are distinctive marks which enable customers to identify those products and services. *For the trade mark to be able to fulfil this role, it must offer a guarantee that all goods bearing it have been produced under the control of a single undertaking which is accountable for their quality.*" [Emphasis supplied.]

7-136   Later, in *Ideal Standard*, a case which concerned the voluntary division of registered trade marks in various Member States, the CJEU expanded on the former limb, namely the meaning of "economically dependent". It said:

> "[34]   This principle, known as exhaustion of rights, applies where the owner of the trade mark in the importing State and the owner of the trade mark in the exporting State *are the same or where, even if they are separate persons, they are economically linked.* A number of situations are covered: *products put into circulation by the same undertaking, by a licensee, a parent company, a subsidiary of the same group or by an exclusive distributor.*"[172] [Emphasis supplied.]

7-137   The court then went on to say:

> "[37]   ... As was held in *HAG II*: 'For the trade mark to be able to fulfil [its] role, it must

---

[169] (144/81) [1982] E.C.R. 2853 at [25].
[170] (C-10/89) [1990] E.C.R. I-3711. This case is discussed at para.7-214.
[171] See para.7-209.
[172] (C-9/93) [1994] E.C.R. I-2789 at [34]. The court derived this principle from the passage quoted earlier in this chapter in *Centrafarm v Winthrop*, see para.7-031.

offer a guarantee that all goods bearing it have been produced under the control of a single undertaking which is accountable for their quality' (paragraph [13]). In all the cases mentioned, control was in the hands of a single body: *the group of companies in the case of products put into circulation by a subsidiary; the manufacturer in the case of products marketed by the distributor; the licensor in the case of products marketed by a licensee.* In the case of a licence, the licensor can control the quality of the licensee's products by including in the contract clauses requiring the licensee to comply with his instructions and giving him the possibility of verifying such compliance. The origin which the trade mark is intended to guarantee is the same: *it is not defined by reference to the manufacturer but by reference to the point of control of manufacture...*

[38] *It must further be stressed that the decisive factor is the possibility of control over the quality of goods, not the actual exercise of that control.* Accordingly, a national law allowing the licensor to oppose importation of the licensee's products on grounds of poor quality would be precluded as contrary to Articles [34] and [36]: *if the licensor tolerates the manufacture of poor quality products, despite having contractual means of preventing it, he must bear the responsibility.* Similarly if the manufacture of products is decentralised within a group of companies and the subsidiaries in each of the Member States manufacture products whose quality is geared to the particularities of each national market, a national law which enabled one subsidiary of the group to oppose the marketing in the territory of that State of products manufactured by an affiliated company on grounds of those quality differences would also be precluded. Articles [34] and [36] require the group to bear the consequences of its choice.

[39] Articles [34] to [36] thus debar the application of national laws which allow recourse to trade mark rights in order to prevent the free movement of a product bearing a trade mark *whose use is under unitary control.*" [Emphasis supplied.]

In a later case, in the context of trade mark cases involving parallel imports, the CJEU has suggested that what is important is that the IPR owner has the right to *control* the initial marketing in the EU of goods protected by the IPR. As the CJEU said: **7-138**

"[21] Furthermore, in adopting Article 7 of the Directive, which limits exhaustion of the right conferred by the trade mark to cases where the goods bearing the mark have been put on the market in the Community (in the EEA since the EEA Agreement entered into force), the Community legislature has made it clear that putting such goods on the market outside that territory does not exhaust the proprietor's right to oppose the importation of those goods without his consent and *thereby to control the initial marketing* in the Community (in the EEA since the EEA Agreement entered into force) of goods bearing the mark. That protection would be devoid of substance if, for there to be exhaustion within the meaning of Article 7, it were sufficient for the trade mark proprietor to have consented to the putting on the market in that territory of goods which were identical or similar to those in respect of which exhaustion is claimed."[173]

The above suggests that the concept of consent and control are very closely related. If the IPR owner has the right to control the marketing of goods by an entity and that entity places the goods on the market, then they can be considered to have consented to their marketing. Put another way, an IPR owner can only consent to the marketing of goods where it has the ability to control their marketing. In the case of economically linked undertakings, it is the possibility of de facto control and in **7-139**

[173] *Sebago and Maison Dubois* (C-173/98) [1999] E.C.R. I-4103 at [21].

the case of legally linked undertakings, it is the possibility of de jure control. Moreover, it is important to emphasise that it is the right of control over the products *in casu*.[174] Thus, as discussed below, it is not sufficient to argue that the IPR owner has consented to the marketing of the goods by having originally assigned the rights. They must be able to control the marketing of the goods *in casu*.

7-140 The above jurisprudence was developed earlier in time to the principle developed by *Davidoff* and *Makro* that in the case of implied consent, such must be unequivocally demonstrated. As discussed above, a legitimate question is whether the fact that goods were marketed in the EEA by persons who were legally or economically linked to the registered proprietor (or other persons which the registered proprietor had the possibility of control over the marketing of the goods *in casu*) is determinative of the issue of exhaustion of rights or merely part of the inquiry as to whether implied consent to the marketing has been *unequivocally demonstrated*. In an English case, *Mastercigars*,[175] the Court of Appeal favoured the latter approach. It said in the context of a submission that any sale by a Cuban company cannot be done without the consent of the Cuban government (who owned the rights in various trade marks for cigars) and thus the Cuban company must be considered to have consented to the marketing of the cigars:

> "[29] Either of these theories would do for Mr. Hobbs' purpose, which is contained in a grandiose submission about the structure and nature of the Cuban economy starting with references to the Cuban constitution. I do not think I am oversimplifying the argument to summarise it as this: everything in Cuba is controlled by the State. So all the acts of HSA, and of the Casa, must be regarded as legally and economically linked. Hence if a Casa sells to a foreigner in Cuba knowing that he intends to resell in the EU consent must be taken to have been given by HSA, whether or not HSA consents or even knows of the transaction or the type of transaction.
>
> [30] I do not accept this argument. It is just too theoretical. The Court of Justice has identified the 'point of control' as being what matters. I think one must focus on what is really happening, on actual knowledge and actual, practical control *or the right of control* by the trade mark owner. In this case this means concentrating on the acts of HSA and its legal and de facto powers of control. Do they, taken overall, lead to the *unequivocal conclusion* that HSA consented to the sale of the consignments in Europe?" [Empahsis supplied.]

7-141 However, the facts were unusual and the central question was not whether the marketing by the defendant of goods in the EEA meant that the claimant had exhausted its rights by reason of the legal and economic linkage between the two. However, the CJEU appears to favour the former approach (i.e. it is determinative of the issue). Thus, as said by the CJEU in *Coty Prestige Lancaster Group GmbH v Simex Trading AG*[176]:

> "[29] Extinction of the exclusive right results *either* from the proprietor's consent, whether express or implied, to a putting on the market in the EEA or from the putting on the market in the EEA *by the proprietor himself or by an operator with economic links to the proprietor, such as, in particular, a licensee*. The proprietor's consent and the putting on the market in the EEA by him or *by an operator with economic links to him*, which are *both* equivalent to the renunciation of the exclusive right, thus both constitute a decisive factor in the extinction of that right... ." [Emphasis supplied.]

---

[174] See *Sebago and Maison Dubois* (C-173/98) [1999] E.C.R. I-4103.
[175] *Mastercigars Direct Ltd v Hunters & Frankau Ltd* [2007] R.P.C. 24; [2007] E.T.M.R. 44.
[176] (C-127/09) [2010] E.C.R. I-4965; [2010] E.T.M.R. 41; [2010] F.S.R. 38.

Such suggests that the marketing by an operator with economic links to the **7-142** proprietor of the goods *in casu* is determinative of the issue of exhaustion of rights. In the author's view, this is right. It would be wrong for the requirement of "unequivocal consent" to permit a dilution of the principle of the doctrine of exhaustion of rights. For instance, where a company in a multi-national conglomerate has marketed the goods *in casu* where the rights are owned by another company in the same multi-national, it would be wrong to impose an obligation on the parallel importer to prove that the IPR owning company has unequivocally consented to the associate marketing company placing the goods on the market *in casu*. Provided that the IPR owner company had the ability to control the marketing of the goods *in casu*, then it is submitted that the IPR owner has exhausted its rights (assuming that the marketing was within the EEA). Put another way, an ability to control the marketing of the goods *in casu* would mean that the IPR owner is deemed to have consented to the marketing of those goods (save perhaps in exceptional circumstances).

The above view has strong support from the Court of Justice's judgment in **7-143** *Schweppes SA v Red Paralela*.[177] Here, a well-known mark was voluntarily divided between two parties in the EU. A parallel importer bought from the assignee and imported into the assignor's territories. However, after the assignment, the assignor and assignee co-operated very closely with each other, in particular to maintain a common brand image for the mark. The Court of Justice held that the concept of "economic links" refers to a substantive and not formal criterion.[178] Therefore, where the assignor and assignee *"co-ordinate their commercial policies ...so that it is possible for them to determine, directly or indirectly, the goods to which the trade mark is affixed and to control the quality of those goods"*, then the assignor cannot exercise its rights against products placed on the market by the assignee.[179] The decisive fact is however not one of actual control but the possibility of control.[180] Thus, as Stix-Hackl AG said, in *Davidoff*, that, in relation to the meaning of consent in the Community:

> "it must be assumed that both the aspect of economic linkage and that of control ultimately relate only to one and the same criterion, namely that of control over the initial distribution within the EEA."[181]

Licensees

The essence of a grant of a licence is the grant of the right by the IPR owner to **7-144** the licensee to carry out acts that would otherwise infringe the IPR. In most cases, it will be clear that the IPR owner is consenting to products falling within the IPR being placed on the market and in such circumstances, the IPR owner will thus have exhausted their rights.

However, some licences do not confer the right to place the product on the **7-145** market. Thus, a sub-contracting manufacturing agreement between a sub-contractor and an IPR owner clearly does not give the sub-contractor the right to place the manufactured products on the market in the EEA. In all circumstances,

---

[177] *Schweppes SA v Red Paralela SL* (C-291/16) ECLI:EUI:C:2017:990.
[178] See [46].
[179] See [46]–[51]
[180] See [45].
[181] *Zino Davidoff SA v A&G Imports Ltd* (C-414/99) [2001] E.C.R. I-8691; [2001] E.T.M.R. 67 at [91].

an inquiry into the exact contractual terms of the licence is required. Thus, an arrangement with an importer to market a batch of products bearing a trade mark in the EEA does not amount to consent to market *all* batches of products bearing the same trade mark.[182]

7-146   In general, the inquiry is that of proving consent to the marketing of the goods. However, as seen in *Ideal Standard*, discussed below, consent is not the only criterion. Thus, in the case of trade mark rights, goods marketed by the assignee of a trade mark to that owned by the registered proprietor of a parallel trade mark in another country does not exhaust the rights of the latter because of the lack of common control. The fact that by the assignment, the latter has consented to the marketing of goods protected by the trade mark is not sufficient for the doctrine of exhaustion of rights to apply. It will be apparent to the reader that in substance, there is little to distinguish between an outright assignment and a bare licence (i.e. one with no terms including quality control) for 100 years of a registered trade mark. Thus, many would say that it would be illogical if a distinction was made between an outright assignment and such a licence. Yet on the other hand, many would say that it is plain that goods marketed in the EEA pursuant to a 100-year licence (regardless whether there exists quality control provisions) exhausts the rights of the trade mark proprietor/licensor because there is clear and unequivocal consent to the goods being marketed in the EEA and that in such circumstances, it is irrelevant whether the licensor has actual control over the marketing of the products.

7-147   How can one reconcile such arguments? What distinguishes a 100-year licence with no quality control provisions from an assignment when considering whether there is exhaustion of rights? The short and obvious answer is that the licensor owns and thus controls the registered mark whereas (after assignment) the assignor does not. The IPR owner can (even if it amounts to a breach of the terms of the licence) rescind the right of the latter to place the product on the market. In such circumstances, it can be said that the IPR owner does have the possibility of control over the marketing of the goods.[183] Whilst the ability to control the marketing of the products via unlawfully breaching a licence may seem an unattractive argument, it should be remembered that it is rare that an IPR owner can actually control the marketing of each and every product. Even in trade mark licences, it is rare for a trade mark proprietor to have the right to check every product placed on the market by the licence. There will often be quality control provisions which permit termination of a licence if such are breached but that is all. In patent and know-how licences, often there are no quality control clauses and thus there is no real control over the marketing of licensed products. As discussed below, there seems no basis for extending the doctrine of *Ideal Standard* to assignments of patents, know-how and other IPRs which do not act as guarantee of trade origin.

Economically-linked parties

7-148   As can be seen from the excerpts quoted above at paras 7-135 to 7-141, the CJEU originally held that the marketing of goods by a person economically *dependent* on the registered proprietor meant that there was exhaustion. Such might suggest that the requirement is simply that the IPR owner must be able to control the company

---

[182] *Sebago Dubois* (C-173/98) [1999] E.C.R. I-4103.
[183] Although a court could in certain circumstances decline to grant any injunctive relief to restrain any acts which, absent the licence, amount to an infringement on the basis that the breach was blatant and unjustifiable.

marketing the goods. However, in *Ideal Standard*, the CJEU held that such would apply where the undertaking was economically *linked* with the proprietor. A parent company is linked to a subsidiary. Yet, a parent company is not under the control of a subsidiary.

So what degree of economic linkage is necessary? The answer comes from *Ideal* **7-149** *Standard* itself. The registered trade mark and the products bearing the trade mark must be under *unitary control* but not necessarily the control of the registered proprietor. Such an approach considers the entity that has ultimate *control* over the IPR rather than is merely the legal owner of the IPR. In effect, it requires a court or tribunal to determine whether there is an undertaking which has ultimate control over on the one hand, the ownership and exercise of the IPR *in casu* and on the other hand, the entity which has placed the product *in casu* on the market. If such is in common control, then it is submitted that there is exhaustion. In *Schweppes SA v Red Paralela SL*,[184] the Court of Justice, endorsing the approach in *Ideal Standard*, where it said that an economic link exists where the owner of the mark "or the entity of which that proprietor is part" can control the quality of the goods to which the mark is affixed.[185] Thus, where the goods are put on the market by a parent company of the owner of the trade mark, there is an economic link and hence exhaustion of rights.[186] The Court of Justice also said that the concept of economic linkage is a substantive and not a formal one. Consequently, there may be economic linkage where, despite two parties not being part of the same group of companies or indeed having any shareholdings in each other, co-ordinate their commercial policies in such as manner as to give themselves the possibility of controlling the goods and the quality of the goods to which a trade mark is affixed.[187]

Assignees

What is the position where an IPR owner divests themselves of certain rights to **7-150** third parties via assignment? Has the assignor "consented" to the placing on the market and subsequent export of protected goods by the assignee? What is the situation where O, the owner of the parallel rights in Member States A and B, assigns the rights in B to X, the assignee, and then seeks to prevent the import by a parallel importer into O's territories of the protected goods marketed by X in B?

Originally, in *HAG I* the CJEU held in a case where registered trade marks had **7-151** been in common ownership but were then compulsorily divided (as the result of war legislation), that such was fatal to an action for infringement. However, the CJEU reversed its position on this in *HAG II*. The rise and fall of the doctrine of common ownership is discussed later in this chapter. Plainly, where there has been a compulsory division of IPR as a result of wartime legislation, it is impossible to say that there has been effective consent to the division and thus, as a consequence, any consent by one party to the other party marketing products under the IPR.[188]

However, such arguments are not valid where there has been *voluntary* division **7-152** of parallel rights. This came up in the *Ideal Standard* case. The facts were that the owner of a parallel German and French registered trade mark, "Ideal Standard", as-

---

[184] *Schweppes SA v Red Paralela SL* (C-291/16) ECLI:EUI:C:2017:990.
[185] *Schweppes SA v Red Paralela SL* (C-291/16) ECLI:EUI:C:2017:990 at [44].
[186] *Schweppes SA v Red Paralela SL* (C-291/16) ECLI:EUI:C:2017:990 at [44].
[187] See [46].
[188] Thus, the CJEU has held that the marketing of a product pursuant to a compulsory licence does not exhaust the rights of the IPR own. See para.7-198.

signed the latter mark to a third party with whom it had no legal or economic connection. Subsequently, goods bearing the French mark were imported into Germany, whereby the owner of the German mark sought to exercise his trademark rights against the importer. The CJEU, ruling in favour of the German trademark owner, rejected a submission by the Commission that by assigning the French trade mark to a third company, the German trade-mark owner gave consent to that third company to put goods bearing the mark into circulation in France and, therefore, could not prevent the marketing in Germany of goods bearing the assigned mark. The CJEU said that:

> "[43] ... The consent implicit in any assignment is not the consent required for application of the doctrine of exhaustion of rights. For that the owner of the right in the importing State must, directly or indirectly, be able to determine the products to which the trade mark may be affixed in the exporting State and to control their quality. That power is lost if, by assignment, control over the trade mark is surrendered to a third party having no economic link with the assignor.
>
> [44] The insulation of markets where, for two Member States of the Community, there are separate trade-mark owners having no economic links is a result that has already been accepted by the Court in *HAG II*. However, since that was a case where unitary ownership was divided following sequestration, it has been submitted that the same result does not have to be adopted in the case of voluntary division.
>
> [45] That view cannot be accepted because it is contrary to the reasoning of the Court in *HAG II*. The Court began by noting that trade-mark rights are an essential element in the system of undistorted competition which the Treaty seeks to establish (paragraph 13). It went on to recall the identifying function of trade marks and, in a passage cited in paragraph 37 above, the conditions for trade marks to be able to fulfil that role. The Court further noted that the scope of the exclusive right which is the specific subject-matter of the trade mark must be determined having regard to its function (paragraph 14). It stressed that in that case the determinant factor was absence of consent of the proprietor of the trade mark in the importing State to the putting into circulation in the exporting State of products marketed by the proprietor of the right in the latter State (paragraph 15). It concluded that free movement of the goods would undermine the essential function of the trade mark: consumers would no longer be able to identify for certain the origin of the marked goods and the proprietor of the trade mark could be held responsible for the poor quality of goods for which he was in no way accountable (paragraph 16)."[189]

7-153   The above excerpt makes it clear that in the case of registered trade marks, the assignment of a parallel registered mark to a third party with no economic links to the assignor does not amount to consent to market goods under that mark in those countries where the assignor has retained registered marks. The rationale is that in such circumstances, the proprietor of the mark is not responsible for the poor quality of the goods of the assignee and such would undermine the essential function of the trade mark. Thus, trade marks protect the interests of not only of the IPR owner but also the public.[190]

7-154   Prima facie, this reasoning does not apply to other forms of intellectual property where the essential function doctrine has no part to play. Thus, in patent and know-how licences, often such will not have quality control provisions because there is

---

[189] (C-9/93) [1994] E.C.R. I-2789; [1994] 3 C.M.L.R. 857 at [43]-[45]. *HAG II* concerned the division of marks that had a common origin as the result of an act of state expropriation. It is discussed at para.7-209.

[190] Jacobs AG in (C-436/93) [1996] E.C.R. I-3457 at [72].

no danger of confusion between the licensor's products and the licensee's. Indeed, in many cases, the licensor will not be active on the market.

Thus, the critical issue is whether the reasoning in *Ideal Standard* applies to as- **7-155** signment of all forms of intellectual property? Is it relevant to other forms of IPRs that the owner of such rights can or can not directly or indirectly determine the products marketed by the assignee where such an act of marketing is a restricted act under the relevant IPR?[191] This can be examined by considering four different types of patent licences and assignments in the context of O being the initial owner of parallel patents in Germany and Italy.

Example A
O assigns the Italian patent to B.

Example B
O grants B a perpetual, royalty-free, irrevocable licence under the Italian patent to market patented products in Italy.

Example C
O grants B a 10-year bare licence under the Italian patent to market patented products in Italy subject to the payment of royalty.

Example D
O grants B a 10-year licence under the Italian patent to manufacture and market patented products in Germany and Italy, subject to O's right to unilaterally prevent the marketing of any product manufactured by B.

In the above examples, it can be seen that only Example D truly gives the **7-156** patentee O the right to determine marketing of *any* product on the market by the licensee. In the case of Example A and B, superficially, there is no difference of substance. Even in the case of Example C, O does not have the right to control the marketing in the 10-year period of *any* product by B. O has, for a period of ten years, renounced his right to control the marketing of products in Germany and Italy by B, provided he is paid a royalty.

What, then, is the correct approach? It has already been submitted that in the case **7-157** of licences, the fact that O can rescind the licence (even if such amounts to a breach of the licence) means that O does have the possibility of control of marketing.[192] Thus, there is in fact a difference of substance between Example A and Examples B-D. Ultimately, if O rescinded the licence, it could sue for infringement of its IPR.[193]

What is the position where there is an assignment of a patent? In such **7-158** circumstances, there plainly is no possibility of control. Despite this, it is submitted that the reasoning of the CJEU in *Ideal Standard* should be confined to the difficulties that arise where an identical or confusingly similar trade mark can be applied to products or services which originate from independent undertakings. In effect, there are special considerations because of the essential function of a trade mark and the need to prevent consumer confusion.

However, without such special considerations, no fundamental distinction should **7-159** be made between an assignment and a licence. In each case, it is submitted that the

---

[191] See (C-9/93) [1994] E.C.R. I-2789 at [43].
[192] See para.7-144.
[193] However see *Van Doren + Q GmbH v Lifestyle Sports Sportswear Handelsgesellschaft mbH* (C-244/00) [2003] E.C.R. I-3051; [2003] E.T.M.R. 75.

court should only consider whether there has been consent to a particular act. Clearly, in the case of an assignment of a patent, there is consent to all future exploitation of that patent by the assignee. In the case of a 1000-year licence, there is consent to exploitation for 1000 years by the licensee. To find that there is no consent in an assignment but there is in a 1000-year licence where special considerations such as the protection of consumer play no part would be artificial, overly generous to the assignor, overly restrictive on the free movement of goods, and goes beyond the specific subject-matter of a patent which is to recompense the creative effort of the inventor. The market value of an assignment of a patent will clearly be determined by the market value of the exclusive rights in the countries of assignment until the expiry of the patent. To permit the patentee to prevent importation of products placed on the market by the assignee would be to permit the patentee to partition the Community, having already received reward in relation to the marketing of such products. This does not strike the correct balance between arts 34-36. The exercise of rights in such circumstances would not be justified under art.36.[194] Thus, it is submitted that in the case of assignments of patents, know-how, registered designs and copyright where the specific subject-matter is to reward the creator of the right, the consent in assignment is indeed sufficient to exhaust the right of the assignor to prevent the importation and marketing of goods by the assignee in countries where the assignor owns rights.

7-160 Such reasoning would not apply in reverse where the assignor exports to the assignee's territories. In such circumstances, the assignee has not been rewarded for the placing of the products on the market in the assignor's territory.[195]

7-161 The above considerations become even more complicated when both assignor and assignee have subsequently assigned their rights to others. For instance, can a third-generation assignor and a third-generation assignee prevent the importation of each other's goods into their territories? For instance, where the owner X of parallel patents in Member States A and B assigns the latter patent to Y, who subsequently assigns it to Z, can X exercise his patent rights against a parallel importer into Member State A of products marketed in Member State B by Z? In the *Ideal Standard* case,[196] the trade-marked products *in casu* had been placed on the market in France by a subsequent purchaser of the assigned French mark.[197] In general, it submitted that the above arguments apply equally to situations where the rights having initially been assigned are then devolved onto other persons. Thus, X, having been rewarded for the assignment of the patent to Y, should not be able to complain about imports into X's territory by Z. Vice versa, if X had assigned his patent in Member State A to a third party, Y should be able to object equally to

---

[194] See G. Tritton, "Articles 30 to 36 and Intellectual Property: Is the jurisprudence of the CJEU now of an Ideal Standard" [1994] E.I.P.R. 423. G.F. Kunze, "Waiting for Sirena II-Trade mark Assignment in the Case Law of the CJEU of Justice" (1991) 3 *International Review of Industrial Property and Copyright Law* 319, 328 states that once assignment has taken place, there is no further need for consent and that the assignment cannot be construed as implying such consent for the future. Accordingly, he concludes that in the case of trade marks, it cannot be said that the assignor or assignee have consented to the marketing of each other's goods after assignment has taken place. Strictly speaking, this is correct, but there is no doubt that the assignor has "permitted" the marketing of protected goods by another when, before, such was not permitted. In the author's opinion, the nature of assignment is a once-and-for-all act and, as such, is a single event that gives consent to the assignee for all future products to be marketed by the assignee in his territories.
[195] See R. Joliet, "Trade Mark Law and the Free Movement of Goods: The overruling of HAG I" (1992) 3 I.I.C. 317, 319.
[196] (C-9/93) [1994] E.C.R. I-2789; [1994] 3 C.M.L.R. 857.
[197] For the facts of the case, see para.7-225.

products placed on the market by the third party in Member State A and imported into Member State B as well as by those marketed by X in Member State A.

Assignment and continuing control

In the above discussion, it has been assumed that the assignment is a "clean" assignment, i.e. that there is no continuing legal or economic links between the assignor and assignee. However, an assignment of IPR may be accompanied by overt or covert collateral agreements such that when viewed overall, it cannot be said that there is no continuing co-operation between the parties. For instance, in a bad case, there may be an overt assignment but a secret collateral agreement between assignor and assignee governing the marketing of products under the mark. In such circumstances, the court or tribunal must look to the substance and not the form of the agreement. In a UK case, *Doncaster v Bolton Pharmaceuticals*,[198] Astra Zeneca, the well-known pharmaceutical company owned the registered trade mark KALTEN for hypertension in Spain and England. It sold the Spanish mark to a Spanish company, Teofarma and the English mark to Bolton Pharmaceuticals. Doncaster began importing KALTEN hypertension drugs which had been placed on the market in Spain into England. Bolton sued for trade mark infringement and sought summary judgment on the basis that there was no arguable case that Bolton had exhausted its rights. However, on appeal, the Court of Appeal reversed the judgment. The Court of Appeal accepted that there was no evidence of "conventional control" by Astrazeneca over Teofarma. However, the court held that there was an arguable case that the assignments of the mark had been done for the purpose of artificial partitioning of the markets and furthermore that there were continuing economic links between the various parties.[199] This case emphasises the fact that courts will look behind assignments of intellectual property rights to determine whether in fact there has been a genuine surrender of control over the placing of products on the market by the assignee. Moreover, it suggests that even if there has been a surrender of control, if the assignments have been done for the purpose of artificial partitioning the market, then such would be contrary to art.36(2) and thus the exercise of rights would not be permissible.

7-162

In *Schweppes SA v Red Paralela*,[200] which concerned the well-known tonic brand Schweppes, the mark for some Member States was sold by Cadbury Schweppes to Coca Cola. A parallel importer sought to take advantage of price differences and import the tonic into Spain. An exclusive licensee of the assignor brought proceedings in Spain for trade mark infringement of the Spanish trade mark. It adduced evidence of continuing close commercial co-operation between the assignor and assignee, including a marketing policy designed to ensure the appearance or image of a single global trade mark. The Court of Justice held in such circumstances, where the parties were able to determine, directly or indirectly, the goods to which the trade mark was affixed and to control the quality of those goods, then the predecessor provision to art.15 TMD precluded enforcement of the Spanish trade mark.[201]

7-163

Schweppes SA makes clear that when considering whether there is exhaustion,

7-164

---

[198] *Bolton Pharmaceutical Co 100 Ltd v Doncaster Pharmaceuticals Group Ltd* [2006] E.T.M.R 65; [2007] F.S.R 3 CA.

[199] See [79]–[80].

[200] *Schweppes SA v Red Paralela SL* (C-291/16) ECLI:EU:C:2017:990.

[201] See [44]–[46].

the court will look at the substantive and not the formal relationship between assignor and assignee.[202] It does not answer the question whether in the absence of any continuing linkage between the parties after the assignment, there is any room for arguing that there is exhaustion. For example, where the purpose of the assignment was to partition the EU. *Doncaster* suggests that there may be. An example of this might be where a pharmaceutical company has sold some of its marks in certain EU countries to third parties because of the erosion of profits caused by parallel imports. Here the difficulty arises as the parties will have not any possibility of control over the marketing of each other's goods and thus, the essential function of each mark would be compromised if goods bearing those marks were allowed to be marketed into the territories of other parties. In such circumstances, it is suggested that the better approach is to consider whether the assignments were contrary to art.101.[203]

When and where is a product first placed on the market?

7-165   Under the doctrine of consent, a rights owner has exhausted their rights in a protected product once a product on the market in the EEA has been placed on the market by the owner or with their consent. This raises two issues, both of which are important. First, in what circumstances, is a product "placed on the market"? Secondly, *where* is a product placed on the market? The second question is important because the CJEU has held that, in relation to arts 34-36 and art.15(1) of the Trade Mark Directive, which incorporates the principle of exhaustion of rights, there is no European Union principle of exhaustion of rights if the product is placed on the market outside the EEA.

In what circumstances is a product put on the market?

7-166   The issue as to what is meant by "placed on the market" came up in *Peak Holding v Axolin-Elinor AB*.[204] In that case, the trade-mark proprietor imported some clothing bearing a registered trade mark into the EEA. The clothes were then offered for sale by the proprietor within the proprietor's chain of shops. Remainder stock was then sold to a French company with the stipulation that 95 per cent of the clothes were to be sold outside the EEA and the other 5 per cent were to be sold in France. The clothing ended up being offered for sale by a Swedish retailer who said that it had no notice of the contractual restrictions. It was common ground that the goods never left the EEA. On reference to the CJEU as to whether such acts exhausted the right of the trade-mark proprietor, the CJEU considered the three factual situations of: (i) importing into the EEA, (ii) offering for sale in the proprietor's shops, and (iii) selling to a third party with the contractual restraint. The CJEU held that in the first two situations, there was no exhaustion of rights because the goods had not been placed on the market but that in the third situation, there was exhaustion of rights as they had been placed on the market with the consent of the trade mark proprietor.

7-167   The CJEU said that a sale which allows the proprietor to realise the economic value of their trade mark exhausts the exclusive rights conferred by the Directive, more particularly the right to prohibit the acquiring third party from reselling the

---

[202] See [46].
[203] C.Stothers, *Parallel Trade in Europe* (Oxford: Hart Publishing, 2007).
[204] *Peak Holding v Axolin-Elinor AB* (C-16/03) [2004] E.C.R. I-11313; [2005] E.T.M.R. 28.

goods. However, an act of importation and offering for sale did not because:

> "Such acts do not transfer to third parties the right to dispose of the goods bearing the trade mark. They do not allow the proprietor to realise the economic value of the trade mark. Even after such acts, the proprietor retains his interest in maintaining complete control over the goods bearing his trade mark, in order in particular to ensure their quality."[205]

It is submitted that the underlying concept is one of surrender of control over the goods.[206] This ties in with the principle that there is no exhaustion of rights unless the goods have been placed on the market under the control (or the possibility of control) of the owner of the rights. Clearly, this occurs in a situation where title in the goods transfer, e.g. in a sale.   **7-168**

In *Coty Prestige Lancaster Group GmbH v Simex Trading AG*,[207] the trade mark owner provided perfume "testers" to its dealers which stipulated that the testers remained the property of the claimant. The testers also contained statements on the packaging declaring that they were "not for sale". The defendant, Simex, which was not part of the claimant's network of authorised dealers, sold the claimant's testers to third party retail outlets in Germany. As regards the origin of these testers, the trade mark owner said that they were originally first put on the market in Singapore. The defendant (the wholesaler Simex) also put forward a second set of facts, namely that the testers were initially supplied by Coty to one of its authorised dealers in the EEA.[208] The CJEU considered that *Peak Holdings* was irrelevant as it was concerned with whether certain acts carried out by a trade mark owner or an operator with economic links to it could be classified as "putting on the market".[209] Therefore it viewed the real issue as one of consent and thus whether Coty had renounced its exclusive right.[210] It held that when determining this, "a decisive factor" against finding consent was that the perfume bottles had said "Not for Sale". It also held that that even if Simex was correct in stating that the perfume bottles had been initially supplied to one of Coty's authorised dealers in the EEA, this would not amount to "putting on the market" within the meaning of the Trade Mark Directive, as the statement "Not For Sale" precluded such a finding.[211]   **7-169**

However, what is the legal analysis where a trade mark owner retains title in goods? Can they avoid the effect of the exhaustion of rights principle because, legally speaking, they have not surrendered control? Is one concerned with de facto or de jure control? Put another way, is one concerned with market realities or an arid dry legal analysis? This issue came up in two decisions of Member States. In   **7-170**

---

[205] See [42].
[206] See T. Hayes and P. Hansen, "Silhouette is not the Proper Case upon which to decide the Parallel Importation Question" [1998] E.I.P.R. 277, where the authors examine the meaning of "first put on market". The authors make a distinction between parallel imports and other acts, such as re-importation. They emphasise that the correct test is whether or not the owner has parted control with the products in issue.
[207] (C-127/09) [2010] E.C.R. I-4965.
[208] For the latter set of facts, see [44]—although it would appear that Simex conceded that the first act of "putting on the market" of the testers was through their sale of them to the retailers—[34].
[209] See [33].
[210] See [36]–[37].
[211] See [44]–[45]. Of course, on Simex's alternative account of facts and matters, here the Court of Justice was considering the issue of "putting on the market" (as opposed to consent). It is thus surprising that on this alternative set of facts, the Court of Justice did not consider *Peak Holdings* as here, the issue was not one of consent but whether Coty had placed on the market the perfume bottle testers when initially supplying them to its authorised specialist dealers.

a Belgian decision, *Xerox Corp v Improv Europe BVBA*,[212] the Brussels Court of Appeal had to consider whether there was exhaustion of rights where toner cartridges were sold by Xerox under a maintenance agreement which provided that the cartridges remained the property of Xerox until they were expended. If the end user did not use them, they were contractually obliged to return them but were not compensated for doing so (and the end user had paid for them in full when taking possession). Unsurprisingly, many end users sold their surplus stock to Impro Europe who marketed them in the secondary market. Xerox brought trade mark infringement proceedings against Impro and the issue was whether there was exhaustion of rights under the predecessor to art.15(1) Trade Mark Directive. The Brussels Court of Appeal held that the toner cartridges were supplied within the scope of a maintenance agreement for a specific machine and with a retention of title. Accordingly, it held that they had not been placed on the market by Xerox.

7-171   This decision contrasts with the judgment of the Bundesgerichtshof in *Parfum-stester*[213] where it held that exhaustion cannot be excluded by agreement between the EUTM owner and the end user.

7-172   The author confesses to having their doubts that the Belgian Court of Appeal was right. The end user had paid for the toner cartridges and therefore they were free to use them for printing. These two facts mean that Xerox had realised "the economic value" of the goods. De facto, there was a transfer of control over the cartridges and the end user was entitled to dispose of them (in the sense of using them). In such circumstances, the "retention of title" clause and indeed the modus operandi of Xerox strikes the author as a mechanism for avoiding the economic effect of the exhaustion of rights principle to "downstream" dealings in branded goods by customers of the brand owner. In much the same way in *Peak Holdings v Axolin-Elanor*, the brand owner sought to do so. Whilst some might say that the real attack should be that the maintenance agreements between Xerox and the end user were anti-competitive and thus contrary to art.101, the Court of Justice has shown no hesitation in finding that the exhaustion of rights principles developed under the free movement of goods provisions of the TFEU override any contractual downstream restraints.

7-173   There is no placing on the market when goods are simply moved internally within a group's internal field of operation. Thus, the Bundesgerichtshof, applying the CJEU 's judgment in *MEMBRAN & K-TEL v GEMA*[214] held that, where a German importer imported records from its English sister company which had acquired a licence from the Mechanical Copyright Protection Society to distribute the records in Great Britain, there was no question of the applicability of arts 34-36 in the case of mere movements within a group of enterprises and where the goods have not yet left the group's internal field of operation.[215]

---

[212] (2013/AR/2763).
[213] I ZR 63/04 *Parfumtester*. Although this decision predated *Coty v Simex*. The facts were very similar to *Coty v Simex*.
[214] (55-57/80) [1981] E.C.R. 147; [1981] 2 C.M.L.R. 74, CJEU; [1981] 1 C.M.L.R. 680, 687, Bundesgerichtshof.
[215] The court said that this accorded with the CJEU's judgment in (15/74) [1974] E.C.R. 1147; [1974] 2 C.M.L.R. 480. It is of note that this finding was despite the fact that the importer had paid a licence fee in the United Kingdom to distribute the records in Great Britain.

Goods in transit through the EU

In *ADDI v Rioglass*,[216] the CJEU had to consider the situation where goods were   **7-174**
in transit from Spain to Poland (then, not a EU country). The goods were seized in
France by French custom authorities under Reg.3295/94 which permitted the
seizure of goods where such infringes intellectual property rights.[217] There was no
dispute that the goods were not intended to be placed on the market in the EU. The
Cour de Cassation referred the matter to the CJEU as to whether such was
permissible. The first issue was whether arts 34–36 was applicable. It was argued
by the French government that they were not because those Articles were only
relevant to intra-EU trade and such was not the case. The CJEU rejected this saying that arts 34–36 were of direct application where goods were moving through
one Member State.[218] The second issue was whether the detention of the goods was
justifiable under art.36 on the grounds of protection of industrial and intellectual
property. The CJEU said that as the goods were not placed on the market in France,
no resort could be had to intellectual property laws. In particular, the court said that
as arts 34–36 did apply, resort could be had to intellectual property laws only for
the purpose of safeguarding rights which are the subject-matter of the intellectual
property. In that case, which concerned registered trade marks,[219] the subject-
matter of trade marks was the right to first market goods bearing the mark. Thus,
as the court said, the implementation of such protection is linked to the marketing
of those goods. As the goods were only in transit to a non-Member State, such
activities were not liable to infringe the specific subject-matter of the trade mark.

As said in *Montex v Diesel*, a subsequent judgment applying *Rioglass*, the mere   **7-175**
risk that the goods could fail to reach their destination and be marketed in a Member
State where there was protection is not sufficient to mean that the goods were placed
on the market in the state of transit. Only where the act of transit "necessarily
[entails] their being put on the market in [the Member State of transit]" can the
proprietor of the trade mark in the state of transit exercise its rights. That case was
different to *Rioglass* because the ultimate destination was actually a Member State
of the EU (Ireland) but the registered proprietor had no trade mark protection in that
state.[220]

In *Class International BV v Colgate-Palmolive*,[221] a container load of toothpaste   **7-176**
bearing the Aquafresh mark were brought into Rotterdam container port from South
Africa using the "external transit" procedure. Under the Customs Code, such goods
were not free for release into the European Community. A reference was sought
from the Dutch courts as to whether the goods had been imported into the EU for
the purpose of the predecessor provision to art.11(3)(c) of the Trade Mark Directive and were thus infringing European trade marks of Colgate-Palmolive. The
CJEU held that the trade mark proprietor cannot oppose the mere physical entry of
the goods into the EU under the external transit procedure. However, where such
goods were within the EU under the external transit procedure, the proprietor could

---

[216] *Administration des Douanes et Droits Indirect v Rioglass* (C-115/02) [2003] E.C.R. I-12705; [2006]
     1 C.M.L.R. 12.
[217] Reg.3295/94 is a predecessor regulation to Reg.608/2013 discussed in Ch.16.
[218] See [20].
[219] Although as Mischo AG pointed out, some goods were seized on suspicion of infringing certain
     registered designs.
[220] *Montex Holdings v Diesel SpA* (C-281/05) [2006] E.C.R. I-10881.
[221] *Class International BV v Colgate-Palmolive Company, Unilever NV, SmithKline Beecham Plc,
     Beecham Group Plc* (C-405/03) [2005] E.C.R. I-8735.

oppose the offering for sale of such goods where "it necessarily entails the putting of those goods on the market in the Community".[222] However, such does not arise merely by the absence of a final specified destination for the goods in a third country outside the EEA.[223]

7-177   In *Nokia v Revenue and Customs*[224] the CJEU held that goods which were merely in transit through the EU could not be classified by reason of that fact as counterfeit goods or pirated goods under various EU custom Regulations, as such required it to be shown that they would be put on the market in the EU. That could be shown where the destination of the goods is not declared, the lack of precise or reliable information as to the identity or address of the manufacturer of the goods, a lack of co-operation with the customs authorities or the discovery of documents demonstrating that there is liable to be a diversion of those goods to EU consumers.

7-178   Therefore, it can be safely said that the free movement of goods provisions of the TFEU are not engaged when goods are in transit through the EU as they are not placed on the market in the EU. Equally, because of this, there is no infringement of national or EU intellectual property rights in the EU.

Trade Mark Directive

7-179   The case law that goods in transit did not engage the free movement of goods provision or infringe registered trade marks was considered by many to hamper the fight against counterfeit goods. Accordingly, the current EU Trade Mark Regulation introduced a provision whereby goods in transit through the EU bearing an identical mark can be seized even if there is no intention to place those goods on the market in the EU. The conditions that need to be satisfied in order for a trade mark owner to do this are discussed further in Ch.3.[225]

Where is a product first placed on the market?

7-180   It will often be important to determine where a product is first placed on the market. In particular, if a product is first placed on the market in the EEA, then the rights of owners of harmonised IPRs or unitary EU rights will be exhausted. However, this is not the case if the product is first placed on the market outside the EEA. In *Music Machine, Discover Enterprise and TWS v IFPI*,[226] a case involving parallel imports, the issue of what is meant by "first sale in the European Union" was considered by a Belgian court in a case whereby goods were sold from inside the EU but delivered outside the EU. The Tribunal de Commerce at Brussels held that "first sale" meant the activity whereby the products are lawfully marketed. This concept had to be assessed, taking into account the reasoning behind the protection of phonograph producers' neighbouring rights (the rights in issue). Phonograph producers were granted protection under the new Belgium Act, since they were the necessary economic channel through which the works of authors, artists and performers were made available to the public. Consequently, "first sale" did not

---

[222] See [61].
[223] See [50].
[224] *Koninklijke Philips Electronics NV v Lucheng Meijing Industrial Co Ltd; Regina (Nokia Corpn) v Revenue and Customs Comrs (International Trademark Association intervening)* (C-446/09 & C-495/09) [2011] E.C.R. 12435; [2012] E.T.M.R. 13. This is discussed in Ch.16 in the context of EU customs regulations at para.16-011.
[225] See para.3-584.
[226] *Music Machine, Discover Enterprise and TWS v IFPI* [1996] 1 E.I.P.R. D-8.

refer to the place where the sales contract was drawn up or where the phonogram producer gave their consent, but where the product was actually marketed.

In *Peak Holding v Axolin-Elinor AB*,[227] which has been discussed above, Peak **7-181** Performance, the licensee of the registered proprietor, Peak Holding, sold the trademarked goods to COPAD, an undertaking established in France with the stipulation that the consignment was not to be resold in European countries with the exception of 5 per cent which could be sold in France. The CJEU held that where there is a contract of sale between the proprietor of a trade mark and an operator established in the EEA (even with a prohibition on reselling in the EEA), this did not mean that the goods had not been placed on the market in the EEA such that there was no exhaustion of rights[228]. It will be appreciated that here, the critical factor appears to be that COPAD was established in France. After all, if Peak Performance had sold to a company established in the Ukraine with a stipulation that the goods only be sold outside the EEA, there can be no basis for finding that the goods were placed on the market in the EEA. What would be the position if the company was a Ukrainian company whose main business activity was fashion distribution in France? Would the result in *Peak Holdings* have been different if the goods were sold to a US company which was the parent of COPAD? What would have been the position if a Ukrainian company had sold the goods to a French company for the purpose of distributing in the Ukraine? It would be surprising if the place of establishment of the French company was determinative of the issue such that the Ukrainian company would be deemed to have exhausted its rights if such goods were circulated in the EEA by third parties. Yet is such a set of facts so different to that in *Peak Holdings*? In both cases the intention and agreement was that the goods *in casu* be marketed outside the EEA. It can be seen that such questions demonstrate that the issue of determining whether goods were first placed on the market within or without the EEA can be difficult. In the author's view, it is unfortunate that the fact of place of establishment of the purchasing company can be considered determinative of where the goods were marketed. In the global world that one lives in, such facts are often very incidental. A Panamanian company who is the registered proprietor of a trade mark may sell trade-marked goods manufactured in Vietnam to a UK company for them to distribute in Australia and New Zealand. In these cases, the fact that the UK company is established in the EU seems almost irrelevant. It would be surprising if the Panamanian company could not exercise its trade mark rights to prevent the unauthorised circulation without the EEA of such goods.

It is suggested that a multifactorial test is required to determine in substance **7-182** whether goods were first put on the market in the EEA or not. This would include consideration of factors such as place of establishment of the seller and buyer, where their principal markets are, whether the goods contain indicia that they are intended to be marketed in the EEA, and other factors which suggest that the locus of the purchaser's business activities with regards to the goods *in casu* is that of the EEA. The Court of Justice has adopted a multifactorial "targeting" test for whether online selling of branded goods infringe the rights of an owner of a registered trade mark in the EU. There seems no reason why it should not do so when determining where goods were first placed on the market.

When considering where a product is placed on the market, a distinction should **7-183**

---

[227] *Peak Holding v Axolin-Elinor AB* (C-16/03) [2004] E.C.R. I-11313; [2005] E.T.M.R. 28.
[228] See [56].

be drawn between a parallel import and a direct import into a Member State. Sometimes, this is not done. Thus, in *Ideal Standard*,[229] the CJEU treated a case concerning direct exports to Germany by a French company as a case of parallel imports. In fact, the goods were never placed in circulation in France, and thus, arguably, the case was never concerned with genuine parallel imports.[230] Strictly speaking, a parallel importer buys goods in one country and exports to another, whereas with a direct export, there is no purchase in the country of export. The difference is important. If a person directly exports from one Member State to another Member State, they have not placed the product on the market in the former Member State.

Goods marketed in Member State where there is no IPR protection

7-184   An IPR owner may not have parallel and equal protection for their rights throughout the EU. This may arise because of differences in national legislation. Alternatively, it may be because they have not sought protection in all Member States. In such circumstances, can an IPR owner who has marketed products or consented to their marketing in Member State A, where it has no rights or lesser rights object to the subsequent circulation of such goods into Member State B where it has rights or a higher level of protection?

7-185   Where there are differing or no levels of protection and the product has been placed on the market by a third party in a Member State where no protection or weak protection exists, the CJEU has repeatedly emphasised that the IPR owner who has no economic links with the third party cannot be deemed to have consented to the marketing of such goods in these countries.[231]

7-186   Conversely, where goods have been placed on the market in an EEA state by the IPR owner or with their consent, the IPR owner cannot prevent further circulation of those goods into other EEA states even though no protection existed in the first EEA state. In other words, the axiomatic criterion is whether the IPR owner has consented to the marketing of the goods and not whether it has marketed the goods in a Member State where it has IPR protection such as to be able to benefit financially from the protection afforded by IPR.

7-187   In particular, the CJEU has considered the above issue in *Merck v Stephar*[232] and *Merck v Primecrown*.[233] In *Merck v Stephar*, the CJEU was concerned with whether a Dutch patentee could prevent the importation into the Netherlands of pharmaceuticals protected by the Dutch patent, where he had placed the pharmaceuticals on the market in Italy where, at that time, protection for pharmaceuticals was not available.

7-188   The CJEU said that:

> "[11]   It is for the proprietor of the patent to decide, in the light of all the circumstances, under what conditions he will market his product, including the possibility of marketing it in a Member State where the law does not provide patent protection for the product in question. If he decides to do so he must then accept the consequences of his choice as regards the free movement of the product within the

---

[229] (C-9/93) [1994] E.C.R. I-2789; [1994] 3 C.M.L.R. 857.
[230] G. Tritton, "Articles [34] to [36] and Intellectual Property: Is the jurisprudence of the CJEU now of an Ideal Standard" [1994] E.I.P.R. 423.
[231] See the next section on constructive consent at para.7-198. See also para.7-070.
[232] (187/80) [1981] E.C.R. 2063; [1981] 3 C.M.L.R. 463.
[233] (267–268/95) [1996] E.C.R. I-6285.

Common Market, which is a fundamental principle forming part of the legal and economic circumstances which must be taken into account by the proprietor of the patent in determining the manner in which his exclusive right will be exercised."

This decision was criticised for applying the principle of exhaustion of rights **7-189** without regard to the specific subject-matter of a patent, namely the right of reward for first marketing.[234]

In *Merck v Primecrown*,[235] the CJEU was asked to reconsider the principle in **7-190** *Merck v Stephar* and, by implication, the whole approach to consent where there were differing levels of protection in Member States for a particular product. The facts in *Primecrown* concerned the parallel importation from Spain and Portugal into the UK of pharmaceuticals that had been placed on the market in those countries by the patentee or with his consent. Originally, Spain and Portugal did not permit patent protection for pharmaceutical patents. However, following their accession to the EC, they were obliged to provide such protection. However, for a transitional period, it was provided that the rule in *Merck v Stephar* was not to apply to pharmaceutical products during this period. The transitional period continued until the end of the third year, after Spain and Portugal had made the products patentable. Thus, for that period, patentees could exercise their rights. Thereafter, they could not. As patents cannot be granted for products that have been marketed prior to the date of application for a patent, after the transitional period, the patentees were unable to obtain patent protection in Spain and Portugal for pharmaceuticals for which they had patent protection in other Member States.

It was argued by the pharmaceutical companies that *Merck v Stephar* was bad **7-191** law. It failed to give account of the specific subject-matter of a patent which is namely to have the exclusive right to first market a patented product. In effect, as recorded by Fennelly AG:

"The strongest argument in favour of the pharmaceutical companies' interpretation of *Centrafarm v Sterling Drug* is that, since the specific subject-matter consists of the exclusive right of first marketing the patented product, a rule permitting parallel imports of such products marketed by the patentee in a Member State where no patent protection exists and where, consequently, the patentee was subject to potential competition at the first marketing stage, would empty that exclusive right of much of its significance, i.e. the patentee must at least have had the opportunity of obtaining monopoly profits in the exporting Member State before its national rights in the importing Member State can be said to have been exhausted. This, of course, was the principal submission of Merck and the intervening Member States which was rejected by the Court in *Merck v Stephar*."

Fennelly AG essentially accepted this argument and advised that *Merck v Stephar* **7-192** should not be followed. In a passage which bears setting out in full, he said:

"It is clear from Article [36] of the Treaty that national industrial property rights are not inherently incompatible with the freedom of movement of goods within the Common Market. In the absence of harmonized Community rules, they remain unaffected by Community law. Community law is, however, legitimately concerned with the activities of owners of parallel patents which have the effect of partitioning national markets. National industrial property laws have traditionally discriminated between domestic and foreign marketing by the proprietor of the right. Thus, whereas marketing on the national territory would generally preclude the proprietor of a patent from further controlling the

---

[234] See discussion of this at paras 7-060 to 7-066.
[235] (267–268/95) [1996] E.C.R. I-6285.

domestic marketing of the protected product, this would not usually follow in the case of units marketed abroad. This difference permitted the proprietors of parallel patents to compartmentalize national markets in the hope of extracting monopoly profits from each controlled marketplace. It is self-evident that such discriminatory treatment can no longer be tolerated in a Community whose fundamental aims include the establishment of a single market without internal frontiers. However, *Merck v Stephar* goes further by applying the same treatment to imports not so controlled. The sole rationale for this is the supposedly voluntary act of marketing.

I am not convinced that an import restriction granted in favour of a patentee constitutes an arbitrary restriction on intra-Community trade simply because the products concerned were marketed voluntarily in another Member State without the benefit of patent protection. The effect of *Merck v Stephar* is to export not merely the product but also the commercial consequences of the legislative choice made by the exporting State to the importing State because the patentee has made a commercial choice to sell the product even in a less protected environment. The effect of the rule would be that, in order to avoid damage to the value of its national patent rights in those Member States which protect them, the patentee is encouraged to partition the Common Market in a different way, i.e. through refusing to supply units of its products to the markets of those Member States where his rights are not recognized: the product will therefore not be available for parallel traders and the patentee may in any event rely on his patent rights in other Member States to oppose any parallel imports of unauthorized copies manufactured in unprotected markets. In other words, it would favour commercially irrational decisions to withhold products from the markets of such States, where sales of the product would hold out some prospect of profit.

One undesirable result that would flow from the exercise by the plaintiffs of the 'choice' recognized by paragraph 11 of the Court's judgment in *Merck v Stephar* would be that Spanish and Portuguese patients would be restricted to using unauthorized locally-produced copies of medicinal products patented in other Member States. I do not think this approach tends to contribute either to achieving an internal market in pharmaceutical products or to 'ensuring a high level of human health protection.

In my view the reliance on the notion of free consent to marketing in *Merck v Stephar* unacceptably glosses over the logical fallacy that a patentee can be said to have exhausted his rights by choosing to market units of the protected product in Member States where no patent protection exists. Accepting, as I do, the Court's definition of the specific subject-matter of a patent, I do not consider that commercially rational marketing of a protected product in a Member State where no protection exists is accompanied by the crucial element guaranteed by that specific subject-matter. In *Merck v Stephar* the Court described the 'substance of a patent right' as lying 'essentially in according the inventor an exclusive right of first placing the product on the market' which 'enables the inventor, by allowing him a monopoly in exploiting his product, to obtain the reward for his creative effort without, however, guaranteeing that he will obtain such a reward in all circumstances."[236]

7-193   The Advocate-General said that a formal application of the doctrine of consent gave rise to clear absurdities.[237] The Advocate-General considered such results unsatisfactory and said that:

"I am satisfied that it is only an approach based on whether or not the exclusive first marketing principle applies which can avoid the "erratic results" inherent in a formalist

---

[236] See [107]–[110].
[237] He referred to *Pharmon v Hoechst* and *Musik Vertrieb* and the absurdities between the two cases at [123] of his Opinion. These two cases are discussed in the next section at para.7-198.

application of the consent test and which permits the focus to be placed on the economic substance of the exclusive rights."[238]

Later on, in his Opinion, the Advocate-General endorsed the approach that the **7-194** exhaustion doctrine is based on the availability of parallel prerogatives in both the country of exportation and that of importation, and that a decision applying the doctrine in the absence of such parallelism would be tantamount to lowering the protection available in the country of importation to the level of the less protective legislation of the country of exportation. Thus, he considered that there was no good reason why the previous Spanish and Portuguese policy of refusing to recognise the patentability of pharmaceutical products should have been imposed upon other Member States who had abandoned that policy many years before.[239] Furthermore, he considered that the case of *Warner Bros v Christiansen* was also difficult to reconcile with *Merck v Stephar*.[240]

The Advocate-General's approach is difficult to criticise. Unfortunately, the **7-195** CJEU chose not to adopt the reasoning of the Advocate-General. Rather, it affirmed the general principle of *Merck v Stephar* and took a formalistic approach in applying the doctrine of consent. Thus, it said:

> "The Court held, finally, in paragraphs 11 and 13 of Merck that it was for the holder of the patent to decide, in the light of all the circumstances, under what conditions he would market his product, including the possibility of marketing it in a Member State where the law did not provide patent protection for the product in question. If he decides to do so, he must then accept the consequences of his choice as regards free movement of the product within the common market, this being a fundamental principle forming part of the legal and economic circumstances which the holder of the patent must take into account in determining how to exercise his exclusive right. Under those conditions, to permit an inventor to invoke a patent held by him in one Member State in order to prevent the importation of the product freely marketed by him in another Member State where that product was not patentable would cause a partitioning of national markets contrary to the aims of the Treaty."[241]

Thus, as discussed earlier in this chapter, consent is the axiomatic doctrine when **7-196** considering exhaustion of rights and not the specific subject-matter.[242] Finally, it should be noted that the cases of *Merck v Stephar* and *Merck v Primecrown* concerned situations where patent protection was not available in Member States. What is the position where the differing levels of protection arise because patent protection was not sought voluntarily in a particular Member State by the patentee? Clearly, in such circumstances, the lack of protection arises because of the

---

[238] See [127]. See also P. Demaret, "Industrial Property Rights, Compulsory Licences and the Free Movement of Goods under Community Law" (1987) 2 I.I.C. 161, 176–177, where the author emphasises that where a patentee markets a product in a country where he has no protection, he has not obtained the substance of the exclusive rights, i.e. the specific subject-matter that flows from the patent.

[239] See [135].

[240] In the author's opinion, this was the one part of his Opinion which was not correct. *Warner Bros* is considered elsewhere in this chapter, at para.7-255. It is submitted that the CJEU in *Merck v Primecrown* was correct in finding that *Warner Bros v Christiansen* was essentially concerned with the distinction between the sale right and the rental right, and not differing levels of protection (see [42]). On this point, see *Foreningen af danske Videogramdistributører v Laserdisken* (C-61/97) [1998] E.C.R. I-5171.

[241] See [32].

[242] See paras 7-060 to 7-066.

patentee's actions or inaction. It might be said that, in such circumstances, a distinction should be drawn between cases where a differing level of protection existed because of difference in national laws, as opposed to a failure by the patentee to seek protection throughout the EU. Clearly, given the decision of the CJEU in the two *Merck* cases, at present, it would not affect the outcome. Marketing by a patentee in a state where they do not have patent protection exhausts their rights, regardless of the reason for the lack of protection. It might be said that, if the court was to re-visit this area, then a distinction should be drawn and that only where the patentee chose not to obtain protection in a Member State should the patentee be protected from exercising its rights if it chose to market goods in that Member State.

7-197   In *Merck v Primecrown*,[243] the pharmaceutical companies who had marketed their pharmaceuticals in Spain and Portugal submitted that, in reality, they had no option but to market their pharmaceuticals because of legal requirements and the ethical obligation that such companies had to nationals of Member States. The CJEU stated that where there was a legal obligation to market goods, then such did not exhaust the patentee's rights as, following *Merck v Stephar*, the patentee had to be able to take his decision freely and in full knowledge of all the circumstances.[244] In relation to the ethical obligation, the CJEU was rather dismissive of this, and said that:

> "such considerations are not, in the absence of any legal obligation, such as to make it possible properly to identify the situations in which the patentee is deprived of his power to decide freely how he will market his product. Such considerations are, at any rate in the present context, difficult to apprehend and distinguish from commercial considerations. Such ethical obligations cannot, therefore, be the basis for derogating from the rule on free movement of goods laid down in *Merck*."[245]

Consent and compulsory licences

7-198   This section considers the approach that will be taken by the CJEU to arguments by parallel importers that, although a party has not expressly consented to the placing on the market in the EU of IPR-protected products (or indeed placed it on the market personally), they must be deemed to have consented to such acts and thus their rights are exhausted. As already discussed in this chapter, in the field of trade marks, the CJEU has held that as consent which is tantamount to the proprietor's renunciation of their exclusive rights, constitutes the decisive factor in the extinction of those rights, it must be unequivocally demonstrated.[246] There is no reason to suppose that any different approach would be taken to other intellectual property rights. This principle is clearly diametrically opposed to any notion of constructive consent.

7-199   This section considers the CJEU's approach to goods marketed pursuant to compulsory licences. These can be granted for a variety of reasons, e.g. failure to work a patent. When a patent or other right is subject to a compulsory licence, it is arguable that the patentee, by obtaining a patent in that Member State, accepts all possible legislative consequences, including the possibility that their patent may be subject to compulsory licenses. However, as seen below, the CJEU has not ac-

---

[243] (C-267–268/95) [1996] E.C.R. I-6285.
[244] See [49].
[245] See [53].
[246] See para.7-035, et seq.

cepted this argument but applied a formalistic approach to such issues which give rise to absurdities (as expressly discussed by Fennelly AG in *Merck v Primecrown*).[247]

Thus, in *Musik Vertrieb*[248] sound recordings were manufactured in England, placed on the market in England with the consent of the copyright owner and a parallel importer imported them into Germany. However, such consent had been against the background whereby, under English legislation, a party could obtain a statutory licence to manufacture sound recordings on payment of 6.25 per cent. Accordingly, 6.25 per cent represented a ceiling on negotiated royalty rates. In such circumstances, the copyright owner agreed to a licence at a rate of 6.25 per cent as the licensee was entitled to such. Under German law, sound recordings produced in Germany were subject to a higher royalty which was collected by GEMA, the German collecting society. GEMA sought to exercise sound-recording rights in Germany on behalf of the author against the parallel importer. The CJEU held that GEMA could not exercise its rights, because the rights owner had consented to the marketing of the recordings in England. The court said it was for the owner to decide under what circumstances he could market the goods. The court refused to take into account that in substance, the copyright owner had simply bowed to the inevitable in granting a licence. If it had in fact refused to grant a licence and left the licensee to apply for a compulsory licence, then GEMA would have been so entitled to prevent the importation of the sound recordings into Germany as seen in *Pharmon v Hoechst* discussed below. Such suggests a fundamental fault in the jurisprudence of the CJEU. It simply cannot be right in a logical and coherent legal system that the legal consequences of granting voluntarily a licence knowing that if such licence is not volunteered, a regulatory authority will grant an identical licence, should be different to the latter licence.

7-200

In a later case, *Pharmon v Hoechst*,[249] Hoechst owned a process patent in Germany, the Netherlands and the UK. DDSA Pharmaceuticals obtained a compulsory licence pursuant to UK legislation.[250] Just prior to the expiry of the patent, DDSA decided to ignore an express export prohibition in the compulsory licence and sold directly a large consignment of the patented pharmaceuticals to Pharmon in the Netherlands (where no such compulsory licence was available). Hoechst brought infringement proceedings. Despite the opinion of Mancini AG, the CJEU held that the patent proprietor was entitled to exercise his patent rights because he had not consented to the activities of DDSA. It said that to find otherwise would be to deprive the patent proprietor of his right to determine freely the conditions under which he markets his products. This finding was despite the fact that as discussed earlier in this chapter, the specific subject matter of a patent which is subject to a compulsory licence was held by the CJEU in *Allen & Hanbury v Generics*[251] to have changed from the right to first market to the right of reasonable remuneration.[252]

7-201

In conclusion, no support can be found in the CJEU's decisions supporting any notion of constructive consent where the IPR owner has been remunerated for

7-202

---

247 See paras 7-060 to 7-066.
248 (55/80) [1981] E.C.R. 147; [1981] 2 C.M.L.R. 44.
249 (19/84) [1985] E.C.R. 2281; [1985] 3 C.M.L.R. 775.
250 The Patents Act 1977 permitted third parties to obtain compulsory licences of patents whose length of protection had been extended, by the Patents Act 1977, from 16 to 20 years for the last four years.
251 (19/84) [1985] E.C.R. 2281; [1985] 3 C.M.L.R. 775.
252 See para.7-049.

exploitation of an IPR. Indeed, if anything, the emphasis now is not only on show-ing consent but unequivocal consent as the only criterion relevant to the determina-tion of exhaustion of rights and constructive or deemed consent has no part to play in European jurisprudence.

International or EU-wide exhaustion of rights principle?

7-203   The case law of the CJEU has meant that the courts of Member States must recognise the principle that, once a protected product has been placed on the market in a Member State by the rights owner or with their consent, the rights owner has exhausted their rights. This raises the question as to whether there is exhaustion of rights under EU law where a product is placed on the market outside the EEA. In order to answer this question, one must distinguish between the situation on the one hand, where the EU doctrine of exhaustion of rights has been codified in a EU Directive which harmonises a particular IPR within the EU or in a EU regulation which creates a unitary EU IPR and on the other hand, a non-harmonised sector of intellectual property.

7-204   In the 1st edition of this book, it was submitted that, in the case of the Trade Mark Directive, there was no discretion on behalf of Member States to retain an international exhaustion of rights principle, because the predecessor to art.15(1) of the Directive which provided for exhaustion where the branded product was first placed on the market in the EU, was intended to exhaustively legislate in this field. Happily,[253] this prediction proved right and the CJEU in *Silhouette v Hartlauer*[254] so held. This is discussed in the chapter on Trade Marks.[255] The CJEU has equally found that an international exhaustion of rights principle is not permissible in other areas where the law is harmonised, e.g. copyright.[256] Thus, where the principle of exhaustion of rights has been incorporated into a EU Directive or Regulation, the placing of a product by the IPR owner, or with their consent, in a country outside the EEA will not exhaust the IPR owner's rights. Moreover, although an IPR owner can consent to such products being imported into the EEA, this will only be the case where such consent is express or can be implied unequivocally from the factual circumstances.[257]

7-205   Where there is no harmonisation, Member States are free to retain a doctrine of exhaustion of rights at a domestic level. For the purposes of EU law, the CJEU has emphasised that, generally, importation by a third party of a product placed on the market in a non-EU state by the IPR owner, or with their consent, will not normally prevent the IPR owner from exercising their rights. Generally, such exercise would not affect trade between Member States and, accordingly, arts 34–36 would be inapplicable. This is discussed elsewhere in this chapter.[258]

---

[253] For the author, if not parallel importers and consumers!
[254] (C-355/96) [1998] E.C.R. I-4799.
[255] See para.3-616.
[256] e.g. See *Laserdisken v Kulturministeriet* (C-479/04) [2006] E.C.R. I-8089 at [27] where the court held that art.4(2) of Dir.2001/29 (the distribution right is not to be exhausted in respect of the original or copies of the work, except where the first sale or other transfer of ownership in the Community of that object is made by the right holder or with their consent) prevented application of an international exhaustion of rights principle. See para.4-320.
[257] See para.7-123.
[258] See para.7-104.

INDIVIDUAL TYPES OF INTELLECTUAL PROPERTY

In the previous sections, the doctrines developed by the CJEU, the Commission **7-206** and national courts in relation to arts 34–36 were examined. Apart from the unharmonised fields of patents and unregistered design rights, the exhaustion of rights principle developed by the CJEU has been introduced into harmonising legislation for trade marks, registered designs,[259] copyright and plant variety rights. As discussed earlier, in general, where the EU has introduced harmonising secondary IPR legislation, direct resort to arts 34–36 is generally not permissible but the provisions dealing with exhaustion must be interpreted in a manner consistent with the free movement of goods provisions of the TFEU.[260] Accordingly, it is common for the CJEU when interpreting provisions in secondary legislation dealing with exhaustion to consider its decisions when considering the interrelationship of the enforcement of unharmonised IP laws of Member States with arts 34–36 TFEU. As said earlier in this chapter, a striking example of this is in the field of repackaging of pharmaceuticals.[261] Another example is in the field of copyright, the continued reference by the CJEU when considering exhaustion of rights issues in secondary legislation to rely upon the "specific subject matter" principle discussed earlier.[262]

Accordingly, this section looks at case law of the CJEU of a particular IPR prior **7-207** to the enactment of legislation which harmonised the law in Member States of that IPR. Thus, the diligent reader who wishes to understand fully the development of the law of exhaustion of rights as it relates to, e.g. trade marks should read the paragraphs above in this chapter, the following section on trade marks and then read the relevant section in the Trade Marks chapter for the development of such principles following the enactment of the Trade Mark Directive and European Union Trade Mark Regulation.[263]

Trade marks

In this section, we look more closely at the historical approach of the CJEU to **7-208** trade marks under arts 34–36 prior to the introduction of the Trade Mark Directive and Community Trade Mark Regulation in the following three areas:

(a) the rise and fall of the "common origin" doctrine;
(b) assignments of registered trade marks; and
(c) additional distinguishing matter.

Common origin and trade marks

In the 1970s, the CJEU considered the exercise of trade mark rights against **7-209** imports, where the mark on imports and that used by the trade-mark owner has once been in common ownership but in which ownership of the mark had been divided as a result of wartime legislation.

---

[259] Including the Community unregistered design right.
[260] See paras 7-059 and 7-093.
[261] See para.7-011.
[262] See para.7-047.
[263] For this, see para.3-590.

HAG I[264]

7-210 **Facts** HAG AG invented decaffeinated coffee. It marketed the coffee under the trade mark "HAG", which it had registered in various countries, including Luxembourg and Belgium. These latter countries' marks were owned by Cafe HAG SA, a subsidiary of HAG AG. In 1935, the international registration of HAG was struck out in relation to Belgium and Luxembourg and new registrations of HAG in those states were effected in the name of Cafe HAG SA. From then on until 1944, Cafe HAG SA produced decaffeinated coffee for the Belgo-Luxembourg market under the "HAG" trade mark. In 1944, all the shares in Cafe HAG SA were sequestrated as enemy property and sold to the Van Oevelen family. In 1971, the HAG marks were assigned to the firm Van Zuylen Frères. HAG AG subsequently acquired registrations in Belgium and Luxembourg in the Cafe HAG marks of its own accord. In 1972, HAG AG decided to export decaffeinated coffee under the mark "HAG" to Luxembourg. Van Zuylen Frères brought trade-mark infringement proceedings and a parallel action to cancel HAG AG's registrations in Belgium and Luxembourg.

7-211 The matter was referred to the CJEU on the question as to whether the predecessor provision to art.101 (art.81) and arts 34–36 prohibited Van Zuylen Frères from bringing an infringement action, given the fact that, though the parties in the action had no legal, economic, financial or technological ties between each other, the trade marks had a common origin.

7-212 The CJEU held in a short judgment:

> "It could not therefore be accepted that the exclusiveness of the trade mark right, which can be the consequence of the territorial limits of the national laws, should be relied on by the holder of a mark with a view to prohibiting trading, in one Member State, in goods lawfully produced in another Member State under an identical mark which has the same origin. In fact such a prohibition, establishing the isolation of the national markets would come into conflict with one of the fundamental aims of the Treaty, the fusion of the national markets into one single market. While in such a market, the indication of the origin of a trade-marked product is useful, informing consumers thereon can be done by means other than those which would affect the free circulation of goods.
>
> Therefore to prohibit trading in one Member State in a product which lawfully bears a trade mark in another member-state, for the sole reason that an identical mark, sharing the same origin, exists in the first State is incompatible with the provisions laying down the free circulation of goods within the Common Market."[265]

7-213 The court, thus, held in the formal part of the judgment that:

> "To prohibit trading in one Member State, in a product which lawfully bears a trade mark in another Member State, for the sole reason that an identical mark, sharing the same origin, exists in the first State, is incompatible with the provisions laying down the free circulation of goods within the Common Market."

---

[264] *Van Zuylen Frères v HAG AG ("HAG I")* (192/73) [1974] E.C.R. 731; [1974] 2 C.M.L.R. 127.
[265] Point 15 in the judgment.

HAG II

The decision in *HAG I* which gave rise to the doctrine of "common origin", was **7-214** severely criticised.[266] The judgment is short and unhelpful. Clearly, it took no notice of the essential function of a trade mark. In relation to this, the court merely said that:

> "while the indication of the origin of a trade-marked product is useful, informing consumers thereon can be done by means other than those which would affect the free circulation of goods."[267]

It took 16 years for the CJEU to recognise the suspect reasoning in *Van Zuylen* **7-215** *Frères v HAG AG*. This was done ironically in a case[268] concerning the successor-in-title to Van Zuylen Frères (SUCAL), who started to export decaffeinated coffee under its mark "HAG" to Germany. This was opposed by HAG AG, who brought trade-mark infringement proceedings against SUCAL. Thus, the boot was on the other foot. The CJEU stated that the decision in *Van Zuylen* (now known as *HAG I*) had to be reconsidered in the light of the subsequent case law.

Jacobs AG delivered a lengthy Opinion for the case. He initially reviewed the **7-216** relevant Treaty provisions, the principles established by the court in relation to intellectual property, and the nature and function of trade marks. He then went on to consider the *HAG I* case and confessed that he did not find the reasoning at all convincing. In particular, he criticised the judgment in that the court did not explain anywhere why the fact that the trade marks were of common origin was relevant in the absence of any market-sharing arrangement.

He concluded that the doctrine of common origin was not a legitimate creature **7-217** of Community law. He noted that the doctrine had been developed when the court's case law on intellectual property had been in its infancy and before the court had established the doctrine of the specific subject-matter and essential function of a trade mark. Furthermore, he found that the case of *Pharmon v Hoechst*, a case analogous but pertaining to patents was irreconcilable with *HAG I*.[269]

Having dismissed the proposal that confusingly-similar trade-marked goods **7-218** should be distinguished by additional matter as not feasible,[270] he concluded that the owner of a trade mark must be allowed to exclude from his territory goods, on which an identical trade mark had been placed by another, an unrelated person who is the owner of the mark in another Member State, and that such a view was justified by both the specific subject-matter of the right and the essential function of the mark. Finally, he recognised that there were differences between *HAG I* and *HAG II*, and that the injustice in *HAG II* was more obvious but considered it healthier to

---

[266] For criticism of the logic of *HAG I*, see C. Morcom QC, "Trade marks in the European Community after Cafe HAG II" (1991) *Trademark Reporter*, Vol.81(5), 534. Also see the discussion of *HAG I* in Jacobs AG's Opinion in *HAG II*, discussed below. See also R. Joliet, "Trade Mark Law and the Free Movement of Goods: The Overruling of the Judgment in HAG I" (1992) 3 I.I.C. 317 and the list of reviewers at fn.2, and G.F. Kunze, "Waiting for Sirena II-Trade mark Assignment in the Case Law of the CJEU of Justice" (1991) I.I.C. 319.

[267] See [14].

[268] (C-10/89) [1990] E.C.R. I-371; [1990] 3 C.M.L.R. 571.

[269] (19/84) [1985] E.C.R. 2281; [1985] 3 C.M.L.R. 775, which concerned patented goods that had been compulsorily licensed in the UK and directly exported to Holland without the consent of the owner of the Holland and UK patents. Thus, a common origin existed. This case is discussed elsewhere— see para.7-201.

[270] See para.7-083 of the 4th edn of this book.

recognise that *HAG I* was wrongly decided rather than make spurious distinctions between the two cases.

7-219   The court in effect, followed the Advocate-General's Opinion. It said that it was necessary "to reconsider" the interpretation given in *HAG I* in the light of the subsequent developments in the case law in the field of industrial and commercial property in relation to the free movement of goods provisions. The court emphasised the doctrine of consent, the specific subject-matter of the trade mark, and the essential function of a trade mark as a guarantee to the consumer of the identity of origin of the product. The court then went on:

> "[15] In assessing in the light of the foregoing considerations a situation such as that described by the national court, the decisive fact is the absence of any element of consent, on the part of the owner of the trade mark right protected by national legislation, to the marketing in another Member State, under a mark which is identical or may cause confusion, of a similar product manufactured and marketed by an enterprise which has no tie of legal or economic independence with that owner.
>
> [16] Under these circumstances the essential function of the mark would be compromised if the owner of the right could not exercise his option under national law to prevent the importation of the similar product under a name likely to be confused with his own mark because, in this situation, consumers would no longer be able to identify with certainty the origin of the marked product and the bad quality of a product for which he is in a way responsible could be attributed to the owner of the right.
>
> [17] This conclusion cannot be altered by the fact that the mark protected by national legislation and the similar mark borne by the imported product pursuant to the legislation of the Member State of provenance originally belonged to the same owner, which was dispossessed in one of the marks as a result of expropriation by one of the two States in question before the Community was established.
>
> [18] In fact since the date of expropriation and in spite of their common origin, each of the marks has independently fulfilled within its own territorial limits, its function of guaranteeing that the marked products come from a single source."

7-220   The court, thus, concluded that:

> "Articles [34] and [36] of the EEC Treaty do not preclude national legislation from allowing an undertaking which is the holder of a trade mark in a Member State from opposing the importation from another Member State of similar products lawfully bearing an identical trade mark in the latter State or liable to confusion with the protected mark even though the mark under which the contested products are imported originally belonged to a subsidiary of the undertaking which opposes the importation and was acquired by a third undertaking as a result of the expropriation of that subsidiary."

7-221   Thus, the doctrine of common origin was annulled in respect of expropriated marks. It was finally laid to rest in *Ideal Standard*,[271] in which the court held, in concluding that the free movement of the goods *in casu* would undermine the essential function of the trade mark, that its reasoning equally applied to the splitting of the market whether through the act of a public authority or as a result of a voluntary contractual assignment.[272] Thus, it can now be said that the fact that a trade mark has a common origin is now irrelevant in considering the application of arts 34–36 to the exercise of trade mark rights.

---

[271] (C-9/93) [1994] E.C.R. I-2789; [1994] 3 C.M.L.R. 857.
[272] See [45]–[46].

To the above, must be added a note of caution. An undertaking may assign a **7-222** registered trade mark to an ostensibly independent undertaking but in fact retain a degree of control over the assignee and the placing of the products on the market by the undertaking. This is discussed earlier in this chapter.[273] Furthermore, it should be noted that if the assignment is carried out for the purposes of market-sharing, then such will be prohibited under art.101.[274]

Assignments of a trade mark

A detailed analysis of the CJEU's approach to the interrelationship of the doctrine **7-223** of exhaustion of rights in the context of the assignment of IPRs has already been discussed in another section in this chapter.[275] This section should be read in conjunction with that section.

In *Terrapin v Terranova*,[276] the court stated that a trade mark owner cannot **7-224** exercise their rights against imports from another state when the right relied on was a result of the sub-division, whether by voluntary act or as a result of public restraint of a trade-mark right which originally belonged to one and the same proprietor.[277] It said that in such cases, the basic function of the trade mark, i.e. that of a guarantee of origin, had been undermined. The reasoning suggested that once a mark had been assigned, a trade mark owner could not exercise their rights against imports bearing the assigned mark from another Member State.

In *Ideal Standard*,[278] the CJEU re-considered the issue of the assignment of trade **7-225** marks in the context of arts 34–36. The facts of this case were that until 1984, the American Ideal Standard group held, through its French and German subsidiaries— Ideal Standard GmbH ("IS Germany") and Ideal-Standard SA ("IS France")—the trade mark "Ideal Standard" in Germany and France for sanitary fittings and heating equipment. In July 1984, IS France, which had been in financial difficulties, sold the "Ideal Standard" French trade mark for heating equipment (retaining it for sanitary fittings) to Société Générale de Fonderie ("SGF"), who later assigned the mark to Compagnie Internationale de Chauffage ("CICh"). CICh had no legal or economic links with American Standard or its German subsidiary. CICh continued to manufacture heating equipment and marketed it under the "Ideal Standard" trade mark.

IHT, a German company, began importing heating equipment made by CICh in **7-226** France, its parent company, and bearing the "Ideal Standard" mark in Germany. IS Germany brought proceedings for trade mark infringement against IHT. The Landgericht Dusseldorf found in IS Germany's favour. It held that there was a risk of confusion between the use of the mark on sanitary fittings and heating equipment. IHT appealed to the Oberlandesgericht, which referred under art.234, to the CJEU the following question:

"Does it constitute an unlawful restriction of intra-Community trade, within the meaning of Articles [34]–[36] of the EEC Treaty, for an undertaking carrying on business in Member State A which is a subsidiary of a manufacturer of heating systems based in Member State B to be prohibited from using as a trade mark the name 'Ideal Standard'

---

[273] See para.7-162.
[274] See para.8-435.
[275] See para.7-150.
[276] (119/75) [1976] E.C.R. 1039; [1976] 2 C.M.L.R. 482.
[277] See [6] relying on *HAG II*.
[278] (C-9/93) [1994] E.C.R. I-2789; [1994] 3 C.M.L.R. 857.

on the grounds of risk of confusion with a mark having the same origin, where the name 'Ideal Standard' is lawfully used by the manufacturer in its home country by virtue of a trade mark registered there which it has acquired by means of a legal transaction and which was originally the property of a company affiliated to the undertaking which is opposing, in Member State A, the importation of goods marked Ideal Standard?"

The CJEU held that, in such circumstances, arts 34–36 did not prevent the exercise of trade mark rights. The decisive factor was whether the trade mark owner had the possibility of control over the quality of the goods.[279] It also rejected the Commission's argument that the owner of a trade mark who assigns the trade mark in one Member State while retaining it in others, must accept the consequences of the weakening of the identifying function of the trade mark following from that assignment. It said that the argument failed to take account of the fact that, since trade mark rights are territorial, the function of the trade mark is to be assessed by reference to a particular territory.[280]

7-227   *Ideal Standard* was followed recently but distinguished by the Court of Justice in *Schweppes SA v Red Paralela*.[281] In this case, the assignor and assignee continued to maintain close commercial links with each other to ensure that there was a single brand image. This case is discussed earlier in this chapter.[282]

Patents

Role of patents

7-228   Unlike trade marks, patents do not have an essential function. Patents only exist to reward the inventor for their creative efforts and to encourage innovation in technology. Thus, patents merely have a specific subject-matter. Furthermore, unlike trade marks, until the Unitary Patent comes into force, there has been little harmonisation of patent law *at EU level*.[283]

Specific subject-matter

7-229   As discussed earlier, the CJEU has said that the specific subject-matter of a patent is:

"inter alia to ensure to the holder, so as to recompense the creative effort of the inventor, the exclusive right to utilise an invention with a view to the manufacture and first putting into circulation of industrial products, either directly or by the grant of licences to third parties, as well as the right to oppose any infringement."[284]

7-230   Thus, the specific subject-matter of a patent is similar to that of a trade mark. Once goods bearing the mark have been marketed by the trade mark owner or with

---

[279] In making this statement, the court was following a proposal put forward in R. Joliet, "Trade Mark Law and the Free Movement of Goods: The overruling of HAG I" (1992) 3 I.I.C. 317. Coincidentally, the Rapporteur in the case was a Professor René Joliet—a case of a self-fulfilling prophecy! See G. Tritton, "Arts 34–36 and Intellectual Property: Is the jurisprudence of the CJEU now of an Ideal Standard" [1994] E.I.P.R. 423 for discussion on the *Ideal Standard* case. See para.3-069, et seq. where the concept of control is discussed in relation to the essential function of a trade mark.
[280] See [47] and [48].
[281] *Schweppes SA v Red Paralela SL* (C-291/16) ECLI:EUI:C:2017:990.
[282] See para.7-162.
[283] See para.2-503.
[284] *Centrafarm v Sterling* (15/74) [1974] E.C.R. 1147; [1974] 2 C.M.L.R. 480 at [9].

their consent, the owner has exhausted their rights in such products. Thus, the doctrine of consent applies to patents.[285]

Care must be taken in seeking to apply the doctrine of specific subject-matter to all issues concerning the compatibility of the exercise of patent rights and arts 34–36. This was seen in *Generics BV v Smith Kline & French*,[286] a case originating from the Netherlands. Generics submitted the drug cimetidine to the Register of Pharmaceutical Products for the purpose of obtaining regulatory approval whilst the patent for cimetidine which was owned by Smith Kline French, was still in force. Smith Kline French issued proceedings for patent infringement, claiming that submission to the Register of a patented drug did not fall within the fair dealing provisions of the Dutch Patents Act 1910. As the registration process took approximately 14 months, it sought an injunction preventing Generics from marketing the drug until 14 months after the expiry of the patent. This was granted by the Dutch court. On appeal, Generics argued that such a provision and the injunction granted thereon were contrary to arts 34–36, as they constituted a quantitative restriction within art.34. The Hoge Raad referred a number of questions on the legitimacy of such relief to the CJEU. In particular, it was argued by Generics that the specific subject-matter of a patent was confined to the right to place on the market and, therefore, the mere submission of samples for regulatory approval could not fall within the specific subject-matter of a patent where no marketing occurred. **7-231**

The CJEU dismissed this argument and held that the use of samples made in accordance with a patented process for a medicinal product for the purpose of obtaining a marketing authorisation without the consent of the patentee fell within the specific subject-matter of the patent right. There was nothing to suggest that the Netherlands law was discriminatory in nature or that it sought to favour domestic products over those from other Member States. Accordingly, the patentee was justified under art.36 in obtaining the relief sought. Furthermore, such relief (i.e. an injunction) was not a disproportionate form of relief. In effect, the CJEU confirmed the right of a patentee to prevent acts of infringement even if they extended beyond the mere prevention of the marketing of a patented product. This case cautions against over-reliance on the specific subject-matter test, which was developed in the context of a case concerning marketing. As Jacobs AG said in his Opinion, the "specific subject-matter" test is not intended to be used to solve all detailed aspects of the scope of patent protection and that the formulation itself had no "vocation to be exhaustive".[287] This decision confirms the principle that, in the absence of harmonisation, the nature and protection of an IPR is a matter of national law, but must not directly or indirectly discriminate against goods or nationals of another Member State.[288] **7-232**

---

[285] See (15/74) [1974] E.C.R. 1147, [1974] 2 C.M.L.R. 480; *Merck v Stephar* (187/80) [1981] E.C.R. 2063, [1981] 3 C.M.L.R. 463; and *Pharmon v Hoechst* (19/84) [1985] E.C.R. 2281, [1985] 3 C.M.L.R. 775.
[286] (C-316/95) [1997] E.C.R. I-3929; [1998] 1 C.M.L.R. 1.
[287] See [30].
[288] See para.7-070, et seq.

Copyright and industrial design

Introduction

7-233   Until recently, copyright and industrial design laws were the least harmonised sectors of intellectual property law in the EU. Certainly, in the field of industrial design, the protection conferred on industrial products has varied greatly in the EC. Even now, despite the introduction of the Information Society Directive, the Design Directive, the Term Directive and other Directives, there is still some variation. Thus, there is considerable variety in Member States as to what type of photographs are protected under copyright law, particularly those which cannot be said to have any "intellectual creation", i.e. a snapshot. Therefore, it is useful to review the Court of Justice's approach in the early days regarding the enforcement of copyright and design right.

Copyright materialised in goods

7-234   The phrase "for the protection of industrial and commercial property" in art.36 applies to goods subject to artistic and literary copyright.[289] Thus, rights in sound recordings,[290] industrial designs,[291] and video cassettes[292] have all been held to be subject to arts 34–36. Indeed, the CJEU has said, in so far as the commercial exploitation of a copyrighted work is concerned, there is no reason to make any distinction between copyright work and other forms of industrial and commercial property.[293]

Specific subject-matter

7-235   It was in *Deutsche Grammophon*, a case concerning sound recording rights, that the CJEU created the doctrine that art.36 only admitted the exercise of intellectual property rights where such is justified for the purpose of safeguarding the specific-subject-matter of such property. In *Musik Vertrieb*,[294] the CJEU acknowledged that copyright comprises both moral and economic rights and that in relation to its economic function it was not to be treated differently to other industrial and intellectual property rights. In *Phil Collins*, the CJEU said, referring to *Musik Vertrieb*, that:

> "[20]   The specific subject-matter of those rights, as governed by national legislation, is to ensure the protection of the moral and economic rights of their holders. The protection of moral rights enables authors and performers, in particular, to object to any distortion, mutilation or other modification of a work which would be prejudicial to their honour or reputation. Copyright and related rights are also

---

[289] *Musik-Vertrieb* (55/80) [1981] E.C.R. 147; [1981] 2 C.M.L.R. 44, CJEU at 64 and *CODITEL II* (262/81) [1982] E.C.R. 3381; [1983] 1 C.M.L.R. 49.

[290] *Deutsche Grammophon* (78/70) [1971] E.C.R. 487, [1971] C.M.L.R. 631; (55/80) [1981] E.C.R. 147, [1981] 2 C.M.L.R. 44; *Polydor Ltd and RSO Records Inc v Harlequin Records Shops Ltd and Simons Records Ltd* (270/80) [1982] E.C.R. 329, [1982] 1 C.M.L.R. 677; *EMI Electrola GmbH v Patricia Im und Export* (34/87) [1989] E.C.R. 79; [1989] 2 C.M.L.R. 413.

[291] (144/81) [1982] E.C.R. 2853; [1983] 2 C.M.L.R. 47.

[292] *Warner Bros v Christiansen* (156/86) [1988] E.C.R. 2605; [1990] 3 C.M.L.R. 684.

[293] See *Dansk Supermarked v Imerco* (58/80) [1981] E.C.R. 181, [1981] 3 C.M.L.R. 590; *Musik Vertrieb* (55/80) [1981] 2 C.M.L.R. 44 at [11]–[12].

[294] See [12].

economic in nature, in that they confer the right to exploit commercially the marketing of the protected work, particularly in the form of licences granted in return for payment of royalties."[295]

The CJEU still has resort to the doctrine of specific subject-matter for the purpose of interpreting copyright Directives and the provisions dealing with exhaustion of rights. An interesting example is in *UsedSoft* which was concerned with whether the licence of a computer program which was downloaded from the Internet exhausted the right of the owner of copyright in the computer program so that the licensee could sell on the "licence" in the same way that undoubtedly, they could do if they had bought a computer program on a CD-ROM or DVD.[296] In finding that licensee was entitled to sell on "the licence", the CJEU said that to allow the copyright holder to control the resale of copies downloaded from the Internet and to demand further remuneration on the occasion of each sale, even though the first sale of the copy had already enabled the right holder to obtain an appropriate remuneration, "would go beyond what is necessary to safeguard the specific subject matter of the intellectual property concerned".[297]

7-236

Essential function

The CJEU has periodically referred to the "essential function" of copyright. Thus, in *TV Listings*, a case concerning art.102 TEFU, the CJEU referred to the essential function of copyright being to protect the moral rights and reward the creative effort of the author.[298] It will be apparent that unlike trade marks, where there is a clear distinction between the essential function and specific subject-matter of trade marks, there is no distinction at all between the essential function and specific subject-matter of copyright. However, in general, although the specific subject-matter of an IPR is closely related to the exclusive right to first place a product subject to the right on the market, it can be understood that in the case of moral rights, there may be reason to exercise such rights even after the copyright owner has received appropriate reward for a copy of their work being placed on the market.

7-237

Exhaustion of rights

The CJEU has confirmed that the doctrine of exhaustion of rights applies in the field of copyright and industrial design, and has held that neither a copyright owner nor a copyright management society acting in the owner's or licensee's name, may rely on the exclusive exploitation right conferred by copyright to prevent or restrict

7-238

---

[295] (C-92/92). See also Darmon AG's Opinion in *EMI Electrola GmbH v Patricia Im- und Export Verwaltungsgesellschaft mbH* (341/87) [1989] 2 C.M.L.R. 413 at 418. See also, in England, Foster J's judgment in *British Leyland Motors v Armstrong Patents* [1982] 3 C.M.L.R. 603 at [4], where he states that the specific subject-matter of copyright was, in the case of industrial design drawings, to ensure that the skill and effort of the draughtsmen were rewarded by the grant of an exclusive right to copy and make for sale three-dimensional reproductions by the grant of licences and to prevent others from infringing that right.

[296] *UsedSoft GmbH v Oracle International Corp* (C-128/11) ECLI:EU:C:2012:407.

[297] See [63] citing, to that effect, *Metronome Musik GmbH v Music Point Hokamp GmbH* (C-200/96) [1998] E.C.R. I-1953, [2000] E.C.D.R. 11 at [14]; *Foreningen af Danske Videogramdistributorer (FDV) v Laserdisken* (C-61/97) [1998] E.C.R. I-5171, [2000] E.C.D.R. 139 at [13]; and *FA Premier League v QC Leisure* (C-403/08 & C-429/08) [2012] F.S.R. 1 at [106]. See also para.7-044, et seq. where the subject matter doctrine is discussed in detail.

[298] (C-241–242/91P) [1995] E.C.R. I-743 at [28].

the importation of sound recordings which have been lawfully marketed in another Member State by the owner personally or with their consent.[299] Thus, once the owner has placed their work on the market, the owner cannot prevent the importation, distribution or sale of that good in another Member State. It should be noted that the CJEU will not permit a party to consent to the placing of a product on a market only for a particular Member State. Thus, a contractual stipulation that a party may only place a copyright product on the market in a particular Member State does not entitle the copyright owner to bring copyright infringement proceedings against the importation of such products into another Member State.[300]

7-239 The principle of exhaustion of rights has now been implemented in a number of Directives in the field of copyright and allied rights including Directives harmonising the law and harmonising the distribution right for copyright works and copyright law in sound recordings, films, recordings of performances and broadcasts, databases, semi-conductor topographical right and computer software.[301] In each case, the relevant provision states that the rights are unenforceable once a product incorporating the right has been put on the market in the EU or with the owner's consent. The CJEU in *Laserdisken v Kulturministeriet* has confirmed that art.4(2) of the Information Society Directive (which provided for a EU-wide exhaustion of rights principle) precludes Member States from legislating for an international exhaustion of rights principle.[302] Thus, any doubt that the decision in *Silhouette v Hartlauer* was confined to the law of trade marks no longer remains.[303] In contrast to the Trade Mark Directive which permits a trade mark proprietor to exercise their rights even where they have placed a product bearing the mark on the market in a Member State provided that the trade-mark proprietor has "legitimate reasons" to do so, there is no such equivalent provision in the Information Society Directive. However, a copyright owner may be able to exercise their moral rights to prevent acts occurring to copyright works that have been placed on the market by the author or with their consent. An obvious example would be where the name of the author is over-stickered. In such circumstances, there should be no reason why the author should be prevented from exercising such rights.[304]

Broadcast, performance and communication to the public copyright

7-240 For the purposes of the TFEU, a distinction is drawn between on the one hand, the exclusive rights of reproduction and other rights relating specifically to goods or tangible media, e.g. the distribution right and on the other hand, the exclusive rights of performance, broadcast and communication to the public of copyright works. These rights of performance, broadcast and communication to the public differ materially from the rights embodied in goods because they are not concerned

---

[299] (78/70) [1971] E.C.R. 487, [1971] C.M.L.R. 631; (55/80) [1981] E.C.R. 147, [1981] 2 C.M.L.R. 44, CJEU at [15]. See also (58/80) [1981] E.C.R. 181, [1981] 3 C.M.L.R. 590; (C-61/97) [1998] E.C.R. I-5171 at [13].

[300] (58/80) [1981] E.C.R. 181; [1981] 3 C.M.L.R. 590; *Peak Holding AB v Axolin-Elinor AB* (C-16/03).

[301] art.5 Dir.87/54 (semi-conductor topographical Directive); art.4(c) Dir.91/250 (computer software Directive); art.9 Dir.92/100 (Rental Right Directive); art.5 Dir.96/9 (database Directive); art.4 Dir.2001/29 (Copyright Directive). These are discussed in Ch.4.

[302] (C-479/04) [2006] E.C.R. I-8089. Generally, see para.4-320.

[303] See para.3-616.

[304] It is of note that the Information Society Directive does not seek to affect the moral rights of an author—see Recital 19.

with goods but more specifically the provision of services. As such, they do not fall within arts 34–36 but arts 56–57, which concern services.[305] The CJEU has confirmed that the same principles that apply to arts 34–36 and intellectual property rights apply to arts 56–57.[306]

Theoretically, there can be any number of performances of a work. Thus, a discotheque can play a tape-recorded work as many times as it wishes. With goods subject to copyright, the reward in relation to the reproduction right is based on the number of goods sold. In relation to the performance rights, the reward for the author is based on the number of performances and the size of the audience. Thus, the performance right is materially different from the reproduction right. **7-241**

Article 56 TFEU provides that: **7-242**

"Within the framework of the provisions set out below, restrictions on freedom to provide services within the Union shall be prohibited in respect of nationals of Member States who are established in a Member State other than that of the person for whom the services are intended.

The European Parliament and the Council, acting in accordance with the ordinary legislative procedure, may extend the provisions of the Chapter to nationals of a third country who provide services and who are established within the Union."

Article 57 states that: **7-243**

"Services shall be considered to be 'services' within the meaning of the Treaties where they are normally provided for remuneration, in so far as they are not governed by the provisions relating to freedom of movement for goods, capital and persons.

'Services' shall in particular include: (a) activities of an industrial character; (b) activities of a commercial character; (c) activities of craftsmen; (d) activities of the professions.

Without prejudice to the provisions of the Chapter relating to the right of establishment, the person providing a service may, in order to do so, temporarily pursue his activity in the Member State where the service is provided, under the same conditions as are imposed by that State on its own nationals."

The first case in which the CJEU had to consider the question of copyright in public performances, in relation to arts 56–57, was *Coditel v S.A. Ciné Vog Films ("CODITEL I")*.[307] **7-244**

In this case, Ciné Vog had the exclusive distribution rights in Belgium to the film *"Le Boucher"*, which it obtained from a French company called *Les Fils la Boétie*. Coditel was a Belgian cable television distribution service. Its central aerial in Belgium picked up a transmission of the film *"Le Boucher"*, which was being broadcast in Germany by German television. This broadcast was with the consent of the original owner of the copyright in the film but confined under contract to Germany. Coditel then transmitted the film on its cable network in Belgium. At the time of transmission, Ciné Vog was showing the film in cinemas. It was stipulated in its contract with *Les Fils la Boétie* that the right to transmit the film by television could not be exercised until 40 months after the first showing of the film in Belgium. Only seven months of this period had expired before the events in question occurred. **7-245**

---

[305] See *CODITEL I* (62/79) [1980] E.C.R. 881; [1981] 2 C.M.L.R. 362 and (262/81) [1982] E.C.R. 3381; [1983] 1 C.M.L.R. 49. See also *FAPL v QC Leisure* (C-403/08) in relation to broadcasts.

[306] See *CODITEL I*, at 903; [1981] 2 C.M.L.R. 362; and L. Defalque, "Copyright-Free Movement of Goods and Territoriality: Recent Developments" [1989] 12 E.I.P.R. 435, 435.

[307] (62/79) [1980] E.C.R. 881; [1981] 2 C.M.L.R. 362.

7-246   Ciné Vog sued Coditel for infringement of copyright. The Cour d'Appel then referred to the CJEU the question as to whether, in the light of such facts, Ciné Vog was prohibited from exercising its rights against Coditel by virtue of arts 56–57 (ex-arts 49–50).

7-247   The CJEU stated that:

> "[12]   A cinematographic film belongs to the category of literary and artistic works made available to the public by performances which may be infinitely repeated. In this respect the problems involved in the observance of copyright in relation to the requirements of the treaty are not the same as those which arise in connection with literary and artistic works the placing of which at the disposal of the public is inseparable from the circulation of the material form of the works, as in the case of books or records.
>
> [13]   In these circumstances the owner of the copyright in a film and his assigns have a legitimate interest in calculating the fees due in respect of the authorisation to exhibit the film on the basis of the actual or probable number of performances and in authorising a television broadcast of the film only after it has been exhibited in cinemas for a certain period of time."[308]

7-248   The CJEU said that the essential function of copyright in performances was to require fees for any showing of a film. Imputing the wording of art.36 to art.56,[309] it then continued:

> "[15]   Whilst Article [56] of the Treaty prohibits restrictions upon freedom to provide services, it does not thereby encompass limits upon the exercise of certain economic activities which have their origin in the application of national legislation for the protection of intellectual property, save where such application constitutes a means of arbitrary discrimination or a disguised restriction on trade between Member States. Such would be the case if that application enabled parties to make an assignment of copyright to create artificial barriers to trade between Member States."[310]

7-249   Thus, they held that Ciné Vog was entitled to exercise its exclusive distribution right against Coditel, as the fact that the broadcast was limited to Germany was not incompatible with the Treaty of Rome, as it was often impracticable to impose any other limitation. In *CODITEL II*,[311] the CJEU confirmed that arts 56–57, and not arts 34–36, were applicable but that the distinction underlying art.36, between the existence and exercise of a right, applied equally where the right is exercised in the framework of the provision of services.[312]

7-250   In *CODITEL I*, the CJEU stated that art.56 does not prohibit the imposition of a geographical limit on any licence to broadcast. However, in *FAPL v QC Leisure*,[313] a case decided 20 years later, the CJEU had to consider the position under arts 56–57 regarding where public houses in England showed English premier football league games using decoders which were intended to decode satellite broadcasts for the Greek market. The decoders were considerably cheaper than those for the English market. FAPL granted exclusive territorial broadcasting licences on a

---

[308] (62/79) [1980] E.C.R. 881; [1981] 2 C.M.L.R. 362 at [12] and [13].

[309] See also *Ministère Public v Tournier; Lucazeau v SACEM* (395/87, 110/88 and 241–242/88) [1989] E.C.R. 2521; [1991] 4 C.M.L.R. 248 at [10]–[15].

[310] See also *Ministère Public v Tournier; Lucazeau v SACEM*, at [15].

[311] (262/81) [1982] E.C.R. 3361; [1983] 1 C.M.L.R. 49.

[312] See [13].

[313] *FAPL v QC Leisure* (C-403/08) [2012] 1 C.M.L.R. 29; [2011] E.C.R. 9083.

Member State basis. The CJEU held that the case was, in substance, concerned about the right to receive the encrypted broadcasting services and thus was concerned with art.56 TFEU.[314] It held that in determining whether such was reasonable, one should have regard to the economic value of the service provided and the actual or potential number of persons who enjoy or wish to enjoy the service.[315] In finding that English legislation which prohibited the use of the decoder devices was contrary to art.56, it distinguished *CODITEL I*. It held that the CJEU had held in *CODITEL I* that in principle, the Treaty of Rome (the predecessor to TFEU) did not constitute an obstacle to the geographical limits which a party to a contract of assignment of IPR could agree upon in order to protect the author and his assigns. Such however was made in a context which was different to that of the facts in *FAPL* as the cable television broadcasting companies had no authorisation from the right holder in the Member State of the place of origin of the broadcast and had paid no remuneration to that entity. In contrast, in *FAPL*, the Greek broadcasters whose broadcasts were received in England did have authority from the right holders.[316] Whilst this is undoubtedly true, the CJEU had said in *CODITEL I* that the rights owner was entitled to charge fees according to how many performances there were of the film. By way of analogy, it could be said that a rights owner is entitled to charge fees according to how many people watch a broadcasted event. Furthermore, in *CODITEL I*, the broadcast which CODITEL picked up was a legal transmission by German television. There is little distinction between that situation and English public houses being able to pick up a broadcast intended clearly only for Greece. Whilst it is true that the English public houses were not themselves cable television broadcasting companies (but instead end-users), the effect was the same. In truth, in *FAPL*, the CJEU was again asserting the importance of the single market and that parallel traders were entitled to take steps which undermined attempts by companies to partition the single market with different pricing structures. In substance, the CJEU saw no distinction between the facts of *FAPL v QC Leisure* and the right of parallel importers to import goods of an undertaking from one Member State where they were placed on the market by the undertaking at a low price into another Member State where they were placed on the market at a high price.

Copyright in works for hire or rent

Many copyright works can be rented out or lent out by libraries. In general, the rental of a copyright work is a restricted act for which permission is required from the copyright owner.[317] It will be apparent that the rental of a work is similar in nature to the performance of a copyright work in that it is capable of being repeated an infinite number of times. Thus, it is not surprising that the approach of the CJEU to exhaustion of the rental right is similar to its approach to exhaustion of the performance right, namely that such cannot occur. However, unlike the performance right, the CJEU has chosen to consider the rental right under arts 34–36. This can be seen from *Warner Bros v Christiansen*, which is discussed below, where the

7-251

---

[314] See [84].
[315] See [108]–[109].
[316] See [120].
[317] Indeed, following the Rental Right Directive, all Member States provide for a rental right.

CJEU said that laws providing for a rental right are justifiable under art.36.[318] *Warner Bros v Christiansen* was decided after *CODITEL I* and thus it might have been thought that the CJEU would have decided the matter under arts 56–57. However, in *Warner Bros*, the questions referred to the CJEU by the Danish court concerned the interpretation of arts 34–36. Moreover, in *Warner Bros v Christiansen*, the issue was whether the marketing of videocassettes in the UK exhausted the right to prevent the rental of the same video cassettes in Denmark. Thus, the case did indirectly concern the importation of goods.

Exhaustion of reproduction rights does not exhaust performance and rental rights

7-252   In the application of the doctrine of exhaustion, the CJEU distinguishes between differing rights in the protected good. The marketing of a copyright product by the owner of the right, or with their consent, in one Member State does not exhaust the owner of a performance or quasi-performance right (e.g. a rental right) in another Member State from enforcing such a right. This is so, even if the law of the first Member State does not provide for the performance right in question. This can be seen in the context of the CJEU's decisions on performance rights and rental rights.

Performance rights

7-253   In *Basset v SACEM*,[319] the CJEU was concerned with the collection of a supplementary mechanical right royalty from a French discotheque owner when he played sound recordings in his nightclub. Under French law, a copyright owner or his assigns can authorise reproduction to a specific end. Thus, reproduction can be authorised for private purposes only. If the work is publicly performed then the permission of the owner of the reproductive right is required and a further royalty can be levied. This is called the supplementary mechanical right royalty. This should be distinguished from the performance right, which also exists under French law. Thus the author or their assigns (in *Basset*, it was the French copyright company, SACEM) can receive two types of royalty when a sound recording subject to copyright is publicly performed. In *Basset*, the owner of the discotheque refused to pay the supplementary right royalty on the grounds, inter alia, that the supplementary mechanical right royalty did not exist in other countries, notably the UK, where many of the records were produced. On reference to the CJEU, the court ruled that the supplementary right royalty could be described as forming part of the royalty payment for the public performance of a recorded musical work.[320] Thus, even if the records which the discotheque played had been manufactured in a Member State where no such right existed, the right which applied to both domestic and national products was not exhausted, as it was a performance-type right and not embodied in a product.[321]

---

[318] See [15]–[16].

[319] *Basset v SACEM* (402/85) [1987] E.C.R. 1747; [1987] 3 C.M.L.R. 173.

[320] The royalty was calculated on the basis of the discotheque's turnover and not on the number of discs purchased.

[321] It seemed that, if the supplementary right royalty had been declared exhausted, SACEM would have increased the performance royalty to compensate for the shortfall. Thus, the effect would have been negligible.

Basset v SACEM[322] was followed in *Ministère Public v Tournier* and *Lucazeau* **7-254**
v SACEM.[323] In the joined cases, Mr Tournier and Mr Lucazeau, the complainants,
felt that it was a real injustice that they were paying considerably higher royalties
for the playing of a largely Anglo-American repertoire than they would have done
in the UK. The complainants relied upon the CJEU's judgment in *Musik Vertrieb
v GEMA*[324] that a copyright management society cannot seek to prevent the marketing of a recording which had been lawfully placed on the market in another Member
State, even if its practice was to levy a higher royalty rate than effectively done in
the Member State in which it was placed on the market. The CJEU held that a
distinction between the reproduction and performance right must be maintained and
held that the rate of royalty charged by copyright management society was not a
matter for arts 34–36 or arts 56–57 but must be appraised in relation to the competition rules contained in arts 101 and 102.[325]

Rental rights

In *Warner Bros v Christiansen*,[326] video cassettes of a film were imported by a **7-255**
Danish trader from England where they had been marketed by the copyright owner.
Danish copyright law, unlike UK law at that time,[327] conferred on the author the
exclusive right to rent as well as to place the video on the market. The Danish trade
offered the videos for hire and the owner of the exclusive rights to hire in Denmark
sued for infringement. The case was referred to the CJEU on the issue of whether,
in such a situation, arts 34–36 prohibited the owner of the rental right in Denmark
from exercising his rights against the renter of the video cassette.

In *Warner Bros v Christiansen*,[328] the Advocate-General had proposed that the **7-256**
CJEU find that arts 34–36 did prevent the holder of the Danish exclusive rental right
from suing for infringement. He held that rental rights cannot be assimilated to
performance-type rights. He put much emphasis on the fact that, in the UK, there
was no rental right and relied upon the *Musik Vertrieb v GEMA*[329] case in that the
owner of a right who has put his work into circulation may not take advantage of
the:

> "disparities which continue to exist in the absence of any harmonisation of national rules
> on the commercial exploitation of copyrights so as to impede the free movement of goods
> in the Common Market."[330]

The CJEU did not follow the Advocate-General. It stated that the two essential **7-257**
rights of the author, namely the exclusive right of performance and the exclusive
right of reproduction, are not called into question by the rules of the Treaty.[331] The
court noted that there was a specific market for the hiring-out of video cassettes.

---

[322] (402/85) [1987] 3 C.M.L.R. 173.
[323] See also (395/87), (110/88) and (241–242/88) [1991] 4 C.M.L.R. 248.
[324] (55/80) [1981] E.C.R. 147; [1981] 2 C.M.L.R. 44.
[325] See para.8-409, et seq., and para.12-290.
[326] (156/86) [1988] E.C.R. 2605; [1990] 3 C.M.L.R. 684.
[327] The situation had now changed in the UK—see Copyright Designs and Patent Act 1988 s.8(2). See
also the Directive on Rental Rights, Lending Rights and Allied Rights, which provides for a rental
right for Member States—see para.4-145.
[328] (156/86) [1988] E.C.R. 2605; [1990] 3 C.M.L.R. 684.
[329] (55/80) [1981] E.C.R. 147; [1981] 2 C.M.L.R. 44.
[330] *MEMBRAN* and *K-TEL v GEMA* (55–57/80) [1981] E.C.R. 147; [1981] 2 C.M.L.R. 44 at [26].
[331] (156/86) [1988] E.C.R. 2605; [1990] 3 C.M.L.R. 684 at [12].

Furthermore, the collection of royalties on sales could not provide remuneration to the author which reflected the number of occasions on which a video cassette had been hired out. The CJEU rejected the contention by the importer that a maker of a video cassette who has offered it for sale in a Member State where there is no exclusive right of hire must accept the consequences of his choices and the exhaustion of his right to restrain hiring-out in any other Member State. The CJEU said that such a submission would render the right to hire-out worthless. Thus, the marketing of a video cassette in a Member State which did not protect the right to rental did not exhaust the right of the author granted to him by the laws of another Member State to oppose the rental in the latter state.

7-258   *Warner Bros v Christiansen* was followed in *FDV v Laserdisken*.[332] In this case, laserdiscs were being imported from the UK into Denmark. The owner of the rental right had implicitly consented to the renting out of the laserdiscs in the UK.[333] Laserdisken lawfully bought laserdiscs in the UK, imported them into Denmark and began renting them out. The Danish rental right-holder brought proceedings against Laserdisken for infringement of the rental right. Laserdisken claimed that the rental right was exhausted because consent to its rental had been given in the UK. The Vestre Landsret decided to refer the matter to the CJEU on this issue. The court, following *Warner Bros*, confirmed two principles. First, the release into circulation of a copyright work does not constitute consent to acts of exploitation to the work which are different in character, such as the performance or rental of that work.[334] Secondly, it held that the exclusive right to hire out various copies of the work contained in a video film can, by its very nature, be exploited by repeated and potentially unlimited transactions, each of which involves the right to remuneration. In such circumstances, the court said that the specific right to authorise or prohibit rental would be rendered meaningless if it were held to be exhausted as soon as the object was first offered for rental.[335]

CONSUMER PROTECTION AND UNFAIR COMPETITION LAWS

Introduction

7-259   Generally speaking, unfair competition laws have two objectives. First, they are to protect the consumer against confusion in the market place; secondly, they are to protect the trader against other traders' business practices that are intent on, or have the effect of, damaging the trader's business other than those founded on free-market economics. Consumer protection laws also are intended to protect the consumer against confusion in the marketplace but will rarely be concerned with protecting the interests of traders.

7-260   Article 10 of the Paris Convention for the Protection of Industrial Property 1883[336] defines "unfair competition" as any act of competition contrary to honest industrial or commercial practice. In particular, art.10*bis* states that [as part of the

---

[332] (C-61/97) [1998] E.C.R. I-5171.

[333] The CJEU said that it was apparent from the reference that the copyright holders had implicitly authorised the rental of the laserdiscs in the UK but not in Denmark. It is not clear whether this meant that the copyright-holder has implicitly authorised the rental of the laserdiscs for payment or not.

[334] See [17].

[335] See [18]. See also *Metronome-Musik v Hokamp* (C-200/96) [1998] E.C.R. I-1953, where the validity of the rental right in Dir.92/100 was confirmed by the CJEU.

[336] As revised in Stockholm on 14 July 1967 (amended on 28 September 1979).

general obligation of the countries of the Union to assure effective protection against unfair competition] that the following are prohibited:

"[i]   All acts of such a nature as to create confusion by any means whatever with the establishment, the goods, or the industrial or commercial activities, of a competitor.

[ii]   False assertions, in the conduct of business, which might discredit the establishment, the products, or the industrial or commercial activity of a competitor.

[iii]   Indications or allegations the use of which in the course of trade is liable to mislead the public as to the nature, the manufacturing process, the characteristics, the suitability for the purpose, or the quantity, of the goods."

EU countries all have laws, whether by statute or case law, that implement such **7-261** obligations. In the UK, which, unlike the civil laws of other Member States, has no comprehensive law of unfair competition, there are piecemeal provisions of which the most important are the common law actions of passing-off,[337] trade libel, and malicious falsehood.[338] These areas are now sufficiently developed so as to encompass most acts which constitute unfair competition in civil-law countries.

From the intellectual property practitioner's viewpoint, the law of unfair competi- **7-262** tion is important. Often a distinctive[339] attribute of a good or service is not adequately protected by copyright, patent, trade-mark or industrial design laws. This is especially so in the get-up, design and shape of products. The enforcement of unfair competition laws can often result in an enterprise owning a monopoly in a particular name, get-up or design. The CJEU has dealt with the problems of unfair competition and the free movement of goods provision mainly in relation to well known national brand names and shapes of food and wine products.

The main difference between this area and intellectual property is that unfair **7-263** competition laws generally do not fall within the meaning of "protection of industrial and commercial property" in art.36. There is no presumption that such a law is for the protection of industrial or commercial property, unlike traditional IPRs such as trade marks, design rights, copyright and patents. As has been commented on, this has led to rather artificial distinctions being made between, e.g. design rights where art.36 is engaged and laws of unfair competition aimed at protecting slavish imitation where art.36 is not engaged.[340]

The court has developed the following principles in relation to art.34 in the realm **7-264** of unfair competition law and consumer protection laws.

---

[337] Five characteristics must be present in order to create a valid cause of action for passing-off, see per Lord Diplock in *Warninck v Townend ("Advocaat")* [1980] R.P.C. 31 at 93:

"(1) a misrepresentation (2) made by a trader in the course of trade (3) to prospective customers of his or ultimate consumers of goods or services supplied by him (4) which is calculated to injure the business or goodwill of another trader (in the sense that it is a reasonably foreseeable consequence) and (5) which causes actual damage to the business to goodwill of the trader by whom the action is brought or (in a quia timet action) will probably do so".

[338] There is also statutory protection in various forms.

[339] "Distinctive" is used in the sense of indicative of trade origin or of a particular product.

[340] See *Industrie Diensten Groep v Beele Handelmaatschappij* (6/81) [1982] E.C.R. 707; [1982] 3 C.M.L.R. 102 (slavish imitation) and (144/81) [1982] E.C.R. 2853; [1983] 2 C.M.L.R. 47 (copying of a design). In D.T. Keeling, "Intellectual Property Rights in EU Law", Vol.1 (Oxford: Oxford University Press, 2004), p.38, Keeling points out that there is no logic in such a distinction.

The "Dassonville" principle

7-265   In the case of *Procureur du Roi v Dassonville*,[341] the CJEU was concerned with criminal proceedings instituted in Belgium against traders who had duly acquired a consignment of Scotch whisky in free circulation in France and imported it into Belgium without being in possession of a certificate of origin from the British customs authorities, thereby infringing Belgium rules. It transpired that a trader wishing to import whisky from a country other than the producer country could only obtain such a certificate with great difficulty. The CJEU ruled that such a provision was contrary to arts 34–36. It went on to say that:

> "All trading rules enacted by Member States which are capable of hindering, directly or indirectly, actually or potentially, intra-Community trade are to be considered as measures having an effect equivalent to quantitative restrictions."[342]

This is called the *"Dassonville"* principle.

The "Cassis de Dijon" principle and exceptions

7-266   A few years after *Dassonville*, the CJEU re-visited the problems of the compatibility of national laws for consumer protection and arts 34–36. *Cassis de Dijon*[343] concerned a German law which provided that fruit liqueurs could only be sold in Germany if they contained a minimum of 32 per cent wine-spirit. Certain beverages were exempted from this law. A trader attempted to import *"Cassis de Dijon"* liqueur, a well-known French fruit liqueur but whose alcoholic strength was below 32 per cent, from France. Thus, the German provision prevented the sale of *Cassis de Dijon* in Germany. The trader sought a ruling from the CJEU that the measure was contrary to art.34 in that it prevented the import of drinks traditionally and lawfully produced in another Member State. The CJEU stated that:

> "In the absence of common rules[344] relating to the production and marketing of alcohol it is for the Member State to regulate all matters relating to the production and marketing of alcohol and alcoholic beverages on their own territory. Obstacles of movement within the Community resulting from disparities between the national laws relating to the marketing of the products in question must be accepted in so far as those provisions may be recognised as being necessary in order to satisfy mandatory requirements relating in particular to *the effectiveness of fiscal supervision, the protection of public health, the fairness of commercial transaction and the defence of the consumer.*" [Emphasis supplied.]

7-267   The italicised exceptions are called the *"Cassis de Dijon"* exceptions. The German Government argued that it was in the interests of the consumer for the latter to know that fruit liqueurs were of a certain alcoholic content and to prevent unfair trade practices developing.[345] However, the CJEU said that labelling of products and stating their alcoholic content, would suffice to ensure that consumers were not

---

[341] *Procureur du Roi v Dassonville* (8/74) [1974] E.C.R. 837; [1974] 2 C.M.L.R. 436.

[342] *Dassonville*, point 5.

[343] (120/78) [1979] E.C.R. 649; [1979] 3 C.M.L.R. 495.

[344] This is interpreted as meaning "in the absence of comprehensive (or exhaustive) legislation"—see *Criminal Proceedings against Karl Prantl* (16/83) [1984] E.C.R. 1299; [1985] 2 C.M.L.R. 238.

[345] This latter argument was based on the fact that the lowering of the alcohol content secures a competitive advantage in relation to beverages of a higher alcoholic content, because alcohol, being taxed heavily, is by far the most expensive constituent of such beverages.

confused. Thus, the German law was not necessary. It therefore concluded that the German measures did not serve the general interest and did not take precedence over the requirements of the free movement of goods. Such an argument applied even though the German law applied to both domestic and imported products.[346] Thus, the *"Dassonville"* principle extends beyond mere prevention of discrimination between domestic and imported goods to removing any internal barriers to trade in goods lawfully placed on the market in a Member State unless such are justified by reference to the *"Cassis de Dijon"* exceptions. This is called the *"Cassis de Dijon"* principle.

The *"Cassis de Dijon"* principle has often been cited by the CJEU.[347] Thus, in **7-268** *Keck v Mithouard*, the CJEU reformulated the principle as follows:

> "It is established by the case law beginning with *Cassis de Dijon* that in the absence of harmonisation of legislation, obstacles to free movement of goods which are the consequences of applying to goods coming from other Member States where they are lawfully manufactured and marketed, rules that lay down requirements to be met by such goods (such as those relating to designation, form, size, weight, composition, presentation, labelling, packaging) constitute measures of equivalent effect prohibited under Article [34]. This is even if those rules apply without distinction to all products unless their application can be justified by a public-interest objective taking precedence over the free movement of goods."[348]

Application of the "Dassonville" principle

In certain cases, it will be obvious if a trading rule is capable of directly or **7-269** indirectly hindering trade between Member States. Thus, if a national measure intentionally discriminates between imported products and domestic products, it is contrary to art.34.[349] If the national measure discriminates against nationals of other Member States, then it is contrary to art.18 TFEU. If the procedural requirements of a national measure are such as to cause discrimination then this is contrary to art.34.[350]

However, in many cases, it is not so obvious that a national law or legal provi- **7-270** sion has the effect of hindering trade between Member States. This is especially the case where the relevant provision applies equally to both domestic and imported products. Thus, a national law that states that all eggs must be sold in six-egg boxes does not appear to be a law capable of hindering trade between Member States. However, whilst in England, the sale of eggs in such containers is commonplace, it may not be so in other Member States. Thus, producers of eggs in those countries would have to bear additional costs in packaging eggs for the UK market so as to

---

[346] National laws will be presumed to apply without distinction to domestic and imported products unless the contrary is shown. See *Industrie Diensten Groep v Beele* (6/81) [1982] E.C.R. 707; [1982] 3 C.M.L.R. 102.

[347] This principle has been applied often by the CJEU, e.g. see *Industrie Diensten v Beele* (6/81) [1982] E.C.R. 1625, [1982] 1 C.M.L.R. 102; *Robertson* (220/81) [1982] E.C.R. 2349, [1983] 1 C.M.L.R. 556; and *Oosthoek* (286/81) [1982] E.C.R. 4575, [1983] 3 C.M.L.R. 428. One must also include "protection of the environment" in the *Cassis de Dijon* exceptions—see *Re Disposable Cans: EC Commission v Denmark* (302/86) [1989] 1 C.M.L.R. 619.

[348] *Merck v Primecrown* (267–268/91) [1995] C.M.L.R. 101 at [15].

[349] See *Allen & Hanburys Ltd v Generics (UK) Ltd* (434/85) [1988] E.C.R. 1245, [1986] 1 C.M.L.R. 101; see also *Gilli and Andries* (788/79) [1980] E.C.R. 2071 and *Re Irish Souvenirs: EC Commission v Ireland* [1982] E.C.R. 4005.

[350] See *Dassonville* which, as discussed above, was concerned with the procedure for obtaining a certificate of authenticity for whisky.

comply with UK law. They would thus be competing unfavourably with domestic UK egg producers. Similarly, UK egg producers would be at a disadvantage with French producers if there was a French law which provided that eggs must be sold in circular containers. In these cases, the importer or the foreign producer is disadvantaged as compared to the domestic producer.

7-271   In applying the *"Dassonville"* principle, the CJEU has widely applied art.34 and prohibited national trading laws which make marketing more difficult for suppliers of products from other Member States. The CJEU's application of the *"Dassonville"* rule is now considered in a number of cases.

Criminal proceedings against Karl Prantl[351]

7-272   Section 17 of the Wein-Verordnung 1971 stated that only wine produced in Franconia could be marketed in a traditional bottle known as the Bocksbeutel (a bulbous-shaped bottle). This legislative measure was actually enacted in Germany because the Bundesgerichtshof had originally found that the Bocksbeutel was an indirect indication of geographical origin and, thus, its use might mislead consumers if used for wine which was not produced in Franconia. As a result of this, anyone who marketed Bocksbeutel not containing wine from Franconia was guilty of a criminal offence. Mr Prantl imported Italian red wine into Germany which had been traditionally bottled in a bottle virtually identical to the Bocksbeutel. The matter was referred to the CJEU as to whether such a provision was contrary to arts 34–36. The court held that:

> "A provision such as section 17 of the Wein-Verordnung, allowing a specific shape of bottle to be used only by certain producers of domestic wine, has protective effects inasmuch as it favours those producers compared to producers in other Member States who traditionally bottle their wine in bottles of identical or very similar shape."[352] [Emphasis supplied.]

7-273   Thus, the court said that, although the legislation applied to national and imported products alike, in practice it had protective effects. Therefore, it came within the scope of the prohibition of art.34.

Theodore Kohl AG v Ringelhan & Rennett SA[353]

7-274   Ringelhan and Rennet was an old German company who used the logo "r+r". It had a French subsidiary, Ringelhan and Rennett SA (R&R). However, in 1982, the German company was wound up and the French subsidiary was sold to a third party. The French company carried on using the logo for their pharmaceutical equipment in Europe. Theodore Kohl, another pharmaceutical equipment manufacturer, brought an action against R&R under a provision in German unfair competition law which prohibited misleading statements. It alleged that the use of the mark without a clarifying statement misled customers into believing that R&R were connected with the defunct German company (who had an excellent reputation). On reference to the CJEU, it was held that, although the German provision applied to both German and imported products, it had been interpreted and applied by the German courts in such a way as to discriminate against imported products. Thus, the CJEU extended the concept of discrimination even further than in *Prantl*, because

---

[351]   (16/83) [1985] 2 C.M.L.R. 238.
[352]   (16/83) [1984] E.C.R. 1299; [1985] 2 C.M.L.R. 238, point 22.
[353]   *Theodor Kohl KG v Ringelhan und Rennett* (177/83) [1984] E.C.R. 3651; [1985] 3 C.M.L.R. 340.

it ruled that even if a law does not have a protective effect per se, it can be contrary to art.34 if it is applied so as to give a de facto protective effect.[354]

Criminal Proceeding against Keck and Mithouard[355]

In this case, the CJEU attempted to narrow the application of the *"Dassonville"* **7-275** principle. This followed an increasing tendency of traders to invoke art.34 as a means of challenging any rule whose effect was to limit their commercial freedom, even where such rules had no ostensible effect on trade between Member States. This tendency had been encouraged in the light of decisions by the CJEU, which were inclined to find that apparently innocuous measures infringed art.34 merely because they directly or indirectly made free trade more difficult.[356]

In *Keck & Mithouard*, the applicants were prosecuted for reselling products in **7-276** an unaltered state at prices lower than their actual purchase price, contrary to French law. The CJEU re-visited much of its law. It said as follows:

"[14] In view of the increasing tendency of traders to invoke Article [34] of the Treaty as a means of challenging any rules whose effect is to limit their commercial freedom even where such rules are not aimed at products from other Member States, the Court considers it necessary to re-examine and clarify its case law on this matter.

[15] It is established by the case law beginning with '*Cassis de Dijon*' ... that, in the absence of harmonisation of legislation, obstacles to free movement of goods which are the consequence of applying to goods coming from other Member States where they are lawfully manufactured and marketed, rules that lay down requirements to be met by such goods (such as those relating to designation, form, size, weight, composition, presentation, labelling, packaging) constitute measures of equivalent effect prohibited by Article [34]. This is so even if those rules apply without distinction to all products unless their application can be justified by a public-interest objective taking precedence over the free movement of goods.

[16] By contrast, contrary to what has previously been decided, the application to products from other Member States of national provisions *restricting or prohibit-*

---

[354] As the headnote to the C.M.L.R. says, this ruling should be analysed with care. In appearance it is extremely wide. It appears, from both the Advocate-General and the court, that the section had never been applied in a purely domestic context. Thus, it is the practical application of the German law and not the actual legislation which appeared to have determined the issue.

[355] (267–268/91) [1993] E.C.R. I-6097; [1995] C.M.L.R. 101.

[356] In particular, the court's severe application of the *"Dassonville"* principle can be seen in its case law, condemning national legislation that regulates prices where such legislation clearly did not have the intention of preventing imports, e.g. see *Cullet v Sodinord & Sodirev* (231/83) [1985] E.C.R. 0305; [1985] 2 C.M.L.R. 524, CJEU (fixed minimum price of petrol in France prevented importers of petrol of lower cost price from passing on the competitive advantage to consumers and, thus, contravened art.36); *Tasca* (65/75) [1976] E.C.R. 291 (fixed maximum prices forced importers of more highly-priced goods to cut their profit margins or be forced to sell at a loss); *Procureur General v Buys* (5/79) [1979] E.C.R. 3203 (national price freeze rules induced dealers of products to prefer domestic products to imported products, because of the generally higher prices of imported products); *Buet* (C-283/89) [1989] E.C.R. 1235 (French law against door to door selling of educational material was prohibited under art.34); *Aragonesa de Publicidad Exterior v DSSSG* (C-1/90 and C-176/90) [1991] E.C.R. I-4151; (C-126/91) [1993] E.C.R. I-2361 (German legislation prohibiting price comparisons was caught by art.34). In contrast, see *Blesgen v Belgium* [1982] (75/81) E.C.R. 1211 (Belgian law outlawing the sale of strong alcoholic beverages in bars and restaurants not caught by art.34); *Quietlynn v Southend BC* (C-23/89) [1990] E.C.R. I-3509 (prohibition of sale of pornographic material not caught by art.34). See D.T. Keeling, "Intellectual Property Rights in EU Law", Vol.1 (Oxford: Oxford University Press, 2004), pp.13–14), See E.L. White, "In search of the limits to Art.[34] of the EEC Treaty" [1989] C.M.L.R. 235 and Opinion of the AG in *Keck & Mithouard*.

> ing certain selling arrangements is not such as to hinder directly or indirectly, actually or potentially, trade between Member States within the meaning of *Dassonville*... so long as those provisions apply to all relevant traders operating within the national territory and so long as they affect in the same manner, in law and in fact, the marketing of domestic products and of those from other Member States.
>
> [17] Provided that those conditions are fulfilled, the application of such rules to the sale of products from another Member State meeting the requirements laid down by that State is not by nature such as to prevent their access to the market or to impede access any more than it impedes the access of domestic products. Such rules therefore fall outside the scope of Article [34] of the Treaty."

7-277   Thus, the CJEU distinguished between laws governing selling arrangements and those governing the composition and presentation of goods. The former do not fall within the *Dassonville* principle but the latter do and thus will only be lawful if covered by the *Cassis de Dijon* exceptions. Furthermore, it means that little reliance can be placed on previous decisions of the CJEU in this area. The distinction between the former and the latter is difficult to justify per se. Rather, the underlying rationale must be that selling arrangements are much less likely to have an appreciable effect on imports and exports than laws relating to the composition and presentation of goods. Thus, Jacobs AG in *Leclerc v Siplec*[357] said that:

> "The effect of the *Keck* judgment is still uncertain: perhaps it is best understood as excluding from the scope of Article [34] only measures of an entirely general character which do not preclude imports, which operate at the point of sale, and which have no effect on trade other than to reduce the overall quantity of goods sold and which in doing so affect imports and domestic products alike."[358]

7-278   Therefore, the Advocate-General proposed a de minimis test: does the legislative measure prevent substantial access of an undertaking to the whole of the Community. This approach has much to commend itself although as commented earlier in this chapter, the CJEU has rejected a de minimis approach to arts 34–36 in contrast to that of arts 101 and 102.[359]

Modern approach

7-279   The court's approach in *Keck* has been followed and endorsed to the present day.[360] Unfortunately, the CJEU has not adopted the approach of the Advocate-General since *Keck v Mithouard*. Rather, it has often rather aridly considered whether a legislative measure does or does not concern selling arrangements. Thus, in *Ditlev Bluhme*,[361] the CJEU held that national legislative measures prohibiting the keeping on an island of any species of bee other than the subspecies *Apis mellifera mellifera* could not be regarded as a selling arrangement and, thus, the principle set out in *Keck v Mithouard* did not apply. Accordingly, it was a quantita-

---

[357] *Leclerc v Siplec* (C-412/93) [1995] E.C.R. I-179.
[358] See [34].
[359] See para.7-020.
[360] e.g. see *Schutzverband gegen Unlauteren Wettbewerb v TK-Heimdienst Sass GmbH* (C-254/98) [2000] E.C.R. I-151 at [23]; *Deutscher Apothekerverband eV v 0800 DocMorris NV* (C-322/01) [2003] E.C.R. I-14887 at [68]; *Herbert Karner Industrie Auktionen GmbH v Troostwijk GmbH* (C-71/02) [2004] E.C.R. I-3025 at [34]–[37]; *Burmanjer* (C-20/03) [2005] E.C.R. I-4133 at [22]–[24]; and *A. Punkt v Schmidt* (C-441/04) [2006] E.C.R. I-2093 at [21]; *Commission v Spain (Marketing of Chocolate)* (C-12/00) [2003] E.C.R. I-459, [2005] 2 C.M.L.R. 33.
[361] *Ditlev Bluhme* (C-67/97) [1998] E.C.R. I-8033.

tive restriction which fell within art.34.[362] It is highly debatable whether such a measure which is plainly not concerned with the presentation or composition of products should be treated less favourably than selling arrangements. Both are very tenuously linked to products. Similarly, in *VFZ v Heinrich Bauer*,[363] the CJEU held that a ban on the selling of periodicals containing games or competitions was a ban relating to sales promotion and was not concerned with selling arrangements—a distinction which is difficult to understand. However, it has extended the principle of "selling arrangements" to marketing methods.[364]

A good example of the CJEU's approach to rules relating to the composition and presentation of goods since *Keck* can be seen in *Criminal Proceedings against Jean-Pierre Guimont*.[365] In that case, criminal proceedings were brought against a trader selling Emmenthal cheese without a rind, which was contrary to a provision of French law. On reference to the CJEU, the court held that the fact that the rule was applicable equally to both imported and domestic products was irrelevant, because it was "likely to make marketing more difficult from other Member States".[366]   **7-280**

In *Fachverband der Buch–und Medienwirtschaft v LIBRO Handelgesellschaft mbH*,[367] the CJEU considered a case which was concerned with fixing of retail prices rather than the labelling or packaging of products. It was concerned with Austrian law which permitted the fixing of retail prices for books. Austrian law permitted the publisher or importer of books to fix and publish a retail price for books which he published or imported. However, in relation to imported books, the importer could not fix a price below the retail price fixed or recommended by the publisher in the territory of another Member State. It was argued that this discriminated against imported books because it prevented importers and foreign publishers from fixing minimum retail prices according to the conditions of the Austrian market whereas Austrian publishers were free to fix themselves the minimum retail prices for the Austrian market. In other words, if the retail price recommended in another Member State was too high to permit effective marketing in Austria, such would disadvantage their sale in Austria where publishers would fix the prices having regards to market conditions in Austria.[368] The CJEU considered that such arrangements were selling arrangements within the meaning of *Keck & Mithouard* but held that despite such, the arrangements created books from other Member States less favourably and thus was unlawful.[369]   **7-281**

The difficulties caused by an arid application of *Keck v Mithouard* were discussed in Maduro's AG Opinion in *Alfa Vita Vassipolous*.[370] He pointed out that in fact, in certain cases, the application of *Keck* by the CJEU had treated packaging condition as selling arrangements and vice versa, advertising rules as relating to products.   **7-282**

---

[362] However, the court found that the national law was permitted under art.36, as it was for the protection of the health and life of animals.

[363] *VFZ v Heinrich Bauer* (C-368/95) [1997] E.C.R. I-3689.

[364] *Tankstation 't Heukske vof and J.B.E. Boermans* (C-401/92 and C-402/92) [1994] E.C.R. I-2199 at [12]–[14]; *Schutzverband gegen unlauteren Wettbewerb v TK-Heimdienst Sass GmbH* (C-254/98) [2000] E.C.R. I-151 at [24]; *Criminal proceedings against Marcel Burmanjer, René Alexander Van Der Linden and Anthony De Jong* (C-20/03) [2005] E.C.R. I-4133 at [25] and [26]; and *A-Punkt Schmuckhandels GmbH v Claudia Schmidt* (C-441/04) [2006] E.C.R. I-2093 at [16].

[365] *Criminal Proceedings against Jean-Pierre Guimont* (C-448/98) [2000] E.C.R. I-10663.

[366] *Applying Smanor* (298/87) [1988] E.C.R. 4489 at [12].

[367] (C-531/07) [2009] E.C.R. I-3717; [2009] 3 C.M.L.R. 26.

[368] See in particular, at [35] where this point was accepted by the CJEU.

[369] See [19]–[21].

[370] *Alfa Vita Vassipolous* (C-158 and C-159/04) [2006] E.C.R. I-08135; [2007] 2 C.M.L.R. 2.

The Advocate-General considered that the pragmatic approach by the court to the application of *Keck* had given rise to uncertainty and inconsistency.

7-283   Ultimately, the CJEU's refusal to discuss at a level of policy the whole approach of arts 34–36 to consumer protection laws is most unsatisfactory. As said by Maduro AG, the real debate can be encapsulated as follows:

> "Is Article [34] of the Treaty a provision intended to liberalise intra-Community trade or is it intended more generally to encourage the unhindered pursuit of commerce in individual Member States?"[371]

7-284   Finally, it should be noted that there is a line of authority that where the legislative measure is wholly internal to a state, arts 34–36 are inapplicable. Thus, in *Glocken*,[372] the CJEU, in considering the compatibility of an Italian law on pasta products, said that it was only concerned with the extension of law to imported products and that EU law did not require the legislature to repeal the law as far as pasta producers established on Italian territory were concerned.[373] This can lead to situations whereby national producers are reverse discriminated against foreign producers, i.e. imported products need not comply with the rules as they are contrary to arts 34–36 but domestic products do.

Application of the "Cassis de Dijon" exceptions

7-285   As discussed earlier, the court in *Cassis de Dijon* said that if the national measure can be justified on the grounds of public interest, it is permissible. After *Cassis de Dijon*, the Commission sent a letter to the Member States containing some policy conclusions.[374] In that communication, the Commission said that where products are manufactured according to a customarily and traditionally accepted way, then exceptions to the principle of free movement of such products would only be admissible under strict conditions. These conditions were that the rules:

(a)   were necessary, in order to satisfy mandatory requirements;

(b)   served a purpose in the general interest which was compelling enough to justify an exception to the principle of free movement of goods; and

(c)   were proportionate.

7-286   The CJEU has adopted the approach of the Commission to the application of *Cassis de Dijon*. First, where the restrictive effect on the free movement of goods is out of proportion to its purpose, then the measure is not permissible.[375] Secondly, where the same objective can be attained by other means which are less of a hindrance to trade, then the measure is not permissible.[376] These principles have been especially applied in the field of food and alcoholic drinks, where the court

---

[371]   Citing Tesauro AG in *Hünermunde* (C-292/92) [1993] E.C.R. I-6787.

[372]   *3 Glocken GmbH and Gertraud Kritzinger v USL Centro-Sud and Provincia autonoma di BolzanoGlocken* (407/85) [1988] E.C.R. 4233.

[373]   See [25]. For an overview of the CJEU's jurisprudence in this area, see C. Ritter, "Purely Internal Situations, Reverse Discrimination, Guimont, Dzodzi and Article 234" [2006] 31(5) E.L. Rev., 690–710.

[374]   Communication from the Commission concerning the consequences of the judgment given by the Court of Justice on 20 February 1979 in *Cassis de Dijon* [1979] OJ C256/2.

[375]   e.g. *Commission of the European Communities v Kingdom of Denmark* (302/86) [1988] E.C.R. 4607, [1989] 1 C.M.L.R. 619.

[376]   See Van Themaat AG in *Industrie Diensten Groep v Beele* (6/81) [1982] E.C.R. 707; [1982] 3 C.M.L.R. 102. Slynn AG again emphasised the principle of alternative means in *Re the Packaging*

has constantly held that if labelling can prevent confusion of the consumer, then a national measure prohibiting imports of certain types of food or drinks, on account of their naming, packaging or bottling on the grounds of danger of public confusion is contrary to art.34.[377]

However, where a marked or packaged good is imported that is misleading to consumers, then an action for a misleading statement will not be contrary to arts 34–36 if the importer has failed to counteract the confusion.[378] The court has upheld the above principles of necessity and proportionality, in several cases concerning art.34, that a generic name for a product cannot be reserved by means of national laws for a national variety to the detriment of other varieties lawfully produced in other Member States.[379] A Dutch rule prohibiting slavish imitation of someone else's product if there is no compelling practical reason for such imitation and the imitation causes confusion was held to fall within the scope of the *Cassis de Dijon* exceptions to be reasonable.[380] A rule of the UK Pharmaceutical Society, requiring dispensing chemists to dispense medicines only as named by the doctor and not to substitute therapeutically-identical brands, was held to fall within art.34 but was covered by the public health grounds in art.36.[381] A provision in German unfair competition laws, which prohibited the circulation of goods with the symbol ®,

7-287

---

of Margarine: EC Commission v Belgium (341/82 and 189/83) (this case was settled after he delivered his Opinion).

[377] e.g. *Prantl* (16/83) [1984] E.C.R. 1299, above; *Cassis de Dijon*, above; *Miro BV* (182/82) [1985] E.C.R. 3731; [1986] 3 C.M.L.R. 545: sale of low-alcohol *"Genever"*, lawfully and traditionally marketed in Belgium could not be prohibited in Netherlands as confusion could be prevented by labelling; *Walter Rau Lebensmittelwerke v De Smedt* (261/81) [1982] E.C.R. 3961, [1983] 2 C.M.L.R. 946: Belgium rules, which required all margarine to be sold in cuboid shapes so as to distinguish it from butter, were contrary to art.34, as other means such as labelling were less harmful to inter-state trade; *Re the Use of Champagne Bottles: EC Commission v Germany* (179/85) [1986] E.C.R. 3879, [1988] 1 C.M.L.R. 135: German legislation, allowing the use of champagne bottles and stoppers only for sparkling wines, could not be invoked to prevent the import of *"Petillant de Raisin"*, which was not a sparkling wine but had been traditionally marketed in champagne-style bottles, as labelling would prevent confusion; *Re German Purity Requirements for Beer: EC Commission v Germany* (128/84) [1985] E.C.R. 3281, [1988] 1 C.M.L.R. 780: German legislation, restricting the use of the word *"bier"* for beer produced according to strict rules which were only met by German manufacturers, was contrary to art.34, as labelling could protect German public expectations; *Ministére Public v Deserbais* (286/86) [1988] E.C.R. 4907, [1989] 1 C.M.L.R. 516: French provision, which prevented EDAM cheese being marketed with a fat content of less than 40 per cent could not be invoked against German EDAM cheese, as consumer confusion could be prevented by labelling. NB. EDAM admitted not to be an indication of origin; *Re German Sausages: EC Commission v Germany* (274/87) [1989] E.C.R. 229, [1989] 2 C.M.L.R. 733: ban on import of low-fat sausages, contrary to art.34, as confusion could be prevented by labelling; *Re Low Fat Cheese: EC Commission v Italy* (196/89 and 210/89) [1990] E.C.R. I-3697, [1992] 2 C.M.L.R. 1: Italian provision that dairy products whose fat content was lower than 45 per cent could not be called cheese (*"formaggio"*) was contrary to art.34, as consumer confusion could be cured by labelling.

[378] See the decision of the Oberlandesgericht Köln in *Re labelling of Dutch poultry* [1990] 2 C.M.L.R. 104: Dutch poultry sold in Germany bore labels specially translated into German that gave consumers the impression that the poultry was local and not foreign. There was no other indication on the get-up to counteract such an impression and this constituted a misleading statement and was not covered by art.34.

[379] e.g. see *"Sekt"* und *"Weinbrand"* case, *EC Commission v Germany* (12/74) [1975] E.C.R. 181, [1975] 1 C.M.L.R. 340; *EC Commission v Italy* (the "vinegar case") (193/80) [1981] E.C.R. 3019, (286/86) [1989] 1 C.M.L.R. 516.

[380] *Industrie Diensten v Beele* (6/81) [1982] E.C.R. 707; [1982] 3 C.M.L.R. 102.

[381] *R. v Pharmaceutical Society of GB Ex p. Association of Pharmaceutical Importers* (C-266/87) [1989] E.C.R. 1295; [1989] 2 C.M.L.R. 751. In this case, the CJEU did not consider whether the provision fell within the *Cassis de Dijon* exception of public health, but there seems little reason why this would not have applied.

where the mark was not protected, was held to be contrary to art.34 and not justifiable under the principles established in *Cassis de Dijon*.[382]

7-288   In *Fachverband der Buch—und Medienwirtschaft v LIBRO Handelgesellschaft mbH*,[383] (which has been discussed above) it was argued that the Austrian law which permitted the fixing of retail prices for the sale of books was in the public interest because books could be considered to be cultural assets and that an erosion of profit margins would mean that it was not possible to finance the production and marketing of more demanding but economically less attractive works. Also, small booksellers which normally offer a wide choice of such books would be driven out of the market by the large booksellers who sell primarily commercial books (such as airport novels). The CJEU, held that the protection of books as cultural objects could not constitute a justification for measures restricting imports within the meaning of art.36[384] but then went on to say (somewhat contradicting its previous statement) in considering the *Cassis de Dijon* exceptions that the protection of books as cultural objects could be considered as an overriding requirement in the public interest but only where the measures were appropriate for achieving the objective of protecting books as cultural objects and did not go beyond what was necessary to achieve such a purpose. It held that a less restrictive measure was appropriate whereby foreign publishers could fix a retail price for the Austrian market which takes the conditions of the Austrian market into account.[385]

Ancillary principles

7-289   The *Dassonville* and *Cassis de Dijon* principles are subject to the following three ancillary principles:

(1)   Member States cannot take or enact any measures which are contrary to or frustrate legislation implemented by the EU pursuant to the EU objectives. Thus, if the EU has introduced a comprehensive and exhaustive regime of legislation in a particular sphere, then Member States have no powers to enact or maintain legislation in that sphere.[386]

(2)   Unfair competition and consumer protection laws usually exist to prevent consumer confusion. As such, it need only be applicable when goods are offered for sale. Thus, the importation per se of goods lawfully marketed in another Member State would not be classified as an unfair practice. The CJEU has recognised this and has held that the actual fact of importation cannot be considered an improper or unfair act which would thus permit derogation from the free movement of goods provisions.[387]

(3)   Measures which prima facie impede imports will not fall within the *Cassis*

---

[382] *Pall v Dahlhausen* (C-238/89) [1990] E.C.R. 4827.

[383] (C-531/07) [2009] E.C.R. I-3717; [2009] 3 C.M.L.R. 26.

[384] See [32] relying upon *Association des Centres distributeurs Édouard Leclerc and Thouars Distribution* (C-229/83) [1981] E.C.R. 1.

[385] See [34]–[36].

[386] e.g. see *Pigs Marketing Board v Raymond Redmond* (83/78) [1978] E.C.R. 2347, [1979] 1 C.M.L.R. 177; *Prantl* (16/83) [1984] E.C.R. 1299; *Re Low Fat Cheese: EC Commission v Italy* [1992] 2 C.M.L.R. 1. See also para.7-093 on EU secondary legislation.

[387] This principle was established in *Beguelin* (22/71) [1971] E.C.R. 181; [1972] C.M.L.R. 81 and applied in *Dansk Supermarket v Imerco* (C-58/80) [1981] E.C.R. 181; [1981] 3 C.M.L.R. 590 at [16].

de Dijon exceptions, if they constitute a means of arbitrary discrimination or a disguised restriction on trade between Member States.[388]

Exhaustion and unfair competition

An important residual question is whether the doctrine of exhaustion applies to the enforcement of unfair competition laws? It should be remembered that this doctrine arose out of the interrelationship between intellectual property and arts 34–36. Often, the importer will not be sued by a private party but by a state organisation responsible for trading standards. In those cases, the laws are not enforced by persons who could be said to have consented to the placing of the product on the market, and so the issue of consent is irrelevant. However, where a claimant is seeking to bring a private action for unfair competition against an importer, does it matter if they originally placed the complained of goods on the market in another Member State?   **7-290**

In *Industrie Diensten v Beele*,[389] a case concerning Dutch laws on slavish imitation and their validity under art.34, Industrie Diensten was seeking to import cable ducts from Germany which were a slavish imitation of a Swedish product whose patent had just expired. The CJEU commented that there was no indication of an agreement or of dependence between Beele and Diensten, the plaintiff and defendant.[390] This observation implies that, where legal and/or economic ties do exist between the parties, then Beele would not have been able to prevent the imports and that if Beele had placed the imitation product on the German market, it would have been deemed to have consented to its marketing in Belgium.[391]   **7-291**

It is arguable that the principle of consent plays no part in the enforcement of consumer protection and unfair competition laws that are concerned with the protection of the consumer. Thus, consumer confusion between two products is no less a concern where two products are placed on the market by the same undertaking than where placed on the market by different independent undertakings. However, in trade mark cases, the CJEU has generally subordinated the need to prevent consumer confusion to the doctrine of consent. Thus, if a trade mark proprietor has applied the mark to goods of differing quality or composition in different Member States, they cannot prevent the circulation of those goods even if such would give rise to consumer confusion.[392] In the author's opinion, in a private action to enforce unfair competition laws, the doctrine of exhaustion of rights is applicable. In short, as with trade marks, the undertaking who wishes to bring proceedings must accept the consequences of their acts of marketing within the EEA.   **7-292**

Unfair competition laws and GIO legislation: arts 34 or 36?

Certain laws of unfair competition are similar to trade marks and have the same objective, namely the prevention of consumer confusion. For instance, laws often   **7-293**

---

[388] *Dassonville* (C-8/74) [1974] E.C.R. 837; [1974] 2 C.M.L.R. 436 at [7].

[389] (6/81) [1982] E.C.R. 707; [1982] 3 C.M.L.R. 102.

[390] See [12].

[391] The decision is somewhat unsatisfactory, because it does not make it clear that art.36 cannot be relied upon in such circumstances.

[392] A trade-mark proprietor, who permits products of differing quality to be placed on the market in the EU under a single brand, must accept the consequences of their actions, even if this gives rise to consumer confusion. See para.3-079.

provide for protection of geographical indications of origin ("GIOs") which are distinct from trade marks. In such circumstances, a party seeking to enforce such provisions against a defendant may well argue that the enforcement of these laws is for the purpose of protection of the consumer and/or for the protection of industrial or commercial property, and justified by art.36. Being able to rely upon art.36 affords more protection for the rights owner than proving that the national measures fall within the *Cassis de Dijon* exceptions under art.34. This is because there are no conditions under art.36 that the law or its enforcement must be necessary, proportionate and that there are not less restrictive ways of preventing consumer confusion.[393] In other words, if an unfair competition law falls within art.36, then its enforcement is permissible without further examination of these criteria. The CJEU has considered in a number of cases whether a law of unfair competition is to be considered under art.34 or art.36. In general, these cases tend to be concerned with the alleged unlawful use of GIOs or traditional speciality guaranteed ("TSG"). The EU has legislated exhaustively in the field of GIOs and TSGs and this is discussed in the Trade Marks chapter (GIOs having similarities with trade marks). Also discussed in that chapter is whether national laws relating to GIOs (including unfair competition laws) are precluded by reason of the exhaustive EU legislation on GIOs and TSGs.[394] This section focuses on the enforceability of unfair competition laws which are exercised against GIOs and TSGs under art.34 or art.36.

7-294   In *Theodor Kohl KG v Ringelhan und Rennett*,[395] a case which has been discussed above, the court held that the protection of the consumer does not fall within art.36.[396] Thus, Jacobs AG said, in *Warsteiner*,[397] that art.36 must be interpreted strictly and cannot be extended to objectives such as protection against unfair competition and consumer protection which are not expressly mentioned therein.[398] Thus, the mere fact that a law is intended to prevent consumer confusion is not sufficient to bring it within art.36 and such laws and their enforcement must be justified in accordance with the *Cassis de Dijon* principles.

7-295   However, insofar as the unfair competition laws specifically relate to GIOs or TSGs, the CJEU's decisions have tended to suggest that such laws would fall to be considered by reference to art.36 and not art.34. In *Sekt und Weinbrand*,[399] an early case in the 1970s, the CJEU was concerned with the lawfulness of German law which attempted to reserve the appellations *"Sekt"* and *"Weinbrand"* to German

---

[393] A rule of proportionality has been held to exist before a state can avail itself of the protection of the "human health" exemption in art.36—see *Criminal Proceedings against Sandoz BV* (174/82) [1983] E.C.R. 2445; [1984] 3 C.M.L.R. 43. However, this should be seen as a condition precedent before art.36 is applicable. It therefore would not appear to pertain to intellectual property rights where it is established that such do not fall within art.36.

[394] See para.3-914.

[395] (177/83) [1984] E.C.R. 3651; [1985] 3 C.M.L.R. 339.

[396] (177/83) [1984] E.C.R. 3651; [1985] 3 C.M.L.R. 339 at [18] and [19].

[397] *SUW v Warsteiner Brauerei* (C-312/98) [2000] E.C.R. I-9187.

[398] *Citing Commission v Ireland* (113/80) [1981] E.C.R. 1625 at [7] and [8], and (177/83) [1984] E.C.R. 3651; [1985] 3 C.M.L.R. 339 which overruled earlier case law of (12/74) [1975] E.C.R. 181, in particular the Opinion of Warner AG at 208. The CJEU in *Warsteiner* did not rule on this point because the question from the national court was merely whether a simple geographical indication fell within the ambit of Reg.2081/92 (now replaced by Reg.1151/2012 (traditional specialities guaranteed), and was thus impermissible. The court held that the regulation did not cover such indications. For discussion on Reg.2081/92 and its successor regulations, see para.3-855, et seq.

[399] *European Commission v Federal Republic of Germany* (12/74) [1975] E.C.R. 181; [1975] 1 C.M.L.R. 339.

sparkling wines with certain qualities. The European Commission brought proceedings on the grounds that the law was unlawful as the appellations were generic which the German legislature had attempted by means of a legislative measure to transform into indirect indications of origin. The Commission argued that as a result, the laws were contrary to arts 34–36. In doing so, it referred to EC Dir.70/50[400] which held that measures which "confine names which are not indicative of origin or source to domestic products only" were to be regarded as contrary to arts 34–36.[401] The CJEU concluded that the terms "*Sekt*" and "*Weinbrand*" were not indications of geographical origin and, therefore, were not protected by art.36. However, in doing so, the CJEU implied that true indications of origin could be protected under art.36. Thus, the court said:

> "[15] The fact that the terms '*Sekt*' und '*Weinbrand*' do not constitute 'indications of origin' signifies that the measures in issue which are included in the legislation on vine products cannot be justified under Article [36] of the Treaty on grounds of the protection of industrial and commercial property."[402]

In *Prantl*,[403] the court suggested that one could not resort to art.36 regarding GIOs   **7-296** relating to bottle shapes where the imported goods had been bottled in accordance with a fair and traditional practice.[404] Again, such suggests that generally, art.36 *is* applicable to GIOs. This was confirmed when, in *Exportur*,[405] the CJEU indicated that signs of provenance (i.e. geographical indications used for products in circumstances where the goods were not dependent for their quality on the geographical region) fell within the meaning of "industrial and commercial property" in art.36. The case concerned the use of the name "*Turron de Alicante*" or "*Turron de Jijona*" for nougat. Under a French-Spanish bilateral agreement, these names had been reserved to nougat from Spain, which complied with Spanish legislation. Two French companies based in Perpignan had produced nougat called, variously, "*Touron Alicante*", "*Touron Jijona*", "*Touron Catalan Type Alicante*" and "*Touron Catalan Type Jijona*". Exportur, the Spanish nougat association, brought proceedings before French courts to prohibit such use under French legislation enacted pursuant to the French-Spanish bilateral agreement. On reference to the CJEU as to whether such laws were compatible with arts 34–36, the CJEU stated that the issue under art.36 was whether the prohibitions contained in the Franco-Spanish Convention were justified by the safeguard of rights which constitute the specific subject-matter of the indications of provenance and designations of origin. The French companies argued that "*Turron de Alicante*" and "*Turron de Jijona*" were not genuine indications of geographical origin in that their quality owed nothing to the geographical areas. They said that the products were, to all intents and purposes, the same. Thus, they said that there could be no recourse to art.36. The CJEU rejected this submission (which was also adopted by the Commission) and said:

> "[37] The aim of the Convention is to prevent the producers of a Contracting State from using the geographical names of another State, thereby taking advantage of the reputation attaching to the products of the undertakings established in the regions

---

[400] Dir.70/50 [1970] OJ C13/29.
[401] art.2(3)(s) Dir.70/50.
[402] See [15].
[403] (C-16/83) [1984] E.C.R. 01299.
[404] See [38].
[405] *Exportur SA v Lor SA and Confiserie du Tech* (C-3/91) [1992] E.C.R. I-5529.

or places indicated by those names. Such an objective, intended to ensure fair competition, may be regarded as falling within the sphere of the protection of industrial and commercial property within the meaning of Article 36, provided that the names in question have not, either at the time of the entry into force of that Convention or subsequently, become generic in the country of origin."

7-297   Thus, the enforcement of national laws relating to what is now known as Protected Geographical Indications ("PGI") as well as Protected Designations of Origins ("PDO") falls to be considered under art.36.[406]

7-298   Subsequent to *Exportur*, the CJEU had to consider, in *Warsteiner*,[407] a situation which was the converse of *Exportur*, namely the enforceability of national legislative consumer protection laws which were aimed at preventing inappropriate use of geographical names. A German brewery, which was based in the town of Warstein in Germany, sold a Pilsener ale called Warsteiner. It acquired a brewery in Paderborn, which was situated 40 km from Warstein. It began to sell pilsener-type beer from this brewery under the same mark. It was common ground that beer brewed in Warstein had no special features attributable to the locality. The reputation of Warsteiner beer derived from the quality of the beer and promotion of the mark. A German consumer association for fair trading brought an action under German unfair trading laws against the brewery on the basis that the mark "Warsteiner" could not be used for beer brewed in the Paderborn brewery as such had no connection with the town Warstein. The brewery responded by saying that it had built up the reputation in Warsteiner beer and that the mark was not a geographical reference but merely an indication of trade origin and the beer owed nothing to the particular characteristics of the area.

7-299   The German courts referred to the CJEU the issue whether the GIO regulation (then Reg.2081/92),[408] precluded the application of a national law which prohibited the potentially misleading use of a "geographical indication of source" (i.e. use of a geographical name where there is no connection between the characteristics of the product and its geographical provenance). The issue of whether EU GIO legislation precludes national laws relating to GIOs (and their misuse) is discussed in Ch.3, the "Trade Marks in Europe".[409] For the purpose of this chapter, it suffices to know that EU GIO legislation is intended to be exhaustive and thus precludes protection of GIOs via national legislation.

7-300   However, in this case, the Advocate-General also considered that it was necessary to reflect upon whether the German law which prohibited geographical indications of source (where the goods did not originate from the place of the geographical name) was compatible with arts 34–36. He said the following:

> "[51]   ... Whether or not simple geographical indications of source such as those at issue in *Exportur* can sensibly be considered to be on a par with mainstream intellectual property rights such as patents, trade marks and copyright, it is none the less clear that in that case the applicant was seeking to enforce a right of at least an analogous nature conferred on it (or its members) by the Convention; it was also clearly regarded as significant by the Court that the protected names and the products manufactured by the undertakings there established had a reputation of

---

[406] For further discussion of PDOs and PGIs, see para.3-855. It should be said that the French–Spanish bilateral agreement would not probably now be enforceable precisely because the EU has legislated exhaustively in the field of PGIs. See para.3-914.

[407] (C-312/98) [2000] E.C.R. I-9187.

[408] Reg.2081/92 and its successors are discussed at para.3-855.

[409] See para.3-914.

which the defendant manufacturers *were taking advantage*. In this case in contrast the applicant, which has no right of any sort to use the geographical indication of source at issue, is seeking to prevent its use by the undertaking which has itself built up the reputation which the name enjoys. *It seems to me that it strains accepted use of Community law concepts to regard the legislation pursuant to which such an action is brought as falling within the scope of 'the protection of industrial and commercial property' within the meaning of Article 36.*

[52]   Moreover, the Court in its case-law on the scope of that derogation has consistently ruled that Article 36 admits derogations from the free movement of goods only to the extent to which they are justified for the purpose of safeguarding rights which constitute the specific subject-matter of such property. The Court has given guidelines as to what constitutes the specific subject-matter of particular types of intellectual property: in the case of patents, for instance, it is the guarantee that the patentee, to reward the creative effort of the inventor, has the exclusive right to use an invention with a view to manufacturing industrial products and putting them into circulation for the first time, as well as the right to oppose infringements; in the case of a trade mark, it is the guarantee that the owner of the trade mark has the exclusive right to use that trade mark for the purpose of putting products protected by the trade mark into circulation for the first time; the guarantee is intended to protect the owner against competitors wishing to take advantage of the status and reputation of the trade mark by selling products illegally bearing the mark. The object of national legislation such as Paragraph 127(1) of the *Markengesetz* is manifestly not to safeguard any comparable rights in connection with indications of source; indeed the Bundesgerichtshof is at pains to stress that, in the absence of an allocation of the indication of source to a specified exclusive holder, it is inappropriate to speak in terms of intellectual property rights. *In my view, the principles developed by the Court in the context of industrial and commercial property in the strict sense of alienable rights such as patents, trade marks and copyright are an inherently inappropriate framework for assessing the lawfulness of national legislation on simple geographical indications of source.*

[53]   Finally I would note that the facts in *Exportur* arose in an entirely different historical and legislative context from those in this case. In *Exportur* the Court was considering a Convention with a much broader aim than that of the national legislation at issue in this case: the Convention sought to protect designations of origin, indications of source and names of certain products, none of which at the time of the facts giving rise to the main proceedings was protected at Community level. *I am not persuaded that the Court's general statement that the objective of that Convention 'may be regarded as falling within the sphere of the protection of industrial and commercial property within the meaning of Article 36' should apply to the much narrower field of simple geographical indications of source, all the more so now that designations of origin are within the scope of the Regulation and protected at Community level pursuant thereto.*

[54]   I accordingly conclude that national legislation such as Paragraph 127(1) of the *Markengesetz* does not fall within the derogation for measures for the protection of industrial and commercial property within the meaning of Article 36 of the Treaty." [Emphasis supplied.]

It is clear that the Advocate-General considered that the fact that the German **7-301** unfair competition law was not seeking to protect the reputation of a GIO to remove it from the scope of art.36 whereas in *Exportur*, the legislation measure in issue was specifically concerned with the protection of the "*Turron*" GIO. In the judgment of the CJEU, it did not consider this issue but merely the referred question and held that Reg.2081/92 did not preclude the application of national legislation which prohibited the potentially misleading use of a geographical indication of source where there was no link between the characteristics of the product and its geographical provenance.[410]

7-302   The interaction of GIO legislation, national laws protecting geographical names and arts 34–36 was also considered in *Budejovický Budvar, národní podnik v Rudolf Ammersin GmbH*.[411] This case concerned the lawfulness under European Union law of a bilateral convention for the protection of designations of the source of agricultural and industrial products between Austria and the Czech Republic which protected the word BUD for beer from the Czech Republic. An Austrian distributor marketed American beer called BUD produced by an American brewery. Budvar, a Czech brewer of "Budweiser Budvar" beer brought proceedings inter alia based on breach of the bilateral convention. It was common ground that BUD was not a designation which fell within EU legislation on GIOs. The Austrian courts referred a number of questions to the CJEU.

7-303   The first question was whether the then EU regulation on GIOs, namely Reg.2081/92, precluded the application of the bilateral convention. The CJEU said that Reg.2081/92 did not preclude the application of the bilateral convention under which "a simple and indirect indication of geographical origin" from that Member State is accorded protection whether or not there is any risk of consumers being misled.[412] This was on the basis that Reg.2081/92 covered only designations of products for which there was a specific link between their characteristics and their geographic origin. It was common ground that BUD was not such a designation. It should be mentioned that subsequent EU legislation now extends protection to "geographical indications of origin". The reader is referred to Ch.3, "Trade Marks in Europe" as to the exhaustive nature of current GIO legislation.[413]

7-304   More importantly, for the purpose of this chapter, was the second question referred by the Austrian court which was whether the bilateral convention was compatible with arts 34–36. The CJEU held, applying *Exportur*, that legislation which sought to protect producers of a state from using the geographical names of another state and thereby taking advantage of the reputation of the products of undertakings established in the regions or places indicated by those names fell within the sphere of protection of industrial and commercial property within the meaning of art.36 provided such had not become generic.[414] It said that:

> "[101] Therefore, if the findings of the national court show that according to factual circumstances and perceptions in the Czech Republic the name Bud designates a region or a place located on the territory of that State and its protection is justified there on the basis of the criteria laid down in Article [36], that does not preclude such protection from being extended to the territory of a Member State such as, in this case, the Republic of Austria (see, to that effect, *Exportur*, paragraph 38)." [Emphasis supplied.]

7-305   However, it held that if the bilateral agreement sought to protect a name which did not directly or indirectly refer to the geographic source of the product that it is designated, such was prohibited by art.34.[415]

7-306   The CJEU's ruling on this case was reconsidered in a subsequent case between

---

[410] This was the actual question referred to the CJEU by the German court.
[411] (C-216/01) [2003] E.C.R. I-13617.
[412] See [78].
[413] See para.3-914.
[414] See [99].
[415] See [111].

the same parties.[416] By this time, Reg.2081/92 had been replaced by Reg.510/2006. The CJEU found that such precluded the bilateral Austria-Czech Republic convention.[417] However, as it had been referred, the CJEU clarified para.101 set out above and confirmed that designations of origin fell within the scope of industrial and commercial property rights.[418] The CJEU held that to determine whether such name was a designation of origin, the national court:

> "[94] ... must ascertain whether, according to factual circumstances and perceptions prevailing in the Czech Republic, that designation, even if it is not in itself a geographical name, is at least capable of informing consumer that the product bearing that indication comes from a particular place or region of that Member State."

Such was to be determined by the national court if necessary by reference to a consumer survey.[419]

In summary, the following can tentatively be said: **7-307**

(1) Sui generis national legislation which seeks to regulate the use of GIOs will generally be unenforceable as the EU has legislated in this area in an exhaustive manner. European legislation on GIOs and the permissibility of national laws in the field of GIOs is discussed in Ch.3, "Trade Marks in Europe".[420] It should be noted as discussed in that chapter that if the GIO is not *registrable* under EU GIO legislation, then it would appear that national law governing the use of that GIO is permissible.

(2) Where national laws protecting geographical indications are not precluded from enforcement by exhaustive EU legislation relating to geographical indications of origin, then art.36 and not art.34 is applicable. Thus, it is not necessary to demonstrate that whether such a measure is proportionate or whether a measure which was less restrictive would achieve the same aim.

(3) Where national legislation seeks to prevent the use of a name which does not directly or indirectly refer to the geographic source of a product then national legislation protecting such is not permissible under arts 34–36.

ARTICLE 101, ASSIGNMENTS AND TRADE MARKS

Article 101(1) TFEU prohibits all agreements between undertakings, decisions   **7-308**
by associations of undertakings and concerted practices which may affect trade between Member States and which have as their object or effect the prevention, restriction or distortion of competition within the Common Market.[421] Prima facie, it is not apparent how the mere exercise of an intellectual property right falls within art.101. Indeed, unsurprisingly, the CJEU has held that a patent by itself does not constitute an agreement or concerted practice but results from a grant by a state.[422]

---

[416] *Budejovický Budvar, národní podnik v Rudolf Ammersin GmbH* (C-478/07) [2009] E.C.R. I-7721.
[417] This is discussed at para.3-914.
[418] See [110].
[419] See [89].
[420] See para.3-914.
[421] The relationship of art.101 and intellectual property to licensing agreements is discussed in depth in Ch.8.
[422] *Parke, Davis and Co v Probel* (24/67) [1968] E.C.R 81; [1968] C.M.L.R. 70.

Similarly, the court has ruled the same in relation to trade marks[423] and industrial design rights.[424]

7-309   However, the CJEU has consistently ruled that the exercise of a right may fall within art.101(1) if it is the object, the means or the result of an agreement, decision or concerted practice whose object or effect is to distort competition within the Common Market.[425] This is discussed elsewhere in this book.[426] This aspect of art.101 is not contentious. Clearly, the effect of art.101 would be undermined if the exercise of intellectual property rights could defeat a finding that there was an anti-competitive practice.[427] Its effect is that parallel imports of goods subject to intellectual property rights cannot be prevented even if such goods were not placed on the market by the rights owner or with their consent.

7-310   In this section, there is discussed some early CJEU authorities which appeared to suggest that in the context of assignments, art.101 could be invoked.

7-311   Thus, in a case in the 1970s, the CJEU in *Sirena v Eda*[428] sought to prevent the exercise of trade-mark rights by recourse to art.101, which had a common origin and which had the effect of establishing rigid frontiers between Member States. The *Sirena* case and its consequences for parallel imports are discussed below, and in particular, whether the "common origin" doctrine has survived under art.101. This doctrine and its demise has already been discussed within the context of arts 34–36.[429]

Sirena v Eda[430]

7-312   Rights to a trade mark in Italy had been assigned by the original American proprietor in 1937 to Sirena. Subsequently, a German company was permitted to use the mark in Germany by the American proprietor. A parallel importer imported goods from Germany bearing the trade mark into Italy. Sirena sought to exercise its trade-mark rights against the parallel importer but the national court referred to the CJEU the question of whether the exercise of the rights was contrary to arts 101 and 102.

7-313   The CJEU held that the simultaneous assignment to several concessionaires of national trade mark rights for the same product if it has the effect of re-establishing rigid frontiers between Member States may prejudice trade between Member States and distort competition. It held that:

> "[11]   Article [101] therefore is applicable[431] to the extent to which trade mark rights are invoked so as to prevent imports of products which originate in different Member

---

[423] *Sirena v Eda* (40/70) [1971] C.M.L.R. 260; [1971] E.C.R. 69. Also (51/75) [1976] 2 C.M.L.R. 235 at [26].

[424] *Keurkoop v Nancy Kean* (144/81) [1982] E.C.R. 2853, [1983] 2 C.M.L.R. 47 at [27].

[425] *Sirena v Eda* (40/70) [1971] C.M.L.R. 260; [1971] E.C.R. 69 at [9]. This has been reiterated in several judgments of the CJEU, e.g. *Deutsche Grammophon v Metro* [1971] 1 C.M.L.R. 631 at [6]; (15/74) [1974] 2 C.M.L.R. 238 at [38]–[41]; *EMI v CBS* (51/75) [1976] E.C.R. 811, [1976] 2 C.M.L.R. 235, point 27; *Nancy Kean v Keurkoop* (144/81) [1982] E.C.R. 2853, [1983] 2 C.M.L.R. 47 at [27].

[426] See paras 8-435 and 14-013.

[427] As recognised by the CJEU in (C-56/64) [1966] E.C.R. 299; [1966] C.M.L.R. 418.

[428] (40/70) [1971] E.C.R. 69; [1971] C.M.L.R. 260.

[429] See para.7-209.

[430] (40/70) [1971] E.C.R. 69; [1971] C.M.L.R. 260.

[431] It has been suggested that the word "applicable" here should be read in the context of [9]–[12] of the case to mean that such an assignment is capable of being prohibited under art.101 but is not

States, which bear the same trade mark by virtue of the fact that the proprietors have acquired it, or the right to use it, whether by agreements between themselves or by agreements with third parties. Article [101] is not precluded from applying merely because, under national legislation trade mark rights may originate in legal or factual circumstances other than the abovementioned agreements, such as registration of the trade mark, or its undisturbed use."

The decision fits uneasily into the framework of art.101. It appears to prohibit any exercise of trade mark rights which have a common origin against products bearing the same trade mark and origin. As has been commented on, neither the Advocate-General nor the court ever really examined the true nature of an outright trade-mark assignment in the context of the provisions of art.101.[432] This may be of importance because there may be legitimate reasons for the division of trade mark rights.[433]   **7-314**

The CJEU's decision in *Sirena* has been criticised and distinguished by subsequent courts and Advocate-Generals. The difficulties that the *Sirena* case gives rise to can be illustrated as follows. Suppose Sirena had sued a genuine pirate, as well as the parallel importer, who illegally affixed the "Prep" mark to shaving-foam products. As art.101 was applicable against the parallel importer, then art.101(2) meant that the assignment was void, being the only voidable agreement in issue. Thus, the pirate could argue that, as the assignment was void, the Italian undertaking did not have title to the Italian trade-mark rights. In reality, there was no underlying anti-competitive agreement which the court could point to as being anti-competitive.   **7-315**

In *HAG I*,[434] Mayras AG said in relation to *Sirena* that: **7-316**

"in the case of assignment pure and simple of the trade mark right, it is more difficult to discern, in the absence of special circumstances, an agreement which has the object or effect of restricting competition. It is in fact of the very nature of such an assignment to constitute a total transfer of the right and to confer on the transferee the very prerogatives held by the transferor."

He thus considered that the court in *Sirena* had gone too far, and concluded that it seemed that there were certain factual elements in the court file which revealed the presence of concerted practices condemned by art.101.[435]   **7-317**

In *EMI v CBS*,[436] the court again considered whether art.101 could prevent the exercise of rights by one party against another, where both derived their rights from a common origin. The assignments which had brought about a division of rights had occurred a long time before the Treaty of Rome came into force. Warner AG said that he found the decision of *Sirena* difficult to understand and that, if it had been decided at the date of giving his opinion, it would have been decided under arts 34–36. He held that the prohibition in art.101 could not extend to an agreement made   **7-318**

---

necessarily so prohibited–see G.F. Kunze, "Waiting for Sirena II-Trade Mark Assignment in the Case Law of the CJEU of Justice" (1991) I.I.C. 319, 331.

[432] See C. Morcom, "Trade Marks in the European Community After Cafe HAG II" in *Trade Mark Reporter*, Vol.81, No.5 (USTA), p.549. See also G.F. Kunze, "Waiting for Sirena II-Trade Mark Assignment in the Case Law of the CJEU of Justice" (1991) I.I.C. 319.

[433] e.g. liquidation of subsidiary companies of trade mark owner.

[434] (192/73) [1974] E.C.R. 731; [1974] 2 C.M.L.R. 127.

[435] This concern is seen in the approach under EU law to assignments of IPRs under arts 34–36 where there is evidence of continuing co-operation or concerted practices—see para.7-162.

[436] (51/75) [1976] E.C.R. 811; [1976] 2 C.M.L.R. 235.

and terminated before the entry into force of the Treaty, because the Treaty did not have retroactive effect nor could it extend to the mere consequences of such an agreement such as the exercise of trade mark rights. The court agreed with the Advocate-General and held that:

> "For Article [101] to apply to a case, such as the present one, to agreements which are no longer in force, it is sufficient that such agreements continue to produce their effects after they have formally ceased to be in force.
> An agreement is only regarded as continuing to produce its effects if, from the behaviour of the persons concerned, there may be inferred the existence of elements of concerted practice and of co-ordination peculiar to the agreement and producing the same result as that envisaged by the agreement.
> This is not the case when the said effects do not exceed those flowing from the mere exercise of the national trade mark rights."[437]

7-319   Thus, *Sirena* was tacitly overruled[438] in relation to assignments which occurred before the Treaty of Rome entered into force. In *Ideal Standard*,[439] the CJEU stated that:

> "where undertakings independent of each other make trade mark assignments following a market sharing agreement, the prohibition of anti-competitive agreements under Article [101] applies and assignments which give effect to that agreement are consequently void. However, before a trade mark assignment could be treated as giving effect to an agreement prohibited under Article [101], it was necessary to analyse the context, the commitments underlying the assignment and the intention of the parties and the consideration for the assignment."[440]

7-320   Obiter dicta, such a ruling means that an assignment per se can never be allowed to result in an adverse finding under art.101 where one party seeks to exercise its trade mark rights against the import of products bearing the same mark from another Member State. As such, the decision would appear to tacitly overrule *Sirena* in its entirety.[441] Only where the assignments are carried out as the instrument of an anti-competitive agreement in order to partition the single market or insulate national markets will it be contrary to art.101.

7-321   More difficult issues arise where the owner of the trade mark unilaterally decides to assign a trade mark to a third party because of the difficulties that parallel imports is causing to the profitability of their enterprise.

Example
The UK owner of parallel trade marks for a pharmaceutical decided to assign the registered trade mark for Spain to a Spanish concern with which it has no legal or economic connections. The UK owner does so because they want to insulate the UK from the Spanish market where pharmaceutical prices are much less than in UK. It makes more economic sense to sell the registered trade mark than to licence its use for the Spanish

---

[437] At 267.
[438] See also Jacobs AG in *HAG II* (C-10/89) [1990] E.C.R. I-3711; [1990] 3 C.M.L.R. 571, where he said that the rule in *Sirena* had been importantly modified by the CJEU's decision in *EMI v CBS*. See also C. Morcom, "Trade Marks in the European Community After Cafe HAG II", *Trade Mark Reporter*, 81(5) (USTA); and G.F. Kunze, "Waiting for Sirena II-Trade Mark Assignment in the Case Law of the CJEU of Justice" (1991) I.I.C. 319.
[439] (C-9/93) [1994] E.C.R. I-2789; [1994] 3 C.M.L.R. 857.
[440] See [59].
[441] See G. Tritton, "Articles 28 to 30 and Intellectual Property: Is the jurisprudence of the CJEU now of an Ideal Standard" [1994] E.I.P.R. 423.

market because the former option means that parallel imports cannot occur. After the assignment, neither the UK nor the Spanish concern engage in any form of concerted practice or co-operative behaviour.

Analysis

The intention of the trade mark proprietor is to partition the market and prevent damaging parallel imports. However, such is a unilateral intention. Thus, although there is an agreement to assign, there is no agreement between the Spanish and the UK concern to engage in anti-competitive activities, i.e. artificially partition the EC. Such partitioning arises because of the assignment but not because of a prior market-sharing agreement (see *EMI v CBS*). In such circumstances, it is submitted that art.101 is inapplicable.[442]

FREE TRADE AGREEMENTS COUNTRIES

Historically, countries entered into Free Trade Agreements ("FTAs") with the EU **7-322** prior to joining it. Such agreements were seen as stepping stones to joining the EU. They were not intended to provide a single market but to remove certain barriers to trade. Thus, the aim of the agreements was more limited than that of the European Treaties which was intended to create a single market and common customs union. In the case of *Polydor Ltd v Harlequin Records*,[443] gramophone records had been lawfully made in Portugal by licensees of the copyright owner. These records were exported to the UK, where the British licensee sought to prevent such imports as being unlawful under British copyright law. At that time, Portugal was not a member of the EU but had an FTA with it. Articles 14(2) and 23 of the FTA were virtually identical to arts 34 and 36. However, the CJEU held that the case law on arts 34–36 was peculiar to the EU and did not apply to third countries, who were the subject of an FTA agreement with the EU. In particular, the FTA did not have as its purpose the creation of a single market reproducing, as closely as possible, a domestic market.[444] Similarly, courts in FTA countries have held that the doctrine of consent is not applicable to FTA.[445] Accordingly, the CJEU held that the copyright owner was entitled to prevent the importation of the gramophone records from Portugal and that it had not exhausted its right. This approach was also initially taken by the EFTA Court in *Mag Instrument, Inc v California Trading* where it held that the EEA Agreement did not establish a customs union and thus, EFTA states were free to adopt an international exhaustion of rights principle.[446]

In general, when considering provisions in FTAs which are similar to those in **7-323** the TFEU, the approach of the CJEU in *Polydor* must be applied with care. Although the interpretation of provisions in the TFEU cannot be applied by way

---

[442] It is not sufficient that there is an agreement between the parties—see para.8-080 and *Unipart Group Ltd v 02 (UK) Ltd* [2005] E.C.C. 9 CA. It should be noted that the exercise of rights in such circumstances might also be considered contrary to art.36(2): see para.7-086. In contrast, see *Bolton Pharmaceutical Co 100 Ltd v Doncaster Pharmaceuticals Group Ltd* [2006] E.T.M.R 65; [2007] F.S.R. 3 CA (England and Wales) discussed at para.7-091 where the Court of Appeal considered a similar situation where it was argued that the divesting by a British company of its Spanish registered trade mark to avoid the effect of substantial parallel imports from Spain into the UK was contrary to arts 34–36 but not under art.101.

[443] (270/80) [1982] E.C.R. 329; [1982] 1 C.M.L.R. 677.

[444] See [18].

[445] See *Bosshard Partners Intertrading AG v Sunlight AG* [1980] 3 C.M.L.R. 664 (Switzerland) and *Austro Mechana v Gramola Winter & Co* [1984] 2 C.M.L.R. 626 (Austria which at the time was a FTA country).

[446] *Mag Instrument, Inc v California Trading Co Norway* (E-2/97) [1998] 1 C.M.L.R. 331; [1998] E.T.M.R. 85, EFTA Court. However, it then reversed its position—see para.7-334.

of simple analogy to the corresponding provisions of a free-trade agreement, such an approach must be seen in its proper perspective and it is not intended to encourage or justify in general terms divergent interpretations of the TFEU and the corresponding rules in free-trade agreements to which the EU is a party. In substance, the CJEU's approach in *Polydor* constitutes no more than the application of a general principle of legal interpretation, as seen in the Vienna Convention on the Law of Treaties, whereby a rule is to be interpreted in the context in which it appears. Thus, whilst it is true in principle that an interpretation given by the court in the context of the TFEU is not automatically applicable in the context of an agreement with a non-Member State, it is also equally true that, when faced with provisions drafted in substantially identical terms and laying down rules of fundamental importance in the context either of the EC Treaty or of an FTA, it is still necessary to determine the specific reasons which may lead to a divergent interpretation.[447]

7-324   Thus, in *Eurim-Pharm GmbH v Bundesgesundheitsamt*,[448] a parallel importer, Eurim-Pharm, wished to import Adalat R, a pharmaceutical product, placed on the market in Austria into Germany by Bayer AG. It made an application to the German health authority (*Bundesgesundheitsamt*) for authorisation to market Adalat R in Germany. This was refused on the grounds that Eurim-Pharm had not supplied the necessary documentation even though Bayer AG had supplied such already in relation to Adalat R. It was accepted that under the authority of *De Peijper*, it was contrary to arts 34–36 to make the grant of market authorisation subject to the production of documents which had already been supplied to the relevant health authority by the manufacturer.[449] Although, at the time, Austria was not a member of the EU, the EEC (as it then was) had entered into an agreement with Austria of which arts 13 and 20 were essentially identical to arts 34–36 which was the subject matter of a Council Regulation.

7-325   Thus, the main issue in the proceedings referred to the CJEU was whether arts 13 and 20 of the EEC-Austria agreement (i.e the Council Regulation) meant that the approach in *De Peijper* which derived from a consideration of their mirror provisions in the EU treaties should apply to imports from Austria. Submissions were made by the UK, Italy and the European Commission that such an approach could not apply to the free trade agreement as the latter made no provision for harmonisation of legislation or for administrative co-operation in the pharmaceutical sector. In short, the EEC-Austria agreement was far less integrationist than the EU Treaties and had much more modest aims. However, in a short judgment, the CJEU rejected this submission and held that such a submission would deprive the rules "of much of their effectiveness."[450]

7-326   It is difficult to reconcile *Eurim-Pharm* with *Polydor* unless one takes the view that the doctrine of exhaustion of intellectual property rights developed under art.36 is intimately linked to the notion of a common customs union and single market whereas *De Peijper* and *Eurim-Pharm* were simply concerned with the legitimacy of quantitative restrictions under art.34. As discussed later, the EFTA Court now takes the view that the EEA is sufficiently similar in its objectives to the EU to war-

---

[447] Tesauro AG in *Eurim-Pharm Bundesgesundheisamt* (C-207/91) [1993] E.C.R 3723 at [15]–[16]. See also C. Worth, "Free Trade Agreements and the Exhaustion of Rights Principle: Eurim Pharm v Bundesgesundheitsamt" [1994] 1 E.I.P.R. 40, 41.

[448] See (C-207/91) [1993] E.C.R. 3723.

[449] *De Peijper* (C-104/75) [1976] E.C.R. 613.

[450] See [25].

rant the same approach to the interpretation of secondary EU IP legislation providing for EU exhaustion of rights—see para.7-344.

TRANSITIONAL PROVISIONS FOR ACCEDING STATES

In many cases, there will be transitional provisions for countries that accede to the EU. These provisions will seek to provide a gradual transition so that EU law is not instantaneously applicable in relation to the acceding state. This is particularly the case in relation to the application of the doctrine of exhaustion of rights to products protected by IPRs. Furthermore, art.351 of the TFEU (ex-art.307 EU Treaty) stipulates that: **7-327**

> "The rights and obligations arising from agreements concluded before 1 January 1958 or, for acceding States, before the date of their accession, between one or more Member States on the one hand, and one or more third countries on the other, shall not be affected by the provisions of the Treaties.
>
> To the extent that such agreements are not compatible with the Treaties, the Member State or States concerned shall take all appropriate steps to eliminate the incompatibilities established. Member States shall, where necessary, assist each other to this end and shall, where appropriate, adopt a common attitude."

In such cases, it may be that the application of the provisions of arts 34–36 and their case law are delayed or suspended. In *Budejovický Budvar, národní podnik v Rudolf Ammersin GmbH*,[451] which has been discussed above,[452] the CJEU had to consider whether a bilateral agreement entered in 1976 into between Austria (not then a Member State of the EU) and the Czechoslovakian Republic (also then not a Member State) by which the appellation "BUD" was protected for Czechoslovakian beer could be relied upon even if the bilateral agreement was contrary to arts 34–36. It held that in principle, art.351 applied to the bilateral convention. However, a complicating factor was that the Czechoslovakian Republic had split into the Czech Republic and the Slovakian Republic. The CJEU noted that in accordance with the second paragraph of art.351 (set out above) that Member States are required to take all appropriate steps to eliminate incompatibilities between an agreement entered into prior to the Member State's accession and the EU treaties and such would require the Member State (Austria) to ascertain whether the incompatibility could be avoided by interpreting the bilateral convention in a manner as to be inconsistent with EU law. However, it held that if this was "impracticable" such that it "encounters difficulties which makes adjustment of an agreement impossible" (which could include denouncing the agreement), then the bilateral convention applied "insofar as it contains obligations which remain binding on that state under international law".[453]   **7-328**

In *Generics (UK) Ltd v Smith Kline and French Laboratories*, the UK Court of Appeal referred to the CJEU as to whether a ban in a compulsory licence against pharmaceutical imports from Spain and Portugal, was contrary to arts 34–36. Although both were Member States, arts 47 and 209 of the Acts of Accession of Spain and Portugal expressly permitted the holders of pharmaceutical patents in the EU to exercise their rights against products from Spain and Portugal, even if the products had been placed on the market by the patentee or with the patentee's   **7-329**

---

[451] (C-216/01) [2003] E.C.R. I-13617.
[452] See para.7-302.
[453] See [170]–[173].

consent, provided such rights were exercised prior to the expiry of the third year after Spain or Portugal had made pharmaceutical products patentable. The CJEU held that terms of the licence may, on the basis of those provisions, prohibit the licensee from importing from Spain and Portugal a patented pharmaceutical product if national law conferred upon the patent owner the right to prevent imports and if the proprietor demonstrated an intention to exercise the right conferred upon them by arts 47 and 209.[454]

7-330   In *Merck v Primecrown*,[455] the CJEU held that the transitional provisions relating to the Accession of Spain and Portugal to the EC should be interpreted so as to ensure the earliest application of the free movement of goods, being exactly three years after pharmaceutical products became patentable.[456] Thus, the transitional periods expired on 6 October 1995 for Spain and 31 December 1994 for Portugal.

7-331   In a case referred to the CJEU by the English Court of Appeal in 2013, *Merck Canada Inc v Sigma Pharmaceuticals Plc*[457] the court was concerned with the interpretation of similar provisions in the Treaty of Accession applicable to the following Member States who acceded in 2004—Czech Republic, Estonia, Cyprus, Latvia, Lithuania, Hungary, Malta, Poland, Slovakia, and Slovenia. As with Spain and Portugal, in 2004, a number of these states had not historically permitted the patenting of pharmaceutical products. Although by 2004, all of these states did permit the patenting of pharmaceutical products, this meant that pharmaceutical companies had historically been unable to obtain patents for some of these accession countries although they had patents in other Member States. Thus, as patents could not be obtained retrospectively and patents were not obtainable in 2004 (because of prior marketing of pharmaceutical products), despite the change in law, pharmaceutical companies were unable to obtain patents in these accession countries. Accordingly, a specific derogation from arts 34–36 was negotiated as part of the accession arrangements and this is called the "Specific Mechanism."[458] This was written in a very similar manner to arts 47 and 209 of the Act of Accession of Spain and Portugal. It provided for a derogation from the doctrine of exhaustion of rights. However, it stipulated that any person intending to import or market a pharmaceutical product into a Member State where such had been placed on the market in the accession countries by the holder of a patent in that Member State had to give one month's prior notification to the holder of the patent of owner of a supplemental protection certificate. An issue was raised in the Court of Appeal that a proper interpretation of the Specific Mechanism meant that not only had notification to be given to the patentee but also that the patentee had to inform the notifying parallel importer that it objected to the importation of the products. This was based upon the fact that in *Generics (UK)* (discussed above) similar provisions in the Act of Accession of Spain and Portugal had been interpreted by the CJEU to require the patentee to notify its objection.[459]

7-332   The Court of Appeal considered that it was not acte clair as to whether the

---

[454] See *Generics (UK) Ltd v Smith Kline and French Laboratories Ltd* (C-191/90) [1992] E.C.R. I-5335; [1993] 1 C.M.L.R. 89; [1993] F.S.R. 592 at 615. See also *The Wellcome Foundation Ltd v Discpharm* [1993] F.S.R. 433 (a UK decision on similar facts) and its' Case Comment by J. Jones, "Exhaustion of Rights: Pharmaceutical Marketed in Spain-a Wellcome Exception" [1993] March E.I.P.R. 107.

[455] (267–268/95) [1996] E.C.R. I-6285.

[456] Applying (C-191/90) [1992] E.C.R. I-5335 at [41].

[457] [2013] 3 C.M.L.R. 17 CA (England).

[458] See Annex IV, Chapter 2 to the Act of Accession.

[459] See *Generics (UK) v Smith Kline & French*, at [42].

patentee or SPC owner had to notify the parallel importer of its objection once it had received notice from the parallel importer. This was important to the case because the parallel importer had notified the patentee in writing of its intention to import but upon receipt of that, the latter had failed to notify the former of its objection. It thus referred this issue to the CJEU. The Court of Appeal also referred to the CJEU the issues regarding which organisation had to make the notification and to whom the notification had to be made. In *Merck v Sigma*, notification had been made by the applicant for regulatory approval in the Member State into which the products were to be imported (as opposed to the importer itself) and notification had been made to the operating company which was the subsidiary of the holder of the patent.

In its judgment[460] the Court of Justice held, following *Generics (UK) Ltd & Harris Pharmaceuticals v Smith Kline & French*, that the Specific Mechanism did not impose a legal obligation on the SPC holder or patentee to give notification of its intention to oppose the proposed importation within one month of notification. However, if it did not do so, it could not rely upon its rights to prevent parallel imports carried out before such an intention was indicated. Here, the Court of Justice strikes a balance by deeming the right holder as having forfeited the right to compensation for parallel imports imported and marketed *prior* to the notification of its opposition but being able to oppose future importation and marketing of the goods once it has indicated its intention to oppose such parallel imports.   **7-333**

The Court of Justice also held that notification had to be given to the patentee, SPC holder or beneficiary of the patent or SPC: such term being used to designate any person enjoying the rights conferred by law on the patent or SPC, i.e. a licensee. However, it held that it was not necessary for the person intending to import or market the pharmaceutical product in question to give notification themselves, provided that it was possible from the notification to identify that person clearly.[461]   **7-334**

THE EEA, FREE MOVEMENT OF GOODS AND INTELLECTUAL PROPERTY

The EEA Agreement is discussed generally in Ch.1. In terms of integration, the objectives of the EEA Agreement must be considered to fall between the limited aims of the Free Trade Agreements between the EU and individual countries and the fully-integrative objectives of the EU Treaties.   **7-335**

Articles 11–13 of the EEA Agreement are identical in substance to arts 34–36 of the TFEU but apply to all Contracting Parties to the EEA. Thus, art.11 provides quantitative restrictions on imports and all measures having equivalent effect are prohibited between contracting states. Article 13 contains the same derogation from art.11 as art.36 does to art.34 of the TFEU.   **7-336**

Article 8(2) of the EEA Agreement provided that *unless otherwise specified*, arts 11–13 of the EEA Agreement (those that correspond to arts 34–36 of the TFEU) only apply to goods "originating" in the territory of contracting parties. Such a provision does not have its counterpart in the TFEU. The reason for this provision of "origination" is that the EEA does not entail a customs union but simply a free trade area. EFTA countries are free to maintain their own commercial policies   **7-337**

---

[460] (C–539/13) EU:C:2015:87.
[461] See [50].

including customs tariffs with third (non-EEA) countries.[462] The EEA Agreement has complex and detailed provisions as to the meaning of "origination".[463] In general, the main principle is that a product can be considered to be originating in the EEA if it is specified in art.4 of Protocol 4 or products are obtained in the EEA *"incorporating materials which have not been wholly obtained there, provided that such materials have undergone sufficient working or processing in the EEA"*. Therefore, contracting parties to the EEA are free to impose restrictions on trade in non-EEA originating goods between EEA states.

7-338   Against these general provisions, the EEA Agreement also has provisions that deal with intellectual property. Hence, as discussed in Ch.1, Annex 17 contains a list of EU IP Directives that the EEA has adopted as *acquis communautaire*.[464] As these EU IP Directives include exhaustion of rights which are limited to the EU, Annex 17 (through the mechanism of Protocol 1 EEA on Horizontal Adaptations) substitutes the wording of the territories of the Contracting Parties to the EEA for the EU. Thus, the exhaustion of rights provisions in the EU IP Directives is extended from being EU-wide to EEA-wide.[465]

7-339   Article 62(2) of the EEA Agreement states that Protocol 28 and Annex 17 contain specific provisions and arrangements concerning intellectual, industrial and commercial property which "unless otherwise specified, shall apply to all products and services".

7-340   Finally, Protocol 28 to the EEA Agreement on Intellectual Property provides as follows:

"Article 1
1. For the purposes of this Protocol, the term "intellectual property" shall include the protection of industrial and commercial property as covered by Article 13 of the Agreement.
2. Without prejudice to the provisions of this Protocol and of Annex XVII, the Contracting Parties shall upon the entry into force of the Agreement adjust their legislation on intellectual property so as to make it compatible with the principles of free circulation of goods and services and with the level of protection of intellectual property attained in Community law, including the level of enforcement of those rights.
3. Subject to the procedural provisions of the Agreement and without prejudice to the provisions of this Protocol and of Annex XVII, the EFTA States will adjust, upon request and after consultation between the Contracting Parties, their legislation on intellectual property in order to reach at least the level of protection of intellectual property prevailing in the Community upon signature of the Agreement

Article 2
1. To the extent that exhaustion is dealt with in Community measures or jurisprudence, the Contracting Parties shall provide for such exhaustion of intellectual property rights as

---

[462] T. Blanchet, R. Piipponen, M. Westman-Clément, *The Agreement on the European Economic Area* (Oxford: Oxford University Press, 1994), p.52.
[463] See Protocol 4 to the EEA Agreement.
[464] This is often added as the EU adopts new IPR Directives and regulations.
[465] It should be noted that in Annex 17, for the first Trade Mark Directive, this was done expressly by art.4 to Annex 17. However, art.4 has now been deleted and with the adoption of Dir.2008/95/EC (the penultimate Trade Mark Directive), art.9h to Annex 17 no longer includes this provision as the same result is achieved through Protocol 1 (Horizontal Adaptations). See *L'Oréal Norge AS v Per Aarskog AG and Nille AS; L'Oréal Norge AS and L'Oréal SA v Smart Club AS* (E-9/07 & E-10/07) at [34] where the EFTA Court explains how the EU-wide exhaustion of rights principle for the Information Society Directive (Dir.2001/29) is extended to the EEA via point 8, Protocol 1 EEA and for other Directives.

laid down in Community law. Without prejudice to the future developments of case law, these provisions shall be interpreted in accordance with the meaning established in the relevant rulings of the Court of Justice of the European Communities given prior to the signature of the Agreement.

2. As regards patent rights, its provision shall take effect at the latest one year after the entry into force of the Agreement."

Finally, under art.6 of the EEA Agreement, insofar as they are identical, the EEA Articles must be interpreted in conformity with rulings given by the CJEU prior to 2 May 1992 in relation to arts 34–36.[466] In relation to judgments given by the CJEU after that date, the EFTA Court must pay "due account" of them.[467] **7-341**

The above legal framework makes it clear that under the EEA Agreement, there is an EEA-wide exhaustion of rights principle. As all EU Member States are contracting parties to EEA Agreement, that is why the national legislation, e.g. trade mark law extends the exhaustion of rights principle to goods placed on the market in the EEA by the trade mark owner or with its consent. **7-342**

However, for some time there was considerable debate on the following three issues: **7-343**

- Does the EEA-wide exhaustion of rights principle extend to goods that do *not* "originate" (within the technical meaning discussed above) from within the EEA but are placed on the market in the EEA by the registered proprietor of the IPR or with his consent?
- Are EEA states not members of the EU obliged under the EEA Agreement to exclude an international exhaustion of rights principle?
- Does the principle of EEA-wide exhaustion of rights extend to unitary rights such as the EU Trade Mark or Community Design?[468]

On the first and second issue, within the context of the exhaustion of rights principle in the Trade Mark Directive, this was resolved by the EFTA Court in *L'Oréal Norge AS v Per Aarskog AS*.[469] Overturning its earlier decision in *Mag Instrument Inc v California Trading Company Norway*,[470] it held that a proper interpretation of the EEA Agreement and in particular, art.65(2) EEA (which applied to all goods regardless of their origination), Protocol 28 and that the differences between the EEA Agreement and the EC Treaty (as it then was) were not sufficient to constitute compelling grounds for divergent interpretation of the exhaustion of rights provision in the Trade Mark Directive, meant that the EEA precluded EEA states from adopting an international exhaustion of rights principle for trade marks regardless of the origin of the goods in question. Thus, on the first two issues, there is exhaustion if the goods are placed on the market in the territory of the EEA by the trade mark owner or with their consent and there is no exhaustion if the goods are placed outside the EEA. The EFTA Court's reasoning **7-344**

---

[466] art.6 EEA Agreement. The date of 2 May 1992 is when the EEA Agreement was signed (see art.6).
[467] art.3(2) ESA/Court Agreement. See para.1-142.
[468] e.g. see F. Prändl, "Exhaustion of IP Rights in the EEA Applies to Third country Goods Placed on the EEA Market" [1993] 2 E.C.L.R. 43, D.T. Keeling, *Intellectual Property Rights in the EU, Vol.1: Free Movement and Competition Law* (Oxford: OUP, 2004), and M. Abbey, "Exhaustion of IP Rights Under the EEA Agreement does not Apply to Third Country Goods" [1992] 6 E.C.L.R. 231.
[469] *L'Oréal Norge AS v Per Aarskog AG and Nille AS; L'Oréal Norge AS and L'Oréal SA v Smart Club AS* (E-9/07 & E-10/07).
[470] (E-2/97) [1997] EFTA Ct. Rep. 129, EFTA Court.

is applicable to any EU IP harmonising Directive which provides for an EU-wide exhaustion of rights principle.[471]

7-345   On the third issue, until recently, none of the unitary EU regulations, e.g. the EU Trade Mark Regulation, the Community Design Regulation nor the Community Plant Variety Regulation provided for an EEA-wide exhaustion of rights principle. Instead, they provided for EU-wide exhaustion of rights principle. However, the new EUTM Regulation now provides for a EEA-wide exhaustion of rights principle despite the EUTM only having territorial effect in the EU.[472] Thus, the owner of a EUTM who placed a product bearing a EUTM in a EFTA state cannot prevent its importation into the EU or its subsequent circulation in the EU (of course, the EUTM owner has no rights under the EUTM in EFTA states as a EUTM does not extend to such countries).

7-346   Nevertheless, no such change has yet been made to the Community Design Regulation[473] nor the Community Plant Variety Right Regulation. The question is then whether the owner of these EU unitary rights who places a product bearing the protected design in a EFTA country (i.e. a non-EU, EEA country) with its consent exhausts its right to prevent their circulation throughout the EU (its rights necessarily only extending to the EU). The Agreement on the UPC also does not have an EEA-wide exhaustion of rights principle for European patents. It only extends to the EU. It should be said that this is not a EU legislative measure.

7-347   It has been said that there cannot be any doubt that the proprietor of such unitary rights exhausts their rights throughout the EEA whenever the proprietor consents to the marketing of goods subject to such rights in any state belonging to the EEA.[474] Certainly, under the principle of *Merck v Stephar*, the fact that a rights owner does not have rights in the country where they first market a product does not prevent the doctrine of exhaustion of rights principle from applying.[475]

7-348   In favour of there being no exhaustion is that the wording of the various legislative measures conferring a unitary right (other than the EU Trade Mark Regulation) is clear—it is a EU-wide exhaustion of rights principle and not a EEA-wide exhaustion of rights principle. Given that the case law of the Court of Justice has precluded the adoption of a wider international exhaustion of rights principle where IP Directives and regulations refer to a EU-wide exhaustion of rights principle, one might have thought that the matter is fairly clear as EFTA states are not members of the EU. Moreover, as has been said, it is unsurprising that the provisions of the various EU unitary right regulations were not extended to Norway, Iceland or Lichtenstein as these regulations were enacted pursuant to EU legislation and not EEA legislation and thus are not binding on the EFTA states.[476]

7-349   There are two arguments against the above interpretation. First, the EU is itself

---

[471] e.g. see *L'Oreal Norge AS*, at [34].

[472] art.15 Reg.2017/1001 (the change was implemented by the amending Reg.2015/242). Regulation 2017/1001 is a codifying regulation.

[473] art.21 Reg.6/2002.

[474] D.T. Keeling, *Intellectual Property Rights in the EU, Vol.1: Free Movement and Competition Law* (Oxford: OUP, 2004), p.118, citing A.M. Tobio Rivas, *Comentarious a los reglamentos sobre la marca communitaria* (Barcelona: Rústica, 1994), Vol.1, p.179. Cf. D. Keeling, D. Llewelyn, J. Mellor, QC, T. Moody-Stuart, I. Berkeley, *Kerly's Law of Trade Marks*, 15th edn (London: Sweet & Maxwell, 2011), where the authors take the opposite view.

[475] See para.7-184.

[476] M. Heritage, S. Tracey and P. Tonna, "How strong is Fortress Europe? Big brands and the exasperated state of EEA exhaustion" *World Trademark Review*, February/March 2014.

a member of the EEA Agreement.[477] Therefore, as discussed above, the EEA Agreement requires contracting parties to provide for a EEA-wide exhaustion of rights. It could be said that the EU itself is obliged to ensure that its IP unitary right legislation provides for an EEA-wide exhaustion of rights principle. However, the reality is that the EU has not implemented this provision (save for the EUTM) and the obligation to do so cannot be relied upon in an action between two private undertakings. Secondly, *Merck v Stephar* might be interpreted as suggesting that the mere fact that the EU trade mark owner has no protection for a EUTM in a EFTA state does not preclude a finding of exhaustion of rights if it markets a good bearing the trade mark in that state and it is then imported into the EU. Thus, as there are equivalent free movement of goods and intellectual property provisions in the EEA Agreement (as discussed above), it might be said that it should equally apply to marketing by a EUTM owner of goods bearing a trade mark in EEA countries. This is a seductive argument. However, although there are equivalent and parallel provisions in the EEA Agreement and the TFEU, this does not mean that the EEA and EU should be treated as the same territory or override the clear wording of the exhaustion of rights principle in the Community Design Regulation or the Community Plant Variety Regulation. For a EEA-wide exhaustion of rights principle to be introduced for EU unitary rights, the author's view is that the EU must (as with the EUTM Regulation) amend these regulations expressly to so provide for the same.

---

[477] The EU (then the European Community) signed the EEA Agreement on 2 May 1992 and it came into force on 1 January 1994.

CHAPTER 8

INTELLECTUAL PROPERTY AND ARTICLE 101

TABLE OF CONTENTS

INTRODUCTION

Article 101(1) of the TFEU[1] prohibits agreements and concerted practices **8-001** between undertakings which may affect trade between Member States that prevent, restrict or distort competition within the EU. Such agreements are void and unenforceable unless they satisfy art.101(3) which requires that the agreement contribute to improving the production or distribution of products or to promoting technical or economic progress whilst allowing consumer a fair share of the resulting benefits and which do not impose restrictions to the attainment of these objectives and do not permit the undertakings to eliminate competition in respect of a substantial part of the products concerned.

This chapter considers art.101 and its application to intellectual property in **8-002** general. As art.101 is concerned with agreements and concerted practices, it is not concerned with the unilateral exercise of IPRs. Its primary relevance is to intellectual property licences. However, before considering this, it is necessary to consider the relationship between IPRs per se and competition laws. IPR laws are principally concerned with encouraging innovation whereas competition laws are principally concerned with regulating the conduct of undertakings on the marketplace. Thus, in the 1990s, it was said that:

> "it is not easy to marry the innovation bride and the competition groom and some have argued that such a marriage will unavoidably lead to divorce."[2]

---

[1] It was previously art.81 in the European Community Treaty and in the Treaty of Rome art.85.

[2] Commission Evaluation Report. *Transfer of Technology Block Exemption*. No.240/96, para.27.

8-003   However, the fears of divorce have proven wrong and indeed the bride and groom are happily married and in love of a common goal—the promotion of consumer welfare and a dynamic market. As said in the Commission's 2014 Guidelines on the Application of art.101 to Technology Transfer Agreements:

> "7.   The fact that intellectual property laws grant exclusive rights of exploitation does not imply that intellectual property rights are immune from competition law intervention. Article 101 of the Treaty is in particular applicable to agreements whereby the holder licenses another undertaking to exploit its intellectual property rights. *Nor does it imply that there is an inherent conflict between intellectual property rights and the Union competition rules. Indeed, both bodies of law share the same basic objective of promoting consumer welfare and an efficient allocation of resources.* Innovation constitutes an essential and dynamic component of an open and competitive market economy. *Intellectual property rights promote dynamic competition by encouraging undertakings to invest in developing new or improved products and processes. So does competition by putting pressure on undertakings to innovate. Therefore, both intellectual property rights and competition are necessary to promote innovation and ensure a competitive exploitation thereof.*" [Emphasis supplied.]

8-004   A similar approach is taken in the US.

> "Consequently, antitrust and intellectual property are properly perceived as complementary bodies of law that work together to bring innovation to consumers: antitrust laws protect robust competition in the marketplace, while intellectual property laws protect the ability to earn a return on the investments necessary to innovate. Both spur competition among rivals to be the first to enter the marketplace with a desirable technology, product, or service."[3]

8-005   Thus, it has been said that contemporary antitrust jurisprudence recognises that innovation may often be fuelled by the prospect and proper exercise of market power.[4] The value of IPRs is directly related to the power that they confer on their owner to exercise in a particular market. The more valuable that power is, the more incentive there is to innovate to acquire IPRs which confer such a power.

8-006   On the commercial plane, there are two central cornerstones to the EU. The first cornerstone is the attainment of a single internal market without barriers between Member States which, at the economic and commercial plane, is intended to ensure, where possible, that trading in the EU is no different to trading in a single country. The second cornerstone is an effective competition policy within the internal market. These two cornerstones can be considered the Castor and Pollux of the EU commercial policy.[5] Thus, art.3 of the Treaty of the European Union[6] states:

> "3.   The Union shall establish an internal market. It shall work for the sustainable development of Europe based on balanced economic growth and price stability, a highly competitive social market economy, aiming at full employment and social progress, and a high level of protection and improvement of the quality of the environment. It shall promote scientific and technological advance."

---

[3]   See *Introduction to Antitrust Enforcement and Intellectual Property Rights: Promoting Innovation and Competition* (2007), US Department of Justice, p.2.

[4]   N.W. Netanel, "Copyright and Market Power in the Marketplace of Ideas" in F. Lévêque and H.A. Shelanski (eds), *Antitrust, Patents and Copyright: EU and US Perspectives* (Cheltenham: Edward Elgar, 2005), Ch.7, p.149.

[5]   For the uninitiated, Castor and Pollux were inseparable twin brothers in Greek mythology.

[6]   The Treaty on the European Union ("TEU") is the sister treaty to the Treaty on the Functioning of the European Union and have the same legal value (see art.1 TEU).

There is no doubt that since its early beginnings in the 1950s, the EU has gone **8-007**
very far in achieving these goals. The European Commission has been aggressive
in tackling anti-competitive abuses in the EU. Furthermore, allowing for the inherent barriers of language, culture and society between Member States, the internal
market is a living entity that businesses now take for granted. However, innovation is the "engine" of the modern economy in the EU. A single internal market and
strong competition policy cannot create an economy but only police it. Put another
way, it is important to ensure that the EU does not have the engine of a lawn mower
and the brakes of a Rolls Royce.[7] The EU faces strong competition from the emerging economies and it is recognised that it cannot compete with them in relation to
the production of commodities and staple products. Thus, the European Commission has recognised the need for innovation and has devoted considerable resources
towards it. Notwithstanding this, the EU is outperformed in innovation by the US
and Canada (although it is catching up) but South Korea and Japan are "pulling
ahead" and China is showing the fastest progress amongst international
competitors.[8] Strong protection of innovation via IPRs plays a very valuable role
in ensuring that the EU's innovation policy is effective[9].

It is perhaps not surprising given the above discussion that in the 21st century, **8-008**
the competition policy of the EU has become more favourable to intellectual
property rights than previously existed. There has been a subtle rebalancing on the
scales of IPR vs. competition. The suspicion that competition law had of intellectual property rights has largely disappeared. They are now recognised as a very
important cornerstone in EU commercial policy. This favourable approach is
particularly evident in relation to IPR licences. The European Commission's approach to IPR licences in the 20th century which was to consider many contractual
restraints in such licences as anti-competitive per se has been replaced in the 21st
century by a favourable approach to licensing in the EU.

This is reflected in the 2014 Technology Transfer Guidelines which recognise that **8-009**
the great majority of licences are compatible with art.101.

> "[9] In assessing licensing agreements under Article 101 of the Treaty, the existing
> analytical framework is sufficiently flexible to take due account of the dynamic
> aspects of technology rights licensing. There is no presumption that intellectual
> property rights and licence agreements as such give rise to competition concerns.
> *Most licence agreements do not restrict competition and create pro-competitive
> efficiencies. Indeed, licensing as such is pro- competitive as it leads to dissemination of technology and promotes innovation by the licensor and licensee(s).* In addition, even licence agreements that do restrict competition may often give rise to
> pro-competitive efficiencies, which must be considered under Article 101(3) and
> balanced against the negative effects on competition. *The great majority of licence
> agreements are therefore compatible with Article 101.*" [Emphasis supplied.]

The modern approach to the effect on competition of licences is to adopt a "rule **8-010**
of reason" approach which adopts an economics-based approach whereby the effect of the licences on geographic and product markets are considered. For example,
it is most likely that competition concerns are raised where licensing is between

---

[7] A saying in the popular UK TV series, *Yes Minister.*
[8] The European Commission publishes a useful "European Innovation Scoreboard" which is updated
annually. See *https://ec.europa.eu/growth/industry/innovation/facts-figures/scoreboards_en* [Accessed
23 January 2018].
[9] Although as said in Ch.1, para.1-008, there are now concerns that IPRs have "over reached"
themselves and to some extent, stifle innovation.

actual or potential competitors. Whilst licensing has the effect of giving undertakings access to technologies they would not otherwise have, licensing between compettitors can reduce competition on the market if the licensed technology replaces the licensee's existing technology.

Structure of this chapter

8-011   In this chapter, the reader is introduced to competition law and its interaction with intellectual property. Article 101 is then discussed and its requirements. Then art.101's application to licences in general are considered. At this point, the reader should note that three chapters then follow. The first concerns IP and Technology Transfer licences. This is concerned with patent/technical know-how licences and other types of industrial licences for the manufacture of goods. The 2014 Technology Transfer Block Exemption and Guidelines are considered in that chapter. The second is IP and Vertical Agreements. This is primarily concerned with IP licences in the context of distribution and supply of goods and services. It focuses on franchises. The Vertical Agreements Block Exemption and Guidelines are considered in that. The third is IP and Horizontal Agreements. This is concerned with agreements between competitors at a horizontal level. It focuses on IP licences in that context, in particular in the context of joint ventures, standardisation agreements and patent pools. The Horizontal Cooperation Guidelines are considered in that together with the Research and Development Block Exemption and Specialisation Block Exemption (as these agreements tend to be at a horizontal level). In this chapter, the competitive effect of individual clauses in licences are considered as often, their effect on competition is independent of the nature of the type of licence. Although, if the reader is interested in a particular type of clause, they should cross-check the analysis of such a clause in this chapter with one of the other three chapters where such is found in a technology transfer agreement, vertical or horizontal agreement.

8-012   This chapter then considers special types of agreements which do not fall easily into any of the three chapters. These are: (i) litigation settlement agreements, (ii) collecting society agreements, (iii) sub-contracting agreements, (iv) mergers and acquisitions involving IPRs, and (v) agreements for SEP (Standard Essential Patents).

8-013   Finally, the interaction of art.101 with the *exercise* of IPR is considered.

COMPETITION LAW AND INTELLECTUAL PROPERTY: PRINCIPLES

Introduction

8-014   The principle of unfettered competition between businesses is one of the sacred cows of today's democratic economies. The theory is that a market economy based on genuine competition benefits the consumer by preventing artificially high prices and encouraging the development and availability of high quality goods and services. The economic primacy of Western market economies has clearly been proven over the last 15 years over economies whose hallmarks are bureaucracy, centralisation, substantial interference in private individuals' economic freedom and substantial state intervention in the marketplace. Whilst such economic models have worked relatively well in bygone eras, which were technologically simpler and the demands of the populace were more rudimentary, their rapid demise in recent years has shown the limits of such systems and their inability to cope and adapt to change.[10]

However, what is meant by a truly competitive economy is far from clear.[11] **8-015** Competition suggests almost a Darwinian struggle for superiority where the fittest survive and the weak fail. Competition law is based on the fact that an individual's selfish desire to better himself is likely to improve the lot of mankind. As said by Adam Smith in the *Wealth of Nations*[12]:

> "It is not from the benevolence of the butcher, the brewer, or the baker that we expect our dinner, but from their regard to their own interest."

Competition law's aim is to ensure that there are enough butchers, brewers and **8-016** bakers so that man can buy as much meat, beer or bread as he wants and of the quality that he wants at a reasonable price. In general, optimal competition conditions exists where on a particular product market, there are a large number of suppliers; consumers have perfect information about market conditions; resources can freely flow from one area of economic activity to another; there are no "barriers to entry" which might prevent the emergence of new competition; and there are no "barriers to exit" which might hinder firms wishing to leave the market. Generally, such conditions do not exist although with the rise of globalisation (which increases the number of suppliers) and the internet (which improves the flow of information), many markets are approaching or have reached optimal competition.

Optimal competition will normally be achieved by ensuring that there are no **8-017** artificial restraints on man's selfish desire to better himself. It is not surprising therefore that a primitive approach to competition law concentrates on prohibiting restraints in contracts between parties, e.g. exclusivity. Historically, as will be seen, the concern of EU competition law was to prohibit restraints of any form on a person's economic freedom, i.e. the right of that person to choose how they behave in a particular market. Such an approach was fundamentally flawed because it failed to consider what the competitive position would have been prior to the agreement being entered into. As is often described, the EU's historical approach was *ex post* and not *ex ante*.[13] Moreover, such an approach can be taken to absurdity. Thus, if A contracts to pay £1,000 to B for X widgets, then B is restricted from selling those widgets to another for a greater price and A is restricted from buying the same number of widgets from another cheaper supplier. Yet no one doubts the need for legally binding agreements as such encourage business relations and provide for certainty in business, ultimately facilitating the supply of widgets to the consumer.

However, a competitive marketplace alone is unable to confer the benefits of **8-018** technology and progress on society. A peasant economy based on bartering can be truly competitive yet still backward. Technological and artistic progress is deemed important by most societies. Indeed, it has been said that progress is *more important*

---

[10] On the other hand, there is a growing counter feeling that wholly unfettered globalised market economies are increasing the gap between the wealthy and the poor and permit companies to avoid their responsibilities to mankind by being able to move their resources around the world to countries where the cost of living is low and where there is minimal legislative interference (in particular, in the financial, employment and environmental fields).

[11] A detailed analysis of the theory of competition and the role of competition law is given in R. Whish and D. Bailey, *Competition Law*, 7th edn (Oxford: OUP, 2012) which is an excellent and jargon free guide to competition law.

[12] Scottish philosopher economist 1723–1790.

[13] See para.8-047 for explanation of these terms.

than competition. Thus, some commentators, such as Schumpeter,[14] have argued with the prevailing view that "perfect" competition was the way to maximise economic well-being. Under perfect competition all firms in an industry produced the same or similar goods, sold it for the same or similar prices and had access to the same technology. Schumpeter saw this kind of competition as relatively unimportant. He wrote:

"In capitalist reality as distinguished from its textbook picture, it is not [price] competition which counts but the competition from the new commodity, the new technology, the new source of supply, the new type of organization…competition which commands a decisive cost or quality advantage and which strikes not at the margins of the profits and the outputs of the existing firms but at their foundations and their very lives."[15]

8-019 One way that this can be achieved is by the grant of legal monopolies to investors and authors for particular products or technologies, i.e. intellectual property laws. The monopolies provided by patents, copyright, design rights, plant breeder rights, etc. are nowadays generally justified as being essential to encourage progress in the fields of science and foster talent in the arts. Without such protection, companies would not invest time and money into research as, if the invented widget is reproduced by others who have not spent such time and money, the company which invented the widget will be financially worse off than the imitators (the problem of "free-riders"). This is often termed the "public justification" for intellectual property. Similarly, artists or authors would be less likely to pursue careers in their chosen artistic field if plagiarisers could prevent them from receiving sufficient remuneration for their endeavours. However, the monopoly is granted for a fixed term. The theory behind granting a monopoly for a fixed term rather than in perpetuity is that the carrot (the fixed term) need only be long enough so as not to impair technological and artistic innovation. Thus, the lure of a 20-year manufacturing monopoly in an invented product is usually enough for a business to deem it worthwhile committing funds for research and development with the hope of inventing a commercially lucrative invention.[16] Once the fixed term monopoly has expired, the widget can be exposed to market forces.

8-020 The "public justification" theory is rather Anglo-Saxon and utilitarian in concept. Another justification for IPRs is as a "reward" for the inventor's own creativity and endeavours. This is called the "reward" theory or "private justification" theory. Thus, the award of a patent to an inventor is a measure of society's gratitude for their inventiveness. Similarly, copyright can be justified in such a way as well. In continental Europe, much more emphasis is given to the "reward" theory. In France, copyright is known as "author's right" and is based on the right of reward.

8-021 Another justification for IPRs is, in accordance with fundamentals of Lockean property theory, a creation that can be thought of as belonging naturally to its

---

[14] An important and influential Austrian economist in the 19th/20th century who took a particular interest in the dynamics of innovation.

[15] J. Schumpeter, *Capitalism, Socialism, Democracy* (London: Harper, 1943), p.84.

[16] However, in very large-scale, long term projects, clearly such a period will not be long enough and state-assisted collaborative ventures are needed, e.g. the development of artificial intelligence. Also, pharmaceutical firms often have to delay placing a drug on the market because of the extensive need to test the drug. Thus, the EU has introduced a regulation to permit the extension of the period of protection for patents where there has been a substantial delay in placing a product on the market because of the need for governmental approval. See Ch.2, para.2-603.

creator.[17] Thus, one of the first intellectual property disputes in the UK, in the Dark Ages, involved the theft and intention of St Columba to copy the psalter of his old teacher, the Abbot Finian. The King ruled in favour of Abbot Finian by saying:

"to every cow, her calf and to every book, its copy."

Nowadays, analysis of IPRs from a competition law perspective tend to emphasise the public justification theory of IPRs to demonstrate that there is no conflict between IPRs and competition law. However, many products and works are not created because of the lure of IPRs. The invention of the paperclip, which requires five minutes of inspiration yet involves no perspiration, is deemed worthy of a 20-year monopoly. Thus, it has been said that it is somewhat puzzling that in general intellectual property law offers a common protection standard to all creations that are judged worth of some level of protection.[18] As commented on, such normally means that the protection offered will often be excessive for the purpose of innovation efficiency.[19] Why then are the same exclusive rights conferred on an inventor without regard to the degree of investment and risk required? Indeed, why is not a right to remuneration rather than exclusive rights granted which many would argue would be more likely to maximise the welfare of consumers? **8-022**

The answer is that the costs of tailoring the exclusive right or level of remuneration to the magnitude or importance of the creation is so uncertain that it adds extra costs to innovation.[20] This increases inefficiencies. For example, is it permissible to take into account the cost of past failures in calculating a reasonable royalty for a successful invention? A refusal to do so could jeopardise future innovation, as firms would be less willing to embark in high risk research and development, preferring to wait for competitors to innovate and obtain compulsory licences from them.[21] Moreover, the grant of exclusive rights lets the innovator determine the best route to appropriate the full value of the innovation.[22] It can be concluded from the above that competition is usually best served by an exclusive right system and not an equitable remuneration system. Of course, the system sometimes breaks down. For instance, most countries' patent laws provide for a system of compulsory licences if a patent is not worked. Clearly, in such circumstances, the justification for a patent, namely to encourage the bringing of inventions onto the marketplace, has failed. However, generally if the exploitation of an invention is commercially feasible, it will be exploited. **8-023**

---

[17] R. Watt, "Adverse Selection and the Legal Protection of Intellectual Property Rights" in F. Lévêque and H.A. Shelanski (eds), *Antitrust, Patents and Copyright: EU and US Perspectives* (Cheltenham: Edward Elgar, 2005), Ch.6, p.127.

[18] R. Watt, "Adverse Selection and the Legal Protection of Intellectual Property Rights" in F. Lévêque and H.A. Shelanski (eds), *Antitrust, Patents and Copyright: EU and US Perspectives* (Cheltenham: Edward Elgar, 2005), Ch.6, p.127.

[19] R. Watt, "Adverse Selection and the Legal Protection of Intellectual Property Rights" in F. Lévêque and H.A. Shelanski (eds), *Antitrust, Patents and Copyright: EU and US Perspectives* (Cheltenham: Edward Elgar, 2005), Ch.6, p.127.

[20] R. Watt, "Adverse Selection and the Legal Protection of Intellectual Property Rights" in F. Lévêque and H.A. Shelanski (eds), *Antitrust, Patents and Copyright: EU and US Perspectives* (Cheltenham: Edward Elgar, 2005), Ch.6, p.128.

[21] Thus, in the 2014 Guidelines on Technology Transfer Agreements, para.8, they suggest that the innovator should be normally free to seek compensation for successful projects that take into account failed projects.

[22] This can be seen as a subtle application of Adam Smith's maxim that a person by pursuing his own interest is more likely to promote society's interest than when society seeks to promote its own interest (which indeed may explain the failure of communism in the latter 20th century).

8-024   Trade marks differ from other types of intellectual property. They are primarily concerned with product-differentiation rather than product-innovation. Trade mark law, by making it illegal for imitators to put a trade mark on products of competitors, reassures the public that a product with the affixed trade mark comes from the same trade source. However, trade marks are also pro-competitive. First, by permitting product-differentiation, they permit effective inter-brand competition. Indeed, it has been said that they are: "nothing more nor less than the fundament of most market-place competition".[23] Secondly, they reward a trader who has developed a reputation in a particular mark by protecting it. This encourages a trader to improve the quality of his goods. The fundamental difference between rights such as patents and trade marks is that the latter will not enable a trader to obtain a monopoly in a particular product market.[24] Nevertheless, trade marks indirectly encourage product-innovation by allowing customers to identify the goods of one undertaking from another and thus spurring them to innovate.

8-025   Thus, in summary, it can be seen from the above that IPR and competition laws both share the same common purpose of promoting innovation and enhancing consumer welfare.[25] It is against that background that the competitive effect of licensing of IPRs can be discussed. However, before doing so, it is necessary to introduce the reader to the basic *analytical tools* of competition law.

The competition law "toolbox"

8-026   In this section, the reader is introduced to certain linguistic "tools" that are used for the purpose of competition analysis.

Inter-brand and intra-brand competition

8-027   Competition can exist at various levels. First, there can be competition between businesses which deal with a product made or sourced from one manufacturer. Thus, wholesalers or retailers can compete with each other on price to sell Widget X. This type of competition is called *intra-brand* competition. Secondly, competition can also exist between different products, i.e. Widget X and Widget Y. This is called *inter-brand* competition. Inter-brand competition is normally between different economic concerns although it is a well-known fact that some washing powder manufacturers create their own inter-brand competition by selling differently branded washing powders that they also manufacture. A competitive market will normally have both effective inter-brand and intra-brand competition.

Inter-technology and intra-technology competition

8-028   This is similar to inter-brand and intra-brand competition. However, here one is concerned with competition between technologies (inter-technology competition)

---

[23]   *HAG GF AG v SA CNL-SUCAL NV* (C-10/89) [1990] 3 C.M.L.R. 571, per Jacobs AG at 583.

[24]   Although a very strong brand will often command substantial market share, it is never impossible for another trader to attack that market share.

[25]   D.L. Rubinfeld and R. Maness,"The Strategic Use of Patents: Implications for Anti-Trust", in F. Lévêque and H.A. Shelanski (eds), *Antitrust, Patents and Copyright: EU and US Perspectives* (Cheltenham: Edward Elgar, 2005), Ch.4, p.85. See also *"Antitrust Guidelines for the Licensing of Intellectual Property"* (January 2017) issued by the US Department of Justice, p.2 citing *Atari Games Corp v Nintendo of Am., Inc* 97, F.2d, 1572, 1576 (Fed. Cir., 1990) and *Intergraph Corp v Intel Corp* 195 F.3d 1346, 1362 (Fed. Cir., 1999). See *https://www.justice.gov/archives/opa/blog-entry/file/925906/download* [Accessed 23 January 2018].

and competition in a particular technology, i.e. between licensees for a licensed technology. This is called intra-technology competition.

Variables of competition-price, quality, service, etc.

At a pure intra-brand level, the goods are all the same and therefore quality is an irrelevant factor. Thus, the price of the product and its availability on the market become important when considering the level of effective competition. However, at an inter-brand level, consumers are interested in the quality of goods as well. Some consumers may place more emphasis on price, others on quality. Thus, a competitive market should provide a range of high quality, high-priced products as against low quality, low-priced products to maximise consumer choice. Also, in the case of complex or luxury goods, consumers are often interested in other factors like after-sales service, customer relations, "brand image", geographical location, etc. As these are important to a consumer, then they constitute areas in which competition can exist. Thus, competition can exist in relation to many variables in relation to a product.

8-029

Horizontal and vertical relationships

Generally speaking, competition is between parties at one level of trading. Thus, manufacturers may compete with each other, distributors may compete with each other and retailers may complete with each other. Such persons are in a horizontal relationship with each other because they are in the same position on the manufacturing and distribution chain. On the other hand, a manufacturer and a distributor are in a vertical relationship with each other because they are positioned in different levels on the manufacturing and distribution chain. Generally, parties in a horizontal relationship will be actual or potential competitors of each other. Parties in a vertical relationship will generally not be actual or potential competitors although parties who are competitors can enter into vertical relationships, e.g. a manufacturer may agree to distribute the goods of another manufacturer because they have a much better distribution network.

8-030

Agreements which restrict competition between parties in a horizontal relationship are considered to give rise to greater competitive concerns than where the parties are in a vertical relationship. These agreements could have as their object price-fixing or other collusive behaviour. Agreements between parties in a vertical relationship are normally less capable of affecting competition at either party's level, i.e the wholesale or retail level. However, where either party has a large market share in the relevant market, vertical agreements can affect third parties who supply the same or substitutable goods as those which form the subject matter of the vertical agreement. Thus, an obligation on a distributor to buy all of their goods from one manufacturer may *foreclose* other manufacturers and lead to a lack of competition in downstream markets.

8-031

Relevant market

In any analysis of the competitive effects of an agreement or licence, it is necessary to evaluate the relevant product and geographical market or other markets that the agreement or licence will affect. This is called the relevant market. In considering the relevant product market, account must also be taken of whether the protected products are interchangeable with other products on the marketplace and whether

8-032

it is relatively easy for undertakings to enter the market. However, it is also necessary to consider *elasticity of demand* and *supply-side substitutability*. This considers whether undertakings that are not actually competing on the market would enter the market if there was a small non-transitory increase in price ("SNIP") for the licensed products.

Technology market

8-033   In the field of technology licensing, it is usually necessary to consider the technology market. This requires considering the nature of the licensed technology and whether there are other competing technologies. Analysis of the technology market is more difficult than the product market. Often, analysis is done by considering in a particular product market, the market shares of products which incorporate a particular technology.[26]

Innovation market

8-034   Furthermore, where the parties to an agreement have R&D capacity, it is sometimes necessary to consider the *innovation market*. The innovation market is concerned with how many numbers of independent "poles of research" there are in a particular field of technology. This analysis originates from American antitrust law and is based on the fundamental principle that innovation is best served by the existence of a number of independent R&D poles. The European Commission has adopted such an approach in relation to the competitive analysis of the effect of research and development agreements.[27]

SNIP/SSNIP

8-035   An economic test that is often applied is the SNIP which stands for Small Non-Transitory Increase in Price. Economists will often hypothetically assume a SNIP for a particular product and hypothesise about the effect such would have on the market. If the market is a competitive market so that demand is elastic, this will normally mean that customers will move some of their custom to other products and suppliers. Often, the test is that of a Small but Significant Non-transitory Increase in Price ("SSNIP").

8-036   The use of the SSNIP test is used in conjunction with the "hypothetical monopolist" test to determine the relevant product market. In essence, the tribunal is seeking to determine the smallest product group that a hypothetical monopolist controlling that product group could profitably sustain above competitive prices, i.e. prices that are at least a small but significant amount above competitive levels. One starts with the products under question, e.g. the products that a party supplies and apply the SSNIP test. If the party can raise the prices of those products by 5 to 10 per cent above competitive levels, then such suggests that the products are the relevant market. If this cannot be done, then the tribunal must repeatedly widen the inquiry into other products and carry out the same test until a group of products have been found for which it is profitable for the hypothetical monopolist to sustain prices 5 to 10 per cent above competitive levels. Unfortunately, this test is of little practical use because it is very difficult to predict what will happen in the

---

[26]   This analysis is done in the 2014 Technology Transfer Guidelines, para.25. See para.9-025.
[27]   See Ch.10, para.10-020.

marketplace if a SSNIP was applied to a set of products and undertakings are not surprisingly loathe to carry out a SSNIP on their products simply for the purpose of gathering economic data. Thus, inquiry tends to be more based on considerations of what goods on the market are interchangeable with each other.

Elasticity of demand

This term measures the responsiveness of a change in demand for a good or service to a change in price of that good. In a highly elastic market, a small rise in the price of a particular good will cause sales to drop off markedly and sales of competing goods to rise to the same amount. It might also suggest that factors other than price are relevant, e.g. quality, after-sales service. **8-037**

This concept of elasticity of demand has other economic labels, namely interchangeability and demand substitutability. All three terms have been used by the CJEU and Commission and essentially mean the same.[28] **8-038**

Supply-side substitutability

This term measures the ease that undertakings can switch to supplying a product that they are not already supplying. Thus, the mere fact that a product has no competitors on the market does not necessarily mean that the relevant product market should be considered as only that product. If manufacturers could switch to producing that product with relative ease and at a reasonable cost, the relevant market may include those other products. Thus, if suppliers or manufacturer switched to producing competitive products to a product if the latter experienced a SSNIP, such suggests high supply-side substitutability. **8-039**

Barriers to entry

In a *relevant market*, there may exist certain factual or legal barriers which prevent undertakings from entering the market. Thus, IPRs may cover the relevant market such that a licence of those rights would be required to enter the market (sometimes called "gateway" IPR). Alternatively, there may be factual barriers such that the cost of investment is prohibitively high. For instance, the cost of becoming a manufacturer of cars is so significant that it is not surprising that in Europe, there are no new car manufacturers. The existing manufacturers have benefitted from a legacy of investment over many decades. **8-040**

"Rule of reason" approach

In investigating the competitive effect of an agreement, the most logical approach is to consider the economic situation on the relevant market with and without the agreement or behaviour. If a detailed economic analysis shows that the agreement or behaviour increases competition, then it should not be prohibited under anti-competition laws. This approach is termed the "rule of reason" approach. It **8-041**

---

[28] See *United Brands v Commission of the European Community* (C-27/76) [1978] E.C.R. 287; [1978] 1 C.M.L.R. 429 at [22]–[28] where all three terms are used. If there is a difference, it is that interchangeability is used more often in relation to the characteristics of products and cross-elasticity of demand is used in relation to the effect that price variations have on sales of similar competing products.

emphasises an economic analytical approach to facts and avoids a formalistic approach which concentrates on whether the parties' contractual freedom has been restricted. In other words, it favours an *ex ante* and not an *ex post* approach.[29]

Ancillary restraints

8-042   When applying a "rule of reason" approach, it will often be necessary for a party to an agreement to impose conditions on another party which ostensibly restrict the trading freedom of parties to an agreement in order to ensure that the transaction is commercially viable. These are called "ancillary restraints". A good definition of "ancillary restraints" come from the Guidelines on the application of art.101(3). It says:

> "In European Union competition law the concept of ancillary restraints covers any alleged restriction of competition which is directly related and necessary to the implementation of a main non-restrictive transaction and proportionate to it. If an agreement in its main parts, for instance, a distribution agreement or a joint venture, does not have as its object or effect the restriction of competition, then restrictions which are directly related to and necessary for the implementation of that transaction also fall outside art.101. These related restrictions are called ancillary restraints. A restriction is directly related to the main transaction if it is subordinate to the implementation of that transaction and is inseparably linked to it. ... If on the basis of objective factors, it can be concluded that without the restriction the main non-restrictive transaction would be difficult or impossible to implement, the restriction may be regarded as objectively necessary for its implementation and proportionate to it."[30]

8-043   Thus, where the goodwill of a firm is sold, a clause restraining the vendor from competing for a period of time with the purchaser is normally necessary so that the vendor cannot, in effect, undermine the sold business. Equally, a clause which confers exclusivity for a particular territory to a particular distributor so as to incentivise the potential distributor to make an appropriate investment into setting up the distribution network and thereby protect the potential distributor from other distributors "free riding" on their initial investment in developing a particular brand is often a necessary ancillary restraint. It can be seen from the above discussion that the ancillary restraints approach is really a specific application of the "rule of reason" approach. If entry into the agreement by an undertaking is likely to increase competition in a relevant market, then if an ancillary restraint is necessary and proportionate in order to make the agreement sufficiently attractive to persuade an undertaking to enter into that agreement; a rule of reason approach would mean that the agreement is not *in toto* anti-competitive.

Foreclosure

8-044   Often agreements between two parties may increase competition in the licensed technology but have the effect of reducing competition in third party technologies or products not covered by the IPRs of the licensor. Thus, an agreement between a licensor and a licensee whereby the latter is obliged not to use competing technologies will "foreclose" the supply of third party competing technologies to licensees. Similarly, an obligation on a licensee to buy certain products not covered by the

---

[29] See para.8-047.
[30] Guidelines on the application of Article 101(3) of the TFEU [2004] OJ C101/97–118, paras 29–31.

IPRs from the licensor will foreclose third parties from supplying the unprotected products to the licensee. Generally, the effect of this is only serious where the licensor or licensee has considerable market power.

Sunk costs

In economic jargon, costs that have already been incurred are called sunk costs. These are normally contrasted to variable costs which will change depending on a particular course of action. In the 2014 Guidelines on Technology Transfer Agreements, they are described as: **8-045**

> "The risks facing a new licensee may therefore be substantial, in particular since promotional expenses and investment in assets required to produce on the basis of a particular technology are often sunk, that is to say, that upon leaving that particular field of activity the investment cannot be used by the licensee for other activities or sold other than at a significant loss."[31]

Ramsey pricing

This rather exotic term is used to describe the optimal approach to pricing for any monopoly. In brief, the price markup is inverse to the price elasticity of demand for a particular customer. Ramsey pricing is used by regulators to determine prices for the supply of services such as telecommunication networks to customers. The idea is that for those markets where there is low price elasticity of demand (i.e. demand does not significantly drop for a significant increase in price), the price markup is higher than for those where there is high elasticity of demand. According to economic theory, this gives rise to allocative efficiencies. In short, charge more to those who can afford more! **8-046**

Ex post/Ex ante

Traditionally, an *ex post* analysis of the competitive effect of an agreement consists of comparing the competitive position after creation of the relevant IPR when the agreement is in place rather than an *ex ante* analysis which consists of considering competitive the position at the time when the decision is made to invest to create the technology or work that is protected by the right.[32] However, sometimes the phrase *ex ante* and *ex post* is used in the analysis of the competitive effect of a contractual restraint to distinguish between an inquiry which considers whether, *in toto*, competition would have been greater in the absence of any licence (*ex ante*) as opposed to whether competition is increased if the offending contractual restraint is void but the licence otherwise remains valid (*ex post*). **8-047**

Gateway IPRs

IPRs (usually patents) which permit undertakings to monopolise a technology or other input that is essential for entry into a particular product market are called "gateway" IPRs. Thus, a patent which gives exclusive rights in an industry **8-048**

---

[31] 2014 Guidelines on Technology Transfer Agreements, para.126.
[32] See V. Korah, *Intellectual Property Rights and the EU Competition Rules* (Oxford: Hart Publishing, 2006), pp.1–2.

technological standard which is indispensable for operating in a particular technological market is a "gateway" patent.

INTELLECTUAL PROPERTY LICENCES AND COMPETITION

Introduction

8-049   In general, licensing is pro-competitive.[33] It will often permit parties to a licence to provide complementary resources and skills so as to permit the efficient exploitation of technology or works protected by the IPR. Most licences are vertical agreements between non-competitors. Such licences rarely give rise to competition concerns. They tend to promote production efficiency by assigning production and sales to the firm with the lowest local costs and/or highest local expertise and lead to diffusion of knowledge throughout the EU.[34]

8-050   In 2001, the European Commission commissioned a report on the then current Technology Transfer Block Exemption. That research indicated the following trends:

- a widening of the range of technologies licensed and an increase in the number of licences granted for the same technology;
- an increase in R&D costs that royalties help to abate;
- an increase in structured patenting strategies for the purpose of maintaining market position including "gateway" patents and "blocking strategies"[35];
- the reduction of public access to knowledge by resort to copyright, database rights, etc. combined with a tendency of educational establishments actively to seek IPRs for their innovations, i.e. the "privatisation" of knowledge;
- globalisation of licensing; and
- an increase in "package licences" and technology pools whereby IPRs from a number of sources is placed into a "basket" to be licensed to each other or third parties. This occurs particularly in complex technological areas.[36]

8-051   In a further report which preceded the current 2014 Technology Transfer Block Exemption, the authors noted that the majority of licences are exclusive and 13 per cent involve cross-licensing. Licensing tends to be seen primarily in the chemical, electronic and computer industry which can be traced to the relative effectiveness of patent protection in those sectors.[37] With the adoption of the Modernisation Regulation and the adoption of the Technology Transfer Block Exemption and the sophisticated Technology Transfer Guidelines, the Commission tends not to consider, as it did in the past, specific technology licences. Thus, the Commission no longer devotes its resources to traditional vertical licences between parties who

---

[33] 2014 Technology Transfer Guidelines, para.8.

[34] *Assessment of potential anti-competitive conduct in the field of intellectual property rights and assessment of the interplay between competition policy and IPR protection* (November 2011) Regibeau and Rockett (report commissioned by European Commission), p.11). See: *http://ec.europa.eu/competition/consultations/2012_technology_transfer/study_ipr_en.pdf* [Accessed January 23 2018].

[35] i.e. the use of "gateway" patents to prevent competing or downstream technologies from being exploited.

[36] Commission Evaluation Report. *Transfer of Technology Block Exemption* No.240/96, paras 61–73.

[37] Regibeau and Rockett report, p.12.

are not actual or potential competitors but towards more horizontal arrangements, such as, patent pools whereby competitors pool their patents.[38]

Before considering in more detail the EU approach to licensing under art.101, it is useful to discuss three types of clauses in licences.   **8-052**

Permissive clauses

Clauses which partially lift the prohibitive effects of an IPR monopoly are permissive clauses. Thus, clauses which limit a licensee to exploiting a patent in a particular way (i.e. manufacture, sale, distribution); limit the quantity of patented products to be exploited; limit the period of exploitation; limit the territory where exploitation is permissible; and limit the field of application are all permissive clauses. Whilst certain clauses, such as a limit on the quantity of products a licensee can manufacture, appear ostensibly as a restriction on the licensee, they are properly characterised as permissive clauses.   **8-053**

Once it is accepted that the existence of the intellectual property monopoly is immune to the rules of competition law, permissive clauses should rarely be considered anti-competitive. This principle is known as the "limited licence" principle. This principle is based on the concept that a rights owner is not obliged to create competition within their protected technology and that if they do they are free to determine the extent of that competition. A licensor could quite clearly refuse to license the protected product and limit its exploitation to themselves. By granting a person the right to partially exploit an invention which otherwise they are prohibited from doing, one is introducing one more competitor at an intra-brand level in the market for the patented product. Thus, such permissive clauses in licences will generally increase competition when compared to the absence of the licence. The main exception to this approach is where licensing is between competitors. Whilst such licences facilitate the diffusion of technology, they can reduce innovation and result in the consolidation of a particular technology in a particular market thereby increasing the licensor's market power. In particular, whilst cross-licensing between competitors with substantial market share can provide pro-competitive benefits by integrating complementary technologies, reducing transaction costs, clearing blocking positions and avoiding costly infringement litigation, they can have anticompetitive effects, particularly when combined with downstream restrictions such as joint marketing or market division.[39]   **8-054**

Restrictive clauses

Licences will often contain clauses that restrict the licensor and/or licensee which are not permissive. For instance, examples of such restrictions that bind the licensee are no-challenge clauses (which prevent the licensee from challenging the validity of the licensed right), tying-in clauses, grant-backs of improvement created by the licensee, etc. In each case, the clause is not merely partially lifting the monopoly of the IPR.   **8-055**

In particular, clauses such as tying-in have the ability to affect markets not   **8-056**

---

[38] In B. Bird and A. Toutongi, "The New EU Technology Transfer Regulation: One Year On" (2006) 28(5) E.I.P.R. 292, para.296, they noted that the Commission was not investigating any technology transfer agreements other than some patent pools.

[39] e.g. see section 5.5 of the *Antitrust Guidelines for the Licensing of Intellectual Property* (US Department of Justice, 2017).

protected by the IPR. Thus, tying-in clauses can affect the market for the tied-in product and foreclose third party suppliers of the third-party product.

8-057   An agreement which provides for exclusivity is a restrictive clause. In such circumstances, the exclusivity restricts the right of the *licensor* to exploit its own technology. Prior to the grant of the licence, no such restriction would have existed and thus it cannot be regarded as a merely permissive clause. Indeed, the licensor may be in a better position to exploit the technology than the licensee and in which case, competition is likely to be adversely affected. However, this is unusual as it is not in the self-interest of the licensor to grant such licences.

8-058   To determine whether a restrictive clause is anti-competitive, it is necessary to conduct a rule of reason approach to the restraint to determine whether the clause can be considered an ancillary restraint[40]. In particular, restrictive clauses which affect products or technologies outside the IPR, e.g. in a tying-in clause require particular scrutiny.

Downstream clauses

8-059   In many licences, the licensor seeks to regulate the market which the licensee will operate in by banning sales to a particular class of customers, or, requiring the licensee to sell goods at a particular price. In general, competition law considers such attempts to meddle in downstream markets as particularly objectionable. Thus, price fixing is considered by both the EU and US as anti-competitive per se. This might be thought somewhat surprising. For instance, a licensor may be concerned about experiencing too much competition from an economically powerful licensee and wish to restrict what he perceives to be unfair competition. By fixing the minimum price that licensee can sell the licensed products, he may be incentivised to license the licensee. However, if he is not allowed to fix the price, then such may discourage him from licensing the licensee. The net result is that there is less rather than more competition. However, there are signs that the Commission's approach to downstream restrictions such as resale price maintenance and customer allocation as being objectionable per se is changing.[41]

The US approach to licensing of IP

8-060   In modern times, there has been considerable convergence between the EU approach to licences and that of the US. Historically, the EU took a rather formalistic approach to contractual restraints in licences, finding that many were void simply because they restrained the freedom of the licensee or licensor. Such was classic *ex post* analysis. However, the European Commission and competition legislation now adopts a full "rule of reason" approach to the analysis of the competitive effects of a licence. This is discussed in more detail later in this chapter.

8-061   It is helpful to consider the US approach as it tends to be more advanced than that of the EU. Although, nowadays, it is fair to say that the EU and US approach has converged. Perhaps the greatest difference is that currently, under US antitrust law, resale price maintenance is no longer considered illegal per se but is subject to analysis under the rule of reason approach.

8-062   The existing US approach to licensing and antitrust laws is set by the Depart-

---

[40]   For the meaning of "ancillary restraint", see para.8-042.
[41]   See para.8-294 in relation to resale price maintenance.

ment of Justice. In January 2017, it published "*Antitrust Guidelines for the Licensing of Intellectual Property*".[42]

The following represents a distillation of the US Department of Justice's antitrust approach to intellectual property licensing:

8-063

1) Intellectual property laws and antitrust laws share the common purpose of promoting innovation and enhancing consumer welfare.
2) The US applies three general principles for antitrust analysis of intellectual property:
   a) The US apply the same analysis to conduct involving IPRs as to conduct for other forms of property, taking into account the specific characteristic of a particular property right. In this regard, IPR is characterised by an ease of misappropriation.
   b) The US does not presume that IPRs create market power for the purpose of antitrust analysis. If IPRs do confer market power, that by itself does not offend antitrust laws nor impose on the IPR owner an obligation to license its use. However, the IPR owner could use the IPR to engage in anti-competitive conduct.
   c) IPR licensing allows firms to combine complementary factors of production and is generally procompetitive. Field-of-use, territorial and other limitations on IPR licences may be procompetitive by allowing the IPR owner to exploit the IPR efficiently and effectively.
3) The exercise of IPRS is neither particularly free from scrutiny nor particularly suspect under antitrust law. Generally, an IPR owner is not obliged to create competition in its own technology.
4) Antitrust laws do not impose liability upon a firm for refusing to assist its competitors as this would undermine incentives to innovate and invest.
5) IPR licences may give rise to antitrust concerns, e.g. where they divide markets amongst undertakings that would have competed using different technologies or merge the activities of two competitors in research and development.
6) Antitrust analysis involves the analysis of the IPR licences on three markets:
   a) the market for the licensed goods;
   b) where technology is licensed separately from goods embodying the IPR, the market for the licensed technology; and
   c) the market in research and innovation. This will apply where the licensed IPR may affect the poles of independent R&D.
7) In most cases, restraints in IPR licences will be evaluated under the rule of reason. This involves an inquiry into the anti-competitive effects of the restraint and then asking whether it is reasonable or necessary to achieve the procompetitive benefits and whether these outweigh the anti-competitive effects. Restraints in licensing arrangements between parties in a horizontal relationship may increase the risk of co-ordinated pricing, output restrictions or the maintenance or acquisition of market power.
8) Some restraints are per se unlawful, being "naked" price-fixing,[43] output restraints and market division amongst horizontal competitors.

---

[42] *https://www.justice.gov/archives/opa/blog-entry/file/925906/download* [Accessed 23 January 2018].
[43] Although resale price maintenance in vertical licences is not per se unlawful but it will be examined under the rule of reason—see Guidelines, para.5.2.

9) In general, the US adopts (like the EU's approach in block exemptions) a "safety zone" whereby absent extraordinary circumstances, the US Department of Justice will not challenge a licensing arrangement which does not contain per se unlawful restraints and:
   a) is between parties with an aggregate market share of the relevant market no more than 20 per cent;
   b) in the case of the effect on technology markets, there are four or more independently controlled technologies in addition to the licensed technology; and
   c) in the case of the effect on a R&D market, there are four or more independently controlled undertakings who do or can engage in R&D that is a close substitute of the R&D activities of the parties to the licence.

10) The enforcement of invalid IPRs may give rise to antitrust concerns, in particular sham litigation to enforce IPRs.

11) Acquisition of IPR is best analysed by applying the principles and standards used for mergers.

8-064   As said, the US and EU approach to the analysis under competition law of IPR licences has markedly converged. Perhaps the most notable difference now is that the US does not treat resale price maintenance as unlawful per se whereas the EU generally does.[44] In the authors' opinion, there are two main differences:

Intra-technology competition

8-065   The US approach to intra-technology restrictions is more lenient than that of the European Commission. As said above, in general, the US will not require the owner of intellectual property to create competition in its own technology. The IPR owner is entitled to appropriate the value of its IPRs as it sees fit.

8-066   In contrast, the European approach is more suspicious of such clauses, particularly those which represent customer allocation or quantitative restrictions. In particular, EU competition law focuses much more on intra-brand competition, i.e. competition *in the licensed products*. Thus, in the 2014 Technology Transfer Guidelines, when considering *intra-technology competition*, the Guidelines make it clear that the critical question is not whether the licensor or licensee would not have entered into the whole licence in the absence of the restraint (i.e. a "package deal" or "all or nothing" argument) but whether:

> "given the nature of the agreement, and the characteristics of the market, a less restrictive agreement would not have been concluded by *undertakings in a similar setting*."[45] [Emphasis supplied.]

8-067   This step is absent in the US approach. It is difficult to justify the European approach and indeed appears to discourage licensing because a licensor should be free to choose the amount of competition that it wishes to create in its protected technology. The European method suggests that an objective approach is required

---

[44]   The US used to, but in *Leegin Creative Leather Products, Inc v PSKS, Inc*, 551 U.S. 877 (2007), the Supreme Court overruled its previous judgment in *Dr Miles Medical Co v John D. Park & Sons Col*, 220 U.S. 373 (1911). See US Guidelines, para.5.2 and fn.64 thereto. For EU approach, see para.8-294.
[45]   See the 2014 Technology Transfer Guidelines, para.12.

which requires the tribunal to determine the least restrictive restraints that a reasonable licensor and licensee would have entered into. Thus, if a licensor and licensee agree ancillary restraints that go beyond the bare minimum necessary to make the licence commercially viable, then it is anticompetitive even if it is established as an objective fact that in such circumstances, the licensor would not have entered into the licence (the *ex ante* approach). This is redolent of the historical *ex post* analysis by the Commission. The European approach is that the owner is not required to create competition in their own technology (intra-brand competition) but if the owner chooses to do, then they are obliged to create as much intra-brand competition as is consistent with a commercially viable agreement. This makes little sense.

Single market and EU

More significantly, the EU, unlike the US, is a patchwork of different sovereign **8-068** countries and thus, in the EU, there is a need to prohibit agreements which artificially partition the EU in which there is a positive obligation to promote and integrate the single market. Thus, it has been said that art.101 of the TFEU constitutes a fundamental provision which is essential for the accomplishment of the tasks entrusted to the EU and, in particular, for the functioning of the internal market.[46] This goal means that arrangements to partition national markets or prevent parallel imports within the EU tend to be viewed very unfavourably. Thus, why the European Commission now accepts that exclusivity is often a necessary ancillary restraint in a licence to incentivise a licensee to promote the licensed goods, services or technology and prevent "free riding", attempts to provide absolute territorial protection and thus inhibit the right of the internal market to arbitrage price differences between Member States are invariably prohibited under art.101.

We now turn to consider EU competition law in more detail. **8-069**

Article 101

The competition provisions of the TTFEU are contained in arts 101 and 102. **8-070**
Article 101 is concerned with anti-competitive agreements and states that:

"The following shall be prohibited as incompatible with the European Union:

1. All agreements between undertakings, decisions by associations of undertakings and concerted practices which may affect trade between Member States and which have as their object or effect the prevention, restriction or distortion of competition within the European Union, and in particular those which:
    (a) directly or indirectly fix purchase or selling prices or any other trading conditions;
    (b) limit or control production, markets, technical development or investment;
    (c) share markets or sources of supply;
    (d) apply dissimilar conditions to equivalent transactions with other trading parties, thereby placing them at a competitive disadvantage;
    (e) make the conclusion of contracts subject to acceptance by the other parties of supplementary obligations which, by their nature or according to commercial usage, have no connection with the subject of such contracts.
2. Any agreements or decisions prohibited pursuant to this Article shall be automatically void.

---

[46] *Eco Swiss China Time Ltd v Benetton International NV* (C-126/97) [1999] E.C.R. I-3055 at [36].

    3.   The provisions of paragraph 1 may, however, be declared inapplicable in the case of:
-   any agreement or category of agreements between undertakings;
-   any decision or category of decisions by associations of undertakings;
-   any concerted practice or category of concerted practices;
-   which contributes to improving the production or distribution of goods or to promoting technical or economic progress, while allowing consumers a fair share of the resulting benefit, and which does not:
    (a)   impose on the undertakings concerned restrictions which are not indispensable to the attainment of these objectives;
    (b)   afford such undertakings the possibility of eliminating competition in respect of a substantial part of the products in question."

8-071   The four essential elements of art.101(1) are:

(1)   an agreement, concerted practice or decision;
(2)   between undertakings;
(3)   which affects trade between Member States; and
(4)   has as its object or effect the prevention restriction or distortion of competition within the EU.

These elements are discussed in detail below.[47]

Agreement, decisions and concerted practices

8-072   Loosely put, art.101 only applies if the conduct of which complaint is made arises from a course of action which involves forms of collusion between two or more parties.[48] Unilateral conduct is only relevant under art.102. Thus, a refusal to license by an undertaking will only be actionable under art.102.[49]

8-073   Generally, it is clear if there is an agreement. Such represents a formal meeting of minds about an agreed course of conduct. It does not need to be in writing. It can be oral. Furthermore, a decision of an association of undertakings is not difficult to understand.[50] The concept of "concerted practice" is more difficult. It encompasses co-operative behaviour which falls short of an actual agreement. It is discussed below. Moreover, there is often a fine line between genuine unilateral conduct and conduct of one party done with the tacit consent or agreement of another. This boundary is considered below.

8-074   Where an agreement is no longer in force, art.101(1) will apply if it continues to produce effects.[51] With regard to assignments of intellectual property where there

---

[47]   For further reading on the law relating to art.101 in the English language, see V. Rose and D. Bailey, *Bellamy and Child, European Union Law of Competition*, 7th edn (Oxford: OUP, 2013); *Butterworth's Competition Law* (looseleaf-continually updated); R. Whish and D. Bailey, *Competition Law*, 7th edn (Oxford: OUP, 2012); and J. Goyder and A. Albors-Llorens, *EU Competition Law*, 5th edn (Oxford: OUP, 2009).

[48]   e.g. see *T-Mobile Netherlands BV v Raad van bestuur van de Nederlandse Mededingingsautoreit* (C-8/08) ECLI:EU:C:2009:343 at [23].

[49]   Although a refusal to license except on unreasonable terms may arguably constitute a breach of art.101 if combined with an exercise of IPRs, see para.14-029.

[50]   e.g. see *IAZ International Belgium SA v Commission of the European Communities* (96/82) [1983] E.C.R. 3369, [1984] 3 C.M.L.R. 276. See also *Nintendo Co Ltd v Commission of the European Communities* (T-13/03) [2009] E.C.R. II-947, [2009] 5 C.M.L.R. 4; *CISAC Agreement, Re* (COMP/C2/38.698) [2009] 4 C.M.L.R. 12.

[51]   *Binon & Cie SA v SA Agence de la Presse* (243/83) [1985] E.C.R. 2015, [1985] 3 C.M.L.R. 800;

is no evidence on continuing co-operation, the European Court of Justice ("CJEU") has said that an agreement is only regarded as continuing to have effects if, from the behaviour of the persons concerned, there may be inferred the existence of elements of concerted practice and of co-ordination peculiar to the agreement and producing the same result as that envisaged by the agreement but that such was not the case when the assignee merely exercised their trade mark rights.[52] Certainly, an assignment per se does not bind the assignor after the event and in itself cannot be evidence of co-operative behaviour.[53]

Concerted practices

The meaning of "concerted practices" was explained in the *T-Mobile* case as: **8-075**

"a form of co-ordination between undertakings by which, without it having been taken to the stage where an agreement properly so-called has been concluded, practical co-operation between them is knowingly substituted for the risks of competition."[54]

As said by the Court of Justice, the notion inherent in the Treaty provisions on **8-076** competition is that each undertaking must determine independently the policy which they intend to adopt on the common market.[55] This does not mean that undertakings may not adapt themselves intelligently to the existing or anticipated conduct of their competitors. However, it does preclude direct or indirect contact between competitors where the object or effect of such is to create conditions of competition which do not correspond to the normal conditions of the market in question, regard being had to the nature of the products or services offered, the size and number of the undertakings involved and the volume of the market.[56]

In many cases, undertakings will meet to exchange information to enable trad- **8-077** ers to know each other's marketing strategies including pricing. If such exchanges reduce or remove the uncertainty as to the operation of the market in question, they are likely to restrict competition, e.g. by allowing an undertaking to adopt a pricing strategy in the knowledge of the pricing strategy of other undertakings in the same market.[57] It is not necessary that there is a direct connection between the exchange of information and the prices adopted by undertakings. Rather, if the exchange of information has an indirect effect on pricing, it is sufficient to engage art.101. This is because art.101 is designed to protect not only the immediate interests of competitors or consumers but also the structure of the market.[58]

By itself, an exchange of information or other collusion between undertakings **8-078**

[ ] *EMI Records Ltd v CBS United Kingdom Ltd* (51/75) [1976] E.C.R. 811, [1976] 2 C.M.L.R. 235.

[52] (51/75) [1976] E.C.R. 811; [1976] 2 C.M.L.R. 235 and in UK, *Doncaster v Bolton* [2006] E.T.M.R. 65; [2007] F.S.R. 3 CA. See para.7-308, et seq.

[53] See *IHT Internationale Heiztechnik GmbH v Ideal Standard GmbH* (C-9/93) [1994] E.C.R. I-2789; [1994] 3 C.M.L.R. 857.

[54] *T-Mobile*, at [26]. This is settled law—see Joined Cases. *Suiker Unie v Commission* (40/73) to (48/73), (50/73), (54/73) to (56/73), (111/73), (113/73) and (114/73) [1975] E.C.R. 1663 at [26], and Joined Cases *Ahlström Osakeyhtiö v Commission* (C-89/85), (C-104/85), (C-114/85), (C-116/85), (C-117/85) and (C-125/85) to (C-129/85) [1993] E.C.R. I-1307 at [63].

[55] *Suiker Unie v Commission*, at [173]; *Züchner* (172/80) [1981] E.C.R. 2021 at [13]; *Ahlström Osakeyhtiö v Commission*, at [63]; and *P. Deere v Commission* (C-7/95) [1998] E.C.R. I-3111 at [86]; *T-Mobile*, at [32].

[56] *T-Mobile*, at [33].

[57] *T-Mobile*, at [34]–[35].

[58] *T-Mobile*, at [36]–[39].

is not objectionable under art.101. It must be shown that it gives rise to actual effects on the marketplace. In other words, there must be a causal link between the collusion and adverse effects in the marketplace. However, there is a presumption, subject to proof to the contrary by the undertakings concerned, that the undertakings take account of information exchanged between them in determining their conduct on the marketplace. This is all the more the case where undertakings meet together on a regular basis over a long time.[59] Thus, if there is an exchange of information between undertakings which would allow the same to co-ordinate market activity, there will be a presumption that the undertakings have co-ordinated their market activity.

8-079   Often evidentially, it is difficult for a competition authority to prove that there was an exchange of information or collusive activity by way of secret meetings. Thus, the authority may seek to infer the same by parallel conduct of undertakings in a market. However, parallel conduct is not itself proof of concertation unless concertation constitutes the only plausible explanation of such conduct. Thus, it is necessary to ascertain whether that conduct, taking account of the nature of the products, the site and the number of the undertakings and the volume of the market in question, can be explained otherwise than by concertation.[60] Evidence of a concerted practice is strong if the parallel conduct leads to conditions of competition which one would not expect in the normal conditions of the market.[61] A concerted practice will be readily inferred if parallel behaviour in the market is established and contact between the parties is proved. In such cases, parties must put forward evidence to explain why such parallel behaviour was not the result of a concerted practice.[62] Expert economic analysis in this regard will often be invaluable.[63]

Unilateral conduct and licences

8-080   What is the position where a manufacturer imposes measures on distributors or wholesalers which they do not resist to? Can it be said that there is an agreement or concerted practice? This difficult area is clearly relevant to licences where the licensor imposes certain measures on its licensees. Where such measures are agreed to by the licensees, there can be no dispute. However, what is the position where anti-competitive instructions, e.g. export bans are communicated by the licensor to its licensees? Is there an agreement if the licensee complies with those instructions? Tacitly acquiesces? Continues economic relations with the licensor? Fails to protest against the instructions?

8-081   Historically, the Commission and the CJEU have readily inferred that apparently unilateral action is pursuant to some "understanding" between undertakings.[64] Thus, where Konica, a manufacturing company, sent a circular to its distributors

---

[59]   P. Hüls v Commission (C-199/92) [1999] E.C.R. I-4287 at [61]–[63]; T-Mobile, at [51].
[60]   Solvay SA v EU Commission (T-30/91) [1995] E.C.R. II-1775; [1996] 5 C.M.L.R. 57.
[61]   (48/69) [1972] C.M.L.R. 557 at [65]–[68].
[62]   e.g. see Petrofina v EU Commission (T-2/89) [1991] E.C.R. II-1087 at [128] (one of the Polypropylene cases).
[63]   e.g. see A. Ahlström Osakeyhtiö v EU Commission ("Woodpulp") (89/85) [1993] E.C.R. I-1307; [1993] 4 C.M.L.R. 407 at [73]–[127], where the court overturned a Commission's finding as to a concerted practice between parties as a result of expert evidence.
[64]   e.g. AEG Telefunken v EU Commission (107/82) [1983] E.C.R. 3151, [1984] 3 C.M.L.R. 325; Metro-SB-Großmärkte v EU Commission (26/76) [1977] E.C.R. 1875, [1978] 2 C.M.L.R. 1. See also Commission Decision No.74/634 Franco-Japanese Ballbearings [1975] F.S.R 221; [1975] C.M.L.R. D8

requiring them not to export its products from the UK to Germany, such was held to be an offer by Konica and that compliance with it by its distributors amounted to an agreement by the distributors and thus was an agreement or concerted practice which fell within art.101.[65]

The whole issue of unilateral conduct was the subject of judicial discussion in **8-082** *Bayer v Commission*.[66] Bayer, the well-known pharmaceutical company, traded via subsidiary companies in the EU. It sold medicinal products for cardio-vascular ill-nesses under the mark ADALATE or ADALAT. The price of such products is gener-ally fixed by competent national authorities. Between 1989 and 1993, the price of ADALAT in France and Spain was much lower than in the UK. This caused a flourishing market in parallel imports from Spain and France into the UK. This caused the UK subsidiary to suffer a very substantial loss in turnover. As a result, Bayer changed its supply policy and refused to meet all the orders placed by French and Spanish wholesalers in an effort to reduce the parallel imports into the UK. The particular practice objected to was that Bayer permanently reduced the medicinal products delivered to wholesalers if they exported medicinal products to the UK. This threat led to the wholesalers becoming reluctant to comply with the export ban. The French and Spanish wholesalers complained to the European Commission that Bayer was refusing to supply them with ADALAT. In 2000, the Commission fined Bayer for operating an export ban through an agreement with the French and Span-ish wholesalers contrary to art.101(1). This was annulled by the General Court on the grounds that the Commission had failed to prove that there was an agreement to limit parallel imports.

The CJEU upheld the decision of the General Court. It made it clear that a **8-083** unilateral policy aimed at preventing parallel imports from wholesalers did not amount to an agreement within art.101.[67] It clarified also the position regarding "tacit acceptance" of unilateral conduct which had previously been mentioned in case law of the CJEU. Thus, in *Sandoz*,[68] a multinational pharmaceutical company had sent invoices to its customers (wholesalers, pharmacies, etc.) which said, "export prohibited". *Sandoz* denied that such amounted to an agreement with its customers. The General Court disagreed saying that the repeated orders for the products and the successive payments without protest by the customer amounted to a "tacit acquiescence" and that taken as a whole, there had been an agreement between its customers.[69] Thus, in *Bayer v Commission*,[70] the Commission argued that the Spanish and French wholesalers had also tacitly acquiesced and such was sufficient. However, the CJEU distinguished *Sandoz* and said:

> "[102] For an agreement within the meaning of art.[101] of the Treaty to be capable of being regarded as having been concluded by tacit acceptance, it is necessary that the manifestation of the wish of one of the contracting parties to achieve an anti-

at [25], where the Commission held that where an undertaking "voluntarily undertakes to limit its freedom of action with regard to the other", such constitutes an agreement. However, in that case, it was clear that the apparently unilateral action resulted from a series of correspondence and meet-ings between the parties. Accordingly, the Commission concluded that there was in principle an agreement.

[65] Commission Decision. *Konica* [1988] OJ L78/34; [1988] 4 C.M.L.R. 848.

[66] *Bayer AG v Commission of the European Communities* (C-2/01P & C-3/01P) [2004] E.C.R. I-23; [2004] 4 C.M.L.R. 13.

[67] See [101].

[68] *Sandoz Prodotti Farmaceutici* (C-277/87) [1990] E.C.R. I-45.

[69] See (C-277/87) [1990] E.C.R. I-45 at [160]–[161].

[70] (C-2/01P & C-3/01P) [2004] E.C.R. I-23.

> competitive goal constitute an invitation to the other party, whether express or implied, to fulfil that goal jointly, and that applies all the more where, as in this case, such an agreement is not at first sight in the interests of the other party, namely the wholesalers."

8-084   The CJEU held that such was not the case. It distinguished *Sandoz* by saying that the insertion by the manufacturer of the words "export prohibited" on invoices amounted to a demand for a particular line of conduct which the wholesalers tacitly accepted.[71]

8-085   It might be thought hard to reconcile *Sandoz* and *Bayer*. It was no doubt a significant fact that in *Bayer*, the Spanish and French wholesalers were unlikely to agree to the unilateral conduct as it was not in their interests and indeed they had complained about it to the Commission whereas in *Sandoz*, it was in their interests. However, in reality, the Spanish and French wholesalers adopted an export ban under threat by Bayer not to supply them. There was no "meeting of minds" to operate an export ban. Rather, the wholesalers adopted the course against their will and desire to export. In short, an undertaking with an economic "gun at its head" may adopt a course of action that the holder of the gun wishes it to adopt but that does not mean that it has agreed willingly and voluntarily to do so. However, the facts of *Bayer* must be seen as an outlier. It should be distinguished from the case where a manufacturer includes anti-competitive terms in its wholesaler terms and conditions and refuses to remove them and as a result, the wholesaler reluctantly agrees to them.

8-086   Further, it is of note that a facile argument that an agreement had been reached within the meaning of art.101 simply because the wholesalers were in a commercial arrangement with the manufacturer was rejected by the CJEU in *Bayer*:

> "[141] In that respect, it is important to note that this case raises the question of the existence of an agreement prohibited by art.[101(1)] of the Treaty. The mere concomitant existence of an agreement which is in itself neutral and a measure restricting competition that has been imposed unilaterally does not amount to an agreement prohibited by that provision. Thus, the mere fact that a measure adopted by a manufacturer, which has the object or effect of restricting competition, falls within the context of continuous business relations between the manufacturer and its wholesalers is not sufficient for a finding that such an agreement exists."[72]

Thus, as said by an Advocate-General in a later case, where a manufacturer unilaterally imposes a measure restricting competition on its wholesalers, the mere continuation of commercial relations does not amount to tacit acquiescence by the wholesalers to that measure.[73]

8-087   In *Microsoft Leader*, the Commission rejected a complaint from a French software company which purchased French-language Microsoft software in Canada and attempted to import them into France. The company complained of proceedings brought by Microsoft together with the French customs authorities to prevent such imports. The French company alleged that such acts were contrary to arts 101

---

[71] (C-2/01P & C-3/01P) [2004] E.C.R. I-23 at [104].

[72] See on this point, a UK case *Unipart Group v O2 (UK)* [2005] E.C.C. 9, where the Court of Appeal made it clear that there must be an agreement about the anti-competitive conduct of which complaint is made and not merely an agreement, at [97] per Jonathan Parker LJ.

[73] *Eturas v Lietuvos Respublikos kokurencijos taryba* (C-74/14) ECLI:EU:C:2015:493 at [64] citing *Bayer AG v EC Commission* at [141].

and 102 of the TFEU because they constituted concerted practices designed to prevent by illegal means the import of products into the EEA and thus to maintain artificially high prices in the EEA. The Commission said that Microsoft's actions were justified as computer programs were protected by copyright and their actions could not be regarded as resulting from an agreement or concerted practice between it and its resales agents to enforce copyright against imports from outside the EU or an attempt fix resale prices.[74]

Undertakings

The word "undertaking" which is not defined in the TFEU, has been given a **8-088** broad meaning by the Commission and the court. It includes any type of person, natural or legal, whose activities are of an economic or commercial nature. This does not necessarily mean that the activity must be profit-orientated.[75] Member States themselves are not as a rule considered undertakings for the purposes of art.101.[76] However, this is construed narrowly and reflects the fact that many activities of Member States are concerned with the performance of administrative and non-commercial duties. Thus where a public body or even a government department is involved in a commercial or economic enterprise, it may be deemed to be an undertaking.[77] Conversely, where a public body is merely carrying out its public duties and awarding public service contracts to private concessionaires, then the public body is not an undertaking for the purposes of art.101.[78] Where the activity of a public authority consisted of storing data in a database which comprised information supplied pursuant to statutory obligations, the fact that the authority permitted interested persons to search for that data did not constitute an economic activity which rendered the public authority an undertaking within the meaning of art.102 TFEU. Furthermore, the fact that the public authority prohibited the use of

---

[74] *Micro Leader/Microsoft* Annual Report on Competition, 1998, p.166. The dismissal of Micro Leader's complaint was appealed by Micro Leader to the General Court which rejected the appeal in relation to art.101 but held that the Commission had not carried out sufficient investigation under art.101 (*Micro Leader Business v Commission of the European Communities* (T-198/98) [1999] E.C.R. II-398).

[75] See *Heintz van Landewyck Sarl v EU Commission* (209–215/78 and 218/78) [1980] E.C.R. 3125; [1981] 3 C.M.L.R. 134 CJEU; *Re Cast Iron and Steel Rolls* [1984] 1 C.M.L.R. 694; *Interpar v Gesellschaft zur Berwetung von Leistungsschutzrechten mbH* [1982] 1 C.M.L.R. 221. Also see decision of *Film Purchasers by German TV stations* [1989] OJ L284/36, at 41. A "one-off" inventor who forms a company to exploit his invention commercially and to which he gives a licence to work his patent is himself an "undertaking" for the purposes of art.101 in addition to his company—*H. Vaessen BV v Alex Moris* (79/86) [1979] 1 C.M.L.R. 511. See also Commission Decision *Reuter/BASF* [1976] 2 C.M.L.R. D44; [1976] OJ L254/40.

[76] art.86 (ex-art.90) of the TFEU governs the competitive behaviour of Member States. See Commission Decision No.82/896 *AROW/BNIC* [1982] OJ L379/1; [1983] 2 C.M.L.R. 240 (a decision by a government commission laying down minimum prices for sale of cognac was not a decision given by an undertaking).

[77] e.g. see The 9th Annual Report on Competition Policy, points 114–115 (*French State/Suralmo*) where a patent licence agreement between a French government department and Suralmo was deemed to fall within art.101. See also *BNIC v Clair* (123/83) [1985] E.C.R. 391; [1985] 2 C.M.L.R. 430, at points 16–19, where the European Court stated that the classification given to an agreement by a Member State's law was irrelevant in relation to the applicability of art.101 (agreement between two associations of undertakings done under the aegis of an institution of public law did not take the agreement outside art.101).

[78] *Bodson v PFRL* (30/87) [1988] E.C.R. 2479; [1989] 4 C.M.L.R. 984.

that data by reference to harmonised EU IPR legislation did not render that authority an undertaking.[79]

8-089   For the purposes of arts 101 and 102, "undertaking" designates an economic unit rather than a legal person.[80] Thus agreements between legal persons which form a single economic unit will not fall within art.101. In the 1960s and 1970s, the Commission emphasised that the criteria for determining whether they do form an economic unit is whether competition is possible between the parties.[81] In the 1980s, the CJEU refined this by saying that:

> "With regard to the applicability of Article [101] to relations between holders of concessions belonging to the same group of undertakings it must be borne in mind that, as the Court has held (Case 15/74, *Centrafarm v Sterling Drug*),[82] that provision is not concerned with agreements or concerted practices between undertakings belonging to the same concern and having the status of parent company and subsidiary, if the undertakings form an economic unit within which the subsidiary has no real freedom to determine its course of action on the market, and if the agreements of practice are concerned merely with the internal allocation of tasks as between the undertakings."[83]

8-090   However, even where an agreement is between two non-economically linked undertakings, this does not mean per se that they are two undertakings for the purpose of art.101. Often their relationship will be such that one undertaking effectively stands in the shoes of the other. This may be the case in an agent-principal relationship where the agent acts on behalf of the principal to sell products or services to third parties (e.g. a sales agent) rather than being in an arm's length commercial relationship. When considering whether an agreement between an agent and its principal is an agreement between undertakings for the purpose of art.101, the Court of Justice has held that this is only the case where the agent is to be regarded as an independent economic operator. Here, the decisive factor is whether there is an assumption by the agent of a non-negligible financial and commercial risks linked to sales of goods to third parties. The tribunal must take account of the "real economic situation rather the legal categorisation of the contractual relationship in national law".[84] Care must be taken here. Article 101 is inapplicable in relation to downstream restrictions on the agent selling the principal's goods into the marketplace. In such circumstances, the agent and principal stand in each other's shoes. However, there may be clauses governing the very relationship between

---

[79]   *Compass-Datenbank GmbH v Republik Österreich* (C-138/11) ECLI:EU:C:2012:449.
[80]   See *Hydrotherm Geratebau GmbH v Compact de Dott Ing. Mario Andreoli & C.S.A.S.* (170/83) [1984] E.C.R. 2999; [1985] 2 C.M.L.R. 244. Also see decision of Commission in *Re Racal Group Service* [1990] 4 C.M.L.R. 627. See also A. Jones, "The Boundaries of an Undertaking in EU Competition Law" *European Competition Journal*, August 2012, 301–331.
[81]   See *Christiani and Nielsen* [1969] C.M.L.R. D36 (EC Commission) and *KODAK* [1970] C.M.L.R. D19.
[82]   *Centrafarm v Sterling Drug* (15/74) [1974] E.C.R. 1147; [1974] 2 C.M.L.R. 480.
[83]   *Bodson v Pompes Funèbres des Régions Libérées* (30/87) [1988] E.C.R. 2479; [1989] 4 C.M.L.R. 984. See also *Parker Pen Ltd v EU Commission* (T-77/92) [1994] E.C.R. II-549; [1995] 5 C.M.L.R. 435 and *Viho Europe BV v EU Commission* (C-73/95P) [1996] E.C.R. I-5457; [1997] 4 C.M.L.R. 419 where the CJEU re-affirmed this approach by stating that even if art.101(1) was read in conjunction with arts 2, 3(c) and (g) of the EC Treaty, art.101(1) did not apply to agreements between parents and subsidiaries, even if such agreements would affect the competitive position of third parties.
[84]   *CEPSA Estaciones de Servicio SA v LV Tobar e Hijos SL* (C-279/06) ECLI:EU:C:2008:485 at [36].

agent and principal ensuring that they do not offer competing products. Article 101 is applicable to those.[85]

The phrase "association of undertakings" applies to regulatory bodies, e.g. trade **8-091** associations, which can affect the trading behaviour of their members.

An undertaking need not be resident in the EU for art.101 to be applicable. It is **8-092** sufficient that such an undertaking is responsible for anti-competitive behaviour within the EU.[86]

Effect on trade between Member States

Article 101 only applies where the agreement, decision or concerted practice has **8-093** an effect on trade between Member States. This aspect of art.101 is often described as a jurisdictional one. The CJEU in *Commercial Solvents v EU Commission*[87] said the expression is intended to define the sphere of application of EU rules in relation to national laws. Thus, the Modernisation Regulation provides that where an agreement which does have an effect on trade between Member States does *not* fall within art.101, national competition law may not find to the contrary.[88] Conversely, once an agreement is found to have an effect on trade between Member States, art.101 applies to the exclusion of national competition law. Thus, if an agreement[89] only affects trade in one Member State, then it is a matter for the relevant national competition authorities and art.101 is inapplicable. The Commission has published a Notice for undertakings to determine whether their conduct is capable of having an effect on trade between Member States.[90] This gives detailed guidance to the determination of this issue to a particular set of facts.

In *Consten & Grundig v Commission*,[91] the court stated in respect of this condi- **8-094** tion that:

> "it is necessary to know whether the agreement is capable of endangering, either directly or indirectly, in fact or potentially, freedom of trade between Member States in a direction which could harm the attainment of the objects of a single market between States."

This formula which was originally stated in *Technique Minière v Maschinenbau* **8-095** *Ulm*[92] has been reiterated many times by both the court and the Commission. The court and Commission have demonstrated in their decisions that they will readily conclude that the above criteria have been fulfilled, especially where it is clear that

---

[85] *CEPSA Estaciones de Servicio SA v LV Tobar e Hijos SL* (C-279/06) ECLI:EU:C:2008:485 at [40]–[42] applying *Confederación Española de Empresarios de Estaciones de Servicio* (C-217/05) [2006] E.C.R. I-11987.

[86] The CJEU has ruled that according to EU law, jurisdiction is established against undertakings responsible for anti-competitive behaviour in the EU, regardless of whether or not they are established inside the EU.

[87] *Commercial Solvents Corp v EU Commission* (6/73 and 7/73) [1974] E.C.R. 223; [1974] 1 C.M.L.R. 309 CJEU, 342. This was a decision on art.102 but both Articles contain the same condition.

[88] art.3(2) para.8 Reg.1/2003. Commission Notice. Guidelines on the effect on trade concept contained in Articles 101 and 102 of the Treaty [2004] OJ C101/07. Clearly, it is an academic issue whether an agreement that does fall within art.101 is also contrary to national competition law.

[89] Hereinafter the phrase "agreement" is used to refer to agreements, concerted practices and decisions.

[90] Guidelines on the effect on trade concept contained in Articles 101 and 102 of the Treaty [2004] OJ C101/07.

[91] *Consten & Grundig v EU Commission* (56 & 58/64) [1966] E.C.R. 299; [1966] C.M.L.R. 19.

[92] *Technique Miniere v Maschinenbau Ulm* (56/65) [1966] E.C.R. 235; [1966] C.M.L.R. 357.

the object of the agreement was to restrict competition.[93] Thus, agreements between undertakings of one Member State which ostensibly are intended to restrict competition in that Member State will often be found to have anti-competitive repercussions on patterns of trade and competition in the EU.[94]

8-096   An alternative formula was stated in *Commercial Solvents*.[95] The court stated that the prohibitions of arts 101 and 102 must be in fact interpreted and applied in the light of the then art.3(g) EC Treaty.[96] It went on to say:

> "The European Union authorities must therefore consider all the consequences of the conduct complained of for the competitive structure in the European Union without distinguishing between production intended for sale within the market and that intended for export. When an undertaking in a dominant position within the European Union abusively exploits its position in such a way that a competitor in the European Union is likely to be eliminated, it does not matter whether the conduct relates to the latter's exports or its trade within the European Union, once it has been established that this elimination *will have repercussions on the competitive structure within the European Union.*"[97] [Emphasis supplied.]

8-097   Trade between Member States is capable of being affected even where some or all of the undertakings who are party to the agreement or concerted practice are not resident in the EU. The test is still the same regardless of the locations of the economic seats of the undertakings concerned.[98] This test is often called the "effects" doctrine. If the effect of the agreement is to affect trade between Member States, then art.101(1) is capable of being applicable, even if the economic seat of an undertaking is outside the EU.[99] Thus, the CJEU said the following:

> "It should be observed that an infringement of Article [101], such as the conclusion of an agreement which has had the effect of restricting competition within the European Union, consists of conduct made up of two elements, the formation of the agreement, decision or concerted practice and the implementation thereof. If the applicability of prohibitions laid down under competition law were made to depend on the place where the agreement, decision or concerted practice was formed, the result would obviously be to give

---

[93]   e.g. *BNIC v Clair* (C-123/83) [1985] E.C.R. 391; [1985] 2 C.M.L.R. 430 at 425, the court stated that any agreement whose object or effect is to restrict competition by fixing minimum prices for an intermediate product is capable of affecting intra-EU trade, even if there is no trade in that intermediate product between the Member States, where that product constitutes the raw material for another product marketed elsewhere in the EU.

[94]   *Publishers Association v Commission* (T-66/89) [1992] E.C.R. II-1995; [1992] 5 C.M.L.R. 120.

[95]   (6 and 7/73) [1974] E.C.R. 223; [1974] 1 C.M.L.R. 309. See also *Greenwich Film Production v SACEM* (22/79) [1979] E.C.R. 3275; [1980] 1 C.M.L.R. 629 (EC Commission) which applied this doctrine to a performing rights' society's behaviour under art.102.

[96]   This provides that the activities of the EU shall include the institution of a system ensuring that competition in the EU is not distorted. Although this article is not replicated per se in the TFEU, the principle of non-distortion of competition clearly exists—see, e.g. art.3 TEU.

[97]   (6 and 7/73) [1974] E.C.R. 223; [1974] 1 C.M.L.R. 309.

[98]   *Re Woodpulp Cartel* (89/95) [1988] E.C.R. 5193, [1988] 4 C.M.L.R. 901; (51/75) [1976] E.C.R. 811, [1976] 2 C.M.L.R. 235, CJEU (a restrictive agreement between traders within the EU and competitors in non-member countries that would bring about an isolation of the EU as a whole, thus reducing the supply of products originating outside the EC, could be of such a nature as to affect adversely the conditions of competition within the EU—at point 28); see also *Beguelin Import v GL Import Export* (22/71) [1971] E.C.R. 949, [1972] C.M.L.R. 81, ("the fact that one of the undertakings which are parties to the agreement is situated in a third country does not prevent the agreement of [art.101] since the agreement is operative on the territory of the European Union").

[99]   For instance, in a country which has entered into a free trade agreement with the EU, *Re the LdPE Cartel* [1990] 4 C.M.L.R. 382.

undertakings an easy means of evading those prohibitions. The decisive factor is therefore the place where it is implemented."[100]

Agreement ostensibly affects trade only outside the EU

Furthermore, art.101 and art.102 may apply even where the agreement was **8-098** between undertakings located outside the EU. For them to apply, it must be shown that *either* the alleged anti-competitive conduct was implemented in the EU or that the conduct will have "immediate, substantial and foreseeable effect in the European Union."[101]

Appreciable effect

Pursuant to case law from the CJEU, art.101 does not apply to agreements whose **8-099** effect is de minimis. This requires consideration: (a) whether the agreement has an appreciable effect on trade between Member States, and (b) whether the agreement has an appreciable effect on competition. Historically, little distinction was made between these two criteria. However, because of the Modernisation Regulation which rescinds the effect of national competition law, where the agreement does have an effect on trade between Member States, it has become necessary to distinguish between the two.[102] Thus, an agreement may have hardcore anti-competitive clauses but be very local in nature. Conversely, the effects of an agreement may be felt throughout the EU but only have marginal effects for competition. Article 101 is only capable of applying to the second but not the first situation. The Commission Guidelines on the effect on trade concept contained in arts 101 and 102 are a very useful guide to the principles developed by EU courts on the concept of appreciability in the context of trade between Member States.[103] These guidelines make it clear that the issue of whether an agreement appreciably affects trade between Member States is a distinct concept to whether an agreement has an appreciable effect on competition.[104] The 2014 Commission Notice on Agreements of Minor Importance is the relevant guide when considering the issue of what constitutes an appreciable restriction on competition.[105]

Appreciable effect on trade between Member States

An agreement will not fall within art.101 if it has no appreciable effect on trade **8-100** between Member States.[106] These days this is often put in the negative, i.e. that

---

[100] *Re Woodpulp Cartel* (C-89/95). For a commentary on the effect of this case, see *EU Jurisdiction in Antitrust Matters: The Wood Pulp Judgment* (Fordham Corp Law Institute, 1989).

[101] *Intel v European Commission* (T-286/09) ECLI:EU:T:2014:547 at [243]–[244]. Upheld by the Court of Justice in *Intel Corp v European Commission* (C-413/14P) ECLI:EU:C:2017:632.

[102] Guidelines on the effect on trade concept contained in Articles [101] and [102] of the Treaty [2004] OJ C101/07, para.4.

[103] See Guidelines above.

[104] Guidelines, at [4]; See also Commission Notice on agreements of minor importance which do not appreciably restrict competition under Article 101(1) of the Treaty establishing the European Union (de minimis) 2014/C 291/01 [2014] C291, para.4.

[105] Commission Notice on agreements of minor importance which do not appreciably restrict competition under Article 101(1) of the Treaty establishing the European Union (de minimis) 2014/C 291/01 [2014]. See para.8-111.

[106] See, e.g. (56/65) [1966] E.C.R. 235, [1966] C.M.L.R. 357 CJEU; *Volk v Vervaecke* (5/69) [1969]

art.101 does not apply if it only has an insignificant effect on the market.[107] This requirement must be assessed by the effect of the agreement or clause on the competitive structure of the EU in the relevant product and geographic market.[108] In determining whether there is an appreciable effect on trade between Member States, it is the market shares of the undertakings in the relevant market that are of importance rather than the actual level of imports or exports in the relevant goods between Member States that is capable of being restricted by the agreement.[109] Thus, if at least one of the undertakings has a large market share in the Member State in a product, an agreement with an undertaking in another Member State prohibiting imports into the former's country will have an appreciable effect on trade between Member States, even if the latter's imports were negligible prior to the agreement.[110] However, the Commission and CJEU will sometimes consider the level of trade between Member States rather than the market share of the undertakings in question. Thus, it held that a contract which affected 10 per cent of French exports in a particular good to Germany had an appreciable effect on trade between Member States.[111] When considering whether or not there is an appreciable effect on trade between Member States, the Commission has tended to construe the relevant product or service market restrictively.[112]

8-101   The doctrine of appreciable effect must be viewed in the context of the *Consten & Grundig* doctrine whereby agreements may fall within art.101 if they are capable of having a potential effect on trade.[113] Thus, where a British manufacturer granted a Dutch dealer the exclusive right to use its trade mark in Holland and imposed an export ban on its British dealers, the Commission held that the agreement could fall within art.101 and have an appreciable effect on trade between Member States, even

---

E.C.R. 295, [1969] C.M.L.R. 273 CJEU; (22/71) [1971] E.C.R. 949, [1972] C.M.L.R. 81 CJEU; *Expedia v Autorité de la Concurrence* (C-226/11) ECLI:EU:C:2012:795 at [16].

[107] *Expedia*, at [16].

[108] For further information on the determination of the relevant market, see Commission Notice on Definition of Relevant Market for the Purposes of European Union Competition Law [1997] OJ C372/3 which is discussed at para.12-037.

[109] e.g. see *Miller v EU Commission* (19/77) [1977] E.C.R. 131; [1978] 2 C.M.L.R. 334 which involved an agreement between a German record manufacturer (Miller) and its French distributor in Alsace-Lorraine that prohibited the latter from exporting to other countries. There was no discussion of the potential export market share from Alsace-Lorraine but only Miller's market share in records in Germany. See also *Distillers v EU Commission* (30/78) [1980] E.C.R. 229; [1980] 3 C.M.L.R. 121 which concerned an agreement which related to a particular alcoholic drink which had minimal sales outside the UK. The court stated at point 28 that:

> "although an agreement may escape the prohibition in art. 81(1)) when it affects the market only to an insignificant extent, having regard to the weak position which those concerned have in the market in the products in question, the same considerations do not apply in the case of a product of a large undertaking responsible for the entire production. In those circumstances there is no reason to distinguish between Pimm's and the other drinks produced by the applicant."

> Thus, it is not the market share in the goods only subject to the agreement but in the relevant market which the goods fall within.

[110] See *Compagnie Royale Asturienne des Mines SA v EU Commission* (29/83) [1985] 1 C.M.L.R. 688 CJEU at [28]–[30]. See also Notice on Agreements of Minor Importance [2001] OJ C368/13, para.8-111. As for the determination of market share and the concepts of relevant product and geographic market, see para.12-037, et seq.

[111] *Société de Vente de Ciments et Bétons de l'Est SA v Kerpen & Kerpen GmbH & Co KG* (319/82) [1983] E.C.R. 4173.

[112] See *Fisher Price/Quaker Oats-Toyco* [1988] OJ L44/4; *Jourdan* [1989] OJ L35/31.

[113] See para.8-094.

though the known quantities of parallel imports were small because the restriction on potential competition was considerable.[114]

Conversely, where there is no normal pattern of trade between Member States that can be disrupted and there is no likelihood of trade between Member States in the absence of the competitive agreement, then there is no appreciable effect on trade between Member States. Thus, where a Swedish supplier refused to supply spare parts to a London service/repairer, there was no effect on trade between Member States because the latter would not find it in his interests to buy spare parts from other Member States.[115]

8-102

The Commission will be more likely to conclude that an agreement is capable of having an appreciable effect upon trade between Member States when the agreement or concerted practice has as its object (i.e. price-fixing or export bans) the restriction of trade.[116] Thus, where an undertaking had a market share of 3.75 per cent in value but 5 per cent in quantity of the German market in records, then an agreement with an undertaking in another Member State which included an export ban to the former Member State fell within art.101.[117] Where an agreement between two undertakings whose market share in hi-fi equipment was below 5 per cent in the EU but the undertakings had a greater share of a fragmented market than most other competitors, this was held to be capable of having an effect on trade between Member States.[118] At the other end, if a manufacturer holds less than 1 per cent of the market share in a product in a Member State then an exclusive concession agreement between manufacturer and distributor will invariably fall outside art.101(1).[119] However, this is not a hard and fast rule.

8-103

An agreement or concerted practice is not viewed in isolation. Thus, if there are a series of agreements whose cumulative effect is to cause an appreciable effect on trade between Member States, then the agreement will fall within art.101.[120] One need not show that each individual clause in an agreement is capable of affecting intra-EU trade. Rather, only if the agreement as a whole is capable of affecting trade is it necessary to examine which are the clauses of the agreement which have as their object or effect a restriction or distortion of competition.[121]

8-104

Where a distribution agreement was concerned with the marketing of branded goods in non-EEA states but sought to impose bans on the marketing of such goods outside the contract territories (including into the EEA), the CJEU has said that such an agreement may, in particular, have an appreciable effect on trade between Member States where:

8-105

---

[114] *Tepea v EU Commission* (28/77) [1978] E.C.R 1391; [1978] 3 C.M.L.R. 392.

[115] *Hugin Kassaregister v EU Commission* (22/78) [1979] E.C.R. 1869; [1979] 3 C.M.L.R. 345.

[116] e.g. see (19/17) [1978] E.C.R. 131, [1978] 2 C.M.L.R. 334, points 11–12; *Wilkes v Theal NV and Watts Ltd* (77/129) [1977] 1 C.M.L.R. D44.

[117] (19/17) [1977] E.C.R. 131; [1978] 2 C.M.L.R. 334 CJEU. Export bans are generally considered "hard core" restrictions incapable of exemption under art.101(3).

[118] *Musique Diffusion Francaise SA and Pioneer v EU Commission* (100–103/80) [1993] E.C.R. 1825; [1983] 3 C.M.L.R. 221.

[119] (5/69) [1969] E.C.R. 295; [1969] C.M.L.R. 273, CJEU. Volcke had 0.2 per cent and 0.05 per cent of the market in washing machines in Germany in 1963 and 1966, respectively.

[120] See (56/65) [1966] E.C.R. 235; [1966] C.M.L.R. 357 CJEU; also (30/78) [1980] E.C.R. 2229; [1980] 3 C.M.L.R. 121. See also *Re the "Toltecs" and "Dorcet" Trade Mark* [1983] 1 C.M.L.R. 412, points 51–53 (EC Commission). In this case, BAT had entered into similar trade mark settlement agreements with numerous other firms besides the complainant. The Commission held that it was entitled to consider the cumulative effect of these arrangements on competition. See also *Stergios Delimitis v Henninger Bräu* (C-234/89) [1991] E.C.R. I-935; [1992] 5 C.M.L.R. 210.

[121] *Windsurfing International v EU Commission* (193/83) [1986] 3 C.M.L.R. 489 at [96].

"the [European Union] market in the products in question is characterised by an oligopolistic structure or by an appreciable difference between the prices charged for the contractual product within the [European Union] and those charged outside the [European Union] and where, in view of the position occupied by the supplier of the products at issue and the extent of the supplier's production and sales in the Member States, the prohibition entails a risk that it might have an appreciable effect on the pattern of trade between Member States such as to undermine attainment of the objectives of the [European Union]."[122]

Effect on trade between Member States: Commission Notice

8-106   In the Commission Guidelines on the effect of trade concept,[123] the Commission sets out the market shares and turnover thresholds which need to be surmounted for the Commission to take the view that trade is appreciably affected.

"52.   The Commission holds the view that in principle agreements are not capable of appreciably affecting trade between Member States when the following cumulative conditions are met:

(a)   The aggregate market share of the parties on any relevant market within the Community affected by the agreement does not exceed 5%, and

(b)   In the case of horizontal agreements, the aggregate annual Community turnover of the undertakings concerned (39) in the products covered by the agreement does not exceed €40 million. In the case of agreements concerning the joint buying of products the relevant turnover shall be the parties' combined purchases of the products covered by the agreement.

In the case of vertical agreements, the aggregate annual Community turnover of the supplier in the products covered by the agreement does not exceed 40 million euro. In the case of licence agreements the relevant turnover shall be the aggregate turnover of the licensees in the products incorporating the licensed technology and the licensor's own turnover in such products. In cases involving agreements concluded between a buyer and several suppliers the relevant turnover shall be the buyer's combined purchases of the products covered by the agreements."

8-107   Where such thresholds are exceeded, there will not be a positive presumption that such agreements do affect trade unless they are agreements which by their very nature affect trade, e.g. because they concern imports or exports.[124]

8-108   However, even if an agreement has as its object the prevention, restriction or distortion of competition, such an agreement falls outside art.101 if it is not capable of appreciably affecting trade between Member States.[125]

8-109   The 2014 Notice discussed below also says that agreements between small and medium-sized undertakings ("SMEs") as defined in the Annex to the Commission Recommendation of 6 May 2003 are normally not capable of appreciably affecting trade between Member States. SMEs are defined as enterprises which have fewer than 250 employees and have either an annual turnover not exceeding €50 million or an annual balance sheet total not exceeding €43 million.[126]

---

[122] *Javico v Yves St Laurent* (C-306/96) [1998] E.C.R. I-1983 at [28]. See para.8-098.
[123] [2004] OJ C101/81.
[124] See [53], e.g. see (319/82) [1983] E.C.R. 4173 where an agreement between a French producer and a German distributor which covered more than 10 per cent of exports of cement from France to Germany was held to have an appreciable effect on trade between Member States.
[125] 2014 Notice, para.4.
[126] *Commission Recommendation concerning the definition of micro, small and medium-sized*

Appreciable effect on competition

It is settled case law that an agreement of undertakings falls outside art.101 if it has an "insignificant effect on the market". It is only where an agreement has the object or effect of perceptibly restricting competition within the common market *and* is capable of acting trade between Member States that it will fall within art.101.[127] An agreement which has an anti-competitive "object" and affects trade between Member States, is deemed to have an appreciable effect on competition.[128] **8-110**

Commission Notice on Agreements of Minor Importance[129]

Periodically, the Commission issues notices on Agreements of Minor Importance which do not appreciably restrict competition under art.101(1). The latest is its 2014 Notice. It should be read together with the Commission Working Document which sets out which restrictions of competition "by object" which, if in an agreement, will prevent it from benefitting from the 2014 Notice.[130] **8-111**

Being Guidelines, the 2014 Notice has no force of law. Therefore, courts and NCAs may take them into account but are not bound to do so.[131] Nevertheless, the 2014 Notice provides valuable guidance and is relied upon by national competition authorities, the European Commission and national courts. In particular, as regards the Commission, the Notice says that it will not institute proceedings either upon application or on its own initiative where cases are covered by the Notice. Also, it says that it will not impose fines on agreements which undertakings assume in good faith are covered by this notice. The Notice also states that it is intended to provide guidance to the courts and authorities of Member States in their application of art.101.[132] Moreover, as said by the Court of Justice in *Expedia*, the Commission may not depart from the Notice without being in breach of general principles of law, in particular that of equal treatment and the protection of legitimate expectations.[133] **8-112**

The criteria for an agreement to fall within the 2014 Notice are: **8-113**

(a) where the aggregate market share held by the parties to the agreement does not exceed 10 per cent on any of the relevant markets affected by the agreement where the agreement is made between undertakings which are actual or potential competitors on any of these markets; *or*

(b) where the market share held by each of the parties to the agreement does not exceed 15 per cent on any of the relevant markets affected by the agree-

---

enterprises [2003] OJ L124/36.

[127] *Expedia Inc v Autorité de la Concurrence* (C-226/11) ECLI:EU:C:2012:795 at [15]–[16] and cases cited thereto.

[128] *Expedia*, at [37].

[129] Notice on agreements of minor importance which do not appreciably restrict competition under Article 101(1) of the Treaty establishing the European Union (De Minimis Notice) 2014/C/291/01 For an examination of this doctrine, see M. Laurila, "The De Minimis Doctrine in EEC Competition Law: Agreements of Minor Importance" [1993] 3 E.C.L.R. 97–102 (although this must be viewed with care in so far as the Commission Notice on Agreements of Minor Importance has been amended since this article).

[130] Guidance on restrictions of competition "by object" for the purpose of defining which agreements may benefit from the De Minimis Notice, 25 June 2014 C(2014) 4136.

[131] *Expedia*, at [29]–[31].

[132] See para.4.

[133] *Expedia*, at [28].

ment, where the agreement is made between undertakings which are not actual or potential competitors on any of these markets.[134]

8-114   Where in a relevant market, competition is restricted by the cumulative effect of agreements for the sale of goods or services, then when considering the market shares above, they are reduced to 5 per cent for agreement between both competitors and non-competitors. A cumulative foreclosure is unlikely to exist if less than 30 per cent of the relevant market is covered by parallel networks of agreements having similar effects.[135] In cases where it is difficult to classify the agreement as either an agreement between competitors or non-competitors, the 10 per cent threshold applies.[136]

8-115   Agreements which contain blatant anti-competitive practices (i.e. price-fixing, market sharing and customer restrictions) which are considered to restrict competition "by object" are not covered by the 2014 Notice. As said above, where such agreements have an appreciable effect on trade between Member States, they will be deemed to appreciably affect competition.[137] In 2014, alongside the 2014 Notice, as said above, the Commission issued supplementary guidance on what restrictions it considers are "by object" those that an agreement which includes such restrictions will not benefit from the 2014 Notice.[138]

8-116   Undertakings will need to determine the relevant market. The Commission Notice on the Relevant Market should be relied upon for determining the relevant market for the purposes of this Notice.[139]

Jurisdictional aspects of art.101

8-117   It has already been stated that an agreement can affect trade between Member States, irrespective of whether the undertakings to the agreement are situated inside or outside the EU or whether the effects of an agreement are intended to take place outside the EU.[140] This has raised certain questions as regards the Commission's jurisdiction with regard to undertakings situated outside the EU. The jurisdictional aspect should be distinguished from the "effects" doctrine. The latter is concerned with whether certain behaviour is capable of satisfying the conditions under art.101. It is concerned with whether a cause of action under art.101 exists even if the undertakings to the agreement are established outside the EU. The former is concerned with the jurisdictional competence of the Commission or national courts to make findings under art.101 against undertakings resident outside the EU. In general, the CJEU and Commission take the view that it has jurisdiction against undertakings resident outside the EU where their activities affect trade in the EU. However, such does not mean that courts of non-Member States recognise the jurisdiction of the EU institutions in this regard. Such difficulties are often only of interest if there is nothing in the EU on which the EU institutions can enforce judgments. Therefore in practice, fines are enforceable against non-EU companies because they will invariably have substantial assets in the EU.

---

[134] See para.8.
[135] See paras 10.
[136] See para.7.
[137] See above at para.8-110. See also *Expedia v Autorite de la Concurrence* (C-226/11) ECLI:EU:C:2012:795 at [37].
[138] Guidance on restrictions of competition "by object" for the purpose of defining which agreements may benefit from the De Minimis Notice, 25 June 2014 C(2014) 4136.
[139] [1997] OJ C273/5. This is discussed in para.12-037.
[140] See para.8-098.

The CJEU has dealt with this sensitive issue in a number of ways. First, the CJEU **8-118** has decided that the behaviour of a subsidary can be imputed to a parent company.[141] Thus, where an undertaking established outside the EU has a subsidiary within the EU, the establishment of jurisdiction against the parent member undertaking is not based solely on the effects of actions committed outside the EU but also on activities attributable to the undertaking by virtue of its subsidiary being situated within the EU.[142] Secondly, the CJEU has said that the EU's jurisdiction to apply its competition rules to such conduct is covered by the territoriality principle as universally recognised in public international law.[143] The effect of this is to legitimise any enforcement action against non-EU institutions whenever an agreement has an anti-competitive effect in the EU. Therefore, if the "effects" of the agreement are felt in the EU, the EU institutions have jurisdiction over the undertakings concerned regardless of their location.

Inevitably, such a finding gives rise to enforcement problems. Will non- **8-119** Member States' courts recognise any decisions of the Commission in such cases? This will be a matter for the relevant national court. However, from the point of EU law, the CJEU has held that the Commission cannot be denied the right on the basis of public international law to safeguard its measures against conduct distorting competition in the EU, even where those responsible for the said conduct are resident outside the EU. Thus, where the Commission served complaint proceedings against a Swiss undertaking at its Swiss address, this was held to be valid service in accordance with EU law, even if it was not according to Swiss law.[144] The Commission has fined several undertakings situated outside the EU for anticompetitive behaviour.[145]

The court has held that the existence of Articles prohibiting restrictive practices **8-120** in Free Trade Agreements between the EU and a non-Member State did not oust the EU's jurisdiction under arts 101 and 102.[146]

Object or effect: the prevention, restriction or distortion of competition within the EU

Under this provision, it is necessary to distinguish between agreements which **8-121** have as their *object* the prevention, restriction or distortion of competition within the EU and those which merely have the *effect*. A full economic analysis of the effects of agreement is only conducted where there is no finding that the agreement has such as its object. Thus, is considered first.

Object of agreement is anti-competitive

The court has distinguished between the phrase "object or effect" in art.101. **8-122** Agreements which have as their object the restriction, distortion or prevention of competition fall within art.101(1) without further analysis (provided they have an

---

[141] See (48/69) [1972] E.C.R. 619, [1972] C.M.L.R. 557, 629; *Continental Can v EU Commission* (6/72) [1973] E.C.R. 215, [1973] C.M.L.R. 199.

[142] See *Geigy AG & Sandoz AG v EU Commission* (52/69) [1972] C.M.L.R. 640, point 51.

[143] See *A. Ahlström Osakeyhtiö v Commission ("Woodpulp")* (89/85) [1993] 4 C.M.L.R. 407 at [16]–[18].

[144] See *Geigy AG and Sandoz AG v Commission* (52–53/69) [1972] C.M.L.R. 637.

[145] e.g. see Commission Decision 86/398 *Re the LdPe Cartel* [1986] OJ L230/1.

[146] See (89/85) [1993] 4 C.M.L.R. 407 at [30]–[31].

appreciable effect on trade between Member States[147]). Other agreements are examined more carefully to determine whether or not they are anti-competitive. Both the EU and the US have adopted an approach whereby certain "hard core" restrictions such as market price-fixing, market division, and group boycotts can be regarded as unlawful per se without the need for market analysis.[148] Where the object of the agreement is to restrict competition, then one does not need to look at the effects of the agreement in order to establish that it falls within art.101.[149]

8-123 The CJEU has said that certain types of co-ordination between undertakings reveal a "sufficient degree of harm to competition that it may be found there is no need to examine their effects".[150] In order to determine this, regard must be had to the content of its provisions, its objectives and the economic and legal context of which it forms a part. When determining that context, it is also necessary to take into consideration the nature of the goods or services affected, as well as the real conditions of the functioning and structure of the market or markets in question.[151]

8-124 For an agreement to have as its "object" the restriction of competition, it is not necessary to show that this was the intention of the parties to the agreement, although such will be usually taken into account.[152]

8-125 A useful summary of case law and the approach by the Commission regarding whether an agreement has as its object the restriction of competition is set out in the Commission's publication "Guidance on restrictions of competition 'by object' for the purpose of defining which agreements may benefit from the De Minimis Notice".[153] The guidance distinguishes between agreements between competitors and non-competitors. The approach to the latter is unsurprisingly more tolerant. As regards competitors, the following will invariably be considered "hard core" and restraints "by object".

8-126 *Competitors*

- price fixing,
- output limitations,
- market sharing,
- bid rigging (whereby two or more companies agree that one or more than will not submit a bid),
- collective boycotts whereby a group of competitors agree to exclude and actual or potential competitor,
- information sharing between competitors of price and market data, and
- restrictions on carrying out R&D or use of one's own technology (save in the context of JVs).

---

[147] See para.8-093.
[148] In relation to the US approach to "hard core" restrictions, see, *Sherman Act & National Society of Professional Engineers v United States* (1978) 435 US 679, 692. See also the Department of Justice 2017 Guidelines discussed at para.8-060.
[149] (58 and 58/64) [1966] E.C.R. 299; [1966] C.M.L.R. 418 CJEU.
[150] *Groupement des cartes bancaires v European Commission* (C-67/13P) ECLI:EU:C:2014:2204 at [50] and case law cited thereto.
[151] (C-67/13P), at [53] and case law cited there.
[152] *T-Mobile Netherlands* (C-8/08) [2009] E.C.R. 4529 at [27]; (C-67/13P), at 54.
[153] C(2014) 4136..

Non-competitors

In the case of non-competitors, "downstream" restraints restrictions on buyers **8-127** and licensees, e.g. as to whom they may sell (customer restraints), where they may sell (territory restraints) and the price they may sell their goods (resale price maintenance) are generally considered "by object" hard core anti-competitive restraints. However, the guidance sets out a number of exceptions. Thus, it is inherent in many distribution networks (e.g. exclusive and selective distribution networks) that downstream restraints such as territory allocation are necessary as ancillary restraints to incentivise distributors to promote and build up markets in the bought or licensed goods in the allocated territory. Here, the guidance follows and draws heavily upon what restraints are considered "hard core" restrictions in block exemptions in, e.g. the Technology Transfer and Vertical Agreements Block Exemptions. In other words, a hardcore restriction in a block exemption which removes the "safe harbour" of these regulations is also deemed anti-competitive restraint "by object". Thus, if a restraint "by object" appears in an agreement, it will be very difficult to have that agreement exempted under art.101(3). The block exemptions for technology transfer agreement (i.e. licences) and vertical agreements (i.e. distribution agreements) are discussed in Chs 10 and 11.

Effect of agreement is anti-competitive

If there is no finding that the agreement has an anti-competitive objection, then **8-128** it is necessary to consider the effect of the agreement. Such requires a full economic analysis. Thus, as the General Court said in *O2 (Germany) v EU Commission*[154]:

"In order to assess whether an agreement is compatible with the European Union in the light of the prohibition laid down in [Article 101(1)] it is necessary to examine the economic and legal context in which the agreement was concluded (Case 22/71 *Béguelin Import* [1971] ECR 949, paragraph 13), its object, its effects, and whether it affects intra-European Union trade taking into account in particular the economic context in which the undertakings operate, the products or services covered by the agreement, and the structure of the market concerned and the actual conditions in which it functions (Case C-399/93 *Oude Littikhuis and Others* [1995] ECR I-4515, paragraph 10).

That method of analysis is of general application and is not confined to a category of agreements (see, as regards different types of agreements, Case 56/65 *Société Minière et Technique* [1966] ECR 235, at 249–250; Case C-250/92 *DLG* [1994] ECR I-5641, paragraph 31; Case T-35/92 *John Deere v Commission* [1994] ECR II-957, paragraphs 51 and 52; and Joined Cases T-374/94, T-375/94, T-384/94 & T-388/94 *European Night Services and Others v Commission* [1998] ECR II-3141, paragraphs 136 and 137).

Moreover, in a case such as this, where it is accepted that the agreement does not have as its object a restriction of competition, the effects of the agreement should be considered and for it to be caught by the prohibition it is necessary to find that those factors are present which show that competition has in fact been prevented or restricted or distorted to an appreciable extent. The competition in question must be understood within the actual context in which it would occur in the absence of the agreement in dispute; the interference with competition may in particular be doubted if the agreement seems really necessary for the penetration of a new area by an undertaking (*Société Minière et Technique* at 249–250)."[155]

Despite such a statement, the matter is complicated by the fact that art.101 is split **8-129**

---

[154] *O2 (Germany) v EU Commission* (T-328/03) [2006] E.C.R. II-1231; [2006] 5 C.M.L.R. 5.
[155] See [66]–[68].

between art.101(1) and art.101(3). Prior to the Modernisation Regulation, only the European Commission could exempt agreements under art.101(3). Analysis of the competitive effect of agreements under art.101 was often rather formulaic. Thus, where an agreement had had both pro-competitive and restrictive provisions, analysis tended to be done within the context of art.101(3).[156] However, this approach ill-fits with the examination under art.101(1) which requires an examination of the impact of the agreement on existing and potential competition with and without the agreement.[157] With the adoption of the Modernisation Regulation and the ability of courts and tribunals to apply art.101 in its entirety, it might be thought that it matters little now whether an agreement falls within art.101(1) and is exempted under art.101(3) or falls entirely outside art.101. However, art.101(3) requires fulfilment of certain conditions which can be difficult to prove, e.g. indispensability. Moreover, where an agreement falls within art.101(1), the onus is on the parties to the agreement to prove that it should benefit from exemption.[158]

8-130 Léger AG said in the late 1990s case, *Wouters v ARNOA*,[159] that in a number of decisions, the CJEU has effectively applied a "rule of reason" approach to art.101(1). In effect, it has drawn up a "competition balance sheet" and found where the balance is positive, that the clauses of which complaint were made were necessary to perform the agreement and thus fell outside art.101(1).[160] Therefore, it is a well-established doctrine of the CJEU that certain contractual restrictions are necessary to increase competition or facilitate its growth in the future and make transactions commercially viable.[161] Hence, art.101(1) permits contractual restrictions in a trade mark licence which are necessary to protect a licensee against active competition from other licensees to persuade a licensee to take the risk of marketing products.[162] For example, the court has ruled that certain clauses restrictive of competition in a distribution franchise agreement were essential to the working of the franchise.[163] Thus, where a sauce-making business was assigned, the court held that a clause preventing the assignor from trading in sauces for 10 years did not have

---

[156] *Pronuptia v Schillgalis* (161/84) [1986] E.C.R. 353, [24]; *Matra Hachette v Commission* (T-17/93) [1994] E.C.R. II-595 at [48], and *European Night Services v Commission* (T-374/94, T-375/94, T-384/94 and T-388/94) [1998] E.C.R. II-3141 at [36]. As said by the court in *Van den Bergh v EU Commission* (T-65/98) at [107], art.101(3) of the Treaty would lose much of its effectiveness if such an examination had already to be carried out under art.101(1) of the Treaty (see, to that effect, *Montecatini v Commission* (C-235/92 P) [1999] E.C.R. I-4539 at [133]; *Montedipe v Commission* (T-14/89) [1992] E.C.R. II-1155 at [265]; *Tréfilunion v Commission* (T-148/89) [1995] E.C.R. II-1063 at [109]; and also *M6 v Commission* (T-112/99) [2001] E.C.R. II-2459 at [72]–[74]). See also 2014 Guidelines on the application of Article 101 of the TFEU to technology transfer agreements, para.18.

[157] (C-234/89) [1991] E.C.R. I-935 at [21] and the competition situation in the absence of the agreement; *Société* (56/65) [1966] E.C.R. 235, 249–250; *O2 (Germany) v EU Commission* (T-328/03) at [69]–[70].

[158] art.2 Reg.1/2003.

[159] *Wouters v ARNOA* (C-309/99) [2002] E.C.R. I-1577; [2002] 4 C.M.L.R. 27. See para.8-154 for the CJEU's approach to licencing being a "rule of reason".

[160] See [103] citing a number of decisions including in the field of intellectual property: *Nungesser and Eisele v Commission* (258/78) [1982] E.C.R. 2015 at [54]–[58]; and (161/84) [1986] E.C.R. 353 at [14]–[27].

[161] e.g. see (56/65) [1966] E.C.R. 235, [1966] C.M.L.R. 357; (258/78) [1982] E.C.R. 2015, [1983] 1 C.M.L.R. 278; *Coditel v Ciné Vog Films (No.2)* (*"CODITEL II"*) (262/81) [1982] E.C.R. 3381, [1983] 1 C.M.L.R. 49; *Remia v EU Commission* (42/84) [1985] E.C.R. 2547, [1987] 1 C.M.L.R. 1; (161/84) [1986] E.C.R. 353, [1986] 1 C.M.L.R. 414.

[162] *Babyliss v EU Commission* (T-114/02) [2003] E.C.R. II-1279, [2004] 5 C.M.L.R. 1, [424]; (258/78) [1982] E.C.R. 2015, [57]; and (262/81) [1982] E.C.R. 3381 at [15].

[163] (161/84) [1986] E.C.R. 353; [1986] 1 C.M.L.R. 414.

as its effect the restriction of competition. Without such a clause, it was held that the assignment would be devoid of any value, as the assignor could effectively prevent the assignee from building up a client base. However, 10 years was held to be too long.[164]

In the Guidelines on the application of art.101(3), the Commission seeks to distinguish between restrictions which can be considered to be "ancillary restraints" and other restrictions. Recognising the fact that the CJEU has found in a number of decisions that certain overtly restrictive clauses fall within art.101(1) and not art.101(3), it has said that: **8-131**

> "In European Union competition law the concept of ancillary restraints covers any alleged restriction of competition which is directly related and necessary to the implementation of a main non-restrictive transaction and proportionate to it. If an agreement in its main parts, for instance, a distribution agreement or a joint venture, does not have as its object or effect the restriction of competition, then restrictions which are directly related to and necessary for the implementation of that transaction also fall outside art.101. These related restrictions are called ancillary restraints. A restriction is directly related to the main transaction if it is subordinate to the implementation of that transaction and is inseparably linked to it. ... If on the basis of objective factors, it can be concluded that without the restriction the main non-restrictive transaction would be difficult or impossible to implement, the restriction may be regarded as objectively necessary for its implementation and proportionate to it."[165]

Thus, the Commission draws a distinction between restrictive clauses which are ancillary restraints and those which are not. The permissibility of the latter category must be done in the context of art.101(3). **8-132**

Vertical and horizontal agreements

Both vertical and horizontal agreements can fall within art.101.[166] This is important, as usually a vertical agreement will involve undertakings who do not compete against each other whereas a horizontal agreement will invariably be between competing undertakings. Thus, it is not surprising that horizontal agreements are far more likely to fall within art.101(1) and not be exempted under art.101(3) than vertical agreements. In the case of vertical agreements between non-competitors, the inquiry is to determine what level of foreclosure there is of third parties. Thus, in the context of a beer supply agreement which had an exclusive purchasing obligation on the owner of a café in Germany, the CJEU has said that two cumulative conditions must be met. First, it must be shown that having regard to the economic and legal context of the agreement at issue, it is difficult for competitors who could enter the market or increase their market share to gain access to the national market for the distribution of beer in premises for the sale and consumption of drinks. The second condition is that the agreement in issue must make a significant contribution to the sealing-off effect brought about by the totality of those agreements in their economic and legal context. This normally involves investigation of the market share of the supplier and the length of the agreements.[167] **8-133**

---

[164] (42/84) [1985] E.C.R. 2547; [1987] 1 C.M.L.R. 1.
[165] Guidelines on the application of Article 101(3) of the TFEU [2004] OJ C101/97–118, paras 29–31.
[166] See (58 and 58/64) [1966] E.C.R. 299; [1966] C.M.L.R. 418.
[167] *Stergios Delimitis v Henninger Bräu* (C-234/89) [1991] E.C.R. I-935; [1992] 5 C.M.L.R. 210.

The Commission has issued a Block Exemption for Vertical Agreements and accompanying Guidelines. This is discussed later in Ch.11.

Inter-brand and intra-brand competition

8-134   For the purposes of art.101, both inter-brand and intra-brand competition must be considered.[168] A vertical agreement which restricts intra-brand competition does not necessarily fall outside art.101(1), even if it might increase inter-brand competition.[169]

Need to attain a single market

8-135   Article 26 of the TFEU states that one of the tasks of the EU is the adoption of measures with the aim of establishing or ensuring the functioning of the internal market. Thus, it has been said that art.101 of the Treaty constitutes a fundamental provision which is essential for the accomplishment of the tasks entrusted to the EU and, in particular, for the functioning of the internal market.[170] As a result, the CJEU has held that any agreement which reinforces the compartmentalisation of the markets of the Member States thus preventing the economic interpenetration of national markets falls within art.101(1).[171]

Cumulative effect of agreements

8-136   Agreements are not viewed in isolation. Thus, if an agreement is one of a series of agreements whose cumulative effect is such as to restrict competition, then the agreement will fall within art.101(1).[172] This principle is applied widely so that where an agreement is similar to many other agreements concluded between different undertakings, i.e. reflects a trade practice, then the competitive effect of the agreements *in toto* will be considered when appraising the competitive effect of the agreement *in casu*.[173]

Types of competition

8-137   The CJEU has accepted that competition can occur in several ways. The obvious one being price. However, competition can also occur in other areas, e.g. with regards to the quality of service to customers.[174] Therefore, where a manufacturer operates a selective distribution system such that resellers are only eligible if they

---

[168] *Grundig v Commission* (58 and 58/64) [1966] E.C.R. 299; [1966] C.M.L.R. 418.

[169] (58 and 58/64) [1966] E.C.R. 299; [1966] C.M.L.R. 418. However, this must be seen in the light of the decision of the CJEU in (258/78) [1983] 1 C.M.L.R. 278. See para.8-157.

[170] *Courage v Crehan* (C-453/99) [2001] E.C.R. I-6300; (C-126/97) [1999] E.C.R. I-3055 at [36]. See also (58 and 58/64) [1966] E.C.R. 299, [1966] C.M.L.R. 418; *Vereeniging van Cementhandelaren v EU Commission* (8/72) [1972] E.C.R. 977, [1973] C.M.L.R. 7.

[171] See (58 and 58/64) [1966] E.C.R. 299, [1966] C.M.L.R. 418; (8/72) [1972] E.C.R. 977, [1973] C.M.L.R. 7.

[172] See (56/65) [1966] C.M.L.R. 357. It does not matter if different undertakings are involved in each agreement-see *Brasserie de Haecht v Wilkin* [1967] E.C.R. 407 (concerning the widespread practice in the brewery industry to provide financial support to a trader in return for imposing an obligation on the trader to buy its beverages from the brewery). See also (30/78) [1980] E.C.R. 2229; [1980] 3 C.M.L.R. 121 and (C-234/89) [1992] C.M.L.R. 5 at 216.

[173] (C-234/89) [1991] E.C.R. 935; [1992] C.M.L.R. 5.

[174] See para.15 of the 2014 Guidelines on Technology Transfer Agreements where the Guidelines refer

have suitable technical qualifications and premises so as to be able to provide a high quality after-sales service to the consumer, then such an agreement will fall outside art.101(1), as the quantitative restriction on competitors is outweighed by the qualitative increase in competition in terms of high quality service.[175]

Thus, a restriction in potential competitors may be compatible with art.101 if there is a corresponding increase in quality.   **8-138**

Effect of finding that an agreement is contrary to art.101

In the case of art.101, art.101(2) provides that "any agreements or decisions   **8-139** prohibited pursuant to this Article shall automatically be null and void". A finding of nullity is retrospective and, thus, any agreement is unenforceable. However, in *Technique Minière v Maschinenbau Ulm*[176] the CJEU held that a finding of nullity only applies to:

> "those elements of the agreement which are subject to the prohibition, or to the agreement as a whole if those elements do not appear severable from the agreement itself".[177]

In the operative part of the decision, it said that the consequences of nullity on   **8-140** those contractual provisions which are not incompatible with art.101(1) are not the concern of Community law. Accordingly, it is a matter for the domestic law of Member States to discover the legal consequence of a finding that a provision is null and void on the agreement as a whole. In England, *Technique Minière* was discussed in *Chemidus Wavin Ltd v TERI*.[178] In an important judgment, Buckley LJ in the Court of Appeal said:

> "So the position appears clearly to be this, that where in a contract there are certain clauses which are annulled by reason of their being in contravention of Article [101], paragraph (1), of the Treaty, one must look at the contract with those clauses struck out and see what the effect of that is in the light of the domestic law which governs the particular contract. In the present case, we have to consider what effect the invalidity, if any, of the clauses in the licences agreement by reason of Article [101] would have upon that contract as a whole. Whether it is right to regard the matter as one of severance of the contract or not, I do not think it is necessary for us to consider now. I doubt whether it is really a question of severance in the sense in which we in these courts are accustomed to use that term on considering whether covenants contained in contracts of employment and so forth are void as being in restraint of trade, and if they are to any extent void, whether those covenants can be severed so as to save part of the covenant, although another part may be bad. It seems to me that in applying Article [101] to an English contract, one may well have to consider whether, after the excisions required by the Article of the Treaty have been made from the contract, the contract could be said to fail for lack of consideration

---

to licences having negative effects on prices, output, innovation or the variety or quality of goods.

[175] See (26/76) [1977] E.C.R. 1875; [1978] 2 C.M.L.R. 1 (cash-and-carry wholesaler excluded from selective distribution because unable to meet requirement); see also (107/82) [1984] 3 C.M.L.R. 325. The court stated that the entry requirements of a selective distribution system must be based on objective criteria. See also (161/84) [1985] C.M.L.R. 446, which concerned a franchise agreement.

[176] *Technique Minière v Maschinenbau Ulm* (56/65) [1966] E.C.R. 235; [1966] C.M.L.R. 357. See also *Société de Vente de Ciments et Betons de l'Est v Kerpen and Kerpen* (319/82) [1983] E.C.R. 4173; [1985] 1 C.M.L.R. 511 at [11]–[12]. For application of these principles see in the UK, *Bookmakers Afternoon Greyhound Services Ltd v Amalgamated Racing Ltd* [2008] EWHC 1978 (Ch).

[177] (56/65) [1966] E.C.R. 235; [1966] C.M.L.R. 357.

[178] *Chemidus Wavin Ltd v TERI* [1976] 2 C.M.L.R. 387; [1978] 3 C.M.L.R. 514 CA.

or on any other ground, or whether the contract would be so changed in its character as not to be the sort of contract that the parties intended to enter into at all."[179]

8-141　Goff LJ gave a concurring judgment. He endorsed Salter J's judgment in *Putnam v Taylor*[180] that:

> "If a promisee claims the enforcement of a promise, and the promise is a valid promise and supported by consideration, the court will enforce the promise, notwithstanding the fact that the promisor has made other promises, supported by the same consideration, which are void, and has included the valid and invalid promises in one document."

8-142　Both judgments suggest that one should "blue pencil" (i.e. excise) the offending provisions. However, only Buckley LJ's judgment goes on to consider whether the agreement as a whole is valid or not. This approach accords with the CJEU's decision in *Technique Minière*, which requires the court to consider whether the "blue pencilled" clauses are severable. Clearly, if they are not, it is submitted that the whole agreement is void. Accordingly, it would appear that Buckley LJ's judgment provides a more complete guide as to the validity of an agreement as a whole.

8-143　A finding of automatic nullity can be relied on by anyone and subsequent courts are bound by it.[181] The finding of nullity is effective *erga omnes* and not merely inter partes. Thus, the provision has no effect and cannot be set up against a third party.[182] This is important from an IPR practitioner viewpoint because, if an assignment of rights is found void, it will mean that the assignee has no rights to assert against third parties. Furthermore, the finding that the offending provision is null and void means that it was void ab initio and, therefore, is "capable of having a bearing on all the effects, either past or future, of the agreement or decision concerned".[183]

Article 101(3) and exemption

8-144　Article 101(1) may be inapplicable by virtue of art.101(3). Historically, exemption could only be granted by the European Commission. However, following the Modernisation Regulation,[184] courts of Member States and competition authorities are entitled to apply art.101(3). The Commission has issued Guidelines on the application of art.101(3).[185] Moreover, as discussed later, certain agreements which fall within Block Exemptions will automatically be exempted and such agreements cannot be held invalid by national courts, by national competition authorities or courts of Member States.[186]

8-145　Under art.101(3), the onus is on the parties to the agreement to prove that it should benefit from exemption.[187]

8-146　The distinction between art.101(1) and (3) is sometimes difficult to draw. The

[179] *Chemidus Wavin Ltd* [1976] 2 C.M.L.R. 387; [1978] 3 C.M.L.R. 514 CA at [18].
[180] *Putnam v Taylor* [1927] 1 K.B. 639.
[181] *Portelange SA v Smith Corona Marchant International SA* (C-10/69) [1969] E.C.R. 309 at [10]; (C-453/99) [2001] E.C.R. 6297 at [22].
[182] *Béguelin Import Co v Import Export SA GL* (C-22/71) [1971] E.C.R. 949 at [29]; (C-453/99) [2001] E.C.R. 6297 at [22].
[183] *Brasserie de Haecht SA v Wilkin-Janssen (Brasserie de Haecht II)* (C-48/72) [1973] E.C.R. 77 at [26]. Re-affirmed in (C-453/99) [2001] E.C.R. 6297 at [22].
[184] Reg.1/2003.
[185] Guidelines on the application of Article 101(3) of the TFEU [2004] OJ C101/97–118.
[186] art.3.2 Reg.1/2003; Guidelines on the application of Article 101(3) [2004] OJ C101/97–118, para.2.
[187] art.2 Reg.1/2003.

Commission is firmly of the view that art.101(1) is concerned with determining whether an agreement has an anti-competitive object or effect whereas art.101(3) is concerned with weighing the pro- and anti-competitive benefits of the agreement.[188] However, as said above, the CJEU has considered ancillary restraints which do restrict the freedom of licensees in the context of art.101(1).[189] Ultimately, it is rather artificial to say that an agreement does have anti-competitive effects but that *in toto*, it has benefits for consumers and is thus pro-competitive. As said by Jacobs AG in the context of art.102, it is important not to lose sight of the fact that the primary purpose of art.102 is to prevent distortion of competition—and in particular to safeguard the interests of consumers—rather than to protect the position of particular competitors.[190]

8-147 It might be thought that with the ability of courts and national competition authorities to apply both art.101(1) and art.101(3) that the distinction does not matter. However, where an agreement is found to fall within art.101(1), the burden of proof lies on the parties to the agreement to show that it should benefit from exemption under art.101(3).[191]

8-148 The Commission's Guidelines on the application of art.101(3) of the TFEU provides detailed guidance to art.101(3).[192] However, when considering intellectual property licences, better guidance can be obtained from the 2014 Technology Transfer Guidelines. This is discussed in the chapter on IP and Technology Transfer Licences.

Article 101(1) and Licences

8-149 Following the publication of the first Commission *Guidelines on Technology Transfer Agreements* ("2014 Guidelines") and the *Technology Transfer Block Exemption* ("TTBE") in 2004, it was clear that EU law's approach to the competitive analysis of intellectual property licences became one of rigorous economic analysis of the effects of an intellectual property licence on the relevant market. This approach contrasts from its historical approach in the 1970s to 1990s whereby a more formalistic approach was taken whereby contractual restraints were ritually found to infringe art.101(1) and a "rule of reason" approach was only relevant under art.101(3).

8-150 The focus shifted from a number of legal "rules" about what was lawful and unlawful in licences which gave certainty to parties and their advisors but were often arbitrary to an approach that emphasises a rigorous full-blown economic analysis which gives rise to considerable uncertainty but is intended to be more just. Neither approach is wholly satisfactory but there is no perfect solution. The real benefit of the current approach is that it will be rare for art.101 to apply to licences between small and medium-sized undertakings because of the market share thresholds in the various block exemptions that provide a "safe harbour" for such entities subject to the non-inclusion of hard core restrictions in the licences. Thus, those who cannot afford full economic and legal analysis are the ones who will rarely need it, whereas, the large concerns who need to be more careful will be able to afford their own economic analysis. With the inability to obtain the "safe

---

[188] Guidelines on the application of Article 101(3) [2004] OJ C101/97–118, para.11.
[189] See para.8-128.
[190] *Oscar Bronner v Mediaprint* (C-7/93) [1998] E.C.R. I-7817 at [58].
[191] art.2 Reg.1/2003.
[192] [2004] OJ C101/97–118.

harbour" of individual exemption of agreements under art.101(3), the onus is on undertakings of substantial size to implement their own regime for ensuring compliance with art.101.

8-151   As analysis of the effect of art.101 on licences depends very much whether the licence is a technology transfer licence, a licence in a horizontal agreement between competitors, a licence in the context of research and development or manufacturing specialisation, or a licence in a distribution agreement, e.g. a franchise, these types of licences are considered in subsequent chapters. However, this chapter considers the effect of art.101 on licences and also typical clauses that appear in IP licences.

No limited licence approach

8-152   EU law does not endorse a "limited licence" approach whereby the rights owner is entitled to determine the exact nature and extent of economic activity where such activity falls within the exclusive rights of the intellectual property. The limited licence approach distinguishes between permissive clauses which partially lift the monopoly of the IPR and those which extend beyond that. Thus, a clause imposing a maximum output on a licensee would be unobjectionable under US law because the US take the view that a rights owner is entitled to determine the extent of competition in the licensed IPR. However, in general, the approach in the EU is that such restrictions may fall within art.101(1). Thus, in the case of output restrictions, although the Commission recognise that the licensor should "normally be free to determine the output produced with the licensed technology by the licensee" if the licensor is a producer and does not want competition from their own licensee, the focus is on whether such output restrictions are "necessary".[193] Thus, if sales restrictions on the licensee selling into a reserved territory of the licensor, then output restrictions may be anti-competitive. As said by the European Commission in its 2014 Guidelines:

> "[12] …The question is not whether the parties in their particular situation would not have accepted to conclude a less restrictive agreement, but whether, given the nature of the agreement and the characteristics of the market, a less restrictive agreement would not have been concluded by undertakings in a similar setting. Claims that in the absence of a restraint the supplier would have resorted to vertical integration are not sufficient. Decisions on whether or not to vertically integrate depend on a broad range of complex economic factors, a number of which are internal to the undertaking concerned."

8-153   In other words, where a licensor chooses to license, it may be obliged to impose only those restrictions on output, territory, etc. if it can justify that such a restriction was objectively necessary rather than simply answering that in the absence of such restrictions, it would not have licensed the technology. Yet, if a licensor chooses to integrate vertically rather than grant licences with output or sales limitations which are unacceptable under EU law yet which otherwise allow a third party to compete on the marketplace, no attack on that licensor can be made under art.101. The excerpt above suggests that the EU Commission is reluctant to embark on an *ex ante* comparative analysis of whether the IPR owner would have not licensed "but for" the unacceptable output or sales limitations—no doubt because of the difficulty in assessing such for each licensor. It is easier to have a set of rules

---

[193] 2014 Guidelines on Technology Transfer Agreements, para.178.

about restraints in IPR licences which apply to all licences rather than ones which are dependent on economic factors peculiar to each licensor.

CJEU's approach to intellectual property licensing

The CJEU has had to consider the competitive effects of intellectual property licences in a number of important decisions. These are *Nungesser v EU Commission ("Maize Seed")*[194]; *Ciné Vog v CODITEL (No.2) ("CODITEL II")*[195]; *Bayer v Sullhöfer*[196]; *Pronuptia v Schillgalis*[197]; *Windsurfing v EU Commission*[198]; and *Louis Erauw Jacquery Srl v La Hesbignonne Societé Cooperative*.[199] The aforementioned are fairly old 20th century cases from a time when the approach to IPR licences was more restrictive than it is now and there was considerable more suspicion of vertical agreements with contractual restraints than there is now. Moreover, these days the existence of the Technology Transfer Block Exemption means that many technology licences—in particular, those between undertakings who do not have large market shares—benefit from its safe harbour provisions. In short, today there is much more tolerance and certainty of the applicability of art.101 to IPR licences.

8-154

The approach by the CJEU and General Court to art.101(1) and licences is substantially to apply a "rule of reason" approach. Thus, the court has accepted that exclusive licences, i.e. a restriction on the licensor not to license others in a designated territory, may be necessary to the dissemination of technology.[200] However, it has tempered this approach with the need to attain a single market. Thus, licences which seek to provide too much territorial protection between licensees, licensor and licensee are not permitted. In *Windsurfing*, a case in the 1980s, the CJEU sought to apply the "specific subject matter" doctrine developed in the context of arts 34–36 to a patent licence. At the time, this doctrine was very much in fashion when considering the interaction of arts 34–36 to the exercise of IPRs. As commented on in Ch.7, "Intellectual Property and Free Movement of Goods", it no longer plays such an important role in the arts 34–36 jurisprudence. In the context of art.101, it no longer appears to play any significant role for the purpose of analysing the effect of art.101 on licences although it is occasionally referred to.

8-155

It is convenient to consider *Nungesser, Louis Erauw Jacquery, CODITEL II* and *Pronuptia v Schillgalis* together as all four are concerned with contractual restraints in licences where it was argued that such were necessary "ancillary restraints" to make the agreements workable.

8-156

Nungesser

In *Nungesser v EU Commission*, a French botanical institution, INRA, had developed varieties of maize seed capable of being cultivated under temperate climactic conditions. Mr Eisele was a supplier of seeds in Germany. In 1961, INRA

8-157

[194] (258/78) [1982] E.C.R. 2015; [1983] 1 C.M.L.R. 278.
[195] (262/81) [1982] E.C.R. 3381; [1983] 1 C.M.L.R. 49.
[196] (C-65/89) [1988] E.C.R. 5249; [1990] 4 C.M.L.R. 182. See also *Adobe Systems Inc v Netcom Online.co.uk Ltd* [2012] EWHC 446 (Ch).
[197] (C-161/84) [1986] E.C.R. 352; [1986] 1 C.M.L.R. 414.
[198] (193/83) [1986] E.C.R. 611; [1986] 3 C.M.L.R. 489.
[199] (27/87) [1988] E.C.R. 1919; [1988] 4 C.M.L.R. 576.
[200] See (258/78) [1982] E.C.R. 2015, [1983] 1 C.M.L.R. 278 and (262/81) [1982] E.C.R. 3381, [1983] 1 C.M.L.R. 49; (161/84) [1986] E.C.R. 353, [1986] 1 C.M.L.R. 414.

assigned the breeder's rights in Germany for four varieties of maize seed to Mr Eisele. Mr Eisele successfully achieved registration of these varieties with the Bundessortenamt (the Plant Varieties Register in Germany). In 1965, INRA and Eisele entered into a new agreement relating to six varieties of maize seed. INRA granted Mr Eisele an exclusive licence to produce and market a hybrid maize seed in Germany. This agreement conferred on Mr Eisele the exclusive right to produce and distribute INRA varieties in Germany. Furthermore, INRA undertook to do everything in its power to ensure that INRA maize varieties were not exported to Germany other than through Mr Eisele. These rights were then assigned to Nungesser KG but the registrations remained in Eisele's name.

8-158   Eisele sought to prevent parallel importers of INRA seeds into Germany by threatening action for infringement of breeder's rights. Eventually, a parallel importer lodged a complaint to the Commission.

8-159   The Commission held that the exclusive nature of the licence granted by INRA to Eisele infringed art.101(1) as it deprived the licensor of the right to issue licences to other undertakings in the same territory. Similarly, it held that the obligation on INRA to prevent parallel importers was contrary to art.101(1). It refused to grant an exemption under art.101(3). This is a good example of the Commission's historical approach to restrictive clauses in licences whereby it interprets them *ex post* rather than *ex ante*.

8-160   On a preliminary reference to the CJEU, the court overruled the judgment in part. The CJEU distinguished between an "open" and a "closed" exclusive licence. The first allows parallel imports of the protected product into the designated territory whereas the second provides for absolute territorial protection.

8-161   The CJEU upheld the (by then) well-established principle that the exercise of an industrial or commercial property right cannot be used to prevent genuine parallel imports and thus ensure absolute territorial protection.[201] This principle, it should be remembered, arose from the decision in *Consten & Grundig*, where it was held that trade mark rights could not be exercised to render ineffective a finding that an exclusive distributorship agreement was void under art.101. Thus, it held that a "closed" exclusive licence fell within art.101(1). The court then went on to consider whether the grant of an "open" exclusive licence fell within art.101(1). It stated that:

> "In fact, in the case of a licence of breeder's rights over hybrid maize seeds newly developed in one Member State, an undertaking established in another Member State which was not certain that it would not encounter competition from other licensees for the territory granted to it, or from the owner of the right himself, might be deterred from accepting the risk of cultivating and marketing that product; such a result would be damaging to the dissemination of a new technology and would prejudice competition in the European Union between the new product and similar existing products."[202]

8-162   Such an approach is indicative of a "rule of reason" approach by the CJEU. It acknowledges that an "open" exclusive licence is a necessary ancillary restraint to persuade an undertaking to take a commercial risk on promoting a product in a particular territory and thus increase competition at the inter-brand level.[203]

8-163   Why did the court make the distinction between "open" and "closed" licence

---

[201] See (58 and 58/64) [1966] E.C.R. 299, [1966] C.M.L.R. 418; (51/75) [1976] E.C.R. 811, [1976] 2 C.M.L.R. 235; (28/77) [1978] E.C.R. 1391, [1978] 3 C.M.L.R. 392.

[202] (258/78) [1982] E.C.R. 2015; [1983] 1 C.M.L.R. 278, point 57.

[203] See 2014 Guidelines on Technology Transfer Agreements, para.12(b) which acknowledges Nungesser when discussing the compatibility of ancillary restraints in licences with art.101(1).

when it came to contemplating the question of whether an exclusive licence had a pro-competitive effect? In certain situations, licensees might be deterred from taking a licence unless they can be assured of absolute territorial protection. This would especially be the case where transport costs would be negligible (as would be the case for seeds) and which would thus undermine the effect of an "open" exclusive licence. Some commentators have stated that where there is a new technology, it is desirable to have some intra-brand competition (i.e. via parallel imports) as it is unlikely that there will be effective inter-brand competition (because it is a new technology).[204] Thus an "open" exclusive licence achieves a compromise. The counter-argument is that if a potential licensee is deterred from taking a licence, then both inter- and intra-brand competition will be adversely affected.

It is clear that this was too large a step for the court to take. First, the court said **8-164** that arts 34–36 did not allow a licensor to exercise IPRs to prevent parallel imports from licensees' territory. Thus, to enable a licensor to prevent parallel imports via contractual restraints, as opposed to the exercise of rights, would be clearly wrong. Secondly, the court said that it was well-established since *Consten & Grundig v EU Commission* that absolute territorial protection amounts to artificial maintenance of separate national markets and distorts competition.[205] It is unfortunate that it sought not to distinguish *Consten* and others as being trade mark cases which did not concern new technologies and significant investment.[206] Thus, the court declined to analyse the effect on competition in *Nungesser* by the grant of a closed exclusive licence.

Ultimately, the judgment may be seen as one of policy. It balances its "rule of **8-165** reason" approach with a desire to avoid partitioning of the EU. The compromise is to condone the "open" exclusive licence but to condemn the "closed" exclusive licence.

Coditel No.2

In *Ciné Vog v CODITEL (No.2)* *("CODITEL II")*,[207] a French film producer **8-166** granted to a Belgian film distributor (Ciné Vog) the exclusive right to exhibit a film in Belgium for seven years. Various Belgian cable television companies picked up transmission of the film in Germany (where it had been lawfully transmitted by the German licensee) and distributed it by cable in Belgium. Ciné Vog sued CODITEL, a cable company, for copyright infringement in Belgium. The matter was referred to the European Court as to whether an exclusive right granted to Ciné Vog was compatible with art.101(1).[208]

---

[204] See D. Hoffmann and O. O'Farrell, "The 'Open' Exclusive Licence-Scope and Consequence" [1984] 4 E.I.P.R. 107.

[205] However, the court in special circumstances has ruled that absolute territorial protection is not contrary to art.101(1), see (262/81) [1982] E.C.R. 3381, [1983] 1 C.M.L.R. 49; *Louis Erauw-Jacquery v La Hesbignonne* (27/87) [1988] 4 C.M.L.R. 576.

[206] The cases which established the principle that industrial and commercial property rights could not be used to provide absolute territorial protection were cases which concerned trade marks (see (58 and 58/64) [1966] E.C.R. 299; (28/77) [1978] 3 C.M.L.R. 392). It is much more difficult to argue that the grant of an exclusive "closed" trade mark licence is pro-competitive than that of a similar patent or plant breeder's right, where often considerable investment and money must be made by the licensee before they can expect to reap any financial rewards.

[207] (262/81) [1982] E.C.R. 3381; [1983] 1 C.M.L.R. 49.

[208] This matter also went to the European Court on the question of whether Ciné Vog was prevented from enforcing its copyright against CODITEL by virtue of arts 34–36 See *Ciné Vog v CODITEL*

Reischl AG's Opinion

8-167   The Advocate-General noted that if there were several distributors in one territory, each would undercut the other in endeavouring to find buyers and would be unable to pay the original owner of the rights earnings equal to those the owner could have obtained by exploiting the film personally. He thus said that first, seen in such a way, it was possible to say that the:

> "specific subject matter of the copyright in a film covers not only the exclusion of unauthorised outsiders from exploiting it, but also where necessary, exploitation by a single person, whether the owner of the right himself or an exclusive licensee, to whom the right is assigned against payment."[209]

8-168   He also pointed out that often distributors advanced sums of money so that the film could be made in return for being granted an exclusive licence. Secondly, films often involved considerable expenditure on publicity and dubbing before being brought to the market. Thus, if the practice was to cease, he noted that film production would largely cease, as distributors would not be prepared to take anything other than an exclusive licence. Thus, he drew a parallel with *Nungesser* and held that art.101 did not apply to the assignment of exclusive performance right for a new film.

CJEU

8-169   The CJEU broadly followed the Advocate-General's Opinion. It held that such a right did not infringe art.101(1). It said that:

> "[15]   The mere fact that the proprietor of a film copyright has granted to a single licensee the exclusive right to exhibit the film in the territory of a Member State, and therefore to prohibit its diffusion by others, for a specified period, is not sufficient however for a finding that such a contract must be considered as the object, means or consequences of an agreement, decision or concerted practice prohibited by the Treaty.
>
> [16]   Indeed the characteristic features of the cinematograph industry and markets in the European Union, particularly those relating to dubbing or subtitling for audiences belonging to different languages, to the possibilities of television broadcasting, and to the system for financing film production in Europe, show that a licence for exclusive exhibition is not in itself likely to prevent, restrict or distort competition.
>
> [17]   Although, therefore, the copyright in a film and the right, arising from the copyright, to exhibit a film do not by their nature fall within the prohibitions of Article [101], the exercise of such rights may nevertheless, under economic or legal circumstances which have the effect of substantially restricting the distribution of films or distorting competition in the film market having regard to its special characteristics, fall within those prohibitions."[210]

(No.1) (62/79) [1980] E.C.R. 881; [1981] 2 C.M.L.R. 362 and Ch.7, "Intellectual Property and Free Movement of Goods".

[209]   (262/81) [1983] 1 C.M.L.R. 49 at 62.

[210]   See [15]–[17].

Louis Erauw-Jacquery (Plant Breeders)

In *Louis Erauw-Jacquery v La Hesbignonne*,[211] the licence was concerned with **8-170**
the propagation of basic seeds. Under the licence, the propagator was prohibited
from selling E2 basic seeds to anyone other than the farmer propagating them.

Mischo AG held that "basic seeds" are comparable to a manufacturing process **8-171**
protected by a patent as it is merely the vehicle for producing what are called first
and second-generation seeds which are intended to be marketed.[212] He went on to
say that:

> "[12] The situation of the breeder or his agent therefore in some respect resembles that
> of a franchisor, of whom the Court has said that 'he must be able to communicate
> his know-how to the franchisees and provide them with the necessary assistance
> in putting his methods into effect, without running the risk that this know-how and
> assistance will aid his competitors, even directly'. It thus follows that those clauses
> which are essential to prevent this risk do not constitute restrictions of competi-
> tion in the sense of Article [101(1)] (citing *Pronuptia*)."

The court placed a different emphasis and said: **8-172**

> "On this point it should be emphasised that, as the Court found in Case 258/78, Nungesser,
> the development of basic lines may involve considerable financial sacrifices. Conse-
> quently, it should be accepted that anyone who makes considerable investments in
> developing basic seed varieties, which may be the subject of plant breeder's rights, must
> be able to obtain protection against improper handling of those seed varieties. For this
> purpose the breeder must have the right to reserve propagation for the propagating
> establishments chosen by him as licensees. To that extent, the clause prohibiting the
> licensee from selling the exporting basic seeds does not come within the prohibition laid
> down by Article [101(1)] of the Treaty."[213]

Pronuptia

In *Pronuptia de Paris v Schillgalis*,[214] a case which was a franchise agreement **8-173**
and thus can be considered as one of a trade mark licence with ancillary restraints
aimed at ensuring a proper functioning of the franchise agreement, the CJEU had
to rule on the compatibility of art.101 and franchising agreements.

The case was a reference from the Bundesgerichtshof in a German action. Thus, **8-174**
the Commission had not examined the agreement. The franchise agreement in question was a business format agreement (although the franchise was called a distribution franchise by the CJEU) for the distribution of wedding dresses and other
clothes under the "Pronuptia" name. Litigation had occurred regarding non-
payment of fees based on sales figures. The Bundesgerichtshof referred two main
questions to the CJEU. The first question was whether or not art.101(1) applied to
franchise agreements. The second question was whether such agreements, if they
did fall within art.101(1), were covered by Reg.67/67 (the then current block
exemption for exclusive dealing agreements).

The actual franchise agreement gave Mrs Schillgalis the exclusive right to use **8-175**

---

[211] (27/87) [1988] 4 C.M.L.R. 576.
[212] See Opinion of Mischo AG in (27/87) [1988] 4 C.M.L.R. 576.
[213] (27/87) [1988] 4 C.M.L.R. 576 at [10].
[214] (161/84) [1986] E.C.R. 353; [1986] 1 C.M.L.R. 414. This case is discussed in detail at para.11-
022.

the mark PRONUPTIA in the areas of Hamburg, Oldenburg and Hanover. The franchisor agreed to provide training and assistance to the franchisee. The franchisee agreed to: only trade under the name "Pronuptia" in the shop specified in the agreement; to purchase 80 per cent of its wedding dresses and accessories from the franchisor; to pay an initial fee and a 10 per cent royalty on all sales; and to refrain from any act of competition, including opening any business with an identical or similar purpose and a ban against assignment of the franchise.

8-176   The court held that distribution franchise agreements similar to *Pronuptia* were nsot per se restrictive of competition.[215] It stated that:

> "In a distribution franchise system such as this, an enterprise which has established itself as a distributor in a market and which has thus been able to perfect a range of commercial methods gives independent businessmen the chance, at a price, of establishing themselves in other markets by using its mark and the commercial methods that created the franchisor's success. More than just a method of distribution, this is a manner of exploiting financially a body of knowledge without investing the franchisor's own capital. At the same time this system gives businessmen who lack the necessary experience access to methods which they could otherwise only acquire after prolonged effort and research and allows them also to profit from the reputation of the mark. Distribution franchise agreements are thus different from either dealership agreements or those binding approved resellers appointed under a system of selective distribution which involve neither use of a single mark nor application of uniform commercial methods nor payments of royalties in consideration of the advantages thus conferred. Such a system, which permits the franchisor to take advantage of his success, is not by itself restrictive of competition. For it to function two conditions must be satisfied."

8-177   It stated that in order for the franchise to operate effectively the franchisor must be able:

(1)   to communicate its know-how to the franchisees and provide them with the necessary assistance in putting its method into effect without running the risk that the know-how and assistance would aid its competitors; and

(2)   to take appropriate measures to preserve the identity and reputation of the network which is symbolised by the mark.[216]

8-178   It then set out the restrictions which were necessary to be included in a franchise agreement so as to enable the franchisor to fulfil these requirements. It concluded that all restrictions, bar the requirement that the franchisee only trade under the franchise name at the location specified in the agreement, were necessary ancillary restrictions designed to ensure that the franchise system was successful. Thus, such clauses fell outside art.101(1). However, it held that the ban on the franchisee opening other shops in conjunction with the exclusivity clause resulted in a kind of market partitioning between the franchisor and a franchisee and between franchisees themselves. Thus, such an obligation fell within art.101(1).[217] The court stated that a prospective franchisee might not want to take the risk of taking a

---

[215]   (161/84) [1986] E.C.R. 353; [1986] 1 C.M.L.R. 414 at [15].

[216]   (161/84) [1986] E.C.R. 353; [1986] 1 C.M.L.R. 414 at [16].

[217]   The court followed its decision in (58 and 58/64) [1966] E.C.R. 299; [1966] 19 C.M.L.R. NB. The court followed that decision because the PRONUPTIA mark was well known ("*répandu*") as in *Grundig*. Where the mark is not well known, the Commission's view is that an exclusive trade mark licence of such a mark may not have an appreciable effect on competition—*Moosehead/Whitbread* [1990] OJ L100/32; [1991] 4 C.M.L.R. 391 (Commission-mixed trademark/know-how manufacturing licence).

franchise if their business was not afforded a certain amount of protection from other franchisees and/or the franchisor but that was a matter for exemption under art.101(3).

This judgment again demonstrates a rule of reason approach to contractual restraints in vertical agreements.   **8-179**

In *BabyLiss v EU Commission*,[218] a case which concerned the permissibility of a merger, certain commitments were given by an undertaking, following its acquisition of Moulinex, a French company. A particular commitment protected licensees from active competition from other licensees. The General Court held, in applying *Nungesser*, that such restrictions were permissible as otherwise licensees might not be prepared to accept the risk of marketing products bearing the Moulinex trade mark.   **8-180**

Article 101 and specific subject-matter

Although little referred to nowadays, historically, the court and Commission sought to import the concept of "specific subject-matter" doctrine which was developed in the context of arts 34–36 by the CJEU to determine the interplay between art.101 and IPR licences. In Ch.7, "Intellectual Property and Free Movement of Goods", it can be seen that this concept is highly fluid in nature and often appears cited without much explanation.[219] Indeed, as discussed in that chapter, the CJEU appears to define the specific subject matter so as to reject the restrictions that the CJEU wish to exclude rather than as an instrument of analysis.[220]   **8-181**

The high water mark of the application of the specific subject matter doctrine to IP licences in the context of art.101 was in *Windsurfing*, which was a case in the 1980s. This is now discussed.   **8-182**

Windsurfing

In *Windsurfing v EC Commission*[221] an American company had invented a rig for a sailboard. Patents were applied for in several countries. In Germany, a patent was applied for and granted which was deemed to be for a rig for a sailboard. Licences were entered into by the patentee with two German undertakings for the exploitation of the German patent. These non-exclusive licences had several clauses which restricted the freedom of licensees. The Commission brought proceedings under Reg.17 against the patentee.   **8-183**

At the heart of the dispute was that many restrictions imposed on the licensees by the patentee concerned the sailboard rather than the rig. The Commission took the viewpoint that the evidence strongly suggested that the patent only related to the rig and not the sailboard (although this was disputed by the patentee).   **8-184**

Commission

The Commission found that certain clauses, inter alia, fell within art.101(1)[222]:   **8-185**

(a)   The obligation on the licensees to exploit the invention only for the purposes

---

[218] (T-114/02) [2003] E.C.R. II-1279; [2004] 5 C.M.L.R 1.
[219] See para.7-044.
[220] See para.7-054.
[221] (C-193/83) [1986] E.C.R. 611; [1986] 3 C.M.L.R. 489.
[222] No.83/400/EEC *IMA AG v Windsurfing International* [1984] 1 C.M.L.R. 1.

of mounting the patented rig on certain types of board specified in the licence and the accompanying obligation to submit for the licensor's approval, prior to their being placed on the market, any new board types on which the licensees intended to use the rigs. Windsurfing International (WSI) submitted that such was an assertion of the right to exercise quality control over board and rig combinations. The Commission held that such a right could only be recognised as forming part of the specific subject matter of the patent right if it was confined to the protected rig.

(b) The obligation on the licensees to only sell the rig in conjunction with the board, i.e. as a complete sailboard. The Commission held that such restricted the right of licensees to act as distributors of rigs to third parties and did not fall within the specific subject matter of the patent.

(c) The obligation to affix to the manufactured sailboards a notice stating, "licensed by Windsurfing International (the patentee)". The Commission held that this gave rise to the erroneous impression that the boards were covered by industrial property rights.

(d) An obligation on the licensees to restrict production of the licensed product to a specific manufacturing plant in Germany coupled with the right of the patentee to terminate the license if the licensee changed its production site. The Commission held that this prevented licensees from manufacturing in countries where there was no patent protection. It said that it was not part of the specific subject matter of the patent if conditions were so formulated as to secure for the patentee a reward for invention even in places where the patentee does not enjoy any patent protection at all.

(e) An obligation on the licensee not to challenge the validity of the licensed patents or the trade marks. The Commission held as it had done several times before that such clauses were not in the public interest and therefore restricted competition.

(f) An obligation to pay royalties calculated on the net selling price of the complete sailboard. This obligation applied even if the licensees chose to sell the rig and sailboard separately such that it was punitive to attempt to sell rigs or sailboards separately as the royalty charged was still based on the sale of a complete sailboard. The Commission held that such an arrangement meant that producers of boards were prevented from selling their boards as complete boards with rigs, and licensees were forced to sell boards and rigs as combination only even though there was a demand for the two parts separately.

8-186   In each case, the Commission was concerned that the above provisions were an attempt to extend the scope of the patent monopoly and thus did not fall within the specific subject matter of the patent. Whilst it did not in its decision expand on what is meant by the specific subject matter, it would appear that it saw it as meaning the right of a patentee to remuneration for the exploitation of the protected product (i.e. the rig) and also the right to exercise quality control over production of the protected product.

8-187   On appeal, the court agreed with the Commission's view that the patent only covered the rig and not the sailboard. It went on to state that:

"The clauses contained in the licensing agreements, in so far as they relate to parts of the sailboard not covered by the German patent or include the complete sailboard within their terms of reference, can therefore find no justification on grounds of the protection of an industrial property right."[223]

Court of Justice

The court, on all but a few points, upheld the Commission's decision. Thus, it said the following: **8-188**

"The controls in Clause (a) (which were said by the patentee to be quality controls) did not fall within the subject matter of the patent unless they related to a product covered by the patent since their sole justification is that they ensure that the technical instructions as described in the patent and used by the licensee may be carried into effect. Furthermore, such controls had to be effected according to quality and safety criteria agreed upon in advance and on the basis of objectively verifiable criteria."[224]

The obligation in clause (b) was not indispensable to the exploitation of the patent. Accordingly, Windsurfing's argument that such a restriction was covered by the specific subject matter of the patent failed.   **8-189**

Clause (c) was covered by the specific subject matter of the patent provided that the notice is placed on the components covered by the patent.   **8-190**

The principle reason behind clause (d) was to prevent licensees from manufacturing in countries where no patent existed. The patentee cannot rely on the specific subject matter of the patent in order to gain the protection afforded by the patent in a country where there is no patent protection.   **8-191**

Clause (e) clearly did not fall within the specific subject matter of the patent in view of the fact that it is in the public interest to eliminate any obstacle to economic activity which may arise where a patent was granted in error.   **8-192**

Clause (f) restricted competition with regard to the separate sale of boards but not rigs as it was accepted that it was equitable for the patentee to charge a higher royalty rate in its new agreements based on the selling price of rigs alone as opposed to the complete sailboards."   **8-193**

In relation to clause (c), the CJEU said: **8-194**

"It should then be noted that such a clause may be covered by the specific subject matter of the patent provided that the notice is placed only in components covered by the patent. Should this not be the case, the question arises whether the clause has as its object or effect the prevention, restriction or distortion of competition."[225]

This last statement is interesting. It means that if a clause falls within the subject matter of the right, then even if it does restrict or distort competition, it falls outside art.101(1). Thus, it is a condition precedent to the application of art.101(1) and not a factor to be taken into account in weighing up the pro- and anti-competitive effects of the agreement.   **8-195**

What is precisely meant by the specific subject-matter of an IPR in relation to licenses and art.101 has never been clarified. The doctrine was borrowed from the CJEU's jurisprudence under arts 34–36 in the context of parallel imports of protected products. Its use as an analytical tool in relation to arts 34–36 has been   **8-196**

---

[223] At point 36.
[224] This test of objectively verifiable criteria for quality controls has been applied in relation to selective distribution networks—see (26/76) [1977] E.C.R. 1875; [1978] 2 C.M.L.R. 1.
[225] At point 72.

much criticised.[226] A fortiori, such criticism applies to its application to art.101. Indeed, commentators have said that the "CJEU defines the specific subject matter to as to exclude the restrictions the CJEU wishes to exclude".[227] In truth, there is no underlying theory to the concept of the specific subject matter. It is simply a synonym for lawful conduct.

8-197   Similarly, its suitability to the competitive effect of individual clauses in licences is questionable. The court gives the impression in *Windsurfing* of applying the "specific subject matter" doctrine only to clauses that relate either to remuneration for the exploitation of the patented product alone or which are necessary for the proper exploitation and manufacture of the patented product.[228] As such, it must be considered a poor substitute for a detailed "rule of reason" approach to licences and clauses in licences.

8-198   The real force of the CJEU's judgment in *Windsurfing* is as authority for the proposition that licences, which require licensees to bundle the licensed product with a product not part of the licensed IPR or which seek to otherwise control the downstream marketing of a product, can and will often fall within art.101(1).

Specific subject matter and the modern approach

8-199   In the 21st century, the court and Commission have resorted to the doctrine of specific subject matter much less in deciding whether an agreement or concerted practice is contrary to art.101 which involves IP licensing. *Windsurfing* was a 1980s case and since then, the approach to the relationship of IP and art.101 has matured as can be seen in the 2014 Technology Transfer Guidelines. The approach is to consider whether the IP licence has an anti-competitive effect *in toto* rather than consider whether the restraint in issue falls within the specific subject matter and only if it does not, to consider art.101. However, occasionally, resort is still made to this fluid doctrine. Thus, in the 2014 Technology Transfer Guidelines, it is mentioned once where it is said that a non-challenge clause is not part of the specific subject matter of an intellectual property rights.[229] Overall, it can be safely said that whilst the doctrine is still resorted to in relation to the free movement of goods provisions of TFEU,[230] its role in the analysis of IP licensing under art.101 is very residual.

Plant breeder's rights

8-200   Plant breeder's rights give rise to particular concerns when considering art.101. Thus, they are considered here. Plant varieties are protected in most industrialised countries by appropriate sui generis legislation.[231] The general requirement is that

---

[226] See para.7-044.
[227] N. McFarlane, C. Wardle and J. Wilkinson, "The Tension between National Intellectual Property Rights and Certain Provisions of EU Law" [1994] E.I.P.R. 525, 527.
[228] In (262/81) [1982] E.C.R. 3381; [1983] 1 C.M.L.R. 49, Reischl AG said that the specific subject-matter of copyright in a film covers not only the exclusion of unauthorised outsiders from exploit-ing it but also, where necessary, exploitation by a single person whether the owner of the right himself or an exclusive licensee, to whom the right is assigned against payment (at 62 in C.M.L.R.).
[229] See [243].
[230] See Ch.7.
[231] See Ch.6, "Plant Variety Rights in Europe".

the plant variety must be new, distinct, uniform and stable.[232] The holder of a plant breeder's right has the exclusive right to sell, offer or expose for sale the "reproductive material" for their plant variety and to produce such reproductive material for the purpose of selling it.[233] When considering the competitive aspects of plant breeder's licences, due regard must be paid to art.39 of the TFEU which states:

"The objectives of the common agricultural policy shall be:

(a) to increase agricultural productivity by promoting technical progress and by ensuring the rational development of agricultural production and the optimum utilisation of the factors of production, in particular labour;

(b) thus to ensure a fair standard of living for the agricultural community, in particular by increasing the individual earnings of persons engaged in agriculture;

(c) to stabilise markets;

(d) to assure the availability of supplies;

(e) to ensure that supplies reach consumers at reasonable prices."

A distinction must be made between "basic" seeds intended only for the use in production of plants (usually cereals) and "certified" seeds which are intended to be sold on the market. Basic seed is seed which is not intended for sale to farmers for sowing but is intended solely for producing additional seed.[234] It must be propagated for about eight years under very stringent conditions before it finds its definitive form and only then can be sold on the open marketplace. It is produced under the responsibility of the breeder according to accepted practices for the maintenance of a variety and is intended for the production of certified seeds (i.e. for direct or indirect sale to farmers for sowing).[235] Certified seed is seed which is generally intended for sale to farmers for sowing. It is of direct descent from basic seed and is generally intended for purposes other than the production of seeds. Certified seeds must exhibit characteristics of uniformity, distinctness and stability in order to be entitled to protection under plant breeder's rights. Finally, there is what is called "technical seed". This is certified seed, which in some countries may lawfully be used to produce new certified seed, whereas in other countries, it may only be sold to farmers. **8-201**

BLOCK EXEMPTIONS

In the 1960s, after the enactment of Reg.17 which only permitted the Commission to exempt agreements under art.101(3), the Commission received a flood of notifications of agreements. Many of these agreements related to intellectual property, especially patent licences and many contained the same similar clauses. It became apparent to the Commission that it was desirable to declare by way of regulation that certain categories of these agreements were exempted without the need for individual notification. To this end, the Council passed two empowering regulations that allow the Commission to issue "block exemptions" to certain categories of agreements. Regulation 19/65[236] empowers the Commission to issue **8-202**

---

[232] See para.6-077, et seq.

[233] e.g. in UK, see Plant Varieties and Seeds Act 1997.

[234] See *Annual Report on Competition Policy* 1998, p.161.

[235] See *Annual Report on Competition Policy* 1998, p.161; *Re Comasso* [1990] 4 C.M.L.R. 259; [1990] OJ C6/3 at [12]–[13], where the Commission sets out its definition of basic and certified seed.

[236] Reg.19/65 [1965–66] OJ, at 35 as amended by EU Reg.1215/1999 [1999] OJ L148/1.

block exemptions in relation to:

> "(a) categories of agreements which are entered into by two or more undertakings, each operating, for the purposes of the agreement, at a different level of the production or distribution chain, and which relate to the conditions under which the parties may purchase, sell or resell certain goods or services;
>
> (b) categories of agreements to which only two undertakings are party and which include restrictions imposed in relation to the acquisition or use of industrial property rights, in particular of patents, utility models, designs or trade marks, or to the rights arising out of contracts for assignment of, or the right to use, a method of manufacture or knowledge relating to the use or to the application of industrial processes."[237]

8-203   Regulation 2821/71[238] similarly empowers the Commission to issue block exemptions in relation to whole categories of agreements relating to the research and development of products and exploitation of the results thereof and specialisation. Such block exemptions must state what types of restrictive clauses must not be included in an agreement ("black-listed") and other conditions which must be satisfied for agreements falling within the above two categories to benefit from a block exemption enacted pursuant to Reg.19/65 or Reg.2821/71. Block exemptions must only be for a finite period.

8-204   Regulation 2821/71 permits multi-partite licences in IP licences unlike Reg.19/65. Thus, the Technology Transfer Block Exemption only applies where there are two parties. In contrast, the Research and Development and Specialisation Block Exemption apply to IP licences where there are a number of parties.

8-205   The Commission has since issued numerous block exemptions. Of relevance to the reader are the block exemptions relating to technology transfers,[239] specialisation,[240] research and development agreements,[241] vertical agreements,[242] and mergers.[243] These block exemptions have played an invaluable role for businesses that have neither the time nor resources to individually notify agreements yet need to know that their agreements are valid.

8-206   These block exemptions play an invaluable role in providing certainty to businesses. It is often said that block exemptions act as a "safe harbour". If an agreement falls within a block exemption, it is immune from attack under art.101 by the Commission, national competition authorities or in proceedings before national courts.[244] However, the fact that an agreement falls outside a block exemption does not mean that it is void under art.101(2) or valid under art.101(3). Thus, for agreements which fall outside block exemptions, it is necessary to consider the competitive effects of the agreements ab initio.

8-207   Historically, now defunct block exemptions, such as the Patent and Know How Block Exemption, set out a list of permissible and prohibited clauses. The legal advisor need only run a check list of the clauses in their agreement and determine whether such benefitted from the block exemption. With the introduction of the Vertical Agreements Block Exemption and the first Technology Transfer Block

---

[237] art.1 (as amended).
[238] Reg.2821/71 OJ L285/46 as modified by Reg.2743/72 [1972] OJ L291/144.
[239] Reg.316/2014 [2014] OJ L93/17. This is discussed in Ch.9.
[240] Reg.1218/2010 [2010] OJ L335/43. This is discussed in Ch.10.
[241] Reg.1217/2010 [2010] OJ L335/36. This is discussed in Ch.10.
[242] Reg.330/2010 [2010] OJ L102/1. This is discussed in Ch.11.
[243] Reg.139/2004 [2004] OJ L24/1.
[244] Reg.1/2003 art.3(2).

Exemption, the approach changed from one concentrating on specific clauses to that of market share of the parties to the agreement and the prohibition of hard core anti-competitive clauses.

INDIVIDUAL CLAUSES IN IP LICENCES

Introduction

In this section, particular clauses which appear in intellectual property licences are considered. As discussed above, apart from hard core restrictions, the analysis as to whether a particular clause has the effect of restricting competition requires a full economic analysis under both art.101(1) and (3). Often, it is only possible to consider the competitive effect of a particular clause in the context of the overall agreement. **8-208**

Nevertheless, it is useful to consider the Commission and court's approach to particular clauses where those clauses raise particular concerns about competition in innovation, technology and product markets. It is also useful to consider the approach of the US to individual clauses in IP licences. In the chapters on IP and Technology Transfer, IP and Vertical Agreements and IP and Horizontal Agreements, we consider IP licences in the context of technology transfers, vertical agreements and horizontal agreements. In particular, those chapters consider the relevant block exemptions and the Commission's guidelines relevant to such agreements. **8-209**

However, regardless of the context of IP licences, it is a useful exercise to consider in this chapter the approach under art.101 to individual clauses which feature in many IP licences regardless of their context. Thus, exclusive licences are common in all types of IP licences. Thus, in the following section, the approach of EU law to individual types of clauses is considered. The reader who wishes to have a thorough understanding of the possible anti-competitive effects of such clauses should read this chapter and then consult the relevant chapter. Thus, if the reader is interested in tie-in clauses in a technology licence, they should read the section on tie-in clauses and then consult the section on tie-in clauses in the Ch.9, "IP and Technology Transfer Licences". **8-210**

It should be said that the greatest guidance to individual clauses in IP licences comes in the context of technology transfer licences. Thus, in this chapter, there will be considerable reference to the 2014 Technology Transfer Guidelines[245] as much of their guidance is applicable to all types of IPR although it should be remembered that such do not have the force of law. Furthermore, the 2014 Guidelines represent the most current thinking of the Commission on art.101 and IP licences. Decision of the CJEU and General Court have force of law and, indeed, where they are in conflict with the Guidelines (but not the relevant Block Exemption), they will prevail over the Guidelines.[246] **8-211**

Accordingly, for each type of clause, the following is discussed: **8-212**

(a) The case law of the CJEU and General Court: because of the lack of cases

---

245 [2014] OJ C89/3.
246 Indeed, the CJEU and General Court have often shown a marked reluctance to follow the Commission Guidelines in their decisions. See (T-374, 375, 384 & 388/94) [1998] E.C.R. II-3141 and *Langnese-Iglo GmbH v Commission* (T-7/93 & 234/99) [1995] E.C.R. II-1533. However, these decisions concerned the *Commission Notice on Minor Agreements*. In *Métropole Télévision (MG) and Commission* (T-112/99) [2002] E.C.R. II-2459, the General Court placed considerable weight on the guidelines concerning the construction of the Merger Regulation.

referred to the CJEU on technology transfer agreements following the introduction of the Modernisation Regulation and the fact that these decisions tend to be as the result of references from national courts, these decisions have been principally concerned with art.101(1).

(b) The approach of Commission as seen in the 2014 Guidelines (and where appropriate, the Technology Transfer Block Exemption) and its case law. However, many of its decisions are old decisions and the Commission's approach to licences has been one of evolution from a rigid formalist approach to that of a full rule of reason approach. Thus, these old decisions are considered briefly.[247]

(c) The approach of the US. The EU is considerably influenced by US antitrust law and the approach in the US to antitrust law in the context of IP licences is a mature one.

Exclusivity and sole licences

8-213 A simple exclusive licence merely imposes an obligation on the licensor not to exploit the IPR personally in a designated territory and not to license others to exploit that right in a particular territory. However, exclusivity can be granted not only for a territory but also for a particular field-of-use or product market. In contrast, a sole licence is one where the IPR owner agrees not to license any other party but does not exclude itself from exploiting the IPR. This section focuses on exclusive licences which are more common than sole licences: these are referred to as *open* exclusive licences.

8-214 However, an IPR owner may seek to confer greater protection on a licensee in relation to the licensed goods or services. Thus, a licensor may wish to grant protection to a licensee from sales from licensees established in other territories and indeed from the licensor personally. This could be done by further contractual restraints banning other licensees and themselves from selling directly into the territory. The licensor could distinguish between active selling campaigns by other licensees and themselves whereby the licensor and they carry out marketing campaigns in the licensee's territory as against bans on passive sales, e.g. other licensees meeting unsolicited orders from the licensee's territory. However, even that will not protect licensees from parallel imports. Thus, the licensor might try to prevent parallel imports by contractual means, e.g. placing a quantity limit in the licence so that the licensee is only allowed to supply local demands. In all these cases the licensor is seeking to provide varying degrees of absolute territorial protection. In this section, these are called *closed* exclusive licences but it should be appreciated that the degree of protection may differ. Thus, the most extreme type of *closed* licence can be considered one which seeks to prevent competition between licensees in respect of direct sales (both active and passive) and parallel imports.

8-215 Before considering the CJEU's decisions, it will be apparent that a bare exclusive licence of long duration is practically indistinguishable from an assignment of the right. Thus, where the term and geographical extent of the licence is the same as that of the right (including parallel rights in other countries), no practical distinc-

---

[247] For the reader interested in a more detailed analysis of these historic Commission decisions should consult the 2nd edn of this book.

tion can be made.[248] To find such an exclusive licence to be anti-competitive is, in reality, to attack the grant of the IPR itself. If an assignment of an IPR is not assailable under art.101 (and generally, it is not), how can an exclusive licence be assailable? This question is discussed at the end of this section on exclusive licences.[249]

From a EU viewpoint, where the patentee has many parallel patents or other rights in different Member States, exclusive licences in each country may contribute to greater market partitioning than if the patentee manufactured the patented products personally in the EU. This is particularly the case where the exclusive licence is closed.

8-216

European Court

Open exclusive licences

The CJEU has adopted a "rule of reason" approach to open exclusive licences. Thus, in *Nungesser*, the CJEU, reversing the Commission's decision in part, held that in the context of plant breeder's rights and a new product, an "open" exclusive licence might be necessary so as not to deter an undertaking from accepting the risk of cultivating and marketing the product and would thus fall outside art.101(1).[250] In *CODITEL II*,[251] which concerned the grant of an exclusive exhibition right, the court adopted a "rule of reason" approach to such exclusive licences. It held that given the characteristic features of the cinematographic industry and markets in the EU and the requirement of dubbing or subtitling and the system of film financing, the grant of an exclusive licence did not "as such" infringe art.101(1). However, the court stated that national courts had to consider whether "exercise of the exclusive right"[252] to exhibit a cinematograph film would create artificial unjustified barriers having regard to the requirements of the film industry, the possibility of excessive royalties and whether the geographical scope and duration of the exclusive right was excessive and thus likely to prevent, restrict or distort competition.[253] It is clear that the court had in mind the fact that distributors were required to make considerable advance investment in financing films, dubbing them and marketing them.[254] In the later case of *Pronuptia*,[255] a case concerned with retail franchises providing a combination of wedding goods and services, the court appeared to resile from an entirely "rule of reason" approach and held that the combination of the grant of an

8-217

---

[248] See AG's Opinion in *Coditel SA, Compagnie générale pour la diffusion de la télévision v Ciné-Vog Films SA ("CODITEL II")* (C- 262/81) [1982] E.C.R. 3381; [1983] 1 C.M.L.R. 49, where he rejected a submission from the UK government that no distinction can be drawn between an assignment and an exclusive licence and that such a distinction depended on whether the licence was shorter than the right and who bore the risk of exploitation. Thus, it is implicit in his reasoning that if the exclusive licence was the same length as the period of protection, it would be equivalent.

[249] See para.8-230.

[250] (258/78) [1982] E.C.R. 2015; [1983] 1 C.M.L.R. 278 at [57]–[58]. The court held that plant breeder's rights were not conceptually different from other rights. *Nungesser* is discussed in detail at para.8-157.

[251] See above. This case is discussed in detail at para.8-166.

[252] The court used this expression which is normally used to describe the bringing of infringement proceedings. However, it is clear from the context that the court was concerned with whether or not in practice an exclusive licence could be contrary to art.101(1).

[253] (262/81) [1982] E.C.R. 3361; [1983] 1 C.M.L.R. 49 at [18]–[19].

[254] See Reischl AG's remarks, at 62.

[255] (161/84) [1986] E.C.R. 353; [1986] 1 C.M.L.R. 414. This case is discussed in detail at paras 8-173 and 11-072.

"open" exclusive licence and the obligation on a franchisee only to trade from the premises stipulated in the contract would result in artificial partitioning of the EU and could thus only be exempted under art.101(3), even if such protection was required to persuade undertakings to enter into the franchise.[256] However, this can be seen as underlining the CJEU's concerns of market partitioning which is not inherent in normal open exclusive licences.

8-218   In the 21st century the CJEU continues to adopt such a rule of reason approach to the examination of open exclusive licences. Thus, it said in *FAPL v QC Leisure*. applying *CODITEL II*, that the mere fact that a right holder has granted to a licensee the exclusive right to broadcast protected subject matter during a specified period was not sufficient to justify a finding that the agreement has an anti-competitive effect.[257]

Closed exclusive licences and restrictions on parallel imports

8-219   However, where parties seek to impose additional restrictions in licences designed to insulate and isolate national markets of one Member State from another and thus frustrate the TFEU's objective of achieving integration of those markets through the establishment of a single market, then such restraints will tend to be regarded as agreements which have as their object the restriction of competition under art.101 and are thus prohibited per se without the need for analysis of their effects on the relevant market.[258] This has been the approach since *Consten v Grundig v Commission* in the 1960s where the CJEU condemned contractual restraints which sought to prevent parallel trade in products protected by a registered trade mark.[259] In *Tepea v Commission*,[260] an English undertaking who was the inventor of a grammophone cleaning device entered into a number of exclusive distributorship contracts throughout the EU. In the Dutch contract, it was agreed that the English undertaking would not fulfil any orders received from customers in the Netherlands but would pass them onto the Dutch exclusive distributor (Tepea). The Commission held that such was contrary to art.101 and, on appeal, the CJEU agreed. It is of note that the court considered that such a practice was intended to provide absolute territorial protection even though it was not aimed at preventing parallel imports but simply direct sales.[261] Blanket bans on exports from a licensee's territory into other territories are considered to be per se objectionable under art.101(1) as the agreed purpose of the contracting parties is to endeavour to isolate a part of the market.[262] An argument that an export ban has not been implemented was unsuccessful because its existence might create a visual and psychological effect which contributes to the partitioning of the market.[263] The circumstances of the case may mean that absolute territorial protection arises merely

---

[256] See para.11-072.
[257] (C-403/08) [2011] E.C.R. I-9083 at [137], [141].
[258] See para.8-121 for discussion as to "object" and "effect" in art.101.
[259] (C-56/64) and (C-58/64) [1966] E.C.R. 299.
[260] (28/77) [1978] E.C.R. 1391; [1978] 3 C.M.L.R. 392.
[261] See also (T-77/92) [1994] E.C.R. 549; [1995] 5 C.M.L.R. 3435 where a ban on a German distributor from distributing outside his territory was held to fall within art.101(1) by the General Court.
[262] (19/77) [1978] E.C.R. 131; *A. Ahlström Osakeyhtiö v Commission ("Woodpulp")* (C-89/85), (C-104/85), (C-114/85), (C-116/85), (C-117/85) and (C-125/85 to C-129/85) [1993] E.C.R. I-1307 at [176].
[263] (T-77/92) [1995] 5 C.M.L.R. 3435.

by the grant of an exclusive licence. Such was the case in *CODITEL II*[264] where the grant of exclusive broadcasting rights amounted to de facto absolute territorial protection and was thus held unlawful. This was reiterated in *FAPL v QC Leisure*, where the CJEU held that although the grant of exclusive licences for the broadcasting of English premier league football matches was not covered by art.101, the additional obligations on the licensees not to supply decoding devices enabling access to the broadcasts by persons outside the licensed territory had as its object the restriction of competition as such enabled each broadcaster to be granted absolute territorial exclusivity.[265] In *Pierre Fabre Dermo-cosmétique SAS*,[266] a case which concerned the marketing of branded cosmetic and personal care products via a selective distribution contract, the contract prohibited Internet selling of these products, the CJEU held that such had as its object the restriction of competition, in particular because it considerably reduced the ability of an authorised distributor to sell the contractual products to customers outside the contractual territory.[267]

However, sometimes, the CJEU has relaxed its approach to attempts to restrict **8-220** parallel imports. Thus, in *Sot Lélos kai Sia*, which concerned attempts by GlaxoSmithKline to refuse to fulfil orders for pharmaceuticals sent to it by wholesalers on account that those wholesalers were involved in parallel exports of these products to other Member States, the CJEU held, following the Advocate-General's Opinion, that it was not an infringement of art.102 to refuse to meet orders which were out of the ordinary in the light and size of the Member State which the wholesalers were based in.[268] The court was concerned that the effect of state intervention on the price of pharmaceuticals in Greece meant that the opportunity for parallel trade was so great that the only commercial choice for GSK was not to supply the Member State at all as the level of parallel imports represented a real threat to GSK's commercial interests.[269] Whilst this was a case under art.102, the CJEU's decision suggests that no different result would be achieved under art.101.[270] Thus, such could open the door to arguments that contractual restraints which seek to restrict parallel imports on traders in exceptional circumstances are permissible under art.101.

Commission

2014 Technology Transfer Guidelines

The 2014 Guidelines distinguish between exclusive licensing between competi- **8-221** tors and non-competitors in the context of technology transfer licences. In the context of the latter, it says that insofar as such are caught by art.101(1) (citing *Nungesser*), they are likely to fulfil the conditions of art.101(3).[271] It states:

"[194] ...The right to grant an exclusive licence is generally necessary in order to induce the licensee to invest in the licensed technology and to bring the products to

---

[264] (262/81) [1982] E.C.R. 3381; [1983] 1 C.M.L.R. 49.
[265] (C-403/08) [2011] E.C.R. I-9083 at [139]–[142]. See also *Sot. Lélos kai Sia* (C-468/06 to C-478/06) [2008] E.C.R. I-7139 at [65] and cases cited thereto, and *GlaxoSmithKline Services v Commission*, at [59] and [61].
[266] (C-439/09) [2011] E.C.R. 9419.
[267] See [38], [47].
[268] (C-468/06) [2008] E.C.R. I-7139.
[269] See [67]–[77].
[270] e.g. see [65]–[69].
[271] See [194].

market in a timely manner. This is in particular the case where the licensee must make large investments in further developing the licensed technology. To intervene against the exclusivity once the licensee has made a commercial success of the licensed technology would deprive the licensee of the fruits of his success and would be detrimental to competition, the dissemination of technology and innovation. The Commission will therefore only exceptionally intervene against exclusive licensing in agreements between non-competitors, irrespective of the territorial scope of the licence."

8-222   The application of the Guidelines to exclusive licences to technology transfer licences are considered in more detail in Ch.9.

Historical approach of the Commission

8-223   In the 1970s, the Commission consistently ruled that exclusive licences of any type fell within art.101(1) as they restricted the licensor's freedom to compete and to grant licences to other competitors in the relevant territory.[272] Similarly, clauses which had the effect of granting an exclusive licence were held to infringe art.101(1). Thus, an obligation on a patentee/licensor not to exploit its rights in a Member State where the licensee was active constituted an infringement of art.101(1).[273]

8-224   Following *Nungesser*, it was hoped that the Commission would take a more liberal approach to exclusive licences. This proved not to be the case. In *Velcro/Aplix*,[274] Velcro was a Swiss company that had been founded by a Mr Mestral who had invented the "Velcro" fastener. Velcro granted Aplix an exclusive manufacturing and exploitation right in the patents in France. In 1977, the basic patents expired although the certain improvement patents were still in force. Under the licence, inter alia, Aplix was obliged to sell all products derived from the patent under the mark VELCRO. The Commission held that the exclusive licence was contrary to art.101(1) in as far as it related to the period after the expiry of the basic patents. It held that the exclusive licences could only fall outside art.101(1) if it concerned the introduction and protection of new technology following *Nungesser*. Thus, it continued to favour the interpretation of art.101(1) in terms of whether the trading freedom of parties was restricted or not.[275] The Commission did sporadically show that it would conduct a detailed analysis of the effect of the agreement on market

---

[272] *Re Agreement of Burroughs AG and ltablissements Delplanque et Fils, J.O. L.* (13/50) (1972), [1972] C.M.L.R. D67; [1972] F.S.R. 467; *Re the Agreement of Burroughs and Geha-Werke GmbH* [1972] C.M.L.R. D73; *Re the Agreement of the Davidson Rubber Co* [1972] C.M.L.R. D52; *Re the Agreement of A. Raymond & Co* [1972] C.M.L.R. D45, [1972] F.S.R. 443; *Bronbemaling v Heidemaatschappij* [1975] C.M.L.R. D67; *Re Kabel's Agreement* [1975] C.M.L.R. D40; *AOIP v Beyrard* [1976] C.M.L.R. D141; *Re the Peugeot-Zimmern Agreement* [1977] C.M.L.R. D22; Trade marks *Re the Agreement of Davide Campari-Milano Spa* [1978] 2 C.M.L.R. 397.

[273] "Re the Complaint by Yoshida Kogyo KK Commission Press Release!" 9 June 1978; [1978] 3 C.M.L.R. 44.

[274] *Velcro SA v Aplix SA* [1985] OJ L233/22; [1989] 4 C.M.L.R. 157.

[275] For Commission decisions where exclusive licences were found to infringe art.101(1), see *Knoll/Hille, 13th Annual Report on Competition Policy*, p.91, (exclusive manufacturing and distribution rights for various furniture designs); *Re the Agreement between Boussois SA v Interpane* [1985] 4 C.M.L.R. 124 (patent/know-how exclusive licence); *Re the Agreement between JusRol and Rich Products Corporation* [1988] 4 C.M.L.R. 527 (exclusive know-how licence); *Re Agreement between DDD Ltd and Delta Chemie* [1989] 4 C.M.L.R. 535 (exclusive know-how licence); *Re the Agreements between BBC Brown Boveri and NGK Insulators Ltd* [1989] 4 C.M.L.R. 610 (exclusive joint research and development know-how licence); *Re German TV Films* [1989] OJ L284/36, [1990] 4

conditions.[276] Where the Commission cleared an exclusive licence, it was because it had applied either the ruling in *Nungesser*,[277] that an exclusive licence was often required to encourage the establishment of new technologies in territories or the ruling of the court in *CODITEL II*,[278] where the court sanctioned an approach that took into account the fact that an exclusive licence was often granted to the licensee where the latter needed to make a significant investment before the product could be marketed. The application of these two criteria is examined below.

The Commission interpreted the "new technology" requirement in *Nungesser* as meaning ground-breaking technology. Thus, in *Re the agreement between Jus-Rol and Rich Products Corp*,[279] Rich Products granted Jus-Rol an exclusive know-how licence for the manufacture of frozen yeast dough products. The Commission held that as other processes existed which provided the means for freezing the yeast, the licence was not concerned with the introduction of new technology necessitating territorial protection. Therefore, the licence fell within art.101(1). **8-225**

In *Pripps/Tuborg*[280] the Commission showed its antipathy to long-term exclusive arrangements. Tuborg (part of the Danish Carlsberg group) had exclusively licensed Pripps (a Norwegian/Swedish company) to make Tuborg beer in Sweden since 1975. Pripps was the leading brewer in Sweden. Carlsberg, the other major brand of the Carlsberg group, was made and sold by a Swedish company, Falcon, which Carlsberg owned shareholdings in. Following the accession of Sweden to the EU, this agreement was notified to the Commission. The Commission informed the parties that the long-term exclusive co-operation between competitors with its likely foreclosure effects gave rise to serious concern regarding its compatibility with art.101 of the ECT. Other restrictions on Pripps (including inter alia an obligation not to co-operate with certain foreign brewers and a guarantee that Tuborg would be the largest foreign brand in Pripps' portfolio) had already been withdrawn by the parties following their initial discussions with the Commission. Following the Commission's intervention, the exclusivity was broken and a second licensee was appointed in Sweden, namely Falcon. In order to avoid an abrupt negative impact on Pripps' production capacity, it was agreed that Tuborg would buy back a steadily decreasing quantity of Tuborg Class III beer from Pripps in the event of the latter failing to sell a minimum volume on the market. As a result, the Commission gave a comfort letter to the parties. **8-226**

The approach in *Pripps/Tuborg* emphasises that where parties are competitors with large market shares in a horizontal agreement which is likely to have foreclosure effects on third parties' ability to penetrate the market, the grant of an exclusive licence will unlikely to be permitted as exclusivity is not required to penetrate a market and is likely to result in less competition. On the one hand, it might be said that the grant of an exclusive licence in a territory (i.e an exclusive licence) is better than no grant at all and that there should exist no obligation on the **8-227**

C.M.L.R. 841 [exclusive television rights in Germany]; *Moosehead/Whitbread* [1990] OJ L100/32, [1994] 4 C.M.L.R. 391 (exclusive trade mark/know-how brewing licence). In contrast, the grant of exclusive licences was cleared in *Spitzer/Van Hool* reported in the *12th Report on Competition Policy*, para.86; *RAI/Unitel* reported in the *12th Report on Competition Policy*, (exclusive performance contracts for opera singers) where the Commission took a favourable view of an exclusive licence once Unitel agreed to waive its exclusive rights for important cultural events.

[276] e.g. see *Re German TV Films* [1989] OJ 1284/36; [1990] 4 C.M.L.R. 841, discussed at para.8-228.
[277] (258/78) [1982] E.C.R. 2015, [1983] 1 C.M.L.R. 278.
[278] (262/81) [1982] E.C.R. 3381; [1983] 1 C.M.L.R. 49.
[279] Decision 88/143/EEC [1988] OJ L69/21; [1988] 4 C.M.L.R. 527.
[280] *Annual Report on Competition Policy* (1998), p.148.

brand owner to create more intra-brand competition than it desires. On the other hand, it could be said that Pripps' role as the leading brewer in Sweden combined with its right to manufacture and sell Tuborg exclusively in Sweden was likely to reduce inter-brand competition, as Pripps would be unlikely to develop its own brand to compete with Tuborg. Such arguments appeared to have played little part in the Commission's informal dealings with the parties. Instead, it was clear that the parties were keen to accommodate the Commission's concerns. Thus, if the *realpolitik* is that a licensor will be prepared to license two persons in order to obtain a favourable decision, the Commission will force that on the parties. In Pripps/Tuborg, the Commission was keen to break up what was seen as a rather cosy arrangement between two competitors.

8-228 The Commission also was reluctant to follow the CJEU's lead in *CODITEL II*[281] and consider whether exclusive licences that involve significant initial investment by licensees fell outside art.101(1). In two cases, it did take the issue of significant investment into consideration.[282] In applying the criteria of "significant investment", the Commission showed that it will also consider whether the length of the exclusive licence is justified under art.101(1). In *Re German TV Films*,[283] the Commission considered the application of *CODITEL II* to an agreement whereby one of the world's leading film producers granted a group of German broadcasting organisations exclusive television rights within Germany and surrounding German-speaking areas to a selection of films from its library and all new ones produced for 15 years. The Commission held that the number of films involved in the agreement was too many and that the duration of the exclusive licence was too long. Such was disproportionate and would result in an artificial barrier to others.[284]

The US approach

8-229 According to the 2017 Guidelines, exclusive licences will generally only raise antitrust concerns where there is a horizontal relationship between licensor and licensee. The Department of Justice says that exclusive licensing may give rise to antitrust concerns where there is cross-licensing between competitors that collectively have market power, grantbacks and acquisitions of IPRs.[285] The Department of Justice takes the view that the grant of exclusivity by a licensor to licensees is similar to those outside IPR licences, e.g. exclusive distribution agreement but exclusivity may be justified more easily because of the ease of misappropriation of intellectual property.[286] Thus, the Department of Justice recognises that exclusive

---

[281] (262/81) [1982] E.C.R. 3381; [1983] 1 C.M.L.R. 49.
[282] See *Knoll/Hille* reported in the *13th Report on Competition Policy*, para.90, et seq; *Spitzer/Van Hool* reported in the *12th Report on Competition Policy*, para.72.
[283] *Re German TV Films* [1989] OJ 1284/36; [1990] 4 C.M.L.R. 841.
[284] para.44. See also *Knoll/Hille* reported in the *13th Report on Competition Policy*, p.91, where the Commission had serious doubts as to whether an exclusive licence which related to furniture "programmes" covered by a mixture of patents, registered designs, trade mark and copyright was valid since neither the "newness" of the product nor the amount of investment seemed to indicate that the exclusivity granted was indispensable to the launching of the product in the relevant market, at any rate not for the length of time originally envisaged (eight years).
[285] See para.4.1.2.
[286] See para.4.1.2.

licences may promote competition by encouraging the licensee to develop and promote the licensed product in the face of uncertain demand.[287].

Assignment and exclusive licences

As discussed earlier, there is often little in substance to distinguish between an assignment and an exclusive licence.[288] Where the holder of parallel patents assigns a patent to an undertaking, this has very similar effects to granting an exclusive licence to the undertaking for the lifetime of the patent. Indeed, such is recognised by many countries in that an exclusive licensee as well as the owner is given the right to sue infringers.[289]   **8-230**

Technically, an assignment is an agreement between two undertakings and is thus capable of falling within art.101(1). Generally, where rights are assigned, it is doubtful whether such an assignment per se is capable of falling within art.101(1).[290] An assignment of intellectual property amounts to a mere change in ownership of the right. Without more, it is difficult to see how such affects competition. The only exception to this is where it forms part of a merger or acquisition and can be said to increase the dominance of the assignee in a particular product, service or technology market in such a manner as to have an adverse effect on competition.   **8-231**

The approach of the Commission and the CJEU to assignments and exclusive licences is to consider the substance of the agreement and not its form. Thus, an assignment which also involves long-term co-operation between the assignor and the assignee is, in substance, akin to an exclusive licence for that term[291]. The European Court will look at the assignment in the context of the economic and legal relationship between assignor and assignee. If it amounts to, in economic terms, an exclusive licence then it will be construed as such. Thus in *Nungesser*,[292] INRA authorised Mr Eisele to register himself as owner of the relevant breeder's rights of INRA in Germany. There were three contracts. First, there was the contract of 1960 which initiated co-operation between INRA and Eisele; secondly, there was the 1961 contract which assigned the plant breeder's rights; and thirdly the contract of 1965 which concerned the distribution of INRA seeds in Germany. The court said that the agreement formed an indivisible whole and that in economic terms Mr Eisele was an exclusive licensee.[293] Similarly, where an assignment of intellectual property continues to produce effects, such an assignment will be considered more in the nature of an exclusive licence. This will rarely be the case, unless there is evidence of continuing co-operation between the assignor and assignee.[294] For instance, where the assignee is contractually bound in any way whatsoever post-   **8-232**

---

[287] See Example 7 of NewCo and BigCo.

[288] See para.8-215.

[289] e.g. in the UK, see Patents Act 1977 s.67; also see Copyright Designs and Patent Act 1988 where s.101 states that "an exclusive licensee has, except against the copyright owner, the same rights and remedies in respect of matters occurring after the grant of the licence as if the licence had been an assignment".

[290] See Ch.7, para.7-308.

[291] This approach is similar to the exercise of trade mark rights against parallel imports where a mark has been divided in ownership in the EU but the assignor and assignee maintain economic links with each other. See para.7-162.

[292] (258/78) [1983] 1 C.M.L.R. 278.

[293] See also *Moosehead/Whitbread* [1990] OJ L100/32; [1991] 4 C.M.L.R. 391, where an assignment by a Canadian brewing firm of the trade mark to Whitbread and Moosehead jointly was treated by the Commission as being, in fact, an exclusive licence.

[294] See (51/75) [1976] E.C.R. 811; [1976] 2 C.M.L.R. 235. In general, as to whether a rights owner can

assignment, such an assignment continues to produce effects and is thus capable of falling within art.101(1). Thus, where there is a ban against further assignment, it is submitted that the true situation is more analogous to an exclusive licence.

8-233   Vice versa, a bare exclusive licence for the duration of the right for the whole of the protected territory is more akin to an assignment. In *Coditel II*,[295] Reischl AG said it was certainly possible to justify the view that the specific subject-matter of copyright in a film covered not only the exclusion of unauthorised outsiders from exploiting it but also, if necessary, exploitation by a single person, whether they were the owner of the right or an exclusive licensee.[296]

8-234   Another situation is where the rights owner makes a number of assignments of parallel rights to differing independent undertakings in different territories within the EU. Such may be held to be for the purpose of partitioning the market rather than for legitimate purposes. In such cases, the cumulative effect of such assignments will be held to fall within art.101(1).[297]

Territorial restrictions

8-235   Licensors will often seek to restrict licensees from manufacturing goods or supplying services outside the territories for which they are expressly licensed to manufacture those goods or supply such services. These restraints are considered. They should be differentiated from restrictions which seek to prevent sales of goods by licensees or licensors into each other's territories which have been considered in the context of exclusive licences (such will rarely exist without a grant of exclusivity).

8-236   These clauses can be divided into two categories: (a) where the licensor possesses parallel rights in territories outside the designated territory; and (b) where no such parallel rights exist. In the case of the existence of parallel rights, if exclusive licences have been granted to other licensees, then a ban on manufacturing in the territories or supplying services in the territories of these licensors or licensees is the corollary of the grant of the exclusive licence limited to a particular territory. However, what is the position where there are no licences in the other territories or only non-exclusive licences have been granted in other territories?

European Court of Justice

8-237   Where no parallel rights exist, the CJEU has held in *Windsurfing*[298] that such restrictions are not of the essence of the patent and fall within art.101(1).[299] Even on a rule of reason approach, it is difficult to see how a prohibition can be justified

---

enforce their rights in the context of assignments, see para.7-308.
[295] (262/81) [1982] E.C.R. 3381; [1983] 1 C.M.L.R. 49.
[296] At [62].
[297] See (58 and 58/64) [1966] E.C.R. 299, [1966] C.M.L.R. 418; (40/70) [1971] E.C.R. 69, [1975] C.M.L.R. 1; (28/77) [1978] E.C.R. 1391, [1978] 3 C.M.L.R. 392; (51/75) [1976] E.C.R. 811, [1976] 2 C.M.L.R. 235. See also *Advocaat Zwarte kip* [1974] 2 C.M.L.R. D79 (EC Commission).
[298] (193/83) [1986] 3 C.M.L.R. 48; [1986] E.C.R. 611.
[299] For discussion of (193/83) [1986] 3 C.M.L.R. 48; [1986] E.C.R. 611, see para.8-183. See also the Commission's decision in *Velcro SA* [1985] OJ L233/22; [1989] 4 C.M.L.R. 157, where it held that a restriction in a patent licence, which was a mixture of basic and improvement patents (the former having expired), that prevented a licensee from manufacturing products for which the patents had expired outside its designated territory fell within art.101(1), as it prevented the licensee from making the expired patent product in the Member State where it could manufacture most advantageously.

as it may put the licensee in a worse position than other potential competitors in the relevant market. It is difficult to see how such restrictions could ever be justified under art.101(3).

Where there are parallel rights, in *Pronuptia*,[300] a distribution franchise case **8-238** whose essence is a trade mark licence, the CJEU was concerned about clauses banning a franchisee from opening a second shop outside the designated territory. The franchisor had trade mark rights throughout the EU. The court held that a restriction on a franchisee only to trade from the outlet permitted in the franchise when coupled with clauses preventing other franchisees from opening a second shop outside the designed territory resulted in an artificial partitioning of the EU and infringed art.101(1) where the mark was well known. It said that such a consideration is relevant only to an examination of the agreement in the light of the conditions laid down in art.101(3).[301] Here, the real concern was of market partitioning. It is obviously permissible to limit a licence to a particular territory.

2014 Technology Transfer Guidelines

The 2014 Guidelines do not provide specific guidance on territorial restrictions **8-239** where there exist parallel rights but no exclusive licences have been granted.

Historical approach of the Commission

In *Boussois/Interpane*,[302] the Commission demonstrated that it will consider ter- **8-240** ritorial restrictions in manufacturing and selling patent/know-how licences as falling within art.101(1), even where parallel patents exist. In this case, Interpane, a German undertaking granted to Boussois, a French firm, an exclusive mixed know-how and patent manufacturing licence in France but no other country for the first five years and thereafter on a non-exclusive basis for an indefinite period. Interpane possessed parallel patents in various other European countries but not all. Interpane gave Boussois an exclusive sales licence in France for five years and thereafter on a non-exclusive basis. Outside France, Boussois had a non-exclusive sales (but not manufacturing) licence for an indefinite period but this was without prejudice to the right of Interpane (who at that time had not licensed anyone else besides Boussois) to grant exclusive sales licences to other undertakings in other territories in the future (and thus thereby terminate the non-exclusive sales licence of Boussois).

The Commission held that the prohibition on Boussois manufacturing outside **8-241** France restricted potential sales in other EU countries because the cost of transportation increased the sales price of the protected product and thus fell within art.101(1). Certainly, where Interpane had no parallel rights, as discussed above, it would have been somewhat bizarre if they were not allowed to manufacture in that territory. However, no distinction was made between those territories where parallel patents existed and did not exist. The Commission also held that the prohibition on sales outside France if, in the future, Interpane appointed an exclusive licensee, fell within art.101(1) as it prevented Boussois from supplying such territories.[303]

In considering art.101(3), the Commission's view has been if that geographical **8-242**

---

[300] (161/84) [1986] E.C.R. 353; [1986] 1 C.M.L.R. 414.

[301] (161/84) [1986] E.C.R. 353; [1986] 1 C.M.L.R. 414.

[302] *Agreement between Boussois and Interpane mbH* [1987] OJ L50/30; [1988] 4 C.M.L.R. 124.

[303] See also Re the Agreements between *Jus-Rol Ltd and Rich Products Corp* [1988] OJ L69/21; [1988] 4 C.M.L.R. 527, where a similar clause fell within art.101(1). For the purposes of this book, this is

restrictions on manufacturing or supply of services are necessary so as to encourage would-be licensees to take licences, then such territorial restrictions will be exempted.[304] In particular, this will apply where the demand for the licensee's product or services is concentrated in a small number of undertakings who will be well informed about the market and thus able to shop around.[305]

The US Approach

8-243   The 2017 Guidelines recognise that territorial limitations may serve pro-competitive ends by allowing the licensor to exploit its property as efficiently and effectively as possible. They also recognise that such limitations can give a licensee the incentive to invest in the promotion and distribution of licensed products by protecting the licensee against free-riding by other licensees or indeed, the licensor.[306]. However, the US does not have the same "single market" integrationist policy of the EU.

Duration of licence

8-244   In general, licensors are free to determine the duration of a licence. Clearly, there can be no obligation to license a licensee until the expiry of the licensed IPR. Bans on the use of licensed technology after the expiry of a licence, provided that the IPR of the licensed technology remains valid and in force, are considered by the Commission to be generally not restrictive of competition within the meaning of art.101(1).[307] Clearly, such is the corollary of a licence for a limited period and proceeds on the basis that, without a licence, the activities of the licensee would infringe the licensor's IPR. Conversely, bans on using the licensed technology where the IPR has expired must be generally considered anti-competitive.

Court of Justice

8-245   In *Ottung v Klee*,[308] the CJEU said that a clause prohibiting the manufacturing of licensed products after termination of the agreement and when the licensed IPR has expired:

> "would put the licensee at a competitive disadvantage in relation to its competitors, who may freely manufacture the products concerned after the patent has expired."[309]

---

not a geographical restriction but a sales restriction.

[304] See *Agreement between Boussois and Interpane mbH* [1987] OJ L50/30; [1988] 4 C.M.L.R. 124 and *Re the Agreements between Jus-Rol Ltd and Rich Products Corp* [1988] OJ L69/21; [1988] 4 C.M.L.R. 527.

[305] *Agreement between Boussois and Interpane mbH* [1987] OJ L50/30; [1988] 4 C.M.L.R. at [20].

[306] See para.2.3.

[307] 2014 Guidelines on Technology Transfer Agreements, para.183.

[308] (320/87) [1989] E.C.R. 1177; [1990] 4 C.M.L.R. 915; [1991] F.S.R. 657.

[309] See [18]. It is of note that although the court said that the clause may, depending on the economic and legal context, restrict competition, such a remark was made in the context of whether the licence was liable to appreciably affect trade between Member States. If it did, there seems little doubt that the court took the view that such a restriction would fall within art.101(1).

2014 Technology Transfer Guidelines

The 2014 Guidelines also suggest that such a restraint will fall within art.101(1).[310] Such restraints should not be confused with obligations to pay royalties beyond the lifetime of the IPR. This is discussed in the next section. Such provisions permit exploitation of the technology but upon payment.

8-246

Historical approach of the Commission

A licensor may seek to prolong a licence by stipulating that it will terminate upon the expiry of the last patent or additional know-how. An obligation that a licence remains in force until expiry of the most recent improvement patent will usually fall within art.101(1) unless the licensee has a right to terminate.[311] Thus, in *Velcro SA v Aplix SA*,[312] the Commission said that:

8-247

> "the automatic extension of the term of the licensing agreement, on condition only that Aplix defrays the cost of maintaining in force the improvement patents it desires to use, denies the licensor the possibility of escaping the restrictive obligations upon him at the end of the statutory period of protection for the basic patents. The restriction of competition resulting from the denial of this possibility to Velcro is all the more serious in that the agreement does not provide a right of early termination, except for serious breach of contract."

Moreover, the Commission considered that it will be rare that such is capable of exemption under art.101(3).[313]

8-248

Therefore, if the licensee wishes to only exploit the basic patents and does not wish to exploit the improvement patents, the licensee cannot be tied involuntarily into the licence. Similarly, a licensor who only wants to license the basic patents is not forced to license the improvements.

8-249

Royalties

Remuneration in licences by way of royalty payments represents the traditional method of payment and as such does not fall within art.101(1).[314] An obligation to pay royalties for the use of secret know-how after the termination of a licence will generally fall outside art.101(1).[315] In terms of legal analysis, the licence may have been formally determined but the IPR is still being exploited pursuant to a de facto licence.

8-250

However, competition concerns can arise in the following situations:

8-251

(i)   Royalties are charged beyond the lifetime of the IPR.
(ii) Royalties are charged on products not covered by the licensed IPR.

These are now discussed.

---

[310] See para.183(c).
[311] *AOIP v Beyrard* [1976] 1 C.M.L.R. D14; *Re the Agreement between Peugeot and Zimmern* [1977] 1 C.M.L.R. D22; *Velcro* [1985] OJ L233/22, [1989] 4 C.M.L.R. 157.
[312] *Velcro* [1985] OJ L233/22, [1989] 4 C.M.L.R. 157.
[313] *Velcro* [1985] OJ L233/22; [1989] 4 C.M.L.R. 157 and *AOIP* [1976] 1 C.M.L.R. D14.
[314] See *4th Report on Competition Policy*, para.21 and *AOIP* [1976] 1 C.M.L.R. D14.
[315] *Re Kabelmetal's Agreement* [1975] OJ L222/34, [1975] 2 C.M.L.R. D40; *Constructions Cartoux v Terrapin Overseas Ltd* [1981] 1 C.M.L.R. 182.

European Court of Justice

Obligation to pay royalties beyond lifetime of IPR

8-252   The European Court has adopted a tolerant approach to an obligation to pay royalties after the expiry of the licensed intellectual property. In *Ottung v Klee*,[316] the Maritime and Commercial Court of Copenhagen was concerned with proceedings for the recovery of royalty payments under a licence. The patentee had licensed the licensee to manufacture and sell two control devices for brewery tanks. Under cll.1 and 2 of the agreement, the licensee undertook, for an indeterminate period, to pay a royalty for each device sold. Under cl.5 of the agreement, as amended by an addendum, the agreement could only be terminated by the licensee giving six months' notice expiring on 1 October of any year. When such termination took effect, the licensee was permitted to manufacture only a number of devices corresponding to the orders received as at the date of expiry of the agreement, less the number of devices, if any, in stock.

8-253   The agreement was entered into after a patent application had been filed in respect of one of the control devices, fitted with a non-return valve for the admission of air. However, this was ahead of the patent being granted in Denmark. During the years following the grant of the patent, the licensee paid the agreed royalty. The Danish patent expired on 12 April 1977 and the last patent in respect of the licensed devices granted in a Member State expired on 15 March 1980. As from the end of 1980, the defendants in the main proceedings ceased paying the royalty, on the ground, inter alia, that all the patents had expired.

8-254   In proceedings brought for recovery of royalties, the Maritime and Commercial Court of Copenhagen referred to the CJEU questions concerning the compatibility of such contractual obligations with art.101. The court held that:

> "[11]   The possibility cannot be ruled out that the reason for the inclusion in a licensing agreement of a clause imposing an obligation to pay royalty may be unconnected with a patent. Such a clause may instead reflect a commercial assessment of the value to be attributed to the possibilities of exploitation granted by the licensing agreement. That is even more true where, as in the main proceedings, the obligation to pay royalty in respect of two devices, one being patented after the agreement was entered into and the other being complementary to the first, was embodied in a licensing agreement entered into before the patent was granted.
>
> [12]   Where the obligation to pay royalty was entered into for an indeterminate period and thus purports to bind the licensee even after the expiry of the patent concerned, the question arises whether, having regard to the economic and legal context of the licensing agreement, the obligation to continue to pay royalty might constitute a restriction of competition of the kind referred to in Article [101(1)].
>
> [13]   An obligation to continue to pay royalty after the expiry of a patent can result only from a licensing agreement which either does not grant the licensee the right to terminate the agreement by giving reasonable notice or seeks to restrict the licensee's freedom of action after termination. If that were the case, the agreement might, having regard to its economic and legal context, restrict competition within the meaning of Article [101(1)]. *Where, however, the licensee may freely terminate the agreement by giving reasonable notice, an obligation to pay royalty throughout the validity of the agreement cannot come within the scope of the prohibition contained in Article [101(1)].*
>
> [14]   For the purpose of the national court's assessment of the legality of the clause at

---

[316]   (320/87) [1989] E.C.R. 1177; [1990] 4 C.M.L.R. 915.

issue, it is irrelevant that the licensor is bound by a clause preventing him from terminating the agreement."

In *Genentech Inc v Hoechst GmbH*,[317] the Court of Justice had to consider **8-255** whether it was contrary to art.101 for a licensee to be obliged to pay royalties on patented products when, after the licence was entered into, one of the licensed patents was revoked but not others (a European patent was revoked but not parallel US patents). A French arbitral tribunal referred a question to the Court of Justice as to whether it was compatible with art.101 for a licensee to be obliged to pay royalties where patents are revoked (ab initio). There was considerable dispute as to the admissibility of the reference as it was said that the proceedings only concerned the US patents which had not been revoked. Despite its doubts, the Court of Justice decided to admit the reference. Applying *Ottung v Klee*, in substance, it held that there was no difference to be drawn between an expired patent right and a revoked patent.[318]

It might be said that there is a difference in principle between *Ottung v Klee* and **8-256** *Genentech*. If a patent is revoked, it is revoked ab initio whereas a patent that expires does not. This would mean that in a single patent licence, a licensee has unnecessarily paid royalties over the period of the agreement yet will be unable to recover those royalties. Whilst this approach is superficially attractive, it ignores commercial reality. When two parties enter into a patent licence or indeed any registered IPR licence, there is always a risk that the patent may be revoked. Often, instead of seeking to revoke the patent itself, the licensee chooses the "easier road" of entering into a licence. It can be said to have done that with its eyes open. In short, it is important to take an *ex ante* approach to the determination of whether the licence is anti-competitive, i.e. as of the date when the licence was entered into and not an *ex post* approach based on hindsight. It is plainly in the interests of robust trade and the dissemination of technology through licensing that patent owners are not inhibited from entering into licences through fear that they may have to repay licence fees if the patent is subsequently revoked. Equally, a licensee cannot complain if it chose the "easier road" rather than fight a patent revocation action. This is commercial reality.

More generally, in both cases, the ability of the licensee to terminate the agree- **8-257** ment upon reasonable notice was critical to the finding of the Court of Justice that the obligation to pay royalties after the expiry or revocation of a patent was not contrary to art.101. Yet if a licensee is free to terminate an agreement the moment a patent has expired or been revoked, the patent owner will of course be deprived of the right to receive royalties after the expiry or revocation of the patent. In *Ottung v Klee*, the Court of Justice took the view that the obligation to pay royalties may be unconnected with the patent (see excerpt above). Thus, it could be related to the licensing of other IPR, e.g. know-how or indeed the provision of ongoing help by the licensor. Yet, in many cases, the obligation to pay royalties will be wholly related to the existence of the patent and the fear of the licensee that it wishes to carry out an infringing activity. In such circumstances, is the Court of Justice's approach correct?

For example, where a patent has 10 years to the date of expiry and the patented **8-258** technology has not been hitherto commercially exploited, it may appeal to a licensee to pay x per cent royalties over 20 years rather than 2x per cent over 10 years. If at

---

[317] (C-567/14) ECLI:EU:C:2016:526.
[318] See [40]–[41].

the time of entering into the licence, the licensed technology is commercially unknown, its exploitation is risky and the profit margin on the licensed technology is low, a licensor and licensee may see the sense of the licensee paying a lower royalty for a longer period. However, if having agreed in good faith the x per cent royalty route for a longer period clause, the licensee can terminate the licence after the expiry of 10 years and have no further obligation to pay royalties, it would be plainly a windfall for the licensee. *Ottung v Klee* and *Genentech* mean that a well-advised licensor will have no alternative but to reject the x per cent licence during negotiations however much commercial sense it makes and indeed may be critical to a licensee deciding whether to enter into a licence or not. Moreover, as made clear in the 2017 US Guidelines, once a patent has expired, there are no barriers to entry for third parties competing with the licensee and thereby ensuring healthy competition.[319]

Obligation to pay royalties on products not covered by the IPR

8-259   The issue as to compatibility of clauses requiring the payment of royalties on products not protected by the licensed IPR with art.101 was considered by the CJEU in *Windsurfing*.[320] This case has already been discussed (above).[321] In that case, the patent licence required that the licensee pay royalties for the sale of unpatented sailboards as well as the patented rigs on the basis of the fictitious net selling price of the complete sailboard.

8-260   The CJEU upheld the Commission's finding that such a clause distorted competition in sailboards but not in the rigs. It pointed out, by way of a preliminary remark, that it was not one of those cases which made it difficult to calculate a royalty based on the patented item. The rig was not incorporated in the board and there was a separate demand for the rig. It held that the royalty calculation on the whole board was uncompetitive, appearing to accept the Commission's submission that it forced the licensees not to sell boards of competitors. However, the CJEU held that the royalty charged did not affect competition in the rigs because it was equitable to charge a higher royalty if the remuneration was calculated on the price of the rigs alone. Thus, it held that the method of calculation restricted competition with regards to the sale of *boards* but not *rigs*. In this decision, the CJEU is foreshadowing the 2014 Technology Transfer Guidelines which emphasise that methods of payments of royalties on unpatented items which need to be used in conjunction with the patented item can cause foreclosure issues.

2014 Technology Transfer Guidelines

8-261   The 2014 Technology Transfer Guidelines comment on royalty obligations.[322] They recognise the freedom of parties to a licence agreement to determine the royalty payable by the licensee and its mode of payment without being caught by art.101. It says that such can take the form of a lump sum payment, a percentage of the selling price or a fixed amount for each product incorporating the licensed

---

[319] See para.8-266.
[320] (193/83) [1986] E.C.R. 611; [1986] 3 C.M.L.R. 489.
[321] See para.8-183.
[322] See [184]–[187].

technology. For software, royalties based on either the number or users or per machine are generally compatible with art.101(1).

Royalties beyond the lifetime of the IPR

The 2014 Guidelines take a benevolent view of obligations to pay royalties   **8-262** beyond the lifetime of the licensed IPR and says that such will normally not fall foul of art.101(1).[323] It says that once these rights expire, third parties can legally exploit the technology and compete with the parties to the agreement. Such actual and potential competition will normally suffice to ensure that the obligation in question does not have appreciable anti-competitive effects. It is of note that contrary to the case law of the Court of Justice, the 2014 Guidelines do not say that the licensee must have the right to terminate the agreement. Historically, the Commission had viewed an obligation to pay a royalty throughout the term of the agreement regardless of the expiry of IPR or the know-how entering the public domain as caught by art.101(1), unless the licensee was able to freely terminate the licence.[324]

Royalties on products not covered by the IPR

The 2014 Guidelines say that in the case of agreements between non-competitors,   **8-263** arrangements for royalties to be paid on the basis of products produced with the licensed technology and products produced with technology licensed from third parties, may facilitate the metering of royalties.[325] However, they say that such could cause foreclosure by increasing the costs of using third party inputs and have effects similar to a non-compete obligation.

Minimum royalties

The 2014 Guidelines make it clear that obligations to pay minimum royalties or   **8-264** produce a minimum quantity of products incorporating the licensed technology will generally fall outside art.101(1).[326]

Historical approach of the Commission

The Commission has shown that it will interfere if the charging of royalties   **8-265** discriminates directly or indirectly against imports as opposed to domestically produced goods. Discrimination on the grounds of nationality is not permissible under the TFEU. Thus, where all manufacturers of television sets in Germany had pooled their patents on a royalty-free basis so that the practical effect was that only

---

[323] See [187].
[324] See *UARCO* reported in the *14th Report on Competition Policy*, point 93 and Reg.2349/84 art.3(4) (the defunct Patent Block Exemption).
[325] See para.188. See also para.102 where the Guidelines say that royalties calculated on the basis of all product sales may fulfil the conditions of art.101(3) where it may be concluded that in the absence of such a clause, it would be impossible or unduly difficult to calculate the royalty payable the licensee, for instance because the licensor's technology leaves no visible trade on the final product and practicable alternative monitory methods are unavailable.
[326] See para.183(e).

imports were subject to royalties, such a practice fell within art.101(1).[327] Similarly, the Commission intervened to prevent national performing right societies from charging royalties to manufacturers of records which were based upon the average retail price of records rather than the manufacturer's published selling price.[328] The Commission said that such meant that manufacturers had to pay widely differing royalties, depending on the country of sale, as retail prices differed markedly from state to state. Such a practice also prevented the cost or price advantages that arose in the country of manufacture from being passed on to consumers in the country of sale.

The US Approach

8-266   The case law in the US has focussed on obligations to pay royalties on IPR after it has moved into the public domain. In a Supreme Court decision, *Brulotte v Thys Co*,[329] the US Supreme Court condemned an agreement in which the licensor demanded royalties for practicing an invention beyond the life of its patents as per se patent misuse. However, *Brulotte* did not involve an antitrust claim. This decision was criticised in *Dolby Laboratories v Scheiber* where Posner J said that:

> "a licensee...to go on paying royalties after the patent expires does not extend the duration of the patent...because...if the licensee agrees to continue paying royalties after the patent expires the royalty rate will be lower."[330]

8-267   In *Kimble v Marvel Entertainment Inc*,[331] the Supreme Court revisited the doctrine in *Brulotte* but refused to overturn it, largely on the common law doctrine of stare decisis.[332] The 2017 Guidelines have little to say on this issue other than to cite that *Brulotte* allows a licensee to defer payments for pre-expiry use of a patent into the post-expiry period although it does bar royalties for using an invention after it has moved into the public domain.[333] In the 2007 Guidelines, cited in the 2017 Guidelines, the Department of Justice takes the view that it is possible that collecting royalties over a longer term than the patent grant will reduce the deadweight loss associated with a patent monopoly and allow the patent holder to recover the full value of the patent, thereby preserving innovation incentives.[334]

8-268   Where the licensee is obliged to pay royalties based on total sales of a licensee's product, regardless of whether it was made using the licensed technology, such may

---

[327] See *IGR/Stereo TV* reported in the *11th Report on Competition Policy*, para.62 and *14th Report on Competition Policy*, para.75.

[328] *Re Performing Right Societies* [1984] 1 C.M.L.R. 308; Press Release IP (84)7, 9 January 1984.

[329] *Brulotte v Thys Co* 379 US 29 (1964).

[330] *Dolby Laboratories v Scheiber* 293 F.3d 1014, 1017 (7th Cir., 2002), per Posner J. The 7th Circuit felt compelled to follow it and hold the patent license agreement at issue unenforceable. The US Court of Appeals for the Seventh Circuit invited the Supreme Court to reconsider the matter. See at 1018 ("[W]e have no authority to overrule a Supreme Court decision no matter how dubious its reasoning strikes us, or even how out of touch with the Supreme Court's current thinking the decision seems."). However, the Supreme Court declined to grant certiorari. *Scheiber v Dolby Labs, Inc*, 537 US 1109 (2003).

[331] 135 S.Ct 2401, 240.

[332] Whereby a court is bound by decisions of earlier courts of the same or higher level.

[333] 2017 Guidelines, fn.90.

[334] *Introduction to Antitrust Enforcement and Intellectual Property Rights: Promoting Innovation and Competition* (2007), US Department of Justice, Ch.6.IV.

increase the cost to a licensee of substituting alternative technologies and thus be anti-competitive and amount to an implied "tie in".[335]

Field-of-use

Generally, field-of-use restrictions do not fall within art.101(1) unless it is shown **8-269** that they are the result or means of implementing an agreement to eliminate competition between licensees.[336] Field-of-use restrictions are restrictions whereby a licensee is limited to one or more technical fields of application or one or more product markets or industrial sectors. Thus, a licensee may be restricted to using the licensed technology to manufacture cars rather than aeroplanes, or even more limited, e.g. diesel cars. Generally, field-of-use restrictions should be considered as falling outside art.101. The IPR owner should be entitled to determine the nature and extent of exploitation of the IPR. Thus, where several fields of use are covered by IPR, the IPR owner should be free to decide which fields of use are to be exploited and which are to be reserved to them alone or other licensees. If the licensor cannot choose the fields of use which it wishes to license, then there would be a disincentive for the licensor to license.

2014 Technology Transfer Guidelines

In the case of licences between non-competitors, the 2014 Guidelines consider **8-270** that field-of-use restrictions are permissible, being generally non-restrictive of competition or efficiency enhancing. They promote dissemination of new technology by giving the licensor an incentive to license for exploitation in fields in which they do not want to exploit the technology personally.[337]

Greater concerns arise where the parties are actual or potential competitors and **8-271** in particular concerns arise in the context of reciprocal licences. The concern is that the licensee ceases to be a competitive force outside the licensed field of use,[338] in particular, where there are cross licences between competitors which provide for asymmetrical field of use restrictions. A field of use restriction is asymmetrical where one party is permitted to use the licensed technology within one field of use and the other party is permitted to use the other licensed technology within a different field of use. If such causes the licensees to reduce output *outside* the licensed field of use (e.g. because it is tooled up to produce the licensed technology and cannot easily swap over), then the Guidelines suggest that competition concerns arise. It is difficult to understand the concern here. Any undertaking must be entitled to choose where to commit its industrial resources and to which field of use, the commitment of those resources is most profitable. If the different fields-of-use represent different product markets and competition is effective in both, then a licensee's decision to commit its resources to one market rather than other will have no effect on the other market if there is effective competition (i.e. another competitor will take its place in that second market). In other words, if an undertaking is operating in one product market but cannot enter another product market because of the lack of

---

[335] See *Complaint in United States v Microsoft Inc* Civ No.94–1564 (D.D.C. filed 15 July 1994); *Competitive Impact Statement*, id (filed 27 July 1994).

[336] See *4th Report on Competition Policy*, para.28.

[337] See paras 208–215 and in particular para.212.

[338] See para.213. This is difficult to understand if the field of use restriction relates only to the licensed IPR rather than all competing technologies.

a licence,[339] then the grant of a licence should be seen as pro-competitive and not anti-competitive. The mere fact that it scales down its operations in the other market should not be objectionable. No undertaking can be required to compete in a particular product market.

8-272   In contrast to asymmetrical field-of-use licences, the 2014 Guidelines say that symmetrical field-of-use restrictions, i.e. reciprocal licences in the same field-of-use are unlikely to fall within art.101(1).[340] A field-of-use restriction combined with an exclusive licence may restrict the licensor's ability to exploit its technology but such, as the Guidelines say, will tend to be analysed in the context of exclusive licences.

Historical approach of the Commission

8-273   A requirement that the licensee should only use the licensed know-how solely for the purposes of manufacturing the licensed product was held to fall outside art.101(1).[341] Such a requirement can be considered a very specific field-of-use restriction.

The US approach

8-274   The 2017 Guidelines take a beneficial view about field-of-use restrictions.[342]

Output restrictions

8-275   A licence often includes restrictions on the quantity of products that can be produced by the licensee. These can either be restrictions on the minimum or maximum number of products which a licensee can manufacture or sell. From a theoretical viewpoint, restrictions on the maximum number of products that can be manufactured would fall within the "limited licence" doctrine as constituting a partial lifting of the prohibitive effect of intellectual property. If a person cannot be compelled to license, then licensing someone to produce a maximum of 100 licensed products should not be objectionable. After all, 100 is better than none. Thus, such should be unobjectionable. To object to such restrictions is to give the licensor two choices: do not licence or give a licence to produce as many products as you wish. Such an approach in itself may give concern because the licensor may not wish to generate too much intra-brand competition and thus be deterred from licensing at all. Such considerations would favour allowing output restrictions.

2014 Technology Transfer Guidelines

8-276   In general, the Commission's view as set out in the 2014 Guidelines is that output limitations produced on a licence in agreements between non-competitors are unobjectionable. They are exempted in the TTBE. In recognition of the arguments above, the Guidelines say:

"As a supplier of technology, the licensor should normally be free to determine the output

---

[339] Or is able to compete more effectively in that product market by the grant of a licence.

[340] See para.213.

[341] See *Re the Agreements between Jus-Rol Ltd and Rich Products Corp* [1988] OJ L69/21; [1988] 4 C.M.L.R. 527 at [35].

[342] e.g. see Example 1 in the Guidelines where they refer to no objections arising merely because of a subdivision of the licensor's intellectual property amongst different fields of use and territories.

produced with the licensed technology by the licensee. If the licensor were not free to determine the output of the licensee, a number of licence agreements might not come into existence in the first place, which would have a negative impact on the dissemination of new technology."[343]

However, such remarks ill-fit with other observations that output restrictions may give rise to anti-competitive concerns as such reduces intra-technology competition between licensees. The Guidelines say that:　　　　　**8-277**

> "[205] ... The main anti-competitive risk flowing from output restrictions on licensees in agreements between non-competitors is reduced intra-technology competition between licensees. The significance of such anti-competitive effects depends on the market position of the licensor and the licensees and the extent to which the output limitation prevents the licensee from satisfying demand for the products incorporating the licensed technology."

The immediate paragraph above can be seen as an illustration of the general principle set out in the 2014 Guidelines that if a licensor decides to license, it can only impose contractual restraints such as output restrictions if they are objectively justifiable and that it is not sufficient for the licensor to say that it would not have entered into the licence if the output restrictions had not existed.[344] Indeed, the tension between the above two excerpts is ultimately a mere example of the tension between the two competing principles, namely that a licensor is free to determine how much competition it creates in technology protected by IPRs and the Commission's insistence that when considering *intra-technology* competition between licensor and licensees, only restraints which be objectively justified are permissible.　　　　　**8-278**

It should be noted that under the 2014 Guidelines, *minimum* output obligations will usually be treated as pro-competitive.[345]　　　　　**8-279**

Historical approach of the Commission

Finally, it should be noted that the Commission's stance has changed over the years. Historically, the Commission's approach to output restrictions was hostile. In the 1970s, in the context of a patent licence which restricted the licensee's capacity, the Commission said that it was:　　　　　**8-280**

> "not of the essence of his rights as patent-holder. There might be justification for differences in royalties but there is none for a restriction of capacity."[346]

This formalistic approach clearly now has no place in the Commission's approach to output restrictions.　　　　　**8-281**

The US approach

The 2017 Guidelines emphasise that when evaluating licensing restraints, output restraints have been found to be unlawful per se.[347] The Guidelines go onto say that if a restriction appears to be of a kind that would always, or almost always, tend to　　　　　**8-282**

---

343 See para.207.
344 See para.12(b) of the 2014 Guidelines.
345 See para.183.
346 See *Zuid-Nederlandsche Bronbemaling en Grondboringen BV v Heidemaatschappij Beheer NV* [1975] 2 C.M.L.R. D67 at [18].
347 See para.3.4.

reduce output, it is likely to be challenged without elaborate analysis.[348] However, although not wholly clear, it would not appear that the 2017 Guidelines were advocating a different approach to that of the 1995 Guidelines. Therefore, it is suggested that the important consideration here is whether the restraint gives rise to a reduction of the *aggregate* output of all products in the relevant market in which the licensed products find themselves.

Tie-in and bundling clauses

8-283   A tying arrangement occurs when a licensor "ties in" a licensee an intellectual property licence with an obligation on the licensee to take a second product or service ("the tied-in product") from the licensor or an appointed third party when making the licensed products ("the tying product"). In general, the quantity of purchases of the tied-in product is proportionate to the level of exploitation of the licensed IPR. The obvious example of this is where a component of a product manufactured under a licence is obliged to be sourced from the licensor or their appointed third party.

8-284   A bundling arrangement occurs when a licensed product is required to be sold together with another product, again, sourced from the licensor or an appointed third party. Tying and bundling give rise to the same concerns and thus it is convenient only to refer to tying-in.

8-285   Tying-in clauses give rise to concerns about foreclosure of third parties who are operators in the tied-in product market. If the licensee has substantial market power, then the tie-in clause may often give rise to competitive concerns in the market for the tied-in product. This effect will depend on the size of the market for the tied-in product and the demand by the licensee for the tied-in product. If the demand for the tied-in product by the licensee is a small fraction of the total market for the tied-in product, then it is unlikely that there will be any anti-competitive effect even if the licensor has substantial market power in the tying product.

8-286   In general, a distinction needs to be made between tie-in clauses which are necessary for quality control purposes as opposed to those which are purely intended to increase the profit of the licensor.

2014 Technology Transfer Guidelines

8-287   The 2014 Guidelines say that the main restrictive effect of tying is foreclosure of competing suppliers of the tied product. The Guidelines state:

> "[223]   The main restrictive effect of tying is foreclosure of competing suppliers of the tied product. Tying may also allow the licensor to maintain market power in the market for the tying product by raising barriers to entry since it may force new entrants to enter several markets at the same time. Moreover, tying may allow the licensor to increase royalties, in particular when the tying product and the tied product are partly substitutable and the two products are not used in fixed proportion. Tying prevents the licensee from switching to substitute inputs in the face of increased royalties for the tying product. These competition concerns are independent of whether the parties to the agreement are competitors or not. For tying to produce likely anti-competitive effects the licensor must have a significant degree of market power in the tying product so as to restrict competition in the tied product. In the absence of market power in the tying product the licensor can-

---

[348] See para.3.4.

not use his technology for the anti-competitive purpose of foreclosing suppliers of the tied product. Furthermore, as in the case of non-complete obligations, the tie must cover a certain proportion of the market for the tied product for appreciable foreclosure effects to occur. In cases where the licensor has market power on the market for the tied product rather than on the market for the tying product, the restraint is analysed as non-compete or quantity forcing, reflecting the fact that any competition problem has its origin on the market for the 'tied' product and not on the market for the 'tying' product."

However, where the tie-in is necessary for quality control or for efficiency, then **8-288** tie-ins may be pro-competitive. According to the Guidelines:

"[224] Tying can also give rise to efficiency gains. This is for instance the case where the tied product is necessary for a technically satisfactory exploitation of the licensed technology or for ensuring that production under the licence conforms to quality standards respected by the licensor and other licensees. In such cases tying is normally either not restrictive of competition or covered by Article 101(3). Where the licensees use the licensor's trademark or brand name or where it is otherwise obvious to consumers that there is a link between the product incorporating the licensed technology and the licensor, the licensor has a legitimate interest in ensuring that the quality of the products are such that it does not undermine the value of his technology or his reputation as an economic operator. Moreover, where it is known to consumers that the licensees (and the licensor) produce on the basis of the same technology it is unlikely that licensees would be willing to take a licence unless the technology is exploited by all in a technically satisfactory way.

[225] Tying is also likely to be pro-competitive where the tied product allows the licensee to exploit the licensed technology significantly more efficiently. For instance, where the licensor licenses a particular process technology the parties can also agree that the licensee buys a catalyst from the licensor which is developed for use with the licensed technology and which allows the technology to be exploited more efficiently than in the case of other catalysts. Where in such cases the restriction is caught by Article 101(1), the conditions of Article 101(3) are likely to be fulfilled even above the market share thresholds."

Historical approach of the Commission

Historically, the Commission considered the question of tie-in clauses in a pat- **8-289** ent licence in *Vaessen BV v Moris*.[349] This concerned a patent relating to a process and device for manufacturing meat sausages. The patent that existed only in Belgium, was owned by Mr Moris and licenced to ALMO, a company of which Mr Moris was principal shareholder. ALMO manufactured and sold synthetic casings for all types of sausages but these casings were not protected by patents. ALMO sub-licensed others to work the patent. The right to use the process was royalty-free provided that the sub-licensees undertook to obtain all their supplies of casing from ALMO. Vaessen, a rival manufacturer of synthetic sausage casings similar to those sold by ALMO in Belgium complained to the Commission that its attempt to penetrate the Belgian market had been impeded by the exclusive purchasing commitment in ALMO's sublicenses. The Commission held that such a clause had the object and effect of restricting competition, since it deprived the sub-licensee of its business freedom to obtain supplies from other undertakings perhaps on more favourable terms. The Commission has also held that an obligation on a

---

[349] (79/86) [1979] OJ L19/32; [1979] 1 C.M.L.R. 511.

patent licensee to obtain manufacturing equipment for making the patented product from a named third party falls within art.101(1).[350] In this case, whilst such did not recompense the patent owner, the patentee had given the third party the responsibility for developing the equipment for manufacturing the patented product on the implicit promise that it would include an exclusive purchasing clause in its licences.

8-290   In trade mark/manufacturing licences, the Commission will generally permit tie-in clauses where such are necessary to maintain the reputation of the mark. Thus, in *Campari*,[351] the Commission considered such a licence. The facts were that manufacturing licensees of the well-known drink "Campari" were obliged to restrict the manufacture of the drink to plants which were capable of guaranteeing the quality of the product. The Commission cleared such a condition as "maintenance of the quality is referable to the existence of the trade mark right."[352] Similarly, obligations to purchase albumin and bitter orange essence from manufacturers who were capable of providing such products of a sufficiently high standard and to purchase colouring matter and herbal mixtures from the licensor fell outside art.101(1). The Commission said that it was a legitimate concern of the licensor to ensure that the product manufactured under licence had the same quality. The composition of the two products determined the characteristic of BITTER CAMPARI and being a trade secret, the licensor could not be required to reveal it to its licensees.[353] In *Moosehead/Whitbread*,[354] which concerned a trade mark/know-how licence regarding the brewing of MOOSEHEAD beer between a Canadian brewery (Moosehead) and an English brewery, the Commission held that an obligation to purchase yeast from Moosehead or a third party designated by it fell outside art.101(1), as it was necessary to ensure a:

> "technically satisfactory exploitation of the licensed technology and a similar identity between the lager produced originally by Moosehead and the same lager produced by Whitbread."[355]

8-291   If a tie-in clause was found to infringe art.101(1), historically, it was not capable of exemption.[356]

The US approach

8-292   In *Illinois Tool Works Inc v Independent Ink*,[357] the Supreme Court revisited the historical hostility of US law to tying in clauses. As the judgment said, over the years, the Supreme Court's strong disapproval of tying arrangements had diminished. In the past, it had said that tying arrangements "serve hardly any purpose beyond the suppression of competition". It noted that the historical approach, that tying arrangements were per se unlawful, was no longer the law. Rather, it noted that in *Jefferson Parish*,[358] the essential characteristic of an invalid tying arrangement "lies in the seller's exploitation of its control over the tying product

---

[350] See *Velcro* [1989] 4 C.M.L.R. 157.
[351] *Re the Agreements of Davide Campari-Milano SpA* [1978] 2 C.M.L.R. 397.
[352] *Re the Agreements of Davide Campari-Milano SpA* [1978] 2 C.M.L.R. 397 at [61].
[353] *Re the Agreements of Davide Campari-Milano SpA* [1978] 2 C.M.L.R. 397 at [62].
[354] *Moosehead/Whitbread* [1990] OJ L100/32; [1991] 4 C.M.L.R. 391.
[355] *Moosehead/Whitbread* [1990] OJ L100/32; [1991] 4 C.M.L.R. 391 at 398.
[356] (79/86) [1979] OJ L19/32; [1979] 1 C.M.L.R. 511 at [23].
[357] 547 U.S. 28 (2006).
[358] *Jefferson Parish Hospital Dist. No.2 v Hyde*, 466 U.S. 2, 9.

to force the buyer into the purchase of a tied product that the buyer either did not want at all, or might have preferred to purchase elsewhere on different terms". As it said, that requires the seller to have market power to force the purchase to do something that they would not do in a competitive market. In other words, tying-in arrangements do not give rise to concerns unless the IPR owner has market power. The Supreme Court in *Illinois Tool Works* departed from earlier decisions and held that IPRs do not by themselves confer market power upon their owner nor could such be presumed.[359] The approach of the Supreme Court in *Illinois Tool Works* is reflected in Title 25 of the United States Code following its amendment by the America Invents Act. This says that no patent owner shall be denied relief where there are tying-in arrangements unless, in view of the circumstances, the patent owner has market power in the relevant market for the patent or patented product.[360]

The 2017 Guidelines adopt the same approach to tying-in clauses as in the 1995 **8-293** Guidelines which were followed in *Illinois Tool Works*. They are most likely to give rise to concern where: (1) the seller has market power in the tying product; (2) the arrangement has an adverse effect on competition in the relevant market for the tied product; and (3) efficiency justifications for the arrangement do not outweigh the anti-competitive effects.[361] Applying *Illinois Tool Works*, the 2017 Guidelines make it clear that the Department of Justice will not presume that a patent, copyright or trade secret by itself confers market power upon its owner.

Resale price maintenance

Commission

In general, the approach of the Commission as set out in the 2014 Guidelines is **8-294** that any attempt to fix prices that the licensee sells downstream are considered objectionable per se.[362] Thus, the TTBE treats them as hard core even for agreements between non-competitors. However, where agreements are between non-competitors, maximum price and recommended price clauses are permissible.

However, in the Guidelines on Vertical Restraints, it is acknowledged that resale **8-295** price maintenance may be helpful during the introductory period of expanding demand to induce distributors to better take into account the manufacturer's interest to promote the product. Thus, it says that RPM may provide the distributors with the means to increase sales efforts and if the distributors are under competitive pressure, this may induce them to expand overall demand for the product. It also says that RPM may be necessary for a short period in franchise systems or similar distribution systems to co-ordinate a short-term low price campaign and to permit retailers to provide additional pre-sales services in particular in the case of experience or complex products. Such would avoid "free riding" by retailers who do not provide such services.[363] This approach is not seen in the 2014 Technology Transfer Guidelines but the logic would seem applicable to technology transfer licences or indeed any licences involving IPR.

---

[359] *Illinois Tool Works* was primarily concerned with whether market power could be presumed where such involved a patent on the tying good. The Supreme Court took the opportunity to endorse the 1995 Guidelines that a patent does not confer market power upon its owner nor could such be presumed.

[360] 35 U.S. Code, s.271(d).

[361] para.5.3.

[362] See para.99.

[363] See para.225 of the Guidelines on Vertical Restraints. See para.11-059.

8-296   In contrast, the 2014 Guidelines considers that the provision of a list of recommended prices to or the imposition of a maximum price on the licensee by the licensor is not considered in itself as leading to fixed or minimum selling prices.[364]

The US approach

8-297   In *Leegin Creative Leather Products v PSKS Inc*,[365] the Supreme Court overruled its nearly 100 years old opinion in *Dr. Miles Medical Co v John D. Park & Sons Co*[366] that resale price maintenance was per se unlawful. It said that they must be evaluated under the rule of reason. This is reflected in the 2017 Guidelines which say that RPM will apply a rule of reason approach and in doing so, will analyse such on a case-by-case basis.[367]

Downstream sales restrictions

8-298   It is often that the licence will seek to restrict the freedom on the licensee as to whom, where and how it sells the licensed products. Thus, the licence may seek to restrict the customers to whom the licensee sells or alternatively seek to restrict the territories into which the licensee can sell. These sales restrictions can take many forms—passive sales bans into territories outside the licensed territory which are concerned at preventing the licensee from meeting unsolicited orders (e.g. Internet sales bans); active sales bans which are concerned at preventing the licensee from embarking on an active promotional campaign in the territories reserved to other licensees; and restrictions on the markets that the licensee can sell, e.g. only sell the licensed products in the automobile market.

8-299   Restrictions of sales into territories of other licensees will often appear in exclusive licences to provide greater territorial protection than a mere open exclusive licence would confer. In this context, this has already been discussed.[368]

CJEU

8-300   In *Windsurfing v EU Commission* (which has been discussed at para.8-183) which concerned a patent for a particular rig, the licence contained inter alia two terms: (1) to fit licensed rigs only to approved boards; and (2) to market the rigs only in combination with boards as complete sailboards. The CJEU held that such would arbitrarily place on the licensee the ability only to sell the patented product in conjunction with a product outside the scope of the patent and thus was not indispensable to the exploitation of the patent.[369] Accordingly, it found that both provisions were caught by art.101(1). In *Intel v Via*,[370] an English case which concerned allegations of anti-competitive practices by Intel, the well-known chip maker, and which is discussed in more detail in the chapter on art.102, the Court of Appeal said that *Windsurfing* was clear authority for the proposition that a licence infringed art.101(1) if it sought to regulate the commercial market by controlling not only what is made with the licensed technology, but also the use which was

---

[364] See para.118 of the Guidelines.
[365] 551, U.S. 877 (2007).
[366] 220 U.S. 373 (1911).
[367] See para.5.2.
[368] See para.8-219.
[369] (193/83) [1986] E.C.R. 611; [1986] 3 C.M.L.R. 489 at [59].
[370] *Intel Corp* [2003] F.S.R. 33 CA at [72].

made of it thereafter. Whilst such is a possible interpretation of *Windsurfing*, in the 21st century, this would state the principle too widely as, e.g. captive use restrictions are permissible[371]; and some downstream passive and active sales bans are permissible in technology transfer licences.[372]

2014 Technology Transfer Guidelines

In general, where the parties are competitors, restrictions on the class of customers or markets that a licensee can sell to are considered hard core restrictions in the Technology Transfer Block Exemption and Vertical Agreements Block Exemption.[373] There are exceptions to these which are discussed in Chs 9 and 11. Thus, in certain circumstances, active and passive sales bans are permissible. Furthermore, captive use and field of use restrictions are permissible.   **8-301**

The 2014 Guidelines make it clear that a more tolerant approach is taken to sales restrictions on licensees and licensors where they are not competitors than where they are.[374]   **8-302**

The US approach

Customer allocation between competitors is also generally considered objectionable per se in the US.[375]   **8-303**

Grantback clauses

A grantback is an arrangement under which a licensee agrees to license back   **8-304**
("grant back") the right to exploit its own improvements to the licensed technology to the licensor or other licensees. Generally, non-exclusive grantbacks will be pro-competitive in the field of the licensed technology as they will result in a greater number of parties being able to exploit technological improvements which have been developed by only one party. Concerns about grantbacks particularly arise where:

(a) the grantback is an exclusive grant back and thus the party who developed the improvement is unable to exploit the technology itself; or

(b) there is a substantial reduction in competition in the relevant innovation market (i.e. the competitiveness of parties who can innovate in the relevant field of technology).

Invariably, exclusive grantbacks restrict competition because they do not allow   **8-305**
competition in the licensed technology (and products incorporating the licensed technology) between licensor and licensee. Furthermore, and more importantly, they discourage research and development by licensees (if licensees are not able to reap the fruits of their R&D efforts, there is little incentive to carry out such).

In contrast, more detailed analysis is required to consider whether a non-   **8-306**
exclusive grantback will decrease competition in the relevant innovation market. Where the undertakings are not competitors in the innovation market (i.e. one of

---

[371] See para.8-323.
[372] See para.9-043.
[373] See para.9-035, et seq. and para.11-061.
[374] See paras 197–203.
[375] *US Antitrust Guidelines for Intellectual Property* [1995], para.5.1.

them is not or does not have the ability to carry out R&D in the relevant technology market), it is unlikely that such will have any material effect on the innovation market. More analysis is required where the agreement is between two competitors who have R&D capacity. In these cases, proper analysis of the competitive effects of such clauses and in particular the need to balance the likely increase in competition in the *product* market (as both licensor and licensee will be able to manufacture products using the improvements) as against a possible decrease in the *innovation* market, i.e. the desire of any party to gain a competitive edge in technology against each other.[376]

2014 Technology Transfer Guidelines

8-307   The Commission has always considered exclusive grant backs as restrictive of competition. As said in the 2014 TT Guidelines:

> "[129] … An obligation to grant the licensor an exclusive licence to improvements of the licensed technology or to assign such improvements to the licensor is likely to reduce the licensee's incentive to innovate since it hinders the licensee in exploiting the improvements, including by way of licensing to third parties. An exclusive grant back is defined as a grant back which prevents the licensee (which is the innovator and licensor of the improvement in this case) from exploiting the improvement (either for its own production or for licensing out to third parties). This is the case both where the improvement concerns the same application as the licensed technology and where the licensee develops new applications of the licensed technology."

8-308   In contrast, non-exclusive grant backs are permissible even if non-reciprocal but if between competitors, they may have negative effects on competition as such would prevent a competitor from gaining a competitive lead over another.[377]

8-309   It should be noted that in the previous Guidelines, a distinction was drawn between exclusive grant-backs of severable improvements and non-severable improvements. However, this distinction no longer applies in the 2014 Guidelines. Many have criticised this on the basis that non-severable improvements cannot be exploited without the permission of the licensor. However, this criticism ignores the fact that many IPRs cannot be exploited without the permission of another IPR owner. An improvement patent is a classic example. As said in the previous edition of this book, the previous Guidelines ignored the need to incentivise licensees to innovate and improve the licensed technology regardless of whether it is severable or non-severable. Furthermore, non-severable improvements, if they give rise to valuable IPR (including know-how), give the licensee leverage with the licensor and thus do act as an incentive for the licensee to innovate. The licensor may be interested in the improvements but knows that they cannot use them without

---

[376] The competitive effects of grantback clauses are considered in detail in a 2011 study commissioned by the European Commission: P. Regibeau and K. Rockett, "Assessment of potential anticompetitive conduct in the field of intellectual property rights and assessment of the interplay between competition policy and IPR protection" November 2011 (COMP/2010/16). This study is an in-depth review of US and EU law and the advantages and disadvantages of grantback clauses. It makes a valuable distinction between grantbacks of severable improvements and non-severable improvements (a severable improvement is one that can be exploited independently of the licensed technology). It focusses (perhaps too much) on the effect of such clauses on future innovation as opposed to increased competition arising from exploitation of the improvements.

[377] See paras 131–132.

permission of the licensee. In such circumstances, one would expect the negotiation of a cross-licence with the payment of royalties. Clearly, if the licensee has to assign or exclusively license the licensor, the licensee has no incentive to do so and thus will not embark on programmes designed to improve the licensed technology. The previous edition suggested that the then guidelines be changed to reflect this and this has now happened.[378]

Historical approach of the Commission

From an early stage, the Commission has held that an obligation on a licensee to assign or grant-back an exclusive licence in improvement patents or know-how developed during the licence to the licensor falls within art.101(1).[379] Conversely, an obligation on a licensee to grant a non-exclusive licence to the licensor and other licensees will generally fall outside art.101(1).[380] **8-310**

In certain cases, the Commission had taken the view that, as discussed above, non-exclusive grantbacks gave rise to concerns about their effect on the relevant innovation market. Thus, the Commission took the view that an obligation to grant back non-exclusive licences may restrict competition in a oligopolistic market as such would prevent one party ever gaining a competitive advantage over another, which might result from such improvements and thus discourage any efforts which the company might normally make to obtain such an advantage.[381] Thus the Commission held that provisions in a patent/know-how licence, granting the two chief producers of zips in the EU the use in a substantial part of the EU of all future patents and know-how developed by the licensor, who was a major competitor, infringed art.101(1) as it helped the two manufacturers to secure a broader control in the field of zip technology.[382] In the context of joint ventures, the Commission, in a patent cross-licensing co-operation agreement between two large undertakings with big market shares, found that an obligation on each to license the other for new, independently developed processes infringed art.101(1), as neither of the two firms would be able to obtain a competitive advantage over the other in research nor could either gain individually by keeping research results to itself.[383] Where a major US glass manufacturer of optical fibres entered into a number of joint ventures with European manufacturers, which required them to grant back on a non- **8-311**

---

[378] A similar point is made in P. Regibeau and K. Rockett, "Assessment of potential anti-competitive conduct in the field of intellectual property rights and assessment of the interplay between competition policy and IPR protection" November 2011 (COMP/2010/16), whereby it called in question the differing treatment under competition analysis of grantback clauses for severable and non-severable improvements. As the authors say, in the absence of a grant back clause, one would expect licensor and licensee to bargain over the use of the non-severable improvement and that would allow the profits (total surplus) from exploiting the improvement to be distributed between licensee and licensor. Thus the authors say *"This calls into question the common reasoning according to which the licensor 'controls the use of non-severable improvements anyway' so that there is nothing to worry about in such a case"* (pp.49–50). It is likely that this report led to the European Commission abandoning the distinction that it made in the previous guidelines.

[379] See *Re the Agreement of Raymond & Co* [1972] C.M.L.R. D45.

[380] See the *Agreements of Davidson Rubber Co* [1972] OJ L143/31, [1972] C.M.L.R. D52; *Re Kabelmetal's Agreement* [1975] OJ L222/34, [1975] 2 C.M.L.R. D40; *Re the Agreement between Jus-Rol and Rich Products* [1988] 4 C.M.L.R. 527 (know-how); *Re the Agreement between Boussois SA and Interpane* [1988] 4 C.M.L.R. 124 (know-how).

[381] See *Re Kabelmetal's Agreement* [1975] OJ L222/34; [1975] 2 C.M.L.R. D40 at [33].

[382] *Re the Complaint by Yoshida Kogyo KK, Press Release of the Commission*, 9 June 1978; [1978] 3 C.M.L.R. 44.

[383] *Re the Agreement between Bayer AG and Gist-Brocades NV* [1976] 1 C.M.L.R. D94.

exclusive basis to the US manufacturer any improvement in the licensed technology which would then be licensed to all joint venture companies, this was held to infringe art.101(1) as it substantially eliminated competition between the joint ventures because technology was a key element in competition between optical fibre producers.[384] These decisions[385] can be seen as constituting implicit recognition of the importance of maintaining competition in the innovation markets. It is clear from the above that grantbacks between competitors in a horizontal relationship are more objectionable than in a standard licence between non-competitors.

The US approach

8-312   In the US, grant back clauses in technology licences are not considered unlawful per se.[386] The Department of Justice will consider the competitive effect of grant back clauses under a "rule of reason" approach. In its 2017 Guidelines, it states:

> "The Agencies will evaluate a grantback provision under the rule of reason, considering its likely effects in light of the overall structure of the licensing arrangement and conditions in the relevant markets. An important factor in the Agencies' analysis of a grantback will be whether the licensor has market power in a relevant technology or research and development market. If the Agencies determine that a particular grantback provision is likely to reduce significantly licensees' incentives to invest in improving the licensed technology, the Agencies will consider the extent to which the grantback provision has offsetting procompetitive effects, such as (1) promoting dissemination of licensees' improvements to the licensed technology, (2) increasing the licensors' incentives to disseminate the licensed technology, or (3) otherwise increasing competition and output in a relevant technology or research and development market. In addition, the Agencies will consider the extent to which grantback provisions in the relevant markets generally increase licensors' incentives to innovate in the first place."

Non-compete (exclusive dealing) clauses

8-313   Licences may impose restrictions on a licensee from dealing with the products or services of competitors or competing technologies. These are known as "non-compete clauses" or in the US, "exclusive dealing obligations". A particular type of non-compete clause is a tying-in clause which prohibits the licensee from buying components from third parties. These raise similar concerns to non-compete clauses but tend to be treated separately.[387]

2014 Technology Transfer Guidelines

8-314   The 2014 Guidelines take a rule of reason approach to non-compete obligations. It recognises that such can produce pro-competitive effects by promoting the dissemination of technology, in particular, by reducing the risk of misappropriation of the licensed technology, particularly in relation to know-how. Also, such may be necessary to ensure that the licensee focusses on dissemination of the licensed

---

[384] Decision 86/405/EEC *Corning/Optical Fibres* OJ [1986] L236/30. Generally, in relation to joint ventures, see Ch.9.

[385] A review of these decisions can also be seen in the Regibeau and Rockett study, pp.43–p.44.

[386] *Transparent-Wrap Machinery Corp v Stokes & Smith Co*, 329 U.S. 637, 645-48 (1947).

[387] See para.8-283.

technology.[388] However, it may be that such can be achieved by less restrictive alternatives, e.g. minimum output or royalty obligations.[389]

The main concerns are that non-compete obligations can result in significant **8-315** foreclosure of competing technologies. This is particularly significant where a substantial proportion of licensees are subject to such non-compete clauses.[390]

Historical approach of the Commission

Where a licensor sought to impose a blanket non-competition clause on a licensee **8-316** prohibiting them from dealing with other parties, this was held to fall within art.101(1).[391] In the case of an exclusive performance contract, whereby various well known opera singers had entered into exclusive contracts with a German company for the production of *Don Carlos* by Verdi and where they had agreed not be involved in any film about the same opera with anyone other than the German company, the Commission took a favourable position on such a clause as its duration was not intended to be long.[392] A non-compete obligations was held to infringe art.101(1) in know-how/trade mark licences.[393] Similarly, clauses in a patent licence which had the effect of restricting a licensee to only manufacturing the licensor's patented product were held to infringe art.101(1).[394] The Commission has historically treated such clauses as not capable of exemption.[395] The historic approach set out in these decisions would no longer appear to be applicable judging by the 2014 Guidelines.

Restrictions on competition and transfer of business

Although not strictly about licences, it is helpful to consider the Commission's **8-317** approach to non-compete obligations in the transfer of a business. Clauses prohibiting the seller of a business competing with the purchaser after sales will normally fall within art.101(1) unless they are necessary to preserve the worth of the transferred business and to protect the purchaser.[396] Thus a non-competition clause in an agreement to sell a business which involved the transfer of know-how and goodwill did not fall within art.101(1).[397] However, a personal non-competition clause was held to be more restrictive than was justified when it covered non-

---

[388] See paras 231–232.
[389] See para.232.
[390] See paras 228–229.
[391] See *4th Report on Competition Policy*, para.30; *AOIP* [1976] 1 C.M.L.R. D14; *Neilson-Hordell/Richmark* reported in the *12th Report on Competition Policy*, point 89.
[392] *RAI/Unitel* reported in the *12th Report on Competition Policy*, point 90 (Unitel undertook to ensure that the making of a film was not delayed unnecessarily so that the non-competition clause was not overly extended). See Commission Decision 78/516/EEC *RAI/UNITEL* [1978] OJ L157/39 which gives the background information to this case (although it was only concerned with a request for information).
[393] *Re the Agreements of Davide Campari-Milano SpA* [1978] 2 C.M.L.R. 397; *Moosehead/Whitbread* [1990] OJ L100/32, [1991] 4 C.M.L.R. 391.
[394] See *Re the Agreements on Video Cassette Recorders* [1978] 2 C.M.L.R. 160. A patent licence obliged licensees to observe particular technical standards for the manufacture and distribution of video cassette recorders and video cassettes which meant that licensees could only manufacture VCR equipment which constituted the licensed technology.
[395] See *AOIP* [1976] 1 C.M.L.R. D14.
[396] See (42/87) [1985] E.C.R. 2547; [1987] 1 C.M.L.R. 1.
[397] *Reuter v BASF AG* [1976] 2 C.M.L.R. D45.

commercialised research in the field concerning the transferred technological rights as it was not necessary to safeguard the worth of the transferred business.[398]

8-318   The period of non-competition must not exceed what is necessary for the preservation of the transferred business. Factors to be taken into account for determining the duration of the non-competition clause on the transfer of know-how are the nature of the transferred know-how, the opportunities for its use and the knowledge possessed by the purchaser. Such a clause must not extend beyond the relevant geographical market in which the seller was active before the transfer.[399] However, if a ban on competition would have the effect of closing down the seller's business, the seller may be allowed to manufacture within the area in which they were previously active provided the goods are intended for direct export only outside the area.[400] Such covenants are often necessary to ensure that the agreement is commercially viable.[401] Finally, it should be mentioned that the CJEU has also considered non-compete clauses in the context of sales of business.[402]

Non-competition and research and development

8-319   In the context of research and development joint ventures, where parent companies have licensed a joint venture company, the Commission has held that a clause prohibiting the parents of a joint venture from competing with the joint subsidiary in the field covered by their cooperation fell within art.101(1).[403] Similarly, restrictions on the right to exploit know-how belonging to a joint venture subsidiary after withdrawal from the joint venture fell within art.101(1).[404] For further discussion of the compatibility of art.101 and research and development agreements, the reader is referred to the chapter on IP and Horizontal Agreements.

The US Approach

8-320   In the US, the 2017 Guidelines[405]make it clear that exclusive dealing (non-compete) clauses are evaluated under a rule of reason. It says:

"In determining whether an exclusive dealing arrangement is likely to reduce competition in a relevant market, the Agencies will take into account the extent to which the arrangement (1) promotes the exploitation and development of the licensor's technology and (2) anti-competitively forecloses the exploitation and development of, or otherwise constrains competition among, competing technologies.

The likelihood that exclusive dealing may have anti-competitive effects is related, inter alia, to the degree of foreclosure in the relevant market, the duration of the exclusive dealing arrangement, and other characteristics of the input and output markets, such as concentration, difficulty of entry, and the responsiveness of supply and demand to changes in price in the relevant market. If the Agencies determine that a particular exclusive dealing arrangement may have an anti-competitive effect, they will evaluate the extent to which the restraint encourages licensees to develop and market the licensed technology (or specialized applications of that technology), increases licensors' incentives to develop

---

[398] *Reuter* [1976] 2 C.M.L.R. D45 at [49].
[399] *Reuter* [1976] 2 C.M.L.R. D45 at [47].
[400] *Sedame and Precilec* reported in the *11th Report on Competition Policy*, point 95.
[401] See (42/84) [1985] E.C.R. 2547; [1987] 1 C.M.L.R. 1.
[402] (161/84) [1986] E.C.R. 353; [1986] 1 C.M.L.R. 414.
[403] *Re Carbon Gas Technologie GmbH* [1984] 2 C.M.L.R. 275.
[404] *Re Carbon Gas Technologie GmbH* [1984] 2 C.M.L.R. 275 and [9].
[405] The 2017 Guidelines repeat verbatim the 1995 Guidelines.

or refine the licensed technology, or otherwise increases competition and enhances output in a relevant market."

The 2017 Guidelines give a helpful example of the approach that the Department of Justice would take to a particular case: **8-321**

"NewCo, the inventor and manufacturer of a new flat panel display technology, lacking the capability to bring a flat panel display product to market, grants BigCo an exclusive license to sell a product embodying NewCo's technology. BigCo does not currently sell, and is not developing (or likely to develop), a product that would compete with the product embodying the new technology and does not control rights to another display technology. Several firms offer competing displays, BigCo accounts for only a small proportion of the outlets for distribution of display products, and entry into the manufacture and distribution of display products is relatively easy. Demand for the new technology is uncertain and successful market penetration will require considerable promotional effort. The license contains an exclusive dealing restriction preventing BigCo from selling products that compete with the product embodying the licensed technology.
   Discussion: This example illustrates both types of exclusivity in a licensing arrangement. The license is exclusive in that it restricts the right of the licensor to grant other licenses. In addition, the license has an exclusive dealing component in that it restricts the licensee from selling competing products.
   The inventor of the display technology and its licensee are in a vertical relationship and are not actual or likely potential competitors in the manufacture or sale of display products or in the sale or development of technology. Hence, the grant of an exclusive license does not affect competition between the licensor and the licensee. The exclusive license may promote competition in the manufacturing and sale of display products by encouraging BigCo to develop and promote the new product in the face of uncertain demand by rewarding BigCo for its efforts if they lead to large sales. Although the licence bars the licensee from selling competing products, this exclusive dealing aspect is unlikely in this example to harm competition by anti-competitively foreclosing access, raising competitors' costs of inputs, or facilitating anti-competitive pricing because the relevant product market is unconcentrated, the exclusive dealing restraint affects only a small proportion of the outlets for distribution of display products, and entry is easy. On these facts, the evaluating Agency would be unlikely to challenge the arrangement."[406]

Captive use restrictions

Captive use restrictions are restrictions where the licensee is obliged to limit their **8-322** production of the licensed product to the quantities required for the production of their own products and for the maintenance and repair of their own products.[407] Thus, the licensee is not entitled to sell the licensed products by themselves or (if components) for incorporation into the products of other producers.

2014 Technology Transfer Guidelines

The 2014 Guidelines distinguish between captive use restrictions between **8-323** competitors where the licensee supplied components to third parties prior to the licence and where they did not. In the former case, its concern is if the effect of the captive use restriction is to cause the licensee to tool up to use the licensor's technology and thereby reduces the use of its own technology and thus to be a component

---

[406] Example 7, p.22.
[407] See para.216 of the 2014 Guidelines.

supplier, then such may have anti-competitive effects.[408] Here the concern is that the market for components (which the licensee may be exiting) suffers as compared to the market in finished products (which the licensee may be entering). In the latter case, the Guidelines say that the captive use restriction does not change anything compared to the pre-existing situation.

8-324   In the case of non-competitors, it says that there are two main competitive risks: (i) a restriction of intra-technology competition on the market for the supply of inputs; and (ii) an exclusion of arbitrage between licensees enhancing the possibility for the licensor to impose discriminatory royalties on licensees.[409] The meaning of this second point is far from clear.

8-325   The 2014 Guidelines continue by recognising the principle that a licensor is entitled to determine the level of competition concerning their own technology by saying that captive use restrictions may be pro-competitive if it can be established that the licensor would not have granted the licence because otherwise they would create direct competition to themselves on the component market.[410] Care must be taken in applying this because as said earlier in the Guidelines, when considering the issue of intra-technology competition, it is not simply sufficient for the licensor to simply say that they would not have entered into the licence but for the captive use restriction. It must be shown that other undertakings in a similar setting would not have accepted a lesser restraint.[411] Such uncertainty about the validity of captive use guidelines is very unsatisfactory and indeed may deter licensors from entering into captive use licences which would be detrimental to the market.

Miscellaneous clauses

8-326   This section deals with a number of miscellaneous clauses which will rarely give rise to any competitive concerns.

Commission

8-327   The 2014 Guidelines make it clear that the following obligations are considered generally not restrictive of competition within the meaning of art.101(1):

"(a)   confidentiality obligations;
(b)   obligations on licensees not to sub-license;
(c)   obligations not to use the licensed technology after the expiry of the agreement, provided that the licensed technology remains valid and in force;
(d)   obligations to assist the licensor in enforcing the licensed intellectual property rights;
(e)   obligations to pay minimum royalties or to produce a minimum quantity of products incorporating the licensed technology; and
(f)   obligations to use the licensor's trade mark or indicate the name of the licensor on the product."[412]

Historical decisions of the Commission

8-328   The above reflects the Commission's decisions and earlier block exemptions where such clauses were stated not to be caught by art.101(1). Thus, an obligation

---

[408] See para.217.
[409] see para.218.
[410] See para.219.
[411] See para.12(b) of the 2014 Guidelines.
[412] See para.183.

not to sub-licence was held to safeguard the right of the licensor to select its licensees.[413] In know-how licences, a ban on assignment and sub-licensing was important in order to control the dissemination of the know-how.[414] A clause stipulating that the licensor will not grant other licences on terms more favourable than that applying to the licensee was held to fall outside art.101(1).[415] However, where such terms are so onerous that the licensor might find it difficult to find other licensees, such a term may constitute a restriction of competition within art.101(1).[416]

Know-how presents its own problems in the case of licensing. The licensing of know-how is only of value to the licensee provided the know-how has not entered the public domain. Thus, it is of paramount concern to a licensor that it ensures that know-how does not enter the public domain, even after the expiry of the licence. The Commission considers that the clause in know-how licences (which require the licensee to maintain the secrecy of technical know-how during or after the termination of the licence) do not fall within art.101(1) if the know-how has not fallen into the public domain.[417]   **8-329**

No challenge clauses

A no-challenge clause is an obligation on the licensee not to contest the validity   **8-330**
of the intellectual property of the licence. It used to be the case that under US law a licensee was estopped from challenging the validity of the right. This rule has now been abolished in the US on the grounds that it is not in the national interest to prohibit the challenge of a possibly invalid patent and that licensees are often the only individuals with enough economic incentive to challenge the patentability of an inventor's discovery.[418]

A variation on the no-challenge clause is one where the licensee is entitled to   **8-331**
challenge the validity of the IPR but without prejudice to the right of the licensor to terminate the licence.

The validity under competition laws of no-challenge clauses are problematic.   **8-332**
This is because there are competing policies in play. On the one hand, there is the public interest that invalid patents are revoked as they stifle innovation rather than promote it. On the other hand, there is a public interest that technology is licensed.

---

[413] *Re the Contract of Burroughs AG and Geha-Werke* [1972] OJ L13/53, [1972] C.M.L.R. D72; *Re the Contract of Burroughs AG and Delplanque* [1972] OJ L13/50, [1972] C.M.L.R. D67; *Re The Agreements of Davidson Rubber Co* [1972] OJ L143/31; [1972] C.M.L.R. D52; *Re the Agreements of Davide Campari-Milano SpA* [1978] 2 C.M.L.R. 397. See, however, the *French StateSuralmo* reported in the 9th Report on Competition Policy, point 114, where an obligation that a patent licensee obtains the licensor's consent for sub-licensing for military purposes existed, no such consent being required for civil use, fell within art.101(1) as it was discriminatory.

[414] See *Re the Agreements of Davidson Rubber Co* [1972] OJ L143/31; [1972] C.M.L.R. D52. Thus, an obligation on the licensee not to divulge know-how communicated by the licensee constitutes in effect a ban on sub-licensing the know-how. Such an obligation is considered generally not restrictive of competition—art.2.1(1) old TTBE.

[415] *Re Kabelmetal's Agreement* [1975] OJ L222/34; [1975] 2 C.M.L.R. D40.

[416] *Re Kabelmetal's Agreement* [1975] OJ L222/34; [1975] 2 C.M.L.R. D40.

[417] *Re the Agreement of Burroughs Ag and Deplanque et Fils* [1972] OJ L13/53, [1972] C.M.L.R. D72; *Re the Agreement between Jus-Rol Ltd and Rich Products* [1988] 4 C.M.L.R. 527; *Re the Agreement between Boussois and Interpane* [1988] 4 C.M.L.R. 124; *Re the Agreement between DDD Ltd and Delta Chemie* [1988] 4 C.M.L.R. 535.

[418] See *Lear v Adkins* 23 L, Ed. 2d. 610, [12] (US Supreme Court). See also *MedImmune, Inc v Genentech, Inc*, 127 S. Ct. 764, 777 (2007). See also para.8-350.

If a licensor is deterred from granting a licence for fear that a licensee will seek to revoke the licensed patent, then this may prevent the dissemination of technology via licensing. In particular, a licensor may fear that a licensee will be best placed to determine whether a patent is valid. Equally, there is the public interest that licences negotiated between undertakings are respected as they allow and facilitate exploitation of technologies. A potential licensee always has the choice to take a licence for a patent or alternatively, to seek to revoke a patent (whether proactively or by way of counterclaim in infringement proceedings). The public interest that agreements are respected becomes much stronger when a no challenge clause is included in a settlement agreement against the background of patent litigation. There is a strong public interest that patent litigation is settled, particularly where such replaces years of uncertainty with licences to defendants alleged to infringe patents.

8-333   As with many other restraints in licences, historically, EU law viewed such with suspicion. However, with the 2014 Guidelines, the European Commission takes a much more nuanced approach to them which takes onboard the competing policies highlighted above.

European Court of Justice

8-334   In *Windsurfing*,[419] the CJEU said:

"It must be stated that [a no-challenge] clause clearly does not fall within the specific subject matter of the patent, which cannot be interpreted as also affording protection against actions brought in order to challenge the patent's validity, in view of the fact that it is in the public interest to eliminate any obstacle to economic activity which may arise where a patent was granted in error."[420]

8-335   Similarly, the CJEU held that a clause which required licensees to acknowledge the validity of Windsurfing's trade marks infringed art.101(1).[421] The same approach was taken in *BAT Cigaretten-Fabriken*.[422] Such was ostensibly a trade mark settlement agreement but the view was taken (probably rightly so) that the agreement so little reflected the parties' relative strengths in the litigation that it could not truly be considered to be a bona fide settlement agreement.

8-336   In *Bayer AG v Süllhofer*,[423] the CJEU reconsidered the question of no-challenge clauses in the context of a bona fide litigation settlement. In 1967, Süllhofer had applied and obtained a utility model and applied for a patent for the manufacture of polyurethane foam-based panels. In 1967, Süllhofer issued warnings to Hennecke, a wholly-owned subsidiary of Bayer, that it was infringing its utility model. Hennecke sought a declaration that the utility model was invalid and issued opposition proceedings against the patent. In 1968, both parties reached a settlement whereby Süllhofer granted Hennecke a non-exclusive free licence to use the patent and utility model and the right to sub-license. Conversely Bayer granted Süllhofer a non-exclusive and non-transferable licence subject to payment of royalties for the manufacture of foam panels under a German patent it held. Further, it

---

[419] (193/83) [1986] E.C.R. 611; [1986] 3 C.M.L.R. 489.
[420] (193/83) [1986] E.C.R. 611; [1986] 3 C.M.L.R. 489 at [92].
[421] See (193/83) [1986] E.C.R. 611; [1986] 3 C.M.L.R. 489 at [81].
[422] *BAT Cigaretten-Fabriken GmbH v EU Commission* (35/83) [1985] E.C.R. 363; [1985] 2 C.M.L.R. 470 upholding *Re the "Toltecs" and "Dorcet" Trade Marks* OJ L379/19; [1983] 1 C.M.L.R. 412.
[423] (65/86) [1988] E.C.R. 5249; [1990] 4 C.M.L.R. 182.

undertook not to challenge the validity of Süllhofer's patents and to withdraw its legal proceedings. Later on, further disputes arose and Süllhofer sought to terminate the agreement for fraudulent misrepresentation. The matter eventually went to the CJEU as to whether a no-challenge clause was incompatible with art.101(1).

The Commission submitted that such a clause should not be incompatible with **8-337** art.101(1) if the following conditions were fulfilled:

(1) The clause was included in a settlement putting an end to litigation pending before a national court.
(2) There were no other clauses restricting competition.
(3) The clause related solely to the right in issue.
(4) That right was manifestly unlikely to be revoked.

The court rejected the Commission's argument. It stated that art.101(1) made no **8-338** distinction between settlement agreements and other types of agreements. It went on to say that no-challenge clauses may fall within art.101(1), depending on the legal and economic context. However, it would not restrict competition when the licensee paid no royalties or when the licence was granted subject to payment of royalties, although related to a technically outdated process which the undertaking accepting the no-challenge clause did not use. Such examples rather suggested that in general, a no challenge clause in a settlement agreement *would fall* within art.101(1).[424]

As it was a preliminary reference, it was left to the national court to determine **8-339** whether the no-challenge clause did infringe art.101(1). Indeed, it could be said that in reality, the CJEU gave no real guidance at all other than that no-challenge clauses in a settlement agreement should be treated no differently than in a normal licence. In this respect, it is submitted that the CJEU was wrong. No-challenge clauses in a settlement agreement are normally the essence of such agreements and are not ancillary. In the majority of intellectual property litigation, an attack is made on the validity of the right by the defendant. A no-challenge clause is no less important than a clause not to continue or bring infringement proceedings.

2014 Technology Transfer Guidelines

The 2014 Guidelines provides rather mixed messages as to the permissibility of **8-340** no-challenge clauses in licences. On the one hand, it says that (in explaining why they are excluded restrictions in the Technology Transfer Block Exemption) that licensees are normally in the best position to determine whether or not an intellectual property right is valid.[425] It says that invalid IPR stifles innovation rather than promoting it.[426] It says that art.101(1) is likely to apply to such clauses where the licensed technology is valuable. However, and echoing *Bayer v Süllhofer*, it says that art.101(1) would not apply where the licensed technology is a technically outdated process which the licensee does not use or if granted for free.

It then discusses clauses where the licensor may terminate the licence in the event **8-341**

---

[424] For an application of these principles in national proceedings, see *Knorr-Bremse v Haldex Brake Products* [2008] EWHC 156 (Pat) (parties to a no-challenge clause were part of an oligopoly in the field of braking systems for commercial vehicles, trade conducted throughout EU, no free licence, technology was not outdated—there was a good arguable case that the no challenge clause was void under art.101 TFEU).

[425] See para.134.

[426] See para.134.

of a challenge to the validity of the IPR. On the one hand, it says that the licensee may be deterred from challenging the validity if it would risk termination of the licence and face significant risks which go far beyond its royalty obligations.[427] On the other hand, it acknowledges the public interest in strengthening the incentive of a licensor to license out by not being forced to continue dealing with a licensee that challenges the very subject matter of the licence but says that such must be balanced against the public interest to eliminate any obstacle to economic activity which may arise where an IPR was granted in error. Taking these factors into account, the Guidelines state that the right to terminate in the event of a challenge to the IPR can have the same effect as a no-challenge clause where switching away from the licensor's technology would result in a significant loss to the licensee. The Guidelines identified two particular concerns: where the patent is a standard essential patent and where the licensor has a significant market position.[428] This approach was taken in a decision of the EU Commission adopted the same year as the 2014 Guidelines, *Motorola Mobility*[429] which concerned a no challenge clause in a SEP licence. The Commission held that a "terminate if challenge" clause is only justified where the licensee has the possibility to make use of competing technology and is not dependent on a dominant licensor. Such did not exist where the patent is a SEP and there are no viable substitutes.

8-342   Outside such scenarios, the 2014 Guidelines say that a "termination for challenge" clause will often not provide a significant disincentive to challenge and therefore not give rise to the same effect as a no-challenge clause.[430]

8-343   In the case of exclusive licences, it says that clauses which give the licensor the right to terminate in the event of a challenge are less likely on balance to have anti-competitive effects.[431] It says that in such circumstances, the licensor may "find itself in a particular situation of dependency".

8-344   In relation to know-how, the 2014 Guidelines takes a favourable view of blanket no-challenge clauses because it allows weaker licensors to license stronger licensees without fear of a challenge once the know-how has been absorbed by the licensee.[432]

Comment

8-345   It is relatively clear from the above that the Commission is conflicted between two strong competing principles: the need to encourage IPR owners to license and the need for invalidly registered IPR to be invalidated. Its distrust of "terminate where challenged" clauses in IPR licences where there is a significant cost for the licensee in switching away from the licensor's technology is somewhat odd. After all, if the licensee is prepared to take a risk in challenging the validity of the IPR, it presumably takes the view that the IPR is invalid and thus may use the licensed technology without fear rather than switch away from it. It is of course accepted that in the real world, it will often take a few years of legal proceedings to determine if the licensed IPR is invalid. A licensee may say that it wishes to challenge the validity of the IPR but does not want to risk that if it is wrong and the IPR is found

---

[427] See para.137.
[428] See para.136.
[429] Case AT. 39985 *Motorola -Enforcement of GPRS standard essential patents* (C(2014) 2893). A copy of the decision can be found at: *http://ec.europa.eu/competition/antitrust/cases/dec_docs/39985/39985_928_16.pdf* [Accessed 28 January 2018].
[430] See paras 136–137.
[431] See para.139.
[432] See para.140.

valid, it ends up without a licence and having to incur significant costs in switching to other technologies. For the licensee, that would be the worst of both worlds. Yet, there is a sense here of the licensee "having its cake and eating it". For instance, if a licensee, instead of seeking to revoke an existing patent enters into a patent licence, and then, within months of the grant of that licence, seeks to revoke the patent knowing that it will be free to use the licensed technology whether it wins (because the technology will then be in the public domain) or loses (because the licensor cannot terminate the licence if there are no competing technologies available to the licensee), the incentive for a licensee to do this is strong as there is no "downside". However, this very fact would act as a powerful deterrent to a licensor licensing in the first place.

Historical approach of the Commission

In the 1970s and 1980s, the Commission consistently held save in one case that **8-346** no-challenge clauses in patent and know-how licences,[433] trade mark licences,[434] copyright,[435] and plant breeder's rights[436] infringed art.101(1). Such rulings were based on the grounds that public policy required that everyone including the licensee ought to be able to bring proceedings for the revocation of patents which had been wrongly granted.[437] Alternatively, it was said that the clause was a restriction on the licensee's freedom of action which did not come within the monopoly granted by the patent right.[438] The one exception was *Re Penney Trade Mark*[439] where, in a trade mark settlement dispute, the Commission held that a no-challenge clause which was limited in duration for five years (constituting the period which in most countries was reasonable for establishing use under the Paris Convention and where the likelihood of the trade marks being liable to be struck off was remote) did not have an appreciable effect on competition.

In *Moosehead/Whitbread*,[440] the Commission considered the question of a trade **8-347** mark no-challenge clause in a trade mark/know-how licensing agreement for the brewing of MOOSEHEAD beer by Whitbread, the English brewers, in England. The agreement stipulated that Whitbread could not challenge the validity or ownership of the registered trade mark MOOSEHEAD. The Commission distinguished between ownership and validity. In the case of a ban on challenging ownership, it stated that such a clause does not fall within art.101(1) as:

---

[433] See *Re the Agreements of the Davidson Rubber Co* [1972] C.M.L.R. D52; *Re the Agreement of Raymond & Co* [1973] C.M.L.R. D45; *Re the Agreement between Kabel AG and Luchaire* [1975] 2 C.M.L.R. D40; *Re Bayer AG and Gist-Brocades* [1976] 1 C.M.L.R. D94 (joint venture specialisation agreement); *AOIP* [1976] 1 C.M.L.R. D14; (79/86) [1979] 1 C.M.L.R. 511; *Ateliers de Construction de Compiegne v Fabry* [1979] 3 C.M.L.R. 77; *Zoller + Fröhlich/Télémecanique* reported in the *8th Report on Competition Policy*, point 109.

[434] See *Re the "Toltecs" and "Dorcet" Trade Marks* [1982] OJ L379/19, [1983] 1 C.M.L.R. 412 upheld on appeal by the CJEU—see (35/83) [1985] E.C.R. 363, [1985] 2 C.M.L.R. 470; *Goodyear Italiano* [1975] 1 C.M.L.R. D31 (Commission).

[435] See *Neilson-Hordell/Richmark* reported in the *12th Report on Competition Policy*, point 89.

[436] See *Royon v Meilland* [1985] OJ L369/9; [1988] 4 C.M.L.R. 193.

[437] See *AOIP* [1976] 1 C.M.L.R. D14 at [24].

[438] See *Re the Agreement of Raymond & Co* [1972] OJ L143/49; [1973] C.M.L.R. D45.

[439] *Re Penney's Trade Mark* [1978] 2 C.M.L.R. 100.

[440] *Moosehead/Whitbread* [1990] OJ L100/32; [1991] 4 C.M.L.R. 391.

"whether or not the licensor or licensee has the ownership of the trade mark, the use of it by any other party is prevented in any event, and competition would thus not be affected."[441]

8-348   This approach is reflected in the 2014 Guidelines.[442]

No-challenge clauses in settlement agreements

8-349   Settlement agreements are discussed below. However, it is common in IPR litigation for settlement agreements to include a no-challenge clause. Their inclusion raises different issues to the inclusion of a no-challenge clause in a simple licence. As the 2014 Guidelines say, it is inherent in such agreements that the parties agree not to challenge the IPRs covered by the agreement as the very purpose of the agreement is to settle existing disputes and/or to avoid future disputes.[443] The approach in the 2014 Guidelines is considerably more tolerant of no-challenge clauses in litigation settlement agreements than that taken by the CJEU in *Bayer v Süllhofer* (which as discussed above, drew no distinction in principle between such clauses in settlement agreements or not). These clauses may be caught by art.101(1) as a restriction on the freedom to challenge IPRs and are not part of the specific subject-matter of IPR (echoing the CJEU's judgment in *Windsurfing*) but it is clear that those circumstances are limited. Thus, they say that a no-challenge clause may infringe art.101(1) where the IPR was granted following the provision of misleading or incorrect information. This again echoes the CJEU's judgment in *Astrazeneca v Commission*.[444] The 2014 Guidelines also say that scrutiny of such clauses may be required where the licensor induces the licensee not to challenge the validity of the IPR, financially or otherwise or if the technology rights are a necessary input for the licensee's production. This alludes to "pay for delay" clauses, this refers to the decision by the Commission and General Court in *Lundbeck* and is discussed later in this chapter in the context of litigation settlement agreements.[445] Finally, the Guidelines expresses the concern that where the licensor has a very significant market share, termination of the licence where the licensee challenges the validity of the licensed IPRs may cause the licensee to have real difficulty finding an alternative technology.[446] Whilst this may be true, if the licensee has the courage of its convictions that the IPR is indeed invalid, then presumably it would be entitled to carry on using the licensed technology on the basis that if invalid, such is in the public domain.

---

[441]   *Moosehead/Whitbread* [1990] OJ L100/32; [1991] 4 C.M.L.R. 391 at 398. In fact, a challenge as to ownership may result in the mark being struck off the register rather than the mark being assigned to the owner. Thus, in the UK, pursuant to s.5(4)(a) of the Trade Marks Act 1994 (which enacts art.4(4)(b) of the Trade Mark Directive), a party who owned substantial goodwill in the mark as at the date of filing of the registered mark may seek to revoke the mark on the basis that normal and fair use of the mark as of the date of filing on the goods or services specified in the application as of the date of filing was liable to deceive a substantial number of persons into believing that there was a connection in the course of trade between the applicant for revocation and the owner of the registered mark contrary to fact. In such circumstances, the mark will be struck off the register and not assigned to the applicant for revocation.

[442]   See para.135.

[443]   See para.242.

[444]   *AstraZeneca v Commission* (C-457/10P) ECLI:EU:C:2012:770. This was a case under art.102 and is discussed at para.12-314.

[445]   See para.8-366.

[446]   See para.8-341.

The US approach

In *Lear v Adkins*,[447] the Supreme Court of the USA said that there was a strong   **8-350**
federal policy favouring the full and free use of ideas in the public domain. Thus,
in *MedImmune v Genentech*,[448] an American court held that a licensee is not
required to break or terminate its licence agreement before seeking a declaratory
judgment that the underlying patent is invalid, unenforceable or not infringed. This
is really a judgment repudiating the "licence estoppel" rule discussed at the beginning of this section. However, it shows an antipathy towards anything that prevents
licensees from challenging the validity of an IPR whilst still a licensee. In *Baseload
Energy Inc v Roberts*,[449] the Federal Circuit[450] held that no challenge clauses in settlement agreements are enforceable even in the absence of prior litigation. It
distinguished *Lear* on the grounds that it was not concerned with a no challenge
clause and emphasised the strong public interest in settling litigation as such
promotes certainty and avoids the costs of litigation. It has been said that the reasoning in *Baseload* applies to all no challenge clauses regardless of whether they form
part of a settlement agreement or not.[451] Yet, outside the case law of the Federal
Circuit, in *Rates Technology Inc v Speakeasy Inc*[452] the Second Circuit held that a
no challenge clause was unenforceable, applying *Lear*, as the importance of
discovering invalid patents outweighed the high costs that arose from patent litigation and the risk imposed on the licensor. It has been said that there is considerable uncertainty how the Supreme Court would approach no challenge clauses
nowadays.[453]

In the predecessor to the 2017 Guidelines, the 2007 Guidelines were generally   **8-351**
opposed to no-challenge clauses. Thus, they say:

> "Invalid patents impair competition, and as a matter of patent policy, challenges to their
> validity are encouraged. As the Solicitor General recently urged, [w]hile patent licensing
> in general should be encouraged because it allows the efficient exploitation of technol-
> ogy and promotes competition and innovation, public policy strongly favors ridding the
> economy of invalid patents, which impede efficient licensing, hinder competition, and
> undermine incentives for innovation. Public policy also concomitantly favors the swift
> resolution of patent litigation on terms not harmful to competition."[454]

The 2017 Guidelines do not mention no challenge clauses. Instead, the focus is   **8-352**
on the enforcement of invalid IPRs as antitrust violations.[455] It is not clear why the
2017 Guidelines chose to drop the 2007 guidance on no-challenge clauses. There
appears no suggestion in the 2017 Guidelines that in fact, the approach in the 2007
Guidelines do not apply.[456]

---

[447] See (1969) 395 Supreme Ct. 653.
[448] See (2007) 127 Supreme Ct. 764.
[449] 619, F.34 357 (Fed. Cir., 2010).
[450] The Federal Circuit has exclusive jurisdiction over appeals in patent cases.
[451] M.S. Gal and A.D. Miller, "Patent Challenge Clauses: A New Antitrust Offense" (2017) *Iowa Law Review*, Vol.102, 1476, 1485.
[452] 685 F.34, 163 (2d Cir., 2012).
[453] M.S. Gal and A.D. Miller, "Patent Challenge Clauses: A New Antitrust Offense" (2017) *Iowa Law Review*, Vol.102, 1488.
[454] Ch.IV s.II.
[455] See para.6
[456] To the contrary, they are referred to a number of times in the 2017 Guidelines outside the context

LITIGATION SETTLEMENT AGREEMENTS

Introduction

8-353   Litigation is more often settled than pursued to trial. Settling litigation play a vital part in a country's economy by relieving pressure on courts and clarifying at an early stage each party's rights. Litigation is costly and the outcome often uncertain. A lack of certainty is economically damaging. For instance, a party may choose not to launch a product because of concern that it infringes a patent. In the vast majority of cases, where a bona fide settlement of an IP dispute occurs, where the negotiations are conducted at arm's length and is between well-funded undertakings who are able to afford litigation costs, it would be surprising if such a settlement was open to attack under competition law. It would impose an unreasonable burden on the parties seeking to settle IPR litigation to have to second guess the outcome of a hypothetical attack under competition law of any settlement agreement (which hypothetical action will no doubt involve determining what the outcome of the underlying IPR proceedings would have been). It would merely trade one form of uncertainty for another form of uncertainty.

8-354   By reason of the above analysis, it will be the exception that a litigation settlement agreement will be found to be anti-competitive. The overwhelming advantages of encouraging settlement (particularly if such allows the defendant to market the patented technology) will normally outweigh anti-competition concerns.

8-355   But are there any "bright lines" when considering the application of art.101 to IP litigation settlements? One argument that has been deployed is that if the settlement does not to seek to restrain the behaviour of the defendants beyond the scope of protection of the IPR (normally patents), then competition law should not intervene. This is called the *"exclusionary potential"* argument. In short, the argument is that only where the settlement seeks to restrain the defendant parties from carrying out acts *outside* the exclusionary potential of the IPR should competition law intervene.

8-356   As attractive as this principle may appear, this doctrine has been rejected in both the US and EU, in the US Supreme Court case of *Federal Trade Commission v Actavis* and also in the General Court case, *Lundbeck v European Commission*. Both cases involved "pay for delay" agreements whereby patent litigation was settled by generic manufacturers being paid to keep out of the market. It is perhaps unsurprising that this principle was rejected in such cases. "Pay for delay" agreements whereby a generic manufacturer is guaranteed money (for doing nothing) by a patentee clearly benefit both the patentee and generic manufacturer but not the consumer or end-user. In essence, the patentee can afford to pay the generic manufacturer to keep off the market because it knows that in entering into such agreements, it can maintain higher prices for its products (normally pharmaceuticals) than it would have done if there had been competition. At an economic plane, it amounts to little more than an agreement between potentially competing undertakings to maintain high prices for a product. The loser is the consumer who has to pay the high prices. Against this, it might be said that if the generic manufacturers were found to infringe the patent, then the patent owner would be able to maintain the same high prices by having a monopoly (through the patent) for the products protected. This is superficially an attractive argument. However,

---

of no-challenge clauses (it is referred to as the 2007 Antitrust-IP Report).

where a patent owner agrees to pay defendants to stay off the market, the strong inference is that the patent owner perceives the patent as weak. This is because normally, if the patent was found to be valid and infringed, the generic manufacturers would pay the patent owner (by way of damages) rather than the other way around. An offer to pay an alleged infringer distorts the normal dynamic of litigation because it removes any incentive on the alleged infringer (the defendant) to fight the litigation. Why fight patent infringement proceedings if you will be as well as off entering into an agreement than winning the action? Indeed, the offer to pay represents a guarantee of monies as opposed to a hope or expectation of making a profit in an uncertain market.

Historically, the CJEU and Commission have been suspicious of IP litigation agreements whilst paying some lip service to the recognition that settlement agreements are pro-competitive. However, in the 2014 Technology Transfer Guidelines, a mature approach is adopted. This is discussed below. **8-357**

Decisions of CJEU

In *Bayer v Süllhofer*, a case which concerned the validity of a no-challenge clause in a settlement agreement has already been discussed,[457] the CJEU has said that for the purposes of art.101(1), no distinction should be drawn between an agreement whose purpose is to put an end to litigation and those concluded with other aims in mind.[458] However, such a remark is not to be interpreted as meaning that one disregards the fact that there has been prior litigation. It means that when considering a settlement agreement, the analysis must be one of a rule of reason and in particular, one must consider the position in the absence of an agreement.[459] Clearly, in the absence of a litigation settlement agreement, an IPR owner might obtain judgment to enforce the patent. Moreover, uncertainty has its own anti-competitive effects. A party who is unsure of the legality of his actions may choose not to compete in a particular market. **8-358**

In *BAT v EU Commission*,[460] the CJEU considered the question of delimitation agreements. The facts were that BAT, the second-largest tobacco firm in Germany was the registered owner of the trade mark DORCET for raw tobacco, tobacco products and cigarette paper. This trade mark had not been used for more than five years and was thus liable to be struck off the register. Segers, a small Dutch firm, owned the trade mark TOLTECS SPECIAL" and had it registered internationally, including in Germany, for raw tobacco and tobacco products. Segers sought to take advantage of the growing market in Germany for fine cut tobacco (used for rolling one's own cigarettes). BAT challenged the registration of TOLTECS SPECIAL in Germany as being confusingly similar under German law to DORCET. The two parties entered into an agreement which provided that: (a) Segers would not use or promote its TOLTECS SPECIAL mark as being suitable for rolling cigarettes, (b) Segers would not challenge the validity of BAT's DORCET mark; and (c) BAT would withdraw its opposition to the grant of protection to the Segers' TOLTECS SPECIAL mark. **8-359**

The Commission held that such an agreement fell within art.101(1) and was not **8-360**

---

[457] See para.8-336.
[458] (65/86) [1988] E.C.R. 5249; [1990] 4 C.M.L.R. 182, [15]. See also (258/78) [1982] E.C.R. 2015; [1983] 1 C.M.L.R. 278.
[459] (35/83) [1985] E.C.R. 363; [1985] 2 C.M.L.R. 470.
[460] (35/83) [1985] E.C.R. 363; [1985] 2 C.M.L.R. 470; [1985] F.S.R. 532.

capable of exemption under art.101(3). The Commission acknowledged that delimitation agreements can promote competition but held that in the instant case, this was not so, especially as it included a no-challenge clause. It stated:

> "In the present state of European Union law, in cases where the products are similar, there is a serious likelihood of confusion and the owner of the prior mark is therefore more likely to be a position to prevent registration and use of the later mark, restrictions on the use of a later mark do not restrict competition within the meaning of [Article 101(1)], for in accordance with the case law of the Court of Justice the right to prevent marketing relates to the existence of the prior mark.
>
> However, the greater the difference in the product or the less likely the risk of confusion, the more the agreement must take account of the overriding goal of the European Union unity. Of all the possible solutions to the conflict, the parties therefore have to adopt that which least restricts the use of both marks throughout the whole of the European Union. This includes agreements to reproduce the disputed mark only in a certain way (colour, form of lettering, inclusion of trade name, etc.) or possibly to use it for certain products only."[461]

8-361 On appeal, Slynn AG advised that the correct approach is to consider the following two key factors:

> "The two key factors are (1) whether there is a genuine dispute between the parties concerning the use of a trade mark and (2) whether, in compromising the dispute, the terms of the agreement impose obligations that are reasonable in the light of the nature of the dispute and the extent to which the trade mark right could reasonably be expected to have been upheld."

8-362 The CJEU, upholding the Commission, held that:

> "it recognises the legality and usefulness of so-called 'delimitation agreements' under which in the reciprocal interests of the parties the respective spheres of application of their marks are defined in order to avoid confusion or conflicts. But that view does not mean that the application of Article [101] of the [TFEU] to such agreements is excluded if they are also for the purpose of market-sharing or other restrictions of competition. As the Court has already stated in *Consten*, it is incompatible with the European Union competition system to allow the improper use of rights under any national trade mark law in order to frustrate the European Union's law on cartels."[462]

8-363 The court upheld the Commission's decision principally on the grounds that the agreement was not a genuine delimitation agreement and in effect served no other purpose than to enable BAT to control and prevent distribution of tobacco produced by Segers in Germany. As the court said, it was a contrived conflict, in particular because the trade mark "Dorcet" was obviously invalid.[463]

8-364 The CJEU and Commission both considered that the unequal bargaining strengths of the parties had meant that an agreement had been foisted on Segers and did not reflect a genuine attempt to resolve differences and consequently increase competition. If the object of the agreement is to restrict competition, then the EU provisions of free movement of goods and competition may take priority over

---

[461] (35/83) [1985] E.C.R. 363; [1985] 2 C.M.L.R. 470; [1985] F.S.R. 532 at [40]–[41].

[462] (35/83) [1985] E.C.R. 363; [1985] 2 C.M.L.R. 470; [1985] F.S.R. 532 at [33].

[463] See [37]. See also *World Wildlife Fund v World Wrestling Federation* [2002] F.S.R. 32, High Ct, at [29] per Jacob J, where he said that *BAT v Commission* was a good example of an obviously invalid right being used to justify a contractual restraint.

national trade mark law. Thus, Slynn AG said that the Commission:

"is entitled, in my view, to scrutinise critically a delimitation agreement to see whether it is regulating a real dispute in a reasonable way or whether in essence it is restricting competition. If the agreement is essentially to prevent the entry of a competitor on to the market, that is to be considered in the light of the rules on European Union competition law, *whatever the position may be in terms of national trade mark law*". [Emphasis added.]

Such an opinion would appear to mean that even if a party can legally exclude by the lawful exercise of trade mark rights, the entry of a competitor onto a national market, a delimitation agreement which has the same effect may still fall within art.101(1). It is submitted that this must be wrong. Moreover, it should be said that trade mark rights do not prevent per se a competitor entering a market. They merely require the competitor to use a different brand. **8-365**

Pay for delay

In *Lundbeck A/S v European Commission*[464] the General Court was concerned with the lawfulness of "pay for delay" clauses whereby generic manufacturers were paid by the owner of an expired basic patent to stay out of the market. The European Commission held that Lundbeck had infringed art.101 by entering into the "pay for delay" agreements with generic manufacturers. The General Court dismissed the appeal. It is now on appeal to the Court of Justice. **8-366**

Lundbeck is a Danish pharmaceutical company. It manufactures and markets a pharmaceutical for treating depression which uses the active ingredient citalopram. Lundbeck originally had a patent for citalopram. The protection afforded by this patent and any relevant SPCs (Supplemental Protection Certificates) had expired at various times between 1994 and 2003 in Member States. However, Lundbeck had obtained second-generation process patents for the manufacture of citalopram for various methods which were granted in the late 1990s and early 2000s. In 2002, it entered into six agreements with suppliers of generic citalopram. These companies were powerful generic manufacturers capable of providing real competition to Lundbeck. Each agreement was somewhat different and some were against the backdrop of threatened or actual patent litigation. However, in broad terms, they all provided for Lundbeck to pay substantial sums of monies to the generic suppliers for them to cease marketing citalopram for the duration of the agreements. In broad terms, the sums of money corresponded to or exceeded the profit that the generic companies would have made from supplying the citalopram for the period of time that the agreements were in force. In some cases, the obligations not to market citalopram went beyond the scope of the patents (as the existing patents only protected a method of manufacture of citalopram as opposed to the pharmaceutical itself). None of the agreements contained any commitment from Lundbeck to refrain from bringing patent infringement proceedings against the generic company after the expiry of the agreements. **8-367**

The European Commission took the view that, in substance, Lundbeck had "bought off" competition from generic manufacturers in citalopram and that this was to the detriment of consumers as it meant that there was no effective competition and therefore prices for citalopram would be kept artificially high. It levied fines against Lundbeck amounting to approximately €90 million. It held that such **8-368**

---

[464] (T-472/13) ECLI:EU:T:2016:449. It is on appeal to the Court of Justice, (C-591/16P).

agreements had the *object* of restricting competition and therefore there was no need to conduct an "effects" analysis of the agreements on the market for citalopram.[465]

8-369 Lundbeck appealed the decision and the fines levied relying upon numerous arguments, some very specific to the facts of the case. The General Court dismissed all of the pleas. The ones of more general application are now considered. Many of the arguments relied upon a central theme—namely that patent litigation settlement agreements are immune from scrutiny under art.101 where they are bona fide settlements of actual or threatened patent litigation and where the restrained conduct goes no further than the exclusionary potential of the patents in issue. If such was the case, Lundbeck argued that it was irrelevant that generic manufacturers were paid to stay off the market. Broadly, these were the same arguments that were dismissed by a majority of the Supreme Court of the US in *FTC v Actavis*.[466]

8-370 Lundbeck deployed a number of arguments which were all dismissed. First, it argued that the generic manufacturers were not potential competitors because they infringed Lundbeck's patents. The General Court rejected this argument, saying that it was based on the erroneous premise that the manufacturers *did* infringe Lundbeck's patents and that the patents would have withstood claims of invalidity. It said that the mere fact that patents are presumed valid until they are revoked, cannot equate to a presumption of illegality of generic products.[467] Here, the General Court was clearly right. The mere fact that the agreements were entered against a threat of patent litigation agreement does not mean that there were not "real concrete possibilities" for the generic manufacturers to enter the relevant market (being the relevant test). Indeed, as the General Court said, the very fact that Lundbeck entered into the agreements was a strong indication that it perceived those undertakings as potential competitors.[468]

8-371 Secondly, Lundbeck argued that the Commission was wrong to find that the agreements were anti-competitive by object.

8-372 The General Court reiterated existing case law that where certain types of co-ordination between undertakings reveal a sufficient degree of harm to competition, such rendered it unnecessary to consider the anti-competitive effects of the agreement.[469]

8-373 The General Court held that the Commission had been right to find that where a reverse payment is combined with an exclusion of competitors from the marketplace, it was possible to consider that such a limitation did not arise exclusively from the parties' assessment of the strength of the patents but was rather an attempt to buy off competition. It made it clear that not all patent settlement agreements with reverse payments fell within art.101.[470] However, in the instant case, the disproportionate nature of the payments (corresponding to the profit that the generic manufacturers would have made); the absence of provisions which made it clear that they could launch their product after the expiry of the agreement without having to fear infringement proceedings; and the presence of restrictions going beyond the scope of Lundbeck's patents (as they were not restricted to method-of-

---

[465] For discussion of the "object" and "effects" principles, see para.8-121.
[466] Discussed at para.8-402.
[467] See [121].
[468] See [181].
[469] See [339]. Agreements which are "by object" anti-competitive are discussed at para.8-121.
[470] See [354].

manufacture) meant that they did have as their object the restriction of competition.[471]

Thirdly, the General Court dismissed Lundbeck's argument that the restrictions were objectively necessary for Lundbeck to protect their intellectual property rights.[472] It said that an agreement may be regarded as having a restrictive objective even if it does not have the restriction of competition as its sole aim.[473] It also said that even if they were objectively necessary for protecting their intellectual property rights, they were nevertheless disproportionate to the achievement of that objective.[474]   **8-374**

Fourthly, and most importantly, the court also rejected the argument that art.101 was only relevant where the agreement sought to restrain the behaviour of undertakings that went beyond "the scope of the patent".[475] In particular, it held that the test was problematic from a competition law perspective where there had been no adjudication that the generic medicines did infringe a valid patent. It said that "the scope of the patent" test is based on a subjective assessment of the patent as opposed to one by a national court or authority.[476] It also relied upon the US Supreme Court's rejection of the "scope of the patent" (*exclusionary potential*) test in *Actavis*. It said that it was doubtful that the agreements at issue resolved the underlying patent disputes[477] but said that even if such was the case, as the agreements had as their objective an anti-competitive effect, as they amounted to "buying off" potential competitors, it was for Lundbeck to prove under art.101(3) that the agreements benefitted consumers and competition. Thus, it said that the relevant test was not whether the exercise of IPRS fell within art.101(1) only in exceptional circumstances but rather whether the agreement had as its object the restriction of competition.[478]   **8-375**

With the above, the General Court is making it clear that there are no specific rules or presumptions when considering the compatibility of IP litigation agreements with art.101 as opposed to mere commercial agreements. All matters must be considered ,and the fact that the agreement was entered into against the threat of patent litigation is merely one matter to be taken into account. In particular, it is clear from the judgment that there is no room for the "scope of patent" test whereby if it is *arguable* that the restrained activities fall within the scope of the patent, the agreement is immune from attack under competition laws. As said above, this is called the *exclusionary potential* argument.   **8-376**

In the author's view, and despite criticism of the decision, the General Court was right to dismiss the appeal. The arrangements were entered into in circumstances when the basic patent for citalopram had expired and Lundbeck was seeking to prolong its life via second-generation method-of-manufacture patents of dubious validity. Competition for generic manufacturers is vital to ensure that consumers and health services do not pay "patent monopoly" prices beyond the lifetime of the patent for medicines based on the active ingredient. "Buying off" generic manufacturers so that the patentee can maintain artificially high prices is clearly   **8-377**

---

[471] See [354].
[472] See [458].
[473] See [459].
[474] See [460].
[475] See [490].
[476] See [491].
[477] See [497].
[478] See [499].

detrimental to the public, particularly in the case of a pharmaceutical recognised as having good effectiveness in combating depression. However, the author would not want *Lundbeck* to be seen as authority for the proposition that patent litigation settlement agreements should be routinely examined for their anti-competitive effects. Rather, "pay for delay" agreements should be seen as an application of the principle established by the Court of Justice under art.102 TFEU that in exceptional circumstances, IP litigation settlement agreements can work against the interests of the wider public. Whilst this approach was expressly rejected as the correct test,[479] there is little doubt that "pay for delay" agreements are a very extreme way of settling patent disputes and inevitably raise properly grounded fears that the predominant purpose of the agreement is to prevent market entry of competitors rather than to protect IPRs. Patent owners cannot expect carte blanche to enter into any agreement, however detrimental to consumers and society, merely by relying upon the fact that such was against the backdrop of threatened enforcement of patents.

8-378   Despite Lundbeck's protestations, there was every reason to believe that the "pay for delay" agreements were entered into precisely because the generic manufacturers had little to fear from patent litigation and everything to gain from the agreements. After all, such agreements represented a *guarantee* of the profit for the generic manufacturers that they had forecast that they would make on the marketplace for the relevant period. Equally, for Lundbeck, they did not mind making such payments because they knew that the entrance on the marketplace of the generic manufacturers would cause the price of citalopram to drop dramatically. Thus, the cost of these payments was small compared to the drop in profits (by reason of the price drop caused by the entry on the marketplace of generic competition) that Lundbeck would have encountered.

8-379   Seen in such a light, the real losers were consumers and health services of Member States (where they subsidise prescriptions for consumers). In such circumstances, the author's view is that the General Court was right to put the burden on Lundbeck under art.101(3) to prove that in fact, the pre-existing price for citalopram would have been maintained in the marketplace if the agreements had not been in place. It is very doubtful that they could have shown this.

English cases

8-380   In *Apple Corp Ltd v Apple Computer Inc*,[480] the court was concerned with the validity of a trade mark delimitation agreement five years after it was entered into. Apple Corp (the company which managed the business affairs of the Beatles) owned a number of registrations in the music field. Apple Computer Inc, an American company, was the well-known Apple Mac computer company and was primarily interested in computers. It sought registrations of a number of marks for "Apple" primarily in the computer industry. Difficulties were caused by the fact that computers were beginning to enjoy multimedia functionality. A trade mark delimitation agreement was entered whereby, broadly put, the parties agreed to limit their business activities and trade marks to the fields of respectively music and computers. The parties entered into a delimitation agreement which contained no-challenge clauses of the claimant's (Apple Corp) marks. However, later Apple

---

[479] See [499].
[480] *Apple Corp Ltd v Apple Computer Inc* [1991] 3 C.M.L.R. 49 CA.

Computer sought to break the delimitation agreement and argued that it was anti-competitive. Apple Corp brought proceedings for breach of the delimitation agreements. At trial, Apple Computers began cross examining witnesses of the claimant on the basis that the registered marks were invalid. The judge held that it was not open to argue such on the pleadings as they stood. However, the defendant served an amended pleading where it was argued that the no-challenge clauses were an unreasonable restraint of trade because in relation to many national trade marks, Apple had no legitimate interest in the subsistence of the registrations (as they had not been used).

On appeal, the Court of Appeal considered whether the amended pleading gave rise to a defence. Neill LJ said: **8-381**

> "[80] It is plain that in order to enforce either the 'field of use' restrictions or the 'no-challenge' restrictions in the 1981 agreement it will be necessary for Apple to prove that they have used the marks at the relevant times in the course of their businesses. The actual use of the marks by Apple will be one of the central issues for the court to determine. Having examined the nature and extent of the use (and any likely use) of the marks the court will then consider whether this use could be regarded as a legitimate interest which required protection and whether the restrictions or restraints were no more than were reasonably necessary in order to protect that legitimate interest.
>
> [101] The registration of the marks in various jurisdictions may enable Apple to take advantage of local remedies to protect the marks, but the legitimacy of Apple's interest in the marks in the context of the present case depends on the use of the marks and not on the fact or the validity of any registrations."

Thus, the Court of Appeal took the view that the validity of the registrations was irrelevant. The court considered *BAT v Commission* and *Bayer v Süllhofer* and said: **8-382**

> "[89] Mr. Carr referred us to a number of other authorities, including in particular the decisions in *BAT v. E.C. Commission* and *Windsurfing International v Commission. The effect of these decisions, however, is to show that under European law, as under English law, the court is concerned to examine the actual facts and is not concerned, except perhaps to a very slight extent, with the validity of any particular registrations according to the rules of the individual countries.* Indeed, as was pointed out to us in the course of argument, the rules which govern the validity of a registration may vary from country to country:
>
> [112] In the present case that approach dictates an investigation of what, in fact, was the scope of the parties' business in 1981 and what was the use being made by them of their respective versions of the APPLE name and the apple device. An agreement which, having regard to the nature and extent of their businesses and their use of the confusingly similar marks, does no more than avoid confusion or conflict between the parties is useful and lawful. Such an agreement would not be one whose object or effect was to distort 'competition.' In this regard, under European Union law as much as under English law, the cancellation issue is irrelevant. The plaintiffs' case is not stronger because under one law, say, Danish law, their registrations were impregnable, or weaker because under the law of another member-State, say, Germany, their registrations were vulnerable. What is material is what was actually happening on the ground, not what was the plaintiffs' entitlement to effect or maintain registrations under particular national trade mark laws. Accordingly, under European Union law as under English law, time and money should not be spent and wasted on an investigation, with the assistance of foreign lawyers, of what are the national requirements for the registration or cancellation of trade marks." [Emphasis supplied.]

The Court of Appeal in *Apple v Apple* considered that it was irrelevant that Ap-   **8-383** ple Corp had valid or invalid registrations when considering the validity of agreements under art.101 or the English doctrine of restraint of trade. It said that one must have regard to the *business interests* when defending the legitimacy of a settlement agreement and not the *legal position*. It is very doubtful whether this is right under art.101. The ability of a party to prevent a course of action in the absence of a trade mark delimitation agreement by the lawful exercise of their trade mark rights must be relevant to the reasonableness of restraints in such an agreement. For instance, if a trade mark proprietor, who had not used a registered mark but such was not liable for revocation for non-use (because less than five years had lapsed from the date of registration), wished to prevent a competitor using their mark, the effect of the Court of Appeal judgment in *Apple Corp v Apple Computers* is to force the trade mark proprietor to proceed to judgment rather than enter into a trade mark settlement agreement. If the trade mark proprietor pursued the latter path, they would have difficulties in justifying restraints, e.g. no-challenge clauses or territorial delimitations on the basis that he had no *legitimate interest* to protect. Yet, if the trade mark proprietor proceeded to judgment, they would be entitled to a permanent injunction regardless whether they had used the mark or indeed, intended to use the mark after the expiry of the five-year period. However, it may be that in fact, the Court of Appeal's approach was driven by the fact that Apple Corp had chosen to justify the delimitation agreement by reference to its use of the marks rather than its legal ability to prevent Apple Computers to bring trade mark infringement proceedings.[481]

8-384   On a more general note, Taylor LJ said that in considering the reasonableness of a restraint in a settlement agreement, one should take into account the following factor:

> "[149] First, this was a settlement agreement. It was made on the footing that each party had some legitimate interest in its trademarks and logos which it wishes to protect. The agreement was drawn up specifically so as to avoid challenges and contests in a host of countries. It was implicit in such a settlement that the parties were not attempting a finite assessment of all their rights country by country. They adopted a broad-brush approach. If one party to such an agreement, dissatisfied with his bargain, can by challenging its enforceability require the court to explore and adjudicate upon the validity and strength of the other's rights country by country, then such an agreement would totally fail to achieve its object of avoiding disputes and litigation. A settlement agreement would settle nothing. It would merely set the stage for the very lengthy and expensive litigation sought to be avoided."

8-385   The emphasis on the need to uphold settlement agreements was followed in *World Wildlife Fund v World Wrestling Federation*,[482] an English case. In this case, a trade mark settlement agreement was entered into between the two parties over the use of the initials "WWF". It was common ground that the World Wrestling Federation committed a number of breaches of this agreement by using the initials. The Federation argued that the settlement agreement was a restraint of trade and thus it was for the Fund to justify it. This argument relied in principal on the English common law principle of restraint of trade whereby any restraint of trade is void unless it can be shown to be reasonable by the party relying on the restraint. The judge said that restraints in the context of actual or threatened actions for infringe-

---

[481] See [150] where Taylor LJ referred to the "plaintiff's main case" turning upon use of the mark to justify a legitimate interest.
[482] *WWF* [2002] U.K.C.L.R. 388; [2002] E.T.M.R. 53; [2002] F.S.R. 33.

ment of IPRs must inevitably be considered in the context of an independent pre-existing restraint imposed by the IPR itself.[483] Moreover, in deciding what is a reasonable restraint, it clearly would be wrong to re-litigate in a hypothetical trial whether the acts restrained in the settlement agreement would have amounted to an infringement of the IPR of the other party. Thus, the judge posed the following three-part test to determine whether a restraint is unreasonable:

(a) the restraint actually imposes a real fetter on his trade;
(b) the restraint goes beyond any reasonably arguable scope of protection of the IPR in issue. However, if this condition cannot be satisfied, the restrainor may nonetheless justify by showing; and
(c) that the restraint nonetheless provides a protection which he reasonably needs.

As the judge explained, in relation to (c), there may be cases where the restrainor **8-386** can justify the restraint independently of or in conjunction with any IPR. The ultimate question is whether the restraint is reasonable in all the circumstances. The restrainor's IPRs are not necessarily the sole determinant of this.[484] It should be noted that the judge was doubtful that a different approach should be taken under art.101. The judge thus upheld the validity of the settlement agreement. On appeal, the Court of Appeal dismissed the appeal and upheld the "threshold" test of Jacob J in condition (b) whereby it must be shown by the restrained party that the restraint obviously extends beyond the monopoly of the IPR in issue. This echoes the US Supreme Court's approach in *FTC v Actavis* (discussed below). They endorsed Taylor LJ's remarks in *Apple* which are cited above. In doing so, they were implicitly not endorsing the approach in *Apple* of considering the restraints in the settlement agreement by reference to the parties' business interests rather than the ability of the IPR owner to succeed in litigation on IPR in the issue.

The need to uphold settlement agreements was also emphasised in *Intel v Via* **8-387** *Technologies*[485] where the judge at first instance said that, in applying *WWF v WWF* the party alleging invalidity of a settlement agreement would need to show a "convincing case" that the agreement is contrary to art.101 if it resulted from a bona fide settlement of court proceedings.[486]

Pharmaceutical patent settlement agreements

In 2009, the Commission published a report on the pharmaceutical sector which **8-388** in particular focussed on the need for innovation and competition.[487] It highlighted a number of concerns such as patent-filing strategies (e.g. filing numerous patent applications for the same medicine); delay in generic entries following expiry of patents; drawn out patent prosecution techniques, e.g. divisional filings which cause excessive delays in filing patents; and the cost and uncertainty of patent litigation. Against that background, the European Commission discussed patent settlements in the pharmaceutical sector. It noted that in approximately half of settlements, the generic company's ability to market its medicine was restricted and a significant

---

[483] *WWF* [2002] U.K.C.L.R. 388; [2002] E.T.M.R. 53; [2002] F.S.R. 33 at [25].
[484] *WWF* [2002] U.K.C.L.R. 388; [2002] E.T.M.R. 53; [2002] F.S.R. 33 at [29].
[485] *Intel Corp* [2002] Eu. L.R. 502; [2003] F.S.R. 12.
[486] See [146]. This issue was not discussed in the Court of Appeal judgment.
[487] *http://ec.europa.eu/competition/sectors/pharmaceuticals/inquiry/communication_en.pdf* [Accessed 28 January 2018].

proportion of these settlements contained a "value transfer" from the patentee to the generic company, either in the form of a direct payment or a licence, distribution agreement or "side deal". Direct payments occurred exceeding €200 million. It also noted that pharmaceutical patentees were intervening in market authorisation requests by generic companies. The Commission's report concluded that generic entry was not happening as early as possible.

8-389   The Commission started to take a tough stance on "pay for delay" agreements. The *Lundbeck* litigation being an example of this, is discussed above. From 2009 to 2015, the Commission published yearly reports on patent settlement agreements in the pharmaceutical sector. These reports were primarily focussed on understanding the nature of these agreements and monitoring the number of "pay for delay" agreements. In the latest (7th) report, it distinguished between agreements that: (a) do not restrict the generic company's ability to enter the market (Category A); (b) those which do restrict their ability but they are not paid to do so (Category B.I); and (c) those which do include a "value transfer" to the generic company (Category B.II).

8-390   The Commission says that Category A settlements are unproblematic. Category B.I settlements are generally unproblematic unless they restrain conduct outside the exclusionary zone of the patent or where the patent owner knows that the patent does not meet the criteria for patentability, i.e. the patent was granted following the supply of incorrect, misleading or incomplete information. In contrast, it said that Category B.II agreements will attract the highest degree of antitrust scrutiny. They noted that out of 70 patent settlement agreements considered in 2015, 26 per cent were Category A, 64 per cent were Category B.I and 10 per cent were Category B.II. It was also noted that despite the Commission's announcement it would scrutinise Category B.II agreements and stakeholders' concerns that the Commission's approach would force them to litigate patents. In fact, such fears have proved to be unfounded and there had been a "strong increase" in pharmaceutical patent settlement agreements. A marked drop in Category B.II agreements was also noted. This suggests that the Commission's tough approach to Category B.II agreements was justified.

2014 Technology Transfer Guidelines

8-391   The "Settlement Agreements" section of the 2014 Technology Transfer Guidelines acknowledges that these types of agreements are in principle a legitimate way to find a mutually acceptable compromise to bona fide legal disagreements. As said:

> "[235] Settlement agreements in the context of technology disputes are, as in many other areas of commercial disputes, in principle a legitimate way to find a mutually acceptable compromise to a bona fide legal disagreement. The parties may prefer to discontinue the dispute or litigation because it proves to be too costly, time-consuming and/or uncertain as regards its outcome. Settlements can also save courts and/or competent administrative bodies effort in deciding on the matter and can therefore give rise to welfare enhancing benefits. On the other hand, it is in the general public interest to remove invalid intellectual property rights as an unmerited barrier to innovation and economic activity.
>
> [236] Licensing, including cross licensing, in the context of settlement agreements is generally not as such restrictive of competition since it allows the parties to exploit their technologies after the agreement is concluded. In cases where, in the absence of the licence, it is possible that the licensee could be excluded from the market,

access to the technology at issue for the licensee by means of a settlement agreement is generally not caught by Article 101(1)."

However, the 2014 Guidelines make it clear, following *Bayer v Süllhofer*, that **8-392** licensing in the context of settlement agreements are treated in the same way as other licence agreements and thus it is necessary to assess whether the parties are potential or actual competitors.[488] In particular, it said that pay-for-delay settlement agreements may be caught by art.101 (citing its decision in *Lundbeck*). It also says that when cross licensing occurs between undertakings with significant market power and the agreement imposes restrictions that clearly go beyond what is required in order to unblock blocking technologies, then particular concerns arise under art.101.[489] Such cross-licensing arrangements between competitors can give rise to concerns about the parties' incentive to innovate being reduced and thus affecting an essential part of the competitive process.[490]

The Commission's approach in the 2014 Guidelines is largely to be welcome. It **8-393** is a shame that there was no greater emphasis that save in exceptional circumstances (e.g. sham settlements), settlement agreements should be considered pro-competitive. There must be a strong presumption that in a bona fide settlement, the parties have determined that any contractual restraints in the settlement agreement arise by reason of a careful appraisal by the parties of the risks posed to their freedom to operate by the IPR litigation. Thus, a party to patent litigation is unlikely to enter into a settlement agreement restraining it from operating in certain Member States unless there was a reasonable prospect that it would be so prevented in the litigation. This presumption combined with the strong public interest that settlement agreements should be upheld, precisely because they are intended to bring certainty to an uncertain situation and that trade is best served by certainty are compelling arguments that settlement agreements should be upheld save in exceptional circumstances, e.g. where the contractual restraint was induced by substantial financial incentive as in *Lundbeck* or there are undesirable "spill over" effects, e.g. foreclosure of third party products.

No challenge clauses in litigation settlement

In the 2014 Guidelines, it is said that generally, no-challenge clauses in settle- **8-394** ment agreements fall outside art.101(1).[491] As said by the Commission, it is inherent in settlement agreements that no-challenge clauses are included because the purpose of the agreement is to prevent further litigation and without a no-challenge clause, such is not achieved. However, the Commission said that they can fall inside art.101(1), e.g. where the patent was granted by reason of misleading information or where the party accepting the no-challenge clause has been financially induced.[492] No-challenge clauses outside litigation settlements have already been discussed earlier in this chapter.[493]

---

[488] See para.237.
[489] See para.240.
[490] See para.241.
[491] See para.242.
[492] See para.243.
[493] See para.8-349.

Historical decisions of the Commission

8-395   Historically, the Commission's approach to settlement agreements has been one of gradual acceptance of the importance that such agreements have in commerce and industry and that such agreements will often open up trade and prevent the waste of time and resources in fruitless litigation.

8-396   In the 1970s and early 1980s, the Commission took a strict view of settlement agreements. Agreements which restricted circulation of goods or partitioned markets infringed art.101(1). The Commission paid scant regard to the actual effects of litigations and the possible outcome. For example, the Commission held that an agreement between an English and French firm who possessed the trade marks SIRDAR and PHILDAR which prevented each from selling its goods under its trade mark in the other's territory fell within art.101(1). The Commission said in that case even if the trade marks were similar and likely to be confused, this did not justify market sharing.[494] Parties were under a duty at EU law to settle any dispute in a way which was least restrictive of competition and the free movement of goods.[495] When looking at the competitive effects of a delimitation agreement, the Commission was more likely to conclude that an agreement was anti-competitive when it was clear that the strong party had forced the agreement on the weaker, as was the case in *BAT v Commission*.[496]

8-397   Conversely, the Commission has ruled that agreements which generally foster competition by allowing each party to freely circulate their trade-marked goods and thus avoid market partitioning will fall outside art.101(1), even if there are ancillary restraint clauses. Thus, where two competing enterprises held identical trade marks but in different countries such that neither was capable of marketing goods under the trade mark in the other's countries, a clause in a settlement of a litigation agreement which was generally pro-competitive but prohibited one undertaking from challenging for five years the other's registration, fell outside art.101(1).[497] Similarly, an agreement between two owners of a trade mark with a common origin which permitted the circulation of each owner's trade-marked products in the other's territories subject to distinctive colouring being used, fell outside art.101(1).[498] Where a German firm obtained an injunction against a Japanese firm for the latter's use of a trade mark confusingly similar to the former's trade mark, according to German law, an agreement that the Japanese company could use its mark unchanged for three years and then, only in conjunction with its own name, was held not to infringe art.101(1).[499] In *Hershey/Schiffers*,[500] an American company, Hershey Foods Corporation, which owned the mark HERSHEY for

---

[494] *Re the Agreement of Sirdar Ltd* [1975] 1 C.M.L.R. D93, [21]. The Commission held that the agreement was not capable of exemption under art.101(3). See *Sirdar Ltd v Les Fils de Louis Mulliez* [1975] 1 C.M.L.R. 378, High Ct, where the High Court of England refused to grant an interlocutory injunction brought by Sirdar for trade mark infringement and breach of contract based on the agreement as the agreement, as the Commission had found it was void under art.101(2). See also *Re the Persil Trade Mark* [1978] 1 C.M.L.R. 395 (the Commission held that concerted practice between two undertakings owning a trade mark PERSIL in different territories (the two trade marks being of common origin) to prevent exports of their trade-marked goods to each other's territories fell within art.101(1)).

[495] e.g. see *Bramley/Gilbert* reported in the *10th Report on Competition Policy*, point 128; *Zoller + Fröhlich/Telemecanique* reported in the *8th Report on Competition Policy*, point 109.

[496] (35/83) [1985] E.C.R. 363; [1985] 2 C.M.L.R. 470.

[497] See No.78/193/EEC *Re Penney's Trade Mark* [1978] 2 C.M.L.R. 100 (EC Commission).

[498] See No.78/193/EEC *Re Penney's Trade Mark* [1978] 2 C.M.L.R. 100 (EC Commission).

[499] *Tanabe Seiyaku Company v Bayer AG* reported in the *8th Annual Report on Competition Policy*,

chocolate products worldwide, and a Dutch company, Schiffers, which owned the mark HERSCHI for drinks settled prolonged litigation whereby Schiffers sold their mark to Hershey and in return, received a renewable exclusive licence for five years for a defined group of products. Furthermore, Schiffers undertook not to introduce new products with the trade mark and not to use HERSCHI as a corporate name for a certain number of years. The Commission held that the agreement fell outside art.101(1) as it was designed to avoid confusion and did not artificially partition the EU.

In *Syntex/Synthelabo*,[501] Synthelabo and Syntex came to an agreement to prevent **8-398** confusion whereby the marks SYNTHELABO or SYNTHELAB would not be used in the UK and certain non-Member States. The Commission held that as the risk of confusion between Synthelabo's trade marks and Syntex's trade marks (the former owning SYNTHELABO and the latter owning SYNTEX, SYNTREX, SYNDREX, SYNODEX and SYNLEXAN) was not such as to justify the partitioning of the market and because of the size of the companies, the agreement fell within art.101(1).

However, it did say that: **8-399**

"In principle national jurisdictions usually have the right to decide on issues where there is risk of confusion between differing trade marks. However, Article 101(1) is applicable to trade mark delimitation agreement in cases where it is *not evident* that the holder of the earlier trade mark could have recourse to national law to prevent the holder of a later mark from using it in one or more Member-States."[502] [Emphasis added.]

The above excerpt suggests that the Commission would have considered the **8-400** likely outcome of legal proceedings in considering whether the settlement was restrictive of competition. This has come to happen with TT Guidelines where they say that one should consider whether it was "likely" that in the absence of the licence, the licensee would have been excluded.

In the context of patent litigation, the Commission has interfered in a settlement **8-401** dispute relating to the ownership of a patent as the interests of the party could have been protected in ways less restrictive of competition.[503] The Commission considered that a patent compromise settlement in which a French concern gave a German concern a licence to manufacture under the patent in exchange for the latter withdrawing its revocation action could not be interpreted as preventing the German company exporting its licensed products to France.[504]

The US approach

The 2017 Guidelines have little to say about the approach of the Department of **8-402** Justice to IP litigation settlement agreements. However, they do state that settle-

---

point 125 (EC Commission).

[500] Press Release IP (90) 87.

[501] Commission Press Release, 23 February 1989; *The European Union v Synthex and Synthelabo* [1990] 4 C.M.L.R. 343; *19th Report on Competition Policy*, point 59.

[502] Commission Press Release, 23 February 1989; *The European Union v Synthex and Synthelabo* [1990] 4 C.M.L.R. 343; *19th Report on Competition Policy*, para.5.

[503] *Bramley/Gilbert* reported in the *10th Report on Competition Policy*, point 128.

[504] *Zoller + Fröhlich/Telemecanique* reported in the *8th Report on Competition Policy*, point 109. By reason of arts 34–36 (ex-arts 30–36), the French concern would not have been able to prevent imports of goods from the German licensee into France.

ments involving cross-licensing can be an efficient means to avoid litigation and, in general, courts favour such settlements.

8-403   In *FTC v Actavis*,[505] the Supreme Court of USA had to consider a pay-for-delay settlement agreement. Like the *Lundbeck* case (discussed above), proceedings for patent infringement were brought against a generic manufacturer. The latter alleged that the pharmaceutical patent was invalid which was disputed. The matter was settled by the generic manufacturer agreeing not to promote its own product but agreeing to promote the patentee's pharmaceutical in exchange for a very substantial payment. The Federal Trade Commission alleged that the agreement contravened US antitrust law. The Supreme Court held that the agreement did indeed contravene antitrust law even though the patent had not expired. This decision (which overturned the decisions of the courts below) was a majority decision of five to three and it is clear that the reason for the division of opinions in the Supreme Court was that by the settlement agreement, the generic company had not agreed to do anything which exceeded *the exclusionary potential* of the patent. In other words, the prohibited conduct in the agreement fell within the monopoly of the patent if such were not invalidated in proceedings. The majority took the view that antitrust law was applicable even if the agreement's anti-competitive effects fell within the exclusionary potential of the patent. As said by Breyer J:

> "Solvay's patent, if valid and infringed, might have permitted it to charge drug prices sufficient to recoup the reverse settlement payments it agreed to make to its potential generic competitors. And we are willing to take this fact as evidence that the agreement's "anti-competitive effects fall within the scope of the exclusionary potential of the patent. 677 F. 3d, at 1312. But we do not agree that that fact, or characterization, can immunize the agreement from antitrust attack."

8-404   It said that both antitrust law and patent policies are relevant in determining the scope of the patent monopoly.[506] It made the point that in pay-for-delay agreements, the patentee and challenger win but the consumer loses.[507] Finally, it held, in rejecting the FTC's submission, that a rule of reason approach should apply rather than a per se rule apply.

8-405   In contrast, the powerful dissenting opinion said that antitrust law is only applicable where the settlement agreement goes *beyond the exclusionary potential of the patent*. As said in the dissenting opinion,

> "The key, of course, is that the patent holder—when doing anything, including settling—must act within the scope of the patent. If its actions go beyond the monopoly powers conferred by the patent, we have held that such actions are subject to antitrust scrutiny... . If its actions are within the scope of the patent, they are not subject to antitrust scrutiny, with two exceptions concededly not applicable here (1) when the parties settle sham litigation... (2) when the litigation involves a patent obtained through fraud on the Patent and Trademark Office
> Thus under our precedent, this is a fairly straightforward case. Solvay paid a competitor to respect its patent—conduct which did not exceed the scope of its patent. No one alleges that there was sham litigation or that Solvay's patent was obtained through fraud on the PTO. As in any settlement, Solvay gave its competitors something of value (money) and, in exchange, its competitors gave it something of value (dropping their legal claims).

---

[505]   570 US 2013; 17 June 2013.
[506]   See 9.
[507]   See 15.

In doing so, they put an end to litigation that had been dragging on for three years. Ordinary, we would think this is a good thing."[508]

Summary—IP settlement agreements

The majority judgment and dissenting judgment illustrates the real debate in rela- **8-406**
tion to competition law and patent settlement agreements (or indeed any registered IPR settlement agreement). Thus, insofar as the settlement agreement does not prohibit conduct on behalf of the generic manufacturer that fall outside the scope of the patent monopoly or beyond its expiry, i.e. its exclusionary potential, it is difficult to disagree with the dissenting opinion. After all, if the generic manufacturers had agreed to the prohibited conduct and to pay damages to the patentee, it would be like thousands of patent settlement agreements and such agreements must be considered immune from competition law. Does the fact that the money flows from the patentee to the generic manufacturer make any difference? In these two situations, the consumer is unaffected by whether Company A pays to Company B or vice versa. It is thus tempting to say indeed that there should be a presumptive rule that where the prohibited conduct in a settlement agreement does not extend beyond the exclusionary potential of the patent,[509] competition law should not intervene unless it is clear that the patent is manifestly invalid (but then such might suggest that the action or settlement was a sham). When settling a patent action and in circumstances where the contractual restraints in the settlement agreement extend no further than the remedies that a court could award in a patent infringement action and there is a non-negligible risk that such remedies would be granted in the proceedings if not settled, parties should not have to look over their shoulder at competition law. Any other approach is, as said at the outset of this section, to trade one uncertainty (the patent proceedings) with another uncertainty (antitrust proceedings) and such would cause substantial business paralysis.

On the other hand, it is equally tempting to say that there is a natural "suspicion" **8-407**
of pay-for-delay agreements that generic manufacturers have been "bribed" not to attack a manifestly weak patent. After all, why would a patentee pay a generic manufacturer not to infringe a strong patent? Surely, they would just continue the patent litigation? If there is a public interest in revoking invalid patents and the undertakings with the greatest incentive to bring revocation actions are, in effect, "bought out", then it can be legitimately said that the public interest is not being served. Invalid patents will remain on the register. As said by the Supreme Court, the patentee and challenger win—the consumer loses.

In the author's view, when considering the competition concerns of litigation set- **8-408**
tlement agreements, there are two competing policies—the public policy of finality in litigation and respecting the pro-competitive effect of settlement agreements and the public policy that invalid patents (particularly where health is concerned) should be revoked. The majority's view in *Actavis* ignores the powerful nature of the "exclusionary potential" argument whilst the minority's view ignores the public interest that invalid patents should be struck off the register. The public interest is not served if those with the commercial motive to bring proceedings to revoke patents are "bought off". However, of these two policies, it is considered that the public policy of finality is the stronger by some distance. After all, anyone can bring an action to revoke a patent (including if necessary, governmental organisations)

---

[508] Dissenting Opinion of Roberts CJ and Scalia and Thomas JJ, at 3.
[509] i.e. beyond the claims and not beyond the expiry of the patent.

and in any event, it is unlikely that an unrevoked patent will cause significant detriment to consumers in a market where there exist substitutable technologies. If this is not the case, then the owner of the patent is likely to be in a dominant position and in which case, art.102 comes into place and thus the patent owner may be obliged to license.

NATIONAL COLLECTING SOCIETIES AND AGREEMENTS

8-409   All EU States have collecting societies who are responsible for the enforcement of copyright in music, films, books, etc. and the collection of royalties on behalf of their members. Often, the copyright is assigned to collecting societies. In other cases, the society merely acts as agent for the copyright owner. The system works to the advantage of authors and users. The copyright owner does not have to police their own rights and negotiate individually with users. Conversely, the user does not have to seek out a large number of rights owners for the purpose of exploiting the rights and generally will be able to use the protected works upon payment of a simply calculated fee without seeking consent from the copyright owner. Such arrangements facilitate the efficient management, administration and exploitation of artistic, musical, dramatic and literary works to the benefit of the public and the artiste.

8-410   Within each state there may be a number of collecting societies who are responsible for particular rights in a work. Thus, a DVD of a music video will normally incorporate a number of copyrights, e.g. musical copyright, literary copyright in the lyrics, sound recording right in the track, film copyright in the film, and performance right in the performances of the artistes. Furthermore, these rights are capable of being infringed in a number of ways—copying, public performance, broadcasting, cable transmission, rental, etc. Unsurprisingly, the landscape of collecting societies can be complex, with different collecting societies administering the exploitation of certain copyrights or certain ways of exploiting such rights.

8-411   On several occasions the CJEU and European Commission have had to consider agreements and practices of these societies. Whilst the legal role of each of the societies is to grant licences of its members' rights to potential users in return for money, generally, anyone who wishes to make use of the members' works are able to do so provided they pay a royalty fee. Thus, the system is akin to a compulsory licence system whereby the user need only pay the payment set by the collecting society in order to make use of the protected work. As such, the case law on the compatibility of the societies' practices must be considered sui generis.

8-412   Generally, collecting societies will not individually negotiate terms with users. Such would be too time consuming and difficult to manage. Instead, they will impose fixed tariffs and royalties. Often, the royalty is based upon monies not directly referable to the work being exploited. Thus, in the case of public performance of audio works in discotheques, it may be based upon turnover of the discotheque.[510] In many cases, the user must take a global licence for all the works whose IPRs are owned by the collecting society rather than a licence for selected works. Such practices often cause unpopularity with users. It is not surprising therefore that disputes between collecting societies and users have raised concerns about whether or not such conduct is anti-competitive. These concerns fall under

---

[510] This was the case in the Joined Cases of *Ministère Public v Tournier; Lucazeau v SACEM*—see para.8-415, et seq.

both arts 101 and 102 (abuse of a dominant position). In general, the courts will have to weigh up the benefits of such policies which are generally adopted for the purpose of effective management of copyright and for ease of use by users as against the user's freedom of choice and decide whether the disputed practices of the collecting society are absolutely necessary for the attainment of the objects of the society.[511] This mirrors the approach taken by the courts in the US which favours a "rule of reason" approach to the practices of collecting societies such as "blanket licensing".[512]

Generally, the concern is that the collecting society is abusing its dominant posi- **8-413** tion by charging unfair prices or royalties. Such concerns are considered elsewhere in this book.[513] Article 101 may be relevant where national collecting societies seek to impose conditions on users which directly or indirectly discriminate between Member States or their nationals. This can be seen in the following examples:

Custom pressing: Re GEMA (Commission)[514]

GEMA, the German copyright collecting society, sought to impose royalties on **8-414** all custom pressing of records carried out in Germany. Custom pressing is the term used to describe the manufacturing of records by independent pressing firms which are working to order and on account of sound recorders. No other copyright collecting society had such a practice. Generally, the supplier rather than the custom presser was required to obtain a licence from a EU collecting society and was free to have the record pressed in any EU state. The Commission took the view that it was for the supplier to obtain the licence to manufacture and not the pressing firm. Accordingly, it held that a separate requirement to pay royalties to the national copyright protection society having "jurisdiction" over the place of manufacture would, in practice, mean the re-erection of national barriers by contractual means. Furthermore, as GEMA only sought royalties from custom pressers where the supplier had obtained a licence from a copyright protection society other than GEMA means that such course of action constituted discrimination against licences granted by copyright collecting societies of other states. GEMA took heed of the Commission's stance and abandoned its practice.

Refusal by copyright-management society to grant access to its repertoire to user established in another Member State: Ministère Public v Tournier and Lucazeau v SACEM (CJEU)[515]

These combined cases concerned complaints by French discotheque owners **8-415** about the royalties charged by SACEM, the French national copyright collecting society. Various complaints under arts 34–36, 49–50 and 101 and 102 were made. For present purposes, we are concerned with the complaint made under art.101 by

---

[511] See Joint Opinion of Jacobs AG in *Ministère Public v Tournier; Lucazeau v SACEM* (395/87, 110 & 241–242/88) [1989] E.C.R. 2521 at [44]–[49] applying CJEU's judgment in *BRT v SABAM* (127/ 73) [1974] E.C.R. 313; [1974] C.M.L.R. 238 at [8].

[512] See decision of Supreme Court in *Columbia Broadcasting System v BMI and ASCAP* (441, US 1, 60 1 Ed. 2nd 1, 99 Sup. Ct 1551) referred to in Opinion of Jacobs AG in (395/87, 110 & 241–242/ 88) [1989] E.C.R. 2521.

[513] See paras 12-274 and 12-290.

[514] *Re GEMA Notice of the Commission*, 6 February 1985; [1985] 2 C.M.L.R. 1.

[515] (395/87, 110 & 241–242/88) [1989] E.C.R. 2521; [1989] E.C.R. 2811; [1991] 4 C.M.L.R. 248.

the discotheque owners. National collecting societies entered into reciprocal agreements whereby each society granted other societies the right to grant within the territory for which they were responsible the requisite authorisations for any public performance of copyright works of the former's repertoire. French discotheque owners were generally charged a blanket royalty rate considerably in excess of the blanket royalty rate charged by collecting societies of other Member States. Furthermore, they generally played foreign Anglo-American repertoires whose rights were unsurprisingly held by US or UK collecting societies. However, the discotheques were unable to obtain licences from the UK or US collecting societies, who refused to license them and were thus forced to obtain licences from SACEM. The French courts referred inter alia the question as to whether such a set of reciprocal representation agreements between national collecting societies in the countries of the EEC, which enabled a national copyright-management society pursuing its activities in a Member State to fix under a standard form contract a comprehensive royalty which had to be paid by users before they could exploit foreign works, constituted an agreement or concerted practice within the meaning of art.101.

8-416   The CJEU said that reciprocal representation contracts have a two-fold purpose. First, they are intended to make all protected musical works, whatever their origin, subject to the same conditions for all users in one Member State and, secondly, they enable copyright management societies to rely, for the protection of their repertoires in a state, on the organisation established by the copyright-management society operating in that state, without being obliged to add to that organisation their own network of contracts with users and their own local monitoring arrangements.[516] Thus, the court held that such contracts cannot be considered to be: "in themselves restrictive of competition in such a way as to be caught by art.[101(1)] of the Treaty". The court held that the position would be different if societies undertook not to allow direct access to their repertoires by users of recorded music established abroad. However, the collecting societies had removed such clauses at the request of the Commission. However, as noted by the Commission, removal of these clauses had not resulted in any change in the conduct of the collecting societies, who still refused to grant their repertoire to anyone other than the society where the user was established. The court held that if such conduct was proven to be the result of concerted practice between the collecting societies, then this was equally restrictive of competition and capable of affecting trade between Member States. However, the court said that concerted practice cannot be presumed because each collecting society may refuse, not due to a concerted practice but because of the difficulties in the management and monitoring licences in another country.[517] The CJEU said that it was up to the national court to determine whether this was the case.[518]

---

[516] See [13].

[517] Even if there is no concerted practice, it may be that the refusal to license a party on the basis of their nationality constitutes an abuse of a dominant position or abuse of a collective dominant position—see Ch.12.

[518] Following these judgments, the Commission resumed its investigations but eventually rejected the complaint on the grounds that there was no EU interest in pursuing the matter, as the matter was essentially a French problem. This led to proceedings brought by the French discotheque owners for annulment of the Commission decision which was dismissed in large part by the General Court (*BEMIM v Commission* (T-114/92) [1995] E.C.R. II-0147).

Collecting societies and single-state licences: CISAC

In proceedings brought by the Commission against 24 national collecting socie- **8-417** ties of the EU, the Commission complained of the practice whereby licences were only granted to users by each collecting society for the Member State which it represented and also where authors were obliged to use the collecting society of the Member State of which they were a national. A complaint was made by multi-platform broadcasters about the refusal of the collecting societies to grant EU-wide licences. It was clear that the practice of the national collecting societies in a modern multi-jurisdictional world was inappropriate. The Commission found that the CISAC members were guilty of a concerted practice in dividing up the territories and prevented authors and copyright owners from choosing collecting societies other than their domestic one for the licensing of their repertoires. Furthermore, users could not choose which national collecting society to deal with when seeking a multinational licence and was forced to deal with only one collecting society for each Member State. The Commission held that such practices were restrictive of competition within art.101 and fell outside art.101(3). The collecting societies then appealed to the General Court arguing that the Commission were wrong to find that the national collecting societies were guilty of a concerted practice. This is discussed earlier in this chapter.[519] The General Court found that there was not sufficient evidence of a concerted practice.[520] The General Court did not thus consider the interesting argument that the territorial limitations existed to avoid a "race to the bottom" with regard to royalties.[521] This argument was somewhat refuted by the fact that a number of collecting societies had already entered into agreements allowing for a single multi-territorial licence to be granted in respect of Internet broadcasting. Thus, the Commission had exempted an agreement by a number of collecting societies whereby multi-territorial simulcasting (the simultaneous transmission by radio stations and television channels via the internet of sound recordings included in their television or radio broadcasts) licences could be obtained.[522] There was also evidence of other one-stop multi-territorial online agreements between collecting societies.[523]

It should be said that in February 2014, the EU adopted a Directive on collect- **8-418** ing management of copyright-related rights and multi-territorial licensing of rights in musical works for online uses in the internal market. This is discussed in Ch.4, "Copyright in Europe".[524] This imposes obligations on collecting societies which reduce the need to rely on art.101.

Sub-contracting Agreements

Often, undertakings, especially small and medium-sized ones, will, for financial **8-419** reasons, prefer to sub-contract out the manufacture of goods or the supply of services rather than manufacture themselves. If intellectual property is involved, this will usually involve licensing the sub-contractor to manufacture the goods.

In 1979, the Commission issued a Notice on the Application of art.101(1) to **8-420**

---

[519] See the Commission Decision in COM/C2/38.698 *CISAC* (16 July 2008). See para.8-075.
[520] *CISAC v Commission* (T-442/08) [2013] E.C.R. 0000; [2013] 5 C.M.L.R. 15.
[521] COMP/C2/38.698 Decision of Commission dated 16 July 2008.
[522] *IFPI/Simulcasting* [2003] OJ L107/58.
[523] e.g. see [35]–[38] of the General Court's decision.
[524] See para.4-399.

certain Sub-contracting Agreements[525] in which it states that:

"The Commission considers that agreements under which one firm, called the 'contractor, whether or not in consequence of a prior order from a third party, entrusts to another called the subcontractor', the manufacture of goods, the supply or services or the performance of work under the contractor's instructions, to be provided to the contractor or performed on his behalf, are not of themselves caught by the prohibition in Article [101(1)]."

8-421   Thus, in the Commission's view, art.101(1) does not apply to clauses which:

(a)   restrict the use of technology or equipment provided by the contractor except for the purposes of the sub-contracting agreement;

(b)   prohibit the making available of technology or equipment provided by the contractor to third parties; or

(c)   "tie-in" the sub-contractor to supplying the goods or services resulting from the use of such technology or equipment to the contractor;

if, and only if, such technology or equipment is necessary to enable the sub-contractor under reasonable conditions to manufacture the goods or supply the services.[526]

8-422   The Notice provides that such restrictions are not justifiable where the sub-contractor could, under reasonable conditions, obtain access to the technology or equipment needed to produce the goods or provide the services. Generally, this will be the case where the contractor provides no more than information which merely describes the work to be done, as in such circumstances, the restrictions could deprive the sub-contractor of the possibility of developing their own business in the fields covered by the agreement.

8-423   The following obligations are also considered by the Notice to fall outside art.101(1): an obligation on the sub-contractor not to disclose confidential information or know-how; a ban on use of know-how after the expiry of the agreement; and an obligation to licence back on a non-exclusive basis any improvement know-how or patents.[527] A contractor may forbid a sub-contractor to apply the former's trade mark or get-up on goods or services which are not to be supplied to the contractor.[528]

8-424   The 2014 Guidelines endorse the approach in the Notice and confirms its applicability in 2014 despite its age.[529] It also points out that the Technology Transfer Block Exemption covers sub-contracting. However, the 2014 Guidelines take the view that other restrictions such as a restriction on the contractor doing R&D may be caught by art.101.[530]

8-425   The most significant omission from the Notice is a sub-contract whereby the principal exclusively licenses another undertaking to make all its goods. Such contracts are fairly common, with the sub-contractor insisting on exclusivity

---

[525] Notice on the Application of art.101(1) to certain Sub-Contracting Agreements [1979] OJ C1/2.

[526] *Notice on Sub-Contracting Agreements* [1979] OJ C1/2, para.2.

[527] *Notice on Sub-Contracting Agreements* [1979] OJ C1/2, para.3. The undertaking may be exclusive in so far as improvements and inventions made by the sub-contractor during the currency of the agreement are incapable of being used independently of the contractor's secret know-how. However, any ban on the right to dispose of results of their own research and development where such results are capable of being used independently may restrain competition.

[528] *Notice on Sub-Contracting Agreements* [1979] OJ C1/2, para.4.

[529] 2014 Guidelines on Technology Transfer Agreements, para.64.

[530] See para.64.

because it needs to know that it will obtain substantial orders to justify investment in manufacturing capacity. Such will be covered by the TTBE if the market shares are sufficiently low. However, if the market share of the sub-contractor or principal in the contract product is such as to remove the protection of the TTBE, analysis of the competitive effect of this type of agreement will most likely depend on the degree of foreclosure to third parties that such an arrangement has. Thus, if the principal and the sub-contractor both have very considerable market power, third parties may be foreclosed from access to the relevant market. Indeed, competitors to the principal (i.e. those owning competing technologies) may be foreclosed from finding appropriate manufacturing facilities for their technologies thus causing an adverse effect of inter-technology competition and equally, competitors to the sub-contractor may be foreclosed from manufacturing the sub-contracting products to the principal such that there is not effective intra-technology competition.

MERGERS AND ACQUISITIONS INVOLVING IPRs

In certain circumstances, an agreement to merge two undertakings can restrict **8-426** competition.[531] In recent times, the Commission has become very active about the anti-competitive effects of mergers and acquisitions which significantly reduce competition in the relevant market and thus constitute an infringement of arts 101 and 102. Whilst IPRs are relevant, they merely represent one integer of the factors that the Commission will take into account when considering whether the merged entity wields too much market power in the relevant market. Often, the merging parties will have IPRs which can result in an unacceptable concentration of IPR such that there is a strengthening of a dominant position. In such cases, the Commission may ask the parties to divest themselves of IPR or require them to license other competitors in the relevant market. The analysis under competition law of mergers and acquisitions is outside the scope of this book.

ARTICLE 101, STANDARD ESSENTIAL PATENTS AND FRAND

In Ch.12, "Abuse of a Dominant Position", the competition concerns that arise **8-427** where the owner of a SEP ("Standard Essential Patent") refuses to license the SEP or refuses to license the SEP on fair terms, reasonable and non-discriminatory (FRAND) is discussed.[532] In particular, there are acute concerns where the owner of a SEP has undertaken to license it on FRAND terms to a technological standard setting institute and as a result of that undertaking, a technological standard has been adopted which incorporates the patented technology. Article 101 may be engaged where a SEP owner has entered into a licence for the SEP. Equally, art.101 may be engaged where a technological standard is agreed. Invariably, such are entered into between undertakings who are actual or potential competitors. In the Guidelines on Horizontal Agreements discussed in Ch.10, "Intellectual Property and Horizontal

---

[531] See (6/72) [1973] E.C.R. 215; [1973] C.M.L.R. 199. Generally, see Ch.11 and A. Bavasso, *Butterworth's Competition Law Handbook* (London: LexisNexis, 2013); V. Rose and D. Bailey, *Bellamy and Child on European Union Law of Competition* (New York: OUP, 2013). The acquisition of intellectual property via a merger may constitute an abuse of a dominant position, see para.12-301.

[532] See para.12-216.

Agreements,"[533] the Guidelines set out the competition concerns under art.101 concerning the anti-competitive effect of technical standardisation agreements entered into by undertakings. In particular, it sets out the anti-competitive concerns where IPRs protected technical standards and the owner of the IPR refuses to license that IPR on a fair, reasonable and non-discriminatory basis.

8-428   In an English case, *Samsung v Unwired Planet and Huawei*,[534] the Court of Appeal had to consider the application of art.101 to an assignment of SEPs from Ericsson to Unwired Planet. Ericsson had given undertakings to the European Telecommunications Standard Institute ("ETSI") to offer its SEPs on FRAND terms. Unwired Planet, which was a patent troll (i.e. it did not practise the patented technology) was seeking to enforce these SEPs against Samsung in patent litigation. Samsung alleged that the assignment pursuant to a master sale agreement ("MSA") was void under art.101 for a number of reasons and therefore Unwired Planet was not entitled to enforce the SEPs against Samsung.

8-429   There were three main arguments, two of which the first instance judge accepted gave rise to "a properly arguable" case that ought to go to trial. These were that: (i) The MSA divided up the SEP portfolio so that Samsung had to deal with both Ericsson and Unwired Planet and such had the object and effect of restricting competition. It said that this was anti-competitive because Ericsson retained a right to a substantial share in the licensing revenue and was required to transfer to UP a substantial body of patents at their discretion and UP was a patent troll. (ii) The MSA imposed a minimum payment by Unwired Planet to Ericsson and thus imposed a minimum royalty likely to be agreed by Unwired Planet with third parties.

8-430   The third argument was rejected by the first instance judge as not being properly arguable. Here, Samsung argued that the MSA did not fully transfer the undertaking given by Ericsson to ETSI. This argument consisted of three strands: (i) the MSA agreements did not require Unwired Planet to give FRAND undertakings, (ii) even if Unwired Planet was required to give FRAND undertakings, third parties could not enforce that obligation, and (iii) the MSA agreements did not limit Unwired Planet to the obtaining of licence terms that were no more favourable than those that Ericsson could itself secure.

8-431   On appeal, Samsung accepted that the MSA did contain obligations on Unwired Planet to give FRAND undertakings in relation to the five SEPs alleged to be infringed in the proceedings. However, it maintained that the judge had wrongly rejected the other two strands. The Court of Appeal dismissed the appeal against the second element as being wholly artificial because Unwired Planet had indeed pleaded and said that the FRAND undertaking was enforceable by Samsung and any other potential licensee.[535] However, it allowed the appeal on the third point. In essence, this point was that where a SEP owner assigns some of its SEPs to third parties, all licences entered into between owners of the SEPs at any time and whether between the assignor and the third party or the assignee and the third party, must be on the same terms to avoid discrimination.

8-432   The Court of Appeal, with some misgivings, considered that this point was properly arguable (relying on the Commission's decision in *Google/Motorola*

---

[533] See para.10-087.
[534] [2016] EWCA Civ 489.
[535] See [37].

Mobility[536]). In short, it considered that Unwired Patent could charge significantly higher licence fees than those charged by Ericsson. This would be discriminatory compared to Ericsson's existing licences, in addition to being detrimental to consumers.

In the author's view, the Court of Appeal was right to find that this was *properly* **8-433** *arguable* as a breach of art.101. The law concerning SEPs, FRAND undertakings and enforcement of SEPs is an evolving area and striking them out as unarguable would be wrong. However, there does seem to be a highly artificial aspect to the non-discrimination argument. Whilst one may not like patent trolls, Unwired Patent had agreed to give FRAND undertakings to anyone and was obliged to do so under the MSAs. Insofar as Unwired Planet had the opportunity to offer licences at a different royalty to those offered by Ericsson, they still had to be *fair* and *reasonable*. Accordingly, it is thus highly unlikely that they would have caused any anti-competitive effects. The Court of Appeal did not appear to take this point into account when saying that the licence fees could be significantly higher.

Commission Guidelines

Following the UK decision in *Huawei v ZTE*, the Commission has issued a **8-434** Notice entitled "Setting out the EU approach to Standard Essential Patents".[537] The Notice is aimed at ensuring a "balanced, smooth and predictable framework for SEPs".[538] Whilst the Guidelines are not binding on courts or tribunals, they are based on a public consultation, analysis of best practices, studies and national case law[539] and thus should be highly persuasive. The following important principles are in the Notice:

- FRAND licences should bear a clear relationship to the economic value of the patented technology and should not in principle include any element derived from the SEP being included in a technological standard.
- To avoid royalty stacking, an individual SEP should not be considered in isolation. Parties need to take into account a reasonable aggregate rate for the standard, assessing the overall added value of the technology.
- SEP licensing should be on a portfolio basis and efficient. A country-by-country approach to SEP licences may not be efficient and in line with recognised commercial practices in the sector. However, whilst portfolios can include non-SEP patents, SEP holders must not require a licensee to accept a licence for other patents.
- To be FRAND, licence negotiations should relate to all SEPs and not based on individual SEPs. However, portfolios should not include competing technologies, only complementary technologies.[540]
- Patent Assertion Entities[541] should be subject to the same rules as any other SEP holder, including after the transfer of SEPs from patent holders to them.

---

[536] Case No. COMP/M.6381.
[537] COM (2017) 712, 29 November 2017.
[538] See p.2.
[539] See p.6.
[540] This is also mentioned in the 2014 Technology Transfer Guidelines, pp.250–255.
[541] Often known as "patent trolls".

EXERCISE OF IPRS CONTRARY TO ART.101

8-435   Primarily, EU law's concerns about the validity of enforcement of IPRs to prevent imports of goods focus on the free movement of goods provisions (arts 34–36) and to a certain extent, the exercise of IPRs by a dominant undertaking (art.102). During the 1960s to 1980s, when understanding of the effect of arts 34–36 on the exercise of IPRs was imperfect, it was argued in certain cases that art.101 prevented the exercise of IPR per se. Again, this is dealt with in Ch.7, "Intellectual Property and Free Movement of Goods".[542] Briefly put, the *mere* exercise of rights does not infringe art.101(1).[543] This is unsurprising because there is no underlying agreement or concerted practice. However, if there is an agreement or restrictive practice between undertakings which infringes art.101(1) and is thus void, then the CJEU has said that the use of IPRs in furtherance of implementing such an illegal restrictive practice is also prohibited. In this case, the prohibition of the exercise of IPRs should be considered as an effective remedy that national courts or regulatory authorities require to restrain the implementation of the anti-competitive agreement rather than as being in itself, contrary to art.101(1).

8-436   The ability of a defendant to rely upon art.101 as a defence to an action for enforcement of IPRs is considered in Ch.14, "EU Defences to Exercise of IPRS".[544]

---

[542] See para.7-308.
[543] See *Parke Davis v Probel* (24/67) [1968] E.C.R. 55, [1968] C.M.L.R. 47; (51/75) [1976] E.C.R. 811, [1976] 2 C.M.L.R. 235.
[544] See para.14-013.

CHAPTER 9

INTELLECTUAL PROPERTY AND TECHNOLOGY TRANSFER LICENCES

INTRODUCTION

In Ch.8 the application of art.101 to licences and individual clauses in licences **9-001** was considered. This chapter focuses on licences which involve the transfer of technology to licensees. The reader who is unfamiliar with art.101 should read the previous chapter. This chapter considers the application of the Commission's 2014 Technology Transfer Guidelines ("the 2014 Guidelines") and the 2014 Technology Transfer Block Exemption ("TTBE") to technology transfer licences.

The European Commission is responsible for the introduction of the 2014 **9-002** Guidelines and the TTBE. They synthesise 30 years of the Commission's experience in dealing with competition issues raised by technology transfer licences. In the 1970s and 1980s, a number of IP licences were notified to the European Commission for individual exemption under the then art.85(3) Treaty of Rome. By 1979, 63 per cent of all agreements notified to the Commission had been patent licences and thus there was a need for a block exemption.[1] This number of notifications led the Commission to realise that many of the patent licences had similar provisions. Thus, in 1985, and following the CJEU's decision in *Nungesser v EC Commission*,[2] the Commission issued the Patent Block Exemption.[3] This block exemption took a "check list" approach to individual clauses whereby such were either white listed (permitted) or black listed (prohibited). Shortly after the Patent Block Exemption, a Know How Block Exemption was introduced in 1989. These block exemptions were then replaced by a Technology Transfer Block Exemption which combined the two in 1996.[4] This still took a "formalistic and rigid exemption approach" to restraints.[5] By 2000, it was clear that the TTBE's approach was outdated and not in keeping with the new economics-based approach that the Commission

---

[1] *9th Report on Competition Policy*, paras 20–27.
[2] (C-258/78) [1982] E.C.R. 2015.
[3] Reg.2349/84 [1984] OJ L219/15.
[4] Reg.240/96.
[5] F. Carlin, S. Pautke, "Last of Its Kind: The Review of the Technology Transfer Block Exemption Regulation, The Symposium on European Competition Law" *Northwestern Journal of International Law & Business* [2004] 24(3), 601–618.

was adopting. In 2001, the Commission published an Evaluation Report[6] in which the Commission openly admitted its shortcomings and promised a radical, more liberal, economics-based approach to technology transfer which was in line with other block exemptions in the field of vertical agreements, specialisation and research and development. In 2004, the Commission published Guidelines on Technology Transfer licences and also a new Technology Transfer Block Exemption was adopted.[7] The approach taken in the 2004 TTBE was radically different to the previous TTBE. Instead of the "check list" approach, agreements between undertakings whose market shares were under a specific threshold were permitted unless they contained certain "hard core" restrictions such as price fixing. Where the market share of the undertakings exceeded that threshold, the TTBE was inapplicable and individual exemption was necessary although there was no presumption that such fell within art.101 at all.

9-003   The 2004 TTBE expired in 2014 and has been replaced by the 2014 TTBE. Furthermore, the Guidelines have been updated. With both the TTBE and the 2014 Guidelines, the changes are relatively modest and the philosophy is the same.

Structure of chapter

9-004   This chapter considers first the 2014 Guidelines as such sets out the Commission's overall approach to technology transfer licences and art.101. The TTBE is then considered. The 2014 Guidelines provide specific advice on the TTBE and its application and thus that aspect of the guidelines is considered "inline" with the TTBE. Whilst the 2014 Guidelines also consider litigation settlement agreements and patent pools, the former is considered in Ch.8 and the latter (being a form of horizontal co-operation) are considered in Ch.10, "IP and Horizontal Agreements".

9-005   A detailed analysis of individual clauses in IPR licences including technology transfer licences is done in Ch.8. This chapter includes consideration of the 2014 Guidelines as they apply to individual clauses. Thus, if the reader wishes to read about the application of art.101 to specific clauses in an IP technology transfer licence, this chapter will inform the reader whether such a clause falls within the TTBE. If it does not, the reader is recommended to read the relevant section in Ch.8 which will give them a detailed discussion of such a clause by reference to CJEU's decisions, the 2014 Technology Transfer Guidelines and Commission decisions and also the US approach.

2014 TECHNOLOGY TRANSFER GUIDELINES

Overview

9-006   In 2014, the Commission published Guidelines on the Application of art.101 to Technology Transfer Agreements.[8] These Guidelines accompanied the publication of the 2014 Technology Transfer Block Exemption.

9-007   The Guidelines can be divided into five parts: (i) General principles applicable to art.101 and IPRS, (ii) guidance as to the application of the TTBE, (iii) the ap-

---

6   Commission Evaluation Report on the *Transfer of Technology Block Exemption* Regulation No.240/96.
7   Reg.772/2004 [2004] OJ L123.
8   Guidelines on Technology Transfer Agreements [2014] OJ C89/3.

plication of art.101 to IP licences outside the TTBE and consideration of individual clauses, (iv) art.101 and settlement agreements, and (v) art.101 and technology pools. As said in the introduction to this chapter, the last two are not considered in this chapter but in the Chs 8 and 10. Furthermore, the approach to individual clauses in the 2014 Guidelines is considered in Ch.8.

Thus, in this chapter, consideration is given to the general approach in the Guidelines to technology transfer licences and then its assistance in relation to the TTBE. The latter is contemplated when considering the TTBE. **9-008**

Licences covered by 2014 Guidelines

The 2014 Guidelines are a comprehensive guide to the Commission's approach to technology licensing. The name of such Guidelines indicates that they prima facie only apply to intellectual property licences which involve the licensing of technology so as to permit the licensee to produce a product. Thus, the Guidelines say that they apply to patents, utility models, design rights, plant breeder's rights, topographies of semiconductor rights, supplementary protection certificates for medicinal products and software copyright.[9] However, the approach taken in the Guidelines is equally applicable to copyright licences (but not licences for performance rights) which are considered in the Guidelines to be similar to technology licences.[10] However, they are not applicable to pure trade mark licences which are considered more akin to distribution agreements. Thus, such should be considered under the Vertical Agreements Block Exemption and their Guidelines.[11] The Guidelines (and indeed the TTBE) are however applicable to technology transfer agreements even if the principal interest lies in exploiting the trade mark rather than the technology.[12] **9-009**

The Guidelines do not have the status of law. Thus, they are expressed to be without prejudice to the interpretation of art.101 by the General Court and CJEU.[13] **9-010**

In general, because of the Commission's conversion to full "rule of reason" analysis, care must be applied in considering old Commission decisions. However, in certain cases, recourse is useful.[14] **9-011**

Principles to be applied to technology licences

There can be no substitute for reading the 2014 Guidelines to obtain a good understanding of the approach of the Commission to technology transfer licences. In recent years, the decisions of the General Court and CJEU on IP licences and art.101 are few and far between. Thus, the 2014 Guidelines are extremely valuable. This is no doubt testimony to the fact that the 2014 Guidelines and TTBE and its predecessors have worked well to provide certainty. The following is distilled from the 2014 Guidelines and can be considered a "potted guide": **9-012**

---

[9] 2014 Guidelines, para.44.

[10] 2014 Guidelines, para.48.

[11] 2014 Guidelines, para.50. The Vertical Agreements Block Exemption and Guidelines are considered in Ch.11, "IP and Vertical Agreements".

[12] 2014 Guidelines, para.47. This revises the previous stance taken—see *Moosehead/Whitbread* [1990] OJ L100/32 and the 2004 Guidelines, para.50; [2004] OJ C101/2.

[13] 2014 Guidelines, para.4.

[14] e.g. in the context of plant breeder's rights, these raise particular issues such as preservation of plant lines—*SICASOV* [1995] 5 C.M.L.R. 100.

(a) The fact that IPRs grant exclusive rights of exploitation does not make them immune from competition law intervention.

(b) Both bodies of law share the same basic objective of promoting consumer welfare and an efficient allocation of resources. Innovation constitutes an essential and dynamic component of an open and competitive market economy. IPRs promote dynamic competition by encouraging undertakings to invest in developing new or improved products and processes. This is the same with competition which puts pressure on undertakings to innovate. Both IPRs and competition are thus necessary to promote innovation and the competitive exploitation of that innovation.[15]

(c) The creation of IPRs often entails substantial investment and these are frequently risky endeavours. Thus, innovators should not be "unduly restricted in the exploitation of IPRs that turn out to be valuable" and should thus be free to seek "appropriate remuneration for successful projects that is sufficient to maintain investment incentives, taking failed projects into account".[16]

(d) In assessing licensing agreements under art.101, the existing analytical framework is sufficiently flexible to take due account of the dynamic aspects of technology licences. There is no presumption that intellectual property licences give rise to competition concerns.[17]

(e) The vast majority of licence agreements do not restrict competition and indeed most create pro-competitive efficiencies. Licensing is pro-competitive because it leads to dissemination of technology and promotes innovation. Licences which do restrict competition may often give rise to pro-competitive efficiencies which must be considered under art.101(3) and balanced against the negative effects on competition. Thus, the "great majority" of licence agreements are compatible with art.101.[18]

(f) The assessment of whether a licence restricts competition must be made in the actual context in which competition would occur in the absence of the agreement with its alleged restrictions. In making this assessment, it is necessary to take account of the likely impact of the agreement on *inter-technology competition* (i.e. competition between undertakings using competing technologies) and on *intra-technology* competition (i.e. competition between undertakings using the same technology).[19]

(g) In assessing the effect of the agreement on *inter-technology* competition, it is necessary to determine whether the licence agreement restricts actual or potential competition that would have existed *without the contemplated agreement*. If so, the agreement may be caught by art.101(1). In making this assessment, it is necessary to take into account competition between the parties and competition from third parties.[20] Cross-licensing between competitors is of particular concern as such would prevent a competitor from gaining a technological lead over the other.[21] Licensing between competitors

---

[15] 2014 Guidelines, para.7.
[16] 2014 Guidelines, para.8.
[17] 2014 Guidelines, para.9.
[18] 2014 Guidelines, paras 9 and 17.
[19] 2014 Guidelines, para.11.
[20] 2014 Guidelines, para.12(a).
[21] 2014 Guidelines, paras 170–171.

may also facilitate collusion, particularly in concentrated markets.[22] Restraints that foreclose third parties are also of concern.[23]

(h) In assessing the effect on *intra-technology* competition, it is necessary to consider whether the agreement affects competition in the licensed technology *without the contemplated restraint*, i.e. a licence with and without the restraint.

(i) When considering such a restraint, the question is not whether the parties in their particular situation would not have accepted to conclude a less restrictive agreement but whether given the nature of the agreement, and the characteristics of the market, a less restrictive agreement would not have been concluded by undertakings in a similar setting.[24] Restraints which are "objectively necessary for the existence of an agreement of that type of that nature" are permissible.[25]

(j) Where a licence contains certain "hard core" restrictions such that it can be concluded they "have such a high potential for negative effects on competition", then such agreements can be considered to have as their *object* the restriction of competition and it is not necessary to demonstrate any actual effects on the market.[26] The restrictions are those contained in art.4 of the TTBE. Hardcore restrictions are unlikely to satisfy art.101(3).[27]

(k) Where agreements do not have as their object the restriction of competition, it is necessary to consider whether the licences have actual or potential effects on competition. For licence agreements to have anti-competitive effects, they must affect actual or potential competition to such an extent that on the relevant market, negative effects on prices, output, innovation or the variety of quality of goods and services can be expected with a reasonable degree of probability.[28]

(l) Particularly relevant factors are the nature of the agreement, the market position of the parties, the market position of the competitors, entry barriers and the maturity of the market.[29]

(m) In general, where there are four or more independently controlled technologies in addition to the technologies controlled by the parties to the agreement that may be substitutable for the licensed technology at a comparable cost to the user, art.101 is unlikely to be infringed.[30]

(n) Such effects must be appreciable.[31] This is likely to occur when one of the parties has or obtains some degree of market power and the agreement contributes to the creation, maintenance or strengthening of that market power or allows the parties to exploit such market power. Market power is the ability to maintain prices above competitive levels or to maintain output

---

[22] 2014 Guidelines, para.171.
[23] 2014 Guidelines, para.172.
[24] 2014 Guidelines, para.12(b).
[25] See 2014 Guidelines, para.12(b) where the restrictions can then be considered necessary ancillary restraints. See Ch.8, especially para.8-042.
[26] 2014 Guidelines, para.14. See para.8-121 about difference between "object or effect".
[27] 2014 Guidelines, para.18.
[28] 2014 Guidelines, para.15.
[29] 2014 Guidelines, para.159.
[30] 2014 Guidelines, para.157.
[31] 2014 Guidelines, para.15.

in terms of product quantities, product quality and variety or innovation below competitive levels for a not insignificant period of time.

(o) For the purpose of analysing restrictions of competition, it is necessary to define the relevant market and to examine the nature of the products and technologies concerned, the market position of the parties, the market position of competitors, the market position of buyers, the existence of potential competitors, the maturity of the market, and the level of entry barriers.[32]

(p) When considering the relevant market, one needs to consider the technology, product and innovation markets.[33]

(q) In general, licences between competitors pose a greater risk to competition than those between non-competitors.[34] In considering whether parties are potential competitors, one must consider whether on the basis of a SNIP[35] of the licensed products, a party could and would have entered the market without infringing the IPRs of the other party within one to two years.

(r) Where a licence contains restrictive anti-competitive clauses, such may also produce pro-competitive effects in the form of efficiencies. Analysis of such takes place under art.101(3). An undertaking that relies on art.101(3) must demonstrate by means of convincing arguments and evidence that the conditions for obtaining an exemption are satisfied.[36]

TECHNOLOGY TRANSFER BLOCK EXEMPTION

Introduction

9-013   As discussed above, in April 2014, the 2014 Technology Transfer Block Exemption[37] ("TTBE") replaced the 2004 TTBE. The changes to the 2004 TTBE arise from the results of a public consultation on the 2004 TTBE initiated in 2013 by the European Commission. As with all block exemptions, an agreement that falls within it is deemed to comply with art.101.[38] Furthermore, they are also immune to challenge from national competition laws of the Member States.[39]

9-014   The 2014 Guidelines provide help in interpreting and applying the TTBE. As with any other block exemption, they have direct effect and a block exempted agreement cannot be prohibited under art.101 by national courts in the context of private litigation.[40] The fact that a technology transfer agreement falls outside the TTBE does not give rise to a presumption that it falls within art.101(1) and/or does not satisfy the conditions of art.101(3).[41]

9-015   As with other current block exemptions, the approach is to permit technology transfer agreements between undertakings whose market share (combined or individual depending whether they are competitors) falls below a certain threshold

---

[32]   2014 Guidelines, para.16.
[33]   2014 Guidelines, paras 19–26. For further discussion of what these markets are, see para.8-032.
[34]   2014 Guidelines, para.27.
[35]   See para.8-035 for an explanation of this term.
[36]   2014 Guidelines, para.174.
[37]   Commission Regulation No.316/2014 of 21 March 2014 on the application of art.101(3) of the Treaty on the Functioning of the European Union to categories of technology transfer agreements [2014] OJ L93/17.
[38]   See para.8-202 in relation to block exemptions.
[39]   See Reg.1/2003, art.3(2); 2014 Guidelines, para.40.
[40]   Reg.1/2003 art.3(2); Guidelines on Technology Transfer Agreements [2014] OJ C89/3, para.34.
[41]   Guidelines on Technology Transfer Agreements [2014] OJ C89/3, para.37.

provided that such agreements do not contain certain hard core restrictions. Where the market share exceeds that threshold, then the TTBE does not apply and the undertakings to the agreement must either seek individual exemption from the European Commission or self-certify the agreement as being compliant with art.101.

Sphere of application of TTBE

The TTBE does not apply to all licences of intellectual property. It is primarily **9-016** intended to deal with licences where intellectual property of a technological nature is licensed (or in the case of technical know-how, communicated) to the licensee so that the licensee can manufacture products or use the technology in a manufacturing process. Although the expression "technology transfer" is used, this can be seen as misleading. It is not necessary that any actual information is transferred to the licensee (this will happen in know-how licences). Rather, it is intended to cover any "technical licence" whereby technical subject matter which is subject to IPR protection is used in a manufacturing process. Thus, as said in the 2014 Guidelines, it also covers agreements whereby the licensor agrees not to assert rights against the licensee and thus covers non-assertion agreements and settlement agreements.[42]

Therefore, the TTBE is said to apply to licences relating to technology rights.[43] **9-017** "Technology rights" are defined as meaning patents, utility models, design rights, topographies of semiconductor products, supplementary protection certificates, plant breeder's certificates, and software copyright.[44] It also includes know-how.[45] In relation to software copyright, the 2014 Guidelines distinguishes between licensing of software copyright for the purpose of mere reproduction and distribution, i.e. for resale and where the licensed software is incorporated by the licensee into the contract products. The former is not covered by the TTBE but the latter is.[46] Other than the above IPR, the TTBE is inapplicable. Thus, it does not cover trade mark or non-software copyright licence. These may have to be considered individually or may fall within the Vertical Agreements Block Exemption.

However, where a licence consists of a number of IPRs, some of them falling **9-018** within the definition of "technology rights" and some which do not, then the TTBE will apply to a licence of the other rights provided that "those provisions are directly related to the production or sale of the contract products". Unlike the 2004 TTBE, it is not necessary that the "technology rights" be the primary object of the agreement. Thus, a mixed knowhow/trade mark licence agreement will be covered by the TTBE even if the principal interest of the parties lies in the exploitation of the trademark rather than the technology.[47]

Furthermore, the following conditions must also be satisfied for the licence to fall **9-019** within the TTBE.

---

[42] 2014 Guidelines, para.53.
[43] art.1.1(c), art.1.1(b).
[44] art.1.1(b).
[45] This must be secret, substantial and identified (see art.1.1(b) and 1.1(i)). It is said that the know how must be "a package of practical information resulting from experience and testing"—art.1.1(i). It is not said that such must be technical but insofar as it is commercial information (e.g. business know how), it is difficult to describe such as being agreements for the transfer of technology—see the 2014 Guidelines, para.44 and is likely to be covered by the Vertical Agreements Block Exemption—see para.11-041.
[46] 2014 Guidelines, paras 62–63.
[47] See 2014 Guidelines, para.47 and fn.12.

(i)   The technology transfer agreement is only between two undertakings.[48] It thus excludes agreements establish technology pools.[49]

(ii)   The agreement must concern the production of products or services produced with the licensed technology ("the contract products").[50] This will apply where the licensed technology is used in either the production process or where it is incorporated in the product itself.[51] The TTBE does not apply to pure licence agreements which permit sublicensing.[52] The TTBE also covers licence agreements whereby the licensee can be considered a sub-contractor.[53]

Relationship with other block exemptions

9-020   A technology transfer licence may exist in a number of contexts. It is probably wrong to say that there is any typical technology transfer licence such as an inventor licensing a manufacturer to use their patent. IPR licences often exist in research and development agreements and manufacturing specialisation agreements. In this context, there are two block exemptions, the R&D Block Exemption and the Specialisation Block Exemption. These are discussed in the chapter on IP and Horizontal Agreements. The TTBE does not apply to any agreements that fall within these block exemptions.[54] The reader should consult these but the R&D Block Exemption covers agreements whereby parties agree to carry out R&D and to jointly exploit the results. The Specialisation Block Exemption is concerned with undertakings agreeing that one shall manufacture for the other. It should be emphasised that these block exemptions are concerned with arrangements inter partes. Because such tend to be horizontal relationships between competitors, where there are licensing provisions, they tend to raise particular concerns, e.g. reduction of innovation between the parties. However, the TTBE does apply to licensing arrangements between these parties and third parties. For instance, a joint venture company set up by the R&D agreement may end up owing IPR generated by the joint venture and license it to third parties for them to produce products. As said by the 2014 Guidelines, the TTBE (and the Guidelines) apply to such licences.[55]

9-021   The 2014 Guidelines also distinguishes between the TTBE and the Vertical Agreements Block Exemption ("VABE"). The TTBE applies to agreements for manufacturing products under a technology licence whereas sales by the licensee of the contract products to third parties is in essence a distribution agreement and is covered by VABE and its Guidelines.[56] However, the matter is somewhat complicated because the TTBE covers "downstream sales" restrictions imposed by the licensor on the licensee in technology transfer licences. In order to comply with those obligations, the licensee may need to enter into contractual arrangements with

---

[48]   art.1(1)(c) TTBE; Guidelines on Technology Transfer Agreements [2014] OJ C89/3, para.38. NB. This means undertakings who are economically independent of each other—see art.1.2.

[49]   See the 2014 Guidelines, para.56; Patent pools are discussed at para.10-094.

[50]   art.2, art.1.1(c) and art.1.1(f) TTBE; Guidelines on Technology Transfer Agreements [2014] OJ C89/3, para.58.

[51]   2014 Guidelines, para.64.

[52]   2014 Guidelines, para.60.

[53]   2014 Guidelines, para.64.

[54]   art.9 TTBE; 2014 Guidelines, para.70.

[55]   2014 Guidelines, para.74.

[56]   2014 Guidelines, para.76.

retailers or distributors of the contract products. Those agreements will need to be, as discussed above, considered by reference to the Guidelines on Vertical Agreements and VABE.[57] Thus the legal advisor will need to consider the lawfulness of "downstream" clauses in technology transfer licences under both VABE and TTBE.

Therefore, it can be appreciated that a number of block exemptions need to be considered. This is best considered by an example: **9-022**

Example
A and B decide to collaborate to research a new form of propulsion engine for near space. They enter into a joint research and development agreement and agree that the results of the R&D agreement will be licensed by company C which is owned 50 per cent: 50 per cent by A and B. This stage is governed by the R&D Block Exemption. The R&D results in some important patents and know how. Company C licenses a large manufacturing aerospace company D to manufacture the propulsion engines. This stage is governed by the TTBE. D manufactures them and enters into a number of hire-lease or purchase agreements with leading airplane manufacturers. This stage is governed by the Vertical Agreements Block Exemption.

Market power

The TTBE only applies to agreements between undertakings which do not have substantial market power. In essence: **9-023**

(a) For technology transfer agreements between *competitors*, the TTBE will only apply where the *combined* market share on the relevant market does not exceed *20 per cent*.

(b) For technology transfer agreements between *non-competitors*, the TTBE will only apply where the *individual* market share on the relevant market of either party to the agreement does not exceed *30 per cent*.[58]

The exemption provided by the TTBE will continue to apply where the above market shares are initially at or below the above levels for a period of two consecutive calendar years from the date when the 20 or 30 per cent threshold was first exceeded.[59]   **9-024**

Relevant technology and product market

The above market share requirements first necessitate the identification of the relevant technology and product market. In this regard, general economic analysis is required. The Commission has issued a Notice on the identification of the relevant market for the purpose of EU competition law.[60] The technology market is the market which encompasses the licensed technology and any other technologies that are regarded by licensees as interchangeable with or substitutable for the licensed technologies by reason of the technologies' characteristics, their royalties and their intended use.[61] The product market is concerned with the market which encompasses, first the licensed products that incorporate the technology, or, have been   **9-025**

---

[57] 2014 Guidelines, para.77.
[58] art.3.1, art.3.2 TTBE.
[59] art.8(e).
[60] See para.12-035, et seq.
[61] See art.1.1(n) which is concerned with the definition of "competing undertakings".

made with the technology, and, secondly products that are interchangeable or substitutable for such products.

Calculation of market shares

9-026   Following identification of the relevant technology and product market, it is necessary to determine what is the market share of the parties to the agreement in those markets. This can be somewhat difficult because the calculation of the market share for the technology market is created by reference to the product market in which the licensed product that incorporates the licensed technology competes in. Thus, in determining market shares in both markets, consideration is only given to the product market in which the licensed products operate in. Detailed guidance with worked out examples is given in the 2014 Guidelines as to the calculation of market shares.[62]

Competitors or non-competitors

9-027   As is clear from the determination of the market share thresholds, the TTBE distinguishes between undertakings who are competitors and those which are not. The TTBE defines this expression. It distinguishes between the technology market and the product market. In the case of the technology market, the TTBE is only concerned with actual competitors. In the product market, it is concerned with undertakings who actually compete against each other or which would on realistic grounds and not just as a mere theoretical possibility, in response to a small and permanent increase in relative price, be likely to undertake, within a short period of time, the necessary additional investments or other necessary switching costs to enter the relevant market (i.e. potential competitors).[63]

Exemption

9-028   Provided that the above conditions of sphere of application and market power are satisfied, then any technology transfer licence is exempted by the TTBE.[64] However, the exemption only applies provided that the IPRs, which have been licensed, have not expired, or, the know-how has not entered the public domain.[65]

9-029   However, it is necessary to consider whether the agreement contains certain clauses called "hard core restrictions" and "excluded restrictions". If an agreement contains a hard core restriction, the effect is that the TTBE will not apply to the *whole* agreement. If an agreement contains an "excluded restriction", then the TTBE will not apply to *that restriction*.

Hard core restrictions

9-030   Article 4 of the TTBE sets out the hard core restrictions. These restrictions can be considered as being terms which have their object of restricting competition and

---

[62] paras 79–93.
[63] art.1.1(n). See also the 2014 Guidelines, paras 27–39 where further guidance on this is given.
[64] art.2.
[65] art.2.2.

thus do not require analysis of their economic effect.[66] When considering hard core restrictions, it is necessary to distinguish between:

(a) agreements between competing undertakings and those between undertakings who do not compete. In essence, and not surprisingly, the TTBE takes a harder line with restrictions between competing undertakings. This is because it is more difficult to identify pro-competitive efficiencies when competing undertakings choose not to compete; and

(b) reciprocal agreements and non-reciprocal agreements. A reciprocal agreement is a technology transfer agreement where two undertakings grant each other licences in technologies that compete *or* can be used for the production of competing products.[67] An agreement is not reciprocal simply because there are grant back obligations or license-back obligations concerning improvements in the licensed technology.[68] A non-reciprocal agreement is where such conditions are not satisfied.[69] It is not necessary that the reciprocal licences are entered into simultaneously. If a second licence is entered into between the same parties, the parties may have to revise the first licence in order to avoid the agreement containing a hard core restriction.[70] The TTBE's approach is harder on reciprocal agreements.

When considering the hard core restrictions, the focus is on substance and not form. Thus, the focus is not on the form of the terms but the aim of the agreements. Therefore, the examination is whether the agreements have the aim or object, directly or indirectly, in isolation or in combination with other factors under the control of the parties, of price fixing, customer allocation, etc.[71] With such in mind, there are categories of agreements which are defined as removing exemption under the TTBE. Article 4.1 deals with those agreements between competitors. Article 4.2 deals with agreements between non-competitors. Where undertakings are not competitors at the time of entering into the agreement but subsequently become competitors, then they are treated as non-competitors unless the agreement is subsequently amended in any material respect.[72] **9-031**

Hard core restrictions for competing undertakings

Price restrictions

This provision prohibits any agreement between competitors that has as its object the fixing of prices for products sold to third parties.[73] As the 2014 Guidelines say, it is immaterial whether the agreement concerns fixed, minimum, maximum or recommended prices.[74] The focus is on the aim rather than the mechanism. The 2014 Guidelines say that in the case of royalties, reciprocal running royalties can co-ordinate and/or increase prices on downstream product markets. However, the 2014 Guidelines say that such will only be treated in this manner if they are void **9-032**

---

[66] Guidelines on Technology Transfer Agreements [2014] OJ C89/3, para.94.
[67] art.1.1(d); Guidelines on Technology Transfer Agreements [2014] OJ C89/3, para.98.
[68] Guidelines on Technology Transfer Agreements [2014] OJ C89/3, para.98.
[69] art.1.1(e)
[70] 2014 Guidelines, para.78.
[71] See the introductory wording to arts 4.1 and 4.2.
[72] art.4.3.
[73] art.4.1(a).
[74] 2014 Guidelines, para.99.

of any pro-competitive purpose or do not constitute bona fide licensing arrangements—in other words, they are sham arrangements.[75]

9-033   The 2014 Guidelines also say that there is an objectionable price restriction where royalties are calculated on the basis of all product sales regardless of whether the licensed technology is used.[76] It is difficult to see this as price fixing although it is clear that such could give rise to foreclosure of third parties and also restrict the licensee's ability to use its own technology.[77] However, it may be that such a restraint would fulfil the conditions of art.101(3) in an individual case, in particular where there are not available practicable alternative monitoring methods.[78]

Output restrictions

9-034   Any restriction on output is not permitted except where they are imposed on the licensee in a non-reciprocal agreement or imposed on only one of the licensees in a reciprocal agreement.[79] An output restriction should normally be unobjectionable as an IPR owner should have the right to determine how much competition it wishes to create. However, in the case of reciprocal licences with reciprocal output restrictions, the object and likely effect is to reduce output in the market.[80] Where the limitation is only one-way, the Commission's view is that it is likely to lead to a real integration of complementary technologies or an efficiency enhancing integration of the licensor's superior technology with the licensee's productive assets.[81]

Allocation of markets or customers

9-035   The TTBE prohibits allocation of markets or customers between competitors save in certain circumstances. These are:

(i)   The obligation on the licensor and/or the licensee, in a non-reciprocal agreement, not to produce with the licensed technology rights within the exclusive territory reserved for the other party and/or not to sell actively and/or passively into the exclusive territory or to the exclusive customer group reserved for the other party.

(ii)   The restriction, in a non-reciprocal agreement, of active sales by the licensee into the exclusive territory or to the exclusive customer group allocated by the licensor to another licensee provided the latter was not a competing undertaking of the licensor at the time of the conclusion of its own licence.

(iii)   The obligation on the licensee to produce the contract products only for its own use provided that the licensee is not restricted in selling the contract products actively and passively as spare parts for its own products.

(iv)   The obligation on the licensee, in a non-reciprocal agreement, to produce the contract products only for a particular customer, where the licence was

---

[75]   2014 Guidelines, para.100.
[76]   2014 Guidelines, para.101.
[77]   The latter point is made at para.101 of the 2014 Guidelines.
[78]   2014 Guidelines, para.102. See also para.8-250, et seq. where these type of royalty clauses are considered.
[79]   art.4.1(b).
[80]   2014 Guidelines, para.103.
[81]   Guidelines on Technology Transfer Agreements [2014] OJ C89/3, para.104.

granted in order to create an alternative source of supply for that customer.[82]

The first two exceptions are concerned with the ability of the licensor and licensee (where they are competitors) to provide territorial or customer group protection between licensor and licensee. The mere grant of exclusivity will not provide absolute territorial protection unless accompanied by sales bans between licensor/licensee or licensee/licensee. In Ch.8, "IP and art.101", the approach of the CJEU and Commission to *open* and *closed* exclusive licences has been discussed with the latter generally considered impermissible.   **9-036**

A distinction is drawn between active and passive sales bans between licensor and licensee and licensee/licensee active and passive sales bans. Whilst in relation to the former, passive sales bans are permitted, they are not in relation to the latter. The definition of active and passive sales bans is that set out in the Guidelines on Vertical Restraints.[83]   **9-037**

The third exception is concerned with captive use restrictions.[84] The fourth condition (the "second supply" exception) speaks for itself and such a restriction has always been viewed favourably by the Commission. It is not dissimilar in nature to that of a sub-contracting arrangement which is generally viewed favourably the European Commission.[85]   **9-038**

Restriction on licensee exploiting their own technology and doing R&D

Any restraint which has as its object the restriction of the licensee's ability to exploit its own technology or the restriction of the ability of any of the parties to the agreement to carry out research and development is considered a hard core restriction (where between competing undertakings) unless such latter restriction is indispensable to prevent the disclosure of the licensed know-how to third parties. As said in the 2014 Guidelines, the licensee must be unrestricted in the use of its competing technology provided that it does not make use of the technology rights licensed from the licensor.[86]   **9-039**

The Commission takes a broad view of what clauses restrict a licensee's ability to exploit its own technology. Thus, it does not include just express terms in an agreement. It covers any agreements whose effect is to discourage a licensee from using their own technology. Therefore, the charging of royalties on the licensee's products, regardless as to whether they use the licensed technology, would fall foul of art.4(1)(d).[87]   **9-040**

Hard core restrictions for non-competing undertakings

Where licences are entered into between undertakings that do not compete, unsurprisingly, a more relaxed approach to hardcore restrictions is taken by the TTBE.   **9-041**

---

[82]   art.4.1(c).
[83]   See 2014 Guidelines, para.108.
[84]   2014 Guidelines, para.111. These are discussed in more detail para.8-322.
[85]   See para.8-419.
[86]   2014 Guidelines, para.116.
[87]   Guidelines on Technology Transfer Agreements [2014] OJ C89/3, para.101.

Price fixing

9-042   Unlike with price fixing clauses between competitors, whilst the TTBE bans attempts by undertakings to a technology transfer licence to restrict the other party's ability to determine prices, such is without prejudice to the possibility of imposing a maximum sale price or recommending a sale price, provided that the latter does not amount to a fixed or minimum sale price as a result of pressure from, or incentives offered by, any of the parties. The risk of co-ordination of pricing between non-competitors is less than for competitors as indeed is the consequence.

Sales restrictions

9-043   The TTBE's approach to sales restrictions is to generally permit such provided that market share requirements are satisfied. Thus, active sales restrictions on licensor and licensee are permitted. This is justified on the basis that active sales restrictions promote investments, no-price competition and improvements in the quality of services provided by the licensees by solving free rider problems and hold-up problems.[88]

9-044   However, when it comes to passive sales, the TTBE reverses its position. Thus, passive sales are prohibited save in certain specific circumstances. The 2014 TTBE represents a hardening of the Commission's stance from the 2004 TTBE which permitted passive sales bans between licensees during the first two years in which licensees sold products manufactured under licence. This exception has been removed. In fact, the old provision was not fit for purpose. It is the new licensee into a particular territory who needs protection from established mature licensees in other territories. With the advent of the Internet, this is a real threat. If such obligations exist, then it is likely that the undertakings will need to seek individual exemption or self-certify.

9-045   Thus passive sales restrictions (whether into territories or to customers) are prohibited save in the following five circumstances:

(i)   the restriction of passive sales into an exclusive territory or to an exclusive customer group reserved for the licensor,

(ii)   the obligation to produce the contract products only for its own use provided that the licensee is not restricted in selling the contract products actively and passively as spare parts for its own products,

(iii)   the obligation to produce the contract products only for a particular customer, where the licence was granted in order to create an alternative source of supply for that customer,

(iv)   the restriction of sales to end-users by a licensee operating at the wholesale level of trade, and

(v)   the restriction of sales to unauthorised distributors by the members of a selective distribution system.

9-046   The first exception is justified on the grounds that such restraints promote pro-competitive dissemination of technology and integration of technology into the production assets of the licensee. It is not necessary for the licensor to be actually producing with the licensed technology in the territory or for the customer group

---

[88]   2014 Guidelines, para.120.

in question.[89] Thus, the licensor is entitled to preserve the territory or customer group for later exploitation.[90] What is the position once that reserved territory is then subsequently licensed to another licensee? Does the passive sales ban on the first licensee cease to be lawful? It is tempting to say that the deliberate removal of the exception in the 2014 TTBE for passive sales between licensees means that such would indeed remove the protection of the TTBE. However, it is precisely the new licensee (i.e. the one subsequently licensed by the licensor) who needs protection from the established licensee. The safe route is for licensors to provide that upon allocation of a territory reserved to a licensor to another licensee, the first licensee is entitled to carry out passive sales into that new licensee's territory (even if such is commercially undesirable because of the vulnerability of the second licensee to the first licensee's competition).

The second exception is a captive use restriction.[91] The Commission has always **9-047** seen captive use restrictions as a special category and permitted them. Captive use clauses are discussed in general in Ch.8.[92] The proviso is that the licensee should be entitled to actively and passively sell the contract products as spare parts for the products that it has manufactured once such go on the market. It mirrors the same provision for competitors.

The third exception concerns "second supply" which the Commission has again **9-048** always taken a favourable approach to. Once more, it mirrors the same provision for competitors.

The fourth exception reflects the CJEU's decision in *Metro (I)*[93] whereby a licen- **9-049** sor can assign a wholesale function to a licensee as opposed to a retail function.[94] This ensures that the licensed manufacturer-wholesaler concentrates on distributing to retailers rather than to end-users. It should be emphasised that an agreement between distributor and retailer will be governed by the Vertical Agreements Block Exemption regardless of whether the distributor is a manufacturer of the contract goods whereas the agreement between licensor and distributor-manufacturer is covered by the TTBE. As discussed earlier (at para.9-021), this can mean that the "downstream" sale restrictions on a licensee in a manufacturing agreement are covered by the TTBE whilst the implementation of those restrictions by agreements between manufacturer-wholesaler and retailers will be governed by the Vertical Agreements Block Exemption (and its Guidelines).

Selective distribution systems

The fifth exception mirrors that in the Vertical Agreements Block Exemption and **9-050** ensures the integrity of a selective distribution system. It is inherent in such systems that only authorised distributors may distribute products which meet the requirements for a selective distribution system. The fifth exception needs to be read in conjunction with art.4(2)(c) which prohibits restraints whose object is the restriction of active or passive sales to end-users by a licensee which is a member of a selective distribution system and which operates at the retail level, without prejudice to the possibility of prohibiting a member of the system from operating out of an

---

[89] 2014 Guidelines, para.121.
[90] 2014 Guidelines, para.121.
[91] 2014 Guidelines, para.122.
[92] See para.8-322.
[93] (C-26/76) [1977] E.C.R. 1875.
[94] 2014 Guidelines, para.124.

unauthorised place of establishment. Thus, as said in the 2014 Guidelines, this prevents a selective distribution system being combined with exclusive territories or exclusive customer groups if such would lead to a restriction of active or passive sales to end users. The reader who digests these provisions may be forgiven for believing that they are more relevant to analysis of distribution agreements under the Vertical Agreements Block Exemption. It should be remembered that the TTBE only applies where the licensee produces contract products. It is rare that a licensee who operates at the retail level will be a manufacturer. Furthermore, as discussed above, arrangements between a licensee and third parties are governed by the Vertical Agreements Block Exemption.[95]

Excluded restrictions

9-051   The following restrictions are called "excluded restriction". Their effect is not to remove the protection of the TTBE *in toto* but rather that protection does not extend to the restrictions themselves.

Exclusive grantbacks

9-052   Any obligation on a licensee to grant an exclusive licence or to assign rights to a licensor in its own improvements or new applications of the licensed technology is excluded.[96] In the 2004 TTBE, this restriction only applied to *severable* improvements, i.e. improvements that could not be exploited without infringing the IPR in the licensed technology. This distinction has been removed. As said by the 2014 Guidelines, such reduces the licensee's incentive to innovate. Criticism has been made of the failure to retain the distinction between severable and non-severable improvements. However, in the author's view, this is not a valid criticism. Whether severable or non-severable, exclusive grant backs of improvements made by a licensee act as disincentives to the licensee to innovate the licensed technology. Grant backs are discussed more generally in Ch.8.[97]

No challenge clause

9-053   Any "direct or indirect obligation on the licensee not to challenge the validity of intellectual property rights which the licensor holds in the EU, without prejudice to the possibility, in the case of an exclusive licence, of providing for termination of the technology transfer agreement in the event that the licensee challenges the validity of one or more of the licensed intellectual property rights" is an excluded restriction.[98] No challenge clauses have been discussed at length in Ch.8.[99] The material change from the 2004 TTBE is that the exception for the right to terminate in the event of a challenge now only applies where the licence is exclusive. Previously, no distinction had been drawn between whether the licence was exclusive or not. The 2014 TT Guidelines sets out the reasoning for this. As it says, licensees are generally in the best position to determine whether or not an IPR is valid. Thus, no challenge clauses stifle innovation because invalid IPRs should be eliminated.

---

[95]   See para.9-021.
[96]   art.5(1)(a).
[97]   See para.8-304.
[98]   art.5.1(b).
[99]   See para.8-330.

It says that the right to terminate in the event of a challenge can have the same effect as a no-challenge clause, in particular where switching away from the licensor's technology would result in a significant loss to the licensee.[100] However, in the case of exclusive licensors, their reliance and dependence on the exclusive licensee makes them peculiarly vulnerable to a strong licensee being able to challenge the IPR.

Restriction on licensee exploiting their own technology and doing R&D

Where the undertakings party to the agreement are not competing undertakings, **9-054** any direct or indirect obligation limiting the licensee's ability to exploit its own technology or limiting the ability of any of the parties to the agreement to carry out research and development, unless such latter restriction is indispensable to prevent the disclosure of the licensed know-how to third parties, is treated as an excluded restriction.[101] This clause is similar in effect to art.4.1(d) where a similar provision in an agreement between competing undertakings amounts to a hard core restriction. As explained in the 2014 Guidelines, in the case of agreements between non-competitors, the licensee normally does not own a competing technology. Thus, concerns on restricting the licensee from exploiting its own technology should not exist (otherwise they would be competitors). However, it is clear that the Commission recognised that there was a lacuna in its approach. This is because under the TTBE, undertakings are not treated as competitors in the technology market unless they both license out substitutable technology rights.[102] Thus, a licensee who uses its technology only in-house for producing its own products is not treated (under the TTBE) as a competitor on the technology market with the licensor. The effect of the licensee being restricted from exploiting its own technology could adversely affect the downstream market of products incorporating substitutable technologies. Thus, the Commission has taken the safe route of requiring individual examination of such restrictions rather than including them in the TTBE.

Withdrawal in individual cases

In certain situations, the Commission and national competition authorities may **9-055** withdraw the benefit of the block exemption where in a particular case, the technology transfer block exemption has effects which are incompatible with art.101(3) in particular where:

(a) Access of third parties' technologies to the market is restricted. For instance, by the cumulative effect of parallel networks of similar restrictive agreements prohibiting licensees from using third parties' technologies.

(b) Access of potential licensees to the market is restricted. For instance, by the cumulative effect of parallel networks of similar restrictive agreements prohibiting licensors from licensing to other licensees or because the only technology owner licensing out relevant technology rights concludes an

---

[100] paras 134–136.
[101] art.5.2.
[102] 2014 Guidelines, paras 34 and 142.

exclusive license with a licensee who is already active on the product market on the basis of substitutable technology rights.[103]

Transitional provisions

9-056   The 2014 TTBE differs in certain significant respects from the 2004 TTBE—passive sales bans, grant backs and no challenges being the three key changes. These changes represent a hardening of the Commission to technology transfer licences and thus, some licences may fall within the safe harbour provisions of the 2004 TTBE but without the safe harbour provisions of the 2014 TTBE. Thus, the 2014 TTBE stipulates that where agreements satisfied the 2004 TTBE as of 30 April 2014 and were in force then, then they shall enjoy the benefit of the 2004 TTBE until 30 April 2015. Thereafter, all agreements must comply with the 2014 TTBE.[104]

INDIVIDUAL CLAUSES IN TECHNOLOGY TRANSFER LICENCES

9-057   As well as providing general advice as to the approach of the Commission to technology transfer licences under art.101, the 2014 Technology Transfer Guidelines provide detailed guidance to specific clauses including royalty obligations; exclusive and sales licences; sales restrictions; output restrictions; field of use restrictions; captive use; tying and bundling; and non-compete obligations. The advice here whilst primarily relevant to technology transfer agreements is also of general application. Accordingly, these are discussed in Ch.8.[105]

---

[103] art.6 TTBE.
[104] art.10.
[105] See para.8-250, et seq.

CHAPTER 10

INTELLECTUAL PROPERTY AND HORIZONTAL AGREEMENTS

TABLE OF CONTENTS

INTRODUCTION

This chapter considers the approach of competition law to issues concerning **10-001** intellectual property in horizontal agreements. By horizontal agreements, one normally means agreements entered into between undertakings who are actual or potential competitors.[1] However, it is also used to mean agreements entered into between persons *at the same level in the supply chain* (i.e. between two manufacturers). In the author's view, the proper definition of horizontal agreements is agreements which are entered into between undertakings to co-ordinate their business activities *at a particular level in the supply chain*. Normally these undertakings will be actual or potential competitors.

Such agreements often give rise to greater concerns than vertical agreements **10-002** precisely because they are co-ordinating behaviour between undertakings who are typically actual or potential competitors. Thus, if three undertakings competed head-to-head in a product market, then it is likely that such will produce fierce competition. If suddenly two of those undertakings entered into a co-operation agreement, this is most likely to have the effect of co-ordinating their behaviour and lessening competition between them in the product market. However, horizontal agreements can be pro-competitive where they combine complementary activities, skills or assets.[2] Such permits the sharing of risk, saving costs, increasing investments and increasing innovation. It will be appreciated that such is more likely to be the case where undertakings with small market shares wish to co-

---

[1] See Horizontal Cooperation Guidelines [2011] OJ C11/1, para.1. The imprecision in which the phrase is used is evident indeed in para.1. It refers to horizontal agreements being between actual or potential competitors but then goes on to say that one can have horizontal agreements between non-competitors—being two companies active in the same product market but in different geographic markets. This definition could include a domestic manufacturer and foreign distributor operating in the same product market who would not normally be considered in a horizontal relationship.

[2] Guidelines, para.2.

operate so as to permit them to develop a product that is beyond their individual resources. However, if two undertakings with large market shares enter into the same arrangements, it is much more likely that this will have anti-competitive effects because these undertakings are much more likely to have the resources to develop the products independently and thus the effect of horizontal co-operation is to reduce the number of different products coming onto the market.

10-003   The purpose of this chapter is not to consider in full the anti- or pro-competitive effects of horizontal agreements. Such is beyond the scope of this book. Instead, it focuses on agreements which are likely to have a significant IP element to them. In particular, it considers research and development agreements and manufacturing specialisation agreements where the generation of IP and IP licensing plays a central role. However, other horizontal co-operation agreements which involve IP can also cause issues. For instance, parties may "pool" their patents or other technological IPRs to license them as a package of IPRs to third parties. Such ventures may unlock technologies and thus be pro-competitive (e.g. where a technology is protected by overlapping IPRs owned by a number of parties). In other cases, they may cause excessive co-ordination on the marketplace. This chapter also looks at the very real competition issues generated by the development via horizontal co-operation of technological standards. In particular it considers IPR issues arising out of the adoption (de jure or de facto) of technological standards in a particular industry and the emphasis in EU competition law on owners of "gateway" IPR to those technological standards permitting access to them via "FRAND" (Fair, Reasonable and Non-discriminatory) licensing.

10-004   Whilst IPR issues in agreements will often be of particular importance, it would be wrong to suggest that clauses relating to IPR are decisive in the determination of whether an agreement complies with EU competition law. Analysis of the competitive effect of horizontal co-operation agreements must be done as a whole. It may be that IPR clauses are necessary ancillary restraints to ensure that a generally pro-competitive agreement works.[3] Thus, an IPR clause in one agreement may be objectionable but in another agreement, permissible.

10-005   This chapter considers the EU competition approach to horizontal agreements generally. In this regard, the EU Commission has published Guidelines to Horizontal Co-operation Agreements which provide detailed guidelines to the approach of competition law to such agreements. In particular, the Guidelines consider agreements concerning technological standards. The guidance that the Guidelines provide on the formation of technological standards should be read together with the guidance from the 2014 Technology Transfer Guidelines on patent pools. They are thus discussed together at the end of this chapter.

10-006   There are two relevant block exemptions—the Research and Development Block Exemption and the Specialisation Block Exemption. Both were introduced in 2010 to replace earlier expired block exemptions. Furthermore, there are a number of old Commission decisions concerning R&D agreements. In recent times, the existence of the Modernisation Regulation (which permits courts to exempt agreements) and the publication of detailed guidelines plus block exemptions has meant that the need for companies to seek individual exemption has substantially reduced. Accordingly, there are very few cases now from the European Commission whereby individual exemption is granted or refused. Whilst the old cases provide some guid-

---

[3]   For "ancillary restraints", see para.8-042.

ance as to the analysis to be taken, it must be remembered that the Commission's approach to the analysis of the competitive effects of agreements has matured substantially over the decades and is now firmly rooted in economic analysis. In earlier days of the EU, a more formalistic approach was taken to the determination of the competitive effects of such agreements. Thus, not too much reliance should be placed on such decisions.

HORIZONTAL CO-OPERATION AGREEMENTS

The Commission has now developed considerable experience in assessing the **10-007** competitive effects of horizontal co-operation agreements ("HCA"). In 2001, it issued Guidelines on the applicability of the then art.101 to Horizontal Co-operation Agreements ("the Guidelines").[4] This in turn has now been replaced in 2010 by the current version of its Guidelines on Horizontal Co-operation Agreements.[5] The Guidelines provide detailed guidance about the approach to the competitive analysis of HCAs. Where a HCA is a R&D agreement or a specialisation agreement, it should be read in conjunction with the block exemptions which apply to such agreements. New block exemptions for both of these types of agreement were published in 2010—in the same year as the Guidelines. The Guidelines and the block exemptions provide a very full and detailed guide to the competitive analysis of such agreements.

Many HCAs take the form of a joint venture. From the outset, it is necessary to **10-008** distinguish between concentrative joint ventures and co-operative joint ventures. Where undertakings set up a fully functional autonomous economic entity which is intended to operate on a lasting basis, then the undertakings have, in effect, merged their efforts into an independent third party rather than chosen to co-operate (these are known *as full-function joint ventures*). This is important from the competition lawyer's viewpoint because concentrative joint ventures are considered differently by EU law and the Commission to co-operative joint ventures. In short, concentrative joint ventures are treated, for the purpose of analysis, as a merger. Thus, they are governed by the Merger Regulation.[6] Therefore, when considering a joint venture, it is important from the outset to determine whether it is concentrative or co-operative. This chapter does not consider IP issues in the context of mergers.

HCAs which are JVs come in many shapes and sizes. From the IPR lawyer's **10-009** viewpoint, the most important JVs are as follows:

(a) joint R&D;
(b) joint production;
(c) joint marketing; and
(d) a combination of the above.

In the case of pure joint marketing JVs, such are not considered in this chapter **10-010** as they will rarely involve any licensing of IPR other than trade marks. It is rare to have pure joint marketing JVs. When considering HCAs which are JVs,

---

[4] Notice on Guidelines on the Applicability of Article 81 to Horizontal Cooperation Agreements [2001] OJ C3/02. This replaced the previous Notice—Notice on the Assessment of Cooperative Joint Ventures [1993] OJ C 43/2, para.3.
[5] See Horizontal Cooperation Guidelines [2011] OJ C11/1.
[6] Reg.139/2004 [2004] OJ L24/1–22 art.3(4).

competition/IPR lawyers should carry out the following checklist:

(1) Is the JV concentrative or co-operative? (If concentrative, the Merger Regulation 139/2004[7] may apply.)

(2) Could the JV infringe art.101(1)? If in doubt, examine the Guidelines on Horizontal Cooperation.

(3) If yes or in doubt as to whether it infringes art.101(1):
   (a) Does the Research and Development Block Exemption apply?
   (b) Does the Specialisation Block Exemption apply?
   (c) Does the Technology Transfer Block Exemption apply?

(4) If not, it will be necessary to conduct an individual analysis of the competitive effects of the HCA by reference principally to the Guidelines.

10-011 Aside from joint venture agreements, undertakings will often enter into agreements for the setting up of a technological standard and to this end, will pool their patents or other IPRs to permit third parties who wish to make use of the standard to obtain as a one-stop-shop a bundle of licences. Standardisation agreements and patent pools are considered at the end of this chapter.

CONCENTRATIVE JOINT VENTURE?

10-012 In the Merger Reg.139/2004 art.3(4) states:

"The creation of a joint venture performing on a lasting basis all the functions of an autonomous economic entity shall constitute a concentration within [the meaning of the Merger Regulation]."

10-013 Generally, this will require notification to the Commission under the Regulation.[8] The Commission has issued a Consolidated Jurisdictional Notice[9] which explains the difference between full-function joint ventures and co-operative joint ventures. In essence, for the determination of whether a joint venture is full-functioning and thus to be considered under the Merger Regulation, careful consideration must be paid to whether the JV has sufficient resources to operate independently on the market, its activities go beyond taking over a specific function of the parents' business activities and how lasting the JV is intended to be.[10] As said in the Consolidated Jurisdictional Notice:

"(92) Article 3(4) provides in addition that the creation of a joint venture performing on a lasting basis all the functions of an autonomous economic entity (so called full-function joint ventures) shall constitute a concentration within the meaning of the Merger Regulation. The full-functionality criterion therefore delineates the application of the Merger Regulation for the creation of joint ventures by the parties, irrespective of whether such a joint venture is created as a 'greenfield operation' or whether the parties contribute assets to the joint venture which they previously owned individually. In these circumstances, the joint venture must fulfil the full-functionality criterion in order to constitute a concentration.

(93) The fact that a joint venture may be a full-function undertaking and therefore

---

[7] [2004] OJ L24/1.

[8] A detailed examination of EU law relating to mergers and acquisitions is outside the scope of this book.

[9] Commission Consolidated Jurisdictional Notice under Council Regulation (EC) No 139/2004 on the control of concentrations between undertakings [2008] OJ C95/1.

[10] Consolidated Jurisdictional Notice, paras 94–109.

economically autonomous from an operational viewpoint does not mean that it enjoys autonomy as regards the adoption of its strategic decisions. Otherwise, a jointly controlled undertaking could never be considered a full-function joint venture and therefore the condition laid down in Article 3(4) would never be complied with.[11] It is therefore sufficient for the criterion of full-functionality if the joint venture is autonomous in operational respect."

The General Court has also considered the predecessor to art.3(4), namely **10-014** art.3(2) in the old Merger Regulation. In *Assicurazioni Generali SpA & Unicredito v EC Commission*,[12] the General Court said that:

"it follows from the wording of Article 3 that the creation of a joint venture is covered by Regulation No 4064/89 only if it enjoys operational autonomy and its creation does not have as its object or effect the co-ordination of the competitive behaviour of the undertakings concerned. If one of those conditions is not satisfied, the joint venture is classified as co-operative and is treated as an agreement."[13]

CO-OPERATIVE HCAs AND ART.101

General approach taken by the Commission

This section is concerned with whether HCAs which do not amount to full- **10-015** function joint ventures—in particular R&D, production and commercialisation agreements between undertakings—will fall within art.101. Whilst not law, the Guidelines to Horizontal Cooperation Agreements[14] must be the advisor's primary reference material. They represent the Commission's approach to such agreements and the distillation of decades of experience in considering the competitive effects of such agreements. Decisions of the Commission are also of assistance, although the older they are, the less reliable they are as a guide. This is because the Guidelines represent the current approach taken by the Commission to reflect the greater reliance on economic criteria that the General Court and CJEU have placed in their decisions.[15] Old decisions of the Commission tended to show rather more formalistic approaches to contractual restraints in JV agreements.

The Guidelines say that they are concerned with agreements between undertak- **10-016** ings which are actual or potential competitors.[16] The Guidelines state that main areas of concern are where HCAs limit competition by: limiting the possibility of the parties competing against each other; requiring the parties to contribute such assets that their decision-making independence is appreciably reduced; or affecting the parties' financial interests in such a way that their decision-making independence is appreciably reduced.[17] However, as acknowledged by the Guidelines, HCAs in the field of R&D and specialisation can be pro-competitive by permitting complementary skills or assets to be the source of substantial efficiencies in R&D and specialisation agreements. In simple terms, HCAs which permit the parties to the agreements to "unlock" technologies, product markets, research capabilities, etc. are

---

[11] The Guidelines here cite *Cementbouw v Commission* (T-282/02) [2006] E.C.R. II-319 at [62].
[12] *Assicurazioni Generali SpA & Unicredito v EC Commission* (T-87/96) [1999] E.C.R. II-0203.
[13] See [67].
[14] *Horizontal Cooperation Guidelines* [2011] OJ C11/1.
[15] See para.8-154, et seq.
[16] See Horizontal Cooperation Guidelines [2011] OJ C11/1, para.1. However, note the imprecision of the decision—see fn.1.
[17] See [33].

viewed positively whereas HCAs which simply reduce the number of effective competing undertakings in a particular product or service market by allowing such parties to co-operate rather than to compete are viewed negatively.

Research and Development Agreements

10-017   The Guidelines provide detailed guidance as to the approach to be taken to the competitive analysis of R&D agreements where such are not fully-functioning JVs. As they say, R&D agreements vary in form and scope and range from outsourcing R&D activities to the joint improvement of existing technologies and co-operation concerning R&D and the marketing of completely new products. The Guidelines apply to all forms of R&D agreements, including R&D agreements which concern the production or commercialisation of the R&D results (i.e. downstream restrictions).[18]

10-018   As with all forms of analysis under competition law, it is important to identify the markets that will be affected or potentially affected by the R&D agreements. R&D agreements not only may affect product markets but may also affect technology markets and competition in innovation (sometimes called the "innovation market"). If the R&D agreement is limited in ambition and concerned with the improvement of existing products, it is necessary to identify the relevant product market for existing products and close substitutes for those products.[19] In this sense, the analysis of the anti-competitive effects is fairly orthodox. Of importance is whether the proposed improvements to those products will in themselves be in the same product market as the unimproved products. However, even if the improved product is a radical improvement on existing products, the product may not compete with existing products but may still be used in an existing product market. Thus, the Guidelines give an example of the development of a new type of engine to be used in cars. In such cases, if the parties to the R&D agreement have market power for cars as well as engines (i.e. there is vertical integration), analysis may need to consider the engine market (and the new engine may be such an improvement as not to compete with existing engines, e.g. electric engines vs. internal combustion engines) as electric cars may compete with internal combustion engine cars.[20]

10-019   As well as the product market, it is necessary to consider the technology market. R&D agreements are often concerned with the development of new technology. Such technology may be used in products but may also be marketed separately from the products to which they relate. For instance, the R&D agreement may be concerned with a new efficient process for manufacturing steel. In such cases, it may be that the parties are more interested in licensing the technology (e.g. if they are not steel manufacturers). In such circumstances, the technology market will consist of the IPRs that are licensed and close substitutes to that technology, e.g. in the above example, processes that will compete with the improved method for manufacturing steel.[21]

10-020   Finally, and unique to R&D agreements, R&D co-operation may not only affect competition in product or technology markets but may also affect competition in innovation and the development of new product markets. Competition law is concerned with the development of new technologies. The Guidelines give two

---

[18]   Guidelines, para.111.
[19]   Guidelines, para.113.
[20]   Guidelines, para.115.
[21]   Guidelines, para.116.

scenarios. In the first scenario, it refers to the pharmaceutical industry and the fact that in that industry, it is possible to identify at an early state competing R&D "poles". Thus, the pharmaceutical industry may be focussed on developing a drug for curing a particular disease. In such circumstances, the concern is that there are a sufficient number of independent R&D poles. This analysis is complex because it may be that without the R&D agreement, neither party would be able to sustain their own independent R&D poles (e.g. because of blocking IPRs or individually, the parties lack the resources to carry out an expensive and long-term R&D program). Where however, both businesses have credible R&D research programs, the R&D agreement may reduce the number of competing R&D poles working to the same or similar goal. The R&D program may act as a disincentive to development of new cures because it would mean (if the results are to be shared) that neither party has any fear of what the other party may develop in the field of R&D. Thus, such analysis is complex but considering the effect of the agreement on the number of credible R&D poles and also potentially on a new product market which the results of the R&D program may create.[22] In the second scenario, the Guidelines say it may not be easy to identify R&D poles. In such circumstances, the Guidelines say that the Commission will not try and assess the impact on the R&D agreement on the innovation market but will restrict analysis to existing product and/or technology markets.[23]

The Guidelines set out the main competition concerns for R&D agreements as follows: **10-021**

> "127. R&D co-operation can restrict competition in various ways. First, it may reduce or slow down innovation, leading to fewer or worse products coming to the market later than they otherwise would. Secondly, on product or technology markets the R&D co-operation may reduce significantly competition between the parties outside the scope of the agreement or it may make anti-competitive coordination on those markets likely, thereby leading to higher prices. A foreclosure problem may only arise in the context of co-operation involving at least one player with a significant degree of market power (which does not necessarily amount to dominance) for a key technology and the exclusive exploitation of the results."

They elaborate on the above. They say that most R&D agreements do not fall   **10-022** under art.101 and this is particularly true of agreements relating to co-operation in R&D at an early stage far removed from the exploitation of possible results.[24] Moreover, they say that R&D co-operation between non-competitors does not generally give rise to restrictive effects on competition.[25] The Guidelines say that in general a distinction has to be drawn between pure R&D agreements and agreements providing for more comprehensive co-operation involving different stages of the exploitation of results (that is say, licensing, production or marketing).[26] These can be considered "downstream" restrictions. The Guidelines also say that R&D agreements are only likely to give rise to restrictive effects on competition where the parties to the co-operation have market power on existing markets and/or competition with respect to innovation is appreciably reduced.[27] The Guidelines also

---

[22] Guidelines, paras 120–121.
[23] Guidelines, para.122.
[24] Guidelines, para.129. See also para.132.
[25] Guidelines, para.130.
[26] Guidelines, para.137.
[27] Guidelines, para.133.

give guidance on the application of art.101(3) to R&D agreements found to fall within art.101(1).[28] Helpfully, the Guidelines give examples of certain hypothetical factual situations and the analysis that would be brought to bear on those examples under art.101.[29]

10-023 In summary, as is its modern approach, the Commission will adopt a "rule of reason" approach to HCAs which involve R&D. The mere fact that there are contractual restraints which formally restrict the freedom of the parties is not sufficient to cause the HCA to fall within art.101. Generalising somewhat, the Commission's approach to such agreements as set out in the Guidelines is as follows:

(a) HCAs between non-competitors or competitors without sufficient resources to carry out independently the objectives of the R&D agreement will rarely fall within art.101.

(b) R&D agreements by undertakings with small market shares in product or technology markets are likely to be viewed more favourably.

(c) In certain structured markets where there are clear R&D poles, the Commission is concerned to ensure that there is a "critical mass" of credible R&D poles and will examine carefully the ability of those undertakings with those R&D poles to carry out independent R&D in the subject matter of the R&D agreement without the need for co-operation.

10-024 Not all R&D agreements between HCAs are likely to contain significant IPR provisions. Thus, this chapter concentrates on the types of JVs which are likely to contain significant IPR provisions and be of interest to the IPR advisor: R&D agreements (including the development of technical standards) and joint production JVs. The formation of JVs to license as a package (e.g. "patent pools") IPR belonging to the parent undertakings is discussed later in this chapter.[30]

IPR licensing provisions in R&D agreements

10-025 R&D JVs will invariably have substantial licensing provisions. These will relate to both existing IPR rights owned by the participating undertakings and also to the ownership and exploitation of IPR rights generated by the JV. As the Guidelines make clear, the prevailing analysis must be an economic one. In that sense, consideration of licensing provisions will not take place *in vacuo*. The Guidelines make it clear that IPR licensing is one part of the competitive analysis. However, certain principles can be established from historic decisions of the Commission as to licensing arrangements in R&D HCAs. The Guidelines are less clear on the effect of individual IPR clauses than these decisions and it is helpful to see how the Commission has approached individual IPR clauses in R&D and HCAs.

Licensing relationship between parent undertakings and JVC

10-026 Where the parties to a R&D agreement set up a JVC, the agreement will often contain licensing provisions between the parents and the JVC. In practice, parent companies will often have to license a JVC set up for the purposes of R&D and exploitation. This in itself will not constitute a restriction of competition. Often, the parent firms will seek to grant exclusivity in the relevant technological field on the

---

[28] Guidelines, paras 141–146.
[29] Guidelines, paras 147–149.
[30] See para.10-108.

JVC so as to make it commercially viable and prevent the parent companies from competing with it.

The Commission has said that the grant of the exclusive right to exploit know-how of the parent companies to a JVC to manufacture a new product for the life of the joint venture is not caught by art.101(1) where: **10-027**

- the existing know-how of both parents plus further R&D are necessary to develop, manufacture and market the new product as well as the machinery and technology linked to it;
- there are no explicit restrictions on the joint venture's activities with respect to pricing, volume, customers and territory, even though the new product may compete to some extent with the output of one of the parents; and
- the exclusivity is limited to the narrowly defined field relevant to the manufacture of the new product and the parents are free to develop closely related and possibly competing products.[31]

Restrictions on the licensing by the JVC of results generated by the R&D project back to the parent companies are often permissible to ensure the proper working of the joint venture. Thus, restrictions on a JVC from licensing its parents where such use was likely to conflict with the purposes of the JVC was not anti-competitive.[32] In another case, the Commission exempted an arrangement whereby the JVC granted back to the parent companies geographic-specific exclusive licences of the results of the R&D so that the European partner was given an exclusive licence for the Community and America.[33] **10-028**

Often, a R&D agreement will cater for the use of technology transferred to a JVC or generated by the JVC upon termination of the R&D agreement. In this regard, the Commission is keen to ensure that the parents are not denied use of technological know-how or rights that they previously had access to. Thus, a ban on parties who withdrew from a JV exploiting for five years know-how belonging to the JVC, including know-how that the retiring party had transferred to the JVC, was held to restrict competition because it made it more difficult for the party to compete in the field of co-operation once it had left the joint venture.[34] Conversely, a more limited restriction on parent companies that upon the breakup of the JVC, they would only be able to use the other party's know-how in the field of the R&D agreement, was held to be a necessary consequence of such an agreement and thus fell outside art.101(1).[35] A prohibition on a parent who withdraws from a R&D JV from using the technology generated by the JV will normally constitute an ancillary restriction necessary for the existence of the JV. Finally, the reader should be aware that **10-029**

---

[31] *ODIN* [1990] OJ L209/15; [1991] 4 C.M.L.R. 832 at [30]–[31]. The judgment is somewhat confusing (see [32]) as to whether the parent companies granted exclusive or non-exclusive licences to the joint venture company. In fact, within the field of the agreement, the parents granted exclusive rights to the joint venture company.

[32] *ODIN* [1990] OJ L209/15; [1991] 4 C.M.L.R. 832 at [30].

[33] *Re the Agreements between BBC Brown and Boveri and NGK Insulators Ltd* [1988] OJ L301/68; [1989] 4 C.M.L.R. 610.

[34] *Carbon Gas Technologie* [1983] OJ L376/67; [1984] 2 C.M.L.R. 275. However, the provision was exempted as it afforded a limited degree of protection against competition from former shareholders or from outside companies without which the object of the co-operation could not have been attained—see [15].

[35] *ODIN* [1990] OJ L209/15; [1991] 4 C.M.L.R. 832 at [33].

if the JV is a full-functioning JV, independent of the parents, then the competitive effect will need to be considered under the Merger Regulation.[36]

Payment of royalties between participating undertakings in a joint venture

10-030   Agreements will sometimes provide for the cross-payment of royalties between undertakings for exploitation of the technology generated by the R&D efforts. In effect, this amounts to co-operation at the market stage and the Commission is suspicious of too much co-operation at the marketing stage. In *Beecham/Parke-Davis*,[37] the Commission took the view that equal contributions to joint research expenditure did not necessarily justify sharing the profit from mutual marketing exploitation and insisted on the removal of a clause which provided for fixed royalties to be paid by one party to the other for sales of the licensed product. The Commission said that it might be fair for one party to pay royalties to the other where one party is unable, particularly for technical reasons, to exploit the results. The Commission held that as both parties manufactured and sold world-wide, there was no reason why results should not be exploited by both parties and thus such cross-royalty payments were unnecessary. If the cross-royalty payments are so structured as to be likely to result in the partitioning of markets, then such a provision will fall within art.101(1) and be unexemptable.[38] Certainly, obligations to share royalties received from third parties can be anti-competitive where the parties individually license out the results of the R&D as such an obligation acts as a disincentive to competitive licensing between the participating parties and punishes the party best able and/or who makes the greatest effort to exploit the licensed technology via licensing.

Restrictions on licensing of third parties

10-031   The Commission generally disapproves of restrictions on the parties licensing third parties. A general limitation on a party's freedom to grant licences to third parties for patents developed through R&D JVs has been held to infringe art.101(1).[39] This will be invariably the case where one party requires the consent of the other in order to license third parties. The anti-competitive effect of such restrictions will be enhanced in an oligopolistic market where there are few manufacturers in the relevant product market. However, each case will depend on its facts. Thus in *EMI/Jungheinrich*,[40] EMI, a manufacturer of electronic control systems, and Jungheinrich, a manufacturer of bulk handling systems, entered into a joint R&D agreement for the development of electronic control devices for use by Jungheinrich in the field of driverless[41] tractor and forklift systems. Under the agreement, Jungheinrich was to make financial contributions to research undertaken by EMI.

---

[36]   See para.10-012.

[37]   *Beecham/Parke Davis* [1979] OJ L70/11; [1979] 2 C.M.L.R. 157.

[38]   *Research and Development* [1971] C.M.L.R. D31 (parties obliged to pay royalties to each other if they marketed R&D products in territories reserved to the other).

[39]   See *Henkel/Colgate, 8th Report on Competition Policy*, paras 89–90. For original decision granting exemption, see *Henkel/Colgate* [1972] OJ L14/14. See also, *Beecham/Parke Davis* [1979] OJ L70/11, [1979] 2 C.M.L.R. 157; *Continental Gummi-Werke and Michelin* [1988] OJ L305/33, [1989] 4 C.M.L.R. 920.

[40]   *EMI/Jungheinrich* [1978] 1 C.M.L.R. 395, Press Release, 2 December 1977.

[41]   It would appear that any third party interested in obtaining a licence for the RHT (flat tyre) which

The Commission approved a provision that EMI would not be able to grant licences to third parties without Jungheinrich's approval in relation to patents which would be obtained from the joint development for use in the field of driverless tractor and forklift systems, but disapproved of such consent being required for use outside such a field. In *Continental Gummi-Werke and Michelin*,[42] the Commission held that where a JVC in a R&D agreement was required to consult with both parent companies before it granted licences to third parties, such had the practical effect of ensuring that the consent of both parties was required before a third party was licensed, and thus fell within art.101(1), although it was exempted under art.101(3) as it meant a simplification of administrative procedure.

Commission decisions

Owing to the case-by-case analysis, it is helpful to consider the Commission's approach to R&D agreements between parties with substantial market power. This can be done by examining actual cases of the Commission and also four examples given in the Guidelines. It should be emphasised that the reasoning of the Commission in old cases is not necessarily a guide to how the Commission would now consider such cases. In particular, the reasoning tends to be somewhat formalistic without real economic analysis. The *ODIN* case study is a useful case for intellectual property advisors because of the licensing provisions in that JV. **10-032**

Beecham/Parke-Davis[43]

Two large pharmaceutical firms entered into a collaborative venture for the development of a product to control the impairment of blood circulation. The Commission held that the collaboration between the parties at every stage of the R&D meant that neither party could obtain a competitive advantage over the other at any point in the innovative cycle. **10-033**

Bayer/Gist-Brocades[44]

Two large companies involved in penicillin manufacture notified a hybrid R&D/ specialisation agreement to the Commission. The Commission held that an obligation on both parties to the agreement to license each other for new, independently developed processes (as opposed to pursuant to the agreement) restricted competition because it prevented either of the two firms from obtaining a competitive advantage over the other in research.[45] **10-034**

---

was the subject of the joint venture would have had to obtain licences from the parent companies as well, and thus in any event, the consent of the parents was necessary. See also, *Re the Agreements between BBC Brown and Boveri and NGK Insulators Ltd* [1988] OJ L301/68; [1989] 4 C.M.L.R. 610, where a provision requiring the consent of the parties before sub-licences were granted was exempted—discussed at para.10-045.

42 [1988] OJ L305/33; [1989] 4 C.M.L.R. 920.
43 [1979] 2 C.M.L.R. 157.
44 [1976] 1 C.M.L.R. D98.
45 The practical consequence of cross-licensing provisions in an agreement is that they will discourage parties from conducting their own R&D programme. They will thus infringe art.101(1)—see *Henkel/Colgate* reported in the 8th Report on Competition Policy [1972] OJ L14/14, paras 89–91 (an obligation on a party to communicate the results of its own research to the other party in an agreement between parties who were amongst the largest washing powder/detergent manufacturers

ICI/Enichem[46]

10-035   An Italian and a British company concluded an agreement establishing a joint venture company for research, development, production and distribution of PVC. The main reason for the agreement was that it allowed the activities of the parent companies to be rationalised in the PVC sector. The joint venture company set up (EVC) was barely independent of the parent companies. There was no transfer of assets to EVC and each parent company retained full ownership of production facilities, patents, know-how and research centres. Thus, the effective co-operation of the joint venture company was highly dependent upon the close co-operation of the parent companies. This restricted the parent companies' ability to maintain effective independent research efforts and thus fell within art.101(1).

Alcatel Espace/ANT[47]

10-036   Alcatel and ANT were rival manufacturers of satellite communications equipment. They entered into a co-operation agreement providing for joint R&D, production and marketing in this field. Essentially, the agreement was to ensure that the parties did not duplicate their R&D efforts and combined their resources for the exploitation of the results through rationalisation of manufacturing, servicing and testing of such systems as well as co-operation in bidding and negotiations for contracts in the field. Both parties agreed to license all necessary patents and know-how to each other on a royalty-free and non-exclusive basis. Exploitation of the results was to be on a co-operative basis, including one party sub-contracting to the other party as much as possible. The parties' combined market share was less than 20 per cent of the Community product market. The Commission held that the effect of the agreement was to:

> "alter the previously autonomous position of the parties relating to planning, financing, R&D, production and marketing of the equipment covered by the agreement, the parties no longer being able to act independently."

SOPELEM/Vickers[48]

10-037   This concerned a R&D between undertakings with small market shares, where both parties manufactured a wide range of microscopes, of which some were competing with each other but most were complementary. There was overlap of the parties' instruments only at an elementary level. However, the Commission held that both parties were capable of extending their range of activities and becoming competitors. The parties' combined market share of microscopes in the Common Market was about 3.5 per cent. Furthermore, competition in the field of microscopy was strong, with three manufacturers holding a combined market share of 50 per cent in the Common Market. The parties set up a joint venture agreement which was aimed at establishing technical co-operation, as well as a future common means of distribution. Furthermore, the parties agreed to standardise their microscopes so that their parts were interchangeable. SOPELEM would have abandoned the production of microscopes if the agreement with Vickers had not been entered into. Each party continued carrying out concurrently its own R&D activities.

---

prevented one party from obtaining a competitive advantage over the other).
[46]   [1988] OJ L50/18.
[47]   [1990] OJ L32/19; [1991] 4 C.M.L.R. 208.
[48]   [1978] OJ L70/47; [1978] 2 C.M.L.R. 146.

The Commission held that the technical co-operation and exchange of expertise **10-038** in R&D would eliminate inter-brand competition between the parties in R&D. It thus infringed art.101(1). However, the Commission exempted the agreement holding that such an agreement would enable SOPELEM and Vickers to secure the development and maintenance of a more comprehensive and advanced range of microscopes. Furthermore, the agreement prevented the parties duplicating each other's results. The distribution system helped rationalise the parties' own distribution costs, which were disproportionately high because of the parties' small market shares. Such would lead to a reduction in costs of the microscopes and this would benefit the consumer. The Commission noted that both parents were free to exploit the results of the R&D without restriction after the termination of the agreement. Due to the presence of other manufacturers, the agreement did not eliminate competition in a substantial part of the relevant product market.

ODIN[49]

Non-competing undertakings set up a R&D JVC. Elopak and Metal Box were **10-039** manufacturers of food packaging containers. Elopak primarily supplied cartons for use in the dairy and food industries and integrated systems equipment for filling, packaging and handling these cartons. Metal Box was active in the canning business. The two parties entered into an agreement establishing a joint venture company, ODIN, to carry out R&D of a container with a carton base and separate closure which could be filled by an aseptic process with UHT processed foods. ODIN was also to undertake production and distribution of the new containers and their filling machines. Both parent companies granted licences to ODIN to exploit all their intellectual property rights relevant to the agreement and ODIN was granted an exclusive licence for those rights relating to ODIN's project. The parents were entitled to obtain from ODIN non-exclusive licences but could not use such licences in the field where ODIN was active. The market for the proposed new package was oligopolistic in structure with several undertakings with large market shares and resources.

The Commission held that Elopak and Metal Box were not competitors in activi- **10-040** ties outside the joint venture and were highly unlikely to develop the proposed product on their own. Furthermore, the Commission held that the existence of other substantial undertakings in the product market meant that there was little risk of foreclosure to third parties. The Commission considered the compatibility of certain clauses in the agreement in order to determine whether such clauses were necessary ancillary restraints designed to ensure the starting up and proper functioning of the joint venture. In relation to the licensing clauses, the Commission held that the licensing provisions including the grant of exclusivity to ODIN by the parent companies were necessary and did not go beyond what was required, as there were no restrictions on the joint venture in respect of pricing, volume, customers and territory, and because the exclusivity was limited to the narrowly defined field relevant to the manufacture of the new product.[50] In particular, it distinguished the grant of exclusivity in the joint venture from that of the grant of an exclusive licence in a

---

[49] *ODIN* [1990] OJ L209/15; [1991] 4 C.M.L.R. 832.
[50] *ODIN* [1990] OJ L209/15; [1991] 4 C.M.L.R. 832 at [30]–[31].

licensor/licensee situation or where the licensor was a partner in a joint production venture which competed directly.[51]

Continental/Michelin[52]

10-041   This concerned a R&D agreement between companies with large market shares. Michelin and Continental entered into a co-operation agreement to develop a new run-flat tyre system-the RHT (Reverse Hook Tyre). The agreement was limited in scope, merely providing for exchange of information and division of R&D efforts. Each party was to remain the owner of its own work products. However, the agreement did envisage the setting up of a common entity whose sole function was to exploit the patents and know-how that resulted from the R&D. Each party was to have a worldwide non-exclusive licence covering all such patents and know-how. Third parties would be granted a licence upon request by one of the parties and after consultation. The parties submitted that the purchasing power of the motor vehicle industry being so great and the latter's insistence upon having several independent sources, meant that, in practice, licences would be granted upon reasonable terms. The parties' combined share of the market was over 20 per cent and thus it was not covered by the then current Research and Development Block Exemption.

10-042   The Commission held that the agreement fell within art.101(1), because without the agreement, both parties might have proceeded to develop competing run-flat systems themselves and because of the intended co-ordination on the marketing of the product and the grant of licences to third parties. The parties managed to convince the Commission that joint research was necessary and that Continental alone would not have been able to solve the numerous technical problems. Also, the Commission accepted the fact that the motor vehicle industry would not tolerate a single supplier so as to avoid supply bottlenecks, so that even if Continental had produced the RHT themselves, they would have had to grant a licence to Michelin. The Commission did not consider that there would have been any difference if Continental had developed the RHT alone and licensed Michelin. Either way, the consumer benefitted from the introduction of a run-flat tyre.

10-043   The agreement provided for two different periods of co-operation. The Commission exempted in relation to the R&D agreement a provision that extended the agreement for five years after the first marketing of the RHT, with automatic annual renewal unless terminated. In relation to the exploitation of the RHT, the Commission considered that two years after first marketing was the longest period necessary for attainment of the objectives of the agreement, as the two parties were competitors with strong market positions and co-operation must be restricted particularly strictly to the period essential for the implementation of the programme.

10-044   There was no risk of the elimination of competition in respect of a substantial part of the products in question, as the RHT tyre would compete with other conventional tyres produced by other manufacturers and it was not certain that RHT tyres would replace conventional tyres. Furthermore, the demands of the motor vehicle industry meant that the parties would offer licences to all interested competitors on reasonable terms.

---

[51]   i.e. see *Re the Agreement between Boussois and Interpane mbH* [1987] OJ L50/30, [1988] 4 C.M.L.R. 124; *Mitchell Cotts/Sofiltra* [1987] OJ L41/31, [1988] 4 C.M.L.R. 111.
[52]   *Continental Gummi-Werke and Michelin* [1988] OJ L305/33, [1989] 4 C.M.L.R. 920.

BBC/Brown Boveri[53]

This was a high risk R&D agreement between a German company (BBC) and a **10-045** Japanese company (NGK) setting up a Joint Venture (NEWCO) to develop sodium-sulphur high performance batteries. These batteries were to be used for powering cars and for providing off-peak power in power stations. BBC was the main party, having brought the sodium-sulphur battery to an advanced stage. Such batteries included ceramic parts which BBC was unable to manufacture satisfactorily. Thus, it sought to co-operate with NGK, which was experienced in ceramics. Each parent company granted NEWCO an exclusive licence for existing patents and know-how in the R&D field. NEWCO then granted NGK an exclusive sub-licence for patents and know-how for Japan and the Far East and a similar exclusive sub-licence for BBC in the Community, America and some other countries, both for 15 years. These included active sales bans in each other's territory for 10 years. The granting of sub-licences in each party's territory was subject to the prior consent of the other party which could not be refused without reasonable grounds. NGK and NEWCO were prohibited from carrying out R&D with third parties without BBC's consent.

The Commission exempted the agreement. The co-operation was aimed at **10-046** developing a fundamental technological innovation which could be done more quickly and cheaply on a collaborative basis. The consumer's quality of life would be enhanced, as electrically-driven cars were beneficial to the environment and the battery would play an important role in power stations. The ban on third party R&D was exempted as being necessary to secure the benefits from the joint R&D. The exclusive sub-licence to BBC was deemed indispensable because of the high-risk in marketing the batteries successfully. Competition was not substantially eliminated as electrically driven cars competed with conventional cars.

Asahi/Saint Gobain[54]

Two major glass manufacturers set up an R&D JV to research and develop bi- **10-047** layer (glass/plastic) laminates primarily for the purpose of making improved safety windows. The primary market for this was car manufacturers. The agreement set up a JVC and all relevant technology was exclusively licensed to the JVC. The JVC was not a full functioning entity but the medium in which the parties co-ordinated their activities. The JVC was to have the exclusive rights to license the results of the R&D to third parties or back to the parent undertakings. The co-operation was to extend to joint exploitation of the results, including setting up two pilot factories to manufacture the safety glass. The JV Agreement stated that nothing would prevent or restrict SG and A.G. from engaging in competition with each other in connection with the manufacture, marketing or sale of bi-layer products; however, it restricted the parties from constructing another plant for the production of bi-layer film prior to the construction of the first and second pilot plants and from expanding existing capacity without the prior consent of the other shareholder. The JV agreement lasted for five years after the establishment of the second pilot factory.

The Commission took the view that both undertakings were strong competitors **10-048** in the field of safety glass and both could have carried out the R&D independently.

---

[53] *Re the Agreements between BBC Brown and Boveri and NGK Insulators Ltd* [1988] OJ L301/68; [1989] 4 C.M.L.R. 610.
[54] [1994] OJ C93/3.

The Commission exempted the agreement because of the substantial nature of the JV, the substantial financial risks that were involved and because the automotive industry had strong commercial power which would not permit large profits to be made. Originally, the agreement was to last for 30 years and the JVC would have exclusive licensing rights for the duration of the patents. The Commission took the view that this was too long and thus took the view that five years joint exploitation of the results was sufficient and that, thereafter, the JVC should be dissolved.

Examples in Guidelines

Impact of joint R&D on innovation markets/new product market

10-049   *Situation*

A small research company (Company A) which does not have its own marketing organisation has discovered and patented a pharmaceutical substance based on new technology that will revolutionise the treatment of a certain disease. Company A enters into an R&D agreement with a large pharmaceutical producer, Company B, of products that have so far been used for treating the disease. Company B lacks any similar expertise and R&D programme and therefore would not be able to build such expertise within a relevant timeframe. For the existing products Company B has a market share of around 75 per cent in all Member States, but the patents will expire over the next five years. There exist two other poles of research with other companies at approximately the same stage of development using the same basic new technology. Company B will provide considerable funding and know-how for product development, as well as future access to the market. Company B is granted a licence for the exclusive production and distribution of the resulting product for the duration of the patent. It is expected that the product could be brought to market in five to seven years.

Analysis

The product is likely to belong to a new relevant market. The parties bring complementary resources and skills to the co-operation, and the probability of the product coming to market increases substantially. Although Company B is likely to have considerable market power on the existing market, that market power will be decreasing shortly. The agreement will not lead to a loss in R&D on the part of Company B, as it has no expertise in this area of research, and the existence of other poles of research are likely to eliminate any incentive to reduce R&D efforts. The exploitation rights during the remaining patent period are likely to be necessary for Company B to make the considerable investments needed and Company A has no marketing resources of its own. The agreement is therefore unlikely to give rise to restrictive effects on competition within the meaning of art.101(1). Even if there were such effects, it is likely that the conditions of art.101(3) would be fulfilled.

SME enters into R&D agreement with monopoly producer

10-050   *Situation*

A small research company (Company A) which does not have its own marketing organisation has discovered and patented a new technology that will revolutionise the market for a certain product for which there is a monopoly producer (Company B) worldwide as no competitors can compete with Company B's current technology. There exist two other poles of research with other companies at approximately the same stage of development using the same basic new technology. Company B will provide considerable funding and know-how for product development, as well as future access to the market. Company B is granted an exclusive licence for the use of the technology for the duration of the patent and commits to funding only the development of Company A's technology.

Analysis

The product is likely to belong to a new relevant market. The parties bring complementary resources and skills to the co-operation, and the probability of the product coming to market increases substantially. However, the fact that Company B commits to Company A's new technology may be likely to lead the two competing poles of research to abandon their projects as it could be difficult to receive continued funding once they have lost the most likely potential customer for their technology. In such a situation no potential competitors would be able to challenge Company B's monopoly position in the future. The foreclosure effect of the agreement would then be likely to be considered to give rise to restrictive effects on competition within the meaning of art.101(1). In order to benefit from art.101(3) the parties would have to show that the exclusivity granted would be indispensable to bring the new technology to the market.

R&D between undertakings with substantial market share to improve existing technology in competitive environment

Situation   **10-051**

Two engineering companies that produce vehicle components agree to set up a joint venture to combine their R&D efforts to improve the production and performance of an existing component. The production of that component would also have a positive effect on the environment. Vehicles would consume less fuel and therefore emit less CO_2. The companies pool their existing technology licensing businesses in the area, but will continue to manufacture and sell the components separately. The two companies have market shares in the Union of 15 per cent and 20 per cent on the Original Equipment Manufacturer ("OEM") product market. There are two other major competitors together with several in-house research programmes by large vehicle manufacturers. On the world-wide market for the licensing of technology for those products the parties have shares of 20 per cent and 25 per cent, measured in terms of revenue generated, and there are two other major technologies. The product life cycle for the component is typically two to three years. In each of the last five years one of the major companies has introduced a new version or upgrade.

Analysis

Since neither company's R&D effort is aimed at a completely new product, the markets to consider are those for the existing components and for the licensing of relevant technology. The parties' combined market share on both the OEM market (35 per cent) and, in particular, on the technology market (45 per cent) are quite high. However, the parties will continue to manufacture and sell the components separately. In addition, there are several competing technologies, which are regularly improved. Moreover, the vehicle manufacturers who do not currently license their technology are also potential entrants on the technology market and thus constrain the ability of the parties to profitably raise prices. To the extent that the joint venture has restrictive effects on competition within the meaning of art.101(1), it is likely that it would fulfil the criteria of art.101(3). For the assessment under art.101(3) it would be necessary to take into account that consumers will benefit from a lower consumption of fuel.

Introduction

10-052 In 2010, the Commission introduced a new R&D Block Exemption to replace the old R&D Block Exemption,[56] which was introduced in 1985.[57] The new block exemption builds upon the old block exemption but does not radically alter it. As with all block exemptions, the purpose is to provide a "safe harbour" for R&D agreements that fall within it by exempting such agreements if such agreements did fall within art.101(1). It should be read in conjunction with the Guidelines on Horizontal Cooperation Agreements which has already been discussed above.[58]

10-053 The basic framework of the block exemption is that R&D agreements are "block exempted" under art.101(3) unless they contain hard core anti-competitive provisions. In this sense, the block exemption is similar to the Technology Transfer Block Exemption and the Vertical Agreements Block Exemption which are discussed in other chapters.[59] However, where the market shares of the participants to the R&D agreement exceed 25 per cent and they are competing undertakings, then the block exemption is inapplicable and individual exemption must be sought. Furthermore, a more restrictive approach is taken to contractual terms which restrict the commercial exploitation of the R&D results.

10-054 The legislative mechanism for the R&D Block Exemption is Reg.2821/71[60] which permits block exemptions in the field of research and development. Unlike the other enabling regulation,[61] this is not restricted to agreements between two parties.

10-055 The recitals mirror the approach in the Guidelines. Where relevant, the Recitals are referred to below in relation to the provisions of the block exemption.

10-056 The R&D Block Exemption will expire on 31 December 2022.[62]

R&D agreements

10-057 The basic provision of the R&D Block Exemption exempts "research and development agreements". These are defined as follows:

> (a) "research and development agreement" means an agreement entered into between two or more parties which relate to the conditions under which those parties pursue:
> (i) joint research and development of contract products or contract technologies and joint exploitation of the results of that research and development;
> (ii) joint exploitation of the results of research and development of contract products or contract technologies jointly carried out pursuant to a prior agreement between the same parties;

---

[55] Reg.1217/2010 [2010] OJ L335/36.
[56] Reg.2659/2000 [2000] OJ L304/7.
[57] Reg.418/85 [1985] OJ L 53/5. This expired in 1997 but was extended until 31 December 2001 by Reg.2236/97 [1997] OJ L306/12.
[58] See para.10-017, et seq.
[59] See Chs 9 and 11.
[60] [1971] OJ L285/46.
[61] See para.8-202.
[62] art.9.

(iii)   joint research and development of contract products or contract technologies excluding joint exploitation of the results;

(iv)   paid-for research and development of contract products or contract technologies and joint exploitation of the results of that research and development;

(v)   joint exploitation of the results of paid-for research and development of contract products or contract technologies pursuant to a prior agreement between the same parties; or

(vi)   paid-for research and development of contract products or contract technologies excluding joint exploitation of the results.[63]

This definition makes it clear that the block exemption applies even if the R&D **10-058** agreement seeks to control the "downstream" exploitation of the R&D results.[64] A change from the previous block exemption is the introduction of the concept of "paid-for" R&D agreements. This is defined as R&D whereby the R&D is carried out by one party and financed by a financing party.[65] The financing party must not be a party carrying out any of the R&D activities itself.[66]

Scope of R&D Block Exemption

The R&D Block Exemption states that it applies to R&D agreements contain- **10-059** ing provisions relating to the assignment or licensing of IPRS to one or more of the parties or an entity established by the parties to carry out the joint R&D, paid-for R&D or joint exploitation of the results *provided that those provisions do not constitute the primary object of such agreements but are directly related to and necessary for their implementation.*[67]

Where such is not the case, it is likely that the Technology Transfer Block **10-060** Exemption will need to be considered. This is intended to cover agreements where the primary focus is the licensing of technical IPRs. However, the distinction is not clear cut. Thus, the R&D block exemption does apply to joint exploitation of the results of R&D which were the subject of a prior agreement.[68] Thus, there may be overlap between the two block exemptions and it may be necessary to consider both.[69] However, if the agreement falls within the R&D Block Exemption, then the Technology Transfer Block Exemption is inapplicable.[70]

Conditions for exemption

The R&D Block Exemption sets out a number of conditions for R&D agree- **10-061** ments to benefit from the block exemption. Thus, if the agreement is a pure R&D agreement, then all parties must have access to the final results and any IPRs and

---

[63]   art.1(a).
[64]   "Research and development" is itself defined at art.1(c).
[65]   art.1(p).
[66]   art.1(q).
[67]   art.2(2).
[68]   See para.10-058—art.1(a)(v). See also art.3(4) which refers to joint exploitation only pertaining to results which are protected by IPRs or constitute know how which is indispensable for the manufacture of the contract products or technologies. Thus, it might be said that in such circumstances, the IPRs are central to the joint exploitation of the results and yet will be covered by the R&D Block Exemption.
[69]   See Ch.9.
[70]   See para.9-016.

know-how covering those results.[71] If this is the case, then all parties must be granted access to any pre-existing know-how of the other parties if such is indispensable for the purpose of exploitation of the results.[72] If the R&D agreement covers joint exploitation, it can only cover the joint exploitation of results which are protected by IPRs or constitute know-how which is indispensable to the manufacture of the contract products or technologies.[73] If one party is charged with the manufacture of the contract products by way of specialisation, then that party must be required to fulfil orders for the contract products from other parties to the agreement except where the agreement also provides for joint distribution or where the specialising party is also charged with distributing the contract products.[74]

Non-competing undertakings

10-062   If the parties are not competing undertakings,[75] then the exemption applies for the duration of the agreement. However, if the results are to be jointly exploited, then the exemption only applies for seven years from the date that the contract product or products are first put on the market in the EU.[76] However, provided that the combined market share of the parties does not exceed 25 per cent on the relevant product or technology markets after the expiry of this seven-year period, the block exemption continues to apply.[77]

Competing undertakings

10-063   If two or more of the parties are competing undertakings, then a distinction is drawn between R&D agreements where one party is the financing party and where such is not the case (the former being called "paid-for" R&D agreements).[78]

Non-paid for R&D agreements

10-064   In the case of non-paid-for R&D agreements, then the period of exemption provided for in relation to non-competing undertakings applies but only if the *combined* market share of the parties to the agreement did not, at the date of entry into the R&D agreement, exceed 25 per cent on the relevant product and technology markets.[79]

Paid-for R&D agreements

10-065   In the case of paid-for R&D agreements, then the period of exemption provided for in relation to non-competing undertakings applies but only if, as of the date of entry into the R&D agreement, the *combined* market share of the financing party and all the parties with which the financing party has entered into R&D agree-

---

[71]   art.3(2).
[72]   art.3(3).
[73]   art.3(4).
[74]   art.3(5).
[75]   Defined at art.1(r).
[76]   art.4(1).
[77]   art.4(3).
[78]   NB. the definition of "paid for research and development" means that the financing party cannot also be carrying out the R&D activities—see art.1(q).
[79]   art.4(2)(a).

ments relating to the same contract products or technologies did not exceed 25 per cent on the relevant product and technology markets.[80] This means that it is necessary to consider the market share of undertakings to *other* R&D agreements that the financing party has entered into which relate to the same contract products or technologies.[81] It should be noted that this does not require consideration of *competing* products or technologies. The justification for this approach is set out in the Recitals where it says that anti-competitive foreclosure effects could arise where one party finances several R&D projects carried out by competitors with regard to the same contract products or technologies, in particular where it obtains the exclusive right to exploit the results vis-á-vis the third parties.[82]

Hard core restrictions[83]

The block exemption sets out a number of contractual terms whose "objects" are considered "hard core" by the Commission and will cause the R&D agreement *in toto* to fall outside the block exemption (and be unexemptable, even if individually notified) if such are included in the agreement. The following objects are not permissible. **10-066**

Non-compete outside JV technological field

Where an object of the agreement is the restriction of the freedom of the participating undertakings to carry out research and development independently or in co-operation with third parties in a field unconnected with that to which the research and development relates, or after the completion of the joint research and development or the paid-for research and development, in the field to which it relates or in a connected field, such is considered a hard core restriction.[84] Thus, the only permissible restriction on R&D outside the agreement is during the R&D phase *and* in a connected field. If these two conditions are not satisfied, the restriction on R&D outside the field of the agreement is a hard core restriction. **10-067**

Limitation of output or sales

The block exemption treats as hard core restrictions any agreement which attempts to limit manufacturing output or product sales. This is not defined as being limited to the contract products or services (i.e. those which embody the results of the R&D agreement) but any products or services.[85] There are a number of exceptions to this which include the setting of production targets and sales targets; practices constituting specialisation (i.e. where one party agrees that the other shall manufacture the contract products); and importantly, the restriction of the freedom of parties to manufacture, sell, assign or license competing products, technologies or processes which compete with the contract products or technologies for the period which the parties have agreed to jointly exploit the results.[86] **10-068**

---

80 art.4(2)(b).
81 See Recital 17 which makes this clear.
82 Recital 17.
83 art.5.
84 art.5(a).
85 art.5(b).
86 art.5(b)(i)–(iv).

Fixing of prices

10-069   Any fixing of prices for the contract products or the licence fees for the contract technologies is treated as a hard core restriction. However, the block exemption permits the fixing of prices or licence fees to respectively "immediate customers" or "immediate licensees" where the joint exploitation of the results includes the joint distribution of the contract products or joint licensing of the contract technologies.[87]

Territorial or customer restrictions

10-070   Any attempt to restrict the territories in which or the customers to whom the parties may *passively* sell the contract products or license the contract technologies is treated as a hard core restriction with the exception of a requirement to exclusively license the results to another party.[88]

10-071   In relation to *active sales* restrictions relating to the contract products or contract technologies, such are prohibited unless they relate to territories which or customers who have been exclusively allocated by one of the parties by way of "specialisation in the context of exploitation".[89] The phrase "specialisation in the context of exploitation" is a defined expression and means in essence that one party has been allocated with the task of production or distribution and because of which restrictions are imposed upon the other regarding the exploitation of the results of the R&D agreement such as restrictions in relation to territories, customers or field of use and includes a scenario whereby one party produces and distributes the contract products on the basis of an exclusive licence granted by the other party or parties.[90] Thus, where such allocation has occurred, an active sales restriction on the party or parties who have not been allocated the task of production or distribution is permissible. The distinction between passive and active sales is set out in detail in the Guidelines on Vertical Agreements.[91]

Attempts to interfere with parallel imports

10-072   Any provision that seeks to impede parallel imports within the EU is also treated as a hard core provision.[92] This provision is reinforced by the black-listing of an obligation whereby parties to the agreement are required to refuse demand from customers in their own territories or customers allocated to them even where it is known that those customers will market the contract products in other territories within the EU.[93]

Excluded restrictions

10-073   The R&D Block Exemption also treats the following as excluded restrictions. The inclusion of these in a R&D agreement does not cause the R&D agreement to

---

[87]   art.5(c). "Immediate" is not defined but presumably means the customers that the R&D parties actually contract with rather than the customers of those customers.

[88]   art.5(d). See also art.5(f) which also prohibits passive sales ("demand from customers") where those customers would sell in territories outside the parties' respective territories. It is not clear what further restrictions this adds to art.5(d) as the latter appear to cover all types of passive sales. See also, as regards the exception for results, Recital 11.

[89]   art.5(e).

[90]   art.1(1)(o).

[91]   See para.11-041.

[92]   art.5(g).

[93]   art.5(f).

fall outside the block exemption but does cause the block exemption to be inapplicable to the clauses themselves.

No challenge

Any obligation which restricts a party from challenging after completion of the **10-074** research and development phase or after the expiry of the R&D agreement the validity of IPRs that the parties hold in the EU which are relevant to, or arise from result of the R&D agreement is prohibited but without prejudice to the right of a party or parties to terminate the agreement in the event of a challenge by the other parties.[94] This mirrors the approach in the Technology Transfer Block Exemption to no-challenge clauses but it will be noted that in the latter, only an exclusive licensor is entitled to terminate in the event of challenge to the validity of the IPRs.[95]

Ban on licensing third parties where R&D results not worked

"An obligation not to grant licences to third parties to manufacture the contract **10-075** products or to apply the contract technologies unless the agreement provides for the exploitation of the results of the joint research and development by at least one of the parties and such exploitation takes place in the internal market vis-à-vis third parties" is an excluded restriction.[96] Thus, if the agreement is a pure R&D agreement, then such obligations are black-listed. However, if the agreement extends to commercialisation of the results of the R&D and such commercialisation is in the EU, then bans are permissible. It is not clear what the expression "vis a vis third parties" means but it is probable that it indicates that if the third parties can be supplied with the contract products by the party or parties entrusted with the exploitation of the results, then this is permissible but not otherwise.

PRODUCTION VENTURES

Many undertakings enter into joint production ventures whereby the parties agree **10-076** to manufacture and market the products together. Like R&D joint ventures, these will often involve licensing of IPR to the production joint venture. Also, similarly to R&D joint ventures, the Guidelines on Horizontal Cooperation Agreements are the primary referential tool. In this part, we consider decisions of the Commission in production joint ventures and then the Specialisation Block Exemption (which ought really to be called the Joint Production Block Exemption).

Production joint ventures can take a number of forms. Thus, undertakings who **10-077** compete in a market may agree that only one party should manufacture a particular product in return for supplying the product to the other. Alternatively, a party could agree the exclusive supply of a product to one party in return for the other exclusively purchasing from the former party. Such agreements will often involve technical co-operation and technology licensing. Often, the parties will be actual or potential competitors.

The Guidelines on the Applicability of art.101 to HCAs have a particular sec- **10-078**

---

[94] art.6(a).
[95] See para.9-053.
[96] art.6(b).

tion devoted to such types of agreements.[97] Generally, licensing provisions are very secondary to the objectives of the agreements and, therefore it is not proposed to consider such agreements in any detail.

Commission decisions: production JVs

10-079   Case studies are given here of production joint ventures where a substantial degree of licensing existed.

Mitchell Cotts/Sofiltra[98]

10-080   This was a joint venture between Mitchell Cotts, a UK company, and Sofiltra, a French company, for the establishment of a joint venture in the UK for the manufacture of high efficiency air filters. The parties competed on a distribution level but not on a manufacturing level because Mitchell Cotts did not have the technological know-how and capability to manufacture such air filters. The joint venture was granted an exclusive manufacturing licence in the UK and an exclusive sales licence in the UK, Ireland and seven non-EC countries. The combined market share of the parties was 17 per cent. The Commission held that the exclusive manufacturing licence infringed art.101(1) but granted exemption for a 10-year period (the duration of the joint venture), as the exclusivity was required to enable the joint venture to establish itself without experiencing competition from its parent companies or other licensees.

Optical Fibres[99]

10-081   Corning Technology was the owner of optical fibre know-how. It entered into three production joint ventures, one in each of France, Germany and the UK, to manufacture fibres using its technology. Each of the partners was already an experienced specialist cable manufacturer and had already been working with Corning. Between the three parties, they owned 48 per cent of the total EC production capacity. Territorial protection was granted to each joint venture by the grant of exclusive sales licences. The Commission considered that such an agreement fell within art.101(1) but granted exemption on the condition that:

(a)   the exclusive sales licences were diluted to non-exclusive licences so that Corning itself could sell or manufacture within the EC;

(b)   each joint venture was given the right to make active sales in the territories of other joint ventures; and

(c)   each joint venture was obliged to sell its products to all users without discrimination.

10-082   The Commission considered the agreement made available high technology to EU undertakings, and that sufficient competition between the parties was possible once the amendments to the agreement were implemented.

---

97   See [150]–[193].

98   [1987] OJ L41/31; [1988] 4 C.M.L.R. 111.

99   [1986] OJ L236/30 (Commission).

SPECIALISATION BLOCK EXEMPTION

The agreements might benefit from the Specialisation Block Exemption.[100] This **10-083** block exemption applies to agreements whereby two or more undertakings agree to enter into arrangements for the manufacture of products which amount to "specialisation agreements". This is defined as being a unilateral specialisation agreement, a reciprocal specialisation agreement, or a joint production agreement. These terms are defined as follows:

(a) "unilateral specialisation agreement" means an agreement between two par- ties which are active on the same product market by virtue of which one party agrees to fully or partly cease production of certain products or to refrain from producing those products and to purchase them from the other party, who agrees to produce and supply those products;

(b) "reciprocal specialisation agreement" means an agreement between two or more parties which are active on the same product market, by virtue of which two or more parties on a reciprocal basis agree to fully or partly cease or refrain from producing certain but different products and to purchase these products from the other parties, who agree to produce and supply them; and

(c) "joint production agreement" means an agreement by virtue of which two or more parties agree to produce certain products jointly.[101]

Such agreements are block exempted provided that the combined market share **10-084** of the participating undertakings does not exceed 20 per cent of the relevant market.[102] As with the R&D Block Exemption, the inclusion of hard core restric- tions in the agreement such as price-fixing, limitation of output on sales (save in certain circumstances, e.g. provisions on the agreed amount of products in the context of unilateral or reciprocal specialisation agreements or the setting of sales targets in the context of joint distribution), or the allocation of markets or custom- ers or sales will remove the protection of the block exemption.

As with the R&D Block Exemption, the block exemption applies provided that **10-085** the IPR licensing provisions in the agreement do not constitute the primary object of that agreement but are directly related to and necessary for the implementation of the R&D provisions.[103]

There is some overlap with the R&D Block Exemption. Prima facie, that ap- **10-086** plies to joint production where such is coupled with an agreement to carry out R&D, i.e. the joint production relates to the results of the R&D phase. Indeed, the R&D Block Exemption specifically deals with specialisation of production within the context of an R&D Agreement.[104] Thus, prima facie, the Specialisation Block Exemption is only relevant if there has been no co-operation at the R&D phase.

---

[100] Reg.1218/2010 on the Application of Article 81(3) of the TFEU to certain categories of specialisa- tion agreements [2010] OJ L335/43. This replaces the previous Specialisation Block Exemption— Reg.2658/2000.

[101] art.1.1.

[102] art.3. Article 5 provides more detail as to the calculation of market shares.

[103] art.2(2).

[104] See para.10-057.

STANDARDISATION AGREEMENTS

10-087   Increasingly, in a technologically complex world, there is a need for undertakings to enter into agreements whose goals are the development of technical standards. Technical standards are complex technical specifications which are typically open and transparent and will govern an area of technology, e.g. mobile telephony or DVDs. They are particularly relevant where manufacturers need to ensure that their products are interoperable with other products on the market or services. To take an example, in the field of DVDs, it is important that DVD players are technically compatible with DVDs. Similarly, mobile telephones must be able to communicate with the cell masts of mobile telephone companies. The Guidelines identify four possible markets that standardisation agreements may affect: the product or service market; the technology market; the market for standard-setting (if different standard-setting bodies exist); and a market for testing and certification.[105]

10-088   The Guidelines state the following as regards the pro- and anti-competitive effects of standardisation agreements:

"263.   Standardisation agreements usually produce significant positive economic effects, for example by promoting economic interpenetration on the internal market and encouraging the development of new and improved products or markets and improved supply conditions. Standards thus normally increase competition and lower output and sales costs, benefiting economies as a whole. Standards may maintain and enhance quality, provide information and ensure interoperability and compatibility (thus increasing value for consumers).

264.   Standard-setting can, however, in specific circumstances, also give rise to restrictive effects on competition by potentially restricting price competition and limiting or controlling production, markets, innovation or technical development. This can occur through three main channels, namely reduction in price competition, foreclosure of innovative technologies and exclusion of, or discrimination against, certain companies by prevention of effective access to the standard."

10-089   Of particular relevance to IPR practitioners is that the Guidelines provide guidance where those standards may involve IPRs. In such circumstances, the exercise of IPRs may prevent access by third parties to the technological standard in issue. It will be appreciated that if the owners of those IPRs did indeed exercise such rights and a technological standard became the de facto standard in a particular field of technology, that the IPR owners would gain a monopoly in a particular product or technological market.[106] Thus, the Commission is particularly sensitive in this area. The Guidelines say the following:

"267.   In the context of standards involving intellectual property rights ('IPR'), three main groups of companies with different interests in standard-setting can be distinguished in the abstract. First, there are upstream—only companies that solely develop and market technologies. Their only source of income is licensing revenue and their incentive is to maximise their royalties. Secondly, there are downstream-only companies that solely manufacture products or offer services based on technologies developed by others and do not hold relevant IPR. Royalties represent a cost for them, and not a source of revenue, and their incentive is to reduce or avoid royalties. Finally, there are vertically integrated companies that both develop

---

[105]   Guidelines, para.261.
[106]   Indeed, in such circumstances, the IPR owner or owners will be in a dominant position and art.102 becomes engaged—see para.12-216.

technology and sell products. They have mixed incentives. On the one hand, they can draw licensing revenue from their IPR. On the other hand, they may have to pay royalties to other companies holding IPR essential to the standard. They might therefore cross- license their own essential IPR in exchange for essential IPR held by other companies.

268. *Third, standardisation may lead to anti-competitive results by preventing certain companies from obtaining effective access to the results of the standard-setting process (that is to say, the specification and/or the essential IPR for implementing the standard).* If a company is either completely prevented from obtaining access to the result of the standard, or is only granted access on prohibitive or discriminatory terms, there is a risk of an anti-competitive effect. *A system where potentially relevant IPR is disclosed up-front may increase the likelihood of effective access being granted to the standard since it allows the participants to identify which technologies are covered by IPR and which are not.* This enables the participants to both factor in the potential effect on the final price of the result of the standard (for example choosing a technology without IPR is likely to have a positive effect on the final price) and to verify with the IPR holder whether they would be willing to license if their technology is included in the standard.

269. Intellectual property laws and competition laws share the same objectives of promoting innovation and enhancing consumer welfare. IPR promote dynamic competition by encouraging undertakings to invest in developing new or improved products and processes. IPR are therefore in general pro- competitive. *However, by virtue of its IPR, a participant holding IPR essential for implementing the standard, could, in the specific context of standard-setting, also acquire control over the use of a standard. When the standard constitutes a barrier to entry, the company could thereby control the product or service market to which the standard relates. This in turn could allow companies to behave in anti-competitive ways, for example by 'holding-up' users after the adoption of the standard either by refusing to license the necessary IPR or by extracting excess rents by way of excessive royalty fees thereby preventing effective access to the standard. However, even if the establishment of a standard can create or increase the market power of IPR holders possessing IPR essential to the standard, there is no presumption that holding or exercising IPR essential to a standard equates to the possession or exercise of market power. The question of market power can only be assessed on a case by case basis."* [Emphasis supplied.]

It will be appreciated from the above emphasised passages that where IPR **10-090** protects a technical standard, there are complex considerations. It does not automatically follow that the owners of IPRs which protect a standard must license their rights on a FRAND basis to third parties. However, if that standard gives the owners of IPRs considerable market power (or indeed a dominant position) in a relevant market, then the anti-competitive concerns of a refusal to license on a FRAND basis become substantial.

Safe harbour

Thus, the Guidelines state that where standard setting agreements risk creating **10-091** market power, compliance with the conditions set out below will normally cause such agreements to fall outside art.101(1). Owing to the importance of such, these conditions are set out verbatim. Compliance with them can be seen as a "soft" safe harbour akin to that provided by a block exemption.

"280. Where participation in standard-setting is *unrestricted* and the procedure for adopting the standard in question is *transparent*, standardisation agreements which contain *no obligation to comply* with the standard and provide *access to the standard on fair, reasonable and non-discriminatory terms* will normally not restrict competition within the meaning of Article 101(1).

281. In particular, to ensure *unrestricted participation* the rules of the standard-setting organisation would need to guarantee that all competitors in the market or markets affected by the standard can participate in the process leading to the selection of the standard. The standard-setting organisations would also need to have objective and non-discriminatory procedures for allocating voting rights as well as, if relevant, objective criteria for selecting the technology to be included in the standard.

282. With respect to *transparency*, the relevant standard-setting organisation would need to have procedures which allow stakeholders to effectively inform themselves of upcoming, on-going and finalised standardisation work in good time at each stage of the development of the standard.

283. Furthermore, the standard-setting organisation's rules would need to ensure effective *access to the standard on fair, reasonable and non discriminatory terms*.

284. In the case of a standard involving IPR, *a clear and balanced IPR policy adapted to the particular industry* and the needs of the standard-setting organisation in question, increases the likelihood that the implementers of the standard will be granted effective access to the standards elaborated by that standard-setting organisation.

285. In order to ensure effective access to the standard, the IPR policy would need to require participants wishing to have their IPR included in the standard to provide an irrevocable commitment in writing to offer to license their essential IPR to all third parties on fair, reasonable and non-discriminatory terms (*'FRAND commitment'*). That commitment should be given prior to the adoption of the standard. At the same time, the IPR policy should allow IPR holders to exclude specified technology from the standard-setting process and thereby from the commitment to offer to license, providing that exclusion takes place at an early stage in the development of the standard. To ensure the effectiveness of the FRAND commitment, there would also need to be a requirement on all participating IPR holders who provide such a commitment to ensure that any company to which the IPR owner transfers its IPR (including the right to license that IPR) is bound by that commitment, for example through a contractual clause between buyer and seller.

286. Moreover, the IPR policy would need to require *good faith disclosure*, by participants, of their IPR that might be essential for the implementation of the standard under development. This would enable the industry to make an informed choice of technology and thereby assist in achieving the goal of effective access to the standard. Such a disclosure obligation could be based on ongoing disclosure as the standard develops and on reasonable endeavours to identify IPR reading on the potential standard. It is also sufficient if the participant declares that it is likely to have IPR claims over a particular technology (without identifying specific IPR claims or applications for IPR). Since the risks with regard to effective access are not the same in the case of a standard-setting organisation with a royalty-free standards policy, IPR disclosure would not be relevant in that context.

FRAND Commitments

287. FRAND commitments are designed to ensure that essential IPR protected technology incorporated in a standard is accessible to the users of that standard on fair, reasonable and non-discriminatory terms and conditions. In particular, FRAND commitments can prevent IPR holders from making the implementation of a standard difficult by refusing to license or by requesting unfair or unreasonable fees (in other words excessive fees) after the industry has been locked-in to the standard or by charging discriminatory royalty fees.

288. Compliance with Article 101 by the standard-setting organisation does not require the standard-setting organisation to verify whether licensing terms of participants

fulfil the FRAND commitment. Participants will have to assess for themselves whether the licensing terms and in particular the fees they charge fulfil the FRAND commitment. Therefore, when deciding whether to commit to FRAND for a particular IPR, participants will need to anticipate the implications of the FRAND commitment, notably on their ability to freely set the level of their fees.

289. In case of a dispute, the assessment of whether fees charged for access to IPR in the standard-setting context are unfair or unreasonable should be based on whether the fees bear a reasonable relationship to the economic value of the IPR. In general, there are various methods available to make this assessment. In principle, cost-based methods are not well adapted to this context because of the difficulty in assessing the costs attributable to the development of a particular patent or groups of patents. Instead, it may be possible to compare the licensing fees charged by the company in question for the relevant patents in a competitive environment before the industry has been locked into the standard (*ex ante*) with those charged after the industry has been locked in (ex post). This assumes that the comparison can be made in a consistent and reliable manner.

290. Another method could be to obtain an independent expert assessment of the objective centrality and essentiality to the standard at issue of the relevant IPR portfolio. In an appropriate case, it may also be possible to refer to *ex ante* disclosures of licensing terms in the context of a specific standard-setting process. This also assumes that the comparison can be made in a consistent and reliable manner. The royalty rates charged for the same IPR in other comparable standards may also provide an indication for FRAND royalty rates. These guidelines do not seek to provide an exhaustive list of appropriate methods to assess whether the royalty fees are excessive.

291. However, it should be emphasised that nothing in these Guidelines prejudices the possibility for parties to resolve their disputes about the level of FRAND royalty rates by having recourse to the competent civil or commercial courts."

Patent disclosure

It will be appreciated that the Commission places reliance on IPR disclosure **10-092** when setting technical standards. This is to avoid what is commonly called "patent ambush" whereby a standard is set and then having been set, an undertaking discloses IPR that is essential for access to the technical standards. Paragraph 327 of the Guidelines give an example of how standardisation agreements would be analysed under art.101 where there is not an obligation of IPR disclosure.

Situation
A private standard-setting organisation active in standardisation in the ICT (information and communication technology) sector has an IPR policy which neither requires nor encourages disclosures of IPR which could be essential for the future standard. The standard-setting organisation took the conscious decision not to include such an obligation, in particular considering that in general all technologies potentially relevant for the future standard are covered by many IPRs. Therefore, the standard-setting organisation considered that an IPR disclosure obligation would, on the one hand, not lead to the benefit of enabling the participants to choose a solution with no or little IPR and, on the other, would lead to additional costs in analysing whether the IPR would be potentially essential for the future standard. However, the IPR policy of the standard-setting organisation requires all participants to make a commitment to license any IPR that might read on the future standard on FRAND terms. The IPR policy allows for opt-outs if there is specific IPR that an IPR holder wishes to put outside the blanket licensing commitment. In this particular industry there are several competing private standard-setting

organisations. Participation in the standard-setting organisation is open to anyone active in the industry.

Analysis

In many cases an IPR disclosure obligation would be pro-competitive by increasing competition between technologies *ex ante*. In general, such an obligation allows the members of a standard-setting organisation to factor in the amount of IPR reading on a particular technology when deciding between competing technologies (or even to, if possible, choose a technology which is not covered by IPR). The amount of IPR reading on a technology will often have a direct impact on the cost of access to the standard. However, in this particular context, all available technologies seem to be covered by IPR, and even many IPRs. Therefore, any IPR disclosure would not have the positive effect of enabling the members to factor in the amount of IPR when choosing technology since regardless of what technology is chosen, it can be presumed that there is IPR reading on that technology. IPR disclosure would be unlikely to contribute to guaranteeing effective access to the standard which in this scenario is sufficiently guaranteed by the blanket commitment to license any IPR that might read on the future standard on FRAND terms. On the contrary, an IPR disclosure obligation might in this context lead to additional costs for the participants. The absence of IPR disclosure might also, in those circumstances, lead to a quicker adoption of the standard which might be important if there are several competing standard-setting organisations. It follows that the agreement is unlikely to give rise to any negative effects on competition within the meaning of art.101(1).

10-093   Other examples are given in the 2010 Guidelines which illustrate the approach by the European Commission to the competitive analysis of standardisation agreements.

PATENT POOLS

Introduction

10-094   Increasingly, businesses "pool" together their patents and know-how. This could be simply for the purpose of cross-licensing each other or in addition, for licensing to third parties. Such are called technology pools and permit third parties to operate in a particular field of technology with just one licence.

10-095   Technology pools will often be set-up for the purpose of creating technological standards or for the purpose of permitting the easy exploitation of a standard. The 2007 US Guidelines give a number of case histories. One particular one is the technology pool for the MPEG-2 technology standard.

10-096   MPEG-2 pool is a digital video compression technology used in many different products and services, including DVDs and telecommunications, as well as cable, satellite, and broadcast television. When making products that meet the MPEG-2 standard, an undertaking could infringe the patent rights of many different rights holders. As a result, firms interested in adopting the MPEG-2 standard hired an independent patent expert to search for the patents that were "essential" to its implementation. Nine companies that held 27 essential patents among them, along with one other company, formed MPEG LA, which acts as the pool's licensing administrator. MPEG LA retains an independent technical expert to determine whether other patents are essential to the MPEG-2 standard. MPEG LA assembles and offers a package of hardware and software licenses to the pool members' patents that are "essential" to comply with the MPEG-2 standard and distributes royalty income among the contributing patent holders on a per-patent basis. Pool members and third parties can challenge the "essentiality" of patents in the pool, i.e. whether access to the patents in the pool is indeed necessary to manufacture products in compliance with the standard. The pool license agreement also requires every licensee to grant back licenses to the pool's members on all MPEG-2-related patents the licensee may have or develop.

The MPEG-2 pool is an example of a pro-competitive technology pool that **10-097** permits the exploitation of "gateway" technology, namely the MPEG-2 standard, by third parties via a "one-stop shop". Not surprisingly, the Department of Justice in clearing the above found that the above arrangements were pro-competitive giving rise to significant cost savings for both licensors and licensees. The restriction of the patent pool to essential patents and the use of an independent technical expert reduced the risk that the patent pool would reduce rivalry between competitors and also reduced the risk that third party licensees were paying for technologies that they did not need.[107]

In general, technology pools where the technologies are complementary rather **10-098** than competing and where the technologies are essential for operating in a particular field or market are pro-competitive whereas technology pools where the technologies are competing (i.e. substitutable) and in the case of standards, consist of inessential patents (i.e. patents which are not required to produce products or provide services that comply with the standard) are anti-competitive. However, in each case a full rule of reason analysis is required.

Guidelines and block exemptions

Regulation 19/65 only permits the enactment of block exemption for technol- **10-099** ogy licensing where there are only two parties.[108] Thus, the 2014 Technology Transfer Block Exemption does not cover technology pools. These are thus dealt with in the 2014 Guidelines. These guidelines provide detailed guidance on technology pools. Thus, they must be considered the primary referential document. However, as discussed above (at para.10-007), the Commission has also published Guidelines on Horizontal Cooperation Agreements which may be relevant, e.g. where two or more parties decide to develop a technological standard. The adoption of a technological standard will often require patent pooling of essential patents.

2014 Technology Transfer Guidelines

The 2014 Guidelines make the important point that there is no "inherent link" **10-100** between technology pools and standards, but the technologies in the pool often support, in whole or in part, a de facto or de jure standard.[109] Standardisation agreements have been discussed above.[110] The 2014 Guidelines recognise that technology pools have pro-competitive effects and that indeed different technology pools may support competing standards. Patent pools play a beneficial role in the implementation of pro-competitive standards.[111] However, the Guidelines also state

---

[107] See Business Clearance letter from Department of Justice dated 26 June 1997 at *http://www.usdoj.gov/ atr/public/busreview/215742.pdf* [Accessed 5 May 2018].
[108] Reg.19/65 art.1(b).
[109] para.245 of the 2014 Guidelines.
[110] See para.10-087.
[111] para.245 of the 2014 Guidelines.

that technology pools can also be restrictive of competition. As it says, the creation of a technology pool necessarily implies joint selling of the pooled technologies which in the case of pools composed solely or predominantly of substitute technologies amounts to a price fixing cartel.[112] Also, it says that in addition to reducing competition between the parties, technology pools may also support an industry standard or establish a de facto industry standard which may result in a reduction of innovation by foreclosing alternative technologies.[113]

10-101   The Guidelines emphasise that open participation in a standard and the creation of patent pools (i.e. all interested parties are open to join) is more likely to result in technologies being included on the basis of price/quality rather than when a pool is set up by a limited group of technology owners.[114] The Guidelines say that two basic distinctions can be drawn in patent pools: (a) technological complements and technological substitutes; and (b) essential and non-essential technologies. Complemental technologies are defined as technologies which are both required to produce the product or needed for the process. Substitute technologies are those where either can be used to produce the product or are used in the process. An essential technology is one which is needed to produce a particular product or carry out a particular process, i.e. there are no viable substitute technologies for producing the product or for use in the process. In the case of a technical standard, a technology is essential if it constitutes a necessary part of the pooled technologies needed to comply with the standard supported by the technology pool. As the Guidelines say technologies that are essential are by necessity also complements (to each other).[115]

10-102   The Guidelines take the approach that the inclusion of substitute technologies in the pool generally restricts inter-technology competition since it can amount to collective bundling and lead to price fixing between competitors. The Guidelines say that the Commission takes the view that the inclusion of significant substitute technologies in the pool constitute a breach of art.101 and are unlikely to be exempted under art.101(3).[116] The Commission takes this view notwithstanding the parties are free to license independently.[117]

10-103   In the case of standards, the desire is that the standard only has technologies which are essential to that standard. The determination whether a technology is essential to a standard is a complex matter and the Commission favours the appointment of independent experts to determine such. It may be that there are a number of substitutable technologies, of which use of one (but any one of them) is essential to have access to the standard. In such cases, it may be that more than one technology pool of essential technologies can be assembled with each pool containing only complementary technologies but the pools competing with each other as each pool contains a substitutable essential technology. Thus, in 2002, the Commission gave clearance to five separate technology pools, each of them permitted access to the 3G mobile telephone standard. Initially, the idea was to have a single patent pool but the Commission was concerned about the lack of competition. It was accepted that the 1MT-2000 3G standard comprised five different technologies, each

---

[112] para.246 of the 2014 Guidelines.
[113] para.246 of the 2014 Guidelines.
[114] para.249 of the 2014 Guidelines.
[115] para.252 of the 2014 Guidelines.
[116] para.255 of the 2014 Guidelines.
[117] para.255 of the 2014 Guidelines.

of which could be used to produce 3G equipment. The Commission cleared the setting up of the five technology pools which would compete against each other.[118]

Safe harbour

The 2014 Guidelines set out a soft "safe harbour" for technology pools similar **10-104** to that for standardisation agreements which if all the following conditions are satisfied would mean that it would be unlikely for the technology pool to fall within art.101(1).

"261. The creation and operation of the pool, including the licensing out, generally falls outside Article 101(1) of the Treaty, irrespective of the market position of the parties, if all the following conditions are fulfilled:
(a) participation in the pool creation process is open to all interested technology rights owners;
(b) sufficient safeguards are adopted to ensure that only essential technologies (which therefore necessarily are also complements) are pooled;
(c) sufficient safeguards are adopted to ensure that exchange of sensitive information (such as pricing and output data) is restricted to what is necessary for the creation and operation of the pool;
(d) the pooled technologies are licensed into the pool on a non-exclusive basis;
(e) the pooled technologies are licensed out to all potential licensees on FRAND terms;
(f) the parties contributing technology to the pool and the licensees are free to challenge the validity and the essentiality of the pooled technologies, and;
(g) the parties contributing technology to the pool and the licensee remain free to develop competing products and technology."[119]

Outside the safe harbour, the Guidelines make it clear that the inclusion of patents **10-105** for non-essential or substitutable technologies in a patent pool are likely to give rise to competition concerns. As they make it clear, once such is included in a patent pool, licensees are likely to have little incentive to license a competing non-essential technology (it amounts to, in effect, a free bundled technology and thus forecloses third parties who can supply substitute technologies). Furthermore, the inclusion of non-essential patents means that the licensee may end up paying for technology that it does not require. Thus, the inclusion of non-essential patents are likely to give rise to a finding of infringement of art.101(1) if the patent pool has a significant position on any relevant market.[120] However, the 2014 Guidelines takes a rule of reason approach to the inclusion of non-essential but complementary technologies in a patent pool and will consider the reasons for including such; whether the licensees are free to license their respective technologies independently; whether the pooled applications have different applications some of which do not require use of all of the pooled technologies; and whether the pooled technologies are available only as a single package or whether a licensee may license part of the package.[121]

If the agreement to set up a technology pool does not infringe art.101, then the **10-106** next step is to assess whether the standard licence from the technology pool to third

---

[118] Commission Press Release IP/02/1651 (12 November 2002).
[119] para.261 of the 2014 Guidelines.
[120] para.262 of the 2014 Guidelines.
[121] para.264 of the 2014 Guidelines.

party licensees falls within art.101. It might be thought that the approach to such would not differ to that under the TTBE or more typical licences. After all, if the formation of the technology pools does not infringe art.101(1), it might be thought that it is little different to an undertaking licensing a number of patents. In some cases, the formation of the technology pool means that it gives the parties to that pool a dominant position in a market. This may be unavoidable if certain complementary patents are essential patents to a technical standard. In such cases, art.102 TFEU becomes engaged.

10-107   The 2014 Guidelines set out the main principles that will govern the assessment of licences between the pool and third party customers. First, the stronger the market position of the pool, the greater the risk of anti-competitive effects. Secondly, the stronger the market position of the pool, the more likely that agreeing not to license to all potential licensees amounts to discriminatory licensing and is contrary to art.101; the pools should not foreclose third party technologies or limit the creation of alternative pools and they should not contain any hard core restrictions.[122] The 2014 Guidelines emphasise that undertakings setting up a technology pool are free to negotiate and fix royalties for the technology package (unless they have committed to license on fair, reasonable and non-discriminatory terms, FRAND). The 2014 Guidelines also emphasise that licensors and licensees should be free to develop competing products and standards; grant back obligations should be non-exclusive and limited to developments that are essential or important to the use of the pooled technology and there should be no no-challenge clauses (or the right to terminate if a challenge is made).[123]

Commission decisions: patent pools

10-108   The Commission has had some experience of technology pools or multi-lateral licences. Thus, in *Concast/Mannesmann*,[124] where two market leaders, who between them held 60 per cent of the market share in continuous casting technology, the Commission held that a know-how pooling arrangement eliminated competition between them and, in effect, forced purchasers to purchase from the two concerns because of the substantial amount of know-how that the two owned. In *IGR/Stereo TV*[125] where two German research institutes, who together owned the patents for stereo television, assigned their patents to a pool of firms who were all German TV manufacturing firms such that foreign firms were excluded from importing TV sets with stereo into Germany, such a practice constituted an infringement of art.101(1).[126]

10-109   In *Re Video Cassette Recorders*,[127] Philips marketed video cassette recorders using the VCR system that it had developed. Other manufacturers of video cassette recorders were interested in marketing the equipment and had decided to use

---

[122] See [266].

[123] See [270]–[272].

[124] *11th Report on Competition Policy*, point 92.

[125] *11th Report on Competition Policy*, point 92 and *14th Report on Competition Policy*, point 76.

[126] The Commission withdrew its opposition when a licence was granted to the complainant (a Finnish firm). However, the matter later came to the Commission's attention when there were further complaints that royalties being raised by the poll system on foreign manufacturers constituted a type of import tax. The royalties were then drastically reduced, such that the Commission held that there was no appreciable effect on competition.

[127] *Re Video Cassette Recorders* [1978] OJ L47/42; [1978] 2 C.M.L.R. 160.

Philips' VCR system. The parties agreed to grant each other royalty-free, non-exclusive and non-transferable licences under their patents and patent applications where such was required to ensure compatibility between the parties' goods. Other manufacturers of VCR machines were free to become parties to the agreement. In the event of termination by a party, that party forfeited any licence for the patents of the other parties granted under the agreement but the remaining partners retained their licences granted by the terminating partner. The Commission held that the termination arrangements fell within art.101(1). It stated that if a party was contemplating manufacturing another system after withdrawing from the agreement, that party's decision was rendered more difficult by the knowledge that it would no longer be able to use investments it had already made for the manufacture of the VCR system and that its patents which might be of use in manufacturing another system would be exploited free of royalties by its former partners.[128] In view of the pre-eminent position of Phillips on the market, the restrictions were particularly marked and would effectively dissuade the parties from any attempt to adopt another system. The Commission also refused to exempt the agreement as it felt that it led to the exclusion of other, perhaps better systems.[129]

In *Philips/Matsushita*,[130] a number of substantial European and Japanese **10-110** electronic product manufacturers agreed to pool their patents on a non-exclusive non-transferable licence basis for the purpose of developing and manufacturing DCC (digital compact cassette) and DCC players. Philips was authorised on an exclusive basis to grant non-exclusive 10-year licences in respect of all the partners' IPR to third parties for the purpose of manufacturing DCC products. Philips had the right to refuse to grant a licence if the prospective licensee had committed acts of copyright piracy. The Commission considered that the pooling of patents and know-how, the exclusive licensing and the standardisation of specifications infringed art.101 but merited exemption under art.101(3) because it would contribute substantially to technical progress and serve the interests of the consumer.

In *Sony/Philips/Matsushita*,[131] Sony, Matsushita and Philips agreed to cross- **10-111** license their patents and know-how relating to optical disk technology for the purpose of development and exploitation of a minidisk system which was a new portable, recordable, digital audio system. The Commission took the view that such pooling of patents and know-how, together with standardisation of specifications, was restrictive of competition but considered that there were sufficient grounds for an exemption under art.101(3).[132]

The decision of *Concast/Mannesmann* demonstrates that in an oligopolistic **10-112** market, the Commission is concerned that there is effective competition between undertakings and that incentives to gain a technological advantage on a competitor are not removed.[133] Similarly, the decision in *Video Cassette Recorders*[134] shows

---

[128] *Re Video Cassette Recorders* [1978] OJ L47/42; [1978] 2 C.M.L.R. 160 at [24].

[129] *Re Video Cassette Recorders* [1978] OJ L47/42; [1978] 2 C.M.L.R. 160 at [29].

[130] *Philips/Matsushita* DCC (IV/33.847) [1992] OJ C333/8.

[131] 1995 Annual Report on Competition, p.123.

[132] This agreement can be a considered a joint venture research, development and exploitation agreement.

[133] For the Commission's approach to obligations in oligopolistic situation, see also *Re Kabelmetal's Agreement* [1975] OJ L222/34, [1975] 2 C.M.L.R. D40; *Re Bayer & Gist-Brocades* [1976] 1 C.M.L.R. D98; *Re the Complaint by Yoshida Kogyo KK*, Press Release of the EU Commission, 9 June 1978; [1978] 3 C.M.L.R. 44.

[134] *Re Video Cassette Recorders* [1978] OJ L47/42; [1978] 2 C.M.L.R. 160.

the concern that the Commission has in ensuring that there is not too much co-operation in a particular technological field if such will substantially reduce inter-brand competition. *Philips/Matsushita* and *Sony/Philips/Matsushita* demonstrate the Commission's favourable approach to patent pools which permit the development of new technologies and standards.[135]

US approach

10-113   The 2017 US *Antitrust Guidelines on Intellectual Property* says the following about cross-licences and pooling arrangements:

"Cross-licensing and pooling arrangements are agreements of two or more owners of different items of intellectual property to license one another or third parties. These arrangements may provide procompetitive benefits by integrating complementary technologies, reducing transaction costs, clearing blocking positions, and avoiding costly infringement litigation. By promoting the dissemination of technology, cross-licensing and pooling arrangements are often procompetitive.

Cross-licensing and pooling arrangements can have anticompetitive effects in certain circumstances. For example, collective price or output restraints in pooling arrangements, such as the joint marketing of pooled intellectual property rights with collective price-setting or coordinated output restrictions, may be deemed unlawful if they do not contribute to an efficiency-enhancing integration of economic activity among the participants.

Settlements involving the cross-licensing of intellectual property rights can be an efficient means to avoid litigation and, in general, courts favor such settlements. When such cross-licensing involves horizontal competitors, however, the Agencies will consider whether the effect of the settlement is to diminish competition among entities that would have been actual or potential competitors in a relevant market in the absence of the cross-license. In the absence of offsetting efficiencies, such settlements may be challenged as unlawful restraints of trade."[136]

---

[135] See also para.10-087.
[136] See para.5.5.

CHAPTER 11

INTELLECTUAL PROPERTY, VERTICAL AGREEMENTS

TABLE OF CONTENTS

INTRODUCTION

This chapter considers competition issues that may arise in the context of verti- **11-001** cal agreements such as franchises and selective distribution agreements. Vertical agreements are agreements which are entered into between parties who are at different levels in the supply chain, i.e. manufacturer and distributor and distributor and retailer. In many cases, technology licences will be vertical agreements but equally could be between competitors. This chapter does not consider vertical agreements which consist of technology transfer licences (e.g. patent or know how licences). They are considered in Ch.9. Furthermore, this chapter does not consider exhaustively competition issues that arise from vertical agreements such as distribution and supply agreements which are outside the scope of this book.

The focus is on two types of vertical relationships which involve the licensing **11-002** of brands, namely franchise and selective distribution networks. In both cases, this will normally involve the licensing of a brand which has a reputation in the marketplace. A franchise agreement (particularly franchises for the supply of a service) will often involve the licensing of know-how. A selective distribution system is mainly deployed for luxury brands where preserving the reputation and luxury image of the brand is important.

When considering the competitive issues raised by vertical agreements, the **11-003** principal reference is the Vertical Agreements Block Exemption ("VABE") and their accompanying Guidelines.[1] As said above, these do not apply to technology licences which are covered by the 2014 Technology Transfer Block Exemption and their Guidelines—discussed in Ch.9. VABE and the Guidelines cover the distribution of goods and services. In such circumstances, there will often be accompanying IPR licence provisions. Such licences are covered by VABE and the Guidelines provided that such are not the primary focus. In other words, they will apply if such licensing provisions are intended to facilitate what can be properly characterised as a distribution or supply agreement.

---

[1] Reg.330/2010 [2010] OJ L102/1; Guidelines on Vertical Restraints OJ [2010] C 130/01.

11-004   Both franchise and selective distribution agreements are governed by VABE and the Guidelines.

Structure of this chapter

11-005   In this chapter, franchise and selective distribution networks are considered, followed by VABE and the Guidelines to Vertical Agreements. The reader is recommended to read Ch.8 for an introduction to art.101 and licences ahead of reading this chapter.

Franchises

11-006   The expression "franchise" is often used to cover a multitude of different types of vertical agreements. This chapter is only interested in those agreements where the franchisor licenses a franchisee to use the franchisor's trade name, trade mark and know-how for the sale of goods or provision of services and where the franchisor exercises continuing control over the franchisee's business. These are called "business format" franchises. Other agreements which are sometimes called franchise agreements are "pure" distribution agreements, where goods are distributed by a distributor. Both of these agreements will, save in exceptional circumstances, fall to be considered under VABE and the Guidelines.

11-007   From a commercial viewpoint, a business format franchise is a very efficient way of exploiting a marketing concept or scheme developed by the franchisor. From a legal viewpoint, a business format franchise agreement has, in essence, four features:[2]

   (1)   the independence of the franchisor and franchisee;
   (2)   the existence of a contractual licence for the use of the franchisor's trade name, trade mark, emblems, symbols, etc.;
   (3)   the provision of continuing assistance to the franchisee by the franchisor; and
   (4)   contractual control by the franchisor over the way in which the franchisee conducts the business (so that there is uniform presentation by all franchisees).

11-008   In many cases, particularly service franchises, there will also be considerable communication of commercial and technical know-how.[3] However, know-how licences in business format franchises for the sale of goods tend to be minimal.[4]

11-009   "Business format" franchise agreements can be for goods or services. Where they concern goods, they will tend to be retail distribution franchises, whereby trademarked goods of the franchisor are sold through special outlets. The franchise agreement will usually ensure that these franchise outlets provide a uniform method of selling the goods and ensure that ancillary services are provided to their

---

[2]   See *VerLoren van Themaat AG's Opinion* in (161/84) [1986] E.C.R. 353; [1986] 1 C.M.L.R. 414. Also, generally see J.N. Adams, K.V. Prichard Jones, J.J.B. Hickey, *Franchising, Practice and Precedents in Business Format*, 5th edn (London: Butterworths, 2004).

[3]   Although in the author's experience, much of the commercial know-how is often little more than a guide to running your own business.

[4]   Often, there will be substantial manuals. However, normally on analysis, the information in these manuals cannot be characterised as know-how (i.e. a body of substantial confidential information), merely methods of doing business in accordance with the franchisor's house style.

customers. The advantage of such systems of selling is that the customer can go to any franchised outlet and know that the standard of goods and ancillary services will be consistent. Service franchises concern the provision of services under a trade name. Invariably, they will include the communication of technical know-how to the franchisee. Fast-food chains, estate agencies, holiday agencies, maintenance and service of domestic appliances and picture-framing franchises are all examples of service franchises. Remuneration of the franchisor in both types of franchises is usually by an initial joining fee and then by way of royalty payments or management fees or service fees.

FUNDAMENTAL ASPECTS OF BUSINESS FORMAT FRANCHISES

From a competition viewpoint, it is clear that the principle of franchising can **11-010** foster competition. The CJEU in *Pronuptia*,[5] a case concerning a retail business format (but called a distribution franchise), said:

"In a distribution franchise system such as this, an enterprise which has established itself as a distributor in a market and which has thus been able to perfect a range of commercial methods gives independent business men the chance, at a price, of establishing themselves in other markets by using its mark and the commercial methods that created the franchisor's success. More than just a method of distribution, this is a manner of exploiting financially a body of knowledge, without investing the franchisor's capital. At the same time, this system gives business men who lack the necessary experience access to methods which they could otherwise only acquire after prolonged effort and research and also to profit from the reputation of the mark. Such a system which permits the franchisor to take advantage of his success, is not itself restrictive of competition."

The Commission said of franchises in its 2010 Guidelines on Vertical Restraints: **11-011**

"Franchise agreements contain licences of intellectual property rights relating in particular to trade marks or signs and know-how for the use and distribution of goods or services. In addition to the licence of IPRs, the franchisor usually provides the franchisee during the life of the agreement with commercial or technical assistance. The licence and the assistance are integral components of the business method being franchised. The franchisor is in general paid a franchise fee by the franchisee for the use of the particular business method. Franchising may enable the franchisor to establish, with limited investments, a uniform network for the distribution of his products. In addition to the provision of the business method, franchise agreements usually contain a combination of different vertical restraints concerning the products being distributed, in particular selective distribution and/or non-compete and/or exclusive distribution or weaker forms thereof.[6]"

Contractual controls, which ensure the quality and uniformity of the network and **11-012** thus maintain the reputation and goodwill of the franchise's trading name, are necessary ancillary restraints because it is precisely the attraction of setting up business under a name which possesses a substantial reputation that encourages persons to take out franchises.[7] If such controls were held to be anti-competitive and hence illegal, then the franchise's reputation would fragment because of the inability of the franchisor to impose effective quality control measures and other control measures

---

[5] (161/84) [1986] E.C.R. 353; [1986] 1 C.M.L.R. 414.
[6] Guidelines, para.189.
[7] For the meaning of the expression "ancillary restraints" in the context of competition law—see para.8-042.

to maintain the identity and reputation of the franchise network. Such would discourage potential franchisees and the franchisor from franchising and ultimately harm the franchise.

Franchises and other distribution agreements

11-013 In assessing the competitive effects of a franchise, it is appropriate to compare franchise networks with other distribution arrangements, in particular, exclusive distribution and selective distribution agreements. The CJEU has said that retail franchises can be distinguished from other distribution agreements because the former use a single mark, the application of uniform commercial methods and payment of royalties in consideration of the advantages such a system confers.[8] Franchise agreements are predominantly characterised by the effort, by means of licences for trade names, marks and know-how and contractual controls, to assimilate the commercial practices of the franchisee as closely as possible to those of the franchisor or its subsidiaries, whilst maintaining the economic independence of the parties. Exclusive supply and purchase obligations play a subordinate role and, from the point of view of competition policy, can only be assessed in the context of the objective pursued, namely the thorough integration of franchisees in the franchisor's network. In contrast, licensing arrangements in exclusive distribution agreements are subordinate to the grant of exclusivity.[9] In particular, exclusive distributions are rarely concerned with the transfer of know-how to the franchisee. However, at a broad level, there are similarities. Thus, a franchise agreement can be characterised as a vertical agreement, as can other distributor agreements. The franchisee will rarely be an actual or potential competitor of the franchisor. Furthermore, a business format franchise is normally concerned about the provision of goods or services at the retail level. These similarities have caused the Commission to include business format franchises as a special type of vertical agreement for the supply or resale of goods or services in its Guidelines on Vertical Restraints and to include business format franchises in its Vertical Agreements Block Exemption.

11-014 Franchises also have similarities with selective distribution agreements. Both seek to distribute products or provide services through selected outlets in order that stringent quality control can be maintained in the area of ancillary services related to the sale of goods or supply of services. Thus, a company might wish only to supply its goods to outlets which can provide an adequate level of after sales repair and maintenance of its goods. Selective distribution agreements will often be used for luxury or high-value goods or services where the brand is important. Thus, like franchises, the trade mark licence is a central element to many selective distribution agreements. In the 1990s, the Commission said the following about franchises in its follow up to the Green Paper on Vertical Restraints:[10]

"Franchising, while being covered, will not be given any preferential treatment in the Block Exemption regulation as it is a combination of vertical restraints. Usually franchising is a combination of selective distribution and non-compete obligations in relation to goods which are the subject-matter of the franchise. Sometimes, other elements like a location clause or territorial exclusivity are added."

---

[8] (161/84) [1986] E.C.R. 353; [1986] 1 C.M.L.R. 414.
[9] See VerLoren van Themaat AG in (C-161/84) [1986] E.C.R. 353; [1986] 1 C.M.L.R. 414 at 437.
[10] Com/98/0544 Communication from the Commission on the application of the Community competition rules to vertical restraints—follow up to the Green Paper on vertical restraints [1998] OJ C365/3.

The CJEU and Commission view favourably selective distribution agreements **11-015** if it is established that the properties of the products in question necessitate the establishment of such a system, in order to maintain the quality of the products and ensure their proper use. Distributors are chosen on the basis of objective criteria of a qualitative nature, relating to the technical qualifications of the distributor and their staff, and suitability of their trading premises, and that such conditions are laid down uniformly for all potential distributors and are not applied in a discriminatory fashion.[11]

The main difference is that a franchise is a far more highly-developed and **11-016** sophisticated arrangement than a selective distribution, although the two can be considered as part of a continuum from bare distribution agreements to selective distribution agreements to franchise agreements, each arrangement representing a more sophisticated method of distribution. Selective distribution is considered in detail later in this chapter.[12]

Franchise agreements and trade mark licences

From the intellectual property practitioner's viewpoint, a business format **11-017** franchise will invariably consist of a trade mark or name and a know-how licence between two independent undertakings with supplementary contractual controls. In fact, it could be said that a franchise licence represents the ideal registered trade mark licence, because it ensures by means of quality control provisions that the trade mark does not lose its reputation or distinctiveness.[13] With a bare trade mark or service mark licence, differing standards of service and manufacturing may be applied by licensees and thus, the function of a trade mark as an indicator of quality will be compromised.

In terms of ownership of goodwill of the franchise brand, in the absence of **11-018** contractual provisions, it might be thought that the goodwill in a franchise is fragmented amongst the various franchisees, despite the fact that the brand is owned by the franchisor. In the UK, the law regards franchises as akin to a lease of the goodwill in the brand for a period of time.[14]

A typical business format franchise will confer exclusivity on a franchisee for a **11-019** defined territory. Historically, the Commission has held the view that the grant of an exclusive licence infringes art.101(1) because it prevents the licensor from licensing others in the same territory.[15] However, its view, as will be discussed later in this chapter, is now much more favourable to the grant of exclusive franchises.

---

[11] *Metro v EC Commission* (26/76) [1977] E.C.R. 1875, [1978] 2 C.M.L.R. 1; *L'Oréal v De Nieuwe* (31/80) [1980] E.C.R. 3775, [1981] 2 C.M.L.R. 235; *Lancôme v Etos* (99/79) [1980] E.C.R. 2511, [1981] 2 C.M.L.R. 164; *Hasselblad v EC Commission* (86/82) [1984] E.C.R. 883, [1984] 1 C.M.L.R. 559. See the AG's Opinion in (161/84) [1986] E.C.R. 353, [1986] 1 C.M.L.R. 414 at 430–431. For a typical Commission decision exempting a selective distribution, see *Yves Saint Laurent* [1993] 4 C.M.L.R. 120 (selective distribution network for cosmetic goods); see also, *Pierre Fabre Dermo-Cosmétique SAS v Président de l'Autorité de la Concurrence* (C-439/09).

[12] See para.11-036.

[13] As suggested by J.N. Adams, K.V. Prichard Jones, J.J.B. Hickey, *Franchising, Practice and Precedents in Business Format*, 5th edn (London: Butterworths, 2004), p.25, fn.4.

[14] *Dyno-Rod v Reeve* [1999] F.S.R. 148 (HC).

[15] *Re the Agreements of Davide Campari-Milano SpA* [1978] OJ L70/69; [1978] 2 C.M.L.R. 397 (exemption renewed—see *Campari* [1989] IV/139). It is usually arguable that an exclusive licence is not anti-competitive when compared to no party being licensed but historically, the court and Commission did not adopt such an analysis. However, it must be recognised that the Commission's current approach is much more economics-oriented than when this decision was made.

The CJEU has said that exclusivity is considered to fall outside art.101(1) if absolute territorial protection from parallel imports or customers outside the territory is not intended or does not occur. Therefore, only where a franchise contributes to market sharing will art.101(1) be applicable.[16]

Franchise agreements and know-how licences

11-020   Franchises will often contain the communication of know-how. This can be technical, commercial and/or marketing know-how. In some franchises, this know-how is crucial to the proper operation of the franchise (i.e. instant development of photographs, framing of pictures). In many cases, it is insubstantial and peripheral (i.e. retail goods business format franchises). It is important to distinguish between true know-how and manuals which set out the modus operandi of a franchise. The latter may appear like know-how but really represents a method of imposing a uniform trading style on the franchise network and forms part of the contractual controls that a franchisor imposes on its franchisees. Thus, often there will be a contractual provision that requires franchisees to operate their franchise in accordance with the manual.

11-021   The Commission places considerable emphasis on franchises involving the transfer of know-how. Thus, it has said that vertical restraints in franchises will be easier to justify where the know-how transferred is important.[17] However, as said earlier, if the transfer of know-how is the primary focus, then it is a know-how licence rather than a franchise agreement and will not be covered by VABE or the Guidelines.[18]

EU LAW AND FRANCHISES

Pronuptia v Schillgalis[19]

11-022   The CJEU in *Pronuptia de Paris v Schillgalis*[20] had the opportunity to rule on the compatibility of art.101 and franchising agreements. It observed that the compatibility of distribution franchise agreements with art.101(1) could not be assessed in the abstract but depended on the clauses contained in such contracts. The case was a preliminary reference from the Bundesgerichtshof in a German action. Thus, the Commission had not examined the agreement.

Facts

11-023   The franchise agreement in question was a business format agreement (although the franchise was called a distribution franchise by the CJEU) for the distribution of wedding dresses and other clothes under the "Pronuptia" name. Litigation had occurred regarding non-payment of fees based on sales figures. The Bundesgerichtshof referred two main questions to the CJEU. The first question was whether or not art.101(1) applied to franchise agreements. The second question was whether

---

16   (161/84) [1986] E.C.R. 353; [1986] 1 C.M.L.R. 414 at [24].
17   Guidelines on Vertical Restraints OJ 2010/C 130/01, para.190.
18   See Guidelines, para.44. However, in such circumstances, the Commission will generally apply the principles set out in VABE and the Guidelines to such arrangements.
19   (161/84) [1986] E.C.R. 353; [1986] 1 C.M.L.R. 414.
20   (161/84) [1986] E.C.R. 353; [1986] 1 C.M.L.R. 414.

such agreements, if they did fall within art.101(1), were covered by Reg.67/67 (the then current block exemption for exclusive dealing agreements).

The actual franchise agreement gave Mrs Schillgalis the exclusive right to use **11-024** the mark PRONUPTIA in the areas of Hamburg, Oldenburg and Hanover. The franchisor agreed to provide training and assistance to the franchisee. The franchisee agreed to only trade under the name "Pronuptia" in the shop specified in the agreement; to purchase 80 per cent of its wedding dresses and accessories from the franchisor; to pay an initial fee and a 10 per cent royalty on all sales and to refrain from any act of competition, including opening any business with an identical or similar purpose and a ban against assignment of the franchise.

Court's judgment

The court held that distribution franchise agreements similar to *Pronuptia* were **11-025** not, per se, restrictive of competition.[21] It stated that:

"[15] In a distribution franchise system such as this, an enterprise which has established itself as a distributor in a market and which has thus been able to perfect a range of commercial methods gives independent businessmen the chance, at a price, of establishing themselves in other markets by using its mark and the commercial methods that created the franchisor's success. More than just a method of distribution, this is a manner of exploiting financially a body of knowledge without investing the franchisor's own capital. At the same time this system gives businessmen who lack the necessary experience access to methods which they could otherwise only acquire after prolonged effort and research and allows them also to profit from the reputation of the mark. Distribution franchise agreements are thus different from either dealership agreements or those binding approved resellers appointed under a system of selective distribution which involve neither use of a single mark nor application of uniform commercial methods nor payments of royalties in consideration of the advantages thus conferred. Such a system, which permits the franchisor to take advantage of his success, is not by itself restrictive of competition. For it to function two conditions must be satisfied."

It stated that in order for the franchise to operate effectively, the conditions must **11-026** be met:

"[16] First, the franchisor must be able to communicate its know-how to the franchisees and provide them with the necessary assistance in order to enable them to apply his methods without running the risk that the know-how and assistance might benefit his competitors, even indirectly... .

[17] Secondly, the franchisor must be able to take the necessary measures for maintaining the identity and reputation of the network bearing his business name or symbol... ."[22]

It then set out the restrictions which were necessary to be included in a franchise **11-027** agreement so as to enable the franchisor to fulfil these requirements. It concluded that all restrictions, bar the requirement that the franchisee only trade under the franchise name at the location specified in the agreement, were necessary ancillary restrictions designed to ensure that the franchise system was successful. Thus, such clauses fell outside art.101(1). However, it held that the ban on the franchisee opening other shops in conjunction with the exclusivity clause resulted in a kind

---

[21] (161/84) [1986] E.C.R. 353; [1986] 1 C.M.L.R. 414.
[22] (161/84) [1986] E.C.R. 353; [1986] 1 C.M.L.R. 414.

of market partitioning between the franchisor and a franchisee and between franchisees themselves. Thus, such an obligation fell within art.101(1).[23] The court stated that a prospective franchisee might not want to take the risk of taking a franchise if their business was not afforded a certain amount of protection from other franchisees and/or the franchisor but that was a matter for exemption under art.101(3).

11-028   The court further stated that franchise agreements concluded between enterprises in the same Member State may affect trade between Member States if they prevent franchisees from setting themselves up in another Member State.

Exemption: Commission's decisions post-Pronuptia

11-029   In *Pronuptia*, the court was not able to examine whether art.101(3) was applicable to the agreements, as the agreements had not been notified to the Commission.[24] Soon afterwards, the Commission issued several exemptions in relation to notified franchise agreements.[25] All these decisions must now be seen in the light of the Guidelines on Vertical Agreements and the Vertical Agreements Block Exemption.[26]

11-030   The Commission's decision after *Pronuptia* followed the guidelines set out in that case as to whether a franchising clause was necessary for "an effective transfer of the business formula".[27] All the franchises notified were found to fall within art.101(1), mainly because the franchise agreements imposed a protected zone for each franchisee which led to artificial partitioning of the market. The following two cases are given by way of example of the Commission's approach to franchise agreement shortly after *Pronuptia*. However, it should be recognised that the Commission's views on the application of art.101 to franchise agreements varies over time. The best guide to its current approach is its views contained within the 2010 Guidelines.

Yves Rocher: "business format" goods franchise[28]

11-031   This was the first "business format" franchise to be exempted by the Commission. Yves Rocher was a well-known cosmetic manufacturer. It held a 7.5 per cent market share in France, 6 per cent in Belgium and, elsewhere in the Community its share was less than 5 per cent. However, there were many competitors and the largest firm held 15 per cent of the European market. It sold by mail order

---

[23] The court followed its decision in *Etablissements Consten & Grundig v EC Commission* (56/64) [1966] E.C.R. 299; [1966] 19 C.M.L.R. Note that the court followed that decision because the PRONUPTIA mark was well-known ("*répandu*") as in *Grundig*. Where the mark is not well known, the Commission's view is that an exclusive trade mark licence of such a mark may not have an appreciable effect on competition—*Moosehead/Whitbread* [1990] OJ L100/32; [1991] 4 C.M.L.R. 391 (Commission—mixed trade mark/know-how manufacturing licence).

[24] At the time, only the Commission could exempt agreements under art.101(3).

[25] *Re the Franchise Agreements of Yves Rocher* [1987] OJ L8/49, [1988] 4 C.M.L.R. 592; *Re the Franchise Agreements of Computerland Europe* [1987] OJ L222/12, [1989] 4 C.M.L.R. 259; *Re the Agreements of Pronuptia de Paris* [1987] OJ L13/39, [1989] 4 C.M.L.R. 355 (exemption granted to Pronuptia franchise); *Re the Franchise Agreements of ServiceMaster* [1988] OJ L332/38, [1989] 4 C.M.L.R. 581; *Re the Franchise Agreements of Charles Jourdan* [1989] OJ L35/31, [1989] 4 C.M.L.R. 591.

[26] See paras 11-087 and 11-041.

[27] See *Computerland Europe* [1987] OJ L222/12; [1989] 4 C.M.L.R. 259 at 269.

[28] *Yves Rocher* [1987] OJ L8/49; [1988] 4 C.M.L.R. 592.

and through franchised retailers. It selected its franchisees in the light of their personality, aptitude and their performance in a training programme. Furthermore, it chose the exact location of the franchisee's shop after careful study. Each franchisee was granted an exclusive right in a defined marketing area to exploit Yves Rocher's trade marks. Considerable know-how and assistance, both commercial and technical was provided by Yves Rocher to its franchisees. It recommended resale prices to its franchisees but these were not binding. Sale to resellers was not permitted but was (after amendment) permitted between franchisees. Franchisees were not permitted to carry on a competing business for the duration of the franchise or for a year after termination of the contract. Payment was by way of an initial joining fee and royalties on sales.

The Commission held that only the agreements' effects of restricting one **11-032** franchisee per given territory fell within art.101(1). In particular, it held that the ban on sale to resellers did not fall within art.101(1) as it would completely devalue the reputation and originality of the Yves Rocher franchise network if resellers could sell goods bearing the franchisor's marks without constraint.[29] Interestingly, it considered the horizontal anti-competitive effects of the Yves Rocher network to see whether it was capable of freezing the structures of distribution and thus, rendering access to the market appreciably more difficult to competing producers, but concluded that there was no appreciable effect.

The Commission exempted the agreements. It held that the franchise contracts **11-033** contributed to improving distribution of the goods, since they helped the producer to penetrate new markets without having to undertake any investment. Furthermore, it held that development of a chain of identical retail outlets strengthened competition vis-à-vis large retail organisations with a branch network. Consumers benefitted from the know-how passed on by the franchisor. The contractual obligations, especially those of exclusivity, were indispensable, as franchisees would be unlikely to have taken up their franchises without a certain amount of protection from other franchisees or the franchisor itself. Competition in the field of cosmetics was not substantially eliminated either at an intra-brand level. This was because the areas allotted were sufficiently small, there was also a mail order service, and the fact that franchisees could sell to any customer or at an inter-brand level because of the smallness of Yves Rocher's market share.

ServiceMaster: "business format" service franchise[30]

This franchise concerned the supply of housekeeping, cleaning and maintenance **11-034** services to commercial and domestic customers and the supply of ancillary goods related to those services. The Commission stated that service franchises showed strong similarities to distribution franchises. However, it considered that the know-how element of services franchises was often more important than in distribution franchises. There were many provisions similar to those in *Yves Rocher* which fell outside art.101(1) as they related to the protection of know-how and the safeguarding of the common identity and reputation of the network. Particular provisions included the obligation to buy products from ServiceMaster or approved third party

---

[29] Note that in *Computerland Europe* [1987] OJ L222/12; [1989] 4 C.M.L.R. 259, the ban on sale to resellers was held to fall within art.101(1) because, in that case, the franchisor did not manufacture the franchise goods and the franchise was effectively a service franchise which provided to the customer computer products of many different manufacturers.

[30] *ServiceMaster* [1988] OJ L332/38; [1989] 4 C.M.L.R. 581.

suppliers and the franchisee's obligation to resell homecare products only with the consent of ServiceMaster and only to customers serviced by the franchisee. Both were held to fall outside art.101(1).[31]

11-035   The Commission held that the ban on the franchisee setting up outlets and conducting an active sales policy (but not passive) outside the franchisee's territory fell within art.101(1) as such amounted to market partitioning. The Commission held that whilst ServiceMaster, at the time of the decision, only had a substantial market (6 per cent) in the UK, it was envisaged that its EC share would exceed 5 per cent in the future. Thus, the Commission held that there was a sufficient probability that the restrictions in the agreements would affect trade between Member States. It exempted the agreement for 10 years upon similar grounds as given in *Yves Rocher*.[32]

SELECTIVE DISTRIBUTION: TECHNICAL AND LUXURY PRODUCTS

11-036   Selective distribution systems are a special type of distribution system. They are often used for the distribution of goods which are either complex technical goods or luxury goods where it is important to maintain a luxury image. They will often involve the licensing of a brand well-known in the marketplace. In the case of the former, a feature of such distribution systems is that wholesalers and retailers will need to have experienced and trained personnel who understand the technology and can answer accurately inquiries from traders and end-users. In the case of the latter, the primary desire of the brand owner is to ensure that the method of distribution and sale of the goods is done in a manner that does not undermine the luxury image of the brand used in relation to the goods. To achieve this, manufacturers and brand owners will normally only choose wholesalers and retailers who meet certain qualitative criteria to sell the goods. Once chosen, they will usually impose contractual restrictions aimed at maintaining the luxury image, e.g. how the goods are to be presented in shops or online so that the luxury image is not impaired. Often, in the case of luxury brands, this will include restrictions on what Internet sites the goods are offered for sale.

11-037   In *Metro v Commission*,[33] the Court of Justice held that for certain types of goods, selective distribution systems are compatible with the predecessor provision to art.101 provided that re-sellers are chosen on the basis of objective criteria of a qualitative nature relating to the technical qualifications of the re-seller and their staff. Also, the aptness of the trading premises and other conditions will be laid down uniformly for all potential re-sellers and should not applied in a discriminatory fashion.[34] In *L'Oréal v PVBA De Nieuwe AMCK*,[35] the Court of Justice had to consider the lawfulness of a selective distribution system for hair care products. It held that it is necessary to consider whether or not the characteristics of the product in question necessitate a selective distribution system in order to preserve its qual-

---

[31]   The second provision acts as a ban against sales to resellers. Whereas in *Computerland Europe* [1987] OJ L222/12; [1989] 4 C.M.L.R. 259, another service franchise, such a provision was held to fall within art.101(1), the Commission stated in ServiceMaster that such a restriction was based on the legitimate concern that the franchisee concentrated on the primary business, which was the provision of services: *ServiceMaster* [1989] 4 C.M.L.R. 581, 588.

[32]   See para.11-031.

[33]   *Metro v Commission* (C-26/76) [1977] E.C.R. 1875.

[34]   See also *CEAHR v Commission* (T-712/14) ECLI:EU:T:2017:48 at [52].

[35]   (C-31/80) ECLI:EU:C:1980:289.

ity and ensure its proper use, and also whether the contractual restraints exceeded the requirements of a selective distribution system.[36]

In *Copad SA v Christian Dior Couture SA*,[37] the Court of Justice had to consider **11-038** whether it was an infringement of a registered trade mark for a distributor in a selective distribution network to sell luxury branded goods to discount stores. (This case is discussed in the Ch.3, "Trade Marks".[38]) There was no issue as to whether art.101 applied to the network. Nonetheless, the Court of Justice, having held that the unauthorised sale of goods bearing a registered trade mark in a manner which was likely to impair the aura of luxury would infringe a registered trade mark for luxury goods, then went on to consider whether the sale of perfume to and then by discount stores would impair that image. It held that the characteristics and conditions of a selective distribution system for luxury goods ensure that goods are displayed in sales outlets that enhance their value and aura of luxury.[39] In *Coty Germany GmbH v Parfümerie Akzente GmbH*,[40] the Court of Justice considered for the first time, whether a selective distribution system for luxury goods designed to preserve the luxury image of those goods was compatible with art.101.[41] The Court of Justice held that provided that the conditions as set out in *Metro v Commission* (i.e. objective criteria of a qualitative nature, non-discrimination, and open to all, etc.) are complied with, a selective distribution system designed, primarily, to preserve the luxury image of goods, is compatible with art.101(1). In doing so, it endorsed what the Court of Justice had said in *Copad* (discussed above) that selective distribution systems contribute to maintaining the aura of luxury. The main significance of *Coty Germany* was that the Court of Justice opined on the compatibility of contractual bans on distributors to third-party websites[42]

In *CEAHR v EU Commission*,[43] the General Court confirmed that selective **11-039** distribution systems for high quality and high technology products necessarily affect competition in the internal market. However, as there are legitimate requirements, such as the maintenance of a specialist trade capable of providing specific services as regards these products, this may justify a reduction of price competition in favour of competition relating to factors other than price. Thus, it held that selective distribution systems which pursue a legitimate goal capable of improving competition in relation to factors other than price are in conformity with art.101.[44]

From these authorities can be derived the following principles concerning the **11-040** compatibility of art.101(1) with selective distribution systems:

- Selective distribution systems for goods that meet certain criteria, e.g. technically complex goods or goods with an aura of luxury are lawful under art.101.

---

[36] See [16].
[37] *Copad SA v Christian Dior Couture SA* (C-59/08) ECLI:EU:C:2009:260.
[38] See para.3-619.
[39] See [29].
[40] (C-230/16) ECLI:EU:C:2017:941.
[41] It was argued that in *Pierre Fabre Dermo-Cosmétique* (C-439/09 EU:C:2011:649), which is discussed at para.11-074, that the Court of Justice had held that the preservation of a luxury image could not justify a selective distribution system but the Court of Justice held in *Coty Germany*, that no such principle could be taken from it (see *Coty Germany*, at [33] and [35]). *Metro* and *CEAHR* concerned technical products.
[42] This is discussed below at para.11-074.
[43] (T-712/14) ECLI:EU:T:2017:48.
[44] See [52] citing *AEG-Telefunken v Commission* (C-107/82) EU:C:1983:293 at [33] and *Pierre Fabre*, at [40].

- Members of a selective distribution network must be chosen on the basis of objective criteria and there must be no discrimination in their selection.
- Restraints in a selective distribution network must be proportionate to the rationale for the network, e.g. the maintenance of a luxury image or the provision of services for technically complex products.

THE VERTICAL AGREEMENTS BLOCK EXEMPTION

Introduction

11-041   In 2010, the Vertical Agreements Block Exemption ("VABE")[45] became law. The history to this block exemption is discussed in previous editions of this book. It applies to vertical agreements for the supply and resale of goods and services. The structure of the VABE is to exempt vertical agreements between undertakings where *both* the market share of the supplier and buyer does not exceed 30 per cent of the relevant goods or services provided that certain hard core restrictions are not included in the agreement. If the market share conditions are not satisfied, then the agreement will fall outside VABE but there is no presumption that such agreements fall within art.101.[46]

11-042   VABE is intended primarily to apply to agreements between non-competing undertakings, although it does cover, to a limited degree, agreements between competing undertakings. In the following sections, the provisions of VABE are considered and where relevant, further clarification of the provisions in The Guidelines.

Definition of vertical agreements

11-043   A vertical agreement:

> "means an agreement or concerted practice entered into between two or more undertakings each of which operates, *for the purposes of the agreement* or the concerted practice, at a different level of the production or distribution chain, and relating to the conditions under which the parties may purchase, sell or resell certain goods or services; ... ."[47] [Emphasis supplied.]

11-044   It will be appreciated from the definition that it is not necessary that the undertakings are for all intents and purposes operating on different levels. It is only necessary that for the purpose of the agreement, they are. Thus, a manufacturer who enters into a distribution agreement with another undertaking for the latter to distribute its goods is a vertical agreement even if the latter also manufactures. A good example would be Apple and Samsung. Apple competes against Samsung in the mobile telephone marketplace but also Samsung makes and supplies parts to Apple. The agreement for the latter falls to be defined as a vertical agreement for the purpose of VABE even though they are also competitors.

---

[45]   EC Reg.330/2010, [2010] OJ L102/1.
[46]   Guidelines, para.23.
[47]   art.1(a).

Application of VABE

VABE applies to vertical agreements but not where their subject matter falls **11-045**
within the scope of other block exemptions.[48] Thus, if an agreement falls within the
Technology Transfer Block Exemption, it yields to such unless the block exemption states to the contrary.

Market share

VABE only applies if the market share held by the supplier on the relevant market **11-046**
in which it sells the contract goods or services does not exceed 30 per cent *and* the
market share of the buyer does not exceed 30 per cent of the relevant market in
which it *buys* the contract goods or services.[49] If the agreement in issue is a
multipartite contract with three or more parties and one undertaking agrees to buy
from one undertaking and sell to another, then when considering the market share
of the intermediary undertaking, one must consider the market share of the
intermediary both as a buyer and as a seller.[50] VABE provides further provisions as
to the calculation of market share.[51] More guidance as to the determination of
market shares is given in the Guidelines.[52]

Competing and non-competing undertakings

Whilst VABE applies to vertical agreements even if they are between competi- **11-047**
tors, VABE is less forgiving where the undertakings to an agreement are competing undertakings. "Competing undertaking" is defined as follows:

"... an actual or potential competitor; "actual competitor" means an undertaking that is
active on the same relevant market; "potential competitor" means an undertaking that, in
the absence of the vertical agreement, would, on realistic grounds and not just as a mere
theoretical possibility, in case of a small but permanent increase in relative prices be likely
to undertake, within a short period of time, the necessary additional investments or other
necessary switching costs to enter the relevant market;... ."[53]

IPR provisions must be ancillary to distribution or supply of goods or services

The Guidelines make it clear that VABE only applies where the main object of **11-048**
the agreement is the purchase or distribution of goods or services.[54] It does not cover
agreements concerning the assignment or licensing of IPRs for the manufacture of
goods or a pure licensing agreement.[55] It gives a number of examples where VABE
does not apply:

"(a) agreements where a party provides another party with a recipe and licenses the other
party to produce a drink with this recipe;

---

[48] art.2(5).
[49] art.3(1).
[50] art.3(2).
[51] art.7 and art.8. These are particularly relevant where the market share of the relevant undertaking increases or decreases over a number of years.
[52] Guidelines, paras 93–95.
[53] art.1(c).
[54] Guidelines, para.32.
[55] Guidelines, para.33.

(b)   agreements under which one party provides another party with a mould or master copy and licenses the other party to produce and distribute copies;

(c)   the pure licence of a trade mark or sign for the purposes of merchandising;

(d)   sponsorship contracts concerning the right to advertise oneself as being an official sponsor of an event; and

(e)   copyright licensing such as broadcasting contracts concerning the right to record and/or the right to broadcast an event."

11-049   In all of the above examples, the supply of goods or services is not the primary object of the agreement. In contrast to the examples where VABE does not apply, the Guidelines also give examples of where IPR licensing provisions are directly related to the supply of goods and services within the meaning of art.2(3) VABE such that the block exemption applies. It says that this will generally be in the following three areas: trade marks, copyright and know-how.[56] Thus, VABE will only apply where the IPR provisions are ancillary to the distribution or supply of goods and services. Thus art.2(3) VABE states that:

"3.   The exemption provided for in paragraph 1 shall apply to vertical agreements containing provisions which relate to the assignment to the buyer or use by the buyer of intellectual property rights, provided that those provisions do not constitute the primary object of such agreements and are directly related to the use, sale or resale of goods or services by the buyer or its customers. The exemption applies on condition that, in relation to the contract goods or services, those provisions do not contain restrictions of competition having the same object as vertical restraints which are not exempted under this Regulation."

11-050   This excludes technology transfer licences where the licensee will manufacture goods. It also excludes pure trade mark licences whereby a brand owner licenses a manufacture to make and sell goods bearing the trade mark. The IPR must be ancillary to the resale of goods or services.

11-051   Section 2.4 of the Guidelines on Vertical Restraints gives further guidance on the application of this important provision. This states that VABE will only apply where five conditions apply:

"(a)   The IPR provisions must be part of a vertical agreement, that is, an agreement with conditions under which the parties may purchase, sell or resell certain goods or services;

(b)   The IPRs must be assigned to, or licensed for use by, the buyer;

(c)   The IPR provisions must not constitute the primary object of the agreement;

(d)   The IPR provisions must be directly related to the use, sale or resale of goods or services by the buyer or its customers. In the case of franchising where marketing forms the object of the exploitation of the IPRs, the goods or services are distributed by the master franchisee or the franchisees;

(e)   The IPR provisions, in relation to the contract goods or services, must not contain restrictions of competition having the same object as vertical restraints which are not exempted under the Block Exemption Regulation."

11-052   There is no doubt that VABE applies to selective distribution systems. The Guidelines clarify that the above five guidelines will usually be fulfilled in the case of franchises:

"as under most franchise agreements, including master franchise agreements, the

---

[56] Guidelines, para.38.

franchisor provides goods and/or services, in particular commercial or technical assistance services, to the franchisee. The IPRs help the franchisee to resell the products supplied by the franchisor or by a supplier designated by the franchisor or to use those products and sell the resulting goods or services. Where the franchise agreement only or primarily concerns licensing of IPRs, such an agreement is not covered by the Block Exemption Regulation, but it will be treated in a way similar to those franchise agreements which are covered by the Block Exemption Regulation."[57]

Therefore, a franchise which permits a franchisee to select goods to be sold under **11-053** a trade mark will be unlikely to fall within the VABE. Greater difficulty may arise when considering a service franchise. Where the services which are provided by a franchisee are not a direct result of know-how communicated to the franchisee, it is doubtful that the agreement will fall within the VABE. In such circumstances, it is difficult to say that the franchisor has provided anything in the way of services to the franchisee. Thus, if the franchise was an office-cleaning franchise, whereby franchisees were given particular territories by the franchisor and permitted to use a well-known brand, it is unlikely that such would fall within the VABE because, properly characterised, the agreement is merely a trade mark licence which would generally fall outside VABE. Most service franchises do include the communication of some know-how but often this can be fairly thin in substance. In such cases, a proper examination is required. However, where a service franchise provides for the purchase of ancillary goods necessary for the working of the franchise from the franchisor or a nominated supplier, such would probably fall within the VABE[58]

Trade mark

The Guidelines state that a trade mark licence to a distributor may be related to **11-054** the distribution of the licensor's products in a particular territory. If it is an exclusive licence, the Guidelines say that the agreement amounts to exclusive distribution.[59]

Copyright

Resellers of goods covered by copyright (books, software, etc.) may be obliged **11-055** by the copyright holder only to resell under the condition that the buyer, whether another reseller or the end user, shall not infringe the copyright. Such obligations on the reseller, to the extent that they fall under art.101(1) at all, are covered by VABE. Similarly, the Guidelines say that agreements under which hard copies of software are supplied for resale and where the reseller does not acquire a licence to any rights over the software, but only has the right to resell the hard copies, are to be regarded as agreements for the supply of goods for resale for the purpose of the Block Exemption Regulation. Under this form of distribution, the licence of the software only takes place between the copyright owner and the user of the software. This may take the form of a "shrink wrap" licence, i.e. a set of conditions included in the package of the hard copy which the end user is deemed to accept by opening the package. Similarly, buyers of hardware incorporating software protected by copyright may be obliged by the copyright holder not to infringe the copyright, for example not to make copies and resell the software or not to make copies and use

---

[57] Guidelines, para.44.
[58] Thus, VABE will apply where the supplier of a concentrated extract licenses the buyer to dilute and bottle the extract before selling it as a drink—Guidelines, para.36.
[59] Guidelines, para.39.

the software in combination with other hardware. Such restrictions, and the extent to which they fall within art.101(1) at all, are also stated to be covered by VABE.[60]

Know-how

11-056   Where know-how is communicated for the purpose of marketing goods in the context of a distribution agreement, then it is ancillary to the distribution agreement. The Guidelines state that franchise agreements, with the exception of industrial franchise agreements, are the most obvious example where know-how for marketing purposes is communicated to the buyer. Franchise agreements contain licences of intellectual property rights relating to trade marks or signs and know-how for the use and distribution of goods or the provision of services. In addition to the licence of IPR, the franchisor usually provides the franchisee during the life of the agreement with commercial or technical assistance, such as procurement services, training, advice on real estate, financial planning, etc. The licence and the assistance are integral components of the business method being franchised.

Hard core provisions

11-057   Vertical agreements will not benefit from exemption under the VABE if the agreement contains provisions whose objects are "black listed". Where a clause is so black-listed, the effect is that VABE is inapplicable to the whole agreement. Interesting, the Guidelines state that whilst hard core restrictions will cause the agreement to fall outside VABE, in certain circumstances, undertakings may be able to demonstrate that such have pro-competitive effects and that the agreement should thus benefit from individual exemption under art.101(3).[61] This demonstrates a softening of the Commission's approach to such provisions.

Blacklisted objects

11-058   Article 4 set outs the blacklisted objects:

"(a)   the restriction of the buyer's ability to determine its sale price, without prejudice to the possibility of the supplier to impose a maximum sale price or recommend a sale price, provided that they do not amount to a fixed or minimum sale price as a result of pressure from, or incentives offered by, any of the parties;

(b)   the restriction of the territory into which, or of the customers to whom, a buyer party to the agreement, without prejudice to a restriction on its place of establishment, may sell the contract goods or services, except:

(i)   the restriction of active sales into the exclusive territory or to an exclusive customer group reserved to the supplier or allocated by the supplier to another buyer, where such a restriction does not limit sales by the customers of the buyer,

(ii)   the restriction of sales to end users by a buyer operating at the wholesale level of trade,

(iii)   the restriction of sales by the members of a selective distribution system to unauthorised distributors within the territory reserved by the supplier to operate that system, and

(iv)   the restriction of the buyer's ability to sell components, supplied for the purposes of incorporation, to customers who would use them to manufacture the same type of goods as those produced by the supplier,

---

[60]   Guidelines, paras 40–42.
[61]   Guidelines, para.47.

(c)   the restriction of active or passive sales to end users by members of a selective distribution system operating at the retail level of trade, without prejudice to the possibility of prohibiting a member of the system from operating out of an unauthorised place of establishment;

(d)   the restriction of cross-supplies between distributors within a selective distribution system, including between distributors operating at different level of trade;

(e)   the restriction, agreed between a supplier of components and a buyer who incorporates those components, of the supplier's ability to sell the components as spare parts to end-users or to repairers or other service providers not entrusted by the buyer with the repair or servicing of its goods."

These provisions are considered in more detail:

Resale price maintenance

Save in exceptional cases, resale price maintenance ("RPM") clauses are not permitted but recommendations to price are. The Guidelines amplify on this provision. They point out that RPM can be achieved through indirect means such as agreements fixing distribution margin, maximum level of discount, making rebates subject to observance of certain price levels, etc.[62] However, the mere provision of a list of recommended prices to buyers is not in itself considered RPM.[63] Recommended prices must not be accompanied by any pressure or incentives for them to be treated as such.[64] Previously to the 2010 Guidelines, RPM was strictly prohibited. However, interestingly, the 2010 Guidelines make it clear that RPM can sometimes be justifiable under art.101(3). Thus, it says that where a manufacturer introduces a new product, RPM may be helpful during the introductory period of expanding demand to induce distributors to take better account of the manufacturer's interest to promote a new product.[65] The Guidelines specifically refer to certain circumstances which, it is permissible for RPM to be included in franchises:

> "Similarly, fixed resale prices, and not just maximum resale prices, may be necessary to organise in a franchise system or similar distribution system applying a uniform distribution format a coordinated short term low price campaign (2 to 6 weeks in most case) which will also benefit the consumers."[66]

11-059

This softening of approach to RPM mirrors that of the US where RPM is now no longer unlawful per se but is subject to analysis under the rule of reason.[67]

11-060

Territorial and customer restrictions

In general, art.4(b)–(e) blacklists customer or territorial restrictions on distributors. The general principle is that downstream restrictions on buyers are blacklisted. Buyers should be free to choose where and to whom they may sell their goods or services. However, there are important exceptions. In large part, these exceptions arise from two concerns:

11-061

---

[62]   Guidelines, para.48.
[63]   Guidelines, para.48.
[64]   Guidelines, para.255.
[65]   Guidelines, para.225.
[66]   Guidelines, para.225. Here, it would be necessary to show that the "low price" was lower than the normal price.
[67]   See para.8-294.

- The need to incentivise new distributors to invest in promoting and selling the bought goods in a territory by protecting them to a limited extent from other sellers (e.g. established distributors).
- In the case of selective distribution networks, the need to maintain the integrity of the same.

11-062   These exceptions are now considered in detail together with the guidance from the Guidelines. Furthermore, because of the problems caused by online sellers who are often able to free-ride on the promotional efforts of distributors or, in the context of selective distribution systems, inappropriate selling can damage the luxury image of a brand, the position regarding Internet is considered separately.

Restriction on wholesalers selling to end-users

11-063   Article 4(b)(ii) VABE permits restrictions on wholesalers selling to end-users. This is justified in the Guidelines as permitting a supplier to keep wholesale and retail levels of trade separate and distinct.[68] Interestingly, the Guidelines permit a supplier to prohibit sales to all end users other than "bigger end users".[69]

Passive and active sales

Definition of active and passive sales

11-064   The rules concerning whether passive and active sales bans are allowed are somewhat complex. Some relate only to selective distribution systems whereas others apply to all vertical agreements. These expressions are not defined in VABE but are defined in the Guidelines. In essence, active sales require actively approaching individuals by direct mail, advertisements, promotions, etc. Passive sales mean responding to unsolicited requests from individual customers for goods or services.[70] However, the Guidelines make a distinction between targeted advertisements and general advertising—the latter is considered passive selling provided that such is incidental to reaching customers outside territories reserved to other distributors or the supplier.[71]

Passive sales and Guidelines

11-065   In certain circumstances, a passive sales ban, although its inclusion will cause the agreement to fall outside VABE, will be unobjectionable. Thus, the Guidelines give the example of where it is necessary to protect a new distributor and the investment that it will need to make to penetrate the market allocated to that distributor. Thus, it says that where substantial investment needs to be made, passive sales bans necessary to recoup that investment will generally fall outside art.101(1) during the first two years that the distributor is selling the contract goods or services.[72]

---

[68] Guidelines, para.55.
[69] Guidelines, para.55.
[70] Guidelines, para.51.
[71] Guidelines, para.51.
[72] Guidelines, para.61.

Selective distribution systems

In the case of selective distribution systems, VABE is more hard-nosed about **11-066** downstream restrictions than in more open-ended distribution systems. This is no doubt because a selective distribution network *inherently* restricts intra-brand competition (i.e. competition between buyers of the goods distributed through the selective distribution network). A "selective distribution system" is defined as:

> "a distribution system where the supplier undertakes to sell the contract goods or services, either directly or indirectly, only to distributors selected on the basis of specified criteria and where these distributors undertake not to sell such goods or services to unauthorised distributors within the territory reserved by the supplier to operate that system."[73]

For selective distribution systems, the effect of art.4 is that selective distribu- **11-067** tion agreements:

- May prevent sales to unauthorised distributors in the territory reserved to the supplier.[74]
- May *not* prevent supplies between authorised distributors within the network regardless of whether they are wholesalers or retailers.
- In the case of retailers in a selective distribution network, may *not* prevent any form of marketing (whether active or passive) to end users.[75]

The Guidelines say that selective distribution systems cannot be combined with **11-068** exclusive distribution systems within the same territory.[76] It is said that this is because such would lead to a hard core restriction of active or passive selling by the dealers under art.4(c) VABE. It is not clear why this is the case because art.4(c) is concerned with restrictions in selective distribution networks from selling to end-users by authorised distributors operating at a retail level. A selective exclusive distribution system (i.e. one whereby only one distributor is appointed in a particular territory within the framework of a selective distribution system) does not per se amount to a restriction on that distributor from selling to end-users either actively or passively.

Internet sales restrictions

VABE itself does not expressly deal with bans on selling online or via third party **11-069** Internet sites. In the case of Internet selling, the Guidelines provide detailed guidance on what type of Internet selling amounts to passive selling as opposed to active selling. In general, the Guidelines emphasis that it is a "powerful tool to reach a greater number and variety of customers than by more traditional sales methods" and that "in principle, every distributor must be allowed to use the Internet to sell products".[77] In general, Internet selling is considered a form of passive sales.[78] The mere fact of offering different language versions on a website is not considered to

---

[73] art.1(1)(e).
[74] Although it is generally accepted that selective distribution systems may prevent supplies to unauthorised distributors regardless of which territory they are based. This is a common feature of selective distribution networks.
[75] But without prejudice to a requirement that they operate out of approved retail premises. This includes professional end users (i.e. businesses)—see Guidelines, para.15.
[76] Guidelines, para.57.
[77] Guidelines, para.52.
[78] Guidelines, para.52.

change the passive character of Internet selling.[79] Attempts to limit Internet selling by, e.g. preventing customers from outside the distributor's territory from accessing the website; refusing to process credit cards which reveal an address outside the distributor's territory; agreements to limit the distributor's overall sales via the Internet; and agreements that impose a higher price on online sales as opposed to offline sales are considered bans on passive sales.[80]

11-070 However, there are important exceptions to this. Thus, a supplier may require a distributor to sell a certain absolute amount (in value or volume) of its products offline to ensure an efficient operation of its brick and mortar shops. Such absolute amounts of offline sales can be the same for all buyers or determined on the basis of objective criteria, e.g. the buyer's size in the network or its geographical location.[81] Also, a supplier can impose a fixed fee to support the latter's online or offline sales efforts.[82] These "carve outs" from the general ban on Internet selling recognise that Internet selling can be cannibalistic. Readers will be all too familiar with the practices of consumers (and no doubt themselves) of looking at products in shops and then buying those goods on an Internet site which sells them at a cheaper price. Internet sellers do not have the overheads of bricks and mortar and thus can "free ride" on the promotional efforts of bricks and mortar sellers. Thus, in a franchise agreement, a distributor of showers may have showrooms where the goods are displayed in situ and provide face-to-face assistance and guidance to potential consumers. These outlets will have overheads associated with providing such costs. The Internet seller will not have these overheads and thus can free-ride on such efforts and ultimately undermine the commercial feasibility of bricks and mortar outlets. Thus, the Guidelines state that suppliers can require that its distributors have one or more bricks and mortar shops or showrooms as a condition for becoming a member of its distribution system.[83] In order to maintain standards, e.g. quality standards in the case of luxury brands or technical products, the supplier can require that the Internet site adheres to certain quality standards. Indeed, it can require that where distributors use third party platforms that they distribute the contract products only in accordance with certain defined standards and conditions agreed between the suppliers and its distributors for the latter's use of the Internet. For instance, the supplier may require that the customer does not visit the distributor's website through a site carrying the name or log of the third-party platform.[84]

11-071 Furthermore, the Guidelines however make it clear that the use of the Internet can amount to active selling (and therefore its ban can be permitted under VABE). Thus, restrictions on online advertisements specifically targeting customers are permissible. In particular, a ban on a distributor paying a search engine or online advertisement provider to have advertisements for the distributor's website displayed specifically to users in a particular territory outside the distributor's territory would be permissible as such amounts to active selling.[85]

11-072 It is of note that outside the application of VABE to bans on Internet selling, the Guidelines specifically recognise the problem caused by free-riding whereby one

---

[79] Guidelines, para.52.
[80] Guidelines, para.52.
[81] Guidelines, para.52.
[82] Guidelines, para.52.
[83] Guidelines, para.54.
[84] Guidelines, para.54.
[85] Guidelines, para.53.

distributor may free-ride on the promotion efforts of another distributor.[86] In particular, this may occur where costs are incurred in promotion of the contract goods or services at the buyer's premises, generally at a retail level, which attracts customers for competitors. This is clearly relevant to Internet "cannibals". However, the Guidelines make it clear that this must be a "real free-rider" issue and that generally, the product will usually need to be relatively new or technically complex, or the reputation of the product must be a major determinant of the demand (i.e. reasonably high value) for such to be an issue.[87]

Selective distribution networks and Internet selling

The Guidelines make it clear that dealers in a selective distribution system should **11-073** be free to sell both actively and passively to all end users with the help of the Internet.[88] This includes restrictions on selling to certain persons via the Internet where such restrictions are not overall equivalent to those imposed on sales from bricks and mortar shops.[89] However, the Guidelines state that this does not mean that the criteria imposed for online sales must be the same as for offline sales. Rather they should pursue the same objectives and achieve comparable results. Thus, restrictions on appointed dealers on selling more than a given quantity to individual end-users may be imposed to prevent their onward sales to unauthorised dealers. This may be stricter for online sales than for offline sales as it is easier for an unauthorised dealer to obtain such via the Internet.[90]

Court of Justice and Internet sales bans in selective distribution systems

The approach in VABE and the Guidelines as to the prohibition on restrictions **11-074** in selective distribution systems to selling on the Internet has been considered in two Court of Justice cases, *Pierre Fabre Dermo-Cosmétique SAS v Président de L'Autorité de la Concurrence*[91] and *Coty Germany GmbH v Parfümerie Akzente GmbH*.[92] In *Pierre Fabre*, the French Court of Appeal referred to the CJEU the issue of whether a ban on Internet sales of cosmetic and personal care products by pharmacies was contrary to art.101 and the predecessor to VABE (Reg.2790/1999). The distribution contracts required sales to be made only in a physical space in which a qualified pharmacist was present which thus excluded Internet sales. The French Competition Authority issued proceedings on the ground that this was contrary to art.101. The CJEU held that such a clause fell within art.4(c) of Reg.2790/1999.[93] The CJEU did recognise that a ban on Internet sales might be objectively justified but that such did not apply to a need to maintain the prestigious image of the products at issue,[94] and to the need to provide individual advice to the

---

[86] Guidelines, para.107.
[87] Guidelines, para.107(a).
[88] Guidelines, para. 56
[89] Guidelines, para.56.
[90] Guidelines, para.56.
[91] (C-439/09) [2011] E.C.R. I-9419.
[92] (C-230/16) ECLI:EU:C:2017:941.
[93] Which corresponds to art.4(c) of the current block exemption and is identically worded. See [54] of the judgment.
[94] See [45].

customer and ensure against incorrect use of products.[95] The CJEU also rejected an argument that the proviso to art.4(c) (namely it does not apply to prohibitions on members operating out of an unauthorised establishment) was applicable on the basis that a ban on selling Internet products was equivalent to such a ban. It held that a ban on Internet selling could not be interpreted as an "unauthorised establishment" and could not be construed as meaning the Internet.[96]

11-075   However, in *Coty Germany*, which followed *Pierre Fabre*, the Court of Justice had to consider whether in the context of a selective distribution system for luxury goods, a ban on selling these goods on third party Internet platforms (here Amazon) was compatible with art.101(1) and if not, whether it fell foul of art.4(b) and (c) of VABE. It held that in contrast to *Pierre Fabre*, which was an absolute ban on Internet sales, the restriction was simply against selling on third party Internet platforms. It also noted that the selective distribution system allowed, under certain conditions, authorised distributors to advertise via the Internet on third party platforms and to use online search engines. It said that a ban on sales through third party Internet sites could harm the luxury image and indeed the character of the goods.[97] Finally, it noted a Commission report that showed that most online distribution was through distributors' own online shops.[98] Accordingly, it held that even though it restricted a specific kind of Internet sale, the prohibition did not amount to a restriction of customers of distributors within the meaning of art.4(b) VABE or a restriction of passive sales to end users within the meaning of art.4(c) VABE.[99]

Other hard core restrictions

11-076   The other hard core restrictions speak for themselves. Further guidance on them is provided in the Guidelines.[100]

Excluded restrictions

11-077   VABE also blacklists certain "excluded restrictions." However, unlike the hard core provisions, the incorporation of such into a vertical agreement does not take the *whole* agreement outside VABE but only the restriction itself. These provisions are set out in art.5 and provide as follows:

> "1.   The exemption provided for in Article 2 shall not apply to the following obligations contained in vertical agreements:
>   (a)   any direct or indirect non-compete obligation, the duration of which is indefinite or exceeds five years;

---

[95]   See [44] applying *Deutscher Apothekerverband* (C-322/01) [2003] E.C.R. I-14887 at [106], [107] and [112]; *Ker-Optika* (C-108/09) [2010] E.C.R. I-0000 at [76].
[96]   Judgment, at [58].
[97]   See [49].
[98]   See [54]. The significance of this report is somewhat ambiguous. The report (Final Report on the E-Commerce Sector Inquiry COM (2017) 229 10 May 2017) says that more than 90% of respondent retailers use their own online shop when selling online ([39(i)]). As stated in the report, this shows that marketplace bans do not prevent the effective use of the Internet as a sales channel ([41]). Thus, the report held that absolute third-party platform bans should not be considered hard core bans under VABE ([42]). However, the report also says that online marketplaces are important for SME retailers. Thus, third party platform bans favour the large retailers and therefore, it must be said, concentration of market power in a few, large retailers.
[99]   See [65]–[69].
[100] Guidelines, paras 55–59.

(b)   any direct or indirect obligation causing the buyer, after termination of the agreement, not to manufacture, purchase, sell or resell goods or services;

(c)   any direct or indirect obligation causing the members of a selective distribution system not to sell the brands of particular competing suppliers.

For the purposes of point (a) of the first subparagraph, a non-compete obligation which is tacitly renewable beyond a period of five years shall be deemed to have been concluded for an indefinite duration.

2.   By way of derogation from paragraph 1(a), the time limitation of five years shall not apply where the contract goods or services are sold by the buyer from premises and land owned by the supplier or leased by the supplier from third parties not connected with the buyer, provided that the duration of the non-compete obligation does not exceed the period of occupancy of the premises and land by the buyer.

3.   By way of derogation from paragraph 1(b), the exemption provided for in Article 2 shall apply to any direct or indirect obligation causing the buyer, after termination of the agreement, not to manufacture, purchase, sell or resell goods or services where the following conditions are fulfilled:

(a)   the obligation relates to goods or services which compete with the contract goods or services;

(b)   the obligation is limited to the premises and land from which the buyer has operated during the contract period;

(c)   the obligation is indispensable to protect know-how transferred by the supplier to the buyer;

(d)   the duration of the obligation is limited to a period of one year after termination of the agreement.

Paragraph 1(b) is without prejudice to the possibility of imposing a restriction which is unlimited in time on the use and disclosure of know-how which has not entered the public domain."[101]

Further guidance on these provisions is given in the Guidelines.   **11-078**

Non-compete covenants

Article 5(1)(a) blacklists non-compete covenants which exceed five years or are   **11-079**
indefinite. Non-compete covenants are defined in VABE as follows:

"direct or indirect obligation causing the buyer not to manufacture, purchase, sell or resell goods or services which compete with the contract goods or services, or any direct or indirect obligation on the buyer to purchase from the supplier or from another undertaking designated by the supplier more than 80% of the buyer's total purchases of the contract goods or services and their substitutes on the relevant market, calculated on the basis of the value or, where such is standard industry practice, the volume of its purchases in the preceding calendar year;"[102]

Guidance is given on the interpretation of this in the Guidelines.[103] As is made   **11-080**
clear by art.5(2), such does not apply to non-compete covenants where the goods or services are sold by the buyer from premises owned or leased by the supplier provided that such does not extend beyond the period of occupancy. The Guidelines state that the reason for this is that it would normally be unreasonable to expect a supplier to allow competing products to be sold from premises and land owned by

---

[101]   art.5 VABE.
[102]   art.1(1)(d).
[103]   Guidelines, para.66.

the supplier.[104] It might be said that this equally applies where the premises are not owned or leased by the supplier.

11-081   It should be said that even if a non-compete covenant exceeds five years or more and therefore be an excluded restriction, such may fall outside art.101(1). Thus, for a franchise agreement, a restriction on the franchisee's ability to sell competing goods is necessary to preserve the identity and reputation of the network which is symbolised by the mark. Such restrictions have been found by the court in *Pronuptia* to fall outside art.101(1). Furthermore, the Guidelines consider that clauses which oblige the franchisee not to engage in any similar business fall outside art.101(1).[105] This can be said to apply to a ban on selling goods or selling services which compete with the franchise goods or services. Thus, although non-compete clauses for the duration of the franchise will be considered an excluded restriction if they last (or could last) for longer than five years, the only effect is that such a clause will not itself fall within VABE. As such clauses are considered generally to fall outside art.101(1), there is no cause for concern and franchisors should feel comfortable in having such clauses in a franchise.

11-082   In the case of selective distribution systems (which franchise networks will often be), art.5(1)(c) prohibits any obligation (direct or indirect) not to sell the brands of *particular* competing suppliers. This however should not be a problem because most franchise agreements would not contain discriminatory non-compete clauses but blanket non-compete clauses. The Guidelines make it clear that it is only non-compete clauses that target "one specific competitor or certain specific competitors" from using these outlets which are objectionable, as such would amount to a "collective boycott".[106]

Post-termination non-compete covenants

11-083   Many business format franchises will seek to prevent the misappropriation of the goodwill of the franchise by the franchisee after termination. A typical clause would be to prevent the franchisee from providing competing services or goods in the franchised territory for a period of one year. This is normally sufficient to ensure that there is some protection for an incoming franchisee from an outgoing franchisee who may have built up a considerable reputation trading under the franchisor's name.[107]

11-084   The combined effect of arts 5(1)(b) and 5(3) is to permit non-compete obligations for a maximum of one year after termination, provided the four conditions set out in art.5(3) are fulfilled. Unfortunately, in most business format franchises, it will be difficult to satisfy two of the four conditions, namely art.5(3)(b) and (c). Article 5(3)(b) means that the franchisee can set up shop next door to the franchised premises and carry on trading. This will do nothing to protect misappropriation of the goodwill of the franchise because the goodwill of the franchise is clearly not limited to the shop premises. This is particularly the case where the franchise is

---

[104] Guidelines, para.67.
[105] para.45(a). See also the example at para.191 which refer to a covenant in a sweet shop not to sell other sweets and the analysis in the Guidelines that such a provision would fall outside art.101(1) as it would be necessary to prevent competitors from benefitting from its trade name.
[106] Guidelines, para.69.
[107] In the UK, see *Dyno Rod Plc* [1999] F.S.R. 148 (HC); *ChipsAway International Ltd v Kerr* [2009] EWCA Civ 320.

concerned with the provision of services rather than the sale of goods. Equally, art.5(3)(c) will normally be difficult, if not impossible, to satisfy. It will be very difficult to justify a post-termination restraint of trade on the basis that it is indispensable to protect know-how transferred during the period of the agreement. In certain cases, this could be achieved by a non-disclosure and non-use of the know-how provision of unlimited duration, as suggested by the relevant provision.[108] Moreover, it ignores the fact that in many business format franchises, the know-how transferred is trivial or not important.[109] In reality, it is the misappropriation of *the goodwill* generated by the trading name and not the *know-how* that a post-termination restraint of trade covenant seeks to protect.[110] Thus, a post-termination restraint of trade covenants is normally limited to the specific geographical area in which the franchisee has been operating. Such demonstrates that a franchisor is not concerned about use of know-how, but misappropriation of goodwill, in a particular territory. The franchisor is not normally concerned if the franchisor sets up somewhere else using the transferred know-how.

11-085   Therefore, in most circumstances, a post-termination covenant will not benefit from VABE. However, there are good grounds for saying that such a provision is nevertheless not prohibited under art.101(1) or is capable of individual exemption under art.101(3). Such is necessary to protect the goodwill of the brand and its misappropriation by an ex-franchisee. Whilst it might be said that such can be achieved by simply preventing the ex-franchisee from using the franchise brand, the ex-franchisee who trades in the same area selling the same goods and services and has used the brand during the currency of the franchise to obtain trade and custom will be able to exploit such goodwill generated by the brand even after the termination of the franchise.[111]

Withdrawal of block exemption

11-086   The Commission may by regulation, withdraw the benefit of the VABE where it finds, in any particular case, that parallel networks of similar vertical restraints cover more than 50 per cent of a relevant market.[112]

11-087   As seen from the previous section, the Guidelines amplify and clarify VABE in two ways. First, they clarify when VABE will be applicable. Secondly, where VABE is not applicable, they provide guidance as to how the Commission and courts

---

[108] Although in England, it is generally recognised that a non-competition obligation of limited duration is permissible to protect confidential information communicated to a franchisee because it is difficult to draw the line between information which is confidential and that which is not, and furthermore it is difficult to prove a breach—see Denning MR in *Littlewoods v Harris* [1977] 1 W.L.R. 1472 CA.

[109] Thus, in many business format franchises, it is unlikely that there is sufficient know-how to satisfy the definition of "know-how", that it must be secret, substantial and identified, art.1(1)(g). See also para.68 of the Guidelines where it emphasises that the know-how must include information which is "significant and useful to the buyer for the use, sale or resale of the contract goods or services".

[110] *Dyno-Rod v Reeve Plc* [1999] F.S.R. 148 (High Court, England and Wales). Cited with approval in *ChipsAway International Ltd v Kerr* [2009] EWCA Civ 320 (Court of Appeal, England and Wales)

[111] e.g. see *Dyno-Rod v Reeve Plc* [1999] FSSR 148, 155 quoted in *ChipsAway International Ltd v Kerr* [2009] EWCA Civ 320.

[112] art.6.

would analyse the competitive and anti-competitive effects of vertical agreements. Much of the guidance is common to all types of vertical agreements and not just franchises. In large part, where relevant to IPRs, they have been considered in the previous section. In this section, certain aspects of the Guidelines are considered which are relevant to IPR practitioners including those advising on franchises.

11-088 The Guidelines set out a detailed and clear approach to the individual analysis of vertical restraints.[113] They point out the positive and negative effects of vertical restraints. In general, they comment that vertical restraints are generally less harmful than horizontal restraints.[114] The main negative effect can be foreclosure of other suppliers and the softening of competition between the supplier and its competitors.[115] They also point out that in general, vertical restraints for non-branded goods are less harmful than for branded goods because branding tends to increase product differentiation leading to a reduced elasticity of demand and an increased possibility to raise prices.[116]

Franchises

11-089 In the context of franchises, the Guidelines make it clear that the following clauses are necessary to protect the franchisor's intellectual property rights and thus are covered by VABE even if they did fall within art.101(1):

(a) an obligation on the franchisee not to engage, directly or indirectly, in any similar business;

(b) an obligation on the franchisee not to acquire financial interests in the capital of a competing undertaking, such as would give the franchisee the power to influence the economic conduct of such undertaking;

(c) an obligation on the franchisee not to disclose to third parties the know-how provided by the franchisor as long as this know-how is not in the public domain;

(d) an obligation on the franchisee to communicate to the franchisor any experience gained in exploiting the franchise and to grant it, and other franchisees, a non-exclusive licence for the know-how resulting from that experience;

(e) an obligation on the franchisee to inform the franchisor of infringements of licensed intellectual property rights, to take legal action against infringers or to assist the franchisor in any legal actions against infringers;

(f) an obligation on the franchisee not to use know-how licensed by the franchisor for purposes other than the exploitation of the franchise; and

(g) an obligation on the franchisee not to assign the rights and obligations under the franchise agreement without the franchisor's consent.[117]

11-090 This approach might be considered a hangover from the original Franchise Block Exemption where certain clauses in franchises were "white listed" as not falling within art.101(1) or if they did fall within art.101(1), falling within art.101(3). In any event, it is of assistance because insofar as a franchise does not fall within VABE, it provides useful guidance that such clauses are, in principle, unobjectionable under art.101.

---

[113] Guidelines, para.96, et seq.
[114] Guidelines, para.98.
[115] Guidelines, para.100.
[116] Guidelines, para.104.
[117] Guidelines, para.45.

Helpfully, the Guidelines set out various justifications for vertical restraints **11-091** including: (a) solving the free-rider problems, (b) opening up new markets, (c) the need to encourage investment, (d) encouraging retailers to maximise sales, e.g. by maximum resale price impositions, (e) encouraging economies of scale, and (f) uniformity and quality standardisation.[118] In particular, the Guidelines provide specific guidance on the analysis of the competitive effects of franchises.[119] They provide helpful analysis of a particular franchise example which is set out below.

"A manufacturer has developed a new format for selling sweets in so-called fun shops where the sweets can be coloured specially on demand from the consumer. The manufacturer of the sweets has also developed the machines to colour the sweets. The manufacturer also produces the colouring liquids. The quality and freshness of the liquid is of vital importance to producing good sweets. The manufacturer made a success of its sweets through a number of own retail outlets all operating under the same trade name and with the uniform fun image (style of lay-out of the shops, common advertising etc.). In order to expand sales the manufacturer started a franchising system. The franchisees are obliged to buy the sweets, liquid and colouring machine from the manufacturer, to have the same image and operate under the trade name, pay a franchise fee, contribute to common advertising and ensure the confidentiality of the operating manual prepared by the franchisor. In addition, the franchisees are only allowed to sell from the agreed premises, to sell to end users or other franchisees and are not allowed to sell other sweets. The franchisor is obliged not to appoint another franchisee nor operate a retail outlet himself in a given contract territory. The franchisor is also under the obligation to update and further develop its products, the business outlook and the operating manual and make these improvements available to all retail franchisees. The franchise agreements are concluded for a duration of 10 years.

Sweet retailers buy their sweets on a national market from either national producers that cater for national tastes or from wholesalers which import sweets from foreign producers in addition to selling products from national producers. On that market the franchisor's products compete with other brands of sweets. The franchisor has a market share of 30% on the market for sweets sold to retailers. Competition comes from a number of national and international brands, sometimes produced by large diversified food companies. There are many potential points of sale of sweets in the form of tobacconists, general food retailers, cafeterias and specialised sweet shops. The franchisor's market share of the market for machines for colouring food is below 10%.

Most of the obligations contained in the franchise agreements can be deemed necessary to protect the intellectual property rights or maintain the common identity and reputation of the franchised network and fall outside Article 101(1). The restrictions on selling (contract territory and selective distribution) provide an incentive to the franchisees to invest in the colouring machine and the franchise concept and, if not necessary to, at least help maintain the common identity, thereby offsetting the loss of intra-brand competition. The non-compete clause excluding other brands of sweets from the shops for the full duration of the agreements does allow the franchisor to keep the outlets uniform and prevent competitors from benefiting from its trade name. It does not lead to any serious foreclosure in view of the great number of potential outlets available to other sweet producers. The franchise agreements of this franchisor are likely to fulfil the conditions for exemption under Article 101(3) in as far as the obligations contained therein fall under Article 101(1)."

---

[118] Guidelines, para.107.
[119] Guidelines, para.189, et seq.

Selective distribution systems

11-092   The Guidelines gives detailed guidance as to the competition analysis of selective distribution agreements.[120] It draws a distinction between "qualitative selective distribution" and "quantitative selective distribution" networks. The former selects dealers on the basis of objective criteria. These will generally fall outside art.101 provided that: (a) the nature of the products necessitates a selective distribution system; (b) resellers are chosen on the basis of objective qualitative criteria; and (c) the criteria do not go beyond what is necessary. Quantitative selection distribution networks impose quantitative caps, e.g. a maximum number of resellers. These do not benefit from the presumption that they fall outside art.101. The Commission's concerns of selective distribution systems principally occur where inter-brand or intra-brand competition is appreciably restricted. Factors which are taken into account include:

- whether the supplier has a strong market position;
- the number of selective distribution networks in the relevant market;
- the degree of inter-brand competition to the goods being distributed under the selective distribution agreement;
- the risk of foreclosure of more efficient distributors; and
- foreclosure of other suppliers of competitive products, particularly where there is a dense network of selective distribution systems and they have non-compete "single brand" covenants.

11-093   The Guidelines give two examples of selective distribution agreements, one which is likely to be unobjectionable under art.101 and one which is objectionable under art.101.

---

[120] Guidelines, paras 174–188.

CHAPTER 12

ABUSE OF A DOMINANT POSITION

INTRODUCTION

According to general economic theory, the behaviour of a monopolist must be **12-001** scrutinised. This is because a monopolist is able to maximise the profit on the product it sells. Thus the price of the monopolist's product will usually be higher than the marginal selling price (i.e. the cost of the product plus a sufficient profit margin to encourage the investor but no more than necessary) which could exist in a perfectly competitive market. A dominant undertaking can be inefficient and still be able to make a profit. The theory is that such inefficiency benefits only the monopolist and not the consumer, the consumer's welfare or the economy in general. The reasoning is that a monopoly is an unnatural economical condition brought about by factors other than market forces and is generally detrimental to an economy.[1] However, in reality, a monopoly may be a natural market condition. For instance, in a particular market, it may be that a minimum efficient scale of operation is achieved only by an undertaking with a market share of more than 50 per cent because of the need to recoup high capital investment, substantial fixed running costs, etc. In these circumstances, a suspicion of undertakings with large market shares is unjustified. Equally, dominance in a particular market may have been achieved because a highly advanced technological product created after a costly and risky research and development programme has no actual or potential substitutes. It thus creates its own market. In such circumstances, although dominance in a particular market has been achieved, consumers have benefitted by the advancement of technology.

Article 102 of the TFEU (previously art.82 EC Treaty and originally art.86 of the **12-002** Treaty of Rome) prohibits the abuse of a dominant position by one or more undertakings within a substantial part of the internal market in so far as it affects

---

[1] Generally, see R. Whish and D. Bailey, *Competition Law*, 7th edn (Oxford: OUP, 2012).

trade between Member States. Both arts 101 which is concerned with anti-competitive agreements and art.102 complement each other. They are the two primary provisions of the Treaty that reflect the fact that the EU has exclusive competence in the establishment of competition rules necessary for the functioning of the internal market.[2] Where anti-competitive measures do not affect the functioning of the internal market, then the TFEU is inapplicable and national competition laws of Member States are relevant.[3]

IPR monopolies and dominant position

12-003   Although intellectual property rights such as patents confer a monopoly on their owners, they do not themselves create market power yet alone dominance in a market. Whilst they create a monopoly for, e.g an invention (patent) there will often be actual or potential close substitutes to products or processes incorporating the said invention.[4] The public is interested in products and services and not intellectual property. Intellectual property in itself does not create a market for a product but is capable of protecting that market. Its ability to protect the market share of products or services which are the subject of IPRs is often described as representing a "barrier to entry" to other suppliers producing the protected product or service.

12-004   In considering whether an IPR can act as a barrier to entry to a particular market, the nature of the IPR is relevant. Different IPRs protect at different levels in a particular market. For instance, if one considers the market for videoscreens, the following hierarchy of IPRs apply:

Product/technology	Relevant IPR
Bus/chipset technologies which have become technological standards for videoscreens	"Gateway" patents
Type of screen: e.g. LCD, CRT, plasma	Patents/know-how
Design of screen: e.g. black plastic/modern-looking/retro-looking	Registered and unregistered designs
Brand: e.g. Dell, Acer, ViewSonic	Trade marks

12-005   It can be seen from the above that apart from patents, IPRs do not play an important role in assisting an undertaking to achieve a dominant position in a relevant market. Thus, in the above example, if the bus/chipset technologies of a particular undertaking have become a technological standard for videoscreens such that incorporation of them into videoscreens are indispensable for all manufacturers, then a licence for the patents which protect those technological standards would be necessary for an undertaking to operate in the videoscreen market. These patents are called Standard Essential Patents ("SEPs"). The organisation responsible for setting a technological standard will often, prior to incorporating the protected technology into the standard, require an undertaking from the SEP owner that the SEP will be licensed on FRAND (fair, reasonable and non-discriminatory) terms. The Court

---

[2]   art.3(b) TFEU.
[3]   See para.13-015.
[4]   See para.2, 2017 *Antitrust Guidelines for the Licensing of Intellectual Property*, Department of Justice.

of Justice has held that it is an abuse of a dominant position for a SEP owner who has given an undertaking to license a SEP not to give such a licence.[5]

When considering the type of screens, it may be that the market for LCD screens **12-006** is clearly separate and distinct from that for CRT or plasma screens because of the qualities, price, etc. of such screens. In that case, patents which protect LCD screen technology will allow its owner to be dominant in the market for LCD screens. However, if CRT or plasma screens compete with LCD screens (in the sense that a significant price increase for LCD screens will increase demand for CRT or plasma screens), then a patent for a LCD screen will not confer sufficient market power on its owner to give the owner dominance in the market for screens.

However, it will be extremely rare for design rights or trade marks to act as a bar- **12-007** rier to entry to a particular market. This is because undertakings that cannot use the protected design for a screen or a particular trade mark are still capable of compet- ing against the owner of such design rights or trade marks by using different designs and trade marks.

This chapter is therefore concerned with the use of IPRs by an undertaking which **12-008** is in a dominant position in a relevant market. In particular, it is concerned with the exercise of IPRs where that exercise allows the dominant undertaking to maintain or strengthen its dominant position.

The obligation of a dominant undertaking not to exercise its IPRs but license **12-009** them instead cannot be discussed without regard to the wider debate concerning the behaviour in the marketplace of market power by dominant undertakings. In particular, are dominant undertakings under a special responsibility not to maintain or enhance their monopoly power? Is there a presumption that the exercise of market power by a dominant undertaking is anti-competitive? It is this issue which is highly contentious. One school of thought is inherently distrustful of dominant undertakings where it is assumed that a dominant undertaking will inevitably seek to take advantage of its dominant position to the detriment of consumers. Another school of thought has no such distrust and indeed takes the view that a dominant undertaking may well be dominant precisely because it was more competitive (in providing superior products at low prices) than their competitors.

In the US these two ideologies are known as the Harvard and Chicago schools.[6] **12-010** In the late 20th century, the Chicago school became the prevailing theory. It mandates a thorough economics-based evidential approach to any allegation of abuse of a dominant position with the focus being on the effect of the alleged abusive conduct on consumer welfare. However, in recent times, the pendulum has swung back towards a synthesis of the Harvard and Chicago schools.[7] This arises for two reasons. First, there is a recognition that markets do not behave in the perfect manner that the Chicago school believed that they did, such that a dominant position will only be temporary. In short, it may be that once an undertaking becomes dominant, it becomes impervious to competition. In such circumstances, antitrust action may become warranted.[8] For instance, software such as Microsoft® Windows® may be dominant not because it is better than other operating systems

---

[5] See *Huawei Technologies Co Ltd v ZTE Corp* (C-170/13) ECLI:EU:C:2015:477. See para.12-216

[6] For a thorough review of these two schools of thought, see T.A. Piraino, "Reconciling the Harvard and Chicago Schools: A New Antitrust Approach for the 21st Century" (2007) 82(2) *Indiana Law Journal*, article 4.

[7] T.A. Piraino, "Reconciling the Harvard and Chicago Schools: A New Antitrust Approach for the 21st Century" (2007) 82(2) *Indiana Law Journal*, 362.

[8] T.A. Piraino, "Reconciling the Harvard and Chicago Schools: A New Antitrust Approach for the 21st

but rather because it has a large installed base and is compatible and integrated into other application programs.[9] Such monopolies becomes self-perpetuating and make it very difficult for effective competition. Secondly, a thorough economics-based evidential approach is difficult to predict and enforce. Therefore, an economic approach requires analysis as to whether the conduct of dominant undertakings is merely the dominant undertaking reaping the benefits of its superior products or acumen.[10] This type of analysis is problematic and very expensive. In particular, where the onus lies on the claimant to prove that the conduct of the dominant undertaking has an anti-competitive effect. This may be very difficult to prove.

12-011 In recent years, it has been recognised that antitrust law has failed and that the US economy has failed the many and enriched the few. As said by the Nobel prize winning economist, Joseph Stiglitz, antitrust law has been taken over by an army of economists and lawyers with their strong presumptions that the market is in fact naturally competitive and places the burden on the complainant who contends otherwise. They argue that one need not worry about monopoly power because it is only temporary. Yet, as he says, economic theory and evidence has laid waste to such claims.[11]

12-012 Thus, it has been said that the US is moving away from a false dichotomy between per se anti-competitve conduct (e.g. price fixing) and other conduct which needs to be subject to a "rule of reason" full economics-based approach to one which combines the Harvard and Chicago schools. This post-Chicago school of thought argues that certain market structures and competitive conduct are more likely to have anti-competitive consequences. If a "quick look" considers the nature of the conduct and the market power of the undertaking and if it raises a prima facie case that the conduct is anti-competitive, the burden of proof shifts to the defendant to demonstrate that the conduct favours competition.[12] Indeed, the Supreme Court has favoured such an analysis whereby the degree of inquiry is "meet for the case" and that "quality of proof required should vary with the circumstances".[13]

12-013 In relation to intellectual property, the approach of the US Department of Justice to licensing of IPRs is in its 2017 Guidelines.[14] Whilst focussed on whether IPR licences are anti- or pro- competition, it states a number of general principles. First, it says that intellectual property and antitrust laws share the common purpose of promoting innovation and enhancing consumer welfare.[15] They then say that there are three principles when considering conduct relating to intellectual property: (i) the analysis of conduct involving intellectual property is the same as conduct

---

Century" (2007) 82(2) *Indiana Law Journal*, 365 citing *United States v E.I.DuPont de Nemours & Co* 96 F.T.C 653, 751 (1980).

[9] T.A. Piraino, "Reconciling the Harvard and Chicago Schools: A New Antitrust Approach for the 21st Century" (2007) 82(2) *Indiana Law Journal*, 365.

[10] For instance, economic analysis would involve consideration whether the prohibition of the alleged abusive conduct would deter undertakings from adopting supracompetitive market strategies which allow them in the first place to become dominant in a marketplace.

[11] J. Stiglitz, "America has a Monopoly Problem—and It's Huge" *The Nation*, 23 October 2017.

[12] T.A. Piraino, "Reconciling the Harvard and Chicago Schools: A New Antitrust Approach for the 21st Century" (2007) 82(2) *Indiana Law Journal*, p.365. *California Dental Association v Federal Trade Commission*, 526 U.S. 756 (1999).

[13] *California Dental Association v Federal Trade Commission*, 526 U.S. 756 (1999) at 780–781.

[14] Care must be taken with these guidelines because they are concerned more with the anti-competitive effects of licences rather than the exercise of IPRs or a refusal to license by a dominant undertaking.

[15] para.1 citing *Atari Games Corp v Nintendo of Am., Inc*, 897 F.2d 1572, 1576 (Fed. Cir., 1990) and *Intergraph Corp v Intel Corp*, 195 F.3d 1346, 1362 (Fed. Cir., 1999).

involving other forms of property; (ii) there is no presumption that intellectual property confers market power; and (iii) intellectual property licensing is usually pro-competitive. It continues to say that antitrust laws do not impose liability upon a firm for a unilateral refusal to assist its competitors because doing so may, in part, undermine incentives for investment and innovation. It says that the exercise of IPRs is neither particularly free from scrutiny nor particularly suspect under antitrust laws.[16] The 2017 Guidelines say that even if an IPR owner lawfully acquires or maintains market power, the owner could still engage in anti-competitive conduct in connection with such IPR.[17]

In the EU, the approach to the exercise of IPRs by a dominant undertaking or a **12-014** refusal to license by a dominant undertaking has been to avoid applying too rigorous a theoretical approach. Rather, its approach is that the exercise of IPRs or a refusal to license by a dominant undertaking is not per se objectionable but that, in "exceptional and clearly defined circumstances", it may infringe art.102.[18] Therefore, the Court of Justice has favoured a "case-by-case" approach which is typical of common law countries. This case-by-case approach looks at particular factual circumstances, e.g. the exercise of rights by the owner of a SEP patent[19] or where the exercise of a right by a dominant undertaking in one market allows it to leverage its power into another market.[20] Thus, the Court of Justice has said that "due account must be taken of the specific legal and factual circumstances in the case".[21] The focus is on whether the conduct of a dominant undertaking uses methods different from those governing normal competition in products or services which have the effect of hindering the maintenance of the degree of competition or indeed the growth of that competition.[22] The focus is on the effect of the behaviour on consumers and end-users rather than a desire to have a number of competitors in a particular marketplace. If the latter were to prevail, it would mean that an undertaking dominant in a market would be required to take action to allow competitors to compete effectively with it. Thus, in cases involving a refusal to license IPR by a dominant undertaking, even where such may eliminate or weaken competition, it is a legitimate answer by the dominant undertaking to say that an obligation to license IPRs would act as an disincentive to innovate and thereby create the very IPRs that a defendant may argue it should be compelled to license. This is a classic and legitimate *ex ante* argument.[23]

Space elevator

In order to understand the above, it is helpful to consider an example of the **12-015** development of a space elevator.

A consortium of transport companies undertakes the very risky venture of researching into nanofilament technology for the purpose of providing a space elevator from earth to

---

[16] para.2, 2.1.

[17] para.2.2.

[18] See *Huawei Technologies Co. Ltd v ZTE Corp* (C-170/13) ECLI:EU:C:2015:477 at [62].

[19] As was the case in *Huawei*.

[20] *Microsoft Corp v EC Commission* (T-201/04) [2007] E.C.R. II-3601. This is discussed at para.12-198.

[21] *Huawei*, at [56] citing *Post Danmark* (C-209/10) EU:C:2012:172, at [26] and case law cited thereto.

[22] *Huawei*, at [45].

[23] The difference between *ex ante* and *ex post* competitive analysis is considered at para.8-047. Thus, in *Microsoft Corp v EC Commission*, Microsoft made such an argument but it failed on the facts.

geostationary orbit.[24] They agree that if the research is successful, they will compete against each other but not license any third parties with any resulting IPR. Ultimately, such is a successful venture and a number of elevators are established on the equator for hauling goods into orbit. They obtain patents which mean that others cannot build the nanofilament elevators. The success and ease of transport ensures that rocket-propelled haulage of goods becomes obsolete being far too expensive as well as being very unenvironmental. Thus, they own "gateway" IPR[25] as the only economically viable way of transporting products to space is via the space elevators. The consortium of transport companies chooses not to provide the facility or license the technology to other transport companies, including those who declined to invest. Accordingly, the consortium has a collective monopoly over the transport of goods from Earthside to space. A third party transport company who wishes to transport goods from Earthside to space applies for access to the space elevator or alternatively applies for a compulsory licence of the patented nanofilament technology so that it can build its own space elevator.

12-016   The patented space elevator technology can be considered as an "essential facility" necessary for any operator who wishes to compete in the earth-to-space transport market (whether such is transport of freight or people). Transport operators are obliged to use a space elevator for the purpose of transporting freight or people into space. Competitors cannot build competing space elevators because of the patents. Equally, they cannot economically use rocket-propelled haulage of goods into space as it is far cheaper to use a space elevator rather than rockets.

12-017   In such circumstances, some economists may consider that either these transport companies should be permitted to use the space elevators for the purpose of transporting the goods of their customers from Earthside to space or alternatively obtain a licence to build competing space elevators (in either case upon FRAND terms). These economists would argue that it is detrimental to the interests of the consumers and businesses for a consortium of transport companies to retain complete control of technology critical for competing in a market and also the market that such technology protects. They would argue that the cost of research and development of the transport companies can be taken into account when considering the monetary terms of the licence.

12-018   On the other hand, other economists would argue that it would be wrong to oblige the consortium to grant access to its space elevator network to third party transport companies or to license its technology to such entities. They would say that the consortium is simply reaping the reward of its risky investment and that even though access to the technology is indispensable for anyone who wishes to compete in the market of space transport services, it is justified in refusing access to third parties, especially those who were not prepared to embark upon the risky venture. To permit such persons to obtain compulsory licences, they would say, would ultimately encourage free-riding and discourage risky innovative long-term research. Thus, even if the consortium were charging prices that were the maximum that the market could afford,[26] they would say that there should be no interference as without such a consortium, there would be no space elevator business at all.

12-019   The Chicago school would consider that such dominance has been achieved as the consequence of a superior product, business acumen and investment and

---

[24] This sounds science fiction but is currently been researched. It was inspired by Arthur C. Clarke's book "Fountains of Paradise". A case of fiction inspiring fact.

[25] See para.8-048 for meaning of gateway IPR.

[26] i.e. the price which if increased would make use of the space transport services uneconomic for the vast majority of undertakings and thus make the use of rocket-propelled haulage economic.

therefore the dominant undertaking should not be penalised.[27] Consequently, it would say that the conduct of the consortium should be immune from attack under antitrust or competition laws. The Harvard school would view the dominance of the consortium with concern and impose upon it a special responsibility not to hinder competition by those outside the consortium.

The EU approach does not grant immunity to undertakings whose dominance has **12-020** been gained by business acumen, research or investment. Rather, it is more nuanced. It would weigh up the advantages of an increase in competition by giving competitors access to the technology versus whether such would disincentivise undertakings to carry out research and innovation[28]. Put another way, it would consider whether the increase in competition in the *technology market* by permitting competitors to have access to such an essential facility would have a detrimental effect on the *innovation market*.

In the case of the space elevator, it might well be said that the huge risk in **12-021** researching and development of it would only have been undertaken if investors were confident that market dominance for a substantial period would be obtained. In other words, they only invested in the hope that if successful, they could get a good return on their investment by reason of the ability to make supra-competitive profits for a substantial period by reason of them being the only persons who could operate a space elevator. Furthermore, it could be strongly contended that other haulage companies were given the opportunity to invest and declined. To allow access would be to allow "free riders" who were averse to risk. Put baldly, as they would not have shared in the loss if the project had failed, why should they share in the success? This would be a strong argument against allowing undertakings access to the space elevator technology (at least for a substantial period).

TRIPS, international treaties and abuse

International treaties on intellectual property laws have recognised that the grant **12-022** of IPRs does not always work in the interests of the consumer. Of the international treaties, the most relevant for the purpose of this chapter is TRIPS. Thus, in the general provisions of TRIPS art.8(2) states:

"2.   Appropriate measures, provided that they are consistent with the provisions of this Agreement, may be needed to prevent the abuse of intellectual property rights by right holders or the resort to practices which unreasonably restrain trade or adversely affect the international transfer of technology."

In the field of copyright, art.13 TRIPS states that: **12-023**

"Members shall confine limitations or exceptions to exclusive rights to certain special

---

[27]   See T.A. Piraino, "Reconciling the Harvard and Chicago Schools: A New Antitrust Approach for the 21st Century" (2007) 82(2) *Indiana Law Journal*, 361 and *United States v Grinnel Corp* 384 U.S. 563 (1966). In the 2017 Department of Justice Guidelines, it cites this case in saying that where an asset (which could be IPR) enables its owner to obtain significant supra-competitive profits by reason of a superior product, business acumen or historical accident, this does not violate antitrust laws (see para.2.2). The author finds it difficult to consider why a monopoly obtained by historical accident should be immune from antitrust investigation as it is not, ex hypothesi, the result of the endeavours and investment of an undertaking.

[28]   See Commission Decision relating to Article [101] of the [TFEU] (COMP/C-37.92) at [713]–[729]. On appeal, the General Court upheld the Commission's approach *Microsoft Corp v EC Commission* (T-201/04) [2007] E.C.R. II-3601 at [688]–[712]. This aspect of the case is discussed later in this chapter at para.12-215.

cases which do not conflict with a normal exploitation of the work and do not unreasonably prejudice the legitimate interests of the right holder."

12-024   In the field of patents, there is a similar provision. Article 30 of TRIPS provides that:

"Members may provide limited exceptions to the exclusive rights conferred by a patent, provided that such exceptions do not unreasonably prejudice the legitimate interests of the patent owner, taking account of the legitimate interests of third parties."

12-025   Article 31 stipulates that where the law of a Contracting Party allows for other use of the subject-matter of a patent without the authorisation of the right holder, including use by the government or third parties authorised by the government, certain provisions must be respected. For example, art.31(l) provides that where a patent ("the second patent") cannot be exploited without infringing another patent ("the first patent"), a Contracting Party may permit the grant of a compulsory licence of the first patent if the following conditions apply:

"(i)   the invention claimed in the second patent shall involve an important technical advance of considerable economic significance in relation to the invention claimed in the first patent;

(ii)   the owner of the first patent shall be entitled to a cross-licence on reasonable terms to use the invention claimed in the second patent; and

(iii)   the use authorized in respect of the first patent shall be non-assignable except with the assignment of the second patent."

12-026   Finally, art.40 TRIPS states as follows:

"1.   Members agree that some licensing practices or conditions pertaining to intellectual property rights which restrain competition may have adverse effects on trade and may impede the transfer and dissemination of technology.

2.   Nothing in this Agreement shall prevent Members from specifying in their legislation licensing practices or conditions that may in particular cases constitute an abuse of intellectual property rights having an adverse effect on competition in the relevant market. As provided above, a Member may adopt, consistently with the other provisions of this Agreement, appropriate measures to prevent or control such practices, which may include for example exclusive grantback conditions, conditions preventing challenges to validity and coercive package licensing, in the light of the relevant laws and regulations of that Member."

12-027   The purpose of setting out the above provisions is that it can be seen that TRIPS has considered carefully the issue of compulsory licensing of IPRs and determined the conditions where the exercise of rights could be restrained. In *Canada-Patent Protection of Pharmaceutical Products*,[29] the WTO Panel had to consider the effect of art.30. It said that the second and third condition in art.30 had to take account of the economic impact of an exception. In particular, the Panel said that "third parties" included consumers. In other words, art.30 is concerned with the economic impact and the effect on consumers—the same aim as competition law.

12-028   The above matters are raised simply to show that the legislators of TRIPS have considered carefully when the exercise of IPRs should not be permitted. TRIPS arose from prolonged negotiations between WTO members and thus it can be

---

[29] *Canada-Patent Protection of Pharmaceutical Products* WT.DS114/R (Decision of WTO Panel dated 17 March 2000).

presumed that the exceptions have been carefully considered and that the provisions strike a fair balance between the interests of IPR owners and the wider interests of society, economy and the consumer. Such being the case, then it might be suggested that competition law should be very reluctant to intervene in determining the conditions when a dominant undertaking should not be allowed to exercise its rights. For instance, if one considers art.31(l) TRIPS (set out above), such sets out the conditions to be applied to the grant of a compulsory licence of a "blocking" patent which prevents the exploitation of another patent. This includes a requirement that the "blocked" patent must involve an important technical advance of considerable economic significance in relation to the "blocking" patent. Should competition law prohibit the exercise of rights by the owner of the "blocking" patent if it is in a dominant position where such conditions are not satisfied? Would such be TRIPS-compliant?

In the author's opinion, the provisions of TRIPS should infuse, at the very least, **12-029** the consideration by a court or tribunal as to whether the exercise of IPRs is unlawful under competition law, particular art.102. As is often said, IPR law and competition law serve the same aim, namely the wider public interest and consumer welfare.[30] Thus, any court or tribunal applying art.102 should consider TRIPS and its provisions when considering the issue of whether a dominant undertaking is exercising its rights in an abusive manner. It could be said that art.8(2) TRIPS expressly recognises that rights can be exercised abusively where such unreasonably restrain trade or the international transfer of technology and that thus TRIPS implicitly recognises that where the exercise of rights is an abuse of a dominant position under art.102, such can be restrained. However, if an issue arose whether a dominant undertaking who owned a "blocking" patent should be permitted to exercise its rights against an undertaking who is seeking to exploit an invention which is the subject of a blocked patent, it would be surprising if consideration as to whether there is an abuse under art.102 does not involve careful consideration of art.31(l) TRIPS and whether if the conditions in art.31(l) are not satisfied, it would be right to find an abuse of a dominant position.

However, as seen later in this chapter, the European Court has been resistant to **12-030** arguments that TRIPS must be taken into account when considering whether there has been an abuse of a dominant position even though the EU is a member of TRIPS.[31] Thus, although EU intellectual property legislation must be interpreted in the light of the aims and objectives of TRIPS,[32] the European courts have resisted the consideration of such in the context of art.102.[33] In the author's view, this is unfortunate. Whilst recognising that the provisions of the TFEU are clearly the highest form of EU law and that an international treaty such as TRIPS cannot be accorded equal status even if the EU has ratified it, provisions such as art.31(l) address very particular situations and it would be surprising if due weight is not given to such an article which has been subject to very considerable negotiation.[34]

---

[30] e.g. see paras 8-001 to 8-025.
[31] See para.12-135, et seq.
[32] See para.1-180.
[33] See para.12-135.
[34] In this regard, valuable assistance can be obtained from D. Gervais, *The TRIPS Agreement; Drafting History and Analysis*, 4th edn (London: Sweet & Maxwell, 2012).

PLAN OF CHAPTER

12-031   One cannot understand the application of art.102 to intellectual property without first studying its general principles as developed by the court and Commission. Thus, each aspect of art.102 is examined first, on a general level and secondly with regard to intellectual property.

ARTICLE 102

12-032   Article 102 states that:

"Any abuse by one or more undertakings of a dominant position within the internal market or in a substantial part of it shall be prohibited as incompatible with the internal market in so far as it may affect trade between Member States. Such abuse may, in particular, consist in:

(a)   directly or indirectly imposing unfair purchase or selling prices or other unfair trading conditions;
(b)   limiting production, markets or technical development to the prejudice of consumers;
(c)   applying dissimilar conditions to equivalent transactions with other trading parties, thereby placing them at a competitive disadvantage;
(d)   making the conclusion of contracts subject to acceptance by the other parties of supplementary obligations which, by their nature or according to commercial usage, have no connection with the subject of such contracts."

The above list, as suggested by the wording, is not exhaustive of what may constitute an abuse.

12-033   The requirements of art.102 can be categorised as follows:

(a)   dominant position;
(b)   abuse;
(c)   which affects trade between Member States;
(d)   in a substantial part of the internal market; and
(e)   by one or more undertakings.

12-034   Unlike art.101, art.102 has no equivalent of art.101(3) and, thus, an abuse of a dominant position cannot be exempted. However, in the context of determining whether there is an abuse, many of the factors that are considered under art.101(3) will be considered under art.102.[35]

DOMINANT POSITION

Market definition

12-035   In order to determine whether an undertaking has a dominant position, it is necessary to define the relevant market in which it is alleged to be dominant. Thus, one must define the relevant product and geographic market. Normally, one is concerned with a product market but the relevant market may be a technology market or an

---

[35]   Guidance on the Commission's enforcement priorities in applying Article 82 EC Treaty to abusive exclusionary conduct by dominant undertakings OJ [2009] C45/7, paras 28–31 where the Guidance sets out the factors to be taken into account where the dominant undertaking claims its conduct is justified.

innovation market.[36] The issue of what is the relevant market is of crucial importance in art.102 proceedings. However, it is also relevant in any situation where a tribunal is seeking to determine whether there has been anti-competitive conduct. Therefore, it is also relevant to investigations into anti-competitive conduct under art.101. The Commission has issued a Notice on the Definition of Relevant Market for the purposes of EU competition law which is a very helpful, clear and practical guide for competition lawyers and economic advisors.[37] It sets out in detail how the Commission will apply the concepts of relevant product market and relevant geographic market. It represents a distillation of the Commission's experience and knowledge in countless decisions in defining such concepts, in particular, in relation to cases concerning mergers and acquisitions where the definition of such concepts is crucial to any finding of dominance. It thus provides a valuable guide not only to the Commission's methodology but also for courts in disputes in national proceedings concerning anti-competitive conduct.

The Commission explains in the Notice why the definition of the relevant market **12-036** is important:

> "Market definition is a tool to identify and define the boundaries of competition between firms. It serves to establish the framework within which competition policy is applied by the Commission. The main purpose of market definition is to identify in a systematic way the competitive restraints that the undertakings involve face. The objective of defining a market in both its product and geographic dimension is to identify those actual competitors of the undertakings involved that are capable of constraining those undertakings' behaviour and of preventing them from behaving independently of effective competitive pressure. It is from this perspective that the market definition makes it possible inter alia to calculate market shares that would convey meaningful information regarding market power for the purposes of assessing dominance or for the purposes of applying Article [101]."[38]

Relevant market

The definition of the relevant market must be done with the utmost care and in **12-037** investigative proceedings, evidence is required. A failure to properly define the relevant market will put any findings of abuse into jeopardy. Thus, the CJEU annulled a decision of the Commission where it failed to state in detail the peculiarities which distinguished three markets from each other, that of the market for light containers for preserved meat; the market for light containers for preserved fish; and the market for metal closures for the canning industry.[39] In *Tierce Ladbroke SA v Commission*,[40] the General Court summarised the test for determining the relevant product market as follows:

> "According to settled case law, for the purposes of applying Article [102] of the Treaty, the relevant product or service market includes products or services which are substitutable or sufficiently interchangeable with the product or service in question, not only in

---

[36] *United Brands Co v EC Commission* (27/76) [1978] E.C.R. 287; *Hoffmann La Roche v EC Commission* (85/76) [1979] E.C.R. 461. For the meaning of "technology market" and "innovation market" see paras 8-033 and 8-034.

[37] Commission Notice on the Definition of Relevant Market for the Purposes of Community Competition [1997] OJ C273/5.

[38] Commission Notice on Definition of Relevant Market [1997] OJ C273/5, para.2.

[39] (6/72) [1973] E.C.R. 215; [1973] C.M.L.R. 199 at [33].

[40] *Tierce Ladbroke SA v EC Commission* (T-504/93) [1997] E.C.R. II-923 at 953.

terms of their objective characteristics, by virtue of which they are particularly suitable for satisfying the constant needs of consumers, but also in terms of the conditions of competition and/or the structure of supply and demand on the market in question."[41]

Product interchangeability

12-038   The ability of consumers to switch easily to available substitute products constitutes the most immediate and effectively disciplinary force on the suppliers of a given product. If the effect of an undertaking raising the price of the products that it supplies is to cause consumers to switch to other substitutes on the market, then clearly there is competition between the various products. Thus, the relevant product market will include those products which are substitutable for the product in issue. In *Hoffmann La Roche v EC Commission*,[42] the court said that:

> "The concept of the relevant product market in fact implies that there can be effective competition between the products which form part of it and this presupposes that there is a sufficient degree of interchangeability between all the products forming part of the same market."[43]

12-039   This concept of interchangeability has other economic labels, namely cross-elasticity of demand and demand substitutability. All three terms have been used by the court and Commission and essentially mean the same.[44] One way of determining the substitutability of products is to postulate a hypothetically small, lasting change in relative prices and evaluate the likely reaction of customers to that increase.[45] This exercise is sometimes known as the SSNIP test ("Small but Significant Non-transitory Increase in Price"). A large increase in sales of other substitutable products means that there is a high degree of cross-elasticity of demand and thus they can be considered interchangeable to a large degree. In this regard, the Commission says as follows:

> "The question to be answered is whether the parties' customers would switch to readily available substitutes or to suppliers located elsewhere in response to a hypothetical small (in the range 5% to 10%) but permanent relative price increase in the products and areas being considered. If substitution were enough to make the price increase unprofitable because of the resulting loss of sales, additional substitutes and areas are included in the relevant market. This would be done until the set of products and geographical areas is such that small, permanent increases in relative prices would be profitable. The equivalent analysis is applicable in cases concerning the concentration of buying power, where the starting-point would then be the supplier and the price test serves to identify the alternative distribution channels or outlets for the supplier's products... ."[46]

---

[41] See also *L'Oréal v De Nieuwe AMCK PVBA* (31/80) [1980] E.C.R. 3775 at [25]; *Nederlandsche Banden Industrie Michelin NV v EC Commission* (322/81) [1983] E.C.R. 3461 at [37]; *AKZO Chemie v EC Commission* (C-62/86) [1991] E.C.R. I-3359 at [51]; *Hilti v Commission* (T-30/89) [1991] E.C.R. II-1439 at [64]; and *Tetra Pak v Commission* (T-83/91) [1994] E.C.R. II-755 at [63].

[42] (88/76) [1979] E.C.R. 461; [1979] 3 C.M.L.R. 211.

[43] (88/76) [1979] E.C.R. 461; [1979] 3 C.M.L.R. 211 at [28].

[44] See (27/76) [1978] E.C.R. 287; [1978] 1 C.M.L.R. 429 at [22–28] where all three terms are used. If there is a difference, it is that interchangeability is used more often in relation to the characteristics of products and cross-elasticity of demand is used in relation to the effect that price variations have on sales of similar competing products.

[45] Commission Notice on Definition of Relevant Market [1997] OJ C273/5, para.15.

[46] Commission Notice on Definition of Relevant Market [1997] OJ C273/5, para.17.

Thus, the Commission gives a practical example relating to soft-drink bottlers.[47] **12-040**
In order to determine whether different flavours of soft drinks belong to the same
market, the question to be asked would be whether consumers of Flavour A would
switch to other flavours when confronted with a permanent price increase of 5–10
per cent for Flavour A. If a sufficient number of consumers did swap to Flavour B,
then the relevant product market would include Flavour B.

The use of the SSNIP test is used in conjunction with the "hypothetical **12-041**
monopolist" test to determine the relevant product market. In essence, the tribunal
is seeking to determine the smallest product group in which a hypothetical
monopolist controlling that product group could profitably sustain supra-
competitive prices, i.e. prices that are at least a small but significant amount above
competitive levels. One starts with the products under question, e.g. the products
that a party supplies and applies the SSNIP test. If the party can raise the prices of
those products by 5–10 per cent above competitive levels, then such suggests that
the products are the relevant market. If such cannot be done, then the tribunal must
repeatedly widen the inquiry into other products and carry out the same test until a
group of products have been found for which it is profitable for the hypothetical
monopolist to sustain prices 5–10 per cent above competitive levels.[48] Unfortunately, this test is of little practical use because it is very difficult to predict what
will happen in the marketplace if a SSNIP was applied to a set of products and
undertakings are, not surprisingly, loathe to carry out a SSNIP on their products
simply for the purpose of gathering economic data. Thus, inquiry tends to be more
based on considerations of what goods on the market are interchangeable with each
other.

Whether or not a product is interchangeable with others will depend principally **12-042**
upon a number of factors: the characteristics of the actual product, the perceived
nature of the product by consumers, the availability of the product, the market
awareness of the product, and the price of the product. A good illustration of the
factors which will be taken into account in considering the interchangeability of a
product is in *United Brands*.[49] In that case, the issue was whether other fruit
products competed with bananas. The Commission maintained that there was a
demand for bananas which was distinct from the demand for other fresh fruit
produce. Features of the banana were that:

(a) It was an all-year fruit as it could be ripened at any time. Thus there was no
unavoidable seasonal substitution with other fruits.
(b) It had certain characteristics, e.g. appearance, taste, softness, lack of seedls,
easy handling and a constant level of production which enables it to satisfy
the very young, the old and the sick.

These characteristics distinguished the banana from other fruits and this was **12-043**
borne out in surveys which showed that the seasonal arrival of other fruits did not
appreciably affect demand for bananas. Further, it was found that because of the
flexible way in which imports were controlled and their marketing was adjusted,
the price of bananas was also not seasonally affected. Thus, the court held that fresh

---

[47] Commission Notice on Definition of Relevant Market [1997] OJ C273/5, para.18.
[48] This test was set out in *Attheraces Ltd v British Horseracing Board* [2006] E.C.D.R. 13; [2006]
F.S.R. 20 at [135–136] and is taken from the *OFT's Guidelines on Market Definition* (paras 2.5–
2.10).
[49] (27/76) [1978] E.C.R. 287; [1978] 1 C.M.L.R. 429.

fruit was only to a very limited extent substitutable for bananas and that the banana market constituted a market sufficiently distinct from other fresh fruit markets.

Secondary market—consumables, spare parts and maintenance and support

12-044   Many products that are sold need to be repaired, maintained or supported. Therefore, in the case of cars, over their lifetime, they will need to be serviced, maintained and repaired. In the case of inkjet printers, the user will need to buy inkjet cartridges over the lifetime of the printer. Buyers of hardware and licensees of software will normally enter into annual support and maintenance contracts for the hardware and software. Often, an issue will arise as to whether this "aftersales" market is a separate market to the primary market for the goods or services sold. This is often relevant where a supplier seeks to leverage its market strength in the primary market into the aftersales market. For instance, let us take an example.

Consumables

12-045   In a competitive market with many independent manufacturers of inkjet printers, a manufacturer of Brand X inkjet printers sells its own Brand X inkjet cartridges for use with its Brand X printers. An independent manufacturer who sells inkjet cartridges compatible with Brand X inkjet printers takes the stance that the manufacturer of Brand X inkjet printers is charging unfair prices or unfairly enforcing IPRs against independent manufacturers of inkjet cartridges compatible with Brand X printers. The independent manufacturer therefore alleges that the Brand X manufacturer is abusing a dominant position. It says that the relevant market is the aftersales market for Brand X inkjet cartridges. The inkjet manufacturer of Brand X inkjet printers says that there is no distinct aftersales market for Brand X inkjet cartridges. It explains that when a consumer decides whether or not to buy Brand X inkjet printers, that consumer considers the "whole life" cost of using that printer, i.e. the total cost of the printer *and* inkjet cartridges over the lifetime of the printer and not merely the cost of the printer. Hence, it argues that if it were to raise its prices significantly for Brand X inkjet cartridges then consumers would buy Brand Y inkjet printers instead. Consequently, it argues that as the market for inkjet printers is fragmented with many different brands, it does not have a dominant position in the relevant market. In contrast, the independent manufacturer of inkjet cartridges which are compatible with Brand X inkjet printers says that there is a "single brand" aftersales market and that when the consumer buys a Brand X printer, they do not take into account the cost of inkjet printers.

12-046   It will be appreciated that whether there is a separate aftersales market is highly fact-dependent. Thus, it is probably right to say that consumers do take into account when buying inkjet printers, the cost of inkjet cartridges and consequently they make a "whole lifetime cost" decision. Equally, because cars are known to break down and require regular servicing, a buyer of a car model probably also takes into account how often that model is known to break down and the degree of servicing that it requires. However, it is probably wrong to say that when a company takes a licence for a software product, it factors into that decision the cost of maintenance and support of that software. Equally, when a buyer buys a mobile telephone, it is also probably wrong to state that a buyer factors in the "whole lifetime" cost of servicing and repairing that mobile phone. This is due to the fact that most buyers buy mobile phones on contract and therefore expect to upgrade that phone within two or three years and mobile phones do not tend to break down during that period.

Spare parts

In a case in the 1970s, *Hugin Kassaregister v EC Commission*,[50] a London firm, **12-047** Liptons, which repaired cash registers, complained to the Commission that Hugin, a manufacturer of cash registers, had refused to supply them with spare parts for its machines as they were not part of Hugin's dealer network. The court, upholding the Commission,[51] said that the relevant product market was that of Hugin spare parts, as these were not interchangeable with spare parts of cash registers of other makes.[52] Hugin had argued that the supply of spare parts could not be considered a separate market but rather an essential parameter of competition in the market for cash registers as a whole. The court also distinguished between the market for the provision of services relating to maintenance and repair work and that of the product market for spare parts. In *Volvo v Veng*,[53] a case in the 1980s, which concerned body panels for Volvo cars, Mischo AG was of the clear view that the relevant market was the market made up of body panels sold by Volvo and components which were capable of being substituted for them. As it was necessary for the body panels to have exactly the same shape as the original body panels produced by the manufacturer and these parts were protected by a registered design, it meant that Volvo had a dominant position.

In its 1997 Notice, the Commission has stated that a narrow definition of market **12-048** for secondary products, for instance, spare parts, may result when compatibility with the primary product is important.[54] Thus, problems of finding compatible secondary products together with the existence of high prices and a long lifetime of the primary products may render relative price increases of secondary products profitable

In *CEAHR v Commission*,[55] the Commission investigated the spare parts sector **12-049** for luxury watches. A complaint was made by the independent watch repairing sector trade organisation that a consortium of Swiss watch manufacturers were abusing a collective dominant position in the market of spare parts for their watches. The complaint was dismissed by the Commission who said that following investigation, it could not be concluded that there were two separate markets: one for watches and one for spare parts for watches. It thus held that the Swiss watch manufacturers did not have a dominant position. The independent trade organisation appealed to the General Court. In a decision which repays careful examination, the General Court held that the Commission's analysis of the relevant market was flawed in a number of ways. One issue was whether the relevant market could be compartmentalised into a series of single-brand spare part markets. The General Court considered that the Commission's analysis that such did not exist was flawed. For instance, it had not shown that the consumer was concerned about the price of

---

[50] *Hugin Kassaregister v EC Commission* (22/78) [1979] E.C.R. 1869; [1979] 3 C.M.L.R. 345.
[51] Although it reversed the Commission's decision on other grounds.
[52] (22/78) [1979] 3 C.M.L.R. 345 at [7]. See also (T-30/89) [1991] E.C.R. II-1439; [1992] 4 C.M.L.R. 16, where the General Court held that the Commission's finding that a relevant product market was nails produced for a specific nail gun manufactured by Hilti was correct. This was upheld on appeal (C-333/94P) [1994] E.C.R. I-667.
[53] (238/87) [1988] E.C.R. 6211; [1989] 4 C.M.L.R. 122.
[54] Commission Notice on Definition of Relevant Market [1997] OJ C273/5, para.56.
[55] (T-427/08) [2010] E.C.R II-5865.

spare parts when it bought a luxury watch and thus would have bought a different brand watch if the price of spare parts for a particular brand was increased (applying the SSNIP test[56]). It also held that the Commission had committed a manifest error in finding that there was not a separate spare parts market.[57] The matter was then remitted back to the European Commission who held that the primary and secondary (aftersales) markets were separate and distinct. Therefore, as regards repairs and maintenance, there was limited substitutability for repair services across brands so there were separate markets for each brand.[58]

Repair and maintenance

12-050   This approach was followed in the European Commission's decision in *IBM*.[59] The case concerned IBM's dealings with undertakings who supplied repair and maintenance services for IBM mainframes. These undertakings needed access to certain "inputs" from IBM (both hardware and software) to permit them to carry out these services. Thus, an issue arose as to what was the relevant market. Was there a separate aftermarket to the market for IBM mainframes? The Commission identified that there were two potential aftermarkets—the market required for the "inputs" for maintaining IBM mainframes and also the provision of IBM mainframe hardware and operating system maintenance services. It said that the issue of whether these aftermarkets were separate markets to the primary market depended on the likely reaction of consumers to moderate price increases in the aftermarket. If increases in the prices of "inputs" for a particular brand did not cause consumers to switch brands in the mainframe market, then the two markets could be considered separate. The Commission said that when applying *CEAHR* it would be appropriate to consider that a single-brand "input" aftermarket was the relevant market if switching to other secondary products (i.e. the inputs) from other brands was not possible and there were high switching costs for the primary product (i.e. the IBM mainframe). The Commission's preliminary assessment was that the relevant market was "inputs" for IBM mainframes or maintenance/repair services for IBM mainframes.[60]

Relevant product markets and legal monopolies

12-051   Where an undertaking has a legal monopoly for the manufacture of certain goods or for the supply of certain services, there has been a tendency for the Commission and the Court to define the relevant market restrictively. An illustration of this can be seen in *British Leyland Plc v EC Commission*.[61] In this case, by operation of law, a person in the UK seeking to import a British Leyland car had to obtain a certificate of conformity from British Leyland certifying that the vehicle conformed to a previously approved type vehicle. A trade had developed in the re-importation of Metro cars from Belgium due to the price difference between the two countries. The Commission claimed that British Leyland was operating its monopoly in an abusive manner.

---

[56] For SSNIP, see para.8-035.
[57] See [110]–[121].
[58] *CEAHR v Commission* (T-712/14) ECLI:EU:T:2017:478 at [13]–[14]. It should be noted that despite this finding, the Commission held that there was no abuse under art.102.
[59] COMP/39.692—*IBM Maintenance Services* [2012] OJ C18/6.
[60] See [20]–[24].
[61] *British Leyland Plc v EC Commission* (226/84) [1987] 1 C.M.L.R. 185.

The CJEU held that the relevant market was that of services which were **12-052** indispensable to dealers who wished to sell the vehicles manufactured by British Leyland in a specific geographical area. In such circumstances, there was clearly no interchangeability between certificates for British Leyland cars and other makes of cars. Similarly, other manufacturers could not provide certificates for British Leyland cars. Thus they could not enter into the market. This analysis favoured the conclusion of a restrictive relevant market.[62] However, it is submitted that such analysis is overly artificial. Consumers are not interested in the purchase and sale of legal certificates but in cars. It is submitted that the proper analysis would have been to determine the relevant product market by reference to British Leyland cars. Such would have meant that British Leyland did not have a dominant position. However, such would not have meant that the practice of British Leyland would have been permissible because it would have amounted to an unjustified quantitative restriction to trade between Member States and, thus, be unlawful under art.34 TFEU.[63]

Relevant product market and raw materials

The relevant product market does not have to be a market for a finished product. **12-053** Competition and thus product markets are capable of existing at all levels of a manufacturing process. In *Commercial Solvents v EC Commission*,[64] the applicants manufactured nitropropane and aminobutanol which were intermediary products for the manufacture of ethambutanol. The latter was used as an anti-tuberculosis drug and was in competition with other drugs. The matter came to the Commission's attention because the applicants had refused to sell aminobutanol to a competitor because the applicants themselves wished to enter the market for the derivative product, ethambutanol.

The court, upholding the Commission, held that for the purposes of defining the **12-054** relevant product market, it was in fact possible to distinguish the market in the raw materials, nitropropane and aminobutanol, from the market on which the product is sold, i.e. anti-tuberculosis drugs of which ethambutanol was but one of several. Clearly, if there were raw products which went to make up nitropropane and aminobutanol, then the relevant product market would be the raw products if the issue of supply of those raw products was at issue. Thus, there may exist many levels of product markets in a manufacturing chain.

Supply substitution

It may be that a product is not interchangeable with other products or that the **12-055** evidence establishes a limited degree of substitutability with other products (i.e. large price increases are required in order to cause customers to switch their allegiances). In such circumstances, the next stage of the inquiry is to ask whether there are any barriers to other undertakings to producing the preferred product. Clearly, if there are no effective barriers, undertakings would start to manufacture the product in issue if there were small and permanent increases in the price of the

---

[62] See also *General Motors Continental NV v EC Commission* (26/75) [1975] E.C.R. 1367; [1976] 1 C.M.L.R. 95, where the court had previously upheld a finding of a similar relevant product market on similar facts.

[63] See Ch.7.

[64] *Commercial Solvents v EC Commission* (6–7/72) [1974] E.C.R. 223; [1974] 1 C.M.L.R. 309.

product. Such would have a disciplinary effect on the competitive behaviour of the companies involved. As the CJEU said in *Michelin v EC Commission*:[65]

> "for the purposes of investigation, the possibly dominant position of an undertaking on a given market, the possibilities of competition must be judged in the context of the market comprising the totality of the products which, with respect to their characteristics, are particularly suitable for satisfying constant needs and are only to a limited extent interchangeable with other products. However, it must be noted that the determination of the relevant market is useful in assessing whether the undertaking concerned is in a position to prevent effective competition from being maintained and behave to an appreciable extent independently of its competitors and customers and consumers. For these purposes, therefore, an examination limited to the objective characteristics only of the relevant products cannot be sufficient: the competitive conditions and the structure of supply and demand on the market must also be taken into consideration."[66]

12-056 Thus, in *Continental Can v EC Commission*,[67] the European Court stated that:

> "a dominant position in the market for light metal containers for canned meat and fish cannot be decisive in so far as it is not proved that competitors in other fields in the market for light metal containers cannot, by a mere adaptation, enter this market with sufficient strength to form a serious counterweight."[68]

12-057 The ability of companies to switch production to the relevant products and market them without incurring significant additional costs or risks in response to small and permanent changes in relative prices is a measure of the "supply-side substitutability". This is often called "elasticity of supply". If there is a high degree of supply-side substitutability, then the relevant product market will take into account the products that are easily substitutable by switching production.

12-058 This is best illustrated by way of an example given by the Commission in its Notice on the Definition of Relevant Market.

Example
Paper is usually supplied in a range of different qualities from standard writing paper to high quality paper to be used, for instance, in producing art books. From a demand substitutability viewpoint, these papers are not substitutable. One cannot use standard writing paper to produce an art book. However, from a supply-side substitutability, paper plants can re-orientate their manufacturing plants in a short time-frame from one type of paper to another. In the absence of particular difficulties in distribution, paper manufacturers are able therefore to compete for orders of the various types of paper quality. In such circumstances, the Commission would not define a separate market for each quality of paper and its respective use. Rather, the various qualities of paper are included in the relevant product market and the sales of those qualities of paper are taken into account to determine total market value of the relevant product market.[69]

---

65 (322/81) [1983] E.C.R. 3461; [1985] 1 C.M.L.R. 282.
66 (322/81) [1985] 1 C.M.L.R. 282 at [37].
67 (6/72) [1973] E.C.R. 215; [1973] C.M.L.R. 199.
68 (6/72) [1973] C.M.L.R. 199 at [33]. Thus, at [36], the court said that there was contradictory evidence in the Commission's file as to whether competition by other undertakings in producing metal containers had been ruled out because of the size of the investment necessary for integrated production facilities and the technological lead of Continental Can in this area. It said that such confusion was further evidence as to the Commission's uncertainty regarding the delineation of the markets.
69 Commission Notice on the Definition of Relevant Market [1997] OJ C372/5, para.22.

Barriers to entry

There will be limited supply-side substitutability when there are considerable **12-059** obstacles in the way of manufacturers on the one hand switching production and on the other hand, supplying the product in issue. In relation to the first category, such obstacles may consist of: the purchase of costly plant machinery, difficulty of exploiting particular manufacturing technologies, lack of expertise in the manufacturing area, etc. In relation to the second category, these may include: difficulties in establishing distribution channels, delays in getting brand onto market (advertising and product testing), uncertainty in the market about unknown suppliers, transport costs, and legal barriers, in particular, IPRs.

These factors which prevent manufacturers or suppliers from switching supply **12-060** to producing or supplying the product in issue are often called "barriers to entry". Where there is low supply-side substitutability, there are high barriers to entry and it will be uneconomic, unfeasible or unlawful for manufacturers to start supplying products the same or similar to the relevant product. Where there is high supply-side substitutability, it will cost little for competing manufacturers to produce identical or competing goods. The expression "barriers to entry" is often used in the context of determining the market power of an undertaking in a particular relevant market. However, it is equally useful in determining the relevant market.

Supply-side substitutability and demand substitutability

As stated earlier, demand substitutability is a more immediate and effective form **12-061** of analysis of the relevant market than supply-side substitutability. Demand substitutability represents the first filter. If the results of the filter are that the relevant market is wide and there is no concentration of market share in any one undertaking, analysis need go no further. If the results of the filter are that prima facie, there is little demand substitutability, and consequently, the relevant market is likely to be drawn narrowly, then market analysis must concentrate on the second filter, namely supply-side substitutability. Often the lack of substitutes will indicate that there are substantial barriers to rival producers or suppliers supplying competitive products. Thus, often low demand substitutability will indicate low supply-side substitutability. Conversely, a large number of competitive products will often indicate a high degree of supply-side substitutability.

However, in some cases, the two concepts of demand-side (i.e. interchange- **12-062** ability) and supply-side substitutability can serve as important complementary analytical tools. This is illustrated in *Michelin v EC Commission*.[70] In this case, the Dutch subsidiary of Michelin brought an appeal against a Commission finding that it had abused its dominant position in the market for replacement tyres for lorries, buses and other heavy vehicles. It argued that the Commission had defined the relevant market:

(a) too widely in that it failed to distinguish between the market for differing types and sizes of tyre which were not interchangeable in the eyes of the consumer; and

(b) too narrowly in that it had excluded car and van tyres although they occupied similar positions on the market.

---

[70] (322/81) [1983] E.C.R. 3461; [1985] 1 C.M.L.R. 282.

12-063   The Commission defended its position in respect of the above arguments by saying that:

(a) it was not possible to distinguish between the differing types and dimensions because the elasticity of supply between differing types and dimensions must be taken into account; and

(b) the criteria of interchangeability and elasticity of demand allowed a distinction to be drawn between the market in heavy vehicles and the market in car tyres owing to the structure of demand and the presence of experienced trade buyers in the case of tyres for heavy vehicles.[71]

12-064   The CJEU, whilst generally upholding the Commission, found also that there was no supply-side substitutability between tyres for heavy vehicle and car tyres, owing to significant production techniques and plant and tools needed for their manufacture. Interestingly, overruling the Commission, the court also held that there was also no supply-side substitutability between different types and dimensions of tyres for heavy vehicles due to differences in the conditions of productions. However, and as a warning to the over-application of minute, detailed technical analysis, it said that neither that nor the absence of interchangeability (demand substitutability) meant that the relevant product market should be construed more narrowly. Instead it said, harking back to *United Brands*,[72] that, in view of the fact that no undertaking specialised in manufacturing a particular type or dimension, such differences were not crucial in assessing the market position of the undertaking because, in view of their similarity and the manner in which they complemented one another, the conditions of competition on the market were the same for all types and dimensions.

12-065   A similar approach was taken in *Elopak v Tetrapak* where a high degree of sophisticated analysis using both the concept of demand substitutability and supply-side substitutability were applied by the Commission in determining the relevant product market.[73]

Potential competition

12-066   It might be thought that potential competition would be taken into account when defining markets. Indeed, when considering the issue of supply-side substitutability, one is considering the issue of potential competition on the relevant product market by suppliers switching to producing competing products to those in issue. Leaving aside such considerations, the Commission has said that potential competition is not to be taken into account, since the conditions under which potential competition will actually represent an effective competitive constraint depend on the analysis of specific factors and circumstances related to the conditions of entry. However, potential competition may be carried out at a subsequent stage once the position of the companies involved in the relevant market has been ascertained.[74]

Evidence to define relevant product market

12-067   An analysis of the product characteristics and intended use will allow the Commission, as a first step, to limit the field of investigation of possible substitutes. The

---

[71] (322/81) [1983] E.C.R. 3461; [1985] 1 C.M.L.R. 282 at [36].
[72] (27/76) [1978] E.C.R. 287; [1978] 1 C.M.L.R. 429.
[73] Commission Decision 88/501/EEC *Elopak/Tetrapak* OJ [1988] L272/27; [1990] 4 C.M.L.R. 47.
[74] Commission Notice on Definition of Relevant Market [1997] OJ C273/5, para.24.

Commission will take into account: evidence of substitution in the recent past; econometric and statistical tests; views of customers and competitors;[75] market surveys about consumer preferences; and barriers to switching demand to potential substitutes such as regulatory barriers, knowledge of other substitutes, uncertainty about the reputation of other suppliers, etc.[76] The Commission will generally obtain evidence by contacting the main customers and the main companies in the industry, relevant professional associations and sometimes, companies active in upstream markets.[77]

Relevant geographic market

Although products may be substitutable, it may be that the problems of **12-068** geography, i.e. transport costs, mean that there is no real competition between substitutable products in a particular area. Such suggests that one must also consider the concept of the geographical extent of a market. The idea that art.102 requires consideration of geography is also shown in the fact that it must be shown that an undertaking is dominant in a substantial part of the internal market. Thus, the CJEU said in *United Brands v EC Commission*:[78]

"The opportunities for competition under Article [102] of the Treaty must be considered having regard to the particular features of the product in question and with reference to a clearly defined geographic area in which it is marketed and where the conditions of competition are sufficiently homogeneous for the effect of the economic power of the undertaking concerned to be able to be evaluated."[79]

In *United Brands*, the court later said: **12-069**

"The conditions for the application of Article [102] to an undertaking in a dominant position presuppose the clear delimitation of the substantial part of the Common Market in which it may be able to engage in abuses which hinder effective competition and this is an area where the objective conditions of competition applying to the product in question must be the same for all traders."[80]

Determination of relevant geographic market

In its Notice on definition of relevant market, the Commission has said the **12-070** following:

"[28] The Commission's approach to geographic market definition might be summarised as follows: it will take a preliminary view of the scope of the geographic market on the basis of broad indications as to the distribution of market shares between the parties and their competitors, as well as a preliminary analysis of pricing and price differences at national and *European Union* or EEA level. This initial

---

[75] However, as the General Court said in (T-30/89) [1991] E.C.R. II-1439; [1992] 4 C.M.L.R. 16, the mere fact that consumers refer to price as a decisive factor without elaborating on the impact which a change in price would have on the choice of products cannot prove that there is a high degree of cross-price elasticity, particularly where the choice of the consumer depends to a large extent on unquantifiable circumstances (at [75–76]).

[76] Commission Notice on Definition of Relevant Market [1997] OJ C273/5, paras 36–42.

[77] Commission Notice on Definition of Relevant Market [1997] OJ C273/5, para.33.

[78] (27/76) [1978] E.C.R. 287; [1978] 1 C.M.L.R. 429.

[79] (27/76) [1978] E.C.R. 287; [1978] 1 C.M.L.R. 429 at [11].

[80] (27/76) [1978] E.C.R. 287; [1978] 1 C.M.L.R. 429 at [44].

view is used basically as a working hypothesis to focus the Commission's enquiries for the purposes of arriving at a precise geographic market definition.

[29]   The reasons behind any particular configuration of prices and market shares need to be explored. Companies might enjoy high market shares in their domestic markets just because of the weight of the past, and conversely, a homogeneous presence of companies throughout the EEA might be consistent with national or regional geographic markets. The initial working hypothesis will therefore be checked against an analysis of demand characteristics (importance of national or local preferences, current patterns of purchases of customers, product differentiation/brands, other) in order to establish whether companies in different areas do indeed constitute a real alternative source of supply for consumers. The theoretical experiment is again based on substitution arising from changes in relative prices, and the question to answer is again whether the customers of the parties would switch their orders to companies located elsewhere in the short term and at a negligible cost.

[30]   If necessary, a further check on supply factors will be carried out to ensure that those companies located in differing areas do not face impediments in developing their sales on competitive terms throughout the whole geographic market. This analysis will include an examination of requirements for a local presence in order to sell in that area the conditions of access to distribution channels, costs associated with setting up a distribution network, and the presence or absence of regulatory barriers arising from public procurement, price regulations, quotas and tariffs limiting trade or production, technical standards, monopolies, freedom of establishment, requirements for administrative authorizations, packaging regulations, etc. In short, the Commission will identify possible obstacles and barriers isolating companies located in a given area from the competitive pressure of companies located outside that area, so as to determine the precise degree of market interpenetration at national, European or global level.

[31]   The actual pattern and evolution of trade flows offers useful supplementary indications as to the economic importance of each demand or supply factor mentioned above, and the extent to which they may or may not constitute actual barriers creating different geographic markets. The analysis of trade flows will generally address the question of transport costs and the extent to which these may hinder trade between different areas, having regard to plant location, costs of production and relative price levels.

[32]   Finally, the Commission also takes into account the continuing process of market integration, in particular in the Community, when defining geographic markets, especially in the area of concentrations and structural joint ventures. The measures adopted and implemented in the internal market programme to remove barriers to trade and further integrate the Community markets cannot be ignored when assessing the effects on competition of a concentration or a structural joint venture. A situation where national markets have been artificially isolated from each other because of the existence of legislative barriers that have now been removed will generally lead to a cautious assessment of past evidence regarding prices, market shares or trade patterns. A process of market integration that would, in the short term, lead to wider geographic markets may therefore be taken into consideration when defining the geographic market for the purposes of assessing concentrations and joint ventures."[81]

12-071   Therefore, in *United Brands*, the court upheld the Commission's decision that the relevant geographic market was Germany, Denmark, Ireland, the Netherlands, Belgium and Luxembourg as the banana markets in these countries were completely free of state intervention and although the applicable tariff provisions and transport

---

[81]   Commission Notice on Definition of Relevant Market [1997] OJ C273/5, paras 29–32.

costs were necessarily different but not discriminatory, in substance, the conditions of competition were the same for all. On the other hand, France, Italy and the UK were excluded because of special circumstances relating to import arrangements and trading conditions and the fact that bananas of various types and origin were sold there. A significant factor which will affect the determination of the relevant geographic market is the cost of transport of the relevant product.[82]

In *TV Listings*,[83] Radio Telefis Eireann ("RTE"), the Irish State Television, was **12-072** accused of abusive behaviour by bringing actions for infringement of copyright against independent publishers of weekly TV listings. The relevant geographic market was held to be the area to which the programmes could be broadcast. However, the area in which the abuse itself occurs, rather than where it is capable of operating, may determine the relevant geographic market.[84]

A party accused of a dominant position will often be caught between trying to **12-073** define the relevant geographical market as small as possible, to show that it does not constitute a substantial part of the internal market, and as widely as possible, to show that it does not have a dominant position in such an area.

Evidence for defining relevant geographic market

The types of evidence that the Commission will consider relevant for defining **12-074** the relevant geographic market are past evidence of diversion of orders to other areas in response to change in prices; basic demand characteristics such as national preferences, language, culture and life style; views of customers and competitors; geographic pattern of purchases; trade flows and pattern of shipments and barriers; and switching costs to divert orders to companies in other areas, in particular, transport costs and transport restrictions arising from legislation.[85]

Intellectual property and relevant market

In general, intellectual property plays little part in the determination of the **12-075** relevant market. Analysis of the relevant market concentrates on the product or service in issue. This requires analysis as to whether there exist on the market substitutable products or services. This analysis is not concerned with whether the product in issue or the substitutable products are protected by IPRs. As commented on by the United States Department of Justice in its 2017 *Antitrust Guidelines for the Licensing of Intellectual Property*, there will often be sufficient

---

[82] *Eurofix-Bauco v Hilti AG* [1988] OJ L65/19; [1989] 4 C.M.L.R. 677 (EC Commission)—high value of product and low transport costs-relevant geographic market held to be the EC (upheld on appeal in (T-30/89) [1991] E.C.R. II-1439; [1992] 4 C.M.L.R. 16); *Napier Brown-British Sugar* [1988] OJ L284/41 (EC Commission)—high transport costs of sugar and other factors led Commission to hold that relevant geographic market was Great Britain. In *Re Italian Flat Glass* [1990] 4 C.M.L.R. 535, the Commission held that where the cost of transport is an important factor and sources of supply in a Member State are controlled by local groups, then the relevant geographical market is the territory of a Member State (at [77]).

[83] *Radio Telefis Eireann v EC Commission* (T-69/89) [1991] E.C.R. II-0485; [1991] 4 C.M.L.R. 586; *BBC v EC Commission* (T-70/89) [1991] C.M.L.R. 669; *Independent Television Publication Ltd v EC Commission* (T-76/89) [1991] C.M.L.R. 745. Upheld on appeal to CJEU (C-241–242/91P) [1995] E.C.R. I-0743; [1995] 6 C.M.L.R. 718.

[84] See *Suiker Unie v EC Commission* (4/73) [1975] E.C.R. 1663; [1976] 1 C.M.L.R. 295.

[85] Commission Notice on Definition of Relevant Market [1997] OJ C273/5, paras 45–50.

actual or potential close substitutes for products or processes subject to IPRs to prevent the exercise of market power.[86]

12-076   If there are no or few competing products with the products in question, a tribunal will consider the supply-side substitutability/elasticity of supply of the product in issue. It is here that intellectual property plays an important role. If there is little elasticity of supply, such will generally suggest that there are barriers to entry to competitors providing competing products. Intellectual property will often be a insurmountable barrier to entry. It is important to distinguish between IPR being a barrier to entry to the protected technology or products and to the relevant market. Obviously, IPR will be a barrier to entry to the protected technology or products. However, that is irrelevant if there are competing technologies or products which are not the subject-matter of such IPR.

Relevant market and IP licences

12-077   It has been urged, essentially in cases involving a refusal to license, that the relevant product market is in licences granted by the rights owner. Clearly, any such finding would make it difficult for the intellectual property owner not to have a dominant position. In the UK, there have been several cases where one party has submitted that the relevant market is that of granting licences under a patent. This submission is normally coupled with an argument that the rights owner's refusal to license is an abuse of a dominant position.

12-078   The English courts have been reluctant to conclude that the relevant product market is that of licences granted by the patentee.[87] Thus, the English Court of Appeal in *British Leyland v Armstrong Patents*[88] rejected a submission that the relevant market was licences to make car exhausts as opposed to exhausts.[89] The defendants had argued that the granting of licences under a patent was analogous to the granting of certificates pursuant to a statutory monopoly.[90] In doing so, the defendants sought to draw an analogy with *General Motors Continental NV v EC Commission*.[91] In that case, the CJEU had held that General Motors had a dominant position in the grant of certificates of approval for its cars, as Belgium law required that certificates were to be provided by each manufacturer in respect of their vehicles. The Patents Court rejected a submission that General Motors was similar to a patentee granting licences, as a patentee was not required to grant licences. In the Court of Appeal, the argument that the market was in licences to make exhausts was described as "entirely artificial".[92] In *Philips v Ingman*,[93] the judge said:

> "[53]   It can be said that the defendants' pleading does not assert directly that the plaintiff's patents give rise to a per se dominant position. Instead it alleges that the plaintiff owns a dominant position in the market for licensing the patented technology. But it seems to me that this is a matter of semantics only. Whenever an IPR exists there is a correlative potential market in licences to exploit it. It is

---

[86]   Antitrust Guidelines for Intellectual Property, 12 January 2017, para.2.2.
[87]   See *British Leyland* [1984] 3 C.M.L.R. 102 (CA); *Chiron Corp v Organon Teknika Ltd* [1993] F.S.R. 324; *Intergraph Corp v Solid Systems CAD* [1998] Eu. L.R. 223; *Philips Electronics v Ingman Ltd* [1999] F.S.R. 112.
[88]   [1984] 3 C.M.L.R. 102.
[89]   *British Leyland* [1984] 3 C.M.L.R. 102 CA.
[90]   *Intergraph Corp* [1998] Eu. L.R. 223.
[91]   (26/75) [1975] E.C.R. 1367; [1976] 1 C.M.L.R. 95.
[92]   See [100] per Oliver LJ.
[93]   *Philips Electronics* [1998] 2 C.M.L.R. 839; [1998] Eu. L.R. 666; [1999] F.S.R. 112.

the ability to grant or refuse such licences which constitutes the right in the first place. This is only an alternative way of saying that the proprietor owns exclusive rights which he can exploit, if he wishes, by licensing."[94]

However, one judge has held that it is arguable that the relevant product market **12-079** could be the grant or transfer of patent licences.[95]

It is submitted that the court in *British Leyland v Armstrong* and *Phillips v Ing-* **12-080** *man* was right. It is artificial to determine a market as that of licences granted by a licensor of rights owned by the licensor. Licences are not sold, marketed, traded in or subject to the marketplace.[96] They are purely legal in nature. Consumers are interested in the licensed products and not the licences per se. To find that the relevant market is that of licences granted by the patentee is, ipso facto, to find that a patentee has a dominant position by the very nature of owning the patent and thus the market in licences. This is contrary to the CJEU's clear approach that IPRs per se are not conclusive of a dominant position.[97] However, in the case of collecting societies, discussed below, it may be that the relevant market is the licensing of, e.g. musical works.

Collecting societies

Where the undertaking concerned is a copyright collecting society, different **12-081** considerations may apply. The European Commission has considered the relevant market in a case where copyright collecting societies were accused of abuse of a dominant position. Thus, in *CISAC*[98] the Commission had to consider certain contractual terms between European collecting societies that dealt with the licensing of public performance rights of musical works of authors that had assigned the right to the collecting societies to collect royalties on their behalf. The Commission considered the issue of relevant market. It held that the first relevant product market was the market for the provision of copyright administration services to right holders regarding public performance of rights.[99] The second relevant product market was the market for provision of copyright administration services by one collecting society to another regarding public performance rights.[100] The third product market was the market for licensing of public performance rights to commercial users for satellite, cable and Internet use.[101] In relation to the third product market, the licences are indeed the "commodity" which is provided. In England, the English Court of Appeal in *British Leyland v Armstrong* said obiter dicta that there

---

[94]   *Philips Electronics* [1998] 2 C.M.L.R. 839; [1998] Eu. L.R. 666; [1999] F.S.R. 112 at [53].
[95]   *Intergraph Corp* [1998] Eu. L.R. 223 (HC) (the allegation was that Intergraph was using its copyright in its computer programs to stifle competition in ancillary markets, namely the sale of second-hand Intergraph equipment and hardware maintenance). However, it is submitted that in fact the market was that of second-hand Intergraph equipment and/or maintenance services. The licences merely attached themselves to such equipment (rather like a certificate of authenticity may be attached to a second-hand car to indicate that it is a genuine product).
[96]   In the case of computer programs, it is sometimes said that one is trading in licences. However, in reality, one is trading in the copies of a computer program to which the licence attaches.
[97]   See para.12-130.
[98]   COMP/C2/38.698—*CISAC* (Commission Decision of 16 July 2008).
[99]   See [51].
[100] See [52].
[101] See [54].

are no doubt cases (e.g. the granting of licences for musical works) where the licensor can be said to be engaged in the provision of a service.[102]

Dominant position in relevant market

12-082 Once the relevant product and geographic market have been established, one must ascertain whether the relevant undertaking has a dominant position. The CJEU said in *United Brands*:

> "The dominant position referred to in this Article relates to a position of economic strength enjoyed by an undertaking which enables it to prevent effective competition being maintained on the relevant market by giving it the power to behave to an appreciable extent independently of its competitors, customers and ultimately of its consumers."[103]

12-083 The definition of a dominant position has been reiterated in several important subsequent cases on art.102.[104]

12-084 It is not necessary that there is a complete absence of competition in order for an undertaking to have a dominant position. As said in *Michelin*:

> "it is not a precondition for a finding that a dominant position exists in the case of a given product that there should be a complete absence of competition from other partially interchangeable products as long as such competition does not affect the undertaking's ability to influence appreciably the conditions in which that competition may be exerted or at any rate to conduct itself to a large extent without having to take account of that competition and without having to take account of that competition and without suffering any adverse effects as a result of its attitude."[105]

12-085 To prove that an undertaking is in a dominant position, many factors must be taken into account. Principally, one must examine the undertaking's market share of the relevant market. An undertaking with a small market share will never be able to dictate market conditions. Where an undertaking has a substantial market share, it may be in a position to dictate market conditions. Whether this is so will depend on how difficult it is for other undertakings to enter the relevant market. There may be many obstacles like the initial cost of plant and machinery; IPRs and the need to set up distribution networks. These are called "barriers to entry". If these barriers are high, then an undertaking with a substantial market is likely to be able to behave independently of others and thus be in a dominant position.

Market shares

12-086 The existence of a dominant position may be inferred from several factors which taken separately are not necessarily determinative. Among these factors a highly important one is the existence of very large market shares. As said in *Hoffmann La Roche v EC Commission*:

> "Furthermore although the importance of the market shares may vary from one market

---

[102] *British Leyland* [1984] 3 C.M.L.R. 102 at [100].
[103] (27/76) [1978] 1 C.M.L.R. 429 at [65]–[66]. See also *Gøttrup-Klim Grovvareforeninger v Dansk Landsbrugs Grovvareselskab AmbA* (C-250/92) [1994] E.C.R. I-5641, 5690
[104] (85/76) [1979] E.C.R. 461; [1979] 3 C.M.L.R. 211; (322/81) [1983] E.C.R. 3461; [1985] 1 C.M.L.R. 287; *CEAHR v Commission* ECLI:EU:T:2017:478 (T-712/14) at [122].
[105] (322/81) [1985] 1 C.M.L.R. 282 at [48]. See also (85/76) [1979] E.C.R. 461; [1979] 3 C.M.L.R. 211 at [39].

to another the view may legitimately be taken that very large shares in themselves, and save in exceptional circumstances, are evidence of the existence of a dominant position. An undertaking which has a very large market share and holds it for some time, by means of the volume of production and the scale of the supply which it stands for—without those having much smaller market shares being able to meet rapidly the demand from those who would like to break away from the undertaking which has the largest market share—is by virtue of that share in a position of strength which makes it an unavoidable trading partner and which already because of this, secures for it, at the very least during relatively long periods, that freedom of action which is the special feature of a dominant position."[106]

What precise percentage amounts to a "very large market share" is unclear. In **12-087** *Hoffmann La Roche*, the court and Commission considered the markets for different groups of vitamins.

(a)   The court held that Roche's market share in vitamin B2, which was 86 per cent, was so large as to be in itself evidence of a dominant position.

(b)   In the vitamin B6 and H category, the court said that even on Roche's figures of 65–70 per cent market share, this would nevertheless be so large as to "prove the existence of a dominant position".

(c)   In the vitamin C market, a 65 per cent market share was "evidence" of the existence of a dominant position which was "confirmed" by the gap between Roche's shares and those of its next largest competitors (14.8 per cent and 6.3 per cent).

(d)   In the vitamin E group, Roche held an agreed market share of 54–64 per cent over three years. Roche's competitors' market shares were estimated at 16 per cent, 6 per cent and 1 per cent and 19 per cent for importers. In this case, the court held that:

> "Such a position as that which has been established conforms even more typically than that established in the case of Vitamin A to the pattern of a narrow oligopolistic market in which Roche's share is much larger than the combined shares of the two largest competitors. Therefore, the Commission was right to find that there was a dominant position on this market."[107]

Therefore, the relative market strength of an undertaking compared to other **12-088** undertakings is an important indicator of market strength. In *Michelin*,[108] the court held that a market share of 57–65 per cent when compared with its main competitors' market shares of 4–8 per cent constituted a "valid indication of Michelin NV's preponderant strength in relation to its competitors".[109] The court found that Michelin did have a dominant position, although the existence of several barriers to entry was important to its finding.

In *United Brands*,[110] the court held that a market share of 40 per cent did not **12-089** permit the conclusion that an undertaking had control of the market but that one must have regard to the strength and number of competitors.[111] In this case, the court said that as United Brands' share was several times greater than that of its nearest competitor, that, along with other factors, afforded evidence of its preponderant strength.

---

[106]   (85/76) [1979] 3 C.M.L.R. 211 at [41].

[107]   (85/76) [1979] 3 C.M.L.R. 211 at [66].

[108]   (322/81) [1983] E.C.R. 3461; [1985] 1 C.M.L.R. 282.

[109]   (322/81) [1983] E.C.R. 3461; [1985] 1 C.M.L.R. 282 at [52].

[110]   (27/76) [1978] E.C.R. 287; [1978] 1 C.M.L.R. 429.

[111]   (27/76) [1978] 1 C.M.L.R. 429 at [109].

12-090   It would seem that where a market share is below 60 per cent, other factors must exist before there will be a valid finding of dominance. In the vitamin B market, Roche held market shares of 28.9 per cent, 34.9 per cent and 51 per cent in the period from 1972–74. Such figures were held not to be a "factor sufficient" to establish the existence of a dominant position. The court said that as the Commission had not indicated what other additional factors might establish a dominant position, its finding that a dominant position existed was unsustainable. Thus, it has been held in English proceedings that 40 per cent does not by itself indicate market dominance, but might be indicative of market dominance if all other competitors were very weak.[112]

12-091   Although not binding, the Commission has said in its Notice on Guidance in its enforcement properties in applying art.82[113] that it considers that dominance is not likely if the undertaking's market share is below 40 per cent in the relevant market.[114] However, it points out that there may be specific cases below that threshold where competitors are not in a position to constrain effectively the conduct of a dominant undertaking, e.g. where they face serious capacity limitations and such cases will deserve the attention of the Commission.[115] Conversely, in the same Notice, the Commission has said that the higher the market share and the longer the period of time over which it is held, the more likely it is that it constitutes

> "…an important preliminary indication of the existence of a dominant position, and in certain circumstances, of possible serious effects of abusive conduct, justifying an intervention by the Commission under Article [102]. However, as a general rule, the Commission will not come to a final conclusion as to whether or not a case should be pursued without examining all the factors which may be sufficient to constraint the behaviour of the undertaking."[116]

Barriers to entry

12-092   Once it is established that an undertaking has a substantial market share, one must establish whether there are any barriers to entry. As has been seen, where an undertaking has a very large market share, that will be evidence of a dominant position without more. On the other hand, where an undertaking does not have a substantial market share, it is very unlikely that it will be in a dominant position, even if there are high barriers to entry preventing further competitors from joining the relevant market. Thus, the consideration of the issue of barriers to entry must be subsidiary to the issue of market shares. However, the court and Commission frequently refer to the existence of barriers to entry and they must be considered as important evidence in establishing whether an undertaking has a dominant position when its market shares can be said to be neither very large nor insubstantial. The following are examples of barriers to entry.

---

[112] *Philips Electronics* [1998] 2 C.M.L.R. 839; [1999] F.S.R. 112 (HC) at [76] cited in *Sandvik Aktiebolag v K.R. Pfiffner (UK) Ltd* [2000] F.S.R. 17 (HC).
[113] [2009] OJ C45/7.
[114] para.14.
[115] para.14.
[116] para.15, Commission Notice.

Capital investment

Where a potential competitor has to invest large capital sums before it is able to **12-093** manufacture the relevant product, this is a barrier to entry.[117]

Economies of scale

Certain products may have to be manufactured and distributed on a large scale **12-094** before they become profitable commodities. Thus, potential competitors would have to undergo a period of unprofitability if they wished to enter the relevant market, until their manufacture of the product was sufficiently considerable to make a profit. This is a barrier to entry. It is somewhat controversial because the alleged dominant undertaking may often have undergone the same period of unprofitability as well. However, in such circumstances, there will usually be an advantage to being first on the market. Thus, an undertaking will have more incentive to undergo a period of unprofitability if the market is young and immature, i.e. in the case of a developing technology. Once the market has become mature and consumer demand is being supplied, then a considerable deterrent to new players entering the market will normally exist if profitability is only guaranteed after the attainment of a substantial market share.

Technological lead

If an undertaking has a substantial technological lead in the products in ques- **12-095** tion, which is a result of investment and research, then this will constitute a barrier to entry. Clearly, if a competitor has to commit itself to a substantial and lengthy investment and research programme, this will mean that there will be a lag time before it can start to manufacture the product in issue.[118] Again, as with economies of scale, this is a cost which the alleged dominant undertaking will presumably have undergone as well and thus, it could be argued that it is unfair to penalise the alleged dominant undertaking for being first on the market. However, as argued in the previous paragraph, a new entrant to the market is more likely to be deterred from investing in such a research and development programme if the market is already mature and consumer demand is being satisfied.

Distribution networks

The existence of a distribution network, with commercial contacts which give the **12-096** undertaking concerned direct access to end users, facilitates the sale of goods. If a competing undertaking does not have access to such a network, they may have to invest considerable sums of money setting up such a network. Furthermore, this may be difficult if the alleged undertaking has exclusive contracts with existing dealers. Distribution and dealer networks are very important for a product which requires after-sales support and maintenance.[119]

Marketing barriers to entry

Some markets require much more advertising and promotion than others. Thus, **12-097** the beer, clothing and cigarette market is very dependent on the promotion of image.

---

[117] (27/76) [1978] E.C.R. 287; [1987] 1 E.M.L.R. 429 at [122].
[118] (322/81) [1983] E.C.R. 3461; [1985] 1 C.M.L.R. 282 at [55].
[119] (322/81) [1983] E.C.R. 3461; [1985] 1 C.M.L.R. 282 at [58]–[59].

Also in some markets, the existence of brand name products is much more important than in other markets. In these markets, a potential competitor will have to spend substantial sums of money promoting its product in order to gain market share. This is another barrier to entry.[120]

Market saturation

12-098   Where the relevant market concerns the sale of capital items as opposed to perishables, then, if a market has become saturated (i.e. all or nearly all consumers have already purchased the capital item), it will be more difficult for a newcomer to enter the market. Thus in relation to a case concerning the supply of milk packaging machinery, the Commission held that, as most dairies were already equipped with packaging machinery which had an average life span in excess of 10 years, it made it difficult for newcomers to enter the market, since in order to sell their products, they had either to compete in the limited market for renewing old equipment or persuade dairies to replace existing equipment.[121]

Legal monopolies

12-099   The existence of a legal monopoly for the manufacture and sale of a product or supply of a service in a relevant market will obviously be an insuperable barrier to entry for the period of its duration. This area is clearly of importance to the intellectual property practitioner. If the legal monopoly is co-terminous with the relevant product or service market, then the undertaking who owns the legal monopoly has a dominant position. If the legal monopoly is not co-terminous and only covers one particular product or service in the relevant market, it will not be particularly relevant to any finding of any dominance, as competing suppliers can supply interchangeable products which are not covered by the legal monopoly. Where there is limited interchangeability between goods in a product market, then a legal monopoly in a preferred good may be relevant as a barrier to entry.

Behaviour suggesting dominance

12-100   Certain behaviour by an undertaking may be evidence of a dominant position. Thus, if it makes excessive profits on the sale of products, this may be evidence that it is in a dominant position. However, it is not a substitute for proper analysis.[122]

12-101   The fact that an undertaking does not make excessive profits does not bar a finding of dominance. Thus, in *United Brands*, the court held that, despite United Brands having made losses on its banana sales, the fact that the customers continued to buy more goods from it and it was the dearest seller was more significant and, in fact, a particular feature of a dominant position.[123]

Intellectual property and dominant position

12-102   The existence of IPRs does not necessarily mean that the owner has a dominant position. Whilst such rights give their owner absolute power in the protected

---

[120] e.g. see (27/76) [1978] E.C.R. 287; [1978] 1 C.M.L.R. 429 at [122].
[121] *Elopak v Tetra Pak* [1988] OJ L272/27; [1990] 4 C.M.L.R. 47 at [44]. On appeal to the CJEU, see *Tetra Pak Rausing S.A. v EC Commission* (T-51/89) [1991] 4 C.M.L.R. 334.
[122] *Sandvik* [2000] F.S.R. 17.
[123] (27/76) [1978] E.C.R. 287; [1978] 1 C.M.L.R. 429 at [128].

product or service, rarely will that product or service be the only product or service in the relevant product or service market. As the CJEU said in *Deutsche Grammophon v Metro*:

"A manufacturer of recordings who has a protection right analogous to copyright does not however have a dominant position within the meaning of Article [102] of the Treaty merely because he exercises his exclusive right to market the protected articles."[124]

In *Sirena Srl v Eda Srl*,[125] the court said, in the context of trade marks, that for a **12-103** dominant position to be proved, it is necessary to show that:

"the trade mark owner should have the power to prevent the maintenance of effective competition in a considerable part of the market in question, taking into account, in particular, the possible existence and the position of producers or distributors who market similar or substitute products."[126]

This doctrine has been re-iterated several times. Thus, in *EMI Records Ltd v CBS* **12-104** *(UK) Ltd*,[127] the CJEU emphasised that in the context of trade marks, where there are several competing undertakings whose economic strength is comparable to that of the owner of the mark and who operate in the market for the products in question, the existence of trade mark rights for a particular product does not imply the existence of a dominant position.[128] The CJEU in *TV Listings*[129] has re-emphasised that, so far as dominant position is concerned, mere ownership of an IPR cannot confer such a position.[130]

The above approach is mirrored in the US, where the Department of Justice has **12-105** said at para.2.2 of the 2017 Guidelines:

"Market power is the ability profitably to maintain prices above, or output below, competitive levels for a significant period of time. The Agencies will not presume that a patent, copyright, or trade secret necessarily confers market power upon its owner. Although the intellectual property right confers the power to exclude with respect to the specific product, process, or work in question, there will often be sufficient actual or potential close substitutes for such product, process, or work to prevent the exercise of market power."

Intellectual property, licensees and market share

IPRs are not relevant in considering the market share of an undertaking in a **12-106** relevant market. However, when considering the market share of an IPR owner who supplies goods protected by the IPR, should the market share of licensees who supply products onto the market under a licence of the IPR be taken into account in calculating the market share of the IPR owner?

In this regard, it is necessary to distinguish between the relevant technology **12-107** market and the relevant product market.[131] In relation to the product market, provided licensees are independent undertakings and not economically or

---

[124] (78/70) [1971] E.C.R. 487; [1971] 1 C.M.L.R. 631 at [15].

[125] *Sirena Srl v Eda Srl* (40/70) [1971] E.C.R. 69; [1975] C.M.L.R. 1.

[126] (40/70) [1971] E.C.R. 69; [1975] C.M.L.R. 1 at [16]. See also, Mischo AG's Opinion in (238/87) [1988] E.C.R. 621; [1989] 4 C.M.L.R. 122.

[127] *EMI Records Ltd v CBS (UK) Ltd* (51/75) [1976] E.C.R. 811; [1976] 2 C.M.L.R. 235.

[128] (51/75) [1976] E.C.R. 811; [1976] 2 C.M.L.R. 235 at [36].

[129] (C-241–242/91P) [1995] E.C.R. I-0473; [1995] C.M.L.R. 718.

[130] (C-241–242/91P) [1995] E.C.R. I-0473; [1995] C.M.L.R. 718 at [46].

[131] For a discussion as to the difference between technology and product markets, see paras 8-033 to

financially connected with the party being investigated, their market share should not be taken into account. In *British Leyland v Armstrong*,[132] Foster J held, in an English case concerning British Leyland bringing proceedings for copyright infringement against manufacturers of spare parts for its exhausts, that if the relevant market was restricted to the after-sales market for British Leyland exhausts then there was no dominant position where British Leyland had a 24 per cent market share while its four licensees had a total of 36 per cent and the market was highly competitive and, on several occasions, the manufacturer had to reduce the price of its exhausts in order to remain competitive.[133] However, if the licensees have to pay a substantial royalty to the licensor, such may mean that there is limited competitiveness between the parties. However, if the licensees have substantial market share vis-à-vis the licensor, such will normally suggest that there is effective intra-brand competition between them.

12-108   However, if one is considering whether an undertaking has dominance in a particular technology market, then as the licensees in a technology transfer licence will be using the same technology, it makes sense to consider the combined market share of licensor and licensees. Thus, in the 2014 Technology Transfer Block Exemption, the determination of the market share of a licensor is calculated on the presence of the licensed technology rights on the relevant technology market taking account of the sales data relating to both licensor and licensee.[134]

12-109   It may be that a licensor and its licensees would be considered to be in a position of collective dominance.[135]

Intellectual property as barriers to entry

12-110   In considering market power, IPRs are relevant, as they can constitute a barrier to entry. Intellectual property, as with any legal monopoly, may constitute a barrier to entry in a particular market. Thus, the General Court has emphasised that art.102 applies where dominance in a relevant market is achieved as a result of national legislation which prevents competition with the activities of the undertaking concerned.[136] When considering whether IPRs act as a barrier to entry, it is helpful to consider the different types of intellectual property. As discussed in the Introduction, the nature of the IPR is important when considering the ability of that IPR to act as a barrier to entry.[137]

Spare parts and design rights

12-111   It will be rare that design IPRs represent a barrier to entry to a market. However, in the field of spare parts, the relevant market may be construed narrowly as spare parts for a particular single-brand product.[138] Often, the design of the spare parts will be protected by design rights. In such circumstances, the rights owner will have a

---

8-034.

[132] *British Leyland* [1982] 3 C.M.L.R. 603.
[133] *British Leyland* [1982] 3 C.M.L.R. 603 at [15].
[134] art.8(d), Reg.316/2014. See para.9-013, et seq. for discussion of the Technology Transfer Block Exemption.
[135] See para.12-333, et seq.
[136] *Centre belge d'études de marché—Télémarketing (CBEM) v SA Compagnie luxembourgeoise de télédiffusion (CLT) and Information publicité Benelux (IPB)* (311/84) [1985] E.C.R. 3261.
[137] See para.12-004.
[138] See para.12-047.

dominant position, as these rights constitute an insuperable barrier to entry in the relevant market.[139] It should be noted that there is still not harmonisation of the laws of Member States as to what protection is afforded under the laws of registered designs to spare parts.[140]

Trade marks

In general, trade marks cannot act as a barrier to entry to a particular market as **12-112** they do not control technologies. However, the existence of a registered trade mark with a high quality reputation may be treated as a barrier to entry. In *United Brands*,[141] the existence of the CHIQUITA trade mark was seen by consumers as a guarantee of high quality bananas. Thus, consumers were prepared to spend 30–40 per cent more for Chiquita bananas than unlabelled and 7–10 per cent more than for other brand names.[142]

Technological lead and patent/know-how rights

A technological lead can constitute a barrier to entry. Such a lead will often **12-113** comprise know-how which other competitors will not have access to. The existence of a body of know-how will thus constitute a barrier to entry.[143] Furthermore, such a lead could be protected by the existence of patents or could be the result of expired patents.[144] If an undertaking does not have a technological lead, the existence of know-how and patents becomes less important because of the interchangeability of other products in the relevant product market.

ABUSE

The CJEU sought to define what an abuse of a dominant position was in **12-114** *Europemballage Corp (Continental Can) v EC Commission*.[145] The facts were that Continental Can Co Inc of New York, via a holding company, Europemballage Corp, acquired 91.07 per cent of the shares in a Dutch company, Thommassen. The Commission held that Continental Can had a dominant position in the market in light containers for preserved meat and other products and also in the market for metal closures for glass containers through its previous acquisition of an 85.8 per cent holding in a German company. It alleged that the acquisition of the shares in the Dutch company was an abuse of a dominant position in that such an acquisition eliminated competition in a substantial part of the internal market. The court

---

[139] See AG's Opinion in (238/87) [1988] E.C.R. 6211; [1989] 4 C.M.L.R. 122; *CICRA v Régie Nationale des Usines Renault* (53/87) [1990] 4 C.M.L.R. 265. In neither case did the court have to decide the question as to whether a rights owner had a dominant position in its spare parts market.

[140] See para.5-177, et seq.

[141] (27/76) [1978] E.C.R. 287; [1978] 1 C.M.L.R. 429.

[142] (27/76) [1978] E.C.R. 287; [1978] 1 C.M.L.R. 429 at [88].

[143] See *Re United Brands* [1976] 1 C.M.L.R. D28 (EC Commission) at [85]. This decision was appealed in (27/76) [1978] E.C.R. 287; [1978] 1 C.M.L.R. 429, but no mention was made by the court of the know-how.

[144] As was the case in (88/76) [1979] E.C.R. 461; [1979] 3 C.M.L.R. 211, 278. See also *Elopak* [1988] OJ L272/27; [1990] 4 C.M.L.R. 47 at 70 (EC Commission) upheld in (T-51/89) [1990] E.C.R. II-0309; [1991] 4 C.M.L.R. 334.

[145] (6/7) [1973] E.C.R. 215; [1973] C.M.L.R. 199.

interpreted art.102 in the light of art.3(g) of the EC Treaty[146] which provides for the establishment of a system which will protect competition in the internal market from distortion and, thus, held that there may be abusive behaviour if an undertaking in a dominant position strengthens that dominant position so that the degree of control achieved substantially obstructs competition.[147]

12-115 The court in *Hoffmann La Roche* refined the above concept. It said that:

> "The concept of abuse is an objective concept relating to the behaviour of an undertaking in a dominant position which is such as to influence the structure of a market, where as a result of the very presence of the undertaking in question, the degree of competition is weakened and which, *through recourse to methods different from those which condition normal competition in products or services on the basis of the transactions of commercial operators*, has the effect of hindering the maintenance of the degree of competition still existing in the market or the growth of that competition."[148] [Author's emphasis.]

12-116 This definition of abuse is now settled law.[149] It appears to suggest that the dominant undertaking must have recourse to *methods* that would not be available to it if it were not in a dominant position. This is somewhat problematic. For instance, a patent holder could seek to exercise its rights against a competitor whether or not it is in a dominant undertaking. Indeed, in many cases, the conduct which is alleged to be abusive could be precisely conduct that the dominant undertaking could do even if it were not dominant, e.g. a refusal to supply or offer loyalty rebates. The obvious conduct which it would not be able to do if it were not in a dominant position would be to sell goods at unfair prices. If the undertaking were not dominant, competitive restraints would prevent it from doing so. One must therefore conclude that the Court of Justice does not mean this definition to be taken too literally. Put another way, whilst the enforcement of a patent can be carried out by an undertaking, whether or not it is dominant, the *effect* of this where the undertaking is dominant, may be to foreclose competition. Whereas if the undertaking were not dominant, it would not do so. Thus, in truth, the "method" must be interpreted as meaning both the mechanism deployed (exercise of patent rights) and the effect that it has on the market (foreclosure of competition).

12-117 Moreover, there is another strand of Court of Justice decisions concerning dominant undertakings. This is that the dominant undertaking has a "special responsibility" not to allow its conduct to impair competition in the relevant market.

12-118 In *Michelin*, the CJEU said:

> "the finding that an undertaking has a dominant position is not in itself a recrimination but simply means that irrespective of the reasons for which it has such a dominant position, the undertaking concerned has a *special responsibility* not to allow its conduct to impair genuine undistorted competition on the market."[150] [Author's emphasis.]

12-119 Indeed, it has been said by the General Court in *ITT Promedia NV v European*

---

146 The predecessor to the TFEU. There is no equivalent provision of this in the TFEU but see art.3(1)(b) which confers on the EU the exclusive competence for the establishment of competition rules necessary for the functioning of the internal market.

147 (6/7) [1973] E.C.R. 215; [1973] C.M.L.R. 199 at [26].

148 (85/76) [1979] E.C.R. 461; [1979] 3 C.M.L.R. 211 at [91]. See for a recent statement of this principle, *Huawei v ZTE* (C-170/13) ECLI:EU:C:2015:477 at [45].

149 e.g. see *Huawei Technologies v ZTE Corp* (C-170/13) ECLI:EU:C:2015:477 at [45] citing *Hofmmann-La Roche* and *Tomra Systems v Commission* (C-549/10P) EU:C:2012,221 at [17].

150 *Nederlandsche Banden Industrie Michelin ("Michelin I") v Commission* (322/81) [1983] E.C.R. 3461, [57]; *Tetra Pak v Commission ("Tetra Pak II")* (T-83/91) [1993] E.C.R. II-755 at [114]; *ITT Promedia v Commission* [1998] (T-111/96) E.C.R. II-2937 at [139]; *Irish Sugar v Commission* (T-

Commission,[151] that:

> "... undertakings in a dominant position may be deprived of the right to adopt a course of conduct or take measures which are not in themselves abuses and which would even be unobjectionable if adopted or taken by non-dominant undertakings."

In *Intel v Commission*[152], the Court of Justice confirmed that the purpose of **12-120** art.102 is not to prevent an undertaking from acquiring, on its own merits nor to ensure that competitors less efficient than the dominant undertaking should remain on the market.[153] However, the Court of Justice went on to confirm the principle of special responsibility, namely that a dominant undertaking must not allow its behaviour to impair genuine, undistorted competition on the internal market.[154]

This special responsibility may include refraining from carrying out acts that **12-121** would be unobjectionable if a dominant undertaking was not dominant.

The Commission Guidelines on the Commission's enforcement priorities in ap- **12-122** plying art.102 to abusive exclusionary conduct by undertakings also emphasise the special responsibility of a dominant undertaking not to allow its conduct to impair undistorted competition on the internal market.[155] However, as a check to taking this principle too far, the Court of Justice has said several times that the degree of market strength is, as a general rule, significant in relation to the effects of the conduct of the undertaking concerned rather than whether an abuse as such exists.[156]

For the purposes of this book, it is not intended to examine in detail abuses which **12-123** do not relate to intellectual property. The following acts have been found to be abuses of a dominant position.

Merger/acquisition

The merger/acquisition of another undertaking by or with a dominant **12-124** undertaking.[157]

Unfair prices

Charging excessive prices in relation to the economic cost or value of the product **12-125** or service provided.[158] The imposition of differing prices in different Member States by a seller when selling its products to an intermediate based on the market conditions that apply to the market that governs the sale of those goods to the consumer.[159] Where a dominant undertaking lowers its prices for a period so as to

---

228/97) [1999] E.C.R. II-2969 at [112]; and *Michelin v Commission ("Michelin II")* (T-203/01) [2003] E.C.R. II-4071, [97]; *Microsoft v EC Commission* (T-201/04) at [229].

[151] *ITT Promedia NV v European Commission* [1998] E.C.R. II-2941.

[152] (T-286/09) ECLI:EU:T:2014:547.

[153] See [132]–[133] citing *Post Danmark* (C-209/10) EU:C:2012:172 at [21] and the case-law cited.

[154] See [135] and the case law cited thereto.

[155] Communication from the Commission—Guidance on the Commission's enforcement priorities in applying Article 82 of the EC Treaty to abusive exclusionary conduct by dominant undertakings [2009] OJ C45/7, paras 1 and 9.

[156] *CEAHR v Commission* (T-712/14) ECLI:EU:T:2017:478 at [122] and cases cited thereto.

[157] (6/72) [1973] E.C.R. 215; [1973] C.M.L.R. 199.

[158] (27/76) [1978] E.C.R. 287; [1978] 1 C.M.L.R. 429; (26/75) [1975] E.C.R. 1367; [1976] 1 C.M.L.R. 95. In relation to unfair prices in the context of intellectual property, see para.12-274.

[159] (27/76) [1978] E.C.R. 287; [1978] 1 C.M.L.R. 429 at [227]–[230]. In this case, *United Brands* on

force another undertaking out of business (known as "predatory pricing"), this constitutes an abuse.[160]

Refusal to supply

12-126   Refusal to supply is in effect the refusal to sell essential raw material to a competitor.[161] Similarly, in the context of services, a dominant undertaking that refuses for no good reason to supply a service to another undertaking and reserves the service for itself constitutes an abuse of a dominant position.[162] An undertaking may not stop supplying a long-standing customer, even if the latter has engaged in conduct which is against the interest of the dominant undertaking, as sanctions must be proportionate to the circumstances and will normally fall short of a cessation of supplies.[163] However, in *Sot. Lélos kai Sia EE v GlaxoSmithKline AEVE Farmakeftikon Proïonton*[164] the CJEU held that a dominant undertaking could refuse to supply orders to a customer if such orders were out of the ordinary and which were essentially destined for parallel exports.[165] In a case where each Swiss clock manufacturer had been found to have a dominant position in the aftersales market for their brands, the General Court held that the Commission was entitled to reject a complaint from independent watch repairers, where despite a refusal to supply, this would not impair competition because they had put in place a network of authorised repairers who competed against each other and this network was open to any repairer who wished to join them.[166] The concept of refusing to supply also covers a refusal to licence interface information[167] or a refusal to grant access to an essential facility.

Resale restrictions

12-127   A blanket prohibition on distributors of a dominant undertaking reselling goods to anyone other than retailers.[168]

---

the basis of information fed to it by local representatives of market conditions in a country, would fix the sale price of bananas by them to the intermediate ripener/distributor.

[160] *ECS/AKZO* [1985] OJ L374/1; [1986] 3 C.M.L.R. 271 (EC Commission). See also *Tetra Pak SA v EC Commission* (333/941) [1996] E.C.R. I-5951.

[161] (6–7/72) [1974] E.C.R. 223; [1974] 1 C.M.L.R. 309.

[162] *Centre belge d'études de marché—Télémarketing (CBEM) v SA Compagnie luxembourgeoise de télédiffusion (CLT) and Information publicité Benelux (IPB) (IPB)* (311/84) [1986] 2 C.M.L.R. 558. This case concerned the refusal by IPB, the advertising arm of CLT, which ran a television station in Belgium, to allow CBEMT to conduct telemarketing sales on its channel.

[163] (27/76) [1978] E.C.R. 287; [1978] 1 C.M.L.R. 429 at [182]–[194]. The offending distributor/ ripener was an exclusive distributor for another banana supplier and had advertised for a rival competitor of United Brands.

[164] (C-468/06) to (C-478/06) [2008] E.C.R. I-7139, [2008] 5 C.M.L.R. 20.

[165] See [71].

[166] *CEAHR v Commission* (T-712/14) ECLI:EU:T:2017:478 at [94]–[98].

[167] *Microsoft v Commission* (T-201/04) [2007] E.C.R. II-3601. This case is discussed at paras 12-192 to 12-215. See also, Guidance on the Commission's enforcement priorities in applying Article [102] of the EC Treaty to abusive exclusionary conduct by dominant undertakings, para.78.

[168] (27/76) [1978] E.C.R. 287; [1978] 1 C.M.L.R. 429 at [152]–[162].

Tying-in arrangements

A clause stipulating that a purchaser buy exclusively from a dominant **12-128** undertaking.[169]

Loyalty rebates

The application of a fidelity rebate whereby loyal customers who purchase all or **12-129** most of their goods from the dominant undertaking receive financial advantages constitutes an abuse of a dominant position because it in effect ties-in the purchaser.[170] This should be contrasted with a quantity discount which is linked solely to the volume of purchases from the manufacturer concerned which is not an abuse.[171] In deciding whether the discount system operated is an abuse, the court will have regard as to whether:

> "in providing an advantage not based on any economic service justifying it, the discount tends to remove or restrict the buyer's freedom to choose his sources of supply, to bar competitors from access to the market, to apply dissimilar conditions to equivalent transactions with other trading partners or to strengthen the dominant position by distorting competition."[172]

INTELLECTUAL PROPERTY AND ABUSE UNDER ART.102

Introduction

Where dominance in a particular market is the result wholly or in part of the grant **12-130** of a legal monopoly in a particular product or service, does the dominant undertaking have to act towards third parties in such a manner so as to ensure that competition is not unduly affected in the relevant market including, where necessary, licensing third parties to carry out economic activities that fall within the monopoly? In other words, is the dominant undertaking obliged in particular circumstances not to prevent competition in the product or service market that is protected by the legal monopoly?

In the cases of *General Motors Continental NV v EC Commission*[173] and *British* **12-131** *Leyland v EC Commission*,[174] both General Motors and British Leyland were exclusively responsible by operation of law for the issue of certificates that entitled cars respectively made by them to be driven on, respectively, Belgian and British roads. In both cases, it was held that they had a dominant position in the relevant market, namely the issue of those certificates. Also, in both cases, it was held that they had abused their dominant position by not charging prices which related to the economic value of the service provided. In neither case did the CJEU consider the alleged abuse in the light of the nature of the legal monopoly. The issue of abuse was treated independently from the fact that a national law had purposively given an undertaking a monopoly which resulted in a dominant position in the relevant market.

---

[169] (85/76) [1979] E.C.R. 461; [1979] 3 C.M.L.R. 211.
[170] (4/73) [1975] E.C.R. 1663; [1976] 1 C.M.L.R. 295; (88/76) [1979] E.C.R. 461; [1979] 3 C.M.L.R. 211; (322/81) [1983] E.C.R. 3461; [1985] 1 C.M.L.R. 282 at [62]–[86].
[171] (322/81) [1983] E.C.R. 3461; [1985] 1 C.M.L.R. 282 at [71].
[172] (322/81) [1983] E.C.R. 3461; [1985] 1 C.M.L.R. 282 at [73].
[173] (26/75) [1975] E.C.R. 1367; [1976] 1 C.M.L.R. 95.
[174] (226/84) [1986] E.C.R. 3263; [1987] 1 C.M.L.R. 185.

12-132   Applying the above authorities to intellectual property, a superficial argument would be that the fact that dominance that has been achieved as a result of the indulgence of the state rather than the undertaking's own activities does not mean that a different approach should be taken to the issue of abuse in a market protected by IPRs. In other words, intellectual property is merely one example of a legal monopoly and should be treated no differently.

12-133   In the author's opinion, there are a number of reasons why intellectual property should not be treated like the above legal monopolies for the purposes of art.102.

(i)   Intellectual property monopolies are often justified in that they are there to reward the author. Other legal monopolies exist usually in order that some duty can be carried out efficiently.

(ii)   The owner of an intellectual property is not statutorily bound to commercially exploit it for the benefit of others. Other legal monopolies usually impose (impliedly or expressly) a duty to operate the monopoly for the benefit of others.

(iii)   The owner of an intellectual property is entitled to choose who it licenses. Other legal monopolies normally impose (expressly or impliedly) a duty not to discriminate between third parties.

(iv)   Intellectual property monopolies exist to encourage further creative work in the artistic field and investment in research and development in industry.

12-134   Although it has not expressly said so, it is no doubt for these reasons that EU law has not sought to assimilate IPRs with other legal monopolies when considering art.102. Instead, it has developed its own body of law with regard to the exercise of IPRs by a dominant undertaking. These are now considered.

International IP treaties and abuse under art.102

12-135   In the Introduction to this chapter, we discussed the interaction of competition law and international treaties for intellectual property. Thus, we discussed the fact that art.31(l) of TRIPS only permits the compulsory licence of a basic patent blocking the exploitation of an invention claimed in an improvement patent where it involves an important technical advance of considerable economic significance over the invention in the blocking patent.[175] It would thus arguably be contrary to TRIPS if competition law permitted the lowering of this threshold on the basis that the blocking patent was an indispensable input for the exploitation of the blocked invention, even though the latter was not an important technical advance.[176] The obvious rebuttal of this is that art.31(l) is intended to apply to all owners of blocking patents regardless of whether they are in a dominant position in a relevant market and that art.102 is dealing with a particular situation—where the owner is in a dominant position.

---

[175]   See para.12-022.

[176]   As discussed later, competition law can apply where IPRs protect an essential facility necessary to operate in a particular market. In particular, abuse is more readily found where the IPRs can be used to prevent the development of new products in a secondary market. In the case of art.31 invention which, by reason of the fact that it represents an important technical advance, the invention will invariably be in a different market to the invention protected by the blocking patent as it is unlikely that the technologies would be substitutable in such circumstances. A good example would be patents that protected normal film cameras which would be indispensable for the exploitation of inventions relating to digital cameras. Digital cameras are an important technical advance and film and digital cameras are unlikely to be considered substitutable.

In *TV Listings*, the broadcasting companies argued that the grant of a compulsory **12-136** licence was contrary to the Berne Convention.[177] They said that since all Member States were parties to the Berne Convention, it must be regarded as forming part of EU law. Article 9(2) of the Berne Convention permitted the reproduction of literary and artistic works in certain specific cases, provided that such reproduction did not conflict with a normal exploitation of the work and did not unreasonably prejudice the legitimate interests of the author. The companies argued that the grant of a compulsory licence was incompatible with art.9(2). In particular, the companies relied upon art.351 TFEU (ex-art.307 of the EC Treaty) which stated that rights and obligations entered into before the entry into force of the EC Treaty between Member States and third countries should not be affected by the EC Treaty.

The General Court rejected this argument on the basis that art.351 only affects **12-137** obligations entered into by Member States towards non-Member States and could not be relied upon with regard to relations between Member States in order to justify restrictions on trade within the EU.[178] Thus, the General Court said that the broadcasting companies could not rely upon them to justify restrictions on the system of freedom of competition established and implemented by arts 101 and 102.[179] In relation to treaty provisions entered into after accession by a Member State to the EU, it said that international rules cannot set aside rules arising out of the EU Treaty by the conclusion of an international agreement or convention.[180] The CJEU upheld the General Court's reasoning on both these points. It said that it was appropriate to observe that the EU was not a party to the Berne Convention. It said that the provisions of an international treaty cannot be relied upon in intra-EU relations if the rights of non-Member States are not involved.[181] It is of significance that the Advocate-General took a different approach. He said:

> "[166] I do not believe that anything more can be inferred from Article 9(2) than that the Convention does not preclude the possibility that in special cases the exclusive right to reproduce the work may be restricted and that it is left to the countries of the Union in their legislation and in accordance with the conditions set out in that provision to determine how they wish to avail themselves of that possibility. It cannot be contrary to that provision to conclude that a general competition provision constitutes the necessary legislative basis."

This reasoning could be applied to art.8(2) TRIPS which permits contracting **12-138** states to legislate appropriate measures to prevent the abuse of intellectual property rights by right holders or the resort to practices which unreasonably restrain trade or adversely affect the international transfer of technology.[182] Following *TV Listings*, the EU became a member of TRIPS.[183] In *Microsoft v EC Commission*, before the General Court, Microsoft criticised the Commission for interpreting art.102 in a way that was inconsistent with art.13 TRIPS.[184] Microsoft argued that EU law, including art.102, must be interpreted in the light of binding international agree-

---

[177] The Berne Convention is discussed in Ch.4, para.4-012.

[178] General Court decision citing inter alia *EC Commission v Italy* (10/61) [1962] E.C.R. 1; [1962] C.M.L.R. 187 CJEU at [102].

[179] General Court decision citing inter alia (10/61) [1962] E.C.R. 1; [1962] C.M.L.R. 187 CJEU at [103].

[180] General Court decision citing inter alia (10/61) [1962] E.C.R. 1; [1962] C.M.L.R. 187 CJEU at [103].

[181] Citing *Ministère Public v Déserbais* (286/86) [1988] E.C.R. 4907 at [18].

[182] art.8(2) TRIPS is discussed at para.12-022.

[183] It ratified TRIPS in 1995 after *TV Listings* was heard. See para.1-179.

[184] art.13 is discussed at para.12-023. It permits limitations or exceptions to copyright in special cases which do not conflict with a normal exploitation of the work and do not unreasonably prejudice the

ments such as TRIPS (even though Microsoft did not claim that TRIPS had direct effect). The General Court rejected the argument. It said that in reality, Microsoft was challenging the legality of the decision on the ground that it was contrary to art.13 TRIPS. It stated that it was settled case-law that WTO agreements were not in principle among the rules in the light of which the EU judicature could review the legality of measures adopted by the EU institutions.[185] The General Court maintained that it is only where the EU has intended to implement a particular obligation assumed under WTO or where the EU measure refers expressly to specific provisions of the WTO agreements that the EU judicature must review the legality of the EU measure in the light of the WTO rules.[186] It also said that this clearly did not apply to the Commission's decision wherein it was found that Microsoft was guilty of abuse of a dominant position.[187]

12-139   However, as discussed in the earlier section, there seems good reason why even though art.102 was not enacted to implement TRIPS, the considerations underlying TRIPS and the exceptions that it permits to the exercise of rights should be taken into account when considering whether there has been an abuse.[188]

Exceptional circumstances

12-140   As discussed earlier in this chapter, a dominant undertaking has a special responsibility not to allow its conduct to impair genuine undistorted competition on the market.[189] This means that it may be deprived of a course of conduct which would have been unobjectionable if carried out by an undertaking which was not dominant.[190] Thus, it would not be a good argument under EU law to assert that the exercise of IPRs by a dominant undertaking is incapable of being the subject of scrutiny under art.102. The special responsibility of a dominant undertaking may require it not to exercise its IPRs if such would impair residual competition in the market in which it is dominant or other markets. For example, it will be apparent that the consequence of the exercise of IPRs will often be to limit production, markets or technical development of products by competitors. If such is to the prejudice of consumers, this would prima facie fall within art.102(b). Such arguments favour the imposition of a duty on a dominant undertaking to license the activities of competitors that would infringe its rights.

12-141   However, and equally, an obligation on a dominant undertaking not to exercise its rights and thus, as a consequence, be compelled to license other competitors strikes at the very heart of IPRs. IPRs are the result of national and EU legislative measures. They are not mere accidents of the marketplace. Thus, it is equally arguable that even a dominant undertaking should be entitled to exercise its IPRs to prevent infringement of its rights.

12-142   This tension between two fundamental principles has been discussed in the

---

legitimate interests of the right holder.

[185] *Microsoft v EC Commission* (T-201/04) at [801] and cases cited there, being *Portugal v Council* (C-149/96) [1999] E.C.R. I-8395 at [47]; *Omega Air* (C-27/00 and C-122/00) [2002] E.C.R. I–2569 at [93]; *P. Petrotub and Republica v Council* (C-76/00) [2003] E.C.R. I–79 at [53]; and *Biret International v Council* (C-93/02) [2003] E.C.R. I-10497 at [52].

[186] See [802] citing *Portugal v Council* (C-149/96) [1999] E.C.R. I-8395 at [49] and *Biret International v Council* (C-93/02) [2003] E.C.R. I-10497 at [53].

[187] See [803].

[188] See para.12-029.

[189] See para.12-114.

[190] See para.12-119.

introduction to this chapter.[191] It has been the subject of considerable case law in the EU and national courts.

In *Parke Davis v Probel*,[192] for the first time, the CJEU had to consider whether **12-143** the exercise of patent rights could be an abuse of a dominant position. It held that the exercise of patent rights could be an abuse if "it were to degenerate into an abuse" of the protection afforded by a patent.[193] Such did little to advance understanding of when the exercise of patent rights was an abuse. Moreover, at the time of this decision, competition law was in its infancy. In *Hoffman-La Roche v Centrafarm*,[194] in a very brief judgment, the court said that the exercise of trade mark rights could be an abuse of a dominant position if such was used as an "instrument of abuse". Such wording, although not elaborated on, suggested that the use of IPRs to implement an abusive practice could be prohibited. It suggested that an abusive practice be identified without reference to the exercise of the IPR. If such could be done, then if the exercise of IPRs was done to implement such a practice, it could be prohibited. It was not until the late 1980s that the CJEU had to properly consider the issue in *Volvo v Veng*[195] and *CICRA v Renault*.[196] The subject-matter of these cases were essentially the same. Thus, it is only necessary to consider *Volvo v Veng*.

In *Volvo v Veng*, Erik Veng was a UK company which imported automobile body **12-144** panels for sale to the automobile repair market in the UK. In particular, it imported from Italy and Denmark front wing body panels for the Volvo 200 series, which had been manufactured without Volvo's authority. Volvo commenced proceedings against Veng alleging infringement of its UK-registered design in the front wing body panel. Veng's defence alleged that Volvo's refusal to grant a licence to the defendant or others constituted an abuse of a dominant position when Veng and others were willing to pay a reasonable royalty. Furthermore, it contended that the front wings were sold by Volvo at exaggeratedly high prices although this point was not at issue before the CJEU.

As the relevant product market was considered to be that of Volvo spare parts **12-145** which were protected by the registered designs, Volvo was held to have a dominant position.[197] Thus, the critical question was whether the exercise of the rights in the registered design which would have the effect of preventing any manufacturer other than Volvo or its representatives from supplying body panels for Volvo cars was an abuse of a dominant position. The Advocate-General noted that the substance of a registered design was the exclusive right to market products bearing the design. He also noted that IPR legislation only permitted the grant of compulsory licences in exceptional cases such as non-exploitation of the patent. He accordingly concluded that the refusal to grant a licence, i.e. the straightforward exercise of the right associated with a registered design could not *in itself* amount to an abuse of a dominant position. He held that there must be a further circumstance or element, e.g. a refusal to supply spare parts to independent repairers or unfair prices. Thus, he distinguished between the exercise of a right in itself and such playing "a rôle in connection with the abuse".

---

[191] See para.12-130, et seq.

[192] (24/67) [1968] E.C.R. 81; [1968] C.M.L.R. 47.

[193] (24/67) [1968] E.C.R. 81; [1968] C.M.L.R. 47 at [4].

[194] (102/77) [1978] E.C.R. 1139; [1978] 3 C.M.L.R. 217.

[195] (238/87) [1988] E.C.R. 6211; [1989] 4 C.M.L.R. 122.

[196] (53/87) *CICRA v Renault* [1988] E.C.R. 6039; [1990] 4 C.M.L.R. 265; [1990] F.S.R. 544.

[197] As to whether the relevant market can be spare parts for a single-brand, see paras 12-044 to 12-049.

12-146   The court adopted the Advocate-General's opinion and emphasised that an obligation to grant to third parties a licence for the supply of products incorporating the design would lead to the proprietor being deprived of the substance of the exclusive right and that a refusal to grant such a licence cannot in itself constitute an abuse of a dominant position.[198] However, following the Advocate-General, it said that the exercise by the proprietor of an exclusive right in a registered design in respect of car body panels may be prohibited by art.102 if it involved, on the part of an undertaking holding a dominant position, certain abusive conduct such as the arbitrary refusal to supply spare parts to independent repairers, the fixing of prices for spare parts at an unfair level, or a decision no longer to produce spare parts for a particular model even though many cars of that model are still in circulation, provided that such conduct was liable to affect trade between Member States.[199]

12-147   In *TV Listings*,[200] the General Court and CJEU considered whether the exercise of copyright in television programme listings could amount to an abuse of a dominant position. The facts were that various television broadcasting companies were responsible for the compilation and publication of information about programme listings. They permitted use of such information for the publication of a comprehensive *daily* programme listings programmes in newspapers. Furthermore, they published magazines which only contained weekly programme listings of their own channels. However, they did not permit the publication of a *comprehensive* weekly listing magazine. They were able to prevent third parties from compiling information from each company's magazine by the enforcement of copyright as under Irish law, copyright vests in compilations. They adopted a vigorous policy of suing anyone who did for infringement of copyright. One undertaking, Magill, sought to produce a comprehensive weekly list incorporating all the channels' programmes. It complained to the Commission that the broadcasting companies' refusal to supply the scheduling information coupled with the threat of proceedings for copyright infringement amounted to an abuse of a dominant position. Its argument was that the refusal to supply the information was analogous to the refusal to supply spare parts to independent repairers in *Volvo v Veng*. Moreover, it considered the fact that the companies published their own weekly listing and allowed comprehensive daily listings to be published by third parties meant that the refusal was arbitrary and discriminatory.[201]

12-148   The Commission found that there had been an abuse of a dominant position. On appeal to the General Court, the court held that whilst the exercise of the exclusive right to reproduce a protected work was not in itself an abuse, that did not apply when, in the light of the details of a particular case, it was apparent that the right was being exercised in such ways and circumstances as in fact to pursue an aim *manifestly contrary* to the objectives of art.102.[202] The General Court considered that the broadcasting companies' conduct had the effect of preventing the production and marketing of a new product for which there was consumer demand.

---

[198] (238/87) [1988] E.C.R. 6211; [1989] 4 C.M.L.R. 122 at [8].

[199] (238/87) [1988] E.C.R. 6211; [1989] 4 C.M.L.R. 122 at [10].

[200] (T-69/89) [1991] E.C.R. II-0485, [1991] 4 C.M.L.R. 586; (T-70/89) [1991] C.M.L.R. 669; (T-76/89) [1991] C.M.L.R. 745. The three cases were decided by the same Chamber and rely on almost identical analysis. The cases are thus not discussed separately. Citations always refer to the first case, *RTE v EC Commission*. The decisions of the General Court were appealed to the CJEU (C-241–242/91P) [1995] E.C.R. I-0743; [1995] 6 C.M.L.R. 718. The CJEU dismissed the appeal.

[201] The television companies authorised the publication of its weekly listings in other Member States without charging royalties.

[202] See [71].

Thereby they excluded all competition in the market of television magazines for which there was no justification and which amounted to an abuse. It thus agreed with the Commission's view that such was comparable to the example in *Volvo v Veng* of an arbitrary refusal by a car manufacturer to supply parts to an independent repairer carrying on its business in the derivative market of automobile maintenance and repair.[203]

On appeal to the CJEU,[204] the CJEU confirmed the General Court's decision. It **12-149** said that it was clear from *Volvo v Veng* that the refusal to grant a licence, even if the act of an undertaking holding a dominant position, could not in itself constitute abuse of a dominant position.[205] However, it said that it was also clear from *Volvo v Veng* that the exercise of an exclusive right may *in exceptional circumstances* involve abusive conduct.[206]

In considering the facts, the CJEU held that the companies' refusal to provide **12-150** basic information by relying on national copyright provisions thus prevented the appearance of a new product, a comprehensive weekly guide to TV programmes, which the companies did not offer and for which there was consumer demand. The CJEU said that such refusal constituted an abuse under heading (b) of the second paragraph of art.102 (limiting production, markets or technical development to the prejudice of consumers). Secondly, the CJEU further held that there was no justification for such a refusal. Thirdly, the CJEU confirmed the General Court's analysis that the companies had reserved to themselves the secondary market of weekly television guides by excluding all competition on that market since they denied access to the basic information which was the raw material indispensable for the compilation of such a guide.[207]

The CJEU also confirmed that the Commission was entitled in order to ensure **12-151** that its decision was effective to require the television companies to provide the information if necessary on payment of royalties.[208]

The requirement that the exercise of IPRs by a dominant undertaking will only **12-152** be abusive in exceptional circumstances must be considered the only fundamental principle to be applied in this area.[209] As said by the Court of Justice in 2015 in *Huawei v ZTE*,[210] it is settled law that the exercise of IPRs by a dominant undertaking cannot in itself amount to an abuse of a dominant position but may in exceptional circumstances involve abusive conduct for the purpose of art.102.[211]

Since *TV Listings*, EU and national courts have had to consider the application **12-153** of this principle to a particular set of facts. Because the CJEU found in *TV List-*

---

[203] See [74].
[204] (C-241–242/91P) [1995] E.C.R. I-0743; [1995] 6 C.M.L.R. 718.
[205] (C-241–242/91P) [1995] E.C.R. I-0743; [1995] 6 C.M.L.R. 718 at [49].
[206] See [50].
[207] (C-241–242/91P) [1995] E.C.R. I-0743; [1995] 6 C.M.L.R. 718 at [54]–[56]. The third reason was based on the decision of the CJEU in (6–7/72) [1974] E.C.R. 223; [1974] 1 C.M.L.R. 309. See para.12-153, et seq.
[208] (C-241–242/91P) [1995] E.C.R. I-0743; [1995] 6 C.M.L.R. 718 at [88]–[94].
[209] See *Intel Corp v Via* [2003] Eu. L.R. 85; [2003] F.S.R. 33, where the Court of Appeal of England and Wales rejected a submission by Intel that "exceptional circumstances" could only arise if all the conditions in *TV Listings* or *IMS v NDC* were satisfied. Thus, the Court rejected the submission that the result of the refusal to licence must be: (a) the exclusion of an entirely new product from the market (*TV Listings*); and (b) the elimination of all competition to the patentee (*IMS*). See also, *Microsoft v EC Commission* (T-201/04) [2005] E.C.R. II-1491 at [331]. See also Commission Notice on art.102, para.78, fn.50 citing *TV Listings* and *IMS v NDC* (C-418/01) [2004] E.C.R. I-5039 at [35].
[210] *Huawei Technologies Co. Ltd v ZTE Corp* (C-170/13) ECLI:EU:C:2015:477 at [46]–[47].
[211] See [46]–[47].

ings that there was an abuse because it concerned the prevention of a new product in a neighbouring market which had the effect of reserving to the companies the secondary market of weekly television guides, parties' legal representatives have in subsequent cases submitted such are *necessary* conditions before an abuse could be found. However, neither the CJEU nor the General Court ever said so. They are simply *sufficient* conditions for an abuse to be found but not *necessary* conditions.[212] Thus, as the European Commission said in *Microsoft/Interoperability*,[213] having reviewed much of the case law in this area, there is no *"persuasiveness to an approach that would advocate the existence of an exhaustive checklist of exceptional circumstances"*.[214] On appeal, the General Court endorsed the Commission's approach that, in certain circumstances, a refusal to supply on the part of a dominant undertaking may constitute an abuse of a dominant position when it is not objectively justified. It confirmed the general principle that it is only in exceptional circumstances that the exercise of IPRs may give rise to a finding of abuse.[215] The General Court also held that when considering the interplay of EU IPR Directives and the application of art.102, the latter was a provision of "higher rank" than such Directives.[216]

12-154 In considering whether there are exceptional circumstances, it has been said that extraneous abusive conduct must be identified that is over and above the mere exercise of IPR.[217] Thus the abuse cannot be the normal result of enforcing the IPR in a market in which the undertaking is dominant, i.e. reserving an economic monopoly to the owner of the IPR. It must bring about some other effect which is anti-competitive or exploitative *and* which harms consumers.[218] Thus, it has been said that this other conduct must be *in itself* an abuse.[219] If one can identify an extraneous abusive conduct, then the use of IPRs to implement such conduct will itself be an abuse.

12-155 Is it possible to determine a conceptual framework as to when the exercise of rights by a dominant undertaking will amount to exceptional circumstances or must each case be determined on its facts? Without prejudice to the general principle that it is only in exceptional circumstances that the exercise of IPRs may amount to an abuse of a dominant position, it is possible from EU and national decisions to say that there are certain situations where a dominant undertaking *may* be prohibited from exercising its rights:

---

[212] e.g. see (T-504/93) [1997] E.C.R. II-923 at [115]; *Intel Corp* [2003] Eu. L.R. 85; [2003] F.S.R. 33. In *IMS v NDC* (C-418/01) [2004] E.C.R. I-5039, the CJEU set out three conditions which it said was sufficient for a licence to be granted—see para.12-194, et seq.

[213] Commission Decision of 24 March 2004 (Case COMP/C-37.92).

[214] Commission Decision of 24 March 2004 (Case COMP/C-37.92), at [555].

[215] See *Microsoft v EC Commission*, at [331].

[216] *Microsoft v EC Commission*, [227]. Thus, it said that the issue was not whether the concept of interoperability in the Commission's decision was consistent with the concept envisaged in the Computer Directive but whether the Commission determined correctly the degree of interoperability in the light of the objectives of art.102.

[217] J. Temple Lang and C. Stothers, "The End of Exclusivity: Abuse of Intellectual Property Rights in the EU" [2002] E.I.P.R. 86.

[218] J. Temple Lang, "Chapter 3: The Application of the Essential Facility Doctrine to Intellectual Property Rights under European Competition Law", in F. Lévêque, H.A. Shelanski (eds), *Antirust, Patents and Copyright: EU and US Perspectives* (Northampton, Mass: Edward Elgar, 2005), p.67.

[219] J. Temple Lang, "Chapter 3: The Application of the Essential Facility Doctrine to Intellectual Property Rights under European Competition Law", in F. Lévêque, H.A. Shelanski (eds), *Antirust, Patents and Copyright: EU and US Perspectives* (Northampton, Mass: Edward Elgar, 2005), p.67.

(a) Where the IPR permits its owner to "leverage" its power in one particular market into a neighbouring market.

(b) Where the IPR controls an "essential facility" which is indispensable to operating in a particular market. This will look particularly at where the IPR, being a patent, is a standard essential patent ("SEP") relating to a technology embodied in a technological standard which standard undertakings must have access to in order to compete in a particular market.

(c) Where the IPR is incidental or the background to abusive conduct by the dominant undertaking, i.e. the charging of unfair prices for products protected by IPRs.

It should be said that often it is not possible to draw a clear distinction between **12-156** "leveraging" cases and "essential facility" cases. Leveraging cases are principally concerned with a situation where there are two distinct markets and the dominant undertaking is using its dominance in one market to obtain dominance in another market. In particular, in the context of intellectual property, it allows a dominant undertaking in one market where its IPRs act as a barrier to entry to obtain market power in another market.[220] Essential facility cases are concerned about where an undertaking has control over an essential facility or input which it is necessary for other parties to have access to in order to provide products or services in a particular market. It is not necessary that there be two markets. However, sometimes it is said that there is one market in the facility/input and another in the market which that facility or input relates to. These scenarios are now considered.

Leveraging

In *TV Listings*, as discussed above, the CJEU held that the exercise of copyright **12-157** by television broadcasting companies to prevent comprehensive television guides was an abuse of a dominant position because the broadcasting companies had prevented the appearance of a new product for which there was consumer demand and reserved to themselves the secondary market of weekly television guides thereby excluding all competition in that market. Thus, *TV Listings* sets out markers as to when a refusal to license may constitute an instrument of abuse. These are:

(a) a new product for which there is consumer demand;

(b) no justification for refusal to license; and

(c) reservation to the rights owner of a secondary market.

Although it was not clear whether these requirements were cumulative, the court **12-158** of *IMS v NDC* made it clear that that they were.[221] Many commentators characterise *TV Listings* as a case where the broadcasting companies were "leveraging" their dominance in one market (programme scheduling information) into another market, namely that for weekly magazines. Although they did not use such dominance to provide a comprehensive weekly magazine themselves (which would have required co-operation between all companies), they were content to force customers to buy a magazine from each broadcasting company in order to determine what was on television.

---

[220] Whilst it is tempting for the purpose of simplicity to consider leveraging as a case where the IPR protection does not extend to the neighbouring market, this is not necessarily so as can be seen from *TV Listings*.

[221] See (C-418/01), at [38].

12-159   In the US, abusive leveraging is an accepted abuse but leveraging intellectual property is considered presumptively legal.[222] However, care must be taken in applying US law as to leveraging under EU law as US law can proscribe any behaviour which amounts to maintenance of a dominant position.[223]

12-160   *TV Listings* has its origin in a non-intellectual property case. In *Télémarketing*,[224] the CJEU held in the declaratory part of its judgment:

> "[27] It must therefore be held in answer to the second question that an abuse within the meaning of Article [102] s committed where, without any objective necessity, an undertaking holding a dominant position on a particular market reserves to itself or to an undertaking belonging to the same group an ancillary activity which might be carried out by another undertaking as part of its activities on a neighbouring but separate market, with the possibility of eliminating all competition from such undertaking."

12-161   The facts of *Télémarketing* were that a Benelux broadcasting company which had a dominant position in the Belgian broadcasting market had entered into a contract with a telemarketing company whereby the former agreed that it would grant exclusive rights to telemarketing on its broadcasting channels. It thus informed advertisers that it would not accept advertisements which involved an invitation to make a telephone call unless that telephone number was that of its agent. Third party telemarketing companies complained. The national court held that telemarketing activities constituted a separate market from that of the chosen advertising medium. It was against this factual background that the CJEU gave the ruling set out in the above excerpt. The CJEU's decision was in part based upon *Commercial Solvents*.[225] In that case, the applicants manufactured nitropropane and aminobutanol which were intermediary products for the manufacture of ethambutanol. The latter was used as an anti-tuberculosis drug and was in competition with other drugs. The matter came to the Commission's attention because the applicants had refused to sell aminobutanol to a competitor because the applicants themselves wished to enter the market for the derivative product, ethambutanol. The court held, in upholding the Commission, that such was an abuse.

12-162   Both *Télémarketing* and *Commercial Solvents* are examples of an undertaking leveraging its dominance in an upstream market to obtain dominance in a downstream market. In *RTT v GB-Inno-BM SA*,[226] it was held to be an abuse of a company operating a public telecommunications network to set technical standards for telephone equipment and be responsible for checking compliance for such equipment when it too was operating in such a field. In short, it was leveraging its power in relation to telephone equipment and networks into the market for checking of compliance. *TV Listings* can be considered as a case where the broadcasting companies were leveraging their dominance in a market for raw materials (programming scheduling information) to obtain dominance in the market for the finished product (weekly television listings).

12-163   However, difficulties arise in applying *Commercial Solvents*, *RTT* and *Télémar-*

---

[222] For a useful review of the issue of leveraging of intellectual property in US law, see M. Paterson, "When is Property Intellectual? The Leveraging Problem" (2000) 73 *Southern California Law Review* 1133.

[223] This point was made in *Getmapping Plc v Ordnance Survey* [2002] Eu. L.R. 464; [2003] I.C.R. 1; [2002] U.K.C.L.R. 410, [2002] EWHC 1089 (Ch).

[224] (311/84) [1985] E.C.R. 3261; [1986] 2 C.M.L.R. 558.

[225] (6–7/72) [1974] E.C.R. 223; [1974] 1 C.M.L.R. 309.

[226] *RTT v GB-Inno-BM SA* (C-18/88) [1991] E.C.R. I-5941.

keting to IPRs. The nature of IPRs is that they are intended to confer exclusive rights to their owners irrespective of what market those rights may be relevant to. Thus, IPRs may result in an undertaking having control over more than one market. Therefore, it is an inevitable consequence of the conferring of copyright on programme schedules that a broadcasting company will have exclusive rights in those programme schedules whether they appear in daily, weekly, monthly or annual television listings regardless of whether there are separate markets for daily, weekly, monthly or annual television listings or not. In *Télémarketing*, the broadcasting company could *only* obtain dominance in the telemarketing market by leveraging its dominance in the broadcasting market. In *TV Listings*, in fact, the broadcasting companies could collectively achieve dominance in the weekly television market by simply exercising their copyright. The fact that they were dominant in the market for programming information or daily listings was irrelevant. Thus, even if they had published the weekly programme schedules sufficiently early and encouraged fierce competition in the daily television listings market, they could have still prohibited Magill or anyone else from publishing comprehensive weekly television guides. In reality, the companies were not leveraging their dominance in one market into another market. They were simply enforcing their copyright in two markets—daily and weekly television listings—so as to control both markets.

For *TV Listings* to have been a genuine "leveraging" case, it would have been **12-164** necessary to show that the broadcasting companies were seeking to leverage their dominance in a particular market for which they had IPRs into a *market where there existed no protection under their* IPRs. IPRs can cover more than one market.[227] Perhaps mindful of this, the General Court in *TV Listings* sought to liken the TV station's refusal to supply the programme schedule information to Magill as analogous to the example given in *Volvo* of a refusal of a car manufacturer to supply spare parts to independent repairers thereby reserving the market for repairs and maintenance of its cars to itself. However, as has been commented on, such is not a proper analogy. In *Volvo v Veng*, the car companies sought to extend their design right to the derivative market of automobile maintenance where Volvo or Renault had not been granted exclusive rights. In *TV Listings*, there was no extension of market power to an adjacent market in which the broadcasting companies did *not* enjoy the protection of an exclusive IPR.[228]

This distinction is made in the US where attempts by independent service **12-165** organisations to argue that manufacturers of photocopiers and printers who have sought to leverage their market power into the market in repair and servicing of their photocopiers and printers by refusing to supply spare parts to independent organisations have generally failed where they have patent protection for the parts.[229] Thus, in *re Independent Service Organisation Antitrust Litigation*,[230] the Federal Circuit has emphasised the need to show that the patent holder is using its statutory right to refuse to sell patented spare parts to gain a monopoly in a market *beyond the scope of the patent*. In contrast, in *Intergraph Corp v Solid Systems CAD*, an English case which was decided after *TV Listings*, the judge held that it was arguable that

---

[227] In the US, there has been explicit recognition of this—see *In Re Independent Service Organisations Antitrust Litigation* 274 F.Supp. 2d 743 discussed below.
[228] See A. Reindl, "The Magic of Magill: TV Program Guides as a Limit of Copyright Law?" I.I.C. 1993 1, 60 at 76.
[229] These cases are often characterised as "essential facilities" cases and are discussed at para.12-179.
[230] Discussed at para.12-192. See also the "pay for delay" cases where the "exclusionary potential" argument was consdiered in the context of art.101—para.8-366.

the refusal of the owner of copyright in computer programs to license third parties in the adjacent maintenance market and secondhand markets was by analogy to *TV Listings*, an abuse of a dominant position.[231] This is despite the fact that it is virtually impossible to operate in these markets without infringing the copyright in the computer software.[232] It is submitted that in these circumstances, applying the principle argued above, it would not be an abuse for the software owner to reserve such a market for itself, as the market is protected by the IPR belonging to the software owner. This permits the software owner to decide on the distribution of remuneration between the primary sales of the software and the support and maintenance of the software. Thus, in the computer software industry, often the real money is made in the maintenance and support market, with the software being sold at a relatively low price. This can be pro-competitive because often the charges in the maintenance and support market are proportionate to the number of licensees or usages. This permits allocative efficiencies because it ensures that those who intend to use the software only for themselves can afford the software.[233]

12-166   Although in many respects, the decision in *TV Listings* is intuitively correct as plainly the interests of consumers were prejudiced by the deliberate refusal to permit the publication of comprehensive weekly television guides with no real attempt by the broadcasting companies to justify such conduct, there are a number of other unsatisfactory aspects of *TV Listings*. First, we have already mentioned the fact that it is not a genuine leveraging case like *Télémarketing*. Secondly, although it was clear that there was consumer demand for a comprehensive weekly television guide, the reality was that the consumer was able to obtain information in the weekly television listings market by buying each broadcasting companies' weekly magazine. Thus, as Gulmann AG said, who recommended that the General Court decision be overturned, the Commission accepted that a comprehensive weekly television guide would compete with the broadcasting companies' guides. As he said, a comprehensive weekly television guide would both be cheaper and give a better overview but it would basically meet the same consumer needs as may be met by buying weekly television guides for the individual television broadcasting organisations. In those circumstances, he considered that the interests of the copyright proprietor should prevail over the interests of consumers as there was no new product in a sense that may be relevant for the application of art.102.[234] Indeed, although its decision is ambivalent on this point, at one point in its judgment, the General Court appeared to accept that the comprehensive weekly television guide would compete with RTE's own magazine.[235] In short, and taking the "spare parts" analogy of *Volvo v Veng*, the broadcasting companies were supplying consumers' needs in the separate market of weekly listings. The fact that they were not supplying those consumers' needs in the most convenient form hardly merits a finding of exceptional circumstances.

12-167   It is thus difficult to deduce any fundamental principle from *TV Listings* other

---

[231] *Intergraph Corp* [1998] Eu. L.R. 223.

[232] The maintenance and support of computer programs invariably requires reproduction and alteration of the programs which is an act exclusively reserved to the IPR owner.

[233] The same pricing theory applies to printer markets whereby the printers are sold cheaply and the ink cartridges are comparatively expensive. This gives rise to efficiencies whereby the charge is proportionate to the level of usage so that a large number of persons can afford to buy the printer.

[234] See [98], Opinion.

[235] See [73]. However, see [62] where the General Court appear to reach the conclusion that the relevant product market was comprehensive weekly television guides which suggest that it did not view magazines only listing one channel as substitutable products.

than that the exercise of rights by a dominant undertaking will only amount to an abuse in exceptional circumstances. In truth, *TV Listings* was merely an example of exceptional circumstances. Jacobs AG in *Oscar Bronner* (a case concerning "essential facilities")[236] said:

"The ruling in *Magill* [*TV Listings*] can in my view by explained by the special circumstances of that case which swung the balance in favour of an obligation to license. First, the existing products, namely individual weekly guides for each station, were inadequate, particularly when compared with the guides available to viewers in other countries. The exercise of the copyright therefore prevented a much needed new product from coming on to the market. Secondly, the provision of copyright protection for programme listings was difficult to justify in terms of rewarding or providing an incentive for creative effort. Thirdly, since the useful life of programme guides is relatively short, the exercise of the copyright provided a permanent barrier to the entry of the new product on the market. It may incidentally be noted that national rules on intellectual property themselves impose limits in certain circumstances through rules on compulsory licensing."[237]

In truth, *TV Listings* was a potpourri of individual facts which in totality **12-168** amounted to exceptional circumstances. Indeed, the second factor in the excerpt above is in truth an attack on the IPR itself rather than its enforcement. It is a finding that the extension of copyright by Irish law to material such as programme listings was an ingredient of the abuse.

In the author's opinion, there are two unusual factors about the facts of *TV* **12-169** *Listings*. First, the nature of copyright is that it is not an absolute monopoly. It prevents copying but does not prevent a designer creating an identical product by way of independent design. It is not intended to give a true monopoly but is intended to prevent a person from misappropriating the skill, labour and effort of another.[238] In *TV Listings*, copyright existed in the weekly programme schedule information because Irish law deemed that the skill and labour expended in compiling the listings from the raw material was sufficient to make the listings original works. However, because the television companies also had a de facto monopoly in the raw material and the actual selection procedure which led to the listings, they were able to prevent third parties like Magill who were clearly prepared to spend considerable sums of money from independently compiling the listings themselves. In effect, the exercise of copyright by the TV companies transformed the qualified monopoly of copyright (which merely prevents copying) into a monopoly only associated with registered rights. Secondly, copyright is not intended to protect pure information. Yet, in *TV Listings*, it did. In a real sense, the broadcasting companies leveraged the power of copyright to obtain total protection over published programme listings. Thus, as said by Laddie J in *Philips v Ingman*,[239] *TV Listings* was concerned with, in reality, a refusal to divulge information about television programmes. These two factors are, in the author's view, the exceptional circumstances of *TV Listings*.

Whatever criticism can be made of the reason in *TV Listings*, it set a judicial **12-170** precedent for finding an abuse where there was a refusal to license IPRs in a leveraging situation. It has been relied upon in a number of subsequent European

---

[236] See para.12-187.
[237] *Oscar Bronner v Mediaprint* (C-7/97) [1998] E.C.R. I-7791.
[238] See Ch.4.
[239] *Philips Electronics* [1999] F.S.R. 112; [1998] Eu. L.R.

and national cases involving a unilateral refusal to license. Often, the dominant undertaking has submitted that one or more of its three conditions have not been satisfied and thus there can be no abuse. However, as discussed above, the three conditions in *TV Listings* are sufficient but not necessary conditions for a finding of abuse. Thus, the mere absence of a condition is not fatal to a finding of abuse. In this section, we look at leveraging cases subsequent to *TV Listings*. In the next section, we look at how the three conditions have been interpreted in cases involving an undertaking seeking access to an "essential facility".

12-171   In *Tiercé Ladbroke*,[240] French horse racecourses refused to give Ladbroke, a company that owned betting shops in Belgium, the right (which was protected by copyright) to transmit live pictures of French races in Ladbroke's betting shops in Belgium. Ladbroke then complained to the Commission who dismissed the complaint. On appeal to the General Court, the General Court dismissed the appeal. Ladbroke argued that the case was similar to *Télémarketing*, *Commercial Solvents* and *TV Listings*. However, the facts were far from those cases. The upstream market was audiovisual services relating to French horse races whereas the downstream market was the betting market in Belgium. Clearly, Ladbroke was not prevented from operating in the Belgian betting market. It simply considered that it could provide a better service if it had access to live broadcasts. Not surprisingly, the above cases were distinguished. *TV Listings*, *Commercial Solvents* and *Télémarketing* had no application because Ladbroke (unlike Magill) was and the French race courses (unlike the broadcasting companies) were not operating on the downstream secondary betting market.[241] Thus, the General Court distinguished the leveraging cases such as *Télémarketing* and *Commercial Solvents* because the French race courses were not seeking to reserve the betting market in Belgium to themselves. In short, the French race courses were not seeking to leverage their dominance in an upstream market of horse racing into the downstream market of betting.

12-172   The General Court interpreted *TV Listings* as meaning that the refusal to supply the applicant could not fall within the prohibition laid down by art.102 unless:

(i)   it concerned a product or service which was either essential for the exercise of the activity in question, in that there was no real or potential substitute; *or*

(ii)   there was a new product whose introduction might be prevented, despite specific, constant and regular potential demand on the part of consumers.[242]

12-173   In relation to the first requirement, it was clear that French live broadcasts were not essential to the operation of Ladbroke on the betting market (it merely improved the quality of their operation). Importantly, this requirement foreshadows the doctrine of "essential facilities" which is discussed in the next section.

12-174   In relation to the second requirement, having stated the principle, the General Court never actually made a finding whether the introduction of live broadcasting of French races in Belgian betting shops was a new product or service. Certainly, it had not been provided before in Belgium. It might have been thought as a desirable new service in the same way that in *TV Listings*, a comprehensive weekly television guide was more desirable than buying separate guides only containing the listings for one channel. There is some suggestion in the reference to "specific,

---

[240] (T-504/93) [1997] E.C.R. II-923 at [131].
[241] (T-504/93) [1997] E.C.R. II-923 at [130].
[242] (T-504/93) [1997] E.C.R. II-923 at [131].

constant and regular potential demand" that Belgian betters did not consider it to be so. It is difficult to see why the introduction of live broadcasting of French races in Belgian betting shops is not as much a new product as comprehensive weekly listings. The CJEU in *TV Listings* never made it a condition that the new product was indispensable to consumers on the basis of no actual or potential substitutes and plainly, as discussed above, comprehensive weekly lists were in competition with single channel listings. In any event, care must be taken in applying this aspect of the General Court's judgment. In *IMS v NDC*, they interpreted the conditions in *TV Listings* as cumulative conditions.[243] Although the court in *IMS* said that they were not necessary but only sufficient conditions, it would be surprising if the mere prevention of a new product for which there was consumer demand amounted per se to an abuse of a dominant position. In short, if a product that was in actual or potential substitution with the new product that was already being provided on the secondary market by any party, then this should be sufficient defence.

In *Sun/Microsoft*,[244] Sun Microsystems lodged a complaint before the EC Commission concerning Microsoft's practice of not disclosing fully information concerning the interface of its PC operating system (i.e. Windows) with operating systems for workgroup servers. Initially, Microsoft did disclose information on the interface to its competitors. This ensured that there was a development of third party applications software and rival workgroup operating systems. Then, once it had obtained about 30 per cent market share for its workgroup server operating system, it reduced the level of disclosure of information to achieve interoperability. This meant that customers and software houses shifted their allegiance to Microsoft's workgroup operating software because of concerns about lack of compatibility of rival workgroup operating software. As a result, the market tips in favour of Microsoft's operating system: rival products are marginalised and competition is eliminated.[245] In short, the Commission found that Microsoft had leveraged its dominance in the client PC operating market to the work group server operating system market.[246] **12-175**

On appeal, the General Court upheld the Commission's decision.[247] This case is considered in more detail in the section on essential facilities. This is because although characterised by some as a leveraging situation, in truth, the identified abuse was the prevention of access to interoperability information, an input necessary for the workgroup server market. **12-176**

Care must be applied in applying the leveraging doctrine. In *Getmapping Plc v Ordnance Survey*,[248] Getmapping produced and supplied detailed digital colour images of the UK to complement maps. Ordnance Survey was responsible for the official definitive surveying and topographic mapping of Great Britain and did so with the assistance of public funding. In particular, it had created the basis for a digital **12-177**

---

[243] See [38].

[244] Commission Decision of 24 March 2004 (COMP/C-37.92) [2007] OJ L32/23.

[245] Generally, see F. Lévêque, "Innovation, Leveraging and Essential Facilities: Interoperability Licensing in the EU Microsoft Case" in F. Lévêque, H.A. Shelanski (eds), *Antitrust, Patents and Copyright: EU and US Perspectives* (Northampton, Mass.: Edward Elgar, 2005).

[246] Commission Decision of 24 March 2004 (Case 4 COMP/C-37.92) at [533], [1063]. See J. Temple Lang, "Essential Facility Doctrine, IP Rights and European Competition Law" in F. Lévêque, H.A. Shelanski (eds), *Antirust, Patents and Copyright: EU and US Perspectives* (Northampton, Mass.: Edward Elgar, 2005), where he says that Microsoft is a leverage case and not an essential facility case.

[247] (T-201/04) [2007] E.C.R. II-3601.

[248] *Getmapping Plc* [2003] I.C.R. 1.

mapping product that consisted of several layers and themes of data such as roads, waters and boundaries. Ordnance Survey announced that it would provide a "one-stop shop" website whereby it would offer digital colour imagery which had not hitherto been seen on maps. This meant that it would be in direct competition with Getmapping who offered such a service. Getmapping brought proceedings for breach of s.18 of the Competition Act 1998 contending that Ordnance Survey was in a dominant position for the supply of such digital imagery and that by cross-subsidising its own imagery from its map business and setting up the one-stop-shop, thereby using public funds to sell the imagery, it was abusing its dominant position in the UK map market. Getmapping sought an interlocutory injunction in the English courts obliging Ordnance Survey to put Getmapping's digital imagery on Ordnance Survey's website.

12-178   Getmapping argued that Ordnance Survey was unfairly leveraging its market power in the mapping market in which it was plainly dominant to gain a competitive advantage in the "imagery" market in which it was not dominant. The unfairness was that Ordnance Survey was publicly funded. The court pointed out that the concept of "leveraging" was developed in the US which proscribes obtaining a dominant position rather than the abuse of a dominant position. The judge said that it was difficult to see how cross-subsidisation amounted to an abuse in competition law. The judge said the mere use of financial muscle to move into a new market could not amount to an abuse.[249] The court concluded that Getmapping's case was very weak and declined to grant the injunction.

Essential facilities

Introduction

12-179   In certain cases, an undertaking will have control over an "essential facility" which is necessary for a competitor to operate in a particular market. In the US, this led to the development of the "essential facilities" doctrine whereby vertically integrated companies which had control over an essential facility were compelled to give access to it to competitors. Thus, in *United States v Terminal Railroad*,[250] a group of railway companies owned a key bridge over the Mississippi river and an accompanying railway and refused to permit use of the bridge to competitor railway companies. They were ordered to give access. In *MCI v AT&T*,[251] a telephone network operator refused to give a telephone company access to its telephone exchanges for the purpose of making long distance telephone calls. The 7th Circuit held that where the following four conditions were satisfied, namely:

(1)   control of the essential facility by a monopolist;
(2)   a competitor's inability practically or reasonably to duplicate the essential facility;
(3)   the denial of the use of the facility to a competitor; and
(4)   the feasibility of providing the facility,

then the owner of the essential facility is obliged to provide access to the facility

---

[249]   Relying upon *UPS v European Commission* (T-175/99) [2002] E.C.R. II-1915 at [20].
[250]   *United States v Terminal R.R. Assocn* 224 US 383 (1912).
[251]   *MCI Commn. Corp v AT&T* 708 F.2d 1081 (7th Cir., 1983).

on reasonable and non-discriminatory terms.[252] An essential facility is sometimes described as an input into a market, i.e. some component that must be used to provide a competitive product or service. Often, it is said that for the essential facility doctrine to apply, it must have the effect of foreclosing competition in a downstream market and thus of helping the owner of the essential facility to acquire or maintain a monopoly in that market.[253] This characterisation of the "essential facility" doctrine is to treat it as simply one of leveraging market power in an upstream market into a downstream market as discussed in the previous section. Thus, in *Intergraph Corp v Intel Corp*,[254] the Federal Circuit said that the essence of an essential facilities claim was that there was an attempt of the defendant to use control of such a facility to gain an unfair advantage in a downstream market in which both the defendant and claimant competed. Thus, the Federal Circuit said that:

> "*The courts have well understood that the* essential facility theory is not an invitation to demand access to the property or privileges of another, on pain of antitrust penalties and compulsion; thus the courts have required *[as a condition of finding that the doctrine of essential facilities apply]* anti-competitive action by a monopolist that is intended to eliminate competition in the downstream market".[255]

In *Intergraph Corp v Intel Corp*, Intel cut off the supply of microprocessors and **12-180** proprietary information to Intergraph who made computer workstations using Intel architecture and microprocessors. Intel's response was in reaction to Intergraph's threat to sue Intel's customers for violating Intergraph patents. Intergraph argued that access to Intel's chips and technical know-how was indispensable to its business. On reversing the district court, the Federal Circuit held that as Intergraph and Intel did not compete at all, Intergraph could not possibly make out an essential facilities claim.

However, in many cases, there is no active upstream market in the facility itself **12-181** and it is better simply considered as an essential input into a particular market. In layman's terms, access is indispensable to operating in a particular market. Thus, in *Terminal Railroad*, it is artificial to talk about a market in bridge services over the Mississippi river. The only relevant market was that of railway services. The bridge was an essential input for that market.

The owner of an essential facility has four choices: (1) not to permit anyone to **12-182** use it; (2) to reserve its use to itself; (3) to permit some but not all to use it; and (4) to permit all to use it on non-discriminatory reasonable terms. *Intergraph* appears to suggest that the doctrine only applies if the second condition is made out. In *Intergraph*, Intel was not involved in the workstation market yet its chips were indispensable to operating in that market. Its conduct did not eliminate competition in the workstation market, it simply eliminated Intergraph's involvement in the

---

[252] In general, for US law on essential facilities, see H. Hovenkamp, M.D. Janis and M.A. Lemley, "Unilateral Refusals to License in the US" in F. Lévêque and H.A. Shelanski (eds), *Antitrust, Patents and Copyright: EU and US Perspectives* (Northampton, Mass.: Edward Elgar, 2006); M. Furse, "The Essential Facilities Doctrine in EU law" [1995] 8 E.C.L.R. 470; D. Ridyard, "Essential Facilities and the Obligation to Supply Competitors under UK and EC Competition Law" [1996] 17 E.C.L.R. 438, and A. Overd and B. Bishop, "Essential Facilities: The Rising Tide" [1998] E.C.L.R. 183.

[253] H. Hovenkamp, M.D. Janis and M.A. Lemley, "Unilateral Refusals to License in the US" in F. Lévêque and H.A. Shelanski (eds), *Antitrust, Patents and Copyright: EU and US Perspectives* (Northampton, Mass.: Edward Elgar, 2006), p.19.

[254] 195 F.3d 1346 (Fed. Cir., 1999).

[255] At 1357.

market. It was thus, in truth, discriminatory conduct, but for which it might be said that there was justification. If Intergraph had been the only operator in the workstation market, then it would have the effect of preventing workstations from being produced which would have been plainly detrimental.

12-183   In *Aldridge v Microsoft Corp*,[256] the court, having re-stated the test in *MCI*, said that the essential facilities doctrine only applied where access to the facility was essential and that the monopoly was a natural or government-supported monopoly. In that case, Aldridge complained that Microsoft had disabled access to its disk caching program on Windows 95 although its disk caching program did work on previous versions of Windows. Microsoft supplied its own disk caching program for Windows 95. The court rejected the claim on the basis that Microsoft's operating system was neither essential nor a natural or government-supported monopoly.

12-184   The essential facility doctrine has been criticised in the US and in a decision of the Supreme Court, the court has said that it has never recognised such a doctrine.[257]

12-185   In summary, the "essential facilities" doctrine in the US is difficult to differentiate from the principle of a competitor in one market leveraging its dominance in that market into another market. As said by the Federal Court in *Intergraph*:

> "[42] Although the viability and scope of the essential facility theory has occasioned much scholarly commentary, no court has taken it beyond the situation of competition with the controller of the facility, whether the competition is in the field of the facility itself or in a vertically related market that is controlled by the facility. That is, there must be a market in which plaintiff and defendant compete, such that a monopolist extends its monopoly to the downstream market by refusing access to the facility it controls. See *TV Communications Network, Inc. v. Turner Network Television, Inc.*, 964 F.2d 1022, 1025 (10th Cir., 1992) (relevant market must be proven for an essential facilities claim); *Consul, Ltd. v. Transco Energy Co.*, 805 F.2d 490, 494 (4th Cir. 1986) ("The fact remains that a relevant market must be proven under any of these theories [including denial of access to an essential facility]). Absent such a relevant market and competitive relationship, the essential facility theory does not support a Sherman Act violation."

The EU

12-186   In the EU, the CJEU and European Commission have developed an essential facility doctrine. Thus, in *Port of Genoa*,[258] the undertaking had a monopoly of dock work in the Port of Genoa. The Port refused to allow ships to unload using modern technology and engaged in other practices such as demanding payment for services which had not been requested. The CJEU held that such was abusive conduct of a dominant position as the Port was an essential facility for those who wished to ship to and from Genoa. This was a classic "essential facilities" case. In *Stena Sealink v Sealink Harbours*,[259] one of the first Commission decisions to refer to the "essential facilities" doctrine, the Commission said:

> "An undertaking which occupies a dominant position in the provision of an essential facil-

---

[256] 995 F.Supp 728 (S.D.Tex., 1998).

[257] *Verizon Communications v Law Offices of Curtis V Trinko* 540 US 398 (2004). This has been described as a "bit of revisionist history"—H. Hovenkamp, M.D. Janis and M.A. Lemley, "Unilateral Refusals to License in the US" in F. Lévêque and H.A. Shelanski (eds), *Antitrust, Patents and Copyright: EU and US Perspectives* (Northampton, Mass.: Edward Elgar, 2006), p.20.

[258] [1991] E.C.R. I-5889.

[259] Decision 94/19 Relating to A Proceeding Pursuant to Article 86 EC (Sea Containers v Stena Sealink-Interim Measures), [1994] OJ L15/8.

ity and itself uses that facility (i.e. a facility or infrastructure, without access to which competitors cannot provide services to their customers), and which refuses other companies access to that facility without objective justification or grants access to competitors only on terms less favourable than those which it gives its own services, infringes Article [102] if the other conditions of that Article are met. An undertaking in a dominant position may not discriminate in favour of its own activities in a related market. The owner of an essential facility which uses its power in one market in order to protect or strengthen its position in another related market, in particular, by refusing to grant access to a competitor, or by granting access on less favourable terms than those of its own services, and thus imposing a competitive disadvantage on its competitors, infringes Articles [102]."

In *Oscar Bronner v Mediaprint*,[260] Mediaprint distributed its newspapers via a **12-187** well-established delivery network in Austria. Oscar Bronner wished to use the delivery network and claimed that Mediaprint's refusal to allow it access to that network was an abuse of a dominant position. Jacobs AG considered the doctrine of "essential facilities" as developed in the US.

He said that it will apply where the following five conditions can be satisfied: **12-188**

"First [there exists] an essential facility controlled by a monopolist. A facility will be regarded as essential when access to it is indispensable in order to compete on the market with the company that controls it … . Secondly, a competitor is unable practically or reasonably to duplicate the essential facility. It is not sufficient that duplication would be difficult or expensive, but absolute impossibility is not required. Thirdly, the use of the facility is denied to a competitor. That condition would appear to include the refusal to contract on reasonable terms. Fourthly, it is feasible for the facility to be provided. Fifthly, there is no legitimate business reason for refusing access to the facility. A company in a dominant position which controls an essential facility can justify the refusal to enter a contract for legitimate technical or commercial reasons. It may also be possible to justify a refusal to contract on grounds of efficiency".[261]

The Advocate-General said that intervention of the kind in *Magill* was only **12-189** justifiable in terms of competition policy where the dominant undertaking has a genuine stranglehold on the related market. It was not sufficient that the undertaking's control gave it a competitive advantage.[262] The CJEU said in *Oscar Bronner* that exceptional circumstances could apply where:

(a) the refusal of the home delivery service was likely to eliminate all competition in the daily newspaper market *on the part of the person requesting the service*;

(b) such refusal was incapable of being objectively justified; and

(c) the service was *indispensable* to carrying on that person's business inasmuch as there is no actual or potential substitute in existence for that home delivery scheme.[263]

However, such did not assist Oscar Bronner. The CJEU said that the mere fact **12-190** that there was only one nationwide home delivery system did not mean that Mediaprint had control of an essential facility. It said that it would have to be shown that it was not economically viable for a second home delivery scheme to be

---

[260] (C-7/97) [1998] E.C.R. I-7791.
[261] See [47], Opinion.
[262] (C-7/97) [1998] E.C.R. I-7791 at [65], AG's Opinion.
[263] (C-7/97) [1998] E.C.R. I-7791 at [41].

created. It was irrelevant that for Oscar Bronner, it was not economically viable to establish such by reason of the small circulation of newspapers that they had. It would have to be shown that it was not economically viable for the distribution of daily newspapers with a circulation comparable to that of Mediaprint.[264]

12-191   It will be noted that in *Oscar Bronner* the parties were in competition with each other in the field of newspaper publishing. Thus, the declaratory part of the judgment ruled that it was not an abuse to prevent a publisher of a rival newspaper from having access to the home delivery scheme of an undertaking with a very large share of the daily newspaper market.[265] It was thus debateable whether *Oscar Bronner* extended the doctrine of essential facilities to where the parties were not in competition, i.e. where the owner of the essential facility had control over an essential input into a market but did not compete in that market. As seen in the discussion of the US cases, it is a requirement that the parties be in competition and the Advocate-General's formulation of the essential facilities doctrine was based on US law.

IPR and essential facilities

12-192   The above cases did not concern essential facilities where IPR controlled access to the essential facility. Before considering the EU approach to the essential facilities doctrine where IPRs are involved, it is a useful exercise to review the US approach to the application of the doctrine where the injured party is inter alia seeking a licence to the IPRs that control access to an essential facility. In general, the US courts have been resistant to the application of the essential facilities doctrine to IPR infringement actions. The real concern is that requiring a company to license its IPR "would significantly chill innovation".[266] Whilst this observation is not without its importance, it can be overstated. For instance, some companies have a deliberate policy of obtaining "patent thickets" to file a multitude of patent applications that claim minor variations on a *competitor's* existing technology.[267] In the author's experience, some printer companies appeared to have a policy of patenting a multitude of trite features surrounding the "interface" between printers and printer cartridges so as to make it as difficult as possible for third parties to supply ink cartridges compatible with printers without infringing patents. Attempts by companies to control the servicing market for these machines have been the subject of a number of US decisions concerning essential facilities. In *re Independent Service Organisation Antitrust Litigation*,[268] a group of ISOs that serviced Xerox machines sued Xerox for violating the antitrust laws because Xerox refused to sell parts to them or their customers. Xerox only supplied spare parts to end-users that serviced the machine themselves or to end-users who hired Xerox to perform the service. This had the effect of Xerox reserving the servicing market to itself. Xerox counterclaimed for patent and copyright infringement claiming that it had IPRs on a number of its parts and copyright in its service drawings. Xerox argued that it was entitled to unilaterally refuse to sell patented or copyrighted products to ISOs. The

---

[264] See [42]–[47].

[265] See [47].

[266] *In re Microsoft Corp Antitrust Litigation* 274 F.Supp 2d 743, 745.

[267] See D.L. Rubinfeld, R. Maness, "The Strategic Use of Patents: Implications for Antitrust" in F. Lévêque and H.A. Shelanski (eds), *Antitrust, Patents and Copyright* (Northampton, Mass.: Edward Elgar, 2006).

[268] 203 F.3d 1322 (Fed. Cir., 2000).

Federal Circuit held that a patentee's right to refuse to license its IPR was limited only in certain circumstances: where the patent was obtained through fraud, where a lawsuit to enforce the patent was a sham, or where the patent holder used its statutory right to refuse to sell patented parts to gain a monopoly in a market beyond the scope of the patent. The Federal Circuit noted that a patent could cover more than one market and it held without explanation that Xerox's parts patents entitled it to control the market for service of Xerox copiers as well.[269]

In *Data General v Grumman Systems Support*,[270] ISOs repaired computer **12-193** hardware manufactured by Data General. To do so, they needed access to Data General's copyrighted diagnostic software. Data General cut off access to this software to increase its own share in the servicing market of its computers. The ISOs obtained access to the diagnostic software and Data General sued for copyright infringement. Grumman counterclaimed for violation of antitrust law. The Federal Court rejected the submission of Data General that there should be an irrebuttable presumption that a unilateral refusal to license was never an abuse. However, it held that there was a strong presumption that a refusal to license was valid in the absence of evidence of immediate harm to consumers. It is of note that the court did not seek to find antitrust law superior to copyright law or vice versa. Thus, it sought to read the two statutes in the light of each other. The court found that the presumption applied as the copyrights were valid, the software was innovative and the courts were unwilling to inquire into the motivation of Data General in enforcing the copyright. In contrast, in *Image Technical Services v Eastman Kodak*,[271] Kodak suddenly decided not to supply ISOs in the photocopier industry after years of co-existence. The ISOs sued for antitrust. Kodak did not sue for patent or copyright infringement until very late in the litigation. The court upheld a jury finding of antitrust liability. The court endorsed the approach in *Data General* of a rebuttable presumption of lawfulness. However, it found that the presumption was rebutted as only a very small minority of parts were patented and because Kodak's reliance on its IPR was a pretence and had no part to play in the refusal to supply the parts. In this sense, unlike the court in *Data General*, the court did inquire into the motivation of Kodak. Indeed, it said that:

"neither the aims of intellectual property law, or the antitrust laws justify allowing a monopolist to rely upon a pretextual business justification to mask anti-competitive conduct."

In Europe, the seminal case on IPR and essential facilities is *IMS Health Inc v* **12-194** *NDC Health GmbH*.[272] In that case, IMS, a pharmaceutical marketing company had developed a geographical data "brick" structure used for the purpose of determining sales of pharmaceuticals in Germany. The brick structure divided Germany into 1860 areas. This map benefitted from copyright protection in Germany. IMS sold pharmaceutical sales information based on the 1860 areas to pharmaceutical companies. After a period, the 1860 map became a de facto standard and pharmaceutical companies insisted on the 1860 map being used. Such was protected by copyright. A competitor wished to provide market information but because the

---

269 See H. Hovenkamp, M.D. Janis and M.A. Lemley, "Unilateral Refusals to License in the US" in F. Lévêque and H.A. Shelanski (eds), *Antitrust, Patents and Copyright: EU and US Perspectives* (Northampton, Mass.: Edward Elgar, 2006), p.28.
270 36 F.3d 1147 (1st Cir., 1994).
271 125 F.34 1195 (9th Cir., 1997).
272 (C-418/01) [2004] E.C.R. I-5039; [2004] 2 C.M.L.R 28; [2004] E.C.D.R. 33.

"brick" structure had become the de facto standard for pharmaceutical market sales information, it required a licence of the brick structure. It requested a licence and it was turned down. It made a complaint to the European Commission. At the heart of the dispute was whether an application of *TV Listings* meant that it was a *necessary* condition for a finding of an abuse that IMS's conduct was preventing the emergence of a new product on the market for which there was consumer demand. IMS said that the conditions in *TV Listings* were cumulative and as it was supplying sales information itself, it was not preventing the emergence of a new product. The Commission did not consider that such was an essential requirement for an abuse to be found. It made an interim decision requiring IMS to grant a licence to NDC. The Commission interpreted *TV Listings* and *Oscar Bronner* as requiring that:

(a) the refusal of access to the facility is likely to eliminate all competition in the relevant market;

(b) such refusal is not capable of being objectively justified; and

(c) the facility itself is indispensable to carrying on business inasmuch as there is no actual or potential substitute in existence for that facility.[273]

12-195   The Commission's finding is a classic statement of the "essential facilities" doctrine. Although *TV Listings* had referred to the prevention of an emergence of a new product, *Oscar Bronner*, although not an IPR case, did not make such a requirement. On appeal to the General Court, in *IMS Health v European Commission*,[274] the President granted a stay pending a final decision on the interim order. IMS said that the essential facilities doctrine requires that a refusal to licence must prevent the appearance of a new product on a market separate from that on which the undertaking in question is dominant (which was not the case in *IMS*). The President said that this raised a serious legal question. However, in 2003, the Commission withdrew its interim measures decisions as NDC had entered into contracts with some big customers without using the 1860 structure (thereby rather undermining its argument that access to the 1860 brick data structure was indispensable).

12-196   Meanwhile, in copyright infringement proceedings in Germany, the German courts referred to the CJEU preliminary questions as to whether IMS's copyright infringement action was an abuse of a dominant position. In *IMS v NDC*,[275] the CJEU elaborated on what the defendant needs to show that access is indispensable for the purpose of competing on the market. In particular, it said that the cost of developing an alternative structure was a legitimate factor to take into account. It then reviewed the case law (principally *TV Listings*) and said:

"[38] It is clear from that case law that, in order for the refusal by an undertaking which owns a copyright to give access to a product or service indispensable for carrying on a particular business to be treated as abusive, it is *sufficient* that three *cumulative* conditions be satisfied, namely, that [1] that refusal is preventing the emergence of a new product for which there is a potential consumer demand, that

---

[273] COMP D3/38.044, *NDC v IMS (Interim Decision), EC Commission* [2002] 4 C.M.L.R. 111 at [70] (Commission).

[274] (T-148/01) [2002] 4 C.M.L.R. 2, [2001] E.C.R. 3193. This decision was upheld on appeal to the CJEU, see (C-481/01P) [2002] E.C.R. I-3401, [2002] 5 C.M.L.R. 1.

[275] *IMS Health GmbH & Co OHG v NDC Health GmbH & Co KG* (C-418/01) [2004] E.C.R. I-5039; [2004] 4 C.M.L.R. 28; [2004] E.C.D.R. 23.

[2] it is unjustified and [3] such as to exclude any competition on a secondary market."[276] [Emphasis supplied.]

These three conditions are discussed below. A number of preliminary remarks can **12-197** be made. First, the CJEU retained the requirement that the refusal to the essential facility was preventing the emergence of a *new* product. Such arose from the need to balance the interests of protection of IPR and the economic freedom of its owner against the interests of free competition.[277] Thus, it is not sufficient for the party seeking access to the essential facility intending to limit itself essentially to duplicating the goods or services provided by the IPR owner.[278] Secondly, there is no requirement that the owner of the essential facility be a competitor on the secondary market. As seen above, this is an important feature in the US cases and it was unclear in *Oscar Bronner* whether such was a condition.[279] Thirdly, It is important to note that the court in *IMS v NDC* was not saying that the three conditions were *necessary* for a finding of abuse but simply that they were *sufficient*.[280] Thus, its judgment did not resolve the issue in the Commission proceedings as to whether NDC had to show that IMS's conduct was preventing the emergence of a new product. Fourthly, the CJEU said that it was not necessary that there be a primary market in which the owner of the essential facility was active and by which it was seeking to leverage into the secondary market. As said by the CJEU, it was sufficient that one could identify a potential or hypothetical market and that such was the case where the products or services of the owner of the right were indispensable to carry on a particular business.[281]

IMS v NDC was considered in *Microsoft v EC Commission*[282] where the General **12-198** Court considered the line of authorities from *Magill* to *IMS v NDC* and held that exceptional circumstances must apply where:

(a) the refusal relates to a product or service *indispensable* to the exercise of a particular activity on a neighbouring market;

(b) the refusal is of such a kind as to exclude any *effective* competition on that neighbouring market; and

(c) the refusal prevents the appearance of *a new* product for which there is potential consumer demand.[283]

It can be seen from these authorities that there are a number of conditions which **12-199** are *sufficient* for a finding of abuse. These conditions are now considered.

Indispensable

In *IMS v NDC* the CJEU said that it must be shown that any alternative structure **12-200** to the 1860 structure is such as:

---

[276] The numbers in square brackets are not in the original judgment.
[277] See [48].
[278] See [49].
[279] Although it should be said that in *IMS v NDC* that the parties were competitors.
[280] A point made by Lloyd J in *Wireless Group Plc v RAJAR* [2005] Eu. L.R. 307, [46]. See also, *Microsoft v EC Commission* (T-201/04) [2005] E.C.R. II-1491 at [332].
[281] See [44].
[282] (T-201/04) [2007] E.C.R. II-3601.
[283] See [332].

"to rule out any economic viability of business on a scale comparable to that of the undertaking which controls the protected structure."[284]

12-201   Therefore, it is not sufficient simply to show that there are less advantageous solutions but that there are technical, legal or economic obstacles capable of making it impossible or at least unreasonably difficult for any undertaking seeking to operate in the market to create, possibly in co-operation with other operators, the alternative products or services.[285] This requirement was considered in *Microsoft v EC Commission*. Microsoft argued that the Commission's decision contained an error of law because its interoperability information could not be characterised as indispensable if it was "economically viable" for competitors of a dominant undertaking to develop and market their own products without having access to the technology. It said that the case law did not require "optimal access" to the market to be granted.[286] It argued that various methods could be deployed by the workgroup servers to achieve interoperability with its PC operating systems which although not providing "perfect substitutability" did make it possible to achieve "the minimum level of interoperability...required for effective competition."[287] The Commission said that the indispensability criterion required an examination of the degree of interoperability necessary to remain as a viable competitor on the market and whether the withheld information was the only "economically viable" source for achieving that degree of interoperability.[288] The General Court held that the Commission's approach was correct and that the requirement of "economic viability" was the correct criterion for determining whether the supply of information was indispensable.[289] It also rejected Microsoft's argument that it was not necessary for competitors to be supplied with the information to remain viable on the market on the grounds that in this regard, the Commission's decision was based on complex economic assessment and was not manifestly incorrect.[290]

Prevents emergence of a new product

12-202   The requirement that the exercise of rights must prevent the emergence of a new product arises from the need to maintain a balance between the rights of the owner of IPR and that of free competition. This was a point made by Tizzano AG in *IMS v NDC* which the CJEU accepted saying the latter could only prevail where the refusal acted to the detriment of consumers.[291] Thus in *Microsoft v EC Commission*, the General Court noted that the requirement that the refusal to present the appearance of a new product for which there is potential consumer demand only appeared in case law on the exercise of IPRs.[292] This requirement means that in essence, the dominant undertaking has the right to choose whether to satisfy the demand for the new product (whether by manufacturing itself or licensing the IPRs to a third party to so do) or alternatively risk not being able to exercise the IPRs itself. It also means that the essential facilities doctrine as developed by the CJEU

---

[284]   See *IMS v NDC*, at [29].
[285]   See *IMS v NDC*, at [28].
[286]   See [339].
[287]   See [345].
[288]   See [352].
[289]   See [377] and [229].
[290]   See [378]–[380].
[291]   See *IMS v NDC*, at [48].
[292]   *Microsoft v EC Commission* (T-201/04) [2005] E.C.R. II-1491 at [334].

cannot be considered a true "essential facilities" doctrine whereby the owner of an essential facility (e.g. a gateway patent) which protects a relevant market is obliged to license any third party who wishes to enter that market.

How "new" does the product need to be? In *IMS v NDC*, the CJEU said that such **12-203** would only be the case where the complainant does not intend:

> "[49] ... to limit itself essentially to duplicating the goods or services already offered on the secondary market by the owner of the intellectual property right, but intends to produce new goods or services not offered by the owner of the right and for which there is a potential consumer demand."

Such a statement suggests that provided the new good or service differs *materi-* **12-204** *ally in certain key characteristics* from the equivalent characteristics of products placed on the market by the IPR owner or with its consent, it does not matter if the "new" good or service *would compete* with the good or service provided by the IPR owner. In other words, it is not sufficient for the dominant undertaking to say that it supplies a competing product with the defendant's product. Such is reinforced by the opinion of Tizzano AG in *IMS v NDC* where he said that it would be abusive to prevent the appearance of goods or services which:

> "although in competition with those of the owner of the right, answer *specific consumer requirements* not satisfied by existing goods or services."[293] [Emphasis supplied.]

This approach appears to follow the approach of the CJEU in *TV Listings* where **12-205** the CJEU held, in not following the Opinion of Gulmann AG, that it was suf-ficient for an abuse to be made out if the broadcasting companies exercised their rights to prevent the appearance of a new product which they did not offer and for which there was a potential consumer demand.[294]

The Commission takes the same view. In the Commission Notice on art.102,[295] **12-206** the Commission emphasises that for an abuse to be made out, it is sufficient that there is demand from potential purchasers and that a potential market for the input at stake can be identified.[296] It is suggested that if such a condition is satisfied, it matters not whether the alleged "new" good or service competes with other goods or services on the secondary market.

Two further points can be made. First, in the Commission's Notice on art.102, **12-207** it says that it is not necessary for there to be an actual refusal—"constructive refusal" is sufficient. Thus, it says that such could take the form of unduly delay-ing or otherwise degrading the supply of the product or involving the imposition of unreasonable conditions in return for the supply.[297] Secondly, in *Microsoft v EC Commission*, the General Court reiterated that conduct which prevented the appear-

---

[293] See [62], Opinion.
[294] See [54], decision of CJEU. At [98] of the Opinion of Gulmann AG, he said that there was no new product because such would compete with the respective weekly television guides of the broadcast-ing companies and although comprehensive weekly television guides would be cheaper and give a better overview, they would "basically meet the same consumer needs as may be met by buying weekly television guides". In such circumstances, the interests of the copyright proprietor should prevail over the interests of the consumer. The CJEU did not reject this approach expressly but it would appear implicitly rejected in the judgment of the CJEU.
[295] See fn.162.
[296] See [79] citing *IMS v NDC*.
[297] See [79]. Although said in the context of refusing to supply actual products, there is no reason why such reasoning cannot be transposed to the grant of a licence—i.e. unduly delaying the grant of a licence or making its term subject to unreasonable conditions.

ance of a new product fell to be considered under art.102(b). It then pointed out that art.102(b) also mentioned technical developments. Thus, it was sufficient to show that the conduct prevented technical developments.[298] Therefore, it upheld that the Commission's finding that Microsoft's refusal to provide interoperability information had "discouraged its competition from developing and marketing work group server operating system with innovative features to the prejudice, notably, of consumers".[299] Thus, it is not necessary to show concretely that a new product has been prevented from appearing on the market but that the *market condition* which could lead to such occurring must also not be prevented. As said by the CJEU, art.102 covers not only practices which prejudice consumers directly, but also those which indirectly prejudice them by impairing an effective competitive structure.[300]

12-208   In some cases, an undertaking will own an IPR for a technological or industry standard. In such circumstances, the fact of standardisation means that there is a market barrier to the creation of a new product. For instance, in the German case, *Standard Spundfass*,[301] the industry had adopted a particular barrel for carrying chemicals which became the industry standard such that it was not commercially feasible to market a barrel which did not comply with this standard. The barrel was protected by patents. In such circumstances, the "new product" requirement would have been fatal to any application for a compulsory licence. The Bundesgerichtshof made a finding of abuse on the basis that de facto standardisation protected the patent holder and the patented technology from having to face competition from superior technologies. The "new product" requirement was not applied but it would appear that the defendant was being discriminated against. It might be thought that the new product rule should not apply where not only the undertaking has a dominant position but there exists a de facto or de jure standard. However, *IMS v NDC* was concerned with a de facto standard and IMS' copyright protected that standard.

Exclude competition in a secondary market

12-209   Two issues arise under this condition. Is there a need for two distinct markets? This is a requirement of leveraging but does it apply to an "essential facility" argument? Secondly, must the defendant establish that the exercise of IPRs eliminates *all* competition or competition from the defendant?

12-210   On the first point, a major plank of IMS's argument in *IMS v NDC* and the Commission proceedings was that art.102 only applies where a dominant undertaking seeks to exclude the appearance of a new product in a secondary market rather than the market in which the dominant undertaking operates in and was dominant. In other words, IMS was seeking to argue that it was necessary to show that the dominant undertaking was seeking to leverage its power into *another* market. IMS said that NDC was seeking to operate in the same market that it was operating and dominant in, namely market research.

12-211   The court, following *Bronner*, did not accept this submission. It said that it was sufficient to identify a *potential* or even a *hypothetical* "upstream" market, i.e. the

---

[298] *Microsoft v EC Commission* (T-201/04) [2005] E.C.R. II-1491 at [647].
[299] *Microsoft v EC Commission* (T-201/04) [2005] E.C.R. II-1491 at [653] citing Recital 694 of Commissioner's decision.
[300] *Microsoft v EC Commission* (T-201/04) [2005] E.C.R. II-1491 at [653] citing Recital 694 of Commissioner's decision.
[301] *KZR* 40/02 (13 July 2004, Bundesgerichtshof).

market in data brick services. In doing so, it followed Tizzano AG's Opinion. Thus, it said that it was:

> "determinative that two different stages of production may be identified and that they are interconnected, inasmuch as the upstream product is indispensable for the supply of the downstream product."[302]

In reality, the court is accepting that it is only necessary to show that an input for **12-212** operating in a particular market is indispensable. This is done by the legal fiction of a hypothetical upstream market in the essential facility. In *Microsoft v EC Commission*, the General Court also said that it was necessary to distinguish two markets but said that it was not necessary that the indispensable product or service was marketed separately.[303]

On the second issue of what amount of competition must be excluded, the **12-213** requirement in *IMS v NDC* that the dominant undertakings behaviour be such as to exclude *any* competition is capable of being interpreted as meaning that provided that there is at least one competitor on the market, then this condition is not satisfied. In *Intel v Via*,[304] the English Court of Appeal made the point that in *Oscar Bronner*, it was not a requirement that there be total elimination of competition but rather elimination of competition *from the person requesting the service*. Also, the summary of the law by the President in *IMS v Commission* had to be read in such a light. Moreover, as the Court of Appeal of England and Wales said, were it otherwise, liability under art.102 could be simply avoided by the grant of a licence to an unenergetic rival.[305] The author's view is that this is correct and that such reasoning applies equally to the decision of *IMS v NDC*.[306] In any event, if a licence had been granted to an unenergetic rival, then the refusal to grant a licence to another may amount to discriminatory conduct without objective justification. Generally, dominant undertakings are required not to discriminate.

In *Microsoft v EC Commission*, the General Court held that art.102 does not ap- **12-214** ply when there is *no* competition on the market. It said that what matters is whether the refusal at issue "is liable to, or is likely to, eliminate all *effective* competition on the market".[307] Thus, it said that a marginal presence in certain niches by competitors was not sufficient.[308]

Unjustified

The court said in *IMS Health* that it is for the national court to examine whether **12-215** refusal of a request for a licence is justified by objective considerations.[309] It did not expand on what these could be. In *Microsoft v EC Commission*, Microsoft sought to put forward various justifications for the exercise of its copyright. These were:

> *The need to protect IPRs*—Unsurprisingly, as the essence of an art.102 case

---

[302] (C-418/01) [2004] E.C.R. I-5039; [2004] 4 C.M.L.R. 28; [2004] E.C.D.R. 23 at [45].

[303] *Microsoft v EC Commission* (T-201/04) [2005] E.C.R. II-1491 at [335].

[304] See [2003] Eu. L.R. 85; [2003] F.S.R. 33 CA.

[305] *Intel Corp* [2003] F.S.R. 33 CA at [49].

[306] In particular, *IMS v NDC*, at [47] the court refers to the refusal to grant the licence as being "capable of excluding all competition on the market for the supply of German regional sales pharmaceutical products". Thus, the test is whether the alleged essential facility is capable of excluding all competition rather than whether the owner of the facility has made use of such capability.

[307] *Microsoft v EC Commission* (T-201/04) [2005] E.C.R. II-1491 at [563].

[308] *Microsoft v EC Commission* (T-201/04) [2005] E.C.R. II-1491 at [563].

[309] (C-418/01) [2004] E.C.R. I-5039; [2004] 4 C.M.L.R. 28; [2004] E.C.D.R. 23 at [51].

is whether it could be abusive to exercise IPRs, the CJEU did not accept that the need to protect IPRs could be an objective justification.[310]

Effect on innovation—Microsoft argued that the grant of a licence would act as a deterrent for innovation which would outweigh the pro-competitive effects of a grant of a licence. In economic speak, the argument is that the detriment to the innovation market would outweigh the benefit to the product or technological market. This argument was considered on its merits. Thus, the Commission, upheld by the General Court, found that Microsoft had not sufficiently established that if it were required to disclose the interoperability information, there would be a significant negative impact on its incentives to innovate.[311] It also pointed out that when considering the requirement of objective justification, such was against the background that it had already been found that there were exceptional circumstances which justified not permitting the undertaking to enforce its rights and that an argument per se that the interoperability information was protected by IPRs could not in itself amount to objective justification because such would mean that the exception never applied.[312] It followed on by saying that it is inherent that if a dominant undertaking holds IPRs such are innovative or original because patents cannot be granted if there is no invention and copyright will not arise unless the work is original.[313] Thus, it seems fairly clear that although such an argument is open to the dominant undertaking to make, persuasive and cogent evidence will be required to establish it.

Protection of secrets—In a technical know-how licence, a licence would involve the disclosure of confidential, valuable information to the applicant and there was a real risk that the applicant would not keep it confidential. It might be thought that in a case whereby a party seeks to protect confidential information, such would be a legitimate justification. However, as pointed out by the CJEU in *Microsoft*, where such an argument was deployed, the argument that the technology to which a third party requires access is secret and of great value did not advance any argument per se because if such information was not secret, then the abuse could not arise and the requirement of indispensability necessarily meant that the information is of "great value" to competitors.

Commercial interests—Where the circumstances concern the enforcement of a patent which protects a technological standard (a SEP patent) and the SEP owner has committed to license its SEP on FRAND terms, the European Commission has said that a SEP holder is entitled to take reasonable steps to protect its interests by seeking interim and permanent injunctions against a potential licensee where: (i) the licensee is in financial distress and unable to pay its debts; (ii) the licensee's assets are in jurisdictions that do not provide for adequate means of enforcement of damages; and (iii) a potential licensee is unwilling to enter into a FRAND licence.[314] These conditions emphasise that a complainant is not entitled to a "free licence" but merely a licence which

---

[310] *Microsoft v Commission*, at [690]; Case AT.39939 *Samsung* (EC Commission Decision, 29 April 2014) at [66].
[311] *Microsoft v EC Commission* (T-201/04) [2005] E.C.R. II-1491 at [697].
[312] See [690]–[691].
[313] See [695].
[314] Case AT.39939—*Samsung* (EC Commission Decision, 29 April 2014) at [67].

ensures reasonable compensation to the dominant undertaking. If the circumstances are such that such is unlikely to happen, then the commercial interests of the undertaking prevail. Thus, the complainant must not only be prepared to enter into a FRAND licence but also ensure that such is not merely a "piece of paper".

In *Syfait*,[315] the Greek Competition Commission referred to the CJEU the question of whether a dominant pharmaceutical undertaking could, in order to limit parallel trade, refuse to meet in full the orders which it receives from pharmaceutical wholesalers. As is well known, in Europe, there is very considerable state intervention regarding the prices that a company can charge for pharmaceuticals. This leads to a very substantial parallel trade. Such can have the effect of reducing the profit margins so markedly on pharmaceuticals so as to amount to a deterrent to research and development. Although the case did not go to the CJEU, Jacobs AG held that a restriction of supply to limit parallel trade is capable of justification as a reasonable and proportionate measure in defence of its commercial interest.[316] Subsequently, in *Sot Lelos kai Sia EE v GlaxoSmithKline AEVE Farmakeftikon Proionton*,[317] the CJEU held that it was not an abuse of a dominant position for a pharmaceutical manufacturer to refuse to meet out-of-the-ordinary orders from a distributor in a Member State which were plainly intended for parallel trade. This was because the manufacturer was entitled to protect its commercial interests where there was considerable disparity in pricing and the orders placed were out of the ordinary. These judgments are to be welcomed. Excessive parallel imports where price disparity arises from state intervention as opposed to matters in the control of the pharmaceutical company can substantially erode profits to a level that harms the ability to carry out R&D.

However, the justification of "defence of commercial interests" clearly should only apply in exceptional circumstances. Most exercises of IPRs, even by a dominant undertaking, will be done to further the commercial interests of the undertaking. Such does not stop their exercise from being an abuse. It is suggested that this defence is confined to circumstances where very unusual market conditions apply.

Burden—In *Microsoft v EC Commission*, the General Court held that the burden lies on the dominant undertaking to raise any plea of objective justification and to support it with arguments and evidence.

Technological standard and Standard Essential Patents ("SEPs")

As discussed in Ch.10, "Intellectual Property and Horizontal Agreements", **12-216** technology companies often seek to develop technical standards for a particular field of technology. This can be pro-competitive if the standard is open and transparent because it permits third parties to develop products to a standard which would have gained industry and consumer acceptance. However, it follows that if a standard

---

[315] *Syfait v Glaxosmithkline AEVE* (C-53/03) [2005] E.C.R. 4609; [2005] 5 C.M.L.R. 1, Jacobs AG. The case went to the CJEU but it was rejected on a preliminary point, namely that the Greek Competition Commission was not a court or tribunal entitled to make use of the preliminary reference procedure.

[316] (C-53/03) [2005] 5 C.M.L.R. 1 at [100].

[317] (C-468/06) [2008] E.C.R. I-7139.

becomes a de facto or de jure standard in a particular product or technology market such that without access to it, a party cannot compete on that market, then such a standard can give rise to competition concerns if third parties are not permitted access to it. The Guidelines to Horizontal Cooperation Agreements set out competition concerns that may arise under art.101 where the standard is not open and transparent and where IPRs protect the standard, such are not licensable on FRAND terms.[318]

12-217   Of particular concern are SEPs (Standard Essential Patents). A SEP is a patent that is essential to a standard established by a standardisation body, rendering its use indispensable to all competitors which envisage manufacturing products that comply with the standard to which it is linked.[319] A feature of the adoption of a technological standard is that a patent will often only become a SEP where the SEP owner gives an irrevocable undertaking that it is prepared to license the SEP on FRAND (fair, reasonable and non-discriminatory) terms. Standardisation bodies are understandably reluctant to adopt a standard which incorporates a patent where no undertaking is given. This would obviously confer unacceptable power on the patent holder.

12-218   Article 102 can become engaged if an undertaking owns a SEP patent. The owner of a SEP patent is not obliged merely because it protects a standard to license it per se. The CJEU has rejected a straightforward "essential facility" doctrine. As seen in the case of *IMS v NDC* which concerned a de facto marketing standard, for there to be an abuse, it must prevent the emergence of a new product for which there is consumer demand. In the CJEU's view, such struck the right balance between free competition and IPRs.[320]

12-219   However, although there is no obligation on a SEP owner to license its patent, such may exist where the SEP owner has permitted or encouraged the adoption of the standard which its SEP covers without either disclosing its SEP or expressly or impliedly representing that it would license its SEP if the standard was adopted. This is often called "patent ambush". The Court of Justice has now made it clear that where a SEP owner has given such an undertaking to a technological standard, a subsequent refusal to grant that licence will, in principle, constitute an abuse within the meaning of art.102.[321]

Injunctions and mechanism for agreeing FRAND terms

12-220   In the case of a SEP patent, the Court of Justice in *Huawei v ZTE*[322] has now given guidance as to how FRAND licences should be concluded. This arose out of a reference from the German courts. To understand fully the judgment of the Court of Justice, it is necessary to consider the earlier decisions of the German courts concerning offers to take a FRAND licence by infringers of a SEP.

12-221   In *Standard-Spundfass*[323] the leading companies in the chemical industry, which belonged to the Verband der Chemischen Industrie e.V. ("VCI"), had demanded a plastic barrel with an improved residue draining capability and, once they had

---

[318] See para.10-087, et seq., where this is discussed.
[319] *Huawei v ZTE Corp* (C-170/13) ECLI:EU:C:2015:477 at [49]; AT.39939—*Samsung* (EC Commission Decision, 29 April 2014), at [27].
[320] See para.12-202.
[321] *Huawei v ZTE Corp*, at [53].
[322] *Huawei v ZTE Corp* (C-170/13) ECLI:EU:C:2015:477.
[323] Federal Court of Justice, decision of 13 July 2004—*Standard-Spundfass II*, WuW DE-R 1329, 1331.

chosen a technology, adopted it as the industry standard in the "VCI General Conditions". The inventor of this technology refused to grant a licence to a barrel manufacturer who was interested in acquiring a licence. The barrel manufacturer claimed that such conduct was contrary to German competition law which is similar to art.102.[324] The Bundesgerichtshof held that the existence of market dominance does not give rise to a duty to licence but if there were additional circumstances, it did.[325] The Bundesgerichtshof held that de facto standardisation protected the patent holder and the patented technology from having to face competition from superior technologies. Therefore, it held that a refusal to license would be an abuse.

Following this decision, in *Orange-Book*,[326] which concerned a SEP, the defend-   **12-222** ant rejected the patentee's standard licence terms and sought to obtain more favourable terms whilst continuing to use the patented invention. The Bundesgerichtshof held that a defendant can only rely upon a FRAND defence against an application for injunctive relief if a number of strict requirements are satisfied where the IPR owner is in a dominant position. These are:

(1) the defendant/licensee offers the *claimant* an unconditional licensing agreement, which the defendant is bound by. The defendant cannot offer the licence under the condition that the court does find the patent to be *valid and infringed*.[327] The *claimant* in return is not allowed to reject the offer if it inequitably obstructs the defendant or discriminates him against other licensees; *and*

(2) the defendant has to act as if the offered licence would have already been accepted, in case the defendant has already used the patent before the *claimant* has accepted the offer (i.e. accounting the use of the patent in question, calculate the royalties and make payment according to these calculations into an escrow account).

This was criticised for making it very difficult for defendants to raise a success-   **12-223** ful defence of abuse.[328]

In the German proceedings leading up to the reference in *Huawei v ZTE*,[329] ZTE,   **12-224** the defendant, had neither made an explicit unconditional offer nor any payment to the claimant, the owner of a SEP. However, the German court felt the need to refer to the CJEU on whether such conditions were too restrictive for the defendant to be able to invoke the FRAND defence. ZTE had been seeking to negotiate with Huawei FRAND terms for a period of time. In particular, the German court felt the need to do so because of a Statement of Objections by the European Commission to Samsung that the seeking of an injunction could constitute an abuse of a dominant position where the holder of IPRs had given a commitment to license on FRAND terms and where the company against which an injunction is sought is willing to negotiate a FRAND licence.[330]

---

[324] Gesetz gegen Wettbewerbbeschränkungen ss.19 and 20.

[325] Citing *IMS v NDC*.

[326] BGH *KZR* 39/06.

[327] Cf. the different approach taken by the European Commission, see *Press Release of European Commission*, 20 April 2014 commenting on *Samsung* and *Motorola* decisions.

[328] See, e.g. H. Ullrich, "Patents and standards—a comment on the German Federal Supreme Court decision Orange Book Standard" [2010] IIC 41(3), 337–351.

[329] *Huawei v ZTE, Landgericht (Dusseldorf)* 4b O 104/12 (12 March 2013).

[330] AT.39939 *Samsung*. See para.12-235.

12-225   In its judgment in *Huawei v ZTE*, the Court of Justice gave guidance as to the mechanism to be used by an infringer in order to found a valid defence under art.102 to the exercise of a SEP against it:

- Prior to bringing an action, the SEP owner proprietor must first alert the alleged infringer of the infringement complained about and specify the way in which it has been infringed.
- If the alleged infringer expresses a willingness to conclude a FRAND licence, the SEP owner must present a specific, written offer for a licence on FRAND terms in accordance with the undertaking given to the standards body setting out in particular the amount of the royalty and the way in which it is to be calculated.
- If the alleged infringer does not accept the offer, it must respond to that offer in writing:
  - — in accordance with recognised commercial practices in the field;
  - — in good faith;
  - — not using delaying tactics; and
  with a counter-offer that corresponds to FRAND terms.
- If the alleged infringer is "using the teachings of the SEP" before concluding a licensing agreement, it must provide appropriate financial security, e.g. a bank guarantee which corresponds to the number of past acts of use of the SEP and it must be able to render an account in respect of those acts.
- If no agreement is reached, the parties may, by common agreement, request that the amount of royalty is determined by an *independent* third party by decision without delay.
- As a standardisation body does not check whether the SEP is valid or essential to the standard, an alleged infringer is entitled to challenge, *in parallel* to the negotiations for a FRAND licence, the validity of the patent and/or the essential nature of the patents to the standard or reserve the right to do so.

12-226   It will be appreciated that the guidance that the Court of Justice gives is detailed. However, inevitably, the real issue is whether the offer by the SEP owner or the inevitable counter offer by the alleged infringer is on FRAND terms. Whether a licence is on FRAND terms is an objective matter but the offers made by the SEP owner and the alleged infringer will be their own assessment of what FRAND is. It is also inevitable that both sides will seek to bargain. For instance, it may be that a FRAND licence is one whereby the royalty is 5 per cent. A SEP owner may offer a licence at 5.5 per cent and the alleged infringer may counter offer with a royalty rate of 4.5 per cent expecting the usual "horse trading". If there is only *one* FRAND royalty rate, namely 5 per cent, then as a matter of fact, neither side has offered a licence on FRAND terms. The alleged infringer could therefore argue that the first breach of the Court of Justice guidance was by the SEP owner and thus the fact that it too has not offered a FRAND royalty rate does not mean that it is not an abuse.

12-227   The effect of *Huawei v ZTE* was considered in an English case, *Unwired Planet v Huawei*.[331] In particular, one issue was whether there could be more than one FRAND set of terms. Allied with this issue was whether, if there is more than one FRAND set of terms, could the alleged infringer rely upon art.102 as a defence to

---

[331] [2017] EWHC 711 (Pat), 5 April 2017.

an assertion of a SEP against it if it offered another FRAND-compliant licence to a FRAND-compliant licence offered by the SEP owner?

The court held that that there is only a single set of FRAND terms.[332] The court **12-228** went on to say that the solution to the problem of parties presenting FRAND terms is simple enough. In short, the court decides what terms would be FRAND and give declarations to that effect. A patentee who refuses to accept "those" terms would be in breach of its FRAND undertaking. Equally, an infringer who refused to accept "those" terms would be injuncted.[333] Parties are obliged to take a "FRAND" approach to negotiation and this allows parties to negotiate in good faith and allow for starting offers which leave room for negotiation. However, "extreme offers" and "taking an intransigent approach which prejudice fair, reasonable and non-discriminatory negotiation" is not a FRAND approach.[334] Thus, in practice, both the SEP owner and the alleged infringer must seek to negotiate in good faith and that will inevitably involve making non-FRAND offers (as the chance of them offering a licence which exactly accords with what a court or tribunal subsequently determines is the one, true FRAND licence is negligible). However, provided that both the SEP owner and the alleged infringer respectively offer and offer to be bound by a licence on "FRAND" terms *in general terms*[335] to be agreed or alternatively determined by the court would mean that the SEP owner could not enforce its SEP against the infringer. In other words, an infringer should ensure that in the event that its offer is not accepted, it agrees to be bound by a court or tribunal's determination of what is a FRAND licence.

Assessment of what is FRAND

The English court gave guidance as to how to assess what is a FRAND licence. **12-229** The following are principles extracted from a very long and thorough judgment.

- A FRAND licence is that which in the relevant circumstances, a willing licensor and willing licensee would agree upon without holding out or holding up.
- Decisions of other courts will be useful and persuasive.
- To the extent that they are available, other licences may be deployed as comparable as these are evidence of what real parties in real negotiations have agreed upon.
- Another useful approach is a "top down" approach. This starts with a number representing what the appropriate aggregate royalty burden will be for a given standard (T). Starting from this figure (T), one then shares out the royalty across all licensors in proportion to the value of each licensor's patent portfolio to the total relevant patent portfolio to the technical standard (S). The FRAND rate is the product of the two (T x S).

Stating the principles is relatively easy. Applying them is very difficult as **12-230** evidenced by the very substantial evidence in the *Huawei/Unwired Planet* case.

One large issue in the *Huawei/Unwired Planet* case was whether a FRAND **12-231** licence would be restricted to acts in the UK or worldwide. Unwired Planet wanted to grant a worldwide licence but Huawei only wanted to take a licence under

---

[332] See [155].
[333] See [164]–[168].
[334] See [163].
[335] See [744(ii)].

Unwired Planet's UK portfolio. It was argued that the offer of a worldwide licence was anti-competitive because it gave rise to foreclosure of competition.[336] In part, this was based on the fact that Unwired Patent did not have patents in every country in the world[337] and where it did, some of them were being litigated upon. In the end, the court, no doubt persuaded by the fact that most licences were entered into on a worldwide basis because they reduced transactional costs, was not contrary to competition law and also was FRAND. It thus held that a refusal to take a worldwide licence was not FRAND.[338]

Damages

12-232   In *Huawei v ZTE*, the Court of Justice also held, in response to a separate question, that the SEP proprietor is not guilty of an abuse of dominant position under art.102 from bringing an action for infringement against the alleged infringer and seeking financial compensation for past acts. As said by the Advocate-General, an action for damages does not lead either to the exclusion from the market standard-compliant products or the acceptance by a potential licensee of unfavourable licensing terms.[339] It is not clear whether the Court of Justice is saying that in such circumstances, damages should be assessed on a compensatory but non-FRAND basis because no FRAND licence was in place at the time of the acts of alleged infringement and negotiations to grant a FRAND licence had not started. The decision envisages that FRAND licences can be granted to apply to acts prior to the conclusion of a FRAND licence as well as afterwards. However, if the alleged infringer has knowingly infringed a SEP without seeking to obtain a FRAND licence, in the authors' view, there is a good argument consistent with the need for ensuring a high level of protection for IPRs[340] that the SEP proprietor is entitled to damages on the normal basis. Such will incentivise the alleged infringer to enter into negotiations with the SEP proprietor and thereby respect its legitimate interests

12-233   The Commission takes a hardline approach to patent ambushes. A number of cases other than Huawei are now considered.

Rambus

12-234   In August 2007, the Commission brought proceedings against Rambus Inc. Rambus had participated in the setting of an industry-wide standard for DRAM (dynamic random access memory) chips.[341] By 2008, the standard covered more than 96 per cent of DRAM sales. The standard required disclosure of all issued and pending patents by members of the standard but Rambus failed to disclose the existence of patents under which it subsequently attempted to claim royalties. Indeed, it was said that it had used information gained from participating in the setting of

---

[336] The argument was primarily one based on tying established on *Microsoft Corp* (T-201/04) [2007] E.C.R. II-3619 where the General Court proposed a fourfold test as to when a tying practice is an abuse. In other words, by forcing Huawei to pay royalties on a worldwide basis, when it did not have patents throughout the world, was anti-competitive (see [524]–[526]).

[337] Its portfolio of SEPs covered most of Europe, Russia, Turkey, China, Japan but not all of south east Asia, USA, Canada, Australia, India and Mexico and limited coverage in Africa, South America and eastern Europe.

[338] See [524]–[572].

[339] See [102].

[340] See [57].

[341] COMP/38.836—*RAMBUS*.

the standard to tailor its patent applications. The evidence suggested that if it had disclosed its patents, the standard would have chosen alternative patent-free technologies. The Commission concluded that Rambus had abused its dominant position by intentionally breaching the standard policy and also breaching the duty of good faith. The Commission said that such behaviour undermined confidence in the standard-setting process which was a pre-condition to technical development and the development of the market to the benefit of the consumer.

Samsung

In this case, Samsung owned a worldwide portfolio of patents in particular, SEPs **12-235** which it had declared to a standard-setting institute, the European Telecommunications Standard Institute ("ETSI"). By reason of being an ETSI member, Samsung had committed to inform ETSI of SEPs relating to a future standard and license these SEPs on FRAND terms during the standard setting process carried out by ETSI in relation to the Universal Mobile Telecommunications Services ("UMTS") standard. ETSI had been appointed by the EU to approve a UMTS standard. Samsung started proceedings for patent infringement of its UMTS-SEPs against Apple in various countries. The Commission considered, applying the "exceptional circumstances" requirements that Samsung had abused its dominant position by such conduct. Furthermore, it considered that such conduct was unjustifiable.[342] In the end, Samsung offered commitments not to seek injunctive relief and to offer licences for its SEP patents on FRAND terms.[343]

Motorola/Apple

This was a case where the Commission took the view that although Motorola had **12-236** offered to license its SEP on FRAND terms when a standard was being set, a refusal to license Apple who was willing to enter into a FRAND licence was an abuse of a dominant position.

In relation to both decisions, the Commission has stressed that SEP owners are **12-237** not obliged to license SEPs. However, it takes the view that there is an abuse where they have given a commitment to license a SEP and the defendant is willing to enter into a FRAND licence. Significantly, the Commission has said that it does not affect such a finding if the defendant wishes to challenge whether the patent is valid, essential to the standard or indeed that it does not infringe the SEP. Thus, a defendant is entitled to offer to enter into a "conditional" FRAND licence.[344]

Finally, although strictly not applicable to art.102, it is considered that the **12-238** Guidelines on Horizontal Cooperation Agreement are a useful guide to whether there has been an abuse of a dominant position by a SEP owner. The concerns expressed in the Guidelines are easily translatable to art.102 as they are concerned

---

[342] This is discussed at para.12-215.
[343] A copy of the decision can be found at *http://ec.europa.eu/competition/antitrust/cases/dec_docs/39939/39939_1501_5.pdf* [Accessed 29 January 2018].
[344] See *Press Release of European Commission*, 29 April 2014 commenting on *Samsung* and *Motorola* decisions. NB. This differs from the German approach—see the section on German decisions at paras 12-221 to 12-224.

with competitive concerns over limitation of production, markets and technical developments to the prejudice of the consumer which appears at art.102(b).[345]

Essential facilities: UK

12-239   In the UK, courts have had to consider allegations of leveraging and refusal of access to an essential facility, although rarely where such involves the exercise of IPRs.

12-240   In *Philips v Ingman*,[346] Philips, the well-known Dutch electronics manufacturer, was the proprietor of a number of patents relating to the design and manufacture of CDs. Importantly, Philips entered into an agreement with Sony whereby the two companies agreed to co-operate in the development of industry standards for CDs. It was agreed that any patents that were obtained would be pooled and enforced only by Philips. It was also agreed that the patents would be licensed on standard terms and that Philips would pursue infringers.

12-241   Patents did result from this co-operation agreement. In particular, Philips and Sony set out actively to ensure that their method of producing CDs became the industry standard. They succeeded in this. The Philips/Sony standard for CD-Audio and CD-Rom were accepted as industry standards by CENELEC (European Committee for Electrotechnical Standardisation). Thus, these patents were important "gateway" patents because, as a result of international standardisation, anyone wanting to make CDs needed a licence of the patents.[347] In short, anyone who wanted to be a supplier in the CD product market needed a licence.

12-242   The defendants were manufacturers of CDs. They declined Phillips' offer of its standard form licence, asserting that the terms were unfair. Phillips then brought an action for infringement of its CD patents against Ingman.

12-243   Ingman alleged that Phillips was abusing its dominant position in the CD market contrary to art.102 and s.18 of the Competition Act 1998 and was seeking to force defendants to enter into agreements which were contrary to art.101. This latter defence is discussed elsewhere.[348] Of interest is the art.102 defence. It was pleaded that Philips was charging excessive prices and acting in a discriminatory fashion. This is also discussed later in this chapter. For the purpose of this section, of interest is the court's approach to the unilateral refusal to license (save on terms alleged to be abusive).

12-244   Ingman argued that they were entitled to a licence on reasonable terms because of the dominance of Philips/Sony in the CD-Audio and CD-ROM market. The grant of a licence was the sole means by which a prospective entrant to the market could produce such disks. In essence, this was an essential facilities claim. Philips sought to strike out the defence. Considering matters of principle, the court considered the judgments of *Volvo v Veng* and *CICRA v Renault* and *TV Listings*. The court said that such judgments showed that it was permissible to exploit the exclusive rights to maintain exclusivity even though such eliminated competition. The court emphasised that it was not an abuse for the owner of an IPR to refuse to enter into a licence for a reasonable royalty. Furthermore, the court said that these decisions showed that an IPR cannot per se confer a dominant position in a particular product

---

[345] Recital 29. The Guidelines are discussed in Ch.10.
[346] *Philips Electronics* [1998] Eu. L.R. 666; [1999] F.S.R. 152.
[347] The phrase "gateway" patent is used to indicate a patent for which a licence is required by any undertaking who wishes to compete on a particular product, service or technology market.
[348] See Ch.14, para.14-031.

market. Although it was not made expressly clear, this remark must be seen against the background that the IPR controlled an essential facility, namely a technological standard. The defence was struck out on the grounds that there was no arguable case of dominance but also on the grounds that in reality, the complaint was not that Philips was refusing to license but rather that the terms on which it was seeking to impose were unreasonable.[349]

In *Attheraces Ltd v British Horseracing Board*,[350] the court was concerned with **12-245** a situation similar to TV Listings but which was characterised as an "essential facilities" claim which shows how similar are, in certain respects, a leveraging claim to an essential facilities claim. The British Horseracing Board ("BHB") had sole possession of valuable information (pre-race data about British horse races). It supplied that information to companies who were interested in operating horse betting services for a fee. This fee was a percentage of the gross profits of bookmakers made on their horserace betting businesses.

Initially, it was thought that such data benefited from database rights. However, **12-246** in *BHB v William Hill*,[351] it was held that the pre-race data did not benefit from database rights. However, because, like the Irish television companies, BHB had contractual control over the supply of pre-race data as it was not readily accessible. Thus, in practice, the ruling that no database rights existed in the pre-race data made little difference. Bookmakers and other providers of race information needed to enter into contracts with BHB.

Attheraces ("ATR") was a broadcaster of horseracing. It supplied websites, **12-247** television channels, etc. with content relating to British racing. It complained about the charges that BHB made. There was no real dispute that BHB provided an essential facility, namely pre-race data without which organisations such as ATR simply could not provide their services. As said by the Court of Appeal about the pre-race data and BHB, "there is no substitute for it and it has no competitor".[352] Pictures of horses without the pre-race data were not sufficient for the purpose of bookmakers or punters.[353]

The judge found that: **12-248**

(a) the pre-race data was an essential facility for ATR for the purpose of the doctrine of "essential facilities";

(b) the application of the "essential facilities" principle did not require that the dominant supplier should be in competition with the purchaser;[354] and

(c) the terms proposed to ATR were unfair and not objectively justified.

The judge's decision was appealed but in essence, only on the finding that the **12-249** price was unfair. This is discussed later in this chapter. It is of note that the judge did not find it necessary to find that there was an "upstream" market in pre-race data. However, it must be noted that because of the finding of the CJEU in *Wil-*

---

[349] See [55].

[350] *Attheraces Ltd v British Horseracing Board Ltd* [2006] E.C.C. 24; [2006] Eu. L.R. 654; [2006] F.S.R. 20; (2006) 29 I.P.D. 29,011; [2006] Info. T.L.R. 423; [2006] U.K.C.L.R. 167; [2006] E.C.D.R. 13; [2005] EWHC 3015; On appeal, [2007] E.C.C. 7; [2007] EWCA Civ 38 CA.

[351] *BHB v William Hill* (C-203/02) [2004] E.C.R. I-10415; [2005] 1 C.M.L.R. 15; [2005] R.P.C. 13; [2005] E.C.D.R. 1.

[352] See [48].

[353] See [51]. Interestingly, the converse (i.e. pre-race data but not pictures of horses) was held to be sufficient in *Tiercé Ladbroke*.

[354] Cf. In the US, see *Intergraph v Intel* where such was held to be an element of an essential facilities claim as discussed at para.12-180.

liam Hill v BHB which was delivered at the same time, the judge was not concerned with a case about refusal to license IPRs as pre-race data was not found to be of such a nature as to enjoy database rights.[355]

12-250   In *Intel Corp v VIA Technologies*,[356] Intel, the well-known manufacturer of microprocessors, brought two actions for patent infringement against VIA Technologies in relation to CPUs and chipsets that the latter made for computers. Intel enjoyed by a wide margin a dominant position. It had 75 per cent of the worldwide market in chipsets for x86 CPUs and 80 per cent of the market for x86 CPUs between 1998 and 2000. VIA was a Taiwanese manufacturer of chipsets and microprocessors. It was a competitor of Intel.

12-251   Intel's two patents were "gateway" patents. They governed the protocols which enabled a CPU to communicate with a chipset. These patents effectively prevented the development of independent technology which was compatible with Intel microprocessors because the patents related respectively to the interface of the chipset with the CPU and the interface of the CPU with operating software. These patents had resulted in a change of the "open architecture" of early PCs into proprietary systems governed by Intel patents.[357]

12-252   VIA and Intel had a number of disputes. This led to Intel producing a licence which contained two provisions that VIA objected to:

(a)   a provision that limited its application of the licensed technology to the manufacture of chipsets compatible with Intel's Pentium 4 CPUs. This meant that if Intel produced an improved version of the Pentium 4 CPU, VIA could not use the licensed technology to make a chipset compatible with the improved version (the "Market Division" term); and

(b)   a provision whereby VIA was obliged to grant to Intel a licence for the unrestricted use of all its patents and technology in exchange for a licence from Intel limited to its chipset and in that respect, that limited it to connection with chipsets compatible with Pentium 4 CPUs (the "Asymmetric Licence").

12-253   VIA denied the validity of the patents and that it had infringed the patents. It also raised defences under art.101 and art.102 and the corresponding provisions in the UK Competition Act 1998 asserting that the bringing of the proceedings was an abuse of the exercise of the IPRs. It claimed that Intel was abusing a dominant position by bringing the action and that its refusal to license VIA was abusive, particularly, because it formed part of a plan to withdraw products from the market for which there was a continuing demand forcing users to adopt more expensive technology, namely Pentium 4 technology.

12-254   In particular, VIA pleaded that the refusal to grant a licence on lawful or reasonable terms was an abuse as it:

(a)   prevented the emergence of new types of x86 compatible chipsets;

(b)   partitioned the market in x86 compatible chipsets by relegating licensees to trailing edge technology;

(c)   prejudiced consumers and users by preventing VIA and others from the development of new improved products and/or lower prices from those supplied by Intel; and

---

[355] See para.4-255.
[356] *Intel Corp* [2003] Eu. L.R. 85; [2003] F.S.R. 33.
[357] In 1981, IBM introduced the PC on an "open architecture" basis by publishing its specification and encouraging other manufacturers to make similar PCs.

(d) in the case of CPUs, would lead to the elimination of certain interfaces such as the "Socket 370" which permits consumers to upgrade inexpensively their CPUs without forcing them to buy expensive Pentium 4 technology.

At the core of VIA's complaint was that Intel owned "gateway" patents which controlled essential interfaces and was using such IPRs to force consumers to upgrade their computers to expensive Pentium 4 technology rather than more cheaply upgrade their computers using VIA technology. **12-255**

The arts 101 and 102 defences were struck out by the High Court and VIA appealed to the Court of Appeal. The art.101 defences have been considered in another chapter.[358] **12-256**

The Court of Appeal contrasted the proposition set out in *ITT Promedia NV v European Commission*[359] where the CJEU said that: **12-257**

> "It follows from the nature of the obligations imposed by Art.[102] of the Treaty that in specific circumstances, undertakings in a dominant position may be deprived of the right to adopt a course of conduct or take measures which are not in themselves abuses and which would even be unobjectionable if adopted or taken by non-dominant undertakings,"

with the CJEU's statement in *Volvo v Veng* that:

> "It must also be emphasised that the right of the proprietor of a protected design to prevent third parties from manufacturing and selling or importing, without its consent, products incorporating the design constitutes the very subject-matter of his exclusive right. It follows that an obligation imposed upon the proprietor of a protected design to grant to third parties, even in return for a reasonable royalty, a licence for the supply of products incorporating the design would lead to the proprietor thereof being deprived of the substance of his exclusive right, and that a refusal to grant such a licence cannot in itself constitute an abuse of a dominant position."

The Court of Appeal said that the basic issue was where the dividing line lay between these two principles. It said that the only test of general application was that stated in *Magill* that the exercise of an exclusive right may *in exceptional circumstances* involve abusive conduct under art.102. **12-258**

The Court of Appeal then considered *Volvo v Veng*, *Magill*, *Tiercé Ladbroke*, *Oscar Bronner*, and *IMS Health*. As a result, the court rejected a submission by Intel that "exceptional circumstances" could only arise if all the conditions in *Magill* or *IMS* were satisfied. Thus, the court rejected the submission that the result of the refusal to licence *must* be the exclusion of an entirely new product from the market (*Magill*) or the elimination of all competition to the patentee (*IMS*). The Court of Appeal said that other circumstances could be regarded as exceptional and that the court in *Magill* and *IMS* were simply indicating the circumstances in which, on the facts before them, there would be exceptional circumstances. The court said that it was at least arguable that the CJEU would assimilate its jurisprudence to the "essential facilities" doctrine in the US.[360] Indeed, the Court of Appeal made the point that in *Oscar Bronner*, it was not a requirement that there be total elimination of **12-259**

---

[358] See para.14-031.

[359] [1998] E.C.R. II-2941.

[360] It is unclear whether any reference was made to the US essential facilities cases involving IPR which have been discussed earlier in this chapter and which severely limit the application of the doctrine where IPRs protect the essential facility.

competition but rather elimination of competition from the person requesting the service and that the summary in *IMS* had to be read in such a light. As the Court of Appeal said, were it otherwise, liability under art.102 could be simply avoided by the grant of a licence to an unenergetic rival.

12-260   The court thus held that it was arguable that the matters pleaded did indeed amount to exceptional circumstances. In short, the Court of Appeal considered that it was arguable that Intel's enforcement of its "gateway" patents was potentially abusive as such controlled the x86 compatible chipset market and that Intel was using its patents to exclude from the market both the Socket 370 and EGBA format.

12-261   Importantly, in both *Intel v VIA* and *Philips v Ingman*, the court was concerned with patents which protected gateway or bottleneck technologies. Any undertakings who wished to compete in the product markets of respectively, on one hand, microprocessors and chipsets and on the other hand, CDs simply could not compete without access to these technologies and thus it was indispensable to them to obtain licences for the gateway patents.

12-262   Other cases in the UK focus on the individual requirements of *Oscar Bronner* and *IMS v NDC*. In a UK case, *Claritas (UK) Ltd v The Post Office*,[361] Claritas, a lifestyle consumer information company, sought an interim injunction against the Post Office and its subsidiary, Postal Preference Service, preparing them from despatching seven million direct mail questionnaires by Postal Preference Service under the Royal Mail brand and logo. Claritas, which also sent out consumer information questionnaires, stated that such was an abuse of a dominant position by the Post Office and its subsidiary, because use of the Royal Mail logo by its subsidiary, gave it an unfair advantage (in effect, it was seen as more "official" by consumers who were thus more likely to answer the questionnaires). It was argued that the case was analogous to the right of access to an "essential facility" (i.e. the Royal Mail logo). However, the judge held that such could not apply where Claritas had full access to the postal facilities of the Post Office. In other words, as the judge said, the argument was really that the Post Office had an unfair advantage in its brand and such could not be considered an abuse.

12-263   In *Wireless Group Plc v Radio Joint Audience Research Ltd*,[362] the claimant complained that the defendant, RAJAR's method of compiling radio listening audiences was defective. Such was done on the basis of a diary system whereby individuals were asked to record what they listened to. The claimant complained that such a methodology was seriously inaccurate and under-recorded the audience for the radio station operated by its subsidiary. The claimant argued that the defendant had abused its dominant position in relation to the market for radio audience ratings surveys by refusing to abandon the diary system and using audiometers. RAJAR applied to strike out the case. However, the court said that it is clear from the law that conduct which is objectively justified cannot amount to an abuse.[363] The court then went on to consider whether RAJAR's conduct was objectively justified and found it to be so.[364]

---

[361] *Claritas (UK) Ltd v The Post Office* [2001] E.T.M.R. 63.
[362] *Wireless Group Plc* [2005] Eu. L.R 307.
[363] Applying *Oscar Bronner*.
[364] As the application was for summary judgment, the court found that the claimant had no real prospect of showing that it was not objectively justified. The main point was that RAJAR was still trying to decide between two different types of audiometers to use. As the judge said, "that is a rational commercial approach", at [71].

Essential facility: France

In *SAEM & NMPP v Conseil de la Concurrence*,[365] the Cour d'Appel de Paris **12-264** dismissed an appeal from the Conseil de la Concurrence that had ordered a nationwide distributor to grant another nationwide distributor access to its computer programme ("Presse 2000"). The Conseil considered that such was an essential facility for the distribution of newspapers and magazines for the whole of France as distributors and retailers would not switch to other computer programmes. It was argued that ordering the owner of Presse 2000 to grant access to its programme would infringe its IPR in the computer programme. However, the Cour d'Appel held that as it had already permitted access to another nationwide distributor, it therefore had to grant access to others on equitable and non-discriminatory terms. The French competition law is a domestic equivalent to art.102.[366]

This decision (which can be considered analogous to *Oscar Bronner* where the **12-265** distribution facility is protected by IPR) was handed down prior to *IMS v NDC*. It departs dramatically from the conditions in *IMS v NDC* because the applicant was not proposing to introduce a new service on the market. Rather, it simply wished to provide the same service as others (namely newspaper distribution services). It will be recalled in *IMS v NDC* that the court considered that a balancing of the interests of competition law and IPR law required that the applicant must be intent on introducing a new product or service. However, the decision is a classic application of the essential facilities doctrine albeit in the context of an IPR case. Alternatively, it can be considered as authority for the proposition that once an essential facility is licensed to one, it must be licensed to all upon FRAND terms.

Essential facility: Germany

Germany has considered in *Standard-Spundfass*, *Orange-Book* and *Huawei* when **12-266** and in what circumstances, a refusal to license IPRs protecting technological standards amounts to an abuse of a dominant position. These have been discussed above.[367]

Essential facilities: summary

It is too early to say that a pure "essential facilities" doctrine now exists in EU **12-267** law in the case of IPRs. It is clear that such exists outside the field of IPR in EU law. In seeking to strike a balance between IPRs and free competition, *IMS v NDC* says that it is sufficient if the exercise of IPRs prevents the emergence of a new product on a market for which there is consumer demand but it is not sufficient if the product is essentially duplicative of the dominant undertaking's products. Apart from this additional requirement, *IMS v NDC* must be considered an application of the "essential facilities" doctrine as developed in the US for physical facilities to a case involving IPRs. In this sense, it could be said that EU law is more interventionist than US law in the case of compulsory licences of IPRs where, as discussed already, the US courts have largely resisted the application of the "essential facilities" doctrine to IPRs. In particular, the CJEU in *IMS v NDC*, jettisoned the idea that there must be two separate active markets. In effect, it is sufficient if there is

---

[365] Cour d'Appel de Paris, 12 January 2004.
[366] art.L-420-2 Code du Commerce.
[367] See para.12-220, et seq.

one market for which there is an indispensable "input". In *Microsoft v EC Commission*, the essential "input" was the interface information necessary for suppliers of workgroup networks to ensure that their networks could interface with Microsoft's PC operating system. Furthermore, in *Microsoft v EC Commission*, the General Court diluted the requirement that the exercise of rights must be preventing a new product from coming onto the market. It was sufficient if it prevented the technical conditions which would *enable* new products and services to come onto the market. In *Huawei*, there was no doubt that access to Huawei's SEP was indispensable for any operator who wished to enter the market. However, even in *Huawei*, the Court of Justice confined itself to considering the position where the SEP holder had given an irrevocable undertaking to the standardisation body to grant licences on FRAND terms.

12-268   Therefore, EU law has come close to a "pure" essential facility doctrine when considering the exercise of IPRs by a dominant undertaking. However, the current state of law is that it is not sufficient merely to establish that the enforcement of IPR by a dominant undertaking would prevent access to an "input" which is indispensable for an undertaking to operate in a particular market. Some further abusive conduct must be proven. The cases suggest that such would be satisfied if there is substantial detriment to customers or consumers. Thus, in the case of *IMS v NDC* and *TV Listings*, it was the prevention of a new product or service for which there was demand. In *Volvo v Veng*, it was the denial of spare parts to customers who owned Volvo cars and needed them to repair or maintain their cars. In *Huawei*, as made clear in the judgment, if the SEP holder had not given the undertaking to license its SEP to the standardisation body, the latter would not have incorporated the technology protected by the SEP and sought an alternative technology. However, if this did not exist, they would have stopped work on the adoption of the standard.[368] Therefore, the giving of the undertaking by the SEP holder had resulted in a technological standard which incorporated the technology protected by the SEP. The undertaking thus allowed the SEP holder to hold a dominant position by ensuring the adoption of the technological standard and then by enforcing its patent. This was an abuse.

12-269   Thus, where an IPR holder controls an essential input into a marketplace, the cases suggest that something more is required to prove an abuse. If the IPR holder in a dominant position ensures that demand for products protected by the IPR at a fair price, then it is unlikely that an abuse will be found. For instance, in *CEAHR II*,[369] the Commission found that although each Swiss watch manufacturer held a dominant position in the aftersales market for repairs of their own watches, the fact that it had set up a network of authorised repairers was sufficient to avoid a finding of abuse as it meant that there was sufficient competition and therefore it was not an abuse to refuse to supply independent repairers. In most cases, the focus is on the detriment to the consumer and the end-user rather than the behaviour of a dominant undertaking to an actual or potential operator in the market of which the undertaking is dominant.

Collateral abusive conduct and exercise of IPRs

12-270   In certain cases, IPRs are incidental to the control of the essential facility. For instance, in a legal article, commentators pose the question of what would have been

---

[368] *Huawei*, at [17].
[369] *CEAHR v European Commission* (T-712/14) ECLI:EU:T:2017:748.

the position if, in the landmark US case, *MCI v AT&T*, (where the court held that the telephone lines in the old Bell phone system were an essential facility that had to be provided to those who wished to supply long-distance telephone services), Bell had patents on its telephone switches.[370] In such cases, permitting MCI to have access to the telephone lines would have necessitated an incidental licence under the patents. It has been said that the law should distinguish between those cases where the IPR is the facility to which the complainant wants access to and those where the IPR exists but is incidental to the control of the facility. In *Image Technical Services v Kodak*, the IPRs were very incidental to the refusal to supply spare parts to independent service organisations.[371]

In many cases, the complaint is that the dominant undertaking is guilty of abusive **12-271** conduct which may be connected with the exercise of IPRs. Thus, it might be alleged that the dominant undertaking has charged excessive prices for products subject to the IPR; charged excessive royalties; discriminated against the complainant with regard to terms on which the licence is granted; imposed onerous clauses in licences, etc. In such circumstances, the primary focus is on whether the collateral conduct is abusive. Thus, in *Volvo v Veng*, the CJEU identified that the exercise of design rights "if it involves, on the part of an undertaking holding a dominant position, certain abusive conduct" such as the arbitrary refusal to supply spare parts to repairers, the charging of unfair prices for spare parts or a refusal to manufacture spare parts for old models could amount to an abuse of a dominant position.[372]

Here the CJEU is identifying that the exercise of IPRs may be prohibited if as- **12-272** sociated with abusive conduct. This necessitates a two stage inquiry. First, is the alleged conduct abusive *in its own rights*? For instance, are the prices charged by the IPR owner for its products unfair? Secondly, is there sufficient *nexus* between the proven abusive conduct and the exercise of IPRs such that the latter may be prohibited under art.102. In the following section, we consider the first issue. The issue of *nexus* is discussed comprehensively in Ch.14, "Euro-Defences".

Against the background of the above discussion, we now turn to consider specific **12-273** collateral abuses such as unfair pricing, refusal to supply, etc. Here, the reader should be aware that it is beyond the scope of this book to consider all types of abusive conduct. Such is the province of a book on competition. The focus below is on those areas where such conduct is often combined with the exercise of IPRs or where, e.g. charging of excessive royalties, such occurs in an IP context.

Unfair prices

Article 101 prohibits the imposition of unfair prices by a dominant undertaking. **12-274** In *United Brands*,[373] the CJEU said that:

> "[250] In this case, charging a price which is excessive because it has no reasonable relation to the *economic value* of the product supplied would be an abuse
>
> [251] This excess could inter alia be determined objectively if it were possible for it to be calculated by making a comparison between the selling price of the product

---

[370] H. Hovenkamp, M.D. Janis and M.A. Lemley, "Unilateral Refusals to License in the US", in F. Lévêque, Howard and A. Shelanski (eds), *Antitrust, Patents and Copyright* (Northampton, Mass.: Edward Elgar, 2006), p.25.

[371] See para.12-193.

[372] *Volvo v Veng*, at [9].

[373] (27/76) [1978] E.C.R. 207.

in question and its cost of production, which would disclose the amount of the profit margin.

[252] The questions therefore to be determined are whether the difference between the costs actually incurred and the price actually charged is excessive and, if the answer to this question is in the affirmative, whether a price has been imposed which is either unfair in itself or when compared to competing products."

12-275 In *Attheraces v BHB*,[374] the English Court of Appeal has said that the judgment poses two questions. Is the difference between the costs actually incurred and the price charge excessive? If so, is it unfair?

12-276 The CJEU and the Commission have not resiled from applying the prohibition of unfair prices under art.102 to goods or services protected by IPRs. In *Volvo v Veng*, it was held that the exercise of the IPR may be an abuse by a dominant undertaking if associated with the fixing of unfair prices for spare parts for cars. In explaining what may constitute unfair prices, the court said in *CICRA v Renault* that:

> "With reference more particularly to the difference in prices between components sold by the manufacturer and those sold by the independent producers, it should be noted that the Court has held (Case 24/67 *Parke Davis*) that a higher price for the former than for the latter does not necessarily constitute an abuse since the proprietor of protective rights in respect of an ornamental design may lawfully call for a return on the amounts which he has invested in order to perfect the protected design."[375]

12-277 In *Volvo*, Mischo AG concluded from *Parke Davis v Probel*[376] that an inventor was entitled to recover not only its production costs in the strict sense and a reasonable profit margin but also its research and development expenditure.[377] The Advocate-General stated that, as regards the bodywork components sold as spare parts, there was an unusual aspect in-so-far as part of that expenditure had probably already been recovered from the sale of new cars. However, he said that he did not, in principle, see any reason why a manufacturer should be prohibited from charging the amortisation to income both from new vehicles and from spare parts, provided that the apportionment is equitable. He said that such was a question to be decided by the national court.[378]

12-278 The whole meaning of "unfair prices" was considered in *Attheraces v BHB* whose facts have already been discussed.[379] This case technically did not involve the exercise or threatened exercise of IPRs.[380] A central issue was whether the charges of BHB were so excessive as to amount to an abuse of a dominant position. In particular, it was complained that the price charged was considerably in excess of the cost to BHB producing the pre-race data.

12-279 It was held by Etherton J, applying *United Brands*, that the "economic value" of

---

[374] *Attheraces* [2006] E.C.C. 24; [2006] Eu. L.R. 654; [2006] F.S.R. 20; (2006) 29 I.P.D. 29.011; [2006] Info. T.L.R. 423; [2006] U.K.C.L.R. 167; [2006] E.C.D.R. 13; [2005] EWHC 3015. On appeal, [2007] E.C.C. 7; [2007] EWCA Civ 38 CA.

[375] (53/87) [1988] E.C.R. 6039; [1990] 4 C.M.L.R. 265; [1990] F.S.R. 544 at [17].

[376] (24/67) [1968] E.C.R. 55; [1968] C.M.L.R. 47.

[377] (238/87) [1988] E.C.R. 6211 at [32]. See also *Deutsche Grammophon Gesellschaft mbH v Metro-SB-Großmärkte* (78/70) [1971] E.C.R. 487; [1971] C.M.L.R. 631 at [19].

[378] (238/87) [1988] E.C.R. 6211; [1989] 4 C.M.L.R. 122 at [33]. In fact, the allocation of manufacturing costs of a product to consumables or spare parts can give rise to allocative efficiencies—see fn.237.

[379] See para.12-245.

[380] Although initially it did, see para.12-245.

the data was the cost of BHB of producing its database (about £5 million) together with a reasonable return of that cost (termed the "cost+" approach). Etherton J held that because the charges to ATR were vastly in excess of that, such charges amounted to an abuse of a dominant position.

BHB appealed this finding. On appeal, BHB's main point was that in determin- **12-280** ing the "economic value" of the pre-race data in accordance with the meaning in *United Brands*, account should also be taken of its value to ATR and how much ATR could benefit from this data as a source of income. In this regard, BHB relied upon an earlier decision of *BHB v Victor Chandler*[381] where the High Court had held, in striking out a defence of excessive profits that value did not mean cost+. Thus, the product was a revenue-earning opportunity for ATR with profitable bill-ing opportunities for bookmakers. BHB also said that the judge failed to consider that the pre-race data was a by-product or secondary formula dependent on the primary activity of horseracing and that revenue was needed to maintain the primary activity. Revenue from BHB was channelled back into horseracing. Thus, BHB said that the relevant costs were not just the costs of compiling the data but also the costs of the primary activity of horseracing.

ATR said that "economic value" could not mean what the consumer was prepared **12-281** to pay. It said that such would undermine competition law. It said that the charge of 50 per cent of net profits proposed by BHB would give BHB a stranglehold on ATR and strip it of its profit.

The Court of Appeal accepted BHB's argument that economic value did not **12-282** equate to cost+. On the one hand, the Court of Appeal realised that "economic value" cannot mean simply what the market will bear because the whole premise of art.102 is that the seller has a dominant position which permits it to distort the market. On the other hand, the Court of Appeal accepted the central contention of BHB that there was no reason why the "economic value" of the product should not be its value to the purchaser rather than cost+. The Court of Appeal held that on the facts of the case, there was nothing to show that ATR's competitiveness on the overseas market had been materially compromised by the terms of the arrange-ments with or specified by BHB. In short, the price charged by BHB did not affect ATR's ability to provide a service to overseas customers. It simply affected the profitability of those services. As discussed later in this chapter, when considering what is reasonable remuneration in a compulsory licence, the Court of Appeal's ap-proach mirrors that taken when determining what is reasonable remuneration in compulsory licences granted under intellectual property legislation (e.g. failure to work the inventions), in the UK and US.[382]

In cases where products were protected by IPRs, English courts have accepted **12-283** that unfair prices for such products can amount to an abuse of a dominant position.[383] An English court has held that a net profit of 15.7 per cent cannot be in any way regarded as unreasonable in the context of whether the price of a product was unfair within the meaning of art.102.[384]

The concept of what is an unfair price in relation to products covered by IPR is **12-284**

---

[381] *BHB v Victor Chandler* [2005] EWHC 1074.
[382] See para.12-325.
[383] See, e.g. *Pitney Bowes Inc* [1990] 3 C.M.L.R. 466 (HC). See also, *Chiron Corp* [1993] F.S.R. 324 (Pat Ct) where the court rejected an argument that as it was not an abuse to exploit a patent, it was not an abuse to charge a particular price for a patented article, citing *Volvo* as authority for the proposition that charging excessive prices could amount to an abuse of a dominant position.
[384] *Hoover Plc v George Hulme (STO) Ltd* [1982] 3 C.M.L.R. 186 (HC).

a difficult concept. In general, the owner of IPRs is entitled to appropriate the maximum value of its IPR by charging whatever price it chooses. Yet, where the IPR owner is a dominant undertaking, such an argument is difficult to distinguish from an argument that a fair price is any price that the market will bear. In short, where an IPR owner is dominant, the IPR owner has a special responsibility. If the IPR owner acted to appropriate the maximum value of its IPR, then the IPR owner will, by reason of its dominance, be extracting the maximum value that it can from the market in which it is dominant.

12-285   In *Attheraces*, BHB submitted that unless the court started from the ratio of cost to price, such was "tearing up European" competition law.[385] Certainly, a cost+ approach is indicated in *Volvo v Veng* and *Parke Davis v Probel*. The problem was discussed acutely in relation to a hypothetical example posed by the court of a monopoly wholesale supplier of a delicacy to a supermarket who charges to the supermarket its cost plus a moderate margin but finds that the supermarket is marking up the supplier's product by 500 per cent. BHB submitted that the supplier would be abusing its dominant position if it raised its price to more than it could get in a competitive market regardless of what the supermarket was charging. Attheraces submitted that the supermarket had established the economic value of the product and there was nothing to stop the producer securing as much as he was able to. The Court of Appeal preferred the latter approach. The Court of Appeal recognised that such might lead to the:

> "realistic possibility of a monopoly supplier not quite killing the goose that lays the golden eggs but coming close to throttling her"[386]

and did not exclude that such could be held to be abusive. However, as it said, art.102 is not a general provision for the regulation of prices but seeks to prevent the abuse of a dominant market position with the object of protecting and promoting competition.[387]

12-286   It is submitted that the Court of Appeal was right to concentrate on the detriment to the consumer and not merely the price charged by BHB to Attheraces. If there is a large profit element to be made by the purchaser, then there is no reason that such profit should not be split between seller and buyer. Moreover, a cost+ approach fails to recognise that often the price of a product bears little relationship to the cost of manufacture *even in a competitive market*. For instance, the price of luxury branded products such as perfume often bear little relationship to the cost of creating the product. Moreover, it is worth pointing out that if the buyer is making a large profit in a downstream market, it may suggest that competition in *that* market is poor and that demand is inelastic. It is easily argued that it would be somewhat hypocritical for a buyer or licensee to retain large profits (i.e. a rate of return which is not cost+) and yet argue that the upstream supplier or licensor is only entitled to a cost+ rate of return because it has no competitors.

12-287   Even if a cost+ approach is the correct approach, it is important that the approach does not discourage innovation. Thus, many attempts to innovate fail. If there is a failure to take into account the cost of failures, this will discourage innovation. It is of note that in the Guidelines on Technology Transfer Agree-

---

[385] *Attheraces Ltd* [2006] E.C.D.R. 13; [2006] F.S.R. 20 at [209].
[386] *Attheraces Ltd* [2006] E.C.D.R. 13; [2006] F.S.R. 20 at [217].
[387] *Attheraces Ltd* [2006] E.C.D.R. 13; [2006] F.S.R. 20 at [217].

ments under art.101, they specifically refer to the need to take into account failures.[388]

Discriminatory pricing

It is clearer that an abuse has occurred where a rights owner conducts discrimina- **12-288** tory pricing. Article 102(c) makes it clear that treating undertakings in a discriminatory manner is an abuse of a dominant position. In an action for infringement of a dominant undertaking's copyright in spare parts relating to the fork lift industry, the English Court of Appeal held that where an instruction had been given to the dominant undertaking's agents to charge full retail price to traders selling spare parts for the dominant undertaking's fork lift trucks so that the traders would be unable to make an ordinary commercial profit, that such did disclose a defence under EU Law.[389] In a patent infringement action, the English High Court permitted the defendant leave to amend its defence to plead that the patentee was infringing art.102 by exporting protected products at a lower price than it sold the products for in its home market.[390]

Abusive pricing and refusal to supply

It might be thought that if it was not an abuse for a dominant undertaking to **12-289** refuse to supply an undertaking with its products or services, then a fortiori it could not be an abuse to charge excessive or unfair prices. In other words, better a product at an unfair price than no product. This has led to arguments that if the refusal to supply products or services was not abusive, then the charging of unfair or excessive practices where an undertaking chooses to supply such products or services cannot be abusive. However, the CJEU has rejected this approach, finding it unduly restrictive.[391]

Unfair/discriminatory royalties

The discussion above on unfair prices is equally applicable to the charging of **12-290** unfair royalties. Royalties are normally used as a financial mechanism to ensure that the licensee has no fixed charges and that its charges are proportionate to the level of exploitation (i.e. profit) that it is making.

The issue of unfair or excessive royalties has been considered in the royalties **12-291** charged by collecting societies. Thus, in *Basset v SACEM*,[392] the CJEU said that:

> "it was possible that the level of the royalty fixed by a copyright society is such that Article 101 may be applied."[393]

This was said in a case where the applicant was arguing that a "supplementary **12-292**

---

[388] See Guidelines on Technology Transfer Agreements [2004] OJ C101/2, para.7. Thus, a cost+ approach which does not take into account failures has been described as a "heads I only make a [reasonable] profit and tails, I lose my investment", V. Korah, "Case Comment" [1988] 12 E.I.P.R. 381.

[389] *Lansing Bagnall Ltd v Buccaneer Lift Parts Ltd* [1984] 1 C.M.L.R. 224. See also *Pitney Bowes* [1990] 3 C.M.L.R. 466 (discrimination against smaller customers by unjustifiably charging high prices can amount to an abuse).

[390] See *Pitney Bowes* [1990] 3 C.M.L.R. 466 (HC) at [5], [13].

[391] *Konkurrensverket v TeliaSonera Sverige AB* (C-52/09) [2011] E.C.R. 527 at [47]–[59].

[392] *Basset v SACEM* (402/85) [1987] E.C.R. 1747; [1987] 3 C.M.L.R. 173.

[393] (402/85) [1987] E.C.R. 1747; [1987] 3 C.M.L.R. 173 at [19].

mechanical reproduction royalty" should not be charged in France for the performance of UK records, as no such right existed in the UK. The court held that the mere existence of such a fact did not mean that art.102 applied and the royalty complained of was akin to a performance royalty. Thus, the complainant was in reality complaining about the level of royalty. In *Ministère Public v Tournier and Lucazeau v SACEM*,[394] the CJEU ruled that a national copyright-management society, which has a dominant position in a substantial part of the internal market and imposes trading conditions, would be guilty of an abuse of a dominant position where the royalties which it charges to discotheques were appreciably higher than those charged in other Member States. However, it stated that such would not be the case if the copyright-management society was able to justify differences by reference to objective and relevant dissimilarities between copyright-management in the differing Member States.[395] Thus, it is clear that the CJEU is prepared to find that an excessive royalty is an abuse of a dominant position. In a patent case, it was held that a demand by the patentee for an "excessive royalty" where an undertaking was entitled to a compulsory licence was an abuse of a dominant position.[396] The English Court of Appeal has appeared to accept that unreasonable royalties can amount to an abuse of a dominant position but held that no case had been made out.[397]

12-293 In *Der Grüne Punkt*, a German undertaking, DSD, had a dominant position in the provision of services for the taking back of packaging from customers (who were required to arrange for the taking back of such packaging pursuant to German law) and entered into agreements with customers for the taking back of all packaging bearing DSD's well known trade mark (*"Der Grüne Punkt"*). The agreements contained a provision whereby licence fees were chargeable in respect of all sales packaging brought on the German market, irrespective of whether DSD actually provided the take back service. The Commission held that such foreclosed other competitors as it would mean that where the licensee used another competitor, he would have to pay both the competitor and DSD. The General Court and CJEU upheld the decision.[398]

12-294 In *Kanal 5*,[399] STIM, a Swedish collecting society, was an association which enjoyed a de facto monopoly in Sweden for making available copyright-protected music for television broadcasts. The members of STIM were composers and music publishers. Under its agreements with composers and music publishers, the right

---

[394] *Ministère Public v Tournier and Lucazeau v SACEM* (395/87, 110/88 & 241-242/88) [1989] E.C.R. 2521; [1991] 4 C.M.L.R. 248.

[395] (395/87), (110/88) and (241-242/88) [1989] E.C.R. 2521; [1991] 4 C.M.L.R. 248 at [46].

[396] (T-30/89) [1991] E.C.R. II-1439; [1992] 4 C.M.L.R. 16 upheld on appeal (C-53/92P) [1994] E.C.R. I-667. However, it should be noted that in compulsory licence of rights proceedings, a royalty reflecting that which would have been negotiated between a willing licensor/willing licensee will be set by the tribunal in absence of agreement. Thus, the abuse for an excessive royalty must be seen in the context that the licensee was entitled to a licence for a reasonable royalty.

[397] *British Leyland* [1984] 3 C.M.L.R. 102 at [101]–[105]. The Court of Appeal held that a "blanket" royalty rate, whereby a royalty was charged on British Leyland's exhausts regardless as to whether they were protected by copyright or not, was not an abuse because it constituted a convenient way of calculating a royalty of 7 per cent on infringing items—see [105]. However, a blanket royalty rate can distort competition and be prohibited under art.101—see para.8-260.

[398] Competition Policy Newsletter, DG Comp, June 2001, pp.27–29; on appeal *Der Grüne Punkt (Duales System Deutschland GmbH v EC Commission* (T-51/01) [2007] II-1691; appeal to CJEU dismissed, *Der Grüne Punkt—Duales System Deutschland v Commission* (C-385/07P) [2009] E.C.R. I-6155). The application of "blanket" royalties may also infringe art.101. See para.8-260.

[399] *Kanal 5 Ltd v STIM* (C-52/07) [2008] E.C.R. I-9275.

to remuneration for public performances and recording and duplication rights were assigned to STIM. In its agreements with commercial television broadcasters such as Kanal 5, STIM stipulated that, in return for licences for these rights, remuneration should correspond to a percentage of the revenue derived from television broadcasts directed at the general public or subscription sales. However, in its agreement with the public service channel (Sveriges Television), STIM was paid a lump sum agreed in advance. Kanal 5 considered that STIM's treatment of it amounted to an abuse of a dominant position. In short, it said that the method of remuneration was unfair and the differential treatment of private undertakings and the public sector was discriminatory. It was accepted that STIM was in a dominant position. The Swedish courts referred the matter to the CJEU. The CJEU realised that the "metering" of use was not a simple matter. Relying in large part on its decisions in *Basset* and *Tournier*, it said that when considering the method and amount charged by a dominant collecting society, it was appropriate to seek appropriate suitable balance between the interests of composers of music protected by copyright to receive remuneration for the television broadcast of their works and those of the television broadcasting companies to broadcast those works.[400] Relying upon *Tournier*, it said that a flat-rate royalty approach could only be criticised if:

"other methods might be capable of attaining the same legitimate aim, namely the protection of the interests of authors, composers and publishers of music, without thereby increasing the costs of managing contracts and monitoring the use of protected musical works".[401] It thus said that there was no abuse if the remuneration model whereby a royalty was charged on the revenue of the channels was proportionate overall to the quantity of musical works protected by copyright actually broadcast or likely to be broadcast "unless another method enables the use of those works and the audience to be identified more precisely without however resulting in a disproportionate increase in the costs incurred for the management of contracts and the supervision of the use of those works."[402]

On the issue of discriminatory treatment, the real concern was whether such **12-295** conduct fell within art.102(c) (application of dissimilar conditions to equivalent transactions thereby placing a party at a competitive disadvantage). The CJEU said that it did not matter for the application of art.102 that the discriminatory treatment distinguished between the private and public sector. It said a copyright management organisation is likely to exploit in an abusive manner its dominant position within the meaning of that article if it applies with respect to those companies dissimilar conditions to equivalent services and if it places them as a result at a competitive disadvantage, unless such a practice may be objectively justified.[403] On the issue of objective justification, it said that the national court should consider the fact that the public service channel did not have advertising, whether they were competitors and also the method of financing public service television.[404]

Refusal to supply

Under art.102(b), a refusal to supply goods or services by a dominant undertak- **12-296** ing is an abuse. This is regardless of whether or not the goods or services are

---

[400] See [31].
[401] See [33].
[402] See [41].
[403] See [48].
[404] See [42]–[48].

protected by IPRs. Therefore, a refusal by a dominant undertaking to supply spare parts for cash registers to an existing customer because the customer had an independent business in the repair and servicing of the undertaking's product was held to be abusive even though the spare parts were themselves the subject of UK design rights.[405]

12-297   Equally, a refusal to supply information can amount to an abuse of a dominant position. Thus, in *TV Listings*,[406] the CJEU held that it was an abuse for television companies to refuse to supply basic information relating to programme scheduling to third parties who wished to prepare weekly listings covering all channels which the companies did not offer and for which there was a clear demand.[407] Similarly, in *IBM*,[408] the Commission objected to IBM's refusal to supply technical information to other manufacturers which was needed to make their systems interface with IBM's technology.[409] In a later IBM case, *IBM*,[410] the Commission was concerned about trading conditions imposed on third party maintainers (TPMs) of IBM mainframes. The Commission had, in a preliminary decision, determined that the relevant market was software and hardware inputs for the repair and maintenance of IBM mainframes. The Commission took the preliminary view that IBM was imposing unreasonable supply conditions to the supply of these inputs that might amount to a "constructive" refusal to supply.[411] In *Microsoft v EC Commission*, which has already been discussed, the Commission and the General Court considered that Microsoft's refusal to supply interoperability information for its PC operating system was an abuse of a dominant position because it was indispensable to undertakings that operated in the workgroup server market.

Arbitrary refusal and objective justification

12-298   The CJEU said in *Volvo v Veng* that where a dominant undertaking "arbitrarily" refuses to supply spare parts to independent car repairers, the exercise of registered designs rights may be prohibited by art.102.[412] What amounts to an "arbitrary" refusal? It is suggested that here "arbitrary" means without objective justification. As discussed in relation to the section on "essential facilities", it is a defence to an

---

[405] *Hugin Kassaregister* (22/78) [1979] E.C.R. 1869; [1979] 3 C.M.L.R. 345. The CJEU appeared to accept the Commission's submission that Hugin could use the UK Design Copyright Act 1968 to prevent independent manufacturers from making the required spare parts. Generally, see para.12-047 for discussion of whether the relevant market should be defined as the market for spare parts for a single brand.

[406] (C-241-242/91P) [1995] E.C.R. I-0743; [1995] 6 C.M.L.R. 718.

[407] (C-241-242/91P) [1995] E.C.R. I-0743; [1995] 6 C.M.L.R. 718 at [54].

[408] *IBM* [1984] 3 C.M.L.R. 147; [1984] OJ L118/24.

[409] IBM subsequently gave undertakings to meet the Commission's objections.

[410] COMP/39.692—*IBM Maintenance Services*. This has already been discussed in relation to the determination of relevant market—see para.12-050.

[411] See [32], applying *Clearstream* (T-301/04) [2009] E.C.R. 3155 at [151] which held that excessive delays in supplying could amount to an abusive refusal to supply.

[412] (238/87) [1988] E.C.R. 6211; [1989] 4 C.M.L.R. 122; (53/87) [1990] 4 C.M.L.R. 265 and repeated in (T-69/89) [1991] E.C.R. II-0485; [1991] 4 C.M.L.R. 586; (T-70/89) [1991] C.M.L.R. 669; (T-76/89) [1991] C.M.L.R. 745. See also *IBM Maintenance Services*, where the Commission said in relation to IBM's practices that the fact that IPR covered the inputs "may be insufficient to justify the conduct"— at [40].

allegation of abuse that there is objective justification for the alleged abusive conduct.[413]

Under art.101, the Commission has permitted franchisors to choose their retail **12-299** franchisees, as the former are entitled to turn down applicants who do not have the personal qualities and business qualifications they deem important and, thus, to decide to whom it supplies its trade-marked goods.[414] Such a sanction clearly envisages that a refusal to supply those who do not meet such criteria would be permissible. Whilst arts 101 and 102, although complementary, are independent of each other,[415] it would be strange if a dominant undertaking was not permitted to refuse to supply to parties who did not meet its requirements (applied in a non-discriminatory fashion) on the basis that such constituted an abuse of a dominant position.[416] Thus, in the field of spare parts, the above reasoning would entitle a dominant undertaking to refuse to supply a repairer where the latter was not capable of providing the necessary standard of repair service. Similarly, where a dominant undertaking refuses to meet demands from undertakings that are intent on exploiting price differences for a single-brand pharmaceutical between Member States which exist because of state intervention, this may be justified if such requests are out of the ordinary.[417]

Where a dominant undertaking has arbitrarily refused to supply protected spare **12-300** parts, this will not necessarily result in a court granting a compulsory licence. Generally, the principle of proportionality means that the burdens imposed on undertakings in order to bring an infringement of competition law to an end must not exceed what is appropriate and necessary to attain the objective sought, namely re-establishment of compliance with the rules infringed.[418] Therefore, it is submitted that where such an abuse has been found by a court, the dominant undertaking should be merely ordered to cease and desist its abusive behaviour. This permits the dominant undertaking to decide whether they will supply spare parts or license the repairer.

Acquisition of IPRs and licences ancillary to mergers

In *Elopak v Tetra Pak*,[419] the Commission held that an undertaking had abused **12-301** its dominant position when it purchased via the acquisition of a group an exclusive licence which strengthened its position in the relevant market. Such a finding must be seen as an application of the general rule established in *Continental Can*[420] that an abuse under art.102 is that which strengthens the dominant undertaking and substantially weakens the residual competition.[421]

The Commission has issued a Notice on restrictions ancillary to concentra- **12-302**

---

[413] The CJEU's approach to "objective justification" is discussed at para.12-215.

[414] *Re the Franchise Agreements of Yves Rocher* [1987] OJ L8/49; [1988] 4 C.M.L.R. 592.

[415] See (T-51/89) [1991] 4 C.M.L.R. 334.

[416] Selective distributorship agreements which exclude distributors who are unable to fulfil certain objective qualitative criteria are considered generally not to infringe art.101—see *Metro-SB-Grossmärkte v EC Commission* [1977] E.C.R. 1875, [1978] 2 C.M.L.R. 1; (31/80) [1980] E.C.R. 3775, [1981] 2 C.M.L.R. 235; *Lancôme v Etos* (99/79) [1980] E.C.R. 2511, [1981] 2 C.M.L.R. 164; *Hasselblad v EC Commission* [1984] E.C.R. 883, [1984] 1 C.M.L.R. 559. See Ch.12.

[417] See para.12-215.

[418] (C-241–242/91P) [1995] 8 C.M.L.R. 718, CJEU, [93]. See also (C-62/86) [1991] E.C.R. I-3359; [1993] 5 C.M.L.R. 215. In the UK, see *Sandvik* [2000] F.S.R. 17.

[419] *Elopak* [1988] OJ L272/27; [1990] 4 C.M.L.R. 47. On appeal, (T-51/89) [1991] 4 C.M.L.R. 334.

[420] (6/72) [1973] E.C.R. 215; [1973] C.M.L.R. 199.

[421] See also para.12-114.

tions[422] which sets out their approach to restrictions which often accompany mergers and acquisitions. In particular, it sets out the Commission's approach to licences of IPRs in such a context:

"*B. Licence agreements*

27. The transfer of an undertaking or of part of it can include the transfer to the purchaser, with a view to the full exploitation of the assets transferred, of intellectual property rights or know-how. However, the vendor may remain the owner of the rights in order to exploit them for activities other than those transferred. In these cases, the usual means for ensuring that the purchaser will have the full use of the assets transferred is to conclude licensing agreements in his/her favour. Likewise, where the vendor has transferred intellectual property rights with the business, she/he may still want to continue using some or all of these rights for activities other than those transferred; in such a case the purchaser will grant a licence to the vendor.

28. Licences of patents, of similar rights, or of know-how, can be considered necessary to the implementation of the concentration. They may equally be considered an integral part of the concentration and, in any event, need not be limited in time. These licences can be simple or exclusive and may be limited to certain fields of use, to the extent that they correspond to the activities of the undertaking transferred.

29. However, territorial limitations on manufacture reflecting the territory of the transferred activity are not necessary to the implementation of the operation. As regards licences granted by the seller of a business to the buyer, the seller can be made subject to territorial restrictions in the licence agreement under the same conditions as laid down for non-competition clauses in the context of the sale of a business.

30. Restrictions in licence agreements going beyond the above provisions, such as those which protect the licensor rather than the licensee, are not necessary to the implementation of the concentration.

31. Similarly, in the case of licences of trademarks, business names, design rights, copyrights or similar rights, there may be situations in which the vendor wishes to remain the owner of such rights in relation to activities retained, but the purchaser needs those rights in order to market the goods or services produced by the undertaking or part of the undertaking transferred. Here, the same considerations as above apply."

Therefore, if the concentration is permissible, then so are the above ancillary licences and assignments.

Defensive registration of trade mark

12-303   In *Renault*,[423] the CJEU said that the mere fact of registration of a design could not constitute an abuse. However, the Commission has held that where a firm in a dominant position registers a trade mark which it knew or ought to have known was already being used by a competitor in another Member State, this may constitute an abuse of a dominant position.[424]

---

[422] Commission Notice on restrictions directly related and necessary to concentrations [2005] OJ C56/24.

[423] (13/87) [1988] E.C.R. 6039.

[424] *OY Airam A.B. v Osram GmbH* [1982] 3 C.M.L.R. 614; *11th Report on Competition Policy*, para.66 (EC Commission).

Imposition of unduly onerous clauses in agreements

Where an undertaking is in a dominant position, it will usually be in a position **12-304** to dictate terms to parties who wish to do business with it. This is true in the area of intellectual property as in any other. Often these clauses will be prohibited under art.101 and thus the application of art.102 will be irrelevant. Where an undertaking threatens infringement proceedings, unless it enters into a licence which is contrary to art.101, such may constitute an unlawful act under art.101.[425]

However, in other circumstances, the imposition of clauses by a dominant **12-305** undertaking which are permissible under arts 101(1) or 101(3) may constitute an abuse of a dominant position. In such cases, the permissibility of such clauses under art.101 is irrelevant to its consideration under art.102.[426] In many respects, the compatibility of unduly onerous clauses in licences is similar to the issue of excessive royalties and the reader is referred to that section.[427] An example of an unduly onerous clause can be seen in the Commission's decision in *Eurofima*[428] to withdraw proceedings under art.102 against an organisation which had a dominant position as a buyer of railway rolling stock. The undertaking had a requirement that as a condition of a contract for the development of a new type of rolling stock with its contractors, it was to have unlimited right of use of the resultant patent rights without payment of additional compensation to the contractors. Upon the Commission bringing proceedings under art.102, it withdrew the requirement. The Commission held that it was "materially improper" that the dominant undertaking was free to give licences for future patent rights to third parties without consulting or giving additional compensation to the contractor.

Threats and conduct of infringement proceedings

It will be rare that the mere initiation per se of infringement proceedings will **12-306** amount to an abuse of a dominant position. If the enforcement of IPR is an abuse of a dominant position, then clearly the proceedings are liable to be dismissed. However, if they are not an abuse of a dominant position, it would be surprising if a court was to find that, despite such merit, the issuing of proceedings amounted to an abuse, as, generally, rights are exercised by the bringing of infringement proceedings. Thus, if the exercise of rights is permissible under art.102 then the *means* of exercising those rights should be permissible.

However, will the making of threats to litigate amount to an abuse of a dominant **12-307** position? An English court has said that the making of threats will rarely amount to an abuse, even if such were made in bad faith.[429] It is debateable whether such a statement is compatible with the approach by the CJEU in *AstraZeneca* which ap-

---

[425] See para.14-031.
[426] *Elopak* [1988] OJ L272/27; [1990] 4 C.M.L.R. 47, upheld on appeal (T-51/89) [1991] 4 C.M.L.R. 334. However, it may be that the bringing of proceedings to force a defendant to enter into an agreement that is contrary to art.101 is in itself contrary to art.101—see para.14-031.
[427] See para.12-290.
[428] *Re Eurofima* Press Release IP (73) 67, 16 April 1973, [1973] C.M.L.R. D217 (EC Commission).
[429] *Pitney Bowes* [1990] 3 C.M.L.R. 466 (HC) at [16]. Mr Justice Hoffmann said that if such threats were made in bad faith, it would merely have amounted to a threat to commit an independent tort (malicious prosecution) unrelated to a dominant position. In the US, an infringement action brought by a claimant where he knows that the rights are invalid may violate US antitrust laws—see [6], US Antitrust Guidelines for Intellectual Property, issued by the Department of Justice, 6 April 1995 [1995] E.I.P.R. 7 Supp.

pears to impose an obligation on a dominant undertaking to behave in good faith to third parties by reason of the special responsibility that a dominant undertaking has.[430] However, *AstraZeneca* was not concerned with the threat of infringement proceedings before national courts. It is tempting to conclude that unjustified threats made by dominant undertakings where it is clear that the case is unarguable or very weak should be dealt with under national laws relating to the bringing of frivolous or vexatious cases rather than under art.102.[431] In *Hoover Plc v George Hulme*,[432] Mr Justice Whitford said that:

> "If the conduct of the plaintiffs in connection with this or any other litigation were such as to amount to an abuse it could be and would be dealt with as an abuse of the process of the court. The consideration of litigation against persons infringing statutory rights and the institution and conduct of such litigation cannot, however, be an abuse within Article [102]."[433]

12-308   In an early case, the Commission held that where the commencement of actions for patent infringement against a competitor by a dominant undertaking was suspended on condition that it entered into a restrictive agreement contrary to art.101 with the dominant undertaking, such actions constituted an abuse of a dominant position.[434] However, the Commission did not say what the situation would have been if the dominant undertaking had merely continued its patent infringement actions. This decision preceded the General Court's decision in *Tetra Pak Rausing SA v EC Commission*[435] which held that arts 101 and 102 are independent of each other. English courts have held that the issuing of proceedings to force a party to enter into an anti-competitive agreement arguably gives rise to a defence under arts 101 and 102.[436]

Refusal to license save on unreasonable terms

12-309   In *Philips v Ingman*,[437] a UK case, the court said, having discussed *Volvo v Veng* and *CICRA v Renault*:

> "[55]   Based on the cases referred to above, it is not an abuse of a dominant position to refuse to licence an intellectual property right on reasonable terms. Even if the royalties sought by the plaintiff are objectively unreasonable and have the effect of destroying the competitiveness of the defendant, it is not an abuse of a dominant position defined by reference to the existence of the intellectual property right. Indeed the proprietor may offer terms which no reasonable competitor could accept. *It is difficult to see how that can be worse, or commercially different, to offering no terms at all—i.e. to refusing a licence—a course the rights owner is entitled to take.*" [Emphasis supplied.]

---

[430] See para.12-314.
[431] Under UK law, making unjustified threats to bring proceedings is actionable as a statutory tort in the field of trade marks, patents and registered designs. A threat is unjustified if the acts do not constitute an infringement of a valid right. Thus, the issue of belief that such is so (whether objective or subjective) is irrelevant.
[432] *Hoover Plc* [1982] 3 C.M.L.R. 186.
[433] *Hoover Plc* [1982] 3 C.M.L.R. 186 at [86].
[434] *Re the Complaint by Yoshida Kogyo KK* [1978] 3 C.M.L.R. 44, *Press Release of the Commission*, IP (78) 111, 9 June 1978.
[435] (T-51/89) [1991] 4 C.M.L.R. 334.
[436] See para.14-031.
[437] Discussed at para.12-240.

Other UK courts have adopted such an approach.[438] The logic of the court is dif- **12-310** ficult to fault. However, care must be taken here. The reasoning of the court depends on the exercise of the rights themselves being unobjectionable if no licence was offered at all. As is clear, in exceptional circumstances, such may indeed be an abuse. Secondly, it may be that the threat of proceedings to force a person to enter into an agreement which is contrary to art.101 may be an infringement of arts 101 and 102. Certainly, it has been held that such is arguable in UK proceedings.[439]

Tying

Article 102(d) prohibits the conclusion of contracts subject to acceptance by the **12-311** other parties of supplementary obligations which by their nature or according to commercial usage have no connection with the subject of such contracts. In *Microsoft v EC Commission*, which has already been discussed with regards to the failure of Microsoft to disclose interoperability information,[440] the Commission was also concerned about Microsoft's practice of bundling its Windows Media Player with its operating system. The Commission said that as a matter of principle, tying the sale of a product with another product would be an abuse of a dominant position where:

(a) the undertaking concerned is dominant in the tying product market;
(b) the tying and tied goods are two separate products;
(c) the undertaking concerned affords consumers no choice to source the tying product without the tied product;
(d) tying forecloses competition; and
(e) there is no objective justification for the tying.

In *Microsoft*, the Commission concluded that such conditions were satisfied. In **12-312** particular, it found that the ubiquity of including Windows Media Player on its Windows operating systems meant that content providers and software tended to rely on and use Windows media technology, particularly because supporting technologies generated significant additional costs. As a result, the Commission ordered Microsoft to provide a version of Windows which did not include Windows Media Player. This finding was upheld on appeal.

In the Commission Notice on art.102,[441] the Commission has said that tying[442] **12-313** may lead to anti-competitive effects in the tied market, the tying market or both at the same time. Its main concern is foreclosure of competitors by such provisions.[443]

---

[438] See *Chiron Corp* [1993] F.S.R. 324 (Pat) at 335. See also *Pitney Bowes Inc v Francotyp Postalia* [1990] 3 C.M.L.R. 466 (HC) at [20].
[439] See para.8-240.
[440] See *Intel v VIA* [2003] F.S.R. 33 at [87].
[441] Communication from the Commission—Guidance on the Commission's enforcement priorities in applying Article [102] of the EC Treaty to abusive exclusionary conduct by dominant undertakings [2009] OJ C45/7.
[442] Defined as where customers which purchase one product are forced to purchase another product— see [48].
[443] See [53].

Improper conduct in applications for IPRs

12-314   In *AstraZeneca v Commission*,[444] the Commission found that AstraZeneca, the pharmaceutical manufacturer, had abused its dominant position for proton pump inhibitors for treatment of ulcers by making misleading representations to patent offices in various Member States to obtain SPCs (supplemental protection certificates) for Omeprazole, which it had a patent for, so as to keep manufacturers of generic products away from the market.[445] The facts are complicated but in essence, the allegations against AstraZeneca were that it had conducted itself improperly before the patent offices by suppressing information which it was aware would, if put forward, have been fatal to the grant of the SPCs. The CJEU held, in dismissing an appeal from the General Court, that art.102 prohibited a dominant undertaking from eliminating a competitor and thereby strengthening its position by using methods other than those which come within the scope of competition on the merits.[446] It held that the conduct of AstraZeneca was manifestly not consistent with competition on its merits. Also, this finding can be considered an example of the specific responsibility that lies on a dominant undertaking not to prejudice, by its conduct, effective and undistorted competition within the EU.[447]

12-315   Under US law, unfair conduct in prosecuting an application for a patent or trade before the USPTO may amount to an anti-competitive act where it involves knowing and wilful fraud. Furthermore, the enforcement of patents which have been obtained unfairly may also be anti-competitive even if they fall short of fraud.[448]

Article 102 and defences under EU IP legislation

12-316   In *Microsoft v EC Commission*, a fundamental issue was what level of information was required by those operating in the workgroup server market to ensure interoperability with Microsoft's PC operating systems. The Computer Software Directive[449] provides for a specific defence of "interoperability". Under this defence, it is not an infringement when acts are carried out to obtain information necessary to achieve the interoperability of an independently created computer program provided that certain conditions are met.[450] On appeal to the General Court against a finding of abuse under art.102 in failing to provide sufficient interoperability information, Microsoft argued that the Commission had taken too broad a view of the interoperability provisions in the Computer Software Directive and therefore the remedies that it had ordered for the provision of interoperability information were outside the scope of the Directive. In particular, Microsoft argued that the information it had been ordered to provide would permit competitors to clone features of its own workgroup server operating systems rather than provide functional equivalence. It argued that the Commission had taken too broad a view of the Computer Software Directive's requirements as to interoperability.

---

[444] *AstraZenecaAB v European Commission* (C-457/10P) [2012] E.C.R. 0000.

[445] SPCs are discussed in Ch.2. In broad terms, they extend the period of protection for patents where there has been delay in marketing authorisation of a pharmaceutical.

[446] See [75].

[447] See [98].

[448] *2017 Antitrust Guidelines for the Licensing of Intellectual Property*, Department of Justice (12 January 2017).

[449] Dir.91/250 [1991] OJ L122/42. This has now been replaced by a codified version (Dir.2009/24 [2009] OJ L111/16) but no substantive changes have been made. This is discussed in Ch.4.

[450] art.6 Dir.2009/24.

Although the General Court considered that the Commission's concept of **12-317** interoperability was consistent with the Computer Software Directive,[451] it deemed that it was not necessary when judging whether there was an abuse under art.102 to be too troubled by the exact extent of the interoperability provisions in the Directive. As it said, art.102 was a provision of "higher rank" than the Computer Software Directive and the question was not whether the concept of interoperability in the contested decision was consistent with the concept in that Directive but whether the Commission correctly determined the degree of interoperability that should be attainable in the light of the objectives of art.102.[452] It said that the Commission's approach, namely to determine the degree of interoperability required to permit developers of non-Microsoft work-group server operating systems to remain viably on the market was the real issue and not whether such was consistent with the interoperability provisions of the Computer Software Directive.[453]

Such an approach suggests that when considering the issue of art.102 in the **12-318** context of a refusal to licence IPRs, the court or tribunal will not pay much attention to defences in harmonising EU IP Directives or EU legislation—even where it could be argued that the defence is intended to deal with the specific abuse that is alleged against the IPR owner. In the author's view, on the one hand, it would be wrong in principle not to give "due weight" to the existence of specific IP defences when considering whether an abuse has occurred. As discussed earlier in this chapter, IP defences have often been the product of considerable negotiation at an international treaty level and are intended to strike a fair balance between competing policies.[454] On the other hand, if the exercise of IPRs (and the mirror image of that, being a refusal to license the same IPRs) may amount to an abuse of a dominant position in exceptional circumstances, it cannot be determinative under art.102 that there is not a defence under IP legislation to the exercise of those rights. This would amount to a trite and facile argument that if the rights can be successfully exercised (i.e. there is no defence to them), they cannot amount to an abuse of a dominant position. This is clearly wrong.

REMEDIES FOR ABUSE

Where a court determines that an abuse has occurred under art.102 and that thus **12-319** the exercise of rights are prohibited, it will usually have a range of remedies at its disposal. Thus, it could order an injunction to restrain the abuse, order damages, etc.[455] In Commission proceedings, it has the power to order the undertakings to cease the abuse and in this respect impose any behavioural or structural remedy it sees fit.[456] It can impose periodic penalty payments for failure to comply with orders and impose fines.

Where the court determines that the exercise of rights is prohibited under art.102, **12-320** it does not follow that the defendant can exploit the IPR for free. The proportionate remedy may be that the IPR holder must grant a licence on fair reasonable and non-discriminatory FRAND terms. Thus, in *TV Listings*, the Commission ordered that the broadcasting companies provide third parties on request on a non-

---

[451] See [225].
[452] See [227].
[453] art.229.
[454] See in the context of TRIPS, para.12-022, et seq.
[455] See Ch.15.
[456] art.7 Reg.1/2003.

discriminatory basis with their individual advance weekly programme listings. The order said that if they choose to supply and permit reproduction of the listings by means of licences, they were able to charge a reasonable royalty. Furthermore, it said that the licences could include terms that were necessary to ensure comprehensive high-quality coverage of all their programmes including those of minority and/or regional appeal, and those of cultural, historical and educational significance. Rather than set out those terms in detail, the Commission ordered the parties to submit proposals for approval by the Commission within two months.[457] In *Microsoft*, the Commission ordered Microsoft to disclose the interface information upon reasonable and non-discriminatory terms including that of reasonable remuneration for the production of the documentation and for IPRs affected by the decision. In the case of the Windows Media Player tying abuse, it ordered that Microsoft provide a version of Windows without Windows Media Player.[458] In the context of abuses concerning refusals to license SEPs, it goes without saying that any licence granted to an undertaking who wishes to have access to the technical standard is on FRAND terms and not free.

12-321   The most difficult issue is what is the appropriate level of remuneration for a compulsory licence granted under art.102? As discussed above, in the section on unfair prices, the Court of Appeal in *Attheraces v BHB* held, in a case which did not involve IPRs but did involve the supply of indispensable information on races to downstream markets, that it was not right to approach the issue on the basis of costs + a reasonable return (the "cost+") approach. The Court of Appeal considered that it was right to take into account the economic value to the licensee.[459] This approach is consistent with the approach in *United Brands* that prices are unfair (i.e. unreasonable) if they bear no relationship to the economic value of the product but, in the context of IPR, is somewhat at odds with *Parke Davis* and *CICRA v Renault* which seem to indicate a cost+ approach.[460]

12-322   A pure cost+ approach must be wrong because it fails to take into account the cost of failed projects. The Guidelines on the application of art.101 to technology transfer agreements make it clear that an innovator should be free to seek compensation for successful projects that is "sufficient to maintain investment incentives, taking failed projects into account".[461]

12-323   It is tempting to conclude that the correct approach is the royalty that would be agreed if the licensor was not in a dominant position and was entering into bona fide willing negotiations with a licensee. In *Microsoft*, the Commission said that the remuneration should not reflect the "strategic value" stemming from Microsoft's market power in either PC or workgroup operating systems.[462] Such suggests considering the matter as if the dominant undertaking was not dominant. This is called the willing licensor/willing licensee approach. It requires the court to determine the result of negotiations between a willing licensee and a willing licensor. In an English case, this approach was taken to the determination of a

---

[457]   See art.2 of the Commission Decision (discussed at *TV Listings* (T-69/89) [1991] E.C.R. II-485 at [14] and [15]).

[458]   Although it did not prohibit Microsoft from also offering a bundled version of Windows including Windows Media Player which rather negates the effect as generally, consumers will want to have a bundled package.

[459]   See paras 12-278 to 12-285.

[460]   See paras 12-278 to 12-285.

[461]   Guidelines on the application of Article 101 of the [TFEU] to technology transfer agreements [2014] OJ C89/3, para.8. These are discussed in Ch.9.

[462]   para.1008(ii).

FRAND royalty in circumstances where a SEP owner had given an undertaking to a standardisation body to grant licences on FRAND terms.[463]

12-324 It is one of the 15 *Georgia-Pacific* factors used in the United States for determining a reasonably rate in calculating damages in patent infringement actions.[464] The 15 *Georgia-Pacific* factors are:

- The royalties received by the patentee for the licensing of the patent in suit.
- The royalty rates paid by the licensee for the use of other patents comparable to the patent in suit.
- The nature and scope of the license (e.g. exclusive vs. non-exclusive or restricted vs. non-restricted).
- The licensor's established policy regarding the licensing (or non-licensing) of its patents.
- The commercial relationship between the licensor and licensee (e.g. whether they are competitors).
- The extent of derivative or convoyed (i.e. ancillary) sales.
- The duration of the patent and the term of the license.
- The established profitability of the patented product and its commercial success.
- The utility and advantages of the patented product over other modes or devices.
- The nature of the patented invention and the benefits to those who have used the invention.
- The extent to which the infringer has made use of the invention and evidence of the value of that use.
- The portion of the profit or selling price of the invention that may be customary to allow for the use of the invention or analogous inventions.
- The portion of the realisable profit credited to the invention as distinguished from non-patented elements.
- The opinion of qualified experts.
- The amount a willing licensor (such as the patentee) and a willing licensee (such as the alleged infringer) would have agreed upon at the time of the infringement if both had reasonably and voluntarily attempted to reach an agreement.

12-325 In the UK, a willing licensor-licensee approach is used for the purpose of determining what is reasonable remuneration in compulsory licences which are granted pursuant to patent legislation, e.g. for failure to work the invention where the proprietor is not a WTO national.[465] Where the proprietor is a WTO proprietor, art.31 of TRIPs which governs the circumstances where compulsory licences may be granted, requires that the "the right holder shall be paid adequate remuneration in the circumstances of each case, taking into account the *economic value*" of the

---

[463] See para.12-229.
[464] The range of acceptable value is the minimum the licensor would have been willing to accept and the maximum that the licensee would have been willing to pay. More generally, see *Georgia-Pacific Corp v US Plywood Corp*, 318 F. Supp. 1116, 1120.
[465] Patents Act 1977 s.50(1)(b); *Allen & Hanburys Ltd (Salbutamol) Patent* [1987] R.P.C. 327; *Smith Kline & French Laboratories Ltd (Cimetidines) Patent* [1990] R.P.C. 203, 236; *American Cyanamid Co's (Fenbufen) Patent* [1991] R.P.C. 409.

licence.[466] This mirrors the approach by the CJEU in *United Brands* discussed earlier in the context of unfair prices.[467] Often, there will be comparable licences on the market which give an indication of the market rate. In the absence of such information, tribunals often use the "profits available" approach which takes into account the profit that the licensee will be likely to make and apportions that profit, normally on a 50:50 per cent basis between licensor and licensee.[468] Certainly, the requirement to take the "economic value" of the licence to the licensee into account favours a "division of profits" approach. Indeed, now that the EU is a member of TRIPS, there is much to be said that art.31 of TRIPS is the correct approach to determining reasonable remuneration in licences granted under art.102.[469]

12-326 However, it is right to point out that there are a number of possible other approaches to the "division of profits". First, it could be simply the maximum royalty that potential licensees are prepared to pay α. This would take the "profits available" route but the split would be 100-x:x per cent where x is the threshold profit at which the licensee deems it commercially worthwhile taking a licence.

Example

A licensee considers that he could sell a product protected by IPR on a particular market for €100 per item. He can make it for €20. Accordingly, his available gross profit is €80. If he considers that the bare minimum profit for which it is worthwhile manufacturing (taking into account overheads and the overall risk of the venture) is €30, then $\alpha = €50$ (80 – 50).

12-327 It has been said that this royalty rate would give the IPR owner the highest level of incentive to innovate and thus this rate "exactly mimics what intellectual property law is supposed to achieve."[470] The difficulty with this approach is that it fails to take into account the opposite, namely the lowest level of remuneration that the non-dominant IPR owner would be prepared to accept (ß).

Example

A non-dominant IPR owner can make the product protected by his IPR for €20 gross profit. However, he has no manufacturing facilities and setting up his own manufacturing facility would be costly such that his net profit would be considerably lower. He is thus prepared to license it for any sum exceeding €5 per item. ß=€5.

If ß is less than α, then one would expect in hypothetical negotiations that a mid-point between ß and α would be reached. It would be difficult to say that such was not reasonable remuneration. However, α does have its attractions where the IPR owner has gained its dominance by creating a product for which there is consumer demand and which is so technologically advanced that it has no competitor products such that it creates its own market. Often, such products are the result of risky R&D programmes. There is much to

---

[466] In D. Gervais, *Analysis of the TRIPS Agreement*, 4th edn (London: Sweet & Maxwell, 2012), he draws attention to the fact that art.31 was one of the most controversial sections. Many countries lobbied for "fair and equitable" rather than "adequate" remuneration (p.496, fn.703).

[467] See para.12-274.

[468] e.g. *Cabot Safety Corp Patent* [1992] R.P.C. 39. Although the "profits available" approach was criticised in *Smith Kline & French Laboratories (Cimetidine) Patent* [1990] R.P.C. 203 per Lloyd LJ, 244 as being not the statutory test and should thus be an approach of last resort, such a decision predates the introduction of TRIPS art.31 into the Patents Act 1977 which expressly refers to "economic value" of the patent where the patentee is a WTO national. The "economic value" of a patent clearly involves consideration of the profit that the licensee will make on the sale as the Court of Appeal recognised in *Attheraces* [2006] E.C.D.R. 13; [2006] F.S.R. 20.

[469] See para.12-022, et seq.

[470] F. Lévêque, "Innovation, Leveraging and Essential Facilities: Interoperability Licensing in the EU Microsoft Case" (2005) *World Competiton* 28(1), 71–91.

be said that in such circumstances, it would be wrong to disregard the need to encourage such R&D programmes, i.e. it would be wrong to penalise the undertaking for obtaining dominance. In such circumstances, the payment of an α royalty permits access to that market for licensees and yet provides maximum encouragement to undertakings to innovate sufficiently so as to "go for markets", i.e. make sufficient investment in R&D programmes so as to create a product sufficiently differentiated from products already on market that the advanced product creates its own market.

FRAND royalty rates

The owner of a Standard Essential Patent ("SEP") to a technological standard will normally give an undertaking to the standardisation body to license the SEP on fair, reasonable and non-discriminatory ("FRAND") terms. The determination of that has been discussed earlier in this chapter.[471]   **12-328**

WHICH AFFECTS TRADE BETWEEN MEMBER STATES?

This condition of art.102 is shared with art.101 and has been discussed in Ch.8.[472]   **12-329**

It should be remembered that the complainant must show that the alleged abuse affects trade between Member States.[473] Accordingly, in an infringement action, it is not sufficient to show that the relief sought affects trade between Member States. In a patent infringement action where the defendant alleged that the charging of high prices amounted to an abuse of a dominant position, it was not sufficient to show that the relief sought (i.e. an injunction) would affect trade between Member States.[474]   **12-330**

SUBSTANTIAL PART OF THE INTERNAL MARKET

The question as to what amounts to a substantial part of the internal market[475] is ultimately a question of fact. The two factors that are important are the land area where the abuse is operative and the density of the population in that area. Furthermore, the court will have regard to the patterns and volume of production and consumption of the said product as well as the habits and economic opportunities of vendors and purchasers. The court has held the following to be a substantial part of the internal market: **12-331**

(a)   Eire and a small part of Northern Ireland;[476]
(b)   Belgium and Luxembourg;[477]
(c)   Southern Germany;[478] and
(d)   The Netherlands.[479]

In *Suiker Unie v EC Commission*, the court, having stated that Belgian consump-   **12-332**

---

[471]   See para.12-229.
[472]   See para.8-093.
[473]   See (238/87) [1988] E.C.R. 6211; [1989] 4 C.M.L.R. 122.
[474]   *Chiron v Murex* [1994] F.S.R. 187 CA at 198, per Staughton LJ.
[475]   In the previous version of art.102, the phrase "common market" was used but it is not thought that such makes any substantive difference.
[476]   (T-69/89) [1991] E.C.R. II-0485; [1991] 4 C.M.L.R. 586.
[477]   (4/73) [1975] E.C.R. 1663; [1976] 1 C.M.L.R. 295.
[478]   (4/73) [1975] E.C.R. 1663; [1976] 1 C.M.L.R. 295. This finding was made when there were only the original six members in the Common Market.
[479]   (322/81) [1983] E.C.R. 3461; [1985] 1 C.M.L.R. 282.

tion of sugar was 350,000 tonnes against EU consumption of 6,500,000, said that such market shares were sufficiently large for the alleged abuses of Suiker Unie to be said to be operating on a substantial part of the internal market.[480] Thus, in considering whether the abuse occurs in a substantial part of the internal market, the Commission and courts will consider many economic matters other than the actual territory in which the abuse operates.

ONE OR MORE UNDERTAKINGS

12-333   This section deals with two issues. First, what is the precise meaning of "undertaking" for the purpose of art.102? Secondly, in what circumstances can two undertakings enjoy a collectively dominant position?

12-334   In relation to the first issue, it is a settled case that for the application of EU competition law, an undertaking is any entity engaged in an economic activity, irrespective of its legal status and the way it is financed. Even a state organ may act as an undertaking. However, where a state organ merely exercises its public powers which are not of an economic nature to justify the application of the TFEU rules of competition, such an entity is not an undertaking for the purpose of EU competition rules. In certain circumstances, the discharge of the public powers and the economic activity of the entity may be capable of sufficient differentiation that the public entity may be regarded as an undertaking in relation to part of its activities. However, where a public entity exercises an economic activity which cannot be separated from the exercise of its public powers, then those activities must be considered to be connected with the exercise of public powers and thus immune from scrutiny under EU competition laws.[481]

12-335   These principles were applied in *Compass-Datenbank GmbH v Republic of Austria*.[482] The Republic of Austria operated a company register database service for Austrian companies' information and appointed several firms which did not include Compass-Datenbank as billing agents for access following a public procurement procedure. In 2001, Austria began an action against Compass-Datenbank for infringement of database right seeking to prevent it from using data from the company register. Compass-Datenbank counterclaimed claiming inter alia that Austria was an undertaking and that it was thus obliged to provide the information pursuant to the "essential facilities" doctrine. The Supreme Court of Austria referred to the CJEU the question concerning whether Austria acted as an undertaking for the purpose of art.102. Having recited the principles in the previous paragraph, it said that a data collection activity which was conducted on the basis of a statutory obligation fell within the exercise of public powers and that such an endeavour was not an economic activity even though consumers were charged for accessing the data.[483]

12-336   If the parent company can exercise effective control over the activities of its subsidiary, then the parent and subsidiary will be treated as one economic unit for the purposes of art.102.[484] Separate undertakings might be treated for a particular purpose as a single economic unit. This could be in the case of joint ventures, where actual control vests in the parents.

---

[480] (4/73) [1975] E.C.R. 1663, [1976] 1 C.M.L.R. 295 at [371].
[481] The above principles are conveniently set out in [35]–[38] of *Compass-Datenbank GmbH v Republik Österreich* (C-138/11) ECLI:EU:C:2012:449.
[482] *Compass-Datenbank GmbH v Republik Österreich* (C-138/11), at [35]–[38].
[483] See [40].
[484] *Béguelin* [1971] E.C.R. 949; *Centrafarm v Sterling* (C15–74) [1974] E.C.R. 1147; (6–72) [1974]

On the second issue, art.102 suggests that two or more undertakings can abuse **12-337** a dominant position.

In *Airtours v Commission*,[485] the General Court held that there were three condi- **12-338** tions for a finding of collective dominance: (i) each member of the alleged dominant oligopoly must have the ability to know how other members are behaving in order to monitor whether or not they are adopting the common policy; (ii) there must be tacit co-ordination over time and there must be adequate deterrents to ensure that there is a long-term incentive not to depart from the common policy; and (iii) the foreseeable reaction of current and future competitors and consumers must not be able to jeopardise the results expected from the common policy.[486]

E.C.R. 223.

[485] (T-342/99) ECLI:EU:T:2002:146.

[486] See [62]. This test has been cited in other cases, e.g. *Independent Music Publishers and Labels Association (Impala) v Commission of the European Communities* ECLI:EU:T:2006:216 at [247]; on appeal, (C-413/06P) [2008] E.C.R. I-04951 at [121]–[124] See also, F.E. Mezzanotte, "Using Abuse of Collective Dominance in Article 102 TFEU to Fight Tacit Collusion: The Problem of Proof and Inferential Error" (2010) 33(1) *World Competition*, 77–102.

CHAPTER 13

ENFORCEMENT OF COMPETITION LAW IN THE EU

INTRODUCTION

This chapter is concerned with how EU competition law, primarily arts 101 and **13-001** 102 of the TFEU, is enforced in the EU—by the European Commission, national competition authorities of Member States and the national courts. It also examines the division of enforcement between the EU institutions and Member States. It is not intended to be exhaustive or complete but rather to give the practitioner in intellectual property law in the EU, a reasonable understanding of how competition law is enforced in the EU. Indeed, it may legitimately be asked why there is such a chapter in this book. The answer is that as will be appreciated from other chapters, intellectual property and competition law have for many years been closely related. Indeed, the enforcement of intellectual property rights is, as seen in other chapters, capable of being prohibited and has been prohibited under both arts 101 and 102. Furthermore, both ultimately serve the same aim—the improvement of consumer welfare. Thus, an intellectual property practitioner should be familiar with how competition law can be enforced in the EU.

The subject of Euro-defences is considered in a separate chapter. By "Euro- **13-002** defences", one means defences which are not contained specifically in IP legislation but defences which arise by reason of direct application of the articles of the TFEU or of secondary legislation which is not peculiar to the IPR in issue.

First it is necessary to consider the various bodies that can enforce EU competi- **13-003** tion law. These are the European Commission, national competition authorities ("NCAs") and national courts—all have different but overlapping roles, for the purpose of enforcing arts 101 and 102.

DG Competition

The Competition Directorate-General ("DGCOMP"), one of the Directorate- **13-004** Generals of the European Commission is responsible for the establishment and implementation of an effective and coherent competition policy for the EU. It derives this responsibility from the EU Treaty (primarily the TFEU) and secondary legislation, primarily Reg.1/2003[1] which is known as "the Modernisation Regulation".

13-005   In furtherance of this responsibility, DGCOMP has two distinct roles: first it acts as an investigative authority; and secondly acts as a first instance tribunal, whereby it determines whether activities of undertakings are compatible with EU competition law. It also has a role under the TFEU to put forward legislative proposals to give effect to arts 101 and 102 to the European Parliament.

13-006   In furtherance of its investigative role, DGCOMP can act on its own initiative or following complaints from states, firms or individuals, or where agreements are notified by individuals. It has legal powers to gather evidence, including the conduct of "dawn raids", the compulsory disclosure of documentation and the compulsory answering of questions. In furtherance of its judicial role, DGCOMP has the power to order the parties to cease and desist; to fine the undertakings concerned; and to impose periodic penalty payments. In the carrying out of its legislative role, it is the initiator of all Community competition legislation.

13-007   It is important to emphasise that DGCOMP is concerned only with the enforcement of Articles of the TFEU concerned with competition. It is not concerned with the enforcement of the Articles on free movement of goods which feature strongly in intellectual property disputes. Another Directorate-General for the Internal Market is responsible for harmonisation of the internal market but it has no equivalent investigative/judicial capacity to DGCOMP.

National competition authorities ("NCAs")

13-008   Following their accession to the TFEU and its predecessor Treaties, Member States have slowly aligned their national laws on competition with those of the TFEU. Thus, the UK has enacted the Competition Act 1998, whose main provisions mirror arts 101 and 102 but substitute the need to show an effect on trade between Member States with the need to show an effect on trade in the UK. Not only are national competition laws aligning themselves to EU law but, in certain Member States, NCAs will be responsible for the enforcement of EU law and national law. Therefore, in certain circumstances, anti-competitive conduct may affect trade between Member States but principally affect only one Member State. In such circumstances, the Commission may leave the issue of enforcement of EU law to the national competition authority on the basis of subsidiarity. In the UK, as from April 2014, the new Competition and Markets Authority ("CMA") will become the UK NCA and it combines the previous roles of the Office of Fair Trading and the Competition Commission.

National courts

13-009   With the introduction of the Modernisation Regulation, national courts now play an important and increasing role in the enforcement of EU competition laws. Unlike the European Commission and NCAs, courts can award damages to a party who is the victim of conduct which infringes arts 101 or 102. Only they can

---

[1]   Reg.1/2003 on the implementation of competition laid down in arts 81 and 82 of the Treaty [2003] OJ L1/1 as amended by Reg.411/2004 [2004] OJ L68/1.

determine the effect on contractual relationships where a term or terms is found to be void under art.101(2). They are often better placed to take interim measures.[2] They can combine a claim under competition law with a claim under national law. Finally, courts can award legal costs to the successful applicant but such is not possible in administrative procedure before the Commission.[3] In particular, the Modernisation Regulation now permits them to consider whether conduct which infringes art.101(1) is exempt under art.101(3).

However, the major benefit of a complaint to the EC Commission or an NCA is **13-010** that if they are sufficiently interested, they will investigate the complaint at no cost to the complainant. Furthermore, they will usually have better experience and resources than individuals to investigate a complaint properly. Courts are essentially passive and can only referee disputes between private undertakings or individuals.

Modernisation Regulation

On 1 May 2004, the Modernisation Regulation came into force.[4] This repealed **13-011** Reg.17/62. It radically changed the enforcement of arts 101 and 102. The major change is that agreements which satisfy the conditions of art.101(3) are not prohibited under art.101(2) without the need for a decision from the European Commission or indeed any authority.[5] Indeed, parties can no longer notify agreements to the European Commission for the purpose of obtaining exemption.[6]

The main reason for this fundamental change was because the Commission's **13-012** monopoly on exempting agreements under art.101(3) was a significant obstacle to the effective application of art.101 by national competition authorities and national courts. In short, when weighing up the validity of an agreement under art.101, it did not make sense to ignore half the equation, namely the pro-competitive gains from an agreement which had prima facie anti-competitive restraints in court proceedings or otherwise "in one go".

Other reasons for the Commission relinquishing the exclusive right to exempt **13-013** under art.101(3) were as follows. First, the notification system rarely revealed agreements that were seriously anti-competitive. Secondly, the notification system imposed a significant burden on industry by increasing compliance costs and preventing companies from enforcing their agreements without notifying them to the Commission. This was particularly detrimental to SMEs. Thirdly, the reservation of the power to exempt worked well for a community of six Member States where there was little competition culture. However by the 21st century, a mature competition culture had developed in both the Community and Member States. The Commission had much less to fear about inappropriate and non-uniform application of art.101(3) by national courts and NCAs. Fourthly, the European Commis-

---

[2] The EC Commission can only take interim measures where there is a risk of serious and irreparable damage to competition. It cannot do so on the basis of a complaint: art.8 Reg.1/2003; Commission Notice on the handling of complaints by the Commission under Articles 81 and 82 of the EC Treaty [2004] OJ C101/65, para.80. It should be noted that NCAs are often well placed to adopt interim measures.

[3] Notice on Handling Complaints [2004] OJ C101/65, para.16.

[4] Reg.1/2003 [2003] OJ L1/1 as amended by Reg.411/2004 [2004] OJ L6811.

[5] art.1(2) Reg.1/2003.

[6] art.10 Reg.1/2003 only permits the Commission to declare an agreement to satisfy art.101(1) or art.101(3) of its own motion and where there is a "Community public interest".

sion needed to prioritise its own resources to investigating serious anti-competitive conduct and such was not helped by the burden of being the only organisation that could exempt agreements under art.101(3).

13-014   The effect of the Modernisation Regulation is to simplify the enforcement of arts 101 and 102 both at an EU and national level. However, the inability to obtain formal exemption of an individual agreement via notification to the EC Commission increases uncertainty. Coupled with the more economics-based approach that typifies current competition law, it places the burden on legal and economic advisors to undertakings to ensure that agreements and conduct of companies are not contrary to arts 101 and 102. In general, this should not trouble legal and economic advisors of small or medium-sized companies as agreements between such entities now benefit from block exemptions which favour exemption up to certain defined market thresholds. Furthermore, detailed advice in the way of Notices from the Commission mean that there is considerable transparency as to the approach that should be undertaken in analysing the competitive effect of agreements or behaviour of an undertaking. Thus, courts can approach the application of EU competition law with considerable confidence.

Relationship between arts 101 and 102 and national competition laws

13-015   It is inevitable that both national competition laws and arts 101 and 102 will be applicable to certain types of anti-competitive conduct if the effect of that conduct is felt in the EU. Indeed, many countries have amended their competition laws so as to provide for a domestic version of arts 101 and 102. Thus, an anti-competitive agreement which affects business in the UK, France and Germany will be prohibited under both EU and the national laws of the three countries.

13-016   The Modernisation Regulation seeks to regulate the application of national competition law by NCAs and national courts where the alleged conduct of the parties may affect trade between Member States. As was discussed in Ch.8, "Intellectual Property and Art.101", the requirement of "may affect trade between Member States" is a jurisdictional one which determines the application of art.101. If conduct only affects trade in one Member State, then art.101 has no application.[7]

13-017   Where an agreement or conduct may have an effect on trade between Member States within the meaning of art.101, then the following principles apply:

- NCAs or national courts must apply art.101(1) in parallel with national competition law[8];
- if the agreement or conduct is *not* prohibited under art.101 (either because it falls outside art.101(1) or fulfils the conditions under art.101(3)), then national competition law may not prohibit such agreements[9];
- if the agreement or conduct is *does* perceptibly restrict competition within the EU and *not* fulfil the conditions under art.101(3), then NCAs may apply in parallel national competition law[10]; and

---

[7]   See para.8-093.
[8]   art.3.1 Reg.1/2003; *Expedia v Droit de la Concurrence* (C-226/11) ECLI:EU:C:2012:795 at [18], *Toshiba Corporation* (C-17/10) ECLI:EU:C:2012:72 at [77].
[9]   art.3.2 Reg.1/2003; *Expedia v Droit de la Concurrence*, at [19].
[10]   *Expedia v Droit de la Concurrence*, at [20]. It might be thought that if an agreement is prohibited under art.101, it is academic if it is also prohibited under national competition law. However, the remedies for breach of national competition laws may be different to that under art.101.

- if the provisions of national law "predominantly pursue an objective different from that pursued by Articles 101 & 102", then NCAs are not precluded from applying them.[11]

In relation to art.102, where the alleged abusive conduct may have an effect on trade between Member States as defined in art.102: **13-018**

- NCAs must apply art.102 as well as national competition law[12]; and
- NCAs may apply stricter national laws which prohibit or sanction *unilateral* conduct engaged in by undertakings. Thus, if unilateral conduct, which may affect trade between Member States, is found not to be contrary to art.102, NCAs may determine that it is contrary to equivalent measures in their own national competition law.[13] As seen above, the opposite applies for art.101.

Neither NCAs nor courts can rule that an alleged anti-competitive practice does *not* breach art.102. Only the European Commission can grant such negative declaratory relief.[14] Thus, if in the process of investigating an alleged breach of art.102 and the equivalent provision under national competition law, the NCA concludes that no breach of art.102 has occurred, they are limited to saying that there are no grounds for action on its part.

Where conduct is limited to one Member State and thus does not affect trade between Member States, then only national competition law applies. As many countries have aligned their competition laws to provide for a domestic version of arts 101 and 102, then in effect, such will involve consideration of the same matters, issues and law but without the need to establish that the conduct of which complaint is made may affect trade between Member States. **13-019**

Relation Between NCAs, European Commission and National Courts

Often, there will be parallel proceedings where NCAs, national courts or the Commission are seeking to apply art.101 and/or art.102 to the same conduct. The Modernisation Regulation regulates what may happen in those circumstances. **13-020**

National courts

The basic rule is that national courts cannot take decisions "running counter" to a decision adopted by the European Commission.[15] Furthermore, they must avoid giving decisions which would conflict with a decision contemplated by the European Commission.[16] Thus, a national court must assess whether it is necessary to stay its proceedings, pending resolution of the dispute by the European Commission, although it may always make a preliminary reference to the CJEU if it sees fit.[17] **13-021**

The Modernisation Regulation makes provision for co-operation between **13-022**

---

[11] art.3.3 Reg.1/2003.
[12] art.3(1).
[13] art.3(2).
[14] art.5; art.10 Reg.1/2003. *Prezes Urzędu Ochrony Konkurencji i Konsumentów v Tele2 Polska sp. z o.o., devenue Netia SA* (C-375/09) [2011] E.C.R. I-3055.
[15] art.16.1.
[16] art.16.1.
[17] art.16.1.

national courts and the Commission including the answering of questions and the transmission of information.[18]

NCAs

13-023 Similarly, NCAs cannot take a decision which would run counter to a Commission decision.[19] NCAs and the European Commission are required to work in "close co-operation".[20] Detailed provisions are made as to how this should be done.[21] However, once the Commission has initiated proceedings in relation to the same subject matter, NCAs are relieved of their competence to apply arts 101 and 102.[22] However, if an NCA is already acting on a case, then, vice versa, the Commission can only initiate proceedings after consulting with the NCA.[23]

ENFORCEMENT OF ARTS 101 AND 102 BY THE EUROPEAN COMMISSION

Investigative powers

13-024 The European Commission can investigate conduct which is suspected of infringing arts 101 or 102. It can do this either of its own motion or if a complaint is made by a third party. In this regard, it has a number of investigative powers. These are:

(i)   The ability to inspect undertakings including carrying out inspections of premises, land, the examination of books, and the taking of copies.[24] If an order for inspection is taken by a decision of the Commission, then undertakings are required to submit to such inspections.[25] The decision must set out the penalties payable for failure to submit to the inspection.[26]

It can inspect home premises where it has a "reasonable suspicion" that books or other records are being kept at such premises.[27] It must take a decision in this regard which is capable of being reviewed by the CJEU.[28] To carry out a home inspection, a national judicial authority of the Member State concerned must give prior authorisation. This cannot be refused unless the measures envisaged are arbitrary or excessive, having regard to the seriousness of the suspected infringement, the importance of the evidence sought, the involvement of the undertaking concerned, and the likelihood that business books and records relating to the subject matter of the inspection are kept in the premises for which authorisation is

---

[18]   art.15.
[19]   art.16.2.
[20]   art.11.1.
[21]   arts 11 and 12 (exchange of information between Commission and NCA).
[22]   art.11.6.
[23]   art.11.6.
[24]   art.20.
[25]   art.20.4.
[26]   art.20.4; art.24.1(e). See *Hoechst AG v EC Commission* (46/78R) [1987] E.C.R. 1549; [1988] 4 C.M.L.R. 430, where *Hoechst* refused to submit to a decision ordering an investigation of the company on the basis that it was seeking an annulment of the decision. The Commission carried out the investigation a month later and fixed a periodic penalty payment of 55,000 ECU representing 55 days of delay. This was upheld by the CJEU.
[27]   art.21.
[28]   art.21.2.

sought.[29] The national judicial authority cannot call into question the necessity for the inspection nor demand that it be provided with information in the Commission's file.[30] The right to privacy and family life as provided by art.8(1) of the European Convention on Human Rights cannot prevent the Commission from carrying out an investigative raid at business premises, even if that happens to be someone's home.[31] It may be that the party being investigated can claim the privilege of self-incrimination.[32] Equally, the party may be able to claim legal privilege over documents discovered in the raid.[33] An appeal to the CJEU for an interim order temporarily suspending the decision of the Commission is unlikely to succeed.[34]

The CJEU has indicated that the Commission will not be entitled to use papers or documents, taken in the course of an investigation pursuant to a decision by the Commission which is then subsequently annulled by the CJEU under art.230, for the purposes of establishing an infringement of arts 101 or 102.[35] During an investigation, the Commission considers that there is a positive duty on the undertakings to assist the Commission officials in the carrying out of the investigation, including the identification of relevant documents.[36] It is not sufficient for a representative of the investigated undertaking to refuse to produce documentation on the basis that they cannot disclose them without the authority of a more senior officer of the undertaking.[37] Undertakings do not have the right to have a lawyer present during the investigation. However, the Commission will allow the undertakings time to summon their lawyers unless there are in-house lawyers present, upon appropriate undertakings as to non-interference with business records.[38]

(ii) The Commission may request undertakings to provide all necessary information.[39] It can either make a simple request or a decision. If it makes

---

[29] art.21.3.

[30] art.21.3.

[31] *Dow Benelux NV v EC Commission* (46/78R) [1987] E.C.R. 1549, [1988] 4 C.M.L.R. 430; *Dow Chemical Iberica SA v EC Commission* [1987] E.C.R. 1549, [1988] 4 C.M.L.R. 430 at 465.

[32] See para.13-036.

[33] See para.13-034.

[34] (46/87R) [1987] E.C.R. 1549, [1988] 4 C.M.L.R. 430 (Interim Order of President of Court of Justice); *Dow Chemical Nederland BV v EC Commission* (87/87R) [1988] 4 C.M.L.R. 439 (Interim Order of President of Court of Justice). The court said that it would be difficult to say that irreparable harm would be caused by such a decision (a condition for the award of interim relief) and would amount to pre-judging a decision on the main issue of the case.

[35] (87/87R) [1988] 4 C.M.L.R. 439.

[36] Commission Decision. *Fabbrica Pisana et al.* (80/334/EEC) [1980] OJ L75/30; [1980] 2 C.M.L.R. 354.

[37] Commission Decision. *FNICF* (82/756/EEC) [1982] OJ L319/12; [1983] 1 C.M.L.R. 575.

[38] *National Panasonic v EC Commission* (136/79) [1980] E.C.R. 2033, [1980] 3 C.M.L.R. 169. Also see *Hoechst AG v EC Commission* (46/87) [1989] E.C.R. 2859, [1991] 4 C.M.L.R. 410; *Dow Benelux NV v EC Commission* (85/87) [1989] E.C.R. 3137, [1991] 4 C.M.L.R. 410; *Dow Chemical Iberica SA v EC Commission* (97/87) [1989] E.C.R. 3167, [1991] 4 C.M.L.R. 410 at [16], where the CJEU held that the Commission must respect the right to legal representation as from the preliminary inquiry stage.

[39] art.18.

a decision, then a refusal to comply with that decision can, if specified in the decision, give rise to a liability to pay periodic penalty payments.[40]

(iii) The Commission may take statements from witnesses who consent to be interviewed for the purpose of collecting information relating to the subject matter of an investigation.[41]

13-025   Because the Commission acts as judge and executioner (i.e. it makes the decision for inspection and then carries it out), and there is no need for judicial approval of a decision by the Commission to order inspection,[42] the General Court has given guidance as to what must go in a decision to inspect. Therefore, the Commission must:

- Set out the presumed facts which it intends to investigate (but this does not extend to disclosing all the information that it has as its disposal concerning the alleged infringement).
- Identify with sufficient but not absolute precision the business sectors covered by the alleged infringement, so as to enable the undertaking to assess the scope of its duty to co-operate with the Commission.
- Identify with sufficient precision the product and geographic markets that form the subject matter of the investigation.[43]

13-026   However, within those bounds, and provided that the Commission decision to grant an order for inspection is properly reasoned and based on facts and matters that have come to its attention to give rise to a reasonable suspicion, the General Court will not interfere lightly in such a decision. For example, on the basis that such was disproportionate as there was a lack of evidence that an undertaking would destroy or not disclose documents and it would have been proportionate merely to request information from the undertaking.[44]

Interim remedies

13-027   In cases of urgency, the Commission may, by decision, on the basis of a prima facie finding of infringement, order interim measures.[45] This can be accompanied with the imposition of periodic penalty payments if the undertaking refuses to comply.[46]

13-028   Prior to the Modernisation Regulation, the court had said that a decision granting interim relief can only be made when it is shown that: (i) the need for such an order is urgent; (ii) the acts complained of are likely to cause serious and ir-

---

[40]   art.18.2, art.24.
[41]   art.19.
[42]   See *Deutsche Bahn AG v Commission* (T-289/11, T-290/11 and T-521/11) ECLI:EU:T:2013:404 where the General Court rejected a complaint that an inspection decision which was not linked or tied to a prior judicial order infringes art.7 (right of privacy) of the Charter of Fundamental Rights and were thus disproportionate.
[43]   *Prysmian SpA and Prysmian Cavi e Sistemi Energia Srl v European Commission* (T-140/09) ECLI:EU:T:212:597 (a judgment of the General Court concerning whether an order for inspection should be annulled). The General Court annulled the decision insofar as it related to certain group of products.
[44]   *Deutsche Bahn AG*, at [185]-[224].
[45]   art.8 Reg.1/2003.
[46]   art.24.1(b).

reparable damage; or (iii) the behaviour complained of is intolerable to the public.[47] Damage which is purely financial is not serious and irreparable for the purposes of interim measures, unless, in the event of success in the main action, it cannot be recouped.[48] The relief ordered must be temporary and conservatory, and restricted to what is required.[49] The Commission has said that such an order must not exceed the framework of the Commission's powers to make such an order in a final decision.[50] The party requesting interim measures may be required to give a cross-undertaking as to damages to the party against which interim measures are sought if, at a later stage, the latter party was found not to infringe arts 101 or 102. The Commission has considerable discretion as to whether or not to grant interim relief and the General Court will be reluctant to interfere in the exercise of that discretion.[51]

Final remedies

If a finding of an infringement of arts 101 or 102 is made, the Commission has **13-029** a number of options:

(i) It can order the undertakings concerned to bring the infringement to an end. For this purpose, it may impose on them any behavioural or structural remedies which are proportionate to the infringement committed and necessary to bring the infringement effectively to an end.[52] However, structural remedies can only be imposed when there is no equally effective behavioural remedy or where any equally effective behavioural remedy would be more burdensome for the undertaking concerned than the structural remedy.[53] The above orders can be accompanied by the imposition of periodic penalty payments to compel undertakings to abide by the order of the Commission.[54]

Instead of imposing such remedies, the undertakings concerned can, prior to the Commission adopting a formal decision, offer "commitments" to meet the concerns expressed by the Commission in its preliminary assessment.[55] The Commission may then by decision make those commitments binding on the undertakings. This decision can impose periodic penalty payments if the undertaking refuses to comply.[56]

(ii) The Commission may impose fines where the conduct found to infringe arts 101 or 102 has been done intentionally or negligently.[57] Such fines must not exceed 10 per cent of the total turnover of the undertakings in the preceding business year.[58] An amount of the fines is determined by the

---

[47] *Camera Care Ltd v EC Commission* (792/79R) [1980] E.C.R. 119, 131; [1980] 1 C.M.L.R. 334.
[48] *Cargill v EC Commission* (229/88R) [1989] 1 C.M.L.R. 304 CJEU.
[49] (229/88R) [1989] 1 C.M.L.R. 304 CJEU.
[50] *Brass Band Instruments Ltd v Boosey & Hawkes Plc* [1987] OJ L286/36; [1988] 4 C.M.L.R. 67.
[51] *Cosimex GmbH v EC Commission* (T-131/89R) [1990] II-1 E.C.R.; [1992] 4 C.M.L.R. 395.
[52] art.7.1 Reg.1/2003.
[53] art.7.1.
[54] art.24.
[55] art.9.
[56] art.24.1(c).
[57] art.23.2.
[58] art.23.2.

gravity and duration of the infringement.[59] Thus, in the *Microsoft* decision,[60] the Commission imposed a fine of $2 million on Microsoft. The Commission may impose fines on a punitive basis (provided it does not exceed the legal limit) so as to deter others from breaking the rules on competition in the TFEU.[61] Ignorance of arts 101 or 102 is no excuse where it is clear that the behaviour complained of has had as its object the restriction of competition.[62] Ultimately, the question of fines is very much at the discretion of the Commission.[63] In 2006, the Commission issued a Notice setting out its approach to fining undertakings which provides a very helpful guide to the likely amount that the Commission will fine.[64]

Limitation periods

13-030   The imposition of fines is subject to limitation periods. This is five years for substantive infringements and three years for certain procedural infringements.[65] Time begins to run on the day on which the infringement is committed but where the infringement is repeated or continuing, time runs on the day on which the infringement ceases.[66] Thus, in the case of an anti-competitive agreement, the relevant date will be the date when the undertakings concerned ceased to implement the agreement.[67]

13-031   Where any action is taken by the Commission for the purpose of the preliminary investigation or proceedings in respect of an infringement, this will start time running afresh.[68] However, even allowing for interruptions, the Commission cannot impose fines for substantive infringements which occurred greater than 10 years earlier.[69] Time is suspended (as opposed to interrupted) where the Commission's decision is subject to appeal to the CJEU.[70]

---

[59]   art.23.3.
[60]   *Microsoft* [2005] 4 C.M.L.R. 19. This was upheld on appeal—*Microsoft Corp v Commission of the European Communities* (T-201/04) [2007] 5 C.M.L.R. 11; [2007] E.C.R. II-3601.
[61]   See *Musique Diffusion Française v EC Commission* (100/80) [1983] E.C.R. 1825; [1983] 3 C.M.L.R. 221. See also *KME Germany AG v European Commission* (C-389/10P) [2011] E.C.R. 0000.
[62]   *Miller v EC Commission* (19/77) [1978] E.C.R. 131; [1978] 2 C.M.L.R. 334.
[63]   e.g. see *NV Koninklijke KNP BT v EC Commission* (C-248/98P) [2000] E.C.R. I-9641, where the CJEU summarises the approach to be taken to fining parties which includes a consideration of who is the "ringleader" in a cartel and emphasises that normally it will be based on turnover of the offenders.
[64]   Guidelines on the method of setting fines imposed pursuant to art.23(2)(a) of Reg.1/2003 [2006] OJ C210/2-5.
[65]   Reg.1/2003 art.25.1(a)-(b).
[66]   art.25.2. In *Montecatini SpA v EC Commission* (C-235/92P) [1999] E.C.R. I-4539, the CJEU held that, although the concept of a continuous infringement has different meanings in the legal orders of the Member States, it comprises a pattern of unlawful conduct implementing a single infringement, united by a common subjective element, see [195]. See also *Siemens AG Österreich v European Commission* (T-122/07) [2011] E.C.R. II-793 where the General Court dismissed an appeal from the European Commission based on art.25.2 that there were two distinct stages of infringement on the grounds that the two stages formed part of a single and continuous infringement (see [101]). This is on appeal to the CJEU.
[67]   See *Re the "Toltecs" and "Dorcet" Trade Marks* (82/987/EC) [1983] OJ L379/19; [1983] 1 C.M.L.R. 412.
[68]   art.25.3 and art.25.5.
[69]   art.25.5.
[70]   art.25.6.

The Modernisation Regulation also imposes a five-year limitation period for the **13-032** enforcement of penalties.[71]

Professional secrecy

Article 339 TFEU requires institutions of the Community not to disclose informa- **13-033** tion of the kind covered by an obligation of professional secrecy. This is respected in the Modernisation Regulation of which art.28 imposes two obligations in this regard:

(i) The Commission can only use information that it collects for the purpose for which it was acquired.[72]
(ii) The Commission cannot disclose information acquired or exchanged by them which is covered by an obligation of professional secrecy.[73] A failure of the Commission to comply with such obligation may give rise to a liability in damages under art.339 TFEU.[74]

Legal privilege

During the carrying out of its investigations, the Commission must have regard **13-034** to the rights of the defence.[75] Thus the CJEU has held that a form of legal privilege applies to communications between a lawyer and their client in relation to possible or actual proceedings against the latter under the now defunct Reg.17.[76] Such communications must be made for the purposes of the client's defence and emanate from an independent lawyer.[77] Thus, privilege will apply to all communications entered into between an independent lawyer and the client after the initiation of an administrative procedure which may lead to a decision on the applicability of arts 101 and 102 and earlier written communications which have a relationship to the subject-matter of that protection.[78] Communications between an "in-house" lawyer and the client will not attract privilege from the Commission's investigation.[79]

---

[71] art.26.
[72] Although this is without prejudice to its right to disclose to NCAs or national courts under arts 12 and 15.
[73] art.28.
[74] *Adams v EC Commission* (145/83) [1985] E.C.R. 3539; [1986] 1 C.M.L.R. 506.
[75] See *Nederlandsche Banden-Industrie Michelin NV v EC Commission* (322/81) [1983] E.C.R. 3461, [1985] 1 C.M.L.R. 282 at [7]; *Hoechst AG v EC Commission* (46/87, 85/87 and 97/87) [1989] E.C.R. 2859, [1991] 4 C.M.L.R. 410; *Akzo Nobel v EC Commission (interim measures)* (T-125/03R and 253/03R) [2004] C.M.L.R. 15.
[76] *AM&S v EC Commission (155/79)* [1982] E.C.R. 1575; [1982] 2 C.M.L.R. 264; (46/87) [1989] E.C.R. 2859; [1991] 4 C.M.L.R. 410 at [16].
[77] *Hilti AV v EC Commission* (T-30/89) [1990] E.C.R. II-163; [1990] 4 C.M.L.R. 602, CFI applying (155/79) [1982] E.C.R. 1575; [1982] 2 C.M.L.R. 264. This rule differs from the English rule where communications between solicitor and client are privileged regardless of the purpose of the communication.
[78] (T-30/89) [1990] E.C.R. II-163; [1990] 4 C.M.L.R. 602 at [13], [14].
[79] (C-155/79) [1982] E.C.R. 1575; [1982] 2 C.M.L.R. 264. See also *Akzo Nobel v EC Commission* (C-550/07P) [2010] E.C.R. I-8301 where the CJEU made it clear that such communications will not benefit from legal privilege and that Reg.1/2003 had not affected the principle set out in *AM&S v EC Commission* (155/79) [1982] E.C.R. 1575; [1982] 2 C.M.L.R. 264.

However, internal documents confined to reporting the text or the content of external independent legal advice are subject to privilege.[80]

13-035   The independent lawyer must be qualified under a Member State's laws.[81] Whilst the communications must be in relation to the initiation of proceedings, this will be interpreted widely.[82] The undertaking may be required to show documentation to the Commission which confirms that it is privileged.[83] Generally, where there is a dispute about the application of legal privilege to documentation, the documents should be sealed and argument on them adjourned to a later date.[84]

Privilege of self-incrimination

13-036   The Commission does not recognise the right to self-incrimination which is an Anglo-Saxon legal concept.[85] However, in the context of Reg.17 which the Modernisation Regulation replaces, the CJEU has, in *Orkem SA v EC Commission*,[86] considered whether an undertaking has the right to remain silent in the face of a request for information under art.11(5) of the defunct Reg.17. It held that:

> "Accordingly, whilst the Commission is entitled, in order to preserve the useful effect of Article 11(2) and (5) of Regulation 17, to compel an undertaking to provide all necessary information concerning such facts as may be known to it and to disclose to it, if necessary, such documents relating thereto as are in its possession, even if the latter may be used to establish, against it or another undertaking, the existence of anti-competitive conduct, it may not, by means of a decision calling for information, undermine the rights of defence of the undertaking concerned.
>
> Thus, the Commission may not compel an undertaking to provide it with answers which might involve an admission on its part of the existence of an infringement which it is incumbent upon the Commission to prove."[87]

13-037   The above right is narrower than the English right against self-incrimination. The latter provides a right to remain silent if the answer would be likely to expose a person to criminal proceedings, whilst the former only provides a right to remain silent if the answer would involve an admission. Thus, in *Orkem & Solvay*, a case which concerned suspected cartels in the PVC trade, the CJEU held that questions which related to meetings of the producers, which were intended only to discover the circumstances in which the meetings were held, the capacity in which the participants attended them and as to what price level measures were taken and how they were to be implemented, were permissible. However, it held that questions which sought an acknowledgment of the undertakings' involvement in price-

---

[80] (T-30/89) [1990] E.C.R. II-163; [1990] 4 C.M.L.R. 602 at [18].

[81] (C-155/79) [1982] E.C.R. 1575; [1982] 2 C.M.L.R. 264. Thus, communications with a lawyer qualified in, e.g. the US, will not qualify for legal privilege.

[82] In (C-155/79) [1982] E.C.R. 1575; [1982] 2 C.M.L.R. 264, the court held that legal privilege attached to communications in 1972 prior to the UK's accession in relation to proceedings started by the Commission in 1979.

[83] (C-155/79) [1982] E.C.R. 1575; [1982] 2 C.M.L.R. 264.

[84] *Akzo Nobel v EC Commission (interim measures)* (T-125/03R and 253/03R) [2003] E.C.R. II-4771; [2004] C.M.L.R. 15.

[85] See *17th Annual Report on Competition Policy*, p.55.

[86] *Orkem SA v EC Commission; Solvay & CIE v EC Commission* (374/87 and 27/88) [1989] E.C.R. 3283; [1991] 4 C.M.L.R. 502.

[87] (374/87 and 27/88) [1989] E.C.R. 3283, [1991] 4 C.M.L.R. 502 at [34]-[35]. See also (46/87R) [1987] E.C.R. 1549, [1989] 4 C.M.L.R. 439; (85/87) [1989] E.C.R. 3137, [1991] 4 C.M.L.R. 410; (97/87) [1989] E.C.R. 2859, [1991] 4 C.M.L.R. 410.

fixing and production-control agreements were not permissible.[88] It will be appreciated that the distinction between questions designed to elicit facts and those designed to elicit admissions will often be a fine one. A request by the European Commission that called on an undertaking to describe the object of and what occurred at meetings in which it participated and also the results or conclusions of those meetings where it is suspected that the object of the meetings was to restrict competition, was impermissible as they were liable to compel the undertaking concerned to admit its participation in an infringement of the Community competition rules.[89]

Article 6(1) of the European Convention on Human Rights

The European Court of Human Rights held in *Funke* that art.6(1) of the ECHR **13-038** (right to a fair trial, etc.) contained an unconditional right to remain silent.[90] In such circumstances, it may be that the authority of *Orkem & Solvay* is in conflict with the ECHR where there is no privilege of self-incrimination.

However, the ECHR has said that it is permissible to take into account a party's **13-039** silence where the situation clearly calls for an explanation from the party.[91]

Moreover, the General Court has said the following in relation to such arguments: **13-040**

"However, it must be emphasised that Community law does recognise as fundamental principles both the rights of defence and the right to fair legal process (see *Baustahlgewebe v Commission*, cited above, paragraph 21, and Case C-7/98 *Krombach* [2000] E.C.R. I-1935, paragraph 26). It is in application of those principles, which offer, in the specific field of competition law, at issue in the present case, protection equivalent to that guaranteed by Article 6 of the Convention, that the Court of Justice and the Court of First Instance have consistently held that the recipient of requests sent by the Commission pursuant to Article 11(5) of Regulation No 17 is entitled to confine himself to answering questions of a purely factual nature and to producing only the pre-existing documents and materials sought and, moreover, is so entitled as from the very first stage of an investigation initiated by the Commission.

The mere fact of being obliged to answer purely factual questions put by the Commission and to comply with its requests for the production of documents already in existence cannot constitute a breach of the principle of respect for the rights of defence or impair the right to fair legal process. There is nothing to prevent the addressee of such questions or requests from showing, whether later during the administrative procedure or in proceedings before the Community courts, when exercising his rights of defence, that the facts set out in his replies or the documents produced by him have a different meaning from that ascribed to them by the Commission."[92]

The reluctance to transpose ECHR jurisprudence to Commission investigations **13-041**

---

[88] See [38]–[41].

[89] *Raiffeisen Zentralbank Österreich AG v Commission* (T-259/02) [2006] E.C.R. II-5169 at [540].

[90] *Funke v France* [1993] 1 C.M.L.R. 897; [1993] 16 E.H.R.R. 297.

[91] *Murray v United Kingdom* [1996] 22 E.H.R.R. 29 at [47]. Generally, see R. Clayton QC and H. Tomlinson QC, *The Law of Human* Rights (Oxford: Oxford University Press, 2000), para.11.211 where the authors discuss the freedom from self-incrimination. See also W.B.J. Overbeek, "The Right to Remain Silent in Competition Investigations: the Funke decision of the Court of Human Rights makes revision of the CJEU's case law necessary" [1994] 15 E.C.L.R. 127 and G. Cumming, "Procedural comment—Privilege Against Self-Incrimination Bernard Crehan v (1) The Inntrepreneur Pub Company (IPC) and (2) Brewman Group Ltd (2004)" 2005 E.C.L.R. 26(7), 375-379.

[92] *Mannesmannröhren-Werke AG v EC Commission* (T-112/98) [2001] 5 C.M.L.R. 1. Upheld on appeal *Salzgitter Mannesmannröhren-Werke AG v EC Commission* (C-411/04P) [2007] E.C.R. I-959; [2007] 4 C.M.L.R. 17. See also *Raiffeisen Zentralbank Österreich A.G. v Commission* (T-259/02)

was reinforced on the appeal of this case to the CJEU (*Salzgitter Mannesmannröhren-Werke AG v EC Commission*),[93] where it was argued by the undertaking that the Court of First Instance (CFI) had been wrong to admit an incriminating document from a source which wished to remain confidential and thus whose identity was not disclosed to the appellant as such was contrary to ECHR. The CJEU said:

> "[42] However, as the Commission rightly claims, the case-law of the European Court of Human Rights cited by the appellant is not decisive in the present case. As the Advocate General observed at points 54 to 56 of his Opinion, that case-law concerns in particular evidence in criminal proceedings, whereas the present case concerns a written document in the context of a proceeding under Article 81 EC. In Community competition law cases, oral evidence plays only a minor role, whereas written documents play a central role.
>
> [43] As the Advocate General also observed at points 57 to 60 of his Opinion, the taking of evidence in Community competition law cases is characterised by the fact that the documents examined often contain business secrets or other information that cannot be disclosed or the disclosure of which is subject to significant restrictions.
>
> [44] In those conditions specific to the Commission's investigations into anti-competitive practices, the principle that everyone has the right to a fair legal process cannot be interpreted as meaning that documents containing incriminating evidence must automatically be excluded as evidence when certain information must remain confidential. That confidentiality may also relate to the identity of the authors of the documents and also to persons who transmitted them to the Commission."

Hearings and rights of defence

13-042   The CJEU has recognised the general principle of EU law that everyone is entitled to a fair legal process.[94] Before the Commission takes any adverse decision, it must give the undertakings concerned the opportunity of being heard on the matters to which the Commission has taken objection.[95] The Commission can only base its decision on objections which the parties concerned have been able to comment.[96]

13-043   Furthermore, the Modernisation Regulation says that the rights of defence of the parties concerned shall be "fully respected".[97] Thus, they are entitled to access to the Commission's file subject to the legitimate interests of undertakings in protection of their business secrets.[98] However, the rights of access do not extend to confidential information and internal documents of the Commission or NCAs.

---

at [539].

[93]   See previous note.

[94]   *Baustahlgewebe v EC Commission* (C-185/95P) [1998] E.C.R. I-8417 at [21] (applied by *KME Germany AG v European Commission* (C-272/09 P) [2012] in cases file); *Netherlands and Van der Wal v EC Commission* (C-174/98P and C-189P) [2000] E.C.R. I-1 at [17]; *Eurofood IFSC* (C-341/04) [2006] E.C.R. I-3813 at [65]; *Salzgitter Mannesmannröhren-Werke AG v EC Commission* (C-114/04P) at [40]-[41].

[95]   art.27.

[96]   art.27.

[97]   art.27.1.

[98]   art.15 Reg.773/2004. See *Soda Ash Appeal* (C-109/10P) [2011] E.C.R. I-10329; [2012] 4 C.M.L.R. 1. The CJEU annulled a decision of the General Court which refused to overturn decisions of the European Commission in relation to a company's alleged breach of competition rules where the Commission had not allowed access to the file. The CJEU said that the right of access to the file

These principles embody considerable case law of the CJEU developed under Reg.17/62.

Where the Commission intends to accept commitments or, for reasons of EU public interest, adopts a decision clearing the undertaking, then it must publish a concise summary of the case and interested third parties may submit their observations within a fixed time limit.[99] **13-044**

The procedure for taking an adverse decision is set out in Reg.773/2004.[100] In brief, the Commission must initiate formal proceedings no later than when it issues a preliminary assessment that an undertaking's conduct is contrary to arts 101 or 102.[101] Once it does, then the Commission must issue a Statement of Objections.[102] At the same time, it must set a time limit within which these parties may inform it in writing of their views. The undertakings concerned must file full written submissions in their defence and attach relevant documents.[103] The Commission must consult the Advisory Committee before taking an adverse decision.[104] **13-045**

Undertakings who are the subject of a Statement of Objections have a right to an oral hearing to develop their arguments.[105] Oral hearings are conducted by a Hearing Officer who is fully independent.[106] **13-046**

Complaints

A person or Member State may apply to the Commission complaining about an infringement of arts 101 or 102 by a third party asking them to issue a "cease and desist" order.[107] A person (natural or legal) may only apply if they have a "legitimate interest".[108] However, as the Commission may, on its own initiative, take proceedings following a complaint, it may be sufficient just to alert the Commission, in which case the requirement of legitimate interest becomes academic. **13-047**

Any complaint must contain certain information as prescribed in the implementing regulations.[109] The Commission has published a Notice setting out the Commission's handling of complaints.[110] **13-048**

A complainant does not have the right to demand that the Commission give a *final* decision on the existence or otherwise of the alleged infringement.[111] Upon receipt of the complaint, the Commission has a duty to examine the facts put **13-049**

---

meant that the Commission had to provide undertakings with the opportunity to examine all of the documents in the investigation that might be relevant for its defence including both inculpatory and exculpatory documents with the exception of business secrets.

[99] art.27.4.

[100] Reg.773/2004 relating to the conduct of proceedings by the Commission pursuant to arts 101 and 102 of the EC Treaty [2004] OJ L123/18.

[101] art.2 Reg.773/2004; art.9(1) Reg.1/2003.

[102] art.10 Reg.773/2004.

[103] art.10.3.

[104] art.11 Reg.773/2004; art.11 Reg.1/2003.

[105] art.12 Reg.773/2004.

[106] art.14 Reg.773/2004.

[107] art.7.1 Reg.1/2003.

[108] art.7.2 Reg.1/2003; art.5.1 Reg.773/2004.

[109] art.5.1 Reg.773/2004 [2004] OJ L123/24. NB. Form C (which is referred to in art.5(1) and sets out the information required) is annexed to the PDF but not HTML version.

[110] Notice on the handling of complaints by the Commission under Articles 101 and 102 [2004] OJ C101/65.

[111] *GEMA v EC Commission* (125/78) [1979] E.C.R. 3173, [1980] 2 C.M.L.R. 175 at [17]; *Rendo v EC Commission* (T-16/91) [1992] E.C.R. II-2417 at [98]; *EMC Development AB v European Commission* (C-367/10P) [2011] E.C.R. I-46 at [73].

forward by the complainant in order to decide whether they indicate behaviour likely to distort competition in the Common Market.[112] Even where the behaviour complained of may infringe art.101, the Commission has a discretion as to whether or not to take action. By art.105 TFEU, the Commission is entrusted with the task of ensuring the application of the principles laid down in arts 101 and 102 and is responsible for defining and implementing the orientation of Community competition policy. In order to perform that task effectively, it is entitled to give differing degrees of priority to the complaints brought before it.[113]

13-050   In exercising its discretion as to whether to initiate an investigation, the Commission will give a higher priority to matters which raise a substantial "Community interest".[114] In considering the Community interest, there is a balance between the significance of the alleged infringement and the extent of the investigative measures required for the Commission to perform under the best possible conditions its task of making sure that arts 101 and 102 are complied with. If the alleged anti-competitive effects are confined to the territory of a Member State and there are proceedings before the national competition authority, the Commission will usually reject the complaint for a lack of Community interest.[115] It should be noted that it would appear that the "Community interest" factor has become elevated to a rule of law. Thus, in one case, it was submitted by an undertaking that the Commission was *not* entitled to bring proceedings against it because there was no Community interest.[116] The General Court rejected the argument by referring to the Commission's finding that the export ban complained of was capable of affecting trade between Member States to an appreciable extent.[117] However, it was implicit that the Commission would not have been entitled to initiate investigative proceedings if there had been no Community interest.

13-051   Factors which are relevant to the determination of whether there is a Community interest in further investigation by the Commission are:

(i)   the complainant can bring an action to assert its rights before national courts;

(ii)   the seriousness and duration of the infringements;

(iii)   the effect of the alleged infringement as regards the functioning of the common market;

(iv)   whether the practices have ceased; and

(v)   whether the undertakings concerned have changed their conduct.[118]

13-052   The Commission is not obliged to take into account circumstances that have not been brought to its attention by the complainant and that it could only have

---

[112] See *Demo-Studio Schmidt v EC Commission* (210/81) [1983] E.C.R. 65, [1984] 1 C.M.L.R. 63; *EMC Development AB v European Commission* (C-367/10P) at [74]; *CICCE v EC Commission* (298/83) [1985] E.C.R. 1105, [1986] 1 C.M.L.R. 486; *Automec Srl v EC Commission (No.2)* (T-24/90 and T-28/90) [1992] E.C.R. II-2223, [1992] 5 C.M.L.R. 431, CFI at [78], [79].

[113] *Delimitis v Henninger* (C-234/89) [1991] E.C.R. I-935 at [44]; *UFEX v EC Commission* (C-119/97P) [1999] E.C.R. I-1341, [2000] 4 C.L.M.R. 268 at [88]. Commission Notice on Handling Complaints [2004] OJ C101/65 at [41].

[114] (C-119/97P) [1999] E.C.R. I-1341, [2000] 4 C.M.L.R. 268; (T-24/90) [1992] E.C.R. II-2223, [1992] 5 C.M.L.R. 431. See also Commission Notice on Handling Complaints [2004] OJ C101/65 at [28], [41]-[45].

[115] *BEMIM v EC Commission* (T-114/92) [1995] E.C.R. II-0147, [1996] 4 C.M.L.R. 305.

[116] *Parker Pen Ltd v EC Commission* (T-77/92) [1994] E.C.R. II-549, [1995] 5 C.M.L.R. 435.

[117] (T-77/92) [1995] 5 C.M.L.R. 435.

[118] Commission Notice on Handling Complaints [2004] OJ C101/65 at [44] and cases cited thereto.

uncovered by the investigation of the case.[119] Provided the Commission has properly considered the complaint prior to rejecting it, it can issue a decision rejecting the complaint at any stage. It does not have to issue a Statement of Objections or initiate a formal procedure pursuant to taking an adverse decision against the complainant.[120]

If the Commission considers that, on the basis of the information in its posses- **13-053** sion, there are insufficient grounds for acting on the complaint, either because the information contained in the complaint does not sufficiently substantiate the allegations or because the Commission decides that there is not sufficient Community interest, it must inform the complainant of its reasons and fix a time limit for them to submit any further comments in writing.[121] If the complainant makes known its view within the time limits and its written submissions do not lead to a different assessment of the complaint, the Commission must reject the complaint by decision.[122] If the complainant fails to make known its views within the time limit, the complaint is deemed to have been withdrawn.[123]

The CJEU has emphasised that the Commission must consider attentively all the **13-054** matters of fact and of law which the complainant brings to its attention.[124] Furthermore, complainants are entitled to have the fate of their complaint settled by a reasoned decision of the Commission against which an action for judicial review may be brought.[125] A failure to act by the Commission is reviewable under art.265 TFEU.[126] The reasons stated must be sufficiently precise and detailed to enable the General Court to review effectively the Commission's use of its discretion to define priorities.[127] The purpose of review by the General Court is to ensure that the decision at issue is not based on materially incorrect facts, and not vitiated by any error of law, manifest error of assessment or abuse of power.[128]

Full details about the Commission's procedure on handling a complaint includ- **13-055** ing the complainant's right to become involved with proceedings against a third party which are instigated as a result of the complaint are set out in the Notice on Handling Complaints.[129]

---

[119] Commission Notice on Handling Complaints [2004] OJ C101/65 at [47] citing *FENIN v EC Commission* (T-319/99) [2003] E.C.R. at [43].

[120] *ANCIDES v EC Commission* (43/85) [1987] E.C.R. 3131; [1988] 4 C.M.L.R. 821.

[121] art.7(1) Reg.773/2004 [2004] OJ L123/18. See also (T-24/90) [1992] E.C.R. II-2223 at [82]; Commission Notice on Handling Complaints [2004] OJ C101/65 at [47].

[122] art.7.2 Reg.773/2004. See also *EMC Development AB v European Commission* (C-367/10P) at [75].

[123] art.7.3.

[124] (C-119/97P) [1999] E.C.R. I-1341, [2000] 4 C.M.L.R. 305; *Demo-Studio Schmidt v EC Commission* (C-210/81) [1983] E.C.R. 3045 at [19]; *CICCE v EC Commission* (C-298/83) [1985] E.C.R. 1105 at [18]; and *BAT and Reynolds v EC Commission* (142/84 & 156/84) [1987] E.C.R. 4487 at [20]; *EMC Developments v EC Commission* (C-367/10P) at [74]. See also Commission Notice on Handling Complaints [2004] OJ C101/65 at [47], [53].

[125] *Guérin Automobiles v EC Commission* (C-282/95P) [1997] E.C.R. I-1503 at [36]. It would not appear that this has to be a formal decision—see*Koelman v EC Commission* (C-59/96) [1997] E.C.R. I-4809; [1996] 4 C.M.L.R. 636.

[126] See para.1-086.

[127] *Rendo v EC Commission* (C-19/93P) [1995] E.C.R. I-3319 at [27]; (142/84 & 156/84) [1987] E.C.R. 4487 at [72]; and *VBVB and VBBB v EC Commission* (43/82 & 63/82) [1984] E.C.R. 19 at [22].

[128] *ITT Promedia NV v EC Commission* (T-111/96) [1998] E.C.R. II-2937.

[129] Commission Notice on the handling of complaints by the Commission under Articles 81 and 82 of the EC Treaty [2004] OJ C10/65-77.

Judicial review of the Commission

13-056   As discussed in the introductory chapter to this book, pursuant to art.263 TFEU, the CJEU and the General Court can review the legality of the acts of a Community institution, including the European Commission.[130] Furthermore, pursuant to art.264, where the Commission fails to address an act to a natural or legal person and such constitutes an infringement of the EC Treaty, they may bring an action before the courts to have it so established.

13-057   Any review of the Commission's decision will usually lie to the General Court. The General Court has jurisdiction in the following circumstances:

(i)   to annul decisions of the Commission imposing fines and cease and desist orders;

(ii)   to annul conditions imposed in decisions otherwise favourable to the applicant;

(iii)   to annul decisions favourable to third parties;

(iv)   to determine the lawfulness of rejection of complaints by the Commission; and

(v)   to review the Commission's failure to act under art.265.

13-058   The four categories in art.263 TFEU which allow the General Court or CJEU to review a decision of the Commission, are: lack of competence, infringement of an essential procedural requirement, infringement of the EU Treaty, or infringement of any rule relating to its application or misuse of powers.[131] As art.264 merely empowers the General Court and CJEU to judicially review the Commission's decision, the court will not approach the matter as a re-hearing. However, the General Court has shown that it is prepared to examine, in detail, evidence used by the Commission in reaching its decision, and will check meticulously the nature and import of such evidence that is taken into consideration by the Commission.[132] The General Court has found there to be good grounds for review where: the Commission has not afforded an undertaking the right to be heard;[133] has failed to give adequate reasoning;[134] has made an error of law;[135] or where the facts as established are not capable of supporting the Commission's decision.[136] It would seem that failure by the Commission to observe any of the procedural requirements would amount to an infringement of an essential procedural requirement.[137]

ENFORCEMENT OF ARTS 101 AND 102 BY NATIONAL COMPETITION AUTHORITIES

13-059   Under the Modernisation Regulation, as discussed, NCAs are also competent to apply arts 101 and 102. Where anti-competitive conduct of an undertaking or

---

[130] See para.1-081.

[131] See para.1-081.

[132] *Re Italian Flat Glass v EC Commission* (C-89/93) [1990] 4 C.M.L.R. 535 at [95].

[133] (100/80) [1983] E.C.R. 1825; [1983] 3 C.M.L.R. 221.

[134] *Re Noordwijks Cement Accoord* (8-11/66) [1967] E.C.R. 75, [1967] C.M.L.R. 77 CJEU; *Remia v EC Commission* [1985] E.C.R. 2547, [1987] 1 C.M.L.R. 1. Article 253 of the EC Treaty stipulates that decisions must be reasoned.

[135] *Suiker Unie v EC Commission* (4/73) [1975] E.C.R. 1663; [1976] 1 C.M.L.R. 295.

[136] *Metro-Großmärkte v EC Commission* (26/76) [1977] E.C.R. 1875.

[137] Gand AG in *ACF Chemiefarma v EC Commission* (41/69) [1970] E.C.R. 661, considered that a failure by the Commission to consult the Advisory Committee on Restrictive Practices and Monopolies pursuant to art.10 of Reg.17 would justify annulment of its decision.

undertakings does not have any effect on trade between Member States and is confined to one Member State, then the conduct will not infringe arts 101 or 102 and the European Commission will not become involved. In other cases, the conduct may have an anti-competitive effect in several Member States but is still not of sufficient interest for the European Commission to become involved. In such circumstances, several NCAs may be investigating the same conduct. The Commission has issued a Notice on Cooperation within the Network of Competition Authorities[138] which provides guidance as to the allocation of work. In principal, the Commission encourages NCAs to allocate a case to a single NCA so that such one NCA has principal conduct of the investigation. In general, an NCA will be "best placed" to deal with a case where first, the agreement has substantial direct actual or foreseeable effects on competition in the territory of that NCA, and is implemented within or originates from its territory; secondly, the NCA is able to bring the entire infringement to an end; and thirdly, it can gather, with the assistance of other NCAs if needed, the evidence required to prove the infringement.[139] However, in certain cases, NCAs can work in parallel, e.g. a market sharing agreement restricting activities of two companies to the Member State of location.[140] The Notice sets out provisions for the sharing of confidential information and evidence.

As discussed above, where the European Commission initiates proceedings in **13-060** relation to the conduct of which complaint is made, then this relieves all NCAs of their competence to apply arts 101 and 102 in relation to that conduct.[141] This applies even if the NCA has already initiated proceedings. However, the Commission will only do this in certain circumstances, e.g. where there is a danger of conflicting decisions from NCAs.[142]

ENFORCEMENT OF ARTS 101 AND 102 BY NATIONAL COURTS

As discussed at the outset of this chapter, the effect of the Modernisation Regula- **13-061** tion is to allow national courts to apply in private actions (and also on appeal in regulatory proceedings) arts 101 and 102 in their entirety, including the ability to exempt agreements under art.101(3). Both these articles have been held to create direct rights in respect of individuals, which the national courts must safeguard.[143] Articles 101 and 102 have direct effect and are directly applicable in Member States.[144] National courts have the right to award damages to the injured party where there has been a breach of arts 101 or 102.[145]

In general, the procedural conditions for the enforcement of EU competition rules **13-062** by national courts are a matter of national law. However, where there is an infringement of arts 101 or 102, national law must provide for sanctions which are effec-

---

[138] Commission Notice on cooperation within the Network of Competition Authorities [2004] OJ C101/43.
[139] Notice on cooperation within Network Competition Authorities [2004] OJ C101/43, para.8.
[140] Commission Notice on cooperation within Network Competition Authorities [2004] OJ C101/43, para.12.
[141] art.11(6) Reg.1/2003; [2004] OJ C101/43, para.51.
[142] Commission Notice on cooperation within Network Competition Authorities [2004] OJ C101/43, para.54.
[143] *BRT v SABAM (127/73)* [1974] E.C.R. 51, [1974] 2 C.M.L.R. 238; *Courage v Crehan* (C-453/99) [2001] E.C.R. 6297.
[144] (C-127/73) [1974] E.C.R. 51, [1974] 2 C.M.L.R. 238; (C-453/99) [2001] E.C.R. 6297.
[145] (C-453/99) [2001] E.C.R. 6297 at [26]–[27].

tive, proportionate and dissuasive.[146] National procedural rules must not make the enforcement of arts 101 or 102 excessively difficult or practically impossible *(principle of effectiveness)* and must not be less favourable than the rules applicable to the enforcement of equivalent national law *(principle of equivalence)*.[147]

13-063   Directive 2014/104/EU on Antitrust Damages Action was adopted by the European Parliament on 26 November 2014 and published in the Official Journal on 5 December 2014. Member States were required to adapt their national laws by 27 December 2016. The Directive seeks to harmonise the approach in Member States to the award of damages in actions based on the competition provisions of the TFEU as follows:

- The basic right to make a claim whether in "follow on" or "stand-alone" cases.
- A minimum limitation period of five years.
- Common rules on joint and several liability.
- A rebuttal presumption that cartel infringements cause harm.
- Ability of claimant to request a court to order a defendant or third party to disclose relevant evidence.
- A prohibition on disclosure of leniency statements.

Parallel proceedings: courts and EC Commission

13-064   A national court cannot take a decision "running counter" to a decision on conduct which has already been the subject of a Commission decision.[148] However, this is without prejudice to its right, where it doubts the legality of the Commission's decision, to seek a ruling to the contrary from the CJEU.[149] Where proceedings have been initiated by the Commission, national courts must avoid giving decisions which would conflict with the Commission's decision.[150] To that effect, the national court may assess whether it is necessary to stay its proceedings.[151] To help with its decision, it may ask the Commission about the progress of the proceedings and the likelihood of a decision.[152] However, if it does order a stay, it may and indeed it has an obligation to consider whether it is necessary to order interim

---

[146] *Commission v Greece* (C-68/88) [1989] E.C.R. 2965 at [23]–[25]; Commission Notice on cooperation between the Commission and the courts of the EU Member States in the application of Articles 101 and 102 EC [2004] OJ C101/54, para.10.

[147] *Rewe v Hauptsollamt Kiel* (158/80) [1981] E.C.R. 1805, [1982] 1 C.M.L.R. 449; *Palmisani v Istituto Nazionale della Previdenza Sociale (INPS)* (C-261/95) [1997] E.C.R. I-4025; *Amminnistrazione della Finance dello Stato v San Giorgio* (199/82) [1983] E.C.R. 3595; see also *REWE v Landwirtschaftkammer fur der Saarland* (33/76) [1976] E.C.R. 1989, [1977] 1 C.M.L.R. 533; *Comet v Produktschap voor Siergewaassen* (45/76) [1976] E.C.R. 2043, [1977] 1 C.M.L.R. 533; *Just v Ministry for Fiscal Affairs* (68/74) [1980] E.C.R. 501, [1981] 2 C.M.L.R. 714, [1977] 1 C.M.L.R. 533; *Amminnistrazione della Finance dello Stato v MIRECO* [1980] E.C.R. 2559; (C-453/99) [2001] E.C.R. 6297 at [29] and *Manfredi v Lloyd Adriatico Assicurazioni* (C-295/04) [2006] E.C.R. I-6619, [2006] 5 C.M.L.R. 17. See also Commission Notice on cooperation [2004] OJ C101/54, para.10(c).

[148] art.16 Reg.1/2003.

[149] See also Notice on cooperation between the Commission and the courts of the EU Member States in the application of Articles 101 and 102 EC [2004] OJ C101/54, para.13; *Firma Foto Frost v Hauptzollamt Lubeck-Ost* (C-314/85) [1987] E.C.R. 4199 at [12]–[20].

[150] art.16 Reg.1/2003.

[151] art.16 Reg.1/2003. See also decisions prior to art.16, (C-234/89) [1991] 1 E.C.R. 935, [1991] 4 C.M.L.R. 329; *Masterfoods Ltd (t/a Mars Ireland) v HB Ice Cream Ltd* (C-344/98) [2000] E.C.R. I-11369 at [51].

[152] See also Notice on cooperation [2004] OJ C101/54, para.12.

measures in order to safeguard the interests of the parties.[153] As well as referring the matter to the CJEU on a point of interpretation of EU law, a national court may ask the Commission for its opinion on questions concerning the application of EC competition rules or on economic, factual or legal matters.[154]

Courts vs. Commission

When considering whether a party who considers itself the victim of anti- **13-065** competitive behaviour contrary to arts 101 and 102 should bring proceedings before the Commission or in the national courts, the following matters should be borne in mind:

(i) The Commission cannot award damages to an injured party but can only fine the infringing party.

(ii) It is possible to combine a claim in EU law with a claim under national law.

(iii) Courts have the power to award costs to the successful applicant.

vs.

(i) A complaint to the European Commission or NCA is usually cheap and often anonymous.

(ii) The Commission or NCA can take a pro-active role in establishing unlawful conduct.

(iii) The Commission's fact-finding powers are much greater than an individual's or those available under national procedures.

(iv) The legal and financial power of the Commission and the ability to impose large fines will often have the effect of causing a party to end the alleged anti-competitive practice.

(v) The privilege against self-incrimination and the right to legal privilege is more restricted in Commission proceedings.

Defences under arts 101 and 102

The availability of defences under arts 101 and 102 is considered in Ch.14, **13-066** "Euro-Defences".[155]

Introduction

Under the EEA Agreement, a system must be set up which ensures that its **13-067** competition rules are equally respected.[156] During the negotiations of the EEA Agreement, one central issue was who would enforce the EEA competition laws and how to divide the competencies. The negotiators finally opted for a two-pillar system, allocating the enforcement of the EEA competition laws between the EC

---

[153] See also Notice on cooperation [2004] OJ C101/54, para.14; (C-344/98) [2000] E.C.R. I-11369, para.58.

[154] Notice on cooperation [2004] OJ C101/54, para.27. (C-234/89) [1991] E.C.R. I-93 at [53].

[155] See Ch.14.

[156] art.1(2)(e) EEA Agreement.

Commission and EFTA Surveillance Authority ("ESA"). The actual allocation of responsibilities as set out in the EEA is quite complicated.

13-068   In summary, they are as follows:

(a)   In relation to cases falling under art.53 of the EEA (the provision equivalent to art.101):

Pure cases—"EFTA" pure cases, where only trade between EFTA states is affected, are dealt with by the ESA[157]; "EU pure" cases, where only trade between Member States is affected, do not fall under the EEA Agreement and will be dealt with by the EC Commission solely on the basis of art.101 TFEU.[158]

Mixed cases—"Mixed cases", where there is both trade between Member States and trade between the EU and one or more EFTA states is affected, such are dealt with by the Commission if the effect on trade between EU Member States is appreciable.[159]

Turnover of undertakings is 33 per cent or more in EFTA countries—The EFTA Surveillance Authority has jurisdiction on cases where the turnover of the undertakings concerned in the territory of the EFTA states equals 33 per cent or more of their turnover in the territory covered by the agreement.[160] However, this does not apply if the agreement also appreciably affects trade between EU Member States.[161]

(b)   In relation to cases falling under art.54 of the EEA (the provision equivalent to art.102):

(i)   cases where the dominance only exists within the EFTA territory will be dealt with by the ESA;[162]

(ii)   cases where the dominance exists only in the EU will be dealt with by the EC Commission;[163] and

(iii) cases where the dominance exists within both EU and EFTA territories the rules concerning mixed cases set out above in relation to art.53 will apply.[164]

Procedural rules of the ESA

13-069   Under Protocol 21 to the EEA Agreement, the ESA, in effect, is entrusted with equivalent powers and similar functions to those of the EC Commission. Under art.3 of Protocol 21 to the EEA Agreement and Protocol 4 to the ESA/Court Agreement, the procedural EU Regulations relating to the enforcement of arts 101 and 102 are incorporated into the EEA Agreement.[165] Accordingly, the enforcement of

---

[157] art.56(1)(a) EEA Agreement.

[158] art.56(1)(a).

[159] arts 56(1)(c) and 56(3).

[160] art.56(1)(b).

[161] art.56(1)(b); art.56(1)(c). In such circumstances, regard needs to be paid to art.58, Protocol 21, Protocol 23 and Annex XIV of the EEA Agreement.

[162] art.56(2).

[163] art.56(2).

[164] art.56(2), final sentence.

[165] This Protocol is changed as the equivalent EU Regulations are changed and readers are advised to read Protocol 21 which can be accessed via the EFTA website (*http://www.efta.int* [Accessed 15 June 2018]).

EEA competition laws by the ESA will be very similar to that of the EC Commission which has been described earlier in this chapter.

Co-operation between the EU Commission and the ESA

The EEA Agreement provides for close co-operation between the ESA and the **13-070** EC Commission.[166] This co-operation extends to the handling of both individual cases and general policy issues. Protocol 23 to the EEA Agreement sets out detailed rules as to the co-operation between EFTA and EC Commission.

---

[166] art.58.

CHAPTER 14

EU DEFENCES TO EXERCISE OF IPRS

INTRODUCTION

In an action for infringement of IPRs, the legislation that confers the IPR will **14-001** normally also provide for a number of specific defences. For example, in an action for trade mark infringement, there are a number of specific defences, e.g. the use of one's own name and address in accordance with honest practices or exhaustion of rights. These defences are contained within the relevant legislation, i.e. in the case of harmonised IPR, the Directive or Regulation.

However, sometimes a defendant considers that it would be contrary to some **14-002** provision of EU law which is not found within the harmonising directive or in the case of EU unitary rights, the regulation which confers such a right. For instance, the defendant may consider that the exercise of the IPRs is contrary to provisions of the TFEU (or historically, its predecessors). Alternatively, the defendant may consider that the enforcement is contrary to an international convention or some fundamental principle of EU law (e.g. the exercise of the IPRs is abusive and thus contrary to the EU principle of *abus de droit*). Alternatively, the defendant may argue that the enforcement of IPRs is contrary to its human rights and rely upon the Charter of Fundamental Rights or the European Convention of Human Rights.

This chapter considers these type of defences—often known as "Euro" defences **14-003** but better termed, EU defences. At the outset, it is important to distinguish a EU-defence from an argument that EU IPRs legislation, e.g. the Trade Mark Directive or domestic legislation must be interpreted in the light of an international convention such as TRIPS. Such international conventions cannot in themselves provide a defence to the exercise of intellectual property rights pursuant to a harmonising EU directive because in the hierarchy of a Member State law, EU law is supreme. Thus, whilst EU law and domestic IP law must be interpreted in accordance with TRIPS, and even though the EU is a signatory to TRIPs, ultimately, TRIPS is not of an equal or superior status to a harmonising Directive, an EU Regulation let alone the Treaty provisions of the TFEU. The requirement to interpret IPRs legislation in the light of international conventions is discussed in the introductory chapter of this book. What this chapter considers are actual defences under EU law to actions for infringement of IPRs regardless of whether such a right is conferred as a result of EU legislation (i.e. a harmonising IP Directive or Community regulation) or is merely the result of the domestic laws of a Member State.

14-004   Historically, prior to the harmonisation of national IPRs legislation of Member States via harmonising Directives, the CJEU established in a series of landmark cases that where goods embodying the IPR had been placed on the market in the EU by the right holder or with consent, the exercise of IPRs was contrary to what are now arts 34–36 TFEU—the free movement of goods provisions. This is discussed in Ch.7, "Intellectual Property and Free Movement of Goods". However, the significance of arts 34–36 became much less once the CJEU's doctrine of exhaustion of rights was "internalised" within the harmonising IPRs Directives by such Directives expressly providing a defence of Community-wide exhaustion of rights. Following such internalisation, there was no need to resort to arts 34–36. Indeed, the CJEU developed the doctrine that direct reliance on arts 34–36 was impermissible where there existed a harmonising Directive.[1] Thus, the significance of arts 34–36 waned as a defence to an action for EU IPRs infringement. However, they are still relevant to patent infringement actions as such not harmonised within the EU by reason of EU legislation.[2]

14-005   Moreover, in the 1960s to 1980s, when the understanding of the effect of the predecessors to arts 34–36 TFEU on the exercise of IPRs was imperfect, it was said by the CJEU that in certain cases normally involving parallel imports that art.101 could prevent the exercise of IPR.[3] However, by the mid-1970s, the CJEU had recognised that arts 34–36 were the more appropriate provisions for introducing a doctrine of exhaustion of rights applicable to parallel imports rather than art.101. As will be seen, the CJEU has made it clear that art.101 still has an important role to play as a EU-defence to an action for infringement of IPRs. In the case of art.102, its development as a defence to an IPR action took considerably longer. This was primarily because it was not until the 1990s that the CJEU had to consider whether or not the exercise of IPRs could be an abuse by a dominant undertaking and thus provide a defence to an action for infringement of IPRs.[4] In the case of art.102, the nexus between the exercise of rights and art.102 is much stronger than for art.101. Thus, where an undertaking has a dominant position and the alleged abuse is a refusal by it to license third parties, the exercise of IPRs (threatened or actual) is the obvious consequence of a refusal to license. In the case of art.101, the nexus would appear to be that the exercise of IPRs must be the "purpose, means or consequence" of an anti-competitive agreement, i.e. the mechanism for enforcing an anti-competitive agreement.[5]

14-006   As well as the free movement and competition provisions of TFEU, there are other categories of EU defences to the exercise of IPRs. Consequently, the EU has enacted the E-Commerce Directive which confers in defined circumstances, defences to information society service providers. These can be considered "standalone" EU legislation aimed at dealing with the difficulties that information

---

[1]   This is discussed at paras 7-059 and 7-093.

[2]   Although patent law is harmonised by the European Patent Convention, it is not EU legislation but a regional European treaty. However, see para.2-503, et seq., on the Unitary Patent (not yet in force).

[3]   See *Parke Davis v Probel* (24/67) [1968] E.C.R. 55, [1968] C.M.L.R. 47; *Consten & Grundig v Commission* (56/64 & 58/64) [1966] C.M.L.R. 19; (51/75) [1976] E.C.R. 811, [1976] 2 C.M.L.R. 235.

[4]   Generally, see para.12-140, et seq.

[5]   See para.14-013.

society service providers find themselves. Furthermore, are there human rights defences, e.g. under the Charter of Fundamental Rights of the EU which is an integral "pillar" to the EU treaties?[6] Finally, it is necessary to consider the EU doctrine of *abus de droit* which is not IP-specific but concerns the use of EU legislation for purposes manifestly contrary to what they were intended.

This chapter considers the following: 14-007

(1) Defences under arts 101 and 102.
(2) Defences under arts 34–36.
(3) The *abus de droit* doctrine.
(4) Defences based on infringement of human rights.
(5) E-Commerce Directive defences for information society service providers.

However, before doing so, it is important to recognise that a mere allegation of **14-008** breach of a provision of EU law will not, even if proven, per se amount to a defence to an action for infringement of IPRs. It is necessary that there is a sufficient connection between the unlawful activity and the exercise of those rights to provide a defence to an action for infringements of IPRs. This is often called the "nexus" requirement and is now discussed.

NEXUS

In some cases, the IPR owner may be engaged in conduct that is a breach of EU **14-009** law or the law of a Member State. However, by itself, that does not mean that there is a defence to the exercise of IPRs by the IPR owner. For instance, the IPR owner may be engaged in price fixing with its competitors. This is far removed from the enforcement of a patent against an infringer. The breach of EU or national law may not be linked at all to the enforcement of IPRs or be too remotely linked to the exercise of rights to confer a defence. It would be wrong, in principle, to deny the claimant the right to enforce its rights.

At both national and EU law, it is often said that there must be a sufficient **14-010** "nexus" between the exercise of IPRs against an undertaking and the unlawful activity of the IPR holder. An obvious case of sufficient nexus is where a dominant undertaking with a SEP patent to a technological standard has undertaken to license the SEP on FRAND terms to any undertaking which wishes to make use of the technological standard. In such circumstances, if it refuses to license the SEP, then this is likely to be an abuse of a dominant position.[7] Thus, the enforcement of a SEP against the undertaking would be plainly the result of the refusal to license the SEP.

In contrast, the owner of a registered trade mark may have entered into a **14-011** franchise distribution agreement with franchisees which contains anti-competitive clauses. If an independent third party started using the same or a similar trade mark for its franchise, it is difficult to see why such should disentitle the trade mark owner from bringing an action against the third party for trade mark infringement. The effect of an anti-competitive agreement under art.101 is that the agreement (or the relevant provision) is void but that is all. The voidness of the relevant provisions (or indeed the agreement) can have no effect on an action for trade mark infringement. There is no *nexus* between the two.

---

[6] See para.14-055.
[7] For when a refusal to license a SEP can be an abuse of a dominant position contrary to art.102 TFEU, see para.12-216.

14-012   However, what would be the position in the above example if the action was against an ex-franchisee who was a party to the anti-competitive agreement. Let us assume that the ex-franchisee breached the anti-competitive terms and as a result, the franchisor terminates the agreement for breach. The ex-franchisee considers that such a term was anti-competitive and unenforceable. If the ex-franchisee continued using the franchise trade mark, should the fact that the termination of the franchise which would include the licence to use the trade mark was due to breach of an anti-competitive term provide a defence to an action for trade mark infringement? In this example, the *nexus* between the two is much closer than the previous example. It might be said that in such circumstances, the franchisor had no right to terminate on the basis of breach of illegal terms. However, if the agreement has been terminated (rightly or wrongly), the fact is that the use of the trade mark by the ex-franchisee is no longer under the control of the franchisor. Thus, the essential function of the trade mark, which is to guarantee that use of a mark is under *unitary* control, will be compromised. Consumer confusion will ultimately arise and damage will occur to the reputation of the trade mark. Thus, it could be argued that the *proportionate* approach should be that the ex-franchisee can sue for damages for breach of art.101 and breach of contract but not rely upon the anti-competitive agreement as a defence. Indeed, if the ex-franchisee can be compensated for loss of profits (past and future) for wrongful termination, then there is no need for it to provide a defence and thus cause confusion in the marketplace.

ARTICLES 101 DEFENCES TO EXERCISE OF IPRs

Court of Justice

14-013   In the 1960s, in *Consten & Grundig v Commission*,[8] the CJEU held that an exclusive distributorship coupled with export bans (so as to provide absolute territorial protection) fell within art.101(1) and that accordingly the exercise of trade mark rights to enforce such absolute protection was invalid. In the 1970s, in *Tepea BV v EC Commission*,[9] a British manufacturer had an exclusive distributorship agreement with a Dutch dealer. The agreement included the grant of an exclusive licence to the Dutch dealer to use the former's trade marks in Holland and was supported by export prohibitions on the British manufacturer's dealers in the UK. All orders received by the manufacturer for Holland were to be passed on to the Dutch dealer. It was apparent from the evidence that the object was to create absolute territorial protection for the Dutch dealer from internal or external competitors and that the Dutch dealer was to exercise trade mark rights in order to achieve such an aim. On appeal from a finding by the European Commission of infringement of art.101, the CJEU held that such absolute territorial protection has as its object or effect the prevention of competition within Holland and thus fell within art.101(1). The CJEU said that:

> "[44]   *The skilful use of the trade mark law has in this way strengthened the territorial protection* given by the exclusive distribution agreement, the existence of which is admitted, the combined effect of these two techniques securing absolute and permanent protection.
> [45]   The original agreement cannot therefore be examined without taking into account the concerted practice which ensured its efficacy." [Emphasis supplied.]

---

[8]   (56/64) and (58/64) [1966] C.M.L.R. 19.
[9]   (28/77) [1978] E.C.R. 1391; [1978] 3 C.M.L.R. 392.

Thus, where trade mark rights are exercised "in tandem" with an anti-competitive **14-014** agreement to achieve an anti-competitive aim, their exercise is itself anti-competitive and unlawful under art.101.

In *Nancy Kean v Keurkoop*,[10] the proprietor of design rights under the law of one **14-015** Member State sought to enforce those rights against an undertaking which imported such products from another Member State where the design was not protected by legal rights. It was held that such enforcement was permissible subject to a number of conditions, one of which was that there was no relevant agreement or concerted practice in breach of art.101. The court said, at [26] and [27]:

"[26] Furthermore, the proprietor of an exclusive right may not rely on his right if the prohibition on importation or marketing of which he wishes to avail himself *could be connected* with an agreement or practice in restraint of competition within the Community contrary to the provisions of the Treaty, in particular to those of Article [101].

[27] Although a right to a design, as a legal entity, does not as such fall within the class of agreements or concerted practices envisaged by Article [101(1)], the exercise *of that right may be subject to the prohibitions contained in the Treaty when it is the purpose, the means or the result of* an agreement, decision or concerted practice." [Emphasis supplied.]

It will be appreciated from this passage that [26] is very general about when **14-016** art.101 can be relied upon as a defence ("could be connected") whereas [27] is more specific—it is a defence where it is "the purpose, the means or the result" of an anti-competitive agreement. It is not clear from the above passage whether the test in [27] is intended to demonstrate exhaustively when art.101 can be a defence to an action for infringement of IPR or should be considered as a specific example of the type of conduct that can be considered to be connected with an anti-competitive agreement as set out in [26] such as to provide a defence to a defendant to an action for infringement of an IPR. Certainly, to the author's knowledge, the circumstances where art.101 has been held to provide a defence to an infringement action appear limited to the circumstances set out in [27]. This does not appear to be because [27] is read as setting out exhaustively the conditions but rather because it appears difficult to conceive of *other* circumstances where the exercise of IPRs are indeed connected with an anti-competitive agreement or practice. It might be thought that the CJEU was suggesting that there had to be some *causality* between the exercise of the IPR and the anti-competitive agreement. Thus, "purpose, means or result" suggests that the anti-competitive agreement has caused the exercise of the rights.

At the same time as *Nancy Kean v Keurkoop*, the Court of Justice considered the **14-017** lawfulness of the enforcement of copyright in a film where there were allegations that the copyright owner was involved in market partitioning in the EU. In *Ciné Vog v CODITEL (No.2) ("CODITEL II"),*[11] a French film producer granted to a Belgian film distributor (Ciné Vog) the exclusive right to exhibit a film in Belgium for seven years. Various Belgian cable television companies picked up transmission of the film in Germany (where it had been lawfully transmitted by the German licensee) and distributed it by cable in Belgium. Ciné Vog sued CODITEL, a cable company, for copyright infringement in Belgium. The matter was referred to the Court of Justice as to whether inter alia the exercise of copyright was compatible with

---

[10] *Nancy Kean v Keurkoop* (144/81) [1982] E.C.R. 2813; [1983] 2 C.M.L.R. 47; [1983] F.S.R. 381.
[11] (262/81) [1982] E.C.R. 3381; [1983] 1 C.M.L.R. 49.

art.101(1).[12] The court considered that the nature of the cinematograph industry meant that it was unlikely that the grant of exclusive territorial licences restricted to a Member State was contrary to art.101. However, it said that it was appropriate for a national court to ascertain whether in a given case, the manner in which the exclusive right was exercised was subject to arrangements, whose object was to prevent or restrict the distribution of films or to distort competition in the cinematographic market.[13] Again, this suggests that the Court of Justice is concerned with whether the exercise of IPRs was to implement an anti-competitive arrangement.[14]

14-018   In the *TV Decoder* cases,[15] an action was brought under domestic UK intellectual property legislation which implemented the Conditional Access Directive. The object of that action was the prevention of importation into the UK of satellite broadcast decoder cards which had been placed on the market in Greece. Such devices permitted the viewing of Greek broadcasts of UK premier league football. The decoder cards were used to watch these broadcasts in English pubs. The broadcasts were encrypted and therefore the decoder device was required in order to view the Greek broadcasts. Pursuant to an exclusive broadcasting licence, the Greek broadcasters were prohibited from supplying the decoder devices for use in the UK. The claimants alleged that the decoder cards were not in free circulation in Greece because of the presence of national rights in Greece *and* because of the export restriction. Consequently, as held by the judge at first instance in the UK proceedings, it was important to the action under the domestic legislation which implemented the Conditional Access Directive and an action for copyright infringement whether the export restriction was lawful. If it was void under art.101 (as was alleged by the defendants), then the action for infringement of the Directive and copyright infringement (in the broadcasts) failed.[16] There was no challenge by the defendants that the mere grant of an exclusive licence was contrary to art.101 but it was argued that the addition of the export ban turned the contract from an "open" to a "closed" exclusive licence whose object was contrary to art.101.[17] A number of issues were referred to the CJEU including whether the export ban was contrary to art.101. In its judgment, the CJEU found that the closed exclusive licence did constitute a restriction on competition prohibited by art.101.[18] Accordingly, the action based on breach of domestic legislation based on the Conditional Access Direc-

---

[12]   This matter also went to the European Court on the question of whether Ciné Vog was prevented from enforcing its copyright against CODITEL by virtue of arts 34–36. See *Ciné Vog v CODITEL (No.1)* (62/79) [1980] E.C.R. 881; [1981] 2 C.M.L.R. 362 and Ch.7.

[13]   See [15]–[20].

[14]   At [15], the court refers to the mere fact of the grant of an exclusive right to a sole licensee to exhibit that film in a Member State and thus to prohibit others from showing the film was not sufficient to find that such a contract was "the purpose, the means or the result" of an anti-competitive agreement.

[15]   *Football Association Premier League Ltd v QC Leisure; Murphy v Media Protection Services Ltd* (C-429/08 & C-403/08) [2011] E.C.R. 9083. This case is discussed at para.8-219.

[16]   *FAPL v QC Leisure* [2008] F.S.R. 32 (High Court) at [344]. This was the judgment whereby Kitchin J referred a number of questions to the CJEU including the issue of whether art.101 applied to such a restriction. Upon its return from the CJEU, it appears to have been conceded that following the CJEU's judgment, there was no right to bring an action under the copyright-circumvention device provisions of UK law.

[17]   See [349]. The distinction between an open and closed exclusive licence and its effect on competition is discussed at para.8-213.

[18]   See [146].

tive failed. Here, it can be seen that there was a clear nexus between the art.101 defence and the allegation of breach of the Conditional Access Directive.

English cases

The issue of nexus in a Euro-defence based on art.101 has been considered in a **14-019** number of English cases. Thus, in the 1980s, in *British Leyland v Armstrong Patents*,[19] British Leyland, the British motor manufacturer, sued the defendant who manufactured motor car exhausts for infringement of the former's design copyright. The defendant pleaded inter alia that British Leyland was debarred from exercising its design copyright against it because it had entered into licences with third parties which were void under art.101(2). The Court of Appeal rejected this defence, relying upon the judgment of Megarry VC in *ICI v Berk Pharmaceuticals*[20] where he struck out a defence based on art.102. The court in *British Leyland* interpreted that judgment as requiring a nexus between the abuse pleaded and the right claimed by the defendants and considered that the requirement of nexus also applied to art.101.[21]

In *Sandvik Aktiebolag v Pfiffner*,[22] the patentee, Sandvik, licensed a Chinese **14-020** company, ZCC, to manufacture certain articles which arguably fell within the exclusive rights of the patent. The defendants imported the articles into Germany. In proceedings before the High Court, it was argued inter alia that the licence between Sandvik and ZCC contained unlawful, disguised customer restrictions and territorial restraints which debarred Sandvik from exercising its rights against the defendants. The effect of the restraints was to prevent the Chinese company marketing or selling the patented goods to EU countries. On a preliminary hearing, the judge held that the patentee was not debarred from claiming relief for infringement of the patent, because there was no nexus between such an action and the unlawfulness of the disguised customer restriction "even if a case under Article [101(1)] was made out".[23] It is submitted that in the facts of the particular case, there was a good argument for saying that there was sufficient nexus. The customer restraint in effect prevented ZCC from exporting or marketing the goods in the EU. Assuming that the customer restraint was unlawful and thus null and void, it is clearly arguable that ZCC could have marketed the goods in the EU. In such circumstances, there was a strong argument for saying that Sandvik, as patentee, should have been treated as having consented to the marketing of the goods in the EU. If such had been found, then there would have been no infringement and, accordingly, there would have been a complete nexus between the infringement proceedings and the unlawful customer restraint.

In a UK case, *Sportswear v Stonestyle*,[24] Sportswear, an Italian manufacturer of **14-021** branded premier STONE ISLAND clothing had entered into a distribution agreement with its UK distributor. The agreement contained a number of prima facie hard core restrictions which appeared to be intended to prevent parallel imports. The Italian manufacturer used garment codes which permitted the manufacturer to identify

---

[19] *British Leyland v Armstrong Patents* [1984] 3 C.M.L.R. 102 CA. This went on appeal to the House of Lords but not on the Euro-defence—[1986] A.C. 577 HL.

[20] *ICI v Berk Pharmaceuticals* [1981] F.S.R. 1; [1981] 2 C.M.L.R. 75. The art.102 defence is discussed at para.14-036.

[21] *ICI v Berk Pharmaceuticals* [1981] F.S.R. 1; [1981] 2 C.M.L.R. 75 and [93].

[22] *Sandvik Aktiebolag v Pfiffner* [2000] F.S.R. 17 (High Ct).

[23] *Pfiffner* [2000] F.S.R. 17 (High Ct) at [62].

[24] *Sportswear Co SpA v Stonestyle Ltd* [2006] F.S.R. 11 CA.

the distributor to which the garments had been sold. The purpose of these codes was disputed but it was argued by the defendant that they were for the purpose of preventing parallel imports. A UK retailer who had bought Sportswear clothing on the gray market sold the clothing with the codes removed from the labels and swing tags so that Sportswear could not identify the trader which the UK retailer had bought them from. The defendant said that if it did not remove them, then Sportswear would take steps to strangle supplies to the source. Sportswear brought proceedings for trade mark infringement on the grounds that although the clothing had been placed on the market in the EU with its consent, it had "legitimate reasons" to prevent the further circulation of the clothing because the defacement and mutilation of the clothing was detrimental to the reputation of a premier brand such as STONE ISLAND. The Court of Appeal, in upholding an appeal whereby a defence based on art.101 was struck out, held that it was arguable that such facts gave rise to a defence under art.101 to a trade mark infringement action on the basis that proceedings were being brought to enforce an anti-competitive agreement.

14-022   However, in contrast, in *Oracle v M-Tech*,[25] the Supreme Court of England and Wales granted an application for summary judgment. In this case, which concerned parallel imports from outside the EU M-Tech raised a number of defences under arts 34–36, art.101 and the doctrine of *abus de droit*. It is an important case albeit not an authority of the CJEU or General Court.

14-023   In a nutshell, M-Tech argued that Oracle (which bought the Sun server business) was engaged in anti-competitive conduct, namely the elimination of competition from the independent sector in the EU. They were doing this by a combination of: (i) enforcing their trade mark rights against parallel imports in Sun-branded servers; and (ii) withholding provenance information which would allow the independent sector to distinguish between Sun-branded servers first placed on the market outside the EEA (unlawful parallel imports) and those first placed on the market inside the EEA (lawful parallel imports). The nature of the secondary market in Sun-branded servers (they were traded many times, brokers were globally based and often Internet based,[26] suppliers were reluctant to reveal their sources and the lack of any markings on Sun-branded servers to indicate whether they were first placed on the market in the EEA or outside the EEA) meant that the independent sector was not able to determine whether they were buying lawful or unlawful Sun-branded servers. However, Oracle/Sun had a database which allowed them (using the serial numbers) to determine whether the servers were first placed on the market by Sun within or outside the EEA. However, the independent sector was not allowed access to this. Therefore, any trader in the independent sector who wanted to deal in Sun-branded servers in the secondary market either: (i) did not deal in them at all, *or* (ii) dealt in them knowing that there was a substantial risk that they were dealing in unlawful parallel imports and risk being sued by Oracle/Sun. Furthermore, Oracle had an authorised network which was not allowed to buy from the independent network.

14-024   M-Tech was an independent trader who was sued by Oracle/Sun for trade mark infringement. M-Tech pleaded that the enforcement of the trade marks was contrary to arts 34–36, art.101 and amounted to an *abus de droit*. Oracle sought summary judgment saying that there was no arguable defence under these provisions. The matter was referred to the Supreme Court. For this hearing, it was assumed that the

---

[25]   *Oracle America Inc v M-Tech* [2013] F.S.R. 14 (Supreme Court).
[26]   Thus, a New York trader would trade in EEA Sun-branded servers.

allegations made in M-Tech's defence was that Oracle's object and intent was to eliminate lawful parallel imports as well as unlawful parallel imports. For the purpose of the art.101 defence, it was said that Sun has two tactics for eliminating the independent secondary market, one was withholding information of provenance of Sun servers from the independent sector and the other was aimed at preventing its own network from dealing with the independent sector. It was thus said by M-Tech, that the two "worked in tandem".[27]

The Supreme Court granted summary judgment. Having considered and rejected **14-025** the defences under arts 34–36,[28] it went onto consider the defence under art.101. It accepted that there are undoubtedly circumstances where art.101 prohibited the enforcement of trade marks where there "is a sufficient nexus between the exercise of the right and the agreement or concerted practice in question".[29] It said that the test was whether the exercise of rights was the "subject, the means or the result of a restrictive practice". The Supreme Court held that the exercise of the trade mark rights was not the "subject, the means or the result" of an anti-competitive agreement which contravened art.101.[30]

Oracle v M-Tech was considered by the Court of Appeal in *FAPL v Luxton*.[31] In **14-026** that case, FAPL brought an action against the owner of a Welsh pub for infringement of copyright. The owner was playing broadcasts of football matches which were broadcast by Sky TV, a licensee of FAPL. The broadcasts were encrypted and thus access to the broadcasts were enabled, on the payment of a subscription, by the provision of "decoder cards" supplied by Sky TV. The owner of the Welsh pub had bought a satellite decoder card from a Danish broadcaster, Viasat. It was a Danish licensed broadcaster. The subscription for the Danish satellite decoder was a "domestic use" subscription, i.e. one that could not be used for playing broadcasts in pubs and public places. In previous proceedings which went to the Court of Justice, *FAPL v QC Leisure*,[32] the Court of Justice had held that UK national legislation which restricted the importation of foreign decoding devices was a restriction of art.56 TFEU (freedom to provide services). Mr Luxton, the Welsh pub owner, argued that the copyright infringement proceedings were an unlawful attempt on the part of FAPL to preclude the use of a foreign decoder device and that FAPL was acting pursuant to a mutual understanding between FAPL and its exclusive licensee, Sky TV to ensure that customers could not receive and decode broadcasts from foreign broadcasters. The effect, it was argued, was to isolate the UK from the continental market. It was said that this was contrary to arts 101 and 56 TFEU.

The Court of Appeal held, applying *Oracle v M-Tech*, that there was no suf- **14-027** ficient nexus between the enforcement of copyright by FAPL and the alleged anti-competitive conduct. This finding of lack of nexus was primarily because even if Mr Luxton had bought a decoder in UK whose subscription was only for domestic use, he still would not have been able to broadcast the football matches in his pub.[33] The court also held that the exercise of copyright was not linked sufficiently to the alleged anti-competitive conduct whereby FAPL and its licensees sought to parti-

---

[27] See [31].
[28] See Ch.7, "Free Movement of Goods" at para.7-101.
[29] See [30] citing *Sirena Srl v Eda Srl ((40/70)* [1971] E.C.R. 69at [9] and *Keurkoop BV v Nancy Kean BV* (C-144/81) [1982] E.C.R. 2853 at [27]).
[30] See [32].
[31] [2016] EWCA Civ 1097 CA.
[32] *FAPL v QC Leisure; Murphy v Media Protection Services* (C-403/08 & C-429/08) ECLI:EU:C:2011:631.
[33] See, e.g. [48].

tion the markets by restricting the reception of the broadcasts to the territories of their licensees.[34] It would appear from the facts of the case that Mr Luxton had tried to obtain a foreign decoder card which had a commercial use subscription but had been unsuccessful in doing so. He had ended up buying, unbeknownst to him, a decoder card with a domestic (home) subscription. However, the court held that this did not help because there was no distinction drawn by Mr Luxton between a pub owner who deliberately sought a foreign "home use" card and one who was accidentally supplied with one.[35]

14-028   There is a feeling in *FAPL v Luxton* that the real abuse was that FAPL and its licensees were making inter-state trade in the EU in decoders for "commercial use" very difficult. The first instance judge considered that there was a prima facie case that FAPL and its licensees were still seeking to make the importation of foreign decoding devices (whether for domestic or commercial use) difficult and that this was therefore an anti-competitive practice.[36] Thus, Mr Luxton had ended up with a "home use" decoder. Thus, FAPL accepted that if Mr Luxton had imported a card for commercial use, he would have had an arguable defence to the copyright infringement claim notwithstanding it was a foreign decoder card.[37] So would Mr Luxton have had an arguable defence to the copyright infringement claim if he had tried but failed to obtain a foreign commercial use card (because of continuing anti-competitive practices between FAPL and its licensees in the Member States) and in desperation, installed a decoder card for "home use" (whether he bought the same in the UK or in another Member State)? Or was his sole remedy to bring an action under art.101 that FAPL and its licensees were carrying out an anti-competitive practice and seek damages? In the authors' view, this raises difficult points of law. To what extent can a victim of anti-competitive practices take steps to mitigate the effects of the same? No doubt an action for breach of art.101 would have been very difficult for a Welsh pub owner to bring. These take a long time, are notoriously expensive (if court proceedings) and largely beyond the means of small business owners. Perhaps he should have bought a UK decoder device which had a commercial subscription and sought not to pay the difference between the UK subscription rates for commercial decoders and those in other EU countries. Here, if his subscription had been terminated and he had carried on showing the broadcasts in his pub for which FAPL brought an action for copyright infringement, he could have argued that the termination of his licence was unlawful, as it was intended to put into effect an anti-competitive practice. Therefore the exercise of IPRs (which could only succeed because he no longer had a licence) was itself unlawful.

Exercise of right to compel defendant to enter into an agreement contrary to art.101

14-029   In certain cases, a powerful rights owner may offer to interested licensees the opportunity to enter into a licence which contains onerous anti-competitive provisions as an alternative to infringement proceedings. Prima facie, it would be surprising if infringement proceedings which were brought where the potential licensee refuses to enter into an anti-competitive agreement would *themselves* be contrary to art.101. This is because not only is there no concluded agreement but the par-

---

[34]   see [50].
[35]   See [55].
[36]   See [7]–[14].
[37]   See [14].

ties to the litigation are antagonists rather than collaborators. Therefore, it cannot be said that there is any concerted practice.

Furthermore, there is a logical difficulty. In general, a defendant relies upon such **14-030** an anti-competitive practice to claim that an injunction restraining the infringement should not be granted. In effect, the defendant is claiming that the court should grant a compulsory licence on reasonable (i.e. competitive) terms. However, if the parties *had entered* into an anti-competitive agreement, then the anti-competitive terms would be void. If such restrictions were not severable from the entire agreement, so that the whole agreement was void, then there would be no licence.[38] Accordingly, it would be odd if the alleged infringer is treated more favourably by rejecting the agreement than by entering into it.

These arguments have been ventilated in a number of English cases. In *British* **14-031** *Leyland v T.I. Silencers*,[39] British Leyland was seeking to enforce copyright in the drawing for exhaust systems against an unlicensed manufacturer of replacement parts. British Leyland was prepared to offer licences to such manufacturers on standard terms but it was alleged by T.I. Silencers that the terms were unreasonable and contrary to art.101. An application was made to strike out the Euro-defence but this failed. On appeal, the Court of Appeal held that the court would not lend countenance to an argument that the ordinary use of copyright included a use which enabled the owner of the copyright to flout EU law. In *Holleran v Daniel Thwaites*,[40] the claimants were tenants of two tied houses. They refused to enter into revised tenancy agreements which they alleged were contrary to art.101. The landlords issued notices to quit against the claimants. The High Court held, in an interlocutory application, that the court had power to restrain a landlord from abusing his contractual right to terminate a tenancy if such was to procure a breach of EU law. Similarly, in *Philips Electronics v Ingman Ltd*,[41] the court said, in following these two decisions, that where the purpose of infringement proceedings was to force the defendant to enter into standard licences which offended against the TFEU, it was arguable that the court may decline to give the relief sought in its infringement proceedings.[42] In *Intel Corp v Via Technologies*,[43] it was held that it was arguable that this could amount to a defence. In this case, when considering the "essential facilities" doctrine,[44] Intel, the well-known maker of semi-conductor chips, owned certain "gateway" patents for chipsets and CPUs in personal computers. Any manufacturer of such parts effectively required a licence of these gateway patents to compete on the market. Intel offered licences to manufacturers which it was alleged contained anti-competitive provisions contrary to art.101.[45] The Court of Appeal in following *Philips v Ingman* said that such a defence was arguable. The Court of Appeal were plainly concerned about the "common sense" argument discussed above that Via Technologies would be in a worse position if it entered into the anti-competitive licence than if it did not.[46] However, the Court of Appeal held that it was arguable. In support of this finding and because

---

[38] As for the test of severability, see Ch.12.

[39] *British Leyland v T.I. Silencers* [1981] C.M.L.R. 75 CA.

[40] *Holleran v Daniel Thwaites* [1989] 2 C.M.L.R. 917 HC.

[41] *Philips Electronics v Ingman Ltd* [1999] F.S.R. 112 HC.

[42] *Philips Electronics* [1999] F.S.R. 112 HC at [93].

[43] *Intel Corp v Via Technologies* [2003] F.S.R. 12 HC; [2003] F.S.R. 33 CA.

[44] See para.12-250.

[45] These provisions are discussed at para.12-240.

[46] It is of note that Via Technologies argued that the proper comparison was between no licence and a lawful licence rather than no licence and an unlawful licence.

there was an art.102 plea as well, the Court of Appeal said that if the willingness to grant licences but only on terms which involve breaches of art.101 was part of the abusive conduct of which complaint is made, then it saw no reason why those facts could not be relied on both for the purposes of the defence under art.102 and as a free-standing defence under art.101.[47]

14-032   Ultimately, it is submitted that in such circumstances, it is difficult to understand how infringement proceedings can be defended by reference to art.101 where there is no concluded agreement or concerted practice. Such is a fundamental condition of art.101. In *Bayer v EU Commission*,[48] the CJEU emphasised the need to show an agreement or concerted practice for conduct to fall within art.101 where ostensibly the anti-competitive conduct was unilateral.[49] The reasoning given by the Court of Appeal is not convincing but it must be remembered that there is an English principle that defences will very rarely be struck out in an area of developing law. Of course, it may be an abuse of a dominant position to exercise (or threaten to exercise) rights in order to force undertakings to enter into an anti-competitive licence. However, in such circumstances, the analysis is under art.102 and not art.101 if the undertakings refuse to enter into the licence. After all, where there is no dominant position, the refusal to enter into anti-competitive agreements should not materially affect competition in the marketplace because there will be ex hypothesi substitute goods, services or technologies.

Exercise of intellectual property rights is contrary to art.102: nexus

14-033   In the case of a Euro-defence under art.102, the matter is somewhat different to that under art.101. It is necessary to distinguish between two situations.

- Where the Euro-defence alleges that the exercise of rights is *in itself* an abuse of a dominant position. Here, nexus is not an issue because clearly, if the exercise of rights is an abuse, then they cannot be exercised and the defendant has a complete defence to an infringement action. Thus, the reader is referred to Ch.12, "Abuse of a Dominant Position" for a full discussion of whether the exercise of rights by a dominant undertaking can *in itself* be an abuse.[50] It should be said that a refusal to license can be considered the other side of the coin to the exercise of rights. A refusal to license necessarily involves a threat to exercise the rights to which the refusal to license relates.
- Where by reason of collateral conduct of the dominant right holder (i.e. conduct other than the exercise of rights/refusal to license), it is alleged that the exercise of rights is abusive. For instance, it might be argued that where a dominant right holder charges unfair prices for products protected by the right,[51] it would be abusive for the right holder to exercise rights against

---

[47]   See [87].

[48]   See (C-2/01P & C-3/01P) [2004] E.C.R. I-23.

[49]   See para.8-082.

[50]   As seen in that chapter, the answer is that in exceptional circumstances, it can amount to an abuse. See para.12-140.

[51]   The charging of unfair prices by a dominant undertaking is a specified example of abuse under art.102. See para.12-274.

those who manufactured the products protected by the right. Here, nexus is important and cases on this are now considered.

European Court of Justice

Most of the jurisprudence of the Court of Justice on the relationship between the **14-034** exercise of IPRs and art.102 has concerned whether the exercise of IPRs themselves or a refusal to license is itself an abuse of a dominant position. This is the first situation discussed above. As regards the second situation, the leading authority is *Volvo v Veng* which is discussed in Ch.12, "Abuse of a Dominant Position".[52]

In that case, the CJEU held that the exercise of rights could be prohibited by the **14-035** proprietor of a registered design in respect of car body panels under art.102, where it involved abusive conduct such as the arbitrary refusal to supply spare parts to independent repairers, the fixing of prices for spare parts at an unfair level or a decision no longer to produce spare parts for a particular model, even though many cars of that model were still in circulation.[53] This suggests that where the exercise of rights is being used *together with* other abusive conduct, e.g. the maintenance of unfair prices, then there is an abuse of a dominant position. It also suggests that if an action was brought by the owner of such rights and the defendant could prove, e.g. the maintenance of unfair prices, then rights holder could not enforce its rights where the defendant has manufactured spare parts or commissioned the same to avoid paying unfair prices.

English cases

In an early case concerning an art.102 Euro-defence in intellectual property **14-036** proceedings, *ICI v Berk Pharmaceuticals*,[54] an action was brought in passing off against pills which copied the shape and colour of the claimant's equivalent pills. It was alleged that the claimant company occupied a dominant position in the common market and was abusing that dominant position by charging excessively high prices for the pills in question, thereby reducing the competitiveness of the defendant and entitling it to adopt the same get-up as the claimant's pills. An application was brought to strike out the Euro-defence. A central plank of the claimant's argument was the lack of any nexus between the alleged breach of art.102 and the passing off action. The defendant argued that it could only compete with the claimants by adopting the get-up of the claimant's pills because patients had become so accustomed to that get-up that they would reject any other tablets. Megarry VC agreed with the claimant. He said:

> "[9] ...Article [102] prohibits any abuse which falls within the ambit of the Article. Many other acts by the plaintiffs are also prohibited, whether by statute, common law or equity, or under the Treaty. I do not think that it could be said that a person in breach of some statutory or other prohibition thereupon becomes an outlaw, unable to enforce any of his rights against anyone. If the plaintiffs are imposing unfair selling prices in that they charge too much for their product, I cannot see why this breach of the prohibition of Article [102] means that the Defendants are thereby set free from any liability to the plaintiffs, if they, the defendants, commit the tort of passing off (or indeed, any other tort) against them... ."

---

[52] *Volvo v Veng* (C-238/87) ECLI:EU:C:1988:477 at [9]. See para.12-144.
[53] *Volvo v Veng*, [7]–[11].
[54] *ICI Ltd v Berk Pharmaceuticals* [1981] F.S.R. 1; [1981] 2 C.M.L.R. 75.

14-037   In *British Leyland v Armstrong Patents*,[55] which has been discussed in relation to Euro-defences based on art.101, British Leyland, then a thriving car manufacturer, owned copyright in spare parts for cars. It offered licences to spare parts manufacturers which included a "blanket" royalty of 7 per cent on all parts, regardless of whether or not such were the subject of copyright. Armstrong, a manufacturer of spare parts, declined to take a licence and manufactured spare parts which it was alleged infringed the copyright. Armstrong pleaded a Euro-defence in relation to an action for infringement of copyright based, inter alia, on art.102. In particular, it argued that the blanket obligation to pay royalties on any spare part was an abuse.[56] The court rejected the defence on the basis that such was merely a practical method of assessing royalties on infringing parts.[57]

14-038   In *Lansing Bagnall Ltd v Buccaneer Lift Parts Ltd*,[58] an action for breach of copyright in 85 spare parts was brought against the defendant who claimed that the claimant was abusing a dominant position under art.102. It was accepted that the claimant had a dominant position as manufacturers of fork lift trucks. The defendant dealt in spare parts for fork lift trucks and thus had supplied spare parts for the claimant's fork lift trucks which it was alleged infringed the claimant's copyright. The defendant pleaded a Euro-defence under art.102, relying on the actions of the claimant in restricting the number of agents who could sell spare parts, whilst charging excessive prices for the spare parts and most importantly, instructing its agents to charge retail prices to other traders in spare parts who were not authorised by the claimants. The defendant said that the effect of such was that it was unable to make an ordinary commercial profit in the course of trade in spare parts. The claimant brought an application to strike out the Euro-defence on the grounds that it was simply enforcing its copyright. The first instance judge held that the allegations in the Euro-defence were not linked in any relevant way with art.102, relying upon *ICI v Berk Pharmaceuticals* and struck out the Euro-defence. On appeal, this decision was reversed. The court considered that there was sufficient nexus for the Euro-defence to go to trial. It distinguished *ICI v Berk* as being a passing off case and that it could not be an abuse of a dominant position to stop someone passing off. Here, we see collateral abusive conduct as arguably giving rise to a Euro-defence under art.102. Interestingly, one of the appellate judges (Templeman LJ) said:

> "If the enforcement by the plaintiffs of their copyright monopoly, including enforcement by means of the present litigation against the defendants, amounts to an infringement of the European Community Treaty, the English court will be faced with the dilemma of preventing that infringement or upholding the copyright monopoly granted to the plaintiffs by the national law. In the present case, if that dilemma ever presents itself as a result of the evidence and findings of the judge at the trial, it is possible that the English court may be able to resolve the dilemma by declining to grant an injunction to enforce the copyright monopoly, awarding damages in lieu of an injunction so as to give effect to the law and damages to a reasonable royalty on the infringing articles so as to prevent the plaintiffs abusing their copyright protection in such a way as to infringe the European Community Treaty."[59]

14-039   This could be described in modern parlance as prescribing a proportionate

---

[55] [1984] F.S.R. 591 CA.
[56] See para.8-259 as to whether such is contrary to art.101.
[57] In doing so, the Court of Appeal showed considerable prescience. The 2014 Technology Transfer Guidelines generally are of the same view—see para.8-263.
[58] *Lansing Bagnall Ltd v Buccaneer Lift Parts Ltd* [1984] 1 C.M.L.R. 224 CA.
[59] *Lansing Bagnall Ltd* [1984] 1 C.M.L.R. 224 CA at [14]. Reiterated in *Ransburg-Gema AG v*

response to the allegation of abuse. Thus, in the modern world, it could be said that the proportionate response is simply to state that the defendant had a remedy for damages for breach of art.102 by way of counterclaim. The jurisdiction to award damages for breach of art.102 was not recognised in the 1980s but is now firmly part of European and English law.

Conversely, in *Ransburg-Gema v Electrostatic Plant*,[60] a Euro-defence under art.102 was struck out. The defendant was sued for infringement of copyright in drawings relating to electro-static powder coating equipment. The Euro-defence alleged a number of matters of conduct including: (i) threatening to institute proceedings, (ii) intending by the action to drive the defendant out of business by *inter alia* saying to potential customers that the defendant would have to pay substantial monies and that it was disreputable, (iii) a refusal to sell spare parts to the defendant, (iv) claiming non-compensatory conversion damages, and (v) claiming an injunction to prevent the importation into the UK of goods lawfully marketed in another part of the common market, namely Spain. These were all struck out. The impression in the case was that the defendant simply relied upon a host of grounds which had little relevance to abusive conduct under art.102. Perhaps the closest allegation (mirroring that raised in *Lansing Bagnall*) was the refusal to supply spare parts. However, as said by the judge, art.102 does not have the effect that all refusals to supply spare parts are wrongful. Something more than mere refusal was required and such was not particularised. Thus, some reliance was placed on *Volvo v Veng* that an arbitrary refusal to supply spare parts could be abusive. However, it was held that the defence was not properly particularised.

14-040

In *Pitney-Bowes v Francotype-Postalia GmbH*,[61] which is a case about unfair prices and art.102, an American manufacturer of postal franking machines and its British subsidiary sued a rival German manufacturer for infringing its patents. A Euro-defence was raised and this was the subject of a strike out application. The court held that the allegations that the patentee charged unfairly high prices, discriminated against small customers by charging them unjustifiably higher prices and discriminated against the home market by exporting at lower prices might amount to an abuse of a dominant position. The judge held that that *Volvo v Veng* was authority for the principle that abuses need not be a direct or even an indirect consequence of the relief claimed in the action but that it was sufficient that the existence of the intellectual property right created or buttressed the dominant position which the patentee was abusing and that the remedy contemplated by the CJEU in *Volvo v Veng* was that the patentee may have to be deprived of the means of maintaining its dominant position.[62] In the author's view, care must be taken with this judgment. IPRs will often permit the maintenance or reinforcement of a dominant position. Indeed, the dominance of the right holder may have been achieved by reason of the IPRs and it is established law that the mere exercise of rights by a dominant undertaking is not in itself an abuse,[63] as indeed is the fact that a dominant position is not in itself an abuse. Interestingly, it was argued by the patentee that stripping the dominant supplier of the right to exercise its patent rights

14-041

Electrostatic Plant Systems Ltd [1989] 2 C.M.L.R. 712 (Pat) at [21].
[60] *Ransburg-Gema AG* [1989] 2 C.M.L.R. 712 (Pat) at [23]. This was appealed but not on the Euro-defences.
[61] [1990] 3 C.M.L.R. 466.
[62] See [11].
[63] See para.12-130, et seq.

lacked proportionality but the court considered that this issue should go to trial.[64] In contrast, Euro-defences based on the action being brought in bad faith and malpractices by the patentee's salesmen were not sufficiently connected with the existence of the dominant position and did not amount to an abuse. Here, the judge was ruling whether such conduct in itself could amount to an abuse rather than whether it was an abuse. Such was sufficiently connected with the exercise of rights to give rise to a Euro-defence.[65]

14-042   *Chiron v Murex Diagnostic (No.2)*[66] was concerned with a biotechnological patent where the claimant claimed infringement and the defendant alleged that the claimant was abusing its dominant position by refusing to license, charging unfair prices, etc. The Euro-defence was struck out on the basis that the alleged abuse could not affect trade between Member States. However, the Court of Appeal considered the position if such was not the case. The first instance judge held that there was a plead-able case that the patentee had abused its dominant position by charging excessive prices for its immunoassay kits contrary to art.102. The Court of Appeal then considered the issue of nexus. The first instance judge had found that there was sufficient nexus between the alleged unfair prices and the patent actions. He said that the whole purpose of the action was to ensure that the patentees and licensees had a monopoly and that the grant of injunctive relief would buttress the ability of the patentee to continue its abusive conduct, namely the charging of unfair prices (relying upon *Pitney-Bowes*). The Court of Appeal considered a submission by the patentee that the proper remedy in such circumstances was an action for damages under art.102 or a complaint to the European Commission. The Court of Appeal found favour with this but did not consider that the judge was plainly wrong. However, one of the judges was of the opinion that the "plainly wrong" test was not appropriate, and considered that there was no nexus. He held that the appropriate and proportionate remedy was not to refuse relief even if the abuses were made out. He decided that such was altogether lacking in proportionality. As the judge said, there may be extraordinary cases where the holder of a patent should be refused relief on the ground that such was in breach of art.102 but such was not made out in the case.

Nexus: summary

14-043   The cases above illustrate the difficulty in relying upon arts 101 and 102 as a defence to the exercise of IPRs. In relation to art.101, much of the jurisprudence in this area (e.g. *Consten v Grundig*, *Sirena v Eda Srl* and *Tepea Commission*) arose before it was clear that trade mark or other rights could not be used to prevent parallel imports of goods first placed on the market within the EEA. Thus, even if there was an anti-competitive agreement between the owner of a trade mark and their authorised network in the EU to prevent trade in such goods and partition the EU single market, the owner could not use its trade mark to prevent trade in the same. The parallel importer would have a complete defence under EU trade mark law without the need to rely upon art.101 as a defence. Conversely, if the enforcement of a registered trade mark against goods bearing a trade mark *is justified* under the EUTM Regulation or the EU Trade Mark Directive (e.g. because they are goods

---

[64]   See [13].

[65]   The question whether the threat or bringing of proceedings by themselves can amount to an abuse is discussed at para.12-306.

[66]   *Chiron Corp v Murex Diagnostic (No.2)* [1994] F.S.R. 187; [1994] 1 C.M.L.R. 410 CA.

first placed on the market outside the EEA), does unlawful trade become lawful trade merely because their enforcement is connected with an anti-competitive agreement? Is the trade mark owner not entitled to say that EU trade mark law has conferred a right on it to stop such a trade and that is all it is doing? In essence, that is what the Supreme Court found in *Oracle v M-Tech*.

Yet undoubtedly, in *Oracle v M-Tech*, it was a combination of the enforcement **14-044** of trade mark rights and the withholding of provenance information that meant that the independent sector was unable to trade effectively in both lawful and unlawful branded goods as they could not differentiate between the two and that was the aim and object of Oracle. The undeniable effect was to oust the independent sector from the market in any Sun-branded goods, thereby reserving the same to Oracle and preventing effective competition in the secondary market between the authorised and independent sector. It would be surprising if EU law was too weak and emasculated not to provide a remedy to such actions.

In the case of art.102, *Volvo v Veng* and the authorities subsequent to it suggest **14-045** that the exercise of rights may amount to an abuse of a dominant position where this is itself an abuse (e.g. a patent infringement action for a SEP patent)[67] or this is not itself an abuse but is exercised to enforce or maintain some other extraneous abuse. For example, the maintenance of unfair prices or an arbitrary refusal to supply spare parts. Here, the focus is on the extraneous abuse, e.g. a refusal to supply spare parts to independent repairers. The exercise of IPRs are ancillary to that and in themselves, not an abuse. For instance, in *CEAHR II*, the Court of Justice held that a refusal to supply spare parts for Swiss watches to independent repairers was not an abuse of a dominant position where there existed an authorised network of repairers and there was sufficient competition between them.[68]

The proportionate remedy?

It may be that in truth, the real question is what is the right and proportionate **14-046** remedy? In *Oracle v M-Tech* the Supreme Court was clearly concerned that the defences under the TFEU would deprive the trade mark owner from enforcing his rights even against industrial counterfeiters.[69] Therefore, as said by the Supreme Court:

> "[27] … However, none of the cases go so far as to hold non-existent or unenforceable rights whose exercise would in itself have no impact on trade between member states, merely because they are accompanied by other acts which do. *The law responds to this situation by restraining the acts which do. It does not pull down the whole temple.*" [Emphasis supplied.]

In *Oracle v M-Tech* the proportionate remedy would have been an injunction to **14-047** restrain Oracle/Sun from exercising its rights without permitting the independent sector to distinguish between lawful and unlawful parallel imports. This would have allowed Oracle to deal effectively against unlawful parallel imports and counterfeits whilst allowing a flourishing competitive market in lawful parallel imports. When faced with a similar conundrum in *Van Doren + Q*, the Advocate-General suggested that the trade mark owner should have a duty of co-operation whereby they

---

[67] See para.12-216 for discussion of when the exercise of a SEP (Standard Essential Patent) may be contrary to art.102.
[68] See para.12-269.
[69] See [28] where it was conceded that the defence could be relied upon by industrial counterfeiters.

would mark goods clearly and comprehensibly to make it easier for distributors to determine whether or not the right conferred by the trade mark has been exhausted.[70]

14-048 It is very much hoped that the Court of Justice, which has never had any difficulty in crafting "creative solutions" to difficulties raised when the exercise of IPRs might prevent lawful trade in parallel imports, e.g. in the case of trade in the EU in repackaged pharmaceuticals whereby there is now a set of rules that must be complied with by brand owner and parallel importer, will come up with a similar creative solution. Therefore, in the UK, in *Glaxo v Dowelhurst (Defence Amendments)*,[71] it was argued that there were anti-competitive agreements between pharmaceutical companies to enforce trade marks to deter parallel importers. The pharmaceutical companies argued that such an allegation was bound to fail because even if such was the case, it would not mean that each pharmaceutical company could not *unilaterally* bring proceedings for patent infringement. The judge crafted a creative solution by holding that such defences were arguable, but that:

> "any relief granted will have to be carefully worded to prevent the collaboration but without taking away the right to sue for infringement of trade mark."[72]

14-049 Equally, in *Volvo v Veng* or *CEAHR II* if there had been an arbitrary refusal to supply spare parts to independent repairers and this was found to be an abuse of a dominant position, is the right remedy that those repairers could commission the making of the spare parts without fear of such being found to infringe? Or is the proportionate remedy an injunction which prohibits the Swiss watch makers from exercising their rights unless they supplied spare parts to the independent network? In the authors' view, whilst the Roman doctrine of *ubi jus, ibi remedium*[73] requires there to be an effective remedy, that remedy should be proportionate to the wrong to maintain the delicate balance between the right of a right holder to exercise their IPRs against any undertaking that infringes those rights and the need to prevent anti-competitive conduct.

Exercise of IPRs is contrary to arts 34–36

14-050 The application of arts 34–36 to the exercise of IPRs has been considered comprehensively in Ch.7—in particular, when it can prevent the exercise of IPRs. In short, arts 34–36 can be relied upon as a defence to an action for infringement of unharmonised IPR but recourse to arts 34–36 is not permitted where there is a harmonised right, although the CJEU has been inconsistent in its application of this principle. The reader is invited to read the relevant section in the Ch.7.[74] With regard to the requirement of nexus, there is no concern here with arts 34–36 as the exercise of rights directly engages the free movement provisions of TFEU.

---

[70] *Van Doren + Q v Lifestyle Sports* (C-244/00) ECLI:EU:C:2003:381 at [87]–[100]. This case concerned where the burden of proof should lie on a trader for proving that the conditions of exhaustion had been satisfied, i.e. that the goods in question had been put on the market in the EEA by the trade mark owner or with their consent. The Court of Justice held that where the burden of proof lay on the trader and such would give rise to a real risk of partitioning of the common market, the trade mark owner should have the burden of proof. This case is discussed at para.7-098.

[71] *Glaxo v Dowelhurst (Defence Amendments)* [2000] F.S.R. 371; [2000] E.T.M.R. 118 HC.

[72] See [22]. NB. In *Sportswear v Stonestyle*, it was argued that the judge should have found that such might give rise to a counterclaim for an action for breach of art.101 but could not amount to a defence to trade mark infringement proceedings. The Court of Appeal saw some force in that but declined to decide the point, see [67] per Lloyd LJ.

[73] "For every wrong, the law provides a remedy".

[74] See para.7-059 and para.7-093, et seq.

However, it is important to show that it is the exercise of rights which is contrary **14-051** to arts 34–36 rather than some other conduct. In *Oracle v M-Tech*,[75] which has already been discussed in the context of defences under art.101,[76] M-Tech said that the exercise of rights against unlawful parallel imports from outside the EEA but which had the object and effect of preventing trade in lawful parallel imports (i.e. goods marketed first in the EEA) was contrary to arts 34–36. The Supreme Court held that the unlawful conduct alleged by M-Tech was "collateral" to the particular right which Oracle was seeking to enforce.[77] It held that in fact arts 34–36 were not engaged because they apply only to the movement of goods within the EEA and not the entry of goods into the EEA and that Oracle was seeking to enforce its right to control the first marketing of the goods in the EEA.[78] Ultimately, the view of the Supreme Court was that to prevent Oracle from exercising its rights against unlawful parallel imports because such had the effect (and indeed was Oracle's aim) of preventing traders from dealing in lawful parallel imports was "to pull down the whole temple".[79] Recognising perhaps that the effect of the decision was (on the assumed facts) indeed to allow Oracle to eliminate trade in both lawful and unlawful parallel imports, the Supreme Court held that M-Tech might have a perfectly good cause of action against Oracle based on arts 34–36 for damages for preventing them from selling Sun branded goods by their policy of withholding information about the provenance of the goods. The court held that such was irrelevant to the appeal as it was not about what business M-Tech had been prevented from doing but rather what M-Tech had done in infringement of Oracle's trade marks. As the Supreme Court said in concluding its rejection of the defence based on arts 34–36:

> "[29] ... It is not a defence to proceedings brought on that basis that there is other business that M-Tech have been prevented from doing by Sun's arguably unlawful policy of withholding information."

In some respects, the defence under arts 34–36 raised more difficulties than under **14-052** art.101. This is because it is well recognised that art.101 can be used as a *cause of action* (a sword) as well as a *defence* (a shield). One can bring an action for breach of art.101 claiming damages and injunctive relief. However, it is unclear that arts 34–36 can be relied upon as a sword.[80] Thus, it was not open to M-Tech to sue Oracle for breach of arts 34–36 in relation to its policy of withholding information. The consequence was that unless the exercise of rights was prohibited, on the assumed facts, Oracle was able to achieve its goal of eliminating trade in both lawful and unlawful parallel imports. There was no potential "middle road" whereby Oracle could exercise its rights against the unlawful parallel imports and by counterclaim, M-Tech could bring an action seeking injunctive relief to prevent it from withholding information so that traders were able to trade effectively in lawful parallel imports.

It is of note that *Oracle* has some parallels in *Loendersloot*,[81] a case of the CJEU **14-053** in the 1990s. In that case, Ballantine was a whisky producer. It sold its whisky with

---

[75] [2012] 1 W.L.R. 2026.
[76] See para.14-022, et seq.
[77] See [24].
[78] See [25].
[79] See [27].
[80] To the author's knowledge, there is no case to such an effect.
[81] *Frits Loendersloot v George Ballantine & Son Ltd* (C-349/95) [1997] E.C.R. I-6227.

a trade mark and identification numbers. Loendersloot was a transport and warehousing firm which sold Ballantine whisky. Its customers included parallel traders. Ballantine claimed that Loendersloot removed labels carrying the trade marks from their whisky and re-labelled the products. Proceedings were brought for infringement of registered trade marks.[82] The Hoge Raad referred a number of questions to the CJEU including whether the action for infringement of registered trade marks was contrary to arts 34–36. One particular issue concerned the legitimacy of the removal of the identification numbers. Loendersloot claimed that such was necessary to prevent artificial partitioning of the markets between Member States. In essence, the argument was that identification numbers permitted whisky producers to enable them to determine the dealers who had supplied parallel traders and thereby prevent such conduct so as to eliminate parallel trade. However, Ballantine argued that such were necessary to deal with counterfeit whisky and also recall faulty products. The CJEU accepted that the identification numbers thus could be used for both legitimate and illegitimate purposes.[83] The CJEU thus said where identification numbers have been applied for purposes which are legitimate from the point of view of Community law but are also used to combat parallel trade, it is under the Treaty provisions on competition that those engaged in parallel trade should seek protection against actions of the latter type.[84]

14-054   From the above, it is clear that a real difficulty arises where a trade mark owner exercises its rights for a legitimate and an illegitimate purpose. Does one permit the exercise and thereby permit the trade mark owner to achieve both purposes, to avoid, as Lord Sumption said in *Oracle v M-Tech*, and discussed above, pulling down the whole temple?[85] Alternatively, does one try and find a *via media* (middle way) whereby the trade mark owner is entitled to exercise its rights against unlawful parallel imports and leave the parallel trader to bring counterclaims for breach of TFEU (e.g. seeking injunctive relief to restrain the unlawful conduct, i.e. in *Oracle*, the withholding of information). Or does one deny the trade mark owner the right to enforce its rights at all? Instinctively, the first and third options seem wrong. The second option seems appropriate because it is tailored to preventing the unlawful conduct but it may be difficult to find an appropriate cause of action under the TFEU. However, as discussed above, it is unclear whether a breach of arts 34–36 gives rise to a cause of action. It is tempting to say that where the solution to the difficulty lies with the right holder, it should not be allowed to exercise its rights without taking the steps necessary to prevent the exercise of its rights achieving an unlawful end. Thus, in *Oracle v M-Tech*, the ability to solve this dilemma lay with Oracle. It could have chosen not to withhold information which would have permitted traders to differentiate between lawful and unlawful parallel imports. Having chosen not to disclose such information, then it should live with the consequences and be denied relief.[86] This approach mirrors that suggested in rela-

---

[82]   This case is discussed at para.3-650.
[83]   See [29]–[41].
[84]   See [43].
[85]   See paras 3-129, 14-022 and 14-046. Another colourful expression is that one does not "throw out the baby with the bathwater"!
[86]   In *Van Doren + Q v Lifestyle Sports* (C-244/00) [2003] E.C.R. I-3051, the Advocate-General in her Opinion considered that in cases such as this, a duty lay on the right holder to permit the market to differentiate between lawful and unlawful parallel imports—see [91]–[100].

tion to arts 101 and 102 whereby the court should grant a remedy proportionate to the infringement of the TFEU.

ABUS DE DROIT

The CJEU has developed the doctrine of *abus de droit*. It is a civil law principle **14-055** that has not until recently had any part to play in the common law systems. It came to prominence in the field of tax schemes which complied with the letter but not the spirit of tax laws.

In *Emsland Stärke*,[87] the CJEU set out what has to be established before a court **14-056** can make a finding of "abuse of rights" under Community law. The court held:

"[52]   A finding of an abuse requires, first, a combination of objective circumstances in which, despite formal observance of the conditions laid down by the Community rules, the purpose of those rules has not been achieved.

[53]   It requires, second, a subjective element consisting in the intention to obtain an advantage from the Community rules by creating artificially the conditions laid down for obtaining it. The existence of that subjective element can be established, inter alia, by evidence of collusion between the Community exporter receiving the refunds and the importer of the goods in the non–member country."

As made clear by *Emsland Stärke*, there is a two-stage test. First, an objective **14-057** test whereby the formal application of EU legislation has been observed but such is contrary to the purpose of that legislation. Secondly, a subjective test, whereby the person intends to obtain an advantage of the EU legislation contrary to the purpose of the legislation. If the conduct of which complaint is made has some other explanation other than an abusive one, then it will not fall within the doctrine.[88] In other cases, the principle has been stated more simply—namely that Community law cannot be used for abusive or fraudulent ends.[89] The nature of the abuse was elegantly put in an English case by the Court of Appeal as:

"The abuse occurs when a person formally observes the preconditions to obtaining the right, but in fact the person has taken advantage of the right for a purpose for which the right was not intended when it was created."[90]

The *abus de droit* doctrine was considered in *Budějovický Budvar, národní* **14-058** *podnik v Anheuser-Busch Inc*,[91] a trade mark case. This case, which is discussed in Ch.3, "Trade Marks in Europe",[92] concerned the long-running war between a Czech brewer and a US brewer over the ownership of the trade marks BUD and BUDWEISER for beer. Following a long-running case, on 9 May 2000, the Court of Appeal allowed registration of the mark BUDWEISER by both parties. On 18 May 2005, four years and 364 days after the registration of the parties' BUD-WEISER mark, the US brewer applied to the UK Trade Marks Registry for a

---

[87]   *Emsland Stärke v Hauptzollamt Hamburg-Jones* (C-110/99) [2000] E.C.R. I-11569 at [52]–[53].
[88]   See *Halifax Plc v Customs and Excise Comrs* (C-255/02) [2006] E.C.R. I-1609 at [75].
[89]   See *Halifax* where AG Poiares Maduro traced the development of the concept in the jurisprudence of the CJEU ([62]–[71]) and concluded that no provision of EU law can be formally relied on to secure advantages manifestly contrary to its purposes and objectives. See [74]–[76] of the judgment of the CJEU in *Halifax* where such reasoning was adopted. See also *Diamantis v Greece* (C-373/97) [2000] E.C.R. 1705.
[90]   *Milk Supplies Ltd v DEFRA* [2010] 2 C.M.L.R. 40 CA at [16] citing *Emsland Stärke* and *Halifax*.
[91]   (C-482/09) [2011] E.C.R. I-8701; ECLI:EU:C:2011:46.
[92]   See paras 3-422 to 3-426.

declaration of invalidity based on its earlier trade mark. The significance of this was that if the Czech brewer decided to issue a cross-application based on *its* earlier trade mark, it would have been out of time because of a provision in the Trade Mark Directive which prevents such applications where the applicant has acquiesced for five years or more in the other's trade mark. A number of questions were referred to the CJEU which did not expressly concern the *abus de droit* doctrine.

14-059   A number of Member States (who intervened in the proceedings) submitted that the US brewer's act in applying only one day before the expiry of the five-year period should be classified as an abuse of rights. Thus the Czech and Slovak arguments were that by making the application one day before the expiry of the five-year period so that the Czech brewer *could not*, in its defence, rely upon by way of defence, the five-year acquiescence period but the US brewer *could*, the US brewer deprived the Czech brewer of the possibility of defending itself.

14-060   The Advocate-General decided to deal with the issue although it was not expressly raised by the English Court of Appeal.[93] The Advocate-General noted that EU law had a concept of abuse of rights and had acquired a relatively clearly defined content. She said that it may be simply understood as meaning that EU law cannot be relied upon for abusive or fraudulent ends.[94] However, she rejected that such applied in *Budějovický Budvar, národní podnik v Anheuser-Busch Inc*. She said:

> "[121] ... find that argument unconvincing, as it rests on the questionable basic assumption that the acquiescing party is to be prevented from making full use of the period specified in art.9(1), out of consideration for another party who, generally unlawfully, is using an identical mark. *But the right-holder must be conceded the right to apply the rules of substantive and procedural law in the way that is most to his advantage without laying himself open to an accusation of abuse of rights.*[95]
>
> [122] Regardless of the question already considered in detail of whether the co-existence of the two marks on the basis of the doctrine of honest concurrent use recognised in national law is permissible under EU law, this argument must therefore be countered by stating that it must be possible in principle for an action which is necessary for complying with a time-limit to be done up to the end of the last day. That corresponds both to the principles of the procedural laws of the European Union and its Member States and to the objectives of the directive. The expectation of the proprietor of the later mark that he will be able to use it free from objection by the proprietor of the earlier mark is already adequately protected by the fact that EU law provides for limitation of rights to occur on the expiry of the five-year period of acquiescence. Until that period has expired, the proprietor of the later mark must be prepared for the other proprietor to take countermeasures at any time. The determination of a fixed time-limit of five years, as already explained, promotes legal certainty and effectively protects both parties by creating legal stability. To prevent the proprietor of the earlier mark from asserting his rights under art.4(1)(a) of the directive one day before expiry of the five-year period of acquiescence would ultimately amount to calling into question the validity of that provision. Blurring the fixed time-limit on considerate grounds, as the Czech and Slovak Governments envisage, would be detrimental

---

93   She considered that it had been implicitly referred to by the Court of Appeal.
94   See [119] of the Opinion.
95   In support of this principle, he cited an article (J. Drew and H. Priestley, "Anheuser-Busch and Budvar march on the ECJ" (2010) 5(2) *Journal of Intellectual Property Law & Practice*, 79–81) whose authors said that the right holder must be allowed to apply the rules of substantive and procedural law to his best advantage—see fn.79 to his Opinion.

to the principle of legal certainty and thus not within the intention of the legislature. Their argument must therefore be rejected." [Emphasis supplied.]

The issue of *abus de droit* was not considered by the CJEU as such was not a **14-061** question referred to the CJEU by the national court. It is submitted that the Advocate-General was right. There is no overriding duty that a person must conduct its affairs (including the acts done for the purpose of legal proceedings) in a manner that does not permit them to take full advantage of the law, provided such is not inconsistent with the purpose of the legislation. It is only if such objectively considered acts were done for a purpose manifestly not envisaged by the legislation, that the doctrine of *abus de droit* is potentially engaged. In the *Budějovický* case, the legislation made it clear that until five years had expired, the acquiescence defence did not apply. There was nothing to suggest that an application made just before that period had expired was contrary to the purposes of the Directive, even if in the circumstances of that case such gave the applicant a tactical advantage against its opponent. Any other approach would, as commented on by the Advocate-General, reduce legal certainty and effectively require parties to consider, when deciding upon a particular act, the interests of the opposing parties as well as their own.

The *abus de droit* doctrine was relied upon and referred to in *Oracle v M-Tech* **14-062** which has already been discussed above.[96] In essence, the argument was that the rationale and legislative background to the enactment of the Trade Mark Directive and EU Trade Mark regulation was for the purpose of achieving a single market. Thus, these legislative measures were passed pursuant to powers granted under the predecessor treaty to TFEU to permit the enactment of harmonising directives for the attainment of a single market. It was thus argued that the exercise of rights granted under these measures where such exercise had the *purpose* of partitioning the single market was an abuse of rights.[97] In essence, the argument was that where a party ostensibly exercised trade mark rights against unlawful parallel imports but with also the ulterior purpose (by reason of making it impossible for traders to differentiate between lawful and unlawful parallel imports) of preventing trade in lawful parallel imports, such was an abuse. It will be appreciated that where there is a non-abusive and an abusive aim behind the exercise of IPR, the problem is more difficult. Should a court: (i) prevent the exercise of rights completely (i.e. permit both the lawful and unlawful activities of the defendant), (ii) permit the exercise of the rights so that the right holder can prevent both the lawful and the unlawful acts, or (iii) deal with the matter in another way, e.g. leave the defendant with the right to bring a counterclaim?

The Supreme Court considered the matter acte clair and that there was no abuse. **14-063** It said:

"[35] The rule of EU law which Sun is invoking in the present case is to be found in articles 5 and 7(1) of the Trade Mark Directive. It is beyond argument that the purpose of those provisions was (among other things) to enable the trade mark proprietor to control the first marketing of his trade-marked goods in the EEA. The exercise of that right by Sun did not only satisfy the formal requisites of those articles. It was entirely consonant with their purpose. Even if (contrary to my view)

---

[96] *Oracle America Inc (formerly Sun Microsystems Inc) v M-Tech Data Ltd* [2012] 1 W.L.R. 2026 (Supreme Court). See para.14-023 where this case is discussed.
[97] For the purpose of the hearing, it was assumed that the *object* (i.e. purpose) of Oracle was to partition the markets by preventing legitimate trade in lawful parallel imports.

M-Tech were right to say that by achieving that purpose Sun was enabled to do other things which tended to eliminate independent resellers from the secondary market, that would not make it an abuse of rights."

14-064   In the author's view, the above excerpt effectively amounts to the establishment of a general principle that where rights are exercised for two purposes: one legitimate and the other illegitimate, such cannot amount to an *abus de droit*. M-Tech's argument (and it was part of the assumed facts) was that not only was Sun *enable* to eliminate (lawful) independent resellers from the secondary market but such was their *intention*. On any rational jurisprudential basis, where a party exercises rights which are ostensibly done for legitimate purpose,[98] arranges their affairs[99] so that they can, by the same exercise of rights, pursue an illegitimate purpose,[100] such should be seen as abusive—especially where that purpose actually succeeds.[101] In particular this could be the case where the abusive purpose has as its goal (and succeeds in that goal) the elimination of lawful parallel trade in the European market, which is a fundamental principle of the TFEU. It would be surprising if the *abus de droit* doctrine allowed the use of trade mark rights granted under EU secondary legislation for a purpose manifestly contrary to a fundamental principle of the TFEU itself—namely the attainment of a single market.

EUIPO and abus de droit

14-065   The *abus de droit* doctrine has been argued several times in trade mark disputes between EUIPO and, on appeal, to the General Court and the Court of Justice. Despite some enthusiasm for it by the Boards of Appeal,[102] the General Court and Court of Justice has been dismissive of arguments based on *abus de droit*. For instance, in *ultra air GmbH v OHIM*,[103] an application was brought to declare invalid the EUTM ULTRAFILTER on the grounds that it was devoid of distinctive character and indicative of a characteristic of filters. The Board of Appeal held that the application was an abuse of rights because the applicant itself wanted to use the mark ULTRAFILTER itself and the manager of the applicant had said that the mark was distinctive. The General Court overturned this finding and held that such did not matter and the Board of Appeal should have considered the substance of the application. The Court of Justice dismissed the appeal. However, interestingly, it was argued that the applicant for the declaration of invalidity was engaged in contradictory conduct—*venire contra factum proprium*—and this was an abuse of

---

[98] In *Oracle*, the prevention of imports into the EEA.

[99] In *Oracle*, the case proceeded on the basis that Oracle had withheld provenance information of its products so as to deny the independent sector the ability to differentiate between lawful parallel imports and unlawful parallel imports.

[100] The elimination of trade in lawful parallel imports (i.e. goods placed on the market in the EEA by the right holder or with their consent).

[101] In *Oracle v M-Tech*, the evidence was clear (and the application proceeded on the basis that such was indeed the case) that Oracle had succeeded in destroying a previously thriving independent trading sector in Oracle goods.

[102] e.g. *Alteco Chemical Pte Ltd ("SUPERGLUE")* R 66/2015-2 at [16] (filing an application for an identical mark to one which had previously been refused registration on absolute grounds was an abuse of rights); cf. R-991/2008-1 *RED BULL* where the Board of Appeal rejected an argument of *abus de droit* where an application for revocation against the well-known RED BULL mark was made by an importer of counterfeit clothing articles in response to criminal proceedings brought against it. Such was considered "a legitimate exercise of the right" conferred by the Community Trade Mark Regulation—see [22].

[103] *ultra air GmbH v OHIM* (T-396/11) ECLI:EU:T:2013:284.

rights. The Court of Justice held that this was not the case but interestingly, did not say that there was no scope for the application of the principle.[104] However, in *Castell*, the Court of Justice had to deal with a case whereby a party sought to invalidate the mark CASTEL on the grounds that it was a GIO, then during the proceedings, itself applied to the German Patent and Trade Mark Office to register CASTEL. The Board of Appeal dismissed the application for invalidity. On appeal to the General Court, the intervenor (the owner of the EUTM) argued that it was an abuse of rights for the declarant to seek a declaration of invalidity where it had itself applied for the mark. It thus said that the action was inadmissible. The General Court dismissed this ground. It said that an argument alleging abuse of rights cannot play any part as regards the admissibility of the action.[105] On appeal to the Court of Justice,[106] the court said that EUIPO's role was to assess whether the mark was descriptive and/or devoid of distinctive character and "the motives and earlier conduct of the applicant...cannot affect the scope of that task".[107] It went on to say that the "potential or actual economic interest pursued by the applicant for declaration for invalidity" is not relevant.[108] The Court of Justice here emphasised the public interest in cancelling registered EUTMs contrary to the EU Trade Mark Regulation.

The clear message from the General Court and Court of Justice is that EUIPO **14-066** should not consider the *abus de droit* doctrine. It is an administrator tasked with determining disputes under the EUTMR and its regulations. Yet, it has not been asked to consider an extreme case, e.g. where an applicant seeks to declare invalid a EUTM on the grounds of lack of distinctive character and also, simultaneously, applies to register as a EUTM the identical sign for the identical goods. Let us imagine that this second application is then opposed on the grounds that it is devoid of distinctive character. Can the declarant/applicant make wholly contrary submissions in the two sets of proceedings? This is not so much concerned with motive but rather the applicant's contradictory actions. Such would engage the principle *qui approbat non reprobat*—the sister principle to *veniore contra factum proprium*.[109] Whilst it is easy to say that both applications should be dealt with on their merits, allowing a party at the same time to run contradictory arguments brings the legal system into disrepute.

HUMAN RIGHTS

As discussed in the introductory chapter, the Charter of Fundamental Rights **14-067** forms an integral part of EU law.[110] Accordingly, EU legislation must be interpreted in the light of human rights enshrined in the Charter and the parallel convention, the European Convention on Human Rights. This includes the interpretation of EU intellectual property law. Unsurprisingly, human rights play a limited role in intellectual property law but there is some interaction.

Article 17(2) of the Charter stipulates expressly that intellectual property shall **14-068**

---

[104] *Donaldson Filtration Deutschland GmbH v EUIPO (intervenor ultra air GmbH)* (C-450/13P) ECLI:EU:C:2014:2016.

[105] *Fürstlich Castell'sches Domänenamt Albrecht Fürst zu Castell-Castell v EUIPO* (T-320/10) ECLI:EU:T:2013:424 at [18].

[106] (C-622/13P) ECLI:EU:C:2015:297.

[107] See [43]. citing *Donaldson Filtration*.

[108] See [44].

[109] "One who accepts cannot also reject".

[110] See para.1-038.

be protected. Furthermore, art.1 of Protocol No.1 of the European Convention on Human Rights stipulates that a person is entitled to peaceful enjoyment of his possessions. In *Anheuser-Busch v Portugal*, the Grand Chamber of the European Court of Human Rights held that such applies to intellectual property.[111] It also held that an application for a trade mark amounted to a set of proprietary rights recognisable under art.1 of Protocol No.1.[112]

14-069   The facts of this case merit discussion. In 1981, Anheuser-Busch, an American brewer well known for its BUDWEISER beer, applied in Portugal to register the mark BUDWEISER. The application was opposed by Budějovický Budvar as it owned an earlier appellation of origin, BUDWEISER BIER. In 1989, Anheuser-Busch applied to have the appellation of origin cancelled. This was granted in March 1995. Accordingly, in June 1995, the Portuguese intellectual property office registered BUDWEISER as a trade mark in Anheuser-Busch's name. In February 1996, Budějovický appealed against this decision to the Portuguese Court of First Instance arguing that the registration contravened a 1986 Agreement which entered into force in 1987 and was concluded between Portugal and the Republic of Czechoslovakia concerning the protection of geographical indications of origin. This was dismissed by the Court of First Instance but the appeal was allowed by the Lisbon Court of Appeal which ordered the intellectual property office to refuse to register BUDWEISER as a trade mark. This decision was upheld by the Supreme Court of Portugal. Anheuser-Busch applied to the European Court of Human Rights, arguing that the Supreme Court's decision amounted to an infringement of its rights under art.1 of Protocol 1 of the European Convention on Human Rights.

14-070   The principal argument of Anheuser-Busch was that the Supreme Court of Portugal had deprived it of its possession (i.e. the application for a trade mark) by giving effect to a bilateral treaty which had come into force after it had filed its application to register the trade mark. Having held, as said above, that the application for a trade mark amounted to a possession within the meaning of art.1 of Protocol no.1, the majority of the Grand Chamber found that there had been no unlawful interference with the applicant's rights. The Grand Chamber considered that the case could be distinguished from cases where the legislature had intentionally implemented legislation with retrospective effect (where a breach of human rights had been found). It said that in the instant case, the very question whether the legislation was retrospectively applied was in issue. It held that in such cases, the rightful place for resolution of the dispute was before the domestic courts.[113] The majority therefore concluded that the decision of the Supreme Court was not arbitrary or manifestly unreasonable. A concurring opinion found that an application for a trade mark did not give rise to a legitimate expectation that it would be realised and thus it did not give rise to a right protected under art.1 of Protocol 1. Interestingly, there was a dissenting opinion which held that the US brewer did have a legitimate expectation. This opinion concluded that the majority reasoning was debatable and contradictory. The dissenting opinion concluded that there had been an unlawful interference with the US brewer's legitimate expectation. It accordingly concluded that by applying the 1986 agreement and applying it retroactively, the Portuguese authorities had objectively caused damage to the applicant.[114] In the author's opinion, the criticism in the dissenting opinion of the majority verdict has

---

[111] *Anheuser-Busch v Portugal* (73049/01) [2007] E.T.M.R. 24 at [72].
[112] See [78], judgment of Grand Chamber.
[113] See [85].
[114] paras 9 and 10 of Dissenting Opinion.

much merit. In truth, the Portuguese court had dispossessed the US brewer of its application by the retroactive application of subsequent legislation. The fact that it was debateable whether that legislation was applicable retroactively misses the point. The Supreme Court of Portugal, by deciding that it did apply retroactively, did dispossess the US brewer of its application. The end result is the same as if it was clear that the bilateral agreement did apply retroactively.[115]

The decision emphasises that even if a breach of human rights had been **14-071** determined, such may only give rise to a liability of a party to pay damages for breach of the Convention rather than provide a defence. However, because of the obligation, following the Lisbon Treaty, to construe legislation in the light of the Charter, then such may have been sufficient to permit Anheuser Busch to succeed. Thus, in *Anheuser-Busch v Portugal*, a key issue was whether the Portuguese legislation should have been applied retroactively. If, as found by the ECHR, an application for a trade mark was protected under art.1 of Protocol 1, then such should have been a decisive factor in finding that on a proper interpretation, the bilateral agreement did not apply retroactively because otherwise, it would amount to a breach of the Convention.

In *The Queen v Secretary of State of Health*,[116] the Administrative Court rejected **14-072** an application for judicial review of UK legislation intended to put into effect the Plain Packaging for Tobacco Products Directive on the grounds that the UK state had unlawfully expropriated tobacco companies' registered trade marks contrary to art.1 of Protocol 1 of the European Convention of Human Rights. The judge held that such was a control of use of the tobacco companies' trade marks and not an expropriation of property and the interference was unequivocally in the public interest. It also rejected the argument that UK legislation could not provide derogations from the EUTMR. This was plainly a bold argument given that the UK legislation was derived from the Tobacco Products Directive and to have found otherwise would have meant that an EU Directive was inferior in status to an EU regulation and therefore void.

E-commerce Directive

The E-Commerce Directive[117] was introduced in 2000 to set up an internal market **14-073** framework for electronic commerce. Importantly, it established certain defences for intermediaries in the electronic information sector such as internet service providers ("ISPs") to actions for infringement of intellectual property rights. These are the "conduit", "caching" and "hosting" defences. The underlying purpose of these defences was to ensure that intermediaries who play a valuable role in the information society such as ISPs and Online Market Operators ("OMOs", e.g. eBay) were not rendered liable for innocent or unintended infringements in an online environment. As said in the recitals of the E-Commerce Directive, the development of electronic commerce within the information society offers significant employment opportunities in the EU but that development is hampered by a number

---

[115] Perhaps the better point was that the fact that it was debateable presumably meant that it was not the clear intention of the Portuguese legislature to apply the legislation retroactively and it would appear that the intention of the legislature is important in such circumstances—see [84]. However, the majority did not determine it on the basis that it was not a breach of art.1 of Protocol 1 to introduce *unintentionally* legislation with retroactive effect.

[116] [2016] EWHC 1169.

[117] Dir.2000/31 [2000] OJ L178/1.

of legal obstacles to the proper functioning of the EU market. One of the purposes of the E-Commerce Directive was to ensure that intermediaries were indeed not hampered unduly in the provision of their services by the application of intellectual property laws.

14-074   The defences only apply to those who provide an "information society service". Article 2(a) of the E-Commerce Directive defines such as being services within the meaning of art.1(2) of Dir.98/34 (as amended by Dir.98/48).[118] It defines "information society service" as meaning:

> "any service normally provided for remuneration, at a distance, by electronic means and at the individual request of a recipient of services."[119]

14-075   The three defences of "mere conduit", "caching" and "hosting" are now considered.[120]

Mere conduit and caching

14-076   Articles 12 and 13 of the E-Commerce Directive provide as follows:

> **"Article 12**
>
> ### 'Mere conduit'
>
> **1.**   Where an information society service is provided that consists of the transmission in a communication network of information provided by a recipient of the service, or the provision of access to a communication network, Member States shall ensure that the service provider is not liable for the information transmitted, on condition that the provider:
>
> (a)   does not initiate the transmission;
>
> (b)   does not select the receiver of the transmission; and
>
> (c)   does not select or modify the information contained in the transmission.
>
> **2.**   The acts of transmission and of provision of access referred to in paragraph 1 include the automatic, intermediate and transient storage of the information transmitted in so far as this takes place for the sole purpose of carrying out the transmission in the communication network, and provided that the information is not stored for any period longer than is reasonably necessary for the transmission.
>
> **3.**   This Article shall not affect the possibility for a court or administrative authority, in accordance with Member States' legal systems, of requiring the service provider to terminate or prevent an infringement.
>
> **Article 13**
>
> ### 'Caching'
>
> **1.**   Where an information society service is provided that consists of the transmission in a communication network of information provided by a recipient of the service, Member States shall ensure that the service provider is not liable for the automatic, intermediate and temporary storage of that information, performed for the sole purpose of making more

---

[118] This Directive concerns the provision of information in the field of technical standards and regulations—EC Dir.98/37 [1998] OJ L204/37 as amended by EC Dir.98/48 [1998] OJ L217/18. Now codified at Dir.2015/1535.

[119] See also *Google France SARL v Louis Vuitton Malletier SA; Google France SARL v CNRRH; Google France SARL v Viaticum SA* (C-236–238/08) [2010] E.C.R. I-2417 at [14], [15] and [111].

[120] For those readers familiar with the E-Commerce Directive who are wondering where discussion of the prohibition on general monitoring is discussed in this book, this can be found at para.15-035, et seq. where the ability to grant website blocking injunctions is discussed.

efficient the information's onward transmission to other recipients of the service upon their request, on condition that:

    (a)   the provider does not modify the information;

    (b)   the provider complies with conditions on access to the information;

    (c)   the provider complies with rules regarding the updating of the information, specified in a manner widely recognised and used by industry;

    (d)   the provider does not interfere with the lawful use of technology, widely recognised and used by industry, to obtain data on the use of the information; and

    (e)   the provider acts expeditiously to remove or to disable access to the information it has stored upon obtaining actual knowledge of the fact that the information at the initial source of the transmission has been removed from the network, or access to it has been disabled, or that a court or an administrative authority has ordered such removal or disablement.

2.   This Article shall not affect the possibility for a court or administrative authority, in accordance with Member States' legal systems, of requiring the service provider to terminate or prevent an infringement."

These two defences can be considered together. In the recitals of the **14-077** E-Commerce Directive, it states that the exemptions from liability cover only cases:

> "[42] ... where the activity of the information society service provider is limited to the technical process of operating and giving access to a communication network over which information made available by third parties is transmitted or temporarily stored, for the sole purpose of making the transmission more efficient; this activity is of a mere technical, automatic and passive nature, which implies that the information society service provider has neither knowledge of nor control over the information which is transmitted or stored."[121]

These defences reflect the fact that information service providers such as ISPs **14-078** who are responsible for the transmission of data from one server to a computer (i.e. the technical process whereby a person at a computer views a website stored on a remote server) will inevitably create temporary electronic reproductions of the contents of the website when transmitting such content. Furthermore, it could be said that the act of transmission could be considered a communication to the public of any copyright works on the remote server. Under the Information Society Directive, transient electronic reproductions and acts of communication to the public of copies of copyright works are, if done without the permission of the copyright owner, infringing acts.[122] Thus, the "caching" and "conduit" defences exempt the ISP from liability. In order to benefit from such exemptions, the ISP must not be involved in any way with the information transmitted.[123] Thus, as said by the recitals, they must not modify the information transmitted, other than manipulations of a technical nature which take place in the course of the transmission (as such do not alter the integrity of the information contained in the transmission).[124]

However, there are a number of important safeguards. Thus, where the "conduit" **14-079**

---

[121] Recital 42. See also, *Google v France*, at [113].

[122] Article 5.1(a) Information Society Directive also provided a defence for temporary acts of reproduction which are an "integral and essential part of a technological process" and whose sole purpose is to enable a transmission in a network between intermediaries between third parties by an intermediary. This is similar to the "conduit" and "caching" defences in the E-Commerce Directive but it is only a carve out from the exclusive right of reproduction right and not other exclusive rights of a copyright holder. See paras 4-327 to 4-335.

[123] Recital 43.

[124] Recital 43.

and "caching" defence is relied upon, it is expressed to be without prejudice to the right of a court or administrative authority to order the intermediary service provider to terminate or prevent an infringement. This has opened the door for the application of provisions in the Information Society Directive and Enforcement Directive to permit the grant of injunctions against ISPs to prevent access by users to websites which contain unlawful copyright works as well as injunctions that require the service provider to remove specific offending content. This is discussed in Ch.15, "Procedure and Remedies for Enforcement of IPRs".[125]

14-080   In an interesting case *McFadden v Sony Music*[126] concerning the ambit of the "mere conduit" defence, the CJEU had to consider the liability of a person who provides unprotected free "wi-fi". Mr McFadden ran a business selling and leasing lighting and sound systems in Germany. Using the free wi-fi network provided by Mr McFadden, an infringing musical work was made available on the Internet without the consent of the right holder. Mr McFadden said that he did not commit the infringement but did not rule out the possibility that someone had used his network to make the infringing musical work available. Sony, the right holder, gave formal notice to Mr McFadden to respect its rights over the phonogram. Mr McFadden brought an action for a negative declaration (*negative Feststellungsklage*) before the referring court. This was met with a counterclaim from Sony seeking relief for infringement of their phonogram rights. The German court dismissed Mr McFadden's claims and upheld Sony's counterclaim. Mr McFadden appealed that judgment averring that he was exempt under the "mere conduit" provisions of the E-Commerce Directive.

14-081   On appeal, the German court said that it was inclined not to hold Mr McFadden personally liable on the basis that he was indirectly liable for failing to have secured the network from which the rights were infringed anonymously. However, it was not sure that it could do so by reason of art.12 of the E-Commerce Directive. It accordingly referred a number of questions to the Court of Justice.

14-082   First, the Court of Justice held that the fact that Mr McFadden was providing the Wi-Fi free of charge did not preclude him from relying on art.12(1) as he was an "information service provider" within the meaning of art.12(1).

14-083   Secondly, the Court of Justice held that it was not necessary for the application of art.12(1) that any conditions should apply other than that the access must be "technical, automatic and passive". Therefore, it was not necessary for there to be a contractual relationship between the recipient and provider of the service or for the service provider to advertise the service. Thirdly, the court held that the conditions in art.14.1(b) (the information service provider must act expeditiously to remove or to disable access to illegal information) did not apply to art.12. The court held that hosting (with which art.14 is concerned) consisted of the storage of information and was of a more permanent nature compared to the service of transmitting information which is not normally continued over any length of time. Finally, and importantly, the court considered whether the right holder could claim injunctive relief to prevent the recurrence of the infringement, compensation and costs against a network access provider whose services were used in the infringement.

14-084   Relying upon art.12(3) E-Commerce Directive, the court held that the right holder could seek injunctive relief to prevent the infringement. Furthermore, the

---

[125] See para.15-035.
[126] (C–484/14) EU:C:2016:689.

right holder could seek reimbursement of the costs of doing so. However, they could not recover compensation against the service provider. The referring court was troubled by the grant of injunctive relief which would force Mr McFadden either to terminate the free Wi-Fi connection, password-protect the Internet connection or monitor all communications passing through it. Here, the court had to balance the right to protect intellectual property rights in art.17(2) Charter of Fundamental Rights, the right of Mr McFadden to conduct a business (art.16 Charter of Fundamental Rights) and the right of others to freedom of information (art.11 Charter of Fundamental Rights). It said that in these circumstances, a fair balance had to be struck between the rights. It held, applying its jurisprudence in relation to website blocking injunctions, that the person injuncted was free to decide which measures should be adopted to achieve the result sought (applying *UPC Telekabel Wien*[127]). In *McFadden*, there were only three measures in practice which could be adopted. It held that monitoring was not feasible and that terminating the Wi-Fi would be a serious infringement of the freedom to conduct a business. Accordingly, it said that a measure requesting people accessing the Wi-Fi to use a password was reasonable provided that such persons were required to reveal their identity. The disclosure of identity was necessary to dissuade users from infringing copyright or related rights.

Caching

On first blush, it is not obvious what the difference is between the "mere conduit" **14-085** defence and the "cache" defence. Both are concerned with the automatic, intermediate and temporary storage of information by an information service provider. However, "caching" happens where such is done "for the sole purpose of making more efficient the information's onward transmission to other recipients of the service". It is the technical process that creates temporary but durable "cache" copies of websites and their contents. This is often done by Internet "spiders" such as Google which will create cached copies of websites on servers for ease of searching and speed of transmission (by ensuring that they are stored on servers close to recipients). Indeed, art.13.1(e) deals with the situation whereby an old cached copy of a webpage exists even though the webpage has actually been taken down. If the original webpage has been taken down, the economic consequences of the public being able to access a cached copy of such a webpage becomes much more significant as such will be the only source. In such circumstances, once the ISP has actual knowledge that a computer or server under its control has a "cached" "orphan" which infringes a copyright work stored on it, (in practice, normally provided by a letter to the ISP from the copyright owner or its representatives), the ISP must act expeditiously to remove or disable access to the cached copy.

Hosting

The hosting defence is different in nature to the caching and conduit defence. It **14-086** applies to the storage of information of a "more permanent" nature to those providing access to a communication network.[128] Thus, it is very common in the "cloud" era for businesses to provide remote servers for businesses and people to store data

---

[127] Discussed at para.15-035.
[128] See *McFadden v Sony Music*, at [61].

on. A good example of this can be seen with Google Drive and DropBox[129] whereby these businesses permit the automatic "syncing" of data between local computers and a remote server (often called a "cloud server"). Other examples of hosting can be organisations such as eBay (usually called Online Market Operators) which allow third parties to post advertisements for products on their websites. Those who host information store it in permanent electronic form and such information is normally intended to be on the computer or server for a significant period of time. The hosting defence is in art.14 which provides as follows:

"*'Hosting'*

1. Where an information society service is provided that consists of the storage of information provided by a recipient of the service, Member States shall ensure that the service provider is not liable for the information stored at the request of a recipient of the service, on condition that:
    (a) the provider does not have actual knowledge of illegal activity or information and, as regards claims for damages, is not aware of facts or circumstances from which the illegal activity or information is apparent; or
    (b) the provider, upon obtaining such knowledge or awareness, acts expeditiously to remove or to disable access to the information.
2. Paragraph 1 shall not apply when the recipient of the service is acting under the authority or the control of the provider.
3. This Article shall not affect the possibility for a court or administrative authority, in accordance with Member States' legal systems, of requiring the service provider to terminate or prevent an infringement, nor does it affect the possibility for Member States of establishing procedures governing the removal or disabling of access to information."

14-087   It can be seen from these provisions that the hosting defence only applies where the provider does not have actual knowledge of the illegal activity or information. In relation to a claim for damages, there is no requirement that the hosting entity knows that it is hosting illegal activity or information but merely that it is not aware of facts or circumstances from which the illegal information or activity is apparent. Thus, a hosting entity may have constructive knowledge of the illegal activity or information for the purpose of a claim for damages. However, it will not be liable even if it has such knowledge or awareness provided it acts expeditiously to remove or disable access to such information upon obtaining this knowledge or awareness. This has led to a practice whereby right holders issue "take down" notices to information service providers which the latter must then act upon.

14-088   Article 14(2) provides an important carve-out to the general hosting defence. If the information service provider is responsible (acts under the authority or control of the provider) for posting the unlawful material on the website, etc. then the provider cannot avail itself of the defence. This may be the case in active, interventionist OMOs and is discussed below.[130]

Internet keyword service provider

14-089   In *Google v France*, the CJEU had to consider whether the "hosting" defence applied to Google which provided an Internet keyword service (the well-known Google Adwords). The principal focus of the CJEU was on whether such a service

---

[129] *http://www.dropbox.com.*
[130] See para.14-090.

was "technical, automatic and passive".[131] It held that the mere fact that Google set the payment terms or provides general information to its clients did not deprive Google of the E-Commerce hosting defence.[132] It also held that the fact that there is concordance between the keyword selected and the search term entered in by the internet user was not sufficient to deprive it of the defence.[133] However, it held in contrast, the role played by Google in the drafting of the commercial message which accompanies the advertising link or in the establishment or selection of keywords was relevant.[134] It was up to the national court to determine whether on the facts and the terms of the service provided by Google, the role played by Google was technical, automatic and passive or not.[135]

Online Market Operators

In *L'Oréal v eBay*,[136] the CJEU had to consider the liability of eBay, an online **14-090** market operator ("OMO") familiar to many, where infringing goods were advertised by a customer on its website. In particular, it had to consider whether eBay's services were covered by the "hosting" defence. As a preliminary matter, it considered that eBay was providing an information society service. It held that an OMO could not avail itself of the "hosting" defence where instead of confining itself to providing a service neutrally (by a merely technical and automatic processing of the data provided by its customers), it plays an active role which gives it knowledge of, or control over, that data.[137] Thus, the CJEU considered that where the operator provides assistance which entails optimising the presentation of the offers for sale in question or promoting those offers, it must be considered not to have taken a neutral position between the customer-seller and potential buyers but to have played an active role of such a kind as to give it knowledge of, or control over, the data relating to those offers for sale. In such circumstances, it could not rely on the "hosting" defence.

Knowledge, awareness and remedies against a hoster

Injunctive relief

Under art.14.3, right holders are entitled to seek injunctive relief to end an **14-091** infringement in the courts of Member States against service providers regardless of the provisions of the e-commerce directive. Furthermore, art.14.1(b) and art.14.3 envisage "take down" notices whereby the service provider is required to remove or disable access to infringing material. These notices will generally contain sufficient information so as to make the service provider know or be aware that it is hosting unlawful material. This provision should be read alongside the ability of courts of Member States to order an intermediary to disable access to unlawful

---

[131] Recital 42, E-Commerce Directive.
[132] See [116].
[133] See [117].
[134] See [119].
[135] See [119].
[136] *L'Oréal SA v eBay International AG* (C-324/09) [2011] E.C.R. I-6011.
[137] See [113].

material under the Enforcement Directive regardless of the liability of the service provider.[138]

Damages

14-092   The wording of art.14.1(a) suggests that a hoster may be liable for damages even if it does not have actual knowledge that the material is unlawful. The phrase "not aware of facts or circumstances from which the illegal activity or information is apparent" is not clear but it must mean something less than actual knowledge. Thus, art.14.1(b) differentiates between "knowledge" and "awareness". In *L'Oréal v eBay*, the Court of Justice says that the service provider will be liable where a *diligent economic operator* would have realised that the activity was unlawful.[139] Where this is established, the service provider may be liable for damages if it does not act expeditiously to take down the unlawful material. One difficult area is where there is a bona fide dispute between the right holder and the advertiser or person primarily responsible for the unlawful material being posted on the hoster's website (the recipient). The latter may claim that there is no infringement. The service provider will often be unable to determine who is right. Would the service provider be liable for damages if it decides that the advertiser is correct and not the right holder and does not take down the alleged unlawful material but subsequently, it is shown that the right holder is correct? A diligent economic operator may be wholly unable to determine that the activity was unlawful. Here it is submitted that the hoster will be immune from an action in damages where it bona fide decides that there is no infringement after reasonable investigation. In practice, this is unlikely to happen because in such circumstances, hosters will usually take down the alleged unlawful material as they will have contracts with advertisers that allow them to take down the material where it is alleged on reasonable grounds that it is unlawful. It is then for the advertiser and the right holder to resolve the dispute between themselves.

---

[138] See para.15-035.
[139] See [124].

CHAPTER 15

PROCEDURES AND REMEDIES FOR ENFORCEMENT OF IPRS

TABLE OF CONTENTS

INTRODUCTION

Part III of TRIPS includes a number of important measures in the field of enforcement of intellectual property rights ("IPRs"). Such is recognition that the commercial value of IPRs rests on the ability to enforce them in an effective manner and to obtain within a reasonable period, effective remedies to prevent further infringements and compensation for past acts of infringement. Section 1 of Pt III sets out general obligations that contracting states must comply with in the conduct of proceedings relating to the enforcement of IPRs. Section 2 provides for a minimum level of protection in the civil judicial procedures and the final remedies that courts of contracting states can make. Section 3 provides for a minimum level of protection in the provisional measures that can be ordered by courts of contracting states. Section 4 sets out provisions relating to the seizure of counterfeit and pirate products by custom authorities. **15-001**

Subsequent to contracting states and the EU ratifying TRIPS, in 1998, the Commission published a Green Paper on combating counterfeiting and piracy in the EU.[1] This said that counterfeit and pirate products accounted for 5 to 7 per cent of world trade and that it was creating a *crise de confidence* in the EU. It noted that probably 100,000 jobs in the EU had been lost as a result of such activities. An investigation indicated that more than one third of all computer programs on personal computers were pirate.[2] The Green Paper suggested certain ways of reducing piracy and counterfeiting. This included the use of technical devices, sanctions and other means of enforcing IPRs and administrative co-operation between competent authorities. This was on top of a customs initiative to protect the external frontiers of the EU. **15-002**

At a EU level, these initiatives have resulted in: **15-003**

(a) A Directive on the Enforcement of Intellectual Property Rights ("the Enforcement Directive").

(b) A Regulation for the seizure by customs authorities of counterfeit and pirate goods ("the Customs Regulation").

---

[1] COM 98/569.

[2] See speech by T. Stoll (Head of DG Internal Market), "*L'état du Droit Communautaire*" given on 9 December 2005 published in *L'Efficacité des mesures de lutte contre la contrefaçon: étude compare*, Vol.4 (Paris: Société de Legislation Comparée, Colloques).

In this chapter, the Enforcement Directive is discussed. The Customs Regulation is discussed in Ch.16, "Border Controls".

HARMONISATION OF PROCEDURES AND REMEDIES RELATING TO ENFORCEMENT OF IPRs

15-004   Directive 2004/48[3] ("the Enforcement Directive") is intended to harmonise the measures, procedures and remedies appropriate to, and relevant to, proceedings relating to the infringement of IPRs based on the best practices of at least one Member State's laws. It is also intended to implement the EU's obligations under TRIPS.[4] Thus, when interpreting legislation of Member States which is intended to comply with the Directive, it is legitimate to consider the nature and purpose of the TRIPS provision and interpret the domestic measures in a manner so as to conform to TRIPS.[5] The general objective of the Enforcement Directive is to approximate the legislative systems of the Member States in order to ensure a high, equivalent and homogeneous level of intellectual property protection and to ensure that the IPR owner is not deterred from bringing legal proceedings for infringement of its IPRs.[6] Thus, it has been said that the purpose of the TRIPS Agreement, Paris Convention and the Enforcement Directive is to require Member States to ensure that there are effective legal remedies designed to prevent, terminate or rectify any infringement of an existing IPR.[7] On the other hand, it is not intended to apply to national procedural provisions relating to invalidation of IPRs as such are not concerned with the enforcement of IPRs which, for the purpose of the Enforcement Directive, are presumed to have been lawfully acquired.[8] Equally, it was held not to apply to an action brought by manufacturers of blank data media such as CD and CD-Rs regarding the fair compensation which they had to pay to collecting societies as part of a Dutch "private copying" levy that it levied against such manufacturers.[9]

15-005   The Enforcement Directive can be considered a "high level" directive which requires Member States to ensure that the enforcement of IPRs in Member States meets the above requirements but gives considerable freedom to Member States to decide how such objectives are achieved.

15-006   The Enforcement Directive is not intended to provide an exhaustive code concerning the enforcement of IPRs. Rather, it lays down a minimum standard concerning their enforcement. Thus, Member States are free to lay down measures that are more protective of IPRs.[10]

15-007   The Directive "cherry picked" the procedural provisions, sanctions and remedies of Member States that were effective in preventing counterfeit activities and require all Member States to provide such measures. Not only did that ensure that the fight against counterfeiting was effective but it also meant that there was harmonisation

---

3   Dir.2004/48 on the enforcement of intellectual property rights [2004] OJ L195/16–25.
4   Recitals 4, 5.
5   See para.1-180.
6   *Realchemie Nederland BV v Bayer CropScience AG* (C-406/09) [2011] E.C.R. I-9773 at [49]; Enforcement Directive Recitals 9 and 10.
7   *Bericap Záródástechnikai bt v Plastinnova 2000 kft (intervening party Magyar Szabadalmi Hivatal)* (C-180/11) ECLI:EU:C:2012:717 at [75]; *ACI Adam BV v Stichting de Thuiskopie* (C-435/12) ECLI:EU:C:2014:254 at [61]. See also art.1 Enforcement Directive.
8   *Bericap*, at [76].
9   *ACI Adam BV v Stichting de Thuiskopie* (C-435/12) ECLI:EU:C:2014:254.
10   e.g. see *Stowarzyszenie 'Oławska Telewizja Kablowa v Stowarzyszenie Filmowców Polskichi* (C-367/15) ECLI:EU:C:2017:36 at [23] citing *Hansson* (C-481/14) EU:C:2016:419 at [36] and [40].

of such practices across the EU. The Enforcement Directive is intended to cover all IPRs.[11] It is not intended to harmonise criminal procedures relating to IPRs.[12] Many of the Member States already provided the measures which the Enforcement Directive refers to. Thus, some states such as the UK have had to do little to comply with the Enforcement Directive.

General obligations

Article 41 of TRIPS has a number of general obligations concerning the conduct of proceedings involving the enforcement of IPRs. These include the need to ensure that IPR holders can bring effective action against any act of infringement of IPRs including the grant of expeditious remedies to prevent infringements and remedies. Such proceedings must be fair and equitable, not be unnecessarily complicated or costly, or entail unreasonable time limits or unwarranted delays.[13] Decisions on the merits of a case must be preferably in writing and reasoned. Furthermore, they can only be based on evidence in respect of which parties were offered the opportunity to be heard.[14] A right of appeal must exist.[15] However, there is no obligation to set up a specialist judicial system for dealing with IPR actions.[16] **15-008**

These obligations are contained within art.3 of the Enforcement Directive which provides: **15-009**

> "[1] Member States shall provide for the measures, procedures and remedies necessary to ensure the enforcement of the intellectual property rights covered by this Directive. Those measures, procedures and remedies shall be fair and equitable and shall not be unnecessarily complicated or costly, or entail unreasonable time-limits or unwarranted delays.
>
> [2] Those measures, procedures and remedies shall also be effective, proportionate and dissuasive and shall be applied in such a manner as to avoid the creation of barriers to legitimate trade and to provide for safeguards against their abuse."

The requirement that any measure, procedure or remedy must be effective, proportionate and dissuasive has been considered in a number of cases, European and national. The words are very general in nature and thus clearly give very considerable latitude to Member States and courts to fashion a wide variety of remedies. The courts have resisted changing well-established practices such as the invariable grant of injunctive relief following a finding of infringement of IPRs.[17] **15-010**

---

[11] arts 1 and 2, Recital 13; Press Release by EC Commission 2005/95/EC [2005] OJ L94/37 (although such has no legal force). It is more debateable whether it applies to confidential information (see *Force IndiaFormula One Team v 1 Malaysia Racing Team Sdn Bhd* [2013] EWCA Civ 780 CA at [108] (Lewison LJ was "sceptical" about the application of the Enforcement Directive to technical know-how). Indeed, it is of note that the Trade Secrets Directive (Dir. 2016/943) contains its own provisions on measures, procedures and remedies (art.6 to art.15) which are similar in nature to the Enforcement Directive.

[12] art.2(3).

[13] art.41(2).

[14] art.41(3).

[15] art.41(4).

[16] art.41(5). This addressed the concern of many developing countries that they did not have such resources.

[17] e.g. see in England, *Interflora v Marks & Spencer* where the court was asked to reconsider the practice concerning the grant of injunctions following a finding of infringement but the court declined to do so—[2013] EWHC 1484 at [18], et seq.

Proceedings

15-011   Article 42 of TRIPS amplifies on the meaning of "fair and equitable" procedures in art.41. It requires that defendants have the right to written notice of claims "which is timely and contains sufficient detail, including the basis of the claims". It requires that owners of IPRs, and federations or associations having legal standing to assert such rights, be able to bring proceedings for infringement. It also seeks to respect confidential information.

15-012   Article 4 of the Directive goes further than TRIPS as to the categories of persons that can bring infringement proceedings. Thus, not only do they include the holders of IPRs, intellectual property collective rights-management bodies and professional bodies that are entitled to defend the rights of the IPR owner, but, they also include "all other persons authorised to use those rights, in particular, licensees".

Evidence

15-013   Article 43 of TRIPS imposes obligations on contracting states to permit courts, where a party has presented "reasonably available evidence sufficient to support its claims", to be able to order a party to provide evidence "which is relevant to substantiation of [the] claims" of the other party subject to certain conditions to protect confidential information. Article 43(2) permits courts to make findings based on the evidence of one party if the other party refuses access to appropriate information.

15-014   Article 6 of the Directive implements these obligations.

> "[1]   Member States shall ensure that, on application by a party which has presented reasonably available evidence sufficient to support its claims, and has, in substantiating those claims, specified evidence which lies in the control of the opposing party, the competent judicial authorities may order that such evidence be presented by the opposing party, subject to the protection of confidential information. For the purposes of this paragraph, Member States may provide that a reasonable sample of a substantial number of copies of a work or any other protected object be considered by the competent judicial authorities to constitute reasonable evidence.
> [2]   Under the same conditions, in the case of an infringement committed on a commercial scale Member States shall take such measures as are necessary to enable the competent judicial authorities to order, where appropriate, on application by a party, the communication of banking, financial or commercial documents under the control of the opposing party, subject to the protection of confidential information."

15-015   The ability to order delivery up of banking, financial and commercial documents was inspired by the Mareva ("freezing") injunction available in England. As well as being able to order the provision of bank and financial documents, this injunction permits courts to "freeze" bank accounts and assets of the defendant in cases where there is a strong prima facie case and there is a risk of dissipation of assets. Often, there will be evidence of dishonesty.[18] In France, *saisie-contrefaçon* orders are often made upon the claimant providing a number of copies of alleged infringing works to the court. The last sentence of art.6(1) reflects this practice.

---

[18]   For further reading on Mareva injunctions which are now known as "freezing" injunctions, see S. Gee, *Commercial Injunctions*, 6th edn (London: Sweet & Maxwell, 2016).

Interim preservation orders

Article 50 of TRIPS contains a number of important provisions concerning **15-016** provisional measures. It is thus set out in full:

"[1] The judicial authorities shall have the authority to order prompt and effective provisional measures:
  (a) to prevent an infringement of any intellectual property right from occurring, and in particular to prevent the entry into the channels of commerce in their jurisdiction of goods, including imported goods immediately after customs clearance;
  (b) to preserve relevant evidence in regard to the alleged infringement.
[2] The judicial authorities shall have the authority to adopt provisional measures *inaudita altera parte* where appropriate, in particular where any delay is likely to cause irreparable harm to the right holder, or where there is a demonstrable risk of evidence being destroyed.
[3] The judicial authorities shall have the authority to require the applicant to provide any reasonably available evidence in order to satisfy themselves with a sufficient degree of certainty that the applicant is the right holder and that the applicant's right is being infringed or that such infringement is imminent, and to order the applicant to provide a security or equivalent assurance sufficient to protect the defendant and to prevent abuse.
[4] Where provisional measures have been adopted *inaudita altera parte*, the parties affected shall be given notice, without delay after the execution of the measures at the latest. A review, including a right to be heard, shall take place upon request of the defendant with a view to deciding, within a reasonable period after the notification of the measures, whether these measures shall be modified, revoked or confirmed.
[5] The applicant may be required to supply other information necessary for the identification of the goods concerned by the authority that will execute the provisional measures.
[6] Without prejudice to paragraph 4, provisional measures taken on the basis of paragraphs 1 and 2 shall, upon request by the defendant, be revoked or otherwise cease to have effect, if proceedings leading to a decision on the merits of the case are not initiated within a reasonable period, to be determined by the judicial authority ordering the measures where a Member's law so permits or, in the absence of such a determination, not to exceed 20 working days or 31 calendar days, whichever is the longer.
[7] Where the provisional measures are revoked or where they lapse due to any act or omission by the applicant, or where it is subsequently found that there has been no infringement or threat of infringement of an intellectual property right, the judicial authorities shall have the authority to order the applicant, upon request of the defendant, to provide the defendant appropriate compensation for any injury caused by these measures.
[8] To the extent that any provisional measure can be ordered as a result of administrative procedures, such procedures shall conform to principles equivalent in substance to those set forth in this Section."

Article 50 recognises that in certain cases, e.g. deliberate counterfeiting or piracy, **15-017** there is a need for fast and effective relief against the counterfeit or pirate. Indeed, it recognises that in certain circumstances, it is appropriate to grant such relief in the absence of the defendant and without legal proceedings having been issued. In England, courts are used to granting ex parte Orders prior to the issuing of proceedings for the purpose of preventing infringements and to preserve evidence. In general, such Orders will not be granted unless the evidence presents a strong case against the intended defendants. The applicant for such relief must justify his reason for seeking ex parte relief. If the applicant has delayed in seeking relief, then the courts are unlikely to grant such relief.

15-018   Depending on the severity of the infringement, English courts have at their disposal a wide range of powers that can be crafted to suit the circumstances of the case. At the most extreme is the "Anton Piller" which is now known as a Search and Seize Order.[19] Such an Order requires the defendant to permit the lawyers of the applicant to search premises (sometimes even home premises) to find infringing copies and incriminating evidence. A refusal by a defendant to permit entry to the named premises is a contempt of court punishable, in certain circumstances, by a fine or imprisonment. The Order always requires that a "supervising solicitor" attend the search. They must act in an independent manner, must explain the terms of the Order to the defendant, and must ensure that the applicant's lawyers abide by the terms of the Order. A Search and Seize Order has been described as the "nuclear weapon" of the English court's powers and thus will only be granted where there is a strong prima facie case against the defendant and a real risk that the defendant would not comply with an Order of the court requiring them to preserve evidence.[20]

15-019   Search and Seize Orders will usually contain other provisions such as injunctive relief which takes effect immediately the Order is served. Other less extreme orders are "Doorstep" Orders where the applicant's lawyers are permitted to serve preservation Orders on the doorstep of the premises where it is suspected that incriminating evidence can be found. However, they are not permitted to enter. In other cases, courts will simply order an ex parte Order for preservation of evidence where there is little reason to doubt that the defendant will disobey an Order of the court.

15-020   In France, the equivalent type of Order is a *saisie-contrefaçon*. This permits a court to order the search of premises where counterfeit items are suspected to be present. It would appear that such Orders are more readily ordered in France than the Search and Seize Orders in England and that often, proof of the IPRs relied upon and some of the infringing copies are sufficient to obtain such an Order. Often, the execution of *saisie-contrefaçon* Orders is accompanied by police. This does not occur in England and indeed it is emphasised that the Search and Seize Order is a civil and not a criminal Order. Thus, a defendant who refuses access to premises over which he has control and which are named in a Search and Seize Order is not committing a criminal offence but, as said above, is committing a contempt of court which ultimately, could lead to the court ordering the imprisonment of the defendant.

15-021   Article 50 of TRIPS applies to a wide variety of procedures. Thus, it has been found to apply to *kort geding* provisional measures in the Netherlands. Traditionally, in such circumstances, the court would grant such measures without requiring the claimant to initiate substantive proceedings. Rather, the burden was imposed on the defendant to seek to revoke or vary such measures. In *Hermes v FHT*,[21] the CJEU held that such measures fell within art.50. Thus, Hermes was obliged to issue substantive proceedings and could not rely upon the measures indefinitely. In

---

[19] The name "Anton Piller" comes from the name of a case in the 1970s where the Court of Appeal first approved the practice, *Anton Piller v Manufacturing Processes Ltd* [1976] Ch 55.

[20] For more information on Search and Seize Orders, see S. Gee, *Commercial Injunctions*, 6th edn (London: Sweet & Maxwell, 2016).

[21] *Hermes International v FHT Marketing Choice* (C-53/96) [1998] E.C.R. I-3603.

Schieving-Nijstad v Groenveld,[22] the court had to consider the start date for the 20 working days/30-calendar-day period in art.50(6) TRIPs. The Netherlands court considered that there were three possible alternatives: (i) when the order was made; (ii) when the order was served; or (iii) when the provisional measure became definitive and was no longer capable of being challenged. The CJEU said that the determination of the start date is a matter of national law:

> "provided always that the period thus fixed is reasonable having regard to the circumstances of each case and taking into account the balance to be struck between the competing rights and obligations of the intellectual property right holder and of the defendant."[23]

The CJEU said that this provision was important because a defendant could only lodge an application seeking revocation of the provisional measures on the ground of failure to issue proceedings after the expiry of this period.[24] In the UK, applications to discharge ex parte provisional measures are often made on the basis that the claimant failed to disclose all material matters to the court when seeking the ex parte relief. This is based on the principle that a party seeking ex parte relief, i.e. where the defendant is not at the hearing (*inaudita altera parte*) has a duty to the court to ensure that the case for relief is fairly put and that facts and law and evidence which is unfavourable to the application are presented to the court. **15-022**

Articles 9 and 7 of the Directive implement respectively art.50(1) (a) and (b). Thus, art.9 is concerned with the grant of an interim injunction aimed at preventing infringements pending determination of the substantive issues and art.7 is concerned with orders for the preservation of evidence. **15-023**

The provisions closely follow TRIPS. However, art.9(2) which is not mirrored in TRIPS is of note. It says: **15-024**

> "In the case of an infringement committed on a commercial scale, the Member States shall ensure that, if the injured party demonstrates circumstances likely to endanger the recovery of damages, the judicial authorities may order the precautionary seizure of the movable and immovable property of the alleged infringer, including the blocking of his/her bank accounts and other assets. To that end, the competent authorities may order the communication of bank, financial or commercial documents, or appropriate access to the relevant information."

This provision reflects the Mareva Order (now known as a "freezing injunction") which has been granted for many years in England.[25] **15-025**

Right of information

Article 47 of TRIPS requires that courts of Member States be able to order the provision of information regarding the origin and distribution networks of infringing goods unless such an order would be out of proportion to the seriousness of the infringement. Article 8 of the Directive implements this provision and permits such orders where there is infringement on a commercial scale. Such orders can include **15-026**

---

[22] *Schieving-Nijstad v Groenveld* (C-89/99) [2001] E.C.R. I-5851.
[23] See [65].
[24] See [64]. It is assumed that the court was not intending to mean that the defendant could not lodge an application to revoke prior to the expiry of this period on other grounds, i.e. change in material circumstances.
[25] See S. Gee, *Commercial Injunctions*, 6th edn (London: Sweet & Maxwell, 2016).

the names and addresses of producers, manufacturers, distributors, suppliers and other previous possessors of the goods or services as well as those further down the distribution chain.[26] It can also include information on quantities produced, manufactured, etc.

Disclosure of names and addresses for purpose of bringing IP proceedings

15-027   Article 8 envisages a commonly made order in UK called a *"Norwich Pharmacal"* order.[27] Such an order is made ex parte by the right owner against any undertakings innocently caught up or involved in the wrongdoings of others. The *Norwich Pharmacal* case concerned an action brought by a right holder against the custom authorities in the UK to force them to identify the names and addresses of persons who had imported alleged infringing items into the UK. The court granted the order. Over the years, such has undergone very considerable refinement. Thus, it is now possible to require an ISP (Internet Service Provider) to disclose the names and addresses of persons who have been involved in illegal acts of copyright infringement. Often, the right holder (or an investigator acting on its behalf) will be able to discover the Internet Protocol ("IP") addresses of persons who are involved in unlawful downloading or uploading of copyright material on a P2P site. The IP addresses will disclose which ISP those persons are customers of. The right holder then makes an application to the court requiring the ISP to disclose these names and addresses.[28]

15-028   The nature of such applications is that they involve the disclosure of private information belonging to consumers. Accordingly, they engage art.8 ECHR and in particular, art.8 Charter (right to protection of personal data). In such circumstances, it is necessary for the court to conduct, when exercising its discretion whether or not to grant such orders, a balancing exercise between the rights owner's rights and the right to privacy. The CJEU has considered this in the *Promusicae* case.[29] This case concerned online infringement and whether an ISP should be ordered to disclose the identities and physical addresses of customers who had been using a file exchange program which permitted the exchange of files which infringed the claimant's rights (an organisation of holders of IPRs). The CJEU noted that not only was the Enforcement Directive engaged but so were the Data Protection Directive and the Information Society Directive, as well as fundamental rights to intellectual property, privacy and protection of personal data. The CJEU held that the courts of the Member State must seek to strike a fair balance between such rights.[30] In England, such a balancing exercise will usually result in the order being made if the IPR owner would be denied access to justice by not knowing the names and identities of the defendants.[31] In *Bonnier*,[32] an application was brought in Sweden by publishing companies with exclusive rights in some audio books against an

---

[26]   art.8(2).

[27]   Named after *Norwich Pharmacal v Customs & Excise Commissioners* [1973] UKHL 6.

[28]   e.g. in the UK, see *Golden Eye (International) Ltd v Telefonica UK Ltd* [2013] E.M.L.R. 1 (reversed on appeal in part *Golden Eye (International) Ltd v Telefonica UK Ltd* [2013] R.P.C. 18). See also, *Rugby Football Union v Viagogo* [2012] UKSC 55.

[29]   *Productores de Musica de Espana (Promusicae) v Telefonica de Espana SAU* (C-275/06) [2008] E.C.R. I-271.

[30]   See *Promusicae*, at [70].

[31]   e.g. see *Rugby Football Union v Viagogo*, at [46]. However, as acknowledged by the Supreme Court, it is necessary to consider carefully and with an intense focus, the respective rights without a presumption operating in favour or against. Thus, the Supreme Court at [44] approved the remarks

Internet Service Provider, ePhone, whose internet services had been used for the purpose of unlawful sharing of these audiobooks using a file transfer protocol procedure. The object of the application was an order for disclosure of the names and addresses of subscribers of ePhone who had used a specific IP address for the unlawful file sharing. The application was resisted by ePhone who alleged that the injunction was contrary to the Data Retention Directive (which had not been transposed into Swedish law).[33] It submitted that this Directive precluded the disclosure to persons other than the authorities referred to in that Directive of information relating to a subscriber to whom an IP address had been allocated. The Swedish court referred the matter to the CJEU on the interrelationship of the Enforcement Directive with the Data Retention Directive. The CJEU noted that the domestic provisions which implemented art.8 of the Enforcement Directive in Sweden required that there be clear evidence of an infringement of an IPR, the information could be regarded as facilitating an investigation into the infringement of copyright and that the reasons for the measures outweighed the nuisance or other harm which the measure might entail for the person affected by it. The CJEU said that a court seised of an application for disclosure of personal data must weigh the conflicting interests and take due account of the requirements of proportionality. It held that the Data Retention Directive did not preclude such application and indeed that the Swedish legislation did not fall within the material scope of the Data Retention Directive.

In *Coty Germany GmbH v Stadtsparkasse Magdeburg*,[34] the Court of Justice held **15-029** that a provision of German banking law which entitled a German bank "in an unlimited and unconditional manner" to refuse to disclose the name and address of the bank account into which the proceeds of sales of counterfeit products had been paid was contrary to art.8 of the Enforcement Directive. Subsequently, the Bundesgerichtshof applied this ruling and obliged the court to disclose the identity of the holder of the bank account.

The Court of Justice has confirmed that it is not necessary that the request for **15-030** information be brought in the same proceedings as those for infringement. Thus, a request for information can be brought in separate proceedings.[35]

Final remedies

Article 44 of TRIPS requires that contracting states give their courts the powers **15-031** to be able to grant final orders (i.e. after determination of the merits of the action) preventing acts of infringement. However, states are not required to give the courts such powers where the products subject to the IPR have been:

"acquired or ordered by a person *prior* to knowing or having reasonable grounds to know that dealing in such subject matter would entail the infringement of an intellectual property right." [Emphasis supplied.]

Article 45 TRIPS equally requires contracting states to give their courts the **15-032**

---

of Arnold J in *Golden Eye (International) Ltd*, at [117] that no article has precedence over the other and an intense focus is required on the two articles; the justifications for interfering with or restricting each right must be taken into account and the proportionality test applied to each.

[32] *Bonnier Audio AB v Perfect Communication Sweden AB* (C-461/10) ECLI:EU:C:2012:219.

[33] Dir.2006/24 which amended Dir.2002/58.

[34] (C-580/13) EU:C:2015:485.

[35] *New Wave v AllToys* (C-427/15) ECLI:EU:C:2017:18.

authority to order an infringer to pay the right holder damages adequate to compensate for the injury that the right holder has suffered because of an infringement of that person's IPR by an infringer "who knowingly or with reasonable grounds to know, engaged in infringing activity." It might be thought that these provisions would prevent the award by courts of contracting states of an injunction or damages where the infringer has innocently dealt in infringing goods. However, it must be remembered that TRIPS only imposes a minimum level of protection for IPR holders.

15-033   The Directive has a number of provisions relating to final measures, i.e. measures to be ordered after there has been a decision on the merits of the case. These include the right to have infringing goods delivered or destroyed, the right to injunctive relief, and the right to damages and the recovery of legal costs.

Injunctions

15-034   The Enforcement Directive specifically requires Member States to issue injunctions upon a finding of infringement and also, where provided for by national law, make non-compliance with an injunction subject to a recurring penalty.[36] Some countries, such as the UK, do not provide for recurring penalties if an injunction is not complied with. Rather, the method of enforcement is to bring contempt proceedings against the defaulting parties (and if such is a company, against the directors) for breach of a court order. A finding of contempt can result in a fine and/or imprisonment. The Recitals to the Enforcement Directive envisage the courts not granting an injunction where the acts of infringement were unintentional and the grant of an injunction would be disproportionate and instead ordering pecuniary compensation as an alternative measure.[37] This provision must be aimed at a factual situation where compliance with an injunction would be so financially punitive to the infringer that it would be wrong in principle to grant an injunction. An example would be where there is some infringing code on avionics software which is used in navigation systems in airplanes and compliance with an injunction would involve grounding the airplanes for six months. Another example could be where a building is half-built and it is then adjudicated that the building infringes the copyright in architectural plans.

Injunctions against intermediaries

15-035   A feature of the 21st century is large-scale counterfeiting and piracy. In 2016, IPR crimes were calculated to be worth up to $461 billion.[38] The use of the Internet assists counterfeiters and pirates as it allows for "faceless" crimes where it is hard to identify the people who are responsible for selling counterfeit goods online or for uploading pirate copies of audiovisual works for easy access and download by end users wherever they are resident. Accordingly, the eternal fight against IPR crimes has moved from chasing the criminals to stopping their crimes by denying them access or outlets to the public or end-users. This is done by injuncting intermediaries, e.g. Internet Service Providers ("ISPs"), Online Marketplace Operators ("OMOs") or landlords of markets who allow (usually unknowingly) their custom-

---

[36] art.11.
[37] Recital 25.
[38] "2017 Situation Report on Counterfeiting and Piracy in the European Union" (Europol/EUIPO), Executive Summary, p.6.

ers to access well-known counterfeiting websites, e.g The Pirate Bay or buy counterfeit or pirated goods on a digital or in a physical marketplace.

EU law allows right holders to obtain injunctions against intermediaries whose **15-036** services are being used by a third party to infringe IPRs. This right was first introduced into the Information Society Directive. Article 8(3) permits injunctions to be sought against intermediaries whose services are being used by a third party to infringe a copyright or related right. This right was then extended for all IPRs by art.11 of the Enforcement Directive. These provisions have been used by right holdesr to seek injunctions against ISPs requiring them to block access of its subscribers to well-known third party websites used for downloading pirate copies of audiovisual works and selling counterfeit goods. They have also been used to require landlords and operators of bricks and mortar marketplaces not to grant leases or enter into rental contracts with persons known to be involved in counterfeit and/or piracy activities. Intermediaries such as ISPs, OMOs or landlords generally are sympathetic to right holders but their main concerns are: (i) when the injunction requires active monitoring rather than the implementation of passive technological measures, (ii) overly broad injunctions which interfere with their ability to do business, and (iii) having to bear the cost of implementing such injunctions—their view is that the right holder should bear the costs. These concerns have led to a number of referrals from the courts of Member States to the CJEU for the latter to set out the parameters, conditions and principles to be applied by courts to the grant or refusal of these injunctions.

Before considering the principles established by the Court of Justice, one must **15-037** refer to other EU legislation which bear on the grant of such injunctions. First, it is necessary to consider the E-Commerce Directive which sets out various provisions applicable to information service (including internet service) providers. These include various defences where the provider is merely acting as a conduit for infringing activities, caching electronic infringing copies and hosting unlawful copies. These defences apply to all intellectual property infringements and are discussed elsewhere in this book.[39] Of greatest importance is that art.15 of the E-Commerce Directive prohibits Member States from imposing a general obligation on information service providers to monitor the information which they store or transmit or to actively seek facts or matters indicating illegal activity. Secondly, the Charter of Fundamental Rights comes into play. Article 17(2) protects intellectual property rights; art.16 protects the right to carry on a business; and art.11 confers the right of freedom of expression and information.

Against this legislation framework, the following principles apply to the grant **15-038** of injunctions against intermediaries have been developed by the Court of Justice:

- intermediary injunctions are available against ISPs,[40] OMOs[41] and owners of physical marketplaces[42];
- generally, considerable latitude is given to the courts of Member States regarding how to apply the EU provisions relating to injunctions against intermediaries[43];

---

[39] See para.14-073, et seq.
[40] e.g. *UPC Telekabel Wien GmbH v Constantin Film Verleih GmbH, Wega Filmproduktionsgesellschaft mbH* (C-314/12) ECLI:EU:C:2014:192 at [40].
[41] *L'Oréal v eBay* (C-324/09) [2011] E.C.R. I-6011 at [135]–[144].
[42] *Tommy Hilfiger Licensing v Delta Center a.s.* (C-494/15) ECLI:EU:C:2016:528.
[43] *Scarlet Extended SA v SABAM* (C-70/10) [2011] E.C.R. I-11959 at [32]. See also Recital 23 which

- measures must be proportionate, effective and dissuasive[44] and strike a fair balance between the rights identified above[45] and not create barriers to legitimate trade.[46] Thus measures should be strictly targeted at preventing the acts of infringement and not affect Internet users who are using the ISP's services to lawfully access information[47];
- courts of Member States must be able to take measures which not only bring to an end the proven infringements but also prevent or hinder further infringements of the same kind[48]; and
- a court may not impose measures which require a general obligation on an intermediary to monitor actively all data of its customers.[49]

15-039   Thus, in an English case concerning whether an injunction should be granted against ISPs to prevent access to websites offering for sale counterfeit products, the court said that in that case, there were seven principles to consider: (i) the comparative importance of the rights that were engaged and the justifications for interfering with those rights; (ii) the availability of alternative measures which were less onerous[50]; (iii) the efficacy of the measures which the order required the ISPs to adopt, and in particular whether they would seriously discourage the ISPs' subscribers from accessing the target websites; (iv) the costs associated with those measures, and in particular the costs of implementing the measures; (v) the dissuasiveness of those measures; (vi) the impact of those measures on lawful users of the internet; and (vii) the substitutability of other websites for the target websites.[51]

Costs of implementation

15-040   A matter that has not been ruled upon by the Court of Justice but which has been ruled on by courts of Member States is whether an intermediary ISP should bear the costs of implementing the blocking measures or the right holder.[52] The courts of two Member States (France and UK) have held that the intermediary should bear

---

states that the conditions and procedures relating to such injunctions should be left to the national law of the Member States.

[44]   e.g. *L'Oréal v eBay* (C-324/09) [2011] E.C.R. I-6011 at [136], [141].

[45]   *UPC Telekabel Wien GmbH v Constantin Film Verleih GmbH, Wega Filmproduktionsgesellschaft mbH.*

[46]   *L'Oréal v eBay*, at [140]. Thus, an injunction against an OMO cannot extend to all online goods bearing the trade mark of the trade mark owner.

[47]   *UPC Telekabel Wien GmbH*, at [56], *L'Oréal v eBay*, at [140].

[48]   *L'Oréal v eBay* (C-324/09) [2011] E.C.R. I-6011, at [144].

[49]   *L'Oréal v eBay*, at [139]; *Scarlet Extended SA v SABAM* (C-70/10) [2011] E.C.R. I-11959; *SABAM v Netlog* (C-360/10) ECLI:EU:C:2012:85. In these latter two cases, the CJEU held that an injunction requiring ISPs to install a filtering system which required the ISP to identify all files within its electronic communications relating to P2P (peer-to-peer) traffic and within that traffic, identify the files containing unlawful works and block file sharing was unlawful.

[50]   Here the court considered alternative measures such as "take down" notices; suspension by payment processors such as Visa of the third party website operators' accounts; seizing the domain names; de-indexation of the target websites with search engine providers, e.g. Google; and customs seizure (see [175]).

[51]   *Cartier International AG v BskyB* [2016] EWCA Civ 658 CA (England and Wales) at [127]. See also [100] where the judge identified nine general requirements from the case law concerning the discretion to grant blocking orders.

[52]   Although in *L'Oréal v eBay*, at [139] the Court of Justice said that the measures required of an ISP must not be excessively costly which implies that the ISP should bear those costs. See *Cartier International AG v BskyB* [2016] EWCA Civ 658 CA at [145]–[146] where the court referred to *L'Oréal v eBay* and *UPC Telekabel* as supporting such a conclusion. NB. the dissenting judgment

the costs. The reasoning is largely based on the fact that ISPs are usually large concerns who can afford to bear the costs, they make profits from letting users access infringing sites and everyone including intermediaries must contribute to fighting piracy and counterfeiting.[53] However, the Supreme Court of the United Kingdom has now reversed the English practice and held that right holders must indemnify ISPs for the cost of implementing the website-blocking orders.

Damages

On the issue of damages, art.13 of the Directive provides that: **15-041**

"[1]   Member States shall ensure that the competent judicial authorities, on application of the injured party, order the infringer who knowingly, or with reasonable grounds to know, engaged in an infringing activity, to pay the right holder damages appropriate to the actual prejudice suffered by him/her as a result of the infringement.
      When the judicial authorities set the damages:
   (a)   they shall take into account all appropriate aspects, such as the negative economic consequences, including lost profits, which the injured party has suffered, any unfair profits made by the infringer and, in appropriate cases, elements other than economic factors, such as the moral prejudice caused to the right holder by the infringement; or
   (b)   as an alternative to (a), they may, in appropriate cases, set the damages as a lump sum on the basis of elements such as at least the amount of royalties or fees which would have been due if the infringer had requested authorisation to use the intellectual property right in question.
[2]   Where the infringer did not knowingly, or with reasonable grounds know, engage in infringing activity, Member States may lay down that the judicial authorities may order the recovery of profits or the payment of damages, which may be preestablished."

Minimum level of damages

As made clear by the Court of Justice in *Stowarzyszenie 'Oławska Telewizja* **15-042** *Kablowa' v Stowarzyszenie Filmowców Polskich*,[54] the Enforcement Directive lays down a minimum standard concerning the enforcement of IPRs. Thus, in the case, the Court of Justice held that Polish legislation which allowed, in the case of infringement of IPRs, the right holder to demand a blanket levy (being 1.6 per cent of net income earned from retransmission of infringing works by cable) or to assess damages as being twice or three times the appropriate fee was permissible without having to prove actual loss as not being contrary to the Enforcement Directive. However, care must be taken here. Article 3.1 of the Enforcement Directive requires that any remedy is effective, proportionate and dissuasive. It is implicit in the notion of "proportionate" that an award of damages must not be so high as to be disproportionate to the nature of the infringement. Thus, whilst art.13 sets down a minimum level of damages, any award of damages must satisfy this general

---

of Briggs LJ who, whilst acknowledging *L'Oréal v eBay* and *UPC*, considered that the tradition of English law was that injunctions against innocent intermediaries caught up in the wrongdoings of others should not have to "put his hand in his own pocket" (see [203]).

[53]   *SFR, Orange, Free, Bouygues Telecom v L'Union des Producteurs de Cinema* ECLI:FR:CCASS:2017:C100909; *Cartier International AG v BSkyB* [2016] EWCA Civ 658 CA; [2018] UKSC 28. See also *Twentieth Century Fox Film Corp v British Telecommunications Plc* [2011] EWHC 1981 (Ch), [2011] R.P.C. 28.

[54]   (C-367/15) ECLI:EU:C:2017:36 at [23]

principle. In the authors' view, this allows for very considerable latitude to the courts of Member States. Thus, an award of damages may be substantially in excess of proven loss if such would have a general dissuasive effect on third parties from infringing the rights in issue.

Lump sum payments

15-043   As said in art.13, in appropriate cases, a court or tribunal may set damages as a lump sum. As said by the Court of Justice, this means that a court can award damages that are not precisely proportional to the loss actually suffered by the right holder.[55] Moreover, an award of lump sum damages is appropriate where it is difficult to show a causal link between the acts of the infringement and loss suffered by the right holder.[56]

Punitive damages

15-044   The Enforcement Directive does not impose an obligation on Member States to provide for punitive damages but Member States are free to do so.[57] However, an award cannot "exceed the loss so clearly and substantially that a claim to that effect would constitute an abuse of rights", as such would be prohibited under art.3(2) Enforcement Directive.[58] Furthermore, as discussed above, any award of punitive damages must satisfy the "effective, proportionate and dissuasive" test in art.3(2).

Profits made by infringer

15-045   Article 13.1(a) refers to the "unfair profits" made by the infringer. Such suggests that an infringer can be required to pay over the profits that it has made to the right holder if the damage suffered by the right holder is less than the profit made by the infringer. In the UK, art.13 was considered in *Hollister v Medik Ostomy*.[59] The facts involved a parallel importer of repackaged pharmaceuticals who failed to give notice to the trade mark proprietor.[60] Proceedings were brought against the parallel importer and an account of profits was sought.[61] An account of profits is a traditional English remedy which IPR owners, who are successful in infringement actions, are given the option to seek instead of damages. It is founded on the principle of unjust enrichment and at its simplest, requires the infringer to disgorge the profits made from the infringing activities to the IPR owner. In *Hollister*, the defendant argued that an account of profits was inconsistent with art.13. The Court of Appeal rejected this argument holding that an account of profits was consistent with the Enforcement Directive. In particular, the court noted that Member States had considerable freedom to choose the most appropriate forms and methods to ensure the effectiveness of directives in the light of their objectives. The court held

---

[55]   *Stowarzyszenie 'Oławska Telewizja Kablowa'*, at [26].
[56]   *Stowarzyszenie 'Oławska Telewizja Kablowa'*, at [32].
[57]   *Stowarzyszenie 'Oławska Telewizja Kablowa'*, at [28], Recital 26.
[58]   *Stowarzyszenie 'Oławska Telewizja Kablowa'*, at [31].
[59]   [2013] F.S.R. 24 (CA, England and Wales).
[60]   Where pharmaceutical goods are repackaged, trade mark law requires that inter alia notification is given to the trade mark proprietor that such has occurred—see generally, Ch.3, para.3-624.
[61]   In fact, it was consented to by the defendant.

that the remedy of an account of profits where the repackager had not given notice satisfied the principles of proportionality.[62]

Moral prejudice

In *Christian Liffers v Producciones Mandarina SL*[63] a right holder brought an ac- **15-046** tion for copyright infringement for misuse of an audiovisual work. He sought damages based upon a notional licence fee under art.13.1(b) of the Enforcement Directive and also a higher sum by way of moral prejudice. The issue referred to the Court of Justice was whether art.13.1(a) and (b) were mutually exclusive. Article 13.1(b) does not refer to moral prejudice whereas art.13.1(a) does. The Court of Justice found such interpretation too narrow. As it said, the objective of Dir.2004/48 is to attain a high level of protection for IPRs that takes into account the specific aspects of each given case and is based on a method of calculating damages that addresses those specific aspects.[64]. It considered that art.13.1(b) was concerned with an alternative way of assessing "material damage" only and is not concerned with moral prejudice.[65] Accordingly, the Court of Justice held that a party injured by an intellectual property infringement who sought compensation by way of payment of a royalty fee could also claim compensation for the moral prejudice suffered.[66]

Costs of researching and identifying acts of infringement

Where a right holder is entitled to compensation for loss actually suffered, such **15-047** should include the costs of researching and identifying acts of infringement.[67]

Costs

Article 14 requires that Member States provide that as a general rule, the suc- **15-048** cessful party has his reasonable and proportionate legal costs paid by the unsuccessful party. However, art.3 of the Enforcement Directive and art.41 of TRIPS, which set out the general principles governing IPR litigation, require that proceedings must not be "unnecessarily complicated or costly". Thus in countries such as the UK where costs are very high compared to other countries, this may be a principle that courts must increasingly take into account.

In contrast, as said by the CJEU in *Realchemie Nederland BV v Bayer CropSci-* **15-049** *ence AG*,[68] in order not to deter IPR owners from bringing infringement proceedings to protect their rights, the author of the infringement of the IPR must generally bear *all* the financial consequences of its conduct. Thus, in that case, it was held

---

[62] As noted in that decision, this decision followed the approach of the Bundesgerichtshof in *Zoladex IZR* 87/07 where the Bundesgerichtshof held that on similar facts (i.e. no notice given by a repackager to the owner of the registered trade mark) the registered proprietor was entitled to surrender of the defendant's entire profits.

[63] (C-99/15) ECLI:EU:C:2016:173.

[64] See [24].

[65] See [20], [26].

[66] It might also be said that given that the Enforcement Directive merely imposes a minimum level of damages, such was permissible without the need to consider whether art.13.1(b) expressly mentioned damages by way of moral prejudice. See also *Stowarzyszenie 'Oławska Telewizja Kablowa'*, at [30] (mere payment of a hypothetical royalty not capable of guaranteeing compensation as such does not take into account, inter alia, compensation for possible moral prejudice).

[67] *Stowarzyszenie 'Oławska Telewizja Kablowa'*, at [30]; Recital 26, Enforcement Directive.

[68] (C-406/09) [2011] E.C.R. 9773.

that costs related to an *exequatur* procedure seeking to enforce six orders made in Germany in a dispute relating to infringement of IPRs fell within art.14 of the Enforcement Directive. In *United Video Properties Inc v Telenet*[69], the Court of Justice held that a flat rate scheme for the reimbursement of costs is permissible provided that the rates are intended to ensure that the costs to be borne by the unsuccessful party are reasonable. The scheme must ensure that a "significant and appropriate part of the reasonable costs incurred by the successful party are borne by the unsuccessful party".[70] However, a flat rate scheme cannot be allowed where such would allow recovery at a rate "significantly below" the average rate charged for the services of a lawyer in that Member State.[71] Thus, a national scheme for recovery of costs which caps costs must reflect "the reality of the rates charged for the services of a lawyer in the field of intellectual property" and that "a significant and appropriate part of the reasonable costs actually incurred by the successful party are borne by the unsuccessful party".[72]

Publication of judgments

15-050   Article 15 requires that Member States permit their courts to order publication of judgments. It has been held in England that although art.15 envisages publication of a judgment which adjudicates that the defendant has infringed the IPRs, there is nothing in principle which prevents the ordering of publication of a judgment where the defendant is acquitted of infringing at the unsuccessful claimant's expense.[73]

Destruction or delivery up

15-051   Article 10 of the Enforcement Directive requires Member States to empower courts to order recall of infringing goods from the channels of commerce, definitive removal from the channels of commerce and destruction of infringing goods. Such should normally be done at the expense of the infringer save where particular reasons exist for not doing so. Article 10 also requires the court to consider the need for proportionality between the seriousness of the infringement and the remedies ordered as well as the recurring interests of third parties to be taken into account.[74] The recitals suggest that such should take account, particularly, of consumers and private parties acting in good faith.[75] In English proceedings, it has been said that the purpose of delivery up or destruction orders is that they are a way of making sure that an injunction is obeyed.[76]

---

[69]   (C-57/15) ECLI:EU:C:2016:611.
[70]   At [25].
[71]   At [26].
[72]   At [29]–[30].
[73]   *Samsung v Apple* [2013] F.S.R. 9.
[74]   art.10(3).
[75]   Recital 24.
[76]   *Mayne Pharma v Pharmacia Italia Spa* [2005] EWCA Civ 294 at [4]; *Merck v Sigma* [2013] 3 C.M.L.R. 17 CA at [90]. In *Merck v Sigma*, (a repackaging case), the Court considered that the first instance judge had exercised his discretion by correctly ordering the delivery up of goods despite the fact that the defendant had acted in good faith, they were parallel imports and the effect of the order was to prevent the sale of the products in the UK after the expiry of the relevant IPR (a supplemental protection certificate).

CHAPTER 16

BORDER CONTROLS

INTRODUCTION

Once counterfeit or pirated goods[1] have entered a country, it is often very dif- **16-001**
ficult to prevent such goods being marketed. Upon entry into the country, such
goods are very quickly distributed to a large number of small distributors and
market traders which means that it becomes uneconomic for the right holder to
police such activity and bring numerous proceedings against all such persons. Thus,
the rights holder will naturally want to restrict the movement of any such goods at
the soonest possible opportunity and it is often the port of entry where such restriction is most effective.

Apart from having private investigators posted at each port, and assuming that **16-002**
such a private investigator gets to see the goods in question, restricting or monitoring movements of goods at ports is impossible unless you happen to be the local
customs authority.

It is for this reason that arts 51–60 of TRIPS contain special requirements relat- **16-003**
ing to the seizure of goods by custom authorities. The EU has adopted regulations
specifically to permit the seizure of goods suspected of infringing IPRs. The current regulation is Reg.608/2013 ("Customs Regulation")[2] which mirrors closely but
not completely arts 51–60 of TRIPS. As the EU is a party to TRIPS, the Regulation must be interpreted in the light and purpose of the corresponding provisions

---

[1] These expressions are used colloquially to mean goods which intentionally bear without consent the
brands of others (counterfeit) or intentionally copy the work of others (pirate). They are defined in
art.51 TRIPS and arts 2(5) and 2(6) of the Customs Regulation.
[2] [2013] OJ L181/14. Its predecessors are Reg.1381/2003 [2003] OJ C196/7–14 and prior to that,
Reg.3295/94.

in TRIPS.[3] Thus, the TRIPS provisions are considered when discussing the Regulation.

Overview of the Customs Regulation

16-004 The Customs Regulation is intended to facilitate the seizure of goods suspected of infringing IPRs at borders of Member States (generally external borders). The essential justification for the Customs Regulation is that customs authorities are skilled at detecting infringing material and the seizure of infringing goods is most effective when entering a Member State, i.e. prior to them entering diffuse and diverse distribution chains.[4]

16-005 The basic mechanism is that holders of IPRs are required to lodge applications with customs authorities of Member States which, once those applications are granted, require the customs authorities to monitor goods coming into Member States from outside the customs territory of the EU.[5] If such goods are suspected of being counterfeit or pirate goods, the customs authorities may seize them. As the EU is a common customs union, it is not intended to deal with goods being transported from one Member State to another.[6] The fate of such goods will then depend on whether the right holder and the owner of the goods agree or disagree to the destruction or forfeiture of such goods. If the owner of the goods disagrees with their destruction, then in general terms, the burden lies on the IPR owner to issue court proceedings within a relevant period to determine their fate. If the owner of the goods agrees, the goods are destroyed or disposed of.

16-006 The success of these measures has been significant. For instance, in 2011, customs authorities of EU countries intercepted 115 million infringing items.[7] The Regulation is supplemented by an implementation regulation which sets out precise rules and includes a number of forms to be used.[8] In many cases, Member States have also provided supplemental regulations.[9]

16-007 The Customs Regulation makes a number of key changes from its predecessors.

(a) It now covers a much wider range of IPRs,

(b) it provides for a simplified procedure for destruction of seized goods where the owner of the goods does not object,

---

[3] For the obligation to interpret EU legislative measures in the light and purpose of TRIPS, see para.1-180. See also Recital 11 of the Regulation which refers to TRIPS and the obligation to protect public health and to promote access to medicines for all.

[4] Recital 4.

[5] This may include overseas dependencies of the European Union. For more detail, reference should be made to the comprehensive book O. Vrins and M. Schneider, *Enforcement of Intellectual Property Rights through Border Measures: Law and Practice*, 2nd edn (Oxford: Oxford University Press, 2012).

[6] This reflects the qualification in TRIPS art.51 that it does not apply:

"where a Member has dismantled substantially all controls over movement of goods across its border with another Member with which it forms part of a custom union".

See D. Gervais, *The TRIPS Agreement*, 4th edn (London: Sweet & Maxwell, 2012), p.614 and note (a) of art.51 of 23 July 1990 draft of TRIPS.

[7] Council Resolution on the EU Customs Action Plan to combat IPR infringements for the years 2013–2017, [2013] OJ C 80/01.

[8] Reg.1352/2013 [2013] OJ L/341/10–13 as amended by Reg.2018/582 [2018] OJ L98/4–16.

[9] e.g. in the UK, see The Goods Infringing Intellectual Property Rights (Customs) Regulations 2004 (SI 2004/1473) (amended by SI 2010/324 and SI 2010/992).

(c) there is a simplified procedure for destruction of counterfeit or pirate goods in small consignments, and

(d) there are less restrictions on what IPR owners who have information provided to them by customs authorities may do with such information.[10]

The Customs Regulation is now considered in more detail.

Intellectual Property Rights Covered by the Customs Regulation

The Customs Regulation applies to national or EU registered trade marks, registered designs, copyright, geographical indications, patents, supplemental protection certificates, EU plant variety rights, semi-conductor topographical rights, utility models, and trade names.[11] **16-008**

Goods Covered by the Customs Regulation

The Customs Regulation does not apply to all goods that infringe IPRs. It excludes goods of a non-commercial nature contained in travellers' personal luggage.[12] It also does not apply to goods that have been released for free circulation under the "end-use regime".[13] The Regulation also permits the seizure of any "mould or matrix which is specifically designed or adapted for the manufacture of goods infringing an intellectual property right" provided that such a mould or matrix also infringes the rights of the IPRs owner[14] and devices which are primarily designed for the purpose of enabling or facilitating the circumvention of anti-copying devices.[15] **16-009**

Parallel imports not covered by Customs Regulation

Whilst it is not necessary to establish that the goods are counterfeit or pirate goods but simply that they infringe the relevant IPR, where the goods have been manufactured with the consent of the right holder, they are not covered by the Regulation.[16] Thus, whilst, in relation to a harmonised EU IPR, e.g. registered designs or trade marks, there is no international exhaustion of rights such that the importation of goods from outside the EEA without the consent of the IPR owner would infringe the EU IPR even where their manufacture was done with the consent of the IPR owner, customs authorities cannot seize them under the Customs Regulation. **16-010**

---

[10] For a detailed guide to this area of law, see O. Vrins and M. Schneider, *Enforcement of Intellectual Property Rights through Border Measures: Law and Practice*, 2nd edn (Oxford: Oxford University Press, 2012).

[11] art.2(1).

[12] art.1(4). However, if there are indications that such personal allowances are being used for commercial traffic, it would appear that the regulation is applicable—see Recital (4), art.3(2).

[13] art.1(3). This is a customs procedure whereby goods enter for free circulation in the EU which are given favourable tariff treatment provided they are put to a prescribed use—for more information, see EC Reg.2913/92.

[14] art.1(7)(c).

[15] art.1(7)(b).

[16] art.1.5, Regulation. This exclusion applies even if the authorised person has manufactured in excess of the quantity agreed.

GOODS IN TRANSIT

16-011   Under the Customs Regulation, custom authorities are required to carry out adequate customs controls and proportionate identification measures with a "view to preventing acts in breach of intellectual property laws applicable in the territory of the Union" and "in order to cooperate with third countries on the enforcement of intellectual property rights".[17] In summary, the customs authorities must determine whether or not the goods are intended to be marketed in the EU and that if they were, they would breach the IPRs of an undertaking. The standard of proof is not high, with suspicion on reasonable grounds being sufficient, but there must be something other than the mere fact that the goods are in the physical territory of the EU.[18]

16-012   In determining whether the goods are intended to be marketed in the EU, the following principles can be deduced from the authorities.

- The mere fact that goods are seized by customs authorities of Member States and put into warehouses under customs supervision does not mean that such goods have been put on sale in the EU.[19]
- It is necessary to show that there are some grounds for believing that the goods are destined for the EU. This may occur because:
  — the goods have been the subject of a commercial act directed at EU consumers such as a sale, offer for sale or advertising;[20]
  — the goods have been released from the customs warehouse into a tax warehouse[21]; and
  — the destination of the goods is either unknown or declared in a manner which is unreliable or there are "indications" that the persons involved in shipping the goods are about to direct their goods towards EU consumers.[22] The standard of proof for "indications" to be proven is low. The CJEU has said that it is sufficient that "there be material such as to give rise to suspicion".[23] This may include: the fact that the destination of the goods is not declared; the lack of precise or reliable information as to the identity or address of the manufacturer or consignor of the goods; a lack of co-operation with the customs

---

[17]   art.1.2.

[18]   See also Recital 15 which refers to "where the custom authorities suspect, on the basis of reasonable indications, that goods under their supervision infringe intellectual property rights." The European Commission has published guidelines on the application of these principles in relation to medicines in transit through the EU.

[19]   *Rioglass and Transremar* (C-115/02) [2003] E.C.R. I-12705 at [27]; *Montex Holdings* (C-281/05) [2006] E.C.R. I-10881 at [19]; *Class International* (C-405/03) [2005] E.C.R. I-8735 at [47]; *Phillips v Lucheng and Nokia Corp. v HMRC* (C-446/09 & C-495/09) ECLI:EU:C:2011:45 at [55].

[20]   See *Phillips v Lucheng*, at [57]; *Class International*, at [61].

[21]   *Top Logistics BV and Van Caem International BV v Bacardi & Co* (C–379/14) EU:C:2015:497.

[22]   See *Phillips v Lucheng*, at [60].

[23]   *Philips v Lucheng*, at [61]. It is not sufficient for it to be shown that there is an abstract consideration that fraudulent diversion cannot be ruled out (*Phillips v Lucheng*, at [62]).

authorities; or the discovery of documentation suggesting there is liable to be a diversion of those goods to EU consumers.[24]

EUTM Regulation and Directive

In order to overcome the problems caused by jurisprudence of the Court of **16-013** Justice, the new EUTM Regulation and Trade Mark Directive now deem it an infringement of a EU trade mark or registered trade mark of a Member State for goods in transit through the EU where: (i) the goods would infringe the rights of the owner of the registered trade mark in the country of destination; and (ii) the goods bear a mark the same or which cannot be distinguished in its essential aspects from the registered trade mark.[25]

IMPORTATION INTO EU FOR PRIVATE USE

In *Blomqvist v Rolex*,[26] a Dane placed an order on a Chinese website for a **16-014** counterfeit Rolex watch for his own use. The watch was sent from Hong Kong by post. The watch was seized by Danish customs. A central issue was whether there had an infringement of Rolex's IPRs in the EU such as to entitle the Danish custom authorities to seize the watch under the Customs Regulation. There was no issue that the Dane had not himself infringed these rights by importing the watch into the EU as he was an end-user and not a trader[27]. Thus, the issue was whether the owner of the Chinese website had infringed Rolex's rights in Denmark.

The CJEU said that the mere fact that a website is accessible from Denmark is **16-015** not a sufficient basis for concluding that the Chinese website had targeted Danish consumers.[28] However, it went onto say that IPRs may be infringed where before their arrival into a Member State where the right holder has protection, goods coming from outside the EU, are the subject of a commercial act directed at consumers in that state such as a sale, offer for sale or advertising.[29] It then said that where goods are sold to a customer in the EU, such is its own proof that the goods were intended to be put on sale in the EU. Thus, it held that was not necessary to show that, in addition, prior to the sale, the counterfeit goods had been the subject of an offer for sale or advertising targeting EU consumers.[30] To make sense of this decision, it must be concluded that the owner of the Chinese website had infringed the

---

[24] See [61]. See also, in the UK, *Mastercigars Direct Ltd v Hunters & Frankau Ltd* [2006] E.W.H.C. 410; [2006] R.P.C. 805, HHJ Fysh QC (sitting as a judge of the Chancery Division), reversed on appeal in other respects where the court held that it was clear that if the goods had not been seized, they would be put on the UK market.

[25] art.9(4) Reg.2017/1001; art.10(4) Dir.2015/2436. This is discussed at para.3-584.

[26] (C-98/13) ECLI:EU:C:2014:55.

[27] There can only be trade mark infringement if the alleged infringing sign is used in the course of trade.

[28] Here, the court was applying case law developed under EU trade mark law whereby a trade mark registered in a Member State is infringed by a website that targets that Member State—see *L'Oréal* (C-324/09) [2011] E.C.R. I-6011.

[29] See [32] citing *Philips v Lucheng*, at [78].

[30] See [34].

rights of Rolex in the EU by selling the Rolex watch to the Danish consumer *in the EU*. Where a person places an order on a Chinese website that is fulfilled by a product being shipped to that person from outside the EU, it is doubtful that such is indeed the case. In substance, the buyer has imported the product himself or herself into the EU.

APPLICATION TO CUSTOMS AUTHORITIES BY IPRS OWNER

16-016   For a rights holder to avail itself of the Customs Regulation, it must make an application to the relevant customs authority. As well as rights holders, collecting societies, professional defence bodies,[31] groups of producers of geographical indications, and persons authorised to bring proceedings on behalf of the right holder can also apply.[32] There are two types of application that can be made—a Union application and a national application. A Union application can only be submitted with respect to a unitary right, e.g. an EU Trade Mark, a Community Design or Plant Variety Right. It does not apply to European patents as these are not granted by Union law.[33] A Union application can be made by an exclusive licensee who holds exclusive licences in at least the entire territory of two Member States provided that such persons are authorised to bring proceedings for infringement of the relevant Union right.[34] The fundamental distinction between a national and a Union application is that the latter is transmitted to all relevant customs authorities of Member States of the EU.[35] Detailed provisions are set out in the Customs Regulation as to the procedure and mechanism. If the application is granted, then its effect can only last for the maximum of a year.[36] The successful applicant is defined as the "holder of the decision". In certain circumstances, the customs authorities will take action even if the goods are suspected of infringing IPRs not covered by a decision.[37] In such circumstances, the customs authorities will, where appropriate, request the IPR owner, if they wish to take action, to submit an application.[38]

MONITORING AND SEIZURE OF GOODS SUSPECTED OF INFRINGING IPRS

16-017   Once IPRs are the subject of a decision of customs authorities granting an application under the Customs Regulation, then customs authorities are required to carry out adequate customs controls and take proportionate identification measures in accordance with risk analysis criteria with a view to preventing acts in breach of intellectual property laws in the EU.[39] Clearly, this gives customs authorities very considerable latitude to determine how they should monitor goods coming into customs territories and decide whether they are infringing goods.

16-018   Once customs authorities identify goods suspected of infringing an intellectual property right covered by a decision granting an application, they must then suspend

---

[31] See art.4(1) Dir.2004/48.
[32] art.3.
[33] art.4.
[34] art.3(3).
[35] art.2 (11). Recital 14.
[36] art.11(1).
[37] art.18.
[38] art.18(2).
[39] art.1(2).

the release of those goods.[40] The regulation states that to do so, there must be "reasonable indications" that the goods are prima facie goods which are the subject of an act infringing the intellectual property rights in the Member State of importation.[41] This will be a matter of the substantive law of the Member State of the relevant customs authority. It is not sufficient that the relevant IPR is in a Member State other than that of the customs authority. This may cause difficulties as once inside the EU, there are generally no further checks. In other words, customs checks tend to be carried out on the goods moving into the EU from outside.

Further assistance as to the approach to be taken is given in *Nokia/Phillips* which **16-019** gives guidance as the standard of proof in determining whether goods ostensibly in transit through the EU are intended for the EU.[42] Although such guidance applies to the Customs Regulation's predecessor, there is no reason to suppose that a different approach would be taken to the standard of proof.

Once the goods are seized, the holder of the goods must be notified within one **16-020** working day of that suspension or detention.[43] The holder of the decision (i.e. the IPR's owner) must also be notified on the same day or promptly after the holder of the goods is notified.[44] As mentioned earlier, the customs authorities may detain goods even if they are not the subject of a decision and invite the IPR's owner to make an application.[45] This ex officio action was responsible for 3 per cent of EU-wide customs actions in 2013.[46]

Both the holder of the decision and the goods owner may inspect the goods and **16-021** where the goods are counterfeit or pirated send samples to the holder of the decision.[47] Information on the goods and their characteristics which is sent to the holder of the decision may be used only for: initiating proceedings for infringement, in connection with criminal investigations, to seek compensation from the infringer, to agree with the holder of the goods that the goods may be destroyed, or to agree the amount of the guarantee.[48] Such information can include providing (where requested) the holder of the decision of the names and addresses of the consignee and of the "origin, provenance and destination" of the seized goods.[49]

DESTRUCTION OR FORFEITURE OF GOODS

Where goods have been seized by customs authorities on the grounds that they **16-022** are suspected of infringing IPRs, then those goods may be destroyed under customs

---

[40] art.17(1).
[41] art.2(7). See also Recital 15—suspicion on the basis of reasonable indications is sufficient for the goods to be seized.
[42] See paras 16-011 to 16-013.
[43] art.17(3).
[44] art.17(3).
[45] art.18.
[46] F. Schwab, R. Böckenholt and V. Schmitz-Fohrmann, "Border Seizure Measures in the European Union" *World Trademark Review* 18 May 2017.
[47] art.19.
[48] art.21. As for guarantee, see below at para.16-025.
[49] art.17(4). Under a predecessor regulation, the CJEU held that a rule of national law which prevented the identity of declarants or consignees from being revealed for the purpose of issuing proceedings was contrary to the predecessor customs regulation—see *Adidas* (C-223/98) [1999] E.C.R. I-7081. It has been said that the information cannot be used to allow the rights holder to contact the importer and consent to the importation of the goods as such would demotivate custom authorities—see K. Daele, "Regulation 1383/2003: A New Step in the Fight against Counterfeit and Pirated Goods at the Borders of the European Union" [2004] E.I.P.R. 5, 214–224, 220.

control without any need to determine whether an IPR has been infringed. This can only occur where all of the following conditions are fulfilled:

(i)   The holder of the decision has confirmed in writing to the customs authorities within 10 working days (three working days in the case of perishable goods) of notification of the seizure that "in his conviction", an intellectual property right has been infringed and furthermore his agreement to their destruction.[50] A failure to notify in respect of both will result in the goods being released.[51]

(ii)   The owner of the seized goods has confirmed within 10 working days (three working days in the case of perishable goods) of his agreement to the destruction of the goods. Importantly, if the owner of the goods fails to respond (i.e. neither agrees to their destruction nor objects), then the custom authorities may deem the owner of the goods to have agreed to their destruction.[52]

16-023   If the owner of the seized goods has expressly objected to their destruction or alternatively, if silent, the customs authorities choose not to deem such as implied consent to their construction, then the customs authorities must notify immediately the holder of the decision and the latter must within 10 working days (three working days in the case of perishable goods), initiate proceedings to determine whether an IPR has been infringed.[53] The holder of the decision must notify the customs authorities within the same period of the initiation of legal proceedings to prevent the release of the goods.[54]

16-024   In *Sintax Trading v Maksu-ja Tolliamet*,[55] the CJEU had to consider whether under identical provisions of the predecessor regulation, customs authorities themselves were able to initiate and conduct the proceedings to determine whether there has been an infringement in the absence of any initiative by the right holder. Bottles suspected of infringing a patent were seized by Estonian customs authorities. They requested an opinion from the right holder who confirmed that they did infringe its patent. Accordingly, the Estonian customs authorities found that the goods infringed the right holder's IPRs and thus rejected an application by the import company for the goods to be released. The importer brought an action before the Estonian courts that the customs authorities themselves were not entitled to determine whether the goods were infringing once the owner of the goods had objected to the forfeiture of the goods. The Estonian Supreme Court referred to the matter to the CJEU. The CJEU said that if the right holder had failed to inform the customs authorities within 10 working days of receipt of notification of suspension of release, such did not prevent the customs authorities from bringing proceedings themselves to have to determine whether there has been an infringement of the IPR although they were entitled "to draw the appropriate conclusions from the inac-

---

[50]   art.23.1(a) and 23.1(b). It is not clear what is meant by "in his conviction". It suggests little more than a bona fide belief that the goods are infringing and there being reasonable grounds for such a belief. It is unlikely that the burden is very high because if there is a dispute, it is intended to be resolved by the courts and not the customs authorities.

[51]   art.23.1(c), last paragraph.

[52]   art.23.1(c). This is a change from the previous customs regulation. In effect, it amounts to deemed consent by silence.

[53]   art.23(3). This is extendible by the customs authorities for a further 10 working days on request.

[54]   art.23(5).

[55]   (C-583/12) ECLI:EU:C:2014:244.

tion of the holder of the intellectual property rights concerned".[56] In particular, the CJEU held that there was a public interest in preventing the marketing of counterfeit or pirated goods on the market and such favoured customs authorities bringing proceedings.[57] The CJEU also found that the predecessor customs regulation did not prevent customs authorities from determining the issue of infringement provided that there was a right of appeal. In particular, this followed from art.41(4) TRIPS which required that parties to proceedings should have the opportunity for review by a judicial authority of final administrative decisions.[58]

In the case of design, patent, utility model, semi-conductor topographical right, and plant varieties rights, the holder of the goods may request the customs authorities to release seized goods. In such circumstances, the customs authorities must do so if: (a) the owner of the goods has provided a guarantee sufficient to protect the interests of the holder of the decision, (b) a court has not granted precautionary measures, and (c) all customs formalities have been complied with.[59] This provision no doubt reflects the fact that these rights are in essence, industrial rights, where the holder of the right can be compensated financially for the acts of infringement. Such is not the case in relation to a trade mark where confusion and damage to its reputation in the marketplace may be difficult or impossible to quantify and indeed to redress adequately through financial compensation. In the case of copyrights, special considerations apply because copyright works have a personal element and moral rights come into play.

16-025

Small consignments

The above procedures were considered rather cumbersome and bureaucratic for small consignments of counterfeit or pirate goods. Accordingly, art.26 of the Customs Regulation introduced a "fast track" procedure for such goods. "Counterfeit goods" are defined as goods which, without the consent of the owner, bear a trademark identical to a registered trade mark or "which cannot be distinguished in its essential aspects from such a trademark" and which thus infringes the registered trade marks (whether national or Community marks) of the applicant.[60] This mirrors almost exactly the definition of "counterfeit trademark goods" in art.51 of TRIPS. Thus, it is not intended to cover goods which display a trade mark confusingly similar to a registered trade mark. The reason for this is two-fold: first, it is unlikely that a deliberate counterfeiter would choose anything other than the identical mark. Secondly, it avoids customs authorities from having to make value judgments about whether a trade mark is confusingly similar. "Pirated goods" are defined as goods which are infringing goods and which "are, or contain copies".[61] Again, this mirrors the definition of "pirate copyright goods" in art.51 of TRIPS. Although it is not wholly clear, it is thought that this means an exact copy, i.e. a facsimile copy and not merely a substantial copy of the work. This would ac-

16-026

---

[56] See [37]. It should be noted that the CJEU found support for this finding in two provisions of Reg.1383/2003, namely arts 14(2) and 10. Neither of these provisions are found in the new customs regulation.

[57] See [41]–[44].

[58] See [51].

[59] art.24.

[60] art.1(5).

[61] art.1(6). The provision is rather poorly drafted as it refers to "copies ... of a copyright or related right or design right" rather than "works protected by copyright or related right or design right". One cannot copy a cause of action!

cord with the general approach of the Regulation, namely that it is intended to prevent the release into circulation of goods that are facsimile copies of another work rather than derivative works.[62]

16-027   The "fast track" procedure only applies where: the goods are suspected of being counterfeit or pirated goods (i.e. not merely infringing goods);[63] the goods are not perishable; the goods are covered by a decision granting an application; the holder of the decision has opted in on the "fast track" procedure; and the goods are transported in small consignments.[64] In such circumstances, the customs authorities need only notify the holder of the goods (and not the holder of the decision) once the goods are seized. The holder of the goods then has 10 working days to object or agree to their destruction. A failure to respond can be treated by the customs authorities as consent to the destruction of the goods.[65]

LIABILITY OF CUSTOMS

16-028   Customs authorities are not liable for failing to detect infringing goods or for seizing goods.[66] However, this is without prejudice to the application of national law.[67] The holder of a decision may be liable to the holder of the goods where the procedure initiated by the customs authorities is discontinued; samples taken are not returned or are returned damaged; or a court adjudicates that the seized goods do not infringe. Such is said to be "in accordance with specific applicable legislation" which might suggest that the Customs Regulation does not itself impose any obligation but such must arise pursuant to national law (or perhaps EU secondary legislation).[68]

---

[62]   Generally, see O. Vrins and M. Schneider, *Enforcement of Intellectual Property Rights through Border Measures: Law and Practice*, 2nd edn (Oxford: Oxford University Press, 2012), p.126.

[63]   Pirate and counterfeit goods are defined at art.2.

[64]   art.26(1)(a)–(e). "Small consignment" is defined as a postal or express courier consignment which contains three units or less or has a gross weight of less than 2 kilograms (art.2(19)).

[65]   art.26 (6).

[66]   art.27.

[67]   art.27. See also Recital 23.

[68]   See Recital 24 which refers to the fact that cost and damage suffered by entities other than customs authorities should be governed by the specific legislation applicable in each particular case.

JURISDICTION AND INTELLECTUAL PROPERTY

INTRODUCTION

This chapter is concerned with whether or not a court or tribunal has the power[1] **17-001** to be seized of and determine a dispute whose subject-matter is intellectual property. It is in this sense that one uses the word "jurisdiction" in this chapter. Thus, this chapter is concerned with the determination as a preliminary issue of whether or not a court has jurisdiction to entertain a dispute which has been brought before it by a party to the dispute. It also considers the recognition and enforcement of judgments in Europe. It is clearly in the interests of justice that, where a dispute may, whether by reason of the applicable law or the facts, have an international element, there exists a coherent, concise and clear set of international jurisdictional rules. Disharmony in this field could potentially result in a situation whereby all countries applying their own jurisdictional rules decline jurisdiction in a dispute, thus depriving an injured party of any remedy. For instance, one might have a situation where a potential defendant in an Anglo-French dispute is an English national domiciled in France. If English law held that jurisdiction must be founded on the defendant's domicile and French law held that jurisdiction must be founded on the defendant's nationality, then the claimant would be deprived of any remedy in either country against the defendant. Not surprisingly, therefore, there have existed for many years, international conventions on jurisdiction.

It is suggested that any set of jurisdictional rules amongst a group of countries **17-002** (contracting states) should take account of the following principles:

(1) The rules are clear, precise and predictable.
(2) A dispute should be tried in the court of a contracting state which has the closest connection with the parties to the dispute. This will normally be the contracting state in which the defendant lives or is established.
(3) A court of a contracting state may also try a dispute if the dispute has a close connection with the contracting state.
(4) The court of a contracting state should not determine the competence of the court of another contracting state to hear a dispute but only whether it is competent to hear a dispute.

---

[1] One could equally use the words "authority" or "competence". Thus, in Italian, the word is "*competenza*", in French, "*compétence*", in German "*Zuständigkeit*".

(5) A dispute should only be determined by the court of a contracting state first seized of the dispute unless that court has declined jurisdiction to hear the dispute.

(6) The judgment of the court of one contracting state should be enforceable with relative ease in that of another contracting state.

(7) The rules should have no application to jurisdictional disputes between contracting states and non-contracting states.

17-003 In the authors' view, this represents a set of principles which are indeed coherent, clear and founded on logic. The one area that the authors have doubts about is the rule that a defendant should be tried in the contracting state of residence or establishment. The underlying principle is that the party who is sued rather than suing should be given preferential treatment as they did not choose to litigate. However, this can favour the cynical law-breaker. Ultimately, it is probably right that given the choice between the state most convenient to the claimant or the defendant, the latter should prevail.

17-004 The Brussels and Lugano Convention, the Brussels Regulation and the Recast Brussels Regulation are all considered below. The first two are jurisdictional treaties applicable to Europe whereas the latter two are EU jurisdiction regulations. Nowadays the Recast Brussels Regulation governs jurisdictional issues within the EU and the other three are of limited historical significance.

Brussels Convention

17-005 Article 220 of the Treaty of Rome required Member States to enter into negotiations for the simplification of formalities governing the reciprocal recognition and enforcement of judgments of courts or tribunals and of arbitration awards. It quickly became apparent that a Treaty which sought to regulate and harmonise the recognition and enforcement of judgments in the European Economic Area (as it then was called) would be incomplete if differing jurisdictional rules applied in the EEC. For instance, it was important to ensure that conflicting judgments could not be obtained in differing Member States. Furthermore, it was realised that Member States' rules on jurisdiction often discriminated on the basis of nationality.[2] Accordingly, a working party was set up by the Member States to draft a treaty that standardised jurisdiction and the recognition and enforcement of judgments in the six original Member States. In furtherance of this, they signed the Convention on Jurisdiction and the Enforcement of Judgments in Civil and Commercial Matters, in Brussels, in 1968 ("the Brussels Convention"). This convention was not an EU legislative measure but a regional European one , albeit the only signatories were Member States.

17-006 In 1971, the same signatories entered into a protocol which conferred jurisdiction on the CJEU to interpret the Convention ("the 1971 Protocol"). Since then, the UK, Denmark, Ireland, Greece, Portugal, Spain, Austria, Finland and Sweden have acceded to the Brussels Convention. The countries who joined the EU after the Brussels Regulation came into force have not acceded to the Brussels Convention as the former superseded the latter. The 1968 Convention, the 1971 Protocol and the subsequent amendments to them by the Accession Conventions, are hereafter

---

[2] Thus, art.14 of the French Civil Code permitted French nationals to sue foreigners in the French courts regardless of the absence of any connection between the dispute and France.

collectively referred to as "the Brussels Convention".[3] Following the enactment of the Brussels Regulation (discussed below) and its successor, the Recast Brussels Regulation, the Brussels Convention is now of very limited interest. It covers disputes of certain overseas territories of Member States. It is also of some relevance to jurisdictional disputes concerning EU trade marks and Community designs.[4] However, because the substantive laws of the Brussels Convention, the Brussels Regulation and the Recast Brussels Regulation are largely identical and both have been interpreted by the CJEU, the case law of the former is relevant to the interpretation of the latter two regulations.

Lugano Convention

The Brussels Convention only applied to EU countries. However, interest was **17-007** shown in it by members of the European Free Trade Association ("EFTA"). Accordingly, the EU countries and the EFTA countries entered into the Lugano Convention on Jurisdiction and Enforcement of Judgments ("the Lugano Convention") which is virtually identical to the Brussels Convention and the Brussels Regulation. It governs issues of jurisdiction between EU Member States and Member States of the European Free Trade Association. In 2007, the EU became a signatory to the Lugano Convention on behalf of the Member States of the EU.[5] The EFTA countries which were not members of the EU also signed the Convention. Switzerland (which is neither a EFTA nor EU member) has also acceded to the Lugano Convention. The Convention was last amended in 2007.

The Brussels Regulation

Following the Treaty of Amsterdam, which introduced a section on jurisdiction, **17-008** recognition and enforcement of judgments in civil and commercial matters, in 2001, the EU issued a Regulation on the same matter which, in broad terms, but with certain changes, enacted the Brussels Convention as a EU Regulation ("the Brussels Regulation").[6] The Brussels Regulation, being EU law, superseded the Brussels Convention,[7] in relation to civil jurisdiction and enforcement of judgments in Member States of the EU (save Denmark). Following the accession of Cyprus, the Czech Republic, Estonia, Hungary, Latvia, Lithuania, Malta, Poland, Slovakia and Slovenia to the EU in 2004, they too became bound by the Brussels Regulation.[8] Equally, following their accession in 2007, Bulgaria and Romania also became bound by it.[9]

Readers should be aware that Denmark's position was somewhat anomalous as **17-009** it (along with the UK) has a full opt-out from the justice provisions of the EU Treaties. However, in 2005, it entered into an agreement with the EU which applies in modified form the Brussels Regulation.[10]

---

[3] A consolidated version of the Brussels Convention was published in the Official Journal—[1998] OJ C27/1–27.
[4] See para.17-218.
[5] [2007] OJ L339/3.
[6] EC Reg.44/2001 OJ [2001] L12/1.
[7] art.68 Brussels Regulation.
[8] Act of Accession [2004] OJ L236/33.
[9] EC Reg.1791/2006.
[10] Agreement between Denmark and European Community [2005] OJ L299/62.

Recast Brussels Regulation

17-010   In 2012, the EU enacted a new jurisdiction regulation (Reg.1215/2012) to replace the Brussels Regulation. This is often known as the "Recast Brussels Regulation" which came into force on 10 January 2015.[11] Although broadly the same as the Brussels Regulation (but with numbering changes), it contains some important differences which are highlighted in the relevant section in this chapter. It now applies to all Member States including Denmark.[12] It also applies to all legal proceedings instituted on or after 10 January 2015. Legal proceedings instituted prior to that are governed by the Brussels Regulation.

Jurisdiction and choice of law

17-011   From the outset, it is important to distinguish between jurisdictional considerations as opposed to "choice of law" considerations. Both will be relevant to the litigator and forum shopper. A Member State may have jurisdiction to hear an action but it may be that, under that Member State's conflict of laws, the applicable substantive law should be that of another Member State. In intellectual property disputes, because of the territoriality of intellectual property rights, this will invariably be the domestic law of the state in which the right is registered or is sought to be enforced (*lex loci protectionis*). The substantive law of a dispute should not be confused with issues regarding the choice of the appropriate law to determine an issue regarding its jurisdiction. Thus, a court may often have to decide which law it applies in order to determine an issue relevant to whether it has jurisdiction or not. For example, the Recast Brussels Regulation only applies if the defendant is domiciled in a Member State. If the defendant is a natural person, the issue of domicile is determined by applying the putative *lex domicilis*.[13] Thus, if it is claimed in a French court that the Recast Brussels Regulation applies to a dispute because the defendant is domiciled in Germany, the French court must first determine whether, under French law (*lex fori*), the defendant is domiciled in France. If not, it must apply German domestic law (*lex domicilis*) to determine whether the defendant is domiciled in Germany. However, it may be that French law is applicable to the substantive dispute.

17-012   The EU has enacted two regulations—Rome I and Rome II—which harmonise the private international law of Member States to contractual and non-contractual obligations. These two regulations are considered at the end of this chapter.

Structure of this chapter

17-013   The provisions of the Recast Brussels Regulation are considered in detail insofar as they are relevant to intellectual property litigation. Towards the end, the Rome I and Rome II Regulations are discussed—again, insofar as they are relevant to intellectual property.

---

[11]   Reg.1215/2012 [2012] OJ L/351/1.
[12]   It was implemented by Denmark by Danish Law No.518.
[13]   art.62 Recast Brussels Regulation.

The Recast Brussels Regulation

Introduction

The Recast Brussels Regulation ("RBR") harmonises jurisdictional rules in **17-014** Member States in relation to civil and commercial matters. It does not apply to revenue, customs, administrative matters, certain types of matrimonial proceedings, bankruptcy and insolvency, social security or arbitration.[14] Such areas are known as excluded grounds. The Recast Brussels Regulation splits into two parts. On the one hand, it is concerned with jurisdiction and on the other hand, with the recognition and enforcement of judgments. This chapter is primarily concerned with the RBR's jurisdictional aspects as they apply to intellectual property. However, the enforcement of judgments is examined in outline.[15]

The Recast Brussels Regulation applies to legal proceedings instituted on or after **17-015** 10 January 2015 and "authentic instruments formally drawn up or registered and to court settlements approved or concluded on or after 10th January 2015".[16] It is likely that this is intended to refer to jurisdiction agreements concluded, whether merely contractual or where such is agreed as part of a court settlement. Thus, if proceedings are commenced after 10 January 2015 but there is a jurisdiction agreement agreed prior to 10 January 2015, then the Brussels Regulation will apply (although it is not clear whether the Brussels Regulation will apply *in toto* or merely those aspects which relate to jurisdiction agreements).

The Recast Brussels Regulation is, in large part, the same as the Brussels **17-016** Regulation. However, there are a number of important differences. These are:

(a) Changes to the lis pendens rules where there is a written jurisdiction agreement conferring jurisdiction on a particular court. The Recast Brussels Regulation confers jurisdiction on the designated court under the agreement even if it is not the court first seized. Under the Brussels Regulation, the designated court had to wait until the court first seized declined jurisdiction even if it was obvious that the court first seized had no jurisdiction (the so called "Italian" torpedo[17]).

(b) Expansion of the *lis pendens* rules where the jurisdiction dispute is between a Member State and a non-Member State. It was originally considered that the Brussels Regulation did not apply to such disputes—in part because the *lis pendens* rules of the Brussels Regulation do not cater for such a conflict. However, following the landmark case (and indeed infamous case) of *Owusu v Jackson* it is clear that it does. Accordingly, the Recast Brussels Regulation permits courts of Member States to stay proceedings in favour of a non-Member State in limited circumstances.

(c) Changes to the requirements for written jurisdiction agreements to have effect. In particular, it is no longer necessary that any party to the agreement is domiciled in a Member State.

---

[14] art.1.

[15] See para.17-241. For a detailed analysis of the system of recognition and enforcement of judgments, see A. Briggs, *Civil Jurisdiction and Judgments*, 6th edn (London: Informa Finance, 2015) and P. Torremans, et al. (eds), *Cheshire, North & Fawcett: Private International Law*, 15th edn (Oxford: Oxford University Press, 2017).

[16] art.66.

[17] So called because litigation in Italy is very slow and thus it often takes a long time for Italian courts to conclude that they have no jurisdiction.

(d)   It is made clear that arbitration proceedings are not covered by the Recast Brussels Regulation.[18]

The Brussels Convention, the Jurisdiction Regulations and their interpretation

17-017   When the Brussels Regulation came into force, the Brussels Convention had been in force for more than 30 years and the CJEU had ruled many times on its interpretation. Save where there are clear differences in its text, the Jurisdiction Regulations are to be interpreted in the same way as the Brussels Convention.[19] In this respect, there are a number of official commentaries on the Brussels Convention which have a significant influence on its interpretation and are published in the Official Journal of the EU. These are as follows:

(1)   The report by Mr P. Jenard on the Brussels Convention and the 1971 Protocol ("the Jenard Report").[20]

(2)   The report by Professor Peter Schlosser on the Convention of Accession of The United Kingdom, The Republic of Ireland and Denmark to the Brussels Convention and the 1971 Protocol ("the Schlosser Report").[21]

(3)   The report by Professors Demetrios I. Evrigenis and K. D. Kerameus on the Convention of Accession of Greece to the Brussels Convention and the 1971 Protocol ("the Evrigenis and Kerameus Report").[22]

(4)   The report by Mr Martinho de Almeida Cruz, Mr Manuel Desantes Real and Mr P. Jenard on the Convention of Accession of Spain and Portugal to the Brussels Convention and the 1971 Protocol ("the Cruz, Real and Jenard Report").[23]

17-018   These reports are usually followed although there is nothing in the Brussels Convention or the Brussels Regulation and Recast Brussels Regulation which requires that the guidance in the reports be adopted or indeed used for the purpose of interpretation.[24] In England and Wales, the Jenard and Schlosser Reports may be used as guides to interpretation of the Brussels Convention.[25]

---

[18]   Although, whether or not a dispute should be referred to arbitration when a court is seized of proceedings where the parties have entered into an arbitration agreement is governed by the Recast Brussels Regulation—Recital 12.

[19]   e.g. see *Falco Privatstiftung and Rabitsch v Weller-Lindhorst* (C-533/07) [2009] E.C.R. I-3327 at [49]–[57] (where the CJEU actually expressly ruled that the case law of art.5(1) of the Brussels Convention should continue to be relied upon to interpret the parallel provision in the Brussels Regulation). See also *Zuid-Chemie* (C-189/08) [2009] E.C.R. I-691 at [17] and *eDate Advertising GmbH v X; Olivier and Robert Martinez v MGN Ltd* (C-501/01 & C-161/10) [2011] E.C.R. I-10269 at [39].

[20]   [1979] OJ C59/1.

[21]   [1979] OJ C59/71.

[22]   [1986] OJ C298/1.

[23]   [1990] OJ C189/35.

[24]   See *Norbert Lieber v Göbel* (C-292/93) [1994] E.C.R. I-2535, for an example of where one report was used, though compare this with the case of *Rösler v Rottwinkel* (C-241/83) [1985] E.C.R. 99, where the expressed view of the reporter was departed from.

[25]   Civil Jurisdiction Judgments Act s.3(3).

Fundamental principles of the Recast Brussels Regulation

The legislative rationale behind the Brussels Convention, the predecessor to the **17-019** Brussels Regulation and Recast Brussels Regulation, was to help facilitate the working of the Common Market (now the EU). The rationale behind the Recast Brussels Regulation is the same. Thus, as said in the recitals to it, the Recast Brussels Regulation was adopted to ensure the sound operation of the internal market, to unify the rules of conflict of jurisdiction in civil and commercial matters and to ensure rapid and simple recognition and enforcement of judgments given in a Member State.[26]

There are a number of fundamental principles which apply to the Recast Brus- **17-020** sels Regulation which have been set out by the CJEU in interpreting its predecessor regulation or the Brussels Convention.[27]

Certainty

The Recast Brussels Regulation is intended to strengthen the legal protection of **17-021** persons established in the EU, by laying down common rules on jurisdiction in order to guarantee certainty as to the allocation of jurisdiction among the various national courts before which proceedings in a particular case may be brought.[28] This need for legal certainty has led the CJEU to say that such requires that the jurisdictional rules which derogate from the general rule of the defendant's domicile laid down in art.4 of the Recast Brussels Regulation should be interpreted:

> "in such a way to as to enable a normally well-informed defendant reasonably to foresee before which courts, other than those of the State in which he is domiciled, he may be sued."[29]

The promotion of certainty is a feature that runs throughout the decisions of the **17-022** CJEU on the Recast Jurisdiction Regulation and its predecessors. Sometimes, it can be said that such has been at the expense of coherence and logic.[30] The Anglo-Saxon common law's preference for a large degree of discretion plays a limited part in the application of the Recast Brussels Regulation. Thus, the principle of forum non conveniens plays no part in the RBR.[31] It has been said that this is to prevent the multiplication or fragmentation of jurisdiction where claims arise within a single legal relation.[32] Where there is more than one state with jurisdiction, such will often precipitate the issuing of proceedings in the court of the Member State of the claimant's choice even if that Member State is manifestly less suited to trying the action than another Member State (e.g. if the dispute is to be determined by the substantive law of the latter Member State).

---

[26] Recitals 3 and 4.
[27] For further reading, A. Briggs and P. Rees, *Civil Jurisdiction and Judgments*, 6th edn (London: Informa, 2015).
[28] *Besix SA v Wasserreinigungsbau Alfred Kretzschmar GmbH & Co KG (WABAG)* (C-256/00) [2002] E.C.R. I-1699, [25]; (C-281/02) [2005] E.C.R. I-1383 at [39].
[29] *GIE Groupe Concorde v Master of the Vessel Suhadiwarno Panjan* (C-440/97) [1999] E.C.R. I-6307 at [23]; (C-256/00) [2002] E.C.R. I-1699 at [26]; (C-281/02) [2005] E.C.R. I-1383 at [40]; *Gesellschaft für Antriebstechnik mbH v Lamellen und Kupplungsbau Beteiligungs KG (GAT v LUK)* (C-4/03) [2006] E.C.R. I-6509 at [28].
[30] This can be seen clearly in *Owusu v Jackson* (C-281/02) [2005] E.C.R. I-1383 which is discussed at para.17-228.
[31] See *Owusu v Jackson*, (C-281/02) [2005] E.C.R. I-1383.
[32] A. Briggs and P. Rees, *Civil Jurisdiction and Judgments*, 6th edn (London: Informa, 2015).

17-023   The emphasis on certainty has led to the CJEU fashioning a set of jurisdictional principles in relation to jurisdiction in online IP infringement cases which bear little relationship to the wording of the provisions of the Recast Brussels Regulation. Thus, rather than taking a nuanced approach to e.g. what is meant by "the place where the harmful event occurred" (7(2) RBR) in the context of online infringement, the CJEU has instead chosen simply to substitute what is meant by this phrase with concepts such as where the victim (i.e. IPR owner) has their "centre of interest", or the place of the establishment of the advertiser (i.e. the alleged infringer). This approach has been justified on the grounds of sound administration of justice and the aim of predictability of rules governing jurisdiction.[33]

Autonomous interpretation

17-024   The CJEU has favoured the autonomous interpretation of phrases and words in the Recast Brussels Regulation and its predecessors, the Brussels Regulation and Brussels Convention, rather than permit diverse and varied interpretations by courts of Member States. It has been said that it is settled law that the regulation must be interpreted independently by reference to its scheme and purpose.[34] Thus, in the field of intellectual property, the phrase "proceedings concerned with the registration or validity of patents" has been given an autonomous interpretation.[35]

Trust in legal systems of other Member States

17-025   Another fundamental principle is that the Recast Brussels Regulation is based on the trust which the Member States accord to each other's legal systems and judicial institutions. Thus, they do not permit national courts to take account of apparent or real failings of the legal systems of other Member States, principally, delay. As stated by the CJEU:

> "It must be borne in mind that the Convention is necessarily based on the trust which the Member States to one another's legal system and judicial institutions. It is that mutual trust which has enabled a compulsory system of jurisdiction to be established, which all the courts within the purview of the Convention are required to respect, and as a corollary the waiver by those States of the right to apply their internal rules on recognition and enforcement of foreign judgments of a simplified mechanism for the recognition and enforcement of judgments."[36]

17-026   In *Turner v Grovit*, the CJEU used this principle to justify a finding that the courts of England and Wales were prevented from granting an "anti-suit" injunction against a defendant from bringing mala fides proceedings against a claimant in the courts of Spain. The claimant had brought proceedings in England, and the Spanish proceedings were commenced by the defendant purely for the purpose of

---

[33]   See *eDate Advertising GmbH v X; Olivier and Robert Martinez v MGN Ltd* (C-501/01 & C-161/10) [2011] E.C.R. I-10269. See also para.17-068, et seq. on online infringement.

[34]   See *Zuid-Chemie* (C-189/08) [2009] E.C.R. I-6917 at [17]; *eDate GmbH v X; Olivier and Robert Martinez v MGN Ltd* (C-501/01 & C-161/10) [2011] E.C.R. I-10269 at [39], and cases cited thereto; *Melzor* (C-228/11), at [22]; *Hi Hotel HCF* (C-387/12), at [21]. A. Briggs and P. Rees, *Civil Jurisdiction and Judgments*, 6th edn (London: Informa, 2015).

[35]   *Duijnstee v Goderbauer* (C-288/82) [1983] E.C.R. 3663.

[36]   *Erich Gasser GmbH v MISAT Srl* (C-116/02) [2003] E.C.R. I-14693 at [72].

frustrating the existing proceedings.[37] The CJEU reached this decision despite the English courts characterising the injunction as one operating in personam. In short, the CJEU said that the Spanish courts should hear the proceedings brought in their jurisdiction, even where/when they were plainly an abuse of process. Although the reasoning of the CJEU is understandable if the Recast Brussels Regulation and its predecessors are applied mechanistically, it is clear that the decision may also give rise to real abuse—particularly if the court seized takes an inordinate time in declining jurisdiction. The Recast Brussels Regulation has sought to ameliorate this to some extent, e.g. where a party to an agreement abusively and contrary to a written jurisdiction agreement starts proceedings in a Member State not designated under the agreement. However, these provisions can be seen as a "patchwork" remedy.[38] The Recast Brussels Regulation has avoided introducing a general provision whereby a court which is not the first seized can find that it has jurisdiction if it does have jurisdiction under the regulation and the court first seized manifestly does not have jurisdiction and the earlier proceedings were issued with the predominant purpose of frustrating justice.

Exceptions are construed restrictively

17-027 The fundamental principle of the Recast Brussels Regulations is that a defendant is entitled to be sued in the courts of the Member State in which they are domiciled. The regulations provide for derogations from this principle which either oust this principle or provide supplementary grounds of jurisdiction. However, such derogations must be construed restrictively.[39]

The golden rules

17-028 The *jurisdictional regime* of the Recast Brussels Regulation only applies where the intended defendant is domiciled in a Member State. To this end, it makes a fundamental distinction between defendants who are domiciled in a Member State and those who are domiciled outside the EU. Defendants who are not domiciled in a Member State will be governed by the national jurisdictional rules of the country whose court is seized with the matter, save in the case of consumer and employee disputes; where exclusive jurisdiction is conferred on the courts of a Member State under art.24[40] and where the parties, regardless of their domicile have agreed that a Member State shall have jurisdiction in a written agreement.[41]

17-029 The concept of domicile is central to both issues of whether the Recast Brussels Regulation applies and if it does, which Member State has jurisdiction. The follow-

---

[37] (C-159/02) [2004] E.C.R. I-3565.
[38] Sometimes known in English as a "Band Aid" remedy (Band Aid is a well-known brand of skin plasters). The expression means a remedy for the symptoms of a problem rather than a solution to the underlying problem.
[39] *Kalfelis* (189/87) [1988] E.C.R. 5565 at [19]; *Freistaat Bayern v Blijdenstein* (C-433/01) [2004] E.C.R. I-981 at [25]; *Kronhofer v Maier* (C-168/02) [2004] E.C.R. I-6009 at [14]; *Melzer* (C-228/11) ECLI:EU:C:2013:305 at [26]; *Pinckney v KDG Mediatech* (C-170/12) ECLI:EU:C:2013:635 at [25]; *Hi Hotel HCF* (C-387/12) at [26]. See also A. Briggs and P. Rees, *Civil Jurisdiction and Judgments*, 6th edn (London: Informa, 2015).
[40] art.6. NB. The one relevant exception to this is that art.24(4) confers exclusive jurisdiction in proceedings concerning the registration or validity of IPRs on the court of the Member State where the application for registration was made regardless of the domicile of the defendants—see para.17-117.
[41] art.25. This is discussed at para.17-108.

ing are the golden rules in relation to civil disputes such as intellectual property:

(1) The *jurisdictional rules*[42] of the Recast Brussels Regulation apply only where:

    (a) the court seized of the dispute is in a Member State;[43]

    (b) the intended defendant is domiciled in a Member State; *or*

    (c) regardless of domicile, the court of a Member State has exclusive jurisdiction under art.24 (which includes proceedings concerned with registered IPRs) or the court has jurisdiction by reason of a written agreement (art.25).

(2) If the jurisdictional rules of the Recast Brussels Regulation apply:

    (a) the primary rule is that the intended defendant must in general be sued in the courts of the Member State in which it is domiciled regardless of its nationality (art.4);[44]

    (b) the defendant *may* also be sued in the courts of another Member State where the Recast Brussels Regulation specifically provides for supplementary grounds of jurisdiction (art.7) or where the defendant enters an appearance in the court of another Member State (i.e. does not contest jurisdiction) (art.26[45]); *but*

    (c) where the subject-matter of the dispute is exclusively governed by art.24 (matters where exclusive jurisdiction is conferred on a Member State) or art.25 (written jurisdiction agreements), the action must be brought in the court designated under arts 24 or 25.

(3) If the intended defendant is not domiciled in a Member State, the domestic rules of jurisdiction in force in each Member State, shall apply (art.6) save where a court of a Member State has jurisdiction under arts 24 or 25.[46]

(4) The following are irrelevant to the determination of jurisdiction under the Recast Brussels Regulation:

    (a) the nationality of the defendant;[47]

    (b) the domicile or nationality of the claimant; and

    (c) the applicable law to the substantive dispute.[48]

---

[42] art.6 of the Recast Brussels Regulation (discussed below) states that where the defendant is not domiciled in a Member State, save in limited circumstances, the domestic laws of a Member State shall determine the issue of jurisdiction. Thus, strictly speaking, the regulation does apply to defendants not domiciled in a Member State but only to make it clear that the jurisdictional rules in the regulation do *not* apply.

[43] This condition is often not emphasised (no doubt because it is considered obvious). However, it is clear that the Recast Brussels Regulation does not apply to the court of a non-Member State, even if the defendant is domiciled in a Member State.

[44] For a detailed analysis of this primary rule, see A. Briggs and P. Rees, *Civil Jurisdiction and Judgments*, 6th edn (London: Informa, 2015).

[45] Although this ground cannot be used to confer jurisdiction on a court of Member State where the court of another Member State has exclusive jurisdiction under art.24.

[46] art.6, art.24 and art.25. These rules owe their origin in part to the Jenard Report, Ch.IV, A.1. It is important to realise that, by reason of art.6, the *regime* (if not the detailed jurisdictional rules) of the Recast Brussels Regulation applies even where a person is domiciled in a non-Member State.

[47] See *Group Josi Reinsurance Co SA v Universal General Insurance Co (UGIC)* (C-412/98) [2000] E.C.R. I-5925 at [59]. It should be noted that art.4.2 makes it clear that persons who are not nationals of a state in which they are domiciled must be treated, with regard to jurisdictional rules, as nationals of that state. This ensures that any national rules of jurisdiction (where they apply) do not discriminate between domiciliaries who are nationals of a state and those who are not.

[48] For a good example of the irrelevance of the applicable law, see *Gareth Pearce v Ove Arup* [2000]

(5) Jurisdictional provisions in EU regulations or national law of Member States which are derived from EU Directives "in specific matters" will take priority over the Recast Brussels Regulation.[49] Thus, jurisdictional provisions in the EUTM Regulation or the Community Design Regulation will take precedence over the Recast Brussels Regulation. However, the Recast Brussels Regulation will apply so long as it is not in conflict with the jurisdictional rules of these provisions.[50] The Unitary Patent also has its own jurisdictional rules which "trump" the jurisdictional rules of the RBR.[51]

Domicile of the defendant: fundamental rule

As said above, the fundamental rule of jurisdiction is that the defendant must be **17-030** sued in the Member State in which it is domiciled. Article 4 of the Recast Brussels Regulation provides as follows:

"1. Subject to this Regulation, persons domiciled in a Member State shall, whatever their nationality, be sued in the courts of that Member State.

2. Persons who are not nationals of the Member State in which they are domiciled shall be governed by the rules of jurisdiction applicable to nationals of that State."

Articles 62–63 of the Brussels Regulation sets out the rules for determining the **17-031** domicile of the defendant. The important rules are as follows:

Natural person

Where it is alleged that the domicile of the defendant is that of the Member State **17-032** seized of the dispute, such is determined by the domestic jurisdictional laws of the seized court. Where the defendant is not domiciled in the Member State of the court seized of the dispute and it is alleged that he is domiciled in another Member State, then the domestic laws of that Member State are applied to determine whether they are domiciled in that Member State.[52]

Legal person or association of natural persons

A defendant who is a legal person (e.g. a company) is domiciled in the Member **17-033** State where it has its statutory seat, or central administration or principal place of business.[53] In the case of the UK and Eire, "statutory seat" means the registered office, or in default place of incorporation, or in further default the place under the law of which the formation took place.

Ch. 403; [1999] F.S.R. 525 CA, in which an action commenced in England was held to be validly brought because the defendant was domiciled in England, even though it was an action for infringement of architectural drawings by the construction of a building in The Netherlands and the applicable law was Dutch copyright law.

[49] arts 67–73.

[50] See, for example, *Nürnberger AV v Portbridge Transport BV* (C-148/03) [2004] E.C.R. I-10327 at [17].

[51] art.71. See para.17-223, et seq.

[52] art.62.1, 62.2.

[53] art.63.1(a)–(c).

Trust

17-034   The domicile is determined by the rules of private international law of the seized court.[54]

17-035   It is apparent from the provisions that the Recast Brussels Regulation does not promote a uniform concept of domicile save in relation to legal persons such as companies. This is because, as made clear from the Jenard Report, the idea of defining domicile in the Brussels Convention as an autonomous concept was rejected because this was outside of its scope and properly belonged to a uniform law.

17-036   In considering IPR infringement, there are a number of permutations where jurisdiction is founded on the defendant's domicile:

(1)   the infringement occurred in another Member State, and

(2)   the infringement occurred in a non-Member State (third State).

Infringement occurred in another Member State

17-037   Proceedings for infringement of intellectual property rights are governed by the general rules of jurisdiction set out in the Recast Brussels Regulation.[55] This means that an action for infringement of an intellectual property right ("IPR") can be brought in the courts of the Member State of the domicile of the defendant, even if the infringement occurred in another Member State. This may often mean trying the action in the court of one Member State whilst the court applies the intellectual property law of another Member State (*lex loci protectionis*). Thus, the Schlosser Report makes the point that the fact that foreign law has to be applied does not constitute a sufficient reason for a court to decline jurisdiction.[56]

17-038   Thus, in the UK, the Court of Appeal (upholding the High Court) held that it had jurisdiction to hear proceedings for infringement of Dutch copyright in architectural drawings by the construction of a building in Rotterdam, as the defendant was domiciled in the UK.[57] In the Netherlands, this was never really disputed.[58] This jurisdictional rule is clearly very useful for the claimant where the defendant has committed a number of acts of infringement in various Member States where parallel rights exist. The claimant can sue for all acts in the state of domicile of that defendant and seek pan-European injunctive relief. In a 2014 case, proceedings for declaration of non-infringement of parallel European patents in the UK, France, Spain and Italy were brought and adjudicated on in the UK.[59]

Infringement occurred in a non-Member State

17-039   What is the position where the infringement occurred in a non-Member State but the alleged infringer is domiciled in a Member State? Can a right holder sue a

---

[54]   art.63.3.

[55]   Jenard Report, para.36. *Duijnstee v Goderbauer* (C-288/82) [1983] E.C.R. 3663; [1985] 1 C.M.L.R. 220 at [23].

[56]   See commentary on this in *Gareth Pearce v Ove Arup* [1997] F.S.R. 641, 652 at [78], per Lloyd J (High Court, England and Wales).

[57]   *Gareth Pearce* [2000] Ch. 403; [1999] F.S.R. 525 CA, England and Wales.

[58]   *Expandable Grafts* [1999] F.S.R. 352, Hoge Raad.

[59]   *Actavis UK v Eli Lilly & Co* [2014] EWHC 1511 (Pat). In this case, the defendant was found to have submitted to the jurisdiction of the English court (see [2012] EWHC 3316 affirmed on appeal, [2013] EWCA Civ 517; [2013] R.P.C. 37). However, parallel jurisdiction can be founded on other grounds, e.g. the defendant is domiciled in a Member State.

defendant domiciled in England for infringement of a US patent by, e.g. acts of manufacture in the US? *Owusu*,[60] which is discussed elsewhere in this chapter, makes it clear that provided a defendant is domiciled in a Member State, the fact that the tort (the wrong) sued upon occurred in a non-Member State does not oust the effect of the Recast Brussels Regulation (and accordingly, there was no room for the English jurisdiction rule of forum non conveniens). There is no reason in principle why such reasoning should not apply to intellectual property torts (i.e. infringements). In the UK, the Supreme Court has now held that the modern trend is in favour of the enforcement of foreign intellectual property rights citing both the Brussels and Rome II Regulations (at least where validity is not in issue).[61] Thus, the position in the UK is that its domestic jurisdictional rules permit proceedings for infringement of foreign copyrights to be brought if there is in personam jurisdiction over the defendant (i.e. the claim is justiciable).[62]

Supplemental jurisdictional rules

Introduction

In addition to the primary rule that an action is to be brought in the Member State **17-040** where the defendant is domiciled, the Recast Brussels Regulation also provides for supplementary grounds of jurisdiction *but only if* the defendant is domiciled in *a* Member State (but not necessarily the Member State of the court seized). Thus, the claimant will often have the option of suing in more than one jurisdiction. The principal grounds of interest to the reader of this chapter are as follows:

(1) a person domiciled in a Member State may be sued in another Member State:
   (a) in matters relating to a contract, in the courts for "the place of performance of the obligation in question" which is determined as follows;
      (i)   in the case of the sale of goods, the place in a Member State where, under the contract, the goods were delivered or should have been delivered, and
      (ii) in the case of the provision of services, the place in a Member State where, under the contract, the services were provided or should have been provided;[63]
(2) in matters relating to tort, delict or quasi-delict, in the courts for the place where the harmful event occurred.[64] This is relevant to infringement proceedings and is discussed in detail below;[65]
(3) where there are a number of defendants, a defendant may be sued in the

---

[60] Discussed at para.17-228.
[61] *Lucasfilms v Ainsworth* [2012] 1 A.C. 208 (Supreme Court) at [108]. The Rome II Regulation (which concerns the applicable law to non-contractual obligations) is considered below at para.17-270.
[62] See [105].
[63] art.7(1). In the case of an agreement between parties not to threaten proceedings for patent infringements in the UK, the English courts have decided that the place of performance of obligation in question is the UK. See *Kenburn Waste v Bergmann* [2002] F.S.R. 44. See also para.17-280, et seq., for determination of the applicable law to be applied in determining the place of performance of the obligation. The licence of IPRs is not a contract regarding the provision of services within the meaning of art.7(1)(b)—*Falco v Weller-Lindhorst* (C-533/07) [2009] E.C.R. I-3327.
[64] art.7(2).
[65] See para.17-044.

courts of a Member State where any one of them is domiciled where the claims are related.[66] This provision has played an important role in infringement proceedings on parallel rights (e.g. a European patent) and is discussed below;[67]

(4) in the case of a counterclaim arising from the same contract or facts on which the original claim was based, a person may be sued in the same state as where the original claim is pending;[68]

(5) where a defendant submits to the jurisdiction of a court.[69] Where a defendant enters an appearance at a court other than to contest jurisdiction, then that court has jurisdiction. This rule does not apply where another court has exclusive jurisdiction other than pursuant to a written agreement;[70] and

(6) where provisional or protective relief is sought, the courts of any Member State have jurisdiction, even if under the Recast Brussels Regulation, the courts of some other state have jurisdiction as to the substantive matter.[71] This has relevance to intellectual property practitioners because often interim injunctive relief is sought. This is discussed below.[72]

17-041 In all the above instances, the jurisdictional rules are additional to the primary rules based on domicile. Thus, in relation to a tort committed in a particular Member State by a party, the claimant may sue the party in either the state where the tort was committed or where the party is domiciled. As these rules are an exception to the general rule that the defendant must be sued in the state of his domicile, they are to be interpreted restrictively.[73]

17-042 As more than one state may have jurisdiction over a dispute or a related dispute, it is possible that the courts of more than one Member State can be seized with a dispute or related dispute. The Recast Brussels Regulation thus has a set of rules to deal with such lis pendens. Such provisions are particularly relevant to parallel infringement proceedings and are discussed below.[74]

17-043 These provisions are discussed now in more detail.

Place where harmful event occurred—art.7(2)

17-044 Article 7(2) allows a defendant who is domiciled in a Member State to be sued instead at the claimant's option "in matters relating to tort, delict or quasi-delict, in the courts for the place where the harmful event occurred or may occur". This

---

[66] art.8(1). See para.17-090.

[67] See para.17-094.

[68] art.8(3). Where there is a counterclaim for revocation of a registered right in an infringement action, see para.17-167.

[69] art.26. See para.17-116.

[70] art.26.1, 2nd sentence. In *Taser International Inc v SC Gate 4 Business SRL* (C–175/15) ECLI:EU:C:2016:176 (discussed more fully at para.17-114) the Court of Justice had to consider a reference from the Romanian court concerning the non-performance of a contractual obligation. It held that where proceedings were brought in the courts of a Member State in which the defendant has its seat, the court was validly seized if the defendant did not dispute jurisdiction, even though the contract between the two parties contained a clause conferring jurisdiction on the courts of a third country. In such circumstances, the court could not declare of its own motion that it did not have jurisdiction where the defendant did not contest jurisdiction.

[71] art.35.

[72] See para.17-168.

[73] See para.17-027.

[74] See para.17-184.

ground of jurisdiction is often called the *forum delicti commissi*.[75] This rule is in addition to the primary rule of jurisdiction based on domicile of the defendant. However, it is important not to overlook the fact that art.7(2) only applies if the defendant is domiciled in a Member State. Accordingly, art.7(2) does not confer jurisdiction on an English court to try the infringement of an English patent by a person domiciled in America.[76]

17-045 The term "matters relating to tort, delict or quasi-delict" was present in the Brussels Convention and the Brussels Regulation. It is to be regarded as an autonomous concept which is to be interpreted by reference to the scheme and objectives of the Brussels Regulation in order to ensure the latter is given full effect. Accordingly, it covers all actions which seek to establish the liability of a defendant and which are not related to a "contract" within the meaning of art.7(2).[77] This clearly includes intellectual property infringement actions. As said by the Jenard Report, infringement actions are governed by the general rules of the Brussels Convention and such actions are properly characterised as statutory torts.[78]

17-046 In *Bier BV v Mines de Potasse d'Alsace SA*,[79] the CJEU, when considering the predecessor provision to art.7(2) in the Brussels Convention, held that the expression "place where the harmful event occurred" must be understood as being intended to cover *both* the place where the damage occurred and, if different, the place of the event giving rise to it. Thus, the defendant may be sued under art.7(2) at the option of the claimant, either in the courts of the Member State where the damage occurred or in the courts of the Member State where the place of the event giving rise to the damage occurred.[80] However, care must be taken in interpreting the phrase in *Bier* "where the damage occurred" too liberally. In *Dumez France SA and Tracoba SARL v Hessische Landesbank*,[81] the CJEU said:

> "[20] It follows from the foregoing considerations that although, by virtue of a previous judgment of the Court [*Bier*, referred to], the expression 'place where the harmful event occurred' contained in Art.5(3) of the Convention may refer to the place where the damage occurred, the latter concept can be understood only as indicating the place where the event giving rise to the damage, and entailing tortious, delictual or quasi-delictual liability, *directly produced its harmful effects upon the person who is the immediate victim of that event.*
>
> [21] Moreover, whilst the place where the initial damage manifested itself is usually

---

[75] See the Jenard Report, p.25. NB. In the Brussels Convention, the words "or may occur" were missing.

[76] In practice, this makes little difference because the majority of domestic jurisdictional rules will permit a person domiciled out of the jurisdiction to be sued for acts of infringement occurring within the jurisdiction, e.g. in the UK, see Practice Direction 6B to the Civil Procedure Rules.

[77] *Kalfelis v Bankhaus Schroder Munchmeyer Hengst & Co ("Kalfelis")* (C-189/87) [1988] E.C.R. 5565 at [18]. It has been held by the English Court of Appeal that it is not acte clair on the basis of Kalfelis that art.7(2) includes a claim for unjust enrichment or misuse of confidential information: *Kitechnology BV* [1995] F.S.R. 765 CA. See also *Barclays Bank Plc v Glasgow CC* [1994] 2 W.L.R. 466; [1994] Q.B. 404 (claim for unjust enrichment) referred to in *Kitechnology BV* [1995] F.S.R. 765 CA.

[78] e.g. see P. Jenard, *"Report on the Convention of September 1968 on Jurisdiction and the Enforcement of Judgments in Civil and Commercial Matters"* [1979] OJ C59/1, 36 See also *Napp Lab v Pfizer Inc* [1993] F.S.R. 151.

[79] (21/76) [1976] E.C.R. 1735.

[80] See also *Melzer* (C-228/11) ECLI:EU:C:2013:305 at [25]; *Pinckney v KDG Mediatech* (C-170/12) ECLI:EU:C:2013:635 at [26]. This approach appears to have been foreseen in the Jenard Report, see p.26.

[81] *Dumez France SA Tracoba SARL v Hessische Landesbank* (C-220/88) [1990] E.C.R. I-0049.

closely related to the other components of the liability, *in most cases the domicile of the indirect victim is not so related.*

[22]   It must therefore be stated in reply to the question submitted by the national court that the rule on jurisdiction laid down in Art.5(3) of the Convention *cannot be interpreted* as permitting a claimant pleading damage which he claims to be the consequence of the harm suffered by other persons who were direct victims of the harmful act to bring proceedings against the perpetrator of that *act in the courts of the place in which he himself ascertained the damage to his assets.*"[82] [Emphasis supplied.]

17-047   Thus, the mere fact that a company's financial worth has been damaged by the defendant's activities, and its principal assets are located in a particular Member State is not sufficient to confer jurisdiction on that state.[83] As said in an English court, such arguments, if correct, would amount to a major derogation from the general rule of jurisdiction of the defendant's domicile.[84] Equally, the CJEU has said that the term "place where the harmful event occurred" cannot be construed so extensively as to encompass any place where the adverse consequences of an event can be felt which has already caused damage actually arising elsewhere.[85] As said in *Kronhofer*, when considering the equivalent provision in the Brussels Convention, such would be liable in most cases to give jurisdiction to the courts of the place where the claimant was domiciled and the Brussels Convention does not favour that solution.[86] The English courts have said that *Dumez* and *Bier* distinguish between damage which is directly and indirectly caused. Indirect damage is not within art.7(2), which precludes consideration of the place where financial loss resulting from the damage complained of is sustained or felt by the injured claimant.[87]

17-048   In a later case, *Shevill v Presse Alliance*, the CJEU was concerned with a libel that had been included in a paper that had been distributed in several Member States. The court emphasised that the policy behind the predecessor provision in the Brussels Convention is that:

"[19]   It is settled case law [citing *Bier* and *Dumez*] that that rule of special jurisdiction [i.e. art.7(2)], the choice of which is a matter for the claimant, is based on *the existence of a particularly close connecting factor between the dispute and courts other than those of the State of the defendant's domicile* which justifies the attribution of jurisdiction to those courts for reasons relating to the sound administration of justice and the efficacious conduct of proceedings."[88] [Emphasis supplied.]

17-049   In *Shevill*, the CJEU then went on to consider the application of both the "place where the damage occurred" and "the place of the event giving rise to it" to the instant facts. In relation to the latter condition, it said:

"[24]   In the case of a libel by a newspaper article distributed in several Member States, the place of the event giving rise to the damage, within the meaning of those judgments, can only be the place where the publisher of the newspaper in question is

---

[82]   See also *Netherlands v Ruffer* (814/79) [1980] E.C.R. 3807 per Warner AG; [1981] 3 C.M.L.R. 293; and *Kronhofer v Maier* (C-168/02) [2004] E.C.R. I-6009 at [19].

[83]   *Dumez France* (C-220/88) [1990] E.C.R. I-0049 at [14]. See also *Kitechnology BV* [1995] F.S.R. 765 at 779, et seq.

[84]   *Kitechnology BV* [1995] F.S.R. 765 at 780, per Evans LJ.

[85]   *Kronhofer* (C-168/02) [2004] E.C.R. I-6009 at [20].

[86]   (C-168/02) [2004] E.C.R. I-6009 at [20].

[87]   *Kitechnology BV* [1995] F.S.R. 765 at 779.

[88]   *Fiona Shevill, Ixora Trading Inc, Chequepoint SARL and Chequepoint International Ltd v Presse Alliance SA* (C-68/93) [1995] E.C.R. I-415 at [19].

established, since that is the place where the harmful event originated and from which the libel was issued and put into circulation.

[25] The court of the place where the publisher of the defamatory publication is established must therefore have jurisdiction to hear the action for damages for *all the harm caused by the unlawful act.*

[26] However, that forum will generally coincide with the head of jurisdiction set out in the first paragraph of article 2 of the Convention."

The observation in [19] above that the policy behind art.7(2) is based upon the **17-050** existence of there being "a particularly close connecting factor" between the dispute and the courts of the place where the harmful event occurred is now considered settled law.[89] This principle has been used for the purpose of establishing other principles under art.7(2) relevant to jurisdictional disputes in online infringement.

The observation that the place of establishment of the publisher of a libel is to **17-051** be equated with the "place of the event giving rise to it" is rather far-fetched. For instance, it is far-fetched to say in the case of a French company who decides to publish an English-language libellous publication in UK, Eire and the Netherlands, that the place of the event giving rise to the damage was France. Indeed, the very fact that such does generally coincide with the "domicile of the defendant" grounds of jurisdiction appears to suggest that such is indeed far-fetched. However, as will be seen, this approach has been favoured in relation to jurisdictional disputes under art.7(2) concerning online infringement of IPRs.

In relation to the *Bier* condition—"place where the damage occurred"—the court **17-052** said:

"[29] In the case of an international libel through the press, the injury caused by a defamatory publication to the honour, reputation and good name of a natural or legal person occurs in the places where the publication is distributed, when the victim is known in those places.

[30] It follows that the courts of each contracting state in which the defamatory publication was distributed and in which the victim claims to have suffered injury to his reputation have jurisdiction to rule on the injury caused in that state to the victim's reputation.

[31] In accordance with the requirement of the sound administration of justice, the basis of the rule of special jurisdiction in article 5(3), the courts of each Member State in which the defamatory publication was distributed and in which the victim claims to have suffered injury to his reputation are territorially the best placed to assess the libel committed in that state and to determine the extent of the corresponding damage.

[32] Although there are admittedly disadvantages to having different courts ruling on various aspects of the same dispute, the plaintiff always has the option of bringing his entire claim before the courts either of the defendant's domicile or of the place where the publisher of the defamatory publication is established."

The court then summarised its views on the two *Bier* conditions in the context **17-053** of a libel:

"[33] In light of the foregoing, the answer to the first, secondly, third and sixth questions referred by the House of Lords must be that, on a proper construction of the expression 'place where the harmful event occurred' in article 5(3) of the Conven-

---

[89] e.g. See *eDate Advertising GmbH v X; Olivier and Robert Martinez v MGN Ltd* (C-501/01 & C-161/10) [2011] E.C.R. I-10269 at [40]; *Melzer*, at [26], *Pinckney*, at [27]–[28]; *Hi Hotel HCF*, at [28]. *Pez Hejduk v EnergieAgentur.NRW GmbH* (C–441/13) EU: C:2015:28 at [19].

tion, the victim of a libel by a newspaper article distributed in several Member States may bring an action for damages against the publisher *either before the courts of the Member State of the place where the publisher of the defamatory publication is established, which have jurisdiction to award damages for all the harm caused by the defamation, or before the courts of each Member State in which the publication was distributed and where the victim claims to have suffered injury to his reputation, which have jurisdiction to rule solely in respect of the harm caused in the state of the court seized.*" [Author's emphasis.]

17-054 It will be clear from the above that if jurisdiction under art.7(2) is based on "the place of the event giving rise" to the damage, the court seized of jurisdiction on this basis will have jurisdiction in relation to damage incurred *throughout the EU*. However, if jurisdiction is based solely on the "place where the damage occurred", then the court's jurisdiction is limited to adjudicating on the damage caused in that court's state.[90]

17-055 It is now necessary to consider these general principles as they apply to intellectual property infringement actions.

IPR infringement

17-056 Generally, an act of infringement which occurs in a Member State is only actionable if the claimant has rights under the intellectual property laws of that Member State. Because of the territorial nature of IP laws, ex hypothesi, acts of infringements must occur within the territory of the protected IPR to give rise to a cause of action under that IPR. Put another way, the *forum delicti commissi* must be the same as the *forum loci protectionis*. Thus, in the case of a manufacture of a physical product or operation of a process, the act of manufacture or processing can only infringe a German patent if it occurs in Germany. The application of art.7(2) to such facts is unproblematic. The tort of infringement has occurred in Germany and thus art.7(2) permits an IPR owner to bring proceedings in Germany. In this example, it is clear that there are two close connecting factors to Germany: the place where infringement occurred and the relevant law applicable to that act of infringement.

17-057 As discussed above, art.7(2) could confer jurisdiction on the court of a Member State in two ways: (1) the place of the event giving rise to the damage happened in that Member State, and (2) the place where the damage happened in that Member State. These conditions apply to actions for infringement of IPRs.[91] The first way means that jurisdiction is conferred on the courts of the Member State whose laws give rise to the IPR which is alleged to be infringed. Thus, if a German patent is alleged to be infringed by the manufacture of infringing articles in Germany, then "the place of the event", i.e. the act of infringement must occur in Germany. The second way may give rise to greater difficulties of interpretation. In most circumstances, it would inevitably include the same Member State. Assuming that the patent is exploited is Germany, the manufacture and distribution of the infring-

---

[90] This has its parallel in the EU Trade Mark Regulation and Community Design Regulation, which have their own rules of jurisdiction, whereby it is expressly stated that where a court of a Member State has jurisdiction because acts of infringement were committed or threatened in the state of the court, then the court only has jurisdiction in respects of those acts committed or threatened within the territory of the Member State of the court—see para.17-214, et seq.

[91] In the context of copyright infringement, see *Hi Hotel HCF SARL v Uwe Spoering* (C-387/12) ECLI:EU:C:2014:215, [27]; *Melzer v MF Global UK Ltd* (C-228/11), at [25]. See also, *Coty Germany* (C-360112), at [46]; *Pez Hejduk v Energie Agentur.NRW GmbH* (C-441/13), at [18].

ing goods in Germany will directly affect sales of the patentee in Germany. Even if not exploited, the acts will reduce the commercial value of the monopoly afforded by the German patent and thus, the ability to license it.

However, in certain cases, the infringing act of manufacture in Germany may affect sales of the owner of the German patent in other Member States. For instance, the infringing goods may be imported into France and sold in competition to the German patentee's goods in France. Assuming that it can be shown that the German patentee has lost sales in France by reason of the sales of the infringing goods, it is clear that there is a clear chain of causation and it is irrelevant for this purpose whether or not the German patentee has any parallel French patent. Would French courts have jurisdiction in such circumstances under art.7(2) for infringement of the German patent on the grounds that France was the place (or one of the places) where the damage occurred? There seems no reason to say that it does not. France is the Member State where damage has occurred. But would this depend on whether the German patentee had parallel patent protection in France? Let us assume that it did not. No doubt it would then be strongly argued by the defendant in French proceedings that the absence of any patent protection in France means that the German patentee cannot say that it has suffered damage in France *as a result of patent infringement* and that any damage it has suffered is as a result of lawful competition. However, the CJEU has said that the requirements under art.7(2) are not to be conflated with the requirements of the substantive action so that it is not necessary to show that an infringement had occurred in the Member State when considering whether that state has jurisdiction under art.7(2).[92] Equally it can be said that the sale of the goods imported from Germany and which infringed the German patent caused financial loss to the German patentee and it is irrelevant that the goods could have been manufactured in France lawfully.[93]   **17-058**

Ultimately, it is submitted, on the basis of the authorities cited in the previous section that the courts will need to consider whether France has a particularly close connecting factor with the dispute and whether the acts of infringement of the German patent have "directly produced" their harmful effects in France.[94] This might be satisfied where the infringing articles are manufactured by a German company pursuant to a sub-contract from a French company, i.e. the goods were only intended to be sold in France. On the other hand, it might not be satisfied where the goods were manufactured in Germany and intended for distribution in Germany but a parallel importer obtained them on the secondary market and imported them into France (see below). Another example would be where goods bearing a registered trade mark are exported from one Member State where there is a registered trade mark to another Member State. Under the EU Trade Mark Regulation and the Trade Mark Directive, the act of exporting of goods from Member State A to Member State B bearing unlawfully a trade mark registered in Member State A is an act of infringement in Member State A. However, it will be rare that the owner of the mark will suffer financial loss in Member State A because the act of export per se means that the goods are not placed on the market in Member State A. In such circumstances, the damage would occur in Member State B even if the right holder had no protection in that state.   **17-059**

---

[92] See *Pinckney v Mediatech*, at [41]–[42], discussed at para.17-087.
[93] In general, it is not a defence in an action for damages for patent infringement to argue that lost profits suffered by the patentee as a result of the marketing of infringing goods would have occurred in any event if the defendant had marketed non-infringing alternatives—in the UK, see *Ultraframe (UK) Ltd v Eurocell Building Plastics Ltd* [2006] EHWC 1344.
[94] Applying *Dumez* discussed at para.17-046.

17-060   The CJEU has had to consider the application of art.7(2) where infringing goods have been sold by a wholesaler established in Member State A to a retailer in Member State B (the retailer collecting the goods in Member State A). In such circumstances, the right holder has sought to sue the wholesaler in Member State B even though they did no acts of marketing in Member State B on the grounds that the wholesaler's acts have caused damage in Member State B (via the downstream actions of the retailer). The CJEU has considered these arguments in *Hi Hotel*[95] and *Coty Germany*.[96] The CJEU considered the alternative jurisdictional requirements under art.7(2): (i) the place of the event giving rise to the damage; and (ii) the place where the damage occurred. In *Coty Germany*, proceedings were brought in Germany against a Belgian wholesaler of perfume who sold perfume to a German retailer (the retailer having taken delivery of the goods in Belgium) for breach of German unfair competition law. In *Hi Hotel*, a photographer sued in Germany a French hotel chain for infringement of copyright in his photographs. He had supplied the hotel chain with photographs of the hotel for use in its advertising brochures. The French hotel chain proceeded to supply the photographs to a French publishing company who then forwarded them to its sister German publishing company. That latter company included the photographs in a book on architecture and distributed that book in Germany.

17-061   In both of these cases, the CJEU said that in relation to the first requirement ("place of the event"), such could not apply to the upstream supplier if he is sued before a court within whose jurisdiction he has not "acted".[97] Here, it will be noted that the CJEU is not so much focussing on where "the event" occurred (i.e. the act of unfair competition) but whether *the defendant* has carried out that act (and is therefore responsible for "the event) in the Member State of the court seized with the dispute. In relation to the second requirement ("where the damage occurred"), the CJEU took a liberal view and said that the test was whether the wholesaler's acts in Member State A "caused or may cause damage" in Member State B.[98] The CJEU gave some guidance on the specific facts of the case which suggest that the only condition which needs to be satisfied is one of causation, i.e. did the wholesaler's acts lead to the infringing acts?[99] Ex hypothesi, anyone in a supply chain upstream of the act of marketing will satisfy this test.

17-062   However, there are two further points to be made.

17-063   In *Coty Germany*, the Court of Justice that "... it is for the court seized to assess, in the light of the evidence at its disposal, the extent to which the sale of the 'Blue Safe For Women' perfume to Stefan P, which occurred in Belgium, was capable of infringing provisions of the German law against unfair competition, and *thereby*, of causing damage within the jurisdiction of that court."[100] This statement followed on from an earlier declaration that with regard to damage resulting from infringement of an intellectual and commercial property right, the occurrence of damage in a particular Member State is subject to the protection in that state of the right in respect of which infringement is alleged.[101] This suggests that it is not enough merely to show that the acts have caused damage in the Member State of

---

95   *Hi Hotel HCF SarL v Uwe Spoering* (C-387/12) ECLI:EU:C:2014:215.
96   *Coty Germany GmbH v First Note Perfumes NV* (C-360/12) ECLI:EU:C:2014:1318.
97   *Coty Germany*, at [50]–[51]; *Hi Hotel*, at [32].
98   *Coty Germany*, at [57]; *Hi Hotel*, at [33]–[40].
99   e.g. *Hi Hotel*, at [37]; *Coty Germany*, at [58].
100 See [58].
101 See [55] citing *Wintersteiger* (C-523/10) EU:C:2012:220 at [25], and *Pinckney* (C-170/12)

the court seized but it must also be shown that the defendant infringed a right *of that* Member State.[102] Therefore, it would seem that the court of a Member State would not have jurisdiction where the acts complained of have caused damage in that Member State, but where the cause of action relied upon against the foreign defendant is an infringement of an intellectual or commercial property right in *another* Member State, i.e the only connecting factor with the Member State of the court seized with the dispute is that damage occurred in that state. For instance, if in *Coty Germany*, Coty Germany sought not to rely upon German unfair competition law but merely the infringement of a Belgian national trade mark that would not be enough to bestow jurisdiction upon the German court merely because that act of infringement gave rise to damage in Germany. In such circumstances, it could be said, that there is not a sufficiently close connecting factor with Germany for the courts of Germany to have jurisdiction under art.7(2).

The second point is that whilst a court may have jurisdiction over a defendant **17-064** on the grounds that the latter caused the damage in a Member State, it does not follow that the claimant has a *cause of action* over the defendant in that Member State. For instance, taking the facts of *Coty Germany*, it would be surprising if the Belgian wholesaler was found responsible for breaching German unfair competition law merely by being an upstream supplier and not having committed any act of infringement in Germany. In other words, whilst the Belgian wholesaler may be responsible for the damage in Germany, it has not itself breached German unfair competition law unless it could be said that it was a joint tortfeasor or accessory to the act of marketing by the German retailer.[103] If this is correct, it would indeed be a Pyrrhic victory if the IPR owner could only found jurisdiction on the second *Bier* criterion, namely the place where the damage occurred. If jurisdiction can *only* be founded on this criterion, it must be because the defendant has not "acted" in the Member State of the court seized.[104] Yet, if the defendant has not "acted" in the Member State, then it is difficult to see how there is any cause of action against that defendant for acts carried out in that Member State. (However, the German court may well lack jurisdiction to hear an action for breach of Belgian unfair competition laws.)

In certain circumstances, an argument of joint tortfeasorship or contributory **17-065** infringement by way of being an accessory may be alleged. Thus, in *Mölnlycke*,[105] a patent infringement action, the claimant brought an action in England against related English and American defendants for acts done in England which it alleged infringed its UK patents. It then realised that a German sister company of the defendants had important documentation relating to the action and sought to join that company as a further co-defendant to the action, merely for the purposes of obtaining disclosure against the German company. The claimant put its case on jurisdiction on the predecessor provision to art.7(2) of the Recast Brussels Regulation, on the basis that the German defendant and English defendant had a common intention to infringe in England. The court permitted joinder on the basis that there

---

EU:C:2013:635 at [33].

[102] See also *Hi Hotel*, at [35].

[103] For instance, an accessory to a wrong is liable under German civil law, e.g. s.830 BGB (Bürgerlichen Gesetzbuches).

[104] As if it had acted, then jurisdiction would have been founded on the basis of the first Bier criterion— the place of the event giving rise to the damage (as discussed above).

[105] *Mölnlycke AB v Procter & Gamble Ltd (No.4)* [1992] R.P.C. 21.

was a good arguable case that the German company was a joint tortfeasor. Thus, jurisdiction against both defendants was founded on art.7(2).[106]

Declaration for non-infringement

17-066   Can art.7(2) be relied upon for a declaration of non-infringement? Article 7(2) of the Regulation refers to the place where the harmful event occurred or *may occur*. In most cases, a declaration of non-infringement is sought because if such is favourable to the applicant, it intends to start marketing the product for which a declaration of non-infringement is sought. Although there was some doubt about this, in *Folien Fischer AGv Ritrama*[107] the Court of Justice confirmed that an action for a negative declaration seeking to establish the absence of a tort fell within art.5(3), the predecessor provision in the Brussels Regulation to art.7(2).

Right to fair compensation

17-067   In *AGWU v Amazon*,[108] the Court of Justice had to consider whether the predecessor provision to art.7(2) applied to claims for payment of "fair compensation" under art.5(2)(b) of the Information Society Directive. AGWU was a copyright collecting society which sought to recover fair compensation on behalf of its members against Amazon. Article 5(2)(b) concerns the right to recover compensation for the "private copying" exception, whereby it is allowed provided that right holders receive fair compensation.[109] It sought to recover royalties against Amazon for the sale of image and sound recording devices or media (blank CDs). The Court of Justice held that the fair compensation provisions in art.5(2)(b) exist to compensate authors for the harm that they have suffered as a result of unauthorised copying. As a result, it said that the failure of AGWU to collect remuneration constituted a harmful event within the meaning of art.7(2).

Online infringements of IPRs

17-068   In the world of the Internet, determination of jurisdiction under art.7(2) RBR is problematical. The Internet is everywhere and nowhere. For example, one could have a website owned by a Russian company, which is hosted on a server based in Panama, which advertises infringing digital copies of musical works for downloading. The website is used by a consumer in England to download these copies even though the website appears aimed at Latin America and is thus only in Spanish. The copies are not in fact on the Panama server but obtained via peer-to-

---

[106] The court said that if jurisdiction had been purely on the basis of art.6(1) of the Brussels Convention (now art.8(2) Recast Brussels Regulation), it would have been improper in the circumstances to join the German company, as such disclosure could have been obtained under the 1970 Hague Convention by an application in the Federal Republic of Germany (per Dillon LJ, at 27). This remark is very much obiter dicta, and was made without submissions from counsel for the claimant. As to the 1970 Hague Convention on taking of evidence abroad in civil and commercial matters, see D. McLean, *International Judicial Assistance* (Oxford: Clarendon Press, 1992), p.852. See also *Football Dataco Ltd v Sportradar GmbH* [2011] F.S.R. 10.

[107] (C-133/11) ECLI:EU:C:2012:664. See also *Bayerische Motoren Werke AG v Acacia Srl* (C-433/16) ECLI:EU:C:2017:550 at [43]–[46] where the Court of Justice held that Folien Fischer did not apply to declaration for non-infringement of Community Designs (which has its own jurisdictional rules) but without saying that it did not apply to national IPRs.

[108] (C–572/14) EU:C:2016:286.

[109] See para.4-338.

peer "swarm" means.[110] In such circumstances where is the "place that the harmful event" takes place? Is it one or more of the following: (i) where the server is situated (Panama); (ii) where the persons responsible for the server are situated (Russia); (iii) where the person who downloads the unlawful copy is based (England); (iv) where the website is accessible (everywhere); and/or (v) the countries targeted by the website (Latin America) or somewhere else? The CJEU has considered this in a number of cases which are now considered.

"Centre of interests"

The difficulties caused by tortious acts being committed via the Internet were first **17-069** considered by the CJEU in the joined cases of *eDate Advertising GmbH v X; Martinez v MGN Ltd*.[111] The first case was concerned with a libel on an Austrian Internet site. In that action, the personality affected who was German brought proceedings in Germany for infringement of his personality rights. Jurisdiction was based on the predecessor provision to art.7(2), art.5(3) Brussels Regulation. In *eDate*, the Bundesgerichtshof referred to the CJEU regarding whether the German courts had jurisdiction under this provision. The same issue arose on different facts in the second case, *Martinez*, which was a reference from the French courts. The references gave the CJEU the opportunity to consider de novo the difficult problem of the application of art.5(3) to online torts. The CJEU started by citing *Shevill v Presse Alliance* (which was also a libel case) and that art.5(3) is based on the existence of a particularly close connecting factor with the dispute and courts of the place where the harmful event occurred so as to justify the attribution to those courts of jurisdiction based on sound administration of justice and the efficacious conduct of proceedings.[112] The court then commented that the peculiar nature of the Internet meant that the usefulness of the criterion relating to distribution developed in the earlier cases was reduced. It thus said that the "connecting factor" approach had to be adapted so that the victim could bring proceedings in respect of all damage. It thus held that an appropriate criterion was the place where the alleged victim had his or her "centre of interests".[113] The court justified such on the basis that such a criterion made it easy to identify the court in which he may sue and permits the defendant to reasonably foresee before which court he may be sued.[114] The CJEU said that in general the "centre of interests" corresponds to the victim's habitual residence but may also include where he pursues his professional activities. The CJEU also said that under art.5(3), an action can also be brought in the Member State where the publisher of the content is established. These two grounds were both based on the *Bier* criterion of "place of the event giving rise to the damage".

The astute reader will appreciate that the test of the "centre of interests" of the **17-070** victim is close to conferring jurisdiction on the courts of the Member State of the *claimant's* domicile (assuming such is the same as the state of its residence). It is also at odds with the approach in *Dumez* (see para.17-046) whereby the CJEU was

---

[110] e.g. *BitTorrent*. This permits the aggregation of parts of the file from a network of users all of whom have mirror copies. For more information, see: *http://en.wikipedia.org/wiki/BitTorrent* [Accessed 19 October 2017].

[111] *eDate Advertising GmbH v X; Olivier and Robert Martinez v MGN Ltd* (C-509/09 & C-161/10) [2011] E.C.R. I-10269.

[112] See [40].

[113] See [48].

[114] See [50]. Such an approach emphasises the importance that the CJEU has placed, in interpreting the Recast Brussels Regulation, on predictability and certainty. See para.17-021.

not receptive to arguments based on art.5(3) Brussels Convention which had the effect of conferring jurisdiction on the Member State of domicile of the claimant (on the grounds of indirect damage to its assets). The reader will also appreciate that the CJEU's reasoning was not based so much on a detailed and nuanced interpretation of art.5(3), but rather on a need for victims of online torts to have a "one stop shop" for online infringements. Yet that exists under the Recast Brussels Regulation—they can sue in the court of the defendant's domicile. Thus, it is difficult to see why this is not an appropriate way of dealing with online jurisdictions. The introduction of a "place of claimant" ground of jurisdiction under art.7(2) makes very substantial inroads into the basic principle that the fundamental rule is that a defendant should be sued in the Member State of its convenience and not the claimant's. Equally, the place where the publisher of the content is established is likely to be the same Member State as where the publisher is domiciled.

17-071   The CJEU in *eDate* also said that jurisdiction could be based on the *Bier* criterion of the place where the damage occurred and that in such circumstances, jurisdiction was conferred on the courts of the Member State in the territory of which online content is or has been accessible. In the context of the Internet, this means everywhere. In such circumstances, those courts only had jurisdiction in respect of the damage caused in the territory of the Member State of the court seized.[115]

IP online infringements: "Place where the event gave rise to the damage": Bier One

17-072   *eDate* was not an IP case, but because it concerned online torts (wrongs), it is not surprising that it was followed with some modifications in relation to online IP infringements. In *Wintersteiger*,[116] the CJEU applied its approach in *eDate* to a case involving a cross-border dispute concerning an Adword (Internet keyword). In that case, the claimant, an Austrian company, had a registered trade mark "Wintersteiger" registered in Austria and Germany for ski and snowboard servicing tools. A competing company, Products 4U, which was established in Germany, reserved the keyword "Wintersteiger" as an Adword for Google's top-level German domain name *google.de*. It did not do so for the Austrian Google equivalent. Thus, a person entering "Wintersteiger" into *google.de* would receive an advertising link to Products4U's website.[117] Wintersteiger issued proceedings in the Austrian courts for infringement of its Austrian trade mark and relied upon the predecessor provision to art.7(2) in the Brussels Regulation as the basis for jurisdiction. Products 4U contested jurisdiction and the matter was referred to the CJEU.

17-073   The CJEU held that under the predecessor provision to art.7(2), it was necessary to determine whether Austria was a significant connecting factor with the torts alleged. It considered the two *Bier* criteria: (i) the place where the event giving rise to the damage occurred, and (ii) the place where the damage occurred. In relation to the first *Bier* criterion, it held that in the case of an online advertisement, the event which gave rise to the damage was the "activation by the advertiser of the techni-

---

115 See [51]–[52].
116 *Wintersteiger AG v Products 4U Sondermaschinenbau GmbH* (C-523/10) ECLI:EU:C:2012:220 ; [2012] E.T.M.R. 31.
117 Whether or not this give rise to a cause of action under the Trade Mark Directive is considered at para.3-552, et seq.

cal process displaying" the advertisement.[118] It held that as such was not foreseeable, it should not be the location of the server. Rather, it said that the place where the activation occurred is the place of establishment of the advertiser.[119]"

In a later case, *Pez Hejduk*, (whose facts are considered below) which concerned **17-074** the placing of photographs on a website without the consent of the copyright owner, the Court of Justice adopted the same approach as that taken in *Wintersteiger* when deciding "the place where the event gave rise to the damage". It held that the causal event must be "the activation of the process for the technical display of the photographs on the website".[120] It held that this event must lie in the actions of the owner of the website.[121] It said that this must be the place where the defendant (EnergieAgentur) had its seat since that is where the company took and carried out the decision to place photographs on the website.[122] Here, it will be appreciated that the court is assimilating the act of placing the photographs on the website to the seat of the defendant merely as an evidential presumption. For instance, if the evidence had shown that in fact, an employee of EnergieAgentur had loaded up the photographs onto the website in a Member State other than where it had its seat, presumably the court of that Member State would have had jurisdiction.

IP online infringements: place where the damage occurred: Bier Two

In *Wintersteiger*, discussed above in relation to the second *Bier* criterion ("the **17-075** place where the damage occurred"), the CJEU held that the Austrian court would have to consider the issue of infringement by reference to Austrian law. It then held that the objective of foreseeability and sound administration of justice militated in favour of conferring jurisdiction on the courts of the Member State in which the right at issue is protected.[123] It said that they are best able to assess whether the acts infringed the protected registered trade mark.[124]

In *Pinckney v Mediatech*,[125] the CJEU was concerned with a case where an **17-076** author, who lived in France and owned copyrights in various songs, brought an action against an Austrian company which had made a CD in Austria of his songs. He alleged that such was done without his permission. The CD was then marketed by UK companies and uploaded onto various Internet sites which were accessible from his residence in France. The author brought an action in France alleging infringement of copyright in his songs. The French courts referred to the CJEU whether it had jurisdiction to hear the action. The CJEU considered the ambit of the predecessor provision to art.7(2) to online marketing of infringing copies.

In relation to the *Bier* criterion of "place of event giving rise to the damage", it **17-077** was common ground that such was not France.[126] Thus, the issue in the case concerned whether the French courts had jurisdiction under the *Bier* criterion— "place where the damage occurred."

Before doing so, it made it clear that the issue of jurisdiction was independent **17-078** of whether the copyright was infringed in France. As it said, such belonged to the

---

[118] See [34].
[119] See [36]–[37].
[120] (C–441/13) EU:C:2015:28 at [24].
[121] See [24] by analogy with *Wintersteiger*, at [34]–[35].
[122] See [25].
[123] See [27].
[124] Despite the fact that trade mark law is harmonised at a EU level.
[125] (C-170/12) ECLI:EU:C:2013:635.
[126] See [29].

examination of the substance of the matter whereas art.5(3), the predecessor provision to art.7(2), was merely concerned with whether a harmful event had occurred. Therefore, art.5(3) did not require that the activity of the defendant was "directed" or targeted at the Member State in which the court was seized.[127]

17-079 Having made the above clear, it held, applying *Wintersteiger* to copyright infringement, that jurisdiction was conferred on the court of a Member State if that state protected the copyrights relied on by the claimant *and* that the alleged damage "may occur" within the jurisdiction of the seized court.[128] It said that this arose from the possibility of obtaining a reproduction of the work from an internet site accessible within the jurisdiction of the court seized.[129]

17-080 The CJEU confirmed that if such was satisifed, then the court seized only has jurisdiction to determine the damage caused within the Member State in which it is situated.[130]

17-081 *Pinckney* was concerned with online sales of *physical items* embodying copyright works. In *Pez Hejduk v EnergieAgentur.NRW GmbH*,[131] the Court of Justice considered the jurisdiction of a court of a Member State to hear an action for infringement of a copyright work being made available on a website without permission of the copyright owner. Ms Hejduk was a professional photographer of architecture and had taken photographs of the Austrian architect, Georg Reinberg. At a conference organised by EnergieAgentur, Mr Reinberg used Ms Hejduk's photographs to illustrate his buildings with her consent. However, EnergieAgentur then reproduced the photographs without the permission of Ms Hejduk on their website. Ms Hejduk, who was domiciled in Austria, brought proceedings for copyright infringement against EnergieAgentur, a German company, before the Handelsgericht Wien, an Austrian court.

17-082 The Austrian court referred two questions concerning whether it had jurisdiction under the predecessor provision to art.7(2) RBR to hear the action in Vienna. Considerable debate existed between the parties regarding whether the criteria in *Pinckney* should apply.

17-083 The Advocate-General considered that *Pinckney* could be distinguished on its facts. He said that in *Hejduk*, the damage was very "delocalise'" and as there was no reliable proof that damage had occurred in a Member State, jurisdiction could not be based on the *Bier* criterion of "place where the damage occurred". He went on to say that under the predecessor provision to art.7(2), in such a case, jurisdiction had to be based on the other *Bier* criteria, "place of event giving rise to the damage."

17-084 The Court of Justice declined to follow the Advocate-General's Opinion and strictly applied *Pinckney*. It said that the "place of event giving rise to the damage" *Bier* criterion was not relevant for the purpose of attributing jurisdiction to the Austrian court in *Hejduk*.[132] This was because EnergieAgentur, the company responsible for the activation of putting the infringing photographs onto its website,

---

[127] See [40]–[42]. Where a sign is used in an advertisement or promotion which targets traders or consumers in a particular Member State, then that sign may infringe a trade mark registered in that Member State. See para.3-549.

[128] See [43]. The emphasis on "and" is not in the judgment. It will be rare that an IPR which is infringed in a Member State does not cause damage in that Member State as the act of infringement will reduce the value of the monopoly afforded by the IPR.

[129] See [44].

[130] See [45].

[131] (C-441/13) ECLI:EU:C:2015:28.

[132] See [23].

was not established in Austria.[133] It then went on to consider whether or not the Austrian court had jurisdiction under the second *Bier* criterion ("place where the damage occurred"). In this regard, it followed *Pinckney*. Jurisdiction was thus founded on the basis that: (i) the relevant rights were protected in the Member State of the court seized with the proceedings, *and* (ii) that the website was accessible in that Member State.[134] It also confirmed, following *Pinckney*, that the court of that Member State could only rule on the damage that occurred in that Member State[135] and that it was irrelevant for the purpose of jurisdiction (as opposed to cause of action) whether the website "targeted" the Member State of the court seized with the proceedings.[136]

Targeting: not a jurisdictional requirement

In *Peter Pammer v Reederei Karl Schlüter GmbH & Co KG* and *Hotel Alpenhof* **17-085** *GesmbH v Oliver Heller*,[137] the Court of Justice had to consider whether an Austrian court had jurisdiction in a consumer dispute. This turned on the interpretation of art.15.1(c) Brussels Regulation, which refers to whether an undertaking "by any means, directs [commercial or professional activities]..." when the undertaking advertises or promotes its business through a website. The Court of Justice gave guidance as to when a website can be considered as being directed at a Member State including taking account of factors such as the language, the currency used and any mention of telephone numbers with an international code. In *L'Oréal v eBay*[138] (which is discussed in Ch.3, "Trade Marks"[139]), the Court of Justice adopted the approach taken in *Pammer* and *Alpenhof* regarding whether the offer for sale on an online marketplace of goods bearing an infringing sign infringed the rights of a EU Trade Mark or national trade mark. It held that the correct test was whether the website (here being eBay's website) targeted consumers in the territories covered by the national or EU Trade Marks.

It was thought that the approach taken in *Pammer* and *Alpenhof* and *L'Oréal v* **17-086** *eBay* might apply to the proper interpretation of art.7(2) Recast Brussels Regulation. Some support for this came from *Football Dataco Ltd v Sportradar*.[140] In this case, the CJEU was concerned with where the act of "re-utilisation" of data within the meaning of the Database Directive occurred where a webserver located in Member State A contained data which was downloaded by a person in Member State B at the latter's request. In the proceedings, the claimant had only asserted infringement of UK database right. Consequently, it was an important issue where the act of re-utilisation took place. The Court of Appeal of England and Wales had referred this question to the CJEU. The CJEU took the view that the act of re-utilisation occurred *at least* in Member State B where it could be concluded that there was an intention on the part of the person responsible for the data to "target" members of the public in Member State B.[141] Previously, the CJEU had applied the criterion of "targeting" in relation to the determination of whether a cause of action arose for

---

[133] See [24]–[26].
[134] See [38].
[135] See [36], [38].
[136] See [33].
[137] (C-585/08 & C-144/09) ECLI:EU:C:2010:740.
[138] (C-324/09) ECLI:EU:C:2011:474 at [58]–[67].
[139] See para.3-549.
[140] *Football Dataco Ltd v Sportradar GmbH* (C-173/11) ECLI:EU:C:2012:642.
[141] See [41]–[43], and [47]. It is of note that the Advocate-General's Opinion suggested that the act of

trade mark infringement.[142] Importantly, for the purpose of this chapter, in its judgment, it recognised that the question of localisation of the acts of sending the data at issue was "liable to have an influence on the question of the jurisdiction of the referring court" under art.5(3), the predecessor to art.7(2). This suggested that it was necessary under art.7(2) that the Member State of the court seized had been targeted by the website of the defendant. However, the CJEU's decision did not concern the proper interpretation of the predecessor provision of art.7(2) of the Brussels Regulation[143] and, therefore, its remarks were obiter dicta.

17-087   However, in *Pinckney v Mediatech*, as discussed above, the CJEU did not follow this approach. It clarified that "targeting" was not a necessary requirement for the purpose of determining jurisdiction. Thus, the CJEU said that a distinction must be drawn between the question whether a *cause of action* existed in a Member State and whether the Member State had *jurisdiction* under the Brussels Regulation.[144] It said that the issue of jurisdiction cannot depend on the criteria which are specific to the examination of the substance of the action. Therefore, it said that art.7(2) does not depend on whether the activity is directed to the Member State (an issue going to whether an infringement has taken place).[145] Equally, in *Pez Hejduk*, also discussed above, the Court of Justice held that it was irrelevant for the purpose of art.7(2) that the website on which the infringing photographs were located, was not directed at the Member State of the court seized with the proceedings.[146]

17-088   Hence, whilst targeting is relevant to cause of action, it is not relevant to the issue of jurisdiction.[147] Of course, this may mean that a court that is seized under art.7(2) RBR of a dispute on the grounds that a right is protected in that Member State may go on to find that there is no cause of action because the website did not target that Member State. This would obviously be a Pyrrhic victory.

Online infringement: summary

17-089   The cases of *eDate*, *Wintersteiger*, *Pinckney* and *Pez Hejduk* introduce, a set of sui generis rules to the application of art.7(2) RBR to national IPR infringements that occur online. They can be summarised as follows:

    (i)   A right holder has the option of suing an infringer in the Member State where the place of event giving rise to the damage occurred or (if different) the Member State where the damage occurred (the two *Bier* criteria).

---

    re-utilisation occurred in both Member State A and B. The judgment of the CJEU carefully avoids stating whether Member State A would also have jurisdiction.

[142] *L'Oréal* (C-324/09) [2011] E.C.R. I-6011 at [67]. See para.3-549.

[143] See [29]–[30]. Although *Football Dataco v Sportradar* was also concerned about jurisdiction, the Court of Appeal, in referring the matter to the CJEU, held that the English court did have jurisdiction under art.5(3) over the database infringement claim (see [38]) as it held that a properly pleaded case of joint tortfeasance in England had been made out in its original claim. Strictly, the reference to the CJEU concerned whether there was any arguable cause of action of "re-utilisation" of UK database right (no foreign database right having been alleged). Thus, the reference to the CJEU was purely on the proper interpretation of the Database Directive and not art.5(3) of the Brussels Regulation. If the act of re-utilisation did not occur in the UK, then there was no cause of action (and thus, the UK court had no jurisdiction over the acts).

[144] See [41].

[145] See [42].

[146] *Pez Hejduk*, at [33].

[147] A point apparently missed in J. Smith and A. Leriche, "CJEU ruling in Pinckney v Mediatech; jurisdiction in online copyright infringement cases depends on the accessibility of website content" [2014] 36(2) E.I.P.R. 137–138.

(ii) If jurisdiction is founded on the *Bier* criterion of the "place of event giving rise to the damage", the court of that Member State has jurisdiction to award damage based on *all* damage suffered by the claimant regardless whether such damage was suffered in the Member State of the seized court. If jurisdiction is founded on the *Bier* criterion of the "place where the damage occurred", the court's jurisdiction is limited to considering the damage suffered by the claimant in that Member State.

(iii) The location of the server is irrelevant to art.7(2).

(iv) "The place of the event giving rise to the damage" will primarily be determined by reference to the Member State where the steps were taken to activate the infringing acts, e.g. the uploading of infringing material. This will normally be the place of establishment of the natural or legal person responsible for the same.

(v) "The place where the damage occurred" is any Member State where: (a) the right sued upon is protected, *and* (b) the Internet site of which complaint is made is accessible (in practice, by reason of the nature of the Internet, this will be anywhere in the world).

(vi) Although it is necessary to consider for the purpose of the *cause of action*, whether the Internet site targets persons in the Member State of the seized court, such is not relevant to the issue of *jurisdiction*.

Co-defendants/art.8(1)

Article 8(1) of the Recast Brussels Regulation provides that: **17-090**

"A person domiciled in a Member State may also be sued:

1. where he is one of a number of defendants, in the courts for the place where any one of them is domiciled, provided the claims are so closely connected that it is expedient to hear and determine them together to avoid the risk of irreconcilable judgments resulting from separate proceedings;... ."

Article 8(1) must be construed restrictively.[148] The wording of art.8(1) differs   **17-091**
from its equivalent provision in art.6(1) of the Brussels Convention which did not contain the wording "*provided the claims...separate proceedings*". However, such wording had its origin in the Jenard Report and was imported by the CJEU into art.6(1) Brussels Convention.[149] This wording then found its way into the predecessor provision to art.8(1) of the original Brussels Regulation.

The application of this rule is limited. Thus, where there are two defendants, it   **17-092**
will only apply where both defendants (D1 and D2) are domiciled in Member States and an action has been brought in the courts of the Member State of the domicile of either D1 or D2[150]. Furthermore, even if the court is in the Member State of the domicile of D1 or D2, art.8(1) may not be applicable if the action is under a different section of the Recast Brussels Regulation which precludes resort to art.8(1), e.g. in an employer-employee action relating to contracts of employment.[151] The nature

---

[148] e.g. *Freeport Plc v Arnoldsson* (C-98/06) [2007] E.C.R. I-839 at [35].

[149] *Kalfelis* (C-189/87) [1988] E.C.R. 5565.

[150] See *Réunion Européenne SA and Others and Spliethoff's Bevrachtingskantoor BV and the Master of the vessel Alblasgracht V002* (C-51/97) ECLI:EU:C:1998:509 at [38]–[52].

[151] Such disputes are covered by s.5 of the Regulation which in a surprising decision, the CJEU held

of the link (the connection between the two claims) must be determined independently and is an EU concept.[152] It should also be noted that the wording in art.8(1) mirrors that in relation to the *lis pendens* provisions of the Recast Brussels Regulation. Thus, art.30 RBR permits courts other than the first seized to stay proceedings where "related actions" are pending in the courts of different Member States. Article 30(3) defines "related actions" as when:

> "They are so closely connected that it is expedient to hear and determine them together to avoid the risk of irreconcilable judgments resulting from separate proceedings."

17-093 Indeed, as noted above, it was this wording in the predecessor provision to art.30 RBR in the Brussels Convention that led the Court of Justice in *Kalfelis* to "import" this wording into the predecessor provision in the Brussels Convention to art.8(1) RBR.[153]

Co-defendants and parallel infringement actions

17-094 Article 8(1) is clearly of great importance to IP practitioners. IP litigation is often multi-jurisdictional. A paradigmatic example is where the owner of a European patent wishes to sue defendants which are part of a multi-national conglomerate for infringement of its European patent. The grant of a European patent results in a basket of national patents. Thus, a typical situation could be a pharmaceutical company with parallel patents derived from the same European application in all Member States. A defendant multi-national may have operating subsidiaries in each Member State which make or sell a pharmaceutical which is alleged to be an infringement of parallel patents. It is clearly unattractive for the pharmaceutical company to have to issue parallel proceedings in all Member States for patent infringement. This would mean exorbitantly expensive litigation. More importantly, in such circumstances, the national court of each Member State would be ruling on essentially the same matter—does the defendant's pharmaceutical product fall within the claims of the European patent? The claims of the patents will be identically worded and furthermore, under the Protocol to art.69 of the European Patent Convention, the law relating to the determination of infringement is the same.[154] Therefore, theoretically, assuming that the same facts and matters are put before the courts of every Member State, the result should be the same. However, as is often said, patents are territorial. Although the result should be the same, there is no danger of, *strictu sensu*, irreconcilable decisions. A German court could find infringement of a German patent and a Dutch court find no infringement of a Dutch patent without there being any risk, at a legal plane, of mutually irreconcilable judgments. This is because the finding by the German court of infringement and the Dutch court of non-infringement only extends to acts in Germany and the Netherlands and any relief granted by the German and Dutch courts would only extend respectively, to Germany and the Netherlands. Hence, they are not mutually exclusive.

---

ousted the effect of the predecessor provision to art.8(1)—*GlaxoSmithKline v Rouard* (C-462/06) [2008] E.C.R. I-3965 (heavily criticised in A. Briggs and P. Rees, *Civil Jurisdiction and Judgments*, 6th edn (London: Informa, 2015), para.2.202).

[152] *Kalfelis* [1988] E.C.R. 5565, CJEU.

[153] See [11]–[12], *Kalfelis*

[154] See para.2-320.

In the above example, does art.8(1) allow consolidation of parallel actions on a **17-095** European patent or parallel national rights in the court of one Member State? This issue first arose in *Roche Nederland v Primus*.[155] In that case, the patentees, who were domiciled in the US, brought an action in the Netherlands against Roche Nederland and eight other companies in the Roche group who were established, inter alia, in Belgium, Germany, France, the UK, Austria and Sweden (i.e. they were domiciled in Member States). The patentees claimed that these companies had infringed rights conferred on them by a European patent by placing immuno-assays on the market in countries in which the patentees were established. The companies in the Roche group which were not established in the Netherlands contested jurisdiction. On matters of substance, they denied that they had infringed, and they also contended that the patent was invalid. One of the reasons that the Dutch courts were chosen was because under Netherlands law, Dutch courts were prepared to assert extra-territorial jurisdiction over associated companies if a Dutch company was the "spider in the web".[156] However, because of doubts over the legitimacy of this practice, the Hoge Raad (the Dutch Supreme Court) referred the issue as to whether indeed Dutch courts did have jurisdiction over the non-Dutch companies to the CJEU.

The CJEU considered the critical issue of whether a judgment given on a patent **17-096** granted in one Member State would be "irreconcilable" with that given on a parallel patent in another Member State, where both patents were derived from the same European application. On this issue, the CJEU said, in interpreting art.6(1) Brussels Convention, the predecessor to art.8(1) RBR as follows:

> "[26] As the Advocate General observed, in point 113 of his Opinion, in order that decisions may be regarded as contradictory it is not sufficient that there be a divergence in the outcome of the dispute, *but that divergence must also arise in the context of the same situation of law and fact.*
>
> [27] However, in the situation referred to by the national court in its first question referred for a preliminary ruling, that is in the case of European patent infringement proceedings involving a number of companies established in various Contracting States in respect of acts committed in one or more of those States, the existence of the same situation of fact cannot be inferred, since the defendants are different and the infringements they are accused of, committed in different Contracting States, are not the same.
>
> [28] Possible divergences between decisions given by the courts concerned would not arise in the context of the same factual situation.
>
> [29] Furthermore, although the Munich Convention lays down common rules on the grant of European patents, it is clear from Articles 2(2) and 64(1) of that convention that such a patent continues to be governed by the national law of each of the Contracting States for which it has been granted.
>
> [30] In particular, it is apparent from Article 64(3) of the Munich Convention that any action for infringement of a European patent must be examined in the light of the relevant national law in force in each of the States for which it has been granted.
>
> [31] *It follows that, where infringement proceedings are brought before a number of courts in different Contracting States in respect of a European patent granted in each of those States, against defendants domiciled in those States in respect of acts allegedly committed in their territory, any divergences between the decisions given by the courts concerned would not arise in the context of the same legal situation.*

---

[155] (C-539/03) [2006] E.C.R. I-6535.
[156] For an understanding of the Dutch legal doctrine of "spider in the web" see *Expandable Grafts Partnership v Boston Scientific BV* [1999] F.S.R. 352.

[32]   *Any diverging decisions could not, therefore, be treated as contradictory.*

[33]   In those circumstances, *even if the broadest interpretation of 'irreconcilable' judgments, in the sense of contradictory, were accepted as the criterion for the existence of the connection required for the application of Article 6(1) of the Brussels Convention*, it is clear that such a connection could not be established between actions for infringement of the same European patent where each action was brought against a company established in a different Contracting State in respect of acts which it had committed in that State.

[34]   That finding is not called into question even in the situation referred to by the national court in its second question, that is where defendant companies, which belong to the same group, have acted in an identical or similar manner in accordance with a common policy elaborated by one of them, so that the factual situation would be the same." [Emphasis supplied.]

17-097   As seen from this excerpt, the CJEU was clearly influenced by the Advocate-General's opinion. His view was that there was a clear difference between diverging decisions and irreconcilable decisions.[157] In doing so, he rejected the more liberal approach taken to the meaning of "irreconcilable judgments" to other parts of the Brussels Regulations or Convention where the CJEU had favoured the test of "conflicting decisions" as opposed to "legal consequences being mutually exclusive".[158] He accepted that although the Protocol on art.69 required the same approach to be taken to the substantive scope of protection conferred by a European patent, such was not the same as the *legal* scope of the rights conferred by the holder of a European patent which were governed by different national legislative systems.[159]

17-098   The approach of the CJEU in *Roche Nederland* was criticised for making multinational patent litigation very difficult and expensive.[160] Technically, of course, IP rights being territorial, in the case of national IPRs (as opposed to EU unitary rights such as the EU Trade Mark), the cause of action under a German patent is different to the cause of action under a French patent. Therefore, at a strict legal level, any decision on infringement of the German patent cannot conflict with that of a decision of infringement of the French patent. However, the requirement that the decisions must arise in the context of the "same situation of law and fact" for there to be a risk of irreconcilable judgments imposes a very high threshold. Indeed, it could be said that save in very limited circumstances (e.g. joint debt), the mere fact that an action is pursued against two separate persons means that they are not ex hypothesi concerned with the same situation of law and fact. Yet, art.8(1) is clearly concerned with separate causes of actions against separate persons.

17-099   Fortunately, in subsequent cases, the CJEU has retreated somewhat from the extreme position in *Roche Nederland*. The starting point of that retreat is a non-IP case—*Freeport Plc v Arnoldsson*.[161] This case was a contractual dispute concerning an allegation of monies owed to Mr Arnoldsson. He said that both Freeport Plc (an English company) and Freeport AB (a Swedish company) owed him the monies. An action was brought in Sweden and he argued that the Swedish court had jurisdic-

---

[157]   See [109] of the Opinion.

[158]   e.g. *The Tatry* (C-406/92) [1994] E.C.R. I-5439 relating to art.22 of the Brussels Convention (art.30 of the Recast Brussels Regulation).

[159]   See [120].

[160]   See A. Briggs and P. Rees, *Civil Jurisdiction and Judgments*, 6th edn (London: Informa, 2015), para.2.71 where the authors said that there was nothing wrong with the logic but everything wrong with the result of expensive parallel litigation.

[161]   (C-98/06) [2007] E.C.R. I-839.

tion over Freeport Plc by reason of the predecessor provision to art.8(1) (hereinafter referred to as art.8(1)). Freeport Plc argued that the action against it was contractual, whereas the action against Freeport AB was based in tort and therefore such excluded art.8(1). It is clear from the facts that the courts considered that there were some grounds for believing that the action against Freeport AB (which was not a party to the contract) had been brought purely to found jurisdiction in Sweden under art.8(1) against Freeport Plc. Various questions were referred to the CJEU concerning art.8(1) and its interpretation. The CJEU held that in substance, the Swedish court was asking whether art.8(1) applied only where the two actions had "identical legal bases". In its decision, which skirted around the difficulties caused by *Roche Nederland*, it said that it was "not apparent" from the wording of art.8(1) that such required that the actions against the different defendants "should have identical legal bases".[162]

In *Painer v Standard Verlags*,[163] the claimant sued for infringement of copyright **17-100** in photographs she had taken of Natascha K (the abducted Austrian child). Her photographs were published by Austrian and German companies. Accordingly, she sued for infringement of Austrian and German copyright against both the Austrian and Germany company in Austria. In considering whether art.8(1) permitted the Austrian courts to adjudicate on the German copyright actions, the Austrian court referred the issue to the CJEU. The CJEU said, in following *Freeport*, that the identical legal bases of the actions brought is only a relevant factor for the purpose of art.8(1). It was not an "indispensable requirement for the application of [art.8(1)]" and therefore did not preclude the application of art.8(1) provided that it was foreseeable by the defendants that they might be sued in the Member State where at least one of them was domiciled.[164] It held that the reasoning was stronger when the actions based against the defendants were "substantially identical".[165]

Freeport and *Painer* opened the door for reconsideration of *Roche Nederland* in **17-101** *Solvay v Honeywell*.[166] This case also concerned proceedings for infringement of a European patent. An action was brought by Solvay SA, a Belgium company, in the Netherlands against one Dutch and two Belgian companies in the Honeywell group. The Dutch and one of the Belgian companies were accused of acts of infringement throughout Europe and the other Belgian company was accused of acts of infringement in Northern and Central Europe. During the course of proceedings, an interim claim was brought against the defendant companies seeking provisional relief in the form of a pan-European injunction against further infringement until a decision had been made in the main proceedings. The Dutch court referred a number of questions to the CJEU including the proper interpretation of art.8(1). Before considering that decision, the reader should appreciate that the facts of this case differ to *Roche Nederland* because, based on the alleged facts, defendant companies were claiming to be operating in a number of Member States. Thus, at trial, the court would have had to determine *for a particular Member State* whether *more than one defendant* had infringed the designated European patent for that

---

[162] Somewhat surprisingly, the Advocate-General does not refer to *Roche Nederland v Primus*.

[163] *Eva-Maria Painer v Standard Verlags GmbH* (C-145/10) [2011] E.C.R. 12533.

[164] See [80] and [81]. This was despite at [79], the CJEU said that it was not sufficient that there be a divergence in the outcome of the dispute but that such must arise in the same situation of fact and law. This suggests that the CJEU perceived that the test of "same situation of fact and law" as being a sufficient but not a necessary condition for the application of art.6(1).

[165] See [82]. Indeed, at [83], it appears to suggest that the fact that they are substantially identical actions was a materially relevant consideration for the national court to find that art.8(1) was applicable.

[166] (C-616/10) ECLI:EU:C:2012:445.

Member State. Clearly, here, there is a much greater risk of irreconcilable judgments rather than merely diverging judgments.

17-102   In its decision, the CJEU cited *Freeport* and *Roche Nederland*. It held that in the present case, two courts may be considering the alleged infringements by different Honeywell companies in the same Member State. It said that the national court should, when deliberating whether there is a risk of irreconcilable judgments, take into account the dual fact that first the defendants are separately accused of committing the same infringement with respect to the same products and secondly, such infringements were committed in the same Member State so that they adversely affected the same national parts of the European patent at issue.[167] It will be appreciated that the CJEU did not adversely comment on *Roche Nederland* nor did it seek to restrict it. Rather, it considered *Solvay v Honeywell* distinguishable from *Roche Nederland*, as in *Solvay*, the various companies were operating in the same territories. The Advocate-General was braver about tackling *Roche Nederland*. He commented that it had been strongly criticised[168] and raised squarely the issue whether it should be overturned or not. However, he held that it was possible to adopt a more nuanced approach, carefully circumscribing the scope of the case-law in *Roche Nederland*[169] on the grounds, as held by the CJEU, that unlike *Roche Nederland*, the defendants in *Solvay* were accused of marketing the same infringing products in the same Member States.

17-103   The position is, therefore, unclear. *Roche Nederland* suggests that there must be same situation of law and fact. However, *Freeport* and *Painer* retreats from this position implying that it is not necessary to have identical legal bases. The approach in *Freeport* and *Painer* highlights that the requirement of same situation of law and fact would be a sufficient but not necessary condition for the application of art.8(1). However, if the requirement of identity of cause of action is removed, then it is difficult to see what other factor should prevent consolidation of proceedings of parallel European patent litigation or EU harmonised IP legislation (assuming the facts are the same, i.e. the product accused of infringement is the same throughout the EU). It is clearly undesirable to have different decisions on the same facts where the substantive law (whether EU law or in the case of EPC, pursuant to an exhaustive regional treaty) is the same. Moreover, such causes considerable expense.

17-104   Of course, it may be that the Court of Justice could still maintain its position in *Roche Nederland* that in essence, judgments on parallel patents (whether European or national) in different Member States against different subsidiary companies can never fall within art.8(1) as the *effects* of each judgment would be confined to the

---

[167] See [29]. This can be considered a powerful "steer" to the national court to find that art.8(1) did apply.

[168] He thus cited the following, European Max-Planck Group on Conflict of Laws in Intellectual Property (CLIP), "*Intellectual Property and the Reform of Private International Law: Sparks from a Difficult Relationship*", IPRax, 2007, No.4, p.284; points 78–85, and the case-law cited in point 78 of the Opinion delivered by Trstenjak AG in *Painer*; see also H. Muir Watt, "Article 6", in U. Magnus, and P. Mankowski, *Brussels I Regulation*, 2nd edn (Munich: Sellier European Law Publishers, 2012), p.313, No.25a; M. Noorgård, "A Spider without a Web? Multiple Defendants in IP Litigation", in S. Leible, and A. Ohly, (eds), *Intellectual Property and Private International Law* (Tübingen: Mohr Siebeck, 2009), p.211; C. Gonzalez Beilfuss, "Is there any Web for the Spider? Jurisdiction over Co-defendants after Roche Nederland", in A. Nuyts, (ed.), *International Litigation in Intellectual Property and Information Technology* (The Hague: Kluwer Law International, 2008), p.79.

[169] See [22].

Member State of that court. Yet, in the opinion of the authors, such a narrow interpretation of art.8(1) should not be favoured. As said by the Court of Justice in *Painer*, the fact that there is a difference in legal basis between the actions brought against different defendants does not preclude the application of art.8(1) provided that *"it was foreseeable by the defendants that they might be sued in the Member State where at least one of them is domiciled"*.[170] In the case of parallel actions brought against subsidiary companies with a common parent company based on the same European patent, it is very tempting to say that it is wholly foreseeable that they might be sued in the court of a Member State where one of them is domiciled.

It may be that the above comments make little difference in many cases. This is **17-105** because in relation to European patent litigation, as will be seen and as is discussed in a separate question ruled on by the Court of Justice in *Solvay v Honeywell*, once the defendant raises the question of validity of a patent, a court of a Member State other than where the patent is registered will invariably have to decline jurisdiction to hear the patent infringement action. This is discussed later in this chapter.

Co-defendants, unitary rights and extraterritorial relief

In the case of unitary rights, such as the EU Trade Mark Regulation and the Com- **17-106** munity Design Regulation, such rights are enforceable throughout the EU. As discussed below, these regulations have special jurisdictional rules which amount to a *lex specialis* and thus take precedence over the jurisdictional rules in the Recast Brussels Regulation.[171] However, these regulations do not include provisions concerning jurisdiction over co-defendants. Accordingly, art.8.1 Recast Brussels Regulation applies to determine whether the court of a Member State has jurisdiction in actions for infringement of unitary rights.[172] In *Nintendo v BigBen*, the Court of Justice had to consider the scope and ambit of art.8.1 RBR to proceedings for infringement of various Community Designs against defendants domiciled in differing Member States where they were involved in supplying products infringing the said designs to various Member States via a website. In particular, a German court (the Landgericht Düsseldorf) was seized of an action against a French company (BigBen France) which supplied infringing goods to various Member States including, via a German subsidiary (BigBen Germany) to consumers in Germany and Austria. The Landgericht was unsure about its jurisdiction to make various orders against the French company in relation to acts carried out by the French company other than supplies to the German subsidiary. On reference from the Landgericht, the Court of Justice held that there was no reason why in infringement proceedings under a unitary right such as the EU Trade Mark or Community Design, the jurisdiction of a court of a Member State over a co-defendant domiciled in another Member State should be limited to acts in the Member State of the court.[173]

The decision in *Nintendo* was heavily influenced by the fact that EU unitary **17-107** rights are intended, as a rule, to have effect throughout the EU. However, it is of note that the Court of Justice said there was nothing in the predecessor to art.8(1) RBR or the case law under that provision that courts seized of jurisdiction over a co-defendant should have its jurisdiction limited to acts that happened in the

---

[170] See [81].
[171] See para.17-214.
[172] *Nintendo Co Ltd v BigBen Interactive GmbH* (C-24/16 & C-25/16) ECLI:EU:C:2017:724 at [44].
[173] See [63]–[64].

Member State of the court.[174] Thus, *Nintendo* can be considered authority for the proposition that where a court of a Member State has jurisdiction under art.8(1) RBR in infringement proceedings of national rights over a co-defendant domiciled in another Member State, its jurisdiction is not limited to acts that happened in the Member State of the court. Indeed, the authors' view is that the right approach under art.8(1) is to treat the co-defendant as if they/it were domiciled in the Member State of the court seized with jurisdiction over the "anchor" defendant.[175] Therefore, if the court has jurisdiction over acts outside the Member State of the court and/or grants extra-territorial relief as against the "anchor" defendant, then, in the authors' view, regardless whether the IPR is a unitary or national right, it has a corresponding and co-extensive jurisdiction against the co-defendant over which it has jurisdiction under art.8(1) RBR. Such avoids unnecessary additional litigation.

Written jurisdiction agreements

17-108   Exclusive jurisdiction may be provided by reason of an agreement in writing between the parties to the proceedings. Article 25 of the Recast Brussels Regulation provides:

> "1.   If the parties, regardless of their domicile, have agreed that a court or the courts of a Member State are to have jurisdiction to settle any disputes which have arisen or which may arise in connection with a particular legal relationship, that court or those courts shall have jurisdiction, unless the agreement is null and void as to its substantive validity under the law of that Member State. Such jurisdiction shall be exclusive unless the parties have agreed otherwise. The agreement conferring jurisdiction shall be either:
>
> (a)   in writing or evidenced in writing;
>
> (b)   in a form which accords with practices which the parties have established between themselves;
>   or
>
> (c)   in international trade or commerce, in a form which accords with a usage of which the parties are or ought to have been aware and which in such trade or commerce is widely known to, and regularly observed by, parties to contracts of the type involved in the particular trade or commerce concerned.
>
> 2.   Any communication by electronic means which provides a durable record of the agreement shall be equivalent to 'writing'.
>
> 3.   The court or courts of a Member State on which a trust instrument has conferred jurisdiction shall have exclusive jurisdiction in any proceedings brought against a settlor, trustee or beneficiary, if relations between those persons or their rights or obligations under the trust are involved.
>
> 4.   Agreements or provisions of a trust instrument conferring jurisdiction shall have no legal force if they are contrary to Articles 15, 19 or 23, or if the courts whose jurisdiction they purport to exclude have exclusive jurisdiction by virtue of Article 24.
>
> 5.   An agreement conferring jurisdiction which forms part of a contract shall be treated as an agreement independent of the other terms of the contract.
>   The validity of the agreement conferring jurisdiction cannot be contested solely on the ground that the contract is not valid."

---

[174] See [63].

[175] i.e. the defendant who *is* domiciled in the Member State of the court seized with the dispute.

General principles

A number of principles have been derived in relation to art.25 and its **17-109** predecessors. First, the purpose of the formal requirements in art.25.1 is to ensure that the consensus between the parties is in fact established.[176] Secondly, the formal requirements of it are strict.[177] Thirdly, the party relying upon the written jurisdiction agreement must demonstrate clearly and precisely that the formal requirements are met. Fourthly, EU law governs formality and consensus whereas national law governs scope, effect and interpretation of jurisdiction clauses.[178] Finally, a party is not bound by a jurisdiction agreement unless they were either a party to the agreement[179]; they have succeeded to the rights and obligations of one of the original parties under the applicable national law[180]; or they have accepted the jurisdiction clause relied on against them.[181]

Domicile of parties is irrelevant

Article 25 of the Recast Brussels Regulation differs from its predecessor, art.23, **17-110** in the Brussels Regulation in that it dispenses with the requirement that one of the parties to the jurisdiction agreement must be domiciled in the EU. This is welcome. It would be most odd and an affront to common sense if a court declined jurisdiction based on a written jurisdiction agreement which conferred jurisdiction on the court of a Member State merely because the parties to it were not domiciled in a Member State of the EU.

---

[176] *Powell Duffryn Plc v Petereit* (C-214/89) [1992] E.C.R. I-1745 at [24] citing *Estasis Salotti v Rüwa* (C-24/76) [1976] E.C.R. 1831 at [7] (in relation to the Brussels Convention).

[177] *Benincasa v Dentalkit Srl* (C-269/95) [1997] E.C.R. I-5451; [1997] E.T.M.R. 447 at [26]–[29] (Brussels Convention). However, such does not mean that the document must expressly refer to the state which has jurisdiction if it is possible to identify clearly that country—see *Coreck Maritime GmbH v Handelsveem BV* (C-387/98) [2000] E.C.R. I-9337; [2001] C.L.C. 550 (Brussels Convention) where the clauses "any dispute arising under this Bill of Lading shall be decided in the country where the carrier has his principal place of business and the law of such country shall apply except as provided elsewhere herein" was held sufficient to confer exclusive jurisdiction on the court which satisfied this condition.

[178] *Powell Duffryn Plc v Petereit; Benincasa v Dentalkit Srl* [1997] E.C.R. I-5451; [1997] E.T.M.R. 447 at [25], [31]; *Antonio Gramsci Shipping Corp v Stepanovs* [2011] 1 Lloyd's Rep. 647 (High Court of England and Wales); *Knorr-Bremse Systems for Commercial Vehicles v Haldex Brake Products GmbH* [2008] F.S.R. 30 (High Court of England and Wales)—patent settlement dispute; *Kitechnology BV v Unicor GmbH Plastmaschinen* [1995] F.S.R. 765; [1994] I.L.Pr 568 CA (England and Wales)—the jurisdiction clause in a confidentiality agreement covered claims for misuse of confidential information as well as breach of contract.

[179] *Coreck Maritime GmbH v Handelsveem BV* (C-387/98) [2000] E.C.R. I-9337, [2001] C.L.C. 550; *Standard Steamship Owners P&I Association (Bermuda) Ltd v GIE Vison Bail* [2005] 1 All E.R. (Comm) 618; *Antonio Gramsci Shipping Corp* not following *Knorr Bremse* on the issue as to whether national law or art.25 applies to the determination of who are the parties to the jurisdiction agreement (the issue being as to whether a principal was bound by an agreement by his agent). In *Knorr Bremse*, the issue was whether a parent company was bound by a written jurisdiction agreement entered into by its subsidiary. Under German law, it was so bound. The English court held that EU and not national law applied and accordingly held that the parent was not so bound.

[180] *Coreck Maritime*, at [27].

[181] *Coreck Maritime GmbH v Handelsveem BV* (C-387/98) [2000] E.C.R. I-9337, [2001] C.L.C. 550 at [27]. The issue as to whether the party has accepted a written jurisdiction clause which complies with art.25(1) would be, it is considered, determined in accordance with the applicable national law.

Validity of contract

17-111   Another key change to the Brussels Regulation is that art.25 seeks to deal with an oft-made submission that the jurisdiction agreement has no validity if the agreement *in toto* is not valid. Thus, art.25(5) sets out that jurisdiction agreements shall be treated as an agreement independent of the other terms of the contract and that the validity of an agreement conferring jurisdiction cannot be contested solely on the ground that the contract is not valid. In this respect, it codifies the judgment of the Court of Justice in *Benincasa v Dentalkit*.[182] However, such provisions do not prevent a court from determining whether the jurisdiction agreement is null and void as to "its substantive validity" under the law of the putative designated Member State.[183] That includes any conflict-of-law rules of that Member State.[184] The intention here appears to be to avoid unattractive arguments whereby a party maintains that the jurisdiction clause in an agreement is inapplicable by reason of an argument that the whole contract should be rescinded or avoided when such may be the very dispute between the parties.[185] Yet, in some cases, the issue may be whether the contract including the jurisdictional clause has been agreed between the parties. In these circumstances, it will be very difficult to differentiate between arguments that the contract *in toto* is void and that the jurisdiction clause in that contract is void. The wording of art.25 is unfortunate, but it is suggested that the court seized with the dispute must determine whether the formalities set out in art.25 are satisfied. If so, then it has jurisdiction under art.25 even though if for other reasons, it is contested that the agreement is not valid.

Evidenced in writing

17-112   Although the written jurisdiction agreement cannot be merely a spoken agreement, it is sufficient if the agreement is "evidenced in writing". Therefore, any communication by electronic means which provides a durable record of the agreement is sufficient to confer jurisdiction under art.25.[186]

Written jurisdiction agreements cannot oust art.24

17-113   Article 25(4) means that a written jurisdiction agreement cannot confer jurisdiction court of a Member State in relation to matters for which the court of another Member State has exclusive jurisdiction under art.24. Thus, in patent litigation, art.24(4) (which is discussed below) confers exclusive jurisdiction on proceedings concerned with the validity of a patent on the court of the Member State of registration. A written jurisdiction agreement which seeks to give jurisdiction to the court of a Member State to revoke a patent in another Member State has no effect. However, what is the position if the written jurisdiction clause merely seeks to ask the court of a Member State to determine the issue of validity on an inter partes basis, which would preclude any party from seeking the remedy of revocation of

---

[182] See [21]–[32].
[183] art.25(1).
[184] Recital 20.
[185] This mirrors the position in the UK under the common law where the validity of a jurisdiction agreement is unaffected by rescission of the contract—see *Fiona Trust & Holding Corp v Privalov* [2007] UKHL 40 and *Deutsche Bank AG v Asia Pacific Broadband Wireless Communications* [2008] EWCA Civ 1091.
[186] art.25(2).

the relevant patent? Thus, it is fairly common for disputes about the level of payment of royalties in a patent licence, for a court to have to determine whether a patent claim is valid (as this triggers the obligation to pay royalties). In such disputes, the court is not being asked to revoke the patent but merely to decide validity in order to determine what royalties a licensee should pay. Although there is no Court of Justice judgment on this issue, the courts of England have had little difficulty in finding that a written jurisdiction clause in a patent licence which confers jurisdiction on the English courts allows the court to determine issues of validity of patents where such is relevant to the determination of the payment of royalties.[187]

Written jurisdiction agreements and submission to jurisdiction

A main difference between art.24 (exclusive jurisdiction) and art.25 is that the **17-114** court of a Member State other than that agreed to in accordance with art.25 can obtain jurisdiction by the submission of the defendant to its jurisdiction. By contrast, submission to a court's jurisdiction is ineffective in overcoming another Member State's exclusive jurisdiction under art.24.[188] Thus, in *Taser International Inc v SC Gate 4 Business SRL*[189] Taser International had entered into two non-exclusive distribution agreements with Gate 4, a Romanian company. Prior to these agreements, Gate 4 had registered in its own name, trade marks of Taser International in Romania. Under the agreements, Gate 4 agreed to assign these trade marks to Taser International. The agreements contained clauses conferring jurisdiction on a court in the US. Gate 4 failed to assign the Romanian trade marks and proceedings were issued in Romania by Taser International. Gate 4 did not challenge the jurisdiction and entered an appearance before the Romanian court. However, on appeal, the High Court of Cassation and Justice of its own motion decided to refer to the Court of Justice the issue of whether it had jurisdiction. In particular, the High Court wanted to know whether it should decline jurisdiction by reason of the written agreements conferring jurisdiction on the US. The Court of Justice held that in proceedings concerning non-performance of a contract which had a written jurisdiction clause conferring jurisdiction on a third country, the court was validly seized of the dispute if the defendant did not dispute jurisdiction. It also held that a court could not, in such circumstances, declare of its own motion that it did not have jurisdiction (applying *CPP Vienna Insurance Group*).[190]

---

[187] *Celltech (Adair's) Patent US Patent* [2004] F.S.R. 35; *Celltech v MedImmune* [2004] EWCA Civ 1331; *Chugai Pharmaceutical Co Ltd v UCB Pharma* [2017] EWHC 1216 (Pat) (patent licence dispute, written jurisdiction clause conferring jurisdiction on English court). In all these cases, the English courts held that they had jurisdiction to determine the issue of validity. Care must be exercised here because these cases were not concerned specifically with provisions of the Brussels Regulation or Convention but rather the validity of patents registered in non-Member States. Thus the issue was whether the determination within licence proceedings was contrary to the English doctrine of "act of state" whereby the courts of one state must respect the sovereignty and autonomy of other states (see [61], et seq.). The English courts have held that the "act of state" doctrine does not preclude the determination of validity in infringement proceedings of a foreign court (e.g. see *Chugai*, at [69] citing *Lucasfilms Ltd v Ainsworth* [2011] UKSC 39.

[188] art.31.

[189] (C–175/15) EU:C:2016:176.

[190] (C–111/09) EU:C:2010:290 at [25].

Written agreements conferring jurisdiction on courts of third country

17-115   Finally, in a dispute where a written agreement confers exclusive jurisdiction on a non-Member State, art.25 is prima facie inapplicable. However, it has been said in the Schlosser Report that in these circumstances, such agreements should be enforced according to the national procedural law of the court of the Member State seized with the dispute.[191] Such an approach is often characterised as applying a "reflexive" approach. The "reflexive effects" doctrine is considered later in this chapter in the context of art.24.[192]

Submission to jurisdiction

17-116   Where a defendant "enters an appearance" other than to contest jurisdiction before the court of a Member State, that court will have jurisdiction unless the court of another Member State has exclusive jurisdiction under art.24, e.g. where the proceedings concern the validity of a registered right. The challenge as to jurisdiction must be taken in the defence which is first filed, but can be put forward as an alternative in this defence to other challenges as to procedure.[193]

Exclusive jurisdiction: proceedings concerning the validity of registered IPRs

Introduction

17-117   Article 24 of the Recast Brussels Regulation imposes exclusive jurisdiction on the courts of a particular Member State in certain situations *regardless of the defendant's domicile*. Thus, art.24 applies even where the defendant is domiciled in a non-Member State.[194] If art.24 applies, then jurisdiction based on any other ground, including the defendant's domicile, is excluded. This is so even if the defendant submits to the jurisdiction of a court of the Member State.[195] The provisions of art.24 cannot be overridden by agreement.[196] If a court accepts jurisdiction in breach of art.24, its judgment will not be recognised or enforced in another Member State.[197] Where a court of a Member State is seized of a "claim" which is *principally* concerned with a matter over which the courts of another Member State have exclusive jurisdiction by virtue of art.24, then art.27 requires that it must declare of its own motion that it has no jurisdiction. In the rare instances that ac-

---

[191] See [176] *Report on the Brussels Convention, Schlosser* [1979] OJ C 59/71. The CJEU in *Coreck Maritime GmbH* (C-387/98) ECLI:EU:C:2000:606 were also of the same view, see [19] endorsing Professor Schlosser's view.

[192] See para.17-150.

[193] *Bayerische Motoren Werke AG v Acacia Srl* (C-433/16) ECLI:EU:C:2017:550 at [30]–[36].

[194] art.6(1); art.24. See also A. Briggs and P. Rees, *Civil Jurisdiction and Judgments*, 6th edn (London: Informa, 2015); Professor Jenard's report at s.5; *Dansommer A/S v Andreas Götz* (C-9/98) [2000] E.C.R. I-0393 at [19]; and (C-281/02) [2005] E.C.R. I-1383 at [28].

[195] art.26(1). *Gesellschaft für Antriebstechnik mbH v Lamellen und Kupplungsbau Beteiligungs KG (GAT v LUK)* (C-4/03) [2006] E.C.R. I-6509, [24]. See also *Taser International Inc v SC Gate 4 Business SRL* (C–175/15) EU:C:2016:176 at [22].

[196] art.25(4); *Gesellschaft für Antriebstechnik mbH v Lamellen und Kupplungsbau Beteiligungs KG (GAT v LUK)* (C-4/03) [2006] E.C.R. I-6509 at [24]. See para.17-115.

[197] art.45(1)(e)(ii); *GAT v LUK* at [24].

tions come within the exclusive jurisdiction of several courts, then any court other than the court first seized must decline jurisdiction in favour of that court.[198]

The art.24 grounds are as follows[199]:   **17-118**

"The following courts of a Member State shall have exclusive jurisdiction, regardless of the domicile of the parties:

(1)   in proceedings which have as their object rights in rem in immovable property or tenancies of immovable property, the courts of the Member State in which the property is situated.

         However, in proceedings which have as their object tenancies of immovable property concluded for temporary private use for a maximum period of six consecutive months, the courts of the Member State in which the defendant is domiciled shall also have jurisdiction, provided that the tenant is a natural person and that the landlord and the tenant are domiciled in the same Member State;

(2)   in proceedings which have as their object the validity of the constitution, the nullity or the dissolution of companies or other legal persons or associations of natural or legal persons, or the validity of the decisions of their organs, the courts of the Member State in which the company, legal person or association has its seat. In order to determine that seat, the court shall apply its rules of private international law;

(3)   in proceedings which have as their object the validity of entries in public registers, the courts of the Member State in which the register is kept;

(4)   in proceedings concerned with the registration or validity of patents, trade marks, designs, or other similar rights required to be deposited or registered, *irrespective of whether the issue is raised by way of an action or as a defence*, the courts of the Member State in which the deposit or registration has been applied for, has taken place or *is under the terms of an instrument of the Union or an international convention deemed to have taken place.*

         Without prejudice to the jurisdiction of the European Patent Office under the Convention on the Grant of European Patents, signed at Munich on 5 October 1973, the courts of each Member State shall have exclusive jurisdiction in proceedings concerned with the registration or validity of any European patent granted for that Member State;

(5)   in proceedings concerned with the enforcement of judgments, the courts of the Member State in which the judgment has been or is to be enforced."[200]

The CJEU has construed the predecessor provisions in the Brussels Regulation   **17-119** and Brussels Convention restrictively. Thus, in the case of *Sanders v Van der Putte*,[201] which was concerned with whether a dispute over a lease of a florist's business was within art.16(1) of the Brussels Convention (the predecessor to art.24(1) of the Recast Brussels Regulation), the CJEU held:

"the assignment, in the interests of the proper administration of justice, of exclusive jurisdiction to the courts of one Member State in accordance with Article 16 of the Convention results in depriving the parties of the choice which would otherwise be theirs and, in certain cases, results in their being brought before a court which is not that of the

---

[198]   art.31.
[199]   art.22(1)–(5).
[200]   The underlined parts are new wording introduced by the Recast Brussels Regulation.
[201]   (73/77) [1977] E.C.R. 2383; [1979] 1 C.M.L.R. 331.

domicile of any of them. Having regard to that consideration the provisions of Article 16 must not be given a wider interpretation than is required by their objective."[202]

17-120   This approach has been upheld in a number of cases.[203] It has been said that the rules of exclusive jurisdiction laid down in art.24 seek to ensure that jurisdiction rests with courts closely linked to the proceedings in fact and law.[204]

17-121   Article 24 cannot be considered in isolation. One must also take account of art.27. This provides as follows:

> "Where a court of a Member State is seised of a claim which is principally concerned with a matter over which the courts of another Member State have exclusive jurisdiction by virtue of Article 24, it shall declare of its own motion that it has no jurisdiction."

17-122   As will be seen, art.27 is relevant to proceedings for infringement of registered IPRs where a counterclaim or plea of invalidity of those rights is raised by the defendant.

17-123   Article 24(4) is clearly of most relevance to the IPR practitioner. The Jenard Report gives fruit and vegetable rights as an example of "similar rights" in the predecessor provision in the Brussels Convention to art.24(4).[205] The rationale and scope of art.24(4) and art.27 in relation to patents has been considered principally in three cases of the CJEU: *Duijnstee v Goderbauer*,[206] *GAT v LUK*[207] and *Solvay v Honeywell*.[208] Article 24(4) RBR is not identical in wording to its predecessor provisions, in the Brussels Convention or Brussels Regulation, as it inter alia introduced the wording "... *irrespective of whether the issue is raised by way of an action or as a defence*." This change merely reinforced the earlier view that a court other than one with jurisdiction under art.24(4) does not have power to rule on the validity of a patent even when raised as a defence to infringement proceedings. This was never in doubt.[209]

Autonomous interpretation and rationale for art.24(4)

17-124   Article 24(4) must be regarded as an independent concept, intended to have uniform application in all the Member States.[210] The rationale for art.24(4) is that the courts of a Member State of registration are best placed to adjudicate upon cases in which the dispute itself concerns the validity of the patent or the existence of the

---

[202] See also *Klein v Rhodos Management Ltd* (C-73/04) [2005] E.C.R. I-8667. However, in *Erich Rösler v Horst Rottwinkel* (C-241/83) [1985] E.C.R. 99; [1985] 1 C.M.L.R. 806, the CJEU gave a contrasting, wide interpretation of art.16/art.22(1) on the facts but without making any general statement.

[203] *Reichert and Kockler* (C-115/88) [1990] E.C.R. I-27 at [9]; (C-292/93) [1994] E.C.R. I-2535 at [12]; *Dansommer v Götz* (C-8/98) [2000] E.C.R. I-0303 at [21].

[204] *Gesellschaft für Antriebstechnik mbH v Lamellen und Kupplungsbau Beteiligungs KG (GAT v LUK)* (C-4/03) [2006] E.C.R. I-6509 at [21].

[205] See para.66 of the Jenard Report.

[206] (C-288/82) [1983] E.C.R. 3663; [1985] 1 C.M.L.R. 220.

[207] (C-4/03) [2006] E.C.R. I-6509 at [21].

[208] (C-616/10) ECLI:EU:C:2012:445.

[209] *GAT v LUK*, at [25].

[210] (288/82) [1983] E.C.R. 3663; [1985] 1 C.M.L.R. 220 at [19]. Thus, the suggestion by Schlosser that the various concepts should be decided by reference to the *lex situs* would not seem applicable: see P. Schlosser, *"Report on the Convention of October 9, 1978 on the Accession of the Kingdom of United Kingdom, Ireland and Denmark to the Brussels Convention"* [1979] OJ C59/71, para.168.

deposit or registration.[211] Put another way, the rules of art.24 seek to ensure that jurisdiction rests with courts closely linked to the proceedings in fact and law.[212]

The justification that the courts of a Member State are best placed to adjudicate **17-125** upon cases where registration or validity of its patents are in issue seems a poor one. As has been pointed out, it effectively amounts to saying that justice would be best served if the courts of that nation applied national law as to validity.[213] This truism would apply as much to infringement actions as to questions of validity. Yet, as stated above, infringement actions are subject to the primary rule of the defendant's domicile and clearly do not fall within art.24(4). Thus, courts will often have to apply a foreign law of infringement.

It is probable that the awarding of exclusive jurisdiction to the country of registra- **17-126** tion under art.24(4) was done as a matter of public policy, i.e. so that rights awarded by a system of registration in a state could only be revoked by that state. Thus, the Jenard Report states that the reason that exclusive jurisdiction is provided is because the grant of a national patent is an exercise of national sovereignty.[214] This was acknowledged in *GAT v LUK* which said that exclusive jurisdiction is justified by the fact that the issue of patents involves national administrative authorities.[215] Thus, for the courts of one Member State to order the revocation of a registered right in another Member State can fairly be considered an impeachment of the sovereignty of the latter state. This reasoning would suggest that it is only an order for revocation rather than a mere determination of the validity of the patent inter partes, which would be contrary to the public policy behind the award of exclusive jurisdiction under art.24(4). However, as discussed below even a finding inter partes by a court on the validity of a patent in the context of a declaration of non-infringement of a patent can only be made by the court of the state of registration.[216]

Wide or narrow interpretation of art.24(4)?

The validity of a registered right may be raised or relevant in a number of ways. **17-127** It will be at the heart of an action for revocation of a patent. It will often be raised by way of a defence to an action for patent infringement.[217] In both these examples, it is plainly at the heart of the litigation. An invalid patent cannot be infringed. Furthermore, if a patent is found invalid, then as a matter of public policy of removing invalid patents from registers of patents, an order for revocation should invariably follow.

---

[211] (288/82) [1983] E.C.R. 3663; [1985] 1 C.M.L.R. 220 at [22]; (C-4/03) [2006] E.C.R. I-6509 at [22].

[212] (C-4/03) [2006] E.C.R. I-6509 at [22].

[213] C. Wadlow, "Intellectual Property and the Judgments Convention" *European Law Review* (October 1985), 305 at 310.

[214] See p.36, cited in *Fort Dodge Ltd* [1998] F.S.R. 222 CA and (C-4/03) [2006] E.C.R. I-6509 at [23]. See also *Chugai Pharmaceutical Co Ltd v UCB Pharma* [2017] EWHC 1216 (Pat) at [70]–[74] where the Patents Court of England gives four strong arguments why direct challenges to the validity of patents should only be decided by the courts of the country of registration including citing from A. Briggs, *Civil Jurisdiction and Judgments* (6th edn, (Abingdon: Informa Law, 2015), para.4.09) that "the grant of a patent is closer to an act of sovereign power, than many."

[215] (C-4/03) [2006] E.C.R. I-6509 at [23] citing the Jenard Report, p.36.

[216] See para.17-130.

[217] The new wording in art.24(4) makes it clear that art.24(4) applies whether the issue of validity is raised by way of an action or as a defence. This was never really in dispute and in *GAT v LUK*, the Court of Justice made clear that the reach of art.24(4) did not depend on the stage when validity was raised in proceedings—at [25].

17-128   However, the validity of a patent may be raised in a more peripheral way. For instance, it may be raised by an undertaking who seeks a declaration of non-infringement of a patent on inter alia, on the grounds that the patent is invalid.[218] It may be raised in the context of competition proceedings, where a competition authority asserts that a dominant undertaking is guilty of an abuse as it has sought to enforce patents which are invalidly registered and it knows them to be invalidly registered.[219] It may be raised in the context of litigation of a patent licence where a licensee is obliged to pay royalties on any product covered by a "valid claim" and the latter is contested. Thus, in many of these cases, a party may not be seeking revocation of the registered right, but the validity of the registered right is an issue in the proceedings. We will now consider the "reach" of art.24(4) in these type of disputes.

17-129   The extent of the predecessor provision to art.24(4) was first contemplated in *Duijnstee v Goderbauer*. This case concerned a patent entitlement dispute between the inventor of a mounting for a rail and the liquidator of his employer company. The critical dispute as to the ownership of the patent was the nature of the legal relationship between Goderbauer and the insolvent company.[220] The Hoge Raad considered of its own motion whether it had jurisdiction to hear the action because of art.16(4) Brussels Convention (art.24(4) Recast Brussels Regulation) and made a reference to the CJEU as to whether art.16(4) was applicable to an entitlement dispute. The CJEU said that entitlement proceedings were not concerned with the validity or existence of a registered patent and thus did not fall within art.16(4). In doing so, it said that art.16(4) should be construed restrictively.[221] However, such a statement should be seen in its context. In *Duijnstee*, the issue was whether the proceedings were related to the validity of the patents. However, the issue was ownership and not validity. There was thus no concern about a court of one Member State ordering the revocation of a patent registered in another Member State. In case it is in doubt, it should be said that the mere fact that infringement proceedings of a registered right are brought are not sufficient to invoke art.24(4) merely because such must be predicated on the basis that the rights must be valid.[222]

17-130   However, the wording of art.24(4) is that the proceedings are "concerned with" and not they must have as their object, the registration or validity of registered IPRs. Thus, an overly restrictive view of art.24(4) would be wrong.[223] In *GAT v LUK*[224] and *Solvay v Honeywell*,[225] the issue was whether the predecessor provision to art.24(4) was triggered whenever an issue concerning the validity of a patent was raised. In *GAT v LUK*, LUK alleged that the offer by GAT to a third-party motor vehicle manufacturer to supply mechanical damper springs infringed LUK's two French patents. GAT sought a declaration in Germany that the springs did not infringe the French patent and further or in the alternative, that the French patents

---

[218] As was done in *GAT v LUK* C-4/03 ECLI:EU:C:2006:457.

[219] See para.12-314 as to when this may amount to a breach of art.102.

[220] The patent applications were not derived from a European patent application. If they had been, different jurisdictional rules would have applied—see para.2-345.

[221] See [23].

[222] e.g. see *Mölnlycke AB v Procter & Gamble* [1992] 1 W.L.R. 1112 (Pat); *Napp Laboratories v Pfizer Inc* [1993] F.S.R. 150.

[223] A point made by A. Briggs and P. Rees, *Civil Jurisdiction and Judgments*, 6th edn (London: Informa, 2015).

[224] (C-4/03) ECLI:EU:C:2006:457.

[225] (C-616/10) ECLI:EU:C:2012:445.

were either void or invalid. The Oberlandesgericht Dusseldorf referred to the CJEU the question whether art.16(4) Brussels Convention (the predecessor provision to art.24(4) RBR) was only applicable in proceedings to revoke the patent (with *erga omnes* effect) or whether it applied where the validity of the patent is raised inter partes in the context of proceedings for declaration of non-infringement. The CJEU held that by reason of the scheme of art.16(4) in the scheme of the Brussels Convention.

> "[25] ... the view must be taken that the exclusive jurisdiction provided for by that provision should apply *whatever the form of proceedings in which the issue of a patent's validity is raised*, be it by way of an action or a plea in objection, at the time the case is brought or at a later stage in the proceedings." [Emphasis supplied.]

In doing so, it rejected a submission that as the effects of a judgment indirectly ruling on the validity of a patent are limited to the parties to the proceedings, such was not an appropriate response to that risk. It acknowledged that the determination inter partes of the validity of the patent would limit the effects of the decision to the parties in the proceedings, but said that such a limitation would lead to "distortions" undermining the equality and uniformity of rights and obligations arising from the Convention.²²⁶ **17-131**

GAT v LUK was considered in *Solvay v Honeywell*.²²⁷ The facts have already been discussed in the context of art.8(1) RBR (jurisdiction based on co-defendants) but the salient aspects are repeated here for ease of reference.²²⁸ The proceedings were for infringement of parallel patents derived from the grant of a European patent. The action was brought by Solvay SA, a Belgium company, in the Netherlands against one Dutch and two Belgian companies in the Honeywell group. The Dutch and one of the Belgian companies were accused of acts of infringement throughout Europe and the other Belgian company was accused of acts of infringement in Northern and Central Europe. During the course of proceedings, an interim application was brought against the defendant companies seeking provisional cross-border relief pursuant to the predecessor provision to art.35 RBR pending a decision in the main proceedings.²²⁹ Under Dutch law, such relief did not require the Dutch court to determine whether infringement had occurred but merely to form a view as to the likely outcome. In the course of the interim proceedings, the Honeywell companies raised a defence of invalidity of the patents without having brought or even declared their intention to bring proceedings for the annulment of the patents, or without contesting the competence of the Dutch court to hear the main or interim proceedings.²³⁰ Under Dutch law, interim relief will not be granted to restrain infringement if there is a reasonable, non-negligible possibility that the invoked patent would be declared invalid by the competent court. The Dutch Court referred to the CJEU the question of whether it should decline jurisdiction in the interim proceedings as regards the interim applications relating to the non-Dutch patents. **17-132**

It was clear that the CJEU felt conflicted. It acknowledged that in *GAT v LUK*, **17-133**

---

²²⁶ See [30].
²²⁷ (C-616/10) ECLI:EU:C:2012:445.
²²⁸ See para.17-101.
²²⁹ art.31 confers jurisdiction on the courts of a Member State where provisional or protective measures are sought. Its equivalent in the Recast Brussels Regulation is art.35.
²³⁰ See [15].

the CJEU had interpreted the predecessor provision in the Brussels Convention to art.24(4) widely and that it applied regardless whether or not the issue of validity was raised during the proceedings or whether by way of action or a plea in objection. Thus, in *Solvay*, the CJEU considered that the predecessor provision to art.24(4) RBR was capable of applying even where jurisdiction was founded on the provisional measures provision in art.31 Brussels Regulation[231] However, clearly it was uncomfortable with the notion that in interim injunctive proceedings for cross border relief in any Member State other than the state of registration of the patent, a defendant could derail such proceedings just by raising the issue of validity of the parallel patents. Accordingly, the CJEU held that, as the Dutch court in the interim proceedings would not make a final decision on the validity of the patent but merely determine whether there was a reasonable non-negligible possibility that the parallel patents invoked would be declared invalid, the provision did not preclude the Dutch court from applying art.31 Brussels Regulation (provisional measures). In reaching its conclusion, it held that the reasons why in *GAT v LUK*, the court interpreted the predecessor provision to art.24(4) widely did not apply to the instant case because there was no risk of conflicting decisions. Furthermore, it would not prejudice the decision taken by the court having jurisdiction over the validity of the patent.[232]

17-134   Are *Solvay v Honeywell* and *GAT v LUK* compatible? In both cases, the courts had to consider the issue of validity of foreign patents as a necessary part of the decision making process. If subsequent proceedings had been brought in the courts of the Member State of registration of the foreign patents on the same issue of validity, it is clear that those courts could have reached opposite and accordingly conflicting decisions on the issue of validity to those in the German and Dutch courts. The distinction drawn by the CJEU in *Solvay* appears to be that in *Solvay*, whilst the Dutch court were bound to consider the issue, such would not prejudice the substantive decision by the various courts of the Member States of the parallel patents which were sued upon.[233] However, the same could have been equally said about the German courts in *GAT v LUK* making a finding inter partes on the validity of the patent. Such would not have prejudiced a subsequent decision on the substance of validity in the French courts. The French courts would have been free to agree or disagree with the German courts' view as to validity.

17-135   It could be said that the real distinction is that in *Solvay v Honeywell*, the Dutch court did not have to determine finally whether the patents were valid, whereas in *GAT v LUK* the German courts were being asked to adjudicate specifically on the issue of validity. In *Solvay v Honeywell*, the Dutch court merely had to consider whether there was a reasonable non-negligible possibility that the patents were invalid. If they were, it would not grant the protective measures. This is an attractive argument. Yet if the Dutch courts had held that there was a negligible possibility that the patents would be found invalid and thus granted interim injunctive relief on foreign patents, it has in truth ruled on the issue of validity. Such a decision would be plainly irreconcilable with a later judgment in the court of the Member State of registration of those patents if that court found the patents to be invalid.

17-136   Ultimately, the decision of the Court of Justice in *Solvay v Honeywell* must be

---

[231] See [47]. Now art.35 RBR—see para.17-168.
[232] See [48]–[51].
[233] See [50].

considered one of *realpolitik*. As said by the Advocate-General in *Solvay*, the answer to the referred question should take account of "procedural reality".[234]

In both *GAT v LUK* and *Solvay*, the core issue in the proceedings was whether **17-137** goods infringed a patent. As one cannot infringe an invalid patent, validity is clearly at the heart of infringement proceedings. However, what is the position where a party makes it clear that it is not challenging directly the validity of a patent. For instance, what would have been the position in *GAT v LUK*, if the claimant had sought a declaration of non-infringement of a patent and, in order to keep the proceedings within a court other than the court of the Member State of registration, undertook that it was not challenging the validity of the patent even inter partes. In such circumstances, one would have thought that art.24(4) is not engaged. However, even in infringement proceedings, a court may consider that it needs to consider indirectly the validity of the patent. Therefore, in English proceedings, in *Actavis UK Ltd v Eli Lilly & Co*[235] the claimant sought a declaration of non-infringement in respect of UK, French, Spanish and Italian designations of a European Patent but undertook not to challenge the validity of the patent. The court held that in deciding what was the correct construction of the claim, it was entitled to consider what the consequences of construction would be for the validity of the patent. In *Chugai Pharmaceutical Co Ltd v UCB Pharma*,[236] the Patents Court supported the approach in *Actavis UK Ltd*. It held, obiter dicta,[237] that in infringement-only proceedings, when considering the extent of protection of a European Patent; the Protocol to art.69 of the European Patent Convention may require the court to address the consequences of rival constructions for the validity of a patent, as a construction which could lead to invalidity and may be unfair to the patentee.[238]

What about where the validity of a patent is raised in a dispute over the level of **17-138** royalties owing under a patent licence? Often, the obligation will be that the licensee is only obliged to pay royalties where the product falls within a valid claim.[239] Thus, an issue in the proceedings will be whether the claim is a valid one. The Court of Justice has not ruled specifically on this although its judgment in *GAT v LUK* would suggest that no court other than that of the Member State of registration could adjudicate on the issue of validity. In a number of English cases, where the English courts have been seized of jurisdiction under a jurisdiction clause bestowing jurisdiction on the English courts in the patent licence, and an issue was whether a US patent was valid, they have held that public policy principles which are concerned with respect for the sovereignty of other states did not prevent them from deciding the issue of validity of foreign patents in the context of a patent licence dispute.[240]

---

[234] See [37]. In this regard, he appears to have been swayed by the fact that the raising of the validity of the patents was a delaying tactic (see [42]).

[235] [2014] EWHC 1511 (Pat).

[236] [2017] EWHC 1216 (Pat).

[237] The case concerned a patent licence dispute.

[238] See [32].

[239] This is often inserted because of concerns that an obligation to pay royalty on an invalid claim is anti-competitive as it amounts to an unjustified tie-in. See para.8-283.

[240] e.g. see *Celltech (Adair's) Patent US Patent* [2004] F.S.R. 35 (which concerned a US patent licence); *Celltech v MedImmune* [2004] EWCA Civ 1331 (licence agreement referred to "valid claim"— written jurisdiction clause conferring jurisdiction on English court). See also *Chugai Pharmaceutical Co Ltd v UCB Pharma* [2017] EWHC 1216 (Pat) (patent licence dispute, written jurisdiction clause conferring jurisdiction on English court). In all these cases, the English courts held that they

The right test?

17-139   As discussed above, the Court of Justice has said that the policy behind art.24(4) is that the courts of the Member State of registration are most able to determine issues of validity. This is highly debateable and indeed the Recast Brussels Regulation plainly anticipates that the court of one Member State will often need to apply the law of another Member State. Indeed, in infringement-only proceedings where pan-European relief on a European patent is brought in the courts of the Member State of domicile of the defendant, a court will have to consider infringement potentially under the laws of all Member States. The policy in favour of allowing efficient and cheap litigation should, in most circumstances, trump the above weak argument. Indeed, the better justification for art.24(4) is that an attack on the validity of a patent granted by an intellectual property office of another Member State may in certain circumstances, amount to an attack on the competence of a state to grant a patent and thus an attack on the sovereignty of that state.[241] This must be the case where the court of one Member State orders that a patent granted in another Member State be revoked. However, in many cases, e.g. patent licence disputes, the court is merely required to determine the issue of validity of a patent at an inter partes level and only for determining the level of royalties to be paid. It is a very weak argument to find that, in substance, this is an attack on the sovereignty of another state. Indeed, it is of note that a unitary right granted by EUIPO may be revoked by way of a counterclaim by the court of any Member State.

17-140   Here, it is suggested that the right approach is for a court to consider, by way of analogy with art.27 Recast Brussels Regulation, whether the proceedings as a whole are *principally* concerned with the issue of validity. It is plain that art.27 envisages that there are *some circumstances* where a court of a Member State seized of a claim can adjudicate on a dispute that the court of another Member State has exclusive jurisdiction under art.24.[242] The concept of "principally concerned" should be interpreted fluidly, taking into account all the circumstances and the public policy behind art.24(4) including: (i) how central the issue of validity is to the relief to be granted in the proceedings; (ii) whether the court is being asked to determine the issue of validity inter partes or is being asked to grant relief which will affect third parties (e.g. an order to revoke the patent); (iii) whether there are strong policy factors favouring the court seized, e.g. the will of all parties that the court seized try the issue of validity, e.g. through a written jurisdiction agreement conferring jurisdiction on that court in a patent licence; and (iv) whether the court is being asked to decide the issue of validity at a final stage or merely take it into account as a factor as to whether or not to grant relief at an interim stage (e.g. provisional or protective measures).

EU unitary rights

17-141   Article 24(4) Recast Brussels Regulation includes the wording "the court of the Member State in which the deposit or registration ... is under the terms of an instru-

---

had jurisdiction to determine the issue of validity. Although care must be exercised here because these cases were not concerned with the interpretation of art.24(4) (as the patents were not registered in Member States), these decisions were made on the basis that a decision as to the validity of patent was not an attack on the sovereignty of another country. This public policy ground underpins art.24(4) as well—see para.17-124.

[241] As said by Jenard, see para.17-126.

[242] Although as discussed at para.17-161, some language versions of art.27 do not include the word "principally".

ment of the Union or an international convention deemed to have taken place". "Instruments of the Union", i.e. EU legislation would include unitary EU registered rights such as the EU Trade Mark, Community Design and Community Plant Variety Right. However, none of the regulations creating these unitary rights deem a Member State to be the state of deposit or registration. This is not an issue because all have their own sui generis provisions regarding jurisdiction, which oust the jurisdiction rules of the Recast Brussels Regulation (including that of art.24(4)) by being a *lex specialis*. These are discussed later in this chapter.[243]

European and Unitary Patents

Article 24(4) refers to the courts of each Member State as having exclusive **17-142** jurisdiction regardless of domicile in proceedings concerned with the registration or validity of any European patent granted for *that* state. This provision reflects the fact that once a European patent is granted by the EPO, it leads to a "basket" of national patents in each contracting state of the EPC designated by the holder of the European Patent. This is stated to be without prejudice to the jurisdiction of the European Patent Office under the EPC. Therefore, the EPO has jurisdiction to determine the validity of granted European patents under the post-grant opposition procedure.[244]

In relation to Unitary Patents, when the Agreement on a Unified Patent Court **17-143** ("UPC") comes into force, the UPC has exclusive jurisdiction over validity proceedings relating to unitary patents (and associated Supplementary Protection Certificates ("SPCs"). It also has shared jurisdiction with national courts over the validity of classical European patents where the holder has not "opted out".[245]

Unregistered intellectual property rights

Article 24(4) does not cover unregistrable rights like copyright, unregistered **17-144** design rights or common law rights. Article 24(1) provides that *"in proceedings which have as their object rights in rem in, or tenancies of, immoveable property, the courts of the Member State in which the property is situated"* have exclusive jurisdiction. As said earlier, art.24(1) is construed restrictively. Thus, it was not sufficient merely that an action merely concerned a right in rem in immoveable property. Rather, the action had to have as its object a right in rem and not a right in personam.[246]

Is unregistered intellectual property "immoveable property" within the mean- **17-145** ing of art.24(1)? Neither the Jenard Report nor the Schlosser Report mentions anything about the relationship between the predecessor provision in the Brussels Convention to art.24(1) and intellectual property rights. Nor is there any definition of "immoveable property" in the Brussels Convention or its successors. Under English law, IPRs are considered analogous to immoveables.[247] First, the monopoly has no effect beyond the territory of the state under whose laws it is granted.

---

[243] See para.17-214.
[244] See para.2-452.
[245] The Agreement on the UPC is discussed at para.2-534. The interrelationship between the RBR and the Agreement on the UPC is discussed below at para.17-223.
[246] *Webb v Webb* (C-294/92) [1994] E.C.R. I-1717.
[247] See *Tyburn Productions Ltd v Conan Doyle* [1990] 1 All E.R. 909 (Ch D.) applying *Potter v Broken Hill Pty Co Ltd* [1906] 3 C.L.R. 479, High Court of Australia. See R. Arnold, "Can One Sue in England for Infringement of Foreign Intellectual Property Rights" [1990] 7 E.I.P.R. 255. However,

Secondly, the title to intellectual property rights devolves according to the laws imposed by the state in which it was created.[248] However, critically, the English courts have held that, although a patent is analogous to an immoveable, it is not an immoveable.[249] A fortiori, this must apply to unregistered rights. In the authors' view, copyright and other unregistered rights do not fall within art.24(1). Immoveable property has the characteristic that its location is easily identified. This is not the case with intellectual property. Furthermore, it is difficult to see how one can have a tenancy in intellectual property. This suggests that immoveable property in art.24(1) is concerned with real, and not intangible, i.e. intellectual, property.

IPR is registered in a non-Member State

17-146   Most countries are very reluctant to assume jurisdiction on a dispute which directly determines the validity of a right which has been granted pursuant to legislation in another country.[250] However, the domestic laws of some Member States are less concerned about adjudicating on validity of a foreign intellectual property right in an action for infringement.[251] This is because the decision of a patent examiner to grant a patent is not seen as an "act of state" which is seen as being confined to foreign legislation and governmental acts of officials such as requisition.[252]

17-147   With regards to the Recast Brussels Regulation, art.24(4) is inapplicable because it only confers exclusive jurisdiction on the court of the state of registration where the right is registered in a Member State. As art.24 is interpreted restrictively, it would appear that there is no derogation from the primary rule of domicile. Thus, a literal application of the Recast Brussels Regulation would mean that an applicant could bring a revocation action in the Member State where a patent owner is domiciled even if that patent was registered in a non-Member State.

17-148   However, this would be contrary to the basic principle that the courts of state of

---

it should be noted that in *Lucasfilm v Ainsworth* [2010] Ch. 503, the Supreme Court of England and Wales held that under domestic jurisdictional rules, proceedings could be brought for infringement of foreign intellectual property rights and so care must be applied in considering the above.

[248] See observations of the High Court of Australia in *Potter v Broken Hill Proprietary Company Ltd* [1906] 3 C.L.R. 479 at 494, per Griffith CJ.

[249] *Coin Controls v Suzo* [1997] F.S.R. 60 (HC). In *Gareth Pearce* [1997] F.S.R. 641, Lloyd J did not decide the issue because it was not argued that an action for infringement of copyright fell within art.22(1). The judge said that an action for copyright infringement is not concerned with rights in rem to the copyright; cf. E. Jooris, "Infringement of Foreign Copyright and the Jurisdiction of English Courts" [1996] 3 E.I.P.R. 127, 139 where the author concludes that copyright is an immoveable.

[250] *British South Africa v Companhia do Moçambique* [1893] A.C. 602; *Potter* [1906] C.L.R. 479; *Coin Controls* [1997] F.S.R. 641.]). However, it might be said that the sensitivities identified in *Lucasfilm v Ainsworth* concerning a ruling on the validity of a right granted by another sovereign country are not applicable where a finding of validity is made inter partes and not erga omnes.

[251] *Lucasfilms v Ainsworth* [2012] 1 A.C. 208 (Supreme Court of England and Wales) at [86] per Lords Walker and Collins; *Belhaj v Straw* [2017] UKSC 3 at [73], [161]; see also *Chugai Pharmaceutical Co Ltd v UCB Pharma* [2017] EWHC 1216 (Pat) at [61]-[69] (validity in issue in patent licence dispute).

[252] *Belhaj v Straw*, at [161. As said by Carr J in *Chugai*, at [68], the decision of a patent examiner to grant a patent is not an act of state. Any party may challenge the validity of a patent in court proceedings, and therefore this is very different from an attempt to challenge legislation or government acts such as requisition. This is true but may be somewhat false reasoning as it could be said that the only reason, e.g. a US patent can be revoked in US courts is due to the very same patent legislation that permits the grant of a patent in the US. Such legislation obviously does not extend to the courts outside the US.

registration should have exclusive jurisdiction in proceedings concerned with the validity of registered IPRs. Thus, the public policy ground for conferring exclusive jurisdiction under art.24(4) on the court where the intellectual property is registered, is that these courts are best placed to adjudicate on the validity of a registered right.[253] This reasoning applies equally to non-Member States. Equally, the other policy ground—that the grant of a registered right is an exercise in national sovereignty—applies where the intellectual property is registered in a non-Member State. It is clear that an action for revocation of a foreign right is an impeachment of the national sovereignty of that country. If such an argument is recognised in the Recast Brussels Regulation as the principle underlying art.24(4), it is no less applicable where the right is registered in a non-Member State. In such circumstances, commentators under the Brussels Convention have tended to take the view that the court of a Member State seized with deciding the validity of a right registered in a non-Member State should resort to its national jurisdictional rules.[254] This is an application of the "reflexive" effect which is discussed below.

Ultimately, it must be concluded that the Brussels Convention and the Brussels **17-149** Regulation (original and Recast) failed to foresee this problem, which is a serious omission. In fact, this is unfair on the draughtsmen of both. It is plain that it was never envisaged that the Brussels Convention, the Brussels Regulation or the Recast Brussels Regulation would apply to jurisdictional disputes between a Member State and a non-Member State. Yet, by reason of *Owusu v Jackson*,[255] such an argument no longer succeeds.

Recast Brussels Regulation and the "reflexive" effect

In *Owusu*, which was concerned with the Brussels Convention, it was argued that **17-150** as the rationale for art.24 was that of a very strong connecting factor between the subject-matter falling within this provision and the Member State referred to in the provision, a "reflex" effect would be that if the connecting factor was with a non-Member State, then the Brussels Convention had no applicability. Léger AG referred to this but said that it was unnecessary to decide this.[256]

The doctrine of "reflexive effect" means that if in a particular situation, a **17-151** jurisdictional treaty confers jurisdiction on a particular country by reason of a strong connecting factor or public policy with that country (e.g. it is the country of registration of a patent), then if that strong same connecting factor or public policy is with a third country (i.e. a country not a member of the treaty), then jurisdiction should be conferred on that third country.[257] This principle does not positively confer jurisdiction on the third country, but rather suspends the effect of the jurisdictional

---

[253] See para.17-124.
[254] See P. Kaye, *Civil Jurisdiction and Enforcement of Foreign Judgments* (Abingdon: Professional Books, 1987), p.880; S. O'Malley and A. Layton, *European Civil Practice*, 1st edn (London: Sweet & Maxwell, 1989), p.521, para.20.06.
[255] Discussed at para.17-228.
[256] See [70], [139].
[257] The doctrine of "reflexive" effects owes its origins to a paper by the well-known late jurist Georges A.L. Droz in a paper entitled *"Compétence judiciaire et effets des jugements dans le Marché commun. Etude de la Convention de Bruxelles du 27 Septembre 1968"*, Paris, 1972, p.109: "We believe therefore that if the linking factors appearing in Article 16 are located outside the Community, the contracting courts, which would be competent pursuant to an ordinary ground of jurisdiction, could nonetheless declare themselves without jurisdiction if their common law authorises this". See also *Directorate-General for Internal Policies, "Possibility and terms for applying Brussels I Regulation (recast) to extra-European disputes"* Study for the JURI Committee (2014).

treaty and leaves the issue to the domestic law of the court seized with the jurisdictional dispute. As said by one commentator, the failure of the Recast Brussels Regulation "so obviously to address the full range of issues surrounding cases involving connections with third states, the doctrine of 'reflexive effect' continues to offer an intellectually attractive solution to the problems generated by the largely inward-looking nature of the provisions of Chapter II".[258] As is perhaps unsurprising given the lack of any express reference to the application of the "reflexive" doctrine in the Recast Brussels Regulation, there are considerable arguments for and against it.[259]

17-152   The application of the reflexive doctrine would mean that the Recast Brussels Regulation would defer determination of jurisdiction to the domestic jurisdictional principles of Member States.[260] The Commercial Court of England had to consider this very issue in an English case, albeit in the context of a written jurisdiction agreement conferring jurisdiction on a third country. In *Ferrexpo AG v Gilson Investments Ltd*,[261] it was argued that the Ukraine had exclusive jurisdiction over the subject matter of the litigation by application of a reflexive effect of art.24. After detailed consideration of relevant textbooks and authorities (at both a national and CJEU level), the judge held that the Brussels Regulation did not require the court to assume jurisdiction over litigation when the subject matter fell within art.24 but the court with exclusive jurisdiction was that of a third state.[262] As the judge said, the expression "reflexive application" does not have a precise meaning but as the judge saw it, a reflexive application of the Brussels Regulation did not mean that the Brussels Regulation conferred on the court the power to decline jurisdiction but rather permitted the court of a Member State to exercise its powers under the national law (even though the defendant was domiciled in a Member State).[263] There is no doubt that the judge's approach accords with common sense. It also gains support from the CJEU decision in *Coreck Maritime GmbH v Handelsveem BV*[264] where the CJEU said in relation to art.17 of the Brussels Convention (written jurisdiction agreement) that where a jurisdiction agreement designates a court of a third country such that art.17 does not apply, then a court of the Brussels Convention must assess the validity of the clause according to the applicable law (including its conflict of law rules).[265] The judge held that he could not accept the argument that in *Owusu v Jackson*, the CJEU intended to overturn its decision in *Coreck Maritime*.[266] Subsequent decisions of English courts have also approved the "reflex" doctrine.[267] Although *Coreck Maritime* concerned art.17 of the Brussels Convention, its reasoning is equally applicable to art.24 of the Recast Brussels Regulation.

---

[258] J. Hill and M.N. Shuilleabhain, *Clarkson & Hill's Conflict of Laws*, 5th edn (Oxford: Oxford University Press, 2016), para.2.280.

[259] e.g. see P. Torremans, et al. (eds), *Cheshire, North & Fawcett: Private International Law*, 15th edn. (Oxford: Oxford Univeristy Press, 2017), pp.473-475 where the authors set out the competing arguments. They argue that a discretionary reflexive approach would be the most satisfactory outcome in policy terms but say that it remains to be seen whether the Court of Justice would be open to reviewing certain aspects of its decision in *Owusu* to endorse this approach (see p.475).

[260] See J.J. Fawcett and P. Torremans, *Intellectual Property and Private International Law*, 2nd edn (Oxford: Oxford University Press, 2011).

[261] [2012] EWHC 721 (Comm).

[262] See [140]–[142].

[263] See [127].

[264] (C-387/98) [2000] E.C.R. I-9337.

[265] See [19].

[266] See [131].

[267] e.g. *Plaza BV v Law Debenture Trust Corp Plv* [2015] EWHC 43 (Ch.) citing, in particular *Masri v*

Both articles are concerned with the conferring of exclusive jurisdiction on the courts of a Member State in derogation to the main jurisdictional rules of the RBR.

Infringement proceedings where validity is raised by way of defence

In an earlier section, the exact scope of art.24(4) and its predecessor provision **17-153** in art.16(4) of the Brussels Regulation, was considered and whether it applied to every proceedings where the issue of validity of a patent was raised. As discussed above, the CJEU took a broad view of art.24(4) in *GAT v LUK* and thus even if the validity of a patent is raised inter partes in declarations for non-infringement proceedings, art.24(4) applied. However, in *Solvay v Honeywell*, the CJEU held that it did not apply in the context of interim injunctive proceedings where the issue of validity was only considered for the purpose as to whether or not to grant interim injunctive relief. The position would appear to be that save in relation to interim protective measures, a court cannot rule on the issue of validity of a patent or other right registered in another Member State regardless of the context in which the issue of validity is raised.

However, in infringement proceedings where validity is raised by way of **17-154** defence, what must happen to the *infringement* proceedings? Thus, in a patent infringement action, the alleged infringer will often plead by way of defence that the patent is invalid and counterclaim for revocation of the patent. In such a case, the patent holder will usually have two jurisdictional options—one based on the domicile of the defendant (art.4) and the other based on the location of the harmful event (art.7(2)). The latter will almost always be in the same Member State as that in which the right is registered, but the former may often be in a different Member State. Therefore, where an infringement action is brought in a state other than the one in which one or more of the patents sued upon are registered, is the court of that state prevented by art.24(4) from hearing an action for infringement where validity is put in issue? This requires careful consideration of art.27 which says as follows:

> "Where a court of a Member State is seized of a claim which is principally concerned with a matter over which the courts of another Member State have exclusive jurisdiction by virtue of Article 24, it shall declare of its own motion that it has no jurisdiction." [Emphasis supplied.]

Thus, in deciding whether another court has exclusive jurisdiction under **17-155** art.22(4), the seized court must determine whether the claim is *principally concerned* with proceedings relating to the registration or validity of intellectual property. If it forms the view that such a condition is satisfied, then art.27 suggests that it must decline jurisdiction (as opposed to staying the proceedings).

The Jenard Report states that the seized court is not obliged to declare, of its own **17-156** motion, that it has no jurisdiction if a matter within the jurisdiction of the court with exclusive jurisdiction is raised as a preliminary or incidental matter in the seized court.[268] This suggests that, although a restrictive interpretation of art.24 is to be taken, a broad interpretation of art.27 should be taken.[269] A further difficulty arises

---

Consolidated Contractors International Co SAL [2008] EWCA Civ 303.
[268] *The Jenard Report on the 1968 Convention and the 1971 Protocol* [1979] OJ C59/1, p.39.
[269] e.g. *Coin Controls* [1997] F.S.R. 660 (Pat).

that there is a lack of clarity as to the meaning of art.27, in particular when all language versions are considered.[270]

17-157　At a fundamental level, where the validity of a registered right is raised by way of defence to infringement proceedings, it is difficult to say that the issue of validity is anything other than central to the dispute. One cannot infringe an invalid right. Thus, in England, the Court of Appeal has said, in *Fort Dodge v Akzo Nobel*, that, where questions of infringement and validity both arise, it is often not possible to conclude that there is infringement without validity being determined. It thus gave the example known as the *Gillette* defence, where the alleged infringer's case is that the patent is invalid if the alleged infringing acts fall within the ambit of the claims. Where such a defence is raised, the construction of the patent claims is critical to both validity and infringement, and obviously such a construction must be the same. The Court of Appeal said that, where the defendant raises validity as an issue, art.27 requires the court to *decline* jurisdiction in favour of the court of the Member State or registration.[271] Thus, the Court of Appeal has said that in an action for trade mark infringement where it is alleged that the trade mark is invalid, the court must refuse jurisdiction if it is not the court of the state in which registry the trade mark has been registered.[272] The Dutch courts take a similar view that infringement and validity are indissociably linked to each other since it was impossible to infringe an invalid patent.[273] Such approaches seem sensible and correct and strongly suggest that art.27 is engaged where there are infringement proceedings of a registered IPR and the defendant raises the issue of validity of the registered IPR.

17-158　The CJEU has not ruled specifically on this point. In *GAT v LUK*, which has already been discussed, it did not rule on the issue whether by reason of the predecessor provision to art.27, the declaration of non-infringement proceedings could continue, be stayed or declined.[274] However, it has held in *Gubisch v Palumbo*[275] that an action for enforcement of a contract and a counterclaim for its rescission were concerned with the same cause of action.

17-159　It should be noted that art.27 uses the expression "claim". This has led to the argument that art.27 is not concerned with defences, but simply what is asserted in the claim at the outset of proceedings. Thus, if there is a claim for infringement, that *claim* is not concerned with invalidity at all. Such would mean that if invalidity was raised by way of a defence or counterclaim, the court could not adjudicate on the

---

[270]　As observed by the CJEU in *GAT v LUK* (C-4/03) [2006] E.C.R. I-6509 at [19]. Thus, the German version reads: "*Das Gericht eines Mitgliedstaats hat sich von Amts wegen für unzuständig zu erklären, wenn es wegen einer Streitigkeit angerufen wird, für die das Gericht eines anderen Mitgliedstaats aufgrund des Artikels 24 ausschließlich zuständig ist*". This does not contain a literal equivalent to the word "principally". The French version which includes the phrase "*à titre principal*" can be translated as "primarily".

[271]　*Fort Dodge Ltd* [1998] F.S.R. 222 at 244, citing with approval *Coin Controls* [1997] F.S.R. 660 at 676 where the court said that the issues of validity and infringement are so closely interrelated that they should be treated for the purposes of jurisdiction as one issue or claim. See also *Knorr-Bremse Systems for Commercial Vehicles LDT v Haldex Brake Products GmbH* [2008] F.S.R. 30 (Pat) (England and Wales) where the validity of the patents was raised in proceedings seeking declarations for non-infringement and the court held that the UK court had exclusive jurisdiction over the issue of validity.

[272]　*Prudential Assurance Co. Ltd v Prudential Insurance Co* [2003] 1 W.L.R. 2295 CA at [21] endorsing *Coin Controls v Suzo* [1999] Ch 33.

[273]　*Expandable Grafts* [1999] F.S.R. 352.

[274]　The German court did not refer this question to the CJEU although the Advocate-General did appear to consider this "*de bene esse*"—see [46].

[275]　*Gubisch Maschinenfabrik v Palumbo* (C-144/86) [1987] E.C.R. 4861.

defence of invalidity but art.27 would not preclude it from determining the *claim* of infringement, instead possibly delaying the grant of relief if the claim was successful pending the determination of the invalidity proceedings. A number of arguments can be put forward in support of this. First, where the Recast Brussels Regulation means "issue" as opposed to "claim", it is quite capable of saying so.[276] Secondly, it has been said that jurisdiction should be determinable at the earliest opportunity and should not be dependent on the defences raised or to be raised by the defendant.[277] Thirdly, the Recast Brussels Regulation does indeed, in some circumstances, favour a race to the courts. Thus, arts. 29 and 30 require that the court second seized should decline jurisdiction in favour of the court first seized.[278] Fourthly, it is a fundamental principle of the Recast Brussels Regulation that the claimant must be able to identify the court before which he may bring an action and the defendant reasonably to foresee the court before which he may be sued.[279] A proper operation of the regulation is not possible if jurisdiction is based on the subsequent determination of what the case is about (i.e. the issues) than what is claimed. It requires the claimant to second guess what issues will be raised. Moreover, challenges to jurisdiction are normally required to be done *prior* to the service of a defence.[280] Finally, in *Préservatrice Foncière TIARD SA v Staat der Nederlanden*,[281] the CJEU said in the context of art.1 of the original Brussels Regulation that whether or not a claim fell within art.1 was unaffected by the defence.[282] A similar approach was taken by the court in *Gantner Electronic GmBH v Basch*[283] in relation to the predecessor provisions to arts. 29 and 30 of the Recast Brussels Regulation, when it was held that the proper application of that provision was by reference to the claim, and it was unaffected by the defence. It could be said that a similar approach should be taken to art.27.[284]

To add to the above comments, it should be noted that the Recast Brussels **17-160** Regulation has changed the wording of art.24.4. It now says that the courts of Member State of registration have exclusive jurisdiction in proceedings concerned with the registration or validity of patents, trade marks, designs or other similar rights irrespective of whether the issue is raised by way of an action or "as a defence". Thus, plainly art.24 envisages such a court having exclusive jurisdiction over any defence which raises validity to infringement proceedings based on a registered right. However, by itself, this change does not mean that the claim of *infringement* must *also* be tried by the court of the Member State of registration.

There are powerful arguments against the formalistic approach that art.27 is only **17-161**

---

[276] C. Wadlow, *Enforcement of Intellectual Property in European and International Law* (London: Sweet & Maxwell, 1998), p.183. Thus, the author gives the example of art.33, which states that: "Any interested party who raises the recognition of a judgment as the principal issue in a dispute may ... apply for a decision that the judgment be recognized".

[277] C. Wadlow, *Enforcement of Intellectual Property in European and International Law* (London: Sweet & Maxwell, 1998), p.184.

[278] C. Wadlow, *Enforcement of Intellectual Property in European and International Law* (London: Sweet & Maxwell, 1998), pp.185-186.

[279] *Effer v Kantner* (38/81) [1982] E.C.R. 825 at [6]; *Mulox IBC* (C-125/92) [1993] E.C.R. I-4075 at [11]; *Francesco Benincasa v Dentalkit Srl* (C-269/95) [1997] E.C.R. I-3767 at [28].

[280] e.g. in England, see CPR Pt.12.

[281] *Préservatrice Foncière TIARD SA v Staat der Nederlanden* (C-266/01) [2003] E.C.R. I-4867.

[282] art.1 determines what types of case are covered by the Convention.

[283] *Gantner Electronic GmBH v Basch* (C-111/01) [2003] E.C.R. I-4207.

[284] However, in A. Briggs and P. Rees, *Civil Jurisdiction and Judgments*, 6th edn (London: Informa Finance, 2015), para.2.70, the authors say that an analogy with this case law is unattractive where the proceedings have as their object and are founded on the validity of the right.

concerned with the "claim" as opposed to the "dispute". First, the literal meaning of art.27 is different in the various languages of the RBR. In French, "claim" is "*litige*" which translates as "dispute" or "lawsuit". In German, the word is "*streitigkeit*" which translates as "dispute" or "litigation". Secondly, as commented on in an English case, such would mean that jurisdiction was determined by who managed to commence proceedings first.[285] Thirdly, *GAT v LUK* suggests that it is irrelevant when the claim to validity is raised.[286] Fourthly, the Advocate-General in *GAT v LUK* considered that the argument that art.24(4) only applied if the "principal claim" of a proceedings concerned the validity of patents was unduly formalistic and would make it possible for the claimant to evade the binding choice of forum under art.24(4).[287]

17-162   In the authors' view, it is likely that the CJEU would not be persuaded by formalistic arguments over the meaning of "claim". It would consider the issues of validity and infringement to be ultimately, two sides of the same coin and as the Dutch courts have held, indissociable. That being the case, where validity is raised by way of defence or counterclaim to an action for infringement, the action for infringement cannot be "de-coupled" from the claim of invalidity and thus art.27 is engaged in relation to the claim for infringement. Indeed, in every case where infringement and validity of a patent is in dispute, there is a common issue—namely what is the *proper construction* of the patent claims? Does the infringing act fall within the claims of the patent? Does the prior art render any embodiment that falls within the claims of the patent obvious or not novel? Indeed, as said by the English court and discussed above, where a *Gillette* defence is run, the construction of the claims is critical to both issues. Here the argument is that if the patent claims are to be interpreted narrowly, then there is no infringement but if they are interpreted widely, then the patent is invalid. Yet it must be recognised that in Germany, invalidity proceedings are separate to infringement proceedings even when raised by way of a defence. There, they have no problems with two sets of proceedings in different courts.

17-163   Assuming that the author's view is right, then the question is what the court seized with the infringement proceedings should do? On the literal wording of art.27, there appears to be only one answer. It must decline jurisdiction. The English courts take the view that such must happen.[288] Thus, if infringement of a French patent is raised in infringement proceedings in England and the defendants raise the issue of validity of the French patent, the English court would have to decline jurisdiction over both the infringement and validity proceedings in favour of the French courts. It will be appreciated that such will mean that in multi-jurisdictional patent litigation, the claimant will need to bring parallel proceedings in each of the Member States where it alleges infringement. However, as the validity of each of the parallel patents in such litigation will need to be determined in each of the Member States of registration of those patents, forcing the claimant to bring the corresponding infringement proceedings in those Member States does not in fact increase the number of actions.

---

[285] *Coin Controls v Suzo* [1997] F.S.R. 660 (Pat). However, strictly speaking, this is not an argument against the submission. If invalidity proceedings were issued first and the issue was whether a counterclaim for infringement was principally concerned with the revocation claim, the court could equally find that the counterclaim for infringement was not so principally concerned with validity proceedings and thus simply decline jurisdiction on the claim but not the counterclaim.

[286] This is now true by reason of the amendment to art.24(4) of the Recast Brussels Regulation..

[287] See [38].

[288] *Fort Dodge*; *Coin Controls v Suzo*.

However, it has been suggested that the infringement proceedings could be stayed **17-164** pending the outcome of the validity proceedings. Thus, the Dutch courts have favoured this approach.[289] However, it is difficult to see how such is permitted by art.27. If it is determined that the proceedings (and it is a binary decision YES or NO) are principally concerned with validity, then it requires the court hearing the infringement proceedings to decline jurisdiction. If they are not principally concerned, then the wording of art.27 confers no discretion to decline or stay. It may be that the court could stay under the *lis pendens* provisions if it is the court second seized and forms the view that the infringement and validity proceedings are related proceedings within the meaning of art.30, but that is a separate issue and merits separate consideration.

However, in this regard, it is also right to mention the Advocate-General's **17-165** opinion in *GAT v LUK*. This opinion considered that there were three options: (1) art.24(4) only applied if the principal claim of proceedings concerned the validity of patents; (2) validity and infringement are in practice inseparable and therefore art.24(4) applied to infringement proceedings; and (3) the court indicated in art.24(4) is competent to determine the validity or nullity of a patent and other is-sues concerning patents (e.g. infringement) fall outside of art.24(4).[290] He concluded that the third proposition should be adopted and rejected the other two. In relation to the second option, he held that it must be discarded because art.24(4) is based on a distinction between disputes concerning patent infringements and those of validity and that the latter does not cover infringement proceedings. He then concluded that the court hearing the infringement action could transfer the case completely, stay the proceedings or deal with the case where the defendant acts in bad faith.[291] As attractive as this approach is, art.27 does not permit the staying of proceedings and the Advocate-General does not set out the basis on which the proceedings for infringement could be stayed. Equally, the CJEU has resisted argu-ments that the rules of the Brussels Regulation do not apply where a party issues proceedings in a court of a Member State for mala fide purposes (i.e. to prevent a court which plainly has jurisdiction from hearing a matter until the other court has declined jurisdiction).[292]

In the authors' submission, a proper application of arts 27 and 24(4) is that where **17-166** the validity of a registered right is raised by way of defence to infringement proceedings in the court of a Member State other than that of registration, then the court seized of the infringement proceedings should decline jurisdiction under art.27. The right holder must then re-issue proceedings for infringement in the Member State of registration. Such an approach has many advantages: (i) the same court will determine the issue of infringement and validity in one action; (ii) the court will apply its own law to both issues rather than the law of another Member State; (iii) it avoids potentially conflicting decisions, e.g. if the patent is found infringed but invalid; and (iv) the rule is predictable and certain in its application. Whilst it could be said that such denies the claimant the right to bring multiple proceedings for infringement of parallel registered rights in the court of the Member State of the defendant's domicile (i.e. a one-stop shop), this is essentially academic

---

[289] See *Expandable Grafts Partnership v Boston Scientific BV* [1999] F.S.R. 352 CA (The Hague).
[290] See [36].
[291] See [46].
[292] e.g. see *Turner v Grovit*. See para.17-026.

if, in any event, there must be multiple proceedings concerning validity of those parallel registered rights in the courts of each Member State of registration.

Counterclaim for revocation

17-167   Article 8(3) extends the jurisdiction of the court of the claim to that of the counterclaim where the counterclaim arises "from the same contract or facts on which the original claim was based". It might be thought that art.8(3) gives the court trying the infringement proceedings the right to assume jurisdiction over the counterclaim of invalidity. However, in *Salotti v RUWA*[293] and *Galeries Segoura v Rahim Bonakdarian*,[294] the CJEU held that art.25 (which gives exclusive jurisdiction to the courts of a Member State in cases where the parties have elected a choice of jurisdiction clause) should take precedence over art.8(3). By analogy, it is submitted that art.8(3) should not be allowed to derogate from art.24.[295] Thus, as pointed out by Wadlow, in *Lieber v Göbel*,[296] it was taken for granted that jurisdiction over a counterclaim alleged to fall within art.24(1) was to be decided in the same way as for an independent action. This is particularly so with the change in wording to art.24(4) of the Recast Brussels Regulation whereby it is now made clear that the courts of the Member State of registration have exclusive jurisdiction over any proceedings relating to registered rights regardless of whether they are raised by way of claim or *by way of defence*.

Provisional and protective measures

17-168   Interim measures feature highly in intellectual property disputes. It is common for IPR owners to seek interim injunctions to restrain alleged infringers from marketing or dealing in goods alleged to infringe the IPRs of the claimant. Where the infringements are deliberate, e.g. in the case of counterfeit (trade mark) or pirated (copyright) goods, it is common for IPR owner to take pre-emptive measures including orders obtained without notice to the defendants. These orders may include the seizure of goods from business or domestic premises; orders to preserve property; freezing orders over the assets of defendants and prohibitory injunctions restraining the defendants from dealing in infringing goods.[297] In other cases, the IPR owner may wish to obtain information as to the identities of persons involved in counterfeiting or piracy other than the defendants and/or preserve evidence which can be used against the defendants or third parties.

17-169   With the introduction of the Enforcement Directive, such orders can now be obtained in the courts of all Member States.[298] To help the fight against counterfeiting and piracy, it may be necessary to often seek protective measures in the courts of Member States other than a Member State seized with the proceedings for infringement. To this end, art.35 confers jurisdiction on these courts where provisional and protective measures are sought. It provides that:

"Application may be made to the courts of a Member State for such provisional, includ-

---

[293] (24/76) [1976] E.C.R. 1831; [1977] 1 C.M.L.R. 345.

[294] *Galeries Segoura v Rahim Bonakdarian* (25/76) [1976] E.C.R. 1851; [1971] 1 C.M.L.R. 361.

[295] See also P. Kaye, *Civil Jurisdiction and Enforcement of Foreign Judgments* (Abingdon: Professional Books, 1987), p.1022, fn.331.

[296] (C-292/93) [1994] E.C.R. I-2535.

[297] Breach of these orders may result in the levying of fines or indeed imprisonment.

[298] See Ch.15 as to discussion of the Enforcement Directive (2004/48).

ing protective, measures as may be available under the law of that Member State, even if the courts of another Member State have jurisdiction as to the substance of the matter."[299]

In this section, we look at the right of courts of Member States to grant interim measures in proceedings for infringement of intellectual property rights. **17-170**

Court seized with substantive dispute

Where a court is seized under the Recast Brussels Regulation with proceedings for infringement of IPRs, it also has jurisdiction to order any provisional or protective measures which may prove necessary.[300] Therefore, if a court has jurisdiction under art.4 (defendant's domicile), it has extraterritorial jurisdiction in relation to the substantive dispute and as a result must have a commensurate extraterritorial jurisdiction in relation to provisional or protective measures.[301] Even if the court is seized under art.7(2) which may, in certain circumstances, confine its jurisdiction to matters occurring in that state,[302] there seems no reason why protective measures such as a freezing order should not extend to assets outside the jurisdiction if such is necessary. As said by the Court of Justice in *Van Uden* with regards to the predecessor provision in the Brussels Convention: **17-171**

> "[19]   The first point to be made, as regards the jurisdiction of a court hearing an application for interim relief, is that it is accepted that a court having jurisdiction as to the substance of a case in accordance with articles 2 and 5 to 18 of the [Brussels] Convention also has jurisdiction to order any provisional or protective measures *which may prove necessary*". [Emphasis supplied.]

Moreover, Recital 33 of the Recast Brussels Regulation would appear to support this. It refers to provisional and protective measures which are ordered by a court not having jurisdiction as to the substance of the matter being confined under the Regulation to the territory of that Member State.[303] This implies that measures which are ordered by a court having jurisdiction as to the substance of the matter can have extraterritorial effect.[304] Thus, it would allow a Dutch court to grant, using the *kort geding* procedure, an interim injunction restraining infringement of a patent outside the Netherlands or an English court to grant a worldwide freezing injunction.[305] Such extraterritorial interim orders made by courts of Member States **17-172**

---

[299] NB. the wording of this is subtly different to art.31 Brussels Regulation which included the words "...even if, under this Regulation, the courts of another Member State...". The impact of this change is discussed at para.17-183.

[300] *Van Uden Maritime v Deco-Line* (C-391/95) [1998] E.C.R. I-7091; *Mietz* (C-99/96) [1999] E.C.R. I-2277 at [41]. In *Solvay v Honeywell* the Advocate-General said that this was "settled law"—see [45]. In UK, see *Masri v Consolidated Contractors International (UK) Ltd (No.2)* [2009] 2 W.L.R. 621 (the court hearing the substantive matter retained the power to make orders which were ancillary to the jurisdiction to its adjudication of the merits).

[301] By implication, Recital 33, last sentence.

[302] See para.17-044, et seq.

[303] Recital 33, last sentence.

[304] See also P. Torremans, et al. (eds), *Cheshire, North & Fawcett: Private International Law*, 15th edn (Oxford: Oxford University Press, 2017), p.303.

[305] See also P. Torremans, et al. (eds), *Cheshire, North & Fawcett: Private International Law*, 15th edn (Oxford: Oxford University Press, 2017).

seized with the substantive dispute are intended to be recognised by other Member States.[306]

17-173   However, as discussed earlier in this chapter, the Court of Justice has made it clear that where a court of a Member State has jurisdiction under art.7(2) RBR solely on the grounds that the Member State is the place where the damages occurred (as opposed to the place of the event giving rise to the damage), that jurisdiction of the court is limited to that Member State. It might be thought odd that the court should have the right to grant extraterritorial interim relief by way of provisional or protective measures but not substantive relief after trial which extends beyond the territory of the Member State of the court. Here, art.35 is irrelevant as it is merely a permissive clause, i.e. it makes clear that where the court of another Member State has jurisdiction as to the substance of the matter, the court of another Member State may grant provisional relief. In the authors' view, in the above example, the court cannot grant extraterritorial interim relief if it has no jurisdiction to grant the same by way of final relief.

Court not seized with substantive dispute

17-174   However, where the court of one Member State is seized with the substantive dispute, art.35 will confer jurisdiction on the court of other Member States to grant "provisional including protective measures".[307] Article 35 does not positively confer a power on the court of one Member State to grant such measures. Rather, it simply makes it clear that the mere fact that the court of another Member State has jurisdiction over the substance of the matter is not a bar per se to the grant of interim relief. As an exception to the primary rule of jurisdiction, it is to be interpreted restrictively.[308] In relation to predecessor provisions of art.35 in the Brussels Regulation and the Brussels Convention, the CJEU has said that provisional or protective measures are "by definition, ancillary measures".[309] It has stressed that courts must ensure that it is not used to circumvent the general rules of jurisdiction laid down in the Brussels Regulation. Therefore, courts must ensure that the measures are genuinely protective or provisional.[310] The CJEU has said that the jurisdiction in art.35 is intended to avoid causing loss to the parties as a result of the long delays inherent in any international proceedings.[311]

Nature of the measures

17-175   The CJEU has said that "provisional including protective measures" is to be understood as referring to measures which, in matters within the scope of the Brussels Convention:

---

[306]   See Recital 33 ("...their free circulation should be ensured under this Regulation..."). Special rules apply where the order is made without notice to the defendant.

[307]   See in relation to art.24 Brussels Convention, *St Paul Dairy v Unibel Exser* (C-104/03) [2005] E.C.R. I-3481 at [11].

[308]   (C-104/03) [2005] E.C.R. I-3481 at [11].

[309]   *de Cavel (No. 2)* (120/79) [1980] E.C.R. 731 at [7]. The English Court of Appeal has said that a post-judgment "freezing order" pending final enforcement of a judgment, falls within art.25 Brussels Convention: see *Bassatne* [1989] 2 W.L.R. 232 CA at 249, per Kerr LJ; cf. *Fort Dodge Ltd v Akzo Nobel NV* [1998] F.S.R. 222, where the same court said that art.25 Brussels Convention envisages measures which are "in aid of or as an adjunct to some final determination then in contemplation".

[310]   *Mietz v Intership Yachting BV* (C-99/96) [1999] E.C.R. I-2277 at [47]; (C-391/95) [1998] E.C.R. I-7091 at [46].

[311]   (C-104/03) [2005] E.C.R. I-3481 at [12].

"are intended to preserve a factual or legal situation so as to safeguard rights the recognition of which is otherwise sought from the court having jurisdiction as to the substance of the case."[312]

The Recitals to the Recast Brussels Regulation make it clear that such measures **17-176** would include protective orders aimed at obtaining information or preserving evidence under national legislation which implements arts.6 and 7 of the Enforcement Directive.[313] Prior to this, there had been some doubt whether the predecessor provisions to art.35 covered evidence-gathering orders.[314] It is also fairly clear that these would include interim injunctions, seizure of goods and orders which freeze bank accounts.[315] However, the same recital makes it clear that the notion of "provisional, including protective measures" does not extend to measures ordering the hearing of a witness.[316] It has also been held by an English court not to extend to a *Norwich Pharmacal* order against a third party in support of foreign proceedings.[317]

Article 35 is a jurisdictional measure and does not set out what the interim **17-177** measures are. Therefore, the measures "as may be available under the law of that Member State" are those provided for by the law of the state of the court to which application is made.[318] There is some dispute over whether the phrase such measures "as may be available under the law of that State" in art.35 means that, in deciding what provisional or protective relief is available under the national law of the court seized of the application under art.35, the court must only have regard to the

---

[312] *Reichert and Kockler v Dresdner Bank* (C-261/90) [1992] E.C.R. I-2410 at [34]; (C-391/95) [1998] E.C.R. I-7091 at [37]; (C-104/03) [2005] E.C.R. I-3481 at [13]. In Reichert, at [31], the court held that an action paulienne, whereby a creditor seeks to set aside a transfer of assets by the debtor to a third party on the basis that the transfer was done to defraud them, did not seek to preserve a factual or legal situation so as to safeguard rights. The recognition of this is sought from the court having jurisdiction, but indeed sought to vary the legal situation of an asset and thus was not a provisional or protective measure (for UK practitioners, this is equivalent to the relief available under ss.339, 340 and 423 of the Insolvency Act 1986).

[313] Recital 25. For the Enforcement Directive, see Ch.15. The right to obtain information is, in fact, art.8 of the Enforcement Directive with arts.6 and 7 concerned both with preserving evidence. It is therefore considered that art.35 would also extend to art.8. The obtaining of information relating to the manufacture and supply of infringing items is vital for IPR owners as it allows them to pursue and prevent other parties dealing in infringing goods. This is particularly in the case of pirated and counterfeit goods.

[314] See G.Tritton, *Intellectual Property in Europe*, 4th edn (London: Sweet & Maxwell, 2014), para.16-064. See also *Anan Kasei Co v Molycorp Chemicals* [2016] EWHC 1722 (Pat) whereby the court refused to grant an order for production of evidence in English proceedings for the purpose of supporting the patent owner's case in Germany. As such an order is envisaged by art.6 Enforcement Directive, it is considered that this type of order is now available under the Recast Brussels Regulation provided it is territorially limited to documents located in the Member State of the court seized with jurisdiction under art.35.

[315] These measures are available under art.9 Enforcement Directive (which is entitled "Provisional and precautionary measures").

[316] This reinforces the judgment of the Court of Justice in *St Paul Dairy v Unibel* (C-104/03) [2005] E.C.R. I-3481 under the Brussels Convention where it held that such an order did not fall within art.25 of the Brussels Convention. As said by Recital 25, reinforcing Professor Schlosser's report of the Brussels Convention that such orders fell within the Hague Convention, this exclusion is without prejudice to the application of Reg.1206/2001 (which implements the Hague Convention into EU law) on co-operation between courts of Member States in the taking of evidence in civil or commercial matters. See G.Tritton, *Intellectual Property in Europe*, 4th edn (London: Sweet & Maxwell, 2014), para.16-064.

[317] *AB Bank Ltd v Abu Dhabi Commercial Bank PJSC* [2016] EWHC 2082 (Comm), [2017] 1 W.L.R. 810.

[318] *Van Uden Maritime v Deco-Line* (C-391/95) [1998] E.C.R. I-7091 at [20].

domestic internal law of the concerned state and not its private international law. It is thought that it must mean the former. However, even those domestic rules themselves may allow a court of a Member State to refuse to grant the interim measures if it considers that the court of another Member State should be asked to grant them. Thus, under English law, a court may refuse to grant interim relief if it is exercising an ancillary jurisdiction in support of substantive proceedings elsewhere if it would be "inexpedient" to grant it.[319] The purpose of art.35 is to permit parties to take advantage of a national court's ability to grant interim measures in relation to subject-matter in that court's territory, as if the claimant were bringing the substantive action in the same state.[320]

Measures must be limited to territory of Member State

17-178   Prior to the Recast Brussels Regulation, there was some doubt whether the predecessor provision to art.35 allowed a court of a Member State which had jurisdiction under the same article to grant relief with effect outside its Member State.[321] In *Van Uden*, the court said that the granting of provisional or protective measures on the basis of the predecessor provision to art.35 is conditional on, inter alia:

> "the existence of a real connecting link between the subject-matter of the measures sought and the territorial jurisdiction of the Member State of the court before which those measures are sought."[322]

17-179   Recital 33 now makes it clear that where the court of a Member State does not have jurisdiction as to the substance of the matter, the effect of such measures should be confined under the regulation to the territory of that Member State. In short, the recital makes it clear that the "real connecting link" is that the measures sought must be limited to the territory of the Member State of the court seized under art.35.

17-180   Although not wholly clear, it is considered that Recital 33 means that the ability of a court to grant relief under art.35 is restricted to the territory of the Member State in which it is situated regardless of whether the court *could have had* extraterritorial jurisdiction to the substantive matter under the Recast Brussels Regulation. Therefore, if in IPR infringement proceedings, a defendant is sued in the Member State where the harmful event occurred (art.7(2)) and the claimant seeks interim relief in the courts of the Member State of the domicile of the defendant (art.4 RBR), this would not allow the latter court to grant extraterritorial interim relief under art.35 even though if it had been seized of the substantive dispute, it *could have* had extraterritorial jurisdiction.

---

[319] Civil Jurisdiction and Judgments Act 1982 s.25(2).

[320] This view was espoused by the English courts by Staughton LJ in *Republic of Haiti v Duvalier* [1990] 1 Q.B. 202 CA at 212E, where the judge held that the Brussels Convention required each Member State to make available, in aid of the courts of another Member State, such provisional and protective measures as its own domestic law would afford if its courts were trying the substantive action (cited with approval in *Union Carbide* [1995] F.S.R. 449 (Inner House, Scotland) at [471]) However, see para.17-173.

[321] See G. Tritton, *Intellectual Property in Europe*, 4th edn (London: Sweet & Maxwell, 2014), para.16-066.

[322] (C-391/95) [1998] E.C.R. I-7091 at [40] interpreting *Denilauler*.

Validity raised in interim proceedings

In *Solvay v Honeywell*, the CJEU held that where interim injunctive relief is **17-181** sought in patent proceedings and the defendants raise the issue of validity of the patents, the predecessor provision of art.24(4) does not prevent the national court from having jurisdiction in circumstances where the national court will only grant an injunction if it considers that there is a negligible risk of the patents being found to be invalid. This has been discussed earlier in this chapter.[323]

Defendant not domiciled in EU: another Member State's court seized with substantive action

Does art.35 apply where the defendant is not domiciled in the EU? Under the **17-182** earlier Brussels Regulation, the wording of art.31, its predecessor, was subtly different. It said *"...even if, under this Regulation, the courts of another Member State have jurisdiction as to the substance of the matter"*. In the 4th edn of *Tritton* it was argued that a court would still have jurisdiction under art.31 (the predecessor to art.35) even if the defendant was domiciled outside the Member State. This was because, under the Brussels Regulation, the court of another Member State could be seized with jurisdiction of the substance matter *under the Regulation* even if the defendant was domiciled outside the EU because of art.4 of the original Brussels Regulation. Article 4 (now art.6 RBR) allows the courts of Member State to apply domestic jurisdictional rules where the defendant is domiciled outside the EU.[324] The omission of the wording "under this Regulation" in art.35 of the Recast Brussels Regulation must support this case and must have been intended to remove any argument that the application of art.35 depends on whether the court of another Member State is seized with jurisdiction under the rules of the Recast Brussels Regulation or its own domestic jurisdictional rules. In short, if the court of Member State A is seized with jurisdiction as to the substance of the matter, art.35 confers jurisdiction on the court of Member State B to grant provisional or protective measures regardless of whether the court of Member State A has jurisdiction under the rules of the Recast Brussels Regulation (because the defendant is domiciled in a Member State) *or* the domestic jurisdictional principles of that Member State (because the defendant is domiciled *outside* the EU).

Substantive action not in a Member State

In contrast, it is not thought that art.35 can be invoked where a claimant seeks **17-183** provisional or protective measures when the substantive action is not brought (or will not be brought) in another Member State but a third state. The CJEU has said that its predecessor, art.25 of the Brussels Convention, expressly envisages the case of provisional measures in a Member State where, under this Convention, the courts of another Member State have jurisdiction as to the substance of the matter.[325] However, it must be accepted that there are counter arguments. First, the CJEU has never said that such is a necessary as opposed to a sufficient condition. Secondly, the wording of art.35 is "even if" the courts of another Member State have jurisdiction as to the substance of the matter and not "only if". Thirdly, the CJEU held in

---

[323] See paras 17-132 to 17-133.
[324] See *Intellectual Property in Europe*, 4th edn, para.16-070.
[325] See (143/78) [1979] E.C.R. 1055, 1066; [1979] 2 C.M.L.R. 547.

Owusu that a court has jurisdiction under art.2 Brussels Regulation (domicile of defendant) where the competing jurisdiction is a non-Member State. Therefore, it could be said that art.35 applies even if the court having jurisdiction over the substance of the matter is a non-Member State. It may be academic because it is likely that under domestic jurisdictional rules, the same range of relief is available to a court of a Member State as would be available under art.35.[326]

Lis pendens

17-184   Any jurisdictional regime must have a set of rules as to what a court should do when there are concurrent proceedings relating to identical or related subject matter in the courts of two or more countries. This situation is traditionally called *lis pendens*. There is a clear need to avoid conflicting judgments and hence all jurisdictional treaties have a set of rules to deal with *lis pendens*. In general, a jurisdictional regime favours the court first seized and thus requires the court second seized to decline or stay jurisdiction. However, it will be appreciated that such a set of rules can be abused. For instance, a party may deliberately seek to issue proceedings in one country either knowing that the court of that country has no jurisdiction to hear the matter with the purpose of delaying resolution of the dispute.

17-185   The Recast Brussels Regulation deals with issue of *lis pendens* in arts 29-34. There is a complexity to them and therefore a full review is outside the scope of this book,[327] which focusses solely on issues concerning IPR litigation.

17-186   Article 29 is concerned with proceedings involving the same cause of action and between the same parties. It states as follows:

> "1.   Without prejudice to Article 31(2), where proceedings involving the same cause of action and between the same parties are brought in the courts of different Member States, any court other than the court first seised shall of its own motion stay its proceedings until such time as the jurisdiction of the court first seised is established.
> 2.   In cases referred to in paragraph 1, upon request by a court seised of the dispute, any other court seised shall without delay inform the former court of the date when it was seised in accordance with Article 32.
> 3.   Where the jurisdiction of the court first seised is established, any court other than the court first seised shall decline jurisdiction in favour of that court."

17-187   Article 30 is concerned with related actions and states the following:

> "1.   Where related actions are pending in the courts of different Member States, any court other than the court first seised may stay its proceedings.
> 2.   Where the action in the court first seised is pending at first instance, any other court may also, on the application of one of the parties, decline jurisdiction if the court first seised has jurisdiction over the actions in question and its law permits the consolidation thereof.
> 3.   For the purposes of this Article, actions are deemed to be related where they are so closely connected that it is expedient to hear and determine them together to avoid the risk of irreconcilable judgments resulting from separate proceedings." (Footnote.)

17-188   These Articles are concerned with the difficulties caused where proceedings are

---

[326]   Although if the defendant in the proceedings in a third country is domiciled in a Member State, it might be said that the court of the Member State cannot have resort to its own domestic jurisdictional rules.

[327]   A thorough review of them is in P. Torremans, et al. (eds), *Cheshire, North and Fawcett: Private International Law*, 15th edn (Oxford: Oxford University Press, 2017), p.442, et seq.

issued in more than one Member State. In particular, this can occur by reason of art.4 (domicile) and art.7 (supplementary grounds of jurisdiction). Therefore, infringement proceedings can often be brought in more than one Member State under the RBR. However, arts 29 and 30 will apply even where jurisdiction is founded in another Member State on the grounds of *domestic* jurisdiction rules pursuant to art.4 of the Recast Brussels Regulation.[328] Clearly, the conditions of art.29 will be much more difficult to satisfy than art.30. There must be shown to be an identity of parties and cause of action. Subject to one exception introduced into the RBR, where the second court seized is the court designated by a written jurisdiction agreement,[329] it must decline jurisdiction. The importance of this to the framework of the Recast Brussels Regulation is evident in the fact that the court must act of its own motion in art.29 of the Brussels Regulation, whereas this does not apply in art.30.[330]

The CJEU has held that the second-seized court cannot examine the jurisdic- **17-189** tion of the court first seized.[331] The underlying policy behind arts 29 and 30 is:

"With respect more particularly to Article [29], the Court has repeatedly observed that that provision, together with Article [30] on related actions ... is intended, in the interests of the proper administration of justice within the Community, to prevent parallel proceedings before the courts of different Member States and to avoid conflicts between decisions which might arise therefrom. Those rules are therefore designed to preclude, in so far as possible and from the outset, a situation such as that referred to in Article [45.1(c)], namely the non-recognition of a judgment on account of its irreconcilability with a judgment given between the same parties in the State addressed (see Case 144/86 *Gubisch Maschinenfabrik v Palumbo* [1987] E.C.R. 4861, paragraph 8, and Case C-351/89 *Overseas Union Insurance and Others v New Hampshire Insurance* [1991] E.C.R. I-3317, paragraph 16)."[332]

As with many other provisions of the Recast Brussels Regulation and its **17-190** predecessors, the mechanical nature of the rules and their interpretation are capable of leading to injustice. The court first seized takes precedence over all other courts not only in deciding the substance of the dispute but also in deciding the logically prior question of whether or not it has jurisdiction under the Recast Brussels Regulation.[333] Where art.29 applies, the second court seized must decline jurisdiction once jurisdiction of the court first seized is established, even if the court seized second is of the clear view that the court first seized does not have jurisdiction.

One abuse which the Brussels Regulation and indeed the Brussels Convention **17-191** was ill-equipped to deal with was the issuing of proceedings in a Member State which was not designated between the parties to have jurisdiction under a written agreement. This was often done with the aim of delaying justice as the courts of the Member State first seized would often take time to decline jurisdiction (including appeals). As a result, changes were made to the Recast Brussels Regulation. Article 31.2 and 31.3 of Reg.1215/2012 now require the courts of Member States other than the Member State designated under a written jurisdiction agreement to stay proceed-

---

[328] *Overseas Union Insurance Ltd v New Hampshire Insurance Co* (C-351/89) [1991] E.C.R. 3317. In that case, neither party was domiciled in a Member State.

[329] art.31(2).

[330] e.g. in the UK, see *L.A. Gear v Gerald Whelan & Sons* [1991] F.S.R. 670 (HC).

[331] (C-351/89) [1991] E.C.R. I-3317.

[332] (C-163/95) [1997] E.C.R. I-5451 at [13]. See also *Gubisch Maschinenfabrik KG v Guilio Palumbo* (C-144/86) [1987] E.C.R. 4861 at [8].

[333] *Erich Gasser GmbH v MISAT Srl* (C-116/02) [2003] E.C.R. I-14693.

ings (even if such is the court first seized[334]) until the court designated in the agreement determines whether it has jurisdiction or not. If it determines that it does, then the courts of any other Member State must decline jurisdiction. As said in the recitals, this provision has been provided to avoid abusive litigation tactics.[335]

Same cause of action?

17-192 In *Gubisch v Palumbo*, the CJEU said that art.21 of the Brussels Convention (the predecessor to art.29 of the RBR) applied where two actions were between the same parties and involved the same cause of action and the same subject-matter.[336] The CJEU held that the issue of whether there was a *lis pendens* must be determined in accordance with EU law and the concept must be given an autonomous EU meaning.[337] Thus, the CJEU found that an action for enforcement of a contract between two parties involved the same cause of action and subject-matter as an action for rescission or annulment of the contract, as the question of whether the contract was binding lay at the "heart of the two actions". It said that the concept of subject-matter was not restricted so as to mean two claims which are entirely identical.[338] In *The Tatry*,[339] the CJEU held that an action where the defendant pay damages involved the same cause of action as that for a negative declaration that it was not liable for that loss. In England, it has been held that proceedings for infringement of a trade mark do not involve the same cause of action as that for passing off.[340]

Meaning of "court first seized"

17-193 Article 32.1 RBR deems a court to be seized:

    (a) at the time when the document instituting the proceedings or an equivalent document is lodged with the court, provided that the claimant has not subsequently failed to take the steps he was required to take to have service effected on the defendant, or

    (b). if the document has to be served before being lodged with the court, at the time when it is received by the authority responsible for service, provided that the claimant has not subsequently failed to take the steps he was required to take to have the document lodged with the court.

17-194 Article 32 RBR and its predecessor, art.30 of the Brussels Regulation, amended the position under the Brussels Convention where the question of when a court was

---

[334] See Recital 22.

[335] Recital 22. A good example of this, where the court felt powerless to intervene under the Brussels Regulation, was in *JP Morgan Europe Ltd v Primacom* [2005] EWHC 508 (Comm) at [10] (English High Court).

[336] *Gubisch Maschinenfabrik KG v Guilio Palumbo*, (C-144/86) [1987] E.C.R. 4861 at[14]. This is based primarily on the French and Italian texts, which respectively express the concept of the same cause of action as *le même objet et la même cause* and *il medesimo oggetto e il medesimo titolo*. In the German and English texts, no distinction is drawn between subject-matter and cause of action.

[337] See [9].

[338] See [19]. For further commentary on this, see A. Briggs and P. Rees, *Civil Jurisdiction and Judgments*, 6th edn (London: Informa, 2015), para.2.228.

[339] *The Tatry* (C-406/92) [1994] E.C.R. I-5349.

[340] *Mecklermedia Corporation v DC Congress GmbH* [1998] Ch.40.

first seized was a matter of national law.[341] Difficulties arose because of differences in the laws of Member States. Under the Recast Brussels Regulation, where there are concurrent proceedings and the issue is which court was first seized, it will need to be determined whether the law of the other Member State is an "issue and serve" (art.32.1(a)) or "serve and issue" (art.32.2(b)).

Related actions: art.30

For art.30 to be triggered, the actions must be "related actions". This defines them **17-195** as: "Actions are deemed related where they are so closely connected that it is expedient to hear and determine them together to avoid the risk of irreconcilable judgments resulting from separate proceedings". It will be appreciated that at the heart of art.30 is the concern of the courts of two Member States handing down irreconcilable judgments.

The issue is what is meant by "irreconcilable judgments". Does it have a wide **17-196** meaning of "contradictory"/"conflicting" or a narrower meaning of "mutually exclusive" legal consequences? Before considering this, it should be said that art.45.1(d) RBR prevents a judgment from being recognised if it is irreconcilable with a judgment given in another Member State involving "the same cause of action and between the same parties". Interpreting the predecessor provision to this in the Brussels Convention, the Court of Justice held that "irreconcilable" has a narrow meaning, namely that the judgments must give rise to mutually exclusive legal consequences.[342]

Under the predecessor *lis pendens* provision in the Brussels Convention, the **17-197** meaning of "irreconcilable" was considered in *The Tatry*.[343] The CJEU said that such must be given an independent EU meaning. It was argued that "irreconcilable" meant that the decisions must be given the same meaning as the predecessor provision to art.45.1. The CJEU disagreed. It said that the interpretation of "irreconcilable judgment" in the *lis pendens* provisions of the Brussels Convention must be broader and:

> "cover all cases where there is a risk of conflicting decisions, even if the judgments can be separately enforced and their legal consequences are not mutually exclusive."[344]

The definition of "irreconcilable judgments" in art.30.3 is also mirrored in art.8.1 **17-198** (jurisdiction over co-defendants). This allows the court of one Member State to have jurisdiction over a number of defendants in the court where any one of them is domiciled, provided that the claims over them are so closely connected that it is expedient to hear and determine them together to avoid the risk of irreconcilable judgments resulting from separate proceedings. The predecessor to art.8.1 was interpreted in *Roche Nederland v Primus*.[345] That case which involved litigation on parallel patents arising from the grant of a European patent has been discussed

---

[341] For the historical position under the Brussels Convention, see G. Tritton, *Intellectual Property in Europe*, 3rd edn (London: Sweet & Maxwell, 2007), para.14.052 and A. Briggs and P. Rees, *Civil Jurisdiction and Judgments*, 6th edn (London: Informa, 2015), para.2.232.

[342] *Horst Ludwig Martin Hoffmann v Adelheid Krieg* (C-145/86) [1987] E.C.R. 645 at [22].

[343] (C-406/92) [1994] E.C.R. I-5439.

[344] See [52].

[345] (C-539/03) ECLI:EU:C:2006:458.

earlier in this chapter.[346] The Court of Justice declined to decide whether the predecessor provisions to art.8.1 and art.30.3 in the Brussels Convention should be interpreted the same.[347] This is because it considered proceedings on parallel patents not to give rise to a risk of irreconcilable judgments even if the word "irreconcilable" was given its broad meaning.

17-199 It has been said that the guidance in *The Tatry* is elusive because it is not clear whether the "conflict" must relate to the rulings of the separate courts or observations within the judgment, i.e. does it relate to the actual finding (or order) of the court or go further and relate to the judicial reasoning underpinning those rulings?[348] Further, there is a strong presumption that if there is a risk of irreconcilable judgments, the court second seized should stay the proceedings.[349] However, as art.30 is only engaged where this is the case, such an approach would be close to an automatic stay under art.30—when in fact, it is clear that the court has an unfettered discretion. However, if the judgments were to lead to mutually exclusive consequences as opposed to being merely contradictory or conflicting, then because of art.45.1(d), it is considered that there must be a very strong presumption that the court second seized stay its proceedings.

Meaning of "same party"?

17-200 The English High Court held in *Mecklermedia* that a licensee cannot be regarded as the same party as the licensor.[350] Conversely, in *Berkeley Administration v McClelland*,[351] the English Court of Appeal said that, in the context of art.27 of the Brussels Regulation, it was "wholly unreal" to separate a wholly owned subsidiary from its parent. In an insurance case concerning damage to a ship, it was held by the CJEU that the insurer and insured are not the same party unless it was established that:

> "with regard to the subject-matter of the two disputes, the interests of the insurer of the hull of the vessel are identical to and indissociable from those of its insured, the owner and the charterer of that vessel."[352]

17-201 In the context of intellectual property litigation, it is highly arguable that an assignee of intellectual property rights is the same party as that of the assignor in relation to proceedings for infringement of those rights against a third party. Whilst the *commercial* interests of the assignor and assignee may differ (although often there will be alignment by reason of indemnities), the *legal interests* vis-á-vis the infringing acts would be aligned.[353]

---

[346] See para.17-095.
[347] See [25]. Léger AG considered that the predecessor provision in art.8.1 should be interpreted more narrowly than the predecessor provision to art.30.3.
[348] A. Briggs and P. Rees, *Civil Jurisdiction and Judgments*, 6th edn (London: Informa, 2015), para.2.242.
[349] P. Torremans, et al. (eds), *Cheshire, North & Fawcett: Private International Law* (Oxford: Oxford University Press, 2017), p.457.
[350] *Mecklermedia Corp* [1997] F.S.R. 627 (HC).
[351] *Berkley Administration* [1995] I.L.Pr. 201.
[352] *Drouot v CMI* (C-351/96) [1998] E.C.R. I-3075.
[353] See *Kolden Holdings Ltd v Rodette Commerce Ltd* [2008] Bus. L.R. 1051 (assignment of interests from proceedings from A to C meant that on the facts of the case, the interests of A and C were indissociable and were to be regarded as the same party)—English Court of Appeal.

Lis pendens where court of non-Member State first seized of action

Ostensibly, arts 29 and 30 RBR do not apply where the court first seized of the **17-202** same or related proceedings is the court of a non-Member State.[354] It only applies where proceedings are brought in the "courts of different Member States". It was therefore unclear whether a court of a Member State seized second of a dispute which a court of a third state was first seized could decline or stay jurisdiction or alternatively resort to its own domestic rules, e.g. forum non conveniens in England.

This problem has now been largely addressed by arts 33 and 34 of the Recast **17-203** Brussels Regulation. This deals with issues of *lis pendens* where the earlier proceedings have been brought in a third state, i.e. a non-Member State. Article 33 is concerned with where the earlier proceedings involve the same cause of action and parties (i.e. the counterpart to art.29), whilst. art.34 concentrates on related actions (the counterpart to art.30). In the case of both arts 33 and 34, the court of a Member State second seized has a discretion whether or not to stay. Under art.33, the court of the Member State may only stay if: (i) it is expected that the court of the third state will give a judgment which is capable of recognition and where applicable, enforcement in the Member State, *and* (ii) the court is "satisfied that a stay is necessary for the proper administration of justice". Conversely, the court of the Member State may continue the proceedings if: (i) the proceedings in the court of the third state have been stayed or discontinued, (ii) the proceedings in the court of the third state are unlikely to be concluded within a reasonable time, *or* (iii) continuation of the proceedings is required for the proper administration of justice. In practice, the common factor here, namely whether the stay or continuation of the proceedings is necessary for the proper administration of justice will be the dominant element. This requires a large number of factors to be taken into account. Thus, the only true "threshold" condition is whether the judgment of the court of the third state is recognisable in the court of the Member State. If it is not, then art.33 does not permit a stay.

In the case of related actions, under art.34, a similar discretion comes into play **17-204** as applies to art.30. However, as with art.33, the threshold condition that the judgment of the third state must be capable of recognition in the court of the Member State must be satisfied.[355]

For intellectual property practitioners, the new provisions of arts 33 and 34 are **17-205** important where there are prior infringement or validity proceedings in a third state. For instance, if an action between the same parties to revoke a US patent has been brought in the courts of the US, then it would allow a court of a Member State which is later seized of infringement proceedings of the same US patent to decline jurisdiction on the grounds that there is obviously a risk of irreconcilable judgments if the US patent is revoked.[356] In this sense, it can be said that arts 33 and 34 introduce a principle of discretionary "reflexive effect" into the Recast Brussels Regulation where an issue of the validity of a right registered in a third state is raised

---

[354] A. Briggs and P. Rees, *Civil Jurisdiction and Judgments*, 6th edn (London: Informa, 2015), para.2.248; P. Torremans, et al. (eds), *Cheshire, North & Fawcett: Private International Law* (Oxford: Oxford University Press, 2017), p.457.

[355] art.34.1(b).

[356] As discussed at para.17-039, a UK court may have jurisdiction to hear infringement proceedings of a US patent where the defendant is domiciled in the UK.

in litigation but only if there are prior proceedings in the third state.[357] Similarly, if there are infringement proceedings in the US of a US patent, subsequent infringement proceedings of the same US patent in a Member State would also give rise to a risk of irreconcilable judgments and inevitably, one would expect the court of the Member State to stay jurisdiction under art.34.

Claims for infringement and revocation in different Member States

17-206   An important issue to intellectual property practitioners is whether an action for infringement of a registered IPR and a counterclaim for revocation of the same right fall within arts 29 or 30. To answer this, one must consider whether such actions, if between the same parties, concern the same cause of action and, thus, fall within art.29. If not, or if the actions are between different parties, one must consider whether such actions are related actions for the purposes of art.30. Before considering the issue, it should be pointed out, as discussed earlier in this chapter, that the issue of *lis pendens* may be academic. Only the courts of the Member State of registration can consider the issue concerning the validity of the registered right. If infringement proceedings are brought in another Member State (e.g. based on domicile of defendant), the courts of that Member State may be required to decline jurisdiction in favour of the courts of the Member State of registration on the grounds that, under art.27, the claim is principally concerned with the issue of validity on which it has no jurisdiction. This is discussed above.[358] Thus, this section is only concerned with a situation where contrary to the view expressed at para.17-166, a court hearing an infringement action of a registered right concludes that art.27 does not remove its jurisdiction to hear that action, even though validity proceedings have been brought in another Member State.

17-207   It is generally considered that an action for revocation of a registered right and an action for infringement of that right are related actions but are not the same cause of action. Common sense suggests that they are not the same although they are plainly related. However, in *Gubisch*, discussed above, it was held that an action for enforcement of a contract and a separate action for the annulment of that contract did involve the same cause of action, as the validity of the contract lay at the heart of both disputes.[359] By way of analogy, it could be said that an action for infringement of a registered right and an action for revocation of that registration do involve the same cause of action, because the validity of the registration lies at the heart of both actions. Certainly, a finding of infringement and a finding that a patent is invalid have mutually exclusive legal consequences.

17-208   If infringement and invalidity proceedings are related proceedings (which seems difficult to refute), then one must consider two situations. First, where the action for revocation of a registered right is brought in Member State A and an action for infringement of the same registered right is brought *afterwards* in Member State B (*Example A*). Secondly, where the action for infringement is brought in Member State B *prior* to the action for revocation being brought in Member State A (*Example B*). The latter situation is more common but actually gives rise to more difficulties under the *lis pendens* principles. This is because in Example B, unless art.27 applies, the court hearing the infringement action in Member State B is the

---

[357] See P. Torremans, et al. (eds), *Cheshire, North & Fawcett: Private International Law* (Oxford: Oxford University Press, 2017), p.458.

[358] See paras 17-153 to 17-166.

[359] See para.17-192.

court first seized and thus the *lis pendens* provisions do not apply to it. Yet, the courts of Member State A hearing the action for invalidity cannot decline jurisdiction even though the court second seized as it has exclusive jurisdiction to determine such under art.24(4).

Dealing with Example A, if art.27 is not engaged, on the assumption that the **17-209** proceedings are indeed "related actions", the court of a Member State hearing the infringement action has the option of continuing, staying or declining jurisdiction. Ultimately, this is an issue of discretion which will need to be exercised on the facts of the case. However, in many cases, the issue of infringement and validity will be very closely connected. For instance, both issues may be dependent on the construction of the claims of a patent. This would favour a court declining jurisdiction so as to avoid different courts construing the claims in a different way.

As said above, Example B gives rise to greater problems. The court hearing the **17-210** infringement proceedings is first seized and the court hearing the revocation proceedings, although second seized, cannot decline jurisdiction over the revocation proceedings. No doubt such arguments would "steer" a court to deciding that the infringement proceedings fall within art.27 (i.e. they are principally concerned with validity) and decline jurisdiction in favour of the court hearing the revocation proceedings. If art.27 does not apply, it might be thought that the much better course of action is for the court hearing the infringement action in Member State B to stay its proceedings depending on the outcome of the revocation action in Member State A. However, Articles 29 and 30 do not permit a court first seized to decline jurisdiction or to stay the proceedings. Could the court have recourse to its own domestic inherent jurisdictional rules or case management powers and stay proceedings? In general, the CJEU has not favoured domestic jurisdictional rules supplementing the Brussels Regulation. Thus, in *Owusu*, it held that there was no room for the doctrine of forum non conveniens.[360] Any exercise of the court's power to decline or stay jurisdiction over an infringement action by applying domestic rules is little different from such a court applying a forum non conveniens argument. Ultimately, it must be said that the *lis pendens* provisions do not assist in this example.

Actions for infringement of parallel rights: related actions?

An important issue is whether parallel proceedings in several jurisdictions **17-211** between the same or related parties relating to infringement of parallel intellectual property rights fall within arts 29 or 30. In *Roche Nederland v Primus*, the CJEU held that parallel causes of action in various countries for infringement of a European patent did not give rise to a risk of irreconcilable judgments for the purpose of the predecessor provision in the Brussels Convention to art.8.1 RBR (co-defendant jurisdiction).[361] An issue in those proceedings was whether the approach in *The Tatry* (discussed above), which favoured a broad meaning to the meaning of "irreconcilable" in the predecessor *lis pendens* provision to art.30.3 RBR in the Brussels Convention should be applied to the predecessor provision to art.8.1 in the Brussels Convention. There was considerable argument that such was not permissible. However, the CJEU declined to decide the issue holding that it was

---

[360] This is discussed at para.17-228, et seq.
[361] art.8.1 allows the court of a Member State to have jurisdiction over a number of defendants in the courts where any one of them is domiciled if there is a risk of irreconcilable judgments. This is discussed at para.17-090, et seq.

sufficient to observe that even assuming that the approach in *The Tatry* was applicable to art.8.1, i.e. whether in a broad sense the decisions were contradictory, decisions on parallel patent European infringement proceedings would not be contradictory.[362] On the basis of this authority, art.30.3 is not applicable to parallel patent infringement proceedings based on a European patent as such proceedings are not capable of being contradictory. Thus, where parallel proceedings are brought on a European Patent in Member State A against X for infringing acts in Member State A and then in Member State B against X for infringing acts in Member State B, the courts of Member State B could not stay proceedings pending the outcome of the proceedings in Member State A.

17-212   However, this would be a surprising result given that infringement of European patents in all Member States is governed by the European Patent Convention. Therefore, assuming that the facts are the same in each country,[363] one would expect the result to be the same in each Member State. Indeed, if "irreconcilable" is given a broad meaning of contradictory or conflicting, it seems impossible to say that the parallel actions are not related actions.

17-213   It may be that, as with subsequent IP decisions on art.8.1 following *Roche Nederland* which appear to favour a broader interpretation of art.8.1 that the CJEU will reconsider the approach taken by the CJEU in *Roche Nederland* to arts 29 and 30. Still, as rightly acknowledged by the CJEU in *Roche Nederland*, if validity is raised in the parallel infringement proceedings of each parallel national patent registered as a result of the grant of the European patent, the courts of each Member State would have exclusive jurisdiction over the validity of such and there would be an inevitable fragmentation of the proceedings.[364] It is therefore only in cases where validity is not in issue, that there are compelling public policy arguments based on procedural economy that should allow consolidation of parallel infringement proceedings in one Member State (if the court first seized has jurisdiction to try the parallel actions and the law of the court first seized allows consolidation[365]).

Special jurisdictional rules

17-214   The Recast Brussels Regulation and its predecessors, the original Brussels Regulation and the original Brussels Convention, are intended to provide a clear set of jurisdictional rules to the courts of Member States. However, there are a number of international treaties and also EU legislation that have their own sui generis rules on jurisdiction. Thus, the European Union Trade Mark Regulation and Community Design Regulation include detailed jurisdictional rules regarding where infringement and also invalidity proceedings should be brought, whether by Member States or the EUIPO. Furthermore, regional treaties such as the European Patent Convention have some limited jurisdictional rules, e.g. on entitlement proceedings to a European patent. Equally, the Agreement on the Unified Patent Court has its own jurisdictional rules. The lawmakers of the Recast Brussels Regulation (and its predecessor, the Brussels Convention) have recognised, wisely, that it would be too ambitious to cater for these rules in the RBR. Accordingly, they have chosen to treat these special rules as a *lex specialis* which "trumps" the Recast

---

[362] See [25].
[363] e.g. where the alleged infringing good is the same in all Member States.
[364] *Roche Nederland*, at [40].
[365] See art.30.2.

Brussels Regulation.[366] To this end, art.67 provides:

"This Regulation shall not prejudice the application of provisions governing jurisdiction and the recognition and enforcement of judgments in specific matters which are contained in instruments of the Union or in national legislation harmonised pursuant to such instruments."

The above Article only applies to EU legislation pertaining to jurisdiction. Its **17-215** counterpart for international treaties which have their own jurisdiction provisions is art.71. This provides as follows:

"1.   This Regulation shall not affect any conventions to which the Member States are parties and which in relation to particular matters, govern jurisdiction or the recognition or enforcement of judgments.

2.   With a view to its uniform interpretation, paragraph 1 shall be applied in the following manner:

   (a)   this Regulation shall not prevent a court of a Member State, which is a party to a convention on a particular matter, from assuming jurisdiction in accordance with that convention, even where the defendant is domiciled in another Member State which is not a party to that convention. The court hearing the action shall, in any event, apply Article 28 of this Regulation;

   (b)   judgments given in a Member State by a court in the exercise of jurisdiction provided for in a convention on a particular matter shall be recognised and enforced in the other Member States in accordance with this Regulation.

Where a convention on a particular matter to which both the Member State of origin and the Member State addressed are parties lays down conditions for the recognition or enforcement of judgments, those conditions shall apply. In any event, the provisions of this Regulation which concern the procedure for recognition and enforcement of judgments may be applied."

An important question is whether or not the effect of arts. 67 and 71 are such as **17-216** to oust the rules in the Recast Brussels Regulation in their entirety. This issue arose in *The Tatry* where a specialised convention (the Arrest Convention) contained particular rules on jurisdiction but did not contain specific *lis pendens* rules where two Member States were seized with related proceedings. On reference to the Court of Justice concerning art.67's predecessor, art.57 of the Brussels Convention, the CJEU held on a proper construction of art.57, that where a party is a contracting party to both the Brussels Convention and the specialised convention, the latter precluded the application of the provisions of the Brussels Convention, "only in cases governed by the specialised convention and not in those to which it does not apply". It thus proceeded on the basis that the *lis pendens* rules of the Brussels Convention applied. The wording of arts 67 and 71, although somewhat different to that of art.57, is not sufficient to warrant a different interpretation.

Since they are special jurisdictional rules, they are considered in the relevant **17-217** chapter and not in this chapter.

EU instruments

•   The EU Trade Mark Regulation and the Community Design Regulation have, **17-218**

---

[366] e.g. see *Nintendo Co Ltd v BigBen Interactive GmbH* (C-24/16, C-25/16) at [42]; *Bayerische Motoren Werke* (C-433/16) EU:C:2017:550 at [39]. For their part, the unitary right regulations exclude a large number of the rules of the Recast Brussels Regulation or its predecessors to proceedings concerning the unitary rights but otherwise, state that they apply, e.g. art.79(3) Reg.6/2002.

in essence, identical jurisdictional rules which govern: (i) allocation of jurisdiction to courts of Member States, (ii) the allocation of jurisdiction between courts of Member States and EUIPO, (iii) *lis pendens* rules where there are concurrent proceedings in courts of differing Member States and/or EUIPO, and (iv) provisional or protective measures. They are considered in Ch.3, "Trade Marks in Europe" at para.3-807, et seq., and Ch.5, "Designs" at para.5-195, et seq.

- The Community Plant Variety Right regulation also has its own rules on jurisdiction. They are considered at para.6-148, et seq.

Regional or international treaties

17-219 • There are limited jurisdictional rules in the European Patent Convention. This is because once granted, they lead to a basket of national patents in the designated Member States. Thus, the Recast Brussels Regulation will apply to infringement and validity proceedings of a European patent as they would to national patents granted by national patent offices of Member States. The one exception to this is that the EPC has a Protocol which concerns disputes on ownership of a European patent. This is discussed in Ch.2, "Patents in Europe" at para.2-345.

However, once the UPC Agreement comes into force, the Unified Patent Court will have exclusive jurisdiction or shared jurisdiction with national courts[367] over litigation on "classic" European patents, i.e. European patents which have not been converted into a unitary patent. The jurisdictional rules under the UPC Agreement, which apply to both classic European patents and unitary patents, are considered in Ch.2, "Patents in Europe" at para.2-541. These rules apply to the allocation of jurisdiction (and other rules, e.g. *lis pendens*) between differing divisions of the Unified Patent Court (e.g. local, regional and central). However, they are not aimed at wider jurisdictional issues, e.g. where there are concurrent proceedings on a national (non-European) patent and a unitary or European patent. The Recast Brussels Regulation will govern such jurisdictional disputes (here, the principal concerns will be *lis pendens*). The jurisdictional rules of the UPC Agreement fall within art.71 as a *lex specialis* for infringement and validity proceedings of a classic European patent. However, as there is tension between the Recast Brussels Regulation and the jurisdictional regime in the UPC Agreement (e.g. the latter extends to defendants domiciled outside the EU), Reg.542/2014 has been enacted to ensure that there is a "smooth interface" between the two. This is discussed further below.[368]

European Patent Convention

17-220 Save in relation to entitlement proceedings, the EPC does not expressly contain any jurisdictional provisions which, pursuant to art.71, would take precedence over the Recast Brussels Regulation. As discussed in Ch.2 of this book, under the EPC, once a European patent has been granted, it becomes, in effect, a basket of national patents for the designated states. Once this occurs, art.64(3) of the EPC states that

---

[367] Where the patent owner has opted out of the provisions of the Agreement on the UPC, it is likely that the UPC has no jurisdiction—see para.2-573.
[368] See para.17-223.

"national law" shall deal with infringement. This article has given rise to some argument as to whether art.64(3) meant that a seized court should apply its own *domestic* jurisdictional rules to proceedings relating to a European patent rather than the Brussels Convention. The reasoning is equally applicable to the Recast Brussels Regulation.

In *Fort Dodge v Akzo Nobel*, the English Court of Appeal held that it was acte **17-221** clair that the EPC was not concerned with jurisdiction.[369] However, in its sister case, *Boston Scientific v Cordis*,[370] the Court of Appeal took a different view and decided to refer to the CJEU the issue as to whether arts. 2 and 64 of the EPC were specialised provisions relating to jurisdiction, which overrode the general jurisdictional rules of the Brussels Convention. However, these cases were subsequently settled. In *Gareth Pearce v Ove Arup*,[371] the Court of Appeal held that it was not persuaded that the court in *Boston Scientific v Cordis* was intending to endorse the view that the English court could not entertain a claim for the infringement of a German patent. In a parallel Dutch case, *Boston Scientific v Cordis*,[372] the Court of Appeal in The Hague rejected the submission that art.64 EPC contained a special provision of jurisdiction. It said that art.64(3) is only intended to make it clear that the infringement of a European patent has to be examined, both as to substantial and to procedural law, as an infringement of a patent granted under the national grant procedure.

It is submitted that the decision in *Fort Dodge* is correct, and the matter is acte **17-222** clair. First, from the heading to art.64 EPC, art.64(3) is clearly concerned with the rights conferred by a European patent and not any jurisdictional rule. Secondly, if it could be said that it related to jurisdictional provisions, "national law" in art.64(3) would include the Recast Brussels Regulation as such is an EU instrument with direct applicability in Member States. Thirdly, art.2 of the EPC makes it clear that European patents must be treated like national patents. In the authors' opinion, it is beyond doubt that infringement and validity proceedings relating to European patents are subject to the Recast Brussels Regulation. Neither the Jenard Report nor the Schlosser Report makes any distinction between national and European patents.

Unitary Patents and European patents

As discussed in Ch.2 on Patents, it is likely that in 2019, a new regime for litiga- **17-223** tion of Unitary Patents or classic European patents will come into existence following ratification of the Agreement on the Unified Patents Court ("UPC Agreement").[373] Once this regime comes into effect, litigation of Unitary Patents is governed by the UPC Agreement and proceedings will need to be brought in the Unified Patent Court with a number of divisions (local, regional and central) for litigating the patents. The UPC Agreement has specific jurisdictional rules concerning the allocation of jurisdiction between the three divisions and also has internal *lis pendens*.[374] The UPC Agreement also confers jurisdiction on the UP Court for

---

[369] *Fort Dodge Ltd* [1998] F.S.R. 222 CA at 242.
[370] *Boston Scientific* Unreported 18 November 1997 CA.
[371] *Gareth Pearce* [1999] F.S.R. 525 at 558.
[372] (C-98/11) [2000] E.N.P.R. 87 CA at [13].
[373] See para.2-506.
[374] See para.2-541.

"classic" European patents.[375] The upshot of this is that courts of Member States and the Unified Patent Court may have shared jurisdiction to hear proceedings relating to a European patent.

Regulation 542/2014

17-224 The jurisdictional provisions of the UPC Agreement are a convention which fall within art.71 of the Recast Brussels Regulation as they govern jurisdiction in relation to particular matters, namely jurisdiction concerning litigation over Unitary Patents and classic European patents. However, art.71(2) does not envisage a court other than a court of a Member State having jurisdiction. As the UP Court is not the court of a Member State but a sui generis court set up by the UPC Agreement, there were concerns that the Recast Brussels Regulation would not apply to such a court. Furthermore, the Recast Brussels Regulation does not provide for jurisdiction where the defendant to the litigation is not domiciled in the EU, whereas the UP Court is intended to have jurisdiction over infringement proceedings of the unitary patent or European patents regardless of the domicile of the defendant.[376]

17-225 Thus, it was necessary to amend the Recast Brussels Regulation. This has been done by the enactment of Reg.542/2014[377] which amends art.71 of the Recast Brussels Regulation by the insertion of various articles (arts 71a–71d). These articles are intended to establish the "international jurisdiction" of the UP Court and not the internal allocation of jurisdiction amongst the divisions of the UP Court nor the arrangements laid down in the UPC Agreement concerning the exercise of jurisdiction, including exclusive jurisdiction, during the transitional period provided for in the UPC Agreement.[378]

17-226 Regulation 542/2014 stipulates as follows:

- It deems the UP Court to be a court of a Member State under art.71(2) of the Recast Brussels Regulation for the purpose of the RBR.[379]
- It deems the UP Court to have jurisdiction under the RBR if it has jurisdiction under the UPC Agreement.[380]
- It provides that even though the defendant is not domiciled in a Member State, Chapter Two of the Recast Brussels Regulation (i.e. the jurisdictional rules of the Recast Brussels Regulation) applies to litigation before the UP Court.[381] These provisions ensure that the UP Court is a relevant court for the purpose of art.71 and that its "international jurisdiction" rules are those of the RBR (as opposed to its internal allocation of jurisdiction amongst the divisions of the UP Court).[382]
- It confers jurisdiction on a UP Court to grant provisional and protective

---

[375] See para.2-572.
[376] Although art.71 of Reg.1215/2012 permits derogations from the general provisions of Reg.1215/2012, it appears that it would not apply if the defendant was domiciled outside the EU (see Recital 6, Reg.542/2014 and the wording of art.71(2)(a)).
[377] [2014] OJ L163/1.
[378] Recital 5.
[379] New art.71a; Recital 4.
[380] New art.71b(1).
[381] New art.71b(2); Recital 6. As discussed earlier in this chapter, the jurisdictional rules of the RBR only apply where the defendant is domiciled in a Member State.
[382] Recital 5.

measures even if the courts of a "third State", i.e. a non-Member State have jurisdiction as to "the substance of the matter".[383]

- Where the UP Court has jurisdiction over a defendant in a dispute on a European patent which gives rise to damage within the EU, it also may exercise jurisdiction in relation to damage arising outside the Union from such an infringement. However, this jurisdiction is only established if property belonging to the defendant is located in any Member State which has ratified the UPC Agreement and the dispute has a "sufficient connection" with any such Member State.[384] This provision is intended to deal with a situation whereby the European patent extends to countries that are not members of the EU, e.g. Turkey, Switzerland and Norway.[385]
- The *lis pendens* rules of the Recast Brussels Regulation apply to proceedings brought before the UP Court and a court of a Member State which is not party to the UPC Agreement (e.g. Spain) and also (as discussed above) where the court of a Member State has shared jurisdiction to hear proceedings relating to the infringement or validity of a European patent.[386]
- Judgments of the UP Court are recognisable and enforceable in the courts of Member States.[387]

TRIPS and Paris Convention

The Court of Appeal in England and Wales in *Fort Dodge v Akzo Nobel*[388] held **17-227** that it was acte clair that TRIPS and the Paris Convention had no provisions directly concerned with jurisdiction.[389] Similarly, in *Gareth Pearce v Ove Arup*,[390] a case concerning infringement of copyright, it was held by the Court of Appeal that the Berne Convention did not purport to govern jurisdiction in relation to the infringement of copyright. These cases emphasise that art.71 RBR only applies where there are particular and express jurisdictional rules.

Jurisdictional dispute between courts of a Member State and a third state

In previous editions of this book, it was argued that the purpose of the Brussels **17-228** Convention and the original Brussels Regulation was to regulate jurisdictional disputes between the courts of Member States, and not disputes between the courts of a Member State and a non-Member State. Underlying this argument was that a fundamental objective pursued by the Brussels Convention and Brussels Regula-

---

[383] New art.71b(2), second paragraph. This provision is somewhat difficult to interpret. The UP Court has jurisdiction to grant provisional and protective measures for infringement of a classic European patent and a Unitary Patent. However, the court of a third state, i.e. a state which is not a member of the EU would not have jurisdiction over the same.

[384] New art.71b(3).

[385] See the proposal for Reg.542/2014 COM(2013) 554, pp.6–7. This provision might be said to reduce the scope of the RBR. Therefore, under the RBR, a claimant could bring an action against a defendant domiciled in a Member State even where the damage occurred outside the EU—see *Owusu v Jackson* discussed at para.17-039. The effect of this provision would be only to allow such recovery where the defendant has property within the EU.

[386] New art.71c(1) and (2).

[387] art.71(d).

[388] See *Fort Dodge* [1998] F.S.R. 222 at 242.

[389] See *Fort Dodge* [1998] F.S.R. 222 at 242.

[390] *Gareth Pearce v Ove Arup Partnership Ltd* [1999] F.S.R. 525 at 559.

tion was to ensure the free movement of judgments between Member States. The English Court of Appeal concluded that such was the case in *Re Harrods (Buenos Aires)*.³⁹¹

17-229   However, these arguments are no longer correct. In *Owusu v Jackson*³⁹² there was a jurisdictional dispute between the courts of England and Jamaica. Mr Owusu had suffered a serious accident on a beach in Jamaica. He sued Mr Jackson, the owner of the holiday home that he rented in Jamaica, in England, on the basis that that was where Mr Jackson was domiciled. In all other respects, there was no connection with England. So, not only did the accident occur in Jamaica, but the holiday operators and owner of the beach were Jamaican. The Court of Appeal referred the issue as to whether the Brussels Convention was applicable to jurisdictional disputes between a Member State and a non-Member State to the European Court of Justice (the CJEU). Furthermore, it asked the CJEU to determine whether, if the Brussels Convention was applicable, it was permissible also to have resort to the English jurisdictional rule of forum non conveniens.³⁹³ In this regard, the Court of Appeal pointed out that art.5(3) of the Brussels Convention (art.7(2) of the Recast Brussels Regulation) was inapplicable because Jamaica was not a Member State. Thus, the claimant's jurisdictional options were more tightly circumscribed than if the accident had occurred in a Member State.

17-230   The CJEU held, in an unsatisfactory judgment,³⁹⁴ that the Brussels Convention did apply to such a situation and that the rule of forum non conveniens, being an English domestic rule of jurisdiction, had no application. The reasoning for this decision was so sparse that it hardly merits any real discussion. In short, the CJEU held that, as was clear from Professor Jenard's report, for the Brussels Convention to apply, it was required that there be an international element and such was the case in *Owusu*.³⁹⁵ The CJEU held that, whilst it was not disputed that the Brussels Convention was intended to ensure the smooth working of an internal market, obstacles to such a market could "derive from disparities between national legislations on the subject".³⁹⁶ It therefore held that the Brussels Convention applied to the relationship between courts of a single Member State and those of a non-Member State as well as to relationships between the courts of a number of Member States.³⁹⁷ The CJEU then concluded that there was no room for the doctrine of forum non conveniens as this was a domestic rule of jurisdiction which had not been incorporated into the Brussels Convention.³⁹⁸

17-231   The real difficulty with this judgment is that a study of the various provisions of the Brussels Convention and the Recast Brussels Regulation makes it clear that it

---

³⁹¹ *Re Harrods (Buenos Aires)* [1992] Ch.71.

³⁹² *Owusu v Jackson* (C-281/02) [2005] E.C.R. I-1383.

³⁹³ This rule allows English courts to decline jurisdiction where there is a more suitable or appropriate jurisdiction for trying the action. See para.17-262.

³⁹⁴ A damning indictment of the conclusory nature of this judgment is given in the Preface to A. Briggs and P. Rees, *Civil Jurisdiction and Judgments*, 5th edn (London: Informa, 2009).

³⁹⁵ Logicians will understand the fallacy of this argument, namely that Professor Jenard had stipulated that it was a necessary condition for the application of the Brussels Convention that there be an international element. It does not follow that an international element is also a sufficient condition for the Brussels Convention to apply.

³⁹⁶ (C-281/02) [2005] E.C.R. I-1383 at [34].

³⁹⁷ (C-281/02) [2005] E.C.R. I-1383 at [35].

³⁹⁸ (C-281/02) [2005] E.C.R. I-1383 at [37]. This was an inexorable consequence of the decision that the Brussels Convention was applicable. The question of incorporation of the doctrine into the Brussels Convention had been discussed when it was drawn up but it was rejected—see Professor Schlosser's Opinion [1979] OJ C59/71 at [77]–[78], cited in (C-281/02) [2005] E.C.R. I-1383 at [37].

was not intended to regulate jurisdictional disputes in which one of the countries involved is not a Member State. Article 5 of the Brussels Convention, the supplemental grounds of jurisdiction (now art.7 RBR) only applies where jurisdiction is conferred on another Member State. Similarly, the *lis pendens* provisions of the Convention and Recast Brussels Regulation only apply where the court of another Member State is seized of the action. Similarly, art.25 RBR (written jurisdiction agreement) only applies to oust the domicile rule where the agreement confers jurisdiction on the court of a Member State. It is clear on any objective reading that the Brussels Convention and the Brussels Regulations are only intended to regulate disputes as to the determination and allocation of jurisdiction between the courts of Member States.

The whole jurisdictional framework of the Brussels Convention and its follow-   **17-232** ers, the Brussels Regulation and Recast Brussels Regulation, breaks down if the competing jurisdictions are that of a Member State and that of a non-Member State. Hence, they are all are silent as to the position where proceedings relating to the subject-matter of the dispute have already been commenced in the courts of a non-Member State. What would have been the position in *Owusu* if proceedings had already been commenced in Jamaica? Would the courts of England have been obliged to find jurisdiction under the Brussels Convention on the basis that the Brussels Convention does not permit stay of proceedings where proceedings are already pending in a non-Member State? As the court in *Owusu* made it clear, art.2 of the Brussels Convention is mandatory. The CJEU said there can be no derogation from the principle that it lays down except in the cases it expressly provides for.[399] The failure of the court to deal with the above arguments which were pressed heavily in the proceedings is a signal failure. Furthermore, it is bound to cause real difficulties in subsequent cases. Its emphasis on the need for certainty and standardisation is to be contrasted with a complete lack of discussion of the many absurdities that follow from such an approach.

To be fair to the CJEU, it did identify situations where the Convention was   **17-233** plainly intended to apply even if there was a potential jurisdictional dispute with a non-Member State. Thus, disputes as to immoveable property or intellectual property situated in Member States were governed by the Convention and now the Recast Brussels Regulation even if the defendant is not domiciled in a Member State.[400] Similarly, the Convention and the Recast Brussels Regulation applies even if the claimant is not domiciled in a Member State.[401] However, such points do not really deal with the main point that neither the Convention nor the Brussels Regulations have a satisfactory jurisdictional framework to deal with disputes where it is claimed that a non-Member State has jurisdiction. For instance, neither the Convention nor the Recast Brussels Regulation permit a court of a Member State to decline jurisdiction where the validity of a registered right in a non-Member State is raised. Yet, the whole policy behind art.24(4) RBR is that the court of the state of registration is best placed to determine validity (and indeed, it would be an attack on the sovereignty for a court of one country to order the revocation of a patent granted in a second country). That policy applies regardless of whether the state of registration is a Member State or a third country.

Owusu is highly relevant to intellectual property disputes as often the dispute as   **17-234**

---

[399] (C-281/02) [2005] E.C.R. I-1383 at [37].
[400] arts 6, 24, RBR. See (C-281/02) [2005] E.C.R. I-1383 at [28].
[401] (C-281/02) [2005] E.C.R. I-1383 at [27].

to jurisdiction is only between a Member State and a non-Member State. Let us substitute the tort of infringement of an intellectual property right for the tort of negligence (as it was in *Owusu*). It should be immediately apparent that, taken literally, where, for instance, it is alleged that there has been infringement of a US patent in the USA (assuming no attack on validity) by a company domiciled in England, *Owusu* would found jurisdiction on an English court which it could not decline in favour of the USA on the grounds of forum non conveniens. Indeed, even if the validity of the registered right was raised by way of counterclaim or defence, the Recast Brussels Regulation does not expressly permit the court to decline jurisdiction over the counterclaim where the right is not registered in a Member State.[402] Thus, the apparent effect of *Owusu* is that an English court would be bound under the Convention and the Recast Brussels Regulation to hear an action for infringement of a US patent by reason of acts committed in the US and a counterclaim for revocation of the US patent.

17-235   The Recast Brussels Regulation seeks to ameliorate the effect of *Owusu*, e.g. by introducing certain provisions relating to *lis pendens* where proceedings are pending before the court of a non-Member State. This has already been discussed.[403] However, these are "Band Aid" measures which alleviate some symptoms but do not tackle root and branch the fact that the Recast Brussels Regulation and its predecessors are "inward facing", i.e. concerned with *intra*-EU jurisdictional disputes. The amendments to the RBR do not approach systematically the issue of conflict of jurisdiction between a Member State and a non-Member State.

17-236   Unsurprisingly, the courts of Member States have resisted applying *Owusu* despite its apparent terms. In *Lucasfilms v Ainsworth*, which has been discussed above, an issue before the Court of Appeal and Supreme Court of the UK was whether *Owusu* permitted an English court to have jurisdiction where the defendant (or a defendant) was domiciled in England but the infringement of copyright occurred outside the EU (in that case, the USA). *Owusu* was briefly mentioned in the judgment of the Supreme Court but the court felt no obligation to decide the issue because it held that under English domestic jurisdictional rules, the English court had jurisdiction. Therefore, the issue was academic. However, in the Court of Appeal, it was not an academic issue because the Court was of the view that English domestic jurisdictional rules prevented the hearing of an infringement action of foreign copyright.[404] Thus, *Owusu* was considered. The Court of Appeal (rightly in the authors' view) made many of the points which are made above and in previous books—namely that many of the provisions of the Brussels Regulation make no sense where the dispute was between a Member State and a non-Member State. It made the point that in *Owusu*, the CJEU was concerned with whether the doctrine of forum non conveniens, a jurisdictional principle of English jurisdictional law, was consistent with the Brussels Regulation. The Court of Appeal said that the CJEU was, as a result, not concerned with "subject matter jurisdiction". This being where the subject matter of the dispute was situated outside the EU. The Court of Appeal said:

> "[129] So for all the reasons we have indicated above we think it clear that the Regulation does not create the extra-EU jurisdiction as we have defined it. The Regulation is not setting up the courts of the member states as some kind of non-

---

[402] arts 24, 27.
[403] See para.17-184.
[404] *Lucasfilms v Ainsworth* [2010] Ch. 503 CA.

exclusive world tribunals for wrongs done outside the EU by persons who happen to be domiciled within the EU. That is the sort of thing that is done reciprocally and by an international Convention-it goes well beyond the remit of judges whose job is to interpret the law, not to legislate. We think the point is acte clair and would accordingly not refer it."

The authors consider that the Court of Appeal was wholly right in its views but **17-237** its reasoning is contrary to the findings in *Owusu* and indeed it could be said to be acte clair but the other way around. In substance, these were the same arguments run in *Owusu* and the authors are far from convinced that *Owusu* can be distinguished in such a manner. It is clear that *Owusu* was concerned with a jurisdictional dispute between a Member State and a non-Member State. The whole tenure of the argument of forum non conveniens was that it was more convenient to have the court of a non-Member State to determine the dispute. Indeed, the reasoning raised by the Court of Appeal as to why the Brussels Regulation did not apply to wrongs done outside the EU was, in truth, rejected by the CJEU in *Owusu* when considering the Brussels Convention. This can be seen by considering the question that the CJEU posed to itself and its answer.

> "[23]   In order to reply to the first question, it must first be determined whether article 2 of the Brussels Convention is applicable in circumstances such as those in the main proceedings, that is to say, where the claimant and one of the defendants are domiciled in the same contracting state and the case between them before the courts of that state has *certain connecting factors with a non-contracting state, but not with another contracting state.* Only if it is will the question arise whether, in the circumstances of the case in the main proceedings, the Brussels Convention precludes the application by a court of a contracting state of the forum non conveniens doctrine where article 2 of that Convention permits that court to claim jurisdiction because the defendant is domiciled in that state."

Its answer was unequivocal: **17-238**

> "[35]   It follows from the foregoing that article 2 of the Brussels Convention applies to circumstances such as those in the main proceedings, involving relationships between the courts of a single contracting state and those of a non-contracting state rather than relationships between the courts of a number of contracting states."

In substance the only difference between *Owusu* and an action alleging infringe- **17-239** ment of Jamaican copyright is that the former cause of action is based upon the common law whereas the latter is based on a Jamaican statute. However, such does not permit a meaningful distinction to be drawn.

In the Supreme Court, as said above, they did not decide the effect of *Owusu* as **17-240** it was unnecessary to do so but said that the point might require a reference to the CJEU. In that regard, they must be right. It is of note that national courts have sought to avoid the effects of *Owusu* by arguing that the Brussels Convention and the two Brussels Regulations have "reflexive" effect where the courts of a non-Member State would have exclusive jurisdiction under arts 24 or 25 RBR if they were a party to the Brussels Recast Regulation or its predecessors (i.e. a Member State). The "reflexive effect" doctrine is considered earlier in this chapter.[405]

---

[405] See para.17-150.

Recognition and enforcement of judgments

17-241   The Recast Brussels Regulation contains detailed provisions on the recognition and enforcement of judgments issued in the court of one Member State by the courts of other Member States. Such provisions are a necessary element in any jurisdictional regime. If a court were not to recognise a judgment on the grounds that the court which handed down the judgment lacked jurisdiction, then any such harmonising legislation on jurisdiction would be deficient. Judgments issued by a non-Member State are not dealt with in the regulation and their enforcement will be subject to domestic rules on recognition of judgment.[406] The Recast Brussels Regulation governs the enforcement of judgments given in a Member State *regardless* of the defendant's domicile.[407] Thus, the court of a Member State seized with jurisdiction under art.6 RBR (defendant not domiciled in Member State) will apply domestic jurisdictional rules. However, such does not prevent the RBR applying to the enforcement of such judgments. There is thus a real "asymmetry" here. As has been commented on, the defendant has none of the protection of the careful structure of the jurisdictional rules established by the Regulation but all of the disadvantages.[408]

17-242   In general, judgments given in a Member State must be recognised in other Member States without any special procedure being required.[409] The Recast Brussels Regulation makes it clear that under no circumstances can a foreign judgment be reviewed as to its substance.[410] Moreover, the court in which recognition is sought cannot review the jurisdiction of the court of origin unless it found that it had jurisdiction contrary to art.24.[411] With these points in mind, there are a number of important exceptions to the fundamental rule that judgments given in another Member State must recognise. They are:

(a)   A judgment will not be recognised if it is "manifestly contrary" to public policy in the Member State in which recognition is sought.[412]

(b)   A judgment will not be recognised:

> "where it was given in default of appearance, if the defendant was not served with the document which instituted the proceedings or with an equivalent document in sufficient time and in such a way as to enable him to arrange for his defence, unless the defendant failed to commence proceedings to challenge the judgment when it was possible for him to do so."[413]

(c)   A judgment will not be recognised where it is irreconcilable with a judgment given in a dispute between the same parties in the Member State in which recognition is sought.[414] A judgment is "irreconcilable" where it

---

[406] art.36.

[407] Recital 27.

[408] A. Briggs and P. Rees, *Civil Jurisdiction and Judgments*, 5th edn (London: Informa, 2009), para.7.04. A result described by the authors as "breath-taking".

[409] art.36(1) RBR.

[410] art.52 RBR.

[411] art.45.3, first sentence.

[412] art.45.1(a). This test of "public policy" cannot be relied upon to attack a finding by the court which handed down the judgment that it had jurisdiction to hear the dispute—see art.45.3.

[413] art.45.1(b). Discussed at para.17-248.

[414] art.45.1(c).

entails legal consequences that are mutually exclusive.[415] Irreconcilability arises from the effects of a judgment.[416]

(d) A judgment will not be recognised if it is irreconcilable with an earlier judgment given in another Member State, or in a third state involving the same cause of action and between the same parties, provided that the earlier judgment fulfils the conditions necessary for its recognition in the Member State addressed.[417]

(e) A judgment will not be recognised if it conflicts with art.24 (which confers exclusive jurisdiction on courts of Member State—in particular, in proceedings concerning the validity of registered rights).[418] Whilst this is the only ground where the court in which recognition is sought can review the jurisdiction of the court of origin, it is bound by the findings of fact on which the court of origin based its jurisdiction.[419] Thus, its review of jurisdiction is limited to the application of those findings to the Recast Brussels Regulation (assuming that the court of origin made findings of fact which it may not have done).

A full review of the recognition and enforcement provisions of the Recast Brussels Regulation is outside the scope of this book.[420] This chapter focusses on aspects which are particularly relevant to practitioners in the field of intellectual property. **17-243**

Action for infringement and defence of invalidity

As discussed above, the combined effect of arts 24 and 27 is that where invalidity of a registered right is raised by defence in infringement proceedings, the court of a Member State which is not the court of the Member State of registration should decline jurisdiction over the plea of invalidity. However, it may decide to try the action on infringement on the grounds that that claim is not "principally concerned" with validity and thus art.27 allows it to try the action for infringement. It then hands down judgment finding that the patent is infringed. If the patent has been or is later revoked by the court of Member State of registration, then plainly the judgment is unenforceable and unrecognisable. It would be simply contrary to public policy to recognise a finding of infringement of an invalid right. In itself, this is unproblematic. However, what if the court of a Member State in which recognition of this judgment is sought believes that the court should have declined jurisdiction under art.27 because the infringement action was "principally concerned" with the validity of the registered right on which the infringement action was founded? Here, art.45.3 RBR is relevant. It says that *"Without prejudice to point (e) of paragraph 1, the jurisdiction of the court of origin may not be reviewed. The test of public policy referred to in point (a) of paragraph 1 may not be applied as to* **17-244**

---

[415] *Horst Ludwig Hoffmann v Adelheid Krieg* (C-145/86) ECLI:EU:C:1988:61 at [22] (German judgment ordering a husband to pay maintenance to his wife by reason of being married incompatible with a Dutch judgment pronouncing a divorce).

[416] *Italian Leather SpA v WECO Polstermöbel GmbH & Co* ECLI:EU:C:2002:342 at [44].

[417] art.45.1(d).

[418] art.45.1(e). Article 24 is discussed at para.17-117.

[419] art.45.2, art.45.3.

[420] The reader is referred to A. Briggs, *Civil Jurisdiction and Judgments*, 6th edn (Abingdon: Informa Law, 2015) and P. Torremans, et al. (eds), *Cheshire, North & Fawcett: Private International Law* (Oxford: Oxford University Press, 2017).

rules relating to jurisdiction." Article 45.1(e)(i) is irrelevant.[421] Article 45.1(e)(ii) might be thought relevant as it states that a judgment cannot be recognised if it conflicts with Section 6 of Chapter II. Article 24 is in Section 6. However, art.27 is not in Section 6. Accordingly, the authors' view is that a court of a Member State in which recognition is sought cannot review a decision by the court of origin not to decline jurisdiction on an infringement action under art.27.

Res judicata, common issues and enforcement of judgments

17-245   Often in IP cases, the same issue arises in litigation. Therefore, where the owner of parallel trade marks seeks to enforce them in various Member States against defendants in the same corporate group, courts of Member States may often have to hand down a ruling on an issue that is common to all the parallel proceedings, e.g. likelihood of confusion between Mark A and Sign B. In general, as discussed above, because of the territorial nature of intellectual property rights, there is no danger of "mutually exclusive legal" consequences from the two judgments and therefore, the judgments, although conflicting, are not irreconcilable.[422] Thus, a French court could find that Mark A (protected by a French registered mark) is confusingly similar to Sign B and an English court may find Mark A (protected by a UK registered mark) is not confusingly similar to Sign B. Neither judgments give rise to mutually exclusive legal consequences as both judgments are limited in their effect to the territory of France and the UK.

17-246   Mention should be made here of an English case under the Brussels Convention, namely *Prudential Assurance v Prudential Insurance*.[423] In this case the Court of Appeal of England and Wales was concerned with a trade mark dispute between the claimant, an insurance company based in England who had registered the marks PRU and PRUDENTIAL as UK and CTMs. The defendant, an insurance company based in the USA, applied to register PRUMERICA as a national trade mark in France. This was opposed by the claimant based on its PRU and PRUDENTIAL marks. The French Cour d'Appel rejected the opposition on the grounds that the marks were not confusingly similar. Subsequently, the claimant brought an action in the UK for infringement of its EUTM and UK marks by reason of the use of PRUMERICA and PRUDENTIAL-BACHE by the defendant. In substance, the issue was the same as decided by the French Cour d'Appel in France—were the marks confusingly similar? However, the French court had to decide the issue in opposition and not infringement proceedings. The defendant applied to strike out the claim contending inter alia that the French court's decision that the marks PRUMERICA and PRU/PRUDENTIAL were not confusingly similar was binding on the UK courts. The argument was based in part on art.21 of the Brussels Convention (the *lis pendens* provision[424]). The court was not persuaded that the *lis pendens* provisions were relevant. In its view, the real issue was whether the English court was bound to recognise the judgment of the French court pursuant to art.26 of the Brussels Convention (art.35.1(e) of the Recast Brussels Regulation). The Court of Appeal took the view that the judgment of the French court could not be

---

[421]   art.45.1(e)(i) is concerned with insurance contracts.
[422]   This is discussed earlier in this chapter at para.17-094.
[423]   [2003] 1 W.L.R. 2295.
[424]   The predecessor to art.27 of the Brussels Regulation.

recognised in the UK because the UK court had exclusive jurisdiction over proceedings involving validity and infringement of a national trade mark.[425]

The authors consider that the Court of Appeal reached the correct result but via **17-247** the wrong reasoning. The reality is that the decision of a French court was merely to the *effect* that an application for a French mark by B could be registered on the grounds that it was not confusingly similar with the trade marks of A. That is not irreconcilable in the meaning of exclusive legal consequences with a UK court later finding that the use of a sign by B in the UK infringed the trade mark rights in A. The mere fact that both the UK and French courts had to consider a common issue—likelihood of confusion between two marks—is not enough to trigger a finding of irreconcilability under art.45.1(c) RBR. Thus, even if the French court had to consider whether B's sign infringed A's trade marks in France and found that they did not, this would not mean that such a judgment was irreconcilable with a UK court finding that they did as both courts' findings would be limited to the territories of France and UK.[426] Put another way, the judgment of the French court was plainly recognisable in the UK *for what it was*—namely a decision by the French courts to grant registration of a sign as a registered trade mark in France. That in itself did not oust the jurisdiction of the UK courts to adjudicate on whether there had been infringement of trade marks in the UK.

Ex parte IPR orders

In many intellectual property cases, the owner of IPRs wants urgent relief from **17-248** courts in order to prevent counterfeit or piracy. Often, they seek orders to seize counterfeit or pirate goods or to preserve evidence. For obvious reasons, no notice will be given to the counterfeiter or person pirating that such an order is being sought. Thus, invariably, the defendant will not be served with any notice of proceedings until after an order is granted. Is an ex parte order granted by one Member State without notice to the defendant enforceable in another Member State? In the case of interim ex parte IPR orders, the problem will only arise where a court makes a provisional or protective order which has extra-territorial effect.[427] It can only do so where it has jurisdiction over the substance of the action. It cannot make an order with extraterritorial effect if its jurisdiction is solely based on art.35.[428] So let us take the case where a court seized with a serious counterfeiting case has jurisdiction to grant pan-EU relief as the defendants are domiciled in the Member State where the seized court is located. Without notice to the defendants, the court grants an interim order with effect throughout the EU empowering the claimant to seize counterfeit goods and preserve evidence. Such orders are expressly

---

[425] See [28]. The reasoning was in part based on Laddie J's remarks in *Coin Controls v Suzo* [1999] Ch 33 that infringement and validity of national trade marks has to be determined in the national court in accordance with national law.

[426] It should be said that in the case of EU Trade Marks, this is not the case as relief can be given on a pan-European basis. But the EUTM Regulation has its own jurisdictional rules to prevent conflicting judgments. See paras 17-128 and 3-807.

[427] The "recognition" procedure in the Recast Brussels Regulation is only concerned with the recognition of a judgment given in one Member State by the courts of other Member States—see art.36 RBR.

[428] art.35 allows the court of a Member State to order provisional or protective measures even if the court of another Member State has jurisdiction. See para.17-168.

envisaged in the Enforcement Directive.[429] Can the court in which recognition is sought refuse to recognise such an order on the grounds of art.45.1(b)?

17-249   In *Denilauler v Couchet Frères*[430] the CJEU said that the predecessor provision, art.27(2) of the Brussels Convention,[431] which is similar to art. 45.1(b) of the Recast Brussels Regulation but not the same, clearly prevented ex parte judgments, where the defendant had not been duly summoned, from being enforceable in another Member State. However, the wording of art.45.1(b) which has been set out above is not the same as art.27(2) of the Brussels Convention. Here, the defendant can ask the court in which recognition is sought to refuse to recognise the judgment where he is not served with the document which instituted the proceedings "in sufficient time and in such a way as to enable him to arrange for his defence". Plainly, if the order is made "without notice", the defendant could not have arranged his defence. However, art.45.1(b) provides for a carveout if "... he failed to commence proceedings to challenge the judgment when it was possible for him to do so". Does this mean that if the defendant *does* challenge the judgment within a reasonable time from being served that the ex parte order of the court of one Member State should not be recognised by the court of another Member State? This would plainly be a counterfeiter or pirate's charter as it would allow the same to take steps to destroy or conceal evidence or move counterfeit or pirate goods out of the jurisdiction before the court of the latter Member State makes a later inter partes order.

17-250   On the one hand, it could be said that it is not a counterfeit or pirate's charter as if the right holder wants such type of relief, it should pursue this relief in the court of each Member State where it seeks to enforce the order. In such circumstances, art.45 is inapplicable and the RBR has no role to play. Ex parte extraterritorial orders made without notice to a defendant are draconian in nature and plainly have the ability to breach fundamental rights of a defendant (e.g. the right to a fair and public hearing and the right of defence under art.47 Charter of Fundamental Rights). Therefore, it could be said that if such orders are to be enforced by a court of a Member State, they should be made by the courts of the same Member State.

17-251   On the other hand, forcing a rights holder to bring simultaneous ex parte orders in a number of Member States makes protection of IPRs difficult and costly. Here, one could argue that there is no public policy argument under the RBR from orders made in one Member State being enforceable in the courts of another Member State, whatever their nature. Indeed, it is an integral pillar of the RBR. To safeguard the rights of defendants, one would argue that a proper interpretation of art.45.1(b) is that such ex parte orders are enforceable as and until the defendant successfully applies to discharge the order and provided that if the order is discharged, the defendant is compensated for any damage caused by the wrongful enforcement of the

---

[429]   art.7.1 Dir.2004/48/EC (the Enforcement Directive), which is discussed earlier in this book in Ch.15 expressly empowers courts of Member States to order prompt and effective provisional measures to preserve evidence without the other party having been heard but on condition that the parties affected are given notice, without delay after execution of the measures at the latest. In particular, this would allow the affected parties to ask the court to review whether the measures should be modified, revoked or confirmed.

[430]   (125/79) [1980] E.C.R. 1553; [1981] C.M.L.R. 62 CJEU.

[431]   Which requires a party seeking recognition or enforcement of a judgment given in default to produce a copy of the document that establishes that the party in default was served with the document instituting the proceedings or with an equivalent document.

order. This would be consistent with the approach under the Enforcement Directive.[432]

Finally, it should be said that the type of ex parte orders that courts will make **17-252** varies substantially depending on the Member State. Therefore, it is well known that the courts of England have the discretion to craft highly flexible orders which meet the justice of the case. Such orders may be unknown in other Member States which could give rise to problems of enforcement. The Recast Brussels Regulation caters for this problem by saying that if such a measure is not known in the law of the Member State addressed, that measure or order should be adapted, to the extent possible, to a measure or order known in the latter Member State "which has equivalent effects attached to it and which pursues similar aims and interests".[433] Hence, it is not a ground for refusing recognition that the order or measure is not of a type known under the law of the Member State in which recognition is sought.

Determination of jurisdictional issues under the Recast Brussels Regulation

Where a party disputes on the facts the jurisdiction of a court of a Member State **17-253** under the Recast Brussels Regulation, the criteria for assessing whether the court has jurisdiction is not governed by the RBR but by the substantive law determined by the national conflict of laws rules of the court seized, provided that the "effectiveness" of the Recast Brussels Regulation is not thereby impaired.[434]

In *Effer v Kantner*,[435] a case under the Brussels Regulation, the court said that, **17-254** in relation to art.5(1) Brussel Convention (which gives jurisdiction in "matters relating to a contract, in the courts for the place of performance of the obligation in question"), a court called upon to decide a dispute arising out of a contract may examine, of its own motion, the essential pre-conditions for its jurisdiction having regard to "conclusive and relevant evidence adduced by the party concerned" establishing the existence or the inexistence of the contract.[436] However, in the same case, the CJEU also said that the claimant might invoke the jurisdiction of the court under art.5(1), even where the existence of the contract on which the claim is based is in dispute between the parties.[437]

In England, the courts require that the claimant show that there is a "good argu- **17-255** able" case that the jurisdictional ground on which reliance is placed is made out.[438] In a Privy Council case, *Altimo v Kyrgyz Mobile*, this was said to mean that the party arguing that the court has jurisdiction must demonstrate that it has "a much better

---

[432] art.7.4 Dir.2004/48 envisages precisely this—namely that if a measure to preserve evidence is revoked, judicial authorities shall have the authority to order the applicant, upon request of the defendant, to provide the latter with appropriate compensation for any injury caused by the measures. As said, art.7.1 Dir.2004/48 expressly empowers courts to make orders to preserve evidence without notice to the affected parties. See fn.429.

[433] art.54 RBR.

[434] *Shevill v Presse Alliance*, at [41]. This was a case under the Brussels Convention.

[435] (38/81) [1982] E.C.R. 825. This case predates *Shevill v Presse Alliance*.

[436] (38/81) [1982] E.C.R. 825 at 834–835.

[437] (38/81) [1982] E.C.R. 825 at 834–846.

[438] See *Tesam Distribution Ltd v Schuh Mode Team GmbH* [1990] ILPR 149; *Canada Trust Co v Stolzenberg (No.2)* [1998] 1 W.L.R. 547 CA, upheld by the House of Lords on this point—[2002] 1 A.C. 1 HL; *Konkola Copper Minds Plc v Coromin Ltd* [2006] 1 Lloyd's Rep. 410; *Bols Distilleries BV v Superior Yacht Services Ltd* [2007] 1 W.L.R. 12; *Knorr-Bremse v Haldex Brake Products GmbH* [2008] F.S.R. 30.

argument" than the other.[439] However, the test of "much the better argument" appears to impose too high a burden on the party claiming that a court has jurisdiction if such is to be interpreted as meaning on the balance of probabilities (or indeed higher). It is of note that the Privy Council in *Altimo* cited as authority for this type of approach, the cases of *Canada Trust v Stolzenberg (No.2)* and *Bols Distilleries*.[440] In the former case, Waller LJ referred to the concept of "good arguable case" having flexibility. Indeed, later in the judgment, Waller LJ said that "good arguable case" means something below "on the balance of probabilities" but higher than the "serious question to be tried".[441] In *Bols Distilleries*, the Privy Council held that what amounts to a "good arguable case" depends on what was required to be shown in any particular situation.[442] The Privy Council in *Bols Distilleries* noted that the approach by Waller LJ in *Canada Trust* was considered by the House of Lords in the same case and approved. Therefore, Lord Steyn rejected the approach that in the context of the Brussels Regulation a more stringent approach than "good arguable case" should be applied, namely on the balance of probabilities.[443] The Privy Council in *Bols Distilleries* endorsed the approach of Lord Steyn in endorsing the approach by Waller LJ. Thus, it would appear clear that the Privy Council in *Bols Distilleries* did not favour an approach of "on the balance of probabilities".

17-256   It should be noted that the standard of proof does not depend on whether or not the point will only arise at the jurisdiction stage. Consequently, the issue of domicile of the defendant will normally only arise at a jurisdictional stage and will not be further argued at trial. However, in contrast, the question of whether a contract was formed may be equally applicable to the merits of the action and (if there is a jurisdiction clause) to the issue of jurisdiction. Although there was some doubt as to whether there should be a different approach, it is now clear that in England, there is not.[444]

17-257   This approach in England has been extended to intellectual property litigation. In *Mölnlycke v Procter & Gamble*,[445] the claimant sued English and American defendants for patent infringement. In the course of proceedings, it was realised that a German sister company of the defendants had important documentation in its possession relating to the action. The claimant sought to establish jurisdiction in England against the additional German defendant on the basis that it was a joint tortfeasor of the infringements committed in England, although it was accepted that the only reason was to obtain discovery. The claimant based its application to join the German company on arts 6(1) and 5(3) of the Brussels Convention (arts 8.1, 7.2 RBR). The Court of Appeal held that, as a good arguable case had been established against the German defendant as joint tortfeasor in relation to infringements committed in England, then there was no abuse in joining the German defendant to the action.[446]

---

[439] *Altimo Holdings and Investment Ltd v Kyrgyz Mobile Tel Ltd* [2012] 1 W.L.R. 1804 (Privy Council) at [71]; *Innovia Films Ltd v Frito-Lay North America Inc* [2012] R.P.C. 24 (Pat).

[440] Cited above.

[441] 558F–G.

[442] See [28].

[443] p.13 per Lord Steyn.

[444] *Agrafax Public Relations Ltd v United Scottish Society Inc* [1995] C.L.C. 862; *Canada Trust Co Stolzenberg (No.2)*, at 554–555 overruling observations in *Attock Cement Ltd v Romanian Bank for Foreign Trade* [1989] 1 W.L.R. 1147 by Staughton LJ.

[445] *Mölnlycke* [1992] R.P.C. 21 CA.

[446] *Mölnlycke* [1992] R.P.C. 21 CA at 35, per Dillon LJ. For an application of this principle, see *AMS*

JURISDICTIONAL PROVISIONS OF ENGLISH LAW

If the defendant is not domiciled in a Member State, then art.6 of the Recast Brus- **17-258** sels Regulation permits resort to national jurisdictional rules. This section considers certain English jurisdictional rules.

In *Lucasfilms v Ainsworth*,[447] the Supreme Court of the United Kingdom **17-259** considered in depth the jurisdiction of English courts under domestic jurisdictional rules to adjudicate on infringement of foreign copyright claims (in that case, an allegation of infringement of US copyright). It said:

"[105] We have come to the firm conclusion that, *in the case of a claim for infringement of copyright of the present kind, the claim is one over which the English court has jurisdiction, provided that there is a basis for in personam jurisdiction over the defendant, or, to put it differently, the claim is justiciable*. It is clear that much of the underpinning of the *Moçambique* rule and the decision in *Potter v Broken Hill Pty Co Ltd* [1905] VLR 612 has been eroded. All that is left of the *Moçambique* rule (except to the extent that it is modified by the Brussels I Regulation) is that there is no jurisdiction in proceedings for infringement of rights in foreign land where the proceedings are principally concerned with a question of the title, or the right to possession, of that property. So also article 22(1) of the Brussels I Regulation does not apply to actions for damages for infringement of rights in land.

[106] The basis for what remains of the rule was said by the House of Lords in the *Moçambique* case [1893] A.C. 602, 623 to be that controversies should be decided in the country of the situs of the property because the right of granting it was vested in 'the ruler of the country' and in the *Hesperides* case [1979] AC 508 to be the maintenance of comity and the avoidance of conflict with foreign jurisdictions. It is possible to see how the rationale of the *Moçambique* rule can be applied to patents, at any rate where questions of validity are involved. For example the claims might touch on the validity of patents in sensitive areas, such as armaments, and that no doubt is part of the rationale for article 22(4) of the Brussels I Regulation. But it is very difficult to see how it could apply to copyright. It is true that copyright can involve delicate political issues. Thus in a very different context Brightman J had to deal with the international consequences for copyright protection of the samizdat circulation in the Soviet Union of Solzhenitsyn's August 1914 without having been passed by the Soviet censor: *The Bodley Head Ltd v Flegon* [1972] 1 WLR 680. But such cases can be dealt with by an application of the principles of public policy in appropriate cases." [Authors' emphasis.]

Thus, it is clear that UK courts have jurisdiction to determine foreign copyright **17-260** infringement actions and indeed, any action for infringement of foreign IPRs provided that validity is not an issue. In this sense, English law now mirrors that under the Recast Brussels Regulation. The only requirement is that there must be in personam jurisdiction against the defendant or, as the Supreme Court says, the claim must be "justiciable". There is some opaqueness in the point that the UK court must have jurisdiction over a defendant provided that the claim is justiciable because the Supreme Court did not differentiate between the issue of jurisdiction and justiciability and indeed used the words interchangeably. However, it is tolerably clear that what the Supreme Court meant was that if under domestic

---

Neve Ltd v Heritage Audio S.L. [2016] EWHC 2563 at [50] applying *Canada Trust Co v Stolzenberg (No. 2)* [1998] 1 W.L.R. 547 at 555–9.
[447] [2012] 1 A.C. 208.

jurisdictional rules, a UK court has jurisdiction, the fact that the action was for enforcement of a foreign copyright was no bar to such rules being applicable.

17-261   It is of note that the Supreme Court considered that the *Moçambique* rule could apply to patents where validity is involved and that such was to be decided by the application of the principles of public policy in appropriate cases.

Forum non conveniens

17-262   Under English domestic jurisdictional principals, where a party can show that there is, prima facie, another forum which is clearly or distinctly more appropriate for the trial than the English forum, then the English court will normally grant a stay or decline jurisdiction, unless there are special circumstances by reason of which justice requires that the trial should nevertheless take place in England.[448] Thus, it has been said that in applying the approach in *Spiliada*, that the question of forum is to be approached in two stages: the first stage is to ask whether England is clearly and distinctly the natural forum, i.e. the forum with which the action has the most real and substantial connection, and the second stage is that if England is not the natural forum, whether England is the *appropriate* forum, in particular because there is a real risk that the claimant will not obtain substantial justice in the natural forum.[449] In determining the natural forum, factors which can be taken into account are: (a) the personal connections which the parties have to the countries in question; (b) the factual connections which the events relevant to the claim have with those countries; (c) factors affecting convenience or expense such as the location of witnesses or documents; and (d) the applicable law.[450] In determining whether England is the appropriate forum if it is not the natural forum, it is not normally appropriate to compare the quality of justice available in a foreign forum with that obtainable in an English court, not that English law (both substantive and procedural) may have advantages over the laws of a foreign country.[451] Rather, the correct approach is whether the court is satisfied that "substantial justice" will be done in the available appropriate forum.[452] Where one part of the action needs to be determined in England, this is a compelling reason that it is appropriate that other aspects also be heard in England.[453]

17-263   The Civil Jurisdiction and Judgments Act expressly preserves the doctrine of forum non conveniens, provided that its application is "not inconsistent" with the Brussels Convention.[454] There never has been any doubt that as a domestic jurisdictional principle, it has no part to play where the jurisdictional dispute was between two Member States.[455] However, historically, it was considered not applicable to jurisdictional disputes between a Member State and a non-Member

---

[448] The doctrine of forum non conveniens was reviewed and re-stated in *Spiliada Maritime Corp v Consulex Ltd* [1987] A.C. 460 HL.

[449] *Innovia Films v Frito-Lay* [2012] R.P.C. 24 at [40]. Although other courts have adopted a less refined approach. Thus, in *Conductive Inkjet Technology v Uni-Pixel Displays Inc*, the court said that the fundamental question is a single "is the court satisfied that England is clearly the appropriate forum"; or as it is put in CPR 6.37(3), "the proper place in which to bring the claim?"—see [129].

[450] *Innovia*, at [41].

[451] *Innovia*, at [42] citing *Amin Rasheed v Kuwait Insurance Co* [1984] A.C. 50 per Lord Wilberforce (at 72D).

[452] Lord Goff in *Spiliada v Consulex*, at 482D–F; *Connelly v RTZ Corporation Plc (No.2)* [1998] A.C. 854 at 872G–873A.

[453] *Conductive Inkjet Technology*, at [130].

[454] Civil Jurisdiction and Judgments Act 1982 s.49.

[455] *Re Harrods (Buenos Aires) Ltd* [1992] Ch. 72 at 96, 101.

State.[456] Therefore, the English court took the view that the Brussels Convention was entered into pursuant to art.293 of the EC Treaty, which secured the simplification of formalities governing the reciprocal recognition and enforcement of judgments of courts or tribunals between Member States of the EC. The court supported the view of a commentator that the Brussels Convention was intended to regulate jurisdictional disputes between Member States but not vis-à-vis between a Member State and a non-Member State. The commentator said that the Member States were setting up an intra-Convention mandatory system of jurisdiction. They were not regulating relations with non-Member States.[457] Thus, the Court of Appeal held that, where the jurisdictional dispute was between a Member State and a non-Member State, the principle of forum non conveniens was applicable. Subsequently, the Court of Appeal confirmed this principle, even where the defendant was domiciled in a Member State.[458]

However, the CJEU in *Owusu v Jackson*[459] has held that where an English court **17-264** has jurisdiction under art.2 of the Brussels Convention over a defendant domiciled in the UK, it has no power to stay proceedings on the grounds of forum non conveniens in favour of the courts of a non-contracting state (in that case, Jamaica). *Owusu* has been discussed above in this chapter.[460] Indeed, in that decision, the court specifically rejected the application of the doctrine of forum non conveniens even where a dispute was between England and a non-Member State.

Thus, the doctrine of forum non conveniens has limited application. It is prima **17-265** facie applicable where the defendant is not domiciled in a Member State such that the Recast Brussels Regulation does not apply.[461] However, even where the defendant is not domiciled in a Member State, the doctrine has no applicability if under the Recast Brussels Regulation, exclusive jurisdiction is conferred on a Member State under the regulation. Therefore, under the Recast Brussels Regulation, art.6 (domestic jurisdictional laws apply where defendant is not domiciled in a Member State), does not apply to disputes where a Member State has exclusive jurisdiction (e.g. dispute on validity of patent).[462] Similarly, where a court has exclusive jurisdiction pursuant to special jurisdictional rules that are such as to invoke art.7 of the Recast Brussels Regulation, an English court has held that there is no room for the principle of forum non conveniens. Thus, in *Innovia*, the English court held that exclusive jurisdiction was conferred on a particular country by operation of the EPC's Protocol on Jurisdiction and Recognition of Decisions in relation to an entitlement dispute over a European patent and that there was no room for the application of the doctrine of forum non conveniens.[463]

---

[456] *Re Harrods (Buenos Aires) Ltd.*

[457] L. Collins, "Note on Re Harrods (Buenos Aires) Ltd" [1990] 106 L.Q.R. 535, 538–539.

[458] *Eli Lilly and Co v Novo Nordisk A/S* [2000] I.L.Pr. 73 CA. See also *Ace Insurance SA-NV v Zurich Insurance Co* [2001] EWCA Civ 173 where the Court of Appeal confirmed the validity of this approach.

[459] (C-281/02) [2005] E.C.R. I-3583.

[460] See para.17-230.

[461] L. Collins, A. Briggs, J. Harris, J.D. McClean, C. McLachlan, C.G.J. Morse, *Dicey, Morris & Collins: The Conflict of Laws*, 14th edn (London: Sweet & Maxwell, 2009), para.12–016; *Innovia*, at [83] (although the point was conceded); *Conductive Inkjet Technology v Uni-Pixel Displays Inc* [2013] EWHC 2968 (Ch).

[462] art.4 (1); art.22 and art.23.

[463] *Innovia Films Ltd v Frito-Lay North America Inc* [2012] R.P.C. 24 at [84]–[85]; *Conductive Inkjet Technology Ltd v Uni-Pixel Displays Inc*. In the latter case, (at [87]–[89]), which was also concerned with entitlement to a European patent, the court held that the result was reached not by an applica-

Anti-suit injunctions

17-266   In certain situations, a party may seek to bring an action to restrain another party from bringing an action in a foreign jurisdiction. This is called an "anti-suit injunction". It is outside of the scope of this book to consider the full extent and ambit of this jurisdiction.[464] The general principle is that an English court has jurisdiction to grant an in personam injunction to restrain a respondent from issuing proceedings in the courts of a foreign country. The grounds on which such an injunction will be granted range from the applicant having a legal right not to be sued in a foreign country, e.g. where there is an exclusive jurisdiction clause conferring jurisdiction on England[465] or where it would be oppressive or vexatious for the applicant to be sued there.[466] It has been said that an anti-suit injunction will be granted where the bringing of the foreign action must be considered unconscionable.[467] The basis for the jurisdiction is an in personam one and is not intended to affect the ability of foreign courts to determine whether they have jurisdiction. An anti-suit injunction was granted in an action where a claimant initially brought proceedings for passing off and breach of confidence in England but then sought to abandon such proceedings and sue in New York.[468]

17-267   However, where it is intended to grant an injunction against a party who has brought or intends to bring proceedings in another Member State, such is not permissible. In *Turner v Grovit*,[469] proceedings were brought in England by an employee against his employer but a vexatious action was then brought by the employer against the employee in Spain. There appears to be little doubt that the Spanish action was not bona fide. The English court were minded to grant an anti-suit injunction but referred the issue of whether it had power to do so under the Brussels Convention. The CJEU held that such an injunction was incompatible with the Brussels Convention and that it was tantamount to interference with the jurisdiction of the foreign court.

---

tion of *Owusu* but rather because art.71 of the Brussels Regulation (art.73 Recast Brussels Regulation) takes priority over the general provisions of the Brussels Regulation. As commented on by the judge, *Owusu* was not concerned with issues of exclusive or special jurisdiction. The Protocol is discussed at para.2-347.

[464] A detailed treatise of this subject is considered in A. Briggs, *Civil Jurisdiction and Judgments*, 6th edn (London: Informa, 2015) and P. Torremans, et al. (eds), *Cheshire, North & Fawcett: Private International Law* (Oxford: Oxford University Press, 2017).

[465] An anti-suit injunction was granted in *Continental Bank v Aeokos Cia Naviera* [1994] 2 All E.R. 540, to enforce an exclusive jurisdictional clause. See also *Scripto v Fomento* [1964] R.P.C. 113, in which an English judge granted an injunction restraining patent infringement proceedings being brought in South Africa, where the parties had agreed not to sue third parties for infringement of certain designated patents. See *Apple Corp v Apple Computer* [1992] R.P.C. 70, in which the court granted an interlocutory injunction restraining defendants from proceeding with applications to cancel the claimant's registered trademarks anywhere in the world, as the defendants were party to a contract governed by English law and with an English exclusive jurisdiction clause under which they agreed not to oppose or apply to cancel the claimant's marks: cf. *Fyffes v Chiquita* [1993] F.S.R. 83.

[466] *Fort Dodge Ltd v Akzo Nobel* [1998] F.S.R. 222. Generally, see A. Briggs *Civil Jurisdiction and Judgments*, 6th edn (Abingdon: Informa Law, 2015).

[467] *Midland Bank v Laker Airways* [1986] Q.B. 689 CA.

[468] *Advance Portfolio Technologies v Ainsworth* [1996] F.S.R. 217 HC.

[469] (C-159/02) [2004] E.C.R. I-3565. See para.17-026.

INTELLECTUAL PROPERTY AND PRIVATE INTERNATIONAL LAW

An introduction

The EU has adopted two "choice of law" regulations—one which concerns the **17-268** applicable law to contractual obligations and the other to non-contractual obligations. These are respectively, Reg.593/2008,[470] the "Rome I Regulation", Reg.864/2007,[471] and the "Rome II Regulation". The Rome I Regulation is intended to codify the Rome Convention on the Law Applicable to Contractual Obligations whilst at the same time, modernising it.[472] The Rome II Regulation has no predecessor convention but owes its birth to an EU initiative called the Hague Programme,[473] which called for work to be pursued actively on the rules of conflict of laws regarding non-contractual obligations. The Rome I and Rome II Regulations apply to all Member States other than Denmark.[474]

A full review of the Rome I and Rome II Regulations is outside the scope of this **17-269** book.[475] In this section, we focus on those provisions relevant to intellectual property rights.

Rome II Regulation

Unlike other areas of law, in intellectual property proceedings, it is rare that an **17-270** issue will arise concerning which is the applicable law to deal with alleged acts of infringement of an IPR. This is because IPRs are territorial in nature. For instance, if a multinational company has patents throughout many countries for the same invention and alleges that a defendant has infringed these patents by the making and marketing of a product, only acts in Country A can infringe the patent registered in Country A, etc. Thus, if a court were to have worldwide jurisdiction over the worldwide acts of infringement by the defendant, it would have to consider whether the alleged acts of infringement that happened in each country were an infringement under the patent law of each country. This is usually called the *lex loci protectionis*—the law of the place of protection. Equally, the validity of a patent registered in Country A will be determined by the domestic patent law of Country A—the country which granted the same patent.

The above is recognised in the Rome II Regulation. Article 8.1 confirms that the **17-271** applicable law to infringement of intellectual property rights is the *lex loci*

---

[470] [2008] OJ L177/6.

[471] [2007] OJ L199/40.

[472] Recital 15, art.24 Rome I Regulation; *Proposal for a Regulation of the European Parliament and the Council on the law applicable to contractual obligations* COM (2005) 650. See also P. Torremans, et al. (eds), *Cheshire, North & Fawcett: Private International Law* (Oxford: Oxford University Press, 2017), p.686 which sets out the history behind the Rome I Regulation.

[473] [2005] OJ C 12/1. See also *Proposal for a Regulation of the European Parliament and the Council on the Law Applicable to Non-Contractual Obligations ("Rome II")* COM (2003) 427 (22 July 2003).

[474] Originally, the UK opted out of the Rome I Regulation but it then opted-in—see the Commission Decision of 22 December 2008 [2009] OJ L10/22. This was enacted by the UK adopting The Law Applicable to Contractual Obligations (England and Wales and Northern Ireland) (SI/2009/3064). This disapplies the Contracts (Applicable Law) Act 1990 to matters which would fall within Rome I Regulation—see Reg.2. It also extends the effects of the Rome I Regulation to intra-UK disputes which would not fall within Rome I Regulation (see art.22(2)).

[475] A thorough review of these regulations is in P. Torremans, et al. (eds), *Cheshire, North & Fawcett: Private International Law* (Oxford: Oxford University Press, 2017), Chs 19 and 20.

protectionis.[476] "Intellectual property rights" is not defined but the recital suggests that it should be interpreted broadly.[477] Where a court of a Member State has jurisdiction, by reason of the defendant being domiciled in its Member State, over acts of infringement in several Member States, as said above, the court will have to apply the laws of those Member States to determine whether or not the acts carried out in those states infringe the rights of the right holder.

17-272   However, what about the grant of remedies? Is that governed by the *lex loci protectionis* or *lex fori* (or some other law)? For instance, if a German court has jurisdiction over infringement proceedings on a European patent in Germany, England and France, and has found that the patent is infringed in those countries, what is the applicable law to determine what remedies can be granted? For instance, when deciding the principles concerning the assessment of damages for the acts of infringement that happened in England, should it apply English law (*lex loci protectionis*) or German law (*lex fori*)? This may give rise to very different levels of compensation.[478]

17-273   The answer to this question is that it is the *lex loci protectionis*. Article 15(c) Rome II states that the applicable law (i.e. the *lex loci protectionis*) shall govern not only the basis and extent of liability but also "*the existence, the nature and the assessment of damage or the remedy claimed.*" Article 15(d) also states that the applicable law is "*within the limits of powers conferred on the court by its procedural laws, the measures which a court may take to prevent or terminate injury or damage or to ensure the provision of compensation.*"

17-274   In contrast, art.1(3) states that the Regulation does not apply to evidence and procedure.[479] These provisions were considered in an English case. In this case, the court had to consider whether an application of the Rome II Regulation meant that where declarations for non-infringement of French, Italian, Spanish and UK parallel patents were sought in English proceedings, the procedural conditions which had to be satisfied for the purpose of granting a declaration for non-infringement was determined by reference to the *lex fori* (England) or the *lex loci protectionis* (i.e. France, Spain, Italy). The threshold requirements for obtaining declarations for non-infringement were different under the various national laws. The dispute between the parties was how far the Rome II Regulation governed the nature of remedies and relief sought by parties in IP litigation. Did it apply to the procedural conditions as to whether such remedies were available? The court concluded, in effect, that there was a difference between actual remedies, e.g. injunctive relief and damages and the procedures to request such remedies. It established that the conditions applicable for a declaration of non-infringement fell outside the Rome II Regulation, as it was a matter of procedure.[480]

---

[476] art.8(1) Reg.864/2007 [2007] OJ L199/40. See also P. Torremans, et al. (eds), *Cheshire, North & Fawcett: Private International Law* (Oxford: Oxford University Press, 2017), p.831.

[477] Recital 26. See also Th. C.J.A. van Engelen, "Jurisdiction and Applicable Law in Matters of Intellectual Property", vol.14.3 *Electronic Journal of Comparative Law* (December 2010), p.13.

[478] Whilst the Enforcement Directive provides some harmonisation to the remedies available for IPRs, the assessment of damages is very much left to the courts of Member States to apply in accordance with their own laws—see para.15-041.

[479] Without prejudice to arts 21 and 22 (which include presumptions as to law and burdens of proof).

[480] *Actavis UK Ltd v Eli Lilly & Co* [2014] EWHC 1511 (Pat) at [206]–[236]. Upheld on appeal, *Actavis UK Ltd v Eli Lilly & Co* [2015] EWCA Civ 555. See also G.-P. Calliess, *Rome Regulations: Commentary*, 2nd edn (Arnhem: Kluwer, 2015). The Court of Appeal cited the commentary by Halfmeier in the 1st edn, where he said that the admissibility for the grant of a declaration action was governed

EU unitary right

In the case of infringement of a unitary EU intellectual property right, e.g. a EU **17-275** trade mark or Community Design, art.8(2) states that the law applicable for infringement of unitary EU rights (insofar as it is not governed by the relevant regulation) is the law of the country in which the "act of infringement was committed", i.e. the *lex loci delicti*. In *Nintendo v BigBen*,[481] the Court of Justice has had to consider this provision in the light of acts of infringement of Community Designs carried out a defendant or group of defendants in many Member States. In that case, BigBen France sold accessories via its website to consumers in France, Belgium and Luxembourg, and via its German subsidiary, BigBen Germany, to consumers in Germany and Austria. Nintendo alleged that these accessories infringed its Community designs. An action was brought in the courts of Germany against both BigBen Germany and BigBen France that the accessories infringed the Community Designs. The Landgericht Düsseldorf found that the accessories infringed the Community Designs. It ordered BigBen Germany to cease using the designs throughout the EU and also ("the supplementary claims") that they pay compensation, recall the accessories and reimburse the lawyers' fees incurred by Nintendo. As regards BigBen France, it also ordered it to cease infringing the Community Designs throughout the EU but limited the scope of its supplementary claims to BigBen France's supplies of the goods to BigBen Germany. It held that the applicable law was the place of infringement, being therefore, German, Austrian and French law. On appeal, a number of questions were referred to the Court of Justice. One question concerned what the applicable law was in order to determine what supplementary measures could be ordered where such were not mentioned expressly under Reg.6/2002 ("The Community Design Regulation"). Under Reg.6/2002, this was a matter for the law (including private international law) of the Community Design Court.[482] Accordingly, as the Rome II Regulation forms part of the private international law of Germany, it was necessary to consider the meaning of art.8(2) Reg.864/2007.

The Court of Justice held that in the context of multiple infringements in vari- **17-276** ous Member States and the complexity of IP infringement, that it was necessary to come up with a workable and predictable test. It said that in those circumstances, art.8(2) required the Community Design Court to identify "the event giving rise to the damage occurred". This was to be done, not by referring to each alleged act of infringement but rather to make an overall assessment of the defendant's conduct in order to determine the place "where the initial act of infringement at the origin of conduct was committed or threatened."[483] Therefore, in the context of a website which targeted consumers in various Member States, it was the place where the

---

by *lex fori* but not the substance of the declaration which "certainly" is to be assessed by the *lex causae* (i.e *lex loci protectionis*).

[481] *Nintendo Co Ltd v BigBen Interactive GmbH* (C-24/16, C-25/16) ECLI:EU:C:2017:724.

[482] art.89.1(a)–(c) sets out certain measures that should be ordered (save for special reasons) by a Community Design Court where infringement is found (being orders to prohibit the defendant from carrying out infringing acts, seizure of infringing goods, materials and implements). However, art.89.1(d) states that the Community Design Court can grant other sanctions which "are provided by the law of the Member State in which the acts of infringement or threatened infringement are committed, including its private international law". Article 88(2) states that on matters not covered by Reg.6/2002, a Community Design Court shall apply its own national law, including its private international law.

[483] See [98]–[103].

process of putting the offer for sale online by the operator on its website was activated.[484] This determination of the applicable law under art.8(2) to unitary rights such as the EU trade marks is analogous to the determination of which Member State has jurisdiction under the supplemental ground of jurisdiction provided for in the EUTM Regulation and the Community Design Regulation which confers jurisdiction on the courts of a Member State where the acts of infringement were committed or threatened.[485]

Non-derogation from art.8

17-277   The above rules cannot be derogated from by written agreement.[486] Thus, where two parties find themselves engaged in costly multinational litigation across a large number of countries, e.g. over a pharmaceutical invention that is the subject of patent protection in those countries, the parties cannot agree that, for example, the patent law of Germany will apply to issues of infringement. This is perhaps unfortunate. The reason given in the *travaux préparatoires* is that "freedom of will is not accepted, however, for intellectual property, where it would not be appropriate".[487] As commented on, this is not much of an explanation and the actual reason is presumably that the territorial principle is so important that parties should not be allowed to override it.[488] Therefore, litigation over parallel rights where the right holder alleges acts of infringement in 27 Member States will require consideration of the law in each of those states which will be very expensive and not in the interests of the parties (if they want a single law to be applicable). Also, it is difficult to see what public interest or policy there is against the parties choosing the applicable law.[489]

17-278   It might be thought that this could be "overcome" by parties not putting in evidence of law in other Member States and the court seized with the dispute thereby treating the law of other Member States as the same as that of the *lex fori*. However, this is problematic as art.22 of Rome II says that the applicable law also applies to rules which raise presumptions of law or burden of proof.[490] It is helpful to consider an example here. English law has a rule of evidence. The law of a foreign country is presumed, in the absence of evidence, to be the same as English law. However, where an English court is seized with actions for infringement of parallel rights in a number of Member States, let us say, France, Germany and Spain, such would be to apply the *lex fori* and not the *lex loci protectionis*. In short, the right approach would be for the English court to consider whether under French, German and Spanish law, they have a similar rule of evidence the same as English law.

17-279   In relation to contractual arrangements pertaining to intellectual property, such as licences and assignment, it is necessary to consider the provisions of the Rome

---

[484] See [108].

[485] This is discussed in Ch.3, "Trade Marks in Europe" at para.3-815.

[486] art.8(3) Reg.864/2007.

[487] *Proposal for a Regulation of the European Parliament and the Council on the Law Applicable to Non-Contractual Obligations ("Rome II")* COM (2003) 427 (22nd July 2003).

[488] P. Torremans, et al. (eds), *Cheshire, North & Fawcett: Private International Law* (Oxford: Oxford University Press, 2017), p.835.

[489] See Th. C.J.A. van Engelen, "Jurisdiction and Applicable Law in Matters of Intellectual Property", vol.14.3 *Electronic Journal of Comparative Law* (December 2010), pp.14–15

[490] This is a derogation from the general rule at art.1(3) that Rome II Regulation does not apply to "evidence and procedure". Article 1(3) is said to be without prejudice to arts 21 and 22.

I Regulation[491] which replaces the Rome Convention on the Law Applicable to Contractual Obligations.

Rome I Regulation

The basic provision of the Rome I Regulation is that the parties are free to choose **17-280** the applicable law relating to disputes concerning the contract.[492] If the parties fail to do so, then the applicable law is determined in accordance with art.4 of the Rome I Regulation. Article 4 sets out in relation to specific situations, the applicable law. Of most interest to the readers of this book are the following: a contract for the sale of goods is governed by the law of the country where the seller has their habitual residence[493]; a contract for the provision of services is governed by the law of the country where the service provider has their habitual residence[494]; a franchise contract is governed by the law where the franchisee has their habitual residence[495]; and a distribution contract is governed by the law of the country where the distributor has their habitual residence.[496] Where there are no specific provisions or where the elements of the contract are covered by more than one provision, the contract is governed by the law of the country where *"the party required to effect the characteristic performance of the contract has his habitual residence"*.[497] To these rules, there is an important exception. *If the above rules are capable of application* but it is clear from all the circumstances that the contract is *manifestly more closely connected* with a country other than that indicated in the above provisions, then art.4(3) states that the law of that country shall apply.[498] The requirement of "manifestly more closely connected" sets a high threshold and is intended to ensure that the specific provisions are not easily derogated from. Lastly, where the law applicable cannot be determined by reference to the above rules, there is a general provision that the contract be governed by the law of the country with which it is most closely connected.[499]

It will be noted that there is no specific rule dealing with intellectual or industrial **17-281** property rights. Such was contained in the original Commission's proposal but was deleted for lack of agreement on a single and all-encompassing solution. This is because the variety of types of contracts that can be found in this field make it very difficult to find a rule that would work well for all cases.[500] Thus, the absence of a specific provision means one must consider whether in an IPR licence, there is a characteristic performance of the contract. If there is, then the law will be where the person who has to carry out such a characteristic performance has their habitual residence. If this does not exist, then the applicable law will be the law of the country with which the IPR licence is most closely connected.

---

[491] Reg.593/2008 [2008] OJ L177/6–16.

[492] art.3.

[493] art.4(1)(a).

[494] art.4(1)(b).

[495] art.4(1)(e).

[496] art.4(1)(f).

[497] art.4(2).

[498] art.4(3).

[499] art.4(4).

[500] J.F. Garcimartin Alferez, *The Rome I Regulation: Much ado about nothing* (European Legal Forum (E) 2–2008 61–80), p.I-69, para.42; P.A. De Miguel Asensio, "The Law Governing International Intellectual Property Licensing Agreements (A Conflict of Laws Analysis)" in J. de Werra, *Research Handbook on Intellectual Property Licensing* (Cheltenham: Edward Elgar Publishing, 2013), pp.312–326, para.4.2. See also P. Torremans, et al. (eds), *Cheshire, North & Fawcett: Private International Law* (Oxford: Oxford University Press, 2017), p.730.

17-282   The above provisions depart significantly from those set out in the Rome Convention. They are intended to simplify its rather complicated provisions.[501] They are intended to provide greater legal certainty as to the applicable law.[502] Thus, previous authorities which considered art.4 of the Rome Convention have little application.[503]

17-283   Of importance to intellectual property practitioners is the application of the Rome I Regulation to determining the applicable law of intellectual property licences. In most cases, licences will expressly set out the law to be applied to determining any dispute under the licence. Hence, it is rare that a legal advisor or court will need to consider the application of the Rome I Regulation to disputes on licences. However, the issue may arise in the context of a compromise agreement in intellectual property litigation whereby a party agrees to grant a licence to the other (often in return for withdrawing a counterclaim to revoke the registered right). Also, this may arise in the context of more informal licences where a business arrangement impliedly includes a licence to use a mark. Because of the great variety of contracts which may contain an intellectual property licence, there is no simple rule. Therefore, a franchise contract will often include a right of the franchisee to use the trade mark of the manufacturer. In such circumstances, there is specific provision as to the applicable law namely that of the state of habitual residence of the franchisee.[504] A mere licence whereby the licensor grants the licensee the right to exploit IPRs in return for remuneration is not to be considered a contract for the provision of services within the meaning of art.4(1)(b).[505] In many licences, the licensee will often be required to perform various services, e.g. to promote and market goods protected by the IPR (or in the case of trade mark licences, to promote the brand). In such circumstances, this type of licence may indeed be classified as a contract for the provision of services under art.4(1)(b). However, many licences involve the provision of both services and goods, e.g. a manufacturing and marketing licence which requires the licensee to manufacture goods (the provision of services) and sell such goods (the provision of goods). In these circumstances, where the provisions of art.4(1) do not apply, art.4(2) stipulates that the applicable law will be that of the habitual residence of the party who is required to effect the *characteristic performance* of the licence.

17-284   The assessment of who is the party required to effect the characteristic performance of the contract can be problematic in the framework of IPR licences. It has been said that the prevailing opinion is that the assignor or licensor is the party who is to effect the characteristic performance in a typical assignment or transfer of rights.[506] Certainly, in the context of an assignment which requires a positive step of assigning rights, the assignor actively performs the contract by assigning the

---

[501] J.F. Garcimartin Alferez, *The Rome I Regulation: Much ado about nothing* (European Legal Forum (E) 2–2008 61–80), para.36.

[502] P.A. De Miguel Asensio, "The Law Governing International Intellectual Property Licensing Agreements (A Conflict of Laws Analysis)" in J. de Werra, *Research Handbook on Intellectual Property Licensing* (Cheltenham: Edward Elgar Publishing, 2013), pp.312–326, para.4.1.

[503] e.g. see *Kenburn Waste Management Ltd v Bergmann* [2002] F.S.R. 45 CA.

[504] See art.41(e).

[505] *Falco Privatstiftung* (C-533/07) [2009] E.C.R. I-3227. This was a decision under art.5(1) of the Brussels Regulation but it is to have the same interpretation as art.4(1)(b) Rome I Regulation—see Recital 17 of the latter Regulation.

[506] P.A. De Miguel Asensio, "The Law Governing International Intellectual Property Licensing Agreements (A Conflict of Laws Analysis)" in J. de Werra, *Research Handbook on Intellectual Property Licensing* (Cheltenham: Edward Elgar Publishing, 2013), pp.312–326, para 4.3.

right. Although the assignee will normally pay a sum of money for such an assignment, this type of obligation is universal in most contracts as to indicate that little weight should be placed on it.[507]

However, in the context of a licence, it is problematic to say that the mere grant **17-285** of a licence (which amounts to little more than an agreement not to sue the licensee in relation to acts which would otherwise be infringing acts) amounts to "the characteristic performance" of the contract. Indeed, it is more likely that the licence will contain positive obligations on the licensee whilst the licensor simply agrees not to sue the licensee for carrying out certain acts. However, the official commentary on the Rome Convention (the predecessor to the Rome I Regulation) states that in a bilateral contract whereby one party grants the right to make use of an item of property to another, it is the grantor who effects the characteristic performance.[508] In the author's view, where the licence is a bare licence and contains no other provisions, it is indeed the licensor who is the person effecting the characteristic performance.[509] Put another way, it can be said that the characteristic performance of a bare licence is the non-enforcement of the relevant IPR by the right holder.[510]

Bare licences are unusual. A typical licence will usually contain a number of **17-286** contractual obligations relating to, e.g. payment, marketing, exploitation of the IPRs, and often exclusivity. Here, it is difficult to identify an obligation which represents the characteristic performance of the licence (let alone the person who is to effect it). It has been said that in such circumstances, the exploitation of the IPR is arguably more important than the payment of money and at least as important as the complete or partial transfer of rights and that a single characteristic performance can hardly be identified in the circumstances.[511] Against this view, it might be said that the very phrase "the characteristic performance" imparts a duty on a court to identify an obligation in a contract which is the *most important* in the contract or which is the *defining* obligation and that it is not sufficient for a court to conclude that there are a number of terms which are promising candidates for this title and therefore find that there is no characteristic performance of the contract.

Nonetheless, such an approach appears overly literal and in the authors' view this **17-287** inflexible approach is not to be adopted. For instance, many agreements involving licensing provisions are genuinely reciprocal, e.g. patent pools or trade mark delimitation agreements where parties agree reciprocal obligations not to issue proceedings against each other for infringement of their respective rights and/or to oppose registration of patents or trade marks. Equally, in a contract between an author and a publisher whereby the latter commissions the former to write a book which it will publish, the obligation to publish the book is of equal importance to the obligation to write the book and they must be considered wholly complementary to each other. In these contracts, for the court to determine which obligation in the agreement is the defining obligation is to ask it to conduct an unreal and artificial

---

[507] A. Schnitzer, *Handbuch des Internationalen Privatrechts II*, 4th edn (Basel: Verl. fur Recht und Gesellschaft, 1958), cited at fn.27 of P.L. Torremans, "Licences and Assignments of Intellectual Property Rights under the Rome I Regulation" [2012] 4(3) *Journal of Private International Law*, 397–420.

[508] *Giuliano-Lagarde Report* OJ [1980] C282/1.

[509] See P.L. Torremans, "Licences and Assignments of Intellectual Property Rights under the Rome I Regulation" [2012] 4(3) *Journal of Private International Law*, 13.

[510] Th. C.J.A. van Engelen, "Jurisdiction and Applicable Law in Matters of Intellectual Property", vol. 14.3 *Electronic Journal of Comparative Law* (Dec 2010), 19.

[511] P.L. Torremans, "Licences and Assignments of Intellectual Property Rights under the Rome I Regulation" [2012] 4(3) *Journal of Private International Law*, 14.

exercise. In such circumstances, the more sensible, just and fair route is not to apply the characteristic performance test under art.4(2), but to apply the "closest connection" rule under art.4(3) and art.4(4) as their flexibility is much greater than the "characteristic performance" test. If the "closest connection" rule applies, the court may need to consider a wide host of facts and matters, including place of residence of the parties or their nationality, whether the rights are localised to a particular country or not, where the contract was negotiated and held, and perhaps even the language of the contract.[512] It has been said the application of this principle would mean that, in general, intellectual property contracts would be governed by the *lex protectionis* (i.e. the law of the right which is licensed) but where there is a licence for several countries, the licence contract would be governed by the law of the country of the licensee.[513] However, it is recognised that there is considerable uncertainty in the application of art.4 of the Rome I Regulation to licences. Parties should always endeavour to agree a choice of law clause in licences.

Litigation over licences

17-288   Litigation over the meaning of IP licences is common. Often, the issue that arises will be whether on a proper interpretation of the licence, the acts of the licensee are licensed. If they are not licensed, then if those acts would be acts reserved to the licensor under relevant IP legislation, then they are infringing acts. In such circumstances, the licensor may often bring proceedings not for breach of the licence, but rather to enforce the licensed IPR as if it were an infringement action. Thus, the claim may state that the licensee has infringed the licensor's IPRs and by way of defence, the licensee will often argue that the acts of which complaint are made, are in fact licensed. This can be characterised as a contractual defence to an action based on a non-contractual obligation. Here, one might think that both Rome I and Rome II are engaged. It might be thought that art.15(b) Rome II gives us the answer. It states that the applicable law under the Rome II Regulation shall apply to *"the grounds for exemption from liability, any limitation of liability and any division of liability"*. Here, the defence is that the licensor has given their consent. So accordingly, Rome II would apply and the court seized would have to determine whether a licence is a defence to an infringement action (which clearly it is). However, insofar as the real issue was the proper interpretation of the licence or indeed its validity, it is considered that the applicable law to the interpretation of the licence must be determined in accordance with Rome I.[514] It is likely that where proceedings for infringement of an IPR are brought against a licensee on the grounds that their acts fall outside the licence, the court will need to consider both the Rome I and Rome II Regulations. The example below illustrates this approach.

Example
A French pharmaceutical company brings an action for patent infringement against an Italian licensee on the grounds that the licensee's acts in Italy fall outwith the licence and thus

---

[512] See P.A. De Miguel Asensio, "The Law Governing International Intellectual Property Licensing Agreements (A Conflict of Laws Analysis)" in J. de Werra, *Research Handbook on Intellectual Property Licensing* (Cheltenham: Edward Elgar Publishing, 2013), para.4.4.

[513] See P.L. Torremans, "Licences and Assignments of Intellectual Property Rights under the Rome I Regulation" [2012] 4(3) *Journal of Private International Law*, p.33.

[514] See Recital 7 Rome I Regulation which states that the two Rome Regulations must be consistent. See also P. Torremans, et al. (eds), *Cheshire, North & Fawcett: Private International Law* (Oxford: Oxford University Press, 2017), p.881.

infringe its Italian patent. The licence contains an express choice of law clause. It states that any dispute under the licence is governed by French law. Under art.8 of the Rome II Regulation, the issue of whether, *but for the licence*, the licensee's acts infringe the Italian patent would be determined in accordance with Italian patent law as the *lex loci protectionis*. Article 8(3) of the Rome II Regulation[515] would prevent French law applying to the issue of infringement. However, by reason of art.3 of the Rome I Regulation, French law would apply to determining whether on a proper construction of the licence, the acts of the Italian licensee fall within the licence.

---

[515] art.8(3) forbids derogation from art.8(1) Rome II by way of written agreement. See para.17-277.

INDEX

This index has been prepared using Sweet and Maxwell's Legal Taxonomy. Main index entries conform to keywords provided by the Legal Taxonomy except where references to specific documents or non-standard terms (denoted by quotation marks) have been included. These keywords provide a means of identifying similar concepts in other Sweet & Maxwell publications and online services to which keywords from the Legal Taxonomy have been applied. Readers may find some minor differences between terms used in the text and those which appear in the index. Suggestions to *sweetandmaxwell.taxonomy@tr.com.*